Climber's and Hiker's
Guide to the
World's Mountains
& Volcanos

Michael R. Kelsey

4th Edition

584 Maps & 650 Fotos

Kelsey Publishing
456 East 100 North
Provo, Utah, USA, 84606-3208
Tele. & Fax 801(385 after 2002)-373-3327
Email Addresses--One of these should work!
mrkelsey@utah-inter.net
kelseypublishing@hotmail.com
kelsey@canyoneering.com

First Edition April 1981
Second Edition March 1984
Third Edition May 1990
Fourth Edition June 2001
Copyright © 2001 All rights reserved Michael R. Kelsey
ISBN Number 0944510-18-3
Library of Congress Catalog Card Number 00-093662

Distributors for Kelsey Publishing

Please write to one of these companies when ordering any of Michael R. Kelsey's guide books. A list of his titles is in the back of this book.

Alpenbooks, 3616 South Road, Building C, Suite 1, Mukilteo, Washington, USA, 98275, Website (www.alpenbooks.com), Email (cserve@alpenbooks.com), Tele. 206-290-8587, or 800-290-9898.
Canyon Country Distribution, Box 400034, Thompson Springs, Utah, USA, 84540, Email (archhunter@moci.net), Tele. 435-285-2210, Fax 435-285-2252.
Origin Books, 415 North, Neil Armstrong Road, International Center, Salt Lake City, Utah, USA, 84116, Email (jasay@Qwest.net), Tele. 801-972-8060, or 888-467-4446.
Treasure Chest Books, 1802 West Grant Road, Suite 101, Tucson Arizona, USA, 85745, Website (www.rionuevo.com), Tele. 520-623-9558, or 800-969-9558.

Some of Kelsey's books are sold by the following distributors.

Anderson News, 1709 North, East Street, Flagstaff, Arizona, USA, 86004, Email (lionwing2000 @aol.com), Tele. 520-774-6171, Fax 520-779-1958.
Books West, 5757 Arapahoe Avenue, D-2, Boulder, Colorado, USA, Website (bookswest.net), Email (sbhat@bookswest.net), 80303, Tele. 303-449-5995, Fax 303-449-5951.
Canyonlands Publications, 4860 N. Ken Morey Drive, Bellemont, Arizona, USA, 86004, Email (bookorder@canyonlandsbooks.com), Tele. 520-779-3888 or 800-283-1983.
Crown West Books (Library Service), 575 E. 1000 S., Orem, Utah, USA, 84058, Email (crownwest@enol.com), Tele. 801-224-1455, Fax 801-224-2662.
High Peak Books, Box 703, Wilson, Wyoming, USA, 83014, Tele. 307-739-0147.
Nevada Publications, 4135 Badger Circle, Reno, Nevada, USA, 89509, Tele. 702-747-0800.
Peregrine Outfitters, 105 South Brownell Road, Suite A, Williston, Vermont, USA, 05495, Tele. 802-860-2977 or 800-222-3088.
Recreational Equipment, Inc.(R.E.I.), P.O. Box C-88126, Seattle, Washington, USA, 98188, Website (www.rei.com), Mail Orders Tele. 800-426-4840 (or check at any of their local stores).

For the UK and Europe, and the rest of the world contact:
CORDEE, 3a De Montfort Street, Leicester, England, UK, LE1 7HD, Website (www.cordee.co.uk), Tele. Inter+116-254-3579, Fax Inter+116-247-1176.
For Australia and New Zealand: Macstyle Media, 20-22 Station Street, Sandringham, Victoria, Australia, 3191, Website (www.macstyle.com.au), Email (macstyle@netspace.net.au), Tele. Inter+61-39-521-6585, Fax Inter+61-39-521-0664

Printed by Cushing-Malloy, 1350 North Main, Ann Arbor, Michigan, USA

Front Cover

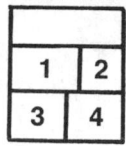

1	2
3	4

Front Cover
1. Kilimanjaro, Tanzania--seen from the Mawenzi Hut.
2. Matterhorn, Switzerland--seen from the east
3. Sajama, Bolivia--looking north at the south face.
4. Pacaya Volcano, Guatemala.

Back Cover

5	6
7	8
9	10

Back Cover
5. K-2, Pakistan--seen from the south near Concordia.
6. Tahat Volcanic Plug, Hoggar Mountains, Algeria--looking north.
7. Rano Raraku, Easter Island, Chile--below statue quarry.
8. Ampato, Peru--from an east side base camp.
9. Ranrapallca, Peru--from the west looking northeast.
10. Masherbrum, Pakistan--from the southeast ridge.

TABLE OF CONTENTS

Chapter 5--Asia..312

Chapter 6--The Pacific..526

Chapter 7--North America..726

Chapter 8--Mexico, Central America, and the Caribbean...........986

Chapter 9--South America..1092

Map Symbols

Village or City..............	□ □
Building, Home..............	□
Hut, Shelter, Refuge..............	△
Campground..............	🏕
Back-Country Campsite..............	▲
Visitor Center..............	🏠
Ranger, Warden Station..............	🏛
Hotel..............	🏨
Buddhist Temple..............	卍 🏠
Christian Church..............	⛪
School..............	🏫
Roads-Paved (mile or kms post)....... 2 3	┼
Roads-Unsurfaced..............	═ ═ ═
Roads-4WD..............	═ ═ ═ ═ ═
Tunnel..............	
Trail..............	─ ─ ─ ─ ─
Route (no trail)..............	• • • • • •
Pass or Col..............	⌣
Viewpoint..............	▲

Lake or Ocean..............	🐚
Peak and Ridge..............	—✕—
Snowfield or Glacier..............	
Spring or Waterhole..............	o
Picnic Site..............	▲
River..............	~~~
Intermittent Stream..............	~ ~
Airport or Airstrip..............	✈
Railroad..............	+—+—+—+
Ski Lift or Tramway..............	⊢——⊣
Grasslands..............	ᵛᵛ ᵛᵛ
Forest..............	❀ 🌲
Mine or Quarry..............	⟋ ⟍
Salt Flats or Salar..............	
Volcano..............	☀
Waterfall..............	
Trailhead Parking..............	Ⓟ
T.V.-Radio Antenna..............	

Map Abbreviations

Hut, Hutte, Hacienda..............	H	Campground..............	CG
Lake, Lago, Laguna..............	L	Picnic Grounds..............	PG
Estancia..............	E	Guard Station..............	GS
River, Rio..............	R	Ranger Station..............	RS
Creek..............	Ck	Quebrada..............	Q
Reservoir..............	R., or Res.	Four Wheel Drive Road or Vehicle..............	4WD
Youth Hostel..............	YH	Two Wheel Drive..............	2WD
Gasoline Station(Iceland)..............	G	Six Wheel Drive..............	6WD
March 17, 1943..............	3/17/1943	Pronounced..............	(Pron.)
October, 1991..............	10/1991		

The author has climbed at least one peak on this map..............	Map 17-1
The author has visited this area, but has not climbed or hiked..............	Map 155-2
The author has not visited or climbed in ths area..............	Map 446-3

Acknowledgements

It's impossible to recall all the thousands of people who in the past 30 years have heped me with information concerning mountains, springs, trails, travel problems, where to find maps or guidesbooks, and so on. Nor is it possible to recall all the friendly people who invited me into their homes during bad weather, or under some other adverse circumstance. There are countless memories of people, much poorer than I, who gave me gifts of food along the way to various mountains, but unfortunately they remain nameless. These people number in the hundreds, and are scattered throughout the 223 countries and island groups I have visited in my traveling & climbing career which officially began in 1970.

Some of those who I do remember because they gave so much of their time are as follow; Steve Tyler, the friend who originally got me interesting in mountaineering, Mitsuo Hiroshima, Luis Fernando Toro, Glenn Galloway, Marc Anderson, Doc Odle, John Greenough, Stan Shepherd, Tom Hendrickson, James Terry, Ralph Cummings, David Taylor, Carlos Zarate & son, Rajan Nair, Asraf Aman, Renato Korell, John McGhee, Shabbir Hussain, Robert Brock, Bill Mahar, Brad Gilbert

Contributors for the 3rd Edition are: Louis Hill, Adam Piños, Greg Horne, George Bell, Dolph Belton, George Headley, James Waganer, John D'Arcy, Richard McGowan, Jerzy Mikulec, Josef Jurak, Brad Solon, Dave Thomas, Ludwig Hendel.

For this 4th Edition some of those who helped were Vladimir Kirianov, Sergay Ageev, and others in the Institute of Vulkanology in Kamchatka; Alex Liveshin, Nigel Jenkins, Bob Villarreal, Greg Horne (again), Martin Tatuch, Greg Frux, Jim Hall, Andreas Wilhelm, Ronald Naar, Andrej Stritar, Scott Patterson, Günther Jüllich, Scott Wilson, Christoph Höbenreich, Richard White, Joe Ollivier, Mark Hall, Val Kerr, Ricardo Hernani, Wayne Federer, Jaume Tort, Graeme Watson, Ulf Carlsson, Yoichiro Kuroda, Troy Hudson, Claudio Cima, and proof reader Sue Fix,

My father, Roland Kelsey, would not be considered a climber, but who at the age of 68 reached the top of Kings Peak, the highest summit in Utah. He died in 1975 while I was in Asia mountain climbing. He never tried in any way to discourage me from climbing solo.

And most important, the person who helped proof-read my manuscripts which took into the hundreds of hours and the person who sent and received my packages while I was overseas, and who helped keep me informed of all developments while traveling, my mother, Venetta B. Kelsey.

The Author

The author was born in 1943, and experienced his earliest years of life in eastern Utah's Uinta Basin, first near the town of Myton, then Roosevelt. In 1954, the family moved to Provo, where he attended Provo High School, and later Brigham Young University, where he earned a B.S. degree in Sociology. Shortly thereafter he discovered that was the wrong subject, so he attended the University of Utah, where he received his Master of Science degree in Geography, finishing that in June, 1970.

It was then real life began, for on June 9, 1970, he put a pack on his back and started traveling for the first time. Since then he has seen 223 countries, republics, islands, or island groups. All this wandering has resulted in a number of books written and published by himself. Here are his books, listed in the order they were first published: *Climber's and Hiker's Guide to the World's Mountains and Volcanos (4th Edition)*, *Utah Mountaineering Guide (3rd Edition)*; *China on Your Own and the Hiking Guide to China's Nine Sacred Mountains (3rd Edition-now Out of Print)*; *Canyon Hiking Guide to the Colorado Plateau (4th Edition)*; *Hiking and Exploring Utah's San Rafael Swell (3rd Edition)*; *Hiking and Exploring Utah's Henry Mountains and Robbers Roost (Revised Edition)*; *Hiking and Exploring the Paria River (3rd Edition)*; *Hiking and Climbing in the Great Basin National Park (Wheeler Peak, Nevada)*; *Boater's Guide to Lake Powell--Featuring Hiking, Camping, Geology, History and Archaeology (4th Edition)*; *Climbing and Exploring Utah's Mt. Timpanogos*; *River Guide to Canyonlands National Park & Vicinity*; *Hiking, Biking and Exploring Canyonlands National Park & Vicinity*; *The Story of Black Rock, Utah*; and *Hiking, Climbing and Exploring Western Utah's Jack Watson's Ibex Country*.

He also helped his mother Venetta B. Kelsey, write & publish a book about the town she was born and raised in, *Life on the Black Rock Desert--A History of Clear Lake, Utah*.

The author's goal, besides updating more editions of this guide, is to climb at least one mountain on every map shown in this book. As of this 4th Edition, he has climbed or attempted peaks on 504 maps, or 86%, of those covered in this book. In addition, he has passed through areas covered by an additional 30 maps making a total of 534, or 91.1%, of the maps in this book the author has first-hand knowledge of.

Help Wanted!

As this 4th Edition goes to press, it will be nearly 31 years since the author first started traveling and gathering information and maps about the mountains of the world. During this time he has made a effort to visit at least one mountain on every map covered in this book. However, even through he has presently (2001) visited 223 countries and island groups, it will be virtually impossible for one person to see and/or climb all the mountains in the world, let alone those featured in this book. It's also impossible to return to previously-climbed mountains to gather updated information.

For these reasons, the author asks hikers and climbers who have been to some of the mountains featured here, to send up-dated information. Also, if you have information on any peak or mountain range which is not covered here, but which you feel should be included in the next edition, please send that information too.

Many European readers have written and ask that I include more information about and/or mountains in Europe. But please keep in mind there are 300 or 400 hiking or climbing guidebooks already written about that part of the world. Since this is a world guide, and one that is leaning toward **volcanos**, the hope is to reveal information about mountains or volcanos that have yet to be *"discovered"* by hikers from the industrialized world.

If your contribution involves significant time spent, the author is willing to reimburse you in US$, or other guidebooks, and will pay for postage and fotographs.

Send information to **Michael R. Kelsey, 456 E. 100 N., Provo, Utah, USA, 84606-3208, Tele & Fax 801(385 after 2002?)-373-3327**, or one of these Email address (mrkelsey@utah-inter.net), (kelseypublishing@hotmail.com) or (kelsey@canyoneering.com).

The Bugaboo Hut at Boulder Camp in Canada's Bugaboo region of the Selkirk Mtns.

Metric Conversion Table

1 Centimeter = 0.39 Inch	1 Mile = 1.609 Kilometers	1 Ounce = 28.35 Grams
1 Inch = 2.54 Centimeters	100 Miles = 161 Kilometers	1 Pound = 453 Grams
1 Meter = 39.37 Inches	100 Kilometers = 62.1 Miles	1 Quart (US) = 0.946 Liter
1 Foot = 0.3048 Meter	1 Liter = 1.056 Quarts (US)	1 Gallon (US) = 3.785 Liters
1 Kilometer = 0.621 Mile	1 Kilogram = 2.205 Pounds	1 Acre = 0.405 Hectare
1 Nautical Mile = 1.852 Kms	1 Metric Ton = 1000 Kg	1 Hectare = 2.471 Acres
1 Kilometer = 5280 Feet	1 Mile = 1609 Meters	

Meters to Feet (Meters x 3.2808 = Feet)

100 m = 328 ft.	2500 m = 8202 ft.	5000 m = 16404 ft.	7500 m = 24606 ft.
500 m = 1640 ft	3000 m = 9842 ft.	5500 m = 18044 ft.	8000 m = 26246 ft.
1000 m = 3281 ft.	3500 m = 11483 ft.	6000 m = 19686 ft.	8500 m = 27887 ft.
1500 m = 4921 ft.	4000 m = 13124 ft.	6500 m = 21325 ft.	9000 m = 29525 ft.
2000 m = 6562 ft.	4500 m = 14764 ft.	7000 m = 22966 ft.	8848 m = 29029 ft.

Feet to Meters (Feet ÷ 3.3208 = Meters)

1000 ft. = 305 m	9000 ft. = 2743 m	16000 ft. = 4877 m	23000 ft. = 7010 m
2000 ft. = 610 m	10000 ft. = 3048 m	17000 ft. = 5182 m	24000 ft. = 7315 m
3000 ft. = 914 m	11000 ft. = 3353 m	18000 ft. = 5486 m	25000 ft. = 7620 m
4000 ft. = 1219 m	12000 ft. = 3658 m	19000 ft. = 5791 m	26000 ft. = 7925 m
5000 ft. = 1524 m	13000 ft. = 3962 m	20000 ft. = 6096 m	27000 ft. = 8230 m
6000 ft. = 1829 m	14000 ft. = 4268 m	21000 ft. = 6401 m	28000 ft. = 8535 m
7000 ft. = 2134 m	15000 ft. = 4572 m	22000 ft. = 6706 m	29000 ft. = 8839 m
8000 ft. = 2438 m			30000 ft. = 9144 m

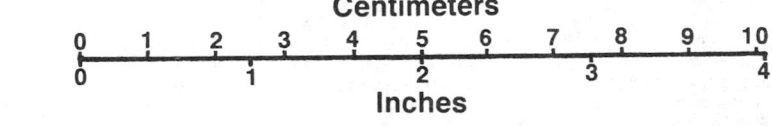

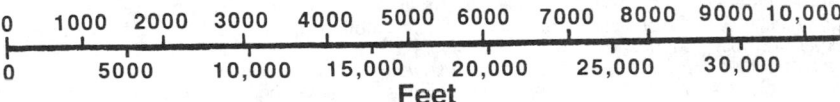

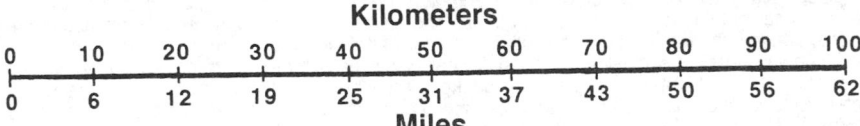

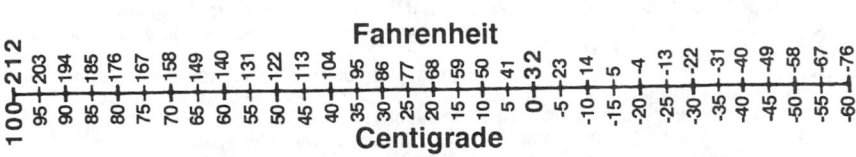

Chapter 1--Introduction

No need to waste space so here arc just a few things to remember while traveling and climbing around the world. This book is not written to be an instruction book. If going to some of the big & difficult mountains, it'll be up to you to prepare yourself for the challenge. Some mountains in this book are obviously difficult and will require lots of experience, good equipment, time, sometimes money and/or being part of a larger group. But most mountains in this book can be climbed by a solo hiker or climber with little climbing experience. However, having some experience traveling will increase your chances of success.

The author's globetrotting days began on June 9, 1970, and throughout that decade, traveled to about 100 different countries. Since it's impossible to return to all those earlier climbs and gather new and up-to-date information, he is now relying on recently-published travel & hiking or trekking guidebooks. About the only things that change are roads which are generally a little better, there are lots more buses, hotels, tour operators, guides, other tourists & climbers, better maps are easier to get, plus cheaper airfares, just to name a few. You're encouraged to buy and use the latest travel guidebooks available, which as time goes on, will help update the information in this book. In the back of this book is a list of the major guidebook publishers. Please consult them about the latest travel guides.

Thieves and Preventing Theft

There will be an introduction to each of 7 different regions of the world in this book. Discussed here will be important messages on a world wide scale. And one of the most important messages to remember while traveling outside of your country will be crimes against travelers. These crimes range from having something taken from a pocket of your pack, to having your entire pack, handbag or camera stolen. These encounters are getting worse every year in the Third World, or developing countries. If you're going to places like Colombia, Peru, Morocco, Kenya, Tanzania, Papua New Guinea or to some of the big cities in the developing world, especially cities in Mexico and Managua, Panama City, Caracas, Nairobi, Jakarta, Bangkok and others just to name a few, pay attention to this part. This evaluation is based on the author's personnel experiences, many from the 1970's, but others from the 1990's and includes over 30 years of traveling and mountain climbing to 223 countries, republics, islands and/or island groups. Virtually every long-term traveler who has been to some of the places mentioned above has had some kind of encounter with thieves.

To save what might be the trip of a lifetime here are some things to do. One of the most popular past times of thieves is to grab something and run; or cut the strap of a handbag with a razor or sharp knife and run; or pick up something left on a counter and quietly walk away. Grabbing small packs or cameras often comes at bus terminals and train stations as trains are pulling away, and many times on poorly-lite streets at night. To prevent some of these things from happening, replace straps of your camera, camera bag, and shoulder bag, with small chains. Also, don't put yourself in harms way-- simply stay in your hotel room after dark.

Pickpocket thieves operate in crowded conditions such as market places or buses, and often times in collusion with partners to create a commotion and/or with lots of pushing, bumping & shoving or jostling to create distractions. If you see this situation coming, grab everything, and perhaps squat down quickly. Avoid those places and/or situations! Another way of protection is to carry your small backpack on your front or chest, instead of on your back, and hold it securely. Make sure all handbags have a shoulder strap and cross the strap across your body so no one can grab it and run. Keep it over your shoulder at all times while in public. Never set anything down while shopping or buying tickets; you may get distracted and walk off without it.

Carry plane tickets, credit card, money and passports concealed in a neck pouch or waist belt, but keep it small or thin and unnoticeable. For carrying an emergency supply of cash, replace the regular belt to your trousers with a money belt with zippered pocket where you can keep up to a dozen or more new US$100 bills folded & wrapped in small plastic bags for moisture protection. In addition to a money belt, sew home-made security pockets into your slightly-oversized trousers for tickets, telefone & credit cards, passport and more money and/or travelers checks. At the same time, always carry small amounts of local currency in a cheap plastic wallet (leave your regular wallet at home) and in a zippered pocket for quick access. Try not to expose your secret hiding places to people in public. Do that in your hotel or a rest room. Using these precautions, the author hasn't carried travelers checks since the 1970's!

Here are more tips. Carry a 2-meter-long chain or cable and bike padlock to secure your pack onto a bus or train luggage rack, or onto a truck. This can also be used at airports or bus & train stations. Lock your pack to a bench right in the middle of a waiting room, then you can buy tickets or something else, or even leave the station to do extra business. This works especially well if you're traveling alone and the cost of storing baggage is high.

Keep your watch band tight, and/or extend your shirt sleeve on your watch arm so grabbers can't get their fingers under the band and run away with it. Don't hang wet clothes on hotel clothes lines; always carry a nylon cord and make a clothes line in your room away from thieves. Also, don't hang clothes or place anything else near an open window, especially at night.

Don't carry irreplaceable valuables in pack pockets. Over the years the author has lost 7 or 8 small flashlights, mostly while flying. To prevent people getting into pack pockets, sew short pieces of nylon cord next to pack pocket zippers, and tie another short piece to the zipper pull itself. When traveling between hotels, tie these together which will slow a thief down enough to keep him honest.

Here's another idea. As far back as the late 1970's in South America, some travelers, mostly French, had placed their large packs inside sacks made for rice or potatoes, then they cut slits for the pack strap, so they could be carried as usual. Wrapping them up this way made them appear to be a sack of produce on top of trucks or buses. It also kept packs clean and made it more difficult for thieves to get into.

If you make these changes and change some old bad habits, it's likely you'll have a good trip. Also, if you have more great ideas about how to keep your valuables from being stolen, please contact the author. He expects to put out more editions of this book and would like to inform future readers of how to make an overseas trip more enjoyable.

One of the original shelters or refugios on Aconcagua. This old rock hut is located at the Confluencia. Aconcagua is to the right or north of this place (Map 571, page 1209).

Chapter 2--Active Volcano Information Sources

The following is a short list of geologic names used by volcanologists when describing volcanos or eruptions. Many are standard textbook terms, others are commonly-used ways to describe eruptions as used by the staff who compile the **Bulletin of the Global Volcanism Network** located in the **Smithsonian Institution** in Washington D.C.

The **Global Volcanism Program** is located in the **National Museum of Natural History, Room E-421, Washington D.C., 20560-0129, USA.** Best way to contact this organization is through the internet at **(www.volcano.si.edu/gvp/)**, or email **(gvn@volcano.si.edu)**, or Tele. 202-357-1511, Fax 202-357-2476. These people are always happy when someone witnesses an eruption, then sends a description or perhaps a fotograph of the event.

Most of the information about volcano eruptions in this edition has come from the book, **Volcanos of the World**, Second Edition, by Tom Simkin & Lee Siebert and published by the **Smithsonian Institution**. This excellent book was compiled in association with the Global Volcanism Program. For a copy contact the American Geophysical Union in the Smithsonian Institution, Tele. 202-462-6900, or in the USA call toll free at 800-966-2481. In Europe call Inter+49-5556-1440. Order by email at (orders@agu.org).

Common Volcanic Terms

Aa A Hawaiian term for a type of basaltic lava flow whose upper surface consists of jagged, tumbled pieces of lava. Such a surface forms because the cooled, brittle outer surface of the flow breaks in response to continued movement of the flow's liquid core.

Active volcano An erupting volcano, or one that has erupted in recorded human history. This writer prefers to call one that is actually erupting a **Live Volcano**.

Airfall deposit Pyroclastic fragments that have fallen from an eruption cloud.

Ash Fine pyroclastic material down to dust size, that's formed by explosive volcanic eruptions.

Caldera A very large basin or depression on a mountain top with steep walls, larger than a crater and usually formed by a cataclysmic or colossal explosive eruption in which the magma chamber is emptied, causing the top of the volcano to collapse in on itself. Crater Lake, Pinatubo and Changbai Shan are good examples.

Cinder Small pieces of volcanic material, usually basaltic and about pea or gravel-sized or smaller, that form when molten magma/lava is ejected into the air from a volcano that is high is gas and/or bubbles. This material cools while in the air during lava fountaining or stromboian-type eruptions. Other names for the same material is **scoria** or **tephra**.

Cinder cone A small conical-shaped volcano composed of cinders. These typically form during a single short-lived eruption, oftentimes with strombolian eruptions, which throws cinders or ash into the air. The down-wind side is always the highest part of the cone.

Columnar jointing Fractures or joints caused by shrinkage, which occurs as thick lava beds cool and solidifiy slowly. These are usually 6-sided columns resembling fence posts or telefone poles or stacked piles of logs. These sites often assume names such as *devil's wood pile*.

Composite volcano Same as **stratovolcano**.

Crater The bowl-shaped depression on top of a volcano where eruptions have occurred.

Crystalline rock A hard rock composed of interlocking crystals, often of igneous origins and caused by heat and/or pressure. Good examples are **granite**, which was originally molten magma, cooled slowly underground allowing the formation of crystals. Another non-igneous crystalline rock is **quartzite**. It starts as sandstone, then transformed with the help of heat and pressure.

Dormant volcano A volcano that is not presently erupting but is likely to erupt sometime in the future.

Extinct volcano A volcano that is not expected to erupt in the future; a dead volcano.

Extrusive Rock that's been erupted or extruded from inside the earth, such as lava. All volcanic rock is extrusive.

Fissure eruption Eruption along a straight line, crack or fault line over a distance of several hundred meters rather from a single vent. Iceland is famous for fissure eruptions.

Flank eruption An eruption from the side of a volcano rather than from the summit crater.

Fountaining This occurs when very fluid or easy-flowing magma/lava comes out of a small vent with great pressure and squirts high in the air for up to 100 meters or more. A good example of this type of eruption is at Kilauea Volcano in Hawaii.

Hot-spot volcanos Volcanos in the middle of a tectonic plate (there are about 12 tectonic plates on the earth's surface), rather than along the edges where most volcanic activity occurs. Hawaii is a hot spot, where as most other volcanos around the Pacific *Ring of Fire* are found along the edge of the Pacific Plate and/or Ocean.

Igneous rocks Rocks formed from the cooling & solidification of magma (intrusive) or lava (extrusive).

Intrusion A rock body formed when molten magma forces its way into surrounding host rocks then cools slowly and solidifies underground. This is how granite is formed.

Intrusive Rock that forms from molten magma but solidifies before reaching the surface, and before it has a chance to be erupted into a volcano. Granite is the best example.

Lahar A lahar forms when loose material on the slopes of a volcano slides or is washed downhill.

Lapilli Round, pyroclastic material ejected from a volcano; from 4 mm to 32 mm in diameter.

Lava This is molten or liquid rock after it comes out of the earth and reaches the surface. Molten rock inside the earth and before it reaches the surface is called **magma**.

Lava block An older block of cold lava thrown out of a volcano during an explosive eruption.

Lava bomb A semi-liquid mass of lava thrown out of a volcano during an eruption. While hurtling & spinning in the air, it normally assumes a round or oblong shape while still semi-liquid. If a cooled lava bomb has a flat spot on one side this means it wasn't totally solid when it hit the ground.

Lava dome A steep-sided and dome-shaped structure which forms inside the crater of a volcano. It is built of very stiff magma that rises slowly from the throat or vent and slowly cools & cracks on the surface. Mt. St. Helens & Bezymianny in Kamchatka have good examples.

Lava lake A lake of molten lava in a volcanic crater; or in solidified or partially-solidified stages.

Lava tube A tunnel formed when the surface of a lava flow cools & solidifies and the still-molten interior lava continues to flows. It's also the hollow tube or **cave** that remains when the interior lava drains away.

Maar A crater formed by a violent explosion but not usually accompanied by igneous extrusion. They are commonly filled by a small circular lake. This is not a commonly used term.

Magma Liquid rock that's inside the earth. When it reaches the surface it's called **lava**.

Magma chamber A region where molten magma rises closer to the earth's surface. It is the area below an active volcano which stores the magma before eruption. If the magma cools before eruption can occur, the chamber forms an intrusive rock such as granite.

Magmatic eruption A volcanic eruption with fresh magma when pressure from beneath forces magma to the surface. It's always accompanied by volcanic quakes and detectable with seismographs.

Metamorphic rock Rocks formed from other rocks when subject to heat and pressure. Examples; sandstone is converted to quartzite, and shale evolves into slate or schist.

Nuée ardente Fast moving, dense glowing cloud of hot volcanic ash & gas erupted from a volcano. This French term was probably first used on the Caribbean island of Martinique referring to the eruption of Mt. Pelée. Same as **pyroclastic flow**.

Obsidian Generally black-colored volcanic glass created by quick cooling lava without crystals.

15

Pahoehoe Hawaiian name for a type of basaltic lava flow whose upper surface is smooth or ropy.

Phreatic (pron. freatic) explosion Caused by hot water and/or steam. An example is after heavy rains, water seeps down to hot rocks near the summit of a volcano, then turns to steam. Something has to give, so it's often a violent explosion. This is what happened on 8/10/1996 at Canlaon Volcano in the Philippines which killed 3 hikers. There was no magma rising from below and no seismic warnings, only a hot water/steam explosion after heavy rains.

Phreatomagmatic eruption An explosion caused by a combination of rising magma and water seeping down to the hot rocks near this magma chamber.

Pillow lava Smooth, rounded, pillow-shaped lava that's extruded underwater with rapid cooling.

Plume A rising column of magma from deep in the mantle responsible for hot-spot volcanos. Or referring to a cloud of ash rising from a volcanic blast or eruption.

Pumice A very light-weight volcanic rock filled with gas bubbles resembling a sponge. In many cases it's light enough to float on water. After Krakatau's big eruption in 1883, ships sailing through the Sunda Straits, reported floating pumice up to 2 meters deep.

Pyroclastics All volcanic material ejected into the air from a volcanic vent. Includes ash, cinders and lava bombs.

Pyroclastic flow A mass of hot, dry rock fragments mixed with hot gases moving down the slope of a volcano at high speeds. This is the same as the French term, **nuée ardente.**

Scoria Small pieces of volcanic material about pea or gravel-sized or smaller, that forms when molten magma/lava is ejected into the air from a volcano. Same as **cinders** or **tephra.**

Sedimentary rocks Rocks which are formed by the accumulation of sediment in the bottom of a lake or sea (limestone, siltstone or shale) or at the land surface (sandstone or conglomerate). These rocks are normally layered having been formed from flat or nearly flat-lying deposits.

Seismometer or **seismograph** An instrument that measures shaking in the earth. It's placed on a volcano and usually radios reports of shaking or tremors to a monitor or laboratory. This gives advanced and/or remote warning of an impending eruption.

Seismology The study of earthquakes, seismic waves, and the structure of the earth's interior.

Shield volcano A very low, rounded & broad-based volcano that was created by very fluid or easy-flowing lavas. Mauna Loa on the big island of Hawaii or Mt. Etna are good examples.

Skylight An opening in the top or roof of an active lava tube caused by local roof collapse.

Spatter cone Similar to cinder cone, but is smaller and very steep-side. It's created by lava fountaining but with low & intermittent ejections of lava which cools or solidifies after it falls to the rim.

Stratovolcano A steep-side cone-shaped volcano built of many layers, often alternating between cinders and lava flows. Another name is **composite cone.** Fujiama, Egmont, Rainier and Kilimanjaro are all stratovolcanos.

Tephra A general term for all airborne material ejected from a volcano. Same as **pyroclastic.**

Throat, volcanic This is the same as vent, vent pipe, neck or conduit of a volcano. After erosion removes outer layers of a volcano or cinder cone, all that may be left standing is the more weather-resistant throat or neck. Peaks in the Hoggar Mountains of southern Algeria, or Devil's Tower, Wyoming, USA, are good examples of the remains of old volcanic throats.

Tilt meter An instrument than measures the slow upward movement or inflation at the surface of a seismically active area. This is caused by the slow upward-moving magma from below which is seeking a way to the surface. This tells volcanologists if magma is close to the surface and if an eruption is eminent.

Tsunami Japanese name for **tidal wave.** A great sea wave produced by a submarine earthquake or volcanic eruptions. These can and do cross the Pacific Ocean and can cause great damage.

Tuff Consolidated volcanic ash or cinders often found on the side of a stratovolcano.

Vent or **vent pipe** The throat or conduit in which magma flows to the surface to be a volcano.

Chemical Composition of Magma/Lava

Chemical compositions that produce thin, easy-flowing magmas or lavas are associated with nonviolent eruptions such as found at Kilauea Volcano in Hawaii; whereas compositions that produce thick, sluggish-flowing magmas correlate with explosive-type eruptions or volcanic events such as found in Indonesia.

Very thin easy-flowing lavas are often **basalt** with roughly 48% to 55% silica. Next is **andesite** between 55% & 60% silica, then **dacite** between 60% & 70% silica. Lavas with the highest content of silica is **rhyolite** at a high 70% to 77%. Rhyolite is generally very thick, sluggish-flowing lavas.

Type of Eruptions & Volcanos

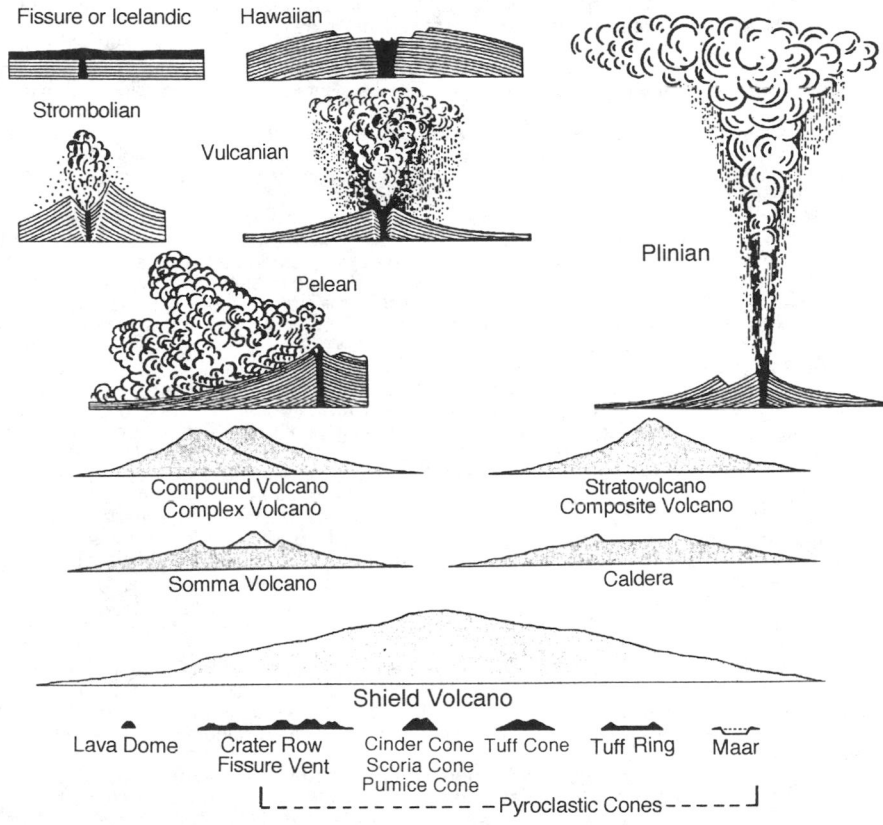

From **Volcanos of the World,** Simkin & Siebert (after A. Holmes & R.J. Pike)

Chapter 3--Europe

This is the first of 7 chapters covering the world's mountains. This part includes all of Europe and has 99 mapped areas. Some of the regions included here are Greenland (because it's a province of Denmark), the Açores and Canary Islands, and from Spitsbergen to Greece. The countries of the former Soviet Union will be included in the Asian chapter.

Most people in the so-called developed world--North America, Europe, Australia and New Zealand, have at least one language which originated in Europe, so language in Europe is not the problem that it can be in other parts of the world. If a traveler has either English, French or German, he or she can usually get by just about anywhere, and if one has all three, then traveling is made very easy. The next best language to have in Europe is Españole or perhaps Italiano. Many people in the north of Europe speak about 3 languages. This is especially true in Der Nederlands, Denmark & Sweden.

It's difficult to make any generalizations concerning climbing here because of the vast distances covered by this chapter. Needless to say, the further north you go, the colder and more miserable the weather becomes. If you are in Iceland, or other North Atlantic islands, rain gear is standard equipment, along with a sturdy tent.

If you're in the Mediterranean region, then it's going to be hot and dry in summer, but cool and wet in winter. There are no glaciers in Spain, Italy (excluding the Alps) or Greece. The majority of the maps in this section cover the Alps. Throughout the Alps you'll see glaciers-- some very small, especially on the southern slopes, but others rather extensive, such as in the Berner and Pennine Alpen of Switzerland. An ice ax & crampons should be standard equipment for all of the Alps; although on some of the easier and more popular peaks, there's a well-beaten path in the snow to the summit and this equipment is sometimes not needed.

In some areas such as the Dolomiti in northern Italy, you'll have little use for ice equipment; but instead may want to take rock climbing gear if you're inclined to do technical routes. The Dolomiti offers some of the best rock climbing in Europe. But there are often easy routes to all summits.

Crimes against travelers are rather unusual in Europe, especially in the northern parts. What is meant here is, someone getting into your tent, or picking your pocket in railway stations, etc. In places like Iceland, the Faroe Islands, Norway, these crimes are almost unheard of. In all the author's travels in Europe he has lost nothing. While most people use huts or refuges in the Alps, the author always camped--but never had anything taken from his tent. However, the author has always taken more precautions in the south. In southern Europe, it's best not to leave a tent for long periods of time. This region is safe when compared to the rest of the world.

While the costs of transportation in Europe is high, it's also possible to travel in this region very inexpensively--that's by hitch hiking. The last time the author traveled there extensively, hitch hiking was very good in the Alps and all over northern and northwest Europe. Areas not so good were the southern regions. But hitching in the 1990's was not as good as it was in the 1960's & 1970's.

For most people living outside the continent, special passes are obtainable for the railway system throughout most of Europe. These are called **Eurail Passes**, and can be bought and used anywhere from 2 weeks to 3 months. If you're visiting all of Europe, these passes are fine, but if you're just going to the Alps, it's best to take an occasional bus or maybe hitch hike in the mountains where no bus service exists. In 1979, the author carried one, 2 or 3 signs; stating the name of the mountain, best-known town in the area of the mountain he wanted a ride to, and distance in kms (especially if the destination was near). Using this method he made 21 ascents in 33 days, beginning with Grossglocker in Austria and finishing with Ecrins in France. Renting a car is best, but expensive. Buses offer another alternative, but these days, almost all travelers drive their own cars.

Typical of all of Europe, whether it be in the north, east, west or south, you can almost always find huts or refuges on the higher and more prominent mountains. This is one area of the world where you can climb without a tent.

Besides huts high on the mountains, Europe has many youth hostels. Most of these are found in the largest cities, but also in most of the important mountain resort towns as well. There's a fee for the membership card, but it's good for a year and allows you to use all International Youth Hostels in the world. Sometimes you can get in without a membership card, but you'll usually pay a slightly higher fee.

Getting good maps of mountains in Europe is easy. Stop at visitor centers at airports and railway stations, and they can give you an address of a local bookstore or map sales office. Or ask which town in the vicinity of where you want to climb caters to climbers or hikers. Go there, to places like Chamonix or Zermatt, and maps are easily available.

As a general rule, the further north you go in Europe, the more expensive everything becomes. The further south, the cheaper things are. However, in the 1990's, prices were equalizing some.

The main street of Zermatt with the Matterhorn rising in the distance. The only vehicles in town are small electric cars or vans.

Young boy milking a goat in a high pasture of Switzerland.

Trails of South Greenland

The area covered by this map is the extreme southern end of Greenland. This region is the warmest and most-heavily populated of all of Greenland. Important towns in the area are Julianehab, the largest, and Narsaq. Other places on the map are much smaller, and are populated almost exclusively by Eskimos. There are almost no roads here so people get from place to place by boat.

For the traveler, the one place of prime importance is the airport at Narssarsuaq. It's the only airfield in the region, and is an important link to the outside world. This airfield was built during World War II by the Americans, and was named Bluey West II. In the 1990's, there was the airport & tourist office, Hotel Nasarsuaq (with small store, restaurant, bar and bookshop), Feldstation & youth hostel, hospital and a small port area. A number of Danish workers live and work there as Greenland is a territory or province of Denmark.

Few really high mountains exist in the area covered by this map, but all rise directly from sea level, making the local relief rather high. For people wanting to travel to the more isolated areas, helicopters or private boats must be hired for such trips. This involves time and/or great expense.

For those who can be satisfied with climbing lower mountains or trekking, this region is excellent. The trails shown, for the most part, are tractor roads or sheep trails, which have evolved over time. In recent years, the DVL (a Danish youth hostel and trekking-type club) has painted stones and made markers or stone cairns along some of the more scenic routes. This same group, with headquarters at Feldstation, also has fixed up old houses and made them into youth hostels in some areas which can be used by anyone for a small fee. For anyone wanting to hike in this area, you must stop at the tourist office for the latest information. No doubt things have changed a lot since the author's visit in 1979. The latest guidebooks will update the author's information.

Here's what the author did. He took a tourist boat from Narssarsuaq across the inlet to Kassiarsuk (Qassiarsuk), which now has a youth hostel, then had a leisurely walk for about 2 1/2 days to Narsaq. There are now (2000) 4 youth hostels along this trek! From Narsaq, he took a state-run ferryboat back to Narssarsuaq in about 1 1/2 hours. This ferry runs once a week. Narsaq now has a youth hostel & 4 hotels.

The author had marvelous weather on his trip, but even in summer, go prepared for cool & wet weather--and mosquitoes! Fly to Greenland from either Iceland (twice weekly) or Denmark (twice weekly), as nothing was going to or from North America as of 2001. Someone at the Hotel Narssarsuaq, youth hostel or airport tourist office can help with the latest information concerning trails, ferries, private boats, the whereabouts of small stores, use of youth hostels,

This is the fjord just south of Kagsiarsuk. Notice the icebergs in the distance.

Map 1-1, Trails of South Greenland

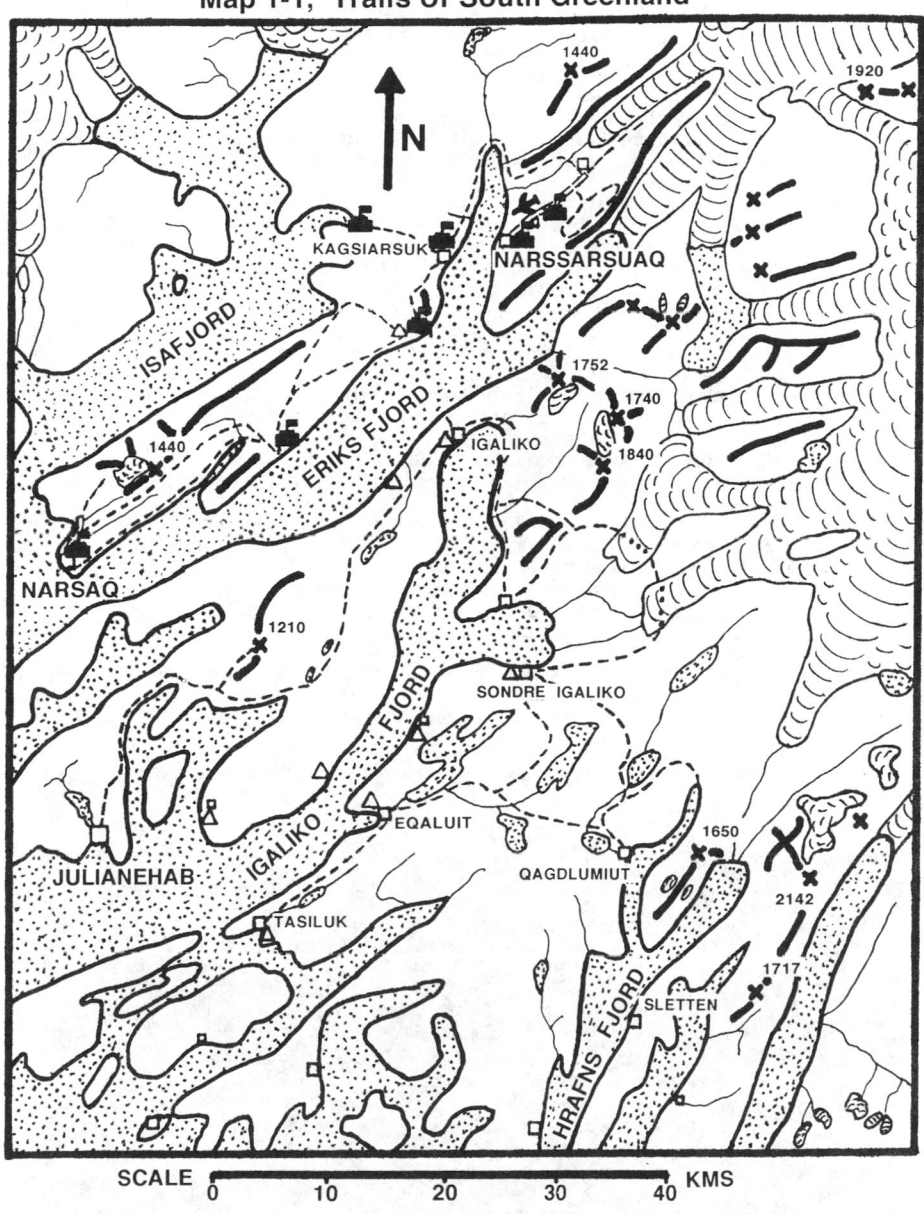

SCALE

| 0 | 10 | 20 | 30 | 40 | KMS |

etc. Consider packing in as much food and supplies as you can on the plane to save money.
Maps Tourist map, *South Greenland*, 1:250,000; and maps in **Atlas-handbog over Gronland**; and the guide *Hiker's Guide--South Greenland* (buy at the airport youth hostel); and travel guidebook **Iceland, Greenland & the Faroe Islands**, Lonely Planet.

Eiriksjokull & Langjokull Icefield, Iceland

In an area about 100 kms northeast of Reykjavik, and just a few kms due north of Geyser and Gullfoss, lies the Langjokull, the second largest ice sheet in Iceland. The highest peak in the region is not on or part of this glacier, however; that honor goes to Eiriksjokull, 1675 meters, located just to the west or northwest of Langjokull.

As with all of Iceland, this area is also of volcanic origin, but there's nothing in the way of new or active volcanos nearby. In the flats immediately northwest of Eiriksjokull is an area called Hallmundarhraun. Somewhere there, is some lava Radiocarbon dated at 925 AD. About 30 kms due east of the northern part of Langjokull is another ice cap called Hofsjokull. Beneath it is a Holocene subglacier volcano.

Unlike some other mountain and glacier regions in Iceland, this area is relatively near some main roads, populated areas, and gasoline stations. For example, a straight line route between Husafell and Eiriksjokull is about 25 kms; the same is true from Gullfoss (the largest and most famous waterfall in the country) to Blafell. This means that the foot traveler or mountain climber can, with a large pack, walk to any point in the region covered by this map. For the foot traveler it would take 2 or 3 days to climb either Blafell or Eiriksjokull, and return to the main roads. The author didn't climb here, but has been in the area. Big volcanic escarpments surround Eiriksjokull, so don't expect that to be an easy climb. Blafell looks a bit easier--on the map--and Thursborg even easier, but that's in the middle of a big glacier with crevasses and poor visibility.

You can hitch hike to Husafell (a bit slow getting out of there) and to Gullfoss. Lots of traffic going to Gullfoss and Geyser, as that area is the premier tourist attraction in Iceland. There's at least one gasoline station with small store at Geyser and Husafell. However, buy all supplies in Reykjavik for better variety and lower prices, if possible.

The track from Gullfoss to Hveravelar is quite good with large buses taking the more rugged *tourists* into that area. Groups can rent 4WD's. The huts shown on the map are available to anyone, but you must contact the Iceland Tourist Board in Reykjavik for reservations and other information concerning their availability and also the latest road (track) conditions. Good maps are available in the large bookstores in Reykjavik.

The worst part of a camping trip to Iceland is the bad weather, especially the high winds. Take a good tent and look for a sheltered spot to place it. Also, take clothing suitable for cold, wet and windy conditions. July, August, and the first part of September are the best months to visit and mountain climb in Iceland.

Maps *Adalkort Blad 5 (Map 5), Mid-Island*, 1:250,000, from Geodœtisk Institit, Copenhagen, Danmark but buy in Reykjavik; also 1:50,000 and 1:100,000 maps available in bookstores in Reykjavik; and the travel guidebook, **Iceland, Greenland & the Faroe Islands**, Lonely Planet.

This is the whaling station on the coast of Iceland not far from Eiriksjokull.

Map 2-2, Eiriksjokull & Langjokull Icefield, Iceland

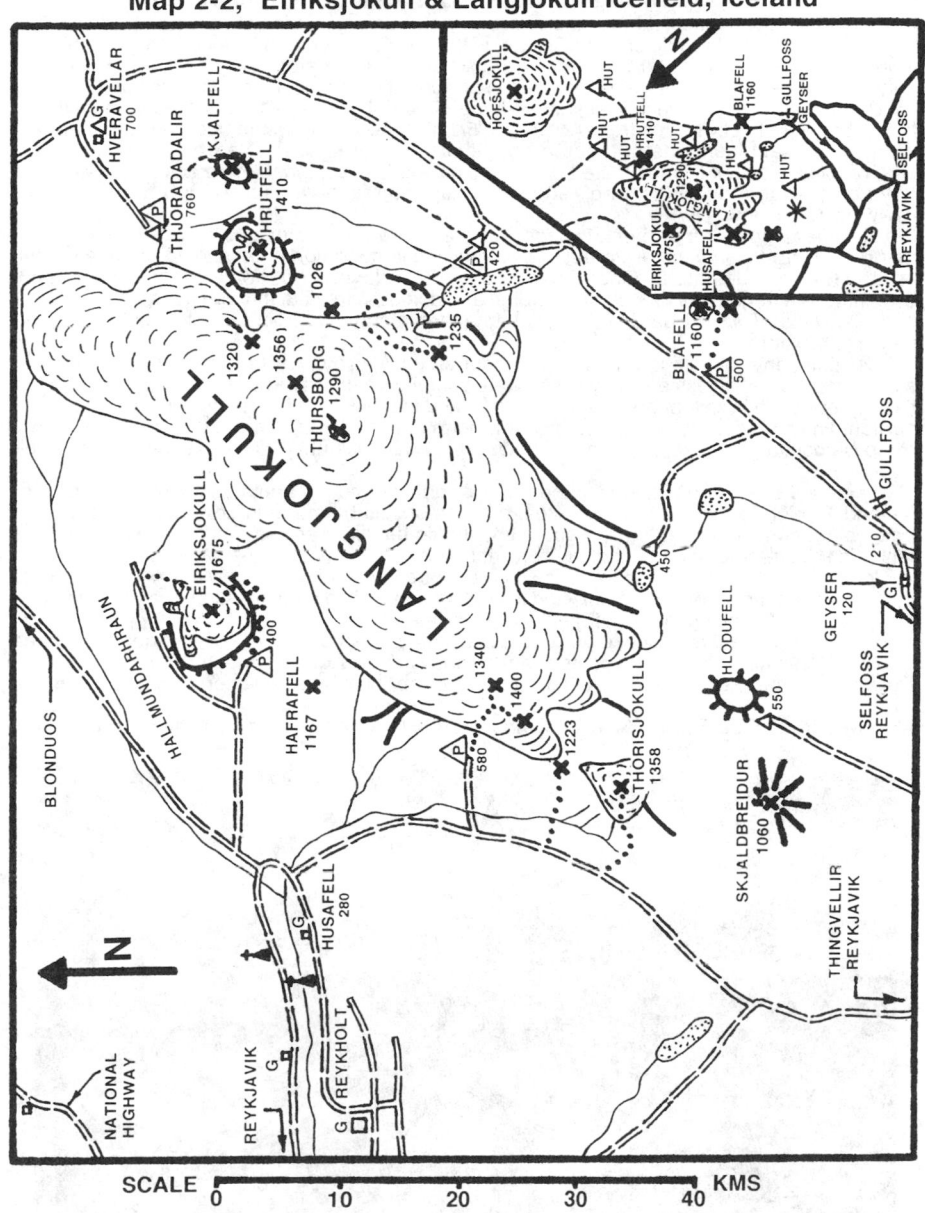

SCALE 0   10   20   30   40   KMS

Bardarbunga & Hofsjokull Ice Sheet, Iceland

Featured on this map is a mountainous region and ice cap in the very center of Iceland. The area surrounding Hofsjokull, or Hofs Glacier, is the most isolated in all the country. The highest mountain in the region is Bardarbunga, approximately 2000 meters. It's located very near the northwest corner or edge of Vatnajokull and is possibly the third highest point in Iceland.

Bardarbunga is a semiactive volcano. In the 1700's, there were 13 recorded eruptions, and the last period of activity was from 12/1902 to 5/1903. According to the book, **Volcanos of the World,** the exact locations of these eruptive sites is not known. Nearby to the south and southwest and just off this map, are Loki-Fogrufjoll and Grimsvotna, 2 more active volcanos that have erupted in the 1980's and 1990's. For updates see websites (www.norvol.hi.is) or (www.volcano.si.edu/gvp/)

The map shows a number of *roads,* but these are undeveloped tracks. This region is uninhabited and distances are great. Only vehicles in good condition should be taken to this area. However, despite the fact these tracks are undeveloped, some are good enough to accommodate large buses which take foreign and domestic tourists throughout the area. Check at the Icelandic Tourist Board in Reykjavik for more information about tour buses heading that way, or about renting 4WD's.

For someone to walk into this region from either Akureyi, Burfell or Reykjavik would be almost impossible, unless a supply cache were somehow set up ahead of time. Iceland isn't that big, but everyone lives around the coastal areas and the middle of the island is uninhabited. The straight line distance from Akureyi to Bardarbunga is about 120 kms. You should be able to climb Bardarbunga in one day from the end of the 4WD track at 1000 meters, as shown on this map.

There are several tourist huts in the area. To get information about using them, contact the Iceland Tourist Board in Reykjavik. Reservations should be made in advance. Regardless of one's plans concerning the huts, a good tent should be taken anyway. If camping, place your tent in a sheltered place and out of the constant wind.

Iceland is notorious for bad weather so go prepared for cold, wet and windy conditions, even in the warmest month of July. Snow and ice equipment should also be taken--ice ax, crampons, goggles, etc.--if climbing the higher peaks is anticipated.

Reykjavik is the best place to get all supplies. Maps can be found in the larger bookstores. 4WD vehicles can be hired or rented, but at heavy cost. Again, consult the tourist office in Reykjavik for the latest conditions of the tracks, availability of huts, weather, where to buy maps, etc.

Maps *Adalkort Blad 5 (Map 5)*, *Mid-Island,* 1:250,000, from Geodœtisk Institut, Copenhagen,

This is near Gullfoss and a rather typical scene of Iceland.

Map 3-3, Bardarbunga & Hofsjokull Ice Sheet, Iceland

Danmark, but buy in Reykjavik; also 1:50,000 and 1:100,000 maps available in Reykjavik; and the travel guidebook, **Iceland, Greenland & the Faroe Islands**, Lonely Planet.

Hekla, Katla & the Myrdalsjokull, Iceland

Talk to anyone from Iceland and they'll tell you the most famous mountain on the island is Hekla. The reason is it's the most active volcano they've got. At 1491 meters, it has perpetual snow and is now building glaciers. Parts of Hekla seem easy to climb, but it appears the more difficult or challenging climb would be Godusteinn at 1666 meters, a part of the Eyjafjallajokull. Another famous peak in the area is Katla, about 1450 meters, the highest point of which is on the southeastern part of the Myrdalsjokull, or Myrdals Glacier.

Since 1104 AD, **Hekla** has erupted 18 times. All activity is along the 5 1/2-km-long fissure called Heklugja, which tends ENE-WSW. Large eruptions of Hekla, have spewed tephra throughout Iceland which make valuable time-markers to date other volcanic eruptions. Hekla is famous for it's huge volumes of lava being extruded via flank fissures. A big explosion on 1/17/1991 sent tephra to the north coast. Large-volume lava flows lasted from 1/1991 through 3/1991. The last eruption started 2/29/2000 and ended on 3/8/2000. On a NASA flight over the area 2/29/2000, the plume extended up to ~13 kms. By 3/1/2000, the new lava had covered 17 sq/kms.

Katla lies beneath the **Myrdalsjokull Icecap**. This subglacier volcano has produced many glacier-outburst floods (jokulhlaups) over the years. Katla is part of an 11x14 km subglacier caldera, with most of it's activity and floods originating from the eastern side. Altogether, there have been 17 eruptions since 930 AD, the most catastrophic was the 1755-56 event which took human lives. Katla had a minor eruption on 6/25/1955, but has been quiet ever since. In this same area are **Vatnafjoll** and **Torfajokull Volcanos** which have seen activity in the last 1200 years or so. For updates see websites (www.norvol.hi.is) or (www.volcano.si.edu/gvp/).

The road running through Vik is the national highway which circles the island. There are several buses a day passing through Vik, but the area is not that far from Reykjavik, so getting a lift is easy, at least up to Vik. Beyond Vik, hitch hiking is more difficult, as traffic thins out. Both Katla and Hekla can be climbed from paved highways in one or 2 days each.

If you're coming directly from Reykjavik to climb, buy your supplies there. However, Vik is the largest settlement around and has several stores, a youth hostel and other bed & breakfast places. Burfell also has a store and places to sleep.

There are several tourist huts in this area that are available. Contact the National Tourist Office in Reykjavik for details on availability, costs, and reservations. They are used mostly on weekends and in summer. Most roads shown on the map, other than those leading to Vik or Burfell, are for 4WD vehicles. The back country of Iceland is uninhabited and wild. Only vehicles in good condition should ply these wastelands.

Good topographic maps are available in the larger bookstores in Reykjavik. The weather in

Fog and mist along the south coast of Iceland near Vik.

Map 4-2, Hekla, Katla & the Myrdalsjokull, Iceland

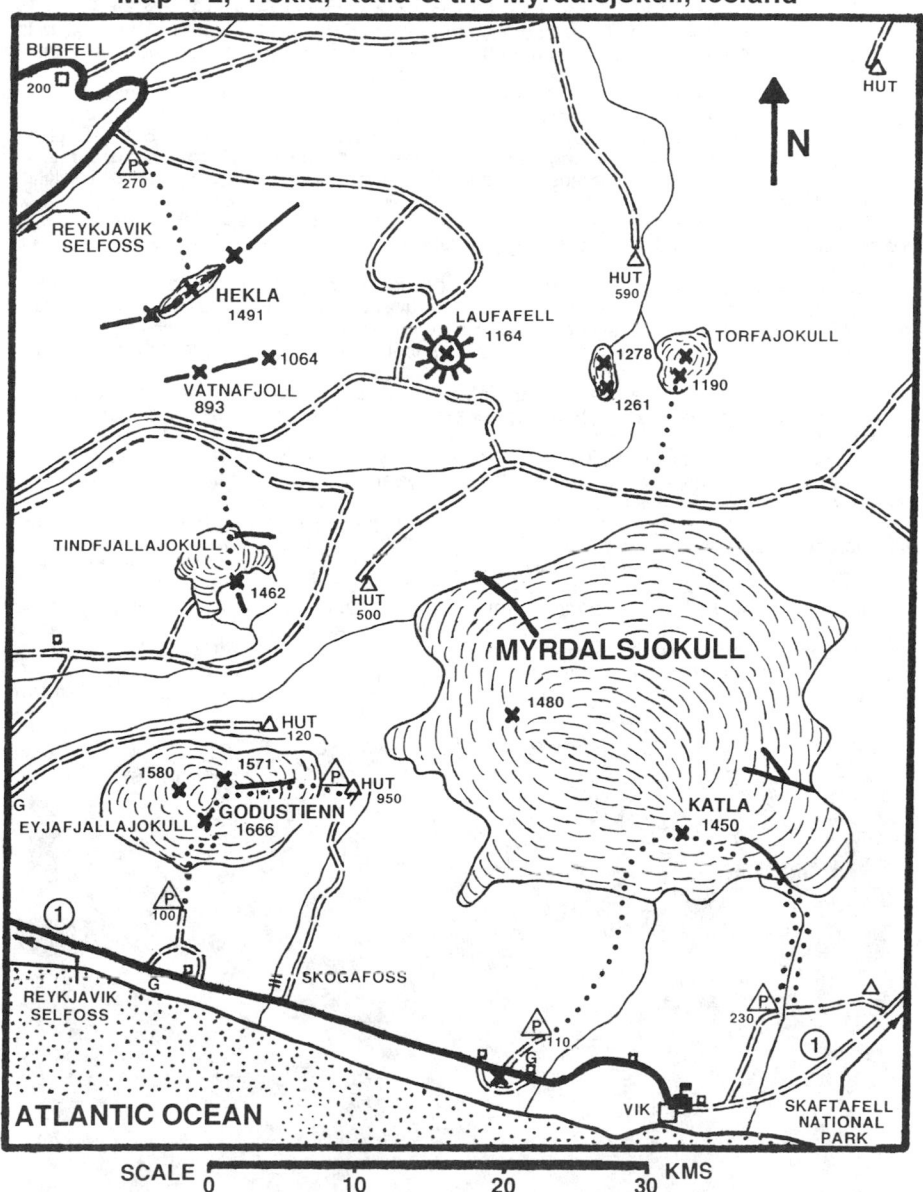

this part of Iceland is the worst in the whole country, as most of the storms come from the southwest. Rain gear is perhaps the most important of all the equipment you can take. You'll also need a good tent, ice ax & crampons.

Maps *Adalkort Blat 6 (Map 6). Midsudurland,* 1:250,000, from Geodœtisk Institut, Copenhagen, Danmark; also 1:50,000 and 1:100,000 maps available in Reykjavik; and the travel guidebook, **Iceland, Greenland & the Faroe Islands**, Lonely Planet.

Hvannadalshnukur, Oræfajokull, Iceland

Near the south coast of Iceland, and at the southern edge of Vatnajokull, Iceland's largest glacier, stands the highest mountain on the island, Hvannadalshnukur, at 2119 meters. This peak is the highest of several summits which ring a very old and eroded volcanic crater or caldera, called Oræfajokull. There are 3 other peaks over 2000 meters on the same crater rim.

Oræfajokull is considered an active volcano. It's last eruptive period was from 8/3/1727 to 5/1/1728, and was located somewhere near the western rim of the caldera.

You can get to this region from Reykjavik by taking public buses, or hitch hiking. But if you plan to hitch hike, better expect to wait for long periods, as there aren't that many cars around. Renting a vehicle is another possibility, but because you can camp and/or climb right from Highway 1, taking a bus might be the better choice.

If you're considering using buses, inquire about getting one of 3 bus passes for Iceland *before you leave home*. They are called *Full-Circle Pass, Omnibuspass,* and *Highland Pass.* See the guidebook below for details.

You can find a good campsite near Sandfell, or maybe camp at the Skaftafell National Park Headquarters Campground a few kms up the road northwest. There are at least 2 stores in the area; one at Skaftafell camp, the other at Fagurholsmyri. No need to bring food all the way from Reykjavik.

From the main highway, which generally follows Iceland's coast, **Hvannadalshnukur** can be climbed in one day (a very long day for some). The best way up begins at a point 1/2 km north of a pasture and one lone tree called Sandfell. There's no trail, so simply follow the hump or hogsback ridge up to the ice, then to the crater rim, and finally north across the caldera basin to the summit. Another longer route is from the petrol station at Fagurholsmyri. Some crevasses exist on both routes, but if climbed in good weather they can easily be avoided. The author felt safe in his solo effort in 1979, but now in his later years, would never do it again! There are other more challenging routes also.

On 7/11/1979, the author climbed to the summit beginning at or near Fagurholsmyri. Near the top he was sinking into snow about 15 cms. He then met about a dozen English hikers and went down a different route--the way they had come up. It took 5 1/2 hours to get up; 81/2 hours round-trip. He then walked and got a ride back to Fagurholsmyri.

Because of the way the mountains in this area are situated, the weather around Skaftafell Park seems to be better than in other parts of Iceland, a country notorious for bad weather. Climbers must have a strong, sturdy tent (as high winds constantly buffet the region), ice ax, crampons, rain gear, and warm cloths suitable for glacier travel.

Good topographic maps can be bought in Reykjavik's bookstores. At Skaftafell Park

Hvannadalshnvkur as seen from the point marked 1848 meters on the map. The distance is about 5 kms.

Map 5-1, Hvannadalshnuker, Oræfajokull, Iceland

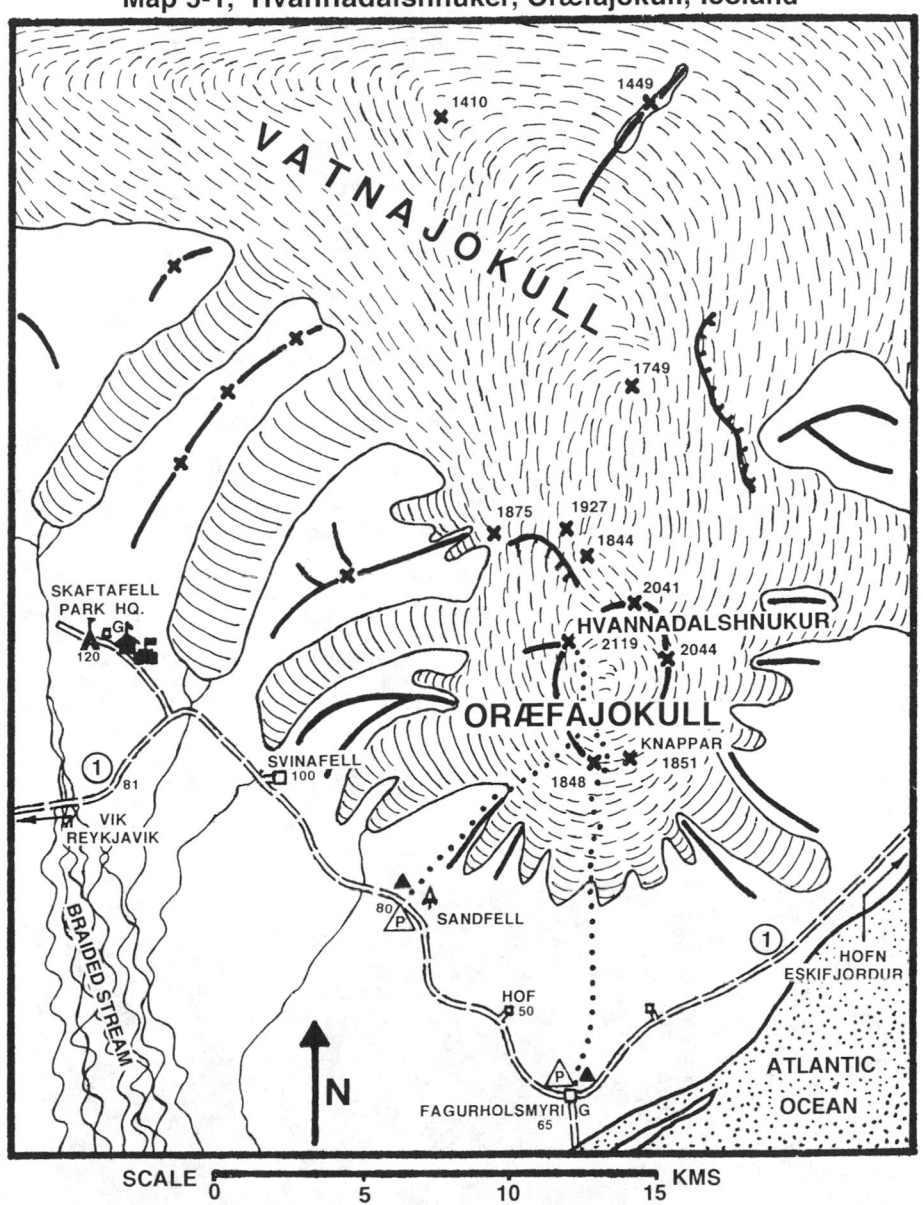

SCALE 0   5   10   15 KMS

Headquarters, there's a visitor center and a hotel nearby. They can give additional information--from maps to weather reports.

Maps *Adalkort Blad 9 (Map 9), Sudausturland,* 1:250,000, from Geodœtisk Institut,Copenhagen, Danmark; also 1:50,000 and 1:100,000 maps available; and the travel guidebook, **Iceland, Greenland & the Faroe Islands**, Lonely Planet.

Snæfell, Askja and Kverkfjoll, Iceland

In southeastern Iceland, just northeast of the large Vatnajokull (Vatna Glacier), stands a rather famous eroded volcano, Snæfell. It's one of the higher peaks in the country at 1833 meters. Because Snæfell stands *behind* the largest glacier in Europe, and is in its *rainshadow,* the snow line here is a bit higher than in the southwest part of Iceland. Also on this map is the volcano and crater named Askja at 1510 meters. It too is on the dry side of Vatnajokull. Also, right on the northern boundary of Vatnajokull is the Kverkfjoll Volcano.

Two of these 3 mountains are considered active volcanos. **Askja** or **Oskjuvatn Caldera** measures 9x14 kms, and inside that is another crater about 3x4 kms in diameter which is filled with Oskjuvatn Lake. A road ends near the lip of the crater lake. Askja has had 8 eruptive periods in the 1900's, most of which were in the inner crater and around the lake. The last eruptive period was from 10/26 to 12/5/1961. **Kverkfjoll** last erupted in 5 & 6/1968. That was somewhere to the northeast of the highest peak. For volcano updates see the websites (www.norvol.hi.is) or (www.volcano.si.edu/gvp/).

To climb **Snæfell**, it would take a 4WD vehicle and a couple of days from the town of Egilsstadir; or if you're using public transport and/or hitch hiking, 3 or 4 days or more would be needed, from somewhere on the national highway, or from the little town of Valthjofsstadur.

If you're interested in venturing further into this cold desert, say for example, to climb Kverkfjoll, at 1920 meters, it would be a serious undertaking; a small expedition in fact. It would either cost a lot of money if you wanted to rent or hire a 4WD vehicle, or it would take a lot of time-perhaps 8 to 10 days if you were to walk! The distance from the national highway near Modrudalur to Kverkfjoll, would be around 100 kms.

There are buses running along the national highway, but no public transport exists on any of the back roads--in fact it's completely uninhabited. Logurinin Lake is somewhat of a resort area with a small forest nearby. Because of the size of the caldera at Askja, it receives some visitors from the Akureyri area. There are also huts near each of these mountains which would make a visit more tolerable.

The weather in these parts is probably the best in all of Iceland, largely because it's on the lee side of the island, and in the *rain shadow* much of the time. However, even in July expect cold and windy conditions and don't forget rain gear. A tough, wind resistant tent is a most important piece of equipment--along with ice ax & crampons.

Look for good maps of various scales in Reykjavik bookstores, and contact the Iceland Tourist Board for information about using the tourist huts in the area. All food can be bought in Egilsstadir or Akureyri, the only real towns in the region. Egilsstadir has a campground, 2 hotels,

This is the elevated roadway across the highly braided river south
of Skaftafell (see previous map).

Map 6-3, Snæfell, Askja & Kverkfjoll, Iceland

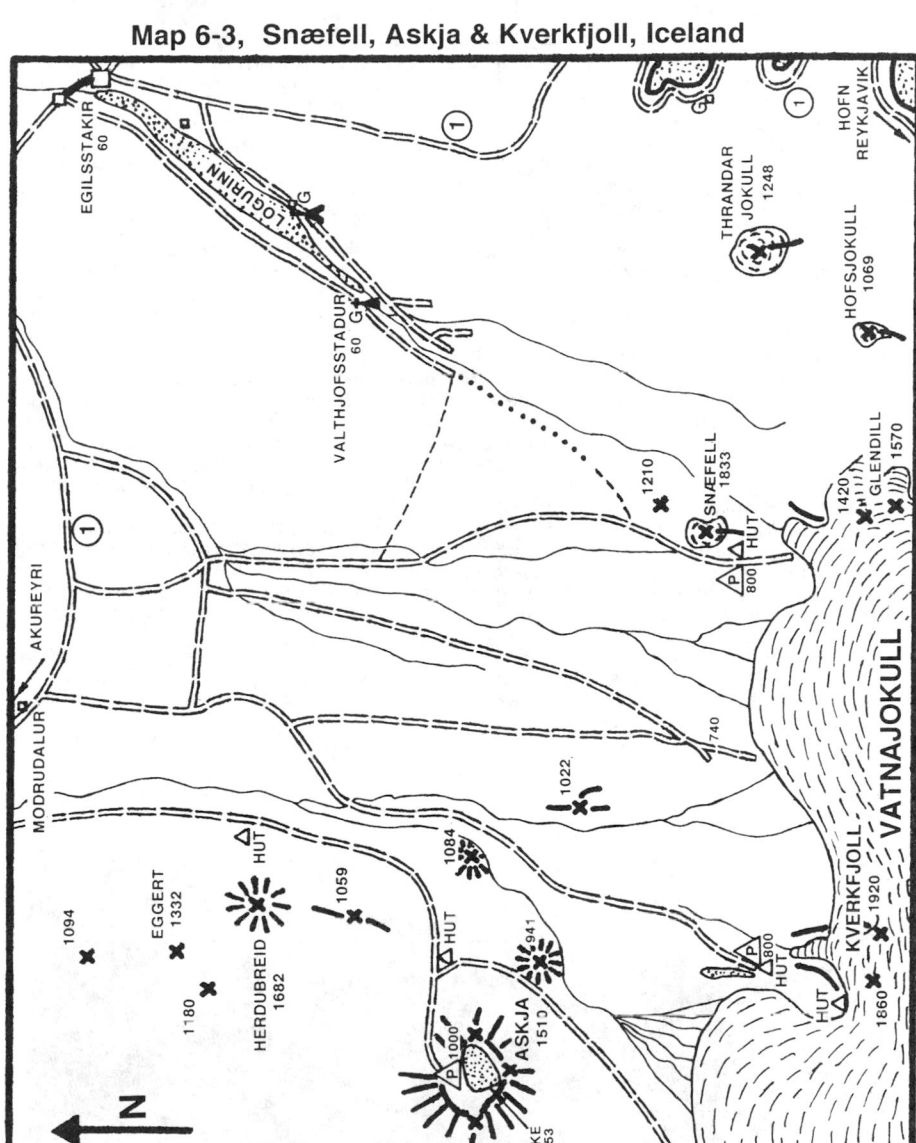

SCALE 0 — 10 — 20 — 30 — 40 KMS

at least one store and a tourist office.
Maps *Adalkort Blad 8 (Map 8), Midausturland,* 1 250,000, from Geodœtisk Institut, Copenhagen, Danmark; also 1:50,000 and 1:100,000 maps available in Reyjkavik; and the travel guidebook, **Iceland, Greenland & the Faroe Islands**, Lonely Planet.

Slættaratindur, Eysturoy Island, Faroe Islands

In the stormy North Atlantic about halfway between Bergen, Norway, Iceland, and Scotland, lie the Faroe Islands. Faroe consists of 18 islands with a land mass of about 900 sq/kms. The islands are made up of very old volcanic lava flows, laid down in layers. Sandwiched between some of the lower levels are coal seams. There are no volcanos in the Faroe Islands.

Getting to Faroe is relatively easy. There's a ferryboat running in the summer months only, between Scrabster, Scotland; Seyoisfjorbur, Iceland; and Bergen, Norway. Air transport is available from Bergen, Copenhagen, and Reykjavik, Iceland. The airport is on the island of Vagar--a long way from nowhere--but the only place in the islands to land a plane. It's also a long way from the capital city of Torshavn.

The highest summit is Slættaratindur, 882 meters, at the northern end of Eysturoy Island. The tendency is, the further north you go, the higher the mountain tops. Most peaks have rather gentle and green, grassy slopes to their summits, but many have at least one side which can challenge any rock climber. For example, the highest headwall in the world is said to be at the north end of Kunoy Island, with a vertical drop of 820 meters. The islands of Vidoy, Kunoy and Eysturoy have most of the highest mountains.

To climb **Slættaratindur**, drive, ride a bicycle, take a bus, hitch hike, or walk to the town of Eidi, at the north end of Eysturoy. From there walk eastward along the main road up to the pass just south of the main peak. Look for the easiest way to the summit, and climb. From the road it will only take an hour or two to reach the top. Nice views from the summit. On 6/18/1979, the author hitch hiked out of Torshavn to Eidi, then walked up the road a ways, hide his big pack, and used the route shown on the map. It only took 1 1/2 hours to reach the flat-topped summit and return to the paved road. He camped nearby for the night.

These islands are small, so getting from place to place doesn't take that long--even to walk. Public transport exists, but hitch hiking is very good, and even walking will get you there in surprisingly little time. Roads are very good--most being paved.

The routes marked as trails on the map are the old paths or ways of getting from place to place. They are marked with stone cairns. Since there are no trees on the islands, walking cross-country is very simple.

The weather is miserable much of the time, so be prepared for very windy and wet conditions. You must camp in sheltered places or risk having the tent ripped by the wind. You can camp literally anywhere, as most grazing areas are public or common lands. The book below lists several official campgrounds around the islands,

Food is easy to get. Each town or settlement of any size has a small store, but the best

Approaching the base of Slættaratindur. This foto was taken on June 18
with some snowdrifts still around on the upper slopes.

Map 7-1, Slættaratindur, Eysturoy Island, Faroe Islands

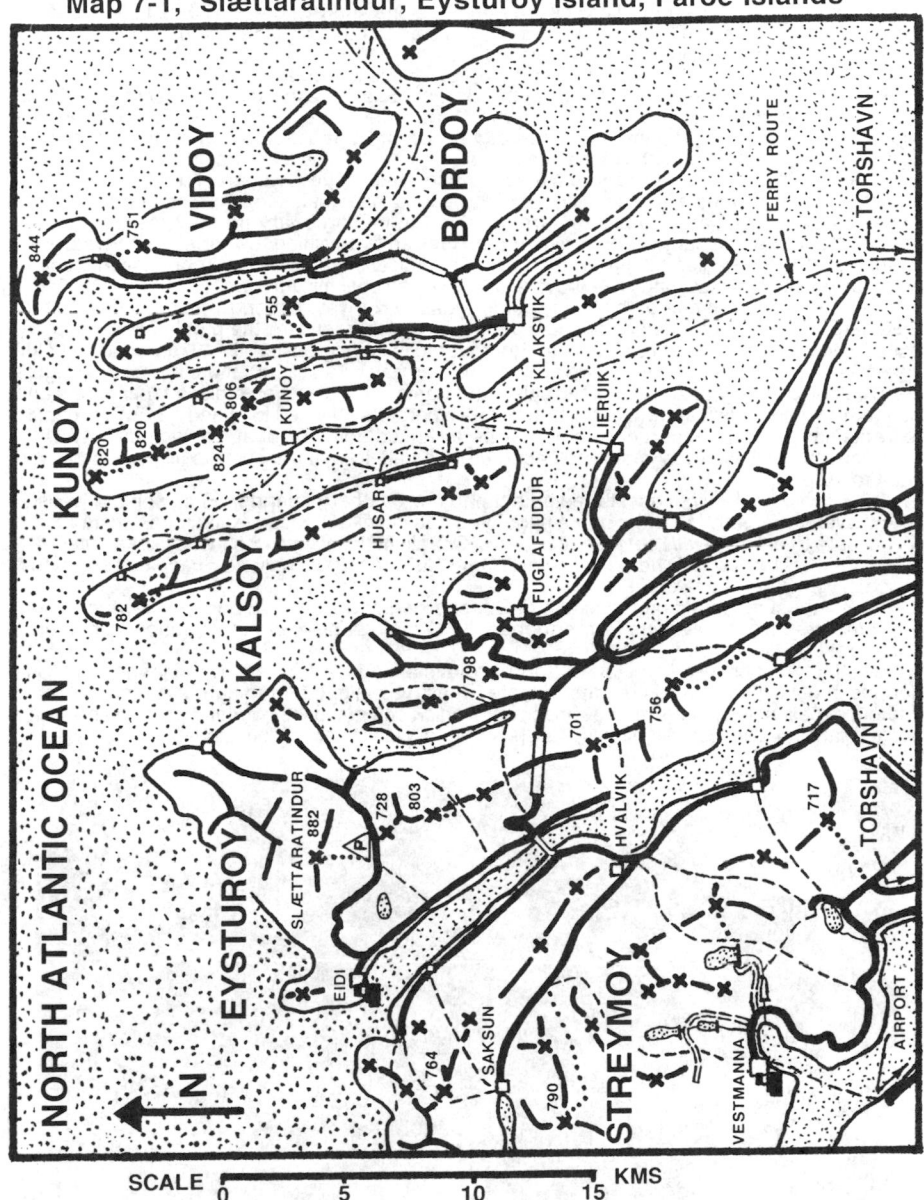

places are obviously the larger towns of Vestmanna, Klaksvik, or the capital, Torshavn. The larger places have youth hostels, and some very expensive hotels.
Maps *Foroyar, North Half,* 1:100,000, Geodœtisk Institut, Danmark; and the travel guidebook, **Iceland, Greenland & the Faroe Islands**, Lonely Planet.

Newtontoppen, Spitsbergen, Svalbard Islands, Norway

Few people have ever heard of Spitsbergen, let alone know where it is. Even fewer people would consider mountain climbing there, but in this age of the airplane, almost any part of the world is open and available to mountaineering.

Spitsbergen Island is the largest of the group of islands known as Svalbard. Svalbard is part of Norway, but is separated by 950 kms of the Barents Sea. These islands lie between 77° and 80° north, and only about 1050 kms from the North Pole. Despite its northerly location, the warm ocean currents keep the islands relatively warm--at least ships are able to anchor at Longyearbyen for 3 to 4 months of the year.

Svalbard has been a territory of Norway since 1925. The Svalbard Treaty, which gave Norway sovereignty of the islands, also gave 41 nations the right to exploit its natural resources. Today, only Norway and Russia (?) are involved in mining coal, the only resource under development. Barentsburg and Pyramiden are Russian coal mining towns, with Longyearbyen the capital, the Norwegian administrative center and location of the only airport. Ny Ålesund is an arctic research station, and Sveagruva is a Norwegian coal mining town.

In looking through one of the travel guidebooks to Norway, nothing was mentioned about Spitsbergen (?). That's strange, because getting to Spitsbergen isn't the problem it used to be, but getting near the highest mountain is. But that too is getting easier. In 1975, regular weekly flights were begun from Tromso, Norway, to Longyearbyen. As of 2000, there are several flights per week by SAS and at least 9 hotels, plus restaurants. There's even a place for campers and budget travelers. Also, there are at least 13 tour operators involved in taking groups of tourists to various places. Transport can somehow be arranged going by boat, snowmobile, 4WD, or even mountain bikes. Presumably someone there can help with transport to any mountain you want to try.

Here is the best way to get started on a trip to the **Svalbard Islands.** First, see the website **(www.svalbard.com)**. After the home page, you can checkout Accommodations, Restaurants, Activities & Events, Travel/Tour Operators, etc. Or call the Norwegian Tourist Office at Inter+47-79-0223-03. That's somewhere in Norway. Or in North America, call the Scandinavian Tourist Office in New York at 212-885-9700.

The highest mountain on the island of Spitsbergen and all of Svalbard, is Newtontoppen, 1717 meters. Not far away is Perriertoppen, 1717 meters also, but is somehow considered number 2 (?).

Getting from Longyearbyen to **Newtontoppen** is a long walk--probably too long. For those serious about climbing in this or other remote areas, you might, for the right-sized pocketbook, find either helicopters, boats or snow machines, which can make the overland journey shorter. If you're planning a serious climbing trip to Spitsbergen, plan for arctic conditions.

Looking north from the area of Mt. Michelsen (Hugo Nunlist foto).

Map 8-3, Newtontoppen, Spitzbergen, Svalbard Islands, Norway

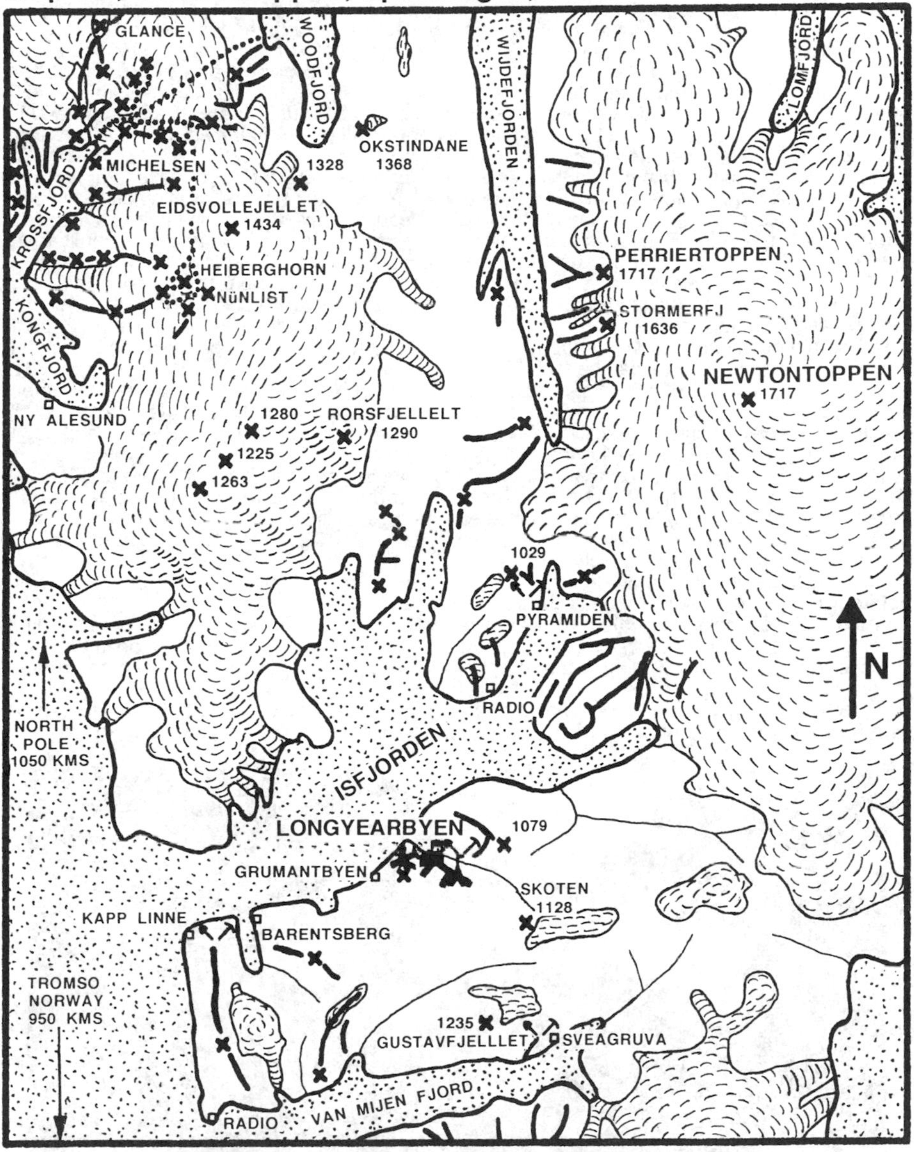

GLANCE

WOODFJORD

WIJDEFJORDEN

LOMFJORD

KROSSFJORD

OKSTINDANE

MICHELSEN 1328 1368

EIDSVOLLEJELLET
✖ 1434

PERRIERTOPPEN
✖ 1717

STORMERFJ
1636

KONGFJORD

HEIBERGHORN
✖ NüNLIST

NEWTONTOPPEN
✖ 1717

NY ALESUND

1280 RORSFJELLELT
✖ ✖ 1290
✖ 1225
✖ 1263

1029

PYRAMIDEN

N

NORTH
POLE
1050 KMS

RADIO

ISFJORDEN

LONGYEARBYEN 1079

GRUMANTBYEN

SKOTEN
1128
✖

KAPP LINNE

BARENTSBERG

TROMSO
NORWAY
950 KMS

1235 ✖
GUSTAVFJELLLET SVEAGRUVA

RADIO VAN MIJEN FJORD

SCALE 0 15 30 45 60 75 KMS

In the area of Krossfjord, the northwest part of the map, are a number of peaks which were first climbed and explored by a Swiss expedition in 1962. Only part of those peaks are shown on this map. One good thing about climbing near coastal areas is, access will be quite good. You could hopefully hire a boat to take you there, then return later to pick your group up.

Maps Svalbard is covered by 1:50,000, 1:100,000, and 1:1,000,000 maps by the Norge Geografiske Offmaling (NGO); and see the book, **Spitsbergen**, by Hugo Nünlist for better maps.

Galdhopiggen & Glittertinden, Jotunheimen, Norway

In the south central part of Norway, and northeast of Bergen, lie most of the higher mountains of Norway. These mountains and many glaciers are located for the most part, at or near the heads of several large fjords, 2 of which are Nordfjorden and Sognafjorden. These are 2 of the longest fjords on the west coast of Norway. This geographic region is called Jotunheimen. The highest summits are Galdhopiggen, 2469 meters, and Glittertinden, 2470 meters. Galdhopiggen usually appears as one meter shorter, but it has a rock summit and is generally considered the highest peak in Norway and in all of Scandinavia. Most rocks here seem to be granite or other metamorphics.

To get there using public transport, take a train north from Oslo, through Lillehammer, and get off at a small town named Otta. From there you'll have to take a bus, or hitch hike, to Lom. From Lom, you'll leave a well-traveled highway and head southwest on a less-used paved road heading toward Fortun. This section of road may or may not have bus service, so you'll need your own car or hitch hike. Stop or be dropped off at Boverdal or Elvesæter.

Both of these high peaks can be climbed easily and from one location, or several. The most normal route up **Galdhopiggen**, is via the Gjuvvas Hytta. Gjuvvas is a hut or refuge with sleeping and food accommodation. From this hut it's an easy half-day climb to the summit via a trail. The mountain can also be climbed from the main highway and Elvesæter (a holiday hotel complex). Still another route can be found from Spiterstulen.

The author hitch hiked into this area in 7/1970. He got information at the Elvesæter hotel, walked south along a trail into a canyon and hid his large pack. From there he headed south straight up the glacier and eventually to the summit. He returned via the Gjivvis Hutte, and got a ride down the mountain--and left his ice ax in that VW bus!

To climb **Glittertinden**, the most normal route is via Spiterstulen and the trail reaching the top. In 2 days, you can climb both of these mountains, from the single base camp of Spiterstulen. Still other ways would be from Visdalsæter and Glitterheim.

The third highest summit in the area is Hurrungane, 2405 meters. It can best be climbed from near the place called Helgedalen.

Most of the summits in this region are not so rugged or difficult to climb Most have been worn down by past glaciation and many easy routes can be found.

All the places marked on the map as towns are hardly that. Most are resort hotels, filling stations, or just *a wide place in the road,* but not real towns. If you're planning to be in the area for several days camping & climbing, buy all your supplies before reaching this mapped area--certainly before leaving Lom.

This area is very wet and cool, so go prepared. The driest months are April, May and June, then heavier rains begin in July. By August, it's the full monsoon. Better have an ice ax &

Just south of Elvesæter. The long glacier is coming down from Galdhopiggen's north slope.

Map 9-1, Galdhopiggen & Glittertinden, Norway

SCALE 0   10   20 KMS

crampons too, sometimes they're needed. Anyone at the hotels or huts can help you with additional route information.

Maps The Joint Operations Graphic (Air JOG) map *Årdal, NP 31, 32-11,* 1:250,000; or other maps at 1:50,000 and 1:100,000 scale from Norges Geografiske Oppmaling (NGO), 3500 Honefoss, Norway; *Norway--Climbing Locations Map*; and the guidebook, **Norway**, Lonely Planet; or the mountaineering guide, **Scandinavian Mountains**, West Col Books.

Romsdal, Romsdalhorn Group, Norway

To hikers and rock climbers around Europe the name Romsdal is familiar. The name Romsdal comes from one very steep mountain called Romsdalhorn. It's nearly vertical on all sides and in some ways resembles the Matterhorn in Switzerland. Because of this one famous peak, the entire region has more-or-less taken on the name of Romsdal. This formerly glaciated mountainous area is located on or near the west coast of Norway, about 175 air kms southwest of Trondheim. It's also about 125 kms northwest of the main north-south highway town of Dombas.

There is only one town of any importance on this map and that's Åndalsnes. Åndalsnes is located at the head of Romsdalsfjorden, and is about 100 kms from the open seas of the west coast. The region has many prominent peaks and summits, but none are above 2000 meters. **Romsdalhorn** itself is only about 1550 meters, but its base is near sea level. The valleys have all been heavily glaciated and are *U shaped*. The rock is mostly granite, with many huge vertical or near-vertical rock faces. This is one of the best rock climbing places in the world. The lower valleys are all green and filled with sheep and cattle during the summer months. The map the author used to create this one is the *Ålesund, 1:250,000 Joint Operations Graphic (JOG)*. It's a good one to use to get an overall look at the entire region. But for greater detail on slopes and trails, it's recommended the four maps listed below be used. Also, for the serious rock climber, use the book listed below from West Col.

Most people reach Åndalsnes via a good paved highway from Oslo by driving their car or possibly hitch hiking. In summer there's a fair amount of traffic. You can also get from Oslo to Åndalsnes by train. Åndalsnes is a small town, but has many food & gasoline stores, hotels, and campgrounds in the area. Food will be cheaper in Oslo.

For rock climbers, there are huts on top of Romsdalhorn, Store Trolftind, and Kongen, and another near Trollstig Pass (Bispen Hut). The locations of these huts indicate the more popular rock climbing areas.

For hikers, there are trails-of-sorts in all valleys, but the most popular hikes are these: From Verma (just off this map south) walk to Reitan (16 kms), located on the south end of Lake Eikesda, take a ferry halfway up the lake, then walk west to Morstol. Also, a 24-km-hike from near Trollstigheiman east to Verma. And one from Berill to near Trollstigheiman. You'll need the *Ålesund* map and the book on *Romsdal* mentioned below to follow these tracks.

June is the driest month in these parts, but during July and August the weather is warmer and still often better than in the Alps or in the UK.

Maps *Romsdalen, Valldal, Åndalsnes, and Eresfjord,* 1:50,000, from Norges Geografiske Oppmaling (NGO), 3500 Honefoss, Norway; *Norway--Climbing Locations Map*; and the guidebook, **Norway**, Lonely Planet; a mountaineering guidebook, **Scandinavian Mountains**; or **Walks and Climbs in Romsdal Norway**, West Col Books.

Andalsnes, with Romsdalhorn in the far left background (tourist office foto).

Map 10-3, Romsdal, Romsdalhorn Group, Norway

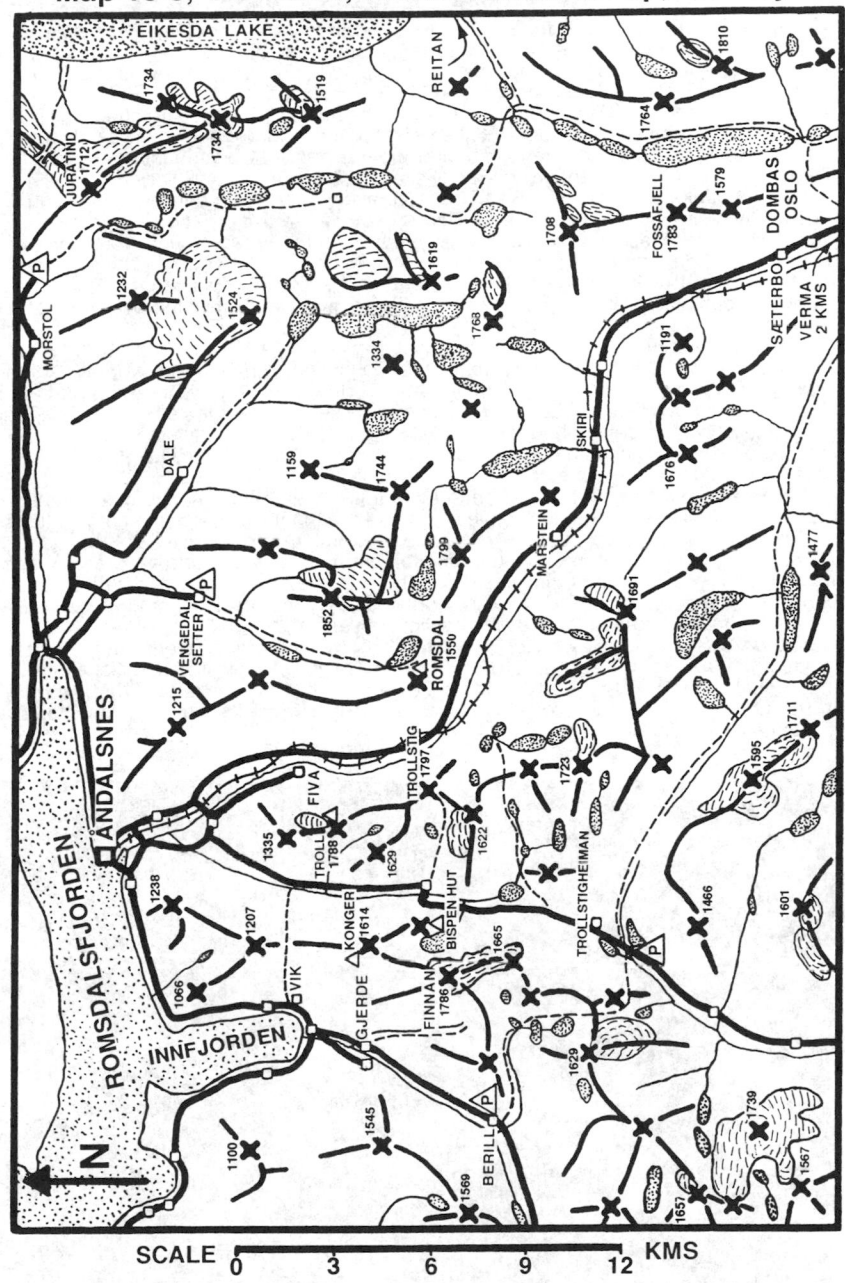

SCALE 0 3 6 9 12 KMS

Kebnekaise, Lappland, Sweden

In northern Sweden, not far from the Norwegian border, and about halfway between Kiruna, Sweden and Narvik, Norway, lies the highest mountain in Sweden, Kebnekaise, at 2117 meters. This part of Sweden is known as Lappland. Because of the latitude, nearly 68° north, one would expect to find a highly glaciated country, and for the most part, this is true. But, since this range in which Kebnekaise is a part, is on the lee or rainshadow side of the watershed, it is noticeably drier than the western side of the mountains which form the border of Norway and Sweden. The peaks on this map are higher than the border mountains, but the amount of precipitation they receive is less. However, there are still many streams, lakes and small glaciers.

Get to Kebnekaise via Kiruna, Sweden. Kiruna is on the main rail line connecting the iron mines in Sweden, with the open port at Narvik. If taking a train, get off at Kiruna, which is a bigger town, and the last place you can do any real shopping. From Kiruna, you should find 2 or 3 buses per day during the summer months making the run all the way to Pirttivuopio and to the end of the road at Nikkaluokta. There isn't much traffic between Kiruna, Pirttivuopio and Nikkaluokta, but hitch hiking may be possible. During July and August there's more traffic going that way.

To climb **Kebnekaise**, walk west along a very good and well-maintained trail from Nikkaluokta for about 18 kms to the Kebnekaise Fjallstation (KFS). From KFS, it's another 7-8 kms along a good trail running generally to the northwest to the top of the mountain which makes this climb very easy. Depending on one's fitness, pack weight, and time of departure, it should take about 2-3 days round-trip from Nikkaluokta. Get an early start from Nikkaluokta if you hope to reach KFS at an early hour. Most will climb Kebnekaise on Day 2, and return all the way to Nikkaluokta on the same day.

There are a few trails in the area, and even a number of emergency-type huts scattered throughout the valleys. If you don't have a tent and are planning to use the huts, better inquire about using and/or reserving them in Pirttivuopio or Nikkaluokta before hiking.

Most of the mountains in this region can be climbed without ice ax & crampons, but it's recommended you take them anyway. Also, be prepared for cold, wet weather, and lots of mosquitoes, especially in early summer. April is usually the driest month in these parts, with more rainfall in July and August, the warmest time of year.

Maps *Kebnekaise, 291, and Abisko, 301,* 1:100,000, from Generalstabens Litografiska Anstalt, Kart Centrum, Vasagatan 16, 11 20 Stockholm; or *Hogfjallskartan Kebnekaise,* 1:20,000, from Lantmateriet Kartforlaget; or perhaps the best map *Abisko--Kebnekaise, BD6/301 Fjallkarten,* 1:100,000; and the guidebooks, **Scandinavia Europe**, Lonely Planet; and **Scandinavian Mountains**, West Col Books.

The southeast face of Kebnekaise during winter (tourist office foto).

Map 11-3, Kebnekaise, Lappland, Sweden

Partetjakka, Sarek National Park, Lappland, Sweden

In northern Sweden, not far south of Narvik, Norway, lie several groups of peaks which are among the highest in Sweden. Included on this map is part of the Sarek National Park, and the highest peak around, Partetjakka, at 2005 meters.

The author still hasn't been to this area, so he isn't sure of the best way to get there. For sure, you'll first have to go to Luleå on the Baltic coast. From there you might take a train heading toward Narvik, Norway, but get off at Murjek (?). From Murjek take a bus to Jokkomokk, then to the small town of Kvikkjokk, which is a tourist camp at the end of the paved road. The other options are to hitch hike or rent a car. Inquire about your options before leaving Stockholm.

Fortunately, **Partetjakka** is the most easily reached of all the higher summits. From Kvikkjokk, simply walk northeast on a trail for about 7 kms, then veer left at the junction; walk another 14 of so kms to a small encampment or group of huts used by park rangers, tourists, and climbers. It's called Pareks Lapplager. On the 1971 map the author used to create this one, there is no marked trail shown to the top of Partetjakka; but there will surely be something there when you arrive. Even with no track or trail, the country is open with no trees, and a route heading northwest should take you to the top with little difficulty.

Most people should be able to make this climb, round-trip from Kvikkjokk, in 3 days. Make sure you get an early start the first day so you make it to the lapplager for your first night.

Another marked trail follows the Tarraatno River. Along this river are a series of huts, primarily set aside for tourists or hikers. The same is true along the Rapaatno River, but maps don't show any trails going that way. There's also a path heading northwest from Kvikkjokk to an unnamed peak marked 876 meters; and another short trail heading east to a lake and peak marked 884 meters.

To reach the area of **Akkatjakka**, 1974 meters, it would be best to follow the Tarraatno River in the direction of Alkavare, where a *rengarda* is located. For other peaks such as **Apartjakka**, 1914 meters, or **Midtjisarki**, 1842, better make inquiries at Kvikkjokk.

Keep this in mind; the entire area is still very wild, and anyone going to the more northerly regions should plan on a small *expedition*. Also, keep in mind river crossings--not all are bridged. Plan ahead by making inquires at Kvikkjokk.

There are some large glaciers in the area, but many summits can be climbed from the south without a lot of equipment. Ice ax & crampons are recommended, however. A good tent,

A typical scene in the Nationalparken Sarek of northern Sweden (tourist office foto).

Map 12-3, Partetjakka, Sarek National Park, Lappland, Sweden

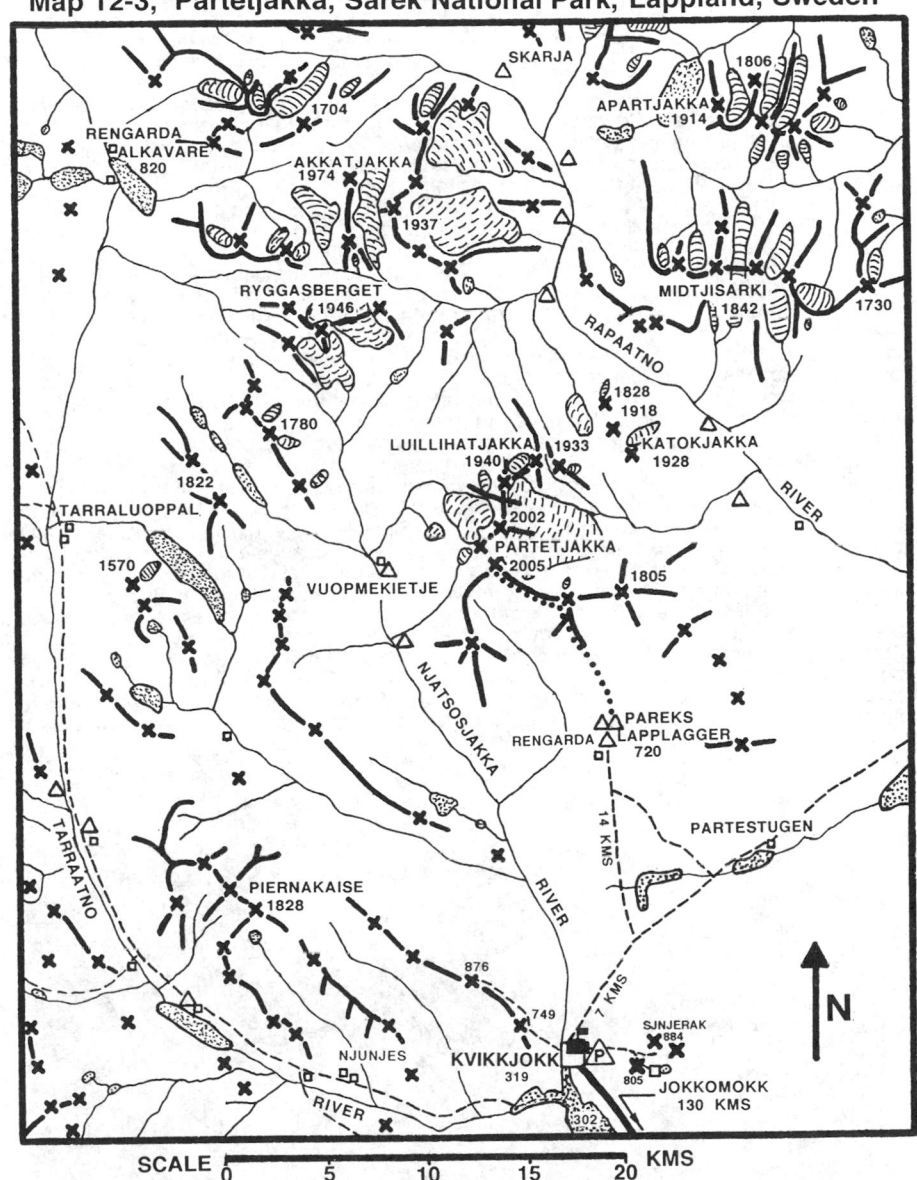

SCALE 0 5 10 15 20 KMS

mosquito repellent and rain gear are necessities. Some food can be found in Kvikkjokk, but it'll be expensive and there wont be much variety. Better to buy all or most of your supplies elsewhere before you arrive in this area. June may have the best weather of the 3 summer months, but July and August is the normal hiking season.

Maps *Sarek, 28H, and Kvikkjokk, 27H,* 1:100,000; from Generalstabens Litografiska Anstalt, Kart Centrum, Vasagatan 16,1120 Stockholm; and the guidebooks, **Scandinavia Europe**, Lonely Planet; and **Scandinavian Mountains**, West Col Books.

Carrauntoohil, Macgillycuddy's Reeks, Ireland

In the extreme southwest corner of Ireland, in Country Kerry, stands a group of mountains known as Macgillycuddy's Reeks. These summits aren't high, but they're the best Ireland has. There are two peaks over 1,000 meters, the highest of which is Carrauntoohil at 1041 meters, the number one peak of Ireland.

Ireland has a number of small mountain ranges scattered about the country, but a few more exist in the southwest, and Country Kerry. It's in this part that the more rugged hills are found. In central and eastern Ireland the mountains are smooth and rounded, worn down during the last glacier age. Other important mountain ranges in Ireland include the *Mourne, Wicklow and Galtee Mountains*. Hill walking is popular in all these areas.

Country Kerry is a tourist area--but it can't be the *paradise* as some call it, as the weather is often terrible. Nonetheless, there are a lot of tourists, especially Americans, who return to their ancestral homeland. Tralee and Killarney are the tourist towns.

The author was in this area on 10/1/1979. That was a Monday and the Pope was in Limerick that day. All stores were closed as it was a declared holiday; and it rained all day. He came in from the north and attemped to climb **Carrauntoohil** from the north and the trail near Auger Lake, but he never quite make it to the highest summit. Be aware that things have surely changed since the author drew this map. For example, Jerzy Mikulec of Krakow, Poland, writes and states that the youth hostel on the north side of the range may not be there any more (?).

To reach this area, first make your way to Killarney, where there are bookstores with the latest guidebooks and maps. Killarney also have a tourist information office, which can update you on the best routes into The Reeks, and the whereabouts of campgrounds and youth hostels.

From Killarney, you can hitch hike to the mountain, or as Mikulec did, rent a bicycle, or motor bike. From Killarney, head west toward Killorglin, but turn south on one of the roads shown. Carrauntoohil can be approached from the east, west, north or south, but the more normal way seems to be via the youth hostel in the Black Valley. There's also another youth hostel, formerly a school, on the north slopes (this is the one that may not exit anymore?). This is the second most used route. However, the most scenic route and one that's amongst the more rugged sections of the mountain, is the approach from the northwest and the Breanlee Bridge.

Please note that the author has indicated routes for the most part, as opposed to actual trails. There are a number of sheep trails on the mountain, which are used by hill walkers, but often times they don't lead you where you want to go. It's not difficult to travel cross-country as the land is open and treeless.

Carrauntoohil can be climbed easily in one day from any direction. Keep in mind that although the mountains aren't big or rugged (except for the Coomlaughara Laugh Cirque), the

Substituting for Macgillycuddy's Reeks is this foto of the Mourne Wall, located in the Mourne Mountains of eastern Ireland.

Map 13-1, Carrauntoohil, Macgillycuddy's Reeks, Ireland

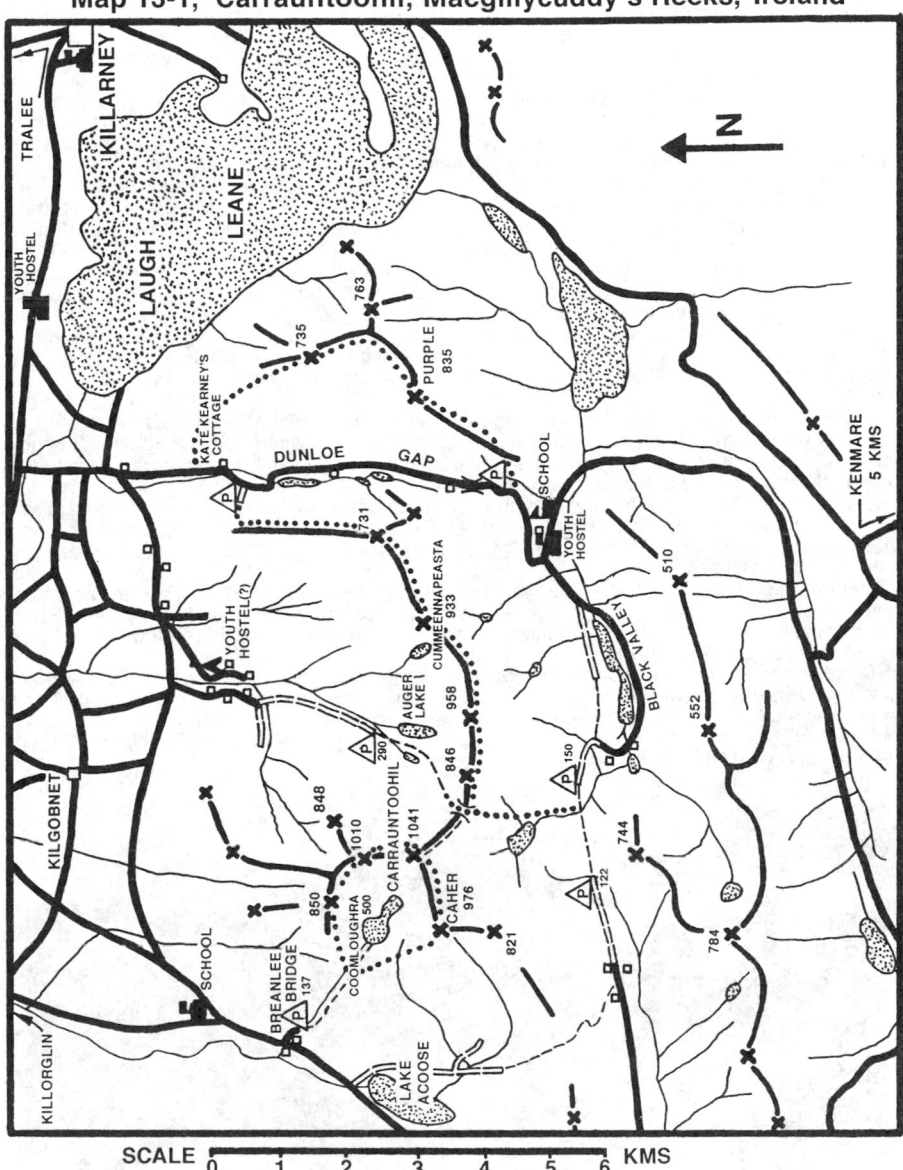

way can easily be lost in the clouds, as the weather in the west of Ireland is typically bad. It's recommended you take a compass, raincoat and rain pants while hiking in this area.

Maps *Dingle Bay, 20*, 1:126,720; or *Kerry, 78*, 1:50,000, Ordnance Survey of Ireland, Dublin; the travel guidebook, **Ireland**, Lonely Planet; and **The High Mountains of Britain & Ireland**, Baton Wicks Publishing. Buy these in Killarney.

Mt. Snowdon, Cambrian Mountains, Wales, UK

In the extreme northwest part of Wales, and in the Cambrian Mountains, lies the highest peak in Wales, Mt. Snowdon, at 1085 meters. Of course it's not a high mountain, but it's one of the most famous in the British Isles, and a lot of people get to the top, either by walking or riding the cog railway.

Mt. Snowdon is now within the boundaries of the Snowdonia National Park. This national park includes a greater part of the Cambrian Mountains, the name of which has geologic connotations. The park was created late in Welch history, so this area is not to be confused with national parks in other parts of the world, which have a more wilderness character.

Here's what the author did. He was heading home from his 1994 trip to Russia, and stopped in the UK to visit Snowdon. He took a bus from London to the small city of Bangor, located not far from **Snowdon**. From there he took a city bus south to Bethesda, but never found the campground he was told about, so he crashed in an empty field. Next morning, 10/8/1994, he hitched a ride to Capel Curig, then got another ride to the trailhead at Pen-y-Pass. There may or may not be any public transport on that route from Bethesda, so hitching seems the only option to driving your own car, or renting one.

From Pen-y-Pass, he took his entire pack up the Pyg Track, passing a lake called Llyn Llydaw, and some rather ancient copper mines and mill buildings along the way. History buffs will surely find this route the most interesting on the mountain. He made it to the summit in about 2 1/2 hours.

From the top, he walked down to Llanberis along the trail which roughly parallels the tracks of the Snowdon Mtn. Railway. From Pen-y-Pass to Llanberis with a full, but lightweight pack, took 5 1/2 hours. If you start in Llanberis, you can walk up the same track; or be a lazy tourist and ride the cog railroad powered by a Diesel engine.

One can also reach the top by starting from the southwest, south and east sides. Trails begin at the youth hostel near Llyn Cwellyn, at Rhyd-Ddu, and from the parking place near Hafed-y-Llan. These are the 5 normal routes up Snowdon. The climb can be made in one day along any of these trails.

Just north of Snowdon, lies a 999 meter summit named **Glyder Fawr**. Further north and southeast of Bethesda is the second highest peak in the Cambrians, **Carnedd Llywelyn** at 1062 meters. There are several trails to near its summit, but you can also climb without a trail from the rescue post on the southwest.

If you're interested in obtaining maps, books or other literature about the Snowdon area, be sure and stop in Llanberis. There you'll find a tourist information office, and a number of bookstores and shops. If you're planning to be camping for a while in the area, best to shop at the Safeway supermarket in Bangor. The author had some great weather for his climb, but bring rain gear as Snowdon is known for its terrible weather.

The eastern slopes of Mt. Snowdon as seen from the eastern shore of Llyn Llydaw. The old buildings on the opposite side of the lake are the ruins of an old copper mine.

Map 14-1, Snowdon, Cambrian Mountains, Wales, UK

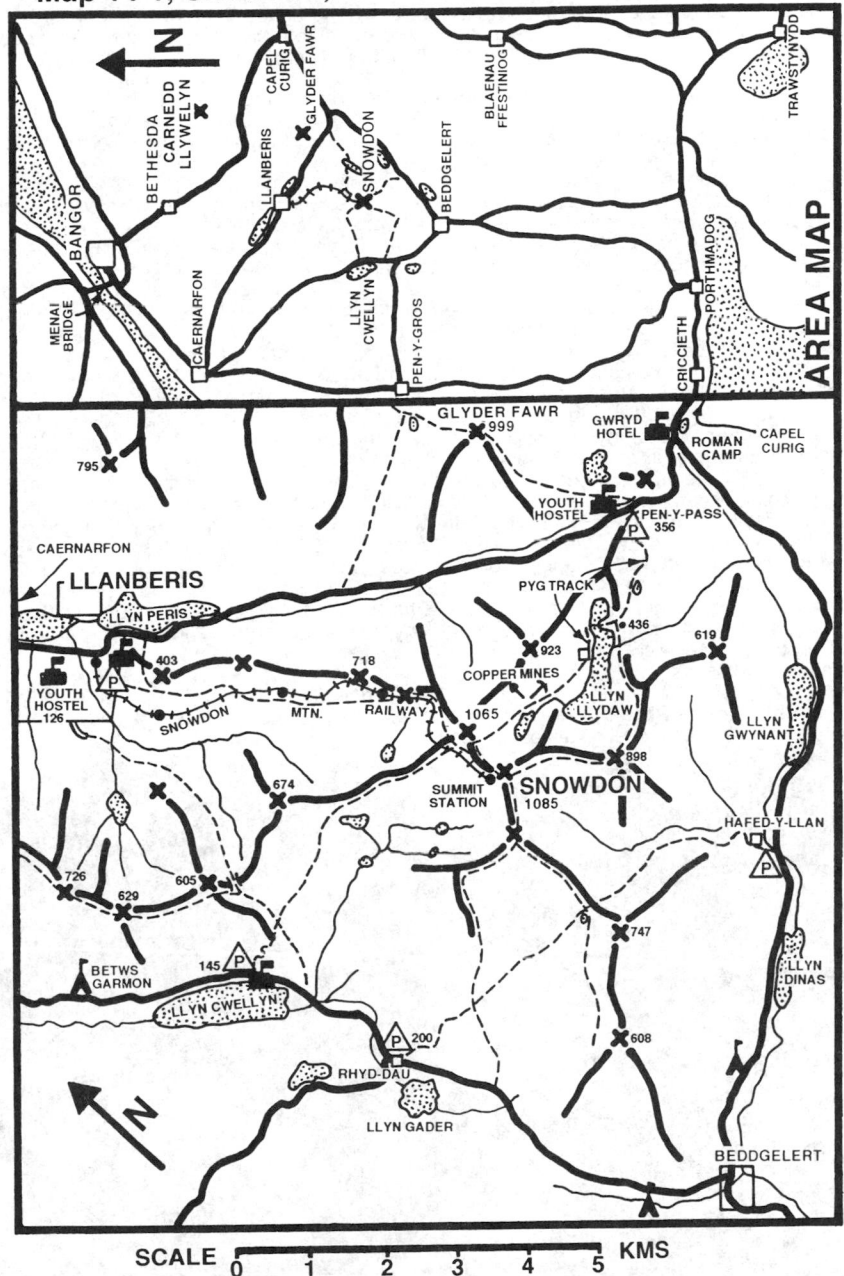

SCALE 0 1 2 3 4 5 KMS

Maps *Snowdonia National Park,* 1:126,720; or *Snowdon & Surrounding Area, 115,* 1:50,000, from Ordnance Survey; and the books, **The High Mountains of Britain & Ireland**, Baton Wicks Publishing; or **Walking in Britain**, Lonely Planet; and the latest travel guidebook to the UK.

Scafell Pike, Lakes District, Cumbrian Mtns., England, UK

This map covers the heart of the area known as The Lakes District. The Lakes District is located in northwest England, not far south of Scotland. More precisely, it's in the area between Motorway 6 (M-6) and the west coast, and south of the city of Carlisle.

These hills are part of the Cumbrian Mountains, and reach their highest point in a peak called Scafell Pike at an altitude of 977 meters. The elevations here are certainly not high by most people's standards, but these are some of the highest and best preserved hill sections in the UK. Other notable summits are Helvellyn, at 949 meters; Stybarrow, 840; Tongue, 856; and Bow Fell, 902 meters.

Getting to the area is quite easy. Since most people in England live in the south, the easiest way to get there is via Superhighway M-6. One could exit at Penrith, east of Keswick; or get off not far south of the town of Windermere, located on Lake Windermere, which is just east of this map. Keswick is probably the most centrally located large town in the Lakes District, but it's also the biggest tourist trap. Windermere is much the same way--very touristic.

These mountains are very subdued because of past glaciation. Most summits are very much rounded over, the valleys are U-shaped, and there are many large lakes like Windermere, Ullswater, Thirlmere, Derwent Water, Wast Water, Crummock Water, and Buttermere, just to name the larger ones. All the region covered by this map is part of The Lakes District National Park. It's different from national parks in other parts of the world, such as in North America, in that much of the area is privately owned. However, most of this private land is in the lower valleys and does not effect those of us who want to hill-walk in the back country. One thing to remember--there are many more trails out there than are shown on this map, and there are closed gates or styles at fenced boundaries. You must always close gates and respect the private land. It seems that the higher and rocky parts, those which have little use to farmers, are held as common land, therefore there are few problems in hiking or walking these regions.

The author's experience on **Scafell Pike** went like this. On 9/11/1979, he hitch hiked to Keswich, stopped to get information at the Tourist Office, then hitched a ride south to Seathwaite. He left his big pack in some bushes, and climbed in the rain and clouds to the summit of Scafell Pike. He finally returned to his pack and camped in a paddock just south of Seathwaite for one night with no problems. He then hitched out the next day. Good hitching.

Any climb on the map can be done in one day from the nearest trailhead. Buy all your food and supplies in Keswich, or perhaps Windermere. Take a waterproof tent and good rain gear. It's nearly always wet.

Maps *Lakes District Tourist Map,* 1:63,360, Ordnance Survey of the UK; and the books, **The High Mountains of Britain & Ireland**, Baton Wicks Publishing; or **Walking in Britain**, Lonely Planet; and the latest travel guidebook to the UK.

About 2 kms south of Seathwaite is the Stockley Bridge on the trail to Scafell.

Map 15-1, Scafell Pike, Lakes District, Cumbrian Mtns., England, UK

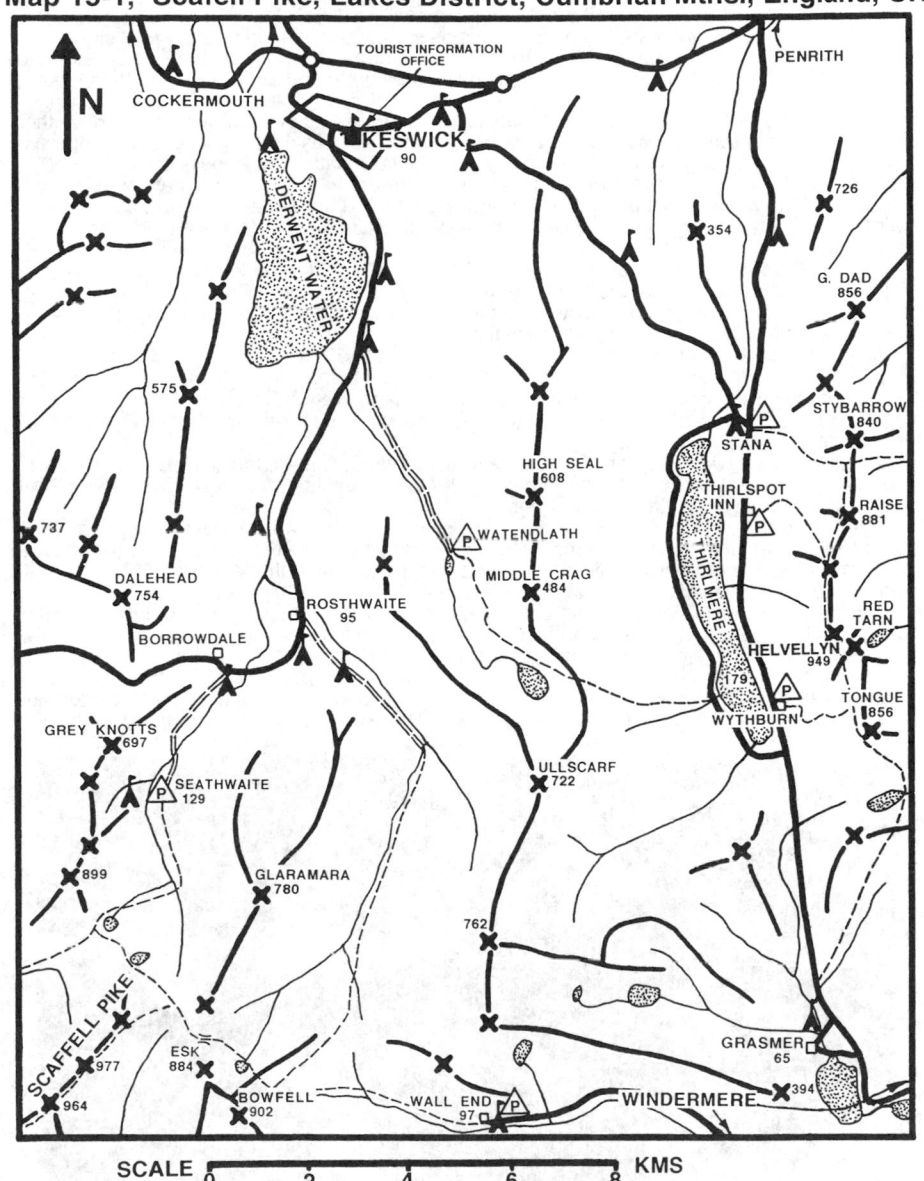

N

TOURIST INFORMATION OFFICE

PENRITH

COCKERMOUTH

KESWICK
90

DERWENT WATER

726

354

G. DAD
856

575

HIGH SEAL
608

STYBARROW
840

STANA

THIRLSPOT
INN

RAISE
881

737

WATENDLATH

MIDDLE CRAG
484

THIRLMERE

DALEHEAD
754

ROSTHWAITE
95

BORROWDALE

RED
TARN

HELVELLYN
949

179

TONGUE
856

WYTHBURN

GREY KNOTTS
697

ULLSCARF
722

SEATHWAITE
129

899

GLARAMARA
780

762

SCAFFELL PIKE

GRASMER
65

ESK
884

977

BOWFELL
902

WALL END
97

WINDERMERE
394

964

SCALE
0   2   4   6   8   KMS

49

Ben Nevis, Grampian Mountains, Scotland, UK

In all of Scotland and Great Britain, the highest summit is Ben Nevis at 1343 meters. This mountain is part of the greater Grampian Mountains system and very near the small city of Fort William, which in turn is located at the head of Loch Linnhe, near the west coast of Scotland. From Fort William, it's about 166 kms to Glasgow to the south, and about 125 kms to Inverness to the northeast.

Getting to Fort William is easy. Most tourists (and there's a lot of them) nowadays, drive their own cars. This should make hitch hiking good, but it's a little slow, as cars are often full of people and baggage. The author hitched rides all over the UK in 1979, but found it slow in these parts.

The other most popular way is by train. There's a new station, complete with shower facilities, at Fort William. A third option is to arrive by bus. Before leaving home and arriving in the UK, check into getting some kind of bus pass or UK train pass. The latest guidebook to the UK will help.

The *tourist route* up **Ben Nevis**, is via Fort William, a farm and parking lot called Achintee, then up a good trail on the west side of the mountain to the summit. One can also get on this same trail from the campground, caravan (trailer) park and youth hostel, as shown on the map. This is one of the most climbed mountains in the world.

To get to the northeast face, and the mountain rescue hut, there's a trail beginning on Highway A-82, just northeast of Fort William. It's this northeast face, with very steep and sometimes icy gullies or couloirs, that has been the training ground for many of the great British climbers. On top is an old observatory, now in ruins, and a number of stone walls or windbreak tent shelters.

The author walked from Fort William to near the youth hostel, but walked into a nearby reforested area and camped. Next morning, 9/23/1979, he climbed Ben Nevis in about 2 1/2 hours. After returning, he hitch hiked to points south.

Even if you're taking the *tourist route*, go prepared for cold temperatures and windy conditions near the top, even in summer. Rain gear and gloves are essential. The west coast of Scotland has some of the worst weather conditions of any place in the world. Because of its northerly latitude, it can snow at the summit year-round.

In the vicinity of Fort William, there are a number of caravan parks, campgrounds and youth hostels. July and August are the warmest months, and that's when most people visit this town and nearby mountains. It's also the most crowded time of year.

The map shows other summits in the region as well. Each peak will have some very easy routes, as well as some more difficult. Fort William has a tourist office at the railway station and bookstores which sell good maps and guidebooks. There are several supermarkets in town as

This steep gully on the north slope of Ben Nevis is a winter challenge.

Map 16-1, Ben Nevis, Grampian Mtns., Scotland, UK

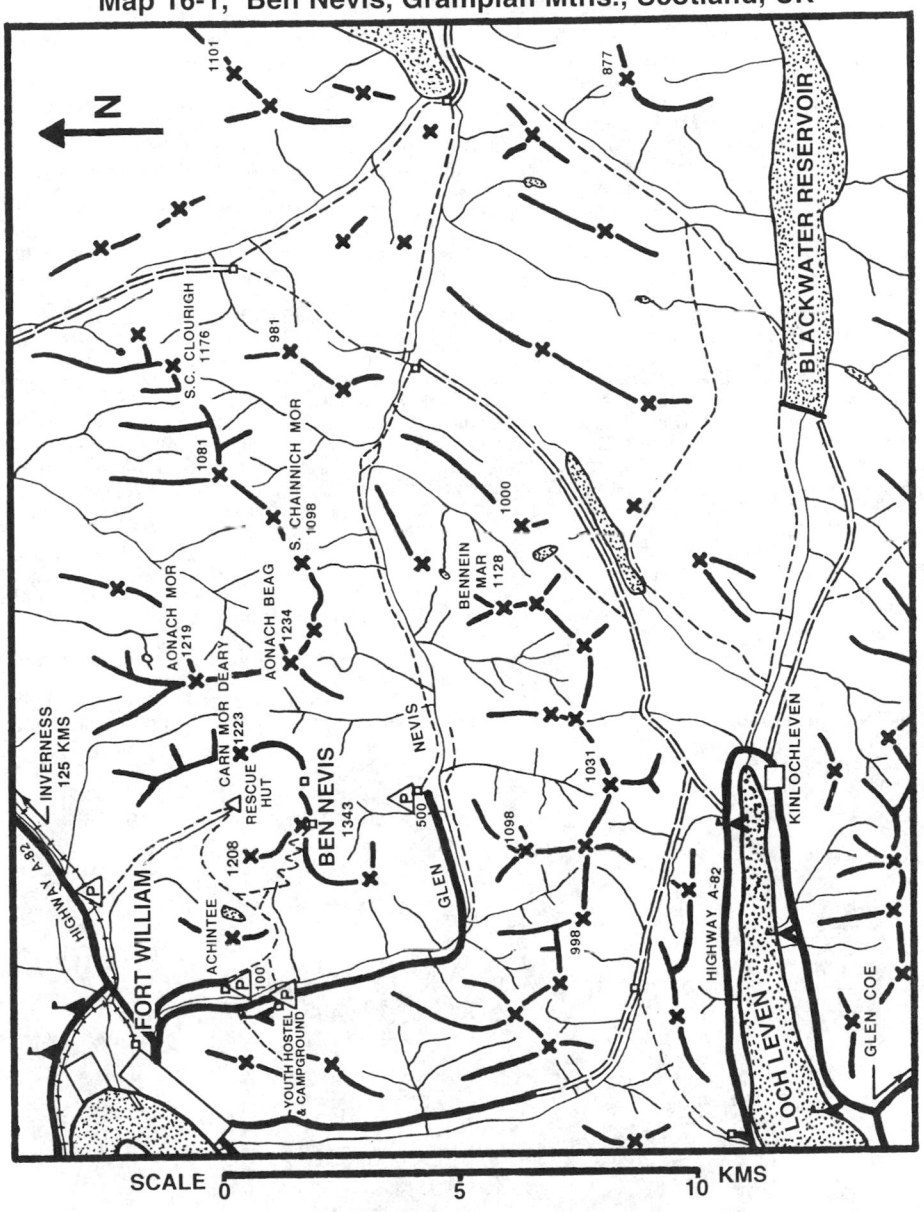

well, so you can buy all your supplies in this one place.
Maps *Ben Nevis & Glen Coe,* 1:63,360, from the Ordnance Survey, Southampton, England; and the books, **The High Mountains of Britain & Ireland**, Butterfield; or **Walking in Britain**, Lonely Planet; and the latest travel guidebook to the UK.

Cairn Gorm, Grampian Mountains, Scotland, UK

If we eliminate Ben Nevis, the highest peaks in all the UK, are in the Grampian Mountains of Scotland. The Grampian Mountains are located in the north of Scotland, not far southeast of the city of Inverness, and west of Aberdeen. Closer to the area are the small towns of Aviemore and Braemar. Both these places are shown on this map.

The best known summit in the region is Cairn Gorm, at 1245 meters, however the highest is Ben Macdui rising to 1309 meters, the second highest peak in the UK. In this same general area we find a number of high tops in excess of 1200 meters. On some maps the name of these high tops in the center of the map is labeled the Cairn Gorm Mountains, but the range as a whole is known as the Grampians.

These mountains are made mostly of granite, but absent are the sheer pinnacles and spires we usually find in association with granite. Instead, these mountains have been rounded and flattened by glaciers. However, there are some steep-sided canyons, mostly in the center of this map. These escarpments or steep gullies, are used by rock climbers, and in the same way the hills around Ben Nevis are used.

The easiest approach to the highest peaks of the Grampians is via Aviemore. It's located on Highway A-9, the main link running between Perth, near Dundee in the south, to Inverness in the north. It's relatively easy to get lifts if you're on foot, and there's bus and train service nearby too. If coming into Braemar, use roads from Perth or Aberdeen. The author hitch hiked all over the UK in 9/1979, but hitching may not be as good today as it was then.

If you want to climb **Cairn Gorm** from Aviemore, walk and/or hitch hike to the base of the ski lifts on the north slope of the mountain, then walk south along one of several trails to the top. At the top of the ski lifts and near the summit is an shelter or inn with food and drinks. On the summit itself is a small met. station. When the author was there on 9/21/1979, it was encrusted with rhime which made a rather eerie scene in the fog. Since this is a relatively small area, you can climb several summits in one day--if the weather holds up.

Even though the elevations aren't that high, this is at 57° north latitude so you must expect very severe weather conditions. Even in summer snow can and does fall on the higher peaks. There's lots of precipitation, strong winds--especially on the high peaks, and cool or cold temperatures. Remember these factors, especially if you're planning to camp out in these mountains overnight.

Between Aviemore and Loch Morlich and through all this valley, and in the area of Braemar, you'll find many hectors of forests. Some are planted coniferous trees and others appear to be the natural vegetation, but this is only in the valley bottoms. Tree line is only about 500 meters altitude. Aviemore and Braemar are both small towns, so it might be best to do most of your

The meteorological station at the summit of Cairn Gorm covered with rhime or hoarfrost.

Map 17-1, Cairn Gorm, Grampian Mountains, Scotland, UK

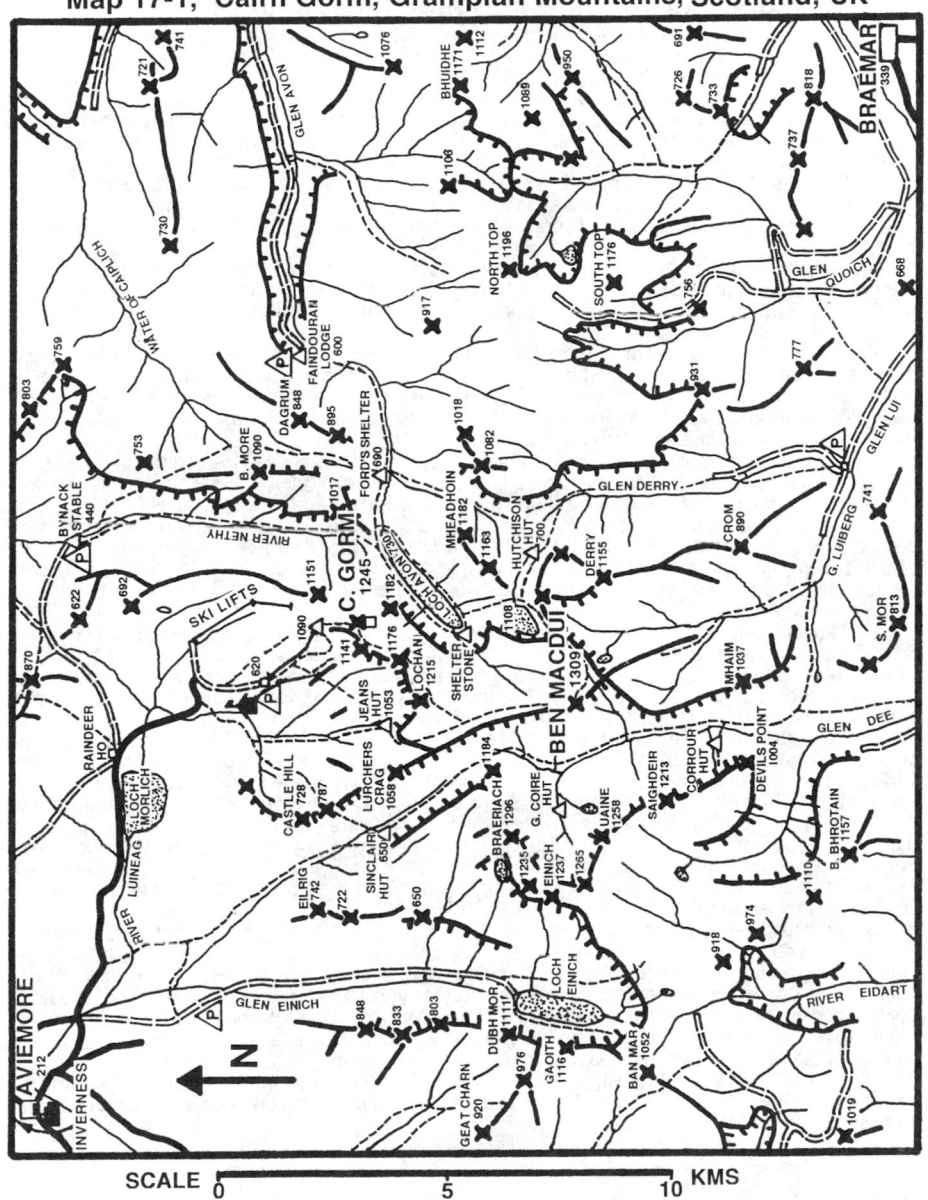

SCALE 0 ————— 5 ————— 10 KMS

shopping elsewhere before arriving in this region.
Maps *High Tops of the Cairngorms,* 1:25,000; or *Grantown and Cairngorm, 36,* and *Braemar, 43,* both 1:50,000, from the Ordnance Survey; and the books, **The High Mountains of Britain & Ireland,** Baton Wicks Publishing; or **Walking in Britain,** Lonely Planet; and the latest travel guidebook to the UK.

Introduction to the Açores Islands, Portugal

The Açores (Azores) Islands are located near the middle of the North Atlantic about 1600 kms due west of Lisboa, Portugal on the mid-Atlantic rift. The group consists of 9 major islands which make one province of Portugal. The language is Portuguese.

The islands are in 3 main groups. In the west are Flores and Corvo; in the east is the most heavily populated island of São Miguel with the provincial capital of Ponta Delgada; and 80 kms due south is the small island or ilha do Santa Maria. The central group consists of 5 islands--Graciosa, Terceira, São Jorge, Pico and Faial. On the island of Terceira is a large joint air base between the USA and Portugal. The highest peak in the Açores is Pico do Pico, at 2321 meters, located on the island of Pico. It and the caldeira (caldera) on Faial are covered in detail on the next page.

One of the nice things about the Açores is that there are few tourists. The main reason being it's an expensive place to get to. From North America, you'll have to fly from Boston on one airline--Air Portugal. A round-trip ticket with dates on both ends costs about the same as a one-way flight. Flights are once a week from Boston, USA. From Europe, you'll have to fly from Lisboa. There are daily flights from Lisboa to Ponta Delgada, and perhaps some direct to Terceira. Some charter flights go straight to Terceira as well.

From Ponta Delgada, you must fly to the central group of islands. There are several flights daily, but the number will depend on the time of year--more in summer, fewer in winter. The flight the author took in late 5/1989, began in Ponta Delgada and stopped at Terceira, then Pico and finally to Faial. There are also flights from Terceira and Horta to Santa Cruz on Flores, but flights change with the seasons. Check with a local travel agent.

If you're going to the Açores to climb, it'll be the peaks on the islands of the central group you'll be most interested in. Expect to fly from Ponta Delgada to Terceira, then to Faial or Pico, then take a ferry boat between these two islands and São Jorge. The most traveled ferry route is from Madalena to Horta. It takes about half an hour and boats run up to 5 or 6 times a day in summer. There are also several boats running daily from either Horta or Madalena, to Velas on São Jorge. That ride takes about 2 hours. There's an occasional boat running from Cais (Roque do Pico?) to Velas too. There's a once-weekly boat from Terceira to Calheta, as well as one from Terceira to Santa Cruz on Graciosa (3 1/2 to 4 hours).

Once on the islands you'll have a choice between renting a car (quite cheap, especially if you have 3 or 4 people in your group), or hitch hiking. Buses are few and far between. There is a once-daily bus running from Ponta Delgada to the east end of São Miguel, and another one running from Horta in a loop around Faial once or twice daily. For the most part this is very inconvenient. The author walked or hitch hiked, which worked well most of the time.

Some of the best hikes or climbs are these. On São Miguel, climb **Pico do Vara** along the southeast ridge from a minor farm road. You can walk around the crater rim of the **Caldeira Das Sete Cidades** from a paved road on the eastern rim. There are farms and lakes inside this crater. On Terceira, climb the highest peak known as **Serra de Santa Barbara** from somewhere on the south side. On São Jorge, the highest point on the island-long ridge is not far from a town called Urzelina. It's called **Esperanza** at 1066 meters. The author was told you can camp near an old church half-buried in lava, then walk, drive or hitch hike up a road crossing over the island. Climb from this road. The author has no information about the smaller hills on Graciosa. Mountains on Faial and Pico are covered on the next map.

Since these islands are in the stormy part of the Atlantic, the best season is during the summer months. The author had lots of rain and clouds at the end of 5/1989, but summer is said to be normally warm, sunny and dry. The Açores have no running water or streams because of the porous volcanic soil, so check on water before climbing or camping (carry extra water bottles for camping). You can get updates on information at the tourist office in Ponta Delgada. That's the best place to get maps too, but try to have some maps with you before you arrive. Ponta Delgada is also the best place to buy food, but Madalena and Horta are larger towns and have some small shops

Maps *Ilha do Açores*, 1:200,000, 1:50,000 and 1:25,000 maps from the Instituto Geografico e Cadastral, Lisboa; TPC map *Azores (Portugal)*, G-24 B, 1:500,000; and the book, **Landscapes of the Azores**, Sunflower Books.

Map 18-1, Introduction to the Açores Islands, Portugal

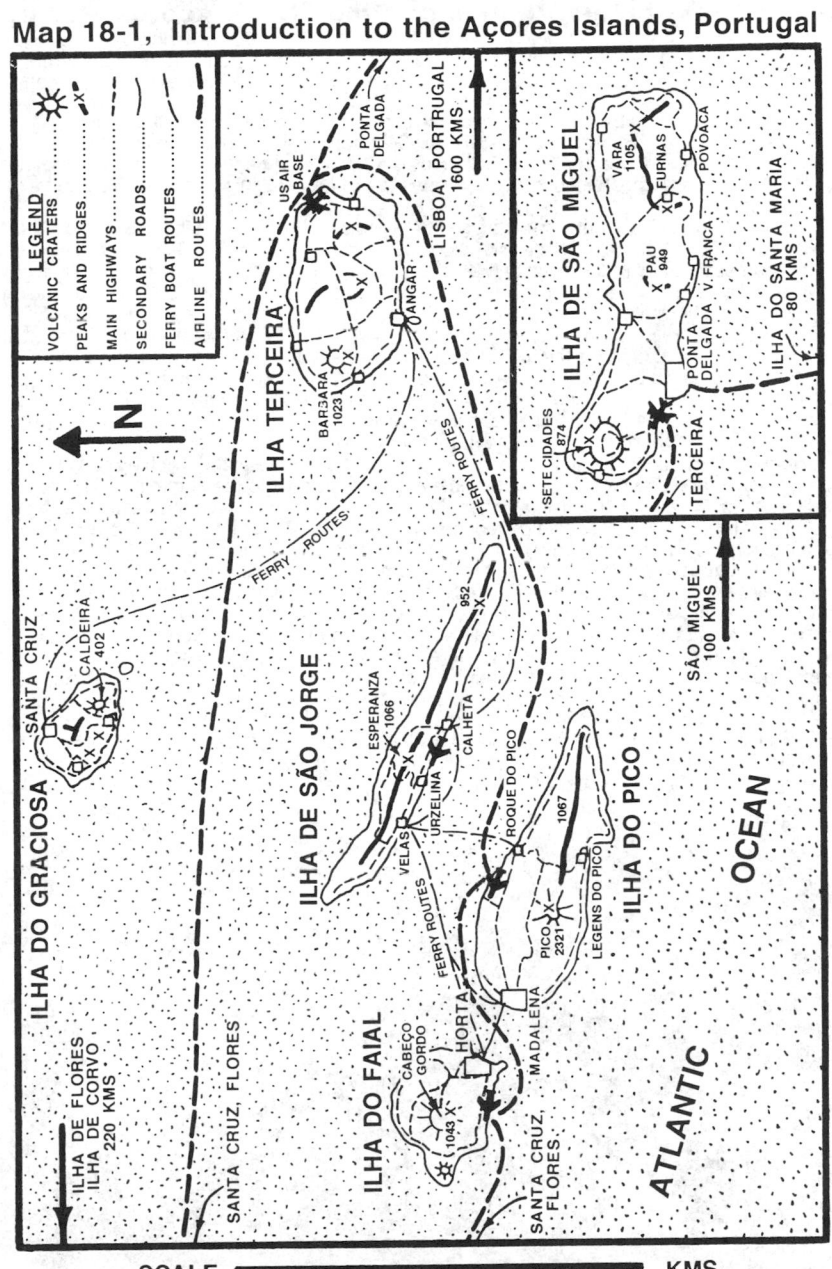

LEGEND

VOLCANIC CRATERS..........
PEAKS AND RIDGES..........
MAIN HIGHWAYS..........
SECONDARY ROADS..........
FERRY BOAT ROUTES..........
AIRLINE ROUTES..........

N

ILHA TERCEIRA

US AIR BASE
PONTA DELGADA
ANGRA
BARZARA 1023
LISBOA, PORTRUGAL 1600 KMS

ILHA DE SÃO MIGUEL

VARA 1105 X
FURNAS
POVOACA
PAU 949 X
PONTA DELGADA V. FRANCA
ILHA DO SANTA MARIA 80 KMS
SETE CIDADES 874
TERCEIRA

ILHA DO GRACIOSA

SANTA CRUZ
CALDEIRA 402

ILHA DE FLORES
ILHA DE CORVO 220 KMS

SANTA CRUZ, FLORES

ILHA DE SÃO JORGE

ESPERANZA 1066
URZELINA
CALHETA
952 X
VELAS
FERRY ROUTES

FERRY ROUTES

SÃO MIGUEL 100 KMS

ILHA DO PICO

ROQUE DO PICO
1067
PICO 2321 X
LEGENS DO PICO
MADALENA

ILHA DO FAIAL

CABEÇO GORDO
HORTA
1043 X

SANTA CRUZ FLORES

OCEAN

ATLANTIC

SCALE 0   25   50   75   100 KMS

Cabeço Gordo (Faial) & Pico do Pico (Pico), Açores, Portugal

Two mountains are discussed here: Cabeço Gordo at 1043 meters, the highest point on the island of Faial; and Pico do Pico at 2321 meters on the island of Pico. Pico is the highest summit in the Açores and perhaps the best hike or climb in the islands. Both are volcanos and both are considered semi-active.

In 1672, there was an explosion and lava flow somewhere on the west flank of Faial's big volcano. Fatalities were reported. Between 9/27/1957 and 10/24/1958, there was limited activity. Pico do Pico's last activity took place between 7 & 12/1720. However, this information from the book, **Volcanos of the World,** may be wrong, because the lava flows the author saw high on Pico seem to be younger than that (?).

To climb **Pico do Pico**, drive or hitch hike from Madalena eastward in the direction of Pico and/or São Roque do Pico. This paved highway runs east just north of the peak. Between Km markers 12 & 13, turn southeast onto a paved country road. You can drive or walk 5 kms from the main highway to the trailhead, as shown on the map. This road gradually deteriorates the further you go, but any car can make it to the beginning of the trail.

From the trailhead walk up the well-used trail toward the furna (spatter cone & cave) and the summit. Along the upper part of the mountain are old cement posts marking the location of the trail. In foggy conditions, you must follow these posts closely. On top and in the middle of an older crater or caldera is a new cone which is the highest peak. There is a good campsite at the furna and probably water at the spring, as shown, as well as at the cement water tanks below. However, in dry periods they may be dry, so you'd better carry your own water supply to the mountain. Expect to take 2-4 hours from the trailhead to the summit, or 4-6 hours round-trip. The author hitch hiked from Madalena to the mountain and camped at the furna; next morning made it to the summit in 1 1/4 hours; 2 1/2 hours round-trip (If you're hitch hiking, better plan to stay one night on the mountain, making it a two-day climb. If renting a car, it should be a one-day climb from Madalena). After the climb, he walked back to the highway, immediately got a lift to Madalena, and got on a ferry to Horta.

To climb **Cabeço Gordo**, hitch hike or drive from Horta to Flamengos, then to Largo Jaime and to the caldeira rim, a popular tourist stop. Hitching is best in the middle of the day when tourists, many from visiting yachts, are out on the road in rental cars. The crater rim is 16 kms from Horta along a paved road. From the car-park, you can walk 400 vertical meters down a very steep trail to the crater floor, or walk the rim of the caldeira. The highest point is Cabeço Gordo which has an communications antenna on top. The author hitch hiked to the crater rim in the afternoon of 5/29/1989 and camped. Next morning, he walked around the crater rim in less than 2 hours (better take water on this hike, as the water in the *caldeira* lakes may not be suitable to drink). Afterwards, the author hitched back down getting a ride with a British yachter. That same man gave the author another lift on Corse (Corsia) later that summer on 7/18/1989. Small world!

Summer is obviously the best time to climb either of these peaks. July is the driest month of the

Camping at the furna on the west side of Pico do Pico.

Map 19-1, Cabeço Gordo & Pico do Pico, Açores, Portugal

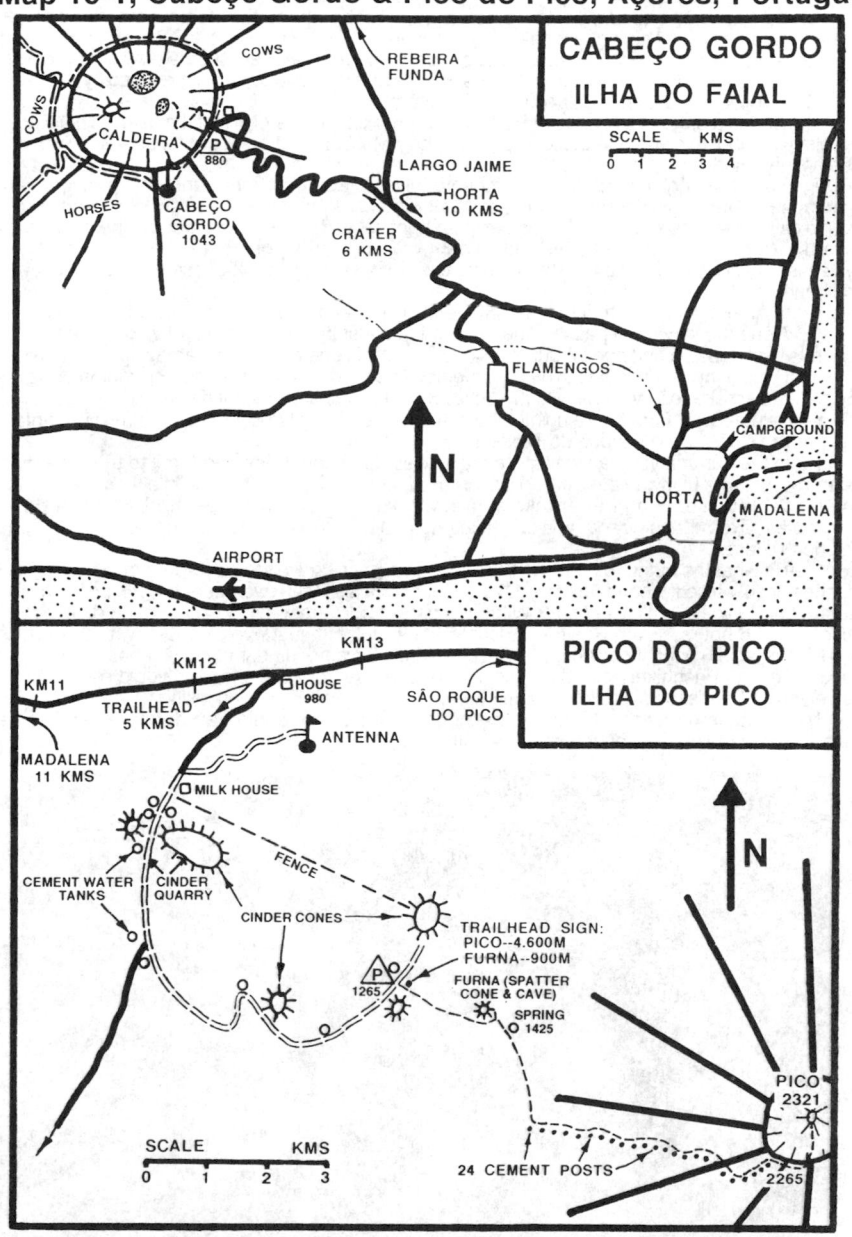

year, followed by June, then August. The Açores get about 70 cms of rain annually. Take rain gear on all climbs. Buy food in Madalena or Horta. Only in winter would an ice ax be needed on Pico.
Maps *Ilha do Açores,* 1:200,000, 1:50,000, or 1:25,000 maps from the Instituto Geografico e Cadastral, buy in Lisboa or probably Ponta Delgada (?); and the travel guidebook, **Landscapes of the Azores**, Sunflower Books.

Pico Ruivo, Madeira Island, Portugal

One of the most rugged mountain areas found anywhere is on the Portuguese island of Madeira, southwest of Lisboa. The highest peak on the island is called Pico Ruivo at 1862 meters. This island was created by volcanism, but all activity ceased long ago, and erosion is now taking place. The normal way to get there is direct from Lisboa with several flights daily. You can also fly there from the UK, Boston--USA, the Canary Islands and elsewhere.

Madeira is a state or province of Portugal and Funchal is the provincial capital. There are many hotels, youth hostels and a tourist office in Funchal, which should be your first stop and your base for seeing the island.

To reach the beginning of the most popular hike, head north from Funchal to Poiso, then to the pausada or hotel on top of Pico Arieiro, at 1818 meters. You can always rent a car and drive, but if you're on foot, take bus 103 which runs between Funchal and the Santana area on the north side of the island. There are at least 4 buses daily, each way. Bus 103 stops at the bar-restaurant at Poiso, which is very near the junction & road running to Arieiro. You can walk or hitch hike the 6.8 kms to the trailhead.

From Arieiro, walk the trail to the northwest. This well-used and maintained path, runs north to Ruivo. Along the way you'll pass through several tunnels and around several vertical walls where the trail has been blasted and carved out of solid rock. This is one of the most amazing trails in the world!

Just below the summit of Ruivo is a refugio where food, drinks and sleeping rooms are available. Be sure and make reservations with the Officina de Turismo in Funchal if you want to stay overnight. It's a 10 minute walk from the refugio to the summit. You can also get to the summit via Santana and the parking place called Achada do Teixeira.

From the summit you can walk on another well-used and maintained trail to the west along the island's crest to a highway pass called Encumeada. Along this trail there is little if any water, so if you intend to stay overnight, better take some with you. The author has marked several possible campsites. From Encumeada, you can take one of 4 or 5 daily buses running between Funchal and the north coast.

Here's what the author did on 6/2/1989. He camped near Poiso, hide some of his baggage in the bushes, then walked & got a ride to Arieiro. It then took less than two hours to walk from Arieiro to the summit of Ruivo, with a large pack. Without a pack, the average hiker is supposed do this round-trip hike in 4 to 6 hours. From Ruivo to Encumeada it took him just over 4 hours, with the same large pack. That was 6 hours from Arieiro to Encumeada. He camped near the pass and hitch hiked out the next morning. Fast hikers could do this in one long day from Funchal, but you'd need someone to drive you up to Arieiro, do the hike, then return to Funchal by bus or hitch hiking.

Most people prefer to hike during the spring season with cooler temperatures and some rain, rather than in the hotter & drier summer months.

Part of the trail to Pico Ruivo runs along this vertical rock face.

Map 20-1, Pico Ruivo, Madeira Island, Portugal

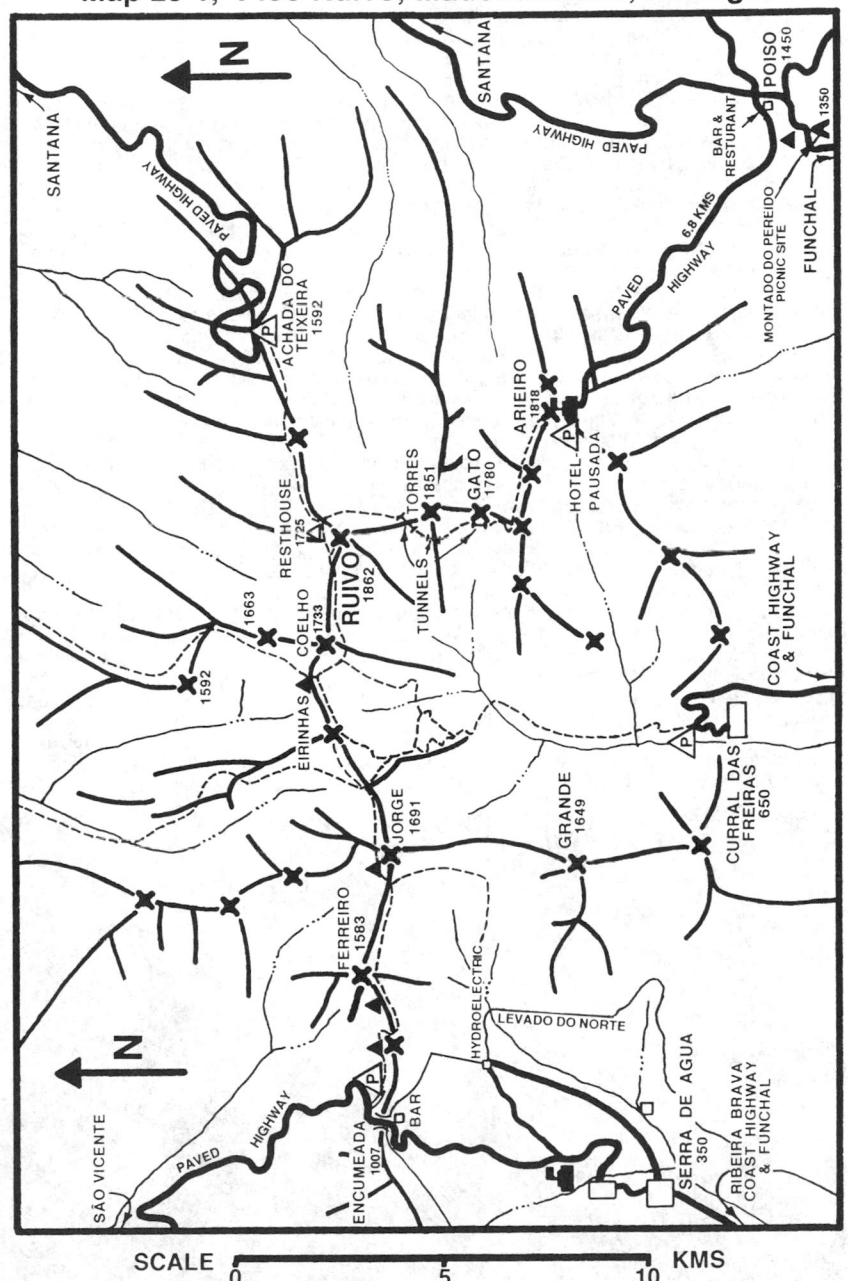

SCALE 0 5 10 KMS

Maps *Two-sheet maps of Madeira*, 1:50,000, from the Instituto Geografico e Cadastral; and the hiking guide **Landscapes of Madeira**, Sunflower Books, buy in bookstores in Funchal.

Caldera de Taburiente, La Palma, Canary Islands, Spain

Featured here is a huge caldera on the island of La Palma, the most westerly of the Canary Islands. This is the Caldera de Taburiente which is a national park. The highest point on the crater rim is 2426 meters. The Canary Islands are located northwest of Morocco in the Atlantic Ocean, and are part of España or Spain.

The Caldera de Taburiente is a very old pine-clad volcano, but there is still some active craters nearby. At the very south end of the island of La Palma is Teneguia crater; it erupted with a VEI-2 explosion between 10/26/1971 & 11/18/1971. It also produced lava flows along with some fatalities.

Get to La Palma by ferry boat or air from the islands of Tenerife and/or Gran Canaria. From the center of Santa Cruz (capital of La Palma and the main ferry boat dock) take a once-every-half-hour mini bus in the direction of El Paso, and get off between Km markers 23 & 24. From that junction, it's a 7 km walk north to a tourist viewpoint on the caldera rim called La Cumbrecita. You can easily hitch hike to this lookout in the daytime hours. This is one main entry point to the caldera and the beginning of hikes along the crater rim.

If you want a good hike to the **crater rim**, instead of going to La Cumbrecita, turn east one km north of the main highway and drive or walk another km to the white church or ermita called *Virgen del Pino*. From the ermita, continue east uphill on an old road another 700-800 meters to the actual beginning of the trail. You can camp there in the *pinos canaria* at the trailhead (carry your own water!). From there, walk up a very good trail to the ridge-top, then turn north and first follow an old road, then another good trail to the Refugio de la Punta de los Roques at about 2050 meters. This rustic refugio will sleep 5-6 people on the floor. It's about 8 kms from the ermita to the refugio, and will take the average hiker 2-3 hours one-way, or 5-6 hours round-trip.

The author got off a bus at the Parque House and walked & got a ride to La Cumbrecita, got lots of fotos, then walked down to the ermita and camped at the trailhead. Next morning, 6/11/1989, he broke camp, hid his big pack, then hurried to Los Roques Refugio in 1 2/3 hours; 3 1/3 hours round-trip.

Another way to the crater rim is to drive from Santa Cruz northeast to the Obervatorio de Astrofisica. This would put you on the highest point of the caldera rim and you could hike along the rim from there. There are no buses on this route except for tour buses. You could hitch hike, but hitching is only fair in the Canaries.

If you'd like to hike inside the caldera, there are a number of trails as shown on the map. Make inquiries regarding national park rules, trails & campsites in Los Llanos city before leaving town. There is a park rangers cabin and a camping area in the center of the crater with good water, but the stream is mostly sulfur tainted. If you're interested in camping, you can also stay at the old campground in the pines south of La Cumbrecita. There's water in a tap across the road. This information is from the author's visit in 1989.

For any hike in this area buy your food in Los Llanos, El Paso or Santa Cruz. Always have water with you and inquire of its whereabouts when you're hiking. You can climb or hike year-round in the Canaries, but the wettest season is from October through January. Summers are very warm and dry.

Looking into the Caldera de Taburiente from the lookout called La Cumbrecita.

Map 21-1, Caldera Taburiente, La Palma, Canaries, Spain

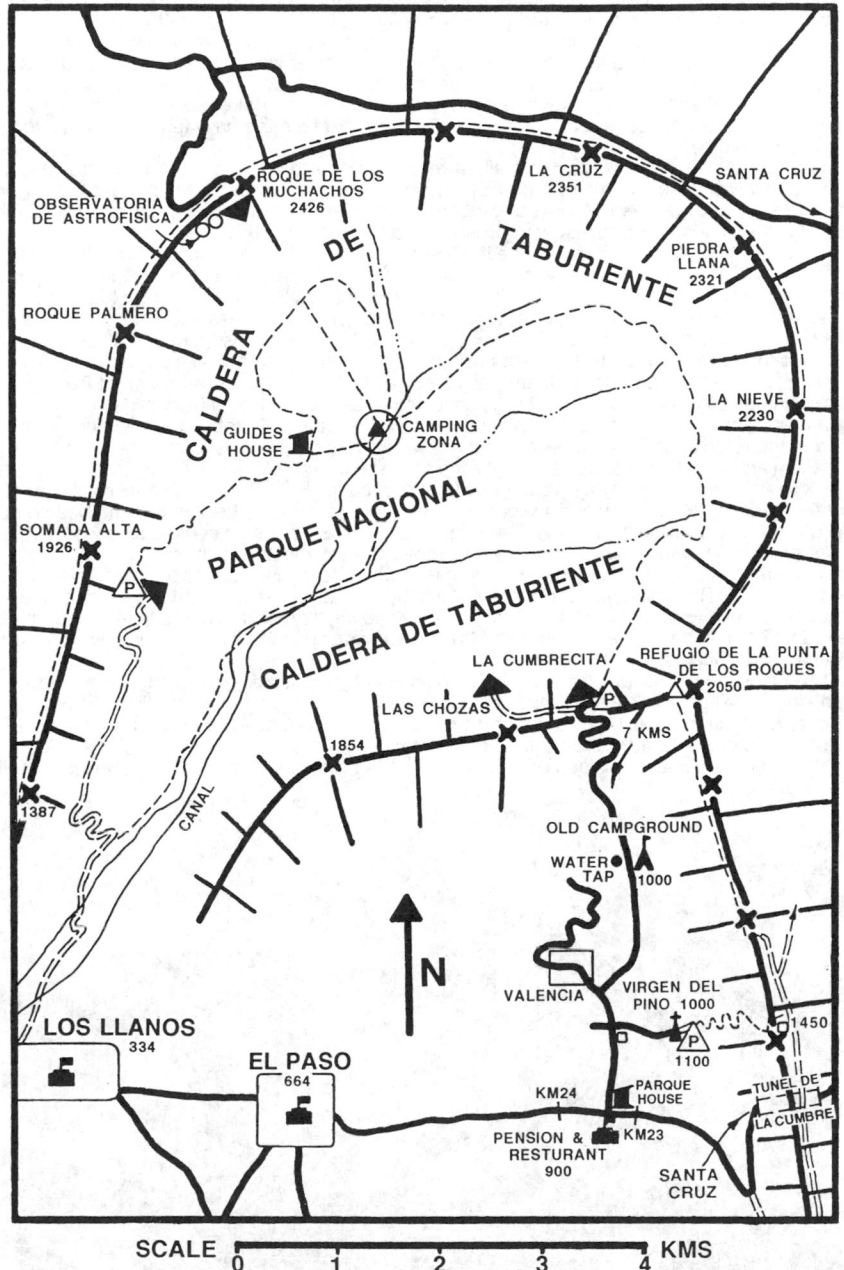

Maps A locally-made map of the parque nacional or other tourist maps; also, *Generalkarte Tenerife (La Palma-Hierro-Gomera)*, 1:150,000, Mairs Geographischer Verlag, Stuttgart; or Spanish topo maps from the Instituto Geografico Nacional; and the latest travel guidebook to the Canary Islands.

Pico de Teide, Tenerife Island, Canary Islands, Spain

The highest peak in Spanish Territory is Pico de Teide, at 3718 meters. It's located on the Canary Island of Tenerife. Teide is considered an active volcano, but it's been a while. While Teide's last eruption was in about 1396 AD, there's been more recent activity on a subsidiary summit called Pico Viejo. This volcano is located about 2 kms just off this map to the west. Viejo's last period of activity was between 11/18 & 11/27/1909. At that time, it had a VEI-2 explosion and issued lava.

Here's how to get there--fly. Most flights to the Canaries originate in Madrid and they land on Gran Canary or Tenerife. If you land on Gran Canary, fly or take the daily ferry to Santa Cruz, the main city on Tenerife.

Many tourists going to this mountain either rent a car or take a tour bus. But you can also hitch hike (a little slow) or take a public bus from Santa Cruz to the central bus station in Puerto de la Cruz. From Puerto de la Cruz, one bus leaves at 8:30am and takes 1 1/2 hours to reach the hotel south of Teide. It stays there all day and leaves for Puerto de la Cruz at 4pm.

Now for **Pico de Teide**. You can take the teleferico to an older crater rim of Teide, then walk the last little ways to the summit (2 readers have written and stated you cannot go above the top of the teleferico or 3500 meters on Teide. Ask about this policy before you climb or you could be fined!). Or you can hike all the way. To do the hike, stop at the road junction marked 2300 meters, with a large sign showing the normal route to the summit prior to 1971. Drivers must park at that junction or the nearby locked gate and walk about 5 kms up an old dirt road to the actual trailhead at about 2750 meters. From there it's an easy walk up a zig zag trail to the Refugio de Altavista, at 3260 meters. This refugio has about 60 beds, some food, and is open year-round. It may be crowded on weekends, especially in summer. In winter, only part is open all the time, the rest is open on weekends only.

From the refugio, continue upwards past a lava tube ice cave on the right. Further on, the trail turns left on an old crater rim and heads to the top of the teleferico. Once there, ask if you can proceed to the summit? From the highway, it's a 6 to 9 hour round-trip climb. There's a small snack bar at the top of the teleferico, which does not give out free water!, and a restaurant at the bottom. Directly south of the peak is a hotel called the Parador Nacional de Las Cañadas. You can eat & sleep, or buy books and get information there. You can also get free water, at least from the restroom.

One of the best places to get fotos of Teide is at the hotel, or just across the road to the west at what they call Los Roques. Another place to get a good view of the peak is from a high point on the old caldera rim called Guajara. To get there, walk or drive south, then east from the hotel to the trailhead (see map). From there, locate an unmarked trail zig zagging up to the rim. Once you find the trail it's easy to follow to Guajara at 2710 meters.

The author hitch hiked from the coast up to the hotel at Las Cañadas, camped nearby out of sight, then on the morning of 6/7/1989 got a ride up to the junction at 2300 meters and climbed from there; 2 1/2 hours to the summit; 5 1/4 hours round-trip. Camped again near Las Cañadas, then climbed Guajara in less than 2 hours round-trip the next morning.

Remember to buy all your food before arriving at the mountain, and take several water bottles

From Guajara, looking north at Pico de Teide center, Viejo left, the viewpoint right.

Map 22-1, Teide, Tenerife Island, Canary Islands, Spain

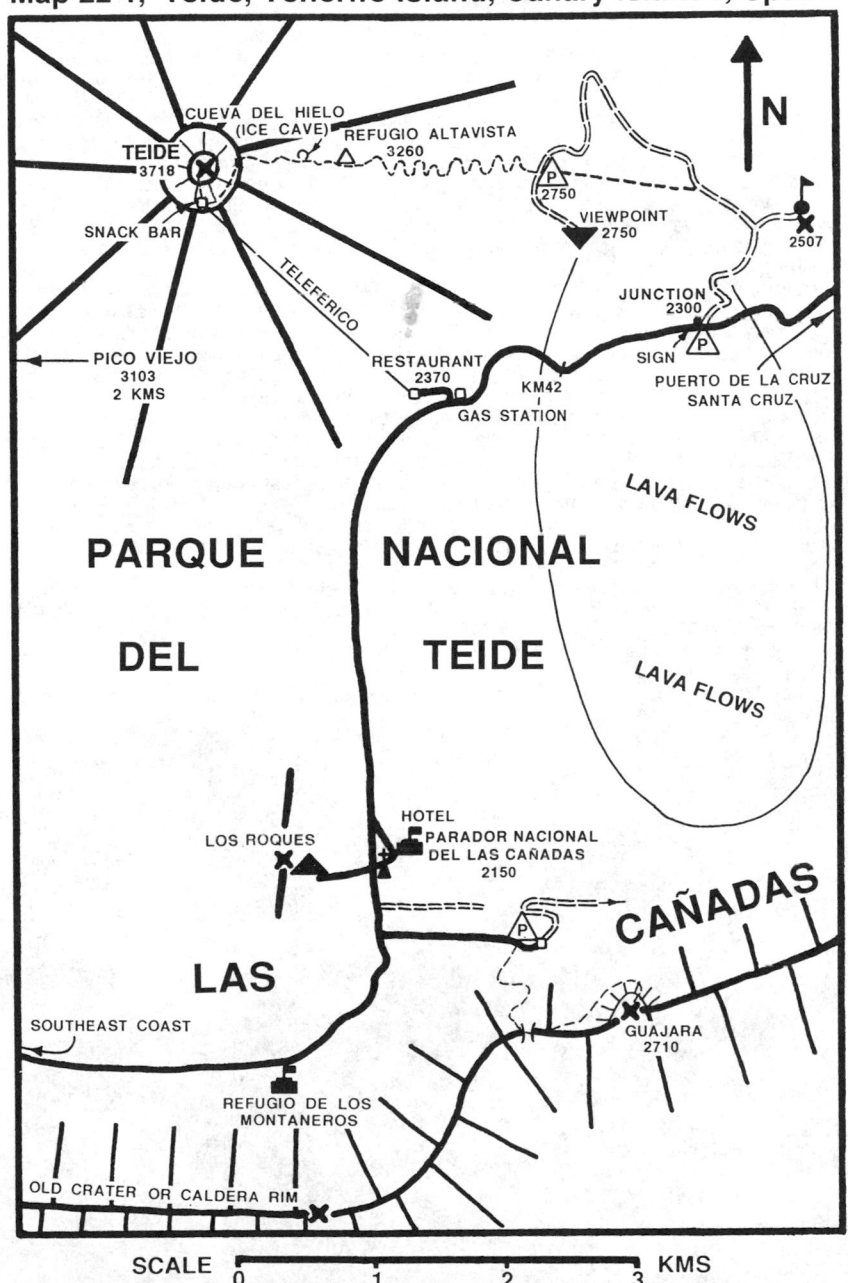

(and keep them full). You can climb Teide year-round, but snow does fall on top in winter. Summer weather is very dry. Camping is prohibited in the national park, so camp out of sight.

Maps *Generalkarte Tenerife (La Palma-Hierro-Gomera),* 1:150,000, Mairs Geographischer Verlag Stuttgart; maps from the IGM, Madrid; or the book, **Landscapes of Tenerife,** Sunflower Books.

The Rock of Gibraltar, Gibraltar, United Kingdom

Most people wouldn't put the Rock of Gibraltar in the same book or category as the Andes or Himalayas, but this magnificent peak has some unusual characteristics which make it an interesting place to visit. The elevation isn't all that high, but its high point at 426 meters does rise nearly vertical from the Mediterranean, making it one of the highest sea cliffs anywhere. The Rock is made of limestone.

Gibraltar is a semi-independent state with very close ties with the UK. The defense is totally in the hands of Downey Street. It has its own currency, but it's interchangeable with the English £S. Long-time citizens speak both English and Spanish, with some speaking Arabia. There are many Arab and Asian merchants living and working there. Gibraltar is a freeport and almost totally dependent on tourism as a source of income. Most tourists come from Spain and the UK.

Most visitors arrive by land via Spain and the border town of La Linea. For many years this was a closed border, but in 1989 it was open. You can also fly in from the UK and Morocco, or take a ferry to or from Tangier.

It's best to stay in La Linea where hotels are much cheaper than inside Gibraltar, then walk across the border and into town (camping isn't permitted in Gibraltar largely because there's no place to put a tent!). It's only about 2 kms from the center of La Linea to the town center of Gibraltar. You can also take one bus from the border into town, or another which makes a complete circle around the Rock itself. Since this map is just an introduction, be sure and stop at the tourist office at the border, or in the middle of town, to get a better map and one of several simple little guidebooks.

To reach the top of the Rock, walk to the center of town, then take the cable car to the top station and walk south from there to the highest peak. For those with more time, head for the bottom of the cable car or lower station, then walk uphill on one of several roads. There are some pedestrian-only trails or tracks at or near the summit ridge. The place with the finest views is on the south side of the highest peak on what is known as the Mediterranean Steps.

The author stayed in a hotel in La Linea, then walked across the border. This was on 7/1/1989. He got so wrapped up in being a tourist, he ended up not having enough time to reach the summit of the Rock. Lots of things to see at Gibralter!

Other things you'll want to see are the upper Galleries (defensive tunnel portals facing Spain), the Moorish Castle, St. Michael's Cave, the water catchment basins and the Barbary apes. In the mid-1980's, there were 67 of these apes, which are actually tail-less monkeys. Since there's not much natural vegetation left for them to live on, the British military garrison has the responsibility of feeding them. Don't leave anything lying around, or the apes may steal it.

Maps Stop at the tourist office or any tourist shop selling books and maps and buy the booklet

From the pedestrian lanes crossing the airport runway looking
south at the north end of The Rock.

Map 23-1, The Rock of Gibraltar, Gibraltar, UK

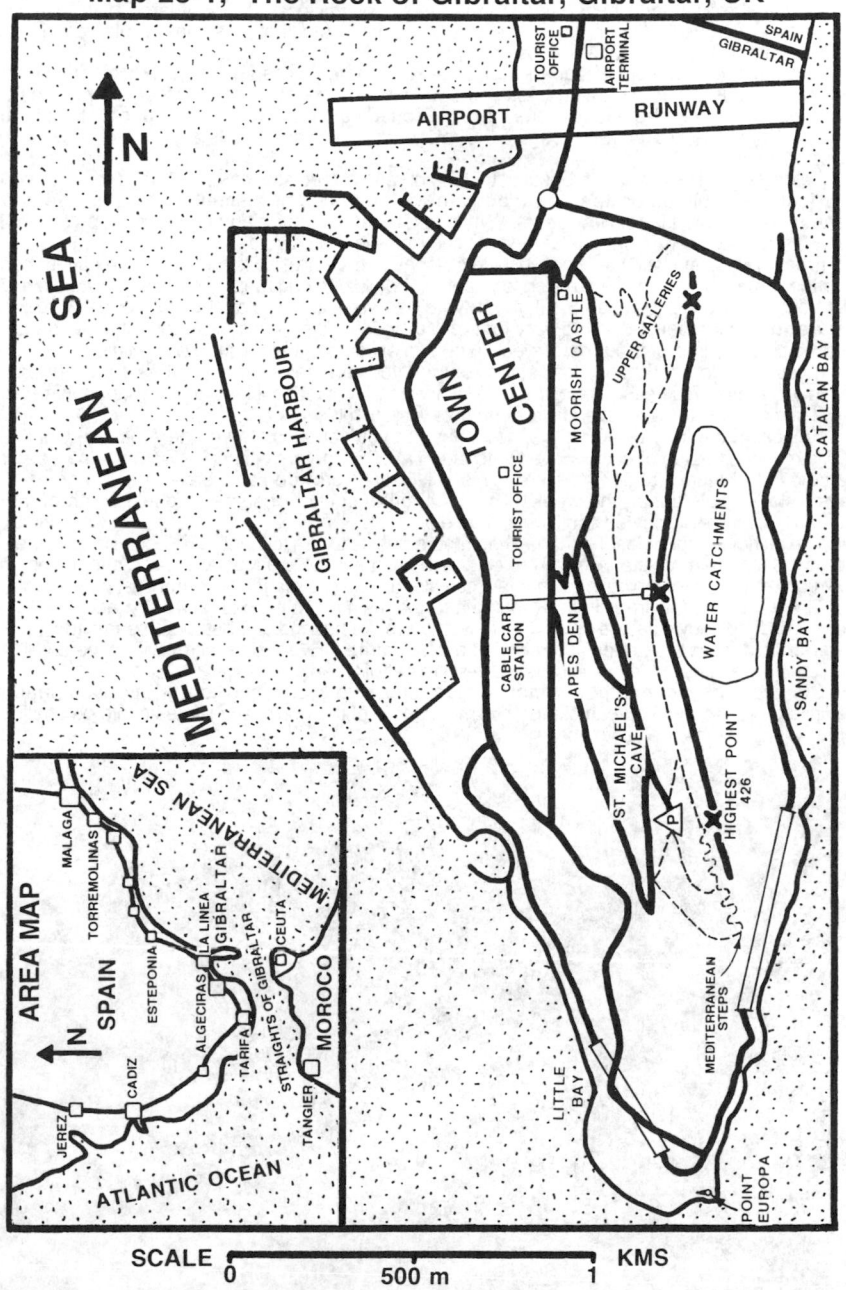

Gibraltar Guide, which includes the Rock's history and a tour map of the colony; and perhaps the latest travel guidebook to España or Spain.

Mulhacén, Sierra Nevada, Spain

Included here is the highest portion of the Sierra Nevada located in southern Spain. The highest peak is Mulhacén, at 3478 meters. These mountains are located not far southeast of Granada and are made of various types of crystalline rock such as quartzite.

To get to the mountain, first go to Granada. From there you can either hitch hike, drive your own car or take a bus up the mountain. Ask someone which bus station you must go to first to catch the right bus. In summer there is one bus leaving Granada at 9am each day. It runs 32 kms to the ski resort of Solynieve, then at 5pm begins the return trip. The road to this area is steep, winding and paved all the way.

Before leaving Granada, it's best to stock up on all the food supplies you'll need for your trip. The only food available on or near the mountain will be at one or 2 small and expensive shops or restaurants at Prato Llano (Solynieve). While in Granada, look for any books or maps of the Sierra Nevada you may need. You may or may not find maps in Prato Llano (?).

From Prato Llano, you can walk up the ski slopes or hitch hike up to the end of the paved road very near the summit of Veleta. If you're on foot, get on the old dirt road running east from just below the top of **Veleta**. This is a good road, so if you have a car, you can drive all the way to the Refugio Felix Mendez or maybe beyond to the very foot of **Mulhacén**. Since this is a high altitude road, it'll be blocked by snowdrifts until July each year. You can of course, walk this route any time.

If you're on foot for the walk past the refugio, you can make a short-cut as shown on the map. When you arrive at the base of Mulhacén, look for an unmarked trail leaving the road running upslope to the summit. On top are several old stone huts without roofs.

You can camp anywhere on the mountain, but you can also stay at the Albergue Universitario (rustic mountain hotel) directly above Prato Llano at 2553 meters altitude. You can also sleep at the Refugio Felix Mendez at 3040 meters. This will likely be crowded on weekends in summer, but will have fewer people during the week. There's another shelter of some kind just south of the peak marked 3201. This is located southwest of Veleta.

The author camped near Granada, then rode a bus up to Pratto Llano, and got a lift up to the end of the paved road near Veleta. He walked east to the summit of Mulhacén and back, and got another lift down and ended up camping in the same place along a small stream a few kms east of Granada.

There are very few trees in this mountain range, as a result it looks rather dry late in the season. However, deep snows do pile up in winter. Summers are hot and dry, but there seems to be plenty of water around, except perhaps at the end of a dry summer. Even if the lakes dry up there will always be water in the canyons, especially near the ski resort of Solynieve.

Summer is of course the normal season for hiking & climbing, but with buses heading for Solynieve year-round, you can climb any time. Some of the north face routes could be challenging, otherwise all climbs are very easy.

Mulhacén in the background, the Refugio Felix Mendez to the right.

Map 24-1, Mulhacén, Sierra Nevada, Spain

Maps *Güejar Sierra*, 1:50,000, Instituto Geografico Nacional, General Ibanez de Ibero, 3, Apartado 3007, Madrid-3; and travel guidebook **Spain**, Lonely Planet; or any other recent guidebook.

Cerrado & Naranjo de Bulnes, Picos de Europa, Spain

The mountains shown here are in the highest part of the range known as Picos de Europa, located between Santander and Gijón near the north coast of Spain or España. They are made of limestone with many difficult climbs as well as some easy hikes. The highest peak is Cerrado at 2648 meters, but there are several others over 2600 meters. The most famous is Naranjo de Bulnes.

The most-used route to this compact range is via the north coast and Santander. From there, head west along the main coast highway, then turn south to Potes and finally west to Fuente Dé. There are several buses daily running from Santander to Potes, then several others making the daily summer run to Fuente Dé, as shown on this map.

The author found hitch hiking moderately good in and out of these mountains during the summer of 1989. He arrived at Fuente Dé on 7/4/1989, and camped in the nearby forest. Next morning he left 2 bags in the bushes and hiked up the trail and camped near Vieja. That afternoon, he climbed Vieja in about an hour then the rain came. Next morning in the rain he walked down to the teleferico and rode it down and hitch hiked out of the area.

At Fuente Dé, you'll find a hotel, restaurant, cafeteria and a campground. Fuente Dé is also a spring at the bottom of a huge bowl, and a former glacier cirque basin.

Here's how to get into the high peaks from Fuente Dé. You can take the teleferico to the top of the bowl, a vertical rise of 800 meters; or walk a trail as shown running under the teleferico to the top of the lift. From there walk up a 4WD road less than a km to a good trail heading off to the left or northwest toward Cabaña Veronica. Then if you like, go over a pass and down to Refugio Ubeda, the refugios at Bulnes and finally to the small town of Arenas on the north side of the range. This would be an easy 2 day hike with backpack.

Within the range, there's a trail to the summit of **Peña Vieja**, a one day hike from Fuente Dé; and an apparently easy route to the top of **Cerrado**, as shown on the map. **Naranjo** has an easy east slope, but the west face is said to be the best technical climb in the range.

If you hike west from Fuente Dé, you'll arrive at Refugio Jermosa and have a chance to climb high peaks in that area such as **Palanca**, **Torres Llambrion** and **Blanca**.

Even through these mountains get heavy snows in winter, there is very little reliable surface water in the high country. The snow melts and the water seeps down into the porous limestone. Go prepared to carry water for camping and ask of the whereabouts of good water in each area. There is water at or near all refugios except Cabaña Veronica. You can also buy some food and sleep at each of the refugios (except Cabaña Veronica).

Santander or Gijón would be the best places to stock up on food, but near the mountain, Potes is a good place. Potes is nearly the same to the Picos de Europa, as Chamonix is to Mt. Blanc. Because this place is so near the coast, count on cloudy weather year-round, especially on the north slopes. Fuente Dé seems to be sunnier than points north. July and August have less precipitation.

The west face of Naranjo de Bulnes (Bustamante de Potes postcard foto).

Map 25-1, Cerrado & N. de Bulnes, Picos Europe, Spain

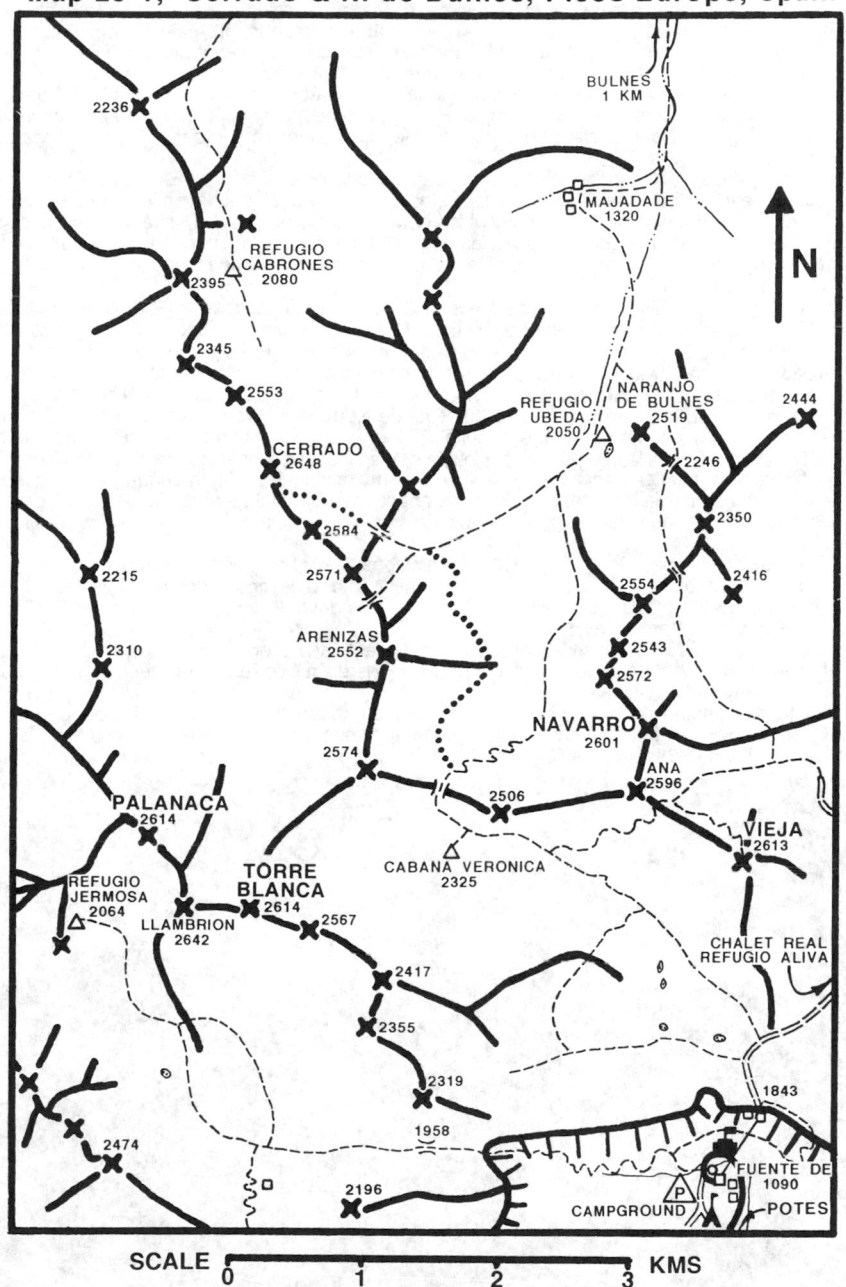

SCALE 0   1   2   3 KMS

Maps *Macizo Occidental and Naranjo de Bulnes,* 1:25,000, Editorial Alpina, Apartado de Carreos 3, Granollers (Barcelona), Spain; and the book, **Picos de Europa**, West Col Books; and perhaps th ⸱ travel guidebook, **Spain**, Lonely Planet.

Massanella, Isla de Mallorca, Baleares Islands, Spain

The mountains shown here are on the island of Mallorca, which is part of the Isles Baleares of Spain or España. This island group is in the Mediterranean just east of Spain. The highest peak is Puig Mayor at 1445 meters, but it has a military installation on the summit and is off limits to hikers. The second highest mountain is the nearby Massanella at 1352 meters.

To get to Mallorca, take a flight from Barcelona, Valencia or Alicante; or a night ferry from these same cities to the capital of the island group, Palma. Many people going to Mallorca end up renting a car and making a tour of the island, but you can also get around and into the mountains via public transportation.

To get to Massanella and the famous monastery at Lluc, go to the Plaza España in Palma, where you can take either a bus or train to a city called Inca. Trains leave about every half hour during day-time hours. From the train station in Inca (which doubles as the bus station) take a bus 15 kms north to Lluc. It seems there are several buses leaving each day, at least in summer. You can also walk about 1 km to the edge of Inca and hitch hike. If you're planning to camp in the mountains, be sure to buy all your food in Inca.

Once in the mountains, and to climb **Massanella**, stop at the gas station-restaurant (marked 585 meters on the map) at the pass near the junction of two major highways just south of the Monasterio de Lluc. From that gas station, walk back down the highway toward Inca about 300-400 meters to a side-road as shown. Walk westward up this zig zag road past a summer home called Comafreda. At the gate and fence turn left and continue up a trail. Later you'll be back on an old road which goes up to 2 cement posts at the Pas de N'Arbona. From there take a trail northwest which zig zags up the south face of Massanella. Higher up the mountain the trail splits; the lower one passes a cave with steps leading down to a fountain or spring and good water (take a flashlight).

At the summit you can return the same way; or climb down a gully on the north face, and make a circuit of the mountain via the Font D'es Prat, the abandoned Canaleta (canal) de Massanella, up over a pass without a trail, then east along an old road back to Comafreda and the main highway. This hike will take a full day.

The author took a night ferry to Palma from Barcelona, stayed one night in Palma, then on 7/9/1989 took a train to Inca, hitch hiked to Lluc and walked the loop hike described above in 7 hours round-trip. He camped near the monastery, then took an 11am bus down to Inca, a train back to Palma and another night ferry to Barcelona.

Seeking adventure? Look into going down the Torrente de Pareis. You'll need ropes, headlamps and a guide and it must be done in spring time when there's a little running water in this very dark & narrow slot canyon.

For those camping, there's a free camp site near the monastery (with a hotel, store & cafe) with tap water, but please inform the church people first and keep the place clean. Once in this area, you can take a number of other hikes. Summers are hot and dry, so the best time to hike is in the spring

The gate at Comafreda and the eastern end of the long ridge extending from Massanella.

Map 26-1, Massanella, Isle de Mallorca, Spain

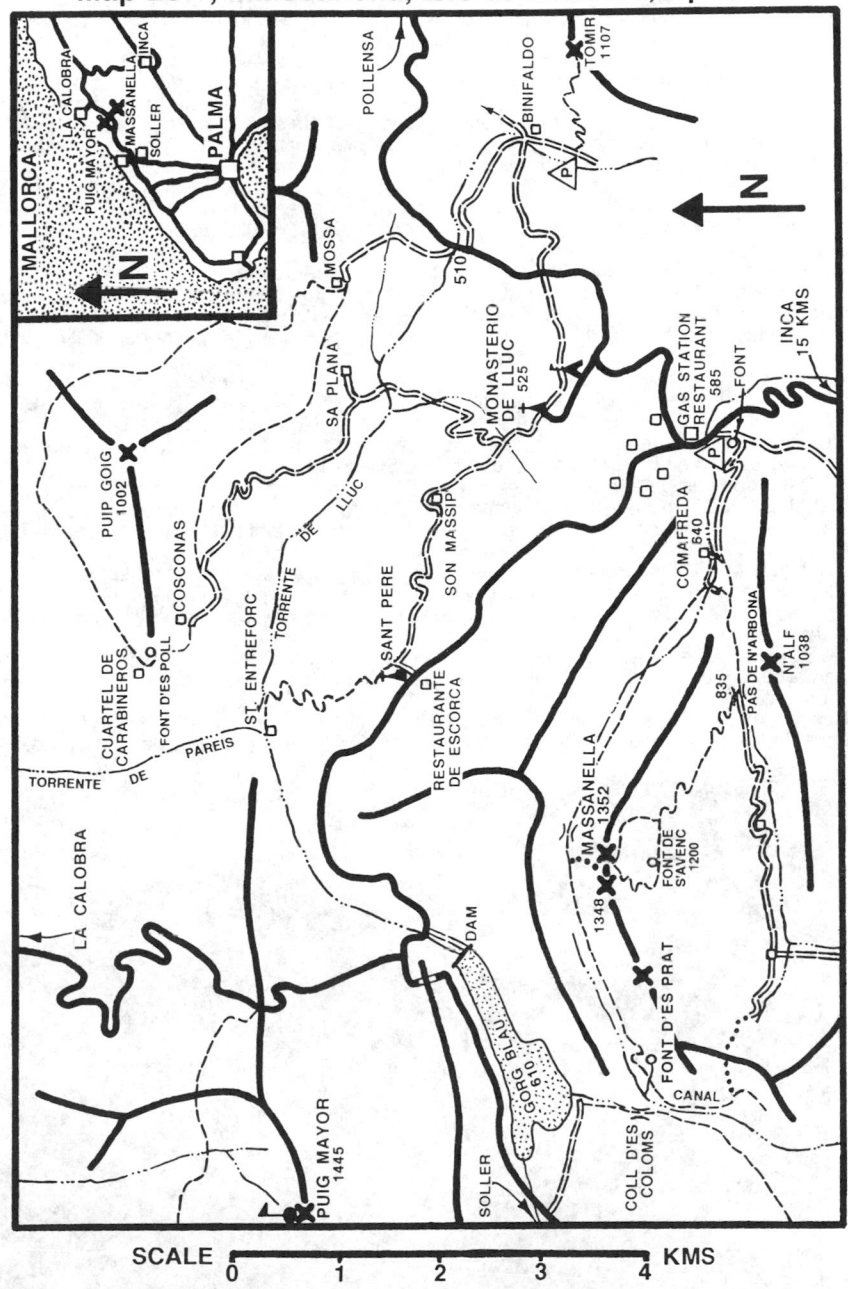

season as well as in fall. Everything is green in the spring, but the chance of rain is also better.
Maps *Lluc Y Su Comarca* (no scale given), from tourist office, Palma; the guidebook, **Landscapes of Mallorca**, Sunflower Books, UK. Upon arrival in Palma, ask someone at the tourist office which bookshop in the city has guidebooks and/or maps for sale.

Vignemale, Pyrenees Mountains, France-Spain

The map shown here is the first of 4 covering the Pyrenees Mountains which form the border between France and Spain (España). Included on this map are: Pic du Mid D'Ossau, 2884 meters, in the western portion; centrally located Balaitous, 3144 meters; and in the eastern part of the map, Vignemale, 3298 meters, one of the better known peaks in the Pyrenees. As with most of the Pyrenees Mountains, the rock make-up in this section is largely metamorphic, like quartzite which is caused by pressure and the folding of the earth's crust.

The western half of this map includes a couple of lower passes, which have good highways built over them and even one railway tunnel (the one beneath the Col du Somport). This area is a skier's paradise, with at least four large resorts, three of which are located on the Spanish side of the border. As a result of these passes, access to the region is good. Any mountain summit included on this map can be climbed in one day from the trailhead at the end of the nearest road.

Access roads, trails and refuges are more developed on the north or French side, than the Spanish side. On this map, there are almost no refugios on the southern slopes. It must be noted too that the most difficult climbing routes are nearly always on the north faces, where snow and glaciers have a chance to accumulate. The southern faces are generally more gently sloping and of course sunnier and drier.

To climb Vignemale, you can approach the mountains from Cauterets and Pont D'Espagne. From Pont, there's a well-used trail to the east face of **Vignemale** and a couple of nearby refuges. This trail is part of the Grande Randonnee (GR), a series of trails linked together to form one long walk along the crest of the Pyrenees from the Atlantic to the Mediterranean. Vignemale can also be reached via Torla on the Spanish side.

Balaitous can be approached about equally well from Gallego on the south, or from Arrens and Migouelo on the north. Like Vignemale, Balaitous has some small glaciers or perpetual snow fields. To help decide which route is best for you, contact people at a nearby refuge--they are normally the best source of information.

Pic du Mid D'Ossau can be climbed from the highway south of Laruns, France. Walk or hitch hike about 6 kms from the highway to find a trail circling the mountain. The author hasn't climbed this peak, but it seems a south face approach may be easiest. Maps don't show a trail to the summit, so it could be a difficult climb (?).

Buy all your supplies before arriving in this area for lower prices and better selections. Cauterets is the largest town on this map. Ice ax & crampons may be needed on a few routes, but not all.

Maps *Pau-Bagneres de Lucho, 70,* 1:100,000, from the Institut Geographique National (IGN), Paris; there are 3 climbing guides to **East, Central and West Pyrenees**, contact Cordee Books.

This is the north face of Vignemale (Walter Pause foto).

Map 27-2, Vignemale, Pyrenees Mountains, France-Spain

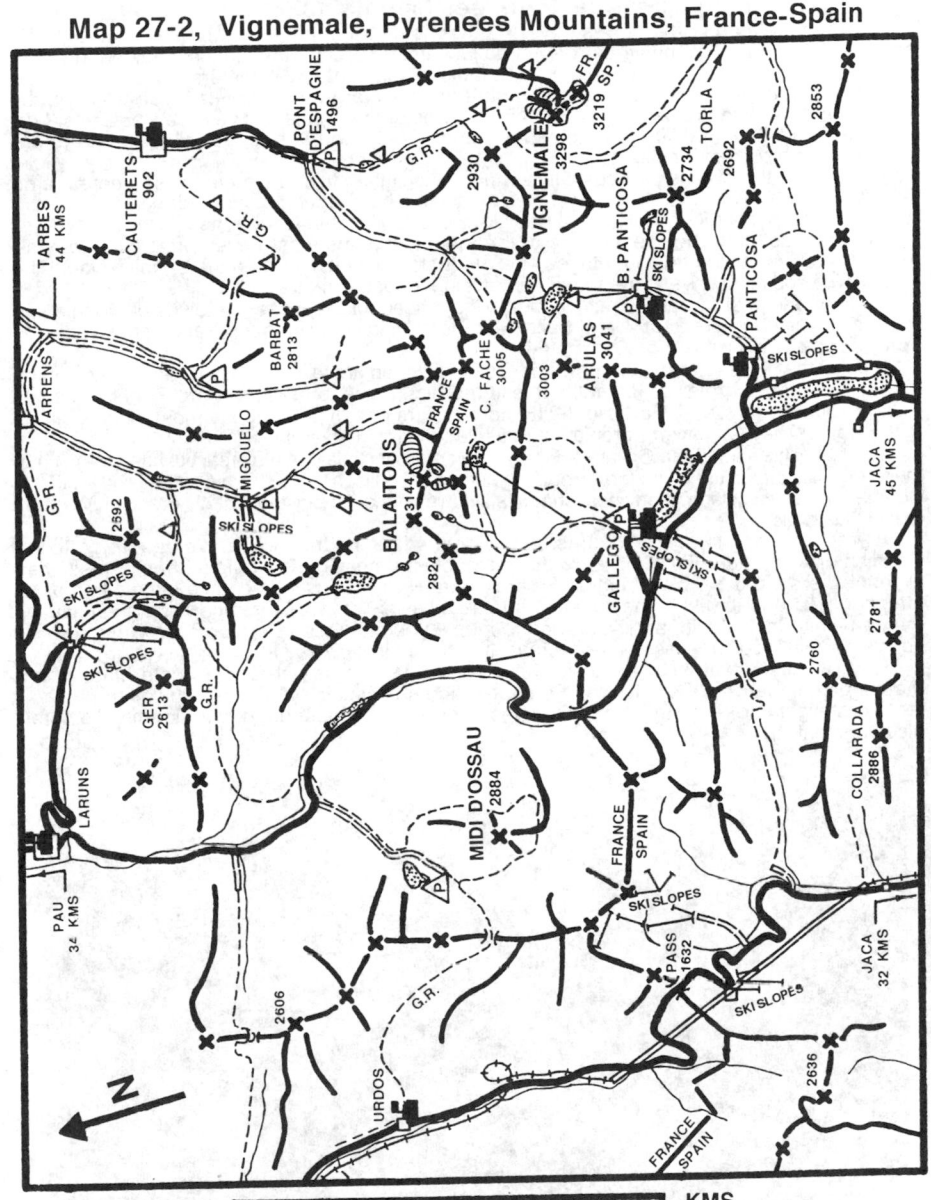

SCALE 0   5   10   15 KMS

Cirque du Gavarnie, Pyrenees Mountains, France-Spain

This second map in the series covering the major summits in the Pyrenees Mountains, includes the peaks surrounding the Cirque du Gavarnie, Perdido (the highest peak on this map and the third highest in the Pyrenees) at 3355 meters, and Long, 3192 meters.

On the south or Spanish side of the mountains, few large settlements exist, while on the north, or French side, there are several larger towns or small cities. They are Cauterets, Luz, Gavarnie, and Saulan. All these towns are built around tourism, especially Cauterets and Gavarnie (the most famous of all).

Getting into this area is perhaps a little more difficult than to some mountains. There are no railways close by, which means your choice is taking a bus, renting a car or hitch hiking. In the late 1970's, the author found hitching a little slow, but he wasn't in a hurry then.

For the most part, the French side of the mountain is the most developed, with many ski resorts, hotels, restaurants, and refuges. Few mountain refugios exist on the Spanish side. The French side seems to have more and better developed roads and trails.

To climb the peaks near the middle of this map, head for the ski resort towns of Mongie and Barges. By climbing south up along trails near the ski lifts, you can easily reach peaks such as **Long** and the summit marked 3091 meters.

Most of the higher and better-known peaks on this map are within relatively easy reach of the tourist town of Gavarnie, so logically, this is the best place to begin a climb. Peaks such as **Taillon**, 3144 meters, and **Marbore**, 3248 meters, form part of perhaps the most famous cirque in the world. They, and even Perdido, can be reached from Gavarnie.

The author hitch hiked into Gavarnie on 9/1/1979 and spent 3 days in the area, but had rain much of the time. He camped out in the forest for 2 nights--probably illegally (?). He did some hiking, but the weather prevented getting to any high summits. However, he did buy most of his French IGN maps there in Gavarnie.

If you're looking for easier routes up the peaks forming the cirque, it's best to go to the Spanish or south side. To climb **Perdido**, the easiest access route would be from Bielsa, then Pineta, where there's a tourist hotel. From Pineta, walk southwest a couple of kms to a pass, then ridge-walk northwest to the summit. Another possibility is via Broto and Torla, then east up the canyon to the refugio, as shown on the map. You can reach Perdido from Gavarnie, but you've got to walk over 3 passes before reaching the summit.

Keep in mind, if you're camping on the French side, a large part of the western half of this map is part of the Parc National des Pyrenees, and camping is forbidden. However, putting a tent up at night and removing it early the nest morning, is condoned. If you do this, discretely hide your tent.

The town of Gavarnie, and the Cirque du Gavarnie to the south in the clouds.

Map 28-1, Cirque du Gavarnie, Pyrenees Mtns., France-Spain

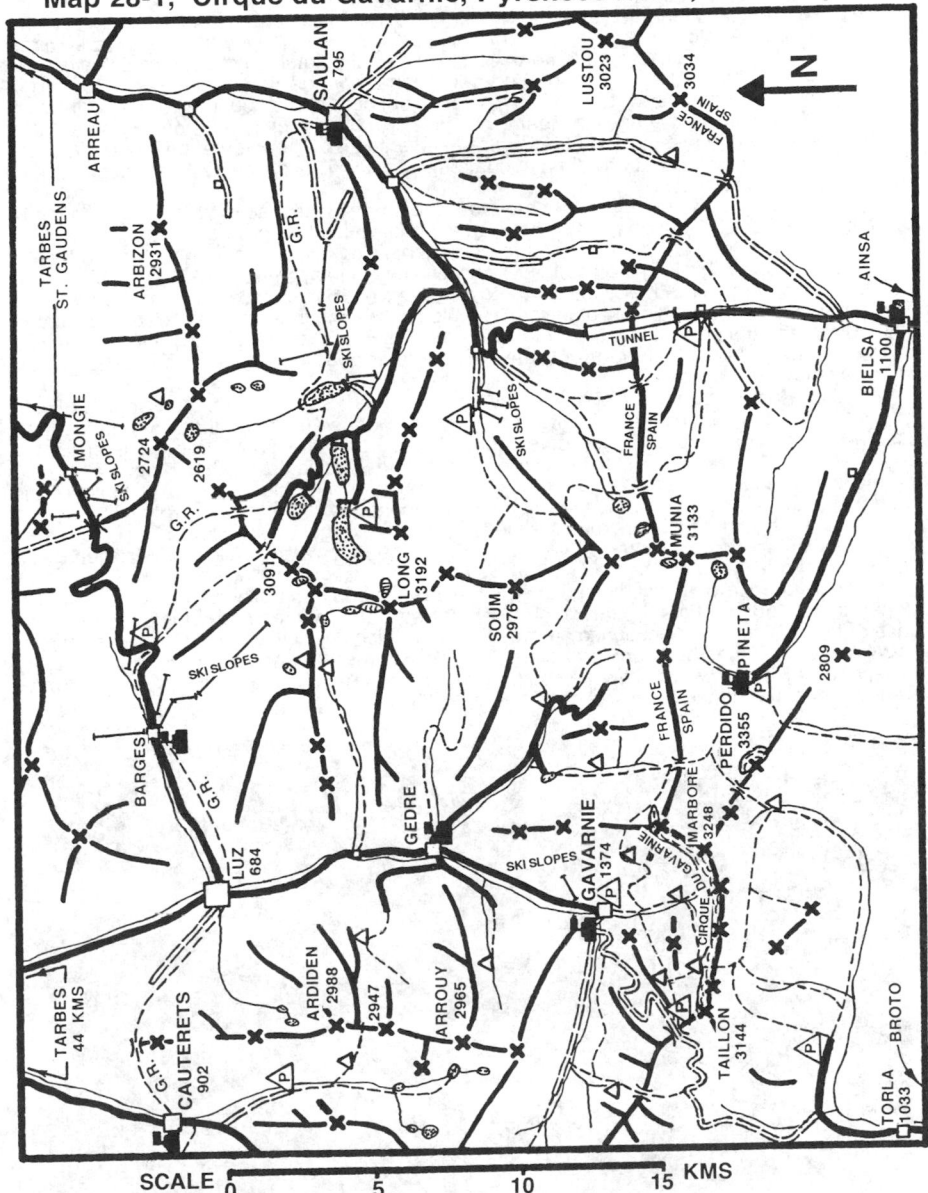

SCALE 0   5   10   15 KMS

If you plan to spend some time in the mountains, buy your food in Luz or Saulan. For the best information concerning trails, refuges, camping and routes, consult the tourist offices in the larger towns, especially Gavarnie, and the refuges in the mountains.

Maps *Pau-Bagneres de Lucho, 70,* 1:100,000, from the Institut Geographique National (IGN), Paris; there are 3 climbing guides to **East, Central** and **West Pyrenees**, contact Cordee Books; and perhaps the latest gravel guidebook to France or Spain (España).

Pico Aneto, Pyrenees Mountains, France-Spain

Very near the geographic center of the Pyrenees Mountains stands the highest summit in the entire range, Pico Aneto, 3404 meters. As one might expect, most of the high peaks are on the boundary line between France on the north and Spain on the south. In most cases this is true, but in the region covered by this map, the international boundary does not follow the line of highest peaks or the natural watershed. In the area of Luchon, the boundary turns north, then east, which puts the Vall D'Aran in Spain, not France. Both Pico Aneto, and Posets, 3375 meters (the second highest peak in the Pyrenees), lie south of the international boundary and the watershed divide and are within the boundaries of Spain. These mountains are composed of quartzite and limestone.

To get to this area from the north, head southeast from Toulouse toward Tarbes, but turn south just west of St. Gaudens, and drive or hitch hike to Luchon or Lés. If coming from the south, head north from Lerida or Barbastro. No trains, and few buses in this area, so having you're own car, or hitch hiking are about your only choices of transport.

The normal route for those climbing **Aneto**, is from the Spanish side via Benasque and the Refugio Renclusa. From this last of several refugios on the mountain, the climb is made in one day. Enroute to the summit, a glacier must be crossed, so an ice ax & crampons will likely be needed. It can also be climbed from the Refugio Cabana, located on the main highway, southeast of the peak.

To climb **Posets**, one has a choice of two routes. There's a trail from the village of Eriste (about 3 kms below Benasque), running to the northwest, then up either the south ridge or the east face of the mountain. Another route begins about 3 or 4 kms above Benasque. This trail begins at an old work camp, and follows the stream to the Refugio del Cantal. From that area to the top is a rough trail up a north facing gully. To climb the south ridge, no special equipment is needed, but the north route may require ice ax & crampons.

The author hitch hiked south from St. Gaudens, and finally got to Oo. He walked up the road a ways and camped. Next morning, 8/30/1979, and in perfect weather, climbed Perdigueru in 3 1/3 hours, then returned and hitched west to Gavarnie.

The only large towns in the immediate area are Benasque and Luchon. These are the best places to buy food and get the latest information about trail, routes and refugios in the area. Each of these towns is big enough to have bookstores which sell detailed maps of the region.

Winter time brings heavy precipitation, but the summers tend to be very dry and sunny. Expect slightly better weather on the southern slopes. One should also expect less-improved roads and facilities on the Spanish side.

The northern slopes of Perdigueru which is south of the town of Oo.

Map 29-1, Pico Aneto, Pyrenees Mountains, France-Spain

Maps *La Vall D' Aran, Maladeta-Aneto, and Posets,* 1:25,000, from Editorial Alpina, Apartado de Coneos 3, Granollers (Barcelona), España (Spain); also, *St. Gaudens-Andorra, 71*, from the Institut Geographique National (IGN), 136 bis, rue de Grenelle, Paris, France, website (www.ign.fr); there are 3 climbing guides to East, Central and West Pyrenees, contact Cordee Books.

Pico D'Estats, Pyrenees Mountains, France-Andorra-Spain

This is the fourth map covering the higher portion of the Pyrenees Mountains. This map is centered on the tiny independent Republic of Andorra, which sits on the mountain top between France and Spain (España). This country uses currency from both its neighbors, and both French and Spanish are the national languages. Nowadays, the entire economy of Andorra is based on tourism.

These peaks are basically of the same geologic makeup as other peaks in the Pyrenees to the west; they're made of mostly sedimentary rocks such as limestone, plus some quartzite.

The highest peak in the area does not border on France and Spain. **Pico D'Estats**, at 3141 meters, is the highest summit east of Pico Aneto. Estats can be reached from the north or south, with the northern route probably being used most, as there are probably more alpinists in France than in Spain.

The northern route to Estats is via Foix, Vicdessos, Auzat, Marc and finally up a road to where water is diverted into an electric plant pipeline. The trail passes several old stone huts, which can be used for free (but often aren't real good shelters, especially when it's raining), then it rises to the top of **Mont Calm** and finally to the summit of Estats. It's a long one day hike from the area around Marc, so most people camp in the higher meadows. Vicdessos or Auzat are both good places to buy food or other supplies.

The author hitch hiked into this area via Foix, Auzat and to Marc. He camped in the nearby canyon, then the next morning, 8/28/1979, walked up a good trail over Mont Calm to Estats and back in 4 1/2 hours round-trip. After lunch, he packed up and walked all the way to Vicdessos before getting a lift out of the area toward Luchon and Oo, both located on the previous map.

From the south or Spanish side, Estats can be climbed via Sort, Alins, Areu and the head of that valley. Trails are shown beginning at the end of the road, but may or may not be in good condition. However, even if there's no trail, it's easy traveling in open country at that elevation.

Not far east of Pic D'Estats, is a high area with three large reservoirs and a number of good peaks. The refuge at the end of the trail above Cayane is a popular place for hikers and climbers. These higher peaks, including **Pic du Port**, 2903 meters, can be climbed most easily from the paved road running between Andorra City and Serret.

Access to most of the higher mountains in the center of this map can be reached best from Andorra. Head for Soldeu, then north to the end of the road. There are a number of medium-sized peaks in that area over 2800 meters.

The city of Andorra is a good place to buy food, locate detailed maps and get the latest information on trails, camping, refuges, etc. There are few, if any, ice or snow routes in these parts, so normally only good boots are needed.

From the summit of Mont Calm we can see Pico D' Estats to the west.

Map 30-1, Pico D'Estats, Pyrenees, Mtns., France-Andorra-Spain

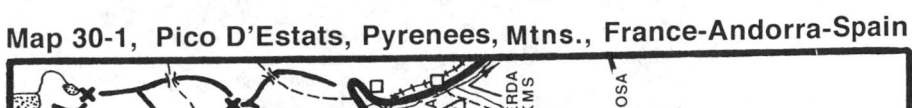

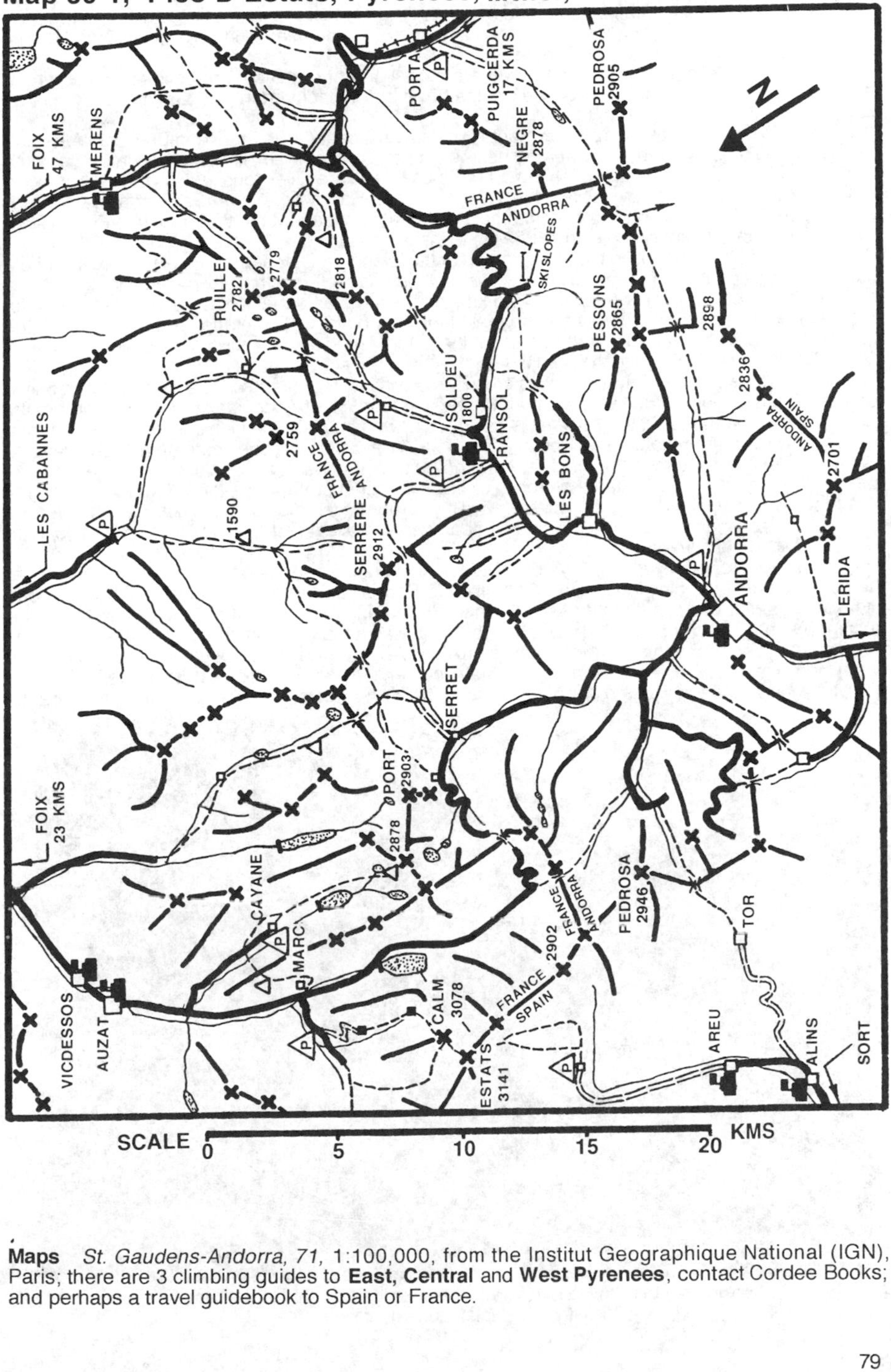

Maps *St. Gaudens-Andorra, 71,* 1:100,000, from the Institut Geographique National (IGN), Paris; there are 3 climbing guides to **East, Central** and **West Pyrenees**, contact Cordee Books; and perhaps a travel guidebook to Spain or France.

Monte Cinto, Corse (Corsica) Island, France

Southeast of France in the Mediterranean lies the island of Corse or Corsica, which is a province of France. Corse is a very mountainous island and one of the premier hiking regions in Europe. The highest peak is Monte Cinto at 2710 meters.

All the higher summits in the Cinto area are composed of granitic-type rocks, either porphyry, rhyolite or gabbro. All the higher cirque basins have been glaciated in the past, but there are no glaciers today.

Getting to Corse is easy. There are flights from several locations in France to Bastia and Ajaccio, but most people get there by ferry boat. These sail from Toulon, Marseille and Nice in France; and from Genova and Livorno in Italia. The main ports on Corse are L'Ile-Rousse, Calvi, Bastia, Ajaccio and Propriano. You can also sail the short distance from Santa Teresa on Sardegna (Sardinia) to Bonifacio on Corse. The boats sailing from Italia used to be cheaper than the French ferries; at least that was the author's experience on his 1989 trip to these parts.

To get to **Cinto**, which is in the northern end of the island, rent a car, hitch hike or possibly take a bus to near a place called Ponte Leccia, which is on the main north-south highway running from Bastia in the north to Ajaccio on the west coast. Two kms north of Ponte Leccia, turn southwest at the sign for Asco and Haut Asco. It's 31 kms from the main highway to Haut Asco at the end of the road in the upper valley. There's not a lot of traffic here, but the author found the hitch hiking good along this road. Lots of Germans driving around the island!

The last place you can buy food is in a grocery store in Asco. Haut Asco is a ski resort with only a restaurant and cabins. When you arrive at the parking lot at Haut Asco, look to the east for the trail running to the summit of Cinto. At first this trail goes down almost to the highway as this paved road makes its last big turn before the ski resort, then the trail heads almost due south up an open canyon. After a couple of kms, turn left or southeast and go up a minor drainage. In places you'll have to pay attention to the painted red marks on rocks to find the way, but there's a lot of foot traffic and you shouldn't have trouble. Up near the last steep wall, you'll turn right and cut to the southwest or west as you angle up to a pass. From the pass, turn left and ridge-walk at first, then drop down a ways, then climb up to the final summit.

The author took an evening ferry from Nice to L'Ile-Rousse on the north coast of Corse; slept at the port, then next morning 7/16/1989, hitch hiked to Haut Asco; hid his pack in the bushes, climbed Cinto in 5 hours round-trip, then got a lift down to Corte and finally on to the Col de Vizzavona (see next map), where he camped in the nearby forest. That was a Sunday and hitch hiking was very good.

You can also make this climb from the Berg. de Manica, or from Calacuccia and Lozzi on the south side of the peak. Early in summer you may need an ice ax & crampons, but not later on. There are other fine climbs in this region too. Consider walking all or part of the way along the Grande

Looking south from Haut Asco into the valley leading to Monte Cinto
which is to the far left and out of sight.

Map 31-1, Monte Cinto, Corse (Corsica) Island, France

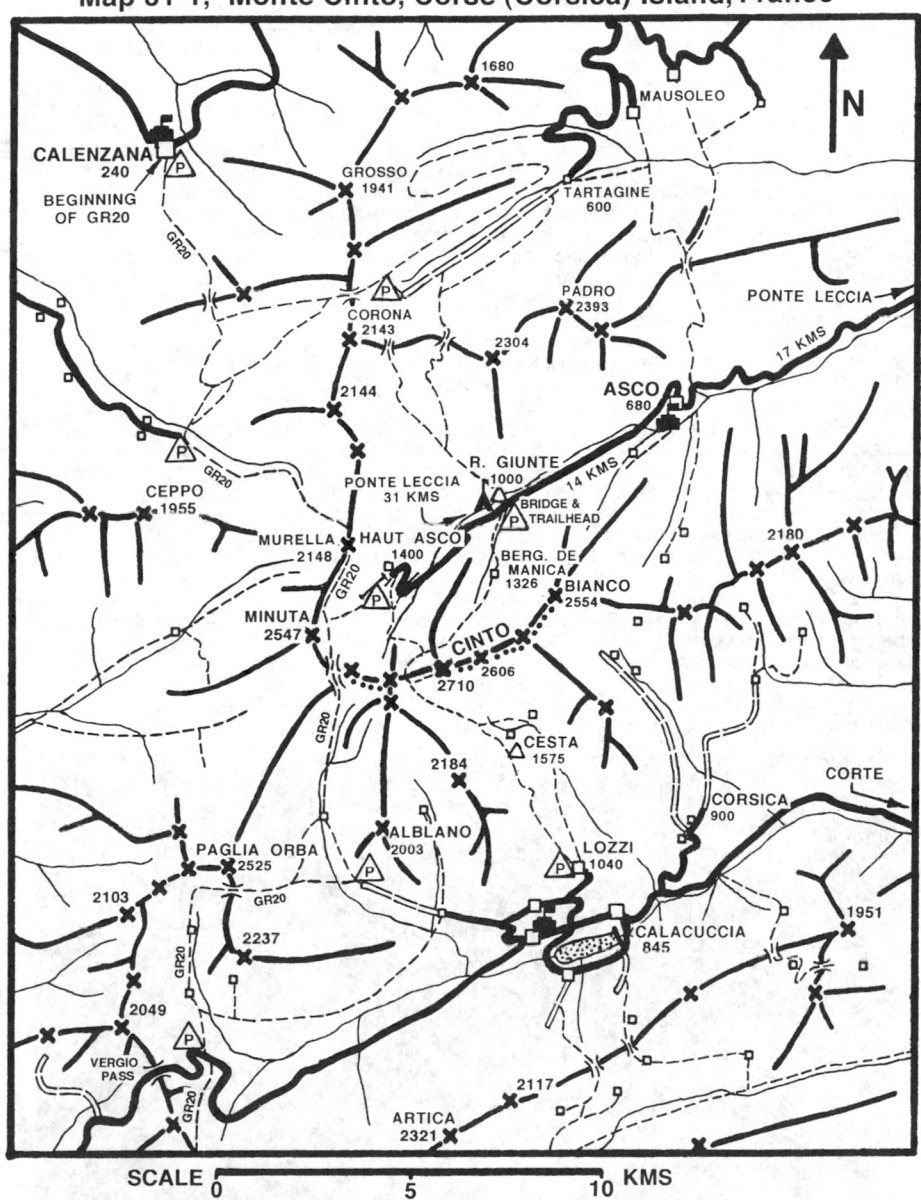

Randonnée (GR20) which extends for half the length of the island.
Maps *Corse Nord, 73,* 1:100,000 (or other maps at 1:50,000 scale), from the French IGN, Paris; also, the climber's guide, **Corsica Mountains**, West Col Books; and the travel guidebook, **Corsica**, Lonely Planet.

Monte Rotondo, Corse (Corsica) Island, France

This map covers most of the higher mountains in the central part of the island of Corse or Corsica. Corse lies southeast of France in the Mediterranean and is a province of France. See the previous map on Monte Cinto on how to arrive in Corse.

The mountains in this region are composed of the same type of rocks as are found in the Monte Cinto area. It's mostly granite of various kinds, both pink and gray. All the higher cirque basins have been glaciated in the past, but there are no glaciers today.

The highest peak here is Monte Rotondo at 2622 meters. However, of more interest to many people is the trail called the **Grande Randonnée 20 (GR20)**, which runs from Calenzana in the north (see Monte Cinto map) to Conca in the south, which is just off this map to the southeast. Many school children of France do all or part of this long hike in summer as part of their education.

To climb **Monte Rotondo**, first go to Corte which is the largest town in the north central part of the island. This is one of the better places to buy food or supplies while in the mountains. From the south end of Corte, turn off the main highway and head southwest. Drive or perhaps hitch hike about 14 kms to the end of the road where the Berg. de Grottelli is located. You'll be able to camp somewhere in the area at the foot of Rotondo.

From the end of the road, walk south up a trail to a couple of lakes where the GR20 dips down to the upper lake. Once on this trail, ridge-walk east and eventually to the summit of Rotondo. You could also route-find up a more direct route to the peak from the area south of Grottelli. Early in the season you'll need an ice ax & crampons for this climb.

Another good climb with very easy access is the peak called **Monte d'Oro**, at 2389 meters. It's located just north of the Col de Vizzavona, which is the high point on the main north-south highway running through the central part of the island. Right at the pass, where you may see domesticated pigs beside the highway begging for food from tourists, locate and follow a minor trail up to an old fort or chateau on the ridge to the north. Once there, locate a good trail running down to the river and the GR20. Once on the GR20, which is marked with red paint, walk west up the canyon to very near the pass, then veer right or east and follow another trail marked with yellow paint. This takes you to the summit of d'Oro.

The author arrived in this area in the evening of 7/16/1989 and camped near the chateau. Next morning, he walked along the GR-20 a ways to the pass west of Oro, then to the summit and returned. The climb took 5 hours round-trip. After lunch, he continued hitch hiking to Ajaccio on the west coast, then immediately got another ride to points south with the same English guy who had given him a ride on the island of Faial back on 5/30/1989 just 2 months previous!

Buy your food before arriving in this area, either at Corte or Ajaccio. By observing the vegetation in this region, it appears to be much wetter than the area around Monte Cinto, so you better take rain

From the top of Monte d'Oro looking northwest at the massive hulk of Rotondo.

Map 32-1, Monte Rotondo, Corse (Corsica) Island, France

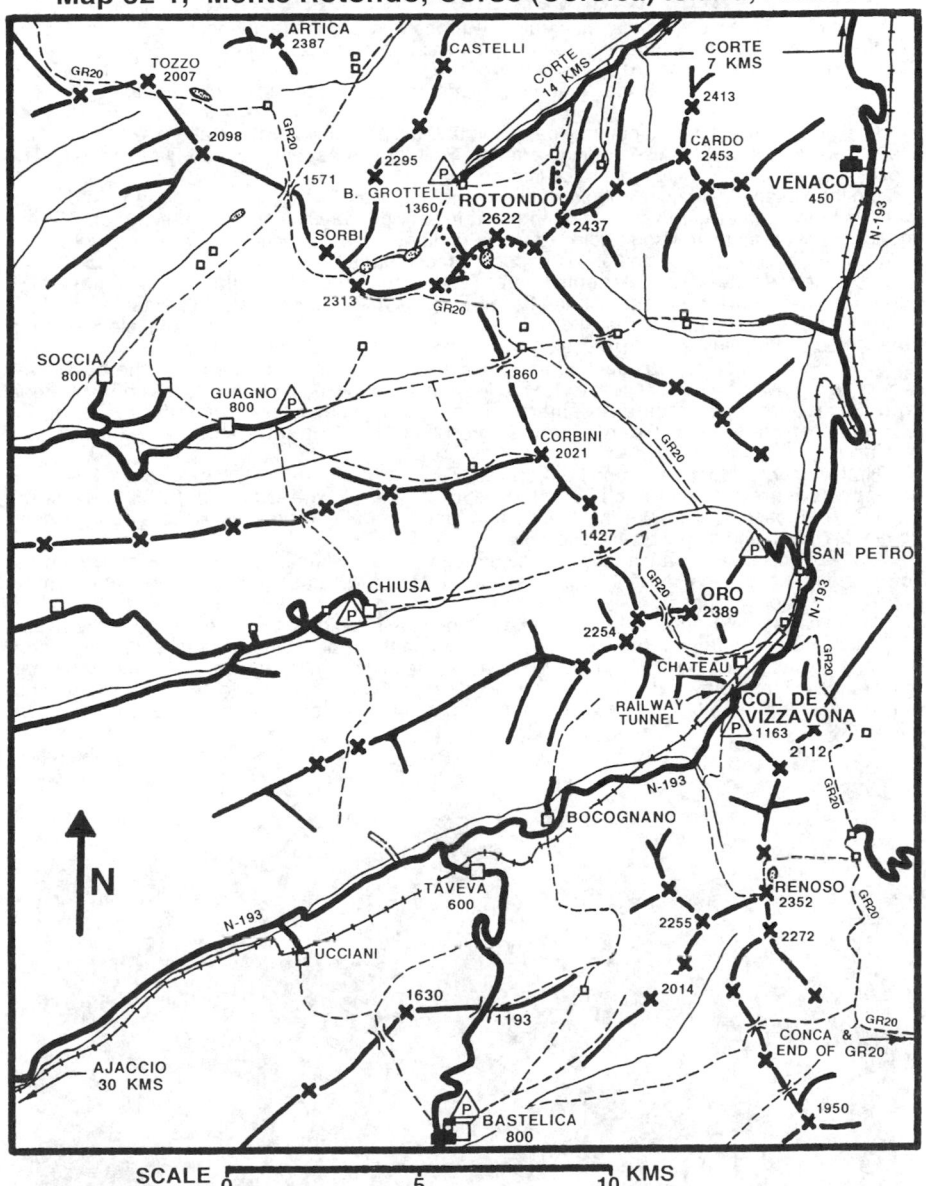

Maps *Corse Sud and Nord, 73 and 74,* 1:100,000 (or some maps at 1:50,000 scale), from the French Institut Geographique National (IGN), 136 bis, rue de Grenelle, Paris, France; also the climber's guide, **Corsica Mountains,** West Col Books; and travel guidebook, **Corsica,** Lonely Planet.

Argentera, Maritime Alps, France-Italy

From Mont Blanc, the highest mountain in Europe (located in the northeast of France), to the Mediterranean Sea, the mountains gradually diminish in size. At a point about 50 kms from the Mediterranean stands the most southerly of the *big mountains* in the Alps. This peak is Argentera, 3297 meters. Between it and the Mediterranean there are no more peaks over 3000 meters.

Getting into this region is not very easy if you're taking public transportation. On the French side, there are probably buses going as far as St. Martin-Vésubie, but surely no further. The closest rail line in France appears to be in Nice.

On the Italian side, buses should still be going as far as Cuneo, but beyond that, and in the direction of Argentera, very likely nothing. Train service may still go as far as Cuneo. Check locally, there might be transport going to Valdieri. Otherwise it's renting a car, driving your own, or hitch hiking. Hitching is rated as fair to poor in these parts.

In the immediate area of **Argentera** are several summits over 3000 meters. These high peaks can be approached best from the Italian side (as the entire mountain lies inside Italy) and the-village of Valdieri, then to the Rifugios Remondino, Bozaro or Morelli--the one closest to the peak. You can also ascend these peaks via Entraque and the Rifugio Genova.

On the French side, you could begin at or near Boreon and hike north, but the better way would be to drive or hitch hike to the Refuge Madone, then walk north toward the Rifugios Soria and Genova, thence north to Argentera. The author isn't aware of the best route up, but someone at the Rifugio Genova can tell you. There should be an easy walk-up route somewhere.

Northwest of Argentera, is another 3000'er, **Matto**, 3088 meters. Climb it from Valdieri. In the southeast part of the map is another group of peaks with **Chafrion**, 3073 meters, the highest. The basin which holds the Refuge Nice and a couple of lakes, would be a good location to place a camp and to make several climbs.

No real glaciers exist in the area, so all summits can be climbed without snow equipment, at least late in the season. Most people stay in refuges/rifugios as very few people camp in the alps. But camping is possible.

There are some definite advantages to climbing in this region. Most climbers go to the higher mountains further north for their holidays, so traffic on the trails in these parts is usually lighter. Argentera itself is fairly well-known however, as it's on all the national highway maps. A second advantage is the good weather in summertime. Long periods of sunny weather can be expected between June and early September. Almost all precipitation comes in the winter months in the

From the top of Chambeyron, looking southeast at Brec Chambeyron and toward the Argentera Group in the far distance (see next map).

Map 33-3, Argentera, Maritime Alps, France-Italy

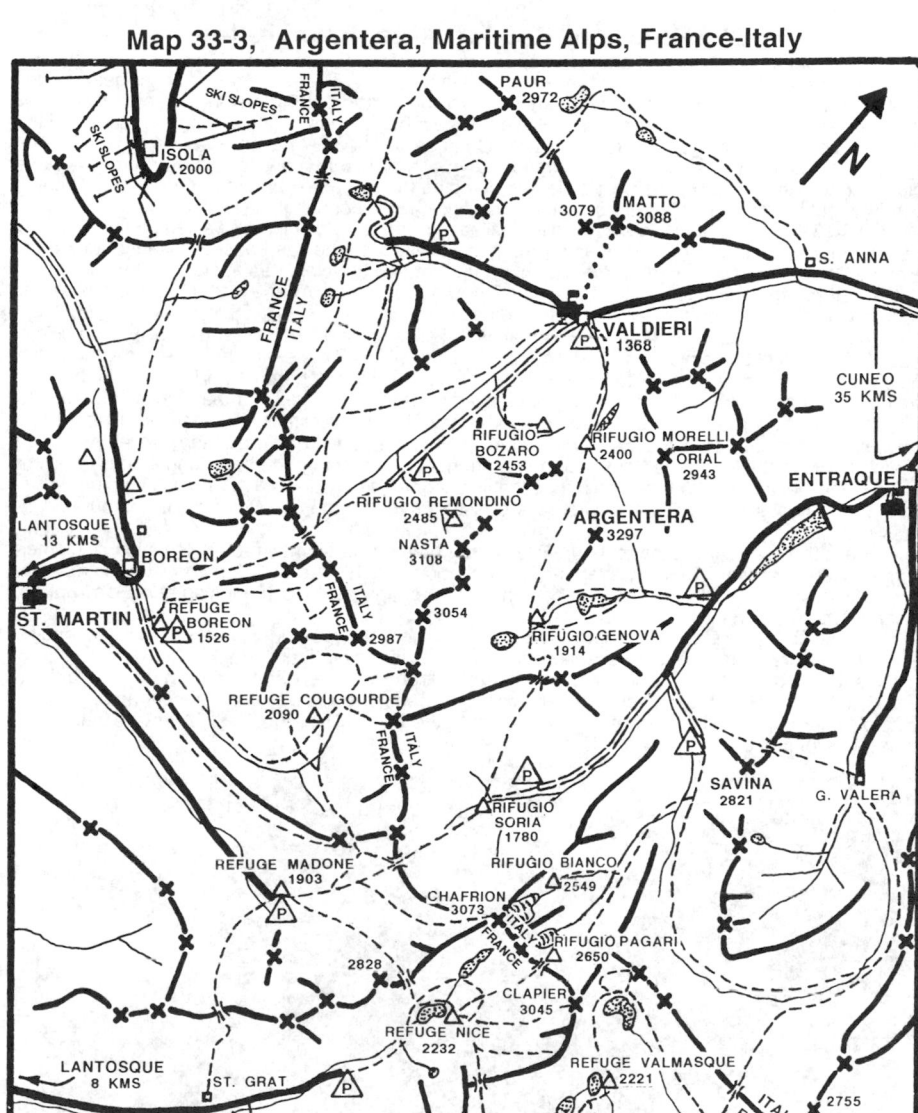

SCALE 0 ... 5 ... 10 KMS

form of snow.

Maps *Haut Pays Nicois, 9,* 1:50,000, from the IGN and Didier Richard, Paris; and the latest travel or hiking guidebook, call Cordee Books, UK. See names, addresses and telefon numbers of companies selling maps and guidebooks at the back of this book.

Chambeyron, Cottian Alps, France-Italy

The mountains on this map are in the southern part of the Cottian Alps. This area is about 100 kms north of the Mediterranean on the French-Italian border. There are no real high peaks in the region, but there are a number of summits between 3000 and 3400 meters. The highest peak is Aiguille de Chambeyron at 3412 meters. However, the most famous and fotogenic mountain, and the perhaps most difficult climb in the region is Brec Chambeyron at 3389 meters.

Get to this immediate area by driving your own car, or by hitch hiking. There are no railways close by, and there may or may not be buses going as far as Barcelonnette or Guillestre. There is surely no public transport over the Col de Larche between Barcelonnette and Cuneo in Italy.

On 7/13/1989, the author hitch hiked to Guillestre, then to St. Paul. He walked up the road and camped near Grande Serenne. Next morning, he walked up the road past Fouillouse and to the Refuge Chambeyron. From there he continued up a trail to the west peak of Chambeyron marked 3328 meters. From his campsite, it took 6 1/2 hours round-trip. After a bath in a cold stream, he hitched out of the area toward Barcelonnette and beyond.

The most popular hiking place on this map is the area around Chambeyron. Drive, hitch hike or walk from St. Paul to the picturesque village of Fouillouse at 1907 meters at the base of the mountain. You'll likely have to park below town, then walk through it to the upper end and turn left at the main trailhead. It's an easy walk on a good and well-used trail to the Refuge Chambeyron, at 2626 meters. It's located in the lower end of a huge cirque surrounded by high summits. The easiest climb is to the western summit of Chambeyron, at 3328 meters. From the refuge head east, then turn left or north at the sign. Go to the Pas de la Sauvagea, then turn right and head up the trail along an easy-to-climb ridge to the western peak. From the refuge to this summit it's only about 1 1/2 hours or less. If you're after the highest summit of Chambeyron, walk east from the refuge, and climb a difficult route on the south face.

The author isn't sure of the route up **Brec Chambeyron**, but it may require technical equipment and experienced climbers. However, most people going to this area are families who make a hike around the Matterhorn-like Brec Chambeyron. Another high peak worth looking at is **Font Sancte** north of Grand Serenne.

The weather in this area is similar to other parts of the Alps, but it does have heavy winter snows, and a longer, warmer, drier summer season than in areas to the north and east.

As for food supplies, Fouillouse and Grand Serenne have restaurants only. St. Paul and Condamine-Chatelard have a small grocery store or two, but the place to find a supermarket will be at Barcelonnette and Guillestre or other larger cities to the west. All or most of the refuges in the area have beds for rent and some kind of food available.

A wide angle view of the Refuge Chambeyron and Chambeyron to the upper left.

Map 34-1, Chambeyron, Cottian Alps, France-Italy

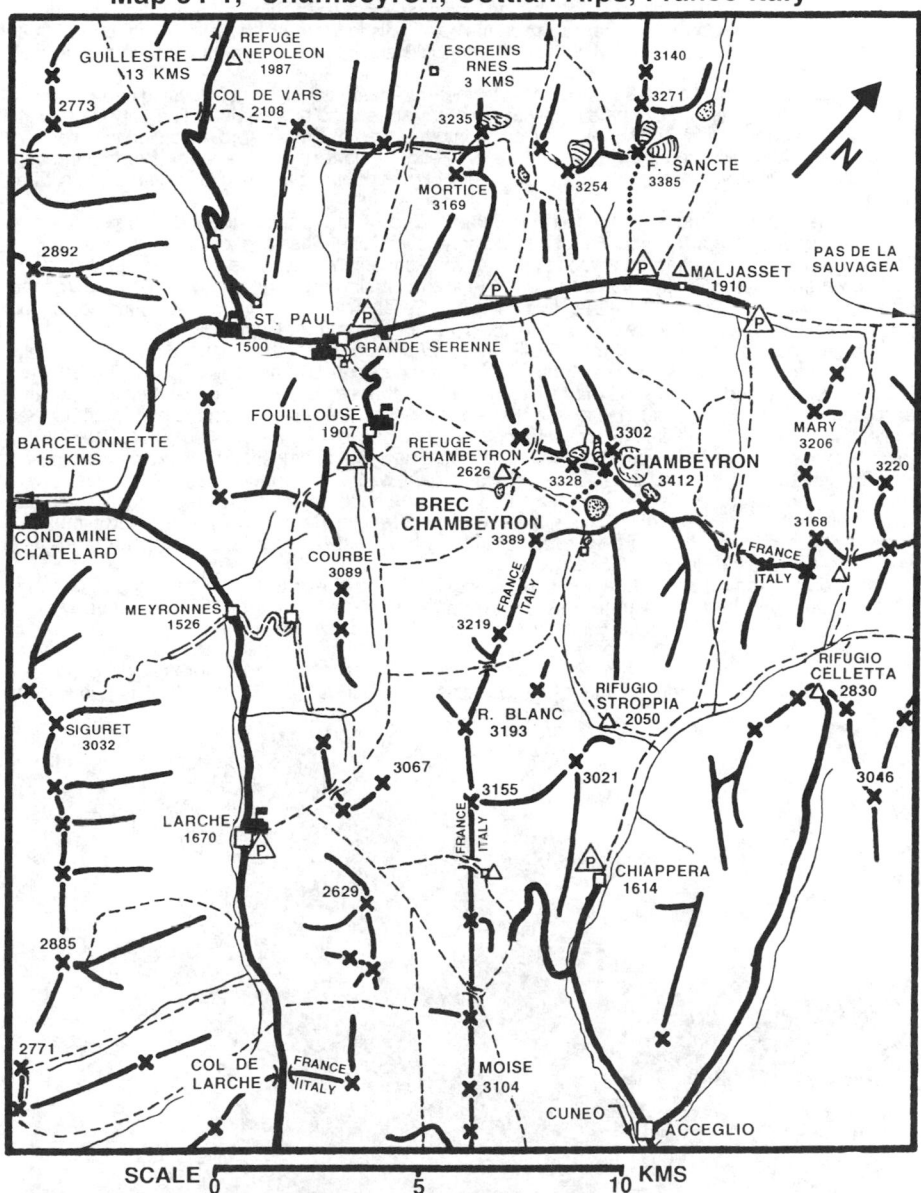

Maps *Queyras and Haute Ubaye, 10,* 1:50,000, from Didier and Richard, or the French Institut Geographique National (IGN), 136 bis, rue de Grenelle, (www.ign.fr), Paris, France; and perhaps the latest travel, climbing or hiking guidebook to this area.

Monte Viso, Cottian Alps, France-Italy

Near the center of the Cottian Alps, that part which straddles the southern French-Italian border, is the highest mountain in the southern European Alps. This is Monte Viso, with an altitude of 3841 meters. The summit lies inside Italia about 2 kms, but part of this map includes mountains and an access route from France.

This part of the Alps is rather isolated; that is, there are no major highways passing nearby and no railway lines. It also appears to be a long way from any scheduled bus service. The only way in is to rent or drive your own car, or hitch hike. Hitching into the area of Crissolo or Casteldelfino is not very good, while hitch hiking on the French side is only slightly better. Carry a small sign stating your destination--a village or mountain, or the number of kms you want to go. This usually helps when trying to get a lift.

One place to park and begin the climb to **Monte Viso**, is at Castello, about 6 kms northwest of Casteldelfino on a rough secondary road leading north over Agnel Pass and toward France. From the trailhead, walk north-northeast on a good trail, then veer to the right toward the south face of Viso.

However, Claudio Cima of Italia, wrote to the author stating the *ruta normal* is to come into the area via Crissolo and the Rifugi Re then to the Rigugio Sella. From there make your way up the south face which is a I or II grade CVIAA and takes 4-5 hours from the RifugioSella.

Still another popular way in is from Guillestre and Abries on the French side. Abries is a popular destination point a few kms north of Monte Viso. From there, drive or hitch hike (good) south toward L'Echalp and the end of the paved road at Roche. The author camped near Abries, then left his camp and got one lift to L'Echalp, then had to walk the rest of the way. He ended up on the pass marked 2820 meters, but didn't have the time to complete the climb and had to return. This was on 7/13/1989. Had he known how far it was, he would have taken his entire pack & equipment and completed the climb.

From the end of that road at 2200 meters, it's an easy walk to the Refuge Baille with a fine view of the northern ramparts of Viso. From this refuge, continue south over the pass at 2820 meters, then eventually to the south face of the mountain. From the French side this could be a 3 day climb. For climbers with experience and the proper equipment, a west face route can be attempted from somewhere above the Rifugio Gagliadone.

This part of the Alps gets heavy winter snows, but being closer to the Mediterranean, summer weather is a little drier and warmer than in the northern or eastern Alps. Viso has several small glaciers and many difficult routes. Better take an ice ax & crampons even on the *route normal*.

You can stock up on food supplies in Crissolo, Casteldelfino or Abries, but none of these small tourist towns have anything approaching a supermarket. Guillestre has larger stores as does Gap and Briançon on the French side. All the refuges/rifugios have food and drinks as well, but of course the

The northern slopes of Monte Viso, with the Refuge Baille in the lower foreground.

Map 35-1, Monte Viso, Cottian Alps, France-Italy

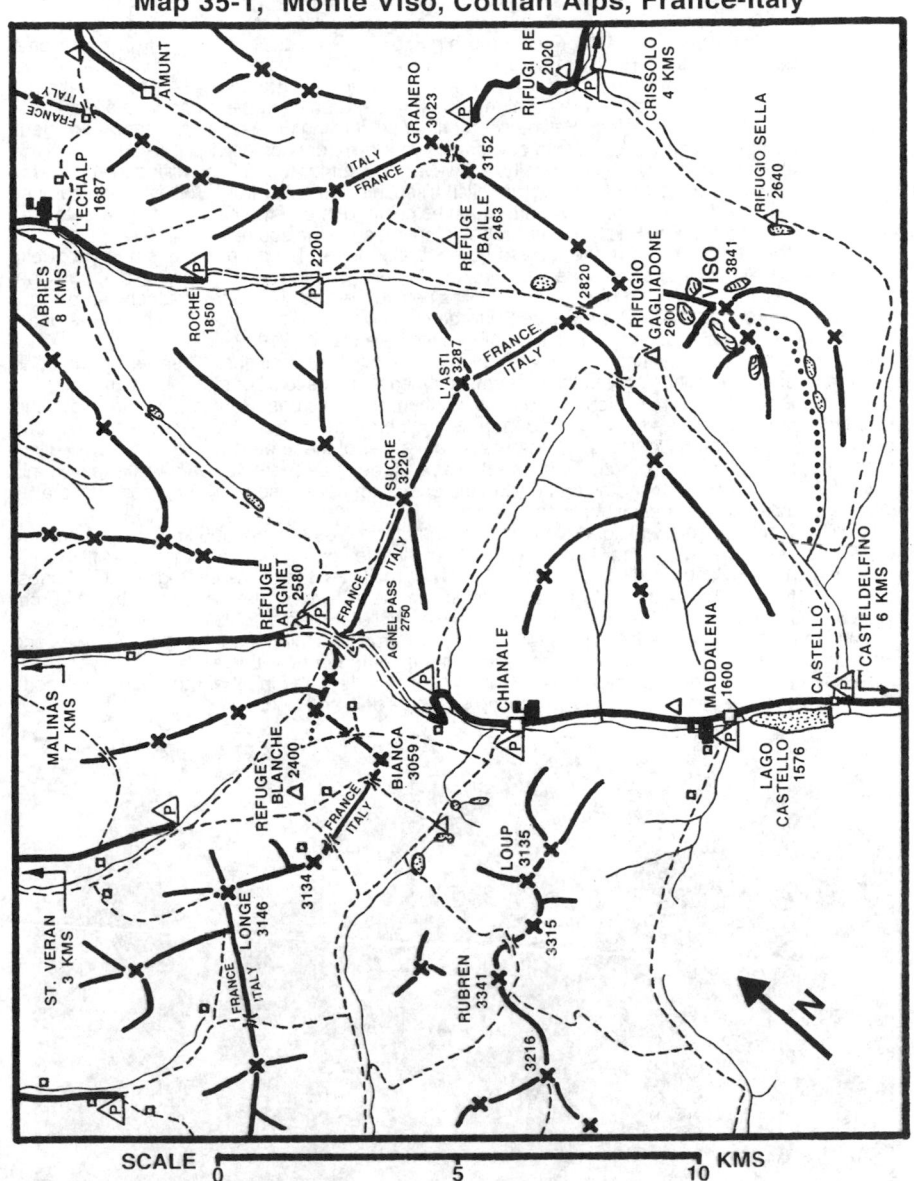

SCALE 0 ————————— 5 ————————— 10 KMS

prices are sky-high.

Maps *Queyras and Haute Ubaye, 10*, 1:50,000, from Didier and Richard and/or the French Institut Geographique National (IGN), 136 bis, rue de Grenelle, (www.ign.fr), Paris, France; and perhaps the latest hiking, climbing or travel guidebook to the area, call Cordee Books, UK.

Rochebrune & Bric Froid, Cottian Alps, France-Italy

Southeast of Briançon and the Massif du Pelvoux, and northwest of Monte Viso, lies the northern section of the Cottian Alps. Included on this map is part of the Parc du Queyras, a French national park. The highest peak here is Rochebrune at 3320 meters, but Bric Froid is perhaps better known at 3302. This area is unknown--most visitors being local French or Italians. The reason it's not particularly well known is that there are no high or famous mountains in the immediate area. Most climbers head for either the Massif du Pelvoux or Monte Viso, leaving Queyras for the family oriented.

Get into this national park by renting a car, driving your own, or hitch hiking. There is no railway nearby and likely no public bus service locally. However, the author found hitch hiking in summer to be moderately good. On 7/12/1989, the author hitch hiked into this valley from Guillestre and camped a couple of days near Abries. That same afternoon he climbed one of the peaks in the Pelvals area which gave him a good look at Bric Froid, as well as Monte Viso to the south.

Probably the best place to make a base camp is at Abries. Located there is a large public campground complete with a small store, washing machines and showers. There is also a municipal campsite about halfway between Abries and Aiguilles next to the river. It seems you can camp about anywhere else near the road. Campers seem to be more welcome here than in other parts of the Alps. This could change a lot however as the author's trip here was in 7/1989.

Most of the peaks on this map are easy hikes, rather than technical climbs. There are some north faces which would be challenging, but there seems to be easy routes to all or most summits.

To climb **Bric Froid**, drive, hitch hike or walk north from Abries past Roux and to the end of the road at the foot of the peak as shown on the map. From there, walk either northwest or northeast and to one of 2 passes marked 2797 or 2706 meters. From either of these passes you can ridge-walk to the summit. The author hasn't actually climbed this peak, but it appeared to be a walk-up from his vantage point to the south. It seems that only in the early summer season will one need an ice ax & crampons to make this or other climbs in the area.

To climb **Rochebrune**, walk or drive north from Chateau-Queyras about 5 kms on an unpaved road. At roads end, walk up the trail to a pass, then route-find left or west to reach the summit.

There are other hiking possibilities, one of which is directly east from the campground in Abries. Locate the bottom of the ski lift, and walk a trail which for the most part runs parallel to the lift. From high on the mountain you can then route-find up the west ridge of **Pelvas** at 2929 meters.

In this immediate area, the best place to buy food and groceries might be Abries, but Aiguilles and Chateau-Queyras are larger communities. Most of the settlements in these upper valleys are ski resorts only. The summer season here is generally less crowded than in other more famous resorts in the Alps. The most-popular climbing and hiking season is July and August.

From the slopes above Abries you can see the south face of Bric Froid.

Map 36-1, Rochebrune & Bric Froid, Cottian Alps, France-Italy

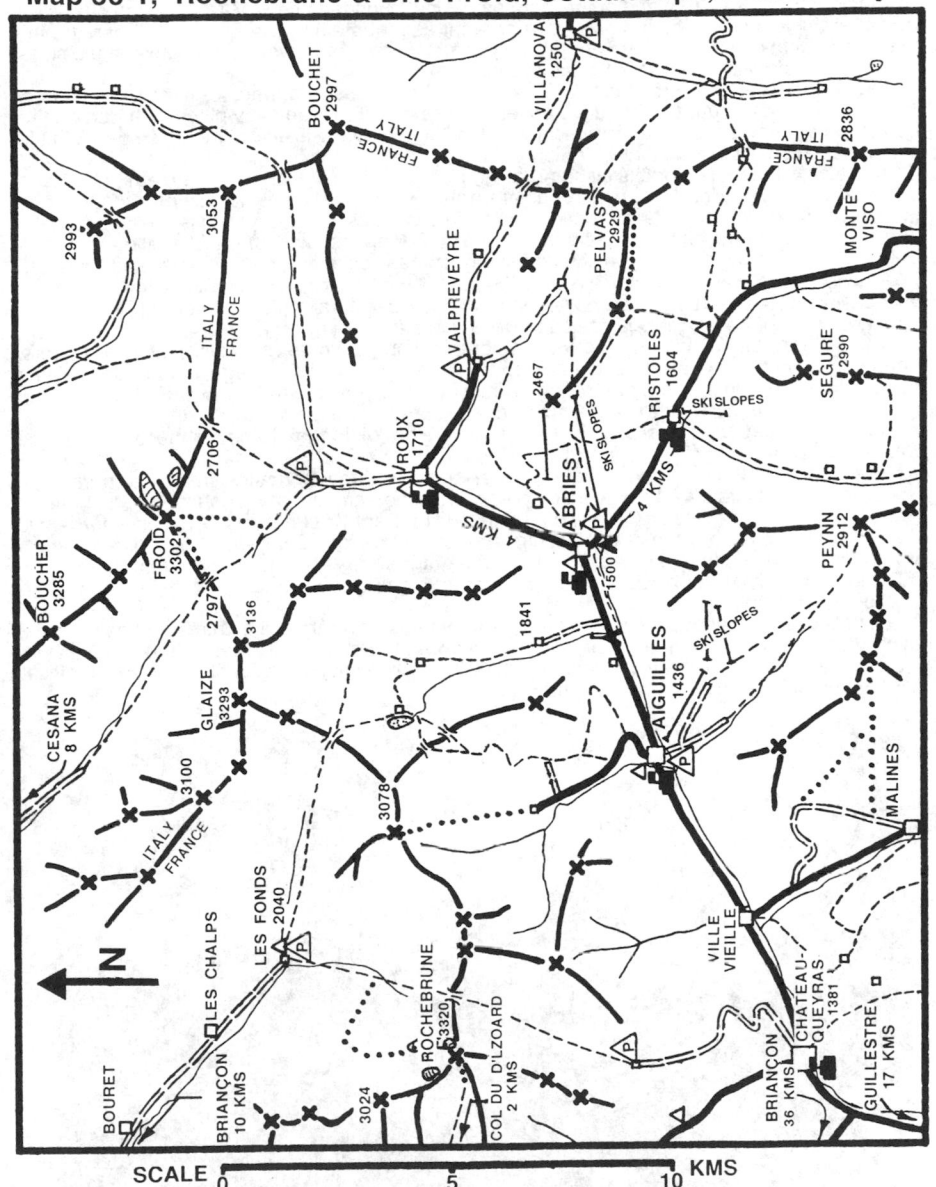

Maps *Queyras and Haute Ubaye, 10*, 1:50,000, from Didier and Richard and/or the French Institut Geographique National (IGN), 136 bis, rue de Grenelle, (www.ign.fr), Paris, France; and perhaps the latest hiking, climbing or travel guidebook to the area, call Cordee Books, UK.

Sirac and Bonvoisin, Dauphine Alps, France

At the extreme southern end of the Dauphine Alps, and the famous Massif du Pelvoux, is an area of small to medium-high mountains--at least as mountains go in Europe. These are the peaks just south of the really high and glaciated summits of the Pelvoux, and between the cities of Gap, Briançon and the large town of Guillestre.

These mountains are far from any railways, the closest stations seem to be at Gap or Briançon. And it's doubtful that public buses can be found to reach any place included on the map. So you'll have to drive your own car or hitch hike. Hitching is only fair in these parts, but in summer one can get around that way.

To get into the middle of this climbing area, head north from Gap, then turn east and head for Orciéres, a huge winter ski complex. There are some interesting peaks just east of Orciéres, but most climbers would prefer to continue north towards Les Auberts, which is due south of Pic du Sirac. Or use the highway running east from St. Fermin heading for La Chapelle or La Clot. With all the ski resorts around, you should have good easy access in both summer and winter.

Probably the best known peak in the area, though not quite the highest, is **Sirac** at 3440 meters. It can be climbed via either La Clot or Les Auberts, and the Refuge Vallonpierre or Refuge Champoleon. Someone at one of the refuges can indicate the *route normal* to nearby peaks.

The highest summit within the boundaries of this map, is **Pic de Bonvoisin**, at 3480 meters. It can be reached from La Clot and the Refuge Chaboumeau. This refuge is perhaps the best place in the region to set up a base camp from which to make several climbs. For most climbs over about 3100 meters ice ax & crampons are required. The author has been in the area, but still hasn't climbed anything yet. Both Sirac and Bonvoisin look to be for more experience climbers.

The climate in these parts is a little warmer and drier than mountains in the northern Alps. While heavy precipitation can be expected in winter, the same is true for sunshine in summer. The glaciers here are small, with few crevasses. The Parc National des Pelvoux, is largely to the north of this map, but does extend south, almost to Orciéres. Camping in the national park is prohibited, but one can legally put up a tent at night then take it down the next morning early. This they call a bivwak or bivouac. The important thing is, keep you tent out of sight during the daytime hours.

Both Gap and Briançon are larger cities, each having several supermarkets and bookstores. If you want additional maps or other information about the mountains, these cities are the best places to get them, especially Briançon, which has an alpin information center and tourist office. July and August are the busy summer months.

On the way to Ecrins is the Refuge Glacier Blanc (see next map).

Map 37-2, Sirac & Bonvoisin, Dauphine Alps, France

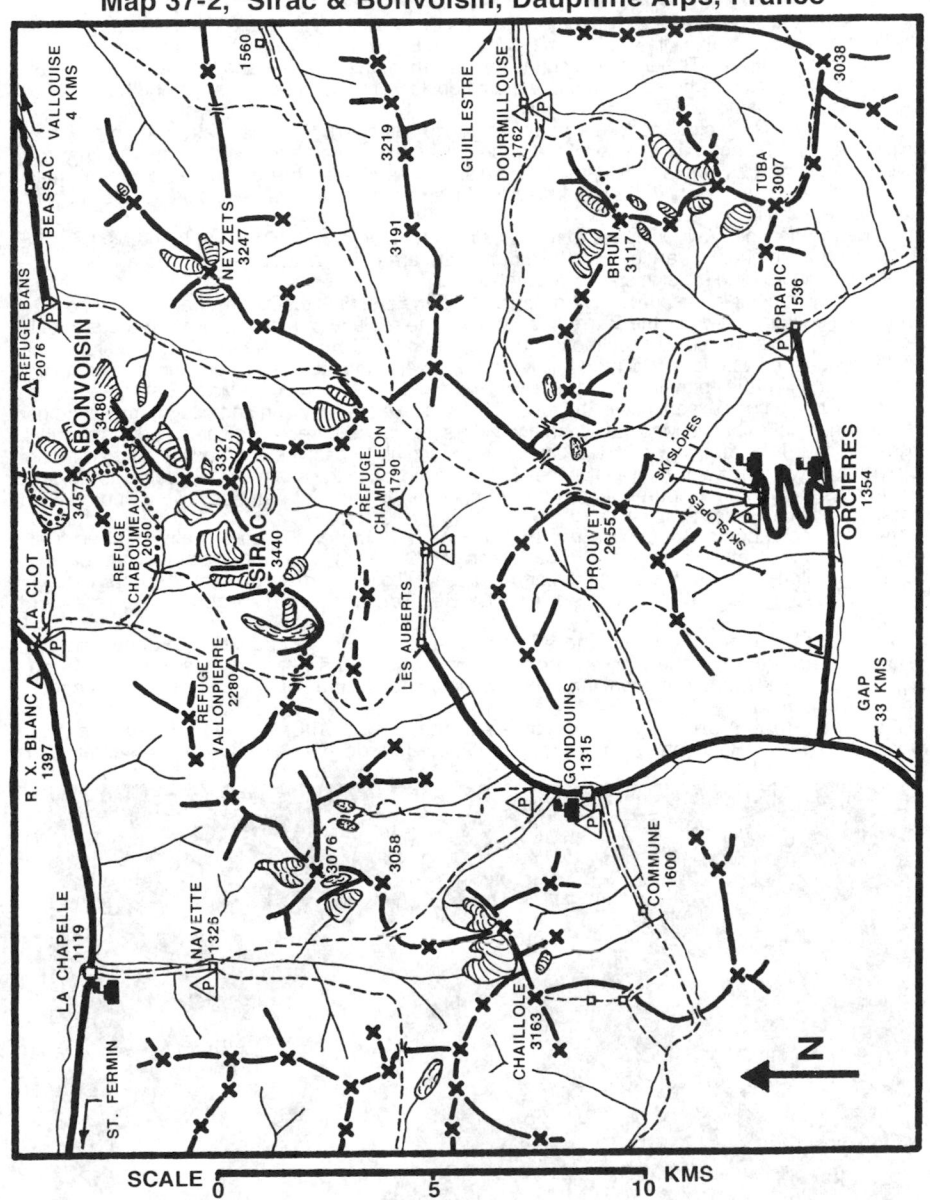

Maps *Gapencais, 7,* 1:50,000, from the French IGN, Didier and Richard, Paris; and perhaps the latest hiking, climbing or travel guidebook to the area. Call Cordee Books about that.

Ecrins, Massif du Pelvoux, Dauphine Alps, France

In the central regions of the Dauphine Alps, lies the Massif du Pelvoux. This high and heavily glaciated mountain complex lies entirely in France; with Briançon on the east, and La Grave and Col du Galibier to the north. This area has abundant high and jagged peaks, and large glaciers with big crevasses. This may be the second best or most-popular climbing area of France--the best may be the area around Chamonix and the Mont Blanc Massif.

You can get fairly close to these peak via public transport. You can take a train as far as Argentiére and Briançon, both east of these peaks. There's also a major highway running from Grenoble east past La Grave to Briançon. There should be buses along that route. From this main highway there are secondary roads running up to Madame Carla, La Berarde and the refuges beyond La Chapelle which is on the south.

Once in Briançon, your choice is to rent or drive your own car, or hitch hike to the peaks. The author found hitch hiking very good in this immediate area, at least for people who appear to be mountain climbers. Make a sign stating destination.

The highest peak in this massif is **La Barre**, 4102 meters. It is the highest point in the group of pinnacles generally known as the **Barre des Ecrins**. The *route normal* to this peak (more precisely the nearby summit which is climbed most often and called the **Dome de Neige**, 4015 meters), is via Madame Carla, the Refuges Glacier Blanc & Caron, several kms across a large glacier, then up the northeast face. This is normally a 2-3 day climb. A more difficult approach is via La Berarde.

Here's the author's experience in the area. He hitch hiked to Briançon and bought maps and got information, then hitched to Madame Carla and hid his tent is some trees. The area had lots of rain & snow that day. Next morning, 8/24/1979, he left early and hiked past the 2 refuges and met climbers coming down who had been in an avalanche. But he continued to the summit of the Dome de Neige in 4 1/4 hours; just under 7 hours round-trip from his tent. It was quite an easy climb and he can't remember any crevasses to speak of.

Another well-known summit is **Mont Pelvoux** at 3946 meters. It's normally climbed from Ailefroide and the Refuge Pelvoux. **Pic Les Bans**, 3669 meters, is climbed from La Berarde and the Refuge Pilatte; or from the southeast and Beassac. To the north is the well-known **La Meije**, 3983 meters. It's usually ascended from La Berarde and the Refuges Chatelleret and Promontorre.

There are too many mountains here to cover in just one page, but keep in mind, there is hardly an easy route in the whole range. All or most routes are across snow and/or ice, requiring a rope, ice ax & crampons and some experience. Some south face routes require rock climbing equipment.

For additional information about routes to these and other peaks, contact the *alpin information office* in Briançon, or the *centre alpin* at La Berarde. Once close to the mountain you

The difficult Le Barre des Ecrins to the left, the Dome de Neige to the far right, which is the summit most people climb.

Map 38-1, Ecrins, Massif de Pelvoux, Dauphine Alps, France

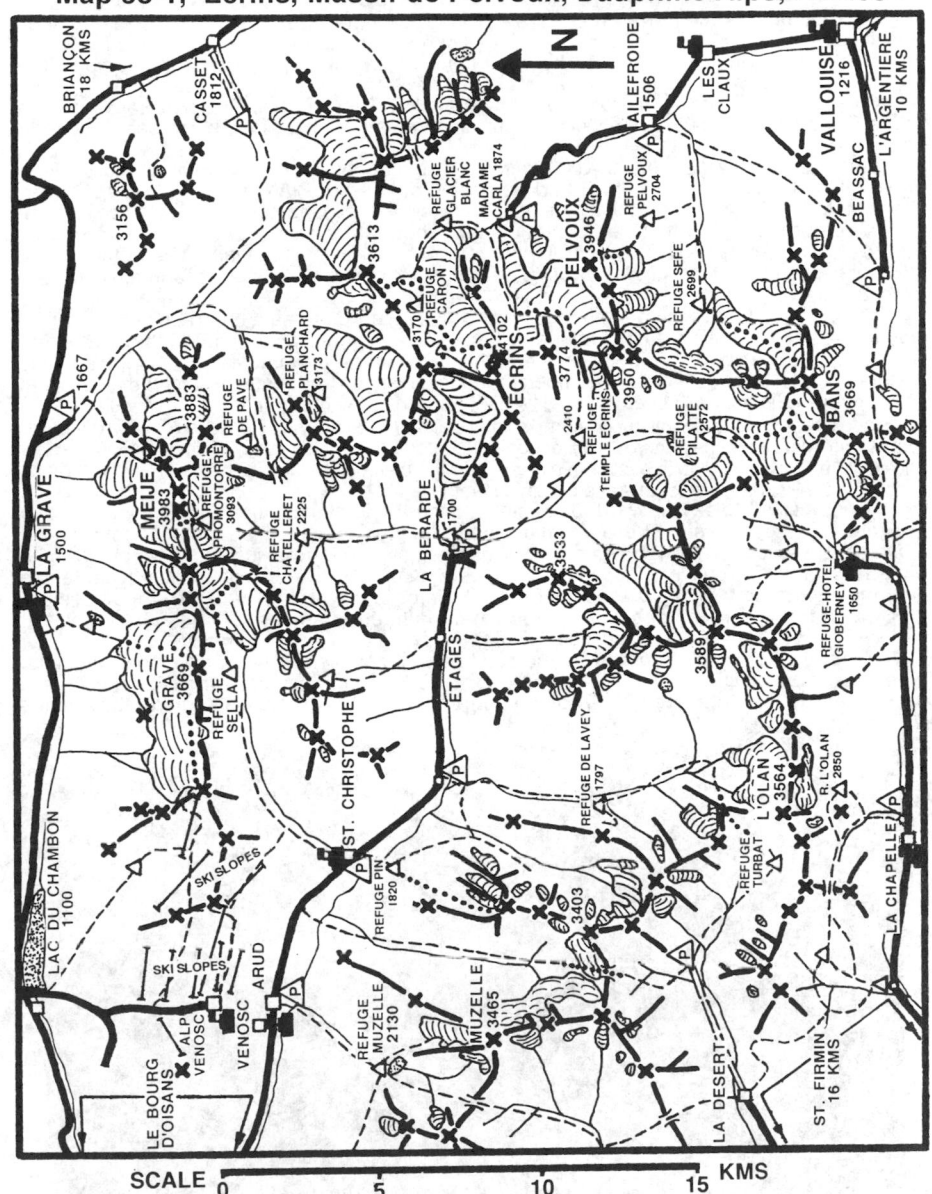

want to climb, contact someone at the nearest refuge, then make final plans for the route of your choice.

Briançon is a good place to buy the best maps of the area, as well as the latest guidebooks. It's also the best place to go shopping for food or other supplies.

Maps *Ecrins Haut Dauphine, 6,* 1:50,000, from Didier and Richard and/or the French Institut Geographique National (IGN), 136 bis, rue de Grenelle, (www.ign.fr), Paris, France; and the guidebook, **Ecrins Park, Dauphine Alps**, contact Cordee Books, UK.

Bayle, Etendard and D'Arves, Dauphine Alps, France

This map covers the northern sections of the Dauphine Alps, which lie between Col du Galibier, L'Alpe d'Huez, and St. Jean. It's also just north of the Barre des Ecrins and Pic Meije, and northwest of Briançon, which is the mountain climbing headquarters for this region. The author passed this way a couple of times but hasn't done any climbing.

Within this area are two main groups of high peaks. They are Les Grandes Rousses, with peaks Etendard and Bayle, in the western part; and Les Aiguilles D'Arves in the east, just north of La Grave.

There are no railways within the boundaries of the map, but one can take a train to St. Jean or St. Michel, located to the north and northeast of D'Arves. A major highway runs from Grenoble to Bourg D'Oisans, then to Briançon, passing Lac de Chambon and La Grave, both of which are good entry points to these mountains. There are surely buses along this highway, otherwise your only choice is either driving your own car or hitch hiking. The author found hitching hiking about fair in these parts, but for someone who looks like a mountain climber it might be better.

This region is popular during summer and winter. There are summer trails and winter ski slopes, mainly in the area east of L'Alpe d'Huez (southwest of Bayle), and north of La Grave. Because there are no really high peaks here, this area is less-known to most climbers, and has little foot traffic. Most experienced climbers head for Briançon and the peaks immediately south of this map. As is the case in all the other Alps, tourism is the only industry in these valleys.

The highest summit on this map is one of the peaks of **Les Aiguilles D'Arves**, at 3510 meters. The normal route to these peaks is via Bonnenuit (located on the main road between Col du Galibier and Valliore, and immediately east of this map), and the Refuge D'Arves. Other routes of approach might be from Rond on the south; or Le Chalmieu on the north.

To the west is **Pic de Etendard**, 3463 meters, and **Bayle** at 3466, the highest summit of Les Grandes Rousses massif. These and other peaks in the group can be reached best from the south and the village of Mizoen near Lac de Chambon and Le Perron, just to the north. If you're one who prefers to sleep in refuges, this is not your mountain. There is only one private refuge near the ski lifts, so camping is required for most climbs in this area. There are some fair sized glaciers in this group, so snow & ice equipment is needed as opposed to climbing in Les Aiguilles D'Arves, where one can usually get by without, at least late in summer.

Food and other simple supplies can be purchased in any of the smaller towns shown on the map, but to buy equipment or books & maps, you must stop in Briançon, Bourg D'Oisans, L'Alpe d'Huez, or St. Jean. Briançon has some supermarkets, plus an alpinists information centre

The north slope of Mt. Pelvoux--see previous map (Walter Pause foto).

Map 39-2, Bayle, Etendard & D'Arves, Dauphine Alps, France

that's worth a visit.
Maps *Ecrins Haut Dauphine, 6,* 1:50,000, from the French IGN, Didier and Richard, Paris; and perhaps the guidebook, **Ecrins Park, Dauphine Alps**, contact Cordee Books, UK.

Mont Thabor and Galibier, Graian Alps, France

This map shows part of the Graian Alps and the area just south of St. Michel and Modane, and immediately east of Col du Galibier. The Cottian Alps are largely in Italy, but overlap into France as far as Briançon. The mountains shown here are Mont Thabor at 3207 meters, perhaps the best-known; and Galibier at 3229 meters. The author has passed by this area but has not yet done any climbing.

Public transportation into this region is good. It's possible for someone to ride a train to La Praz and hike from there; or continue to Modane and begin walking right from the train station.

There's also a major highway running from St. Michel south over the Col du Galibier to Briançon. Also, there is a major highway reaching Bardonecchia, on the Italian side of the border. This is a major summer and winter resort and destination. There will be scheduled bus service on all the routes and towns just mentioned. Your other choice is the train, drive your own car or hitch hike. The author found hitch hiking fairly good on the main highway linking Modane, St. Michel, and the Col du Galibier, but as of the late 1990's it wasn't as good as it once was.

One of the normal routes to the top of **Thabor**, is via Briançon, Nevachi (?) and the refuge at Les Granges de la Vallee Etroite. The high area above Granges and the Refuge de la Valle Etroite, would be a good place to set up a base camp in order to make several climbs. This is on the southeast side of the mountain. It could also be ascended from the end of the road above Modane, or right from the small town of La Praz. Still another starting point would be from the Refuge des Drayeres which is southwest of the peak.

The highest summit in this area is **Galibier**, located 2 kms due east of the Col du Galibier. It could be climbed from the Col itself, from Plan La Cha, and at or near the site at the end of the road called Camp des Rochilles, as shown on the map.

Another access option would be to come in from the Italian side to the small city of Bardonecchia. There is apparently a highway and railway tunnel from there to Modane, but the author has no up-to-date information on that.

This area is surrounded by higher mountains, which makes it a bit drier, than say for example, the region to the west, which receives more precipitation. There are no real glaciers in this area, only a few small perpetual snow fields. Crampons or ice ax are not needed unless you're climbing in seasons other than in late summer. The climate is definitely warmer and drier here than the Alps further north.

The best places to shop and get information are in Modane, which has a good tourist office; or Briançon with its alpin information center. These are both small cities, each having bookstores and supermarkets, and are good places to do all your shopping.

Looking south from near the Refuge La Dent Parrachee toward Thabor.

Map 40-2, Mont Thabor & Galibier, Graian Alps, France

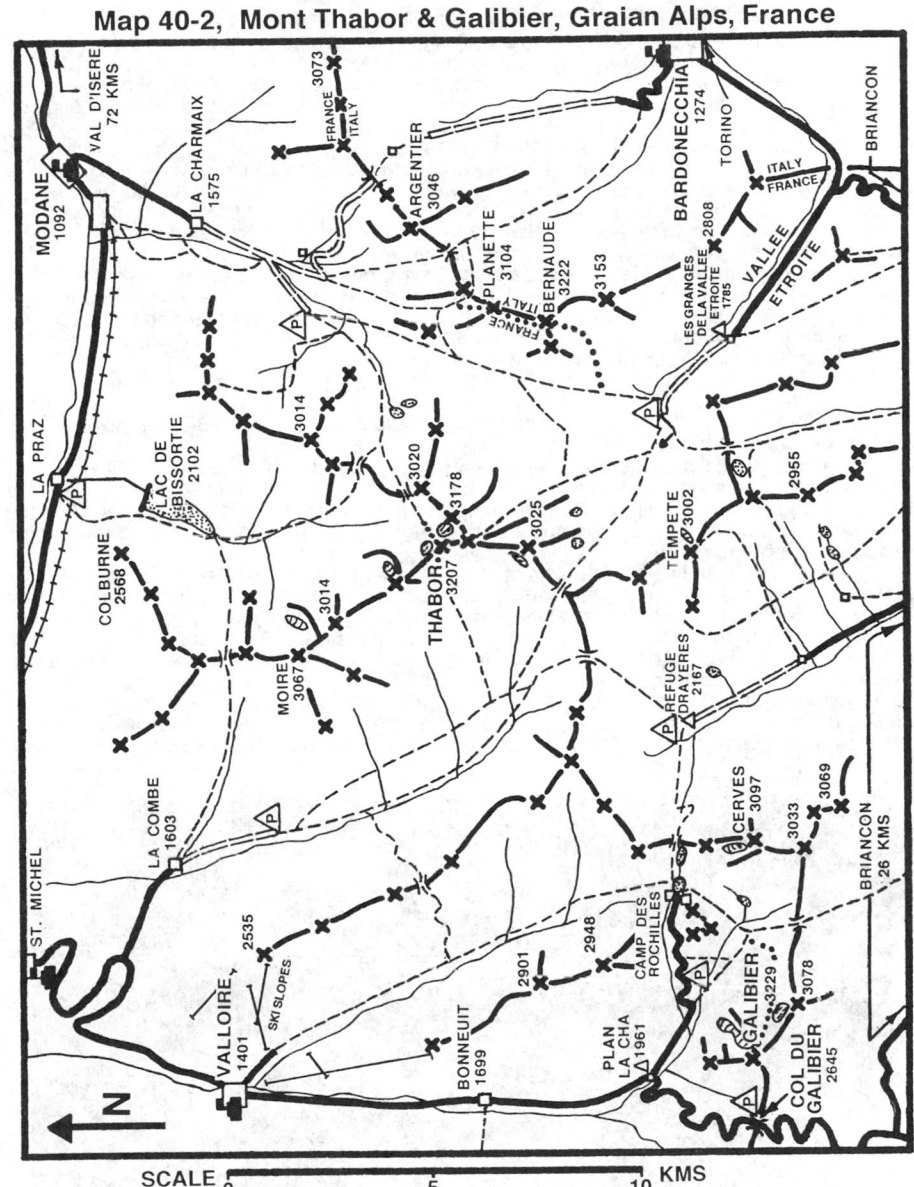

Maps *Ecrins Haut Dauphine, 6,* 1:50,000, from Didier and Richard and/or the French Institut Geographique National (IGN), 136 bis, rue de Grenelle, (www.ign.fr), Paris, France; and perhaps the latest hiking, climbing or travel guidebook to this area. Contact Cordee Books, UK.

La Dent Parrachee, Massif de La Vanoise, France

In the eastern French alps there's a group of high glaciated peaks known as the Massif de la Vanoise. Part of the massif has been set aside as the Parc National Vanoise, and a large section of the park is shown on this map. This is the area immediately north of Modane, west of Termignon, and south of Pralognan. The region has a number of medium to high peaks and one very large glaciated area known as the Glaciers de la Vanoise.

Public transportation is fairly good to this area at least in the southern portion. A rail line stops about 1 km from the center of Modane, and from there one can walk directly to some of the mountains. Presumably there are trains still running on this line (?). Another option is taking a bus. One should be able to reach Termignon and Modane by bus, but probably nowhere else. The author was here in 1979, and did just fine hitch hiking. He carried a sign stating a nearby destination, usually a mountain, or the number of kms and had no trouble.

The highest summit in the area is **La Dent Parrachee** at 3697 meters. It's just west of Termignon and at the south end of the Vanoise Glaciers. It can be reached beginning in Modane; then Aussois, past the ski slopes to the Refuge La Dent Parrachee, and finally along a roughly marked trail northeast to the summit. With care, you may not need any ice ax & crampons, at least in late summer, as there's a trail to the top.

The author hitch hiked into this area from the Val D'Isere side and ended up camping near Aussois at about 1500 meters. Next morning, 8/22/1979, he made it to the Refuge La Dent Parrachee in just over 2 hours; just under 5 hours to the summit. Round-trip from his tent was just under 8 hours in perfect weather.

To climb some of the peaks which form the western edge of the Glaciers de la Vanoise, one could approach from several directions: from the Refuge La Dent Parrachee on the south; the Refuge L'Arpont, on the east; or Refuge Geneph on the west which is approached from the north and Pralognan. There are many summits in this glaciated area over 3500 meters, all requiring ice ax & crampons.

To climb other high peaks northwest of Modane such as **Polset** or **Peclet** (3534 and 3562 meters), you can walk from downtown Modane, past the Refuge L'Orgere and towards the Refuge Polset. This area also has a large glacier system, and the right equipment is needed. The disadvantage to climbing here is that on the western slopes is the large ski resort of Val Thorens. One lift nearly reaches the summit of Peclet! Evidently the glaciers in the Polset-Peclet Massif aren't as dangerous as in other parts (?).

Keep in mind that in France, and probably all countries of Europe, camping within the boundaries of a national park is either frowned on or prohibited. However, one can get around this inconvenience by camping in a very isolated place or by bivouacing; that is, putting up a tent

The southwest slopes of La Dent Parrachee.

Map 41-1, La Dent Parrachee, Massif de la Vanoise, France

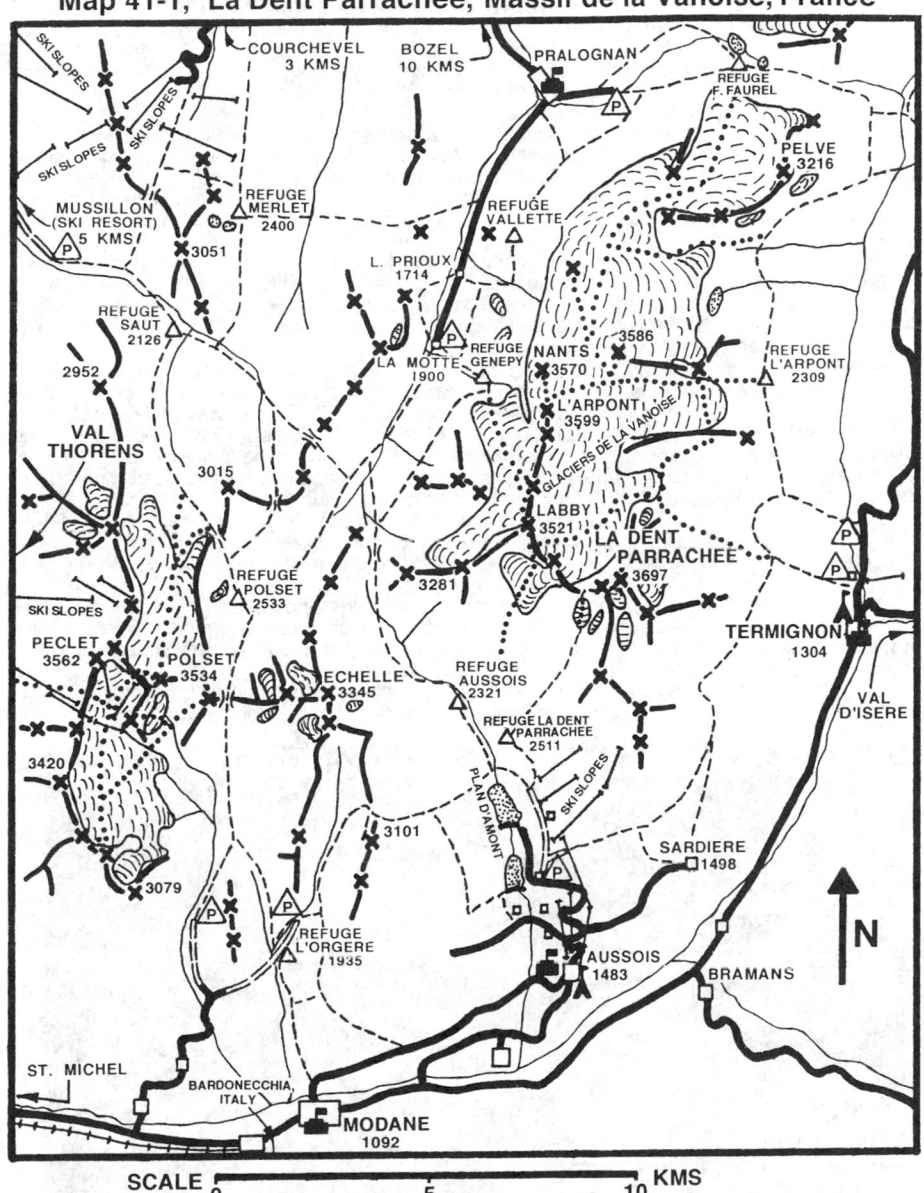

in the evening, and taking it down early the next morning. This is usually legal, but sometimes not convenient. The thing they all dislike is to see a tent in daylight hours.

Make Modane your shopping headquarters, for food, equipment, and more detailed maps or guidebooks.

Maps *Vanoise, 11,* 1:50,000, from the French IGN & website (www.ign.fr) and/or Didier and Richard, Paris; and the guidebook, **Vanoise Park** (?), contact Cordee Books, UK.

Albaron & Charbonnel, Graian Alps, France-Italy

In the area just south of Val D'Isere, perhaps France's most famous ski resort, and east of Col du Mont Cenis, is a group of high mountains, part of which form the French-Italian border. Most of these peaks are part of the Graian Alps, while only the western and northern sections are part of the Massif de la Vanoise, part of which is in a national park of the same name. The author passed this area a couple of times but has not yet done any climbing.

In the area covered by this map there are no railway lines and no train service. However, there is a major highway running from Mont Cenis, through Bessans, over the Col de l'Iseran and to Val D'Isere and beyond. Buses should be running this route. Another choice is hitch hiking. Because there's not a lot of traffic going over the pass between Bassens and Val D'Isere, except in July and August, hitching on that route can be slow. Best of course to have your own car.

The highest mountain on this map is **Charbonnel**, 3752 meters. It's an isolated peak and not so rugged or glaciated as others in the area. As a result, it's not well-known. The most likely route to the summit is via Bassens and the Refuge Averole. Or head south from Bassens to Jaffa and L'Arcelle, and climb east, then up the south face somewhere. Climbing this route will keep you away from glaciers & crevasses.

Some easy climbs can be found to the south of Val D'Isere, in the areas of the ski resort. **Pers**, 3386 meters, is near the ski runs, but can also be approached from the Refuge Carro. **Levanna**, 3619 meters, lies just southwest of the international border and is normally climbed via the Refuge Carro.

Further south, along the French-Italian border, is **Albaron** at 3637 meters. This appears to be the best-known peak in the region. The *route normal* for Albaron appears to be from Bonneval, to L'Ecot and the Refuge Evettes. Or perhaps head due east of Bessans and to a hill-side location called Les Planors. From there continue east and up the west-side glacier of Albaron.

Near the Lac du Mont Cenis, is **Ronce**, known otherwise as **Rocciamelone,** at 3612 meters. This peak could be climbed from the ski slopes above Adroit, then up the northern slopes and a glacier (?); or from the lake and the south slpes which appears to be the *route normal*, and which is an easy scramble.

The snow line is higher here than in parts of the northern Alps, and it's definitely warmer and drier around Bessans and that valley, than say for example the Zermatt, Switzerland region. Even so, most of the higher peaks support fairly large glaciers, especially on their northern slopes. Ice ax & crampons are required on most peaks over about 3200-3300 meters.

Largest settlements in the area include Val D'Isere, Bessans, and Adroit. Food can be bought in any of these towns, but if you're looking for books or more detailed maps of the area, better to look in

The north face of Albaron from the Refuge des Evettes (Walter Pause foto).

Map 42-2, Albaron & Charbonnel, Graian Alps, France-Italy

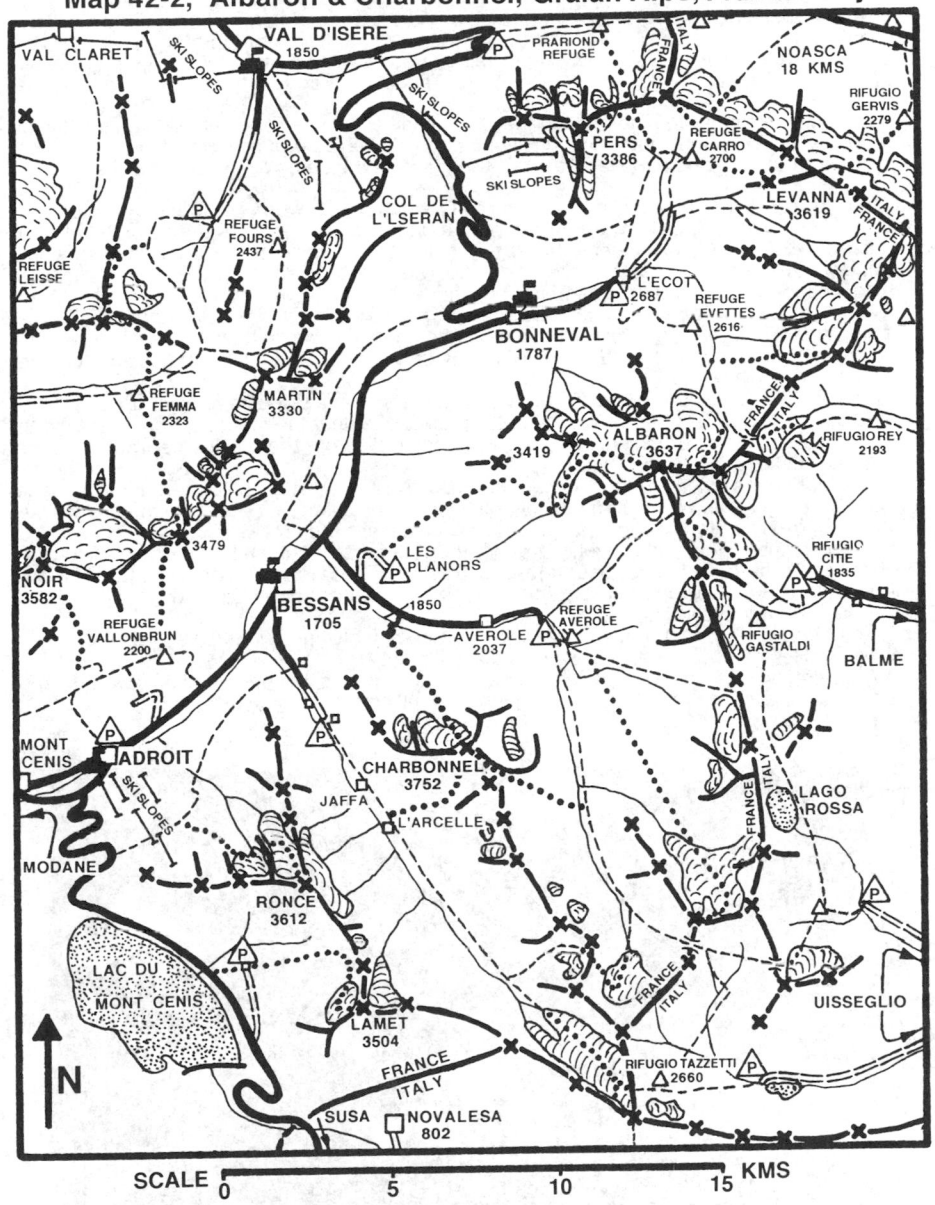

places such as Val D'Isere or Modan (located just off this map to the west).

Maps *Vanoise, 11,* 1:50,000, from the French IGN, see website (www.ign.fr), and/or Didier and Richard, Paris; and book, **Vanoise Park**, contact Cordee Books, UK; and perhaps the latest travel guidebook.

La Grande Casse & Pourri, Parc National Vanoise, France

In the area south of Bourg-St. Maurice, west of Val D'Isere and north of Modane, is the Parc National Vanoise in eastern France. Shown here is the northern portion of the park with the highest peak, La Grande Casse, 3855 meters, located near the bottom of this map. Another well-known peak is Mont Pourri at 3779 meters. These are a couple of the best climbs in the Alps.

The higher and more remote parts of these mountains have all been set aside as a national park. However, the slopes near the highways and towns have been developed into ski resorts The areas around Tignes and Nancroix are the most developed. Winter may be the busiest season in these parts.

One can reach this area by train, with a rail line running between Moutiers and Bourg-St. Maurice, with Landry & Bellentre being the closest the railway comes to the national park boundaries. Buses surely run along this same route. Buses can also be found running along the highway between Val D'Isere and Bourg-St. Maurice stopping in Tignes. Hitch hiking is pretty good too--by French standards which isn't the best.

Getting to **La Grande Casse**, is quite easy. The normal route is via Prolognan and the Refuge Felix Faurel, just southwest of the peak. Another option would be from the north and the route from Champagny, and the Chalet-Refuge de Laisonnay. These are not easy climbs and all routes involve glacier travel.

Just east of Casse is **La Grand Motte** at 3653 meters. What could be another great climb is spoiled by ski lifts (and a telepherique) that takes skiers to near the summit. The existence of skiers indicate that glacier isn't as dangerous as some (?). But there are other routes on the mountain as difficult as any you'll want.

In the northern section stands another fine peak, **Mont Pourri** at 3779 meters. This peak has some very good and difficult routes, but also some easy ones. The *route normal* is via the village of Gurraz, the Refuge Turia, and the north slopes, either on rock or snow, whichever you prefer. The author camped above Gurraz at about 2100 meters, then on 8/21/1979, walked past the Refuge Turia and on to a pass before climbing south. He got to 3430 meters, before realizing he was on the wrong route. By that time it was too late to go back down and climb one of the routes shown on the map.

Another normal route, but much more difficult and involving an icefall, is via Landry, Les Lanche, the Refuge Pourri and the west face glacier.

Weather conditions here are similar to other parts of the Alps, but can be slightly warmer and drier than mountains in Switzerland. Lots of full sized glaciers in this area so have at least an ice ax & crampons with you on all climbs.

Looking south from Mont Pourri to the north slope of La Grand Casse.

Map 43-1, La Grande Casse & Pourri, Parc N. Vanoise, France

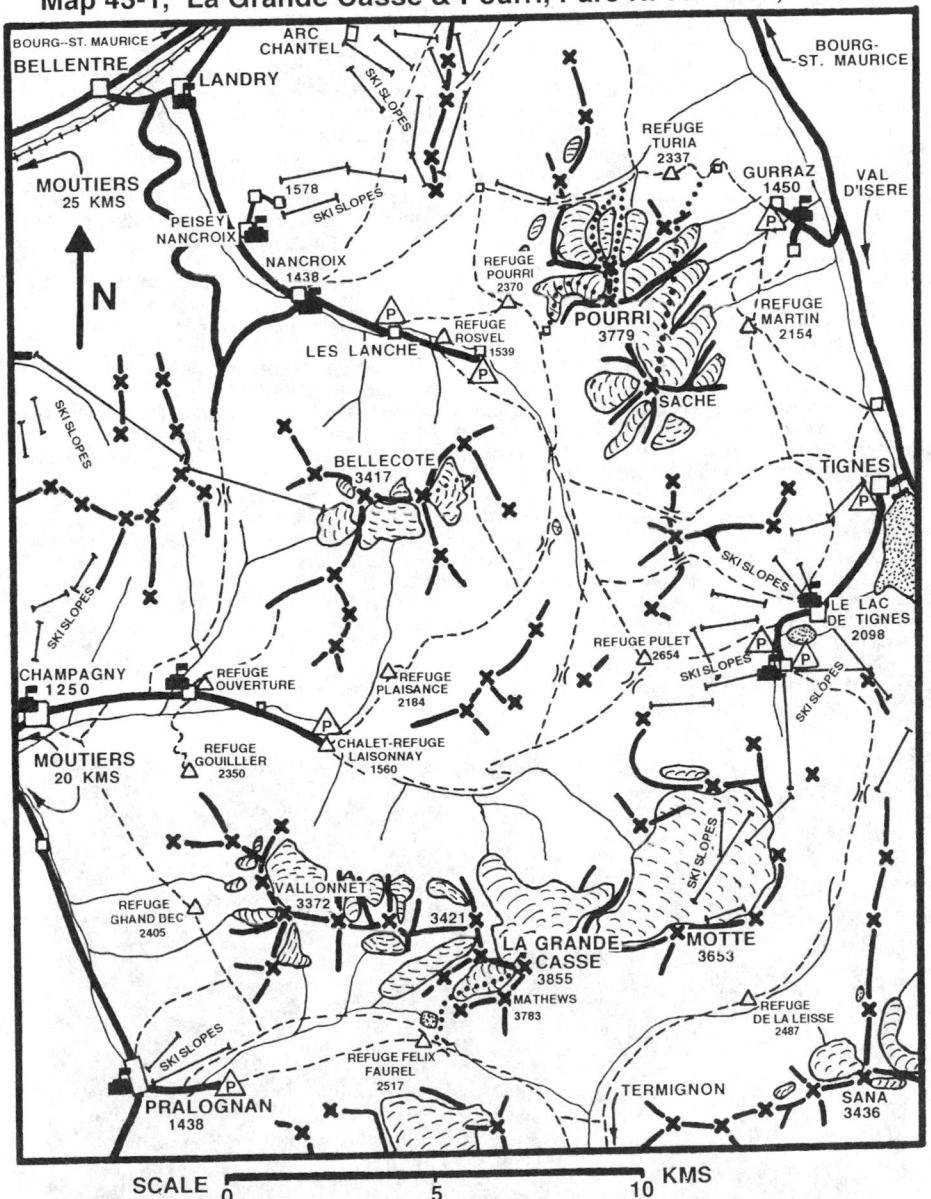

SCALE 0 ____ 5 ____ 10 KMS

For the best information concerning routes to other peaks, contact the custodian or some of the guests at the refuge nearest the peak you want to climb. Most refuges have a good map hanging on a wall. Also, good maps can be found in any of the larger towns in the area, notably, Val D'Isere, Bourge-St. Maurice and Pralognan. Also Tignes or Le Lac de Tignes, would be a good place for information.

Maps *Vanoise, 11,* 1:50,000, from the French IGN, website (www.ign.fr), and/or Didier and Richard, Paris; and the guidebook, **Vanoise Park**, contact Cordee Books, UK.

Grande Sassiere & Testa de Rutor, Alpi Graie, France-Italy

Included on this map is the mountain area north of Val D'Isere, southeast of Bourg-St. Maurice, both in France; and west of Gran Paradiso & southwest of the Italian city of Aosta. All of these peaks are part of the Alpi Graie, and all are either on the French-Italian border, or just inside Italia. The highest peak on this map is Grande Sassiere, 3751 meters. It lies just north of Val D'Isere, on the international border. A second important climbing area is the Glacier or Ghiacciaio del Rutor. The highest summit there is Testa de Rutor at 3486 meters. The author has passed through this area twice, but still hasn't climbed anything.

In the area covered by this map there are no railroads; the closest lines being in the Val d'Aosta, just to the northeast of this map, and at Bourg-St. Maurice. If you plan to spend time in these mountains, Aosta is a good place to make headquarters. Buses can be taken to Val D'Isere, which is an internationally known ski resort, and of course to Aosta. Reaching all other places on this map will require that you drive your own car, hitch hiking, or walk. There may or may not be any bus service into the valley locations southwest of Aosta (?).

Grand Sassiere can be climbed in one long day by a fit climber from either Les Brevieres or Le Fenil. These routes would put you on the northwest glacier before reaching the summit. Others may want to camp one night in the upper valley just below the glacier and do it in 2 days. Another possibility from the French side is to drive, walk or hitch hike east from Nial to B. le Saut and climb a mostly rock route from there as shown on the map. The way shown is actually a winter ski route. There are no refuges on any of these routes to Grande Sassiere.

Southeast of Sassiere is another good mountain, **Tsanteleina** at 3605 meters. It can be climbed by the north ridge, or its south face, with the climb originating from Nial or Val D'Isere; or the Rifugio Benevolo on the Italian side. The most difficult climb in the area according to Claudio Cima is Grande Rousse. It's likely best climbed from Chudana or thereabouts.

In the northern parts are the high summits surrounding the **Ghiacciaio del Rutor**. The peaks in this region can be approached from a number of different ways. From the north via La Thuile, La Joux, and the Rifugio A. Deffeyes. Or from the southeast via Bonne, and the Rifugio Scavarda. From the French side and the southwest, walk from Le Miroir to the Refuge Ruitor, then to the Rutor Glacier.

For information concerning routes to other peaks, contact the tourist office in Bourg-St. Maurice, or Val D'Isere, or the refuge keepers in the area of the mountain you want to climb. In Italia, use Aosta as an information gathering place, as you'll find a good tourist office there. Or contact someone at one of the rifugios on the Italian side.

Use Aosta, Val D'Isere, or Bourg-St. Maurice as shopping and information centers, as there are supermarkets in each place. Maps can be purchased in all these cities.

Maps *Gran Paradiso-Valle D'Aosta, 86,* 1:50,000, from Kompass-Fleischmann, Bozen, Italia; or

The west face of Mont Pourri (see previous map).

Map 44-2, Grande Sassiere & T. de Rutor, Alpi Graie, France-Italy

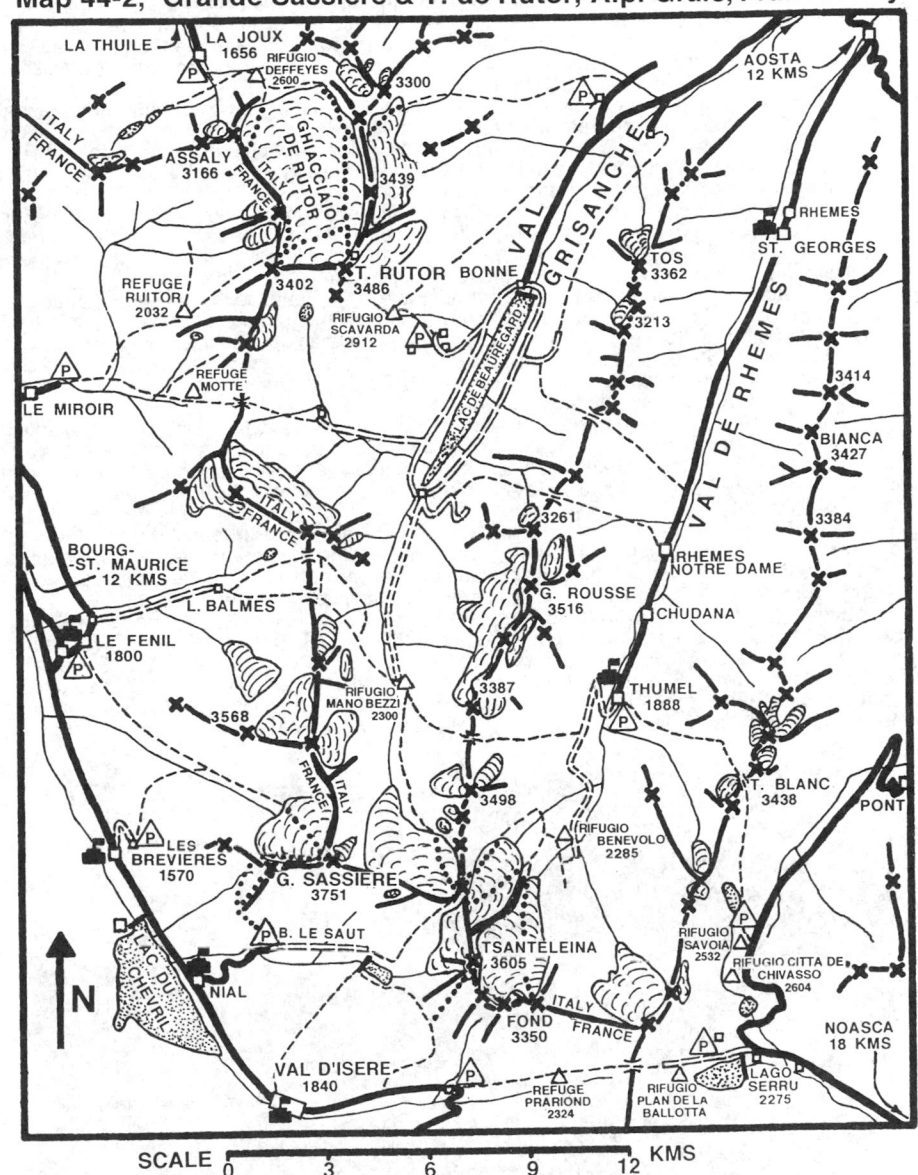

look for a local guidebook to this area in one of the cities mentioned above; or call Cordee Books, UK.

Gran Paradiso and Grivola, Alpi Graie, Italy

In northern Italia due south of Aosta and the Val d'Aosta, is a group of high peaks and large glaciers now included in the Gran Paradiso Parco Nazionale. The highest summit is Gran Paradiso at 4061 meters. It's one of the better known mountains in the Alps. After Paradiso is Grivola at 3969. There are many summits in this area over 3600 meters.

Public transportation is good into and through the Val d'Aosta. There's a busy international highway and a railway running east-west through the valley. To reach Cogne, which is in the valley north of Paradiso, turn off the main valley highway west of Aosta at Sarre, then go south to Cogne. Or turn south off the same main valley highway west of Aosta at Villeneauve to reach Pont, which is the beginning point for the hike up Paradiso.

There may be buses going from Aosta to Cogne, but don't count on any public transportation to these 2 upper valleys. You may have to drive your own car. The last alternative is hitch hiking, which the author found pretty good in the summer of 1979 going up to Pont. Look like a mountain climber and carry a sign stating your destination and you should do OK.

For those climbing **Gran Paradiso**, the normal route is via Pont and the Rifugio Emanuele at 2732 meters, located on the west side of the mountain. From the rifugio, head north on a trail, then follow a path of sorts east up a glacier to a south peak, then north to the main summit. This is an easy hike, a walk-up, but take an ice ax & crampons. Fit climbers can do this in one day from Pont. It can also be climbed from the north and Cogne, Valmaina, and the very small Biv. Carlo Pol, but this route will surely take 2 days.

The author spend a couple of days in Aosta repairing boots, etc, then with a sign Paradiso, got one ride to Pont in the rain. He walked up the trail aways and camped at 2100 meters. Next morning, 8/19/1979, hiked to the Rifugio Emanuele in just over an hour. From there on he had about 10 cms of new snow, plus more coming down. Finally at about 3800 meters, he turned back in a white-out.

The second highest peak in the area is **Grivola**, 3969 meters. Perhaps the normal way (?) to this difficult summit is via Cogne, Valnontey, and the Rifugio Vittoris Sella. There's another small hut and route on the north side, which may be the *ruta normal*. It can also be reached via Creton. **Tersiva** at 3613 meters can be climbed via Cogne and the western slopes.

South of Pont lies **Cliarforon** at 3642 meters. Since it's near Gran Paradiso and the Rifugio Emanuela, use the same route up from Pont to the rifugio, then turn southeast. It can also be ascended from the southeast, via the town of Noasca.

One might think that because Gran Paradiso lies in the *rain shadow*, or on the lee side of Mont Blanc and the French Alps, that it receives less precipitation. But this isn't always true, as the Gulf of Genoa is not far away. Southern winds can push heavy clouds from that direction

The upper west face of the Gran Paradiso.

Map 45-1, Gran Paradiso & Grivola, Alpi Graie, Italy

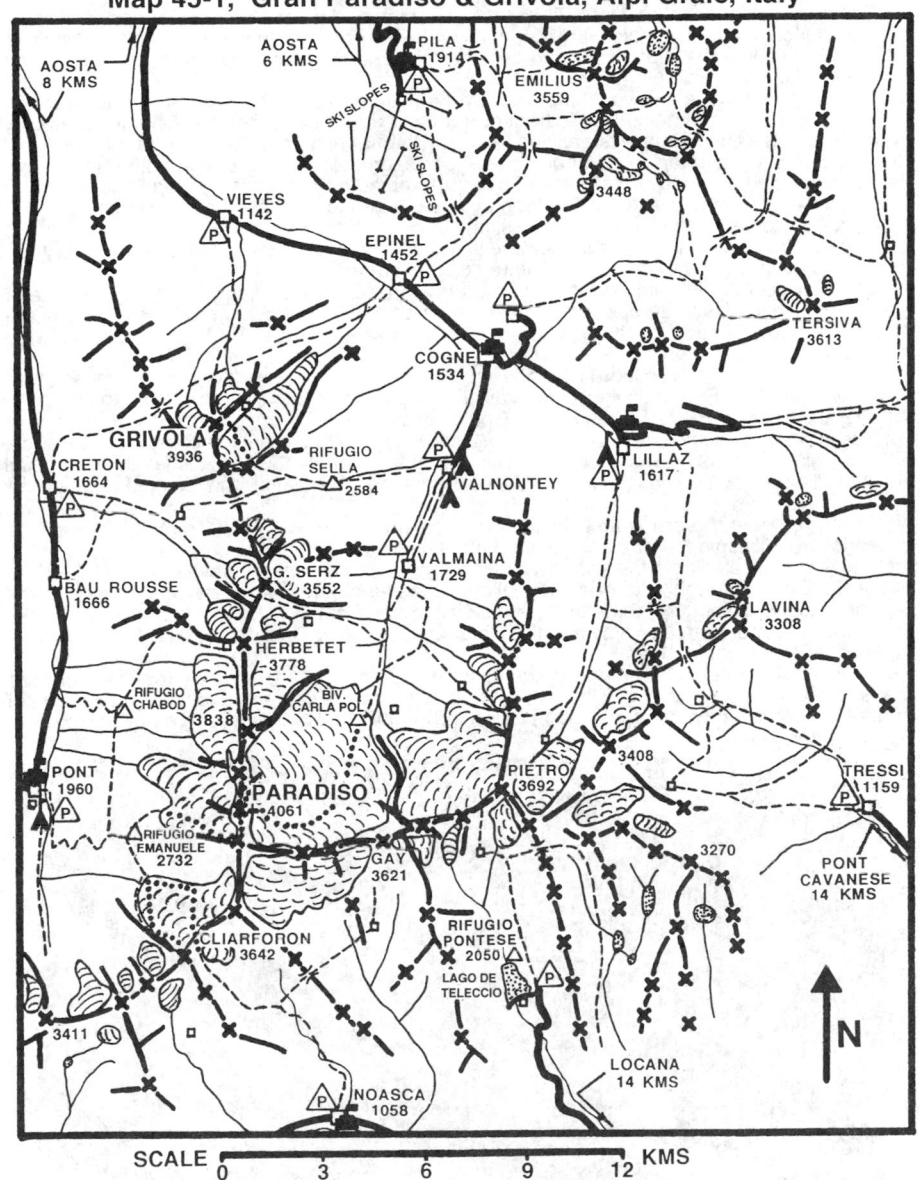

ahead of cold fronts, often bringing heavy rains and snow to this area.
On all summits over about 3200 meters, ice ax & crampons will be needed. Included on the map are only 2 rifugios having food, drinks and beds available. There are, however, many smaller huts or bivouacs--as shown on the map. Aosta is by far the best place to buy supplies, with Cogne second best. At all the campgrounds shown, there are small grocery stores.
Maps *Gran Paradiso-Valle D'Aosta, 86,* 1:50,000, from Kompass-Fleischmann, Bozen, Italia; and perhaps a travel guidebook to the area, contact Cordee Books, UK.

Mont Blanc, Graian Alps, France-Italy

Shown on this map is the Mont Blanc Massif, a high and glaciated group of peaks lying on the boundaries of three countries; France, Italia and Switzerland. Mont Blanc at 4807 meters, is the highest peak in the Alps of Europe and the glaciers here are the biggest in France, and among the largest in Europe.

If you go to this massif, you'll likely end up in Chamonix, located on the northwest and French side of the mountain. Public transportation to this area, especially Chamonix, is very good. There are main highways passing through Chamonix from Italia (through a tunnel) and Switzerland, so getting on a bus shouldn't be a problem. There are also trains running from France and Chamonix into Switzerland. Trains also come from Italia to as far as Pré St. Didier (shown on a 1970 map). Around Chamonix, it would be nice to have your own car, but hitch hiking is easy to nearby trailheads (carry a sign).

The Mont Blanc Massif is a summer and winter recreation center, with lifts in service year-round, and even a cog railway running halfway up the mountain.

Chamonix compares with Zermatt, Switzerland, in size, elevation, and proximity to some of the highest mountains in Europe. It's a real tourist trap, but an interesting place as the climbing on rock or snow is some of the best around. There are also many refuges/rifugios on the mountain.

Here's the normal route to **Mont Blanc**. First make your way to the west end of Les Hoches, then up a trail to the Voza Station on the cog railway. From there walk along the train tracks to the end of the line, and finally up the trail to the Refuge Goûter. Back in 7/1970, the author camped nearby; or you can stay in the refuge. From Goûter, follow a snow ridge to the summit--an easy and safe climb. Some tourists either take a train from St. Gervais, or ride a lift from the Les Hoches area to the rail line, then finally walk from there. On Day 2, the author made the summit and returned to Chamonix that afternoon.

Other peaks in the area can be climbed as follows: **Peuterey**, 3772 meters, is normally ascended from Rifugio Peuterey; **Jorasses**, 4208 meters, from Rifugio Jorasses; **Geant**, 4013 meters, is often scaled from the tramway (connecting Chamonix with Entreves, at the Italian end of the Mt. Blanc Tunnel) and the Rifugio Torino; or the alpinist route via Chamonix and the Refuge Requin; **Dolent**, 3820 meters, is usually climbed from Pre du Bar, and the Biv. Fiorio; **Noir**, 3836 meters, from La Fauly and the Refuge Neuve; and **Chardonne**, 3824 meters, from La Tour, and the Refuge Albert I.

One should stop in Chamonix before climbing. That's where you buy food, equipment, maps, guidebooks--everything. Chamonix has many hotels & campgrounds, a climbing school and tourist office which can give you updated information on routes, reservations of refuges,

The south face of Mont Blanc (Walt Unsworth foto).

Map 46-1, Mont Blanc, Graian Alps, France-Italy

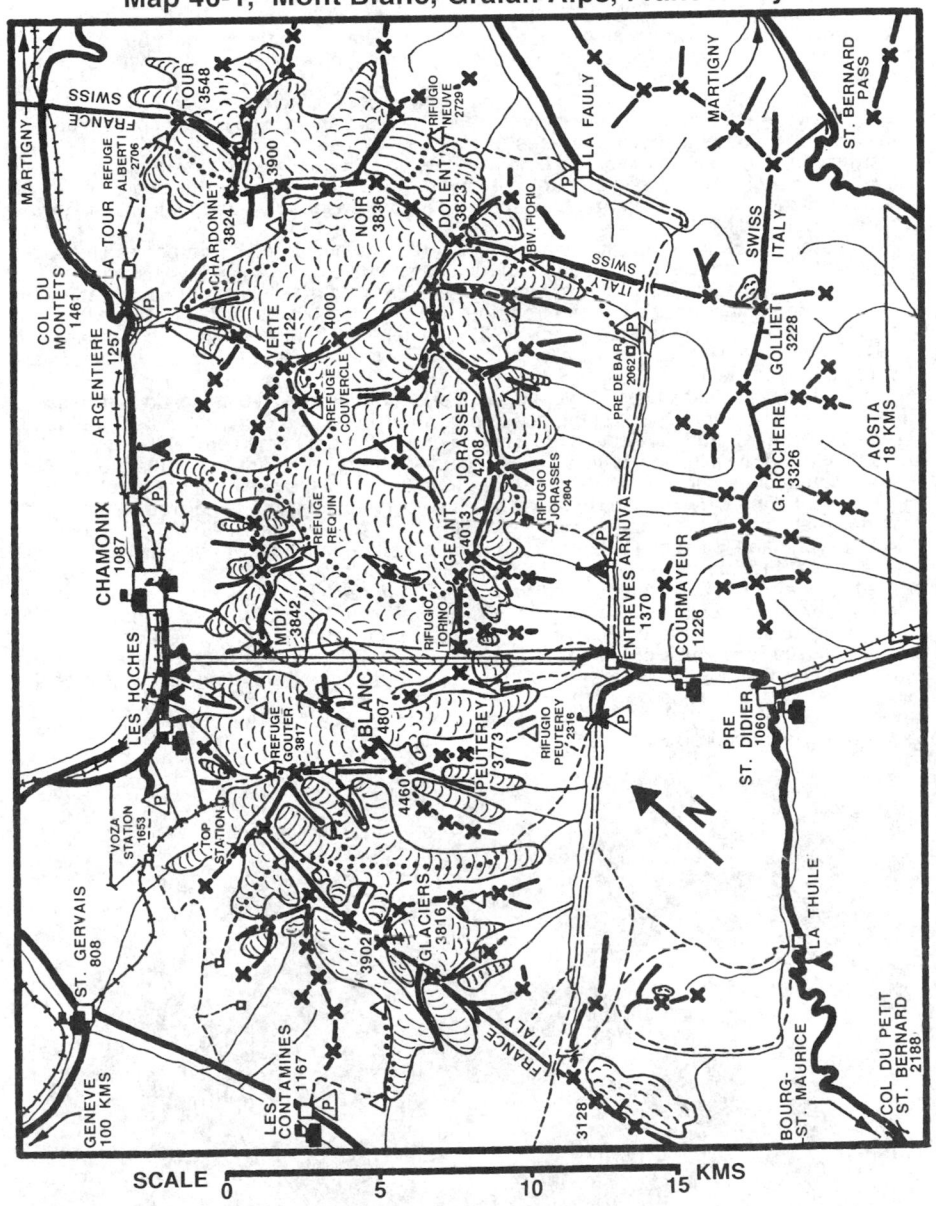

weather, etc.
Maps *Massiccio del Monte Bianco, 85,* 1:50,000, from Kompass, Bozen, Italia; and *Massifs du Mont Blanc-Beaufortain, 8,* 1:50,000, from the French IGN, Didier and Richard, Paris; the book, **Mont Blanc Massiff--100 Finest Routes**, Rebuffet; and the book/map (?) **Mont Blanc Trails--Valley & Huts: Guide & Map,** contact Cordee, UK.

Wildhorn, Berner Alpen, Switzerland

The region covered by this map includes the western end of the Berner Alpen. This is the area northwest of Sion and north of Martigny. By Swiss standards these would be considered small mountains, yet there are a couple of medium sized glaciers beneath the highest peaks. The highest summit is Wildhorn at 3248 meters.

Public transportation to and around the area is pretty good. There's a busy highway running through the valley from Sierre to Martigny. There's also a main rail line running parallel to this highway, so you have a choice of buses or trains. You can climb most of the peaks from somewhere in this valley shown on the bottom of the map; or from the highway running through Les Diablerets. There are also a couple of paved roads running into or through the higher slopes. For the budget traveler on foot, hitch hiking is reasonably good along the highway between Sierre and Martigny.

The normal route to **Wildhorn** is via the Wildhorn Hutte just north of the peak. The usual way to get to this hut is via a secondary road running south from Lenk, which is just off this map to the right. Or you can reach Wildhorn Hutte via Lauenen on a multitude of trails covering the slopes. Wildhorn can also be climbed from the Gelton Hutte, but normally this hut is used for ascents to the peaks around **Arpelistock** at 3035 meters. Wildhorn can also be climbed from the lake, Lac de Tseuxier at 1777 meters. If you have your own vehicle, this is surely the easiest and fastest way to the mountain.

The high massif south of Les Diablerets has a ski resort by the same name. In this massif is **Oldenhorn** at 3123 meters, one of the easier peaks to climb. You can climb it from the upper ski lifts as shown; or from a refuge at the western end of the group marked 2278 meters. That location offers good climbing in the vicinity, including the highest summit of this group, **Tete Ronde**, 3210 meters. Ronde can also be scaled from the top of the ski lifts near Oldenhorn.

To reach **Grand Muveran**, 3051 meters, take the trail running between Leytron or Les Plans. From the pass, turn north to the summit. To climb **Dent de Moreles** at 2969 meters, drive or walk to Leytron and to the end of the road, then take the left-hand trail which goes up to a pass near Moreles. From there route-find to the top. The author hasn't been to these peaks, but has passed this way on 2 occasions. By looking at a topo map, both look easy to climb.

The snow line is a bit lower here than in the east of Switzerland, indicating the region gets more precipitation. It's more exposed to the cyclonic storms coming from the west. Some routes will require ice ax & crampons, but many do not. Except for the glaciers around Les Diablerets and Wildhorn, crevasses hardly exist. Martigny, Sion, Sierre or Aigle would be the best places to shop for supplies.

Maps *Col du Pillon, 41,* 1:100,000, from Eidg. Landestopographie, Bern; and the latest travel and/or hiking guidebook to Switzerland.

Camping east of the Matterhorn (Map 51, page 121).

Map 47-2, Wildhorn, Berner Alpen, Switzerland

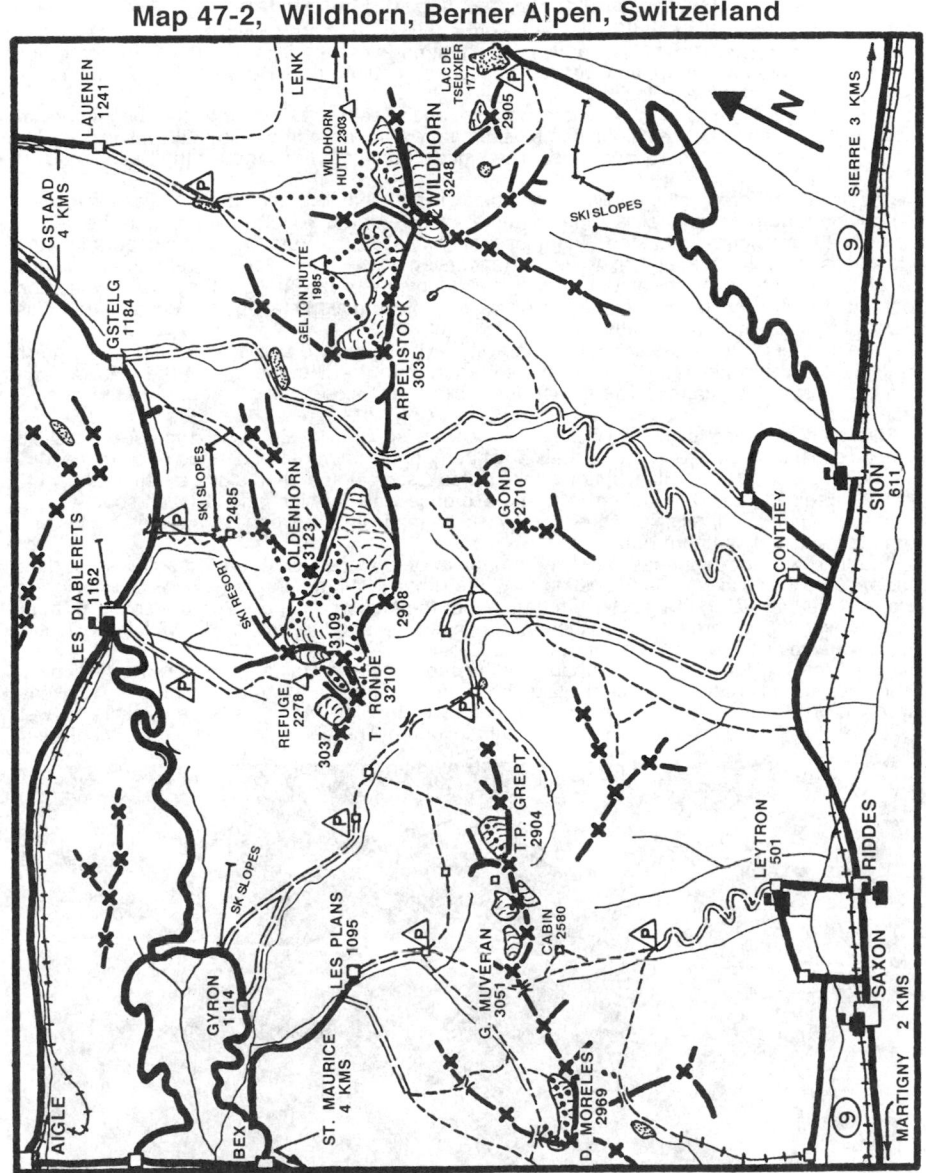

SCALE 0 ———— 5 ———— 10 KMS

Bietschhorn, Berner Alpen, Switzerland

Located north of Visp and Sierre, and south of Bern in central Switzerland, is the middle section of the Berner Alpen. This part is also just northeast of Sion and the Wildhorn group shown on the previous map; and west of the highest portion of the Berner, which contains the famous Jungfrau and Eiger Peaks.

This section contains high mountains, but not on the same scale as those to the immediate east. In this part, the Berner Alpen can be seen narrowing down from about 25 kms in width, to a single ridge about 10 to 15 kms wide. The highest summit on this map is the Bietschhorn at 3934 meters.

Getting to this area using public transportation is quite easy. Running along-side Highway 9 is an important international rail line. Train stations exist at several locations in the valley, including the most important stop, Brig (just east off this map). From Brig one can board a train which runs through a tunnel coming out at Kandersteg on the north slope. There should be bus service to all cities on Highway 9, but likely not along side-roads into the canyons. If you're on foot and hitch hiking up some of these side-valleys, make a sign stating your destination. This usually helps in getting short rides.

The normal route to **Bietschhorn** is to first leave Highway 9 and drive or hitch hike north past Hohtenn to as far as Wiler, then walk east up to the Bietschhorn Hutte. From there continue east to the summit. The author hasn't climbed this one, but go prepared with ice ax & crampons.

On the north slope is another well-known peak called **Blümlisalp** at 3664 meters. To climb it, head south from Switzerland's capital city of Bern, to the town of Kandersteg near the head of the valley. From there walk east to the lake called Öschinensee, then along a trail northeast to the Blümlisalp Hutte. One route from there is to ridge-walk (or climb) south, then southwest to the triple summit of Blümlisalp. Other climbs can be made in that area via Kandersteg, Gastern, and the trail to the Mutthorn Hutte.

Further west, one can easily ascend a number of peaks which surround a flat, snow filled basin, called the Glacier de la Plaine Mort. **Wildstrubel**, 3244 meters, is the highest peak in this group. One can reach the glacier rim from either the Montana ski area on the south; or head south from the Bern area to Lenk, then to the Iffigen Alp and the trail to the Wildstrubel Hutte. From there you have a choice of many climbs & routes.

Don't forget your ice ax & crampons, as the snow line and glaciers in this region are lower than in other parts of the Alps, particularly those areas to the south in Italia. Brig, Visp or Sierre are larger towns, each having cheaper food and other supplies at Migros Supermarkets, as well as several bookstores where hiking maps can be found. There should also be a tourist office in

Bietschhorn in the central part of the Berner Alpen (Walter Pause foto).

Map 48-2, Bietschhorn, Berner Alpen, Switzerland

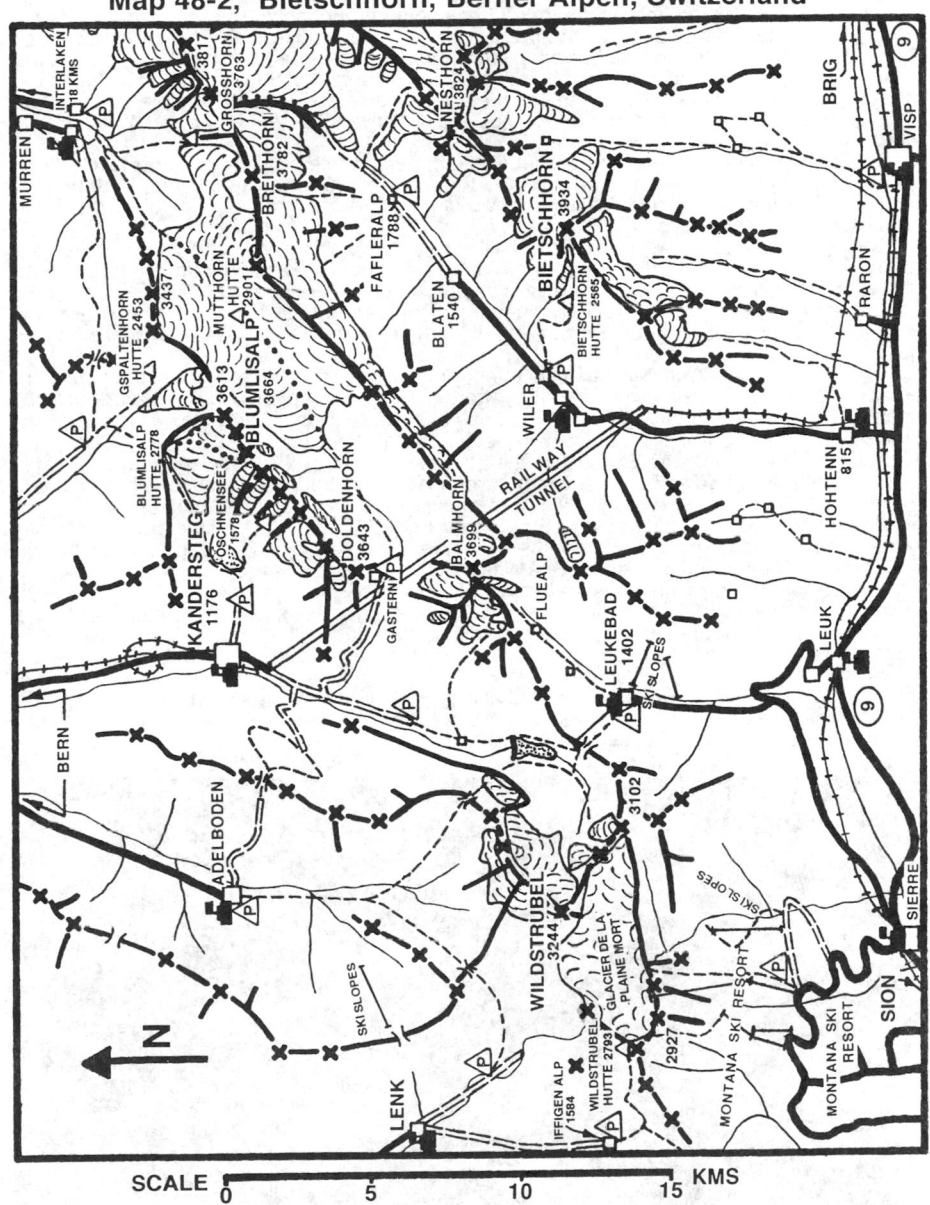

SCALE 0 — 5 — 10 — 15 KMS

each city. Kandersteg on the north slope looks large enough to have good facilities as well.
Maps *Col de Pillon, 41 and Oberwallis, 42,* 1:100,000, Eidg. Landestopographie, Bern; and the latest travel guidebook to Switzerland.

Jungfrau & Eiger, Berner Alpen, Switzerland

The Berner Alpen in central Switzerland has some of the most famous mountains in the world. Names like the Eiger and Jungfrau top the list. Others like Wetterhorn, Schreckhorn, Aletschhorn, and Finsteraarhorn are a bit less famous--but just as, or almost as, challenging. That part of the Berner included on this map is the highest part of the range, and includes the longest glaciers in Europe. The summits here are only a couple of hundred meters lower than the high peaks surrounding Zermatt, but they are directly in the path of the incoming storms, which makes the glaciers larger.

The best-known mountain is the Eiger, 3970 meters, and especially its north face. It and other mountain faces rise abruptly from the lowlands in one giant step with no intervening foothills. Because of this, and the fact that it's in the heart of Europe, it is perhaps the most-famous mountain in the Alps.

Getting to this area is easy. There's a rail line running from Brig and points southwest up the valley to Gletsch and beyond to Andermatt. There's another line running from Interlaken south to Murren and Grindelwald. Busy highways follow these same railways, so bus service should be available on all the major highways shown on this map. Check locally. The author found hitch hiking good in these parts. He had lots of short rides which was just fine because he was going from one mountain to another.

There's a railway which takes tourists to near the top of Eiger, under the summit of Monch, and to a col between Monch and Jungfrau. There stands the Jungfraujoch Hotel at about 3475 meters. To some, this is cheating, but if you use this easy way up, it will get you close to other peaks without having to spend a day or two just getting to a base camp.

An *easy way* to climb the **Eiger** is via the Eismeer Station, or the Mittellegi Hutte, thence to the top. Both **Jungfrau** and **Monch** can be ascended easily from the Jungfraujoch Hotel. Get the latest information on this alpen railway and climbing in Grindelwald or Wengen.

The highest peak in this group is **Finsteraarhorn** at 4274 meters. This one is normally scaled from Finsteraarhorn Hutte; get there from Belalp, Reideralp, or Fiesch. **Aletschhorn**, 4195 meters, is ascended from either Oberaletch or the Konkordia Huttes.

The author hitch hiked into this area, then walked up to Belalp and camped nearby at 2200 meters. Next morning, 8/7/1979, he crossed the glacier, walked past the Oberaletsch Hutte and toward Aletschhorn and tried climbing it on 3 different routes. When he finally found the easy route it was too late, so he missed the summit. Stop and ask the hutte attendent about the route normal before attemping the climb.

Climb **Schreckhorn**, 4078 meters, from Strahlegg Hutte; and the **Wetterhorn**, 3701 meters, from the Glechstein Hutte. In the eastern sections, the routes and trails reaching Dossen, Gulie and Lauteraar Huttes, can be used to climb peaks in that area.

Aletschhorn as seen from the south on the route from Belalp.

Map 49-1, Jungfrau & Eiger, Berner Alpen, Switzerland

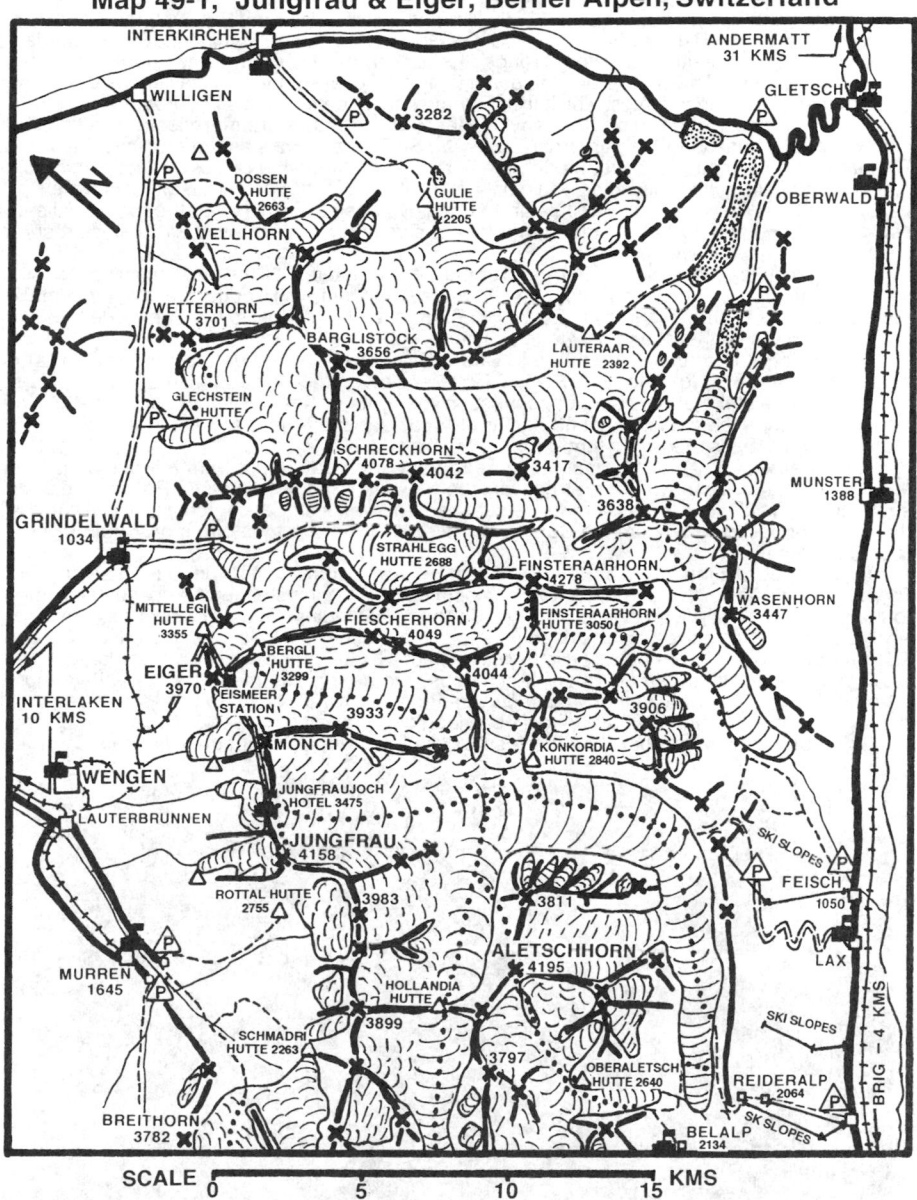

Needless to say, one must be equipped for snow & ice as well as for rock climbing in this entire region. Few climbs are for beginners. Climbing in the heart of this area is as good as any place in Europe. For those who prefer to camp, go prepared for a minor expedition. Make inquiries at the huttes in the area of your climb, for routes up various other summits.
Maps *Brunigpass, 37 and Oberwallis, 42,* 1:100,000, from Eidg. Landestopographie, Bern; also look for a climbing or travel guidebook which can updated the limited information here.

Grand Combin, Pennine Alps, Switzerland-Italy

The area covered by this map is directly west of Zermatt, Switzerland; just north of Aosta, Italia; northeast of St. Bernard Pass; and south of Sion, Switzerland. The international boundary between Switzerland and Italia runs through this area from St. Bernard Pass northeast in the direction of Zermatt. This area is dominated by fairly high peaks and large glaciers, and is at the western end of the Pennine Alps, which include many of the better climbs in Europe.

Some portions of the region are easy to reach, while others are more isolated. There is plenty of public transportation from Aosta, over the St. Bernard Pass and to Martingy and Sion. This includes international rail lines and highways, and some kind of bus service, which the author is unfamiliar with. However, you must have your own car or hitch hike to get into the side valleys from the main arteries. In July and August it's easy to get lifts into the higher valleys, especially if you appear to be a climber. Make a sign stating your destination. If it's a short distance, you should have good luck.

The highest peak in the area is **Grand Combin**, 4314 meters. It's the only summit over 4000 meters in the group. It has 2 normal routes to the summit, but neither one is easy. First, make your way southeast from Martigny to Bourg St. Pierre, then up the trail to the Cabina de Valsore. From there, head northeast and east to the summit.

With a sign, the author hitch hiked to Bourg St. Pierre, walked up the road/trail to 2000 meters and camped. Next morning, 8/15/1979, he walked to the Cabina Valsore in 1 1/2 hours, but made the mistake of not asking directions to the route normal. Even in good weather, he somehow missed the easier way and had to turn back at 3820 meters. On the way down, he found where he made the wrong turn.

The other way up Grand Combin is to head east, then southeast from Martigny, passing through Villetta to Fionnay. From there walk the trail south to the Cabina de Panossiere, then south up the Glacier de Corbassiére to the summit. This looks longer, more difficult & risky than the more normal route up from the Cabina de Valsore. Take ice ax & crampons and maybe a rope & partner.

To climb **Mont Blanc de Cheilon**, 3870 meters, head south from Sion to the Lac des Dix. From the south end of the lake, walk to the Cabina des Dix, then up either the east or west ridge to the summit. This is not an easy climb. **Mt. Collon**, 3667 meters, is usually climbed from Sion, Arolla, then the trail to the Cabina des Vignettes, and up either the west or south ridge. **Gele** at 3518 meters is perhaps the easiest climb on this map. Climb from either side of the border.

If you're interested in making several climbs, the best place might be the valley above Fionnay and in the vicinity of the Cabina de Chanrion. This valley seems less-developed than other places in the Pennine Alps. Go to these mountains prepared for glacier travel.

Or, if you prefer more rock than ice & snow climbing, go to the south or Italian side of the

Monte Velan as seen from the Cabana de Valsore.

Map 50-1, Grand Combin, Pennine Alps, Switzerland-Italy

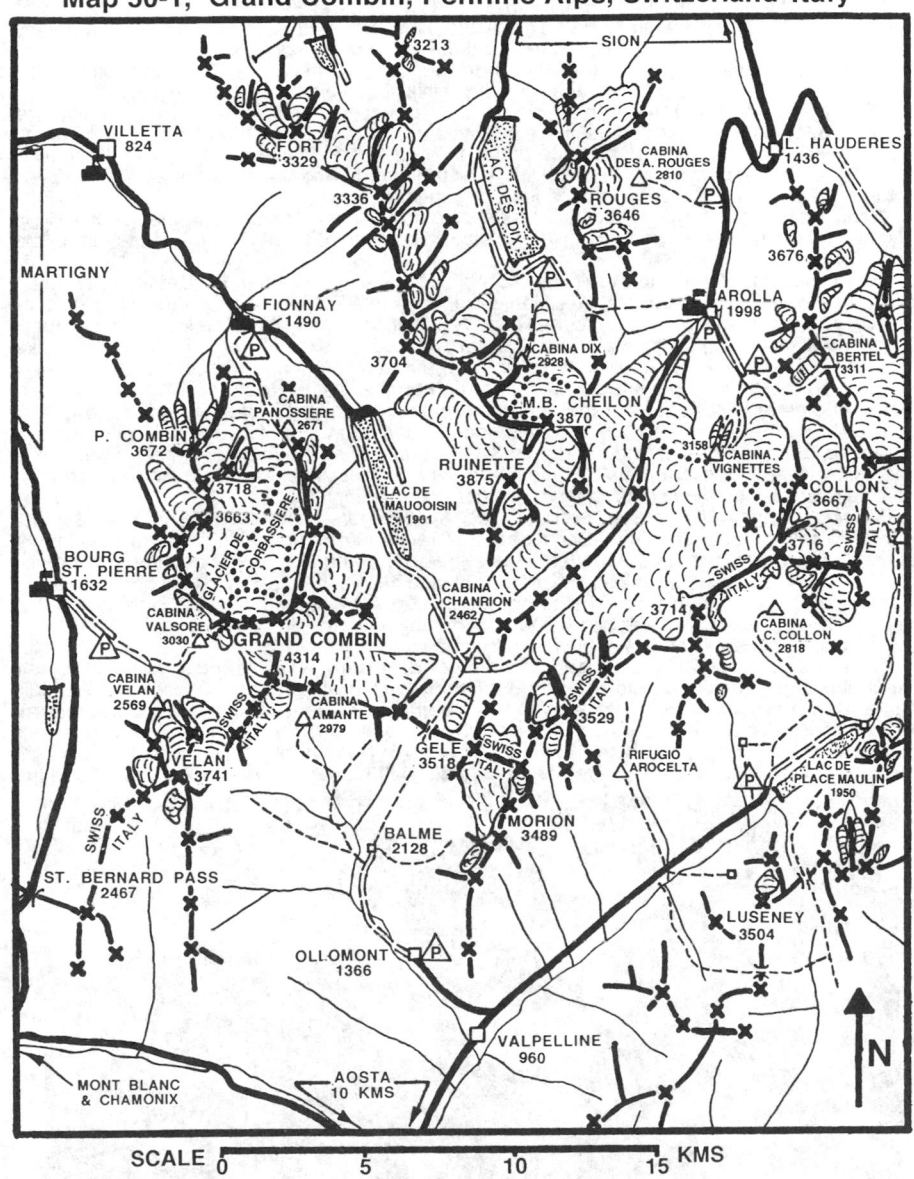

SCALE 0 5 10 15 KMS

border, then head north from Aosta into one of two valleys above Valpelline.

Martigny, Sion and Aosta are the largest cities in the area, so they would be the best places to shop for food, equipment, maps, guidebooks, etc. Each city also has a tourist office which is often helpful. On the mountains, the people who maintain the refuges or cabinas can also be helpful in planning a route.

Maps *Val de Bagnes, 46,* 1:100,000 (1:25,000 and 1:50,000 also available), from Eidg. Landstopographie, Bern; also the latest travel, climbing or hiking book to this region.

Monte Rosa & Matterhorn, Pennine Alpen, Switzerland-Italy

Possibly the premier climbing area in all of Europe is at Zermatt and the surrounding mountains. All the major summits in this circle are over 4000 meters and the glaciers are nearly as large as any in the Alps. Zermatt is perhaps the number one *alpenists trap* in the Alps, and the Matterhorn could be the most fotographed mountain in the world. But even with all the tourists, trekkers and mountaineers, the climbing is still good and the area interesting.

Getting to this region using public transport is very easy. Zermatt is often the first destination for many people. To get there, many take a train to Zermatt, which is the end of the line. Public buses may stop at the edge of town (?). If you're driving a car, turn south about 9 kms east of Brig and drive to Täsch. Park near the station and board a train for Zermatt--no private cars are allowed in Zermatt because of a space problem.

If coming from the south on the Italian side, turn north off the main autostrada about 25 kms east of Aosta and drive, or perhaps take a bus, or hitch hike to Breuil/Cervinia at the foot of the Matterhorn.

The highest mountain in this region is **Monte Rosa**, with its loftiest peak, Dufourspitze, 4634 meters--second highest in Europe after Monte Blanco. From Zermatt, walk southeast up a partly paved trail, or take the cog railway to the Rotboden Station, then walk to the Monte Rosa Hutte, and to the summit from there. With an early start, one could take the train from Zermatt, make the climb, and return to Zermatt on the last train, but that would be a fast climb for the fittest climbers only! Most people stay at least one night in the Monte Rosa Hutte while doing this climb. The author left Zermatt in the afternoon, camped near the end of the cog railway, and climbed Monte Rosa on 8/15/1979. While coming back on the knife-edge summit ridge, his crampons jammed together and he tripped & fell down one side a short distance. That was a close call! Nearby, **Liskamm** at 4527 meters, a very difficult climb, and others in that corner of the basin can also be climbed using the same general approach route.

The **Matterhorn (Mt. Cervino to Italianos)**, 4478 meters, can be ascended from Zermatt and the Hornli Hutte; or from the Italian side from Breuil/Cervinia and (Rifugio Abruzzi no longer exists) 2 small huts high on the mountain as shown. Both normal routes have been modified with ropes, ladders or steel cables, with the Italian side having the most modification. The Italian Route is said to be the easiest. The author camped in some trees below the Hornli Hutte but had a couple of days of bad weather & snow. When he tried the Matterhorn on 8/11/1979, fresh snow made it impossible and no one was on the mountain.

Other mountains can be climbed as follows: **Breithorn**, 4159 meters, from either the Theodul Hutte or Rifugio Mexxelama; **Dent d'Herens**, 4171 meters, normally from the Rifugio Aosta; **Dent Blanche**, 4357 meters, from the Cabina de la Dent Blanche; **Ober-Gabelhorn**, 4063 meters, from the Rothorn Hutte--or direct from Zermatt for the more fit climbers; **Weisshorn**, from Randa and the Weisshorn Hutte; **Nadelhorn**, 4327 meters, from the Mischabel Hutte (and very easy); **Dom & Lenspitze**, 4545 & 4294 meters, from Randa and the

Looking south from near the Rotboden Station at the northern slopes of Breithorn.

Map 51-1, Monte Rosa & Matterhorn, Pennine Alpen, Swiss-Italy

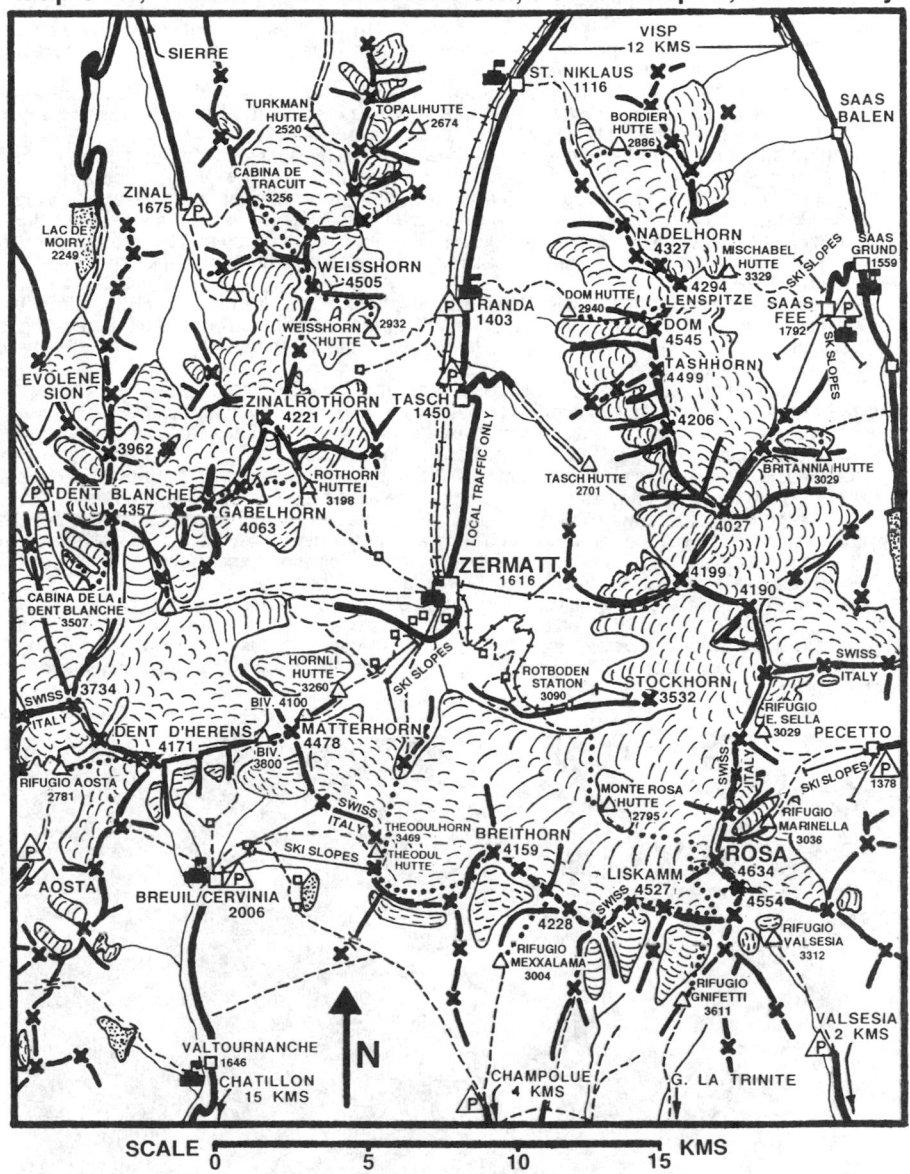

SCALE 0 5 10 15 KMS

Dom Hutte. The author camped above Randa at 2335 meters, then on 8/9/1979, climbed Dom in about 3 2/3 hours; 5 2/3 hours round-trip. For more information about other climbs in the area, contact the tourist or climber's information offices in Zermatt and/or Breuil/Cervinia.

In Zermatt there are several supermarkets and hundreds of sport & bookshops--if better maps are needed. Equipment and guides can also be hired. Lots of hotels too. In Breuil/Cervinia the same situation exits, but the author has never been there.

Maps *Val de Bagnes, 46 and Monte Rosa, 47,* 1:100,000, from Eidg. Landestopographie, Bern; or for peaks south of Zermatt, the map *Breuil/Cervinia-Zermatt, 87,* 1:50,000, from Kompass, Innsbruck; perhaps the book, **Zermatt,** Upton, contact Cordee, UK.

Weissmies, Pennine Alpen, Switzerland

The mountains shown on this map lie just south of Brig and east of Zermatt in south central Switzerland. While parts of northern Italia are shown, the highest summits lie in Switzerland. These peaks and valleys are part of the eastern Pennine Alpen. This group has two summits over 4000 meters, along with some *medium sized* glaciers.

Access to the area using public transportation is fairly good. West of the highest peaks is a paved road running south from Visp which is used primarily by skiers going to the Saas Fee ski resort. This valley has no rail line, and it likely has no bus service (?).

Running through the center of this map, and east of the highest summits, is Highway 9 and the Simplon Pass. There may or may not be bus service on that highway when you arrive, but there is a railway line running through a tunnel under the international border between Varzo, Italia, and Brig and Visp in Switzerland. You can use trains to get to each of these towns, then you'd likely have to hitch hike into nearby valleys. The Simplon Highway and the road running to the Saas Fee area, make for some short access routes to nearly all of the more interesting peaks shown here.

The highest mountain in this area is **Weissmies** at 4023 meters. It's normally climbed from the highway just north of Saas Grund. From the bottom of a tram or ski lift, walk one of 2 trails east up to the Weissmies Hutte, then climb a mostly-snow route up to the southeast and the summit. This is said to be an easy glacier scamble.

From this same hutte, it's also possible to climb the next 2 highest summits in the range; **Lagginhorn**, 4010 meters, and **Fletschhorn**, 3996 meters. The author hasn't climbed here yet. It also appears both peaks can be scaled from the village of Simplon, which is east of the peaks and 8 kms south of Simplon Pass, but Fletschhorn is difficult from that side.

Northeast of Simplon Pass is another smaller and less-known massif, with **Leone**, 3553 meters, the highest in the group and an easy scramble. It can be ascended from the Simplon Pass itself, or from a place on the main highway called Maderalp. Also, one can climb from the Italian side and the town of Varzo, then to the place called Alpe Veglia, located in a central valley among the high peaks.

Still further to the northeast is another small cluster of peaks, with **Helsenhorn**, 3272 meters, the highest. These peaks can be scaled from Binn, Switzerland, or Alpe Veglia, Italia.

Take ice ax & crampons on all climbs in this area. Brig is the best place to buy food, equipment, maps and guidebooks. Brig, in the heart of a great tourist mecca, has all the amenities of a larger city. **Maps** *Oberwallis, 42 and Monte Rosa, 47,* 1:100,000 (and other scales at 1:25,000 and 1:50,000), from Eidg. Landestopographie, Bern; and perhaps the latest hiking, climbing or travel guidebook to Switzerland.

Looking south from Dom at nearby Taschhorn in shadows, and
Monte Rosa in the far distance to the left.

Map 52-2, Weissmiss, Pennine Alpen, Switzerland

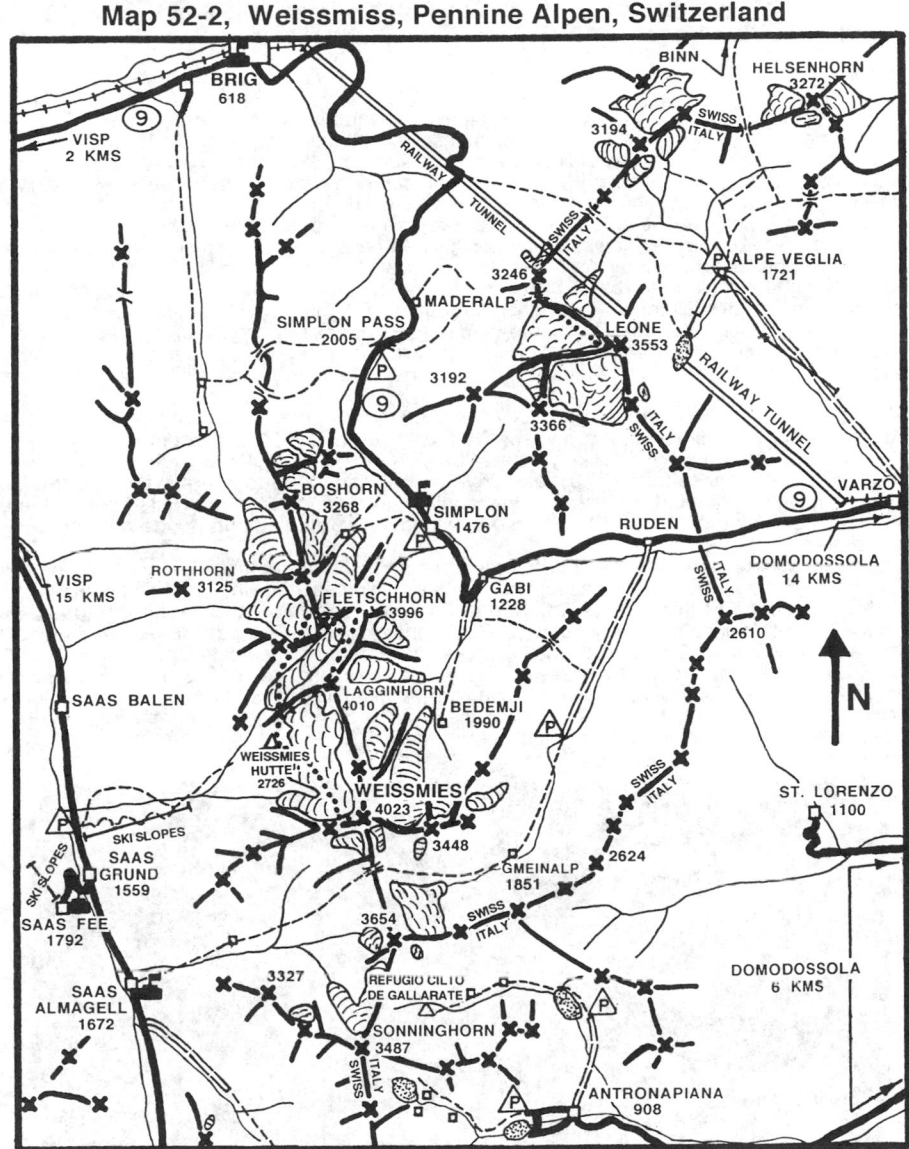

SCALE 0 — 5 — 10 KMS

Blinnenhorn, Lepontine Alpi, Switzerland-Italy

Northeast of the high peaks surrounding Zermatt, and southeast of the Jungfrau-Eiger Massif, is located the most easterly extension of the Pennine Alpen. This map includes the single ridge of medium-high peaks located southeast of Highway 19, and from about Brig to the Furka Pass.

Access to this area is relatively simple, at least from the Swiss side. There's a main rail line running alongside Highway 19 from Brig northeast to Andermatt and beyond. There should be lots of stops in the valley between Gletsch and Brig. There must be some kind of bus service on this route as well. Along Highway 19, hitch hiking can be very good, especially if you carry a sign indicating your destination, and if you're going a short distance.

On the Italian side above or north of Domodossola, there doesn't seem to be much going on, either in the way of summer or winter sports activities, but some say it's a great place to climb. So traffic is light and there may not be any bus service when you arrive(?). Because there are no really high peaks in the area, it's almost a forgotten corner of the Alps. There's not much traffic on the road over Nufenen Pass either, so plan to drive your own car or hitch hike.

For many people this area of small-to-medium sized peaks doesn't sound attractive, but it has some good climbing areas. Just because they're not as high as some nearby mountains, doesn't mean they're all easy. All grades of climbing can be found here, but the area would be classified more for beginners.

The highest peak is **Blinnenhorn**, 3374 meters. To get there, start at the small village named Reckinger just to the northwest. Walk or drive a ways, then ascend the northwest slopes. In late summer this will likely be an all-rock route. If it's a glacier route you want, you could start at or near Nufenen Pass, and drive or walk southwest to a terminal moraine lake, then go straight up the Griesgletcher to the summit. According to the map listed below, there are no rifugios or cabinas in the area, so you'll have to do this climb in one day, or camp somewhere.

Several peaks shown at the bottom of this map may be interesting. They are the peaks surrounding **Helsenhorn**, 3272 meters, and can best be approached via Fiesch and Binn. In the northeast section of this map is **Rotondo** at 3192 meters. You can reach this peak via Oberwald; or by taking a trail beginning in Realp and ending at Rotondo Hutte. Or you could start along a trail about 2 kms southwest of Bedretto and climb up the south face.

There seems to be no ski lifts or resorts in the area, indicating that it's not well-used by skiers or climbers. As a result, the trails are not overly developed, nor is the hut system. For climbers or hikers wishing to leave the crowds behind, this might be the place to go. For the higher peaks one should always have snow & ice climbing equipment.

Glacier and western slopes of Dom (Map 51, page 121).

Map 53-2, Blinnenhorn, Lepontine Alpi, Switzerland-Italy

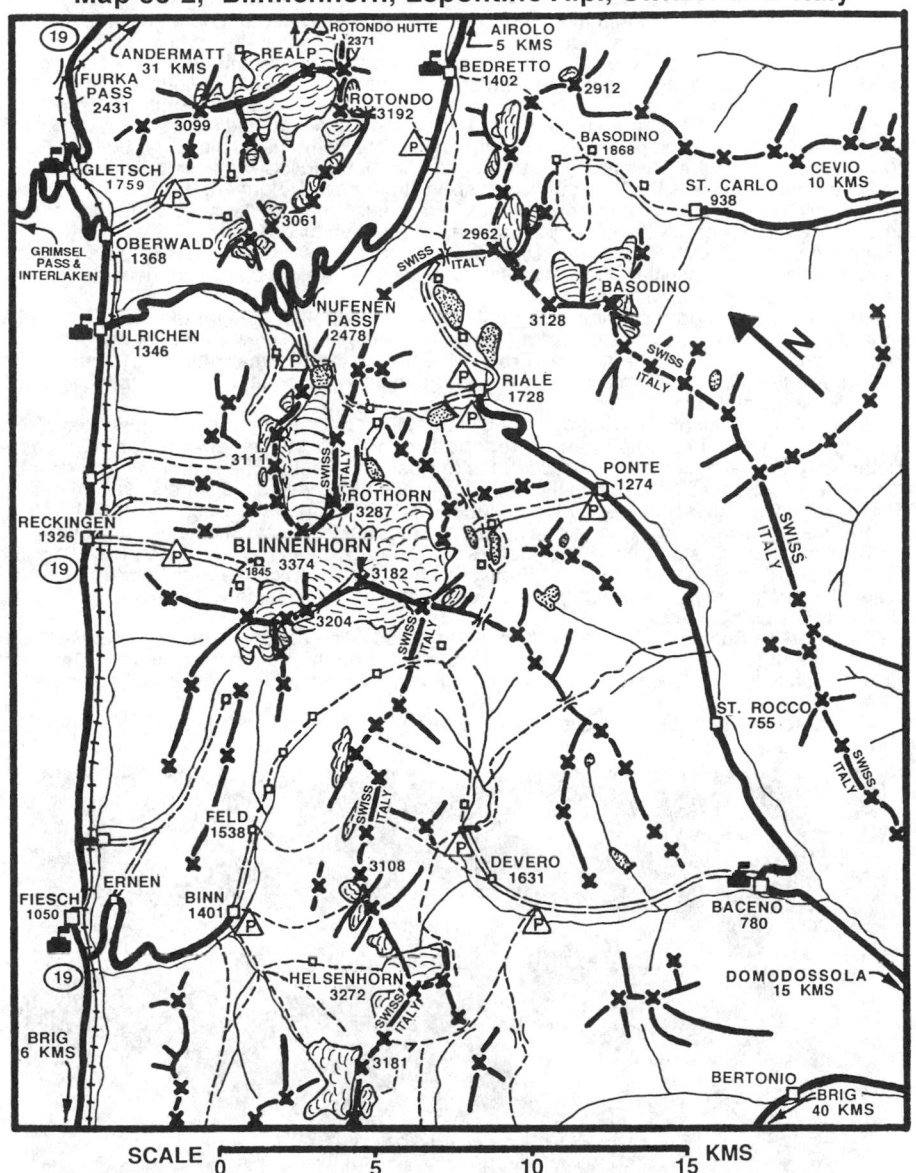

Brig would be the best place to go shopping (there's a big Migros Supermarket located there), to buy maps, or for more information about the area. Airolo and Domodossola are also big towns.

Maps *Oberwallis, 42,* 1:100,000 (maps at 1:25,000 and 1:50,000 also available) from Eidg. Landestopographie, Bern; and perhaps the latest hiking, climbing or travel guidebook to Switzerland.

Dammastock, Urner Alpen, Switzerland

In central Switzerland, south of Luzern, and just west of Andermatt, is an area of medium high mountains with a couple of glaciers that rival the largest in the Alps. Most of these higher summits are on one long ridge called **Winterberg**. Most peaks on this ridge are around the 3500 meter mark, including the highest in the area, Dammastock at 3630 meters.

Access to the region is good. Trains run from Brig over Furka Pass (actually through a tunnel under the pass) and down to Andermatt, then north to Altdorf and the lowlands. This line gives access to the more important towns in the area. The highways running over Susten, Furka and Gottard Passes are busy and surely some kind of bus service will exist to Andermatt (?). However, train service is the best public transport (from near Andermatt, there's now a tunnel and railway line running south to Ariolo, Italia). From Andermatt, to the base of various peaks, hitching is good, especially if you carry a sign stating your nearby destination.

Andermatt and vicinity is a busy place---both in summer and winter. It's in the heart of the Alps and has all the amenities of a first class resort town. Make this place your headquarters for information and shopping while in the area.

Dammastock is normally climbed from the Damma Hutte, located on the east side of the peak. One can drive, hitch hike or walk from Goschenen on the highway north of Andermatt, to the reservoir called Goscheneralpsee. From there hike to the Damma Hutte, then climb up the east face to the summit. Normally, people spend a night in the hutte, then finish the climb and return home the next day.

Another high peak of the Winterberg is **Gallenstock**, 3583 meters. It's an easy climb from the Albert Heim Hutte, which can be reached from the hotel-restaurant complex called Tiefenbach, on the main highway between Furka Pass and Realp. The author hitch hiked from Andermatt to Tiefenbach, walked up the trail a ways and camped at 2185 meters. Next morning, 8/5/1979, he walked past the Albert Heim Hutte, then to the top of Galenstock and Tiefenstock (3515 meters). It must have taken all day, because he slept 2 nights at the same campsite.

Further north, **Sustenhorn**, 3503 meters, can be ascended by the normal way via the Susten Pass, Tierbergli Hutte, and the Steingletscher. But crossing the Stein Glacier could be tricky (?). Another route is from Chelenalp Hutte, which is in the same valley as Damma Hutte. No crevasses on this route.

North of the Susten Pass is another smaller group of mountains, with **Spannort** at 3198 meters, the highest. The normal route to its summit is on the trail that passes the Spannort Hutte, which in turn, is reached via Engelberg. From Engelberg there's a lift to the top of a 3028 meter peak.

For someone interested in glaciers, the Rhone-Trift complex is one of the largest in the Alps.

The east face of Galenstock as seen from near the Albert Heim Hutte.

Map 54-1, Dammastock, Urner Alpen, Switzerland

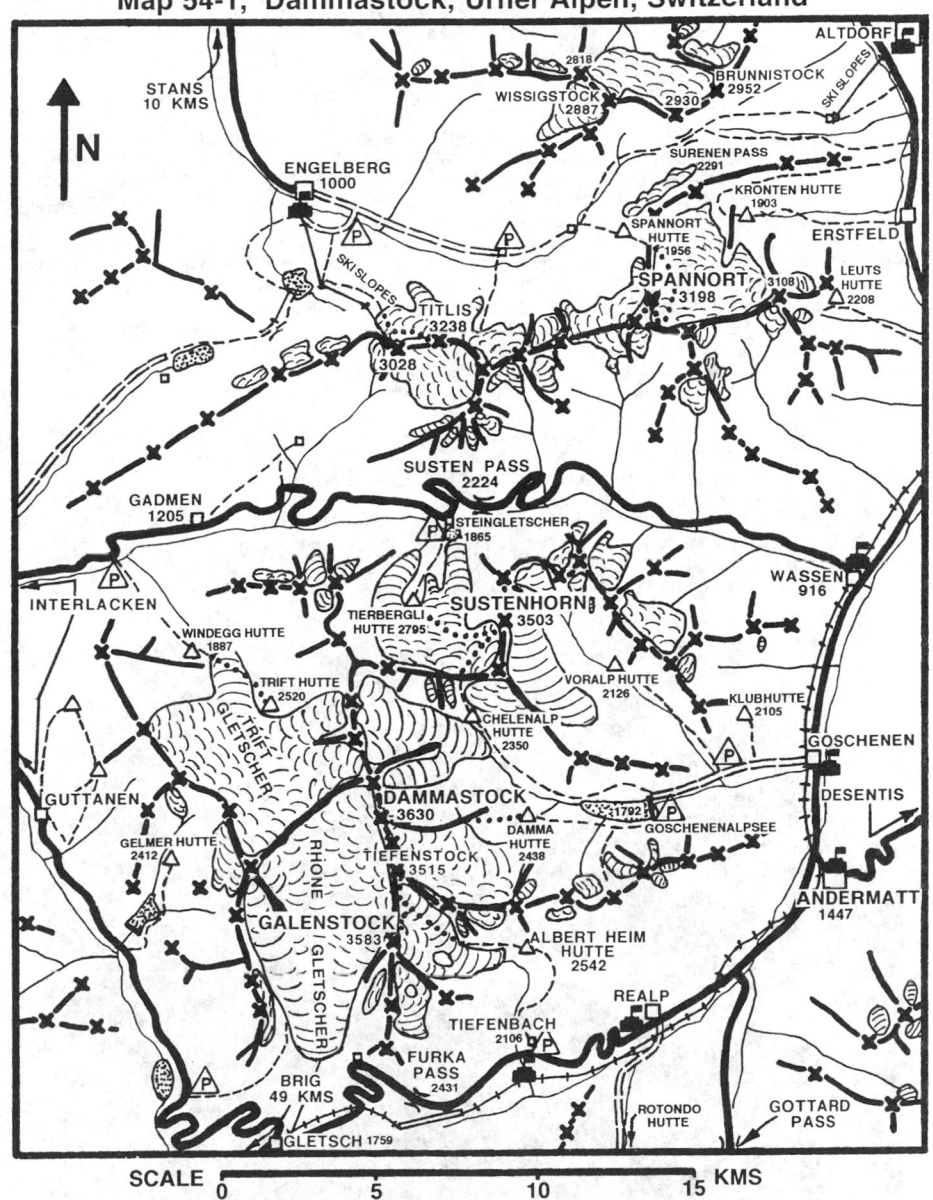

All the higher summits on this map require an ice ax & crampons. At all the huttes mentioned above, there are full-time guardians who can advise climbers of the different routes up nearby peaks. Andermatt is a good place to get local information, as there's a tourist & climber's information office and climber's school located there.

Maps *Brunigpass, 37,* 1:100,000, from Eidg. Landestopographie, 3084 Wabern, Bern; and perhaps the latest hiking, climbing or travel guidebook to Switzerland.

Pic Tödi, Glarner Alpen, Switzerland

In central Switzerland in the area surrounding Disentis Muster, lies the Glarner Alpen. By Swiss standards these mountains would be classed as medium sized. Because of this, the region is not as popular for climbing as other ranges in the country or the Alps.

This area is easily accessible with a rail line passing through Altdorf to Andermatt, then over Oberalppass, to Disentis-M and eastward to Chur. This is a major rail line giving good access to to this main east-west valley. Another rail line comes from the north to as far as Linthal in the northeast part of this map. The road running east-west through Disentis-M, known as Highway 19, is also a major route in the southern part of the country and northern Italia. It seems there should still be some kind of bus service along this route. Years ago, the author had good luck hitch hiking in this area, but most people would prefer to rent a car than stand on the road.

The highest summit in the region is **Tödi** at 3614 meters. The author was told the most-used route for climbing Tödi was to pass through Linthal, then drive and walk to the Gronhorn Hutte at 2448 meters, and finally up the east face and/or ridge to the summit. However, some literature says another route, presumably easy (?), exists as shown on the map--via the Planura Hutte, possibly over the peak marked 3063 (?) to Sandy Pass at 2781 meters, then east up a ridge to the summit.

Other high peaks in the Tödi area are **Bifertenstock**, 3421 meters, climbed from either the Gronhorn Hutte on the north, or the Punteglias Hutte on the south. Also **Clariden Peak** at 3267 meters. That looks like an easy climb from the Planura Hutte then north up the south ridge to the summit.

Tgietschen, 3328 meters, is usually approached from the Cavardiras Hutte, then west across the Brunnifern Glacier. Peaks in the region of the Etxli Hutte can be climbed from that refuge, or even from the south and a place called Bauns at 1936 meters.

South of Disentis-M stands **Medel**, 3211 meters, and another groups of glaciated peaks. Medel is normally approached from Solioa village just south of Disentis-M, the Medel Hutte, then south to the summit. Or possibly from the south and Pass D' Uffiern and a place called Scaleta. This latter route would normally be without snow.

Most climbs in this region involve a combination of snow and rock, depending on the season,

The northeast face of Tödi from above Linthal (Walter Pause foto).

Map 55-1, Pic Tödi, Glarner Alpen, Switzerland

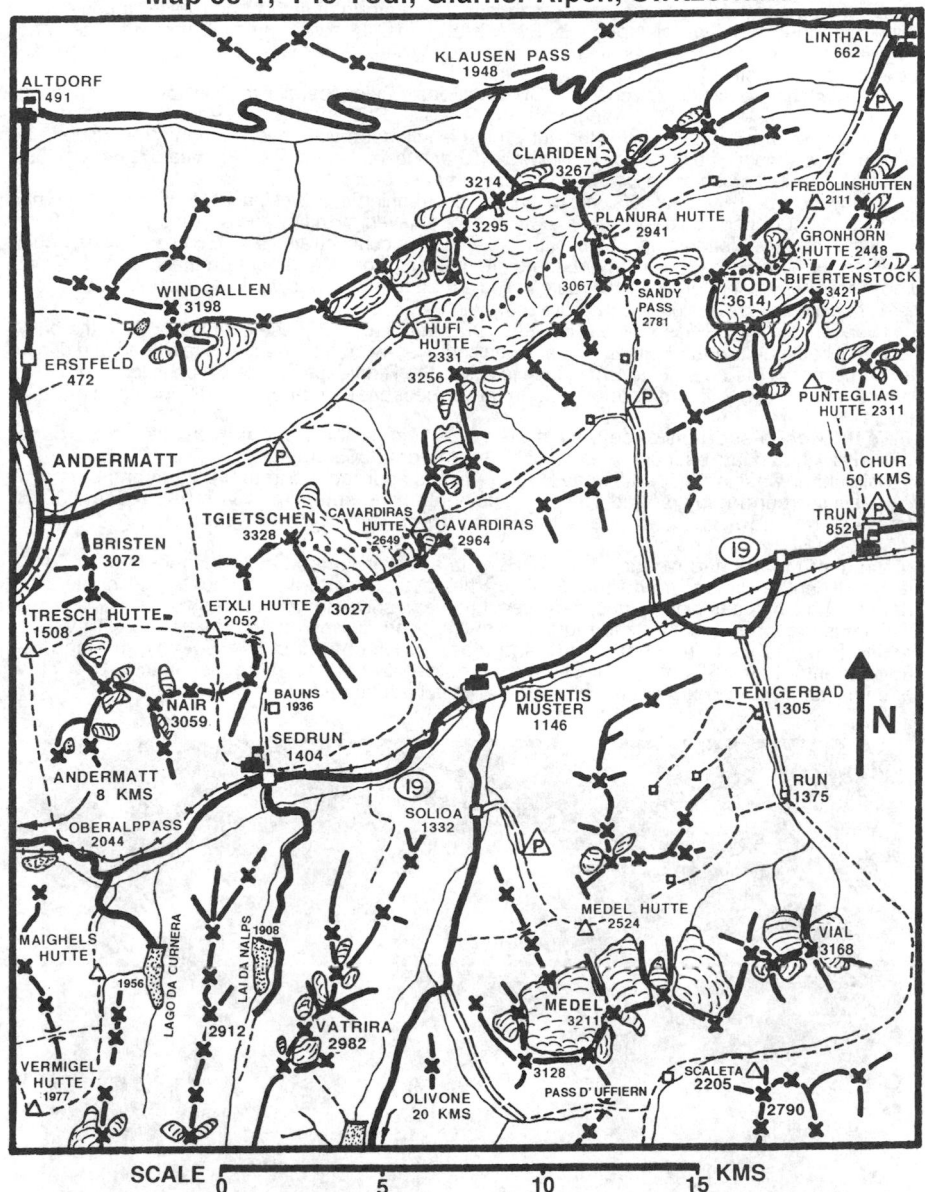

KLAUSEN PASS 1948

LINTHAL 662

ALTDORF 491

CLARIDEN 3267

3214

3295

PLANURA HUTTE 2941

FREDOLINSHUTTEN 2111

GRONHORN HUTTE 2448

TODI 3614

BIFERTENSTOCK 3421

3067

SANDY PASS 2781

WINDGALLEN 3198

ERSTFELD 472

HUFI HUTTE 2331

3256

PUNTEGLIAS HUTTE 2311

ANDERMATT

CHUR 50 KMS

TGIETSCHEN 3328

CAVARDIRAS HUTTE 2649

CAVARDIRAS 2964

TRUN 852

BRISTEN 3072

19

ETXLI HUTTE 2052

3027

TRESCH HUTTE 1508

NAIR 3059

BAUNS 1936

DISENTIS MUSTER 1146

TENIGERBAD 1305

N

SEDRUN 1404

ANDERMATT 8 KMS

19

RUN 1375

OBERALPPASS 2044

SOLIOA 1332

MAIGHELS HUTTE

1908

MEDEL HUTTE 2524

VIAL 3168

1956

LAGO DA CURNERA

LAI DA NALPS

MEDEL 3211

2912

VATRIRA 2982

VERMIGEL HUTTE 1977

3128

PASS D' UFFIERN

SCALETA 2205

2790

OLIVONE 20 KMS

SCALE 0   5   10   15 KMS

so it's important to have an ice ax & crampons. Andermatt, Altdorf and Disentis-M are the largest towns in the area and are the best places to do your shopping. Each of these towns has stores where you can buy better detailed maps or books, as well as food. And each town has a tourist office that can be of assistance in giving directions to mountains and/or routes. There's a mountaineering school & information office in Andermatt, which can also be of help.

Maps *Panixerpass, 38,* 1:100,000, Eidg. Landestopographie, Bern; and perhaps the latest travel, hiking or climbing guidebook to this area.

Ringelspitz, Glarner Alpen, Switzerland

In the area west of Chur in eastern Switzerland, lies a group of smaller and less-climbed peaks which are part of the Glarner Alpen. By Swiss standards, these are small to medium sized and insignificant mountains. However, there are some good climbs & hikes here, including some on ice, snow and small glaciers.

Transportation to this area is good. There's a rail line running parallel to Highway 19, connecting Chur with Disentis Muster and Andermatt, to the west. Still another line ends at Linthal in the northwestern corner of this map. Hopefully there is still good train service along these lines. In addition, there should be bus service on Highway 191 and to the Linthal area (?). Years ago the author had good luck hitch hiking along Highway 19, but that's not a option for everyone.

For the most part, there's one single mountain ridge running east-west, north of Highway 19. This ridge and the surrounding valley area is a winter sports haven, with lifts and ski runs stretching from one end of the valley to the other. Most of the ski areas are concentrated above Flims. As one would expect, along with all the development, there are many dirt roads and trails on these slopes. From almost anywhere along Highway 19, you can find a road running up toward some peak. In addition, there are more trails on the ground than are shown on this map.

There are about 3 Swiss Alpine Club (SAC) huts in the area. These huts are open in the busy months of both summer and winter, and are watched over by an attendant. Usually food and drinks can be bought in the huts. One SAC place is called the Ringelspitz Hutte which is located above Tamins, and on the trail and normal route to the highest peak in the region, **Ringelspitz** at 3247 meters.

To the west a short distance, and in the valley above and west of Vattis, is the Sardona Hutte. It's situated just east and at the foot of **Surenstock**, 3058 meters.

Still further west is the Martinsmad Hutte, which is approached from the north and Elm. It's in a basin surrounded by rugged peaks, including the twin summits of **Vorab**, 3028 and 3018 meters. This mountain can easily be scaled from Flims and the ski trails; or from the Martinsmad Hutte.

South of Linthal and west of Panixer Pass is another summit called **Hausstock** at 3158 meters. It can be climbed from either Panix on the south, or Linthal to the north, and in one day. There are no SAC huts in the Hausstock area, but maps show some kind of shelters.

Chur is the largest town in the region, so make it your shopping headquarters. Or if you're coming from the west, try shopping in Andermatt or Disentis-Muster. Locally, one can get additional information at hotels, the Chur tourist office, or at huttes in the mountains. They may not be needed, but ice ax & crampons should always be taken along anyway.

This is the east ridge of Weisshorn (Map 51, page 121).

Map 56-2, Ringelspitze, Glarner Alpen, Switzerland

Maps *Panixerpass, 38,* 1:100,000, from Eidg. Landestopographie, Bern; and perhaps the latest travel, hiking or climbing guidebook to this area.

Adula/Rheinwaldhorn, Adula Gruppe, Switzerland

In the southeastern corner of Switzerland near the Italian border, and not far north of Bellinzona (Switzerland), is a small and little-known group of mountains called the Adula Gruppe. Several of the peaks are medium size, the others would be classed as small--by Swiss standards. As a result, they're almost unknown, despite the fact there's some good climbing on the higher slopes.

The highest summit in the region is Rheinwaldhorn, 3402 meters. This is the German name, but it's more commonly known locally as Adula, as this is in the Italian speaking sector of Switzerland.

Public transportation is not real good close to these peaks. A rail line passes through Bellinzona and Biasca, then to Andermatt bypassing this mapped area. That line continues to Chur and points north and east.

The main highway through this immediate area is N13, which runs south from Chur, then up & over--or under, St. Bernard Pass, then on to Bellinzona. There is good bus service along this route. The other main road is the highway linking Disentis-Muster in the north to Biasca. There are likely no buses (?)on this road, so your choices may be to rent a car or hitch hike.

Now for climbing. The easiest and shortest way to **Adula** is via Dangio, Sol, and 2 huts on the west side of the mountain. On the map, the northwest ridge looks easy. The author got a ride to Soi and camped at about 1400 meters in the rain. Next morning, 8/2/1979, he climbed for 2 1/4 hours, then it began snowing. In white-out conditions with zero visibility at 3300 meters, he had to return. Never did see the mountain!

You can also approach the mountain from the east side using the trail passing the Zapport Hutte. A north ridge looks easy on a map, but so does the southeast ridge after a walk up the Paradisegletcher. On the north, the trail passing the Lanta Hutte could be used, but this route is not as convenient as the west-side route. On the south you can approach from Dandrio and some kind of shelter high in the valley at 2048 meters. From there, the west ridge looks easy.

The second highest peak is **Güferhorn**, 3383 meters. The easiest way up should be from the Lanta Hutte, using the northern approach. More difficult routes may be found if you were to start at the Zapport Hutte or the Canalalp routes.

For someone wanting to climb a number of peaks from one base, the best cirque basin to operate from would be the one where the Zapport Hutte is found. The glaciers in the area are not big, but the larger ones have some crevasses. It's recommended that climbers always take along an ice ax & crampons.

Most of the larger towns in this mapped area have at least one small store, with Olivone, Malvaglia, Mesocco, and Splugen perhaps the best places to buy food. Bellinzona is about the

Homes with natural slate shingles near the village of Dangio.

Map 57-1, Adula/Rheinwaldhorn, Adula Groupe, Switzerland

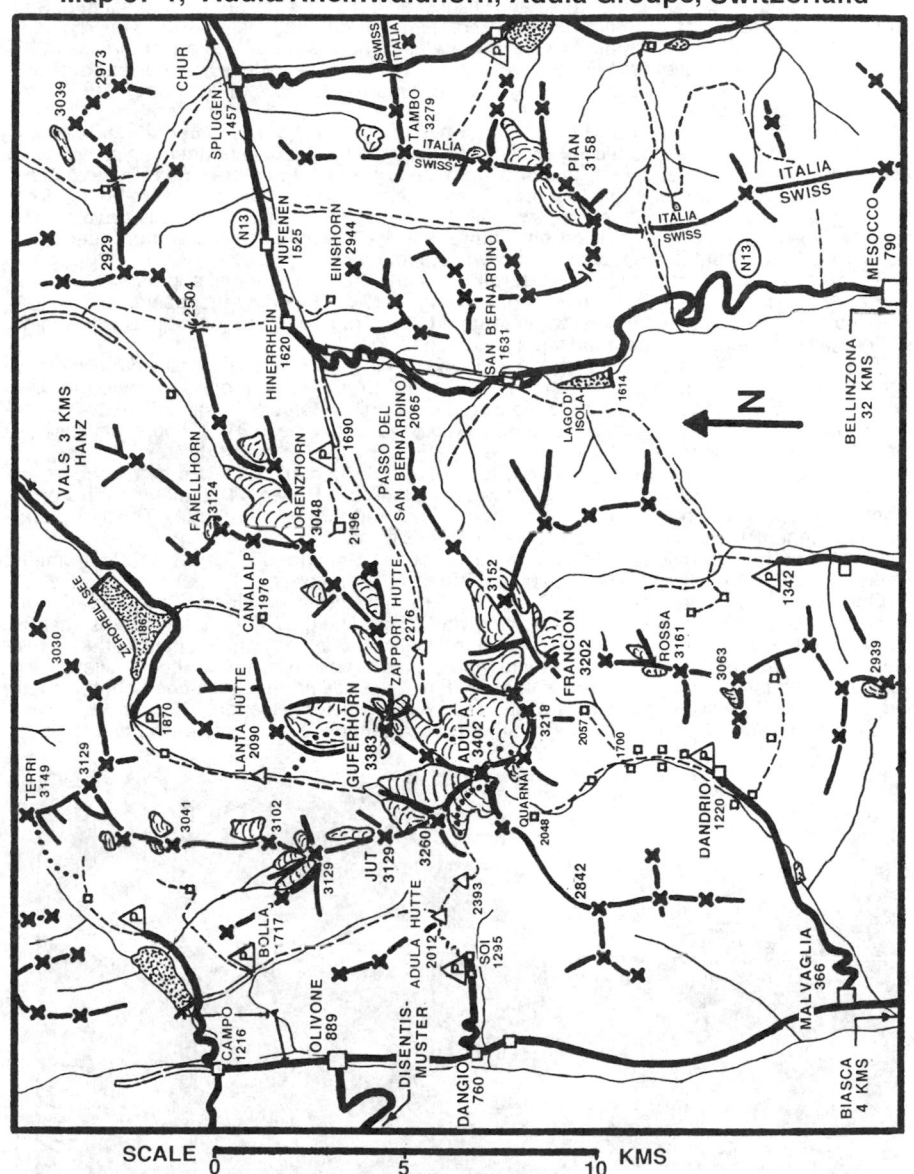

SCALE 0 — 5 — 10 **KMS**

only place in that part of Switzerland where you can find better maps of the area. Or it might be best to do your shopping outside this mapped area in such places as Andermatt, Disentis-Muster or Chur.
Maps *Sopra Ceneri, 43,* and *Panixerpass, 38,* 1:100,000 (1;25,000 & 1;50,000 scales availble), from Eidg. Landestopographie, Bern; and perhaps the latest travel, hiking or climbing guidebook to this area.

Piz Bernina, Bernina Gruppe, Switzerland-Italy

Included on this map are the Bernina and Disgrazia Gruppes. They are located south of San Moritz, Switzerland, north of Sondrio, Italia, and along the international border. This region is considered one of the best climbing areas in the Alps. There are many sharp summits, knife-edge ridges, and large glaciers with big crevasses. While there are a few rather easy routes, many peaks offer difficult and challenging climbs. Among the more difficult ones are: Ferro, Rosso, Roseg and Bernina.

Public transportation to and within the region is fairly good, with an international rail line crossing the Bernina Pass, connecting the Sondrio Valley to the south in northern Italia, with San Moritz. Another rail line reaches San Moritz from the northeast, but there's no railway running southwest of this big winter sports center. Overall, there is good train service to San Moritz. The main highways, especially the ones passing through San Moritz, are heavily traveled and should still have bus service, at least on Highways 3 & 29. Years ago the author found hitch hiking good throughout the area, but you may want to rent a car.

The highest peak on this map is **Piz Bernina**, 4049 meters. The usual approach is via San Moritz, Pontresina and the Bovalhutte. From there, head south, cross the glacier to the east, then south along a ridge, and west to the summit. This is a long one-day climb with a high altitude glacier traverse, and near the top a knife-edge ridge.

The author camped in the rain near the trailhead marked 1896 meters. It rained much of the night, then the next morning, 7/30/1979, he got to the Boval Hutte in one hour and followed tracks of climbers made the day before, up past the Refugios Marco & Rosa, and all the way to the top of Bernina under dark clouds. Round-trip time must have been 8 or 9 hours, because he stayed at the same campsite for 2 nights.

Not far to the east on the same high ridge is **Palu**, 3905 meters. It can be climbed from either the Boval or Diavolezza Huttes. Just west of Bernina is **Roseg**, 3920 meters. This peak is normally climbed from Pontresina, the Roseg Hotel and the Tschierahutte. These 3 peaks and some unnamed summits make some very challenging ice & snow climbing.

On the southeastern flanks of the Bernina Gruppe is **Scalino**, 3323 meters. It's normally ascended via Sondrio, Chiesa, and from either Rifugios Cristina or Zoja.

Southwest of Piz Bernina is the Disgrazia Gruppe with more medium-high peaks and glaciers. **Badile**, 3308 meters, a difficult climb via Masino and the Rifugio Gianetti. Its eastern neighbor, **Ferro**, 3267 meters, is climbed from the south and is easy. One of the better known peaks in the group is **Castello**, 3392 meters, and is an easy climb from the Rifugio Allievi. The highest summit in this gruppe is **Disgrazia** at 3578 meters. It's normally climbed from the south and the Rifugio C. Ponti, then straight up the Preda Rossi Glacier to the top.

Since there are few all-rock climbs in either group mentioned here, you must have ice ax &

Piz Bernina as seen from the glacier below Mt. Palu.

Map 58-1, Piz Bernina, Bernina Gruppe, Switzerland-Italy

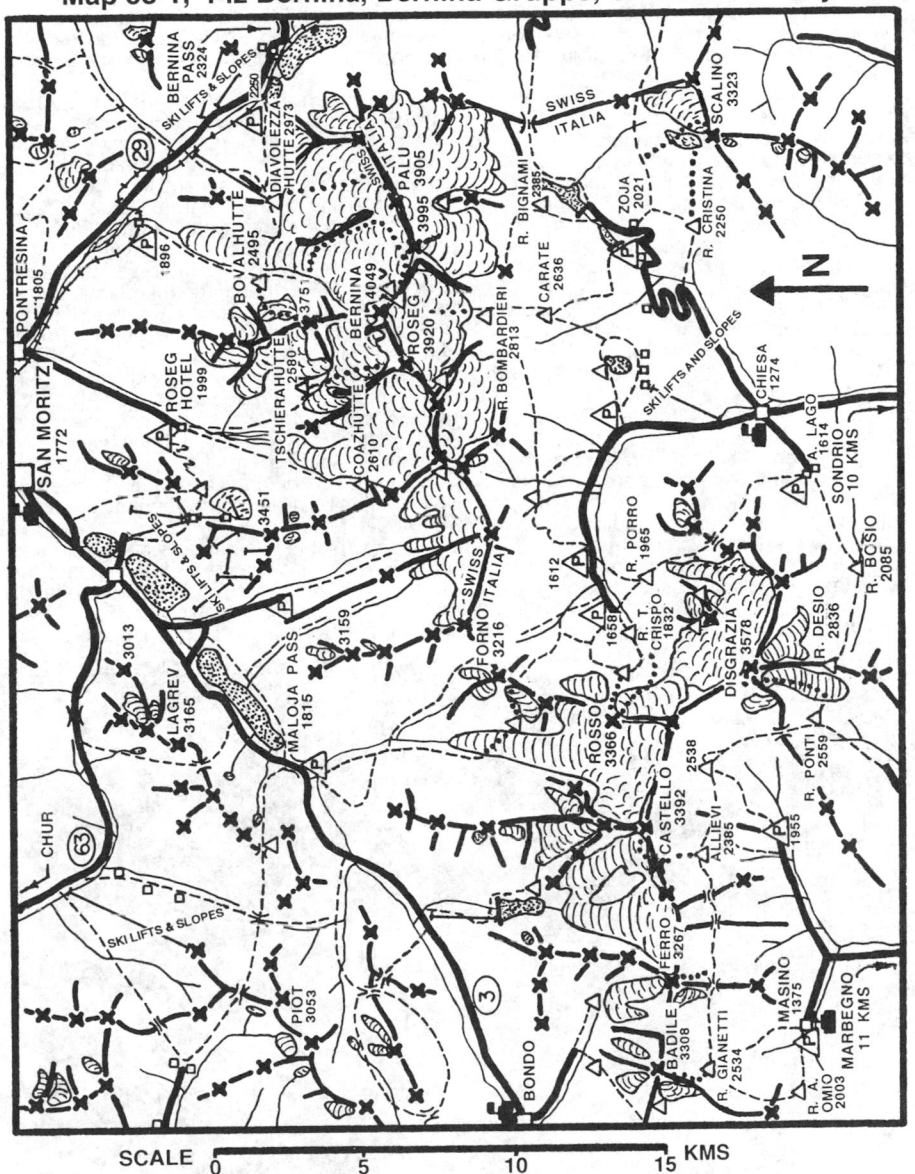

SCALE 0   5   10   15 KMS

crampons on all climbs. Any of the larger towns in the surrounding area will have supermarkets and bookstores where you can buy better maps than this one. Also tourist or alpenists information centers. The larger communities include Sondrio and Tirano, Italia, and San Moritz, Switzerland. San Moritz is for the rich & famous and rather expensive.

Maps *Bernina und Engadiner Alpen, 51,* 1:100,000 (maps at 1:25,000 & 1:50,000 available), from Freytag und Berndt, Wien; and the latest travel guidebook to Switzerland.

Piz Kesch & Calderas, Retiche Alpen, Switzerland

The Retiche Alpen is a rather indistinct mountain mass consisting of 3 higher massifs or groups of peaks. The location of these mountains is northwest of Highway 27, and due north of San Moritz, all in eastern Switzerland. Also included on this map is part of the Languard Gruppe which is southeast of Highway 27.

St. or San Moritz is one of the better known ski vacation destinations in the Alps; unfortunately it seems to cater to the rich & famous. But sometimes people like you and I are allowed in. Getting there using public transport is quite easy. There's a rail line coming in from the northeast from the direction of Davos, and another line coming from Bernina Pass, Sondrio in northern Italia, and from points south. There seems to be good train service into this valley. San Moritz is also on a major highway running north from Milano, and south from Davos. There should be bus service along these major routes. Other options are renting a car, and hitch hiking, which the author found OK back in 8/1979, but which may not be as good today.

The highest and best-known summit in the region is **Piz Kesch** at 3417 meters. This climb is normally made by passing through Bergun to the Kesch Hutte, thence up the glacier to the northeast ridge. This is considered an average climb for the Alps. An alternate way would be to approach the mountain from the southeast and the area around Zouz and the Es-Cha Hutte. There seems to be a route to the east ridge of Kesch from there.

Northeast of Kesch is another massif with **Piz Vadret**, 3229 meters, as the highest peak in that group. One can climb most of the peaks near Vadret from the Grialetsch Hutte at 2542 meters. Enter this area from the Davos side and the Schurlihutte; or from the southeast and Highway 27. This latter route is more convenient to San Moritz, but would be a longer walk.

In the area west of San Moritz and its ski slopes, is another small group of glaciated summits. The highest peak there is **Calderas** at 3397 meters. You can camp near, or use the Jenatsch Hutte, which is in the center of a ring of high summits. This area is perhaps the most easily reached, since you can walk right from downtown San Moritz.

Outside the 3 small groups mentioned, there are many mountains but no other glaciers to speak of. For these 3 higher groups of peaks you will normally need an ice ax & crampons, but if a southern approach is used, they may not be needed. The weather is typical for Switzerland, being no drier or wetter than other parts. July & August is the normal climbing season.

In this area, San Moritz is by far the largest community. Plan to do your shopping there as it

This is the north face of Piz Kesch (Walter Pause foto).

Map 59-2, Piz Kesch & Calderas, Retiche Alpen, Switzerland

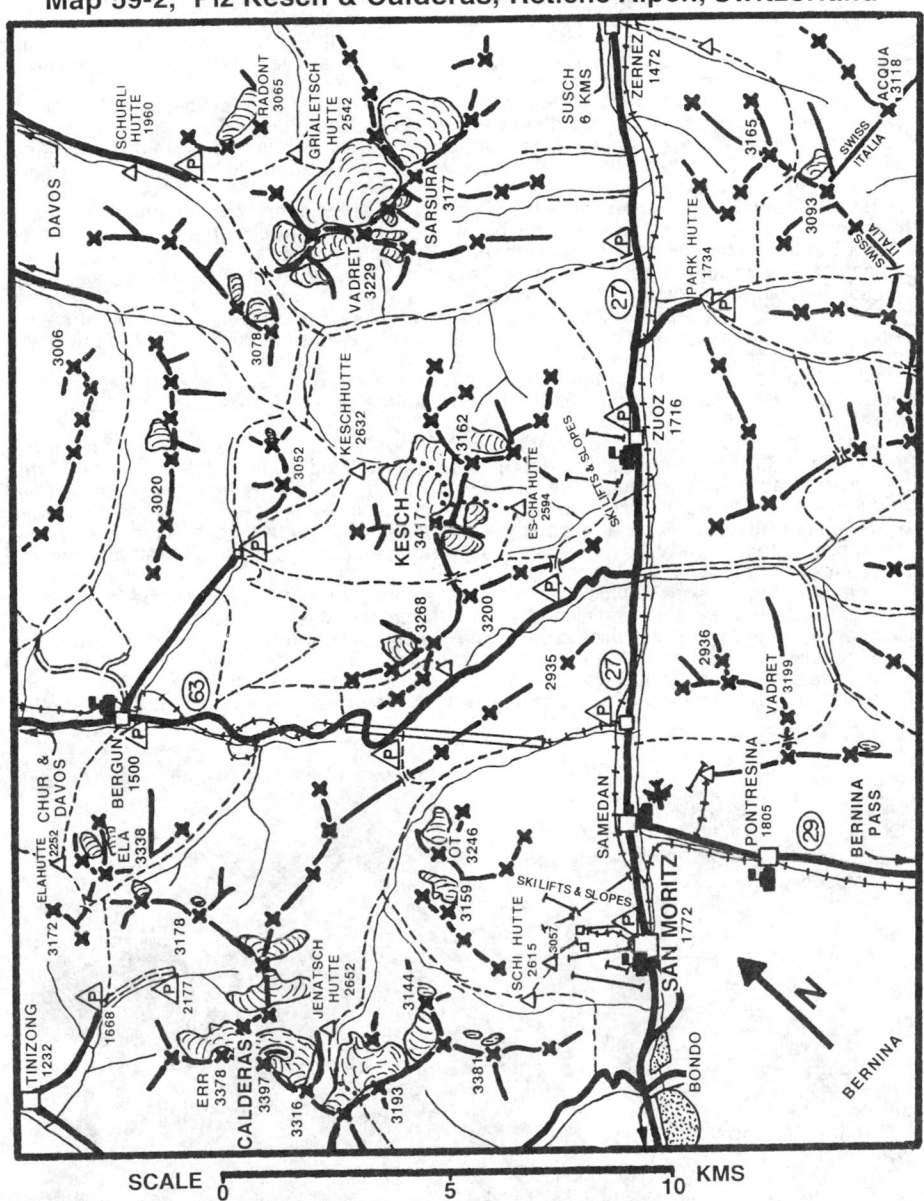

SCALE 0 ——————— 5 ——————— 10 KMS

has supermarkets and bookstores where you can find a good variety of food, books, and maps. San Moritz is also the best place to begin a climb because it's the transportation hub of the area. San Moritz is a rich man's resort town and the cost of living is much higher than in other mountain towns in Switzerland. Shop elsewhere if you can!

Maps *Bernina und Engadiner Alpen, 51,* 1:100,000, from Freytag und Berndt, Wien (one Italiano states Swiss maps are better); and perhaps a travel guidebook to Switzerland.

Gruppos Adamello & Presanella, Italy

The area shown on this map involves two groups of high peaks very near each other. They are the Gruppos Adamello and Presanella. This region is not too far west of Trento, and southwest of Bolzano in northern Italia. Both of these groups are very near, but not actually part of, the Dolomiti system of the Italian Alps further to the east.

One can expect public transportation in the form of buses to be available up to Pinzolo on the eastern side of this map, and on the route from Vermiglio to Edolo. Edolo is the closest city to have a rail line, but the author isn't sure if trains actually still run there. In the summer of 1979, the author hitch hiked into this area but it was slow. Northern Italia is not good for hitch hiking! Best to rent a car if you can afford it.

On the Adamello side, **Adamello** is the highest peak at 3554 meters. The normal routes to this summit are via Lobbia Alto Peak and the Rifugio Cadati Adamello on the east side; or the Rifugio Trento which means a northern approach. Both routes involve long glacier walks. A less popular route is via the Rifugio Predenzini to the south. There are also routes to this peak via the Rifugios Garibaldi or Miller; from the northwest and west.

On 7/28/1979, the author hitch hiked to Edolo and Rino, but because of bad information, literally got on the wrong side of the mountain and never made the summit. Somehow it was more important at the time to get on to the next mountain.

Care Alto at 3462 meters, at the southern end of the group, is usually climbed from the Rifugio Care Alto. **Frati**, 3283 meters, is climbed from the ski resort area above Pont Legno, or the Rifugio Garibaldi.

Just across the valley to the east is the Gruppo Presanella, with its highest summit, **Presanella** at 3556 meters. It can be approached from at least 3 different directions. Perhaps the easiest way is via the Rifugio Presanella. Another possibility is from the Rifugio Stavel (perhaps it has a different name?), located on the north side of the peak. One can also make the climb from Rifugios Bedole and Trento, west of the peaks. By using one of these 2 rifugios, or camping in that upper valley, both Adamello and Presanella can be explored and climbed from the same base camp.

Both of these massifs include glacier travel, so ice ax & crampons are needed on most climbs. There are many ski resorts in the area, particularly at Passo del Tonale. Many of the ski lifts operate year-round. This region is one of the more popular climbing areas in northern Italia.

Generally speaking, the weather in this part of the Alps is better than in the areas further north, therefore climbing is often more enjoyable. The system of trails and rifugios is very good in and around these peaks. People in this entire area speak Italiano, as opposed to other

The northern slopes of Presanella (far left) as seen from near the Rifugio Stavel.

Map 60-1, Gruppos Adamello & Presanella, Italy

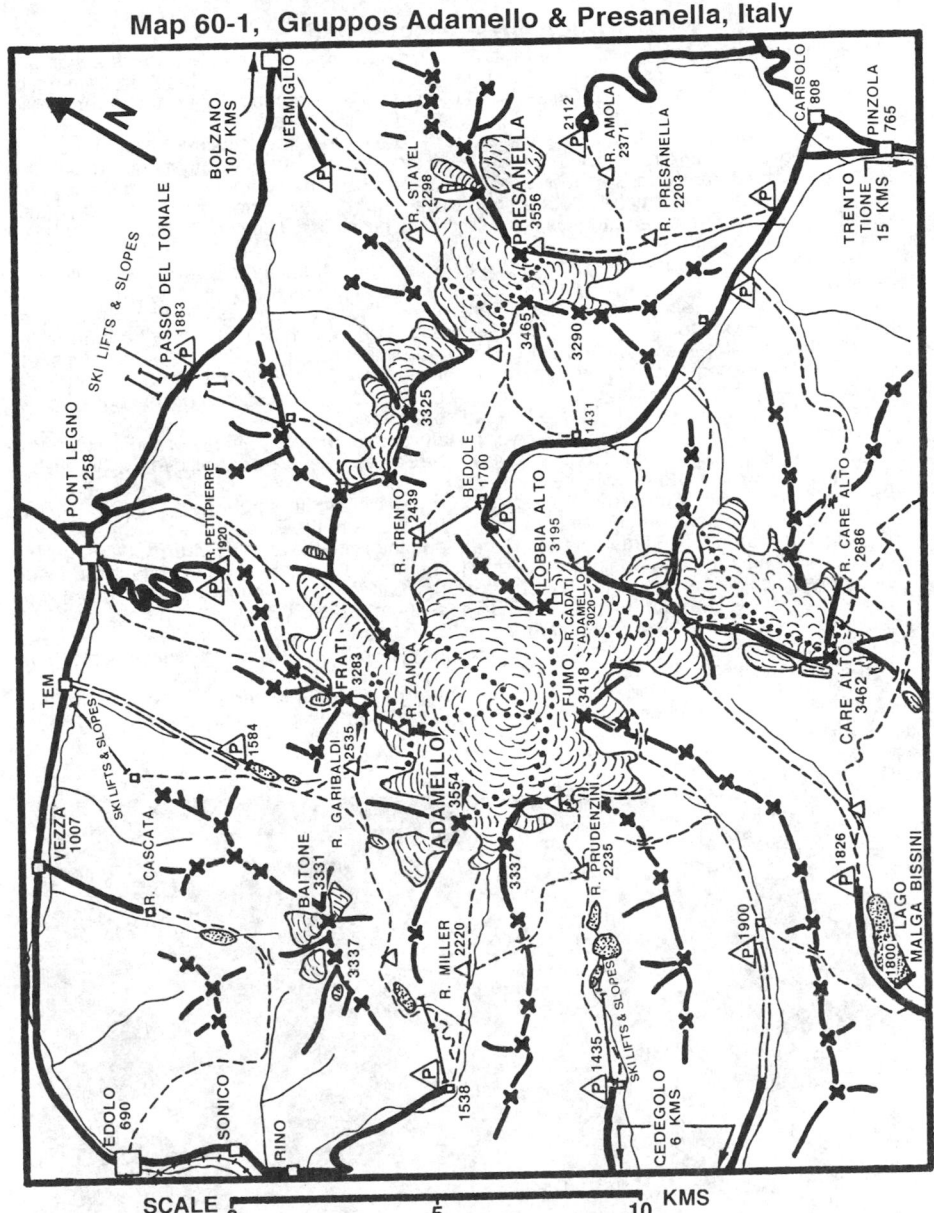

SCALE 0   5   10 KMS

mountain valleys just to the north, where German is often spoken.

The towns of Pinzolo, Edolo and Vermiglio are the biggest communities in the area, so they are the best places to buy food. To buy more-detailed maps and possibly guidebooks, better shop in Trento, a bigger city further to the east. Tione is just south of this mapped area and it's a larger town.

Maps *Brenta-Adamello-Presanella, 50,* 1:100,000, from Freytag und Berndt, Wien (look for Italiano maps); and a travel guidebook to Italia.

Ortler, Ortlergruppe, Italy

In an area west of Bolzano in northern Italia, is located the Ortlergruppe. This is a high and glaciated massif and ranks as one of the best snow and ice climbing places in Italia. The highest peak is Ortler (in Italiano, *Ortles*) at 3902 meters. In addition, there are several other summits in this group at 3700 meters and higher.

Getting to this mountain group is fairly easy. There's a rail line passing through Laas, the only possibility of using train service in the area. In the western part of this mapped area, buses hopefully can be taken from Bolzano to as far as Bormio. The rest of the nearby roads are mountain routes, with holiday travelers driving to various resorts in the area. The author hitch hiked to Trafoi from where he made his climb, but hitch hiking is a little slow in Italia. If you're on foot, rent a car if you can.

Ortler can be climbed from either Trafoi or Sulden, via the Payer Hutte at 3020 meters, located on the north ridge. Beyond this hut, is one section of *iron route*, or steel cables. It's an interesting climb, despite the cables, and is quite easy. After the author camped not far above. Next morning, 7/27/1979, he walked to the Payer Hutte and beyond to the summit. That took 4 hours; 6 1/2 hours round-trip. He spent a 2nd night at the same campsite.

Another nearby peak just southeast across a glacier from Ortler is **Konigs** at 3859 meters. It can be climbed from Sulden and the Schaubachutte (just up the valley to the south); or St. Caterina and the Rifugio Pizzine, situated on the south side of the peak.

Also from the Sulden Valley, one can scale **Vertain Spitze** rising to 3544 meters, located north of the main Ortlergruppe. The normal route passes by the Zaytal Hutte. One can also reach this peak by way of Prud, and **Hochwand** at 3123 meters.

San Matteo at 3684 meters, is another high peak normally ascended from the Rifugio Branca, but other routes can be used; including the one from the Cagolo area. There's also a trail to the top of **Zufall**, 3764 meters from Cagolo and the Rifugio Larcher. **Zufritt**, 3438 meters, is in the northeast, and can easily be climbed from either Zufrittsee, or the St. Gertraud side. Another easy climb is up **Vioz** at 3640 meters. A trail reaches this summit from Cagolo.

The one best valley from which to climb several mountains is Sulden, where a couple of small stores exist. Sulden is a big winter resort, as are many other villages in these high valleys. Many people on the northern side of the Ortlergruppe are German speaking; while people in the other parts speak mostly Italiano.

Being on the southern side of the Alps, the Ortlergruppe generally has better weather than mountains to the north and west. However, there are still lots of big glaciers, so don't forget your ice ax & crampons.

The north ridge of Ortler as seen from the Payer Hutte.

Map 61-1, Ortler, Ortlergruppe, Italy

The biggest cities in the area are Bolzano, Italia, and Innsbruck, Austria. Plan to buy most of your food and other supplies in either of these places before you arrive in this area. If better detailed maps are required, you can find them in either of these cities.

Maps *Ortler, 46*, 1:100,000, from Freytag und Berndt, Wien; Kompass also has good maps of this area; and a travel guidebook to Italia.

Piz Buin and Silvretta, Silvretta Gruppe, Switzerland-Austria

The well-known Silvretta Gruppe is located on the Swiss-Austrian border near the point where these 2 countries and Liechtenstein meet. This group is due east of Davos, and northeast of San Moritz, in extreme eastern Switzerland. It's also south of Arlberg and St. Anton--but you have to drive over or around a couple of mountain ranges to arrive from those places.

Little public transport exists in the immediate area. Your best bet is getting bus service east from Davos to Susch and Scuol; or perhaps there are buses running north from San Moritz (?). About the only way of getting around the immediate area is to have your own vehicle, rent one, or hitch hike. Getting short lifts is easy with a sign stating the number of kms to a nearby destination.

Climbing routes are about equally distributed on both sides of the border, but the Austrian side may offer slightly easier and shorter routes to most of the summits. Northern routes will always involve more snow & ice climbing than from the south slopes.

The highest peak in this group is **Piz Buin** at 3312 meters. It's normally climbed from the Weisbadener Hutte, located on the north slope, but can also be reached from the Shamanna Hutte on the south. **Silvretta** or **Silvrettahorn**, 3244 meters, for which the group is named and most famous peak in the area, can be climbed from either Weisbadener Hutte, or Silvretta Hutte to the west.

Not part of the Silvretta Gruppe, **Fluchthorn** to the east at 3399 meters, can be scaled from either the Jamtal or Heidelberger Huttes; while **Augstenberg** at 3228 meters, is best approached from Jamtal Hutte.

For those wanting only rock to climb, try **Piz Linard**, 3411 meters. It's the highest peak on this map, but not part of the Silvretta Gruppe. Use the route passing through Lavin and the Chamanna (hut) del Linard.

Included on this map, but actually a part of the Sesvennagruppe, is **Piz Lischana**, 3105 meters. There's only one real approach to this peak and that's via Scuol and the Chamanna Lischana. Also included here is a peak which is part of the Albulagruppe. This is the **Flüela Weisshorn**, 3085 meters. Climb this one from Wegehaus or the Flüela Hospiz. Inquire at one of these locations as to the exact route.

In the vicinity, several small towns exist where food supplies can be bought; Susch and Scuol in Switzerland; or St. Gallenkirch, Galtur, and Ischgl in Austria. Best places to find maps of the area would be Innsbruck or St. Anton, Austria; or San Moritz or Davos in Switzerland. These last

The northern slopes and glacier of Piz Buin (Walter Pause foto).

Map 62-2, Piz Buin & Silvretta, Silvretta Group, Switzerland-Austria

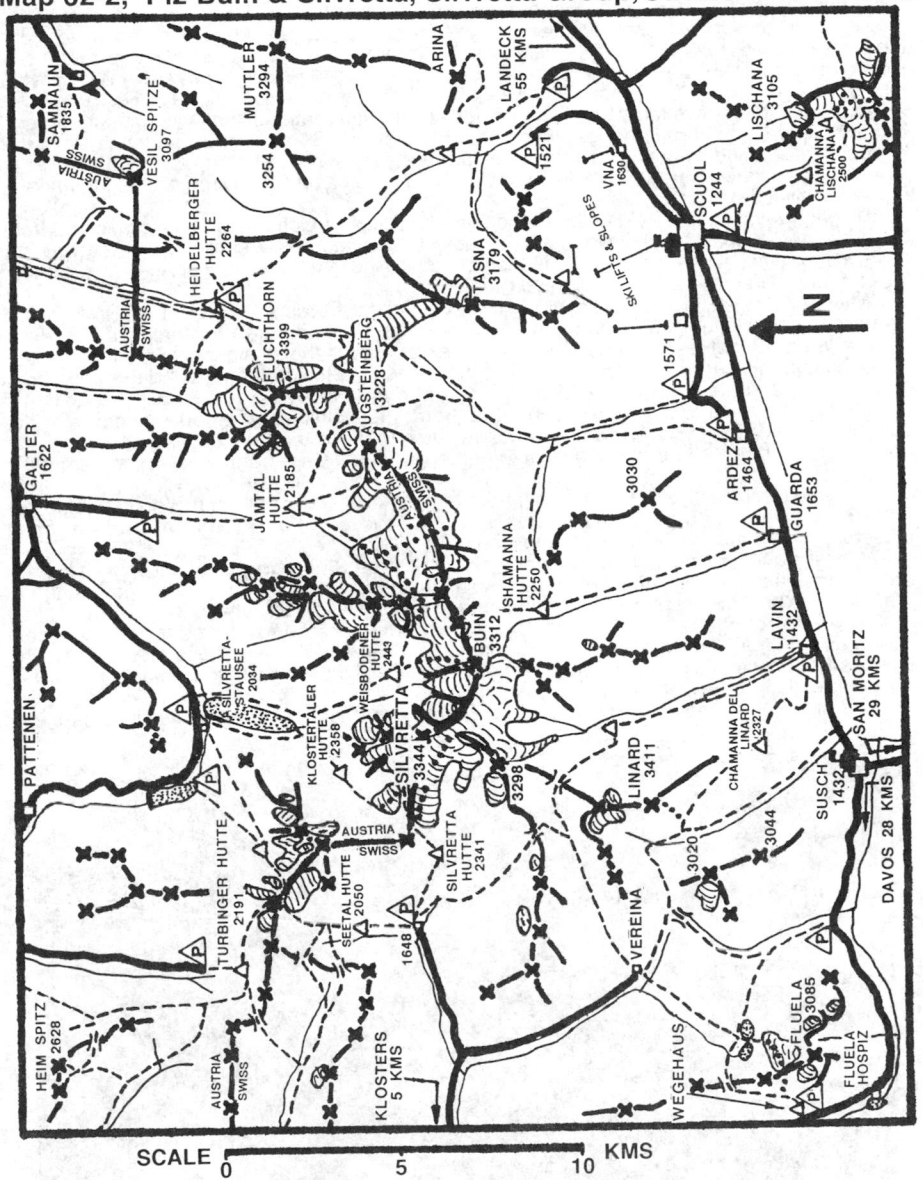

SCALE 0   5   10   KMS

2 cities would be the best places of all to shop for food, maps, guidebooks or information.

For exact routes high on the peaks, consult someone at a nearby hutte. For the most part, any peak over about 3000 meters and climbed from the north, will require ice ax & crampons.

Maps *Ratikon-Silvretta-Verwallgruppe, 37,* 1:100,000, from Freytag und Berndt, Wien; and perhaps a book (?), **Silvretta Alps**, contact Cordee Books, UK; and perhaps a travel guidebook to Switzerland or Italia.

Wildspitze, Otztaler Alpen, Austria

About 72 highway kms southwest of Innsbruck lies the Otztaler Alpen, an area of high and glaciated mountains. The highest and best-known peak on this map is Wildspitze at 3772 meters. It's the second highest peak in Austria. This group, the Otztaler Alpen, is covered in 2 maps. This one includes peaks in the western and northern portions, mostly west of Solden. The next map covers the east and southern parts. The famous 5000 year old Ice Man was found somewhere in these parts.

Access to the area is fairly good, with a not-so-busy international highway running through Solden. There may or may not be buses on that highway. Southwest of Solden is Vent, the most convenient and centrally located village in the region for climbing purposes; but very likely it has no bus service (?). Vent would make the best *base camp* for anyone wishing to make a number of climbs in the region.

The highways leading to Mittelberg and the lake called Speicher Gepatsch branch off from the busy international highway west of Innsbruck. From that main highway you'll likely have to drive your own car, or hitch hike. The author found hitching generally good in Austria; just make a sign stating a nearby destination and you should get a lift quickly.

Wildspitze can be climbed most easily from Vent and the Breslauer Hutte, but also from the Braunschweiger Hutte, located on the north slope. The route up from Vent makes a very easy climb to Wildspitze, at least that was the author's experience in the summer of 1979.

On the morning of 7/22/1979, he got a quick ride from below Solden to Vent, walked about one hour and setup his tent at 2200 meters about halfway up to the Breslauer Hutte. Afterwards, he hiked to the hutte in about an hour, then climbed for another 2 hours to the summit. It took about 4 hours from Vent to the summit; round-trip from camp took less than 5 hours. The northern route starting from Mittelberg is much longer and involves more glacier travel.

From the Hochjoch Hospiz, or at least from that direction, one can climb **Weisskugel**, 3739 meters, or **Dahmann Spitze**, 3401 meters. This seems to be the normal route to each mountain, but the author has no information on route difficulty.

Along a big ridge running north from this main massif is **Glockturm**, 3355 meters. It can be climbed from either Gepatsch Haus or the Hohenzoller Hutte. Along another big north ridge is **Wazespitze**, 3533 meters; it can be ascended from either the Verpeillhutte or Kaunergrat Hutte.

You're not obligated to use these huttes, but they are good places to get the latest information on trail conditions and routes. You can camp anywhere in these mountain for the most part, but hutte keepers generally frown on people camping too close to the shelters.

Besides the climbs just mentioned there are many more in this area, most of which require ice ax & crampons. The area to the left, or the southwest corner of the map, is in Italia. If you

The Breslauer Hutte on the south face of Wildspitze.

Map 63-1, Wildspitze, Otztaler Alpen, Austria

SCALE 0 ———— 5 ———— 10 KMS

climb from that side, you'll have mostly trails and rock climbing; as opposed to snow climbing on the Austrian or northern side.

Solden is a good place to stock up on food, as it's by far the largest town in the immediate area. Innsbruck isn't far away either so shop there is you can. There are also a couple of small stores in Vent, as well as hotels and cafes. Vent is no doubt bigger now than in 1979.

Maps *Otztaler Alpen, 25*, 1:100,000, from Freytag und Berndt, Wien; and perhaps a travel guidebook to Austria.

Hintere Schwarze, Otztaler Alpen, Austria-Italy

The Otztaler Alpen, a large group of high and glaciated peaks southwest of Innsbruck, is covered in 2 maps. The previous map covered the Wildspitze area, while this one shows the southeastern section, which straddles the Italian-Austrian border south of Vent.

Getting to this area is reasonably easy. Your first destination is Solden. To get there from Innsbruck, head west to Telfs, then west again on Highway E17 for 20 kms, then turn south toward Solden, which is immediately north of this mapped area. There may or may not be bus service to Solden (?). From there drive or hitch hike south into one of 2 main valleys. Vent is completely surrounded by high peaks, but Obergurgl is another good access point to high summits.

If you're coming from the south, first go to Bolzano, then head north-northwest toward Merano, then over the border to Solden. Or head to Naturns and Karthaus and beyond. There's no public transport to the valley around Karthaus.

One notable peak on the Italian side is **Lodner Spitze**, 3279 meters. The normal route to this summit is via Partschins, the Lodner Hutte, and the northwest slopes. North of Lodner Spitze, is **Hochwilde** at 3482 meters. It can be approached from either the Italian side via Eisjoch Hutte; or from the Austrian or north side, via the Hochwildehaus or hutte, located southwest of Obergurgl.

Going further west, the next important climb is **Hintere Schwarze**, 3628 meters. It's the highest peak south of the Vent area. The normal route here is via Solden, Vent, the Martin Busch Hutte and either the north or west ridges.

Next in line to the west is **Similaun** at 3606 meters. It can be scaled from the south via Karthaus, Rafein Hutte, Similaun Hutte, and the northwest ridge; or from the north side and Vent, the Martin Busch Hutte, and either a direct approach to the summit or via the Similaun Hutte.

Weisskugel, 3739 meters, can be climbed via the Italian side (see Wildspitze map) or the northeast approach, via Solden, Vent, the Hochjoch Hospiz, over the long Hintereisferner (glacier), and the south ridge.

Only the southern route to **Wildspitze** is shown on this map--for the north approach see Wildspitze (previous) map. The route from Solden, Vent, the Breslauer Hutte, is by far the shortest and easiest to Austria's second highest peak, at 3772 meters.

If you were to choose one valley or town in which to make a *base camp,* it would have to be the village of Vent. Vent has a couple of stores, plus many hotels and cafes.

For directions to other peaks in the area, the best place to get information is at the hutte nearest the mountain you want to climb. Needless to say, with all the glaciers around you'll need an ice ax & crampons on almost every climb. Some routes on the south slopes can be

Looking southwest from Vent with its picturesque church.

Map 64-1, Hintere Schwarze, Otztaler Alpen, Austria-Italy

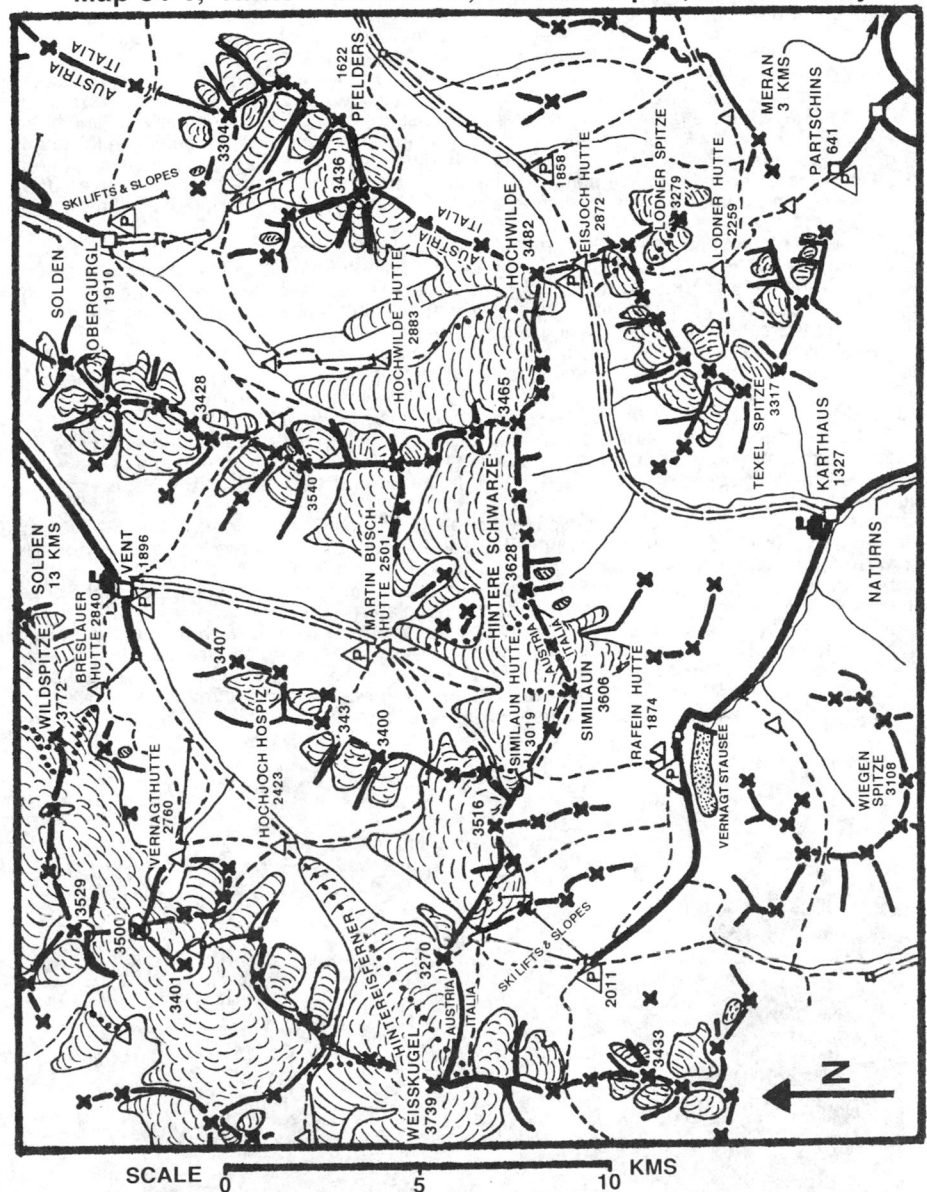

SCALE 0 — 5 — 10 KMS

snow-free in late summer. To buy better maps and perhaps a guidebook to this area, stop in Innsbruck to the north.

Maps *OtztalerAlpen, 25,* 1:100,000, from Freytag und Berndt, Wien; and perhaps a travel guidebook to Austria.

Zuckerhutl & Schrankogel, Stubaier Alpen, Austria

In the region just southwest of Innsbruck, Austria, is a high mountain range called the Stubaier Alpen. This group is immediately east and northeast of both Solden and another group known as the Otztaler Alpen. Those peaks are discussed on the 2 previous maps.

If you're driving from Innsbruck, head west 26 kms to Telfs, then west again on N13 for 20 kms and turn south and drive toward the Solden area. You can also drive north from Bolzano on the Italian side. Or drive due south from Innsbruck, but at Schonberg, veer southwest and head for Ranalt. From the valley above Ranalt you can climb almost all the major peaks on this map. Public transport is probably available to Solden, but there's likely no buses into the Ranalt area (?). Once into these valleys, someone who looks like a mountain climber can hitch hike rather easily, especially if you hold a sign stating a nearby destination, or the number of kms you're going.

There are a number of interesting peaks here with varying degrees of difficulty. The highest of the group is **Zuckerhutl** at 3507 meters. It can be climbed from either Dresdner Hutte on the north, or Hildesheimer Hutte on the southwest slopes. This latter route is the one the author used in 1979, and in good weather, it was a very easy climb following a trail in the snow. But there are crevasses in these north-facing glaciers, so be careful.

Here's what the author did. From his camp on Wildspitze (see previous map), he walked down to Vent and the first car to pass stopped and gave him a lift to Solden. From there he walked a short distance and setup his tent; then with small pack, headed up Zuckerhutl. From camp to summit took 4 hours; 7 1/2 hours round-trip. This was on 7/23/1979.

Wilder Freiger, 3418 meters, is normally climbed from Ranalt and the Nurnberger Hutte, located north of the peak; or from the Italian side and the Becher Hutte high on a ridge just south of the summit. **Feuerstein**, 3285 meters, can be scaled from either the Bremer or the Nurnberger Huttes.

Further north and west of the above mentioned summits, stands **Wilde Leck**, 3361 meters. The normal route to this summit is via Unter and the Amberger Hutte. Still further north is **Schrankogel**, 3486 meters. It can be climbed from either the Amberger or Franz Senn Huttes. Maps indicate this is an easy climb (?). Across the glacier to the northeast is **Ruderhof Spitze** at 3473 meters. Best to climb it from the Mutterbergalm area.

If you want to do a lot of climbing, perhaps the valley of Ranalt, with the Dresdner and Nurnberger Huttes, is the best choice for a making a base camp. One drawback to this valley is the lack of any larger towns for shopping. If you're going there, buy all your supplies in Innsbruck, located only about 30 kms away. If you prefer more detailed maps of the area get those in Innsbruck as well. While in Innsbruck, stop at the Austrian Alpen Club office near the

The northern slopes of Zuckerhutl (Walter Pause foto).

Map 65-1, Zuckerhutl & Schrankogel, Stubaier Alpen, Austria

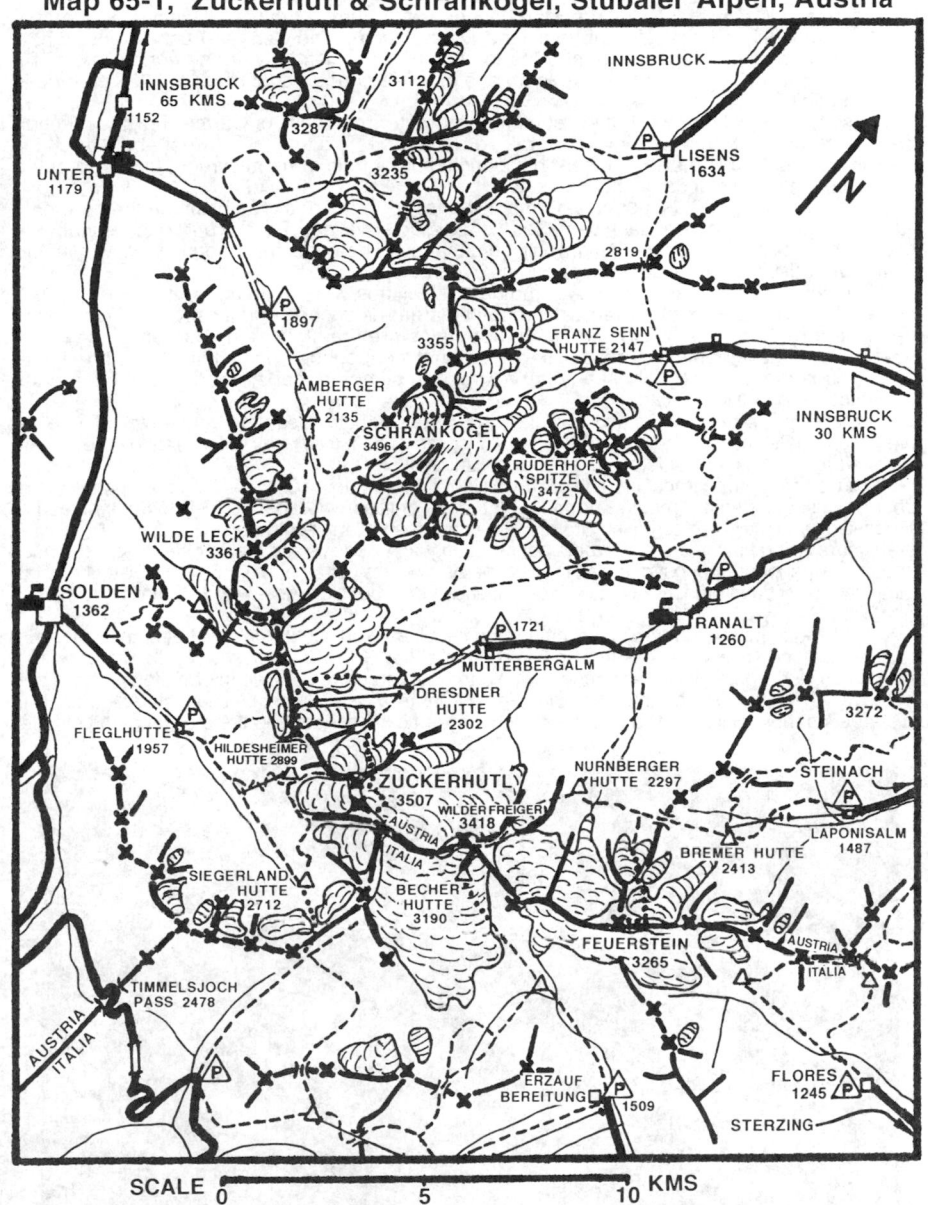

center of town, for further information about routes, huttes, etc.

Most routes on the higher summits in this region involve some snow and glacier travel, so ice ax & crampons are required. On the other hand, if you use one of the normal routes to a popular peak like Zuckerhutl, often times this equipment may not be needed, as the way is very much a *well-beaten path* in the snow right to the summit.

Maps *Stubaier Alpen, 24*, 1:100,000, from Freytag und Berndt, Wien; Cordee Books, UK, lists a book, **Stubai & South Tyrol**, that may updates this information.

Zugspitze, Bavarian Alpen, Germany-Austria

After World War II, those who drew the boundaries in Europe pretty well eliminated the Alps from Germany (those folks call their homeland *Deutschland*). The German-Austrian border now follows the northern-most ridge of the Alps, putting Germany entirely on the *north slope*. The highest summit in Germany therefore, is on one of those ridges. Zugspitze, at 2962 meters, is that high point.

Zugspitze is just southwest of the summer and winter resort city of Garmisch-Partenkirchen (G-P). You can get there by driving, or taking a bus or train south, southwest about 100 kms from Munchen. You can also get there by taking a bus or train from Innsbruck, Austria, located to the southeast, a distance of about 35 kms.

The summit area of this mountain forms a U-shaped valley or cirque basin on the northeast side and was once, not too many centuries ago, a glacier valley. Today you'll find remnants of that glacier but it's pretty small. Also, you'll be unhappy to hear there's a mountain railway to the summit of Zugspitze, but of course you can hike to the top for more merits.

Along with hiking, there are rock climbing possibilities with all degrees of difficulty. Only problem is, it's near a couple of large metropolitan areas--Munchen and Innsbruck. This makes the place a real tourist trap. Since these mountains are the highest in Germany, one would expect a lot of development. And that's exactly what's happened. If you think there are lots of trails on this map, you should see some hiking and climbing maps. Many trails have been eliminated here for simplicity.

This area has many ski lifts and funiculars that are used both in summer and winter. There are even 2 funiculars and one railway to the top of Zugspitze itself (if they're all still operating?). But there are also trails and several different ways to reach summit.

If you're using public transportation, start walking from downtown G-P, or hitch hike up the road to Ober or Eibsee to begin climbing **Zugspitze**. Or drive or road-walk south of G-P to the trailhead at 980 meters, and make the summit by trail from the east, then up the south slopes.

If you're using huts in the area, remember that July and August--and the weekends, are the busy times. Few people camp, but camping may be the best way to get a good night's sleep. Inquire about camping, it may be forbidden--at least in some places. But you might get away with making a bivouac for a night (?).

Little need to mention where you can buy food supplies. You could pick up a better trail guide in a bookstore which specializes in climbing literature in either G-P or Innsbruck. These 2 places also have alpen clubs, with offices and people who can give you more detailed information on trails and routes. Of the warm weather months, early September may be the most pleasant time for outings in this area, as most children and college students are back in school and the crowds much smaller.

Swiss farm houses. This is a common scene throughout the Alps of Switzerland.

Map 66-2, Zugspitze, Bavarian Alpen, Germany-Austria

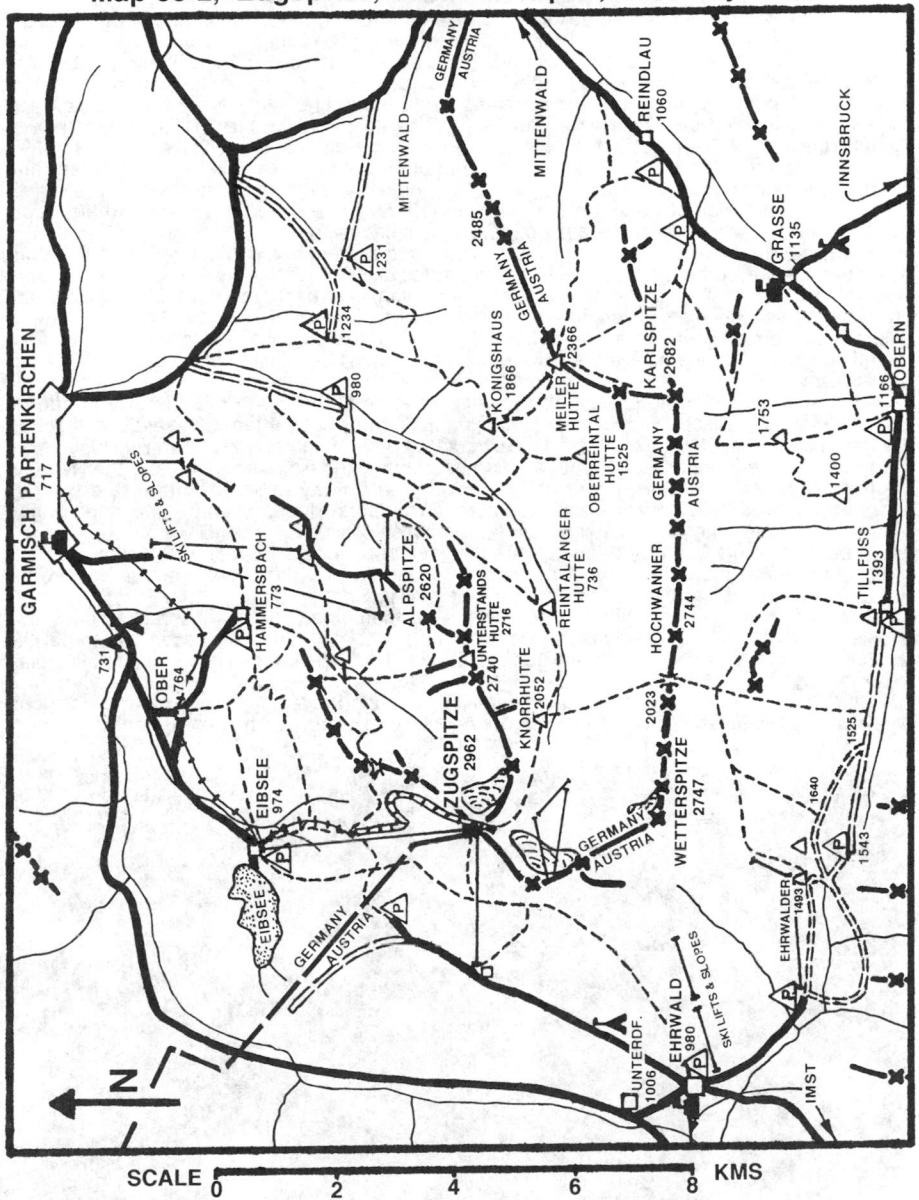

SCALE 0   2   4   6   8 KMS

Little need for snow or ice climbing equipment, at least in late summer or early fall. In early summer you may need an ice ax & crampons however. Or skis in winter.

Maps *Wettersteingebirge, 34*, 1:100,000, from Freytag und Berndt, Wien; and perhaps the guidebook, **Zugspitze Bavaria**, Rother Walking Guide.

Hochfeiler & Olperer, Zillertaler Alpen, Austria-Italy

In an area southeast of Innsbruck lies the Zillertaler Alpen, which has a number of medium sized peaks & glaciers. The highest summit is Hochfeiler, at 3510 meters.

The 2 most common routes of approach to the Zillertaler Alpen are; from the south via Bolzano, Brixen, Bruneck, then to Luttach and Prettau, as shown on this map. There may or may not be bus service into this upper valley. From the north the normal route is from Innsbruck, Wiesing, Zell, and Mayrhofen. Mayrhofen is the best place to make your headquarters if you plan to climb several peaks. To reach the valleys above Mayrhofen, you'll have to drive your own car or hitch hike.

There are no rail lines even close from the south, but there is a line to Mayrhofen, and presumably train service (?). Bus service to Mayrhofen may or may not exist when you arrive. Mayrhofen is the biggest town on this map and it has bookstores and places to buy food; however Innsbruck is the best place to do most of your shopping.

To climb **Hochfeiler** via the normal route, it's best to approach from a different direction than described above. About halfway between Innsbruck and Bolzano is the Brenner Pass on the Austrian-Italian border. Just south of that is the Italian town of Sterzing, which has train and probably bus service. From Sterzing, drive or hitch hike northeast toward the Pfitscher Hutte, a distance of about 18 kms. To actually climb Hochfeiler, make your way to Hochfeiler Hutte first, then the summit. An alternate route is via the Eisbruggjoch Hutte just to the south. This part of Italia is known as Sudtyrol (South Tyrol) and is mostly German speaking.

Along the same high ridge east of Hochfeiler, stands **Moseler** at 3478 meters. It can be climbed from the Furtschagl or Berliner Huttes on the north slope; or the Neveser Joch Hutte on the Italian side. Next to Moseler stands **Turnerkamp** at 3418 meters. It's normally scaled from the north and the Berliner Hutte, but can also be approached from the south and the Neveser Joch Hutte at 2420 meters. East of Turnerkamp are many other prominent peaks with interesting routes and all having some glaciation on the north slopes. Many south slope routes may be rock climbs only, but take an ice ax & crampons for climbing any facing north.

In the northern section of this map sits the 2nd highest peak, **Olperer**, 3480 meters. It's entirely within Austria and can be climbed from the Geraer or Spannagel Huttes. This area is more developed with several ski lifts and is a winter ski resort.

If additional information is needed, contact the Austrian Alpen Club in Innsbruck. That's also the best place to pick up good maps. For any particular mountain, the best place to get the latest information on trail or route conditions, is at one of the alpen huttes near the peak you plan to climb.

Most climbing is done during the months of July through September, but June also has good weather. Early September might be the very best time to climb, as children are back in school

Some high mountain meadows are still trimmed with a sickle.

Map 67-3, Hochfeiler & Olperer, Zillertaler Alpen, Austria-Italy

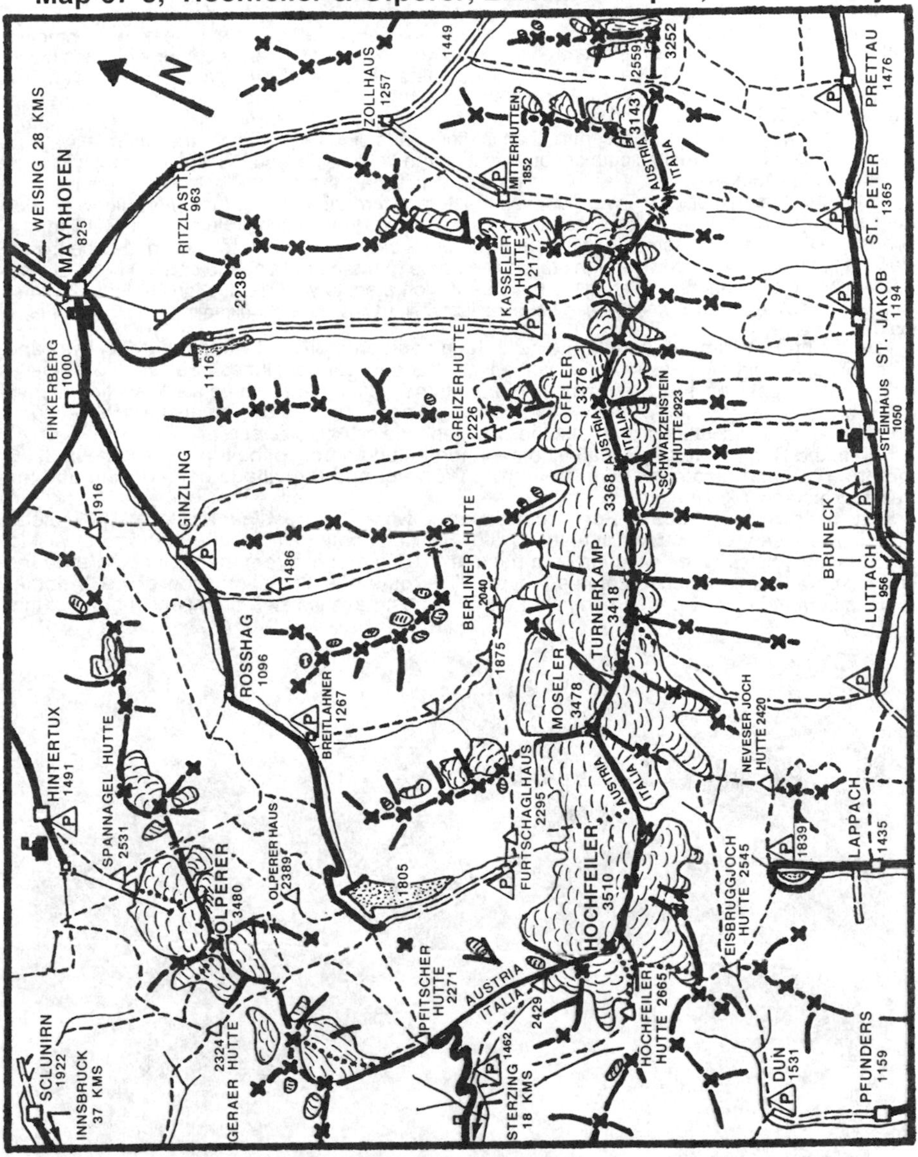

and the crowds smaller.

Maps *Zillertaler Alpen, 15,* 1:100,000, from Freytag und Berndt, Wien; Kompass also makes good maps for climbing; and perhaps a travel guidebook to Austria or Italia.

Hochgall & Ruthner Horn, Rieserfernergruppe, Austria-Italy

Located on the border of northern Italia and southwest Austria, is a small mountain range known as the Rieserfernergruppe. This compact massif is located just southeast of Hochfeiler in the Zillertaler Alpen shown on the previous map; and south of Grossvenediger which is shown on the next map. This is not a large area, but it has a couple of fairly high summits, with many easy routes and a few difficult ones as well. The highest peak is Hochgall at 3435 meters. Ruther Horn, 3377 meters is 2nd highest.

This is a remote area, with less traffic than in other parts of the Alps. There are 2 normal ways to approach this area. From the south or southwest on the Italian side, you must pass through Brixen, Bruneck and to Anterselva; or to Rain on the left side of this map; thence into the higher mountains.

From the Austrian or East Tyrol side, you must pass through Lienz or Matrei on Highway 108, then west up a narrow secondary road to Erisbach and/or the Patscher Hutte. You will find bus service on this road, but sometimes it's faster to rent a car and drive. Hitch hiking may be a little slow. If hitching, always have a sign stating the name of the mountain, and/or town nearest your destination. Or a simply sign stating the number of kilometers to your destination (10 kms, 20 kms, etc.) works well, especially when you're traveling just a short distance. Looking like an alpenist helps too.

Here's how to climb **Hochgall**. Its north face has some difficult routes, but the easy and normal way is from the eastern side, via the Patscher and Barmer Huttes. Below you'll follow a trail, then at a pass east of the summit, the route turns west and has some steep sections. Part of the route is on ice & snow--but it's considered an easy climb. You can also reach Hochgall from the south and southeast and from the Oberseehutte or Antholzersee.

From the Barmer Hutte you can also walk north along a trail to the top of **Lenkstein**, 3236 meters. You can also climb Lenkstein from the west and the village named Rain and the trailhead marked 1733 meters.

Another summit is **Ruthner Horn**, sometimes known as **Schneebiger Nock** at 3377 meters. This is a very easy climb. Start at Anterselva or Schwarz, both to the south. Head northwest to the Gansebichljock Hutte which is on a pass at 2799 meters. From there climb north to the summit on a trail; or at least a marked route. This route has almost no snow or ice. Another route is from the north via the Hochgall Hutte. You must have ice ax & crampons for part of this

A glacier on the northeast part of Hochgall (Walter Pause foto).

Map 68-3, Hochgall, Ruthner Horn, Rieserfernergruppe, Austria-Italy

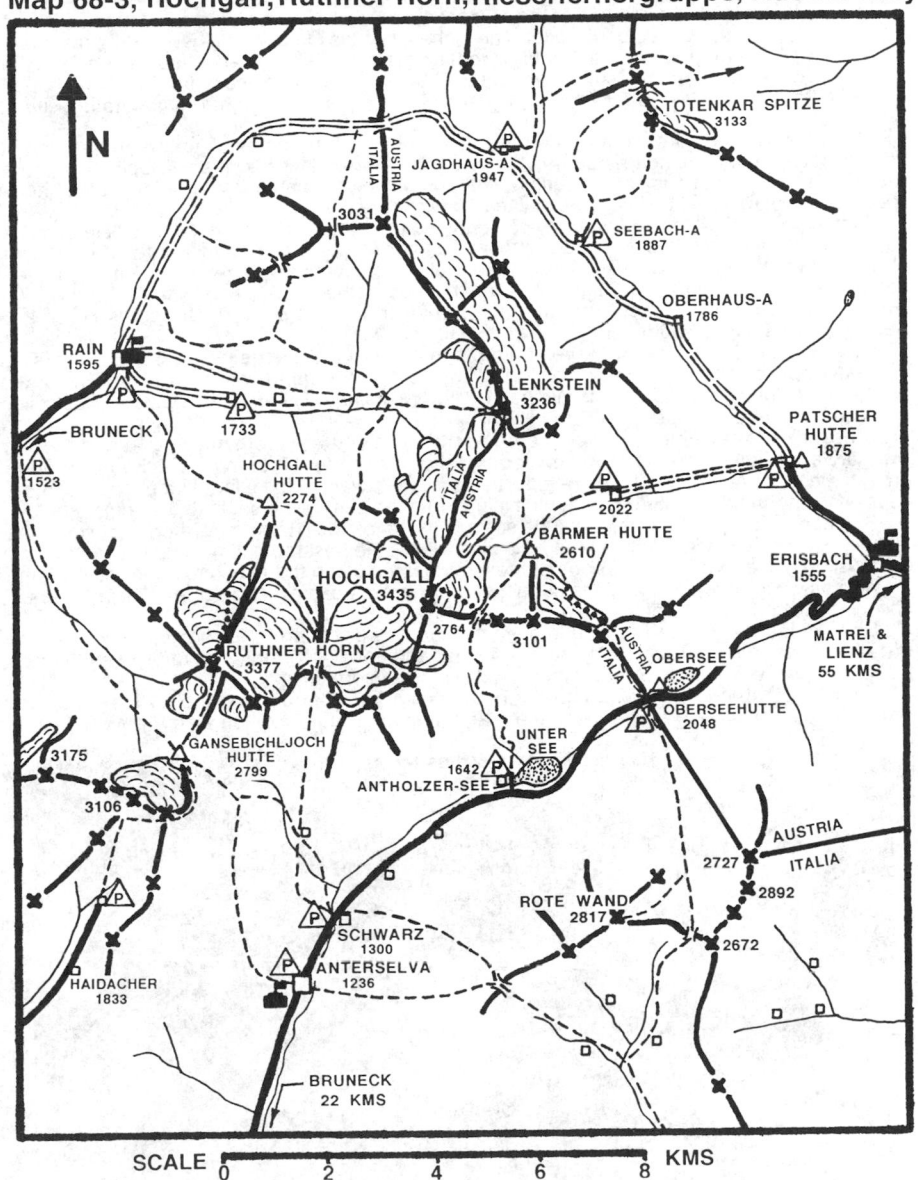

SCALE 0   2   4   6   8   **KMS**

north face climb.

The last places to shop in the area would be Bruneck, Lienz or Matrei. Buy all your supplies before going into these mountains. If you're unsure of the final route on the mountain, the best place to get that information is at the hutte nearest your climb. June, July, August or September are the best months for mountaineering or hiking in these parts.

Maps *Zillertaler Alpen, 15*, 1:100,000, from Freytag und Berndt, Wien; and perhaps a travel or hiking guidebook to Austria or Italia.

Grossvenediger & Rotespitze, Venedigergruppe, Austria

Included on this map are some of the highest peaks and largest glaciers in Austria. This is the area known as the Venedigergruppe. The highest peak is Grossvenediger at 3674 meters.

The top of this map is located roughly 4 to 8 kms south of Krimml and Neukirchen; and the southeastern corner is about 6 kms northwest of Matrei. The southwest corner of this mapped area is part of Italia. It's about 41 kms from Prettau (on this map) to the small Italian city of Bruneck.

There's a rail line coming from the northeast, running through Neukirchen and ending at Krimml, but there may no longer be train service. But there may be buses available (?). There should be some kind of bus service running through Matrei, but not to Prettau. To get into these upper valleys you'll need to drive your own car or hitch hike.

Grossvenediger is located near the center of the group and is surrounded by glaciers, but is rated an easy climb--at least in good weather. The normal route is from the north and the town of Neukirchen, by road to Obersulzbach Hutte, walking to Kursinger Hutte at 2562 meters, then climbing east, then south to the summit. From the south, the *normal weg*, is from the towns of Matrei, Pragraten and Hinterbichl, then up a good trail north past the Johannis Hutte and Defregger Haus; thence north, northwest to the summit.

Other peaks in the area make excellent climbs also. **Grossgeiger** at 3360 meters, is normally approached from the north and the town of Krimml, past Tauernhaus to the Warnsdarfer Hutte. It could also be climbed from the Kursinger Hutte; or the Essener-Rostocker Hutte on the southern slope.

Rotespitze, 3495 meters, lies on the Austrian-Italian border. From the west and the Italian side, drive to Kasern, walk to the Lenkjochl Hutte, thence to the summit via the north ridge. From the east or Austrian side, drive to Hinterbichl, then walk to the Clara Hutte, and up to the pass on the north ridge, where both routes join. From the pass climb south to the summit.

Reichen Spitze, 3303 meters, can be scaled via Gerlos Pass or Krimml, then from either the Zittauer or Richter Huttes. Ask the hutte keepers what's the best route to the summit.

Most people spend a night in one of these huts, then climb to the summit and return home the next day. However, if conditions permit, strong climbers can ascend some of these peaks in one long day from the end of the road.

Some of the last places in which to buy food supplies are Matrei, Neukirchen, or Krimml, as the villages on this map are pretty small. To get additional information and/or maps, stop in Innsbruck, the best place in all of Austria to get climbing information.

If you're climbing during the months of July or August, and using the huttes, avoid the weekends, as local people overcrowd them at that time. Better take ice ax & crampons for all

The northwest face & glacier of Grossvenediger (Walter Pause foto).

Map 69-3, Grossvenediger & Rotespitze, V. Gruppe, Austria

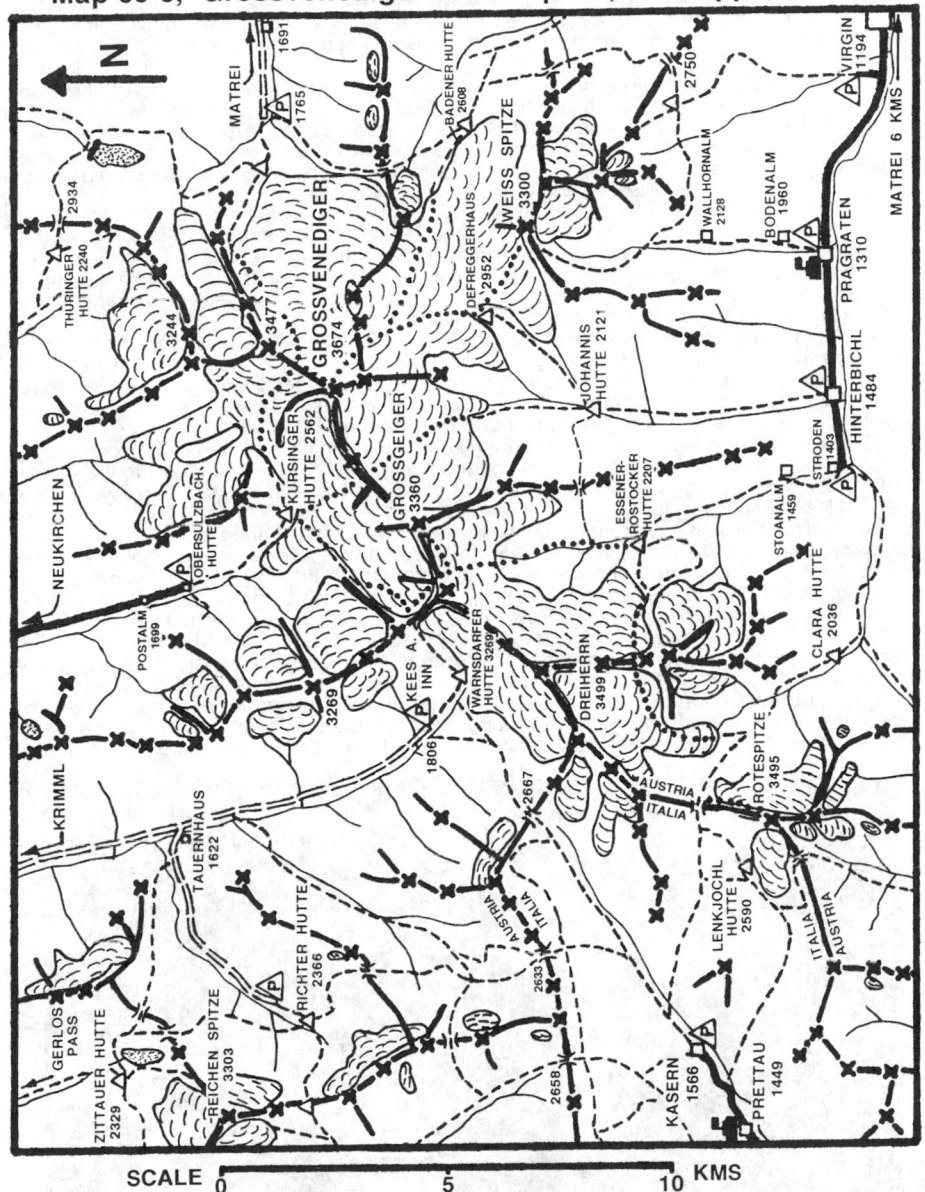

SCALE 0 ____ 5 ____ 10 KMS

the higher peaks. As in other mountain areas in Austria, the easy or normal routes are heavily traveled, so finding the way is generally easy, even on the glaciers.

Maps *Glockner und Venedigergruppe, 12,* 1:100,000, from Freytag und Berndt, Wien; and a travel guidebook to Austria.

Grossglockner, Glocknergruppe, Austria

The highest summit in Austria is a mountain called Grossglockner, with an altitude of 3797 meters. Grossglockner is located in west central Austria about due south of Kitzbühel and Zell am See, and north of Lienz.

You can reach this area by driving Highway 108 which runs south from Kitzbühel to Matrei and Lienz; or Highway 107 which runs between Zell am See & Bruck in the north, past Heiligenblut, to Lienz in the south. There are no rail lines in this immediate area, but trains run east-west in the valley to the north and through Bruck, Zell am See and Mittersill; and to the Lienz area to the south. Hopefully seasonal bus service still runs north-south on the 2 semi-major highways shown on this map. To get to the upper valley sites, you'll either need your own car, or hitch hike.

Grossglockner is one of the better climbs in Austria, and because it's the highest, it's very popular. The normal route or *normal weg,* has been made easy by a trail up a rocky ridge, then by hordes of people walking up a glacier, making a very good path in the snow. There's also a hutte high on the mountain, which encourages some people who ordinarily would not be there, to make the climb. Without the trail, snow path and hutte, this ascent would be more challenging. Elsewhere on the mountain, more difficult routes exist.

The beginning of the trail to **Grossglockner** is at the Hotel Franz Josefs at 2451 meters. At that place there's a 4 or 5 level parking lot needed to accommodate the thousands of tourists visiting the place each week. At this same complex are several small stores selling food and/or souvenirs, as well as prepared meals. There used to be a seasonal daily bus stopping at Franz Josef Hotel on the Zell am See-Heiligenblut-Lienz line (Ludwig Hendel).

From the parking lot, you can ride a lift (or hike) down to the glacier, then walk over the ice to a ridge. There a trail begins and follows first the ridge, then a route over snow to the Johann Hutte at 3454 meters; and finally to the summit. You can also ignore the lift and walk all the way, via the Hofmanns Hutte.

Here's what the author did. He hitch hiked to Heiligenblut, bough food, got information about the climb, then hitch hiked to the Hotel Franz Joseps. It was a miserable day, but he walked down to the glacier up the ridge on the other side and made camp at 2500 meters. Next morning, 7/21/1979, he hurried to the summit which was in the clouds, in just over 2 hours. Later that day, and with a sign reading Wildspitze, got to within a few kms of that peak.

Perhaps the second most important climb in the area is **Gross Wiesbachhorn**, at 3565 meters. It's located a few kms north of Grossglockner, and west of the resort of Ferleiten. The normal way up this peak is from the northwest side and the Schwaigerhaus at 2802 meters.

Both of these mountains and most others in the group, require at least an ice ax & crampons, as this is perhaps the most heavily glaciated area in Austria. Some of the places where food and supplies can be bought are Mittersill, Lienz, Bruck, Zell am See and a place

From near the Hofmanns Hutte looking southwest at Grossglockner.

Map 70-1, Grossglockner, Glocknergruppe, Austria

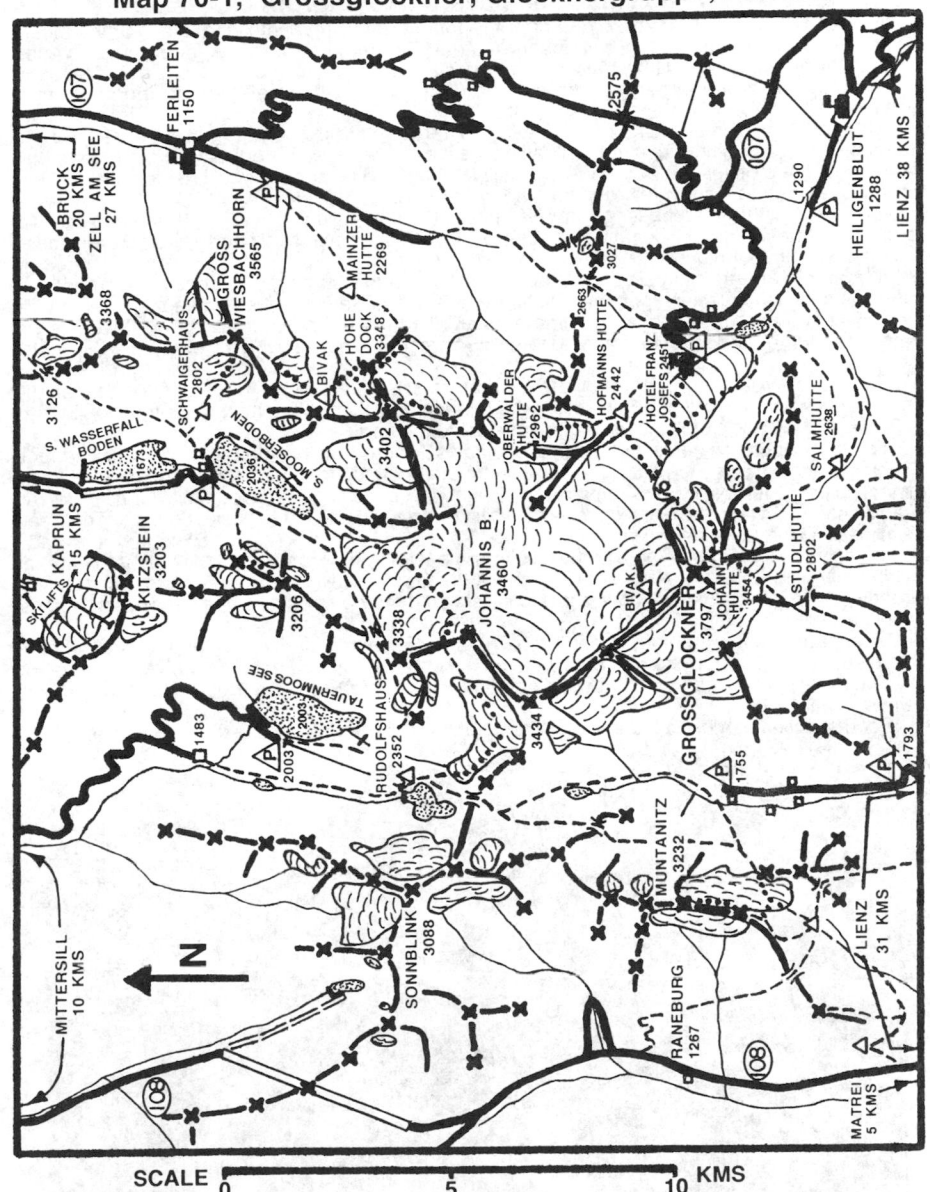

nearest the mountain, and a kind of climber's headquarters--Heiligenblut. This town has only one industry--tourism. It has many hotels, restaurants and small stores. It is to Grossglockner, what Chamonix is to Mont Blanc, and Zermatt is to Monte Rosa and the Matterhorn, only on a smaller scale. For additional information, contact the tourist office in Heiligenblut, or the Austrian Alpen Club in Innsbruck.

Maps *Glockner und Venedigergruppe, 12,* 1:100,000, from Freytag und Berndt, Wien; and for updated travel information, a guidebook to Austria.

Ankogel and Hochalmspitze, Ankogelgruppe, Austria

Almost due south of Salzburg and near the tourist resort town of Badgastein, is the most-easterly of the big glaciated mountains in Austria. The most famous peak here seems to be Ankogel at 3246 meters. However, the highest summit in this massif is Hochalmspitze, 3360 meters. East of Ankogelgruppe, the mountains are much lower elevation, and none have glaciers.

Getting to these mountains is quite easy. There should be both bus and train service to Badgastein, and maybe a rail stop at Mallnitz as well. There is no north-south highway in this same area that crosses the Alps--only the railway tunnel. This means you'll have to drive south from points north to Badgastein and into the upper valleys beyond. From the south you'll have to drive northeast from Lienz, or northwest from the Spittal area which is on Autobahn A10. To reach the eastern side of Hochalmspitze, exit A10 at Gmund and head northwest. Surely there are no buses on that highway, so drive your own car or hitch hike.

Ankogel is an easy climb as there are trails right to the summit. By choosing routes, you can have snow and glaciers, or if the regular route is used, there may be no need for even an ice ax. This of course depends on the time of year. The normal route from the northwest is via Badgastein and the Hanover Haus, located due west of the peak. Head east from the hutte. See map.

If you're approaching from the southwest, there are several ways of getting to the summit. The easiest is via Mallnitz, the Schwussnerhutte, then directly north to the top; or from Mallnitz to Schonberg, then north to Hanover Haus, and east to the peak.

To climb **Hochalmspitze**, you have a choice of 3 routes. If you desire a dry path and rock climbing all the way, use the Mallnitz-Schwussnerhutte route up to a pass called Trippkees at 2862 meters on the southwest ridge. From there head straight up the ridge to the summit. Or take the trail heading northwest from the Grossener Hutte, which is located south of the peak. From the Trippkees Pass, head up the same southwest ridge.

If you like glacier climbing or routes, use the eastern route passing the Villacher Hutte, at 2194 meters. But the more normal route is via the Grossener Hutte, then on the trail heading directly north. It usually has some snow to cross, so it may be best to have ice ax & crampons on this ascent.

Most people spend a night in one of the huts near the mountain, then on the second day, finish the climb and return home. But if you're physically fit and you have your own car, either of the above mountains can be climbed in one long day from one of the trailheads in the valleys below.

Food supplies can be found in Badgastein, Mallnitz or Gmund. If you'd like to buy good trail

If camping, you'll find lots of friendly but curious cows in the Alps.

Map 71-3, Ankogel & Hochalmspitze, Ankogelgruppe, Austria

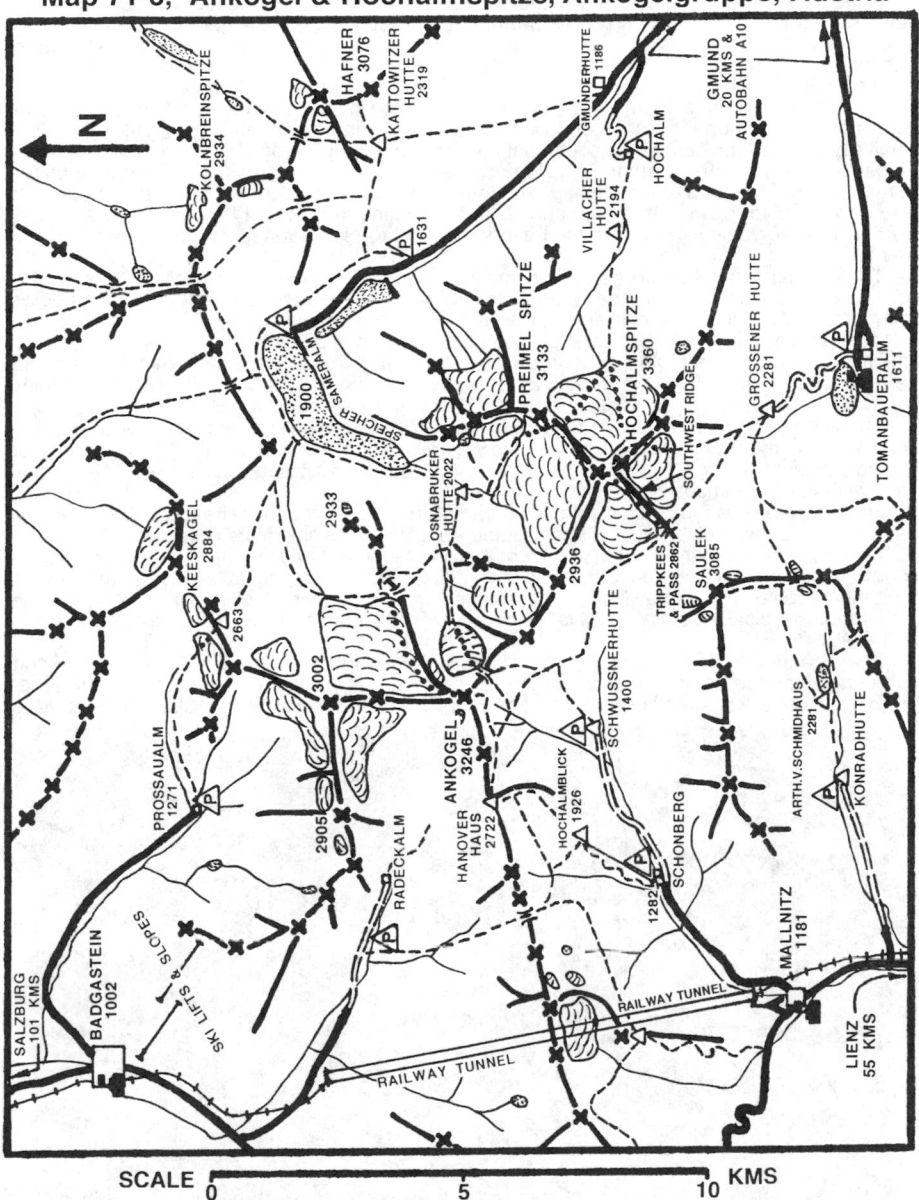

maps they can be found in the larger towns or cities such as Innsbruck, Salzburg, or Badgastein. July, August, September are the normal months for climbing, with September being the least crowded.

Maps *Goldberg-Ankogel, Radstadter Tauern, 19,* 1:100,000, from Freytag und Berndt, Wien; and perhaps a travel guidebook to Austria.

Tosa and Brenta, Gruppo Brenta, Italy

Immediately east of the Gruppo Adamello and Presanella, and just west of Trento in northern Italia, stands the Gruppo Brenta. This rather small cluster of peaks is geologically part of the Dolomiti--most of which lies east of Trento and Bolzano and not far south of the Austrian border. The rock here is dolomite, with many sheer faces. There are no glaciers in the Brenta, but some large snowfields exist.

The Brenta Group is a small area that is surrounded by good highways. Access is easy. Lots of public transport in the form of buses and trains run north-south through Trento which is a small city just 15 kms east of the southeast corner of this map. From Trento, a major highway runs west to Tione, then north to Pinzolo and Madonna di Campiglio. There should be buses from Trento to Madonna, but not many; and they may not exist when you get there. Your best way is to have your own car, or hitch hiking. Hitch hiking in northern Italy is only fair at best. Getting from the main highways to the trailheads is not too far, even if you have to walk all the way.

The highest summit in this group is **Cima Tosa** at 3173 meters. The normal route up this peak is via the trails passing the Rifugio Brentei on the northwest slopes; and the Rifugios Pedrotti & Tosa, both on the east side of the summit. The author isn't sure of the exact route, so ask someone at one of the rifugios. Both routes are probably steep climbs, and are rated more difficult than the normal routes up other peaks in the Alps. For all the author knows, this could be a real rock climb! From the Rifugio Brentei one route involves a very difficult snow couloir (see foto); while the way from Rifugio Pedrotti appears to be entirely on rock.

The second highest summit is **Cima Brenta**, 3150 meters. It can be ascended from the northwest and the Rifugio Tuckett. Maps show a trail running north-south along the east side of Brenta between Rifugio Stoppani in the north, and Rifugios Pedrotti & Tosa in the south. In this area you'll find the famous iron routes.

Just south of Tosa is **Cima Agola** at 2953 meters. A trail reaches the top of this peak via trails passing between the Rifugios Agostini and Apostoli and is said to be a walkup.

If you're climbing in this central portion of the Brenta, an ice ax & crampons should be taken, although they may not be needed, especially in late summer or early fall. Outside this central area there are few if any snowfields. The area is almost entirely rock climbing. The weather in the Brenta is typically *Dolomiti*, that is, with much more sunshine than in the Alps to the north and west.

The area around Madonna di Campiglio, is a winter resort with many ski lifts and runs. Food and equipment can be bought in any of the larger towns. If you need better maps of the area, the best place to buy them is in Trento. The Brenta is criss-crossed with trails, with a lot more

Cimi Tosa left, Crozzon de Brenta right, as seen from near the Rifugio Brentei.

Map 72-3, Tosa & Brenta, Gruppo Brenta, Italy

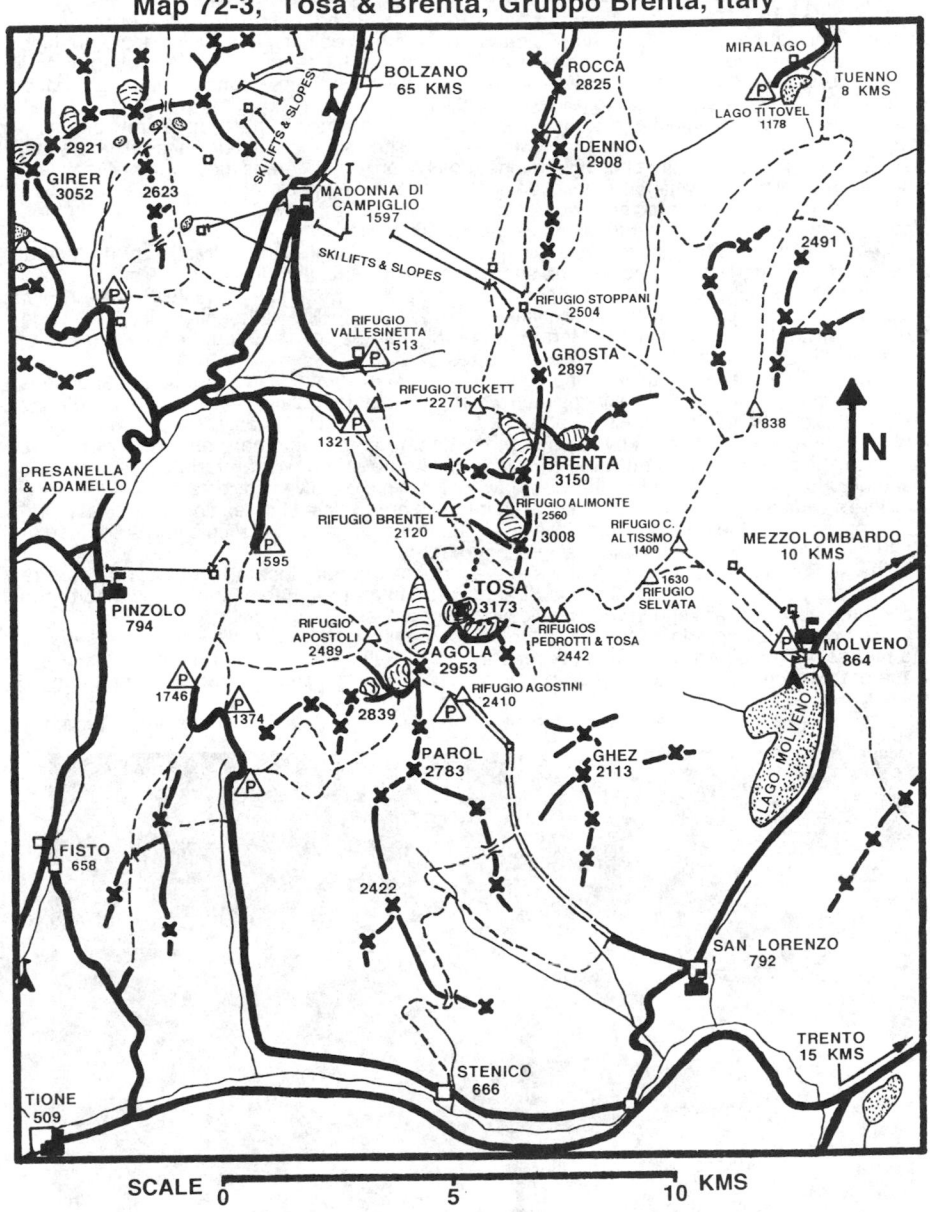

SCALE 0 ————— 5 ————— 10 KMS

than are shown on this simple sketch, so get a more detailed map than this.
Maps *Brenta-Adamello-Presanella, 50,* 1:100,000, from Freytag und Berndt, Wien; Cordee Books, UK, lists 3 guidebooks to this area, maybe more; **Trekking in the Dolomites**, Stedman, and **South Tyrol**, and **The Dolomites**.

Marmolata & Tofana di Mezzo, Dolomiti, Italy

The Dolomiti, or Dolomites, are that part of the Alps lying just south of the present-day Austrian-Italian border; also just east of Bolzano, and north of Belluno. The Dolomiti are not high or glaciated when compared to other parts of the Alps; the highest peak is Marmolata at only 3342 meters. But they have distinctive qualities, which make them among the most attractive mountains in all of Europe for hiking, climbing or skiing.

It's the rock which makes part of the difference--these peaks are made up entirely of a type of rock called *dolomite*, which is similar to limestone. The rock was laid down in ancient seas, then uplifted. To this day, the bedding remains mostly horizontal. Areas most weather-resistant stand as vertical towers with horizontal bedding high above the pine forests.

The weather is another factor. You can count on much better weather in the Dolomiti than elsewhere in the Alps. This is true for both summer and winter.

Keep in mind, this map covers a large area and lacks detail. Only a fraction of the actual trails, roads, and rifugios are shown here, so treat this only as an introduction to the area.

There are no railways into this mapped area, and bus service may be limited, so your best choices are to have your own car, or hitch hike (which is slow). The author hitch hiked into Lago Fadaia from Bolzano and climbed Marmolata in the summer of 1979, but he had some long waits. Renting a car is best if you want to move fast.

In all the Dolomiti, the glacier on the north slope of **Marmolata**, is the largest. Marmolata is normally climbed from the north and the dam which holds Lago Fadaia. There are trails heading up from the dam, but after a ways it's all snow to the summit. This is an easy climb with few if any crevasses. You'll find many ski lifts on that same slope which are apparently used 12 months of the year. A second route comes up from the south which starts at the trailhead marked 2080. This is a snow-free trail all the way. Expect big crowds any time of year!

Here's what the author did. He hitch hiked into this area with a sign reading, *Marmolata*, and was dropped off at the dam on Lago Fadaia. He left his big pack at the rifugio and started up at 10:30 am. The climb took only 2 hours up; 3 hours round-trip.

The second highest cluster of peaks is the Tofana Gruppe, located just west of Cortina. Unfortunately, the highest peak, **Tofana di Mezzo**, 3244 meters, has a lift of some kind to the top. There are also trails and several rifugios in the group, so hiking is still popular.

Just north of Campitello, is another group of high peaks, with **Langkofel**, 3181 meters, being the highest. These peaks can best be reached from Sella Pass at 2214 meters. The north slope of this group has many ski lifts, as well as trails. See a picture of this group on the next page.

It you're a hiker or climber, and plan to be in the area for a while, it's recommended you buy

The north face of Marmolata on a busy weekend.

Map 73-1, Marmolata & Tofana di Mezzo, Dolomiti, Italy

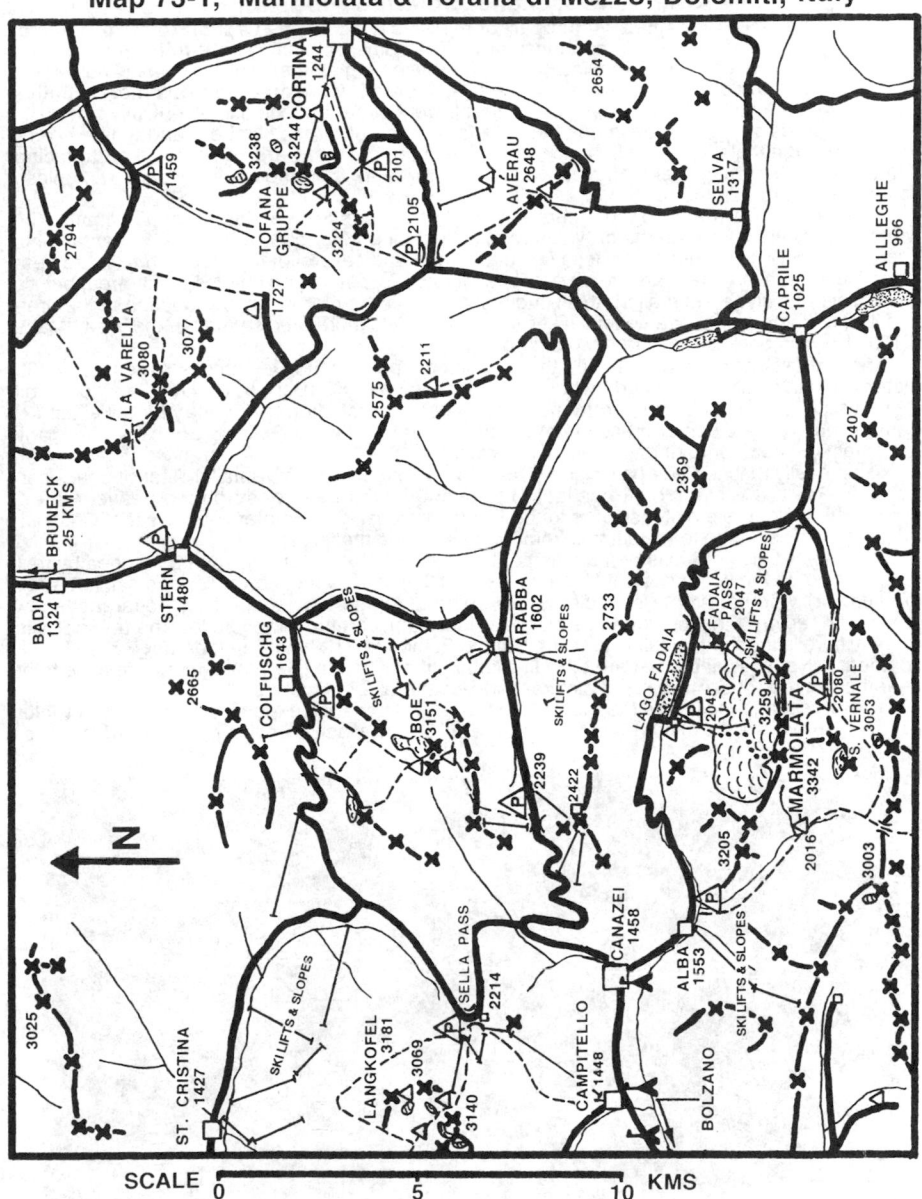

a better map and/or a guidebook of the area. There should be plenty around. The best places to shop are in Canazei and Cortina or sometimes at any of the towns or bigger hotels on this map. Outside the immediate area, Bolzano or Innsbruck are good places to find maps, etc.

Maps *Westliche Dolomiten,16, and Ostliche Dolomiten,17,* 1:100,000, from Freytag und Berndt, Wien; or look for Kompass maps; Cordee Books, UK, lists 3 guidebooks to this area, maybe more; **Trekking in the Dolomites**, Stedman, and **South Tyrol**, and **The Dolomites**.

Antelao & Cristallo, Dolomiti Alps, Italy

The Dolomiti, or Dolomites, is that part of the Alps lying mostly east of Bolzano, south of Bruneck, and north of Belluno, in northeast Italia. The name Dolomiti, comes from a type of rock called Dolomite, which is similar to limestone. There are no granites, schists, or lavas here--only dolomite. The bedding or layers of rock are horizontal, with some portions more weather resistant. As a result, there are many prominent fingers of barren rock rising vertically to the sky above the forests. The Dolomiti has become famous among rock climbers and alpine hikers. There are no real glaciers in this region or on this map, but there are some small north facing snow fields. Generally speaking, you won't need an ice ax & crampons in these parts, unless you arrive in early summer.

Included on this map are the higher summits of the eastern section of the Dolomiti. The western parts are shown on the previous 2 maps featuring *Marmolata* and *Tosa & Brenta*. This map shows only the higher summits, a few main trails, and several of the rifugios which are near these higher peaks. There are literally dozens more trails, peaks and rifugios in the area, but it's impossible to include them all on this simple sketch. This is merely an introduction to the area and it's recommended that a serious hiker or climber buy a more precise map of the area. Maps can be found in bookstores in the towns on this map.

The highest peak in the area, and the 2nd highest peak in the Dolomiti, is **Antelao** at 3263 meters. It can easily be climbed by trail from either Vodo or St. (San) Vito. There's a good trail to a bivacco, or small hut, just north of the main peak, which means this may be a walkup (?) from the hut. Or you can approach from the north and the Rifugio Gallasi. But be warned, any route from the north or northeast is likely technical.

Other easily reached groups include **Cristallo**, 3216 meters. This small cluster of peaks can be reached via the Tre Croci Pass just to the south. One trail goes right up between the 2 highest summits, while a lift ascends to the Rifugio Lorenzi, 2829 meters, just west of Cristallo. There is a difficult route to the summit from the pass or the rifugio (?).

Still another high group is around the peak **Kofel**, at 3192 meters. It can be reached by trail from Giralba on the south or from Moos on the north. There's an old bivacco, or small hut, near the summit. Another high area includes **Sorapiss**, 3205 meters, which has the largest snow field in the region. This peak can be climbed right from Cortina; simply follow the trail or trails roughly paralleling the funicular up to the Rifugio Faloria at 2120 meters, then ridge & trail-walk southeast. Sorapiss and Kofel are difficult climbs. In addition to the above, there are trails to or near the summits of **Froppa**, 2933 meters, and **Lucano** at 2839 meters.

The largest and most important town in the area is Cortina, an expensive summer and winter resort, followed by Auronzo and Pieve. Use Cortina as your shopping & information

Looking northwest from near the summit of Marmolata at Langkofel right, Plait Kofel
far left, and Grohmann Spitze in the center (see previous map).

Map 74-3, Antelao & Cristallo, Dolomiti Alps, Italy

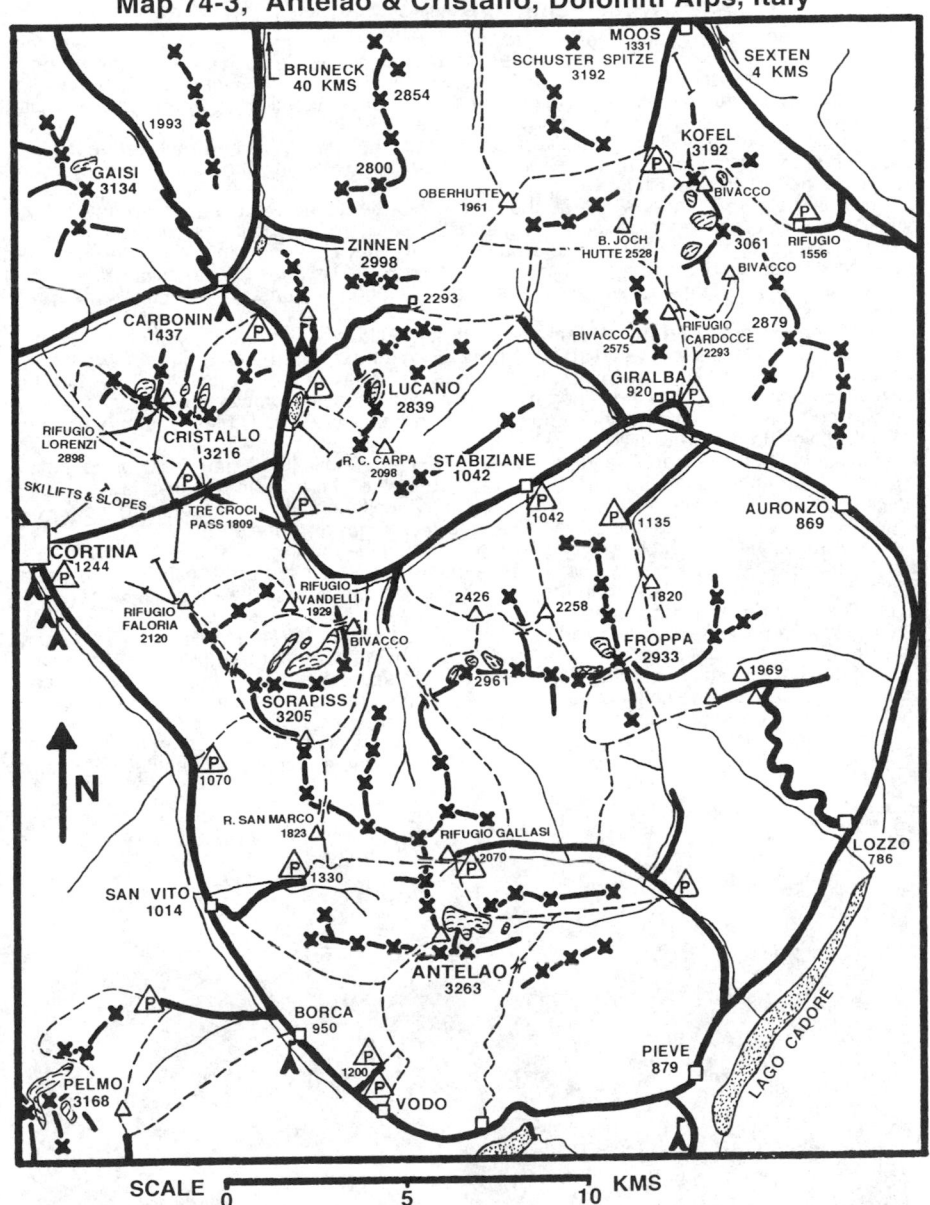

headquarters. Camping is severely restricted in all of the Dolomiti, so hide your tent well; or put up your tent at sunset and take it down early the next morning.
Maps *Ostliche Dolomiten, 17,* 1:100,000, from Freytag und Berndt, Wien; or look for Kompass maps; Cordee Books, UK, lists 3 guidebooks to this area, maybe more; **Trekking in the Dolomites**, Stedman, and **South Tyrol**, and **The Dolomites**.

Triglav, Julijske Alpe, Slovenia

In the extreme northwest corner of Slovenia (which was the northern-most republic of the former Yugoslavia), where the boundaries of Italia and Austria now meet, is the highest mountain in Slovenia and the former Yugoslavia. It's called Triglav, 2863 meters. The mountain is due south of the Austrian city of Villach, and southwest of Jesenice, the largest town in this part of Slovenia. It's also70 kms west of Ljubljana, capital of Slovenia.

Triglav is part of the Julian or Julijske Alpe. This part of the Alps now straddles the Italian-Slovenian border, with about half lying in Italia. This map covers only the eastern or Slovenian part where the highest summits are found.

The Julijske Alpe is rather similar to the Dolomiti further to the west in northern Italia. The rock is largely limestone or dolomite, and is generally considered good for rock climbing.

Four languages can be heard in the area of Triglav; Slavens (local language), Serbo-Croat (one official language of the former Yugoslavia), German and Italiano. On the Italian side of the border, the main languages spoken are German and Italiano. In tourist areas a small amount of English is spoken.

Here's how to get to **Triglav**. From the north and Villach, Austria, drive southwest on the autobahn (E7-14), turn east at Tarvisio, enter Slovenia, continue to a small town called Mojstrana, then go 10 kms southwest to the base of Triglav to a place called Vrata and the Aljazev Dom. From Ljubljana, head northwest to Mojstrana, then southwest to Triglav. There is bus service on the main highway, but no trains. From Mojstrana to Triglav, you may have to hitch hike if you don't have your own car.

In this area there many trails and mountain huts, referred to in these parts as *rifugios, doms or koca*. Most of the kocas or doms, but only about half of the trails in the area, are actually shown as this map, so you must buy a better one. With all the trails and accommodations you know this is a popular area for the Slovenian and former Yugoslav tourists.

There are 2 main approaches to Triglav. One is from the town of Mojstrana, then the place called Vrata and the Aljasev Dom located at the end of the road in the upper valley on the north side of the mountain. Trails lead to the summit on both the east and west sides. There are several kocas or doms on the mountain.

The area can also be approached from Bovec, Soca, and the Trenta Valley & Na Logu and the Dom Zlatorog, but getting to that valley is less-convenient than the route from Mojstrana. Each of these trailheads or starting points is about the same distance from the mountain, and each requires about the same length of time for the climb. A third approach is from Bled and the Dom Savica, but the walk from there is much longer.

If you prefer doms to camping, they are generally open from about July 1, through the end of September (Triglav Dom is open year-round because it has a met. station inside). All major

A postcard picture showing various routes on the north face of Triglav.

Map 75-3, Triglav, Julijske Alpe, Slovenia

JESENICE

MOJSTRANA 10 KMS

RJAVINA 2457

VODMKOVA KOCA 1805

BOHINJ JEZERO (LAKE) 528

BLED

N

DOVSKI KRIZ 2531

VRATA ALJAZEV DOM 1015

DOM STANICA

TRIGLAV DOM 2515

DOM PLANIKA 2004

TRZASKA KOCA 2120

KANJAVEC 2568

KOCA PRI TRIGLAVSKIH 1682

SKRLATICA 2738

BIWAK STENAR 2501

DOM 2952

TRIGLAV 2863

POGACNIKOC

(TRIGLAV LAKES HUT)

2472

BIWAK

KOCA KRNICI 1218

PRISOJNIK 2547

RAZOR 2601

ZDANJICA 725

ZARSAVSKA KOCA 2071

KRANJSKA GORA 2 KMS

NA LOGU 645

DOM ZLATOROG

2348

POSTARSKA KOCA 1611

TRENTA VALLEY

RATECE 2 KMS

DOM TAMAR 1108

2369

943

BAVSKI GRINTAVEC 2344

SOCA 487

(PONCA) VELIKA 2272

SLOVENIA

JALOVEC 2643

BIWAK PELC 2437

1350

SLOVENIJA

ITALIA

RIFUGIO LUIGI 1165

BIVACCO 2259

2678

1669

2343

(BAVSICA) LOGJI 711

LAGHI DE FUSINE 936

2062

GORLOG 620 (LOG POD MANGRTON)

TARVISIO

ITALIA SLOVENIA

GORIZIA

BOVEC 483

FUSINE

SCALE 0 — 5 — 10 KMS

doms offer sleeping and eating accommodations, others are simple shelters called *biwaks*. Buy all food and supplies before arriving at the mountain. Camping is restriction because this is now a national park.
Maps *Julische Alpen, 14,* 1:100,000 (or a new map at 1:50,000 using Slovenian names), from Freytag und Berndt, Wien; or *Julijske Alpe, Vzhodni del (east part)* 1:50,000, or *Triglav,* 1:25,000, both from Planinska Zveza Slovenije (Mountain Club of Slovenia), Ljubljana; and the book, **Julian Alps**, West Col Books; and perhaps a travel guidebook to the former Yugoslavia.

Gerlach, Vysoke (High) Tatry, Slovakia

These mountains are called the Vysoke or High Tatry, located on the Polish-Slovak border. The highest peak is Gerlach at 2655 meters. This mountain is totally inside Slovakia and about 8 kms from the border of Poland or Polska. However, many of the highest peaks to the west are on the international boundary.

To climb the highest peaks, first make your way by train to Poprad, a city south of the range. From the train station catch a bus, or better still an electric train, going to Tatranska Lomnica or Stary Smokovec. These resort towns are at the foot of the Tatry where another train makes many runs daily between Tatranska Lomnica and Strbske Pleso. There are also buses running along the same general route. You can get to the mountains from any one of many entry points along this railway or bus route. Stock up on food supplies in Poprad, as there are few stores selling anything but snacks and drinks near the mountains.

To climb **Gerlach**, you must first go to Stary Smokovec, stop at the tourist office, and locate the climbing club in town. They are supposed to advise you on the problems of climbing this moderately difficult peak and give you official permission to do so. Other climbers have told the author that national park patrol people do issue tickets for those who don't get permission. The normal route seems to be up the east face. One of the big problems for making this climb is bad weather and poor visibility. Once you decide to climb Gerlach, then either walk from Stary Smokovec, or take the train/bus to Tatranska Polianka and hike from there.

If you're not interested in climbing Gerlach, you can climb any one of many other good peaks, apparently without permission. The author was very short on time and the weather was bad, so he walked up a good trail from Stary Smokovec to the summit of Slavkovsky at 2452 meters (2 hours up). This was on 8/13/1989. If you're interested in a quick trip to the top of a high peak just for fotos, you might take the cable car from Tatranska Lomnica to the top of Lomnica Stit at 2632 meters--which could be the 2nd highest peak in the range (?). However, there are no trails leading up or down from the summit, so you'd have to return the same way.

Before you head for the high peaks, stop at a tourist information office somewhere (such as Eurocamp) and get the latest word on exactly where you can or cannot camp in the high country. It seems camping is forbidden up high. It might be you'll have to camp in the valley and go to the mountains for day climbs only. You might also hide your tent in the trees out of sight. Or you can sleep in shelters, but you'll likely have to make reservations ahead of time at Eurocamp, at that time the largest campground in Europe.

Russian and German are good languages to have in this country. However, with the breakup of Czechoslovakia in the early 1990's, expect more western European languages to be taught and spoken in the future. The author did this climb in the summer of 1989, so there may be lots of changes here regarding transport and schedules, facilities, etc., since the national breakup.

If you're coming from the Polish side, head for Zakopane, Poland's equivalent to Chamonix or

Lomnicky (upper right) as seen from the lower east ridge of Slavkovsky.

Map 76-1, Gerlach, Vysoke (High) Tatry, Slovakia

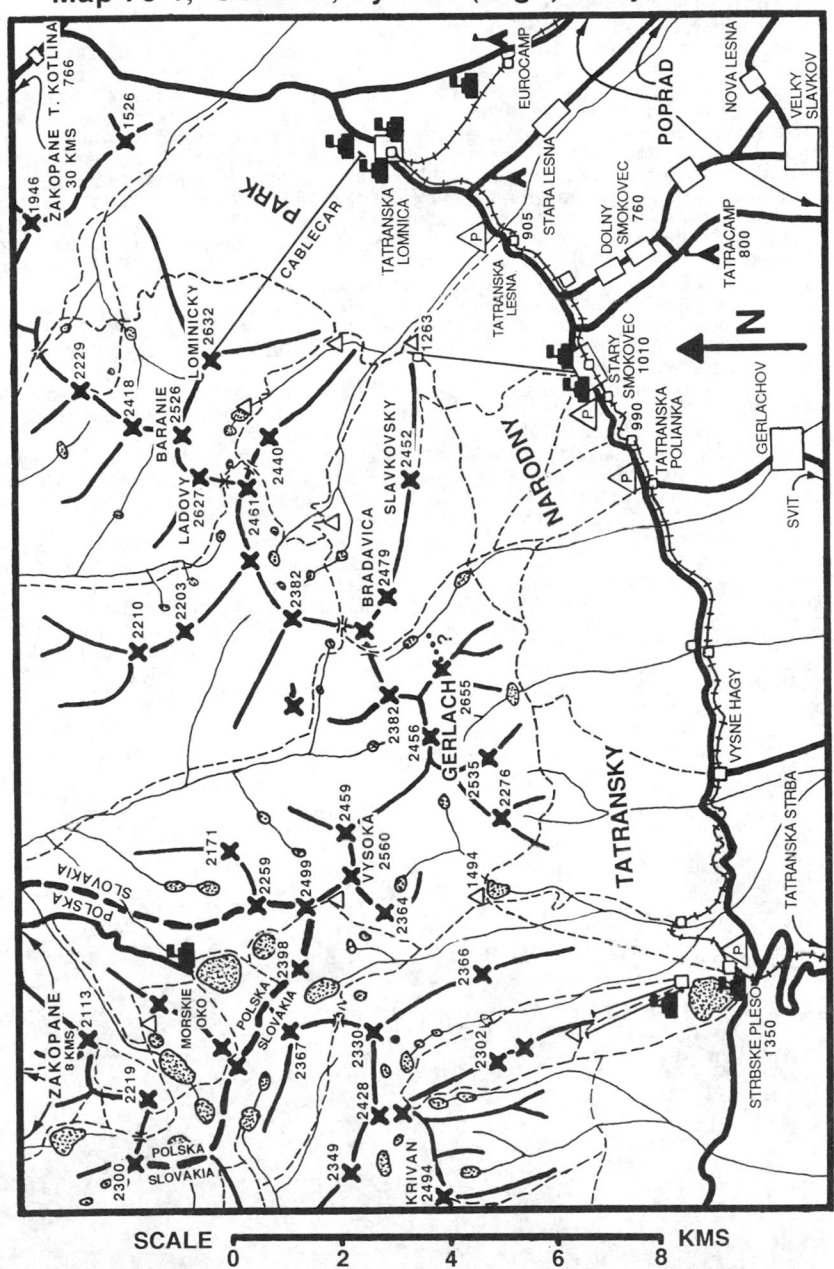

Zermatt. There are lots of hiking opportunities on the Polska side, but climbing Gerlach from that direction would take much longer.

Maps *Vysoke Tatry, Letna Turisticka Mapa, 21,* 1:50,000. Buy this multi-language map in any of the local kiosks; and the latest travel guide to **Eastern Europe**, from Lonely Planet, for updates on travel in Eastern Europe since the breakup of the Soviet Union.

Dumbier, Nizke (Low) Tatry, Slovakia

This map shows the highest part of the Nizke or Low Tatry Mountains of central Slovakia. This granite range runs east-west and parallel to the Vysoke (High) Tatry, which is just across the valley to the north. This range consists of one long single ridge with the highest point being Dumbier at 2043 meters. This mapped area is approximately in the middle of the range, and there are a number of other summits over 1900 meters nearby. Even though these mountains aren't as high as peaks to the north, or in the Alps, they are still alpine, with summits rising above timberline and many ski resorts.

To climb the highest peak, drive or take a train to the city of Mikulas, which is about one hour west of Poprad, which is the city from where you climb Mt. Gerlach, the highest peak in the Tatry. Immediately next to and east of the train station is a large parking area where buses park while dropping off or taking on passengers. From this central hub, buses go in all directions (this is the pattern for what you'll find at all major train stations in Ceska or Slovakia, and all over the former Soviet Union). At this parking lot, look for the bus going to Jasna, a locally famous ski resort located due south of Mikulas. The author faintly remembers the bus being number 3 (?). One leaves about every 45 minutes, at least during the summer tourist season.

Before you leave Mikulas, look around for a supermarket or grocery store and buy all the food you'll need before leaving. There's a small supermarket just east of the bus parking lot, then more shopping areas 4 or 5 blocks south in the city center. At Jasna, there are only expensive hotels & restaurants and small kiosks.

If you intend to camp, better get out of the bus at the campground at the mouth of the canyon near Pavcina Lehota. There are no other official campgrounds further upcanyon. This entire region is part of a national park so things seem pretty heavily regulated, including camping.

The bus runs up to a parking place at Jasna where you'll find a little cafeteria and ice cream kiosk at the bus stop. If you want to camp around Jasna, you'll have to do as the author did--walk out in the forest a ways to put up your tent. Backcountry camping is permitted, but to be safe, take it down during the day and hide it, as the author did on his visit in 1989.

To climb **Dumbier**, you could begin at a trailhead about 3 kms below Jasna and walk south up a canyon to the summit, but the normal route seems to be to climb a subsidiary peak called **Chopok**, then ridge-walk east to Dumbier. To do this, look for the blue cable car running up to the southwest. There's a road-trail beginning at its base which parallels the lift. After a ways the trail veers left or east, and runs through the forest to an intermediate lift station. Follow the signs from there. One trail runs east and joins the first one mentioned heading south, while another runs south to the top of Chopok. From there follow a trail running east along the ridge. The author climbed Chopok in the rain on 8/14/1989, the day after climbing in the Gerlach area. He reached the top in 1 2/3 hours; 2 1/3 hours round-trip, but gave up on Dumbier because of the weather--however, it can easily be done in one day round-trip. Carry plenty of water on this dry ridge route.

Since the breakup of Czechoslovakia, expect some changes in these parts, especially bus service

This picture was taken from the summit of Chopok looking west.

Map 77-1, Dumbier, Nizke (Low) Tatry, Slovakia

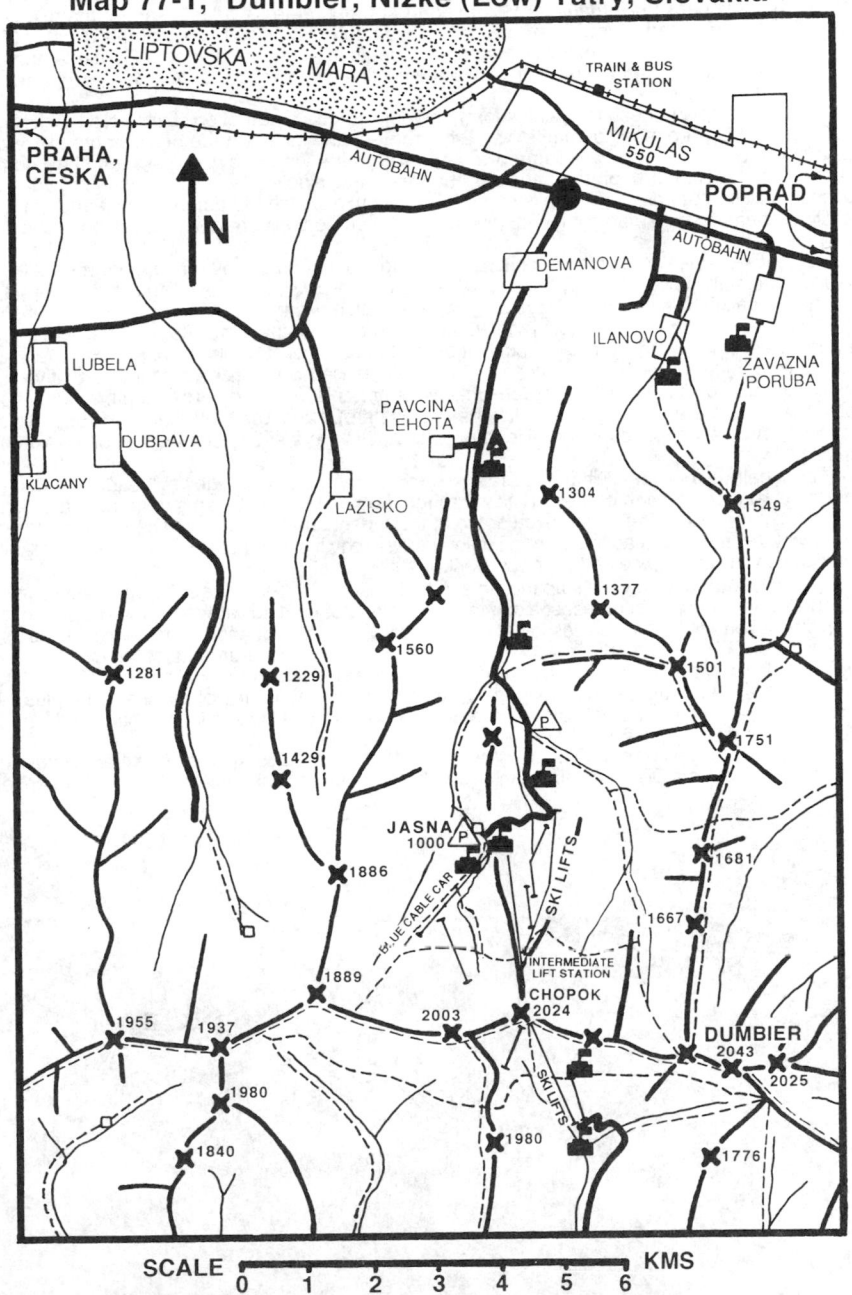

to, and shops at Jasna.

Maps *Nizke Tatry, Letna Turisticka Mapa, 18,* 1:100,000. Buy at any local kiosk or bookstore; and the latest travel guide to **Eastern Europe**, from Lonely Planet, for updates on travel in Eastern Europe since the breakup of the Soviet Union.

Moldoveanu, Muntii Fagaras, Meridonali Carpati, Romania

The highest peak in Romania is Moldoveanu at 2544 meters. It lies in about the middle of a mountain range called Muntii Fagaras or Fagarasului. Fagaras is part of the greater Middle Carpathian or Meridonali Carpati. This range is located in about the center of Romania and about halfway between Sibiu and Brasov, both of which are located north of these mountains. This area is all northwest of Bucuresti.

For the most part, these mountains form one single ridge made of crystalline-type rock running east-west. There are many summits over 2400 meters and all are made of either granite or other metamorphic rock. These are rugged alpine mountains with snow staying until late summer. Running north-south through the middle of the range is a single paved road which provides good access. Readers beware, this map is made from a simple sketch the author drew, and from a non-detailed schematic-type map someone gave him. The proportions are not the best, but it should get you there.

To get there, take a bus, drive or hitch hike along the main highway running between Sibiu and Brasov. The author didn't see any buses on this route in 1989, so if you're using public transport, you may have to hitch hike in areas away from railways! Hitch hiking is something all Rumanians were doing with their tight national budget problems of the 1980's. At that time, Romanians were normally paying drivers who picked them up, about half of what the bus ticket would be, but no one every asked the author for money. Hitching in Romania was rather pleasant and easy at that time, and if you know one of the Latin languages, you'll feel reasonably comfortable in this country (Rumanian is part of the Latin group and they use the Roman alfabet same as here). This was the situation in 1989, but since that time, everything has changed. Hopefully the public transport system will be better when you arrive (?).

About halfway between Sibiu and Brasov, turn south on a paved highway heading to Bilea Lac. This small lake at the north end of a tunnel through the mountain, is 32 kms from the main highway and is a ski resort in winter. When you arrive at the tunnel and lake, you can camp for free nearby. This is not a campground as there are no toilets--everybody just camps where they like. The toilet is everywhere you want it to be and the place stank in 1989!

To climb **Moldoveanu**, walk up the zig zag trail east of Cabana Bilea Lac (where you can sleep or eat) to a pass, then continue east along the well-used trail marked with red & white paint on rocks. At one point you will use iron cables to get over one rough steep spot and at another place you'll see a monument to a Richard Nerlinger. Finally you'll arrive at the twin summits of Moldoveanu. Most climbers do this hike in 2 days, but the author camped near the lake & tunnel and on 8/17/1989 did the climb in 7 1/2 hours, round-trip. Along the way he met several groups of backpackers, plus lots of tents at Lac Capra. Fill a water bottle at Bilea Lac or Lac Capra and take a lunch. Afterwards, he got a ride off the mountain going south.

The second best-known mountain in the area is **Negoiu** at 2535 meters. Get there by taking the trail running west from Bilea Lac above the Turnul (Tunnel) Paltinului. The author hasn't been to this

This foto was taken from near the *Iron Cables* looking east. Moldoveanu is in the center of the picture and in the far distance.

Map 78-1, Moldoveanu, Muntii Fagaras, Carpati, Romania

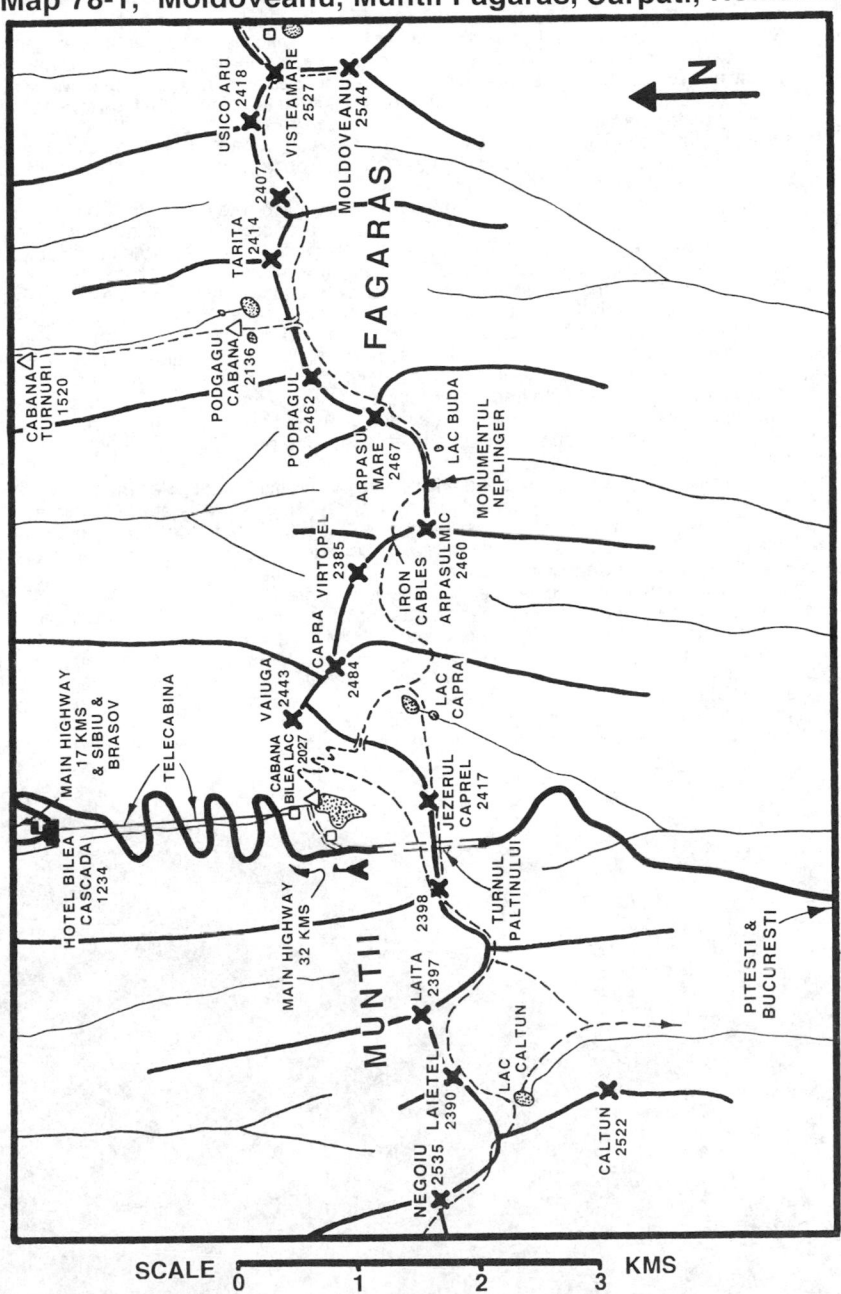

SCALE 0 1 2 3 KMS

peak.
Maps *Sibiu, R-35,* 1:250,000, Army Map Service, UK (this may be a JOG map now?); and a schematic map called *Muntii Fagaras.* Buy this one at the Hotel Bilea Cascada (?); and the latest travel guidebook to **Eastern Europe**, from Lonely Planet, for updates on travel in Eastern Europe since the breakup of the Soviet Union.

Omul, Muntii Bucegi, Meridonali Carpati, Romania

The mountains featured here are in central Romania and the highest point is called Omul at 2507 meters. This small compact range is called the Muntii Bucegi, which is part of the greater Carpathian Mountains or the Meridonali Carpati. This area is on the main rail line and highway running north from Bucuresti and Ploiesti to Sinaia, Busteni, Predeal and to Brasov. The east face of Muntii Costila at 2498 meters, is a vertical rock climb. The author saw lots of conglomerate-type rocks along the trail on this hike to the summit.

Hikers using this map should be aware of some flaws. The author climbed Omul mostly in clouds while using a very poor sketch map from the tourist office to create this one. It should get you there, but it's not as accurate as he would like.

Getting to these mountains and **Omul** is very easy. Drive, hitch hike or take the train to the resort and papermill town of Busteni. From the train station, first walk some distance and look for a better map than this at the tourist office. If they don't have any, check at one of the hotels or kiosks in town. Then walk south along the main street buying any food you'll want for your hike.

Less than one km from the station, you'll see a sign pointing the way to the Hotel Silva which will be to the right. Walk uphill to the west until you reach the hotel. Walk uphill to the west until you reach the hotel. Just behind the Silva is the lower station for the telecabina or gondola, which runs up to the top of a semi-flat region that resembles a plateau more than a mountain. You can take the telecabina to the Cabana Babele, or hike all the way for more merits. From the Hotel Silva, walk southwest up a gravel road to the mouth of the canyon. The road then turns into a well-used trail which runs upcanyon to the Cabana Caraiman where you can buy food and rent a bed or room. From Caraiman, walk west over one of many trails to near the Cabana Babele. This area has been abused and eroded to the point that it's the ugliest site in any mountain range the author has ever seen!

From Cabana Babele, walk north along a road and/or trail with metal poles marked with yellow and white paint. This road goes to a lookout on top of **Virfu (Peak) Costila** at 2498 meters, but you should turn left and continue to the northwest along another old track to the summit of Omul and a cabana with food and beds. To return a different way, locate the trail heading down through the Valea Prin (Prin Valley) and Valea Cerbulul to Busteni.

Here's what the author did. He camped just above the Hotel Silva, then on 8/20/1989, left his big pack at the railway station, and went up the trail past Cabana Caraiman & Babele, then to the top of Omul. Finally it was down the Valea Prin and Valea Cerbulul to the train station in about 6 1/2 hours.

You can camp just above the Hotel Silva or anywhere in the forest, or on the plateau. Busteni and Sinaia are locally famous ski resorts, but in 1989 with the author's visit, the river flowing through the main valley was running black from residue coming from papermills in the area. A nice place otherwise. Look for big changes since the author's visit.

Maps *Sibiu, R-35, 1:250,000, Army Map Service, UK (this may be a JOG maps now?); and Tourist*

Soldiers & alpinists mingle at the Cabana Omul which is next to Omul's summit rock.

Map 79-1, Omul, Muntii Bucegi, M. Carpati, Romania

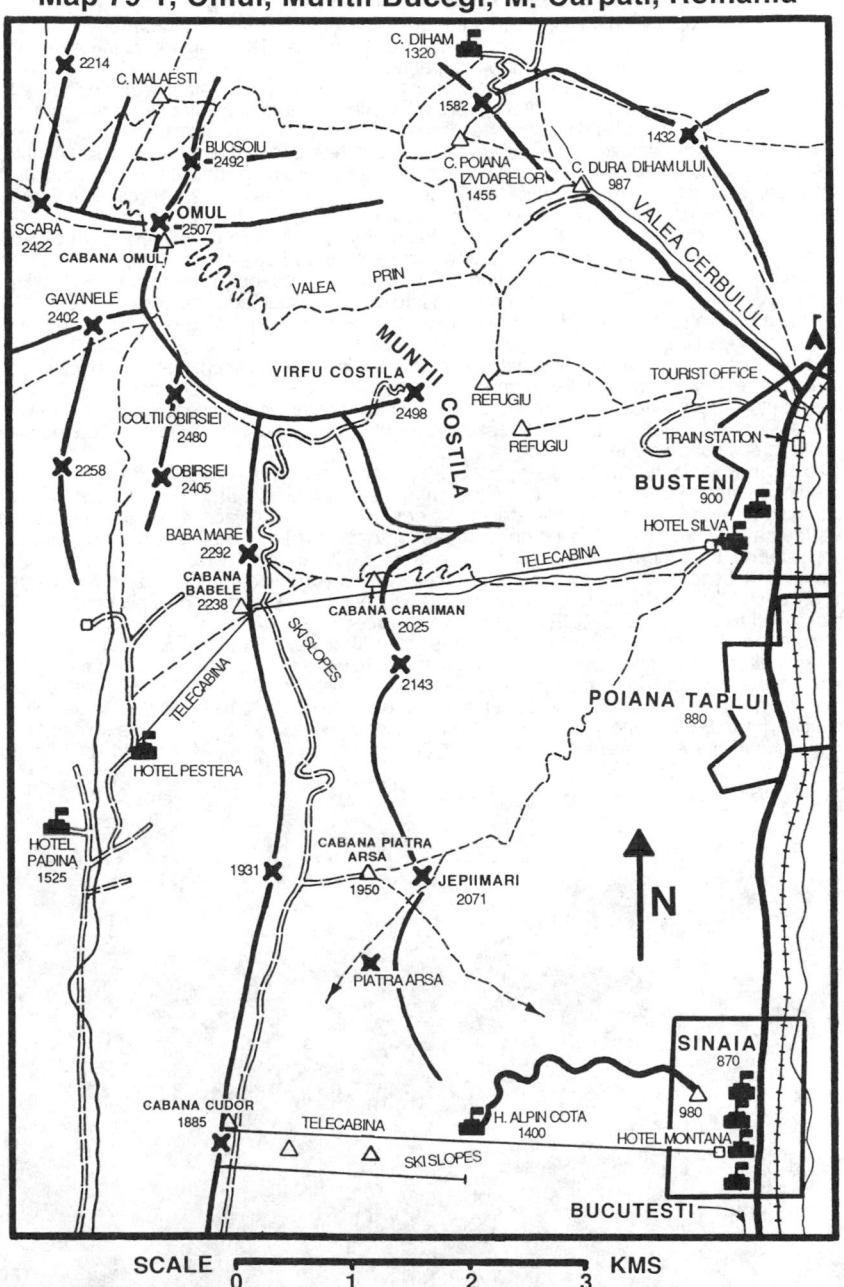

leaflets and maps, *Sinaia and Busteni*. Buy in nearby kiosks or tourist office; and the latest travel guidebook to **Eastern Europe**, from Lonely Planet, for updates on travel in Eastern Europe since the breakup of the Soviet Union.

Musala Vrh, Rila Mountains, Bulgaria

The highest mountain in the Balkans is Musala Vrh (Musala Peak) at 2925 meters. It's located south of Sofia in south central Bulgaria and in the Rila Mountains. This map shows the eastern half of the range, the central core of which is made of granitic-type rock.

If you're coming from Sofia and using public transportation, first talk to someone at a tourist information office, either at the train station, or at the office located one km away in the center of the city. Ask them about maps, and find out the number of the tram which will take you to the correct bus station to get a bus to Samokov. The station is in the southeast part of the city. At that station there are buses leaving about every hour for Samokov which is the jumping off point to the Rila Mountains.

You can also get to these mountains from the south and southwest from the cities of Razlog and Bansko, but the author is unfamiliar with that approach route.

Once at the bus station in Samokov, take a city-type bus to the resort town of Borovec (pronounced *Borovets*). Before leaving Samokov, be sure and buy all the food you'll need for the duration of your trip to the Rila in Borovec--only restaurants and kiosks. The author stayed one night in Samokov, where you'll find cheap accommodation. He paid US$8 to stay in a room in a private home. He did this trip in 1989 before the breakup of the USSR, so some things may have changed (?).

Borovec has several big international-type hotels and some smaller chalet-type lodges or hostels. The author never got involved with getting the prices of these places, but most looked expensive. There are no campgrounds near Borovec, so if you want to camp you'll have to walk out of town to the southwest and put your tent up in the forest out of sight. Like a lot of other expensive ski resorts, they don't like to see people camping for free!

To climb **Musala**, first locate the gondola which takes passengers to the peak called Jastrebec, located due south of Borovec. You can either take the gondola part way up, or walk along the road heading southwest from the lower lift station. When you reach the place where the gondola cables cross the paved road, turn to the left or southeast onto a dirt road. Follow this along the creek for a short distance, then the real trail begins which is marked with red & white paint on rocks or trees. Follow this trail south all the way to an upper basin where you'll find the Musala Dom (Musala Hut). In 1989, one of the 2 buildings there had burned down, but they were starting a new one. Nearby, the author found a campsite full of DDR (East German) hikers.

From the Musala Dom, the trail again heads south toward 2 more upper basins, two lakes, another shelter called Irecek, then to the summit which has the ruins of an old lift of some kind. If you take the gondola up and down you can cut your walk-time by about half. On 8/23/1989, the author hiked from Borovec to the summit in 3 hours, then took the gondola down so he could quickly get to the next mountain. From Borovec, he took a bus to Samakov, then another to Maljovica. See next map.

Maps *Hiking Routes-Borovecs, Bulgaria,* 1:130,000, printed by Bulgarian Association of Tourism and

From the campsite near the Cabana Musala, you can see Musala Vrh in the center background.

Map 80-1, Musala Vrh, Rila Mountains, Bulgaria

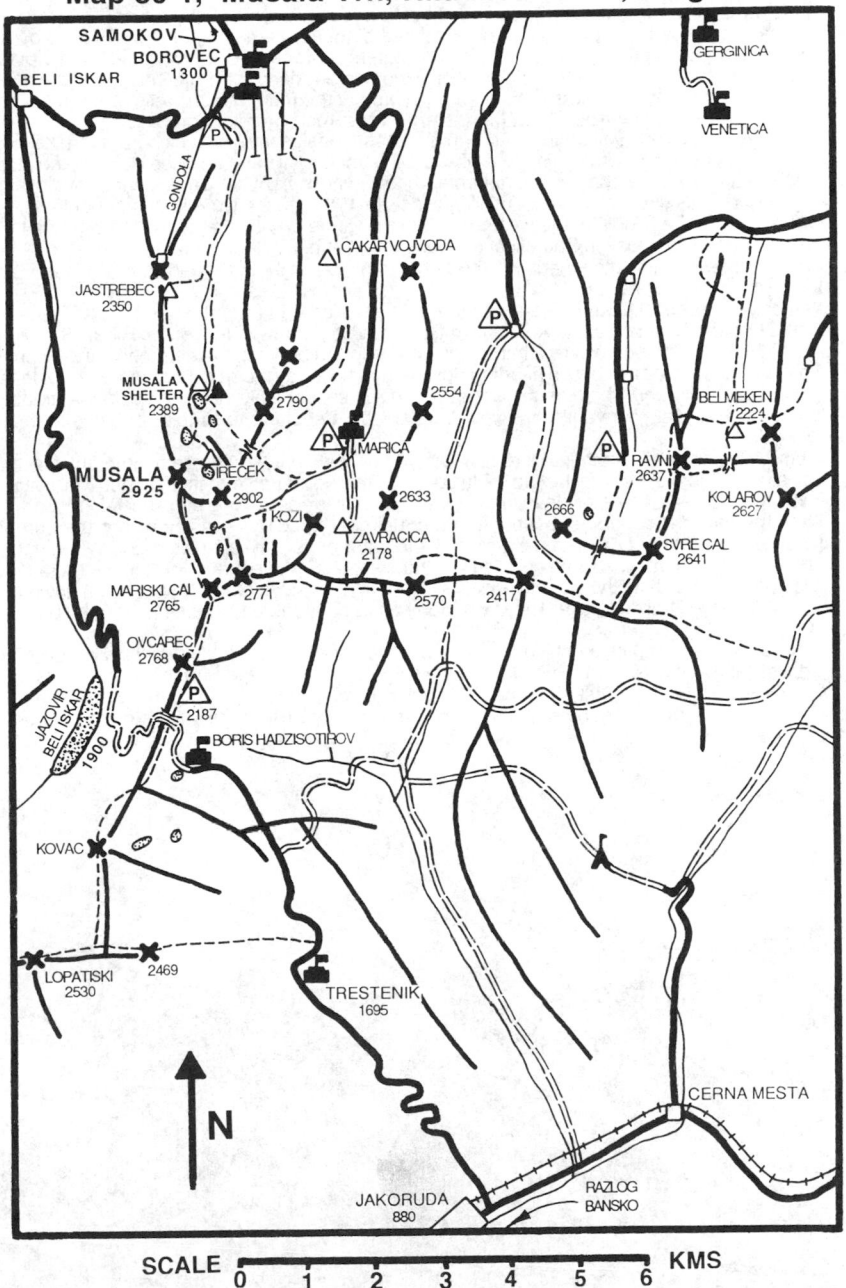

Recreation, Sofia. Buy this map in Boravec or any local kiosk or tourist office, but get the English version in Sofia; and the latest travel guidebook to **Eastern Europe**, from Lonely Planet, for updates on travel in Eastern Europe since the breakup of the Soviet Union.

Maljovica Vrh, Rila Mountains, Bulgaria

This map covers the western half of the Rila Mountains, which is just west of the previous map titled *Musala*, and south of Sofia, Bulgaria. This part of the range has a number of peaks over 2700 meters. The highest is Goljam Kupen, at 2731 meters, but the best known peak is Maljovica Vrh (pron. Mal-o-vit-sa Peak), at 2729 meters. While the eastern part of the Rila has the highest peak in the Balkans (Musala, 2925 meters), this area has some of the more famous religious shrines around, among them the Rilski Manastir (Rilski Monastery). Most rocks here are granite.

If you're coming from Sofia and using public transport, ask someone which tram to take to get to the bus station which has buses going to a city called Samokov. There are buses leaving the station in the southeast part of Sofia about every hour bound for Samokov. At the Samokov bus station look for buses going to the ski resort complex of Maljovica. In 1989, buses were leaving about every hour. This will put you in the middle of the western half of the range and on the north side which is the best entry point. Buy all your food in Samokov, as there are no shops in Maljovica.

Another access road, but perhaps with no public transport, is the one heading south from Beli Iskar toward the lake called Jazouir Beli Iskar.

You can also enter this mapped area via the Rilski Manastir from the southwest. Take a train south out of Sofia and get off at the Kocerinovo Station. Catch a bus from there to Rilski, or walk up the road to the highway junction where other buses can be found heading for the monastery. From Rilski there are about half a dozen buses heading downcanyon per day, so of course there are at least that many going up. This would be during the summer tourist season only. Expect less public transport at other times of the year. The author however, believes it's easier and simpler to arrive at Maljovica from Samokov.

From Maljovica, walk south into the main canyon on a wide trail. You can camp any place along the way after you leave the resort. After only about 3 kms, you'll arrive at the Cabana Maljovica. You can camp in that area as well, or sleep in the small hotel. They sell meals and snack-type food.

From the cabana, continue upcanyon to a couple of high cirque basins where the author saw campers from the former DDR (East Germany) and other parts of eastern Europe. When you arrive at the summit ridge, turn west, then curl north to the summit of **Maljovica**. An alternate route for going down is to head west along the summit ridge trail, then at a low point or pass, walk south down another ridge on a less-used trail to Rilski. There you can camp, buy food and leave the area by bus or hitch hiking.

To give the reader an idea of hike-time and distance, the author took a bus from Borovec, where he had just climbed Musala, to Samakov then Maljovica. He camped up the trail a ways, then on 8/24/1989, walked with his full-sized pack from Maljovica Ski Resort up to the peak and down to Rilski, in 5 hours. Another popular place for hikers is the basin with 7 lakes and the shelter called *Sedemie Ezera* (Seven Lakes). Expect some snowdrifts here throughout the summer, but no glaciers.

Maps *Hiking Routes--Borovecs, Bulgaria*, 1:130,000, Bulgarian Association of Tourism and

Cabana Maljovica, with the north ridge of Maljovica in the background right.

Map 81-1, Maljovica Vrh, Rila Mountains, Bulgaria

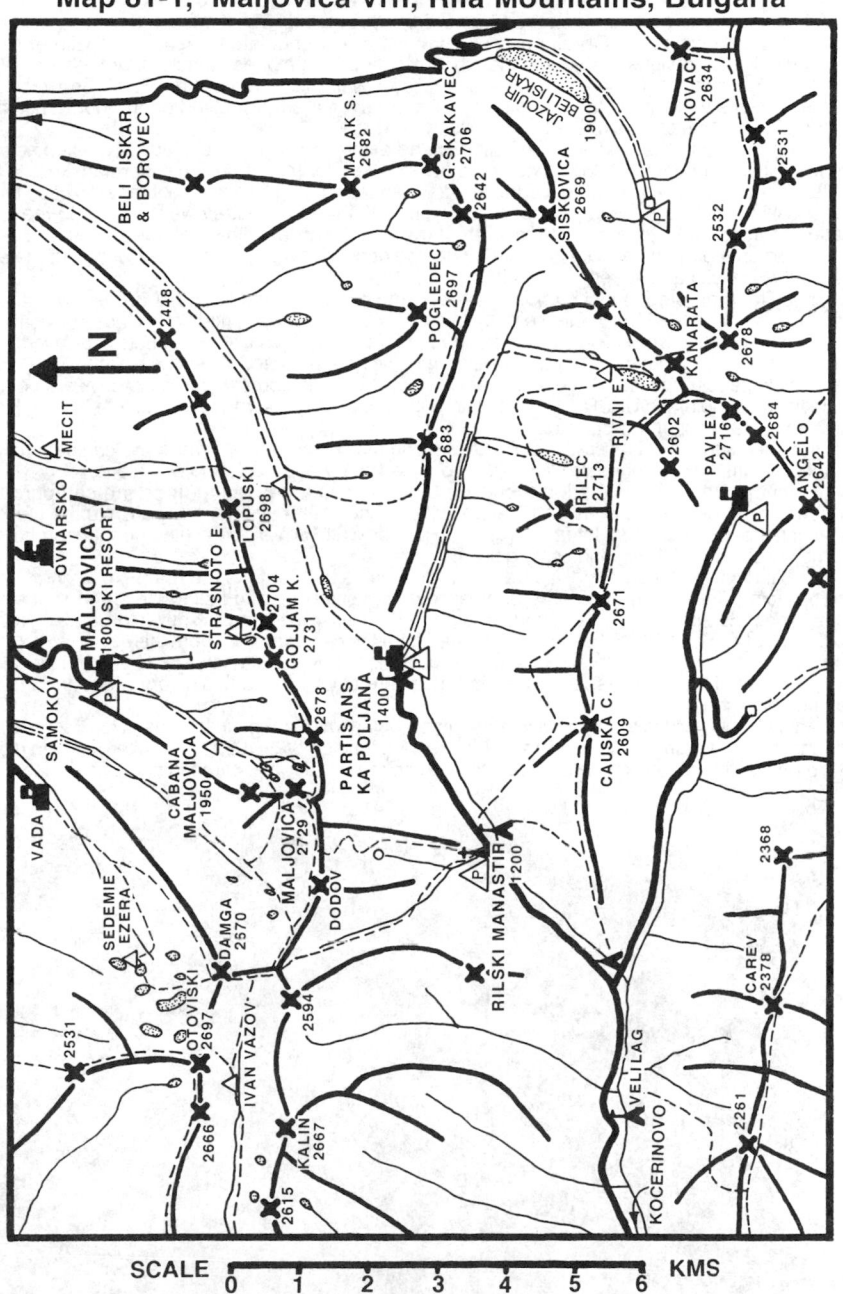

SCALE 0 1 2 3 4 5 6 KMS

Recreation. Buy in any local kiosk or tourist office, but get the English version before leaving Sofia; and the latest travel guidebook to **Eastern Europe**, from Lonely Planet, for updates on travel in Eastern Europe since the breakup of the Soviet Union.

Vihren Vrh, Pirin Mountains, Bulgaria

The area shown here is called the Pirin, or Pirin Mountains. They're located south of Sofia, and about halfway towards the Greek border. They are also immediately south of the Rila Mountains covered in the 2 previous maps, and the city of Razlog. The highest summit is Vihren Vrh (Vihren Peak) at 2914 meters. There are several other peaks over 2800 meters in the Pirin. Snow drifts stay on these peaks throughout the summer and there's even a small icefield on the northeast side of Vihren Cirque. This peak is made of a granitic-type rock.

The author found lots of hikers and climbers here from the DDR (East Germany) when he visited the place in the summer of 1989. One of the favorite treks for the former East Germans was to begin at Bansko, take a bus (or drive) to the trailhead at Bandaritsa, and hike in a southerly direction to Yena Sandanski or Melnik (located just south of this map). From there they went by bus to the railway station of Sandanski, located not far north of the Greek border. This trek takes from 2 to 5 days depending on the route and rate of travel. It can be done in reverse direction as well. But the author only knows Bansko and Vihren.

If you're interested in just climbing **Vihren**, and are taking public transport, begin at the train station in Simitli, located west of these mountains. Walk about one km north to a place just north of the river bridge, which is where you catch a bus bound for Razlog, then Bansko. There are several buses going that way daily, but if there are several of you, hiring a taxi used to be cheap (in 1989). In those days you were required to change so many US$ per/day in the country, but those days are behind us since the breakup of the USSR. Buy all your food for the trip to the mountains before leaving Razlog, as there are fewer shops in Bansko.

In Bansko, there's at least one alpinists lodge in the center of town where you can get a bed in a dormitory room. The author paid US$3.20 for one bed in a 3-bed room, and was alone.

From the Bansko bus station there are 3 or 4 buses a day going up to the campground at Bandaritsa. Buy your ticket as early as possible. Since 1989, it's entirely possible the number of buses on the road may be a lot fewer (?). You can also hitch hike, but getting up the mountain on a thumb will be more difficult than coming down.

At Bandaritsa Campground, locate and walk along a trail (or take the road) south and up to the Vihren Dom (Vihren Hut). From there, hike west up a steep zig zag trail to the summit. Instead of coming down the same way, head north to a pass, then turn east and walk down to Bandaritsa via the northern route. This trail finishes just up the road from the campground where there used to be a hotel, 2 restaurants and a small store. Be sure and use this northern route in order to see the icefield and cirque basin. This is very spectacular for such a relatively low altitude mountain and in such a southerly location.

After climbing Musala & Maljovica, the author took a train to Simitli and buses to Razlog, Bansko & Bandaritsa, and climbed Vihren Vrh in 3 hours round-trip on 8/25/1989. That afternoon, he returned to the Simitli Railway Station and took a train to the Greek border and camped nearby.

This foto shows the northeast face & cirque basin on Vihren Vrh.   Notice the small icefield.

Map 82-1, Vihren Vrh, Pirin Mountains, Bulgaria

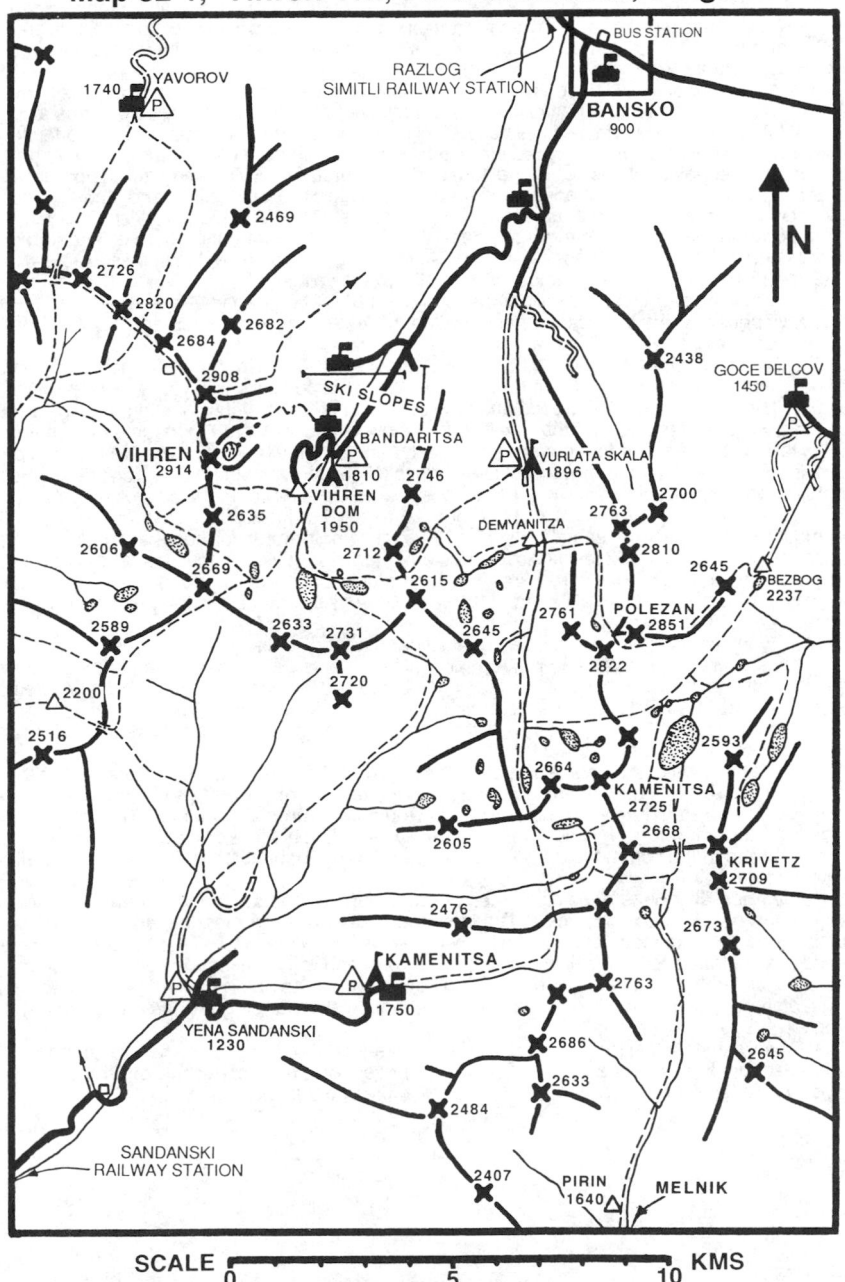

SCALE 0 — 5 — 10 KMS

Maps The author used a map in Bulgarian called *Pirin*, at 1:75,000 scale. For those who can't read the Crylic or Russian alphabet, try to locate an English or German version of the same map at the national tourist office in Sofia; and the latest travel guidebook to **Eastern Europe**, from Lonely Planet, for updates on travel in Eastern Europe since the breakup of the Soviet Union.

Mt. Athos, Monastic Republic of Athos, Greece

Southeast of Thessaloniki, Greece, are three narrow peninsulas protruding into the Egeon Sea. Mt. Athos is at the southeastern tip of the most-easterly of the three peninsulas and reaches an altitude of 2033 meters. The author has not been to this mountain so he's using information from Dubin's book, **Backpacker's Greece**.

Here's a brief history of this region. Mt. Athos is a Christian holy mountain which the Greeks call Ayion Oros (Holy Mountain). The first hermits to settle the peninsula set up living quarters at Karoulia (?) in 963 AD. The leader of this small band of religious monks was St. Athanasios, who founded the monastery of Meyisti Lavra. It's been in existence every since. The group gradually grew and reached its most powerful position in the 15th and 16th centuries during and after the collapse of the Byzantine Empire. During this period of time the population grew to 20,000 and it developed into a parliamentary monastic republic represented by 20 monasteries. When the Turkish Ottoman Empire was in power in the region, from roughly 1518 to 1918, the Order continued to exist and remained independent. When the Ottomans fell in 1918, Athos assumed its present status as a state within the Greek state. Today Athos is to Greece, as the Vatican is to Italia.

One problem with visiting Ayion Oros is that women are not allowed to enter. This custom apparently began with a 12th century edict called the *avaton,* which forbids access to Athos for all female species higher evolved than a bird.

If you want to visit Athos you must first have permission. If you're in Athens, go to your embassy and get a letter of introduction. Then take it to the Aliens Police Station. If you're in Thessaloniki, first go to the Ministry of Northern Greece and get some kind of letter of introduction, then take it to the Aliens Police. It's reported that the number of foreigners allowed into Ayion Oros is 10 per day, so expect to wait a day or two for your papers. In summer you may have to wait a week or more. With permission you can stay a maximum of only 4 days (Nigel Jenkins states they don't often check the entry date when you leave, so you can sometimes stay an extra day or 2 and not get in trouble?).

From downtown Thessaloniki, take bus 10 to the Halkidiki Bus Terminal (this is 1980's information so expect some changes). From there take another bus for about a 3 hour ride to either Iérissos or Ouranópoli, the 2 towns closest to the border. If you stop at Iérissos, take a coastal ferry-type boat called a *caique* to Iveron, 3 kms from the Athonite capital of Karyés. If you go to Ouranópoli, take a boat to Dáfni, which is 8 kms from Karyés. There is one boat per day to each port, except in summer, when more operate.

When you land at either port, police will take your passport and send it to Karyés. You then take a truck or bus or walk to Karyés and pick up your passport plus pay a fee for the number of days you intend to stay and a document which entitles you to board and lodging at any of the 20 monasteries and half dozen skíti (secondary monastery) without further donations. Before leaving Karyés, it's recommended you stock up on lunch-type trail food, as the monasteries don't have any. Or take all of your own food and eat when you like for the 4 days.

From Karyés, walk or take a bus-truck to the port of Dáfni, then locate a coastal trail heading for Símona Pétra, the first of 3 *hanging monasteries.* After Símona Pétra, there is Grigoríou, Ayióu Dionysíou, Avióu Pavlóu, and Ayi' Anna. This would be your last monastery before climbing Mt. Athos. It's about 4 hours walking from Dáfni to Ayi' Anna. This looks like about 15 to 17 kms (?). From Ayi' Anna to the summit and back is an all-day climb. About 250 meters below the summit is a chapel and well.

Remember, all monasteries close their doors at sunset, so late spring or early summer would give you more walk-time. However, Dubin states that's when it's most crowded as thousands of Greeks make this pilgrimage as well. Fall is perhaps the ideal time. Beware too that some meals are served at ridiculous hours, so taking some of your own food might be handy because of your limited time schedule. Here's an alternate to walking both ways on the same trail. If you take a ferry boat from Dafni to Ayi Anna (or vice versa), so you can view the hanging monasteries along the cliffs enroute.

Maps Apparently you can buy pilgrims maps in Ouranópoli, or perhaps Karyés; also, one of these books: **Backpacker's Greece**, Dubin, Bradt Enterprises; or **The Mountains of Greece**, Cicerone Guides; or the latest travel guidebook to Greece for more updated information.

Map 83-3, Athos, Monastic Republic of Athos, Greece

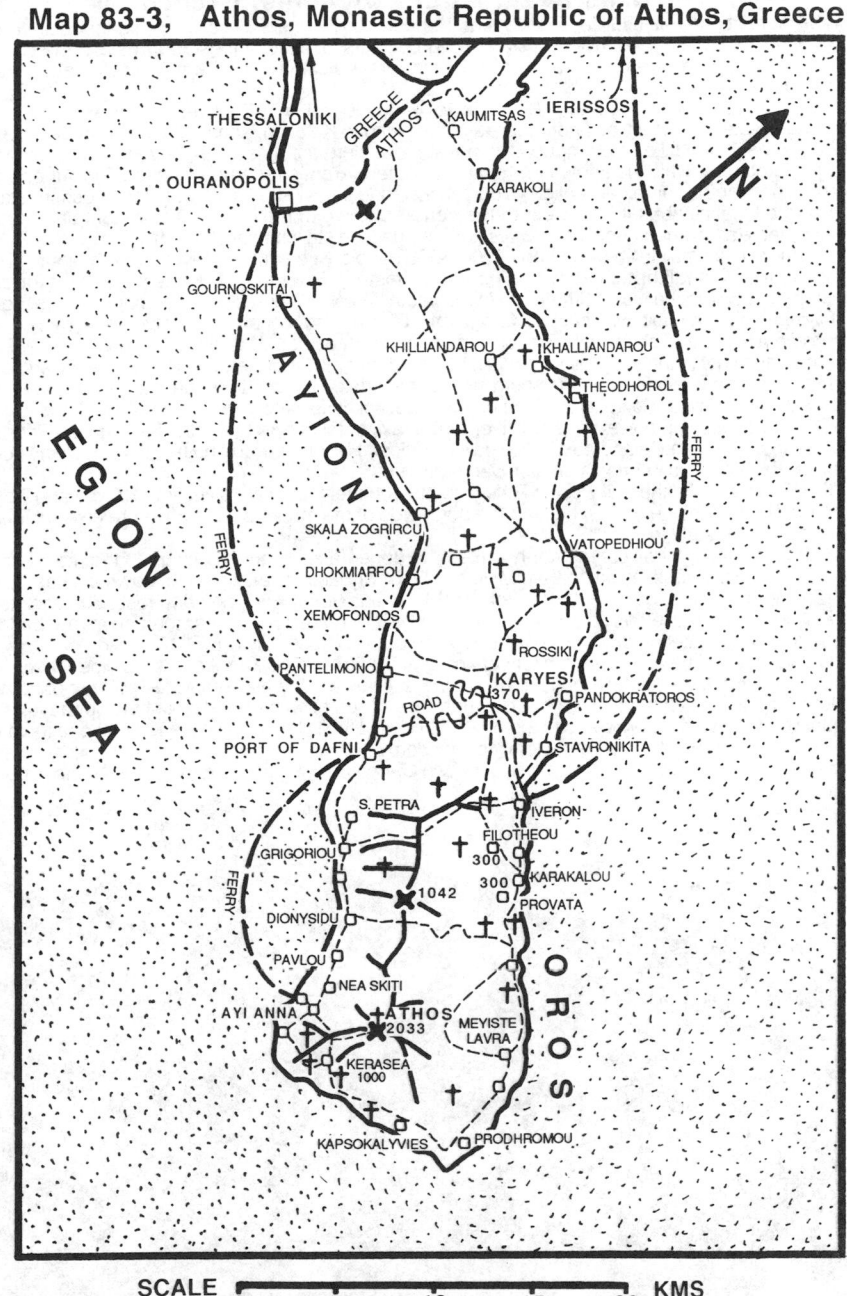

SCALE | 0 5 10 15 20 | KMS

Mytikas Peak, Mount Olympus, Greece

The highest summit in Greece is Mytikas Peak at 2917 meters. This is the highest point on the mythical Mt. Olympus. Because of it's name and because it's the highest mountain in the country, Olympus is climbed often by Greeks and foreigners alike. This entire massif is made of solid limestone.

To get there from the north and Thesslonike, go to the station with buses heading south towards Athens and Katerina. Every half hour there's a bus going to Katerina, about 20 kms north of Litochoro, where you begin the hike to Olympus. From Katerina, there are at least 34 buses daily (in summer) going to Litochoro, which is shown on this map. There are also many buses leaving Athens daily heading north for the same destination. You can also ride a train and get off at to the Litochoro station, then take a local city bus 4 kms west to the center of town at the base of the mountain. If you're camping, there's a campground just a ways north of the train station near a beach.

Litochoro is a small town of perhaps 2000-3000 people who earn their living from tourism. There you'll find many small hotels as well as a youth hostel. From the central square look for signs directing you uphill to the west 300 meters to the youth hostel. They sell books & maps on Greece and Mt. Olympus and can help with hiking information. There's also a good tourist office next to the police station and a number of shops selling books, maps and post cards. This was the situation in 1989.

One way to get to the mountain is to walk to the upper end of town and into the gorge, as shown on this map. There's a good trail on the south side of the creek. It ends at the road further up the canyon near the Ayios Dionyios Monastery. Once on the road, continue west to the trailhead and beyond.

The normal way up however, is to drive, rent a taxi, or hitch hike to the trailhead called Prionia at 1100 meters. If hitching, stand next to the police station. Hitching is good both ways and many people do it. It's about 18 kms to Prionia on a gravel road (1989).

From Prionia, take the trail west to Refuge A at 2100 meters. There's water at Prionia and Refuge A, and at or near Refuge S.E.O. high on the north side of the mountain, but nowhere else--at least in late summer and early fall.

Further up, take a trail cutting north across the upper face; or go directly up to the main summit ridge. Once on the ridge, climb north to Mytikas. From Mytikas, go east straight down a steep gully to the trail, then if you like, go north to the Refuge S.E.O. and head down the northeast ridge back to the road. If you want to use this secondary route, it's best to go down it, rather than climb up, because there's no reliable water enroute. You can sleep and eat at Refuge A or S.E.O.

On 8/27/1989, the author tried hitching and got a quick ride by 7am from the police station on a Sunday morning, then did the loop-hike beginning at Prionia. The hiking part took 6 1/3 hours, while the total time from Litochoro was 8 hours round-trip. Good hitch hiking--at least on Sundays. Most people who are not mountaineers, do the hike in 2 days, usually taking a weekend. Make reservations for a refuge at the tourist office before leaving Litochoro.

Maps Tourist map from the tourist office; or *Mt. Olympus*, 1:100,000, from Greek Alpine Club, 16,

The Refuge S.E.O., with the northeast face of Stefani left, Toumpa right.

Map 84-1, Mytikas Peak, Mount Olympus, Greece

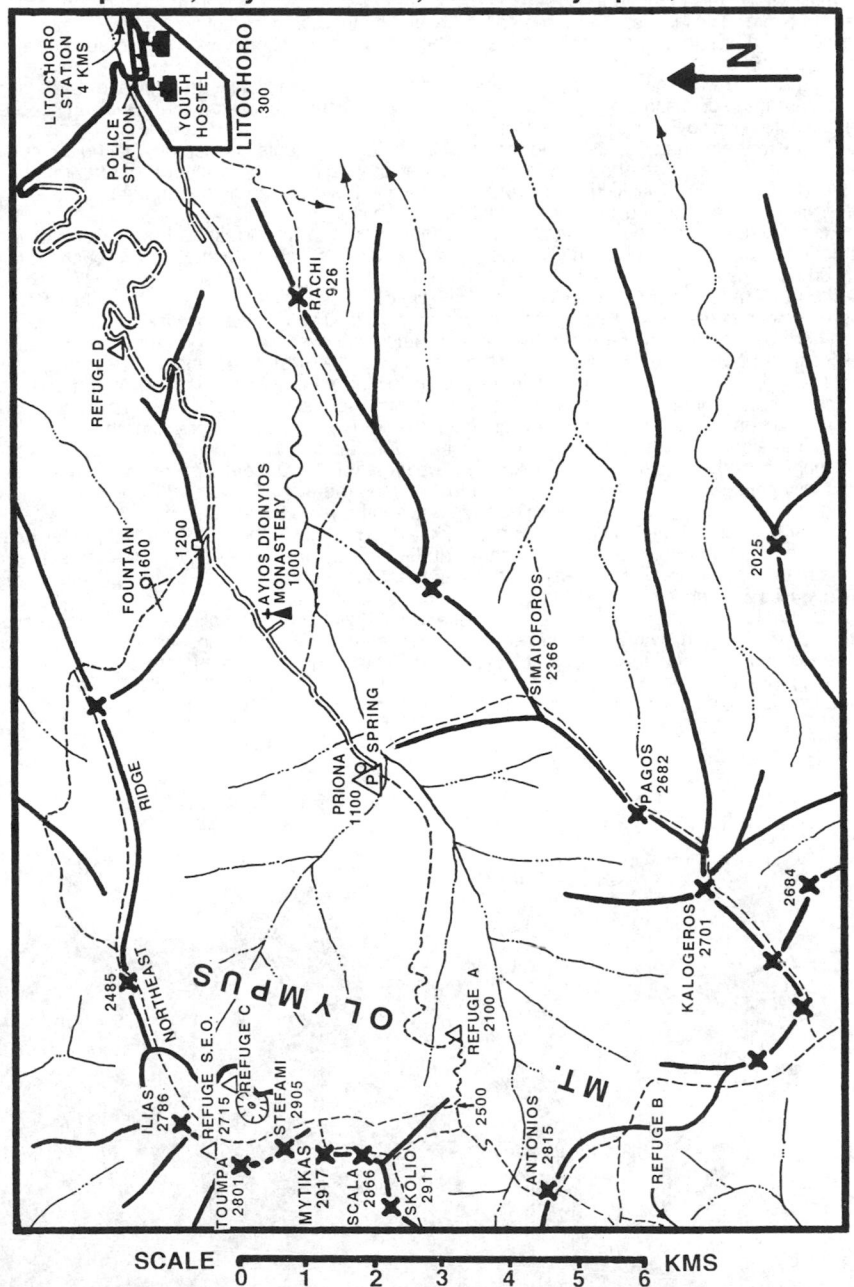

SCALE 0 1 2 3 4 5 6 KMS

Central Square, 136 71 Acharnes, Greece; and one of these books; **Backpacker's Greece**, Bradt Enterprises; **The Mountains of Greece**, Sfikas, Efstathiadis Group; **The Mountains of Greece**, Cicerone Guides.

Pachnes & Samaria Gorge, Lefka Ori, Crete, Greece

Included on this map are the Lefka Ori (White Mountains) and the Samaria Gorge on the Greek island of Crete. The highest peak in the Lefka Ori and on the island is Pachnes at 2453 meters. Keep in mind, this sketch map is rather poor because the author couldn't find a good topo maps on his quick trip there in 1989.

To get there, you can surely fly; or take a ferry from Athens to Hania, the capital of Crete; then a city bus from the docks to the city center. Whatever your plans are, buy all your food and supplies in Hania before going to Pachnes or the Gorge.

To get to the mountains, first go to the main bus station in Hania city center. During the summer tourist season, there are about 4 public buses per day going in the direction of Omalos and the trailhead at Ksilokala (Xyloskalo). Most of these leave in the early morning from about 7am to 10am. There are also many tour buses as well for those who go in a group.

Here's what tourists do. Almost all passengers going to Ksilokala, end up walking down the **Samaria Gorge** to the coast, then take a ferry boat to Hora Sfakion, then another bus back to Hania-- all in one long day.

If you want to climb **Pachnes**, here's what you do. Stay on the bus until it reaches Ksilokala where you can stay in a small hotel and eat in a restaurant. Then instead of walking down the gorge, head northeast on the trail & road to the Kallergi Hut which overlooks the gorge. From there, road-walk east and *downhill* to the base of what the author calls the **First Peak**. At a big sweeping curve in the dirt road, look for a trail marked with red paint. This trail runs to the top of the first peak, then seems to disappear on the ridge. But don't worry, from there simply ridge-walk eastward, gradually veering southeast. You'll be able to see your objective Mt. Pachnes in front of you all the way.

Further along, you'll go down into a valley where you can camp near one of three open wells used by shepherds to get water for their flocks. The well marked 1700 meters is covered with a piece of airplane wreckage and has the best water--at least during the author's trip. Take some iodine tablets (or water filter) to purify it. From the wells, route-find southeast to the summit of Pachnes.

On 8/30/1989, the author carried his big pack from Ksilokala to the top of the first peak where he hid it in some rocks. He then climbed Pachnes and returned, making camp at 1500 meters as shown on the map. That entire day from Ksilokala to camp, took 9 1/2 hours. It takes most people 2 days for this long hike & climb.

To hike the Samaria Gorge, first pay an entry fee at Ksilokala, then walk the 17 kms downcanyon to the coast. Along the way are a number of religious shrines, several springs, and some places to eat at the villages of Samaria, Agia Roumeli and Tarra. The gorge has some interesting narrow places too. In spring, you'll wade in a small creek, but it's apparently dry in summer. Sometimes hundreds of tourists do this hike daily in summer. At the bottom they all catch a boat to Hora Sfakion, then take

Pachnes is seen in the upper left-hand corner, with the Samaria Gorge falling away to the right. Foto was taken from Peak 2010.

Map 85-1, Pachnes & S. Gorge, Lefka Ori, Crete, Greece

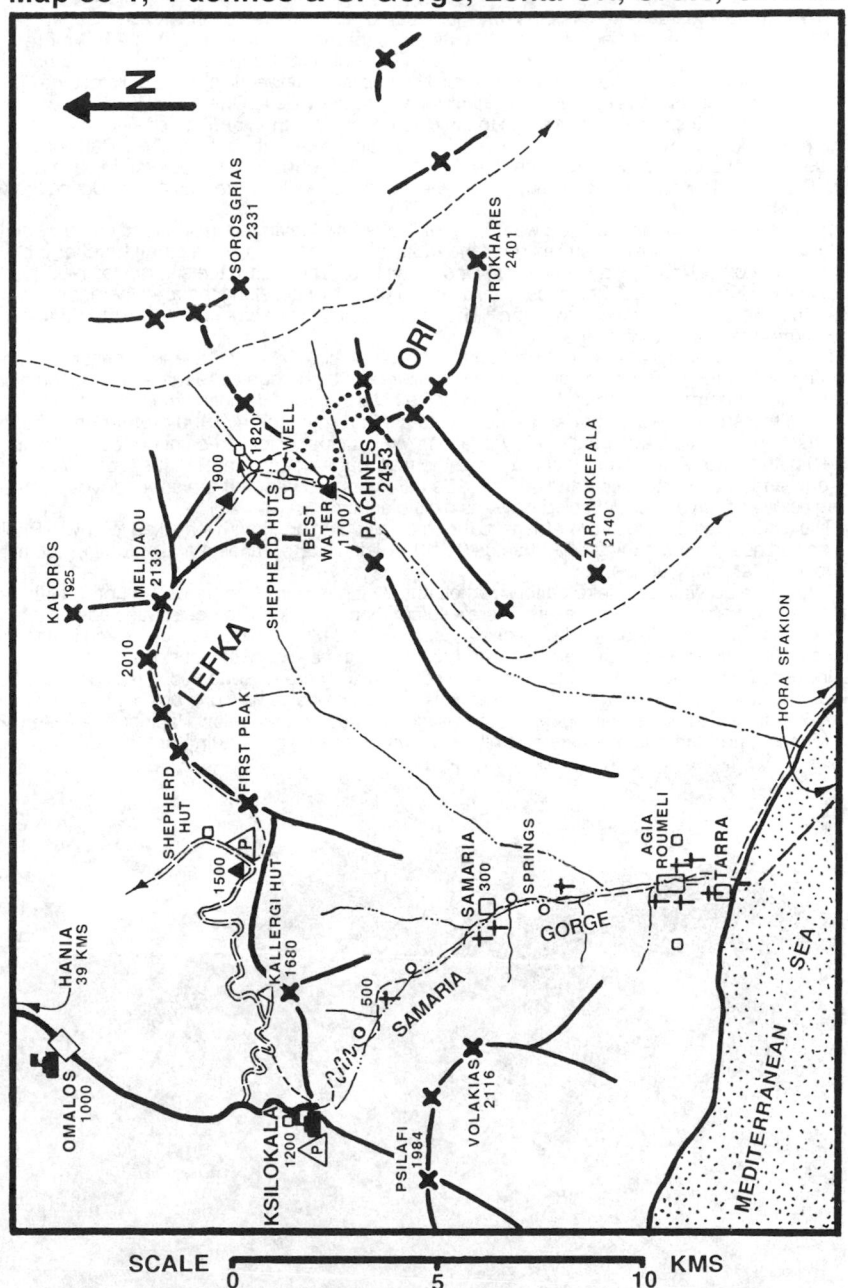

SCALE

0   5   10   KMS

an late afternoon or evening bus back to Hania.

Maps In the books, **The Mountains of Greece,** Sfikas, Efstathiadis Group, Athens; or **Backpacker's Greece**, Bradt Enterprises; or **The Gorge of Samaria**, Iatridis, Self Published, Athens.

Mt. Gamila & Vikos Gorge, Pindos Mountains, Greece

The mountain featured here is probably the best rock climbing region in Greece. Or you can just hike in the area like most people. It's Mt. Gamila (sometimes called Timti) at 2497 meters. It's located in the Pindos Range of northwest Greece. The northern ramparts of this summit has sheer cliffs forming a great wall. The mountain is actually an uplifted plateau-like mass of limestone tilted up to the north, leaving the cliffs exposed and in full view from the valley of the Aoos River.

To climb **Gamila**, drive or take a bus to the city of Ioannina, then another one north to Kalpaki or Papingo Junction. From that junction you may have to hitch hike to the area of the 2 Papingos. There may be a bus or 2 each day going there, but if you arrive at the wrong time, you could be in for a long wait. The author found hitch hiking fairly good, at least on the weekend he was there. During the week there may be less traffic.

Be sure to have all the food you want for your trip before leaving Ioannina, and certainly no later than Kalpaki, as there are no stores near the mountain. There is only a small hotel or inn and a restaurant at Lower Papingo, and nothing in Upper Papingo. This was in the summer of 1989. It's only about one km between the 2 Papingos and it might be best to walk along the road there, then you can easily find one of several places to camp. The best campsite is near a small stream and above the deep *swimming pool* shown on the map.

From Upper Papingo, walk northeast on a very good trail. There are at least 4 drinking fountains or springs along the way before you reach the shelter on a high ridge at 1950 meters. If you want to use the hut, get permission and make payment at the hotel in Lower Papingo before hiking.

From the shelter, walk east *down* the trail to a swampy place at 1800 meters, then continue southeast up a gentle slope east of Mt. Astrakas. Watch closely for red paint on rocks marking the correct path. After 2 or 3 kms, you may lose the trail, but it doesn't matter; just veer to the left 90 degrees, and head northeast to the summit. Be careful not to veer left too soon, or you'll climb the wrong peak, and have to back track a ways, as did the author.

The author took 2 buses from Athens to the Papingo Junction, then hitch hiked to Lower Papingo. He camped near the swimming pool, then on 9/2/1989, left his tent standing and made the summit in 2 2/3 hours; 5 1/2 hours round-trip.

You can also walk to a lake called Drakolimni, which is below some of the upper cliffs of the mountain and northeast of the shelter. There's some good rock climbing possibilities east of this lake. Another easy climb would be to the top of Mt. Astrakas, at 2436 meters. You can climb it via the trail shown, or head southeast from the shelter, and climb it via the easy southeast slope.

Included on this map is the **Vikos Gorge**, a popular hiking area. Read about this one in the books below. Get to Monodhendri by bus from Ioannina. There's probably only one bus per day, so you may have to hitch hike. You can also begin at the village of Vikos, not far below Papingo. Between Vikos and Monodhendri there is at least one trail as shown on the map. Starting at Monodhendri means

From near the top of Gamila, looking west at the east side of Astrakas. The shelter (1950 meters) is on the ridge in the lower right-hand corner.

Map 86-1, Gamila & Vikos Gorge, Pindos Mtns., Greece

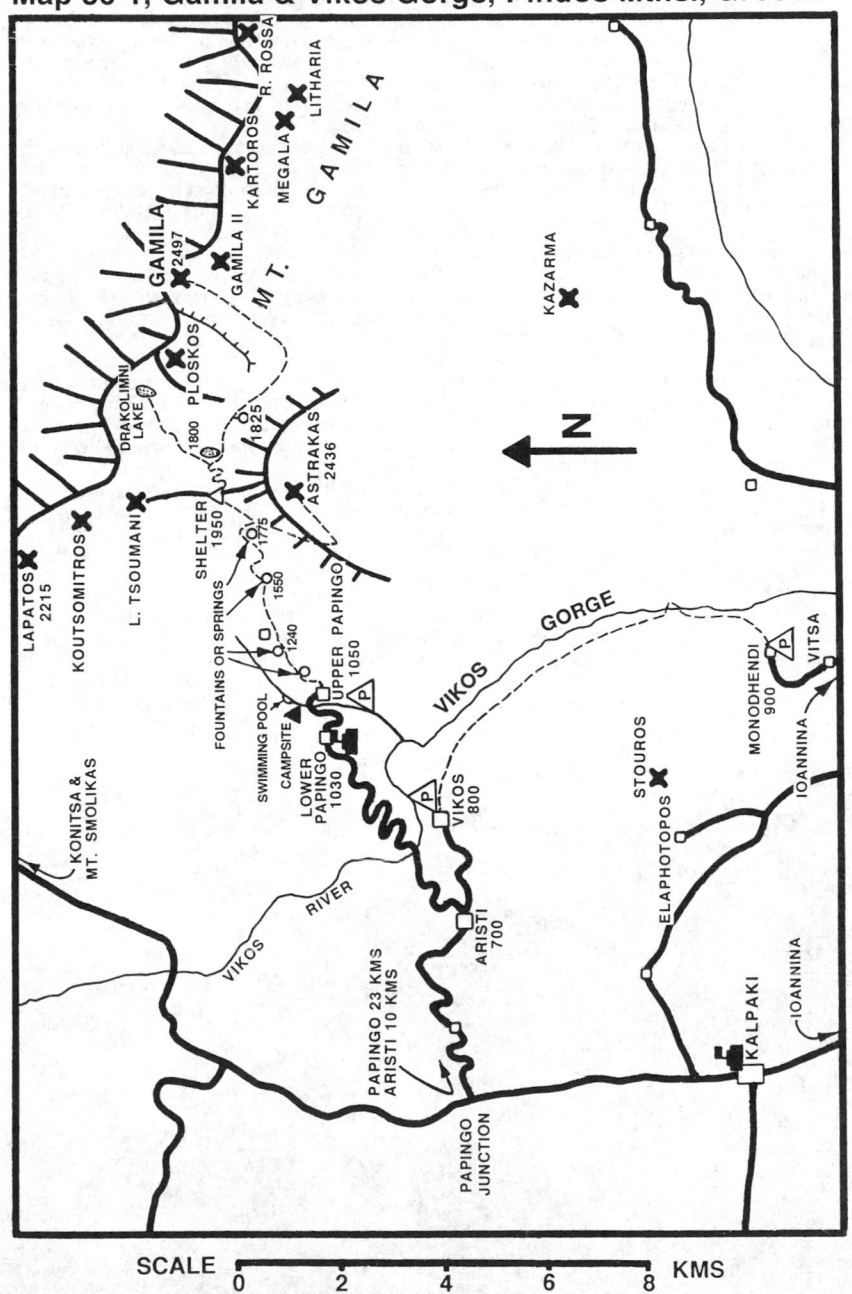

walking downhill.
     Given the elevation of this area, you can hike from May through October, but you may have a harder time getting transportation in the spring or fall.
Maps In the books **The Mountains of Greece**, Sfikas, Efstathiadis Group, Athens; or **Backpacker's Greece**, Bradt Enterprises; or **The Mountains of Greece**, Cicerone Guides.

Mt. Smolikas, Pindos Mountains, Greece

Featured here is the second highest mountain in Greece, Mt. Smolikas at 2637 meters. It's located in the northwest part of the country not far from the Albanian border. It's also directly north of Mt. Gamila (shown on the previous map) and the Aoos River Valley. Of all the mountains the author has climbed in Greece, this one is closest to being a wilderness area. High on the southern slopes are virgin pine forests which were being logged in the summer of 1989. In the meadows above timberline (about 2200 meters) you'll find herds of sheep grazing in summer.

The summit area is made of brown rock with a glassy look, perhaps obsidian or quartzite (?), otherwise the mountains in this region are made of limestone.

Here is the normal way to get to and climb **Smolikas**. The place to start is in the small city of Ioannina to the south. From there take a bus going north to Konitsa, located west of the mountain. At the bus station in the town center, inquire about buses going in the direction of Pades. This village is directly south of Smolikas. There are one or two old dilapidated buses going that way each day; at least that was the situation in the summer of 1989. If you have to wait overnight, there are at least 3 small inexpensive hotels in Konitsa. If you don't want to wait for the next bus, walk up the road a ways and try hitch hiking. There's not a lot of traffic on that road, but the author got a ride to Pades in an old beat-up jalopy carrying pigs in the back after dark one night.

Just as you're arriving in Pades, look to the left or west, and you should see a dirt road signposted for Smolikas. Walk up this road about 200 meters and you'll come to a water trough and fountain. This is a good place to wash or stock up on water. You can also camp in the pine-covered hills nearby. Walk (or maybe get a lift) up this logging road as it zig zags up the slope to the north. If you're on foot you can make shortcuts; or if you have your own vehicle, you can drive halfway up in dry summer weather, which begins sometime in June.

Just beyond the Second Meadow, look for a trail leaving the road as shown. Walk this trail into the upper canyon. At about the point where the trail crosses a creek at 1830 meters, head straight up the ridge to the summit; or continue north to a pass and the lake called Drakolimni at 2220 meters. From the lake, look for a faint trail zig zagging east up the west face of Smolikas. Once you're high on the mountain you can pick you're own route without a trail. The eastern summit appears to be about the same height as the west.

After camping in the forest near Pades, the author hide his pack in the brush and hiked to the summit in 3 hours; round-trip from Pades was 5 1/2 hours. Later that afternoon, he took a bus back to Konitsa and stayed the night in a small hotel for US$8. That day was 9/3/1989.

Konitsa is a nice little town and the best place around to buy camping food or other supplies. You should find a restaurant and one store in Pades, but it's just a village. This mountain has plenty of good water up high and many grassy campsites.

The west face of Smolikas as seen from Drakolimni (Dragon Lake).

Map 87-1, Mt. Smolikas, Pindos Mountains, Greece

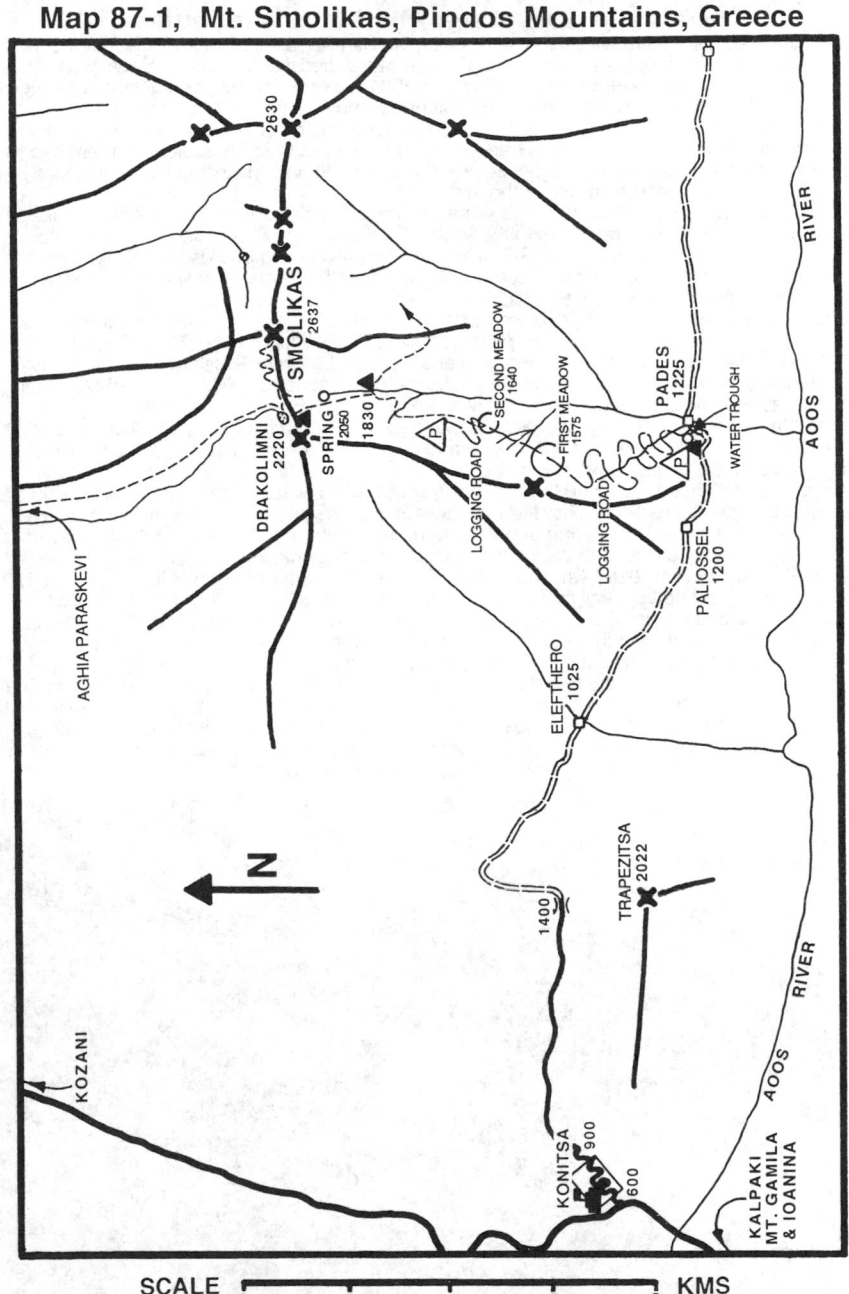

SCALE

0   2   4   6   8   KMS

Maps Try the books, **The Mountains of Greece,** Sfikas, Efstathiadis, Athens; or **The Mountains of Greece,** Cierone Guides; and maybe a travel guidebook to Greece.

Pelister Vrh, Baba Planina, Makedonia

In the extreme southern part of the former Yugoslavian Republic of Makedonia, and not far from the Albanian and Greek borders, is a compact range called the Baba Planina or Baba Mountains. Its highest summit is Pelister Vrh or Pelister Peak, at 2601 meters. This entire highland region east of Bitola is now the Pelister National Park. The mountain range is made of crystalline-type rock.

To get to this area and Bitola from the north, take a bus south from Skopje; or perhaps take a train all or part way. If you're coming from Greece, you'll probably start in Thessalonika, then head west and pass through Edessa and Florina before crossing the border into Makedonia. You can take buses, or hitch hike across the border, as the author did.

This map shows several summer and winter recreation centers. Naselba has a motel-like sports complex with ski runs up the mountain to the south. On the north side of Pleister Vrh, is a place called Kopanke. It too is a ski resort with a hotel. There's a very rough and little-used 4WD-type road to the summit where a microwave station is located, but there are a number of well-marked hiking trails to various parts of the mountain as well.

To climb **Pelister Vrh**, the best place to begin is Naselba. This complex is located due east of Pelister and 10 kms from Bitola, the second largest city in Makedonia. To get there, first go to the train & bus station in Bitola. From there take one of about 5 daily buses to Naselba. But here's a warning, bus schedules may have changed since the author's trip in the fall of 1989. You can also hitch hike from the western side of town where the highway splits.

From the motel at Naselba, walk south and locate a good trail zig zagging up an obvious ridge. At the end of this trail is Golemo Ezero (Big Lake) and an alpinest shelter. You can camp nearby or sleep and buy meals in the shelter which has 45 beds.

From Golemo Ezero, walk up the trail northwest toward Malo Ezero (Little Lake). The trail is marked by painted stones and is easy to follow even in fog. Beyond this second lake, the trail contours along the east face, before heading uphill to the ridgetop where it intersects a 4WD road near the summit. From there walk north to the top with its huge antenna complex.

To return a different route, walk down the east face following the power lines, especially if it's cloudy. There is no apparent trail high on this slope, but further down you'll find many sheep trails. By the time you reach the bottom of the steep slope there is an obvious trail which heads northeast to the mouth of the canyon. The author was here in early September and ate 3 kinds of wild plums, as well as raspberries and blackberries along the lower canyon trail.

The author camped at a municipal campsite in the western end of Bitola for free (but no guards, toilet, or showers!), then on the morning of 9/5/1989, walked half a km west to the highway junction, where he got a short ride on a factory bus. Further up, he hitched to Naselba. He left his pack at the reception desk and did the hike described. From Naselba it took 5 1/2 hours round-trip, but he was in the clouds most of the time. Buy all your food and other supplies in Bitola.

Foto shows the Golemo Ezero (Big Lake) and shelter.

Map 88-1, Pelister Vrh, Baba Planina, Makedonia

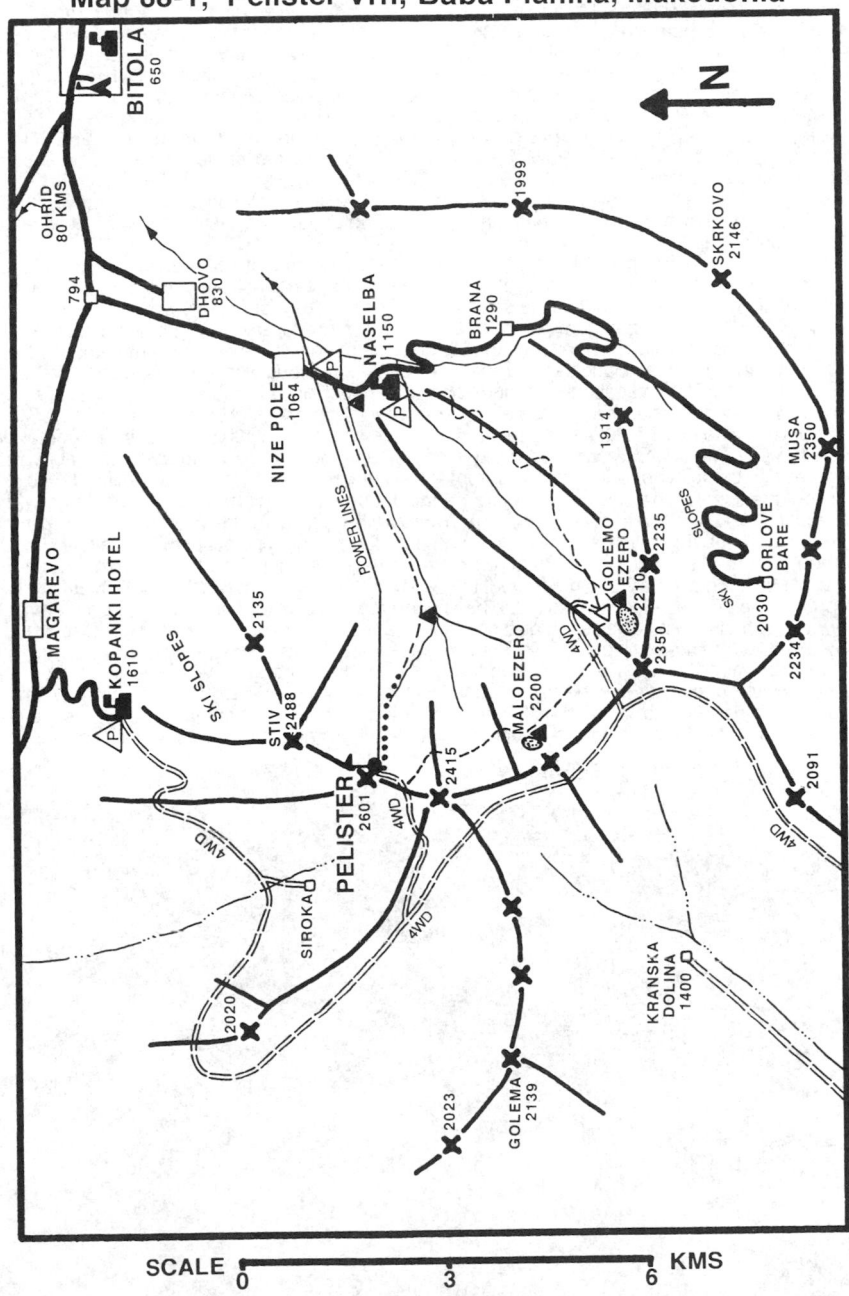

SCALE 0   3   6   KMS

Maps *Resan--Krusevo, 155,* 1:100,000; or DMA map *Tirane, G-1,* 1:250,000, Army Map Service, UK or USA (perhaps it's now a JOG map); and travel guidebook, **Eastern Europe**, Lonely Planet, for updates on changes since the breakup of Yugoslavia.

Titov Vrh, Rudoka Planina, Makedonia

Featured here is what used to be Yugoslavia's second highest summit, Titov Vrh or Titov Peak, at 2748 meters. This peak is now located in the northwestern corner of Makedonia and in the Rudoka Planina or Rudoka Mountains. This small compact range is found immediately west of the city of Tetovo, which is 42 kms west of Skopje, the capital of the Republic of Makedonia. These mountains are made of various metamorphic or crystalline rocks. Included on this map is another mountain range called the Sar Planina which has many peaks over 2500 meters.

Readers beware! The author has drawn this map using a former Yugoslavian 1:250,000 scale military map, and his own sketch drawn in the mist and fog with an altimeter. It should get you there, but it's not as accurate as he, or you, would like.

Getting there is easy. First go to Skopje, then take a bus from the main station to Tetovo. You can also reach this city by bus from the south and Bitola, Ohrid and the Pelister Planina, which is featured on the previous map.

From the bus station in Tetovo, either walk or take a taxi straight south about one km along the main highway out of town. Then turn right or west and after another half km you should be at the base of the gondola which runs straight up the slope to the ski resort town of Popova Sapka.

The gondola was in operation year-round in 1989, but they were closing it down at times in the summer season for repairs and maintenance. During the periods of repairs, they run a bus to Popova Sapka from the base of the Gondola. In September of 1989, the bus went up at 7am and 1pm, and left Popova Sapka for Tetovo at about 9am and 3pm. You could hitch hike, but it might be slow. Or you could walk up the road, which is somewhere between 12 and 14 kms!

Popova Sapka has 3 hotels, some restaurants, many private cabins and ski lifts. The hotel clerks may tell you it's forbidden to camp nearby, so if camping, walk upslope to the southwest above some pine trees and camp out of sight and as far from the ski resort as possible. Take water with you.

From the area of the campsite in the pine trees shown on this map, walk uphill in a westerly direction until you find one of several sheep or hikers trails going up to the peak marked 2500 meters. From that summit, ridge-walk southwest over at least 2 other high points until you reach **Titov Vrh**. On the morning of 9/6/1989, the author left his home-stay room in Ohrid (located in the southeast corner of Makedonia) on a 7:30am bus. Got to Tetovo in 3 hours, but had to wait until 3pm for a bus up to Popova Sapka. He put up his tent in the trees, then raced the setting sun, and in clouds and mist all the way, reached a high point a short distance from the main summit in less than 3 hours round-trip.

The smooth rounded slopes above Popova Sapka are uninteresting, so the adventurous hiker-climber might head for Vesala, which is in the canyon to the north, and walk southwest from there. The northwest slopes appear to be rather rugged with large cirque basins. There should be some kind of public transportation to Vesala. Ask about that at the Tetovo bus terminal. There must be one or more cheap hotels in Tetovo, but the author was in and out fast and camping, and didn't ask.

This is part of Popova Sapka, a ski resort just northeast of Titov Vrh.

Map 89-1, Titov Vrh, Rudoka Planina, Makedonia

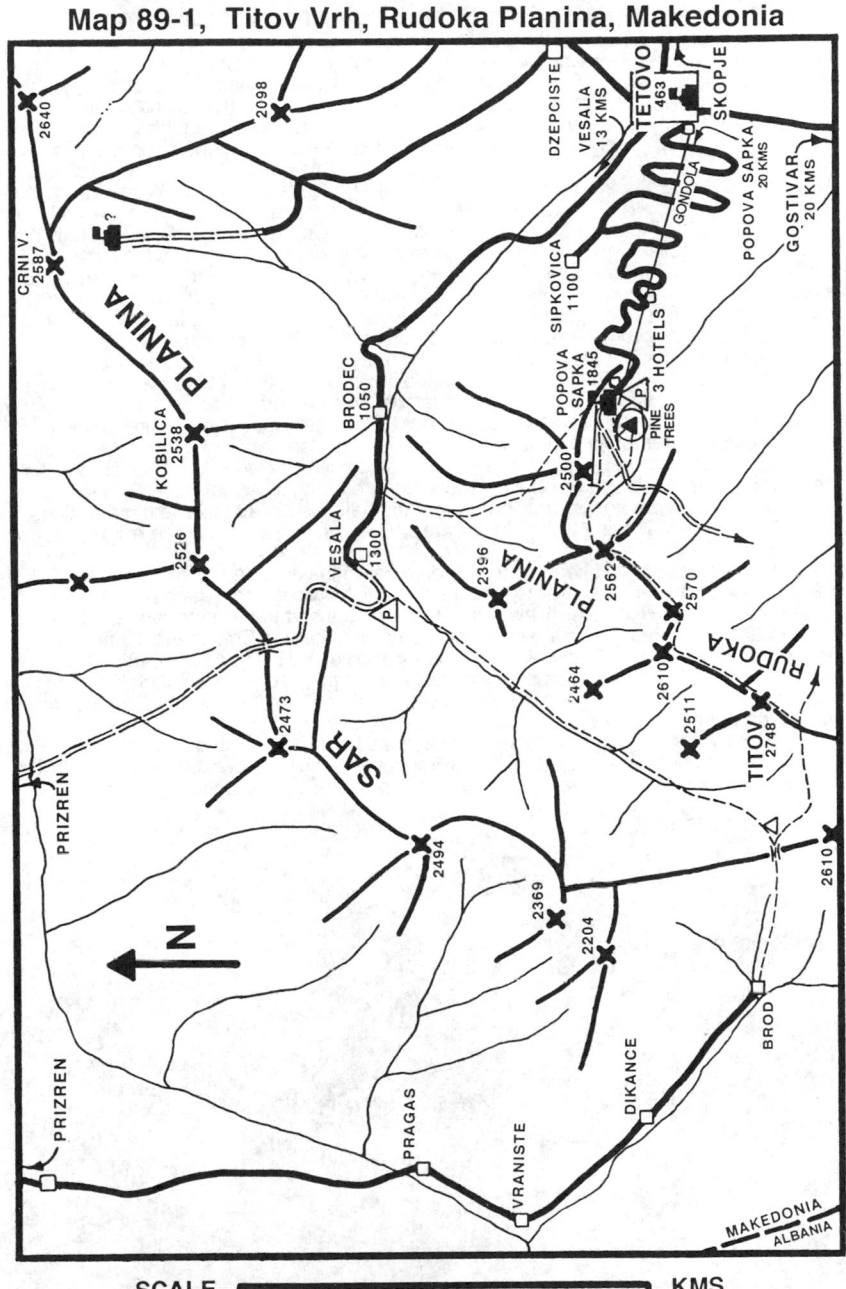

SCALE

0   5   10   KMS

Maps *Sheets 140, 141, 147 and 148,* 1:100,000, Army Map Service (?) or DMA (or maybe JOG) maps *Skopje and Prizren,* 1:250,000; and travel guidebook, **Eastern Europe**, Lonely Planet, for updates on changes since the breakup of Yugoslavia.

Bobotov Kuk, Durmitor Planina, Montenegro-Yugoslavia

This map shows the central portion of the Durmitor Planina or Durmitor Mountains, located in what is now northwestern Montenegro, a (former?) republic of Yugoslavia. These are magnificent peaks and have the appearance of the Alps, although the highest summit, Bobotov Kuk, is only 2523 meters. Next to Triglav in the far north, these might be the best mountains and climbs in all of the former Yugoslavia. There are even some perpetual snow fields on the higher summits. These mountains are made up mostly of limestone. In this range are a number of mountain huts and well-marked trails.

These mountains are located about halfway between Podgorica (formerly Titograd) and Sarajevo. To get there, first go to Podgorica, then take a train, or perhaps bus, north to Mojkovak, located southeast of Durmitor. From the train station, walk half a km to the bus station on the main highway and catch a bus to Zabljak, which is at the northeastern base of the Durmitor. In the summer of 1989, there were 2 buses going that way each morning, 2 more in the late afternoon or evening. This schedule will likely change with the seasons, and perhaps with the breakup of Yugoslavia (?). Zabljak is a year-round hiking, climbing, and ski center. In some ways, Zabljak is similar to Chamonix, Zermatt or Heiligenblut because of its location near a nice hiking area, but much smaller.

From the bus stop in Zabljak, walk west on the main road toward the Hotel Durmitor and the national park headquarters. Before leaving town, do all your shopping. There are several shops with plenty of food. When you reach the park headquarters, be sure and talk to them about various trails, routes, mountain huts or doms, campsites and water. These are limestone mountains with almost no surface or running water, so late in summer you'll have to plan your trip around the availability of water. Also, buy a better map than this one. There's a good one included in a book called, **Durmitor and the Tara Canyon**. This book comes in about 4 different languages, including English.

From the park headquarters, walk southwest on the paved road to Crno Jezera (Crno Lake). There you'll find a newly built (1989) restaurant where you can also buy the map and book just mentioned.

From the Crno Jezera, first head northwest on a trail to the Jacsika Mill, then turn southwest and walk another good and well-used trail to the huts at Katun Lokvice. From there head west over a low pass, then southwest to **Bobotov**. This is one of the most-used trails in the range. The return trip could include Bezimeni Peak and the huts at Stari Katun, then back to Crno Jezera.

The author got a bus from Tetovo & Titov Vrh to a place called Ivangrad and camped in a city park. Next morning, 9/8/1989, he got a bus to Mojkovac, then Zabljak; bought maps, then left his big pack at Crno Jezera and hiked to & climbed Bobotov in 5 hours round-trip. You'll want more time than this-- probably all day for most people.

While Bobotov is a rugged peak, there are others, perhaps more rugged, to the east, all with trails or routes to the summits. In a couple of places, iron routes (cables) have been built to help climbers up. A climb to the summit of Meded will give you some of the best views around. This is the

The Durmitor Planina (D. Mountains) as seen from near the National Park Headquarters. The peak in the center is Meded.

Map 90-1, Bobotov, Durmitor Planina, Montenegro-Yugo.

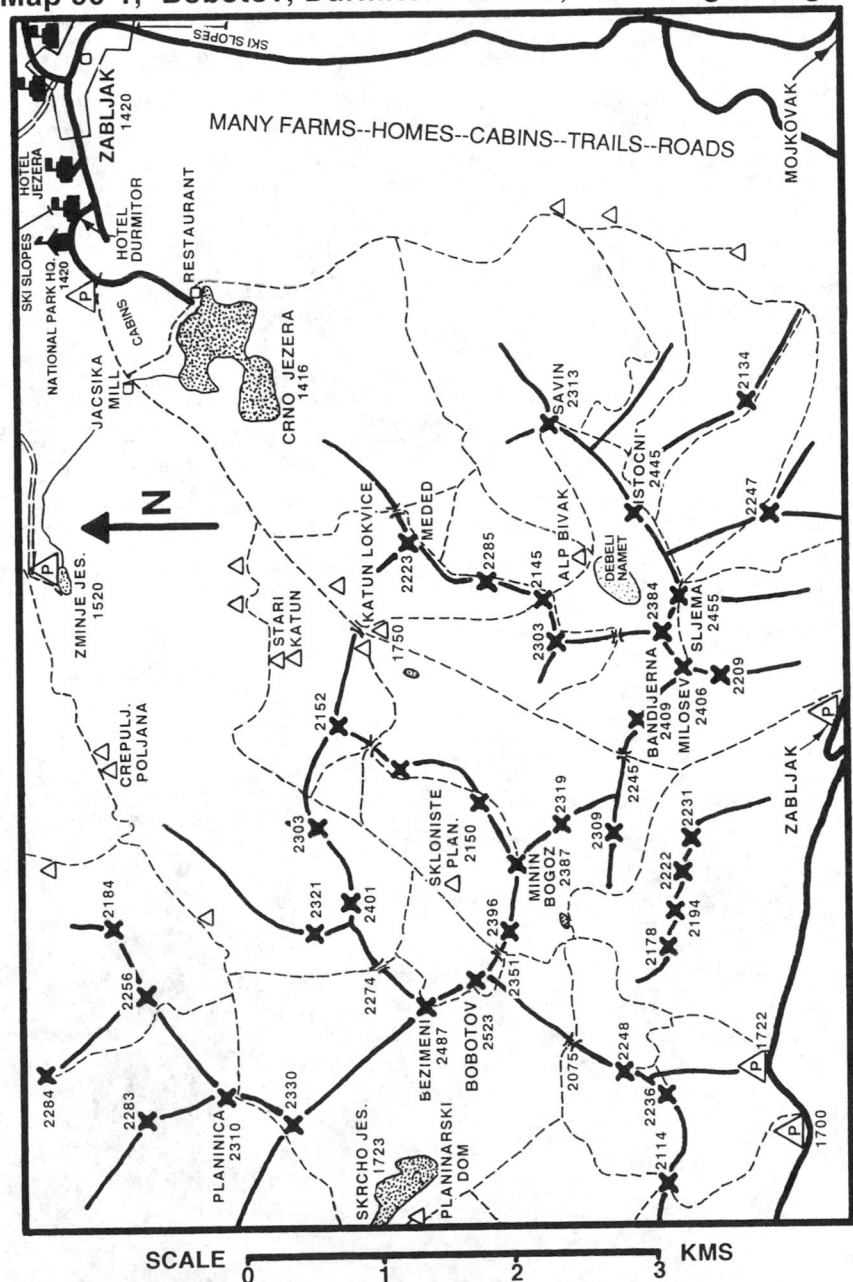

SCALE
0   1   2   3   KMS

prominent peak seen from Crno Jezera. Some of the shelters shown on this map appear to be old shepherd huts.

Maps Excellent map and book, both with the same name, **Durmitor and the Tara Canyon,** 1:25,000, buy locally; and travel guidebook, **Eastern Europe**, Lonely Planet, for updates on changes since the breakup of Yugoslavia.

Corno Grande, Gran Sasso D'Italia, Italy

Located northeast of Roma in the middle of Italia, is a small mountain range known as the Gran Sasso D'Italia. Its highest peak is Corno Grande at 2912 meters. The summits here are truly alpine, but there are no trees on the mountain except for a few that are planted (reforestation) on some of the lower slopes.

To get there, take Autostrada 24 east out of Roma in the direction of L'Aquila. You can also take a bus leaving about once every hour from near the central train station in Roma. Or you can take a train, but the train takes twice as long as buses and costs more. You can also arrive in the area from the east coast of Italia on the same autostrada, but exit at Assergi at the west end of the tunnel.

L'Aquila is a pleasant small city at 900 meters altitude. It has several supermarkets and a tourist office. From there you can either drive or hitch hike to the end of a paved road at a place called Campo Imperatore at 2130 meters. There at the top of a funivia (tramway), is a ski resort and some kind of an osservatore (observatory).

You can also take a city bus from the center of L'Aquila to Assergi. From there walk to the bottom of the funivia, then either take the funivia, or walk up the main trail below the lift. There's a campground at the base of the funivia, or you can camp for free in the planted forest (reforested area) above. If you do this, remove the tent the next morning.

From Campo Imperatore and the top of the funivia, walk up the slope to the west, either to the Rifugio Abruzzi, or along another trail heading directly toward Corno Grande. From the Rifugio Abruzzi, where you'll have a fine view of the mountain, walk due north on a well-used trail to the lower end of the west ridge at 2506 meters, thence east to the summit.

Or you can climb the south face route which is marked with green paint. The south face requires some climbing on all-4's, making it just difficult enough to be interesting. On the north slope of the main summit is a small icefield.

A second way up would be from the north side and the ski resort named Prati di Tivo. At certain times of the year, some of those lifts could be used to reach the 2028 meter mark; then it would be a short hike to the summit.

There are a number of rifugios on and around the mountain. Most sell food and drinks and have beds and rooms for rent. They are much quieter during the week than on weekends or holidays. Lots of people are on this mountain on summer weekends.

Be aware of one minor problem, lack of water. These mountains are made of limestone and very porous, so there's no running water anywhere near the route described above--except maybe in late spring or early summer. Make sure you have enough water with you before leaving Campo Imperatore.

The author took one bus from Roma to L'Aquila, another to Assergi, then walked to and camped in the reforested area. Next morning, 8/5/1989, he hid his big pack in the trees, climbed up the trail below the funivia and on to the summit in about 3 hours. His total round-trip time from his pack & campsite

Corno Grande as seen from the Rifugio Abruzzi.

Map 91-1, Corno Grande, Gran Sasso D'Italia, Italy

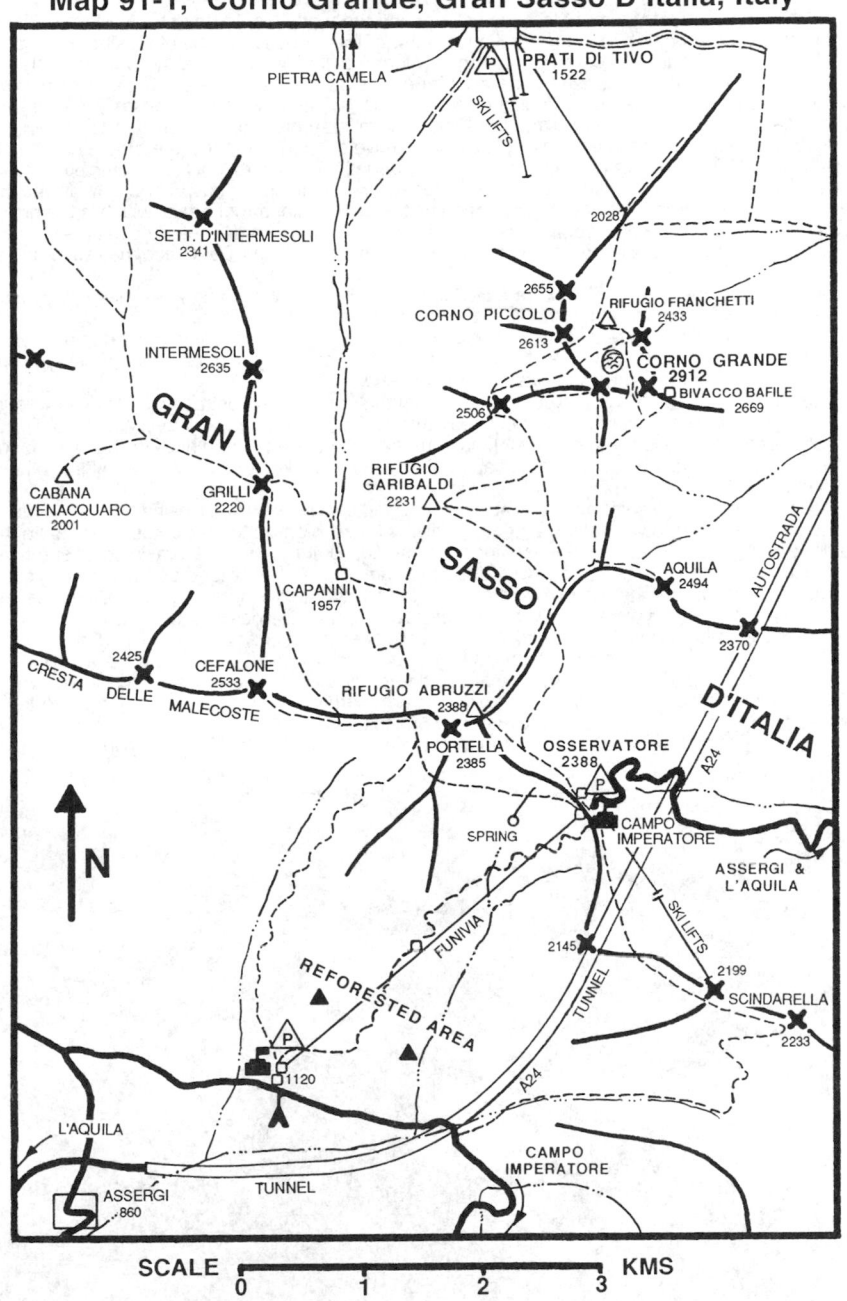

SCALE 0 1 2 3 KMS

was under 6 hours.

Maps *Gran Sasso D'Italia,* 1:50,000, Club Alpino Italiano, buy in L'Aquila, or perhaps at one of the hotels on the mountain (?); and a travel guidebook to Italia.

Monte Vesuvio, Italy

Historically, one of the most famous volcanos in the world would have to be Monte Vesuvio at 1281 meters. It's located in central Italia just east of the Napoli suburbs of Resina and Torre Del Greco. Several thousand years ago, a larger volcano called Mt. Somma, blew up leaving a small caldera. Later, a new composite cone developed inside the older crater; this is the present-day Vesuvio. Its most famous eruption occurred in 79 A.D., which covered and destroyed Pompeii and other nearby villages killing thousands. Later, a big plinian eruption occurred in 1631, which also caused fatalities. Since then a number of lava flows have occurred, with the latest big eruption being in 1944. In 10/1999, there were seismic swarms, the largest in 50 years, so it isn't completely dead yet! For updated volcano information see the websites (www.volcano.si.edu/gvp/) or (www.stromboli.net).

The Vesuvio we know today is surrounded by the old circular rim of peaks which is the rim of the Somma Caldera. This whole complex is located less than 5 kms from a heavily populated region just east of Napoli. When it blows up again, the cities of Resina and Torre Del Greco may suffer the same fate as Pompeii.

Vesuvio and the ruins of Pompeii are big tourist attractions in these parts. As many as a thousand tourists climb this volcano every day in the summer season. Vesuvio has an impressive crater for those who haven't seen a real volcano up close. Most people going there join a group and go to the mountain from Napoli in a tour bus. Many groups have a multi-lingual guide. Others rent cars, while a few hitch hike, as the author did in the summer of 1989.

On 8/2/1989, the author came to the area from the south on Autostrada A3, running west of the volcano. He left his ride at the Torre del Greco exit, walked up the road a ways, and hitch hiked. He remembers the trailhead being about 12 kms from the autostrada (?), and hitch hiking fairly good. He eventually got a lift to the bus parking lot at 1017 meters. He hiked to the rim in 15 minutes then was back at the trailhead in one hour, round-trip.

The topo map of Vesuvio indicates another road to the trailhead from Resina. It's about the same distance from either town to the trailhead. When you get high on the mountain and inside the old caldera, you'll see signs everywhere stating no camping. But if you're on foot you could surely hide a tent in the pine trees for one night. If you decide to camp, take all your food and water with you to the mountain. At the end of the paved road are a couple of dilapidated restaurants and a filthy toilet, as well as a number of open-air vendors selling post cards, books and all kinds of souvenirs.

From the trailhead to the crater rim it's only about one km and can be walked in 15 minutes. Near the top is a ticket booth and everyone has to pay an entry fee of about US$3. This crater is 330 meters deep and very impressive. If one were allowed to climb down, it would have to be with very long ropes. Before the paved highway was built to the mountain, there used a lift or funivia to transport tourists to the crater rim. That's now abandoned and in ruins.

The busy time is summer, that's when the weather is dry and stable. Spring and fall would also

An aerial postcard view of Vesuvio looking north. The older crater rim is in the lower background.

Map 92-1, Monte Vesuvio, Italy

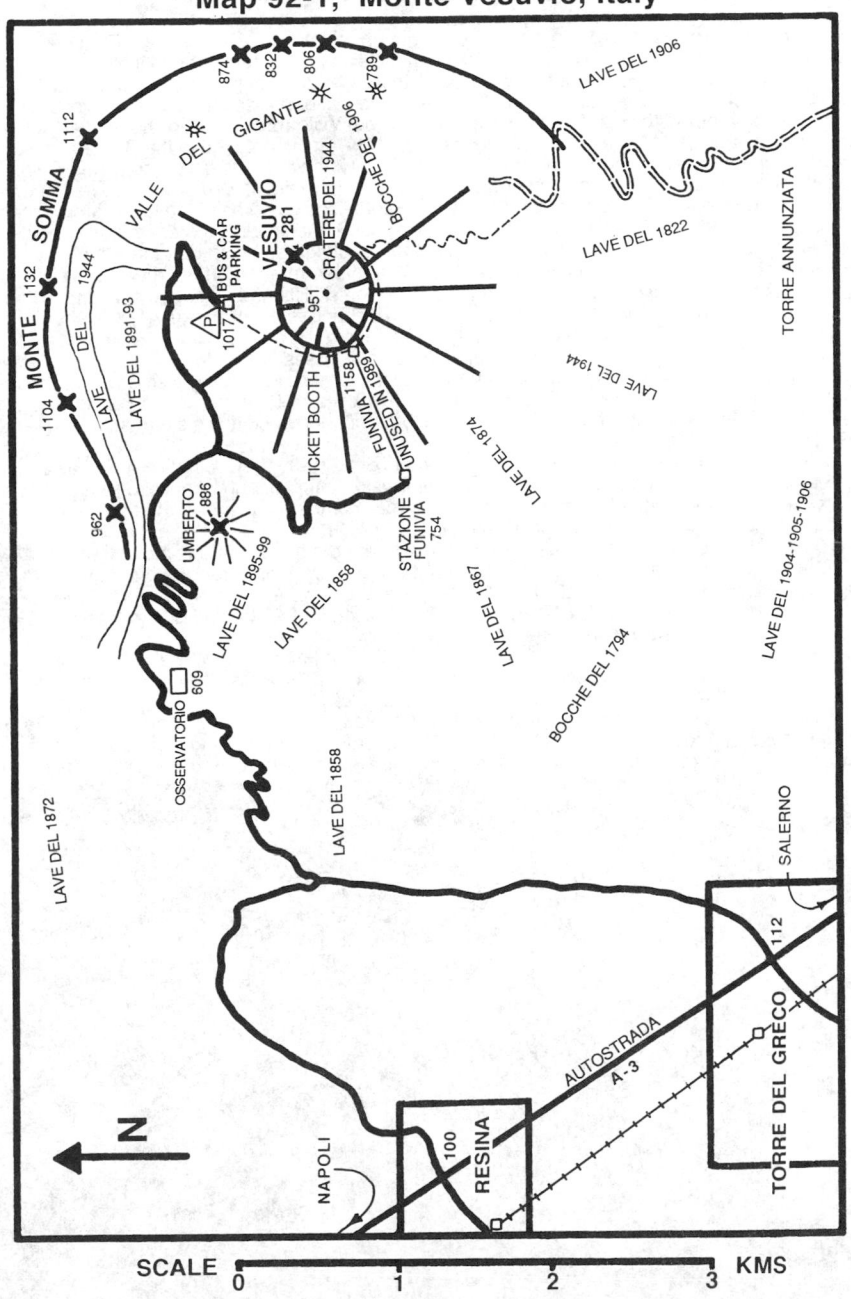

SCALE 0   1   2   3   KMS

be nice. If you're in Napoli, any travel agent can line you up with a tour group and go there in a bus.
Maps *Vesuvio,* 1:25,000, Instituto Geografico de Agostini, S.p. A., Novara, Italia; and a travel guidebook to Italia.

Monte Etna, Island of Sicilia, Italy

The volcano on this map is the huge massive hulk of Monte Etna rising to 3340 (or 3315) meters. It's located on the island of Sicilia just off the southern tip of Italia. For many years Etna has been in almost continuous eruption. The author visited the mountain on 7/28/1989, and found it smoking to the point that fotography was impossible. At that time there was activity in the small Southeast Crater, which blew smoke and molten rock high in the air every few minutes with muffled explosions.

Here's some of the latest information from the **Global Volcanism Network**. On 9/4/1999 there were eruptions from the Voragine Crater, then on 9/20/1999, activity shifted to the Bocca Nova Crater (BNC). Later the activity shifted to the Northeast Crater in October. During that month there was lava fountaining and Strombolian activity in the BNC, and still later, lava flowed down the western slopes for the first time since 1964. Strombolian eruptions were taking place as of the last report which was 6/2000. For updated information see the websites (www.volcano.si.edu/gvp/) or (www.stromboli.net).

Halfway up the southern slopes of Etna, are several buildings located at the top of the ski lifts which were damaged in the lava flows back in 1985. In the summer of 1989, there was some road building going on and it appeared they were going to get the ski lifts and other equipment ready for the following season. This is an ongoing evolution, so expect changes on this very lively volcano.

To climb **Etna** via the route normal, first go to Catania, a large city south of the mountain on the east coast of Sicilia. From there take one of several daily buses to Nicolosi, 18 kms from Catania. The author isn't sure, but there must be a public bus or two each day going all the way to the resort complex called Monte Etna and the Rifugio Sapienza. This is at 1900 meters on the south slope. The author took a bus to Nicolosi, then hitch hiked from there up then back down the mountain. He found hitch hiking good in 1989.

At Monte Etna is a first aid station, several restaurants, many souvenir shops, and at least one hotel called Rifugio Sapienza. These businesses haul water to the mountain, so take some with you or expect to *buy* it there. Bring all your food as well. You can camp near the resort, but do so out of sight. You can also join a group going high on the mountain in 4WD's.

To climb the mountain, either walk up the dirt road toward a rifugio at 2941 meters; or simply walk up along the ski lifts in a more direct line toward the top. Above La Montagnola, look for the trail roughly paralleling an old funivia, cutting off lots of extra walking. At the highest rifugio, you may see signs telling, *go no further*, but of course you can. The reason for the warning is, if you get hurt by lava bombs, the authorities won't be responsible.

From the rifugio at 2941 meters, walk due north to the summit and hope the wind is blowing from the south. The author hid his big pack near the Rifugio Sapienza, then climbed to the top in 2 1/4 hours; round-trip in less than 4 hours. This isn't a very long hike.

If the volcano is alive when you arrive, head up in the afternoon and orient yourself, then stay until after dark for some real fireworks. Take a flashlight to come down with, and tripod for fotos of crater glow and fountaining after the sun sets. Consider camping somewhere in the vicinity of the rifugio at

An aerial postcard view looking west (?) at Monte Etna.

Map 93-1, Monte Etna, Island of Sicilia, Italy

2941 meters for a real night-time light show.
Maps *Monte Etna,* 1:100,000 (also in 1:50,000 scale), Instituto Geografico de Agostini, S.p. A., Novara, Italia; and a travel guidebook to Italia.

Introduction to the Eolie or Lípari Islands, Italy

Most people have heard of the island or volcano of Strombóli, but few people outside of Italia, and even fewer outside of Europe, have ever heard of the Eolie or Lípari Islands. This is a group of volcanic islands located directly north of Sicilia. The group includes one of the most active volcanos in the world--Strombóli at 924 meters. It's been continuously active or alive since anyone can remember, and it's visited every night in summer by perhaps a 100 tourists, maybe more.

If you visit these islands in summer you'll have lots of ferry boats and hydrofoil craft (called aliscafi) to choose from. You can take an aliscafi from Napoli or Messina, but by far the most-used port of departure because of its nearness to these islands, and the port with the cheapest fares, is Milazzo on the north coast of Sicilia. You can get to Milazzo by bus, train, automobile or hitch hiking.

There are several boats leaving Milazzo's port daily with at least 2 companies in competition for passengers. Most of these ferry boats or aliscafi make a quick stop at Porto Levante on Vulcano, then go on to the city of Lípari, the capital of the island group. From Lípari, boats fan out to all the other islands. Salina is the biggest island with lots of inhabitants and visitors. The fourth most visited island is Strombóli. There is one ferry boat visiting Strombóli each day and several aliscafi. For hikers, climbers and volcano hunters, this is the most popular island to visit. All boats going to Strombóli also stop at Panarea. The 2 small islands to the west, Alicudi and Filicudi are visited less often.

Since these islands are small and very mountainous, there aren't many places to camp. However, if you're determined to save the cost of a hotel room, you can always find a place for a tent. The author never did see a campground, except on the island of Vulcano. Also, every night there are campers sleeping on top of Strombóli watching the fireworks.

One big problem you'll have if you're camping on these islands is water. There are simply no streams anywhere and during the long, hot, dry summers, some water is brought in by ship. So each time you get a chance to fill a water bottle for free, do so. Most people end up buying soda pop or bottled water from supermarkets and at ridiculous prices. As you travel around you'll see hundreds of these empty bottles littering the islands.

The season with the best weather is always summer, but it gets pretty warm then and everything gets brown. It seems that April and May, and again in September and October would be the ideal times to climb or hike in these islands. There would be fewer tourists at that time, but fewer scheduled boats as well. The author spent 4 days in these islands between 7/29/1989 and 8/1/1989.

Maps Map and Chart *Isole Eolie o Lípari*, Arte Photo Graphic, Oreste Ragusi, Milazzo. Buy this or a similar map locally at any nearby souvenir shop; also, the latest travel guidebook to Italia for any new information on schedules of ferry boats, hotels, etc.

A postcard view of Salinas Island. Porri to the far upper left, Fossa is in the center left.

Map 94-1, Introduction to the Eolie/Lípari Islands, Italy

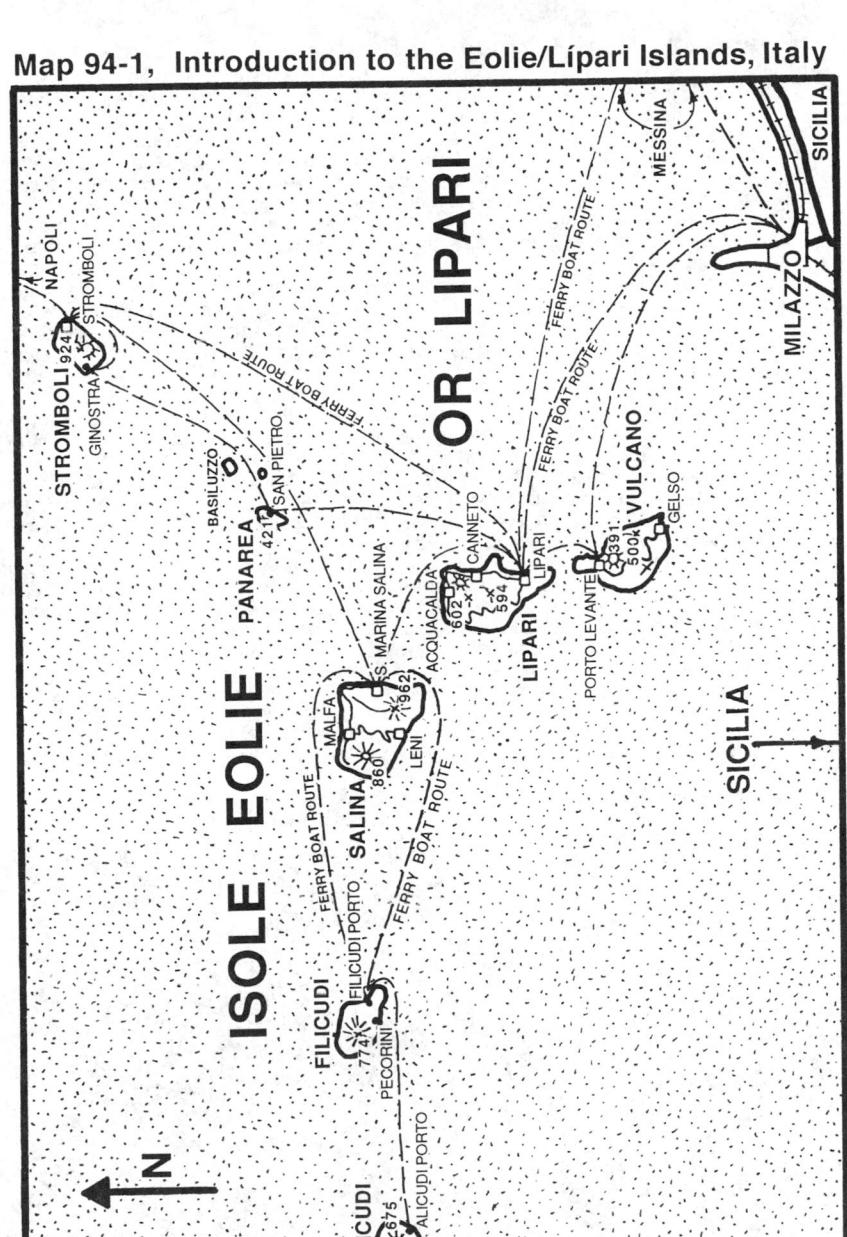

Peaks on Lípari & Vulcano, Eolie & Lípari Islands, Italy

The islands shown here are Lípari and Vulcano, the 2 islands closest to the port of Milazzo on Sicilia. Each island has some very old and eroded volcanos, but on Vulcano there's a young, and an active cone, with many sulfur and steam vents.

The active volcano on Vulcano Island is called Gran Cratere. It last erupted in 1888-90 when meter-sized bombs and lava blocks fell in the area now occupied by the village of Porto di Levante. It was still steaming as of 10/1999. Just north of the port is Vulcanello, the youngest part of the island. It began to form about 2100 years ago as in isolated island that later became connected with the main island. The latest activity of Vulcanello occurred in the 1500's when lava flows, now covered by hotel complexes, were extruded. For updated information see the websites (www.volcano.si.edu/gvp/) or (www.stromboli.net).

Here's how to climb **Gran Cratere**, the highest point on the island of Vulcano. From the docks at Porto di Levante, walk south into the business district of town. From the area of restaurants, continue south for about 200 meters, then turn left onto a cobblestone street. There should be a sign, but if you get confused ask about the trail to the Gran Cratere. This very good and well-used trail first zig zags up the slope, then veers to the right or west. After less than 2 kms, you'll arrive at the crater rim. From there you can rim-walk around the crater and/or walk down into the smoky & steaming basin. There are sulfur vents in the bottom which you can smell from town. The highest point on the rim is 391 meters. From there you have an excellent view of Vulcano, and Lípari Island to the north. From the port, you can do this hike in about 2 hours round-trip. The author was here on 8/1/1989.

Near the port are many restaurants & hotels and some fumaroles & mud pots which are tourist attractions. There's a campground north of the port, and southwest of the younger cone called **Vulcanello**. You could drop a tent (bivwak) for one night about any place on the island where there's no people--just put it up out of sight and don't leave a mess.

The mountains on Lípari are higher, but not as interesting, and nothing active. Here's a suggestion for an all-day hike. Take the once-hourly bus from near the port in Lípari toward Acquacalda on the north coast. At the east end of Acquacalda, and at the first switchback in the highway, begin walking south. A dirt road takes you past the pumice & obsidian mines on the west side of the crater named Pilato. This is the only place on the island that still resembles a volcano.

From there, walk along a road heading southwest to the garbage dump. At the dump, locate a trail running south up the east end of **Chirica** (602 meters). On the other side, another track heads south and toward the east end of Angelo. Along the way are old abandoned farms. On top of **Angelo** is a microwave tower and a cement water catchment basin. From that area, road-walk down to Varesana and Pianoconte and catch another bus back to Lípari and your hotel, the youth hostel in the castle, or a campground.

If you do this hike in summer be sure and take more water than you think you'll need. In the later afternoon of 7/31/1989, the author took his entire pack and camped near the summit of Angelo, after

Looking north toward Lípari Island from the summit of Gran Cratere. Notice the steam & yellow sulfur in the crater.

Map 95-1, Peaks on Lípari & Vulcano, Eolie/Lípari, Italy

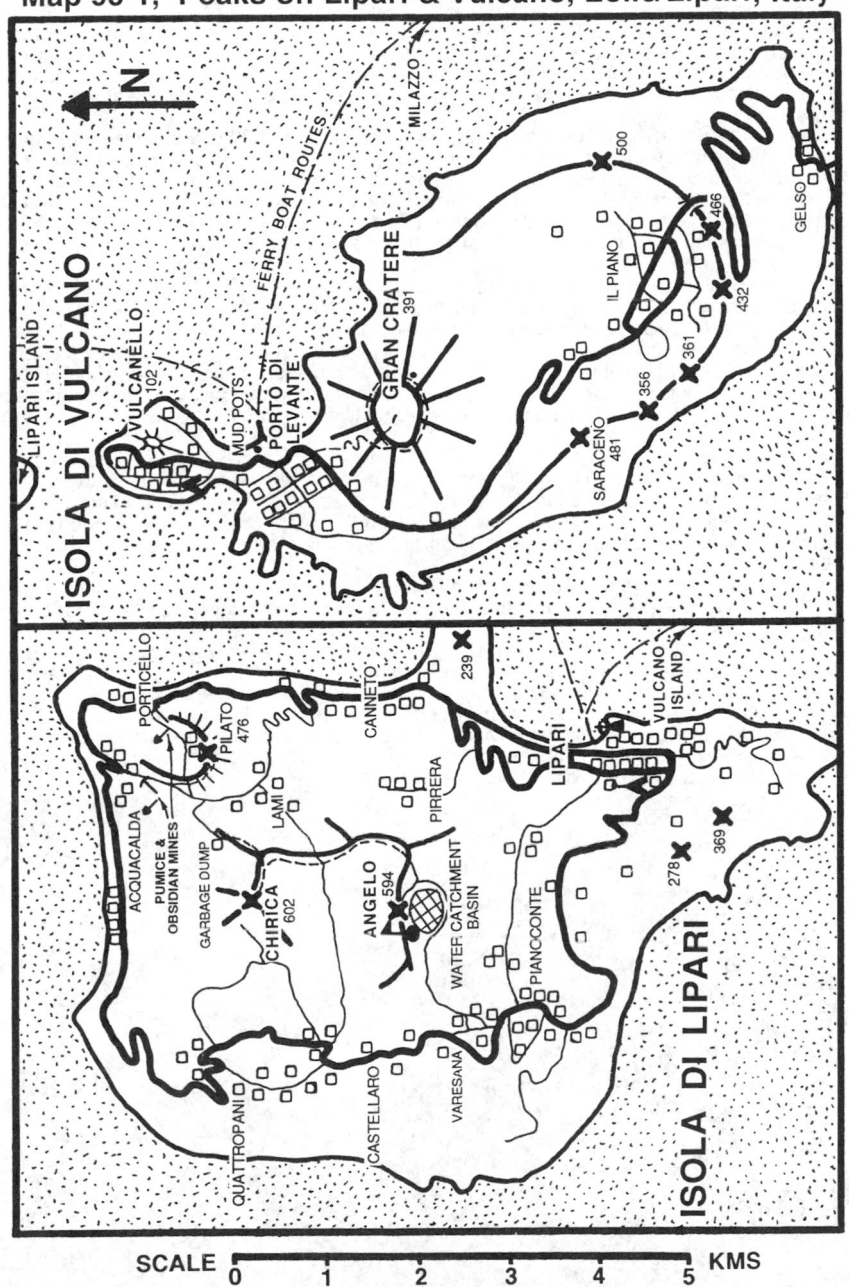

SCALE 0 1 2 3 4 5 KMS

walking from the east end of Acquacalda in 3 hours (in the hot afternoon sun!). He drank between 3 and 4 liters of water in that 3 hours! For most people it would be best to do this in one day from Lípari with a day-pack only. Lípari is the capital of the island group and has the biggest and best supermarkets around.

Strombóli Volcano, Eolie or Lípari Islands, Italy

One of the most active volcanos in the world is on Strombóli, one of the Eolie or Lípari Islands. These islands are just north of Sicilia. This volcano has had gas explosions continuously for many years and has developed into a real tourist attraction. The highest summit is known as **Váncori** at 924 meters. Most people however just climb to the viewing area called Pizzo Sopra La Fossa at 918 meters, for a good look down into the active part of the crater, which is below and at a relatively safe distance.

Strombóli has been in almost continuous eruption for over 2000 years. Its small *Strombólian* explosions, which hurl incandescent scoria above the crater rim, occur several times an hour throughout the day, but larger eruptions are less frequent. This map is similar to what was observed in 6/1999, as featured in the **Bulletin of the Global Volcanism Network**. The active craters are on the northwest part of the volcano and all ejecta rolls down the northwest face called the Sciara del Fuoco, to the sea. For updated information see the websites (www.volcano.si.edu/gvp/) or (www.stromboli.net).

The ferry boat you'll be on will leave from Lípari, first stopping at the island of Panarea, then the town of Ginostra (without docking) on the west end of Strombóli. Small boats come out to exchange empty gaz tanks for full ones, as well as taking on food and other supplies. The ferry then sails to the east end of the island and the village of Strombóli. This is a rather large village with several small hotels, a youth hostel and a number of small restaurants and stores. In 1989, the ferry boat ticket office was very near the port as shown. One ferry comes to this island every day in summer, but several hydrofoil craft (aliscafi) make the trip daily; some from Milazzo, but others possibly from Messina or Napoli.

From the port, walk into the main part of town on narrow streets only wide enough for motor scooters; there are no cars on the island. Somewhere along the way you'll have to stock up on water. If you're taking a big pack and plan to stay on top for the night, you'll need up to 4-5 liters for a 24 hour period (the author used 4 1/2 liters in 20 hours in 7/1989!). Try to climb in the early morning or late afternoon to avoid the heat of the day in summer. Spring or fall might be more comfortable for climbing.

When you have all your supplies, walk north through town and to the trail going up the north ridge as shown. With a large pack the author took 2 1/2 hours up; one hour down the next morning. His trip was on 7/29 & 7/30/1989.

Some people stay in a hotel but climb up in the late afternoon. After seeing the eruptions just after dark, they go down using flashlights. If you plan to do this, it might pay to join a group for a small fee and go with a guide. Most of those returning with the guides use the *return trail* as shown. Don't attempt to go up this trail as you'll never find the beginning at the bottom. In summer, about 100 people a night observe the eruptions. In the daytime, all you'll see is a lot of smoke and flying lava; but at night, this same lava glows red in the dark. This is one of the best place in the world to see, feel, smell and hear a real live active volcano--and live to tell about it.

The smoking Strombóli Volcano as seen from the ferry boat and town of Strombóli.

Map 96-1, Strombóli Volcano, Eolie/Lípari Islands, Italy

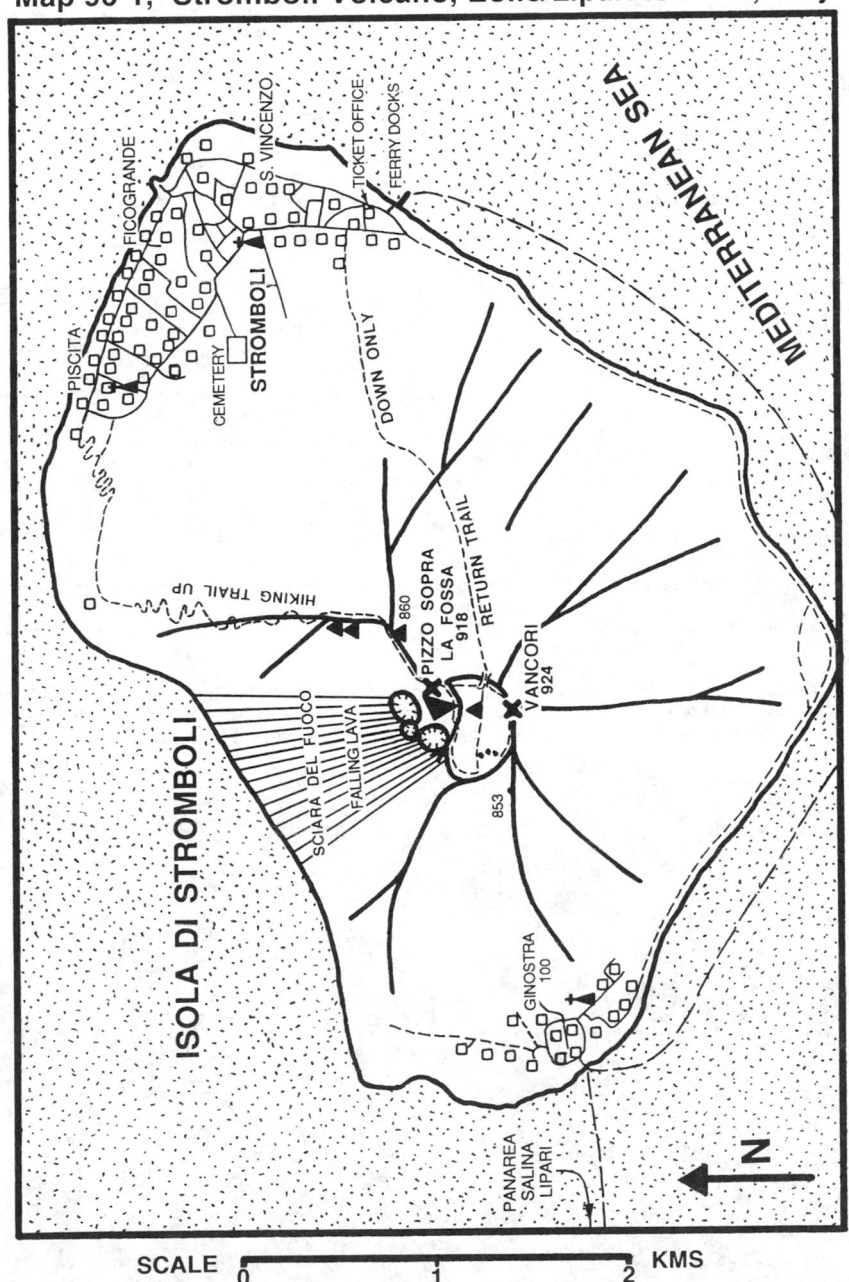

SCALE 0 1 2 KMS

Over the years, a number of small stone wind shelters (no roofs) have been built on the crater rim. Most of these are big enough for 2 or 3 people to sleep in, while some are large enough for a small tent. If you plan to stay the night, it might be best to place your tent back from the observation point a ways to insure a good night's sleep.

Monte Fossa, Salina Island, Eolie or Lípari Islands, Italy

The island on this map is called Isola di Salina, and it's the third largest in the Eolie or Lípari island group located just north of Sicilia (on this map it appears to be the largest?). The highest summit in the entire island group is Monte Fossa, at 962 meters. North of this summit, and on the the main ridge, is a subsidiary peak called Monte Rivi at 854 meters. The other main mountain on this island is called Monte del Porri at 860 meters. Porri still has a conical shape, whereas Fossa is a much older and eroded volcano which has lost much of its symmetrical shape.

The ferry or hydrofoil craft (aliscafi) you'll likely be coming from Lípari, but some arrive from Filicudi, Panarea and Strombóli. All boats dock at San Marina Salina, which is the administrative center of the island.

To climb **Fossa** you'll have 3 possible routes to choose from. To do the first one, walk north from the docks after you fill your water bottles at the little fountain nearby. At the north end of town will be a little canyon called Valle del Castagno. Walk up this deep gully on a dirt road for about one km. At about that point the road gradually disappears, and you continue on a trail which immediately zig zags up to the north out of the canyon and across the upper east face of the mountain. This is a reforested area and the trail may change as they plant or cut pine trees. When you reach the ridgetop, you'll come to a firebreak road. Walk on this old track south along the ridge to the highest peak. The author raced the setting sun and made the summit in 1 1/2 hours using this trail. That was on 7/30/1989. Round-trip was 2 1/2 hours from San Marina.

To climb Fossa via the normal and recommended route, take the once-hourly bus running from San Marina Salina to Leni; or hitch hike, which the author found moderately good. Stop on the pass between Porri and Fossa and where a paved road runs east to the Santuaria del Terzito (a large church half a km east of the highway). Walk to the church, then look for the trail heading straight up the ridge to the east. This will put you on the summit ridge, then walk south on an old road to the highest peak.

The third choice is walk up an old and little-used road to the summit area. This road begins at or near the Santuaria del Terzito church. You may have to ask where this road and/or trail begins. Observe the map carefully.

The author never climbed **Porri** because of the July heat and bushwhacking involved, but he was there looking for a route. He was told of at least 4 different ways up, none of which were trails in 7/1989. Ask someone in Leni about a route or trail to the summit. There must be one somewhere (?). The best place to begin would likely be just across the highway from the area of the Terzito church. The north ridge might be a good choice as well.

In the past, people used to farm terraces high on this mountain, but today farming seem dead as a door nail, and there are no more sheep or goats grazing on the peak; therefore what trails there may have been in the past are now overgrown. So now you may have to work your way up the brushy

From just above the Santuary del Terzito looking west at Monte del Porri.

Map 97-1, Fossa, Salina Island, Eolie/Lípari Islands, Italy

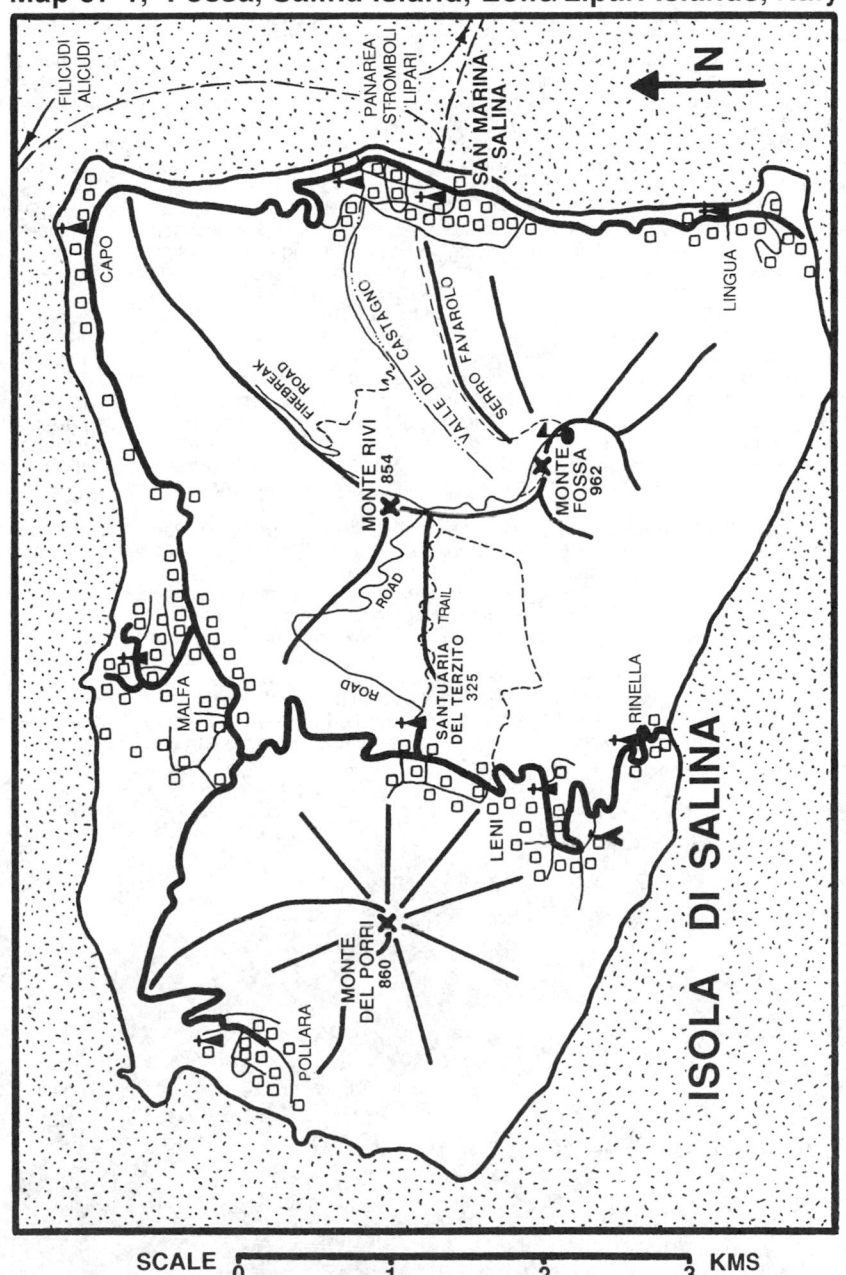

SCALE 0 1 2 3 KMS

slope. It would be best to climb in cooler weather, say in spring or fall, then you'd be more comfortable wearing long pants rather than shorts.

Maps show a campground in the area between Leni and Rinella, otherwise just camp on any flat spot on the mountain that's out of sight and away from private lands or inhabited areas.

Alicudi, Filicudi & Panarea Islands, Eolie or Lípari Islands, Italy

The islands shown here are the three smallest inhabited islands in the Eolie or Lípari group. They're all located just north of Sicilia. Even though these islands are small, the peaks are fairly high. See the introduction map to this island group. If you decide to hike or climb here please buy a better map than this; best to do that in Milazzo, the port on the north coast of Sicilia where most boats to these islands begin. The author has not visited any of these 3 islands, but there shouldn't be any surprises to speak of in climbing to the highest summits on each.

Panarea is halfway between Strombóli and Salina or Lípari and all boats going to Strombóli stop here. From the port of San Pietro, walk in a southerly direction on narrow lanes suitable for motor scooters. About where a church is located, head west and locate, with the help of villagers, a trail winding up the east face of the high peaks. There will surely be many trails, but the map the author used to create this one, indicates one main trail heading up to the pass just north of the highest peak called **Corvo** at 421 meters. If you're camping you can likely find a flat spot high above the village on the east side of the peaks. The only problem with doing that is, you'd have to carry a fair amount of water with you. Otherwise, there should be a hotel of some kind to stay in near the port.

The island with the highest peak is called **Filicudi**. The highest summit is **Fossa Felci** at 774 meters. It's basically a one-mountain island, but there appears to be two younger volcanic craters as shown. Felci seems to have lost most of its symmetrical shape. From the docks at Filicudi Porto, walk in a northwest direction past one church, then left a bit, and continue northwest toward the summit. There are many narrow lanes to choose from so inquire of the whereabouts of the trail heading to the summit of Fossa Felci. The actual trail shown on topo maps begins at about 300 meters altitude and leads to the summit ridge east of Felci. Once on this ridge, it should be an easy walk to the main peak. Besides the trail to the summit, there are other trails going in a northwest direction along coastal areas. The map the author used to create this one, shows a campground near the harbor.

The last island is **Alicudi**, the most westerly of all the Eolie or Lípari Islands. In summer there are ferry boats heading this way 5 days a week, but in winter it's down to 2 a week. They come via Filicudi, Salina, Lípari and Milazzo.

From the docks at Alicudi Porto, walk up the steep slope in a northwest direction. The map shows several route possibilities. One of these improved paths, perhaps an old road, leads to the north side of the mountain called **Montagnole** at 675 meters. At about 550 meters, a real trail heads south to the 2nd highest summit called **Filo dell' Arpa** at 662 meters. This peak, and in fact the entire island, appears overgrown with brush but it still has a conal shape. It also appears from observing the postcard foto below, that a 2nd cone or volcano has grown up inside an older caldera or crater.

One of the biggest problems to camping and hiking on these islands is water. Try to fill you're water bottles on the boat, or with luck at a hostel, otherwise you may have to buy liquids. If using boat

Aerial postcard view of Alicudi, the smallest of the Eolie/Lípari Islands.

Map 98-1, Alicudi, Filicudi & Panarea Islands, Italy

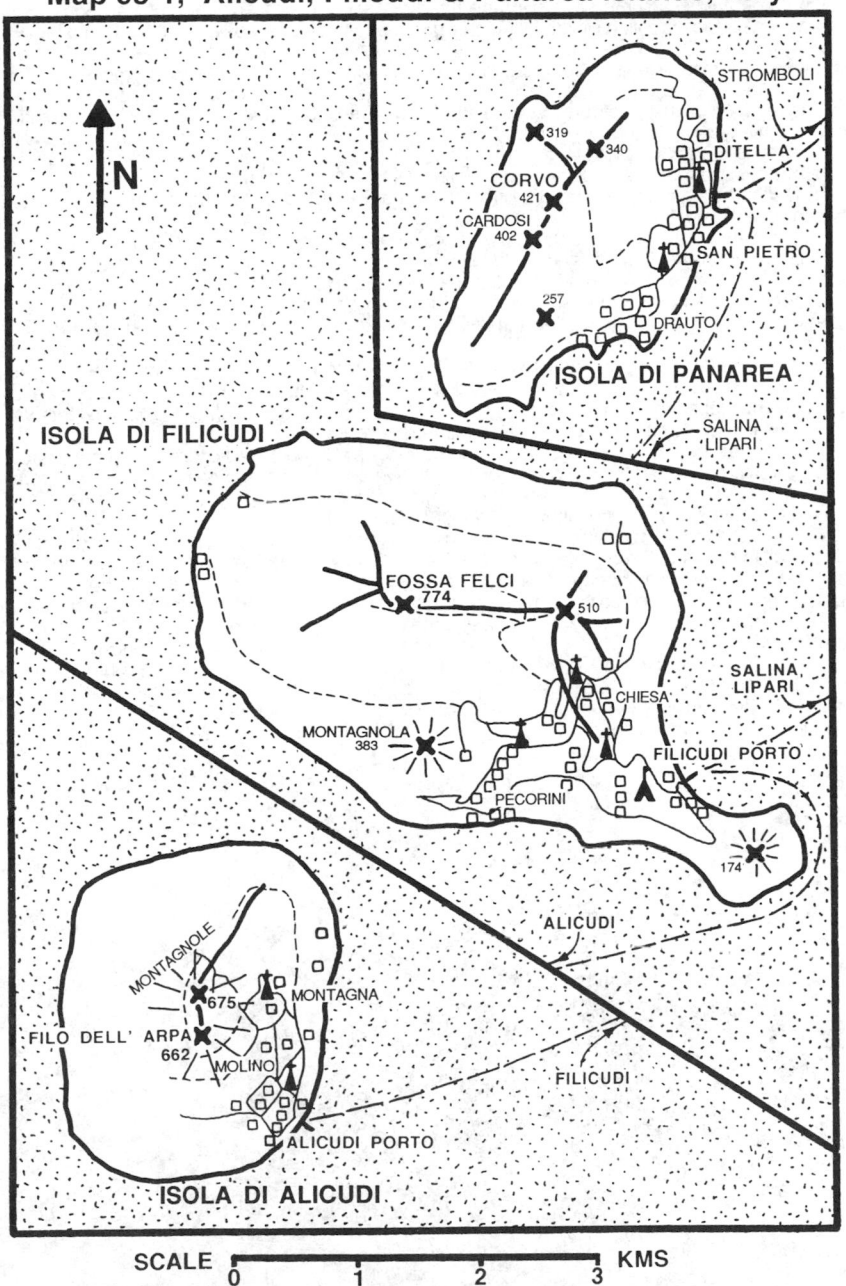

SCALE
0   1   2   3   KMS

water, better have some purification tablets just to be sure. The author was once told water from the ferry boats was not suitable for drinking (?).

Mármora, Monti del Gennargentu, Sardegna, Italy

The mountains shown on this map are the highest on the Italian island of Sardegna (Sardinia). The mountain range is called Monti del Gennargentu and the highest peak is called Punta La Mármora at 1834 meters. The second highest point is called Monti Bruncu Spina. At the summit and on the north face of Bruncu Spina, is the only ski lift on the island. These mountains are made of granite and other metamorphic rock.

These mountains are not rugged, instead they resemble the Scottish Highlands. Climbing here is more like hill-walking in Ireland or the UK. There are sheep & goat and cattle trails all over which makes getting around very easy. The tree line is at about 1200 meters. The valley immediately west of Mármora is used for sheep dairy farming. The bottom 1/3 of this map is not accurate, because the author lost his hiking map and the IGM of Italia apparently had run out of the *Punta La Mármora maps* when the author was there.

Get to Sardegna by flying, or ferry boat from Tunis, Trapani, Palermo, Napoli, Livorno, Genova, and Bonifacio on the French island of Corse or Corsica. Ferries arrive at Santa Teresa, Olbia, Arbatax, Porto Torres and Cagliari. Once there, head for the central part of the island and to the area south of Nuoro. The town to look for is Désulo, one of the highest mountain villages on Sardegna. There are several buses passing through this town daily; or you might try hitch hiking, which was very slow in 1989!

Once you arrive in Désulo, the easiest way to get to **Mármora** would be to drive, or hire a taxi and be driven to the sheep dairy farm at the western base of the peak, then walk east or north up one of the easy-to-climb slopes to either of the high peaks. Another option; you can also walk all the way from Désulo in one long day and feel you've done some mountaineering.

At the north end of Désulo, right on the big curve or switchback, walk north along the dirt road as it contours up the opposite slope or opposite side of the valley to the east. See map. You can camp in the forest one and 2 kms from town near some springs, or fountains, as they're called in Italia. The author camped near a small stream as shown, about one km from Désulo.

From where the author's campsite is shown just northwest of Désulo, walk east and northeast up a good trail to the ridge & road to or near Funti Perdu Porcagiu. At that point cross the road and ridge-walk east up to the main ridge running to **Bruncu Spina**. There are sheep & goat trails everywhere and walking is easy in treeless country. From the summit of Spina, ridge-walk or use sheep trails to reach the top of Mármora, then road-walk all the way back to camp or Désulo. With any luck you'll get a ride part way back. To do this suggested hike is to walk about 30 kms round-trip. The author was on top of Mármora in 3 hours, and back to his camp in just over 6 hours, round-trip. His hike was on 7/20/1989. You'll want more time than this because the author was walking fast; that's partly because the walking is easy. Also, if you decide to camp as the author did, pack everything up in the morning, and hid your big pack in brush covering it with leaves or branches.

From the top of Bruncu Spina looking southeast at the west face of Mármora.

Map 99-1, Mármora, Monti Gennargentu, Sardegna, Italy

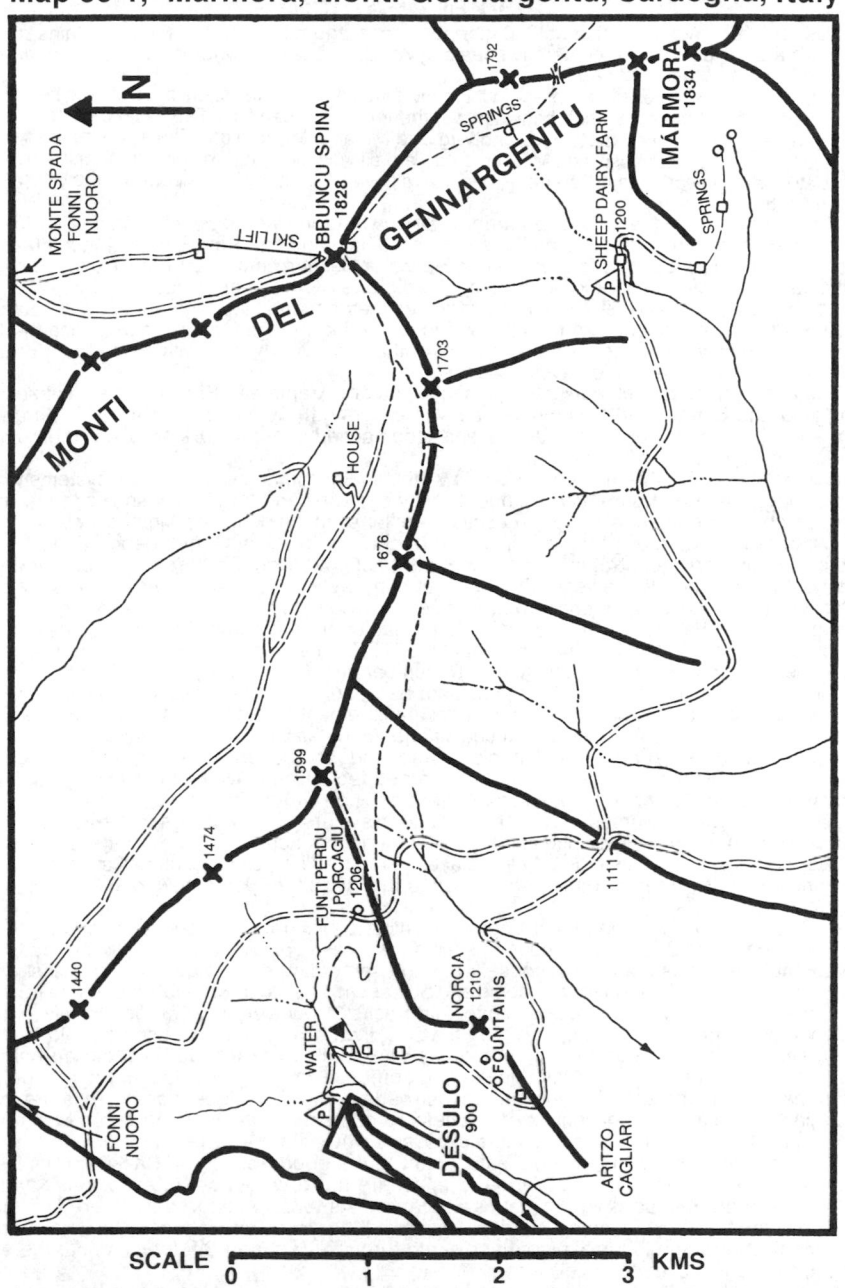

There are many springs in the lower valley, but always carry water on the dry ridges. Summers are warm and dry; winters stormy--with snow.

Maps *Désulo and Punta La Mármora,* 1:25,000, Instituto Geografico de Agostini, S.p. A., Novara, Italia; and the latest travel guidebook to Italia.

Chapter 4--Africa

This chapter covering Africa has 46 mapped areas and all or most major mountains on the continent are included here. Generally speaking Africa has less to offer in the way of mountain climbing than the other continents.

It's difficult to make generalizations about the mountain types in Africa, but if one has to be made it would be that most have had their beginnings in the form of volcanism. The exceptions to this rule would be the Atlas, Ruwensori, The Brandberg and Mulanje Mountains. Other mountains in East Africa, Jebel Marra, the Tibesti, and Mt. Cameroun are all volcanos. In Ethiopia and South Africa, the high plateaus and escarpments are made of old lava flows, and many of the peaks in the Hoggar are volcanic plugs or necks.

The problems with the language barrier are not what they would be if it hadn't been for the colonial period and the efforts of the British, French, Belgians and Portuguese. Much of North, West and Central Africa were formerly under French or Belgian control, so French is used by the native people as their second or international language. Other places such as Egypt, Sudan, East Africa and parts of West Africa use English as their second language. In parts of southern Africa, Portuguese is spoken as both a first and second language, and in South Africa the first language is English. If you speak one or more of these tongues (especially English or French), you'll have few problems while traveling Africa.

Two of the most-spoken native tongues in Africa are Arabia and Swahili. Arabia is spoken throughout the Sahara and points north, as well as along the east coast. Swahili is a trader's language which dominates eastern Africa, and is composed of about 40% Arabia; and 60% from the Bantu group.

The weather in North Africa is controlled by the middle latitude cyclonic storm systems which pass through the area from about October to May. These can bring heavy snows to the Atlas Mountain chain. Southern Africa experiences a similar situation during its winter season.

The central portion of Africa is dominated by the Intertropical Convergence Zone (ITCZ). This is the equatorial jet stream which meanders back and forth, north to south, and normally from west to east, during the year. For the most part, the wet season in Africa follows the sun; that is, when the sun is in the northern hemisphere, which is the northern summer, the rains are normally north of the equator. Mountains on the Equator normally have 2 wet and 2 dry seasons brought about by the north-south movement of the ITCZ. The rainy season for southern Africa is during their summer which is generally from December through February or March.

Generally speaking, most climbs in Africa are easy, but there are exceptions to this rule. For example, climbs in the Ruwensori are about equal to the best peaks in Europe, and Mt. Kenya is barely soloable--but you'll need the right equipment and be an experienced climber.

There are some very good rock climbs in the Hoggar, the Dragensberg and some in the Ruwensori. At least an ice ax & crampons are needed in the Ruwensori, on some routes of Kilimanjaro and maybe Mt. Kenya, and for winter climbing some routes in the Atlas.

Africa is one of the worst places in the world for travelers to have things stolen. Fortunately, most thieft occurs in the larger cities and around tourist beaches. The problem areas are where tourists congregate, such as Morocco and places in East Africa. Other countries such as Sudan, are generally quite safe. See the introduction to this book for tips on how to keep from losing your valuables.

Another generalization; in former English colonies, public transportation is generally good; in the Francafon countries, it's often poor. It seems the British concentrated on building roads and railway lines; whereas the French consentrated on something else. Egypt, Sudan, East Africa and Nigeria all have good railway systems and bus service; while in French West Africa railways are almost non-existent, and roads are often dirt tracks. However, if you've got the will to go to some far away mountain range, you'll find a way. Hitch hiking is good in some parts of North Africa and in the East, but it's not as good as you might think in South Africa, and almost unheard of elsewhere. Generally speaking, if someone stops and gives you a lift, you pay! About the only private vehicles you see on the roads in Black or Subsaharan Africa are those belonging to missionaries, diplomats or business tycoons. For the most part public transport is cheap in the former English colonies, more expensive where the French settled.

There are few youth hostels on the continent, but a good network of Backpacker's Rests exist in southern Africa. In west Africa where there are few tourist, hotels are few and far between, and often expensive. In places where tourists tend to congregate, there are lots of hotels and many are quite cheap. Sudan, Egypt and Morocco (and in most Islamic countries) have many cheap hotels. In Ethiopia and south through East and Southern Africa, there's a good assortment of cheaper hotels too.

Two more thoughts. If you're willing to eat what the locals eat, food can be cheap; but imported or European-type food is very expensive. Throughout eastern Africa, north to south, contact mountaineering clubs or tourist offices in the capital cities for further information about the local mountains.

From the summit of Kibo (Uhuru Point), you have a good look down to the east at Mawenzi. These 2 peaks form the huge mass of Mt. Kilimanjaro.

At about 3000 meters elevation on the west side of the Ruwensori Mountains, you pass through a moss or cloud forest. The trail can be 2 meters deep in moss in some places.

Introduction to Cabo Verde (Cape Verde Islands)

Cabo Verde is the present name of what used to be called in English the Cape Verde Islands. These islands were formerly a colony of Portugal located off the west coast of Africa, but since July, 1975, they have been independent. The population as of 2000 is about 400,000. Cabo Verde consists of 10 major islands, 9 of which are populated, and they're all volcanic in origin. The newest islands are Brava and Fogo with active or semi-active volcanos. The highest peak in the islands is Pico do Antonia at 2829 meters on Fogo. It last erupted in 1995.

There are several ways to reach Cab Verd, as locals call it. Some flights originate from Lisboa, Portugal. Depending on the season, there are one or 2 flights weekly which land at the international airport on Sal. Since there is now a large Cabo Verdean community near Boston, there are also weekly flights from the USA. Cabo Verde used to gets lots of aid from Eastern Europe and the USSR, but that connection is long gone, and so are the flights. However, there are direct flights, some perhaps charter flights, from 8 other cities in Europe bringing lots of tourist to a new complex of hotels on the Sal's south coast. There's also flights from South Africa. Check with a travel agent.

An alternate to landing on Sal, is to first go to Dakar, Senegal, West Africa, then fly into the much smaller airport at the nation's capital of Praia. This small city is located on the most populous island of Santiago. The runway there is much shorter and for smaller aircraft, but they are presently upgrading it and by 2002, hope to be able to land large jets and bring in more tourists direct to Santiago Island.

Most people arrive at Sal, where there are now beach-front hotels and growing numbers of tourists, but many take internal shuttle flights to the other islands. There are daily flights from Sal to São Nicolau and São Vicente. From São Vicente there are less frequent flights to Ribeira Grande on Santo Antão. From this northern group of islands there are daily flights directly to Praia.

Also from Sal, you can take flights direct to Praia on Santiago, or a flight which stops at Boavista and Maio on the way to Praia. From Praia, there are daily flights to Mosterios on the island of Fogo. Make reservations as early as possible and remember to reconfirm your flight within 72 hours of departure, otherwise you'll be put on a standby list.

Most of the planes used are getting old, but considering this is Africa, things work fairly well. Always take some food and water to the airport in case there's a flight delay. Most airports are way out of town and there's often no water--not even to buy; in this very dry country. Take some water to Sal's airport, otherwise you'll have to pay extortion prices to get a drink!

While flights will get you to or from islands a long ways apart, there are also ferry boats serving all islands. Some of these are very slow and cover long distances; others are short hops from neighboring islands. About once a week there's a large cargo vessel--a ferry boat, making a run from Praia which stops at most of the islands before returning to home base. There's another night ferry running every 3 days between Praia and São Filipe on Fogo. This is how most locals get between these 2 islands.

There's an almost-daily boat running from Furna on the island of Brava, to São Filipe on Fogo as well. This links up with the boat heading to Praia. In the north, there's a twice daily boat sailing from Mindelo on the island of São Vicente, to Porto Novo on Santo Antão. This ride takes only about an hour. Most of the ferry boats in Cabo Verde were new in1989 and in good condition. For the most part, service is reliable; but remember, in Cabo Verde you've got one foot in Africa and delays can occur.

To get from town to the mountains you can always hitch hike, which the author found good (but expect to pay the driver); or you can use public transport which is usually good. For the most part vans or small pickup trucks masquerade as buses. These carry both passengers and cargo.

Cabo Verde is located between 15° and 17° north latitude. This is equivalent to the southern fringe of the Sahara Desert so expect a very dry situation almost all the time. The wet season is from July through September. The southern islands get more rain than those in the north. Praia gets 24 cms of rain a year, but Mindelo may get only a third as much, or less. Water is a real problem as you'll see, so plan to take fast showers and conserve. There are desalinization plants at Mindelo and on the island of Sal.

Here are some tips for a good trip to Cabo Verde. First, find a map before leaving home. There are very few available in Cab Verd, and then only in Praia. Also, take several water bottles if you're planning to spend more than one day in the mountains. The only water you'll find will be from tapped springs which are always at or near villages.

On some of the outlying islands, some foods are a little scarce, depending on the season. However, the markets in Praia and Mindelo are full most of the time. Locally grown fruits and vegetables are reasonably priced, but anything imported is rather expensive.

There are hotels or pensions in every larger town on each island. Most of these are clean and reasonably priced. The cheaper ones vary in price from about US$5 to $8 a night for one person (1989), but the author found one comfortable pension in São Filipe, Fogo, for US$2. The larger towns also have more expensive hotels.

Map 100-1, Introduction to Cabo Verde (Cape Verde)

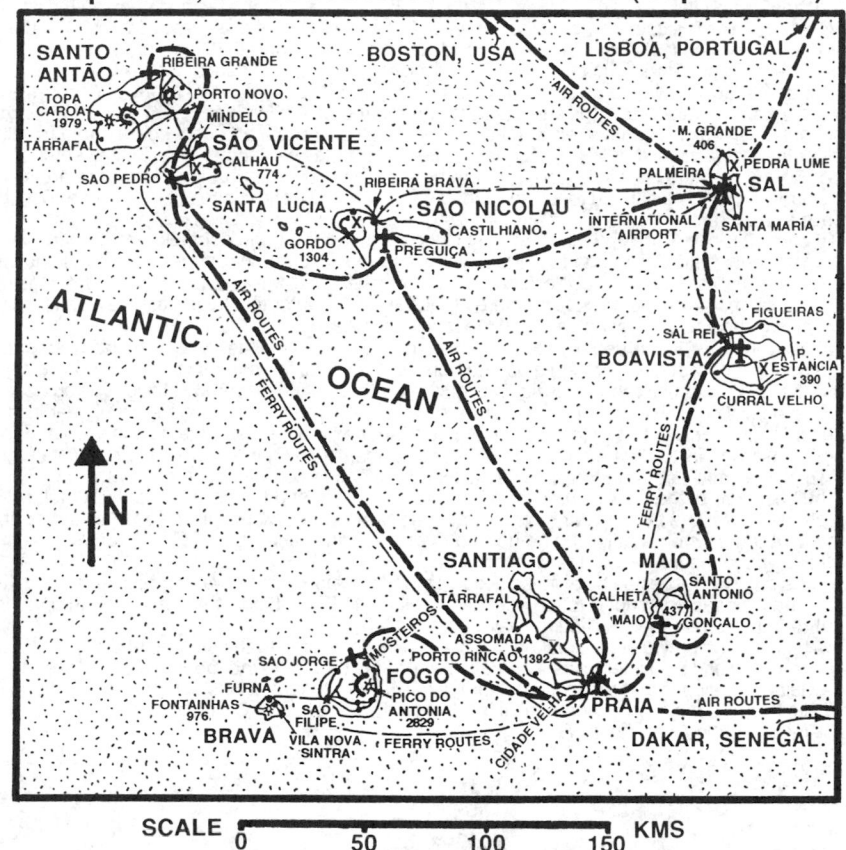

SCALE 0 50 100 150 KMS

The author found the people in Cabo Verde very poor, but very honest and easily as friendly as you are--so smile. He was there 2 weeks and never heard any horror stories about people being robbed or having things stolen. The reason for that is the low population, and lack of a lot of tourists. The people are African and speak Portuguese. If you know a little Spanish or Italiano you can get by in Cab Verd.

For the latest updated information on the islands see these websites (www.caboverde.com) or (www.newafrica.com/travelguides/capeverde.asp).

Maps The TPC map *Cape Verde, K-OA,* 1:500,000, shows all islands on one map, as does the *Mapa Touristico, Cabo Verde,* about 1:500,000 (?), from Direcção-Geral do Turismo, Caixa Postal No. 211, Praia, Cabo Verde. Get individual island maps from the tourist office (Geral do Turismo) in Praia, or IGM maps from Lisboa. Have some maps with you before arriving if possible. It would be a good idea to begin your trip in Praia, get some good maps, then fly out to the other islands for climbing.

Monte Gordo, São Nicolau Island, Cabo Verde

The mountain featured here is Monte Gordo at 1304 meters. It's the highest peak on the island of São Nicolau, which is located in about the center of Cabo Verde. This is an eroded volcano, but barely resembles one. The last activity on this island was sometime in the Holocene, or the last 10,000 years. That activity was likely in the 2 small craters just east and northeast of Monte Gordo.

The only practical way to get to São Nicolau is to fly to Ribeira Brava. From the airport, either walk the 5 kms, or take a taxi (pickup truck) to the main plaza in Ribeira Brava, the administrative capital of the island. As you first enter this town you'll see the small and very comfortable Hotel Sila on the right. It cost the author US$5 a night in 1989. There may be another hotel in the center of town after 1990. Across the dry creek bed from the hotel is the mercado (market) and there are several shops in town for buying canned foods and bread. The variety isn't the best, but it's enough. The hotel also has a restaurant.

To climb **Monte Gordo**, walk west past the park along the main cobblestone road in town; or walk west along the dry creek bed. Further up, the road and creek bed meet. All roads shown as paved on this map are actually cobblestoned. Further to the west, the cobblestone path zig zags up to the little white church on the pass. There are at least 4 public water taps along the way, so fill up your water bottles before you leave the pass and the town of Kashasu.

When you arrive in the upper valley, you'll be in an area called Kashasu. It's a large spread-out village with lots of scattered farms, fields and homes. Get onto the main street or road heading due west in the upper part of Kashasu. It zig zags up the northeast face of Gordo. Higher up you'll pass an old home on the rim of the first of 2 small craters in the area, then just beyond is a trail heading up to the left or south. Follow this path as it zig zags up the main southeast ridge. Soon you'll be on the summit of Gordo. In 1989, they were constructing a small building with perhaps a radio antenna on top. There's a small farm with trees inside a second crater just below the summit as shown.

The best view of the mountain might be on the south side and from a place called Ortelao. The map shows several ways to reach this small village. One is by rough road from just south of Kashasu; another is on a trail running up and over the southeast ridge of Gordo; or you can head straight down the mountain from the summit.

Here's another suggested hike; make a loop around the mountain by walking past Ortelao to Torno d'Agua and Calhaus, then uphill to the east and back to the farms below the summit on the northeast side. From there walk back to Ribeira Brava.

With an early morning start, most people can easily do a climb to the summit of Gordo and return to Ribeira Brava and the Hotel Sila in one day. Fast hikers can climb the mountain and make the loop from Ortelao to Calhaus and return in one long day. Be sure to take a lunch and plenty of water. You can make this hike during any month, as this mountain may get only 10 cms of rain a year! Perhaps less. Any kind of boots or shoes will do.

From just east of Ortelao, one has a good view of the south face of Monte Gordo.

Map 101-1, Monte Gordo, São Nicolau Island, Cabo Verde

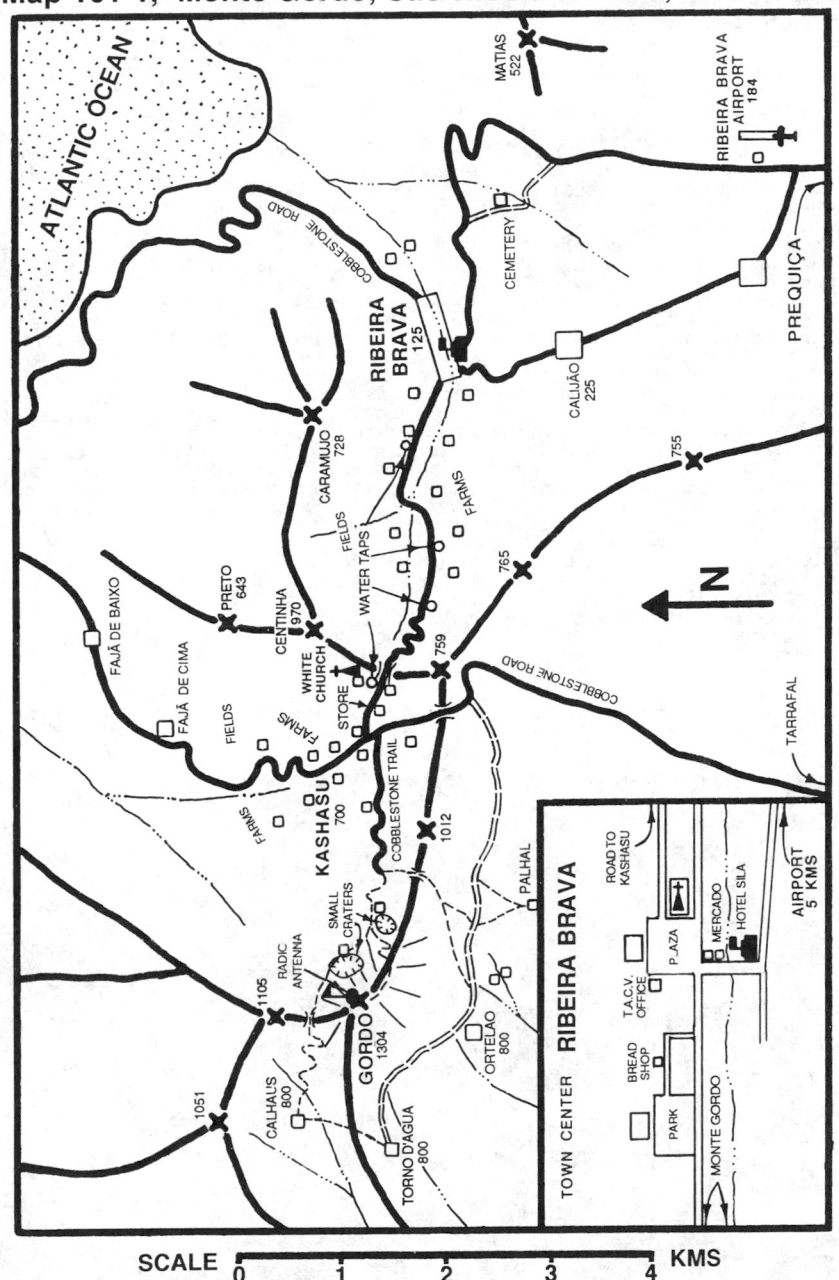

On 6/15/1989, the author climbed the peak and visited Ortelao, but didn't make the loop-hike. He did that in just over 6 hours round-trip from Ribeira Brava. He had a little fog or a cloud deck on the mountain in the morning hours.

Topa Caroa, Santo Antão Island, Cabo Verde

The highest peak on the island of Santo Antão is Topa Caroa, at 1979 meters. Santo Antão is the northern-most inhabited island in Cabo Verde. Besides Topa Caroa, you'll be seeing one of the most impressive and rugged calderas on earth, the Caldeira Das Patas. Swarms of dikes have been exposed by erosion on the walls of this caldera. It's an impressive site. You'll also see several small volcanic craters or cones. All of these date from sometime in the Holocene, or within the 10,000 years.

You can fly to this island, but there aren't many flights; or better still, fly to São Vicente, then take the twice-daily ferry boat from Mindelo, São Vicente Island, to Porto Novo on Santo Antão. That's what the author did. When you get off the ferry, look around for a pickup truck or *carro* heading in the direction of Das Patas. There should be several vehicles heading that way upon the arrival of each ferry. It's about 20 kms from the port to the middle of the caldera. Once there, ask to be let off at Curral Das Vacas--if they're going that far. That will be at the beginning of the trail to the village of Catano and to Topa Caroa.

From Curral Das Vacas, walk up the dirt road and over a minor ridge toward Catano. At the junction about 500 meters before Catano, turn right onto a wide trail which goes straight up the extremely steep face of the crater wall. The Topa Caroa Trail to the rim of the caldera was completed in 1960 and is cobblestoned to the rim. It zig zags up a slope most mountaineers would find difficult if not impossible to climb. It's most impressive piece of trail construction the author has ever seen.

On the crater rim at 1600 meters, look to the west to see the rounded massif of **Topa Caroa** in the distance. Continue on the trail down a ways, over a hill and down again to the flat area known as Chã de Campo Grande. This is a goat grazing area with a number of shepherd huts. From the flats, simply set your sights on the mountain and walk. There's a trail to the summit, and many others on the mountain. From Curral das Vacas to Topa Caroa and back will be a long all-day walk. Carry water from the villages, and camp anywhere outside the caldera.

The author stayed in the Hotel Chave D'Oro in Mindelo for US$6.75, stored 2 extra bags, took the ferry to Porto Novo, got on a pickup to Curral das Vacas, got water, hiked up to the crater rim and camped near the pass at 1600 meters. Next morning, 6/18/1989, climbed Topa Coroa and returned to camp in 3 1/2 hours round-trip; walked down past the Sinta Spring to Salada, then back to Catano and camped. Next morning, climbed Cuvão in 3 hours round-trip, then back to Curral das Vacas, rode a dump truck to Porto Novo and ferried back to Mindelo.

Another interesting trek would be to hike up the Topa Caroa Trail to the crater rim, then rim-walk to the top of **Cuvão**, at 1870 meters; or walk along the caldera rim to **Pico Guda Branco**. These are both easy climbs with fine views.

Another trail, and one the author was impressed with, is along a trail built across the steep caldera face to a spring called Sinta at 1400 meters. From Topa Caroa Pass (1600), head north along the rim. After less than 2 kms is a low point in the rim and a trail zig zagging out across the south face of Guda Branco. This trail passes 2 small springs where villagers get water. It ends on the main caldera road which runs on to Ribeira Cruz and Altomira.

Hike here year-round. It's best to buy your food in Mindelo or Porto Novo, but some can be found in small stores in villages inside the caldera. It seems there are no hotels around, but ask villagers about a room, a place to camp, and where to get drinking water.

Looking down on the Topa Caroa Trail as it snakes its way up to the rim
of the Caldeira das Patas.

Map 102-1, Topa Caroa, Santo Antão Island, Cabo Verde

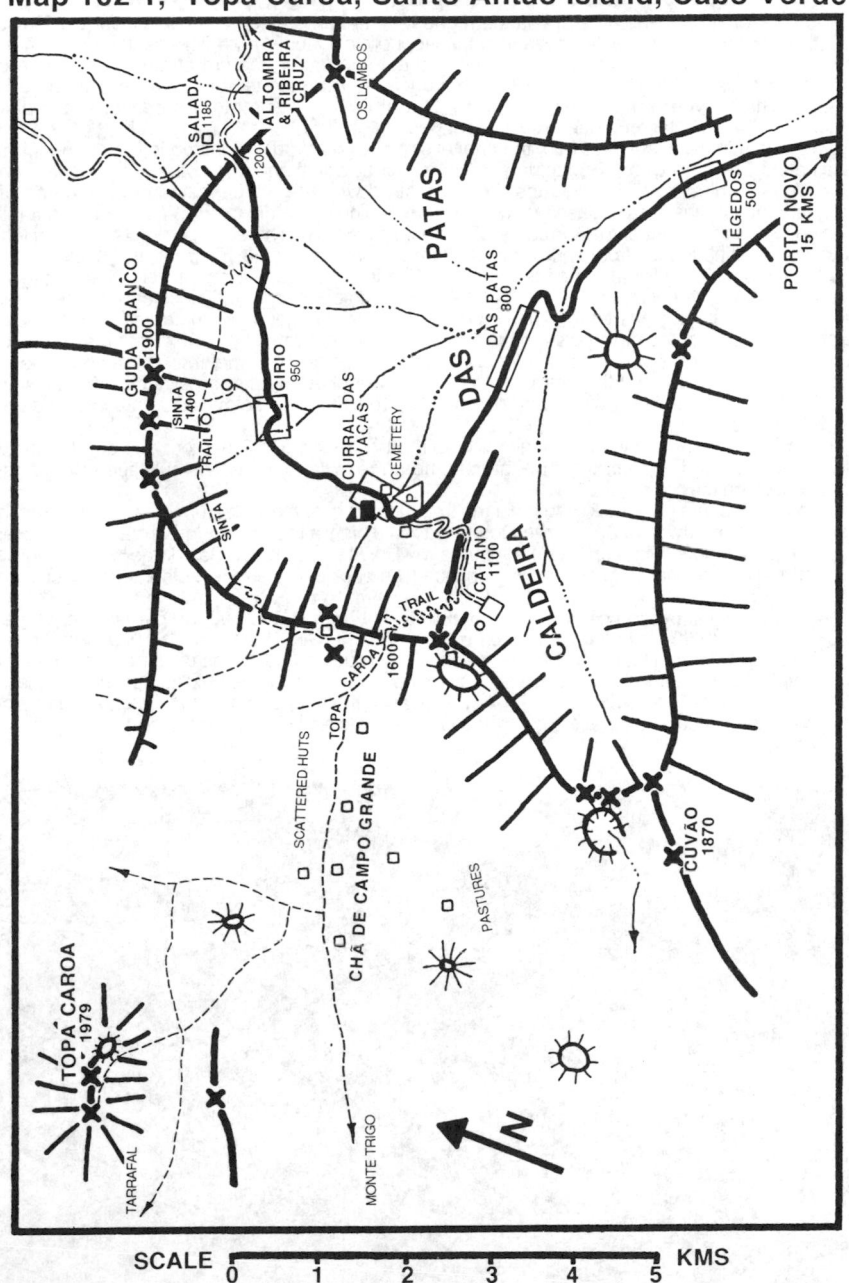

SCALE 0 1 2 3 4 5 KMS

For someone with more time, there's another volcanic crater along with some fairly high mountains about halfway between Ribeira Grande and Porto Novo in the eastern part of the island. See the map *Introduction of Cabo Verde*. As you ride in a bus or truck along that road, get out of the vehicle at the pass, and hike to the east.

Pico de Antonio, Santiago Island, Cabo Verde

Pico de Antonio at 1394 meters, is the highest mountain on the island of Santiago. This is the largest, wettest and most populated island in the Republic of Cabo Verde. This peak has an extremely steep and rugged east face and may be the highest summit on the rim of a very old and eroded caldera. Just east of the peak and within this ancient crater is the small town of São Jorge Dos Orgãos. This is where the President of the Republic has a summer home. There is also an agricultural research station inside this bowl-shaped valley

To get to this peak, start in Praia, the capital city of Cabo Verde. First go to the open-air market place called Sucupira (pron. Sucupida), which is just downhill and northwest of the central part of Praia. At Sucupira, you will see vans driving around with the driver yelling out the name of the destination he intends to take passengers. Find one going in the direction of Assomada, but tell the driver you want to get out at the Mercado (Market) Dos Orgãos. There will be one bus or van leaving about every half hour or so from approximately 6am to 7pm. When the van is full, they leave.

About 34 kms from Praia is the Mercado Dos Orgãos. Get out there and walk west up the valley on a dirt road past many farms. Higher up, the road ends on a ridge and place called Casa Grande, which is also the beginning of a trail running through fields of sugar cane and mango trees. Head for the pass just south of the main peak. Take drinking water with you as you won't find a safe drink until you reach the big grove of junipers just below the pass marked 1040 meters. There you'll find some water in the creek bed, and the entrance to a water tunnel at 890 meters altitude. Walk inside the tunnel to find good drinking water before it's piped to the valley below. This place makes a fine campsite as well.

From the junipers and water tunnel, walk up the trail to the pass, then curve around to the west side of the peak and head straight up the second ridge. Along the way, you'll see wild goats and monkeys high on the peak.

If you'd rather not backtrack, return via the trail running past the water tunnel as shown, then head east downcanyon towards São Jorge Dos Orgãos. This trail runs through a man-made forest of eucalyptus, with more wild monkeys and guinea fowl. When you reach São Jorge, walk 2 more kms to the main highway and wave down a van or hitch hike back to Praia. The author found hitching quite good.

With an early start, you can do this trip in one day from Praia, but camping at the junipers is possible. The author paid US$6.25 for a pensão (hotel), then left Praia on 6/21/1989 at mid-day with his large pack. He didn't know what to expect on the mountain and was thinking he might have to camp one night. He carried his pack all the way to near the summit, then hid it, and finished the climb reaching the summit in less than 3 1/2 hours (this was in the heat of the day!). He ended up camping at the water tunnel that night and enjoyed the cool water. He returned to Praia the next morning.

Pico de Antonio, highest peak on the island of Santiago, as seen from
the village area known as Casa Grande.

Map 103-1, Pico Antonio, Santiago Island, Cabo Verde

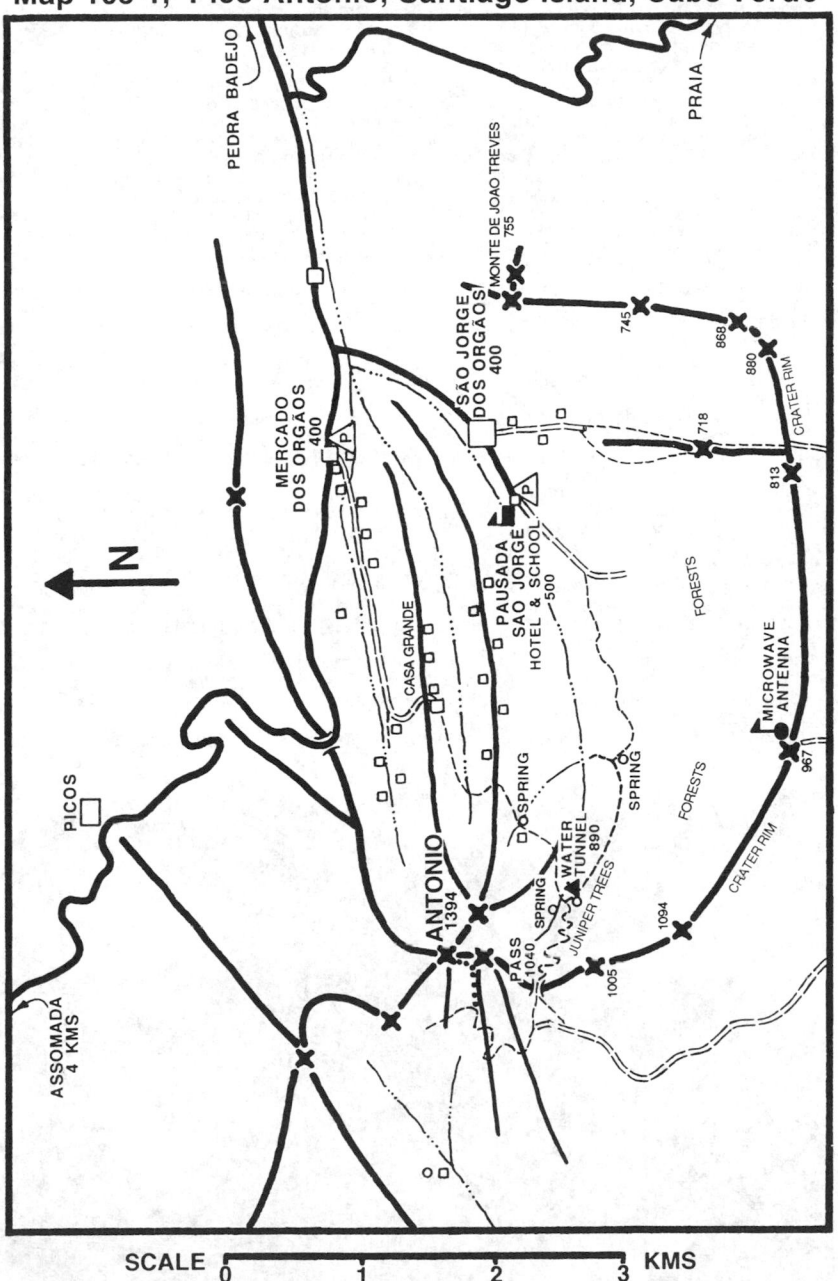

SCALE 0   1   2   3 KMS

Buy all your food before leaving Praia if possible, but you can get some food at the Mercado Dos Orgãos. You can do this hike any time of year, but the rainy season is from about July through September.

Pico da Antonia, Fogo Island, Cabo Verde

Shown on this map is Pico da Antonia, at 2829 meters, the highest mountain on Fogo, and in Cabo Verde. Also included is the island of Brava and it's only mountain called Fontainhas, at 978 meters. Both of these volcanos are considered active or semi-active.

The Global Volcanism Program from the Smithsonian Institution calls this volcano **Fogo**. A new cone they simple call **Pico**, rises from the floor of the Cha Das Caldeira, which is breached on the east. After the Portuguese came in 1500, Pico was continuously active until 1760. During and after that time, including some eruptions from the caldera floor, some lava flows reached the east coast.

The last eruptive period on Fogo was from 4/2/1995 through 5/28/1995. Lava vented at the southwest foot of Pico and covered 6 sq/kms. It flowed over and buried the small settlement of Boca de Fonte and came close to Portela village before stopping. About 1300 people living inside the caldera were evacuated. For volcano undates see the website (www.volcano.si.edu/gvp/)

Here's how to get there. Take the ferry from Praia to São Filipe (one boat every 3 days), then take a pickup truck, or walk from the port to the town center (4 kms) and the mercado (market). Nearby are 3 Pausadas or pensãos (hotels) if you want to stay overnight for US$2. You could also camp at the black sand beach just below town or near the port.

At the mercado, buy all your food and supplies before leaving São Filipe. Then look for a vehicle heading in the direction of Fonte Aleixo, Achada Furna, or better still to the caldera towns of Portela and Bangaeira (they should still be there, but the location of the road has changed since the author was there in 1989 and the eruption of 1995). There are vehicles going to the crater 2 or 3 times a week; or you can hire a taxi-pickup for about US$40. If you miss one of the trucks going to the caldera, then go to Fonte Aleixo or Achada Furna and walk from there. You can shorten this hike by making short-cuts on goat trails along the zig zagging road.

When you arrive inside the Cha Das Caldeira, stop at the western base of the new volcanic cone. You may see a couple of huts in the area used by farmers who care for the grapes and pomegranates. In 1989, there was grape growing and a wine industry inside the caldera at Portela and Bangaeira. The wine is sold under the label *Mańico*.

From the foot of Pico da Antonia, angle up in a northeast direction. Make the climb on the northwest side of the cone for better footing, but come down the fine cinder & ash-covered west face. It'll normally take 2-3 hours to reach the summit (the author did it in 1 1/2 hours), but only about half an hour coming down. Take with you to the caldera all the water you'll need for the duration of your trip.

On the morning of 6/24/1989, the author left Praia on a ferry to Fogo (US$10 & 6 1/2 hours), got an aluguer (pickup) to Fonte Aleixo for US$1.25, and walked from there to the base of Pico da Antonia in just over 4 hours with a huge pack full of water. Next morning, climbed Pico, then got a ride back to São Filipe on top of a dump truck and stayed the night. Next night was on a ferry going to Praia towing an old broken-down ship.

The author isn't familiar with the northern route, but the airport on Fogo is at Mosteiros. If you fly in, look for vehicles heading for the caldera or Achada Grande, or just walk from the airport. Buy all supplies in Mosteiros (best to buy in Praia) before leaving (including water). This map is incomplete on the north side, but there is a road to Bangaeira.

The author has no information about Brava, except there's a ferry almost daily from São Filipe

The author's tent sits beside a small pomegranate tree at the western base of Pico da Antonia, the highest mountain on Fogo and in Cabo Verde.

Map 104-1, Pico da Antonia, Fogo Island, Cabo Verde

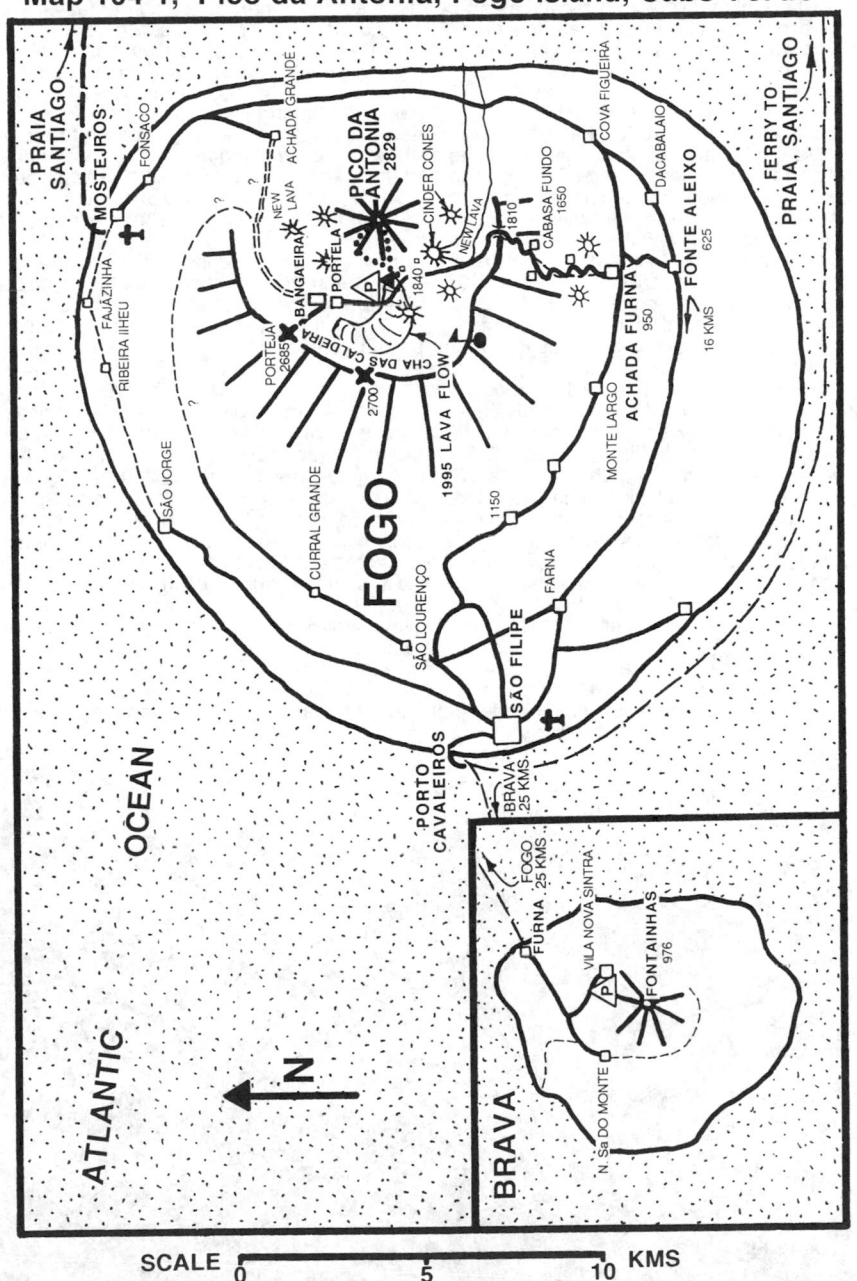

SCALE 0 ___ 5 ___ 10 KMS

(Porto Cavaleiros) to Furna. From the port there should be vehicles going to Vila Nova Sintra. Or just walk from the harbor to the top of **Fontainhas**, a one day climb. Best to buy all your food before arriving on Brava.

Toubkal, Atlas Mountains, Morocco

Most people think North Africa is as arid and dry as the Sahara Desert, but that's not true. There are some places, namely the high Atlas Mountains of Morocco, which have many streams, deep winter snows, and an invigorating climate. One of these places is on the road and trail to Toubkal at 4167 meters. This is the highest peak in Morocco and all of North Africa. The highest part of the Atlas is due south of Marrakech about 65 kms by road. Toubkal and the Atlas are folded mountains with a variety of sedimentary rock formations.

It was November, 1973, that the author visited this peak. If memory is correct (3 months later in Zaire his handbag and diary were stolen!) he started walking from Asni, then got a ride part way to Imlil, which is the end of the road and the starting point for those climbing Toubkal. From Asni, he made the climb in 3 days, up and back to Imlil. He had snow and bad weather on the mountain and met some British troops from Gibraltar at the Refuge Neltner. He got a ride out of the mountains with them in a white Land Rover.

Here's how you get there and climb the mountain. First visit the tourist office in Marrakech to see about buses, the facilities at Asni and Imlil, the huts in the mountains and how much they might cost and in what condition they're in, and perhaps pick up some of the latest maps. Also, stock up on climbing food there too. Then take a bus to Asni, and maybe on to Imlil (?). If there are no buses, collective taxis will be looking for passengers to make the run. Asni has a youth hostel and a couple of hotels, at last report, in case you get stuck there.

The valley from Asni to Imlil is an oasis, with a fine stream of water, irrigated fields, and many trees and small villages. The distance is 17 kms. At Imlil, you'll find several small stores where you can buy enough basic food for the trip. For better variety however, shop in Marrakech. Also at Imlil, is a climber's refuge which sleeps 35 people in separate bunks; anyone can stay there. And there's at least one other hotel, maybe more by 2001.

From Imlil, **Toubkal** can be done easily in 2 days, but a strong climber might do it in one long day. From Imlil, simply walk south up the main canyon. At the western base of Toubkal is the Refuge Neltner at about 3207 meters. It's big enough to sleep perhaps 20 people. You could stay there for free back in 1973, but you'll have to pay now. Ask about using it, and about it's condition, at Imlil. It might pay to take a tent just in case. Normally, people hike from Imlil to Neltner on the first day, then make the climb and return to Imlil on Day 2.

This map shows a number of other peaks, valleys, trails and refuges. If you're interested in seeing the real Morocco, you might take in some of these other mountain valleys.

There are no glaciers in the area, but snow stays late in the summer on the high peaks. The best time to climb is from May or June, through October or even into November. Heavy precipitation is often received in the winter months. The book below indicates there are now 6

This is the scene along the stream valley just below the village of Imlil.

Map 105-1, Toubkal, Atlas Mountains, Morocco

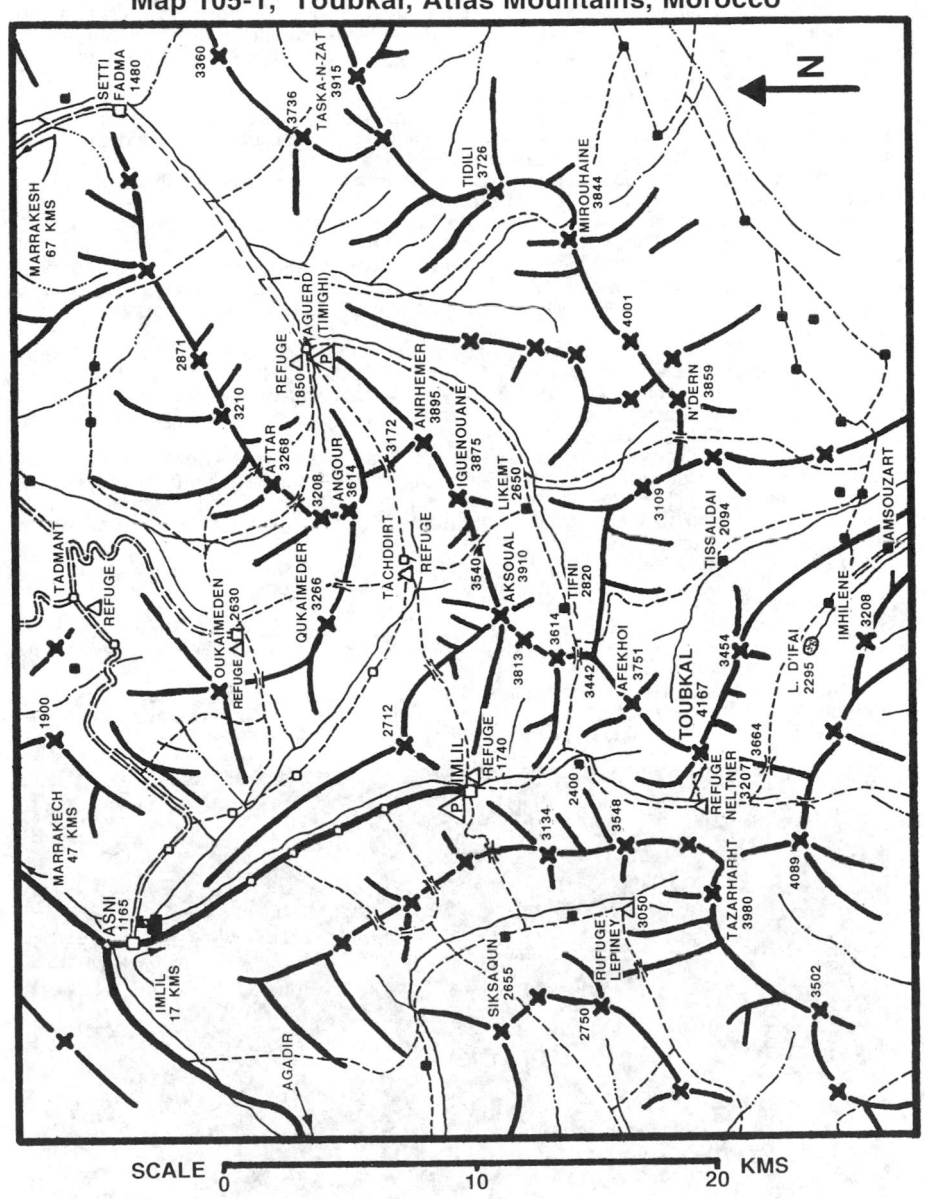

CAF (Club Alpine France) refuges located in the higher valleys of the Atlas.
Maps Michelin Map *169, Maroc,* 1:1,000,000; perhaps DMA map *NH 29-3,* 1:250,000; and 4 maps *Amezmiz, Oukaimeden-Toubkal, Tizi-n-Test and Taliwine,* 1:100,000, from the French IGN; the book, **Atlas Mountains**, West Col Books; and a travel guidebook to North Africa or Morocco.

Lalla Khedidja, Djurdjura Massif, Atlas Mountains, Algeria

Stretching almost halfway across North Africa, from the south of Morocco to Tunisia, are the Atlas Mountains. They reach their highest in Morocco with Toubkal, then gradually become lower to the east. But in the center of northern Algeria, is another high area known as the Djurdjura (pron. Ju-ju-ra) Massif.

The highest peak is Lalla Khedidja, at 2308 meters elevation. Another summit nearly as high is Timedouine, at 2305 meters. It lies west of Khedidja about 12 kms. These mountains are not big by alpine standards, but the higher slopes are forested with a mixture of pine and other trees, and brush. The very highest summits are above timberline.

As the year 2000 rolls around the political situation seems to be improving in Algeria, so shortly it may be safe enough for tourists to return. When that day comes, getting to the Djurdjura Massif is quite easy. Not far north of this mapped area is the main coastal highway linking all of North Africa. This is Highway N12 which connects Algiers to the west, with Bejaia to the east. Take a bus along this highway and stop at Tizi-Ouzou. From there look for buses, or more likely, collective taxis going south along Highway N30 toward M'chedallad. Or try hitch hiking--but there's not a lot of traffic. If someone picks you up, they may ask for money, about the equivalent of the bus fare.

To the south is Highway N5, which runs east-west south of the mountains. It runs from Algiers to Bouira, then bypasses M'chedallad and on to Bordj-bou-Arreridj and Stif in the east. This highway should have plenty of traffic including buses and collective taxis. If you use this route, you may have to get off at the junction 2-3 kms south of M'chedallad and walk or take a taxi. Also, Highway N26 begins or ends just south of M'chedallad, and runs east to Bejaia.

Here's the author's experience on **Lalla Khedidja**. He walked from the town of M'chedallad, up road N30 a ways, then cross-country to Tala-Rana, which is just a goat farm--if the author remembers correctly (?). From there a trail runs north right up to the summit. After the climb, he walked all the way back to M'chedallad on the highway. This was all in one long day in late November or early December, 1973.

One easy way to shorten this long hike would be to first look for a collective taxi heading over the mountain, or hire one for yourself, and get out at the pass at 1600 meters. Or try walking and hitch hiking.

The higher slopes are covered with brush and trees, and there are goats and shepherds. Above Tala-Rana, is a pine forest with troops of baboons, or maybe barbary apes (?). Timber line is around 2100 meters.

M'chedallad is large enough to have several shops and good food selections can be found. There may or may not be a hotel, but the author guesses there's some place to stay (?). This hike is dry, so carry plenty of water. In mid-winter, snows become deep, and in the 3 or 4

Hoarfrost on the highest trees on the south slopes of Khedidja.

Map 106-1, Khedidja, Djurdjura Massif, Atlas Mtns., Algeria

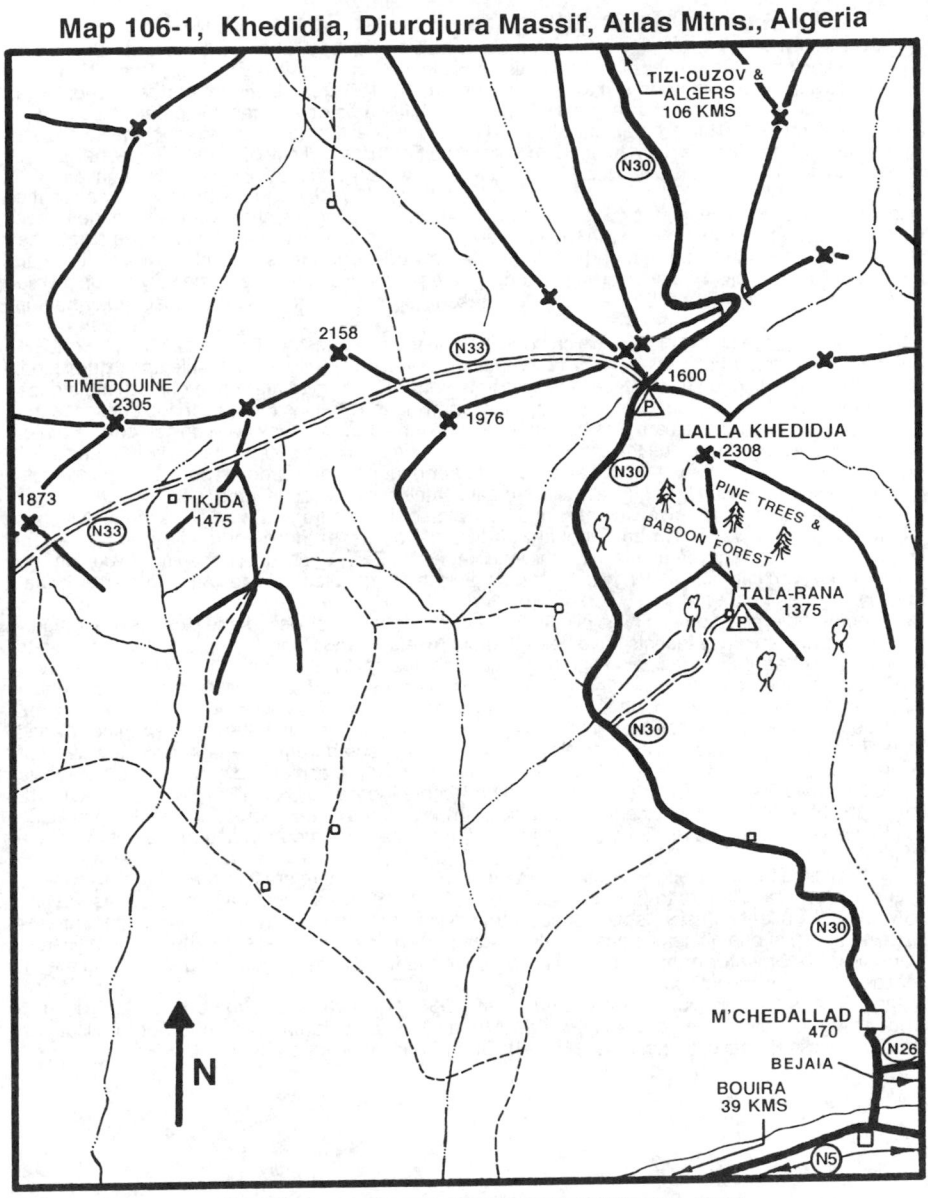

summer months the temperatures are high, making fall or spring the ideal time to hike in the Djurdjura.

Maps Michelin Highway map *Algerie-Tunisie, 172,* 1:1,000,000; DMA map *NJ-31 15,* 1:250,000; perhaps TPC map G-2A, 1:500,000; the French IGN probably has some better maps, perhaps at 1:100,000 scale; and the latest travel guidebook which should update the political situation in Algeria.

Falaise de Bandiagara, Dogon Country, Mali

If you're traveling West Africa, or more precisely Mali, the closest thing you'll find to a mountain is a plateau and an escarpment called the Falaise de Bandiagara or Bandiagara Cliff. This cliff runs in nearly a straight line from northeast to southwest for about 150 kms. In the far northeast (not quite shown on this map), the cliff is as high as 600 meters. In the area of this map, the greatest local relief is about 400 meters. This escarpment is formed by a fault-line; the northwest side up, the southeast side down. This Falaise is located about 100 kms east of the small city of Mopti. Since the author hasn't been to Mali yet, he is using the 2 books listed below as his primary sources of information. There's more to see in the area than the cliff itself. Perhaps the most interesting sites are the villages of the Dogon people who live along the Falaise. The Dogons are a very independent tribe numbering about 250,000. When the Islamic wave swept this region several hundred years ago, the Dogons resisted in this mountain-like stronghold. Few converted to Islam. Along the Cliff are an estimated 700 villages. Some are sitting on top of the escarpment, some are at the very bottom, while others are perched on the cliff-face itself. It's these fotogenic villages that attract so many foreign visitors these days.

The villages are small, most of which constitute only a few houses. The homes on top or at the bottom of the cliff normally sit atop rock outcroppings, so as not to take up valuable agricultural land. Other dwellings cling to the cliff-face in isolated pockets. The homes are made of mud and stones with many small rooms. The roofs are always flat, enabling the Dogons to sleep on top during the hot dry season. Their granaries are also built of mud and stone, but with thatched conical roofs. Both of these structures are built up off the ground on piles of stones, as if on stilts. This not only keeps them high and dry in the wet season, but also helps to keep insects and rodents out. The homes and granaries are surrounded by high walls which create small enclosed courtyards.

If you plan to go to **Dogon Country** and the **Falaise de Bandiagara**, first go to Mopti, which is located about halfway between Timbuktu and Bamako. From there you can either join a tour organized by the Mali government tourist office known as SMERT, or go independently. If you don't go with a group, you can either hitch hike to Bandiagara, the largest town in the immediate area, or get there in a shared taxi.

From Bandiagara, you can hitch hike to Sanga, one of the most visited and picturesque villages. However, since so many tourists have been there in recent years, Sanga may be losing some of its character or charm. Sanga is also one of the strongholds of SMERT, which requires you to hire a guide and pay high prices to visit other villages. For the not-so-hardy traveler it's recommended you take a guide, but it's best to hire one in Bandiagara, rather than in Sanga, which will be less expensive. Because of SMERT's policy about hiring a guide, most independent travelers are visiting villages as far from the jet-set tourists as possible. Some are going south from Bandiagara to the vicinity of Djiguibambo. The distance is said to be about 25 kms, which doesn't quite match this map's scale (?). Other travelers go to Bankas below the cliff and where there's no SMERT office, then walk the 12 kms to the base of the cliff to either Kanicombole or Ende. From Bankas, you could walk to, then along the Falaise to Douro or even Sanga, using one of many trails both on top and at the bottom of the escarpment.

If you intend to take a long hike, buy all your food in Mopti, as there are few good shops elsewhere. You can also ask villagers to prepare meals for about US$1 (this price may be as old as the late 1980's). Take a tent, or ask villagers for accommodation at about US$4 a night. This usually means sleeping on top of one of their homes. Purify all water drawn from their wells, and be aware of Guinea worm in pools of water or in streams. Rainy season is from June to September. This is the off season for tourists and few go there then.

Maps Michelin map *Africa, North and West, 153*, 1:4,000,000; and the books, **Africa on a Shoestring**, Lonely Planet; or **Backpacker's Africa** (West and Central Africa), Bradt Publications. Ask for maps in Bamako, or contact the French IGN in Paris for better maps.

Map 107-3, Falaise de Bandiagara, Dogon Country, Mali

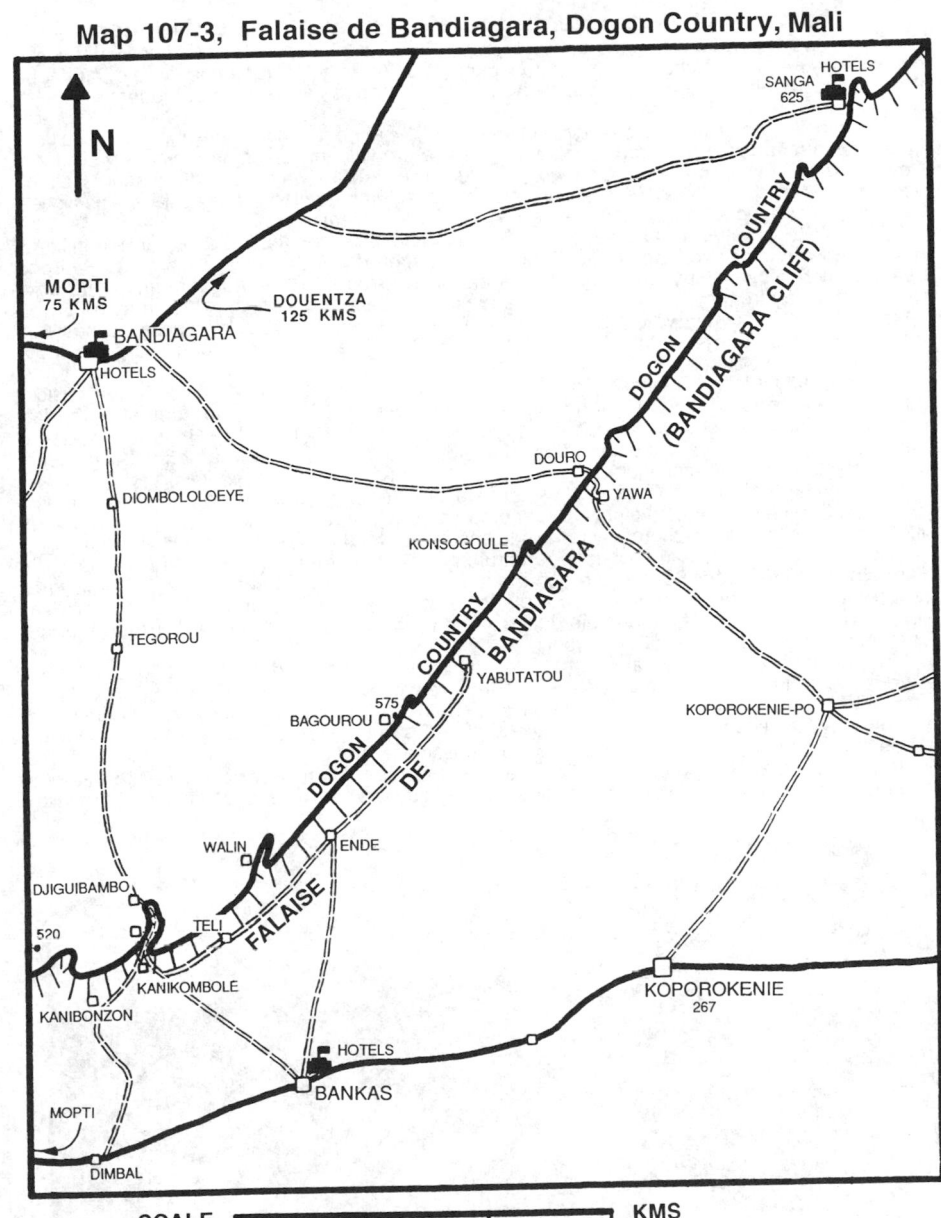

Tahat & Assekrem Hermitage, Hoggar Mountains, Algeria

For the adventurous who wants to climb or hike in unusual places, the Hoggar Mountains in south central Algeria might be what you're looking for. Actually this region is more of a plateau than true mountains, as parts of it appears similar to the spires and buttes of Monument Valley on the Colorado Plateau in the southwest USA.

Intermingled among the flat-lying beds of lava are 2 separate groups of peaks which are actually the remains of ancient and eroded volcanos. These are volcanic plugs or necks very similar to Devil's Tower in Wyoming, USA. One group of plugs is just a little ways north of Tamanrasset; the other group is further north, both east and west of the Assekrem Hermitage or Monastery. The highest peak or volcanic plug is **Tahat**, 2918 meters, just west of Assekrem.

The only town within 700 kms in any direction is Tamanrasset (locals call it Tam), a military, tourist and trading town. Getting to Tam isn't as difficult as it once was. There's an airport nearby which allows many tourists into the area, mainly from France and Germany. There's a road or highway from the north and from the towns Ghadaia and Insalah, which may be paved all the way to Tam when you get there (?). There are buses and trucks, and an occasional private vehicle on this road, but it's difficult to hitch hike. Even if a truck stops and gives you a ride, you'll pay just like on a bus.

There's also a track running south from Tamanrasset to Agades in northern Niger. Trucks use this route regularly, but overland tourists must travel in convoy. The number of tourists visiting this part of Algeria will depend on the political stability. By flying to Tam, it would appear that all the bloody scenes in the north can be avoided. However, by the year 2000, things seem to be getting back to normal again.

The best time to visit this area is in winter. Daytime temperatures then are pleasant, maybe 22° to 25°C, with cool or cold nights, depending on your elevation. The area is so dry, there's little need for a tent; nor is there any reason to check the weather forecast--it's always sunny!

North of Tam is a 190-km-long loop-road running into the heart of the Hoggar Mountains. In Tam, you can hire Land Rovers to reach the mountains, or perhaps join with others to form a group; or walk! Water is found in 3 or 4 places, but it's hardly fit to drink. Take a filter. The Monks who live on top of a mountain called **Assekrem**, get most of their water from tourists. They may give you some if you're back on foot.

The author hitch hiked to Tam on top of a truck from the north and Insalah along with 5 other Americans. That ride took about 2-3 days, but there was no traveling at night. He slept under one lone tree outside of Tam on Christmas Eve, 1973, then with all his food bought in the local suk (market), walked north to Assekrem and about 4/5's of the Hoggar Circle in 4 days, with just a ride at the end. He got most of his water from passing tourists. This was during the Christmas Holidays of 1973; that's when most of the traffic comes to the Hoggar. After the Hoggar adventure, he rode on top of another truck south to Agadez with an American couple. That took

Looking southeast at many volcanic plugs or necks from the hermitage of Assekrem.

Map 108-1, Tahat & Assekrem Hermitage, Hoggar Mtns., Algeria

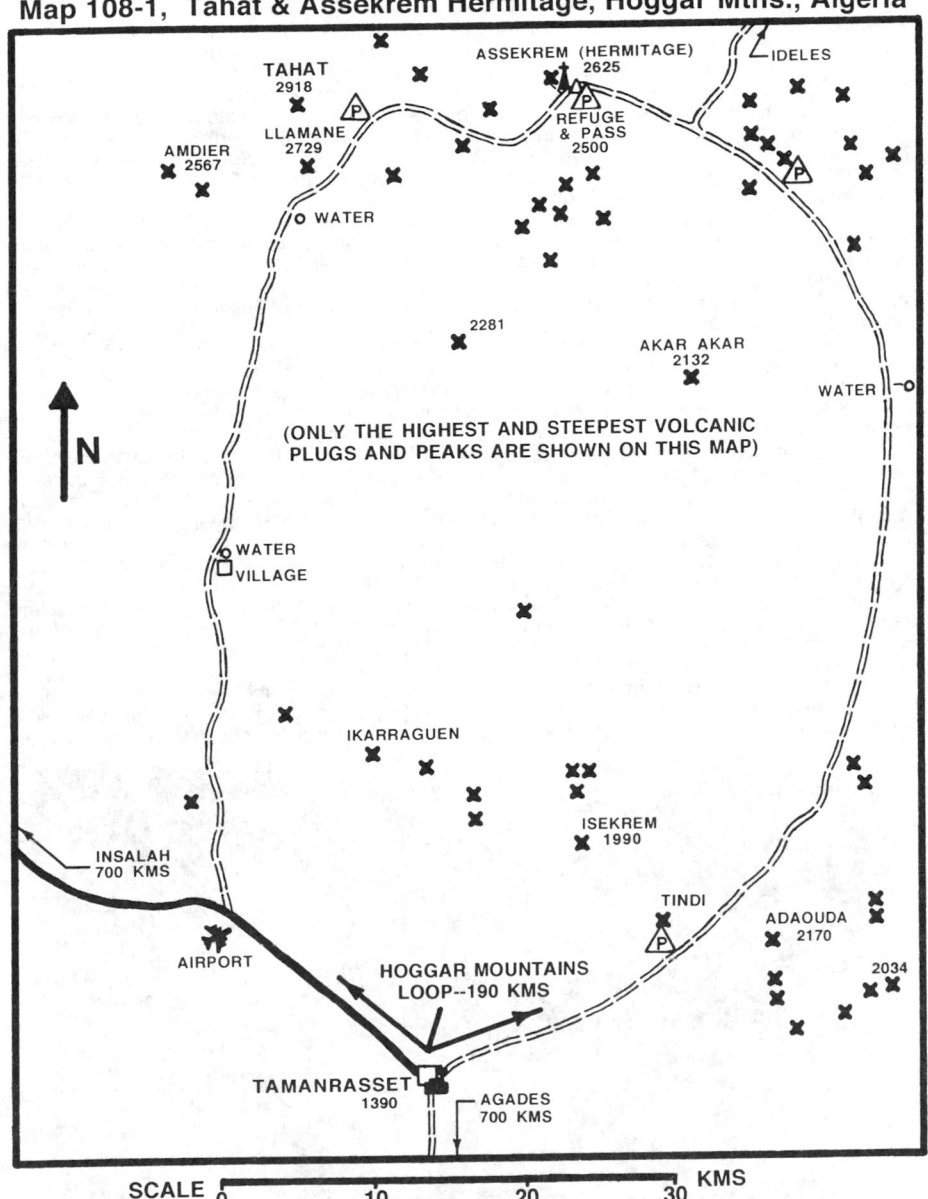

about 3 days.
   Plenty of food can be found in Tamanrasset, including some fresh fruits and vegetables.
There are several hotels and tour agencies in Tam, and they or the tourist office can update this
information. Climbers take note: rock climbing equipment is needed on many or most of the
peaks shown on this map.
Maps Michelin Highway map *Africa North and West, 153*,1:4,000,000; TPC map J-3A,
1:500,000; DMA map NF 31-8, 1:250,000; the French IGN surely has some better maps,
perhaps at 1:100,000 scale (?); and the latest travel guidebook to Algeria or North Africa.

Emi Koussi, Tibesti Mountains, Chad

In the very heart of the Sahara (which means desert in Arabi) and in the extreme north of Chad, is an area called Tibesti. This is a rugged mountainous region with many dry river beds called wadis and a number of relatively high mountains, many of which are volcanos. There are a few people living here, but it's one of the most remote parts of the Sahara.

There is little information about these mountains. The book **Volcanos of the World**, mentions 4 volcanos which are Holocene in age; that is, they had eruptions sometime in the last 10,000 years. The 4 mentioned volcanos include the following. **Tousside** at 3265 meters. It's a new cone in what appears to be an old caldera that measures roughly 25x45 kms. **Tarso (Mt.) Voon** listed at 3100 meters, is a 15-km-wide round caldera.

Somewhere in this group is **Tarso Toh** at 2000 meters, another Holocene volcano, but the author couldn't find it on the IGN maps. And there's the highest point in the Tibesti, **Emi Koussi** at 3415 meters. This is another Holocene volcanic caldera about 11 kms across. The crater floor is about 2600 meters elevation, which means it's over 800 meters deep. Maps show a smaller crater within the caldera which is likely the youngest part of this mountain. Climbing to the rim of this crater is no problem--it should be a walk up, but getting to it is another story.

This map of the Tibesti covers a large area. It's 525 kms from Zouar to Faya Largeau! Distances are long, roads or tracks are never maintained or graded, water and food are scarce, and there have been periodic civil wars that have kept visitors out for many years. The people of the Tibesti are nomadic Moslems, while people in the south of Chad are Black Africans. If and when the political problems are ever settled, you may then visit the area.

There seems to be no public transportation to the Tibesti--as we think of it, but there are cargo trucks which provide that service. Passengers always ride on top. These trucks begin in Fort Lamy, now called N'Djamena, and first proceed to Faya Largeau, where an airstrip is located. That's 948 kms of dust! From there it's on to the 2 most important villages in the Tibesti; Zouar and Bardai. There's a furnished resthouse at Zouar. Further on near Bardai, one can find many caves, cave paintings, hot springs, and other interesting sites. If transportation was better, this region would be a was better, this region would be a marvelous tourist attraction.

The area between Zouar, Bardai, Mouskorbe, and Emi Koussi, is the most rugged area and the part which can only be visited by persons having their own 4WD vehicle or by hiring a Land Rover. Needless to say, you would have to be equipped with extra water, fuel, tools and spare parts, before attempting an expedition to any part of the Tibesti.

The best place to get information, permission, maps, and everything one needs for the trip is in N'Djamena, the capital of Chad. The guidebooks to Africa don't even mention this place, so it will remain a dream for most of us. If you ever get the chance, plan your travels during winter,

Substituting for the Tibesti is this foto of the Tindi volcanic plug, located in the Hoggar Mountains not far north of Tamanrasset. There are dozens of such features in the Hoggar.

Map 109-3, Emi Koussi, Tibesti Mountains, Chad

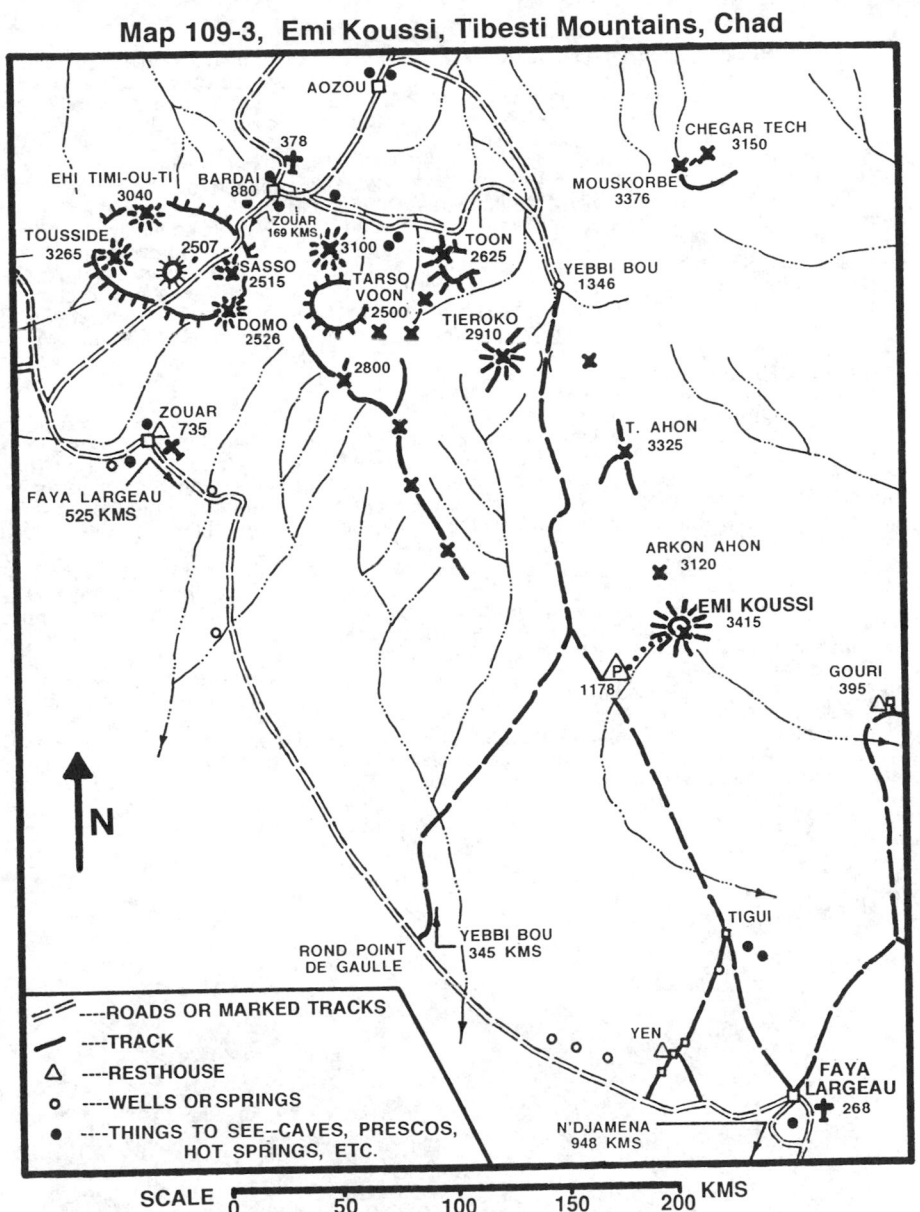

AOZOU

CHEGAR TECH
3150

378

EHI TIMI-OU-TI
3040

BARDAI
880

MOUSKORBE
3376

ZOUAR
169 KMS.

TOUSSIDE
3265

2507

3100

TOON
2625

SASSO
2515

TARSO
VOON
2500

YEBBI BOU
1346

DOMO
2526

TIEROKO
2910

2800

T. AHON
3325

ZOUAR
735

ARKON AHON
3120

FAYA LARGEAU
525 KMS

EMI KOUSSI
3415

GOURI
395

P.
1178

N

TIGUI

YEBBI BOU
345 KMS

ROND POINT
DE GAULLE

YEN

FAYA
LARGEAU
268

N'DJAMENA
948 KMS

═╱═ ----ROADS OR MARKED TRACKS

╱── ----TRACK

△ ----RESTHOUSE

○ ----WELLS OR SPRINGS

● ----THINGS TO SEE--CAVES, PRESCOS,
HOT SPRINGS, ETC.

SCALE ┌────┬────┬────┬────┐ KMS
0   50   100 150 200

December through February.
Maps Michelin Highway map *153, Africa North and West,* 1:4,000,000; and the French IGN maps
Djado NF-33 & (?) NF-34, and Bilma NE-33 & Largeau NE-34, all 1:1,000,000; and the TPC map *J-4A, J-4C & J-4D,* with just a corner of *J-4B,* 1:500,000; and possibily the latest travel guidebook to
Africa for updates on access to this area.

239

Jebel Marra Volcano, Sudan

To the people of western Sudan, Jebel Marra is a region, rather than a single mountain. It includes many villages and stream valleys, which encircle an old, eroded volcano. The southern rim of Jebel Marra's caldera is the highest summit at 3042 meters. The Deriba Caldera holds 2 lakes; one salty, the other fresh water. According to carbon-14 tests conducted in the area, this volcano had its last eruption about 2000 years ago.

The author was in Sudan for 2 months in 1 & 2/1976. He wandered all over the country, mostly by train, finally arriving in Nyala. Beginning on 2/3/1976, he then rode on top of a truck (in Sudan they're called an *arabia*) through Kass, Dibbis, and finally to Kalu Kitting for the Wednesday Suk (market). That particular arabia was hired by the widow and family of a former military office who had been executed a week before, and they were going back home. From the Kalu Kitting Suk (Market), he then hiked north to Trongtunga and west toward the rim of the crater, but wasn't on the right trail and didn't make it. Rough country! He eventually climbed Peak 2799, then returned. His hike took 3 full day & part of another. He found a good stream of water at 1500 meters north of Kalu Kitting, and some water in the villages higher up. Where there's a village, there's water of some kind, but take iodine tablets. On his last day, he walked all the way to Nyama and caught a truck leaving the suk in the middle of the night going back to Nyala, arriving there early in the morning of 2/8/1976.

Later, somewhere in Sudan, he met an American couple who were heading that way to do some trekking. In 3/1976, they sent a long letter from Kenya detailing their *10 day hike* from Nyertete to Guldo, Golo, Killing, Suni, the Deriba Lakes, Trongtunga and Kalu Kitting. They didn't have a good map, so the sketch they made is not accurate in the north. This map shows small villages and waterholes or running water they found. They passed a number of small streams on their trip and bought most of their food along the way. They signed the letter *Snake & Myrriah* from San Francisco--the author never did get their full names or address.

To do any trekking in this region, you must learn a little Arabi, otherwise you won't make it. There are trails, people and villages everywhere, but look for a better map than this, and take a compass & altimeter. Before leaving Khartoum, stop at the Lands and Survey office where topographic maps can be purchased. At the time of the author's visit, the map covering the northern half of the region was out of stock, but surely it's available now (?).

Take a train from Khartoum to Nyala at the end of the railway line; that's the best place to buy food--also the place to find trucks going to Jebel Marra. Nyala has at least 2 hotels and a good daily suk. Things get primitive beyond Nyala, but the people are friendly and helpful.

Getting to the summit of **Jebel Marra** and return will take perhaps 4 or 5 days from either Nyertete on the west, Suni on the northeast, or Kalu Kitting on the south. There are roads to each of these villages with trucks coming and going on market days, mostly from Nyala. At Nyertete is a government experimental fruit farm. It's a green paradise with all kinds of gardens and popo & mango trees. The author's guess is, the route from Nyertete is best--if reaching Jebel Marra's summit is important.

Jebel Marra as seen from the east and villages in the Trongtunga area.

Map 110-1, Jebel Marra Volcano, Sudan

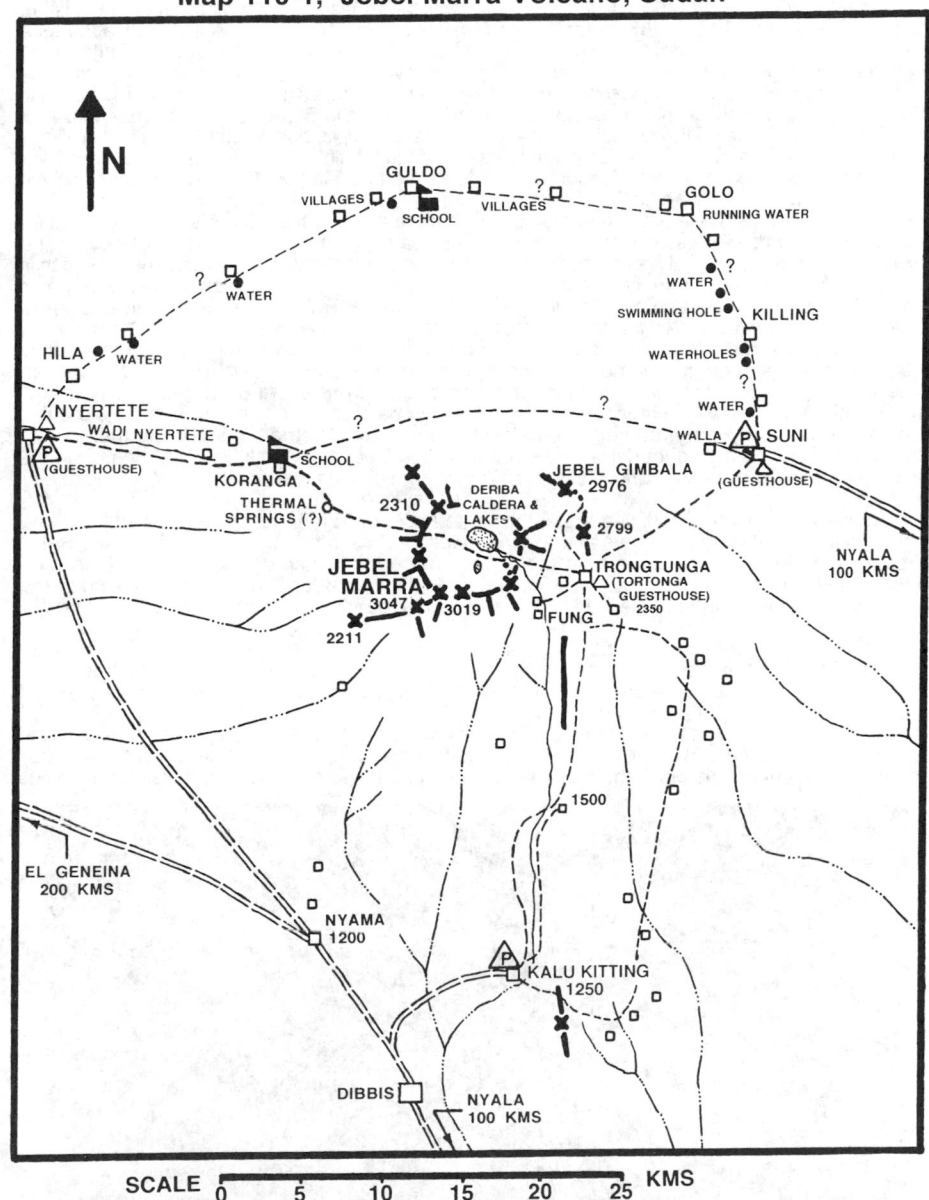

SCALE

| 0 | 5 | 10 | 15 | 20 | 25 | KMS |

Hike here year-around, but the rainy season is June through September. The winter months of December, January & February are perhaps the best time to visit this region as skies are always clear, and you might get by without a tent. Remember, water and heat are the 2 biggest problems to trekking in the Jebel Marra. Always carry 3-4 liters of water between waterholes and continually inquire of its whereabouts.

Maps Michelin Highway map *154, Africa North and East,* 1:4,000,000; look for a TPC if available?; and *ND-35-M & ND-34-I,* 1:250,000, from Lands and Survey Office, Khartoum; and a travel guidebook to Africa or this region.

Jebel Musa & Katherina, Sina Peninsula, Egypt

In the heart of the Sina (Sinai) Peninsula of Masri (Egypt) is a granite mountain the Christian world knows as Mt. Sinai, 2285 meters. The Moslems know it as Jebel Musa. In Arabi, Musa means Moses. Southwest of Musa 7 or 8 kms is the highest summit in Sina, Jebel Katherina at 2642 meters. Both mountains are sacred in Christian mythology and both have chapels on top.

The normal way to get there is to locate the bus station with buses going from Cairo (El Qahira) to Sina. In 1999, it was about one km northeast of the Nile Hilton & the Egyptian Museum in the middle of the Cairo. Depending on the season, there are one or 2 big public buses a day going to the village tourists call St. Katherina--but which is known as Al Milga locally. The tourist office or your hotel manager can give you the latest information. In 1/1999, the bus ride from Cairo to Katherina cost the author US$10 and took 7 1/2 hours.

In the town at the base of the mountains, St. Katherina or Al Milga, are 5 expensive 1st class hotels, and 2 cheaper places where you can camp or sleep in rooms. There's also a bakery, post & telefon office and many small shops where you can buy food--but everything is more expensive than in Cairo. About 5 or 6 kms from the center of town is the Monastery (Deir) of St. Katherina. It has a hostel costing US$10 per bed/per night in a dormitory room. Private rooms are also available, but cost more. You could also drop a tent anyplace, but it would have to be taken down in the day time.

Both **Musa & Katherina** can be climbed in one long day by any person in good condition. Here's what the author did. He got to Katherina after dark in mid-January 1999, and ended up sleeping in his tent about 2 kms below the police & tourist office. At dawn the next morning, 1/21/1999, he walked to the monastery and left his big pack at the hostel. After having a quick look inside the monastery, he headed up the trail to the south (there's a second trail, not as steep, for camels carrying tourists). He went past The Doorway, the little dam, then on to the summit (passing a deceased English tourist along the trail) in just over an hour. You'll want 2 or 3 hours.

From the summit he could see the entire route to Jebel Katherina, so he headed that way; down past several shay (tea) huts and to the enclosed olive trees at Ramada Musa Abu Saiid. From there it was up to the summit of Katherina on a good trail, then back to Ramada Musa and down to town along a tractor road. After buying a few items of food, he walked back up to the monastery. Total round-trip time was 6 1/2 hours. Most people will want 8 to 10 hours, or more for this loop-hike.

However, it's recommended you spend an entire day climbing Musa and making a loop with the camel trail, and seeing all the historic sites in that area. Then on Day 2, climb Katherina, perhaps from the town. There's lots of interesting things to see in this compact little area, so don't hurry as fast as the author did.

Best time to visit Katherina is during spring or fall, from late February through March, and October and November. Winter is nice, but the days are short and nights freezing cold. Mid-day temps in January can be pleasant, but if going then, take a warm jacket and gloves for evenings

St. Katherina's Monastery from the beginning of the trail up Jebel Musa.

Map 111-1, Jebel Musa & Katherina, Sina Pen., Egypt

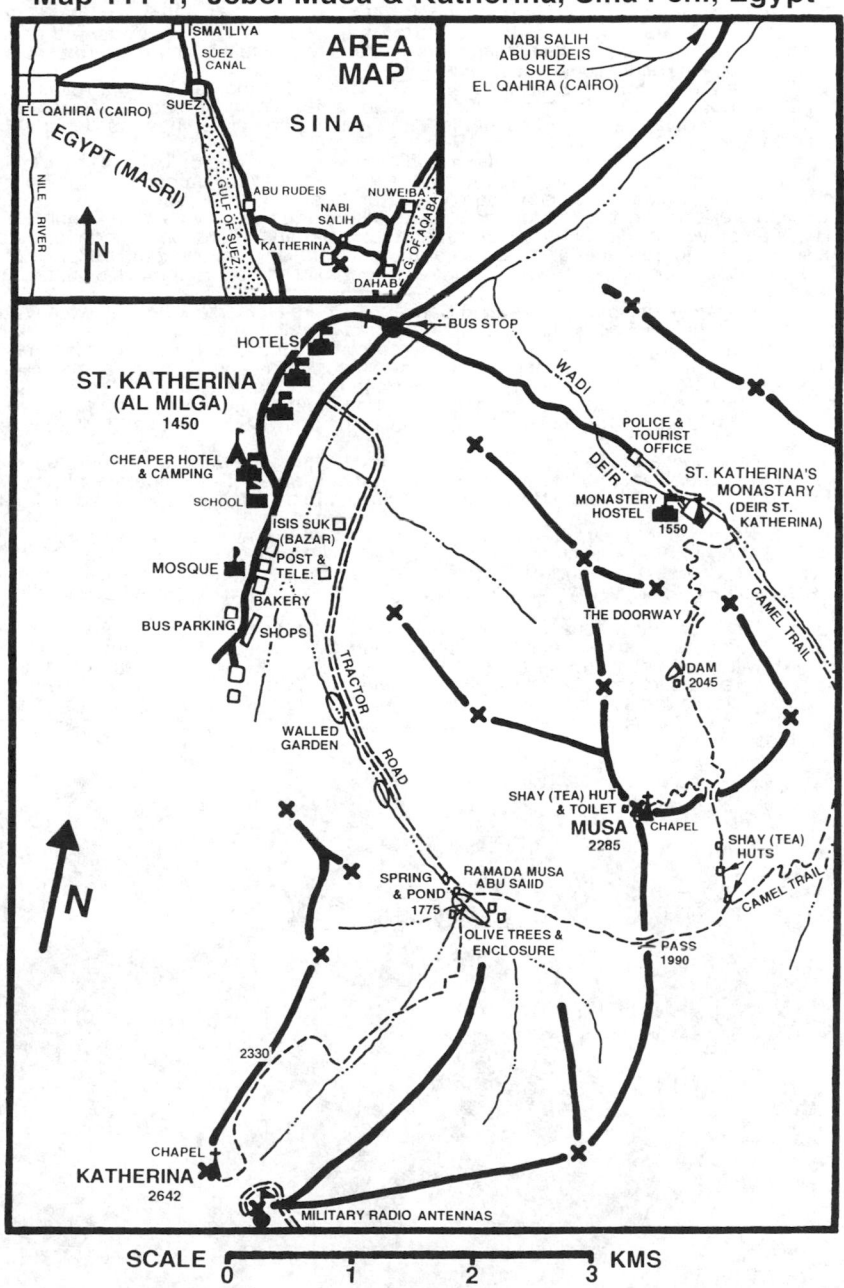

AREA MAP

SMA'ILIYA

SUEZ CANAL

EL QAHIRA (CAIRO)

SUEZ

S I N A

EGYPT (MASRI)

NILE RIVER

GULF OF SUEZ

ABU RUDEIS

NABI SALIH

KATHERINA

G. OF AQABA

NUWE!BA

DAHAB

N

NABI SALIH
ABU RUDEIS
SUEZ
EL QAHIRA (CAIRO)

BUS STOP

HOTELS

ST. KATHERINA
(AL MILGA)
1450

WADI

CHEAPER HOTEL
& CAMPING

SCHOOL

ISIS SUK
(BAZAR)

POST & TELE.

MOSQUE

BAKERY

BUS PARKING

SHOPS

TRACTOR ROAD

WALLED GARDEN

POLICE &
TOURIST
OFFICE

DEIR

MONASTERY
HOSTEL
1550

ST. KATHERINA'S
MONASTARY
(DEIR ST.
KATHERINA)

CAMEL TRAIL

THE DOORWAY

DAM
2045

SHAY (TEA) HUT
& TOILET

CHAPEL

MUSA
2285

SHAY (TEA)
HUTS

N

SPRING
& POND
1775

RAMADA MUSA
ABU SAIID

OLIVE TREES &
ENCLOSURE

CAMEL TRAIL

PASS
1990

2330

CHAPEL

KATHERINA
2642

MILITARY RADIO ANTENNAS

SCALE 0   1   2   3 **KMS**

and on the summits.

Maps *Egypt--Road Map for Sightseeing,* 1:750,000, from Kümmerly und Frey, CH-3001, Bern, Switzerland; or the TPC map *H-5A,* 1:500,000: and the travel guidebook **Egypt**, Lonely Planet, for bus and hotel information.

Ras Dashen, Simien Mountains, Ethiopia

The highest point in Ethiopia is Ras Dashen at 4543 meters. This is the highest point on a high plateau. This area was once the scene of many volcanic outpourings laid down in horizontal beds. Later it was uplifted & tilted, then eroded to create this great escarpment. This area is about 100 kms north, northeast of Lake Tana.

Here's what the author did between 2/17 & 2/27/1999. He took a bus from Addis Ababa north to Gondor; 2 days, 20 hours travel, US$6.62. No traveling at night--bandits. Buses always stop in towns at caravansaries. He bought food in Gondor, then bused north to Debark; 4 1/2 hours, US$1.13.

In Debark, he contacted the national park office at the south end of town. They require a guide & an armed scout, so they assigned an English speaking guide, who took care of organizing the mini-expedition. A scout carrying a Kalishnakof rifle was also assigned. There's a road to Chenek and beyond, but foreign tourists/hikers can ride only as far as Sankaber--to give locals employment. Or you can walk straight from Debark. Plans were made for 6 days; guide, scout, 4WD to Sankaber and a horse or mule & handler all cost about US$210, paid in advance. In Debark, the Simien Hotel cost US$2 a night; Simien Park Hotel, US$3.33, both with hot water.

Next morning everyone rode in a 4WD to Sankaber, where the horse & handler were waiting. All walked to Chenek in 5 hours and camped (by road--Sankaber to Chenek, 28 kms; taking shortcuts, 24 kms). Day 2, everyone walked to Ambikwa in 5 1/2 hours with a long lunch break in Chiro Leba (4 hours actual walk-time). Day 3, the author, guide and Kalishnakof-man climbed **Ras Dashen** in 2 3/4 hours; then returned to Ambikwa in 5 hours total walk-time. After a long lunch and breaking camp, everyone headed for Chiro Leba to camp next to the school. Total walk-time for Day 3 was 6 1/4 hours. Campsites can be anywhere, but must be flat places & near water.

Day 4, everyone walked to Chenek in 2 1/2 hours, looked for a vehicle, but had to walk all the way to Sankaber in more 5 hours (the horse & handler were left in Ambaras). Total walk-time for 4 days was 24 1/2 hours. At Sankaber, all got a ride back to Debark, but the author had to pay US$7.

The author planned on, and paid for 6 days, but it took only 4; however there were no refunds from the total US$217 paid. Part of that money was for the 4WD (400 bir or US$53), but the guide only paid the driver 50 bir (US$6.67), and pocketed the rest. This is what the driver told the author in Amharic. Learn some Amharic (Ethiopian, which has many words from Arabi) quick to prevent cheating & save money.

You can buy your food in Debark, but you'll have better selections in Gondor or Addis. In 1999, there was a war with Eritrea not far north of Ran Dashen, but it had no effect on the author's trip--except there were no flights north from Addis. There were 2 buses daily between Debark and Gondor. One left each place about 5am (11 o'clock Ethiopian time); the 2nd about 11am (5 o'clock Ethiopian time). There were also several daily buses between Gondor and Addis, but on the author's return trip, it took 3 full days (728 kms) because of flat tires. Best time to trek in the Simien Mountains is from October through May.

Looking north from the summit of Ras Dashen, with the required scout & Kalishnakof, and guide.

Map 112-1, Ras Dashen, Simien Mountains, Ethiopia

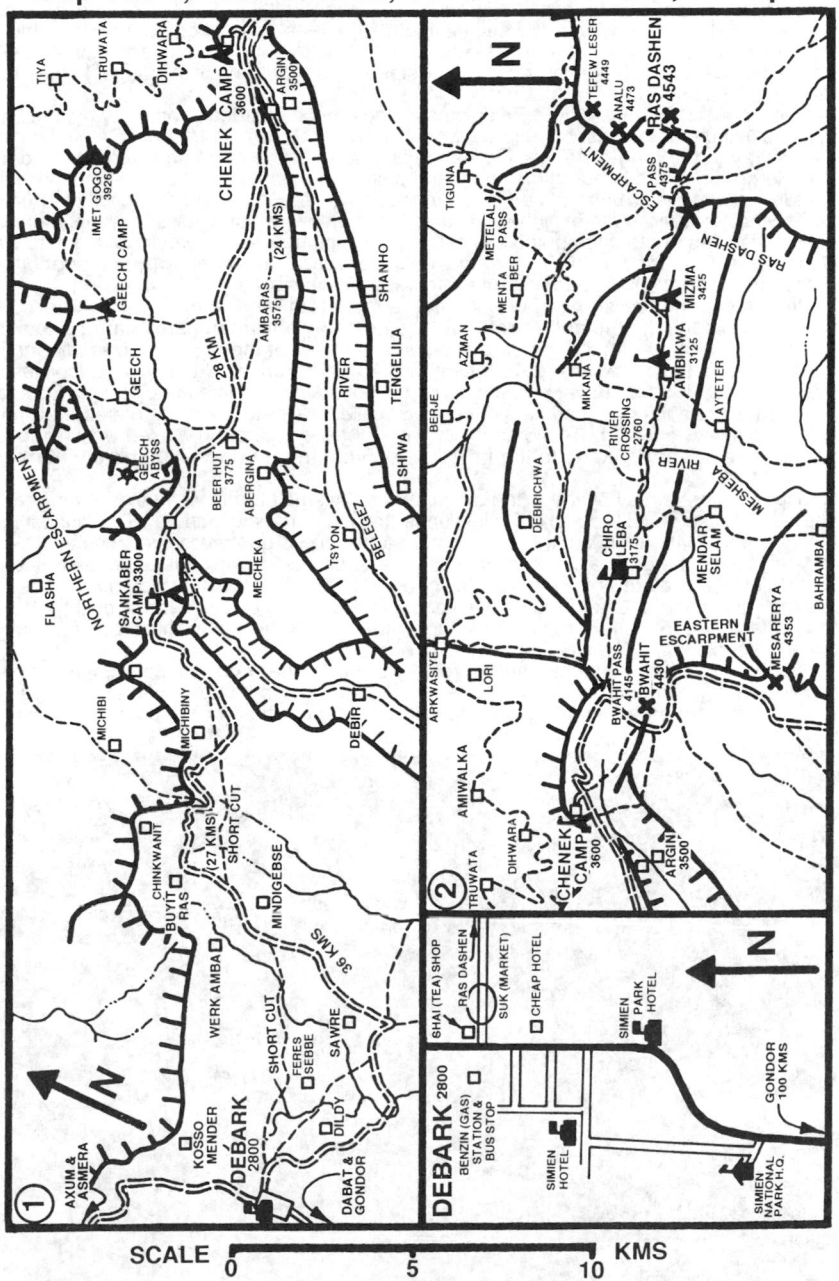

Maps *Simien Mountains Trekking Map,* 1:100,000, Institute of Geography, University of Bern, Switzerland; Michelin Highway map *154, Africa North East & Arabia;* and the latest edition of any travel guidebook to Africa or East Africa; and the book, **Trekking in East Africa**, Lonely Planet.

Mogli Peak, Wuchecha Volcano, Ethiopia

The mountain featured here is the Wuchecha Volcano at 3391 meters, located immediately west of Addis Ababa. However, the second highest peak on the old caldera rim and the most interesting to climb is Mogli, at about 3310 meters. Wuchecha is an eroded volcano, perhaps half a million years old. Mogli, which is rather steep, appears to be the youngest peak, having the look of a lava dome.

Access to **Wuchecha & Mogle Peak** is easy and can be climbed in one day by a fit climber from Addis using public transport. Here's what the author did on 2/14/1999. On his first try, he made his way to the long-distance bus station just north of the mercato (market) in northeast Addis. He got on a bus heading for Ambo and points west, but got off at the junction with the sign stating: *Menagesha Suba State Forest Project, 18 kms.* He walked all the way to Suba with no traffic what-so-ever. With only the TPC map listed below, which shows only the main roads, the author decided not to attempt the summit, not knowing how long it would take; so he walked south and east from the sawmill site, to the main highway near Sabata where he got on a bus back to Addis. Total walk-time for the 34 km trek was 6 hours.

With this experience and a good look at the mountain, and after having gathered more information from locals, the author returned the next day. With an early start, he took a city minibus to the north end of the mercato and just southwest of the big *Tana Department Store*. There he got on a big yellow city (government) bus 26 which runs to Sabata. That took less than an hour and cost US$.08. Private minibuses can be found in the same area going to Sabata.

At Sabata, the author hopped on a donkey cart called *gares* to reach the Meta Beer Brewery, about 3 kms away. He paid US$.40, then right at the brewery gate, he walked west along an old road, across a stream, and up to the next ridge. From there he walked straight north to the summit of Mogli.

Along the way, and all over this mountain, are many small farms with fields & terraces, and native huts. These go all the way up to just under the rim of the old caldera. The highest hut the author saw was at about 3000 meters. And there are sheep & goat trails everywhere. There are even farms inside the old crater which drains to the southwest toward Suba and the Menagesha Forest which was planted by Emperor Zara Yaqob (date unknown). If you have access to a 4WD, and if using the southern route only, you can drive all the way to a lodge built by Mengistu in the 1980's. Nearby is a Forestry Training Center, which the author hasn't seen. For more information, contact the Forestry Department in Addis.

From the summit of Mogli, the author returned via another ridge to the east and along the trail which ends, or begins, at Sabata. See map. Total hike-time from road to road was 4 2/3 hours. He then got on another bus back to Addis. Total trip-time from Addis and the mercato was 8 hours.

Mogli Peak on Wuchecha Volcano as seen from about one km to the southeast. Notice the fields going up to the crater rim.

Map 113-1, Mogli Peak, Wuchecha Volcano, Ethiopia

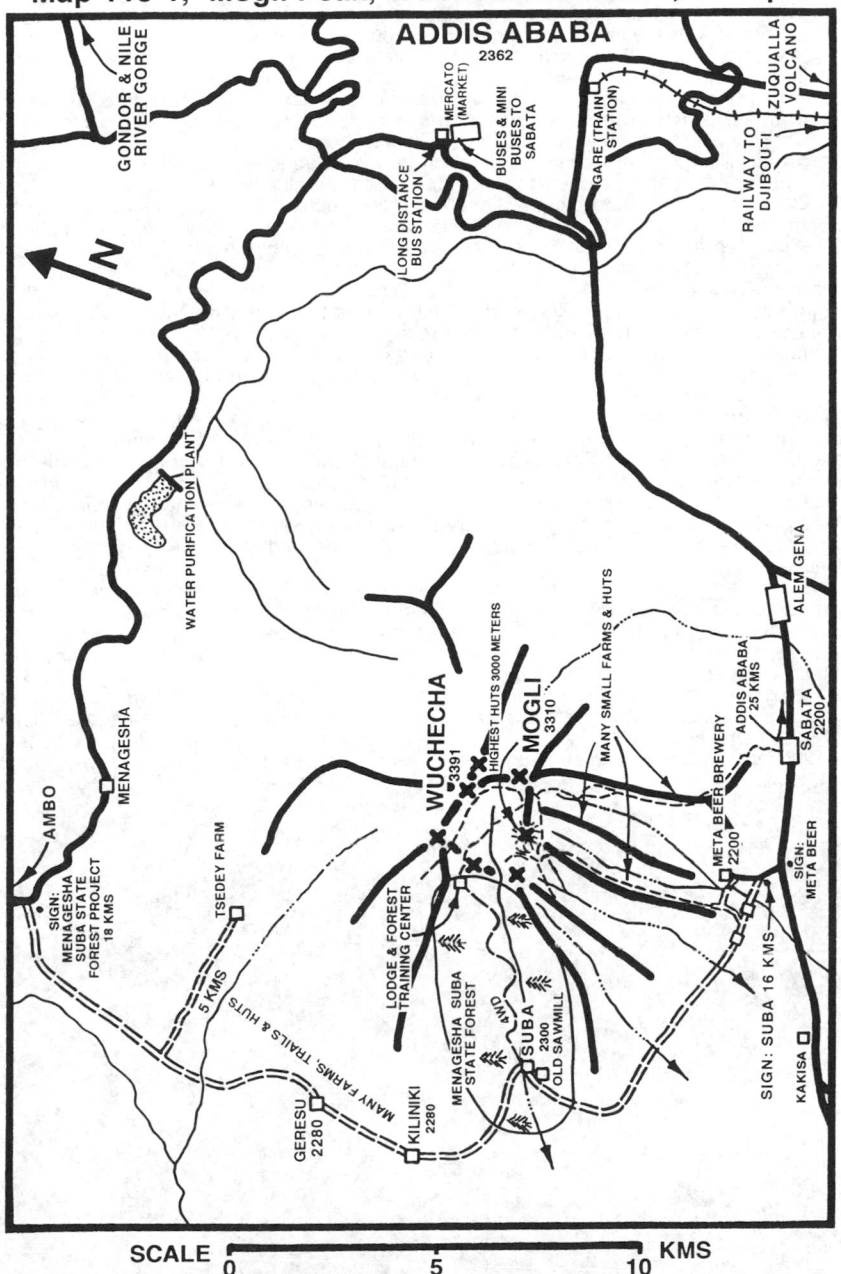

The wet season for Addis is June through September, while the driest months are October through January. February through May is also quite dry.

Maps Michelin Highway map *954, Africa North East & Arabia,* (1:4,000,000); TPC map *K-5C,* 1:500,000; and the latest travel guidebook to Africa, East Africa or Ethiopia.

Zuqualla Volcano, Ethiopia

Shown on this map is Addis Ababa, and about 60 kms to the south, Zuqualla Volcano, rising to 2989 meters. This mountain is a near-perfect cone and is rather young, perhaps Holocene in age. The crater is about 2 kms across and 60 meters deep. Inside the crater is a shallow lake. This mountain is famous because of its monastery and church at the summit. The church was originally built by Gebre Menfes Kidus, but was destroyed by Ahmed Gragn (dates unknown). Ahmed was a fanatical Muslim, who in 1531, left Arabia on a jihad (holy war) against Christian Ethiopia. He conquered much of the country before the Portuguese intervened and Ahmed was killed in 1543. The octagonal church you see today was rebuilt in 1912. Twice each year, in March and October, the *tabot* is taken out of the church and carried around the lake. During these 2 periods, and on weekends, many people make a pilgrimage to the summit.

Here's what the author did on 3/2/1999. He got up quite early and walked to what the locals call the *gare*, or train station in Addis. About one block west of the gare is a small bus station which serves locations south of Addis. He got on a bus bound for Debre Zeyt (pron. Zit), a distance of about 44 kms. It took 1 1/2 hours and cost US$.40. He asked the ticket conductor to be let off at the road going to **Zuqualla**, which is near the center of Debre Zeyt. About 100 meters west of the highway junction is where pickups and 4WD's park while waiting for passengers. There are one or 2 vehicles a day going to Wember, the village at the base of Zuqualla. He waited 2 hours for a truck, then rode 1 1/2 hours on a rough 2WD road to Wember. Cost was US$1.

The author immediately found a small shop & tea house where he left his big pack. He then hurried up the trail to the south. There were many volunteers to be his guide, but they aren't needed. There's a very good trail up to the towns only water source near the Wember Maryam (church). Above that, he continued on a trail as it cuts across the rough road, which zig zags up to the top. It only took about 1 1/2 hours to reach the parking place next to the church. He then walked part-way around the rim to the highest point, then returned. Round-trip from Wember was 3 1/4 hours, but most people will want 5 or 6 hours, depending on how long they stay on the mountain.

The author was told there were some places to sleep in Wember, but there were none. So he had a couple of warm soft drinks (no electricity in town) at one of 3 or 4 small shops, then started walking back toward Debre Zeyt. After one hour, and as he was looking for a place to camp, a small truck came by and he rode back to Debre Zeyt. From there he got on the last minibus (about 7pm) going to Addis.

If using public transport from Addis, better plan on making this a 2-day trip. You can camp on the crater rim, but don't make yourself known! Hide your tent discretely in the trees. Or, stay in one of several hotels in Debre Zeyt, then you can surely get to Zuqualla and back in one day (?). Or if you're with a small group, hire a vehicle for one day in Debre Zeyt. The wet season for

The forested crater of Zuqualla Volcano as seen from the radio antenna. The sacred church and monastery are out of site to the left.

Map 114-1, Zuqualla Volcano, Ethiopia

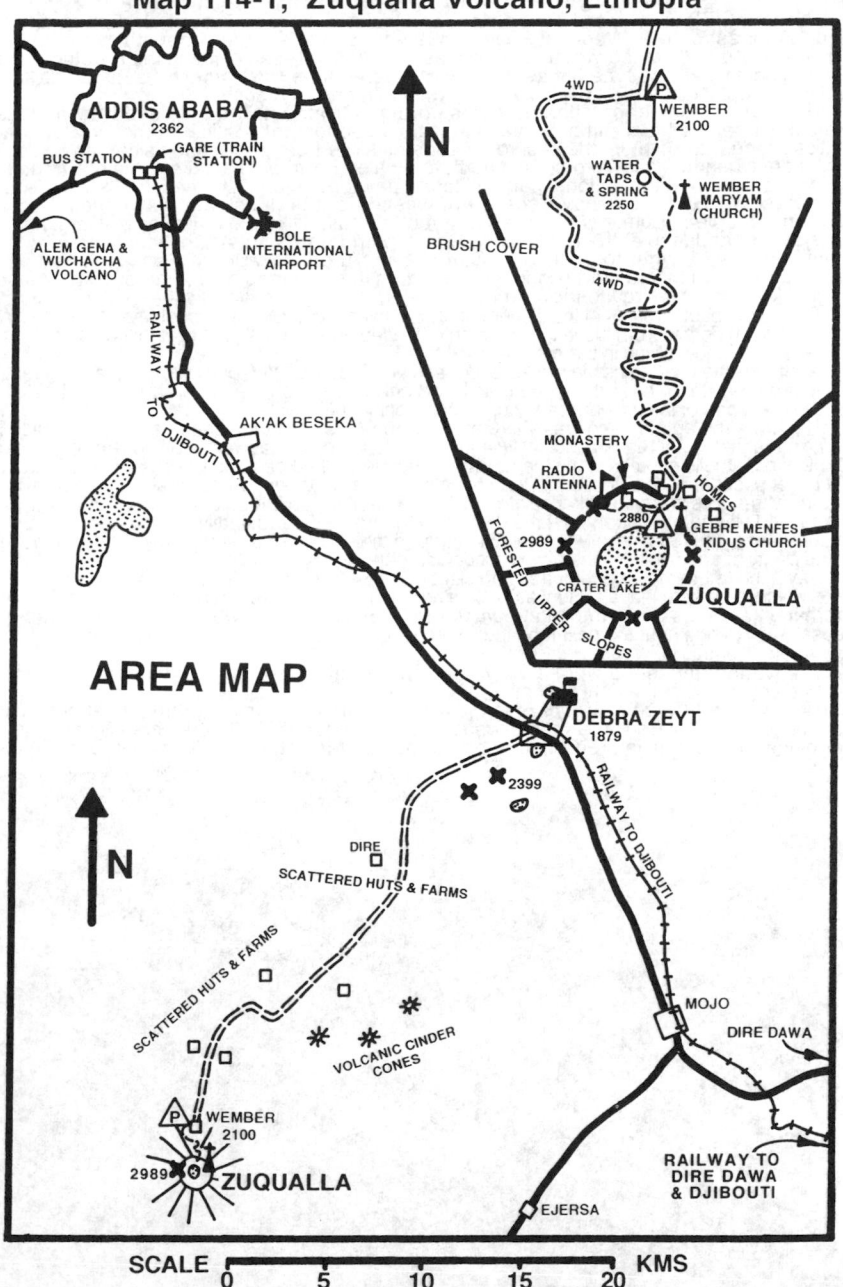

Addis is June through September; while the driest months are October through January. February through May is also quite dry.

Maps Michelin Highway map *Africa--North East & Arabia 954,* 1:4,000,000; TPC map *K-5C,* 1:500,000; and the latest travel guidebook to Africa, East Africa or Ethiopia.

Wagagai Peak, Mt. Elgon, Kenya-Uganda

This is Mt. Elgon, located on the Kenyan-Ugandan border west of Mt. Kenya and Kitala. Elgon's highest peak is Wagagai Peak at 4321 meters. Like many mountains in East Africa, Elgon is an old and eroded volcano, whose last eruption was sometime in the Pleistocene (last 2 million years). At one time it was much higher, because today there's a 11 or 12-km-wide caldera on top, indicating an explosion of epic proportions long ago.

There are a number of different routes up Elgon from both Uganda and Kenya. Over the years most people have climbed routes in Kenya because of political turmoil in Uganda. But politics change; as of 1999, the best route appears to be from the Uganda side. If you decide to climb from Uganda, go to Tororo, then north to Mbale. From Mbale, take a minibus (matatus) to Budadiri and stop at the national park offices to pay fees, etc. Park fees in 1998, were US$60 for 3 days, US$80 for 5 days. Because of washed-out bridges, you may have to walk from Budadiri. People in Bumagabula can show you the trail. Hike past the Sasa River Camp (with porters huts) and stop at the Mude Cave Camp (with porters huts) & national park checkpoint. From Mude, veer right to Jackson's Summit and finally Wagagai Peak (8 kms one-way). Depending on when you start hiking, you could do this is 3 long days, but for some it's best to prepare for 4 or 5 days round-trip from Budadiri.

There are about 4 routes to the caldera on the Kenyan side. One is through the Mt. Elgon National Park, but if you do this, you'll have to pay an entrance fee and use a 4WD to get to the end of the road-- but there's no road walking in the national park!

Another route used to be via Kitale, Endebess and Masara. You can take a matatus to that point. From there be sure to have the guide map listed below to get on the right road and trail. This route goes through part of the national park, but it's apparently OK to walk (?).

The route the author used was via Kimilili. On 6/5/1993, he took one bus from Nairobi to Kitali, then a matatus to east Kimilili, and finally another matatus to Kapsakwany; all in one day. He camped next to the Catholic church. Early the next morning, he walked past the forest station, but had to talk fast to get past the guard. It seems Uganda cattle thieves had been making raids to the Kenyan side, and forest rangers worry for hiker's safety! He then walked up the seldom-used muddy track to the abandoned village of Laboot, past the Austrian Hut (no roof), and finally to the end of the track and beginning of a trail (33 kms in 9 hours). He camped there at 3675 meters, but went down to the west to find plenty of good water in the almost hidden creek.

Day 2, he left camp on a faint trail and climbed Lower Elgon at 4301 meters (camping at Sacred Lake would be a safe place). He was back at camp in 3 1/2 hours, then headed down. He walked another 5 1/2 hours and camped at 5pm in the forest just above Kapsakwany. He was back in Kapsakwany in one hour the next morning. You better plan on 3 full days. There's one little hotel and several small shops in Kapsakwany.

The wettest times are April & May, and from August through November; but it could be climbed anytime with the right clothes.

Maps *Map and Guide to Mount Elgon* (3 maps at different scales), from tourist bookshops in Nairobi, or West Col Books, UK; or *Endebess, Elgoni & Kimilili*, 1:50,000, from Survey of Kenya, Nairobi (army permission required!); and the books, **Mountains of Kenya**, Mountain Club of

Looking west from near the Lower Elgon summit at Sacred Lake and beyond.

Map 115-1, Wagagai Peak, Mt. Elgon, Kenya-Uganda

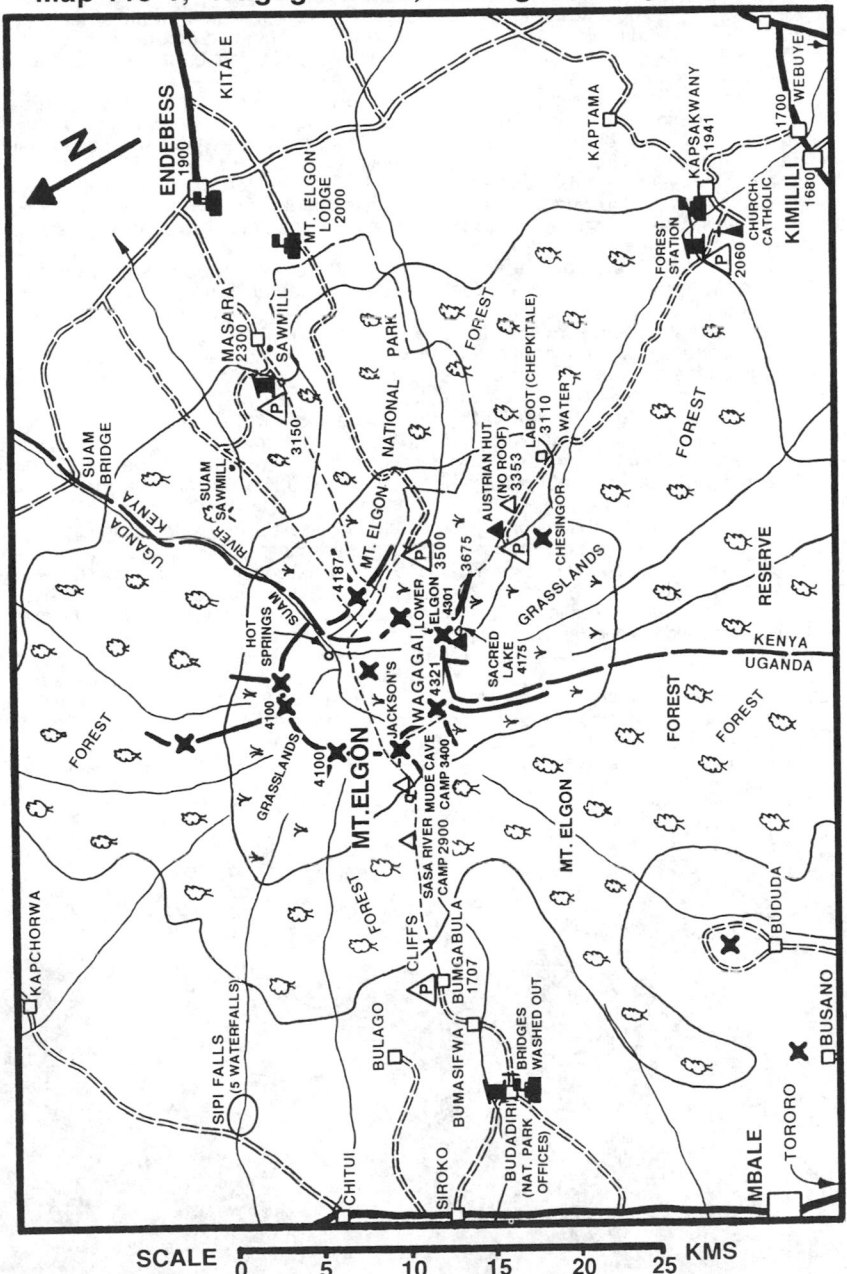

Kenya, Box 45741, Nairobi (Wilson Airport, Tele. 501747); and **Trekking in East Africa,** Lonely Planet.

Batian Peak, Mt. Kenya, Kenya

Mt. Kenya is located due north of Nairobi about 175 kms. Mt. Kenya, with its twin summits, Batian, 5201 meters, and Nelion, 5190 meters, is the second highest mountain in Africa. Like most of East Africa's high mountains, it too is an old and eroded volcano. It's so old that only the throat, neck or plug remains.

Getting to the mountain is easy. There's a very good paved highway running north out of Nairobi, past Nyeri and finally to Naro Moru. It's easier to find a bus from Nairobi to Nyeri, then change to another minibus or matatus to get to Naro Moru. There are several access points to the mountain, but the route from Naro Moru is the most popular.

There are 2 inexpensive hotels and several small shops at Naro Moru Junction. Two kms away is the Naro Moru Lodge where you can find an assortment of rooms at different prices, and a campsite. While you can probably find enough food in this small town, best to buy all your supplies in Nairobi or Nyeri.

From Naro Moru, turn east and head straight for **Mt. Kenya**. About 7 kms from the main highway is the Mt. Kenya Youth Hostel. You can camp or sleep in a dorm there. Many walk to this point, but there are also local matatus running there too. For a few US$ more, you can negotiate with the driver and be driven further, perhaps to the Met. Station.

The road continues east for about another 11 kms to the Mt. Kenya National Park. Everyone pays an entrance fee at the gate. Foreigners paid US$15 a day in 1998--probably more when you arrive! Locals pay nothing, or just a few cents.

From the Park Headquarters & Naro Moru Gate, it's another 8 kms (?) or so to the Meteorological (Met) Station. That's near the end of the rough track, and you can hire vehicles to take you there and just beyond. You can also sleep in a bunkhouse at the Met. Station for US$8 a bed, but pay in advance at the Naro Moru Lodge. You can also camp at the met. station for US$1.

From the Met Station, it's 10 kms on a good trail to the Teleki Lodge, often called MacKinder's Camp. You may sleep in a large hut (40 beds at US$9 each) or camp for US$1. Some go on up to the Austrian Hut with 25 beds, at 4800 meters. For those unacclimatized, you probably won't sleep good at the Austrian Hut because of the high altitude. There are several other huts on the trail which rings the mountain, but most seem to be in poor condition at last report. Most people reaching the mountain are only trekking around the peak and make no attempt at the summit.

Getting to the top Mt. Kenya is for experienced and properly equipped climbers only. On top of Nelion Peak is a 4-person emergency hut. The normal route used by most climbers is from the Austrian Hut, then up the southeast side of Nelion. This is rated a IV, with VI being the most difficult pitch. Most of the routes are rated V. Another route up the southwest face of Batian rates a IV.

On 3/20/1974, the author took a big bus from Nairobe to Nyeri, a matatus to Naro Moru, and somehow slept in a church. Next morning, he and a couple of British hikers walked to Mrs.

Nelion and Batian peaks left, the Lewis Glacier to the right.

Map 116-1, Batian Peak, Mt. Kenya, Kenya

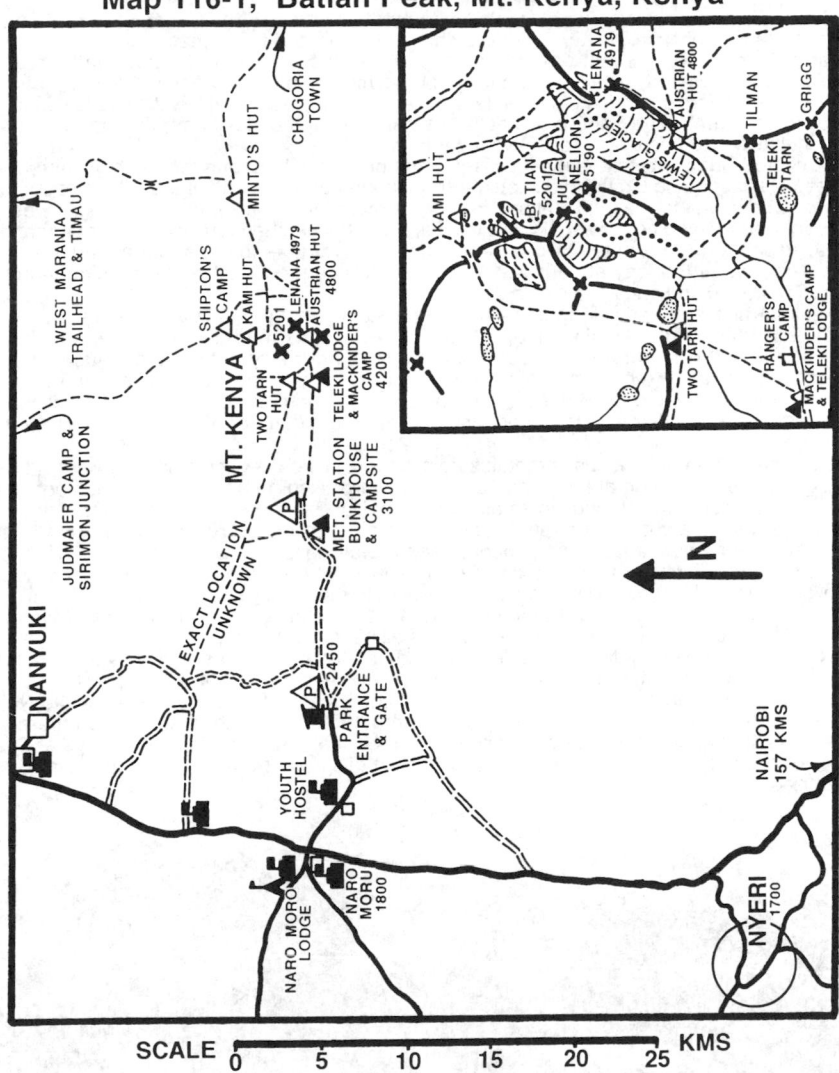

SCALE |0   5   10   15   20   25| KMS

Keneraly's Farm (she is long gone, but the place seems to have been made into a youth hostel?). Baggage was stored there, then he walked up to the Teleki Hut in 6 hours. Next morning it took 2 1/3 hours to reach the Top Hut, or what is now known as the Austrian Hut. That afternoon he walked to the summit of Lenana in the afternoon clouds. Next morning he tried climbing Kenya via 2 different routes but failed, largely because he was heading for the Himalayas via Africa and was wearing Lowa Mt. Everest double boots. After 3 hours, he went back to the hut, loaded his big pack, and in 3 hours was at the met. station. From there, he got a ride to the entry gate, walked 7 kms and slept in a milk shed. Last morning, 3/24/1974, he walked to Mrs. Keneraly's farm, then the highway and with 2 fast rides was back in Nairobe.

Maps *Mount Kenya,* 1:25,000, Survey of Kenya, Nairobi; and *Mt. Kenya Map & Guide* by Mark Savage; the books **Mountains of Kenya**, Robson; **The Mountains of Kenya**, Clarke; **Guide to Mt. Kenya & Kilimanjaro,** Mtn. Club of Kenya, Box 45741, Nairobi (Wilson Airport, Tele. 501747); and **Trekking in East Africa** from Lonely Planet.

253

Longonot & Susua Volcanos, Rift Valley, Kenya

The 2 volcanos on this map are located in the bottom of the Rift Valley of western Kenya not too far northwest of Nairobi. Longonot is a shield volcano and the highest and youngest of the two at 2777 meters. It's last eruption was in 1863. It's also part of a national park which includes Lake Naivasha. The other is Susua, but its highest peak is called Ol Doinyo Onyoke at 2356 meters. There's a much older caldera rim surrounding each peak, with Susua's being the most impressive. Susua had it's last activity some time in the Holocene, or in the last 10,000 years, but its lava dome inside seems younger than that.

To climb **Longonot**, take a minibus (matatus) or hitch hike along the old highway running between Naivasha and Limuru (you could also take the train). Get off at the village of Longonot and make your way to the train station. You can store a large pack there. Then walk west to a good dirt road running northwest. Follow this for about 2 kms, then turn left or west onto another well-used dirt road. From the turnoff, walk another 1 1/2 kms to the national park camp and gate. There you must pay about US$13 for the entrance fee (1993). The road continues for about 300 meters and ends at a picnic spot.

A good trail then heads straight up the mountain to the crater rim. Once on the rim you can walk in either direction to make a loop. The author did this round-trip loop-hike from the park camp in about 2 1/2 hours; and about 3 3/4 hours round-trip from the train station where he stored his big pack. You'll want most of one day if walking all the way. Take your own water from the station. If you don't like the costly entrance fee, there are other route possibilities, like walking cross-country straight from Longonot. There are a number of small hotels, restaurants and shops in Longonot.

To reach **Susua**, take a bus or matatus from Nairobi in the direction of Narok, west of Susua. Have the driver let you off at the village of Susua, which also has a couple of small hotels (but probably not fit for tourists!) and stores and a food stall or 2 masquerading as restaurants. From this village walk straight south. As you get higher on the slope, you'll come to brush, but there are many sheep & goat trails going through it, so the walking is easy and fast.

Once on the old caldera rim, you can see Ol Doinyo Onyoke and the route in front of you. In the old caldera valley, you'll come to a road; follow it to the southwest to the trailhead which can be a campsite with a good view of the inner crater. If you have a vehicle, you can drive to this spot, as shown on the map. From there a good trail heads to the summit.

There are a number of Maasi people living and herding animals inside this caldera, but don't expect to get water from them--take your own. You can camp anywhere. On 7/18/1993, the author did this hike in one long day from Nairobi, but because the last big bus back to Nairobi passes Susua at about 4pm, he didn't quite reach the summit. He later realized there were matatus on the highway too. His hike-time was 6 1/4 hours round-trip from the village of Susua. To be successful, plan to spend at least one night in this area, perhaps at Longonot, or Susua, or camping.

Longonot Volcano in the distance. Notice the prices for residents & non-residents.

Map 117-1, Longonot-Susua Volcanos, Rift Valley, Kenya

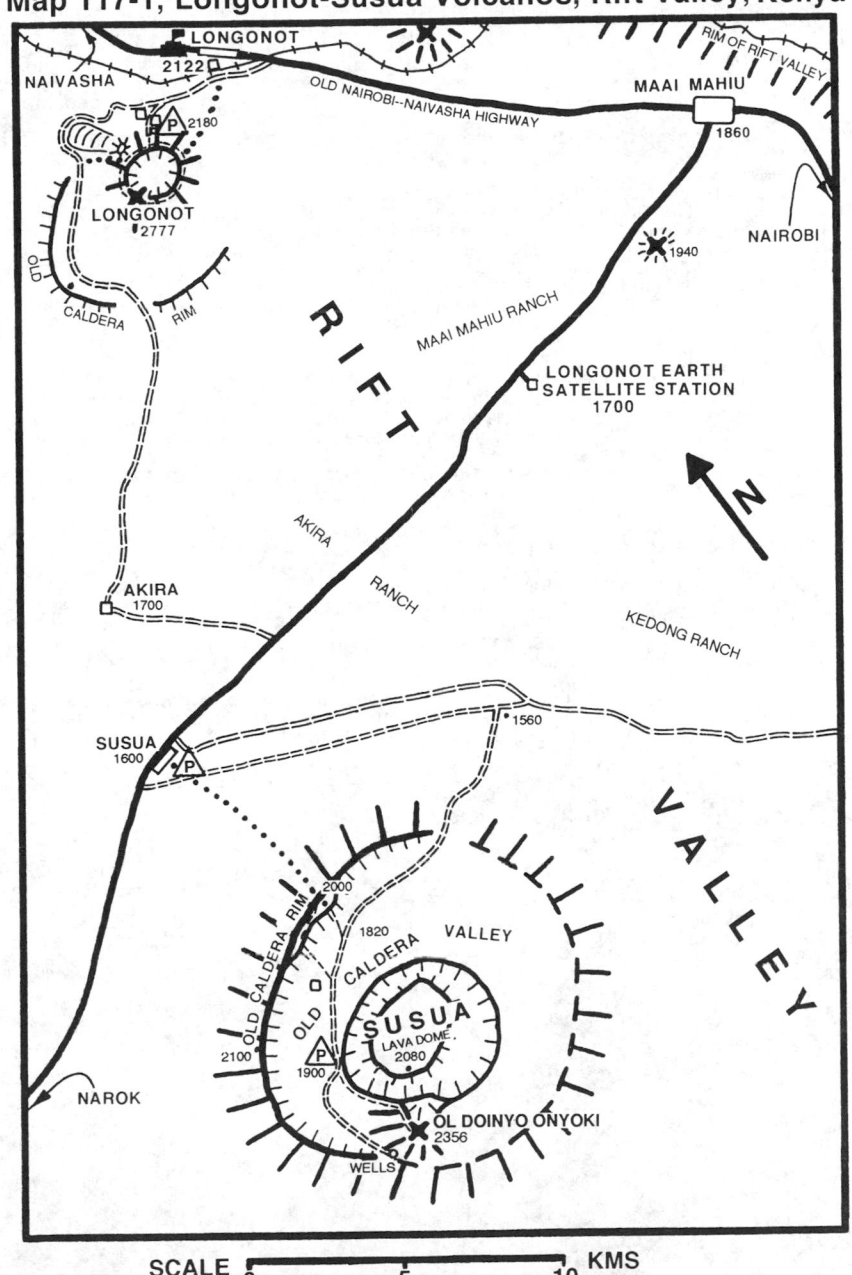

Maps *Longonot & Ol Doinyo Onyoke,* 1:50,000; or *Nyeri & Nairobi,* 1:250,000, from the Survey of Kenya, Nairobi; and perhaps the book, **Mountains of Kenya**, Mountain Club of Kenya, Box 45741, Nairobi (Wilson Airport tele. 501747); and the latest travel guidebook to Kenya or East Africa.

Margherita Peak, Ruwenzori Mountains, Congo-Uganda

One of the most unique cordilleras in the world is the Ruwenzori Mountains sitting on the Congo-Uganda border. The highest summit is Margherita Peak, the highest point on Mt. Stanley which has some real glaciers with crevasses. Smaller glaciers also exist on Mt. Speke at 4890 meters, and Mt. Baker, 4844 meters. If the author remembers correctly, the rocks here are granitic-type or metamorphic. In recent years, the Ruwenzoris have become more popular than ever since Kilimanjaro has become so expensive. Also, because Uganda has become more tranquillo.

These mountains are well-known for their strange animal and plant life. Everything seems to *go crazy* above 3000 meters, as one finds giant groundsel up to 10-12 meters, and earthworms nearly a meter long.

You can climb from Congo, formerly Zaïre, or the Uganda side. Look at the political situation first, then choose. The author climbed from the Zaïre (Congo) side from 2/19 to 2/24/1974 while Idi Amin was head of Uganda. He walked the 40 kms from Beni to Mutsori with Lowa Mt. Everest double boots, then with sore feet, took about 3 days with a huge pack to reach the Moraine Hut. He caught hell on the mountain from guides of another group because he went solo without a guide. He later had to pay for everything, which was about US$25. From the Moraine Hut, he almost reached the summit of Margherita Peak, but with brittle rhime, and cracks--who knows how deep, he didn't quite make it. That climb from the hut took 3 3/4 hours round-trip. The next morning he was in Mutsori and got a lift out to Beni. The author has no late word on climbing routes due to shrinking glaciers.

Greg Horne of Jasper, Alberta, Canada, updates the author's information from 1986. Make your way to Beni, then look for trucks going to Mutsori, headquarters for the Virunga National Park. There you're required to pay a daily park fee, hire and pay for a guide (the park people will make all arrangements) and porter (optional), and pay a hut fee. It appears this cost was about US$100 for one person for about a week in the 1990's. Expect the park and guide fees to be higher when you arrive! The shelters on the Zaïre side were in fair condition in 1986, but there were no stoves or bunks in any of them, and there was no door on the Moraine Hut. Take a little extra plastic to cover windows or doors.

With Congo the way it was in the 1990's, trekking is now (2001) more popular from the Uganda side. Take a bus from Kampala to Kasese, and the Ruwenzori Mtn. Services there can make all arrangements for a trek (for a fee of course!), then you hitch hike or hire transport to the town of Ibanda and park headquarters at the end of the road. You'll pay park entrance fees, but the good news is--guides & porters are apparently **not required!**, at least as of the 1990's.

The Nyamuleju Hut was in poor condition in the late 1990's, but the John Matta & Guy Yeoman Huts are new. Other huts seem OK. Tourists take a week to make a loop from Ibanda, to the Bujuku & Kitandara Huts, but tough-ass climbers can cut that time nearly in half. Trails are boggy on the Ugandan side, better in Congo.

To enter this area from either country and climb one mountain, count on a trip lasting about one week. You will need rain gear, extra dry clothing, ice ax & crampons. Take a tent in case huts are full. Some of these peaks rate about even with the Alps. The drier times to visit are

Margherita Peak, highest part of Mt. Stanley, is completely encased in rhime or hoarfrost.

Map 118-1, Margherita, Ruwenzori Mtns., Congo-Uganda

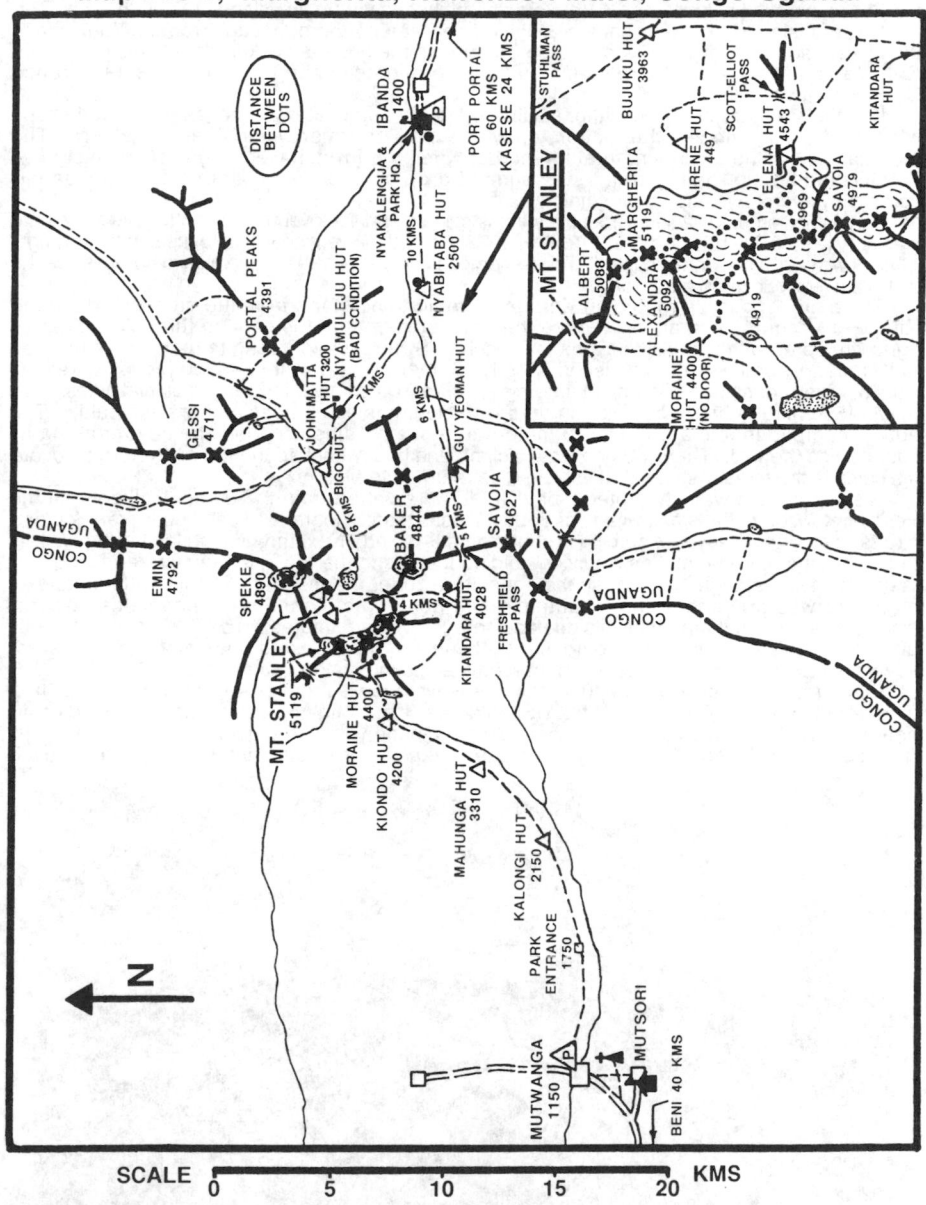

from mid-December to mid-March, and from June to August; but expect wet conditions any time. During the author's trip, he had no rain at all, but there was a fair amount of fog.

Maps *Central Ruwenzori*, 1:25,000; and *Ruwenzori Mountains*, 1:25,000, both from Uganda Lands & Survey; *Ruwenzori* by Wiielochowski--all maps found in Kasese, Kampala and Nairobi, or specialty shops overseas, like Stanfords, London; and the books **Guide to the Ruwenzori**, Osmaston and Pasteurs, from Mountain Club of Uganda, Kampala, & West Col Books; or **Trekking in East Africa**, Lonely Planet; and maybe, **Backpacker's Africa**, Bradt Enterprise.

Kartala Volcano, Grande Comore, Comoro Islands

Shown here is Mt. Kartala, 2361 meters, the highest point on the island of Grande Comore in the Comoro Islands. These islands are located between northern Madagascar and Tanzania in the Moçambique Channel. Fly to Grande Comore on the once-a-week flight connecting Nairobi with Madagascar. Also, there seems to be other flights coming or going direct to France. Consult a travel agent.

Kartala is a large shield volcano, similar to Mauna Loa in Hawaii. It has a rounded shape instead of conal, and is rather flat on top with a smaller crater within a larger caldera. The mountain is covered with a natural forest, but when the French were there, they must have established an old road or trail to the summit area as shown. Now, this old track seems completely overgrown and no one maintains it.

Kartala has erupted 22 times from the summit caldera and flank vents since 1828. Recently there was activity from 9/8/1972 to 10/5/1972. In 4/1977, a SW flank vent sent lava to the sea destroying 3 villages with 4000 people evacuated. The last eruption was 7/11/1991. For volcano updates see the website (www.volcano.si.edu/gvp/).

There are 2 possible routes up **Kartala**. The first one starts from the eastern side of the village of M'Vouni. Ask anyone where the trail begins. It heads east up through a forested agriculture area with many side trails. In French or Swahili, keep asking farmers about the way to Kartala. Upon the author's visit in 6/12/1993, there was a well-used loggers skid trail, as shown, which connected with an old road, which surely dates back to French colonial times.

At 1550 meters, you'll come to an area with clearings, log fences and grazing cattle. The author camped in this area at 1700 meters in a heavy rainstorm, but the next morning he couldn't find the trail. There was no way to climb and bushwhack to the top and return to locate his camp in the forest with no landmarks; so he returned to Moroni.

A second route was attempted 2 days later. In an afternoon, the author walked from the Pension Karibou to the small village of Boboni in less than 3 hours, and camped there. You can hire taxis to go part way, but nothing is cheap on this island. Next morning he left his big pack at the home of a guy who makes his living guiding tourists to the top. He then walked along one main trail going straight up through the agriculture zone. Farms end at about 1200 meters all along the western side of the mountain. Just above the highest bananas fields, the trail disappeared. From there on up, it's due east through virgin rainforest. To do this and keep your bearings, you'll have to use a compass, & altimeter, while looking back along the coast for several small cinder cones. The author missed the summit on this occasion too!

Either route will get you there, but strong perseverance is required. To insure success, hire a guide in M'Vouni or Boboni, at about US$25 a day. It's a long one-day trip, or you could camp near the top. You'll have to carry water if camping, but if you take a guide, he will know where rainwater can be found. The dry season is supposed to be from June through September, but it

A postcard aerial view of the summit area of the Kartala Volcano.

Map 119-1, Kartala, Grande Comore, Comoro Islands

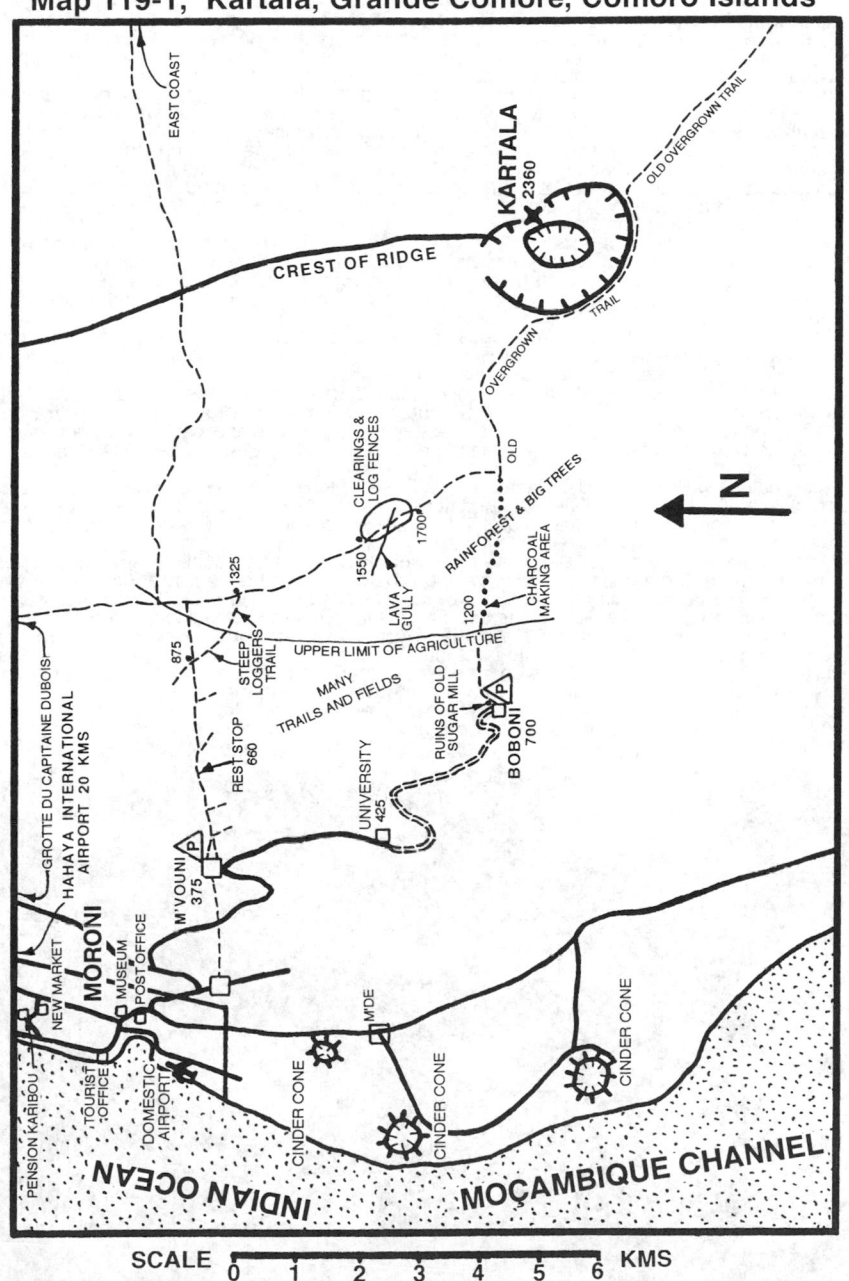

can rain any time.
Maps Old DMA or newer JOG map *SC 38-13, 1501 series,* 1:250,000; (the French IGN probably has better maps); or TPC map *N-6A,* 1:500,000; and the latest travel guidebook to Africa.

Morne Seychellois, Seychelles Islands, Indian Ocean

This maps shows Morne (Mt.) Seychellois, 905 meters, the highest peak on Mahé, the largest island in the Seychelles group. These islands are located due east of Kenya and Tanzania in Africa, and northeast of Madagascar, in the Indian Ocean. There are about 115 islands in this group, 32 of which are made of granite. These are the only mid-ocean granite islands in the world. Since the airport was built in the early 1970's, these islands have finally become accessible to the world. Many flights stop here on their way between Réunion Island and France; others come from Nairobi, Kenya, and perhaps elsewhere.

The author was here first on 4/6/1974. He was sailing on the Indian passenger boat, *State of Hariana* between Mombasa, Kenya, and Bombay, India. There was no port then, so only a few passengers could get there at a time in small boats to look around. The author was there only 2 hours. But between 7/11 & 7/15/1993, he flew from Mauritius to Seychelles and spent 4 days there before flying back to Nairobi.

To climb **Morne Seychellois** in 1993, one had to get special permission from the military. The problem was, President Albert Renè had his home built right at the beginning of the summit trail. Because of that, the trail deteriorated, and almost no one was doing that climb. Permission came too late for the author, but at least he once walked along the road in front of the house.

However, the future looks bright, because at about that time, Renè did move to a coastal home. Whenever the security problem isn't a factor, then the tourist department should re-cut the trail allowing tourists/hikers to make this climb again.

Here are 3 other hikes, all of which the author did in 2 days. Take a bus from downtown Victoria, the national capital, in the direction of Port Glaud. Have the driver drop you off at the trailhead to **Morne Blanc** (667 meters) just above the tea factory. The trail starts out the beginning of the trail at 440 meters. The author went to the summit and back in one hour. There's a nice mossy cloud forest dominating that peak.

After that, he walked with full pack back up the Foret Noire Road to the trailhead for the peak called **Copolia**. He hiked up that trail and camped near the summit. From Copolia, at about 497 meters, one has an excellent view of Victoria and the entire east coast of Mahè Island. The hike from the highway to Copolia and back will take about one hour.

Another popular hike is to take a bus from Victoria up to Sans Souci. Buses are frequent on that route. There another sign points out a short road, then the trail to **Les Trois Freres**, and on to Le Niol. The author climbed to the cross on top of one of the Trois Freres in about 45 minutes, then went on to Le Niol Reservoir. From Sans Souci to Le Niol took 2 1/2 hours.

There are no campgrounds on any of the Seychelles islands--by government decree. They have decided to allow only so many tourists into these islands per month or year. To do this, the government has put strict standards on hotel rooms, and in the process guaranteeing high prices only jet-setters can afford. But you can still camp where the camp symbols are shown on this map. But don't let anyone know, and don't leave a tent up during the day; take it down and hide it in the trees or brush. Hitch hiking is good, but there are lots of buses, even along the Foret Noire Road (about one every hour). The dry season is from June to October, but expect clouds

Substituting for the author's poor fotos on Seychellois is this one of giant groundsels in the Ruwensori Mountains between the Kiondo and Moraine Huts.

Map 120-1, Seychellois, Seychelles Isl., Indian Ocean

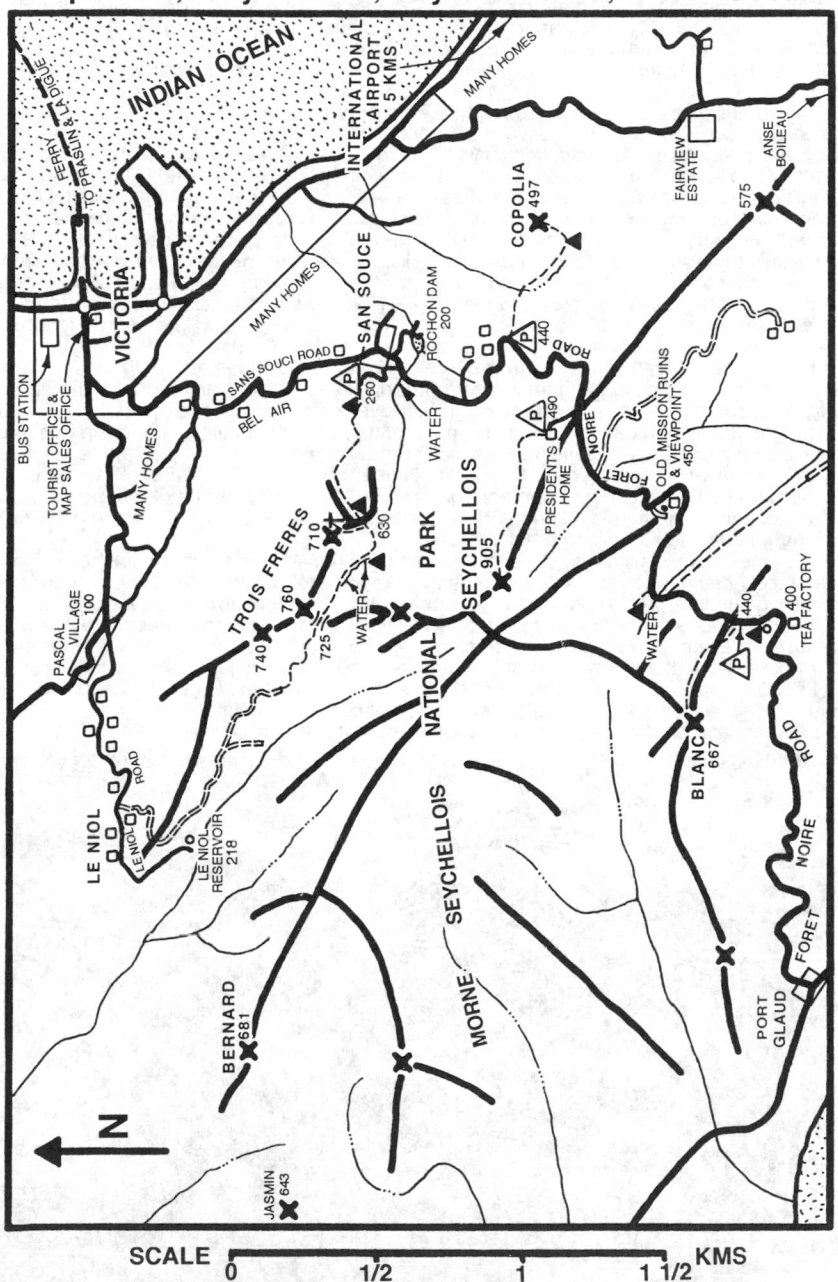

SCALE

0   1/2   1   1 1/2   KMS

over the peaks every day.

Maps *Mahé, 3 & 6,* 1:10,000, from Director of Surveys & Lands, P. O. Box 199, Independence House, Victoria; or Ordnance Survey, UK; and the latest travel guidebook to Africa or the Seychelles Islands.

Tsiafajavona, Ankaratra Massif, Madagascar

The second highest mountain range in Madagascar is the Massif de L' Ankaratra, located south of the capital of Antananarivo (Tananarivo or just Tana for short), and due west of the small city of Ambatolampy. This is a small range with the highest point apparently called Tsiafajavona at 2643 meters. These are folded mountains and if the author recalls correctly, the rock is mostly limestone (?).

To get there, take a bus from Tananarivo south to Ambatolampy, a distance of about 68 kms. Buy food and supplies in either city. There's at least one hotel in Ambatolampy. The road to Ankeniheny, at the eastern base of the Ankaratra Mountains, begins in open fields between 2 parts of Ambatolampy. From there to Ankeniheny it's about 12 kms. At various times each day, you can get a ride to Ankeniheny in a taxi brouse (bush taxi) for less than US$.50, but you may have to wait a long time. Walking to Ankeniheny will take 3 hours, and you can camp in eucalyptus groves along the way. It's a good walk through rice patties that resembles Southeast Asia--yes, these people came from Sumatra! You can buy some snack-type foods or bananas in little shops along the main road in Ankeniheny.

The author took an afternoon bus from Tana to Ambatolampy, walked for 2 1/2 hours and camped in eucalyptus trees. Next morning, 6/29/1993, he walked into Ankeniheny. From there you have a choice of 2 routes to the summit of **Tsiafajavona**. One will be up through the forest reserve which has lots of camping places, but you have to pay about US$9 to use that very old winding 4WD or ox cart road. From the forestry gate to the top is about 20 kms. The author chose this route, because the gate keeper offered to keep his big pack there for the day. From the gate to the highest summit it took him just over 4 hours of non-stop walking in mist and strong winds--a terrible day for hiking. He never did see the mountain! Round-trip from the gate was 7 2/3 hours (after he got his pack he walked toward Ambatolampy and camped in the same place; total walk-time for the day, 11 hours). Higher up, the road deteriorates to the point that vehicles can no longer use it. In an emergency, you could sleep in one of the grass huts about halfway up this road (there's a spring just to the south) at about 2100 meters. For your hike, get drinking water at the sawmill or forestry station.

The other route would be to stay on the main road running west from Ankeniheny. This road undoubtedly deteriorates to a 4WD track near the pass at 2377 meters, because there's little or no traffic going that way. From that pass, north to the highest peak, there's a trail through open grasslands. This is the shortest way up and you won't have to pay the forest entrance fee. The forest reserve occupies only the south slope of the major ridge running east from the highest peak to Lac Froid. It's mostly a forest of introduced trees, such as pines and eucalyptus.

The dry season for Madagascar is June through October, but go prepared for cold temperatures, as this is their winter. And it does get cold in the central highlands!

Maps *Ankaratra,* 1:100,000, from the F.T.M. (Institut National de Geodesie et Cartographie),

Typical homes & Sumatran rice paddies just west of Ambatolampy.

Map 121-1, Tsiafajavona, Ankaratra Massif, Madagascar

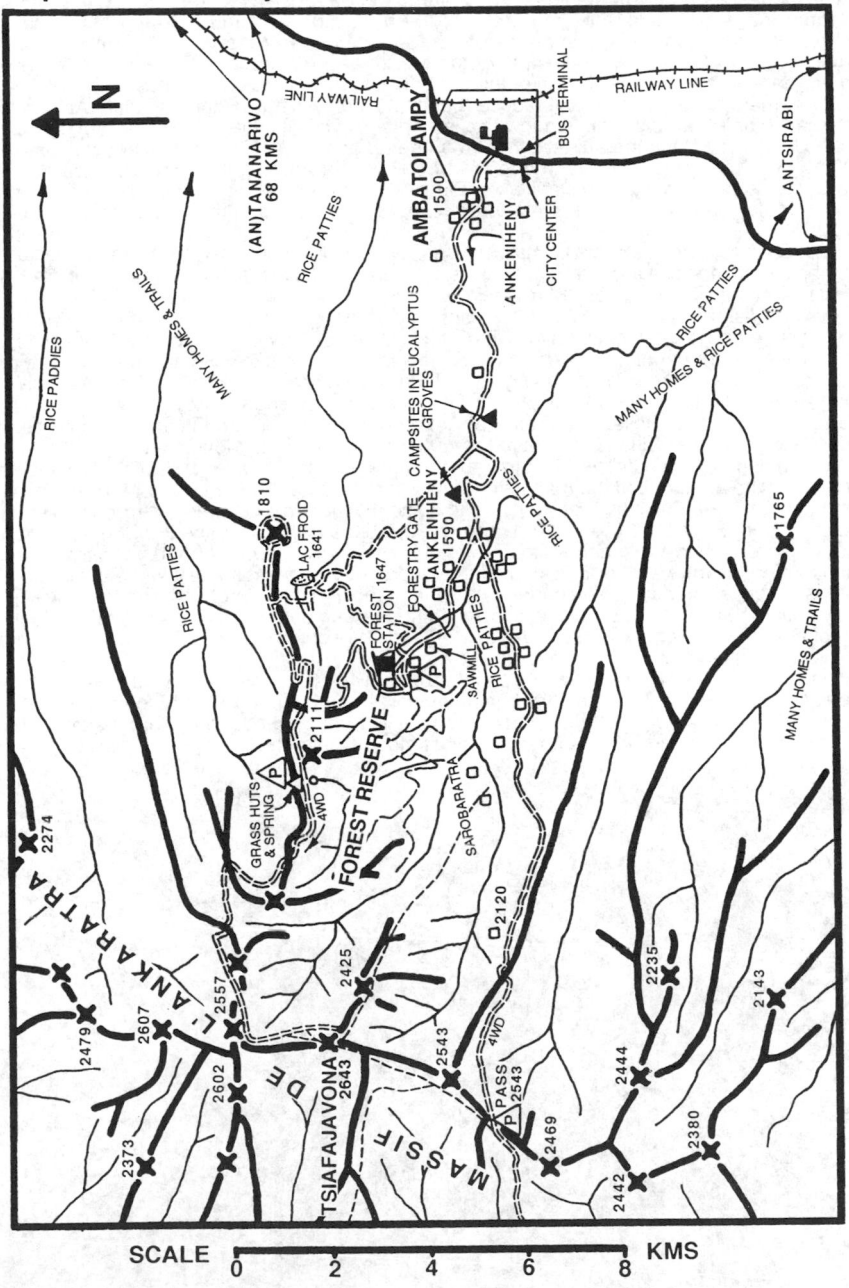

Lalana Dama--NTSOHA, J. J. B., BP 323, Tananarivo, 101, Madagascar; and the latest travel guidebook to Africa or Madagascar.

Maromokotra, Massif du Tsaratanana, Madagascar

The highest mountain in Madagascar is Maromokotra, at 2876 meters. It's in the Massif du Tsaratanana, which is located in the far northern end of the island. Much of this range is covered with a natural rainforest and is protected as a nature reserve. There is no logging or serious erosion here, as in other parts of the Madagascar. These mountains are made up of various metamorphic rock, including granite which makes up most of Maromokotra.

To get there, take a bus, or taxi brouse (bush taxi) northeast from the capital of Antananarivo (Tananarivo or Tana for short), to a town called Antsohihy. This ride in the back of a pickup on a mostly dusty road, took the author 22 hours nonstop and cost US$13.55. That was on 6/21 & 6/22/1993. From Antsohihy, take one of about 3 taxi brouses per day going northeast on a paved road to Bealana(na), a distance of about 130 kms. Bealana is a quiet town (no electricity) with a couple of small hotels and restaurants and a pretty good market. You can buy all your food there.

From Bealana, take one of about 2 taxi brouses per day going northeast 30 kms to the market town of Ambatoria. Ambatoria also has one or two small hotels and many shops, but food that climbers or tourists will be eating is pretty expensive there.

From Ambatoria you must walk to Mangindrano, although it's certainly possible to hire an ox cart--if you're carrying a lot. Head due north toward Mangindrano on an ox cart road as shown, but observe where people are walking and follow them--there's more than one track. Some of these routes have some deep wading. You'll have to wade 5 or 6 streams before arriving in Mangindrano, which is 24 kms from Ambatoria. Between these 2 towns, you'll be walking through a large valley called the Plaine D' Anketraka with pasturelands and rice paddies. On 6/23/1993, it took the author 5 1/2 hours to walk from Ambatoria to Mangindrano.

Not many people live above Mangindrano, but they do graze cattle in the foothills just below the forest. The author used the map below, which shows a trail all the way to **Maromokotra**, but that must have been built by the French, and since they left, it's become overgrown. He barely got into the forest, about 10 kms above town, and gave up. Naturally, the people who guide hikers up aren't going to maintain this trail, so it's strongly recommended you hire a guide in Mangindrano. If you had 4 or 5 days of perfect weather you might make it without, because this route is almost all on a ridge, according to the map, and you could probably find the way (?). But no one could have such good luck in this wettest part of Madagascar. Plan to hire a guide! The cost of a guide was about US$6 per day in 1993, and one guide said the trip takes 5 days round-trip from Mangindrano.

Mangindrano has several small shops, but with only basic foods--so buy supplies elsewhere. There's another trail to Maromokotra from the west via Ambanja and Marotaolana, but it seems a bit more complicated. The drier part of the year is from about June through October, but go prepared for rain, fog and clouds no matter what month you're there.

Oxen pulling a wagon through the Plaine D' Anketraka near Ambatoria.

Map 122-1, Maromokotra, Massif Tsaratanana, Madagascar

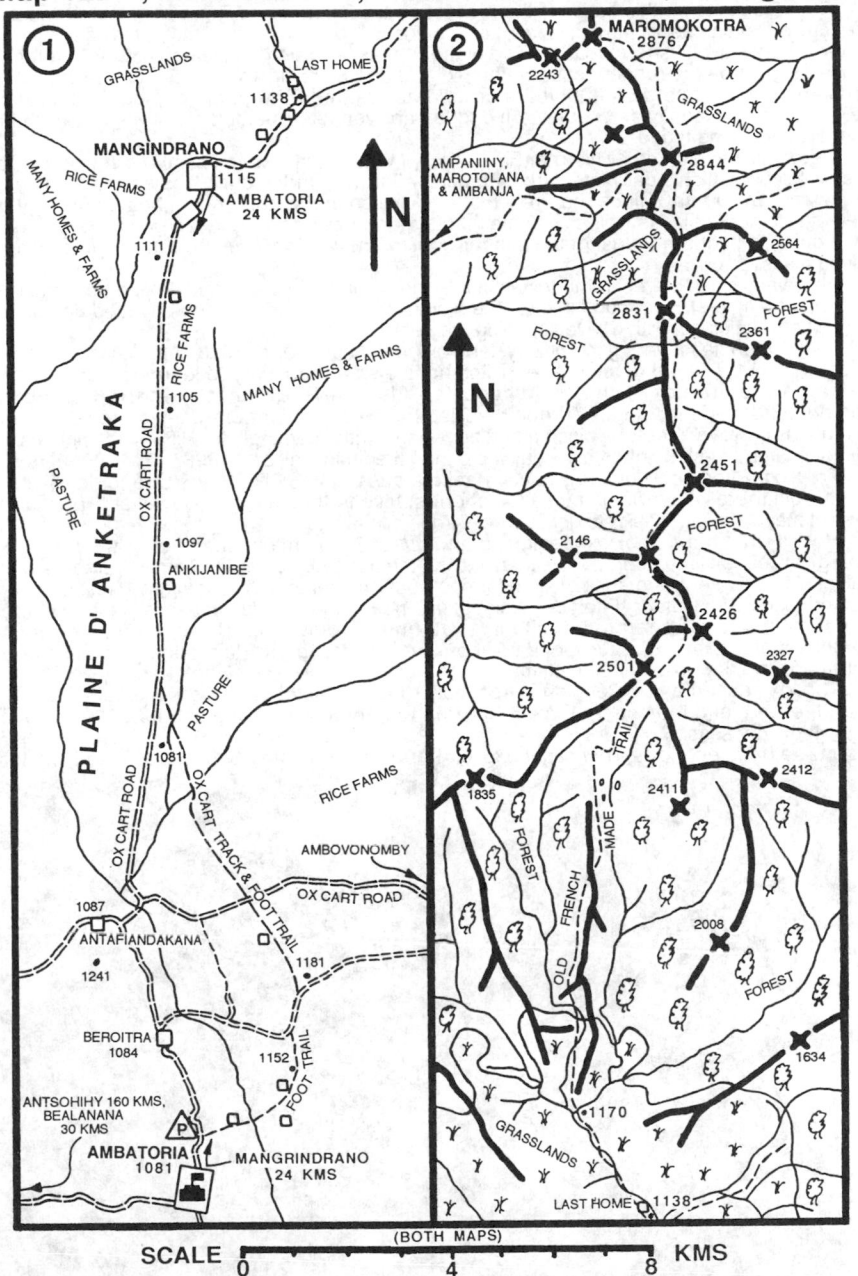

SCALE $\qquad$ KMS

(BOTH MAPS)
0   4   8

Maps *Mangindrano & Marotaolana,* 1:100,000, from F.T.M. (Institut National de Geodesie et Cartographie), Lalana Dama--NTSOHA, J.J.B., BP 323, Tananarivo, 101, Madagascar; and the latest travel guidebook to Africa, or better still, Madagascar.

Piton des Neiges, La Réunion Island, Indian Ocean

The mountains on this map are the highest on the island of La Réunion, which is located in the Indian Ocean east of Madagascar. La Réunion is a department (or state) of France, which is the same as Hawaii is to the USA. The highest peak is Piton des Neiges at 3069 meters. All these peaks are very rugged, and are the old and eroded remains of ancient volcanos. All this erosion over the past 250,000 years or so, has created 3 huge almost identical craters or calderas, known locally as *cirques*. All cirques are very steep-sided making some of the best scenery and hiking found anywhere.

Get to La Réunion by flying from East Africa, Madagascar, Mauritius and elsewhere. There are also several flights daily direct from France. All flights land about 4 kms east of the capital of the island, St. Denis. Since the French like hiking so much, this region has many very good well-maintained trails, as well as mountain huts or refuges known here as *gites*. Before leaving St. Denis, contact the tourist office and the *Maison de la Montagne,* to reserve gites and buy hiking maps.

There are small stores in the towns inside the Cirque de Cilaos and Cirque de Salazie, but bigger supermarkets are found in all of the bigger coastal towns. Best to buy food and supplies in one of these place, with St. Denis, being the best.

La Réunion has a very good bus system, but in the summer of 1993, this may have been the best place in the world to hitch hike. Hitching is also a great way to learn French, which you must learn a little of, or be handicapped. Also on Réunion, there are 6 established campgrounds; one inside the Cirque de Cilaos, the others scattered along the coast. In the mountains however, you can place a tent anywhere, with seemingly few, if any restrictions. The author camped each night on his 6 day trip during the first week of 7/1993.

To climb Piton des Neiges, you could take a bus or hitch hike to the Cirque de Cilaos and climb from there. This would make the shortest hike to the summit. However, transportation wise, it may be a little easier to get into the Cirque de Salazie.

Here's what the author did beginning on 7/2/1993. He hitch hiked from St. Denis to Hell-Bourg inside the Cirque de Salazie, then walked the trail to Bèlouve in about 1 1/2 hours with full pack. He got water there, then walked for one hour and camped for the night. Next morning he walked to the Gite Dufour (Piton des Neiges) in 2 hours and left his big pack. He then hurried to the summit and returned to the gite in 1 1/2 hours, round-trip. From there, he continued southeast and camped at the Col de Bèbour on his way to La Plaine des Palmistes and the active volcano, Le Volcan (see next map).

The dry season on La Réunion is from June through October. This is the cool time on this island, even along the coast. Expect freezing temperatures above about 2000 meters each night in the dry season.

Maps *La Réunion, Carte Touristique, 3615,* 1:100,000, from any bookshop on La Réunion, or

Looking northwest from the summit of Piton des Neiges.

Map 123-1, Piton des Neiges, La Réunion, Indian Ocean

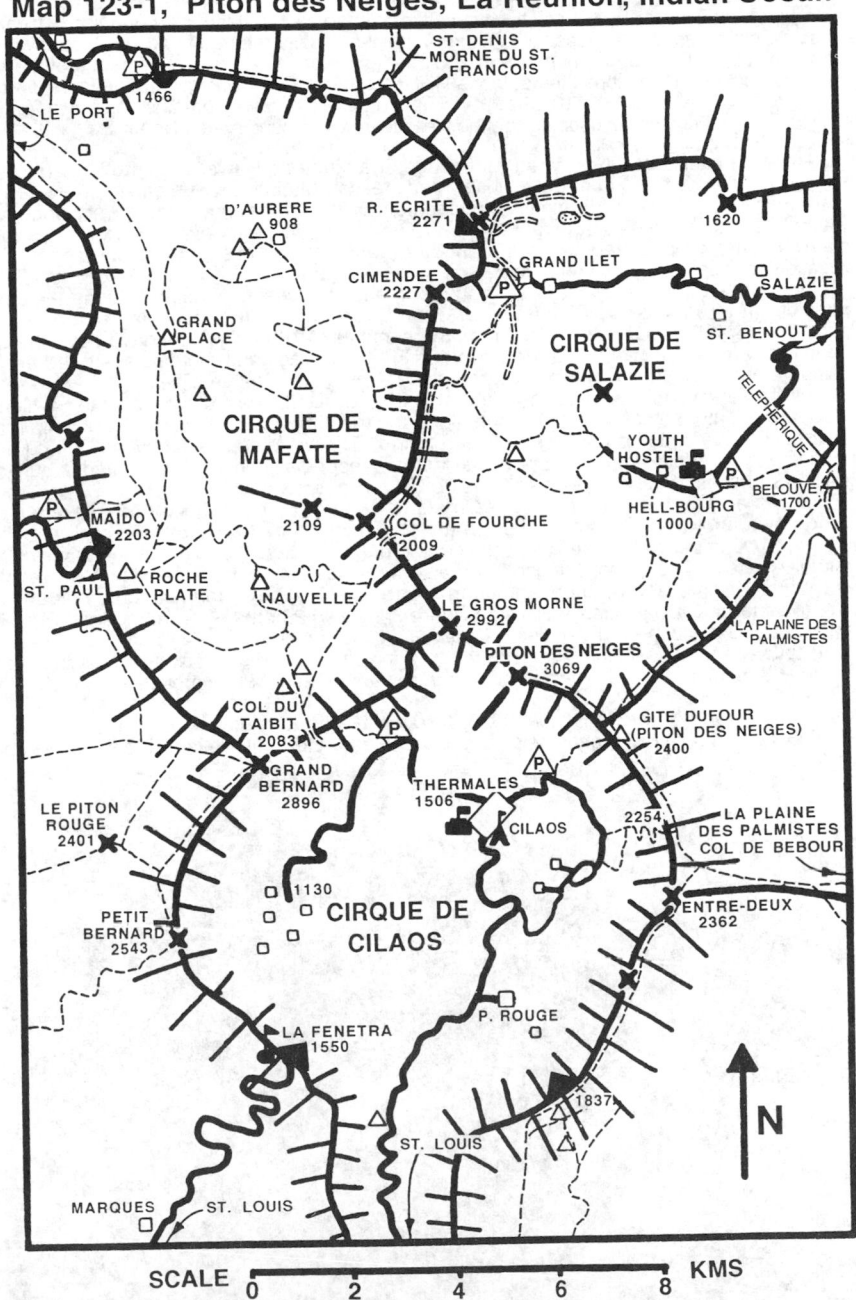

ST. DENIS
MORNE DU ST.
FRANCOIS

LE PORT
1466

D'AURERE
908

R. ECRITE
2271

1620

CIMENDEE
2227

GRAND ILET

SALAZIE

GRAND
PLACE

CIRQUE DE
SALAZIE

ST. BENOUT

CIRQUE DE
MAFATE

TELEPHERIQUE

YOUTH
HOSTEL

BELOUVE
1700

MAIDO
2203

2109

COL DE FOURCHE
2009

HELL-BOURG
1000

ST. PAUL

ROCHE
PLATE

NAUVELLE

LE GROS MORNE
2992

LA PLAINE DES
PALMISTES

PITON DES NEIGES
3069

COL DU
TAIBIT
2083

GITE DUFOUR
(PITON DES NEIGES)
2400

GRAND
BERNARD
2896

THERMALES
1506

LE PITON
ROUGE
2401

CILAOS

2254

LA PLAINE
DES PALMISTES
COL DE BEBOUR

PETIT
BERNARD
2543

1130

CIRQUE DE
CILAOS

ENTRE-DEUX
2362

P. ROUGE

LA FENETRA
1550

1837

N

ST. LOUIS

MARQUES

ST. LOUIS

SCALE 0   2   4   6   8 KMS

the French IGN. This shows the entire island, plus trails and gites. There is also a series of
about 10 very detailed topographic large-scale maps covering the island. They're available from
the IGN, or the Maison de la Montagne, 10 Place Sarda-Garriga, St. Denis; and the latest travel
guidebook to Africa, or La Réunion.

267

Piton de la Fournaise, La Réunion Island, Indian Ocean

Featured on this map is the nearly-always-active volcano on the island of La Réunion, which is in the Indian Ocean east of Madagascar. This mountain is usually referred to as Le Volcan, with the highest peak called Piton de la Fournaise at 2631 meters. For years, this has been one of the most active volcanos around, but upon the author's visit in early 7/1993, it was quiet. The latest eruptive period lasted from 9/28/1999 to 10/23/1999. That consisted of lava fountains and flows from the Dolomieu Crater. For volcano updates see the website (www.volcano.si.edu/gvp/). (www.volcano.si.edu/gvp/).

La Réunion Island is a department of France; the same as Hawaii is to the United States. Get to La Réunion by flying from East Africa, Madagascar, Mauritius; or on one of several flights daily from France. Since the French like hiking so much, this region has many very good well-maintained trails, as well as several mountain huts known here as *gites*. Before leaving St. Denis to begin hiking, contact the tourist office as well as the Maison de la Montagne, to get information on reserving gites and/or to buy good hiking maps.

Before going to Le Volcan, it's best to buy food and supplies in some town along the coast; or possible at La Plaine des Palmistes, or even Bourg Murat, the last village enroute. La Réunion has a very good bus system, but in the summer of 1993, this may have been the best place in the world to hitch hike. La Réunion has 6 established campgrounds scattered around the island, but once in the mountains you can place a tent just about anywhere.

To get to **Le Volcan**, take a bus or hitch hike from St. Denis east & southeast to St. Benoit, then southwest into the center of the island along the main road running toward Le Tampon and St. Pierre. The turnoff to Le Volcan is at Bourg Murat. There are no buses beyond Bourg Murat, but hitching is generally good as there's lots of traffic, especially on weekends, and in July and August. It's 30 kms from Bourg Murat to Pas de Bellecombe.

From the end of this road, or the nearby Gite de las Pas de Bellecombe, there's a trail running down into a large caldera, then to the top of **Piton de La Fournaise** crater. A trail marked with white paint also goes around a couple of new craters, so even if it's foggy, you can do this hike safely. The author climbed Fournaise from his camp behind the gite on consecutive days, but under different weather conditions. The first day it was foggy and he couldn't see much; next morning it was sunny. His times were 3 1/2 and 2 hours each, round-trip. From the top of Fournaise you can see Piton des Neiges.

The dry season on Réunion is from June through October. This is a cool time on the island, even along the coast. Expect freezing temperatures above about 2000 meters each night in the dry season.

Maps *La Réunion, Carte Touristique, 3615*, 1:100,000, from any bookshop on Réunion, or the French IGN. This shows the entire island, plus trails and gites. There is also a series of about

From near the Pas de Bellecombe looking southeast at the very active Le Volcan.

Map 124-1, Piton-Fournaise, Réunion Island, Indian Ocean

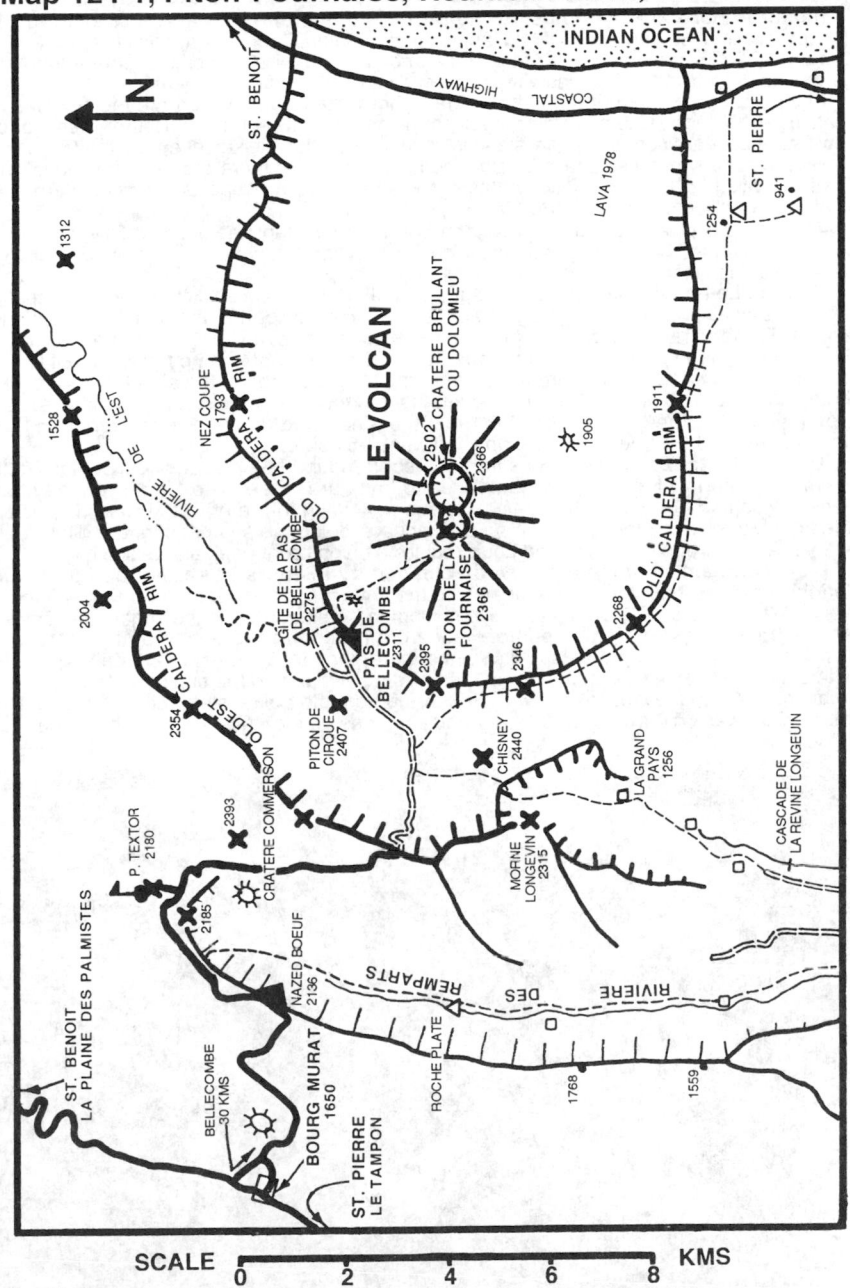

SCALE ⊢————————————————⊣ KMS
0   2   4   6   8

10 very detailed topographic maps covering the island. They're available from the IGN, or the Maison de la Montagne, 10 Place Sarda-Garriga, St. Denis; and the latest travel guidebook to Africa, or La Réunion.

Volcanic Plugs of Mauritius, Indian Ocean

Featured here are 3 maps showing parts of the island of Mauritius, located east of Madagascar and just northeast of La Réunion in the Indian Ocean. Mauritius is a refueling stop on many airline routes between Africa, Asia and the Southwest Pacific & Southeast Asia; so there's lots of air traffic going that way and from a number of different countries.

Shown here are most of the island's Matterhorn-like peaks, which are the remains of old volcanos. They appear to be throats, necks or plugs, or former eruptive fissures, vents or dikes. However, it appears nothing on the island is younger than the Pleistocene Epoch.

Hiking to many of these peaks is rather popular locally and there are trails of various kinds to most. For hiking & trail information contact: Ministry of Youth & Sports, 7th floor, Baroda Bank Building, Sir William Newton St., Port Louis.

There are 2 popular and fotogenic peaks shown on the top map; Le Pouce, 812 meters, and Pieter Both, 823 meters. These altitudes aren't much, but they rise direct from sea level. Both are visible and accessible from the capital city of Port Louis.

To climb **Le Pouce**, start in the city center. Look for Edith Cavell Street and walk southeast toward the peak. As you walk, inquire about Le Pouce Street and the suburb of Tranquebar. Once in Tranquebar, look for one prominent power line tower to the south along the large electric lines. Head for that on a dirt road. From the tower continue up the road, but look for a good trail to the right, shown here at 275 meters. Once you reach the shoulder of the peak at about 600 meters, look for a trail veering left, as the main trail continues straight ahead. It's a good trail right to the summit. On 7/8/1993, the author did this one round-trip from the Bus Station South in 3 1/4 hours. Most people will want 4-6 hours.

To climb **Pieter Both**, take a bus from the south-bound bus station (Bus Station South on this map) going to St. Pierre, and maybe on to La Laura. See Area Map. You may have to road-walk some. From La Laura, ask about the trail going to Pieter Both Peak. This is a very steep climb toward the top, but there's a trail, apparently up the southeast ridge. This will likely take you all day from downtown Port Louis, but it's a magnificent peak and a nice hike.

Lion Mountain, 480 meters, can be climbed by taking a bus from the bus station in Mahebourg, near the international airport, to the town of Pavillon Du Grand Port. One leaves every 15-20 minutes. Get off at the police station and walk north into the sugar cane fields on a cement track, but veer east and later walk a dirt road in the direction of the bottom of the prominent southeast ridge, as shown. Once there, look for some cement stairs going up 30 meters to an old cement platform. From there, it's a steep trail to the summit. You can descend via another trail to the west as shown. Round-trip from the police station took the author 1 2/3 hours. That was on 7/10/1993. The dry and cooler season on Mauritius is from June through October.

From the top of Le Pouce looking east at Pieter Both Peak, the one on the far left.

Map 125-1, Volcanic Plugs of Mauritius, Indian Ocean

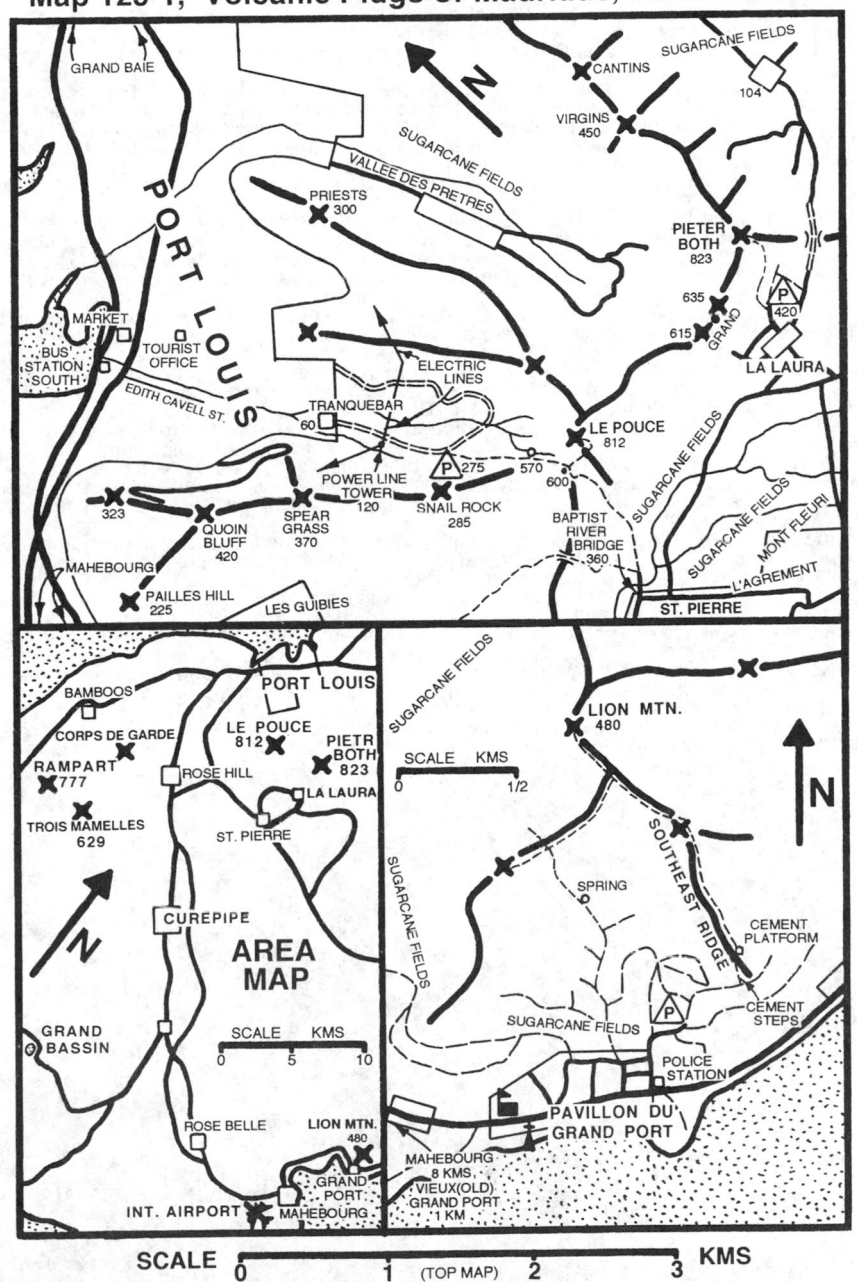

SCALE | 0 | 1 (TOP MAP) | 2 | 3 | KMS

Maps *Port Louis, 4 & Mahebourg, 10,* 1:25,000, from Chief Surveyor, Ministry of Housing, Lands and the Environment, Edith Cavell Street, Port Louis; or from Ordnance Survey, UK; and the latest travel guidebook to Africa or Mauritius.

Kibo and Mawenzi Peaks, Mt. Kilimanjaro, Tanzania

One of the best-known mountains in the world is Kibo, the highest of the 2 summits forming Mt. Kilimanjaro. This mountain is located in northern Tanzania, near the Kenyan border. It rises from the dusty plains at about 1000 meters, up to nearly 6000 meters, in a distance of about 30 kms.

Of the 2 summits on Kilimanjaro, the best known is Kibo, with Uhuru Point, 5963 meters, the highest place on the crater rim. Kili's last volcanic activity was sometime in the last 10,000 years. The other summit on Mt. Kilimanjaro is Mawenzi and Hans Meyer Peak at 5149 meters. Mawenzi is the 3rd highest peak in Africa, after Kibo and Mt. Kenya. Mawenzi's appearance is similar to that of Mt. Kenya; very steep and rugged, and the throat of a very old volcano. It has very little snow on top and no glaciers. The summit area has many pinnacles, most of which are very difficult to climb.

The author was there from 3/8 to 3/12/1974. Here's what he did. Day 1 to Mandara Hut--4 hours; Day 2 to Horombo Hut--3 1/2 hours; Day 3 to Mawenzi Hut--2 1/2 hours & climbed one of Mawenzi's peaks that afternoon; Day 4 from Mawenzi Hut past Kibo Hut and on to Uhuru Point in 5 hours, then walked down to Mandara Hut in 5 2/3 hours; Day 5 down to entrance gate--3 hours. Total walk-time for climbing both peaks was 23 2/3 hours. It's not the distance, but the altitude that hurts.

For this edition, the author has used letters from hikers, and the book, **Trekking in East Africa** to update his information. There are 6 official routes up Kilimanjaro, but the Marangu Route is the easiest to reach, and the most-used trail on the mountain. Since 1991, all climbers were required to hire a private tour company to organize the trip. All groups must have a guide, and each guide must have a porter for his supplies. You are not required to take porters. This is the only *gold mine* Tanzania has, so they are going to take you for all you're worth!

Your tour outfit will arrange transportation to the mountain, pay the park fees, hire porters, etc. As of the late 1990's, the cost for each hiker was around US$400, minimum. That's for the standard 5 day trek up the Marangu Route to Kibo. This slow pace is for you to acclimatization, which is the biggest problem hikers have on this mountain. For strong and acclimatized people, it can be done in 3 or 4 days--to the top of Kibo and back--but you may not find a guide who wants to do it that fast.

In some cases, it might be best to pay a little more than the absolute minimum to get better service. Check with other climbers who have just returned from the mountain, and with different tour operators in Arusha and Moshi for the best deal.

Because a tour operator must be hired to organize your trip, consider going via a different trail than the standard Marangu Route. That will keep you away from the crowds and trashly campsites. If you add one or 2 more days to this hike, you can climb both Mawenzi and Kibo on the same trip, and grab the 1st and 3rd highest summits in Africa.

No special equipment is needed, unless an unusual route is climbed. There are bunks in most huts, but you'll need a stove, extra water bottles, warm sleeping bag & pad, warm gloves and clothes, etc. Ice ax & crampons are not needed to climb Kibo. Consider taking a tent just in case, if you want privacy. Guides will know where water holes are. You may have to melt snow at the Kibo Hut. Best times to climb Kilimanjaro is during the months of December to March, and

Looking west at Kilimanjaro (Kibo) from the saddle between Kibo & Mawenzi.

Map 126-1, Kibo & Mawenzi, Mt. Kilimanjaro, Tanzania

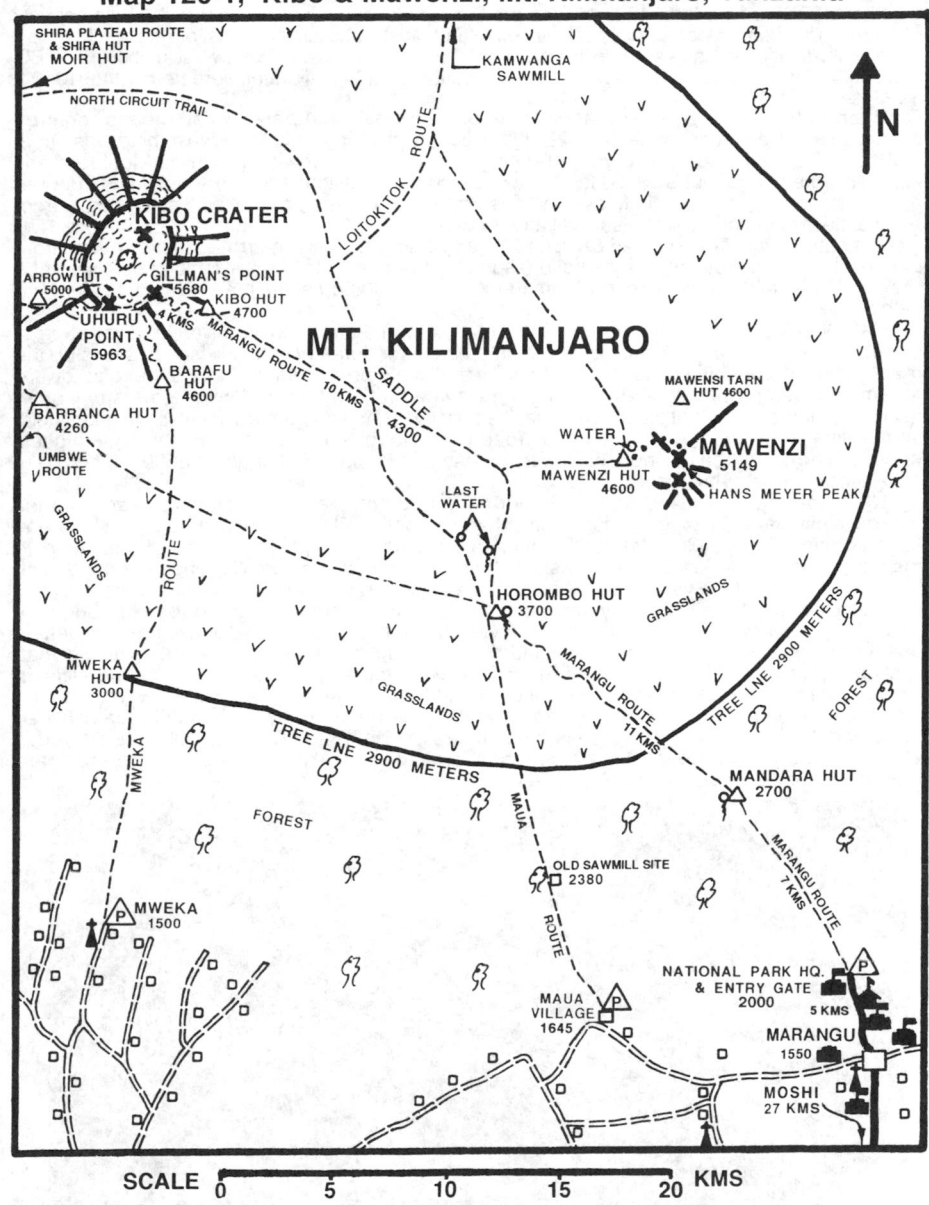

SCALE 0   5   10   15   20 KMS

from June through August.

Maps Tanzania Dept. of Survey maps *56/1, 56/2, 56/3, 56/4,* 1:50,000; British Ordnance Survey map *Kilimanjaro,* 1:100,000; and Wielochowski's *Map & Guide to Kilimanjaro,* 1:100,000; some of these or other maps available in Moshi or Arusha, Tanzania; and the books **Mountains of Kenya**, Robson, and **Guide to Mt. Kenya & Kilimanjaro,** from the Mtn. Club of Kenya, Nairobi; and **Trekking in East Africa**, Lonely Planet; and perhaps the latest travel guidebook for hotel listings, and bus or train information.

Mt. Meru Volcano, Tanzania

Shown here is Mt. Meru, 4565 meters, the 3rd highest summit in Tanzania after Kilimanjaro & Mawenzi. This peak is located west of Kilimanjaro and Moshi, and just northeast of Arusha. Meru is a symetrically-shaped volcano as seen from the west, but it had an east-side blow-out in about 5850 BC, creating a crescent-shaped caldera. The last eruptions inside this crater were from 10/26/1910 to 12/22/1910.

Much of the eastern side of Mt. Meru is part of a national park, which means required entrance fees & a guide. In the late 1990's, the cost of climbing it via the *tourist route* was about US$100 for a 2-day climb and you arrange your own transport and pay a park guide at the Momella Gate. Or about US$160 for 3 days. Or, contact any tour agent in Arusha and they can arrange transport, etc. To climb it via the eastern park route normally takes 2, 3 or 4 days from Arusha, depending on your fitness level and arrival time.

The author was there on 7/26 & 7/27/1993, and discovered another route to the summit from the west completely bypassing the national park. After talking to several local people who had climbed Meru via the west side, and with the *Arusha* 1:250,000 scale map in hand, this is what he did.

He took a local bus from the Arusha bus station running north toward Kenya, and got off at Olmotoni. From there he was lucky to get on a bus to the forestry school which is 3 kms up the road. He bought a bottle of soda pop at one of the little stores, then walked up the road toward the forestry camp of Nadungoro. Along the way he met, and walked with, a forestry worker using the short-cut trail. At Nadungoro, he filled his water bottles from a tap (which is good, cold, spring water). From there, it was up the road past a logging camp, then east into the highest reforested grove of trees in the area, where he camped for the night at about 2600 meters. Day 1 walk-time, a little over 3 hours.

Next morning he walked east, then north along an old vehicle track to a meadow in the natural forest, then zig zagged east on first sheep & cattle trails, then elephant trails, all the way up to treeline at about 3350 meters. From there it was straight up to the summit. From camp, to the summit and back, just over 6 hours. He then walked down toward Nadungoro, but got a lift in a logging truck all the way back to Arusha. The entire trip from Arusha took 27 hours.

Keep in mind there will always be water at Nadungoro, but the logging roads through the reforested areas will change as trees are harvested and replanted. Plan to take one day getting to a high camp, then start early the next morning going up the mountain. Take a compass, map & altimeter. If you had your own vehicle, and knew the route, it's possible to make this climb in one long day from Arusha. However, be prepared for a 3 day trip, especially if walking all the way from Olmotoni. Be aware of elephants which have made many trails in the area between 2800 and 3300 meters. This route is for climbers, not tourists. Dry season is June through October, and December to March. Buy all your food in Arusha, where there are many inexpensive hotels or guesthouses.

Looking east at the west face of Mt. Meru from the *temporary logging camp.*

Map 127-1, Mt. Meru Volcano, Tanzania

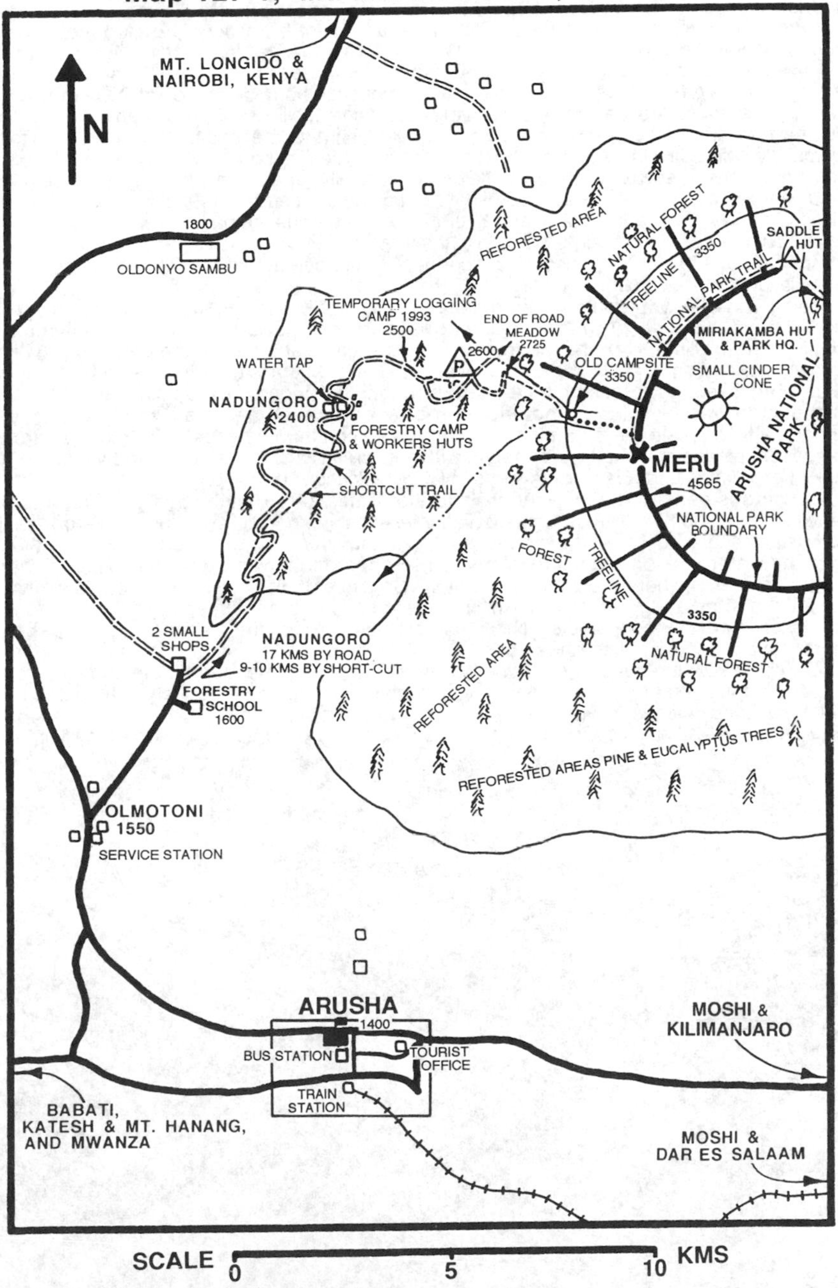

N

MT. LONGIDO &
NAIROBI, KENYA

REFORESTED AREA

NATURAL FOREST

TREELINE 3350

SADDLE
HUT

NATIONAL PARK TRAIL

1800
OLDONYO SAMBU

TEMPORARY LOGGING
CAMP 1993
2500

END OF ROAD
MEADOW
2725

MIRIAKAMBA HUT
& PARK HQ.

WATER TAP

P 2600

OLD CAMPSITE
3350

SMALL CINDER
CONE

NADUNGORO
2400

FORESTRY CAMP
& WORKERS HUTS

MERU
4565

ARUSHA NATIONAL PARK

SHORTCUT TRAIL

NATIONAL PARK
BOUNDARY

FOREST

TREELINE

2 SMALL
SHOPS

NADUNGORO
17 KMS BY ROAD
9-10 KMS BY SHORT-CUT

3350

NATURAL FOREST

FORESTRY
SCHOOL
1600

REFORESTED AREA

REFORESTED AREAS PINE & EUCALYPTUS TREES

OLMOTONI
1550

SERVICE STATION

ARUSHA
1400

MOSHI &
KILIMANJARO

BUS STATION

TOURIST
OFFICE

TRAIN
STATION

BABATI,
KATESH & MT. HANANG,
AND MWANZA

MOSHI &
DAR ES SALAAM

SCALE 0   5   10 KMS

Maps *Arusha, SA 37-13*, 1:250,000, from Survey of Kenya, Nairobi; or map numbers *55/1, 55/2, 55/3 & 55/4*, 1:50,000, from Lands & Surveys, P.O. Box 9201, Dar es Salaam, Tanzania; and the book, **Trekking in East Africa**, Lonely Planet; and perhaps the latest travel guidebook for hotel listings, buses, etc.

Ol Doinyo Lengai, Rift Valley Volcanos, Tanzania

Shown on this map are about 10 volcanos and one granite mountain. The volcanos are in or near the Rift Valley of north central Tanzania, and west & northwest of Arusha. The most famous place here is Ngorongoro Crater & Conservation Area. Ol Doinyo Lengai is the most famous volcano, and it's almost always active. To the east and next to the main highway running from Nairobi to Arusha, is a solid granite mountain named Longido at 2629 meters.

Your first stop is Arusha, with lots of hotels and tourist facilities. To reach any of the volcanos, you'll have to hire a 4WD vehicle, or go on a group safari (trip or expedition). It's possible to reach Ngorongoro (with 3 hotels & campground) by bus, but you can't get out and walk or climb on foot in the conservation area--because of lions & buffalo! So make all arrangements in Arusha. If you go to any of the peaks in the Ngorongoro area, you'll have to pay US$15 per/day (1993 price), but the 3 northern volcanos of Ol Doinyo Lengai, Gelai and Kitumbeime are outside the park boundaries and no fees or permission needed. Periodically, trucks go to the villages of Gelai Lumbwa, Kitumbeime or Engaruka, but who has time to wait! Ask about transport at any tour operator in Arusha. There are many tour agents in town, so look around and bargain.

To climb **Gelai**, you could walk up along the water pipeline on the east side as shown; or perhaps from the north. The Amboseli map listed below shows some kind of track running up from the north. Climb **Kitumbeime** from the village school and maybe the north ridge. Climb **Ol Doinyo Lengai** from a gully on the northwest side--at least that's the route described in the book below. But take a good look at the eastern side, and if you can drive up close climb the east or northeastern face. This is a popular climb among geologists, as it has the world's only carbonate lake inside the summit crater. It's been continuously active for many years with a number of hornitos emitting lava or steam within its crater, and lavas flowing down the northwest flank. For volcano updates see the website (www.volcano.si.edu/gvp/).

Longido is easy to reach, as there's lots of traffic on the highway from Arusha north to Kenya. Get off the bus or truck at the police checkpost in Longido town and walk northeast past the hospital and school. Let the game wardens in their office know of your intentions, then walk up to the water tank on the hill as shown. From there follow the pipeline trail up toward the upper intake area where there's lots of water. Continue up the good ridge trail as shown, then cross the stream and route-find north up buffalo trails to the main summit ridge. From there head east or west to the 2 peaks. This mountain has a cloud forest, so take a compass. Watch out for buffalo--they could be dangerous!

On 7/21/1993, the author got off the bus from Nairobi and headed for the summit, hiding his big pack in brush on the lower slopes (if you do this, be sure no one sees you hide it, and cover it with branches or leaves). Round-trip hike-time was just over 4 hours.

Maps *Amboseli, Arusha, Oldeani & Loliondo*, 1:250,000. In 1993, the author bought the first 2 maps in

Looking west at the West Peak of Longuido.

Map 128-1, Ol Doinyo Lengai, Rift Valley, Tanzania

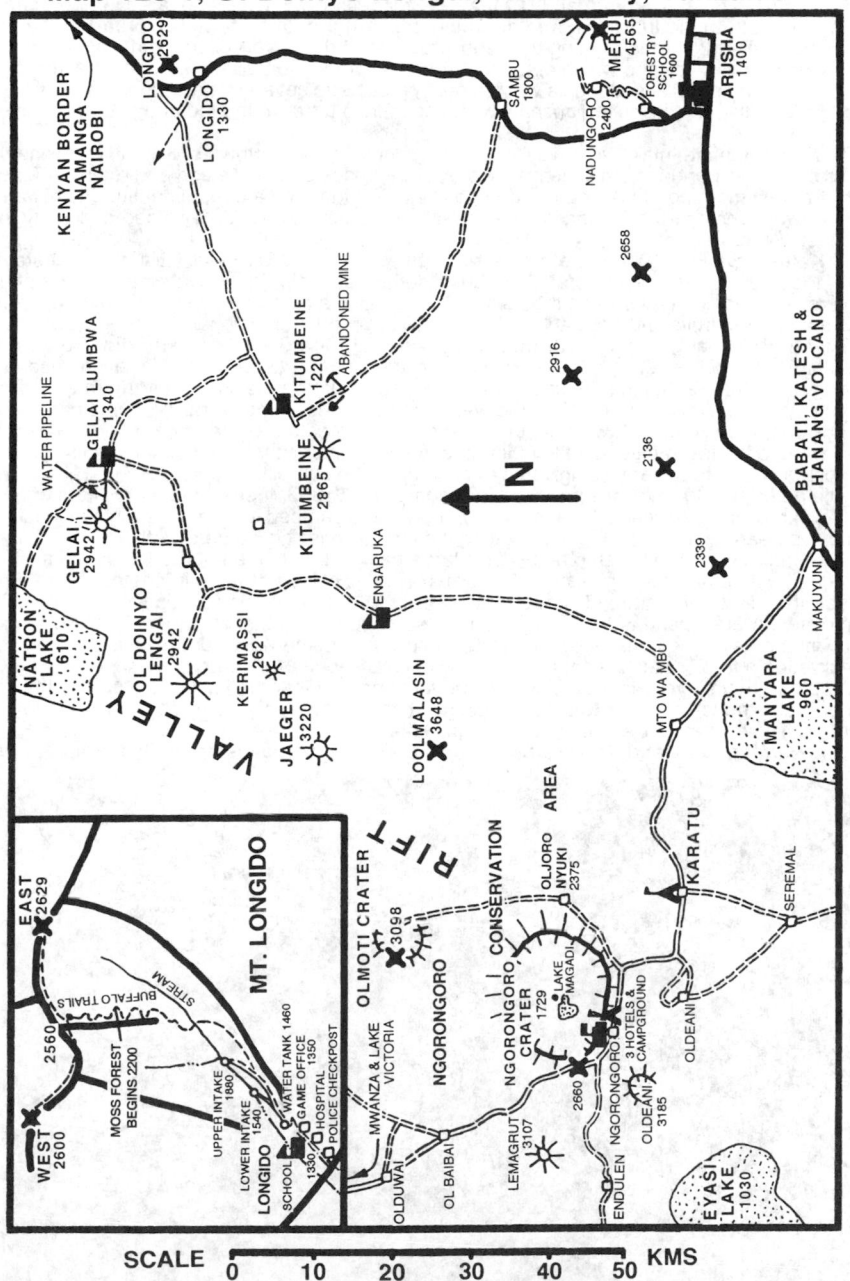

SCALE 0 10 20 30 40 50 **KMS**

Nairobi, Kenya, but Oldeani and Loliondo were unavailable at Surveys and Mapping, Ministry of Lands, Housing and Urban Development, Dar es Salaam, Tanzania; and the book, **Trekking in East Africa**, Lonely Planet.

Hanang Volcano, Tanzania

Shown here is Mt. Hanang, at 3419 meters, a little known volcano located in north central Tanzania south of Ngorongoro, and southwest of Arusha and Mt. Meru. Nearby, the town Katesh is on the main road running between Arusha and the Lake Victoria port city of Mwanza. Hanang is an older volcano which apparently had its south side blown out during the last major eruption. From on top and along its west ridge, you can see several small craters in the vicinity. This is one of the best hikes in Tanzania because there's a trail to the top and you don't have to pay to climb it.

To reach Hanang, make your way to the pleasant little market town of Katesh by taking one of about 5 buses per day from Arusha. Two of these buses stop at Katesh and return to Arusha early the next morning. One or 2 per day go on to Singida, and a couple continue to Mwanza. The highway running from Arusha is paved to as far as Babati, then it's a graded and dusty road to Katesh.

In Katesh are 8 or 10 little hotels or resthouses for about US$1 or $2 a night. If staying there, look the hotels over carefully, because some near the highway are noisy and cater to truckers; with women featured on the menu. There's also a number of small stores and a pretty good market with fruits and vegetables. It's a small town, but the regional gathering place.

To climb **Hanang**, walk north through town and locate the road heading toward the mountain. After one or 2 kms, the road veers northeast. In that area, look for a well-used trail running up to the west along the south face of an embankment as shown on the map near the parking symbol. Walk up that trail to the west, then use one of many trails running north along the obvious ridge coming down from the west side of the caldera. Head north along this main ridge. Above the last hut at about 2000 meters, the ridge steepens and the many trails converge to become one. From there a single trail runs on up to the summit.

The author got to Katesh late in the afternoon of 7/23/1993, then with about 5 liters of good, cold town tap water, he walked for about 1 1/2 hours and camped just above the highest hut. He had 2 good earthquakes that night, indicating the mountain isn't quite dead yet!

Next morning he broke camp and hid his large pack in brush, then hurried to the summit in 2 1/2 hours. He returned to his pack in 2 hours, then was back in Katesh in another hour. From Katesh the climb took about 7 hours total walk-time. This means you could sleep in a little resthouse in Katesh, and with an early morning start, you should be able to make the climb and return in one day. The book below suggests you climb from the west side, but you'd have to hire a vehicle to do that! Katesh seems the only logical place to start a climb.

You can buy all your food in Katesh, but you'll have a little better variety in Arusha. The author drank the town's water without problems; it comes from springs up the canyon before it's polluted. The dry season is from June through October.

Maps *Hanang, 84/4 and Katesh, 103/2,* 1:50,000, bought easiest from Overseas Surveys,

One of several thatched huts on the lower south ridge of Hanang Volcano.

Map 129-1, Hanang Volcano, Tanzania

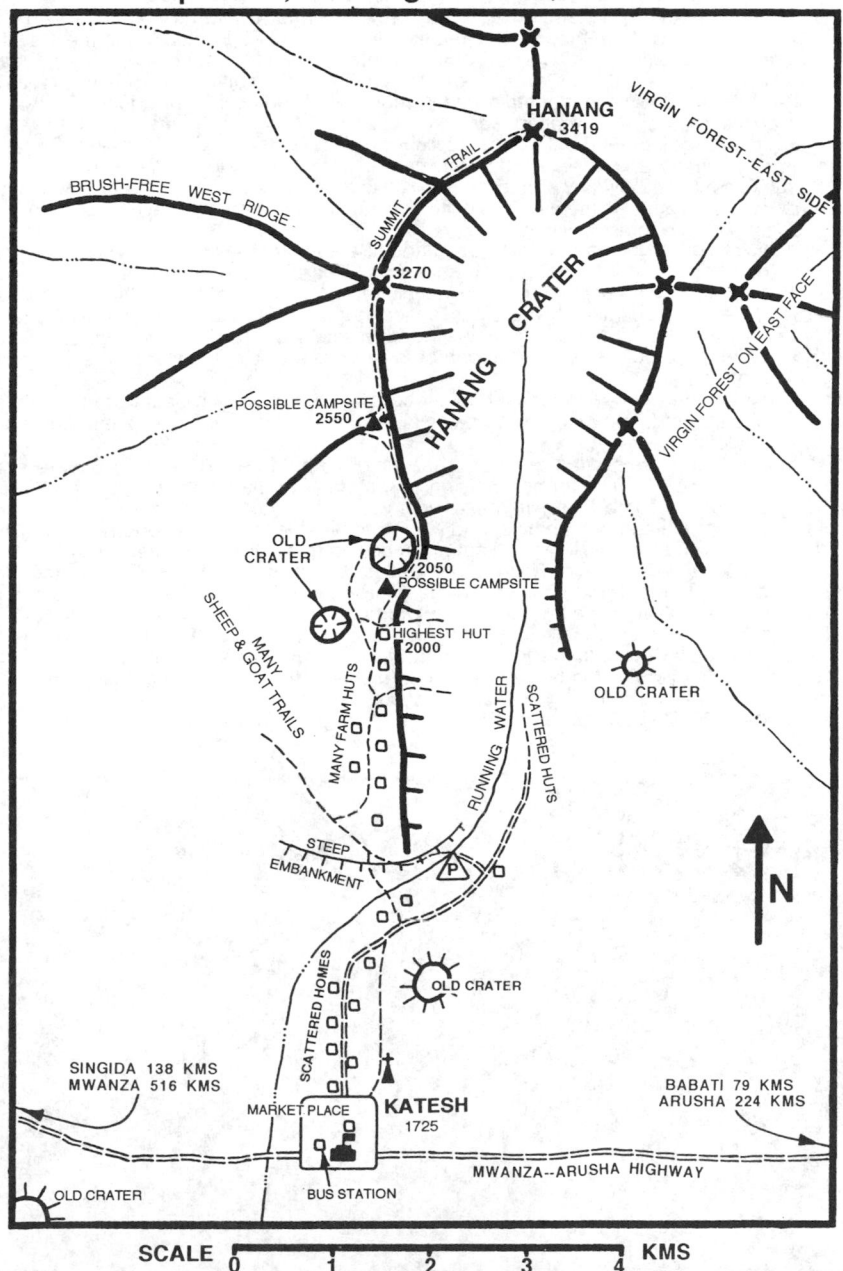

Southampton, UK, or Stanfords in London; or Joint Operations Graphic (JOG Air) map *Singida, SB 36-4,* 1501 Series, 1:250,000, US Defense Mapping Agency & Ministry of Defense, UK; or ask about these maps at the Lands and Surveys, Dar es Salaam; and the book **Trekking in East Africa**, Lonely Planet.

Rungwe Peak, Poroto Mountains, Tanzania

If you're backpacking around Africa and Tanzania and looking for an out-of-the-way mountain to climb, here's one that might interest you. It's Rungwe Peak at 2961 meters. This peak and rather large mountain are part of the greater Poroto Mountains, which are located about halfway between the small city of Mbeya, and the north end of Lake Nyasa in southwestern Tanzania. All the mountains in this region are lined up in or beside the Rift Valley.

This is an old volcano, with what appears to be an ancient caldera rim, plus a number of newer craters or cinder cones inside that. The last eruptions in this area were in about the year 1800, when explosions & lava from Sarabwe & Fetiko craters caused casualties. The author has no idea where those 2 craters are (?). They may or may not be on this map. The mountain is heavily forested all around with a mostly natural rainforest. The north slope appears to have been reforested. Places on the high slopes should be grass covered.

Get to this region by taking the train from Dar es Salaam to Mbeya (on it's way to Zambia), then a bus heading south for Tukuyu or Kyela. Or better still, take one of several daily long distance buses from Dar es Salaam heading in the direction of Kyela at the northern end of Lake Nyasa. These same buses usually carry passengers heading south to Malawi. It might be best to stop at Tukuyu where there are several inexpensive hotels for about US$2 a night, and many shops and a market place. By staying at one of these hotels, you could store excess baggage during your climb.

From Tukuyu, there are many local buses each day heading north past Katabe, Kyimo or Kikota. From either of these places, you can walk to the old mission settlement of Ilolo. With luck you might get a lift.

The former Ilolo mission has a guesthouse which should be available to travelers, and maybe a shop or two (?). The former mission school is now public and is called the Rungwe Secondary School. To climb **Rungwe**, make your way to Ilolo and the secondary school. Ask one of the teachers there about the hike, and he should be able to arrange for one of the school boys to walk with you part way. This will save you getting totally lost in the fields just below the forest. Tip the boy a dollar or two. Each August, school teachers and students hike to the top of Rungwe and keep the trail open, making August through October the best time to climb this mountain. The proximity of Lake Nyasa has a lot to do with heavy rainfall in this region.

The author was here on 8/14/1993, but arrived just in time for an off-season monsoon. He got only about halfway through the forest but turned back to save his camera, in some of the heaviest rains he's ever tried to hike in. It's best to stay in the mission guesthouse one night then get an early morning start. This should help you beat the daily cloud buildup.

Maps *Rungwe, 259/1*, 1:50,000, from Surveys and Mapping, Ministry of Lands, Housing and

A close-up view of the east side of Kilimanjaro (Kibo), with the Kibo Huts in the center
and the summit trail to the left zig zagging up the slope above.

Map 130-1, Rungwe Peak, Poroto Mtns., Tanzania

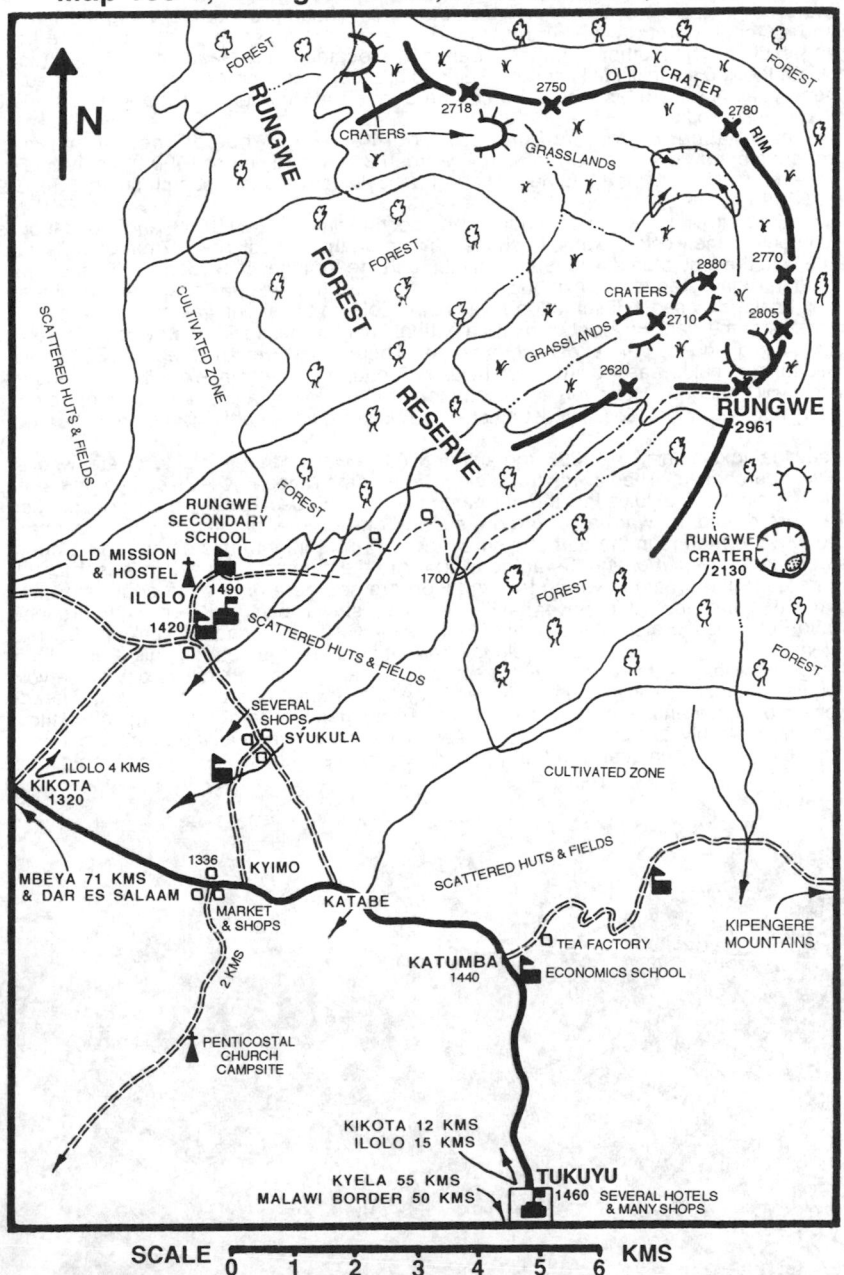

Urban Development, Dar es Salaam, Tanzania; or perhaps from Terra Surveys Limited, Ottawa, Canada; or from Overseas Surveys, Southampton, UK; and the latest travel guidebook to Tanzania or East Africa.

Karisimbi, Virunga Volcanos, Rwanda-Congo-Uganda

Featured here are 6 of the 8 Virunga Volcanos. These are located along the borders of Rwanda, Congo (formerly Zaïre)and Uganda, but the normal approach routes are from the Rwandan side. The 2 other Virunga volcanos are located to the west inside Congo (see next map). Of these 6 summits, Mikeno and Sabinyo are the oldest, most eroded, and rugged. Most of these volcanos were last active sometime during the Holocene, or the last 10,000 years. None are active today.

There are about 6 groups of mountain gorillas within the confines of this map, all approachable from Rwanda. During the Rwandan 3 year civil war of 1990-93, only one group was open for visitations; the one near Diane Fossey's cabins and research station. In 1993, it cost US$125 per visit.

The author arrived in Kigali, Rwanda for the second time on 7/31/1993, and found it possible to climb only in the western part. He chose **Karisimbi**, the highest, at 4507 meters. As it turned out, he was the first to do any mountain climbing in the Virungas in 3 years. He bought most of his food in Kigali, then took a minibus to Ruhengeri. At that time, all shops and businesses in Ruhengeri were closed, but some food was being sold on the streets, as only a few people had returned after the war. He luckily ran into a national park guide, so 2 motorcycle taxis were hired to get to Kinigi and the park supervisor's home. There a park entrance fee of US$13 was paid. A national park guide was required, but it was not required to pay him extra beyond the park fee (but this will change!). However, it's recommended you tip him a couple of US$ or so per day, plus buy his food--which doesn't cost much. The author paid about US$20 for the short two-day trip.

Early the next morning 8/2/1993, the author & guide walked from Kinigi to Bisate, where more food was purchased. Then it was to Visoke and up past Diane Fossey's cabins and along the trail to Karisimbi. The guide lost the normal trail to the hut, because the army commandos who were there during the war had created a second one. Never did find the hut, but camp was made at 3600 meters in the author's small tent. From Kinigi to this camp took 6 hours at a leisurely pace. Next morning the author hurried to the summit and back in less than 2 hours. There's a manned radio tower on top and workers get there on a good south-side trail, but because of clouds the author never saw it. Then a fast walk back to Kinigi in 4 hours, and a lift down to Ruhengeri. He spent the night of 8/3/1993 in Gisenyi, Rwanda, on Lake Kivu.

Here's some tips. Hire a motorcycle taxi (about US$3 per person) or walk & hitch hike from Ruhengeri to Kinigi. Distances are not great, so you can walk from Kinigi to any of the volcanos in about half a day. Sabinyo can be climbed in one day from Kinigi, but 2-3 days are needed for the peaks on either end of the park. Buy food in Ruhengeri, but small small shops exist in Kinigi, Bisate and probably Gasiza. The author used a little French, and a little Swahili in these parts and got by OK. You can camp virtually anywhere on this map. Rain can come anytime in the

Setting up camp on the northeast slope of Karisimbe with Mikeno in the distance.

Map 131-1, Karisimbi, Virungas, Rwanda-Congo-Uganda

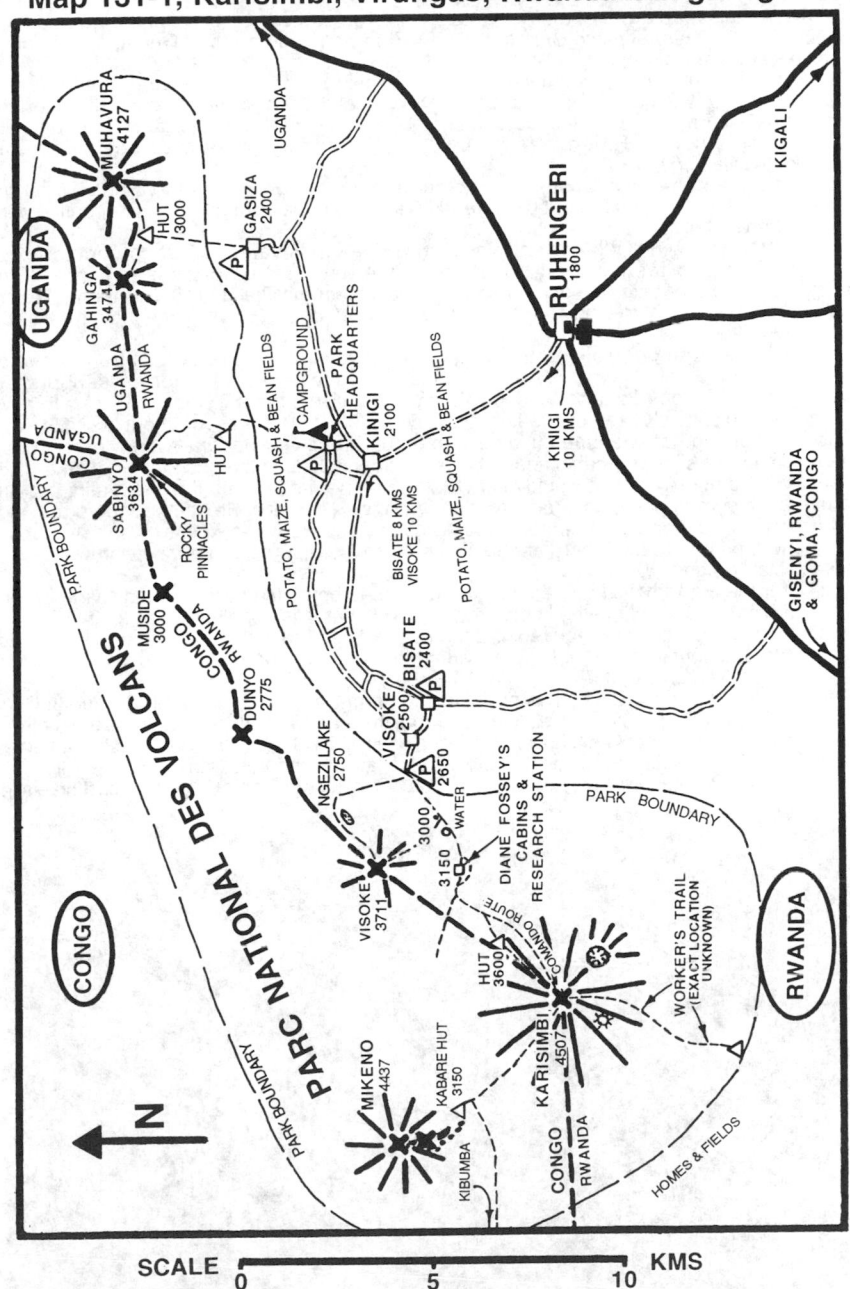

mountains, but June through October is the driest period.
Maps *Rwanda, Sheet 6,* 1:200,000, US Army Map Service, Washington, D.C; and the book
Backpacker's Africa, Bradt Enterprises; and the latest travel guidebook to Africa.

Nyiragongo & Nyamuragira, Virunga Volcanos, Congo

Shown on this map are 2 of the 8 Virunga Volcanos; the others are to the east and on the previous map. These are inside Congo, formerly Zaïre, and due north of Goma, a small city on the north shore of Lake Kivu. Both these peaks are in the Virunga National Park, which stretches north to as far as the Ruwenzori Mountains. In early 8/1993 when the author was there, Nyiragongo was quiet, but on 1/10/1977 a lava lake deep within the summit crater burst out of a flank fissure on the south side and sent very fluid lava downslope at 60 km/hour killing 70 people. It's last eruption was in 4/1995. For volcano updates see the website (www.volcano.si.edu/gvp/).

Nyamuragira is Africa's most active volcano, but most eruptions have been from flank fissures. Flank lava flows in the 1900's extend 30 kms from the summit. It's last eruptive period was in the 2nd half of 10/1998.

To get to this region, it's normally best to arrive via Rwanda. Congo seems to be in perpetual chaos, so the less you travel there, the better. You can also fly into Goma's international airport, or take one of many daily minibuses from Kigali to Gisenyi, then take a taxi or walk across the border to Goma. Goma has a tourist office just north of the main round-about in the center of town.

To climb **Nyiragongo**, walk north along the highway until you're across from the airport runway. Along that highway is where minibuses (usually trucks) stop for passengers. The author ended up on top of a truck loaded with furniture. From there it's about 15 kms to a wide place in the road called Kibati. In 1993, that ride cost 3,000,000 Zaïres, or about US$.65!

Kibati is nothing but one long building with 6 apartments for national park workers, plus a two-room mountain climber's cabin and outside toilet behind. No stores, shops or even a village. In Goma, the author was told it would cost US$20 for a permit to climb this mountain, but when he arrived, the correct price, according to a price list, was US$40. He camped there that night, but changed his mind and returned to Goma. Big mistake! He was told this climb takes about 6 hours round-trip from Kibati. There are 3 small huts on the mountain for those who would like to camp and stay a night.

Still later the author was told he could have climbed both Nyamuragira and Nyiragongo for US$40, and that would include the cost of the guide. If that was, or is, the case, then it would be worth the US$40. Guides are required, but the national park pays them from the entrances fees collected. You of course would have to provide them with food, probably a tip, but that's a small price for 2 big adventures in one.

To climb **Nyamuragira**, take a bus or truck north from Goma on a good paved road to Rugani. Somewhere in that area is a national park office. From there a trail heads west to a shelter at the base of the mountain. This is about an 8 hour hike. Sleep one night in the hut, then climb to the summit and return to Rugani on Day 2. Your guide will carry an elephant gun for protection.

June through October are the driest months. Buy all supplies in Goma. The cheapest hotels there

This slightly outdated sign is next to the one main building at Kibati.

Map 132-1, Nyiragongo & Nyamuragira, Virungas, Congo

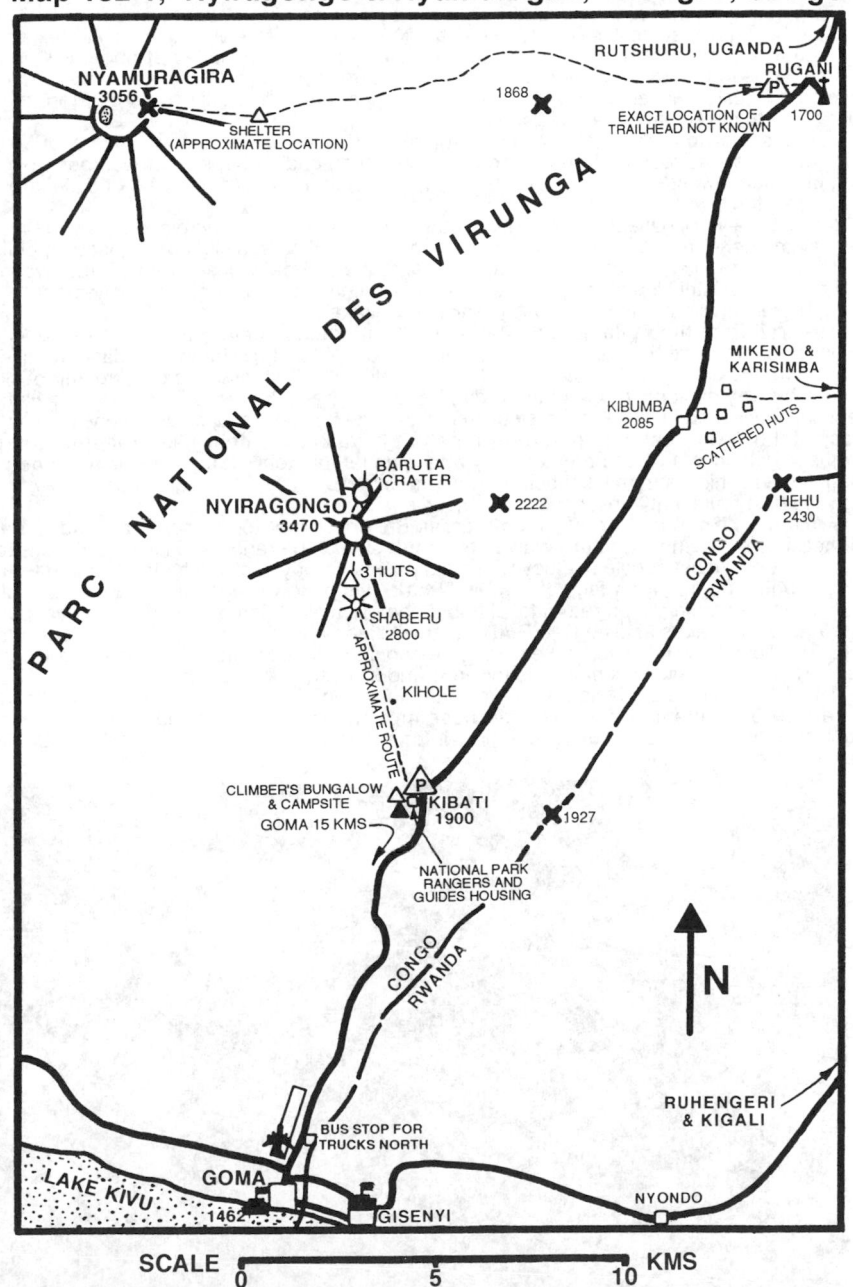

cost about US$20, but the Catholic or Protestant missions are cheapest, if you can get in. Use French or Swahili here.

Maps *Rwanda, Sheet 6,* 1:200,000, US Army Map Service, Washington, D.C.; and the book **Backpacker's Africa,** Bradt Enterprises; and the latest travel guidebook to Africa.

Sapitwa Peak, Mulanje Mountains, Malawi

The Mulanje Mountains in southern Malawi has some of the best hiking and climbing in Africa. The highest summit is Sapitwa Peak at 3002 meters. This elevation may not seem like much, but remember it rises direct from the bottom of the Rift Valley at about 600 meters altitude. This range is the result of an intrusive stock that never did quite break the surface to become a volcano. Instead it froze in place creating a rounded granite plateau. From the Rift Valley floor to the summit is nearly 2400 meters.

The best way to reach this area is to first make your way to Blantyre, the capital of Malawi. Once there visit the tourist office for updated information and perhaps buy food, then go to the long distance bus station in the eastern part of the city and take one of 4 or 5 daily buses heading for the town of Mulanje.

Once there you'll have to decide which route you want to take to the plateau. If you take the trail running north from Mulanje, you could camp at the golf course clubhouse just east of town. Or if you decide to start from Likhubula, then take one of 2 daily buses running that way from Mulanje or the Chitakali Shopping Center. One goes in the morning; another in afternoon. Hitch hiking is pretty good too--from the road junction in Chitakali.

The trail from the Mulanje bus station is the most convenient for those taking public transport, but if you're there in a wet spell, part of this trail can be slippery and dangerous. This is the route the author took on 8/19/1993. He was told it would take one day, up and back, so he took his day pack only. As it turned out, he left the trail just east of the Tele. Box Hut and went up the west ridge. That route is covered with large boulders making walking very slow. He reached the **West Peak** and had to turn back. It was an 11 hour hike from the golf club campsite (which is guarded day & night) where he left his tent. Later he was told about the normal route, which is from Likhubula. If your intention is to climb the highest peak only, that is likely the best route, but transport is less convenient.

From the Likhubula Forest Station, cross the creek just to the south and head east & northeast on the Lichenya Path. Walk to the north side of the range and locate the Red Route Hut. This takes most people one day with a big pack. On Day 2, climb the trail marked with red paint heading up the north face of **Sapitwa Peak**. It's a slow rough hike, but it's possible to climb it in the morning, then return to Likhubula before night. Some may need 3 days, but the average person takes 2. The Red Route Hut will sleep about 5-6 people on the floor and it's free. The Tele. Box Hut is about the same size and it too is free to use. To stay in the Lichenya Hut or Rest House you must make reservations and payment in Likhubula.

The dry season in the Mulanje is from June to October, but you can hike anytime, because there are good huts and trails all over these mountains. Contact expatriate white guys in Blantyre or the golf club in Mulanje for more information. Best place to buy food is in Blantyre, then Mulanje or Chitakali.

From the top of West, looking east to the North Peak. Notice the large granite boulders.

Map 133-1, Sapitwa Peak, Mulanje Mountains, Malawi

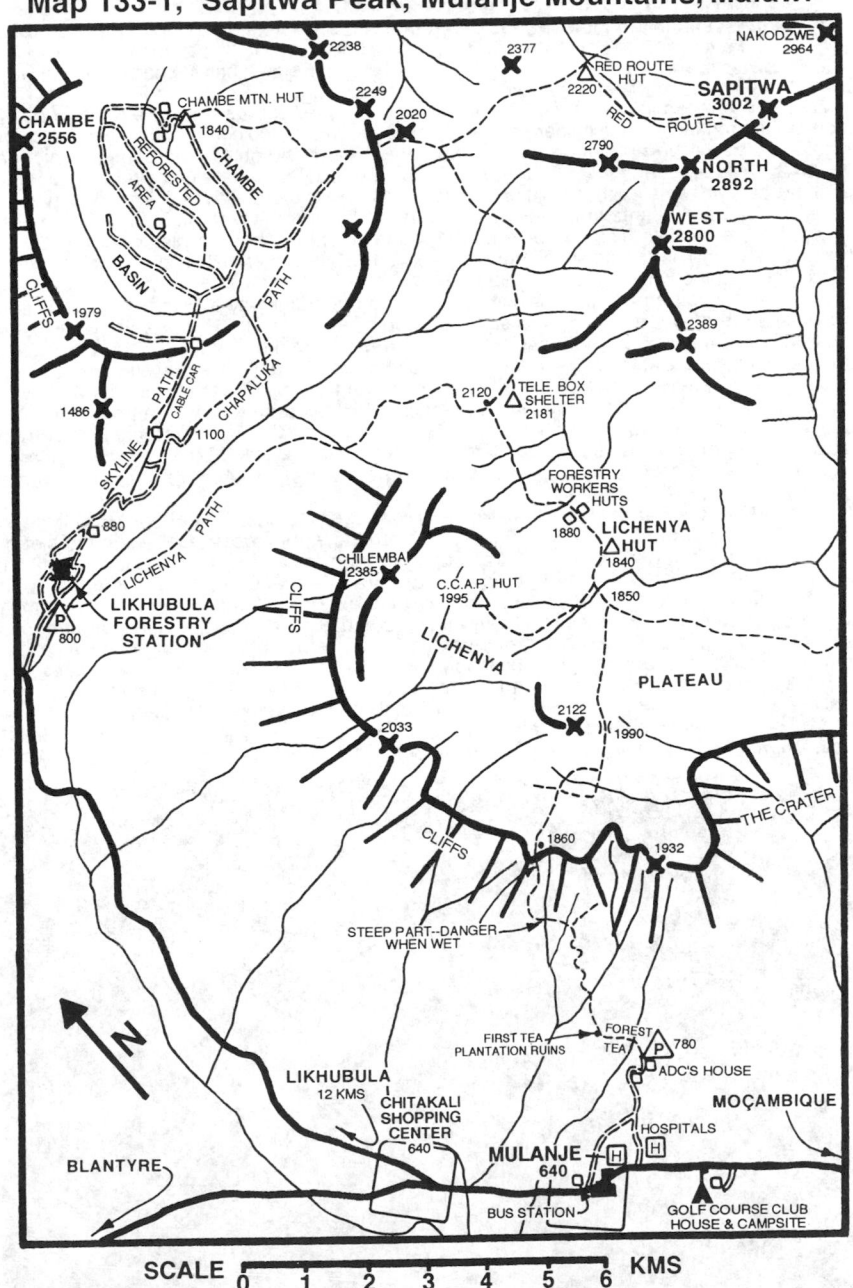

NAKODZWE 2964

2238

2377

RED ROUTE HUT

2220

SAPITWA 3002

CHAMBE MTN. HUT

2249

2020

RED ROUTE

CHAMBE 2556

1840

CHAMBE

2790

NORTH 2892

REFORESTED AREA

WEST 2800

BASIN

2389

CLIFFS

1979

PATH

CHAPALUKA

2120

TELE. BOX SHELTER 2181

1486

1100

SKYLINE PATH

CABLE CAR

FORESTRY WORKERS HUTS

880

LICHENYA PATH

1880

LICHENYA HUT 1840

CHILEMBA 2385

C.C.A.P. HUT 1995

1850

LICHENYA

PATH

LICHENYA

CLIFFS

PLATEAU

LIKHUBULA FORESTRY STATION

P

800

2033

2122

1990

THE CRATER

CLIFFS

1860

1932

STEEP PART--DANGER WHEN WET

N

FIRST TEA PLANTATION RUINS

FOREST TEA

P 780

ADC'S HOUSE

LIKHUBULA 12 KMS

CHITAKALI SHOPPING CENTER 640

MULANJE 640

H

H

HOSPITALS

MOÇAMBIQUE

BLANTYRE

BUS STATION

GOLF COURSE CLUB HOUSE & CAMPSITE

SCALE 0 1 2 3 4 5 6 KMS

Maps *Mulanje Mountain,* 1:30,000, from Map Sales, Department of Surveys, P.O. Box 349, Blantyre; or Stanfords, London; also the book, **Guide to the Mulanje Massif,** Eastwood, Mountain Club of Malawi, P.O. Box 240, Blantyre, Malawi; and perhaps the latest travel guidebook to Africa or southern Africa.

287

Inyangani, Nyanga National Park, Zimbabwe

The highest summit in Zimbabwe is Inyangani at 2593 meters. It's located in the eastern highlands not far north of the city of Mutare. This national park used to be part of the old Cecil Rhodes Estate, then was made into the Rhodes-Inganya National Park. Now it has the name Nyanga National Park. All this area is just west of the border of Moçambique.

Most of the rocks in the eastern highlands are granite, but it seems the main ridge which makes up Inyangani is a much finer grained granitic-type rock geologists call dolerite or diabasic. It's believed these were magmas which didn't quite reach the surface to become volcanos or lava flows. Because they were near the surface, they cooled more slowly than extruded lava, thus the grains are smaller than regular granite, which cools more slowly at a deeper level.

You can get to this area from the capital of Harare by taking a night train to Mutare, or one of many day-time buses. You can also hitch hike very easily, but if a black person stops, he usually asks for money. Hitching is always free from white drivers. This could all change after the troubles with the white farmers in 2000 (?).

If you're coming from Harare, it's best to leave the main highway at Rusape, which is 83 kms southwest of this national park, and a good place to shop. From Rusape, there are several buses daily running to Nyanga, passing the national park visitor center and the Rhodes Hotel along the way. But hitching may be faster because there's usually lots of white folk vacationing in the region. There are occasional buses running north from Mutare to Nyanga as well.

Once into this area, stop at the turnoff to the park visitor center, or the campground which is another km up the road toward Nyanga. Camping is not permitted inside the park, so you'll have to stay in the campground as shown. Camping there cost about US$2 in 1993, which included hot showers--something you'll need in the cooler winter season which is June through September.

From the park visitor center, where you're supposed to sign in, it's about 16-17 kms to the trailhead to **Inyangani**. You can usually get a lift out there, but most tourists tend to sleep late and begin driving that way by 10 or 11am. The author got up early on the morning of 8/24/1993 and walked all the way to the end of the road and trailhead at 2140 meters in about 3 hours. From there he climbed Inyangani in less than an hour; about 1 1/2 hours round-trip from the car-park. He met other hikers on the mountain with cars and got a ride back to the campground. It's recommended you ask at the campground or visitor center for people going that way. There's lots of traffic along the *loop road* on weekends.

Buy all your food in Harare, Rusape, Mutare, or Juliasdale, which is the last place to buy supplies. The dry season is from June through October, but it sometimes gets rather cool, so be prepared with a warm sleeping bag and warm clothes.

Maps *Tourist Map of Nyanga*, 1:63,360; or *Inyangani 1832 B4 & 1833 A3*, 1:50,000, from the

Inyangani with the trailhead at the end of the road one km ahead.

Map 134-1, Inyangani, Nyanga National Park, Zimbabwe

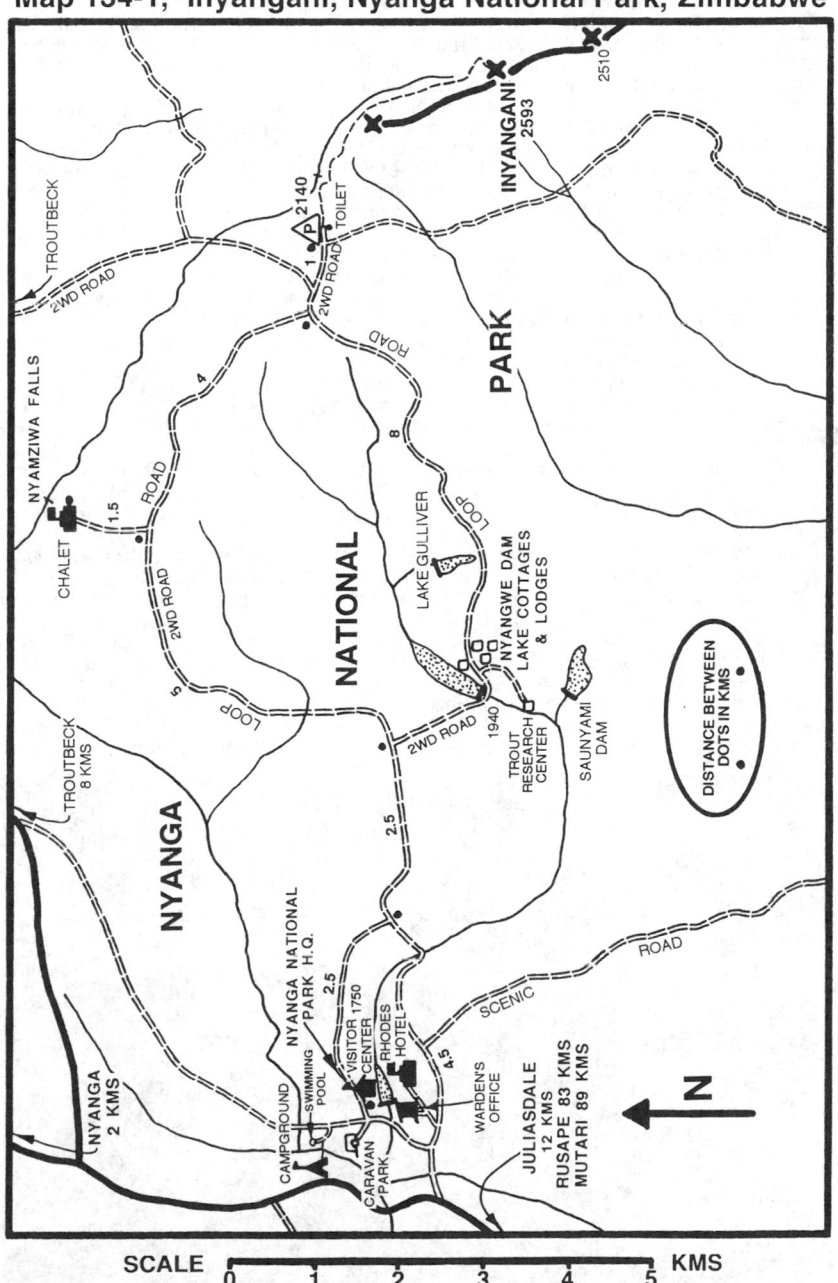

visitor center, or Department of Surveyor General, Electra House, Sanora Machel Ave., Harare; and/or the *Tourist Map of Zimbabwe* by the Automobile Association of Zimbabwe; and the latest travel guidebook of Africa, or southern Africa.

Mt. Binga, Chimanimani National Park, Zimbabwe

Shown here is Mt. Binga, 2438 meters, the second highest peak in Zimbabwe. This summit is found in Chimanimani National Park, the most popular hiking area in the country. Mt. Binga is located south of the large city of Mutare in the eastern highlands and along the border with Moçambique. These mountains are made mostly of Precambrian quartzite, which has been folded and uplifted forming several ridges running north-south. As seen from the hotel in the village of Chimanimani, this uplift is one of the grandest mountain scenes in southern Africa.

To reach this region, take a bus (or a night train) from the capital city of Harare, eastward in the direction of Mutare which is next to the border of Moçambique. Then from the main bus station in the southwest part of Mutare, take one of half a dozen daily buses going in the direction of Chimanimani; or better still, find one going past Chimanimani and on to Tilbury. Most of these buses take 4-5 hours for the trip, so hitching might be faster. Hitch hiking was quite good in Zimbabwe when the author climbed this peak on 8/25/1993.

At Chimanimani, you'll find a large tourist hotel, a campsite next to it, and immediately north of that, the bus station along with several stores and a restaurant. You can buy all your food there, but you'll have better selections in Harare or Mutare. Just down the road east from the hotel is an inexpensive backpackers lodge similar to a youth hostel. These *backpackers rests* are something you'll see all over southern Africa.

If you're on a bus to Tilbury, get off at Charleswood and walk 7 kms east to Base Camp. Or maybe you'll get a lift. If your bus stops at the Chimanimani Hotel, then either wait for a Tilbury bus, or walk and/or hitch hike down the road toward Charleswood and Base Camp. It's 16 kms from Chimanimani to Base Camp.

Base Camp is a campground with hot showers and park ranger station, but there are no stores or food available. Everyone pays a small camping fee of about US$2, plus a park entrance fee of about US$1 (in 1993). Backpackers can then hike and camp for free anywhere in the park.

To climb **Mt. Binga**, walk up the trail to the east. Soon you'll be on the first ridge with the higher peaks to the east in full view. Further to the northeast, and down a little, is a shelter with 2 large dorm rooms with a total of about 30 beds (no mattresses), and a cooking or kitchen area. Sleeping there costs about US$1 per night.

From the hut head downhill to the east, cross the valley and continue on a good trail right to the top of Binga. This trail is well-signposted and easy to follow. There is water at several locations enroute. The author did this hike from Base Camp to Binga and back, in 5 hours. Most hikers will want 7-8 hours to do this round-trip.

You can climb Binga year-round, but the dry season is from June through October, which happens to be their winter as well. If camping in the higher valleys in winter, expect freezing

Looking northwest from the summit of Mt. Binga. Moçambique is on the right.

Map 135-1, Binga, Chimanimani Nat. Park, Zimbabwe

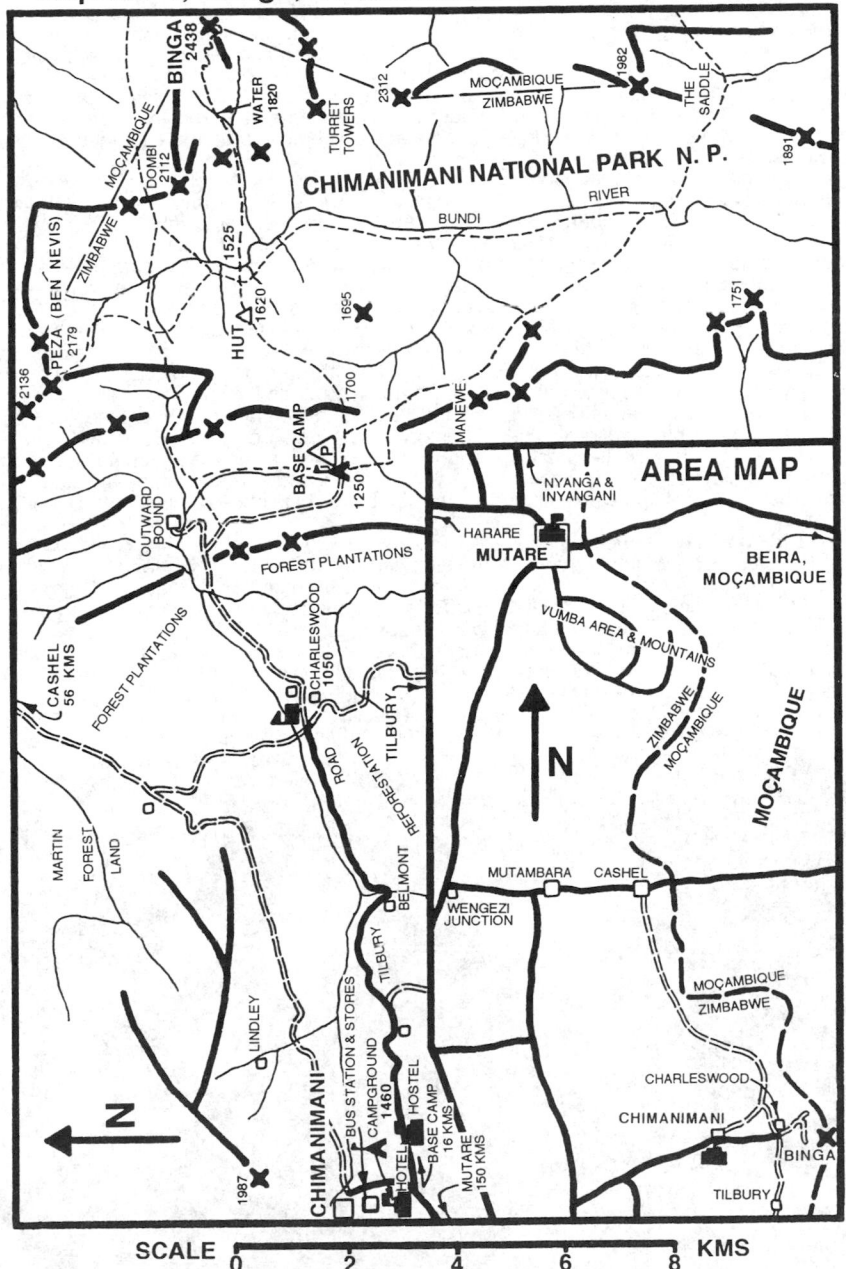

temperatures every night.
Maps *Chimanimani, 1932 D4 & 1933 C1/C3* (one map), 1:50,000, from Map Sales, Department of Surveyor General, Electra House, Sanora Machel Avenue, Harare, Zimbabwe; and the latest travel guidebook to Africa, or southern Africa.

Mont-aux-Sources, Drakensberg, Lesotho-South Africa

Featured on this map is the northern-most part of Southern Africa's Drakensberg Escarpment, and the Royal Natal National Park. Also shown is the highest summit in the region which is Mont-aux-Sources, at 3282 meters. The Drakensberg consists of a rather flat plateau, which is Lesotho; and the highly eroded escarpment which breaks away into South Africa's Natal state, and Qwa Qwa, a black homeland within the boundaries of Orange Free state. The rock forming the top layers of the plateau is old basalt, while underneath that is the Cave Sandstone Formation. It's the erosion of the edge of the plateau which has created the Great Escarpment known otherwise as the **Drakensberg**.

To get there using public transportation, first make your way to Estcourt or Ladysmith, then at either bus station, look for a *black taxi* or *combee* (15 passenger vans or minibuses owned and operated by blacks) heading for Bergville. At Bergville, look for another one going to the visitor center in the national park. Once in the park, stop at the visitor center for updated information on camping and hiking, and for maps and/or guidebooks. Up the northern-most road from the visitor center is the Mahai Campsite. Or turn left at the visitor center and drive or walk up the road to a hutkamp with a number of small huts or cabins for campers.

To climb to the plateau and/or **Mont-aux-Sources**, begin at the trailhead between the visitor center and the campground. This trail (shown as a heavy black line on this map) runs west up to the Witzieshoek Mtn. Resort. From there, road-walk south to the end of the road at 2500 meters. At that point is a second trailhead used by those who drive cars up from Harrismith.

From there an overused trail runs up past the Sentinel to the plateau. One of the 2 routes up the steeper part is via a steep gully; the other is up a chain ladder of maybe 50 meters. Once on top, the trail actually runs to the Natal Mtn. Club Hut, then south along the top of the escarpment. To climb Mont-aux-Sources, walk southwest from the hut; or south from near the top of the chain ladder. There's no trail to the summit and it's really a boring hike once you get beyond the Great Escarpment.

To climb Mont-aux-Sources is a very long all-day hike. For most it's best to do it in 2 days. On Friday, 9/3/1993, the author started in the late afternoon at the visitor center and walked for 2 1/2 hours, camped near the Witzieshoek Mtn. Resort, then climbed Mont-aux-Sources and returned to the visitor center in 7 1/2 hours on Day 2 (he got a ride part-way down along the road to the Mtn. Resort). On Day 2, the author was joined by runners.

On the first Saturday of September each year is the Drakensberg Marathon, a 50 km run from the visitor center to near the Natal Mtn. Club Hut, and back. On the 1993 marathon which was held on 9/4/1993, the best time was 4 hours, 30 minutes, 32 seconds.

The dry season is from June through October, which is their winter with snow possible on top, but hiking can be done year-round. Buy all your food and supplies no later than Bergville.

Hikers waiting to climb the chain ladder to reach the top of the Great Escarpment.

Map 136-1, M. Sources, Drakensberg, Lesotho-S. Africa

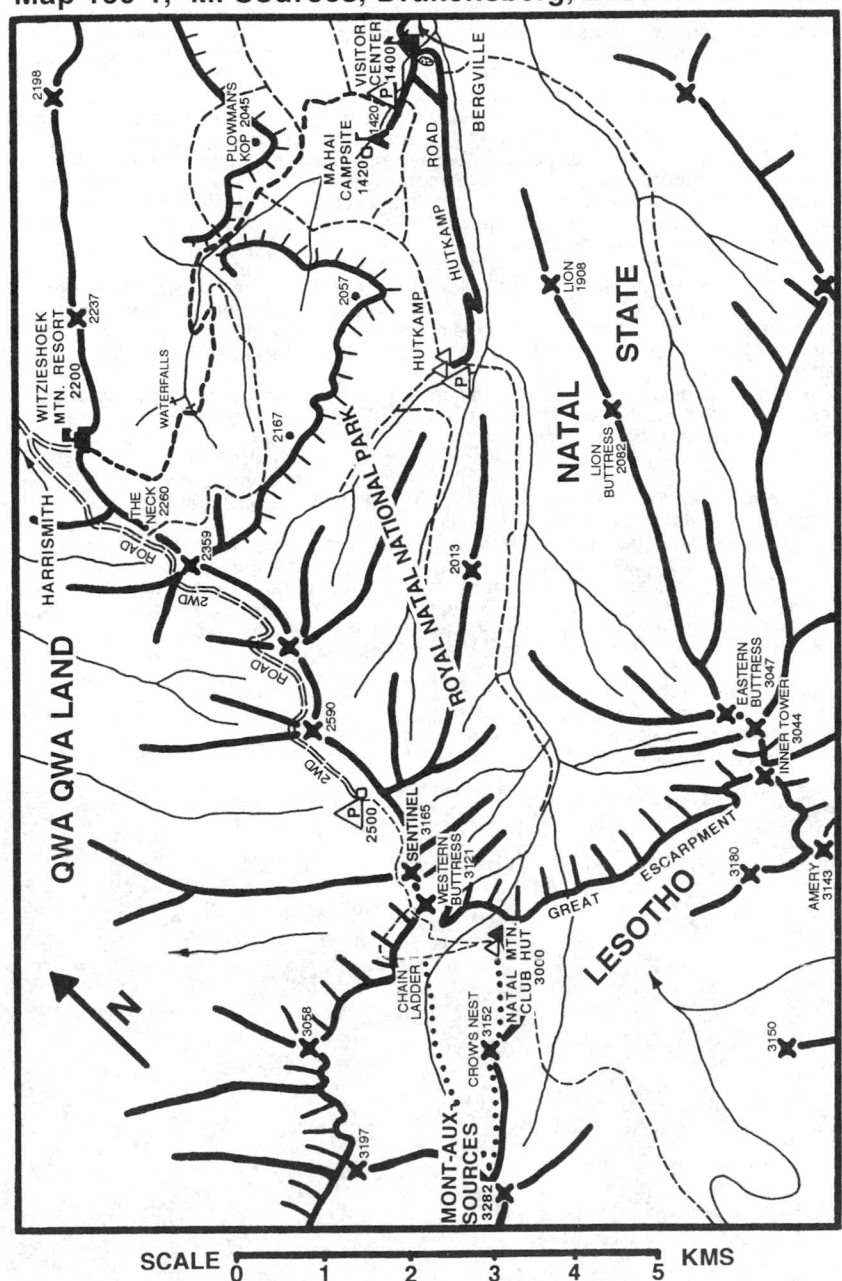

SCALE 0 1 2 3 4 5 KMS

Maps *Drakensberg North,* 1:50,000, Forestry Department, Private Bag X447, Pretoria, or buy at the visitor center; also the book, **Drakensberg Walks,** Bristow, Struik Publishers, 80 McKenzie Street, Cape Town, South Africa; and the latest travel guidebook to Africa or southern Africa.

Cathkin Peak Region, Drakensberg, Lesotho--South Africa

This is the second map featuring the Drakensberg region of South Africa, and one of the most popular mountain areas in the country. Prominent landmarks are Cathkin Peak at 3149 meters; Monk's Cowl, 3234; and Champagne Castle at 3248 meters. All areas on the plateau are part of Lesotho, while the cliffs and crags below the escarpment are in Natal State of South Africa. The highest point in this region is an insignificant hump near the Ship's Prow at 3377 meters. The plateau is capped with old volcanic rock, while the lower levels are sandstone.

To reach this area, make your way to the bus station in Estcourt (or possibly Ladysmith); then look for a *black taxi* or *combee* (15 passenger vans) heading for the Kwa Zulu community of Loskop. From there, look for another combee going to the Champagne Castle Hotel. You could also go from Estcourt to Winterton, then find a combee heading for Champagne. Another option is to leave Estcourt or Winterton and head for the Cathedral Peak & Mike's Pass area just to the north, then hike south to this region. Or vice versa. Buy food and other supplies in Estcourt or Winterton because there are no stores near the escarpment.

From the Champagne Castle Hotel, walk up the road 2 kms to the Monk's Cowl Forest Station, visitor center, campground, and trailhead. The region between the forest station and the top of the escarpment is a wilderness area administered by the national park system of South Africa. Therefore you must register at the visitor center where they sell maps and books. Those people can update this information as well.

There are 2 popular hikes here. One is from the visitor center toward **Champagne Castle**, then either north or south to a trail which runs between The Castle and **Cathkin Peak**. A fast strong hiker could do this loop round-trip in one day.

A second hike would be to use the same approach, but climb to the plateau, making a loop between Gray's and Ship's Prow Passes. To do this in one day would be rather difficult, so 2 days are recommended with a camp, perhaps on the plateau. Inquire at the visitor center about the availability of water on top if you're thinking of camping there. There was a small stream on top on 9/6/1993 during the author's climb which was near the end of the dry season. Otherwise there's good drinking water in most of the streams shown below the escarpment..

On 9/5/1993, the author walked from Mike's Pass Road in the Cathedral Peaks area, southeast on the Contour Trail to the river camp at 1900 meters in 8 1/2 hours. Next morning, he climbed up over **Gray's Pass** to the highest point, then returned to camp--6 hours. Later that day he walked down to the Monk's Cowl Visitor Center in another 2 1/2 hours. He left the area in a combee.

The dry season for all of southern Africa is June through October, which is their winter. You can climb here year-round, but go prepared for possible snow on top in winter. Have warm cloths and a warm sleeping bag if you plan to camp on top.

Maps *Drakensberg North,* 1:50,000, Forestry Department, Private Bag X447, Pretoria; or buy at

Cathkin in the middle (flat top), Monk's Cowl to the right, as seen from the trail to Gray's Pass.

Map 137-1, Cathkin Pk., Drakensberg, Lesotho-S. Africa

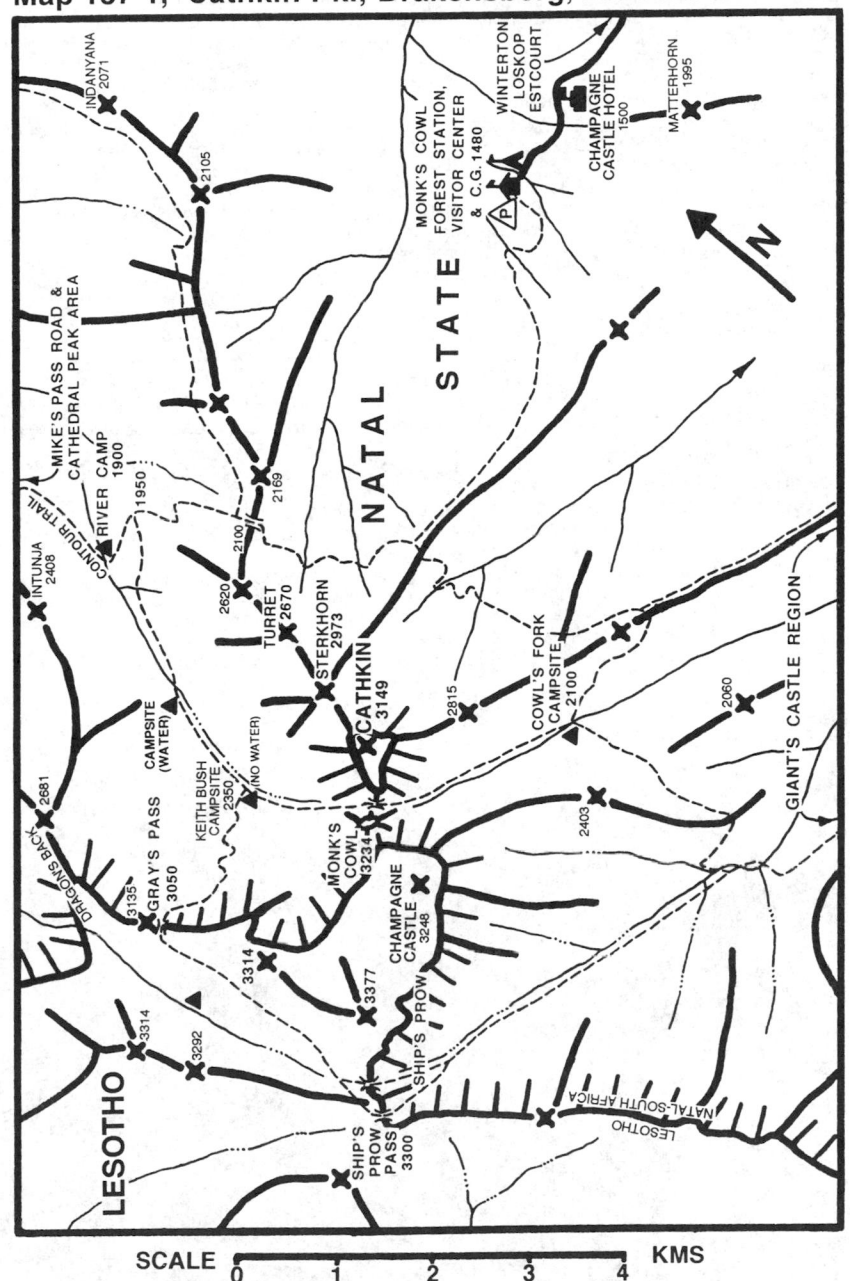

SCALE

0   1   2   3   4   KMS

the visitor center. Also the book, **Drakensberg Walks,** Bristow, Struik Publishers, 80 McKenzie Street, Cape Town, South Africa; and a travel guidebook to southern Afria.

Thabana Ntienyana, Drakensberg, Lesotho

Shown here is the highest mountain in Africa south of Kilimanjaro. It's Thabana Ntienyana, at 3482 meters. This peak or summit is located in the Drakensberg region, but entirely inside Lesotho. It's about 4 kms from the boundary of South Africa. The rocks here are the same as in other parts of the Drakensberg, with old volcanic rocks making up the entire plateau. Below these old lava flows are sandstone formations.

Here's how to get there using public transportation. Make your way to Pietermaritzburg, the capital of Natal. Find the place near the train station where *black taxis* or *combees* park waiting for passengers. Locate one going to Underberg and Himeville, and hopefully to points northeast from there. Three kms east of Himeville is the turnoff to Sani Pass Hotel and Sani Top. In 1993, there was public transport going toward Nottingham Road, but very few combees going to the Sani Pass Hotel on a graveled road. If you don't have your own car, you'll have to start walking from that junction east of Himeville and hope for a lift part way. The author walked, then got 2 short rides to the hotel, then walked again. He camped near Km post 12, then got a lift the next morning to the South African border post at Km post 26, which is open from 8am to 4pm daily. Once through emigration, he walked to Sani Top Village & Sani Pass in 2 hours (8 kms). The Lesotho border post is open from 7am to 5pm.

The village of Sani Top has the Lesotho border post, many rock huts and 2 stores. Everything in the stores comes up from Underberg, and the prices are quite reasonable. Just east of the village is the Sani Pass Chalet, with rooms, restaurant and a small store.

On 9/8/1993, the author started walking from Sani Top Village around mid-day and in just over 3 hours, left his pack at the base of **Thabana Ntienyana**, and hurried to the top in another 30 minutes. He camped beside a small stream at 3200 meters south of the peak.

The trail from Sani Top is very easy to follow; it can be up to 10 trails and 10 meters wide in some places. This is a major route used by local herdsmen. Be sure to have a compass, and head due north from Sani Top for the most part. There is water in several places, but with grazing livestock everywhere, better purify it first. The landscape here is barren--only grass, and is heavily grazed in the warmer half of the year.

The next morning the author walked back to Sani Top in 3 hours, which included a quick skinny dip in ice-covered water in the creek near the village. This was on 9/9/1993 and the total walk-time from Sani Top was about 7 hours, mostly with a big pack. Had he gotten to Sani Top right when the border post opened at 7am, he would have gotten a lift down to Underberg easily. Several 4WD vehicles a day head down starting early. As it was, he waited several hours for the next ride.

The dry season is from June through October. June through August is winter with some snow, but you can normally climb without skies or snowshoes. When conditions are right, South Africans come to the chalet and ski cross-country during this time. The road up to the South

Part of the Sani Top Village located right on Sani Pass.

Map 138-1, Thabana Ntienyana, Drakensberg, Lesotho

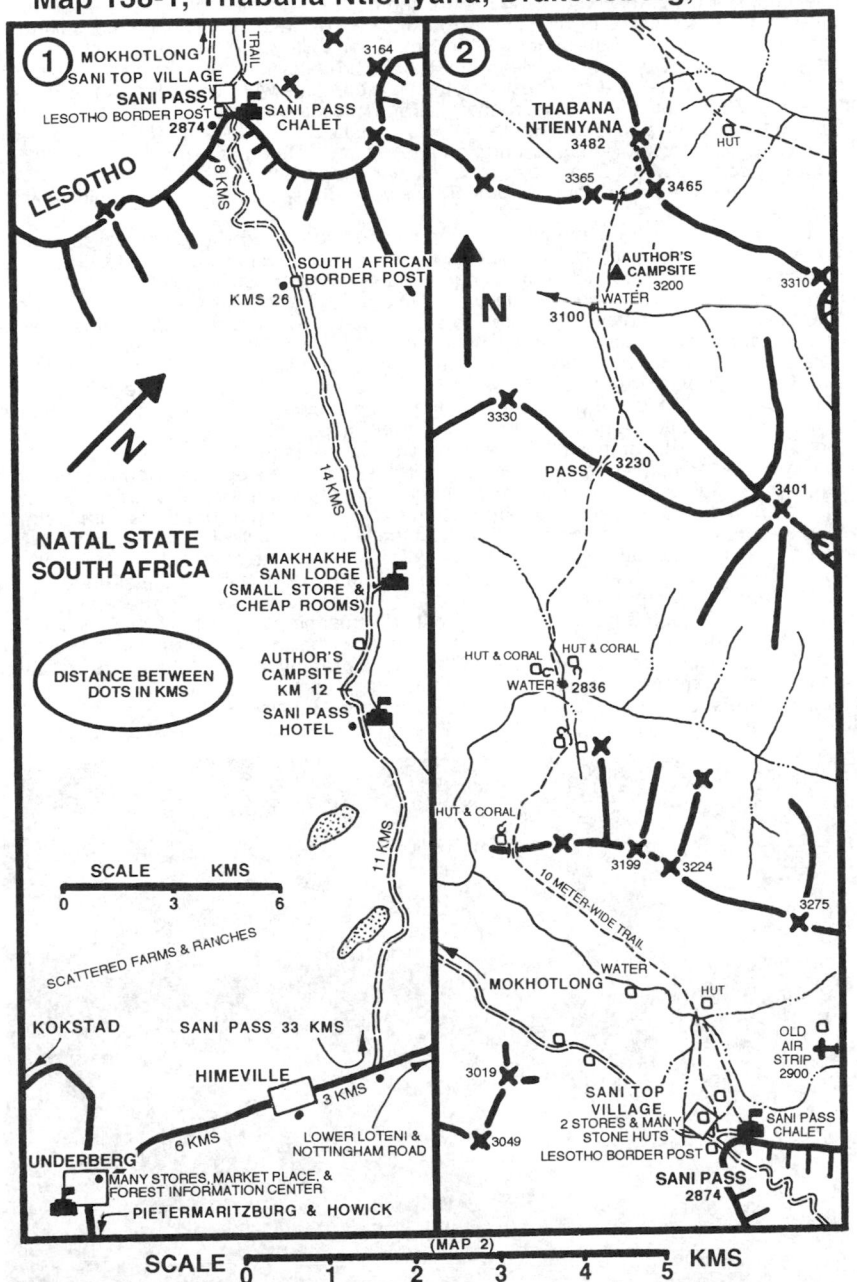

African border post is good for cars, but 4WD's only from there to the pass & Sani Top Village.
Maps *Giant's Castle, 2929AD* and *Sani Pass, 2929CB,* 1:50,000, from Government Printer, Private Bag X85, Pretoria; also any national highway map, perhaps Map Studio's *Road Atlas of South Africa*; and a travel guidebook to southern Africa.

Matroosberg, Hex River Mtns., Cape Province, South Africa

Featured here is Matroosberg, 2249 meters, the highest summit in the Hex River Mountains (Hexriverberg). This range is located about 109 kms east of Cape Town on the main highway to Johannesburg. South of Matroosberg is the Hex River Valley and the grape growing & wine producing town of De Doorns. The Hex River Berg is probably the best climbing area in South Africa next to the Drakensberg. These are folded mountains with rocks of various kinds, but along the route from Lombardi to Matroosberg, all you'll see is quartzite.

Getting there using public transportation was easy in 1993. The author left Cape Town at 9:20am on the daily train to Johannesburg, and got off in De Doorns at 1pm. You can also take *black taxis* or *combees* from Cape Town to Worcester, then another one to De Doorns. Ask any black person near the train station in Cape Town where those combees park while waiting for passengers.

De Doorns is a small town, but it has one pretty good supermarket and several small stores. From the middle of town you'll have to walk or hitch hike northeast along the old highway about 5 kms to the Lombardi Road. At that junction is a store called Bo Valley Winkel, and a sign pointing the way to *Johaan Malan, Lombardi*. From there to Lombardi it's about 2 more kms.

Now the problem! All of these mountains are privately owned by various farmers, therefore to climb you must have permission from a landowner. Luckily for the south side of Matroosberg it isn't a major problem. For permission, you must call Johaan Malan, Tele. (02) 322-2570, ahead of time if possible; or just show up at his house at Lombardi. The reason for the permission requirement is that you must pass through a couple of his gates next to his house to reach the campsites and the hiking route shown on this map.

Along the way to the campsite on the left, you'll pass 2 pump houses, and you can camp anywhere above the canal. To climb Matroosberg, walk up the slope near the prominent little stream valley heading straight for the highest peak. On the lower slopes, you'll have to route-find around some large boulders, but up high, it's an easy walk. From the summit, you look down on ski club huts below to the north. Contact the Mountain Club of South Africa, 97 Hatfield Street in Cape Town, about how and where to get permission to climb from the north side.

On 9/15/1993, it took the author 2 1/2 hours to reach the summit, and just under 5 hours round-trip from his camp near the pump houses. The wetter season in the Western Cape Province is June through September (winter), but you must prepare for snow and icy conditions at that time. Otherwise, October and November may be the best months to climb partly because you'll have good running water in the small streams shown. Summers (December through March) are rather warm and dry, with no running water.

Maps *De Doorns, 3319 BC*, 1:50,000, from Surveys and Mapping, Private Bag X10, Mowbray (suburb of Cape Town), Tele. (021) 685-4070; and perhaps the book, **Western Cape Walks**,

Conical Peak as seen from the summit of Matroosberg.

Map 139-1, Matroosberg, Hex River Mtns., South Africa

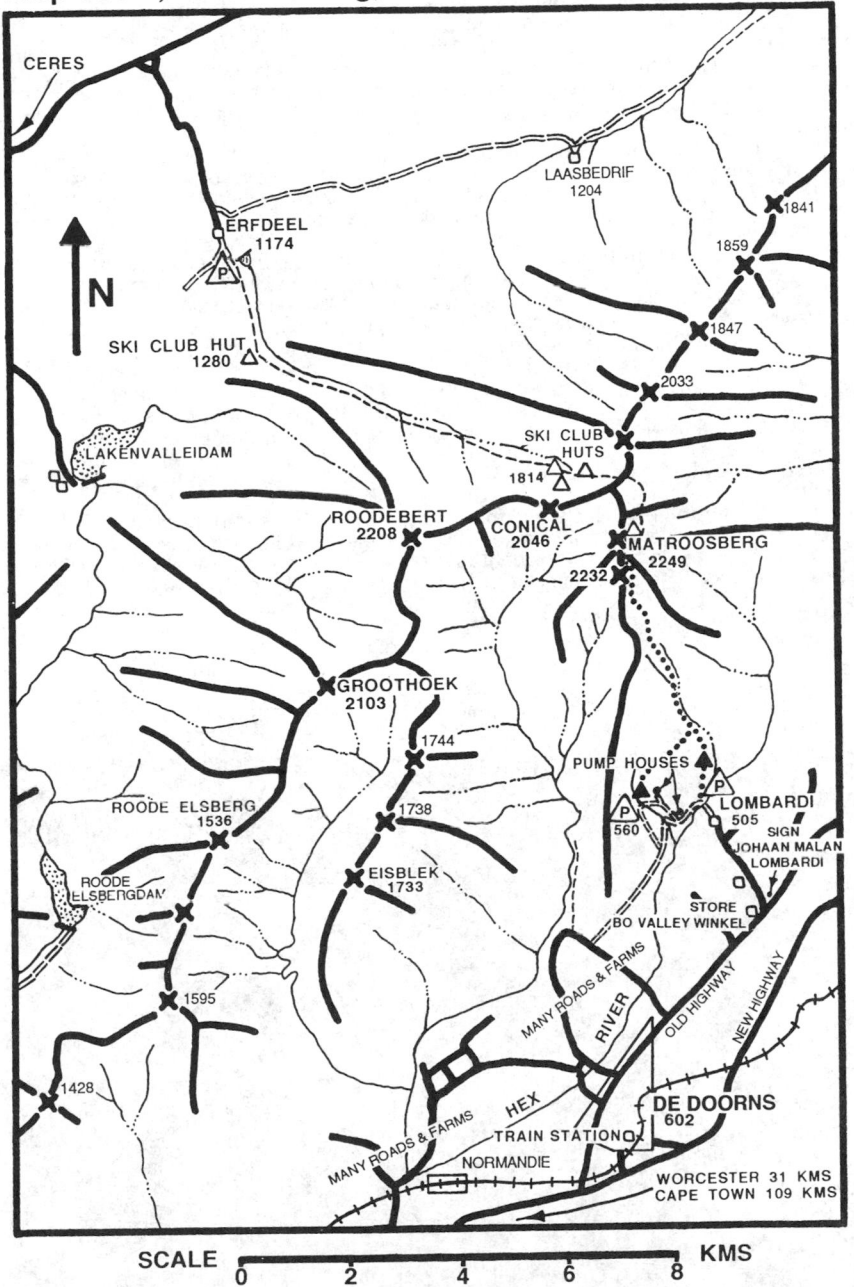

Bristow, Struik Publishers, Cape Town (the 1st edition of this book covers all hikes in the Western Cape, but *not* the Hex River Berg!).

Table Mountain, Cape Province, South Africa

One of the most famous mountains in Africa is Table Mountain (Tafelberg), although it's only 1086 meters high. The reason it's so well-known is because it forms a spectacular scene right behind the famous port city of Cape Town. This city and it's suburbs surround Table Mountain, which is barely 5 kms from the waterfront. This mountain is actually the last remains of an uplifted plateau, with the highest escarpment being on the north side facing downtown Cape Town. The upper-most rock band is made of rather solid limestone, making it very good for rock climbing.

If you want to do serious climbing, or a lot of hiking, it's best to stop at the tourist information center in the same complex as the bus & train stations in the middle of the city. They can help you find the Surveys and Mapping office in the suburb of Mowbray, and the nearby Mtn. Club of South Africa office. These people sell the guide books listed below. Any good bookstore will also sell these books.

To climb **Table Mountain**, leave the downtown area by walking southward along Buitengracht Street, which changes to Kloof Nek Street or Road further up to the south. When you reach the big junction at Kloof Nek, turn left onto Tafelberg Road and following the signs to the cableway. There are several starting points along this paved road.

For an example of time and distance, here's what the author did on 9/12/1993. He walked from his backpacker's hostel near the middle of the city and made it to the lower cableway station in about an hour. He then went up the trail below the cableway, making it to the top station in less than 1 1/2 hours. He had a lunch there at the upper cableway station which is the highest point, bought several post cards from the curio shop, then walked down the good trail in the steep ravine called Platteklip. Near the bottom, he turned left onto the Contour Path and returned to the lower station. From the lower station of the cableway, the hike took 3 hours round-trip.

There are many other routes to the top, some of which are shown here. Some routes are easy, some difficult. Be sure to have a good city map plus the map and book below. If you want to climb **Devil's Peak**, located on the right side of this map, you can climb it via Kloof Nek and the Tafelberg Road; or take a commuter train to the eastern suburb of Mowbray, and walk to the mountain from there. To climb **Lions Head**, in the far northwest corner of this map, walk to Kloof Nek and turn right onto Signal Hill Road. You'll have to look for the trail going up on the east side, which then completely circles this spire to get on top.

The wet season is from about May through September which is their winter. This is the time when cold fronts blow across the Cape. You can climb Tafelberg year-round, as there's never any really cold weather. It's hot and dry in summer--December through March.

Maps *Kaapstad--Cape Town, 3318CD*, 1;50,000, from Surveys and Mapping, Private Bag X10,

From Capetown's waterfront, looking south at Table Mtn. and the highest point on the far right.

Map 140-1, Table Mtn., Cape Province, South Africa

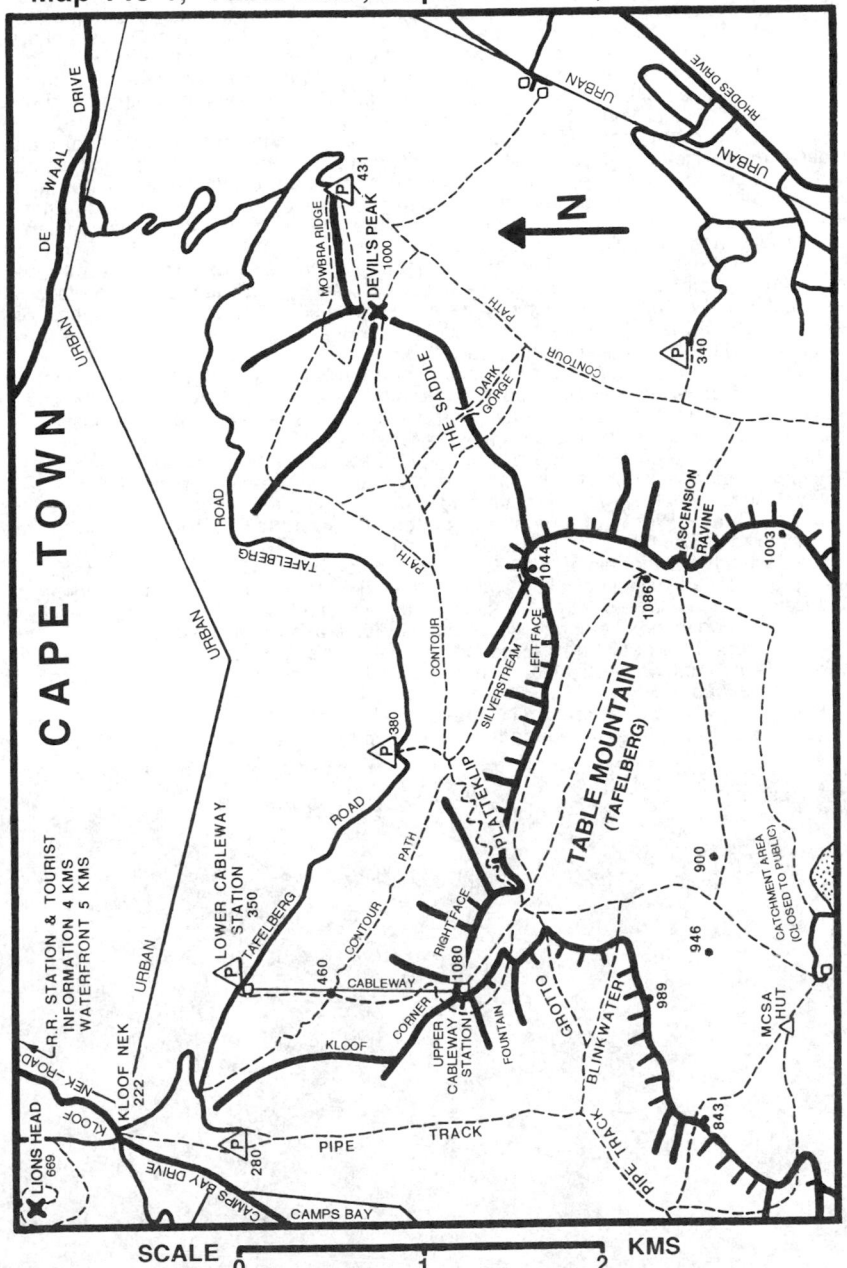

Mowbray; the book, **Table Mountain Guide**, by the Cape Town section of the Mountain Club of South Africa, 97 Hatfield Street, Cape Town; or **Western Cape Walks**, Bristow, Struik Publishers, Cape Town.

Gross (Big) Spitzkoppe, Namibia

This map features a couple of steep monoliths in central Namibia. The highest peak is called Gross (Big) Spitzkoppe, reaching a height of 1728 meters. This peak is west of the town called Usakos and northeast of Swakopmund. It can be seen easily from the main highway running between Swakopmund on the coast, and Windhoek the capital. Like a lot of other mountains in this part of Namibia, Spitzkoppe is a solid light-colored granite intrusion. This is not a high mountain, but it's very fotogenic and on the tourist circuit.

Here's how to get there. There is one large bus running between Swakopmund and Windhoek daily which will let you off at *The Junction* at the bottom of this map. But big buses in Namibia are infrequent and expensive. You can also take a *black taxi* or *combee* along the same route. Or just get out on the highway and flag any vehicle down. If a white guy stops it's a free ride; if a black driver stops, you normally pay about the same as taking a combee. Most Namibians just flag down black drivers and pay.

Once at The Junction marked 1200 meters, you'll have to hitch hike or walk, or a combination of both. If you're looking for a ride, then walk west along the road to Black Range, then turn north. From the main highway, it's about 28 kms to the town of Spitzkoppe. You can walk that in a day with a big pack, but hopefully will get a lift part way. You could also walk to Sandamap and hike north along a 4WD track.

At the village of Spitzkoppe is a school and nearby water tap, a bar, one small store (open only part-time) and a medical clinic--but don't get sick there! From this village, walk along a road toward the mountain. This is a good road and tourists in cars reach this place almost every day. Once at the base of the peak, you can camp anywhere.

The normal route up **Gross Spitzkoppe** appears to be in the gully on the southeast face. However, it's not a walkup. Good climbers can apparently free-climb it, but better take a rope anyway--it doesn't look easy! Just getting up to the steep part requires some route-finding and boulder climbing. Plenty of difficult routes too. Tourists take fotos, but don't climb this Matterhorn-like peak. The author never did make the summit.

Here's what the author did on 9/19/93. He took a combee to The Junction arriving late in the evening. He carried 10 liters of water and walked straight for the mountain in the moonlight for 2 hours; camped near Daniels Ranch. Next morning he walked to the Black Range Ranch, hid his big pack, then continued. Later he discovered the village and water--no one told him about that! He walked around the peak and returned to his pack in the late afternoon, then walked to near the Pforte Ranch and camped; an 11 hour day. Next morning he got a lift to the main highway and on to Swakopmund.

Have several liters of water at all times--this is a desert! Don't expect to get water at the ranches shown; some are abandoned. Buy all food before arriving. Best to hike or climb in

Gross Spitzkoppe, one of several granite spires in the area.

Map 141-1, Gross (Big) Spitzkoppe, Namibia

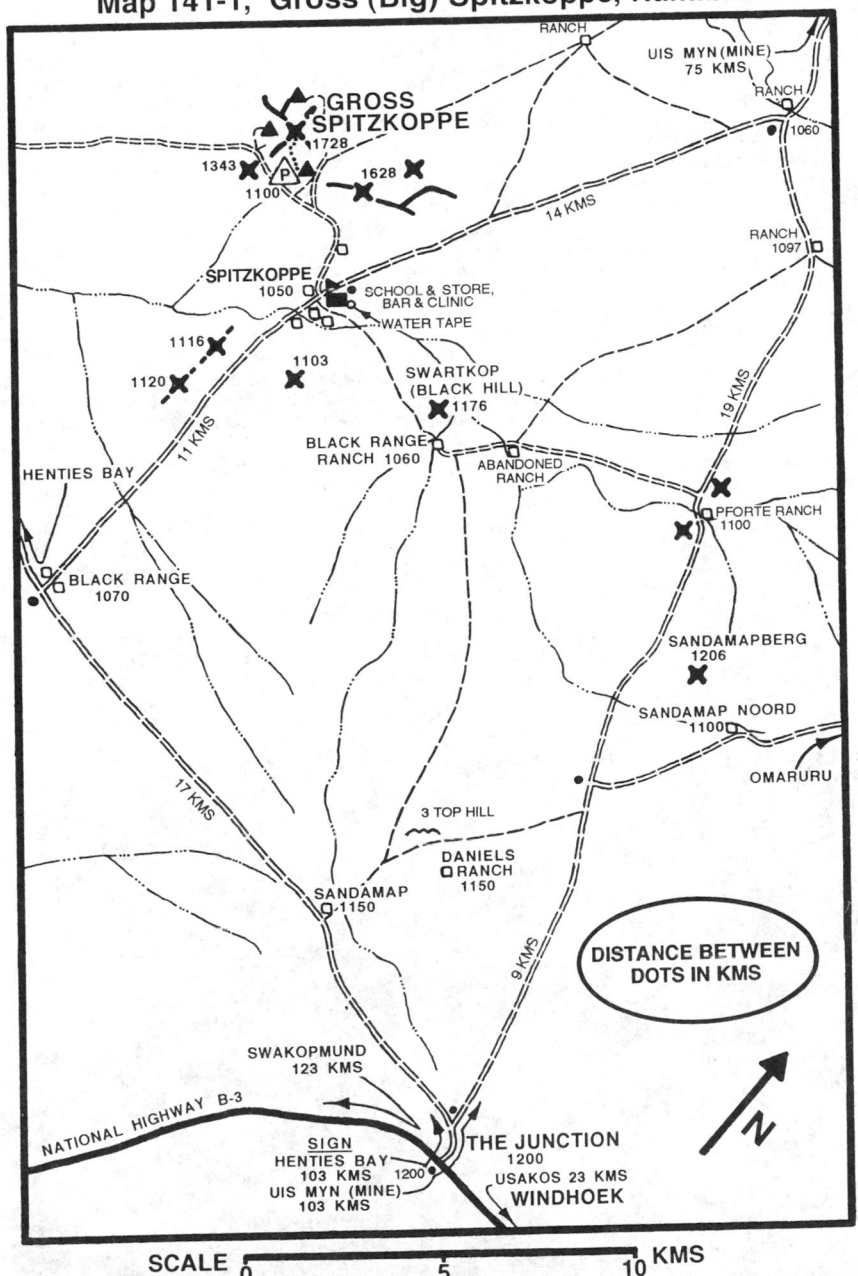

winter--June through August, which is both the cool and dry season.
Maps *Omaruru, 2114,* 1:250,000, and *Spitzkuppen 2115CC & Sandamap 2115CD,* 1:50,000, from the Surveyor General, Justitia Building, Independence Avenue, Private Bag 13182, Windhoek; and the latest travel guidebook to Africa or Southern Africa.

Königstien, Brandberg (Burnt Mountains), Namibia

These maps show the Brandberg, or Burnt Mountains, of Namibia. The highest peak here, and in the country, is Königstien, 2573 meters. These mountains are located due north of Swakopmund and west of the little mining town of Uis. This range is a circular granite intrusion.

Graveled highways lead to this area from the east--Omaruru; from the southeast--Usakos & Spitzkoppe; from the north--Khorixas; and from the south--Swakopmund & Henties Bay. There's a once-a-week bus running from Swakopmund & Henties Bay to Khorixas on Wednesdays, but it's best to just hitch hike to Uis as locals do.

The Uis Mine was closed in about 1990, but the town hangs on, and hitching is remarkably easy going that way. This is real desert country, but if people have room, they'll stop for you. For the most part, the further out in the desert you are, the kinder people are to hitch hikers! The road from Henties Bay to Uis is the busiest of all approach roads to this area.

In 1993, Uis had two parts; the white section in the west had a petrol station, bakery & store, and recreation center with a campground, swimming pool, bar and a golf course made of sand. The black township to the east had 2 small stores and the public school. Some of the teachers were from the US Peace Corps.

Ask around Uis and you'll likely find someone who can drive you out to the White Lady Trailhead for a small fee. You can hitch hike but it would likely take all day. In one full day you could walk to the trailhead, but carrying tons of water 40 kms is no fun! Getting back from the White Lady is quite easy, as there are normally several tourist vehicles going that way each day. There are 3 other routes shown on the area map, but you'll need a 4WD vehicle to reach those trailheads.

From the White Lady Trailhead, where a guide/vendor is camped and sells stones & guide services to tourists, walk up the track to the White Lady Paintings (pictographs) in about one hour. Half a km above that is a big pothole in the dry creek bed, which should have water year-round (?). Above the first pothole it's easy walking for a ways, then the creek bed becomes choked with boulders, making walking hard with a big pack. Further along, you must climb up the south side of the canyon wall to avoid dryfalls. From the *Double Potholes*, you have a choice of 2 routes, each taking about the same amount of time.

Remember, there is no running water in the **Brandberg**, except for short periods during the rainy season--from December through March. Best time to climb is from March to June, because there will be water in potholes as shown--maybe even a real spring or two (?).

On 9/23/1993, the author paid a guy from Uis about US$12 to drive him out to the White Lady Trailhead (30 minutes) with 18 liters of water. Seven liters was left there with the guide/vendor at the trailhead, then he walked up to the 2nd pothole and camped at 900 meters. Next day he climbed Königstien in 4 1/2 hours; 8 1/2 round-trip from his camp making a loop-

Tourists inspect the protected White Lady Paintings near the trailhead in the Brandberg.

Map 142-1, Königstien, Brandberg (Burnt Mtns.), Namibia

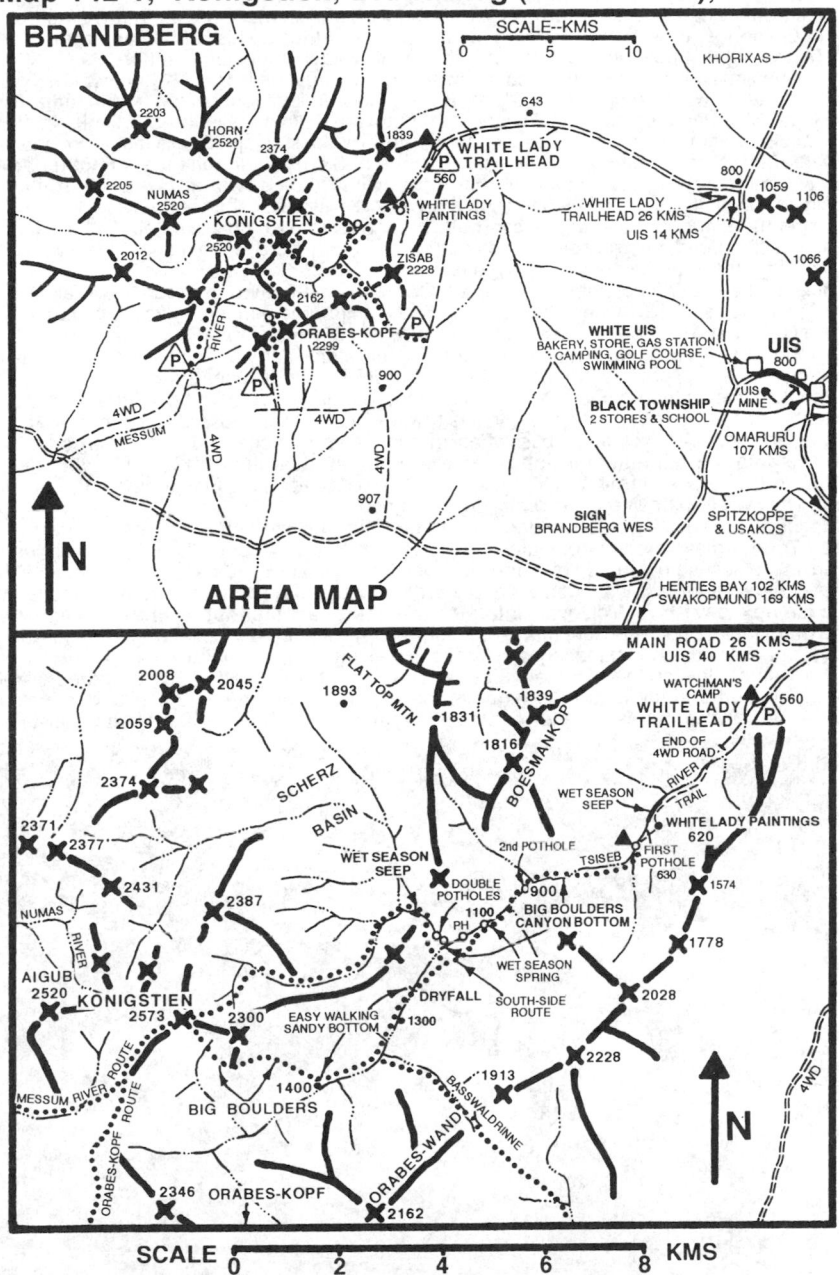

hike using both routes shown. That afternoon he returned to the trailhead--an 11 1/2 hour day. Day 3, he walked out to the main road in 3 1/2 hours, and immediately got a lift back to Uis.
Maps *Brandberg, 2114BA,* 1:50,000; and *Omaruru, 2114,* 1:250,000, from Surveyor General, Justitia Building, Independence Avenue, Private Bag 13182, Windhoek.

Mt. Cameroun, Cameroun

In extreme western Cameroun, very near the Nigerian border and just a few kms from the Gulf of Guinea, stands one of the biggest volcanos in Africa. This a Mt. Cameroun, at 4070 meters, the highest point in West Africa. This huge volcanic massif has more than 100 small cinder cone's on its flanks and surrounding lowlands. An eruption in 2 & 3/1959 produced a large east flank lava flow. An eruption in 10 & 11/1982 produced lava fountaining from a radial fissure 6 1/2 kms SW of the summit and a lava flow that moved 12 kms down the SW flank. In 1989, a minor explosive eruption formed a new crater on the SW flank. Cameroun's last eruption started on 5/29/2000 from 2 southeast flank fissures; one at 3300 meters altitude, the other at 4000 meters. At last report, lava was 4 kms from the village of Bokwango, which is at southern outskirts of Buea. For volcano updates see the website (www.volcano.si.edu/gvp/).

To get there from Douala, take a bus west & north toward Kumba, but get off at the highway junction east of Buea; this may be at mile post 17 (?). From there get in a shared taxi with others for the 5 km (?) ride to Buea along a paved highway.

Buea is the starting point for climbing **Mt. Cameroun**. Located there are several shops, at least 3 places to sleep (between US$5 and US$15 a night) and a market place with many middle latitude fruits and vegetables. Buea is at an altitude of 1000 meters and has a cool climate. This part of Cameroun was once under British control, therefore many people know English as their 2nd language; as opposed to the rest of Cameroun which is French speaking.

People climbing the mountain are required to hire a guide. A guide is definitely not needed as the trail to the top is very good, but this is the way it's done in most of Subsaharan Africa. If you want to take a risk, you might bushwhack around the police checkpoint, but this could lead to problems later on. The author got a way with doing that back in 1/1974, but you probably couldn't today. Get a permit & guide at about US$16/day at the tourist center in the middle of Buea. They will also update the information in this book.

About 3 hours walking above Buea is the first hut and the last year-round spring on this route. You normally must carry water from that point for the rest of the hike. At about 3200 meters is the second hut, made of aluminum, which sleeps about 10 people; it's not fancy, but it keeps out the weather. Most people sleep there one night, then reach the summit and return to Buea the next day. R.E. McGowan informed the author another hut has been constructed at about 3800 meters near the summit (1986 information). The author believes he did this climb in 2 days, but his diaries and handbag were stolen a week afterwards in Zaïre.

Wear shorts low on the mountain, but on top it can be very cold, so go prepared with long pants. The author remembers the winds at the summit being among the strongest he's ever encountered. These winds were felt right at the summit, while about 100 meters below that last

A 1974 foto of the tin shelter at 3200 meters on the eastern slopes of Cameroun.
Ask about its condition before leaving Buea!

Map 143-1, Mt. Cameroun, Cameroun

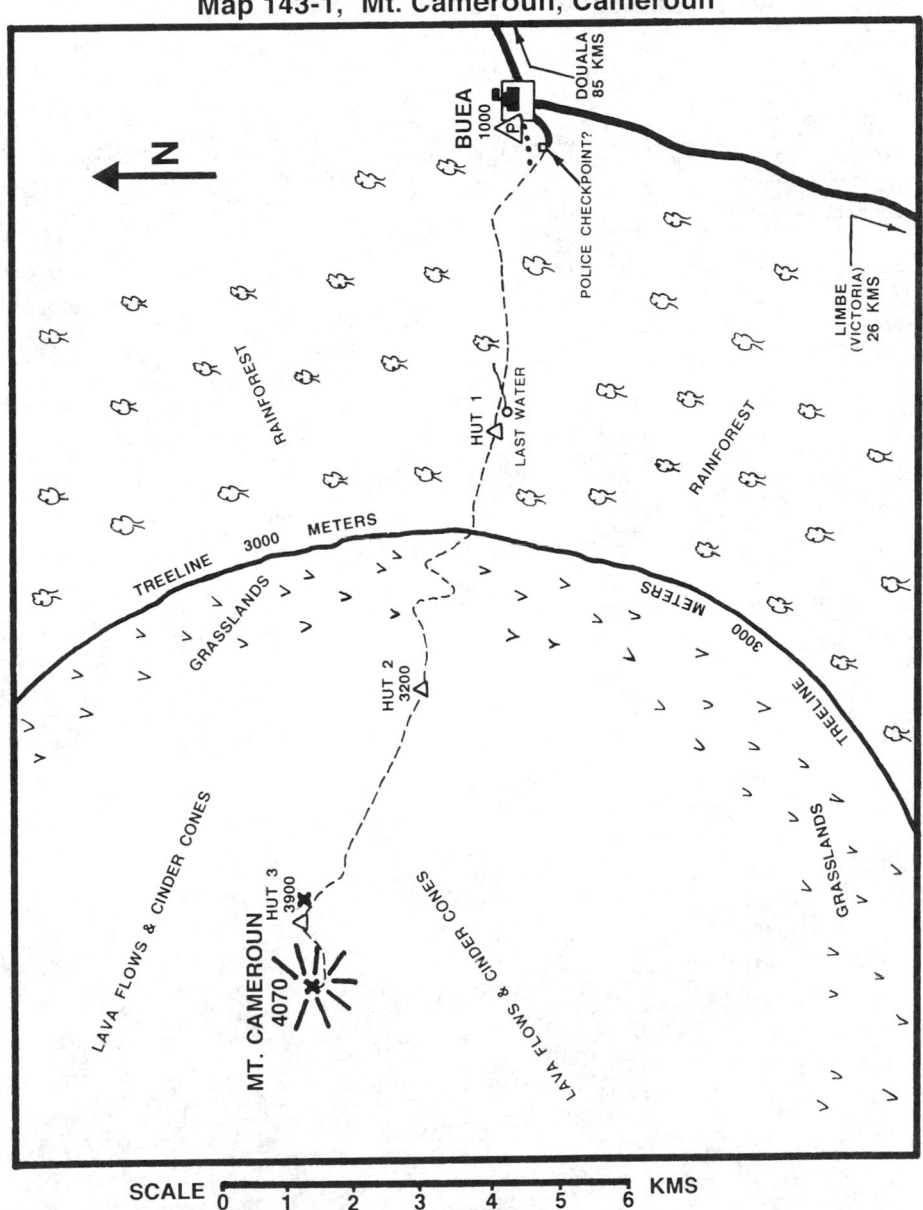

SCALE 0   1   2   3   4   5   6 KMS

cinder cone, there was just a breeze. The climbing and/or dry season is from mid or late
November to mid-May, but expect cloudy conditions on top for 365 days a year!

Maps Michelin Highway map *155, Africa Central and South,* 1:4,000,000; the map *Buea-Douala*
1:500,000, from the Geographique National, Av. Vogt, BP 157, Yauondi, or from car rental firms
in Douala or Yauondi; or TPC map L-3A, 1:500,000. Surely there are better mountain climbing
maps available by the year 2000. Ask at the tourist office in Douala or Buea, or inquire at the
French IGN.

Pico Malabo, Bioco Island, Equatorial Guinea

This island used to be called Fernando Poo when it was a colony of Spain, but today it's called Bioco and is part of the Republic of Equatorial Guinea. Independent Equatorial Guinea consists of the islands of Bioco and Pagal (Annobon) and part of the African mainland long known as Rio Muni. This small nation of 300,000 people has as its capital the small city of Malabo, located at the northern end of Bioco. It had a population of about 35,000 in the late 1990's. The country survives by exporting wood, cacao and coffee.

The first inhabitants of Bioco were migrants from the African mainland. Portuguese explorers seeking a route to India, found the island in 1471. Portugal retained control until 1778, then the island was ceded to Spain. Spain controlled it (with the exception of the period from 1827 to 1843, when Britain established a base on the island to combat slave trade) until 1968. From 1960 until 1968, representatives from Equatorial Guinea were seated in the national parliament in Madrid. From 1968 until 1979 the country and island was ruled by the elected Macias Regime. In that year Macias was overthrown and was later executed after a trial attended by international observers. Since that early stormy period, the situation in the country and island have slowly come back to normal. The official language is Spanish, but some French is spoken.

To go to Bioco, you must first have a visa. Get it at the Equatorial Guinea Mission at the UN in New York, or at the embassy of Equatorial Guinea in Madrid, Paris, Nigeria or Cameroun (perhaps in other nations too?). In Douala, getting a visa takes only one day, and costs about US$60. There are international flights to Malabo. They arrive twice weekly from Douala, Cameroun, and from Madrid, via Lagos, Nigeria. There are daily national flights from Bata on the mainland. There are bush taxis (shared taxis or colectivos) from Malabo to Luba and Riaba. These are the three major towns on the island.

Before you go, begin to take malaria suppressants a week or two in advance, as this is a health problem. Immunization for Yellow Fever is required, and all other available shots are recommended. Remember this is Africa, which was largely bypassed by the 20th Century. There are at least 4 hotels in Malabo. If you have a camera, you may need a permit to take pictures! Ask about that. Bioco has a wet tropical rain forest climate and Malabo gets about 250 cms (2.5 meters) of rain annually, so take an umbrella and/or adequate raingear. Once on the island, be sure to buy most of your food (especially canned foods) in Malabo if you can. Luba and Riaba have limited shopping facilities. Traveling to Bioco is for adventurous people only.

The highest mountain on Bioco is **Pico Malabo (or Santa Isabel)**, at 3011 meters. This is a very large shield volcano with a number of newer cinder cones dotting the surface along the axis running northeast-southwest. It has had 3 historic eruptions somewhere on the southeast flank in 1898, 1903 & 1923. San Joaquin and San Carlos are also shield volcanos which last erupted some time within the last 10,000 years (Holocene).

There is a road to the summit of Malabo as shown on the map. However, there's a radio tower and military installation on the summit and you will need permission to go there--which will likely not be given. See the Foreign Ministry or the radio station in Malabo. It's 15 kms from Malabo to the turnoff from the main highway, then 30 kms of dirt road to the top. In addition, there is an old trail and

Substituting for Bioco is this canyon in the Brandberg with the double potholes (Map 142, page 305).

Map 144-3, Pico Malabo, Bioco Island, Equatorial Guinea

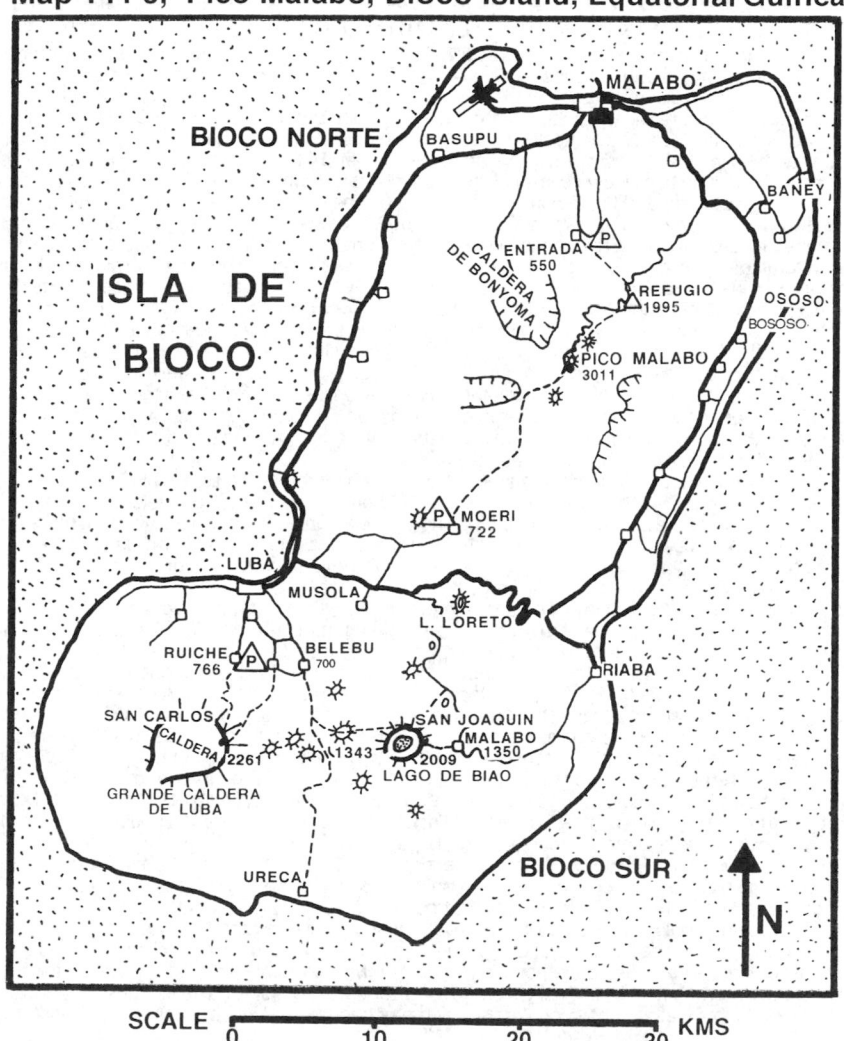

refugio on the north side. This trail begins at a place called Entrada, but the author guesses it will be overgrown because of lack of use. From the summit, another trail runs southwest to the village of Moeri at 722 meters elevation. You may be able to use this one, but better not get too close to the summit.

To climb to the rim of the Gran Caldera de Luba and **San Carlos** at 2261 meters, take a bush taxi to Luba, then either walk or look for a truck or bush taxi going to the village of Ruiche (or perhaps Belebu), a distance of about 6 kms. From Ruiche walk a trail to the eastern summit (a one day climb). From Belebu you can use another trail leading to the top of **San Joaquin** (with crater lake Lago de Biao) at 2009 meters. If you can find a truck going to the small village of Malabo on the eastern slopes of Biao, you can use what appears to be a good trail to the summit from the east (half day hike). The author has no idea how good these trails are, but they are shown on the maps listed below. They surely run through a rain forest and you'll likely need to hire a local to reach the top.

Maps *Isla de Bioco*, 1:50,000, a very good 4-part map; and a good map at 1:200,000 scale, both made by the IGN of Spain, Madrid. Buy or fotocopy any map you can before arriving as good maps may be hard to find locally; and the latest travel guidebook to Africa.

St. Helena, Ascension & Tristan da Cunha Islands, South Atlantic, United Kingdom

The 3 islands shown here are all part of a British colony commonly going under the name St. Helena. Besides St. Helena, Ascension, Tristan da Cunha, and 3 other small islets are part of the group. All these tiny volcanic islands are located in the South Atlantic between Southern Africa and South America. They are widely scattered from north to south, but all are close to 10° west longitude. The administrative capital is Jamestown on the island of St. Helena. The entire population of all the islands was 7200 in 1989. Most of them live on Ascension and St. Helena, with a few more on Tristan da Cunha. The colony has its own currency, the St. Helenian Pound (£S), which is always on par with the British £S. It's defense is the responsibility of the UK. The colony has one AM radio station and no TV--but maybe they have satellite TV now (?). The 550 telefones are linked by HF radio Ascension, then relayed by satellite to the rest of the world. At the ports of Jamestown and Georgetown, lighters are used to unload passengers and supplies. The colony has one passenger-cargo ship, and the only airport is the Wideawake Airstrip on Ascension. This facility has changed greatly since the Falklands (Malvinas) War in 1982, when it became an important stop-over between the UK and the war zone.

The biggest problem to hiking on any of these islands is just getting there. As of 1999, there were two RAF Tri-Star flights per/week from Brize Norton, Oxfordshire, UK, landing at Ascension to refuel for its onward flight to the Falklands Islands. It would seem you could stop there for a few days or a week, then continue on to the Falklands, or return to the UK on the next flight. But the author still has no further information regarding hotels or other accommodation on Ascension. There must be something there; with all the military around during and since the Falklands War, and with the occasional passing yacht--of which there are quite a few of these days.

Getting to St. Helena is a different matter. The man who wrote the article in National Geographic (see below) concerning Napoleon and St. Helena, got there on the R.M.S. St. Helena, which in 1982 provided a regular service between Avonmouth, England, and Cape Town, South Africa. It takes about a month for a one-way journey, stopping at St. Helena, and perhaps Tristan da Cunha (?) and Ascension (?). Since this is such a changing world, you'll have to check this one out; there might be something going there more regularly by now (?).

If you can get there, you should find some interesting walks around the island of Ascension. It's near the equator, so expect a warm climate. The highest summit is called **The Peak**, at 859 meters. It's the highest point on **Green Mountain**. From Georgetown to the end of the road just west of The Peak, is about 11 kms, then another 1 1/2 kms to the top. You may get a ride part way up (?). From the summit, there appears to be many livestock trails going in all directions. All over this island are cinder cones dotting the landscape, but none are active. According to the book, **Volcanos of the World**, the last eruptions on Ascension were sometime in the Holocene, or the last 10,000 years.

St. Helena is the oldest and most rugged island. It's volcanic in origin, but it's very much eroded and has many steep ridges. It's last eruptions were earlier than the Holocene. It receives only moderate amounts of rainfall, as one can see in the fotos in the February, 1982 issue of National Geographic (page 187). The highest summit is **Diana's Peak** at 818 meters. It should be an easy task to climb it from anywhere along the road circling the peak.

The best attraction on St. Helena, and in the entire colony, would be a visit to Longwood, the former residence of the exiled *Napoleon Bonaparte*. Napoleon was defeated by the British at Waterloo Ridge, Belgium, on June 18, 1815. Not long after that he requested asylum from the British. The British granted him asylum, but on St. Helena in the middle of absolutely nowhere! He arrived sometime late in the year 1815, and made his home at Longwood. He had servants and wrote a lot, but during the last 2 years of his life, he didn't leave the house. He died on May 5, 1821, after 5 1/2 years on the island. He was buried there, but in 1840 the French government moved his remains to Paris. A permanent French diplomat looks after Longwood today, which has been turned into a museum. It's also French property.

Tristan da Cunha will be the most difficult island to reach, but if you can manage to get there it should be interesting. Expect to find a few farmers raising sheep and growing potatoes. They have (had) a fish cannery at the only town of Edinburgh. The highest summit on the island, and in the colony, is **Queen Mary's Peak** at 2060 meters. This volcano erupted in about 1700 according to tree ring analysis. That was somewhere on the south flank. Then on 10/10/1961, this stratovolcano blewup somewhere on the north flank. It sent lava northward which did some damage, and everyone on the island was evacuated for a year and a half. Activity ended on 3/15/1962.

Maps   Separate maps of each island are printed by the DOS, at 1:25,000 and about 1:140,000 scale, buy at Stanfords, 12/14 Long Acre, London, Tele Inter+171-113306; also, see the **National Geographic**, February, 1982.

Map 145-3, St. Helena, Ascension & Tristan da Cunha Islands, South Atlantic, United Kingdom

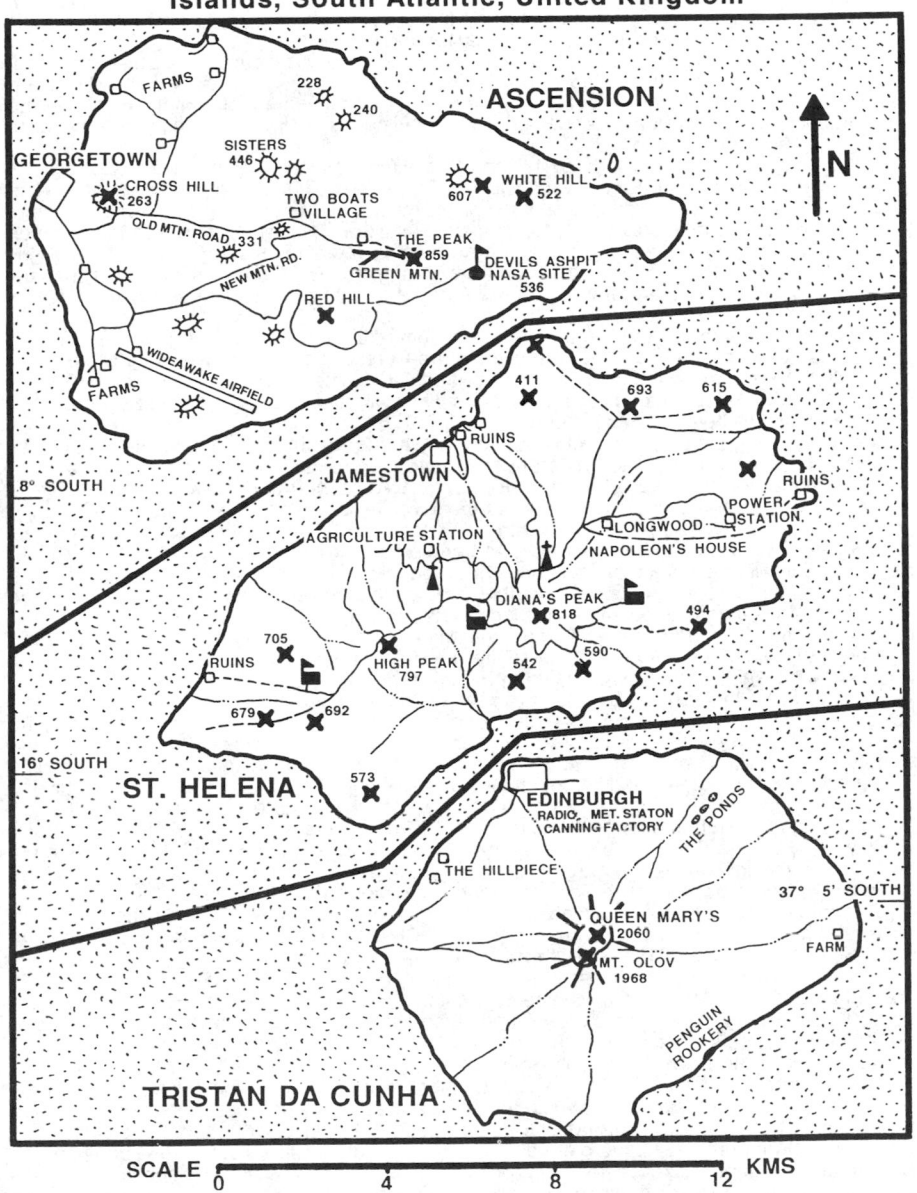

SCALE
0   4   8   12   KMS

Chapter 5--Asia

This chapter on Asia has a total of 93 maps. Included here is everything between Turkey, Russia, Kamchatka, China and Southeast Asia. In this edition, Korea, Japan, Taiwan, Indonesia and the Philippines have been placed in the chapter on The Pacific.

This is such a large area, it's impossible to make any generalizations on the mountain types, but there are some volcanos and a lot of mountain ranges, such as the Himalayas and Karakorum, which are folded and caused by the apparent movement of continents. In Turkey and Iran, there's a mixture of volcanos and crustal folding, as is also the case in the Kavkazian (Caucasus) Mountains of the USSR.

As for language barriers, for some this can be the most difficult region of the world to travel in. However, the Indian Sub-Continent (including Sri Lanka-Ceylon and Myanmar-Burma) were part of the British Empire, so every educated person those places speaks English. Because of the dozen or more languages in India, the Parliament in New Delhi uses English as the common tongue. English speaking travelers have no problem in India. Besides you can learn a little Hindi-Urdu rather quickly too! In Turkey, the second language is German, as a result of so many Turkish men working in Germany. All the rest of the countries involved use English as their second language.

If you're in India and take the time to learn some Hindi (it's Urdu in Pakistan), then it's sometimes useful as one travels to the west in the Persian and Arabic speaking areas. The reason is, there are many common Islamic words between Arabic, Persian, and Hindi-Urdu. It may be that with the revolution in Iran, all signs which western travelers can read, have been taken down, as has been the case in Libya.

As for climbing, the only real problems are in the areas with the very highest peaks such as in China, Tajikistan, Kyrgyzia, Pakistan, India and Nepal. Climbing in many places in the Greater Himalayas and Karakorum, involves getting official permission from one of the governments. For the really big 8000 meter peaks, you're required to have a liaison officer and pay him wages, as well as provide him with tent, food and clothing. All porters you might take above the snow line, must have clothing and equipment provided, as well as food and daily payment. This all requires a great deal of money, something small groups don't often have.

However, there's another way. The author traveled to all these areas by land, learned some of the languages involved, became knowledgeable about the customs, and then went into the mountains--simple as that! In Nepal he got a trekking permit, but went above the ends of trails, as many other people do. In Nepal, there are now many peaks you can officially climb with a trekking permit (see the book, **The Trekking Peaks of Nepal**).

If you're in North America, Europe or Japan, and write to someone in India or Pakistan and ask if permission is needed to trek--they'll probably say yes! But if you're there traveling by land and not importing food there are never any questions asked. The problem lies with those who want to bring food from home and who know nothing about the local language or customs. The author has been climbing in 28 different regions of the Himalayas, Karakorum, Pamirs, Tianshan & Kavkazia (always alone), and has only had permission to go to Concordia (near K-2), a trekking permit in Nepal, a permit to climb Pik Lenina in Kyrgyzia, and in 2 places in North Kavkazia. In other areas he has never been approached by anyone asking to see any kind of permit. This includes 9 other areas he visited in Kyrgyzia, 8 others in Kavkazia. In fact, he has spent many nights at lonely police posts high in the mountains.

Beginning in 1980, China began opening its door to foreign climbers, and the original 8 open mountains has now been expanded to many more. Climbing in Afghanistan looks difficult if not impossible as of 2000, and Iran is on the verge of opening up again.

Things have changed for the better in countries of the former USSR. It's lots easier now to get into all those countries, and now instead of going through a government, you simply contact a private outfitter and pay them to organize an expedition for you; or perhaps they or someone can help you get a visa as did the author. Read more about the author's experiences in the CIS states in the introduction to the former USSR

Stealing from tourists or climbers is *perhaps* becoming more common in Asia, but in Turkey and Korea, you should take extra precaution. The author has never met anyone who has had things stolen from his pack, but has encountered con-men twice--in Istanbul and Delhi. But where ever there are tourists, there are always crooks to follow. In Korea, people attempted to steal from the author on 3 occasions. In recent years, the author has heard some bad stories coming out of India regarding thieves, but SE Asia is normal, China seems OK, and there's few crimes against tourists in the former Soviet states. See the introduction to this book for ideas on how to prevent being a crime victum.

The 52-meter-high statue of The Buddha at Bamiyan, Afghanistan (see Koh-i-Baba Mountains, Map 218, page 476). It was built in the 5th Century AD, and as this books goes to press, and on March 1, 2001, the Taliban leaders of Afghanistan ordered it and other Buddhist treasures to be destroyed. They claim it's an idolatrous image contrary to Islam! If plans go ahead, it will be destroyed with rocket launchers and tanks.

Kazak family & yurt in the valley above Tian Chi in the Bogda Shan of Xinjiang Province of China.

Demirkazik, Aladaglari, Turkey

The mountains featured here are the Ala Mountains, or Ala Dag or Aladaglari, a small compact range within the greater Toros Daglari. The Toros Mountains are in the south central part of Turkey not far from the Mediterranean Coast. The Aladaglari is south of Kayseri and east of the small city of Nigde. The highest peak is Demirkazik at 3756 meters. This range is an uplifted mass of limestone which makes some rugged peaks, and many people enjoy rock climbing here. This is the third most popular climbing area in Turkey, after Agri Dagi and the Kaçkar.

To get there, first make your way to the city of Nigde; either from the coast and Mersin or Adana, or from the north and Kayseri. There are many buses going through this small city. Nigde has many small hotels near the bus terminal. Buy all your food in Nigde. At the bus station, look for one of about 8 or 10 daily buses going to, or passing through the town of Camardi (pron. Chamardi), which is near the western base of the Aladaglari. The distance is about 115 kms.

About 5 kms before arriving at Camardi, have the driver drop you off at the road leading to the village of Demirkazik. Demirkazik is 4 kms uphill to the east. Walk, and maybe get a ride part way. Walk east through Demirkazik and after about one km you'll come to the *dag ve kayak evi* (mountain and ski shelter) at about about 1575 meters. This is a small resort-type hotel open year-round which can accommodate up to about 80 people in various small rooms and will cost from about US$4 to US$12 a night depending on the room. Meals are served in the dining room.

To climb **Demirkazik**, walk south uphill from the dag evi (mtn. shelter) on a rough dirt road. This road passes a livestock watering trough, then some farms. Finally the track passes a water pipe & trough and ends at the mouth of Waterpipe Canyon. This is a good camping area with water entering a piping system from the spring in upper Waterpipe Canyon. Continue up the canyon east on sheep trails. Higher up veer left to avoid a dryfall, then go straight up the former glacier valley. Finally the trail veers north and goes straight up a steep gully. At the top of the gully and at the pass marked 3300 meters, is a cairned trail-of-sorts running northwest along the ridge to the summit. This is steep in places, so if there's snow or ice on this smooth limestone slickrock ridge, it can be dangerous.

On 10/2/1994, the author camped at Waterpipe Canyon, hid his pack and everything behind some rocks, then reached the summit in 2 1/2 hours. He was back at his pack after 4 1/4 hours, round-trip. Most people will want double these times. He now wishes he had gone down to the north past Teke Pinari (spring) and made a loop hike back to his pack.

You can also reach these peaks from the village of Cukurbag. June and July would be the ideal time to climb, with more snow and water around than in late summer or fall. Most trekkers end up in the Seven Lakes Basin, south, southeast of Demirkazik. Guides are available at the Safak Pansion (hotel-US$3 a night) on the highway west of Cukurbag. Expect to find shepherds and sheep in the high valleys. There's only one small shop in Cukurbag and Demirkazik, so buy your food and supplies

Demikazik as seen from the village of Cukurbag.

Map 146-1, Demirkazik, Aladaglari, Turkey

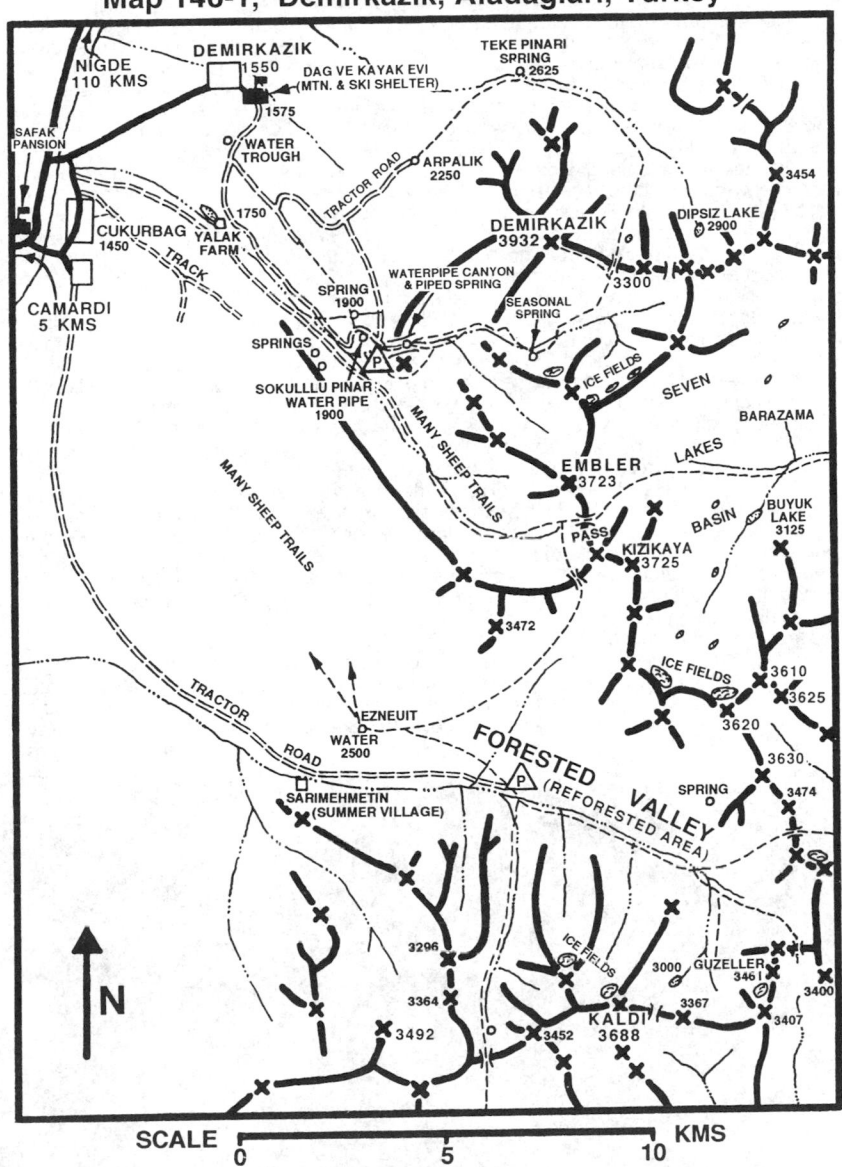

SCALE: 0 — 5 — 10 KMS

N

before arriving in this area.
Maps *Nigde, F-9,* 1:200,000, from the Army Map Service, London; or *Aladaglari, 1:25,000,* by Bozkurt Ergor--buy in Kayseri Tourist Office (?); and the guidebooks, **Trekking in Turkey,** Lonely Planet; and **The Ala Dag**, Cicerone Press.

Ana Doruk Peak, Erciyes Dagi, Turkey

Ana Doruk at 3917 meters, is the highest pinnacle on top of a much larger mountain known as Erciyes Dagi. This is an old and eroded volcano with a number of jagged peaks clustered at the summit area. There are also a number of younger volcanic craters surrounding the mountain. The last eruption from a flank crater was in about 253 AD. This was probably just northwest of Erciyes. This massif is located directly south of the city of Kayseri in central Turkey. Kayseri is on the main rail line and highway running across Asia. It's a tourist destination and the jumping off point to the famous Goreme Valley to the west.

To climb this mountain begin in Kayseri, which has many inexpensive hotels. First, look up the tourist office which is in the city center immediately east of the old citadel. While there, you can get information about buses, hotels, and the map listed below.

There are 2 ways to get to **Erciyes**. One is to take a city bus south about 10 kms to the suburb of Hisarcik. These buses begin from a little bus stand less than half a km southeast of the tourist office and run about every half hour. From the last bus stop in Hisarcik, begin walking, then hitch hike 14 kms up to the dag ve kayak evi (mountain & ski shelter), at about 2150 meters. This mostly-winter ski center consists of at least one large hotel, which is open year-round, and an assortment of other buildings--maybe hotels, a mountaineer's refuge, restaurant, or employee housing (?). The highway from Hisarcik over the mountain to Develi is paved but doesn't have a lot of traffic. A second option would be to take a taxi direct from Kayseri. If you're with a group this would be the best option. The tourist office could help you find a taxi. Buy all your food in Kayseri before leaving.

From the kayak evi (ski lodge), climb west up along the ski lift road. It'll take 2 1/2 hours to get to the top of the lift (with a large pack), then another hour to reach a good campsite at about 2850 meters. There's a spring near this campsite, and another one further up the valley to the west at about 3000 meters; that spring drains into a cement ditch. Otherwise the mountain is dry in late summer, except for perpetual snow & small glacier high on the peak. Because there's normally no running water high on the mountain, it's best to climb between late May and July, so there will be snow to melt for drinking water. The normal route to the summit is from this east-side campsite or the top of the ski lift. Strong climbers can make the ascent in one long day from the kayak evi, but for most it takes 2 days. See the map for the route to the summit. It involves getting up on the southeast ridge, then walking northwest to the summit. Easy climb.

To traverse the mountain, climb north over the ridge & pass at 3340 meters, located west of the campsite & ski lifts, then walk north, then west around another ridge and down to a good campsite with water at 2750 meters; or to a nearby shelter at 2684 meters. From that shelter, a 4WD road heads downhill to the north. At about 2100 meters is a place where water is put into a pipeline. Further down is a gravel quarry where you can likely get a lift down to Sakar and another city bus back to Kayseri.

Beginning 9/29/1994, the author walked from the kayak evi to the summit, then to the dry campsite

Erciyes and north ridge from the author's camp at 2980 meters.

Map 147-1, Ana Doruk Peak, Erciyes Dagi, Turkey

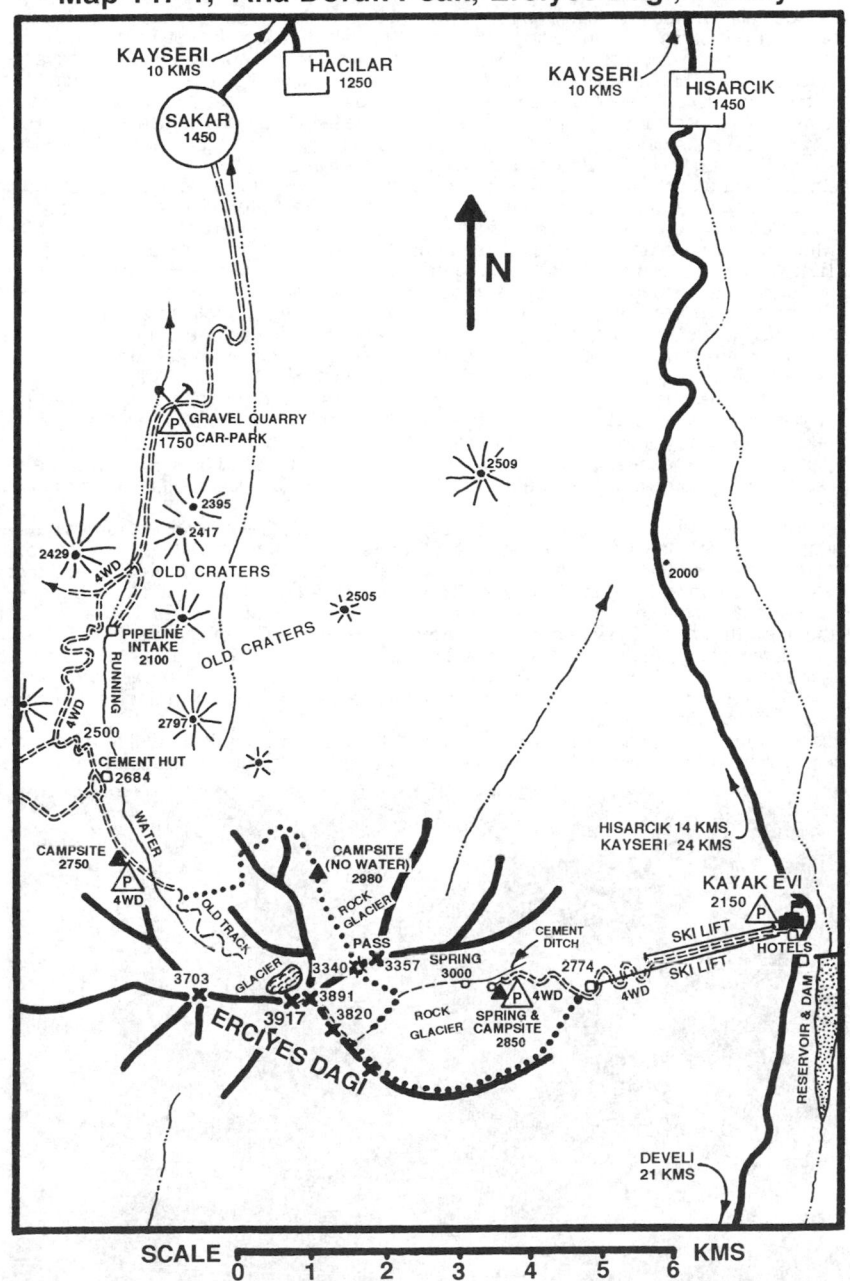

at 2980 meters, all in 7 hours. Next day he walked down to the gravel quarry in 3 hours, and got a lift in a dump truck all the way to Kayseri.

Maps *Erciyes Dagi,* 1:80,000, by Bozkurt Ergor, free from the tourist office in Kayseri; and the guidebook, **Trekking in Turkey**, Lonely Plant; and a travel guidebook to Turkey.

Volkan Nemrut, Turkey

The mountain featured on this map is called Nemrut Dagi at 2935 meters; but because there are 2 mountains with this same name in Turkey, this one will be called Volkan Nemrut, or Nemrut Volcano. The other Nemrut Dagi is in south central Turkey near Adiyaman and Malatya, and is famous for its archeological ruins. This Nemrut is located in eastern Turkey just west of Lake Van and immediately north of the small city of Tatvan. Tatvan is located on the main east-west international railway line which crosses Asia. It's here that trains are rolled onto large ferry boats and carried across Lake Van to the city of Van on the other side. There are many buses going to/from Agri, which is located to the north and on the main international highway running across Asia.

Nemrut is a stratovolcano with a large caldera. Inside are several lakes, the biggest of which has crystal clear water and covers nearly half the floor of the crater. The south rim has more obsidian than any volcano this writer has ever seen. The last eruption was in 1441 AD somewhere on the north flank, but there have been 16 recorded explosions from the crater since 7769 BC. There's a steep 4WD road running up the east side to the crater, and you can hire a 4WD vehicle in Tatvan to take you up. It's about 28 kms by road from Tatvan.

To climb **Volkan Nemrut** directly from Tatvan, make your way to this small city and stay in one of several hotels, the best of which was the *Hotel Ustun*. It was one of the cheapest, and cleanest hotels the author found in Turkey, and a real bargain at US$4.50 a night (9/1994). It's located 150 meters east and downhill from the Post, Telefone & Telegraph (PTT).

Here's what the author did on 9/21/1994. With an early morning start, he walked to the western part of Tatvan and climbed to the top of a limestone hill as shown. From there he could see the route up Nemrut. He then walked straight toward the highest part of the caldera rim. He stayed off the roads, because he was nervous about being kidnapped by members of the PKK! Because of political problems with the Kurds, the mountain was actually off limits to tourists at that time.

Walking to Nemrut cross-country is very easy. There are no trees or forests, so you just set you sights in the top and walk. A little less than 4 hours after leaving the hotel, he arrived on the south rim. Peaks on the north rim seem a little higher. He ate lunch, then followed a good sheep & goat trail down to the biggest lake. The water tasted good, and the lake is big enough so that sheep & goats likely won't pollute it too much. He then returned, arriving at the police checkpoint on the main highway after 7 1/4 hours walk-time. The police were so concerned about the safety of tourists, they held him there a few minutes, while waiting for a police car from Tatvan to come to drive him back to the hotel. They were really bending over backwards making things safe for visitors in those troubled times. However, as of late 2000, things seem calm in Turkey with the capture and trial of the leader of the PKK in 1999.

This is normally a one day climb from Tatvan, but you could camp in the caldera next to the lake with plenty of good water. You will likely get a lift on a tractor or truck along the road

Vulkan Nemrut's caldera lake as seen from the most-easterly of the peaks marked 2900 meters.

Map 148-1, Volkan Nemrut, Turkey

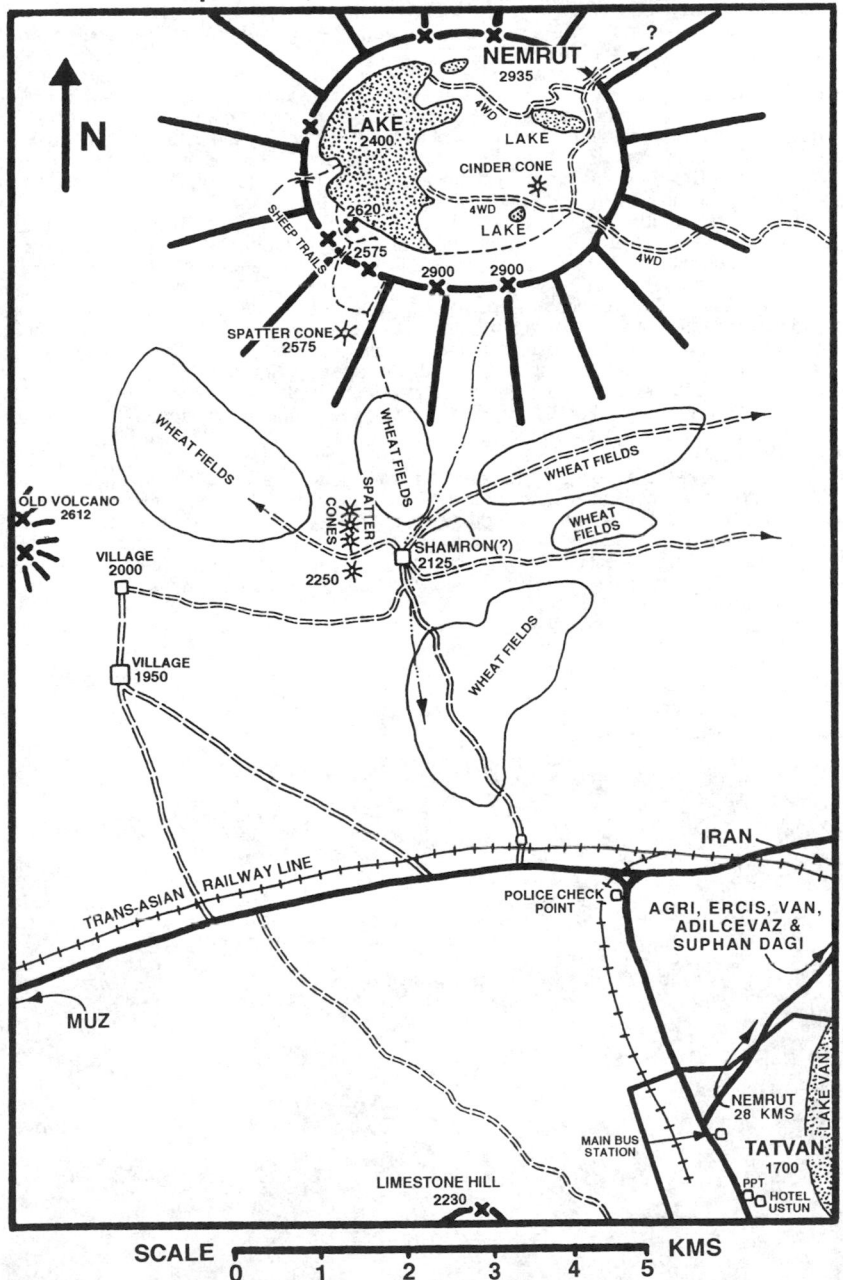

leading to the village of Shamron. Climb here from June though October.

Maps Turkish highway map from any tourist office; and possibly the TPC map *G-4B,* 1:500,000; or DMA or maybe JOG (?) map NJ 38-??, 1:250,000; and a travel guidebook to Turkey.

Suphan Dagi, Turkey

Located in extreme eastern Turkey, not far from the Iranian border and just north of Lake Van, is Turkey's second highest mountain. This is Suphan Dagi at 4434 meters. It's also located about 200 kms southwest of Agri Dagi, or Mt. Ararat.

Suphan Dagi is an old volcano having had it's last eruptions sometime in the Holocene, or in the last 10,000 years. Inside its summit crater is a small snow or ice field, and the most recent or youngest cone; or perhaps a lava dome (?). See the foto below which the author took on 10/13/1975.

You can reach this area by bus from Agri, located to the north on the main Trans-Asian Highway (E-23). There are several buses daily. Get off at Adilcevaz. Or take a bus from the west and the cities of Elazig or Diyarbakir heading to Tatvan, located on the western end of Lake Van. Or take a train to Tatvan. Tatvan is on the main rail line linking Turkey and Iran.

Tatvan is the best jumping-off point for the climb to Suphan Dagi. There you'll find several inexpensive hotels (see the previous map on Nemrut) and a good market place or bazaar. From Tatvan, take a bus in the direction of Agri or other points north or east, and get off a Adilcevaz. 'Cevaz is a larger town with several stores, but probably no hotel (?).

Climbing **Suphan Dagi** is simple. Depending on what time you arrive at the base of the mountain, it should normally take 2 days to reach the summit and return--from Adilcevaz. From just east of 'Cevaz, walk north on a dirt road heading in the direction of the mountain. You might also hire a taxi and save 2-3 hours walking. After about 6 or 8 kms, the road splits. The one on the right goes to a small village at the base of the mountain with a good spring and tap water nearby. This village is named Kef Kalesi, or Yildiz (?) at 2200 meters. The women in this village appear to have just come from the Ukraine or some place to the north, with very light colored skin, and having a Russian peasant look about them.

From this village, there are many sheep & goat trails going in every direction, but just walk north straight toward a minor canyon and the summit. This country is not rugged, nor is it forested. In fact, there's not a tree in sight. Walking cross-country on the grassy slopes is easy.

At about 2800 and 3000 meters, are 2 springs. This is the last or highest water on the mountain. The upper part is steep, but not difficult to climb. Camp as high was possible. *Here's a warning:* there are many sheep & goats on the mountain, usually tended by a very curious teenage boy, so don't leave an unguarded camp, especially at lower altitudes.

Starting on 10/11/1975, the author took a bus from Tatvan to 'Cevaz (2 hours), walked for 1 1/2 hours and camped near a stream at 1900 meters. Day 2, he hiked about 7 hours with 5-6 liters of water up to 3200 meters and camped. On Day 3, he reached the summit in 1 2/3 hours, and returned to camp in 40 minutes, then down to Yildiz in 2 hours, and another 2 1/2 hours walking back to Adilcevaz. About 14 1/2 hours total walk-time round-trip from 'Cevaz. Late that afternoon, he got a lift in a dump truck back to Tatvan.

The summit and lava dome of Suphan Dagi on 10/13/1975.

Map 149-1, Suphan Dagi, Turkey

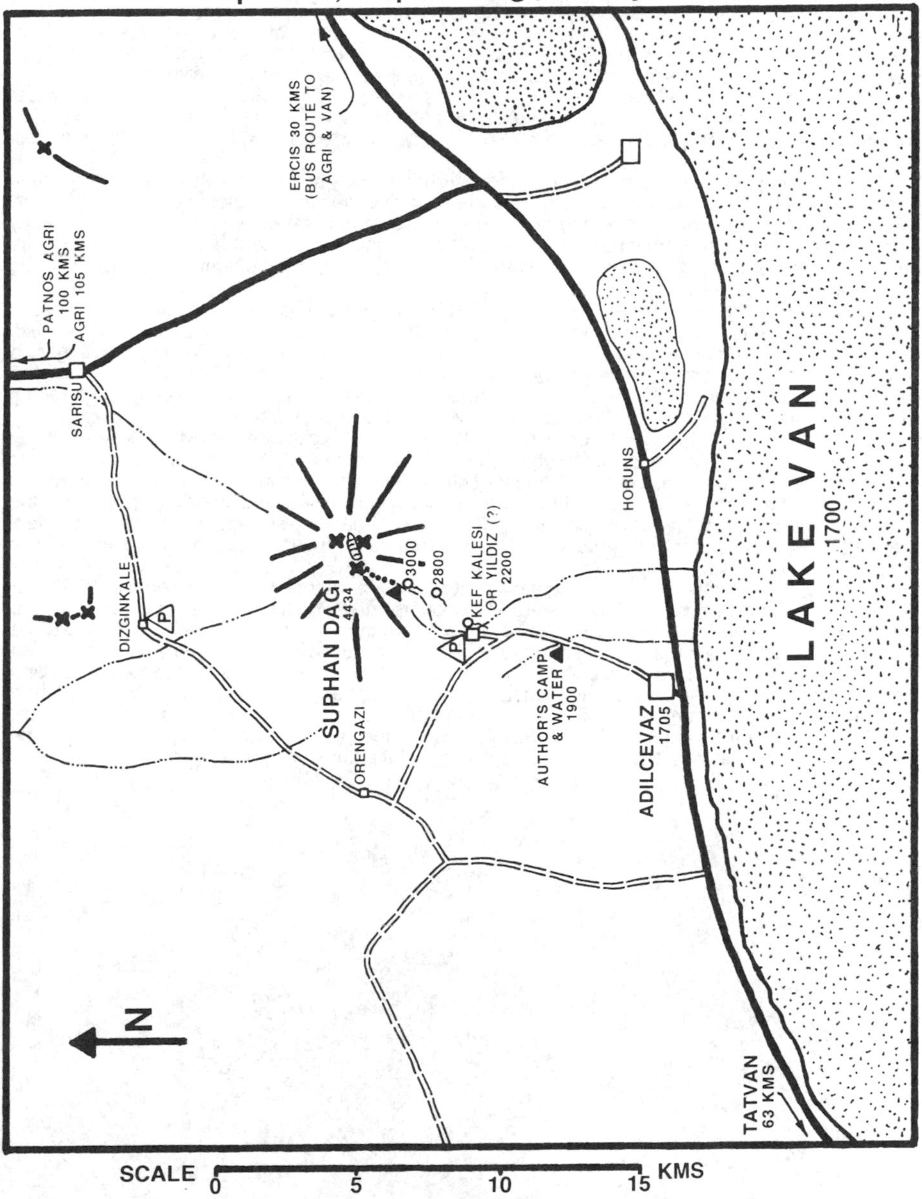

SCALE 0 ... 5 ... 10 ... 15 KMS

LAKE VAN 1700

ERCIS 30 KMS (BUS ROUTE TO AGRI & VAN)

PATNOS AGRI 100 KMS
AGRI 105 KMS

SARISU

DIZGINKALE

SUPHAN DAGI 4434

P 3000

P 2800

KEF KALESI OR YILDIZ (?) 2200

ORENGAZI

AUTHOR'S CAMP & WATER 1900

HORUNS

ADILCEVAZ 1705

TATVAN 63 KMS

N

In winter, this area can have tremendous snowfall, but for the most part, this is a rather dry country. The normal climbing season is from June through October.

Maps TPC map *G-4B,* 1:500,000; or DMA or JOG (?) map *NJ 38-??,* 1:250,000; and the book, **Trekking in Turkey**, Lonely Planet; and the latest travel guidebook to Turkey.

Kaçkar Dagi, Kaçkar Daglari, Turkey

Here is some of the best hiking and climbing opportunities in Turkey. It's in the Kaçkar Daglari (Mountains) of extreme northeast Turkey. They're located due east of Trabzon and Rize, north of Erzurum, and southwest of Artvin. The highest peak is Kaçkar Dagi (Peak) at 3932 meters and the rocks are mostly granite and crystalline-type which can make some challenging climbs.

One thing to keep in mind is that these mountains are near the Black Sea, therefore the northwest side of the range is more humid and a little greener than the eastern slopes. During stable weather conditions, the higher peaks often poke up above the clouds which bank-up against the northwest slopes.

Another thing to be aware of as you wander through these mountains; there are many small temporary shepherd communities in the high pastures during the summer months. Local herdsmen take their livestock (and families) to the high meadows for summer grazing, and at the same time, milk some animals to produce cheese and butter. It's possible you might buy some of their dairy products. Also leave someone guarding your camp while away, or take your tent down and hide everything before climbing.

If you decide to come in from the northwest, first head east from Trabzon and Rize to the town of Camlihemsin near the coast. From there take a bus to the hot springs resort of Ayder. This is a small tourist town with 7 or 8 hotels and several shops where you can buy all or most of your trekking food (it's best to buy supplies in some larger city however). From Ayder, there's normally one truck per day heading upcanyon to the south toward either Yukari Kavron or to near Yukari Caymakcur. However, this is not the recommended approach if you want to climb Kaçkar.

If your goal is to climb Kaçkar, come in from the east side. Take one of several buses per day running from Erzurum to the tourist town of Yusufeli, which has many hotels and shops. In the summer months, there's one minibus (dolmus) each afternoon running from Yusufeli to the village of Barhal (Altiparmak), which has about 2 hotels and 2 shops; then the same dolmus continues on to the village of Yaylalar, just northeast of Kaçkar. In 1994, Yaylalar had one small hotel or pansion above a pretty good little dukon (store). This same dolmus returns to Yusufeli beginning at 7am the next morning.

It's about 12 kms from Yaylalar to the base of **Kaçkar**. The author did this hike on 9/24/1994 in 2 1/2 hours. From the campsite at 2700 meters, it's recommended you climb up the mountain a ways to the south for a good look at the peak & route. Then climb north up along the stream to and beyond the big rock slide east of the summit. Further up, veer left or west, and climb along side a snow field, then up the easy-to-climb east face. You can return via a trail-of-sorts on the west side, and the canyon and stream south of the peak. This climb is easier than it first appears. The author hid his pack, then made the summit in 2 hours; less than 4 hours round-trip from the campsite at the mountain's base. On Day 2, he spent 4 1/3 hours exploring and fotographing the basin & lakes to the east of camp, then walked back to Yaylalar in 2 1/3 hours. Two day total hike-time was just over 13 hours. In early

South side of Kaçkar left and the canyon leading to the its summit in the middle.

Map 150-1, Kaçkar Dagi, Kaçkar Daglari, Turkey

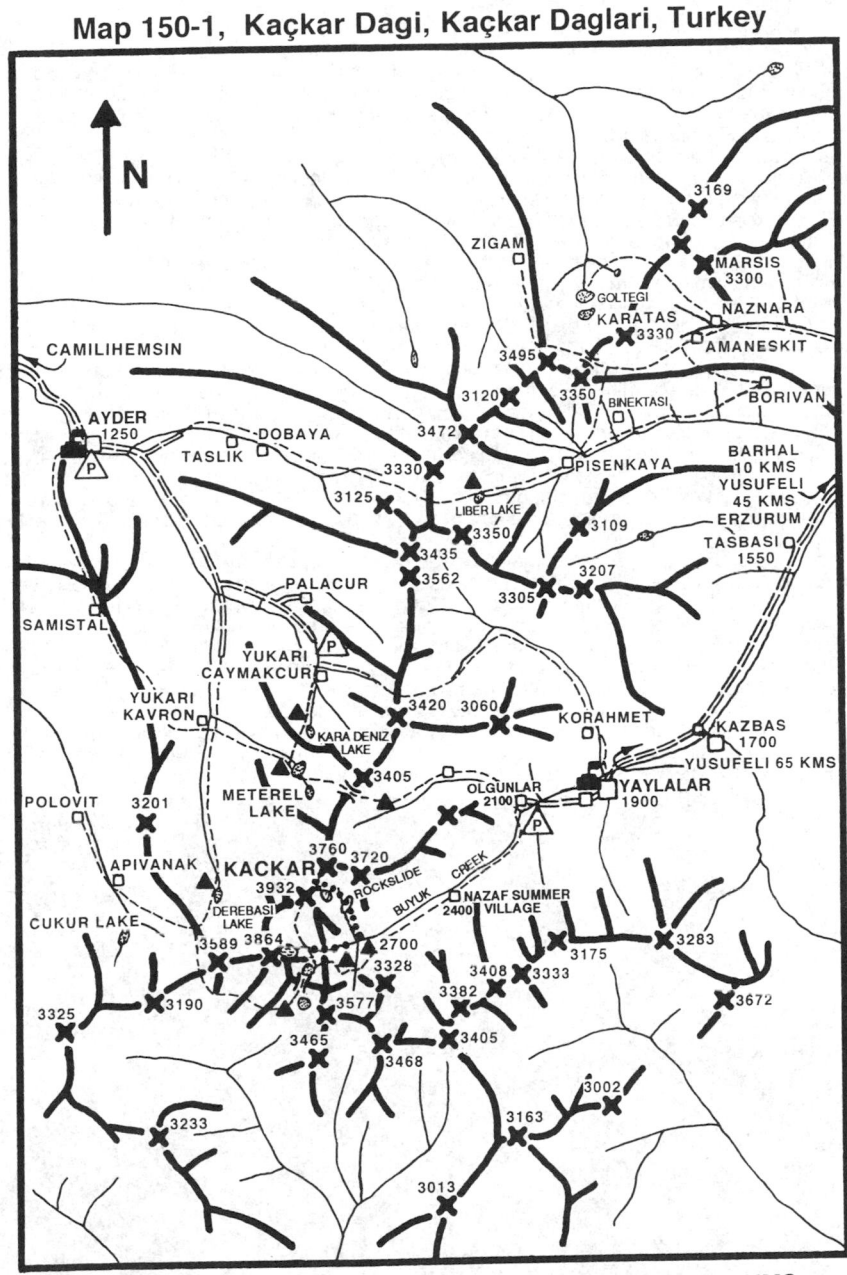

SCALE 0 5 10 15 KMS

summer, you'll need ice ax & crampons. Climb from June through October.

Maps *Kaçkarlar,* 1:80,000, if available; TPC map *F-4D,* 1:500,000; and the book, **Trekking in Turkey,** Lonely Planet; and the latest travel guidebook to Turkey.

Agri Dagi (Mt. Ararat), Turkey

Agri Dagi at 5137 meters, is the highest mountain in Turkey. It's located in the extreme eastern part of the country, only a few kms from the borders of Iran and Armenia. The Christian world knows this mountain as Mt. Ararat. Southeast of Agri Dagi is another symmetrical cone called Kucuk (Little) Agri Dagi at 3925 meters. Both of these peaks are clearly visible to those traveling overland across Asia on the Trans-Asian Highway E-23.

Agri Dagi is a dormant stratovolcano; according to one source it had its last eruption in 1840 (?). However, according to the Global Volcanism Program, the last eruption was sometime during the Holocene. Perhaps there was activity from one of the cinder cones between the 2 main volcanos (?).

Much of this updated information comes from the book by Dubin & Lucas listed below. Because Agri Dagi is located just a few kms from the former Soviet border, it was necessary to secure permission to climb it. By the mid-1990's, apparently the same policy existed as during Soviet times, but hopefully in the near future, the permit system will end.

Here's the latest information the author has. Individuals should first contact the Turkish Embassy in their country. Ask for the one-page, 2 line mountaineer's application (not the 5 page *ark hunter's* questionnaire!). Do this 6 months in advance if possible. The embassy will send it to their Ministry of Foreign Affairs in Ankara. If you end up leaving home without final permission, go to the Ministry of Tourism & Culture or the Ministry of Interior in Ankara. Apparently one of these organization will contact the jandarma (police) in Dogubayazit (Now here's some bad news--as of 10/4/2000, someone at the Turkish Embassy in Washignton DC told the author they haven't been giving out permits lately even though things are rather tranquillo in regards to the PKK, and the cold war is far behind us!).

Another way to get permission to climb, which may be the easiest--but most costly, is to contact one of several tour operators in Istanbul. Trek Travel and Trek Kosmos were 2 operators in the 1980's. The Turkish Embassy should be able to give you updated information and/or tour agents you can contact.

For those on their own, once you get to Dogubayazit, it's necessary to hire a guide, rent a radio and usually pack mules. In former times, one task of the guide was to keep you from spying on the Russians or the NATO spies on the north side of Agri, so everyone must stay together as a group (this information seems a little outdated!). Once everything is secured, you will have to hire a taxi to go 18 kms from Dogubayazit to Ganikor (or thereabouts) and the trailhead. Mules will be found in Ganikor, if you want them. Normally 5 days of food is taken, but it can be done in 3 long days. For 2 people, the total cost will be about US$400, or US$200 each. For 5 people, it'll come to about US$120 each.

Normally it's one day to Camp I, another day to Camp II, one day up and back to either camp, another day back to Dogubayazit--3 to 5 days, depending on your physical condition, ability at higher altitudes and what time you get started. Lots of people are climbing the mountain these days. The author has passed this way 8 or 10 times, but still hasn't climbed it.

Agri Dagi (Mt. Ararat) left, Kucuk Agri Dagi right, as seen from the Trams Asian Highway.

Map 151-2, Agri Dagi (Mt. Ararat), Turkey

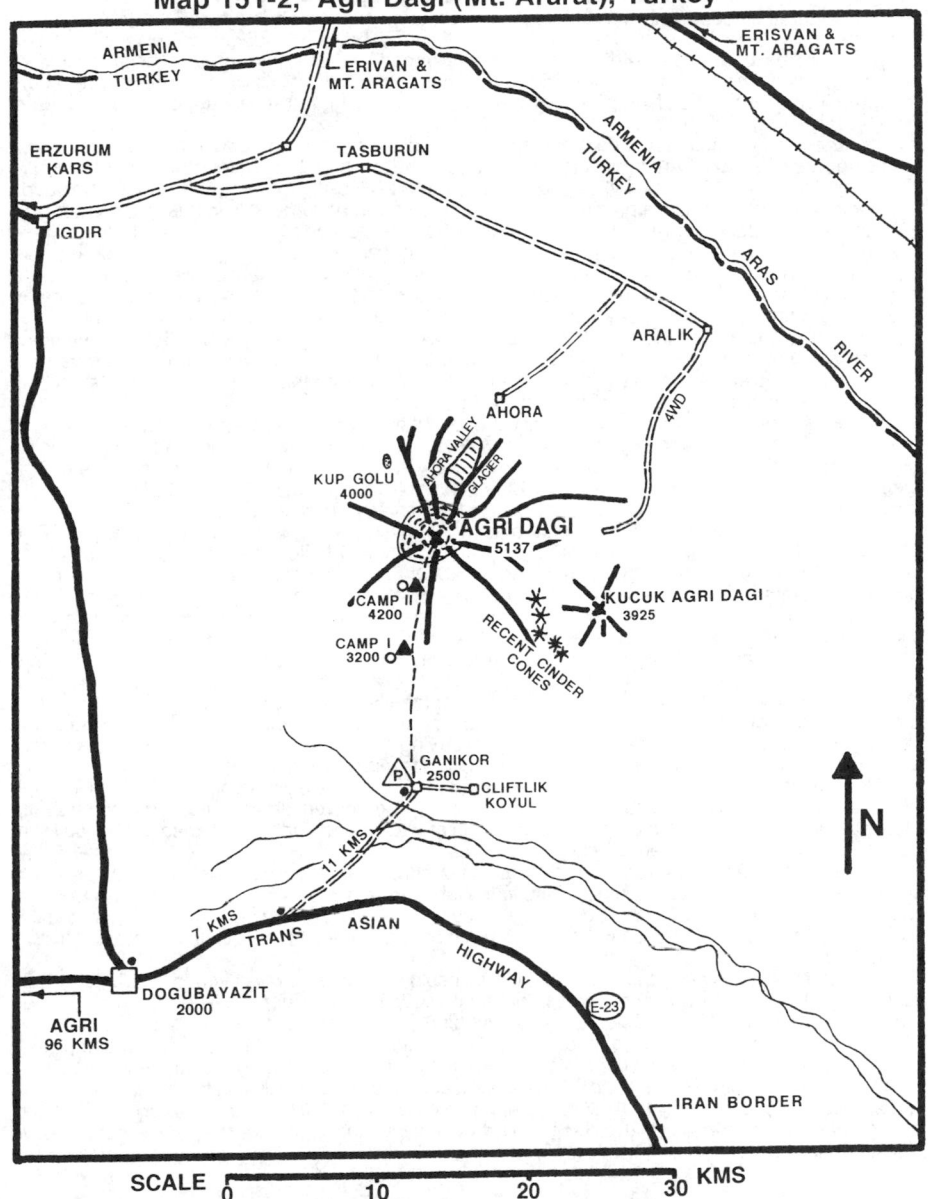

Most climb during July, August and September. This is the wetter season, but it's a dry area, so it can't be that wet. In summer, you'll encounter snow on this southern route halfway between Camp II and the summit. Take an ice ax, boots with a good tread and warm cloths (crampons are generally not needed in summer).

Maps DMA map *Dogubayazit, C-17,* 1:200,000; TPC map *G-4B,* 1:500,000; Turkish tourist highway map; the book **Trekking in Turkey,** Lonely Plant; and the latest travel guidebook to Turkey.

Uludoruk (Resko), Cilo Daglari, Turkey

In the extreme southeastern corner of Turkey are a number of mountains around 4000 meters. The highest peaks are in the Cilo Daglari (Cilo Mountains). They are Uludoruk, sometimes known as Gelyasm (or Resko) at 4136 meters; and Buzul (or Suppadurek) at 4116 meters. These mountains are very rugged with the largest glaciers in Turkey on their northern slopes. Another prominent mountain range is the Sat Daglari, just to the southeast. These ranges appear to be made of sedimentary rocks (?).

As far as real tough and rugged mountains go, these are the best in Turkey, but they are almost unknown. One reason there's so little information about them is they're located in southeastern Turkey, and that part of the country is to Turkey as Siber is to Russia. It's high, wild and undeveloped. Another reason is its close proximity to the borders of Iran and Iraq. It's in this 3-corners region that the dominant population is Kurdish. For many years now, especially since the 1970's through the late 1990's, there has been a war between the Turks & Iraqis and Kurds, and an influx of refugees from both Iran and Iraq. Along with a refugee problem is a separatist movement as well and it has been declared off limits to foreigners since the 1970's. However, with the capture of the Kurdish leader in 1999, there is reason to hope these mountains will again be open to climbers in the early 2000's.

The author hasn't been there but has passed by Lake Van and Agri Dagi just to the north on many occasions. Therefore one of the main sources of information for this area is from the guide book listed below. Problem is, they were in Turkey during the time when this corner was off limits, so their information is 2nd hand. That makes this 3rd hand information!

As far as getting into this area, you'll just have to make inquiries before leaving home and hope to arrive at the right time. Turkish road maps show Highway E-24 as being the second most important highway route between Turkey and Iran & Iraq. However, in times of trouble, it could be that all international traffic across these borders comes to a hault. If traffic is moving, you'll be able to take minibuses or buses into part of this area, at least to Hakkari and Yuksekova.

If you ever get the opportunity to hike or climb, you'll have 2 different ways to enter the **Cilo Range**. Perhaps the easiest is from the northwest. From Van & Lake Van, drive, take a bus or hitch hike toward Hakkari, the largest town in the area. About 20 kms before arriving at Hakkari, stop at a police checkpost called Zap Karakolu. From there cross the Zap River on a bridge and walk upcanyon southeast past the 2 small villages of Diz and Kursin and into the upper valley. This route will put you on the glaciated north slope of **Uludoruk** and **Buzul**.

The second way into the Cilo begins in Yuksekova. After buying all the food you'll need, either take a minibus, hire a taxi or try hitch hiking south and toward the town of Daglica, only 10 kms from the Iraqi border. After riding about 1 1/2 hours get off at the Istazin village bus stop, then walk north to the small village of Serpil. From there, a trail heads northwest over a pass and into the heart of the range. There's also the possibility of entering or leaving the mountains via the village (or summer encampment) of Orisa. Apparently it's possible to hire a taxi in Yuksekova and be driven there.

Once in the mountains, you can either trek around to various valley locations or go climbing. One location that's used as a base camp is near the summer nomadic encampment called Mergan Zoma (Mergan Meadow). From this base, you'll have lots of glacier and north face routes to choose from, but those routes are mostly very difficult.

Apparently the easy normal route to the summit of **Uludoruk** begins with a camp southeast of the peak at a meadow called Gehi Zoma. Getting to Gehi appears to be an easy one day walk from the road on the south via the village of Serpil. While you can spend up to a week just trekking around this range, it appears about 2-3 days will get you to Uludoruk and back to the Istazin bus stop. This will depend on when you arrive.

With the higher elevations and glaciers, there should be plenty of water around. If climbing, take along proper rock and ice climbing equipment, especially if coming in from the north. July through September seems to be the logical time for climbing. During the summer season expect to find shepherds and livestock in the high meadows. This means someone will have to watch camp while climbing; or you'll need to take your tent down and hide everything while on the mountain. You may also be able to buy milk, yogurt, butter, cheese or meat from shepherds while in the mountains.

Maps Map *F-17(no name?)*, 1:200,000, or DMA map *Mosul, 8,* 1:800,000; and possibly the TPC map *G-4B,* 1:500,000; and the book, **Trekking in Turkey**, Lonely Planet; and the latest travel guidebook to Turkey for updates on traveling to this area.

Map 152-3, Uludoruk (Resko), Cilo Daglari, Turkey

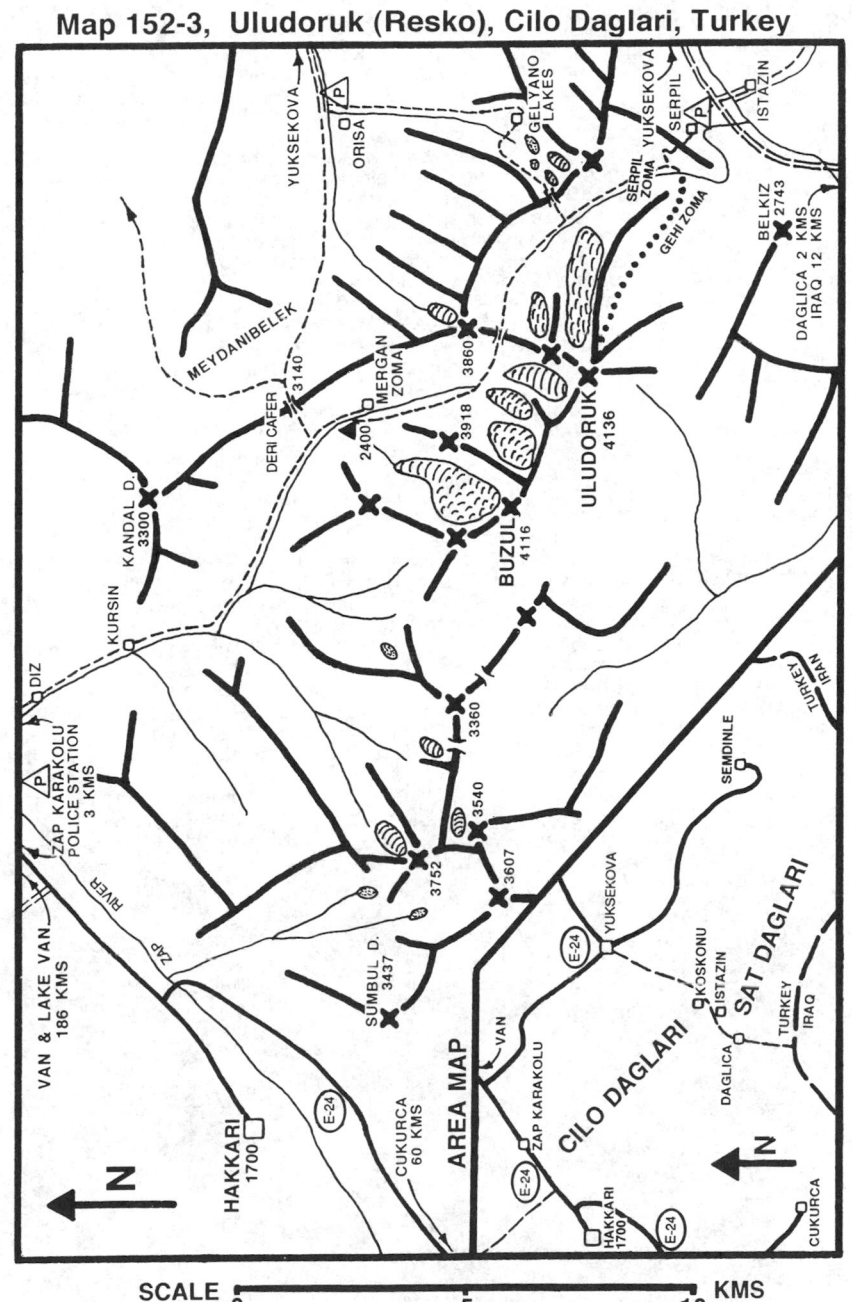

SCALE 0 ———— 5 ———— 10 KMS

Jabal Nabi Shayib, Central Plateau, Yemen

The highest mountain in Yemen and all of Arabia, is Jabal Nabi Shayib rising to 3621 meters. It's located about 25 kms southwest of San'a, the capital of Yemen. This mountain, as well as all the high central plateau of Yemen, is made of old horizontal volcanic lavas. After the volcanic activity stopped, the region was uplifted and erosion created lots of mesa-like mountains. Nabi Shayib is the highest remnant on a high volcanic plateau, but it is not a volcano.

Getting there from San'a is easy and fast. Here's what the author did. On 1/30/1999, he first went to the Bab Al Yemen (Yemen Gate) on the south side of the walled city to find a bus heading west toward Manakha and Hudayda. However, the big long distance buses don't stop at the town of Matnah, so he took a mini bus from near Bab Al Yemen running due west along Az-Zubayri Street. This main street is actually the beginning of the highway running to Manakha and Hudayda.

Right at the western edge of San'a, he stopped at the taxi & mini bus stand called *Taxi Mahatta Asera* (Asera Taxi Station). He soon found a shared or group taxi going to Matnah, about 35 kms away. That ride took 40 minutes and cost about US$1. At Matnah, he had breakfast of chai leban (milk tea), bread and bananas, then walked about 500 meters southwest out of town to a road running up the south side of **Nabi Shayib**. With his full pack (he had no idea how long it would take to climb the mountain), he walked all the way to the village at 3075 meters, then continued west along a good sheep & goat trail across the lower face of the mountain to the villages at 3200 meters (sorry for the lack of names). From there he walked up the good graded road toward the summit. About one km from the top, he hid his big pack in some rocks, and headed up. At the summit is a radar site. Although there were no signs of any kind warning people of this forbidden zone, guards took the film from the author's camera, even though he hadn't taken any pictures in the area. (Two days later, he and one of the guards went to a foto lab in San'a and his film was left there to be developed. He was allowed to pick it up the next day, so he lost nothing in the ordeal).

From the top, the author returned to his pack, reloaded his camera, and walked down the main road to the Bata Shoe Factory on the main highway, taking lots of fotos of the picturesque villages along the way. From Matnah to the summit and back to the highway took 6 2/3 hours, carrying a large pack with several liters of water, most of the way.

The author had planned to camp one night on the mountain, but it's very near the highway, so it can easily be climbed in one day from San'a--even using public transport. Be sure to learn a little arabi and get an early start--lots of traffic in the mornings. Also, take lots of film because the villages are very fotogenic. However, don't attempt to reach the highest peak with the radar. If you discretely climb the southern of the 3 peaks shown at about 3500 meters, you should make it OK without loosing film. Because of **Israel & the Zionist,** no one in Arabia trusts foreigners.

You can climb Nabi Shayib anytime, but there's a wet period from late March through May,

Nabi Shayib, far left in the distance. Near is the village marked 3200, and terraces.

Map 153-1, Jabal Nabi Shayib, Central Plateau, Yemen

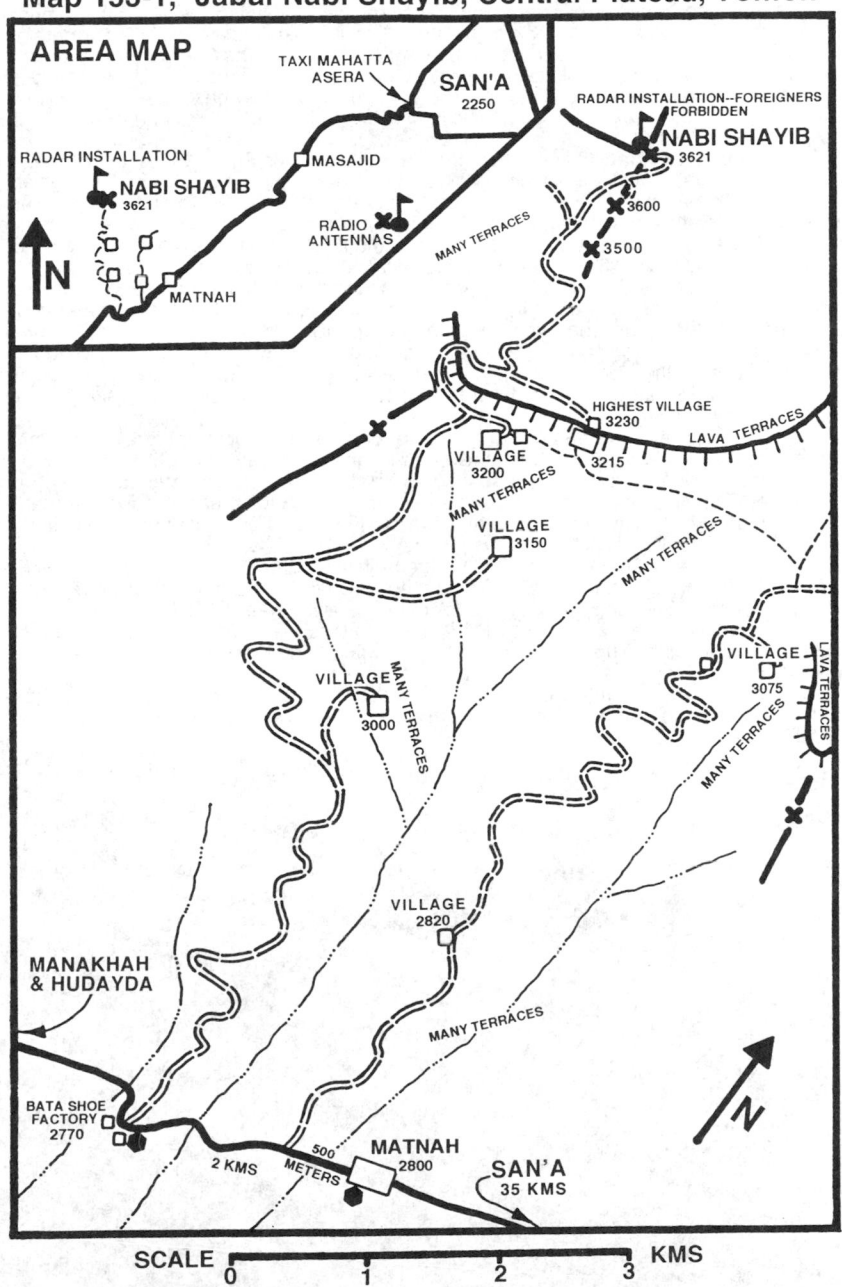

and again in August (when San'a receives 10 cms of rain). But San'a gets only about 25 cms of rain a year, so it's seldom very wet. Buy food in San'a or Matnah.
Maps TPC map *K-6A*, 1:500,000; and the travel guidebook, **Yemen**, Lonely Planet.

Jabal Isbil Volcano, Central Plateau, Yemen

Here's an interesting mountain for volcano watchers; it's Jabal Isbil, which is the remnant of a much larger and higher volcano. The highest point on this old caldera rim is 3191 meters. Isbil Crater is 5 or 6 kms in diameter and has a small village, many farms & terraces and several new cones and volcanos inside the old caldera. Some of the volcanic cones in this area are definitely Holocene in age--less than 10,000 years. The youngest appear to be those near the villages of Halima and Hammat Suliman. This volcanic field is located about 35 kms due east of the central Yemeni city of Dhamar.

Here's what the author did. He left his hotel in San'a early on 2/2/1999. At the Bab Al Yemen (Yemen Gate), on the south side of the old walled city, he got on a large bus bound for Dhamar (1 1/2 hours--US$1.40). He got off in the center of the city at the turnoff to Rada and Al Bayda. One hundred meters away was where shared taxis & minibuses were parking. He bought some food, then took a shared taxi to Sanaban (25 minutes--US$.70). He immediately found a road going in the direction of **Isbil** and started walking (10:30am) carrying a big pack with lots of water for 2 days!

He reached Hammat Suliman said he was going to Halima which was closer to the mountain--so he got a lift in the back of the pickup. At Halima, the author was literally dragged into a wedding reception and was forced to eat a meal with almost all the men of the village who hadn't yet taken their yearly baths. (the only water in these villages is trucked in in barrels as this is a real desert!). After this second lunch, he was allowed to leave. He walked along a road, then a trail, to the peak marked 3150 meters, where he camped for the night.

Next morning, he broke camp, hid his big pack in a ravine out of sight of sheep & goat herders, then walked through the village of Isbil, and on a trail along the south side of the caldera to the second highest peak at about 3180 meters. There's an antenna of some kind on what appears to be the highest summit, so he didn't attempt that for fear of loosing his camera or film. But he did make a big circular loop-hike around the interior of the caldera and observed the many fields & terraces for which Yemen is famous.

He then retrieved his pack and started for the highway. Enroute, he passed the well north of Dayda and had a quick splash-bath, then walked through Dayda and on to the highway. His total walk-time from Sanaban to Isbil and back to the highway was about 11 1/4 hours in 2 days.

You can surely find a minibus or taxi in Dhamar that can take you all the way to the base of the mountain if you like. There are even 4WD pickups around that could take you all the way to the village of Isbil; for a price.

Once on the highway, the author stuck out a thumb and got a ride in the first car to pass. That took him back to Dhamar. He then got in a shared taxi going south to Ta'izz (2 1/2 hours--US$2.80) where he spent that night in a hotel.

From the peak marked 3150, looking west at Isbil village and Jabal Isbil on the far right.

Map 154-1, Jabal Isbil Volcano, Central Plateau, Yemen

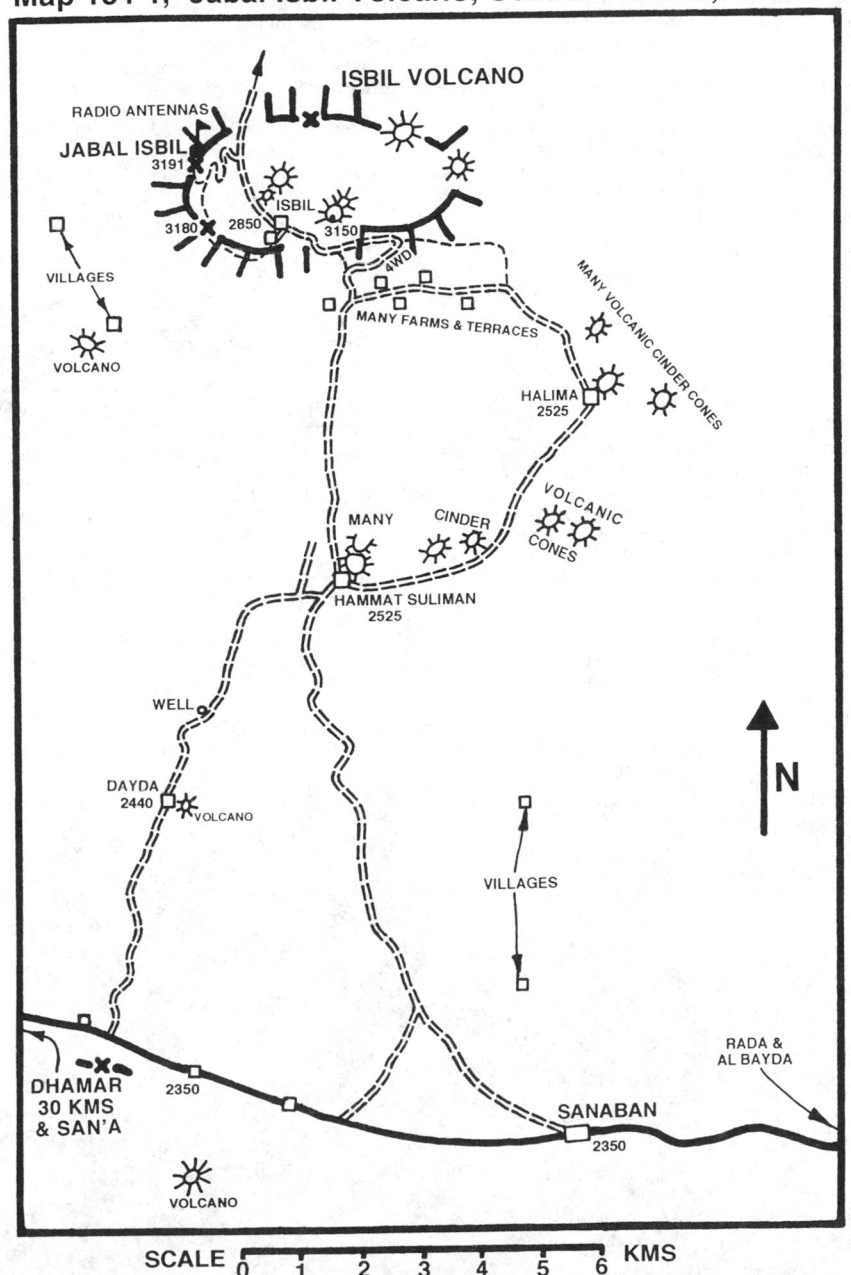

ISBIL VOLCANO

RADIO ANTENNAS

JABAL ISBIL
3191

ISBIL

3180   2850   3150

VILLAGES

VOLCANO

4WD

MANY FARMS & TERRACES

MANY VOLCANIC CINDER CONES

HALIMA
2525

MANY   CINDER

VOLCANIC
CONES

HAMMAT SULIMAN
2525

WELL

DAYDA
2440   VOLCANO

N

VILLAGES

DHAMAR
30 KMS
& SAN'A   2350

RADA &
AL BAYDA

SANABAN
2350

VOLCANO

SCALE 0 1 2 3 4 5 6 KMS

The best time to climb Isbil would be winter, from November through March, when temperatures are rather pleasant. The closest hotels are in Rada and Dhamar, which means you'll have to camp in the Isbil area. Buy food in Dhamar or Sanaban.

Maps TPC map *K-6A*, 1:500,000; and the travel guidebook, **Yemen,** from Lonely Planet.

Manakha Treks, Haraz Mountains, Yemen

This map shows perhaps the most interesting hiking area in all of Yemen. It includes the mountains & ridges south and east of the large town of Manakha. What makes this place so interesting are the dozens of mountain-top or rock-top villages or fortresses. There are no doubt other places just as good, but Manakha is very easy to get to; and in the 1990's, some trekkers have visited the place, so foreigners aren't the novelty they are in more isolated areas. Most of these peaks are granite.

Here's what the author did (a summery of 2 trips to the area in 2/1999). In San'a, he went to the long distance bus stand just west of the Bab Al Yemen (Yemen Gate). There you'll find several daily buses running to Hudayda, but in the mornings only. You can also take a minibus to the west end of San'a, to the Taxi Mahatta Asera, and get a shared taxi to Manakha for about 10% more, but much faster. He got a bus which took about 3 hours and cost US$2 to reach Maghraba, just downhill from Manakha. From there it was into a shared taxi for the 6 km ride up to Manakha (US$.20). He stayed in the Manakha Tourist Hotel for about US$4.50 a night. That place has hot showers and is rather clean, but you sleep on a mattress on the floor.

About 400 meters from the hotel in the center of town, are several chai (tea) houses, and a number of dukons (shops) where you can buy everything. There is also a bakery and a big Saturday suk (market), where you can buy plenty of fruits and vegetables. Near the hotel are several shops selling souvenirs, with lots of old rifles; they also change money. Nice place, and for the most part, the people leave you alone.

On his first trip to Manakha, he walked the road (which was being upgraded and paved at the time) to Hoteb, where you'll find a granite rock-top Muslim religious shrine. You can visit the pilgrim site for a small charge. He returned via Jabil and Khahil, 2 of the more fotogenic villages in the area. Round-trip walk-time 4 1/4 hours.

On this second trip, he walked to Hajarra, Meglet, Ajus, Aleana, Jabil, Khahil and back to the hotel in 6 hours. There are a number of villages, and of course lots of terracing, south of Ajus and Aleana along that prominent ridge.

His third hike was back to Khahil, then Maree and along the prominent ridge southeast of Manakha to Saaoot, then down to Banihalas, and along the road past Jermy, Salon, Vahada, and back to Manakha. That trek took 7 3/4 hours; but most people will want 10 or 12 hours for the same hike.

Here's a warning; don't visit the peak just north of Manakha, or **Jabal Shibam**, the highest local summit--both are military posts with antennas. They're forbidden, as are most of the highest mountains in Yemen (with radio sites), as well as Arabia. Get caught there and you may loose film!

All mountain tops in this area and all of Yemen, have thousands, if not millions, of terraces, where wheat, barley and other grains are grown. Valley sites are too dry; mountains are wetter

Just south of Manakha is the fotogenic rock-top village of Khahil (looking north).

Map 155-1, Manakha Treks, Haraz Mountains, Yemen

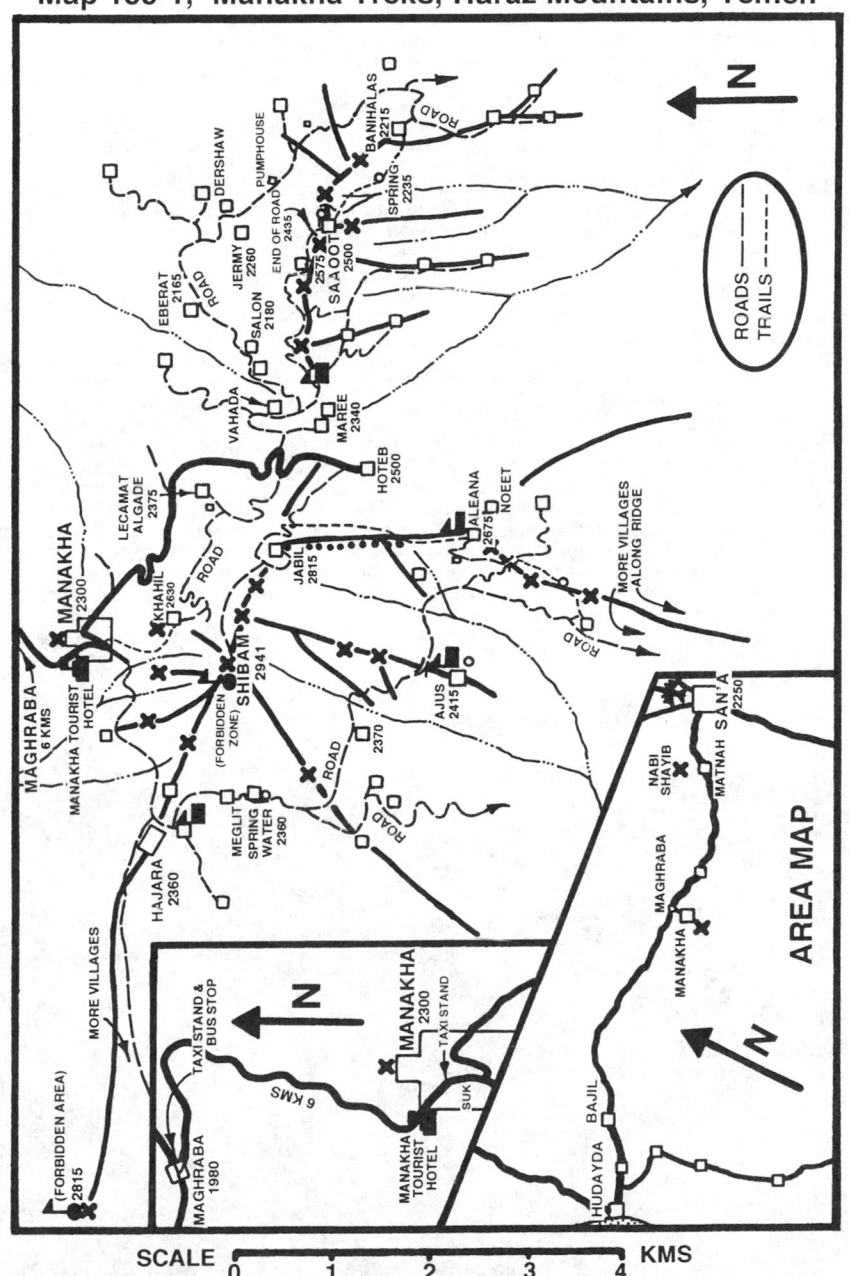

& cooler. While most people in these parts look Mediterranean, some of the not-so-shy girls in Khahil, have skin as white as Nordics! Trek anytime, but there are 2 wetter periods. One is in March, April and May; the other is late July and August. Winter brings clear skies.

Maps TPC map *K-6A*, 1:500,000; and the travel guidebook, **Yemen**, Lonely Planet.

Jabal Shams, Jabal Al Akhdar, Oman

This map shows the highest mountains in Oman, and the highest peaks in Arabia outside of Yemen. This is the Jabal Al Akhdar (or Green Mountains), west and southwest of the capital city of Muscat. The highest peak is Jabal Shams, 3009 meters.

Here's what the author did in late 1/1999. He came by land to Oman from the UAE. He used group taxis and minibuses. He stopped at the Seeb International Airport to change money, then actually camped nearby. The next morning, 1/25/1999, in front of the airport, he got in a commuter minibus heading west along the coastal road, but got out at the Nizwa Fidora (Nizwa Junction). Right at that junction is a group taxi & minibus stand with vehicles heading to Nizwa and beyond. He got in a minibus, and when full, it left heading along a good paved highway toward Nizwa, one of the larger small cities in the desert (2 hours, US$2.62). At Nizwa, he went to a small supermarket and bought most of the food, then to the suk (bazaar) for fruit.

After relaxing for an hour or two in Nizwa, he walked to the taxi & minibus stand which is very near the center of town and right in the mostly-dry wadi (stream channel). He got in a minibus and after 45 minutes (and US$1), was at Hamra Fidora or Fidora Hamra-Bahla, which is only a junction with a gas station. He then got right in a small bus heading for Hamra, which cost US$.50 for the 17 km ride.

In Hamra, he stored some baggage with a Hindustani shopkeeper, and walked along the paved road circling the Hamra Oasis, then up the Wadi Jhooli and later, on the road heading for Jabal Shams. He got a short ride to Rwiah, where he stocked-up on water, then headed straight up the mountain past the 2000-year-old Persian ruins. He camped at 1600 meters.

Next morning he hid his big pack in some rocks; there are sheep & goats and shepherds around-- so beware!, then walked up to the village of Dar A' Sawadi and was stopped at the police gate. From there to a north peak of Jabal Shams, with the radar installation, is forbidden (mamnua), so he had to return. Because of the time of day, and the supplies he had, the author couldn't reach the summit that day--partly because of fear of being arrested. So he went back down the mountain, but had a good chance to see and fotograph the upper part of **Jabal Shams**, and 2 other possible routes. The best way up is shown as *Best Route* on the map. There is a steep place or two on that ridge route, but it's far from the radar installation, and hopefully any trouble. By the way, the steep limestone Wadi Nakhan (Nakhan Canyon) is very impressive and worth a look.

Later, he got a lift back to Hamra with a couple of Hindustanis, got his baggage and water, and walked to a nearby wadi and bathed with 2 liters of water, then camped. Next day it was back to the airport near Muscat.

You can climb in the Jabal Al Akhdar any time of year, but temperatures are more pleasant from November through March when most of the rain falls. May through October is hot and cloudless. Buy food in Muscat, Nizwa or in small shops in Hamra. Hiring a vehicle should be easy in Hamra if you

Looking north and down into Wadi Nakhan. Jabal Shams is to the far right out of sight.

Map 156-1, Jabal Shams, Jabal Al Akhdar, Oman

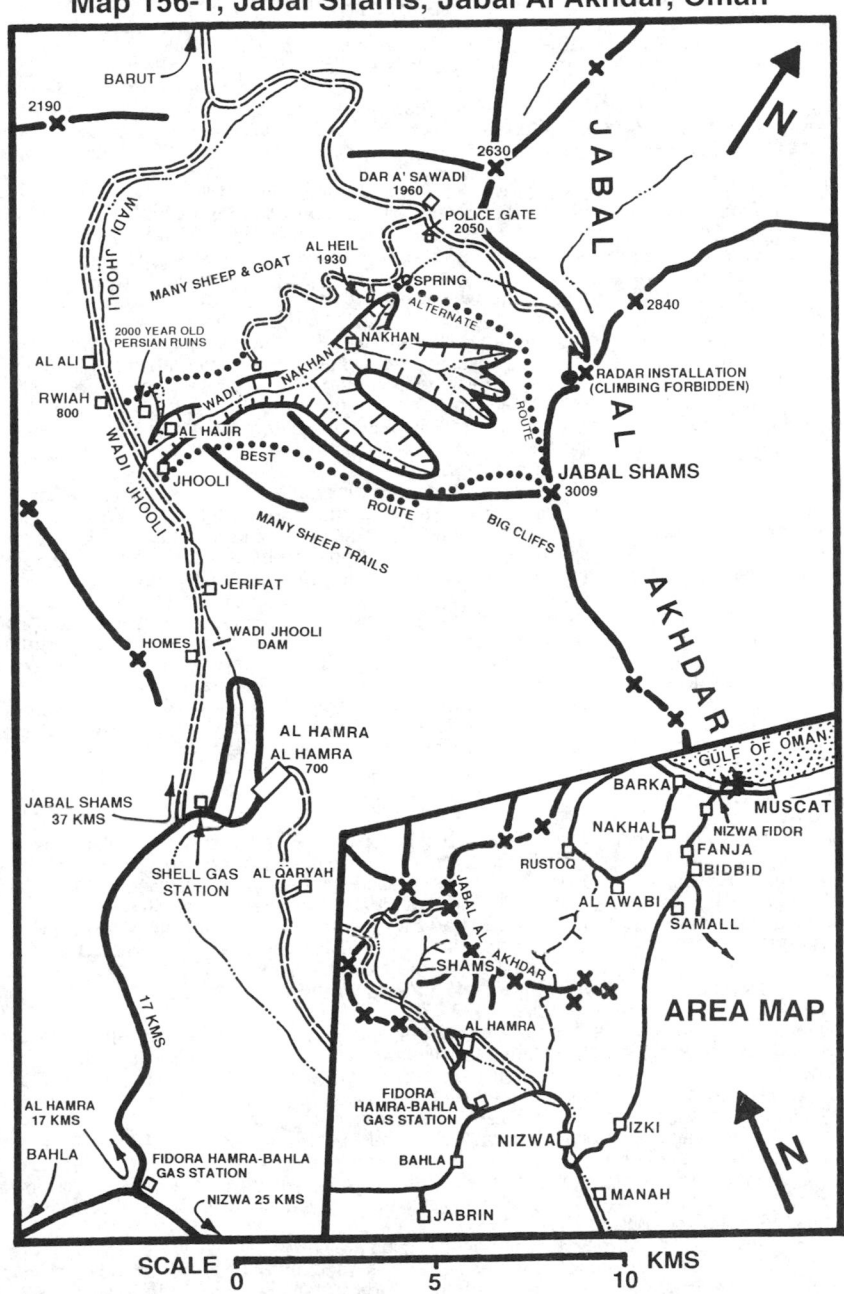

BARUT

2190

JABAL

2630

DAR A' SAWADI
1960

POLICE GATE
2050

WADI JHOOLI

MANY SHEEP & GOAT

AL HEIL
1930

SPRING

ALTERNATE

2840

2000 YEAR OLD
PERSIAN RUINS

NAKHAN

NAKHAN

AL ALI

WADI

NAKHAN

RWIAH
800

AL HAJIR

RADAR INSTALLATION
(CLIMBING FORBIDDEN)

ROUTE

WADI

BEST

JABAL SHAMS
3009

JHOOLI

JHOOLI

ROUTE

MANY SHEEP TRAILS

BIG CLIFFS

AL

JERIFAT

HOMES

WADI JHOOLI
DAM

AKHDAR

AL HAMRA

GULF OF OMAN

AL HAMRA
700

BARKA

MUSCAT

JABAL SHAMS
37 KMS

NAKHAL

NIZWA FIDOR

RUSTOQ

FANJA

BIDBID

SHELL GAS
STATION

AL QARYAH

AL AWABI

SAMALL

17 KMS

JABAL AL

AKHDAR

SHAMS

AREA MAP

AL HAMRA

AL HAMRA
17 KMS

FIDORA
HAMRA-BAHLA
GAS STATION

BAHLA

FIDORA HAMRA-BAHLA
GAS STATION

NIZWA

IZKI

BAHLA

NIZWA 25 KMS

MANAH

N

JABRIN

SCALE

0   5   10

KMS

want to save a little walking. You should be able to beg for water at any of the small villages shown on
this map. Learn some Arabi quick, it'll help.
Maps TPC map *J-7B*, 1:500,000; and the latest guidebook, **Arab Gulf States**, Lonely Planet.

Introduction to Russia and the CIS states (Former USSR)

As everyone knows, there have been many big political and economic changes in that part of the world which was once the Soviet Union. And it seems that more changes will happen in the future. Below are some personal experiences the author had in the summer of 1994 when he spent 3 months in Russia; and in 1995, while he spent 5 months visiting the 3 Kavkazian (Caucasus) and 5 Central Asian Republics. Also, a discussion of (1) Visas, (2) Getting There and Around, (3) Hotels, (4) Maps (Kartas), (5) Guidebooks, (6) Weather, (7) Bears, (8) Climbing Equipment, (9) Politics & Permission--Proposk, and (10) Internet Information Websites & Guide Services.

In the winter of 1993, the author was in communication with a Russian friend in Moskva (Moscow). The friend agreed to get and send a *private invitation* for this writer to 'isit Russia. The friend was paid US$100 dollars for his efforts. With it, the author then paid US$30 to get a visa good for 3 months in Russia. Upon arrival, there were no travel restrictions and he was able to wander freely, without escort or a prearranged or prepaid schedule or itinerary. It was just like traveling anywhere else in the world, but getting the invitation & visa was a bit of a hassle.

With that visa, he flew from Salt Lake, Utah, to Seattle, Anchorage, Khabarovsk (eastern Siber or Siberia) and finally to Petropavlovsk Kamchatsky on the Kamchatkan Peninsula. After climbing and traveling for 3 1/2 weeks there, he flew to Moskva (Moscow) for a short visit, then flew to Mineral'nyye Vody (Min Vody=Mineral Water) north of the Kavkaz (Caucasus) Mountains. He spent 2 months there, visiting 10 different regions in western Kavkazia, then finally took a boat from Novorossiysk to Istanbul. He climbed several peaks in Turkey, then flew home.

In the summer of 1995, the author again got his friend in Moskva to get him a private invitation for a visa to visit Russia. During the spring months, he also sent his passport to the embassies of Armenia, Georgia, Azerbaijan, Turkmenistan and Kyrgyzstan in Washington D.C. and had those 5, plus the Russian visa (which he actually picked up in Istanbul), before starting his next 5 month trip. He flew to Istanbul, then traveled east by bus to Armenia, Georgia and Azerbaijan, where he climbed 2 mountains in each country, during late May and the month of June.

He crossed the Caspian Sea in a big ferry boat (flights available as well) which cost US$75, then used trains and buses to cross Turkmenistan, Uzbekistan, Tajikistan and finally into Kyrgyzstan where he spent 2 months traveling and hiking & climbing in 10 different regions. After that it was into Kazakstan where he hiked into the mountains south of Almaty, the capital. Finally, he took the train north to Barnaul, Russia, then buses south to Pik Belukha, the highest summit in Siber. After this trek in late September, he hurried to eastern Europe where he quickly toured countries he had not visited before, including Albania where no visa was required for Americans, then flew back to the USA from Istanbul.

1. Visas.

Here's the visa situation for **Russia** as of 12/2000 for (North) Americans, most Europeans and anyone from the industrialized world. The biggest headache for getting a visa to Russia has always been you had to have either a **private invitation** from a friend or acquaintance; or make arrangements with a trekking, climbing or travel group, which would issue you an official invitation--or would just get your visa from the government. This is still true, but getting an invitation is much easier than before. For independent travelers who don't want to travel with a group, first contact the **Russian National Tourist Office (RNTO)**. One of their offices is at 130 West 42nd Street, Suite 412, New York, NY, USA, 10036; Tele. 212-575-3431, or toll free in the USA 877-221-7120, or Fax 212-575-3434, or website (www.russia-travel.com) or email (info@russia-travel.com). Major capital cities in Europe and elsewhere should also have an office.

The RNTO **website** states: send or email a completed application form, 3 passport-size fotos, a fotocopy of your passport, **an official invitation (which they will provide for US$50)**, and a self-addressed prepaid envelope to return your visa. Consular fees vary with processing time--US$70 for 2 weeks, or US$120 total. Double or multiply entry visas cost more. The RNTO will hand-carry everything to the nearest Russian Consulate and return the visa to you.

If you make contact with an alpinist travel company such as Alpindustriya Russian Travel Co., Moskva 105037, Izmailovskaya Square 1, Tele & Fax 7-095-367-3183, they will issue you an invitation, then you get the visa from a consulate. But only if you join one of their groups. Alpindustriya is a good contact, because they have guided trekking and climbing groups going to all parts of the CIS. See other *guide services* below.

If you're thinking of going to Kamchatka, keep in mind the people who know the mountains best are the geologists and/or volkanologists. In the early 1990's, their normal pay was disrupted by inflation and government cutbacks, so by 1994 some of the geologists were setting up their own part-time tour agency to make ends meet. They were escorting small groups to the volcanos, as well as doing research. Vladimir Kirianov and others who work out of the Petropavlovsk-Kamchatsky (P-K) Institut Volkanology office, have created and run Alpha Tour, at 27 Abel Street, Suite 42, P-K, 683006, Russia. International Tele & Fax 509-01-640081, or local Tele. 415-00-55050, or email (tour@alpha.

kamchatka.su). These people can arrange transportation and accommodation, and can surely get invitations and/or visas for their clients. The Institut Volkanology in P-K is located at about Km 9 on the main road leading to Elizovo Airport, and about one km short of the Km 10 Avtovakzal (Km 10 Bus Station), which is on the western edge of P-K. The institutes address is: Piip Avenue 9, P-K, 683006, Kamchatka, Russia. As far independent travel to any part of the CIS, if you don't speak any Russian, it's best to go with a group for your first trip. Only experienced travelers, or someone who knows, or who can learn Russian quickly, should travel on his/her own. You won't find many people in Russia speaking a foreign language! Of the foreign languages spoken, English is most used, with German second. French is also spoken in Moskva. For those visiting the Kavkazian or Central Asian republics, Russian is spoken by everyone, so that's the language to learn. Azerbaijan and all the Central Asian states except Tajikistan, speak a dialect of Turkish--but it's not the same as in Turkey!

During the summer of 1995, if you had a Russian visa, you could transit through each of the 5 Central Asian Republics. The author went by boat from Baki (Baku is the Russian name), Azerbaijan, to Krasnovodsk, Turkmenistan. On both sides of the Caspian Sea there were passport checks but beyond that there were few if any *tamozhenas* (customs posts) or passport control points between states. As long as you had a Russian (or Kyrgyzstan) visa and continued going in the same direction, you were allowed 3 days in each country (the same is true as of 1/2001) The author got a stamp in his passport upon entering Turkmenistan, then again at the OVIR (police passport office) in Osh, Kyrgyzstan, but other than those, he has nothing in his passport to show he visited Central Asian. Hotels always want to see your passport, and when you buy train or airline tickets they also want to see your documents. That's the way it was in 1995, and it appears to be the same today. However, as of 2001, there are more border formalities than in '95.

Then there's the old boundary of the former Soviet Union. That one is or was for real and the Russian Pagranichny (border patrol or contingent) still guard (1995) that old exterior boundary, even for the Kavkazian and Central Asian Republics. Once inside that old boundary, you could and still can pretty much wander at will. As long as you don't buy train or airline tickets, or stay in hotels, no one will want to see your passport.

For the Kavkazian or Central Asian Republics of the former USSR, call the nearest embassy or consulate, travel agent or **search the internet under each republic**, for updated visa requirements.

For **Georgia** (or Gruzia), visas are issued by any embassy and now cost US$50 for a one month stay. In 1995, the author wasn't required to have an invitation, but as of 1/2001, you had to have a *letter of invitation* from some travel agent based in Georgia. Contact the RNTO above for suggestions, or call a Georgian embassy as to who can give you an invitation. In Ankara, Turkey, you used to get everything done in 10 minutes! Or check the website (www.georgiaemb.org).

If you're going from Turkey to Armenia, you must first enter Georgia, then Armenia. The author did this, then had to re-enter Georgia a second time, but no one bothered to look at his passport & visa. If you're traveling the same direction as the author did, consider getting a double-entry visa just to be sure. When leaving Georgia no one was around to look at the author's passport, but when he entered Azerbaijan they did.

You can get a 21 day **Armenian** tourist visa for US$60 (as of 1/2001) and you don't have to have an invitation. For the latest information check the website (www.armeniaemb.org).

For **Azerbaijan** in 1995, if you had a visa from a neighboring CIS country and were going in that direction, they would issue you a 3 day transit visa at the border (all CIS countries did the same). To get a tourist visa in 1/2001, you must have a letter of invitation from a tourist agency, private individual or government organization. However, in 1995 the author got several other visas first, then wrote a long letter explaining that he very much wanted to travel freely and climb several mountains in Azerbaijan which would be in the next edition of his World Guide, and couldn't he be given a 2 week visa. Luckily the embassy in Washington DC gave him one without an invitation. A tourist visa now costs US$40. Also, sometimes if you're traveling in a country close to Azerbaijan, the requirements for visas are sometimes more flexible than when you apply from your own home country. This is the case with many countries. Azerbaijan and Armenia were at war in the mid-1990's and still don't have diplomatic relations, so you cannot travel directly between those 2 states. For updated information see the website (www.wtg-online.com).

Here's the visa situation for **Central Asia** as of 1/2001. All of these countries (except perhaps Tajikistan?) have strong ties with Turkey, so you may be able to get a visa at their embassies in Istanbul or Ankara. For a regular tourist visa to **Turkmenistan**, contact Asia Tour at (www.asiatour .org), or email (office@asiatour.org) for the latest information. They charge US$40 for an invitation and US$30 for a visa. But if they help, you have to reserve a hotel, perhaps for just one night (?). In 1995, the author got a 3 week visa for US$30, and no invitation! But if you have a visa to any of the other Central Asian Republics, they will give you a 3 day transit visa at the border. For more information see (www.turkmenistanembassy.org).

The requirements for visas to **Uzbekistan** are the same as the other Central Asian Republics. You'll have to make reservations for at least one night through an agency such as Asia Tour (www.asiatour.org), then they issue an invitation and get you a visa. The cost of a one month visa is US$30 plus US$35 for an invitation.

In 1995, the author never did get an Uzbekistan visa, but since there was no checkpoint at the Turkmen-Uzbek border at the time, and he had visas to Kyrgyzstan and Russia, he visited Bukhara and Samarkand and stayed a total of 5 or 6 days with only a minimum of hassles at bus stations where the local version of the KGB was on the lookout for visa-less wanderers. However, as of 1/2001, border formalities are much better organized.

Kyrgyzstan is a wonderful place to visit. The best country in Central Asia, and one of the best in the world--at least for mountaineers. In many ways it resembles Nepal--nice people, very little or no crime, inexpensive, no travel hassles, and lots of wild & wooly mountains for trekking and/or climbing. The author got a 2 month visa in 1995, with no invitation--but that may have changed. Individual travelers now need to write a *statement of purpose* for going there, or get an *invitation* just like in all the other Central Asian Republics. Call the nearest embassy or see the websites (www.asiatour.org) or (www.kyrgyzstan.agava.ru). You may have to book one night in a hotel to get started. Or see Lonely Planet's guidebook, **Central Asia**, for possible ways to *beat the system*. In talking to the Kyrgyz consular officer in New York on 1/9/2001, the author was told they are flexible on this *invitation* business. Because he had been there before, they would have given him a one month visa on the spot.

In Kyrgyzia in 1995, alpinists had to pay US$100 for permission to climb Pik Pobeda, Pik Lenina or Khan Tangri, and get a trekking permit (US$15) to visit 3 popular canyon trekking areas south of Kara Kol (formerly Przheval'sk). Otherwise you were free to roam, hike or climb anywhere. However, you did have to have proposk (permission) to visit border regions near China or Tajikistan which was easy to get at the OVIR office in Osh, Bishkek (the capital) or Kara Kol.

In 1995, it was a hassle getting a visa to **Tajikistan** because of the continuing border war with rebels from Afghanistan. It's still the same, but if you contact (www.asiatour.org), they can set you up easy. However, at the Tajik Embassy in Askhabat, Turkmenistan, the author was told he could get a one month tourist visa to Tajikistan in just one day--but that was for Dushanbe and points away from the Afghan border. As it turned out, the author, armed with his Russian & Kyrgyzstan visas, and on his way to the Fergana Valley (Uzbekistan) and Osh, sailed right through the northern parts of Tajikistan where there were border stops, but no passport controls. No one ever asked to see his passport, even in the Fergana Valley area, where there are many border crossings between Tajikistan, Kyrgyzstan and Uzbekistan. Late word is that you now need an official transit visa when making the run from Samarkand, Khudzhand, Kokand to Osh. Check that out before going.

In 1995, getting a visa to **Kazakstan** required an invitation, or you could transit through easily with a Russian visa. It's still the same in 2001. Contact the nearest embassy or consulate, or (www.asiatour.org) for the latest. When the author entered Kazakstan from Kyrgyzia, there was no border stop on the Kazak side; as a result he stayed a total of about 7 days and did a couple of day-hikes in the mountains south of Almaty, the capital. But they have a border post there now.

When the author took a train from Almaty to Barnaul, Russia, the train sailed across the border at about 3am non-stop. There were no passport checks what-so-ever, and the author never did get a Russian stamp in his passport, partly because he landed on a Saturday morning. However much later, he was sweating blood on the train leaving Russia for Estee (Estonia). He had all his excuses rehearsed & ready, but the only thing the Russian passport officer said was, *Nyet Problem!*

2. Getting There and Around.

Here are some normal access routes to the mountains of the former USSR. Most flights to Kavkazia, Central Asia, the Altai Region and Kamchatka originate from Moskva. But there are some exceptions. If going to Kamchatka, there are several direct flights from Moskva daily. But you can also take an Aeroflot flight beginning in Seattle, then flying to Anchorage and on to Khabarovsk, an international hub in far east Siber. From there, it's a 3 hour flight to Petropavlovsk-Kamchatsky (P-K), the capital city of the Kamchatka Oblast. As of 1994, there were no international flights direct to P-K. From the capital city, buses run north to Mil'kovo, Esso, Kozyrevsk and to as far as Kluchi, the normal beginning point for those climbing Kluchevskoya.

From Moskva, there are many flights per day south to the Kavkazian city of Mineral'nyye Vody--*Min Vody* for short. From where you leave the airport baggage area, walk 200 meters southeast to find perhaps the busiest avtovakzal (bus terminal) in Kavkazia. From there you can get hourly buses to the mountain gateway and the ethnic autonomous republic cities of Mahachkala, Grozny, Vladikavkaz, Nalchik and Cherkessk. From the bus stations in these capital cities, other buses go to the highest village in every major valley in the Kavkaz Mountains. From Vladikavkaz, there are 6-7 buses per day running south to Tbilisi, Georgia.

In **Georgia**, the starting point for anyone going to the mountains is Tbilisi. From there, some buses go to some of the highest villages, while others go to regional centers, then a change of bus is necessary to reach some of the isolated valleys. Lots of bad roads in Georgia in 1995. And it will likely remain that way for some time. Erevan or Yerevan is where buses fan out to all parts of **Armenia**. Lots of buses and bad roads in Armenia too.

Baki is the capital of **Azerbaijan**, and all bus traffic begins there. Azerbaijan has lots of oil and oil money, so their roads are good, and many buses are new, or nearly so. It's best to go directly to Baki first, and get acquainted with restricted areas before doing any wandering. This writer didn't, and as a result found himself near some military installations quite by accident. He was hauled into police or KGB offices 3 times in 2 days; because they were having a little border war with Armenia at the time.

The last time, he was arrested and hauled off to Baki. With a little help from the USA Embassy, things turned out OK; but remember, there is continuing hostilities between Azerbaijan and Armenia, so things are uptight. Armenia still occupies the entire Nagorno-Karabakh region, and will likely be there for a long time. Stay in the northern parts near the Kavkazian Mountains and you should be OK. But don't go near Kut Kashen, now known as Qabala (Kabala)!

You can get to the **Central Asian Republics** from Russia by bus or train, or by ferry boat from Baki, Azerbaijan. But most people fly into the capital cities of Dushanbe, Tashkent, Biskek (formerly Frunze) and Almaty (Alma Ata) from Moskva. There are also direct flights from Istanbul via Turkish Airlines to Baki, Azerbaijan; Ashkabat, Turkmenistan; Tashkent, Uzbekistan; and to Almaty, Kazakstan. By now, they may be flying to Bishkek, Kyrgyzstan (?). There are surely more flights directly from other countries as well. Check with any travel agent

In **Kazakstan**, the only mountains are just south of Almaty. There are buses leaving from various stations and into those mountains. Locations are detailed in the 2 hikes covered in that section. **Tajikistan** was mostly off limits in 1995, and may be that way for a long time. To climb there, at least on Pik Kommunizma, guided climbing groups were flying in by helicopter direct to base camps from Kyrgyzstan. Whenever things normalize, the starting point will be the capital city of Dushanbe.

Most climbing, hiking or trekking will be in **Kyrgyzstan**. If you're coming from the west by land, the first big place in Kyrgyzia will be Osh, an old Silk Road city. Make Osh your headquarters if going into the mountains in the southwest part of the country, including Pik Lenina. Osh has a great bazaar where everything can be bought for any hike or climb. If climbing Lenina, go to the *futbol statian* in the south part of the city and the Sport Kommitti Buro to pay US$100 for permission, and the OVIR (passport) office for permission to be near the Tajik border. If you're going to areas south of Osh, find buses at the Stary Avtovakzal (Old Bus Station) just across the river south & east of the main bazaar. If you're going by bus to Bishkek, then there's a small enclosed bus parking area across the river and east of the bazaar. These small buses normally leave in the afternoons, but only when they are full. And they do get full! They run through the night and arrive in Bishkek in the morning, after about 18 long hours. Cost in 1995 was US$20. For US$90 you can fly from Osh to Bishkek.

In Bishkek there are buses going to all parts of the country, mostly from the Novey Avtovakzal (New Bus Station) in the northwest part of town. Not far south of that is one big bazaar, called the Osh Bazaar (there are several bazaars in Bishkek). Another large town is Kara Kol, located just east of Issyk Kul (Issyk Lake). Make it your headquarters for hikes or climbs in the eastern third of Kyrgyzia. In the south central part of Kyrgyzia is Naryn, another regional hub with buses going from there to other parts. Near Naryn is At Bashi. Small buses fan out from there too. Kara Kol, At Bashi and Naryn are all about 8 hours away from Bishkek by bus.

3. Hotels.

Here's a quick rundown on **gastinetsas (hotels)** in some of the mountain gateway cities. In **Russian** Kamchatkas **Petropavlovsk-Kamchatky**, there are at least 3 gastinetsas. The cheapest one is the *Geyser* at about US$14 for one person in 1994. It's located about one km southeast of the Institut Volkanology, and about 500 meters south of *Gastinetsa Petropavlovsk* and the main ticket sales office of Aeroflot. Further southeast in the city center is the expensive *Gastinetsa Avacha*. In **Kozyrevsk**, which is west of the highest volcanos in Kamchatka, is a small seismic station with one volcanologist. He doesn't have any accommodation, but you could likely pitch a tent in his fenced compound. In **Kluchi**, the Institut Volkanology has a small guesthouse called the *Gastinetsa Stromboli* which has about 3 large rooms available and which might be able to sleep about a dozen people--plus some on the floor in a pinch. You could also pitch a tent there in the compound if necessary. Down the street there was a sign indicating another gastinetsa in the summer of 1994, but that was never investigated.

In **Russia's Kavkazia**, the most westerly autonomous republic is **Karachay-Cherkessk** and it's capital city **Cherkessk**. The main hotel there is the *Gastinetsa Cherkessk* located at the south end of the city center. The author paid about US$8 a night there, which included a private bath and TV. There's a second hotel about one km to the north, and not far east of the tourist office. The *Gastinetsa Kuban(?)* is the same price, but didn't have a baggage store room. South of Cherkessk, is the city of **Karachaevsk**. It's only hotel for tourists was closed in 1994, but if the wars in the area stop and tourists return, it will reopen. At the mountain resort of **Dombai** there are about 2 hotels you can stay in.

Next ethnic republic to the east is **Kabardino-Balkaria** and it's capital city is **Nalchik**. In the north end of the city is the main long distance Avtovakzal (Bus Station) 1. In the same building is the *Hotel Avtovakzal*. Staying there alone, the author paid about US$10 a night. In the south end of the city next to a big park and lake is the *Gastinetsa Nalt*, at the same price, but maybe a little cleaner. In the city center is the Avtovakzal 2, and immediately across the street to the south is the bazaar, maybe the best in Kavkazia. There are about 3 different numbered buses running between the 2 bus stations, plus marsroute (shared) taxis. About 500 meters to the southwest of the bazaar is the *Gastinetsa Alpinista*. The author paid about US$6 a night there. The bath was shared with one other room (2 rooms, one bath). This was the cleanest and newest hotel he found in Russia. Accommodation in the upper Baksan Valley below Mt. Elbruz is discussed in the individual hikes.

To the east of Kabardino-Balkaria is **Severo (North) Ossetia** and it's capital city of **Vladikavkaz**, which is shown on old maps as *Ordzhonikidze*. In the north end of the city is the main avtovakzal. About 2 kms due south of that, and next to the river, is the expensive *Gastinetsa Vladikavkaz*. About a km south of this hotel is a smaller bazaar, and next to it a parking place on the street for buses running up to Kobi and Kazbegi in Georgia and to the foot of Pik Kazbek. In the southeastern part of Vladikavkaz is the *Gastinetsa Kavkaz* next to the university. It was full when the author arrived, but he was directed 150 meters south down the street to the *Gastinetsa Universitetskaya*. It was very clean, and included the usual private bath & TV for about US$10 a night. If memory is correct, it was electrobus or tram 8, and marsroute taxi and bus 2 (?) making the run between the main avtovakzal and these 2 hotels. It appears this place is open to tourists in the summer only.

In 1994, there was a war going on in Chechen-Ingush (before it was known to the rest of the world), and a cholera outbreak and quarantine in Dagistan, so the author didn't get to climb in the eastern Kavkaz and is unfamiliar with these 2 republics, and their capital cities of Grozny (now in rubble) and Mahachkala. It'll be awhile now before any hikers or climbers go into Chechnya, but you may be able approach the border peaks in that region from the Georgian or Azerbaijan side.

Now the **Kavkazian (Caucasus) Republics**. In Tbilsi and **Georgia**, there are several hotels, the cheapest in 1995 being the *Gastinetsa Kavkaz*, south and across the river from the 300 Aragveli Metro Station. In was occupied by refugees in 1995, and pretty run down, but they stored baggage for the author. It was US$12 a night. There are several others around that are easy to find. Ask taxi drivers about *privatny domas* or private homes, which are cheap and secure. If you're heading for Pik Kazbek, there is an inexpensive hotel in the east end of the town of **Kazbegi**, which is just east of the peak. On the south side of the range and the Elbruz region, is the town of **Mestia**. It has a hotels, but is unknown to the author.

In **Erevan** and **Armenia**, there are several large expensive hotels in the city center, the cheapest of which was the *Gastinetsa Shirak* at about US$16 a night. There may have been other hotels in some of the suburbs but the Shirak is near the Central Bazaar and very convenient to buses and shopping.

In **Baki, Azerbaijan**, there was nothing cheaper than US$20 in 1995. The *Gastinetsa Apsheron* is across the street from the ticket office for the ferry boats going across the Caspian Sea. That's where lots of foreign business men stay and it's a nice place for $25. Expect that price to be higher when you arrive. Near the Metro Station 28 May is the *Gastinetsa Baki* for US$20, but it was a dump for that price. In the small mountain city of **Sheki** is the tall 10-story *Gastinetsa Sabuhe* at US$6 a night. There is also a hotel in **Kusari** which is just east of the highest peaks in the country. See the Tourist Map of Kavkazia listed below. It shows all the towns and cities of Kavkazia, both north and south of the mountains, which have hotels or gastinetsa.

Central Asia. In **Bishkek** (formerly Frunze), **Kyrgyzstan**, there are many hotels to choose from, but the cheaper ones are the *Gastinetsa Pilot* at the corner of Ulitsa (street) Toktogula and Logvinenko at about US$12 a night; and the little summer-time-only *Gastinetsa Sultanet*, at Belinsky #22A, 5th floor, Tele. 21-34-25. This one was for US$6 a night 1995, and located near the corner of Belinsky & Moskovskaya. It's a student boarding house from September to May. The book, **Bishkek Handbook** by Prior, which can be bought in Bishkek, has a larger list of other hotels, as will late editions of travel guidebooks. Or contact Tien Shan Travel, 105 Panfilov Street (Ulitsa), Bishkek, 720035, Tele. (3312) 429 825, Fax (3312) 621 255, or email: tienshan@asiemm.bishkek.su. Those people cater to foreigner travelers and can help you with transport, guide service, hotels, etc.

In **Kara Kol** (formerly Przheval'sk) at the east end of Issyk Kul (Lake) in eastern Kyrgyzstan, is the *Gastenitsa Kara Kol* at US$5 a night. It's in the center of town, 2 blocks from the Little Bazaar. Also near the last bus stop on the road to the Kara Kol Canyon is some kind of alpinist lodge or inn. Also, if you need help, try contacting Global-X, or JS Turkestan, at m-d "Voskhod", 10/50. Tele/Fax Inter+996-3922-59896. Or email psi@glob-X.karakol.su and website www.oasis.fortunecity.com/myrtle/168 This fellow, Sergey Pyshnenko, speaks good English and is in the travel & trekking business.

In **Naryn**, there's the *Gastinetsa Ala Too,* which is about a 15 minute walk west of the avtovakzal, or about 2 astanovkas (bus stops) away on the electric trolley. It's in between the bazaar and the avtovakzal. It cost about US$4 a night in 1995, but there were rooms without private baths for less. In **At Bashi**, there is the *Gastinetsa Koshoy* about 5 minutes walk west of the bazaar, then north one block on a side street. It had an outside toilet and no showers, but you can take water to the toilet for a *bucket bath*. Or ask about the local banya (public bath house). This place was very clean and quiet for US$2 night in 1995.

In **Osh**, the best place to stay was the *Gastinetsa Alai*, located about 2 blocks west of the south end of the main bazaar, and 3 blocks west of the Stary Avtovakzal (Old Bus Station). It was very clean, and inexpensive at US$5 a night in 1995. It's so well located to the bazaar, bus station, etc, that no one would want to go to the more expensive hotel one km to the south (can't remember the name). The Alai stored extra baggage for the author on several occasions. In fact, all of the above mentioned hotels stored baggage for this writer free of charge while he was out climbing.

4. Maps (Kartas).

Before going to any of the CIS states, buy or copy as many maps as you can. Secrecy, and lack of interest and finances, have all contributed to a general lack of maps available in this part of the world. There are some around, but most are where tourists have traditionally visited. If you live near a large university, check out their map collection and copy any map you can get you hands on; this includes cities, highway or topo maps. In Kavkazia, the author found city maps of Nalchik and Pyatigorsk, and tourist maps of the Dombai and Elbruz regions, and nothing more. He was lucky to have had copies of Russian highway maps before leaving home.

Sometime in the early 1990's, the Russian government, as well as most other CIS governments, lifted many if not most topographic maps from the restricted list and are now available to the public. The Soviet government map making organization is usually referred to as the **GUK**(?), or maybe just **G&K**. The full name seems to be the **Geodesi & Kartografiya Rossiyskoy Federatsi**, and it's in Moskva, a little north of the Kurski Metro Stantsiya (Station) and immediately across the street from the Teatr Gogolya. However, they don't sell maps or kartas there; but they will tell you where they're sold when you arrive. In 10/1995, a privatny or chasny magazin (private shop) selling topo maps was located on Ulitsa Kuznetski Most, just west of the Kuznetski Most Metro Station. This is 5 or 6 blocks, or less than one km, due north of the Kremlin and Red Square. The author was told all maps of Kavkazia were sold out and unavailable at that time. However he did buy a set of 8 maps at 1:200,000 scale of the Altay Mountains of southwest Siber (Siberia). That set, which were sold as a unit, only cost about US$5.50.

Maps for other CIS states may still be printed in Moskva, but as time goes on, this may change. Whatever capital city you're in, ask about the location of the **Geodesi & Kartografiya**. In the past, they have printed maps at 1:50,000, 1:100,000, 1:200,000, and 1:500,000 scale, but tight budgets make them hard to find. Some maps, especially those at large scale, or 1:50,000, may still be restricted (?).

In **Kyrgyzstan** and the capital of **Bishkek**, you'll find lots of maps at their G&K office located at #107 Ulitsa Kievskaya. Enter on the west side of that large building marked #107. Ask for the "karta buro", which is upstairs. That office had and sold the complete set of good topo maps at 1:200,000 scale, plus many trekking kartas which outlined popular trekking routes. It's not sure if they have kartas at 1:50,000 scale or not; this writer didn't ask. In 9/1995, he did buy a complete set of 1:200,000 maps for the entire country of Kyrgyzstan at about US$3 each. These are good maps, but printed on poor paper and in the crylic alfabet. Some have been updated to the 1980's, and they work well for getting into any of the mountain areas. Maps can only be bought at that office--no mail orders.

There is another set of maps published by **Vilém Hrdina**, from **Praha, Ceska** (Prague, Czech Republic). This map series (perhaps 25 or 30) covers all or most of Kavkazia, and the mountainous regions of Tajikistan, Kyrgyzstan and Kazakstan. They're all at 1:100,000 scale, printed in the Russian or Crylic alphabet, and all date from the late 1980's. They show the normal routes up major peaks such as Lenina and Pobeda, as well as base camps or alp lagers, tourist facilities, etc. These are really good maps for trekking or climbing, perhaps the best available for the regions they cover. In 1995, the author tried to buy these in Praha, but couldn't make contact on a weekend and isn't sure where you can buy them.

If you're climbing or just traveling around Kavkazia (Caucasus Region), either in southern Russia on the north side of the mountains, or in the 3 Kavkazian Republics, there's one map you should have--if you can find it. It seems to be **untitled** but it shows a generalized road map of the region with important towns and cities. Next to each town's name is a symbol showing gastinetsas (hotels), avto repairs, benzin (petrol) stations, camping sites, tourist bases. It also shows maps of the major cities in the region. It's only in the Russian or Crylic alphabet, and it's outdated some, but if you like wandering to out of the way places, it's one of the best maps or guides you could possibly have. Look for this Soviet era map in any major university map library.

If you're in the USA, Canada, or Great Britain, you might be able to find some 1950's maps at 1:250,000 scale of the Kavkazian region in some university map libraries. These were printed by the **US Army Defense Mapping Agency** (**DMA**) with a little help from the British, and are out of print. They were created by using older Russian and German maps of the area. The author copied many of these and used them much of the time in Kavkazia and Central Asia. They were printed in our English alphabet and still fairly accurate in most cases, but of course anything man-made is outdated by about 60 years.

In recent years, and after the breakup of the USSR, more maps have been printed and are available for tourists and alpinists. In Moskva, a private company called the A.S.S. Co. Ltd. has a 1993 map titled, **Tourist Map-Elbrus and Environs**, 1:50,000, and is in English or Roman letters. This map of Elbrus is the most accurate of any this writer has seen, especially in regards to present-day roads, tracks, trails, priyuts (huts), and shepherd huts. It's been updated over all others. Get this one in Moskva at Alpindustriya, Izmailovskaya Square, 1, Moskva, 105037, Russia. Maybe other places too.

West Col Productions of Goring, Reading, Berks. RG8 9AA, England, UK, has a series of 6 map-guides covering the western half of the Kavkaz Mountains. They are: **1.** Teberda Region, Western Range, 1:100,000; **2.** Mount Elbruz Region, 1:80,000 & 1:210,000; **3.** Bezingi, Sugan, Laboda, Adaikhokh, 1:100,000; **4.** Adaikhokh, Gimarai, Kazbek, 1:100,000; **5.** Caucasus Central, Elbruz to Kazbek, 1:200,000; and **6.** Elbrus Ski/Tourist Map, 1:50,000. They also have 2 maps of Tajikistan/Uzbekistan: Fann Mountains and Pamir Mountains, both at 1:200,000 scale.

Even though these British maps came out in the early or mid-1990's, no one went out to do the footwork in the high mountains. Most tourist facilities shown are fairly accurate, but the roads shown are no more updated than the 1950's DMA maps. Otherwise they are good maps, which also have information on transportation, history of the region, etc. And they're in the Roman alphabet!

For generalized regional maps, and in some cases poor quality hiking maps, you might try some put out by the **US Army Defense Mapping Agency**. While **Joint Operations Graphic** (**JOG**) maps at 1:250,000 are available for the Americas, the best DMA maps available for the old USSR are those titled, **Tactical Pilotage Charts (TPC)**. These are topo maps at 1:500,000 scale which cover the entire world. Here's a list of TPC's for **Kamchatka**; D-9D, E-10B, & E-11A. For the **Altai Region**, E-6C covers Pik Belukha and most of the mountains you might be interested in, but E-6B shows access from the north. For the **Central Asian Republics**, F-6C, & D, & G-6B cover all of Kyrgyzstan and most of Tajikistan. TPC map G-7A has just the eastern part of Tajikistan. In **Kavkazia**, F-4C & D cover all of the Kavkaz Mtns., while G-4B & G-5A cover the extreme southern parts of Armenia & Azerbaijan. There are many sales offices around the world for these maps, but the main office which sells them all, is in the USA at: NOAA Distribution Branch, N/CG33, National Ocean Service, Riverdale, Maryland, USA, 20737-1199. Telefone number is 301-436-6990. The Fax number for Visa or Master Card orders is 301-436-6829. Ask for their catalog.

5. Guidebooks.

By 1994, there were 2 books in English out on the Kavkaz Mtns. They were; **Classic Climbs in the Caucasus**, by F. Bender. It's a translation from German by Diadem Books of London, and Menasha Ridge Press, 3169 Cahaba Heights Road, Birmingham, Alabama, USA. This guide is for experienced mountaineers and technical climbers. The second book is titled, **Trekking in the Caucasus**, from Circerone Press, Milnthorpe, Cumbria, U.K. This was written by 2 Russians and has good hiking maps in the back. This book details and features trekking routes over periwals (passes). Both books are stitch bound, have plastic covers, and both concentrate on the western half of the Kavkaz, with access mostly from the Russian side.

There is also the book, **Trekking in Russia & Central Asia**, by Maier, published by The Mountaineers, 1011 SW Klickitat Way, Seattle, Washington, USA, 98134. In the UK it's published by Cordee, while in Canada it's published by Douglas & McIntyre. It has mostly trekking, but some climbing information for Kavkazia, Central Asia, the Altay Mountains, Kamchatka, and other parts of Siber, plus the Urals, Crimea and Kuril Islands.

There are also travel guides becoming available to individual travelers. These will give updates on buses, trains, hotels, etc. Check with Lonely Planet Guidebooks, and other guidebook publishers, to see their latest updated books on Russia and the CIS region. Look in the back of this book for the names, address, Telefon & Fax numbers, and email addresses of the major guidebook publishers and guidebook & map distributors.

6. Weather.

As one would expect, July and August are the busiest months for climbing or hiking in the **Kavkaz Mtns.**, just like the Alps and Rockies. However, June is also a good weather month, but with lots of winter snow still on the ground. But many tourist facilities aren't always open then. September is also an excellent month, with good weather and dry conditions. However, some facilities close when school starts around September 1st, and there are fewer buses on the road. But that's just fine for those of us who like quiet conditions. Early October is a good time for trekking, but with much cooler temperatures.

In **Central Asia** the climbing season is from July through mid-September. The trekking season in some areas can begin in late June or early July, and end by mid-September, just about like everywhere else in the northern hemisphere. For the major peaks in Kyrgyzia and Tajikistan, the new guide service outfits are in the mountains and have established camps from mid-July until the first week of September. In Central Asia, many people are surprised to find how hot and dry valley locations are, only to find the mountains above about 4000-4200 meters have perpetual snow. Any peak above above 4500 meters will have a real glacier with crevasses on it's north side--maybe on it's south side too! So expect bad weather for about 2-3 days each week, and the usual afternoon cloud buildup each day. The further south you go in the Central Asian mountains, the drier it gets.

The **Altay Mountains** of southwest Siber (Siberia) get more precipitation than in Central Asia. On a map, follow the boundary of Kazakstan. This boundary, for the most part, is also the biological boundary separating the grasslands of Kazakstan, and the Russian or Siberian boreal forest called the *taiga*. There are few grasslands in this part of Siber, just forests. Forests mean more rain and bad weather. So expect wetter weather in the Altay than in the Central Asian Republics.

For **Kamchatka**, there is less rainfall in June, but more winter snow on the ground with some wet camping places. The very best time to hike or climb there is from mid-July through the first week or so of September.

7. Bears.

If you're heading for Kamchatka remember, they have as many medveds (**bears**) as in Alaska, and they're just as big. Not many people have problems with them, but you don't want to surprise a mother and her cubs. It's recommended you carry a small bell of some kind on your pack. By making noise with a bell, or continually talking with friends, the bears will hear you coming and get out of your way. If camping in a forested area, consider hanging food high in between 2 trees. Or wrap it well to keep odors from spreading too much. The author was alone for most of his Kamchatka trip and although he never saw a bear, he saw plenty of big tracks!

In **Central Asia** and **Kavkazia**, there are no bears to speak of, and no problem. When the author was hiking alone into the mountains south of At Bashi, Kyrgyzstan, several people warned him of the dreaded *volks*, or wolves. It's doubtful there are any wolves left in that desert region, so it seems they were just trying to talk him out of going alone. Even if there were wolves around, they certainly are no danger to humans. There doesn't seem to be a bear problem in the **Altay Mountains**, but in less populated and wilderness settings, there are surely some bears around. So be aware of this potential problem.

8. Climbing Equipment.

As for climbing equipment, all the higher mountains in Russia and the CIS have snow and ice and big glaciers. This means you'll need at least an ice ax & crampons, and more technical equipment if you're with a group trying some of the more difficult peaks in Kavkazia or in Central Asia. In these 2 regions, the peaks are as difficult as any on earth, and it takes well-equipped and experienced alpinists to have any success. Even if you're trekking, many of the periwals (passes) you'll be hiking over require an ice ax & crampons, and in some cases even a rope. There are few if any alpinist-made trails in Russia or the other CIS, but there are many trails made by shepherds and their livestock--sheep & goats, cows & horses. These are the trails you'll be using. Some maps may show a trail over some periwal, but often there is little or no trail right on top. It's often times just a route. These are the ones where you may need a ice ax & crampons to get over safely.

In **Kamchatka**, some of the bigger volcanos have glaciers, but there seem to be moderately easy routes around the crevassed areas. The highest volcano there is Kluchevskoya, which has very few glaciers, and no glaciers on the northeast side along which is the *marsroute normalny* (normal route). Perhaps one reason for this might be that it's active, and the heat from within doesn't allow glacier buildup. Also, perhaps high winds keep it off the higher slopes. On all the volcanos take an ice ax & crampons, just in case. In some parts of Kavkazia and Kamchatka there are climber's shelters called priyuts or domas, but for the most part you'll also need a tent, which is standard equipment.

9. Politics and Permission--Proposk.

One problem the author ran into in parts of the Russian **Kavkazia**, was that he had to get *proposk* or permission from the Pogranets Otryad or Pogranechny (Border Guards) to get into the high peaks along the Georgian border. However, this problem seemed to be only in Kabardino-Balkaria (a semi-independent state similar to Chechnya), which includes the Mt. Elbruz region, Bezingi, and the Chegem and Balkaria Valleys. Their patrol camps are shown on the author's climbing maps.

Even though this was a bit of a hassle, the soldiers and the young officers were a friendly bunch, twice inviting this writer into their mess hall for breakfast. But on one occasion it was a free ride back to Nalchik in an army 4WD to get proposk! On that occasion, the English-speaking Lieutenant borrowed the author's DMA maps of Kavkazia which were created by using 1940's German and Red Army maps and took them to Army HQ, where all the big brass got a kick out of seeing those rather-detailed English-language maps of their country!

In Severo Ossetia and Karachey-Cherkessia the author never saw any soldiers in the mountains at all. Why it was that way was never understood, but things will surely change in the future, hopefully with less hassles.

If you plan to climb in Kavkazia and pass through Nalchik, be sure to stop at the *Gastinetsa Alpinist*, located about 500 meters southwest of the main bazaar. Once there, they will direct you to the semi-private, semi-government sponsored **Kabbalkalpinist Association** about 500 meters northwest from the hotel. Look up Vladimir Barashnikov, the general manager (or successor). Someone there will speak English and/or German, and they will help you get permission from the Pogranets Otryad to get into the high peaks. If you want to stay in the any of the alplagers (alp camps) or tourbazes (tourist bases) in Kabardino-Balkaria, they can make the arrangements, because they own or operate most of them. They can arrange transport, guides, everything. Contact this group at: Kabbalkalpinist, Ulitsa Chaikovsky 8, Nalchik, 360000, Kabardino-Balkaria, Russia. Fax 866-22-73510, Tele. 866-22-55916.

In **Kyrgyzstan**, you'll have to get your *proposk* whenever you get real close to any of the border regions. This includes going past Sary Tash on the way to Pik Lenina, or into Maida Aydr on the way to Pik Pobeda, and any other other areas close to the old external boundary of the former Soviet Union. You get this proposk at the OVIR (passport) offices in Osh, Bishkek or Kara Kol. This normally takes one day and is free.

10. Internet Information Websites & Guide Services.

As of 12/2000, just as this book is going to the printers, here are just a few websites you can explore which will get you started on a trip to Russia. Perhaps the first contact to make is the **Russian National Tourist Office**. Their offices are likely in most national capitals in the industrialized world, including New York, at 130 West 42nd Street, Suite 412; Tele. toll-free in the USA 877-221-7120, or 212-575-3431; Fax 212-575-3434; Website (www.russia-travel.com); or email (info@russia-travel.com). Once on this website you can click on tours or visas or whatever and go from there.

In addition to some of the contacts mentioned earlier in this chapter on Russia and countries of the former USSR, here is another contact. It's Pilgrim Tours at website (www.pop@ pilgrimtours.org). These people specialize in taking groups to Mt. Elbrus and other tours. Another contact for Elbrus is email (yurykolomiets@mtu-net.ru). Those who know how to get around the Internet can find lots of sites and information and in different languages. For information on other other CIS countries, click on SEARCH under Armenia, Kyrgizstan, etc.

The author standing on Periwal Koiavgan (Koiavgan Pass) which separates the Adylsu and Adyrsy Valleys (Map 161, page 355).

Along the Balkaria-Stir Digora Hike (Map 164, page 363) is this shepherd
hut with the ruined Severny Priyut in the background to the left.

This is the 6WD Russian Army GAZ truck the author got a lift in up to the Avachinsky
Tourbaze at the base of Koryaksky and Avacha Volcanos (Map 190, page 421).

Arkhiz Region, Kavkaz Mountains, Russia

This map shows the most-westerly high peaks in the Kavkaz or Caucasus Mountains. To the west are few if any peaks over 3000 meters. This is a popular hiking region, but not so popular for climbing. The highest summit is Pshysh at 3790 meters. Next is Sofiya at 3637.

To get to the starting point which is the small town of Arkhiz, first make your way to Cherkessk, the capital of the Karachay-Cherkassia Republic. At the main bus terminal next to the train station in the north end of the city, take one of 2 or 3 daily buses to Arkhiz; or one of several other buses to the small city of Zelenchuk, located halfway to Arkhiz. From Zelenchuk's station, or from the turnoff half a km to the west, take another bus, or hitch hike to Arkhiz. You can also catch these same buses 100 meters south of the Hotel Cherkessk (US$8 a night in 1994). The number of buses depends on the time of year and amount of tourist traffic.

In the past and in Soviet times, there used to be 3 hotels in Arkhiz, but in 1994, it seems there was just one in operation, the Tourbaze Arkhiz, at the beginning of town. You can walk from Arkhiz, or if you like, locate a taxi or private car to take you higher into the mountains. Or just start walking and you'll likely get a lift part way in a milk truck or with other tourists.

To climb **Pshysh**, walk or ride 18 kms from Arkhiz to the end of the road in the Pshysh Valley and continue on a trail as shown. You'll go past a log cabin, then wade a sizable stream on your way to the Pshysh Meadow at the foot of the mountain. The author saw this mountain from the top of **Peak 3200** just west of Sofiya, but still doesn't know the easiest route up. It doesn't look that easy, but there surely is a route up the south or east side. By September, the glaciers aren't as large as they appear on this map, so it'll be mostly a rock climb.

To climb **Sofiya**, walk up the Sofiya Valley past the hiker's priyut (hut) which is now in ruins and unusable, past the dairy & cheese farm to the end of the road. Cross the stream on a log bridge and head south up a livestock trail to the area west of the peak. Higher up, veer right to reach Peak 3200 meters. This is an easy climb and from on top you'll have a good look at Sofiya and Pshysh. There are several route possibilities up the west face of Sofiya. Or you can walk the fairly good trail northwest to and beyond Turquoise Lake, as shown.

The author spent 3 days here, 9/2 to 9/4/1994. Day 1, walked from Arkhiz up Sofiya Valley to 1900 meters--5 hours; Day 2, up to Peak 3200, then down & up past Turquoise Lake, and back to War Memorial--7 1/4 hours; Day 3, walked to Tourbaze at 1675 meters, then back to big pack & Arkhiz--7 1/4 hours.

This map shows a trail in the Kizhych-Bash Valley, but it's in the Teberda Nature Reserve and you may need permission to enter. Inquire at the Tourbaze Arkhiz. Also, the trail there is not so good, with lots of wading, according to the book listed below. Also, the trails over the passes are not all that good or easy and you'll likely need ice ax & crampons to make it over safely. You can buy food in Arkhiz, but it's best to buy all supplies in Cherkessk. Climb or hike here from July into early October.

From the top of Peak 3200 looking southwest at the eastern slopes of Pshysh.

Map 157-1, Arkhiz Region, Kavkaz Mountains, Russia

SCALE 0 2 4 6 8 KMS

Maps Touristskya Karta, *Western Kavkaz--Arkhiz*; buy from any trekking company in Moskva; or DMA map *Gagra, NK 37-3*, 1:250,000; the book, **Trekking in the Caucasus**, Cicerone Press; and read the *Introduction to Russia* for more information.

Dombai Region, Kavkaz Mountains, Russia

Featured here are a number of peaks in the area around the popular tourist & ski center of Dombai. Dombai is near the western end of the Kavkaz or Caucasus Mountains. To the west are peaks south of Arkhiz. As in most parts of Kavkazia, the peaks here are made of granite and crystalline rocks of various kinds. The highest summit is **Dombai-Ulgren** at 4046 meters. The peaks south of Dombai are on the main crest of the range and very rugged. While Dombai is in the forest at 1650 meters, the peaks above are heavily glaciated. Easier climbs can be found to the north of this main ridge. Most of the area on this map is part of the Teberda Nature Reserve, which means more regulations and restrictions than in other parts of Kavkazia. The book below is most helpful.

To get there, it's best to first head to Cherkessk, capital of the Karachay-Cherkassia Republic, and the best place to buy food and supplies. The Hotel Cherkessk, had rooms with TV and private bath for US$8 a night in 1994. From the main bus terminal next to the train station (vakszal) in the north end of the city, take one of many daily buses 108 kms to the health resort town of Teberda, 20 kms from Dombai. In the busiest part of the year, there may be buses going all the way to Dombai from Cherkessk. In summer, there are also direct buses from Mineralny Vody Airport. From Teberda, there are other buses heading for Dombai. By September, there is only one, maybe 2 buses per/day going that way.

Dombai has 3 or 4 hotels, but in the summer of 1994, they were barely running because the old Soviet trade unions were no longer sending members. Only at the Hotel Dombai was there anyone speaking English. It costs about US$10 a night, including 3 meals. Foreigners now apparently pay the same price as Russians. On the south side of the Dombai complex is the worker's housing, with 2 or 3 small magazins (shops). The gondola wasn't working at all in 9/1994, and the ski lifts were taking tourists up the mountain on weekends only.

On 8/27/1994, the author took a bus from Cherkessk to Teberda and camped in the forest just above town. Next morning, he got an early bus to Dombai, then hid his pack in the forest west of the resort. He then hiked to Alibek, an alplager (alpcamp)--but with no alpinists in '94. About US$7 will get you a room and 3 meals a day there. He then hiked further west, but never did find the trails to the 2 nearby passes. He later camped (illegally) in the woods just west of Dombai. Next morning brought heavy rain all day, but he did climb to the top of the ski lift carrying an umbrella. Next day more rain!, so he went back to Cherkessk by bus.

There are several short trails in 3 directions from Dombai, leading to climbing areas, but be warned, these are all rugged peaks. Ice ax & crampons, and more, are required on most routes. About 17 kms east from the main highway is the Severno Priyut (North Hut), with some interesting World War II monuments near the Periwal Khukhor (Khukhor Pass) where Germans and Russians fought. Camping may not be officially allowed near Dombai, but you can--just

One of the big hotels at Dombai with what appears to be Peak 3450 in the background (?).

Map 158-1, Dombai Region, Kavkaz Mtns., Russia

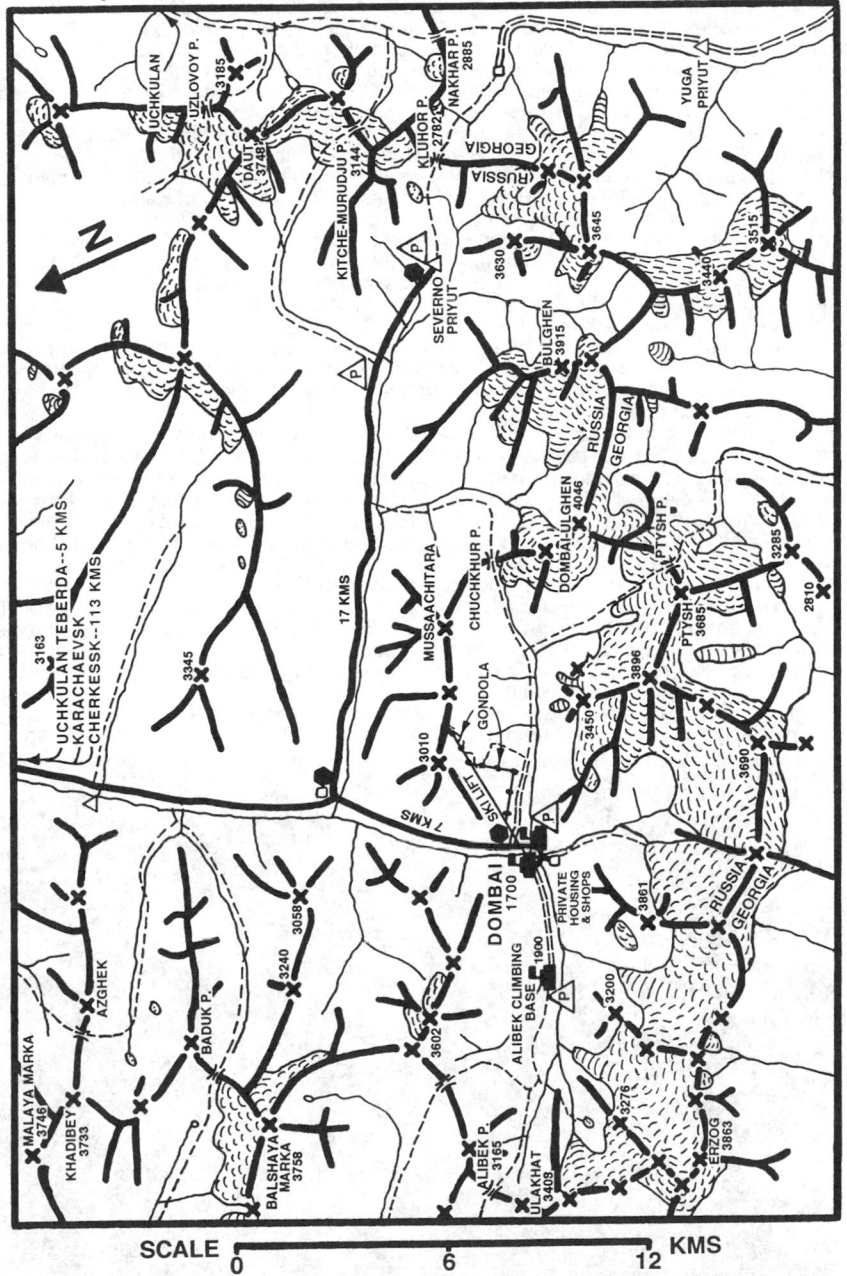

SCALE 0 · · · · · · 6 · · · · · · 12 KMS

your tent down in the morning and hid it.

Maps Turistskaya Karta, *Dombai--Elbruz*, 1:200,000, buy in bookstores in Cherkessk or at Dombai; and the very good book, **Trekking in the Caucasus**, Cicerone Press.

Uchkulan Region, Kavkaz Mountains, Russia

Featured here is the Uchkulan Region, which is between Dombai and Mt. Elbruz. This map includes the villages of Uchkulan and Khurzuk, and the western approaches to Mt. Elbruz, the highest mountain in Kavkazia (Caucasus) and Europe at 5642 meters. If climbing Elbruz without tourists is important to you, then this might be the access route to take. Elbruz is an old stratovolcano, having had an eruption in about 50 AD. But it seems dead as a doornail today. It's in a sea of metamorphic or crystalline rocks of various kinds.

To get there, start at Cherkessk, the capital of the Karachay-Cherkassia Republic, and the best place to buy food and supplies. The Hotel Cherkessk, with TV and private bath, was US$8 a night for one person in 1994. From the main bus terminal next to the train station (vakszal) in the north end of the city, take one of many daily buses south to the city of Karachaevsk. At the main bus station or the city center, get on another bus for Uchkulan or Khurzuk. About 4 buses daily go to Uchkulan, 2 or 3 of which go on to Khurzuk.

Here's what the author did. Beginning on 9/7/1994, he got an early morning bus from Cherkessk to Karachaevsk, then took the 11am bus to Uchkulan--one that didn't go to Khurzuk. He then walked a ways before getting a lift to Khurzuk. At 2pm he started walking and made it just past the farm house at 2000 meters in 4 hours. Next morning he broke camp, hid his big pack, then walked the road, then trail up to about 2700 meters in the canyon southwest of **Elbruz**. Along the way he passed the Voroshilov summer village at 2150 meters (about 8 homes and 25 kms from Khurzuk). In the canyon southwest of Elbruz, he saw a large herd of semi-wild yaks, imported from Tibet.

Later that day he returned to his pack and walked just into the lower end of the Chiryu-Kol Valley and camped; 8 hours walking. Next morning he returned to Ullukam Tourbaze (tourist base) and hid his big pack again, then walked to the shepherd camp above and southwest of the Uzunkol Alplager (Alpinist Camp). He then walked back to Khurzuk and got a lift down to Uchkulan, where he camped nearby; about 10 hours walking. Next morning, took the 6:30am bus back to the cities.

If you're heading for the mountains on the west side of this map, then get off at Uchkulan and walk, or locate a taxi or some private car, to take you up to as far the alplager, about 20 kms away. If going to Elbruz, you could walk or find a taxi or truck and get to Voroshilov summer village, but climbing the southwest slopes of the mountain is probably the most difficult route. It would be best to hire a vehicle, then walk east from Khurzuk to the Periwal Balkbashi (Balkbashi Pass) at 3650 meters, then route-find up from there. The average climber may need up to 5 or 6 days from Khurzuk to complete this climb. Routes on the mountain from this side may or may not be easy--also beware of crevasses! High altitude climbing equipment required.

The peaks along the main east-west Kavkazian ridge are all basically technical climbs. Khurzuk probably has one magazin (store) and Uchkulan 2, but buy your supplies in Cherkessk

Looking south from the shepherd camp at Zamok left and Dalar to the right.

Map 159-1, Uchkulan Region, Kavkaz Mtns., Russia

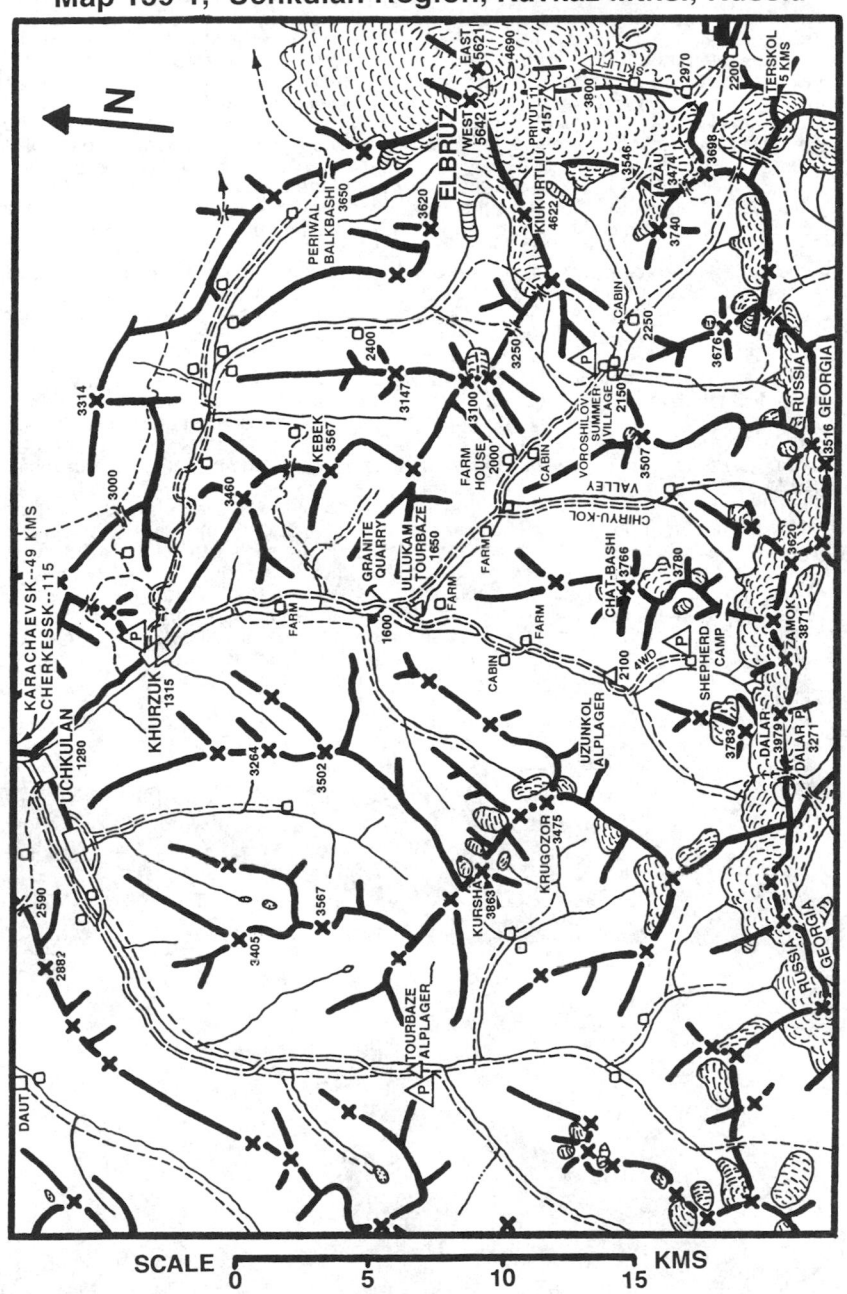

SCALE

0   5   10   15   KMS

or Karachaevsk. Climbing season is July to early September.
Maps *Mount Elbruz Region, Map and Guide,* 1:80,000 & 1:210,000, West Col Books; and the book, **Trekking in the Caucasus**, Cicerone Press

Mt. Elbruz, Kavkaz Mountains, Russia

This map shows the normal route to the top of Europe's highest summit, Mt. Elbruz at 5642 meters. It's located in the western part of the Kavkaz or Caucasus Mountains and southwest of the city of Nalchik, the capital of the Kabardino-Balkaria (K-B) Republic. While most of the Kavkaz has crystalline or metamorphic-type rocks, Elbruz is an old volcano which last erupted in about 50 AD. It still has a conal shape, but it's now considered extinct.

First go to Nalchik. There's a hotel for about US$10 a person at the main long-distance bus station. This is the station where you find buses to Terskol, the small town at the base of Elbruz. In summer there are 7 or 8 buses per day going that way. Also in Nalchik, there is a very clean Alpinists Gastinetsa (Hotel) about 500 meters south of the bazaar & Avtovakszal (bus station) #2. The author paid about US$6 a night there (and they store baggage). Nearby is the alpinist headquarters, where you can hire guides and/or get more information about climbs in K-B. Buy all supplies for your trip in Nalchik's bazaar, the best in Kavkazia.

About 2/3's of the way from Nalchik to Terskol, is the small city of Tyrnyauz. All buses stop there for about 30 minutes next to the bazaar. If you need any more supplies, get off the bus quickly and buy them there, because Terskol has only a couple of small magazins (shops) and the variety is terrible. Most people who live in the upper valley take one of many buses per day from Terskol down to Tyrnyauz to do their shopping.

There are a number of tourist hotels and alplagers (alpinist camps) in the Azau Valley, but no place to officially camp with a tent. To do that, you'll have to go into the Adylsu Valley to the Shkhelda (pron. Shielda) Alplager (right side of map). Or you could just bivouac in the trees (?), but you really need a place to store baggage while climbing. In 1994, some of the alplagers were being used for other purposes because of so few tourists and climbers, so expect changes to this information.

To climb Elbruz, walk northwest from Terskol about 5 kms to the bottom of the gondola & Azau Hotel and either ride up, or walk along the 4WD road & trail (not shown on this map) up to ski slopes above. From the end of the ski lift, continue up the snow field to the Priyut 11 (Refuge of the 11). It was a small hotel sleeping about 200, mostly in rooms for 2, and costing about US$7.50 per night. Unfortunately it burned down in 1999, but as of 7/2000 they were building a new one. Ask about that situation in Nalchik. Or you can camp nearby on the rocky ridge. From Priyut 11, a generally good trail in the snow leads up to Pastukhova Rocks, then up to an abandoned hut in the saddle, then left to the west summit. Along the way you'll step across 3 or 4 small crevasses--no problem. Ice ax & crampons and warm clothes are mandatory, but it's an easy climb.

On 7/24/1994, the author walked from Alplager Cheget Hotel to Priyut 11 in 5 1/4 hours, and camped. On Day 2, he reached the summit in very unsettled weather in less than 3 1/2 hours, then returned to camp. Round-trip time from camp was 5 hours. That afternoon he left the

Elbruz with the old Priyut 11 nearby, and the Pastukhova Rocks beyond to the right.

Map 160-1, Mt. Elbruz, Kavkaz Mountains, Russia

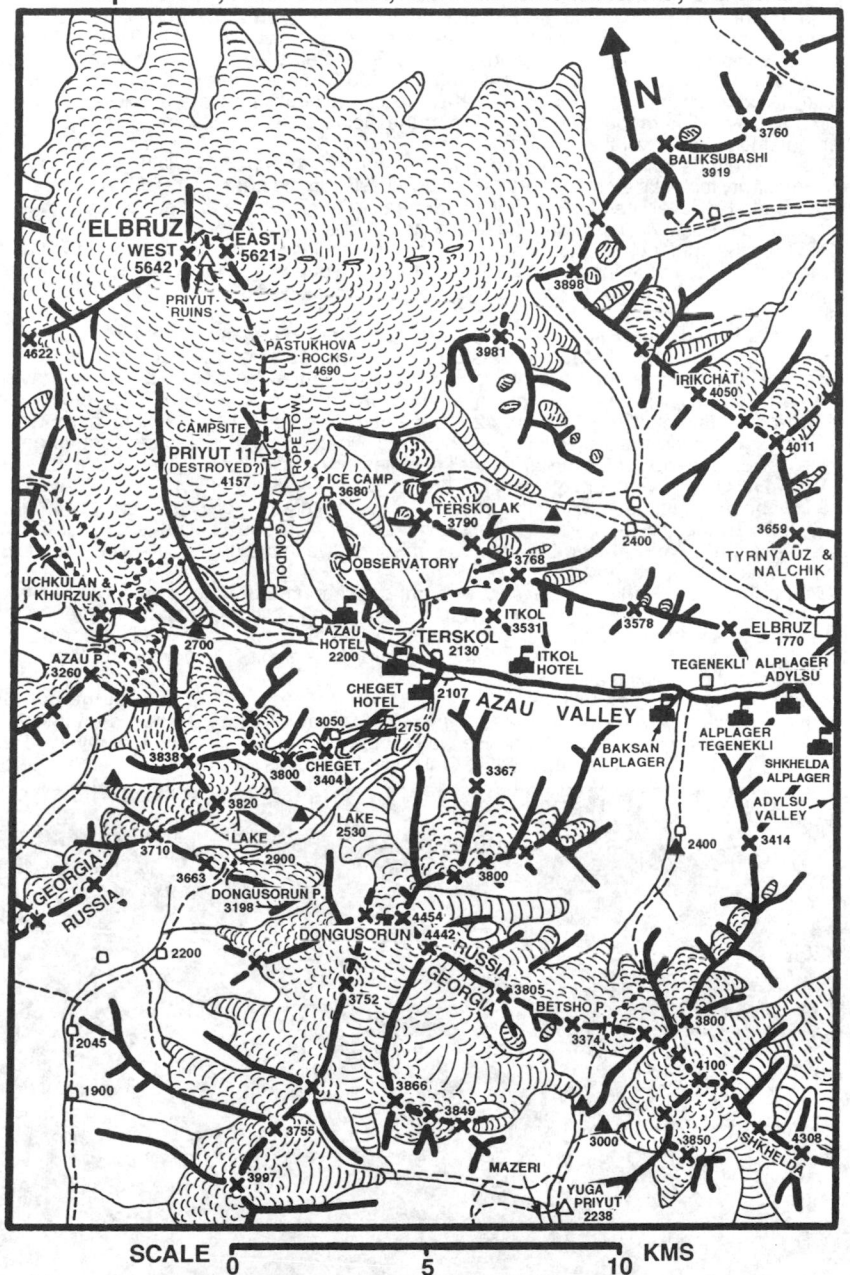

SCALE 0   5   10 KMS

mountain and camped near the base of the gondola & Azau Hotel (2 1/2 hours). Average
climbing times are about double the author's.
Maps *Mount Elbruz Region--Map and Guide*, 1:80,000 & 1:200,000, West Col Books; and the
book, **Trekking in Russia & Central Asia**, Maier, The Mountaineers.

Ushba-Jailik Region, Kavkaz Mountains, Russia-Georgia

The mountains on this map are immediately east of Mt. Elbruz, in the Kavkaz or Caucasus Mountains. The best known peak here is the twin summits of **Ushba** at 4707 & 4694 meters. Not far away is **Shkhelda** (pron. Shielda), or the **Shkhelda Wall**, the highest part of which is 4320 meters. Northeast of Ushba is **Pik Jailik** at 4533 meters. After Elbruz, this is the most popular hiking and climbing region in all of Kavkazia. The peaks here are as rugged and difficult to climb as any in this range, or the world. For the most part, the rocks are all granite, or some other metamorphic or crystalline rock.

The southern half of this map is Georgian territory; the north half Russian. In the past, most climbing activity took place on the north slope, in Russia. In the near future, this may continue to be the trend. However, as of 1994, it was a lot easier to get a visa to Georgia than to Russia. Read the *Introduction to Russia and the CIS* states for the latest on visas.

Because the author came into this region from Russia, all information presented will be from that side. If you do come in from Georgia, then make your way to the Mestia area where you can get the latest information. There are facilities for tourists and climbers, but the author isn't familiar with them.

From the Russian side, first make your way to Nalchik. There's a hotel for about US$10 a person at the main long-distance bus station. This is the station where you find buses to Terskol, the small town at the base of Elbruz. In summer, there are 7 or 8 buses per day going that way. Also in Nalchik, is a very clean alpinists gastinetsa (hotel) about 500 meters south of the bazaar & Avtovakszal (bus station) #2. The author paid about US$6 a night there (and they store baggage). Nearby is the alpinist headquarters, where you can hire guides and/or get more information about climbs in this area. Buy all supplies in Nalchik's bazaar, best in Kavkazia.

About 2/3's of the way from Nalchik to Terskol, is the small city of Tyrnyauz. All buses stop there for about 30 minutes next to the bazaar. If you need any more supplies, get off the bus quickly and buy them there, because there are only a few small magazins (shops) in the upper Baksan Valley and variety is terrible. Most people who live in the upper valley take a bus down to Tyrnyauz to do their shopping.

Get off the bus at Verkhnny Baksan, or a km or two past Elbruz, and walk or hitch hike up either of the 2 main valleys; Adylsu or Adyrsu. There is no public transport into either, but there are hotels and alplagers (alpinist camps) in both. A bed in a small room, plus 3 meals a day at Shkhelda Alplager cost US$5 in 1994. Pitch a tent for $1 a night. The Jantugan Hotel is as low as US$11 a night, including 3 meals.

A popular hike is to go up one valley and down the other. This is what the author did beginning on 7/28/1994. The hike lasted into the 3rd day and took 16 hours total walk-time crossing the Periwal (pass) Koiavgan. He walked from the main highway to highway. He had bad weather except for the first day, so he didn't climb. No easy climbs here! Almost all peaks

The Shkhelda (Shielda) Wall as seen from just above the Shkhelda Alplager.

354

Map 161-1, Ushba-Jailik Region, Kavkazia, Russia-Georgia

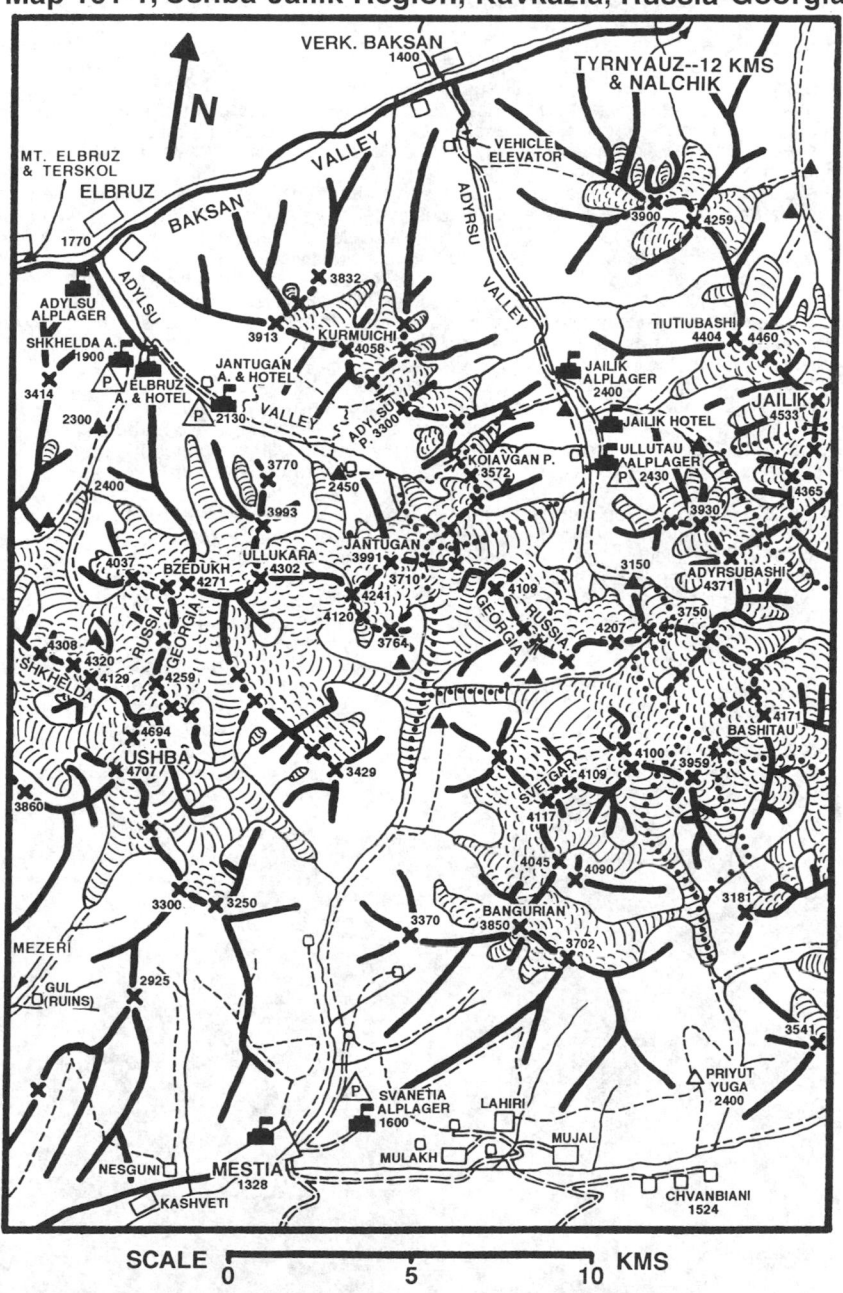

in these parts are for experienced and well-equipped climbers only.
Maps *Mount Elbruz Region--Map and Guide,* 1:80,000 & 1:200,000, West Col Books; and 2 books,
Trekking in the Caucasus, Cicerone Press; and **Classic Climbs in the Caucasus**, Diadem Books.

Chegem Region, Kavkaz Mountains, Russia

Shown on this map are the mountains between the Mt. Elbruz & Ushba area to the west, and the Bezingi Valley & Wall to the east. This is the upper drainage of the Chegem River Basin. This whole area is southwest of Nalchik and is in the Kabardino-Balkaria (K-B) Republic. Like most peaks in the Kavkaz or Caucasus Mountains, these are made of granite and other metamorphic rocks. Only the non-glaciated summits are easy climbing--everything else is difficult. Even the passes here are for experienced and well-equipped climbers.

To reach this area, first make your way to Nalchik. There's a hotel for about US$10 a person at the main long-distance bus station. This station is about 1 km northeast of the bazaar and Avtovakszal (bus station) #2, which is where you find buses to Bulungu, the upper-most town in the Chegem Valley. In the summer of 1994, there were 2 buses per day running from Bulungu down to Nalchik each morning for shoppers; then 2 buses returning to Bulungu each afternoon. Also in Nalchik, is a very clean alpinists gastinetsa (hotel) about 500 meters directly south of the bazaar. The author paid about US$6 a night there. Nearby is the alpinist headquarters, where you can hire guides and/or get more information about climbs in this area. Be sure to stop at the alpinists headquarters to see if you need proposk or permission to climb peaks near the border in this region. Also read the *Introduction to Russia and the CIS States* for more information on climbing in K-B. Buy all supplies for your trip in Nalchik's bazaar, the best in Kavkazia.

In Bulungu, there is one small magazin (shop) right at the main square, but it doesn't have much. From Bulungu there are pretty good roads running 14 kms up the valley to either the Bashil or Chegem Tourbazes (tourist or alpinists bases--TB). There are no buses, but you can either hire a vehicle in Bulungu, or just start walking and you'll probably get a lift part way. At either tourbaze, you can get a room with 3 meals for about US$10 a day. In 1994, there was hardly anyone staying at either one. Nowadays, no reservations are needed, and we pay the same as Russians. Or you can camp near either tourbaze for free. In 1994, just above each tourbaze, was a pagranitzny (border guard) camp. To get past them, you had to have a permit. Get that permit in Nalchik--if it's still required when you arrive (?)

Above the Chegem TB, is the Priyut Severny (North Hut) at the base of **Tikhtengen**, at 4617 meters, the highest peak in the immediate area. That hut was in very poor condition upon the author's visit, but 3 or 4 people could sleep in it. From Chegem, and by using some high and very rugged passes, you could head east to the Bezingi Wall area. From the Bashil TB, you can take trails up to the base of Jailik, or go over other high passes to reach the Adyrsu Valley and Ullutau Alplager (Alpcamp). Tourbazes open in July, close about September 1.

For 3 days beginning on 8/22/1994, the author was at these 2 tourbazes. He got a lift in a Russian army truck to Chegem TB and hiked to the hut above, but couldn't go far above Bashil TB because he lacked proposk.

Looking south at the peaks above the Priyut Severny (North Hut).

Map 162-1, Chegem Region, Kavkaz Mtns., Russia

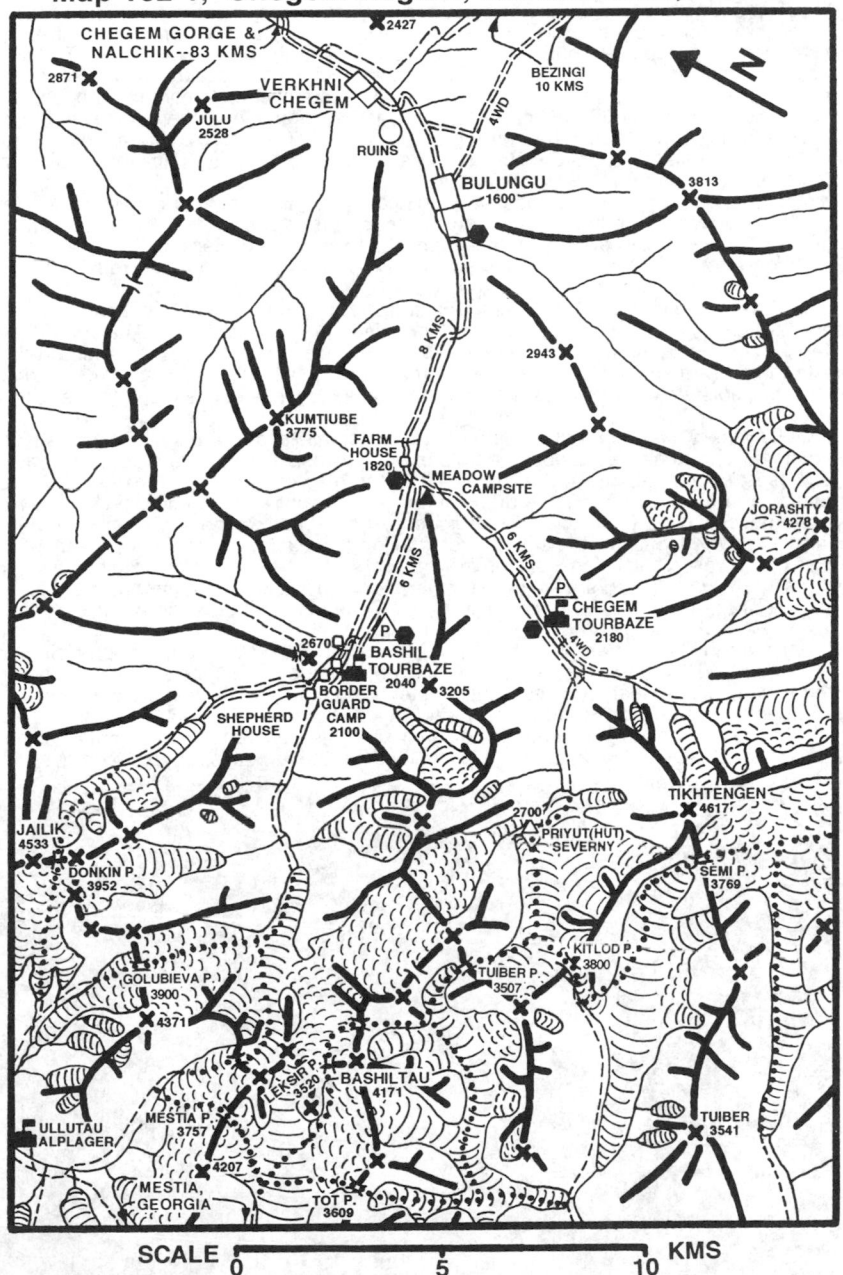

SCALE 0 ——————— 5 ——————— 10 KMS

Maps *Caucasus Central, Elbrus to Kazbek, Map--Guide 5* in the series, 1:200,000, West Col Books; and the books, **Classic Climbs in the Caucasus**, Diadem Books; and **Trekking in the Caucasus**, Cicerone Press.

Bezingi Wall Region, Kavkaz Mountains, Russia

This map shows one of the highest, wildest and most popular snow & ice climbing areas in all of the Kavkaz or Caucasus Mountains. It's known simply as Bezingi Wall, a 15-km-long section of peaks along a high ridge all of which are very near the 5000 meter level. The highest point is Dyktau at 5204 meters. This map shows more 5000 meters peaks than any other part of the range. Most of the rocks here are either granite or some other metamorphic type.

This mapped area is southwest of Nalchik, and in between the Chegem Valley to the west, and the Balkaria to the east. The starting point is Nalchik. Before going further, read the *Introduction to Russia and the CIS* first, in regards to *proposk*. In Nalchik, make your way to the Avtovakszal (bus station) #2, which is across the street from the bazaar. About 500 meters south of the bazaar is the Alpinist Gastinetsa (Hotel), and near that is the alpinist association. Before leaving Nalchik, buy all your food and supplies in the bazaar, the best market in Kavkazia. From the #2 bus station, take the 4pm bus to the town of Bezingi. This takes about 2 or 2 1/2 hours for the 73 km ride. This same bus leaves Bezingi running to Nalchik in the mornings at about 8am, returning each afternoon at 4pm.

There is one little magazin (shop) at the main square in Bezingi, but they don't have much. Most people take the daily bus to Nalchik for shopping. From Bezingi, there's a good dirt road running 18 kms up to the Bezingi Alplager (BA) or Tourbaze at 2100 meters altitude. This alpinists camp has about a dozen buildings; some large homes, others like small dormitories or hotels. It has no shops, but your fee, if you stay there, includes a bed and 3 meals, at US$15 a day.

From BA, there's a good trail running south to a small *kosh* or hut called Misses Kosh at 2450 meters. This kosh sleeps about 4 people, but it's trashy--so take and use your own tent. From Misses Kosh, walk down the good trail to the glacier and head for the rocky medial moraine and continue south. Higher up, veer left or east right at the corner and walk across a crevasse-free section of the glacier. Then get onto a good trail on the lateral moraine heading east to the Jangi Kosh below the south face of **Dyktau**. This hut sleeps up to about 5 or 6 in crowded conditions. Or you can camp anywhere nearby, but keep things in your tent away from the chamois (Asian big horn sheep). In summer, someone at this kosh has radio contact with BA as part of an alp rescue service. The map shows various routes to nearby peaks and passes.

There's another kosh east of Bezingi Alplager. Get there by a good sheep trail along a lateral moraine. The Ulu Kosh is high above the valley at about 3200 meters. The author tried, but never did find it; he learned of its location later. The map shows its approximate site. The author spent 4 leisurely days in this valley region starting on 8/7/1994, and saw 2 of the 3 koshes, but camped nearby instead. He only climbed the peak above the Jangi Kosh. Total walk-time from Bezingi town; 23 hours. To climb any of these peaks, or just to go over any of

Looking southwest from the Jangi Kosh (Jangi Hut) at the Bezingi Wall).

Map 163-1, Bezingi Wall Region, Kavkaz Mtns., Russia

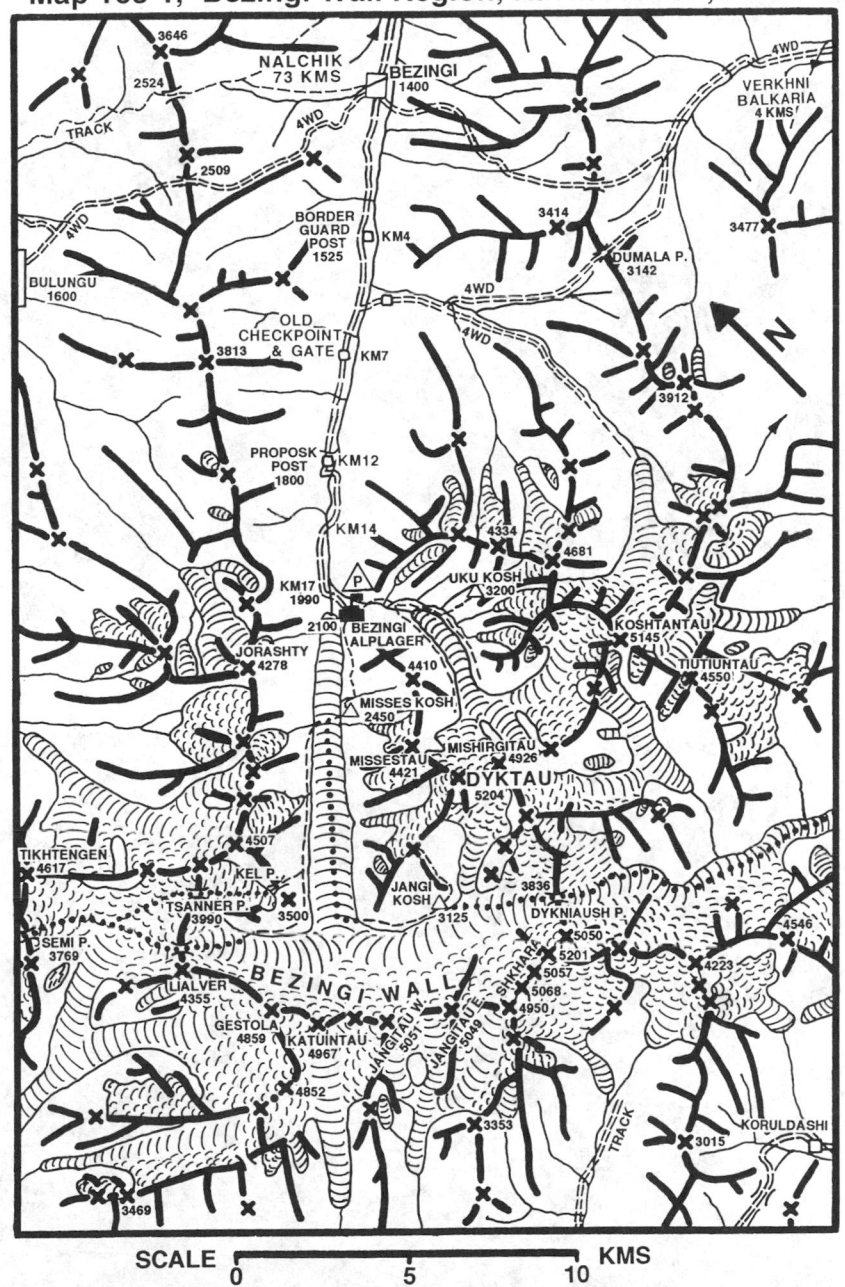

SCALE 0 — 5 — 10 KMS

these passes, requires full alpine snow climbing equipment.

Maps *Caucasus Central, Elbrus to Kazbek, Map--Guide 5*, 1:200,000, or *Bezingi, Map--Guide 3* in the series, 1:100,000, West Col Books; and the books, **Classic Climbs in the Caucasus**, Diadem Books; and **Trekking in the Caucasus**, Cicerone Press, all from the UK.

Looking south from upper Terskol at the north face of Dongusorun (Map 160, page 353).

The upper north face of Dongusorun (Map 160, page 353) as seen from above Terskol.

Looking south at the Bezingi Wall with the Bezingi Alplager on the left.

An upclose look at the Bezingi Wall from where the Bezingi Glacier turns northeast.

Balkaria-Stir Digora Region, Kavkaz Mountains, Russia

This is the 8th map in the series covering the Kavkaz or Caucasus Range of Southern Russia. This one shows the mountains above the small town of Verkhni Balkaria (Upper Balkaria) which is in Kabardino-Balkaria Republic; and the peaks around the small village of Stir Digora, which is in Severo Ossetia (Northern Ossetia). Most peaks here are over 4000 meters and heavily glaciated. The rocks range from granite and metamorphic, to the softer gray shale at the Shtulu Pass, 3326 meters, which is the reason for the east-west valley running between the 2 groups of high summits. Before going further, read the *Introduction to Russia and the CIS States,* for more information concerning **proposk**.

Since this map covers 2 semi-independent republics, there are 2 starting points. To reach Balkaria, go to Nalchik. From the main Avtovakzal 1 (Bus Station 1), take bus 11, 15, or 17 to the Avtovakszal 2 (Bus Station 2), which is next to the bazaar. Buy all your food there, then take one of about 6 daily buses heading for Verkhni Balkaria, 73 kms away. Balkaria has 2 small shops or magazins, but food selections are poor. It's about 28 kms from Balkaria up to the end of a fairly good dirt road in the upper valley ending at the Priyut Severny (north hut). This upper road has little traffic, but if walking, you'll likely get a ride part way. Before leaving Nalchik, be sure to check if proposk (permission) is needed to hike above the border patrol (pagranichny) checkpoint.

To reach Stir Digora, first go to Vladikavkaz. From the main avtovakzal at the north end of the city, take one of about 2 afternoon buses running west to Chikola, Matsuta and ending at Stir Digora, which has the only magazin in the upper valley. In the middle of the summer season, one bus may run on to the Rostovskaya or Digora Tourbaze each day. From there, a pretty good dirt road runs west for about 5 or 6 kms but it has little traffic.

The author took a mid-day bus from Nalchik to Verkhni Balkaria and started walking in the early afternoon of 8/13/1994, Day 1. About mid-day of Day 2, he waded the stream near the shepherd huts (S. huts on the map) at 2340 which was a little tricky. He made it over Shtulu Pass later on Day 2, and was at Stir Digora about noon on Day 3--about 18 hours walk-time.

There are many good peaks on either side of this main east-west valley with many sheep & goat trails going up to meadows at the base of glaciers. This is a great place to simply hike or climb. Shtulu Pass is snow-free in late summer and easy, but for other passes you'll need ice ax & crampons. The route symbols on the map show possible treks. There are many small shepherd huts along the way, but they are being used in summer, or are in terrible condition. Use your own tent! The Severny Priyut was useless in 1994; cows were jumping through the windows and it's full of manure. In summer there are many shepherds tending flocks of sheep, goats and cattle in the upper valleys. In Severo Ossetia, proposk was not needed to hike or climb in 1994; but there were pagranichny (border guards) checking permits above Verkhni Balkaria. Luckily the author had his that time.

From along the Balkaria-Stir Digora Hike looking north at the Sugan-Doppakh area.

Map 164-1, Balkaria-Stir Digora Region, Kavkazia, Russia

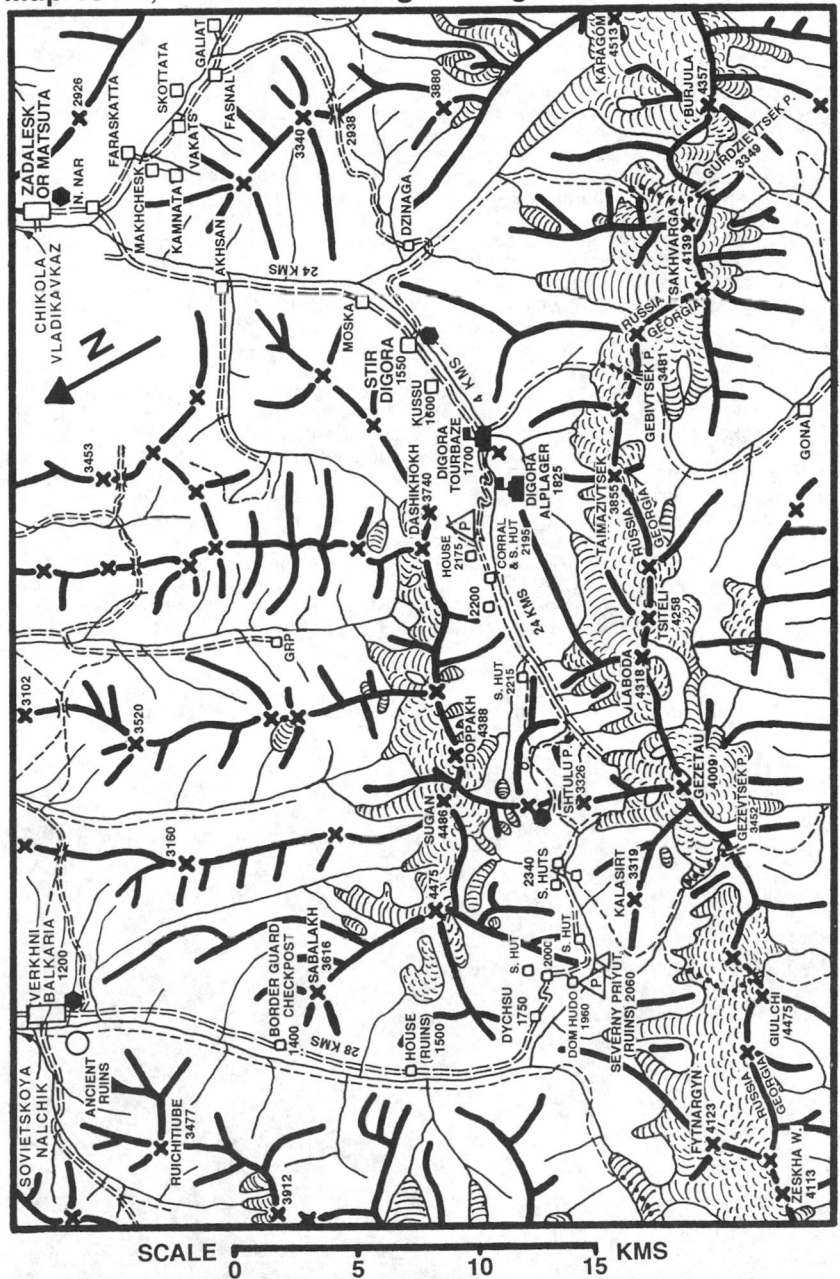

SCALE

0   5   10   15   KMS

Maps *Caucasus Central, Elbrus to Kazbek, Map--Guide 5*, 1:200,000; or *Bezingi, Map--Guide 3* in the series, 1:100,000, West Col Books; and the books, **Classic Climbs in the Caucasus**, Diadem Books; and **Trekking in the Caucasus**, Cicerone Press, all from the UK.

Buron Region, Kavkaz Mountains, Russia

This is the 9th map covering the Kavkaz or Caucasus Mountains on the border of Russia and Georgia. These peaks are located southwest of Vladikavkaz and within the Severno Ossetia Republic (North Osssetia). You can climb from the Georgian side, but all or most of the tourist facilities seem to be north of the border. The small mining community of Buron is the most centrally located town in the area and is the end of normal public bus service to this region. The highest peak is Uilpata at 4646 meters, at the head of the Tsei Valley. In a second group of summits, Tepli at 4431 meters, is the highest. The rocks here are mostly metamorphic or crystalline type.

To get to these peaks, first go to Vladikavkaz. There you'll find a good bazaar not far south of the railway station. This is one of the better places to shop, so buy everything there for your trip. The cheapest accommodation is the Gastinetsa (Hotel) Universitetskaya, located across the street from the university and 150 meters south of the Hotel Kavkaz. From the hotels and the bazaar area are buses and marsroute (group) taxis running to the north end of the city and the main avtovakzal (bus station). From there take one of about 2 daily buses running west to Alagir, then south to Buron. One bus leaves in the morning, one in the afternoon.

At the last bus stop in Buron, which is near the pagranichny (border patrol) traffic checkpoint, ask about a group taxi or truck running west up to the tourist facilities in the Tsei Valley. If business gets better than it was 1994, there may be a daily bus or two. Otherwise, just start walking and you may get a lift.

At Tsei, there are 6 lodging places or hotels; either gastinetsas, tourbazes or alplagers, but in 1994, they weren't doing much business. There were only one or 2 open at that time. Before the USSR broke up, there was at least one magazin or shop selling food, but that was closed too. Just before you cross the second river bridge, turn left and walk up the zig zag paved road to the upper-most facility which is the Torpedo Alplager next to the ski lift at about 2100 meters. This was open in 1994 and there were some Russian hikers around. From there you can walk up the track beneath the ski lift to the bottom of the glacier. Another track continues up to 2550 meters where an old rope tow used to be located.

If you walk up the main valley toward **Uilpata**, you'll pass an 8 or 9 story hotel that was closed in 1994. Beyond that is a 4WD road running for about 2 kms, then a trail up along the lateral moraine of a glacier. The peaks in this area are fairly rugged and heavily glaciated, but aren't quite as difficult to climb as those in the Bezingi or Dombai regions. Be sure to take snow & ice climbing equipment. If it's a quite corner of Kavkazia you're looking for, this might be the place.

The author took a late afternoon bus from Vladikavkaz to Buron, and walked a ways and camped. Next day, 8/20/1994, he walked up to Tsei, then to the ends of both trails mentioned above on a quick tour of the place, but didn't do any climbing. In the afternoon of Day 2, he got

This is the upper part of the ski lift at 2550 meters above Tsei.

Map 165-1, Buron Region, Kavkaz Mtns., Russia

SCALE 0 5 10 15 KMS

a lift part way down to Buron, camped nearby and got a morning bus back to Vladikavkaz.
Maps *Caucasus Central, Elbrus to Kazbek, Map--Guide 5,* 1:200,000; or the *Adai Dhokh-Khalatsa-Kazbek Region, Map--Guide 4,* in the series, 1:100,000, West Col Books. The 2 guidebooks listed for other parts of western Kavkazia don't cover this district.

Gora Kazbek, Kavkaz Mountains, Russia-Georgia

One of the best known climbs in the Kavkaz or Caucasus Mountains is Gora (Mt.) Kazbek at 5047 meters. This peak is located due south of Vladikavkaz and immediately west of the famous Georgia Military Highway, the most-used link between Russia and Georgia. Kazbek is a old eroded stratovolcano. It's last 2 eruptions were about 4000 BC and 750 BC. This volcano sits in a sea of granite and other metamorphic or crystalline rocks.

Kazbek is on the boundary of Russia and Georgia, but is north of the watershed divide. All the streams draining the south slope actually flow east, then north past Kazbek, and on into Russia. This means if you're coming from the Russian side, you'll either have to climb it from a more difficult northern route, from Karmadon or Dargavs; or have a visa to Georgia (a transist visa at the border should do?) and/or perhaps a double entry visa to Russia (?).

The author took a local bus from the small bazaar at the south end of Vladikavkaz up to Kazbegi, did his climb, then returned. Going up, the Russia pagranichny (border guards) waved the local bus through, and it didn't even stop at Georgia Customs. On the way back there was still no stopping on the Georgian side, but the Russians looked more closely. They thought his visa wasn't valid in that region, so after 5 hours, and after driving him back to Vladikavkaz in an army 4WD, the pagranichny finally set him free to wander. As of 1994, it was much easier to get a visa to Georgia than to Russia, so climbing Kazbek via Georgia seems less complicated. Hopefully the Russias can solve this little inconveinance.

There are many buses running south from Vladikavkaz; both local to Kazbegi and Kobi, and international going on to Tbilisi. To use the normal route to **Kazbek**, stop in Kazbegi and walk west up to Gergeti. From there, a steep 4WD road zig zags west up to an old church on the hill above. Near that church, continue southwest up along a good trail on a ridge. Higher up, you'll come to a stream crossing, then along a glacier moraine. Cross the lower end of the glacier to another trail leading up to the abandoned meteostantsiya (meteorlogical station) at 3660 meters. Three or 4 rooms are regularly used, but 50 or more people could sleep on the floor of a dozen more rooms.

The normal way to Kazbek's summit is to walk west on a trail under the south face, then along the moat. Later, veer northwest, then when you're due west of the peak, turn back to the east, *cross 5 or 6 big crevasses* and climb the easy west slopes up to the summit ridge. You could also climb the steeper south face, and east slope above the hut. The author was there in bad weather between 7/17 & 7/20/1994, but did get up to about 4800 meters, and 400 meters from the top, before being turned back by a blizzard. His total walk-time from Gergeti was 19 1/2 hours. His trip involved 2 long days, and about one hour walking on days 1 & 4. He camped his 1st and 3rd nights just above Gergeti. Three full days from Gergeti is normal. There is one little cheap hotel in Kazbegi and several small stores. Ice ax, crampons, and warm clothes are required.

Maps *Caucasus Central, Elbrus to Kazbek, Map--Guide 5*, 1:200,000; or the *Adai Dhokh-Khalatsa-*

Looking east at the eastern side of Kazbek from the meteostantsiya.

Map 166-1, Gora Kazbek, Kavkaz Mtns., Russia-Georgia

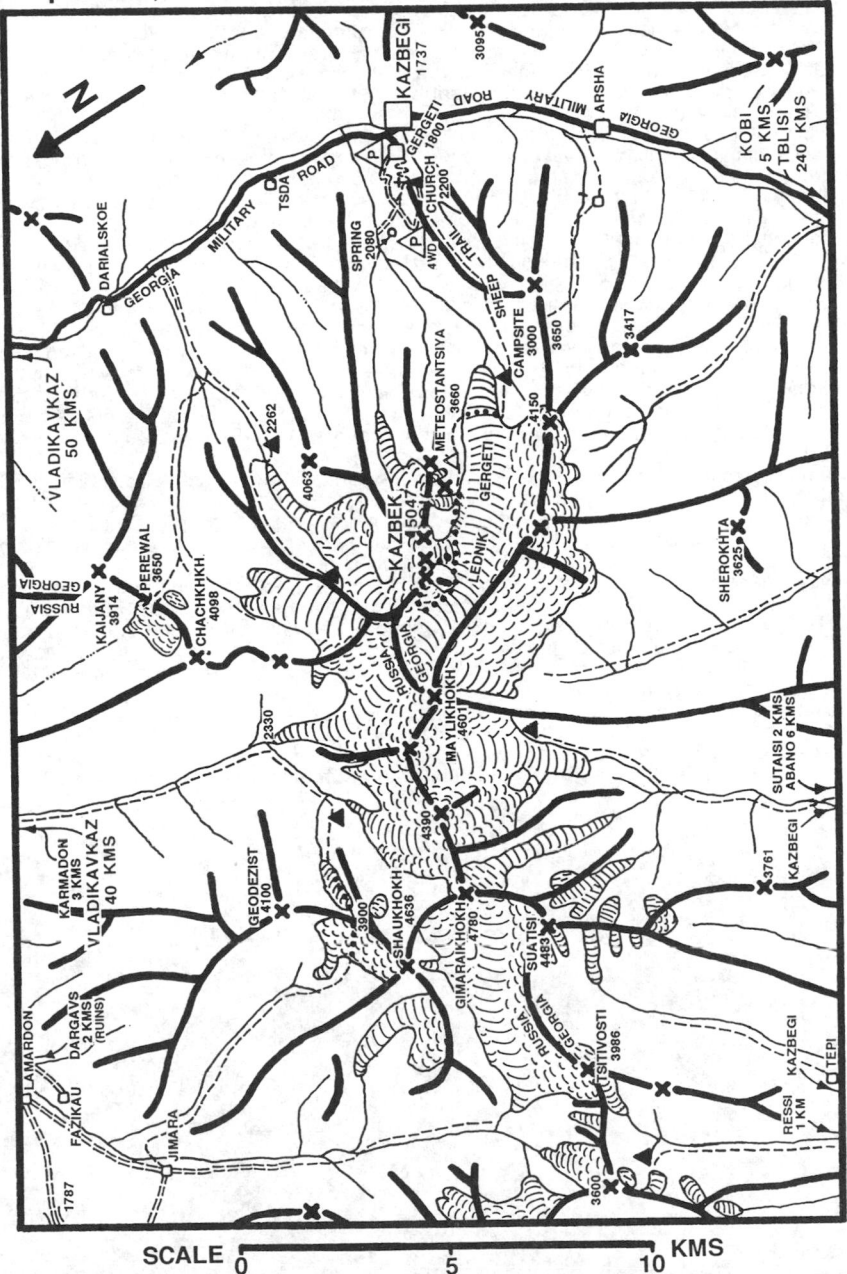

SCALE 0 ___ 5 ___ 10 KMS

Kazbek Region, Map--Guide 4, in the series, 1:100,000, West Col Books; also the guidebooks, **Classic Climbs in the Caucasus**, Diadem Books; and **Trekkihg in Russia & Central Asia**, The Mountaineers.

Sherkota & Keli Plato, Kavkaz Mountains, Georgia

The main focus of this map are some volcanos just south of the high massif of Gora (Mt.) Kazbek. The highest point here is Zilgakhokh at 3856 meters, but more interesting will be the Keli Plato (Plateau) and Sherkota Volcano, 3694 meters. This whole area is in the central Kavkaz or Caucasus Mountains and just south of the Russian-Georgian border. Just up the road about 6 kms off this map is Kazbegi and Gergeti, the normal starting point for climbing Kazbek. See previous map.

On one of the ridges across a glacier south of Kazbek is a rather recent volcano called Gora Sut. South of this and across a valley is the Keli Plato and Sherkota, the peak which looks more like a volcano than any other around. It appears to be 2000 or so years old (?).

While you could get to this area via Vladikavkaz and Russia, the normal route is from Tbilisi, Georgia. In Tbilisi, get on the metro or subway, then get off at the northern station of Didube. On the west side of that metro station is the avtovakzal (bus station) for northern destinations. Take one of several buses per day going the 101 kms to Zemo-Mleta or Mleti, right where the road going over the pass to Kazbek begins to climb. Get a local bus, because the international buses to Vladikavkaz, probably won't stop at Mleti.

From Mleti, locate the old vehicle track running northwest along the southwest side of the river. It ends after 2 or 3 kms, then you continue on the sheep & goat trail which rises to a ridge-top, then eventually to the plato itself. Once on the plato, follow the route symbol north to **Sherkota**. Don't try climbing Sherkota from the Periwal Krestovy (Krestovy Pass)--the author tried it but was stopped by the very steep gorge. You could also approach the plato from from the west and Kvemo-Roka in the southwest corner of the map. Buses should go there from Tbilisi.

To reach Kobi (or Kazbegi and Gergeti), take a bus from the Didube metro station in Tbilisi heading for Vladikavkaz. Many of these buses begin in the late afternoon and arrive in Vladikavkaz in the morning. From Kobi, start walking west along the road to Resi and Tepi. This gives access to **Gora Sut,** and the lava flows south of Zemo Orokana, and trails going over high passes to Kvemo-Roka, and even Sherkota from the north

The author was in this region for 4 days from 6/8 to 6/11/1995, and found lots of snow and bad weather. He camped at 2100 meters just above Shevardeni, then spent 4 hours climbing Gora Sut, round-trip. Next day he hitch hiked from the police check post in Kobi, up to Periwal Krestovy, but couldn't get across the gorge. He finally hitch hiked down to Mleti and walked in from there. He found snow completely covering the Keli Plato, and that, along with terrible weather kept him away from Sherkota.

Expect some difficult climbing on the glaciated peaks shown on the west side of this map. The south slopes are easier than the icy north faces. Routes on the Keli Plato are very easy. Vulkans Sut and Sherkota are easy walk-ups. You'll find sheep & goats here in summer wherever grass grows. Hike or climb from July into September. With all the livestock on the

From the *tourist lookout,* looking northwest at the *steep gorge* and Sherkota.

Map 167-1, Sherkota & Keli Plato, Kavkaz Mtns., Georgia

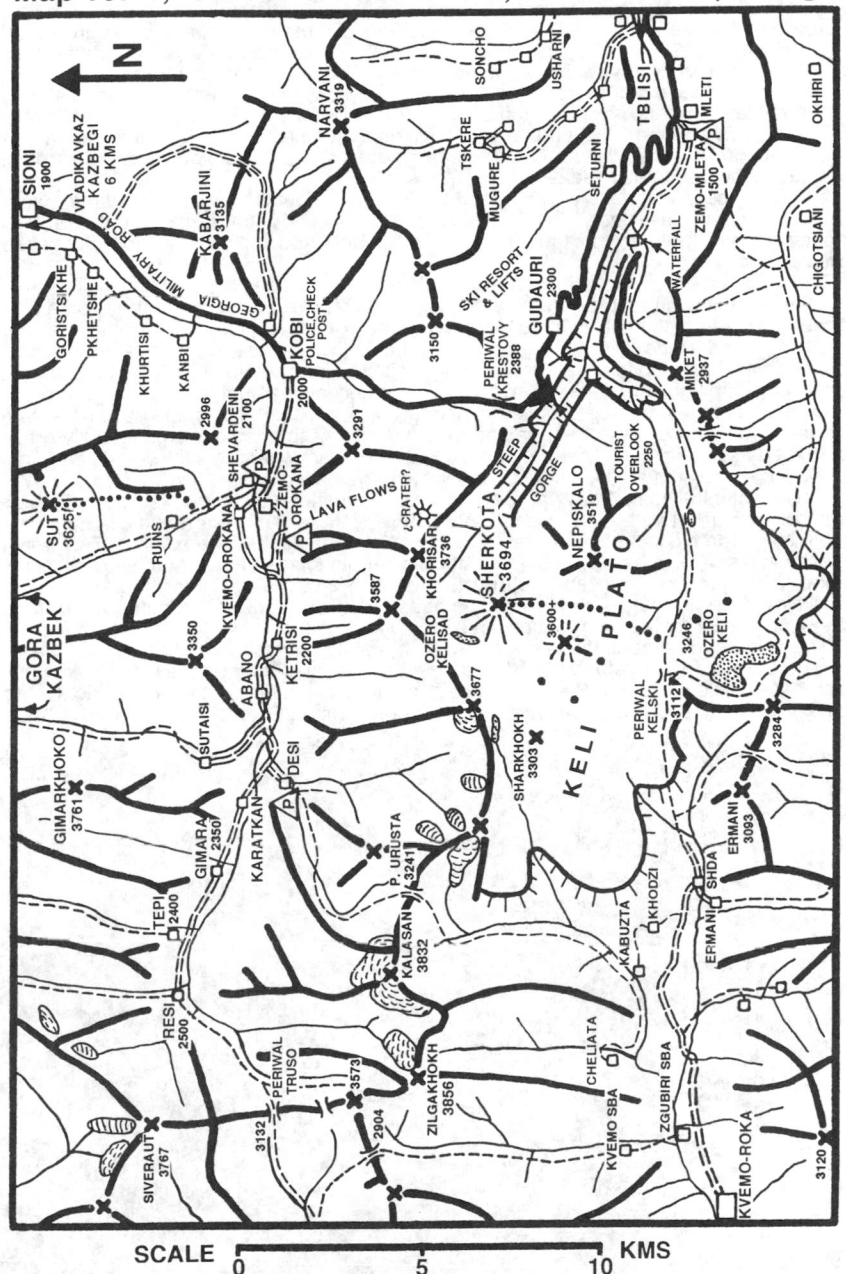

mountain, choose drinking water carefully and don't leave an unguarded camp. This is a forgotten corner of Kavkazia which makes it appealing to adventurers.

Maps TPC map *F4-C,* 1:500,000; DMA map *Gora Kazbek, NK 38-5,* Series 501, 1:250,000; or *Caucasus Central, Elbrus to Kazbek Map--Guide 5,* 1:200,000, West Col Books.

Vulkan Abuli, Georgia

This map shows 2 groups of moderately high mountains in southern Georgia. The highest peak in called Vulkan Abuli at 3300 meters altitude. To the north is a second group with the highest summit at 3285 meters. Its name is unknown. These mountains are located just east of the small city of Akhalkalaki, which is just north of the Armenian-Georgian border.

Abuli is a rather old and eroded volcano, however, in the northern group there are some younger volcanic craters. From the top of Abuli, this writer could see one well-defined crater just to the north between the 2 higher massifs. Also, on top of the northern group, it appeared there were a number of newer, less eroded volcanic cones. The last eruptions were surely in the Holocene or the last 10,000 years.

To climb Abuli, first make your way to Akhalkalaki. About 3 blocks south of the avtovakzal (bus station) is the Gastinetsa (Hotel) Dzhvakhet, the only one in town. It cost only US$2 a night for one person in 1995. It's not the greatest, but it's adequate, and you can store baggage there while climbing.

The normal route to **Vulkan Abuli** is to walk or take a taxi east from Akhalkalaki, across the river, through the suburb of Kartikami, and up a short canyon which cuts through some low hills. On the other side of the hills is the small village of Buzavet. Just north of this village is an old vehicle track and a side road running east. This track gives access to the lower west side of the mountain, which seems to have been part of a military firing range. No one was using it upon the author's visit, but there were old military vehicles and lots of empty shell casings in the area. Once on the steeper slope above the spring, just walk east and up the obvious west ridge. The mountain is covered with grass and the walking is easy. This area is heavily grazed by sheep & goats in summer. There are no trees or brush anywhere to slow you down. The only trees in this entire area are in the reforested sections in the foothills as shown.

Not knowing the normal way up, the author took a bus from the avtovakzal north then east to the small town of Olavert. This was on 5/28/1995. From there, he carried his large pack up to 2350 meters and hid it in some rocks, then in 1 1/2 hours reached the summit. By the time he got back to his pack, it had been 5 hours of hiking--from Olavert to the summit and back to his pack at 2350 meters. He camped on the mountan and the next morning walked back to Akhalkalaki in about 4 hours, which included one hour to climb one of the foothill peaks for fotos. Total walk-time for the 2 days was about 9 hours.

This climb can be done in one long day from the gastinetsa in Akhalkalaki and walking all the way. Or you could hire a taxi to be taken up to Buzavet to shorten the hike. Take your own water, there's little on the mountain. There's a good bazaar in the central square right in front of the gastinetsa. The climbing season is from late May through October.

From the *reforested foothills* looking east at Abuli and the village of Buzavet.

Map 168-1, Vulkan Abuli, Georgia

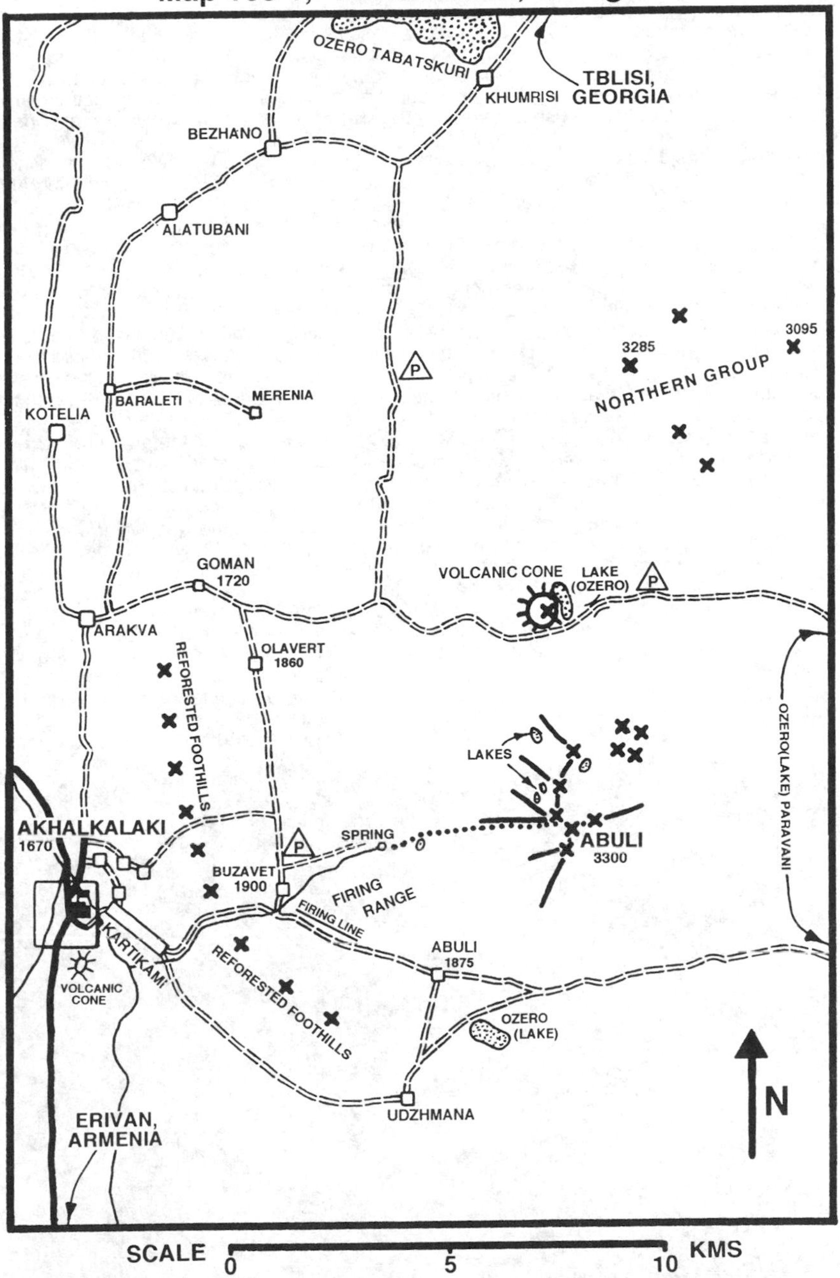

OZERO TABATSKURI

TBLISI,
KHUMRISI GEORGIA

BEZHANO

ALATUBANI

P

3285 3095

NORTHERN GROUP

KOTELIA BARALETI MERENIA

GOMAN
1720

VOLCANIC CONE LAKE
(OZERO) P

ARAKVA

OLAVERT
1860

REFORESTED FOOTHILLS

LAKES

AKHALKALAKI
1670

SPRING

ABULI
3300

P

BUZAVET
1900

FIRING RANGE

FIRING LINE

KARTIKAMI

ABULI
1875

REFORESTED FOOTHILLS

OZERO
(LAKE)

VOLCANIC
CONE

N

ERIVAN,
ARMENIA

UDZHMANA

OZERO(LAKE) PARAVANI

SCALE 0   5   10 KMS

Maps Not very helpful is the TPC map *F-4C*, at 1:500,000. If you're in Tbilisi first, look for the Institut Geodezi & Kartografia, they may have some better maps for sale.

Vulkan Aragats, Armenia

Shown here is Gora or Vulkan Aragats, the highest peak in Armenia at 4095 meters. This name is Armenian, as is the name of it's sister peak south across the Turkish border; that's Mt. Ararat, or as the Turks call it, *Agri Dagi*. Aragats is about 45 kms northwest of Erevan, capital of Armenia.

Aragats is an old and eroded stratovolcano. The summit area has 4 main peaks on the old crater rim. It appears to have had a large explosive eruption in it's dying days which blew out the southeast side of the crater. This volcano, or some flank eruptive center (?), date from the Holocene. There are newer or younger cones in the surrounding valleys.

To get to **Aragats**, take one of 3 daily buses from the Byurakan (pron. Burakan) bus parking area near the central bazaar in the heart of Erevan (you could also catch any bus passing through Agarak, then walk from there). Get off at or very near the last astanovka (bus stop) in upper Byurakan, then either ask about a taxi to take you up to the end of the road and the Institut Physic; or just start walking and hope to get a lift. Byurakan to the Institut facility is about 27 kms and the road is paved all the way. If walking, you can follow an old road along the power lines and cut off many kms. In early summer, there will be water at a number of places along the way. However, in late summer or fall, you'll want to fill a water bottle at one of the buildings near the 2000 meter level.

From the Institut Physic and small reservoir, walk north past the meteostantsiya (meteorological station) directly up the valley as shown. The author did this climb on 5/31 & 6/1/1995, with lots of snow on the upper part of Aragats. He didn't see any trail, but there must be one. He went up the south ridge to avoid snow, descended to a pass, then into the crater and contoured around to the north before walking up the SE ridge to the north peak.

The author missed the first bus to Byurakan, but got another one to Ashtarak and hitch hiked to Agarak, then walked all the way to 2900 meters and camped near the cement hut. Walk-time 6 hours. Day 2, he hid his pack and climbed the north peak, then walked all the way down to the Ski Weekend building and camped nearby. Total walk-time is 10 hours. Next morning, Day 3, he was on the 8am bus from Byurakan back to Erevan. Total walk-time was 17 hours.

If you'd rather not hike near a paved road, ask around Erevan of the whereabouts of a bus to the town of Aragats (or maybe Kaznafar?) on the eastern side of the mountain. There's either a road and/or trail up into the canyon as show on the DMA map listed below. There should be water along that stream because that are waterfalls shown on DMA maps.

Buy all your food in Erevan. Byurakan has a couple of small shops, but without a lot to choose from. If traveling by public transport, better take 3 days supplies and plan for 2 nights on the mountain. With your own vehicle this can be done in one long day from Erevan. There are shepherds and sheep & goats on this mountain from June through October, so be careful about leaving a tent for the day. This would be a great place for ski touring in winter.

Maps The 1950's DMA map *Yerevan, NK 38-11*, Series 501, 1:250,000 may be the best; any

Looking north at the South Peak of Aragats from the lake and Institut Physic.

Map 169-1, Vulkan Aragats, Armenia

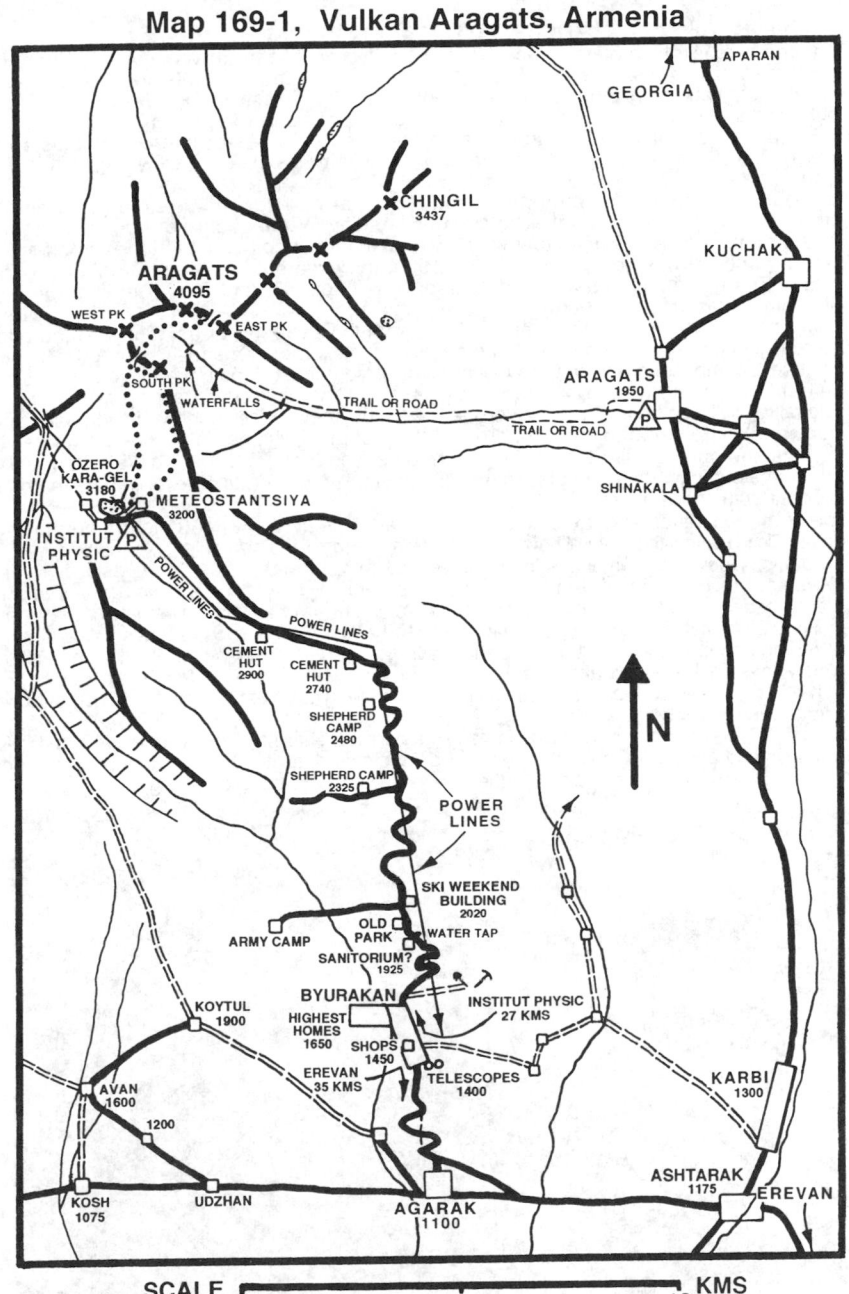

APARAN

GEORGIA

KUCHAK

✕CHINGIL
3437

ARAGATS
4095

WEST PK

EAST PK

SOUTH PK

WATERFALLS

TRAIL OR ROAD

ARAGATS
1950

P

TRAIL OR ROAD

SHINAKALA

OZERO
KARA-GEL
3180

METEOSTANTSIYA
3200

INSTITUT
PHYSIC

P

POWER LINES

POWER LINES

N

CEMENT
HUT
2900

CEMENT
HUT
2740

SHEPHERD
CAMP
2480

SHEPHERD CAMP
2325

POWER
LINES

SKI WEEKEND
BUILDING
2020

ARMY CAMP

OLD
PARK

WATER TAP

SANITORIUM?
1925

BYURAKAN

INSTITUT PHYSIC
27 KMS

KOYTUL
1900

HIGHEST
HOMES
1650

SHOPS
1450

EREVAN
35 KMS

TELESCOPES
1400

KARBI
1300

AVAN
1600

1200

KOSH
1075

UDZHAN

AGARAK
1100

ASHTARAK
1175

EREVAN

SCALE

0   5   10 KMS

highway map; or TPC map *F-4C,* 1:500,000. In Erevan, ask where the Institut Geodezi &
Kartografia is, they may be selling better topo maps.

Vulkan Azhdaak, Armenia

Featured here is a high plateau located about halfway between Erevan, capital of Armenia, and the large lake known as Sevan. The highest peak is Azhdaak at 3609 meters. Azhdaak is one of the youngest craters atop this massive volcanic field. This massif is several million years old, but Azhdaak, shown on some maps by its Turkish name of Kyzyl-Dag, is fairly now. It's officially classed as Holocene In age. It has a crater lake as does a sister summit just to the southeast. The youngest volcano the author saw on his trip was the one just NW of Azhdaak. It might be less than 2000 years old.

To get there, make you way to the central bazaar on Prospect Lenina (old name) in downtown Erevan. From there take the city bus heading for the suburb of Abovian, about 15 kms to the northeast. A bus goes that way every half hour or so. Get off at the turnoff to Zar, and wait for another bus going that way. In 1995, there were 5 buses per day running from Abovian to Zar, beginning at 9am. Last bus leaves at 6pm. The return buses start in Zar at 7:30am, with the last one at 4:30pm.

From Zar, you'll have to walk or hitch hike 7 kms to Sevaberd, or ask about hiring a taxi. Sevaberd is just a village with a school and several small kiosks or magazins (shops). If you're on foot, use a compass and walk from Sevaberd in a southeast direction angling up the slope. This mountain has no trees or brush anywhere so it's very easy walking cross-country. Occasionally, you'll see trails and even vehicle tracks, but they usually don't go in your direction.

In summer, there are Kurdish shepherds on the mountain with herds of sheep & goats, and some cows and horses. They have large white canvas tents and use trucks to move their camps and belongings. In some places, you'll see small diversion ditches or canals to irrigate parts of their summer pastures.

One of the first landmarks to look for will be the 2 hills at about 3100 meters northwest of **Azhdaak**. Once you get there, you'll have a good look at the top of the plateau and Azhdaak.

The author's route is shown on the map. He walked from Zar to Sevaberd and eventually camped at 2900 meters the first night. Walk-time 5 hours. Next morning he hid his tent and big pack in some rocks, and headed for Azhdaak. After the ascent, he returned straight down the mountain, got water at the spring at 2000 meters, and camped near Musakend. Total walk-time 8 1/2 hours. Next morning, he walked one hour and was on the 7:30 bus leaving Zar on the morning of Day 3. Snow almost completely covered the ground above 3000 meters on this early season trip from 6/3 to 6/5/1995. A strong hiker with a 4WD vehicle can do this climb in one long day from Erevan. The way is to walk south from Ozero Kani Gel (Lake Kani Gel).

Buy all your food in Erevan, but Abovian has some small magazins. Plan to be away from Erevan about 3 days and 2 nights. Carry some water from Sevaberd, as it may be scarce by September. Normal climbing or hiking season is from June through October. Beware of leaving an unguarded tent

From one of 2 peaks marked 3100 meters looking southeast at Azhdaak (left).

Map 170-1, Vulkan Azhdaak, Armenia

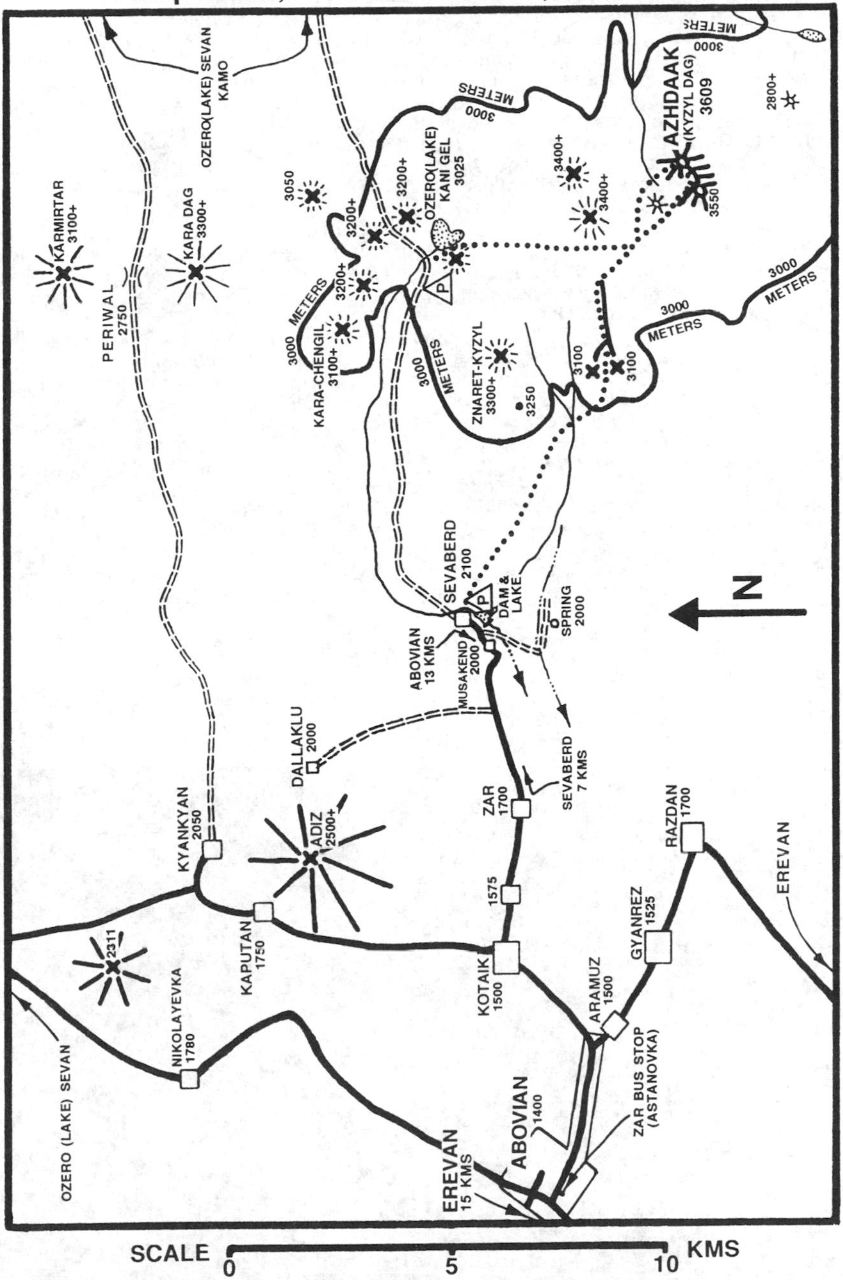

OZERO(LAKE) SEVAN KAMO

METERS 3000

AZHDAAK (KYZYL DAG) 3609

2800+

3550

3000

3200+

OZERO(LAKE) KANI GEL 3025

3400+ 3400+

3050

KARMIRTAR 3100+

KARA DAG 3300+

3200+

3200+

3200+

P

3000 METERS

3000 METERS

PERIWAL 2750

3000 METERS

KARA-CHENGIL 3100+

ZNARET-KYZYL 3300+

3100 3100

3250

METERS

SEVABERD 2100

P

DAM & LAKE

SPRING 2000

N

ABOVIAN 13 KMS

MUSAKEND 2000

SEVABERD 7 KMS

DALLAKLU 2000

KYANKYAN 2050

ADIZ 2500+

ZAR 1700

RAZDAN 1700

EREVAN

1575

GYANREZ 1525

2311

KAPUTAN 1750

KOTAIK 1500

ARAMUZ 1500

NIKOLAYEVKA 1780

ZAR BUS STOP (ASTANOVKA)

OZERO (LAKE) SEVAN

ABOVIAN 1400

EREVAN 15 KMS

SCALE 0   5   10 KMS

for the day--shepherds will be everywhere!
Maps The 1950's DMA map *Yerevan, NK 38-11,* Series 501, 1:250,000 may be the best; any highway map; and the TPC map *F-4C,* 1:500,000. In Erevan, ask where the Institut Geodezi & Kartografia is, they may be selling topo maps.

Gora Nour, Kavkaz Mountains, Azerbaijan-Russia

This map shows a small part of the southeastern Kavkazian Mountains which lay on the border of Russia's Dagistan Republic and Azerbaijan. There are many good hikes or climbs along this border, but this section was chosen because of good facilities for tourists and hikers. Featured here is the most accessible high mountain in the area called Gora (Mt.) Nour at 3644 meters. The highest summit however is Baziki Dag at 3864 meters which is just inside Dagistan. The rocks in these parts are sedimentary, metamorphic or granite.

Getting to **Gora Nour** is quite easy. Once you reach Azerbaijan, make your way to the center of the country to either Yevlak or Agdash. From either place you will find several buses per day running to Sheki, a small city at the foot of the mountains. Sheki is the largest city in the area and during Soviet times was apparently a sizable tourist center.

From the avtovakzal (bus station) in Sheki, walk north up the main street nearly one km to the city center, then turn right about one block to find the Gastinetsa (Hotel) Sabuhe. It's the tallest building in town at 10 stories. This hotel isn't fancy, but very adequate. It cost only about US$6 a night in 1995, and they will store extra baggage for you. The main bazaar is west about half a km. The bazaar has everything you'll need for camping.

From the avtovakzal in Sheki, there should be buses running to the 2 or 3 other valleys shown on the map. It's likely buses come into Sheki bazaar in the morning, then return in the afternoon. There are also roads, then trails, into all canyons throughout this range, because there are shepherds taking sheep & goats to the high mountain meadows in summer.

To get up the valley above Sheki, walk about one block west of the Gastinetsa Sabuhe and ask where the bus running to the small town of Kish parks or picks up passengers. There's a bus about every hour, and it's only about 7 kms from downtown Sheki. From the Kish astanovka (bus stop), walk uphill on the main road west of the small stream. It gradually curves to the northeast. There are several different streets you can take. In upper Kish, you'll drop down a ways and walk past gardens to a former hunting lodge. Just before the lodge, continue east on the tractor road crossing the stream. This track continues up to about 1900 meters at the foot of the periwal (pass). From there veer left, walk past a summertime sheep camp, then pick up a trail that zig zags up the ridge behind. Once at the periwal, walk northwest on the main ridge to the summit of Nour.

On 6/17/1995, the author took an 8am bus to Kish, then walked up to the old hunter's lodge where some Azerbaijani hippies & artists were living. He spent too much time there, then went up the valley described above and camped at 2130 meters at 5pm. Next day he climbed to a subsidiary peak near Nour and returned to his tent in about 6 hours. He then packed up and walked to the Kish bus stop in 3 1/2 hours. This can be done is 2 days for some, 3 for others. The peaks in this region are for the most part easy walk-ups, so you can ridge-walk from Nour in

From the main ridge looking northwest at Nour in the far background.

Map 171-1, Gora Nour, Kavkaz Mtns., Azerbaijan-Russia

SCALE 0 5 10 15 KMS

either direction and come out via a different valley, then catch a bus, or hitch hike back to Sheki.
Maps DMA map *Nukha, NK 38-9*, 1:250,000, Series 501; or the TPC *F-4C* map, 1:500,000; or in the Azerbaijan Hotel in Baki (Baku) buy the good national map *Azerbaican Respublikasi* in Roman letters at 1:500,000.

Bazar-Dyuzi & Shah Dag, Kavkaz Mountains, Azerbaijan-Russia

Shown on this map is the highest peak in Azerbaijan. It's Bazar-Dyuzi Dag at 4466 meters. Bazar-Dyuzi is on the Dagistan or Russian border right where the international frontier dips the fartherest south. It's also very near the southeast end of the Kavkazian Mountains. This area is northwest of Baki (Baku), and west of the 2 small cities of Kusari and Kuba. The rocks here vary from granite and shale; to limestone and sandstone beds which are especially prominent on the west and south slopes of Shah Dag, and the north face of Kyzyl Kiya.

To reach these mountains from Baki, first go to the main avtovakzal (bus station) which is near the sports stadium. There you'll find about 5 buses per day running to Kusari (Kusar or Qusar). The first one leaves about 8am, the last about 4pm. There might be one bus a day going all the way to Kuzun (?), so ask about that at the same station.

There is one small gastinetsa (hotel) in Kusari about one km west of the avtovakzal, and half a km west of the main bazaar, on the main road running toward Kuzun. Best to do all your shopping in Baki, but Kusari has many small magazins or dukons (shops) and a good bazaar. When you arrive in Kusari, get on the daily 4:30pm bus running to Kuzun, 30 kms away.

When you arrive in Kuzun, get off at the most (bridge), and walk up the 4WD road zig zagging up the slope to the south. This road intercepts the other main road which starts between Enik and Zindan-Murak. After about 6 or 7 kms you'll come to the village of Laza at 1650 meters (no dukons in this town). From Laza, walk south along an old road, then trail, into the main canyon, **but don't cross the river**. You'll find lots of sheep, goats, cows & horses as well as shepherd camps all along the way.

Higher up, you'll veer right and go up through a crack in a band of limestone forming a cliff. About 2 kms past that, the valley opens up into a large basin. At the far end straight ahead is **Bazar-Dyuzi**. So you don't have to wade large streams, cross the Shakh Dyuzi river at the rock bridge at 2500 meters as shown, and walk upstream on the north side. Time your arrival to this valley so you can camp at the upper or western end near the periwal (pass) at 3070 meters. You'll need to camp fairly close to Bazar-Dyuzi, in order to climb it in one day along its prominent northeast ridge. This appears to be a very easy climb, but take an ice ax & crampons. The easiest route up **Shah Dag** appears to be the one running up along the stream as shown. **Tufan Dag** looks easy too along a north ridge route.

The author arrived at Kuzun on 6/23/1995 about 6pm, then walked for 1/2 an hour and camped. Next morning he made the mistake of crossing the river near Laza and couldn't get past the waterfalls further up. He lost 5 hours retracing steps. He ended up camping in the lower end of the basin, which made it impossible to reach the summit of Bazar-Dyuzi the next day. He made it to the periwal at 3070, and returned from there. From Kuzun, his walk-time was 24 1/2 hours (or about 20 not counting backtracking time!). Fit hikers will need 3 full days (and maybe part of another morning or evening?) if you want to climb this one peak--one day in,

From a shepherd camp looking north at the southern slopes of Shah Dag.

Map 172-1, Bazar-Dyuzi, Kavkaz Mtns., Azerbaijan-Russia

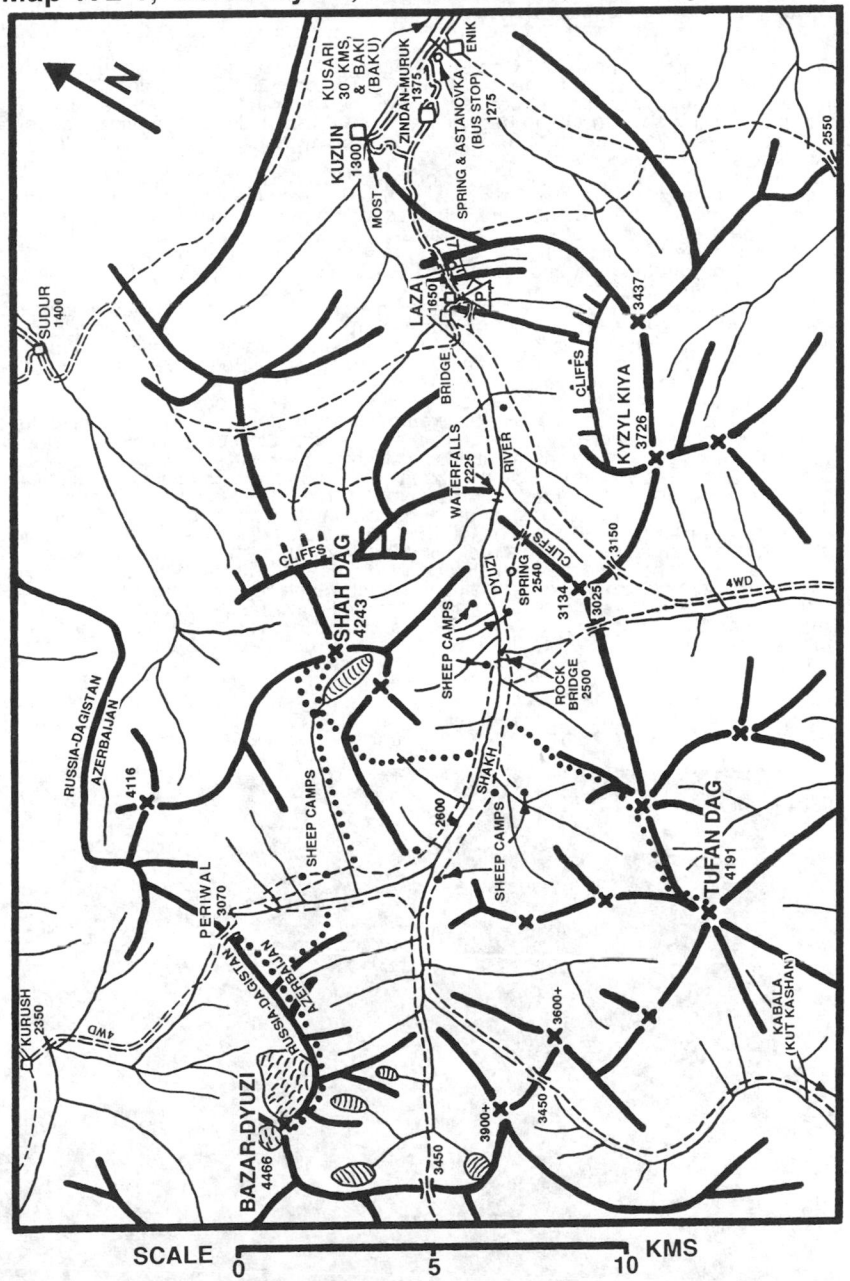

SCALE 0 — 5 — 10 KMS

one day climbing, and one day out, from Kuzun.
Maps DMA maps *Nukha NK 38-9, and Kuba, NK 39-7,* 1:250,000, Series 501; TPC map *F-4C,* 1:500,000; or the map *Azerbaican Respublikasi,* 1:500,000, buy in the Azerbaijan Hotel in Baki.

Kommunizma & Korzhenevskaya, Pamir Mountains, Tajikistan

Featured on this map is the highest portion of the Pamir Mountains of Central Asia. This part is entirely within Tajikistan, but the border of Kyrgyzstan, as well as Sary Tash and Pik Lenina, are just east of this map. The highest mountain here is also the highest in the former USSR. It's Pik Kommunizma at 7495 meters. Nearby is Pik Korzhenevskaya at 7105 meters. It's the 4th highest summit in the former USSR, behind Pobeda (2nd) and Lenina (3rd).

In 1995, the author traveled independently to all the Central Asian republics, including the northern parts Tajikistan. Most of the rest of the country was off limits to outsiders because of the war near the border of Afghanistan. This changed the approach route to Kommunizma, but alpinists were still on the mountain.

The long time normal approach to this region is via Dushanbe, the capital. From there, take a bus or truck to the large village of Dzhirgatal. This trip takes most of one day. Dzhirgatal is the jumping off point for trekking or climbing in this region. In the past you could take a plane from Dushanbe to Dzhirgatal, but flying is sporadic.

According to the book listed below, Dzhirgatal has a hotel, a pretty good bazaar, some magazins (shops) and chai khanas (tea houses). Next to the airport-helipad is a alpinist guesthouse and a free place to camp.

The normal way into the high peaks is by helicopter. But there is an old road running up the valley to the east. It's not certain whether there's any traffic on that road, or whether it's still usable, but you could certainly walk along it. From the last village or farm called Khodoka Tau, there are trails continuing up the valley to the Lednik Fortambek (Fortambek Glacier) and base camps to the above mentioned peaks. If you had transport to Khodoka Tau, then with a light pack it appears to be about a 3 day walk to base camp (?). It's probable you could send most supplies in by helicopter, then hike in. This would help with fitness as well as acclimatization. Walking out would be another way to see the country, but most climbers just helicopter in & out with their guide service, which is how most people climb in these parts these days..

There are 2 standard routes up **Kommunizma**. One is from the Fortambek Alpinist Lager at 4000 meters. From there it's up to the Firnovoye Plato, a 3 x 12 km flat area at about 5800 meters. Then up to the main east-west ridge, and the summit. The second route is up from one of 2 alplagers on the Lednik Moskvina at 4000 & 4200 meters. Then it's south up the Borodkin Ridge to the plato with some technical rock climbing, then the summit. This is a more difficult route, but many like it because they can also climb Korzhenevskaya from the same base camp. The standard route on **Korzhenevskaya** is up the southwest face. Most groups take 3-4 weeks of supplies. Guide services are on the mountain from mid-July to September 1.

Because of the political situation in Tajikistan in 1995, climbers were going to Osh, Kyrgyzstan, then taking buses to the end of the bus route at Daraut Kurgan, then used helicopters to ferry climbers into the base camps.

Maps DMA maps *Khait, NJ 42-4, Nusay, NJ 42-7, Daraut-Kurgan, NJ 43-1, and Kudara, NJ 43-5,* 1:250,000; USSR maps *I-42-23, I-42-24, I-42-35, I-42-36, I-43-13, I-43-25,* (scale unknown?); Ceska map by Vilém Hrdina, *Severo-Zapadniy Pamir,* 1:100,000; and the TPC map *G-6B,* 1:500,000; and the book, **Trekking in Russia & Central Asia**, The Mountaineers.

Substituting for Kommunizma is a foto of the author's camp just north of Kunzukur, with Lenina beyond (Map 176, page 389).

Map 173-3, Kommunizma & Korzhenevskaya, Pamir Mountains, Tajikistan

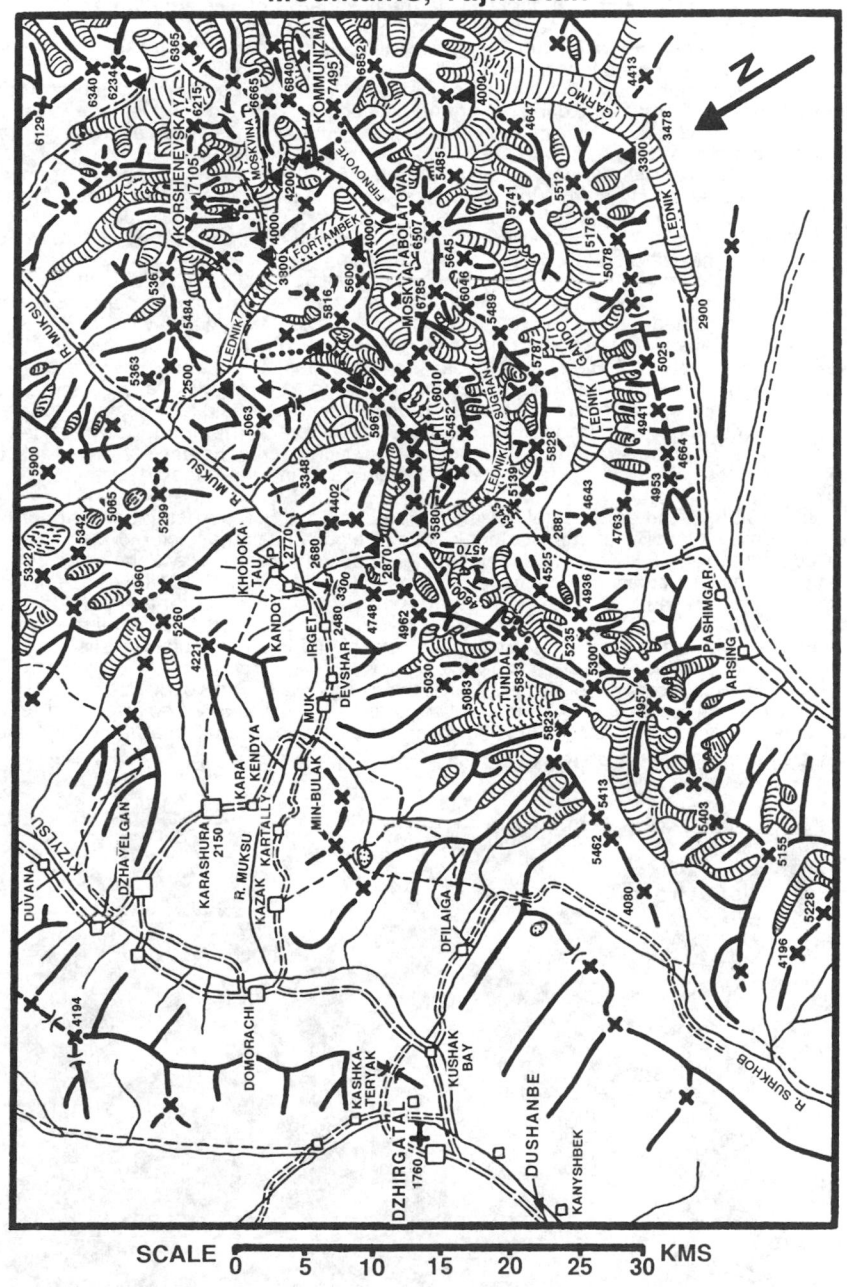

SCALE 0 5 10 15 20 25 30 KMS

Pik Karakyr, Chatkal'sky Mountains, Kyrgyzstan

Here is part of the Chatkal'sky Krebet (Mountains) which are immediately north of the Fergana Valley. This range in entirely inside the boundaries of western Kyrgyzstan, while the valley is part of Uzbekistan. The highest summit is Pik Karakyr at 4306 meters (or 4404 on another map). These are folded mountains with all kinds of sedimentary rocks, including shale, but the author remembers a few granite boulders too.

Get to this area by bus from the Uzbeki Fergana Valley cities of Namangan or Andizhan (Andijan); or *Osh, Kyrgyzstan,* due south of Andijan on the south side of this huge valley. With your Kyrgyz visa, you can transit through Uzbekistan by bus from the novey avtovakzal (new bus station) just north of Osh, going to Ala Buka (and likely other cities nearby) with no political problems (in 1995). The author is familiar with Ala Buka; there you will find a moderately good bazaar just across the street from the avtovakzal, and a small gastinetsa (hotel) about half a km east. That hotel is very clean, but the toilet is outside, and the banya (public bath) is 300 meters east. If you're coming from any of the larger cities mentioned above, buy all your food and supplies there; the selection of food in Ala Buka is not that good.

To climb **Pik Karakyr**, walk north on the main street which is 2 blocks east of the avtovakzal. You'll cross the river just north of town, then it's straight up the road into the canyon. If walking, you'll likely get a ride part way. Or hire a private car or taxi. About halfway to Karakyr is an old hunting lodge called Memek Lager (Memek Camp) which was open for business in 1995. To avoid wading at about 1740 meters, walk up along a bypass trail as shown. Later you'll pass some huge springs which have deposited lots of calcite. You may have to do some wading there. At the campsite marked 1970 meters, cross on the bridge and turn west into the canyon. Further up, turn right and cross over a pass at 3400 meters, then drop down to the foot of Karakyr. Finally, climb straight up the south face, which seems the easiest way. Most of the trails shown here are from the Terek Say map below, but there are many more trails than are shown.

On 7/10/1995, the author took an afternoon bus from Osh non-stop straight across the Fergana Valley to Ala Buka, then started walking. He got a ride on a tractor for 6 or 7 kms, then walked, and camped 2 kms above Memek Lager (2 hours walking). Day 2, he hiked up to near the periwal (pass) marked 3580 meters and camped (8 1/4 hours). Day 3, he climbed along the ridge north to just south of Karakyr, then returned via the valley. Later he hiked down to the main valley and camped at 1970 meters (10 1/2 hours). Day 4, he walked all the way to Ala Buka in 5 2/3 hours and stayed in the gastinetsa one night for US$2. Total walk-time was 24 1/2 hours. Next day he took the 7am bus back to Osh.

There should be some good hiking and/or climbing up the valleys above Ak Tam or Kashka Su as well. The roads above these 2 towns may not be correct as the Terek Say map dates from 1977, and the information earlier than that. You'll find sheep, goats, horses & cows in all the valleys and high

From Peak 4020 looking northeast at Karakyr in the middle background.

Map 174-1, Pik Karakyr, Chatkal'sky Mtns., Kyrgyzstan

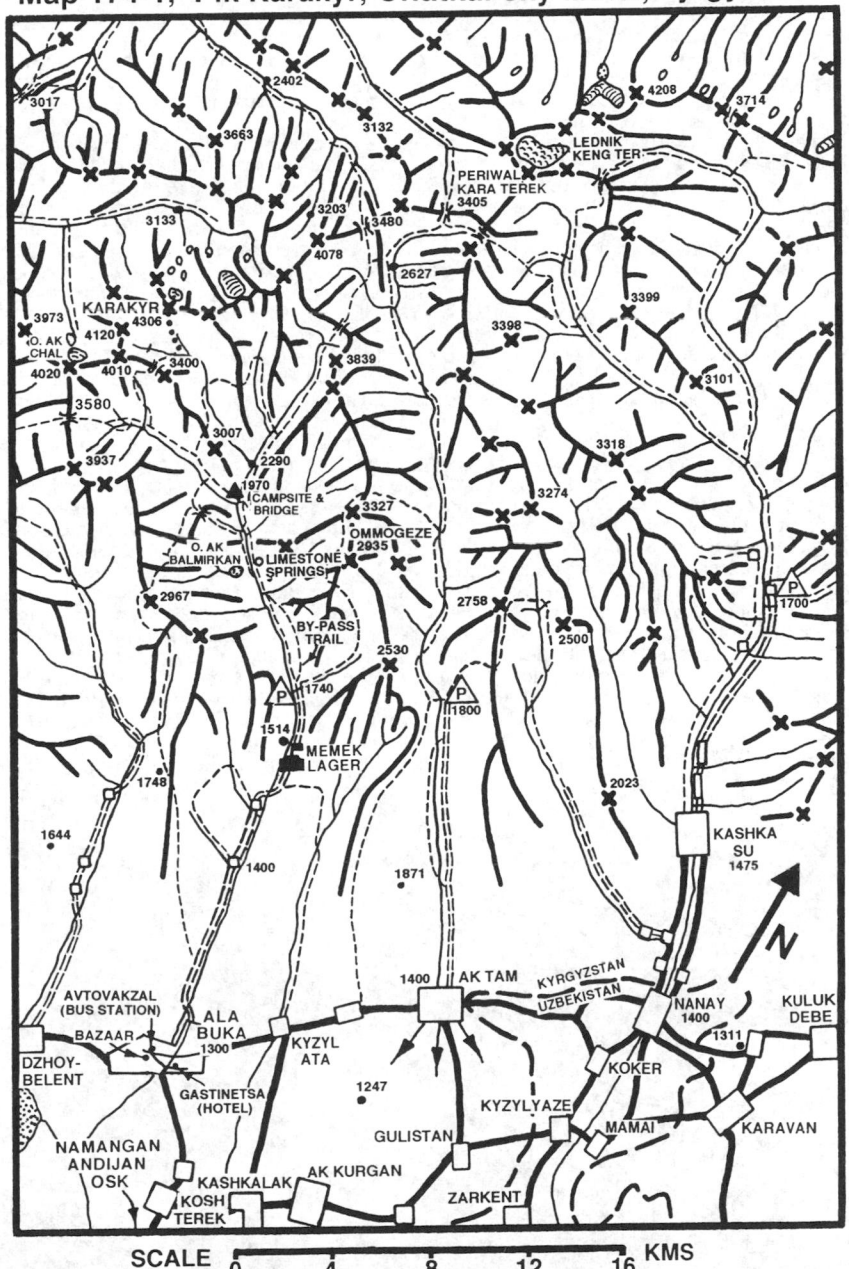

meadows in summer. Climb here from early or mid-July and into September. Take an ice ax & crampons in July, or for north face routes.

Maps DMA map *Kassa Say, NK 42-9,* Series N502, 1:250,000; Kyrgyz Geodesi & Kartografia map *Terek Say, II-42-24,* 1:200,000; the TPC map *F-6D,* 1:500,000; and the latest travel guidebook to Central Asia.

Aksu & Karasu Valleys, Turkistan Mountains, Kyrgyzstan

The crest of the Turkistan Mountains on this map form the boundary between Kyrgyzstan and Tajikistan. This region is located in extreme southwestern Kyrgyzstan but is almost completely surrounded by Tajikistan. While the highest peak in this part of the range rises to 5510 meters, most of the climbers end up rock climbing in either the Karasu or Aksu valleys between soaring granite towers. The central core of this range consists of granite, but along the route in are lots of sedimentary rocks.

To get there, you could join a guided group and fly in by helicopter from Tashkent, but there's a way for adventurers too. First make your way to Isfara, Tajikistan, which is southwest of the Fergana Valley. Your Kyrgyz visa should get you there from Osh. From Isfara, take one of 3 daily buses (10am, and 1 & 3pm) going south to Vorukh, about 32 kms. Ask the driver to let you off in the suburb of Maydan, about 3 kms before the central part of Vorukh. Ask someone there about the road running up the Karavshin Dolina (Karavshin Valley) to Mazar (ruins of an old sheep camp). There are several streets running to the one road which crosses a small river, then skirts around the western end of a low ridge before going west up the main valley. You can hire a motorcycle, tractor or car to take you up about 10 kms to where the road was washed out in 1995.

Along the way to Mazar, you'll pass several abrico (apricot) orchards--ripe in mid to late July, and several places to get clear water. Or you can drink the muddy river water. The first day of this trip is at low altitude and hot; otherwise it's easy walking. It's about 27 kms from Maydan to Mazar, then about another 15 kms to the Aksu Lager (Aksu Camp). If walking, it's about one day to Mazar, then another day to either the Aksu or Karasu lagers. The peaks and pinnacles there are for expert rock climbers only. Other peaks offer difficult snow or glacier routes.

On 7/17/1995, the author had a motorcyclist take him up the road about a km above Maydan, then walked for 2 1/2 hours and camped near the old landslide & lake site. End of Day 2 he camped in the lower part of Karavshin at about 2400 meters. Day 3, he walked to each of the base camps and met climbers from several countries, then camped at an old abrico orchard at 1800 meters. Day 4, walked 8 hours and got a ride the last 3 kms to Maydan (total 4 day walk-time was 32 1/2 hours). He then caught the last bus to Isfara, then quickly jumped on another bus to Batken where he stayed in a gastinetsa (hotel). Next morning he got a bus going directly to Osh along the southern boundary of the Fergana Valley. In those 2 days from Vorukh to Osh he crossed 9 international boundaries and parts of 3 countries, but didn't have to show his passport once. Hopefully the politics will remain tranquillo in the future.

There are many other nearby places to explorer. There will be sheep & goats in the higher valleys, so trails are everywhere, and hopefully bridges too! All large streams are muddy but drinkable; just let it settle awhile. Lots of long-abandoned homes and fruit orchards too. There are several magazins (shops) in Vorukh, but it's best to buy all your food in Osh or Isfara. Isfara's bazaar is one block north of the avtovakzal (bus station). Hike or climb from July into

Some of the granite towers along the east side of the Aksu Valley.

Map 175-1, Aksu & Karasu, Turkistan Mtns., Kyrgyzia

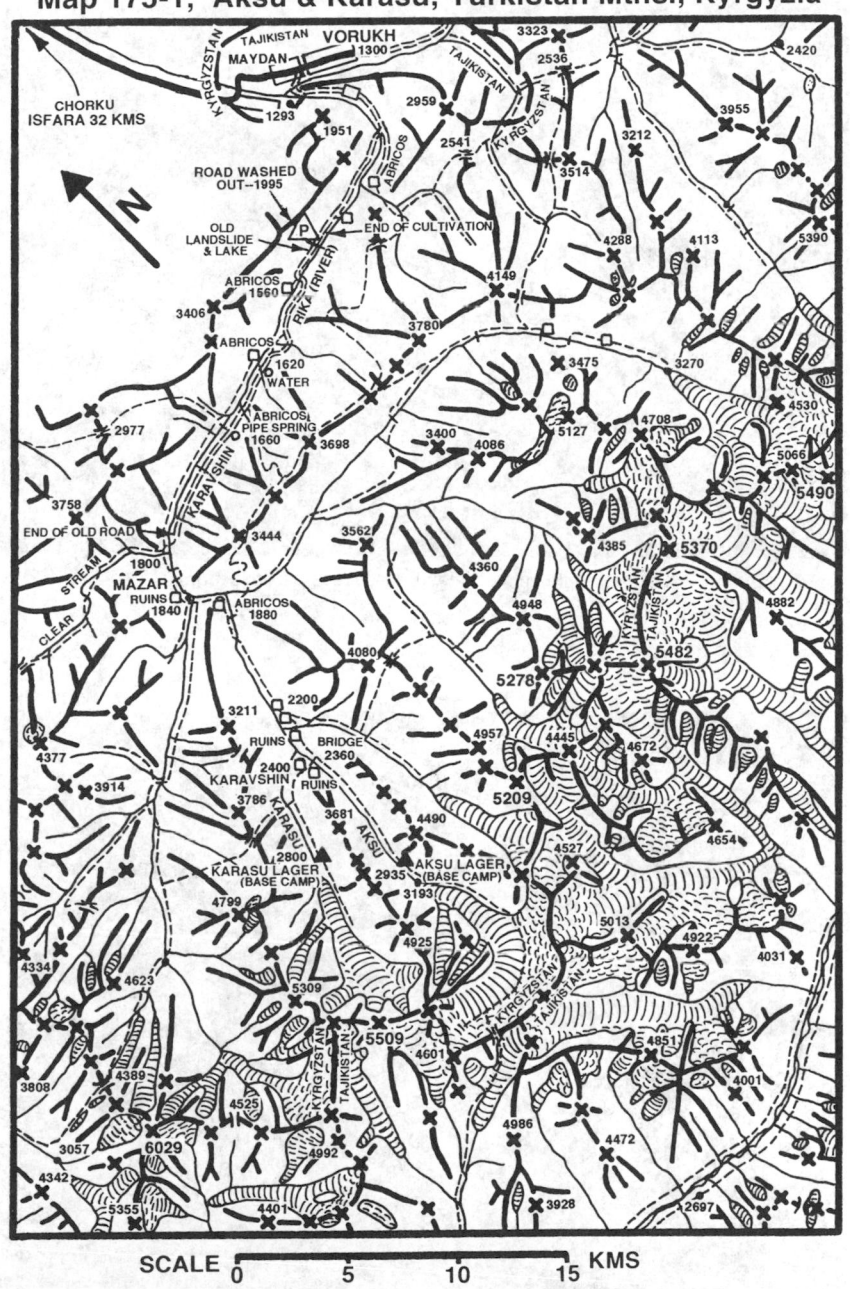

SCALE 0   5   10   15 KMS

September. Guides normally end their services and abandon camps the first week of September.

Maps DMA maps *Garm, NJ 42-3, & Khait, NJ 42-4,* 1:250,000, Series N502; or Kyrgyz Geodesi & Kartografia map *Vorukh, 10-42-05 or J-42-V,* 1;200,000; the TPC map *G-6B,* 1:500,000; and the latest travel guidebook to Central Asia.

Looking south up the Karasu Valley (see previous map)..

Achik Tash Lager with Pik Lenina the highest snow peak on the right (see next map).

Below is Base Camp (Baze Lager) for Pik Lenina, and looking north toward Achik Tash and Sarı Mogol in the far distance (see next map).

From Camp I looking southwest with Pik Lenina in the upper left, and Camp II to the right behind the rock buttress (see next map).

387

Pik Lenina, Zaalaysky Mountains, Kyrgyzstan

Shown on this map is one of the highest, easiest to climb, and most accessible big mountains in Kyrgyzstan and the world. This is Pik Lenina, at 7134 meters. It's the highest point in the Zaalaysky Krebet (Mountains). It's located on the Kyrgyz-Tajik border not far east of Pik Kommunisma, and due south of Osh, the unofficial capital of southwest Kyrgyzstan. In 1995, Lenina was one of about 5 summits in Kyrgyzstan you were required to pay a fee for climbing. The fee was US$100. The rocks on Lenina and nearby summits consist mostly of sedimentary layers, including conglomerate & shales, but also some granite.

It's quite easy to get to Lenina. First, make your way to Osh, the small city on the southeast corner of the Fergana Valley and near the border of Uzbekistan. Before leaving Osh, inquire at the *OVIR (Passport Registration Office)* to see if you still need *proposk (permission)* to get past Sari Tash and on to the mountain which is on the Tajik border. Also, stop at the *Sport Kommittee office* at the south end of the *futball stadian*, and pay US$100 for permission to climb Lenina. Or you can pay on the mountain at Achik Tash.

To get to Lenina using public transport, make your way to the center of Osh and the bazaar. Just across the river to the east and a little south, is the stari avtovakzal (old bus station). This station is about 3 blocks down the hill and east of the Gastinetsa Alai (Alai Hotel). Each morning there's at least one bus making the run to Sari Tash and west to the small town of Daraut Kurgan (Daroot Korgon). Be there at 7am, but the bus usually doesn't leave until 8 or 9am. In 1995, they always had to run around at the last minute looking for benzin (gasoline)!

It takes about 7 hours for the bus to reach Sari Tash, which has at least one small gastinetsa and probably several magazins (shops). From Sari Tash, you can see across the big, wide valley at Pik Lenina, but the exact summit is hard to pick out from there. Three kms southwest of Sari Tash is a traffic checkpoint and Russian Pagranichny (border guards). In 1995, everyone, including Kyrgyz, had to have proposk to get past that point.

It's about one more hour from the checkpoint to Sari Mogol, the jumping off place for Lenina. From the highway at Sari Mogol, walk south along the main street (with one or 2 small magazins) or along the small stream as shown. Cross the Kyzyl Su (Kyzyl River) on the bridge and continue south up the road toward Kunzukur, an old collective farm complex. From there, turn right or west for about one km, then wade a braided stream, the Achik Tash Su, which is easy to cross as it's divided into many small channels. Deepest place, only 30 cms in the morning hours.

Once on the west side, just walk straight toward the opening of the main canyon which is just a little east of due south. The author never did stay on any vehicle track, and only walked along a road as he neared *Achik Tash,* the former *International Climbing Camp Pamir.* A family now runs that place with your own 37 hectors of land nearby. You can buy meals, rent tent/cabins, and/or hire 4WD's to get back out to Sari Mogol or Sari Tash.

From Achik Tash, there is a road and/or trail running south for about 5 kms up to the normal Base Camp (Baze Lager), at Ludkova Polyana, a high meadow at 3735 meters. Lots of people camp there. From Base Camp, a trail heads up a valley, over a pass, down onto a glacier, then up to Camp 1 on a medial moraine. From Camp 1, you cross the glacier heading straight for the summit, while zig zagging up the slope passing crevasses, then veer right and land at Camp 2 at about 5300 meters. This campsite is on gravel and scree. This part of the route can be dangerous because of crevasses, but the guided groups always make and have a good trail marked out. It seems most people don't rope-up in this section. There are lots of people on this climb so it's a good snow trail.

From Camp 2, it's steeper, but easy climbing, up to Camp 3 at about 6100 or 6400 meters, thence along the long summit ridge to the top. Because there are so many people on this mountain, and because it has such easy access, this is one of the most-climbed big glaciated mountains in the world.

After being turned back once at Sari Tash for not having proposk, this writer finally got to Sari Mogol on 7/26/1995, then walked 1 1/2 hours and camped near Kunzukur. Day 1, he made it to Base Camp with a total walk-time of 8 hours from Sari Mogol. Day 2, it was 3 hours walking up to Camp 1. On Day 3 it was just over 4 hours to Camp 2. However, on that part of the climb, while using inadequate sun goggles, he got snow blindness, and the next day had to come down all the way to Achik Tash, where he paid for a ride to Sari Tash, and stayed in the little gastinetsa there taking a bus to Osh the next day.

Most people do this climb in 10 or 12 days, or maybe 2 weeks, but you'd better have 3 weeks vacation altogether. They relay loads from one camp to another, while acclimatizing the best they can. You'll need warm cloths, ice ax & crampons and a good strong tent for Camp 3, which is subject to high winds. Achik Tash is manned from mid-July to the end of August, the normal climbing season. This is a dry region and good weather seems normal in the valley; but up high, afternoon snow showers are common. You can buy all your food for this climb in Osh. Also, take the best & darkest mountaineering goggles you can find, plus sun lotion. This of course is the same on any big mountain.

Map 176-1, Pik Lenina, Zaalaysky Mtns., Kyrgyzstan

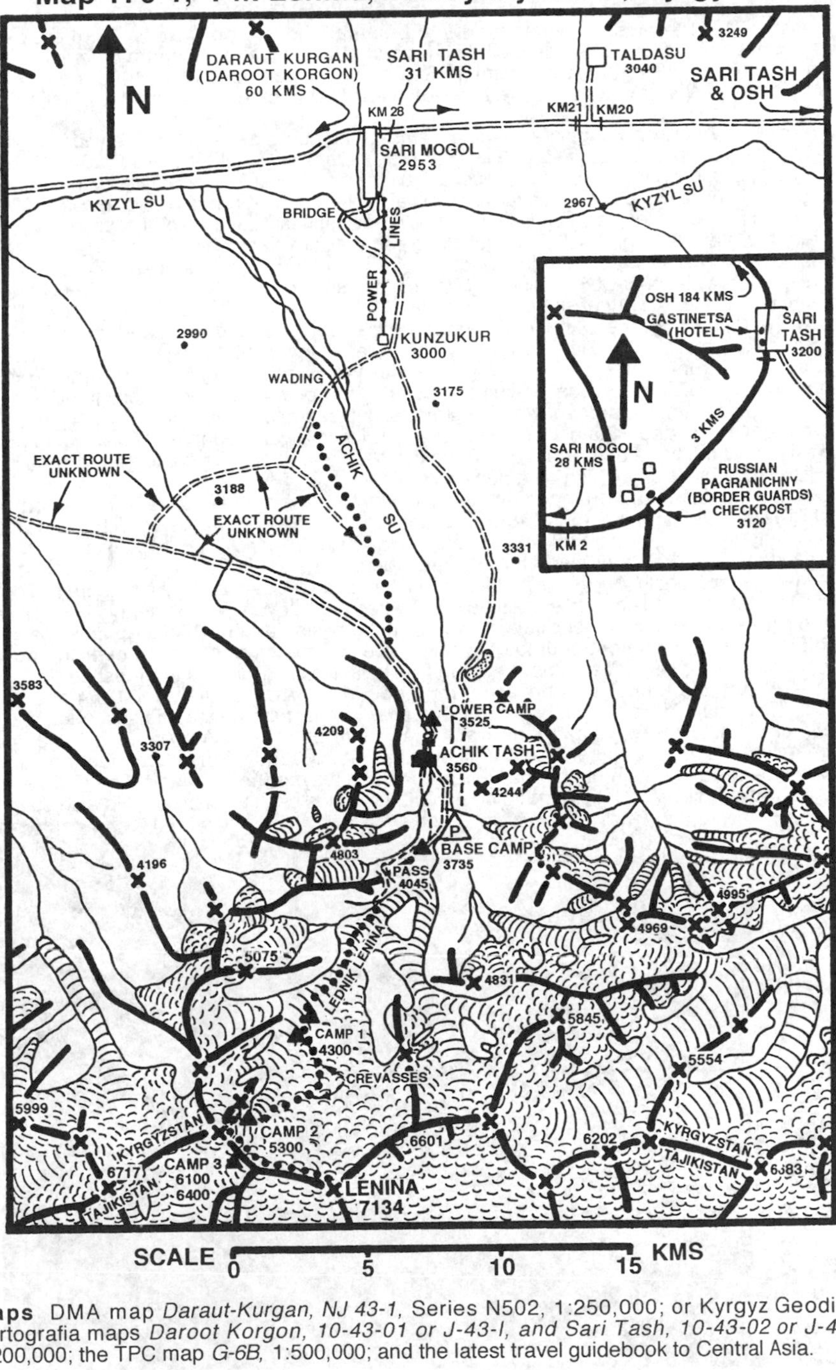

N

DARAUT KURGAN
(DAROOT KORGON)
60 KMS

SARI TASH
31 KMS

TALDASU
3040

3249

SARI TASH
& OSH

KM 28

SARI MOGOL
2953

KM21 KM20

KYZYL SU

BRIDGE

POWER LINES

2967 KYZYL SU

2990

KUNZUKUR
3000

WADING

3175

OSH 184 KMS

GASTINETSA
(HOTEL)

SARI
TASH
3200

N

EXACT ROUTE
UNKNOWN

ACHIK SU

3188

EXACT ROUTE
UNKNOWN

3331

KM 2

SARI MOGOL
28 KMS

3 KMS

RUSSIAN
PAGRANICHNY
(BORDER GUARDS)
CHECKPOST
3120

3583

3307

4209

LOWER CAMP
3525

ACHIK TASH
3560

4244

3735

4196

4803

PASS
4045

BASE CAMP
3735

4995

4969

5075

4831

LEDNIK LENINA

CAMP 1
4300

5845

5554

5999

CREVASSES

6601

6202

KYRGYZSTAN

6717

CAMP 2
5300

TAJIKISTAN

6383

CAMP 3
6100
6400

TAJIKISTAN

KYRGYZSTAN

LENINA
7134

SCALE 0   5   10   15 KMS

Maps DMA map *Daraut-Kurgan, NJ 43-1*, Series N502, 1:250,000; or Kyrgyz Geodise & Kartografia maps *Daroot Korgon, 10-43-01 or J-43-I, and Sari Tash, 10-43-02 or J-43-II*, 1:200,000; the TPC map *G-6B*, 1:500,000; and the latest travel guidebook to Central Asia.

Semyona Tianshanskovo, Ala Archa N. P., Kyrgyzstan

This map shows the peaks directly south of Bishkek, formerly Frunze, the capital of Kyrgyzstan. This range is known as the Kyrgyzski Ala Tou (or Too). However, most people refer to the area as either Ala Archa, because it's part of a national park; or the other river valley known as Alamedin. The highest summit is **Semyona Tianshanskovo** at 4895 meters. The rocks here are mostly granite, but there's lots of quartzite and other metamorphics in the peaks west of upper Ala Archa.

To reach the **Ala Archa Lager** (Ala Archa Camp) using public transport, make your way to the junction of Belinski & Bokonbayeva Ulitsas (Streets) in Bishkek. Wait for bus 11, 26 or 15, at the astanovka (bus stop) on Belinski, which is just across the street west from a Small Bazaar. All these buses go south to the city bus terminal at Chonarik at about Km 13. From there, take bus 171 which goes to the entry gate of the national park at Leshos (Leskhos) near Km 30. You'll have to pay a small entry fee, then start walking. You'll likely get a ride part way, or you can hire a taxi. The alp lager is 11 kms up a good paved road and just past the Km 41 marker. You can sleep there in a small gastinetsa or lodge for about US$6 a night in 1995, or just camp anywhere just up the trail out of sight. anywhere just up the trail out of sight.

From Ala Archa, take the lefthand trail which heads southeast and you'll end up at the Priyut (Hut) Stoyanka Ratseka. This is a popular camping place, or you could sleep in the priyut free, if there is room. From there, hike up the glaciers or the moraines; or if you're really good at climbing and have all the technical equipment, you can try some of the most difficult routes in the world. You'll find 2 small emergency huts higher up, but take a tent anyway!

If you continue up the Rika (River) Ala Archa, you'll find a very rough 4WD track going up to some ski runs at the head of the canyon. From this track you can make some easy climbs to the west. There's another priyut high on a ridge as shown.

To reach the **Alamedin** drainage, make your way to the Alamedin Bazaar in the northeast part of Bishkek. Get on hourly bus 145 which runs to Koytash. From there you'll have to walk & hitch hike, or hire a taxi, up to Tepliye (Garachi or Hot) Kluchi(Spring) Sanitoria. You must make prior reservations to bathe or sleep there. Also, there are 2 sanitoria buses which leave from somewhere on Prospect Chui in the middle of Bishkek at about 8am daily, running up to Tepliye Kluchi. They return at 11am and sometime in the afternoon. If you can locate this bus, it'll save you about walking 11 kms. Most climbers end up in the basin north of **Pik Kyrgyzstan**, another very difficult climb. But most people going here are just trekking; some go over the passes south, then down the Issyk Ata to the Issyk Ata Sanitoria, which is 70 kms from Bishkek.

On 8/5/1995, the author walked, then got a ride to Ala Archa, hiked for 1 3/4 hours and camped. Next day, hid his big pack and walked upcanyon past the meteostantsiya (met. station) and climbed a 4000 meter peak to the west, then returned to near Ala Archa in 9 1/2 hours. Next morning, hid his pack, then hiked to Stoyanka Ratseka and 3 kms beyond in the snow & rain, then returned and with his big pack walked all the way to the park entrance and camped nearby (9 hours walking). Next morning he caught the buses back to Bishkek. He also spent an

A tent camp near Stoyanka Ratseka with Pik Corona in the clouds behind.

Map 177-1, S. Tianshanskovo, Ala Archa N.P., Kyrgyzstan

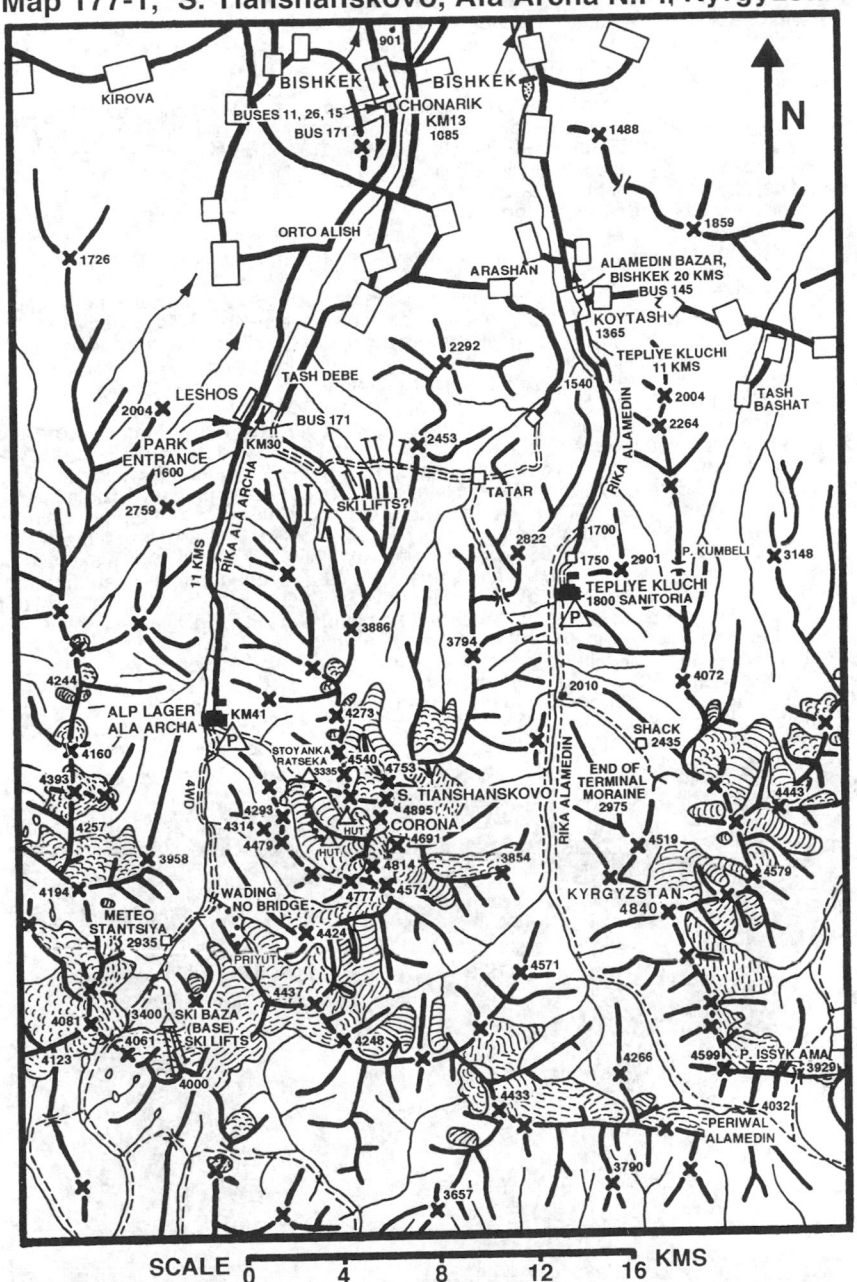

afternoon and morning walking up to near the base of Kyrgyzstan and back to the sanitoria.
Maps Kyrgyz Geodesi & Kartografia maps *Frunze, II-43-09 or K-43-IX, & Chontëbe, II-43-15 or K-43-XV,* both at 1:200,000; the Vilém Hrdina map *Zapadniy v Tian Shan Kyrgyzski Krebet,* 1:50,000, Praha, Ceska; and the TPC map *F-6D,* 1:500,000; and the latest travel guidebook to Central Asia.

Almaty Hikes, Zailiisky Ala Tau Mtns, Kazakstan

Featured here are the mountains immediately south of Almaty, the capital of Kazakstan. This map only shows the 2 most popular and easily accessible canyons nearest Almaty, but there are many other high glaciated peaks both east and west from this mapped area. The rocks here are the usual assortment of metamorphics and granites.

The most popular hiking area is above Medeo, an international skiing and ice skating center. To get there using public transport, make your way to the Central Bazaar in Almaty. One block east of the bazaar, and a little south on Ulitsa (Street) Voshem (Eight) Go Marta, is the astanovka (bus stop) where bus 6 begins. It goes 20 kms to Medeo. Or catch this bus in front of and across the street from the Kazakstan Hotel.

From where the bus stops in **Medeo**, walk up the road past the hotel and skating rink. Just above that is a large flood control & debris dam. Steps take you right up to the top. From there, walk 4 kms along the paved road up to the ski lifts & gastinetsa (hotel) called Chimbulak at about 2220 meters. Or take a taxi.

From Chimbulak there's a dirt road running upcanyon to the south where some homes are located, at least one private hotel and maybe an old alplager(alpcamp)? This very rough track runs up to the end of the valley. Strong hikers who get on the first bus up and the last bus down to Almaty, will have time to day-hike to the end of the valley. If you prefer difficult climbing, walk up a trail along the ski lift to the pass and drop down into the next valley east where there's the Baze Alpiiskaya Rosa (Base Camp Rosa). Lots of snow and ice climbs over there.

To reach the other main valley south of Almaty, make your way to the south side of the city and Ulitsa Al Faribe and the Avtostantsiya Arman (small bus station Arman). This is a major transfer point where suburban and city buses meet. At Arman get on bus 93 which runs up to a sanitoria called **Almarisan** at 1775 meters. There are 16 buses going up daily. The first leaves at 6:20am, the last at 7:40pm. This bus takes you to the end of the road and the beginning of a good trail running up to the Periwal Almaty (Almaty Pass); a long day-hike from Almarisan.

If heading to **Ozerny**, take bus 93, but get off at Kokshoky and walk and/or hitch hike from there. Bus, 93A, runs only to Kokshoky and stops. One man reported to this writer, the road up to Ozerny was all but impassible as of 1995. He drove up about 4 kms in a 4WD and returned. From Kokshoky, it's about 12 kms to the lake where a number of old buildings are located. From the lake to Periwal Ozerny is another 10 or 12 kms. By using Ozerny or Almaty passes, you can hike to Issyk Kul (Issuyk Lake) in Kyrgyzstan. See the next map for that long hike.

On 9/10/1995, the author got on the wrong bus and walked 10 kms to Medeo, then went up past the ski lift for 3 kms or so and returned on the right bus. Next day, he went to Almarisan in the morning, then hiked to within 3 kms of Almaty Pass and returned to Almarisan in 6 hours round-trip. Buy all food in Almaty. Hiking season is from July through late September.

Looking down on Medeo Winter Park from the top of the debris dam.

Map 178-1, Almaty Hikes, Zailiisky Ala Tau, Kazakstan

SCALE 0 ___ 5 ___ 10 ___ 15 KMS

Maps The rather poor DMA maps *Alma-Ata, NK 43-3* and *Rubach'ye, NK 43-6,* Series N502, 1:250,000; or the Kyrgyz Geodise & Kartografia maps *Alma-Ata, II-43-II or K-43-XI, and Talgar, II-43-12 or K-43-XII,* both 1:200,000; the book, **Trekking in Russia & Central Asia,** The Mountaineers; and the latest travel guidebook to Central Asia.

Almaty-Issyk Kul Hike, Kazakstan-Kyrgyzstan

Shown here are the high peaks along the border of Kazakstan & Kyrgyzstan immediately south of Almaty. Emphasized will be trails you can use to access the peaks for climbing, or for trekking from Almaty to the large lake called Issyk Kul. Use this map and information in conjunction with the map & information on the previous page. On that page is information on how to get into the mountains from Almaty. This part shows access from the south, or Kyrgyz side. These mountains are made mostly of granite, plus metamorphics like quartzite.

The starting point is on the north side of Issyk Kul at the large town of Grigoryevka. To get there from Bishkek (Frunze), the capital of Kyrgyzia, start at the novey (new) avtovakzal (bus station) in the northwest part of the city. Buy a ticket on a bus bound for Kara Kol, the unofficial capital of eastern Kyrgyzstan, located just east of Issyk Kul. There are 8 or 10 buses per day making this run using the route along the north side of the lake, called the *severno marsroute* (north route). It's a 6 or 7 hour ride.

In the middle of Grigoryevka is a bazaar, and one block east is the astanovka or bus stop where they'll drop you off. From the astanovka, walk north on the street immediately to the west. After one km you'll be out of town in open fields and on the road into the canyon. You can either walk and hope to get a lift part way; or hire a taxi or *privatny* (private car) from around the bazaar. The road into the canyon crosses the river 4 times, then turns west into the upper valley which has trees, meadows and several summer homes with sheds where cows are milked. There might be 10 vehicles on this road per day, so getting a ride is easy for the first 10 to 15 kms.

Around the area called the *outwash plain,* the road deteriorates to a 4WD track. Still higher, at around 3000 meters, it's just a trail. Later, you'll cross over the Periwal Aksu (Aksu Pass) and down to the north, then west. From along the Chon Kemin River, turn north and cross over either the Periwal Ozerny or Almaty. You probably won't need ice ax & crampons for these 2 passes, but you will to get over the Aksu Pass! About half a days walk from either pass will be transport down to Almaty.

Another less-used route between Grigoryevka and Kazakstan is the one over Periwal Kuganmir, down into the upper Zhongirik Valley, then over the Periwal Talgar, down Talgar Valley to Talgar, and finally by bus to Almaty. Ice ax & crampons are required for this route, as well as a rope for glacier travel. You may have to wade large streams if the shepherds haven't made bridges (?). This may be your biggest problem on this trek.

From above Grigoryevka, the author got a lift to the outwash plain with people gathering gribei (mushrooms). Next day, 8/11/1995, he camped at the pass just north of the Periwal Aksu--9 1/2 hours. He had intended to hike to the Periwal Ozerny and back, but bad weather changed that. Day 3, he walked back to within 6 kms of Grigoryevka & camped--11 hours. Next morning, one more hour to the bus stop. With a large pack you may have trouble getting on a crowed bu

This foto was taken near the shepherd camps at 3066 meters looking west.

Map 179-1, Almaty-Issyk Kul Hike, Kazakstan-Kyrgyzstan

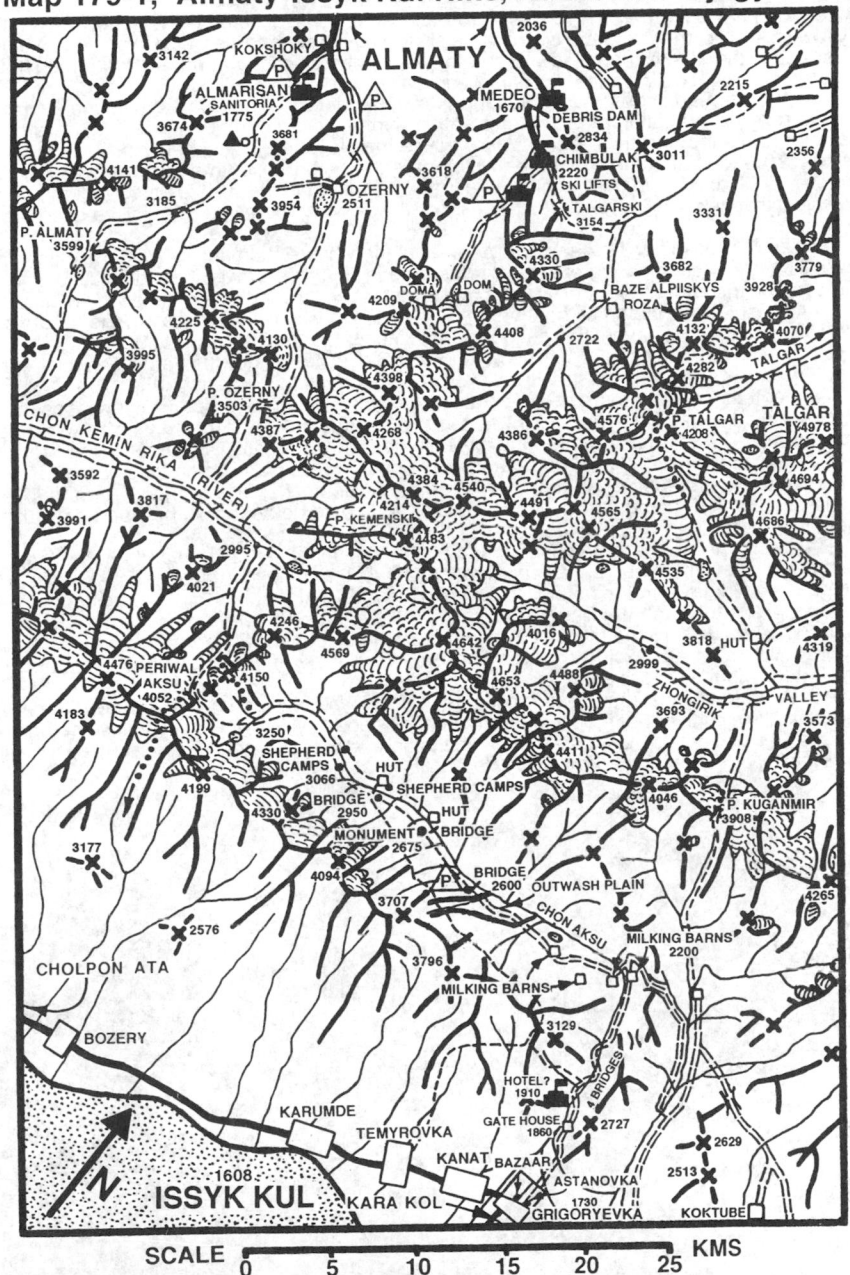

Map 179-1, Almaty-Issyk Kul Hike, Kazakstan-Kyrgyzstan

more buses begin. Buy your food in Bishkek, although Grigoryevka has a good bazaar. Grigoryevka to Almaty is about 4-5 days via the periwals Aksu & Ozerny or Almaty.

Maps The DMA and Kyrgyz maps listed for the previous hike, plus the TPC map *F-6C;* and the book, **Trekking in Russia & Central Asia**, The Mountaineers; and the latest travel guidebook to Central Asia.

At Bashi Mountains, Kyrgyzstan

Shown here is the Khrebet At Bashi (At Bashi Mountains), located in the south central part of Kyrgyzstan just south of the small city of At Bashi, and not far north of the Chinese border. The author mostly used the Kyrgyz map below to create this one, but neither that nor the DMA map had any names for peaks. This indicates it's been overlooked by alpinists.

The Kyrgyz map shows the highest peak is 4786 meters. That map shows many glaciers, but the biggest ones shown are on the south slopes, which can't be correct. Therefore the glacier information here is in error. Also, notice the elevation of the At Bashi Valley, which is roughly 2100 to 2250 meters elevation. Compare that with the south-side empty quarter which is mostly 3500 to 3900 meters. This entire region is drier than the Bishkek area, but the glaciers indicate this range is big enough to create its own weather. The rocks seem to be quartzite with some granite (?).

To get to At Bashi, go to the novey avtovakzal (new bus station) in Bishkek and catch one of several small private morning buses, or marsroute taxis (shared taxis) bound for At Bashi. The author made the return trip in 7 1/2 hours in a marsroutny, for the same price as the buses.

In At Bashi, there's a small gastinetsa (hotel), which will store extra baggage; and a pretty good little bazaar. However, it's best buy your climbing food in Bishkek. Some food prices in At Bashi are double Bishkek prices. The hotel cost US$2 in 1995 and was very clean, but you had to take a bucket bath in an outside toilet. Ask about a banya (public bath).

To reach these mountains from At Bashi, you could get on one bus which passes through Oytersken bound for Uzgorysh to the east; or another one going through Oytersken to Pogranichnik. Both of these leave the At Bashi avtovakzal about 7:30am and 4pm; returning from Uzgorysh and/or Pogranichnik at 9am and 5pm. You can also catch these crowded buses at the astanovka (bus stop) on the main street near the hotel. Or hire a taxi, if there's benzin available. If you're going to the closest peaks, you could do as the author did and walk right from the hotel.

The author arrived here from Naryn and stayed one night in the hotel and bought food from the bazaar. Next morning he walked 4 kms to Oytersken, then into the closest canyon. Taxis can go about 7 kms from the hotel. He used an old road in the Acha Kaindy Canyon, then good livestock trails to reach the base of a glacier. He camped one night, with rain & hail, then climbed one easy 3915 meter peak the next morning. He then walked all the way back to the hotel. Total walk-time, excluding the one climb, was 11 1/2 hours. This shows that distances aren't great and the access easy.

Adventurous people could take a bus east to Pervoye Maya and hike south over the Periwal Bogoshity (Bogoshity Pass) and explore the south slopes, which would likely have some easier ascents. It's glacier and mostly steep rock on the north slopes. Rivers are small and easily waded. You'll find roads in every canyon, then livestock trails to the high meadows.

From the town of Oytersken looking southeast at the At Bashi Mountains.

Map 180-1, At Bashi Mountains, Kyrgyzstan

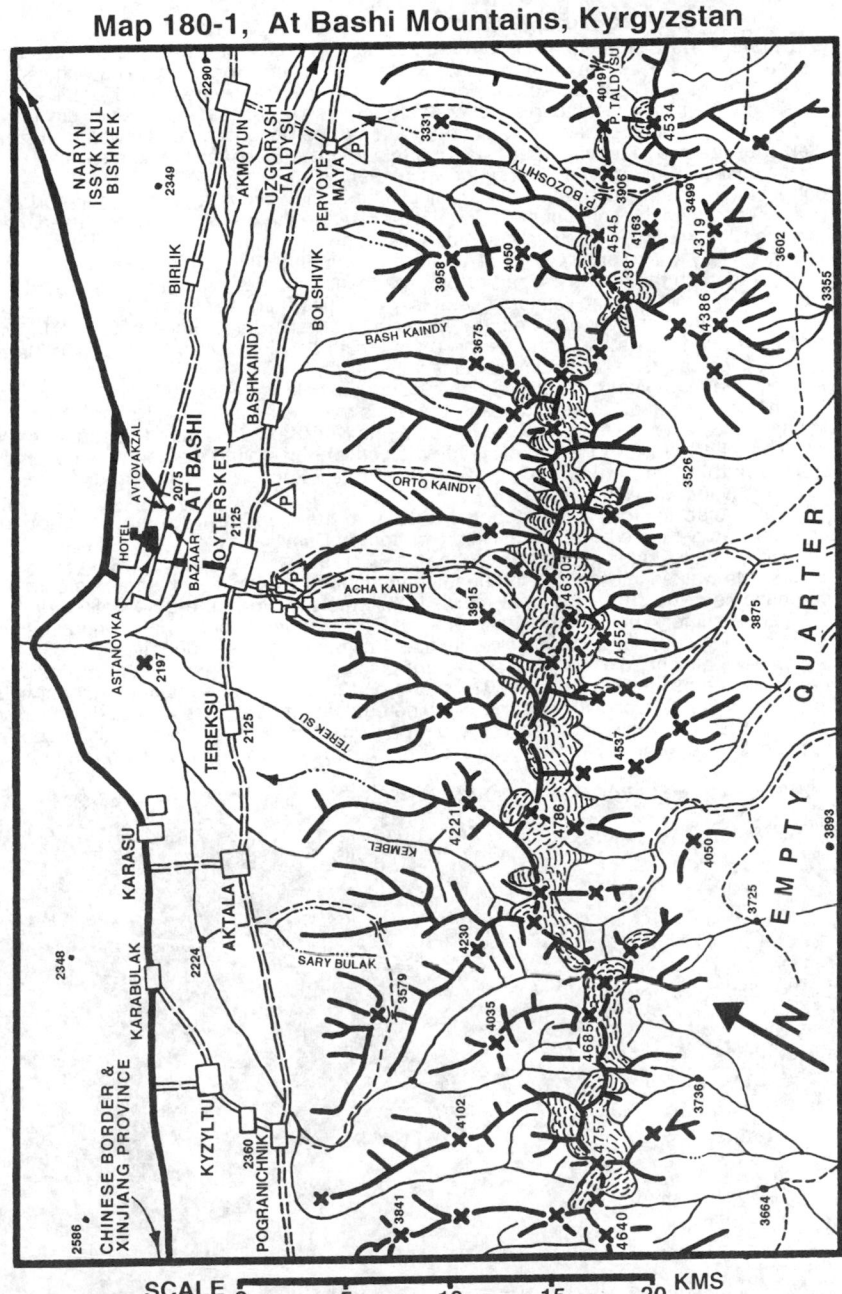

Maps DMA maps *Naryn, NK 43-8, Ak Beit, NK 43-11, Imeni Voroshilova, NK 43-9, and maybe Chong Kara Kol, NK 43-12,* Series N502, 1:250,000; or Kyrgyz Geodise & Kartografia maps *At Bashi, K-43-XXVIII, and Akmuz, II-43-29 or K-43-XXIX,* 1:200,000; the TPC map *F-6C,* 1:500,000; and the latest travel guidebook to Central Asia.

Gora Nura & Gora Naryn Tau, Kyrgyzstan

Shown here are 2 small ranges of moderate height. To the north is Gora Nura, and the highest summit Pik Kokseki at 4444 meters. To the south is the Gora Naryn Tou with its highest summit 4500 meters. The maps below, which the author used, show no names for these peaks.

These mountains are located in south central Kyrgyzstan just east of the small city of Naryn. Naryn has a pretty good bazaar, and all your food can be bought there. However, bazaars in Bishkek offer more, and are cheaper. Naryn has one hotel called the Gastinetsa Ala Too (Tu). This place cost US$4 a night and was rundown in 1995.

Both of these mountain ranges have small glaciers, and difficult routes on their north faces, with easier routes up the south slopes. In the Nura Range the author found some sedimentary rocks along with quartzite and other metamorphics.

To reach Naryn, take one of several small daily morning buses from the novey avtovakzal (new bus station) in the northwest part of Bishkek, bound for Naryn or At Bashi. You can also take a bus from Balikchi at the western end of Issyk Kul (Issyk Lake).

From Naryn, take an 8am or 4pm bus east along the road north of the Rika (River) Naryn to as far as the town of Irisu, a distance of 40 kms. Buses return from there at 10:30am and 5:30pm. This gives easy access to mountains to the north.

To reach the **Gora Naryn**, take a bus from Naryn east along the south side of the river as far as Voroshilova. The author was told buses along this road go as far as Eki Naryn, which doesn't show on the maps below, but it may be the same as Ken-Saz (?). There appears to be some vehicle tracks and livestock trails leading into the canyons east, and the north, then east of this mapped area, but there are no buses. With the maps listed below, trekking or climbing into areas east of Naryn would be interesting.

The south side of Gora Naryn is accessible from the town of Akmuz, but it's not certain whether you can get there by bus from Naryn, or from At Bashi (?).

The author stayed one night in Naryn, then on 9/3/1995, got on the 8am bus and went as far Orto Nura. He walked into the canyon heading straight for **Kokseki** and got a ride on a tractor to the house near the end of the road marked 2670 meters. From there he walked up a good sheep & goat trail for 4 hours to the base of Kokseki. Because of bad weather and fresh snow on the very steep south face of Kokseki, the author climbed an easy 4000 meters peak instead. Next morning, he climbed Peak 4180 and returned to camp in less that 3 hours. He didn't have an ice ax or crampons, so no attempt was made on Kokseki, but normally by August you can climb the steep south face without snow climbing equipment. Later he walked downcanyon to the pass marked 2810, climbed the 3177 meter peak just to the south, then continued down the road to within one hour of Chet Nura and camped. Next morning he was on the first bus to

From Orto Nura looking south at the northern slopes of the Naryn Tau Mountains.

Map 181-1, Gora Nura & Gora Naryn Tau, Kyrgyzstan

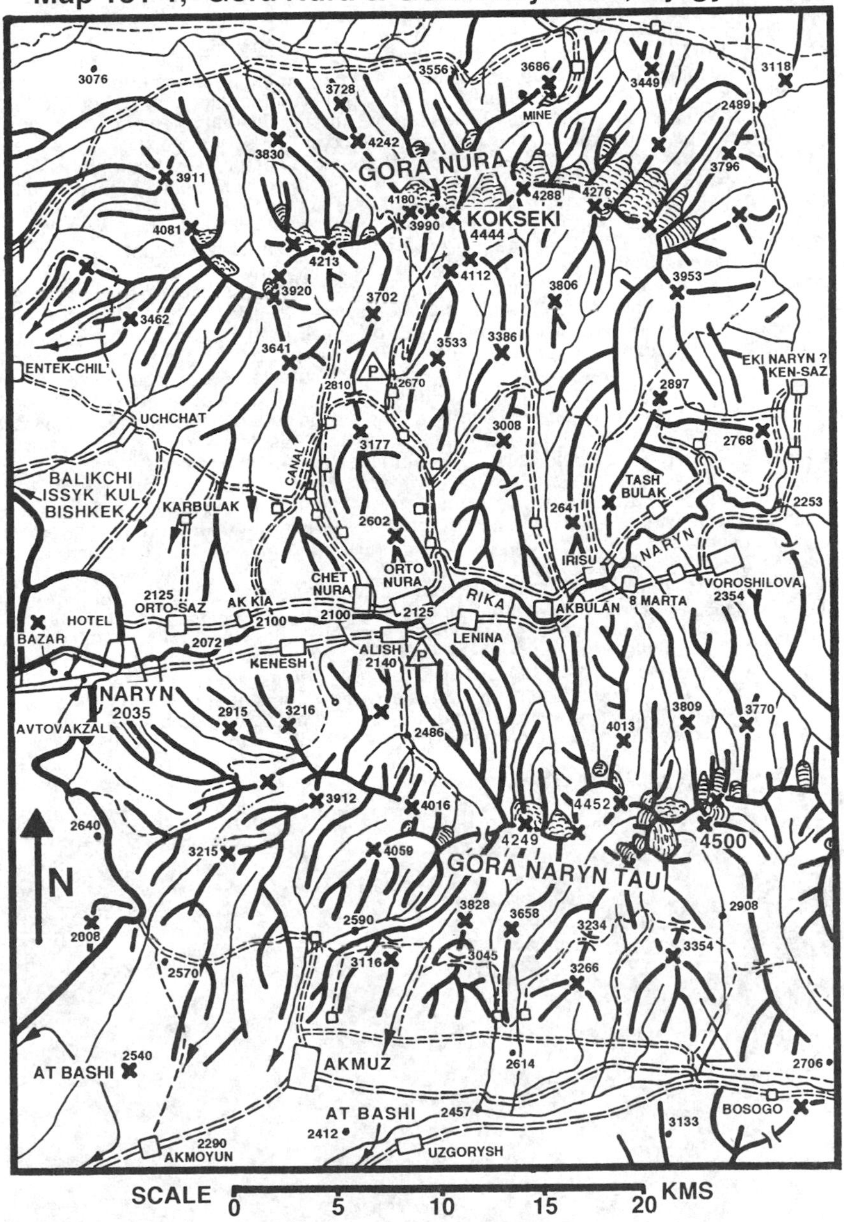

Naryn. Total walk-time for 3 days, just under 16 hours. All sizable villages have one small store, but it's best to buy your food in Naryn.

Maps DMA map *Imeni Voroshilova, NK 43-9*, Series N502, 1:250,000; or the Kyrgyz Geodesi & Kartografia maps *Naryn, K-43-XXIII, and Akmuz, II-43-29 or K-43-XXIX*, 1:200,000; the TPC map *F-6C*, 1:500,000; and the latest travel guidebook to Central Asia.

Aksay Hikes, Terskey Alatou, Kyrgyzstan

Featured here is the 1st of 3 maps covering the mountains immediately south of Issyk Kul (Issyk Lake) in eastern Kyrgyzstan. This part of the Terskey Alatou is southwest of the lake. For those interested in exploring, there is another group of high peaks west of this area and southeast of Kochkorka. The highest peak here isn't named on the maps the author used, but it's altitude is 4762 meters. As in other areas of Central Asia, peaks over about 4200 meters begin to be difficult, so this area has all classes of climbing difficulty. There are a number of glaciers, and the rocks are granite, quartzite and other crystallines.

At the top of this map are several towns and one small city on the main highway linking Bishkek, with Kara Kol, at the east end of Issyk Kul. If coming from Bishkek, take a bus along the yugom marsroute (south route) to Kara Kol. There are about 6 buses per day making this run, plus other local buses running from Balikchi (formerly Rybach'ye) to Kara Kol. There is at least one bus per day running in the morning from the village of Alabash, east to at least Bokombayev and returning in the afternoon. Best to buy food in Bishkek or Kara Kol, but Bokombayev has a good bazaar and a gastinetsa (hotel), the only one on this map; however there are several resort hotels on the south shore of Issyk Kul just to the east.

Depending on where you want to hike, get off the bus at Bokombayev, Aksay, or the astanovka (bus stop) immediately east of Tortkel'. From either of these places, you'll then have to walk, hitch hike on trucks or tractors pulling trailers, or look for a taxi to get you closer to the canyon, peak or periwal (pass) you want to go to. There are old Soviet era roads into all the major canyons, then normally sheep & goat trails on up to the higher summer pastures. The author used mostly the Kyrgyz 1:200,000 maps below to create this one, but some trails shown here may be old vehicle tracks or roads. Those old maps show a trail over the Periwal Konurlen (west side of map), but several people told this writer there was actually a road of some kind.

The author took an afternoon bus from Kara Kol bound for Balikchik and got off at the astanovka east of Tortkel'. He walked southeast to Turasu, got a lift on a tractor for about 3 more kms, and camped. Next morning, 8/28/1995, he started walking, then got a lift on a 1940's truck up to 3000 meters in the valley north of Periwal (P.) Ton. They stopped at a shepherd camp to pickup Kumis, which is fermented mare's milk. After breakfast in a yurta, he walked up the old road, over P. Ton, and down to the deep valley and a good road, then up another rough road to Teshik Kul to a camp. While going over P. Ton, steep ice covered the road, so he had to take the horse trail up the ridge to the east then back down. In early summer this is just steep snow and sheep & goats go over it OK, but by September you may need an ice ax & crampons.

From Teshik Kul, he headed north for the Periwal Koltor, but snow, and lack of ice ax & crampons turned him back. He returned over P. Ton in a blizzard and camped on the road at 2500 meters. Next day, he walked to Kuksay before getting a lift to Aksay. Total walk-time, 25 hours.

This summertime yurta was located in the valley north of Periwal Ton.

Map 182-1, Aksay Hikes, Terskey Alatou, Kyrgyzstan

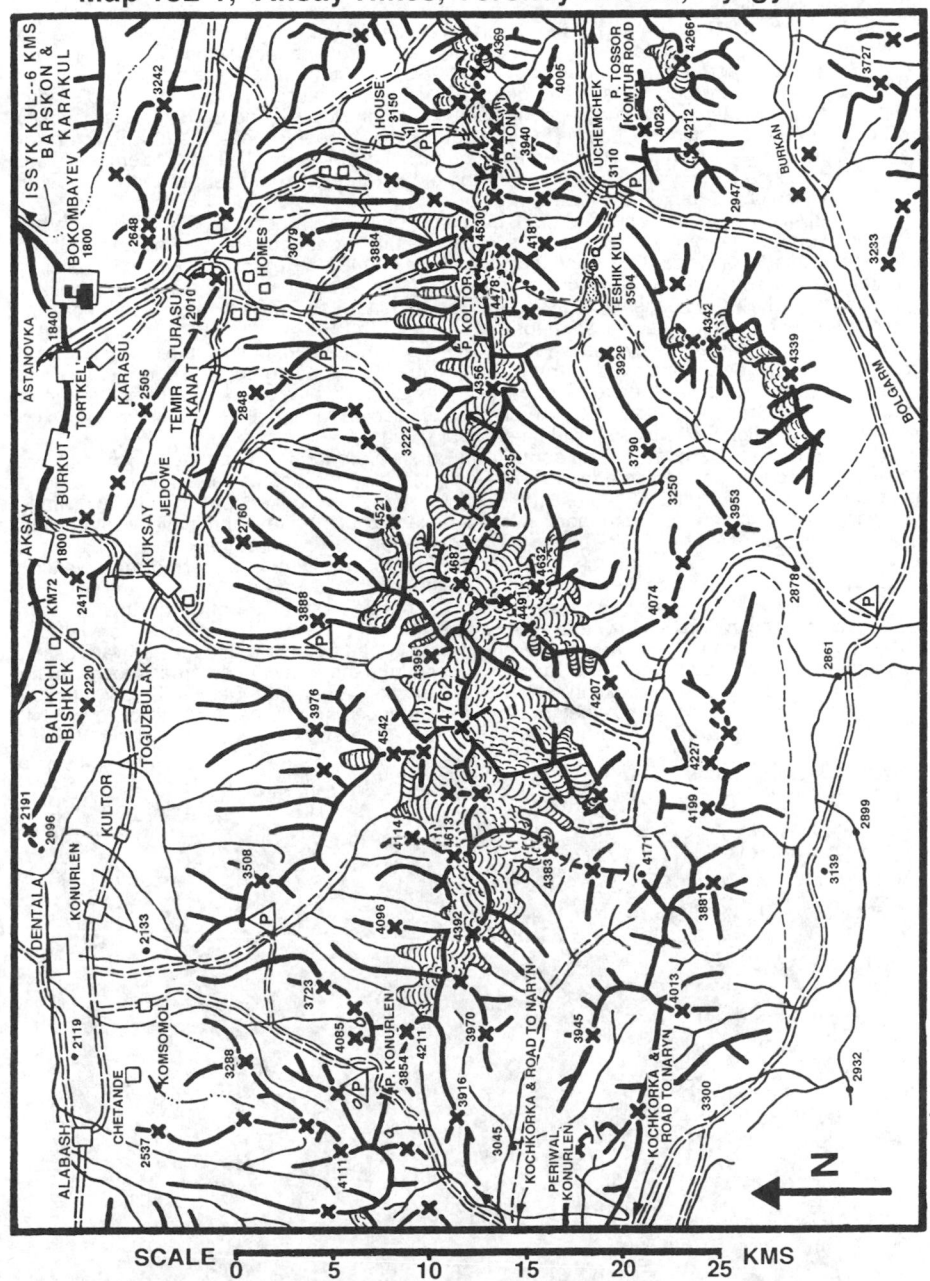

SCALE

0   5   10   15   20   25   KMS

Maps DMA maps *Rybach'ye, NK 43-6,* and *Imeni Voroshilova, NK 43-9,* Series N502, 1:250,000; or Kyrgyz Geodesi & Kartografia maps *Kadzhi-Say, II-43-18* or *K-43-XVIII, Karasay, K-43-XXIV, Rybach'ye, II-43-17* or *K-43-XVII,* and *Naryn, K-43-XXIII,* all 1:200,000; the TPC map *F-6C,* 1:500,000; and the latest travel guidebook to Central Asia.

Barskon Hikes, Terskey Alatou, Kyrgyzstan

The mountains on this map are located immediately south of Issyk Kul (Issyk Lake) in eastern Kyrgyzstan. They are part of the Khrebet Terskey Alatou, which run east-west along the south shore of the lake. The largest town in the area is Barskon, about 60 kms west of Kara Kol.

There are 3 main mountain ridges here. The one to the north and closest to Issyk Kul has some very steep and rugged peaks and made of mostly metamorphic rock. The middle ridge isn't as rugged and there are some easy climbs up the south slopes. The rocks there are mostly granite and quartzite. The 3rd ridge to the south is the *Khrebet Suek*. It's in a much drier setting, therefore glaciation hasn't carved the high points down so much. The glaciers there are more like small ice caps which seem to sit on top of the rounded summits, rather than moving downhill. Those peaks appear to be easy walk-ups.

Get to this area by taking one of about 6 buses per day running between Bishkek & Kara Kol along the south shore of Issyk Kul. This is known as the yugom marsroute (south route). Or take one of several other buses making local runs west from Kara Kol. Buy food and supplies in Bishkek or Kara Kol. Once in this region, the author used Kara Kol and the inexpensive hotel & good bazaar there as his base while hiking into 3 different areas. Barskon has a small bazaar and only a couple of small magazins (shops).

From Barskon, there's a new road (1995) running south, then east and south for 90 kms to a gold mine run by Komtur, a Canadian-Kyrgyz company. It was being upgraded for heavy truck traffic in 8/1995, and is likely paved by now (?). The author saw a Km 43 marker on the road near the Periwal (pass) Barkson. As mine operations become routine, there should be buses on this road; or just hitch hike which should be easy for foreigners.

On 8/23/1995, the author walked south from Barskon along the road a ways, got a lift in a donkey cart and was invited into a farmers home for lunch. After that he walked again and got a lift in a truck up to the big lake 5 kms past Periwal Barskon; then walked the high, dry and windy route east and north to P. Dzhuku, north into the upper Dzhuku Valley, and finally west back to the Komtur Road. Two day walk-time, 13 1/2 hours. On Day 3, he day-hiked west up to the Ozera (Lake) Chunkurkul and back. Walk-time 7 hours. On Day 4 he started road-walking north, then got 2 rides back to the astanovka (bus stop) north of Barskon.

The Komtur Road is your best route of access, but you can also get up or down via the valley road starting in Saru. Today that road is seldom used but will always be good for walking. There's also a road coming up the valley from the west, then heads north over Periwal Tossor. The author saw this road up the valley from Ozera Chunkurkul, and from the Periwal Ton area, shown on the previous map (very good at that point). It surely deteriorates around the Periwal Tossor, but that track will give easy access to the western part of this mapped area. The Arabel Dolina (Arabel Valley) in the empty quarter is so high (about 3600-3700 meters), dry, cold & windy, that it's

Looking south across the Dolina Arabel (Arabel Valley) at the northern slopes of the Krebet Suek (Suek Mountains).

Map 183-1, Barskon Hikes, Terskey Alatou, Kyrgyzstan

SCALE

0   5   10   15   20   25   KMS

almost deserted, except for a handful of shepherds & their herds. But it would be a great place to make some easy climbs, or just trek, in a land that's unknown to alpinists. Lots of livestock in the valleys north of Dolina Arabel.

Maps DMA map *Rybach'ye, NK 43-6,* and *Imeni Voroshilova, NK 43-9,* Series N502, 1:250,000; or Kyrgyz Geodesi & Kartografia maps *Kadzhi-Say, II-43-18 or K-43-XVIII, and Karasai, K-43-XXIV,* 1:200,000; the TPC map *F-6C,* 1:500,000; and the latest travel guidebook to Central Asia.

Kara Kol Hikes, Terskey Alatau, Kyrgyzstan

Shown on this map are the Terskey Alatau (Terskey Mountains) and canyons immediately south of Kara Kol, formerly known as Przheval'sk. This mapped area is immediately east of Issyk Kul (Issyk Lake). Emphasized here will be access points & trekking routes. Most people visiting this region hike rather than climb. The higher peaks are heavily glaciated which makes some very difficult climbing routes. There is lots of granite here, plus quartzite.

To get to Kara Kol from Bishkek, take one of 8-10 buses per day going along the severno marsroute (north route) to Kara Kol. These go along the north shore of Issyk Kul. Or there are about 6 daily buses along the yugom marsroute (south route). In Kara Kol there are 2 good bazaars and the Gastinetsa Kara Kol (Hotel Kara Kol) for about US$5 a night (1995). You can buy all your food for trekking in Kara Kol. Selections there are almost as good as in Bishkek, but the cost of most food is about 15% higher.

The author was told afterwards, that hikers and climbers need a permit to trek in the canyons above Kara Kol, Dzhetyoguz and Teploklychenka. Get it for US$15 (in 1995) at the Buro of Turizm, apparently next door to the Gastinetsa Kara Kol (?).

To hike up Kara Kol Canyon, walk to the center of town next to the Small Bazaar and ask where bus 1 stops. Get on it and ride to the end of a paved road along the Rika (River) Kara Kol. From there, either walk or hire a taxi to get upcanyon another 10 kms or so. This road steadily deteriorates the further up you go. This is true for all canyons shown on this map, as well as all mountain canyons throughout Kyrgyzstan. You may find some bridges washed out, but shepherds or someone should replace most of them in order to take sheep, goats, horses & cows to the high pastures every summer.

From the upper end of the Kara Kol River you can climb glaciated peaks; or hike over periwals (passes) to other river drainages. In 3 days beginning on 8/19/1995, the author walked up the Kara Kol, over the pass marked 3710 meters to the west, then down to Korut, where he got a ride back to Kara Kol. Total walk-time was 22 hours. This time included 2 fast trips (evening & morning), without the big pack, to the upper valley above Korut for fotos.

There are sheep trails wherever there's grass. The trails shown going over periwals with snow or glaciers, are for people who have an ice ax, crampons, and possibly in some cases, a rope. They're not technical, but they're not easy summer strolls either.

To reach the towns of Saru, Pokrovka, Dzhetyoguz or Teploklychenka, all of which are at the mouths of major canyons, go to the avtovakzal (bus station) in the northeast part of Kara Kol. From there a number of buses run along this main road daily. If you're interested in reaching the very high, dry and isolated *empty quarter* south of these mountains, head for Saru or Pokrovka, and hike south from there. The easiest periwal to cross is the one south of Saru, then up the 2nd major canyon to the east, thence over Periwal Kashka Su. There are apparently almost no humans or livestock on the other side because it's so high, dry, cold and inhospitable.

Looking south from the periwal (pass) marked 3710 at the highest peak in the region marked 5216.

Map 184-1, Kara Kol Hikes, Terskey Alatau, Kyrgyzstan

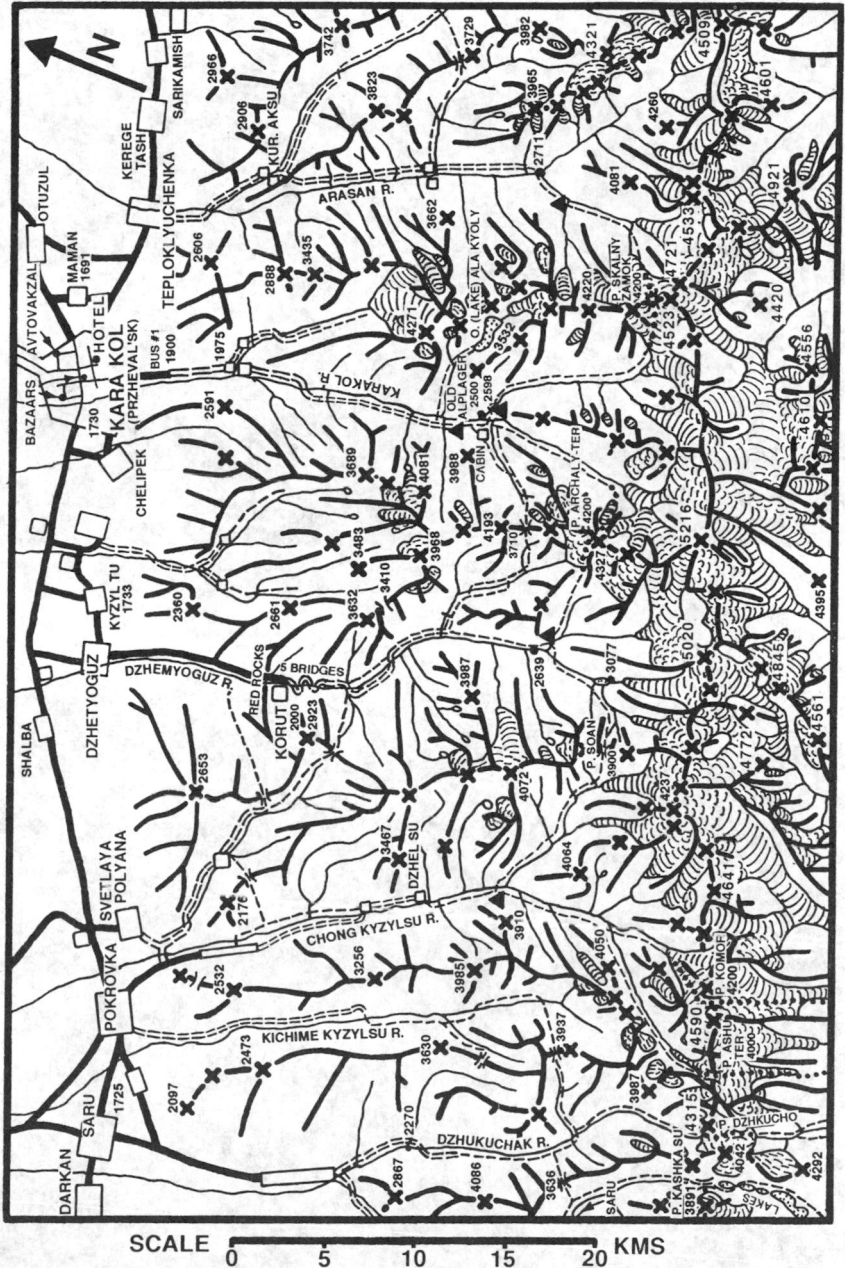

SCALE
0   5   10   15   20 KMS

Maps DMA map *Przheval'sk, NK 44-4*, Series N502, 1:250,000; or Kyrgyz Geodesi &
Kartografia maps *Przhevalsk, II-44-13 or K-44-XIII*, and/or *Uchkoshkon, T-G-148 or K-44-XIX*
(for empty quarter and Akshiypak Mtns.), 1:200,000; or the Russian trekking map *Gorny Turizm-
Tian Shanoo;* the TPC map *F6-C*, 1:500,000; the book, **Trekking in Russia & Central Asia**,
The Mountaineers; and the latest travel guidebook to Central Asia.

From near the Periwal Aksu and the pass marked 4150 meters, looking south at the heavily glaciated northern slopes (Map 179, page 395).

Looking south across the Dolina Arabel and the Komtur Road at the Krebet Suek. These glaciers look more like non-moving ice caps than valley glaciers (Map 183, page 403).

Looking across the river from Tyungur toward the village of Kucherla (Map 186, page 411).

From the meteostantsiya & Lake Akem, looking south at Pik Belukha in the far distance.
(Map 186, page 411).

Pik Pobeda & Khan Tangri, Tian Shan (Mtns.), Kyrgyzstan

This is an introduction to 2 of the highest peaks in Kyrgyzstan located in the Tian Shan (Tian Mountains). They are Pik Pobeda at 7439 meters, the second highest peak in the former USSR (after Pik Kommunizma); and Khan Tangri, 6995 meters. Pobeda is on the Kyrgyz-Chinese granetsa (border), while Khan Tangri, just to the north, is near the Kyrgyz-Kazakstan border. The author hasn't been into this region, but the rocks are likely various metamorphics and granite.

The area map shows the eastern third of Kyrgyzia and the route from Kara Kol (formerly Przheval'sk) to the mountains. Get to Kara Kol by taking one of about a dozen daily buses from the novey avtovakzal (new bus station) in the northwest part of Bishkek. It's about an 8 hour ride. From Kara Kol, the professional guide services normally have their clients either helicopter directly to the end of a rough road and a kind of base camp called Maida Adyr; or they take everyone in with small buses which takes about 5 hours. Maida Adyr has sleeping rooms made from old converted railroad cars, a kitchen-cook building and banya (bath). It's located at about 2475 meters.

It's best to stop and stay in Maida Adyr for one or more nights to help with acclimatization. From there it's about 2 days walking to a camping area called Chon Tash, 2850 meters, near the snout of the Lednik Engilchek (Engilchek Glacier). Chon Tash is on the other side of the river from Maida Adyr, and it was never explained to this writer how hikers get across the river to camp there at a good spring (?). You can also get to Chon Tash by hiking from Dzhergalan as shown on the area map. This 4-6 day hike is described in the book below.

From Chon Tash, it's about 3 more days walking up the Lednik Engilchek along a medial moraine to the baze lager (advanced base camp) at 4160 meters. One campsite along the way is called Merzbacher Glade, located near Ozero (Lake) Merzbacher. Advanced base camp is now privately run and has standup & kitchen tents and a banya for their clients. From advanced base camp it's south up the glacier to Camps 1, 2 and somewhere higher, a 3rd camp. This mountain is for experienced and determined climbers only. The last 4-5 kms is along a ridge all above 7000 meters. Weather conditions have to be perfect for this climb. Because of its northern latitude (42°N), conditions are said to be as bad as on Everest, except you'll have a little more oxygen. Khan Tangri can be climbed from the same baze lager.

If you're interested in doing it without a guide service, go to the Kara Kol Hotel in Kara Kol. Next door is the office of the Kommittee of Turizm & Sport. In 1995, you had to pay US$100 to climb Pobeda and/or Khan Tangri at this office. Since it's on the border of China, you must also get proposk (permission) to be in that area. They can help you get that, or get it yourself at the OVIR (passport) office. There is public transport to Akbulak and Dzhergalan, then you walk--or look for a lift. Or you could inquire about getting on a helicopter starting in Kara Kol, or Maida Adyr. This shouldn't be difficult. Or you could walk in and have supplies flown in to advance base camp. Normally climbers take 3-4 weeks supply of food, etc. Climbing camps are manned by the guide services from mid-July to the first week in September.

Maps DMA maps *Przheval'sk, NK 44-4, and NK 44-5*, Series N502, 1:250,000; the Ceska map *Sentralniy Tian Shan*, 1:100,000, by Vilém Hrdina, Praha; the Kyrgyz Geodesi & Kartografia maps *Dzhergalan, II-44-14 or K-44-XIV, and Pik Pobeda, II-44-15 or K-44-XV*, 1:200,000; and

The author was invited inside this *yurta,* the one shown on Map 182, page 400.

Map 185-1, Pobeda & Khan Tangri, Tian Shan, Kyrgyzstan

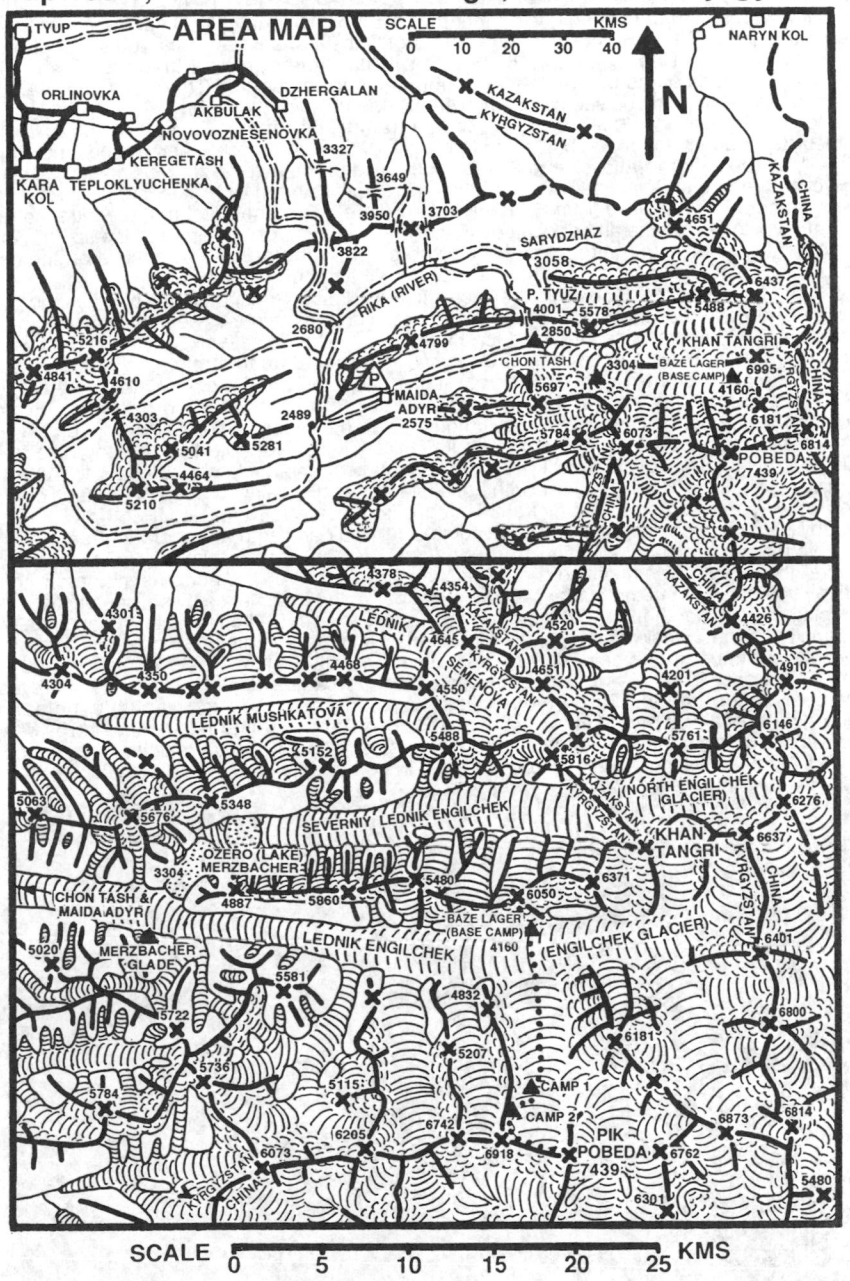

for access, the TPC map *F-6C*, 1:500,000; also the book, **Trekking in Russia & Central Asia**, Maier, The Mountaineers.

Pik Belukha, Altay Mountains, Siber, Russia

Shown on this map is the highest mountain in Siber (Siberia), Pik Belukha at 4506 meters. It's located in the Altay Mountains on the border of Russia and Kazakstan, due south of Barnaul and Novosibirsk. Because it's at 50° north with an abundance of glaciers, this peak has conditions as difficult as on much higher mountains to the south. The rocks in the Altay are quartzite and slate, but you see granite boulders in the valleys.

Here's the author's experience. He took a train from Almaty, Kazakstan to Barnaul. He immediately caught a morning bus south to the city of Gorno-Altaysk, where he bought 5 days of food. In 9/1995, Gorno-Altaysk had 2 hotels; one next to the avtovakzal (bus station). Next day he got on the one and only daily morning bus heading south to Ust Koksa, a 9 hour ride. In the past you could fly to Koksa from Barnaul, but no more. The one hotel at the central square in Koksa was closed, so the author camped in the woods just across the river to the south. There's a foot bridge about 200 meters south from the bus parking area. Right there on the central square are 5 small magazins (shops), but with very little to buy.

On the third morning, 9/18/1995, he hitch hiked the last 64 kms to the town of Tyungur. Later that day, he walked all the way to a campsite located on the main trail west of Periwal Karaturek; walk-time, 7 1/2 hours. Then it rained for 35 hours! On Day 2, he walked to Lake Kucherla and back in 4 hours, all with an umbrella. On Day 3, he walked up the trail to Karaturek Pass and down to the meteostantsiya (meteorological station) next to Lake Akkem. Walk-time 6 1/2 hours. One km south of the met. station is an alplager (alpinists camp) with 3 huts. From the meteostantsiya, he continued for nearly 3 hours down the Akkem River and camped. Day 4, he walked all the way back to Tyungur in about 8 1/2 hours. Not counting the day-hike to Lake Kucherla, his total walk-time from Tyungur to Lake Akkem and back was about 25 1/2 hours.

Tyungur has one small magazin with not a lot to buy. Buy all your food in Barnaul, or maybe Gorno-Altaysk. Across the river from Tyungur is a hunter's lodge at US$30 or $40 a night. Nearby is an baze alplager (alpinist base camp). But you can camp anywhere for free!

If you're serious about climbing **Belukha** (pron. *Beluha*), better take about 2 weeks of food. With all that weight, you might consider flying in. For about US$100 per person (more when you arrive!) you can fly from the hunter's lodge into either of the large lakes by helicopter. The normal climbing route is south from L. Akkem, up the Lednik Akkem (Akkem Glacier) to an icefall, then left and up to the Tomsky Camp, a priyut (hut) at 2957 meters. This takes one day. From Priyut Tomsky, continue up the flat lednik to the base of Periwal Delone, then up a steep 300 meter slope to the pass itself. From Delone Pass, drop down to a glacier plateau with many crevasses, and veer right or south. Finally you'll climb up to the Berelsky Ridge at 3400 meters, then according to Maier's book below, you'll have a Russian Climbing Route Class 3B, with *ten pitches of low-fifth class rock, interspersed with knife-edge snow* before reaching the summit.

The normal climbing season is from mid-July to early September. You'll need all the standard

Pik Belukha as seen from Periwal Karaturek (Pass) through a telefoto lens.

Map 186-1, Pik Belukha, Altay Mtns., Siber, Russia

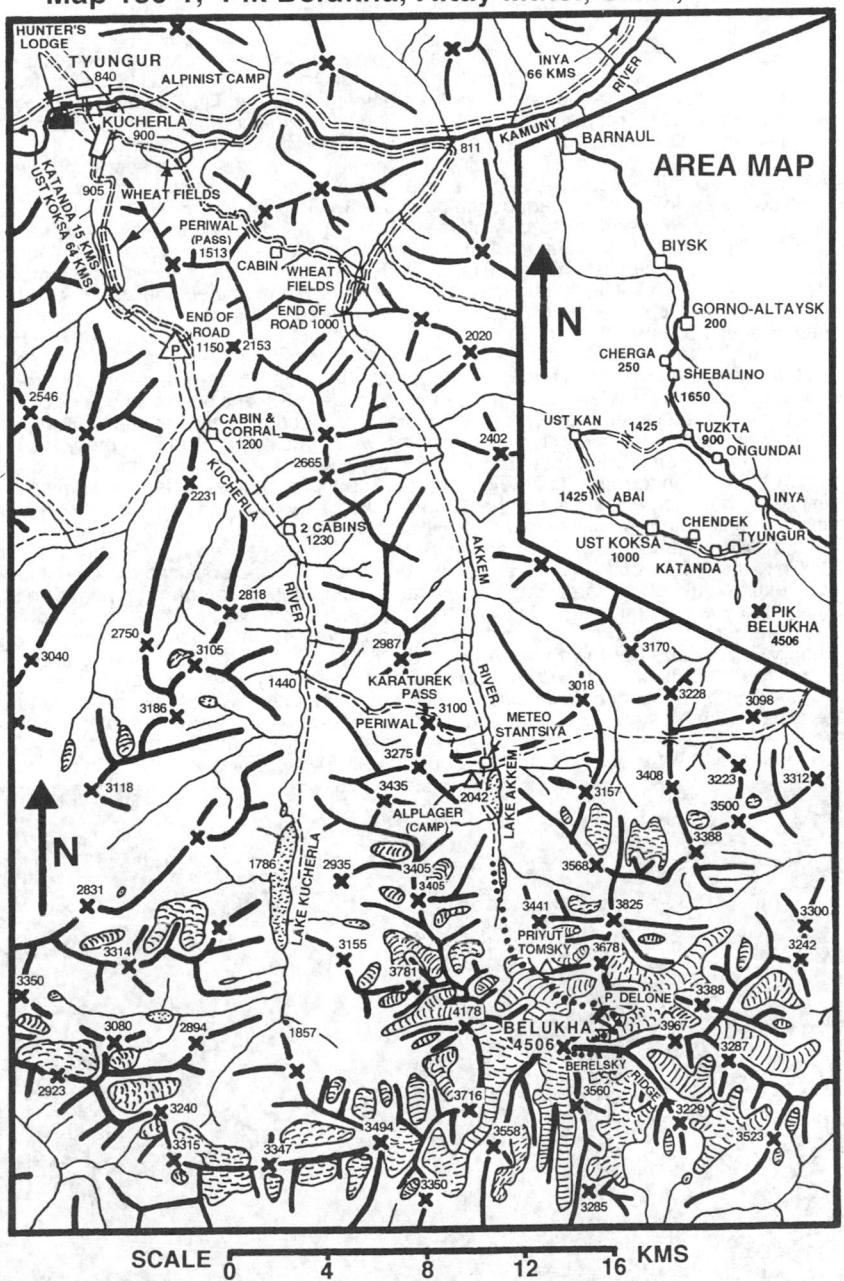

SCALE 0 4 8 12 16 KMS

snow & ice climbing equipment.
Maps For access, TPC map *E-6C*, 1:500,000; and maps *4 & 7, Katanda & Bereli,* from the AQUA 9 map series of the Altay; and the book, **Trekking in Russia and Central Asia**, Maier, The Mountaineers; and the latest travel guidebook to Russia.

Sheveluch, Harchinsky & Zarechny, Kamchatka, Russia

The mountain featured here is called Vulkan Sheveluch, at 3283 meters. It's located about 30 kms north of Kluchi in central Kamchatka. Sheveluch is an old eroded volcano, but it has a new and very active crater on its south side. About 65,000 years ago it exploded, leaving a 9-km-wide caldera. In 1854 & 1964 the younger Molodoy Sheveluch had its biggest historic eruptions that buried the forest for many kms to the south. In the 1990's, there were many eruptions through 7/3/2000. Also included here are 2 other old and extinct volcanos; Harchinsky, about 1500 meters, and Zarechny, at about 770. For volcano updates see website (www.avo.alaska.edu/) or (www.volcano.si.edu/gvp/).

There is one small problem with climbing Sheveluch. There is a highly secret missile base somewhere north of the mountain and the entire area is restricted. Even the geologists at the Institut Vulkanology in Kluchi are required to have special proposk (permission) to visit its active crater. So if you're planning to climb Sheveluch, contact the Institut headquarters in Petopavlovsk-Kamchatky (P-K) ahead of time and ask them for help getting proposk. If for some reason you don't have proposk, but if you're the adventurous type, simply head for the mountain quickly before the KGB has a chance to remind you that it's a restricted zone. Not long before this writer was in Kluchi to climb Kluchevskoy, a Japanese man made it to the mountain and returned without problems. If you're caught climbing it without permission you'll likely be fined.

Here's how to get to **Sheveluch**. Best to hire a 4WD vehicle in Kluchi, then drive to a point 300-400 meters west of the main shopping area, and turn north into the port area. The ferry will take you and/or your vehicle across. On the other side, drive 28 kms north to a point west of the mountain and to a side road as shown. Drive this old track about 8 kms and start walking. If the water is low, you can walk along the stream; otherwise, buskwhack through the trees on the south side of the stream. Once out of the forest at about 900 or 1000 meters, the walking should be easy. Fotos and maps indicated the best route is up along the west side of the new crater to the main east-west ridge, then east to the summit. The Sheveluch part of this map was created with the map below and verbal information, so it's not very accurate.

To climb **Harchinsky**, walk from the Institut Vulkanology and the Gastinetsa (hotel) Stromboli, to the ferry, cross the river, and walk north about 300 meters along the road, then turn left and head up through the forest on the prominent south ridge of **Zarechny**. There's no trail at first, but once you get upon the ridge, a pretty good path begins and runs up to a point where you have to drop down to a pass, then route-find & bushwhack up a south-side ridge to Harchinsky. This can be down in one day from Kluchi. The author climbed Zarechny on 7/1/1994. It was a 4 hour round-trip hike from the ferry. The ferry runs from 9am to 5pm.

All food can be bought in Kluchi, but P-K has better varieties. Climb from mid-July to early September. Take mosquito repellent and a bell for bears; and a tent, crampons & ice ax for Sheveluch. Be sure to read the *Introduction to Russia* for more information.

Maps TPC map *D-9D*, 1:500,000; and the books, **Active Volcanoes of Kamchatka**, Volume I,

Just west of Kluchi looking southwest at Kluchevskoy left and Plosky Bliznaya right.

Map 187-1, Sheveluch, Harchinsky & Zarechny, Kamchatka, Russia

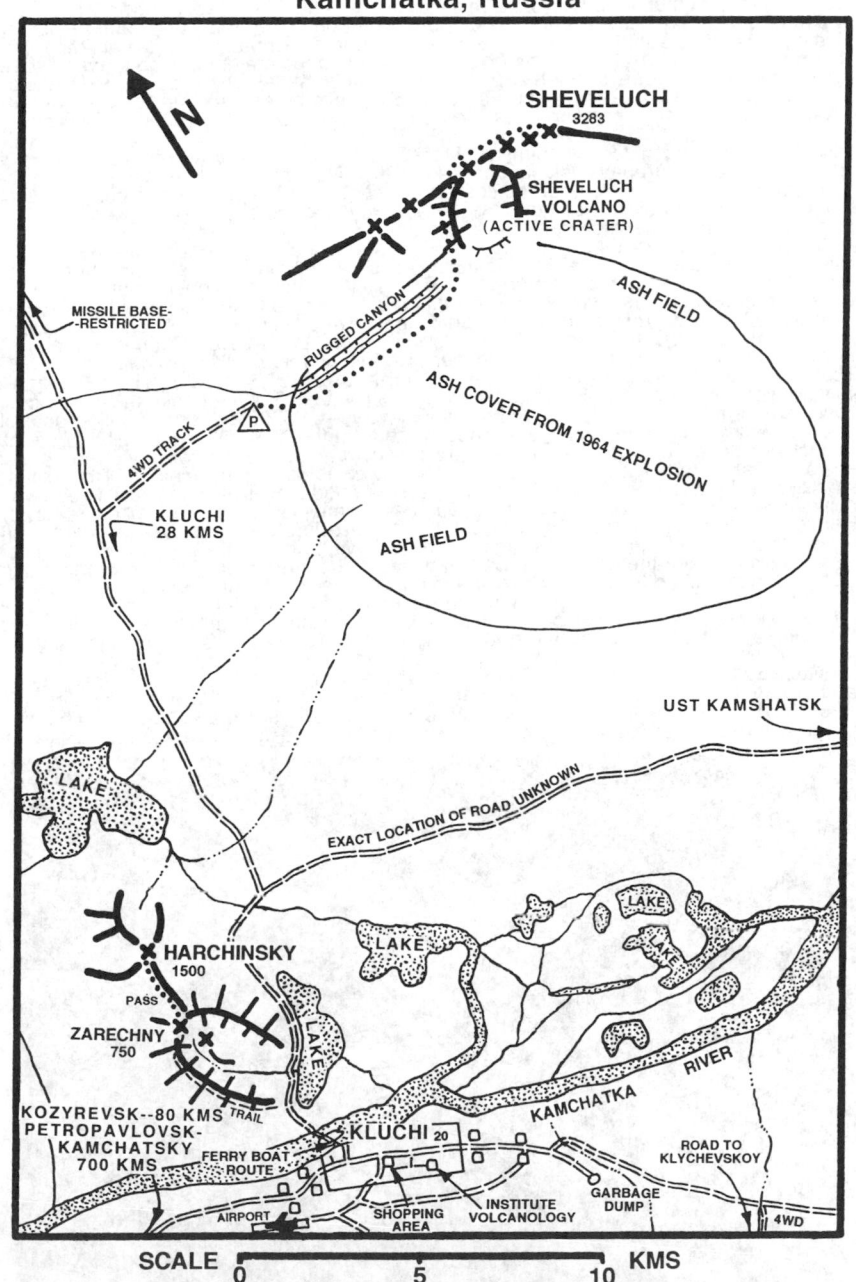

SHEVELUCH
3283

SHEVELUCH
VOLCANO
(ACTIVE CRATER)

ASH FIELD

MISSILE BASE-
-RESTRICTED

RUGGED CANYON

ASH COVER FROM 1964 EXPLOSION

4WD TRACK

P

KLUCHI
28 KMS

ASH FIELD

UST KAMSHATSK

LAKE

EXACT LOCATION OF ROAD UNKNOWN

LAKE

LAKE

HARCHINSKY
1500

PASS

ZARECHNY
750

LAKE

RIVER

KOZYREVSK--80 KMS
PETROPAVLOVSK-
KAMCHATSKY
700 KMS

TRAIL

FERRY BOAT
ROUTE

KLUCHI 20

KAMCHATKA

ROAD TO
KLYCHEVSKOY

AIRPORT

SHOPPING
AREA

INSTITUTE
VOLCANOLOGY

GARBAGE
DUMP

4WD

SCALE 0   5   10 KMS

by the Russian Academy of Science--Institut Vulkanology, Nauka Publishers, Moskva, 1991; and **Trekking in Russia & Central Asia**, The Mountaineers; and the latest travel guidebook to Russia.

Kluchevskoy, Kamen & Bezymianny, Kamchatka, Russia

Featured on this map are Kamchatka's highest and most active volcanos. Kluchevskoy is listed at 4750 meters, but the author believes it's closer to 4900. This *vulkan* is 7000 years old and is almost constantly active. On top is a 700-meter-wide crater, plus it has about 100 flank eruptive centers. The eruption of 1955-56 ended 1000 years of peace for Bezymianny, 3081 meters (or 2882?). That explosion created a horseshoe-shaped crater opening to the east. It's been active with a lava dome through 2000. Kamen at 4632 meters, has not erupted in historic times. Two other high peaks of 4109 and 3945 meters belong to the heavily glaciated Ushkovsky Volcano. For volcano updates see website (www.avo.alaska.edu/) or (www.volcano. si.edu/gvp/).

The normal starting point for climbing all of these peaks is from the town of Kluchi. Get there by taking a bus from Petropavlovsk-Kamchatsky (P-K). It's about 700 kms and private buses run about twice a week. The 20 hour trip cost about US$35 in 1994. Hitching is quite good too. Or fly from P-K about 4 days a week for US$134 one way. Best to buy food supplies in P-K, but Kluchi has a small bazaar and several little shops or magazins, as well as a Volcanology Station about 500 meters east of the town center. They have a small guest house (Gastinetsa Stromboli) you can use, or maybe camp in their enclosure. All the volcanologists speak a little English and are hoping to earn extra money by being guides. They are very helpful.

Leave for the mountains soon after arriving in Kluchi--before the KGB has a chance to tell you Kluchi is a 2nd class restricted zone; even so the airlines may sell you a ticket anyway!; as they did with the author. No major problem, but you could be fined US$50 if you don't have permission to be there. This was a minor problem in 1994, and hopefully it will go away!

To reach **Kluchevskoy,** it might be best to look for a 4WD and be driven 70 kms to Apahonchich seismic station which would allow you to climb all 3 of the best peaks. You could also get there from P-K by helicopter, but that's expensive--US$700 an hour! Another possible route, perhaps walking all the way, is to head south from the military airport. This route has some bushwhacking, then glaciers higher up. The *normal route* however is via the shelters (priyuts or doms) of Podkova, Circum and Scredny. By going this route, it can be climbed in 4-5 days walking all the way from Kluchi. These doms have wood stoves (volcanologists keep wood at each) and were in pretty good condition in 1994 (take some plastic to cover broken windows).

Here's what the author did. On 6/26/1994, with part-time geologist Sergei Ageev, they walked southeast from Kluchi on the road toward Podkova, but took the wrong right turn and it took 2 full days to reach the end of the road. On Day 3, the author left Podkova alone at 7am with full pack and walked to Circum Dom and left his big pack. He then reached 4770 meters (altimeter reading) at 5:15pm. The summit appeared to be about 100 meters above when he had to start back down (take & use old *rock* crampons for the last half km). He arrived at Circum at 10:15 pm, after wandering for one hour in the fog. At 15 1/4 hours this was the author's longest day ever! Next day both walked back to Kluchi, but got a ride the last 9 kms. The author's total walk-time was 46 hours. Two hours after arriving in Kluchi, the KGB finally caught the author and told him it's OK this time, but don't go to Sheveluch! With a 4WD this climb could be made in 2 very long days, or maybe 3 shorter days, from Kluchi. Take ice ax, crampons, compass, bear bell and warm clothes. Climb from mid-July to early September.

From the Podkova dom (house) looking southwest at Kluchevskoy.

Map 188-1, Kluchevskoy, Kamen & Bezymianny, Kamchatka, Russia

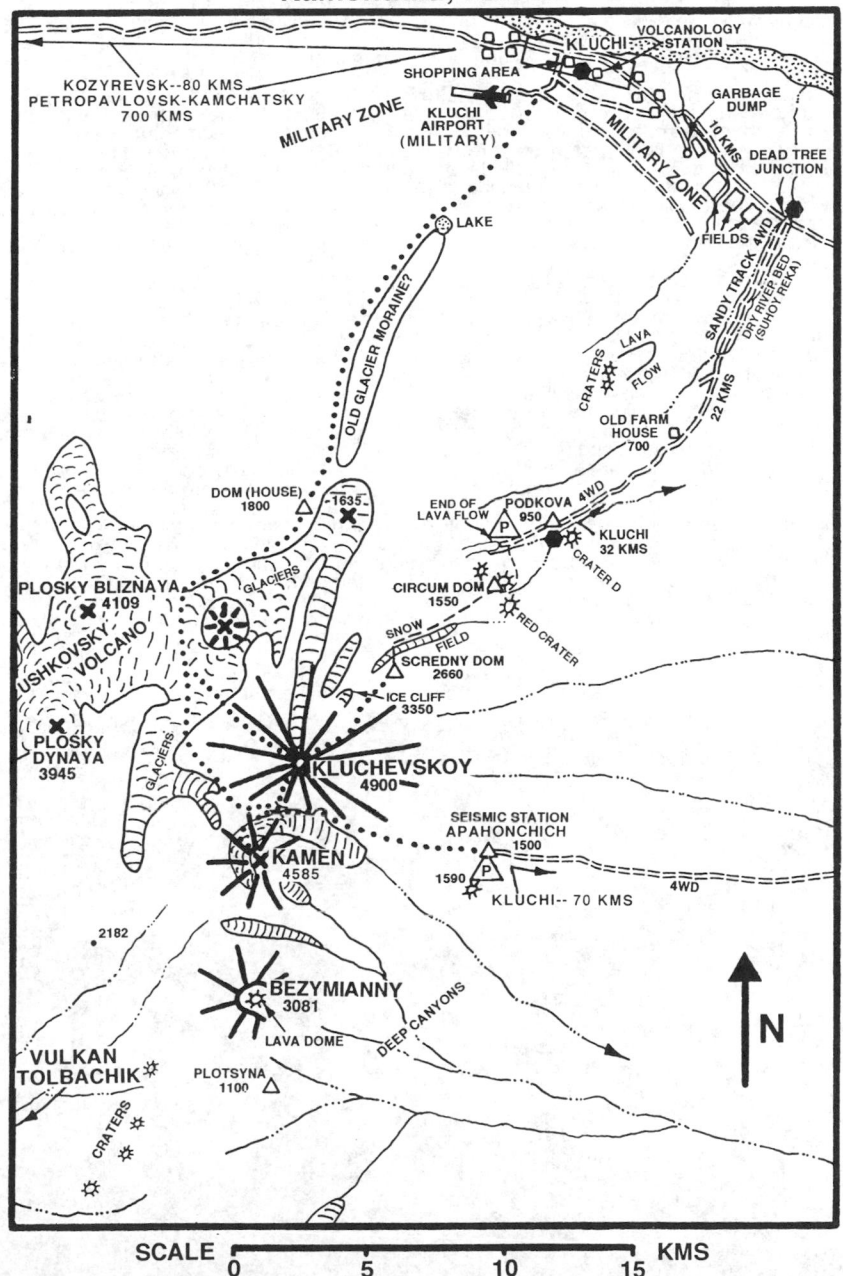

Maps TPC map *E10-B*, 1:500,000; Russian maps are availble, ask at the Institut Vulkanology, P-K, the book, **Trekking in Russia & Central Asia**, The Mountaineers; and the latest travel guidebook to Russia or Kamchatka.

Vulkans Tolbachik, Udina & Zimina, Kamchatka, Russia

Featured here are 3 volcanos immediately south of the Kluchevskoy group. The better known and highest is Tolbachik Ostry at 3682 meters. Immediately east of that peak is a very flat plateau with a 3-km-wide crater. This part is called Ploski Tolbachik. On 2/18/1999, it had a minor steam & gas explosion, but back in 1975-76, it had huge outpouring of basaltic lavas from Ploski and from the rift zones to the south. Also featured here is Bolshay Udina at 2923 meters, and Zimina, 3081.

The normal route to Tolbachik is from the town of Kozyrevsk located to the northwest on the banks of the Kamchatka River. By road, Kozyrevsk is about 80 kms southwest of Kluchi, and 620 kms north of Petropavlovsk-Kamchatsky (P-K). The only way to get there, besides hiring a helicopter out of P-K, is by hitch hiking or by bus. In 1994, there were about 2 buses per week running from P-K to Kluchi; or you could take one of several daily buses running north from P-K to Milkovo, and hitch from there. You could also get on one of about 2 daily buses running from P-K to Esso, located southwest of Kozyrevsk; but get off at the road junction and hitch hike north toward Kozyrevsk. In 1994, there was a new upgraded graveled road running to Kozyrevsk and northward and it may be paved by the time you get there. When it does, expect better bus service.

In the northern part of Kozyrevsk is a seismic or vulkanstansia (volcanology station). The only volcanologist there in 1994 was Kuzma Kirishev, who spoke no English.

From Kozyrevsk, there's a road running through the forest and logging area southeast to a seismic station called Vodapodny (waterfall). Normally there are people with 4WD vehicles you can hire in Kozyrevsk to take you the 45 or so kms to Vodapodny, but that will depend on the availability of benzin (gasoline). When the author arrived, he was told there was no benzin in town and no one could be found who had any. The author was also told there was a maze of logging roads along the way and it would be very difficult for someone unfamiliar with the area to find the right track. For that reason he decided not to attempt Tolbachik. Apparently there is water in only one location along that access road.

There's at least one house or dom at Vodapodny, and another dom of some kind at the meteostantsiya (meteorological station) south of Tolbachik. These are never locked and you can use them without payment, but please keep them clean for the next visitor.

The map shows some possible routes. From Vodapodny, head straight for **Tolbachik** and climb up the south ridge to the highest summit. Fotos show it as fairly steep, but with no crevasses; there will likely be crevasses on the plateau glacier surrounding the crater on Ploski. From Vodapodny, walk due east across the plain with a number of new cinder cones to reach the met. station, then route-find up the west side of **Balshay Udina**. Walk northeast from the met. station to climb **Zimina**. There may be some deep, rugged canyons along the way, so be prepared for a rugged hike. If you were to ride into this area with a 4WD, climb the 3 peaks featured, then walk out, it could take 7-8 days. Consult the vulkanologists in P-K. You can buy your food in Kozyrevsk, but P-K has much better varieties. Take an ice ax & crampons, but you may not need them in late summer. Climb from mid-July to the first week in September.

From a backyard garden in Kozyrevsk looking east at Plosky Dynaya (left), Kluchevskoy, Kamen and Bezymianny on the far right.

Map 189-1, Tolbachik, Udina & Zimina, Kamchatka, Russia

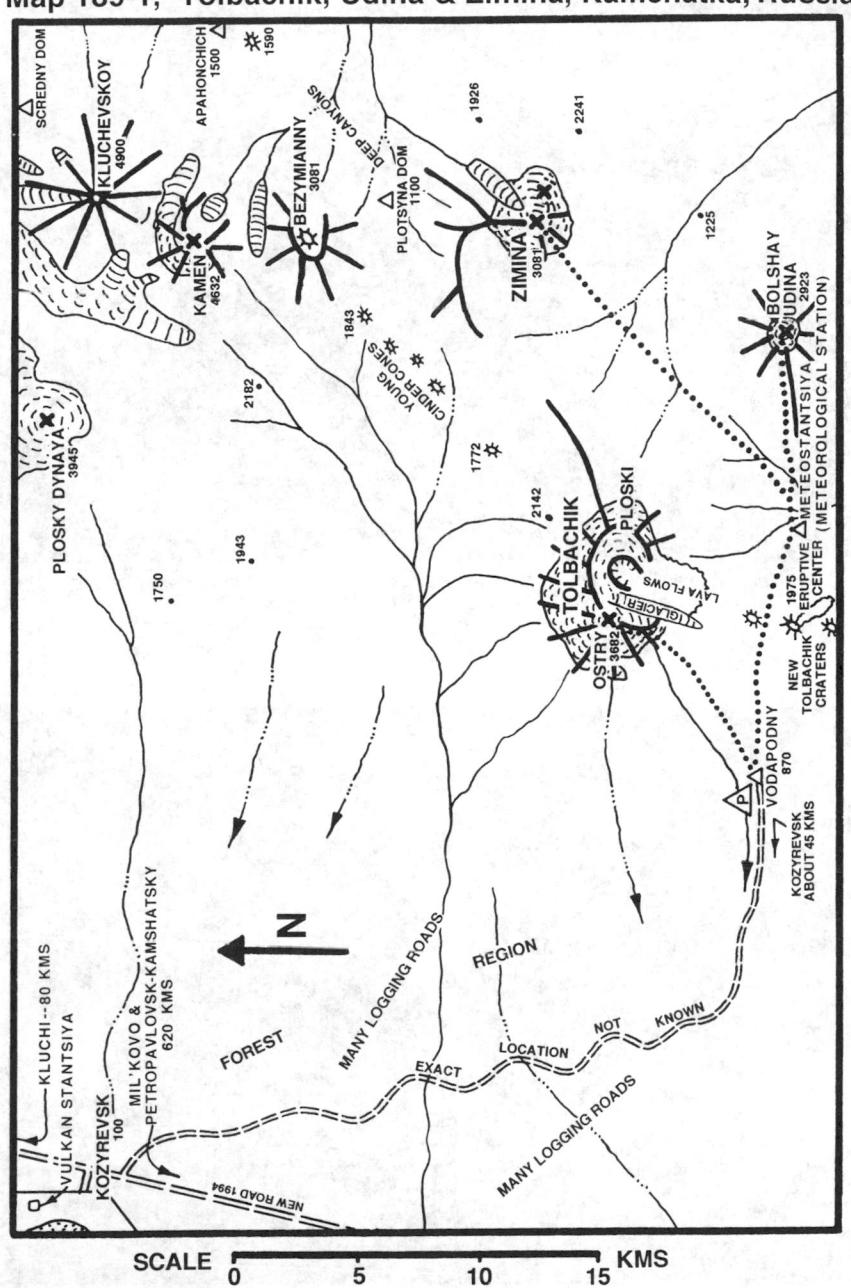

SCALE

0   5   10   15   KMS

Maps TPC map *E10-B,* 1:500,000; and the books, **Active Volcanoes of Kamchatka**, Volume I, by the Russian Academy of Science--Institut Vulkanology, Nauka Publishers, Moskva; and **Trekking in Russia & Central Asia**, The Mountaineers; and the latest travel guidebook to Russia or Kamchatka.

This is the author's camp in the Krebet At Bashi (At Bashi Mountains) which are just south of the town of At Bashi (Map 180, page 396).

From a hill above the city of Petropavlovsk-Kamchatsky (PK), looking north toward Koryaksky on the left, Avacha (Avachinsky) on the right (see next page).

The Circum Dom (Circum House) and Kluchevskoy (Map 188, page 415).

Some buildings at Avachinsky Tourbaze with Avacha behind (see next page).

Koryaksky, Avacha & Zupanovsky, Kamchatka, Russia

The 2 main summits on this map are located immediately north of Kamchatka's capital city of Petropavlovsk-Kamchatsky (P-K). Koryaksky is 3456 meters and Avacha (or Avachinsky) is 2741. Both are *vulkans;* Koryaksky's last eruptive period was from 12/1956 to 6/1957. P-K is built on top of a debris avalanche from Avacha that took place about 30,000 to 40,000 years ago. In 2/1990, Avacha had a big eruption sending tefra up 5 kms; but has been just building a lava dome inside the crater ever since. There are 2 other high peaks to the north in the Zhulapov Mtns. Zupanovsky is highest at 2927 meters. Some maps show these 2 old volcanos as being active also, but they don't appear that way from a distance.

Here's what the author did. He bought 4 days of food while staying in the cheaper Gastinetsa (Hotel) Geyser (about US$14 night in 1994). He then took bus 103 from the Km 10 Avtovakzal (bus station) to the airport at Elizovo. While looking for bus 105, which is supposed to make the loop running between Elizovo and P-K, someone offered him a ride to the beginning of the road to Avacha. He took that, then finally got on the right track and walked only 2 hours before camping. This was on 6/20/1994, and there was running water in the Suhoy Reka (Dry River). Next morning he got a lift in a 6WD army truck heading for the Russian Sports Federation summer ski camp. After that ride, he left his pack in an unused building and climbed **Avacha** in 3 1/2 hours; about 5 1/4 hours round-trip. He slept in the same ski school building for free, which was closed for the summer, then headed for **Koryaksky** the next morning. He was turned back about halfway up because of heavy rain & snow. Later that day he walked down the road following the electric lines to near the summer dachas in 5 hours; and camped. Next morning he hitch hiked back to P-K.

Here are some distances: Km 10 to airport, 20 kms; airport to summer dachas, 8-9 kms; dachas to RSF ski camp, 25 kms. About US$10 will get you from P-K to the dachas in a taxi; or take bus 105 from the Komsomoliskaya Avtovakzal to near the dachas. However this bus seems unreliable. Or take bus 100, 101, 102, or 103 from the Km 10 Avtovakzal to the airport and get a taxi to the dachas. From there either follow the electric lines or the 4WD track along the Suhoy Reka, which has running water in early summer. Five days of food should be plenty for both peaks. There should always be some kind of hut or building open where you can sleep for free at Avachinsky Tourbaze or the ski camp, but you can't buy food there. Take an ice ax & crampons, but in late summer you may not need them.

There is some kind of old vehicle track, running north to the foot of **Dzendzur**, as shown. Hiking maps show priyuts (huts) along the way. From the end of the road at Pinachevo to the **Zhulapov Mtns.** appears to be about 75 kms. A round-trip hike to that region could take 7 or 8 days. From the summit of Avacha, these peaks don't appear to be that difficult, just a long walk. Better take a tent.

Best time to climb is from late July to the first week of September. Take mosquito repellent and rain gear. In P-K, there's a big supermarket in the downtown area near the port and the Gastinetsa Avacha. Buy the tourist map below in the Avacha Hotel.

The summit of Avacha with the lava dome to the left, and Koryaksky to the right.

Map 190-1, Koryaksky, Avacha & Zupanovsky, Kamchatka, Russia

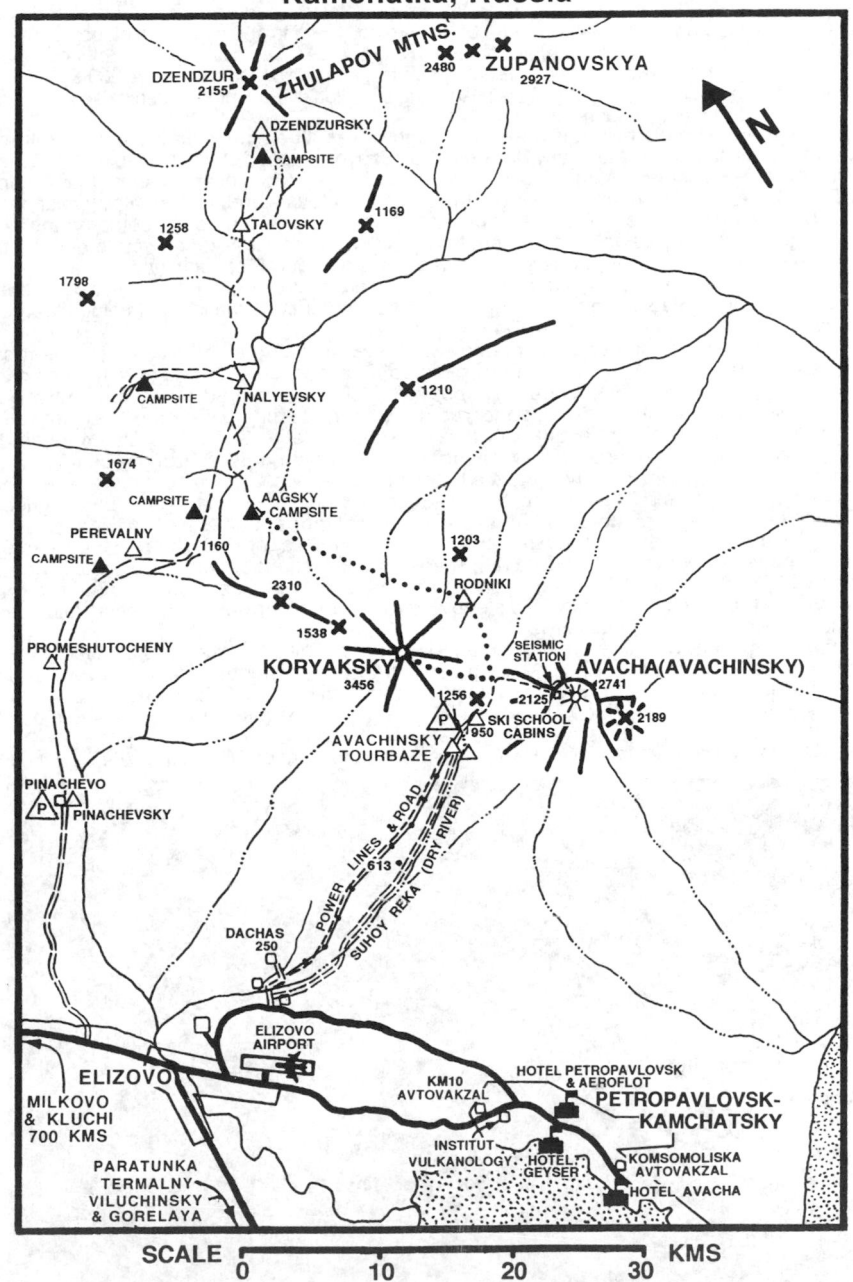

SCALE 0 10 20 30 KMS

Maps *Petropavlovsk-Kamchatsky, N-57-B,* from GUK, Moskva; Russian map *Kamchatskaya Oblast--Turistskaya Karta,* buy in P-K hotels; TPC map *E10-B,* 1:500,000; the book, **Trekking in Russia & Central Asia,** The Mountaineers; and the latest travel guidebook to Russia or Kamchatka.

Viluchinsky, Gorelaya & Mutnovsky, Kamchatka, Russia

The 3 volcanos on this map are south, southwest of Petropavlovsk-Kamchatsky (P-K). Viluchinsky's last eruption was about 5550 BC, but it still retains a perfect conal shape as seen from P-K. Gorelaya blew up big time ~40,000--50,000 years ago ejecting 100 cubic/kms of tephra, making a 9x13.5-km-wide caldera. It's last eruptions were in 8 & 9/1984. Mutnovsky is made of 4 coalescing stratovolcanos. It had it's last lava flow in 1904, but it's last eruptive period was in 12/1960 & 1/1961. It has the highest heat capacity of any vulkan in Kamchatka. Please read the Introduction to Russia and the CIS Countries for more information.

To get there, see the previous map which shows P-K, then make your way to the Km 10 Avtovakzal (bus station) and take any bus going to Elizovo. Buses 100, 101, 102, and 103 make that run every few minutes. At the Elizovo avtovakzal, there's a bus heading south to Paratunka and Termalny about every half hour. From the astanovka (bus stand) in Termalny, the last stop, walk west up one of the streets about 200 meters, and turn left or south on the main road heading toward these volcanos. From there walk and/or hitch hike; or inquire about a taxi or private car to take you there quicker. Hitching is pretty good, especially on weekends. In 1994, there was a good road running all the way to a proposed geothermal power plant at the foot of Mutnovsky. The southern half of that road was under construction and being cleared of snow during the author's visit between 7/4 & 7/ 7/1994.

From Termalny, the author got a lift part way, then walked to a campsite at the west-side base of **Viluchinsky**. The next morning he climbed up a west gully and ridge to the summit in just over 4 hours; about 6 1/2 hours round-trip. Then he walked along the road to the construction worker's huts on the ridge-top as shown, and camped. The next day he walked toward Gorelaya, but only got about halfway before bad weather set in. On Day 4 he started walking back to Termalny, but got a ride most of the way in a 6WD army truck. That ride included a stop at a little military hotel, and a bath in the nearby hot spring swimming pool.

For Viluchinsky, climb any route on the west side. It's best to start in a gully, then higher up use what ever route is easiest. Take an ice ax & crampons, but late in the season it can probably be climbed without. For **Gorelaya**, leave the road at or near the pass marked 950 meters, and walk over the old caldera rim, then climb the younger volcano with several new craters. There's a crater filled with snow and ice on the west side of the summit region of **Mutnovsky**. Fotos show crevasses and steep ridges, but the northwest ridge seems fairly easy. Take ice ax & crampons for Mutnovsky.

If you had your own vehicle, it would be possible to climb all three in maybe 3 days from P-K, but for anyone on foot, hitch hiking and using public transport, better take food for a week. Shop in P-K, but Termalny has several small shops or *magazins* next to the astanovka. Climb from mid-July to the first week of September. Take rain gear, mosquito repellent, a small bell for bears and a tent.

Maps *Petropavlovsk-Kamchatsky (N-57-B)*, from GUK, Moskva; or TPC map *E10-B*, 1:500,000;

From the road worker's camp looking east at Viluchinsky Volcano.

Map 191-1, Viluchinsky, Gorelaya & Mutnovsky, Kamchatka, Russia

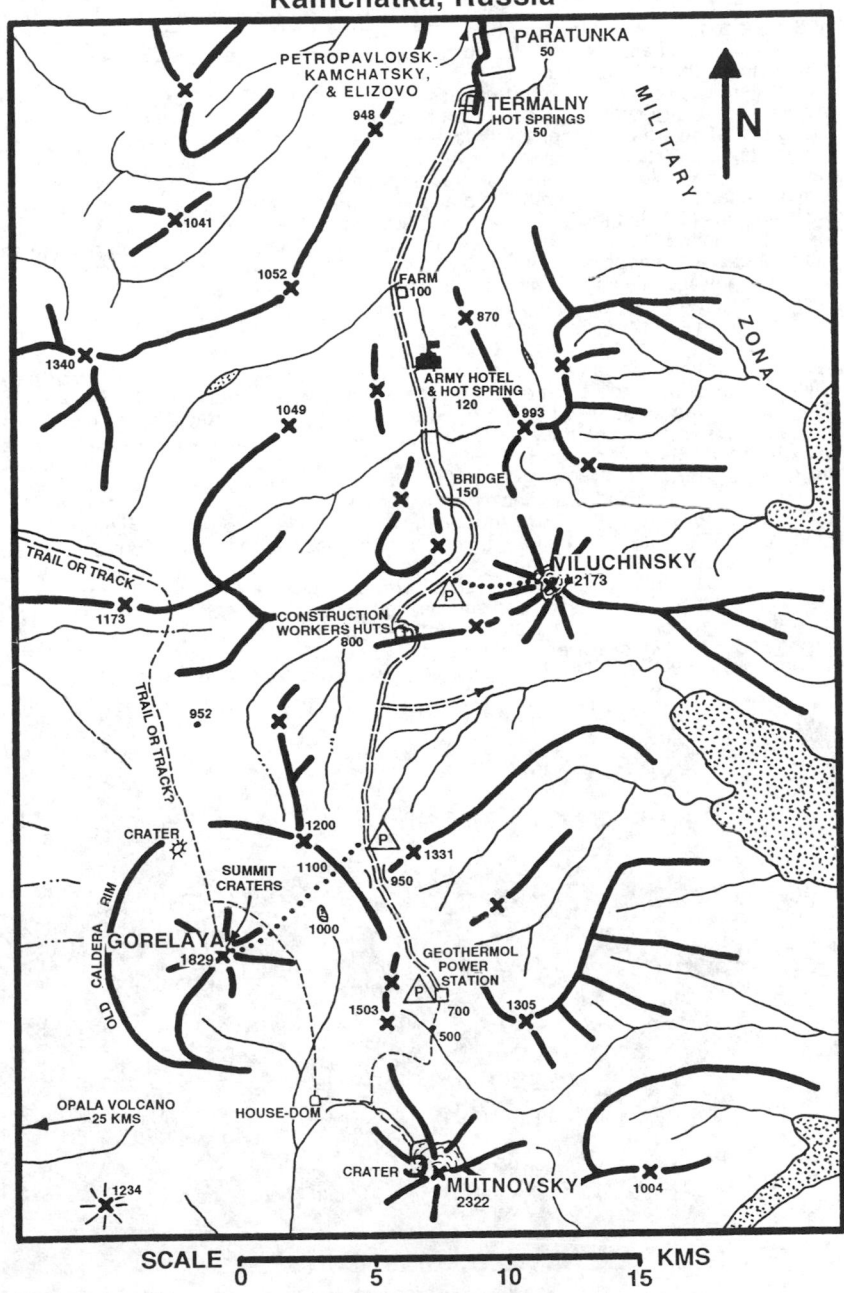

SCALE 0 5 10 15 KMS

and the books, **Active Volcanoes of Kamchatka**, Volume I, by the Russian Academy of Science--Institut Vulkanology, Nauka Publishers, Moskva, 1991; and **Trekking in Russia & Central Asia**, The Mountaineers; and the latest travel guidebook to Russia or Kamchatka.

Kongur and Muztagata, Xinjiang Province, China

The area on this map is in extreme western Xinjiang Province of China. The highest peak is Kongur Shan at 7719 meters. Not far away is Kongur Tiubie, 7595 meters. And to the south is the third highest summit, Muztagata Shan at 7546 meters. This one is the best known of the three. The author still hasn't been to this immediate area so this is just an introduction; nor does he know anything about the geology.

Few western climbers have been here, especially since 1950. Tilman and Shipton were in the area in 1947, and reported rather easy climbing. They approached Muztagata from the west and found soft snow near the top. They failed to reach the summit for various reasons, but came close on just a reconnaissance climb without any real preparation. In July, 1980, an American group was allowed to climb the mountain on skis. Their route is shown on the map. This climb is easy for such a high mountain and apparently doesn't require anything more than ice ax & crampons (?). Better take rope anyway, and remember, it's not for novices.

The author visited China for 5 months in the summer of 1984, and ended up going as far west as Kashgar (all other places were closed at that time). Kashgar is a Uygar city; the Uygars are a Turkish speaking minority in China, but they're a majority in Xinjiang.

Since the 1990's, all parts of Xinjiang have been open to foreigners, new roads have been built, and lots of old archeological sites have been opened, along with many new tourist facilities. See the latest Lonely Planet guidebook, **China**.

If you're really serious about a full-scale assault of any of these peaks, then you *may* have to get official permission to do so and go through a bureaucratic nightmare. But things are changing. If you want to go trekking in the region of **Kongur** or **Muztagata**, you can do so on your own by just taking one or 2 daily buses running along the Karakorum Highway (KKH) bound for Tash Kurgan, or Khunjerab Pass and/or Pakistan, and get off anywhere. Many hikers get off at Little Kara Kul, or Karakuri Lake, and trek from there. At the lake, you can stay in Tajik yurts for US$4-5 night. Meals are also available.

Many tourist-types are trekking with the help of tour or trekking agents in Kashgar. The best known in the 1990's was *John's Information & Cafe* across the street from the Seman Hotel. Owner John Hu can make arrangements for transport and perhaps equipment. They can arrange transport for tourists or a small group of climbers who are interested in a real assault of any peaks. They could transport you and supplies to the base of say Muztagata, then let you go on your way, perhaps picking you up later, or providing guides. With luck, they might get official permission to climb, *if indeed that's still required (?)*. Contact the Chinese Embassy in your country who will give you the latest info on the permission business; or if you're not operating on

Muztagata as seen from the north and the lake called Little Kara Kul. The normal route is up the slopes on the right side (Book-**High Mtn. Peaks of China**).

Map 192-1, Kongur and Muztagata, Xinjiang Province, China

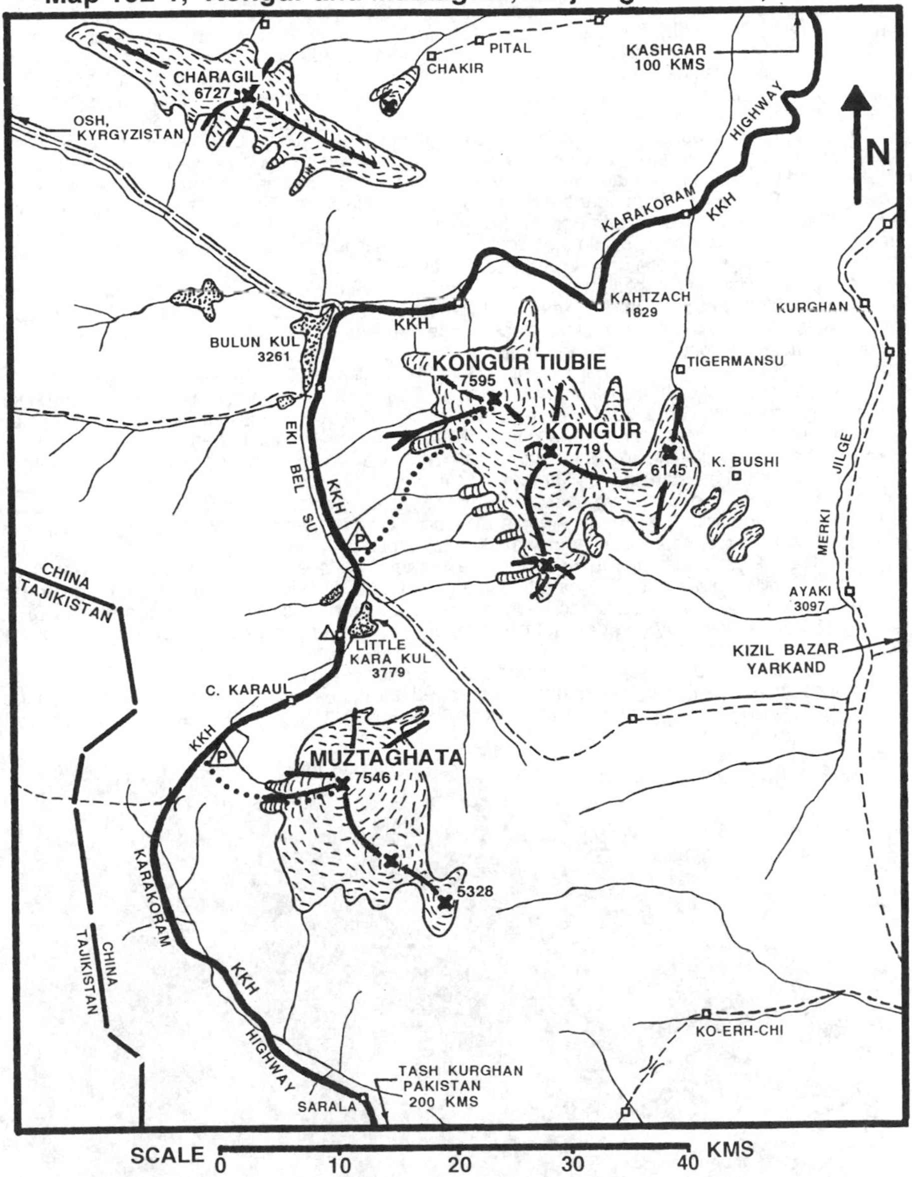

CHARAGIL
6727

PITAL

CHAKIR

KASHGAR
100 KMS

OSH,
KYRGYZISTAN

KARAKORAM

KKH

HIGHWAY

N

BULUN KUL
3261

KKH

KAHTZACH
1829

KURGHAN

KONGUR TIUBIE
7595

TIGERMANSU

EKI BEL SU

KKH

KONGUR
7719

6145

K. BUSHI

MERKI JILGE

CHINA
TAJIKISTAN

P

AYAKI
3097

LITTLE
KARA KUL
3779

KIZIL BAZAR
YARKAND

C. KARAUL

KKH

P

MUZTAGHATA
7546

KARAKORAM

5328

CHINA
TAJIKISTAN

KKH

KO-ERH-CHI

HIGHWAY

SARALA

TASH KURGHAN
PAKISTAN
200 KMS

SCALE   0   10   20   30   40   KMS

a real time schedule, just go to Kashgar and sort things out from there.

Regardless of whether you're trekking or climbing, buy all the food and supplies in Kashgar. July & August and maybe the first week into September is the best time to climb. Lots of fresh fruits and vegetables in Kashgar in late summer-early fall.

Maps DMA maps *NJ-43*, 1:1,000,000, and *NJ-43, 6 & 7*, Series 1302, 1:250,000; TPC map *G-7A*, 1:500,000; and the travel guidebook **China**, Lonely Planet.

Bogda Shan, Tian Shan, Xinjiang Province, China

Bogda Shan is located in the eastern half of the Tian Shan (Heavenly Mountains), in north central Xinjiang Province. The highest peak is Bogda Shan at 5447 meters. The lower slopes are covered with a pine or fir forest but the peak is heavily glaciated. Bogda Shan is within easy reach of all climbers and tourists, foreign and Chinese. The author spent 3 days here beginning 8/24/1984. The book below helped updated his information. At that time there were only a few hikers in the area, but today it's become rather popular.

To get to these mountains and a place called Tian Chi (Heavenly Lake), start in Urumqi, the capital of Xinjiang. There are many tourist hotels in Urumqi and someone at your hotel can tell you where to find buses going to Tian Chi. In the late 1990's, you could find several daily public buses leaving about 9 or 9:30am from near the north gate of Renmin Park. Be there a little early and buy a ticket to insure a seat. Cost was about US$3, round-trip. Private minibuses leave from the same area; or from the Hongshan Hotel. In the summer season buses leave each morning for the lake, then return to Urumqi beginning at 4 or 4:30pm. The ride takes 3 hours each way.

At Tian Chi, which is a cool summer hideout, are many vendors selling food. It's best however to buy your climbing food in Urumqi. There is at least one binguan (hotel) at the bus stop and many tourist boats cruising the lake. It's a nice place as the name indicates, but with too many tourists. It's surely a lot more developed now than in 1984!

To get to **Bogda Shan**, start walking south along the west side of the lake on a very good trail. At the south end of the lake should be an encampment of yurts (nomadic tents). You can stay there for US$5 a night, including 3 meals. There are other real live Kazak nomads in the area, and they may invite you into their yurt for chai (tea) and lodging if you like (but watch out for bed bugs!).

From the south end of the lake, the author walked south, then east to the yurt camp at 3050 meters, then south again. There's another trail or route to the west, but the author hasn't seen it. As you near the big peaks, you'll cross over a pass, then will see the northwest face of Bogda Shan. It's looks pretty steep, icy and difficult, but a tough and experienced climber *might* be able to solo it (?). A strong hiker could make it to or near base camp in the late afternoon of the 1st day (after the bus ride), but for most it will take 2 days from Urumqi to reach a base camp. Horses can be hired at the lake to pack supplies in. It will then likely take 2-3 days to find the right route and climb it, then one long day back to the lake and an afternoon bus back to Urumqi. If you'd prefer to do it all legally, contact the CITS (tourist office). Apparently you can get official permission there in Urumqi. Otherwise, just go trekking and climb what you like.

George Hendley walked south from Bogda Shan's base camp, mostly along the east side of the stream, past the 3 small lakes, and in one day reached a village at the base of the mountains on the south side. There's a road up to that village, but you'll likely have to walk half a day through the desert

North face of Bogda Shan as seen from one of the summits just north of the base camp.

Map 193-1, Bogda Shan, Tian Shan, Xinjiang Province, China

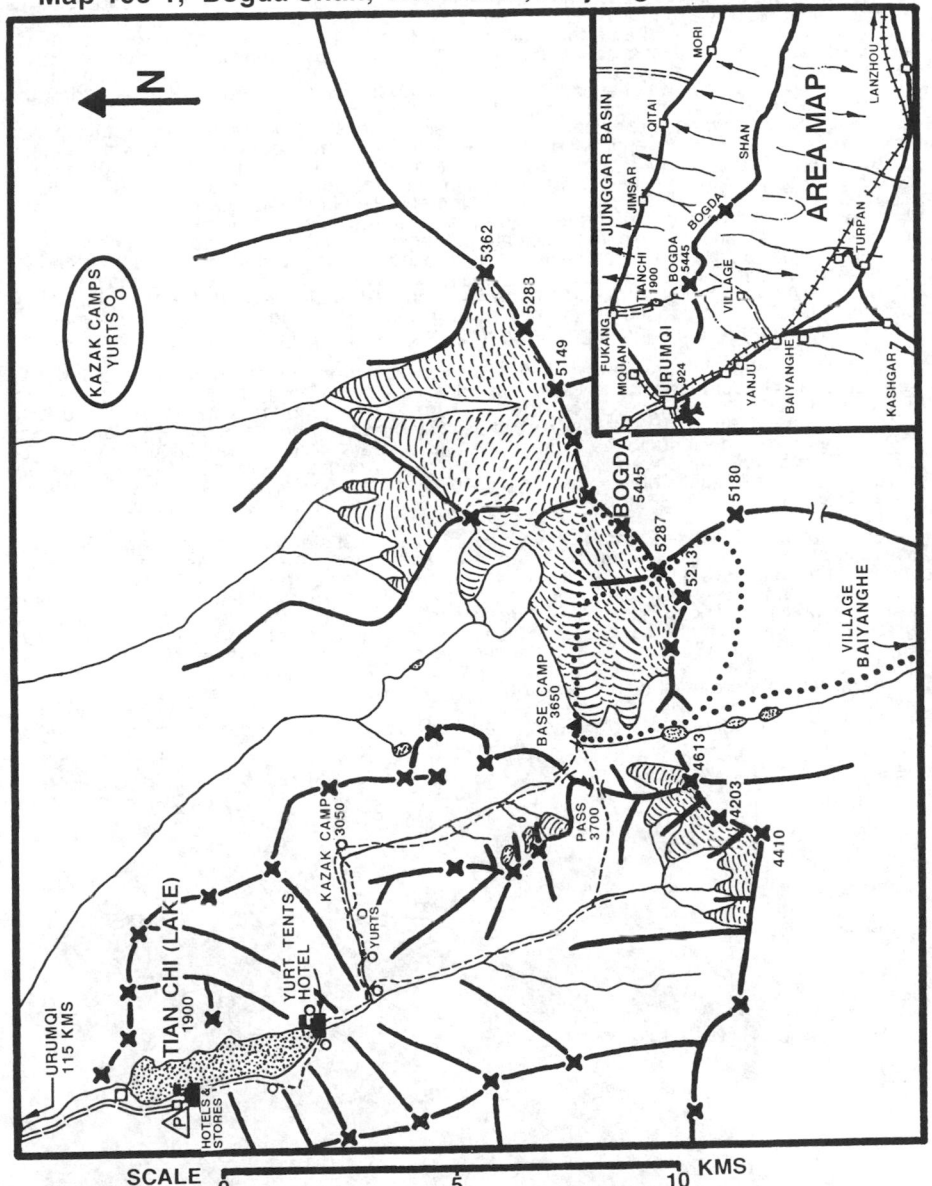

to the main highway (the last water is 1 or 2 hours south of this village!), then hitch hike or stop a bus heading northwest back to Urumqi.

Maps *Mountaineering Map of Xinjiang*, from Xinjiang Mountaineering Assoc., Urumqi (check at CITS tourist office); or the book, **High Mountain Peaks in China**, Chinese Mountaineering Association; TPC map *F-7D*, 1:500,000; and the travel guidebook, **China**, Lonely Planet.

Maqên Gangri, Anyêmaqên Shan, Qinghai Province, China

This map shows one of many high mountains of China now open to foreign climbers. This peak is called Maqên Gangri at 6282 meters. This moderately high mountain lies southwest of Xining in the Anyêmaqên Shan (Mountains) of Qinghai Province. In 1980, there were only 8 mountains open, but today it appears you can go to virtually any mountain in the country, with a permit. This is merely an introduction to the area, so if you get permission to climb it, the authorities will equip you with better maps. The author hasn't been here, and doesn't know the geology, but the rocks are no doubt sedimentary of some kind.

Anyone who has read very much in the mountaineering literature, will recognize Anyêmaqên as the mountain which was reported to be higher than Mt. Everest by several different people or groups. In the 1920's and 30's, several travelers and explorers viewed the mountain and thought the summit to be over 9000 meters. One article was even written up in the National Geographic Magazine. In 1944, an American air crew flying from Chongqing to Burma reported themselves to be flying at 9000 meters, and the summit was several thousand meters above them! But in 1948 an American group went to the region and reported it's height much lower. A Chinese Expedition in 1960, made an investigation and found it's altitude to be what we know it today. They also made the first ascent, coming in from the eastern side of the mountain.

Much of the information here comes from the book, **High Mountain Peaks in China**. That book is in English and Japanese, and has some sketch maps and good fotos. This map is a compilation of that book's very rough sketch map and a National Geographic map of China and the TPC map G-8C.

For the serious climber one first step for obtaining information about going to places like Anyêmaqên is to contact website (**www.expeditiontrips.com**) or in the USA call *Expedition Trips* Tele. 877-412--8527. Or contact an outfit called *Mountain Madness* in Seattle, Washington, at 206-937-8339, or their website (**www.mountainmadness.com**). This company specializes in taking clients to the highest summits on each continent. In 2000, they charged US$89,000 to climb all Seven Summits: Kilimanjaro, Aconcagua, Denali, Elbrus, Carstenz Pyramid, Everest & Vinson Massif. Or contact *Adventure Associates* in Sydney, NSW, Australia, Tele. Inter+61 2-9389-7466, or Fax Inter+61 2-9369-1853, or their website (**www.adventure associates.com**).

Or contact the Chinese Embassy in your country as a first step. Or contact the CITS (tourist office) in Xining if you're only interested in trekking in the area. It appears as of the late 1990's, you might have to have a travel permit to go there, but that can be obtained in Xining.

If you're alone or just a couple of people, then take a train to Xining, a city with lots of western tourists heading to Tibet. There are several hotels in the city. Once there inquire at the CITS office about going to the mountain and if you need a permit of some kind. You can likely go that way by 2000 (?), and trek with a minimum of formalities. Better learn a little Chinese quick too!

From Xining there must be some kind of public transportation going all or part way. If not, you may have to spend a lot of money hiring a 4WD vehicle. Or just get out on the highway and try hitch hiking in the direction of Maqên. You'll certainly need a lot better map & information

This is apparently the northeast face of Anyêmaqên (Book-**High Mtn. Peaks of China**).

Map 194-3, Maqên Gangri, Anyêmaqên Shan, Qinghai, China

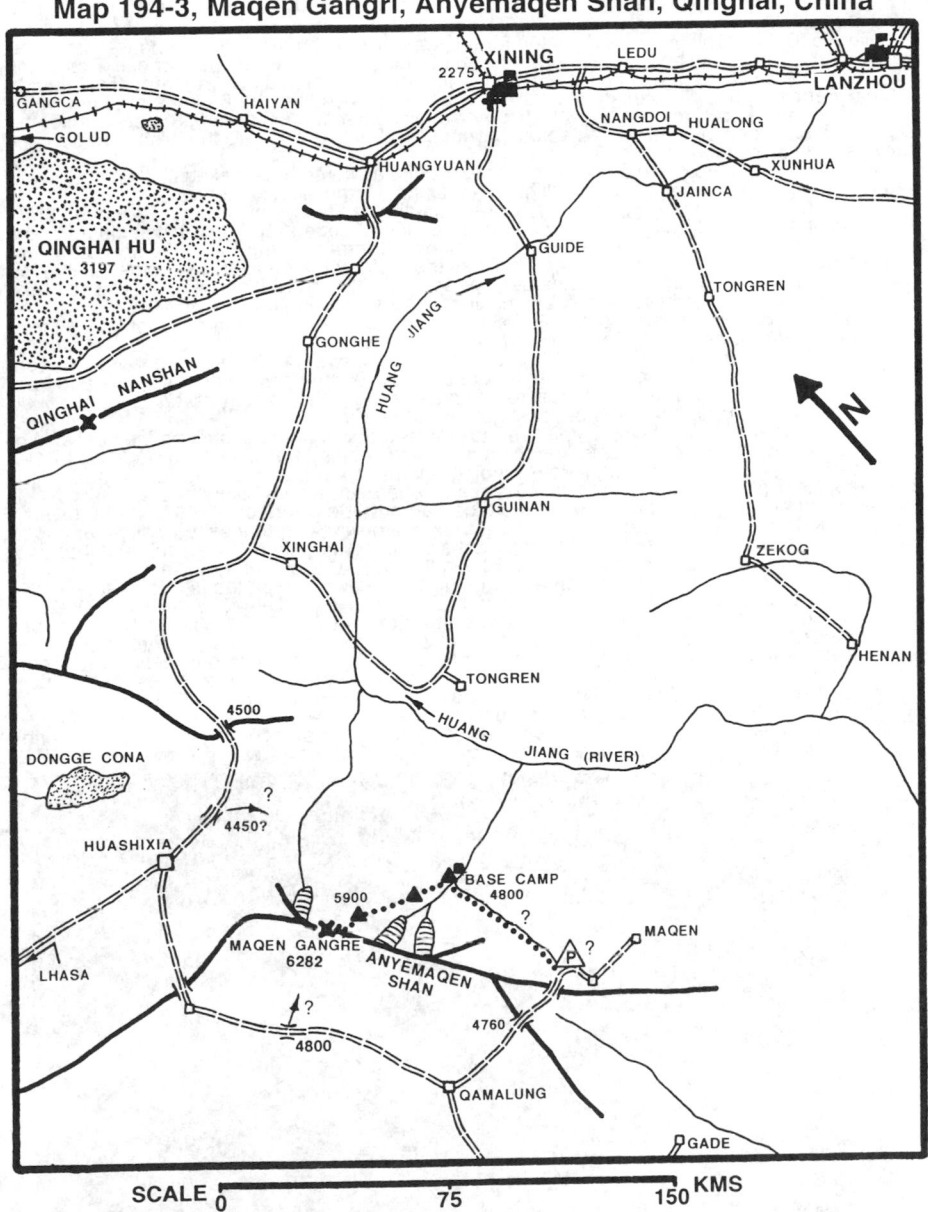

SCALE

| 0 | 75 | 150 | KMS |

than this! If you get that far, stop 30-40 kms short of Maqên and walk north to the area where the Chinese set up a base camp. The Chinese had some minor difficulties, but put 8 climbers on top in one day.

Maps National Geographic Map, *Peoples of China,* 1:6,000,000; TPC map *G-8C,* 1:500,000; the books, **High Mountain Peaks In China**, Chinese Mountaineering Association, ISBN 4-8083-0056-7; and the travel guidebook, **China**, Lonely Planet.

Gongga, Hengduan Shan, Sichuan Province, China

This map shows Gongga Shan at 7555 meters. It's located west of Chengdu in Sichuan Province of China. This map was created for the most part using maps from 3 books; first, **Men Against the Clouds** (The Mountaineers, Seattle), the story of the 1932 American Expedition which conquered Gongga (Minga Konka) on the first try; and the book **High Mountain Peaks in China** (People Sports Publishing House of China). This book lists the 8 peaks of China which were open to foreign climbers in 1980. Today it seems all mountain areas are open. Also, the travel guidebook below has some usefull information about getting into the area especially on the east side of the mountain.

For those hoping to climb Gongga, or Minya Konka as some have called it, it's advised you read the books mentioned above; they'll help to understand the situation there.

The normal route to **Gongga** begins in Chengdu, the capital city of Sichuan Province. From there you'll go by road/bus to Yachow (Yaan), Kangding, Luting (Luding), Tatsienlu, over the pass west of Djezi La (Pass). Then finally by trail over Tsemei La and to the Gompa Lamasery at the southwest base of the mountain. This was the route of the original expeditions, but today there seem to be new names, or the names are spelled differently. It's also likely you can take 4WD's to the trailhead west of Tsemei La, making a lot less walking than in the 1930's!

From the Gompa Lamasery, the route follows the north side of the Gongba (Gongga) Glacier to the col, then southeast up the northwest ridge. This is the route taken by the Americans in 1932 and the Chinese in 1957. There's a difficult pitch or two, but as big mountains go, it's a relatively easy climb. It's also possible to trek to the base of the peak on the east side and from Taitho and Mosimien or Moxi. The local relief on the east side is as high as it gets--about 6000 meters, one of the highest faces or deepest gorges in the world.

In Lonely Planet's guidebook **China**, it states there is now a national park on the east side of the mountain with Hailuogou Glacier the main attraction, it being the lowest glacier in Asia. Get there by taking a bus from Chengdu to Kangding, then another bus to Luting (Luding). Finally, take another bus 50 kms south to Moxi (Mosimien), where you'll find 3 binguans (hotels). When you enter the Hailuogou Glacier Park, you'll pay an entry fee of about US$7, but be given a small book & map (in Chinese). Guides from Moxi are now taking tourists on pony tours up to the glacier and to other destinations on the east side of the mountain. The people at that park will know more about the climbing routes, including the original one, than anyone else.

One step for obtaining information about going to places like Gongga is to contact website **(www.expeditiontrips.com)**, or in the USA call *Expedition Trips* Tele. 877-412--8527. Or an outfit called *Mountain Madness* in Seattle, Washington, at 206-937-8339, or their website **(www.mountainmadness.com)**. This company specializes in taking clients to the highest summits on each continent. In 2000, they charged US$89,000 to climb all Seven Summits: Kilimanjaro, Aconcagua, Denali, Elbrus, Carstenz Pyramid, Everest & Vinson Massif. Or contact *Adventure Associates* in Sydney, NSW, Australia, Tele. Inter+61 2-9389-7466, or Fax Inter+61 2-9369-1853, or their website **(www.adventureassociates.com)**.

The climate is similar to the Himalayas of Nepal. The monsoon begins in mid-June and ends in the last part of September. The dry season is from October through May, with the pre-

Gongga Shan (Minya Konka) from the southwest (Book-**High Mtn. Peaks of China**).

Map 195-3, Gongga, Hengduan Shan, Sichuan Province, China

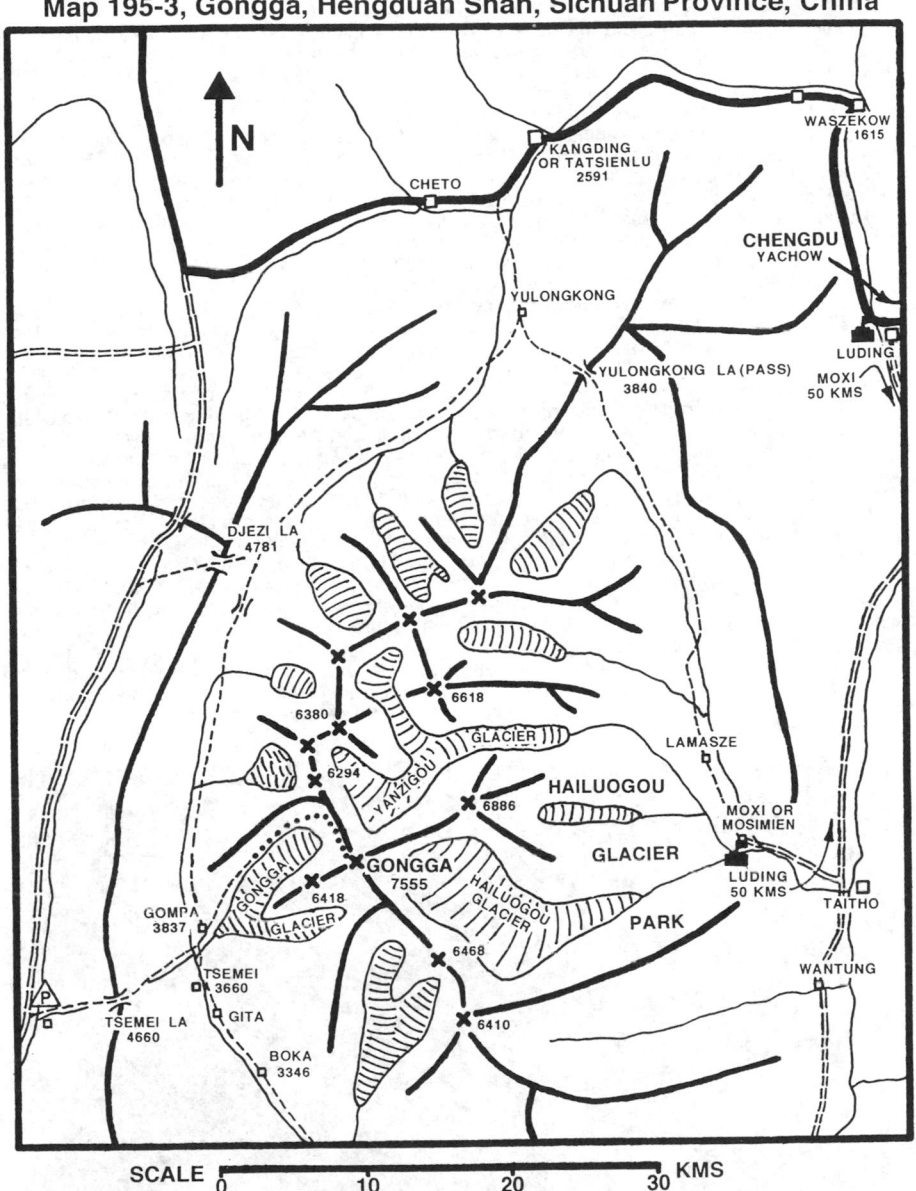

monsoon month of May being one of the warmest, and certainly the driest month. If climbing the mountain, plan to be on top around the 1st of June. The snow line averages 5000 meters, but it's a bit lower than this on the eastern face as a result of more precipitation--a little higher on the dry or western side.

Maps *Hailuogou Glacier Park* map, pick up at Moxi; TPC map *H11-A,* 1:500,000; maps in the above mentioned books; and the latest travel guidebook, **China**, Lonely Planet.

Siguniang, Hengduan Shan, Sichuan Province, China

The small group of peaks shown here are known as Siguniang (Four Sisters). They're part of the Hengduan Shan (Mountains), and are located west of Chengdu in Sichuan Province. The highest of the four peaks is 6250 meters, but there are a number of other high peaks in the area over 5500 meters. The author hasn't seen these mountains, but since they're glaciated, it's a sure bet they're rugged and for experienced and well-equipped climbers only.

Some of the information the author has dates from 1984, but most should still be current. He has updated this book using the latest China guide below. Siguniang is open to foreigners, but you may be required to have a guide or go through a trekking company (?) if you're planning a serious expedition. For some, one thing to do is join a group going to this mountain and/or to the Wolong Panda Reserve. Those who are more interested in climbing or hiking than watching pandas, could first contact the Chinese Embassy in their country. Another way of getting information and/or setting up an expedition-type climb, is to go to the Chinese Mountaineering Association in Beijing. The author was there in 1984, but they surely have an new addresses now, so ask the national tourist office (CITS).

Or contact website **(www.expeditiontrips.com),** or in the USA call *Expedition Trips* Tele. 877-412--8527. Or an outfit called *Mountain Madness* in Seattle, Washington, at 206-937-8339, or their website **(www.mountainmadness.com).** This company specializes in taking clients to the highest summits on each continent, but to other places as well. Or contact *Adventure Associates* in Sydney, NSW, Australia, Tele. Inter+61 2-9389-7466, or Fax Inter+61 2-9369-1853, or their website **(www.adventureassociates.com).** Or see ads in sports magazines such as **Climbing** or the **Sierra Club.**

As of 2000, it's probably best just to go to Chengdu and make arrangements there, which will mean fewer headaches than trying to organize an expedition from Europe or North America. Just contact CITS in Chengdu. If you're more interested in hiking than climbing some difficult peak, then just get on a bus and head in that direction. It's best, according to the China book below, to take a bus to what it calls *Dujiangyan*. This seems to be the same place as *Guanxian*, a place the author went to in 1984 (?). From there take another bus heading west to Wolong Panda Reserve, then on to Rilong. It appears that no permit is needed to travel to Rilong and it is open to foreigners (?).

There may or may not be any hotel or binguan in Rilong (?). From there hike north to the base camps shown, or just start hiking into any of the canyons shown. On the map the author was given, there are 2 routes to the summit of Siguniang, but neither one is very easy, guaranteed! At Rilong, there should be mules or perhaps porters for hire if you have lots of gear and equipment to haul up.

To leave the area, there are, or were in 1984, lots of logging trucks on the road going down to Guanxian (Duijangyan?) so getting transport out shouldn't be a problem. You should hurry and learn some Chinese or *Putonghua* before going into far away places like this.

Go prepared for rain and damp conditions. There is heavy precipitation for 6 or 7 of the warmest

Substituting for Siguniang is a foto of Huang Shan (Map 206, page 453).

Map 196-3, Siguniang, Hengduan Shan, Sichuan, China

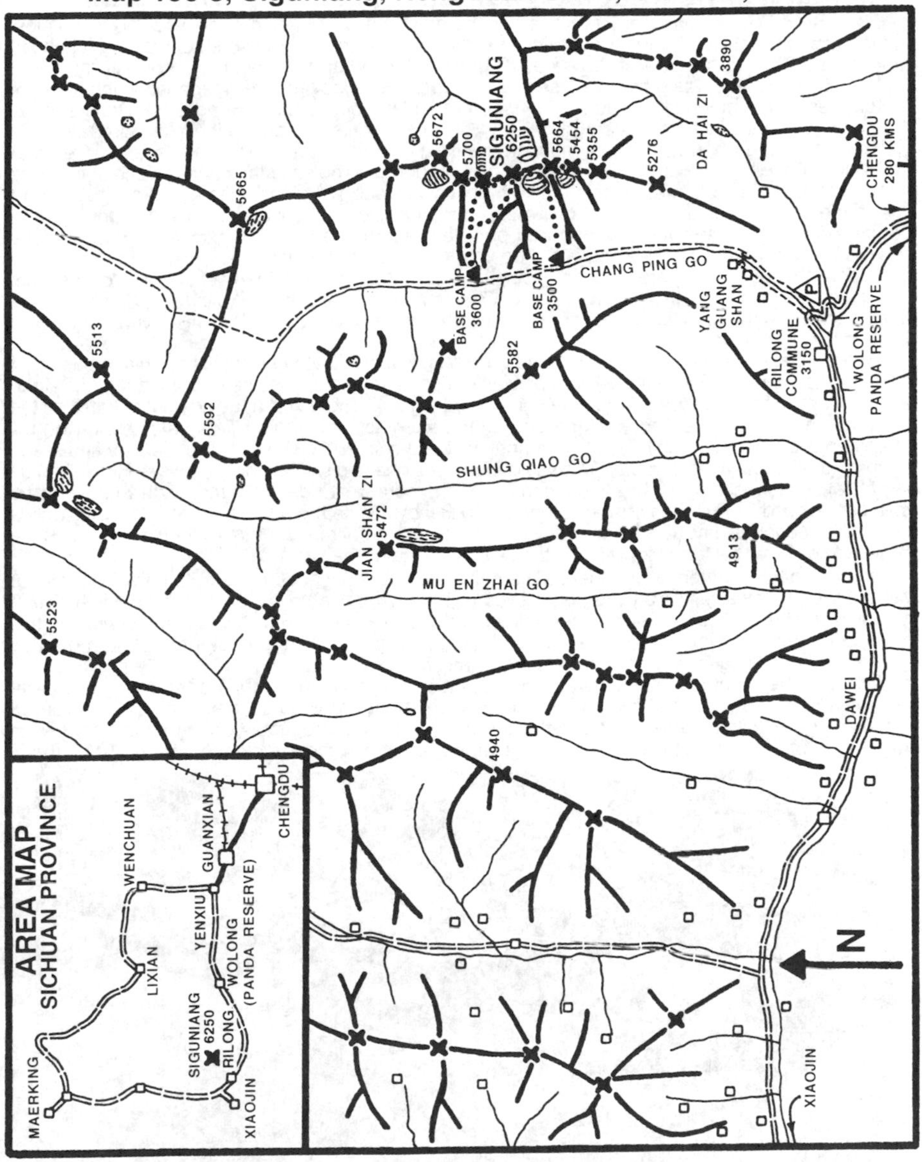

SIGUNIANG
6250
5672
5700
5664
5454
5355
5276
3890
DA HAI ZI
CHENGDU 280 KMS
5665
5513
5592
5523
BASE CAMP 3600
BASE CAMP 3500
CHANG PING GO
5582
YANG GUANG SHAN
RILONG COMMUNE 3150
WOLONG PANDA RESERVE
SHUNG QIAO GO
JIAN SHAN ZI 5472
MU EN ZHAI GO
4913
4940
DAWEI
XIAOJIN

AREA MAP SICHUAN PROVINCE

MAERKING
LIXIAN
WENCHUAN
YENXIU
GUANXIAN
CHENGDU
SIGUNIANG 6250
RILONG
WOLONG (PANDA RESERVE)
XIAOJIN

N

SCALE 0 5 10 15 20 KMS

months of the year, but in Chengdu, August is slightly drier than early summer or the fall season.
Maps The Chinese Mountaineering Association map called *Siguniang*. It's good quality so you know there's a better topographic map of this area available somewhere; TPC map *H11-A*, 1:500,000; and/or any good road map of Sichuan Province--buy locally; and the latest travel guidebook, **China**, Lonely Planet.

Heng Shan Bei (Daoist Mountain), Shanxi Province, China

Heng Shan Bei, or North Heng Mountain, is the most northerly of China's nine sacred mountains; and the first of 5 Daoist (Taoist) mountains in this book. Located not far south of Datong, it rises to 2017 meters. Datong is in Shanxi Province and can be reached by train from Beijing or Taiyuan.

In 1984, this place was officially closed to foreigners because they were reconstructing some of the temples on the mountain. But it's now open. Most people going to Heng Shan Bei first go to Datong where some of the best Buddhist caves in China are located; these are the Yungang Caves.

To reach **Heng Shan Bei**, take a morning bus from Datong. If you can find a bus going directly to the mountain, it will pass Hunyuan on the way, and should drop you off at the parking place at the base of the cliffs at about 1600 meters altitude. A few minutes walk will take you to an amphitheater part way up the mountain where a number of temples and monasteries are located. In 1984, there was no lodging on or near the mountain, so most people made this a one day excursion from Datong. However, it's a dry area, and sleeping out of doors on the mountain is possible.

If for some reason there are no buses going directly to the mountain, then get one bus to Hunyuan, then get another to the south side of the peak. Or, join a group going to the *Xuan Kong Si,* or Hanging Monastery, as some tourists call it. Then walk from there. If you get stuck in Hunyuan, there are hotels in town.

Here's what the author did on 7/15/1984. The bus drivers in Datong wouldn't sell him a bus ticket to Heng Shan Bei because this area was officially closed to foreigners, so he hitch hiked from Datong to Hunyuan and finally to Xuan Kong Si (Xuan Kong Temple). There was a fair amount of traffic on the road, thus hitch hiking was good. After seeing the spectacular Hanging Temple of Xuan Kong, a policeman said he couldn't go beyond the tunnel, so the author walked down to Tao Jazhou and asked some children about another route. They said there was one and showed him the way. He walked on one of several terraced field paths into a canyon on the northwest side of the mountain where several trails come together. He then climbed Heng Shan Bei by this northern route which is used by only a hand-full of people a day. On the way down he visited some of the mountain's temples, then on the highway hitch hiked back to Hunyuan and took a bus to Datong the same day.

If you use this northern route, there's a small spring at about 1500 meters, but always start out with a bottle full of water if it's a warm day. If you use the normal route, expect to find people between the bus stop and the temples, selling food and drinks. Few people actually climb to the summit of this mountain; most just visit the temples instead. These are among the most interesting mountain temples in China because several are under overhanging cliffs.

While in the area don't miss Xuan Dong Si. It's one of the most unique temples anywhere, because it's perched on a cliff face. Many tourists join groups to visit this temple on day-trips out of Datong. You should be able to visit all the temples and climb the mountain in one long day from Datong; if not there are at least 2 hotels in Hunyuan. Can someone please update the author's

This is the Xuan Kong Si (Xuan Kong Temple) located just west of Heng Shan Bei.

Map 197-1, Heng Shan Bei (Daoist), Shanxi Province, China

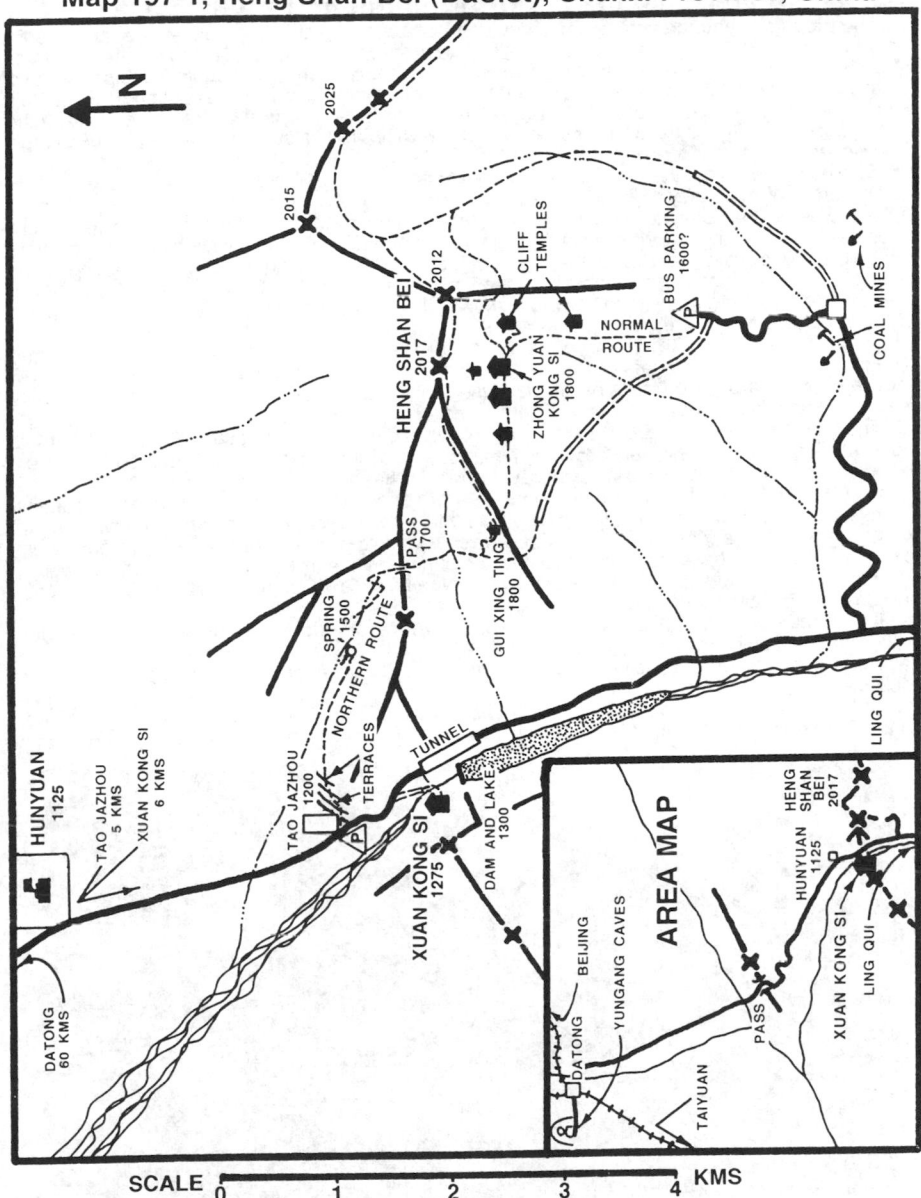

SCALE 0 — 1 — 2 — 3 — 4 KMS

information regarding facilities at the bus parking area at 1600 meters and other sites on the mountain.
Maps   Buy a simple tourist map in Datong, Hunyuan or on the mountain; and the latest guidebook,
China, Lonely Planet. This book discusses the Hanging Monastery, but not Heng Shan Bei!

Tai Shan (Daoist Mountain) Shandong Province, China

The mountain featured here is Tai Shan, at 1524 meters. Tai Shan is one of 5 sacred Daoist mountains in China. It's located on the main rail line running between Beijing on the north and Shanghai to the south, and in Shandong Province. At the base of the mountain is the small city of Tai'an, which owes its existence to thousands, maybe millions(?) of pilgrims visiting the mountain each year. Tai Shan is the most-climbed of all the 9 sacred mountains in China and it could be the most-climbed mountain in the world. Its location on the main rail line puts it within easy reach of most Chinese, as well as most foreign tourists.

Because of its popularity, all trains--even express trains--stop at Tai'an. There are many hotels in Tai'an, and as of 2000, they all accepted foreign visitors. In 1984, only one allowed foreigners to stay; that was the Tai Shan Binguan (hotel) at the beginning of the trail. It's still the best one to stay in. To reach the Tai Shan Binguan, walk out of the train station and turn left. Walk a short distance to where bus 3 stops. This bus will take you to the hotel located near the beginning of the main trail going up the mountain. This same bus also runs between the 2 main trailheads used for climbing Tai Shan. If you have taken the western route (road) down the mountain, catch bus 3 at the bottom of the climb and it will take you back to the hotel via the train station. This is the same bus as in 1984.

To begin the climb up **Tai Shan**, walk a short distance north on the street in front of the Tai Shan Binguan. Soon you'll see a gate which is the beginning of the normal route. You'll pay about US$4 entry fee. The trail is a wide stone-paved staircase all the way up. Along the way are many vendors selling food and drinks, souvenirs, film and fotographs.

The distance is either 7.5 or 12 kms (?), one-way. The elevation at the bottom is about 225 meters and you climb an estimated 6660 steps to the top, according to the book below. There are 2 expensive hotels on the mountain you can stay in now; one halfway up, one on the summit.

On 6/12/1984, the author started at 6am and walked up the staircase or central trail to the summit. On the return trip, he walked down the road to the bottom and bus stop. It took 5 1/2 hours round-trip. He then took bus 3 back to his binguan. Most however, should plan on an all-day trip as there's much to see. Chinese are allowed to spend a night on the summit in one of the *pilgrims shelters*, but not us. We apparently have to stay in the expensive hotel! Non-hikers can ride a bus halfway up, then reach the summit in a cable car or teleferico.

It's recommended you use the western route on the return trip. It begins at Zhong Tian Men, which is the bottom of the cable car and the end of the road. You can walk down the old trail or road, passing a fine waterfall and pool on the way. Remember, it's warm at the base of the mountain and cool on top, so take a jacket.

Climb from April through October. Also visit the Tai Miao (Temple) in Tai'an, one of three palace-style buildings in China (the other 2 are the Imperial Palace in Beijing and the Kong Miao in

Near the summit of Tai Shan with porters carrying wine to the hotels on top.

Map 198-1, Tai Shan (Daoist), Shandong Province, China

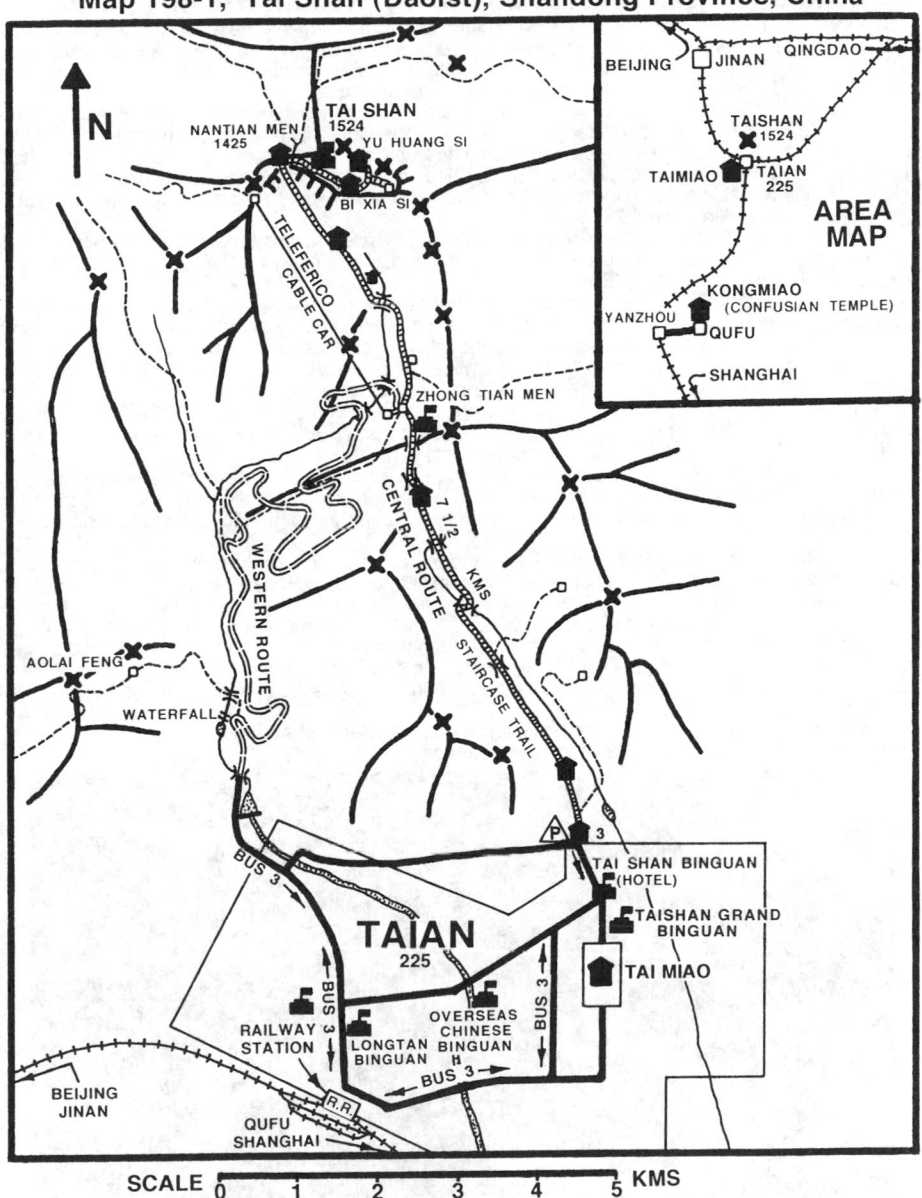

SCALE 0 1 2 3 4 5 KMS

Qufu). Lots of tourist here, so someone at the train station can update this information.
Maps The author found 3 different maps which he bought at the train station and hotel; also, the latest travel guidebook, **China**, Lonely Planet.

Heng Shan Nan (Daoist Mountain), Hunan Province, China

This mountain is called Heng Shan Nan (South Heng Mountain). It's the most southerly of the five Daoist mountains in China. The highest peak or feng is called Zhou Rong Feng with an altitude of 1290 meters. Of the 9 sacred mountains in China, this is perhaps the least interesting, largely because there's a road to the summit instead of the usual staircase.

Heng Shan Nan is located between Changsha and Hengyang in central Hunan Province. The author arrived in Hengyang from Guangzhou on a train, then took city bus 1 to the northern part of the city where the bus station for travelers going north is located. There are many buses, one every half hour or so each day going in the direction of Heng Shan and a town at the base of the mountain called Nan Yui. One can also get off the train in Heng Shan, take a ferry boat across the river and find a bus going south toward Hengyang. See Area Map.

In Nan Yui, you'll be left at the bus station on the south side of town. From there walk north about 400 meters to a large gate which is the beginning of the road leading to the Nan Yui Si (Temple), and the beginning of the way to **Heng Shan Nan**.

On the street between the bus station and the temple are many shops and hawkers selling souvenir pins, umbrellas, maps, and food. You won't need to worry about food as there are food vendors everywhere along the road to the summit. Also, there are several places in which to spend the night--Ban Shan Ting being the largest. Rooms are usually the large dormitory type, but there may be smaller rooms for couples or foreigners (they expect foreigners to stay in the nicer & more expensive rooms!). Dormitory beds are very cheap and bedding is provided. Chinese pilgrims seldom take more than a camera and toothbrush, but everyone takes an umbrella, as this mountain is in that part of China that receives the heaviest amounts of rainfall.

The author took a tent and camped in the rain and fog, but luckily no one saw the tent; otherwise he may have been asked to sleep in one of the pilgrims hotels, which were a little expensive for him at the time. Camping is not recommended as flat campsites are difficult to find. The author was here on 5/1 & 5/2/1984.

From Nan Yui to the top is 12 kms. The round-trip can be done easily in one day. If you're in a hurry and don't want to spend a night on the mountain, it's possible to take a bus or truck from the Nan Yui Si to Ban Shan Ting, at Km 7. From there everyone walks along the old road to the top. If you're spending more time on the mountain, you might visit Nan Tai Si or one of the other temples.

Film sizes 126 and 135 can be bought on the mountain, and B+W film can be developed on the spot in little black boxes along the way. The bottom of the mountain is warm and humid, while the top is cool--dress accordingly. Shorts are accepted in China. There should be at least one hotel in Nan Yui and others in both Hengyang and Hengshan.

Maps Only in Nan Yui can one buy small Chinese maps similar to this one; also, take the latest travel guidebook to China for lists of hotels and bus schedules, etc.

Pilgrims buying souvenir pins at the summit of Heng Shan Nan.

Map 199-1, Heng Shan Nan (Daoist), Hunan Province, China

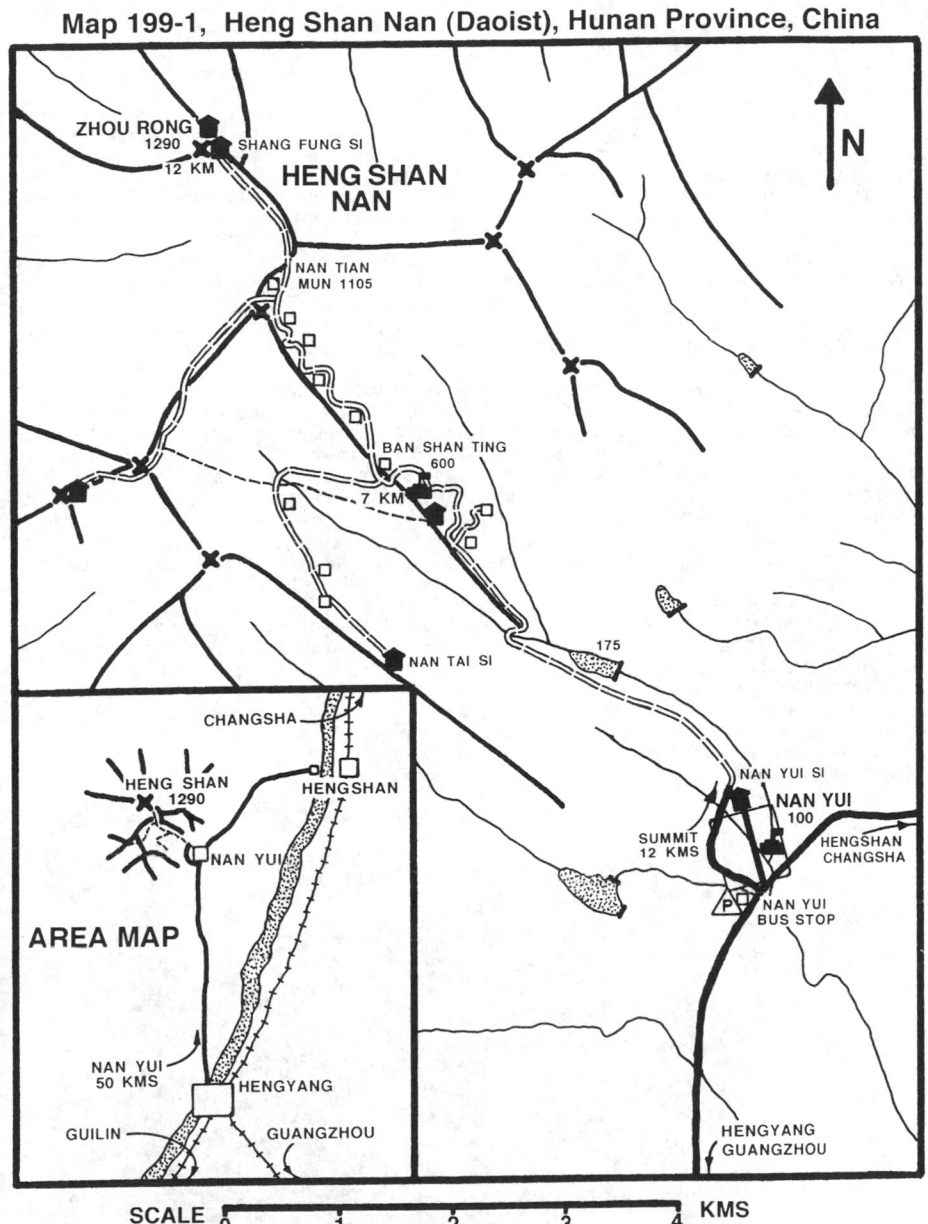

N

ZHOU RONG
1290
12 KM
SHANG FUNG SI
HENG SHAN NAN

NAN TIAN MUN 1105

BAN SHAN TING 600
7 KM

NAN TAI SI

175

NAN YUI SI
NAN YUI
100
SUMMIT 12 KMS
HENGSHAN CHANGSHA

NAN YUI BUS STOP

HENGYANG GUANGZHOU

AREA MAP

CHANGSHA

HENG SHAN 1290

HENGSHAN

NAN YUI

NAN YUI 50 KMS

GUILIN

HENGYANG

GUANGZHOU

SCALE 0   1   2   3   4   **KMS**

Hua Shan (Daoist Mountain), Shaanxi Province, China

Hua Shan is one of 5 sacred Daoist mountains of China. This one is located next to the main rail line running between Xian and Luoyang in Shaanxi Province and very near where the Huang He (Yellow River) makes its eastern turn after running south for so long.

As with most of the 9 sacred mountains of China, Hua Shan is made of solid granite, at least the central core. It may be the most beautiful of the nine, and in many ways is similar to Huang Shan located in Anhui Province. As with all the 9 sacred mountains, this range also has many temples (si) and pavilions (ting) and is visited by thousands of pilgrims each year.

However, with the author's visit in 1984, it was officially closed to some foreigners. Tourists from Hong Kong (or people of Chinese ancestry--Overseas Chinese) were allowed on the mountain, and European and North American workers and students living in China were allowed to climb, but the author, a tourist, was not given permission. The lame excuse given was there had been some bad accidents on the mountain. In places, rock steps have been cut into steep granite walls and chains installed, but in cold weather it can be icy and dangerous, thus the discrimination.

The author went to the base of **Hua Shan** on 7/25/1984, but was told to go to Xian for permission. That permission never materialized and at the end of his journey he didn't have the time to return and climb it illegally.

The map the author used to create this one he bought at the Hua Shan Da Men (Hua Shan Gate). The book on China below updates what the author learned. It states if you're coming by train, get off at the *Mengyuan Station* located 15 kms east of the mountain and the village of Huashan, then take a bus to Huashan, and hike south from there. However, on the author's trip in 1984, **slow trains did stop** at the Huashan Railway Station 2 kms east of the Hua Shan Da Men. He stopped there and walked along the railway tracks to the Hua Shan Gate and had a good look around before continuing on to Xian. Could it be the 2nd generation of China travelers never take the slow trains (?). Check this out before buying a ticket in Xian or Luoyang.

There are several hotels in Huashan Village, where you can store unneeded baggage. There is now an entry fee of about US$6 at the gate for foreigners. From the gate to the Bei Feng (North Peak) is 6 kms, perhaps another 4 or 5 kms to Nan Feng (South Peak). The difficult part to climb, and a bottleneck when crowded, is just below Bei Feng, where it's steep and there are steps cut in the granite and cables to hang onto. There are 4 or 5 hotels on the mountain that foreigners can stay in, but they are overpriced and not too clean, according to the *China* guidebook below.

The Lonely Planet guide also states the highest peak is Nan Feng at 2160 meters. But the map the author bought shows that Zhong Feng at 1997 meters is the highest (?). Can someone please check this out and get in touch with the author--who will likely never go back to China?

Many Chinese people make this climb at night; it seems they get more merits if they see the sun rise from on top. This should be one of the most fotogenic hikes around. You can do this climb in one

Typical scene in the Hua Shan. The core of this mountain is made of granite.

Map 200-1, Hua Shan (Daoist), Shaanxi Province, China

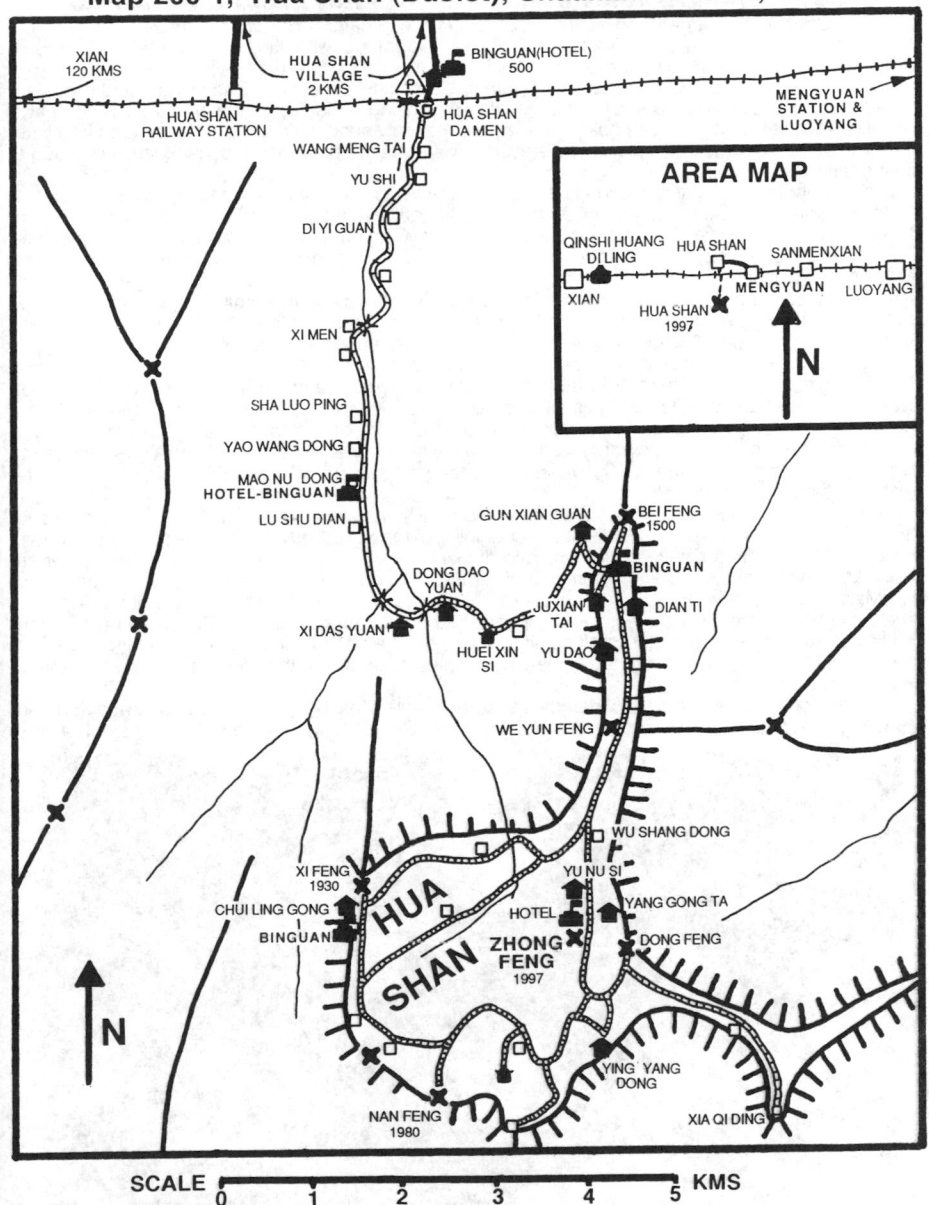

AREA MAP

XIAN
120 KMS

HUA SHAN
VILLAGE
2 KMS

BINGUAN(HOTEL)
500

MENGYUAN
STATION &
LUOYANG

HUA SHAN
RAILWAY STATION

HUA SHAN
DA MEN

WANG MENG TAI

YU SHI

DI YI GUAN

QINSHI HUANG
DI LING

HUA SHAN

SANMENXIAN

XIAN

MENGYUAN

LUOYANG

HUA SHAN
1997

XI MEN

N

SHA LUO PING

YAO WANG DONG

MAO NU DONG
HOTEL-BINGUAN

LU SHU DIAN

GUN XIAN GUAN

BEI FENG
1500

BINGUAN

DONG DAO
YUAN

DIAN TI

XI DAS YUAN

JUXIAN
TAI

HUEI XIN
SI

YU DAO

WE YUN FENG

WU SHANG DONG

XI FENG
1930

YU NU SI

CHUI LING GONG

HOTEL

YANG GONG TA

BINGUAN

ZHONG
FENG
1997

DONG FENG

N

YING YANG
DONG

NAN FENG
1980

XIA QI DING

SCALE 0 1 2 3 4 5 KMS

day from Huashan Village. There are people selling food and drinks all along the way, but at higher prices. Climb between May to October.
Maps Maps should be for sale at the train station(s), in Huashan Village and at stalls at the gate Hua Shan Da Men; also, the latest travel guidebook, **China**, Lonely Planet.

Song Shan (Daoist Mountain), Henan Province, China

Song Shan is the name of an entire mountain range in central Henan Province of China. The range is divided into 2 parts. Tai Shi Shan is north of Dengfeng, with Junji Feng the highest peak at 1494 meters; and Shao Shi Shan located west of Dengfeng and south of Shaolin Si.

Song Shan is located between Luoyang (with the Longmen Caves) and Zhengzhou, and is the 5th of the 5 sacred Daoist mountains in China. Most people going to the Song Shan visit the temples only, with very few climbing any of the peaks. The author met only about a dozen other people on his climb of Junji Feng on 7/23/1984. On his trip, he stayed 2 nights in the Song Shan Binguan (hotel) for US$3 a night--it's now about US$8.

The number one pilgrim attraction in the area is the Shaolin Si (Shaolin Temple). This is perhaps the most famous temple in China. It was founded originally in 495 AD, and is the birth place of Zen Buddhism and the founding location of the martial arts, or Kung Fu. Besides Shaolin Si, the Zhong Yue Miao (Zhong Yue Temple) is deluged with visitors, and the Song Yue Si is the most picturesque temple in the range.

The author climbed Junji Feng on his first day, then the rains came eliminating any more hiking. He was told of some poor quality trails leading into the Shao Shi Shan from the Shaolin Si, but never got the chance to climb. Will someone who has hiked there please send a report to the author.

Most people going to the Song Shan arrive from Luoyang (many buses daily), but some also come from Zhengzhou by bus. There are many local buses carrying pilgrims running between Shaolin Si and Zhong Yue Miao, with Dengfeng as the central hub. In Dengfeng is a newer hotel called the Song Shan Binguan. It has all classes of accommodation and is the best place to stay while exploring the mountains and temples. But when you arrive, there should be more hotels, and more places for foreigners. At last report there is a Wushu Binguan somewhere at or near Shaolin, but it's more expensive than the one in Dengfeng.

This is what the author did. He got an early morning start and walked from Dengfeng to the Song Yue Si, then to Lao Mu Dong, which is at the beginning of the paved stone trail to the top of Junji Feng. At about 1050 meters are several old ruins and drinking water, but at the summit are neither. If you'd like to return a different way, there's another trail following the ridge south to the area of Zhong Yue Miao. The author walked this ridge route to Zhong Yue, then got a bus back to the hotel. The trail on the south end of that ridge is easy to follow except from the farm houses at 1000 meters to Huang Gai Feng, where many trails and small canyons exist, but the general direction is easy to follow. The author's total hike-time from his hotel, to the two temples, the summit, then down to Zhong Yue Miao, was 8 hours.

Carry a bottle or two of water when the weather is hot. Most people should walk straight to Lao Mu Dong and do the hike without seeing the Song Yue Si, as visiting that temple will make it a very

Bronze statues at Shaolin Si located to the west of Song Shan.

Map 201-1, Song Shan (Daoist), Henan Province, China

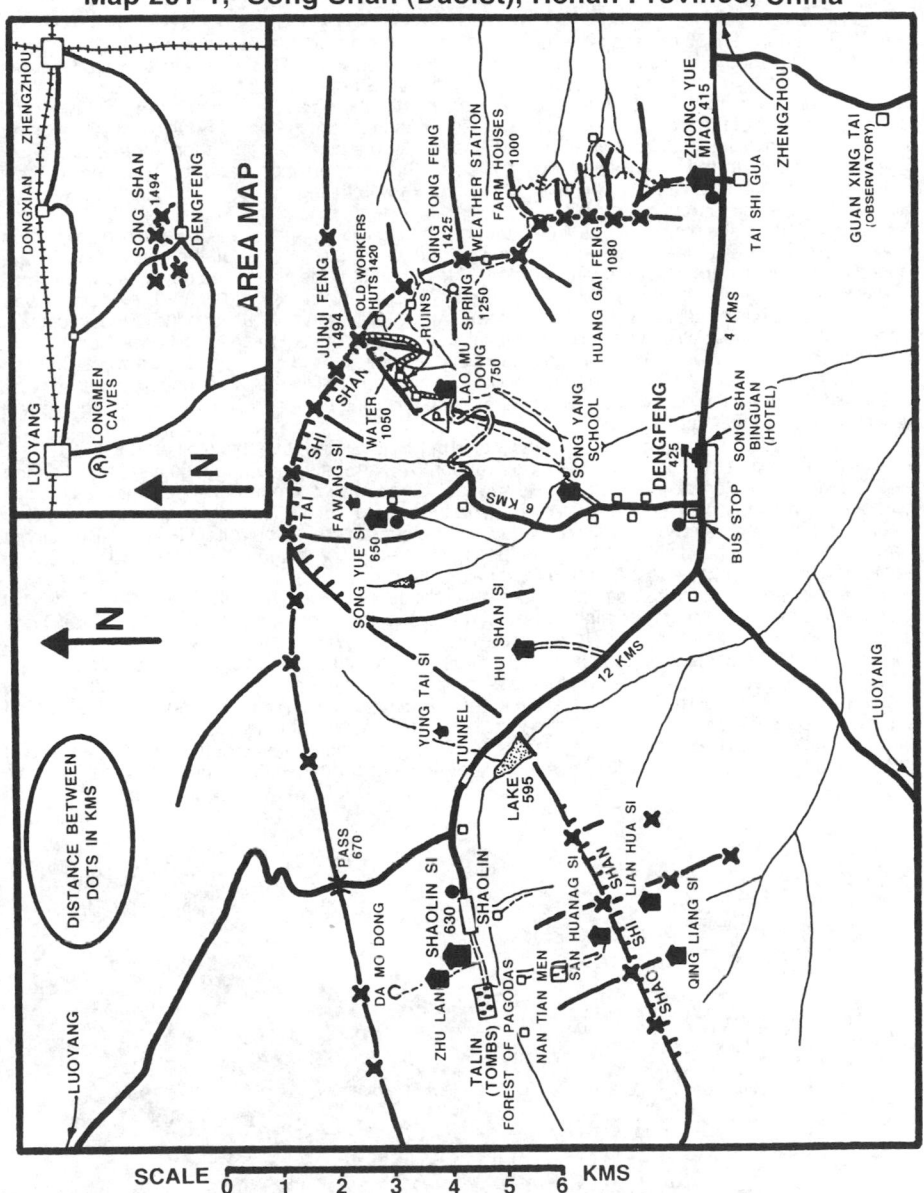

SCALE 0 1 2 3 4 5 6 KMS

long walk. Climb here during the warmer season from April through October.
Maps Buy simple maps at the Song Shan Hotel, Shaolin Si, or Zhong Yue Miao; and the latest travel guidebook, **China**, Lonely Planet.

Wu Tai Shan (Buddhist Mountain), Shanxi Province, China

Wu Tai Shan at 3058 meters, is the most northerly of the 4 Buddhist mountains in China. It's also the second highest of China's 9 sacred mountains, after Emei Shan. This mountain is located 8 hours by bus north of the Shanxi Provincial capital of Taiyuan, and 7 hours west of Beijing by train.

The normal way to **Wu Tai Shan** is to take a train from Beijing or Taiyuan and get off at Xin Xian, a town southwest of the mountain. From there take a bus to the village of Tai Shan (or Wu Tai Shan). Another route involves getting off the train at Fanshi, taking a bus to Shahe, then another bus (?) or hitch hiking south to the mountain. However, doing this northern approach route is more difficult unless you speak a few words of Chinese. One problem with taking this latter route in 1984 was that no one around spoke a word of English.

As of 9/5/1984, the problem the author found in climbing this mountain was it was closed to foreign visitors--except for Overseas Chinese. Here's what the author did. He got off the train at Fanshi and ended up sleeping there at the station overnight. He got off at Fanshi because people in small towns weren't familiar with the government's policy of open and closed areas for foreigners. If you tried to get off a bus or train in a closed area, sometimes a policeman or train conductor would put you back on. At other places they wouldn't sell you a ticket on a bus or train to an unauthorized location. In these situations, if you really wanted to go some place that was closed, you had to learn some Chinese quick, then get out on the highway and hitch hike. During the 1980's, the reasons some places were closed was because they lacked good facilities, English speaking staff, or someone to help the average tourist. Or some other lame excuse.

From Fanshi, the author caught an early morning bus to Shahe, then hitch hiked & walked to the village at the base of the mountain called Tai Shan or Wu Tai Shan. He bought souvenirs and a map and visited the main temple, Ta Yuan Si. He sure got stared at a lot; probably because he was the first barbarian to visit the place! He then walked back up the road to Km 30.5 north of town along the way to Fanshi and camped nearby. It was a rainy day with no one around so he put up his tent just as it got dark. Next morning he climbed the highest peak, Bei Tai Din, returned to the road and hitch hiked back to Fanshi. Later he caught an 11pm night train to Beijing.

The book below, which dates from 1998, states that the (Wu) Tai Shan village is called *Taihuai*. It also has a different name for the highest peak, *Yedoufeng* (the TPC map below lists it Beitai Ding). Their maps indicate there are 5 hotels in the town itself, and 4 others just to the south. There is also a tourist office (CITS) immediately south of town. Those authors also state that you can get there by one daily bus from Datong, via Shahe and the pass marked 2500 meters. There are about 7 buses daily leaving Taiyuan for Wu Tai Shan, all leaving in the morning, an 8 hour trip. No mention of getting off the train close to the mountain and getting a local bus--but that's got to be a good option.

Wu Tai Shan is one of the nine mountains where pilgrims mostly just visit the temples, instead of climbing to the summit. As you use this map, keep in mind about half the temples around Tai Shan

One of many temples in the valley south of Wu Tai Shan.

Map 202-1, Wu Tai Shan (Buddhist), Shanxi Province, China

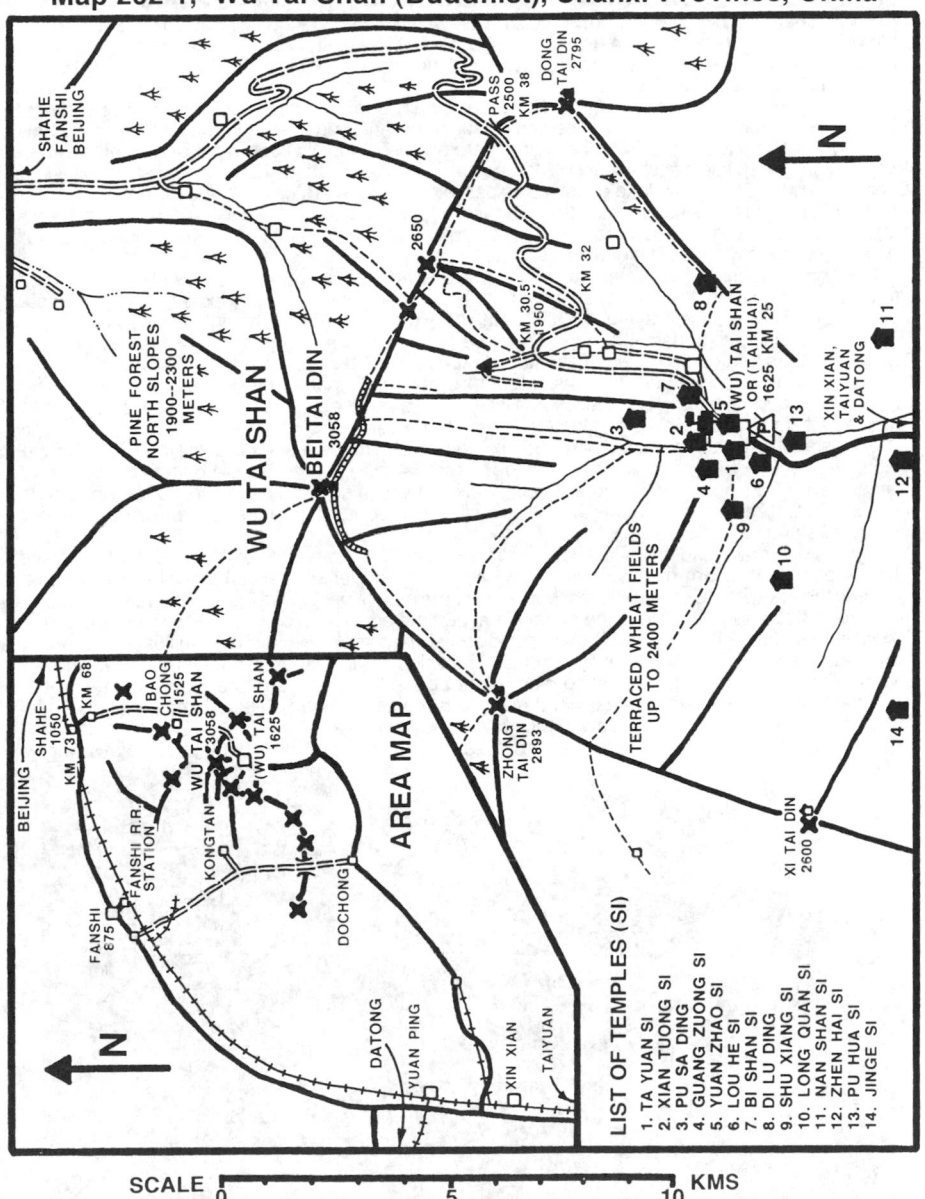

are not in their exact locations. The author created this map from a sketch drawn on a handkerchief which wasn't very accurate. However, the peaks and ridges of the higher summits should be in about their proper places.

Maps Buy maps in Taiyuan, Xin Xian or Tai Shan village shops; perhaps TPC map *G-9B*, 1:500,000; and the latest travel guidebook, **China**, Lonely Planet.

Putuo Shan (Buddhist Mountain), Zhejiang Province, China

Putuo Shan (Pu Island Mountain) is the smallest of the 9 sacred mountains in China, but it's one of the most interesting to visit. Putuo (Pu Island) is located off the east coast of China; east of Ningpo and south of Shanghai. The author visited this island and mountain on 5/28 & 5/29/1984, but used the book below to updated his information.

There are 3 ways to get to **Putuo**. There are 2 daily boats from Ningpo departing at 8:30am & 1:20pm, which takes 3 hours to reach the port of Huang Fo An. Boats leave Putuo for Ningpo at 8am & 2pm daily. The fare is about US$8 one-way. There are also 2 nightly boats from Shanghai, leaving at 4pm & 5pm. Cheap seats cost about US$10 one-way. This takes about 12 hours and saves paying for a nights lodging. Or you can take a faster & expensive boat at 10am daily. It takes 7 hours and costs about US$27. You can also get there from Zhoushan Island. All boats are clean and comfortable. All passengers will be pilgrims, just like yourself. Try to buy your ferry boat ticket a day before departure if possible, especially for a weekend trip.

Once you reach the docks at Huang Fo An, pay an island entry fee and walk in a northerly direction, first on a road, then a cement path to one of the binguans or hotels located in or just west of the village of Puji. The hotel symbols on this map may not be in exactly the right place, as the author used the book below to update this map. There are about 4 places in Puji which accept foreigners, and 2 more binguans located further north and near the base of the highest peak on the island. Prices vary according to day of the week & the season, but *these are not cheap*. The best place to sleep is in a converted nunnery called the Sanshengtang Hotel. Singles start about US$18. There are many street vendors and small restaurants along the market street in Puji.

This island is filled to capacity with Buddhist temples. The best ones are: Puji Si (Puji Temple), lying in the center of Puji, the only town on the island; Fayu Si, located at the bottom of the cement staircase leading to the top of the highest peak; Huiji Si, located near the top of the highest peak at 245 meters; and Dacheng Monastery with a large reclining Buddha. There are numerous other smaller monasteries and pavilions as well.

There's one main road on the island running north-south. One branch of this road winds its way to near the top of **Putuo Shan**. There are a few mini-buses available which take older or handicapped people to the Huiji Si and other temples, but the vast majority of people walk along the road, then climb the cement staircase to the top of the mountain at 284 meters. One could walk from Puji to the top of Putuo Shan and back in a couple of hours, but to see all the temples will require a full day.

There are some good sandy beaches on the east side of the island, but the author saw almost no one swimming. The author actually put up a tent on the larger beach (after dark) just east of the Dacheng Monastery, then took it down early in the morning. No one objected, mainly because few people saw it. You likely won't get away with that when you arrive.

If you use black & white film, there are people on the streets and the cement stairways who will

Vendors selling Chinese soft drinks along the way to the top of Putuo Shan.

Map 203-1, Putuo Shan (Buddhist), Zhejiang Province, China

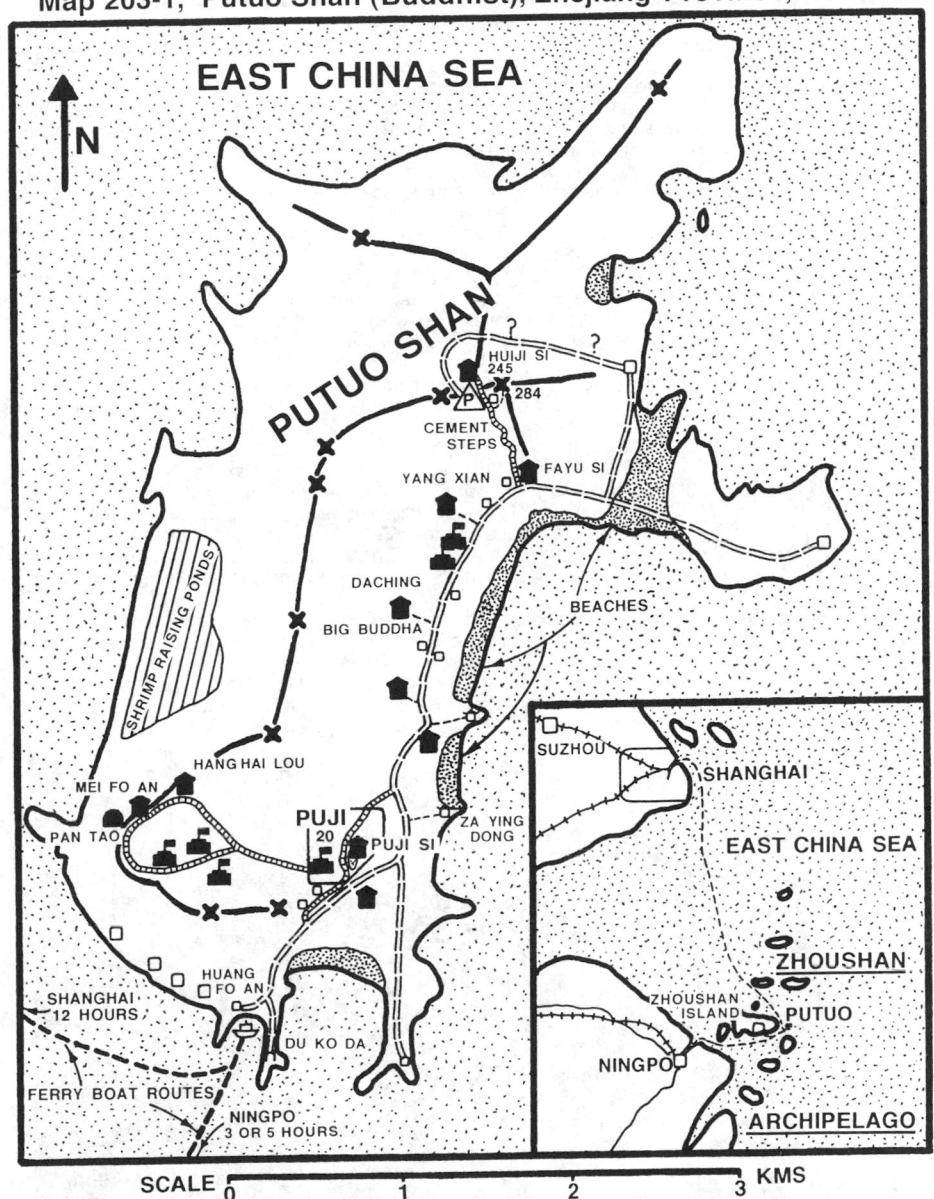

EAST CHINA SEA

N

PUTUO SHAN

HUIJI SI
245
P
284

CEMENT
STEPS

YANG XIAN

FAYU SI

DACHING

BEACHES

BIG BUDDHA

SHRIMP RAISING PONDS

HANG HAI LOU

MEI FO AN

PAN TAO

PUJI
20

PUJI SI

ZA YING
DONG

SUZHOU

SHANGHAI

EAST CHINA SEA

ZHOUSHAN

ZHOUSHAN
ISLAND

PUTUO

HUANG
FO AN

SHANGHAI
12 HOURS

DU KO DA

NINGPO

ARCHIPELAGO

FERRY BOAT ROUTES

NINGPO
3 OR 5 HOURS

SCALE 0   1   2   3 KMS

develop it on the spot in little black boxes. Putuo is a foggy place, so to see it all, you might have to stay more than one day.
Maps Buy maps on the ferry boat, or from vendors in Puji; and the latest travel guidebook, **China**, Lonely Planet.

447

Jiu Hua Shan (Buddhist Mountain), Anhui Province, China

This map shows one of the 4 sacred Buddhist mountains in China, Jiu Hua Shan, with an altitude of 1341 meters. It's located just west of another mountain called Huang Shan, both of which are west of Hangzhou. See Area Map. It's in the southern part of the province of Anhui. Daoist monks built huts on this mountain in the 3rd century AD, but Buddhism gradually replaced Daoism.

There are various ways to get there. One of the most popular is to take a bus from Huang Shan, another nearby mountain also featured in this book. There are at least 2 buses daily making this run (most people arrive at Huang Shan via Hangzhou). Another common route is to take a train south from Nanjing to Tongling, then take one of several daily buses running south to Jiu Hua Shan. If you're boating down the Chang Jiang (Yangtze River), it's possible to get off at Guichi and ride a bus to the mountain.

As is the case with all 9 of China's sacred mountains, **Jiu Hua Shan** (Nine Flowers Mountain) has many temples. The first temples to be visited will be in the area generally known as Jiu Hua Shan town or village. This is where the bus stops and where the binguans or hotels are located. Nearby are 2 interesting temples. The Qi Yuan Si (Qi Yuan Temple) has several very large statues of The Buddha, and the Hua Cheng Si has a very old library as well as many artifacts. Bai Sui Si, located on the ridge east of the Dong Ya Binguan (Dong Ya Hotel), is also interesting. In all, there are over 70 temples on the mountain.

From Jiu Hua Shan village, which has many small souvenir shops and eating places, the normal route to the top is along a stone & cement path running southeast. The trail first crosses over a low pass at 735 meters, then drops down to the main river valley and the small village of Middle Minyuan. From there, the route rises steeply to the crest of the main ridge. In the steeper part, there are about six important temples, all with food & drinks being sold nearby. From Tian Tai Si, walk southwest along the ridge to the top of **Shiwang Feng** (Shiwang Peak) at 1341 meters.

On the return, or perhaps the beginning of the trek, walk along the minor ridge where the Bai Sui Si is found. This is about one km north of the pass marked 735 meters. There seems to be a temple or shrine about every 100 meters or so along this main trail. On the author's trip, he saw more monks on this mountain than on any of the other 8. Maybe that's the reason he felt climbing this mountain was a real pilgrimage.

It's been said that the months of September, October and November are the most colorful, but also the busiest and most crowded. The author was there from 6/4 to 6/6/1984 and the place was very quiet and peaceful. In fact, the trek up Jiu Hua Shan was one of the more pleasant hikes he had in China. You can walk up to the summit and back in 3 or 4 hours, but to see all the temples, plan on taking a full day. There are now at least 4 hotels or binguans in the village which accept foreigners. There is also a cable car running up to the summit of Tian Tai Shan, but it's exact location is not known. Entry fee is

Tian Tai Si, the highest temple on Jiu Hua Shan at the top of the cement staircase.

Map 204-1, Jiu Hua Shan (Buddhist), Anhui Province, China

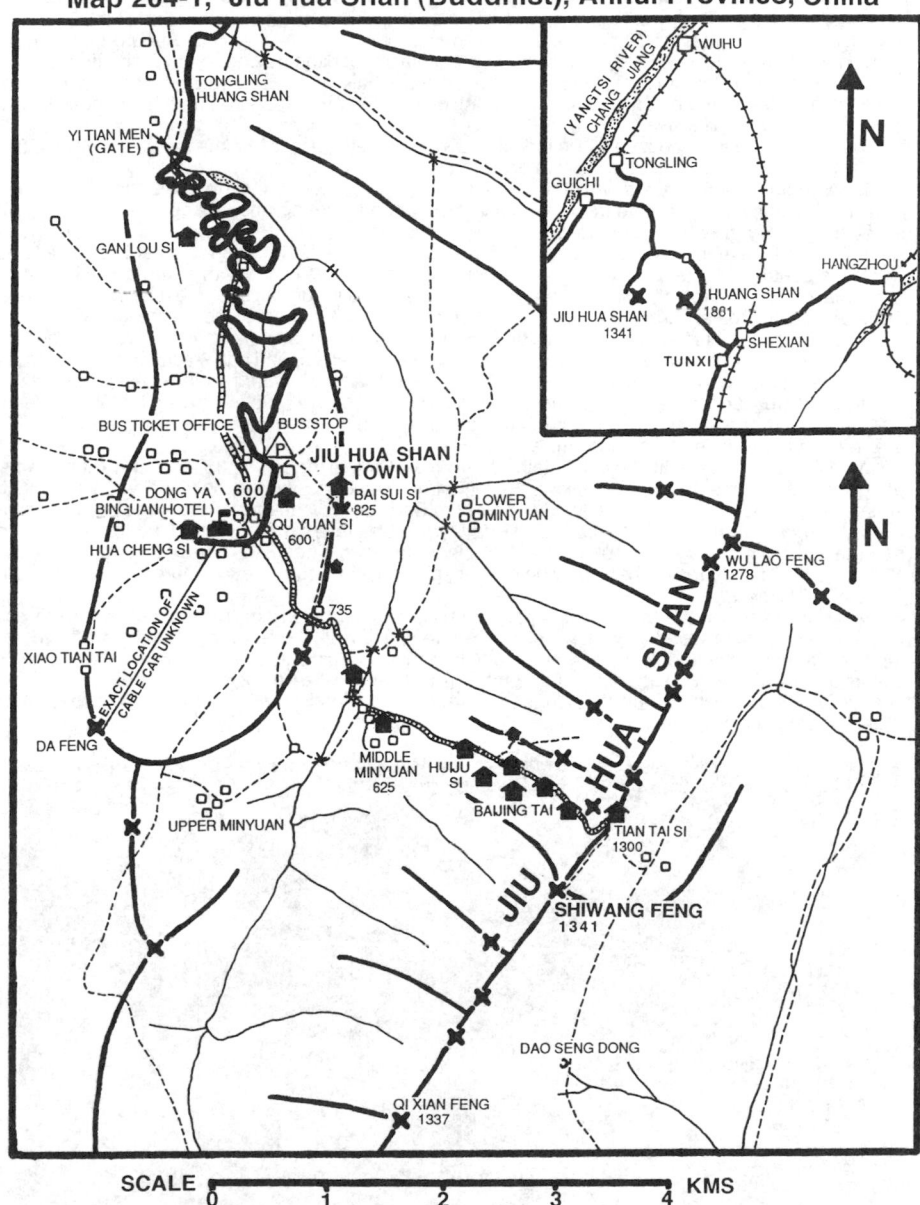

SCALE

0   1   2   3   4   KMS

now about US$6.

Maps There are good maps available along the market street in Jiu Hua Shan village, or at hotels; and the latest travel guidebook, **China**, Lonely Planet.

Emei Shan (Buddhist Mountain), Sichuan Province, China

Emei Shan is probably the best-known of the 4 Buddhist mountains in China; and of the 9 sacred mountains, it's the highest at 3099 meters. On this mountain you'll see the usual Buddhist temples or pavilions, pilgrim shelters all along the way, and thousands of pilgrims on the trail. The first temple was built in the 2nd Century A.D., but most were originally built in the 6th Century. At one time there were 151 temples on the mountain but today many of those have disappeared and the number is now down to 20 that are still active.

The author arrived in the area late in the afternoon of 5/9/1984, and left on the morning of 5/13/1984. He used the book below to update his own information.

Emei (pron. Omei) **Shan** is one of the most popular climbs among foreign tourists in China. One reason for this is its location on the main rail line between Kunming and Chengdu. Buy your train ticket to Emei Shan--which is actually the Emei Station located 3 1/2 kms north of Emei town, as shown on the area map. From the train station take a bus to Emei town, then another bus to the Bao Guo Si, a popular temple, but not the most popular starting point for the climb. Or take a bus from Emei Station or Emei town to Jin Shui on the north side of the mountain and begin hiking from there. Regardless of the route, you will walk along a paved stone staircase most of the way to the top.

The author took his big pack and camped on the mountain illegally, but that's not recommended. What is recommended is to stop in Emei at the main tourist hotel and find out exactly where foreigners are allowed to sleep on the mountain. By the late 1990's, almost every pilgrim shelter, binguan or hotel on the mountain accepted foreigners; so it appears there's no problem finding a place to sleep. Then you can take a very small day pack and eat and sleep in the pilgrim shelters along the way. This is a real cultural experience, so don't miss it.

Maps the author bought show the staircase from Jin Shui to the top as 38 kms, **but that seems exaggerated**. The same map also shows the route from Bao Guo Si to the top as being 55 kms, but it seemed more like 35 or 40. *The author walked from Bao Guo Si to the top with a large pack (most of the way), then returned via Jin Shui in 2 1/2 days.* Most travelers the author talked to were on the mountain about 4 days. The book below states it will take most people 2-3 days if starting from Jin Shui. The time needed will depend on where you begin and end, what time you start the hike, and your own physical fitness.

For non-hikers, or the lazy, it's possible to ride a bus, small van or truck the 49 kms (?) from Emei town to a place called Jieyin Dian at 2540 meters, and walk the few remaining kms from there. Or if you're really lazy and want to cheat, and get no merits at all, you can ride a new cable car from Jieyin Dian to Jin Ding Feng and walk from there to **Wan Fo Feng**. If you can make the proper connections, the mountain could be *climbed* in one day from Emei town. Most people however walk all the way starting at Jin Shui.

Typical eating place along the stone-paved trail to the top of Emei Shan.

Map 205-1, Emei Shan (Buddhist), Sichuan Province, China

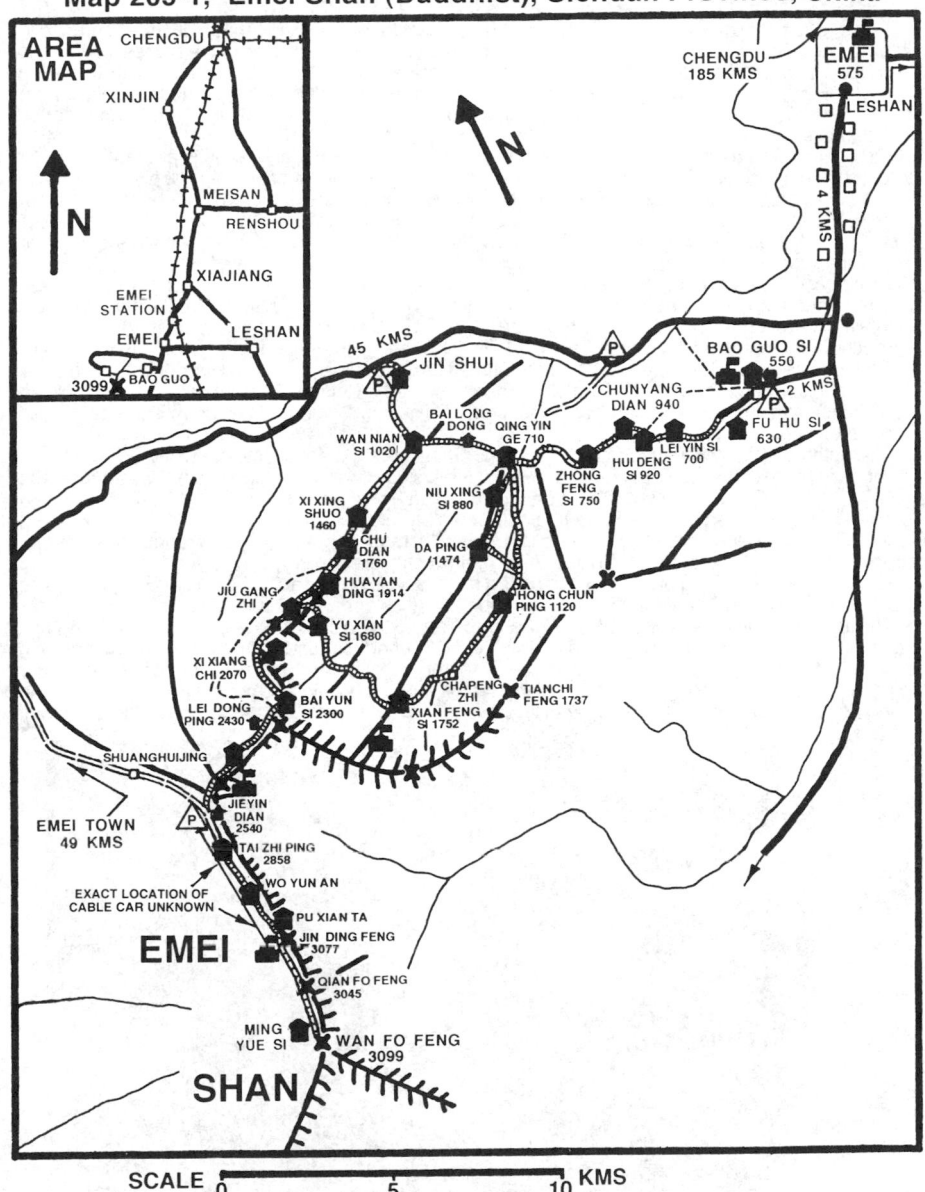

Take an umbrella--it's a wet mountain with lots of fog. Umbrellas and plastic rain covers are sold along the trail. Take as small a pack as possible--all lodging includes bedding. Maybe bed bugs too, so look over your bedding carefully. Food is sold everywhere along the way, but you might stock up on your favorite snack in Emei town.

Maps Buy one of several different maps at Emei, Jin Shui or Bao Guo Si; and the latest travel guidebook, **China**, Lonely Planet.

Huang Shan, Anhui Province, China

Huang Shan (Yellow Mountain) is a small and compact mountain range made entirely of granite in southern Anhui Province. There are 4 major groups of peaks or pinnacles here, the highest of which is Lian Hua Feng at 1860 meters. There's a stone-paved path to the top of this peak, as well as to the top of Tian Du Feng, at 1810 meters. There's another a stone-paved trail to the top of the peak with an altitude of 1820 meters. The 4th group of high pinnacles is south of Tian Du Feng, but cannot be reached by trail.

Of all the small mountain ranges of China covered in this book, Huang Shan is perhaps the most interesting and fotogenic. The combination of clouds & fog, pinnacles & spires, and oddly shaped pine trees make a fairyland-type scene. Even though this is not one of the 9 sacred mountains of China, it is one of the most-visited in the country. Also, the scenery is perhaps the most-used by artists in China. The *Pine in Beckoning Posture,* seen near the Yu Binguan (Yu Hotel), is the most fotographed and painted scene in China, and you'll see pictures of it everywhere as you travel.

In the past, the most common way to approach Huang Shan was to take one of many buses each day from Hangzhou. That trip took 8 hours to reach Tao Yuan, located at the southern base of the mountain. However, sometime after the author's trip in 1984, a new rail line was opened up running from Wuhu in the north to the cities of Shexian & Tunshi (Huangshan) and further south. Now the best way to get there is to take that train and get off at Tunshi and take a bus to Huang Shan. There is also bus service from Tongling and Jiu Hua Shan (one of the 9 sacred mountains in China) to Tao Yuan, the main trailhead. If coming from that direction, you could stop and hike from Tai Ping located on the north end of the massif.

The author made a circular loop-hike of Huang Shan twice, on consecutive days--6/2 & 6/3/1984. You'll understand why when you get there. Hiking the first day was in fog; the second was sunny and clear. It's about a 23 km-loop from Tao Yuan to Lian Hua Feng, Bei Hai Binguan (Hotel), and to Yun Goa Si. From there everyone rides a shuttle bus 7 kms back to Tao Yuan.

This 23 km-long-loop hike can be done in one day by most people. However, some sleep at one of about 9 binguans or hotels for one night. Apparently foreigners can stay in all of these places now. If you're thinking about staying on the mountain for a night, ask someone at the Tao Yuan Binguan in Tao Yuan, where you can stay before starting out. You may want to make reservations, if possible (?).

By far the most interesting part of the trip is from Tao Yuan, to Tian Du Feng, **Lian Hua Feng** and to the Pai Yun Ting. The pathway there is made entirely of granite and cement stepping stones with very few level places. The group of granite spires surrounding the Yu Binguan is most fotogenic. For the person who has more time than the average tourist, there are several other trails in the heart of the Huang Shan. There are food and drink stalls all along the main route, but carry a full bottle of water if

Huang Shan in fog and a typical fairyland-like scene.

Map 206-1, Huang Shan, Anhui Province, China

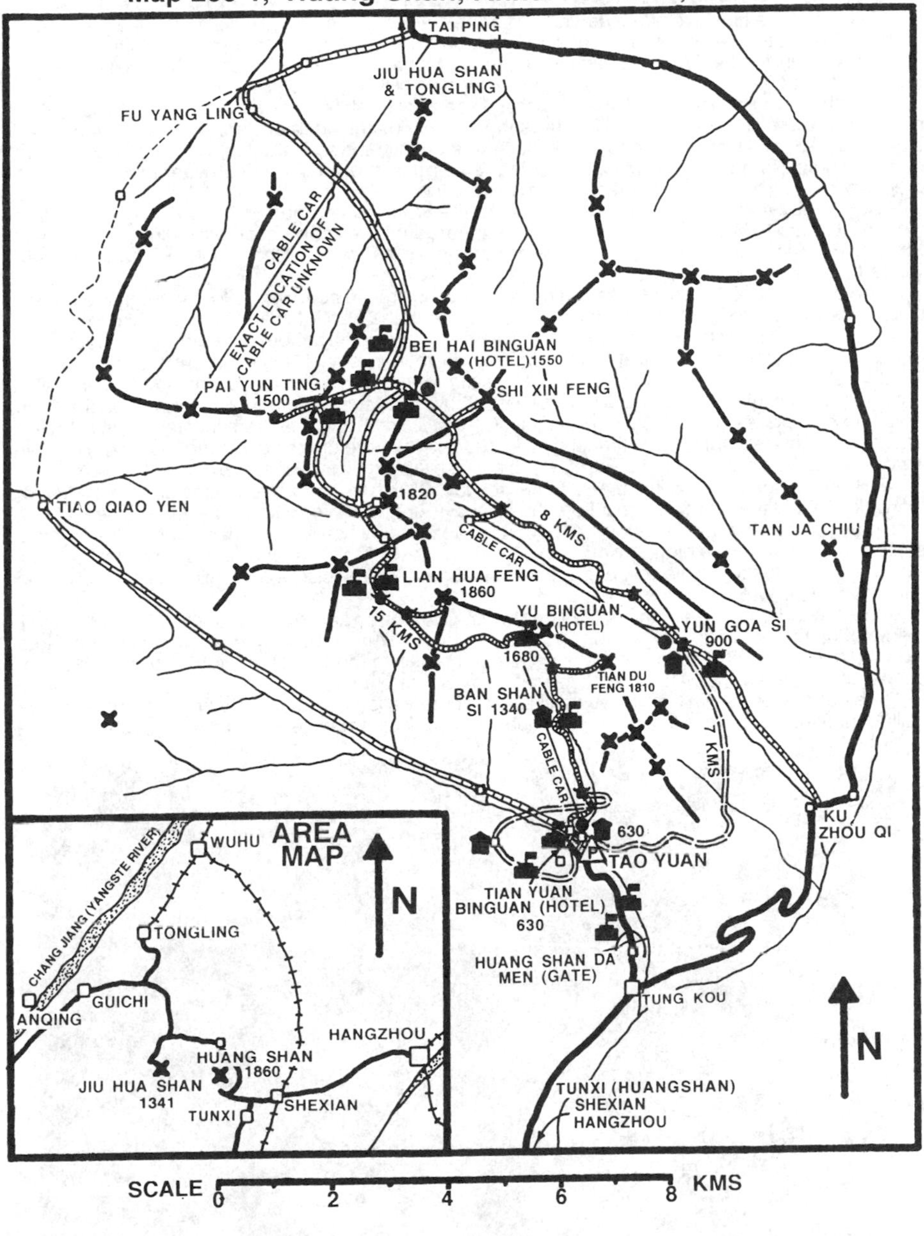

TAI PING

JIU HUA SHAN
& TONGLING

FU YANG LING

CABLE CAR

EXACT LOCATION OF
CABLE CAR UNKNOWN

BEI HAI BINGUAN
(HOTEL)1550

PAI YUN TING
1500

SHI XIN FENG

TIAO QIAO YEN

1820

8 KMS

CABLE CAR

TAN JA CHIU

LIAN HUA FENG
1860

15 KMS

YU BINGUAN
(HOTEL)

YUN GOA SI
900

1680

TIAN DU
FENG 1810

BAN SHAN
SI 1340

CABLE CAR

7 KMS

KU
ZHOU QI

630

AREA MAP
N

WUHU

CHANG JIANG (YANGSTE RIVER)

TAO YUAN

TIAN YUAN
BINGUAN (HOTEL)
630

TONGLING

GUICHI

ANQING

HANGZHOU

JIU HUA SHAN
1341

HUANG SHAN
1860

TUNXI

SHEXIAN

HUANG SHAN DA
MEN (GATE)

TUNG KOU

TUNXI (HUANGSHAN)
SHEXIAN
HANGZHOU

N

SCALE 0   2   4   6   8   KMS

it's a warm day. Carry an umbrella too, as this mountain is in one of the wettest parts of China.
Maps Several maps and booklets can be bought at the Tao Yuan Binguan; and the latest travel guidebook, **China**, Lonely Planet, for possible updates.

The Great Wall Hike, Shanhaiguan, Hebei Province, China

Featured here is a hike along part of the Great Wall of China. This ancient wall snakes its way from east to west across northern China for about 5000 kms. At times throughout history the wall was a continuous unit, but today some parts are missing. Mother nature has taken her toll in places, while in other sites man has carried away stones to be used as building material.

Almost all tourists, including Chinese visitors, see the Great Wall at one of three locations. Most of the big crowds visit the place called **Badaling**, about 60 kms north of Beijing. The wall there has been restored for distances of about 2 or more kms on either side of the highway just for visitors to see. This site is a real gold mine for China, and as of the year 2000, it was announced that preparations are going ahead to preserve and restore more sections of the wall.

Also, many tourists visit the western end of the wall at **Jiayuguan** (Jiayu Pass). This is in western Gansu Province, and is conveniently located on the main rail line running to Urumqi in Xinjiang Province. The third place is at the eastern end of the wall at Shanhaiguan (Shanhai Pass), where the wall meets the sea.

Some adventurous travelers take a late afternoon bus or train from Beijing to Badaling, hike up one side of the wall or the other, and sleep overnight in one of the watch towers; then return to Beijing as the crowds come in for the mid-day viewing. This is all very touristy, therefore perhaps the best place to visit and hike along the wall is at **Shanhaiguan**, where there's a lot less traffic and tourists.

To get there, take a train from Beijing or Tianjin to the northeast and to Shanhaiguan in Hebei Province. You could camp in the hills northwest of town, but there are now 4 hotels in Shanhaiguan which accept foreigners. The Shengyi Binguan (Shengyi Hotel) is not far from the train station, but it's expensive. This is where the author stayed in 1984. Most foreigners stay in the Jingshan Binguan inside the walled city and near the East Gate, otherwise known as the First Pass Under Heaven.

The author spent 2 days in the area. The first day, 6/19/1984, he walked to the sea, via the top of the wall. To find the wall, walk east from the Shengyi Binguan. You'll know it when you see it, as it runs right through the middle of town. Then climb up on top wherever you can. The wall along this section is 7 to 8 meters high, giving one a tree-top view of the city and farms & gardens. Walk southeast along the top to the very end of the the wall, where huge blocks of granite lie scattered on the beach where the wall enters the sea.

The second day, the author walked northwest from town, again on top of the wall, to the peak marked 500 meters. The wall seems to disappear or get smaller as it winds its way northwest into the distant hills. The best part of the wall is from the sea to the first peak at 460 meters. Several people could sleep in the watch tower located at the 260 meter mark.

Besides the Great Wall itself, you must also visit the walled part of the city of Shanhaiguan. The wall around the old town is 8 to 10 meters high and very well-preserved, perhaps the best-preserved

This part of the Great Wall of China is just north of Shanhaiguan.

Map 207-1, Great Wall Hike, Shanhaiguan, Hebei Province, China

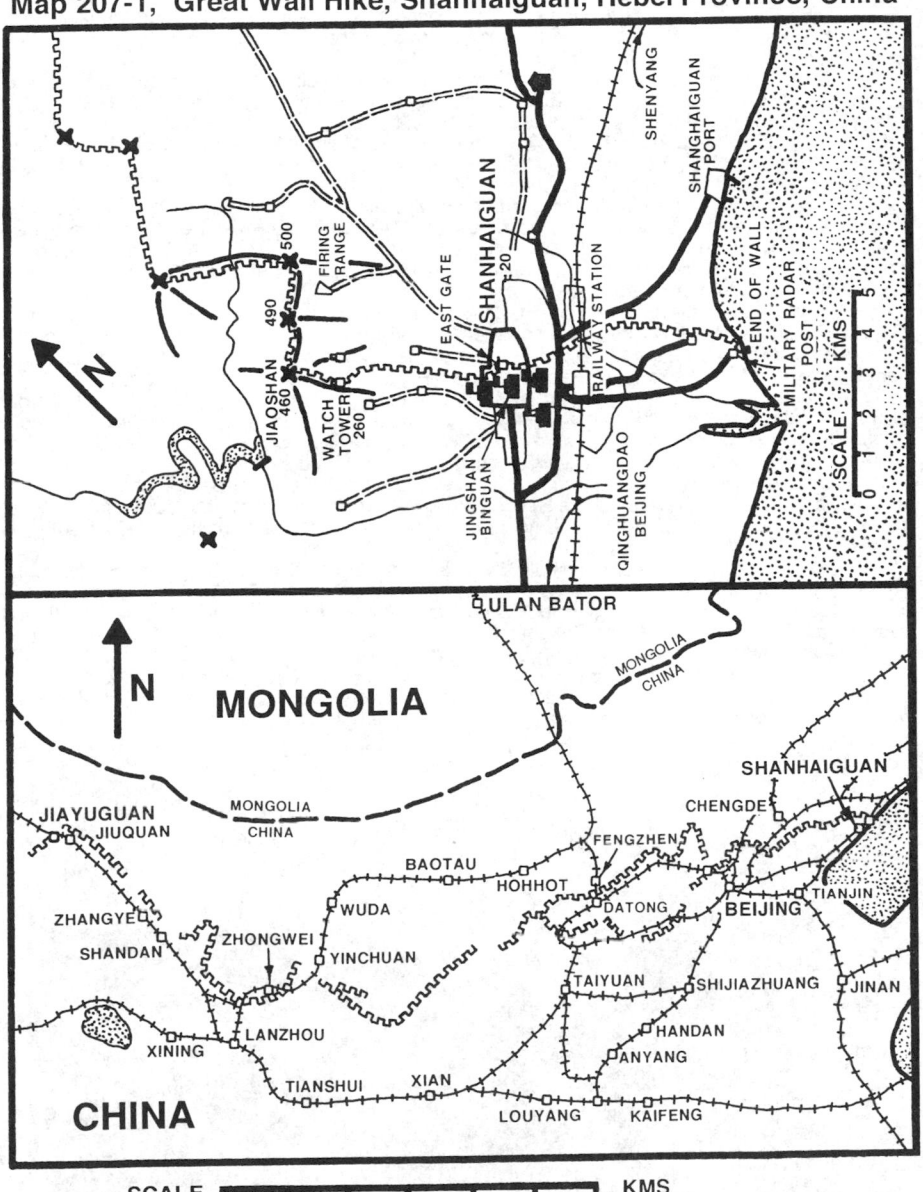

fortress or walled city the author has ever seen.

Maps The map *People of China,* from National Geographic; and map of *Shanhaiguan* (buy at your hotel or train station); also, the latest travel guidebook, **China**, Lonely Planet.

Changbai Shan (Baitoushan), Jilin Province, China-Korea

Changbai Shan lies on the Chinese-Korean border, almost due south of Jilin and Mudanjiang in northeast China. This mountain, lake and giant caldera are called *Baitoushan* in the book, **Volcanos of the World**. Perhaps this is the Korean name (?).

This caldera may have had some kind of volcanic activity in 1668 & 1702, according to the book above, but these were small compared to the colossal explosion that took place in about 1050 AD. That's when it exploded with a ranking of VEI-7 (Volcanic Explosion Index) scale. Only 3 others volcanos have been rated a VEI-7 during human history: Tambora--1815, (Indonesia); Crater Lake--4895 BC (Oregon, USA); and Kikai--4350 BC (Ryukyu Islands, just south of southern Japan). This is an almost identical twin to Crater Lake in the state of Oregon.

The highest point on the caldera rim surrounding the lake is Bai Yun Feng at 2744 meters. The mountain and the lake are about evenly divided between China and Korea. On the Korean side, there's a dirt road running to the rim where a communications station is located. China also has one on the north side of the mountain. There is one outlet to the lake which drains north. Changbai Shan is a Chinese national nature reserve.

The author visited this mountain on 7/1/1984, but lots of things have changed, including names! The book below calls the town the author knew as **Ardo, Baihe**, and it appears that **Shenyang** is now called **Tonghua** (?). Perhaps some of these names are Korean or Chinese (?). On this map, both names are used. Also, it seems permission is no longer needed to visit this region--good news.

There are now 2 normal ways to get to Ardo/Baihe, the starting point for the trip to **Changbai Shan**. One way is to take a train from Jilin to Dunhua where there are plenty of places to stay. From Dunhua, there are about 6 buses a day running to Ardo. The first leaves at 7:45am. You could also get there from Mudanjiang, the border town of Tumen, then Antu, and Ardo/Baihe.

The second normal way is from Tonghua, located to the west. This may be what the author knew as Shenyang (?). From Tonghua, there are 2 daily trains to Ardo; one leaves at 9:05pm, and arrives at 4:36am; the other leaves at 8:45am, arriving at Baihe at 5:15pm. These may change by the time you get there!

In Ardo/Baihe, there are several small, cheap and comfortable Korean-type yogwans (Korean-style hotels) near the train station. To get to Changbai Shan, take one of several daily buses leaving from in front of the train station, beginning at about 6am. Round-trip ticket for the 55 or 40 kms (?) trip cost about US$5 in the late 1990's. The entry fee to the mountain is about US$15, plus another US$5 if you want to climb to the lake called Tian Chi (Heavenly Lake).

On the mountain, there are 3 binguans or hotels; or you could camp, as this is wilderness-type country. There's a trail and a road to the communications or met. station, which is very near one peak of about 2680 meters. Another trail runs upcanyon from the hotels to a 68-meter-high waterfall, then

Tian Chi (Heavenly Lake) fills the caldera on top of Changbai Shan.

Map 208-1, Changbai Shan (Baitoushan), Jilin Prov., China-Korea

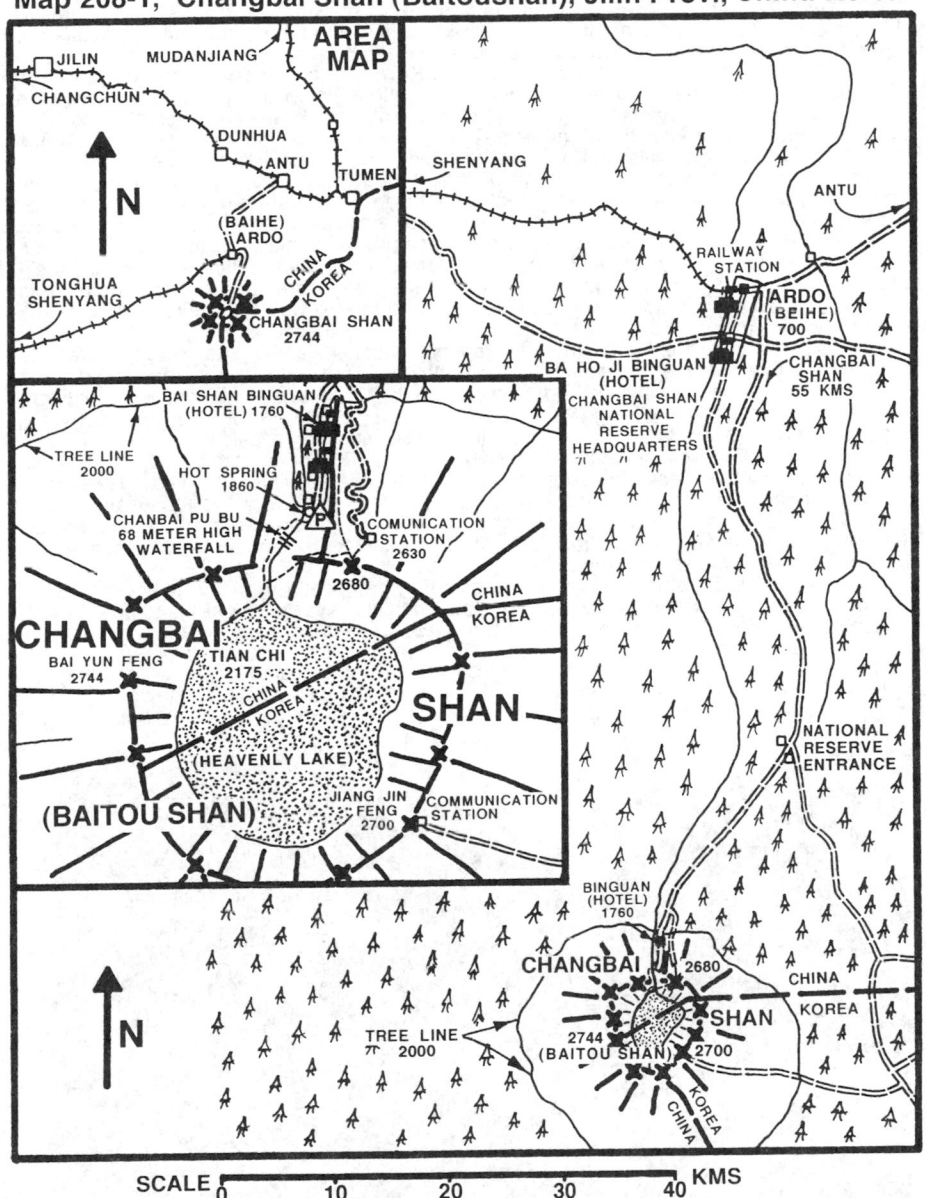

on to the lake. There are small shops selling food near the hotels, but if you plan to stay a while and camp, buy your food in Ardo/Baihe. Visit this mountain only in the months of June to September, the only time transport is available to the mountain.

Maps A booklet with a map can be bought at the railway station or hotels in Ardo/Baihe, or on the mountain; TPC map *F-9C,* 1:500,000, and the latest travel guidebook, **China**, Lonely Planet.

Taech'ongbong Peak, Sorak San, Korea

The Sorak San Massif offers some of the best hiking possibilities in Korea. The highest summit is called Taech'ongbong at 1708 meters. Sorak San and the surrounding peaks are made of granite and other metamorphic-type rocks.

Sorak San is located near the east coast of Korea, not far north of the large city of Kangnung, and just west of Sogcho. Kangnung is on the main rail line and motorway serving the east coast of the country. From Kangnung take one of many buses north along the coast to Daepodong, then west to Sorakdong, at the main entrance to the Sorak San National Park. Bus service exists on almost all roads in Korea, making travel easy. Hitch hiking is pretty good too.

With the economic boom in Asia and Korea in the 1980's & 90's, and with many people owning cars, Sorakdong has become a real tourist trap. Located there are many hotels or yogwans, restaurants and souvenir shops. There's also a cable car to or near the top of a peak called Kwonkumsong, but the trail from there south along the ridge may be closed (?).

Beyond Sorakdong, are many trails, most of which are over-used. During summer, the main trail heading south to the hostel and eventually to **Sorak San**, has a variety of vendors offering food, souvenirs and anything that will sell. Most hikers can easily walk from Sorakdong to Sorak San round-trip in one day, then get a bus from there to the next destination.

The hostel just mentioned is similar to the mountain huts in the Alps and in Japan, with food and beds available. Another hut, marked at 1075 meters, is not as fancy but food can be found there. When the author was in these mountains on 8/22/1977, someone had pitched a tent right on the summit of Taech'ongbong (Sorak San) and was selling soda pop, candy and other goodies. Needless to say, there is no problem finding food in these mountains.

Nigel Jenkins offers some updated information from 1/2000. He went to Osaek Hot Springs, just south of the highest peak, and climbed north from there on a winter day-hike. He returned along a west ridge trail and the Hangyeryong Pass. Lots of public transport to Osaek Yuksa, even in winter, where you'll find several yogwans and one huge hotel with shops and a disco. This place is now part of the national park with entrance fees of about US$2; hopefully this money will be used to keep the place clean.

The mountain tops are generally rounded, as if they had been run over by glaciers, but the main canyon leading to Sorak San from Sorakdong, has many good rock climbing possibilities. Camping is regulated, so you're advised to ask questions before dropping a tent. Beware of leaving a tent unguarded.

All trails which cross difficult places, have been fixed with ladders, ramps and bridges-- something like the Dolimiti of northern Italy. Also, in some of the more remote areas of the park are found several Buddhist temples. The water in streams used to be good, but could get

This foto shows one of the *Iron Routes* in the gorge north of Sorak San.

Map 209-1, Taech'ongbong Peak, Sorak San, Korea

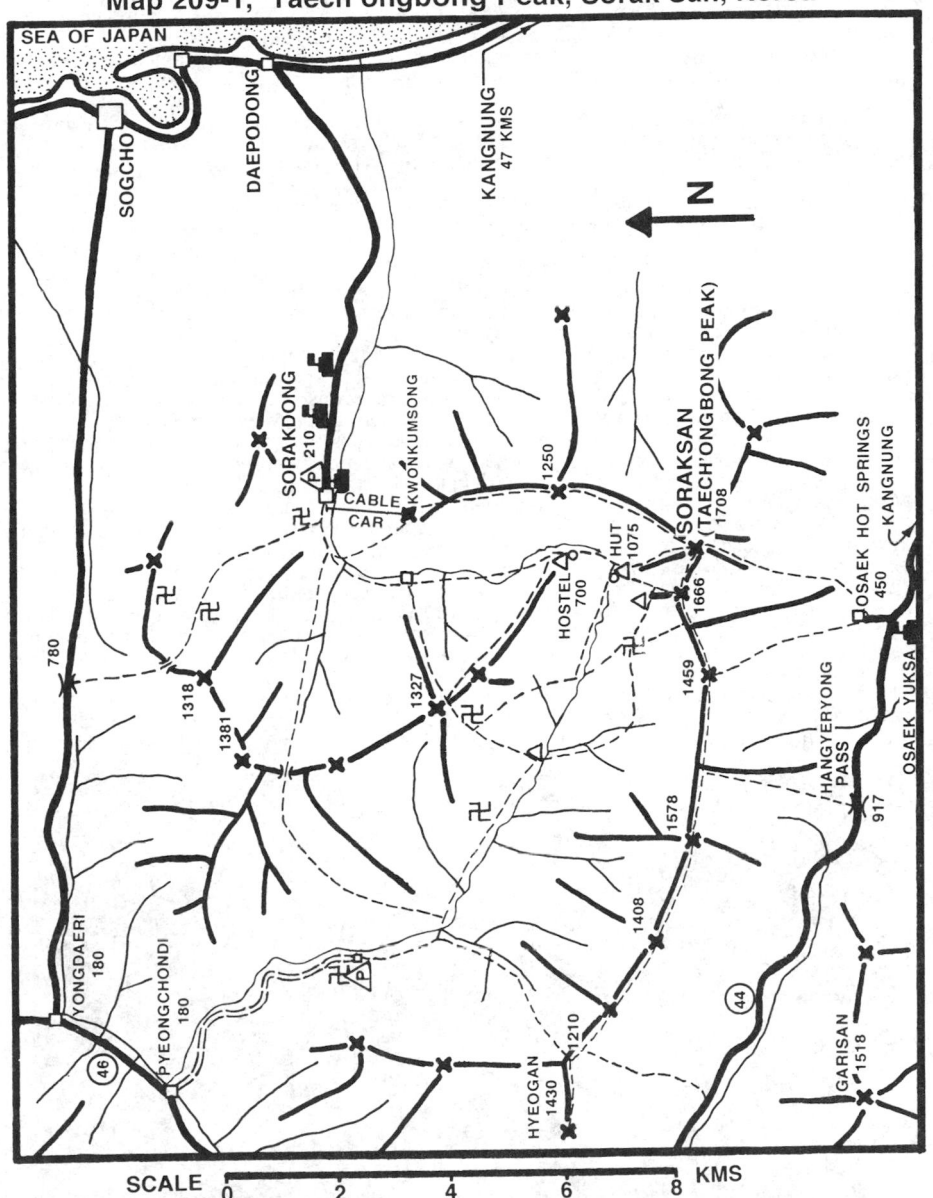

polluted in summer with too many people now. Climb in these mountains from about lake May through October.

Maps *Guide Map of Climbing Mt. Seolag* (Sorak San), 1:75,000, Jung-Ang Map & Chart Service, 125-1, Gongpyeong Dong, Jongro-Gu, Seoul; or the book, **Mountaineering Guide Maps in Korea**, ISBN 89-390-0013-7. Buy these in Seoul; and the latest travel guidebook to Korea.

Pirobong Peak, Odaesan, Korea

Of the 4 mountain areas in southern Korea covered in this book, Odaesan is the shortest at only 1563 meters elevation. It's also possibly the least-visited of the 4. However, that doesn't make it the least enjoyable. In fact, the Buddhist temples in this range are as interesting as in any of the mountains of Korea, with the exception of Sogri San (which is not featured in this book).

Odaesan and the surrounding mountains are heavily forested, from top to bottom. Nowhere in this area do the summits rise above the tree line, with the exception of the last few meters on the highest peak of Odaesan which is called **Pirobong**. This region is now part of the Odaesan National Park.

Odaesan is located just north of the Yeongdong Expressway, the one linking Seoul with Kangnung and the east coast. Hitch hiking on the expressway can be good, but on side roads maybe difficult.

Getting to this area is easy, as with all the mountain areas of Korea. In the past you could get buses only to as far as the bridge about 2 kms north or above Wolchongsa (sometimes called Dongsan Ri), but Nigel Jenkins informs the author that as of 1/2000, you can take local buses all the way to Sangwonsa Temple, even in winter.

If you're coming from Seoul by bus, they'll probably set you off at, or near, the Daegwanryeong ski resort. From there you'll have to catch another bus to Ganpyeongri then north into the main valley to **Odaesan** and the the Sangwonsa Temple, as shown. If you're coming from the Kangnung side, there are many local buses going to the same area.

At Wolchongsa, and up the road for about 2 kms, there are several yogwans (small traditional Korean hotels where you sleep on the floor) and many small shops, eating places, and a large 4-star hotel catering to skiers. According the Jenkins, there's also a ski resort at or near Wolchongsa (?), which wasn't there on 8/20/1977 during the author's visit. This is the last place in the valley where you can surely buy food and accommodation. Further up the road there's a campsite (and possibly a store?).

From the bridge above Wolchongsa, it's a 1 1/2 hour walk (or a short bus ride) to the Sangwonsa (it may be called Sangweon?) Temple. That's where the main trail to the summit of Odaesan, or Pirobong Peak, begins. Enroute, you'll pass 2 more temples before reaching the top. This trail is good, but others in the area may not be as well-used. The late information from Jenkins indicate there are some yogwans and stores open year-round in Odaesan, most specifically around Wolchongsa.

As for camping, you used to be able to camp anywhere, but with national park status and lots more people, you'll probably have to camp in a designated campsite only. However, if you walked up and out of the valley and onto one of the mountain sides, you could surely find a quiet

The trail to the top of Odaesan is forested with many rest stops.

Map 210-1, Pirobong Peak, Odaesan, Korea

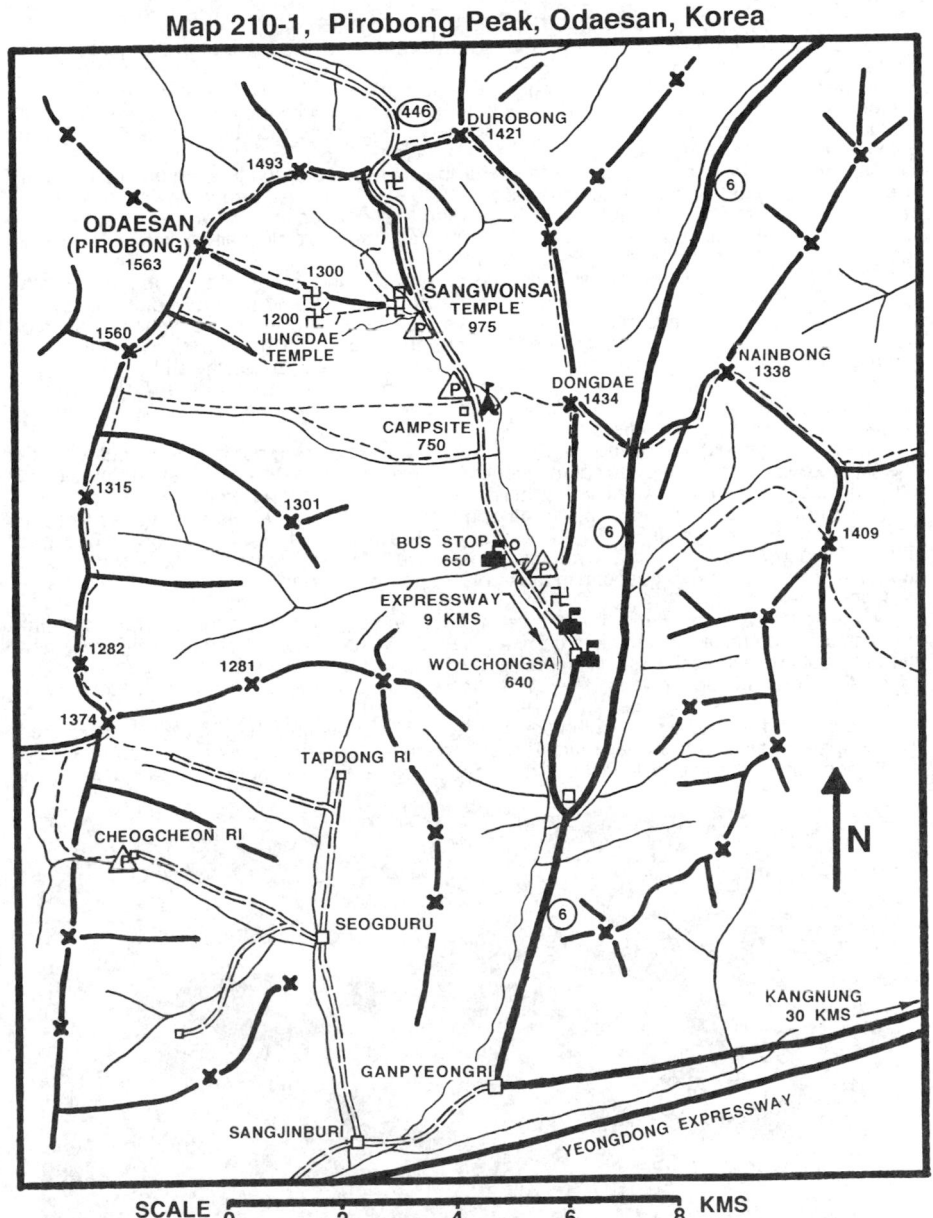

place to bivouac for the night--but never leave an unattended tent in such a situation! Climbing in these mountains is usually from sometime in May through October with the fall colors.

Maps *Guide Map of Climbing Mt. Odae (Odaesan)*, 1:75,000, from Jung-Ang Map & Chart Service, 125-1, Gongpyeong Dong, Jongro-Gu, Seoul; and the book, **Mountaineering Guide Maps in Korea**, ISBN 89-390-0013-7; and the latest travel guidebook to Korea.

Jirisan (Chirisan), Korea

In south central Korea, not far from the south coast, is located one of the largest national parks in the country. Within Jirisan National Park is the second highest peak in South Korea called Jirisan (apparently the one single highest peak is called *Ch'onwangbong*?) at 1915 meters. In some romanized texts, you may see this mountain with the name Chirisan; with Chi replacing the Ji. But the author distinctly remembers the pronunciation being more like *Jidi San*, with the "d" replacing the "r" sound.

As with all national parks in southern Korea, public transportation to even the most remote areas is rather good. With the author's visit on 8/29 & 8/30/1977, there were very few private autos, but that has changed as of 2000, according to Nigel Jenkins. Now many people have cars, but there are still large buses making several daily runs to almost all backcountry villages, including small places inside Jirisan National Park.

There are several ways to reach this national park. The author began in Jinju (on the Namhae Expressway) to the southeast of this mapped area, and took a bus to the town of Jongsan, literally at the base of the mountain. With full pack, he climbed the highest peak, then traversed the main part of the range heading west and finally walked down to Yonggang, then got a bus to Tabri. Later, another bus was taken to the Namhae Expressway and beyond.

You can also approach this mountain area from the north and Gaheding, but it's recommended one of the southern approaches be used, as they are nearer the expressway and probably have better public transport.

The author found hitch hiking good on expressways in Korea, but it was difficult on back roads; however, with more cars, and on weekends, hitching a ride may be faster than taking a bus, especially in mountain areas where there may only be one or 2 buses a day.

Once into these mountains and on **Jirisan**, there are many well-used trails, as Koreans being Buddhists, are great lovers of mountains. There are at least 2 good huts on or near Jirisan. In 1977, they lacked any real sleeping places and are, for the most part, only small stores. Plenty of food can be found in these places, either hot and cooked, or of the packaged or snack variety.

In the valleys or canyons, water is never a problem, as Korea gets a fair amount of rainfall; but higher on the ridges you need to carry a full water bottle. There is always water at or near the huts, but sometimes that is rain water; so if you're there in a dry period you may have to pay for it. Also, with the big crowds in these mountains on weekends, watch out for polluted water. Best to take it from a spring if possible.

Late spring or early fall may be the best time to hike, but the huts may be closed at that time. The summer season and on weekends is the time when Koreans get out on the trails. On the south slope of Jirisan above Jongsan, there's one Buddhist temple complete with monks, which

This is the hut and hut keeper just west of Jirisan.

Map 211-1, Jirisan (Chirisan), Korea

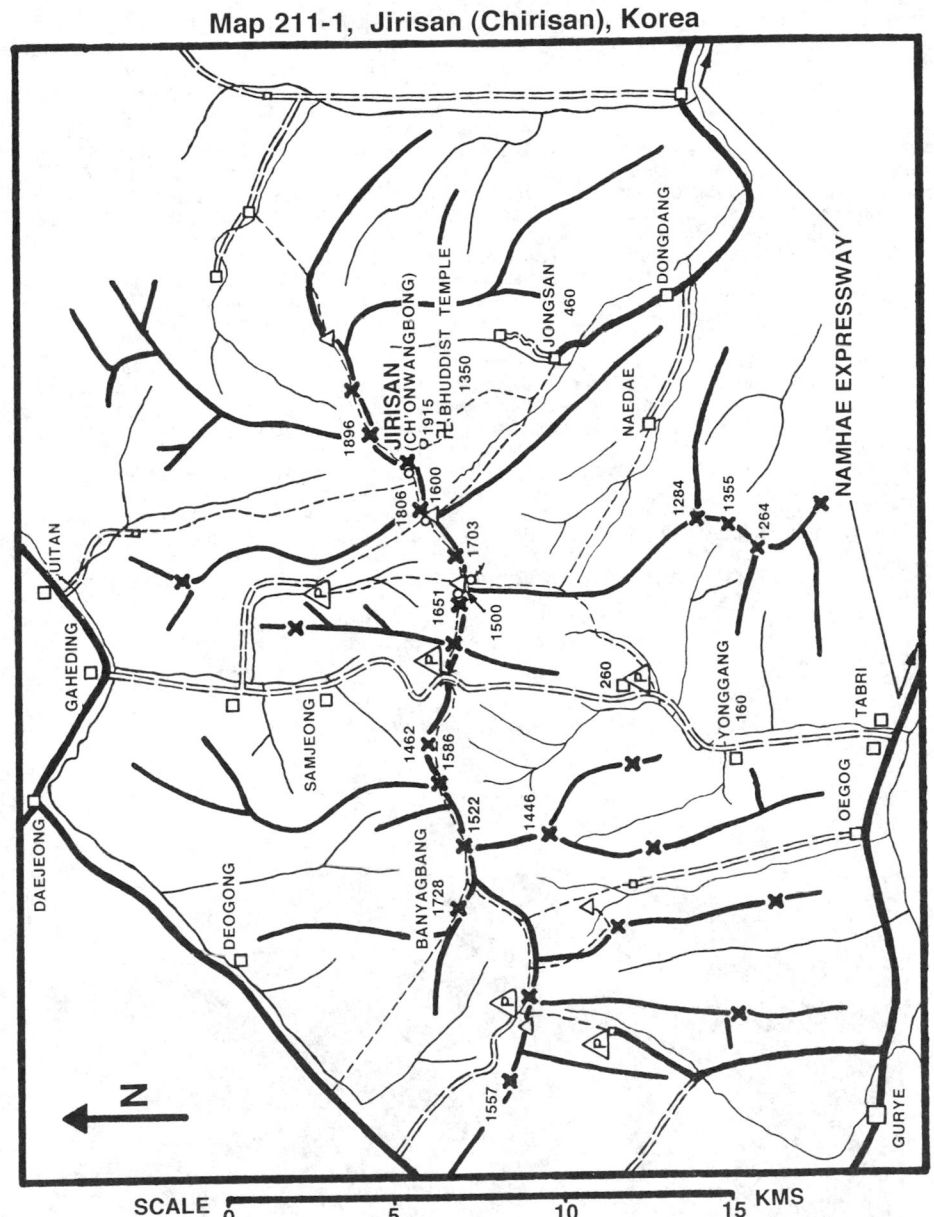

SCALE | 0 .... 5 .... 10 .... 15 KMS

makes the trip more interesting.
Maps *Guide Map of Climbing Mt. Jiri (Jiri San)*, 1:75,000, from Jung-Ang Map & Chart Service, 125-1, Gongpyeong Dong, Jongro-Gu, Seoul; and the book, **Mountaineering Guide Maps in Korea**, ISBN 89-390-0013-7; and the latest travel guidebook to Korea.

Halla San, Chejudo (Cheju Island), Korea

In the channel separating Korea and Japan are many islands, one of which is Chejudo (Cheju Island). The highest summit on Chejudo, and the highest mountain in southern Korea, is Halla San at 1950 meters. Like all the higher mountainous regions in southern Korea, this too is a national park. Like all or most of the islands in that channel, this is volcanic. The surface is pocked with cinder cones, some old, some rather recent. According to the book, **Volcanos of the World**, Halla San has had 2 historic eruptions; one was in 1002 AD, the last in 1007 AD. Both were explosive eruptions from flank vents, but the author doesn't know which vents or craters. This volcano and/or island is certainly not yet considered totally extinct.

There are 2 ways to reach Chejudo. One is by air (unfamiliar to the author), the other is by ferry. One ferry route is from Pusan on the southeast coast of the Korean Peninsula, the other is from the town of Mogpo, located on the southwest corner of the Korean mainland.

From Mogpo, there were two ferries daily in 1977, each taking 7 hours. Cheju City on the north shore of the island is the ferry terminal and a good place to visit. There you will find many yogwans or Korean-style hotels in all price ranges. Expect wetter and warmer conditions on Cheju Island than in the rest of Korea.

From Cheju City, there are many buses running to all parts of the island, and especially to Seogwipo. These buses head south over the hump on the east side of Halla San. Any of these buses can drop you off at either of the 2 trailheads shown along that eastern route. Other buses run south along the west side of the volcano to Jungmun. They too can drop you off at any trailhead.

Halla San can easily be climbed in one day if one of the 2 western routes or the northern route is taken. The 2 other routes, from the east, and the southeast, are longer and some people may require an overnight stay on the mountain, especially if you arrive late in the day.

On the mountain are several huts; some rather good, which you have to pay for; others too not so good and are in need of repairs. At any rate, you can spend a night on the mountain without a tent. At most huts, especially those higher on the mountain, food or meals can also be bought. Most of these huts are similar to those in Japan and Europe.

At the beginning of each trail is a national park building and park entrance gate. Everyone must pay a small entry fee. Someone at the entry gate will give you a small map, and any information needed as to the opening or closing of huts and food availability. If you're there during the summer or holiday months, all huts should be open and serving food. For those wishing to camp, that can be done anywhere. The author camped the night of 9/1/1977 inside the summit or main crater with plenty of water available in 2 nearby ponds.

A wide-angle lens view of the entire crater at the top of Halla San.

Map 212-1, Halla San, Chejudo (Cheju Island), Korea

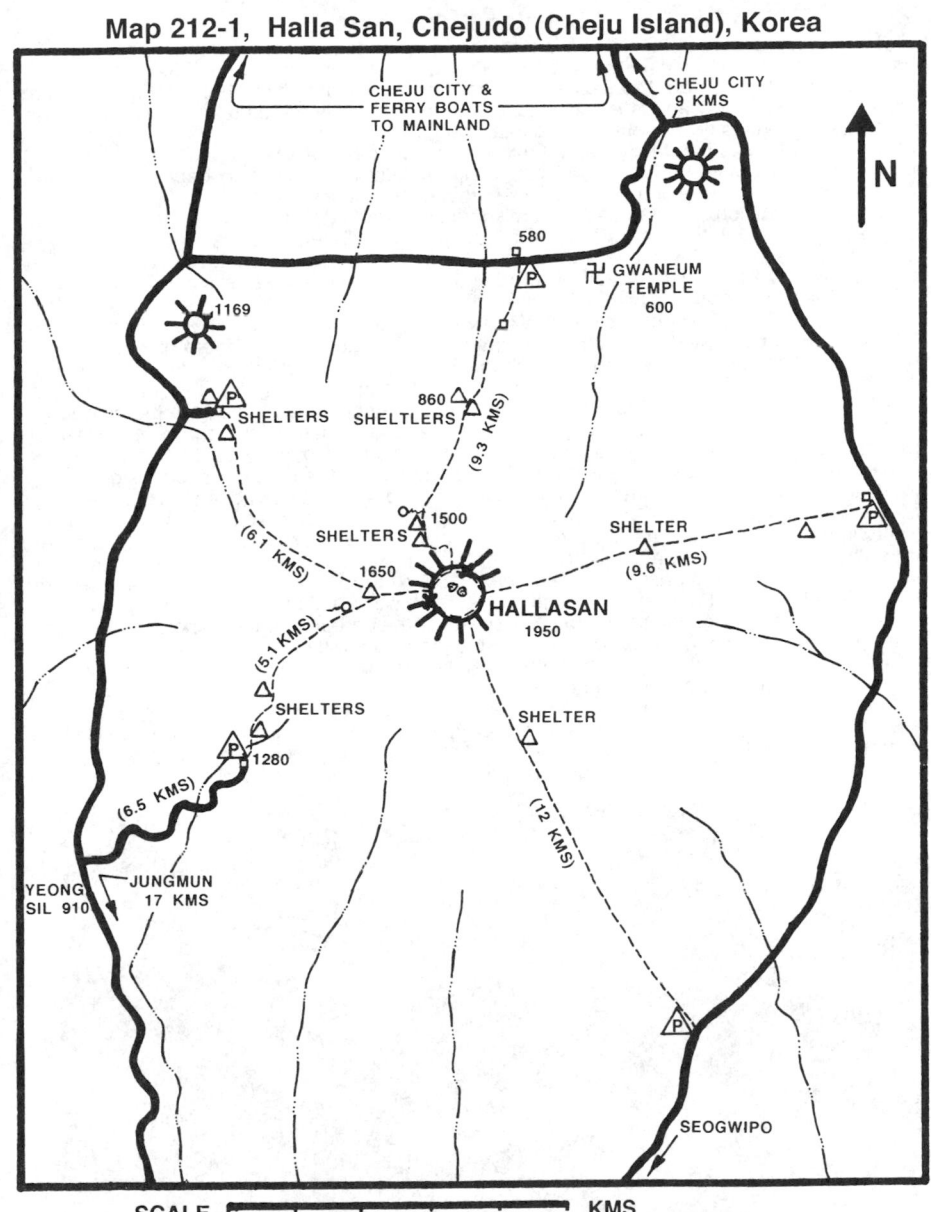

CHEJU CITY &
FERRY BOATS
TO MAINLAND

CHEJU CITY
9 KMS

N

580

P

卍 GWANEUM
TEMPLE
600

1169

P

SHELTERS

860 △
SHELTLERS

(9.3 KMS)

SHELTERS △ 1500

SHELTER
(9.6 KMS)

P

1650

HALLASAN
1950

(6.1 KMS)

(5.1 KMS)

SHELTERS

SHELTER

P
1280

(6.5 KMS)

(12 KMS)

YEONG
SIL 910

JUNGMUN
17 KMS

P

SEOGWIPO

SCALE 0 1 2 3 4 5 KMS

Maps *Tourist Map of Cheju*, 1:100,000, from Jung-Ang Map & Chart Service, 125-1, Gongpyeong Dong, Jongro-Gu, Seoul; and the book, **Mountaineering Guide Maps in Korea**, ISBN 89-390-0013-7; and the latest travel guidebook to Korea.

465

Sabalon Kuh, Iran

The third highest mountain in Iran is Sabalon Kuhn at 4821 meters. Sabalon is a very old and eroded volcano, located in the extreme northwest corner of Iran, not far south of the former USSR border, which is now Azerbaijan. It's also located about halfway between the southern part of the Kavkazian (Caucasus) Mountains and the Elburz Mountains of north central Iran. However, it belongs to neither of these mountain ranges.

The author has no information about this extinct volcano, but a wild guess would be that it last erupted perhaps 40,000 to 50,000 years ago. It still retains a conal shape, but it's highly eroded, with several peaks and one small lake around the summit area.

Getting to Sabalon is quite easy. There's a major highway running south of the mountain from Tabriz to Ardabil, then to Astara, on the Caspian Sea Coast. Another highway skirts the north side of the mountain. There are several buses, and perhaps group taxis, on these roads each day, linking Tabriz with Ardabil. There are also a fair number of trucks and private autos, which makes hitch hiking a possibility.

Here's what the author did beginning 9/27/1974. He made the climb in 4 days from Ardabil, all on foot. He walked west from Ardabil on one of many vehicle tracks. There are a number of very small villages on the way, and many sheep & horse trails all over. But, it's one long walk direct from Ardabil! The author's total walk-time was 32 hours.

What the author is calling *Abegarum* on the map, may be called *Sareiyn* in the guidebook below; if so, there are hot springs and some kind of accommodations there now (not in 1974). You could likely find a taxi in Ardabil to take you there, which would make it a 2-day climb.

Or try a route from either Meshkin Shahr or Nir, towns on the north and south sides of the mountain. Get off a bus at either town and either walk or hire a taxi to get a little closer. The country in these parts is treeless with some rolling hills so it's easy to set your sights on the mountain and walk. There are a number of stream valleys near the peak, and as one gets nearer the mountain, and away from the plain surrounding it, there is plenty of water available.

There are also many trails and a few very small villages in the area, as well as nomadic people, possibly Kurds (?), with their round *yurt* tents. Visiting and seeing these people is one of the best reasons for climbing the mountain. However, be careful about leaving an unguarded, low altitude camp. If your last camp is high on the mountain and in a hidden place, and with no nomadic camps in view, it may be safe; but the author recommends the tent be taken down and hidden while you make the final ascent.

Both Nir and Meshkin Shahr are small places, but both have food shops. Meshkin Shahr has some hot springs. However, do your shopping in either Tabriz or Ardabil. The best time to climb is from June through October. There's a small amount of perpetual snow on the north side of the summit, but no special equipment is needed.

The author and the summit of Sabalon Kuh in the background.

Map 213-1, Sabalon Kuh, Iran

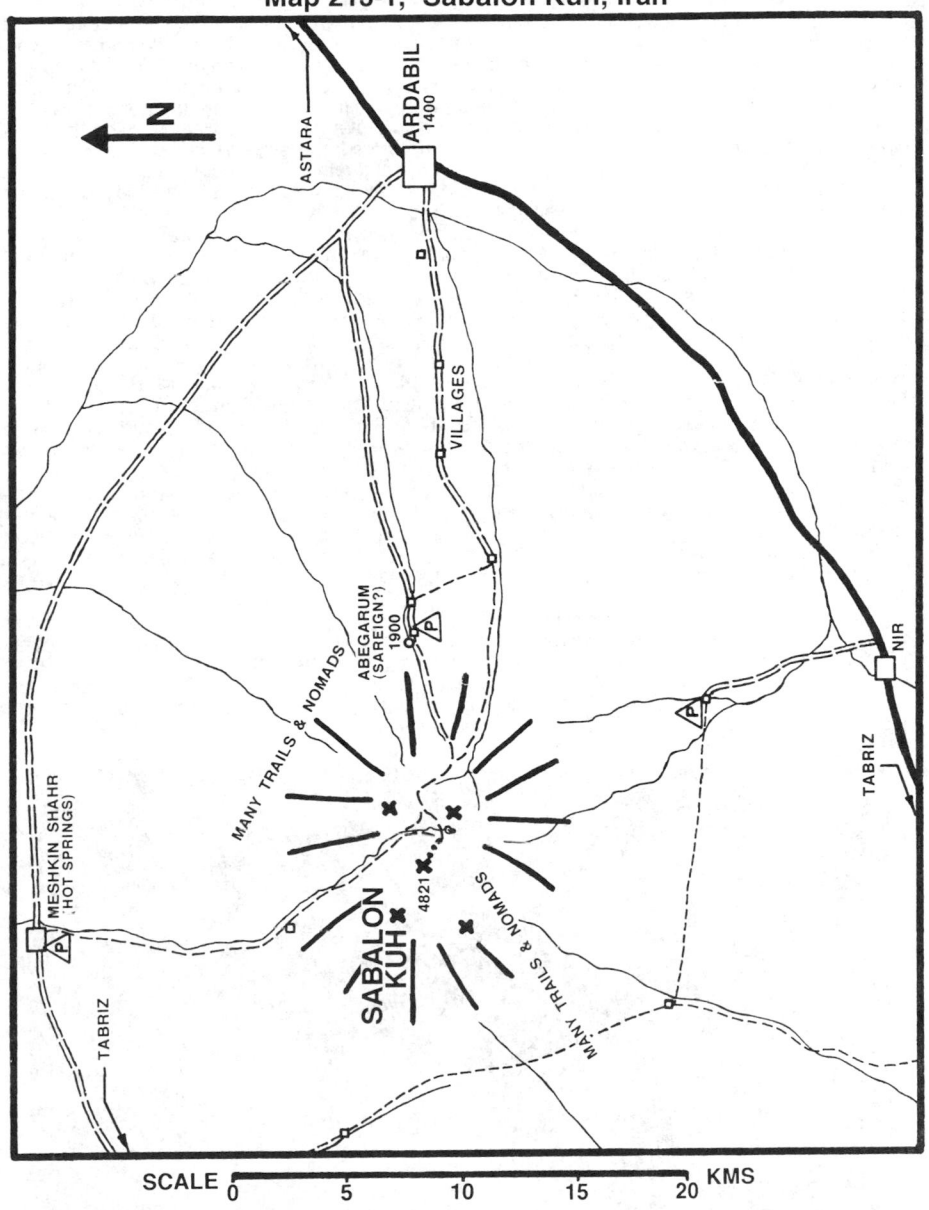

Maps Any *Iran tourist highway map,* 1:2,500,000, from Iranian tourist office; DMA map *NJ-38,* Series 1301, 1:1,000,000; or the better TPC map *G-5A,* 1:500,000; and the travel guidebook, **Iran**, Lonely Planet.

Alum Kuh & Takht-e-Soliman, Elburz Mountains, Iran

The Elburz Mountains (Reshten-ye Alborz), which form an arc around the south end of the Caspian Sea in northern Iran, is a strange mixture of tectonics or mountain building processes. In the center of the range is Damavand, a semiactive volcano. See next map. West of that, and northwest of Tehran, are totally different mountains. This massif, with the highest summit being Alum Kuh at 4840 meters, is an igneous intrusion with granite rocks in the heart of this area.

Alum Kuh is the 2nd highest mountain in Iran, and probably the one which can be the most challenging to climbers. Its north face is one of the more impressive walls outside the Andes and Himalayas. It has about 600 meters of near vertical granite. The second highest summit in this region, and one almost as famous, is Takht-e-Soliman at 4650 meters. This may be the 4th highest summit in Iran, but it is not as difficult to climb as Alum Kuh.

To get there, take a bus west from Tehran on the main international highway. At Karaj, you'll turn north toward the Caspian Sea Coast. At a small town on that highway called Marzanabad, get off one bus and onto another going in the direction of Kelardasht, and with a little luck, one going to Rudbarak. There should be much better transport now than when the author was there in 1974. Kelardasht is a large village, with several shops and stores. The author bought all his food for the climb in 2 of those shops.

From Kelardasht, there's a paved road up the canyon to Rudbarak, where you'll find a mountaineer's bungalow with several rooms for climbers. Check with the *Mountaineering Federation of Iran* (about 200 meters from the old US Embassy in Tehran) for an update on facilities in Rudbarak and a good map. The vicinity of Rudbarak was filling up with new homes in 1974, and now a paved road runs up the canyon several kms to a mine. There's likely some kind of bus service from Kelardasht to Rudbarak. Or look for a taxi, walk or hitch hike.

The author spent 4 days in this area from Rudbarak beginning 9/22/1974. Beyond the mine is a 4WD road, then a trail. At Vandarban, a stream junction with nearby shepherd huts, turn right or west to get into the big cirques on the north side. You can also turn left and follow a stream to Tanakrud, which is likely a shepherd camp with huts. Further up that same valley, you will find some easier routes up the southern slopes of Alum Kuh, plus 2 small huts as shown on the map, according to Andrej Stritar.

There was, apparently as late as in the 1990's, one good shelter named *Sarchal Hut*, which can be used for a fee. Another higher hut was in ruins, wiped out by an avalanche. From that old ruined shelter, head southeast across the glacier (no crevasses) and easily climb **Siah Sang** at 4603 meters. You can hopefully climb **Alum Kuh** from along that east ridge. The northeast face is very technical. Head southwest from the Sarchal Hut to a col between Rostam Nisht & **Takht-e-Soliman**, then climb the north ridge to Soliman's summit.

The north face of Alum Kuh is one of the best rock climbs in west Asia.

Map 214-1, Alum Kuh & Takht-e-Soliman, Elburz Mtns., Iran

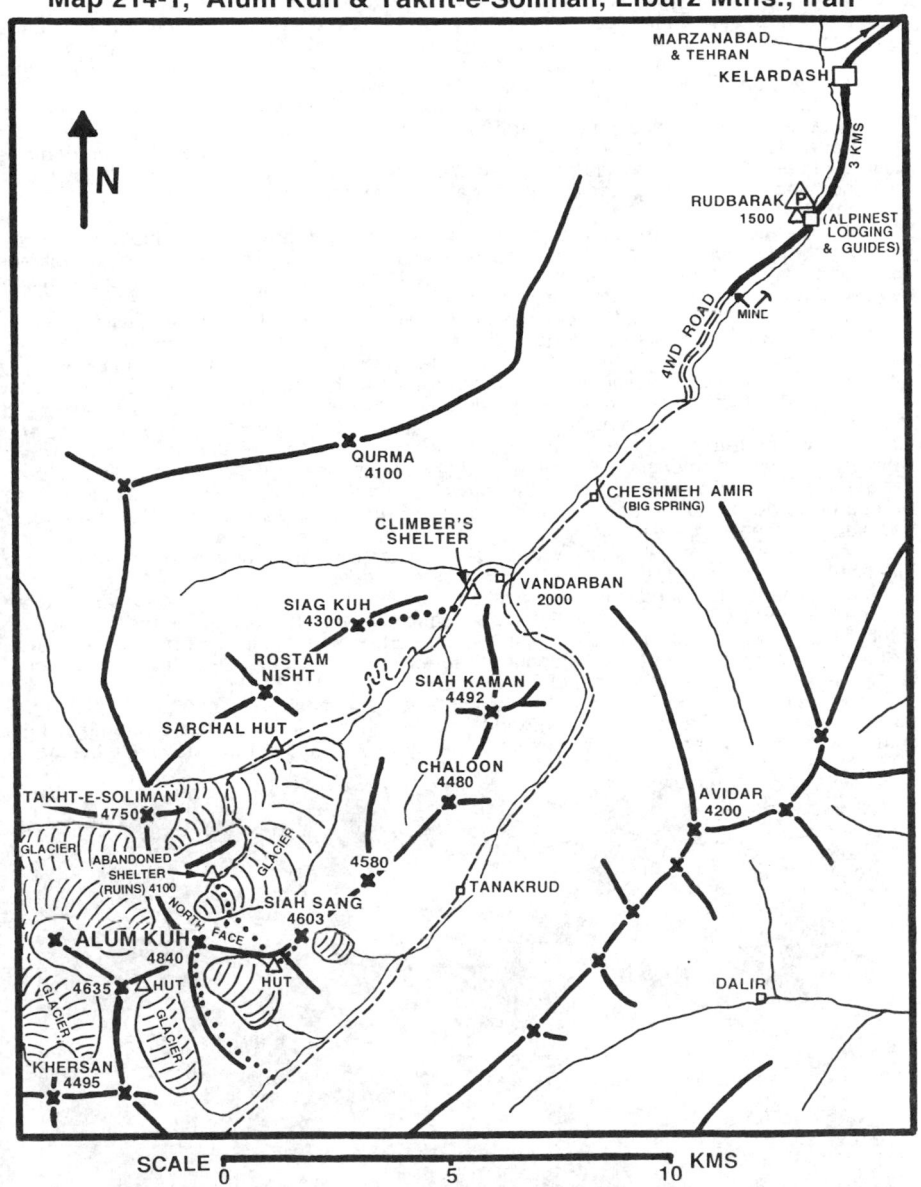

SCALE 0   5   10 KMS

Someone in Rudbarak can update this information. To climb one mountain and return to Rudbarak will take 4 or 5 days--unless a difficult route is taken. The author climbed Siah Sang, but had cold snowy weather and could hardly see any peaks. His 4 day total walk-time was 28 hours.

Maps TPC map *G-5A,* 1:500,000; and the books, **Atlante di Alpinismo nel Mondo**, Mario Fantin, Club Alpino Italiano (shows routes by Italian climbers); and the travel guidebook, **Iran**, Lonely Planet.

Damavand Volcano, Elburz Mountains, Iran

In the central part of the Elburz Mountains (Reshteh-ye Alborz) in north central Iran, is the country's highest mountain, Damavand Kuh at 5671 meters. The Elburz Mountains form a crescent-shaped half moon at the south end of the Caspian Sea and almost all mountains in this area are folded and uplifted. However, Damavand is a volcano.

In the book, **Volcanos of the World**, it states this mountain's last eruption was sometime in the Holocene (within the last 10,000 years). It seems that it must have been sometime rather recent and historic, perhaps within the last 1000 or 2000 years. The author climbed this mountain in 9/1970 (his information has been updated with the help from the book below), and found hot steam and sulfur gases coming out of vents at the summit. It retains a near perfect conal shape.

To climb **Damavand**, take a minibus or shared taxi from Tehran's Eastern Bus Station in the direction of Amol, but get off at Raineh Junction and the road going up to the village of Raineh, just up the southeast slopes. There you'll find a small bazaar, and a few shops where food can be bought; however, it's best to do your shopping in Tehran.

From Raineh Junction, walk or get in a shared taxi going up to Raineh, then walk or hire a taxi to take you to another small village, believed to be called *Gusfan Sarah*, at about 3000 meters. The author found it more of a military camp than village. It had a small store and running water in ditches. Coming down the mountain the author bought food in that shop.

From Gusfan Sarah, there are several roads and many trails, so one should first head up and to the left, in a northwesterly direction. There's a very good trail, used both by shepherds and climbers, which leads to the Iranian Mountaineering Federation Shelter at 4170 meters. However, the beginning of this trail may be hard to find but once on it, it's easy to follow as it zig zags up the slope. Better have 2 or 3 liters of water with you before leaving Gusfan Sarah, as there's none on the lower part of the mountain. It can also be very warm at the bottom depending on the time of year you climb.

At the shelter there should be snow nearby, which can be melted for drinking water--or in the afternoons some running water may be found. For most people with a car, it's a 2-day weekend climb from Tehran, but because of its elevation, some may need 3 days. Take a tent, the hut may be full; and an ice ax & crampons, just in case. May or June might be the best time to climb, because you'd have more snow on the lower part of the mountain, for drinking water. At that time you'd need an ice ax & crampons for sure. Iran is a dry land, with most precipitation coming in the winter. Summers are hot & dry.

Here's what the author did. His climb took 3 days beginning on 9/22/1970. He took a city bus to the outskirts of Tehran and hitch hiked to the Raineh Junction. He started walking, but got a lift up to Gusfan Sarah (but can't remember exactly where Raineh is located? On the map it

This foto of Damavand was taken from the highway south of the mountain.

Map 215-1, Damavand Volcano, Elburz Mtns., Iran

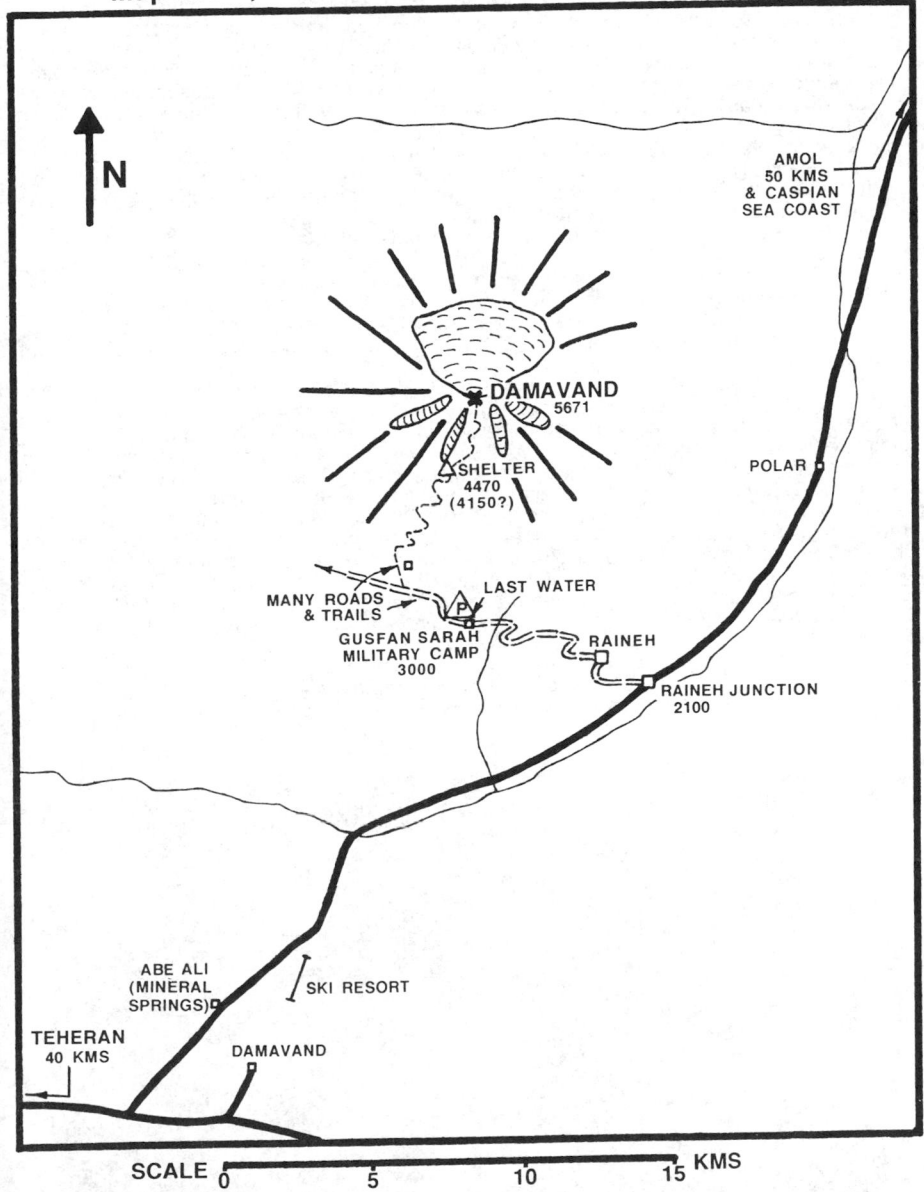

N

AMOL
50 KMS
& CASPIAN
SEA COAST

DAMAVAND
5671

POLAR

SHELTER
4470
(4150?)

LAST WATER

MANY ROADS
& TRAILS

GUSFAN SARAH
MILITARY CAMP
3000

RAINEH

RAINEH JUNCTION
2100

ABE ALI
(MINERAL
SPRINGS)

SKI RESORT

TEHERAN
40 KMS

DAMAVAND

SCALE 0   5   10   15 KMS

may not be in the proper place). Without much water, he hiked up, but couldn't find the trail in the hot afternoon sun, so he just slept on the ground dehydrated and with muscle cramps all night long. Next morning, found the trail and soon was at the hut. He then melted snow, ate breakfast, and was at the summit by 2pm. Slept that night in the hut, then walked down to the highway and hitch hiked back to Tehran at the end of Day 3.

Maps *Tourist Guide Map of Iran*, get in Tehran; TPC map *G-5D,* 1:500,000, and the guidebook, **Iran**, Lonely Planet.

Kuh-e-Zardeh, Zagros Mountains, Iran

In western Iran near the border of Iraq, is one of the most extensive mountain ranges in the world. From the area where the borders of Turkey, Iraq and Iran meet, southeast to the region of Bandar Abbas and the Straits of Hormuz, is one continuous mountain chain. Various groups of peaks are lumped together and called the Zagros Mountains. The part of most interest is the central section where the highest peak in the range, and the 5th highest summit in Iran, is located. This is Zardeh at 4548 meters. This map and limited information is meant to be an introduction only.

Included on this map is the area between Dorud in the northwest, and Isfahan & Shahrkurd in the southeast. This area contains a number of peaks over 4000 meters, all of which have been folded and upturned. The author remembers limestone on his one climb. The stream drainage pattern runs northwest to southeast, between parallel ridges.

The author's personal experience in the area was a climb to near the summit of **Shotaran Kuh**, 4328 meters. His 3 day hike began on 9/30/1975. He rode a train to Dorud, bought 3 days of food, stored extra baggage at the train station, then hitch hiked toward the village of Azna. He left the highway where the vehicle parking symbol is shown. He then climbed a ways and camped just above a village. Day 2, he hiked to above 3000 meters, but was sick, and camped. Next morning, hiked up to a minor summit, but had diarrhea, so he returned to Dorud that afternoon.

This region is dry and has a similar appearance to Nevada's mountains in the western USA, except here in the Zagros there are no trees high on the mountains; at least the author saw none on his climb to Shotaran Kuh. Wooded areas are found along the streams but the mountains are covered with grass and short brush. Walking is easy. Springs and streams can be found near all higher mountains, which makes water less of a problem than in southeastern Iran.

To climb **Zardeh**, and a number of other peaks in that area, the starting place would be Isfahan. Buses run every half hour to the large town of Shahrkurd. From there, take either a minibus, truck or shared taxi to Farsan, then somewhere north to the Kuhrang Dam area (the Kuhrang Dam was very new in the 1970's and is not shown on this map; its exact location is unknown to the author). The hiking route would be on the trail to the south of Raugunsk. It looks like you'll have to walk over one pass, then across a valley before reaching Zardeh's summit. Looks like a long hike, maybe 3 or 4 days, depending on how close you get to the mountain using public transport, or taxis, or maybe a 4WD (?).

Some peaks in this area are fairly rugged, but it appears most can be climbed easily without special equipment (?). Most precipitation comes in winter in the form of snow, with late spring and early summer being the best time to climb. Expect to find lots of sheep & goats in these mountains along with shepherds.

From the small city of Dorud looking southeast at Shotaran Kuh (Camel Mountain).

Map 216-1, Kuh-e-Zardeh, Zagros Mountains, Iran

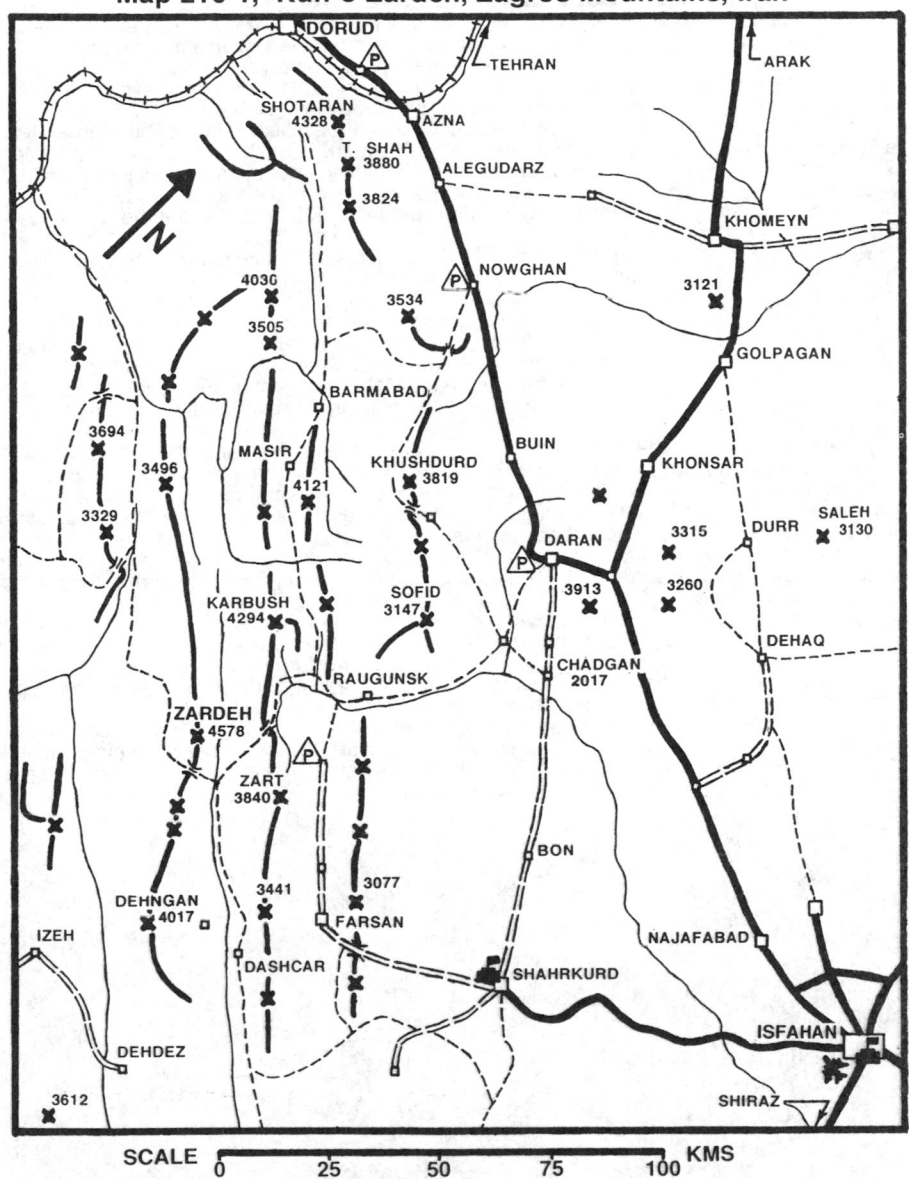

The best place in the area to get additional information, at least about public transport and hotels, etc., is at the tourist office in Isfahan. At that office, ask about a local mountaineering club. If you can find someone there, they would have the best information on how to get to Zardeh or other interesting peaks.

Maps TPC map *G-5D & H-6B*, 1:500,000; and the latest travel guidebook, **Iran** (this book has no information on hiking or climbing in this area, but does discuss some highway routes, hotels, etc.), Lonely Planet.

Hazar, Southeastern Plateau Ranges, Iran

In southeastern Iran are many high mountains, the highest of which is Hazar at 4420 meters. This region is south of the city of Kerman, which is on the main highway crossing central and eastern Iran, and linking Zahedan to Pakistan. This highway from Tehran is paved all the way to Zahedan. The author passed this way several times during his wandering days of the 1970's and has updated his information as much as possible using the book below.

In southeastern Iran are several volcanos, but they are just south of this mapped area. **Kuh-e-Taftan** (Mt. Taftan) at 4050 meters is south of Zahedan, Mirjaveh and Ladiz. From Ladiz, Taftan is near the highway going toward Khash. Taftan may have had an eruption on 4/25/1993 according to press reports, but it's a long ways out there and nothing was available from geologists. Further south from Taftan is **Kuh-e-Bazman**, 3490 meters, another old volcano. This one last erupted in the Holocene.

Here's what the author did. Starting on 3/20/1975 and lasting into the 4th day, and while on his way to Pakistan, he got off a bus at Mahan, where he bought food for the next few days, left a sack of baggage with a shopkeeper, and started walking south towards **Kuh-e-Jupar** at 3962 meters. That was around mid-day. By nightfall he camped near the village of Kanuas. Next day he set up a high camp at the base of Jupar, and reached the top of a 3700 meter peak on the 3rd day. He found lots of snow up high. The final camp was again set up near the village of Kanuas. The morning of the 4th day, he returned to Mahan, and got a bus to Bam on his way to Zahedan and Pakistan. Use the above example as a guide in reaching other mountains in this vast desert.

If given the chance, the author would climb **Hazar** from Khaneh and Rayin; **Lalezar**, 4374 meters, from Mashiz, Nigar, and Azghar. While there may be shared taxis, buses or trucks on the road from Mashiz to Baft (the biggest town in the area away from main highways with a powerline running from Kerman), there surely will not be much traffic between Khaneh to Rayin, if any; in fact there may not be a road! Maybe it's still just a camel track (?)! To get to any of these faraway places, you'll almost have to hire a 4WD vehicle. Ask at any nearby town; or start at the tourist office in Kerman. Most trails shown on the map appear to be rough tracks for trucks or 4WD vehicles.

This part of Iran is very dry with almost no running water, except in the higher mountain canyons. This is the biggest problem with climbing here, but the dry climate also benefits the climber as well. Between mountains and/or villages, it's best to have several bottles of water. Continually make inquiries as to the whereabouts of the next waterhole. The approach routes are made easy as there are no deep gorges, badlands or forests.

There are many buses each day running from Tehran to Kerman. Buses also use the Kerman to Sirjan route; and also to Zahedan. There are 3 trains weekly running between Tehran and Kerman, the end of the line. The Pakistani train from Zahedan to Quetta, now runs 2 times a week; there are buses doing that route as well.

Southwest of Mahan is the village of Kanuas with Kuh-i-Jupar beyond (March foto).

Map 217-1, Hazar, Southeastern Plateau Ranges, Iran

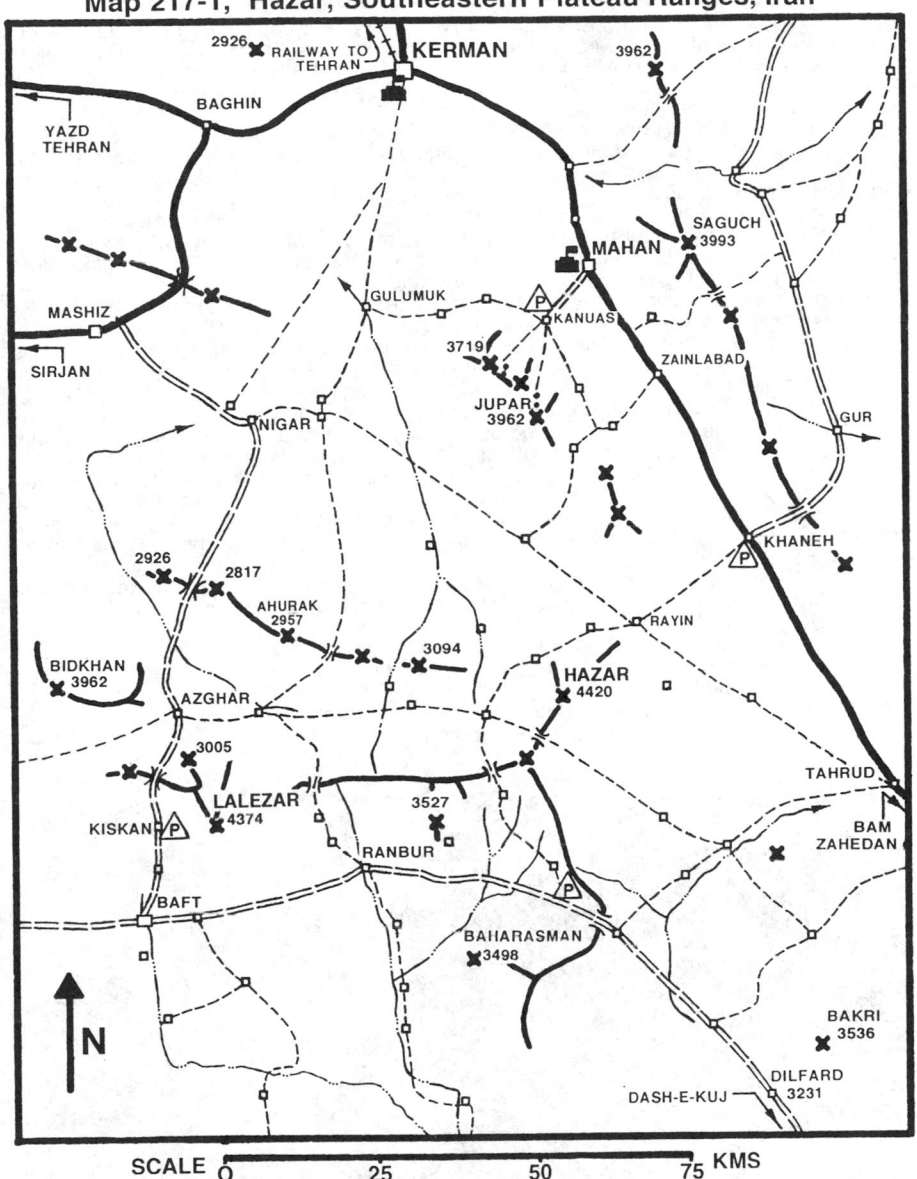

SCALE 0 — 25 — 50 — 75 KMS

The biggest city in the region is Kerman, followed by Mahan. Shop in these places. Villages which will likely still be populated are named on the map; otherwise, symbols indicating villages or buildings, are likely to be abandoned, or shepherd huts (?). Late winter or spring is the best time to wander into this region, as there will be cooler temperatures and generally more water available, at least in the form of snow on the higher peaks.

Maps The latest *Tourist Map of Iran*, from any tourist office; TPC maps *H-7A & (H-7B for Tafton)*, 1:500,000; and for finding rooms, bus information, etc, the travel guidebook, **Iran**, Lonely Planet.

Shah Fuladi, Koh-i-Baba Mountains, Afghanistan

From one location in central Asia, often called the Pamir Knot, several mountain ranges radiate out in different directions. They are the Pamirs, Tien Shan, Kun Lun, Karakorum, Himalayas, Hindu Kush, and finally the Koh-i-Baba. The Koh-i-Baba is the smallest range of the group and has no really high summits, at least compared to the giants to the east. The highest peak in the Koh-i-Baba is Shah Fuladi at 5143 meters.

The author was here between 9/8 & 9/13/1974, on his way home from Pakistan after spending 5 days in a Hunza Valley Hospital, plus 22 more days in the Gilgit Hospital, with hepatitis. He had only a map of Asia and wasn't sure at the time which peak was the highest, or where it was. Also, because his fitness wasn't good at the time, and because he wasn't 100% sure he was cured of hepatitis and wanted to take it easy, he only climbed or hiked about half a day. His total walk-time from Bamiyan for the 6 days was only 27 3/4 hours! But he did climb one lesser peak just north of the main east-west crest. He can't remember the rocks, but it seems like they were light-colored granite (?), plus others.

Getting to the area may or may not be difficult, depending on the political situation at the time. But in times of political stability, you should be able take a bus or truck from the capital of Kabul, and reach Bamiyan in one day. There's also an airport. Bamiyan was, in the 1970's, the number one tourist attraction in Afghanistan. Located there are 2 huge statues of The Buddha (one is 52 meters high) carved out of a cliff face. There are other ruins nearby, perhaps having to do with the raids of Ghengis Khan in 1221 AD, as he was chasing the young Persian Shah Jalal-ud-din to India.

Bamiyan is a large village, with a good bazaar and once had a number of small hotels and eating places. There used to be 1st class accommodations on the hill near the airport (1974 information). Buy all your food in Bamiyan (plan on a minimum of 4 or 5 days), then walk, hire a taxi, or get a ride on the occasional truck or tractor going in the direction of the village of Fuladi. However, this part of the journey is best seen and enjoyed on foot. Along the way are numerous homes and irrigated fields, and some ruins dating back to perhaps the same time period as the statues at Bamiyan.

Beyond Fuladi, which is the final village and the last shop where some basic foods can be purchased, there's a 4WD road for a short distance, then numerous livestock trails. Once in the mountains, forget the sheep & goat trails and make your own way.

From Fuladi village, veer left and walk along the 4WD road as shown, then after 5 or so kms, veer right, or west, and enter the western of the 2 basins shown. That's the route to use to climb **Shah Fuladi**. The author went into the eastern basin and by the time he realized he wasn't going to make the highest summit, he was low on food, and had to return.

The north faces offer some snow & ice climbing and also many rock routes, some of which

The northern slopes of peaks located just east of Shah Fuladi.

Map 218-1, Shah Fuladi, Koh-i-Baba Mtns., Afghanistan

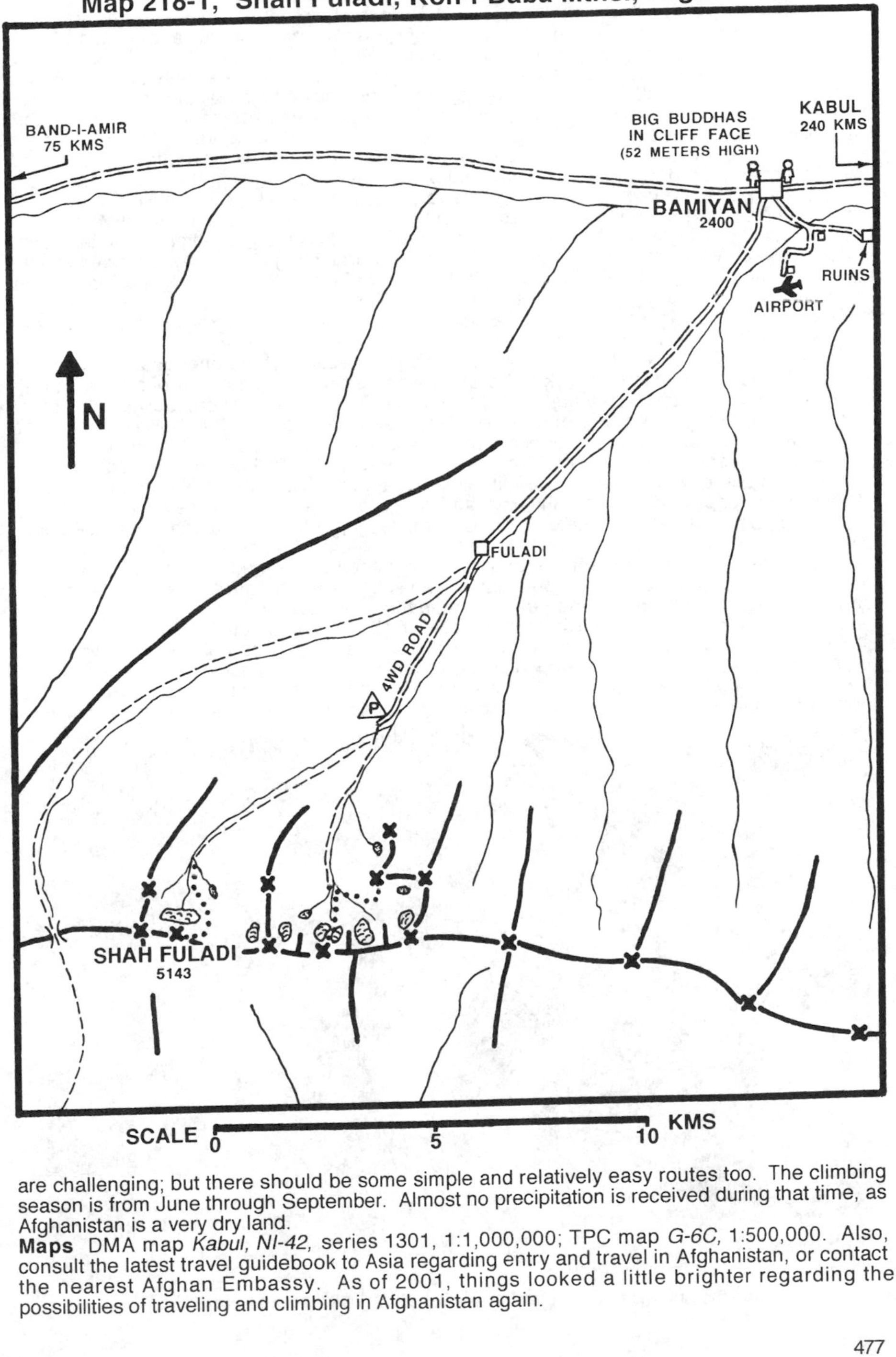

BAND-I-AMIR
75 KMS

BIG BUDDHAS
IN CLIFF FACE
(52 METERS HIGH)

KABUL
240 KMS

BAMIYAN
2400

RUINS

AIRPORT

N

FULADI

4WD ROAD

P

SHAH FULADI
5143

SCALE 0   5   10 KMS

are challenging; but there should be some simple and relatively easy routes too. The climbing season is from June through September. Almost no precipitation is received during that time, as Afghanistan is a very dry land.

Maps DMA map *Kabul, NI-42,* series 1301, 1:1,000,000; TPC map *G-6C,* 1:500,000. Also, consult the latest travel guidebook to Asia regarding entry and travel in Afghanistan, or contact the nearest Afghan Embassy. As of 2001, things looked a little brighter regarding the possibilities of traveling and climbing in Afghanistan again.

Tirich Mir, Hindu Kush Mountains, Pakistan

The Hindu Kush Mountains, for the most part, form the boundary between Afghanistan and Pakistan. The area shown here is northeast of Kyber Pass, north of Chitral, and includes Tirich Mir, 7706 meters, the highest peak of the Hindu Kush.

Getting to **Tirich Mir** is relatively easy. From Peshawar, there are daily flights into the provincial capital of Chitral. There's also a good road, and getting better all the time, which links Chitral with the outside world. You can take one of several daily buses from Peshawar into the Swat Valley, then to Dir, over Lowari Top Pass, and down into the Chitral Valley.

Tirich Mir can be climbed in 2 to 4 weeks from Chitral, depending on one's fitness, and acclimatization prior to the climb. It's one of the most difficult climbs in the entire range, but there are many other nearby summits which are very easy; at least as big mountains go.

From Chitral there's a good 4WD road, heading up the valley eventually linking Mastuj, the Shandur Pass, and finally Gilgit. Each day there are Pakistani jeeps & tractors using this road. Stop at Kurgh, or with luck, a passenger jeep might be found going all the way to Kosht. Or just hire one, as most groups do. From Kosht, which is still the end of the road, a trail begins, which passes the village of Otool (Uthul?), crosses the Tirich Pass (3800 meters), and down to the last inhabited village of Shahgrom. Beyond the fields of Bandok, a climber's trail leads up to a base camp, from which many climbs can be made.

Chitral (with 50,000 people at last report!) has a fine bazaar, where enough good food can be found to make any climb or trek. There are also several hotels of various classes and comforts to choose from. Many are very cheap. There's also a tourist office which can be of assistance in rounding up a jeep or porters. The best place to get porters however, is on the mountain at the end of the road, where local people know the trails better. Ask around.

The author went to Tirich Mir and was alone for 19 days from Chitral starting 6/24/1975, a year after his battle with hepatitis in Gilgit. He took a passenger jeep to Kurgh, then walked slowly over the pass and down to Shagrom and finally to base camp. While acclimatizing, he climbed the peak marked 6665 meters. From there, he went south & southeast and attempted Tirich Mir from the west, but that's not the easiest way, a least for a solo climber who had only a road map of Asia. He later returned unsuccessful. His total walk-time for the 19 days was 116 1/4 hours. It appears the normal route is to climb south from the main glacier east of base camp, and into a basin east of the peak, then up the east face and/or ridge. There are big crevasses on the higher glaciers, which means solo climbers may not return!

The Hindu Kush is normally a *good weather* region. It's in a dry part of the world with good weather the general rule. However, high on the summits the weather always deteriorates in the afternoons. Winter climbing is now done in the Hindu Kush, but normally June to early September is the climbing season. Like elsewhere, monsoon bursts usually arrive sometime in

From the summit of Ghul Laast at 6665 meters, looking east at Tirich Mir.

Map 219-1, Tirich Mir, Hindu Kush Mountains, Pakistan

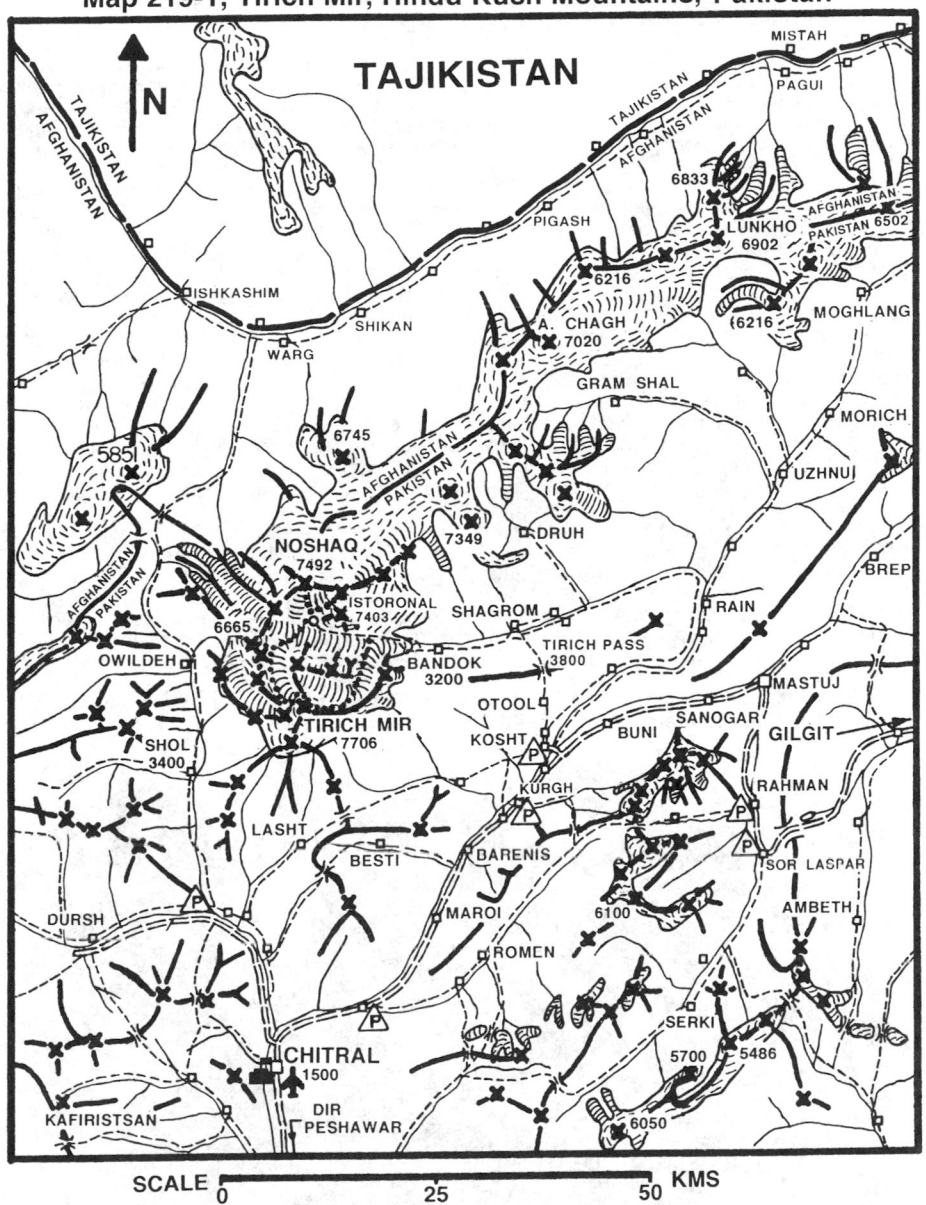

SCALE 0 — 25 — 50 **KMS**

July and lasts until sometime in September.

Maps DMA map *The Pamirs, NJ-42,* 1301 series, 1:1,000,000, or from Lands and Survey of India, New Delhi; TPC map *G-6C,* 1:500,000; and books, **Trekking in the Karakoram & Hindukush**, and travel guidebook **Pakistan,** both from Lonely Planet.

Koyo Zom, Hindu Raj Mountains, Pakistan

The main mountain mass shown on this map is the Hindu Raj. It's located in northern Pakistan, and sandwiched in between the Hindu Kush to the west & southwest, and the Karakorum to the east. Part of the Hindu Kush is shown in the upper left hand corner of the map. For mountaineers, this is an unfamiliar area. Perhaps one reason is, there are no peaks over 7000 meters; the highest being Koyo Zom, listed at 6872 meters. Despite the fact there are no really high mountains in the area, good climbing can be found. It's also an interesting region for trekking, which is more popular than climbing. Both guidebooks listed below cover this area rather well, and they are likely a little more undated than this--*and a lot more detailed.*

When comparing this range with other big mountain areas in Asia, these parts have relatively easy access. By far the easiest way to get there is via Gilgit, located about 20 kms off the map to the southeast. Gilgit can be reached by air from Rawalpindi, or by a good paved road, known as the KKH, or Karakorum Highway. Gilgit is a large town with many government workers and a good bazaar. Everything needed for climbing or trekking can be found there.

From Gilgit, jeeps (or other 4WD's) can be found carrying cargo & passengers to the various valleys of the Hindu Raj. Tractors with trailers are also used, but they're slow, tiresome, & dusty. The Gilgit tourist office can assist in locating transport and can update the author's original information which goes back to the summer of 1974 when he was in the Gilgit hospital with hepatitis. Just before he left Gilgit, he spent a couple of days in this area around Gupis.

Larger towns on the map are Gupis, Pingal, Yasin, Gakuch, and Ishkuman. These and other villages have small shops selling basic goods. Many of the villages have guesthouses, owned and operated by the government, and by now even some little private hotels. These are clean, comfortable and cheap; and if desired, the *chokidar*, or keeper of the resthouse, will prepare Pakistani meals at low prices. Someone in Gilgit can tell you where these guesthouses are and how much they cost.

To reach the highest peak, **Koyo Zom**, look for passenger jeeps going to Yasin, or if you're with a group, hire one. From there, walk to near the village of Nialthi, then turn north. It's possible to get there from the village of Darkot, but a pass would have to be crossed if this route were used. It could also be reached from the north, and from near the village of Pechus. Pechus can be reached by walking from Imit, on the southeast, or Mastuj to the southwest (off this map). The author isn't familiar with the normal route so you're on your own once you get to the mountain. The Afghan border is at the Baroghil Pass, and hopefully you will be allowed onto the northern routes (?). Check that out before leaving Gilgit.

July to mid-September are the best months for climbing; but trekkers have a much longer season. The monsoon rains seldom get this far north, so it's not a big factor. Late summer

The author used this zuk to cross the Shayok River and reach Masherbrum in 1975 (Map 222, page 485). There is now a bridge across that river (?).

Map 220-2, Koyo Zom, Hindu Raj Mountains, Pakistan

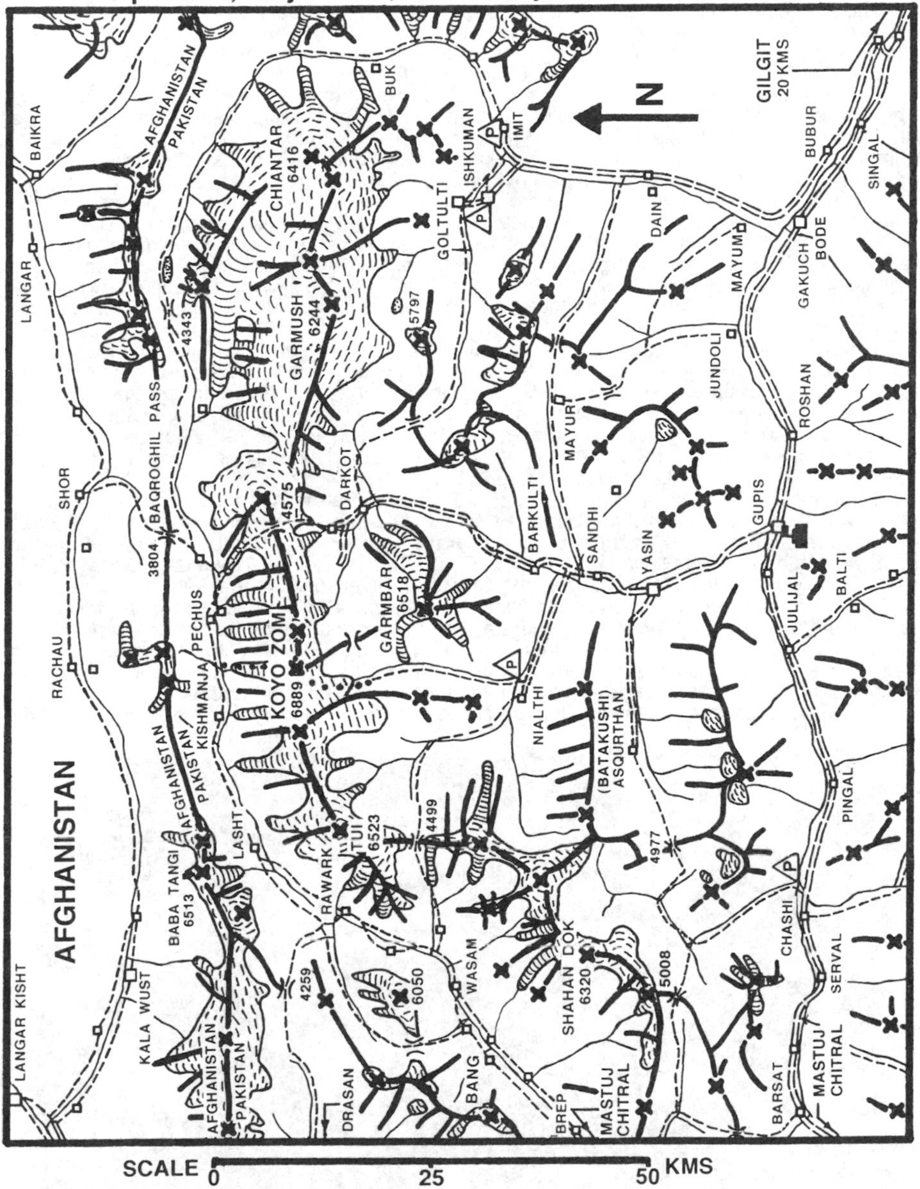

months are best for fruits & vegetables which begin to ripen after July 1.
Maps DMA maps *The Pamirs, NJ-43*, Series 1301, 1:1,000,000; and *NJ-43, 13 & 14,*
1:250,000, also from Lands and Survey of Pakistan (or India?); TPC maps *G-6B & G-6C,*
1:500,000; and the books, **Trekking in the Karakoram and Hindukush**, and travel guidebook,
Pakistan, Lonely Planet.

Rakaposhi, Karakoram Mountains, Pakistan

The area covered by this map is a vast region of northern Pakistan and includes the most northerly and westerly parts of the Karakoram Mountains. In the center of the map is the Hunza Valley with its capital, Baltit. This is only an introduction to the area; you'll have to use the latest travel and trekking guides for the latest information on the area.

Some of these peaks are among the easiest to access of any big mountains in the world. This is a result of the Chinese building the Karakorum Highway (KKH), finishing it in 1978. It's a paved highway from Urumqi in Xinjiang Province of China, into northern Pakistan, through the Hunza Valley to Gilgit, and south through the Indus Valley to Abbottabad. Only since the opening of this route have the peaks east of Hunza been made accessible.

Some of the highest summits in the area include: Kampire Dior, 7142 meters; Batura, 7785 meters; Shispar, 7619; and Ultar, 7398 meters. These are all north of the Hunza Valley. Other peaks south of Hunza are: Rakaposhi, 7788 meters--probably the most famous mountain in the region; Minipin, 7273; Malubiting, 7291; and Haramosh, 7406 meters. East of Hunza are the highest summits on this map: Trivor, 7720 meters; Kunyang Chhist, 7852; and the very highest, Distaghil Sar, 7885 meters. All the mountains in this area, regardless of their elevation, are rugged and challenging climbs!

Today, buses can be found on the highway from Abbottabad, to Gilgit, Hunza, and to Kashgar in Xinjiang, making it convenient to reach many peaks. One of the mountains easiest to approach is **Rakaposhi**. From the village of Jogalot to base camp, on the southwest side of the peak, is a couple of easy days with a large pack. It was first climbed by the southwest ridge. The author made an 11 day solo attempt on this ridge beginning 6/20/1974, but lost a tent pole and had to give up. Later, he made it to Pasu before deciding he had hepatitis, and returned to the Aliabad Hospital in Baltit, and later to Gilgit's Hospital.

Other peaks in the area and their approaches are: **Batura**, from Pasu and the Batura Glacier, or from the west and the village of Taltar; **Shispar**, the highest summit of the Pasu Group, has been climbed from Pasu and the Pasu Glacier, or it could be climbed from the southwest and the Baltit Glacier northwest of Baltit. Peaks such as **Trivor** and **Distaghil Sar** can be approached from the north and the Shimshal River, or from the west and south from Nagir, Hispar and the Hispar River and Glacier. **Kampire Dior** can be approached from the north--from Sost and the Yarz Yarz (if there are no border restrictions(?); or from the west and Imit (see previous map), or maybe from the south and Taltar(?). **Minipin** can be approached from Hunza and Nagir and the northern slopes, or from the southwest and the meadow campsite called Diran. And approach **Haramosh** from the north and Dachi and Barche.

The regional capital of Gilgit has a large bazaar which can supply any expedition with food

From Baltit in the Hunza Valley looking at the northern slopes of Rakaposhi.

Map 221-1, Rakaposhi, Karakoram Mountains, Pakistan

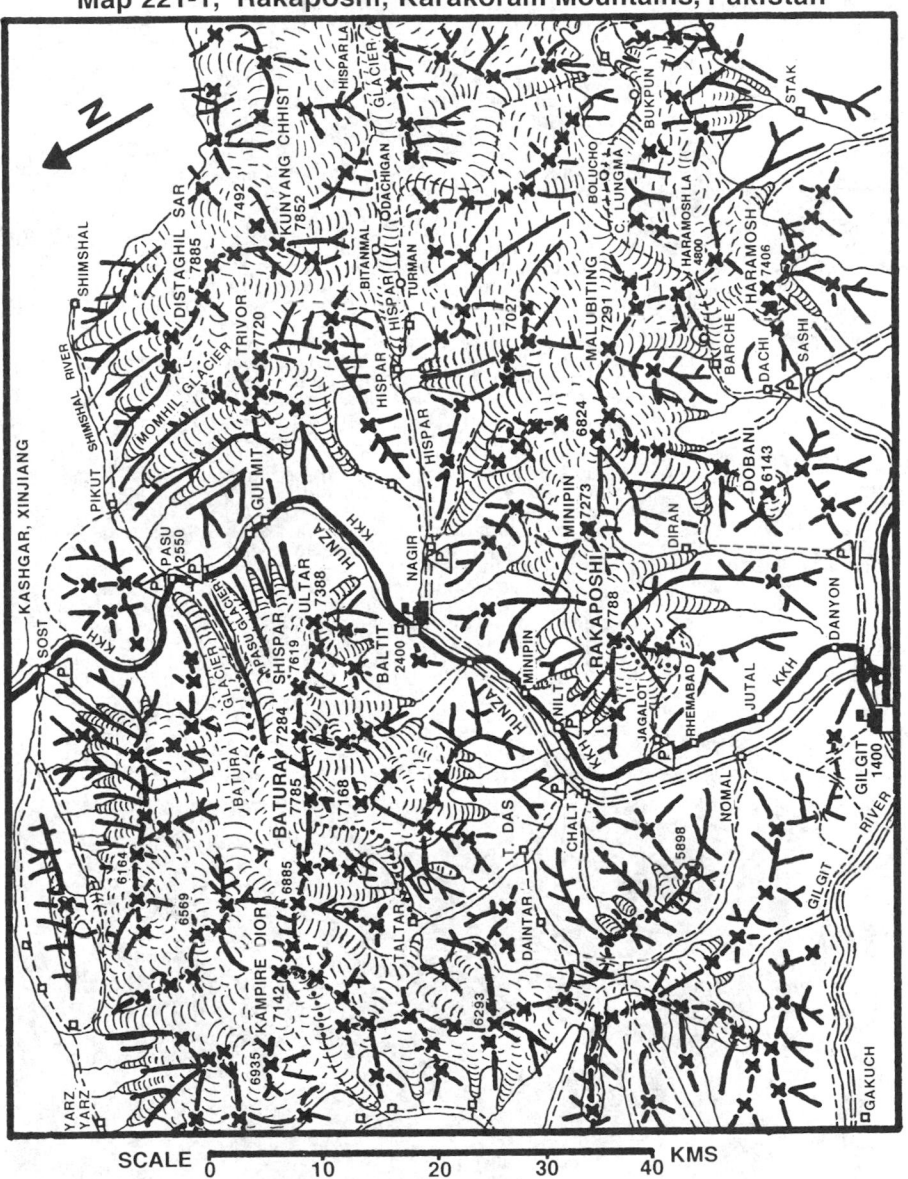

SCALE 0 10 20 30 40 KMS

and supplies. Most climbs in this area are made in July, August and early September.

Maps DMA maps *The Pamirs (NJ-43) and Khasmir (NI-43)*, Series 1301, 1:1,000,000; and NJ-43, 14 & 15, and NI-43, 2 & 3, all 1:250,000; TPC maps *G-6B & G-6C and G-7A & G-7D*, 1:500,000; and the books, **Trekking in the Karakoram & Hindukush**, and travel guide, **Pakistan**, both from Lonely Planet.

K-2 & Hidden Peak, Karakoram Mountains, Pakistan

In northern Pakistan along the Chinese border, stands the Karakorum Mountains. Within this range are 4 of the world's 14 summits over 8000 meters. They are; **K-2**, 8611 meters, 2nd in the world, climbed first in 1954 by Italianos; **Hidden Peak** or **Gasherbrum 1**, 8068, 11th, first climbed in 1958 by Americans; **Broad Peak**, 8047, 12th, climbed first in 1957 by an Austrian team; and **Gasherbrum II**, 8035, 13th, and first climbed by an Austrian group in 1956. All of these summits are within about 30 kms of each other. No other place in the world has so many high mountains so close together. This is merely an introduction to a very large area.

The normal route used to climb all these peaks, and many more in that central region, begins in Skardu. From Skardu, you must hire a jeep for the trip to Thungol. From Thungol, and with porters going at their speed, it's 8 days to Concordia.

The normal camping places start at Thungol, where a police check post is located. From Thungol, the rough road actually continues to Askole, then it's wild country, with the following campsites: Korofon, Bardumal, Piau, Lilihua, Urdukas, Goro and finally Concordia. In the past these campsites had to be used, because there was no fuel for porters to use; in the future it appears you must be prepared to put porters in tents and provide them with stoves & fuel for cooking. If your group provides this equipment, then it might be possible to go at a faster rate of speed (?).

The part between Korofon and Bardumal used to be either a cold wade & death trap; or a long walk upstream to a glacier crossing, but now there are a couple of cables strung across the river and a cable car. You now pay some locales to be helped across a sizable river.

Other important peaks and access routes are: **Masherbrum**, 7820 meters, climbed via Khapalu and Hushi; **Saltoro Kangri**, 7742 meters, from Khapalu, Gama, and the Siachen Glacier (access may be limited by the war with India?); **Chogolisa**, 7654 meters, climbed from Concordia; **Ogre**, 7285 meters, climbed from the Panmah or Biafo Glaciers.

The author bought most of his food in Rawalpindi, where the flights to Skardu originate, but some was purchased in Skardu for his solo attempts of Masherbrum in 1975, and Broad Peak in 1978. For **Masherbrum**, he started with a 50 kg pack, then used zuks (rafts made out of inflated animal skins with a frame of poles on top for rigidity) to be ferried across the Shayok River next to Khapalu (apparently there's now a bridge, and a 4WD road to Hushi). Then it was up past Hushi and onto the glacier and the south face. From Hushi, he had 5 days of perfect weather, but decided to go slow to acclimatize. Bad weather hit at 6850 meters and had to camp there for 5 days. He later moved up to 7300 meters and camped for 2 nights (at the same time deteriorating), but bad weather only allowed him to reach 7350 meters, then headed back. On his way down in a blizzard, he went into 2 crevasses up to his waist. From Khapalu, it took 24 days round-trip between 8/2 to 8/25/1975. Then had to wait through 14 days of bad weather for a flight back to Rawalpindi. Read his story in *Climbing* magazine, #47, March-April, 1978.

For **Broad Peak**, he got official permission in Skardu to study the glaciers around Concordia (but it was really for climbing only!), then with 2 porters jeeped to Dhaso, walked to Askole & Concordia, let the porters return, then explored routes to Chogolisa, found a dead Japanese climb on the glacier, had a good visit with Doug Scott & Chris Bonnington who had just lost Nick Escort on K-2, and attempted Broad Peak. He went up the icy west face, but faulty crampon

From near Concordia we can see K-2 in the center, Broad Peak to the right.

Map 222-1, K-2 & Hidden Peak, Karakoram Mtns., Pakistan

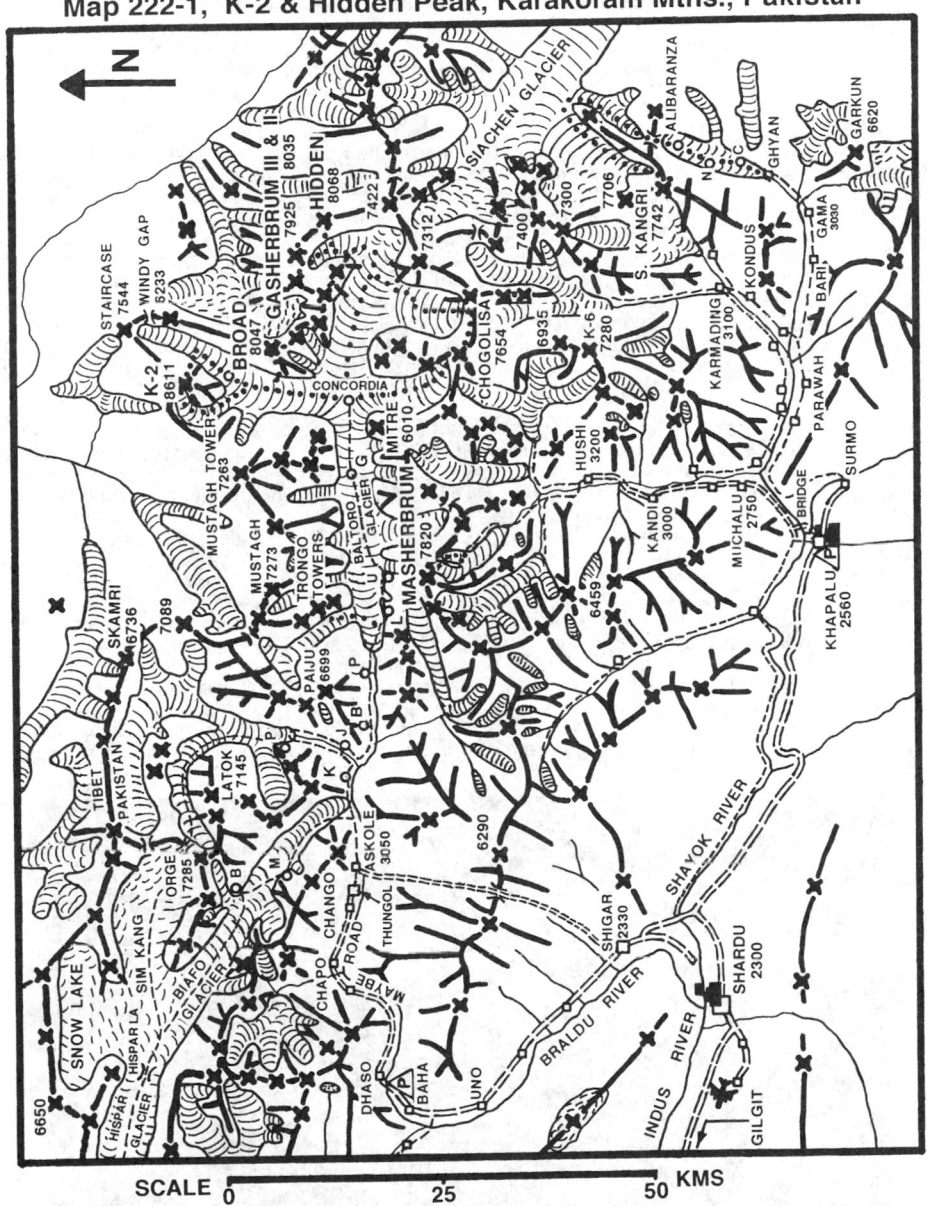

straps put an end to that. While returning near the Urdukas campsite, he nearly drowned in the stream beside the glacier. Got back to Skardu after 31 days. That trip lasted from 5/27 to 6/26/1978.

Skardu has many hotels now and in all price ranges. The tourist office can help find porters and jeeps if needed. Many passenger jeeps reach Khapalu and Shigar and beyond.

Maps DMA maps NJ-43, 15 (and 16?), and NI-43, 3 & 4, 1:250,000; TPC map *G-7D*, 1:500,000; and the book **Trekking in the Karakoram & Hindukush**, Lonely Planet. This book lists a number of other maps, too many to mention here, so check the list of book distributors for other trekking or climbing guidebooks & maps to this area.

Nanga Parbat, Himalayan Mountains, Pakistan

The 9th highest mountain in the world is Nanga Parbat at 8125 meters. It's located in northern Pakistan not far south of Gilgit. Although it's not far from the central Karakorum and the high peaks there, it's not actually part of the Karakorum system. Instead, geologically it belongs to the Himalayas, and is at the extreme western end of the range. It's also the most westerly of all the 8000 meter peaks in the world.

Nanga Parbat was first climbed by a German team in 1953, not long after the conquest of Everest. The route taken by that expedition was from the north and the Rakhiot Bridge on the Indus River at 1194 meters. The route went up to Tato, the last village, onto the Rakhiot Glacier, and to the summit. Greg Horne says in 1985, they were building a new road from near Rakhiot Bridge to Tato on the west side of the drainage. This is now complete, and you can hire jeeps from somewhere near the bridge to take you up to Tato.

Three other routes have since been used to climb the mountain and it appears at least one of the latter routes is the easiest. The second ascent was via Bunar and the Bunar Valley, Zangot, and the Diamir Valley and Glacier. The summit was reached via the northwest face.

The next 2 successful ascents were from the Rupal Valley. One group climbed from the village of Rupal, then up the Bazhin Glacier, and finally up the southeast spur. The other route taken was via Rupal village, southwest up the Rupal Glacier, to the Mazeno Pass, and along the southwest ridge to the summit. Those who made the southwest ridge climb said it is the easiest and safest route on the mountain.

Nanga Parbat is surely the easiest of all the 8000 meter peaks in the world to gain access to. For several years while the Karakorum Highway (KKH) was being built by the Chinese, it was closed to foreigners, but it's been open since 1978. This paved highway starts in Abbottabad (north of Islamabad), and runs along the Indus River to Gilgit, through the Hunza Valley, and into Xinjiang province of China ending at Kashgar.

Buses can be taken from Rawalpindi and Abbottabad to all points along the KKH. From the Rakhiot Bridge south to the original base camp takes only a couple of days. Jeeps can be found at Bunji for climbs originating on the southeast side of the mountain--if your party is small. If it's a larger group, transport will have to be found in either Gilgit or Chilas. The new trekking book below has lots more and updated information on all aspects of hiking in the area, and of course you can use that access information for climbing. The route from Zangot, over Mazeno Pass, to Rupal, is an open route for trekkers, and no permit or guide is required.

All food needed for a climb of Nanga Parbat can be found in Rawalpindi. Abbottabad would be the next best place to shop, with Chilas or Astor the last possible places close to the mountain. Or if you're coming from Gilgit, you'll find a good bazaar and many shops there. Previous expeditions have climbed the mountain in all summer months, from June through

The northwest face of Nanga Parbat as seen from a Gilgit-Rawalpindi flight.

Map 223-2, Nanga Parbat, Himalayan Mtns., Pakistan

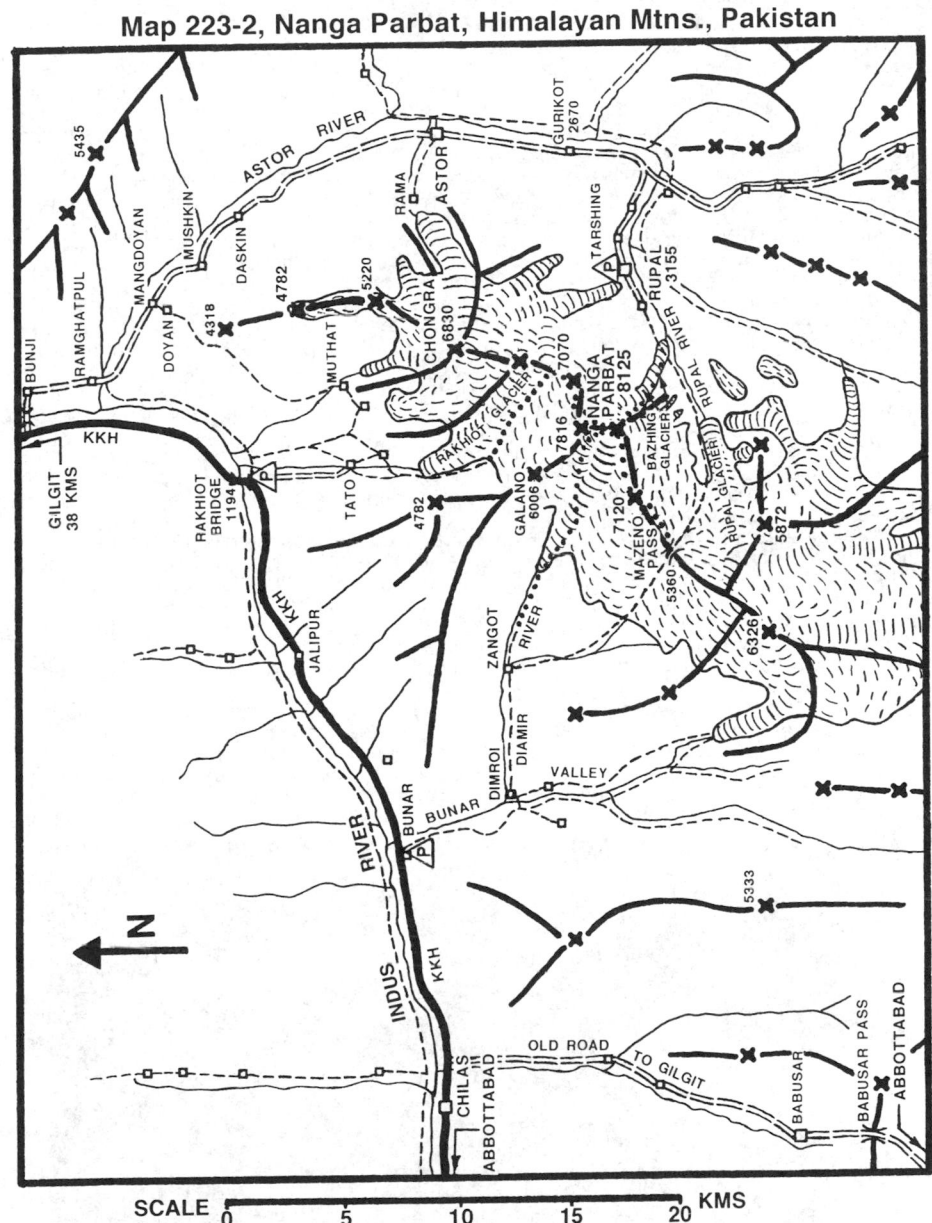

September. The author was in the area on 2 occasions. Once coming from Skardu, he had a good look at it from the Hercules C-130. Another time from Gilgit in a Fokker.

Maps Old DMA or US AMS India and Pakistan Series U502 map *NI 43-6 (or 2?)*, 1:250,000; *Nanga Parbat Gruppe,* 1:50,000, from the 1934 Expedition, now reproduced in Germany; TPC map G-7D, 1:500,000; and the book, **Trekking in the Karakoram & Hindukush**, Lonely Planet; and the latest travel guidebook to Pakistan.

Nun Kun, Himalayan Mountains, India

This map covers that part of India just east of Srinagar and the Vale of Khasmir. The highest peak in the area is Nun Kun at 7135 meters. This part of the Himalayas is totally within the boundaries of India, but political conflicts in the late 1990's could effect access on the northern approach via Kargil. Check with the nearest Indian Embassy.

There are 2 ways to get to **Nun Kun**; from the north and from the south. The author took a bus from Srinagar to Kishtwar, which is south of Nun Kun. This was all before the road from Srinagar to Leh was open to foreigners, so he had to attempt the ascent from the south. Beginning on 5/7/1974, and with a 48 kg pack, it took 12 days to arrive at the mountain's lower slopes at an altitude of 4700 meters, a distance of about 150 kms. Because of bad weather, snow, and low-to-no-visibility, he never even saw the mountain, and frankly never knew exactly where he was! He then hurried back down to Furiabad to cross a river on a snow bridge before it melted. The entire trip took 19 days round-trip from Kishtwar. One reason for the failure was that he went far too early in the season.

If you're using this route to Nun Kun, you'll pass villages of Palmar (the end of the road), Ikhala, Sondar, Hanzal, and Marwa. Then the route continues up the Krish (Kish) Nullah (canyon) past hot springs (Garumpani), and the last inhabited village of Metwan. Further up, at the cemetery of Furiabad, it may be necessary to cross the river on a snowslide if it's early in the season. Metwan villagers, who take sheep & goats into the high meadows in summer, erect a new bridge each year when the water level drops. There are shepherd huts all along the way to the base of the mountain.

From base camp directly south of the summit, the 1953 group headed northwest up a southface glacier, then east on the west summit ridge to the top. You can buy some food in the villages along the way. The author, who was smiling a lot more in those days, was invited into homes on many occasions.

The route from the north was the normal route; until perhaps the late 1990's, but may be closed now because of continued Muslim insurgents in the Kargil area (?). This route begins in Srinagar with buses or trucks heading for Leh. Stop in Kargil, and look for jeeps or other 4WD's traveling south in the direction of Suru (Panikhar) and Parkutse (Parachik). There's little traffic on this mountain road, but if you can find a cargo-passenger carrying vehicle, it'll save a long walk. Or just hire a 4WD. From Parkutse, most expeditions head straight south and up the Parkutse Glacier. This puts climbers on the west side of the twin peaks of Nun, 7135, and Kun, 7077 meters.

It's also possible to continue east to the next village of Guimatung, and climb south from there. This is up the Shafat Glacier, but subsidiary peaks will have to be climbed before reaching Nun Kun. Depending on the road, you might get a 4WD to the east side of the mountain, then trek west over the Chilung La (Pass) to the southern base camp.

As with the southern route, some of these villages along the way can offer some food. Some may have schools and/or resthouses which climbers or trekkers can use. The southern canyons

South of Nun Kun on the Kistwar route. Nun Kun is somewhere to the left.

Map 224-1, Nun Kun, Himalayan Mountains, India

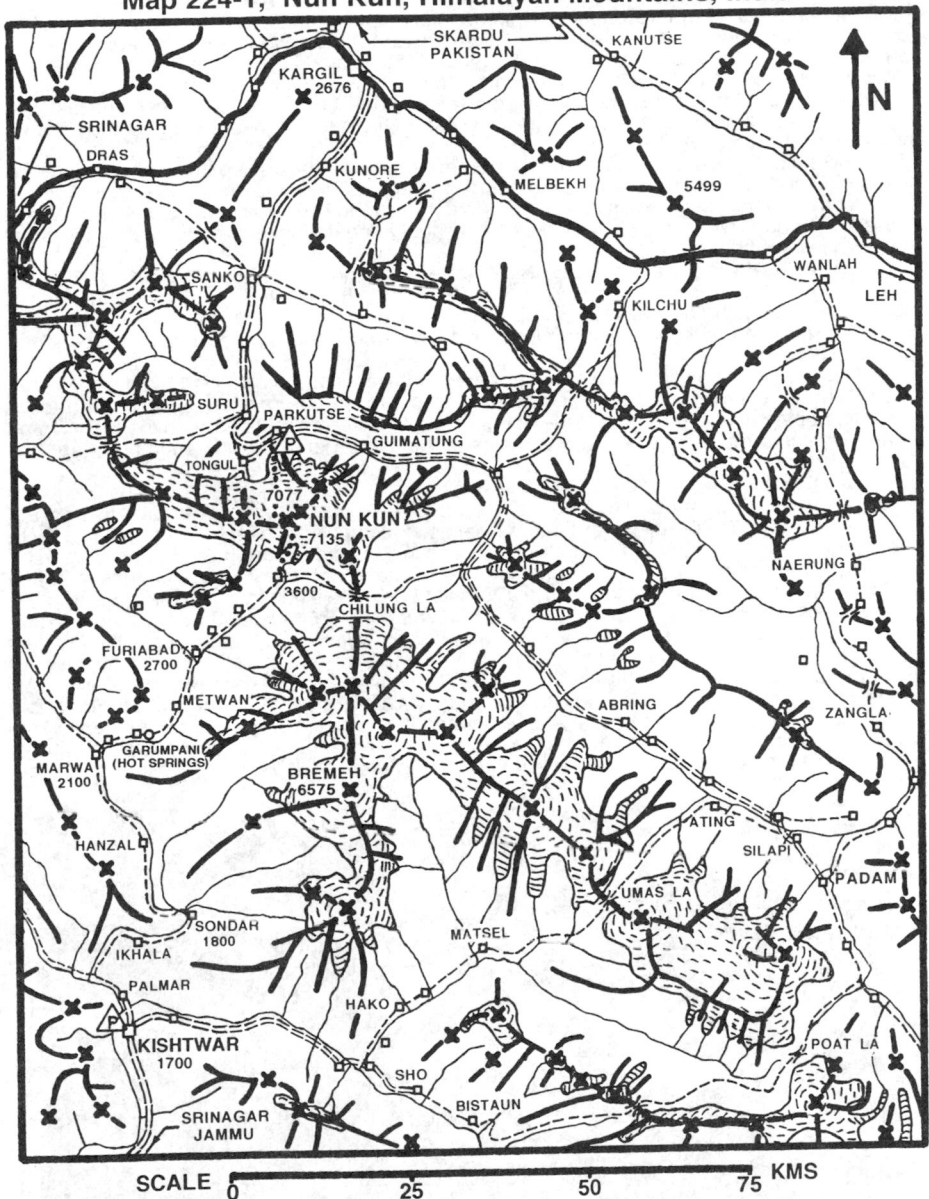

SCALE 0   25   50   75 KMS

are covered with pine trees and much wetter than the northern slopes. The best time to climb is July through mid-September, the monsoon season. Food for the trip can be bought in Kishtwar or Kargil, but Srinagar, Jammu or Delhi are better places.

Maps Leomann *Map 2, Kargil, Zanskar and Nun Kun Area* (scale not known); old DMA or newer Lands and Survey of India maps *NI 43, 7 & 11*, 1:250,000; TPC map *H-9A*, 1:500,000; and maybe the book, **A Mountain Called Nun Kun**, a record of the 1953 expedition, Pierre; or guidebooks **Leh and Trekking in Ladakh**, and/or the **Trekking in the Indian Himalaya** (for the north approach to Nun Kun), both from Lonely Plant.

Nanda Devi & Kamet, Himalayan Mountains, India

Some people are surprised to learn that the highest mountain in India is *only* 7816 meters elevation. That mountain is Nanda Devi. It seems that all the world's 8000 meter peaks, of which there are 14, are for the most part in 2 groups; one is along the Nepal-Tibetian border, the other is in northern Pakistan in the Karakorum. In between is India, with not one 8000'er!

Nanda Devi is located just west of the area where Tibet, Nepal and India meet, and just east of the city of Hardwar. This map of Nanda Devi shows India exclusively, except for the extreme north, which is Tibet.

In 1983, the Sanctuary at the head of the Rishi Gorge was closed due to the lack of firewood for porters, and degradation. It was closed through the 1990's and no one knows when it will be open for trekking/climbing again, but when it is you'll have to take your own stoves and provide porters with fuel. The latest guidebooks below should update that situation, or check with the nearest Indian Embassy.

The Nanda Devi area is rather easy to get to, because not far to the northwest is Badrinath, which is one of the sources of the sacred Ghanges River. Thousands of pilgrims visit the area of Joshimath, Badrinath, the lake Hem Kund, and other area sites to bathe in the holy waters each year. Therefore, to Joshimath at least, it's a well-traveled route, with good public transport, and places to eat and sleep.

Get to **Nanda Devi** from Delhi, or elsewhere, then Hardwar, Joshimath, Lata, Deodi (in the Rishi Gorge), then south, turn back north, and climb the south face. The south face is considered the easiest to climb and the normal route. The same route through the Rishi Gorge is used to climb other well-known mountains in the same general area, such as **Trisul** and **Dunagiri**.

A second way to Nanda Devi is from the south, and the towns of Almora, then by bus as far as Song, just off this map. Coming from the south allows access to **Nanda Kot** and the southern routes of **Trisul**. Along this trail is a series of resthouses which trekkers can use. With the closing of the normal route to Nanda Devi, you might consider **Nanda Devi East**. Get to the east side of the **Nanda Devi & Trisuli Massif** by taking a bus from Almora to Munsyari, then trek to a base camp east of Nanda Devi, via Martoli. See more in the trekking guide below.

Still another famous mountain on this map is **Kamet**. At 7756 meters, it was one of the first really big mountains in the Himalayas to be successfully climbed. The only possible problem with Kamet, is that it's on or near the Chinese border and getting permission to enter the area for the normal route has been difficult or impossible in the past. That normal route is from Joshimath, Lata, Pumg, Kurkuti & Malari--perhaps by 4WD (?), then trekking north to Siunti and up the Kamet Glacier on the east side. About the only climbers into this area for many years were Indian expeditions. But times change, so check at the nearest embassy if they'll let you in. India and China seem to be getting along better lately, so trekking and climbing in the border

Nanda Devi from the northeast showing the north ridge (Joseph Tasker foto).

Map 225-3, Nanda Devi & Kamet, Himalayas, India

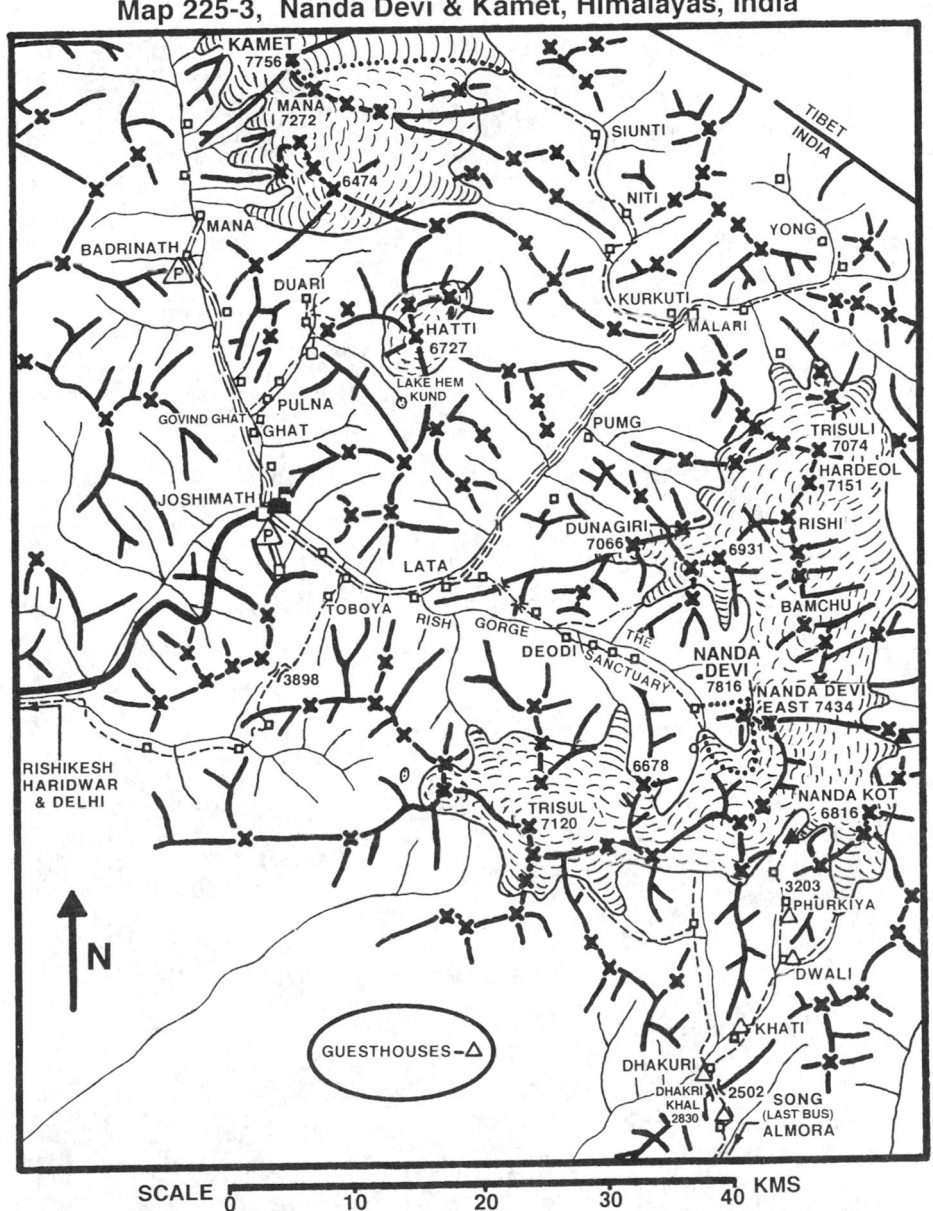

SCALE
0   10   20   30   40 KMS

area may be possible.

Trains can be taken to as far as Hardwar, then buses for the remainder of the journey to Joshimath; or by train east to Bareilly, then bus north to Almora or beyond. If you're trekking, some food may be found at the lower villages. Trekking is not quite as developed here as in Nepal, but can be just as fun and perhaps more interesting.

Maps TPC map *H-9A*, 1:500,000; DMA & Lands and Survey of India map *NH 44-6,* 1:250,000; *Leomann Map 7, Uttar Pradesh (Kumaon)*; and the books **Trekking in the India Himalaya**; and travel guidebook **India Himalaya**, both from Lonely Planet.

Kailas, Gangdise Shan, Tibet, China

Here's a mountain that's never been climbed, and likely never will be. It's **Mt. Kailas** at 6714 meters, located just north of where the borders of Nepal, India and Tibet meet, and immediately north of 2 large lakes, Rakas and Manasarowar. Kailas is famous in Sanskrit literature as the Paradise of Siva and Parvati. This mountain and the lakes are sacred to Tibetans and Hindus, because the 4 rivers; Indus, Sutlej, Ghanges, and Tsangpo (the Tibetan headwaters of the Brahmaputra) all rise within 65 kms of them. Kailas appears in the Mahabharata writings of the Hindus as Kailasa; and is known to Tibetans as Kangrinboqe. It's holier to them than either Gauri Sankar or Chomo Lhari.

Buddhist and Hindu pilgrims alike, attain *great merit* by making the sacred *circuit loop* or **kora** around Kailas. The actual trail, which starts and finishes in Darchen (Tarchen), goes over one high pass of 5630 meters and covers a distance of 53 kms. Pilgrims or trekkers normally accomplish the trek in 3 days. The most fanatical among them carry out the circuit by prostrating themselves; laying down, stretching out their arms and making a mark, then rise, walk to the mark and prostrate themselves again. Those who make the kora this way may take 3 weeks.

Much of the information here is from the **Tibet** book listed below. It appears if you're a Hindu from India or Nepal, you can get to the mountain very easily (there's a road direct from India to Burang & Darchen, but the Tibet guidebook makes no mention of that possibility. It's likely more of a caravan trail than a road (?), but for anyone else, it's a little more difficult. For western trekkers, begin this trip in Lhasa. You'll first need permission or a permit. The authorities there normally give out permits only to groups of half a dozen making the trip in Land Cruisers. They may or may not give this to individuals who are hitch hiking to Kailas. Hitching is possible, but is very, very slow. Some of these people have gotten permits from checkpoints along the way.

However, it's best to check bulletin boards at your hotel in Lhasa, and ask around about tour agents who are making up a group. When you do this, the permit problem will be taken care of. In the late 1990's, the total cost of a trip was about US$600. That's not bad when you consider about 6 people ride in a 4WD, followed by a small truck with gasoline and baggage and another tourist. The round-trip journey from Lhasa takes from 17 to 20 days. The drive to the mountain alone is about 4 days, each way! And there's not much in between!

Take all your food and other supplies, or as much as you can. The only place near the mountain where you can buy supplies is at Darchen (or Tarchen), the only town in the area. At Darchen, is at least one shop or store and 2 guesthouses or binguans, but the toilet is down the road or over a ridge somewhere. This should improve someday!

On the mountain, plan to take your own tent and camp. Two good campsites are shown, plus there are pretty grim guesthouses at the Dirapuk and Zuthulpuk gompas or monasteries. Don't plan to buy any food there--carry everything including a good tent, stove & fuel, and warm clothes & sleeping bag--it'll freeze every night at those altitudes! As foreigners, you'll have to pay a fee at the beginning and the end of the trek.

The north face of Kailas (Stan Armington foto & Lonely Planet **Tibet** guidebook).

Map 226-3, Kailas, Gangdise Shan, Tibet, China

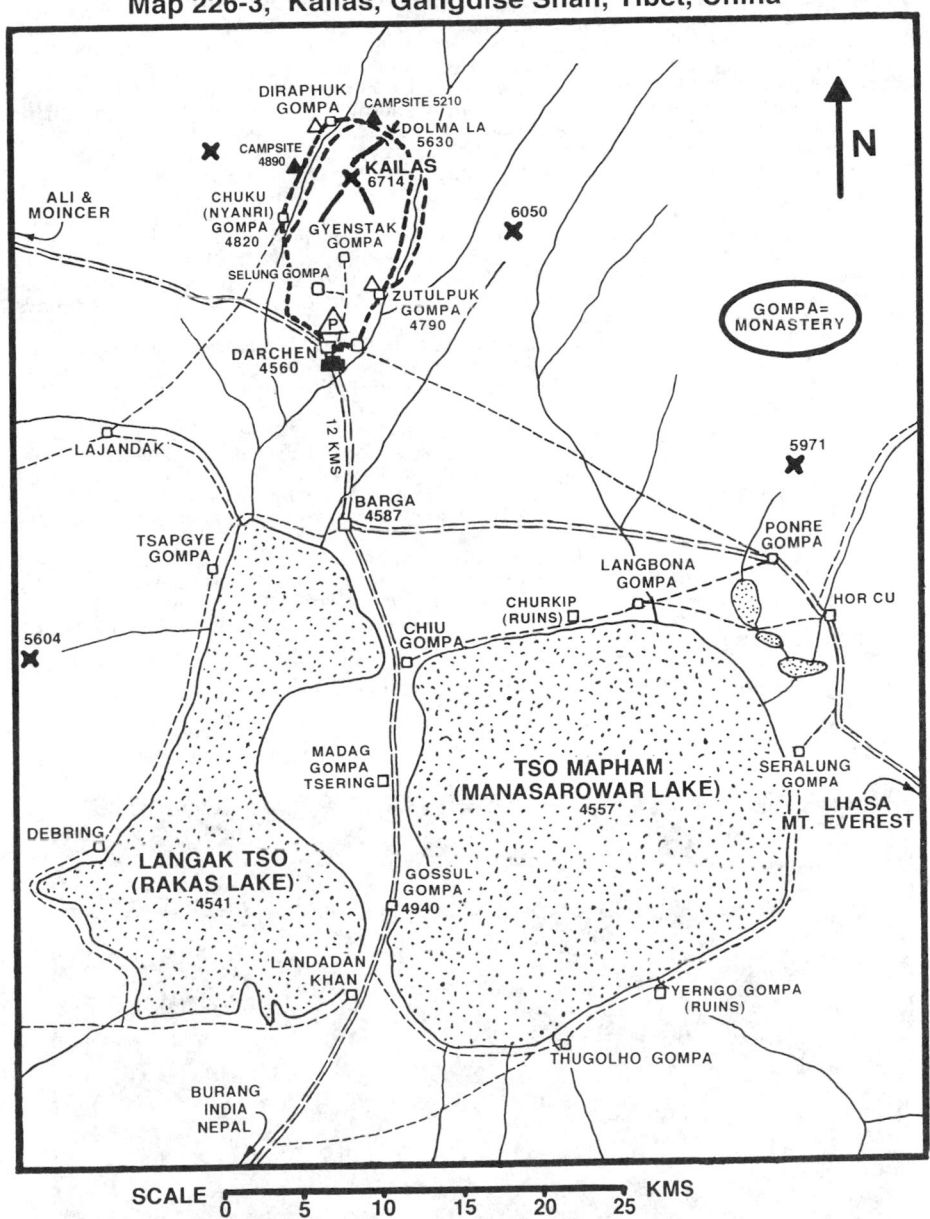

Apparently, very dry Tibet does have enough of a monsoon to matter, because the book below recommends you do this trip in May or June, then in mid-September to early October. The reason is, in mid-summer, when it's warmest, the rivers are running higher, and fording steams is more difficult. As time goes by, bridges are being built, so this should be less of a problem in the future.

Maps DMA maps *NH 44*, 1:1,000,000, 1301 Series, and *NH44-7 & 3*, 1:250,000, if available; or TPC map *H-9A*, 1:500,000; and the latest guidebook, **Tibet**, Lonely Planet (this is by far the best source and devotes a dozen pages to Manasarowar and Kailas treks).

Jumla Trek, Karnali Province, Himalayan Mountains, Nepal

The focus of attention on this map are interesting trekking possibilities in western Nepal's Karnali Province. This isn't to say there are no mountains which will interest climbers, but there are simply no big name mountains around. The highest summit on this map is **Kanjiroba** at about 7045 meters. In the same group are several other peaks just under the 7000 meter mark.

Jumla at 2440 meters, located in the southwestern corner of this map, is the district headquarters for the Karnali Province located in extreme western Nepal. To get to Jumla one must walk about 2 weeks from Pokhara, located to the east; or about one week from the end of the road at Surkhet (get the latest information--maybe that road has been extended?).

Or you can fly to Jumla and save time and body parts! There are regular flights from Kathmandu, but they are difficult to arrange, partly because there aren't that many, and because of weather. However, the author's information is getting old, so things may have changed for the better; airport, communications and facility-wise. If you want to fly into this region and can't get a flight from Kathmandu, you might try other flights originating from Nepalganj, located on the India-Nepal border; or from the before-mentioned town of Surkhet. For most people these days, flying to Jumla seems the only way--in the interest of time.

The eastern part of this map connects to the western part of the Dhaulagiri map at the place called Dune (see next map). If you intend to walk from Pokhara, then you must begin the trek by using the Annapurna map, then the Dhaulagiri, and finally this one. It's a long walk from that side! Best to fly in if you can.

The main reason some trekkers come to Karnali is to see the people and an interesting place called Rara Daha, or Rara Lake. This lake is at a cool and delightful 3000 meters, and the mountain sides are covered with pine, fir, spruce and other trees. This is an area of relatively low population, thus the lake and surrounding hills are now part of a national park. If you want to camp at the lake for several days, then go to the south shore, which has more virgin forest and better camping places.

If you should fly to Jumla, take in as much food and supplies as possible given the weight restrictions. Because this area is so isolated, it's difficult, if not impossible to bring many supplies in. So once there, you'll have to have your own food or buy locally, which has chronic shortages. There is a bazaar in Jumla with rice, wheat, potatoes, beans and other fruits and vegetables in season.

Information from the book, **Trekking in Nepal**, says one should have a tent, as it isn't the custom of the people in these parts to have guests into their homes. While getting a trekking visa in Kathmandu, be sure to get the latest maps and information on roads, flights, food, and hotels before leaving. Trekking weather is good from about March to June, and again from September to November; the pre & post monsoon periods. Winter trekking is possible in the

If you're trekking and *going native* in Nepal, this will be a typical scene.

Map 227-3, Jumla Trek, Karnali Province, Himalayas, Nepal

SCALE 0 10 20 30 40 KMS

lower attitudes. In the middle of summer, streams are high, and sometimes difficult to cross.
Maps *Guide Map of Nepal*, 1:506,880, Natraj Tours and Travel, Kathmandu; or *Nepal*, 1:500,000;
TPC map *H-9A*, 1:500,000; or the books, **Trekking In Nepal**, The Mountaineers; or **Trekking in the Nepal Himalaya**, Lonely Planet; or **Trekking Peaks of Nepal**, Cloudcap.

Dhaulagiri, Himalayan Mountains, Nepal

The 6th highest mountain in the world is Dhaulagiri at 8167 meters. This mountain is located in north central Nepal, not far northwest of Pokhara, and just across the Kali Gandaki River Gorge west of Annapurna. Dhaulagiri was first climbed in 1960 by a Swiss team. Of the fourteen, 8000 meter peaks in the world, only Gosianthan was first climbed at a later date. The normal route to Dhaulagiri's summit is one of the more difficult of all the 8000'ers.

As of 1979 the only route that had been successfully climbed is the one up the northeast ridge. Few others have even been attempted. The route used in getting to the mountain has always been from Pokhara, Tirkhe, Tukuche, the French Col, the Northeast Col and finally up the Northeast Ridge. If you're not into killer mountaineering, you can always enjoy trekking and make a loop around the Dhaulagiri Massif.

The time involved in reaching the Tukuche area would be about a week or a little more, depending on group size, but to get to base camp, which involves going over 2 passes with lots of glacier travel, may take closer to 2 weeks. At the same time of course, you'll be acclimatizing.

Always plan to spend time in Kathmandu. Some of the things you'll have to do there are; get a trekking permit, food--of which there is plenty for any trek, climb or expedition--a small language dictionary and/or phrase book, and additional information from the trekking organizations. Some of the things you'll need to know are the conditions of the trail & bridges on the approach route, and what local foods can be found and in what villages along the way. Also ask about what villages have resthouses or homes where trekkers can stay.

Many people who go trekking now eat local food in villages along the trails, because almost all villages have a tea house and families who rent rooms. Eating along the way means a much smaller pack as well. As time goes on, and as climbing parties get smaller, climbers too are using more local foods. Importing food into Nepal is costly--in time, money and headaches!

For alpinists, the best times to climb are April and May (pre-monsoon), and the end of September and October (post monsoon). For trekking, and at lower elevations, only the months of June, July and August may be rainy and wet on the southern slopes, but much drier in the northern valleys. Some trekkers who stay in the lower valleys, find mid-winter an enjoyable time to visit and trek in Nepal.

There are plenty of buses running from Kathmandu to Pokhara, along with trucks and small aircraft. Pokhara is another fine place to spend a little time, as there's a number of cheap but clean hotels and many food shops and tea houses.

Maps *Pokhara to Jomsom, Trekking Map,* 1:60,000, Kathmandu; *Dhaulagiri Trekking Map,* 1:250,000; TPC map *H-9B,* 1:500,000: and the books, **Trekking In Nepal,** The Mountaineers; **Trekking in the Nepal Himalaya,** Lonely Plant; or perhaps **Trekking Peaks of Nepal,** Cloudcap; and of course the latest edition of any travel guidebook.

From the north with Dhaulagiri left, Tukuchi right (? foto).

Map 228-3, Dhaulagiri, Himalayan Mountains, Nepal

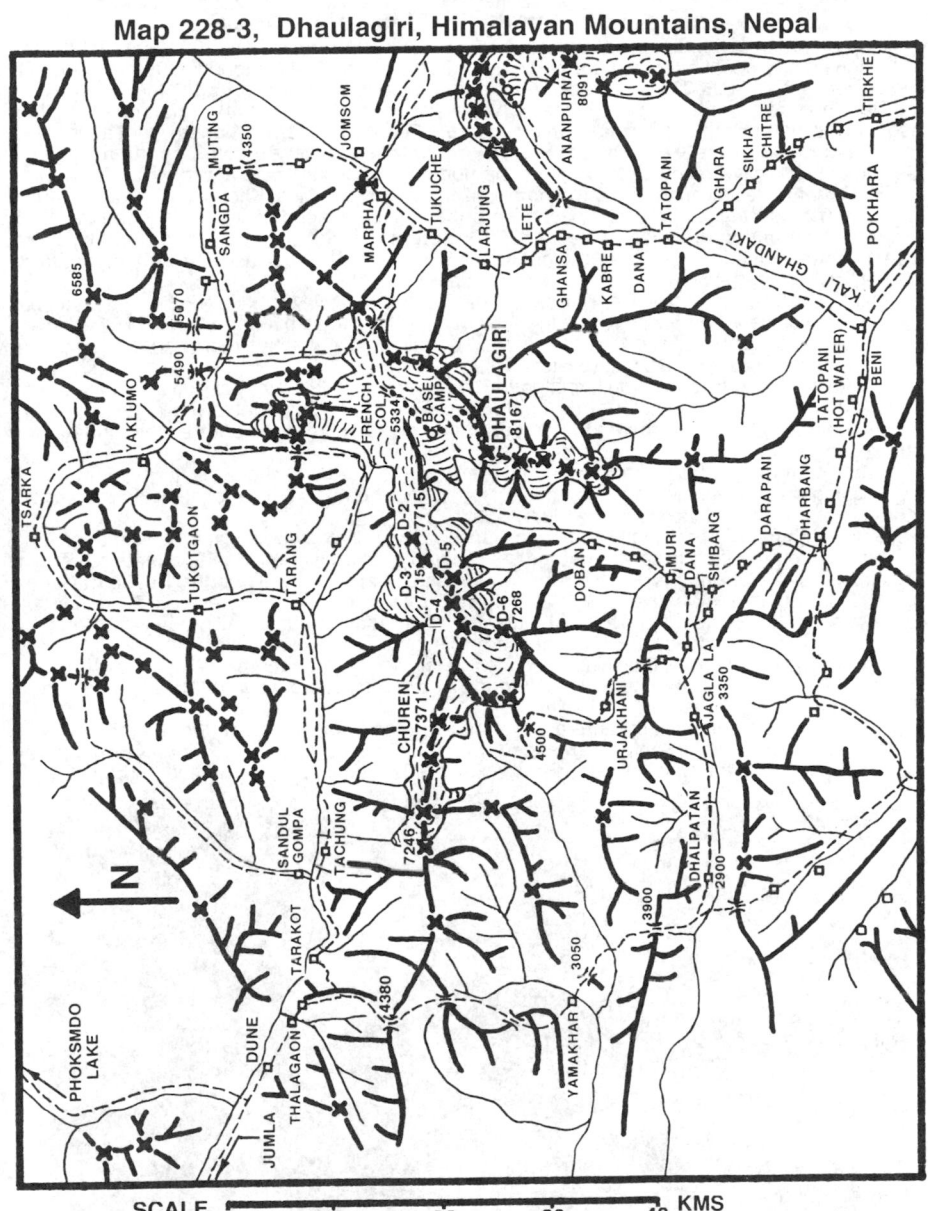

SCALE
0   10   20   30   40 KMS

Annapurna, Himalayan Mountains, Nepal

One of the most famous big mountains in the world is Annapurna at 8091 meters. It's the 10th highest and was the first 8000'er to be conquered. It was first climbed in 1950 by a French Expedition. Of all the 8000'ers in Nepal, Annapurna is the closest to any road or highway.

Here are the 2 normal access routes which have been used to climb Annapurna: The first ascent was made on the north face, which was reached via Pokhara, Ghansa, Choya, and into the Miristi Khola on the western slopes. The route then zigzagged south up the north face. Getting to the former French base camp on the north face will take about a week.

The other route was made from Pokhara, Birethanti, and the Modi Khola, which leads to what is called *The Sanctuary*, a kind of box canyon or horseshoe-shaped basin, surrounded by a wall of mountains, much of which is nearly 8000 meters. It was a British team lead by Chris Bonnington that made one of the first technical climbs in the Himalayas up the southeast face. Getting to this base camp will take less than a week.

Here's what the author did. He left Pokhara on 5/14/1975, with a big pack and headed north, but had a very poor map. He headed for the south face of this massif, but was totally lost in the clouds and rain. He did get up close to a glacier, but doesn't know exactly where--somewhere near Machapuchare (?) He returned 8 days later.

To reach **Annapurna**, you must first go to Kathmandu. While there, get up-to-date maps and information and any last minute food or other supplies. If trekking, that's where you'll get your trekking permit. Ask about the condition of bridges and what villages offer accommodation or shops, etc.

From Kathmandu, take one of many buses going to Pokhara; there are lots of buses and traffic going that way these days. You could also fly, but weather regulates the flying part, so it's more simple and reliable to make the trip by bus.

Solo climbers or other small climbing groups, can usually do some climbing with a trekking permit. There are officially sanctioned peaks ranging from about 5600 to 6650 meters that can be climbed on a trekking permit. See the latest edition of the book, **Trekking Peaks in Nepal**, for more information. Whether you're climbing or trekking, you can buy all your food in Nepal and not be bothered dragging it through customs. Nowadays, you can also buy food along the trails because most villages have a tea house and homes to sleep in.

This is especially true of the villages on the trail circling the Annapurna Range. This is a very popular hike and is known as the *Annapurna Circuit*. The route from Pokhara to Jomsom is another popular hike called the *Jomsom Trek*.

If climbing, May 20 or 25th, and mid-October are the times set aside for summit attempts. Sometime in June to mid-September is the monsoon season. The valleys north of Annapurna are much drier than the south slopes. For trekkers, at low elevations, September through May is

Annapurna as seen from Pokkara.

Map 229-1, Annapurna, Himalayan Mountains, Nepal

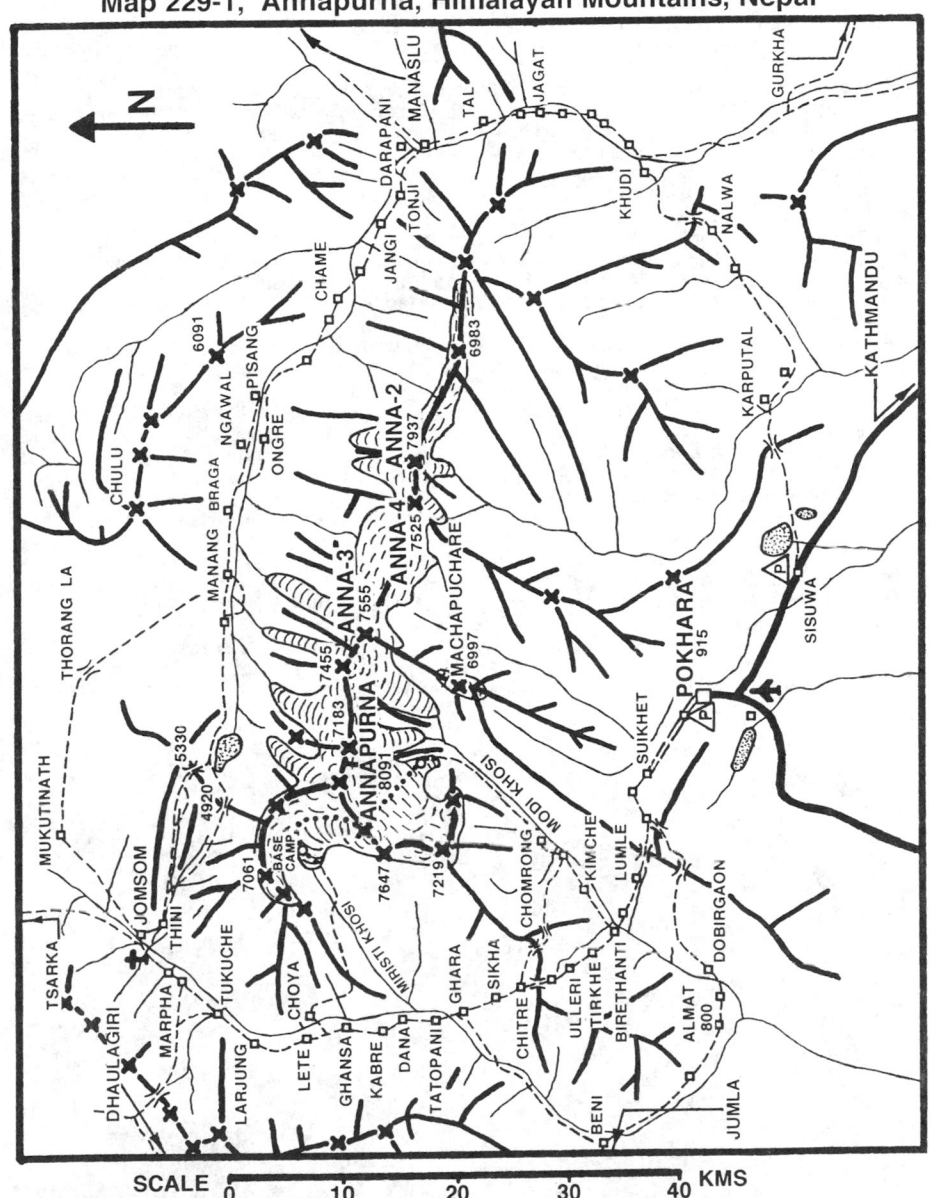

SCALE
0   10   20   30   40 KMS

generally good, but the higher valleys are snowed in during winter. Besides the normal camping gear, a complete rain suit for both you and pack are required--even in the so-called dry season and on the south slopes.
Maps The map *Kathmandu to Pokhara*, 1:60,000, printed in Kathmandu; the Schneider trekking map *Annapurna*, 1:100,000; and books, **Trekking In Nepal**, The Mountaineers; **Trekking in the Annapurna Region**, Trail Blazers; **Trekking in the Nepal Himalaya**, Lonely Planet; **Trekking Peaks of Nepal**, Cloudcap; and the latest travel guidebook to Nepal.

Manaslu, Himalayan Mountains, Nepal

The 8th highest mountain in the world is Manaslu at 8156 meters. It's in north central Nepal, and just south of the Nepali-Tibetan border. If you were to go to a point about halfway between Kathmandu and Pokhara, then go due north to near Tibet, there would be Manaslu.

There are 2 main ways in which to reach **Manaslu**. The route taken by the Japanese who made the first ascent in 1956, was from Kathmandu, Trisuli Bazar, Arughat Bazar and the Buri Gandaki River; then north to Sama and the Manaslu Glacier. The route they took to the summit was southwest up this glacier and the north face, as shown.

From Kathmandu, take a bus or truck to the market town of Trisuli Bazar, shown on the next map, and begin the trek from there. This route puts you on the east side of the mountain and along the Buri Gandaki.

The second approach route is from the southwest and western side and the Marsyandi River. This route starts in Pokhara, or rather Sisuwa on the highway to Pokhara (see Annapurna map), then to Khudi on the Marsyandi River and north to Darapani. From that point, the mountain has been climbed via the southwest slopes and the Dona Khola, with a base camp on the Thulagi Glacier.

A second route beginning in Darapani, has been northeast up the Dudh and Domen Kholas, to the Domen Khola Glacier. The last part of that route was up the northwest face and the west ridge.

If you intend to visit the Dudh Khola and the western approaches to the mountain, then take a bus going toward Pokhara, but get off at Sisuwa. This small town is about 15 kms before, and southeast, of Pokhara. Begin walking from there. This is the same starting point as one would use to make the circle trek around the Annapurna Range. See the previous map of Annapurna.

The route from Pokhara and Sisuwa seems to be the shortest of the 2 approach routes. It will take about 7 to 9 days to reach the mountain from this direction, whereas from the Trisuli Bazaar area, count on about 8 or 10 days. Really fit climbers can do it faster, but if you're using porters, they prefer to go at their pace, which is usually slower (if you pay them per/day).

Kathmandu is the best place to buy food and supplies, but Pokhara also has a good bazaar, where everything needed for a climb or trek can be found. Some of the more basic foods can also be found in Trisuli Bazar.

Going to Manaslu has always been easy, since it's totally inside Nepal with no border problems. Kathmandu is the place to get your trekking or climbing permit, and the last place to get additional information about trails, guidebooks and the latest trekking maps. Don't leave Kathmandu without a language dictionary and phrase book.

Manaslu seen from the east. It was first climbed by a Japanese group (? foto).

Map 230-3, Manaslu, Himalayan Mountains, Nepal

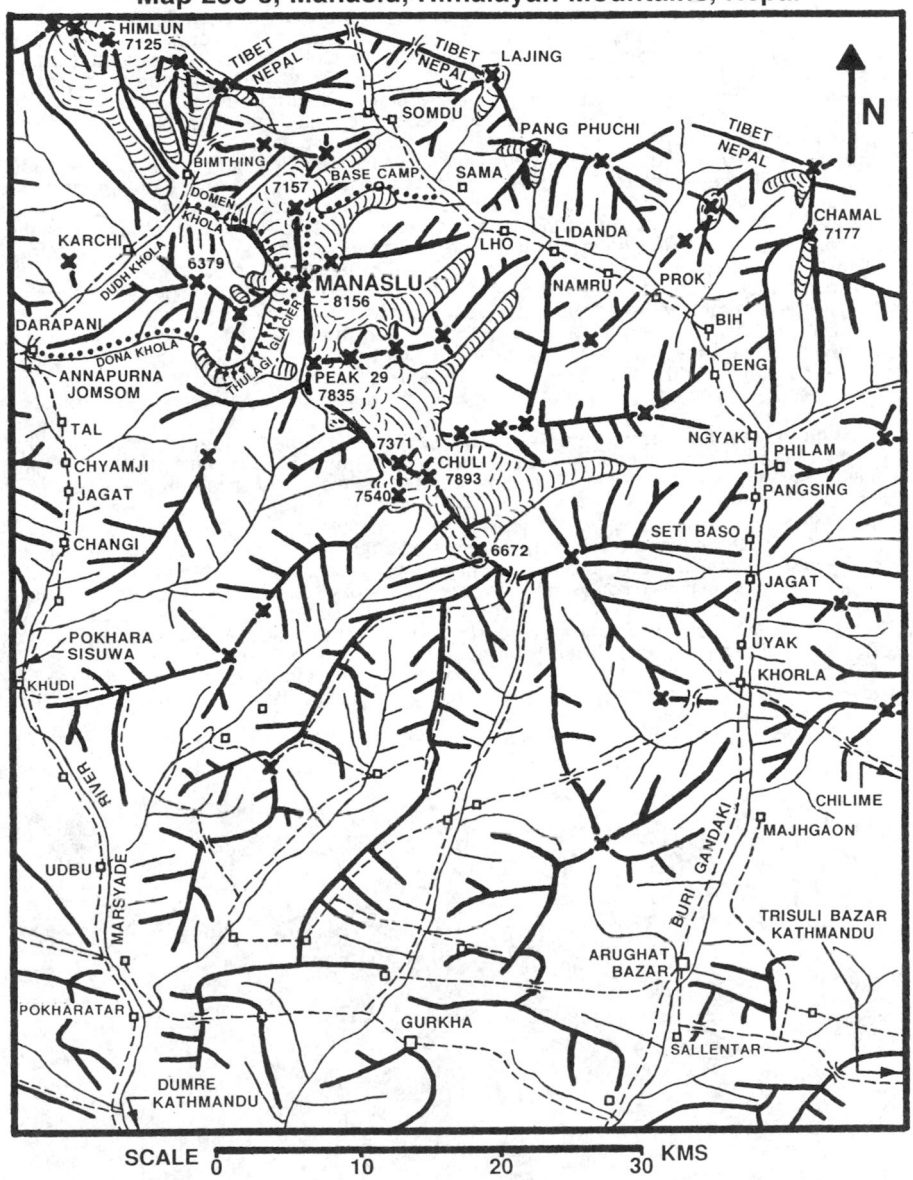

SCALE

0   10   20   30   KMS

Maps *Kathmandu to Pokhara, Trekking Map,* 1:60,000, printed in Kathmandu; the map *Nepal,* 1:500,000; or TPC map *H-9B,* 1:500,000; and the books, **Trekking In Nepal,** The Mountaineers; **Trekking Peaks of Nepal**, Cloudcap; and **Trekking in the Nepal Himalaya**, Lonely Planet.

Xixabangma & Langtang Trek, Himalayas, China-Nepal

The 14th highest mountain in the world is Xixabangma (Shisha Pangma), 8013 meters. This peak is located just inside the Tibetan or Chinese border, perhaps 3 or 4 kms from Nepal. However, this map shows little of the approach to the mountain. Instead, it concentrates on the areas between the Nepal-Tibetan border and Kathmandu. This is a popular trekking area for those with short holidays and who don't have the time to hike for several weeks. Chinese climbers scaled Xixabangma in 1964, via a northeast glacier and ridge. They likely started their climb from somewhere north of Nyalam, on the highway to Lhasa.

Until the late 1970's and early '80's, it was impossible to climb in China or Tibet, but in 1980, Messner was allowed to climb Everest from the Chinese side. There are now no political problems with getting permission to climb this mountain or any other peak.

Besides Kathmandu and some trekking trails between the capital city and the border, this map also features the following mountains; Jugal Himal (Big White), 7083 meters; Langtang Himal (Kyungka Ri), 6979; Langtang Lirung, 7245; and Ganesh Himal, 7150 meters.

You could walk right from downtown Kathmandu to any part of this area, but it's not pleasant walking in the heat at low elevations. The best thing to do is to take a truck or bus to Trisuli Bazar, which is the normal beginning point for the approach route to all the mountains previously mentioned (with the exception of Xixabangma and Big White). Or by taking a truck or bus from somewhere in Kathmandu to Chautara, you can reach the south slopes of Big White. Someone at the tourist information office or one of the trekking outfitters can tell you where to find transport around Kathmandu.

Up until the last few years, there was but one type of climbing expedition; the kind that brought all food supplies from Japan, Europe or North America. But that's slowly changing. Nowadays, any climber or trekker who wants can buy all his/or her food in Kathmandu, or in villages along the way.

Also there are 2 kinds of trekkers; those who hire porters to carry most of their baggage and all their food (which often comes from home); and those who go native. Those who go native, eat local food, purchased at the local tea shops now found in most villages. Many of these trekkers sleep, at least part of the time, in private homes along the way. If one of your objectives in going to Nepal is to meet local people, this is the best way to accomplish that. The point being made here is, one doesn't have to go to all the bother of bringing food from home to trek or to climb in Nepal. Kathmandu has a good selection of foods for any climb, and you can gather it all in one or 2 days.

This information is merely an introduction. When applying for a trekking permit in Kathmandu, all the latest information about routes, food availability along the trails, better maps, bus information, etc., will be made available to you.

Maps Map *Nepal*, 1:500,000; and *Kathmandu Valley*, 1:50,000; TPC maps *H-9B & H-9C*, 1:500,000;

This is Xixabangma as seen from the north (Book-**High Mtn. Peaks of China**).

Map 231-2, Xixabangma & Langtang Trek, Himalayas, China-Nepal

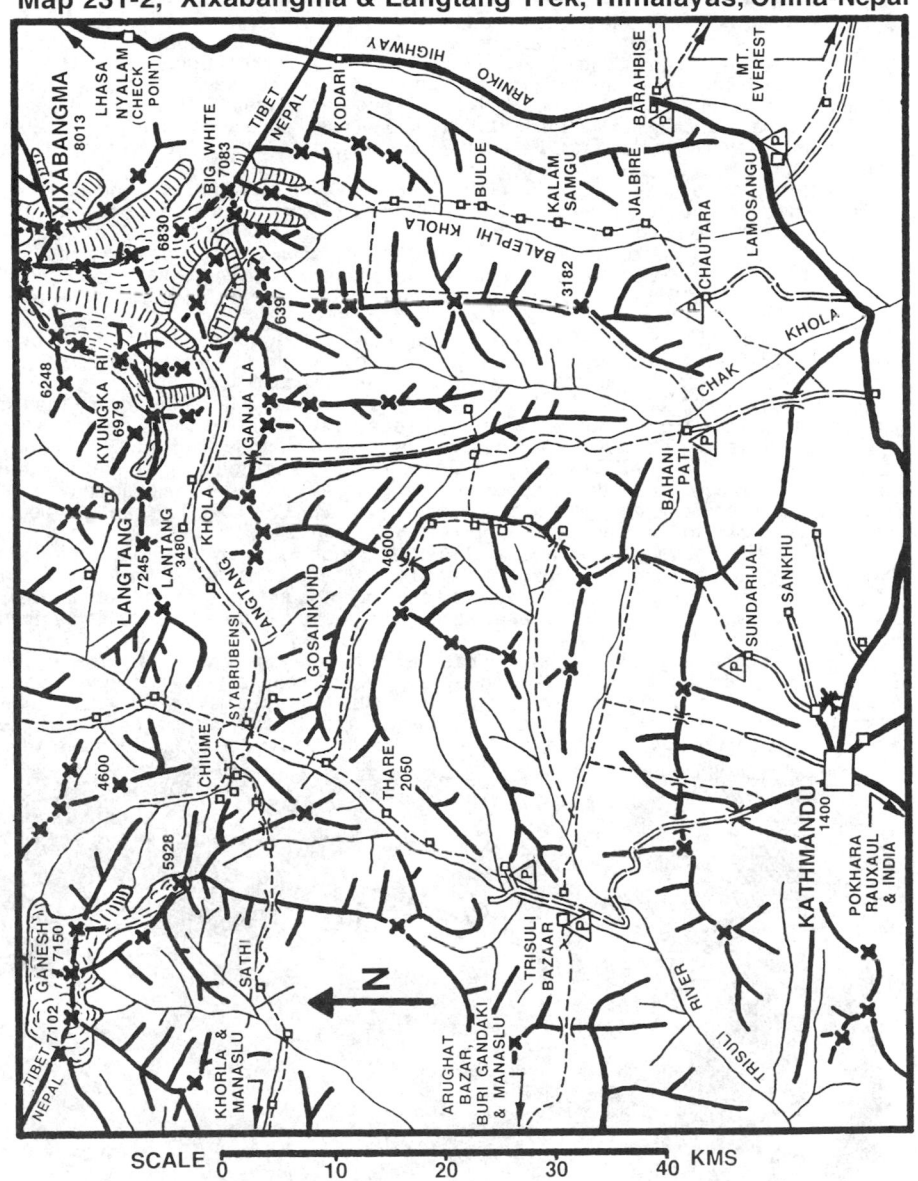

and the books, **Trekking In Nepal,** The Mountaineers; or **Trekking in Langtang**; or **Trekking in the Nepal Himalaya**, Lonely Planet; or **Trekking Peaks of Nepal**, Cloudcap; and any good travel guidebook to Nepal.

Everest & Cho Oyu Treks, Himalayan Mountains, Nepal

This map shows the route that's become famous in mountaineering circles throughout the world. It's the trek that's been used since about 1950 for most expeditions heading to Mt. Everest and vicinity. Today it's used by literally thousands of trekkers from every part of the world who want to set foot on, or have a close look at, the highest mountain in the world. It's not difficult to go to Kathmandu, obtain a trekking permit, and walk to the Mt. Everest Base Camp. Also shown here is Cho Oyu at 8153 meters. To climb this peak, everyone must use the same approach as those going to Everest, but the route splits at Namche Bazar. The next map shows the normal routes up both peaks.

The best time to do these treks and/or climbs is in the months of April, May, September and October. However, if you're out to trek only, and will stay at *lower elevations*, the winter months can also be good. You can also hike in the summer monsoon season, but it's not quite as enjoyable then. For climbing, the months just mentioned; that is, the pre-monsoon and post-monsoon periods, are the best times to summit. Most people now consider the post-monsoon (end of September and October) season to be the most stable, weather-wise. But by October the days are getting shorter.

Anyone with hiking or backpacking experience can make this 2-week-plus walk to the area of Mt. Everest. It's an up-and-down route, requiring more determination than anything else. It's a good way to get in shape and lose weight; about all you need is desire.

Before leaving home, buy one or more of the books and/or maps listed below and familiarize yourself with the situation. Then in Kathmandu get a trekking permit, pick up information booklets at various trekking agents which describe the route in more detail (if you haven't done so), buy a small language dictionary & phrase book, and start learning simple phrases immediately. Also buy food for the trek and/or the climb; and if you desire, make arrangements for porters (all the names and addresses of all these organizations will come to you as you begin the process of getting the trekking permit).

Big expeditions have always carried all their own food, but now little tea houses are scattered along the trail where local food can be found for those alone or with small groups. In Namche Bazar, near Everest's Base Camp, you can find enough good food to climb Everest! Some of this food is leftovers from big expeditions. You can even buy some climbing gear in Namche.

Daily buses can take you from Kathmandu to the start of the trail now at Jiri; this takes one full day. From Jiri to Namche Bazar takes some people up to 9 day, but others do it in about a week. And if you wish, as most do, return by air from Lukla. However, unless they've upgraded the airport radar, you could be waiting days for the weather to clear. Many villages have rooms to rent but take a tent anyway. Take a good pair of boots that don't bother your feet and always

Cho Oyu from the Tibetan side (Book-**High Mtn. Peaks of China**).

Map 232-3, Everest & Cho Oyu Treks, Himalayas, Nepal

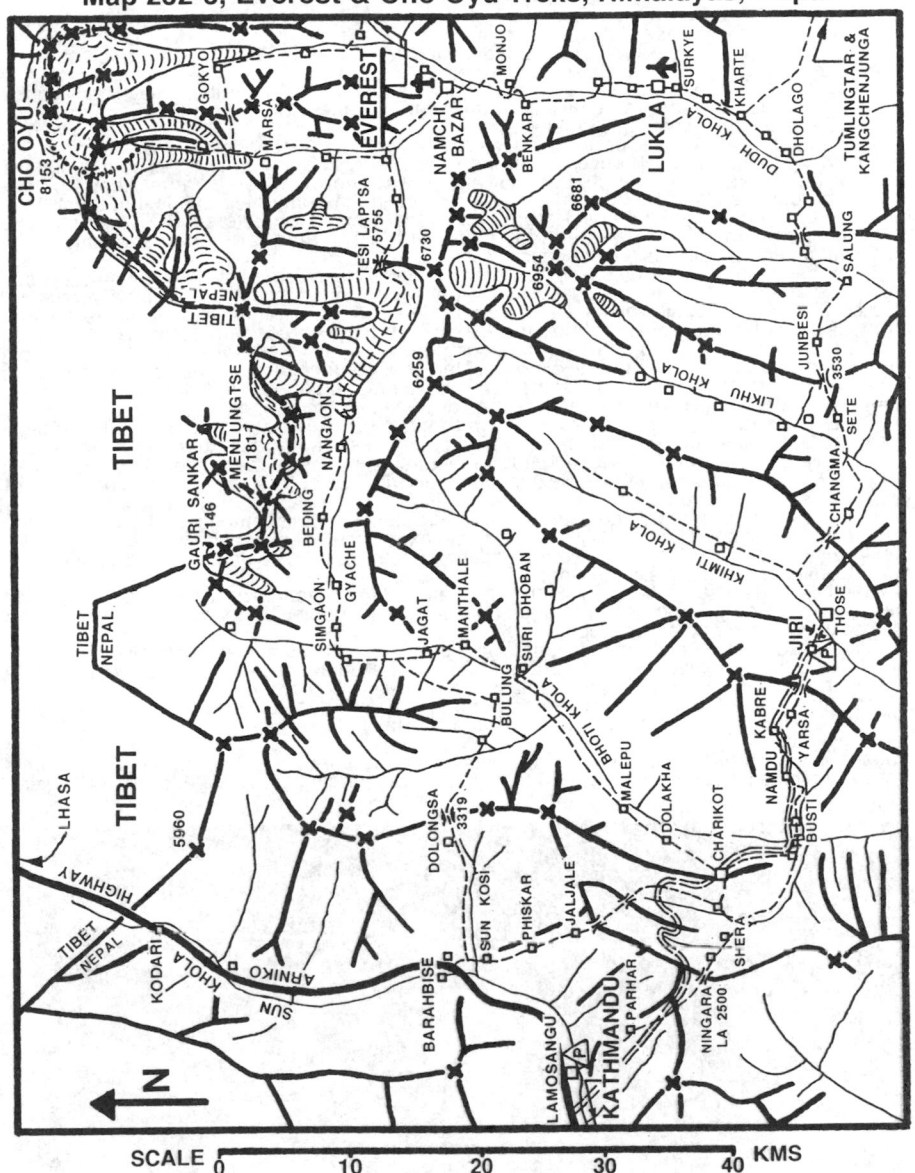

rain gear.
Maps *Lamu Sangu to Mt. Everest Trekking Map,* Kathmandu; or *Khumbu Himal (Everest),* 1:50,000; or *Everest Climbing Routes,* National Geographic; or TPC map *H-9C,* 1:500,000; and the books, **Trekking in the Everest Region**; or **Trekking In Nepal,** The Mountaineers; or **Cho Oyu Himal & Ryajo Ri Himal,** Expo Publishing; or **Trekking the Nepal Himalayas,** Lonely Planet; and **Trekking Peaks of Nepal**, Cloudcap. For hotel and transport information use the latest travel guidebook to Nepal.

Everest & Cho Oyu, Himalayan Mountains, Nepal

The previous map covers the Everest Trek from Jiri to Namche Bazar, located 2 to 3 days walk from the Everest Base Camp. This map covers the area north or above Namche Bazar, and includes the 1st, 4th, and 7th highest mountains in the world. These are Mt. Everest, 8848 meters; Lhotse, 8511; and Cho Oyu, 8153 meters.

To reach any of these mountains, you're required to use the same route in reaching Namche Bazar. From Namche, the route divides, with most foreigners walking in the direction of Mt. Everest Base Camp at about 5350 meters.

Getting to this area is easier now than in previous years. Most people make this 7 to 9 day walk from Jiri to Namche. However, it's now possible to fly in or out of Lukla--a couple of days south or below Namche. Flights begin or end in Kathmandu. Bad weather keeps planes grounded because it's still a visual flight-path airport--no instrument landings, but there have been some improvements in recent years. Helicopters and Twin Otters now fly into this 450 meter-long runway. In bad weather you could wait along time for flight, especially in the monsoon months of June, July and August.

In this immediate area, Namche is the best place (the only place) to stock up on any supplies you'll need at the last minute. You can actually find enough good food here to climb Everest; but all expeditions still bring all their food from Europe, Japan or North America. In Namche you can find roasted nuts and grains, canned foods of all kinds, potatoes and other vegetables (in season), dried milk, ground cereals (for making hot porridge), kerosene, etc. For the latest information about what exactly is available in Namche, contact some of the trekking agents in Kathmandu. You may want to buy some items in Kathmandu, others in Namche. Nowadays, many people who do this trek, eat in tea houses along the trail to Everest.

On **Everest** itself, the normal route is via the Western Cwn and South Col, the original conquest route taken in 1953. Most expeditions have used that route, but other more difficult routes have been pioneered. In the 1990's, almost all summiteers were clients of guides who organized groups for profit. Now only the rich can climb Everest it seems. The expeditions of yesteryear seem to have vanished.

Lhotse, which is actually the south peak of Everest, was first climbed in 1956 by a Swiss group that later climbed Everest while on the same expedition. They reached the summit via the Western Cwm and a coulior on the northwest face. South face routes on Lhotse are some of the most difficult and dangerous in the world.

Cho Oyu was first climbed in 1954 by an Austrian team, along with 2 Sherpas. The route they used involved going over the Nangpa La (Pass), and just into Tibet, then turned east and climbed up a glacier and a west ridge.

Plan to spend time in Kathmandu before your trek to get the latest maps and information.

The traditional expedition to Everest a thing of the past. Today people normally join a outfitter that organizes trips to various places. Here are several organizations you can contact. To start try website (**www.expeditiontrips.com**) or in the USA call *Expedition Trips* Tele. 877-412--8527. They are a *middle man*, lining up clients with guide services.

Or contact *Mountain Madness* in Seattle, Washington, USA, at 206-937-8339, or see their website (**www.mountainmadness.com**). This company specializes in taking clients to the highest summits on each continent. In 2000, they were charging US$89,000 to climb all **Seven**

Mt. Everest left, Lhotse center, Nuptse right (National Geographic foto).

Map 233-3, Everest & Cho Oyu, Himalayas, Nepal

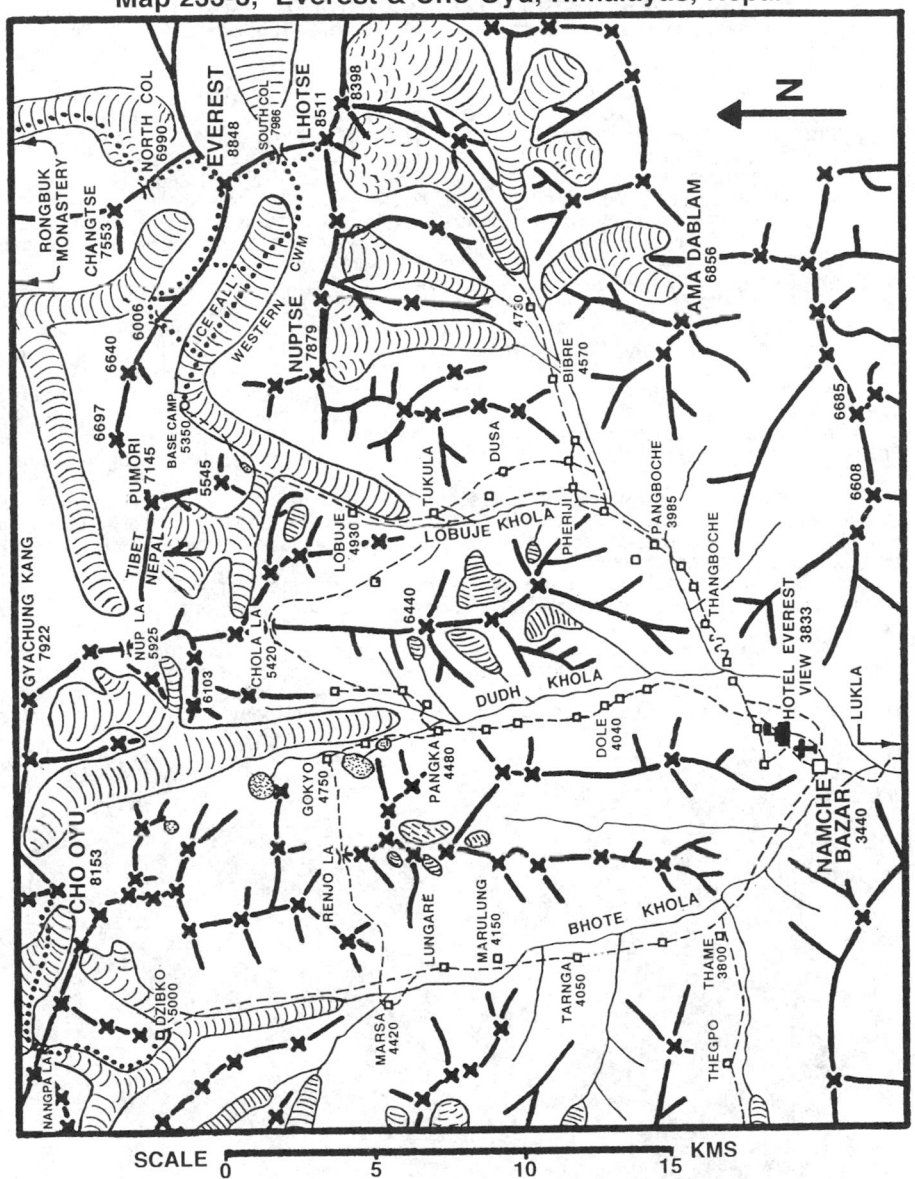

SCALE

			KMS
0	5	10	15

Summits: Kilimanjaro, Aconcagua, Denali, Elbrus, Carstenz Pyramid, Everest & Vinson.
Or contact *Adventure Associates* in Sydney, NSW, Australia, Tele. Inter+61 2-9389-7466, or
Fax Inter+61 2-9369-1853, or see their website **(www.adventureassociates.com)**. For more
outfitters see ads in sports magazines like *CLIMBING*, or the *Sierra Club*.
Maps *Everest Climbing Routes*, National Geographic; *Khumbu Himal (Everest)*, 1:50,000,
Schneider Maps; or *Chomolongma-Mount Everest*, 1:25,000, Freytag und Berndt; and the
books, **Trekking In Nepal,** The Mountaineers; or **Trekking in the Nepal Himalaya**, Lonely
Planet; and/or **Trekking in the Everest Region**, (?).

Makalu, Himalayan Mountains, Nepal

The big mountain just east of Everest and Llotse is Makalu at 8481 meters. This is the 5th highest mountain in the world and it was first climbed in 1955 by a French team.

There are 2 possible routes by which to reach the base of **Makalu**. This map shows the more normal route. It begins in the southern Nepali town of Dharan or Dharan Bazar. The first part of this trail is the same route used to approach Kangchenjunga, located further to the east (see the next map, *Kangchenjunga*, for a look at the beginning of this trek). From Dharan Bazar, to a small village called Hile, where the routes to Kangchenjunga and Makalu split, takes 2 to 3 days, depending on the climber or trekker. Then the route goes to the left and north toward Makalu, all the time following the Arun River Gorge. Higher up this same river gorge, the name changes to the Barun Khola.

A second possible approach would be from Lukla Airport, which is south of Everest. This is an important and well-used airfield and is often used by Everest trekkers or expedition members to get back to Kathmandu without lugging a pack for 2 more weeks!

From Lukla, the trail heads south, then turns east at Kharte and links up with the Dharan-Makalu trail just north of Tumlingtar (see the *Mt. Everest Trek map*). It is here that an airstrip is located. It seems possible that a small aircraft can be hired in Kathmandu to land at Tumlingtar. In fact, there may be some kind of regular air service to that site by now (?). If so, it would be a shorter hike in, or out; when you're tired and trying to get back to civilization in a hurry.

Before going to Dharan Bazar, one must first stop in Kathmandu to get a trekking permit (climbers usually have it before arrival). It doesn't take much time, only a day or two. In the meantime you can go shopping for food, fuel, a phrase book, up-to-date maps, etc. Also, if you're someone which a limited time in Nepal, check out the possibility of flying in or out of Tumlingtar.

Throughout Nepal, most people use kerosene stoves for cooking, and that fuel can be found in many villages. Needless to say, a kerosene stove is the best one to have in Nepal (as well as throughout most of the less-developed world). Or better still, take a stove that burns all fuels and you can always find something to burn.

The climbing months are April and May, the first week of June, end of September, October and in some years, early November. Trekking can be done in winter too, but only in the lower valleys.

Buses can be found in Kathmandu or Rauxal (Indian border), for the ride to Dharan Bazar. Kathmandu has bookstores and other places where you can buy some of the latest maps and get the current information on the trails, food availability and villages where you might find someone renting a room to trekkers along the way, etc. Before leaving home, buy the latest

Makalu is located southeast of Everest (Book-**High Mtn. Peaks of China**).

Map 234-3, Makalu, Himalayan Mountains, Nepal

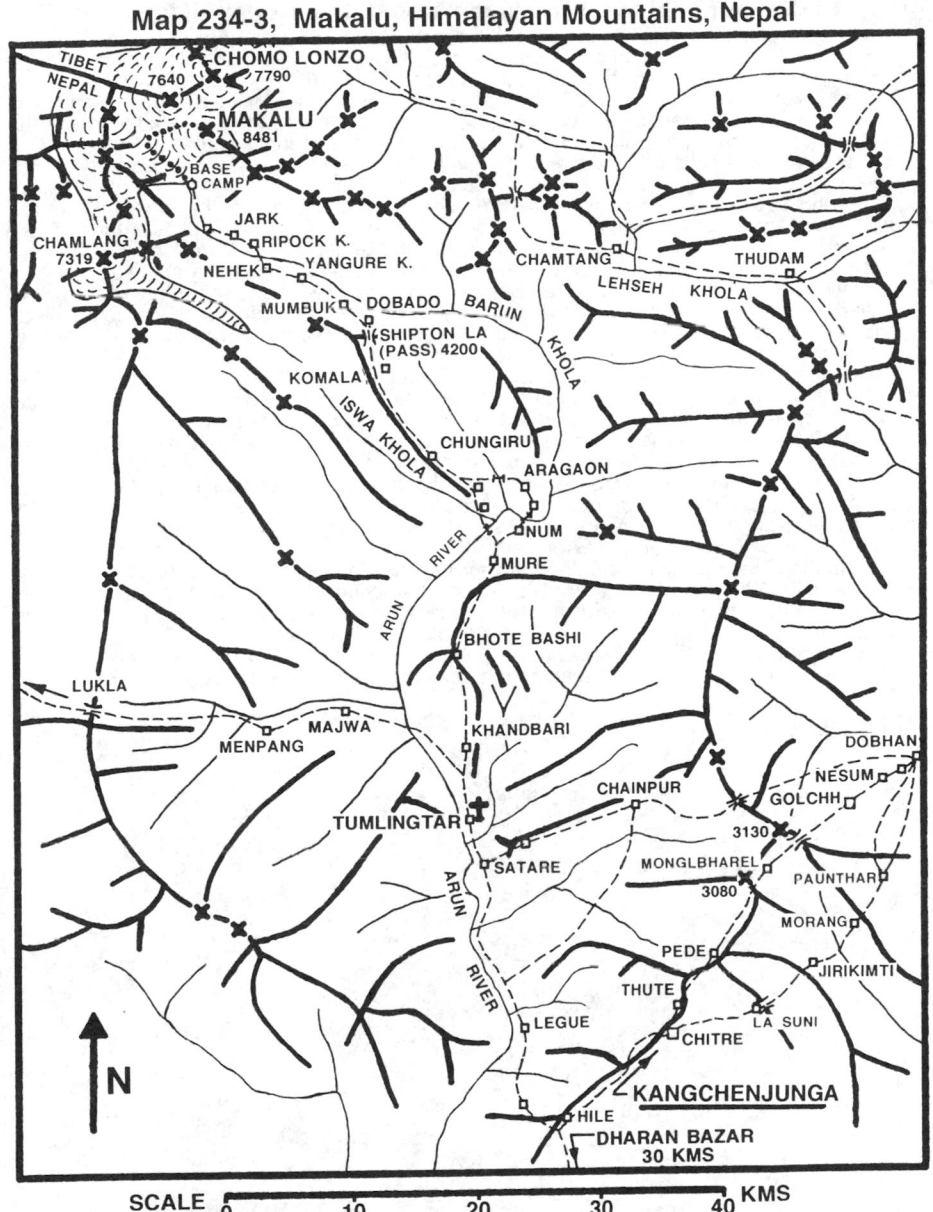

SCALE

| 0 | 10 | 20 | 30 | 40 | KMS |

edition of any trekking guide to updated this information.

Maps The map *Nepal*, 1:500,000, Kathmandu; DMA map *Kangchenjunga,* 1:250,000; TPC map *H-9C*, 1:500,000: and the books, **Trekking In Nepal,** The Mountaineers; or **Trekking in the Nepal Himalaya**, Lonely Planet; and maybe **The Trekking Peaks of Nepal,** Cloudcap.

Kangchenjunga, Himalayan Mountains, Nepal-Sikkim

The third highest mountain in the world is Kangchenjunga, 8598 meters. It's located on the border of Nepal and Sikkim, and just south of Tibet. It's also about 80 kms almost due north of Darjeeling in northern India. Kangchenjunga was first ascended in 1955 by a British team. It is the furthest east of any 8000'ers, and is the last really big peak in the Himalayas going east.

The route to **Kangchenjunga** covered on the map is the one from the Nepal side and the town of Dharan Bazar. One must look at the political situation in India, Nepal and Sikkim, then decide which route will be open or the best for you; this one through Nepal, or a 2nd one from Darjeeling. Politics change and so may be the approach route.

The way used by the 1955 British Expedition was from Darjeeling, but they crossed over the Nepali border and made the ascent from the Yaiung Glacier and the southwest face (the last part of their approach and climb is the same as is shown on this map). That expedition took 10 days to reach the base of the mountain. The route described here may take slightly longer.

Getting to Dharan, or Dharan Bazar, can be done from Kathmandu or the border town of Rauxal (India-Nepal). Small, overcrowded buses make this trip, which is one long ride. You might also catch a truck going that way--sometimes they are better than buses. You can probably fly to Dharan from Kathmandu as well (?).

As for food, that can all be bought in Dharan or Kathmandu. Kathmandu has good enough food selections for climbing any mountain in the world. As one is trekking (or climbing), local food can be bought in tea shops in some villages enroute. This means a smaller pack, especially for trekkers. While it's different than the menu you're accustomed to, it is adequate. *Going native*, is half the fun of being in this part of the world.

If one needs porters, they can be found in Dharan, or at points along the way. Porters do not need special equipment to reach the place called Oktong, but above that, special arrangements must be made for *high altitude porters* (HAP's). This means you supply them with food, tent, ice ax, special clothes & boots and stoves & fuel.

Kathmandu is a necessary stop; not only for the best food selections, but for your trekking permit as well. While there, check with the tourist information office and local trekking outfitters and get the latest information regarding trails, bridges, places where you can buy food along the way, etc.

Best months for climbing or trekking are April and May, early June, the last of September, October and early November. The monsoon season is from June through early September.

The upper south face of Kangchenjunga (Indian Air Force foto).

Map 235-3, Kangchenjunga, Himalayas, Nepal-Sikkim

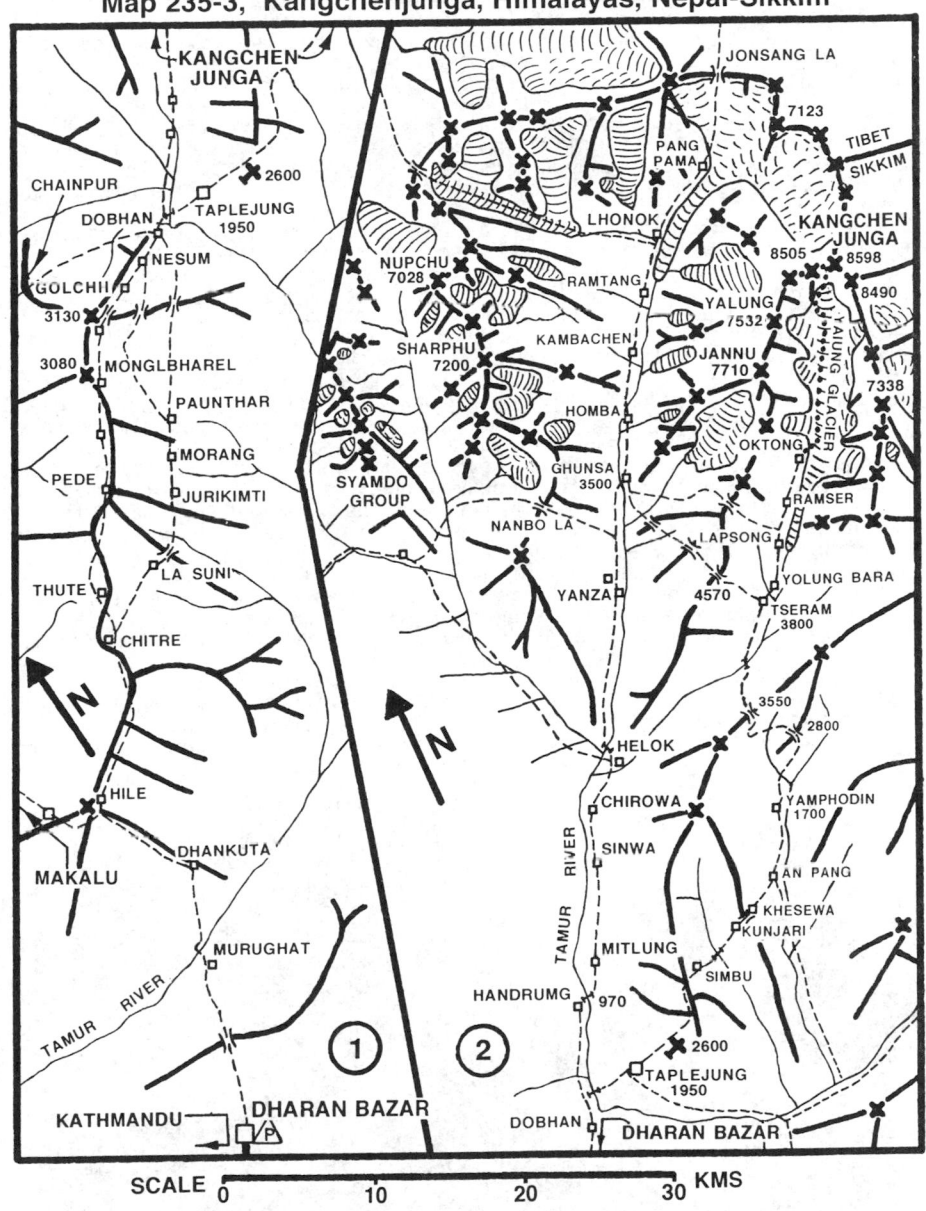

During all months, go prepared for wet conditions, as the Nepali foothills seems to be damp all the time.

Maps The map *Nepal*, 1:500,000; DMA map *Kangchenjunga, NG 45-3,* 1:250,000; TPC map *H-9C,* 1:500,000; and the books, **Kangchenjunga: Trekker's Guide**, (?); **Trekking In Nepal,** The Mountaineers; **Trekking in the Nepal Himalaya,** Lonely Planet; and **Trekking Peaks of Nepal,** Cloudcap.

Adams Peak, Sri Lanka (Ceylon)

One of the easiest, and for sure, one of the most interesting climbs you'll ever make is to the top of Adams Peak on the island of Ceylon (now the country's name is officially called Sri Lanka). Adams Peak at 2233 meters, is a sacred mountain to Buddhists. They believe The Buddha was there and left the impression of his foot in the rock at the summit. Because of this, it's one of the most climbed mountains in the world.

Adams Peak is located northeast of Ratnapura, the gem capital of Sri Lanka, and southwest of Hatton, an important town in the highland region. From Ratnapura and Hatton, there are dozens of buses daily, in fact about one every half hour, going to both Carney and Dalhouse. These places are the trailheads on either side of the mountain. The buses are full of pilgrims making the trip to the mountain.

The shortest walk to the summit is from Dalhouse at 1200 meters. This beginning point is notably higher than the 350 meter altitude at the Carney Trailhead on the south side. From Dalhouse, there's a cement staircase to the summit, complete with hand railings and electric lights for night-time hiking. The trail from the Carney side is not as well developed--at least there's not quite so many cement steps, but it does have electric lights from top to bottom. The reason for the lighting on the paths, is that many people make the pilgrimage at night, when it's cooler. The heat and humidity on this tropical island are terrific!

Along the trails, particularly on the Carney side, are trail-side vendors; people with small shops or refreshment stands. So there's no need to burden yourself by carrying food up the mountain. These people sell both food and soft drinks; all of which is carried up the mountain on someone's back. Naturally the prices are higher than in the towns below.

At several locations, mostly on the Carney side, are pilgrims shelters, used as rest stops. These are large buildings with roofs over cement floors, but with open sides to allow for air movement. There's never a charge for using the shelters, as they seem to be public property, at least that was the case when the author made the climb in 1975. People lay down small mats and rest or sleep a while sometime during the night, but on the author's trip, while he was trying to sleep, others were coming and going all the time.

On the Carney side there are several small streams along the path. Drinking this water shouldn't be a problem because it's nothing but virgin rainforest upstream. On top there's a shrine, covering what is alleged to be the *footprint* of The Buddha, and a place where Buddhist monks live.

The author recommends a traverse of the peak. He started in the late afternoon of 4/20/1975 at Carney carrying a large pack, walked to the shelter named Heremitpana, stayed the night and continued to the summit and down to Dalhouse the next morning. From there he got a bus to Hatton, then Nuwara Eliya. Nothing special is needed for the hike, as thousands do

This foto was taken above Carney on the south-side trail to the summit.

Map 236-1, Adams Peak, Sri Lanka (Ceylon)

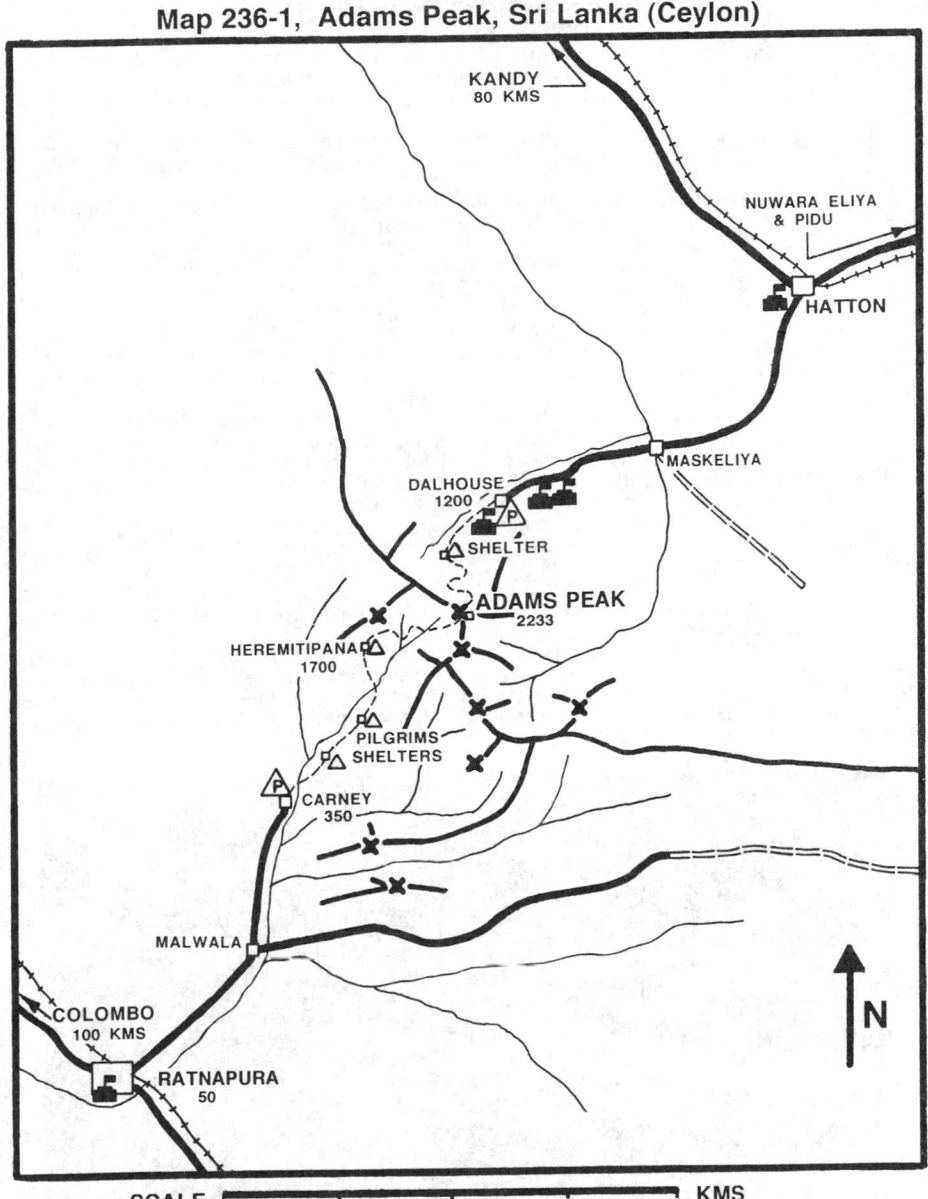

it weekly, including old people, many of whom walk barefoot. The driest months are December through March, and July through September (for Colombo, the capital).
Maps *Ratnapura*, 1:63,360, Survey Department of Sri Lanka; DMA map *NB-44, 2 & 6*, 1:250,000; and the latest travel guidebook, **Sri Lanka**, Lonely Planet; or **Sri Lanka Handbook**, Moon Publications.

Pidurutalagala (Pidu), Sri Lanka (Ceylon)

The mountains on the island of Ceylon, or what is known today officially as Sri Lanka, are not high or rugged, but they are interesting. One of the main reasons for going to the mountains or highland areas, is to get up and away from the tropical heat and humidity. One fine place to do that is to visit the town of Nuwara Eliya and the highest peak on the island, Pidurutalagala at 2524 meters.

Nuwara Eliya is located in the south central part of Sri Lanka, about 70 kms southeast of Kandy, the old capital, and not far east of Hatton, which is on the way to Adams Peak. See the previous map.

Getting to Nuwara Eliya is easy. There are many buses running to this region from every direction, including Kandy, Hatton and Colombo (the capital). Bus service in Sri Lanka is very good, but if you get there with the war still going on with the Tamil Tigers, everything might be disrupted. *In fact, it already has! Since the author's visit in 1975, a TV antenna was installed on top, and because of that and the war, as of 1999, at least the summit area was closed to hiking. If things are quiet when you arrive, you should be able to make this hike.*

Nuwara Eliya is a hill-station at a cool and invigorating 1900 meters, in the middle of one of the most important tea growing areas of the world. Because of its altitude and refreshing climate, it's also a tourist hangout. Most tourists are Sri Lankans, as few foreigners know of the place. At least that was the situation on the author's trip to Pidu on the morning of 4/22/1975.

About 3 kms immediately north of Nuwara Eliya is **Pidurutalagala**, or *Pidu* for short. To climb Pidu, first walk to the north end of town and near a hospital ask someone where the trail to Pidu is. The author's diary states he walked past *St. Xavier's College and the Keena Lodge*. This is a small town and everyone knows where the beginning of the trail is. All educated people in Sri Lanka speak English, so communication is not a problem.

The trail begins at about 1900 meters altitude, and it's only about 5 kms to the summit. This can be completed in a couple of hours, or about half a day, round-trip. The author made it up in about 1 1/2 hours, and was back at his hotel by 10:30am. About 3 hours round-trip.

At one point just beyond the Ramboda Pass is a small stream where good water is found. The final portion of the trail is on grassy slopes, whereas lower on the mountain, you'll walk through a virgin rain forest.

In Nuwara Eliya, there is a variety of accommodations, from the most expensive to very cheap guesthouses. In some cases you might stay in someone's home with rooms for rent. It's not a big place, but it has all that's needed for a pleasant stay. The driest months in the capital of Colombo are December through March, and July through September. This same rainfall pattern is likely the same for Nuwara Eliya.

This is the small stream & spring along the trail up Pidu.

Map 237-1, Pidurutalagal (Pidu), Sri Lanka (Ceylon)

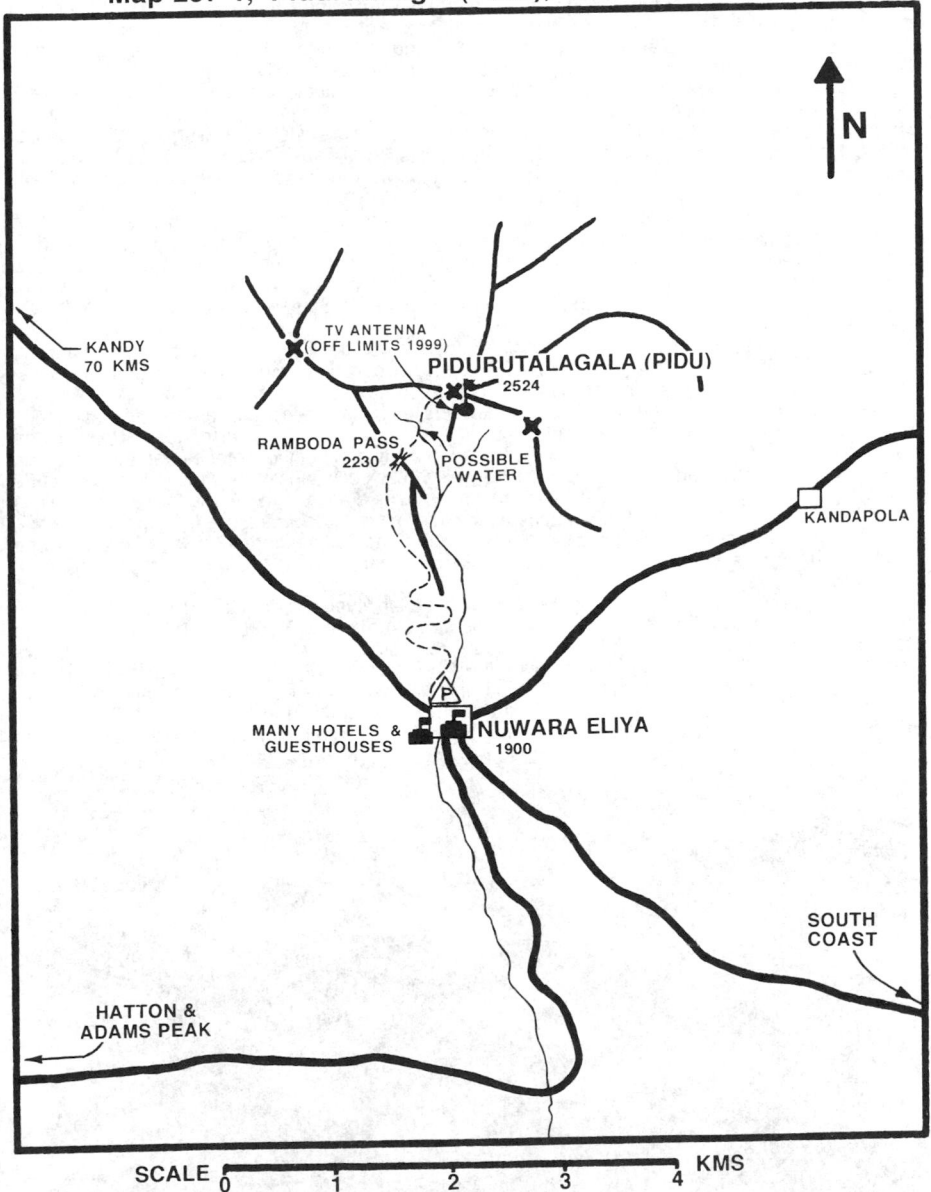

N

KANDY
70 KMS

TV ANTENNA
(OFF LIMITS 1999)

PIDURUTALAGALA (PIDU)
2524

RAMBODA PASS
2230

POSSIBLE
WATER

KANDAPOLA

P

MANY HOTELS &
GUESTHOUSES

NUWARA ELIYA
1900

SOUTH
COAST

HATTON &
ADAMS PEAK

SCALE
0   1   2   3   4   KMS

Maps DMA map *NB-44, 2 & 3*, 1:250,000; and *Nuwara Eliya*, 1:63,360, Survey Department of Sri Lanka; and one of the latest travel guidebooks, **Sri Lanka**, Lonely Planet; or **Sri Lanka Handbook**, Moon Publications.

Popa Taung Volcano, Myanmar (Burma)

Near the geographic center of Myanmar, formerly Burma, is the only volcano of consequence in that part of the world. This is Mt. Popa. It rises from a base of about 500 meters up to 1518. Popa is located southwest of Mandalay, and southeast of Nyaung-U & Bagan, the city of ancient pagodas & stupas. Popa is a stratovolcano which had its last eruption in about 442 BC.

All tourists to Myanmar visit Mandalay & Bagan, and many visit the temple complex at the base of Mt. Popa called Popa Taung Kalat. This site includes the Mahagiri Temple, dedicated to 37 Nats in the upper part of Popa Town; and a lower section, where you'll find lots of shops selling food & souvenirs. Next to this lower section, and on top of a volcanic plug, is **Popa Taung Kalat**. Tourists climb to this temple along a spiral metal & cement staircase. Along the way are lots of monkeys. Watch out, they'll steal food from you!

Here's what the author did. He took an all night bus from Yangon to Mandalay (15 hours & US$5.70), then changed plans and immediately got on another bus to Kyauk Padaung (pron. Chau Padaung). That bus which was heading to Nyaung-U & Bagan, took 5 hours and cost US$3.15. At Kyauk Padaung, he then waited at the *pickup parking--to Popa*. This was late in the afternoon, and there weren't enough passengers to justify making the trip, so the author pitched in about US$3 and away they all went.

As of 2/2000, the only hotel on the mountain for tourists was the Mt. Popa Resort at US$80 a night, so the author was allowed to sleep on the floor of a private room in the Kumara Rama Monastery just north of the volcanic plug. His donation was about US$1.50.

Next morning, 2/13/2000, he had breakfast at a local tea house, then road-walked north to the entry point & little visitor center for Mt. Popa Park. From there he walked up the road to the Mt. Popa Resort Hotel and got more information on the trail up the mountain (in front of the visitor center, there's a map painted on a large signboard). From the hotel, he walked back down the road to the trail shown at 860 meters, then went up the mountain. At 920 meters, he reached another trail which follows power lines to the 2nd highest peak marked 1466 meters. From this 1st peak, he was at the true summit of **Popa** in 18 minutes. He made it to that point in 1 1/2 hours from the 860 meter mark. He returned to Popa Town and the monastery via the trail which starts at 760 meters. Round-trip from the monastary took about 3 1/2 hours.

Lots more buses (pickup trucks) make the run between Kyauk Padaung and Popa Town in the morning hours than in the afternoons. Big tour buses make it to Popa Town (from Bagan) via Momboba (just east of Mt. Popa and north of Popa Town), but if you take one of those, you won't have time to climb the mountain--only to Popa Taung Kalat. The monastery offers bucket baths and rooms with keys, but you'll need your own bedding. Or carry water and sleep in the bamboo shelter at 1100 meters. Or try the government guesthouse near Momboba. Plenty of food available in Popa Town. You can climb Popa any time, but the wet season is June through October; the dry season from

This is the volcanic plug called Popa Taung Kalat, located on the west side of
Popa Volcano. At the base is Popa town, with a temple on top.

Map 238-1, Popa Taung Volcano, Myanmar (Burma)

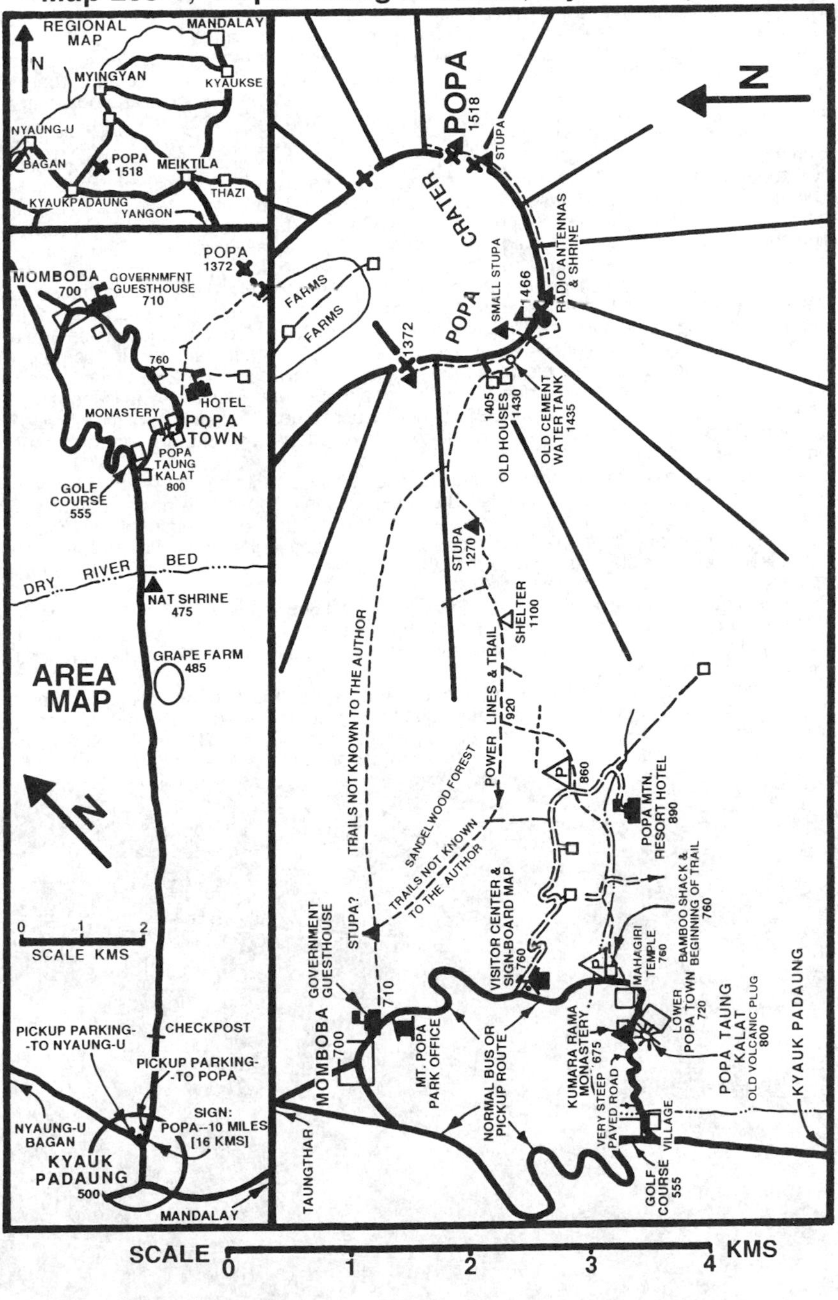

REGIONAL MAP

N

MANDALAY
MYINGYAN
KYAUKSE
NYAUNG-U
BAGAN
POPA 1518
MEIKTILA
KYAUKPADAUNG
THAZI
YANGON

AREA MAP

N

MOMBODA 700
GOVERNMENT GUESTHOUSE 710
POPA 1372
760
HOTEL
MONASTERY
POPA TOWN
POPA TAUNG KALAT 800
GOLF COURSE 555
DRY RIVER BED
NAT SHRINE 475
GRAPE FARM 485

0 1 2
SCALE KMS

PICKUP PARKING- -TO NYAUNG-U
CHECKPOST
PICKUP PARKING- -TO POPA
NYAUNG-U BAGAN
SIGN: POPA--10 MILES [16 KMS]
KYAUK PADAUNG 500
MANDALAY

POPA 1518
POPA CRATER
STUPA
SMALL STUPA
1466
RADIO ANTENNAS & SHRINE
1372
1405
OLD HOUSES
1430
OLD CEMENT WATER TANK 1435
FARMS
FARMS
STUPA 1270
SHELTER 1100
POWER LINES & TRAIL 920
P 860
POPA MTN. RESORT HOTEL 890
BAMBOO SHACK & BEGINNING OF TRAIL 760
MAHAGIRI TEMPLE 760
LOWER POPA TOWN 720
POPA TAUNG KALAT 800
OLD VOLCANIC PLUG
KYAUK PADAUNG
SANDELWOOD FOREST
TRAILS NOT KNOWN TO THE AUTHOR
TRAILS NOT KNOWN TO THE AUTHOR
VISITOR CENTER & SIGN-BOARD MAP 760
P
KUMARA RAMA MONASTERY 675
VERY STEEP PAVED ROAD
GOLF COURSE VILLAGE 555
STUPA?
MOMBOBA GOVERNMENT GUESTHOUSE 700
710
MT. POPA PARK OFFICE
NORMAL BUS OR PICKUP ROUTE
TAUNGTHAR

SCALE 0 1 2 3 4 KMS

November through April or May.
Maps This map and the latest travel guidebook, **Myanmar (Burma)**, Lonely Planet; or **Myanmar (Burma)**, Odyssey Guide.

Golden Rock Pagoda, Kyaiktio, Myanmar

The mountain featured here is Kyaiktio (pron. Chaitio), which means Mt. Kyaikto (pron. Chaito), is 1102 meters elevation. It's located about 80 kms northeast of Yangon, the capital of Myanmar (Burma). It's also near the Myanmar--Thai border. This is another mountain sacred to Buddhist with many people making the pilgrimage to the top every day. The objective is the summit where a large rock is balanced at the edge of a cliff. Over the years it's been painted gold and now has a small shrine or stupa on top. This mountain is made of light colored granite.

Here's what the author did. He bought a train ticket from Yangon to Kyaikto (US$8), then left at 8am on the next morning, 2/9/2000. The railway grade is in such poor condition, it took 5 hours to get to Kyaikto. In front of the railway station were several buses and pickups (with benches in the back and on the roof to carry passengers), and for US$.10 he got a 30 minute--12-km-ride to a small town at the base of the mountain called Kinpun, or Kinpun Camp. This was early afternoon, so he left his pack in one of 2 small hotels and hurried to the summit; a 13-km-walk which took 2 2/3 hours.

He was at the summit area for about an hour, then walked down the cement road to the truck parking area and got on a truck for the ride back to Kinpun for US$.40. That ride was in the dark and he made part of this map with a flashlight and altimeter squatting on a low bench with many other passengers. In Kinpun, he paid only US$3 for a room in the Pann Myo Thu Guesthouse with cement walls, fan and private bath with hot water. It was a nice quiet place, with help from the cement walls.

The next morning, he got on a pickup bound for Bago. That cost US$1.25 and took 2 hours. He walked around town to see 2 big Buddhist temples and a 55-meter-long reclining Buddha. Later he took another pickup to Yangon for about US$.35, but it stopped near the outskirts of the city and he had to take a taxi back to his hotel (US$1). Taking private buses & trucks are much cheaper than government trains in Myanmar.

Going through Kyaikto, the author saw one guesthouse; plus another on the road to Kinpun, and 2 hotels in Kinpun--the Sea Sar and Pann Myo Thu Guesthouses. Kinpun's main street, at the beginning of the trail, is lined with souvenir shops & restaurants. The trail up the mountain has a bamboo shack about every 100 meters with people selling food, drinks and souvenirs. In past years before the road was built, some pilgrims slept at the Dharmshala or the Ye Myaung Gyi Camp, but it's a short hike and there's no need to stay overnight now.

On top is a government guesthouse at US$15 a bed in a dormitory. Or US$36 or $40 for singles. The Golden Rock Hotel 2 kms down the mountain may be cheaper (?). To visit the Golden Rock, you'll have to buy your US$6 ticket in Kinpun, and present it at the fee gate shown. Up to that point you can climb the mountain for free.

Many people now cheat and ride part way up the mountain in trucks to the truck parking area, then walk the last 2 1/2 kms to the summit, even though there's a cement road all the way. Or you can hire 4 porters to carry your lazy ass up in a *sedan chair!* Near the Golden Rock, take off your shoes & socks; this is sacred ground, During the rainy season, which starts in June and runs until the first part

At the summit of Kyaiktio is the balanced Golden Rock & nearby temples.

Map 239-1, Golden Rock Pagoda, Kyaiktio, Myanmar

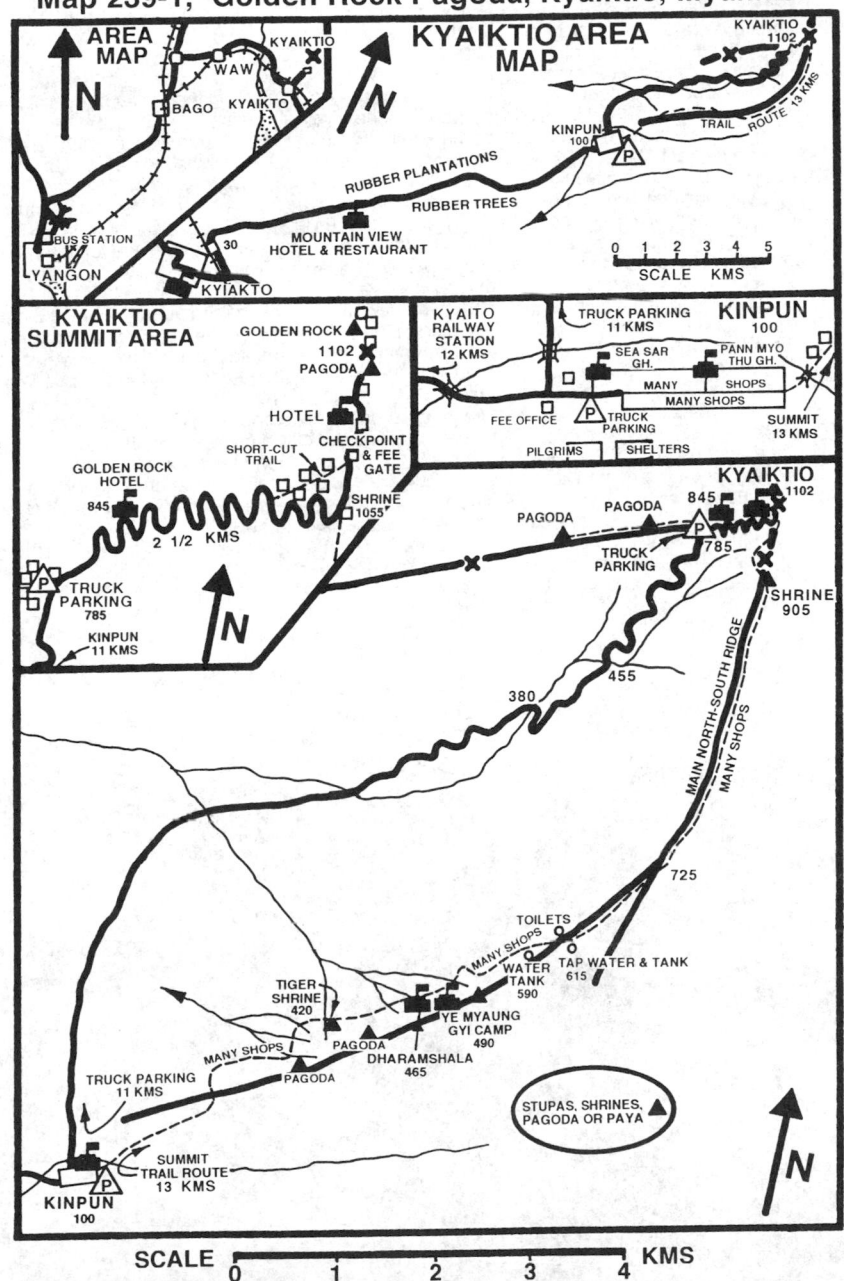

of October, there are few people on the mountain. The trail then is likely muddy & slick in places with the lateritic soil. The dry season is November to May.

Maps This map and the latest travel guidebook, **Myanmar (Burma)**, Lonely Planet; or **Myanmar (Burma)**, Odyssey Guide.

Phu Kradung Doi, Phu Kradung National Park, Thailand

One of the better known & easily accessible mountains in Thailand is **Phu Kradung Doi** (Mtn.). This is actually a plateau, the centerpiece of the Phu (pron. Fu) Kradung National Park. The national park covers 348 square kms, but the top of the plateau is about 60 sq/kms. This nearly flat sandstone mesa, is covered with a grassy savannah & pine trees. The highest point is at the southeastern corner at 1288 meters. The visitor center below is about 330 meters elevation. In the center of the plateau are some canyons and waterfalls. Wildlife in the park includes wild elephants.

Phu Kradung is located 74 kms south of the small city of Loei, and 8 kms west of Highway 201, all of which is in northeast Thailand. If going there from Bangkok, make your way to the Mo Chit or North & Northeastern Bus Terminal which is within walking distance (1 km) of the Mo Chit Skytrain Station. Take a morning bus heading for Loei which runs along Highways 2, then 201. That bus should drop you off at Phu Kradung town as it nears Loei. The author's bus trip took 7 hours and cost US$6.21.

In Phu Kradung, you'll find many shops and places to eat, plus at least one place to stay called the Phu Kradung Guesthouse, which is a group of one-room cottages. The author paid less than US$7 for a clean fan room with attached bath & warm water.

The author arrived in the late afternoon, then the next morning he walked due west along the paved road to the visitor center which is at the beginning of the trail up the mountain. He could have hired a moto (motorcycle taxi) for the ride, but was more interested in making this map, so he walked the 4 kms instead. At the visitor center, he picked up a free information handout which included a map similar to this one.

About 100 meters from the visitor center is a gate where everyone pays about US$.50 for entry to the national park. Then it's straight up to the southeast corner of the mesa, a distance of about 5 kms. The author made this part of the hike in less than 1 1/2 hours. Along the way, are at least 11 places (only 9 are shown on the geology cross-section) where you can stop and eat snacks, full meals or a warm soda pop; or buy souvenirs, post cards or pins. These rest stops are bamboo shacks with tables. Obviously, this is a cultural experience, not a wilderness climb.

On top of the plateau, which measures about 6 x 9 kms, is a maze of trails heading to different viewpoints, waterfalls (wet season only) and the park headquarters, 3 kms from the summit. Nearby is a campground where you can rent a tent & bedding if you'd like to stay a night. Cottages and meals are also available. The author made this climb on Saturday morning, 1/22/2000, and found 500 or more other people, mostly college-age students, going up the trail apparently for the weekend. The author walked to the H.Q., then returned to the visitor center in about 4 hours round-trip. He then hitched a ride back to his hotel. From his guesthouse, the entire outing took a total of about 5 1/4 hours round-trip. Plan to make this an all-day hike.

One information handout states the visitor center is open year-round, but the park (the climb to the top?) is closed from June 1 to September 30, because of the rainy season. However, you may still be

This is one of the main reststops & eating places along the trail to Phu Kradung Doi.

Map 240-1, Phu Kradung Doi, Phu Kradung NP, Thailand

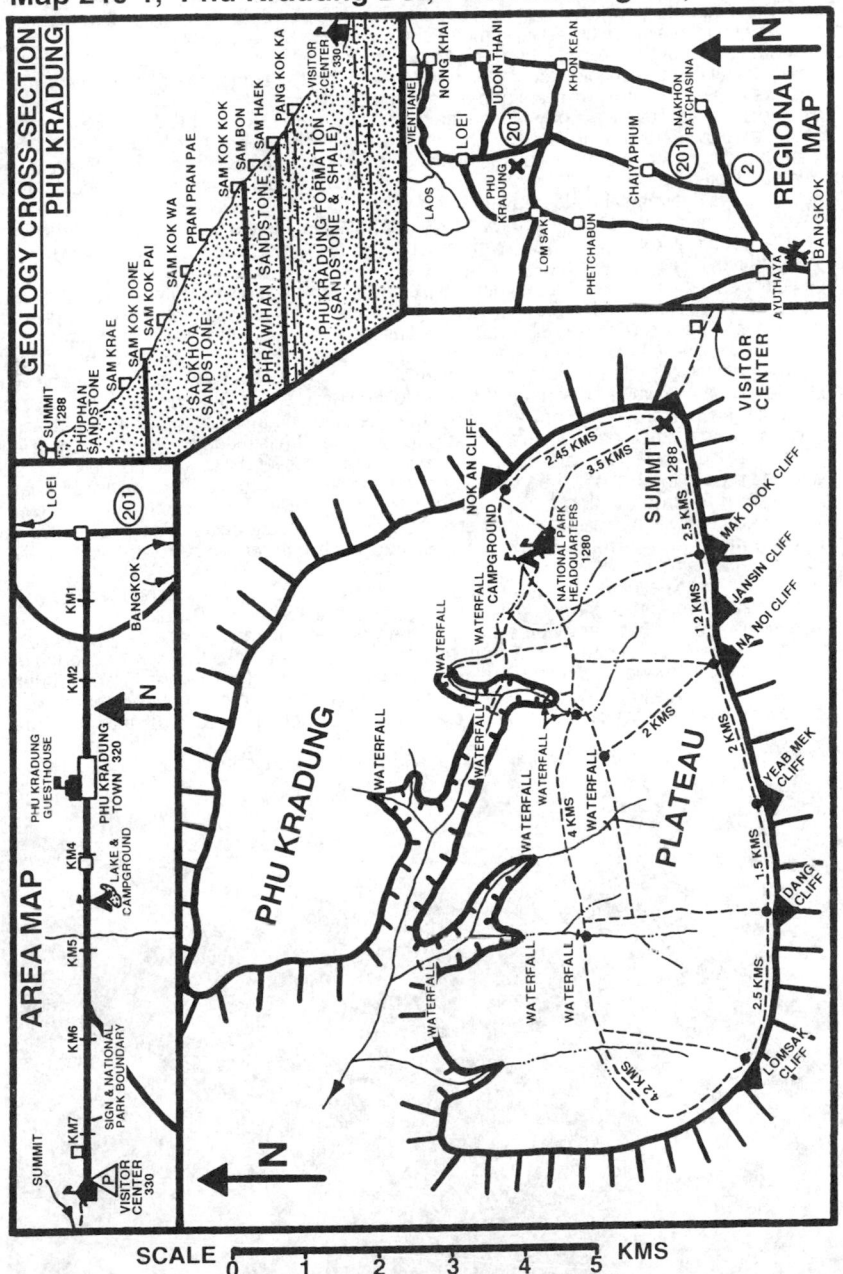

able to make the climb then, but no facilities will be open along the way (?).

Maps This map, which was partly created from a free visitor center handout; and the latest travel guidebook featuring Thailand.

Fan Si Pan, Hoang Lien Son, Vietnam

The highest mountain in Vietnam is Fan Si Pan (Fan Si Peak) at 3143 meters. It's located in the far north of the country along a big ridge or mountain range called Hoang Lien Son. This entire area is just a few kms south of the Chinese border. These mountains are the southeastern tail end of the greater Himalayan Cordillera which are folded and uplifted. On the author's hike, he saw sedimentary rocks such as limestone, siltstone, shale and even some quartzite.

To get to this area, first take a day or night train, or a bus, from Hanoi to the border city of Lao Cai. The author flew into Hanoi around mid-day, then took a night train to Lao Cai costing US$16. Waiting at the Lao Cai station were many mini buses heading to various destinations--including Sapa, a former hill station built by the French at 1500 meters altitude. The author paid less than US$2 and got there in 1 1/2 hours. Sapa has many hotels--maybe 30 or 40, or more! About US$5 will get you a room with private bath, hot water and TV (pay extra for an electric heater). There's also many small restaurants, shops and a good market place. Weekends are busy with various ethnic groups in town wearing traditional clothing; a fotographers dream.

The author arrived in Sapa on the morning of 1/27/2000. It was a cold spell with fog, light mist and 100 meters visibility. He stayed In the Viet Hung Hotel, which doubles as a travel agency, plus has a pretty good map of the area on one wall. That served as the blueprint for this map.

The next 2 days were cold & foggy, with room temperatures between 10°C & 13°C, and no central heating! Everyone in all hotels were huddled over buckets of charcoal trying to keep warm. Finally the author left Sapa and walked down out of the fog to the village of Cat Cat, crossed the bridge to the old & unused French hydroelectric power station, then headed upcanyon to the west. In about 1 1/2 hours, he reached the small log cabin in an area with many new trails made by wood cutters. He was back in the fog at that point so he gave up and returned to Sapa. Never did see the mountain!

Later, he talked to Mr. Hung at the Viet Hung Hotel and was told most *tourists* take 2 or 3 days for the climb of **Fan Si Pan**, making a camp at the stream & water shown on the map. However, somebody who is really fit and calls himself/herself a climber, might be able to do it in one long day--if they knew the way. Or do as most do and make a camp at the *normal campsite*, and finish the climb and return to Sapa the next day.

Since the author experienced several trails in the area of the log cabin, it's recommended you take a guide, at least until you get up the mountain a ways. They cost about US$10 a day.

You couldn't possibly have any worse luck with the weather than the author, so if you can see the mountain, an experienced climber with a campus & altimeter, might make the climb without a guide. There's lots of thick bamboo high on the mountain and the summit ridge to wade through, but a trail does exist. Richard White has written telling the author he went with someone via another more-northerly route shown. He thinks you must have 2 days and a guide because of the many side-trails in that area too.

The rainy season, from June or July through September, brings high water making 2 stream

This is the old French hydroelectric station on the trail to Fan Si Pan.

Map 241-1, Fan Si Pan, Hoang Lien Son, Vietnam

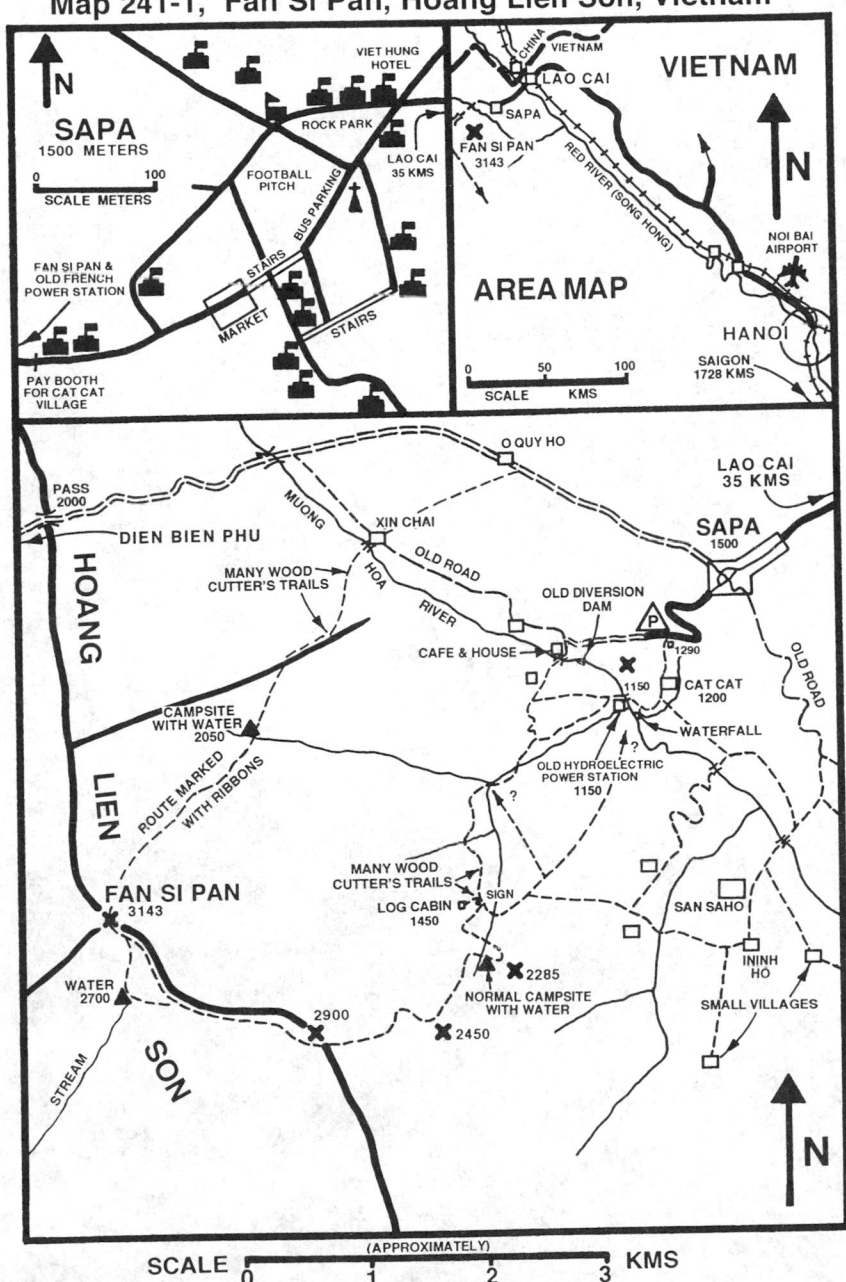

crossings potentially risky. March, April & May, or October & November are the best times to climb. December through February can be rather cold in what is normally considered to be a tropical country.

Maps This map, and one on the wall of the Viet Hung Hotel (other hotels offer guides and possibly have better maps); and the latest travel guidebook to Vietnam.

Nui Ba Den, Vietnam

The mountain shown here is called Nui Ba Den, or Ba Den Mountain. Translated it means Black Lady Mountain. It rises abruptly from the Mekong River plain to an altitude of 986 meters. There are no foothills whatsoever. It's located about 100 kms northwest of Ho Chi Minh City and its major enclave or suburb of Saigon.

As you approach the mountain, it appears to be a volcano, but it's not. Instead it's solid light-colored granite. In places you'll see large crystals like quartz monzonite; in other places it has fine crystals like diorite porphyry. Long ago, magma was forced up from below and it tried to break the surface, but didn't; so the molten magma froze in place to become a granite intrusion. Much later in time, erosion removed the surrounding rock, exposing the granitic-type core.

Nui Ba Den is supposed to be sacred to Buddhists, or at least the temple on the mountain side is. At the very base of the peak is a rather newly developed park area with a small lake, picnic sites and apparently some small cottages. East of that is a new lift or cable car, which takes people up to a temple complex & pilgrimage site at 330 meters. All or most of the complex at the base of this mountain seems to be in private hands and is rather new as of 1/2000. There's a ticket office at the gate and the whole thing seems geared to remove money from your pockets! But you can still walk up to the temple on a very wide path lined with 9 small bamboo structures where souvenirs and soft drinks are sold. Above the temple complex is first a cement staircase, then a regular mountain trail winding up past a couple of caves and through small banana plots to the summit.

Here's what the author did. He arrived in Saigon by train from Hanoi in the early morning of 1/31/2000. He immediately got on a moto (motorcycle taxi) and for about US$1.50 was taken to the northwest part of the city where buses going to Tay Ninh can be found. There's a small bus terminal, but some outfits stop you before the station and put you in their buses. He got in a minibus and after 2 1/2 hours (US$1.50) was let off in the city just south of the Cao Dai Temple. Wrong place! From there he jumped on another moto and for US$1 was taken to the base of **Nui Ba Den**.

He left his large pack at the entry gate at the base of the mountain, then headed up. He was at the summit in 1 1/2 hours; 2 3/4 hours round-trip (One American Vietnam War vet told the author the Americans had control of the summit area on this mountain which they used for communications & observations. They mostly controlled the base of the peak as well. However, the Viet Cong had the middle part of the mountain and were dug in heavily in tunnels. Ask someone about seeing these tunnels). He then got on another moto for US$1.50 and rode to Tay Ninh. He had thought of staying there for one night, but it was still early, so he got on a large bus and headed back to Saigon. That took 3 hours and cost about another US$1.50. Finally for another US$1.50, he took another moto to downtown Saigon and to the area of the *Sinh Cafe* where he got a room with fan & private bath for US$6.

It's best to stay in the area of the Sinh (pron. Sin) Cafe, which is now a travel or tour agency, because of the many hotels nearby. Also at the Sinh Cafe, or other agents nearby, you can book a tourist bus and visit the **Cu Chi Tunnels** (made by the Viet Cong during the American War), Cao Dai Temple and the lower part of Nui Ba Den. But if you want to climb this peak, you'll have to do what the author did; or possibly stay a night in Tay Ninh, or in the cottages at the mountain base. Inquire at the Sinh Cafe in regards to hotels in that area when you arrive. The dry season is from December

The temple on the south side of Nui Ba Den with the summit area in the distance.

Map 242-1, Nui Ba Den, Vietnam

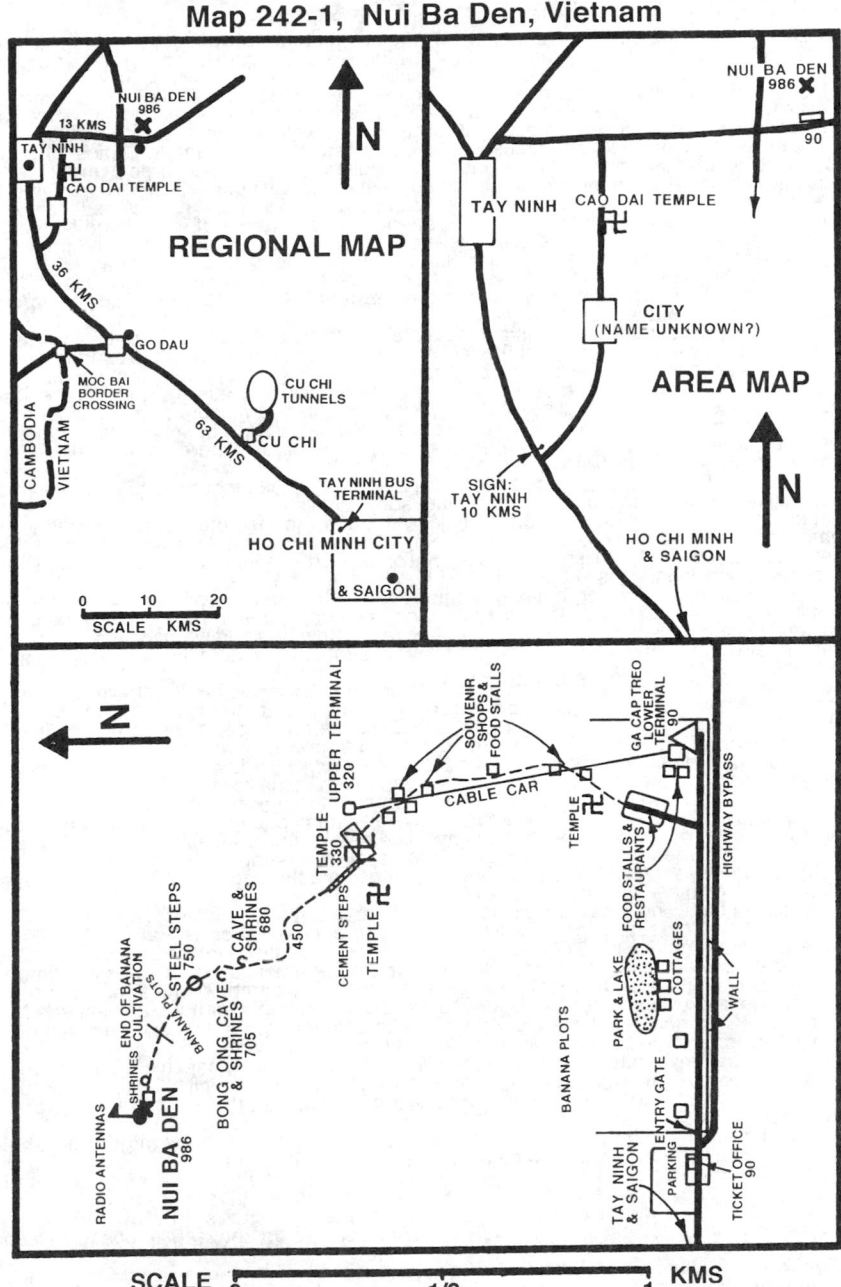

REGIONAL MAP

NUI BA DEN 986 ✗
13 KMS
TAY NINH
CAO DAI TEMPLE
36 KMS
GO DAU
MOC BAI BORDER CROSSING
CAMBODIA / VIETNAM
63 KMS
CU CHI TUNNELS
CU CHI
TAY NINH BUS TERMINAL
HO CHI MINH CITY
& SAIGON

0   10   20
SCALE   KMS

AREA MAP

NUI BA DEN 986 ✗
90
TAY NINH   CAO DAI TEMPLE
CITY (NAME UNKNOWN?)
SIGN: TAY NINH 10 KMS
HO CHI MINH & SAIGON

N

TEMPLE UPPER TERMINAL 320
SOUVENIR SHOPS & FOOD STALLS
CABLE CAR
GA CAP TREO LOWER TERMINAL 90
STEEL STEPS 750
CAVE & SHRINES 680
TEMPLE 330
CEMENT STEPS 450
TEMPLE
TEMPLE
FOOD STALLS & RESTAURANTS
HIGHWAY BYPASS
END OF BANANA CULTIVATION
BANANA PLOTS
BONG ONG CAVE & SHRINES 705
SHRINES
RADIO ANTENNAS
NUI BA DEN 986
BANANA PLOTS
PARK & LAKE
COTTAGES
WALL
ENTRY GATE
TAY NINH & SAIGON
PARKING
TICKET OFFICE 90

SCALE 0   1/2   1 KMS

through April, but highways are paved all the way so you can climb Ba Den even in the wet season of May through November.

Maps This map and the latest travel guidebook to Vietnam.

Chapter 6--The Pacific

This section of the book has a total of 91 maps, covering Taiwan, Japan, The Philippines, Indonesia, Papua New Guinea (PNG), Australia, New Zealand, and a number of islands scattered throughout the central and eastern Pacific.

Most of the mountains in this region are volcanic, a few others are folded and uplifted. All of the summits in Indonesia are volcanic related. Some are old and have lost all their conal shape, others are still active. Indonesia probably has more active volcanos than any country on earth. The Philippines are really an extension of the Indonesian Archipelago, with most of its peaks volcanos as well. Taiwan is made up entirely of sedimentary or metamorphic and folded-type rocks, but with some submarine volcanos located just to the east of the island. Japan is entirely volcanic from north to south with the except of the Kita, Chuo and Minami Alps located in the center of the big island of Honshu. The Japanese Alps are made of folded sedimentary and metamorphic-rocks. PNG has a great deal of volcanic activity too, but Mt. Wilhelm in the Bismarck Range, is made of granite. Granite also forms the core of the Snowy Mountains in Australia and Mt. Kosiusko. New Zealand's North Island is made entirely of volcanics, but the South Island's Southern Alps are similar to the European Alps. All other Pacific islands are volcanic of one age or another.

For anyone speaking English this can be a pleasant part of the world to visit. New Zealand, Australia and Hawaii use English as the mother tongue, while in every other country or island, English is the second language and the only common lingo used by people from various parts of some countries. For example, in PNG there is said to be 717 different languages, so it's important for them to know English. Actually, Pidgin English--a mixture of many languages, is becoming common in PNG, and other island nations today. The dominating language in The Philippines is Tagalog (very similar to Indonesian), but everyone there speaks some English, even people on the street selling bananas.

Because of the script, Japanese and Taiwanese are difficult languages to master in a short period of time, but all school children there learn some English.

In Indonesia, there seems to be one major language; Bahasa Indonesia, but a few people speak Dutch, and even more are now learning English. In virtually every bookstore in the country, you can buy an English-Indonesian dictionary. Their script is the same as ours, and is one of the easiest languages in the world for English speakers to learn.

As for weather, remember that New Zealand and southern Australia are dominated by the movement of cyclonic storms, the same as the middle latitudes in the northern hemisphere. Their winter is the rainiest season, at least in Australia. New Zealand seemingly never has a dry season! Taiwan is humid semi-tropical and Japan is ruled by middle latitude cyclonic storms, plus the remnants of the occasional typhoon.

One thing to remember in the tropics, is that the heaviest rainfall follows the sun. For example, when the sun is at its southern-most point in the sky, it means that it's raining in areas south of the equator; that's in December through about March. Areas north of the equator, have a rainy season, or monsoon, from about May or June through September and into October. Those areas on the equator generally have 2 wet and 2 dry periods during the year. This is the same for Africa and partially true of South America (the Amazon Basin).

There's not much in the way of difficult climbing in this region, but one exception is in the Southern Alps of New Zealand. These peaks have altitudes up to just over 3700 meters, but Mt. Cook has glaciers down to 600 or 700 meters. The best climbs on Cook are as challenging as any in the world, when all factors are taken into account; weather, height of snowline, size of glaciers, avalanches, etc. Outside the Southern Alps, and the snow peaks of Irian Jaya, most climbs in this region are walk-ups.

This part of the world is generally safe for travelers. Not many tourists lose things, and when it does happen, it's usually the traveler's fault. The big exception is **Papua New Guinea**. Between the author's trips in 1977 and 1997, big changes took place, unfortunately for the worst. In cities, every store has one or more security guards, and robberies, usually with machetes, are common. Stay off the Port Moresby's streets at night. When camping in the mountains, never allow locals to know where your tent is, or you could get a midnight intruder, as happened to the author once! Common sense should dictate how to care for your safety and belongings. See **Chapter 1--Introduction** to this book for the ultimate steps in security.

Getting to these various countries is not difficult, but it can be expensive. There are cheap flights from Europe, Hong Kong and North America to Indonesia, the Philippines, Taiwan, Japan, Australia, New Zealand and Hawaii, but to or from places in the central Pacific are very expensive.

Within the islands of Indonesia, there are of course flights between the larger cities, but the cheapest way is by boat. It can also be the slowest, especially if you get on a cargo ship which makes occasional stops. In April & May of 1977, it took the author took 17 days to go from Jayapura in Iran Jaya (western New Guinea) to Surabaya on Java. He jumped ship about midway and found a faster boat. Taking some of these boats is an adventure in travel. However, nowadays it's best to fly, which is what most people do between Indonesians far flung islands.

The Philippines has a very good ferryboat service, but it can be dangerous. You can actually take the same bus from Manila to Davos in the far south, which includes about 4 ferryboat rides. Other ferrys have good sleeping accommodations.

When you're in Hawaii, Tahiti, New Zealand, or Australia, hitch hiking is very good; and probably necessary after paying for your airline ticket to the latter 3 countries. On the major roads in the Philippines, hitching may be good, but it's usually too hot to stand on the road. In PNG, there are many missionaries who will stop for a thumb. If that doesn't work, PMV's (Public

Motor Vehicles) are usually available--though about as expensive as in the industrialized world.
The 2 *cheapest countries* in this region for travelers are the Philippines and Indonesia. Hawaii and Tahiti are among the most expensive places, but there you can camp on beaches and hitch hike, bringing costs down.

The Wilhelm Hut located at Lake Piunde on the trail to Mt. Wilhelm.

Typical scene along the Kokoda Trail of Papua New Guinea. It's a well-maintained trail, but the humidity is very high and your clothing will be soaked all the time.

Yu Shan, Central Range, Taiwan

Yu Shan (Jade Mountain) at 3997 meters, is the highest mountain in Taiwan and all of east Asia. It's built of metamorphic-type rock, as are all the mountains in Taiwan.

When the author was there is 1977, you could only get to this mountain and Alishan by a narrow gauge railway. Since then, there's been a new highway built and that's how most people get to Alishan and the base of the mountain.

You can start on the north side of the mountain at a place called Shuili, but there's only one bus a day heading south to Tatachia (the trailhead) and Alishan. Or hitch hike. But by far the best way to reach Alishan and Yu Shan, is to make your way to Chaiyi (Chaiyahi), located in the lowlands 70 kms by railway due west of Alishan.

Once in Chaiyi, make your way to the railway station. As of the late 1990's, there were 2 trains daily running to Alishan. Both trains leave around mid-day, but they're often full and the tickets cost nearly twice as much as buses. Trains take 3 1/2 hours.

Most people now take a bus from Chaiyi to Alishan. Just outside Chaiyi's train station are 4 bus companies. Look for the Chaiyi County Bus Company terminal. They have about 6 buses per/day to Alishan. The journey by bus takes 2 1/2 hours.

Alishan used to be a lumber town, but it's now a tourist resort sitting at a cool 2274 meters. There you'll find many hotels, youth hostels, eating places, and Buddhists temples. Not far away is the largest tree in Taiwan, but it's dead as a door nail now!

To climb Yu Shan in the late 1990's, foreigners were required to get a **mountain pass or permit**. The reason for the pass is the crowded conditions and ecological damage done in the mountains by too many people. This is the same situation we're starting to see throughout the developed world.

You must get this pass at the **Foreign Affairs Police** in Chaiyi--not Alishan! Or at any Provincial Police Station, or the Provincial Police Administration in Taipei. Ask about this requirement at the tourist office at the airport when you land. They'll direct you somewhere.

To get this pass, you're also supposed to have a group of at least 3 people, and a letter from an Alpine Club in Taiwan. If you're climbing several peaks you might as well get this pass or passes all at once in the same place. While in Taipei, ask about the location of the Taiwan Mountaineering Association, or the Chinese Taipei Alpine Association. Get their current Tele. numbers and addresses at the tourist office in Taipei. You might as well go to one of these clubs to buy good maps as well.

To climb **Yu Shan**, you could walk along the old unused railway grade from Alishan (Km 70) to what the author was told was Yushan Ko (Km 82). It seems that place is now called **Tatachia** (?). But it's easier to hitch hike, or take the irregular once-a-day bus running from Alishan 21 kms along the new Central Highway, and stop at Tatachia (In updating this map, the author is guessing as to the location of this highway because he hasn't seen a new map. It could be running along the old railway grade? So that part of this map is not accurate). Tatachia has a visitor center and two hotels you can stay in, or if full, crash in the forest nearby (take a tent).

From Tatachia, walk 3 kms along an old road to the actual beginning of the trail. The trail heads east below a ridge. At 3520 meters is the Pai Yun Hut. It can sleep about 50 people and has running water and cooking facilities, all for a price. From Pai Yun to the top is a scramble

Near the Pai Yun Hut the trail was blasted out of solid rock.

Map 243-1, Yu Shan, Central Range, Taiwan

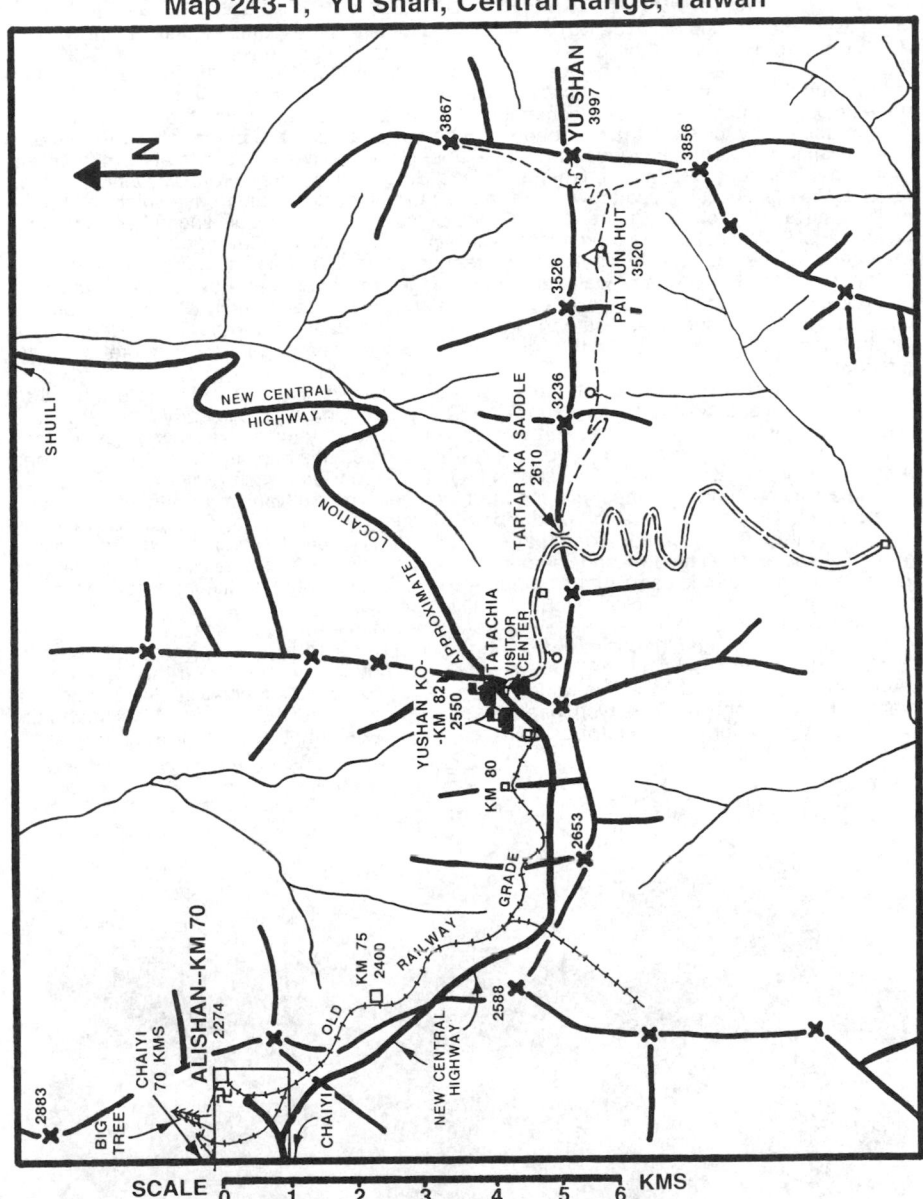

with many trails to choose from. From Alishan, this hike will take 2-3 days, round-trip, depending on your physical fitness and time of departure. Or half this time from Tatachia. The author climbed Yu Shan in 2 days from Alishan beginning on 8/8/1977. From Tatachia, a strong hiker can easily make the climb in one long day, up and back. The months of May, June, October & November are the best months to climb Yu Shan.

Maps DMA map *NF-51-1*, 1:250,000; and Taiwan maps from the tourist office or an alpine club (but they may be in Chinese); or the book, **Walking in Taiwan**, Caves Books Ltd., Taipei; and the latest travel guidebook to Taiwan.

Chilaiju (Chida) Shan, Central Range, Taiwan

Chilaiju (pron. Chida or Chida Su) Shan at 3605 meters is the highest summit in the vicinity of the Hehuan (Hohuan) Shan Ski Resort. This group of high peaks is about 20 & 30 kms southeast of Lishan and the still higher mountains of Hsuih Shan and Nanhuda Shan, Taiwan's second and third highest peaks. As with most or all of Taiwan's mountains, Chilaiju Shan is made up of metamorphic-type rock, something like the Toroka Gorge, just to the northeast.

The usual way to reach the ski resort of Hehuan Shan and the beginning of the hike to **Chilaiju Shan**, is via the east-west running Trans-Island Highway. It starts at Toroka on the east coast, then runs west up the famous Toroka Gorge to Dayuling (pron. Tayuling), 30 kms before Lishan (a mountain resort town). From this main highway, another paved highway heads south from Dayuling toward Wushe. In 1977, the author walked from Dayuling to Hehuan Shan, a distance of 9 kms; but there's more traffic now, and probably buses too (?).

A good trail begins at a big signboard at Hehuan Shan at the beginning of the trail heading southeast. After 5 or 6 kms of walking along a ridge, you'll come to a pass at 2850 meters, separating Hehuan Shan and Chilaiju Shan. Then at another pass marked 3350 meters on this map, the trail splits; one goes south to Nan Feng (South Peak), the other north to Bei Feng (North Peak). The last portion of the trail to Chilaiju Shan is a ridge-walk in some beautiful meadows.

Portions of the trail between the ski resort and the Twin Huts at 2875 meters used be through very tall and overhanging bamboo grass. If you're climbing in the early morning hours, better have some kind of raincoat and waterproof cover for your pack, as you may drench yourself under the wet brush. However, the author climbed this back in 1977, and since then that trail has gotten a lot more use and should be in better condition when you arrive.

The author started to this mountain the morning after climbing Nanhuda Shan and his camp near Suien. He hitched a ride to Lishan, bought food, got more information, hitch hiked to Dayuling, walked 9 kms on a dirt road (paved now) to the Hehuan Shan ski resort, then walked to the first spring along the trail and camped. Next morning, 8/6/1977, he climbed Bei Feng or North Peak, and return to camp in 4 1/2 hours. He walked back to Dayuling, hitched to Chaiyi, and took a train to Alishan (to climb Yu Shan), all in one day.

There were 3 huts along the trail. All were open and free for public use. They were good huts, made of steel and aluminum, but had no furniture or caretaker during the author's visit. This has surely changed since 1977. Streams and springs are found near the huts, and at several other places on the trail. In winter, the area is snow covered, while in late summer the island is hit with typhoons. The typhoons cause landslides on mountain roads, blocking traffic; therefore, May & June, and October & November are usually the best months to climb in Taiwan.

From the north summit of Chilaiju (Chida) Shan looking southwest at Nan Feng.

Map 244-1, Chilaiju (Chida) Shan, Central Range, Taiwan

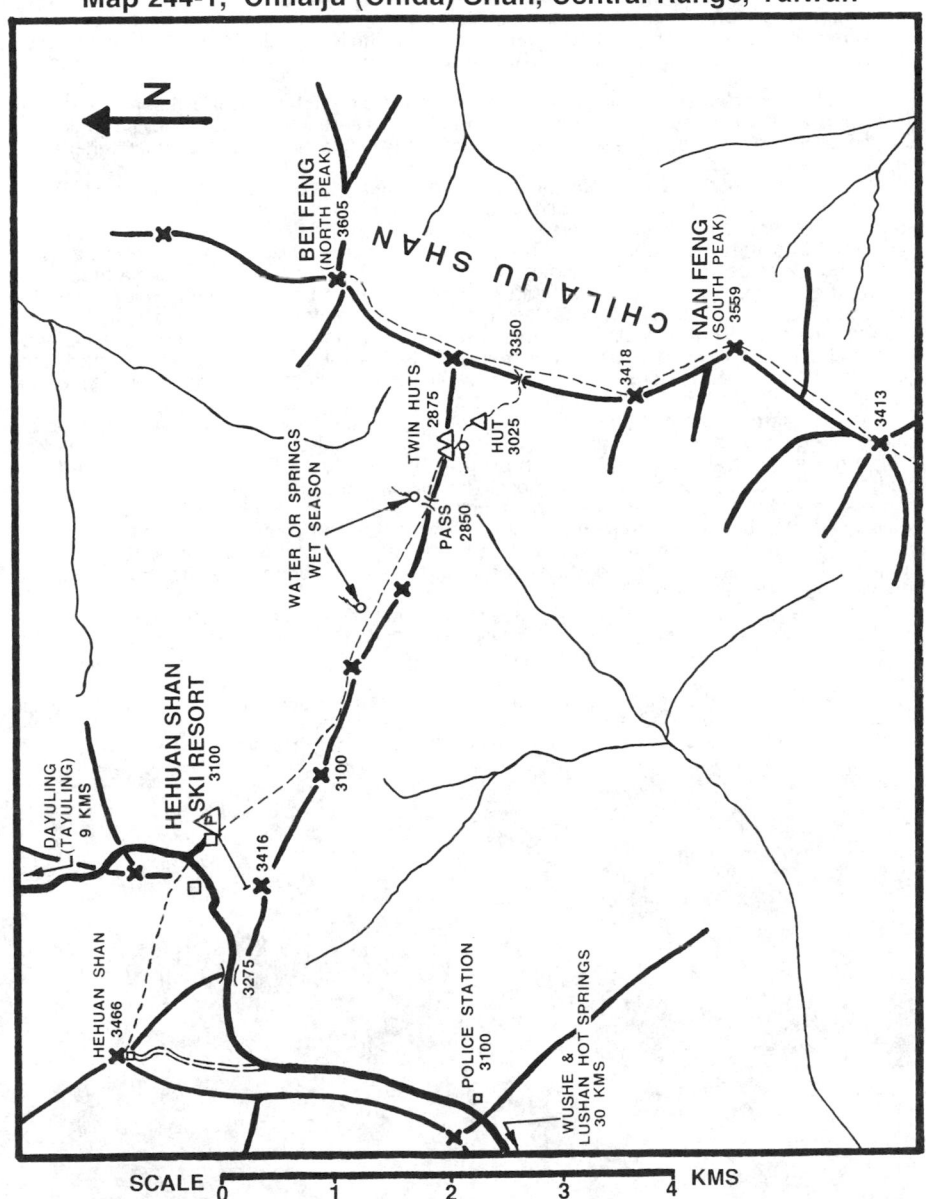

You can buy all your food in Dayuling, 9 kms north of the trailhead; or 30 kms northwest at Lishan. Get to Lishan and Dayuling by bus or hitch hiking. See the Yu Shan map for information about geting a permit to climb mountains in Taiwan.

Maps DMA map *NG-51-13*, 1:250,000; and Taiwanese hiking maps from the tourist office, but they may be in Chinese; or the book **Walking In Taiwan**, Warburten & Haas, Caves Books Ltd., Taipei; and the latest travel guidebook to Taiwan.

Nanhuda (Lam Hoa) Shan, Central Range, Taiwan

In the northern part of Taiwan's Central Range and northeast of Lishan are the 3rd & 4th highest mountains in Taiwan. They are Nanhuda (Lam Hoa) Shan at 3740 meters, and about 5 kms south of that is Jong Yong Gien Shan at 3703 meters. These peaks are made of metamorphic rock of various kinds.

This is another climb where you're supposed to have a mountain permit. It seems climbing all peaks over 3000 meters requires one. See the information under Yu Shan for more details. Also, check with the tourist office when you arrive for any last minute changes and/or where you can get these permits in Taipei.

To reach either of these mountains, you must first reach Suien, located on the main highway connecting the resort town of Lishan, with lowland cities of Ilan and Lotung. On that highway are buses about every hour, and lots of cars for hitch hiking.

From the town of Suien, it used to be a 2 day climb (round-trip) to **Nanhuda Shan** and maybe 3 days to **Jong Yong Gien Shan**. There's a pretty good trail as far as Nanhuda, but beyond that, the trail becomes less-used. Surely the trails have been improved since the author's 1977 trip, so Nanhuda Shan can be climbed in one day from the trailhead.

From Suien, it's a 6.7 km walk to the trailhead at 2300 meters. The beginning of the trail may be difficult to locate. When the author was there, the trail on the left (northeast) side of the road, was marked by colorful ribbons on several small pine trees. On the right was a large pine tree with several small signs in Chinese and ribbons.

Once on the trail, there should be little trouble finding the way, but it was one of the more difficult hikes the author had in Taiwan. Along the way, from the trailhead to the peak marked 3140 meters, the trail was marked with bright ribbons. The problem was with the tall & overhanging bamboo grass. With a large pack, it was difficult to crawl under. Besides that, this tall grass is wet most of the time, so it's important to have a waterproof cover for your pack. You'll be wet too, but largely from perspiration. Carry water from near the trailhead to the hut & spring at 3100 meters. This trail will be in a lot better condition when you arrive. The one aluminum hut is located right at treeline with a spring nearby for good water. The route from the hut to Nanhuda Shan is easy.

On the afternoon of the day the author climbed Hsuih Shan, he walked along the road 3 kms above Suien & camped. The next day, 8/301977, he waded through wet bamboo grass for 5 hours to reach the hut at 3100. Next day, he reached the summit, then walked back to within one km of Suien and camped again.

If you're there from July through September, expect to encounter typhoons; with possible travel delays due to rain and landslides on the mountain roads. Normally, May & June and October & November are the best times to climb. If this is your first climb in the area, buy your

Winter scene on Yu Shan (tourist office foto, Map 243, page 528).

Map 245-1, Nanhuda (Lam Hoa) Shan, Central Range, Taiwan

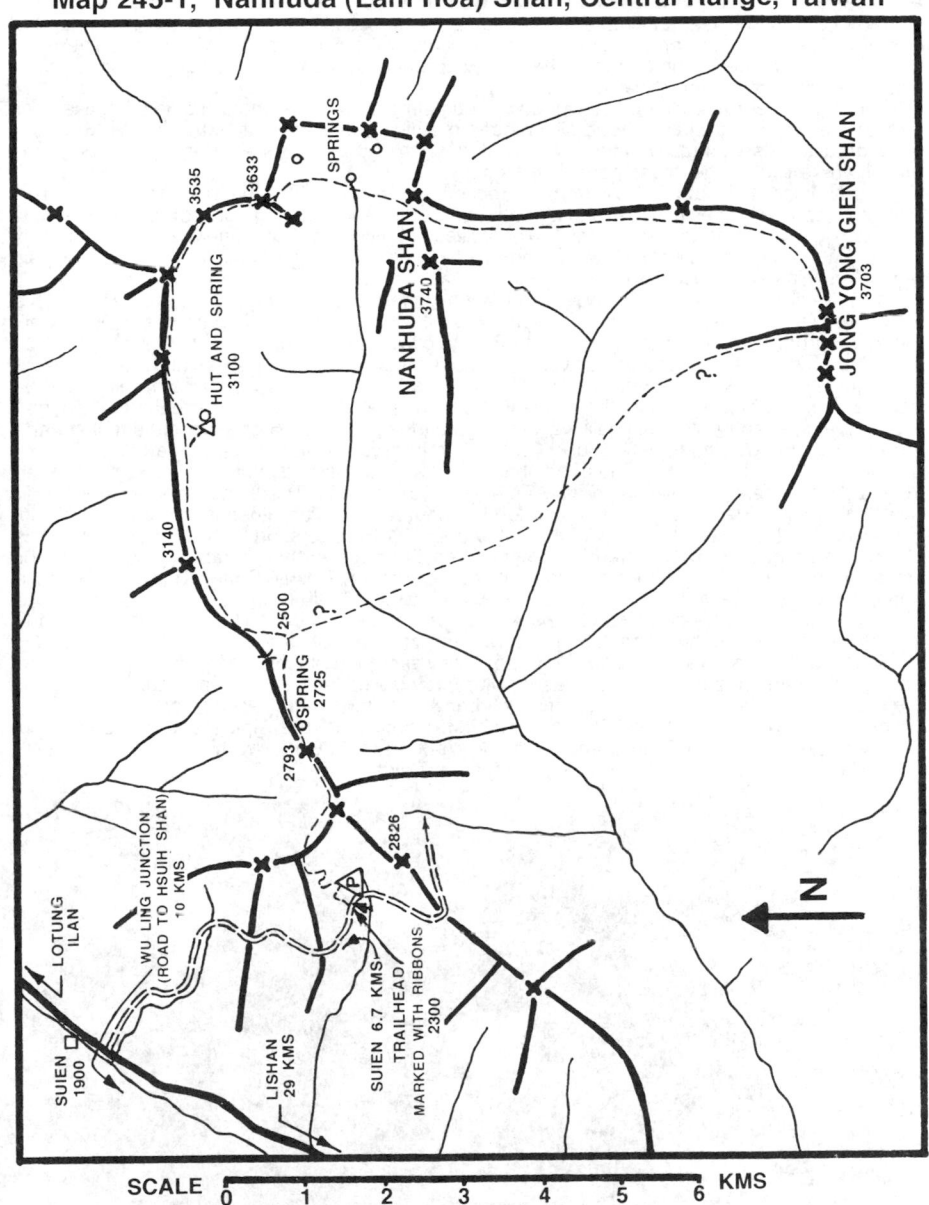

SCALE 0 1 2 3 4 5 6 KMS

food in Taipei; or if coming from the south, buy supplies in Lishan. If coming from Taipei, ask someone at the tourist office where to buy hiking maps of the area.
Maps DMA map *NG-51-13*, 1:250,000; and some Taiwanese hiking maps, but they're in Chinese, buy in Taipei; or the book **Walking In Taiwan**, Warburton & Haas, Caves Books Ltd., Taipei; and the latest travel guidebook for Taiwan.

Hsuih Shan, Central Range, Taiwan

Hsuih Shan (Snow Mountains) at 3884 meters, is the second highest peak in Taiwan, and is one of the most climbed on the island. It's now part of the Shei-Pa National Park. There's a very good trail to the top and none of the tall & overhanging bamboo grass to fight through, as was once common on other nearby mountains.

This is another climb where you'll need a mountain permit. It seems climbing all peaks over 3000 meters requires one of these silly pieces of paper. See information under Yu Shan for more details. Also, check with the tourist office when you arrive for any last minute changes and/or where you can get these permits in Taipei.

The approach to **Hsuih Shan** is from 2 directions. First, from the south and the resort town of Lishan. There are 5 daily buses running between Lishan and Wu Ling Long Chan. The second approach is from the northeast and the lowland cities of Lotung and Ilan. There are at least 2 daily buses from Lotung, and one from Ilan, running directly to Wu Ling Long Chan; plus others on the main highway running every hour or so.

If you're not on a direct bus, stop at the junction where the Wu Ling Farm road begins. This should be about 10 kms southwest of Suien. From there hitch hike or take another bus; or walk the 5 kms from the junction on the main highway to Wu Ling Long Chan which is the last bus stop. Nearby is a campgound and travel service (all this since the author was there in 1977).

About 3 kms north of Wu Ling Long Chan is the trailhead at Wu Ling Farm. Ribbons on trees, and no doubt a sign, mark the trailhead along the road. Or just ask where the trail begins. On the first part of the trail you'll walk through cabbage farms. Higher up is a small stream, then the *Chi Ka Zhuang* (Chi Ka Hut). Chi Ka is a large hut which slept as many as 50 or 75 people in 1977, but by 1985, it had been abandoned and was in bad shape. At last report, in the 1990's, it's still there, but with no caretaker as there was in 1977. There should be water nearby.

From Chi Ka, the trail zig zags up a ridge to about 3200 meters, then it's up and down until you reach the 3-6-9 Hut (San Liu Jiu Zhuang) at about 3175 meters. In both 1977 and 1985, this shelter had a good roof, but there's no caretaker and apparently no water (go up the trail a ways). Beyond the 3-6-9 Hut it's an easy walk to the summit of Hsuih Shan. This climb will take some people two days, but it can be done in one day from Wu Ling Farm. The author took about an hour to reach Chi Ka with full pack; slept there, then on 8/2/1977, took a day-pack and in 3 1/4 hours reached the summit; 5 1/4 hours round-trip from Chi Ka.

Buy your food in Lishan, or elsewhere; not many shopping places in the Wu Ling area. July through September is the typhoon season, with heavy rains, sometimes causing landslides on the mountain highways. May & June, and October & November are the best months to climb.

Maps DMA map *NG-51-13,* 1:250,000; and hiking maps from the Alpine Club of Taiwan, but they're in Chinese, buy in Taipei; and the book **Walking In Taiwan**, Warburton & Haas, Caves Books Ltd.,Taipei; and the latest travel guidebook to Taiwan.

Looking along the east ridge toward the summit of Hsuih Shan.

Map 246-1, Hsuih Shan, Central Range, Taiwan

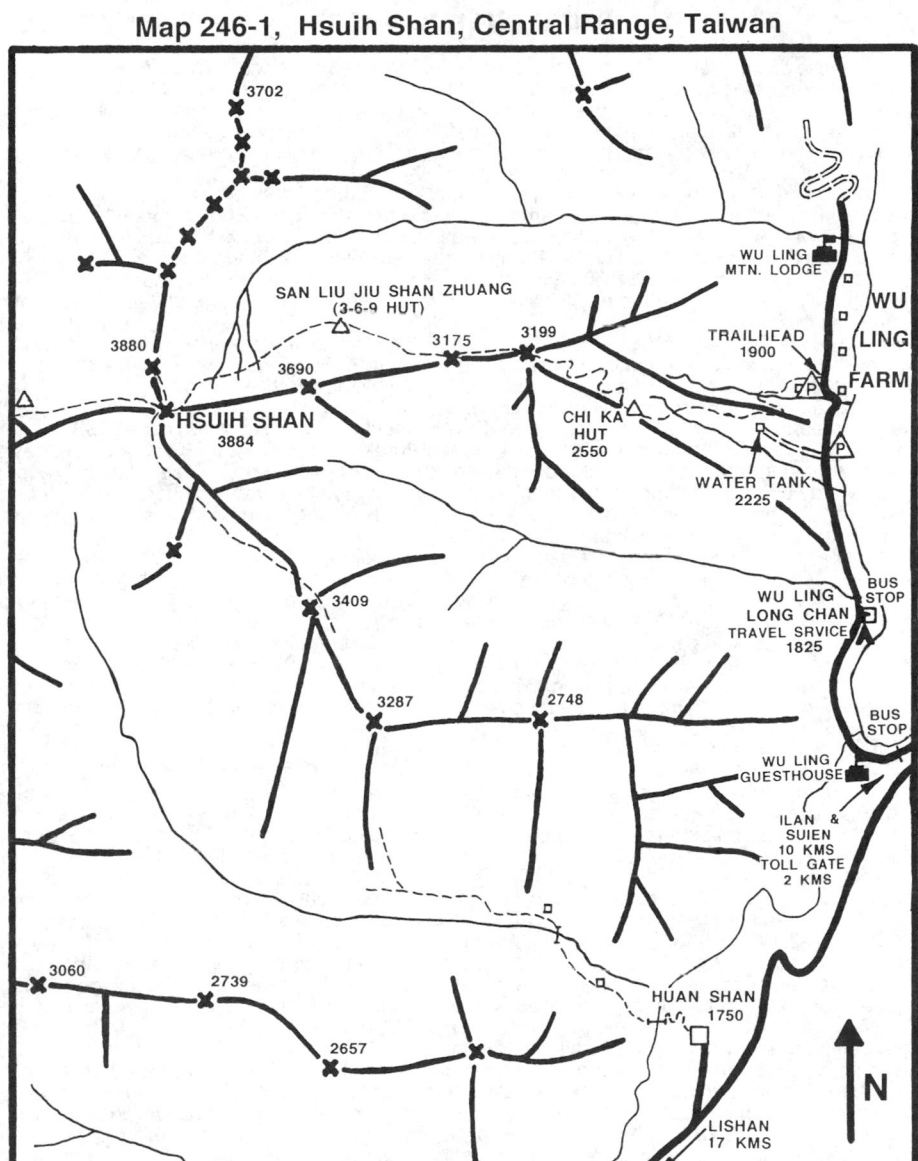

3702

3880

SAN LIU JIU SHAN ZHUANG
(3-6-9 HUT)

3690

3175   3199

HSUIH SHAN
3884

CHI KA
HUT
2550

WU LING
MTN. LODGE

WU
LING
FARM

TRAILHEAD
1900

WATER TANK
2225

3409

3287   2748

WU LING
LONG CHAN
TRAVEL SRVICE
1825

BUS
STOP

BUS
STOP

WU LING
GUESTHOUSE

ILAN &
SUIEN
10 KMS
TOLL GATE
2 KMS

3060

2739

2657

HUAN SHAN
1750

N

LISHAN
17 KMS

SCALE   0   1   2   3   4   5   KMS

535

Introduction to Japan

In September & October, 1977, the author spent 5 weeks in Japan. On that trip, he hitch hiked almost exclusively and visited the 3 Japanese Alps; Kita (North), Chuo (Central), and Minami (South), plus he hiked in Deisetsuzan National Park on Hokkaido. In May and part of June, 1998, he spent just over 4 weeks in Japan. On that trip, he bought 2 Japan Rail Passes (JR Pass) before leaving home, one for a week, the other for 3 weeks. With that extra speed, and an occasional ride on a bus, plus a little hitch hiking, he managed to climb 19 mountains, all volcanos, 3 of which were alive or erupting at the time.

From his 1998 trip, here are some updated facts and information. There is only one good way for foreigners to travel around Japan, and that's with a *JR Pass*. They come in lengths of one, 2 or 3 weeks. In 1998, the cost for adults was ¥27,800 for one week; ¥44,200 for 2 weeks; and ¥56,600 for 3 weeks. The 3 week JR Pass is the best value. With a JR Pass you can travel very quickly, especially on the Bullet trains, all of which are on the *Shinkanzen Lines.*

To get a JR Pass, you must pay for and get a voucher at a travel agent, or Japan National Tourist Office, in your country before leaving home. Upon arrival at Narita Airport, you exchange the voucher for the pass. About 99% of the railway kilometers in Japan are publicly owned, and JP Passes are usable. At some railway stations, Japan Railways also has buses running to various other locations. JR Passes are valid on these buses and you ride for free.

Before leaving home, along with paying for your JP Pass, also contact the *Japan Travel Bureau International* in New York, Chicago, San Francisco & Los Angeles in the USA, or in Toronto, Sao Paulo, London, Paris, Frankfurt/M, Bangkok, Seoul, Hong Kong and Sydney. Inquire at a local travel agent for the latest Tele. number of the nearest office. Japan Travel Bureau can send you an information package with a national highway & railroad map, youth hostel address book & map, JR schedule, emergency Tele. numbers, etc. This is a must if you intend to travel on your own in Japan.

Also before leaving home, get a Japanese phrase book & dictionary and start learning the language. There are lots of dictionary translating Japanese into English. Most big stations in Japan have an information counter with someone speaking English, but not always. *Independent travelers should learn some Japanese quickly!*

Before leaving Tokyo, be sure to buy topo maps of the mountains you'd like to climb. These are from the national mapping agency and the cost was ¥160 each for 1:50,000 scale maps in 1998. You can buy these in the Buyodo Map store near the Tokyo Station. Someone at one of the tourist information booths at the station can get you the correct address. That map store was open from 9am to 7pm, Monday through Friday, and 9am to 3pm, on the 1st & 3rd Saturdays of each month. And closed on the Christian holiday, Sunday.

Also, there is a national tourist information office about 15 minutes walk from the Tokyo Station, where you can pick up lots of information booklets in Romanji (this alphabet). Those people all speak good English, and hopefully several other languages as well. Ask where this office is at one of the information booths at the station. It was in the *International Trade Center.* Also, any new travel guidebook to Japan should have the latest address if it should change.

Another thing to do before leaving Tokyo, is ask someone where a good bookstore is where you can buy a book of maps for Japan titled, **Road Atlas, Japan,** put out by **Shobunsha**, ISBN4-398-20104-1. Their address was 4-2-11 Kudan-kita Chiyoda-ku, Tokyo 102 Japan, Tele. 03-3262-2141. The 1998 bilingual version the author bought had 250 maps (plus kilomage charts, etc.) covering all of Japan. This version had maps in English & Kanji (Japanese characters), and cost ¥2857; and worth every ¥ (pron. En)! Most maps in this indispensable atlas are at 1:250,000 scale and cover all of Japan. The author used this atlas, in addition to national topo maps, to climb all the mountains on his 1998 trip.

When you arrive at nearly all train stations, you will find a bus stand or station within 100 meters. Only at small town stations you may not find a bus to take you to a mountain or elsewhere. Also near each major railway station you'll find a supermarket and the usual fast food places. When you get on a bus, take a numbered ticket, which is your beginning point. As you travel, watch how much you owe on the electronic board above the driver. At your destination, pay the amount indicated on the ¥ information Board.

If you're there to climb volcanos and would like to know which ones are alive or erupting, check these websites for the latest updates (www.volcano.si.edu/gvp/) or (www.kishou.go.jp/).

This is Komagadake on the island of Hokkaido. The signs are on the old caldera marked 900 meters. In the background is the highest peak (Map 252, page 549).

These statues of Buddhist saints are located just south of Step 8 on the west-side trail leading to the summit of Ontake San (Map 262, page 569).

Rishirizan, Rishiri Island, Hokkaido, Japan

Shown on this map is the northern tip of Hokkaido & the small city of Wakkanai; and the circular volcanic island of Rishirito (Rishiri Island) located just to the west in the Sea of Japan. The highest point on Rishirito is Rishirizan (Rishiri Peak), at 1721 meters. This is an old and eroded stratovolcano. Radiocarbon dating indicates there was an explosive eruption somewhere on the island in 3250 BC. By the time the author reached the summit, clouds obscured the mountain and he has no idea where this explosion may have taken place. It may have come from one of several small craters on the south side of the island (?).

To get there, make your way to Wakkanai. The best way is by train. There's one nightly train from Sapporo, and about 3 daytime trains leaving each morning, about noon, and in the late afternoon. Trains returning to Sapporo leave at 7:52am, 12:57pm, 4:02pm and 10:13pm. From the Wakkanai train station you can jump on a waiting bus, or walk about 600 meters to the ferryboat, and save about US$1.25. A one-way ticket to Rishirito costs about US$14 and takes 1 2/3 hours. There are several daily boats running from Wakkanai to Oshidomari and returning, at least in summer.

When you get off the ferry in Oshidomari, walk west up the main road from the port and into town. About 500 meters from the docks will be a sign in *Romanji*, pointing out the paved road to the left running up to the campjo and the beginning of the trail up **Rishirizan**. From the ferry terminal, it's 4 kms to the Hokuroku Campjo, or 3.3 kms from the center of Oshidomari.

Hokuroku Campjo was quite new when the author arrived on 6/1/1998. It had new toilets and a clothes washing area, but no showers. Also, an office with a few food items for sale. Camping at that time was free, but if they install a shower, you will pay. From the upper end of the campjo is the very good and well-used trail up Rishirizan, a distance of 5.6 kms. Along the way is one hut, then the usual shrine at the first summit. A 2nd or highest summit is about 200 meters away. Most people apparently stop at the first peak at 1718 meters.

The author arrived in Wakkanai by train at 6am, road the bus to the ferry terminal, took the boat to Rishirito, bought a couple of things in a small shop in Oshidomari, then walked up to the campjo. He set up his tent, then walked to the summit in 2 hours. The top was in clouds, and he thought the first summit was the top--then returned. Round-trip was 4 1/4 hours.

Later that afternoon, he took a jug of water into the forest and had a bath, then broke camp and walked down the road, getting a ride part way to the ferry. He took the afternoon ferry back to Wakkanai, then waited for the 10:13pm train back to Sapporo. This was all on the same day.

There are 2 small supermarkets near the Wakkanai train station, plus many small shops in Oshidomari to buy food. The 2 consecutive night trains the author took to and from Sapporo were uncrowded and each person had double-facing seats to sleep on. Early summer has less rain than the wettest month of September in Sapporo.

This foto shows the mountain called Rishirizan on Rishirito (Rishiri Island).

Map 247-1, Rishirizan, Rishiri Island, Hokkaido, Japan

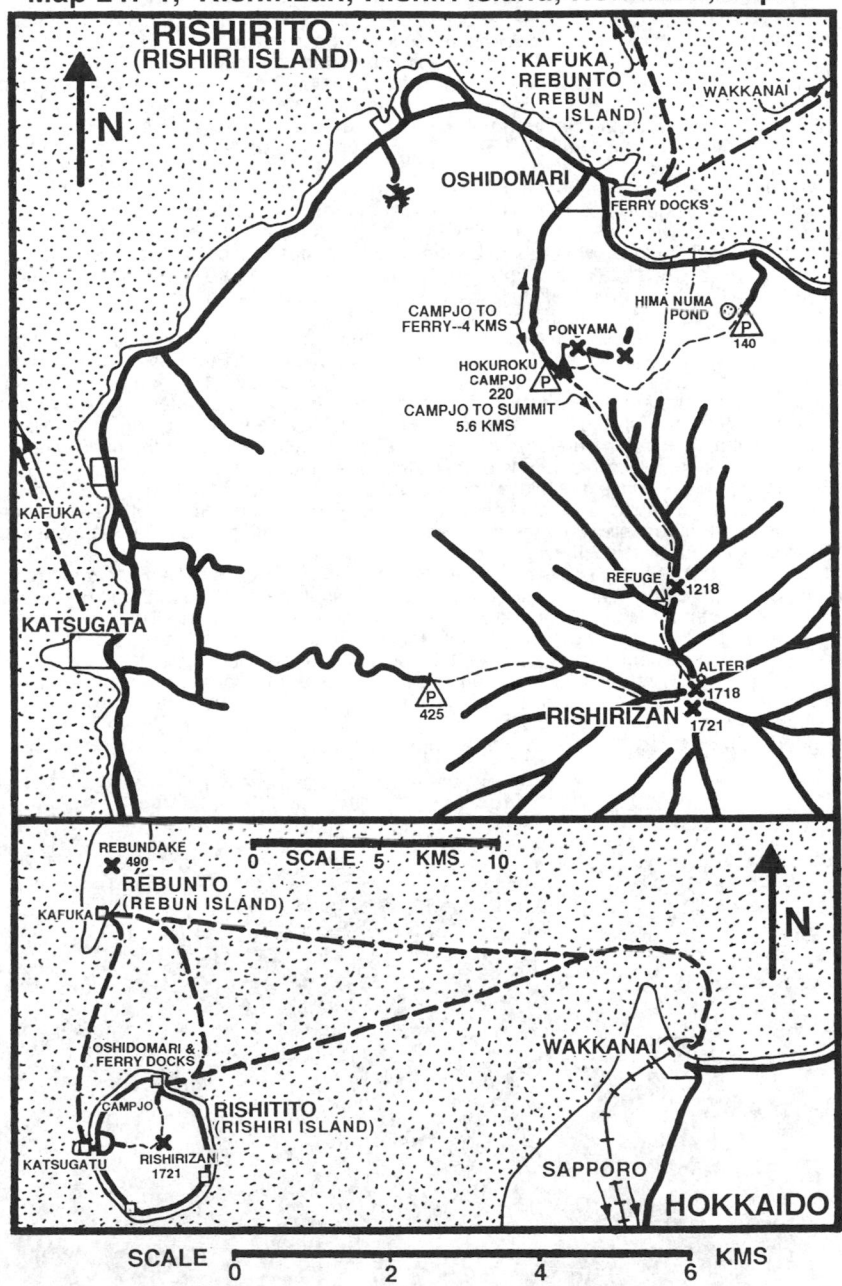

Maps Japanese map *Rishirito, NL-54-17-9,10,13 &14*, 1:50,000; **Japan Road Atlas** in Romanji by Shobunsha; and the latest travel guidebook to Japan.

Asahidake, Daisetsuzan National Park, Hokkaido, Japan

Daisetsuzan National Park, located at the center of Japan's northern island of Hokkaido, has some of the most-popular hiking and scenic attractions of any national park of Japan.
All the peaks in Daisetsuzan N.P. are volcanic, some old, some new. The highest summit is Asahi at 2290 meters. Asahi's last eruption was in about 1400 AD. The most active volcano in this immediate area is Tokachi at 2077 meters, located in the southern part of this map. It had a partial cone collapse in 1926 that led to about 144 deaths and 5000 homes destroyed. It was last active between 12/16/1988 and 5/1989. For volcano updates check these websites (www.volcano.si.edu/gvp/) or (www.kishou.go.jp/).

The high peaks in this national park are surrounded by many access roads, but the most-used entry points are from Sounkyo, Teninkyo, and the resort at the bottom of the lift going part way up Asahi on its west side. If coming by railway, go to Kamikawa on the north, then take a bus southeast to Sounkyo. This has to be the easiest access point to reach with regular bus service. Or on the west, take a train along the rail line running north-south, and get out at Asahigawa or Biei-cho, then hopefully find a bus or hitch hike to Teninkyo. However, there may not be any public buses going to this onzen (hot spring spa).

On 9/18/1977, the author hitch hiked from the south to the onzen at Sounkyo. From there he took his full pack up the mountain along side the lifts and climbed Asahi. He spent 5 days and 4 nights on the ridge-tops heading south. His next to last day saw steady rain from a typhoon and he was totally drenched and freezing with no stove at the time, and no water. He had 2 candles, the only warmth that night against hypothermia. Next day he walked down to Tokachidake Onzen and got a lift out of the area to Asahigawa. The trails he took along the ridges were well-used and signposted, but at that late date, there were no other hikers.

Even though Hokkaido is much less developed than other parts of Japan, there seems to be a lot of development in and around this national park. There are a number of cable cars or lifts in the area, and that, coupled with the hundreds of buses and private cars, brings thousands of people to these mountains each year.

If you intend to backpack in this area, the best place to buy food is in Sapporo supermarkets. Nearer the park, the best place might be Kamikawa or Asahigawa. Within the park are several huts or shelters, similar to those found in other mountains in Japan and Europe. At the huts, some food can be purchased; sometimes hot meals, sometimes snack-type food. The sleeping places are often large communal rooms, with the sleeping area raised above the floor.

Camping is strictly regulated, with nearly all campsites at or near the huts, and always near water. The trails in the Asahi area are so well-used, they are often fenced in, to keep people right on the path. Away from the central area, trails are still good, but not overly used. Always take good rain clothing and a water-proof cover for your pack. Also, expect much cooler

In the distance is Asahidake, the highest summit in Daisetsuzan National Park.

Map 248-1, Asahidake, Daisetsuzan NP, Hokkaido, Japan

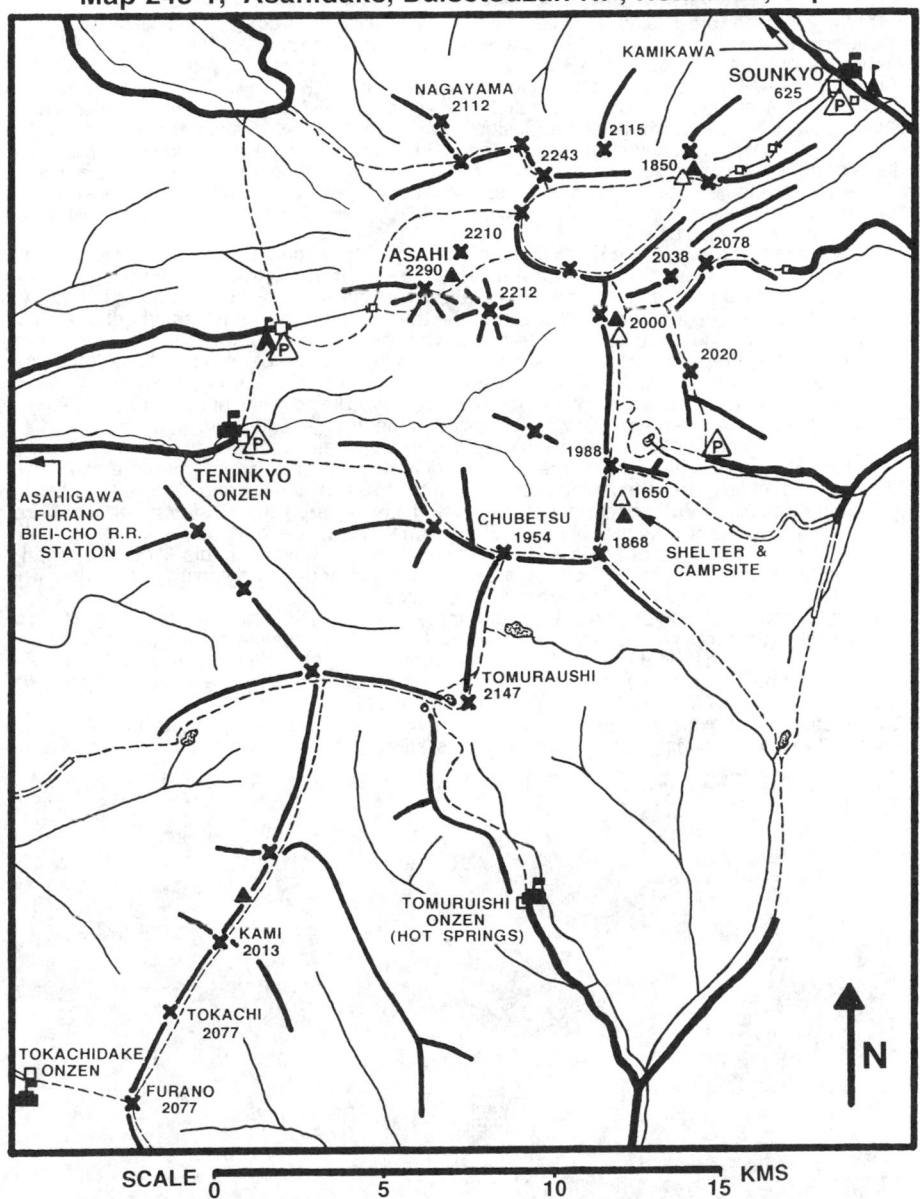

temperatures on Hokkaido, than in other parts of Japan.

Maps *Daisetsuzan National Park*, 1:50,000, printed in Japanese characters called *Kanji*; DMA map *NK-54-9*, 1:250,000; and the book, **Japan Road Atlas** in Romanji from Shobunsha; and the latest travel guidebook to Japan.

Me-Akandake & O-Akandake, Hokkaido, Japan

These 2 volcanos are located in the eastern part of the island of Hokkaido, about halfway between the cities of Kushiro and Abashiri, and in the western part of the Akan National Park. Akan is a 13x24-km-wide caldera that formed about 31,500 years ago. Its caldera lake is surrounded by 4 post-caldera stratovolcanos. While there is no date on the age of O-Akan Peak or Dake (1370 meters) which is rather old, Me-Akandake (1499 meters) is an active volcano. Me-Akan's last major eruption was in 1988, but a smaller phreatomagmatic explosion occurred on 11/9/1998. Upon the author's visit on 5/31/1998, there was a roaring steam vent in the northern crater just below the summit, plus steam was belching out of another vent in the southern crater. In addition, there were dozens of steam vents & fumaroles in a large basin area located just northeast of the main summit. This looked like the *Valley of 10,000 Smokes* in Alaska. For volcano updates, check these websites (www.volcano.si.edu/gvp/) or (www.kishou.go.jp/).

Getting to this area is a little more time consuming than to some other mountains in Japan. It's best to have a Japan Rail Pass and travel by train. If doing that, make your way from western Hokkaido to Kushiro, then take one of about 6 or 7 daily trains heading northeast toward the city of Abashiri, but get off at Mashu. From the train station, walk northwest about one km to the bus station and get a ticket to the resort town of Akankohan, about 40 kms to the west. However, hitch hiking might be faster, if it's good weather. However, to do that, you'd have to walk 2 or 3 kms out of town to a highway junction.

At Akankohan, which is a hot spring resort or onzen, you'll find many hotels and small shops; also a youth hostel and a good campjo, as shown on the map; all within walking distance of the bus station. To climb **O-Akan**, walk, hitch hike or take a bus, east to the eastern end of Akan Ko (Akan Lake). A trail begins right where the stream leaves the lake, and zigs up the southwest side of the mountain. The author didn't climb it, but the trail is well-used and it's a popular hike.

To climb **Me-Akan Volcano**, first find the youth hostel, where you can stay for about US$22 a night (camping at a campjo is a lot cheaper!). From there walk about 200 meters west on the main highway and turn left or south onto a dirt & gravel road. Walk up this secondary road 6 kms (with km posts) to find a big parking area on the right, and the beginning of the trail. The trailhead is in a forest which would make a good campsite.

From the trailhead to the summit is about another 6 kms via a good well-used trail. The trail first goes through an open forest, then gradually rises above the treeline at roughly 1000 meters. On the author's trip, he left the youth hostel at 4:35am, was at the trailhead at 5:30, and at the summit at just before 7am. He walked around the summit crater for a while, then returned to the youth hostel. Round-trip took 4 hours. This was on 5/31/1998.

You can buy all your food in Mashu or Akankohan, but if passing through Kushiro, buy supplies from a supermarket near the railway station. Spring is the driest time of year for

From the top of Me-Akandake looking south at Akanfuji behind the steam.

Map 249-1, Me-Akandake & O-Akandake, Hokkaido, Japan

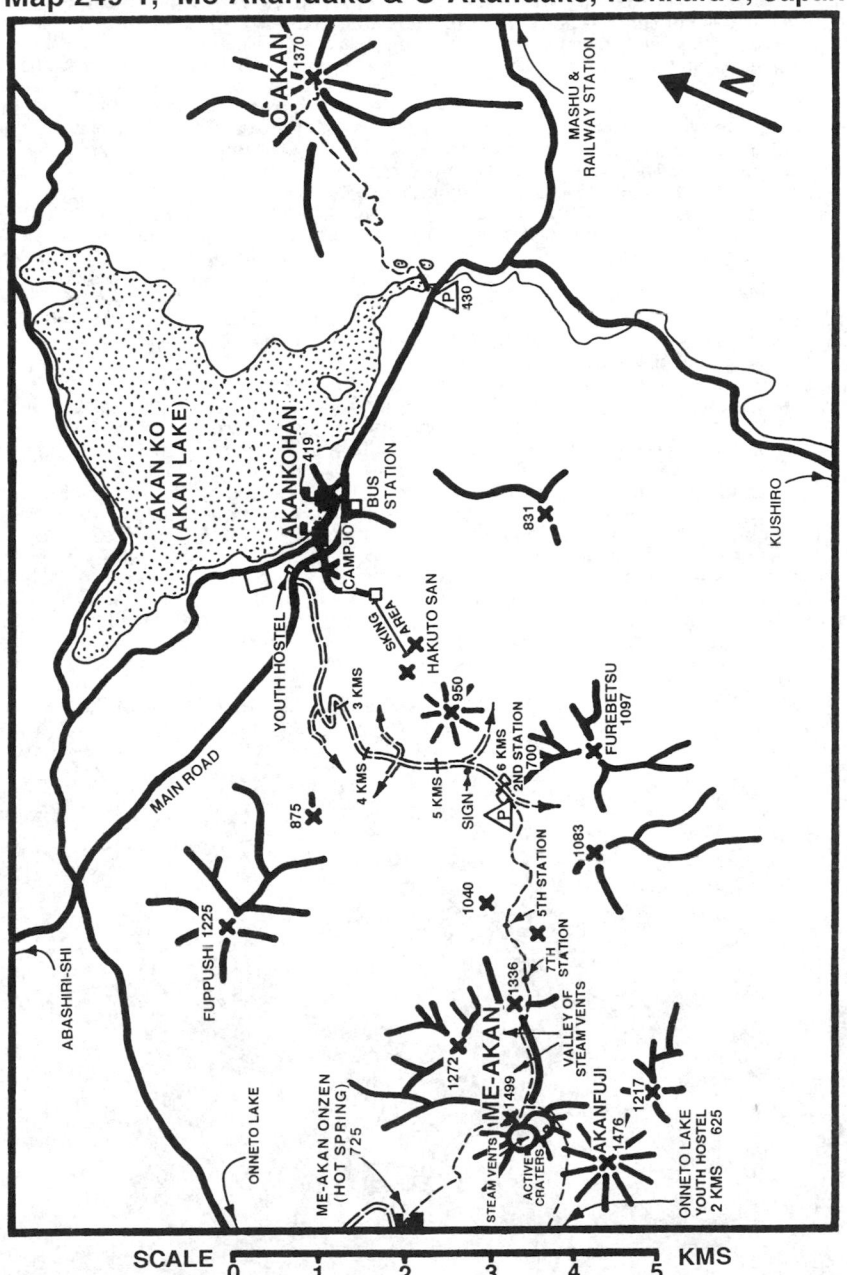

Hokkaido, but June is likely the best month for hiking. September is the wettest month in northern Japan.

Maps Japanese map *Akanko, NK-55-31-16,* 1:50,000; the **Japan Road Atlas** in Romanji from Shobunsha; and the latest travel guidebook to Japan.

Tarumaizan, Fuppushidake & Eniwadake, Hokkaido, Japan

Shown on this map are the peaks and volcanos around a very large caldera with Shikotsu Ko (Shikotsu Lake) occupying the middle. The whole region is generally called Shikotsu, or Shikotsu Ko, and it's similar to Crater Lake in the USA. The 3 highest peaks are Fuppushi Peak or Dake, 1102 meters; Tarumaizan at 1041; and Eniwadake at 1320 meters. Radiocarbon dating of ash indicates Eniwa Volcano's last eruption was from its east-side summit crater in about 110 AD. The book **Volcanos of the World**, has no date on Fuppushidake, but it's the oldest of the 3 major peaks shown. The 13X15 km Shikotsu Caldera, mostly filled by Shikotsu Lake, was formed during one of Hokkaido's largest Quaternary eruptions about 30,000 years ago.

Tarumai is a live one and Hokkaido's most active volcano, having had 35 major eruptions since 1667. It's last eruptive period was in 1981, but it had lots of quakes in 7 & 8/1996. In 1998, it was still alive and steamy as ever. In the middle of its 1 1/2-km-wide summit caldera is a huge lava dome. Nearby were 2 large steam vents seen on the author's visit of 5/29/1998. For volcano updates, check these websites (www.volcano.si.edu/gvp/) or (www.kishou.go.jp/).

There are 4 ways to reach this huge caldera; from Toya Ko on the west; by bus from Sapparo to the north; also by bus from Chitose on the east (4 buses daily). But the best way using public transport is from Tomakomai City (Shi), located to the southeast. The author got off the train at Tomakomai, bought some food in a nearby supermarket (ask about its location at the station information booth), then got on a bus heading to Shikosu Kohan. In summer, there are many buses each day. It's only about 25 kms, but it cost about US$5. You could hitch hike, but Tomakomai is a big city and it's a long way to walk to the edge of town.

At Shikosu Kohan is a hot spring spa or onzen, lots of small shops, tourist office and a youth hostel. The author wanted to climb Tarumai the most, so he walked south on a good trail to the Morappu Campjo and camped on the beach for about US$3.75 (this campjo or campground has a small store, coin operated hot showers, and several small summer-time outdoor cafes nearby). Next morning, he walked up the good road to the trailhead at the 7th Step in 1 1/3 hours. From there it was to the crater rim in 20 minutes. He inspected all parts of the crater; dome, steam vents and the usual shrines, then walked back to the campjo. Round-trip time was 4 1/2 hours.

To climb **Fuppushidake**, walk northwest from Tarumai's highest peak called Higashidake (East Peak), or maybe from 7th Stage (?). Only one map the author saw indicated there were trails to its summit, as shown, but the author didn't checkout either one. He did see a trail heading that way from Higashidake. This is apparently not a popular hike, and likely has only a rough trail to the summit.

To climb **Eniwa Peak**, hitch hike or take a bus to the north side of Shikotsu Ko to the Poropinai Campjo, then use the trail, as shown. One little guide-map the author saw, indicated it would take the average person 3 1/2 hours to reach the summit; fit hikers should do it in half that

This is one of 2 steam vents inside the crater of Tarumaizan. Behind is the lava dome.

Map 250-1, Tarumaizan Volcano, Hokkaido, Japan

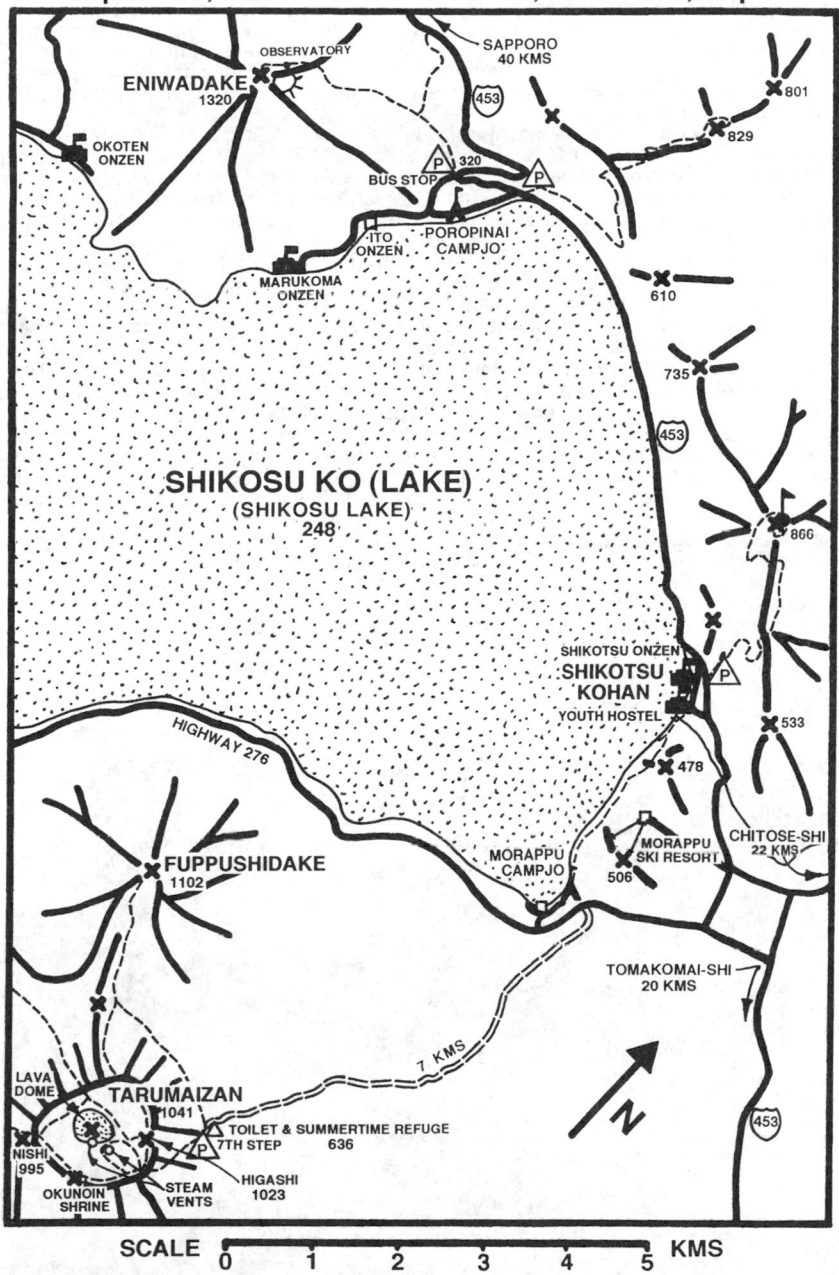

SCALE 0 1 2 3 4 5 KMS

time. Best month to climb in Hokkaido is June; September is the wettest.
Maps Japanese map *Tarumaizan, NK-54-14-12,* 1:50,000; the **Japan Road Atlas** in Romanji from Shobunsha; and the latest travel guidebook to Japan.

Yotaizan Volcano, Hokkaido, Japan

This map shows one of the most perfectly formed volcanic cones found anywhere. This is Yotaizan, or Yotai Peak or Volcano, 1898 meters, located on Japan's northern-most island of Hokkaido. Yotai is located in the western leg or arm of Hokkaido, almost due west of the island's capital of Sapporo. Yotai is a dormant stratovolcano. Radiocarbon dating places the last eruption at roughly 5050 BC. There's at least one hot spring (onzen) in the area located just west of this map.

If you intend to climb any other mountain in Hokkaido, your first stop should be Sapporo, and the main tourist office there. In 1998, it was located about 750 meters south of the main train station (see the latest travel guidebook). Generally speaking, they will have better information and maps, etc., than the main JNTO in Tokyo, which is near the Tokyo Station. Also, near Sapporo's tourist office is a national chain bookstore where topo maps of Hokkaido's mountains can be bought.

This is what the author did when he was ready to leave Sapporo. Since there are no supermarkets in the Sapporo's city center, he got on a commuter train (departs about every 20 minutes) heading west to Otaru, the last city in the greater Sapporo metropolitan area. About 200 meters from Otaru Station, he stocked up on food at a big supermarket nearby, then got on one of about 7 daily trains destined for Oshamanbe, located at the end of that railway line on the south coast. About halfway between Otaru and Oshamanbe is the town of Kutchan. The first stop south of Kutchan is Hirafu, and that's where the author got off. This is closest train station to Yotaizan, and the best starting point for anyone using public transportation.

From Hirafu Station, he walked south about 500 meters to the main road, then headed eastward through scattered farms to the main north-south highway. He turned left, or north for 200 meters, then at the sign and the first paved road to the right, he headed east again. There are no shops whatsoever in Hirafu, so be sure to have all your food and other supplies before arriving!

From the main highway, the author walked east almost to Hangetsu crater lake, then headed north off the paved road and hid his big pack in a reforested area. From there, he continued up the paved road to the trailhead and the beginning of the trail. At the trailhead in 1998, was an undeveloped campsite or campjo, several picnic tables and a toilet. Camping was free.

He then hurried to the summit of **Yotaizan** along a very good and well-used trail. Total walk-time from the train station to the top was just under 3 hours; and just under 2 hours from the trailhead. Round-trip walk-time from the trailhead was 3 2/3 hours. The author camped in the reforested area, then early the next morning, 5/28/1998, walked back to the station in 40 minutes, where he caught the next train back to Sapporo. Total walk-time from the station, to the summit and back was 4 3/4 hours. June might be the best month for climbing in Hokkaido.

One of several small shrines on the rim of Yotaizan Volcano.

Map 251-1, Yotaizan Volcano, Hokkaido, Japan

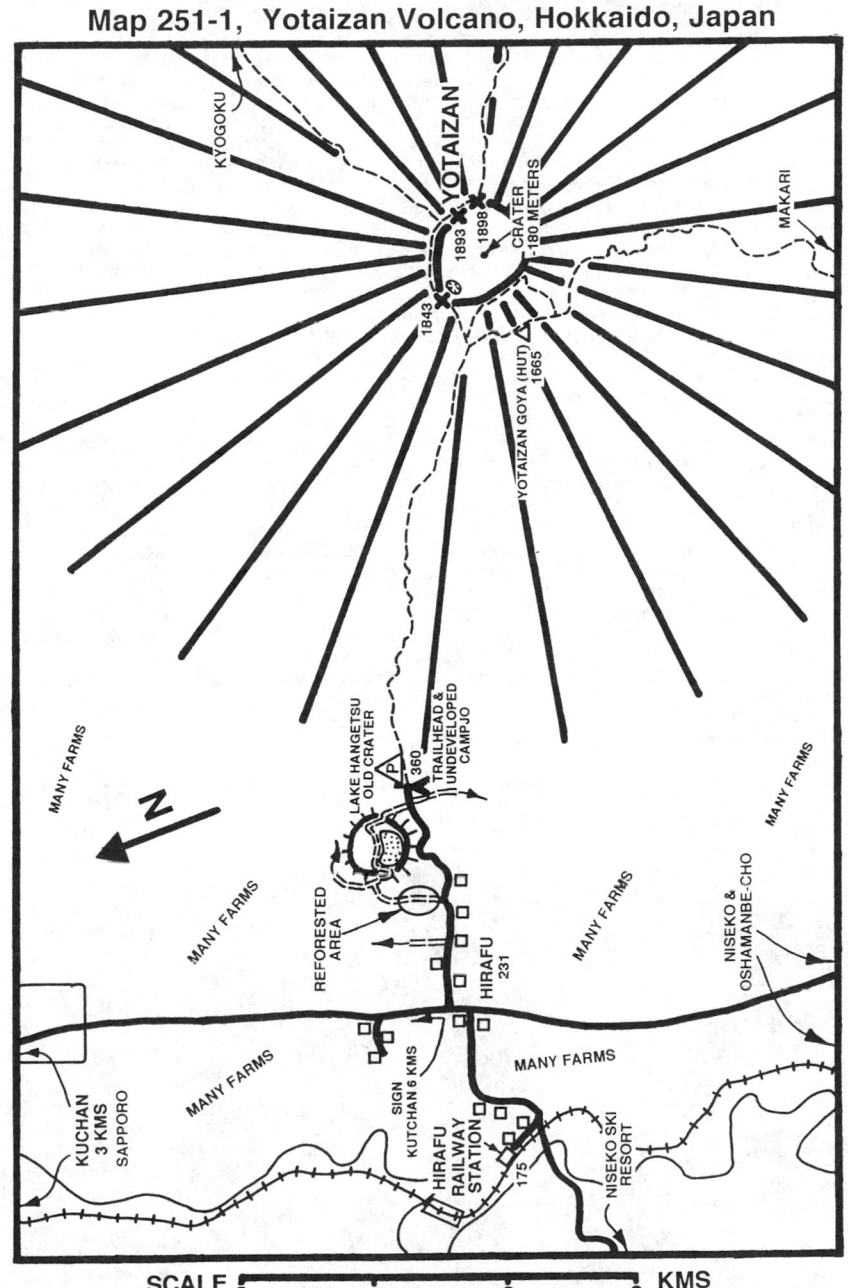

Maps Japanese maps *NK-54-20-3, NK-54-20-4* and *NK-54-20-7*, all at 1:50,000; the **Japan Road Atlas** in Romanji from Shobunsha; and the latest travel guidebook to Japan.

Komagadake & Volcano, Hokkaido, Japan

The mountain on this map is known as Komagadake or Komaga Peak or Volcano, rising to 1121 meters. This doesn't seem very high, but the northern-most peak is barely 6 kms from the sea. This volcano even forms its own peninsula. Komaga is located near the southern tip of the western arm of Hokkaido, and about 30 kms north of Hakodate-shi (Hakodate city).

Komaga is an active andasite stratovolcano with a 2-km-wide horseshoe-shaped crater opening to the east. It has produced some large pyroclastic explosions, including major historical eruptions in 1640, 1856 and 1929. In the 1640 eruption, debris from a partial summit collapse entered the sea resulting in a tsunami that killed 700 people. Although the 1929 eruption was one of the largest 20th century eruptions in Japan, it may not have had clear geophysical precursors (it may have been a phreatic explosion). The next to last eruption was a small scale phreatic (steam or hot water) explosion on 10/25/1998, then another on 9/5/2000--details lacking. Upon the author's visit on 5/26/1998, there was a roaring steam vent in the side of the 1929 crater. It's probably best not to get too close to that crater right after some heavy rains! For volcano updates, check these websites (www.volcano.si.edu/gvp/) or (www.kishou.go.jp/).

Getting to **Komagadake** is easy. The best way is via train and from either north or south. Be sure to ask someone at Hakodate-shi Station, or some town to the north, to help you on a *local train*, and one that stops at either Komagadake or Akaigawa Stations. The faster express trains don't stop at either of these rural towns.

Best starting point is Hakodate. Buy food or other supplies in a supermarket near the train station, then board a *local train* heading north. The author got off at Komagadake Station, walked northeast on a new paved road, then turned south, as shown on the map. A bit later he hid his big pack in some bushes, then continued south, and turned northeast on the road with an arch overhead as you enter a reforested area. Later he walked along the place labeled *double road* and up to the junction at 420 meters, then finally to the real trailhead which had a new toilet facility in 1998. From there it's a very good trail up to the crater rim at 900 meters.

To climb the highest peak, veer left, and head for the obvious summit. This rugged peak is a small part of a much larger former crater rim standing by itself. Stay on the trail which runs north along the eastern base of the peak. Walk beyond the peak, then turn left or west and head up a steep gully. You'll have to climb over the rim and down the other side a ways, before climbing east up another gully to the summit.

The author made it from the train station to the summit in just under 2 1/2 hours; while the round-trip took 4 3/4 hours. On his way back, he found several cars at the trailhead & weather station. They hadn't used the author's route; so he believes they came up the road passing near the Akaigawa Station. Getting to the trailhead may be a little less complicated if you start at the Akaigawa Station (?).

From the summit of Komagadake looking northeast at Sawaradake and the 1925 crater.

Map 252-1, Komagadake & Volcano, Hokkaido, Japan

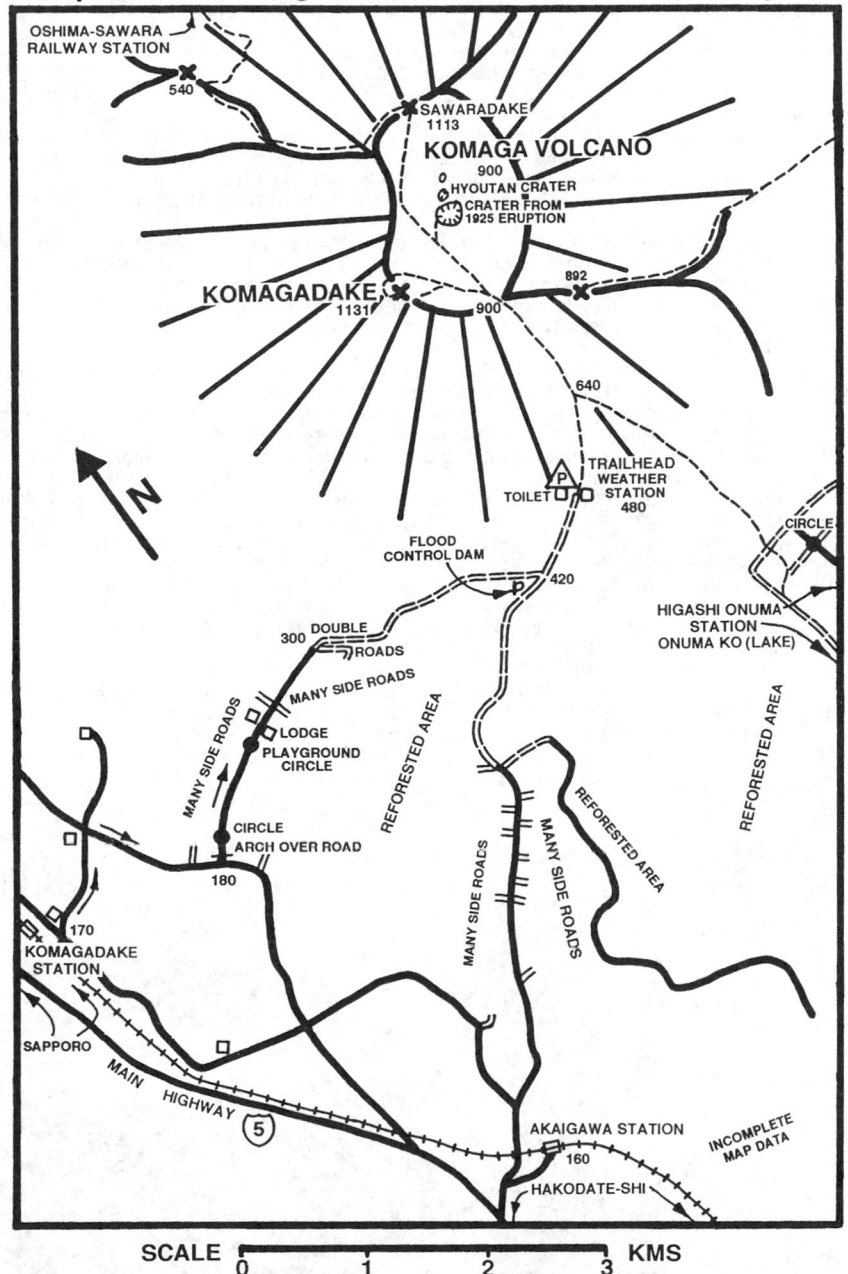

OSHIMA-SAWARA
RAILWAY STATION

540

SAWARADAKE
1113

KOMAGA VOLCANO
900

HYOUTAN CRATER
CRATER FROM
1925 ERUPTION

KOMAGADAKE
1131

900

892

640

TRAILHEAD
WEATHER
STATION
480

TOILET

P

FLOOD
CONTROL DAM

P 420

CIRCLE

300 DOUBLE
ROADS

HIGASHI ONUMA
STATION
ONUMA KO (LAKE)

MANY SIDE ROADS

MANY SIDE ROADS

LODGE
PLAYGROUND
CIRCLE

REFORESTED AREA

REFORESTED AREA

REFORESTED AREA

CIRCLE
ARCH OVER ROAD

180

MANY SIDE ROADS

MANY SIDE ROADS

170

KOMAGADAKE
STATION

SAPPORO

MAIN
HIGHWAY
5

AKAIGAWA STATION

INCOMPLETE
MAP DATA

160

HAKODATE-SHI

SCALE 0   1   2   3 KMS

June has to be the best month for hiking in Hokkaido. If camping on the mountain, you'll have to carry water from either station, or from a local home (?).
Maps Japanese map *NK-54-21-8*, 1:50,000; and the **Japan Road Atlas** in Romanji from Shobunsha; and the latest travel guidebook to Japan.

Odake, Hakkoda Volcanos, Honshu Island, Japan

Near the northern end of Japan's Honshu Island, is a group of stratovolcanos known as Hakkoda, or the Hakkoda Volcano Group. This group is located about 25 road kms south of the provincial city of Aomori, or Aomori-shi. The highest summit is Odake at 1584 meters. This is one of the better known hiking areas in northern Japan. Some of these volcanos date from the Recent or Holocene Period, but apparently there have been no eruptions in historic times. Surely the youngest peaks are the ones with craters; Idodake and Odake.

The 6/1997 issue (2 months behind) of the **Global Volcanism Network**, reported that on 7/14/1997, 3 Japanese soldiers died when they slipped into a depression and inhaled poisonous gases somewhere on the lower northern slopes of Hakkoda. The author has no idea where this was. For volcano updates, check these websites (www.volcano.si.edu/gvp/) or (www.kishou.go. jp/).

Getting to these mountains is easy. First go to the Aomori Railway Station. All trains going toward Hokkaido pass through Aomori, so it's a busy place. At the train station is a good information booth. They had lots of tourist maps of important destinations in northern Honshu & Aomori Province, in Romanji (Roman script). These were all free and they always had a girl there who spoke some English. Near the station will be a supermarket where you can buy all your food and supplies.

Also, right in front of the railway station is the bus terminal. Ask for a bus going to Lake Towada, which is south of Hakkoda. Buses leave this train station about 7 or 8 times a day, at least in the summer season. The author bought food in Aomori, then got on an early morning bus in the rain going to Sukayu Onzen, which is just west of Odake. See map. That ride took 50 minutes, and was free because it was a Japan Railways (JR) bus, and anyone holding a JR Pass rides without charge.

At Sukayu Onzen, the author waited 3 hours for the rain to stop, but it didn't; so he finally walked to the top of **Odake** in 1 1/2 hours, in the rain carrying an umbrella all the way. The wind on top was around 50 kms/hour. He came back the same way because in the clouds and wind he couldn't locate the trail down the south side. Round-trip was about 2 3/4 hours.

About 400 meters from the onzen (hot spring spa) is the Sukayu Campjo, which is open only in the 3 months of summer. There's another campjo on the east side of Hakkoda, but there may not be any public transportation running that way. Hitch hiking, driving a rented car, or walking may be your only choices if going that way (?).

Maps show 2 huts or shelters in the group, both just north and south of Odake. The hut just north of Odake is called Odake Hinan Goya. It was new, unlocked, unoccupied and free to use on the author's visit of 5/25/1998. All these trails seem to get fairly heavy use in summer, but some roads are closed in winter. Only the highest peaks rise above treeline.

Best time to visit this region would probably be June or July. September has the most

This is the hut located between Idodake and Odake, both in the Hakkoda area.

Map 253-1, Odake, Hakkoda Volcanos, Honshu, Japan

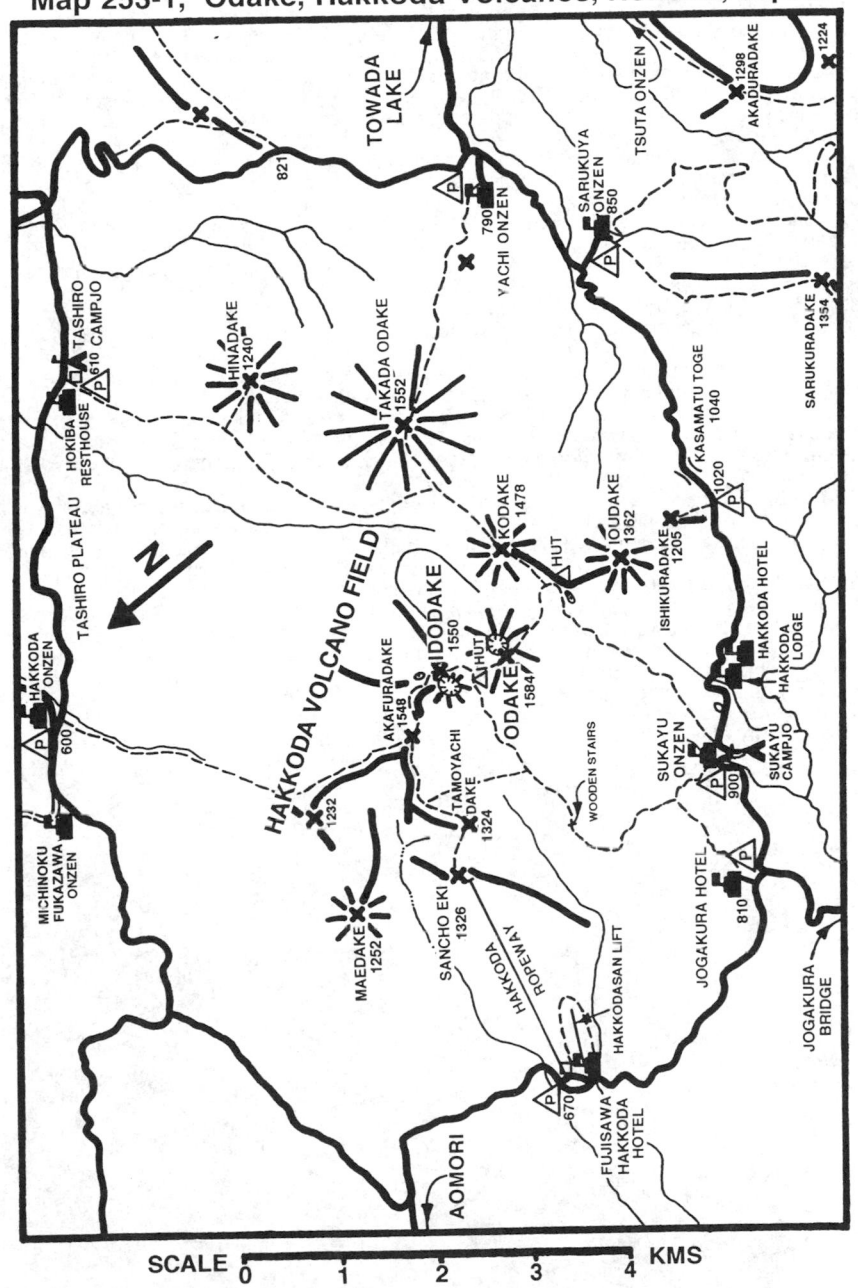

SCALE 0 1 2 3 4 KMS

rainfall of any month in Japan, due to typhoons.
Maps Japanese map *Aomori Tobu, NK-54-23-4 & Hakkodasan, NK-54-24-1,* 1:50,000; the tourist map *Hakkoda,* from the Aomori Train Station; and the **Japan Road Atlas** in Romanji from Shobunsha; and the latest travel guidebook to Japan.

Iwatesan, Honshu, Japan

Iwatesan or Iwate Volcano at 2038 meters, is located in the northern part of Japan's Honshu Island. It's also about 15 kms north, northwest of the city of Morioka and the main train station. Iwatesan is considered an active volcano. Its last major eruption was in 7/1919. That was a phreatic explosion inside the central crater, which can still be seen today. Other historical eruptions took place in 1686, 1687, 1689, 1719 and 1731. These were all explosive eruptions, some having lava flows. For volcano updates, check these websites (www.volcano.si.edu/gvp/) or (www.kishou.go.jp/).

If you climb any mountain or volcano in Japan, you'll find small shrines or Buddhist temples on almost all summits. Around the Iwate's summit crater, are dozens of statues of saints and the usual shine at the summit.

Getting to **Iwatesan** is a little more difficult than to some other peaks in Japan. Best way to get there is to start at the Morioka train station, which was the northern end of the Shinkanzen Line (Bullet Trains) in 1998. From there, take a local commuter train north and get off at the 2nd stop, which is the Takizawa Station. From Takizawa Station, there are no buses going to the base of the mountain, because most of the roads are running north-south. Your options will be to hitch hike (but that won't be easy because you'll be going cross-grain to all the traffic), walk, or take a taxi.

This is what the author did. Right in front of the Takizawa Station is a big sign in Romanji stating, **Taxi** and a telefon number. At that time, the author's Japanese wasn't good enough to speak on the telefone, so he asked someone waiting at the station if he could please call a taxi. Minutes late he was on his way to the Iwatesan Onzen (Iwate Hot Spring Spa). This is near the Iwatesan Jinja (Shrine). These are the best landmarks to shoot for in that area. He paid ¥2260 or about US$17 for the 20 minute ride!

He could have been taken to the trailhead, but chose to stop at the onzen and walk. It was late afternoon, and after a couple of kms, he jumped a fence on the left, and walked into a reforested grove of pine trees. He camped there, hid his pack in brush the next morning, and started walking, but got a lift part-way to the trailhead. That was Saturday morning, with lots of traffic. From the trailhead, which has tap water, toilets and nearby places you could camp (hide your tent--it's not a campjo!), the trail first goes *down* into a gully, then zig zags up a ridge to an old crater rim. Inside the old crater are 2 huts. From the 2nd hut (2 or 3 old ones), the trail heads north to the summit on a younger crater.

There are other trails (and huts) coming up from the west side of the mountain, but they may be more difficult to get to. From the trailhead, the author made it to the summit in 1 3/4 hours; round-trip was 3 1/3 hours. This was about twice as fast as the other hikers that day. From the trailhead he got a lucky ride all the way back to Morioka Station.

Best to buy all your food in Morioka. The author's climb was on 5/23/1998 and there was

Shown here are statues of saints every few meters along the crater rim of Iwatesan.

Map 254-1, Iwatesan, Honshu, Japan

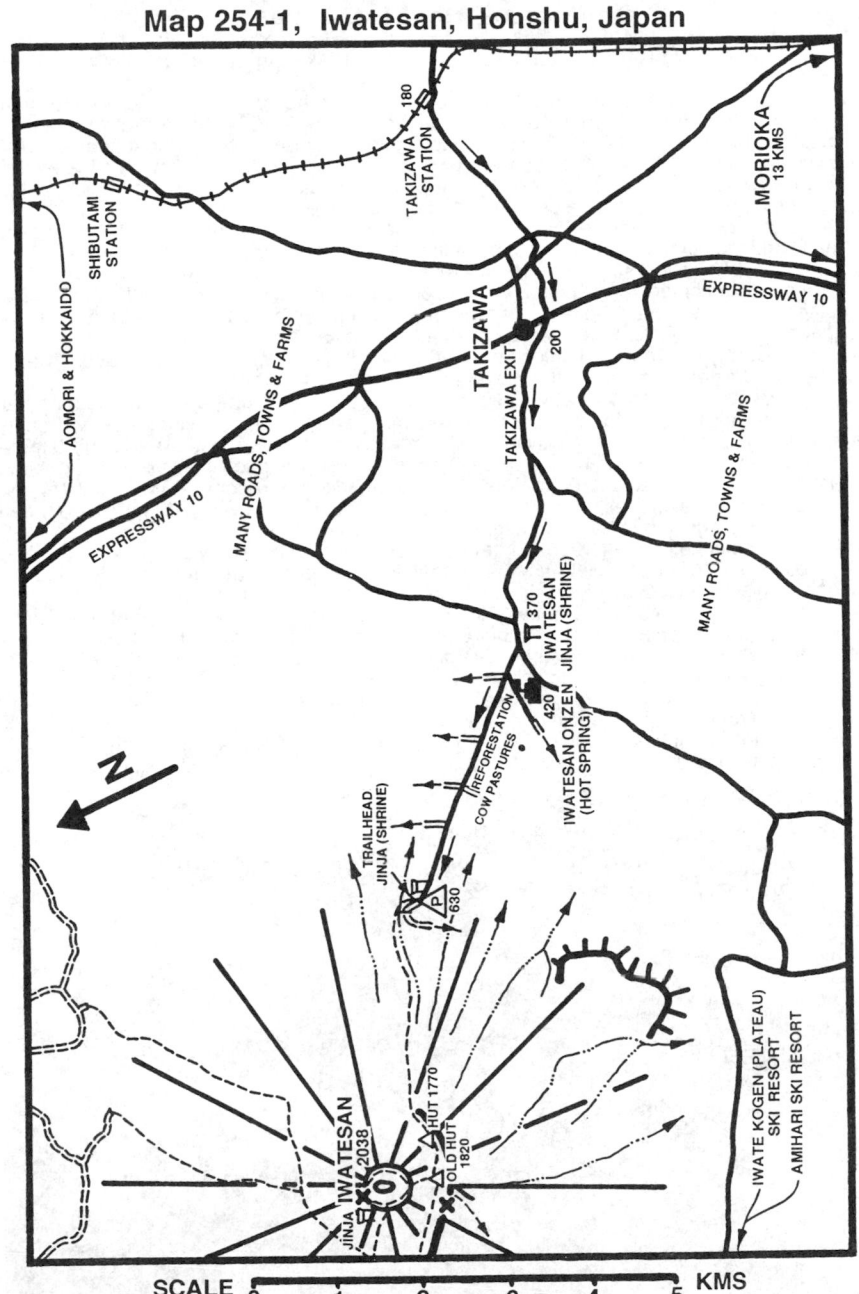

SCALE 0 1 2 3 4 5 KMS

some snow inside the old crater. June is perhaps the best month to climb.

Maps Japanese maps *Numakunai, NJ-54-13-13 & Morioka, NJ-54-13-14,* 1:50,000; and the **Japan Road Atlas** in Romanji; and the latest travel guidebook to Japan.

Chokaisan, Honshu, Japan

Shown here is Chokaisan or Chokai Volcano at 2236 meters. It's located right along the west coast of northern Honshu about halfway between Akita in the north, and Yamagata or Niigata to the south.

Part of Chokaisan is a moderately old volcano, but other parts are quite new or young. Volcanic eruptions have been recorded as far back as 573 AD. Those that old have very incomplete data, but since 1738, all activity has occurred at or near the highest peak. The last activity was during 3 & 4/1974. These were phreatic explosions and mud flows on the east side of Shindake, which is a sizable lava dome on top of Chokaisan. Shindake, the highest point on the mountain, sits inside a much older crater that opens to the north.

Chokaisan also has a crater called Hakusan-Ichige about halfway between the westside trailheads and the summit. The highest point is called **Shogatake** at 1640 meters. The Ohama Shelter is located on the northern rim of this crater.

Getting to **Chokaisan** is reasonably easy. For non-residents, using trains is best. Right after the author climbed Iwatesan, he got on a train from Morioka to Akita, then boarded a *local train--* one that stops at all stations--heading south along the west coast. He got off at Fukura Ike (Station), bought some food in a little supermarket nearby, then walked out to the road heading up to the high western shoulder of the mountain.

There are no buses going that way from Fukura, but there is perhaps one bus a day, plus tour buses, from Kisakate, located north of this mapped area. Hitch hiking seemed best, so that's what the author did. He quickly got a lift and was let off at the restaurant at 1020 meters, got some water, camped in the bush nearby, then after hiding his pack the next morning, headed up from the trailhead marked 1100 meters. He made it to the lava dome summit in 2 1/4 hours, then returned via the villa or hotel at 1140 meters. Round-trip was 4 1/3 hours, trailhead to trailhead. He later got a ride back to Fukura.

His hike was done on 5/24/1998, and there were still lots of big snow drifts on the upper part of the mountain. The Ohama Hut near the crater lake was open for business, but the huts at the Omonoimi Jinja were closed. They surely will be open during the summer.

The trails on Chokaisan are heavily used as this, along with all prominent mountains in Japan, is a popular outing. There are other trailheads to the east and south, but you'll need your own car to use them. The author found several small snow-melt streams west of the crater lake, but in late summer they will likely be dry. Have a bottle full of water to start your hike.

On the author's climb, the slopes near the trailheads were crawling with local people out bushwhacking and picking some kind of new tender chutes (?), so beware of hiding your pack in the bush in late May and early June. Buy all your food in either Fukura or Kisakate. There's lots of traffic on this loop-road on weekends and in summer, which makes hitch hiking good. June is

Shown here is the lava dome and the Omonoimi Jinja located on the top of Chokaisan.

Map 255-1, Chokaisan, Honshu, Japan

probably the best month for hiking.
Maps Japanese maps *Fukura, NJ-54-26-2* & *Chokaisan, NJ-54-20-14*, 1:50,000; the **Japan Road Atlas** in Romanji from Shobunsha; and the latest travel guidebook to Japan.

Bandaisan, Honshu, Japan

This map shows a very popular summer resort & winter ski area in central Honshu. The region is generally known as **Bandai Kogen** (Bandai highland or plateau), and the mountain is Bandaisan at 1818 meters. This area has many lakes and is very scenic. Bandai is an old and rather eroded volcano, but it still has some hot spots and is still considered active. It has an old horseshoe-shaped caldera-like bowl opening to the north, and it seems this is where the activity must be. The first recorded eruption took place in 806 AD, then between 1611 and 1808, there were 5 more recorded periods of activity. The last eruption took place on 7/15/1888 at Kobandai (?), which included pyroclastic flows, plus fatalities. Presumably that was in the old bowl on the north side of the mountain (?). For volcano updates, check these websites (www.volcano.si. edu/gvp/) or (www.kishou.go.jp/).

Getting to this area is quite easy. The best way is by train, so be sure to buy a Japan Rail Pass before you leave home. Start at the Tokyo Station. Get on any one of about 15 or so daily trains running north on the fast Shinkansen Line toward Morioka. Get off at the Koriyama Eki or Station (1 hour, 20 min.), and walk downstairs to the regular train or railway lines. Get on one of 6 or 8 daily trains heading northwest to Bandaisan and the town of Inawashiro. Get off at Inawashiro, and in front of the station get on a bus running toward Bandai Kogen. These buses run about every hour or so and pass through Kawakami, the Kitashiobara village, and on to the Bandai Kogen Eki or bus stop. The author paid ¥630 or about US$4.75 for the ride up to Kawakami; and later paid ¥750 or US$5.65 for the ride from Gosikinuma Iriguchi Eki back to the Inawashiro Station.

To climb **Bandaisan**, you could walk right from the Inawashiro Station toward the mountain and climb from the Inawashiro ski area; or at the Bandai Kokusai ski lifts; or the Ottare Onzen & ski area. But the scenery on the south side of the mountain isn't much to look at. Most people who climb Bandai do so from the northern routes and from somewhere on the Bandai Kogen.

The author stopped at Kawakami and walked up the road a ways, and found a campsite off in the trees. Next morning, he hid his big pack, and hiked up the trail from Kawakami. He made it to the summit in about 1 3/4 hours. That was on 5/21/1998. There were some snowdrifts higher up and water in several places along the way. He returned via the trail passing the *blue huts* at 1225 meters, the Urabandai ski area, and finally to the Bandai Kogen Hotel. Total hike-time from Kawakami Onzen was 3 3/4 hours. From there he walked & hitch hiked back to his pack and campsite. He later walked toward the youth hostel and hid his tent in trees about 500 meters away for one night.

Much of this area is part of a national park with lots of hotels and ski resorts. About 4 kms north of this map are several campjos (campgrounds). Expect to pay about US$20 a night in the youth hostel. The Kitashiobara village has a good tourist office with maps in Romanji (English). Buy all your food in Koriyama or Inawashiro, or from 2 small supermarkets at Bandai Kogen Eki

This is Bandaisan as seen from a hill above Kawakami Onzen.

Map 256-1, Bandaisan, Honshu, Japan

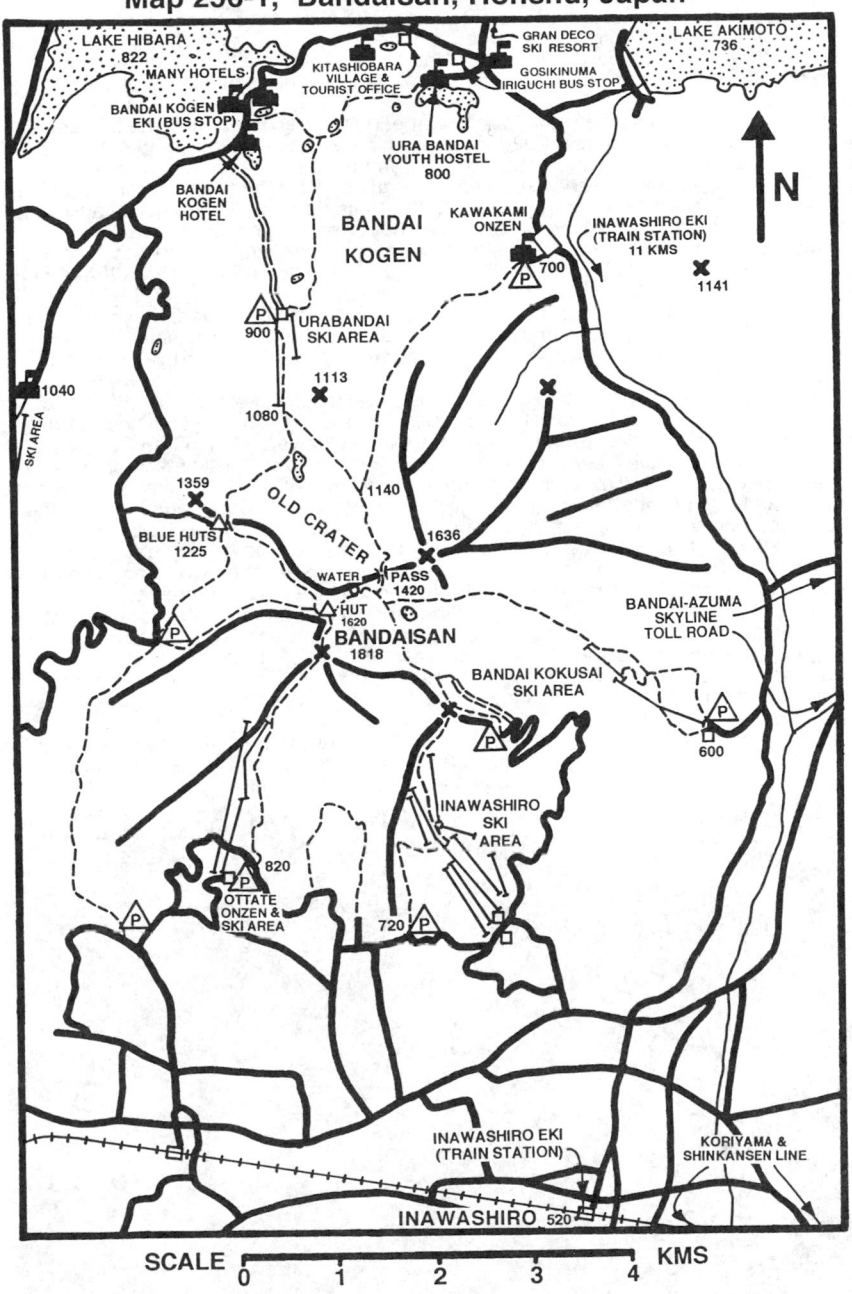

or Kitashiobara. July is the driest month of summer in these parts.
Maps Japanese map *Bandaisan, NJ-54-22-15,* 1:50,000; and the **Japan Road Atlas** i n
Romanji from Shobunsha; and the latest travel guidebook to Japan.

Azumasan & Issaikyoyama, Honshu, Japan

This map features a very large mountain massif called Azumasan, or Mt. Azuma. The highest summit is called Nishiazumasan at 2035 meters. It's located about halfway between Tokyo in the south, and Morioka in the north, and due west of the city of Fukushima, which is on the Shinkansen Railway Line. It's also immediately northeast of Bandaisan, which is featured on the previous map.

Part of Azuma is an active volcano, but that part is far removed from the highest summit. The active part is Issaikyoyama, 2024 meters, located on the eastern end of the massif. It seems to be at or near the crater marked 1949 on this map. Its last major eruption was on 12/7/1977. It was a small phreatic explosion. The author didn't get to that section, and the map he bought, didn't quite show all the area and the trails from the Bandai-Azuma Skyline Toll Road. That part of this map is incomplete. When buying topo maps, be sure to get the 1:50,000 scale map just east of Azumasan. The starting point for Issaikyoyama is from that toll road, but the author isn't showing it correctly on this map. For volcano updates, check these websites (www.volcano.si.edu/gvp/) or (www.kishou.go.jp/).

It seems there is no public transportation on the Skyline Toll Road, so your options are renting a car or hitch hiking. One end of this toll road begins at the Fukushima Railway Station, another begins at the Matsukawa Station. The **Japan Road Atlas** shows these major highways and train stations.

If you're interested in climbing **Azumasan**, then use the previous map to get from Koriyama, Inawashiro and to the youth hostel in the Bandai Kogen area. From the youth hostel, walk out to the main road leading to the fishing village on Lake Onogawa and the Gran Deco Ski Resort. There's no buses--so hitch hike, or walk. It's about 7 or 8 kms to the ski resort on a new paved highway. The author found lots of traffic going as far as the fishing village, then fewer vehicles.

From the huge parking lot in front of the Gran Deco Hotel, locate and head up the main graveled road zig zagging up through a big meadow to the north. Just below where this ski slope road begins to climb & zig zag to the left, take a side road to the right. After 300-350 meters this track ends and a good trail begins. However, this may become overgrown with time, so you could also walk uphill beneath the ski lifts, or continue along the road to the upper-most ski runs at 1550 meters. From a building at the highest lifts, there's a trail running east which connects to the main trail which was there long before Gran Deco. Continue along this trail to the highest summit as shown. Near the highest peak, you'll walk through meadows along raised, wooden walk-ways, which prevent erosion. Nearby is a new hut which sleeps 25 to 30 people. The summit of Nishiazumasan is covered with pine trees making observations of the countryside difficult.

The author bivouacked near the youth hostel, then walked & hitch hiked up to Gran Deco. From there to the top took just over 2 hours; 3 3/4 hours round-trip. There were big snow drifts on top--on 5/22/1998. From the main road junction near the youth hostel, up and back, took 5

This is one of the huts and a raised boardwalk near the summit of Nishiazumasan.

Map 257-1, Asumasan & Issaikyoyama, Honshu, Japan

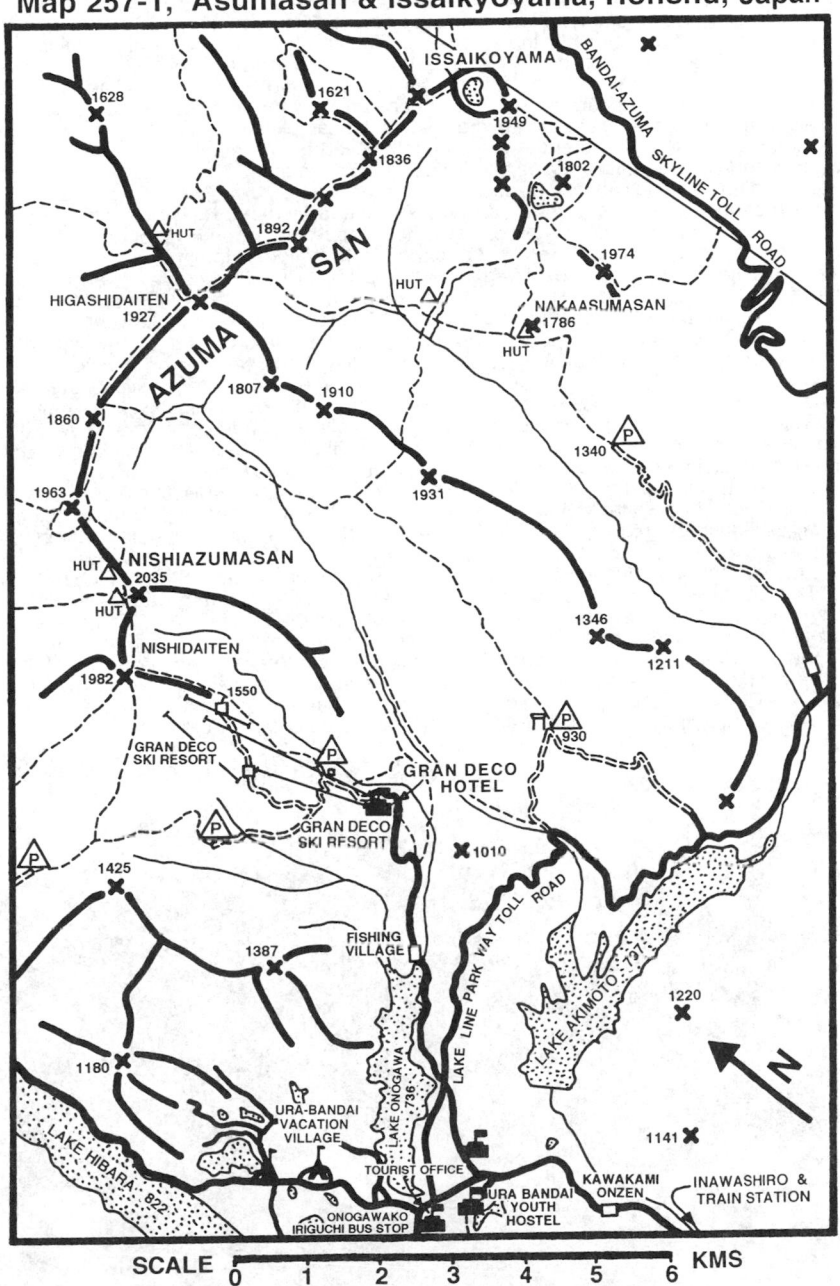

1/4 hours. Good hitch hiking! Buy your food in Koriyama or Inawashiro, if possible.

Maps Japanese map *Bandaisan, NJ-54-22-15 & Azumasan, NJ-54-22-14*, and *the one immediately to the east*, 1:50,000; and the **Japan Road Atlas** in Romanji from Shobunsha; and the latest travel guidebook to Japan.

Nantaisan, Honshu Island, Japan

Shown on this map are a number of medium high peaks located about 120 kms due north of Tokyo. The best known summit in the area is an older volcano by the name of Nantaisan, or Mt. Nantai. Nantai is also located about 11 kms due west of the resort town of Nikko.

Nantaisan is a dormant stratovolcano with an almost perfect conical shape. Its last eruption was sometime in the Holocene or Recent Epoch, which is the last 10,000 years. There are several onzens or hot spring spas in the area, so it's not completely dead yet.

Nikko, Nantaisan and the entire region is a real tourist hangout. It's a pretty place with onzens, waterfalls, Buddhist temples and Shinto jinjas or shrines. There's also a wide range of hotels, youth hostels and camping places.

One reason Nikko is so popular is that it's reasonably close to Tokyo with good public transportation. You can use an expressway or toll road from Utsunomiya, but the best way for foreign tourists is by train. There are 2 separate railway lines running from Tokyo to Nikko. First, there's the Tobu-Nikko Line. It begins at the Asakusa Station in the basement of the Tobu Department Store (?) in Tokyo. Trains run about every half hour, cost ¥2690, and take about 2 hours. For some, this is the best way, because you don't change trains. However, since it's a private railway, Japan Rail Passes are not accepted. So if you have a JR Pass, start at the Tokyo Station and get on one of many Shinkansen (Bullet) trains heading north toward Morioka, but get off at Utsunomiya. From there, walk downstairs and get on a regular *local train* running to, and ending at, Nikko. These run every half hour or so and take 45 minutes.

Once in Nikko, your first stop should be the tourist office located up the main street of town about one km from the train stations, which are near each other. Actually, each train station has some pretty good information pamphlets, but the tourist office has more.

For the budget traveler, there are 2 youth hostels in town. On 6/5/1998, the author stayed in the one just north of town for ¥2450, or about US$18.50, a night. There are also 3 campgrounds or campjos just north of town, plus a big new Lion Do Supermarket within half a km of the train stations.

To reach **Nantaisan**, you could hitch hike, but most prefer the bus. Start at the bus eki (bus stop) located in front of the Tobu-Nikko Station. Ask for a bus going to Nantaisan, Futarasan Jinga, or the Chuzenji Onzen. Cost is about ¥1100, or US$8.25. Get off at the bus stop or terminal at the east end of Lake Chuzenji, as shown. From there, walk west about 15 minutes to the Futarasan Jinja. You must enter this Buddhist Temple to reach the beginning of the trail. For this you pay a fee of ¥500. From there, a good trail zig zags upslope, then follows a road a ways. At a little white shrine, the trail begins again. You'll pass some old & unusable huts and a shrine (jinja), then the summit, with the Ōkumiya Jinja. Round-trip for the author from Futarasan

This is the temple called Futarasan Jinji at the beginning of the trail up Nantaisan.

Map 258-1, Nantaisan, Honshu Island, Japan

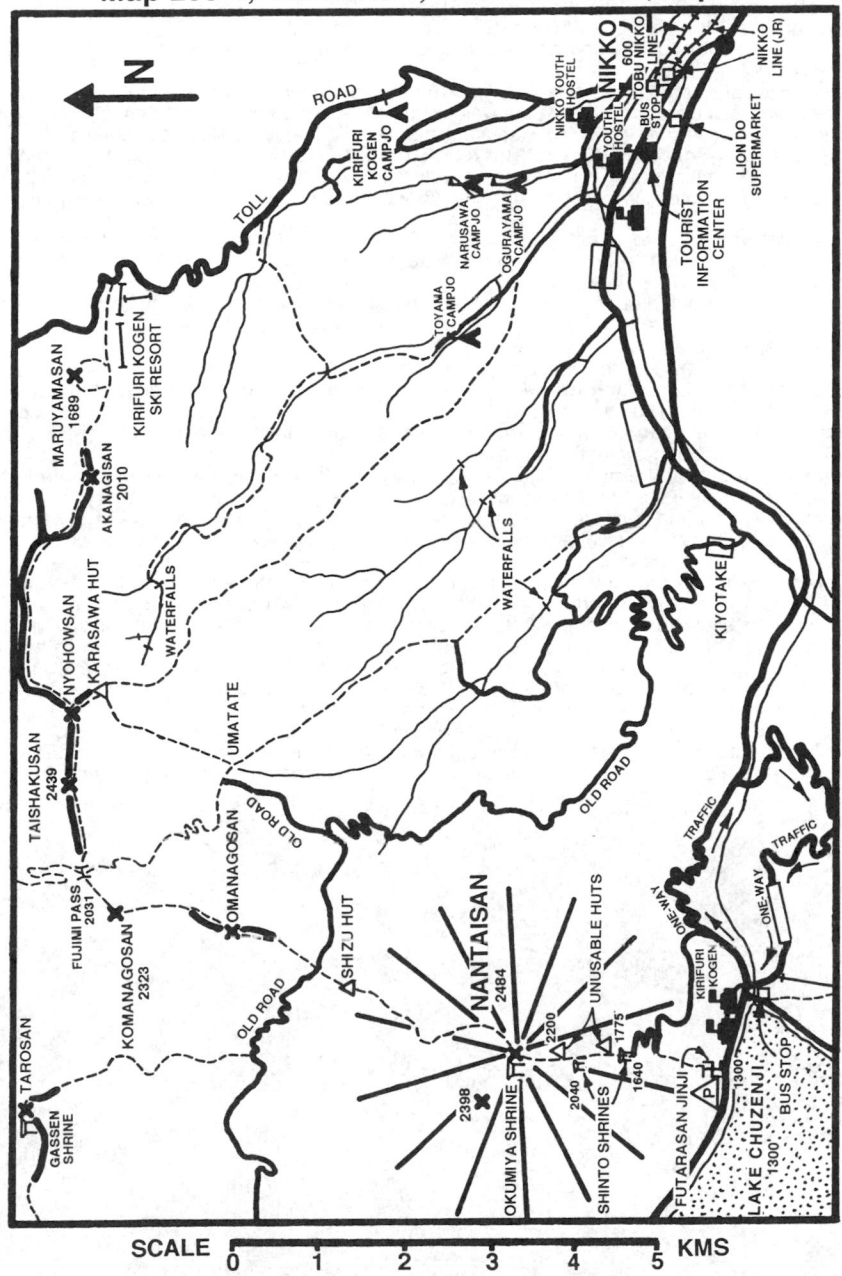

SCALE 0 1 2 3 4 5 KMS

Jinga was just over 3 hours.
Maps *Nikko Hiking Guide*, from the Nikko Tourist Office; and the **Japan Road Atlas** in Romanji from Shobunsha; and the latest travel guidebook to Japan.

Asamayama Volcano, Honshu Island, Japan

Featured here is the most active volcano on the Japanese island of Honshu. It's Asamayama, or Mt. Asama, at 2568 meters. This volcano is located about 130 kms northwest of Tokyo and about 40 kms southeast of Nagano. It dominates the northwest skyline of the small city of Karuizawa.

Asama is considered a complex volcano, with the first recorded eruption in 350 AD. The last major eruption took place on 7/20/1990. It was a small VEI-2 explosion from the central crater. Since then, there have been some periods of steam and tremors. Recorded fatalities have been documented during the following eruptions (years): 1721, 1783, 1900, 1909, 1930 & 31, 1935, 1938, 1947, 1950, and 1961. No wonder the mountain was *officially closed* to hiking when the author climbed it on 5/20/1998! More below. For volcano updates, check these websites (www.volcano.si.edu/gvp/) or (www. kishou.go.jp/).

The best way to get to **Asamayama** is by train, so get your Japan Rail Pass before leaving home. From the Tokyo Station, get on any Shinkansen train bound for Nagano, but get off at the Karuizawa Station. From there, you've got to get to the Nakakaruizawa Station. To do that, you'll have to walk out in front of the station and get on a bus; or get on a private train; one that doesn't accept the JR Pass. The author paid ¥180, or US$1.35 for that short trip on the private train. Or just walk the 4 kms between the 2 stations.

From near or in front of the Nakakaruizawa Station, take a bus going to Asama Pass and a place called Minenochaya. There were 11 buses per day in 1998, which cost ¥630, or about US$4.75. The author rode a bus up, but hitch hiked back. If you intend to take a bus up, ask someone at the Karuizawa Station if the Minenochaya bus starts there, or somewhere nearby (?). If so, forget about going to the Nakakaruizawa Station.

Where you get off the bus at Minenochaya, will be 2 gravel roads veering to the left, or northeast. If you take the road to the right, you'll soon see the volcano observatory from Tokyo University. Walk along this road one km to reach the trail going up the mountain. The author took the one to the left and bivouacked for the night less than one km from the observatory.

The next morning, he broke camp, hid his big pack in the trees & brush, and headed up the mountain on the first road mentioned. From his campsite, to the summit and back, took just under 3 hours. There's a good trail all the way up to the new crater, which is inside an older caldera rim, as shown on the map. Volcanologists ride ATV's up the trail about halfway to check their seismographs. The author met several other people on the mountain, which seemed closed to the public at the time. However, there were no guards or locked gates, even though there was a sign near the observatory (in kanji) which appeared to be telling people of danger or closure. In these situations, you go at your own risk!

Within about one km of the Nakakaruizawa Station are three supermarkets, which are the best places to buy food. There was a campjo as shown on the map, but the author didn't see or use it. There's a good forest on either side of Minenochaya for camping but if you should camp,

In the center of this foto is the beginning of the trail up Asamayama (background left). To the right in the trees is the volcano observatory.

Map 259-1, Asamayama Volcano, Honshu Island, Japan

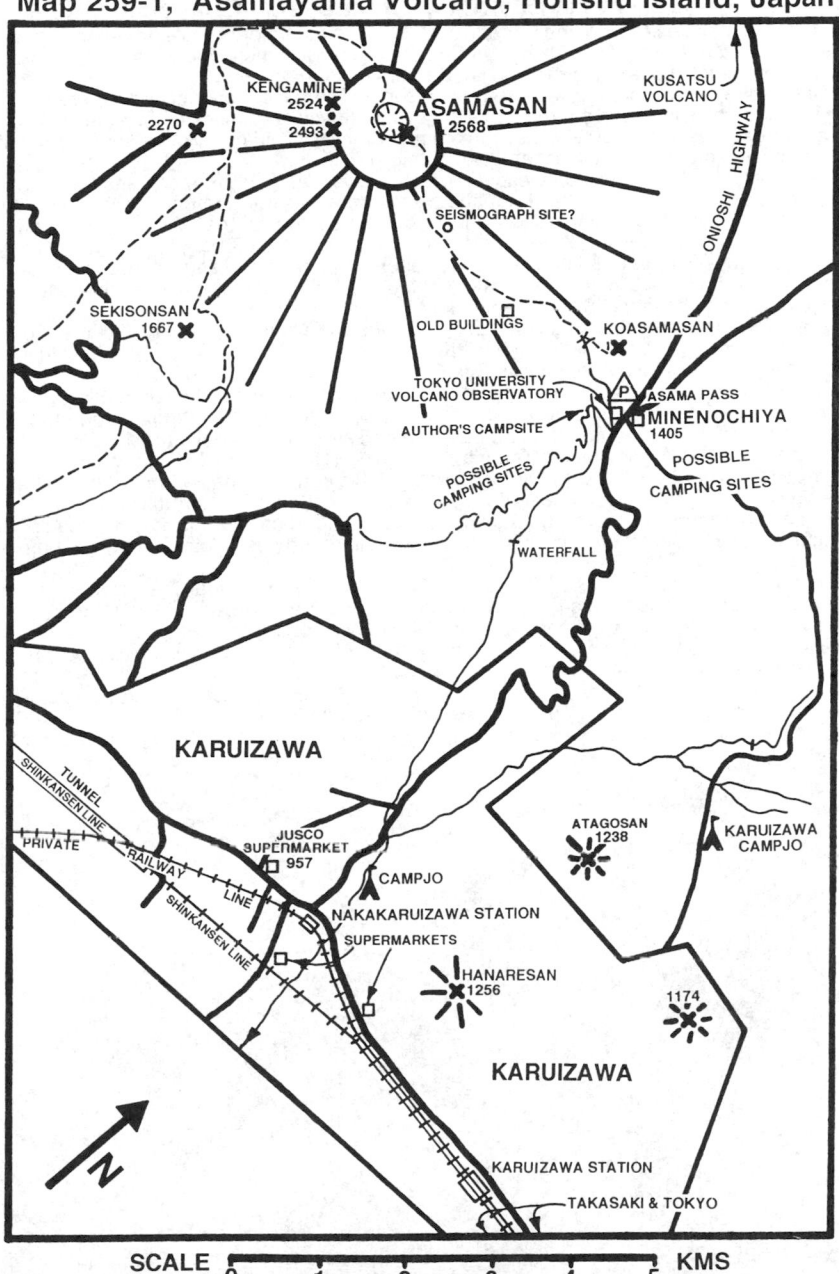

KENGAMINE
2524 ✗
2270 ✗   2493 ✗   ⊙ ASAMASAN
                              2568

KUSATSU
VOLCANO

SEISMOGRAPH SITE?
○

SEKISONSAN
1667 ✗

OLD BUILDINGS □   KOASAMASAN
                                    ✗

TOKYO UNIVERSITY
VOLCANO OBSERVATORY   P ASAMA PASS
                             □ MINENOCHIYA
AUTHOR'S CAMPSITE ←   1405

                                        POSSIBLE
        POSSIBLE   CAMPING SITES
      CAMPING SITES

                    WATERFALL

KARUIZAWA

SHINKANSEN LINE
TUNNEL

PRIVATE   ATAGOSAN
        RAILWAY   1238   KARUIZAWA
              LINE   CAMPJO
    SHINKANSEN LINE   JUSCO
                        SUPERMARKET
                        □ 957

                           ✚ CAMPJO
                        NAKAKARUIZAWA STATION
                        SUPERMARKETS
                          □ HANARESAN
                           ✗ 1256   1174

                                KARUIZAWA

                        KARUIZAWA STATION
                        → TAKASAKI & TOKYO

SCALE 0   1   2   3   4   5 **KMS**

be sure to put a tent up in the evening, and take it down early the next day. There was a
restaurant at Minenochaya, where you could get drinking water. July is the best time to climb
Asamayama.

Maps Japanese map *NJ-54-36-6,* 1:50,000; and the **Japan Road Atlas** in Romanji from
Shobunsha; and the latest travel guidebook to Japan.

Tateyama, Kita Alps, Honshu Island, Japan

This map includes most of the northern half of the Kita or Northern Alps. All the mountains coming under the name *Japanese Alps* are on the island of Honshu; same island as Tokyo and Fujisan. The highest peak in this region is Tateyama at 3015 meters.

The unique thing about the Japanese Alps is, they are folded and uplifted; whereas most or all other mountains in Japan are remnants of new or old volcanos. The author was just south of this area from 10/9 to 10/12/1977, but can't remember what kind of rocks he saw. Undoubtedly they are sedimentary of some kind, and/or metamorphic.

As is the case with all the Japanese Alps, this area is fairly easy to reach and from a number of different directions. To get to the highest peak, the easiest approach is from the area of Toyama to the northwest. First take a JR train to Toyama, then at the Toyama Station switch to a train on the private Toyama-Kamidaki Line heading southeast & east to Bijodaira Tateyama. From there, take a bus, or hitch hike, to the resort of Murodoh. From Murodoh to the top of **Tateyama** is a half-day hike for most. Many of the summits in that region (the ones west of the Kurobe Dam), can be reached in one day from Murodoh.

Another approach to the peaks east of the Kurobe Dam is from Omachi. Get there by train, then take a bus or hitch hike west to Ohgizawa. Getting to Tateyama from the east involves a boat ride across the lake behind Kurobe Dam.

Or if a longer hike is your goal, rather than climbing the very highest peak, a ridge walk might be interesting. From Ohgizawa, you can get to the top of a long ridge running north to the high peak of **Shirouma** at 2933 meters, and the town of Sarukura. To walk this distance is to walk almost half of the total length of the Kita Alps.

Depending on when you start and end the hike, this can be done in 2 or 3 days. Along this ridge you'll find many shelters, most of which are like small hotels. Normally each place has a dorm room for sleeping and you can usually buy either hot meals or snack food. Inquire at the Omachi Railway Station tourist office about which shelters provide lodging and meals before you go.

Near each shelter is usually a place to camp, generally for a small fee. Being on a ridge, water is difficult to find, but the hut keepers catch and store rainwater. When rain is plentiful, drinking water is free, but in dry periods a small fee may be charged.

Another approach might be from the north and the place called Unazuki Onzen. The author never was able to get details, but there's a railway from Unazuki to Keyakaidaira (trains may or may not be running?). If running, it may serve tourists in summer, but if not, you could walk the tracks to reach the trails further up the canyon to the south.

If you're planning to cook your own food, buy it in Omachi or Toyama, or some other larger

From the summit of Hotaka looking north along the ridge toward Yaridake (see next map).

Map 260-3, Tateyama, Kita Alps, Honshu Island, Japan

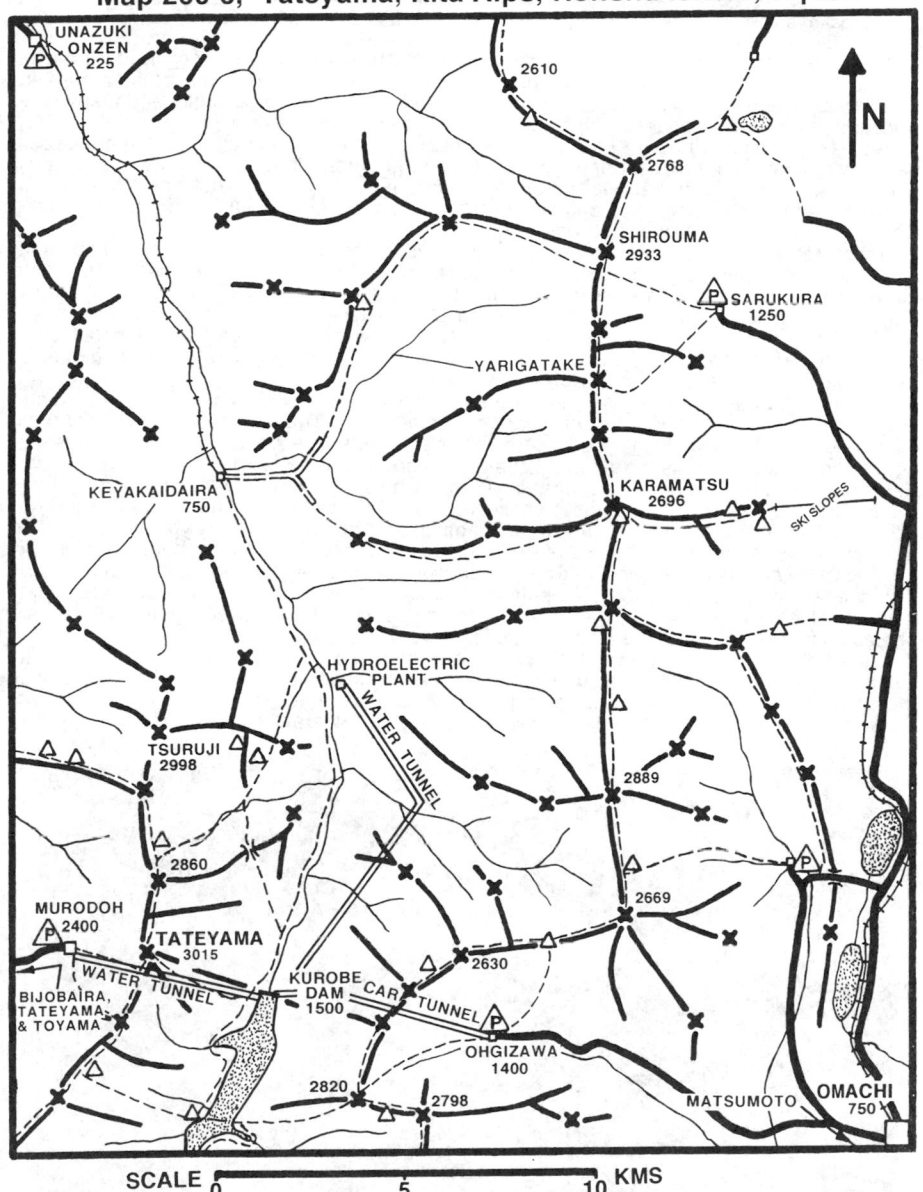

SCALE 0   5   10 KMS

town before reaching the trails. June through mid-October is the hiking season here, with early
October being one of the favorite times because of fall colors.
Maps Japanese map *Kita (North) Alps,* 1:100,000, printed in Japanese characters (kanji); and
the **Japan Road Atlas** in Romanji from Shobunsha; and the latest travel guidebook to Japan.

Yaridake, Kita Alps, Honshu Island, Japan

Yaridake (sometimes spelled Yarigatake) at 3179 meters, is the *Matterhorn* of Japan and one of the most famous mountains in the country. In the same area is Okuho Dake (Okuho Peak) at 3190 meters, Japan's third highest summit. Nearby is Hotaka at 3100 meters, another popular destination.

The Kita or North Alps are folded & uplifted mountains composed mostly of metamorphic-type rocks, as opposed to the rest of the country which is largely made of old, and many new, volcanics. None of the Japanese Alps are volcanic in origin.

Access to these southern Kita Alps is very easy and it is visited by perhaps more people than any other part of the Japanese Alps system. To get there, first make your way to a small city of Matsumoto, located about 180 air kms northwest of Tokyo. Direct train service from Tokyo is via the Chuo Line. You can also reach Matsumoto by train via another branch of the Chuo Line from Nagoya to the southwest.

From Matsumoto, most people take a bus to the resort of Kamikochi, a distance of about 45 kms. Hitch hiking can be good, but only to a point 6 kms below Kamikochi. At that point, private autos are not allowed to pass--only buses. There simply isn't room for parking upcanyon around Kamikochi. Just take a bus! Or you can walk that short distance in just over an hour.

At Kamikochi are many shops, stores, hotels and campsites. It's a beautiful place, but a real tourist trap. From Kamikochi it's hiking the rest of the way. There is a narrow gravel road up to Yokoh, but that's limited to hotel deliveries in small trucks only.

To climb **Yaridake** about 4 days are needed, or maybe 5, depending on when you start and finish. Many make one camp at Yokoh, another higher up. The normal route is right up the main valley above Yokoh, then directly to the summit via the shelters at 2825 & 3050 meters.

To climb **Okuho**, about 3 days are usually enough. Most people doing this hike, camp at Kalasawa (camping is in designated areas only in this national park). For those with more time, the following route is recommended: Kamikochi, Yokoh, Kalasawa, Okuho, **Hotaka**, Yaridake, Yokoh and Kamikochi. This hike would take most people about 5 days, maybe more (?). The ridge top between Okuho and Yaridake is rugged, and probably slow walking, but well-used.

The valley camps have plenty of good water available, but it's rain water at the ridge camps & shelters, sometimes for a fee. Most huts offer everything for the light traveler who wants comfort in the hills. Special equipment must include a raincoat and cover for the pack, as rain comes often. Better take an ice ax & crampons early in the season.

June through October are the favorite months for climbing in the southern Kita Alps, with October being the most colorful and fotogenic; and at times the most crowded. The author was there from 10/9 to 10/12/1977, and spent parts of 4 days/3 nights climbing Okuho and Hotaka. He arrived on a weekend, including October 10th, which is apparently some kind of holiday, and

10/10/1977 holiday camping at the Kalasawa Campjo. Look at all the tents!

Map 261-1, Yaridake, Kita Alps, Honshu Island, Japan

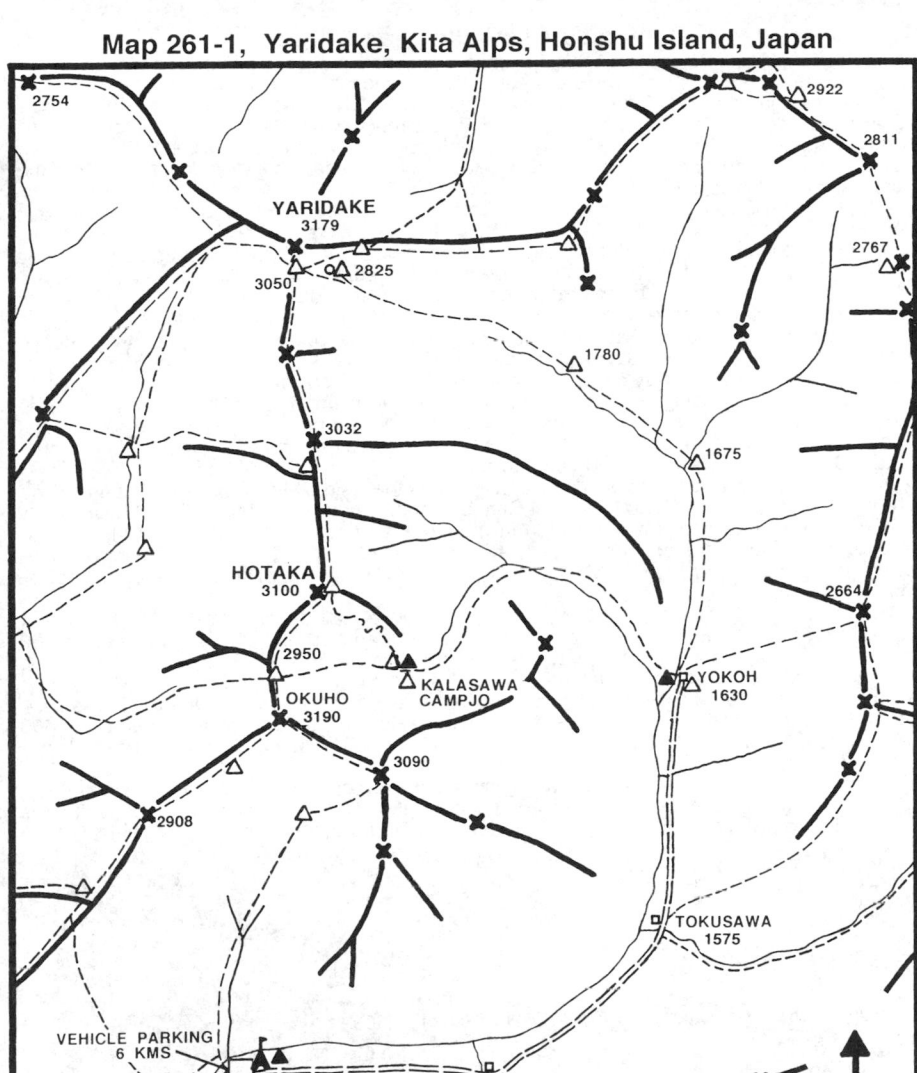

SCALE 0 3 6 9 12 KMS

the place was very crowded.
Maps Japanese map *Kita Alps*, 1:100,000, printed in Japanese characters (kanji); and the
Japan Road Atlas in Romanji from Shobunsha; and the latest travel guidebook to Japan.

Ontake San, Honshu Island, Japan

If you enjoy visiting Buddhist temples & shrines (jinjas) and statues of saints, here's the mountain for you. It's Ontake at 3063 meters, the second highest volcano in Japan after Fujisan. Ontake is located at the southern end of the Kita Alps and just south of the previous map featuring Yaridake. There are no less than 7 starting points and routes up this mountain, and along each are many pilgrim shelters, statues, small jinjas and temples. This place has been a sacred mountain to Buddhists for several centuries, and there are more religious sites and resthouses here than on any mountain the author has climbed in Japan.

Ontake is now considered an active complex volcano, but it's first eruption in recorded history was just recently--on 10/28/1979. Activity lasted until late 4/1980. The 1979 phreatic explosion took place immediately south of the main summit and included ash & lapilli in a pyroclastic flow. The tephra column rose 1500 meters, & acidic water from the new vents killed fish in nearby rivers. The 4 large craters on the mountain today date from 23,000 BC. For volcano updates, check these websites (www.volcano.si.edu/gvp/) or (www.kishou.go.jp/).

Getting to **Ontake** isn't as easy as to some mountains but you can do most of it with public transportation. With your Japan Rail Pass, get on any Shinkansen train and make your way to Nagoya, located about halfway between Tokyo and Osaka. From Nagoya, take one of 15 or 20 regular trains per day going northeast in the direction of Matsumoto and Nagano, but get off at Kisofukushima (KF). Beside the KF station is a good tourist information office where you can get tourist maps, some written in Romanji & English. They can direct you to a supermarket located about 500 meters north and downhill from the station.

To get to the mountain, walk across the street from the train station to a bus company office and buy a ticket to Kiso Onzen (Kiso Hot Springs Spa). In June, there are 5 or 6 buses daily making this run, but in mid-summer, there may be more; and perhaps buses going all the way to Nakanoyu (6th Step), probably the most-used starting point on the mountain. Or there may be buses going all the way to the Ontake Kogen Ski Resort (?), or to the trailhead called Mikasayama (?).

Here's what the author did. He took a bus to Kiso Onzen (21.3 kms for ¥1050 or US$8), and walked up the road 8 kms to the ropeway (lift) and Kunamade Ski Resort. He camped 600 meters below the bottom of the ropeway, then the next morning, 6/4/1998, he hid his big pack & tent, and walked to the end of the paved road, which is the old 6th Step. From there he walked along a well-used trail past 5 more pilgrim resthouses until he reached the summit. There were quite a few snow drifts, but they weren't a problem. Round-trip time from his camp at 1500 meters was 4 3/4 hours. Later, he got a lift part way down to Kiso Onzen where he had a hot bath for ¥500.

Along the trails are many resthouses pilgrims once used before better roads were built; now they seem almost abandoned. There's a big shelter at the 8th Step, plus 2 groups of statues nearby. There are many old shelters at the 9th Step, plus an interesting Shinto jinja. At the

From the summit of Ontake San looking south at the active part and Peak 2940.

Map 262-1, Ontake San, Honshu Island, Japan

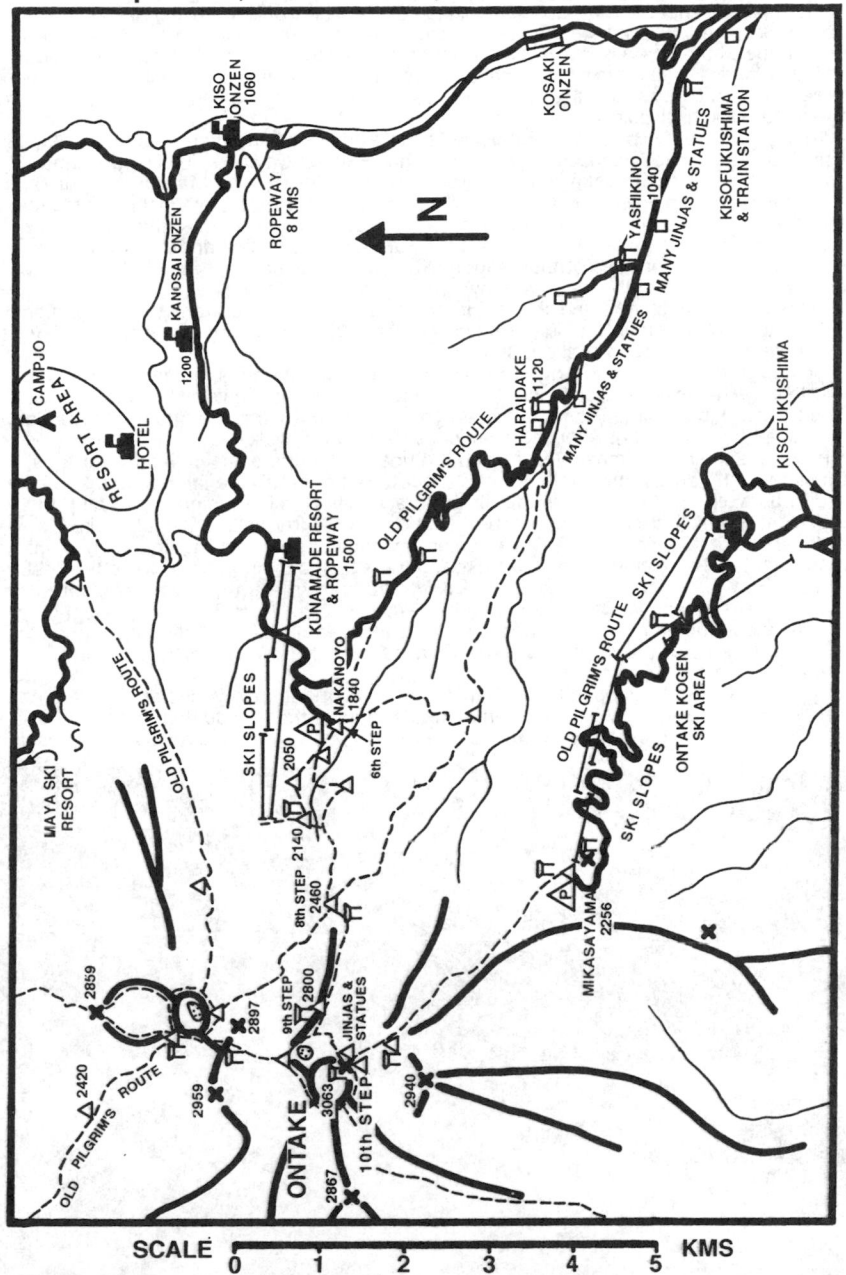

summit (10th Step) are many more shelters and a new jinja, right on top. Because of all these religious sites, Ontake may be the most interesting climb in Japan.

Maps Japanese maps *Ontake San, NI-53-1-9, and Kisofukushima-machi, NI-53-1-5,* 1:50,000; the **Japan Road Atlas** in Romanji from Shobunsha; and the latest travel guidebook to Japan.

Komagadake, Chuo Alps, Honshu Island, Japan

The Chuo or Central Alps of Japan are located on the island of Honshu, just west of the northern Minami or Southern Alps, northwest of Fujisan, and not far south of the city of Matsumoto. The highest summit in the Chuo Alps is Komagadake (sometimes spelled Komagatake) rising to 2956 meters. The Chuo Alps are included in the national park system, which includes all of the high and important mountains in Japan. Like all of the Japanese Alps, these mountains are folded and uplifted and are made of metamorphic-type rocks.

Getting to the region of the highest peaks is quite easy. The normal route of approach is via the small city of Komagane, located next of the Chuo Expressway and Lida Railway Line.

To get there, it's best to take a train; either from the north and Matsumoto; or take any Shinkansen train running between Tokyo and Nagoya, but get off at Toyohashi. From there take one of many regular trains northeast toward Matsumoto, but get off at Komagane. At the train station ask about buses going up the canyon toward a power station and the Komagane Kogen Ski Resort. (The author doesn't remember a ski resort being there in 1977, but the Japan Road Atlas maps indicates there's one there now).

You could also hitch hike, which the author did in 1977. If there aren't too many buses, you may have to walk and/or hitch a ride. It's only 6-7 kms (?) up to what was a locked gate for cars, a power plant, and ski resort at about 850 meters.

Located at the Komagane Kogen Ski Resort are several hotels, eating places, and some small stores. The power station is the end of the road for private vehicles; only tourist buses are allowed beyond that point. From the locked gate to Shirabi Daira--the end of the road and the beginning of the lift & trail--is about 15 kms, or about a 3 hour walk.

If you take the lift like most, you'll finish the ride in a cirque basin called Senjojiki, at about 2600 meters. If you'd rather walk, there's a good trail beneath the lift, which takes hikers to Senjojiki as well. From the top of the lift there are many trails fanning out to all parts of the range, most of which are on the ridgetops. That part of the trail linking Senjojiki with the shelter or hut marked *2800 meters*, is heavily traveled, even by people wearing fine clothes, including business suits! The trail is fenced in to keep all the traffic in line and to save the rest of the mountain from being trampled to death. **Komagadake** is a short walk from the hut just mentioned. The author was here 10/7 & 10/8/1977.

Lodging and food can be found at all locations along the route, including the highest shelter on the mountain, Senjojiki, the ski resort area, and best of all at Komagane, where a supermarket is found.

If you're planning to sleep in the higher shelters, you must have your own sleeping bag and stove (if you're cooking). Meals are sometimes served in these mountain huts, but for a very high price. Camping used to be permitted, but always away from the crowds, or in designated

The top of the cable car at Senjojiki and beginning of the trail to Komagadake.

Map 263-1, Komagadake, Chuo Alps, Honshu, Japan

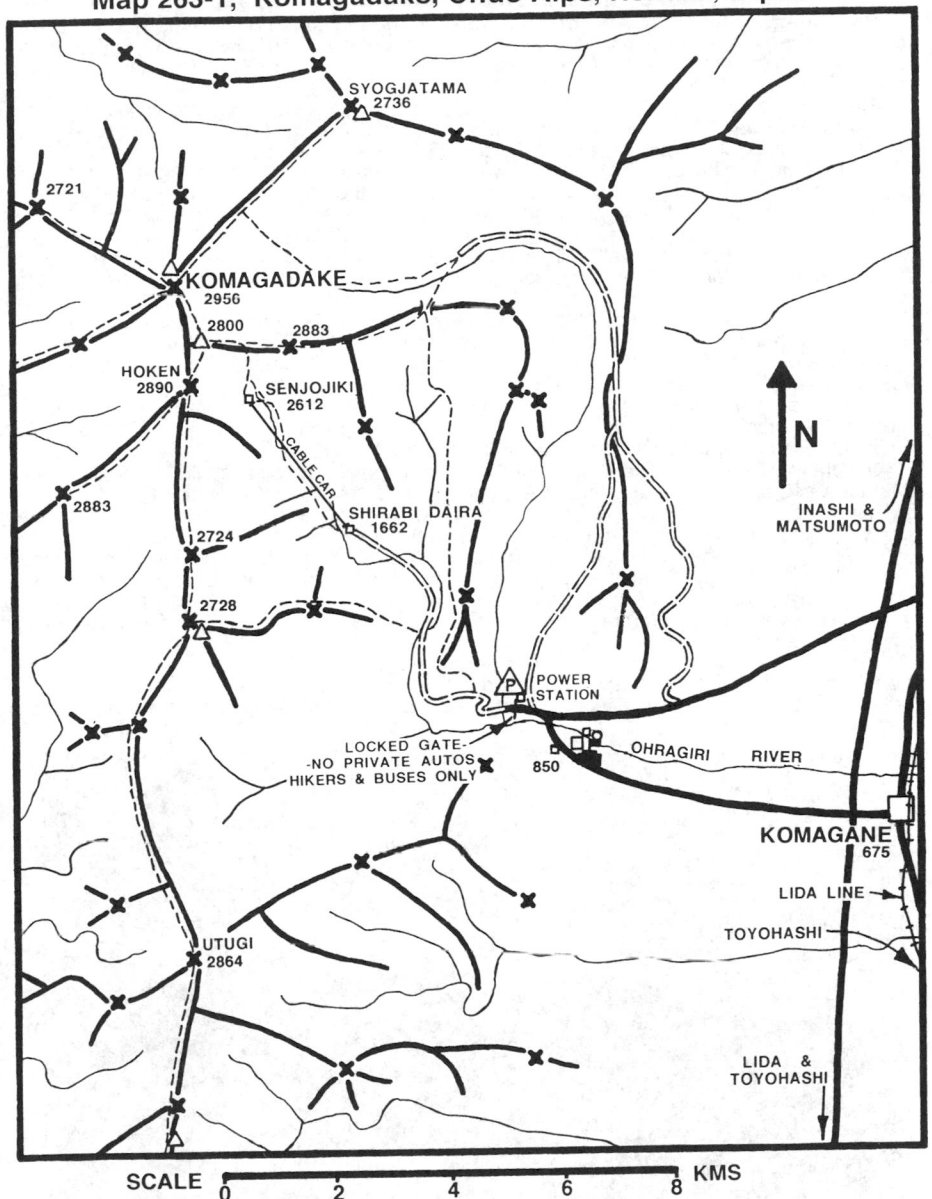

SCALE 0 2 4 6 8 KMS

areas. June through October is the hiking season with October the most colorful month.
Maps Japanese map *Chuo Alps*, 1:50,000, printed in Japanese characters (kanji); the **Japan Road Atlas** in Romanji from Shobunsha; and the latest travel guidebook to Japan.

Kitadake, Minami Alps, Honshu Island, Japan

The Minami or Southern Alps of Japan are on the big island of Honshu (as are all the Japanese Alps). This mountainous region is just west of Kofu and northwest of Fujisan. The highest peak in the entire Minami Alps is **Kitadake** at 3192 meters, making it the second highest mountain in Japan. Only Fujisan is higher.

Getting to this region is fairly easy. If coming from Tokyo, start at the Tokyo Station and get on any train going along the Chuo Line in the direction of Kofu. Get off there and inquire about buses going to Ashiyasu, and hopefully beyond to as far as Hirogawara, or maybe even toward Narada Onzen.

Traffic, including buses, really slows down beyond Ashiyasu, so you may have to hitch hike on the road from Ashiyasu to Hirogawara. It'll depend on the season, but there are no towns or farms in that area, so it will be tourist traffic only--if the author remembers correctly (?)

As for hiking, most people make a traverse along the ridge tops; in fact, you haven't much choice in the matter as almost all trails and shelters or huts are on ridges. These ridge-walks and climbs are fine for sightseeing and fotography, but sometimes bad for camping and finding water.

Here's what the author did. Between 9/28 & 9/30/1977, he hitch hiked from Kofu into Hirogawara, then walked the ridge-top trail from Hirogawara south to Narada. He stayed one night in one of the huts along the big north-south ridge, but can't remember which one. He later walked and hitch hiked out of the area on the 3rd day.

All or most of the huts along the way are in some ways similar to those in Europe. Inside the shelters, the middle section of each large dormitory or sleeping room is for walking and shoes, while the raised outer portions are for sleeping, eating and cooking.

Generally the huts are large enough for 50 to 100 people. You can usually buy snack foods, or order a hot, prepared meal. Most hikers take a small stove and cook for themselves. Each hut has facilities for catching and storing rainwater. Normally they'll give you all the water you want, but in dry periods you may have to pay for it.

The Minami Alps are part of the national park system, so things like camping are regulated in crowded areas. Normally, campsites exist near the huts, but the hut keepers usually charge a fee. If camping, place your tent well, as high winds are common on these ridge tops. Japan is a wet country so a good waterproof tent is required, as is some kind of rain gear for you and your pack.

During the summer season, say from mid-June through October, there are many people in the mountains hiking, taking fotos, etc., especially on weekends. October can be cold on the high peaks, but it's a colorful season, with generally fewer people around because children are in school.

At the summit of Kitadake looking north along the summit ridge.

Map 264-1, Kitadake, Minami Alps, Honshu, Japan

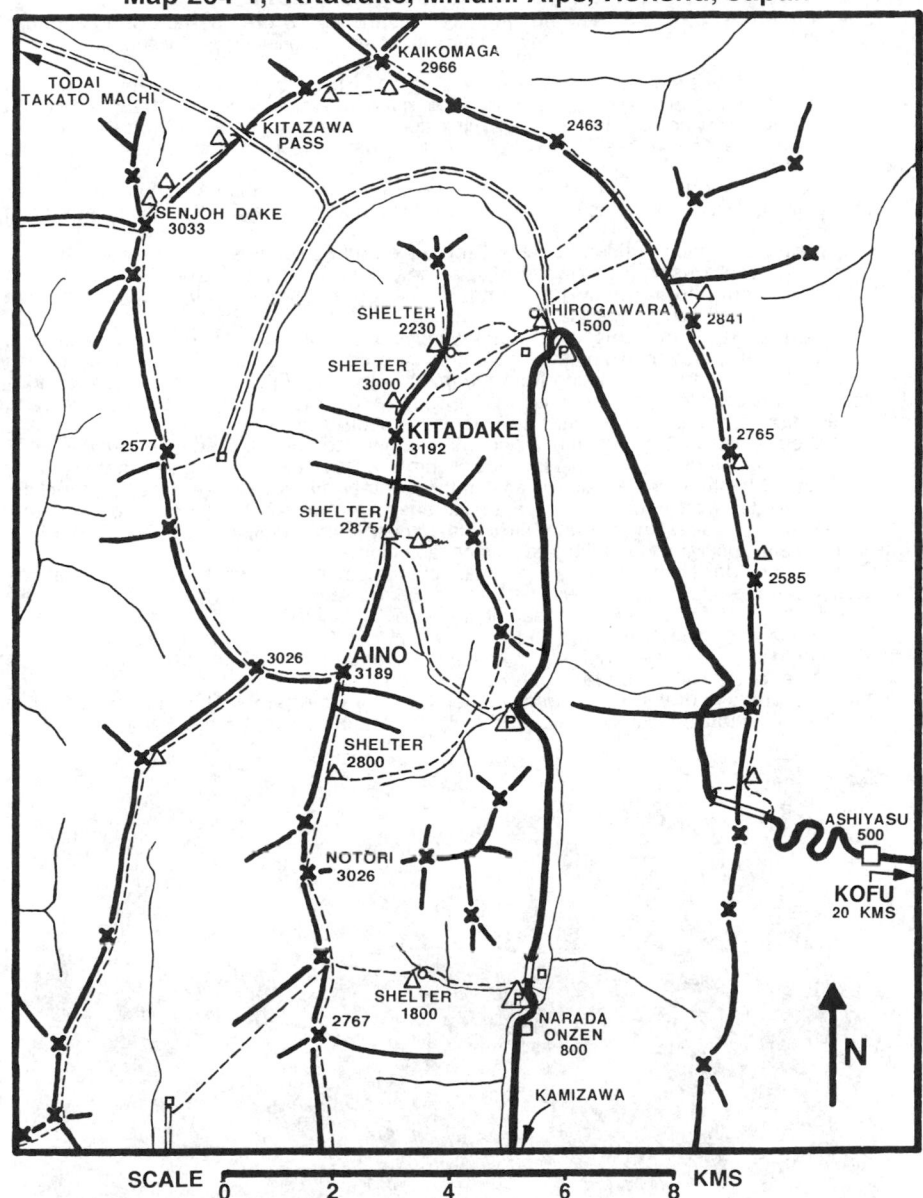

KAIKOMAGA
2966

TODAI
TAKATO MACHI

KITAZAWA
PASS

2463

SENJOH DAKE
3033

SHELTER
2230

HIROGAWARA
1500

2841

SHELTER
3000

2577

KITADAKE
3192

2765

SHELTER
2875

3026

AINO
3189

2585

SHELTER
2800

ASHIYASU
500

NOTORI
3026

KOFU
20 KMS

SHELTER
1800

NARADA
ONZEN
800

2767

KAMIZAWA

N

SCALE 0   2   4   6   8   KMS

Maps Japanese map *Minami Alps*, 1:100,000, printed in Japanese characters (kanji); and **Japan Road Atlas** in Romanji from Shobunsha; and the latest travel guidebook to Japan.

Fujisan, Honshu Island, Japan

One of the most famous mountains in the world and by far the best-known in Japan is Fujisan at 3776 meters. It's located in the south central part of the island of Honshu, not far west of Tokyo.

Fuji is a semi-active stratovolcano which last erupted in 1707, but that was a southeast flank eruption (Hoei Craters). The last certain eruption from the summit area was on 1/25/1033, when the summit crater blew up with a small VEI-2 explosion. At the same time, there was a lava flow from a SSE flank vent (Nishi Asakizuka). Fuji has an almost perfect conal shape and is likely the most-fotographed mountain in the world.

Each year the mountain is climbed by thousands of tourists, climbers, and most of all, Buddhist pilgrims. Few mountains in the world can claim more people reaching the summit each year.

Most people approach **Fujisan** from the Tokyo side and Fujijoshida, via the Chuo (Central) Expressway. If you're using the railways, start at the Tokyo Station and take any train west on the Chuo Line bound for Kofu or Matsumoto, but get off at Otsuki and transfer to a private railway line until you reach Fujijoshida.

From Fujijoshida, the most-used route up the mountain is the *Fuji-Subaru Line*, beginning at the Fuji Visitor Center, as shown on the map. From the visitor center, or train station, buses can be found; or you can try hitch hiking from the main entry gate (it's especially good for non-Japanese). This excellent road leads up to Step 5 at 2270 meters. Step 5 consists of several hotels, restaurants, shops and Buddhist temples and/or shrines (jinjas).

From Step 5, first walk along an old road that contours southeast, then up a well-used trail which zig zags up the mountain. This trail has pilgrim shelters every few hundred meters, many of which have refreshments for sale--at least in the summer hiking season. Most people climb **Fujisan** in one day from Step 5. On top are at least 3 temples and a weather observatory situated at various places on the crater rim. The author climbed Fujisan on 10/14/1977, which was late in the season and found the place almost abandoned.

For those who don't like crowds, you might try other trails from the south, the southeast, and the east. See map. But to get to these trailheads, you may need your own vehicle (?). There's also a trail circling the mountain, at or near the treeline.

Camping is not officially allowed on the mountain, but if you can find a quiet place in the forest, it would not be noticed (leave a clean campsite and no one should ever object). Since this is a volcano, there is no surface water on the mountain. You must take all the water you want to the mountain; or you'll have to buy other drinks or water at very high prices at Step 5. An early morning start is recommended, as the afternoon clouds ruin the view. Normal climbing

Fujisan is perhaps the most visible landmark in Japan and is one of the most-climbed mountains in the world (tourist office foto).

Map 265-1, Fujisan, Honshu Island, Japan

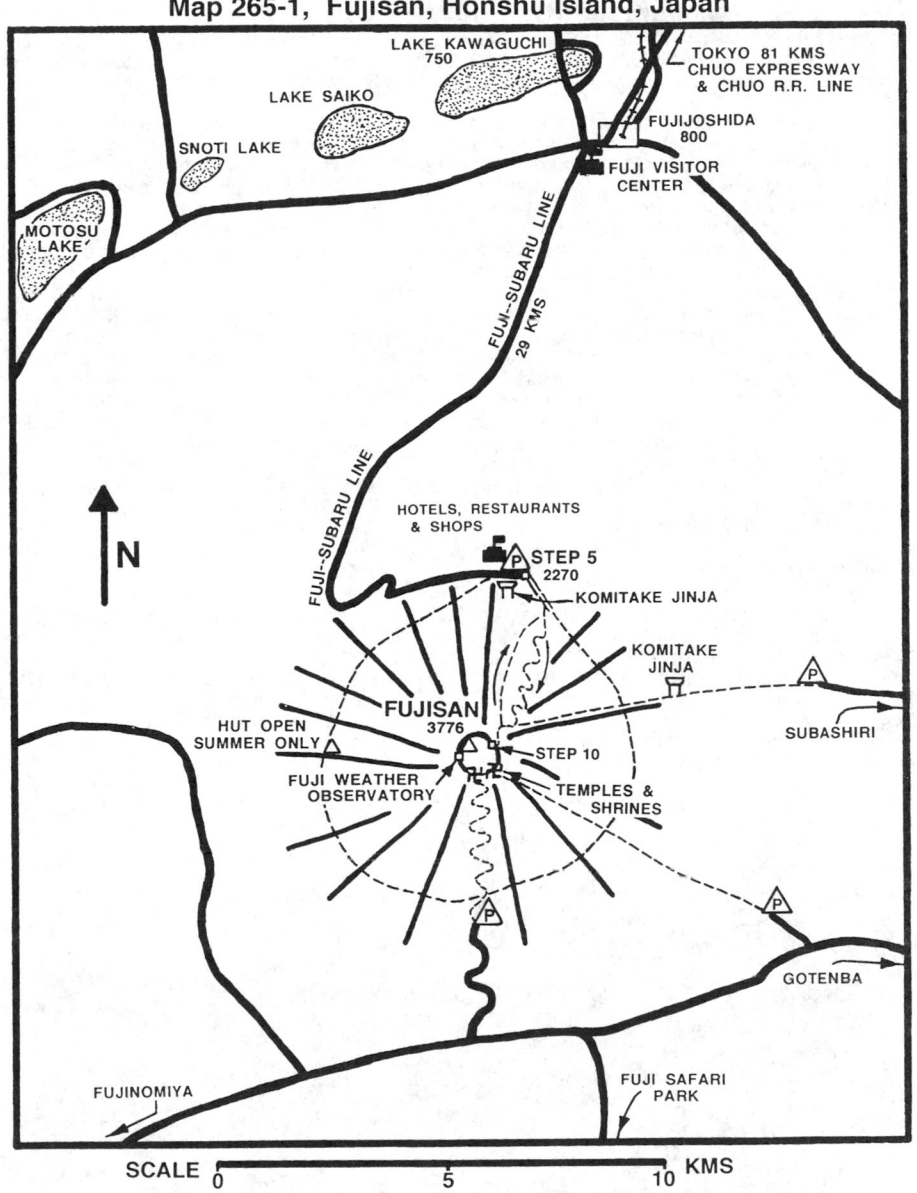

SCALE 0 — 5 — 10 KMS

season is from June to September. If you're there at that time, expect lots of company.
Maps There are a number of good maps available in Tokyo bookstores, including one at 1:60,000 scale, but it's in kanji or Japanese characters; even the **Japan Road Atlas** in Romanji from Shobunsha is good enough to get you there; and the latest travel guidebook to Japan.

Miharasan, Oshima (O Island), Japan

Shown here is the island called Oshima (O Island), located southwest of Tokyo and southeast of the Izu Peninsula. Oshima is small, roughly 10x20 kms, but it has a rather active volcano which is the island's highest mountain. It's called Miharasan, or Mt. Mihara, and it's highest point is about 758 meters.

Mihara's last really big eruption began on 11/15/1986 and lasted about one month. Spectacular lava fountaining shot up as high as 1 1/2 kms, some of the highest ever recorded. The fountaining came from radial fissures within the one-km-wide central crater. Large amounts of lava were extruded as shown on the map. Approximately 12,000 people were evacuated.

There was another 2-month period of activity beginning in 11/1987, and another eruption on 10/4/1990. Both of these were phreatic or steam generated explosions. Since then, almost continuous earthquakes have been recorded all around the area. For volcano updates, check these websites (www.volcano.si.edu/gvp/) or (www.kishou.go.jp/).

When the author climbed the volcano, he found a paved trail to an observatory tower on the south side of the main central crater. Along that trail are a couple of cement bomb (lava bomb) shelters. Within this crater is another smaller crater perhaps 200-300 meters in diameter. This was the scene of the 1987 & 1990 phreatic explosions. The highest summit is on the rim of the smaller crater. All this sits inside a still older and larger caldera measuring roughly 3x4 kms.

Getting to Oshima and **Miharasan** is fairly simple. There are nightly ferry boats running from Tokyo (Takeshiba Port) to Oshima and to either Okata or Motomachi Ports--depending on which way the wind and high waves are coming from. Other ferries begin at Yokohama, Yokosuka, Atami and finally Ito, the most-used mainland port.

From Ito, there are about 3 ferries daily. Some of these ferries make stops at other islands to the south, all of which are volcanic. Between Japan Rail Passes, the author took a 10 hour night ferry from Tokyo to Niijima, south of Oshima, for US$40. After a night on Niijima, he took another ferry to Oshima for about US$8. Two days later he took a 1 1/3 hour ferry boat ride to Ito which cost about US$18.

The author landed at Okata Port and took a bus to Motomachi (¥350-US$2.65), but the driver hand-delivered him to the Tsubakien Campjo & Youth Hostel. He paid ¥500, about US$3.80, for a campsite and cold shower. The next day, 5/18/1998, he walked in the rain up the road a ways, then along the original trail up to Sanchoguchi. From there he spent an hour or so wandering around inside the crater, then returned to the campjo. Round-trip was about 3 2/3 hours. That afternoon, he took a boat to Ito, slept at the train station, and the next morning began his second JR Pass.

There's one supermarket in the middle of Motomachi and a number of small shops. There are buses running between Okata and Motomachi about every hour. They all begin or end right

The beginning of the now-paved trail to Miharasan. Seen are recent lava
flows and to the right the top of the newest crater at 765 meters.

Map 266-1, Miharasan, Oshima (O Island), Japan

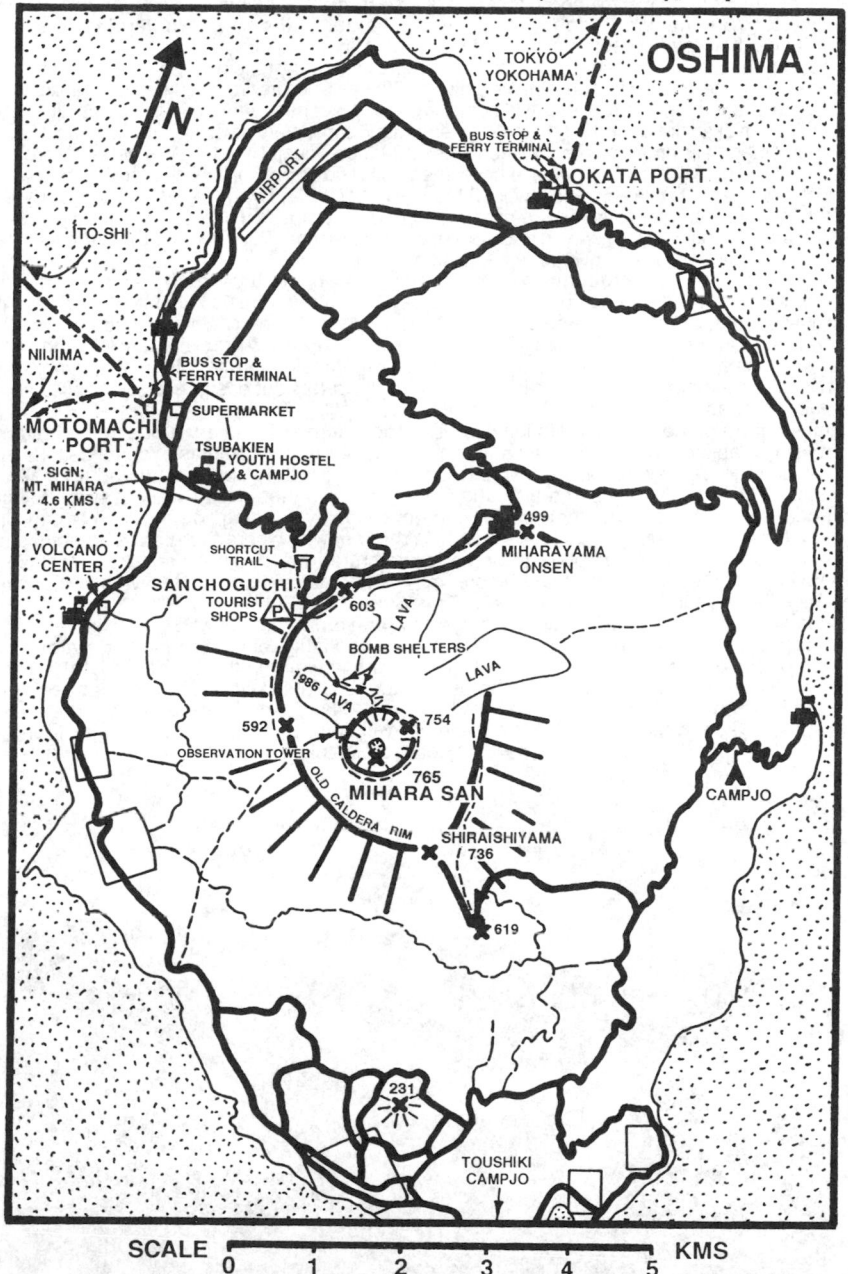

OSHIMA

TOKYO
YOKOHAMA

N

AIRPORT

ITO-SHI

BUS STOP &
FERRY TERMINAL

OKATA PORT

NIIJIMA

BUS STOP &
FERRY TERMINAL

SUPERMARKET

MOTOMACHI
PORT

TSUBAKIEN
YOUTH HOSTEL
& CAMPJO

SIGN:
MT. MIHARA
4.6 KMS.

499

MIHARAYAMA
ONSEN

VOLCANO
CENTER

SHORTCUT
TRAIL

SANCHOGUCHI
TOURIST
SHOPS

603

LAVA

LAVA

BOMB SHELTERS

1986 LAVA

592

754

OBSERVATION TOWER

765

MIHARA SAN

OLD CALDERA RIM

CAMPJO

SHIRAISHIYAMA
736

619

231

TOUSHIKI
CAMPJO

SCALE
0   1   2   3   4   5   KMS

at the ports. There are lots of tour buses, but hitching is reasonably good too because distances are short. The driest summer month is July.
Maps Japanese map *Oshima, NI-54-26-12*, 1:50,000; the **Japan Road Atlas** in Romanji from Shobunsha; and the latest travel guidebook to Japan.

Aso San, Kyushu Island, Japan

One of the more active volcanos in Japan is Aso San. The highest summit on this massif is Takedake at 1594 meters. Aso is located in the center of the southern Japanese island of Kyushu about halfway between the cities of Kumamoto and Oito.

Aso San, namely the Nakadake Crater, has produced more historic explosive eruptions than any other volcano in the world. Nakadake has erupted 165 times since its first documented eruption in 553 AD. Aso is in the middle of a 24-km-wide caldera, with 15 cones forming an east-west line on the caldera floor. Nakadake Crater is 1.1 kms long and has 7 small craters within. Strombolian, phreatic, and phreatomagmatic eruptions are common in the 100-meter-deep Crater 1. It is presently filled by a crater lake (1998). Since 1980, 71 people have been hospitalized due to inhalation of volcanic gases, 7 of whom have died. The latest deaths were 2 tourists in 11/1997. The Japan Meteorological Agency monitors gas concentrations along the rim, and periodically closes it to tourists. Needless to say, keep the wind at your back, when you're on or near this crater rim! For volcano updates, check these websites (www.volcano.si.edu/gvp/) or (www.kishou.go.jp/).

To get there, go to the Kumamoto train station, and locate the Japan Rail (JR) Hohi Line which operates between Kumamoto and Beppu. It's a red train and usually full of tourists. After about 1 3/4 hours, get off at the Aso Eki (Aso Station). At that station is a very good tourist office with maps and information in Romanji & English. They can line you up with a hotel or the youth hostel, which is about 1.3 kms up the road toward the mountain. Further along is a campjo. You might camp on the mountain too, but keep your tent discretely out of sight, a good policy on any mountain in Japan.

Right in front of the Aso train station is a bus stop where you can get a bus to the bottom of the ropeway (cable car or lift) and Nakadake Crater. Or for a more meritas experience hike up.

To reach the peaks on foot, walk across the street from the youth hostel and up a cement road & path. Follow the signs to the Bochu Campjo. From there, road-walk past the toll gate about one km, then get on another narrow cement roadway heading south, which is now used only by hikers. This takes you up to Nishiguchi & the ropeway where there are souvenirs shops and restaurants. From there, follow the road to the crater rim. From **Nakadake Crater**, use a good trail heading east, then north to the summit of **Nakadake** with nearby lava bomb shelters. A few minutes beyond that and to the east is **Takedake**.

Because of bad weather, the author stayed in the youth hostel for ¥2450 or about US$18, then headed up the route described on 5/14/1998. At Nishiguchi, he found the crater closed because of poisonous gases, so he retreated a ways and went up the shortcut route shown on the map. He ended up on the north side of Nakadake Crater with a wind to his back. From there, he headed south to the trail, then walked up to Takedake. He returned via the top of a second ropeway at Kako Higashi. From there he walked back to the youth hostel. Round-trip was just under 7 hours, but an hour was lost because of backtracking.

One of several *lava bomb shelters* along the trail above Kako Higashi.

Map 267-1, Aso San, Kyushu Island, Japan

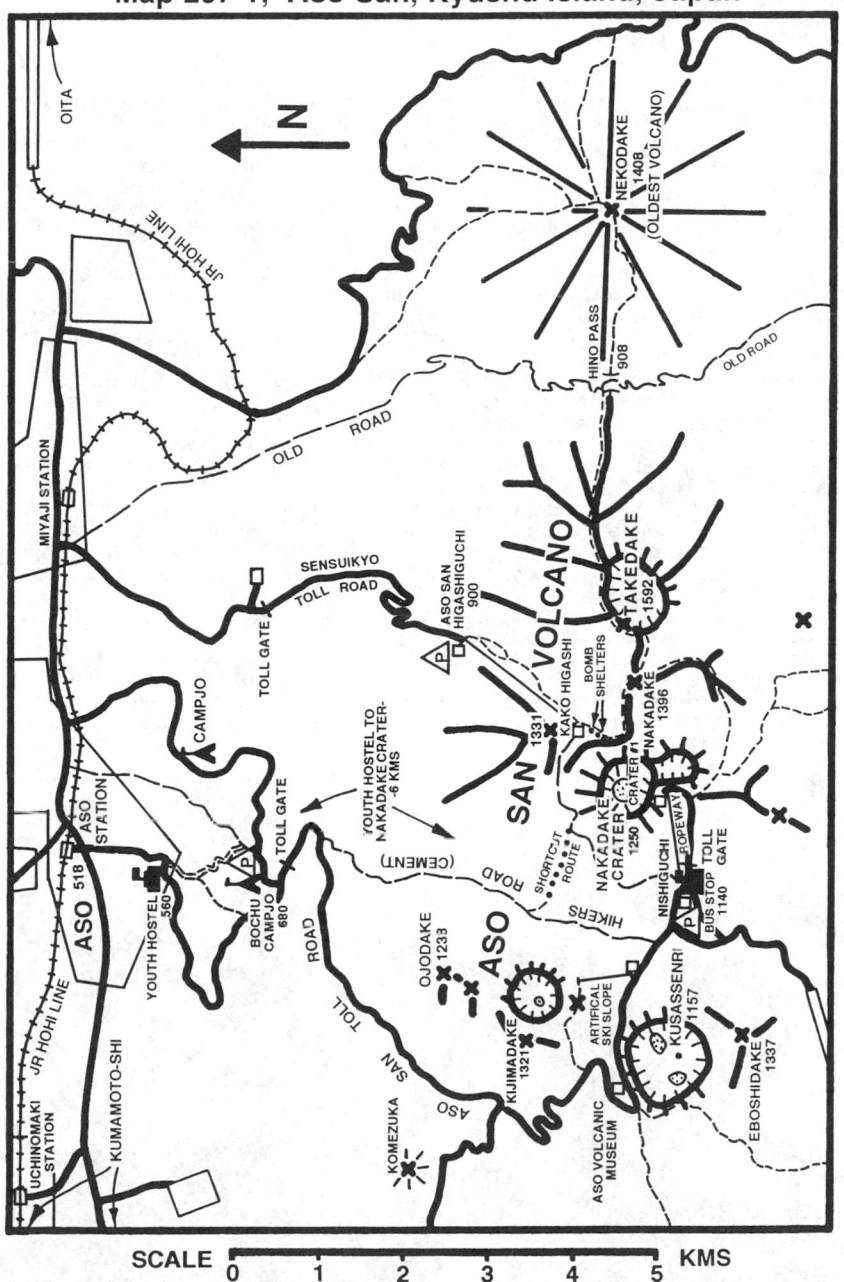

SCALE | 0 1 2 3 4 5 KMS

There are many shops between the train station and the youth hostel. Summers are really wet here, but April, May and October are supposed to be drier.
Maps Japanese map *Aso San, NI-52-5-15*, 1:50,000; the **Japan Road Atlas** in Romanji from Shobunsha; and the latest travel guidebook to Japan.

Karakunidake, Kirishima National Park, Kyushu, Japan

This map shows most of Kirishima National Park located in the southern part of Japan's Kyushu Island, and not far northeast of Kagoshima. The highest peak is Karakunidake at 1700 meters. Next is Takachihodake at 1574 meters. As you can see on the map, there are 5 major summits all lined up from northwest to southeast.

All the peaks in this national park are volcanos. There are 20 eruptive centers spread out on a 20x30-km plateau, and there have been 66 recorded eruptions since 742 AD. The last big eruption in the park was on 2/13/1959. At that time, Shinmoedake had a phreatic or steam explosion where tephra was ejected. Most of that was from a flank fissure on the west side of the crater. A smaller eruption occurred there in 1/1992. According to the book, **Volcanos of the World**, most recorded eruptions in this area took place at Ohachi, which is near the bottom of this map. Karakunidake's last eruption was from a flank vent in 1768, while Takachihodake last exploded about 3050 BC.

Getting to Kirishima is fairly easy using trains and buses. First take a train to either Kobayashi on the northeast, Ebino on the north, Kirishima Nishiguchi on the west, or to Kirishima-cho south of the park. According to the **Japan** travel guide from Lonely Planet, there are more buses from Kirishima-cho to the mountains than from the other stations, but this varies with the season.

The author arrived at Kirishima-cho on 5/11/1998, a little early for most tourists. He found 4 buses a day running from Kobayashi and Kirishima-cho to the main tourist village called Ebino Kogen (Ebino Plateau). However, the bus he got on only went to the hotel at Hayashida Onzen. He finally hitched a ride from there to Ebino in the rain and fog. He dropped a tent in what he thought was a campjo, but it was a picnic site. No problem; no one else was there and the place was fogged in and raining during his entire trip!

The next day, he sat in his tent trying to stay dry until 11am, then got out and climbed **Karakunidake**. Just before arriving at the summit, he was caught in heavy rain with wind & lightning, so he turned back, perhaps 200 meters from the top. Going down, the trail turned into a small river! Round-trip was just over an hour from the road. In good weather, you can walk from Ebino southeast all the way to Takachiho Gawara in about 5 hours, according to the tourist literature. Add another 2-3 hours for a climb up Takachihodake & back. If you do this hike, you'll have to hitch hike back to Ebino, or drive your own rented car.

At Ebino in 1998, were a couple of small stores & souvenir shops, places to eat meals, and a hotel. Between these 2 buildings was a large parking area & bus stop. Nearby was a large open meadow with toilets & picnic sites. About 300 meters from the picnic site was a campjo. As with most other mountain areas in Japan, it's best to visit Kirishima in summer which will

A tourist office foto and aerial view of all the major peaks of the Kirishima National Park looking in a southeast direction. Karakunidake is in the middle.

Map 268-1, Karakunidake, Kirishima NP, Kyushu, Japan

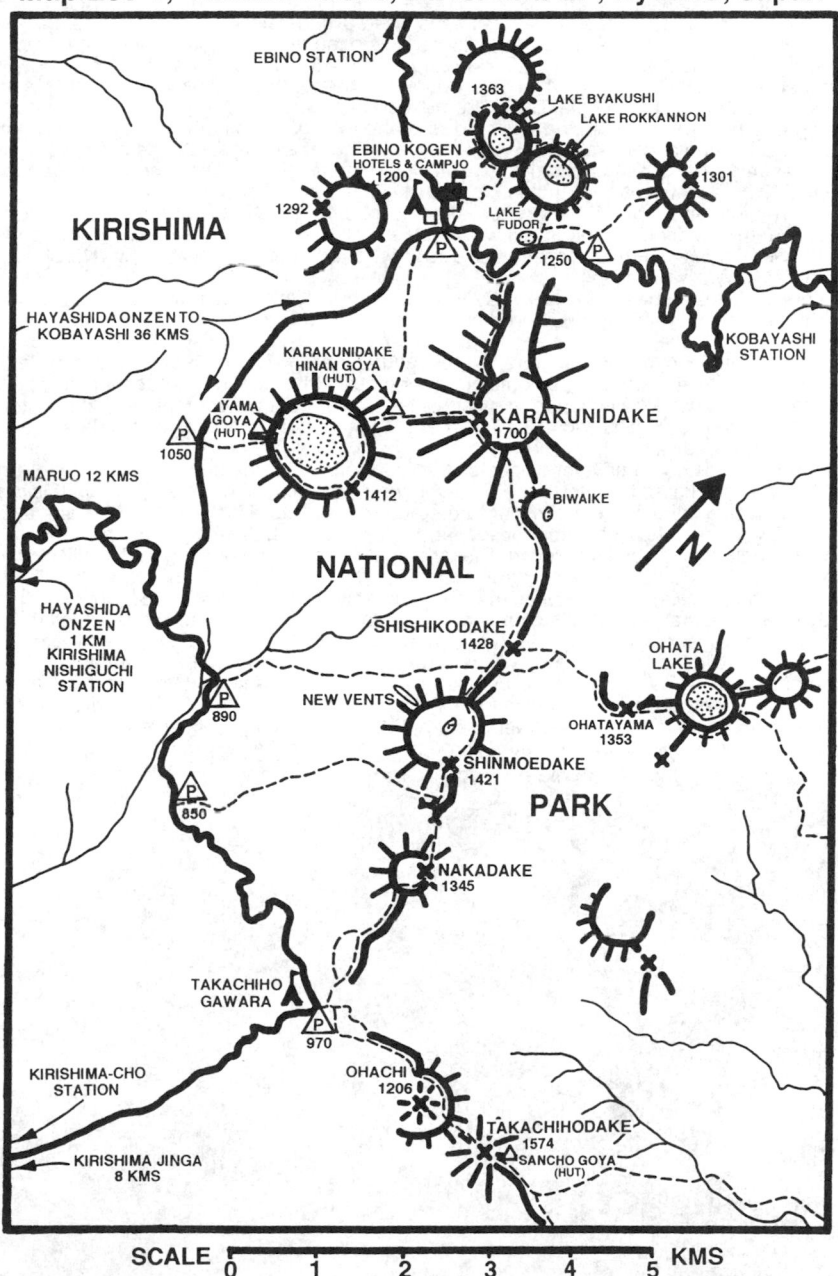

have more public transportation, or traffic for hitching. And hopefully better weather!
Maps There are topo maps at 1:50,000 scale available, but the author used a free tourist handout he got from the *tourist office in Kagoshima;* the **Japan Road Atlas** in Romanji from Shobunsha; and the latest travel guidebook to Japan.

Sakurajima Volcano, Kyushu Island, Japan

The liveliest volcano in Japan is Sakurajima at 1117 meters. This doesn't seem very high, but it soars directly from sea level. Sakurajima is located in the extreme southern end of Kyushu Island, immediately east of the city of Kagoshima, and in the middle of Kagoshima Bay.

The first recorded eruption of Sakurajima was in 708 AD. That was the South Peak or Minamidake. In 1779, there was a large eruption on the northeast flank of the North Peak, or Kitadake. In that one, 140 people died. The next eruption was in 1914, perhaps the biggest of all. It spread lava on the east and west sides of the island, and finally formed a land bridge between the volcano and the mainland. Ever since, it's been a peninsula. The next big eruptive period was in 1946 from Minamidake, and lasted almost a year. The last period of activity started in 1955, and it continues to this day (2001). Notice the map, the lava flows from the 4 biggest eruptions in recorded history are shown. Minamidake is the live one, and because eruptions are explosive, the mountain was officially closed to sightseeing & hiking upon the author's visit on 5/10/1998. For volcano updates, check these websites (www.volcano.si.edu/gvp/) or (www.kishou.go.jp/).

To get to **Sakurajima**, make your way to Kagoshima. On the east side of the main Nishi Kagoshima Station is an information office. At that station are lots of luggage lockers of all sizes. From there, take the tram or any local JR train northeast to the Kagoshima Station. From there, walk south less than 500 meters to the Sakurajima Ferry. In 1998, this 15 minute ferry ride cost ¥150. There were about 3 boats per hour crossing the channel throughout the day.

At Sakurajima, walk half a km to the visitor center just southwest of the ferry docks to see pictures of previous eruptions and get tourist maps & information. For budget travelers, there's a youth hostel not far away.

In the past, you could drive or walk along a road to or near the summit of Kitadake, but in 1998, that was blocked-off somewhere (?). If you were on foot, you could still hike up this road-- if you could locate it; but there are lots of farms and roads around the bottom of the volcano on that side. There are lots of cars, tour buses, and a few regular buses, along the paved highway circling the mountain, so getting around is fairly easy. Even if the mountain is officially closed to hiking, you can still climb it--but at your own risk! The author saw no guards posted anywhere.

Here's what the author did. He left his big pack in the Nishi Kagoshima Station, then made his way to Sakurajima. After getting maps at the visitor center, he walked in the rain all the way to the Yunohiro Observation Lookout. Between showers he had one good look at the mountain and saw a dirt track and a route up the western slopes of Minamidake. Because of rainy weather, he made no attempt to climb, but that route looks good with no bushwhacking. Best to approach from the west side, because if there are explosions or Strombolian activity, the lava bombs appears to be falling on the lower eastern side. If you climb it, observe where the bombs are falling as you approach the top. June through September are very rainy; spring and fall are

Looking east at Sakurajima and the very active Minamidake on the right (tourist office foto).

Map 269-1, Sakurajima Volcano, Kyushu Island, Japan

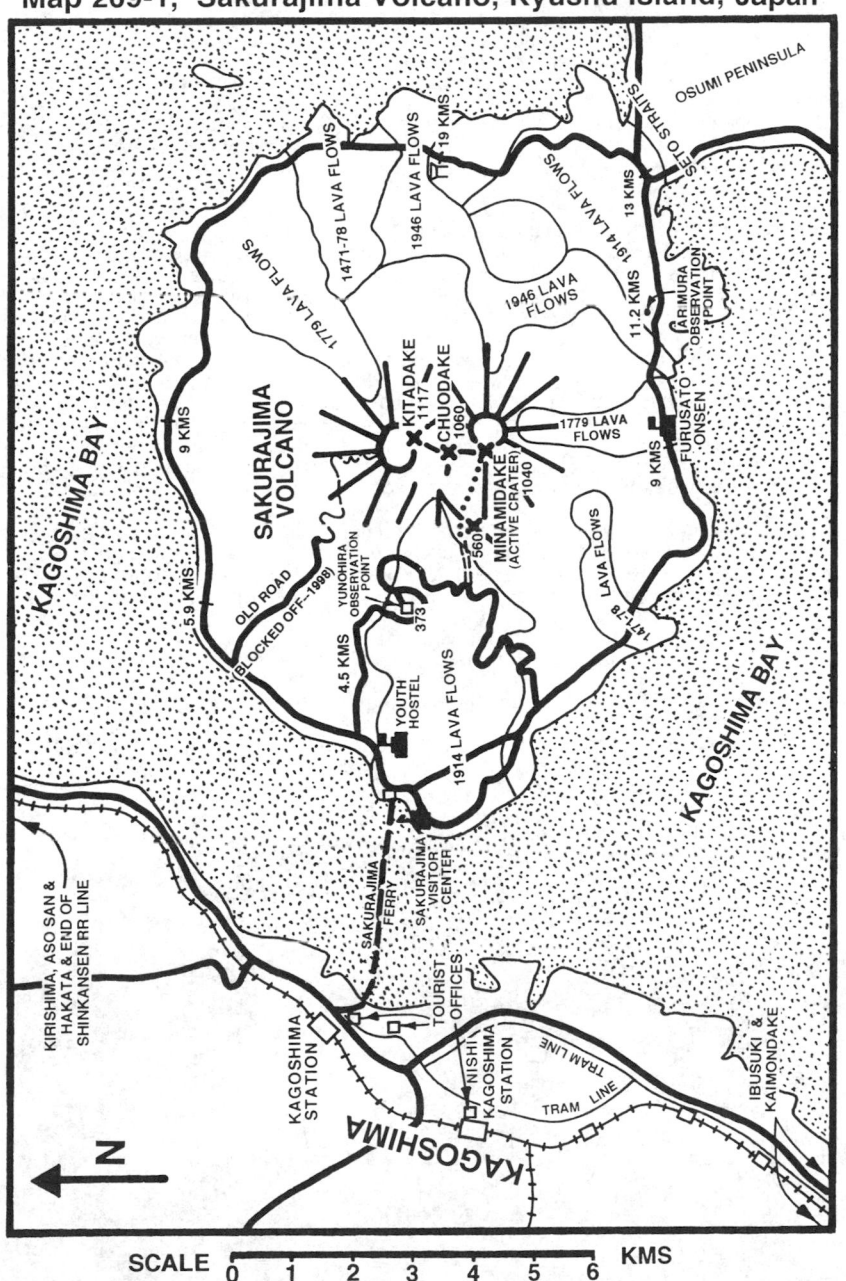

SCALE 0 1 2 3 4 5 6 KMS

drier.
Maps Simple tourist handouts & maps from any of the tourist or information offices shown on the map; and the **Japan Road Atlas** in Romanji from Shobunsha; and the latest travel guidebook to Japan.

Kaimondake, Kyushu Island, Japan

The most southerly Japanese mountain in this book is Kaimondake or Kaimon Peak, or Volcano. Kaimon is not very high, only rising to 922 meters, but it rises directly from the sea, so you've got to climb nearly all that altitude to reach the top.

The last known and/or recorded eruption of Kaimondake was on 8/29/885 AD. That eruptive period lasted for one month. During that time, there was a large VEI-4 explosion with some lava flows, according to the book, **Volcanos of the World**. The author wonders about this explosion, because there doesn't seem to be a crater of any size on top, which would indicate a big explosion (?). There were 4 other recorded eruptive periods between 860 and 885 AD. Presently, Kaimondake seems dead.

Just north off this map is the Ikeda Caldera, filled with Ikedako (Ikeda Lake). This is a 5-km-wide lake-filled caldera which had it's last big eruption in about 2690 BC. It was a very large VEI-5 explosion, and it would seem that was the eruption which created the caldera we see today.

Getting to Kaimondake is quite easy. For those with a JR Pass, take a train to Kagoshima-- see Area Map. From there, get on one of only 3 or 4 commuter trains per/day running south, then west & northwest to Makurazaki-shi. Not too many trains on that line. Get off at Kaimon Eki (Kaimon Station). An alternate to taking a train all the way to Kaimon, would be to take one of many trains to either Ibusuki or Yamagawa, then take a Japan Railway bus to Kaimon. Get off at the bus stop shown. If you're a JR Pass holder, this JR bus ride is free.

From Kaimon railway station, walk east, then south directly toward the mountain. About 2 kms from the station, turn right or west at the sign of a campjo. That place has a large area for pitching a tent at ¥900, or about US$7 a night, which includes a hot shower. They also have rooms and cabins for rent, and a small store in the main office. But be sure to buy all your food in Kagoshima, because the author can't recall seeing any stores along the walking route to the campjo.

To climb **Kaimondake**, first walk east from the campjo, then turn uphill, or south, on a paved road. You'll pass (in 1998) a rollerblade ski slope on your left, then you enter the forest at the trailhead. Once on the trail, you can't get lost. The trail is very well-used, but there's some boulder-hopping on the higher slopes. Near the summit is a steep section with fixed ropes to help hikers get up. At the top is a small shrine or jinja. It took the author only 1 1/4 hours up, while round-trip from the campjo was 2 1/2 hours. This was on 5/11/1998.

The author used a tourist map of the mountain (not a topo map) and the summit was in clouds upon his arrival, so he isn't sure if there's a crater on top or not. Doesn't seem to be (?). Summer is a wet time in southern Kyushu, so spring or fall--April, May and October--may be better months for climbing.

Maps Obtain tourist maps from the tourist office in front of the Kagoshima or Nishi Kagoshima

Looking south at the author's tent at the campjo with Kaimondake Volcano behind.

Map 270-1, Kaimondake, Kyushu Island, Japan

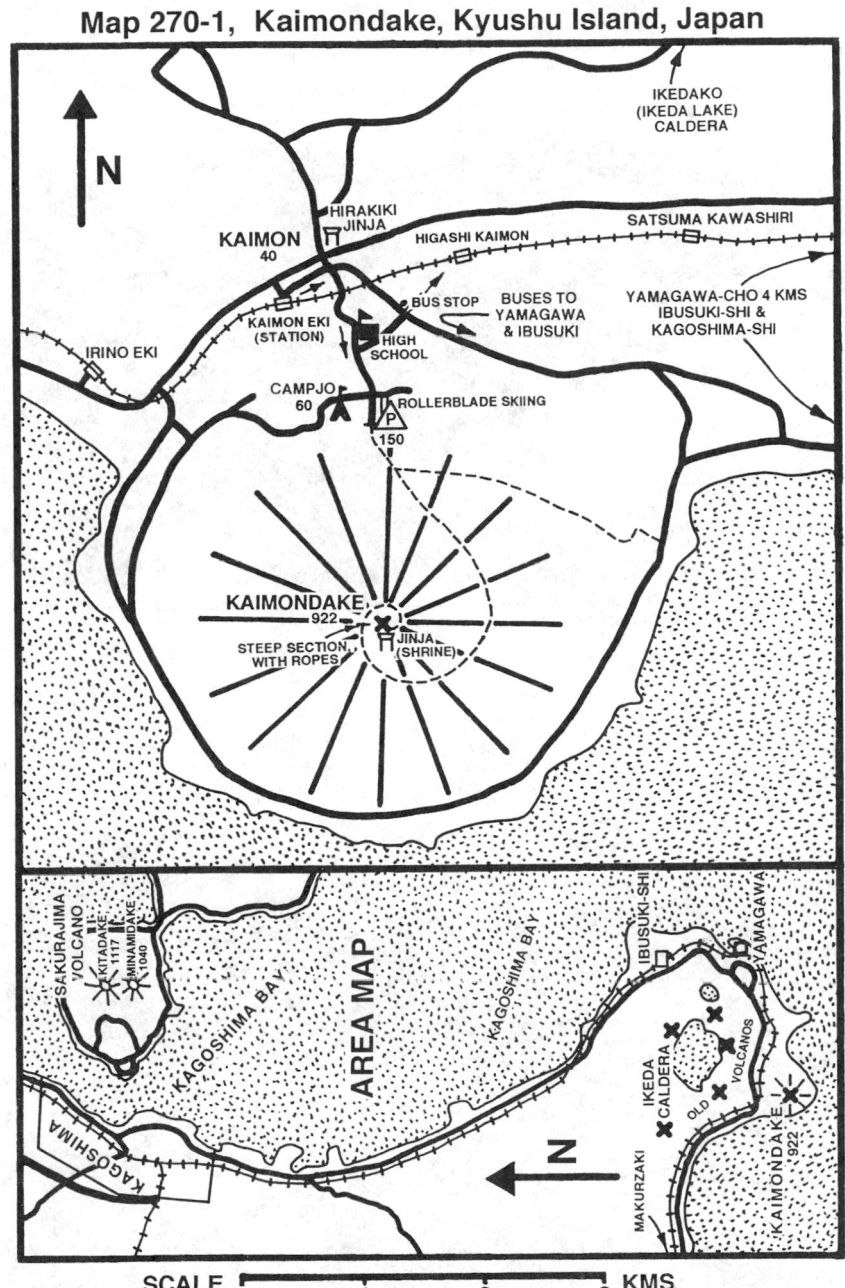

SCALE 0   1   UPPER MAP   2   3 KMS

Stations; topo maps at 1:50,000 scale are also available, but the author arrived in Tokyo on a weekend and couldn't buy any for this part of his trip; also the **Japan Road Atlas** in Romanji from Shobunsha; and the latest travel guidebook to Japan.

This is one of several lava bomb shelters on the trail leading to the summit crater of Miharasan (Map 266, page 577).

From the summit of Lows Peak on Mt. Kinabalu, looking west down on Alexander Peak to the left, with Andrews Peak to the right (Map 280, page 607).

A typical jeepney, the public transport vehicle of choice in the Philippines, seen here carrying native Philippinos called *Negritos*, up the O'Donnell River toward the northern slopes of Pinatubo Volcano (Map 272, page 591).

From the summit of Canlaon Volcano, looking northeast down on the North Crater and nearby peak (Map 277, page 601).

Mt. Pulog, Cordillera Central, Luzon Island, Philippines

For people accustomed to a temperate climate, one of the most interesting and desirable places in the Philippines is the highlands of northern Luzon Island. Interesting places to see are the rice terraces of Banawe, the summer capital of Baguio, the Kabayan Valley, and Mt. Pulog at 2930 meters, the second highest peak in The Philippines.

The place of interest on this map is the Kabayan Valley. Not only will you find 2 of the highest mountains in the Philippines, but some interesting cultures and mummy caves.

To reach this area, first take one of many buses each day running from Manila to Baguio. There you'll find lots of hotels and a cool climate. In Baguio, the tourist office or anyone at your hotel, can tell you where to find the bus heading for Mt. Pulog and Kabayan. Before leaving Baguio, ask if there's a hotel in Kabayan (?).

From Baguio, take the only daily Dangwa Tranco bus running to Kabayan, a distance of 85 kms. This is a morning bus and takes about 6 1/2 hours. Apparently there are still no buses heading north from Kabayan toward Abatan & Bantoc.

If your plan is to climb **Mt. Pulog** first, get off the bus at the Ellet Bridge in Kinayang village. From that point, there's a good trail heading eastward all the way to the top. At first the trail passes rice terraces and farms, then at Ellet, turns right or southeast and goes up a pine-tree-covered ridge (without water) to the village of Ambukot. From that point there's an old road coming from the other side of the mountain, which ends at a pass between 2 hills where the latter part of the trail actually begins. This trail leads to villages on the eastern side of the mountain and to the summit of Pulog.

Above about 2500 meters, the area is almost continually in cloud cover, therefore the trees are draped with moss. Above about 2700 meters, the moss forest is left behind, and open & windy grasslands continue on to Pulog. High on the mountain veer left to the summit. The dry season is from October to May; and water is found only at Ellet Bridge, Ellet, Ambukot, and at a spring at 2625 meters. The author started late in the afternoon of 7/15/1977, camped near Ambukot, then took his huge pack to the summit; then camped again near Ambukot. Next morning, 7/17/1977, he walked back to the road. Pulog can be climbed in one long day from Ellet Bridge--with just a day-pack!

On the mountain sides around Kabayan and in natural caves, are many wooden boxes containing mummified remains of the valley's former inhabitants. Stop at the municipal hall in Kabayan to see a small museum, and get information as to the locations of nearby caves. Someone can show you around to the caves that are still open. For this you'll have to pay a guide, as things have changed since the author's visit in 7/1977. Kabayan is the best place to buy food in the valley, but each village usually has a small store.

To leave the area, you'll have to return to Baguio by afternoon bus; or hike from Pacso or

These skulls are found in the basement of a church in the Kabayan Village.

Map 271-1, Mt. Pulog, Cordillera Central, Luzon, Philippines

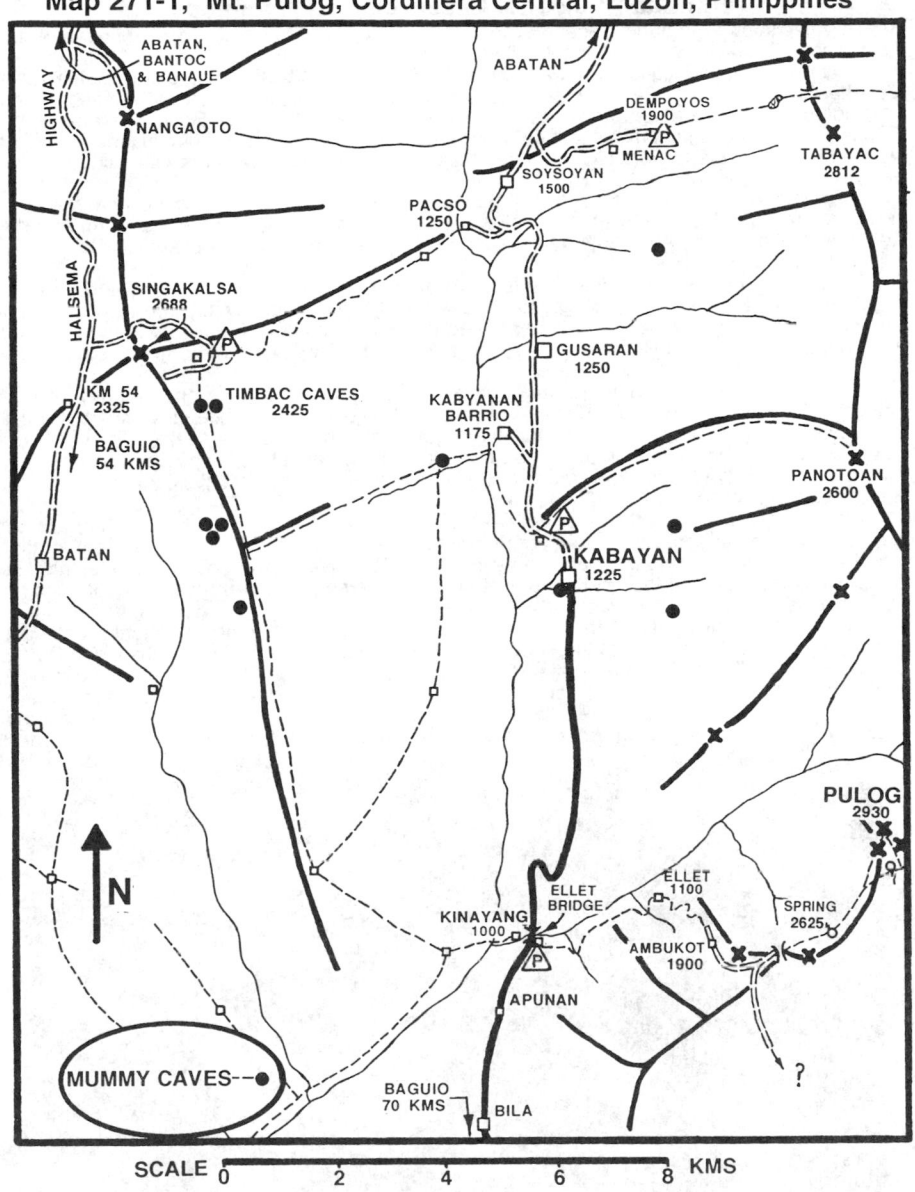

Kabyanan Barrio up to the Halsema Highway, where you can catch a bus going north or south.
Maps DMA map *NE-51-13*, or *Dagupan City, 2507*, both 1:250,000, from the Coast and Geodetic Survey, Manila; any *national highway map* which you can buy in Manila; TPC map *J-12C,* 1:500,000; and the latest travel guidebook to the Philippines.

Pinatubo Volcano, Luzon Island, Philippines

This map shows Pinatubo Volcano at 1383 meters. It's located on Luzon Island northwest of Manila and immediately west of Angeles and the former Clark Air Force Base.

Pinatubo is a stratovolcano which was dormant until 4/1991. On 6/15/1991, it blewup with a violent VEI-6 explosion creating a 2-km-wide crater and burying the surrounding area with ash. About 200,000 people were evacuated, and the US owned Clark Air Force Base was abandoned. Subsequent typhoons sent mud flows or lahars into all surrounding valleys burying many villages. About 700 people died. For volcano updates see the websites (www.phivolcs.dost.gov.ph/) or (www.volcano.si.edu/gvp/).

The author visited Pinatubo twice, in 4 & 5/1998. On both trips, he took a bus from Manila to Dau, the main bus terminal for the Angeles area. From there jeepneys run south to Angeles about every 2 minutes. Angeles may have the best bargains on hotels in the world--aircon, TV, private bath for about US$7.

On his first trip he took a jeepney from Angeles to the village of Sapangbato and was required to hire a guide to go part way up the Sacobia River. Unfortunately that was not one of the 2 main routes to the crater. He later talked to volcanologists in Manila (Quezon City) and was told a route up the O'Donnell River was probably the best way, although a route up the Pasig River is a second normal route.

On his second trip, the author bought his food in Angeles, then took one jeepney north to Capas and another one west to O'Donnell. For just a little extra money, jeepney drivers will take you as far as Santa Julian. At Santa Julian, he got more information at the home of the village head or captain, then walked up the flat outwash lahar floodplain along the O'Donnell River. He had to walk about 12-13 kms to where vehicles must stop--but with a little luck, you can probably get a lift in that section.

Interestingly, all along the river between the Negrito village & the hogback hill, and the beginning of the canyons, are many aboriginal negritos, obviously of African descent, cutting wood and other forest products. Jeepneys from Angeles drive up the O'Donnell to fetch these products almost daily. If they stop and give you a lift, be sure to offer money, about what the passenger jeepneys would charge.

From the last vehicle tracks, the author found a trail the guides use and eventually made it to a campsite at 780 meters. That took about 7 1/2 hours walking from Santa Julian. On Day 2, 5/3/1998, he walked to the crater lake in 40 minutes, then headed back. From his campsite down to the Negrito village took about 4 hours, then he got a lift to O'Donnell and another jeepney back to Angeles. His total 2-day walk-time was about 13 hours, but if you were to hire a jeepney in Angeles or O'Donnell to take you up to the end of the vehicle track, you could

A postcard view of Pinatubo Volcano. The highest peak is on the far side (southwest), while most hikers end up in the gap in the caldera wall to the lower right (Jens Peters foto).

Map 272-1, Pinatubo Volcano, Luzon Island, Philippines

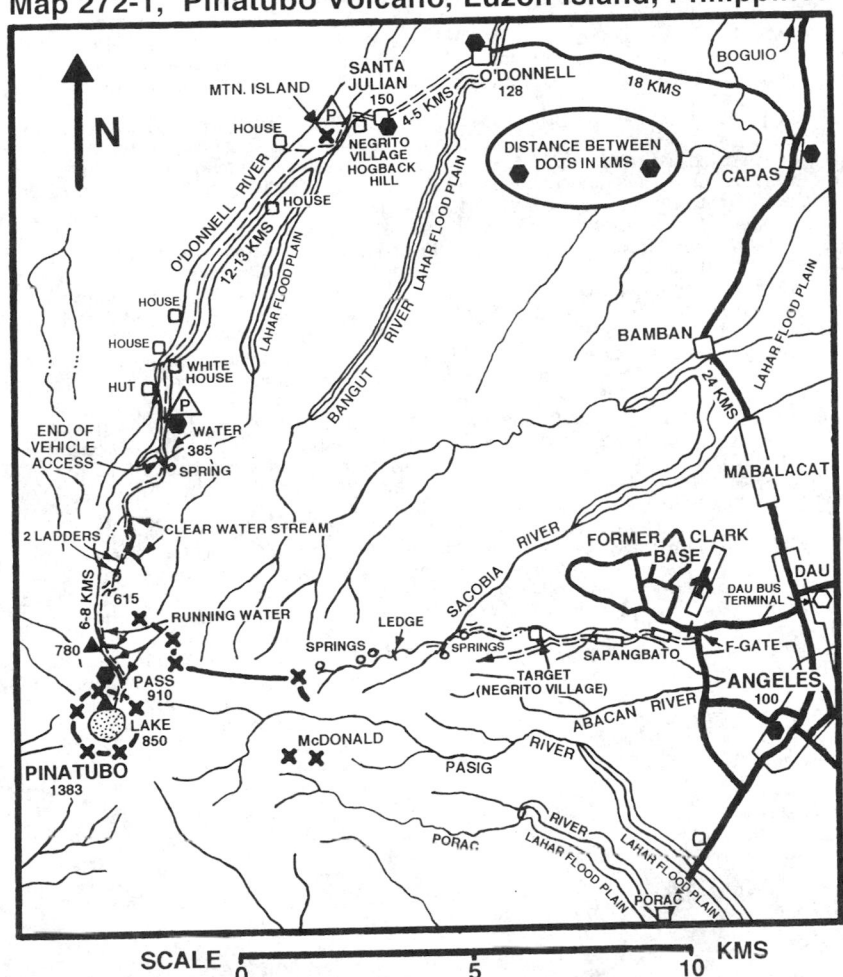

SCALE 0   5   10 KMS

probably day-hike up & back in about 6 to 7 hours--if you don't get lost! Strong hikers who hire a jeepney in Angeles, and with an early start and late return, can do this in one long day. The jeepney would have to wait for you on the mountain.

Here's more trail information for **Pinatubo**. From the end of the vehicle tracks, walk up the main canyon and around 2 big bends, then follow the *clear water stream* south, instead of turning to the right or west. At that point, you may find a hot springs on the right. After another km or so, *turn right away from the clear water stream* and into a small dry side-canyon. You'll climb 2 ladders, or steep sections, pass a spring or two, then drop down into the main canyon again. Follow footprints and/or a trail as shown on this map. In 1998, climbing any peak was risky because of loose deposits. Do this only in the dry season from about January through April.

Maps The 1989 *Mount Pinatubo*, 1:50,000, NAMRIA map is nearly useless--lots of errors, plus changes after the 1991 explosion. Best to see the DMA map *ND 51-1* (or its Philippine equivalent *Tarlac, 2509*, 1:250,000, from the Coast and Geodetic Survey, Manila; or the *Volcano Hazards Map* of Pinatubo from Philvolcs, Quezon City; TPC map *K-11B*, 1:500,000; and the latest travel guidebook to the Philippines.

Taal Volcano, Luzon Island, Philippines

This map features what is generally known as the Taal Volcano, located about 70 kms due south of Manila. This region consists of a huge, very old and eroded caldera which holds Taal Lake at 3 meters above sea level. In the middle of the lake is Volcano Island, which for the most part, is one volcano called Mt. Tabaro. It rises to about 311 meters. Inside its crater is Yellow Lake.

On the northwest corner of the island is Malaki Volcano, while to the southwest is the newest vent which was active between 1965 & 1977. Tabaro Volcano's last eruption was in 1911. That was a large phreatic explosion rated at VEI-4. That eruption, and resultant tsunami, caused fatalities--but things were quiet upon the author's visit on 4/9 & 4/10/1998. For volcano updates see the websites (www.phivolcs.dost.gov.ph/) or (www.volcano.si.edu/gvp/).

From Manila, the author took a bus from one of many bus company terminals, located near the Edsa Light Rail Station, to the small city of Tanauan. That bus, which was bound for Batangas, took about 1 1/2 hours and cost less than US$1. Tanauan is located on the main highway to Batangas and just east of Taal Lake. From the main market in Tanauan, he got in a jeepney going to Talisay (a 20 minute ride), the largest town on the lake and the place where most boats going to Volcano Island tie up.

At Talisay, the author hired a twin outrigger motor boat to Volcano Island which cost about US$13, round-trip. Going alone is always more expensive, but if you can form a small group, the cost per/person is much lower.

Once at San Isidro, the main village & landing site on the island, he left his big pack with the owner of the boat and took a fast day-hike up to and around the crater rim of **Tabaro Volcano**. That trip took nearly 4 hours round-trip on the hottest day of the year for Manila (37°+C)! He then had a bath in the lake and walked inland a ways and camped for the night. The next morning he returned to Talisay.

There are many buses and jeepneys running all day from Manila & Tanauan, to Talisay, where you'll find many hotels or pensions. Most people stay in Talisay, then make a day-trip to Volcano Island. There are no hotels on the island, so if you want to stay overnight, you'll have to camp, which can be done about anywhere. There are some gardens and many cattle & horses on the island, therefore many trails. You could also walk all the way around the island on the trails shown.

In 1998, there were many tourists from Taiwan doing this trip. From San Isidro, they were all riding horses or burros up the main trail to the crater rim. As you approach the island by boat, you can see the main trail going up the north face of Tabaro, so you don't need a guide. On top are many shelters where you can get out of the sun or rain. There are several small restaurants in San Isidro, and many children selling soda pop on the crater rim.

The dry season is from January through April or May, but this one you can do anytime. In

These boats are located at Talisay on Taal Lake. Volcano Island is seen in the distance.

Map 273-1, Taal Volcano, Luzon Island, Philippines

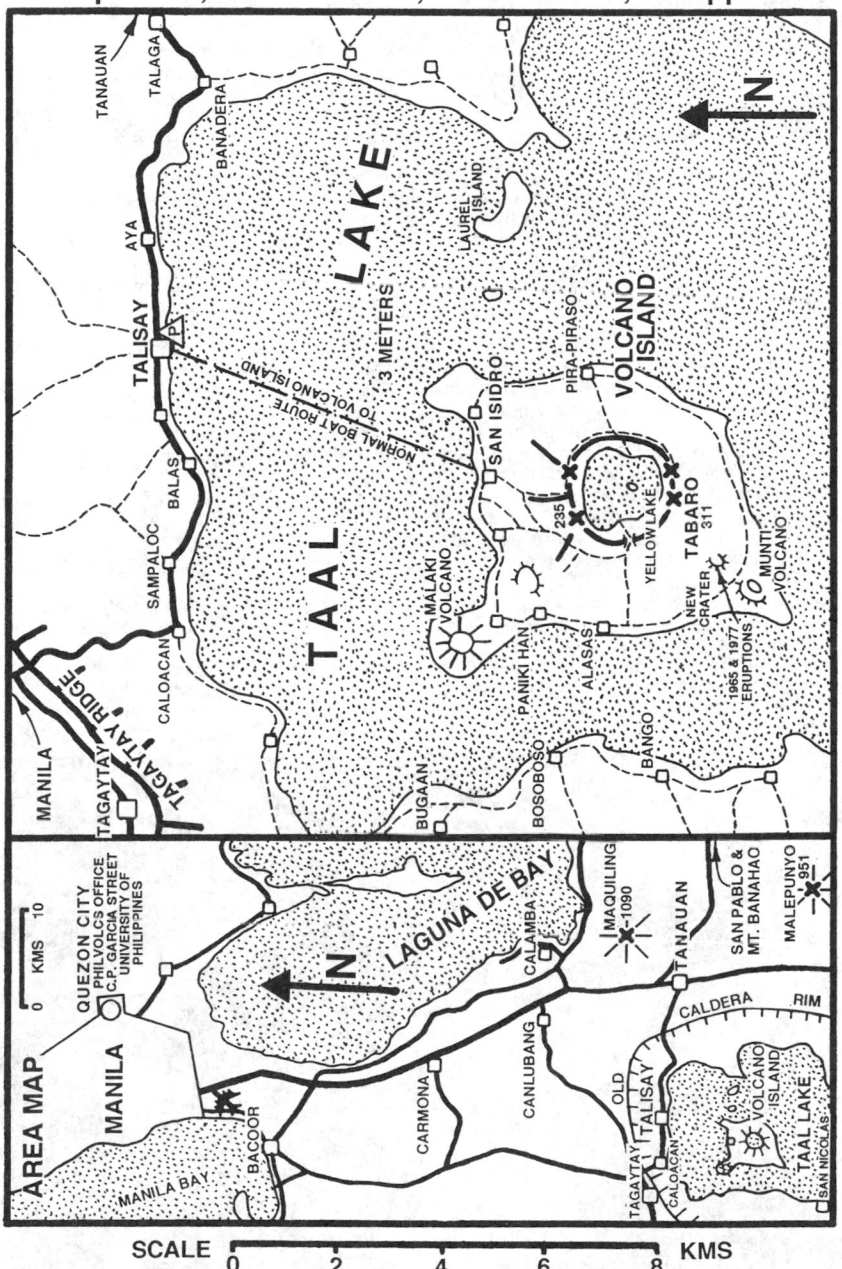

fact, it might be better to hike around Volcano Island in the wet season, as the author found the trails very dusty.

Maps The NAMRIA map *Manila*,1:250,000 is good enough, but there are also maps at 1:50,000 scale available; TPC map *K-11B*, 1:500,000; and the latest travel guidebook to the Philippines.

Banahao Volcano, Luzon Island, Philippines

Banahao (Banahow) Volcano at 2165 meters is located about 75 kms southeast of Manila, and 45 kms east of Taal Lake and its volcano complex.

Banahao is an older volcano covered with a pristine rain & cloud forest. At one time in the distant past, this volcano exploded making a crater with an opening to the south. Since then other nearby mountains have emerged such as Cristobol Volcano to the west, another cone to the east called Banahao de Lucban, and what appears to be a young volcanic plug just southwest of Kinabuhayan. According to the book, **Volcanoes of the World,** the last eruption on Banahao was a mudflow in 1730.

Since the introduction of Christianity to the Philippines, Banahao has become a sacred religious site with an annual pilgrimage during Easter week. At the far eastern end of the town of Kinabuhayan is a religious complex with shrines and is very reminiscent of Buddhist temples on other mountains in Asia. In the nearby dry creek bed is a depression on a rock believed by some to be the footprint of Jesus Christ. During Easter week, there are thousands of people making the pilgrimage to Kinabuhayan. Those who are able, attempt to climb the mountain. After Easter week, there are far fewer people around and less public transport. Weekends are always busier than week days.

The author arrived at San Pablo by bus on Thursday, 4/10/1998 (Easter weekend). He found a jeepney near the town center going to **Banahao** and Kinabuhayan. On the narrow road near Kinabuhayan was a big traffic jam, as there were jeepneys coming and going continually. He bought all his food in the many little shops on the main street of town, then to avoid the crowds and tent camps around Kinabuhayan, hiked halfway to Crystallino Falls and camped. Next morning, he returned to town, left his large pack in a shop for safe keeping (for a small fee), then climbed Banahao via the **Crystallino Falls Route.**

At the summit where everyone was stopping, there was a trail going down into the crater, and people said it ended, or began, at a place called Sarayan (Sarayang). Also, it appeared by peeking through the clouds, there was another, perhaps higher summit, half a km to the northeast. However, there were some huge cliffs and lots of brush in between, and apparently no trail (?).

Going down, the author used a second trail called the **Tatlong Tankas (3 tanks) Route.** He passed the large campsites of Kapatagan and Tatlong Tankas, where some people had set up small shops & eating places for pilgrims.

The ascent took the author about 2 1/2 hours; round-trip 4 3/4 hours. Many people take between 8 and 12 hours round-trip. Always start with 2 or 3 of liters of water, but there should be water at Crystallino Falls and 2 other places above on the normal ascent route. On the way down there is water at Tatlong Tankas and Tres Maria Spring only. Also, eat some salt or salty

Food & souvenir stalls line the street at Kinabuhayan at the base of Banahao. This foto was taken during Easter Week, 1998.

Map 274-1, Banahao Volcano, Luzon Island, Philippines

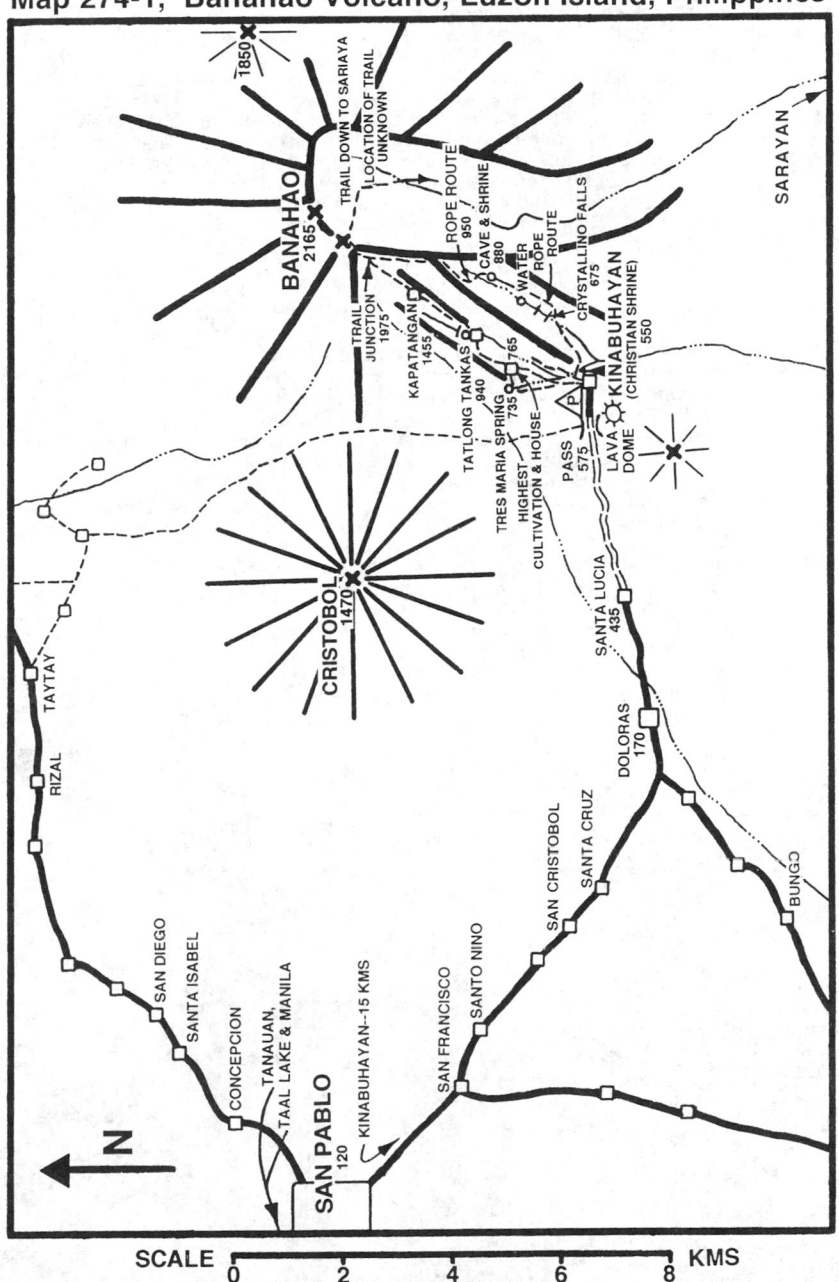

food--you'll sweat a lot. There are many daily buses from Manila or the Taal Lake area running to San Pablo, then jeepneys to Kinabuhayan. The dry season is January through April.

Maps This and the *Manila*, 1:250,000 map from NAMRIA will be enough; TPC map *K-11B*, 1:500,000: and the latest travel guidebook to the Philippines.

Vulcan Mayon, Luzon Island, Philippines

One of the most perfectly formed volcanic cones in the world is located on the southern end of the island of Luzon in the Philippines. This is Vulcan Mayon at 2462 meters, immediately northwest of Legaspi.

Mayon's last eruptions were on 1/5/2000 and 2/23 & 2/24/2000, and into 3/2000. All areas within 7 kms of the summit were evacuated. Historically, on 2/1/1814, there was a huge explosive eruption which buried the village of Cagsawa just to the south. The church was packed with people seeking shelter from falling ash, when the roof collapsed. About 1200 people died. The church's bell tower is still standing and is a major tourist attraction today. For volcano updates see the websites (www.phivolcs.dost.gov.ph/) or (www.volcano.si.edu/gvp/).

You can reach this area and **Volcano Mayon** by bus from Manila. If you're coming from that direction, stop at the town of Ligao and take a bus or jeepney along the road toward Tabaco, but get off at the junction where the road to the resthouse & volcano observatory begins. This paved road runs for 8 kms and you can usually get a lift part-way up to the resthouse. If not, it's an interesting walk past bamboo huts and fields of sugar cane and abaca. If you're coming from Legaspi, take a bus or jeepney to Tabaco or Ligao, then another vehicle as suggested above.

At the volcano observatory is a small museum with an explanation of the tectonics involved in the mountain's upheavals and destruction, and an explanation of the Cagsawa Ruins.

At one time there was a road up the mountain past the observatory for some distance, but now it's overgrown and unusable for vehicles. However, there is a trail along this old road; at least to as far as the Buang Gully. This gully is where rain water races down the mountain during stormy periods, but it also makes an easy route to the summit. At about 1300 meters, there are several potholes in the gully, which generally contain good drinking (rain) water.

At about 1800 meters, are several platforms for camping, but there's no water nearby. However, this climb can be made easily in one day from the observatory so there's no need to camp. A fast climber using this normal route, can climb Mayon is one day from Tabaco; or with your own vehicle, from Legaspi.

On the southeast side of the mountain there's another route to the top, but it may be overgrown in places, and is a much longer walk than from the resthouse. Inquire at the tourist office in Legaspi about that route.

To reach the **Cogsawa Church Ruins** take any jeepney from the middle of Legaspi heading in the general direction of Ligao or Camalig. Ask anyone on the street or a jeepney driver and they'll point out the right vehicle. Get off at the sign and road to Cogsawa, then walk east for 10 minutes. There's a small entry fee, and lots of people selling soda pop and souvenirs. Go in the mornings for a cloud-free look at Mayon beyond the church steeple.

The ruins of the Cagsawa church with Volcan Mayon in the distance to the left.

Map 275-1, Vulcan Mayon, Luzon Island, Philippines

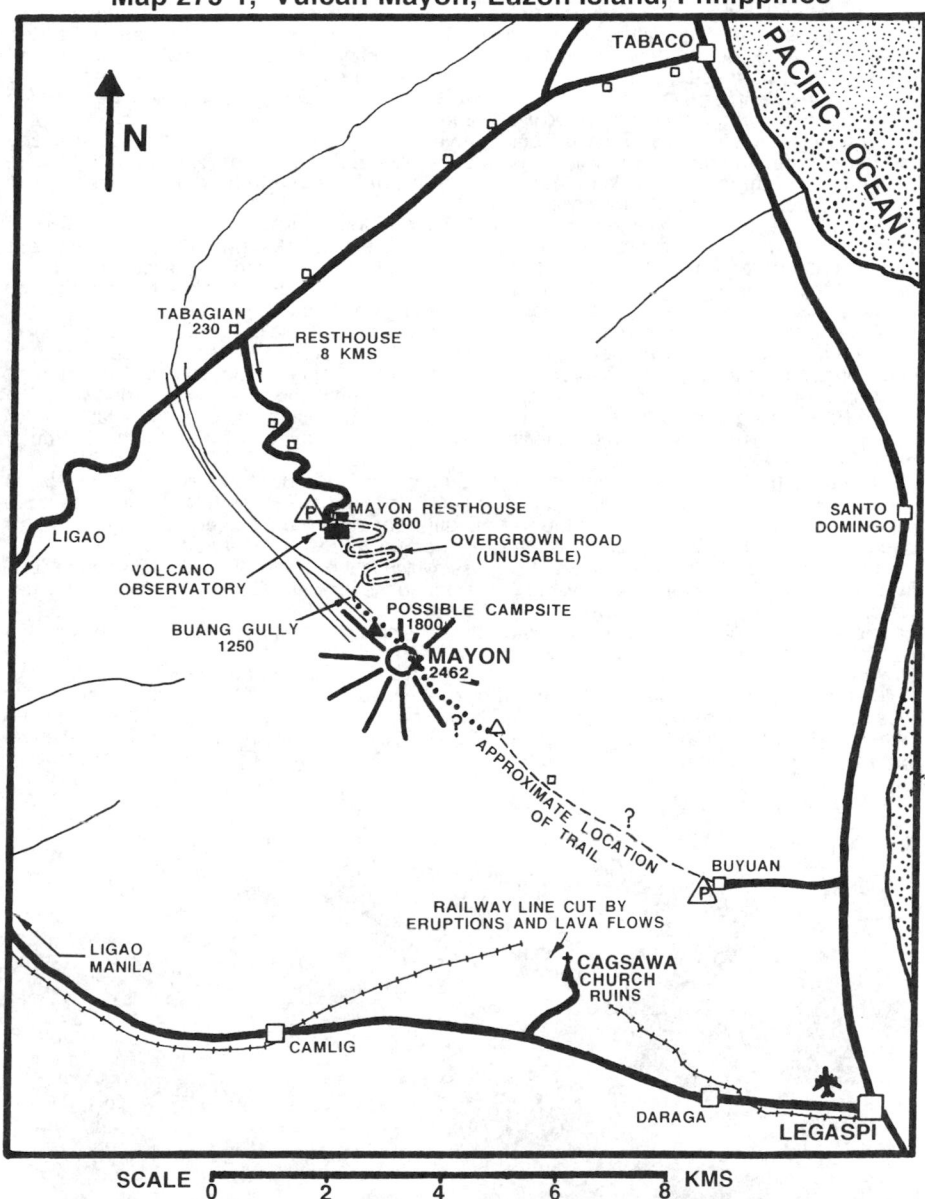

TABACO

PACIFIC OCEAN

N

TABAGIAN
230

RESTHOUSE
8 KMS

LIGAO

VOLCANO
OBSERVATORY

MAYON RESTHOUSE
800

OVERGROWN ROAD
(UNUSABLE)

SANTO
DOMINGO

BUANG GULLY
1250

POSSIBLE CAMPSITE
1800

MAYON
2462

APPROXIMATE LOCATION OF TRAIL

?

BUYUAN

RAILWAY LINE CUT BY
ERUPTIONS AND LAVA FLOWS

LIGAO
MANILA

CAGSAWA
CHURCH
RUINS

CAMLIG

DARAGA

LEGASPI

SCALE 0   2   4   6   8 KMS

Take food & water from Ligao, Legaspi, or Tabaco, as the resthouse may or may not be open when you arrive. The dry season is from December or January through April.
Maps *Legaspi City, 2516*, 1:250,000, or 1:50,000 scale maps, if available, from NAMRIA, Manila; or TPC map *K-11B*, 1:500,000; and the latest travel guidebook to the Philippines.

Bulusan Volcano, Luzon Island, Philippines

Shown on this map is the Bulusan Volcano, located at the very southeastern tip of Luzon Island. Bulusan at 1558 meters, is an active volcano with occasional steam & ash eruptions. The period at the end of 1994 and into 1/1995 was very active. The last phreatic explosion was on 1/28/1995, which sent ash 2 kms high. During the author's visit on 4/18/1998, steam was roaring from a vent in the side of the main summit crater. For volcano updates see the websites (www.phivolcs.dost.gov.ph/) or (www.volcano.si.edu/gvp/).

If coming direct from Manila, take a bus heading for any place south of southern Luzon and the ferry boats at Matnog. You will then get off at Irosin, just south of Bulusan. Or if you're coming from Legaspi and Vulcan Mayon, you'll probably have to take a full-sized bus to Sorsogon, then a jeepney 35-40 kms to Irosin.

Make Irosin your headquarters for climbing **Bulusan**. In the middle of town is a good market where you can buy anything you'll need for the hike. Two blocks away is the St. Michael's Lodge at about US$4 a night. Surrounding the market block will be parking places for jeepneys and motor tricycles going in all directions. Look for jeepneys going to the coastal town of Bulusan; or a tricycle to San Roque, which is the starting point for climbing the volcano.

Once in the village of San Roque, ask where the captain's house is. There are many trails in the area and most people will need someone to lead them through the gardens and up to the beginning of the trail through the forest. An adventurous hiker can probably get to the summit with this map, but the mountain side with the gardens is San Roque communal property and in all the Pacific it's generally understood that hikers need permission and/or a guide, at least for part of the way. The village captain will find a young man or boy to guide you at least through the gardens (always for a fee).

There are many beginning points in San Roque, but one is about 250 meters east of a small stream. Past the village, the trail heads northwest, then northeast up a steep slope to more gardens above. Finally you'll reach the end of cultivation at about 620 meters. From there, it's one trail through the rainforest paralleling a stream below on your right, or north.

Later, you'll enter a big flat area with tall grass, which is the middle of an old crater or caldera. Then it's straight up the tall grass-covered east slope to the summit. On the other side, is a small crater with a pond; and the main active crater. There are 2 places in the old crater where some people have camped. You'll normally find water near each campsite, but take 2 or 3 liters with you from San Roque. Plan on 6 to 10 hours round-trip for this climb from San Roque.

On his first day, the author got off a jeepney above San Roque, then walked 20 minutes to Bulusan Lake. There he found a good trail around the lake, and ruins of an old resort, plus there was some new facilities being built in 1998. The second day, he was required to take a guide up Bulusan. They both reached the summit in just over 3 hours. Returning, the guide stayed at the hut at 620 meters, and the author continued down alone. He paid the guide about US$4.

From the summit of Bulusan looking east down into an old crater and Peak 1220.

Map 276-1, Bulusan Volcano, Luzon Island, Philippines

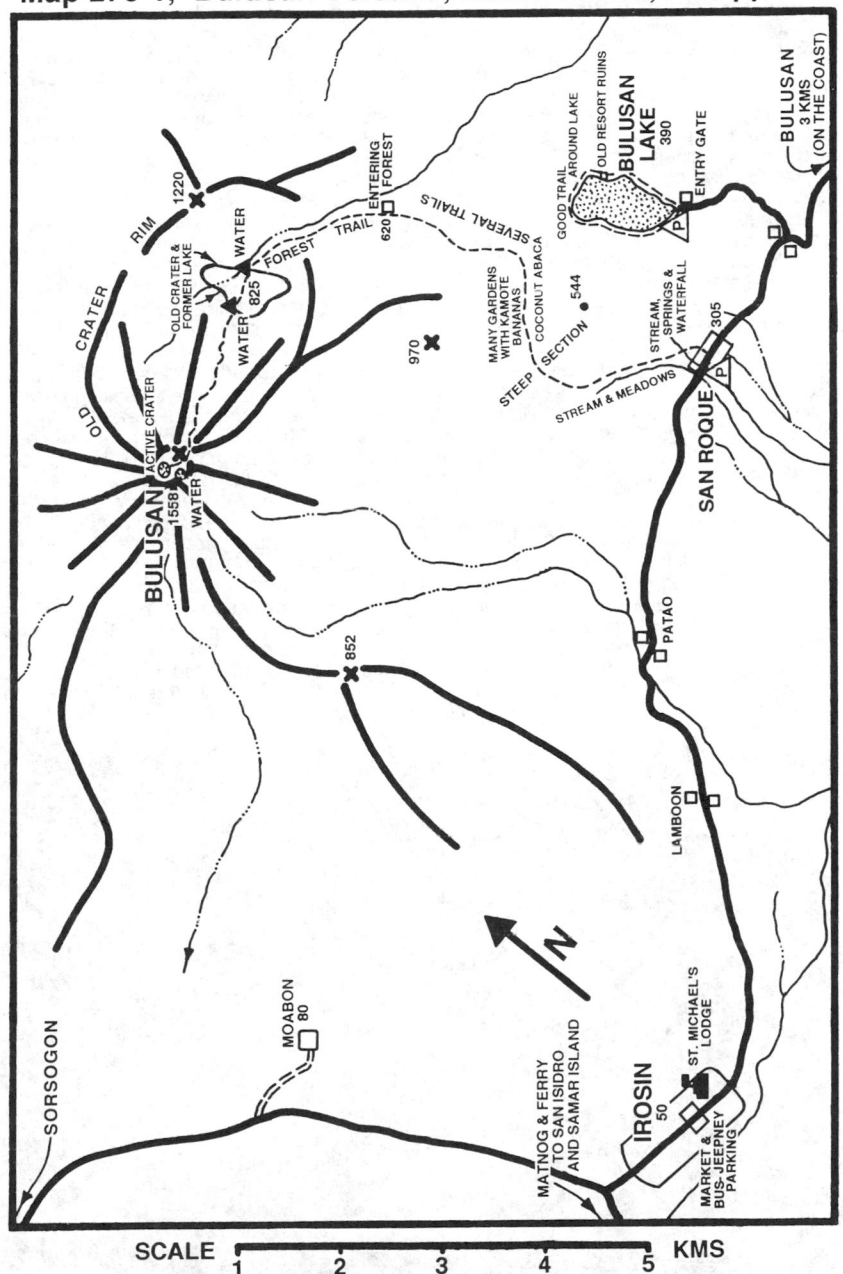

SCALE | 1 | 2 | 3 | 4 | 5 | KMS

Round-trip from San Roque took just under 6 hours.
Maps 1:50,000 scale maps are available, but likely not in stock at NAMRIA (Coast & Geodetic Survey), Manila; or *Bulan, 2519,* I:250,000; or TPC map *K-11B,* 1;500,000; any national highway map; and the latest travel guidebook to the Philippines.

Canlaon Volcano, Negros Island, Philippines

Canlaon (sometimes spelled Kanlaon) Volcano at about 2435 meters, is located on the island of Negros, which is in about the middle of the Philippine Archipelago. Canlaon is an active volcano and the highest peak on Negros. Prior to the author's climb on 4/29/1998, the most recent activity was in 8/1996. This was a single steam generated or phreatic explosion, caused by the heavy rains at that time. The nearby Philvolcs Volcano Observatory had no seismic readings below the volcano that month, indicating it was rainwater seeping down to the top of the hot rocks near the summit that caused the explosion. That explosion on 8/10/1996 at 2:31 pm killed 3 hikers; one British and 2 Filipinos, who happened to be on the crater rim at the time. For volcano updates see the websites (www.phivolcs.dost.gov.ph/) or (www.volcano.si.edu/gvp/).

To get there, first go to Bacalod, Negros, by ferryboat or air from Manila; or from Cebu Island, located just to the east. Lots of ferryboats leave Cebu at Toledo and land at San Carlos, just northwest of Canlaon. From San Carlos, take one of maybe 4 to 6 buses a day going to as far as Canlaon City. They stop there because of a short stretch of privately owned road, as shown on the map. Buses have to pay a fee, so they let passengers off, who then take motor tricycles across. On the other side at Masulog, there are several other buses daily running to Bacalod, the largest city on Negros. If coming from Bacalod, look for a bus going to Magallon, then Masulog.

Upon reaching Masulog, you can stay in a new village guesthouse called the Masulog Pension. The author paid about US$4 for his room. Nearby is a good market selling all kinds of food, plus several shops, and many little food stalls selling rice & meat dishes, etc.

The author reached Canlaon at the end of a terrible drought and the mountain was closed to climbing; but he talked his way into a special permit from the Canlaon City government. The permit required him to take a guide, which he did, but only up through the maze of trails in the gardens to the treeline. The guide was paid about US$5.25, and the author went alone from there. The climb took 6 1/4 hours round-trip from Masulog. With this map, you can likely make it up through the trails and farms to the treeline, then it's one very good trail to the summit. If you should get lost, pay a local farm boy to get you on the right trail.

From the Masulog market, walk north on the paved road as shown, then along a rough vehicle track through lower & upper Mananaowin. The author passed 2 taps with good spring water piped from somewhere above. From the highest huts, you enter the forest, cross one big gully (with pothole water nearby?), then zig zag up the grassy western side of a prominent ridge (with trees on the eastern side). Turn west on the summit ridge to reach the highest crater.

The dry season lasts from December through April or May. Buy all food in Masulog stores. You'll need at least 2, but probably 3 liters of water, for the climb.

Canlaon Volcano. The trail heads up through farms then into the forest and onto the grass-covered ridge to the upper right.

Map 277-1, Canlaon Volcano, Negros Island, Philippines

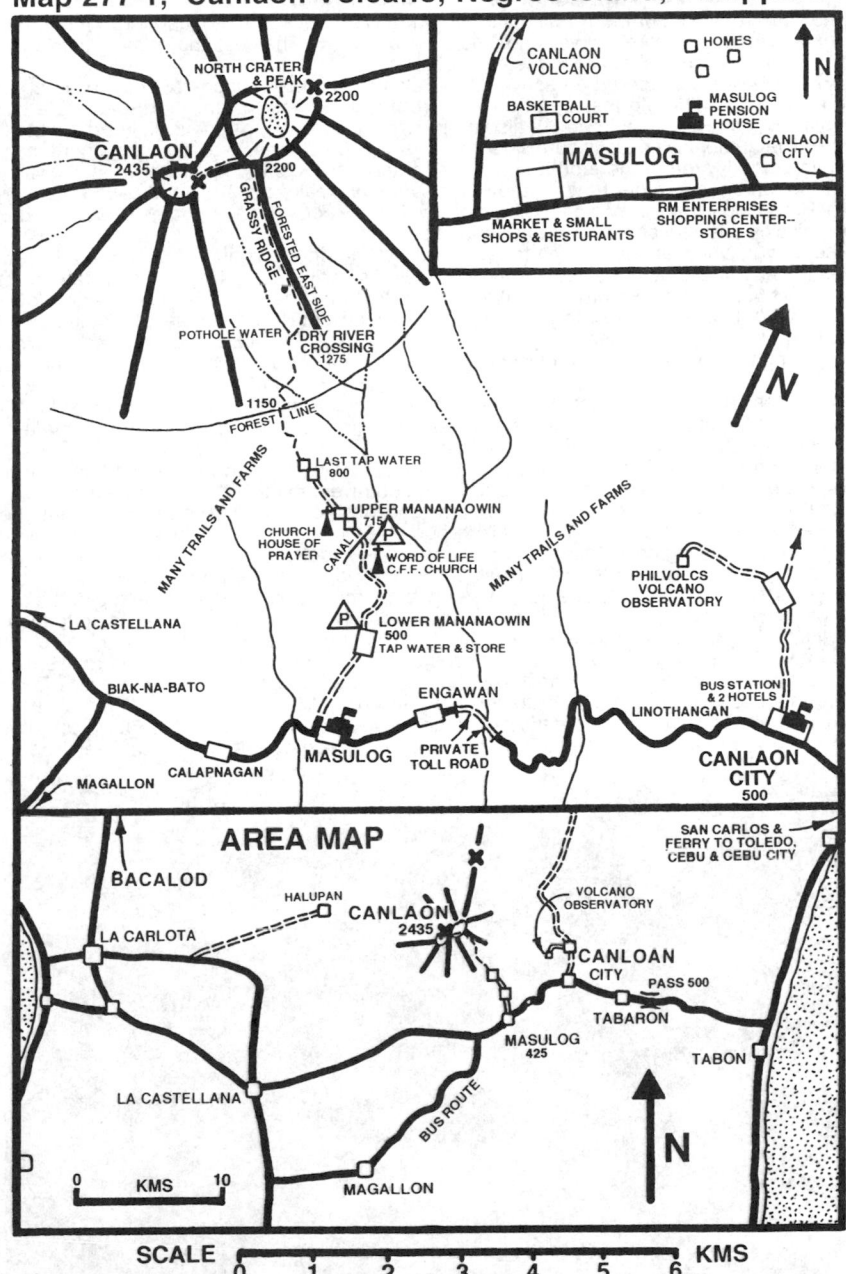

Maps Maps *3651-II* & *3651-III*, 1:50,000; or maps *2528* & *2529,* 1:250,000, from NAMRIA, Manila; or *Kanlaon Volcano Eruption Hazards Map*, 1:50,000 from the Philvolcs Observatory near Canlaon City (or Quezon City); or TPC map *K-11C*, 1:500,000; and the latest travel guidebook to the Philippines.

Hibok Hibok Volcano, Camiguin Island, Philippines

Shown here is the southern Philippine island of Camiguin, located just north of Mindanao. Camiguin is made up entirely of volcanos, both old and new. The best known mountain is Hibok Hibok Volcano, which is about 1310 meters high.

Hibok Hibok is considered an active stratovolcano. Its last episode of activity lasted from 1948 until 1953. The biggest eruption was from a flank vent on the northeast side of the mountain. There were lava flows, but also a moderately large explosion which killed about 2000 people. The author isn't exactly sure where this vent is, but there is a crater on the north side of the main summit area of the mountain. There's another volcano just northwest of the main summit which seems rather new. The highest peak or peaks on the island called Mambajao and/or Timpoong (?) are very old remnants of a volcano. For volcano updates see the websites (www.phivolcs.dost.gov.ph/) or (www.volcano.si.edu/gvp/).

The only way to Camiguin is via ferryboat. First, get to the island of Mindanao. You can start in the city of Cagayan de Oro and perhaps take a hydrofoil boat every other day. Cost is about US$3.50. Or the best way is to take a bus north from Cagayan de Oro to the port town of Balingoan. Or take a bus west from Butuan to Balingoan. At Balingoan, get off at the busy bus station and walk north across the highway to the docks. From Balingoan, there are boats running to either Guinsiliban or Benoni about every hour for about 12 hours a day. Cost is about US$.50.

Regardless of where you land, buses, jeepneys or motor tricycles will be waiting to take you to the town of Mambajao, where a number of hotels and/or pensions exist. In 4/1998, the author paid about US$2.50 for a room with shared bath.

From Mambajao, take any jeepney from the center of town going west toward some tourist hotels, but get off after 2 kms at the road running southwest to the *Ardent Hot Springs*. Walk 5 kms to the hot springs; or maybe jump on a motor tricycle. You'll have to pay a small fee to enter the hot springs compound, then walk through the hotel grounds to the lower end of a very prominent ridge coming down from the summit of **Hibok Hibok**.

From the hotel, walk southeast. You'll be on a good trail while passing through gardens, then across an open field, and finally up a steep slope through rainforest to the top of the ridge. Once on the ridge-top, the trail veers right or southwest, and winds its way straight up to the top. From the first summit, continue west on a trail to a second peak. From there you look straight down into Hibok Hibok's crater on the north side. The author was there on 4/25/1998 and reached the first summit in less than 1 1/2 hours from the hot springs; 3 hours round-trip. Buy soft drinks and cookies near the hotel; otherwise buy food in Mambajao.

While in the area, walk or ride a tricycle or motorcycle 4 or 5 kms up to the Philvolcs Volcano Observatory. Beyond that, the road continues to a place called *Itum* at the very base of

From the summit of Hibok Hibok looking down to the north at another crater.

Map 278-1, Hibok Hibok Vol., Camiguin Island, Philippines

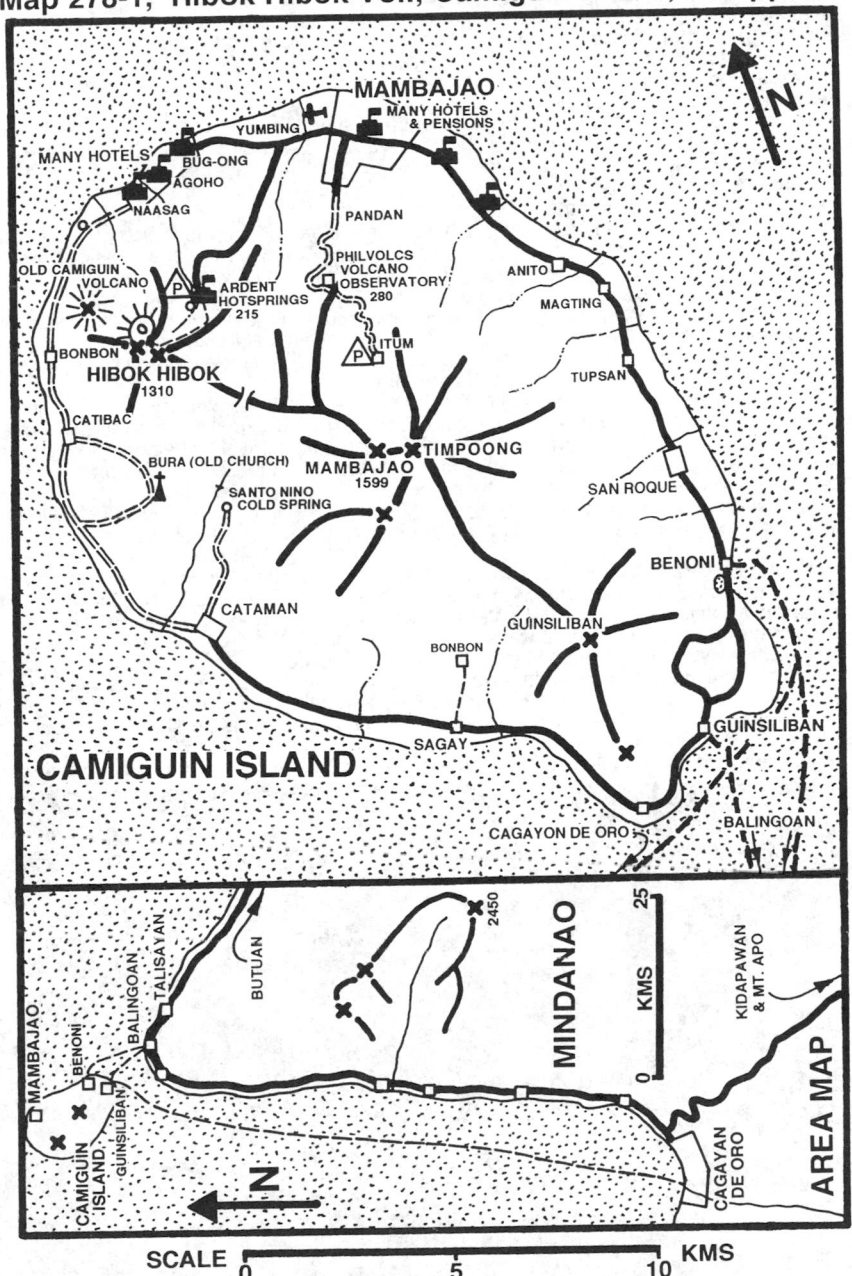

Timpoong (or Mambajao?). There may be a trail up this steep mountain (?). Or hire a young boy as a guide.
Maps There are 4 maps at 1:50,000 covering Camiguin, if you can find them at NAMRIA, Manila; TPC map *K-11C,* 1:500,000; and the latest travel guidebook to the Philippines.

Mt. Apo, Mindanao Island, Philippines

This map features the highest mountain in the Philippines, Mt. Apo, at 2938 meters. Apo is located on the southern Philippine island of Mindanao just southwest of Davao City. Mt. Apo is an old stratovolcano with lots of hot springs and fumarolic activity. If you climb Apo via the normal route, the one from Kidapawan, you'll pass through the Mindanao Geothermal Project. This project began in about 1992 and was partly completed by 1998.

In some ways this geothermal project has made getting to the mountain easier, but in other ways it may be a hindrance. When the author arrived at Kidapawan on one of many buses from Davao (4/22/1998), the mountain was officially closed to hiking because of the severe drought and fears of forest fires. So he went to the city offices, told them of his need to climb the mountain, and was granted a special permit. He had to show that to the guards at the Jaguar Gate to get onto the mountain. However, and it still isn't clear to this writer, even if the mountain is open for hiking, you may have to go to the Kidapawan city offices to get a pass of some kind to get through the geothermal project area. Check this out in Kidapawan before leaving town.

The author got his permit in the afternoon, then the next morning waited for a jeepney going all the way to Lake Agko, at the beginning of the hike. However it looked like a long wait, so he hired a jeepney as a taxi for about US$10. In one hour he was at Lake Agko hot spring, and a national park campsite. To insure success, he hired a boy as a guide (about US$3) to get him past the geothermal project and well onto the mountain.

From Agko, they walked up the road to the Jaguar Gate and after waiting an hour, continued along a road to Site B, the beginning of the trail. From there it was *down* to the Marbel River and after another 2 kms, the boy returned from where the trail left the river. The author continued up to Lake Venado, where he hid his big pack in the forest, and hurried to the summit. From the Jaguar Gate to the top took 4 1/2 hours, mostly with his large pack. He then returned all the way to the Marbel River & hot springs and camped. Next morning it took just over an hour to reach the gate, for a round-trip walk-time of just under 8 hours; about 6 1/2 hours of which was with a large pack.

The water in Marbel River is undrinkable because of hot springs & mineral water on the west side of the mountain, but water from the cold spring is good. See map. Also, there are many campsites in the flats surrounding Lake Venado, and there will always be some water in a small stream and the lake. But purify that water first! Strong hikers can camp at Lake Agko, and with an early morning start, reach the summit and return the same day. With your own vehicle you can climb it in one long day from Kidapawan. Many jeepneys go to Ilomavis each day, but only 2 or 3 go to Lake Agko. Getting a lift from project workers off the mountain is easy. Buy all your food in Kidapawan, where there are several hotels. You'll find some small shops & food stalls near the geothermal project.

Other routes up the mountain begin at Bulatucan, southwest of the peak; and Kapatagan, a

The summit of Mt. Apo and boys catching butterflies on the Lake Venado flats.

Map 279-1, Mt. Apo, Mindanao Island, Philippines

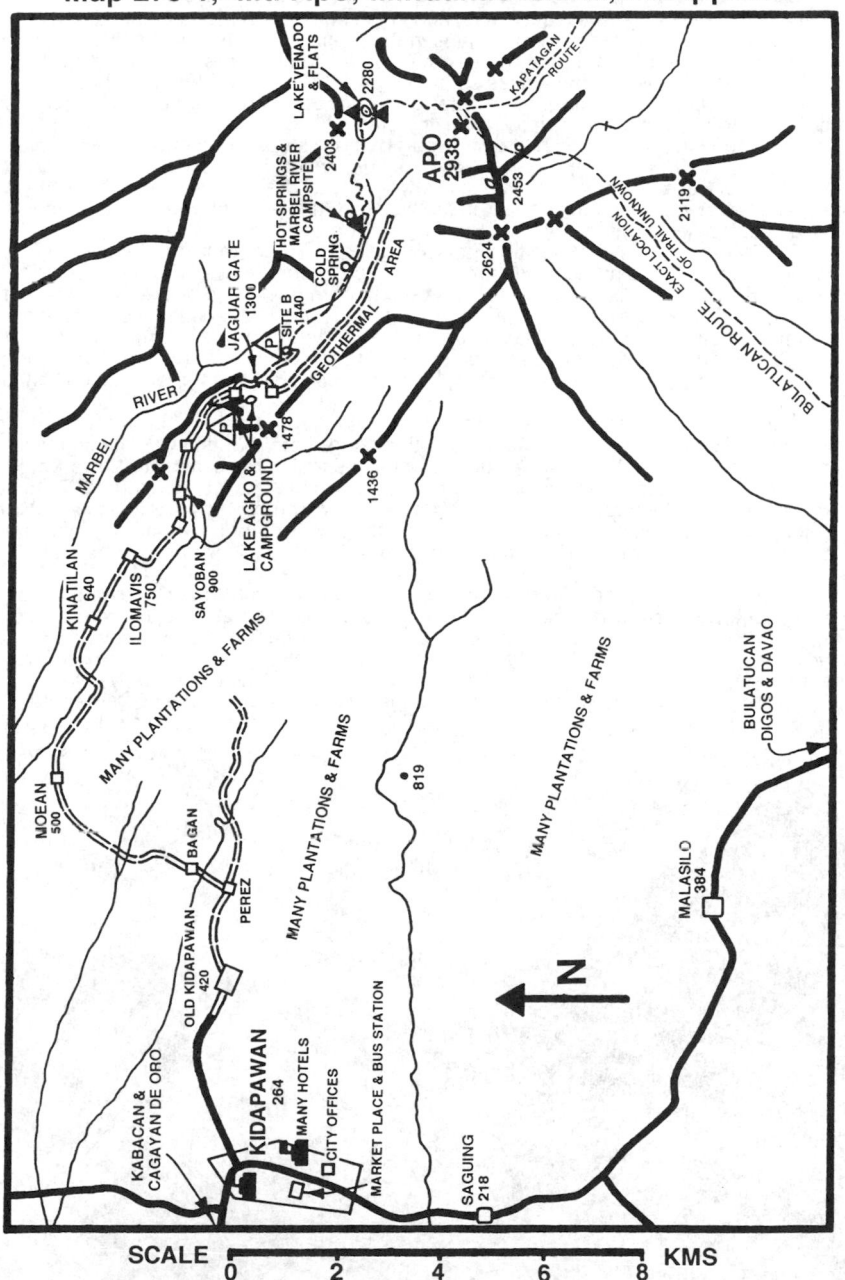

route from the southeast. These are longer routes, but without all the geothermal sites. The dry season is from December through April.

Maps Maps *4041-III, 4041-II, 4040-I, & 4040-IV,* 1:50,000, from NAMRIA, Manila; TPC map *L-12A,* 1:500,000; and the latest travel guidebook to the Philippines.

Lows Peak, Mt. Kinabalu, Sabah Province, Borneo, Malaysia

On the north end of the island of Borneo, and in the Malaysia province of Sabah, stands one of the highest and most impressive mountains in the Pacific. This is Gunung (Mt.) Kinabalu at 4101 meters. This mountain is an igneous intrusion of solid granite, not large by some standards, but impressive in that it rises so high right from sea level and stands all alone. Its sides are very steep with the top somewhat of a plateau, with a number of pinnacles and summits rising from the otherwise smooth granite dome.

North Borneo isn't as remote as it once was. Being the eastern half of Malaysia, you can easily fly there from Kuala Lumpur, Brunei or Bangkok, and perhaps other places. You'll fly to the capital city of Sabah called Kota Kinabalu (KK). KK is a small city with many hotels to fit any budget. There's at least one supermarket in the basement of the Centrepoint Department Store, and hundreds of other shops and stores. Buy all your supplies in KK.

Here's what the author did. He flew from Bangkok & Brunei to KK and stayed one night. Next morning, went shopping, etc, then got on a mini bus from the bus station on Jalan Padang (Padang Street) heading for Ranau. There are many small and large buses going that way all day long. After 1 1/2 hours he was let off at the road leading to the park headquarters about 200 meters off the main highway. He walked up to H.Q. and got his park permit for the next day (about US$10), then hiked 4 kms up the paved road to the power plant to checkout the actual trailhead. He finally returned to the main highway and checked into the Mountain Resthouse. He paid US$2.70 for the night.

Next morning he got up in the dark and at 5am, walked past the guard at the entry gate (nothing was said and no one asked for a permit!) next to Park H.Q. and was at the trailhead at the crack of dawn (5:45am). He walked up the well-used trail to the summit or **Lows Peak** (in T shirt & shorts), a distance of 8.72 kms. He got some fairly good fotos, then returned. The round-trip walk from his resthouse (hotel) took 7 1/4 hours; from the power plant it was a 5 2/3 hour round-trip hike. The record round-trip time from the power plant is 2 hours 42 minutes--but marathoner Jan Holms of the UK, wasn't carrying 6-7 kgs of water, food, extra clothes and cameras, etc!

If you decide to stay in the park facilities, make reservations in KK the day before (Tele. 011-60-88-243629), but there are plenty of little hotels along the highway on either side of the park entrance. You're supposed to take a guide as well, at least if climbing above *Laban Rata Resthouse*, but the author didn't and wasn't hassled (the entry gate next to the power plant is manned during the day so just show him your park permit and tell him you're only going to Laban Rata). During the day, transport to the trailhead is available from Park H.Q. From the Sayat Sayat Huts to the summit there is one long rope lying on the granite--just follow it and you can't

Mt. Kinabalu. From the summit of Lows Peak looking southeast at the Donkey's Ears on the left, and Kinabalu South Peak on the right.

Map 280-1, Lows Pk., Kinabalu, Sabah, Borneo, Malaysia

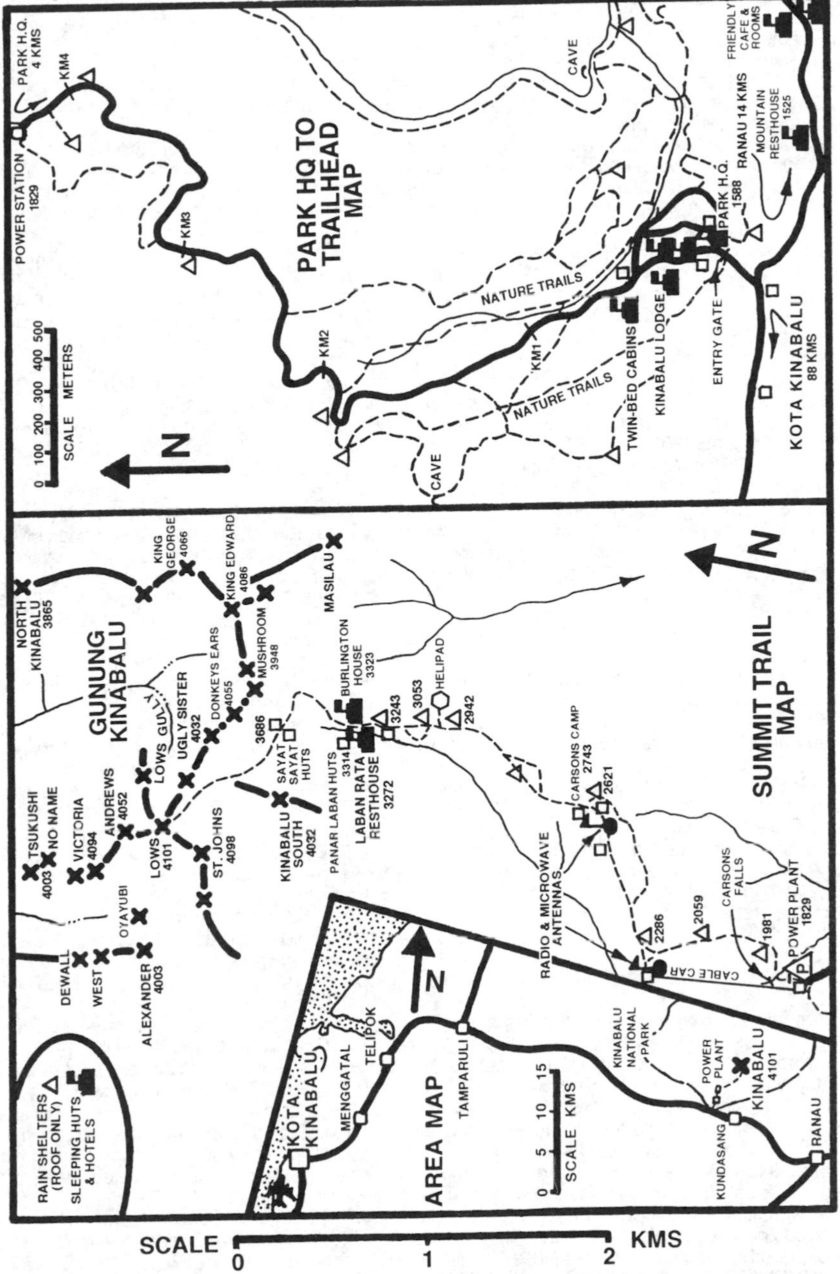

PARK HQ TO TRAILHEAD MAP

PARK H.Q. 4 KMS
KM4
POWER STATION 1829
KM3
KM2
KM1
NATURE TRAILS
NATURE TRAILS
CAVE
CAVE
PARK H.Q. 1588
RANAU 14 KMS
MOUNTAIN RESTHOUSE 1525
FRIENDLY CAFE & ROOMS
ENTRY GATE
KINABALU LODGE
TWIN-BED CABINS
KOTA KINABALU 88 KMS

SCALE METERS
0 100 200 300 400 500

N

GUNUNG KINABALU

NORTH KINABALU 3865
KING GEORGE 4066
KING EDWARD 4086
MASILAU
MUSHROOM 3948
DONKEYS EARS 4055
UGLY SISTER 4032
LOWS GULY
3686
TSUKUSHI 4003
NO NAME
VICTORIA 4094
ANDREWS 4052
LOWS 4101
ST. JOHNS 4098
SAYAT SAYAT HUTS 4032
KINABALU SOUTH 4032
OYAYUBI
WEST
DEWALL
ALEXANDER 4003

BURLINGTON HOUSE 3323
HELIPAD
3053
2942
3243
PANAR LABAN HUTS 3314
LABAN RATA RESTHOUSE 3272
CARSONS CAMP 2743
2621
RADIO & MICROWAVE ANTENNAS
2286
2059
CARSONS FALLS
1981
POWER PLANT 1829
CABLE CAR

SUMMIT TRAIL MAP

N

RAIN SHELTERS (ROOF ONLY)
SLEEPING HUTS & HOTELS

AREA MAP

KOTA KINABALU
MENGGATAL
TELIPOK
TAMPARULI
KINABALU NATIONAL PARK
POWER PLANT
KINABALU 4101
KUNDASANG
RANAU

N

SCALE KMS
0 5 10 15

SCALE KMS
0 1 2

get lost in the fog. There's no real dry season for Kinabalu as it sits almost on the equator. Go anytime, and be prepared for wet conditions. Get an early morning start before clouds build up.
Maps *Mt. Kinabalu Climbing Guide* (free handout & map), from Park H.Q. at the park, or in KK; or call Park H.Q. in KK at Inter+60-88-211881 or 211652; and the latest travel guidebook to Malaysia.

Introduction to Hiking & Climbing in Indonesia

Indonesia probably has more volcanos, and/or active volcanos, than any country on earth. At one time or another, almost all of its 16,000 islands were created or closely associated with volcanism. The author first went to Indonesia in the dry season of 4 & 5/1977 and climbed 7 mountains during his 1 1/2 month stay. After 22 years, he returned during 9 & 10/1999. On that trip, he climbed 23 volcanos, from Sumatra east to as far as Flores, then north and east to northern Sulawesi and to the islands of Tenate and Tidore in the Maluku (Spice) Islands. In these 2 trips he has climbed all the better known volcanos in the country.

Whether you're a professional volcano hunter, or just an average hiker, the best way to get information on active volcanos is to contact the **Volcanological Survey of Indonesia (VSI)** at Jalan Diponegoro No. 57, Bandung, 40122, Indonesia; or see the website (www.vsi.dpe.go.id) or email (igan@vsi.dpe.go.id). Another website to check for active volcano undates is (www.volcano.si. edu/gvp/). See below.

To actually visit the VSI in person and to perhaps buy copies of their maps, the best place to start is in Central Jakarta. From the airport take the Damri Airport Bus direct to the Gambir Railway Station. Most individual travelers stay in the Jalan Jaksa area which is a 12 minute walk south of that station. From Gambir, take one of 20-25 daily trains to Bandung (3 hours). At Bandung Station, ask the tourist information people inside which bemo (minivan) to take to the VSI. Or take a taxi. The people at the VSI can tell you which volcanos are alive or quiet, and will show you maps of active volcanos. For a small price, they will copy their maps for you. Some of their maps are old, but OK. These volcanologists know the active volcanos, including normal routes, better than anyone.

The normal place to buy new topographic maps of Indonesia is at the Bedan Koordinasi Survey dan Pemetaan Nasional **(BAKOSURTANAL)**, Jalan Raya, Jakarta-Bogor, Km 46; Tele. 807-2062, Fax 021-879-3075. This place is located about 10 kms north of Bogor, and 46 kms south of Jakarta on the Raya Highway.

The best way to get there from Jakarta is to start at the Gambir Railway Station. Get on any train heading for Bogor or Bandung. Stop at Bogor Station, and ask about a bemo heading back north on Jalan Raya. You may have to change bemos once. The map facility is near Km 46, on the east side of the highway and back about 250 meters. Look for D wing, 2nd floor. If buying maps, expect to spend 2-3 hours minimum, because of bureaucracy. In 1999, they sold good new maps at 1:25,000 and 1:50,000 scale for about US$2.50 each. The author found no restrictions, as there have been in the past. The problem is, not all regions of the country have been mapped.

Another way to get updated information on Indonesian volcanos, or any active volcano in the world, is to contact the **Global Volcanism Program**, National Museum of Natural History (Smithsonian Institution), Room E-421, Washington, DC 20560-0129, Tele. 202-357-1511; Fax 202-357-3218 or 2476; email (service@volcano.si.edu) or website (**www.volcano.si.edu/gvp/**).

You can also subscribe to the **Bulletin of the Global Volcanism Network (GVN)** for about US$22 ($39 outside the USA) a year. This comes through the American Geophysical Union (2000 Florida Avenue NW, Washington, DC 20009, Tele. 202-462-6900 or 800-966-2481, Fax 202-328-0566; or email: cust_ser@kosmos.agu.org). You can also get the GVN via email (listserv@asu.edu), from Arizona State University.

Besides some pretty good Indonesian topo maps at 1:25,000 and 1:50,000 scale, you might also copy some older maps put out by the **Defense Mapping Agency (DMA)**. These are all at 1:250,000 scale. This agency is the Army Map Service, Corps of Engineers, US Army; but the British helped too. These maps date from the 1940's, 1950's and the early 1960's from information gathered mostly during World War II, or just after. Even through they're pretty old, the mountains are still the same. The only things they lack are new highways and the size of towns & cities. These maps show a good wide-angle view of an area and are better than most people realize. Look for these in university map libraries.

In recent years, **NOAA** (see mapping agencies in the back of this book) has republished and/or upgraded these old DMA maps and they are now called **JOG's--Joint Operations Graphics--**Air. You cannot buy these in the USA, but you can buy similar maps in Indonesia, or other individual countries that were covered by the original DMA 1:250,000 maps. **TPC maps** at 1:500,000, would help, but there's only a couple available which cover parts of Sumatra.

Some good travel maps are also found in the latest edition of the **Indonesia Travel Atlas**, put out by Periplus Editions, Ltd., out of Hong Kong. This atlas is very good and you should carry it with you in your travels to Indonesia. These are in full color and cover the most-widely traveled areas of the country. The only thing they lack is the scale in kms for each map.

The last thing you'll need is the latest travel guidebook to Indonesia. Lonely Planet (LP) puts out one called **Indonesia**, plus they have several others with greater detail dealing with just Bali & Lombok, or other islands. LP has offices in Australia, UK, France and the USA. In the US call Tele. 510-893-8555, or Toll Free at 800-275-8555 or email (info@lonelyplanet.com) or website (www.lonelyplanet.com).

Moon Publishing puts out the **Indonesia Handbook,** and other titles covering the same areas. Contact them in Chico, California, USA. Email (travel@moon.com) or website (www.moon.com).

Or Tele toll free in the USA 800-345-5473, or 530-345-5473.

The best time to visit Indonesia is during the dry season, which corresponds with summer in the northern hemisphere. From sometime in April or May things dry out pretty good over most of the archipelago and this lasts until sometime in October, usually. August is the driest month over most areas, but in Manado and the Malukus, September is the driest. In Sumatra, there is no dry season to speak of, but the wettest time is from sometime in September through December. February and March are the driest in Medan, northern Sumatra. When climbing in Sumatra, always go prepared for rain.

Here's what the author usually took on his climbs. A small camera bag, altimeter watch, compass, medium sized day pack, mini umbrella, a 2 liter water bottle--usually full, some kind of map, small notebook & pen, lunch (always bought locally), and sometimes a long sleeved shirt. He always wore shorts or short pants and a T shirt, low cut hiking shoes and a baseball-type cap with *cancer curtain* sewn on around the back and sides.

Of all the climbs he took on his 1999 trip, his only multiple-day climbs were on Rinjani and Semeru & Bromo. All other climbs he did in one day. For the skinny & fit person and those who walk fast, almost all volcanos in Indonesia can be climbed in one day.

Here's some Indonesian words you should become familiar with: bemo=minibus or van; ojek=single passenger motorcycle taxi; losmen=family run inn or hotel; wurang=food stall; water=air (pron. eye-ear); jalan=road; jalan kacil=little road or trail; jalan jalan=walking, or trip or safari; gunung=mountain; gunung api=volcano; sungai=river; sungai kacil=creek; tenda=tent; pendaki gunung=mtn. climber; mendaki=climbing; desa=village; kapala desa=village head; peta=map; toko=shop; pondok=cottage, cabin or shelter; pasar=market place; mosquito coil=obat nyamok; coffee=kopi; tea=teh; coffee plantation=kebun kopi.

Important short phases are: how much?=barapa; do you have?=punya; where is=demana ada; can I?=boleh. C's are always pronounced as a ch. Summit or Peak=puncak, but is pronounced punchak.

From the crater rim looking down into the bottom of the Bromo Volcano. This active volcano is in the Tengger Caldera just north of Semeru (Map 291, page 631).

Pusuk Buhit, Toba Caldera, Sumatra, Indonesia

This map shows part of northern Sumatra, including the city of Medan and Danau Toba (Lake Toba), the largest lake in southeast Asia. Also shown is a dormant volcano called Pusuk Buhit at 1982 meters. This volcano is inside the giant Toba Caldera, perhaps the world's largest. This caldera was formed about 74,000 years ago by a cataclysmic explosion which blew out an estimated 2800 cubic/kms of rhyolitic magma--the biggest blast ever studied! Compare this to Tambora's 1815 blowout, recent human history's largest eruption, with over 100 cubic/kms of magma ejected.

After Danau's eruption, a lake formed, then later eruptions created the island called Samosir. Pusuk Buhit came much later and is the youngest volcano in the area. On the northeast flanks is a hot spring (panis air) area, indicating the place is not totally dead. Toba is a popular tourist destination.

To reach this area, take a bus or bemo south from Medan; or north from Padang or Bukittinggi. Stop at the tourist town of Prapat on the east side of Toba. Lots of hotels there. Most tourists take a ferry from Prapat to Tuktuk, where you'll find 30-35 hotels or losmen; but if you're going to Pusuk Buhit and Pangururan, it's best to take a ferry from Ajibata to Tomok (30 minutes).

Ajibata is just around the little ridge south of Prapat. You can walk between these 2 ferry docks, or take a bemo. The reason for going to Tomok is there are many more buses waiting for the arrival of each ferry. From Tomok, buses use the northern route to reach Pangururan (one hour), but they bypass Tuktuk. There are at least 2 hotels in Pangururan; the author stayed in the Asido Star Inn for less than US$2 a night on 9/1/1999.

The author stayed in Prapat one night, took an 8am ferry from Ajibata to Tomok, then a small bus to Pangururan. He checked into the Asido Star Inn, then walked north to where the road to the hot springs turns left or west. It's about 2 1/2 kms from Pangururan to the hot springs. There he paid US$.04 to enter the area (where you can bathe in the hot water), then took the trail up **Pusik Buhit** which begins about 100 meters before the entry booth.

He walked the trail to the first farm homes at 1250 meters, then turned west and walked the most-used trail along the top of a big hogsback ridge toward the summit. There are several trails & farms in that area, so you may have to ask someone if this is the *trail to the summit* (jalan kachil ki punchak?). He reached the top or punchak (puncak) in 1 3/4 hours from the hot springs--2 1/2 hours from his hotel.

From the summit he walked northward down an old and unused road past a couple of ponds, down a southwest ridge, then north around the bottom of the volcano to the village complex called Nahulahula. From there he used several trails to get down to the road where he got in a bemo (minibus) heading back to Pangururan. Round-trip from his hotel only took about 5 1/2 hours.

Plan on a full day for this hike. Also, you'll save a lot of time by returning the same way you climbed--the east ridge, rather than going down the old road and circling the mountain. Drier season is from January to August. There are buses every half hour from Pangururan to Tomok, and 7 or 8

Shown here is the northeast slope of Pusik Buhit, with a tomb & rice patties nearby, and the hot springs area (light colored) in the distance.

Map 281-1, Pusik Buhit, Toba Caldera, Sumatra, Indonesia

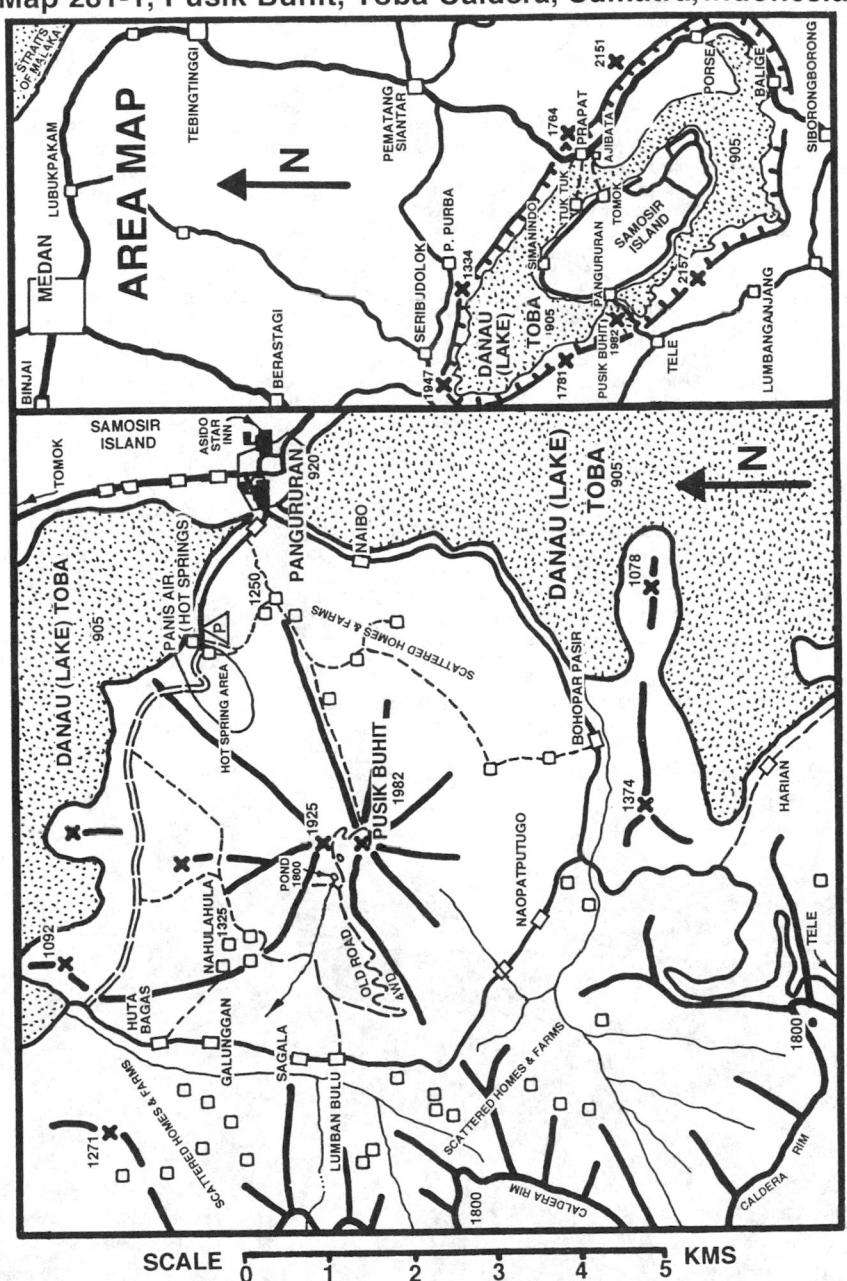

ferries a day between Tomok and Ajibata.

Maps Indonesian map *Pangururan, 0618-61*, 1:50,000; or DMA map *Pangururan, NA 47-6*, 1:250,000; and the latest edition of the map book **Indonesian Travel Atlas** from Periplus; and the latest travel guidebook to Indonesia.

Marapi & Singgalang, Sumatra, Indonesia

The mountain featured here is Gunung Api Marapi (Marapi Volcano) at 2891 meters. Also on this map is the older and extinct Singgalang Volcano at 2877 meters. Both are located in central Sumatra just south of the small highland city of Bukittinggi. The Trans-Sumatran Highway runs between these 2 peaks.

Marapi is a stratovolcano and perhaps Sumatra's most active. It has a broad summit area, with trees & brush covering the highest peak. West of the summit are 5 or 6 small active steaming craters within the 1 1/2-km-wide Bancah Caldera. About 50 small to moderate explosive-type eruptions have been recorded since the late 1700's. The last eruption was on 8/5/1999, less than a month before the author's visit. For volcano updates see the websites (www.vsi.dpe.go.id) or (www.volcano.si.edu/gvp/).

One local person told the author that **Singgalang** was not a popular hike and getting to the top wasn't easy, so with stormy weather and a tight schedule, the author made no attempt to climb it. Old maps do show one trail going to the summit from the north; another from the pass and Kotabaru. Trails may be overgrown and difficult to find without a guide, or a few words in Indonesian, so for more information, check with the tourist office in Bukittinggi, or with one of the tour agents who guide hikers up Marapi.

To climb **Marapi**, make your way to the bus terminal in the southeastern part of Bukittinggi and locate a bemo (minibus) running south to Kotabaru. Tell the driver to let you out at the *Jalan Kachil ki Marapi* (trail to Marapi). That should be at the side-road signposted *Jalan Tantawi*. This road first heads east, then north toward Batupalano. About 100 meters from the main highway is another paved road turning right or southeast. Walk this road about 3 1/2 kms until just before the microwave station, then turn left at the road-side shelter which is the beginning of the trail.

At first, this well-used trail heads east, then north, then east again, passing through farms & gardens until it reaches an old road at 1480 meters. Soon after that, you pass a spring on the left, then cross a gully on a bamboo bridge with the only running water on the mountain. Shortly after that, you'll pass a flat area where on weekends people sell food to hikers. That flat place is the end of the old bulldozed road. Then the trail heads due east up to the plateau with craters.

The author went up a different route. He walked to Batupalano, then headed up an old plantation road as shown. This is a longer route with lots of zig zagging. He made the summit area is 3 hours, then returned to Kotabaru via the normal route described above. Round-trip from Kotabaru was about 6 1/2 hours.

Stay in one of many hotels in Bukittinggi and get an early start. Do it in one day. This region is virtually on the equator and wet year-round; however, the drier time is from January through August. Take an umbrella & rain gear, and a compass so you don't get lost in clouds on the

From the Bangsu Crater rim looking northeast at the highest point on Marapi Volcano. Also seen are 2 other active, steaming craters.

Map 282-1, Marapi & Singgalang, Sumatra, Indonesia

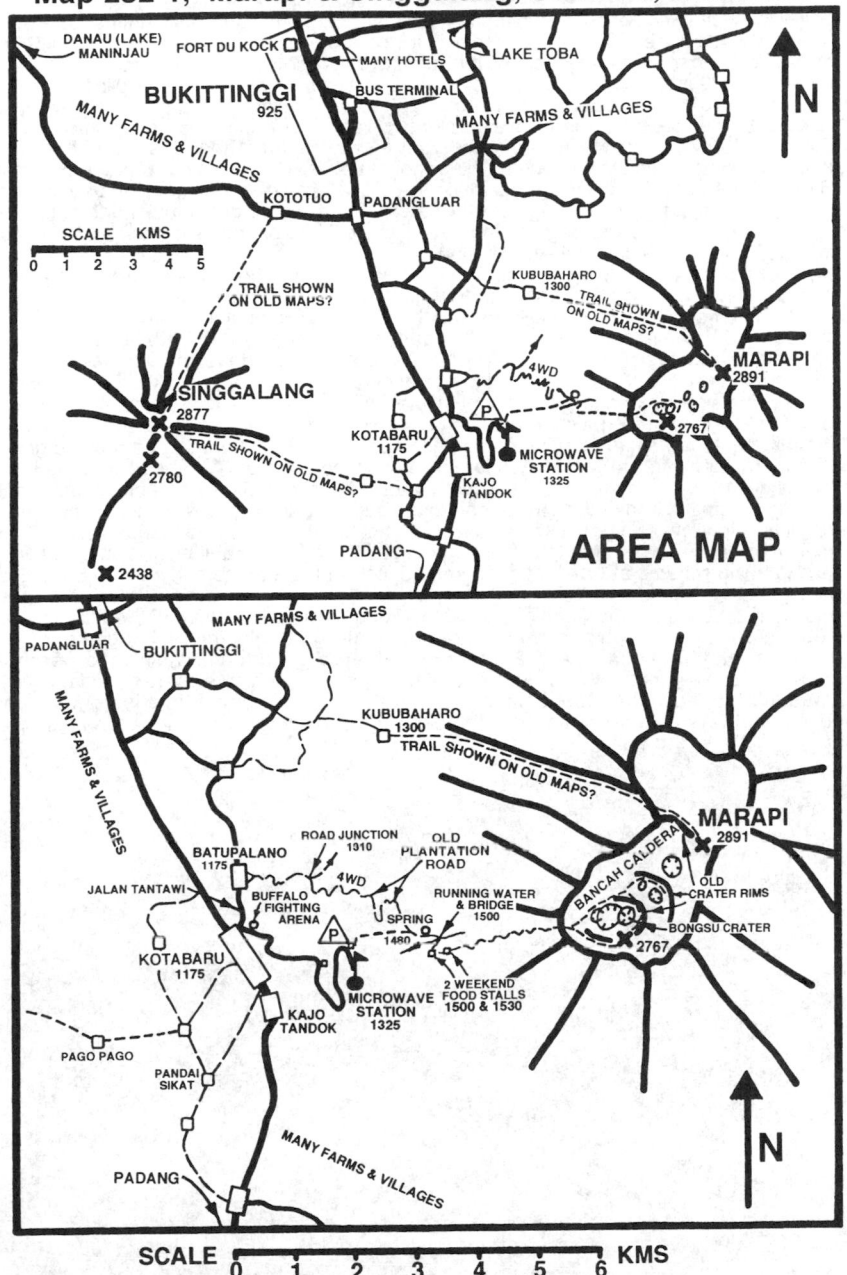

plateau.
Maps *Singgalang Tandikat* and *Marapi,* both 1:80,000 scale, from the VSI, Bandung, Java; or the DMA map *Padang, SA 47-3,* 1:250,000; and the map book **Indonesian Travel Atlas** from Periplus; and the latest travel guidebook to Indonesia.

Kerinci Volcano, Sumatra, Indonesia

The highest mountain and volcano in Indonesia outside of Irian Jaya, is Gunung Api Kerinci or Kerinci Volcano (pron. Kerinchi)) at 3808 meters. It's located in central Sumatra southeast of Padang. Kerinci is one of the more active volcanos on Sumatra and is now part of a national park. It towers from 2400 to 3300 meters above the surrounding plains, and has a 600-meter-wide crater at the summit. The last big explosive eruption was on 7/28/1999, with minor activity continuing into 9/1999. For volcano updates see the websites (www.vsi.dpe.go.id) or (www.volcano.si.edu/gvp/).

To get to **Kerinci** from the north, make your way to Padang, then take a 9 hour bus ride south to Krisik Tuo, which is just south of the mountain. If you're coming from the south along the Trans-Sumatran Highway, stop at Bangko and transfer to a bus or bemo going to Sungaipenuh (4 hours). From Sungaipenuh, catch another bemo or minibus north to Krisik Tuo (1 1/2 hours) where the climb begins. In Krisik Tuo, you'll find about 5 losmen and many small tokos (shops) where you can buy all your food.

Here's what the author did beginning 8/5/1999. He took a 5pm bus from Padang to Krisik Tuo, arriving at 3am. He and 2 other Indonesian hikers spent the rest of the night in a local mosque. Later, he checked into a losmen and the owner took him to the home of a national park employee. They convinced the author that both a free permit, and a guide were required-- because some people couldn't find their way! As it turned out, the losmen owner was a guide and he could take care of everything. How convenient! After that, breakfast and lunch were purchased at a small toko and by 8am, both were on a motorcycle riding through the Kayu Aro Tea Estate to the end of the paved road at 1785 meters. See map.

From there, they walked 10 minutes due north on a rocky road to a big unmanned gateway, where the trail begins. Three minutes later they passed the first of 4 shelters (roofs only--no walls) along the way, then the author hurried ahead of the guide and to the puncak (punchak) or peak alone. From the end of the paved road to the summit took 3 1/2 hours; and just under 6 1/2 hours round-trip. The author walked all the way back to Krisik Tuo and the statue of a tiger on the main highway in 7 1/3 hours total round-trip time. Because the author was so upset with the money-grabbing scheme at Krisik Tuo, he immediately got in a bemo and went to Sungaipenuh for the night.

Along the trail, the author met 4 groups of Indonesian hikers who were not required to have a permit or a guide! You can avoid this scheme by telling people you're just going for a walk through the tea plantation. Take 2-3 liters of water, a good lunch, and get an early start. Perhaps hire an ojek (motorcycle taxi) to get to the trailhead. Most foreigners need from 10 to 12 hours round-trip, but most Indonesians camp one night. The driest time is from January to August--but always take rainrear and a compass. Observe directions and landmarks carefully

Kerinci Volcano as seen from Krisik Tuo and the road junction with tiger statue on the right. This is the road you take to reach the trailhead.

Map 283-1, Kerinci Volcano, Sumatra, Indonesia

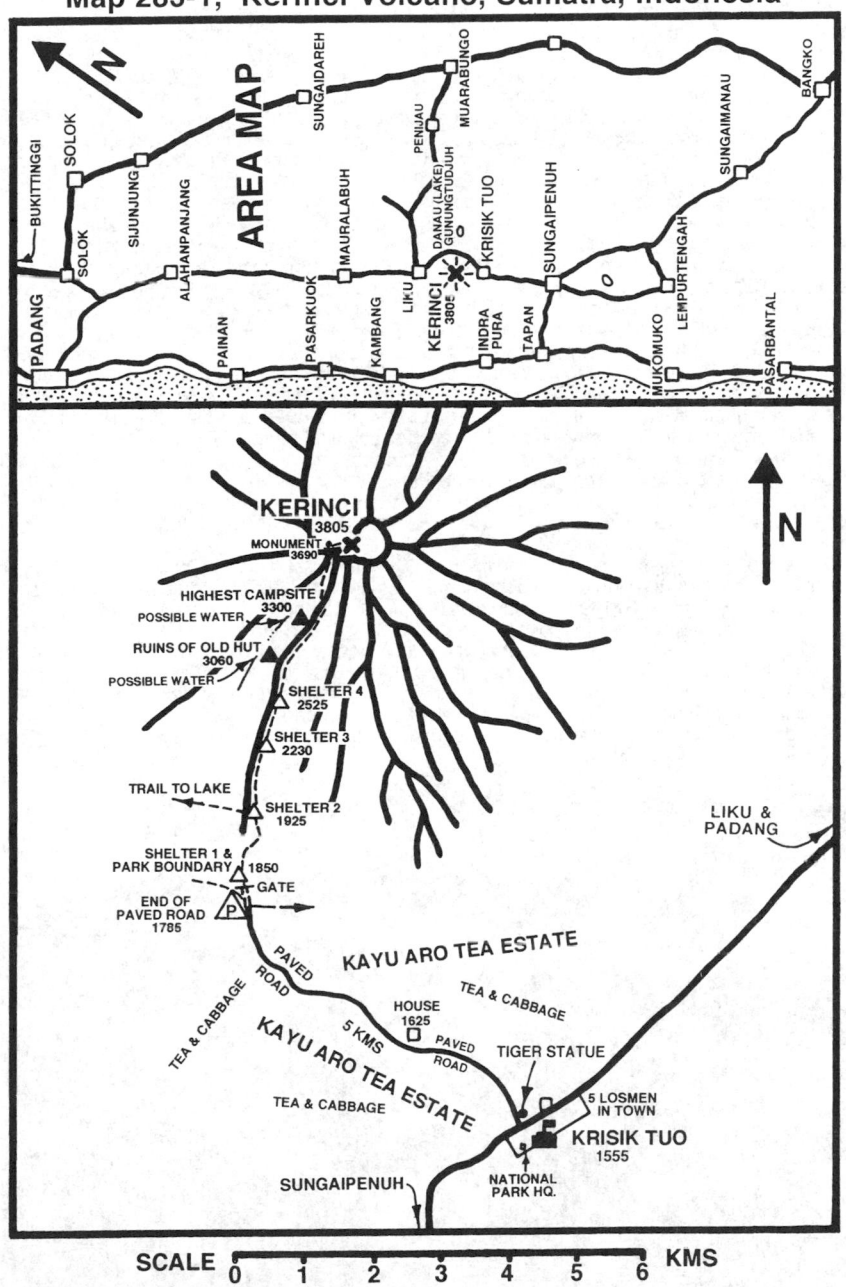

SCALE 0 1 2 3 4 5 6 **KMS**

going up the last 400 meters, so you return along the right trail.
Maps This map is the best; or *Puntjak G. Kerintji,* 1:80,000, from the VSI, Bandung, Java; DMA
map *Painan, SA 48-13,* 1:250,000; and the latest travel guidebook to Indonesia.

Anak Krakatau, between Sumatra & Java, Indonesia

Anak Krakatau, which means *Child of Krakatau*, is a small volcanic island located about halfway between Sumatra and Java. During the author's visit on 9/9/1999, its altitude was determined to be 285 meters, according to his altimeter.

Krakatau Volcano has had a very explosive history. At one time the prehistoric Krakatau (Stage 1) was an island 11 kms in diameter and over 2000 meters high. It exploded leaving 3 small islands and a big hole. Recent geological studies and investigations of ancient religions writings, have led some researchers to believe this may have occurred in 535 AD (?). Later, Rakata became active, along with 2 smaller volcanos approximately where Anak Krakatau is now (Stage 2). They later merged forming an island measuring 9x5 kms. On 8/26 & 27/1883, a series of cataclysmic explosions (rated a VEI-6) occurred which were heard as far away as South Australia and Ceylon (Sri Lanka). The biggest blast generated tsunamis (tidal waves) that killed 36,000 people living along the shores of the nearby Sunda Straits. The tsunamis even registered in the English Channel. Ships passing that way a few days later encountered floating pumice 2 meters deep. Later, underwater eruptions occurred and finally on 8/12/1928, Anak Krakatau emerged from the sea and has been growing above sea level ever since. For volcano updates see the websites (www.vsi.dpe.go.id) or (www.volcano.si.edu/gvp/).

Because the 1883 explosion is considered the 2nd biggest in documented human history (Tambora was the biggest), it has now become an international tourist attraction. To visit and climb **Anak Krakatau**, take one of many buses west from Jakarta to the coastal tourist town of Carita (pron. Charita). You can charter boats to Anak Krakatau from several different towns along the coast, but the place most tourists go to is Carita. Once there, check into a hotel and ask about boats. For sure, someone from one of the little travel agents will contact you right a way.

The author arrived in the late afternoon from Sumatra, and arranged to be in a boat with 4 other Swedish tourists the next morning. Each paid about US$31. In the off season, you may have to wait a day or two for others to make a group--or pay for the entire boat yourself--perhaps as much as US$150! These speedboats are about 6-7 meters long, have twin outboard motors of 40 to 60 hp each, and can carry up to 10-12 passengers.

The author's group left about 8am and it took 1 3/4 hours to arrive at the black sand landing beach as shown. In another 40 minutes or so the author was on top. It was quiet at the time, but earlier in 1999 it was active--until 8/16/1999. On the way back to Carita, the boat stopped just off the east coast of Rakata and the group snorkeled a while on a small reef. Round-trip from Carita took about 6 hours.

You can climb Anak Krakatau about anytime, but the dry season for west Java is from April or May through October. August is the driest month, but it can be hazy. Toward the end of the dry season, strong winds may blow. Buy a lunch in Carita before you leave, and take a liter or two of water, plus a hat for shade and a plastic bag to protect your camera from sea spray.

Maps *Geologic Map of Krakatau Volcano Complex,* 1:25,000, from VSI, Bandung, Java; and the

Aerial postcard view of Anak Krakatau looking west at Sertung Island beyond.

Map 284-1, Krakatau, between Sumatra & Java, Indonesia

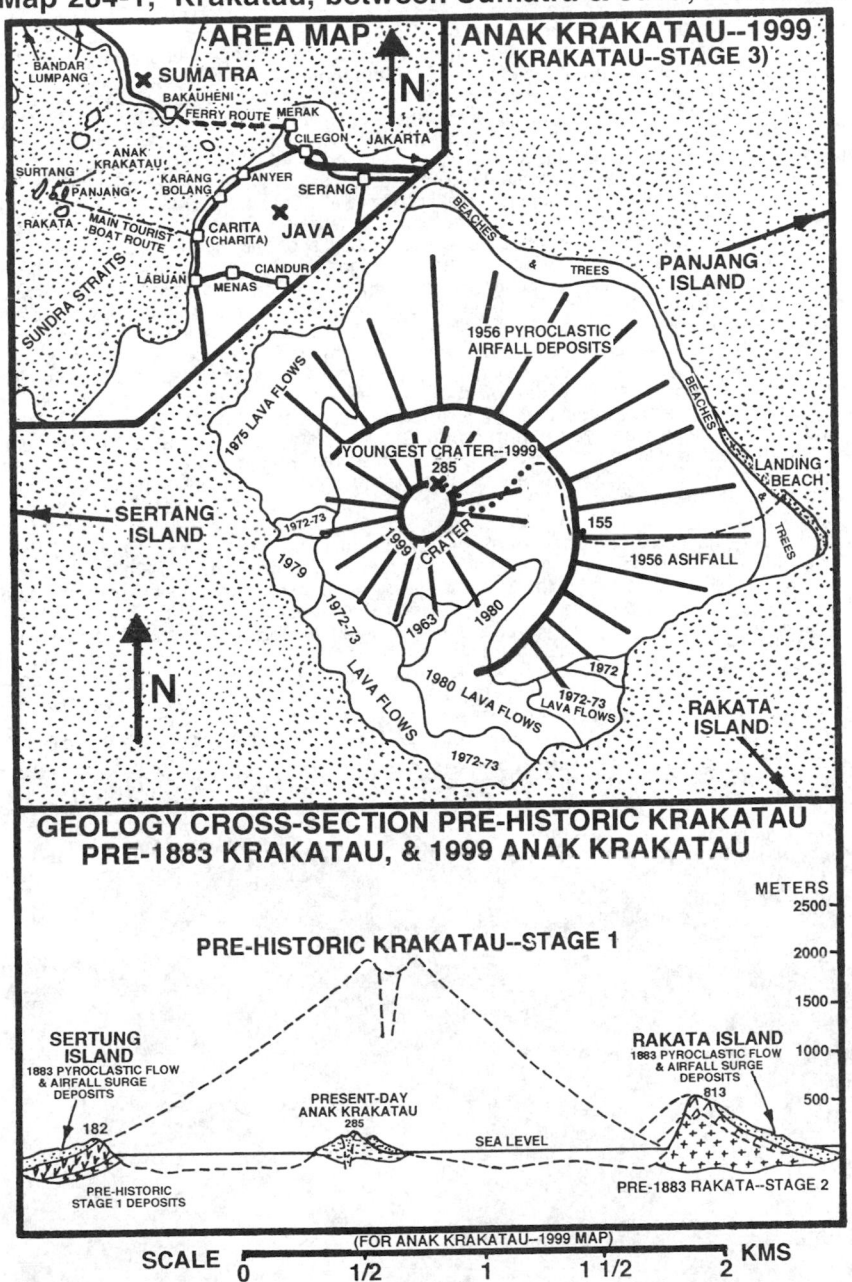

AREA MAP

BANDAR LUMPANG
SUMATRA
BAKAUHENI
FERRY ROUTE MERAK
CILEGON JAKARTA
ANAK KRAKATAU
SURTANG
KARANG BOLANG ANYER
PANJANG SERANG
RAKATA MAIN TOURIST BOAT ROUTE
CARITA (CHARITA) **JAVA**
CIANDUR
LABUAN MENAS
SUNDRA STRAITS

N

ANAK KRAKATAU--1999
(KRAKATAU--STAGE 3)

BEACHES
& TREES
PANJANG ISLAND
1956 PYROCLASTIC AIRFALL DEPOSITS
BEACHES
1975 LAVA FLOWS
LANDING BEACH
YOUNGEST CRATER--1999
285
TREES
SERTANG ISLAND
1972-73
155
1979 1999 CRATER
1956 ASHFALL
1972-73 1963 1980
1980 LAVA FLOWS
LAVA FLOWS 1972-73 LAVA FLOWS 1972
1972-73 **RAKATA ISLAND**

N

GEOLOGY CROSS-SECTION PRE-HISTORIC KRAKATAU
PRE-1883 KRAKATAU, & 1999 ANAK KRAKATAU

METERS
2500

PRE-HISTORIC KRAKATAU--STAGE 1
2000

1500

SERTUNG ISLAND
1883 PYROCLASTIC FLOW & AIRFALL SURGE DEPOSITS
RAKATA ISLAND
1883 PYROCLASTIC FLOW & AIRFALL SURGE DEPOSITS
1000

PRESENT-DAY ANAK KRAKATAU
285
813
500
182
SEA LEVEL
PRE-HISTORIC STAGE 1 DEPOSITS
PRE-1883 RAKATA--STAGE 2

SCALE	(FOR ANAK KRAKATAU--1999 MAP)				KMS
0	1/2	1	1 1/2	2	

booklet, **A Guide to Krakatau**, I.W.B. Thornton, Zoology Dept., La Trobe University, Melbourne, Australia (hopefully you can get both of these at Carita, which the author did, or the VSI); and the latest travel guidebook to Indonesia.

Gede and Pangrango Volcanos, Java, Indonesia

The 2 volcanos on this map are Gede at 2958 meters, and Pangrango at 3019. They're located south of Jakarta, southeast of Bogor, and east of Bandung, in western Java. Both are now part of a national park. Pangrango as seen from the northeast has a forested perfect symmetrically shaped cone which actually sits on top of a much older caldera rim. It's now considered extinct. Gede is inside an older caldera, the rim of which is seen to the south & east. Gede is a younger crater which opens to the northwest. Inside it is a small active crater which last exploded on 3/13/1957. In the 1990's, there was seismic activity, but no eruptions. For volcano updates see the websites (www.vsi.dpe.go.id) or (www.volcano.si.edu/gvp/).

These peaks are in a heavily populated region and because they're higher is altitude and only 75 kms or so from Jakarta, it's a very popular weekend getaway. On the Jakarta-side of Puncak (pron. Punchak), the highway is lined with holiday hotels, resorts, restaurants and warungs (food stalls). Because of this, the trails to these 2 peaks are often overused, especially on weekends.

To get there, take a bus or train from Jakarta to Bogor, then a bemo to the main bus terminal. From there take a bus or bemo heading for Bandung, but tell the conductor to stop in Rarahan at the *jalan ki Cibodas* (road to Cibodas). From the highway junction, jump into one of many small bemos running uphill about 5 kms to Cibodas (pron. Chibodas). There you'll find at least 3 family run losmen (small hotels) and many warungs, especially in the upper end of town near the botanical gardens.

To climb the volcanos, walk to the entry to the gardens, but turn right on the paved road heading up toward a golf course. Halfway there, turn left at the sign and staircase leading up to a ridge top. About 100 meters from the road is a visitor center where you pay an entrance fee at the beginning of the trail.

The trail up to the pass between **Pangrango & Gede** is heavily-used and has a number of old and broken-down shelters. Some may provide shelter from a thunderstorm, but none were fit to sleep in during the author's visit on 9/11/1999; except perhaps the highest one at 2380 meters. But that one may be reserved for park rangers (?). You'll also pass some hot water (panas air) running right across the trail.

From that highest hut, turn left and look for signs pointing the way to Gede. Soon you may see another sign, and trail heading to the right going Pangrango. A couple of minutes later will be another trail junction; take the one to the left to get inside the kawah (crater); or veer right to reach the puncak or summit of Gede. Or take the trail from or near the highest hut to reach the puncak of Pangrango. The view from Gede is excellent, but you can't see a thing from the top of Pangrango because of trees.

From his losmen in upper Cibodas, the author climbed both peaks in about 6 3/4 hours, round-trip. Most hikers will need up to 10-12 hours. Make this climb in one day only and forget about camping. The dry season is from about May through October, but you can climb year-round. Buy all your food supplies in Cibodas. Avoid this place on weekends if possible because of big crowds.

Maps *Tjitjurug, 4323 II* & *Tjiandjur, 4422 IV*, both 1:50,000; get copies of these at the VSI in Bandung;

From the top of Gede, looking at the active crater below and Pangrango in the distance.

Map 285-1, Gede & Pangrango Volcanos, Java, Indonesia

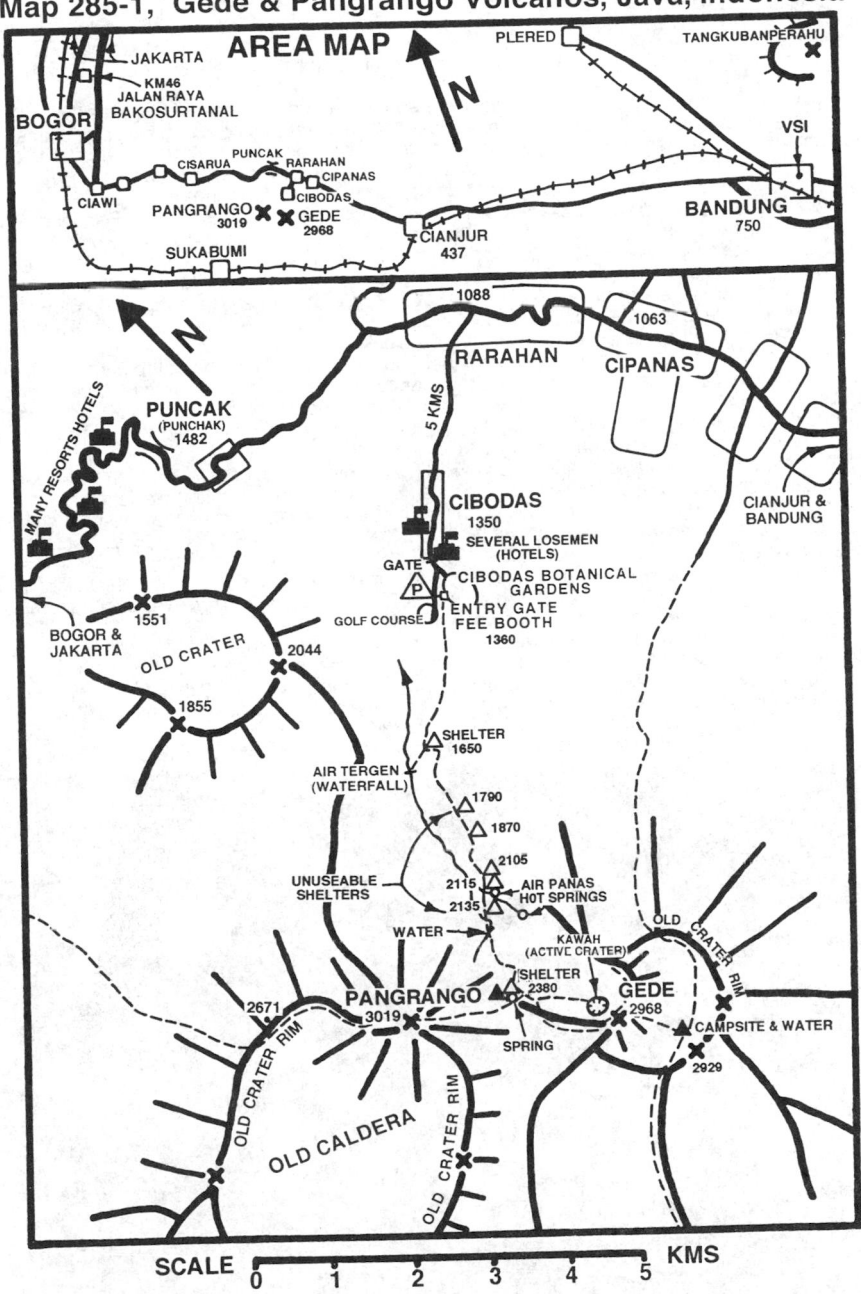

AREA MAP

JAKARTA
KM46
JALAN RAYA
BAKOSURTANAL
BOGOR
CIAWI
CISARUA
PUNCAK
RARAHAN
CIPANAS
CIBODAS
PANGRANGO 3019
GEDE 2968
SUKABUMI
CIANJUR 437
PLERED
TANGKUBANPERAHU
VSI
BANDUNG 750
N

1088
1063
RARAHAN
CIPANAS
PUNCAK
(PUNCHAK)
1482
MANY RESORTS HOTELS
5 KMS
CIBODAS
1350
SEVERAL LOSEMEN
(HOTELS)
CIANJUR &
BANDUNG
GATE
P
CIBODAS BOTANICAL
GARDENS
ENTRY GATE
FEE BOOTH
1360
GOLF COURSE
BOGOR &
JAKARTA
1551
OLD CRATER
2044
1855
SHELTER
1650
AIR TERGEN
(WATERFALL)
1790
1870
2105
UNUSEABLE
SHELTERS
2115
2135
AIR PANAS
HOT SPRINGS
WATER
KAWAH
(ACTIVE CRATER)
OLD CRATER RIM
2671
PANGRANGO
3019
SHELTER
2380
SPRING
GEDE
2968
CAMPSITE & WATER
2929
OLD CRATER RIM
OLD CALDERA
OLD CRATER RIM
N

SCALE 0 1 2 3 4 5 KMS

or at the Bedan Koordinasi Survey dan Pemetaan Nasional (BAKOSURTANAL), Jalan Raya, Jakarta-
-Bogor, Km 46. See its location on this map. And the latest travel guidebook to Indonesia.

Slamet Volcano, Java, Indonesia

This map features Slamet Volcano (Gunung Api Slamet). At 3432 meters, this is the 2nd highest mountain and/or volcano on Java. Slamet is located near the center of the island, directly south of the coastal city of Tegal, and due north of Purwokerto. It's also due west of the twin volcanos of Sundoro and Sumbing.

Slamet has 2 dozen cinder cones on its lower southeast and northeast flanks, plus the Malang II cinder cone near the summit on the east side. The Malang II crater once sent a lava flow 6 kms down the eastern slopes. Slamet also has a small active crater inside a larger crater at the summit. The last eruptive period was from 7 to 9/1999, when ash clouds reached 400 meters above the summit. For volcano updates see the websites (www.vsi.dpe.go.id) or (www.volcano.si.edu/gvp/).

Here's what the author did on **Slamet**. On 9/12/1999, he got an early start from Bandung (west of this area--see the Gede & Pangrango map), which is where the Volcanological Survey of Indonesia is located. He took a long distance bus heading for Semarang, but got off at Tegal. From there he got in a bemo (minibus) heading south. He was let off at Yomani, where he got into a small bus heading for Bumijawa and the hot springs resort town of Guci (pron. Guchi). That entire trip using 3 buses took about 8 hours. On that day, which was Sunday, there were dozens of buses and bemos making the run from Yomani to Guci. Expect fewer vehicles on weekdays.

He checked into the Lestari Villa Hotel for just under US$4 a night, one of the cheaper places in Guci. He walked around town observing a thousand or more Indonesian tourists and hundreds of wurangs (food stalls) selling corn-on-the-cob and other goodies, plus he located the route up the mountain. He also had a bath in the hot water (panas air) spring & pool, along with many others, including some older women who were topless--in Moslem Indonesia(?!).

Next morning, he got a 6am start. He walked up the dirt & cobblestone road for about 3 kms to where it turned right near a blue & white roof-only shelter. He lost 15 minutes wandering around, until he gave some women a small tip to get him on the right trail. **A warning**--in that area are small 1 to 2-meter-high pine trees and corn fields. By 2005 to 2010, those trees may be too large for farmers to grow corn, and the trails may change.

Once on the trail, he went along a ridge, first in the open, then into a pine forest plantation. Higher up, the pines ended and a natural forest began. At 2800 meters, the trees gave way to open lava, and a steep trail marked with stone cairns. Follow the markers closely.

On the crater rim, the author experienced the strongest winds (near 90 kph) he's ever had while climbing. Walking was so difficult he didn't quite reach the highest point on the rim. On the way down he unknowingly took a left turn on a side trail (see map) and lost another 45 minutes. From his hotel, round-trip time was 7 1/4 hours--or about 6 1/4 hours if not counting lost time. Later, he had another hot bath, took a pickup down to Yomani, then a bus to Purwokerto for the night.

Dry season is May through October. Be sure to take a compass so you don't get lost in the clouds

Slamet's summit is in the distance as seen from the blue & white shelter.

Map 286-1, Slamet Volcano, Java, Indonesia

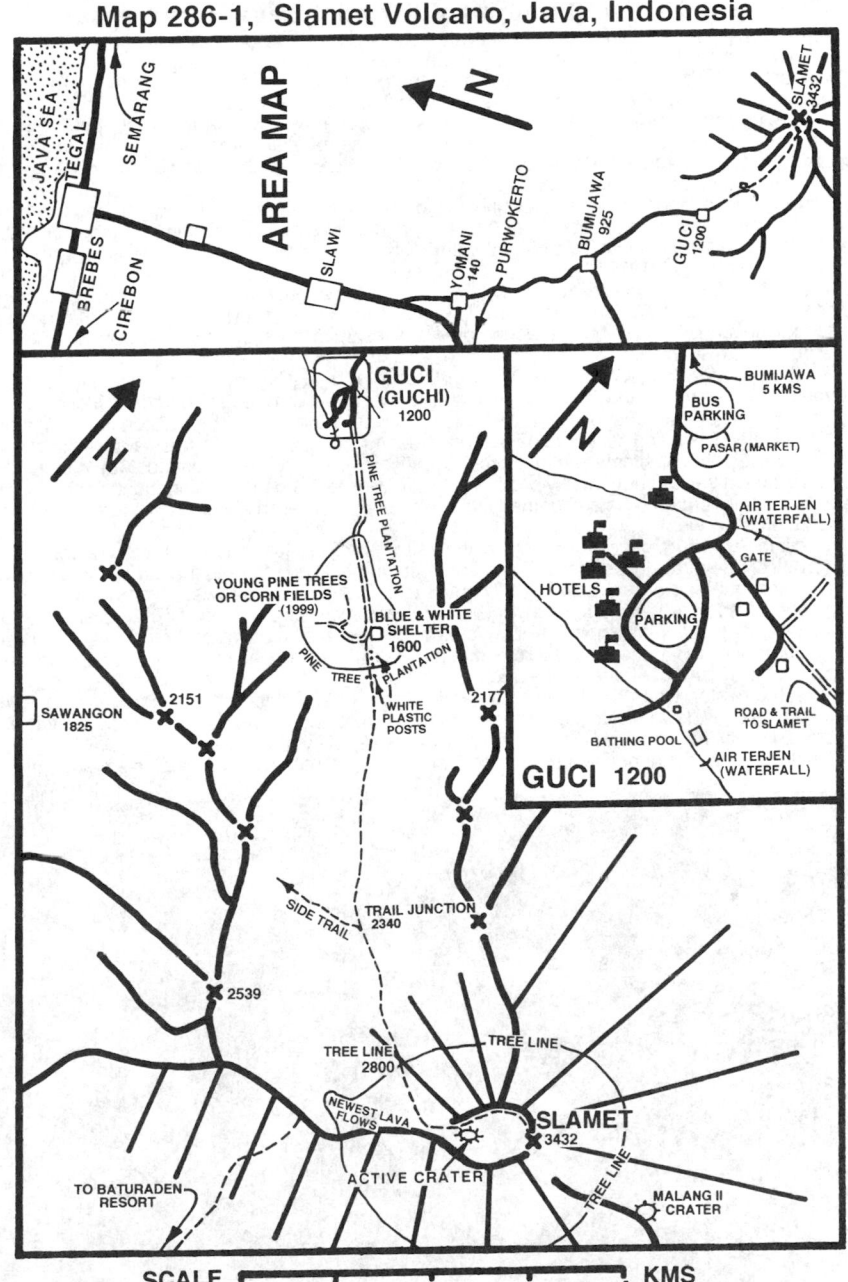

AREA MAP

JAVA SEA

TEGAL

SEMARANG

BREBES

CIREBON

SLAWI

YOMANI 140

PURWOKERTO

BUMIJAWA 925

GUCI 1200

SLAMET 3432

GUCI (GUCHI) 1200

PINE TREE PLANTATION

YOUNG PINE TREES OR CORN FIELDS (1999)

BLUE & WHITE SHELTER 1600

PINE TREE PLANTATION

WHITE PLASTIC POSTS

SAWANGON 1825

2151

2177

SIDE TRAIL

TRAIL JUNCTION 2340

2539

TREE LINE 2800

TREE LINE

NEWEST LAVA FLOWS

SLAMET 3432

TO BATURADEN RESORT

ACTIVE CRATER

TREE LINE

MALANG II CRATER

BUMIJAWA 5 KMS

BUS PARKING

PASAR (MARKET)

AIR TERJEN (WATERFALL)

HOTELS

GATE

PARKING

ROAD & TRAIL TO SLAMET

BATHING POOL

AIR TERJEN (WATERFALL)

GUCI 1200

SCALE 0 1 2 3 4 **KMS**

coming down above the forest, or take a wrong trail. There's no water along the way, so take 3 liters with you. You'll need it.

Maps *Bumiaju, 4821 III,* 1:50,000, from the VSI, or BAKOSURTANAL; and the latest travel guidebook to Indonesia.

Sundoro & Sumbing Volcanos, Java, Indonesia

This map shows 2 of the higher volcanos on Java; Sundoro (locally called Sindoro) at 3151 meters, and Sumbing at 3371 meters. This whole area is northwest of Jogjakarta and east & northeast of Wonosobo, which is the small gateway city to the Hindu archeological sites on the Dieng Plateau. Wonosobo is on the main east-west highway running through central Java.

These are both stratovolcanos. Sumbing's last eruption may have been in 1730, but that's not for sure. Sundoro's last eruption was on 11/9/1971. It was a small category VEI-2 phreatic (steam) explosion, but it's been quiet ever since. For volcano updates see the websites (www.vsi.dpe.go.id) or (www.volcano.si.edu/gvp/).

To climb these mountains, it's probably best to use Wonosobo as a base, which has a number of hotels and/or losmen (from about US$2.50 and up) and a good market or pasar. You can also stay at the Kledung Pass Hotel (with TV and hot water), which was expensive by Indonesian standards at about US$11 a night in 9/1999.

The author stayed in the Wisata Duta Homestay located about one km north of the bus terminal in Wonosobo and on a main east-west street. Near that losmen is where buses begin the run to both Dieng and Kledung. Wonosobo to Kledung by bus takes 30 minutes and the cost was only US$.20 in 9/1999.

To climb **Sundoro**, get out at the Kledung Pass Hotel, or at Kledung village (Kledung desa) about 300 meters to the northeast. Walk northwest through the desa, then along a road for 2 1/2 kms heading straight for the summit. Just beyond where the road ends, turn left at the trail junction. Higher up, you'll go through fields and scattered pine trees. Veer right at one junction, cross a dry gully, then turn uphill just beyond the shelter with a metal roof & hiker's graffiti. Highest fields are 2055 meters. From there, it's a good trail through mostly brush and small trees to the puncak (pron. punchak) or summit, which has a small crater. The author made this climb on 9/15/1999 in about 2 1/3 hours from Kledung; round-trip was 5 hours.

To climb **Sumbing**, get out of the bus at the Jalan Sumbing (Sumbing Road) and Garung desa. At that turnoff are several shops or tokos and one restaurant called *Wurang Makan Susy*. Just up the road is a mosque and a bank and beyond that a microwave or radio tower. Garung is one narrow village about 1 1/2 kms long. At the upper end, turn right and walk along a road into a canyon, cross a normally-dry creek bed, then up the trail which follows a ridge all the way to the puncak. If you come to a confusing junction, there's usually someone around in the fields who can point out the *jalan kacil ki puncak* (trail to summit). At about 2820 meters, the trail veers left to avoid a steep ridge.

Most hikers stop when they reach the kawah (crater) rim instead of walking another 1 1/2 kms along a rough up & down trail to the highest point on the other side. The author reached the kawah on 9/16/1999 in 2 3/4 hours; round-trip from the highway was just over 5 hours.

The trails on both mountains are good, with an occasional metal arrow nailed to a tree pointing the

From the highest fields on Sumbing looking northwest at Sundoro. The white dot on the pass below is the Kledung Pass Hotel.

Map 287-1, Sundoro & Sumbing, Java, Indonesia

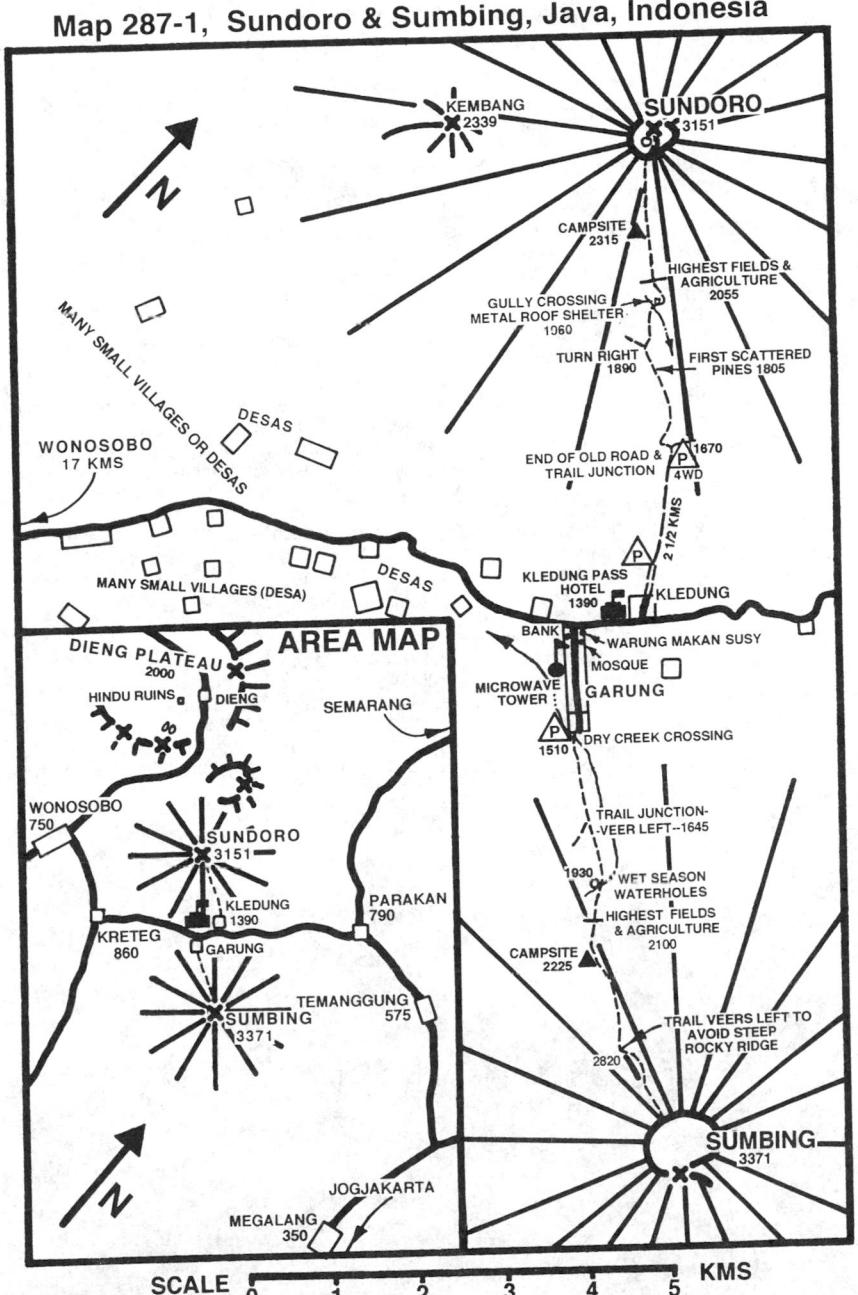

KEMBANG
X 2339

SUNDORO
X 3151

CAMPSITE
2315

HIGHEST FIELDS &
AGRICULTURE
2055

GULLY CROSSING
METAL ROOF SHELTER
1060

FIRST SCATTERED
PINES 1805

TURN RIGHT
1890

MANY SMALL VILLAGES OR DESAS

DESAS

WONOSOBO
17 KMS

END OF OLD ROAD &
TRAIL JUNCTION

P 1670
4WD

2 1/2 KMS

P

MANY SMALL VILLAGES (DESA)

DESAS

KLEDUNG PASS
HOTEL
1390

KLEDUNG

AREA MAP

BANK

WARUNG MAKAN SUSY

DIENG PLATEAU
2000

MOSQUE

HINDU RUINS

DIENG

SEMARANG

MICROWAVE
TOWER

GARUNG

P
1510

DRY CREEK CROSSING

WONOSOBO
750

SUNDORO
X 3151

TRAIL JUNCTION-
-VEER LEFT--1645

1930

WET SEASON
WATERHOLES

KLEDUNG
1390

PARAKAN
790

HIGHEST FIELDS
& AGRICULTURE
2100

KRETEG
860

GARUNG

CAMPSITE
2225

TEMANGGUNG
575

SUMBING
3371

TRAIL VEERS LEFT TO
AVOID STEEP
ROCKY RIDGE

2820

SUMBING
3371

JOGJAKARTA

MEGALANG
350

SCALE 0 1 2 3 4 5 KMS

way to the puncak. Take 2-3 liters of water and a lunch on each volcano. Also, get an early start to beat the clouds. If you're not a fast hiker, it might be best to stay in the Kledung Pass Hotel; that way you'd have more day-light hours for climbing.

Maps *Batur, 4921 II, Temanggung, 5021 III, Magelang, 5020 IV, & Wonosobo, 4920, I*, all at 1:50,000; or DMA map *SB 49-14*, 1:250,000; and the latest travel guidebook to Indonesia.

Merbabu and Merapi Volcanos, Java, Indonesia

Located in central Java are 2 interesting volcanos and hikes. The highest of the two is Merbabu at 3142 meters; and Merapi, 2919 meters. Since these volcanos are so near each other, and the trail to the top of each begins in the same village, one might as well climb both peaks while in the area. The village of Selo, located between the two and at a cool and delightful 1500 meters, is the normal starting point for both climbs. Even if you're not a mountain climber, this is a nice place to get away from the tropical heat.

Merbabu is an older volcano; its last volcanic activity was in 1797. It's now considered dormant. Merapi on the other hand, is one of Indonesias most active volcanos. On 11/22/1994, it sent a pyroclastic flow down the SW slopes killing 41 people who refused to be evacuated. It's last activity was from 3 to 5/1999. At that time, pyroclastic flows raced down the southern slopes for 1.8 kms. No deaths were reported at that time. Activity on Merapi is ongoing. For volcano updates see the websites (www.vsi.dpe.go.id) or (www.volcano.si.edu/gvp/).

To climb both peaks, first go to the tourist town of Jogyakarta, located south of both volcanos. Take a large bus from Jogyakarta to Solo, then another to Boyolali. From Boyolali, take another smaller bus or bemo west to Cepoco (pron. Chepoco), and finally to Selo. Or, in Solo, wait for one of about 4 large buses making the daily run up over the pass to Selo and down to Magelang. Another way there, if coming from the west, is to begin in Magelang. Take one of these large buses toward Solo, and get off at Selo. In Selo, there are several stores, many food stalls called wurangs, and several little family run hotels called losmen or homestays.

An alternative way to climb Merapi is to take a bus or bemo north from Jogyakarta 25 kms to the hill resort of Kaliurang at 900 meters. There you'll find hotels and a trail up the mountain, but that's where the avalanches or pyroclastic flows come down. When the mountain is alive and rumbling, they often officially close this route.

To climb **Merapi** by the normal route, walk from the center of Selo about 2 kms west, then at Jalan Merapi (Merapi Street), turn south. After about 2 more kms the homes and the street end and the trail begins. There are several trails at the beginning, but higher up they combine into one. There's a crater at the top always emitting smoke and fumes from a lava dome. During eruptions, its red lava can be seen at night from Jogyakarta. The last water is from a tap at the junction of Jalan Merapi and the main highway.

To climb **Merbabu**, head east from the town center to Jalan Merbabu and walk north about 2 kms to where the road ends in at couple of small villages. From the end, or near the end of that road, there are several trails going up and west to a ridge top. Once on the ridge, it's easy to find the one single trail going to the summit. When the author climbed these volcanos on consecutive days 5/18 & 5/19/1977, this trail was well-used by local farmers who climbed to the upper slopes to cut wood. On top of this eroded volcano, is a small platform and what appears

The very active Merapi Volcano seen from the summit of Merbabu. Selo is to the left.

Map 288-1, Merbabu & Merapi Volcanos, Java, Indonesia

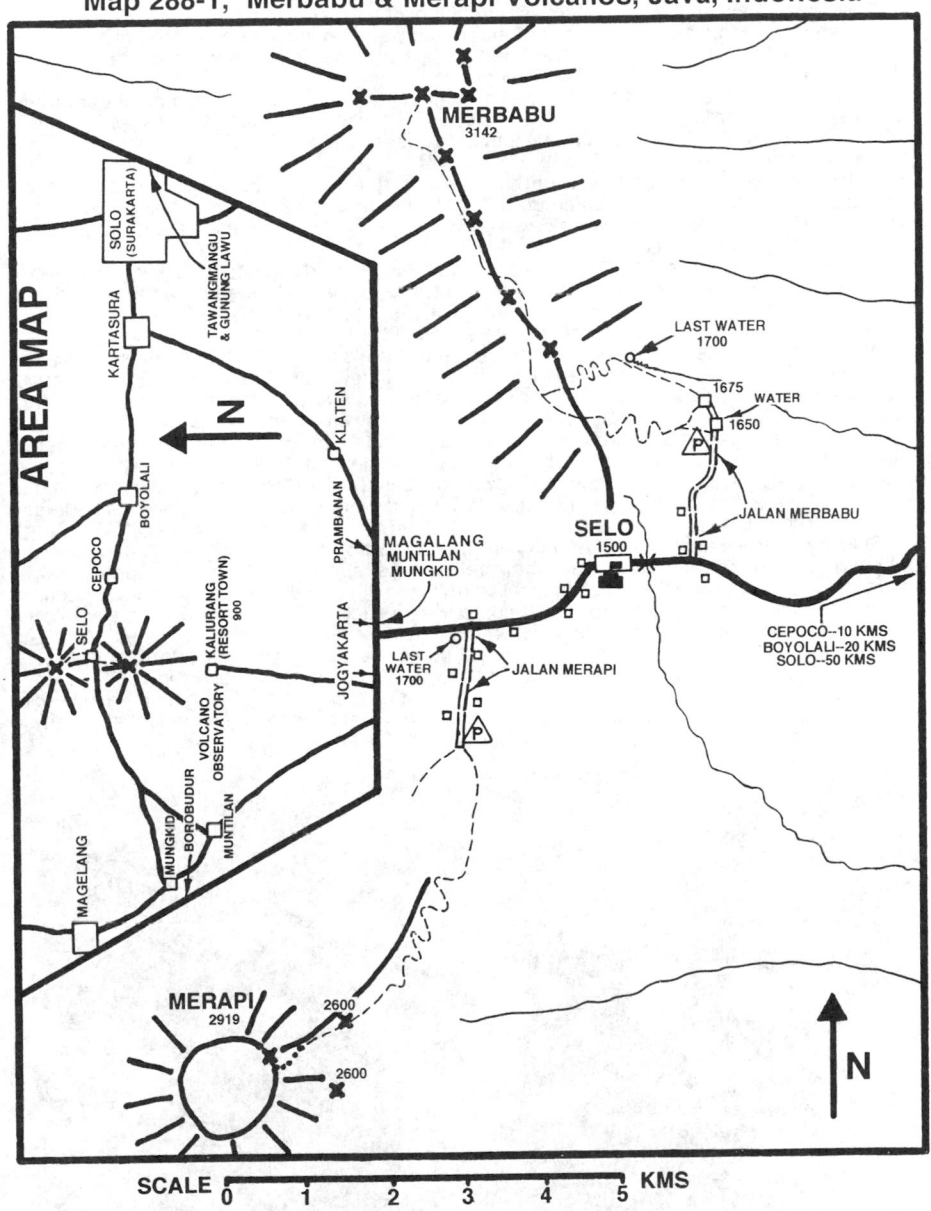

to be a religious shrine.

Maps *Grabag* and *Muntilan,* 1:50,000, from VSI or BAKOSURTANAL; DMA map *Jogjakarta, SB 49-14,* 1:250,000; and the book, **Indonesia Travel Atlas**, from Periplus; and the latest travel guidebook to Indonesia.

Gunung Lawu, Java, Indonesia

Gunung (Mt.) Lawu at 3265 meters, is one of the more interesting mountains on Java. Like many summits on this most-populated of Indonesian islands, it's a heavily forested & eroded volcano but still retains a symmetrical shape. It's last eruptive period was sometime during the Holocene, which is within the last 10,000 years.

Lawu is one of the most important holy mountains on Java. Old Hindu temples are found near the summit and on the lower western slopes. To visit these west-side temples, start in Karangpandan and take a bemo northeast, then hike from the villages of Kemuning and Jenawi to Candi (Temple) Ceto or Candi Sukuh.

Getting to **Lawu** is quite easy. From the west, start in Solo. Take a bus to the hill resort town of Tawang Mangu, then a bemo up and over the pass toward another hill station called Sarangan. Get out at or near Cemoro Sewu (CS). However, there are few if any facilities at CS, so most people stay in Sarangan.

The way most people get to this mountain is from the east side. Start in Madiun. Take a bus to Magetan, then you'll likely have to change to a smaller bemo to reach the tourist resort of Sarangan. During the author's climb on 5/17/1977, there wasn't a lot of traffic between Sarangan and Tawang Mangu, but today there's more.

At Sarangan, located at a delightful 1250 meters, there's a small lake with boats to rent and a large selection of hotels--both cheap and expensive. It doesn't have a large market place, but still there's good a selection of tokos or shops and food stalls to choose from. The author recommends Sarangan as the place to make headquarters while climbing Lawu.

West of Sarangan is Cemoro Sewu, where a couple of TV or radio towers were located. This distance is only 5 kms and can be walked in one hour; or hire a motorcycle taxi called *ojeks*. Immediately west of the bridge, as shown on the map, is the beginning of the trail going to the top. Or use the road heading north past the TV-Radio Antenna, then the trail. It's well-used and in good condition.

This trail is used annually by thousands of people who make the pilgrimage to the Hindu temple & rest stop (darma) near the summit called Argodalam Pondok. Hindu-Buddhism was the religion of Java before the Arabs brought Islam in the 8th and 9th centuries (Hindu-Buddhism still survives today on the islands of Bali & Lombok). Even though Java is mostly Islamic today, many old traditions still survive; one of which is to make offerings on mountain tops. All along the trail, especially at the huts marked on the map, you surely will see offerings of food & flowers. All these huts, except Argodalam Pondok, were bamboo-type shelters in 1977.

There's water at several points along the trail; see the map. From Sarangan, it's a long one-day hike (made shorter by using an ojek), but with the many shelters, an overnight stay can be enjoyed. The rainier season is from November through April.

This is the Argodalam Pondok at the summit of Lawu.

Map 289-1, Gunung Lawu, Java, Indonesia

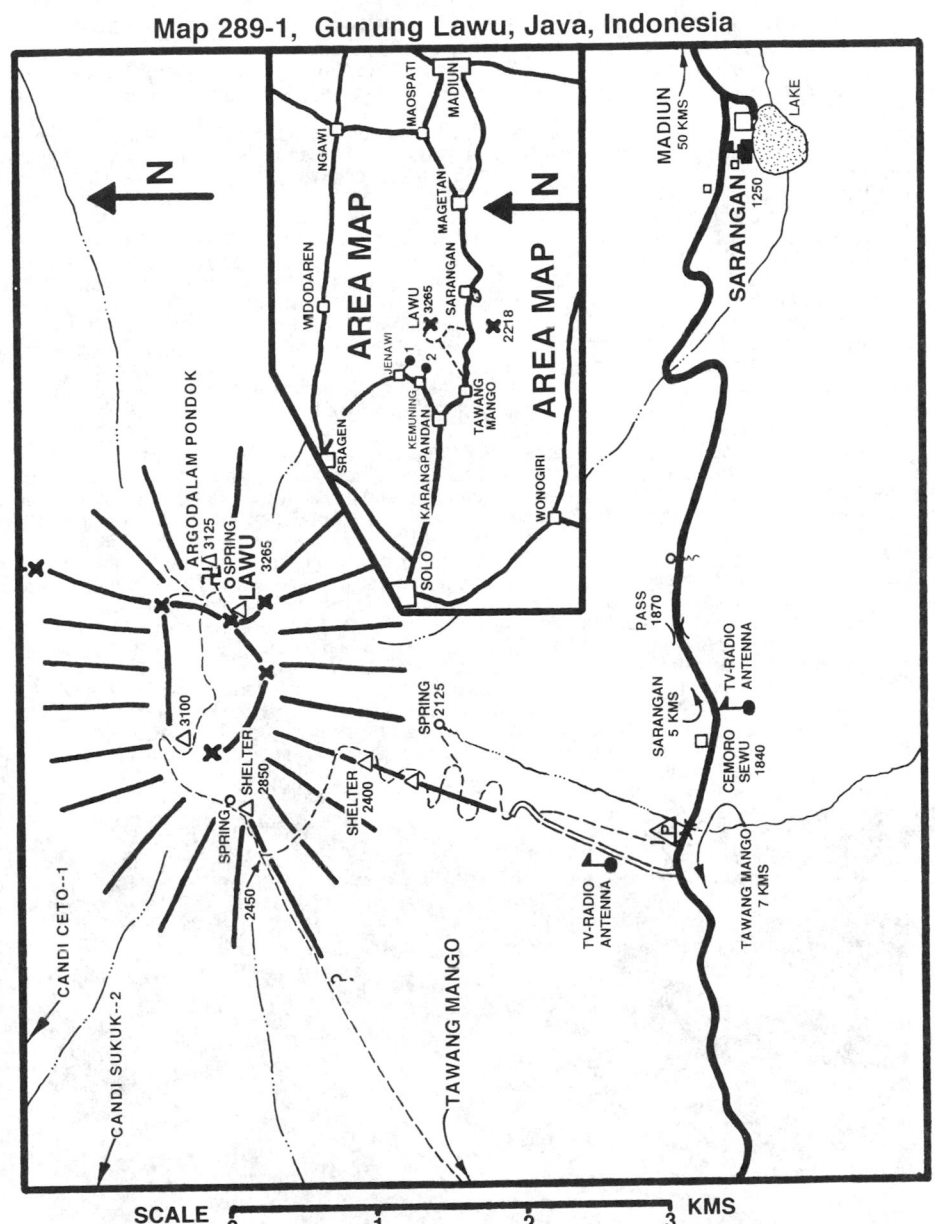

SCALE

0   1   2   3   KMS

Maps *Karangpandan,* 1:50,000, from the VSI or BAKOSURTANAL; or the DMA map *Surakarta, SB 49-15,* 1:250,000; the book, **Indonesia Travel Atlas**, from Periplus; and the latest travel guidebook to Indonesia.

Arjuna, Kember & Welirang Volcanos, Java, Indonesia

Shown on this map are 4 volcanos, all of which are located south of Surabaya in eastern Java. This group of peaks is also the first massif northwest of the Bromo area. The highest and most famous mountain is Arjuna (Arjuno) at 3339 meters. Next is Welirang, 3136; Kember 1 at about 3030; and Kember 2, 3126 meters.

Arjuna is an old, eroded and forested volcano, but the summit area is free of vegetation because of its altitude. The Kembers are also covered with a pine forest. Welirang has the only crater or kawah of the group, and its first historic eruption was in 1952. That activity was only a mud flow 4 kms from the summit somewhere on the NW flank. In 8/1991, a white plume was observed coming from Welirang's summit, where workers mine sulfur inside the old crater.

Transportation wise, the easiest way to reach these volcanos is to take a bemo or bus from the small city of Pandaan up to the hill resort of Tretes at 750 meters, where many hotels or losmen are located. In 1977, the author went to Tretes, started up the trail with full pack and camped near the stream as shown (not on the main trail). Next morning, 5/14/1977, he returned to Tretes, started up again, then hid his big pack in bushes and continued up the well-used trail to the summit of **Welirang**. This trail was heavily-used at the time, mostly by the sulfur miners, who were packing sulfur down the mountain in shoulder baskets. By now it's likely to be overrun by hikers from nearby Surabaya. This took the author one day, something like 8 hours round-trip from just above Tretes, but many camp one night on the mountain. Normally it's a one-day climb from Tretes to Welirang or Arjuna. Strong hikers can do both in one long day.

If you want to climb **Arjuna** from Tretes, you'll have to locate a trail running over the top of the **Kember 1** and down to the pass at 2920 meters. From there, the normal trail runs to the top or puncak (pron. punchak) of Arjuna. Or from or near the miner's camp, walk cross-country south through an open pine forest, then southwest toward the pass between Arjuna and **Kember 2**, thence to the summit.

Another way to reach these peaks is to make your way to Malang, then Batu, located northwest of Malang and south of these 4 volcanos. From there, take a bus or bemo north to the town of Sumber Brantus. This is the route recommended by reader Victor Esbensen, whose information goes back to the 1980's. You can also come in from the north and from the town of Pacet (pron. Pachet), but that route is more complicated than coming from Batu. If you're learning Bahasa Indonesia, then routes off the beaten path are a good way to mingle with the locals and learn the language.

It's not known if there are any hotels of losmen in Sumber Brantas, but there likely is (?), given its cool climate and its proximity to the peaks. From Sumber Brantas, walk, hitch hike or charter an ojek or bemo for 3-4 kms up to the vegetable farming area called Praseng Atas at about 1900 meters. Ask someone there where the trail to Arjuna starts. This should be a well-used route, and an easier and shorter walk to the peaks than from Tretes.

The dry season is from May through October. Be sure to take plenty of water, as that found on the

This 1977 foto shows porters carrying sulfur down to Tretes from a mine near the summit of Welirang.

Map 290-1, Arjuna, Kember & Welirang, Java, Indonesia

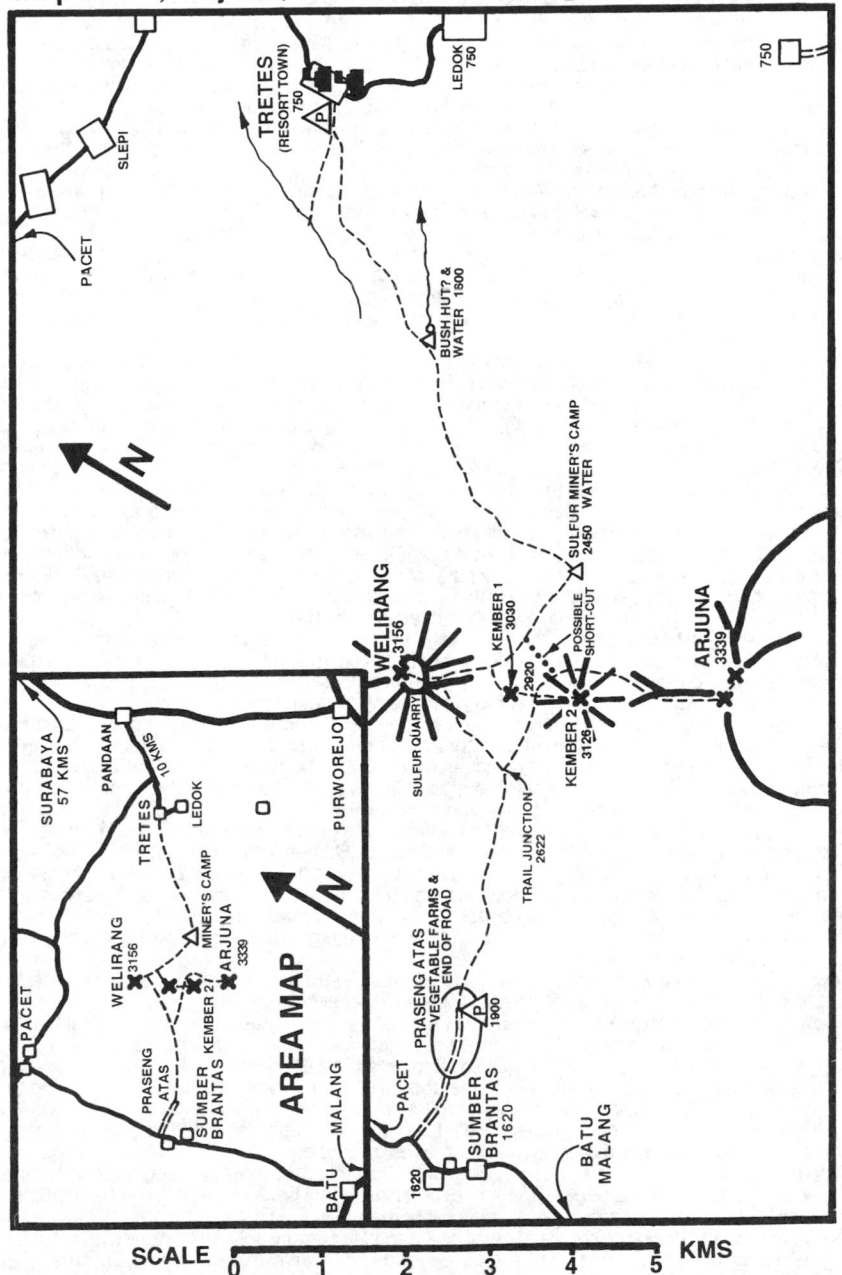

SCALE 0 1 2 3 4 5 KMS

mountain is likely polluted. Indonesians are beginning to enjoy camping, but they usually leave a big mess behind!

Maps *Purwosari,* 1:50,000, from the VSI or BAKOSURTANAL; or the DMA map *Surabaya, SB 49-16,* 1:250,000; the book **Indonesia Travel Atlas** from Periplus; and the latest travel guidebook to Indonesia.

Semeru & Bromo Volcanos, Java, Indonesia

Shown on this map(s) are 2 of the better known volcanos in Indonesia. First is Semeru, the highest peak on Java at 3677 meters. The other is Bromo, 2390 meters. Bromo is actually just an active crater within the much larger Tengger Caldera. The highest point on this old crater rim is 2742 meters. Since these 2 areas are so close together, you can easily visit & climb both on the same trip which can be accomplished in 3 days minimum--but 4 or 5 days for most.

Semeru may be the most active volcano in Indonesia. With the author's first climb on 5/12/1977, it was booming with thundering gas explosions about every half hour. On his 2nd climb of 9/19/1999, it was sending up nearly-silent billowing clouds of ash about every 20 minutes. On 7/27/2000, there was a larger than normal explosion which killed 2 volcanologists from the Volcanological Survey of Indonesia. They were with several foreign geologists who were attending a convention at the time.

Bromo is a small pyroclastic cone which has been historically very active. This no doubt helped create religious myths associated with the region. Immediately north, and at the base of the cone, is a rather new-looking Hindu Temple. Vehicles, mostly 4WD's, take tourists to Bromo and the temple making it the most-visited volcano in Indonesia. Bromo's last activity was in 9 & 10/1995, when it was sending up clouds of ash. For volcano updates see the websites (www.vsi.dpe.go.id) or (www.volcano.si.edu/gvp/).

There are several ways to reach these volcanos. One route to Semeru is from the south. In 5/1977, the author stayed in a church in Pronojiwo (no doubt there's a hotel or losmen there now), then made his way to Supitorang as shown. From there, country roads run to a village called Kamera and up to a spring & running water (carry water from there). He walked a trail up through sugar cane fields to the Kali Besukkobokan (Kobokan Gully). From there it was straight up the gully to a campsite at 1700 meters. That night, there were chunks of red hot lava blocks tumbling down to within 200 meters of his tent. Not much sleep that night! On Day 2 he made the summit and returned. Treeline there is only about 1700 meters because that's where most of the debris from explosions comes down. This way is seldom if ever used by others because it's considered the most dangerous route.

In 9/1999, the author used one of about 4 normal routes to **Semeru**. He stayed one night in Malang, then took a bemo to the bus terminal north of the city. From there he took a small bus 21 kms to Tumpang, bought 2 days supply of food, then got another bemo to Gubugklakah, the end of public transportation. He bought a little more food, then hired an ojek (motorcycle taxi) for less than US$2 for the ride up past Ngados to the caldera rim & road junction called Jemplang. From there he walked a very dusty road for 2 kms, then reached the paved road running down to Ranu Pani and on to Senduro.

Ranu Pani is a cabbage, cauliflower and potato growing area at between 2100 & 2300 meters. This altitude means cold nights so have some warm cloths for mornings and evenings.

He stayed at Pak Tasrip's Family Homestay in lower Rano Pani where 2 meals a day were provided. That afternoon he walked 400 meters past the lake to the national park office (kantor) & shelter (pondok) to get a permit which cost less than US$1. Next morning he got a 5am start and walked about one km past the N.P. kantor to a point immediately before a gate spanning the paved road, then turned right on the new trail, as shown. He walked up the well-used trail to Rano (Lake) Kumbolo (2 hours) where there was a usable shelter. Many Indonesians were camped there. Then south up the very good trail to another shelter at the base of Semeru's cone. From there it was straight up to the puncak (pron. punchak) or summit. He made the puncak in less than 5 hours. From there it was back to Rano Pani at 2pm. Round-trip time was 9 hours. Most hikers will need every minute of daylight, which is about 13 hours. Most people carry water from Kumbolo (boil or purify first) to the shelter or a campsite at the base of Semeru and camp one night, then finish the climb and return to Rano Pani on Day 2.

The author stayed a 2nd night at the Family Homestay--total cost for 2 nights and 4 meals was US$6.29! Now you can stop complaining about your low wages!

Probably the best way to Rano Pani is go to Lumajang which is east of Semeru, and take a bus to Senduro, stay a night in the one hotel there, then get on the daily 8am bus to Ranu Pani.

On the morning of Day 3, the author walked up the road to the Tengger Caldera, then down a good trail with 2 wooden roof-only rest shelters to the bottom of the crater. Then to Bromo, and up to the tourist resort of Cemoro Lawang where there are lots of hotels or losmen and tokos (shops). Walk-time for Day 3 was 4 1/4 hours; total 3-day walk-time was 15 3/4 hours. He then got in one of many bemos heading down to the big bus terminal 5 kms west of Probolinggo.

You can also get to these volcanos from Tosari & Wonokitri, but the most-used route to **Bromo** is via Cemoro Lawang. The easiest way to Semeru and Ranu Pani is via Lumajang and Senduro. If Pak Tasrip is still alive when you arrive, you'll enjoy his home. Several times in the 1990's Pak has seen tigers on the road to Senduro. You can buy all hiking food in Ranu Pani. The dry season in from May through October, but with the good trail and paved roads, you can climb either peak anytime. Take 3 liters of water up Semeru.

Maps *Tumpang, 5518 I* & *Tosari, 5519 II*, both 1:50,000, from the VSI or BAKOSURTANAL; or DMA maps *Surabaya SB 49-16* & *Lumajang SC 49-4*, 1:250,000; the **Indonesia Travel Atlas** from Periplus; and the latest travel guidebook to Indonesia.

Map 291-1, Semeru & Bromo Volcanos, Java, Indonesia

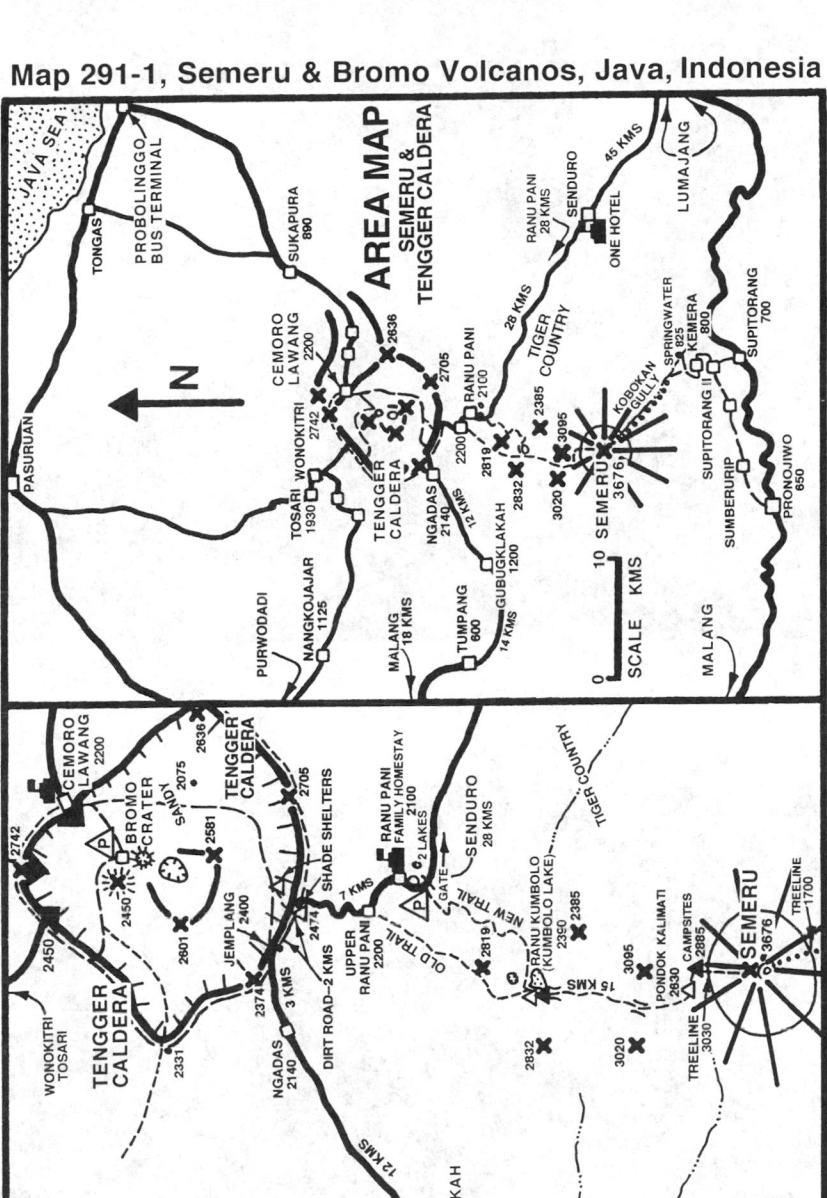

The summit of Semeru in 1977, with Tengger Caldera seen in the distance.

This is a 9/1999 foto of the northern slopes and ash explosion of Semeru as seen from the Pondok Kalimati (Kalimati Shelter or Cabin). This volcano seems continuously active!

Looking toward the east at Ranu Kumbolo (Kumbolo Lake) and the shelter and campsite on its western shore.

This is the Hindu Temple at the northern base of Bromo Crater (looking south).

Raung Volcano & Kawah Igen, Java, Indonesia

At the extreme eastern end of Java are several volcanos, the highest of which is Raung, 3334 meters. The other featured hike is to Kawah Igen. Kawah=crater, so this is *Igen Crater* at about 2386 meters. Other nearby summits are Pendil, 2376 meters; Rante, 2644; Merapi, 2799 and Suket, 2950 meters. The only summits with trails seem to be Igen and Raung.

All these volcanos are on the south side rim of the 20-km-wide Kendeng Caldera. Since 1796, there have been 7 major eruptions at Igen; the largest was in 1/1817. The latest activity were 2 small phreatic explosions on 6/28/1999. Igen has a sulfur mining operation next to its 200-meter-deep lake which has become a tourist attraction. Miners carry sulfur out of the crater and down to Paltuding in shoulder baskets. A dam has been constructed at the outlet of the lake to control possible floods. Raung has a large, deep, 2-km-wide crater, possibly made by a VEI-5 explosion in 1593, with a small active cone inside. It's last significant eruption took place in 6/1997. For volcano updates see the websites (www.vsi.dpe.go.id) or (www.volcano.si.edu/gvp/).

There are 2 ways to reach **Kawah Igen**. The author stayed a night in Bondowoso, then on 9/21/1999, took a small bus 56 kms to the plantation town of Sempol (2 1/2 hours, US$.50). He stayed one night in the Arabica Homestay in nearby Kalisat (US$3.15). Next morning, he hired an ojek (motorcycle taxi, US$2.85) to take him 14 kms to Paltuding. The ojek waited while the author climbed 4 kms to the kawah & sulfur mine, then a quick visit to the dam, and back to Paltuding. The hike took 3 hours round-trip; then the 30 minute ride back to Sempol.

The 2nd, and most-used way to Kawah Igen, seems to be from the coastal city of Banjuwangi. There is public transport to Jambu, but then you'll have to hire an ojek or charter another vehicle, perhaps forming a group to share costs. There are also tour agents in Banjuwangi (?) who organize groups & transport to the crater. There are rooms to rent and a small store & restaurant at Paltuding.

In the afternoon, after his trip to Kawah Igen, the author took a bus back to Sukasari, then an ojek 3 kms to the decrepit losmen (US$1.90) in Sumber Wringle (SW). Next morning at 5:30am, he hired another ojek (US$1.25) for the 6 km ride up to Pos Satu (Pos 1), which is at the end of the good road and one km from the beginning of the trail to **Raung** (Pos Satu is a bamboo hut where a watchman and his family live). The author then hiked a good trail to the crater rim in 4 1/4 hours. The crater rim is very steep and unstable, so walking 2 kms to the highest point would be a major undertaking. He returned to Pos Satu after a total of 7 hours, round-trip.

He then walked the 6 kms back to SW in 1 hour, 10 minutes. Long hike! Most Indonesians camp one night on the mountain--but they have to carry lots of water! Consider arranging to have an ojek pick you up at Pos Satu at the end of the hike, making this long walk more tolerable. There's no water anywhere, so begin with 3 liters from SW. Buy all your food in SW

Shown here are men mining sulfur from the south side of Kawah Igen (Igen Crater). Steam is diverted downward into pipes which helps the sulfur to precipitate out to be collected.

Map 292-1, Raung Volcano & Kawah Igen, Java, Indonesia

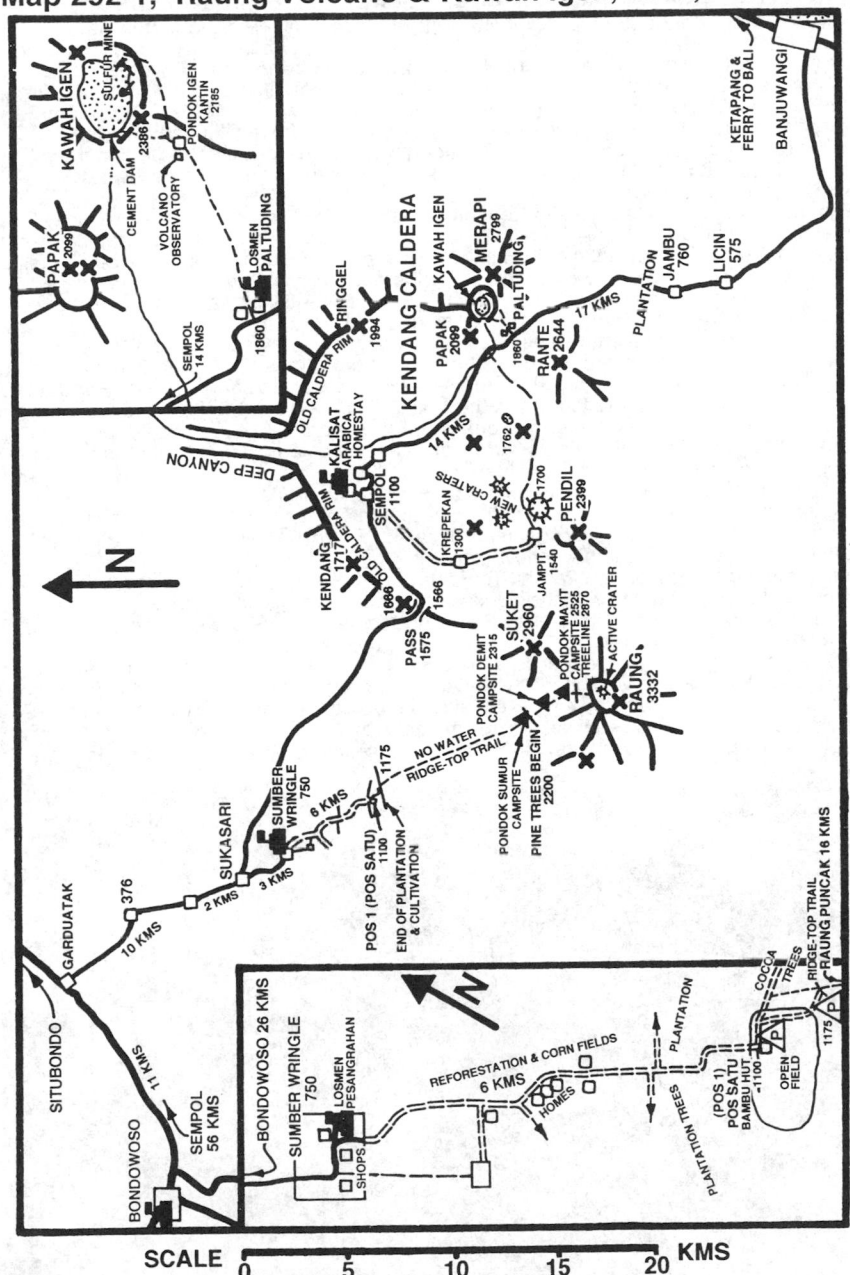

SCALE 0   5   10   15   20 KMS

and/or Sempol.
Maps *Kajumas, 5819 III, Krepekan, 5818 IV & 5719 II,* all at 1:50,000, from Bedan Koordinasi Survey dan Pemetaan Nasional (BAKOSURTANAL); or DMA maps *Bondowoso, SB 50-13 & Singaradja, SC 50-1,* 1:250,000; the **Indonesia Travel Atlas** from Periplus; and the latest travel guidebook to Indonesia.

Batur, Abang & Agung Volcanos, Bali, Indonesia

On this map are 3 of the best-known mountains on Bali. The highest is Agung at 3070 meters. Next is the high point on the Batur Caldera rim called Abang at 2172 meters. Inside the Batur Crater is the new & active Gunung Api Batur (Batur Volcano) at 1730 meters.

Agung is a sacred mountain to the Hindus of Bali, but it's been a deadly volcano. Between 2/1963 & 1/1964 it was very active, but the biggest blast came on 3/17/1963. It killed more than 1000 people, but has been quiet since, except for some fumarolic activity in 1989. Batur Volcano had an explosive eruption in 1974 along with a lava flow; also some minor explosives from 3/1999 through 7/1999. For volcano updates see the websites (www.vsi.dpe.go.id) or (www.volcano.si.edu/gvp/).

To reach the **Batur Caldera** and Penelokan using public transport, make your way to Kuta Corner in Kuta (almost all tourists stay in Kuta), then take one bemo to Tegal Terminal, another bemo to Kreneng, then still another to Batubulan Terminal. From there locate a bus heading for Penelokan, or Kintamani via Penelokan. *Just getting across Denpasar is about the biggest hassle in Indonesia*, so consider asking one of the travel agents in Kuta about tourist transport to Penelokan. It's not that expensive, and you'll save an hour or two just getting across Denpasar!

From Penelokan, there are bemos heading down into the caldera; or just walk to Kedisan or nearby Toya Bungkah, where there are hotels or homestays (losmen). From Juti or Toya Bungkah (village with hotel symbol) there are trails to Batur Volcano. The author did this on 5/6/1977. There are also trails around the lake. Or take a boat to the Terunyan cemetery. Bodies aren't buried, they're just laid out in bamboo cages to decompose, or be eaten by whatever (?). Or stay in Penelokan and walk east on a road, then a trail to the summit of **Abang**. There's a trail all along the caldera rim for those interested in longer treks. It's almost necessary to stay in this area one night or more to do much hiking.

To reach **Agung**, make your way to the Batubulan Terminal and look for a bus to Besakih. Or it might be faster to go to Menanga, then Besakih. There are several losmen at Besakih, and plenty of shops & warungs to buy food. From the Pura (temple) Besakih, take the trail straight up the mountain. You'll pass a 2nd, 11 roof pura along the way. This trail goes to the highest summit. Get an early start to beat the clouds. The author did this on 5/7/1977.

A 2nd way to **Agung** is via the Pura Pasar Agung at 1650 meters. At Batubulan Terminal, take a bus to Selat, then hitch hike or hire an ojek (motorcycle taxi) to reach the pura or Hindu temple at the end of the paved road. At the pura, walk around the left side of the temple and straight up to the top on a very good & well-used trail. This path takes you to the crater rim, but not the highest peak. From the temple, the author made the round-trip climb in 2 3/4 hours; that was on 9/25/1999. With an early start, you can make this climb in one long day from Kuta; but if you get stuck and have to walk down to Selat, the closest hotel is in Sidakaria. Take water from Selat--there's none at the pura.

Batur Lake and Batur Volcano inside the Batur Caldera. The boat is made of reeds.

Map 293-1, Batur, Abang, Agung Volcanos, Bali, Indonesia

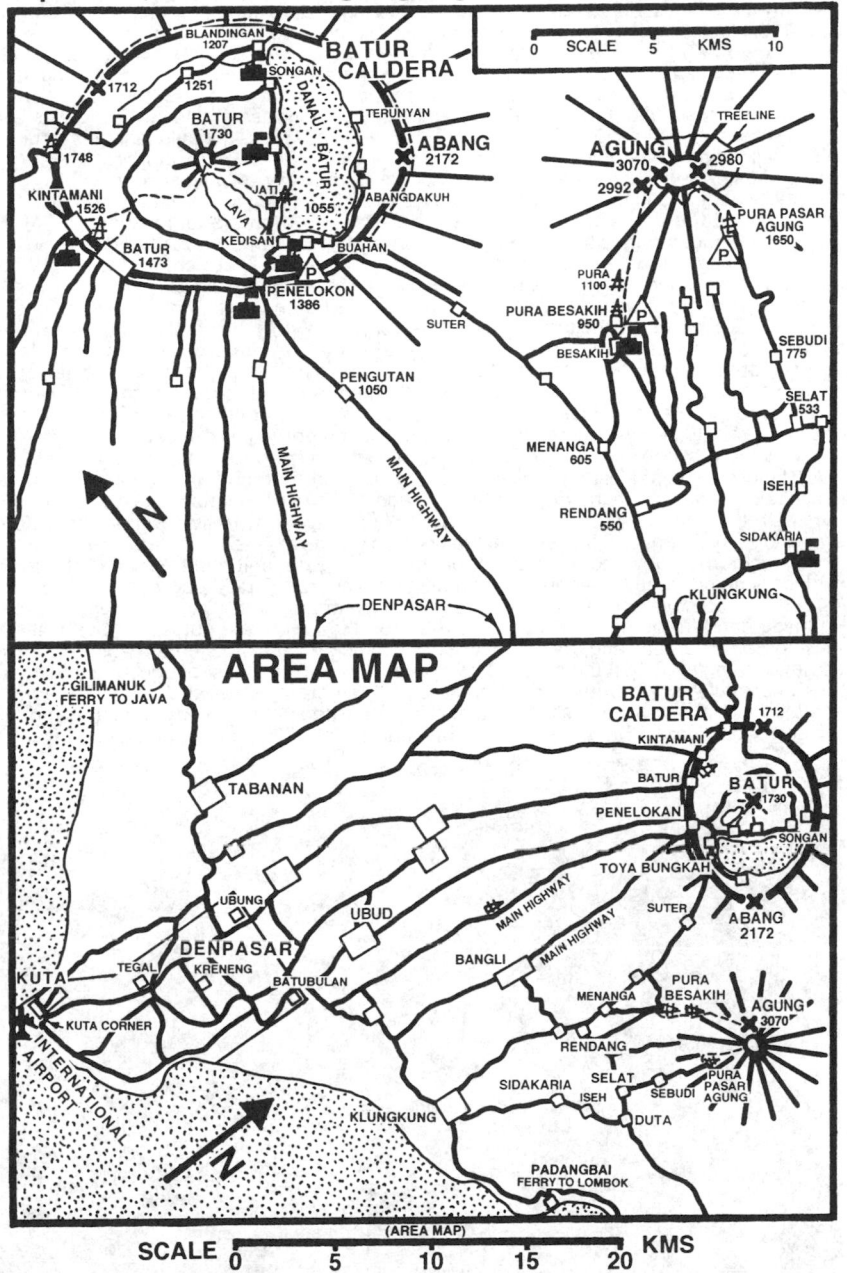

Maps You'll need 6 maps from BAKOSURTANAL at 1:25,000 scale to cover all this area. The numbers are *1707-641, 1707-642, 1707-622, 1707-623, 1707-624 & 1807-413*; or the DMA map *Singaradja, SC 50-1,* 1:250,000; and the **Indonesia Road Atlas** from Periplus; and the latest travel guidebook to Indonesia.

Rinjani Volcano, Lombok Island, Indonesia

Shown here is Rinjani at 3726 meters, the 2nd highest volcano in Indonesia. It's located on Lombok, the first island east of Bali. The summit or puncak (pron. punchak) of Rinjani sits on the eastern rim of a 6-km-wide caldera which is filled with a lake (danau). Just southeast of the highest summit is an old one-km-wide crater, plus there's a new cinder cone growing inside the caldera. This is called Gunung Baru (New Mountain) and rises to 2363 meters. There was activity between 3/28/1966 & 8/8/1966, when it spewed both ash and lava. There was also lava flows and ash clouds from 5/1994 through 11/1995. On 11/3/1994, a cold lahar raced down from the summit killing 30 people who were collecting water in the Kokok Jenggak River (?). For volcano updates see the websites (www.vsi.dpe.go.id) or (www.volcano.si.edu/gvp/).

Here's what the author did on the last 3 days of 9/1999. He started in Mataram, the capital of Lombok located near the west coast. He took a bus north and east to Anyar (2 1/4 hours & US$.60), then a bemo (minibus) up the mountain to near Senaru for about US$.25. He checked into a losmen near the trailhead for about US$1.71 a night. There are 12 losmen or hotels in Batukoq & Senaru and all will store baggage while you're on the mountain.

Next morning he started early and in 4 hours made it to the crater rim at 2600 meters. Along the way are 2 pondoks or shelters--no walls, just roofs. Down in the canyon to the west of each is water. From the pass, he descended to the lake and had lunch. There were lots of local fishermen at the lake, which has a slightly sulfur taste, so he filled up with good water at the cold spring just beyond the hot springs and about 300 meters from the ruins of the old shelters near the lake's outlet. He then walked eastward toward the ridge marked 2639 meters, but found a good campsite at 2200 meters, along with a spring in the gorge just 20 meters below. Watch out of monkey thieves; one came down from a tree and stole a soap dish that afternoon!

Next morning he hid his big pack in tall grass, away from trees & monkeys, and hurried up to the ridgetop, then south to the main northwest ridge of **Rinjani**. He made it to the summit in 2 1/2 hours. On the puncak (summit), he met some Indonesians who had walked from Sembalun Lawang the day before and had slept at the ridgetop campsite at 2725 meters.

He then hurried down to his pack. From there to the summit had taken 4 1/2 hours, round-trip. Finally he returned to Senaru in about another 5 hours. Total 2-day walk-time was about 14 1/4 hours. If you have time, visit the 60-meter-high *air tergen* (water fall) near Senaru.

Or you can hire guides in Batukoq or Senaru. Most of these guides hire vehicles to take clients to Sembalun Lawang, then they walk west along what was to be a road, but construction was never completed. On the map, 10 bridges are shown. The last bridge spans a stream and that's where hikers get water for the camp at 2725 meters. After the summit, they return to Senaru via the lake and the pass at 2600 meters. Most people take 3 days for this climb.

Buy all your food in Batukoq, but Mataram has better selections. Sembalun Lawang has at

From near the summit of Rinjani you have a good look down into the Rinjani Caldera, with a large fish-stocked lake and active volcano called Gunung Baru (New Mountain).

Map 294-1, Rinjani Volcano, Lombok Island, Indonesia

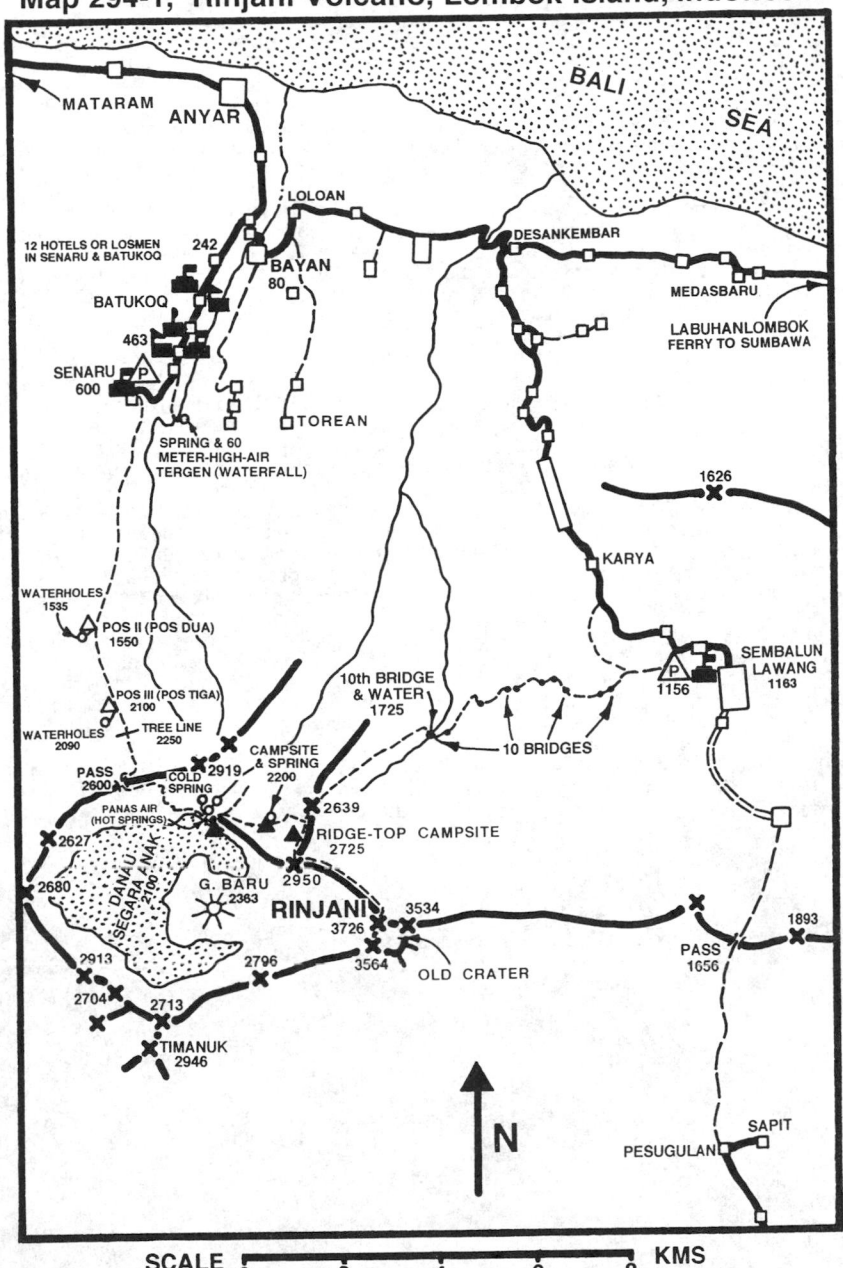

least one hotel. Dry season is April through October. Don't leave an unattended camp at the lake--the place is crawling with locals fishing.

Maps *Bayan, 1807-524, Gunung Rinjani, 1807-522 and Sembalunlawang, 1807-614,* all 1:25,000 scale, from BAKOSURTANAL; the **Indonesia Road Atlas** from Periplus; and the latest travel guidebook to Indonesia.

Tambora Volcano, Sumbawa, Indonesia

One of the most famous volcanos in the world is Tambora, located on Sumbawa, which is 2 islands east of Bali. It's altitude is 2722 meters, according to the new 1998 Tambora maps below.

The reason Tambora is famous is that it had the biggest volcanic explosion in man's recorded history. That eruption took place on 4/11 & 4/12/1815. As many as 10,000 people were killed by the explosion itself, and because it covered most of Sumbawa and Lombok with ash, another 82,000 either died of starvation or disease on these 2 islands. It had a Volcanic Explosivity Index of 7 (VEI-7); only 3 others in the Holocene are ranked so high. They are Changbai Shan, China-Korea; Crater Lake, Oregon, USA; and Kikai, Ryukyu Islands, Japan. The volume of material ejected is estimated to be 100 cubic/kms.

To get to **Tambora** from the east, take a bus from Bima west to Dompu, then another bus to Calabai (pron. Chalabai). There are several buses a day. If coming from the west, take a bus from Sumbawa Besar to Soriutu and wait for another bus to Calabai at the main highway junction.

Or if you want to save a day, here's what the author did on 10/3/1999. He went to the east end of Sumbawa Besar where bemos going to Air Bari (pron. I or eye bari) park, but instead he took an ojek which was faster (US$1.20). From Air Bari, he chartered a speedboat to make the 55 minute run to Calabai, which cost US$14.75.

In Calabai, he could have waited for a bus or bemo to Pancasila (pron. Panchasila) about 4 each day, but used another ojek instead (US$.60). He asked to be taken to the Kepala Desa (chief of village), but was taken to someone else's home. He paid about US$1.75 for a place to sleep and for baggage storage. The author had no idea where to begin the hike, so he paid the man of the house US$1.20 to guide him to the beginning of the trail. They road-walked southeast; then south on a trail crossing a small stream before coming to the private logging road (25 minutes). Follow the map & insert carefully.

Once on that road, they walked fast for 54 minutes to the trail at about 800 meters. About 20 meters from the road on the right are 3 small metal signs marking the trail. They're nailed 3 meters high on some trees. With a compass & altimeter, you can likely find it, but it might pay to hire someone to escort you to that point. Once on the trail, it's hard to get lost.

Going up the trail you'll see signs of a water pipeline, then a pondok or shelter--no walls, just a roof. Then at a hunter's campsite; veer left. Further on you'll come to a small stream and the best place to camp. The author passed 2 more campsites, with small signs pointing to the right or south to *air* ((pron. eye-ear=water). Some hunters were camped at the site marked 1600 meters.

He finally reached the crater rim at 2616 meters in 5 2/3 hours, but felt he didn't have time to go to the highest point, just over a km away to the south. He returned to Pancasila in a total round-trip time of 10 3/4 hours. From Pancasila, he rode an ojek down to Calabai and stayed in the only losmen in the area for US$2.35. Next morning, he was on the 7am bus to Dompu.

This is a long hike, but fast walkers can do it in one day. Start at dawn (5:30am) with 2 liters of water and a good lunch. Best to buy food in Calabai or elsewhere. Dry season is April to October.

Looking east into the Tambora Caldera from the point marked 2616 meters.

Map 295-1, Tambora Volcano, Sumbawa, Indonesia

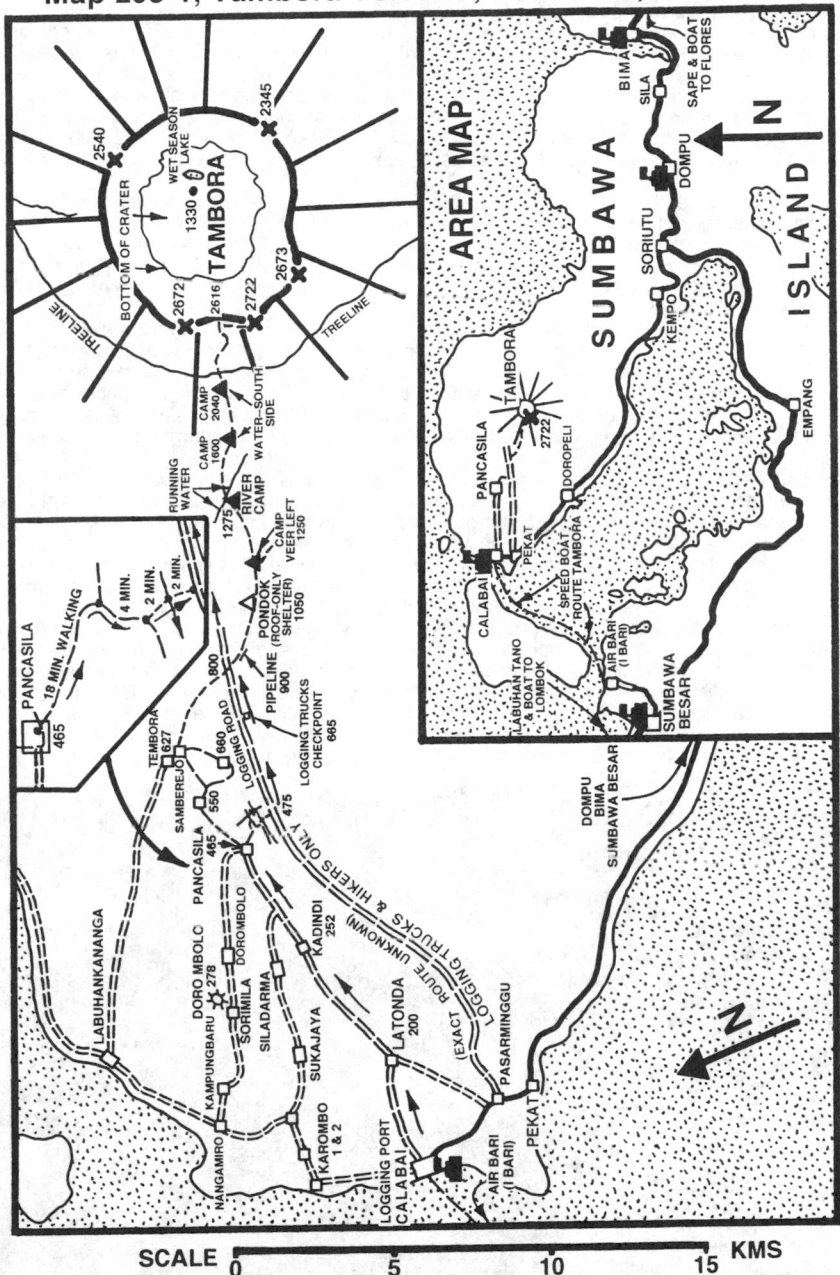

Maps *Calabai, 1907-532, Labuhankananga, 1907-541, and Gunung Tambora, 1907-542,* all at 1:25,000. These new maps don't show the new logging road or trail, so **this map is best**. Also an old 1951 map titled, *Geologi Gunung Tambora, Sumbawa, dan Sekitarnja,* 1:250,000 from the VSI, Bandung; the **Indonesia Road Atlas** from Periplus; and the latest travel guidebook to Indonesia.

Doro Api, Sangeang Island, Indonesia

Featured here is Pulau Sangeang (Sangeang Island), located 7 kms northeast of the larger island of Sumbawa. Sangeang has 2 complex volcanos: Doro Api, 1949 meters, & Doro Mantoi at 1795. Doro Api erupted big time on 7/30/1985 and continued (with lava flows, vulcanian & stombolian explosions, plus a nuée ardente coming down to 200 meters) for 2 1/2 years. Activity ended in 2/1988. In the first 2 days of that eruptive cycle, 1250 residents were evacuated to Sumbawa. Most were from the main village of Sangeang and they settled just across the channel at what is now called New or *Baru Sangeang*. Latest activity was between 3 & 5/1999, when white ash plumes rose 150 meters above Doro Api. For volcano updates see the websites (www.vsi.dpe.go.id) or (www.volcano. si.edu/gvp/).

The author visited the island on 10/6/1999, but didn't get far. First, he took a bus from the big regional market town of Bima to Tawali (56 kms, 2 hours, US$.60). He bought more food at the good pasar (market) next to the bus terminal, then took a bemo 6 kms to Baru Sangeang. Since there were no hotels in Tawali or Baru Sangeang, he contacted the kepala desa (village chief) and ended up staying in his home for one night (US$1.80). The kepala desa also contacted a boat man about going to the island in a kapal or launcha.

Next morning, the author took food and water for one day only, and rode in a 8-meter-long launcha to Sangeang. It had an old 5 liter, putt putt, hot head Diesel engine and it took only 57 minutes to cross. They found a fisherman/farmer at Toro Ponda, then with this so-called guide, headed for the old abandoned homestead at 240 meters. The author let the man go back, then found there was no trail as is shown on the map listed below. At the time he was unaware that the island was unoccupied, so what trails there were formerly, were completely overgrown. Later that afternoon, everyone returned to Sumbawa. Boat rental cost US$12.

If you decide to go to **Sangeang**, here are some tips. Prepare to camp and stay for up to 3 days. Best shopping is in Bima, then Tawali. You'll likely have to stay in Baru Sangeang one night, so ask for the kepala desa; helping visitors is his job. He'll arrange for a boat, which may stay with you for the duration of the trip. Take lots of water; but those people will know where to get more. There are wells near shore, plus spring water seeping out at the high-tide mark in various old village sites. It's suggested you sail around the island looking for breaks in the forest & brush, perhaps at one of the 5 areas where lava has come down close to the sea. You may have to bushwhack, so take long pants.

The areas that look easy may be above old Sangeang village and up a lava flow to **Doro Api**, or on the east side. From what the author could see, the treeline east of **Doro Mantoi** was lower & the climbing easier than from the south or west. Perhaps scout a route the first day, then with an early start, finish the climb on the 2nd day. In October (pre-monsoon), the southeast part of the island will have fewer clouds & better visibility than the NW side because of strong southeast winds. Beware of this map, it's not real accurate! It's a combination of the maps below, plus the author's own limited visual sightings. The bivouacs (bivaks) shown are where geologists have camped over the years. In

From the beach at Baru Sangeang looking northeast at Sangeang Island. On the right is Doro Mantoi.

Map 296-1, Doro Api, Sangeang Island, Indonesia

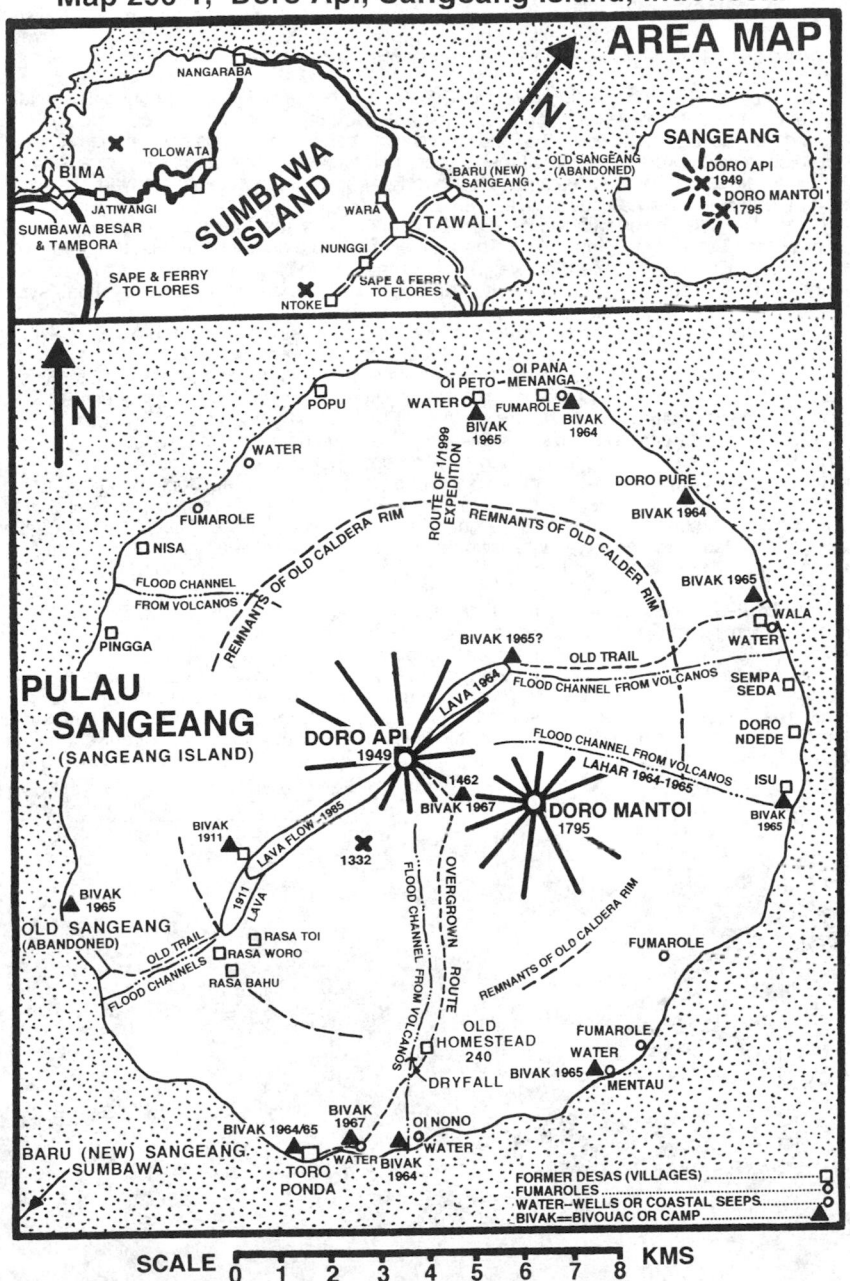

the future, people may move back to the island, and will hopefully rejuvenate trails. Better learn a little Indonesian for this trip!, or hire an English speaker as a guide.
Maps *Sangeang*, 1:50,000, from the VSI; a good area map, but poor otherwise is the DMA map *Bima, SC 50-4*, 1:250,000; and the latest travel guidebook to Indonesia.

Keli Mutu & Tri-Colored Lakes, Flores Island, Indonesia

Keli Mutu at about 1640 meters, is a complex volcano located near the center of the island of Flores. It has 3 craters at the summit or puncak (pron. punchak), each with a different colored lake. It's become quite a tourist place and by 1999, there was a paved road to within a short distance of the craters.

Keli Mutu's big historic eruptions were in 6 & 7/1968, but not much happened. Tiwu Nua Muri Kooh Tai Lake had 30-meter-high water fountains, and later an ash column was emitted. In 5/1995, a search was conducted for the body of a Dutch tourist who had fallen into this same turquoise-blue lake. A portable raft was lowered by ropes and searchers had to breathe bottled oxygen because of strong SO/2 concentrations. The body was never found. For volcano updates see the websites (www.vsi.dpe.go.id) or (www.volcano.si.edu/gvp/).

To get there, take any bus running between Ende to the west, and Maumere on the east, and get off at Moni located just east of the mountain. There's lots of bus and/or bemo traffic on this road. You can fly in or out of Ende or Maumere as well, but you may have to wait a few days for a seat, or fly standby. Those airports & airline offices weren't hooked up to a computer reservations system in 1999 which made flying a problem.

Moni is very small, but has 6 or 8 hotels or losmen to choose from, plus there's a small pasar or market, and a number of small tokos or shops. Most losmen offer meals.

From Moni you have 2 ways to reach **Keli Mutu** and the **Tri-Colored Lakes**. Most tourists hire a driver & vehicle in Moni; or they come into the area in a private or chartered car, then drive the paved road to the old shelters (pondoks) near the craters. From there they walk up an old road to a lookout point at 1630 meters where all 3 lakes can be seen. This is the best place to take fotos.

The other way is to hike. With this map, anyone can do it alone. From the middle of Moni, walk southwest through town and just after you pass the main curve (see map), look for a good trail going down to a small canal, then to the bottom of the air tergen (waterfall). Cross the stream and climb the good trail to the southwest. This trail passes the villages of Nuadepi, Koposili and Manukoko. It finally reaches the paved road and a gate where you'll have to pay a small fee to see the mountain. From there road-walk to the end of pavement, then continue on trails running around the rims of all the craters.

On 10/8/1999, the author did this hike to the lookout in about 2 1/2 hours, then road-walked all the way back to Moni to make this map. From his losmen, the total round-trip time was 6 hours. You can climb this mountain any time, but April or May through October is the dry season.

For anyone interested in real climbing, and who have the time (the author didn't), consider climbing one of the other active volcanos shown on the *Area Map*. **Ambulombo** looks easy to climb from Boawae where there are 2 losmen. Climb **Ija** right from Ende, and **Egon** from Maumere and a hot spring (panas air) northwest of the summit. Climb **Lewotobo** from Maumere, Kedang and the village of Bawalatang (last hotel is in Maumere). If climbing Lewotobo, try to find the volcano watcher

From Peak 1620, looking northwest at 2 of the 3 lakes on top of Keli Mutu.

Map 297-1, Keli Mutu-Tricolored Lakes, Flores, Indonesia

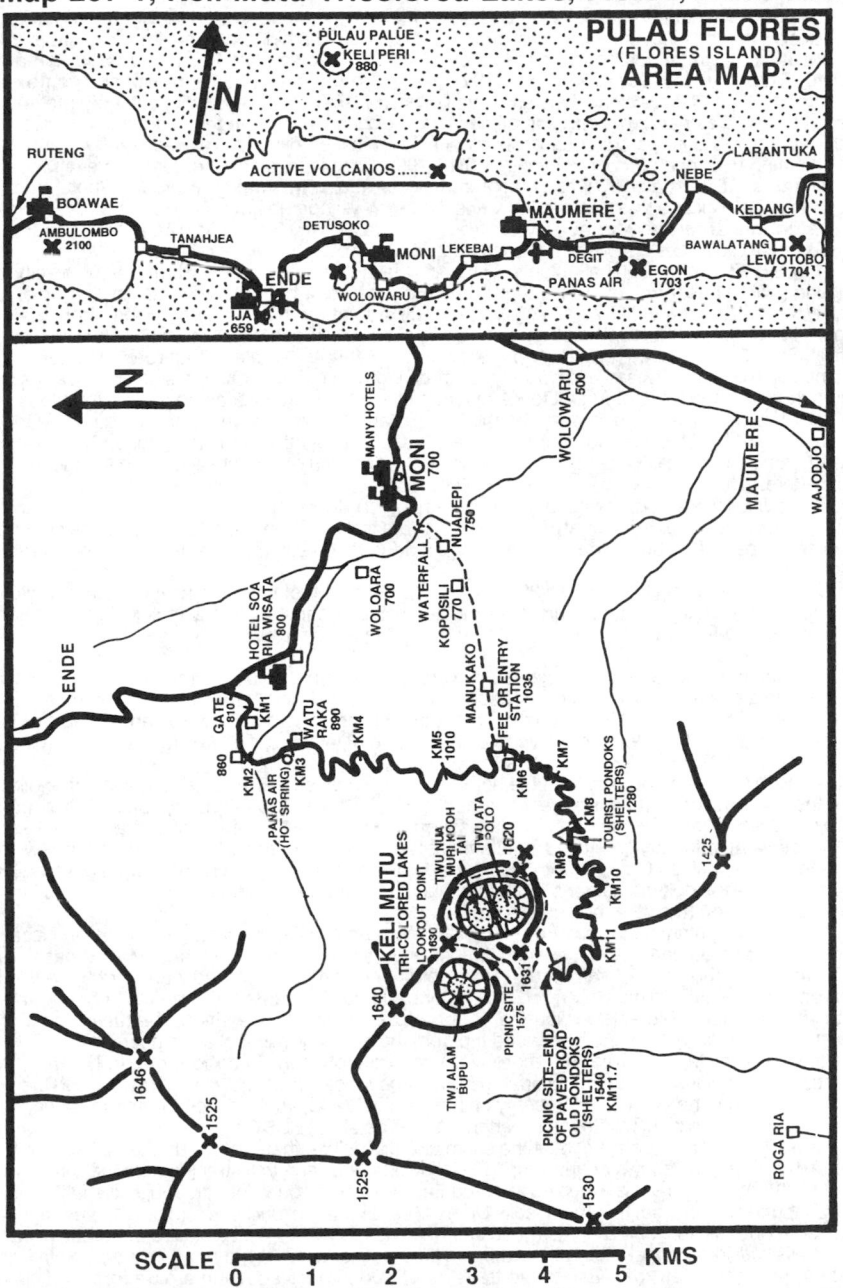

SCALE 0 1 2 3 4 5 KMS

in the village of Bawalatang. He can direct you to the best way or trail (?). At that village, you may have to look up the kepala desa (village chief) for a possible place to sleep.

Maps Nothing available in 1999, but the old 1960 DMA map *Ende*, 1:250,000, gives a good look at the region; and the latest travel guidebook to Indonesia.

Lokon, Klabat & Soputan Volcanos, Sulawesi, Indonesia

The volcanos featured here are located at the extreme northern end of the island of Sulawesi and are just east and/or south of the regional capital of Manado. The highest summit here is Klabat at 1990 meters; it's a dormant volcano whose last eruption is unknown. Next highest is Soputan at 1809 meters. This is an active volcano having had lava flows, some lava dome growth and dome glow in the fall of 1996, and more explosions and lava flows on 7/1/2000. Next is Lokon at 1579 meters. This summit has no crater and was built sometime in the Holocene, but just to the north, between Lokon and Empung, is the active crater called Tompaluan. Its last eruptive period was in 3 & 4/1999. It was still steaming upon the author's arrival on 10/19/1999. The last volcano featured here is Mahawu at 1372 meters. It's last activity was in the summer of 1994, with small geysers, mudpots, and noisy fumaroles. For volcano updates see the websites (www.vsi.dpe.go.id) or (www.volcano.si.edu/gvp/).

Get to this area and Manado by air from Jakarta, Ujung Pandang, Malaysia, Bangkok, the Philippines and perhaps elsewhere. Manado has lots of hotels in all price ranges.

To climb **Klabat** (or Kelabat), start in Manado. Make your way to the eastern side of the city to the Pal Dua (Pal 2) bus terminal. Once there, get into a bemo or bus heading east to Airmadidi (pron. Imadidi or eye/ear/ma/didi). After 19 kms they will stop at the bus terminal. From there walk east about 600 meters to the pos (post) police. Immediately east of the police station, turn northeast or uphill and walk up a paved road toward the mountain. After 300 meters, that road turns left, but you continue uphill. See the insert map. After less than another km, turn right, pass an *old house*, veer left, then right again and walk through a fence and into a coconut plantation along a trail. After less than a km, you'll come to a *cement building* on the left and another trail coming in from the right. Continue uphill. After 10 minutes, you'll pass a *monument & shack*; in another 3 minutes will be *fields & a hut* on the left. As the main trail turns right, locate another trail continuing straight ahead up the mountain and into the forest.

This trail follows a ridge past 2 old woodcutters campsites, then veers right at 3 junctions to reach the foundations of an old shelter at 1050 meters. From there it's one trail all the way to the crater and a popular campsite at 1900 meters. Finally it's up a ridge to the summit. Inside this forested crater is a small lake.

The author tried this climb on 10/22/1999, but got lost. He returned the next day, with a little more information, and finally got to the summit. From the pos police to the puncak took just under 3 hours; 5 1/2 hours round-trip. From his hotel in Manado the entire trip took 7 1/2 hours--lots of bemos on the road and fast rides that day!

To reach the other 3 peaks, make your way to the Karombasan bus terminal in southern Manado and get into a bus going to Tomohon. Get out in Kakaskasan 1 and at the Gereja Pniel (Pniel Church). See insert map. From the church, walk west downhill asking about the Volcano Resort or Happy Flower Homestay. After 400 meters you'll come to both of these places next to each other (plus a 3rd losmen nearby). Rooms there are ~US$5 or $6 a night.

To climb **Lokon**, walk west from the hotels on a dirt road; after 8 minutes turn right for another 7-8 minutes to 3 houses and an intersection; then turn left and walk straight for Lokon. Or start at the Gereja Katolic (Catholic Church) and walk west on one road past a cemetery, 2 gravel quarries, then finally veer right to the dry creek bed. Once there, walk up the creek bed past 5 dryfalls, following foot prints to the Tompaluan Crater. From the east side of that active crater, climb left up a good trail to the summit. This hike took the author 1 2/3 hours; and a total round-trip time of 3 1/3 hours from his hotel, the Volcano Resort (the other homestays are cheaper!).

For **Mahawu**, start in the center of Tomohon. Walk east to the big pasar or market, and locate the place where bemos park. About every half hour there's one going to Tondano, via the pass marked 1100 meters on this map. After about 4 kms, get out right at the pass and walk north on a trail wide enough for a vehicle. This very good trail first heads north, then east, then north again and runs alongside a couple of forested volcanos. After about 3 kms, you'll come to the rim of the Mahawu Crater. The author climbed this one round-trip from the highway in just over an hour.

Next is **Soputan**. In 10/1999, there were several hotels in Tomohon, one in Bawah (Lower) Sonder, but none close to the mountain. There may be a hotel in Langowan in 2001(?). So the author started early from the Samaria Homestay on the east side of Tomohon, got a bemo to Kawangdoan, then was offered a ride to Tau'ure in a chartered bemo for about US$.60!

He was let off at the gereja right at the south end of Tau'ure, then walked up the trail around the left side of the church, as shown on this map. He followed the ox cart trail straight up to the rumah makan (food stall). At that point, be watching the mountain in front of you. Your first objective is to reach the canyon to the right of what the author calls Dome Mtn. There are junctions, but always veer right. Just inside that obvious canyon is another good trail which takes you up past a couple of homes or wayside food stalls, beside a mineral stream and finally to a trail junction at the head of the canyon. At that junction go right or left, because these trails meet 500 meters above in a pine forest. This is the campsite marked 1325 meters. From there, continue south on a good trail as shown. Finally you'll arrive on a ridge with a view of Soputan Volcano just to the southwest.

Continue *down* the trail from 1475 meters to the divide below, then route-find through the brush with many trails (1350 meters). Be observant here as you could get lost going back! Mark your way

Map 298-1, Lokon, Klabat & Soputan, Sulawesi, Indonesia

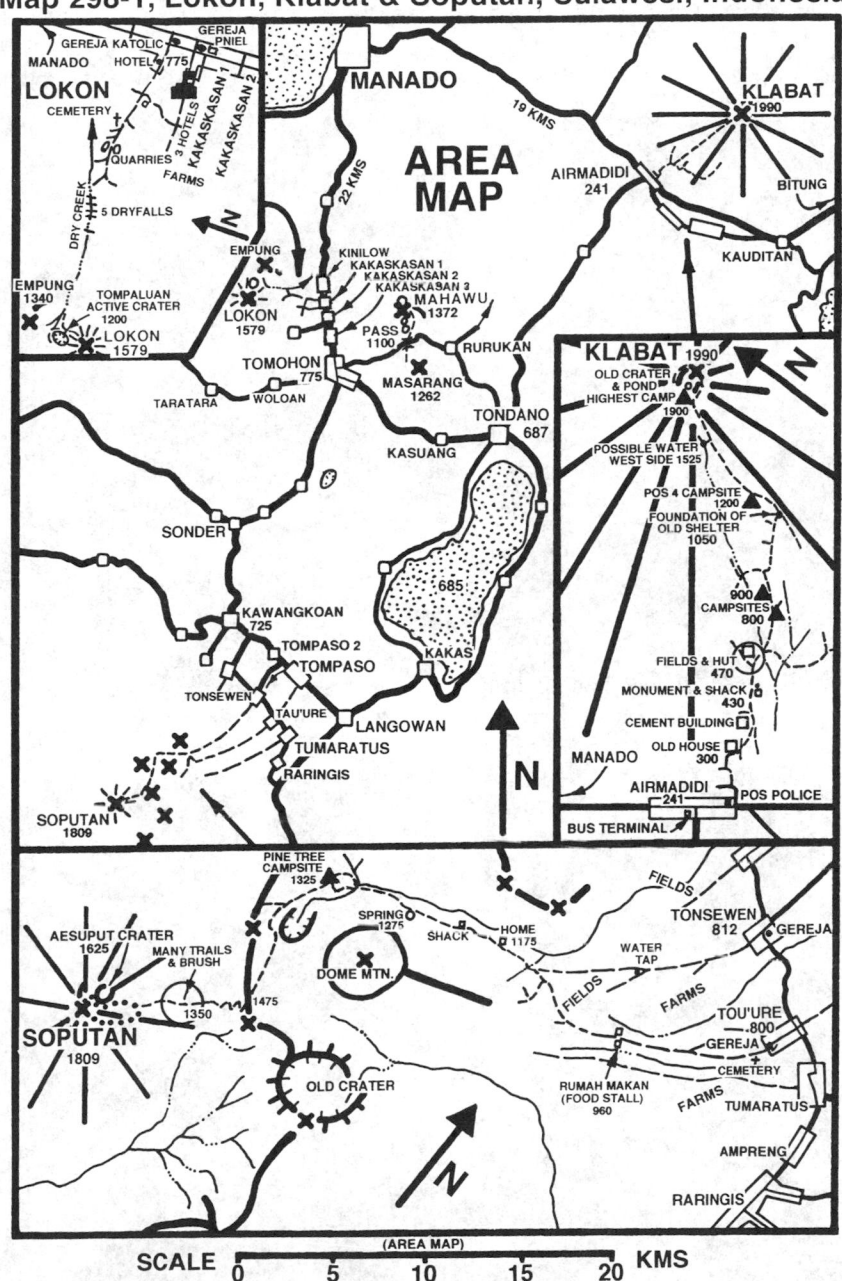

as best as you can for a safe return. From there, the author headed straight up the volcano, but a big storm came with wind & rain, and he didn't quite reach the true summit. Instead, he hurried down hoping to locate his path in the fog. He luckily made it through the brush!

On the way down in the rain, he ended up on another trail or ox cart road, the one passing the water tap and ending in Tonsewen, which is probably the better place to start hiking. From Tau'ure, up and back to Tonsewen took 5 3/4 hours.

Maps *Manado 2417-23, Bitung 2417-24/33, Amurang 2417-12 & Langowan 2417-21,* all at 1:50,000 from BAKOSURTANAL; and *Sulawesi Utara (North),* 1:100,000 from VSI, Bandung; the **Indonesia Travel Atlas** from Periplus; and the latest travel guidebook to Indonesia.

From near the summit of Lokon, looking down into Lokon's active crater, with Empung to the north in the background.

On the southwest side of the crater near the top of Klabat Volcano is the highest campsite on the mountain. On weekends, lots of young Indonesians camp here.

This is Kawah Igen (Igen Crater, Map 292, page 635) as seen from the trail going down to the emergency dam on the lowest part of the crater rim (on the left).

From the speedboat docks at Kota Ternate looking south at the island of Tidore and the highest peak called Keimatubu (see next map).

Ternate & Tidore Volcanos, Indonesia

Shown here are the islands of Ternate & Tidore, located immediately west of Halmahera, the biggest island in the Maluku group. In the west, this group has been known as the *Spice Islands*. Gamalama at 1721 meters, is the volcano on Ternate; and Kiematubu is the highest peak on Tidore at 1730. Kiematubu is a late-Pleistocene volcano, which still has a very steep & breached crater at the summit. Gamalama erupted throughout 1994, once sending ash ~5 kms high. For volcano updates see the websites (www.vsi.dpe.go.id) or (www.volcano.si.edu/gvp/).

The airport on Ternate is the gateway to the Maluku Islands and up to half a dozen flights from Manado land each day. The planes are small 16 passenger Casa 212's.

Climb both mountains from one of many hotels in Kota Ternate (Ternate City). To climb **Gamalama**, make your way to the bemo (minibus) terminal near Fort Oranje and ask about one going to Marikurubu. The distance is 3 kms on a paved road. From where the bemo stops, you'll likely have to walk another 300 meters or so to the *Direktorat Vulkanologi* building shown in the insert map. From there, walk north through or around the small cemetery immediately across the road and locate a good trail beyond the trees on the other side. Once on this trail, head straight up the ridge going northwest toward the summit.

Near the top or puncak (pron. punchak), you'll be in 3-meter-high bamboo grass, then the barren slopes of the new summit cone. From the observatory, the author made it to the puncak in 2 1/3 hours; 4 1/3 hours round-trip.

To climb **Kiematubu**, walk or take a bemo to the south end of Kota Ternate (Ternate City) to where the speedboats to Tidore dock. These 6 to 7-meter-long, 12-14 passenger boats have twin 40hp outboard engines and do the crossing in 8 minutes for about US$.20. You'll land at Rum, with many bemos waiting to take passengers to the bemo terminal in Kota Tidore (US$.20). At the terminal, consider buying food in the pasar (market) next door, then wait for a bemo running up to Gurabunga; or, do as the author did, charter an ojek (motorcycle taxi) for US$1.20 for the 6 km ride.

From the mosque in Gurabunga, walk 100 meters west and turn right, then left, and walk past several homes, the round village wash house, then along a trail. You'll soon pass a garbage heap, 2 graves, then veer left at the major trail junction. That point is 300 meters from Gurabunga. See insert map.

From that junction, head straight up the mountain on a good trail. Along the way you'll climb over 3 farm fences or styles. The highest fields are 975 meters. At 1030 meters, watch closely for a less-used trail veering left. This is about 50-75 meters below a bamboo shack, which is at the end of a well-maintained trail. This less-used trail contours 50 meters southeast, crosses a gully, then heads straight up the mountain. At about 1500 meters, you'll veer right 3 times. Watch closely because of the wild pig trails in that area. You may find running water at 1600 meters, then treeline at 1625 meters. The author made the summit in 1 2/3 hours; just over 3 hours round-trip from Gurabunga.

He got on a bemo going down the mountain and returned to Rum, then a speedboat to Ternate.

From the Ternate Airport, you have a good look at the northeastern slopes
of Gamalama Volcano, with its active crater on the right.

Map 299-1, Ternate & Tidore Volcano, Indonesia

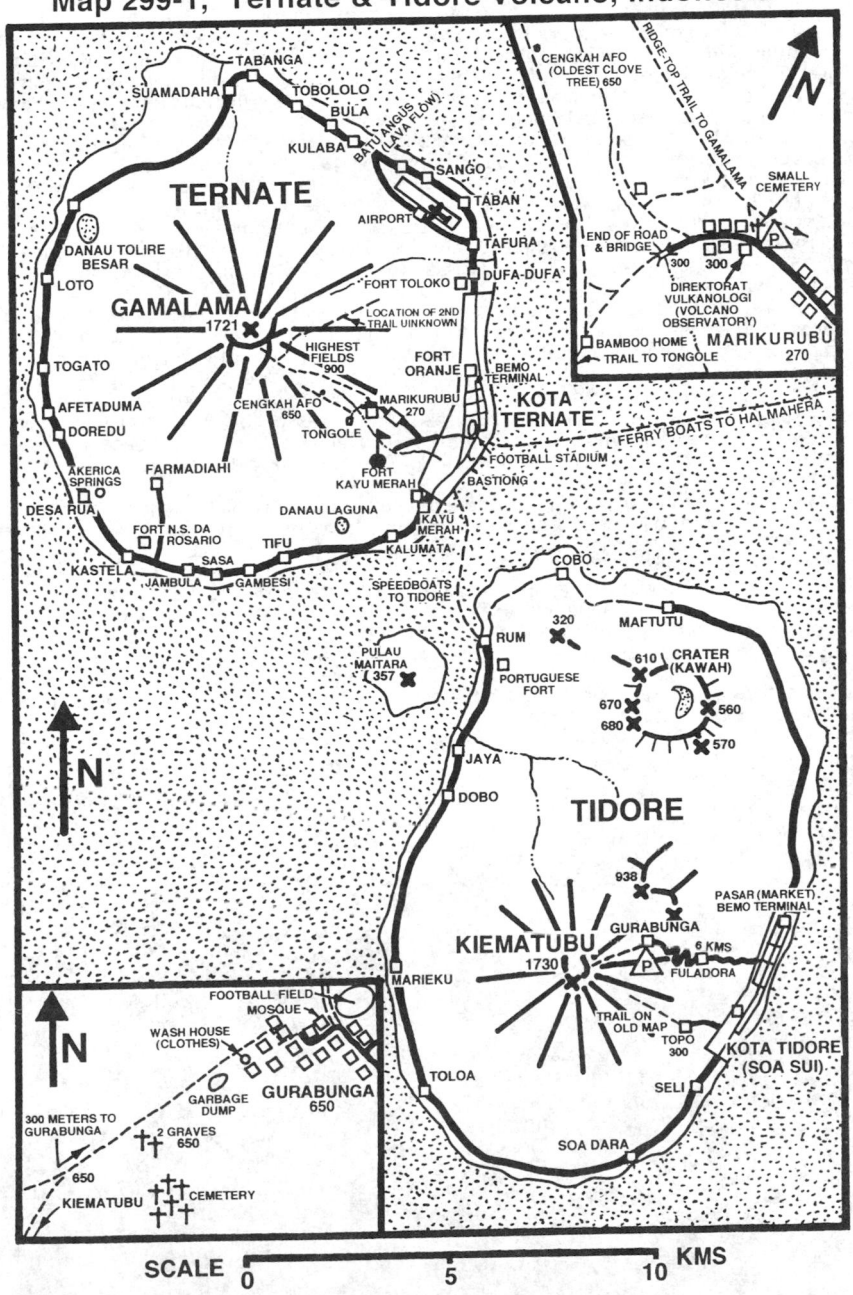

SCALE ⊢————————————————————⊣ KMS
0   5   10

Total round-trip time from Ternate's port was 6 1/2 hours. That included both speedboat trips. Dry season is April through October.

Maps *Ternate dan Hiri,* 1:50,000, and *Tidore,* 1:100,000, from the VSI, Bandung, Java; the **Indonesia Travel Atlas** from Periplus; and the latest travel guidebook to Indonesia.

Puncak Jaya, Sudirman Range, Irian Jaya, Indonesia

Much of the information here comes from Robert Shapiro of Philadelphia, USA. The mountains included on this map are those in the highlands of Indonesia's Irian Jaya--the western half of the island of New Guinea. Apparently the name of these mountains is the Sudirman Range. Some call it the Snowy Range. There are other conflicts concerning the names of the highest peaks The highest summit is now called Puncak (pron. Punchak) Jaya, at 4884 meters. This is the Indonesian name, but in the west we sometimes know it as Carstenz Pyramid.

The second highest summit is called Carstenz Timor (East), or as most say, East Carstenz Top, at about 4880 meters. The 3rd highest peak is Naga Pulu, at 4862 meters. Some sources call this Sukarno Peak. Not only are the names in confusion, but elevations as well. Most maps of the area list Puncak Jaya as 5020 meters, but since the best maps are from the book, **The Equatorial Glaciers of New Guinea**, by G.E. Balkema, those names and elevations are used here. Balkema's maps come from the U.S. Army Joint Operations Graphic (JOG's), Series 1501, *Timika, SB 53-4,* and *Hitalipa, SB 53-16,* at 1:250,000 scale. Balkema also used mountaineering maps to create his.

The normal route into these mountains is from the highland town of Ilaga, which has an airstrip serving a mission. Flights originate from Jayapura, Irian Jaya's capital city located on the north coast near the border with PNG; then from the larger town of Wamena, east of Ilaga, or from Mulia to the north. You might also get there via Nabire, or possibly Timika.

From Ilaga, there are 2 tracks leading west; a northern route, one heading toward Ugimba; and a southern track or the highlands track, which first heads southwest out of Ilaga. This latter route seems the best. Porters can be found in Ilaga for the 4 or 5 day trek to the mountain base. Climbers are forbidden from hiking from the copper mining town of Tembagapura, but if that route is ever opened, it would make an easy one day approach.

Once in the area of the snow peaks, there are both easy and difficult routes. **Naga Pulu** and the peak shown as **4700** meters, can both be climbed from the notch called New Zealand Pass, at about 4500 meters. To climb **Carstenz Timor**, cross over the NZ Pass, and make a camp in the Meren Valley (south of NZ Pass). Then cross over a small ridge and climb up the Carstenz Glacier to the top. The easy route up **Puncak Jaya** is to circle around the mountain ridge to the west and come in from the south face. All easy routes are south face approaches. The North Face of Puncak Jaya is the most difficult route in the range (all rock).

At last report, this area may be closed to climbers because of political problems and guerrilla activity by locals against the copper mine and the cultural invasion by Javanese/Indonesians. The driest time of year is May through October. Bring all supplies into this region, either from your home country, or better still, from Jayapura.

Maps The book, **The Equatorial Glaciers of New Guinea**, Balkema, Rotterdam, 1968?;

The north face of Carstenz or Puncak Jaya, right, and Carstenz Glacier, left.
(Robert Shapiro foto).

Map 300-3, Puncak Jaya, Irian Jaya, Indonesia

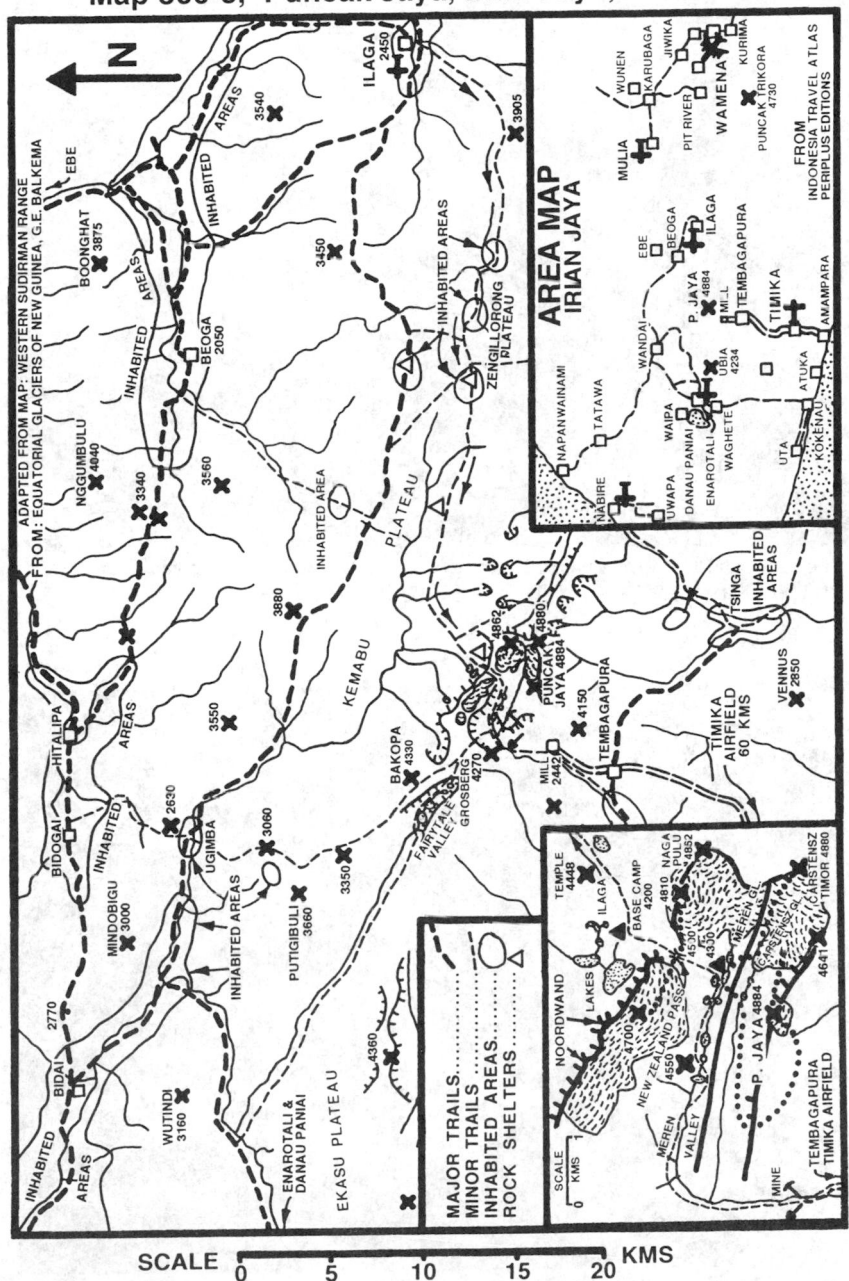

Indonesia Travel Atlas from Periplus; and the maps mentioned above if they're obtainable from the Bedan Koordinasi Survey dan Pemetaan Nasional (BAKOSURTANAL), Jalan Raya, Jakarta-Bogor, Km 46; and the latest travel guidebook to Indonesia.

The black sand landing beach on the northeast side of Anak Krakatau, departing tourists, and a 6-7 meter long speedboat. Everyone has to do a little wading as they land (Map 284, page 617).

This is the Kledung Pass Hotel located on the pass between Sundoro (behind) and Sumbing. The trail to Sundoro begins about 300 meters east of this hotel (Map 287, page 623).

This is the grass airstrip at Sola Airport. To the north is the highest peak on the island of Vanua Lava, more commonly known as Sola (Map 313, page 681).

A night-time foto of the very active Yasur Volcano. It's located on the island of Tanna in the Pacific island nation of Vanuatu (Map 318, page 691).

Mt. Giluwe, Central Range, Papua New Guinea

Mt. Giluwe at 4368 meters, is located in the heart of the highlands of Papua New Guinea (PNG). This is a very old and highly eroded volcano, similar to Mt. Hagen. The author has no information on this volcano's age, but it could easily be 30,000 to 40,000 years since its last eruption. This peak is high enough to have occasional snow showers at the summit and evidence exists of glaciation during the last ice age.

To get to this area, first head to the small city of Mount Hagen, and look for PMV's (small passenger carrying trucks) or buses going to Tambul and probably onward to Mendi. Get off in Tambul town and locate the Christian mission which is just northwest of the Tambul Airfield. The author did this climb in 1977, and was invited into the mission and slept one night before his trek. Regardless of who's there when you arrive, those people can help with information regarding transport up to Kargoba, and perhaps a guide and/or porters--it that's your style.

The normal route to **Giluwe** is via Tambul and Kargoba (a high altitude agricultural station). It's either 18 or 25 kms (?) from Tambul to Kargoba, but in 1977, there wasn't much traffic on that road, so the author walked all the way. By now there should be several trucks, PMV's or buses daily. Along this road, some fruits or vegetables may be purchased from people living in grass huts. If you have to walk, it'll be interesting.

Once at Kargoba, walk along the fenced area in a southeasterly direction, until the forest is reached. The trail should be visible, but if you have difficulty, there is usually someone around the station who can put you on the right path--unless things have changed radically! The author found the first 1 1/2 kms overgrown with grass, but beyond that it was a good trail in the forest. He had no guide, and no problems with finding the way.

The shelters shown on the map are bush huts, not like the climber's hut on Mt. Wilhelm; but you might get through a night in one--it they're still there. A *tent is required* however. The author did this climb in 2 very long days from Tambul on 3/27 & 3/28/1977; walking all the way. Total walk-time was 23 hours! A strong climber, with an early start, could climb Giluwe in one very long day from Kargoba.

Water is no problem on Giluwe, as you'll pass 3 streams between Kargoba and the summit. Raingear will keep you dry from wet undergrowth, if you're there in a wet period. It's recommended a change of clothing, kept dry in a plastic bag, be taken and used at night. The upper part of Giluwe is steep and one has to search a bit for the route, but no great difficulties should be found. Hopefully there will be enough people climbing the mountain to keep the trail open and visible.

The last place to buy food is at Tambul, but Mount Hagen has several supermarkets. Giluwe can be climbed at any time of year, but there is a wetter period from about December through March. May through September is the driest and best time.

Looking south at the upper part of Giluwe. The highest summit is in the middle.

Map 301-1, Mt. Giluwe, Central Range, Papua New Guinea

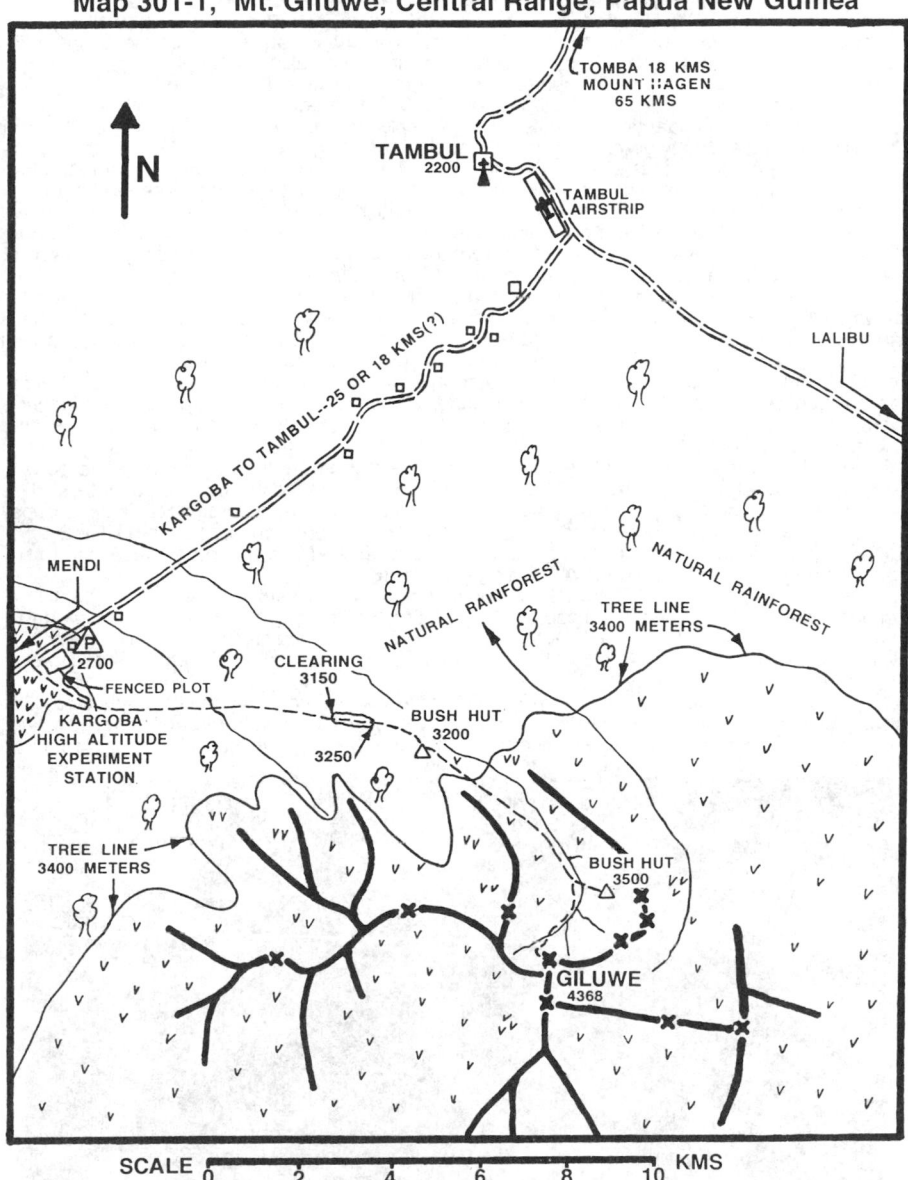

Maps *Mendi, 7685 & Wapenamanda, 7686,* 1:100,000; new JOG (or old DMA) maps *(Lake) Kutubu, SB 54-12,* and *Karimui, SB 5-9,* 1:250,000, from the National Mapping Bureau, Box 5665, Melanesian Way, Port Moresby, Tele. 276465; and the book, **Bush walking In Papua New Guinea**, Lonely Planet; and the latest travel guidebook to PNG.

Mt. Hagen, Central Range, Papua New Guinea

In the heart of the highlands of Papua New Guinea (PNG) stands one of the higher mountains in the country, Mt. Hagen at 3795 meters. This massif appears to be the remnants of a very old volcano. Mt. Hagen is not to be confused with the small city of Mount Hagen, which is about 40 kms east and is the most important settlement in the western highlands.

PNG was a protectorate of Australia up until 1975, with most Australians finally leaving the country by 1978. Since that time, tourists will have replaced the Aussies and will hopefully keep the trail open. It was pretty good when the author climb Mt. Hagen on 3/26/1977.

Getting to the highlands is easy. There are buses taking passengers from Lae and Madang, both on the coast, to Mount Hagen. This is your first stop. Mount Hagen has several hotels or resthouses and by now several supermarkets and a good market place.

From Mount Hagen there are now minibuses to just about everywhere. Or look for PMV's, which are normally pickup trucks carrying cargo and passengers. One may also get a ride with missionaries, of which there are too many in this land of bushmen.

From Mount Hagen, take a bus or PMV westward about 42 kms to the town of Tomba, as shown on this map. Tomba has an Adventist church & mission (SDA) and you should stop there and see if someone can give you updated information regarding the beginning of the trail. Tomba also has several small stores where you can buy more food if needed.

From Tomba, walk or get a lift up the road northwest to Harris and Kakaitomba, about 2 kms. The trail begins at about where the road junction is shown, but you'll have to ask. The location has no doubt changed since 1977. The trail passes several huts (or houses), then a swamp before it enters the forest.

The author found it a muddy trail, used much more at the bottom than the top. There are 2 clearings in the forest before the trail enters the higher grasslands at about 3400 meters. The trail is reasonably good at this point, but again, only climbers (usually foreigners) use the upper sections. The hike can be done in one long day from Tomba, but if you decide to do it in 2 days, plan to camp high on the mountain where water is available. Most of the trail and route to the summit is on a ridge, with no water in the middle sections.

The author made this climb in 8 1/2 hours round-trip from the Adventist Mission in Tomba, but he stopped at the peak just north of the one marked 3778 meters thinking that was the summit. At that time, it seems that was the end of the trail too (?). However, in 1997, on his 2nd trip to PNG, he bought better maps which show the true summit further along the main ridge at 3795 meters. There may or may not be a trail going that way.

The dry season is from about May through October, but expect wet conditions any time. For those afraid of becoming lost, there will be plenty of volunteers to be your guide; however, guides are likely not needed, especially after the 1st km or so. What you might do is hire a boy

The author putting up his tent with a big crowd at the Adventist church in Tomba.

Map 302-1, Mt. Hagen, Central Range, Papua New Guinea

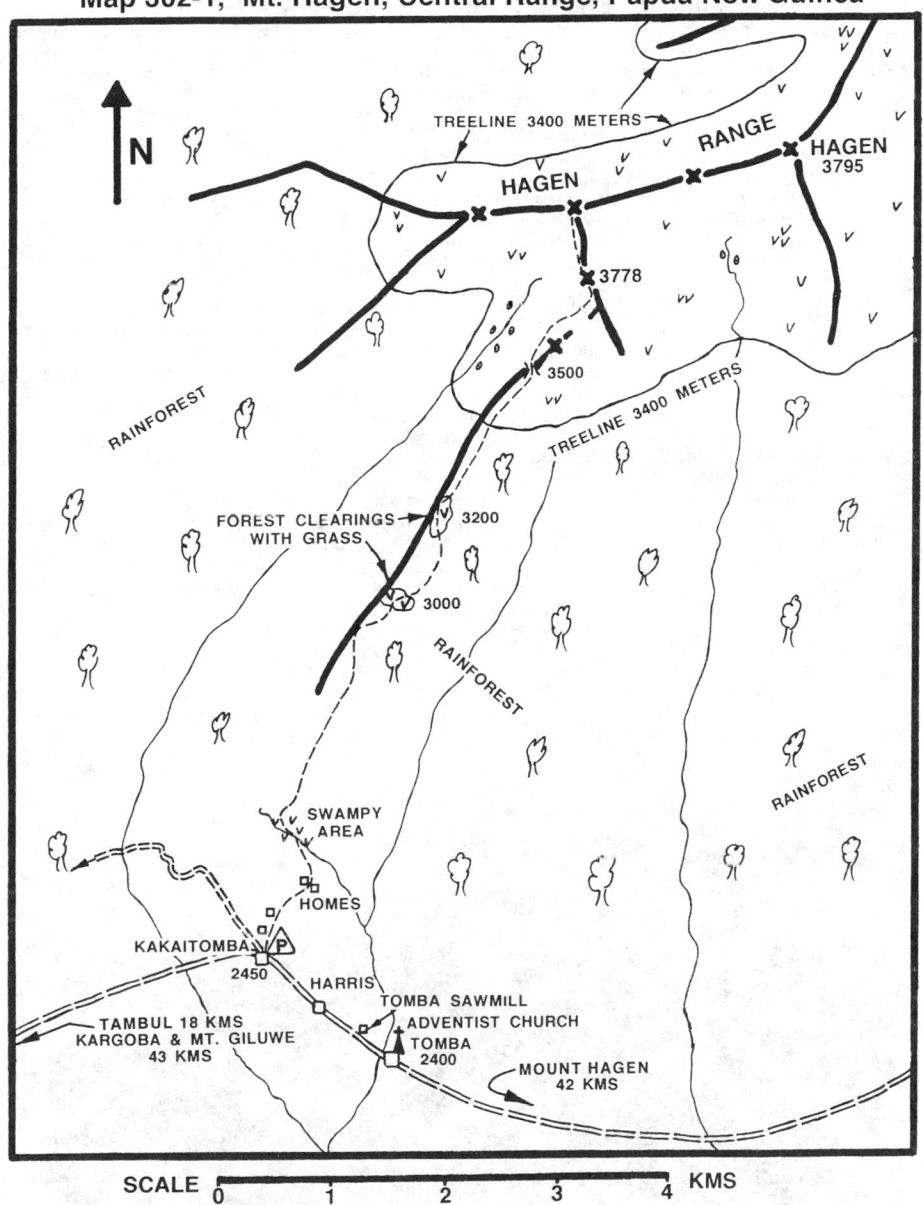

to escort you well into the forest and past the swampy area.

Maps *Hagen, 7786,* 1:100,000; or the new JOG (old DMA) maps *Ramu, SB 55-5,* and *Wabag, SB 54-8,* 1:250,000; from the National Mapping Bureau, Box 5665, Melanesian Way, Port Moresby, Tele. 276465; and the latest travel guidebook to PNG.

Mt. Wilhelm, Bismarck Range, Papua New Guinea

The highest mountain in Papua New Guinea (PNG) is Mt. Wilhelm at 4510 meters. Wilhelm is located in the Eastern Highlands and the Bismarck Range; northwest of Goroka and northeast of Kundiawa. The higher portion of the mountain consists of granitic-type rock (some are calling it gabbro), which could offer some good rock climbing.

Getting to **Wilhelm** is fairly easy. After reaching the eastern highlands and Kundiawa, the capital of Chimbu province, look for a minibus or PMV (Public Motor Vehicle; a pickup carrying people and cargo), or perhaps a missionary heading north in the direction of Keglsugl & airstrip or Toronambanau and the Denglagu Catholic Mission. Before leaving Kundiawa, do all your shopping, as the variety of food there is much better than at the base of the mountain. Or shop in Goroka or Mount Hagen City, which are even bigger places. There's apparently one small store near the mission, another at Keglsugl. There were no hotels in this upper valley, but the book below suggests you might bed down on the floor of an annex next to the store in Keglsugl for a small fee. Or drop a tent near the Keglsugl airstrip.

For the most part, traffic ends at the mission, but there's a road on to Keglsugl airstrip at about 2480 meters elevation. Beyond the airstrip (which is often used by climbers with more money than time) a 4WD road continues to a sawmill and lumbering area (which will change as time passes). In 1977, the road ended at a small stream, and a well-marked and often-used trail began. The trail is maintained by somebody; probably the people running the research station higher up, or people in Keglsugl, who control the climber's hut on the mountain.
The trail runs along a ridge, with no water, until reaching several small bush huts on the terminal moraine of a former glacier at 3200 meters. From that point, it's open grassland up to the climber's hut and High Altitude Research Station.

Lake Piunde is in the first of 2 cirque basins which rank high for their beauty and grandeur. To use the climber's hut, you're supposed to make a payment and pick up the key at the Keglsugl airstrip caretaker's house. If you prefer, it's possible to sleep free in the porters hut behind the research station. However, everyone going to Mt. Wilhelm must take a tent and be prepared to camp.

From the climber's hut there's a well-marked trail leading past the remains of a Japanese warplane near the 12000 ft. (3658 m.) marker. The book below says it's an American plane, but this writer remembers seeing Japanese characters on a propeller (?). From the wreckage, a good trail continues to the summit marked with yellow paint, poles and rocks, so there's little chance of getting lost in the fog. The climb normally takes 2 days from Keglsugl.

The author camped at the mission, then in 3 1/2 hours stopped to camp at Aundi Lake. Next morning, 4/2/1977, he was at the summit in less than 2 hours. Later, he walked 11 kms past the Denglagu Mission to the Sumbaru Mission and camped. This means a strong hiker can climb

High on the slopes of Mt. Wilhelm is the wreckage of a Japanese war plane.

Map 303-1, Wilhelm, Bismarck Range, Papua New Guinea

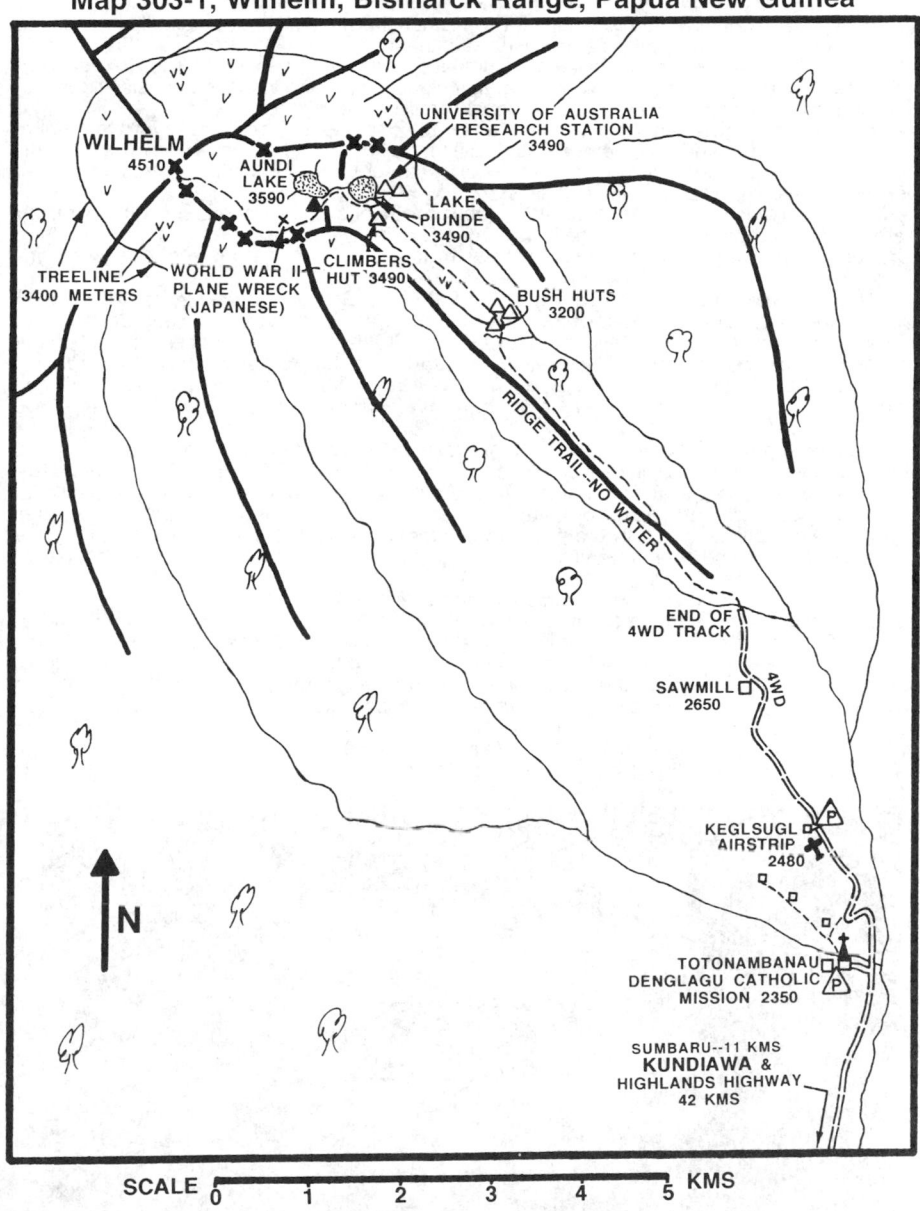

Wilhelm in one full day from Keglsugl. The dry season is from May through October.
Maps *Bundi, 7986,* 1:100,000; or the new JOG (old DMA) map *Ramu, SB 55-5,* 1:250,000; and the book, **Bushwalking In Papua New Guinea**, Lonely Planet; and the latest travel guidebook to PNG.

The Kokoda Trail, Papua New Guinea

The Kokoda Trail of Papua New Guinea, while not classified as a mountain climb, must be covered here, as it's one of the great *adventures* in the world of trekking. This path is a *National Walking Trail,* created by the Australian government during their stay in PNG. The **Kokoda Trail** was a military battleground during World War II; the Japanese were stopped at Imata Ridge, but now it's used by trekkers and by poor local people crossing the island.

From Owen's Corner on the south end, about 48 kms east of Port Moresby, to the rubber plantation town of Kokoda on the north, is 93.6 kms. The trail is very well-marked with signs, stating in kms and hours, the distance to the next water or village. It's all but impossible to get lost. Guides are not required, but being fit is.

Many people doing this hike, fly from Moresby to Popondetta, then take a minibus or PMV (cargo and passenger truck) to Kokoda, where the 5 to 7 day trek begins (or ends). Start at the north end by walking or riding from Kokoda, through the rubber plantation to Kovelo and continue south.

Starting on the south, take an early morning PMV from Gordon's Market in Port Moresby to Owen's Corner; 2 hours, 48 kms, US$3. There are few vehicles passing Owens Corner, so if ending the hike there, it may be necessary to walk the 11 kms to the main Sogeri Road, then get transport to Moresby. *Because of thieves, get an early morning start from either end of the trail and walk as far as possible the first day. On the last night, camp as far from the trail & trailhead as possible. Don't camp near either trailhead, as PNG has become **a den of thieves!** Leave most money in Moresby.*

Food should be bought in Popondetta or Moresby, but there are small stores at Naoro, Menari, Efogi I and Kagi selling canned foods, crackers, etc.; and some fruits and vegetables are available at most villages along the route. At several places along the trail, mainly at the south end, you must be able to carry 1 or 2 liters of water, as pointed out by the signs, to get over several high waterless ridges. There's plenty of water along the way, but as the trail follows the ridge tops, there are no streams, and the heat and humidity are terrific. Pay attention to the trail, and when it begins to rise, fill your water bottle. Take salt tablets, or eat some salt.

Almost all villages have a guesthouse you can use for a fee, and there are some bush huts along the way, but the author recommends a lightweight tent, to keep out the bugs & mosquitos. Perhaps the most important thing to remember is, go with as little weight as possible.

While all streams now seem to have bridges, best not to hike in the wet season because of muddy trails and high water. The drier months are from May through October. Dry clothing to change into at night, should be taken and kept in plastic bags. During the day, the clothes you'll be wearing will be soaked continually from perspiration.

The author started this hike on 3/10/1977. He started in a PMV, then hitched to Owens Corner. He hiked for 1 1/2 days with a 35 kg pack, and returned to Moresby. He air shipped 16 kgs of baggage to

One of many signs along the Kokoda Trail.

Map 304-1, The Kokoda Trail, Papua New Guinea

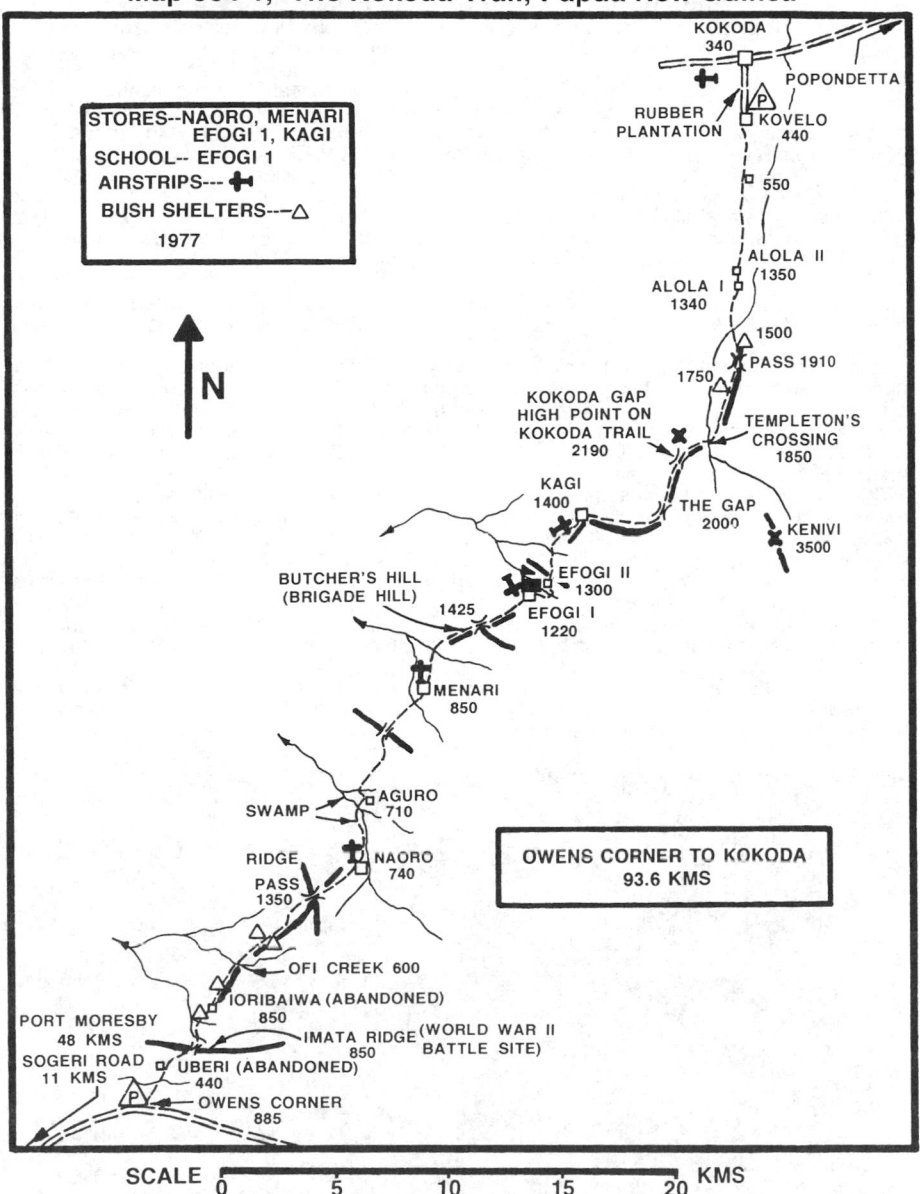

STORES--NAORO, MENARI
EFOGI 1, KAGI
SCHOOL-- EFOGI 1
AIRSTRIPS--- ✈
BUSH SHELTERS---△
1977

N

KOKODA
340

POPONDETTA

RUBBER
PLANTATION

KOVELO
440

550

ALOLA II
1350

ALOLA I
1340

1500

PASS 1910

1750

KOKODA GAP
HIGH POINT ON
KOKODA TRAIL
2190

TEMPLETON'S
CROSSING
1850

KAGI
1400

THE GAP
2000

KENIVI
3500

BUTCHER'S HILL
(BRIGADE HILL)

EFOGI II
1300

1425

EFOGI I
1220

MENARI
850

AGURO
710

SWAMP

RIDGE

NAORO
740

PASS
1350

OWENS CORNER TO KOKODA
93.6 KMS

OFI CREEK 600

IORIBAIWA (ABANDONED)
850

PORT MORESBY
48 KMS

IMATA RIDGE (WORLD WAR II
850   BATTLE SITE)

SOGERI ROAD
11 KMS

UBERI (ABANDONED)
440

OWENS CORNER
885

SCALE   0   5   10   15   20   KMS

Popondetta, then started again in the afternoon of 3/13/1977. He reached Kokoda on the 5th day with a total walk-time of 35 3/4 hours. He averaged about 20 kms for each full day, and camped each night away from villages.

Maps *Kokoda, 8480 & Efogi, 8479,* 1:100,000; *The Kokoda Trail,* about 1:150,000, and the *Longitudinal Cross Section of the Kokoda Trail;* and/or new JOG (or old DMA) maps *Buna SC 55-3* and *Port Moresby, SC 55-7,* 1:250,000, all from the National Mapping Bureau, Box 5665, Melanesian Way, Port Moresby, Tele. 276465; the book, **Bushwalking In Papua New Guinea**, Lonely Planet; and the latest travel guidebook to PNG.

663

Lamington Volcano, Papua New Guinea

On the north side of the island of New Guinea, and on Papua New Guinea's north slope, not far south of the provincial capital of Popondetta, and near the northern end of the Kokoda Trail, is the Mt. Lamington Volcano at 1679 meters.

Lamington is an old, forested and rather weathered stratovolcano, but the summit area has some recently built cones. Carbon dating has put large prior eruptions at 5980 & 4850 BC, but the last big one was on 1/17/1951, with some minor activity lasting until 1956. In that large eruption, which ranked 4 on the Volcanic Explosivity Index (VEI), 2942 people were killed by pyroclastic flows (superheated gas & ash). The debris covered villages on the north slope. The entire European population of Higatura plus many Papuans were killed. It was later estimated the temperature stood at about 200°C and the gas cloud moved downhill at 300 km/h. About 1/10 of the population of the province was left homeless. For volcano updates use email (rvo@datec.com.pg) or see website (www.volcano.si.edu/gvp/).

The author hasn't climbed this mountain, but he was in the area at the end of his Kokoda Trail hike in 3/1977, and nearly got there in 1997. Part of the information here comes from Ben Talai of the Rabaul Volcano Observatory; and part from the Lonely Planet book, **Papua New Guinea**.

Begin in Popondetta. Go to the main town market near the high school, to locate a PMV or minibus. There should be several each day running to Kokoda, or to somewhere along that road. Look for a PMV running up to the Susembata Mission, and maybe on to Kendata, at the end of the road. There should be one going there each day, but there will never be a schedule of any kind, because they usually go when the PMV is full. It'll either be in the morning or afternoon.

Once at the base of the mountain, preferably Susembata Mission, ask the village counselor or chief about the trail and a possible guide. The people at the mission also might be of help. It's likely best to hire a guide from one of the highest villages, perhaps Kendata. For safety sake, look for a room at the mission for one or 2 nights. If you stay there, always make a donation, even if they don't ask for payment. This area, especially along the road to Kokoda, has seen armed robberies in the 1990's. This is now happening all over PNG!

Arrive in the afternoon if possible, hopefully sleep at the mission, then start early the next morning before the afternoon clouds build up. It's only 6 or 7 kms to the top, so for some it could take only 4 or 5 hours round-trip.

In Popondetta are several hotels or guesthouses, plus several missions or Christian training centers you can stay in. You may also stay in a Franciscan Friary, or camp on their grounds, but never leave your tent alone after dark. Please leave a donation if you stay there. Buy all your supplies in Popondetta at one of several small supermarkets or the market place. The dry

This huge spring is right at the shoreline on the northwest coast of Karkar Island off the north coast of PNG. People gather here at Kaviak to bathe and wash clothes (Map 307, page 669).

Map 305-2, Lamington Volcano, Papua New Guinea

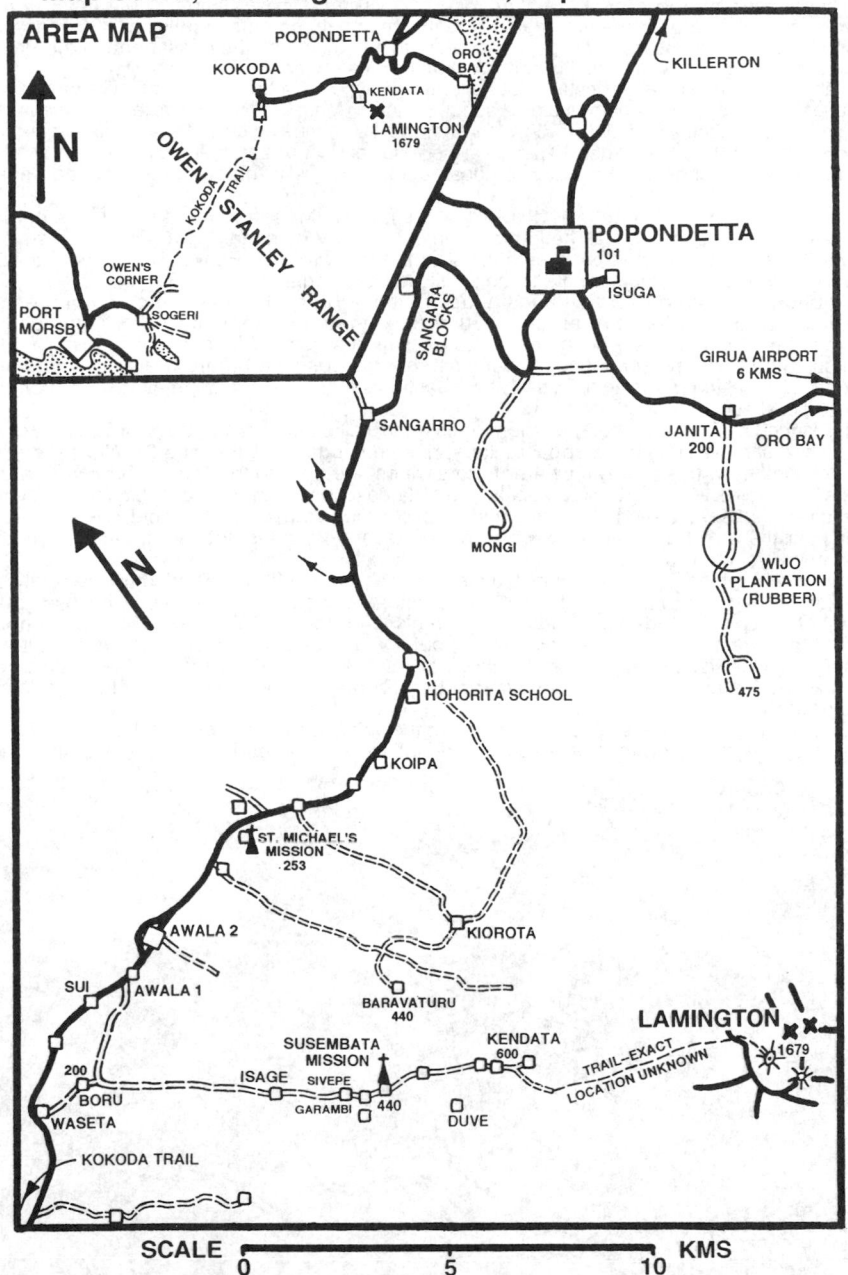

season is from May or June through October.

Maps *Popondetta,* 1:100,000; and/or new JOG (or old DMA) maps *Buna, SC 55-3* and *Port Moresby, SC 55-7,* 1:250,000, all from the National Mapping Bureau, Box 5665, Melanesian Way, Port Moresby, Tele. 276465; and the latest travel guidebook to PNG.

Yabu Volcano, Manam Island, Papua New Guinea

The volcano featured here is called Yabu or Iyabu by local villagers, but most people elsewhere usually refer to the mountain as having the same name as the island. Manam is a small island only 10 kms is diameter. It's located about 15 kms off the coast north of the Papua New Guinea town of Bogia, which is northwest of the small city of Madang.

Yabu has been in a near-constant state of eruption since 1974 and is one of PNG's most active volcanos. Its composite cone contains 2 summit craters (Main and South Craters). Four valleys radiate from the summit and pyroclastic and lava flows are channeled down these. The larger-than-normal eruption of 12/3/1996, killed 13 people in the village of Budua. Latest eruptions were in 11/1999, but it's continually ongoing. For volcano updates use email (rvo@datec.com.pg) or see website (www.volcano.si.edu/gvp/).

The author climbed **Yabu** on 9/18/1997. His started in Madang. From the middle of town and near the main bus terminal, he found a minibus or PMV going to Bogia. There are several PMV's making the trip daily, but they don't start until they're full. Best to buy all your food in Madang supermarkets, but there are some small shops in Bogia, as well as on Manam.

At Bogia he stayed in a little guesthouse in the north part of town, then early the next morning was at the wharf. At around 7:30 or 8am, there are normally 8 or 10 speedboats arriving from Manam. They bring copra and passengers from various villages to Bogia, then take supplies and other passengers back as soon as possible before the daily winds start blowing hard making rough seas. The speedboat the author took was 6-7 meters long, took one hour and cost about US$4.

He landed at Tabela (Tabele) Mission Station and walked east to Dugulaba 1 & 2. There's a school and shop (selling soda pop, crackers, rice and sugar) in Dugulaba 2. While there, he filled his bottles with semi-fresh water from springs seeping up from the shoreline near the villages, but some villagers walk to Tabela and fill large jugs with well water, which tastes better. He then walked east to the bottom of the southeast valley or lava flow channel. He camped in trees near the trail, but you should walk up the mountain a ways and never allow anyone to know where your tent is.

The next morning, he broke camp, hid his large pack in brush, and climbed up the southeast lava flow. It was easy walking until near the summit, then he found it steeper with loose gravel on top of a hard crusted ash foundation. The climb up took 3 1/2 hours; about 6 1/2 hours round-trip. There was lots of steam on top, but it was quiet. About one month later, it was booming again with ash eruptions and night-time crater glow. The next morning he found a boat at Dugulaba 2 and got back to Bogia in about 1 1/2 hours. From there he hitched a ride in a pickup back to Madang in 4 hours.

Best to land at Tabela so you can ask about the volcano from the person who monitors the nearby seismograph. You can also walk around the island on a road & trail. Each larger village

From the highest peak on Yabu Volcano looking north at the main crater.

Map 306-1, Yabu Volcano, Manam Island, P. New Guinea

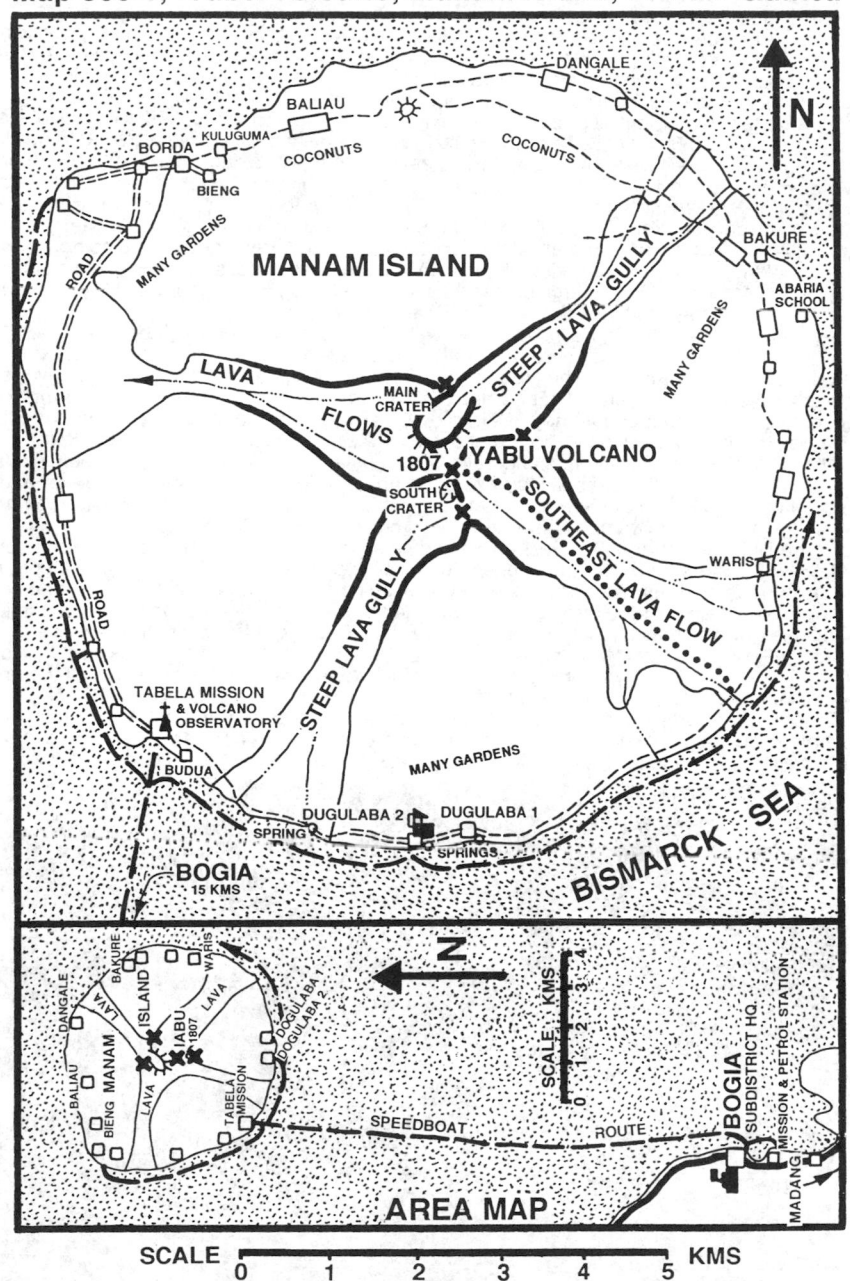

should have a small store of some kind. The dry season is from May or June through October.
Maps *Nubia* and *Manam*, 1:100,000; and the new JOG (or old DMA) map *Bogia, SB 55-1,*
1:250,000, both from the National Mapping Bureau, Box 5665, Melanesian Way, Port Moresby,
Tele. 276465; and the latest travel guidebook to PNG.

Uluman Volcano, Karkar Island, Papua New Guinea

Off the north coast of Papua New Guinea are several volcanic islands, one of which is Karkar. This island forms an almost a perfect circle and is itself one single stratovolcano. The highest point on the oldest caldera rim is 1831 meters, but there is a more recent 3-km-wide crater just to the north. We can assume this volcano was much higher in the not-too-distant past and before at least 2 large explosions took the top off. Within the present crater is Bagia Cone, at about 1320 meters, with a fumarole on its southeastern slope. The last major eruptive period was in 1/1979, with activity lasting through about mid-1980. By 1997, trees were covering the inner crater, but fumarole gases had killed some vegetation in 9/1999. For volcano updates use email (rvo@datec.com.pg) or see website (www.volcano.si.edu/gvp/).

To get to **Karkar**, first go to Madang. In 1997, boats to Karkar docked behind the new Anderson's Supermarket. There are several plantation boats making runs between Karkar & Madang; with at least one boat making the run each day. Be sure to get on one going along the west side of the island. Ask to be let off at the Kulkul Plantation docks if possible, which is about 4 hours from Madang. From there you can walk 3 kms east up to the village of Mom. If you get off at Kinim, you'll have to hire a taxi or motorcycle to get to Mom.

If you go direct to Mom, the village chief will find a place for you to sleep (for a fee). You could likely camp at or near the central gathering place, but you wouldn't have a moment's peace! You could also camp in the grounds of the Kulkul or Marangis Plantation, but never allow anyone to know you're there. That's where the author camped, and at midnight, 4 men with machetes came demanding money or his life. It's a long story, but all they got was a pocket knife! See the *Introduction* to this book on how to hide your cash and avoid being robbed!

Above Mom are lots of gardens and trails and a guide is required. This is the same situation as on all Pacific Islands. Each village owns the rights going up the mountain above, and the village chief will arrange to have one of the boys take you up. The author paid the boy about US$4. You can leave extra baggage in the chief's house.

Above Upper Mom at 290 meters, are gardens up to about 550 meters, then the rainforest. At about 950 meters, and after about one hour's walk, you'll leave the forest and walk up an old lava gully. There should be potholes with water along this section, but it may or may not be drinkable (?). At about 1300 meters, you'll come to the crater rim. At that point the trail basically disappears. Maps show a trail running along the rim to **Kunugui Peak**, but it was a bushwhack on 9/21/1997! If getting to the highest peak is important, inquire about the routes from Wakon or Gamog. However, the volcanologists use the Mom route, which is the best way to the crater. The author and guide hurried to the rim in 1 2/3 hours; 3 3/4 hours round-trip.

Buy all your food in Madang. Catch the boat back to Madang at Kinim if possible, where there are shops, a guesthouse, and a Catholic resthouse with Brother Sabastian. He also had a little store in 1997. Round-trip from Madang will be 3-4 days, depending on boat schedules. The

The required guide and his friends climbing up the lava gully of Uluman Volcano.

Map 307-1, Uluman Volcano, Karkar Island, PNG

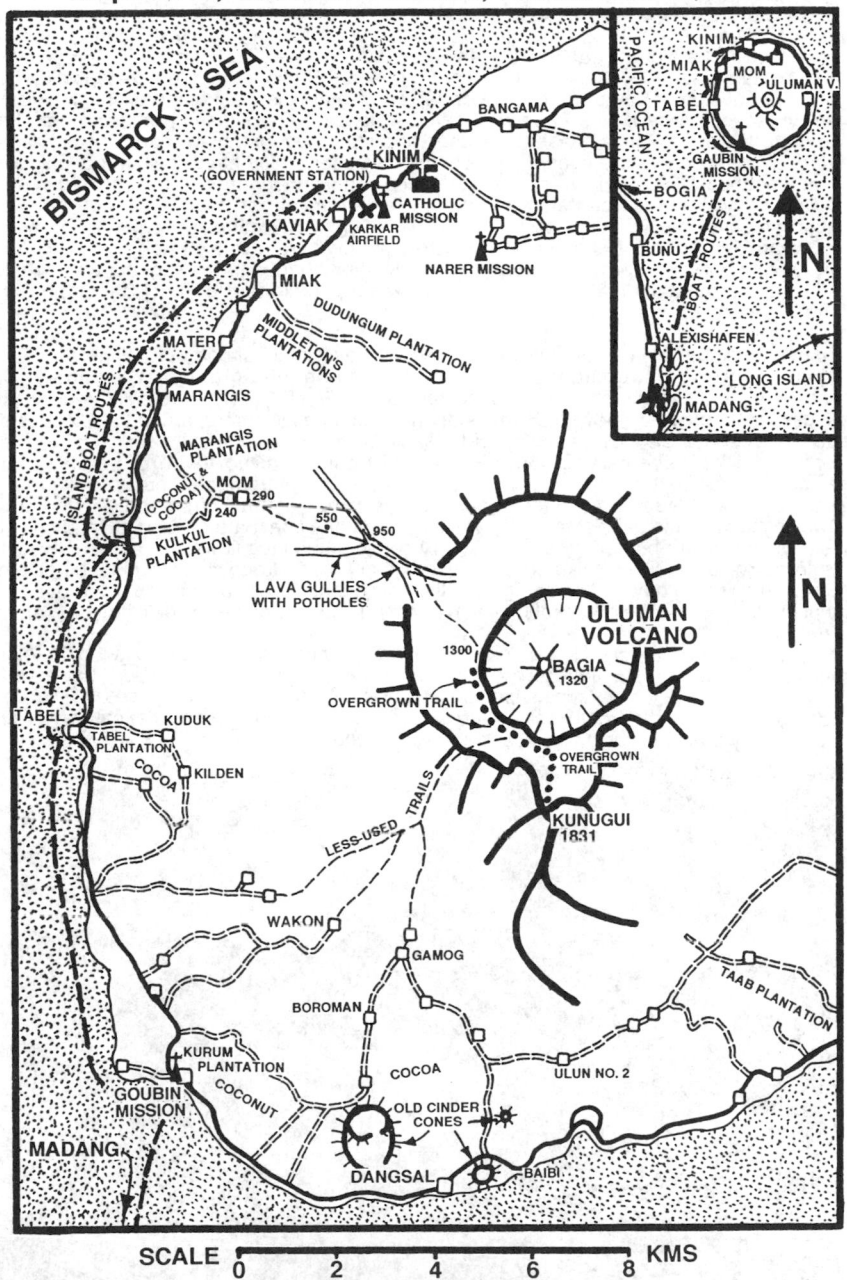

dry season is from May or June through October.
Maps *Karkar* and *Bagabag,* 1:100,000; the new JOG (or old DMA) map *Karkar Island,* 1:250,000; all from the National Mapping Bureau, Box 5665, Melanesian Way, Port Moresby, Tele. 276465; and maybe the latest travel guidebook to PNG.

Talawe & Langila, New Britain Island, Papua New Guinea

Shown here is the extreme western end of the island of New Britain, which was the scene of some big battles during WWII. Featured are several volcanos, one of which might be the most active in PNG. The highest summit is Talawe at 1824 meters. To the south is Tangi at 1481 meters, Awala at about 1080, and Namur at 1092 meters. These are all old forested volcanos.

However, of most interest are the new cones and craters just east of the extinct Mt. Talawe. These are collectively called the *Langila Craters*. As late as 12/1999, and continuing, were the 4 active craters around Gulu. These have been in a state of constant eruption for more than a century. These 4 craters are overlapping composite cones which have spewed out lava to the north and northeast. Some flows have reached the sea, although most eruptions have been of the volcanian type. There is often crater glow at night with strombolian activity. For volcano updates use email (rvo@datec.com.pg) or see website (www.volcano.si.edu/gvp/). Or read the book **Strong Men Armed**, Robert Leckie, a history of World War II in the Pacific.

The author flew into Hoskins, shopped at Kimbe, then headed to Ulawun, but was on a tight schedule and didn't quite make it to Langila. However, he did talk to Ben Talai of the Rabaul Volcano Observatory, and a member of the Airlink Airline staff at Hoskins Airport for this information.

To get there, the only way is to fly to West New Britain's main airport at Hoskins, then get on an Airlink Airlines flight going to various airstrips along the north coast, ending at Cape Gloucester Airport, sometimes called Gloucester Bay. In 9/1997, there were daily flights in small 4 to 6 passenger planes. They left Hoskins at 8am and normally turned around at Gloucester at 11am. The cost was US$100 each way, or US$200 round-trip.

For climbing, it seems you could walk right from the airport where a small volcano observatory is located, but Ben Talai states you could also do it from the Gloucester Patrol Post, or anywhere in between. As you fly in, observe the terrain carefully from the air, and ask the pilot which might be the easiest route for walking. Near the coast are coconut plantations, then grasslands (which are burned off during the dry season) and lava flows, but apparently no rain forest to worry about. Seems like pretty simple hiking (?). A strong climber might be able do it round-trip in one long day, but camping near the active craters would give you some good night fotos of the fireworks. The only problem with camping near the crater is you'll have to carry lots of water.

To get to the older volcanos to the south, you'd have to hire a pickup truck to get to the Aimaga Mission, which would likely be the best starting point. Expect no public land transport; only expensive taxis. Do all your shopping in Kimbe supermarkets, where some of the lowest prices in PNG can be found. Lots of PMV's run from Hoskins Airport (where you'll find one small expensive hotel) to Kimbe. The dry season is from May or June through October.

Leaving Manam Island in a 6-meter-long speedboat (Map 306, page 667).

Map 308-3, Talawe & Langila Volcanos, New Britain, PNG

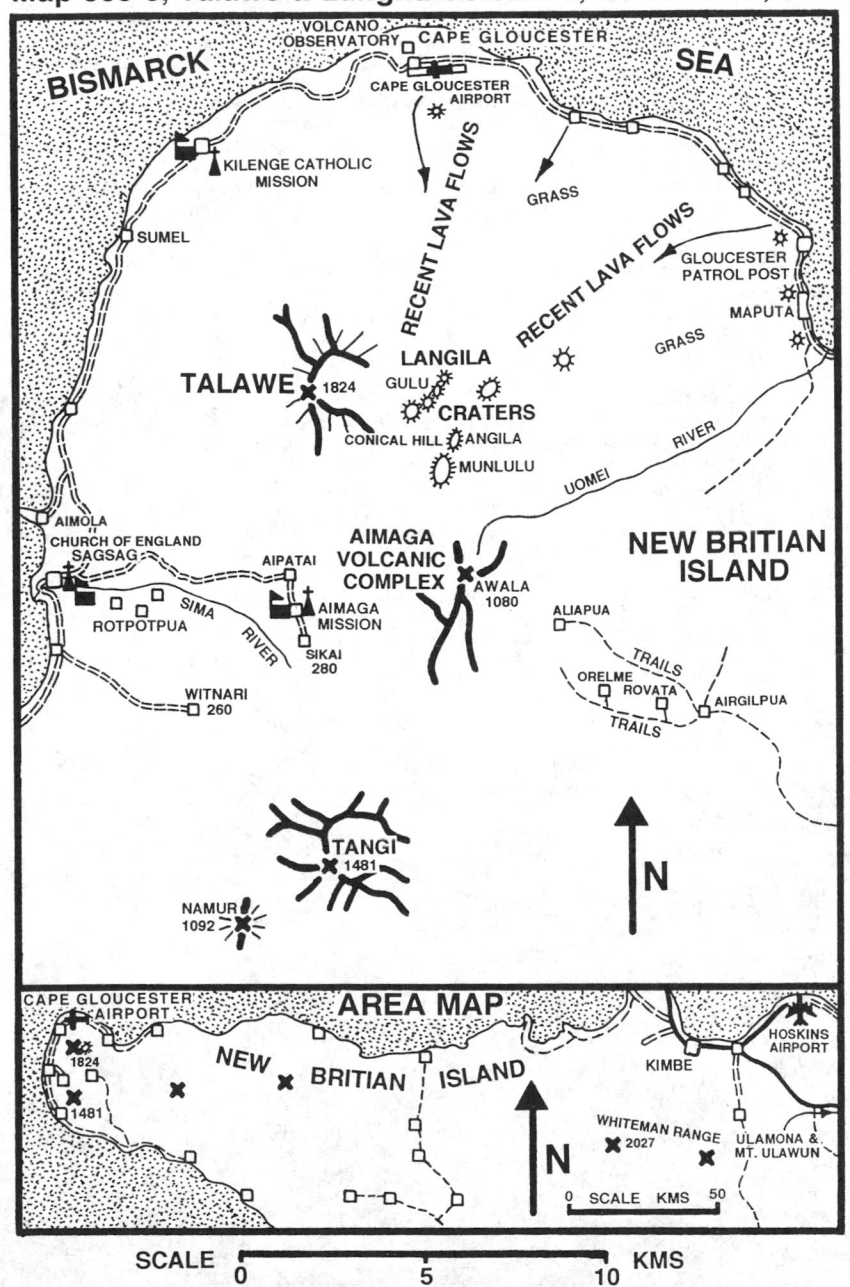

Maps *Gloucester, 8587* and *Talawe, 8586,* 1:100,000; and perhaps the new JOG (or old DMA) maps *Umboi, SB 55-7* and maybe *Andewe, SB 55-8,* 1:250,000; all from the National Mapping Bureau, Box 5665, Melanesian Way, Port Moresby, Tele. 276465; and the website above which is for the **Bulletin of the Global Volcanism Network**.

Ulawun Volcano, New Britain Island, Papua New Guinea

The highest mountain, and one of the most active volcanos on the island of New Britain, is Mt. Ulawun at 2334 meters. It's located in the eastern quarter of the island, very near the north coast, and southwest of Rabaul. It's also about 152 kms east of both the Hoskins Airport and the large market town of Kimbe.

When the author climbed it on 9/14/1997, it was emitting lots of steam. Rocks at the crater rim were very warm, but the mountain was otherwise quiet. Ulawun's last major eruption was on 10/19/1999, but it continually emits steam & vapor and could be this way for years to come. For volcano updates use email (rvo@datec.com.pg) or see website (www.volcano.si.edu/gvp/).

To climb **Ulawun**, you'll first have to fly from either Port Moresby or Rabaul to the main airport for West New Britain which is at Hoskins. Waiting for each flight at the airport will be many PMV's--minibuses or pickups--to take you to Kimbe, the provincial capital. Kimbe has several large supermarkets where you can buy all your food. From the market or the downtown area, catch a bus or pickup heading for Bialla, about 132 kms east. From Bialla, which has several stores, find another PMV, likely a pickup, going to the little mission & sawmill town of Ulamona. There are 3 sizable unbridged & flood-gutted river channels to ford along the last 20 km section, so do this trip only in the dry season, or you may not get to the mountain.

Ulamona sawmill was first constructed in about 1927 by the Catholic Church to make lumber to build churches in PNG. In 1994, the church gave up the sawmill, but they still have the mission and a guesthouse you can use (about US$11 per night). Locally, there are several small shops where you can buy most of the basic foods you want. It's quite a pleasant place. You may be riding in a sawmill-owned pickup when arriving or leaving Ulamona.

Here's what the author did. At the guesthouse, he met the local policeman who wanted to hike part way up the mountain, so they left at 6am and walked northeast along the main road. After 5 kms, and about one km before the Sule Airstrip, they turned south onto one of many old logging tracks (best to have someone show you this road). Then they walked directly toward the mountain for about 3 kms to where floods had deposited lava rocks & gravel creating a tree-less corridor for walking.

From there, the author went alone along an old track for another km or so, then along a narrow ridge between 2 gullies (if this ridge has collapsed, get into the eastern gully and continue climbing). Further up, he walked on the right or west side of the Big Gully, which may have the best footing. Near the top, the footing is loose, but once on the crater rim, it's easy walking. On top is a crater of some kind, but the author never saw it because of steam. The climb up took 5 1/4 hours; round-trip from Ulamona was 10 hours.

This is a long day-climb for the average person, so consider hiring a pickup to take you to the first lava rocks. Or walk there in the afternoon, camp, and climb the next day. Take extra water and leave it near the end of the logging track. Dry season is from May through October.

Ulawun Volcano as seen from the little sawmill town of Ulamona.

Map 309-1, Ulawun Volcano, New Britain, P. New Guinea

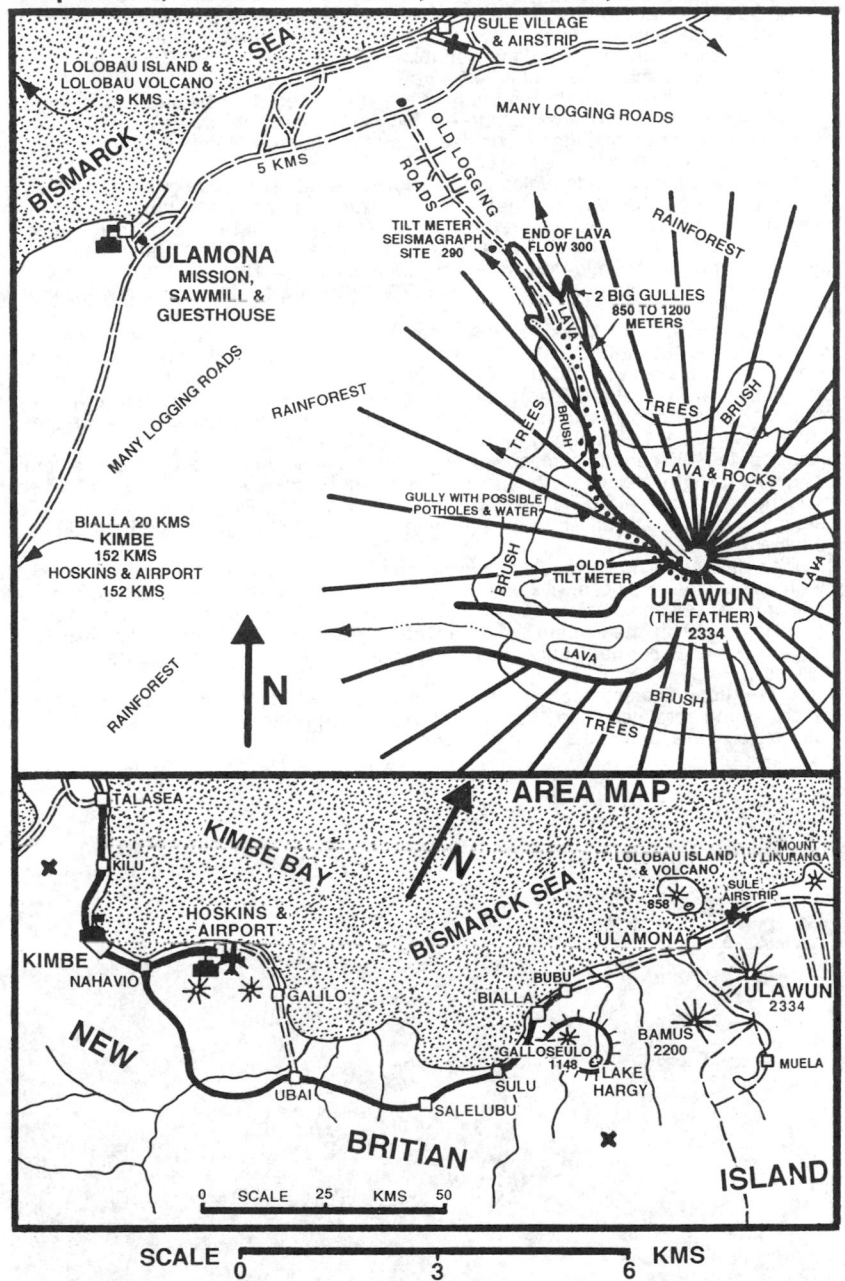

Maps *Lolobau, 9188,* and *Ulawun, 9187,* 1:100,000; and perhaps *Talasea, SB 56-5,* 1:250,000; all from the National Mapping Bureau, Box 5665, Melanesian Way, Port Moresby, Tele. 276465; and maybe the latest travel guidebook to PNG.

Rabaul Volcanos, New Britain Island, Papa New Guinea

Featured on this map are the active and rather lively volcanos surrounding the Simpson Harbor and the small city of Rabaul. Rabaul is located at the extreme northeastern end of the island of New Britain, which is part of the Republic of Papa New Guinea (PNG). New Britain is located northeast of the main island of New Guinea.

The Rabaul or Simpson Harbor is actually a giant caldera now ringed with a number of younger volcanic cones. Two large caldera-forming explosions took place here at about 1550 BC & 540 AD and created this marvelous deep-water anchorage. Most of the new cones you see there now have been built since that time.

Today there are about 6 older volcanos as shown, and 2 very active craters. Two of them really came to life on 9/19/1994. At that time, Tavurvur, or rather the Matupit Crater, erupted first, then Vulcan blew up 1 hour and 12 minutes later. As of 9/11/1997, Vulcan was quiet with no smells or any sign of life. Tavurvur was smoking and there was some crater glow. The last activity on Tavurvur were mild vulcanian eruptions between 10 & 12/1999 and continuing through 6/2000. For volcano updates use email (rvo@datec.com.pg) or see website (www.volcano.si.edu/gvp/).

The eruption of 1994, the first since 1943, literally buried the southern half of Rabaul and its airport under one to 2 meters of ash. The prevailing southeast winds blew the ash northwest from Tavurvur. That part of Rabaul has been abandoned. By 9/11 to 9/13/1997, during the author's visit, there were still 2 hotels operating in the destroyed section, trying to take advantage of the few tourists coming to view the destruction. The biggest headache then was the blowing dust caused by afternoon winds and the El Niño drought.

Because of the 1994 eruption, most people moved to the south side of the giant caldera near Kokopo, a very fast growing small city about 25 kms from Rabaul. Another 12 or so kms east of Kokopo is the new airport at Tokua; that's where you'll land when flying to Rabaul. From Tokua, there are minibuses, locally called PMV's, running to the big Kokopo market. From there you'll catch another PMV to Rabaul.

At Rabaul, the first thing you should do is visit the Volcano Observatory immediately north of the city's market place. You can walk uphill from the road junction shown. There you can talk to Ben Talai or other volcanologists about trails and ways of climbing any of the nearby volcanos. If you're volcano hunting, the **Rabaul Volcano Observatory** should be your first stop in PNG, so you can get the latest information about all active craters. This is the headquarters for volcano observations in PNG.

To get to **Vulcan Crater**, take any PMV running between Rabaul and Kokopo, and get off somewhere on the northwest side of the crater. The only problem in climbing this 200-meter-high cone are possible deep & steep-sided gullies.

These ruins are located at the southeast end of the now-abandoned Rabaul Airport. In the background can be seen the very active Tavurvur Volcano, and Turanguna.

Map 310-1, Rabaul Volcanos, New Britain Island, PNG

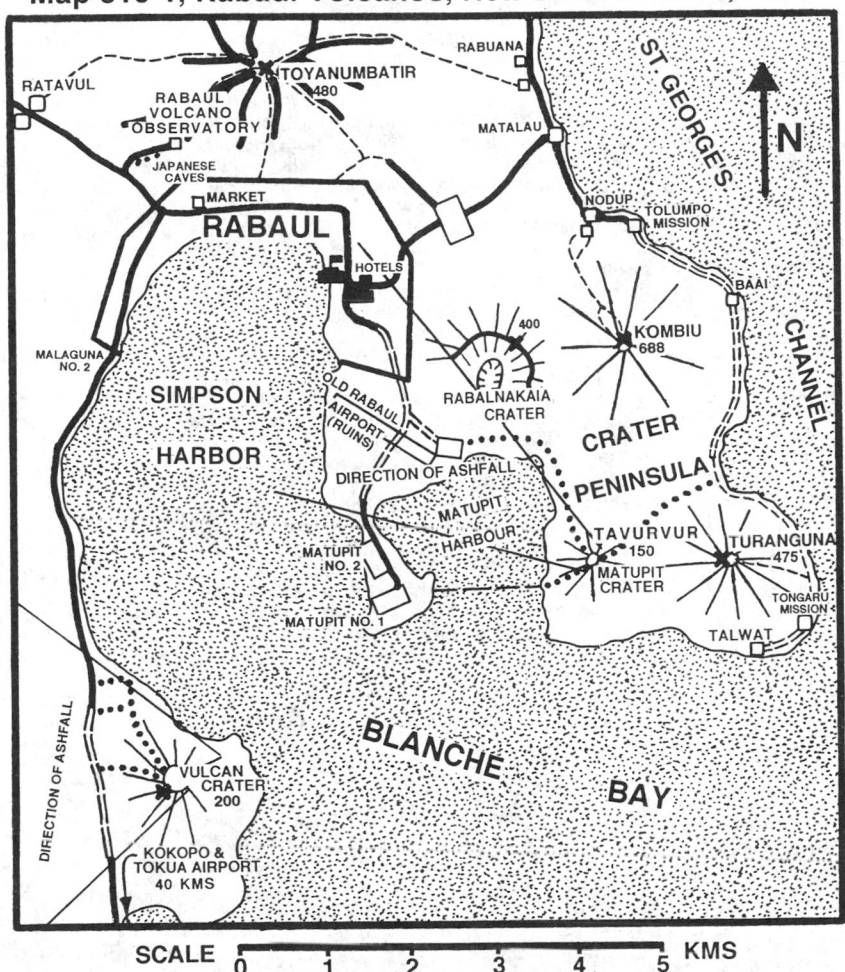

SCALE 0   1   2   3   4   5 KMS

To reach Tavurvur, take a PMV from Rabaul's market place in the direction of Matupit on the Matupit Peninsula. There are no hotels there, but you might be able to camp. Ask around. The author camped there with a good view of Matupit Crater across the bay, but it was quiet that night with no crater glow. To climb **Tavurvur & Matupit Crater**, start at the old airport and walk east then south. But beware, in 1997, there were huge gullies in that area which will be difficult to cross.

To climb **Kombiu** (The Mother) or Turanguna (South Daughter), walk or take a PMV from the middle of Rabaul east to the coast of St. George's Channel and to Matalau, Nodup and perhaps the Tolumpo Mission. Pre-1994 maps show a trail up Kombiu from Nodup as shown. It should still be there, but it might be a bushwhack. To reach **Turanguna**, continue south along the coast of the Crater Peninsula to Tongaru Mission. Maps show a trail from there up to the top where there are some buildings of some kind which were likely not effected by the 1994 blowout. That would be a great place to look down on an active & lively Matupit Crater.

Buy all food in the area of Rabaul's market, which is also where you catch PMV's to Kokopo and the airport. The dry season is from May or June through October.

Maps *Rabaul, 9389,* 1:100,000; and perhaps *Gazelle, SB 56-3,* 1:250,000; all are from the National Mapping Bureau, Box 5665, Melanesian Way, Port Moresby, Tele. 276465; and the latest travel guidebook to PNG for updates on the hotel situation.

Kolombangara Island Volcano, Solomon Islands

Featured on this map are the islands of Gizo and Kolombangara, located in the northwest portion of the Solomon Islands. Kolombangara is an almost a perfect circle made up of one massive extinct shield volcano. There are names for several high points around the 4-km-wide caldera rim, but the map the author bought doesn't indicate which is highest. Other maps show the highest point being 1768 meters. The author didn't quite make it to either island, but talked to several people in Honiara, the capital of the Solomons, to get most of this information.

To climb to the **Kolombangara** caldera rim, you'll almost have to fly to Gizo City on the island of Gizo about 20 kms to the west. The reason for this is, and as of 1997, there was only one flight a week to Ringgi, the administrative & old logging center on Kolombangara. For some, spending a week there might be OK. At Ringgi, you'll have to ask about a possible trail to the top from the end of the road running due north from town. This island was a logging center until 1986, so there are roads through the forest is many locations, mostly along ridges, but not up high in the non-commercial timber.

If you decide on the Gizo route, you'll fly from Henderson Field near Honiara on Guadalcanal, to the second largest town in the Solomon Islands, Gizo. There are several flights a day to Gizo, a main trading & tourist center with many Chinese-run shops and businesses. Also, there are a number of inexpensive hotels and guest or resthouses, only part of which are shown on this map. This is the most-visited place in the Solomons, so the tourist office can help.

Because this is a commercial center, the locals living on western Kolombangara, use small speedboats to take produce to market in Gizo. There is a daily market, as shown, and one person the author talked to in Honiara stated, about 10 boats a day run between Gizo and the towns of Iriri, Vavanga and Ghatere. That same person, also stated there was a trail from Ghatere up the mountain to the summit crater. In the **South Pacific Handbook** by Stanley from Moon Publications, it states you can also climb from Iriri or Vavanga.

The author's experience with speedboats in PNG is that mornings are calm, while afternoons are breezy with rough seas, so the boats likely travel in the mornings only (?). Your first day will be getting to Kolombangara, then you'll likely have to spend one night on the mountain, reaching the summit on Day 2 or 3 (?) You will likely boat back to Gizo on Day 3 or 4.

Buy all your food and supplies in Gizo before leaving, and take proper raingear as the Solomons are wet and humid. The wettest 3 months are January, February and March, while the driest are June through November. Buy a Solomon Islands Airline Pass before you leave home to get cheaper rates for island hopping for up to 30 days.

Maps Two maps, *New Georgia Group, West and Northeast,* 1:150,000. There are also larger scale maps at 1:50,000 available from Lands & Surveys (it used to be behind, or south of the

Substituting for Kolombangara Volcano is this day-time foto inside Yasur Volcano on the island of Tanna in Vanuatu. Notice the ash cloud after the minor explosion (Map 318, page 691).

Map 311-3, Kolombangara Volcano, Solomon Islands

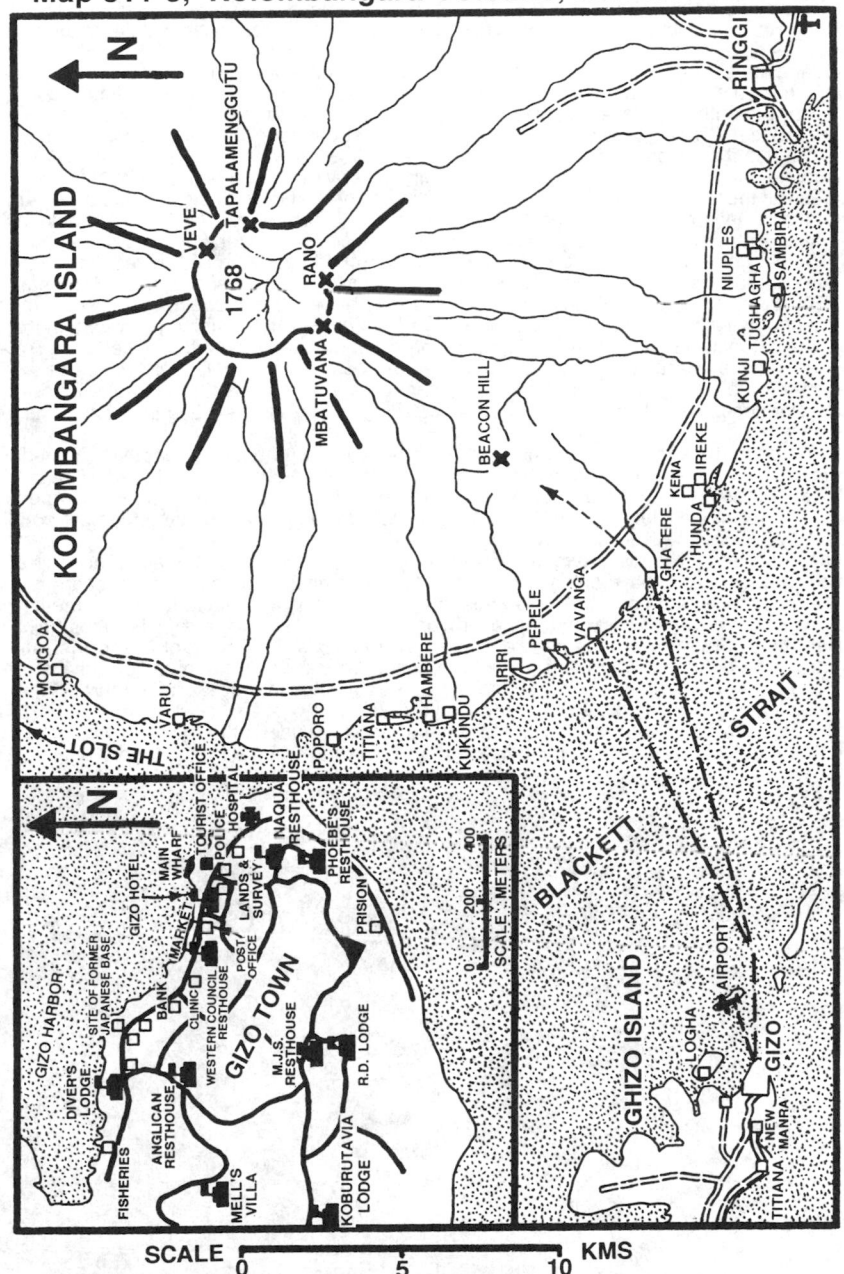

SCALE 0 — 5 — 10 **KMS**

main post office) in Honiara; also the latest travel guidebook to the Solomon Islands, or the South Pacific Handbook (the one mentioned above).

Makarakomburu, Guadalcanal, Solomon Islands

The mountains on this map are located on Guadalcanal, the largest island in the Pacific nation of Solomon Islands. The Solomons are located east of Papua New Guinea and north of Vanuatu and New Caledonia.

Guadalcanal first hit the headlines in 1942. Japan took the island and started building an airfield, then the Americans invaded and took over the area of Honiara and Henderson Field. For several months the Japanese made numerous attempts to retake the island and drive the Americans out. There were several naval battles just offshore, the result of which are many ships lying on the bottom. The sea north of Honiara has since been known as *Iron Bottom Bay*. The airfield originally started by the Japanese, finished by the Americans and called *Henderson Field*, is still there and is now the international airport for the Solomons. The Japanese artillery weapon nick-named *Pistol Pete* by the Americans is still there on display. Most people visiting Guadalcanal are WWII veterans or their children, or divers looking for shipwrecks in Iron Bottom Bay. Before going, the book **Strong Men Armed** by Robert Leckie should be required reading.

The highest peak on the island is Makarakomburu at 2447 meters; second is Popamanaseu at 2330. Some of the original rocks on the island may by volcanic in origin, but most seem to be sedimentary. The hills around Gold Ridge have long been a gold mining area, and in the late 1990's, a big multinational company was building a road to that area and was set to begin large scale operations. Because of that road and mine, access should be a lot better and easier. The author, who passed through Honiara twice on short visits in 9/1997, didn't have time for this climb. Nor does he have reliable information regarding public access along that road or its exact location.

In the past, the normal route to the highest peaks, and/or the south coast via the middle of the island, was through Choruchoru Pass. Information from the 1970's indicate a trip to **Makarakomburu** would be 5 or 6 days, but with a better road, it seems it should now be in the realm of 4 days. It all depends on public access to Gold Ridge, starting time, and the condition of the trails--which are likely not very good.

On most Pacific islands, payment is needed to walk past a village, because the land above belongs to them. After payment, a guide is normally thrown in with no additional charges. That system doesn't seem to apply to Guadalcanal because of its size, lack of development, and a small population. The trails seem to be used very little, especially in these higher mountains.

Because of the wilderness nature of these mountains, first contact the tourist office in Honiara. They can help you find people who know the trails and can give you advice; or can lead you to a guide and where to buy maps. Also look for a tour agent in Honiara. To insure success, a guide is highly recommended, even though it will cost a little. It seems the best route will be via Gold Ridge, then to the top of Popamanaseu. If indeed the trails shown here are for real, that part should be easy; getting to the top of Makarakomburu may be more difficult. The

The author has no fotos of the mountains on Guadalcanal, but this Japanese artillery piece called *Pistol Pete* by the Americans during World War II, can be seen in Honiara.

Map 312-1, Makarakomburu, Guadalcanal, Solomons

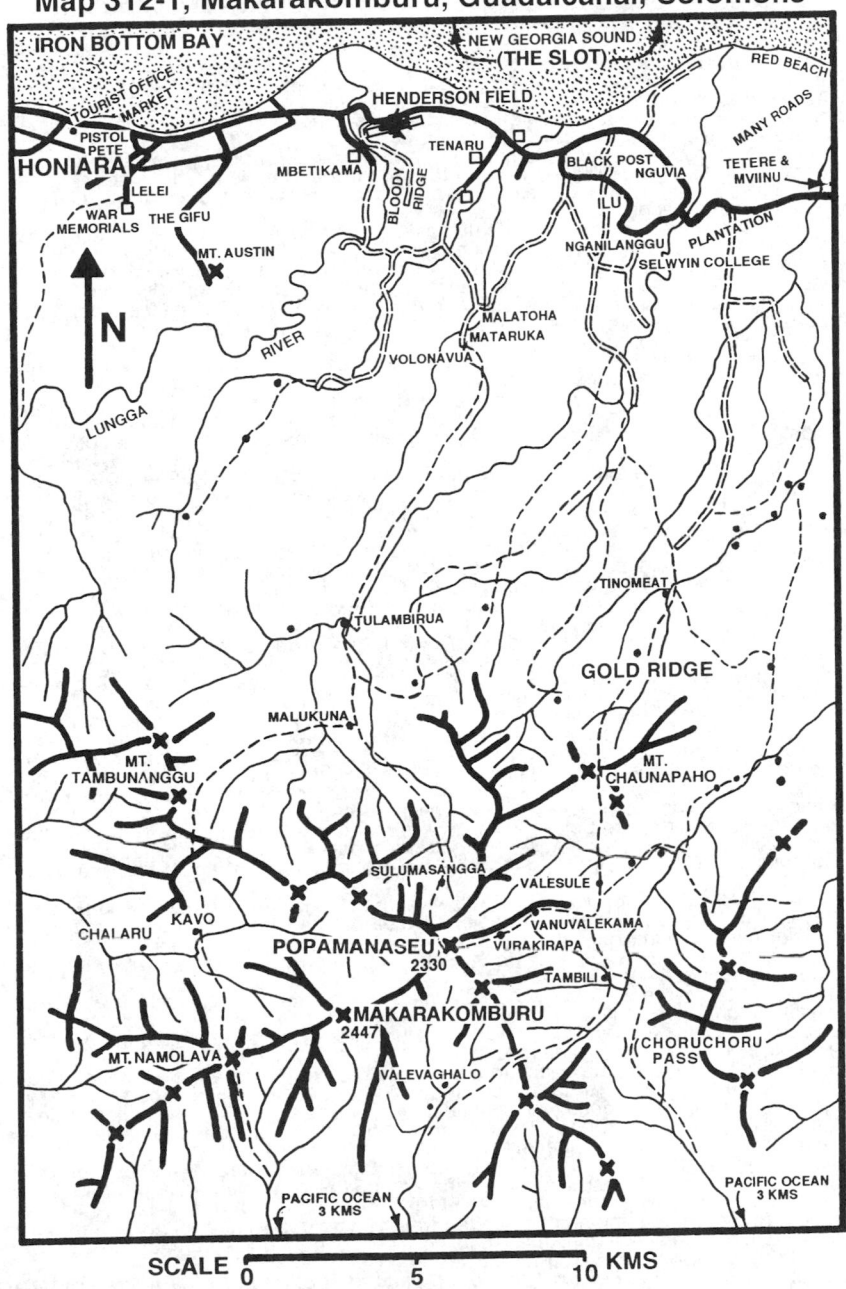

SCALE 0 5 10 KMS

dry season is May or June through October, but it's a wet area year-round.
Maps Maps at 1:50,000 are available, but they don't show trails. The map *Guadalcanal,*
1:150,000 scale, does show trails and is the one the author used to create this one. Also, the
latest travel guidebook to the Solomons.

Sere'ama, Vanua Lava Island & Introduction to Vanuatu

Vanuatu is an small Pacific island nation located north of New Caledonia, west of Fiji, and southeast of the Solomon Islands. In about 1906, the French and English made an agreement for the administration of these islands. They called it the *Condominium* system. Both powers occupied the same territory, but each set up its own police force, schools, administrators, etc. Each school taught either French or English, but a kind of Pidgin English also developed. Independence came in 1980, with 4 official languages--English, French, Pidgin English and the local Melanesian, of which there are 105 dialects.

Vanuatu has 82 islets, but only about a dozen would be considered major islands. All islands are volcanic in origin, but some are very old & eroded and have had limestone added, plus tectonic uplift. Six or 8 islands still have active volcanos. This is one of the best countries in the world to see live volcanos.

Getting to and around Vanuatu is fairly easy, but expensive. There are direct flights from Australia, New Zealand, New Caledonia, Fiji and the Solomon Islands. There are some freighters plying the waters, but most people get around by air; especially tourists on a tight time schedule. Vanair is the domestic airline and they have several flights daily from Port Vila the capital, to Tanna, and Luganville on Espiritu Santo. Everyone refers to the latter city & island as just *Santo*. Most of the rest of the islands have 2 to 3 flights per week. For most people, 2 or 3 days on each island is long enough.

If you intend to spend much time in Vanuatu, be sure to purchase a Vanair Pass with multiple tickets before you leave home. All internal flights are made with 20 passenger Twin Otters. If you intend to visit other island nations in the South Pacific, get in touch with a local travel agent specializing in this region and buy a South Pacific Pass. About half a dozen regional airlines participate in this promotional for tourism. You must buy these and other similar passes before you leave home.

Tourists from most developed or industrialized countries don't need a visa, but all are required to have a passport, return/onward ticket and sufficient funds. There's normally a tourist officer at Bauerfield Airport in Port Vila for incoming international flights, and a good tourist office in downtown Vila. Vanuatu is dependent on tourism, so they try hard to help. Anyone there, or most people around town, can direct you to the Survey Department where you can buy good maps of all islands at 1:50,000 or 1:100,000 scale. See map of MacDonald & Efate. For volcano information, ask for the location of ORSTOM. They are the ones who monitor volcanos in Vanuatu. For volcano updates see the websites (www.metservice.co.nz) or (www.volcano.si.edu/gvp/).

One of the northern-most islands in Vanuatu is Vanua Lava. Its best known peak is Sere'ama (or Soretimeat?) at 921 meters. It's an older and eroded volcano, but it has some hot springs near the summit. On 8/9/1965, it had a pretty good phreatic explosion somewhere on the northwest flank. By 1966, it was normal again.

The administration center for this island is a small town known as Sola; as a result, the entire land mass is usually referred to as *Sola*. To get there, make your way to Santo (Luganville) where there are a number of inexpensive hotels. It's from Santo that Vanair makes its flights northward to the Banks Islands. Normally there are 3 flights per week going to Sola, with stops at Mota Lava, Gaua, and sometimes small airstrips at the northern end of Santo. Each day's flight has different stops, depending on where people are going.

From the grass airstrip at Sola, you can normally catch a pickup into town--for a pretty good price; or walk it in 45 minutes. In town, there is one guesthouse with 5 or 6 little thatched cabins (US$9 a night in 1997), 2 stores--one with a bakery, a dispensary, post office and one card telefon.

Upon arrival, the author was coming down with malaria (apparently picked up on Efate). That evening he started taking the 12-tablets-in-3-days cure. After 36 hours he felt fine, so he took a 7 1/2 hour round-trip hike to Laingetak, but he couldn't make up for the lost day. Normally Sere'ama can't be climbed in one day from Sola, so he turned back failing to reach the summit and had to fly the next day.

Here's how to get there. Leave excess baggage at the Leumerus Guest House, then walk to the airstrip. From there continue north right on the beach. The one stream crossing is normally knee deep; but at high tide, water can be up to your chest. This is not a major problem, but ask locals about high tide before going.

Continue north right on the beach to a point 400 meters from the Fisher Young Education Center, then turn left or north at the old house & garden. Soon you'll be at the edge of a mangrove swamp. In that swamp, which is only 300-400 meters wide, is one stream crossing on a pole bridge. Try to do this in low tide if you can. Occasionally 7-meter-long salt water crocs get in that stream at high tide.

Continue to Laingetak No. II. The author doesn't know the route above, but people in that village told him there was a trail up Sere'ama. Along the way you'll walk beside a hot water stream, then apparently to the summit itself (?). Buy all your food in Sola, or Luganville, if possible. Better plan on one night along the way, maybe in a village (please offer to pay). If you're unsure, or want the summit really bad, consider taking a guide from Laingetak. On other islands, it's about US$9 to $13 a day for guides.

Maps *Iles Banks--Nord, Feuille 2,* 1:100,000; and the national map, *Republic of Vanuatu,* 1:1,000,000. Buy at the Survey Department, Vila; and a the latest travel guidebook to this area.

Map 313-1, Sere'ama, Vanua Lava Island & Introduction to Vanuatu

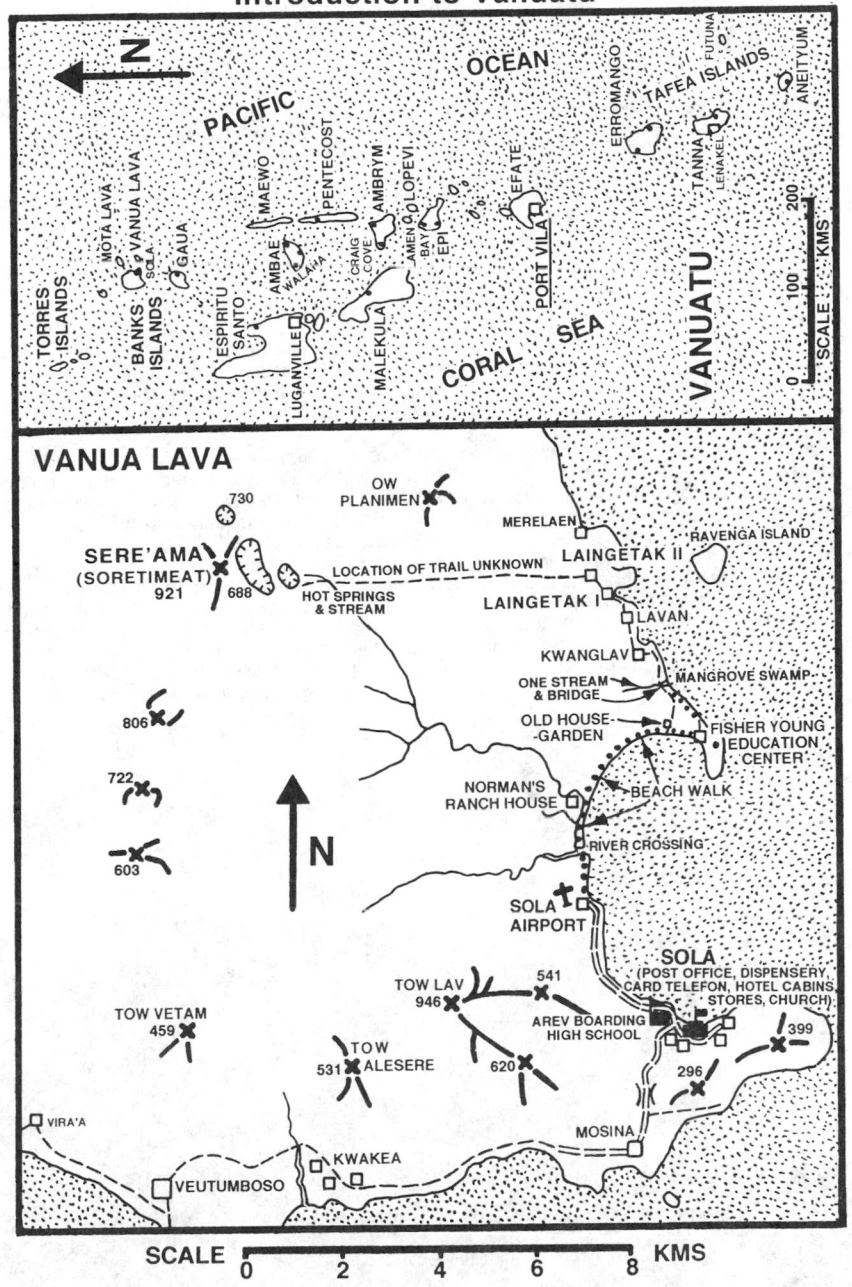

Garet Volcano, Gaua (Santa Maria) Island, Vanuatu

This map shows most of the island of Santa Maria, more commonly known as Gaua; which is in the new Pacific island nation of Vanuatu. It's the island between Sola to the north, and Santo to the south. See previous map. This island is one large active volcano, which has a caldera approximately 10 kms in diameter. Gaua island is only about 20 kms across. Covering half the floor of the caldera is a large fresh water lake, and an active cone known as Garet Volcano, at 797 meters altitude.

Garet was quiet for many years, then in 1962 it came alive. Garet's last significant eruptions of ash were in 7/1981 and 4/1982, but there are occasional phreatic explosions and steam rising from the summit crater all the time. The author was there on 8/29/1997, and saw dead trees on the northwest slopes apparently because of strong fumarolic activity in the summit crater. Lots of steam from the crater was seen by researchers in 9/1999. This island is off the beaten path, so current information about eruptions is hard to come by. For updated volcano information see the New Zealand website (www.metservice.co.nz/) or (www.volcano.si.edu/gvp/).

There are about 3 flights a week to Gaua, all originating from Luganville (Santo). At the airport is a small store, open upon arrivals & departures, and nearby is a man named Stephen Futuna, who has rooms to rent and can direct you to a guide. He is about the only one around who speaks good English, so locate him if he's still alive. You'll likely walk to the beginning of either route up the mountain, as there's only 8 kms of road on the island. There will also be a pickup taxi waiting for passengers at the airport; but it's not exactly cheap!

There are 2 routes to **Garet**, and 2 villages which claim all rights to guide, and collect fees, from hikers. Each island in Vanuatu has the same internal argument, but that's not a problem for climbers to worry about.

About 3 kms northwest of the airstrip is Namasari, which has a clinic, store and English school; but no one speaks English! Learn Pidgin fast! The author camped nearby, then had to pay about US$9 for permission to climb and a guide, plus about US$6 for permission to fotograph (hide your camera while negotiating!). This price is negotiable, but the standard fee for a guide in Vanuatu was between US$9 & US$13 per day in 1997.

Next morning they went up the trail, but the guide thought he was going to the lake only. They returned part way, then the author went alone on another trail circling to the west around the lake. He never did reach the summit, as the trail ran out in thick thorny bushes, and the trails of wild cattle didn't help. Another tourist told about having to wade right along the edge of the lake, avoiding thorny bushes in order to reach the active cone. With the right guide, and moving fast, you should be able to go up and back in one long day. Or perhaps camp near one of the good streams near the lake, as shown. *Tell the guide you want to climb the volcano*, not just go

The Garet Volcano located inside the caldera on Gaua (or Santa Maria) Island.

Map 314-1, Garet Volcano, Gaua (Santa Maria), Vanuatu

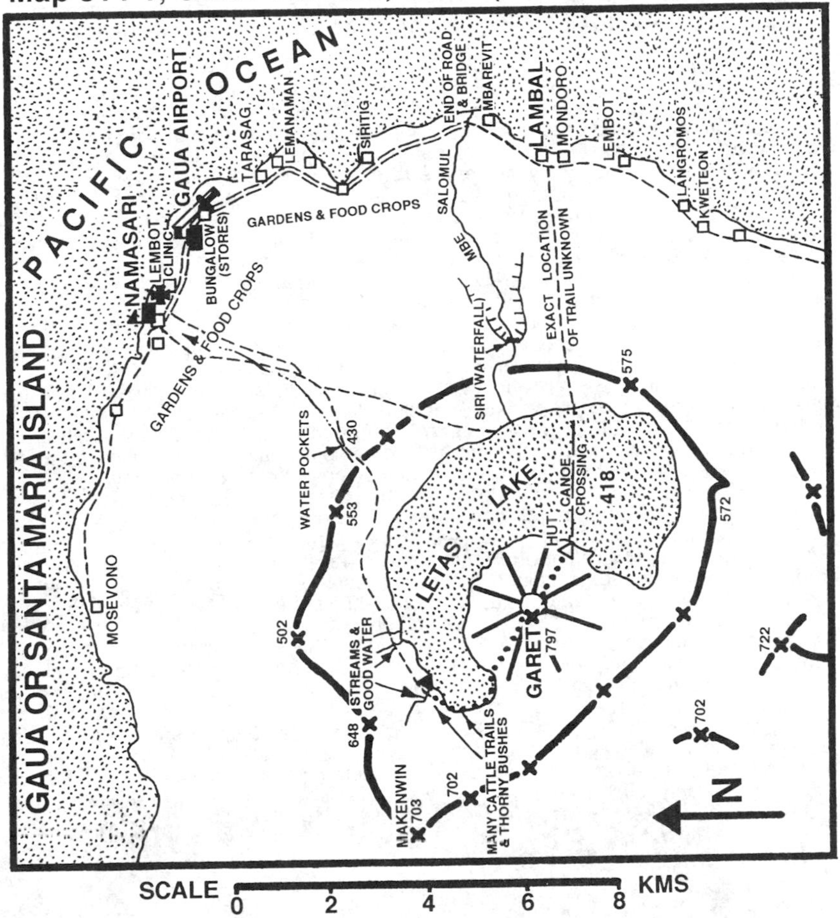

(Map labels: PACIFIC OCEAN; GAUA OR SANTA MARIA ISLAND; NAMASARI; GAUA AIRPORT; TARASAG; LEMANAMAN; SIRITIG; SALOMUL; END OF ROAD & BRIDGE; MBAREVIT; LAMBAL; MONDORO; LEMBOT; LANGROMOS; KWETEON; LEMBOT; CLINIC; BUNGALOW (STORES); GARDENS & FOOD CROPS; GARDENS & FOOD CROPS; MBE; SIRI (WATERFALL); EXACT LOCATION OF TRAIL UNKNOWN; MOSEVONO; WATER POCKETS; 430; 553; 502; STREAMS & GOOD WATER; 648; MAKENWIN 703; 702; MANY CATTLE TRAILS & THORNY BUSHES; LETAS LAKE; HUT; CANOE CROSSING; 418; 575; 572; GARET 797; 722; 702; N; SCALE 0 2 4 6 8 KMS)

to the lake!

   Some French tourists told of a second route. They went to the place south of the airport called Lambal, then with their guide hiked up to the caldera rim and paddled across the lake in a canoe. They slept in a bamboo hut east of Garet, then climbed it the next morning and returned all the way to the village. Contact a Mr. Tembis in Lambal.

   If possible, bring all or most of your food from Luganville, Santo, especially bread and maybe some fruit. The shops on Gaua sell rice, sugar, crackers, cookies (biscuits), lots of canned meat & fish, and that's about all. On flight days, people occasionally sell fruits, vegetables, and peanuts at the airport. You can camp at the airport as well. Dry season is June through October.

Maps *Iles Banks Sud,* 1:100,000; and the national map *Republic of Vanuatu,* 1:1,000,000. Buy these in the Department of Land Surveys, Port Vila; and the latest travel guidebook to Vanuatu or the South Pacific.

Lobenben, Aoba Volcano, Ambae Island, Vanuatu

Shown here is the island of Ambae, located near the center of Vanuatu. Ambae is basically one large basaltic shield volcano called Aoba, with it's highest summit known locally as Lobenben at 1496 meters.

Inside this semi-active forested crater are 3 lakes; the one in the middle has undrinkable water, the other 2 may have water that's acidic. Major eruptions took place in about 1590, 1670, and in the 1870's; the last 2 of which resulted in a loss of life. In 7/1991, there was a minor phreatic eruption which killed trees in the summit area. The dead trees allowed the sun to hit the ground and by 8/1997 it was a jungle of 2-meter-high ferns. For updated volcano information see the New Zealand website (www.metservice.co.nz/) or (www.volcano.si.edu/gvp/).

Here's how to get there. There are 3 corners to the island of Ambae, each with an airstrip. Redcliff is least visited, with Longana second. The busiest airstrip seems to be at Walaha, where there are at least 3 flights per week, all originating from Luganville (locally called Santo). At the airstrip, are 2 tiny stores, a restaurant, and one card telefon. These are open on flight days. Waiting for arrivals will be several old jalopies masquerading as taxis to take you to town, which in this case is the administrative center for West Ambae, Nduindui. You can also walk there in 2 hours. At Nduindui, is a hospital, several small stores, one card telefon, and a tiny restaurant & market, which seems to be open daily. The people on Ambae seem to be better educated, speak more English, and are more industrious than on some other islands.

The author was taken to Noel Tahi, a very good English speaker, who lives near Hukarere. In 1997, he was building a guesthouse for tourists. He found 2 guides to take the author up the mountain past the ORSTOM seismograph and to the crater, but that village's trail was totally overgrown, and they didn't quite make it to a good camping place next to Lake Nanaro Ngoru. This was on 8/26/1997. At that time, guides on Ambae cost about US$9 per day.

Upon leaving the island, Pastor Amos Waki, the postmaster at Loone, informed the author that the village of Lolombingnunga somehow held the rights to take tourists going up the mountain. It seems every village on every island in Vanuatu claims communal land & rights going up to a mountain or volcano! In this case, other people told the author the trail from Lolombingnunga was better maintained, so this is likely the better way to go. Either way, you'll be wandering through village gardens up to about 600 meters or higher, and will need a guide. Even if the trail is well-maintained, you'll need someone to get you through a maze of lower trails in the gardens. You might ask to go alone, but payment to the village and guide is required, as tourism is becoming an important industry in Vanuatu. **Aoba & Lobenben** can be climbed in one long day; or camp one night near Lake Manaro Ngoru, as shown, and climb it in 2 days. Near that campsite is good water.

The volcanologists in Port Vila & ORSTOM later told the author, perhaps the best trail to Lobenben is from the villages of Lolopuepue, Ambanga, and Nduvlara. To get there you'd want to fly into Longana; or walk northeast from Loone past the cliffs as shown. You can buy all your

This is the airport near the village of Walaha on the western end of Ambae Island.

Map 315-1, Lobenben, Aoba Volcano, Ambae Isl., Vanuatu

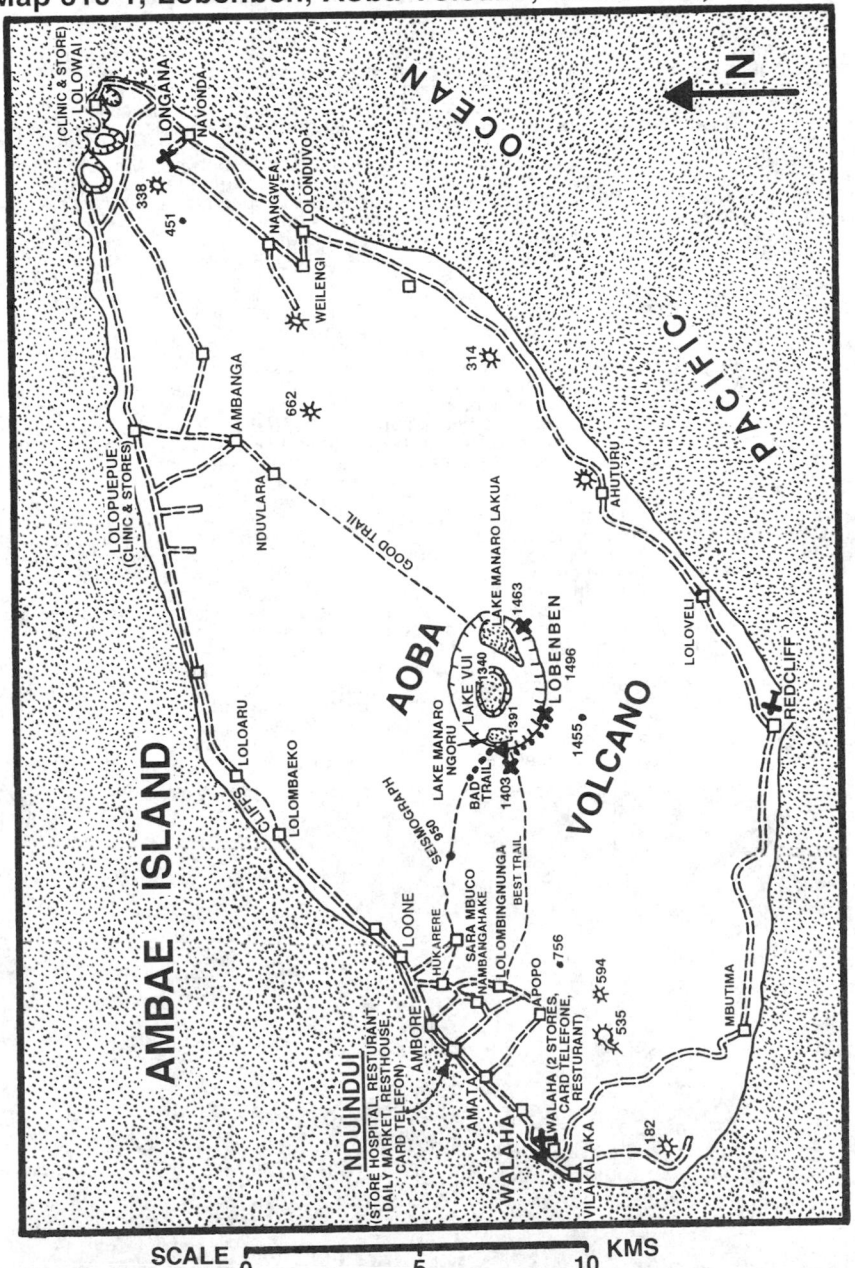

SCALE 0 5 10 KMS

food on Ambae, but better selections are found on Santo. June through October is the dry season.

Maps *Aoba (Omba-Ambae)*, 1:50,000; the national map *Republic of Vanuatu*, 1:1,000,000; and the latest travel guidebook to Vanuatu or the South Pacific.

Benbow & Marum Volcanos, Ambrym Island, Vanuatu

Shown here is a large caldera and several active volcanic craters on the island of Ambrym. In the summer of 1997, Benbow at 1159 meters, was steaming & rumbling, and the 2 small craters immediately southeast of Marum's big crater (1270 meters) were steaming, but quiet. Volcanologists from ORSTOM in Port Vila, have made detailed studies of this 13-km-wide caldera and dated the major lava flows, as shown. Initially, this caldera was created by a major Plinian explosion in about 50 AD which rated a VEI-6. Eruptions continued well into 2000. For updated volcano information see the New Zealand website (www.metservice.co.nz/) or (www. volcano.si.edu/gvp/).

There are flights to Ambrym about 3 times per week, all running between Vila and Luganville (Santo). The landing is the grass airstrip at Craig Cove. There are no facilities at the airstrip, but about one km north is the small settlement of Fali, where a guesthouse and large store are located. All food for climbing can be bought there, including bread.

The normal route to the **caldera** is via the village of Lalinda. To get there, you can walk the 15 kms in 3 or 4 hours, but there will always be a pickup taxi or two at the airstrip waiting for passengers. If you're with a group the cost should be about US$7 per person. In 1997, there was the Milee Guesthouse in nearby Sanesup, but no hotel in Lalinda. Or camp in the lower end of the dry river bed just north of Lalinda. Get water at Sanesup or Lalinda.

Most people climb to the caldera in one day, round-trip. But first, everyone is supposed to pay for permission and a Lalinda guide which was about US$13 in 8/1997; but with this map, experienced climbers could likely make it OK without. *Tourists* should take the guide.

To climb, walk east up the plantation road which begins about 200 meters north of Lalindas dry river bed. After about one km, turn right and enter the gully and follow other people's tracks. At the 2nd dryfall, regress 200 meters, to find a bypass trail on the left. At the 3rd dryfall, turn right into another dry creek bed; do the same at the 4th dryfall. Keep following people's tracks. Higher up, you'll climb up a minor ridge, then drop back to a gully. Altogether, you'll skirt around 6 dryfalls.

Once on the **Ash Plain** in the caldera, head northeast toward the live volcanos. You must have a compass, and maybe an altimeter, so you can find your way back to the trail if the clouds roll in. Also, pay attention to landmarks and trail markers as you hike. You'll first be in a dry channel, then you'll turn left or north to reach **Benbow**. A well-used track leads to the crater rim.

To reach **Marum**, continue northeast in the dry channel, but the final ascent may be next to impossible on the west side. Instead circle around to the southeast side and climb from there. The reason is, Marum was covered with ash and cinders, then erosion created hugh, steep-sided gullies, making it difficult to climb from the west or north. See National Geographic magazine for 11/2000 for some fotographs of these 2 live volcanos.

The author paid his money to someone in Lalinda, then climbed alone on 8/22/1997. He first explored the active cones southeast of Marum, but bypassed its main summit. He then climbed Benbow from the east and returned via the normal route. Round-trip from his campsite near Lalinda was 9 hours. If you plan to explore a lot, do it in 2 days, getting water about one km below the Ash Plain, as shown on this map.

A second route is from the north and the guesthouse at Ranon, but you can only get there by

Postcard view of Benbow to the left, Ambryum right (Adventure Center foto, Vila).

Map 316-1, Benbow & Marum Volcanos, Ambrym, Vanuatu

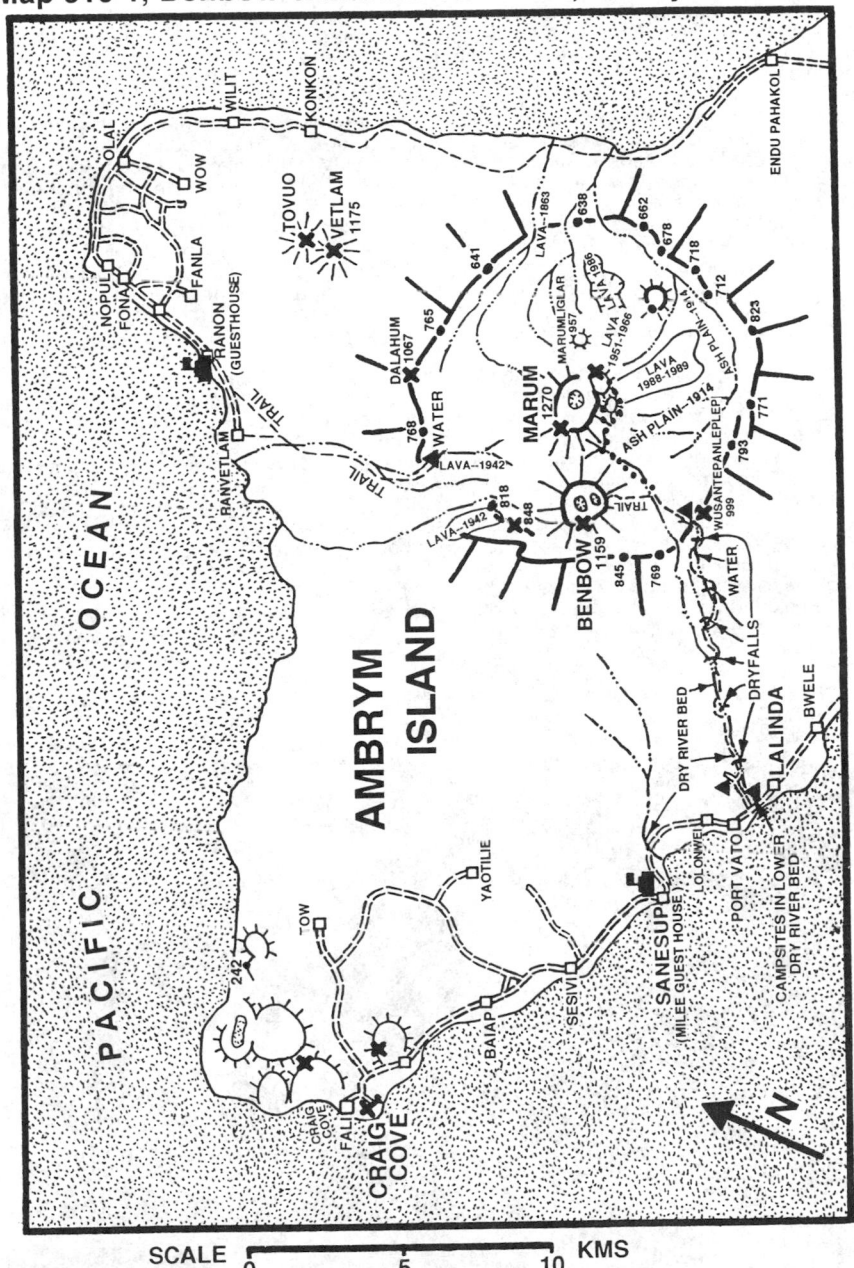

SCALE 0 5 10 KMS

boat from Craig Cove, making it longer & expensive. Dry season is June through October.
Maps *Ambrym,* 1:50,000; and the national map *Republic of Vanuatu,* 1:1,000,000; and the latest travel guidebook to Vanuatu or the South Pacific.

Mt. MacDonald, Efate Island, Vanuatu

This map shows about half of the island of Efate, including Port Vila, the capital of Vanuatu. Locals just call it Vila. Also shown is the approximate location of the tourist office, the Department of Land Surveys where you can buy maps, and ORSTOM, where you can get the latest information on volcanos. The highest peak on the island is Mt. MacDonald at 647 meters. MacDonald is not a volcano, but it's made of old volcanic rock.

Much of this hike is through an undisturbed rainforest at about 500 meters elevation. One attraction for this peak is it can be climbed in one day, or 2, and can be done while waiting for flights to other islands. Another attraction is the trail seems to be maintained and marked once a year for what appears to be an annual trek for many living in Vila. The national electric company, a French-speaking outfit, is the sponsor for the hike. In the month or so before the trek, usually in late August, they send out crews with machetes to open and re-mark the trail.

To walk the entire Bernier Trail or Sentier, and climb MacDonald, it's best to climb from north to south. Here's what the author did on 8/15/1997. He walked from his hotel, the less-expensive Kalfabun Guesthouse, to the major road junction at Tagabe. From there he waved down vehicles until he found one going toward Mele Maat and along the road circling the island. He got a second lift from Mele Maat to Ulei. You'll have to pay for rides in trucks, as *hitch hiking is normally not free.*

From Ulei, he walked back along the road one km to the small cemetery, which is where the road running up to a radio antenna begins. That vehicle track is often used up to the antenna, then it turns into a wild horse trail. As you near the viewpoint shown, you'll enter the rainforest with large trees. From there on, you'll be in the shade of a high canopy.

After the viewpoint, you'll be walking east along a trail that is well-marked with paint on tree trucks or ribbons tied to branches. It's generally easy to follow. In the area south of MacDonald, the author left his backpack at the trail junction (525 meters) with a log frame of a shelter, then hurried north to the summit. That part; to the summit and back to the trail junction, took a little less than 2 hours. The author found about 3 places on the plateau where there was drinking water, either running or in potholes. He camped near the third waterhole he found. Total walk-time on Day 1 was just under 7 hours.

The next morning, and in the rain and carrying an umbrella all the way, he walked down to the end of the road as shown. From there, it was on to Bauer Field, the international airport, and his guesthouse. Walk-time for Day 2 was less than 4 hours; the total 2-day walk-time was 10 2/3 hours, most of which was with a large pack.

Before going, get the latest trail information at the tourist office, or the nearby electric company. If you plan to do this hike in one day, you'll likely have to hire a taxi or rent a car, and get an early start. There are lots of mini buses (vans) from the airport to downtown Vila. Dry

Part of the Bernier Trail, called by the French *Le Piste Bleu*, crossing Efate Island.

Map 317-1, Mt. MacDonald, Efate Island, Vanuatu

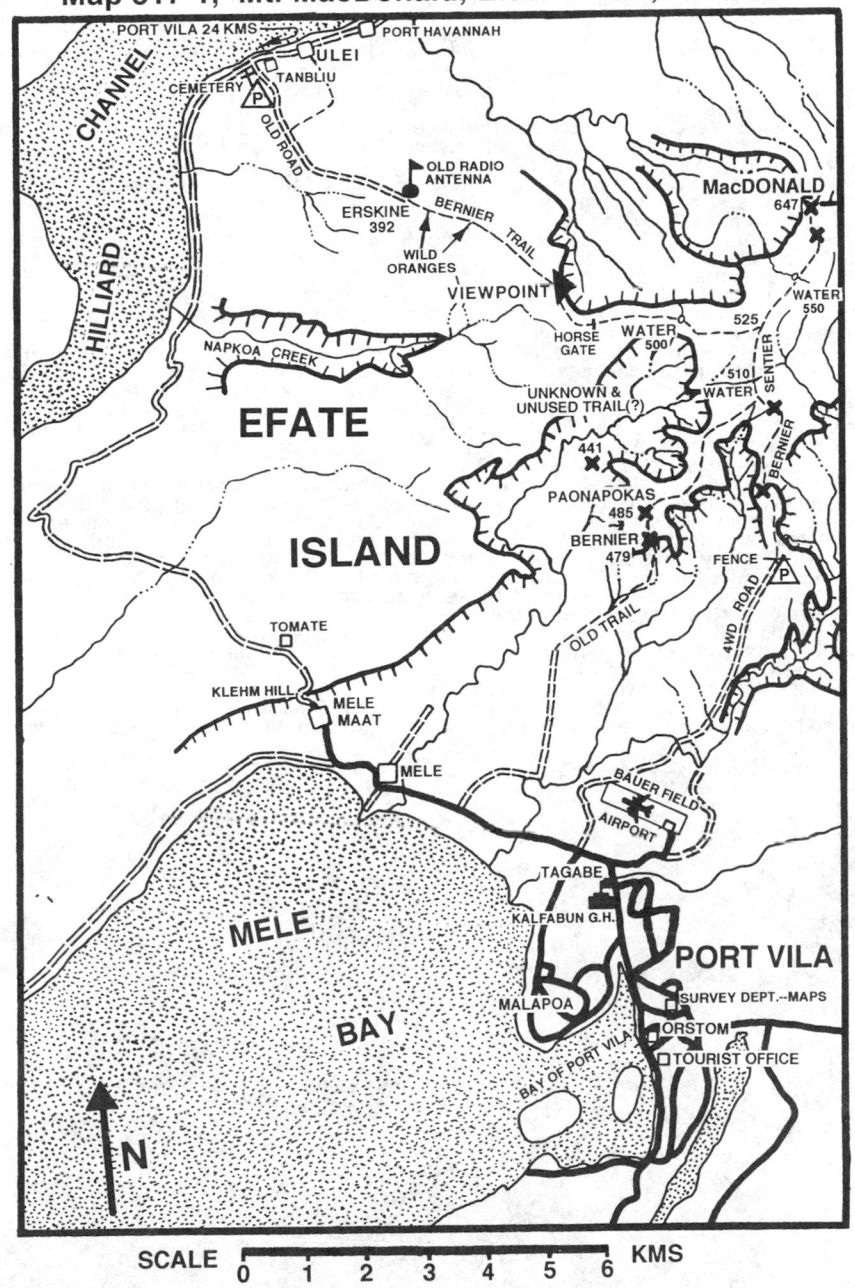

season is from May through October.

Maps *Efate*, 1:100,000; and the national map *Republic of Vanuatu*, 1:1,000,000; and the latest travel guidebook to Vanuatu or the South Pacific.

Yasur Volcano & Tukosmera, Tanna Island, Vanuatu

Featured here is the island of Tanna and the Yasur Volcano, the most active in Vanuatu. Yasur is thought to have begun erupting about 800 years ago, and has been in more or less continuous Strombolian & Vulcanian activity since Captain Cook saw it erupting in 1774. At only 361 meters it is the most-accessible *live volcano* in the world. It's activity is ongoing through 4/2000, and beyond. Also shown is Tukosmera, at 1084 meters, the highest summit on this island. For updated volcano information see the New Zealand website (www.metservice.co.nz/) or (www.volcano.si.edu/gvp/).

Because of Yasur, Tanna is the most-visited island in Vanuatu, and the biggest money-maker for the country. In 1997, there were several flights daily from Port Vila. The planes were 20 passenger Twin Otters and they landed at the grass airstrip just north of Lenakel. However, at that time they were constructing a new intenational airport a few kms north near White Grass. It opened in 1998, and apparently some international flights land there, bypassing the capital of Vila. Check the latest guidebook.

Here's what the author did. Upon landing, he was met by a tourist officer who collected about US$18 for the landing fee & volcano pass. He checked out the once-a-week market and several large stores at Lenakel, reconfirmed his return flight to Vila, then with large pack walked south to the village of Ikeute (pron. Iketi) in about 2 1/2 hours. At Ikeute, is a church, school and water tap. He then walked up to Yenhup, where children escorted him on to the very small village of Yerutana.

Yerutana is on the normal route to **Tukosmera**, so that village has the rights to charge visitors for crossing their communal property. They also maintain the trail; the first half of which is through gardens and a fenced cow pasture, then a nice cloud forest. The author paid about US$13 for permission & guide. He left his big pack in the guide's bamboo hut, then the 2 ran to the summit in one hour (normally it's 2 hours up), had a foggy look down on Yasur, then ran back down. He then walked about halfway back to Lenakel and camped under coconut palms near the coastal road. This was all on 8/18/1997.

Next morning he walked back to Lenakel, and waited for a pickup heading for several villages collectively known as White Sands on the east side of the island and not far from **Yasur**. He was let off before White Sands, but paid about US$3, then walked the rest of the way, which was across a dusty *ash plain*. He filled his water bottles at Isiwi Lake (& purified it!), then climbed the sandy northwest side of Yasur in about an hour. He later camped near the crater rim on the southeast side. At that time, the volcano had 2 live craters, each exploding about every 10 minutes. Getting fotos at night is best. If camping, do so down from the live craters a ways, so you don't get *bombed* in the night!

If you don't like climbing, you can hire a vehicle at any of the many hotels in White Sands, Port Resolution, or Lenakel, and be driven to within about 200 meters of the crater rim. Most tourists are driven there in the late afternoon and stay until just after dark to see the best part-- the red hot lava fireworks shooting high in the sky.

On Day 3, 8/20/1997, the author bathed--then waded across a shallow bay of Lake Isiwi, walked to near White Sands, got a pickup ride back to Lenakel for US$3, and caught a flight to

Yasur Volcano seen from the north. The main trail goes up to the crater rim on the left; or you can wade across the shallow lake and climb up the sandy northwest ridge.

Map 318-1, Yasur Volcano & Tukosmera, Tanna, Vanuatu

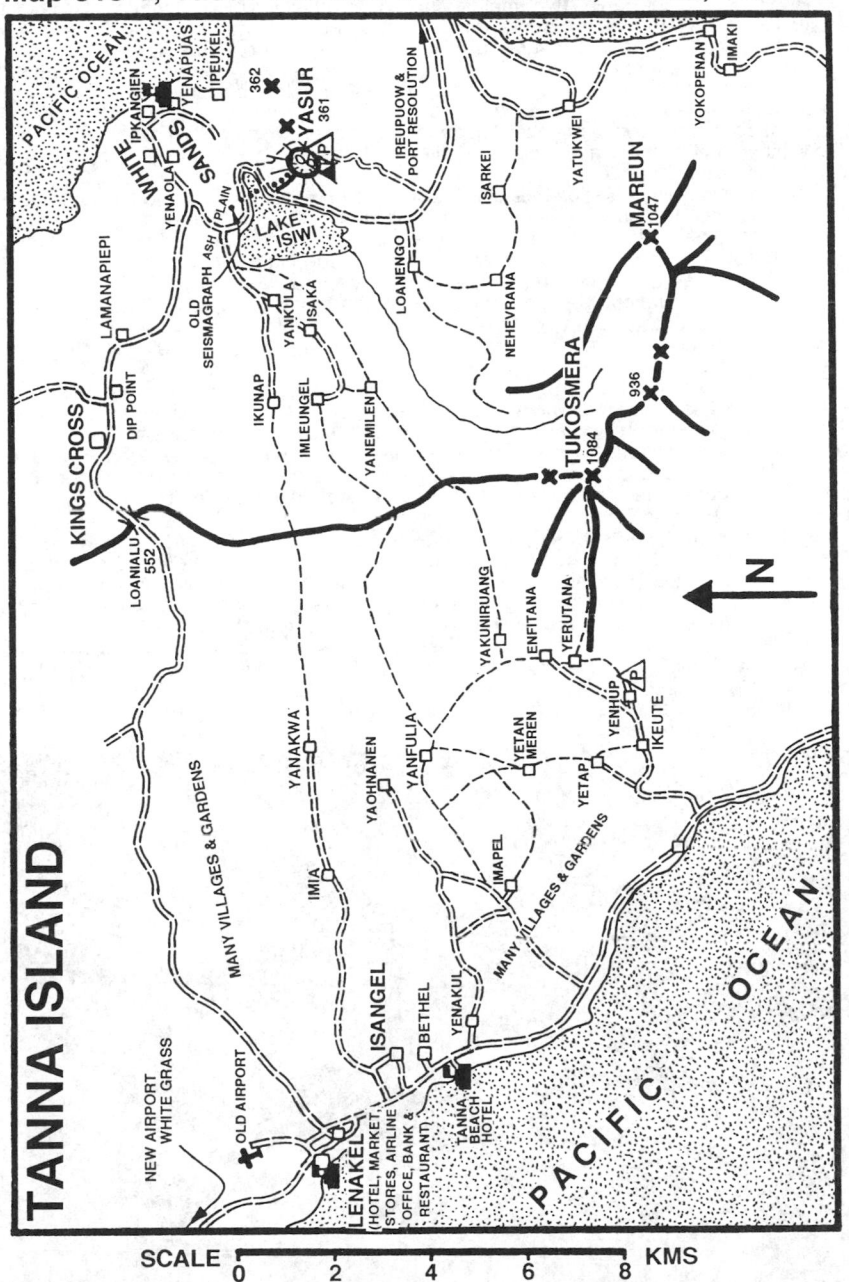

Vila. Best to buy supplies in Vīla, but Lenakel has stores and a restaurant.
Maps *Tanna,* 1:50,000; and the national map *Republic of Vanuatu,* 1:1,000,000; and the latest travel guidebook to Vanuatu or the South Pacific.

Mont Panié, Grand Terre Island, New Caledonia

Shown here is Mont Panié, 1629 meters, the highest peak in New Caledonia. This mountain is located near the northwestern end of the largest island in the group, Grand Terre. *Nouvelle Calédonie* is a state or department of France, and has the same status as Hawaii does to the USA. This island is located east of Australia, and the currency is the French Franc. New Caledonia is perhaps the most expensive place in the Pacific for travelers!

You can fly there direct from France, Australia, New Zealand, Fiji or Tahiti. The international airport is at Tontouta, 45 kms northwest of the capital city of Nouméa. Almost all the French live in the southern half of the island around Nouméa; most of the Kanaks (indigenous Melanesians) live in the northwest,

Hitch hiking is pretty good on this island, but you can also take a bus from Nouméa to most parts of the island. During the daytime, there's a bus about every hour running from the airport to the main terminal in downtown Nouméa. If you plan to take a bus to Panié, start at the main bus terminal in Nouméa, as it may or may not stop on the highway next to the airport. Buy a ticket to the administrative center of Hienghéne (pron. Yen-gan).

Buy all your food before going north if you can; there are no supermarkets anywhere near the mountain. The author found the cheapest place to buy food was in the supermarket located about 350 meters from the airport terminal right where the airport road meets the main highway. It was open on a Sunday morning.

Once in Hienghéne, there may or may not be a bus running northwest along the coast toward Pouébo. Ask someone about buses. The author was there on a Sunday afternoon and hitched a ride in an empty school bus, but had to pay the Kanak drive a small amount. From Hienghéne your choices are; maybe a bus, hitch hike--which is slow on that road; or walk nearly 20 kms from Hienghéne to the trailhead--a long way in the tropical heat. If they ever pave that section of the coastal road, they'll have bus service for sure, and more traffic.

However you get to Panié, aim for the Cascade de Tao near Tao, which is half a dozen homes. Continue north another km to the next stream and second bridge. This is a good place to bathe and/or get good drinking water, or pitch a tent for the night. About 125 meters north of this second bridge, you'll see the good trail on the west side of the road, but no sign.

Once on the trail, you can't get lost. Near the top is a hut or refuge, but it had a wet dirt floor in 8/1997. Nearby is a stream and spring (source). The summit is where the French military occasionally make camp. The author camped next to the road & second bridge, then hid his pack in the brush for his climb. He made it to the top in about 3 1/4 hours; just over 6 hours round-trip. This was on 8/11/1997.

The driest & cooler season is August through October. If you're traveling cheap, you can camp for free in cow pastures near the airport.

This is the hut called the Refuge Caledonie located on the north side of Panié.

Map 319-1, Mt. Panié, Grand Terre Island, New Caledonia

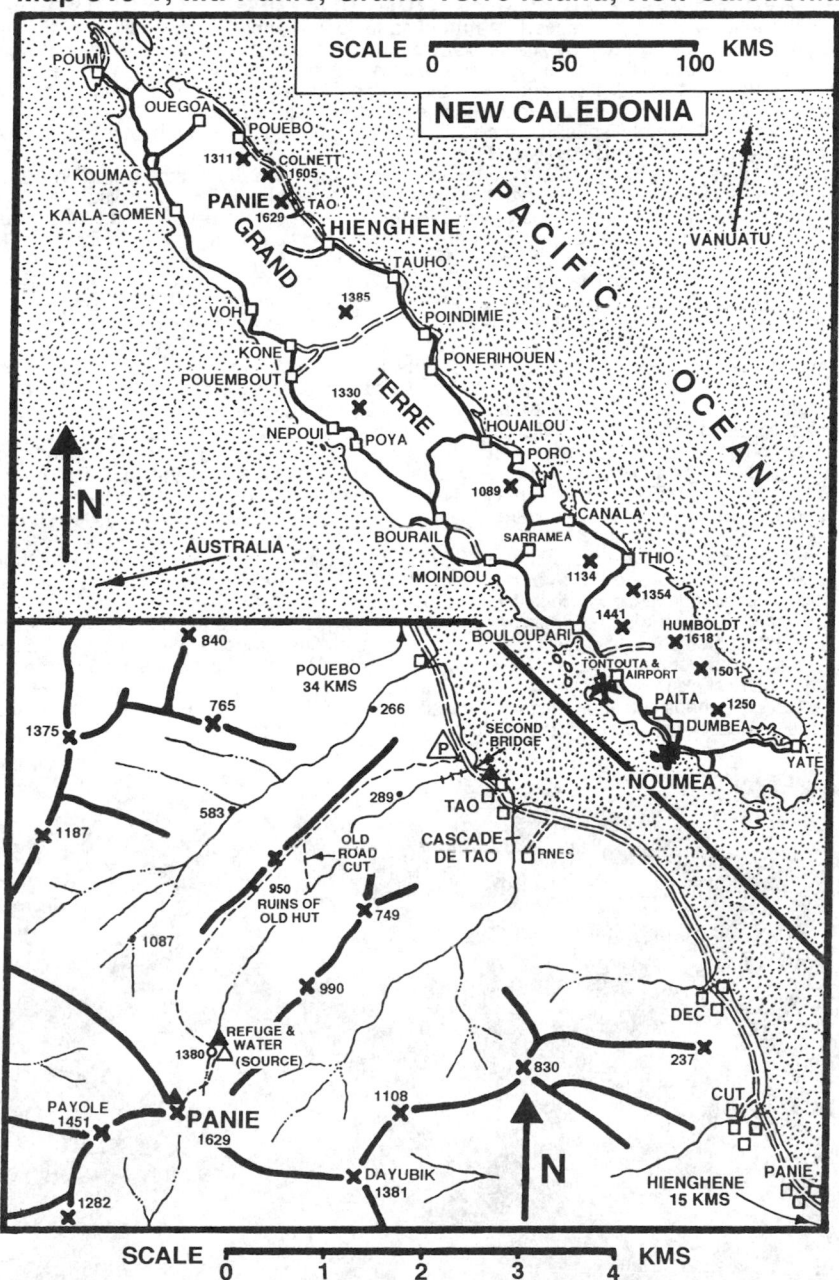

Maps *Nouvelle Calédonie,* 1:500,000; and *Hienghéne, Serie Orange, 4808,* 1:50,000, both from the French IGN (Institut Geographical National), 136 bis, rue de Grenelle, (www.ign.fr), Paris, France; but buy in Nouméa or Hienghéne; and the latest travel guidebook to this area or the South Pacific.

Ayers Rock & The Olgas, Northern Territory, Australia

Featured here is one of the world's largest sandstone monoliths, Ayers Rock (Uluru to the Aborigines) and another group of smaller bluffs or buttes called The Olgas or Mt. Olga (Katatjuta). The top of Ayers Rock is 867 meters altitude, which is 348 meters above the flat, featureless plain. Mt. Olga is 1069 meters elevation, but towers 546 meters above the plain. Both are now part of the Uluru National Park, which is located in the southern part of Australia's Northern Territory.

This area is extremely isolated, being 241 kms west of the turnoff along the Adelaide--Alice Springs highway, and 445 kms from Alice Springs.

Reach Ayers Rock by flying into Connellan Airport from various major centers in Australia. There's a free shuttle bus from the airport to Yulara Village (Ayers Rock Resort), a distance of 6 kms. Or by bus tours from Alice Springs, as well as by regular bus service direct from Adelaide. You can also get there by rent-a-car, and since there are now nearly half a million people visiting Ayers Rock each year, you have a chance to hitch hike. Once you get to the park headquarters at Yulara Village, you can rent a car, scooter or bike, or hire a taxi, or hitch hike out to the 2 major sites. There is also a shuttle bus making the rounds. That bus schedule, as well as all public transport to the area, will vary with the season. You can buy a 3 or 5-day *Rock Pass*, which enables you to ride the shuttle bus anywhere for the length of the pass. You can also fly over Ayers Rock or the Olgas.

Yulara Village is a new development just outside the park boundary which contains a visitor center--Tele. Inter+61-8-8956-3138, 2 international hotels, a budget lodge, campground, bank, post office, gasoline-petrol station, news agency, many restaurants, a supermarket, curio shop, a primary school, police and fire stations, and of course Australians couldn't get by without a pub or two.

Once you get to **Ayers Rock**, you can walk around the monolith on an old road in about 3 hours, taking in all the caves and Aboriginal rock art sites, and best of all, climb to the summit. The trail to the top begins at the western end. To make it safe for the general public, ropes or cables, attached to metal poles, have been installed along the steeper places to form a kind of railing. Thousands climb it annually.

The **Olgas** may be even more interesting than Ayers Rock. They consists of no less than 28 major separate sandstone bluffs or mini-monoliths. You may still pretty much wander at will throughout this strange maze with lots of foto opportunities.

Uluru National Park is in a desert setting, getting only 25 to 30 cms of rain annually. From December through the first part of March it's hot; while from June through early September it's cool to cold. This makes October & November, and March, April & May, the most enjoyable months to visit the area. Carry drinking water if you're hiking on a hot summer day.

Maps Get good maps and information at the visitor center in Yulara Village; also the latest edition of any travel guidebook to Australia, which should update this information.

This is the group of sandstone domes & bluffs known as The Olgas (Katatjuta).
(tourist office foto).

Map 320-3, Ayers Rock & Olgas, N. Territory, Australia

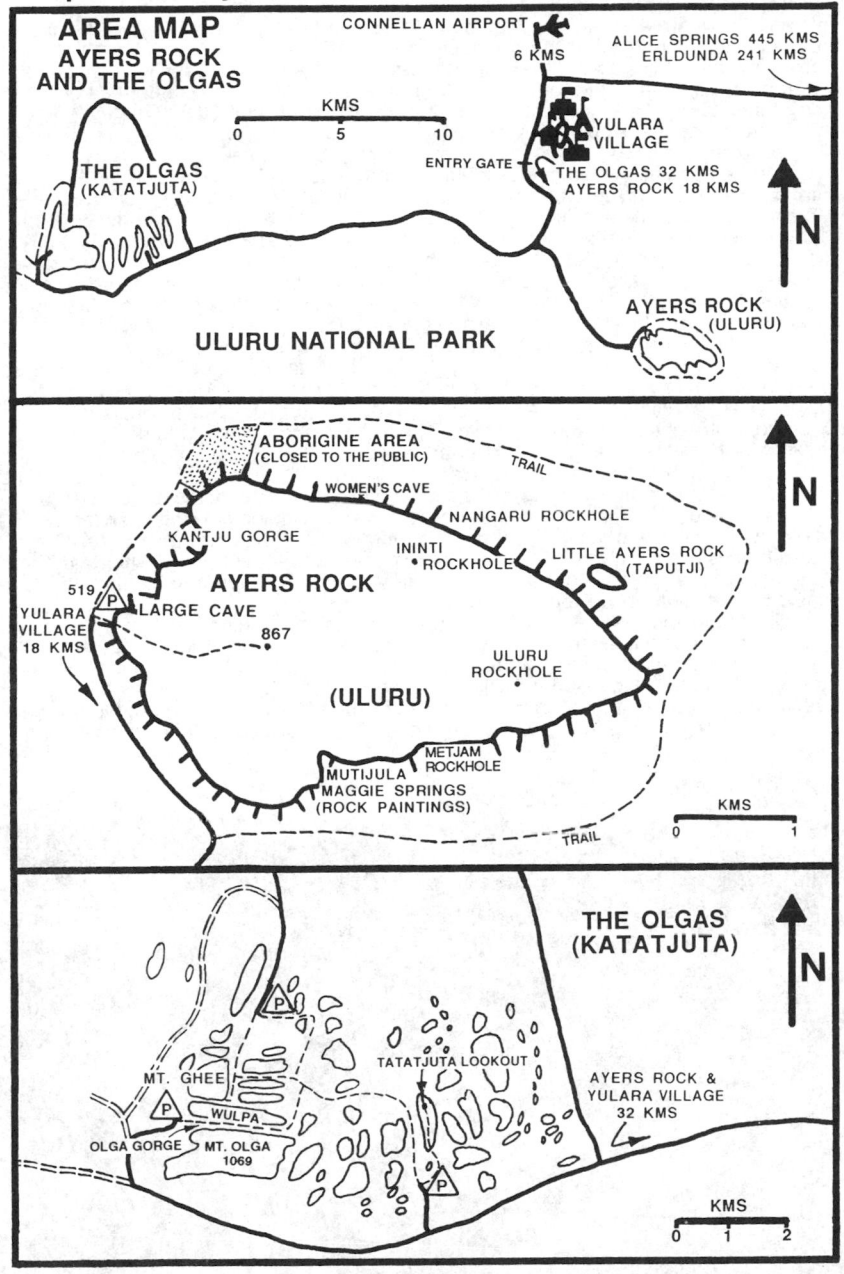

AREA MAP
AYERS ROCK
AND THE OLGAS

CONNELLAN AIRPORT
6 KMS

ALICE SPRINGS 445 KMS
ERLDUNDA 241 KMS

KMS
0   5   10

YULARA
VILLAGE

THE OLGAS
(KATATJUTA)

ENTRY GATE

THE OLGAS 32 KMS
AYERS ROCK 18 KMS

N

AYERS ROCK
(ULURU)

ULURU NATIONAL PARK

ABORIGINE AREA
(CLOSED TO THE PUBLIC)

TRAIL

N

WOMEN'S CAVE

NANGARU ROCKHOLE

KANTJU GORGE

ININTI
ROCKHOLE

LITTLE AYERS ROCK
(TAPUTJI)

519
P

AYERS ROCK

YULARA
VILLAGE
18 KMS

LARGE CAVE

867

ULURU
ROCKHOLE

(ULURU)

METJAM
ROCKHOLE

MUTIJULA
MAGGIE SPRINGS
(ROCK PAINTINGS)

TRAIL

KMS
0   1

THE OLGAS
(KATATJUTA)

N

MT. GHEE

TATATJUTA LOOKOUT

AYERS ROCK &
YULARA VILLAGE
32 KMS

P

WULPA

OLGA GORGE   MT. OLGA
1069

P

KMS
0   1   2

695

Kosciusko, Snowy Mtns., New South Wales, Australia

Australia is the flattest of all continents with almost no mountains, or at least large mountains. There are a few hills in the southern and northern parts of Western Australia, and others scattered throughout the land, but none can compare with the Snowy Mountains.

The Snowy Mountains are located south of Canberra, the national capital, and in the state of New South Wales, not too far north of the Victoria state line. These mountains aren't big by anybody's standards, the highest summit being Mt. Kosciusko, only 2229 meters. There isn't much of a challenge for climbers; it's mostly just trekking or walking, but it's about the best the country has to offer. The rocks in these mountains are a light colored granite.

Most people approach these mountains from the Canberra side. Head due south to Cooma, then southwest to Jindabyne. The region is now a national park and park HQ is in Jindabyne, Tele. from outsite Australia is Inter+61-2-6456-2444 or 6450-5600. From there, you have a choice. First option is drive or hitch hike north about 8 or so kms, then southwest to Perisher Village ski resort, and on to Charlotte Pass. This valley is served by a good paved road which is open year-round. The valley is not only a skier's paradise, but is a summer recreation area as well. From Charlotte Pass, there's a trail (old road) running up to just below the summit of **Kosciusko**. That walk from Charlotte Pass to the summit is about 8 kms one way.

Here's the 2nd option. The main highway running southwest from Jindabyne passes through the Threadbo Village. This ski resort can also be reached via Khankoban, which is north of this mapped area. This is a good highway and open year-round. To climb Kosciusko from Threadbo, locate a trail right in the middle of town (or you can take the lift) which runs up to the ridge top, then straight ahead to Kosciusko. The trail running to the right once you're on ridge top, heads down to Charlotte Pass and Perisher Village. North of Kosciusko are several other rounded summits with a number of trails. Back on 1/26/1977, the author hitch hiked to Perisher, then walked over the top and down to Threadbo, and hitch hiked out of the area.

In the ski season there will be a number of tour bus companies providing transport to the ski resorts, most of which are geared to the weekends. Also, in summer and winter Greyhound Pioneer bus lines has a daily bus running from Sydney and Canberra to Perisher and Threadbo villages. Check this out at a tourist office when you arrive in Australia. Hitch hiking is an alternative to having or renting your own vehicle.

There are hotels in the area open year-round, but one can camp almost anywhere. Ask about that before dropping a tent. A big problem in summer are the millions of bush flies; by far the most ever seen by the author! Jindabyne is the best place to buy groceries and supplies. There are restaurants at the resorts, as well as some small shops, but the prices are high.

Precipitation comes at any time, but the winter months of April through October are the wettest. Heavy rains & snow come at that time. A *fly swatter* is about the only special

Threadbo Village and the ski runs which are just south of Kosciusko.

Map 321-1, Kosciusko, Snowy Mtns., New South Wales, Australia

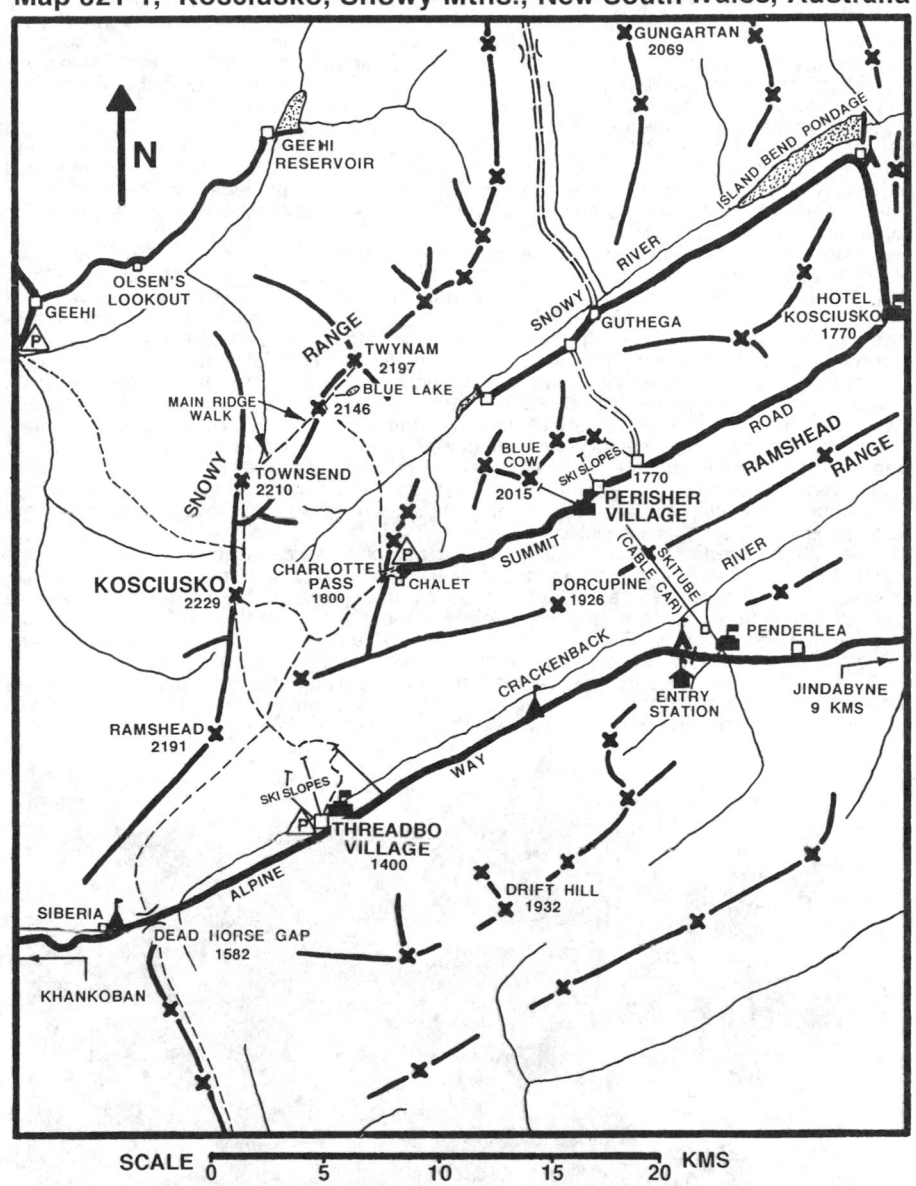

N

GUNGARTAN 2069

GEEHI RESERVOIR

ISLAND BEND PONDAGE

OLSEN'S LOOKOUT

GEEHI

P

RANGE

TWYNAM 2197

BLUE LAKE

MAIN RIDGE WALK

2146

SNOWY

RIVER

GUTHEGA

HOTEL KOSCIUSKO 1770

ROAD

SNOWY

TOWNSEND 2210

BLUE COW 2015

SKI SLOPES

1770

PERISHER VILLAGE

RAMSHEAD RANGE

RANGE

KOSCIUSKO 2229

CHARLOTTE PASS 1800

P

CHALET

SUMMIT

PORCUPINE 1926

SKITUBE (CABLE CAR)

RIVER

CRACKENBACK

PENDERLEA

RAMSHEAD 2191

SKI SLOPES

P

THREADBO VILLAGE 1400

WAY

ENTRY STATION

JINDABYNE 9 KMS

SIBERIA

DEAD HORSE GAP 1582

ALPINE

DRIFT HILL 1932

KHANKOBAN

SCALE 0 5 10 15 20 KMS

equipment you'll need to hike in the Snowy Mountains.

Maps *Snowy Mountains,* 1:250,000, from the Snowy Mountain Hydroelectric Authority, Canberra; better hiking maps are available in Threadbo or Perisher Villages; and the latest travel guidebook to Australia.

Milford Track, Southern Alps, South Island, New Zealand

Featured on this map is one of the better-known hiking or trekking trails in the world. This is the Milford Track, located on the south island of New Zealand. Besides the Milford Track, there are several other well-known walks in the area. They're shown on the map as the *Greenstone, Routeburn, Hollyford, Big Bay* and the *Martin's Bay Tracks*. This map and brief description is only an introduction so see one of the guidebooks below for more detailed information.

Approximately half of this map (western) shows portions of the Fiordland National Park. This national park covers the better part of the southwest coast of the South Island. Fiordland's name tells the story. This part of NZ has many inlets or fiords, and has a climate similar to that of Norway or British Columbia. The reason for all the fiords is the legacy of the last ice age when many glaciers carved great canyons which are now lakes or inlets. There also may be some subsidence occurring in the area.

To get started, make you way to **Te Anau**, a town at the south end of **Lake Te Anau**. Two or 3 daily buses arrive or depart to other parts of the island. There you'll find shops to buy food, and more importantly, the headquarters of the national park and their visitor center, Tele. 03-249-7924 (from overseas dial Inter+64-3-249-7924). Or more importantly, call the **Great Walks Desk at the visitor center** (Tele. 03-249-8514, or Inter+64-3-249-8514) in July to make reservations for the following summer, and especially from mid-December through January. Reservations must be made in advance for independent walkers. The cost of NZ$90 (US$47) includes the use of huts and permit. Everyone must do the trek in 4 days & 3 nights; and everyone must stay in the Neale Burn, Mintaro and Dumpling Huts. Guided groups use different huts and don't mingle with real trampers. No camping and no deviations allowed, even for bad weather! Everyone must walk in one direction, from south to north. This is so regulated it's unbelievable! Telefon calls are cheap these days, so use the numbers above to get the latest information and make reservations as far in advance as possible. Or show up each day at the visitor center and hope for cancellations.

The **Milford Track** is a 4 day, 53 km hike, or *tramp* as it's called in New Zealand. Some begin at the Eglinton Flat Campground, but most now take a bus from Te Anau to Te Anau Downs, then a boat on Te Anau Lake to Glade Wharf & House at the north end of the lake. Then it's one hour to the Neale Burn Hut. At the end of the trek, you'll then take another boat from Sandfly Point to Milford Sound; then a bus back to Te Anau. The transport system is very well organized from ferrys to buses, and there's no need to worry about taking you own car.

Te Anau is a summer tourist spot on the main road leading to the Milford Sound. The very busiest time is from mid-December through January. It's that time when most New Zealanders take holiday. For the hike, beware of bad weather much of the time and take proper rain gear.

This is an aerial view looking north from above Glade House, which is the official starting point for the Milford Track (tourist office foto?).

Map 322-3, Milford Track, Southern Alps, South Island, NZ

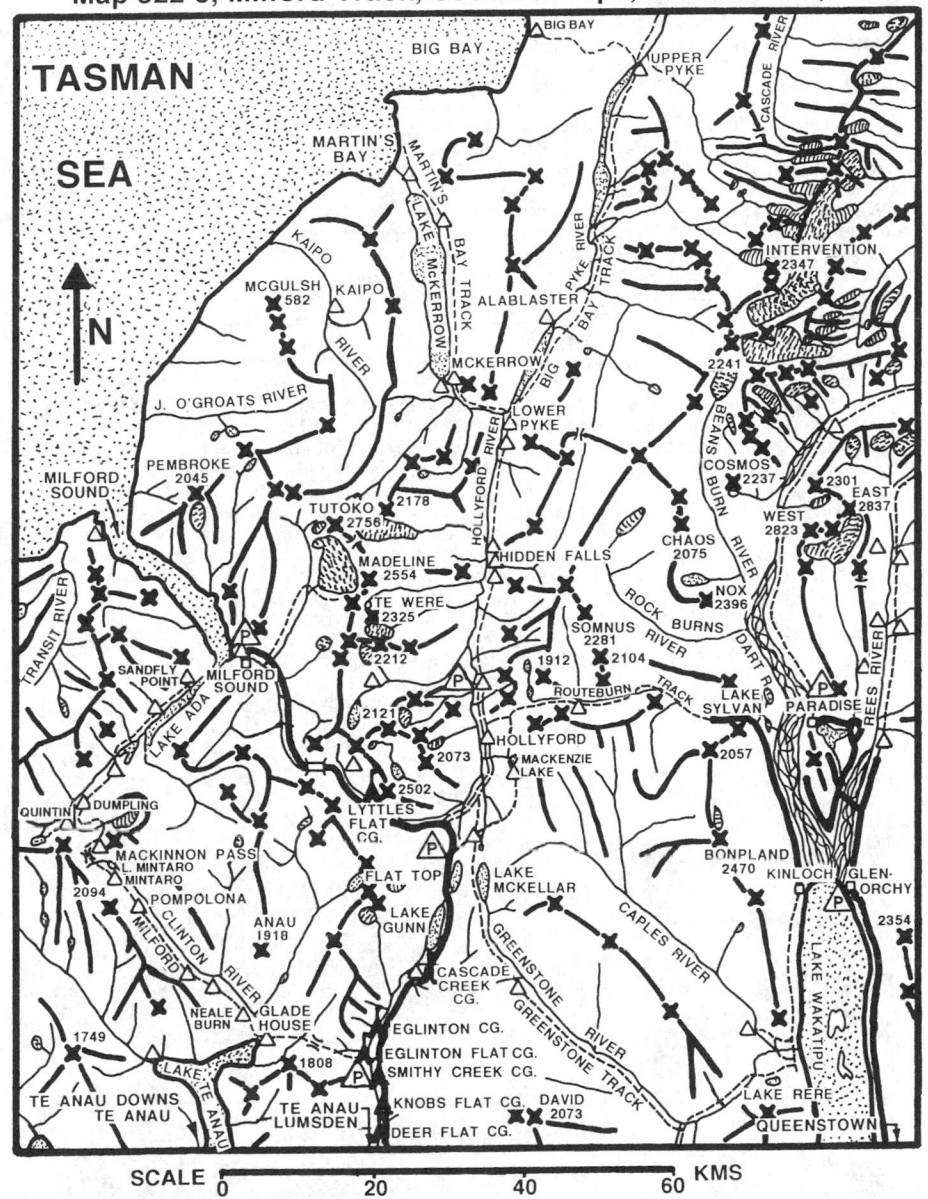

SCALE 0 — 20 — 40 — 60 KMS

Buy all food and supplies elsewhere if possible, but you can also buy everything in Te Anau.
Maps Trackmaps *Milford Track, 335-01*, 1:75,000; or *Fiordland's National Park,* 1:300,000,
Lands and Surveys; and the books **Tramping in New Zealand**, Lonely Planet; or **Milford Trails,**
Anderson, A.W. Reed; other maps or books are available at park visitor center, Te Anau.

Mt. Aspiring, Southern Alps, South Island, New Zealand

Running the full length of New Zealand's South Island is a folded, uplifted, and heavily glaciated mountain range, known as the Southern Alps. They are just as rugged, even more glaciated, and have more bad weather, than the Alps of Europe. In the south central part of this range stands one of the better known peaks in New Zealand, Mt. Aspiring at 3025 meters.

To get to this mountain, first get to Wanaka, located at the south end of Lake Wanaka. Two bus lines serve this town. *Intercity* has daily buses running between Queenstown and Christchurch, via Mount Cook, Haast Pass and Wanaka, with a connection to Dunedin. *Mt. Cook Landline* has daily buses running on a similar route except on Sundays. In some cases it's better to rent a car, or hitch hike (which is still good even since the author's trip back in 12/1976).

Wanaka is the last settlement on the approach route. Wanaka is also the headquarters of the national park in which Mt. Aspiring is the central attraction. Be sure to stop at the Department of Conservation (DOC) Visitor Center on Ardmore Street, for current information, especially that having to do with the use of huts, transportation to the trailhead and the latest weather forecast. They sell maps and guidebooks.

The huts on the mountain are operated by the DOC and reservations are needed for using them, especially during the busy season. The busiest season is from about mid-December through late January. That's when all, or most, New Zealanders take their holidays.

From Wanaka to the end of the main road at the private Raspberry Hut, or to Aspiring Station, is around 54 kms. If you don't have a car, it's a very long walk; but during the summer there's some traffic on this otherwise lonely road, and getting a lift is possible. Or, if you're on foot, a small company called *Mt. Aspiring Express,* part of Wanaka United Travel, can provide a shuttle. In the late 1990's, it cost NZ$25 (US$13) per person to the Raspberry Hut.

The normal route for those climbing **Aspiring** is via the end of the good road at the Raspberry Hut, then walking up a 4WD track to Aspiring Hut, Scott's (Rock) Bivwak, and the Colin Todd Hut. Below Colin Todd, you'll cross the Domar Glacier, so you'll need ice ax & crampons and maybe a rope. From Colin Todd, head east about 3 kms along the Northwest Ridge that's mostly a rock climb. Because of the terrible weather you'll likely encounter, make sure you have a good supply of wool clothing, rain gear, extra food, and the latest weather forecast, if possible.

In times of good weather--which is seldom, & with your own vehicle, it could be climbed in as little 3 days from Raspberry; *but 4 or 5 days is more normal*--without bad weather intervention. However, weather almost never allows for such a quick ascent, so plan on spending time in one of the huts waiting for a break in the weather, then make a run for it.

Late December to early March has the most stable weather. Because of the changeable weather, few people camp on the high mountains; almost everyone uses a hut.

Maps *Mount Aspiring National Park,* or *Aspiring S106,* and *Earnslaw S114,* (scale?), from

One of the best climbs in New Zealand is Mt. Aspiring on the South Island.
(tourist office foto?).

Map 323-3, Mt. Aspiring, Southern Alps, South Island, NZ

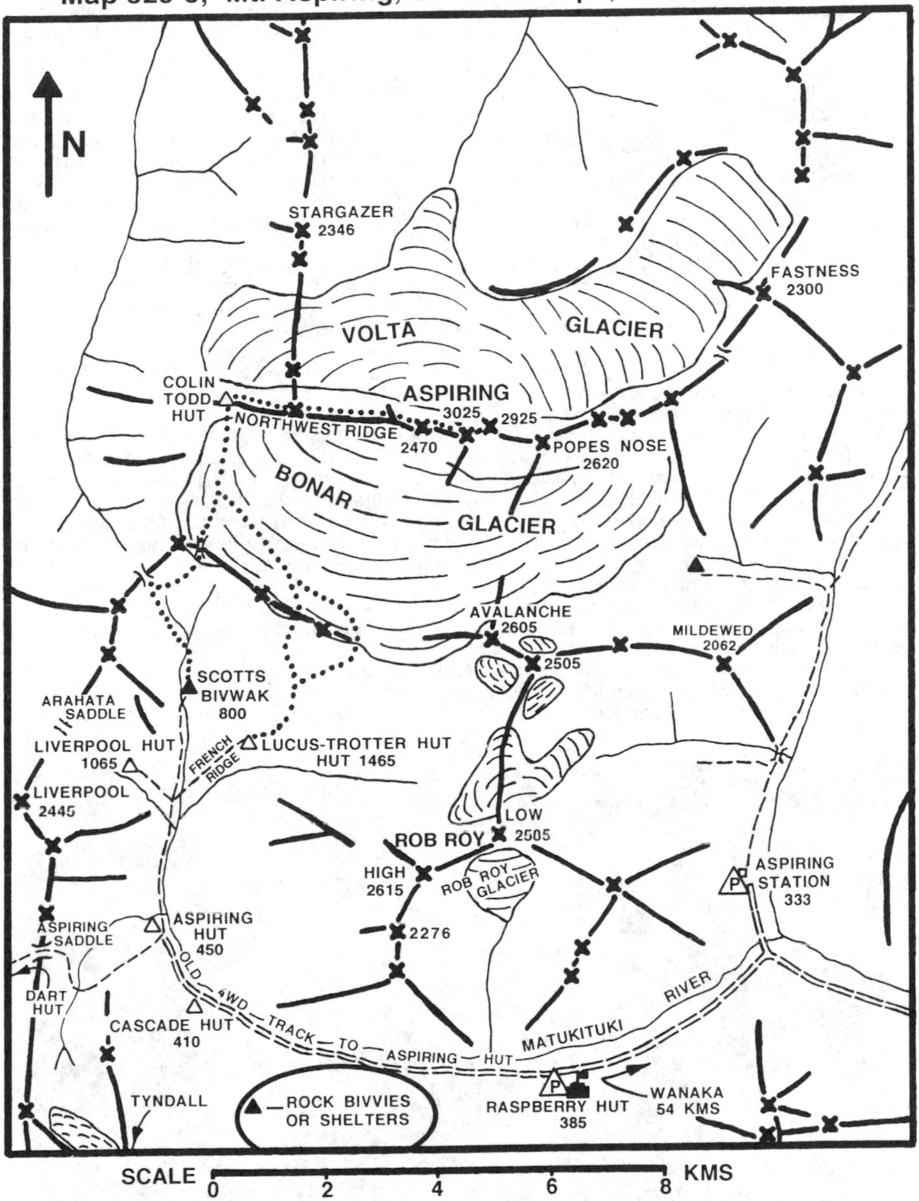

N

STARGAZER
2346

FASTNESS
2300

VOLTA   GLACIER

COLIN
TODD   ASPIRING
HUT   3025   2925
NORTHWEST RIDGE   POPES NOSE
2470   2620

BONAR

GLACIER

AVALANCHE
2605

MILDEWED
2062

2505

SCOTTS
BIVWAK
800

ARAHATA
SADDLE   FRENCH RIDGE
LIVERPOOL HUT   LUCUS-TROTTER HUT
1065   HUT 1465

LIVERPOOL
2445

LOW
ROB ROY   2505

HIGH   ROB ROY
2615   GLACIER   ASPIRING
STATION
333

ASPIRING   ASPIRING
SADDLE   HUT
450

DART
HUT   2276

CASCADE HUT   OLD 4WD TRACK TO ASPIRING HUT
410   MATUKITUKI   RIVER

TYNDALL   ROCK BIVVIES   WANAKA
OR SHELTERS   RASPBERRY HUT   54 KMS
385

SCALE 0   2   4   6   8 KMS

Lands and Surveys; or *Mount Aspiring, 273/02*, 1:150,000; and the book **The Mount Aspiring Region**, Bishop NZAC, Moir's Guide Books; and for approaches, maybe **Tramping in New Zealand**, Lonely Planet.

Mt. Aoraki-Cook, Southern Alps, South Island, New Zealand

Mt. Cook, renamed **Aoraki-Cook** in 1997, is the highest and one of the most challenging mountains in New Zealand. It lies in the central part of the Southern Alps on the South Island, and is not far from the storm-battered west coast. It's almost due west of Christchurch and Timaru. Mt. Cook has been uplifted and is made of granite & metamorphic-type rocks.

To get there, make your way to Oamaru or Timaru, then drive or hitch hike westward to the town of Twizel near the southern end of Lake Pukaki; and finally north to Mount Cook town. *Mt. Cook Landline* (Tele. 03-435-1849) has daily bus service to Mount Cook running between Queenstown, Te Anou and Christchurch. *InterCity* also has daily bus service between Queenstown & Christchurch, stopping at Mount Cook town, located in the valley below Mt. Cook. Mount Cook has hotels, a youth hostel, campground, stores, park headquarters & visitor center and guide services. Food can be bought at Mount Cook, but it's expensive. Best to buy all your supplies in Christchurch, Timaru, or elsewhere.

Don't underestimate **Mt. Cook** and its nearby peaks. Forgetting the ease of access, mountain huts, and low elevation, it is of Himalayan proportions. From the base of the Tasman Glacier to Cook's summit is nearly 3000 meters. The weather is bad most of the time, glaciers are extensive, and there are many crevasses and avalanches to deal with.

If everything is favorable, Cook can be climbed in 4 or 5 days from the end of the good road at Blue Lakes Shelter (day use only); or from Husky Flat (4WD road to that point); but people who have been so fortunate, are few and far between. Most people take up to 10 days of food & supplies, and plan for a long wait for a spell of good weather.

From Mount Cook, drive, walk or hitch hike north to the Blue Lakes Shelter, which is the end of the paved road (or drive up the rough road to Husky Flat). Continue up the Ball Hut (emergency only), and down to the glacier, then after 2 kms, turn left or west and head up to the Haast Hut, then the Plateau Hut at 2300 meters. From there it's west across the upper part of the Hocksetter Glacier, and up to Cook's summit from the north; approximately as shown on the map. The author tried this climb in 12/1976, but missed the summit. Before climbing, be sure to stop at the visitor center/park HQ. at Mount Cook for information on routes, weather and use of/and latest conditions of the huts.

Expedition-type clothing, including wool or the latest fabrics, must be used. For the serious climber, February or March are usually the best months for climbing, but good weather periods can come at any time. Winter climbing is now popular.

Huts are usually equipped with stoves & fuel and often left-over food. Larger huts are furnished with a radio, for communication between climbers and park rangers in the evening of each day. Good maps & guidebooks can be found at park HQ. in Mount Cook, Tele. Inter+64-3-435-1818.

Looking north up the Tasman Glacier from near the Plateau Hut on Mt. Cook.

Map 324-1, Aoraki-Cook, Southern Alps, South Island, NZ

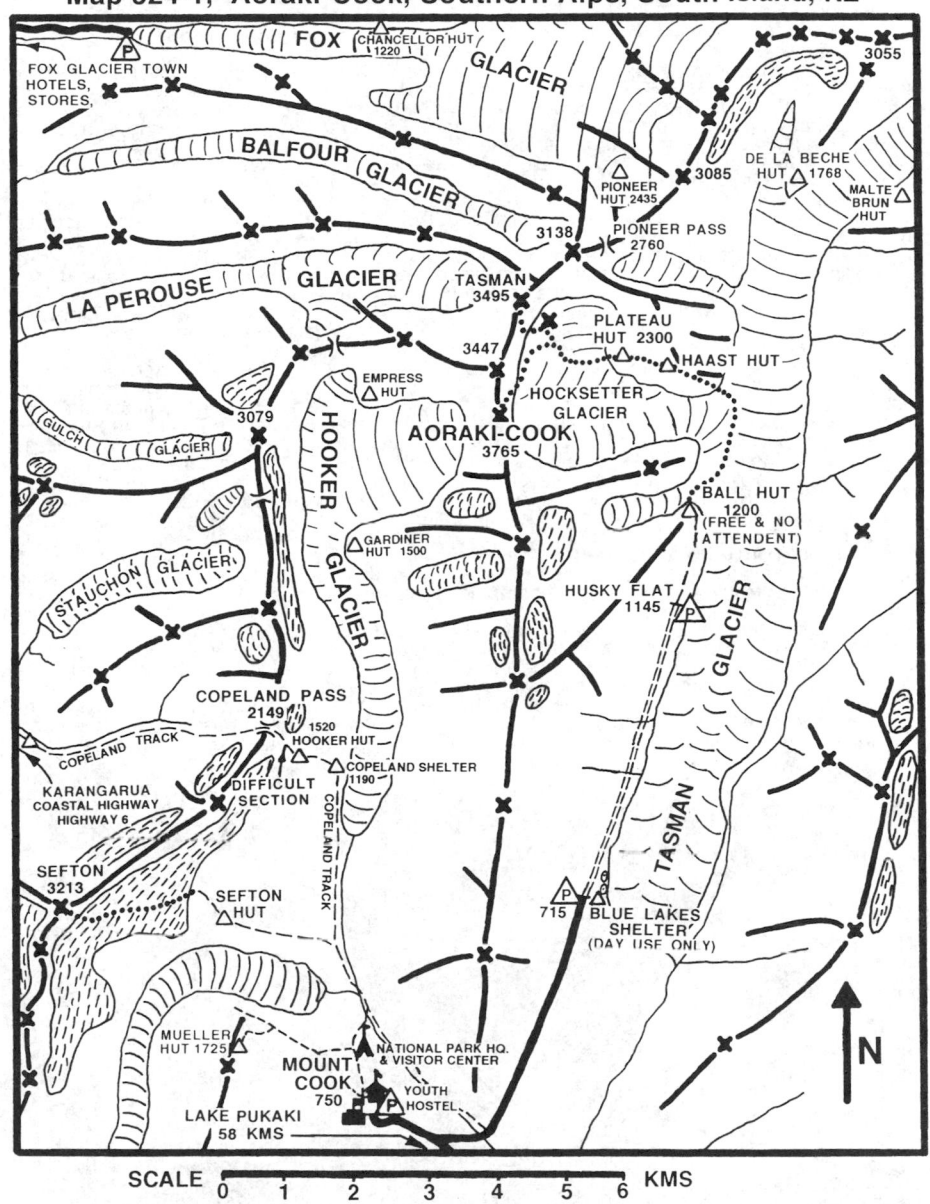

Neaby is a popular walk, the Copeland Track. This tramp begins at Mount Cook and runs over Copeland Pass to the West Coast Highway; a difficult 3-day walk.

Maps *Mount Cook and Westland National Parks,* 1:100,000, Lands and Survey; Topomaps *Mount Cook, H36,* 1:50,000; and the books, **Mount Cook Alpine Regions,** Hewitt & Davidson; or **Mount Cook Guidebook,** Logan, both from NZAC.

Ruapehu, Tongariro, Ngauruhoe, North Island, New Zealand

The 3 peaks featured here; Tongariro, Ngauruhoe and Ruapehu, are all within the Tongariro National Park. As with most (literally all) of the mountains on the North Island of New Zealand, these too are volcanos.

Ngauruhoe at 2291 meters, is an active volcano with a symmetrical shape which had its last explosive eruption on 7/4/1977. Nearby Red Crater last blewup in 1926; Te Mari Crater last erupted in 1896; and the North Crater about 7750 BC. The main summit of Tongariro, as shown on this and other maps, is older than the Holocene. Ruapehu was very active throughout the 1900's, with it's last phreatic eruptions in the fall of 1997. For updated volcano information contact the Institute of Geological and Nuclear Sciences in Wairakei, NZ at website (www.gns.cri.nz/) or (www.volcano.si.edu/gvp/).

All these peaks can best be reached from the highway connecting the hamlet of National Park on the west, and the small city of Turangi to the northeast. Turangi is the best place to organize your trip to these peaks. There you'll find campgrounds, supermarkets, motels, a tourist office, Department of Conservation (DOC) office (Tele. 07-386-8607) where you make reservations for the huts (and possibly campsites?), and purchase a *Great Walk Pass*, if you plan to stay in any of the huts or campsites around Tongariro.

Public transport, *Alpine Scenic Tours* (Tele. 07-378-7412) runs buses from Taupo to Turangi, then shuttle buses from Turangi to National Park via Whakapapa, 3 times daily.

Ruapehu is the highest and most developed mountain of the group having 3 ski resorts on it's slopes with many lodges and campgrounds. At the Whakapapa Village are hotels, National Park Headquarters & Visitor Center, Tele. Inter+64-7-892-3729 or website (www.doc.govt.nz), a store, garage and service station. Tour buses make the rounds, but as in most places in New Zealand, hitch hiking is good along the main highway and on the road to the Top of the Bruce.

Few if any facilities exist at the Tukino Village, and even fewer are at the Turoa Village. Both of these are trailheads and winter ski slopes. Little traffic exists along these back roads.

The author recommends a traverse of the 3 main summits, from north to south (or vice versa), walking from Ruapehu to the Ketetahi Carpark & Trailhead on the north side of Tongariro. You can climb all these major summits along the way in 3 or 4 days. Starting on 12/16/1976, the author hitch hiked to the Ketetahe Trailhead, then walked south over the top of **Tongariro & Ngauruhoe**, then to Whakapapa and Top of the Bruce. He climbed Ruapehu, but sat in his tent for a day before being blown off the mountain. This trip took 4 days. Routes to all these summits are easy. If camping above treeline, about 1000 meters, take a low profile tent!

Food should be bought in Turangi or National Park, but some supplies can be found near the National Park HQ., and at the Top of the Bruce. Streams abound everywhere, so water is no problem. There are many huts you can use, but contact the DOC office in Turangi or Whakapapa Village, or any office in the country, to make reservations

Most trails are *poled,* that is, a pole about 3 meters high is placed on the trail about every 100 meters to help hikers locate the route in foggy conditions. These poled-trails have been prepared everywhere above treeline. The weather is always bad in New Zealand, so take along

A mid-1990's eruption of Ruapehu (Craig Potton Publishing foto).

Map 325-1, Ruapehu, Tongariro, Ngauruhoe, North Island, NZ

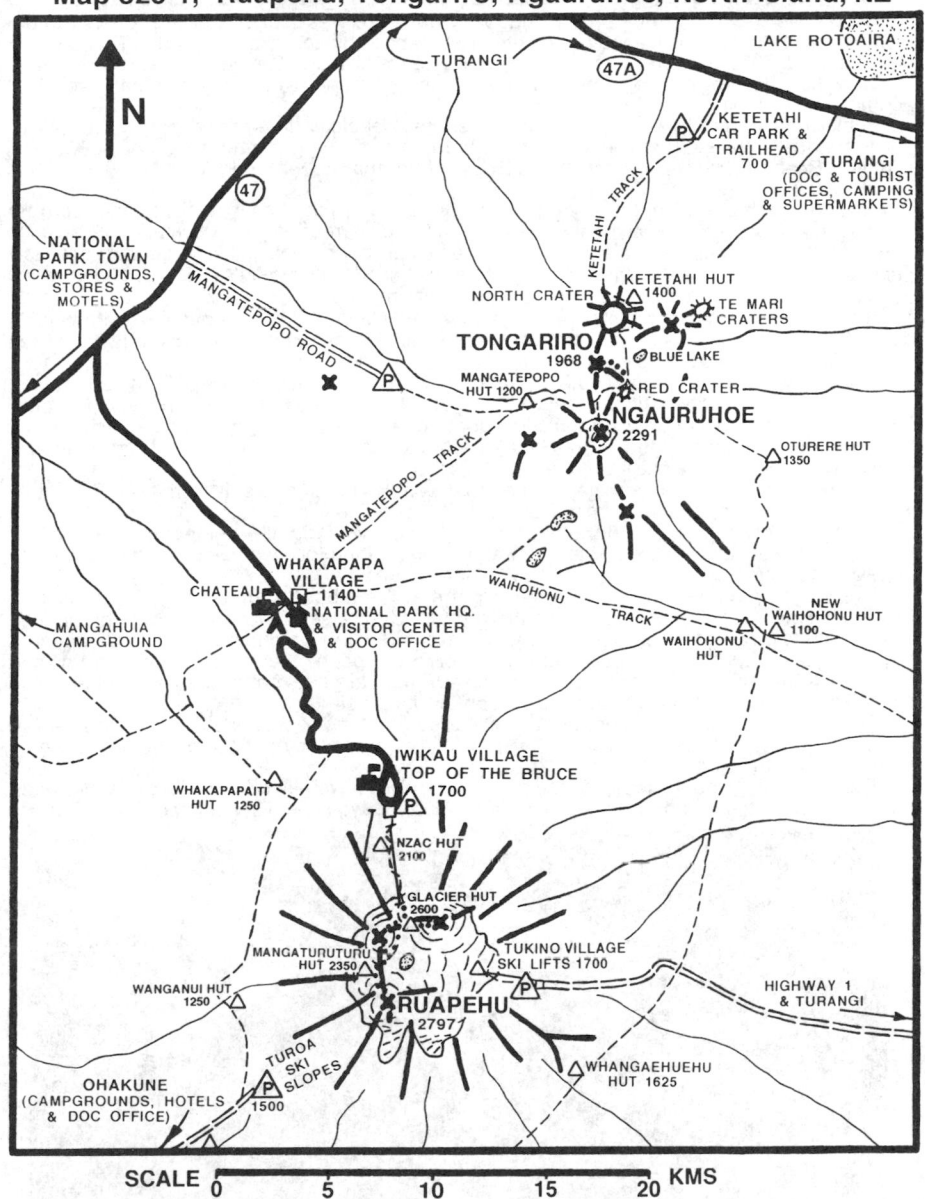

some wool clothing, plus rain gear for you and your pack. The busiest time for hiking is from mid-December through late January. This is when most New Zealanders and Australians take vacations. February or March is perhaps the very best time for trekking or climbing, as the weather can more often be good and there are fewer people. An ice ax & crampons may be needed for Ruapehu, but not for the other peaks unless you're planning a winter ascent.

Maps Parkmaps *Tongariro National Park, 273-04,* 1:80,000; or 4 maps from Topomaps, *T19, T20, S19 & S20,* 1:50,000; buy at the national park HQ. & visitor center, in National Park or Turangi; and the book, **Tramping in New Zealand**, Lonely Planet.

Egmont (Taranaki) Volcano, North Island, New Zealand

On the North Island of New Zealand, very near the west coast and the towns of New Plymouth and Stratford, lies a very symmetrically-shaped volcano. Its name is Mt. Egmont (the Maori name is Taranaki), and it rises from virtually sea level to 2510 meters. Despite its relative low elevation, it's crowned with snow throughout the year and even has some real glaciers at and near the summit.

Egmont last erupted in about 1755, using dendrochronology (tree ring) dating. This was 15 years before white settlers arrived. There was an even bigger blast in about 1655. The southern **Beehive** erupted in about 1250 BC, and **Fanthams Peak** had an eruptive period in about 1350 BC.

Getting to **Egmont** is fairly easy, as climbers have 3 main access roads to choose from. Possibly the most-used approach is the one up from Stratford, reaching the Mountain House Lodge (formerly Stratford House) and the ski resort at Manganui Lodge. Next to the Manganui Lodge is a public shelter for climbers & skiers, open year-round. It used to be free in 12/1976; that's when the author made his summit climb. Who knows what it costs now!

As for climbing, there's a trail up from the Manganui Lodge to the top of the ski lift, then it's onto the permanent snow field and straight to the summit. The author never saw any crevasses on this route, so it's safe. This is perhaps the 2nd most popular route.

Another approach is the road up from Kaponga to Dawson Falls where you'll find a part-time visitor center built by the national park. There you'll find a cheap tramper's shelter, the Konini Lodge; or the expensive Dawson Falls Tourist Lodge. Use the trail passing the Hooker and Kapuni Huts, then on past the Syme Huts (one old & historic, plus a new one) and Fanthams Peaks, and finally make a beeline to the top.

A third approach route, and maybe the most popular for climbers, is from New Plymouth, where a paved 28 km road runs up to North Egmont and The Camphouse. There you'll find the national park visitor center (Tele. 06-756-8710) which sells maps & guidebooks. From The Camphouse, walk up a 4WD road to Tahurange Lodge, then follow a poled-route up the north ridge to the summit.

There's no public transport to these trailheads, exception for Tubby's Tours in New Plymouth, which take trampers up to North Egmont. Otherwise, it's take your own car, or hitch hike--which is pretty good. No matter what route is taken, the mountain can be climbed in one day, start to finish, from either trailhead. However, many people tramp (hike) the loop-trail and take 3 to 4 days in the process. Not shown on this map are huts on the western slopes. The summit can be reached from about any place on this loop-trail.

Egmont is very easy to climb, but there are some steeper sections near the top. A few routes can be found to offer challenges, some of which may be icy. All routes require an ice ax & crampons (maybe not the north ridge?).

The worst thing about this climb, and all the climbs in New Zealand, is the weather; it's often one storm after another. Expect wet conditions and you won't be disappointed. Rain gear for

Mt. Egmont from the northeast and one of many dairy farms in New Zealand.

Map 326-1, Egmont (Taranaki) Volcano, North Island, New Zealand

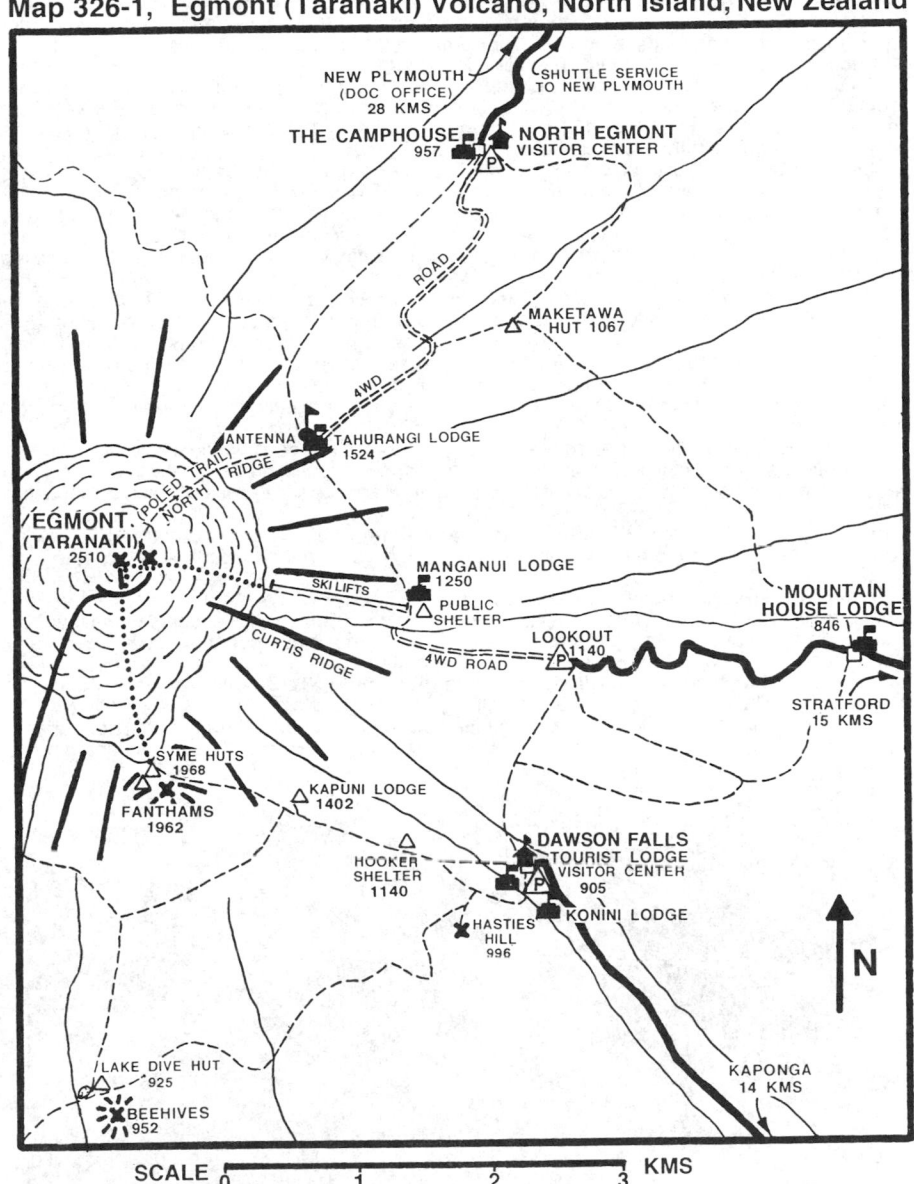

NEW PLYMOUTH
(DOC OFFICE)
28 KMS

SHUTTLE SERVICE
TO NEW PLYMOUTH

THE CAMPHOUSE
957

NORTH EGMONT
VISITOR CENTER

ROAD

MAKETAWA
HUT 1067

4WD

ANTENNA

TAHURANGI LODGE
1524

(POLED TRAIL)

NORTH RIDGE

EGMONT
(TARANAKI)
2510

SKI LIFTS

MANGANUI LODGE
1250

PUBLIC
SHELTER

CURTIS RIDGE

4WD ROAD

LOOKOUT
1140

MOUNTAIN
HOUSE LODGE
846

STRATFORD
15 KMS

SYME HUTS
1968

KAPUNI LODGE
1402

FANTHAMS
1962

HOOKER
SHELTER
1140

DAWSON FALLS
TOURIST LODGE
VISITOR CENTER
905

KONINI LODGE

HASTIES
HILL
996

N

LAKE DIVE HUT
925

BEEHIVES
952

KAPONGA
14 KMS

SCALE 0   1   2   3   KMS

both you and pack is required.
   Do your shopping in the surrounding towns before reaching the mountain; New Plymouth is best. If you're planning to use the shelters take note; the busiest season, when most natives take holiday is from mid-December through late January. Shelters are most crowded at that time. Reserve huts at any Department of Conservation (DOC) office in New Zealand.
Maps Parkmap *Egmont National Park, 273-9,* 1:50,000; or Topomaps *260 Series, Egmont, P20 & New Plymouth, P19,* 1:50,000, buy at the North Egmont Visitor Center or New Plymouth; and the book, **Tramping in New Zealand**, Lonely Planet.

Tomanivi (Mt. Victoria), Viti Levu Island, Fiji

Shown here is an area map covering the northern half of the Fijian island of Viti Levu, and a 2nd map showing the highest summit called Tomanivi. The colonial name was Mt. Victoria. At 1323 meters, it's the highest mountain in the Fijian group.

All travelers to Fiji arrive at the Nadi (spelled Nadi, but pron. Nandi) International Airport. From the airport, take one of many daily buses which run between Nandi and Lautoka. Both small cities have lots of hotels and supermarkets, but Lautoka has more, and that is the starting point for buses going to the north side of Fiji's largest island.

From the bus terminal in downtown Lautoka, take a long distance bus to Tavua. Start in the morning, because there's only one expensive hotel in Tavua, and there seems to be only one bus daily running from Tavua to Navai (at the base of Tomanivi) and on to Nandrau. For sure, there's one bus running from Tavua to Navai about 3pm which transports school children. That same bus makes the return trip very early the next morning carrying school kids. Hitch hiking from Navai to Tavua in the afternoons seems easy.

At Navai, ask someone where the Turanga Ni Koro's (village leader) house is. As in most of the Pacific, you'll have to get permission to climb a mountain from the nearest village, and its leader. The Turanga Ni Koro will likely invite you to sleep on mats in his house, for which you'll have to pay. Expect to pay a small fee to climb the mountain as well. This is how the village chief makes a living. For a 4 year term of office, he is a policeman, judge, priest, etc, and has no time for a regular job. If you prefer to be more private, you can surely get permission to camp on the mountain.

On 8/4/1997, the author paid the chief about US$14.50 which included permission to climb, several cups of kava (the narcotic of choice in the Pacific) at a wedding reception or some kind of party (?), a night's sleep in his house, a couple of Fijian meals, and for storing his big pack while on the mountain the next day.

From the center of Navai, look for the sign pointing out the little road heading toward Tomanivi. This road runs by a stream for a km, then you'll pass through a cattle gate, and continue along this same old road. After another km or so, the road fades into a regular trail. You'll have 2 stream crossings, then you'll be on a minor ridge. In the early 1990's, this mountain was made into a forest reserve, and one of the jobs of Navai's leader is to maintain the trail. From the sign proclaiming the forest reserve, it's a good but steep trail through a moss or cloud rainforest. In places you'll have to pull yourself up using tree branches or roots. When you reach the summit ridge, turn left to the highest point. Start early to hopefully beat the afternoon cloud buildup so you can see something from on top.

Best to buy all your food in Lautoka, because Navai has only one small shop. It sells snack-type food, plus rice and sugar, but no fruits or vegetables. You can do this hike in about half a

From the middle of Navai looking at the beginning of the road/trail to Tomanivi, which can be seen in the distance.

Map 327-1, Tomanivi (Mt. Victoria), Viti Levu Island, Fiji

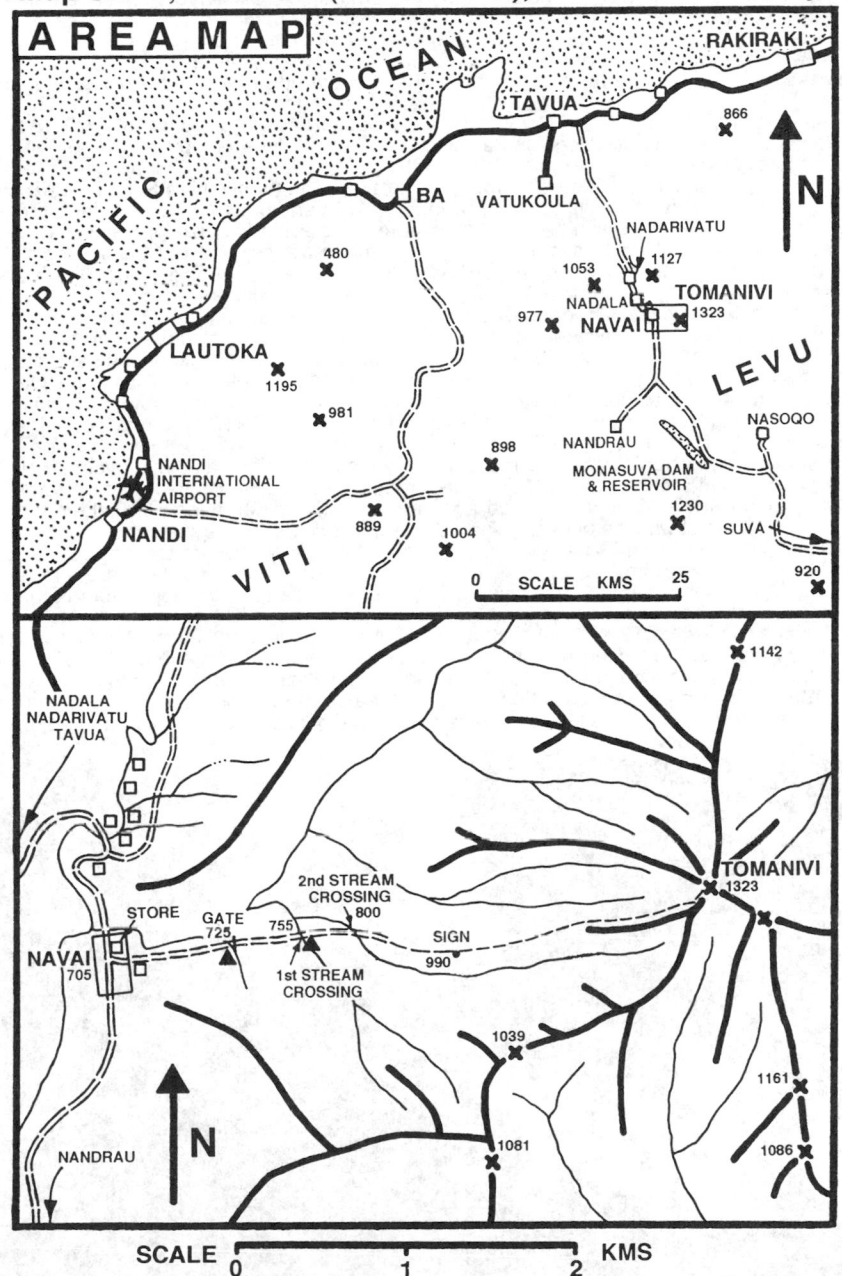

day. The author made it up in about 1 1/3 hours; 2 2/3 hours round-trip. The dry season is from June through September.

Maps *Balevuto, M27,* and *Monasuva, N27,* both 1:50,000; or *Viti Levu,* 1:250,000; buy these maps at Lands & Surveys, Suva, Fiji; and the latest travel guidebook to Fiji or the South Pacific.

Silisili Volcano, Savaii Island, Western Samoa

This map shows the highest mountain in Western Samoa, Silisili Volcano at 1858 meters. It's located on the island of Savaii. Silisili is an old volcano, but the nearby Mata Ole Afi issued lava from 10/30/1902 until 11/17/1902. Also, Matavanu Volcano sent huge amounts of lava northeast right into the sea beginning 8/4/1905. Activity lasted until 11/1911. For volcano updates see the website of the Bulletin of the *Global Volcanism Network* (www.volcano.si.edu/gvp/).

After landing on the island of Upolu, where the capital city of Apia is located, take a bus to Mulifanua and a ferry to Salelologa on Savaii Island. At the ferry wharf, buses will be waiting for passengers, then fan out across the island on the paved circular island highway. Take a bus which goes past the little village of **Aopo**, the starting point for climbing **Silisili**. Stop in the center of town and pay the village leader about US$12 per/day for hiking on village property. They are the ones who maintain the trail, and of course, collect hiking fees for their work.

You'll need about 1 1/2 days for this climb, if using public transport. Best to buy food in Apia, or in big shops near the ferry wharf, as you can only buy snack-type food in Aopo. There are no streams or springs on the trail, so get enough water in Aopo for your entire trip.

From Aopo, go downhill northeast to the track heading south up the mountain. From the highway, it's about 7 kms through gardens and a logged-out area to the end of the road. In 1997, there was an old rusty barrel at the very beginning of the trail. Once on the trail, you'll first pass through cultivated gardens, then rainforest. At about 1500 meters you'll leave the forest as you level off onto a plateau. If there's a break in the clouds, you'll see some volcanic cones. The high one straight ahead will likely be Silisili, but with fog & clouds, you may not get a good look at anything. Carry a compass, and maybe an altimeter.

Follow the trail across grass-covered lava. At a junction, one path goes straight ahead to 2 log & plastic-sheet shelters south of Silisili; the other turns left and goes back into the forest and ends on top of Silisili. The author used an umbrella, altimeter and compass all the way and made it to the top of what he believes was Silisili--unless there's more than one volcano with a plague on top! He made it from the end of the road, where he camped, to the top in 3 2/3 hours. It was about 6 1/2 hours round-trip from the end of the road. The total 2-day walk-time was 10 1/4 hours from Aopo. Summit day was on 7/27/1997. June through September is the drier season, but expect rain & fog anytime.

Buses are scare from Aopo, but hitch hiking is good down to Fatuvalu or Safotu, then there are more buses back to the ferry. Along the way, stop at Samauga and walk or hitch a ride up to Paia, then ask which road goes up to **Matavanu**. From Paia, it's about 7 kms along a pretty good road. Less than one km back from the end of that road, look for a parking place and a trail running east through the brush. Matavanu's crater is about 300 meters from the road, but the author walked right by it!

This foto was taken inside the church at Saleaula. Molten lava flowed inside through the doorway in the middle of the picture.

Map 328-1, Silisili Volcano, Savaii Island, Western Samoa

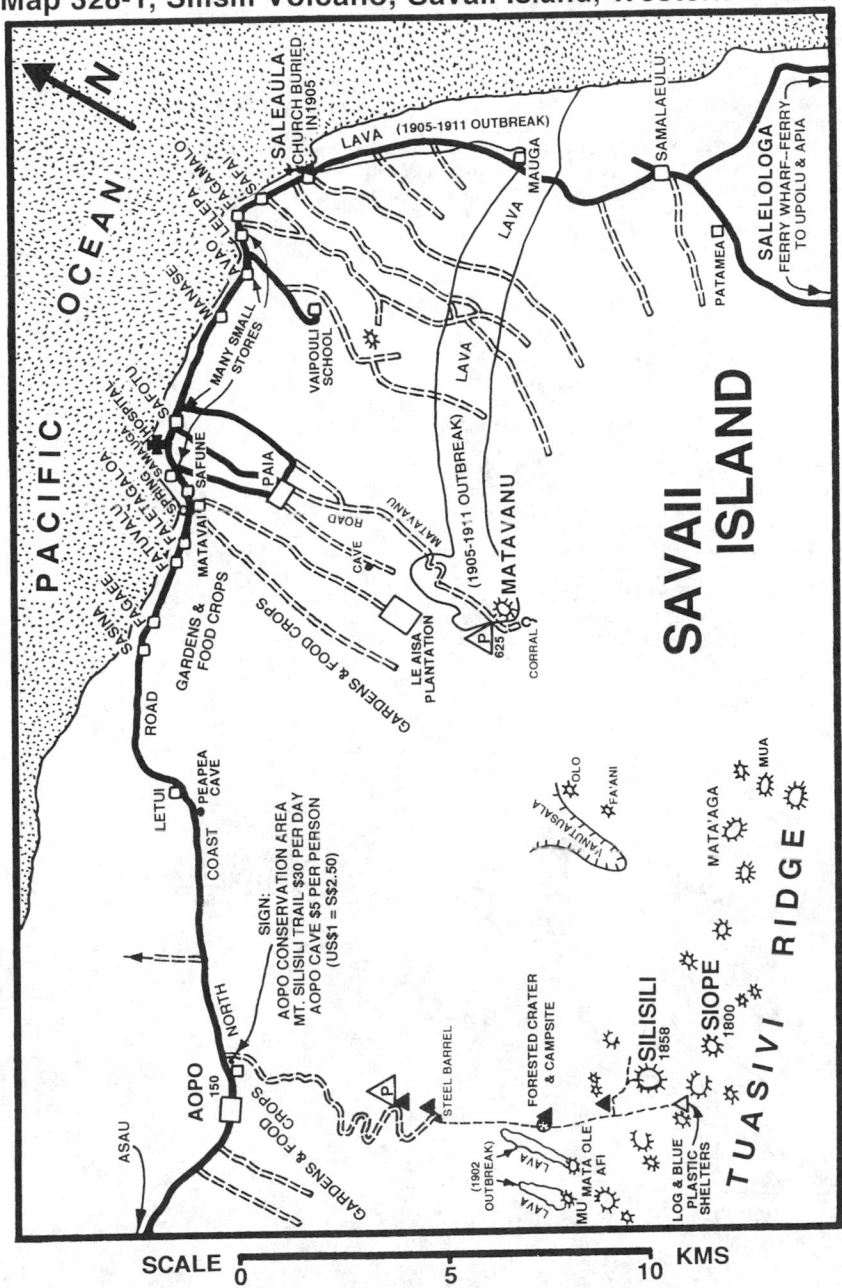

SCALE
0   5   10   KMS

Another site for volcano hunters, is the **church at Saleaula**. It was surrounded and half-buried by lava from Matavanu in 1905. One tongue of lava went right through the front door.
Maps *Fagamalo & Silisili, Savaii, 4 & 7*, 1:20,000; the Hema map *Western Samoa*, 1:235,000, from Lands and Survey, Apia; and the latest travel guidebook to Samoa or the South Pacific.

Matafao, Tutuila Island, American Samoa

Near the middle of the Pacific Ocean and the island group known as Polynesia, is Samoa. Of the 5 or 6 inhabited islands in the Samoan group, only one is part of American Samoa. The 2 larger islands to the west form what is now known as Western Samoa, which is an independent nation. American Samoa, the island of Tutuila, is administered by the USA. Most of this islands population lives around the perimeter of Pago Pago Bay. The seat of government is at Fagatogo. The international airport is called Pago Pago.

This map covers the central part of Tutuila where the higher mountains are located. Like most Polynesian islands, Tutuila is volcanic in origin. Evidence of this is seen in the excellent harbor in Pago Pago Bay. This looks like the remains of an old caldera (?). Just west and southwest of the airport are some Holocene craters, but there hasn't been any volcanic activity in the human history of this island.

Tutuila Island is only about 30 kms long and very narrow. The highest summit is Matafao rising to 653 meters. To some this doesn't seem very high, but this and all other mountains rise directly from sea level; Matafao being only one km from tidewater. Even though this peak is the highest on the island, this area is part of a watershed for drinking water, so there are few trails around. However there is one trail to the summit.

There are 3 possible routes to the top of **Matafao**. The topo map listed below, shows trails beginning at Fagaalu, Fagatogo, and from near the pass marked 181 meters, but doesn't show any going to the summit. However, there is a trail to the top, and it's shown in it's approximate location on this map. The region around Matafao is steep and heavily forested.

The author was in Pago Pago during 10/1976, but he arrived during a very wet period. In that week, he estimated the rainfall at about 3/4's of a meter, or 75 cms! Like a damn fool, he waited for better weather to climb, but it never came. He did however have other people describe the routes in the mountains and presumably to the summit of Matafao. The only mountain he climbed was Alava as shown on this map. If you're planning to climb on Tutuila, just take an umbrella & waterproof camera bag, and be prepared to be drenched!

Another interesting hike is to the top of **Alava**. From the village of Pago Pago, walk or hitch hike up the road to the pass marked 181 meters, then turn right and walk along an old ridge road to the top. At the summit of Alava is a television transmitter and the upper terminal of a cable car which runs from Fagatogo. The transmitter is apparently serviced using the cable car.

There are a couple of other hikes beginning from Pago Pago Bay. One trail goes northeast over a ridge to Vatia; another goes to Afono, both on the north coast. Another trail connects these 2 villages. Making this loop-hike would make a nice one-day outing taking in both villages.

Pago Pago Bay and Matafao as seen from the summit of Alava.

Map 329-1, Matafao, Tutuila Island, American Samoa

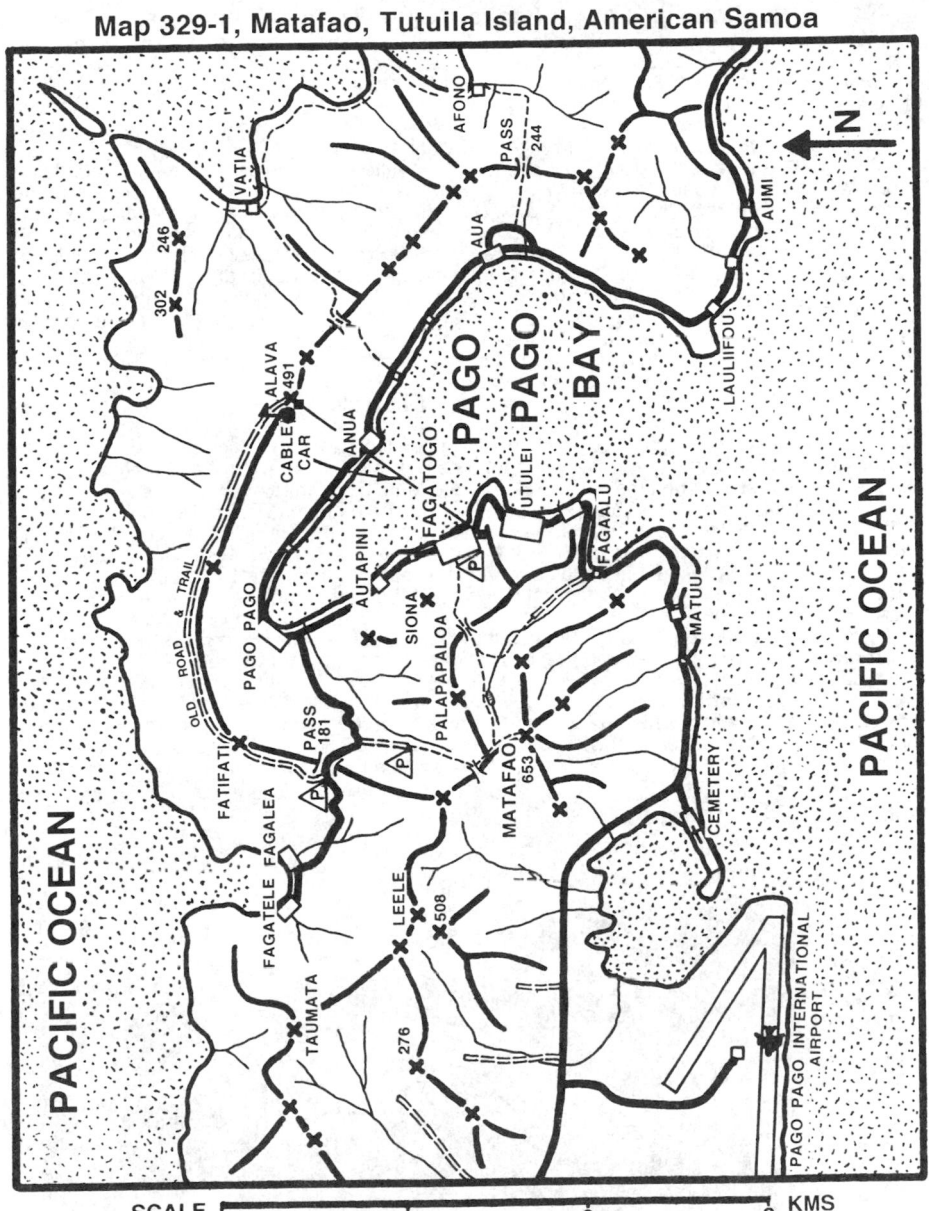

Samoa is warm & humid and receives about *5 meters* of rain each year. August is the driest month; June & July next driest.
Maps *Tutuila Island, American Samoa,* 1:24,000, from the USGS; and the latest travel guidebook to this South Pacific region.

Orohena and Aorai Peaks, Tahiti, French Polynesia

This map shows a small part of the island of Tahiti, including the highest peak, Orohena at 2241 meters. However, in 1997 the most popular hike was to the top of Aorai at 2066 meters.

Sometime in the mid-1990's, there was a forest fire on the slopes of Orohena, which burned the fixed ropes along the route to the summit. Orohena is extremely steep and without those fixed ropes, it's almost impossible to climb, at least for the average hiker. Hopefully, it will be open, upgraded, repaired & climbable by the time you arrive.

To get to **Orohena**, start at the Tourist Information office in Papeete. Get as much updated information there as possible, then drive, hitch hike or take a bus east. The turnoff from the main highway is between Km posts 11 & 12, and next to a police station and near a hospital. From there hitch hike or drive a car. Ask someone about the road going to *Le Paradis* and the trail to *Milli Sources* (1000 Springs). There were lots of new homes being built at Le Paradis on 7/20 & 7/21/1997, so ask where the trail is located. It used to begin at the city water tanks. From there, a blocked-off 4WD track contours along the face of the ridge to a huge spring and small dam. From there the trail goes straight up the mountain. You may need ropes and maybe 2 days to climb this one, so get the latest information on the trail before starting out.

To climb **Mt. Aorai**, locate one of several buses running east from near the tourist office in Papeete. Ask the driver to drop you off at the road going up to Le Belvedere. From the main highway, it's 6.8 kms to the Belvedere Restaurant along an old paved road. You'll have to walk, but you'll probably get a lift part way.

From Belvedere, walk up a very good and well-used trail along the ridge to Aorai, a distance of 10.6 kms. Along the way are 2 huts or refuges. The first is at about 1450 meters and will sleep about 7 or 8 people on the floor. Refuge Fare Mato has two rainwater tanks which collect rain from the roof. It once had solar powered lights, but the batteries were stolen in 1997.

The upper hut, or the Refuge de Fare Ata, is at about 1800 meters. It's a larger hut which still had solar powered electric lights on 7/19 & 7/20/1997. It has 3 rainwater tanks and a veranda nearby for eating. From this refuge, a good trail runs along a knife-edge ridge to the summit of Aorai. From there you'll have some great views of Orohena and other needle-like peaks to the south.

Aorai, can be climbed in one long day, but it's likely best to walk up to one of the refuges in the afternoon, then finish the climb the next morning before the clouds roll in--which happens every day. Near each refuge there are places to put up a tent, and there should be water in the tanks at each hut for drinking. Better purify it first, just in case. With a large pack, the author walked to Belvedere in about 1 1/2 hours, then to the 1st refuge in 2 more hours. He camped there, then rushed to the top in 1 1/3 hours the next morning. He was back at the main highway at 1:20pm that afternoon, walking all the way. Dry season here is June through October. Tahiti

From the *Sommet de L'Aorai*, looking southeast at the very steep Orohena.

Map 330-1, Orohena & Aorai, Tahiti, French Polynesia

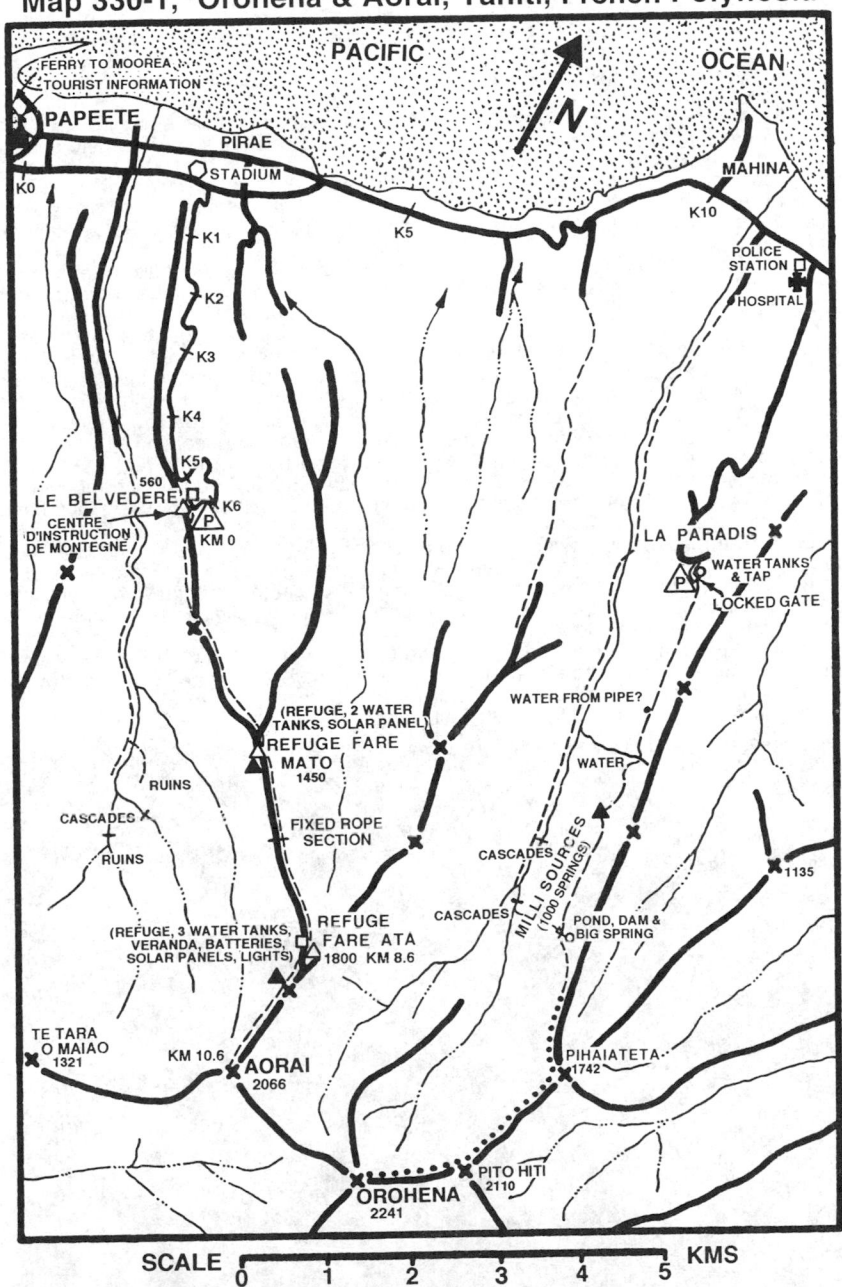

PACIFIC OCEAN

FERRY TO MOOREA
TOURIST INFORMATION

PAPEETE

PIRAE

STADIUM

K0

K1

K2

K3

K4

K5

K5

560

LE BELVEDERE

K6

CENTRE
D'INSTRUCTION
DE MONTEGNE

P

KM 0

MAHINA

K10

POLICE
STATION

HOSPITAL

LA PARADIS

WATER TANKS
& TAP

P

LOCKED GATE

(REFUGE, 2 WATER
TANKS, SOLAR PANEL)

REFUGE FARE
MATO
1450

WATER FROM PIPE?

WATER

RUINS

CASCADES

RUINS

FIXED ROPE
SECTION

CASCADES

CASCADES

CASCADES

MILLI SOURCES
(1000 SPRINGS)

1135

(REFUGE, 3 WATER TANKS,
VERANDA, BATTERIES,
SOLAR PANELS, LIGHTS)

REFUGE
FARE ATA
1800 KM 8.6

POND, DAM &
BIG SPRING

TE TARA
O MAIAO
1321

KM 10.6

AORAI
2066

PIHAIATETA
1742

PITO HITI
2110

OROHENA
2241

SCALE 0 1 2 3 4 5 KMS

is to France, as Hawaii is to the USA; so learn some French.
Maps *Tahiti, Archipel de La Société, 3615,* 1:100,000, Institut Geographique National (IGN at website www.ign.fr), buy in Papeete; and the latest travel guidebook to Tahiti or the South Pacific.

Rotui & Mouaputa, Moorea Island, French Polynesia

This map shows the entire island of Moorea, which is about 21 kms due west of Tahiti, both of which are in French Polynesia. Moorea has a number of needle-like peaks, some of which have yet to be climbed. The highest is Tohiea at 1207 meters, but it's not discussed here because it's extremely difficult to climb. Two of the peaks routinely climbed are Rotui, 899 meters, and Mouaputa at 830.

To reach **Moorea**, you'll first fly to the big island of Tahiti, then take a bus from the airport east into the center of Papeete. There you'll find the Tourist Information office, and about 300 meters north, the docks where the ferry boats depart for Vaiare on Moorea. There are 6 or 7 departures daily going each way. In 1997, the cost was US$7 per/trip which took 30 minutes. Many Mooreans commute daily to Tahiti for work. At the ferry terminal in Vaiare, are buses going around the island in each direction. Bus schedules are timed to the arrivals & departures of ferry boats.

To climb **Mouaputa**, take a bus, taxi, or walk about 5 kms south to Afareaitu. Get off the bus near a hospital and on the road to Atiraa Cascade (Waterfall). This should be near Km 9. Walk northwest up a dirt road half a km, pay the entrance fee of about US$2, then continue another 10 minutes to the end of the road. From there, a trail runs 400 meters to the 100-meter-high waterfall or cascade. About 200 meters below the waterfall, cross the creek and look for the steep trail skirting the falls on the southwest side. Higher up, you'll walk right along the creek above the falls. Still higher, the trail veers left, then back to the right or north, and ascends a ridge. From there it's straight up a steep slope to the summit. There are 7 roped sections, which makes this a fun, but sometimes slippery, climb. Mouaputa is identified by a hole or arch right through the middle of the summit. Where you pay the entrance fee, ask about the possibility of camping below the waterfall--if you're traveling cheap. The author climbed this one in 2 1/3 hours round-trip from the end of the road on the afternoon of 7/21/1997; then camped below the cascade.

To climb **Rotui**, take a bus toward the Moorea Lagoon Hotel. Ask someone there where the trail begins; on 7/22/1997, there were some new buildings going up right at the trailhead. The trail runs south right along a knife-edge ridge. It's hot & dry at the bottom; wet & humid at the summit. It's a good trail, but a little brushy in places. The author climbed Rotui in 3 2/3 hours, round-trip from the highway below.

Here are 2 more interesting hikes. From the ferry terminal, walk 300-400 meters west & south, and turn west. Soon the side-road ends, but you can continue west over a low divide. Part of this trail is an old road. You can walk all the way to Paopao.

From Paopao, walk or hitch hike southwest along a paved road in the direction of Opunohu

This is a postcard picture (Teva Sylvain foto) looking south from above Cook Bay. Mouaputa is on the left, Tohiea in the center.

Map 331-1, Rotui & Mouaputa, Moorea, French Polynesia

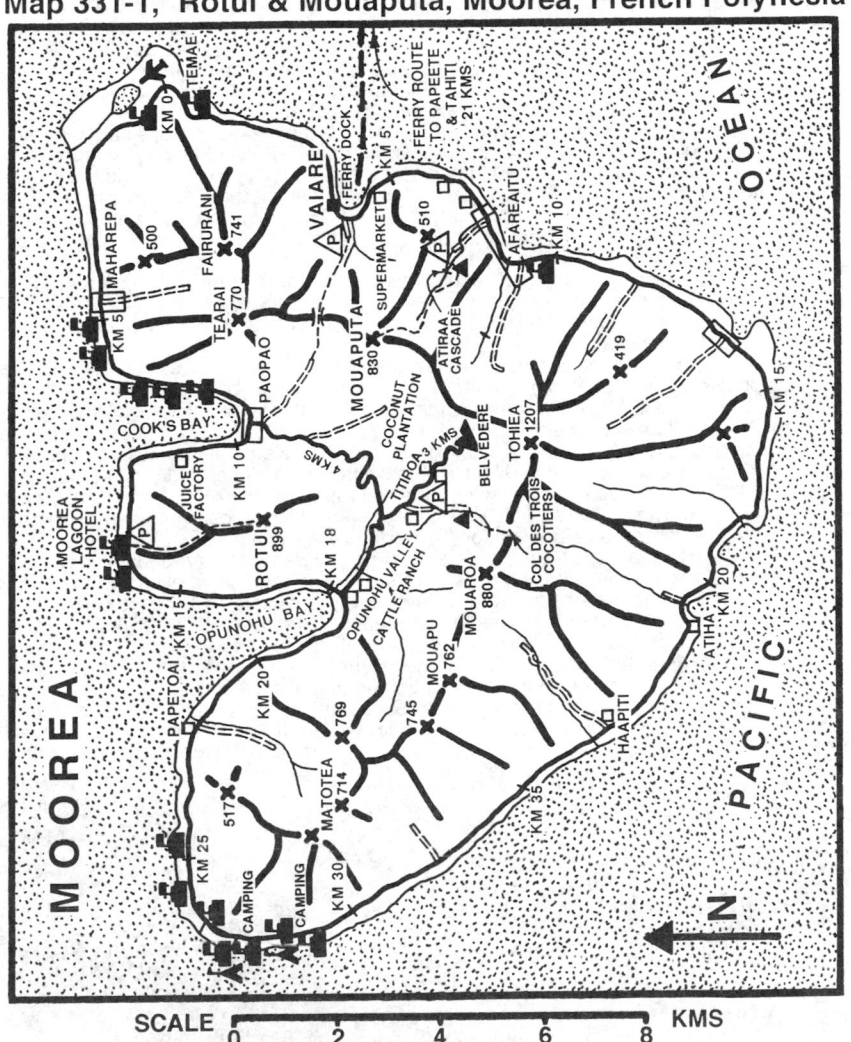

Valley and the viewpoint called Belvedere. It's 4 kms to a road junction, then 3 more to Belvedere. About one km south of the road junction, look for the sign on the right pointing out the way to **Col des Trois Cocotiers**. Walk south along a dirt road past some pig barns. Eventually the road turns into a trail, then goes down to a stream crossing where you could camp, then zig zags up to the col. This is a good rainforest hike.

There are 2 beach campgrounds and several small stores on the northwest corner of Moorea near Km 27 & 28. One km south of the ferry docks is a large supermarket; plus several other stores and people selling fruit near the ferry.

For more hikes on other French Polynesian islands, buy an airline pass which begins in Papeete and island-hop to Moorea, Huahine, Tahaa, Bora Bora and Raiatea, then back to Tahiti. Dry season is June through October.

Maps *Tahiti, Archipel de La Société, 3615,* 1:100,000, Institut Geographique National (IGN website www.ign.fr), buy in Papeete; and the latest travel guidebook to Tahiti or the South Pacific.

Rano Aroi & Rano Raraku, Rapa Nui (Easter Island), Chile

Rapa Nui, Easter Island or Isla de Pascua all refer to the same island located about 3500 kms due west of central Chile. The people here are Polynesian; therefore the name Rapa Nui. This subtropical island belonging to Chile, is built up entirely of volcanic lavas, and has at least 14 volcanic cones. None are very high, the highest being Rano Aroi at 506 meters. The last eruption on the island was sometime during the early Holocene.

There's no running water on Rapa Nui and no native trees (except small scrubby specimens inside the crater of Rano Kau). The island measures about 12 by 22 kms. It's simply a dot in the Pacific, but its archeological ruins are among the most-fascinating in the world. This island is literally an outdoor museum. The story of the people who carved the statues, or *moai*, is one of the great mysteries of our time. Readers should consult Thor Heyerdahl's books **Aku Aku** and **Kon Tiki**, and Peggy Mann's, **Easter Island, Land of Mysteries**. And there might be more book about the island when you arrive.

In 1997, there were 2 weekly flights low season; 4 flights weekly in high season, from Santiago to Rapa Nui by Lan-Chile. Most of these flights run between Santiago and Tahiti. Cost is about $US900 for the round-trip ticket from Santiago. Most food is brought in on supply ships 3 times a year, but some is airlifted.

There are some expensive tourist hotels, plus many family run hotels or residencias, all at Hanga Roa. Cheapest, may be US$10 (?), but there are many at about US$20, and up. You can cut expenses by bringing food for the trip from Santiago, and by camping and walking everywhere. You can also rent cars, 4WD's, motorbikes, or bicycles.

The important archeological sites are as follows: the main statue quarry at *Rano Raraku*; the most interesting place on the island. Next is *Ana Kena* where Heyerdahl erected some of the fallen statues. *Puna Pau* is the quarry where the red top knots were cut. And *Orongo*, where the birdman cult left some ruins. This one is near Hanga Roa, the only town on the island. Many fallen statues and *ahus* (statue platforms) lie along the south coast.

There is a definite scarcity of water here and you must plan a trek around this need. There are lakes inside **Rano Raraku** and **Rano Kau** craters, and a small pond on **Rano Aroi**, but this water must be treated before using as there were horses roaming everywhere on the author's visit between 3/21 to 3/28/1982. Besides at Hanga Roa, there is drinking water only at Rano Raraku from a tank at the ranger's residence. Camp there, and at Ana Kena, but there's probably no water available there. The author remembers water at the estancia (ranch) headquarters at Vai Tea, and at in a livestock trough northeast of Rano Raraku.

Scattered about the island are a number of eucalyptus groves which make fine campsites, but you will need to carry water to camp in these places. If there are lots of camping regulations, drop a tent after sunset, then take it down quickly in the morning and hide it. You'll also find lots

These are some of the carved statues just below the quarry on Rano Raraku.

Map 332-1, Rano Aroi & Rano Raraku, Rapa Nui(Easter Island), Chile

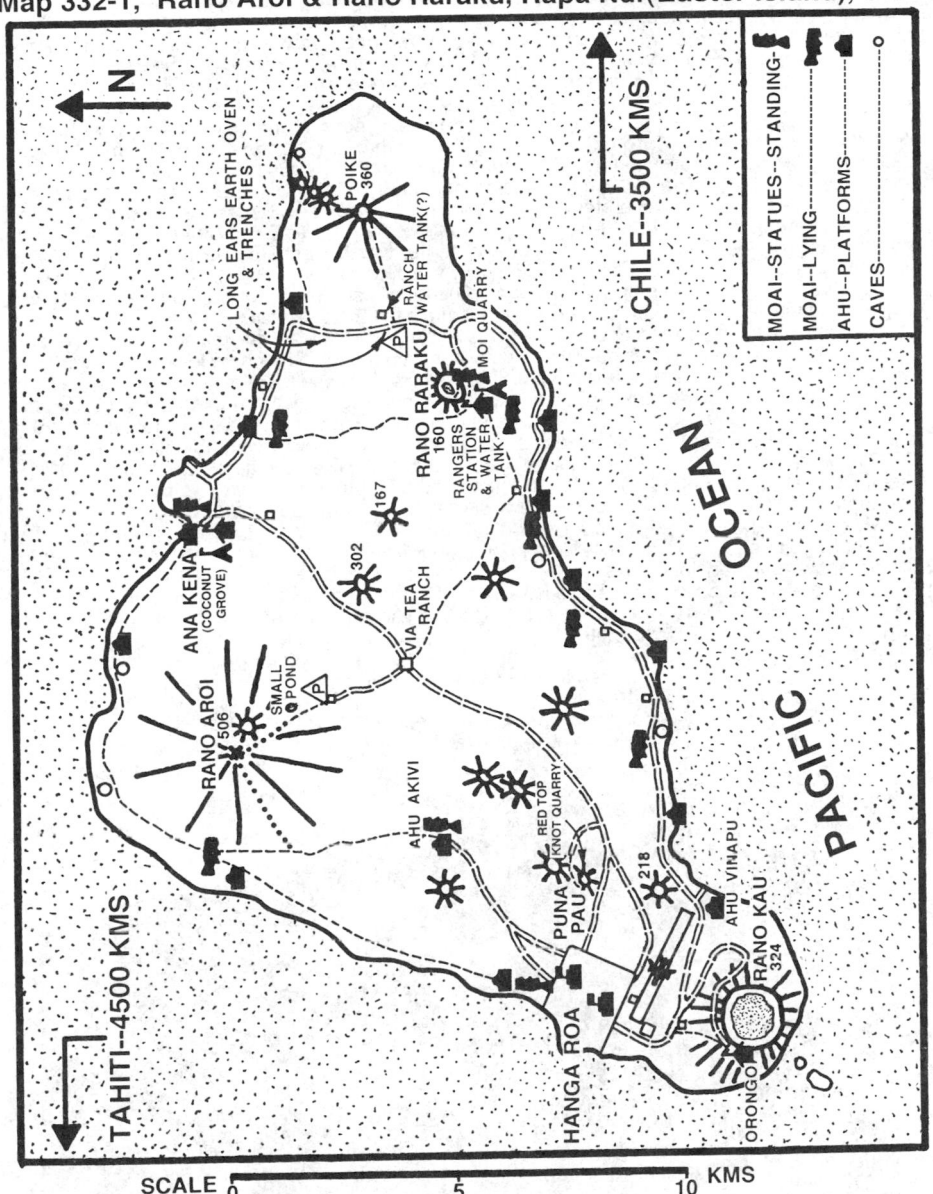

of wild guava bushes in many locations and the fruit is free. The author was there one week and walked around the entire island. Great Trip!

Maps Tourist maps from souvenir shops or office of Parque Nacional Rapa Nui, Hanga Roa; and the latest **South American Handbook**, Footprint Handbooks.

Mauna Loa, Island of Hawaii, Hawaiian Islands, USA

The second highest mountain on the big island of Hawaii is Mauna Loa at 4170 meters. This is a huge shield volcano, which differs from stratovolcanos, in that the lava is very fluid and creates a broad, gentle sloping mountain. These differ from stratovolcanos such as Fuji, Rainier, or Kilimanjaro, which are much steeper and conal shaped. The summit and eastern portions of the mountain are part of the Hawaii Volcanos National Park.

Mauna Loa is an active volcano, erupting every few years, sometimes issuing lava from or near the summit crater, or from the southwest or northeast rift zones. The summit crater is called the Mokuaweoweo Caldera. In recent years big lava flows have taken place in 1942, 1949, 1950 and 1975. The last eruption lasted from 3/25/1984 to 4/15/1984. These flows came from fissures near the summit crater & flowed southwest; also flows ran northeast from the North Pit area; some came from the Dewey Cone and flowed southeast; and other flows began just east of the Red Hill Cabin in an area known as the North East Rift Zone. For updates on volcanic activity in the area see the website (www.volcano.si.edu/gvp/).

There are 2 main routes up **Mauna Loa**. The most-used route for backpackers is the trail beginning at the end of the Mauna Loa Road not far from the Kilauea Crater. However, your first stop should be the national park visitor center just northeast of the Kilauea Crater. There you can get the latest information regarding free permits for huts, camping (no fixed numbers for tent campers), the water situation, fees, etc. Tele. 808-985-6000. They will also have the latest maps and guidebooks.

From the visitor center, drive or hitch hike west along Highway 11 running toward Kona, but turn northwest onto the Mauna Loa Road and drive 21.7 kms to the trailhead lookout at 2031 meters. From there, a good trail winds its way northwest over old lava to the Red Hill Cabin at 3039 meters. This is 12.1 kms and takes about half a day. The next section is from Red Hill to the summit, a distance of 19.5 kms; or 18.7 kms to the Mauna Loa Cabin. Some people stay in the summit cabin overnight which makes the journey longer, but usually more enjoyable.

Most people take 3 or 4 days for this climb from Kilauea. With an early morning start, a strong hiker can get to the summit cabin in one long day--30.8 kms, stay one night, then return the next day. Two very long days!

If you take the Red Hill route, there is rainwater from the roofs of both cabins stored in tanks. It's recommended this water be boiled, or purified. There are no springs on the mountain, so begin your hike with a full water bottle.

A **second route** is for *day-hikers* with their own cars. This route begins at the Saddle Road, or Highway 200, which connects Hilo and Waimea, then it's about 27.5 kms up to the US Weather Observatory where the trail begins. From there to the summit is only about 10.3 kms, or about 2-3 hours hiking. That part of the map is not drawn to scale.

There may or may not be public transportation on Highway 11 that passes the Kilauea

This is the Red Knob Hut located on the northeast slopes of Mauna Loa.

Map 333-1, Mauna Loa, Island of Hawaii, Hawaiian Islands, USA

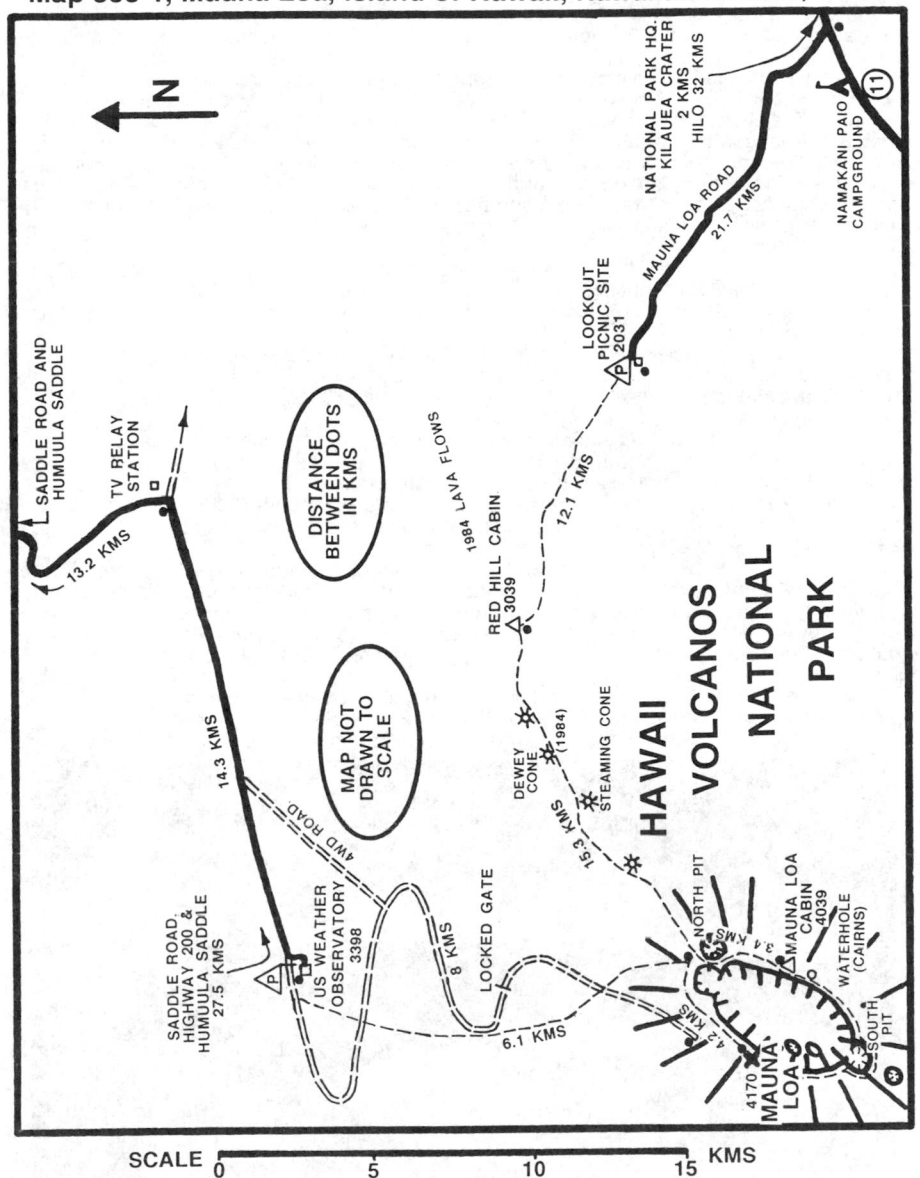

SCALE 0   5   10   15 KMS

Crater; or on the Saddle Road, Highway 200. If you don't have a car, then hitch hiking might be your best bet. Hitching was easy in Hawaii when the author was there during the 2nd half of 11/1976. Buy your food in Hilo or Kilauea. See the park's website (www.nps.gov/havo) for updated informaion on huts, camping, etc.

Maps *Hawaii, 2 & 3,* 1:100,000, from the USGS; any Hawaii state highway map; free park handout maps from visitor center; and the books, **Hawaiian Hiking Trails**, Touchstone Press; **The Backpacker's Guide to Hawaii**, University of Hawaii Press; or travel guidebook, **Hawaii**, Lonely Planet.

Mauna Kea, Island of Hawaii, Hawaiian Islands, USA

The highest mountain in the Pacific Basin, with the exception of peaks on the island of New Guinea, is Mauna Kea at 4206 meters. This is a shield volcano located on the big island of Hawaii.

The entire Hawaiian Island group is made up of volcanic outpourings laid down over the past few million years. The oldest rocks are found in the islands to the northwest; the youngest to the southeast. The newest or youngest island is Hawaii, sometimes known as The Big Island.

Mauna Kea is a huge mountain mass with a number of cinder cones scattered about its summit. At this time the mountain is considered dormant and all the activity has shifted south to its sister shield volcano, Mauna Loa, and to the very active & lively volcano called Kilauea. Mauna Kea's last eruption was from a southside radial fissure at about 3500 meters. That explosive eruption was in about 1650 BC. It's last lava flow was in about 3400 BC, also from a south flank fissure.

This area can be reached from either Hilo on the east coast, or Kona and other towns to the west, via the Saddle Road running between Mauna Kea and Mauna Loa. There is limited bus service on the Saddle Road, so most visitors rent cars. Or try hitch hiking which is generally good all over Hawaii.

Most will be disappointed to find there's a road to the summit of **Mauna Kea** which ends at a world famous astronomical observatory. But, there's also a trail which begins at the picnic site near *Halepohaku Visitor Center*. For more information call 808-961-2180, or see their website (www.ifa.edu/info/vis).

Please sign in at the visitor center so they know who is on the mountain. The trail to the top is good and well-used. At about 3500 meters, there's an old obsidian quarry named Keanskakoi, where native Hawaiians used to mine their ax heads.

The trail ends at a road near the summit. From there, you must walk the last 2 kms on another road leading to the observatory. There are several telescopes at this University of Hawaii facility. The highest point is near the telescopes.

Beginning 11/23/1976, the author walked from the trailhead marked 2031 meters on the south side of Mauna Loa (see previous map), to that summit, then down to the weather observatory. From there he road-walked down to The Saddle, and the next day climbed Mauna Kea. He got a lift back down to the picnic trailhead where he spent his last night on the mountain. The hiking part took 4 full days. On the morning of Day 5, he hitched a ride back to Hilo.

Water can be found at the visitor center at Halepohaku. Stock up there for your hike, there's none along the way or at the top. If you're driving, carry lots of water in your car.

These islands are within the tropics, so any month is a good time to climb; however, from

From the snowy summit of Mauna Kea looking southwest at Mauna Loa. Notice the newer or more recent crater to the right not far away (Richard White foto).

Map 334-1, Mauna Kea, Island of Hawaii, Hawaiian Islands, USA

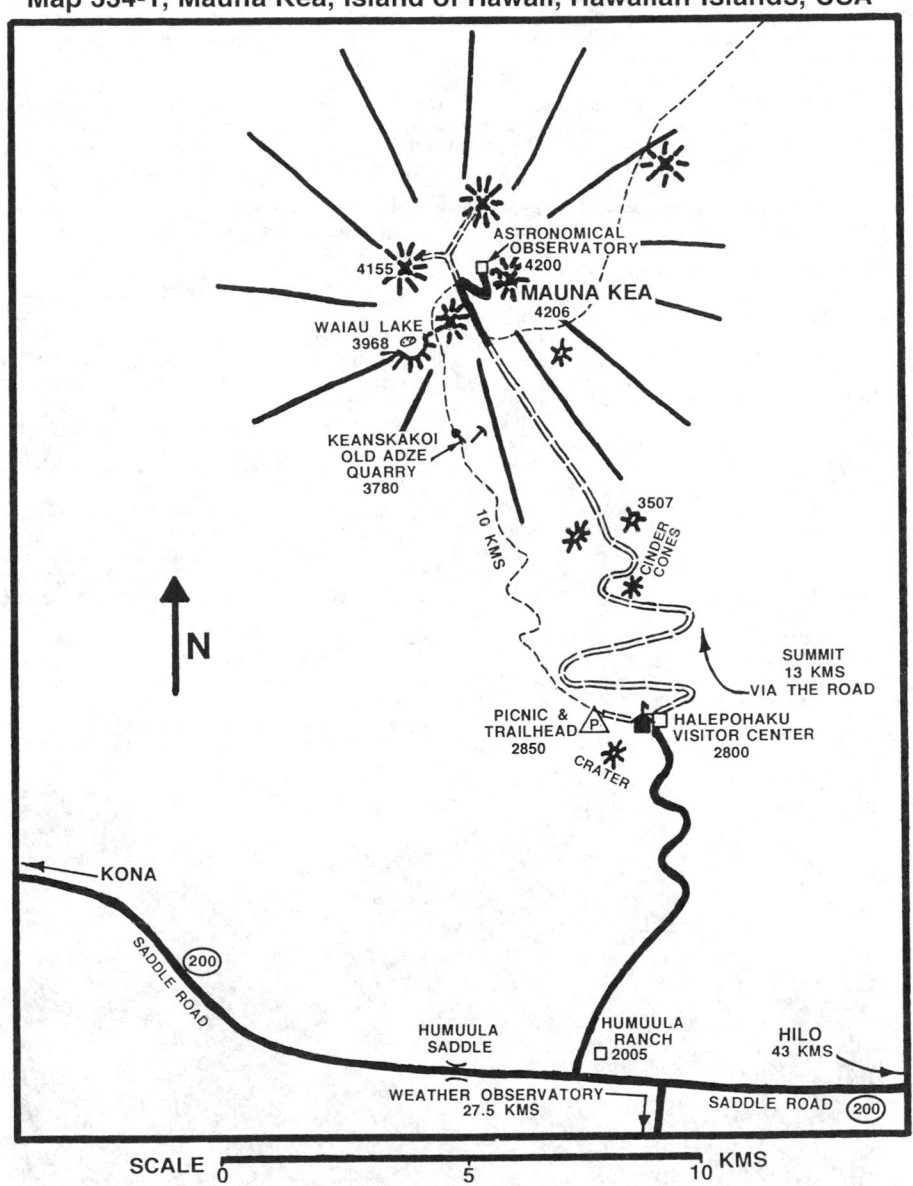

SCALE 0   5   10 KMS

December to February snow may fall at the higher elevations. If you look closely in the summit area, you can see evidence of past glaciation. Also, there is still some permafrost under the surface near the observatory. The best places to buy food for this hike is at Kona or other towns to the west, or Hilo, which is the largest town on the Big Island.

Maps *Hawaii, 2,* 1:100,000, from the USGS; any Hawaii state highway map; and the books, **Hawaiian Hiking Trails,** Touchstone Press; or **The Backpackers Guide to Hawaii,** University of Hawaii Press.

Haleakala Crater, Maui Island, Hawaiian Islands, USA

Featured on this map is the Haleakala Crater located on the Hawaiian island of Maui. This is an old and eroded volcanic caldera. Inside are multicolored cinder cones which form a desolate-looking landscape. The highest point on the rim is the Puu Ulaula Overlook, located on Red Hill, at 3055 meters. Unfortunately, there's a good road to the top.

The entire chain of Hawaiian Islands is made up of volcanic rock of one age or another. The oldest and most eroded islands are in the northwest; with the younger or newer islands in the southeast. The youngest island, and the one with the most recent volcanic activity, is the big island of Hawaii. It's the last island in the chain. The next to the last island, and the next to the youngest, is Maui.

No one has determined when Haleakala blew up, but there are many younger cinder cones inside. These probably date from the Holocene, or within the last 10,000 years. However, the last volcanic activity on this shield volcano was not inside the crater, but along a southwest rift zone at 180 to 360 meters altitude. That was in about 1790 AD. Somewhere just east of this map, there were other lava flows in about 1460 AD. For updates on volcanic activity in the area see the website (www.volcano.si.edu/gvp/).

This entire crater is within the Haleakala National Park, and very much regulated. To get there, drive south from the city of Kahului, and/or the nearby airport, toward Pukaiani. Watch for signs pointing the way up to the Haleakala National Park. There's a good paved road winding up the northwest side of the mountain to the crater rim, which brings thousands of people to the area. At the park HQ. and the rim, are 2 visitor centers where you can get all the information needed for a day-hike or an overnight stay in the crater. Inquire about the use of cabins, camping regulations, availability of water, etc., inside the crater. For the latest information about hiking, cabins, camping, etc, see their website (www.nps.gov/hale) or call 808-572-4400.

Within the crater are some well-used trails and 3 cabins and 2 campsites. To use these cabins, you must call or write to the national park and make reservations well in advance. These are a little expensive. Or pick up a free camping permit (25 people at each site/day) on the day of your hike. Because this is such a popular place, it's recommended you day-hike only down from one of 2 places on the rim, perhaps making a loop-hike. No reservations or permits are need for day-hiking.

If you do get permission to camp or use the cabins, rainwater from the roofs of each cabin is stored in tanks. Boil or purify this water first, and *please conserve*. If you're on foot and don't have to return to the crater rim, you could hike south from the crater down to Kaupo. This can be done in one day from the Paliku Cabin.

Shop in Kahului supermarkets. Be prepared for possible cold and wet weather, and carry a full bottle of water at all times. There's no public transport to the rim, so you'll have to drive your

Inside the desert-like Haleakala Caldera with lots of young craters and weird plants.

Map 335-1, Haleakala Crater, Maui Island, Hawaiian Islands, USA

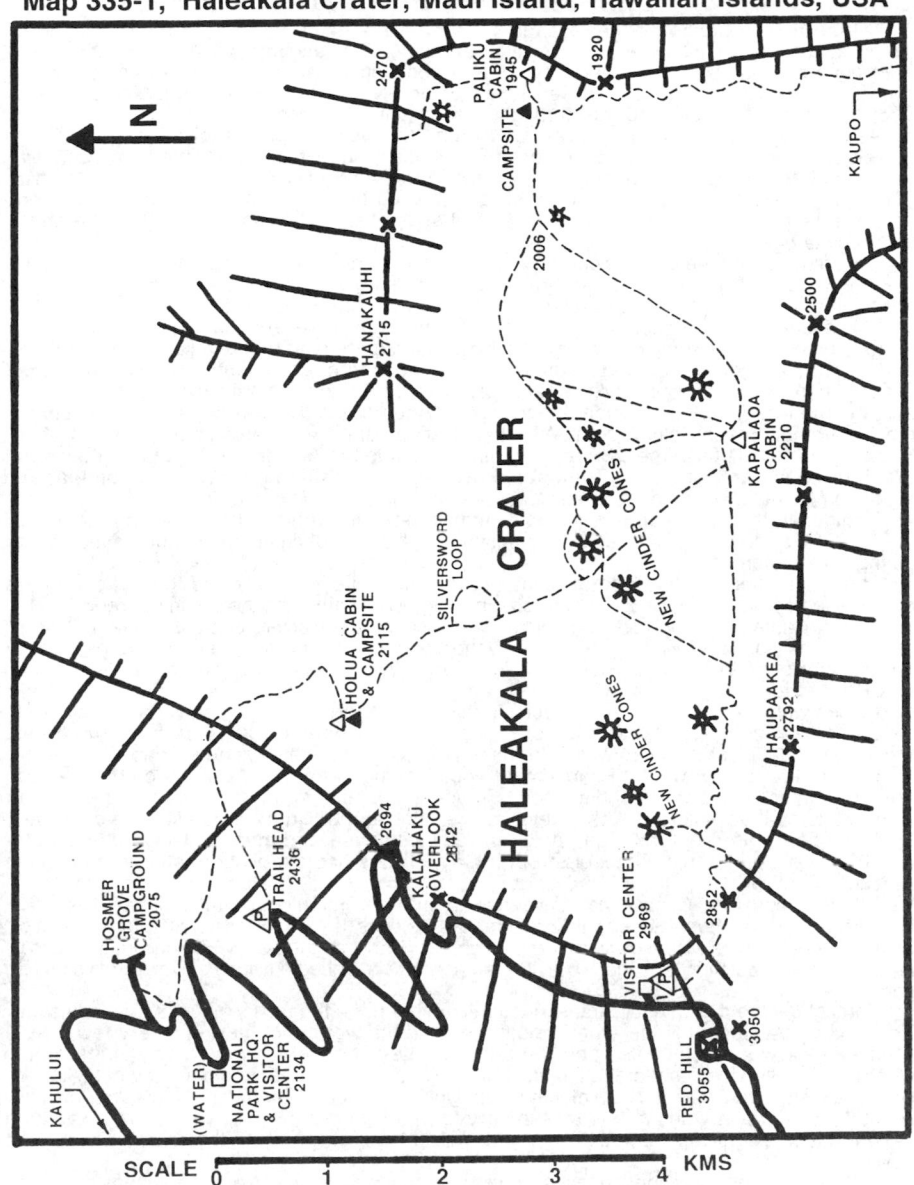

SCALE 0   1   2   3   4   KMS

own car, or hitch hike, which is generally good all over Hawaii.

Maps Maps of *Haleakala National Park* come from Trails Illustrated,1:25,000, and Earthwalk Press, 1:24,000; any *Hawaii state highway map*; and the books, **Hawaiian Hiking Trails**, Touchstone Press; or **The Backpackers Guide to Hawaii**, University of Hawaii Press.

Chapter 7--North America

This section on North America; Canada and the United States, has 126 maps. In this part of the world, the mountain type which dominates are the uplifted and folded variety, caused by the wrinkling of the earth's crust and the movement of continents. There are some volcanic regions, concentrated mostly along the Northwest Coast of the USA, and in south central Alaska, west of Cook Inlet and Anchorage, and west throughout the Aleutian Islands.

As with most folded mountain ranges around the world, many in this region consist of granitic-type rocks at their core. Some of these ranges include the Sierra Nevada of California, Tetons and Wind Rivers of Wyoming, parts of the Purcells of British Columbia, and Mt. McKinley in the Alaska Range. Great limestone ranges include the Canadian Rockies which extend southward into Montana. Ranges composed of quartzite are the Rockies in Colorado and in Utah's Uinta Mountains.

In North America there is basically one language throughout and that's English. In Canada, the province of Quebec is officially French speaking, but most Canadian government documents, with maps as a good example, are in both English and French.

This entire region is under the influence of the middle latitude jet stream and cyclonic storm system, much the same as in Europe. In winter, the storms tend to move south, and at times move from the Pacific onshore to California, then east across the southern USA. A second winter pattern shows storms moving from the Gulf of Alaska, to the Northwest Coast of the USA and into the Intermountain Region, thence east. Another familiar winter pattern sees storms moving through British Columbia and Alberta in Canada, then south along the east slope of the Rockies into the plains of the USA and eventually east to the Atlantic. This pattern leaves the Western USA warm and dry. The coasts of Oregon, Washington, British Columbia, and southern Alaska, are termed the *West Coast Marine Climates*, and are very wet.

In summer, the rainfall pattern is mostly monsoonal, with warm moist air moving north from the Gulf of Mexico ahead of weak frontal passages. Beware of lightning on mountain summits during thunderstorms.

The mountains with the greatest climbing difficulties lie in Alaska and the Yukon. Great names such as McKinley, St. Elias, and Logan dominate all other mountains in the region. This is an area of little population and long distances. The largest glaciers on the continent lie here, making it necessary to use small aircraft to either land on glaciers with men and supplies; or to air drop supplies to climbers waiting on glaciers. Practically every mountain requires an expedition to reach the summit.

Places which stand out as great rock climbing areas, are the Sierra Nevada of California, Tetons of Wyoming, the Sawtooths of Idaho, the Bugaboos of BC, and the Cumberland Peninsula of Baffin Island, Northwest Territories. These are the better known areas.

If you prefer cooler weather and snow & ice climbing, then areas along the USA-Canada border and northward are the best places. If you enjoy hiking on trails and for the most part warm weather, then Colorado, Utah, Nevada, Wyoming and California are best. The southwest USA is a dry region, but the high peaks are always alpine and there's always some water nearby. The months from October through May, always bring snow to the mountains in the American Southwest.

Generally speaking, climbers can leave their camps in the morning and return in the evening to find everything safe. But as the population increases, so does theft. In places like California, be a bit more cautious about leaving a camp all day unattended. However, theft is still very uncommon, and in areas of small population it's unheard of. The author has never had anything stolen from his tent or car.

Throughout the region public transportation is rather poor; the reason is, everyone has a car. The highway system in North America is the best in the world, but there are very few buses. There are railways in the USA and Canada, but they service very few areas of interest to climbers. Bus service is better than trains, but still it doesn't compare to other parts of the world. Simply stated, if you want to climb mountains in North America, you'll have to have your own car or hitch hike--which won't get you there very fast! Foreign travelers who plan to stay long periods of time sometimes buy used cars, which are very cheap, and sell them later. Others rent new cars.

Regarding sleeping accommodations in the mountains, almost all North Americans carry and use a tent while backpacking. There are very few places in the USA where you'll find a refuge or hut to sleep in such as you find in Europe. The same system exists in Canada, but there are a few huts available in the more popular parts of the Canadian Rockies.

Here's a new bureaucratic nightmare to think about if hiking or climbing in the states of Oregon and Washington. As of 2000, you will need a **Northwest Parking Pass** when you park at any Forest Service trailhead in those states. The year pass costs US$30, or it's US$5 a day. Stop at or call any local ranger station for updated information because this policy seems to be spreading to other states and other national forests.

The northern slopes and big cirque basin of Wheeler Peak, which is now a part of the Great Basin National Park (Map 407, page 873).

The north face of Mt Temple as seen from near Lake Louise (Map 369, page 795).

Atigun Pass Region, Endicott Mountains, Brooks Range, Alaska, USA

Shown on this map is a small portion of the Brooks Range of northern Alaska. More specifically, it's the Endicott Mountains, which are right in the middle of this huge range. Also shown is part of the Alaska Pipeline and the nearby Dalton Highway or Haul Road. This highway runs from just north of Fairbanks to the company town of Deadhorse, which is often referred to as Prudhoe Bay. The place where the highway and pipeline cross the mountains is called *Atigun Pass* at 1494 meters. Much of the land west of the highway is part of the *Gates of the Arctic National Park*. There are no big name peaks in this region, but the highest summits are around 2300 meters. These mountains are made mostly of metamorphic-type rocks such as quartzite.

Access to this immediate area is very easy along the Dalton Highway. Tourist agencies may tell you it's possible to drive only to Coldfoot, or Wiseman or Dietrich Camps, but in reality, there are no guards at those places, so those brave enough to drive the 800+ kms of gravel road can indeed go all the way to the Arctic Ocean. The reason it's not closed as some would like, is that public money is spent maintaining the highway and they can't close it completely. However, tourist-type facilities are few and far between, so they try to discourage people from going that way. There are fuel stops and restaurants at the Yukon River Crossing, Coldfoot, and at Deadhorse only. There are no campgrounds except at Coldfoot. At Deadhorse you can buy gas or Diesel, some snack-type food (no milk or bread!), very expensive hotel rooms & meals, and that's about it. A few tourists fly in and are bused around, but there's nothing to see at Deadhorse except caribou on the airport runway. There are very few tourist facilities at Deadhorse.

Buy all your supplies at Fairbanks and have good tires on your car! Once on the graveled part of the road, lower tire pressure about 25%, to prevent puncturing or bruising from sharp stones. Have plenty of mosquito repellent, which you'll need up to where the tundra gives way to all-rocky slopes. Take binoculars to view wildlife, and a bell on your pack (or make noise) to let grizzly bears know you're coming.

The last tree along the road is just south of Chandalar Camp. Above that, and on all the North Slope, there are no trees and just a few small dwarf willows. Walking is usually easy and fast. There are no trails in this country, except for those made by caribou, moose, grizzly bear and Doll sheep. Weather conditions in summer, along with vegetation, make climbing here similar to what you find in the Colorado Rockies above timberline. One difference is the numerous small, north facing cirque glaciers. However, these are small and harmless and you can get by without ice ax & crampons in summer. Just park anywhere along the road and start hiking. Most streams near the pass are small and easy to cross.

On 7/23/1992, the author stopped at the sharp curve just southwest of Atigun Pass and walked due west to the peak and glacier shown with the route symbols. On his return to the car, he hauled several heavy caribou antlers back. That trip took 91/4 hours. The next day he climbed James Dalton Mtn.

A pleasant July day in the mountains just west of Atigun Pass. Keep moving to avoid mosquitos! Also, lots of caribou antlers to gather.

Map 336-1, Atigun Pass Region, Brooks R., Alaska, USA

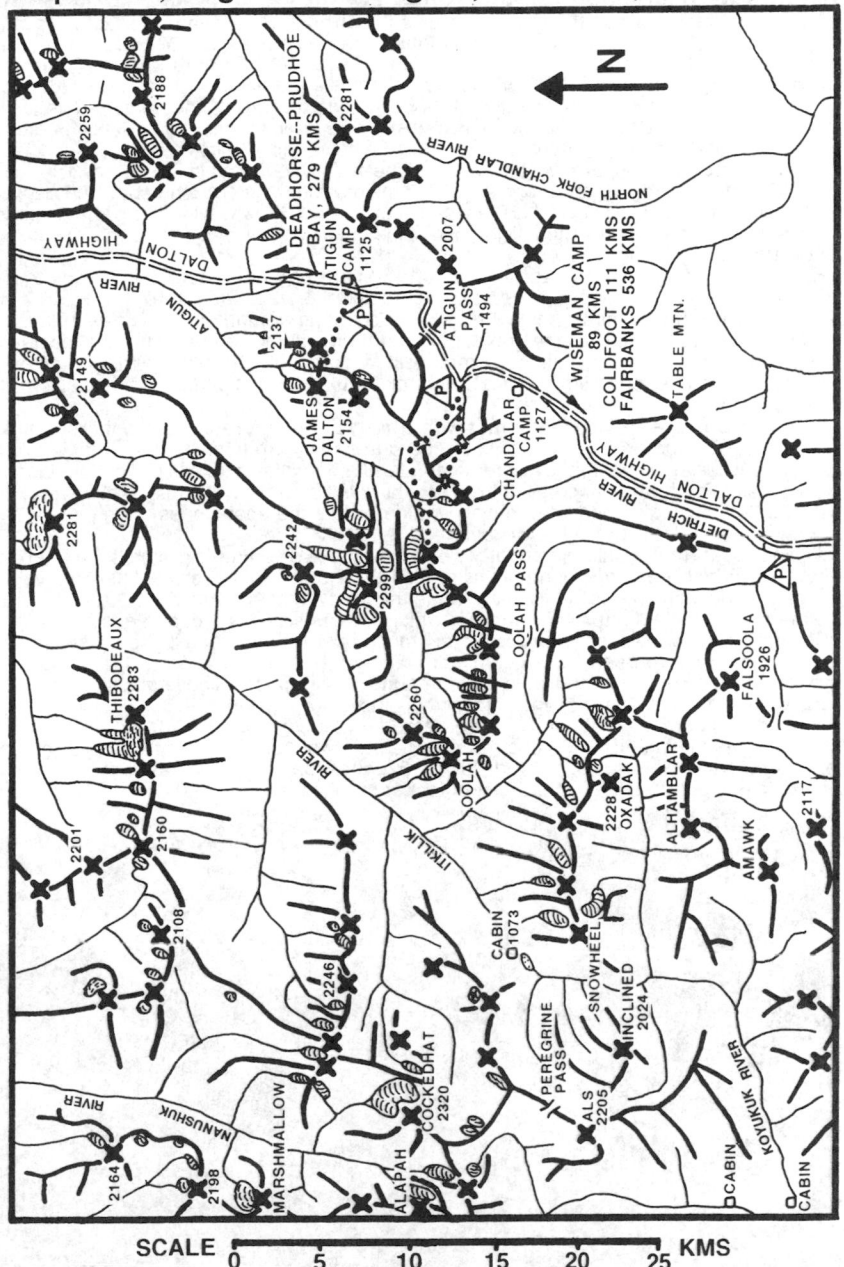

SCALE 0   5   10   15   20   25 **KMS**

from the site of the old Atigun Camp in just over 4 hours, round-trip.
Maps USGS maps *Chandler Lake* & *Philip Smith Mtns,* and perhaps *Chandalar & Wiseman,* all 1:250,000. There are 1:63,360 scale maps available for the serious climber, but the author got by with the first 2 mentioned. Buy at the USGS, 4230 University Drive, Fairbanks, Alaska, 99508-4664, Tele. 907-786-7011; or buy at the national sales office in Denver, Colorado, USA.

Chamberlin, Michelson & Isto, Romanzof Mtns., Brooks R., Alaska, USA

These mountains are in the eastern end of the Brooks Range in northeast Alaska. This group, the Romanzof Mountains, are the highest peaks in the Greater Brooks Range. The highest summit here is Mt. Isto at 2762 meters, while Mt. Chamberlin is 2749, and Mt. Michelson, 2699 meters. Most rocks in these mountains are granite.

The only way into this region is to fly with a bush pilot. In 7/1992, the author drove along the pipeline or Dalton Highway (or Haul Road as it's usually referred to), in his VW Rabbit Diesel to the company town of Deadhorse at Prudhoe Bay. There he contacted *Alaska Flyers* at the airport. They were flying rafters and supplies to various places in the region, so being alone with a flexible schedule on 7/24/1992 he flew into the gravel bar marked 457 meters northwest of **Michelson**. The plane would have been empty, so the author got this flight for half price--or so he was told. The pilot then picked up other people in the area for his return flight. Since the others had reserved the plane, they of course paid full fare of about $330 per/hour of flying time.

From the landing spot, the author walked a leisurely 4 hours with large pack to a pass marked 762 meters and camped. The next day he spent 6 1/2 hours climbing Michelson via the Esetuk Glacier & the southeast summit ridge, and scouting around on **Mt. Tugak**. On Day 3, it took about 3 hours to return to the gravel bar where he was picked up. The total cost for both flights was US$550 (less than half the normal cost, according to the pilot). Strong climbers, with good snow & weather conditions and a day pack, could climb Michelson in perhaps 12 hours from the landing site.

To climb **Chamberlin**, make contact with a *float plane* operator in Deadhorse, and fly to Lake Peters. One possible route would be the one shown, up a west ridge or face. To climb **Isto**, take a *wheeled plane* from Deadhorse and land at the airstrip/gravel bar on the Jago River. Take a small raft or canoe to cross the river to the west side; or walk upstream several kms to locate a safe crossing. One possible way would be from the east slopes, then the south ridge (?). But the author isn't sure of the *route normal*.

Another possible way into this country would be to take a commercial flight from Fairbanks to Kaktovik on Barter Island due north of this region, then look for a bush pilot to shuttle you south from there. The author rates the Brooks Range the best place to climb in Alaska. This is mainly because there is little if any bushwhacking which means travel is fast and easy; lots of visible wildlife (including grizzlies, so take a bell!); and much drier weather than in the coastal regions.

Climbing might be best in August or early September, after the snow has melted. Take plenty of mosquito repellent and ice ax & crampons on all climbs. These glaciers aren't too big but there are some crevasses on the biggest icefields.

For further information about flights contact Alaska Flyers at 907-640-6324 in Kaktovik, or 907-659-2544 in Deadhorse (Prudhoe Bay), or email (waltaudi@aol.com). Some government agencies may say the road to the North Slope-Prudhoe Bay is closed past Coldfoot, but that's not true. The problem is the general lack of tourist facilities, and the 800 kms of gravel road, but

The author's camp at the pass marked 762 meters. Michelson is to the left
out of sight at the head of the Esetuk Glacier.

Map 337-1, Chamberlin, Michelson & Isto, Romanzof Mountains, Brooks Range, Alaska, USA

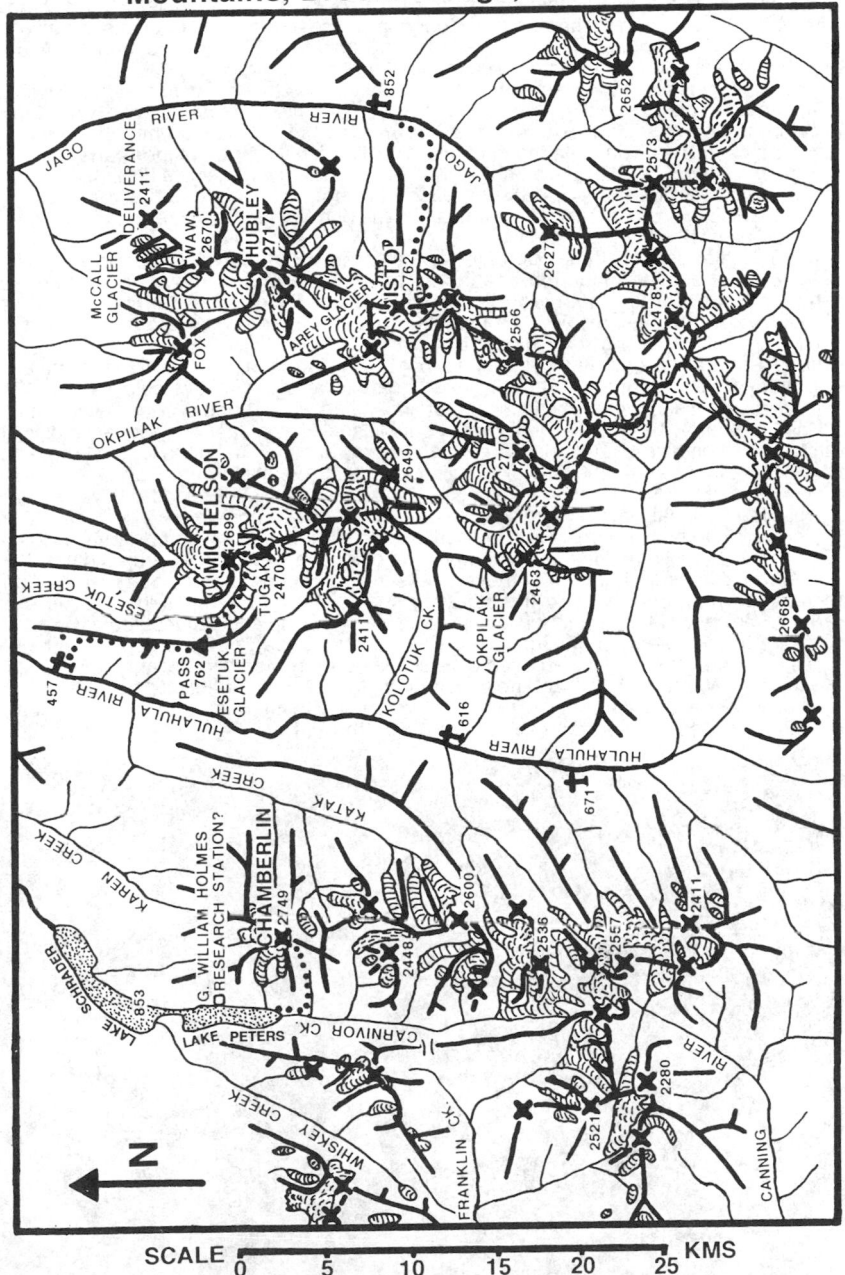

SCALE

0   5   10   15   20   25   KMS

you can drive from Fairbanks to Deadhorse. See previous map.
Maps USGS maps *Demarcation Point* & *Mt. Michelson*, 1:250,000; and *Mt. Michelson B-1 & B-2*, and *Demarcation Point A-5 & B-5*, 1:63,360. Buy at the USGS, 4230 University Drive, Fairbanks, Alaska, 99508-4664, Tele. 907-786-7011.

Igikpak & Arrigetch Peaks, Endicott Mtns., Brooks R., Alaska, USA

The peaks on this map are located toward the western end of the greater Brooks Range, as well as in the western part of the Endicott Mountains. These 2 groups of peaks are also in the Gates of the Arctic National Park. It's believed both **Igikpak** at 2612 meters, and the **Arrigetch Peaks**, the highest being 2192 meters, are made of granitic-type rocks.

Since this region is total wilderness, the only way there is to fly. To do that here's what you do. First head for the Fairbanks International Airport, but go to the east ramp opposite the main terminal on about 3800 University Avenue South. Once there, contact one of several small commuter-type airlines flying into the interior of Alaska. Most of their planes carry 8, 10, or 12 passengers. In 1992, Frontier (Tele. 907-474-0014), Larry's Flying Service (907-474-9169), and Wright's Flying Service (907-474-05020) each had regular flights to a place called Bettles, located about 125 kms southeast of these peaks. The only way to Bettles is to fly. The one-way flights cost about US$90.

Once in Bettles, contact Sourdough Air Service (Brooks Range Aviation) or Bettles Lodge Air Service to get a charter plane into the mountains. They should know the landing places, because there are others going into this region to fish, hike or on rafting trips. Contact Sourdough at Box 10, Bettles, 99726, or call 907-692-5252; or Bettles Lodge Air Service, Box 27, Bettles, or call 907-692-5111, for more information.

This is an area the author hasn't been to, but by looking at the 1:250,000 scale map of the area (Survey Pass), it appears there are trees in the lower river valleys below about 600-650 meters. This means some bushwhacking, but how much will depend on where you land. You could land on Walker Lake or Takahula Lake, but Michael Horan says the normal landing site is at Circle Lake then hike up Arrigetch Creek. Since this is a national park, contact the Gates of the Arctic National Park in the Doyon Building, 201, 1st Avenue, Fairbanks, or call 907-456-0281; or Gates of the Arctic National Park, P.O. Box 30, Bettles, 99707, or call 907-692-5494; or see or call the National Park Service, 2525 Gambell Street, Anchorage, 99503, or call 907-257-2687, for more information. Don't be surprised if some of these telefon numbers have changed.

Buy all your supplies in Fairbanks and plan on at least a week, or maybe 10 days, if you're serious about climbing. Pictures of these peaks indicate some real serious rock climbing on granite, so go prepared for rock, if that's your style. The north slopes involve snow or ice climbing. Employees at the Park Service can help plan your trip and suggest routes.

Be sure to take plenty of mosquito repellent and/or a head net and perhaps a bell to let grizzlies know you're coming. Because of possible bear problems, cook and store food away from your tent. March and April are the best months for skiing. Mid-June to early September is the best time for backpacking, hiking and climbing. August is the rainiest month of the year, and July is the warmest. July might be the best month overall. Early summer has the most

Aerial view of the northern slopes of the Arrigetch Peaks (Michael Horan foto).

Map 338-3, Igikpak & Arrigetch Peaks, Endicott Mountains, Brooks Range, Alaska, USA

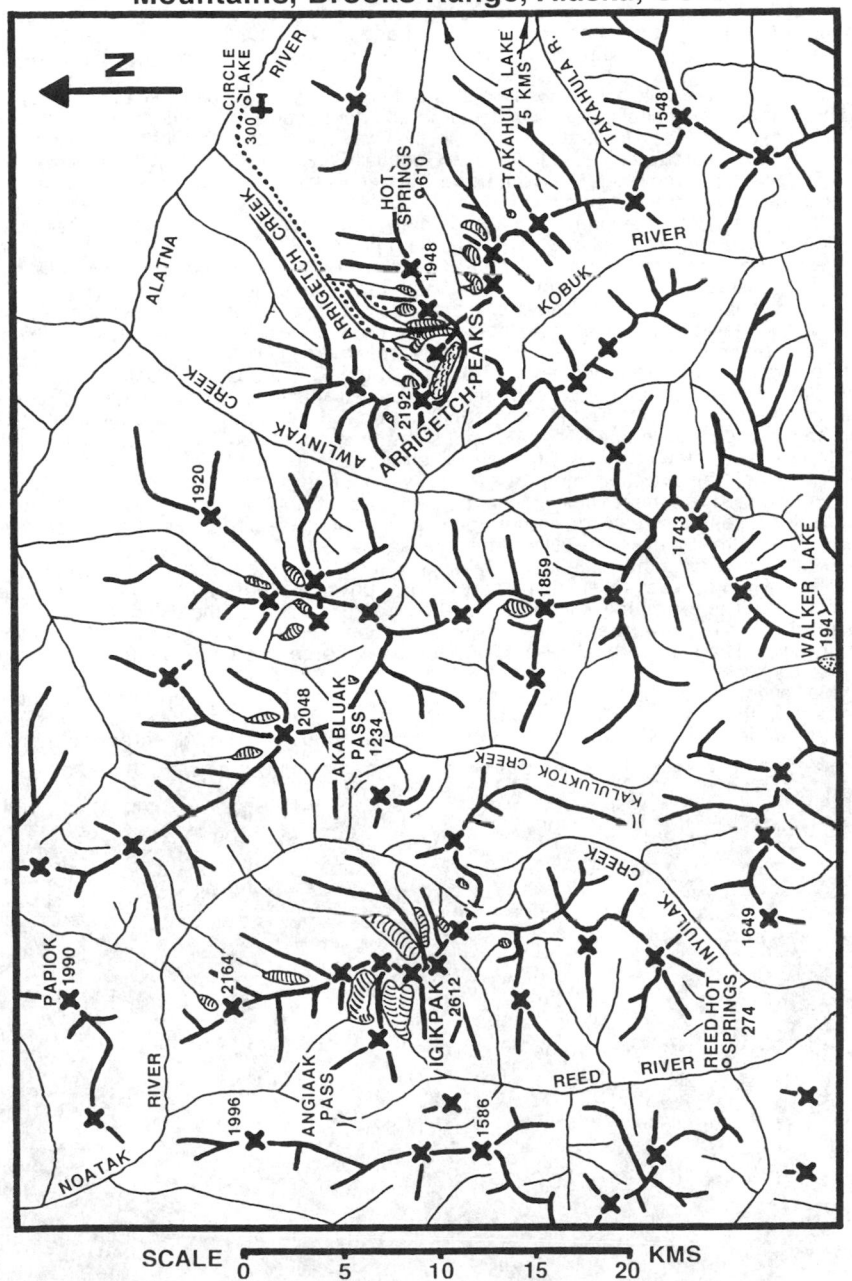

SCALE 0 5 10 15 20 KMS

mosquitos.
Maps USGS map *Survey Pass,* 1;250,000; or *Survey Pass B-3, B-4,* & *B-5,* 1:63,360. Buy at the USGS, 4230 University Drive, Fairbanks, Alaska, 99508-4664, Tele. 907-786-7011.

McKinley, Denali National Park, Alaska Range, Alaska, USA

Mt. McKinley's south peak at 6195 meters is the highest summit in North America. McKinley is part of the Alaska Range which dominates the interior of Alaska. In recent years, a move was underway to change the name of the mountain and the national park in which it lies. Those attempts were half successful. Today Mt. McKinley retains its old name, but is part of Denali National Park.

In the past there have been 2 normal routes up McKinley; one overland from the north; the other from the south using airplanes. If you do it from the north, you'll first have to drive (with special permission) or take the park bus to Wonder Lake, then walk due south across the hazardous & braided McKinley River, past Turtle Hill, then up to McGonagall Pass. From there up the Muldrow Glacier and finishing on Carpe Ridge, then the upper Karsten Ridge. This trip often takes 3 weeks and involves lots of energy and planning.

Starting 7/4/1971, the author and Steve Tyler, drove to Wonder Lake and started walking; made it to McGonagall Pass in 2 days with 38 kg packs. Then to Gunsight Pass, and up the Pioneer Ridge. Somewhere above the 3240 meter mark, Steve's sleeping bag rolled loose down the mountain, and that was the end of that! They returned to Wonder Lake on Day 8.

However, today almost all climbers use the southern approach and the West Buttress Route. This involves taking the train from Anchorage, or driving to the little town of Talkeetna southeast of the mountain. Talkeetna's livelihood is totally dependent on Mt. McKinley. From there you fly with one of 4 or 5 charter airlines to a tributary of the Kahiltna Glacier just outside the park boundary. When the weather is good, there are daily flights to the mountain beginning in April and ending in early July. The airline people set up a base camp at the landing site to help climbers in & out. Also, the NPS sets up a summer camp at about 4325 meters high on the south face just below the West Buttress. Their job is to assist climbers, especially those in trouble. They remove their camp by the first week of July because of bad weather, which corresponds to the summer monsoon in the Lower 48. At that time, the landing site becomes unusable too, and they can't go further up the glacier because park rules forbid landing inside the national park. So everyone pulls off the mountain.

Most people doing this route take 2-3 weeks of food, but if the weather remains good, it can be climbed in 5 or 6 days, depending on your own physical fitness and how long you need to acclimatize. The extra food is for sitting out bad weather, of which there is often plenty! Most people use skis or snowshoes, while carrying their supplies part way up on small plastic sleds or toboggans. The sleds are left at the NPS refuge or camp, then everything is carried up in normal backpacks.

May and June are the best weather months, and that's when most people climb. A good trail develops in the snow at that time. Today, there are also a number of professional guides who assist climbers. Individuals can sign up with one experienced guide, creating a group of

This foto was taken from the lower part of Pioneer Ridge with the North Peak above.

Map 339-1, McKinley, Denali NP, Alaska R., Alaska, USA

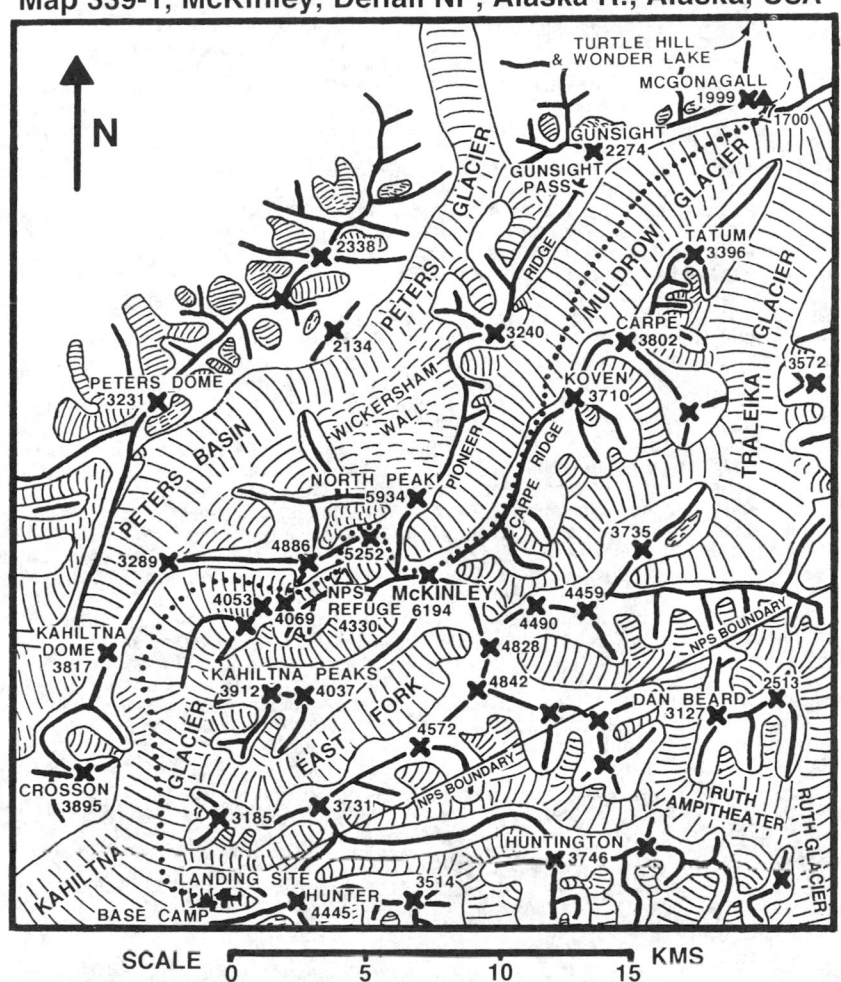

individuals. Most people now do it this way. Some solo climbers are harnessing themselves into an aluminum ladder so they won't fall into crevasses, but this is not a good mountain for solo climbing! The killers on McKinley have always been crevasses and bad weather.

For flights and other information, including transport from Anchorage, contact one of these outfitters: *Talkeetna Air Taxi,* Box 73, Talkeetna, Alaska, 99676, or Tele. 907-733-2218, or toll free from the USA, 800-533-2219; *K-2 Aviation,* Box 545-B, Talkeetna, Alaska, 99676, or Tele. 907-733-2291 (or toll-free in Alaska, 800-478-2291); *Doug Geeting Aviation,* Box 42, Talkeetna, Alaska, 99676, or Tele. 907-733-2366; *Hudson Air Service,* Box 648, Talkeetna, Alaska, 99676, or Tele. 907-733-2321 or 2679. In 2000, the round-trip airfare was about US$275. During the time when the mountain is occupied, there are many flights daily (in good weather), and climbers jump in any available plane. At the end of your climb, simply jump in the first available plane out as the flying outfits all cooperate.

Also, contact the National Park Service (NPS), Talkeetna Ranger Station, Box 588, Talkeetna, Alaska, 99676, Tele. 907-733-2231; or see their website (www.nps.gov/dena). This website will update all the author's information above.

Maps USGS map *Mount McKinley National Park,* 1:250,000; and *Mt. McKinley,* 1:50,000, published by the Museum of Science of Boston & Swiss Foundation for Alpine Research.

Gerdine, Torbert & Spur, Tordillo Mtns., Aleutian Range, Alaska, USA

These 3 moderately high summits are located about 150 kms almost due west of Anchorage in the northern-most part of the Aleutian Range. This entire mass of snow and ice is labeled the Tordrillo Mountains on USGS maps. The author believes all these peaks have volcanic origins. The last to erupt was Mt. Spurr's Crater Peak at 2309 meters. On 6/27/1992 it had a big a VEI-4 explosion. It last erupted on 9/17/1992, but a cloud or steam plume was observed on 3/26/1998. No seismic activity was observed at that time. For volcano updates see websites (www.avo.alaska.edu/) or (www.volcano.si.edu/gvp/).

This is a totally road-less region, so the only way to get there is to fly. Here's what the author did. After making inquires at the University of Alaska's Volcano Observatory, and talking to Tom Miller the head geologist there, he contacted Airlift Alaska, located at 2301 Merrill Field Drive, in Anchorage, 99501 (Tele. 907-276-3809). This is one of the flying services used by the USGS to fly men and equipment to outlying areas and in particular, to Mt. Spur, which had erupted 2 1/2 weeks before the author got there. Arrangements were made with them for a small C-172 to fly the author out early on the morning of 7/15/1992 to a small natural landing site just southeast of Crater Peak. At the time, the cost of that plane was US$125 per/hour.

After landing, the author bushwhacked north through alders for about 300 meters until he came to the lateral moraine of a glacier. Then it was up and down and over the rock & sand covered ice to the other side, where he set up a camp. That afternoon, he climbed straight up to the rim of the cloud-covered **Crater Peak**. The volcano was quiet at the time. The next morning he went up again, hoping to see something, but it was in the clouds again. Round-trip for each climb took about 3 hours. Late that afternoon he was picked up in a C-206 (at US$200 per/hour). The reason a larger plane was needed for the return trip was, the landing site is made of soft dirt requiring more power to get 2 people out. The entire cost of that 2 day trip was US$529. If you have a flexible schedule, you can sometimes cut costs by catching a ride in an empty plane that's going out to pickup someone else; or vice versa.

Climbing Crater Peak is safe to solo, but the main summit of **Spur** at 3374 meters, seems to be *heavily crevassed*--otherwise it's a walkup. **Gerdine** at 3431 meters, and **Torbert**, 3484, are much more rugged, requiring expedition-type equipment and planning. Call ahead of time to inquire about snow conditions and possible landing sites on glaciers. The glacier landing at 975 meters has been used before to climb Gerdine. To climb Torbert, do a glacier landing at about 1100 meters, and approach from the southeast. Or land on a gravel bar at 700 meters, and approach via Harpoon Glacier. In April or May a plane may land on the upper part of Hayes Glacier west of Gerdine, although an approach from the east or south looks easier on the map.

Best weather months are May & June. July & August are rainy. Always take 2-3 days extra food in case the weather turns bad and planes can't fly. If you're camping below snowline, take precaution for bears; carry a bell on your pack to warn them you're coming. Here are 2 float

Unidentified flier at the USGS landing site at 600 meters, looking north at Crater Peak to the left & smoking, and Mt. Spurr above and behind (Bill Doorman foto).

Map 340-1, Gerdine, Torbert & Spur, Tordillo Mountains, Aleutian Range, Alaska, USA

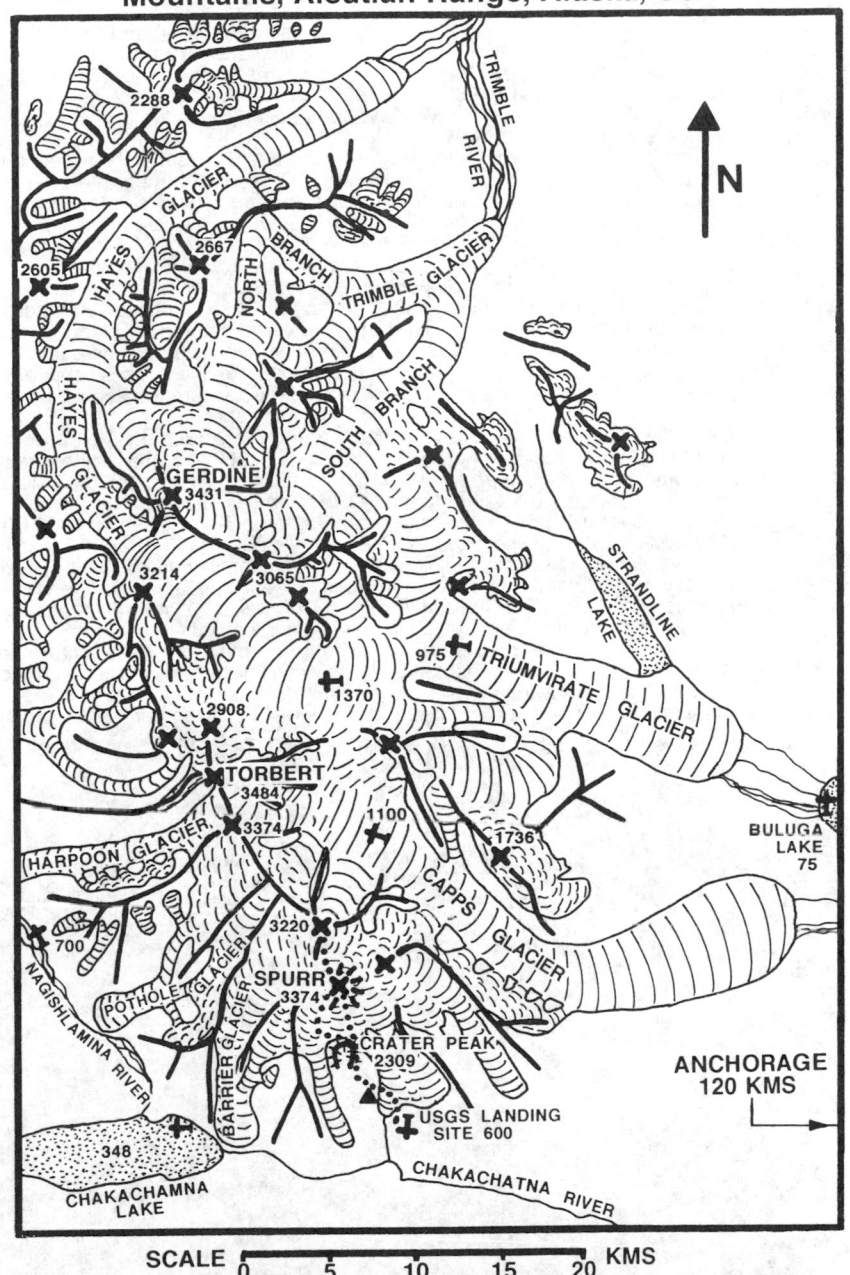

SCALE 0 5 10 15 20 KMS

plane outfitters you might contact; Alaska Air Guides, Box 190989, Anchorage, Alaska, 99519, Tele. 907-243-3669; or Regal Air, Box 190702, Anchorage, Alaska, 99519, or call 907-243-8535.
Maps USGS map *Tyonek,* 1:250,000, shows the entire massif; and/or *Tyonek B-6 & B-7,* and *Tyonek C-6 & C-7,* all at 1:63,360 scale.

Redoubt & Iliamna, Chigmit Mtns., Aleutian Range, Alaska, USA

The 2 volcanos on this map are located southwest of Anchorage on the west side of Cook Inlet opposite Kenai, Soldotna and Homer. This is another of Alaska's roadless areas, so the only way in is to fly. It's a flight of about 100 kms from Kenai to Redoubt, and from Homer to Iliamna. Iliamna is an older volcano but still retains its conal shape. It's last eruption was on 3/1/1953, but there were volcano-tectonic seismic swarms from 8/1/1996 until 3/1/1997. Redoubt's last eruptions were on 12/14/1989 & 6/5/1990. One explosion registered a VEI-3 on the Volcano Explosivity Index or scale. For volcano updates see websites (www.avo.alaska. edu/) or (www.volcano.si.edu/gvp/).

If you're heading this way, do all your shopping in Anchorage if possible, then head for the Kenai Peninsula towns of Kenai, Soldotna or Homer. These are all sizable towns with supermarkets, etc, but Anchorage is still a better place to shop. If you're planning to visit Redoubt, it would be best to contact someone in Kenai or Soldotna. Here are names of several outfitters: *High Adventure Air Charters,* Soldotna, Tele. 907-262-2637, or 2637; *Clearwater Air,* Box 1915, Soldotna, 907-262-5022; or *Kenai Float Plane Service,* Kenai, 907-283-4761. Make contact with one of the pilots in each of these outfits and get his advice on landing sites.

For **Redoubt**, one obvious site would be to land on Crescent Lake in a float plane, but there may be a river bar site closer to the mountain where a wheeled plane could land. Redoubt doesn't seem to have too many flat glaciers, so a ski plane probably wouldn't help unless you were there in April. You might also make high-tide landings on Cook Inlet. There appear to be sportsmen's cabins along the shore, but you'd be in for a long walk from the coast with lots of bushwhacking. Climb Redoubt's eastern slopes to reach the highest peak.

The author flew fairly close to Iliamna when he went to the Augustine Volcano, and it appears an approach up the west face would be the easiest. To get to **Iliamna**, contact some of these outfitters in Homer such as; *Homer Air,* 2190 Kachenak Drive, Homer, 99603, Tele. 907-235-8591. This outfit has wheeled & float planes. Or *Beluga Lake Float Plane Service,* Box 2072, Homer, 99603, or call 907-235-8256; *Kenai Fjords Outfitters,* Box 72, Homer, 99603, Tele. 907-235-6066; or *Kachemak Air Service,* Box 1769, Homer, 99603, Tele. 907-235-8924. These 3 outfitters all use float planes. One good possible landing site near Iliamna would be Hickerson Lake, but it's on the wrong side of the mountain. It would be best to locate someone with a ski plane and land on the upper part of the Tuxedni Glacier. That would put you within easy reach of the west face. April or May would be the best time to do a glacier landing.

May or June has the best weather and is generally the climbing season for Alaska. Depending on where you land and the amount of bushwhacking involved, it will likely take from 3 to 6 days to climb either peak--maybe more (?). Always take 2-3 extra days of food in case bad weather keeps the planes grounded. Lots of bears on the lower slopes so carry bells and make

The northern slopes of Redoubt Volcano showing the active part (Austin Post foto).

Map 341-3, Redoubt & Iliamna, Aleutian R., Alaska, USA

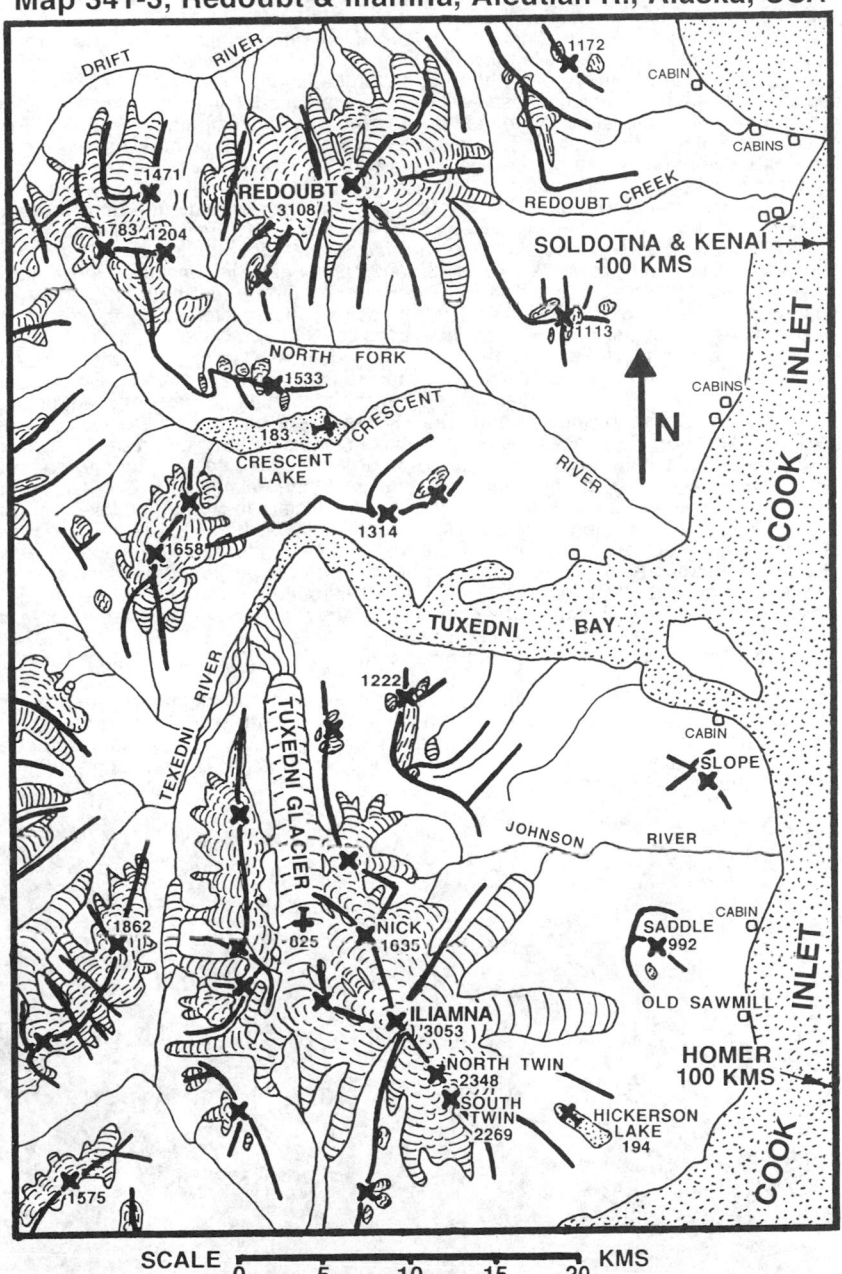

SCALE | 0 5 10 15 20 | KMS

noise! These are glaciated peaks, so take ice ax & crampons and ropes, and maybe skis or snowshoes for early season climbing.

Maps USGS maps *Lake Clark, Kenai, Iliamna & Seldovia*, 1:250,000; or *Kenai C-7 & C-8, and B-7 & B-8* (for Redoubt), and *Lake Clark A-1, Kenai A-8, Iliamna D-1, & Seldovia D-8* (for Iliamna), 1:63,360.

Katmai NP & Augustine Volcano, Aleutian Range, Alaska, USA

This mapped area is southwest of Anchorage, Cook Inlet and Homer, and is at the beginning of the Aleutian Peninsula. Featured here are mountains in Katmai National Park and 3 active or semi-active volcanos. It was **Novarupta** which blew up on 6/6/1912 with a VEI-6 eruption, not Katmai as is commonly thought; but that eruption did cause the crater of Katmai to collapse making a crater lake (see geology cross-section). The last mountain in this area to erupt was Augustine Volcano on the island northeast of Katmai. It last blew up on 3/27/1986, and was active until 8/31/1986. Every named mountain on this map is a volcano of one age or another. For volcano updates see websites (www.avo.alaska.edu/) or (www.volcano.si.edu/gvp/).

To get to **Katmai**, fly on one of several daily flights from Anchorage to King Salmon. The national park HQ is located there. There are many flights between June and September. Contact *MarkAir*, Box 196769, Anchorage, 99519, or call 800-426-6784 (from continental USA), or 800-478-0800 (in Alaska); or contact *Alaska Public Lands Information Center*, 605 W., 4th Avenue, Anchorage, 99501, or call 907-271-2737 or 2599, for more information. *Reeve Aleutian Airways*, 907-243-1112 also has flights to King Salmon. Or contact park HQ, Box 7, King Salmon, Alaska, 99613, Tele. 907-246-3305. Or for quick updated information and a long list of park rules and regulations, see their website (www.nps.gov/katm/).

From King Salmon there are daily charter flights to Brooks Camp, where a visitor center, campground and lodge are located. You can also take a boat from Lake Camp to Brooks Camp. From Brooks Camp, walk or take concessionaire transport along the 37-km-long road running to the **Valley of Ten Thousand Smokes** and **Three Forks Overlook**. From there you can hike to the peaks on the map. Remember, it's windy and cold in this country, go prepared for glacier travel, and have a tent that won't sail away in the wind! Also, take a bell on your pack for bears. Buy all supplies in Anchorage because there's not much at King Salmon or Brooks Camp.

Here's what the author did on 7/12/1992. He flew from Homer to **Augustine Island** in a float plane which was going out empty to pick up fishermen & bear-watchers at McNeil River. He was put off in the evening at the cabin & campsite shown. The next morning he climbed Augustine in about 4 1/2 hours, round-trip. On the third day, he was picked up by another float plane which had just taken other bear-watchers to McNeil River. His round-trip flight cost US$285. If your schedule is flexible, you can cut your flight cost in half by riding in an otherwise empty plane. Contact *Beluga Lake Float Plane Service*, Box 2072, Homer, Alaska, 99603, Tele. 907-235-8256; or *Kachemak Air Service*, Box 1769, Homer, 99603, or call 907-235-8924; or *Kenai Fjords Outfitters*, Box 72, Homer, 99603, Tele. 907-235-6066.

As you're about to land on Augustine, have the pilot point out the little ravine leading up through the alder brush towards the mountain. This is the route you'll take as you start the climb. There is a good campsite 100 meters from the little geologist's cabin in the spruce and alders; or you could stay in the cabin--if you promise to keep it clean! There's good spring water nearby. This mountain & island have no glaciers or bears, but lots of mosquitos. Take 2-3 days

Looking east at Augustine Volcano from the landing side near the cabin.

Map 342-1, Katmai National Park & Augustine Volcano, Aleutian Range, Alaska, USA

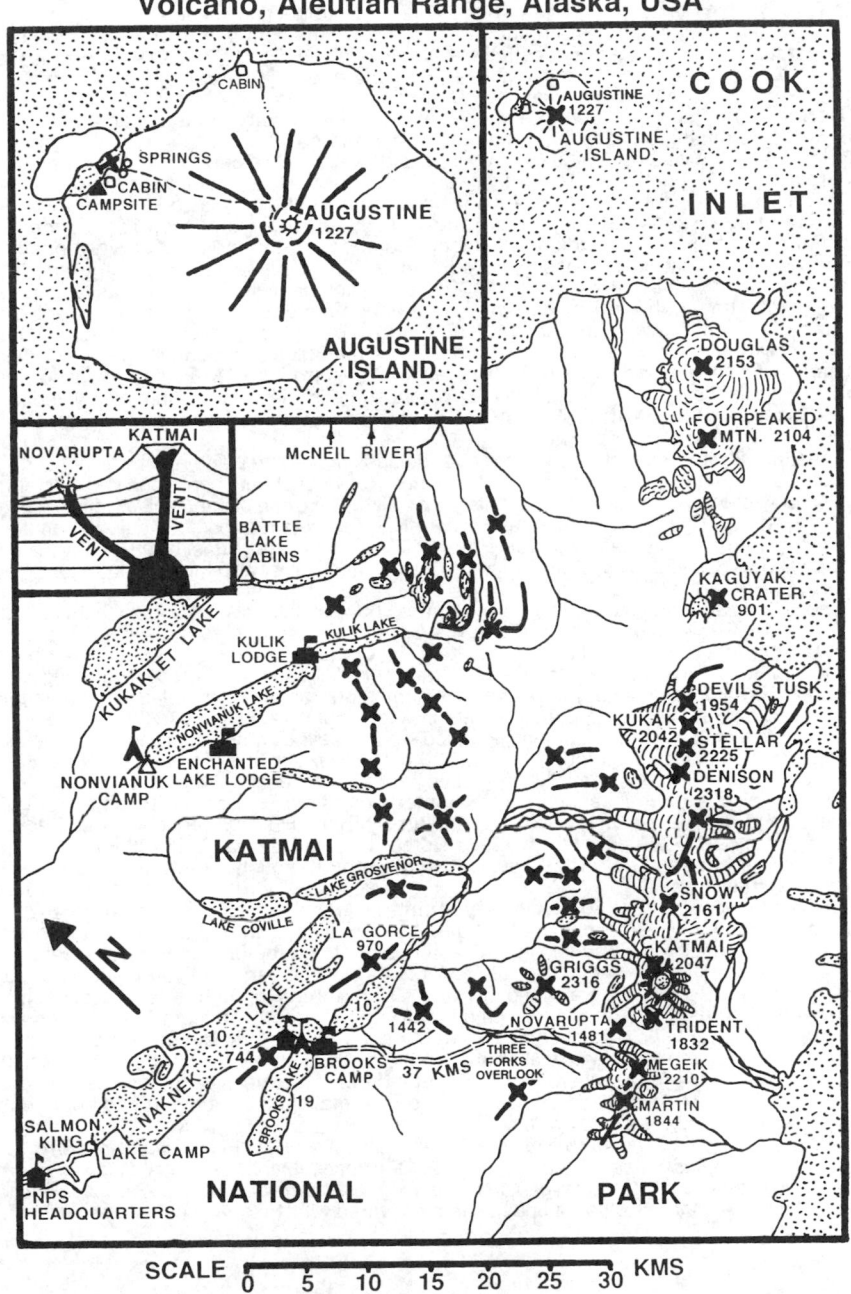

SCALE 0 5 10 15 20 25 30 KMS

extra food in case bad weather keeps the planes grounded.
Maps USGS maps *Iliamna, Afognak, Mt. Katmai & Naknek,* 1:250,000; and *Iliamna B-2,* for Augustine and many other maps for Katmai at 1:63,360 scale.

Introduction to the Aleutian Islands Volcanos, Alaska, USA

The author hasn't been to this area so this is just an introduction to some interesting hikes or climbs in the remote southwestern end of the Alaska Peninsula and to several of the larger islands at the beginning or eastern end of the Aleutian Island chain. This entire region is made up of volcanos, some very old, some active. The entire Aleutian group is volcanic and every mountain on this map is a volcano at one stage or another.

Here's a list of some of the more important & active volcanos on this map and their last eruptions. Beginning on Map 2 & Umnak Island in the southwest; Vsevidof Volcano's last eruption (phreatic) was on 3/11/1957. Okmok's 10-km-wide caldera, one of the more lively volcanos in the Aleutians, started activity on 2/13/1997 and lasted until the end of 4/1997. Makushin Volcano had an explosive eruption on 3/2/1987, but it only lasted one day. Isonotski issued lava in 3/1831, but there are uncertainties on the exact location & time. The symmetrically-shaped Shishaldin is the highest and one of the most active volcanos in the Aleutians; it had phreatic explosions from 9/1999 to 1/2000, and it appears to be ongoing.

On the Alaska Peninsula and on Map 1, Pavlof is another lively one. It had its last eruption on 3/5/1990. Its neighbor, Pavlof Sister, was active between 1762 & 1786. Veniaminof Volcano's last activity was between 7/30/1993 to 12/31/1993, and beyond. Aniakchak has a large caldera which was active on 6/25/1951. The symmetrically-shaped Chiginagak Volcano has had an active fumarole on it's north flank at 1676 meters since 1943; its last venting was in 7/1971. This list covers only about half the volcanos, the liveliest half, in this area listed in the book, **Volcanos of the World**. For volcano updates see websites (www.avo.alaska.edu/) or (www.volcano.si.edu/gvp/).

There are 2 ways to reach this remote and roadless region; by plane and by ferry boat. The easiest, fastest and the most expensive is by plane. Between about June 1 and mid-September, *MarkAir* of Anchorage has daily flights to Adak (near the far west end of the Aleutians and not on this map); almost daily flights to Cold Bay; several daily flights to Dutch Harbor; and daily to Sand Point. For more information contact MarkAir, Box 196769, Anchorage, Alaska, 99519, or call from continental USA 800-426-6784, or from Alaska 800-478-0800. They also run tours to various places including St. Paul in the Pribilof Islands northwest of this mapped region.

Reeve Aleutian Airways also flies this way. They have smaller planes and go to more places than MarkAir. Reeve flies to Attu and Shemya at the far western end of the Aleutians, and to Adak, Dutch Harbor, False Pass, Cold Bay, King Cove, Chignik, and Ivanoff Bay. Their busiest schedule runs from about June 1 through the first week of September. These flights originate in Anchorage, and run almost daily through the 3 months of summer. To update this information, call the Alaska Public Lands Information center in Anchorage at 907-271-2737.

From many of these airports or landing strips, you can either walk directly to the mountain of your choice, or contact a charter company such as *Peninsula Airways*, Tele. 800-448-4226. The local pilots should know of potential landing sites near any of these volcanos.

There is also ferry boat service. From Homer, you can take a boat with stops at Kodiak, Chignik, Sand Point, King Cove, Cold Bay and finally Dutch Harbor. It takes about 3 days for this trip and cost US$240 one-way in 1992. Homer to Cold Bay was US$186, and to Chignik US$116. The boat makes this trip about twice a month, which means anyone on a tight schedule won't use it much.

Be aware that all of this region is very remote, with almost no roads from the towns or airports. It's also very wet almost all the time, so be equipped with good warm clothing, rain gear and wind protection. May and June are supposed to be the drier months in Alaska, plus the weather is warming up then. There are few forests in these parts, but you'll surely find some brush in places, otherwise it's grass and tundra you'll be walking through. Waterproof boots and gaiters would be useful. The higher summits are snowcapped with some moderately large glaciers. Permanent snow line seems to be at about 1500 meters, but that varies. Ice ax & crampons are required on all peaks over about 1500 meters. Better take a rope too. There will be some stores in the towns where you land, but food will be expensive, so take as much with you as possible from Anchorage, or elsewhere on the mainland. Expect to find bears on the Alaska Peninsula, so take a tinker bell.

Maps USGS maps *Ugashik, Sutwik Island, Chignik, Stepovak Bay, Port Moller, Cold Bay, False Pass, Unimak, Unalaska and Umnak*, all at 1:250,000 scale. Maps of other Aleutian islands not covered on this map will be *Samalga Island, Amukta, Seguam, Atka, Adak, Gareloi Island, Rat Islands, Kiska and Attu*. Each area appears to be covered with 1:63,360 scale maps as well.

Map 343-3, Introduction--The Aleutians, Alaska, USA

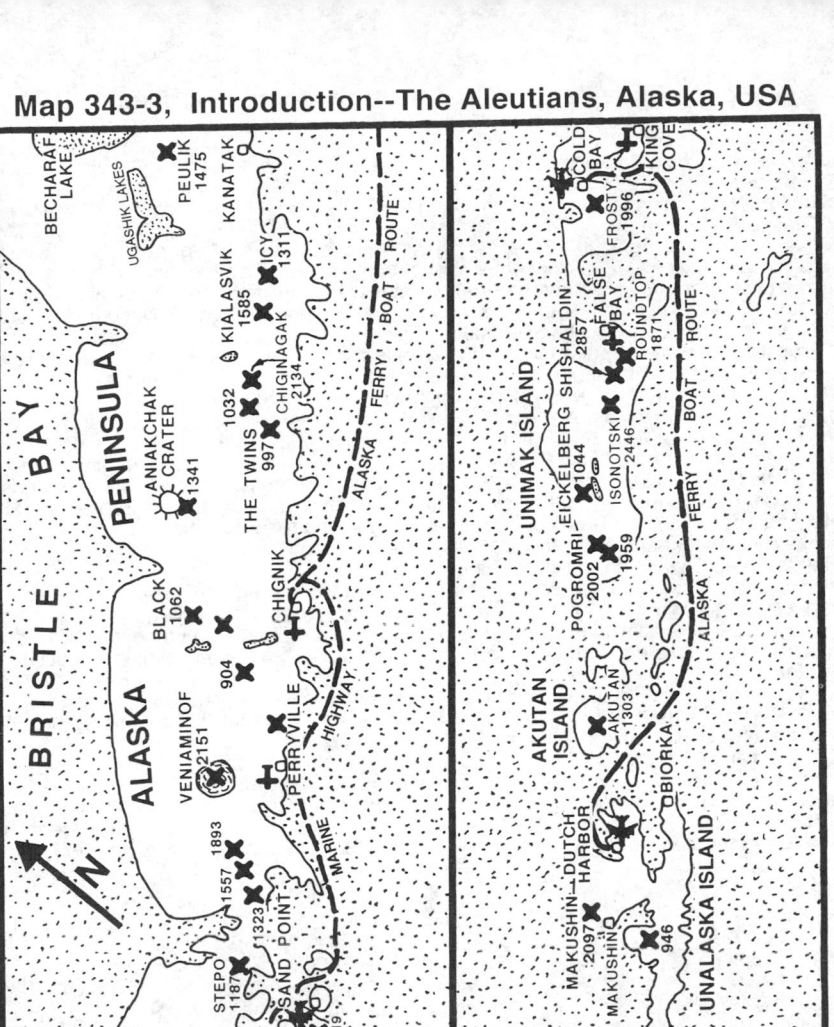

SCALE 0   50   100   150   200 KMS

Chugach State Park Trails, Chugach Mountains, Alaska, USA

Featured here are the mountains directly east of anchorage, Alaska's largest city. These peaks, valleys and glaciers are in the Chugach Mountains which have been made into a state park called the *Chugach State Park*. This is one of the few places in Alaska where you have easy access to hiking, climbing, cross country skiing, etc. To get a good map and other information about this state park, write to Chugach State Park, HC 52, Box 8999, Indian, Alaska, 99540, or call 907-345-5015. Or try the *Alaska Public Lands Information Center* at 605 W. 4th Avenue, Anchorage, Tele. 907-271-2737. If you're in the area south of Anchorage, stop at the Chugach State Park HQ. & visitor center at about mile post 115 on the Seward Highway. There you can pick up maps and other information, at least in summertime. They also have visitor centers on Eagle Creek and near Eklutna Lake. There's also a Chugach National Forest visitor center in Girdwood near Alyeska Ski Resort.

Probably the most popular hike in this area is the trail to Crow Pass. Get to this area by driving southeast out of Anchorage on the Seward Highway in the direction of Seward, Kenai and Homer. Near mile post 90 is a small community called Girdwood. From there, turn north on a paved road running toward Alyeska Ski Resort. When the main road turns east, you continue north on the Crow Creek Road. Girdwood to the Crow Pass Trailhead is 11 or 12 kms. From the trailhead to a hut near Crow Pass, is only about 5 kms. You'll pass an old mining area going up. Up and back can be done in as little as half a day. The author did this hike to the pass and back in just over 3 hours. That was on 7/17/1992. You can rent the state park hut at 1036 meters for about US$20 a night, but you'll have to call and reserve it months in advance. From this pass and shelter are many opportunities for hiking, and rock, ice & snow climbing. All of the region to the east is a large icefield with big crevasses.

From Crow Pass, you can continue north along the Iditarod Trail toward the Eagle River Road Trailhead. To get to that trailhead, drive northeast out of Anchorage on the Glenn Highway. Near mile post 13, turn east onto the Eagle River Road and proceed to its end where a visitor center is located. Each year locals have a marathon-type race along this section of the old Iditarod Trail.

Another popular place is Eklutna Lake and the trail running southeast along its eastern shore. The trail gives access to the Eklutna Glacier and lots of snow & ice climbing possibilities. There's another trail running up Indian Creek and down Ship Creek, but the middle part of this was not a maintained trail in 1992, and you may have to do some bushwhacking (?).

There's a small store in Girdwood, but best to do all your shopping in Anchorage. June is one of the best months weather-wise, but with some snow on the ground. July, August and September have less snow, but it's usually wetter--but each summer is different. Camp anywhere in the backcountry without a permit. Take a tinker bell for bears. The author saw

This old boiler is found along the trail to Crow Pass and not too far below the cabin.

Map 344-1, Chugach Trails, Chugach Mtns., Alaska, USA

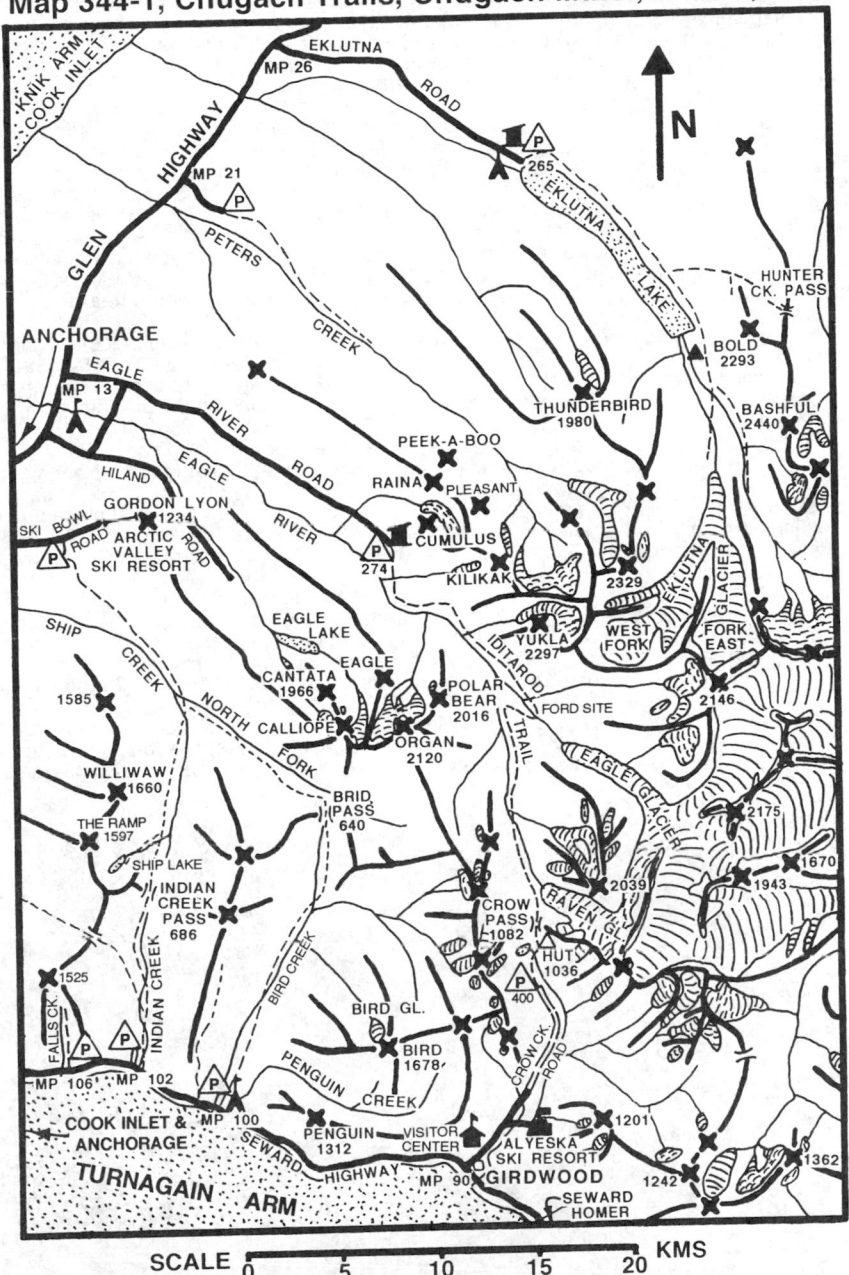

some people carrying .44 magnums on his hike, but the chances of meeting a bear are slim.
Maps USGS maps *Anchorage & Seward,* 1:250,000; or *Seward D-6 & D-7,* and *Anchorage A-6, A-7, B-6 & B-7,* all at 1:63,360 scale; or *Chugach State Park summer guide* map. Buy good maps at the USGS office, Alaska Pacific University, 4230 University Drive, Anchorage, Tele. 907-786-7011.

Marcus Baker, Witherspoon & Thor, Chugach Mountains, Alaska, USA

This map shows some moderately high peaks due east of Anchorage and the Matanuska Valley; and south of the Glenn Highway and Haines Junction. This is the highest and central part of the Chugach Mountains. The highest peak in the range is Mt. Marcus Baker at 4016 meters. Thor is next at 3734, with another well-known summit named Witherspoon at 3661 meters. There are a number of other high peaks along the same summit ridge. These mountains are folded and have been compressed to create mostly metamorphic-type rocks.

There are 2 ways to get into this region; walk or fly. Most prefer to fly. Because these peaks are so close to the Glenn Highway, it's possible to walk right from this main paved road. If you try this route, park somewhere along the highway near the bottom end of the Matanuska Glacier. You can see the glacier right from the highway. It should take about 3 or 4 days, or more, to walk up the glacier to a base camp at the northern foot of Marcus Baker. A guess as to how much time it would take for this climb might be 8 to 10 days round-trip; if you had good weather all the time. Another walk-in possibility would be to drive to Valdez and walk up Mineral Creek or the Valdez Glacier. But climbing from that area wouldn't put you anywhere near the highest peaks.

The best way of getting into the high summits is to fly. The author has put possible landing sites for ski planes on this map. For more information call Mike Meekin at 907-745-6159. The author was told he lives somewhere near mile posts 114 & 115 along the Glenn Highway. He apparently has a wheeled-ski plane which is what you'll need to land on the glaciers. Or if Mike is no longer with us, or out of business, try Ellis Air Taxi, Glennallen Airport, Box 106, Alaska, 99588, Tele. 907-822-3368. Pilots there might be able to help, or know who can.

If none of these people have a ski plane, contact someone at Talkeetna or McCarthy. See Mt. McKinley and Mt. Bona maps for their names and telefon numbers. It would be much cheaper however, if you found someone closer to these mountains. One last place you can contact for more updated information is the *Alaska Public Lands Information Center* at 605 W. 4th Avenue, Anchorage, Tele. 907-271-2737. They should have a current list of bush pilots throughout the region.

Another option would be to fly in, then when you're through with Marcus Baker, and with a lighter pack, you could rather easily (hopefully) walk down to the highway via the Matanuska Glacier. Better check this route out from the air as you fly in; also check out the lower end of the route from the highway with binoculars, or walk in a short distance and checkout that end of the route before going. May or June are the best months for climbing in Alaska. By the time July and August roll around the weather is much worse and the glacier landings become rougher because of icing and open crevasses. For Marcus Baker, the approach from the northeast and the landing site marked 1980 meters appears to be the best. Always take lots more food than you think you'll need; to sit out bad weather, which is the rule, not the exception. Be prepared for

From the main highway east of Palmer you'll have a good look up the Nelchina Glacier.

Map 345-2, Marcus Baker, Witherspoon & Thor, Chugach Mountains, Alaska, USA

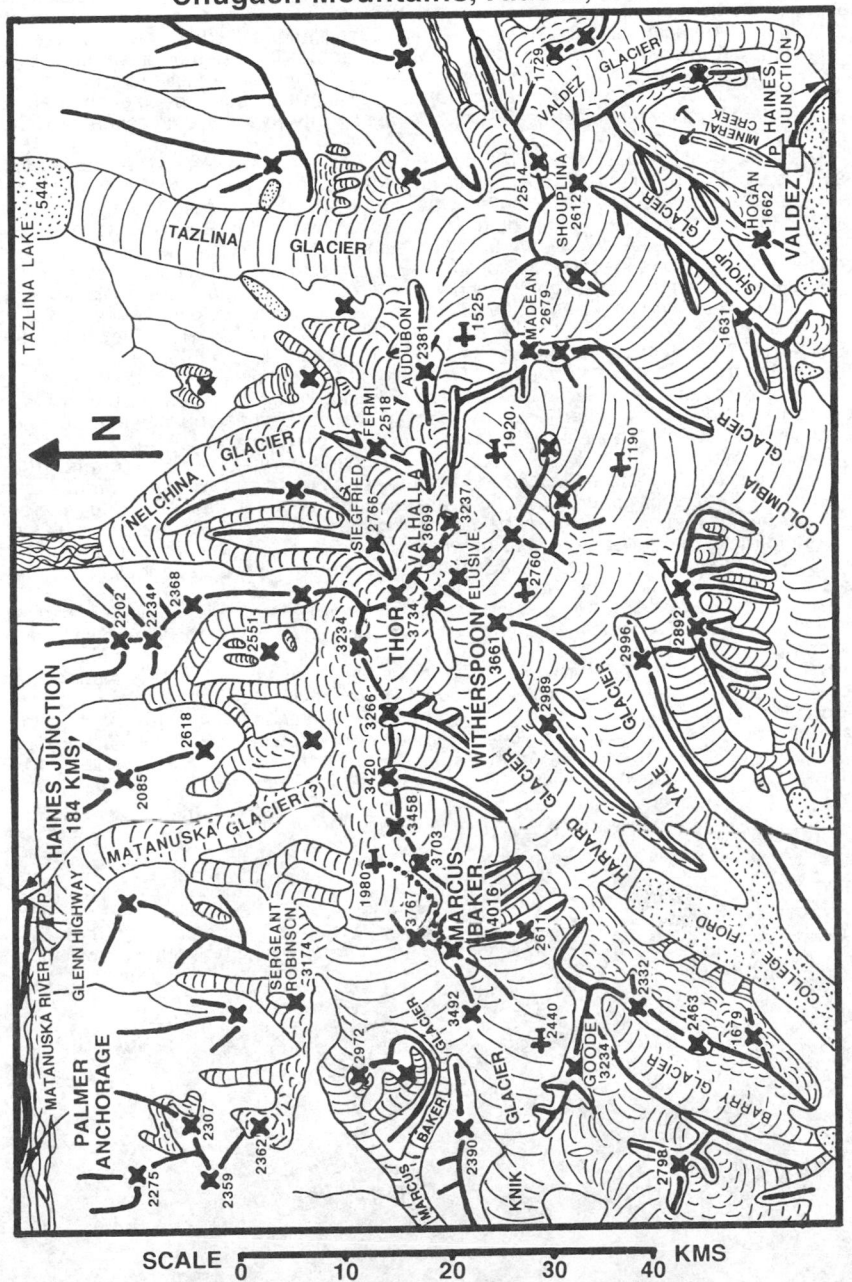

big glaciers, big crevasses, and terrible weather. No place here for beginners!
Maps USGS maps *Anchorage and Valdez,*1:250,000. There are also about a dozen maps at 1:63,360 scale available covering the range.

Drum, Sanford & Wrangell, Wrangell Mountains, Alaska, USA

Shown on this map are 3 of the well-known peaks in Alaska. They are Mt. Drum, 3661 meters; Mt. Sanford the highest at 4949; and Mt. Wrangell at 4317 meters. They're all located in the Wrangell Mountains, and the Wrangell--Saint Elias National Park and immediately east of Glennallen, but the park extends east to the Canadian border. All 3 of these mountains are volcanic in origin, but only Mt. Wrangell is still considered active. Wrangell's last certain eruption was in 1902, but there may have been some activity in 1907. Some people say there is still steam venting from its summit crater. Sanford's last activity was in the Holocene, or within the last 10,000 years.

These mountains are all clearly visible from Glennallen and Gulkana. They seem near and easy to reach, but the roaring Copper River runs between the highway and the mountains and there are no roads what-so-ever going anywhere near the peaks. Until recent times, climbers would do this trip in the spring when the river was frozen; while others used boats to get across. Today however, airplanes are used to transport climbers to or near the base of the mountains. The author was at Gulkana waiting for several days in 7/1992, but had constant rain.

Here's a rundown on how to get to each mountain and the normal route. This according to pilots at Gulkana. To climb **Mt. Drum**, which is the closest, simply go to the Gulkana Airport just north of Glennallen Junction, and make contact with *Ellis Air Taxi*, Box 106, Glennallen, 99588, or call 907-822-3368; or *Gulkana Air Service*, Box 31, Glennallen, 99588, Tele. 907-822-5532. In a wheeled plane, they can fly you out to a dry lake bed southwest of Drum at approximately 1070 meters altitude. In 1992, Lynn Ellis was charging US$235 to transport climbers to the mountain and pick them up later. From the landing site, simply head up the southwest ridge to the summit. Bad weather appears to be the only risk on this route.

To climb **Wrangell**, call ahead and see which flying service has a ski plane. If one is available, you can fly to and land at the saddle between Sanford and Wrangell. From there walk due south to the summit crater. Lots of crevasses on this route! Or if you'd prefer, there are 2 landing sites for wheeled planes west of the mountain. The one at 1675 meters would put you next to the rock-covered Sanford Glacier which should make an easy route to the summit as shown. From the other landing at 1130 meters, you would have a steeper climb up the west face; or perhaps circle around to the south face (?).

The normal way up **Sanford** is to land at the site northwest of the mountain and make the long walk up Sheep Glacier to the summit. This is a relatively easy climb, but with seemly lots of glacier travel and crevasses.

To climb Drum takes 4-5 days minimum; Wrangell, no less than 7-8 days, and for Sanford about the same. However, you must take about twice as much food as you think you'll need--to sit out bad weather; of which there is plenty, which keeps planes on the tarmack. May or June are the best weather months, or maybe as early as April. You can buy food in Glennallen, but it's expensive! Best to shop in Anchorage or Fairbanks supermarkets. Get additional information at the Wrangell--St. Elias N. P. Visitor Center in Copper Center, Box 29 (Glennallen),

Mt. Sanford stands tall as seen from the Tok Cutoff Highway.

Map 346-2, Drum, Sanford & Wrangell, Wrangell Mountains, Alaska, USA

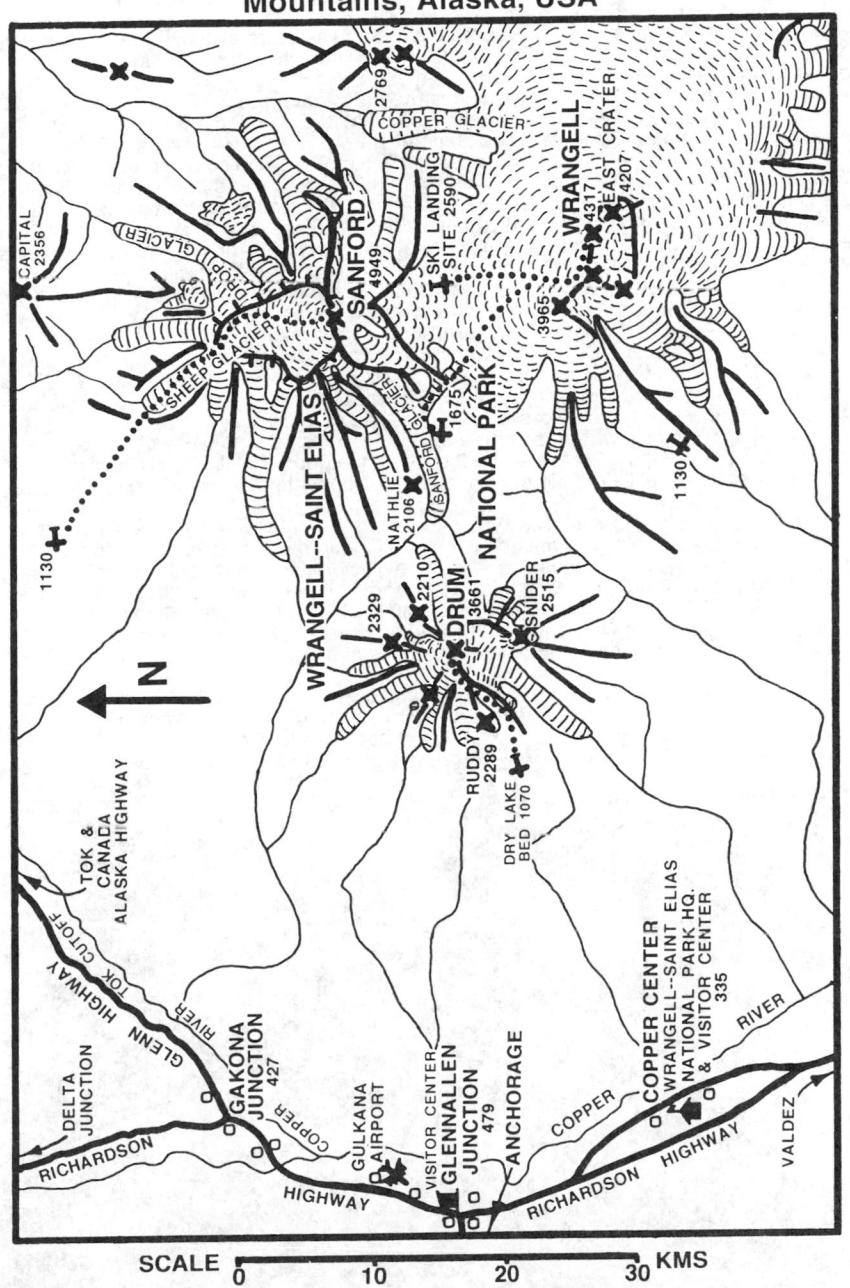

99588, or call 907-822-5235.
Maps USGS maps *Gulkana & Valdez,* 1:250,000, or USGS maps *Gulkana B-1, A-2, A-1, and Valdez D-1,* 1:63,360; see Map 344, page 745 for more addresses.

Mts. Hayes and Deborah, Alaska Range, Alaska, USA

The mountains featured on this map are in the Alaska Range south of Delta Junction, southeast of Fairbanks, and northeast of Mt. McKinley. The 2 best known peaks are Mt. Hayes, the highest at 4216 meters; and Mt. Deborah at 3761. There are also a number of other peaks in the Mt. Hayes area that are higher than Deborah. They are Shand and Moffit. The rocks in these mountains are metamorphic and granitic-types.

One nice thing about these mountains is they are reasonably close to a major road, the Richardson Highway. However, this doesn't mean that it gives good easy access. The access would be good for the eastern part of this mapped area if it weren't for the Delta River. This is a rather large stream of water making wading impossible in summer except for maybe in the area near mile post 210. You could likely find a place to wade across there if conditions were right, but that would mean an unreasonable hike to reach the highest peaks. If you could somehow get across, maybe by using a boat, at or near Black Rapids and mile post 227, then the eastern end of this massif would be within walking distance. Another way to handle this big river problem would be to climb in March or April with the river frozen or with a lot less water.

Another remote possibility would be to drive to Denali from the Denali Highway south of this map, and walk north. But there are big river crossings there too. But by far the best way into the area with all the high peaks is to fly with a wheeled ski plane. There might be someone in Paxson (at the junction of the Richardson & Denali Highways) who can fly you in, but the first person you should contact would be Harvey Wheeler with *Sawmill Creek Air*, Box 885, Delta Junction, 99737, or call 907-895-5040. In 1992, he was charging US$150 per/hour for the smaller Super Cub (one person + gear), and US$180 an hour for his 2 passenger + gear Cessna 180.

He normally has one wheeled ski plane handy and has landed climbers on the upper glaciers in the past. He has landed at the 2 sites on the upper Black Rapids Glacier at 1920 & 1860 meters altitude, but by looking at the map, there appear to be sites on the upper West Fork and Yanert Glaciers as well.

Wheeler is the one who will advise you on where you can land and the best time of year to go. If you go early, such as in April, then you can land in many places; but if you go in June, then you can only land on the upper parts of these glaciers. In summer, the winter snow melts, leaving rough rocky landings. May or June generally have good weather and are the best months to climb. If you're flying in and out, then April or May is the best time to go.

The western slopes of **Deborah** and the south ridge or ridges on **Hayes** look the easiest. The author hasn't climbed here, but did a day-climb just across the highway on the east side of this map.

Whenever you go, be sure to have plenty of food so you can sit out bad weather. This range is a lot drier than the mountains further south, but bad weather is still common. Anchorage or Fairbanks have large supermarkets and are the best places to shop for everything. These are

Mt. Deborah from the south. The normal route is up the left side (Bradford Washburn foto).

Map 347-2, Hayes & Deborah, Alaska R., Alaska, USA

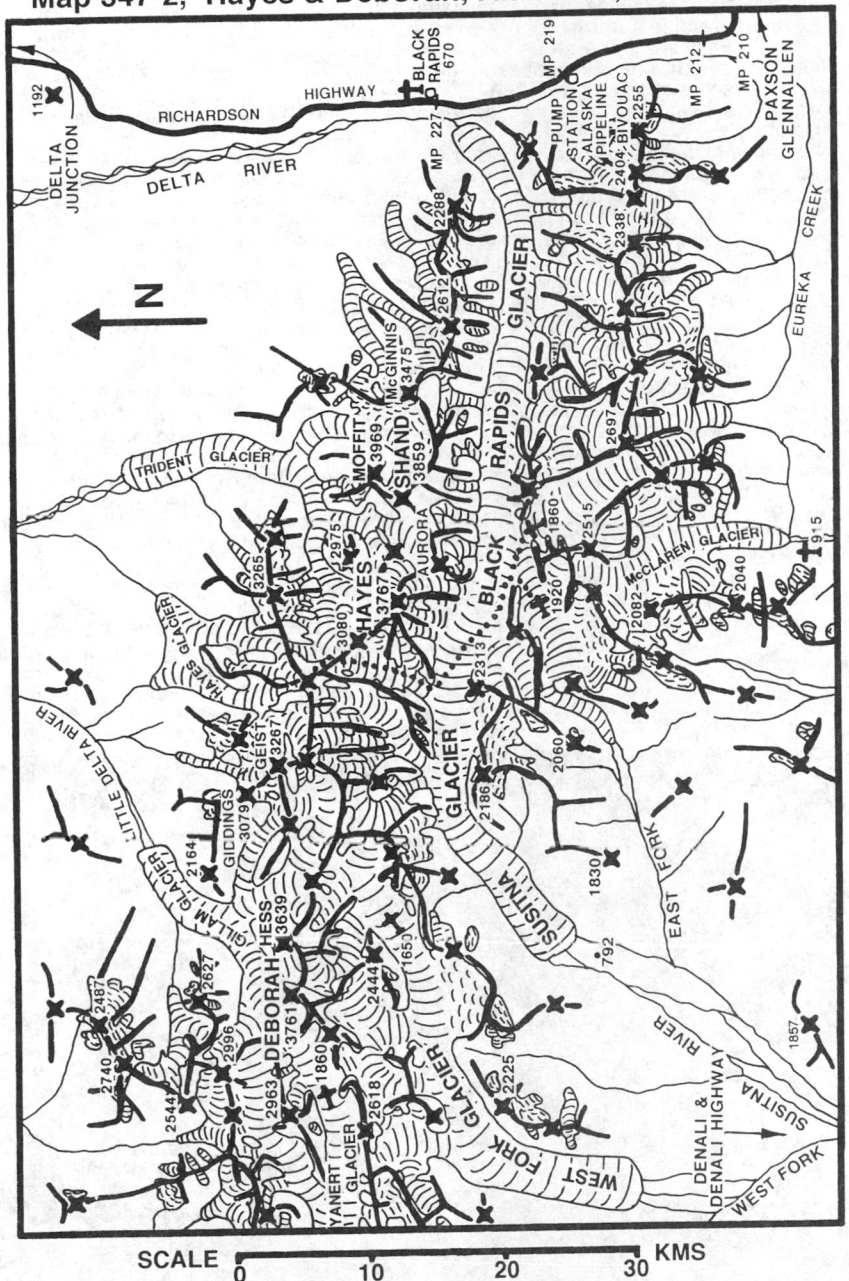

SCALE | 0 | 10 | 20 | 30 | KMS

big rugged mountains, so go prepared for a real expedition.
Maps USGS maps *Healy and Mt. Hayes,* 1:250,000; and/or *Healy C-1,C-2, Mt. Hayes C-5, C-6, B-5, and B-6,* all at 1:63,360 scale.

Silvertip, Gakona & Kimball, Alaska Range, Alaska, USA

This map shows a number of peaks located just east of the Richardson Highway, south of Delta Junction and just northeast of Paxson. Just to the west is another group of peaks featuring Mt. Hayes & Deborah as seen on the previous map. Some of the better known summits here are Silvertip at about 2750 meters; Gakona, 2925, and Mt. Kimball about 3110 meters. For some reason, the 1:250,000 scale maps give very few elevations for these summits, therefore most altitudes given here are estimates. The rocks are either granite or other metamorphics.

This is one of the few mountain areas is Alaska you can drive to and have reasonably easy access. It's the paved Richardson Highway that makes it possible. Here are some possible starting points for those wanting to climb without flying in. Between mile posts 197 & 198 is a side road leading northeast to an old placer mine near the bottom end of the College & Gulkana Glaciers. By parking there, you can reach many of the peaks on the south slope.

By parking at 1100 meters and walking east, in about 4 days (?) you could be at a base camp ready to climb **Kimball**. Look at the 1:63,360 scale maps; there might be a road into Slate Creek (?). Maps indicate a west ridge might be the easiest route (?). Twelve to 14 days should be enough time to climb Kimball, if the weather remains reasonably good. If you try this route, beware of possible river crossings along the way. One way around wading would be to cross on the lower ends of the glaciers, but this might be tough walking!

After walking about 2 days up the Gakona Glacier, you could climb **Gakona** from the south. You should be able to do this one easily with a week of good weather. On 7/28/1992, the author parked at the trailhead marked 1100 meters, then spent less than 6 hours round-trip climbing the peak east of College Glacier marked 1890 meters.

Another starting point would be somewhere between mile posts 216 & 218 and near the bottom ends of the Castner, Eel or Canwell Glaciers. Parking there would give you easy access to **Silvertip** and other peaks in the western or northwestern part of this massif. By walking up the Castner Glacier for one or 2 days, you should be in a good spot to climb Silvertip, perhaps by the east ridge.

If you have the money, but not too much time, you could fly to some of the more remote peaks. Contact Harvey Wheeler, *Sawmill Creek Air,* Box 885, Delta Junction, 99737, or call 907-895-5040; or *Ellis Air Taxi,* Box 106, Glennallen, 99588, Tele. 907-822-3368. In April or May you could likely land on some higher glacier. There are also several airstrips south of Kimball you might be able to fly into.

All these climbs will take expedition-type clothes and equipment. Even though none of these peaks is real high in elevation, few are really easy to climb. However, this area would be a good place to begin climbing in Alaska. The weather here is better that on mountains to the south, at

Substituting for this area is a postcard foto of the Russell Glacier (Map 349, page 755) looking south with Mt. Bona on the left and Mt. Churchill on the right (George Herben foto).

Map 348-1, Silvertip, Gakona & Kimball, Alaska, USA

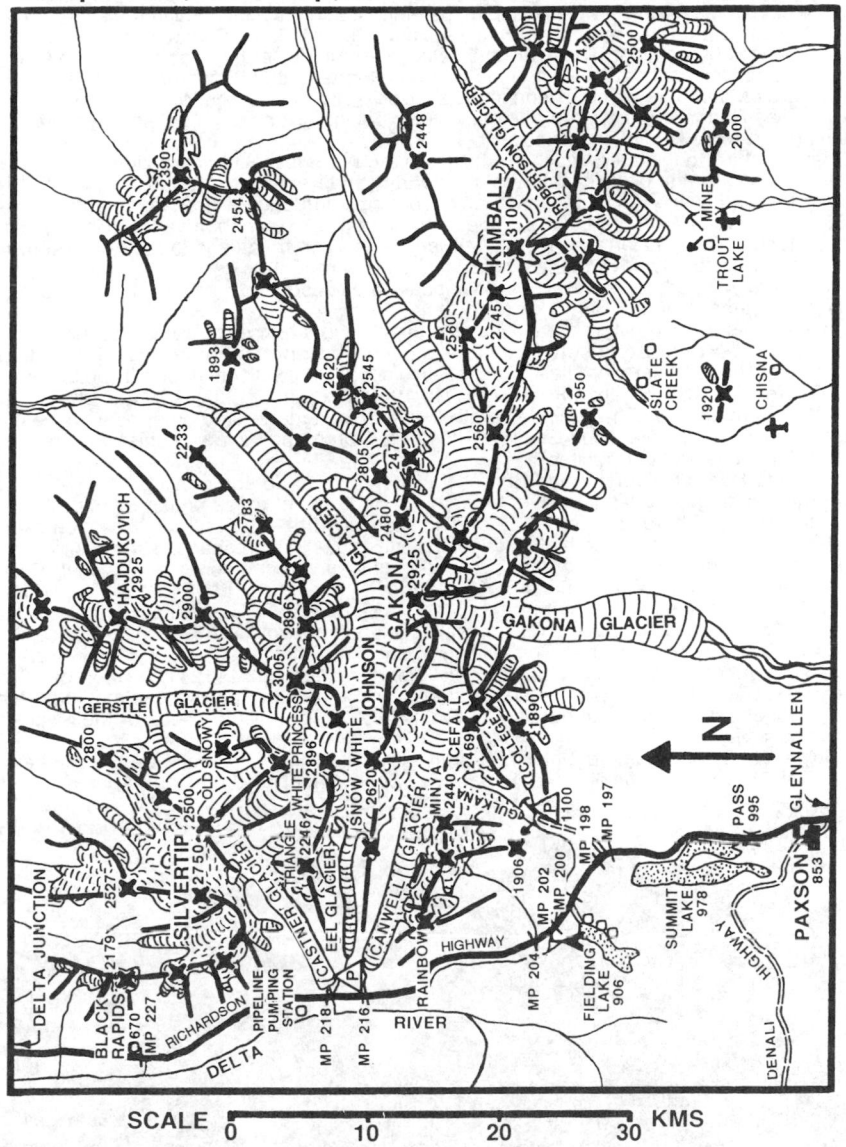

least when compared to the coastal Chugach Mountains. Most mountaineers in Alaska climb in May or June, which generally has better weather than in mid-summer. If you were to go in March or April, you could get up close to the peaks on snowmobiles. Buy all your supplies in Anchorage or Fairbanks.

Maps USGS map *Mt. Hayes,* 1;250.000; or *Mt. Hayes C-3, C-4, B-2, B-3, B-4, and A-2 & A-3,* all 1:63,360 scale. Buy these and other good maps at the USGS office, Alaska Pacific University, 4230 University Drive, Anchorage, Tele. 907-786-7011.

Blackburn, Churchill & Bona, St. Elias Mountain, Alaska, USA

The mountains on this map are among the highest and least climbed in the state of Alaska. Included here is Mt. Blackburn at 4996 meters, plus Rime & Parka Peaks all clustered together in the Wrangell Mountains. These are the peaks north of McCarthy. To the east are Churchill, 4766 meters; University at 4411; and Mt. Bona the highest at 5005 meters. These are part of the St. Elias Mountains which extend into Canada's Yukon. Both the Wrangell Mountains and the St. Elias Range are made up of mostly old volcanics. Bona is an old stratovolcano, while Churchill had some kind of an explosion in about 700 AD.

If you make it to this area, much of which is in the Wrangell--St. Elias National Park, be sure to drive to and visit the old mining towns of McCarthy and Kennicott. McCarthy is where most of the miners lived; while Kennicott is a huge copper smelting plant which was abandoned in the 1930's. This is now one of Alaska's biggest tourist draws. You can drive there in any vehicle, along a road which was formerly the old railway grade. The train used to run from Kennicott to Cordova. You actually drive to the river opposite McCarthy, then use a footbridge to walk into town. Where you park are several hostels or bed & breakfasts and a national park visitor center. Nearby is a campground.

Beyond this copper mining area, things get primitive in a hurry! To climb Blackburn and any of the peaks north of Kennicott, you can simply walk from the copper smelter and up the Kennicott or Root Glaciers. While in the area, you could also walk the good trail up to the mines north of Kennicott on Bonanza Peak. On 7/19/1992, the author did this hike in about 7 hours round-trip from his car. That included a quick visit to the smelter and other nearby sites. You could also fly onto the Nebesna Glacier north of Blackburn and have an easier and shorter trip. See map for possible landing sites.

To climb Bona, University and Churchill, you'll have to do some flying. There are some moderately high glacier landing sites to the north and east of these peaks, which will make a climb fairly easy. There are also many landing sites for wheeled planes as shown on the map. Most of these will get you near the bigger peaks, and above the forest and bushwhacking.

Here are some bush pilots or mountaineering guides you can contact. *Wrangell Mountain Air,* McCarthy, Box MXY, Glennallen, 99588, or call year-round 907-345-1160 (radio fone in McCarthy). Or if you're already there, contact *McCarthy Air* in Glennallen and/or McCarthy. Also, Paul & Donna Claus have a wilderness lodge southeast of McCarthy with air access only. Claus flies parties onto glaciers. Contact him at Box 109, Chitina, 99566, or call 907-823-2233. You also might contact Bob Jacobs, *St. Elias Alpine Guides,* Box 111241, Anchorage, 99511, Tele. 907-277-6867; or see them in person in McCarthy. Jacobs knows these mountains better than anyone! Or call the national park at 907-822-5235 for a list of pilots, or their website at (www.nps.gov/wrst/).

Buy all supplies elsewhere, not in McCarthy! Expect some of the worst weather in the world here. Take 3 weeks of supplies for an otherwise one week or a 10 day trip. April, May & June

This is the historic Kennicott Mill complex just north of McCarthy.

Map 349-1, Blackburn-Bona, St. Elias Mtns., Alaska, USA

SCALE

0   10   20   30   40   KMS

have the best weather. Expect huge glaciers and crevasses. Prepare for arctic conditions and a real expedition to these highest peaks!

Maps USGS map *McCarthy,* 1:250.000, or many others at 1:63.360 scale. In Anchorage, buy maps at the USGS, Alaska Pacific University, 4230 University Drive, 99508, Tele. 907-786-7011.

Bagley Icefield Peaks, Chugach Mountains, Alaska, USA

The peaks and glaciers on this map include those located just west of the Alaska-Yukon border, just north of the Gulf of Alaska, and south of McCarthy (see previous map). These mountains are mostly in the far eastern end of the Chugach Range, but those in the lower right-hand corner are apparently part of the St. Elias Mountains, much of which is in Canada's Yukon Territory. Most of the area on this map is within either the Wrangell--St. Elias National Park, or the Wrangell--St. Elias National Preserve (hunting is allowed in the preserve part).

The mountains featured here are those near the middle of the map and next to the Bagley Ice Field. There are literally hundreds of peaks to choose from, some of which have yet to be climbed. **Tom White, Hawkins, Steller** & **Miller** are some of the higher and better-known peaks. These glaciers & ice fields are some of the largest in the world outside the polar regions.

This is one of the many isolated mountain regions of Alaska accessible by airplane only. The first thing you'll want to do is call one of several air taxi or charter airplane outfitters. These people will give you an idea of what is available and where they are capable of landing. Here's a list of nearby outfitters that can fly you into this region, or will know of others who can. *McCarthy Air,* Box MXY Glennallen, 99588, or in McCarthy, 99588; or *Wrangell Mountain Air,* Box MXY, Glennallen, 99588, or call 907-345-1160 (radio fone); or contact *Ultima Thule Outfitters,* Paul & Donna Claus, Box 109 Chitina, 99566, Tele. 907-823-2233. Paul Claus & wife have a private lodge as shown near the top of the map. They fly people into this lodge for fishing, hunting, rafting, and mountain climbing. Paul is the pilot who takes most climbers onto the glaciers. He also works closely with the *St. Elias Alpine Guides,* Box 111241, Anchorage, 99511, or call 907-277-6867. Bob Jacobs is the owner and knows these mountains better than anyone. Or call the national park at 907-822-5235 for a list of pilots, or their website at (www.nps.gov/wrst/).

When you get to Alaska, your first destination should be the national park headquarters and visitor center at Copper Center just south of Glennallen Junction. From there you can drive your car to Chitina, then along the old railway grade to the Kennicott River opposite McCarthy. If you have a lot of baggage, telefone across the river for a special taxi to carry baggage. You'll most likely fly out of the McCarthy airfield.

Keep in mind, even though these peaks are not as high as McKinley, they still present lots of glaciers & crevasses and weather as bad as anywhere on earth. You'll most likely want 3 weeks of food, just to do about one week of climbing. May and June are the favorite months for climbing. This map shows some of the many landing sites on the glaciers and airstrips for wheeled planes. Buy all your food in Anchorage or elsewhere before arriving here, because there's only a small store or two in McCarthy--plus several lodges and restaurants.

Maps USGS map *Bering Glacier,* 1:250,000, also many maps at *1:63,360 scale* can be found at the USGS, Alaska Pacific University, 4230 University Drive, Anchorage, 99508, Tele. 907-786-

Just east of this mapped area is the eastern face of Mt. St. Elias (Bradford Washburn foto).

Map 350-3, Bagley Icefield, Chugach Mtns., Alaska, USA

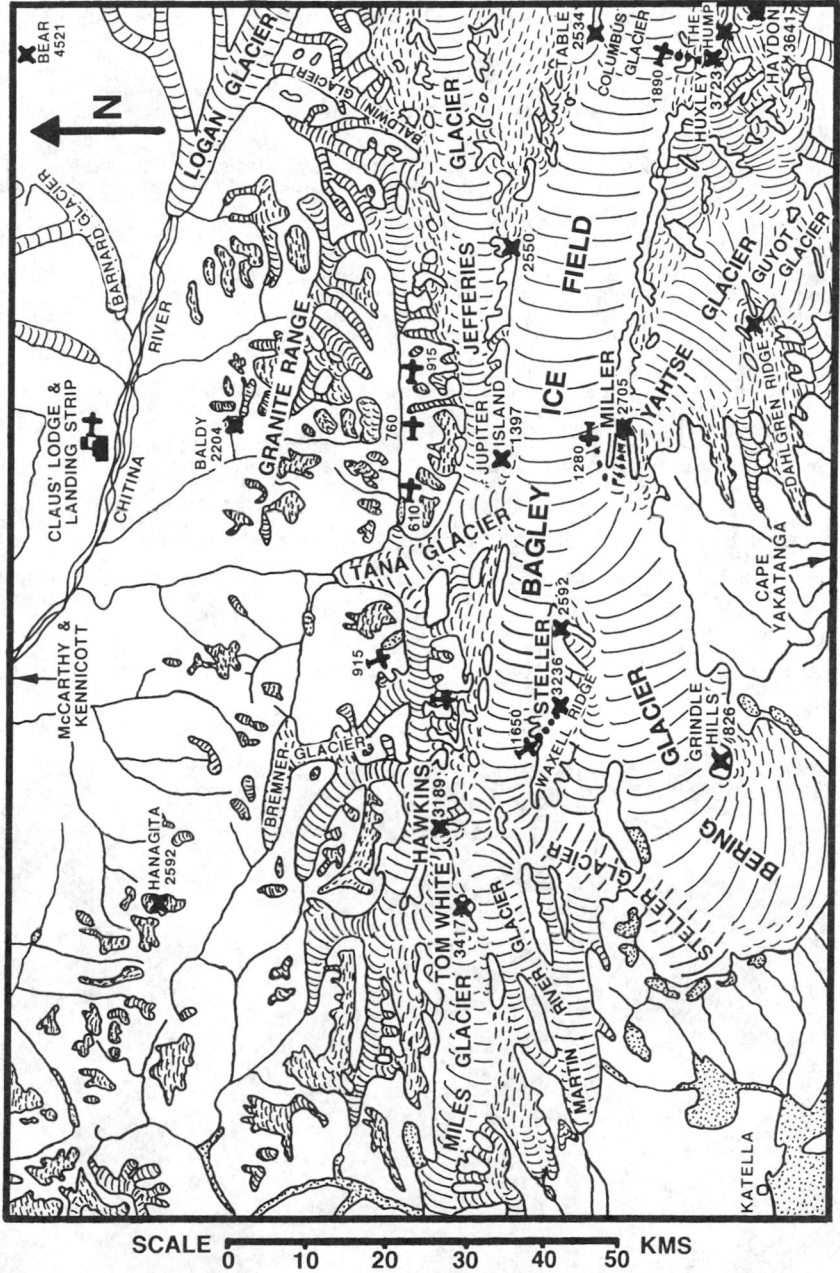

SCALE | 0 10 20 30 40 50 | KMS

7011. Or call the Alaska Public Lands Information Center at 907-271-2737, located at 605 W. 4th Avenue, Anchorage.

Logan, St. Elias, Lucania & Hubbard, St. Elias Range, Yukon, Canada

This very rough sketch map shows the highest peaks in the St. Elias Mountains of the Yukon Territory of Canada. The left side of this map is the border between Alaska and the Yukon. The highest peak here is Mt. Logan at 5950 meters. The next highest is St. Elias at 5488 meters. This peak is right on the border of Alaska and the Yukon. These mountains are not only high and very remote, but they also have some of the biggest glaciers in the world outside the polar regions. In the old days, climbers used to use dog sleds for the long approaches, but those days are long gone. Today, virtually everyone climbing these peaks flies into the area and lands on nearby glaciers.

There are 2 normal routes up **Mt. Logan**, plus an alternate. The most-used is the one up King's Trench. To do this, planes land on the Quintino Sella Glacier west of King Peak. From there, climbers head east up the glacier to the base of Logan at the upper end of the glacier. The other popular route is to land on upper Hubbard Glacier east of Logan, then climb west up the East Ridge. However, this is a more technical climb. A third route would be to land on the Logan Glacier northwest of Logan, and climb up the Ogilvie Glacier as shown. This would be the longest of the 3 routes.

Depending on the route desired, people who climb **St. Elias** either land on the Columbus Glacier, for a north face climb; or on the Newton or Agassiz Glaciers. Some have come up from the Malaspina Glacier as well. To climb **Hubbard** or **Kennedy**, land on the upper Lowell or the Hubbard Glacier. For those going after **Steele** or **Lucania**, the normal approach is to land on the Dennis Glacier, then climb one of the southern routes as shown. The pilots (see below) know where to land and the climbing routes as well.

The author hasn't done any serious climbing here, but on 7/30/1992, he did stop at the Sheep Mtn. Visitor Center at the southeastern end of Kluane Lake, and climbed **Wallace Peak** in 5 hours round-trip. Easy climb.

Before climbing, you'll have to go through some red tape with Kluane National Park at Haines Junction, Yukon Territory, Canada, Y0B 1L0, or call KNP visitor center, 867-634-7207; or the Warden's Office for climbing information at 867-634-7279; or see their website (www. harbour.com/parkscan/kluane). Here are just a few of their guidelines as of 2000; each party must have 4 members, 3/4's of the group must be experienced mountaineers, and each party must have a radio. There are fewer climbers here than on McKinley and the rules seem to be a lot more strict.

For aircraft information contact Whitehorse Chamber of Commerce, 302 Steele St., Whitehorse, Yukon, Canada. They will give you a complete updated list of contacts. Or contact *Icefield Ranges Expeditions*, 59-13 Avenue, Whitehorse, Yukon, Y1A 4K6, or call 867-633-2018. However, from about April to October this outfit is based on the Alaska Highway at Silver City near mile post 1054. Call them there at 867-841-4561. These people have a ski plane and at last report were charging about US$490 per/person to be flown into the King's Trench landing, and about US$410 to be landed at the base of the East Ridge. They'll also rent you radios. See their website (www.icefields.com) for their expanded services as of 2000.

To land on the south slopes of St. Elias, you might contact Mike Ivens, *Gulf Air*, Box 367,

Mt. Logan left, King Peak right, and King Col in the center (Bradford Washburn foto).

Map 351-1, Logan-St. Elias, St. Elias R., Yukon, Canada

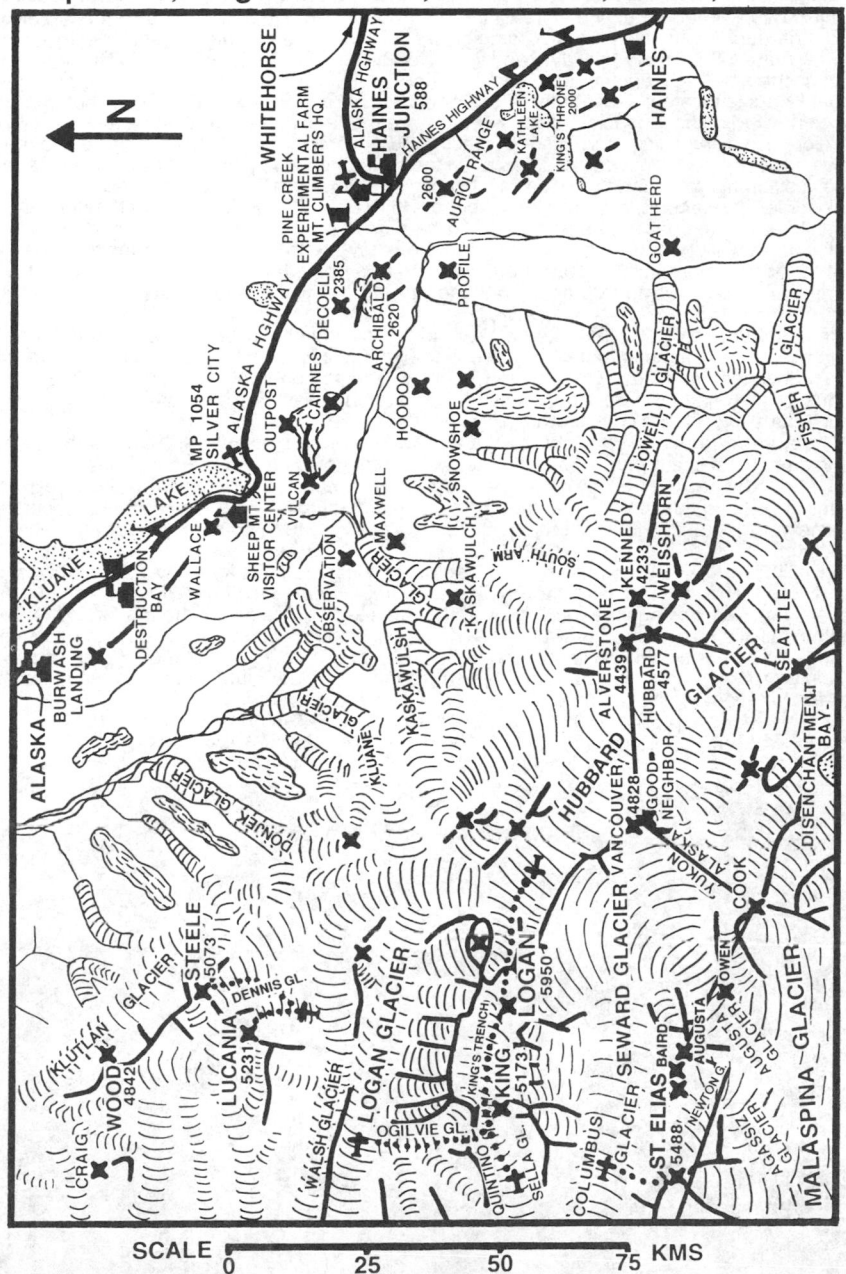

SCALE 0 25 50 75 KMS

Yakutat, Alaska, 99689, or call 907-784-3240. Be ready for a serious arctic-type expedition.
Have all supplies before arriving in the area. Most people climb in May or June.
Maps *Mt. St. Elias, 115 B & 115 C, and Kluane Lake, 115 G & 115 F,* 1;250,000. Buy from
Maps Canada, 615 Booth St., Ottawa, Ontario, Canada, K1A OE9, or see their website
(www.nrcan.gc.ca:80/homepage/maps.shtml) for a list of sales outlets.

Decoeli, Archibald & King's Throne, Kluane Range, Yukon, Canada

For those who prefer alpine style hiking, as opposed to expedition-type climbs up difficult and dangerous mountains, here are some peaks for you. The mountains on this map are very near the Alaska & Haines Highways, and in the foothills of the St. Elias Range. These summits are near the small settlement of Haines Junction (HJ) where the headquarters of the Kluane National Park is located. Most of the hikes or climbs here are easy to moderate, but generally for experienced outdoor people. All these peaks are made of metamorphic-type rock.

Before doing any hiking or climbing, stop at the visitor center in HJ. They have maps and at least 2 guide books for sale. They can update you on trails, weather and bears. HJ also has several small stores, restaurants, gas stations, motels, etc, but buy most of your supplies elsewhere if you can.

To climb **Mt. Decoeli**, drive northwest out of HJ to Bear Creek Pass at 1004 meters altitude and to the old mile post 1004 (KM 1655). Turn southwest and drive up a rough road for about one km, then walk up a hiker's trail along the creek toward the canyon, as shown on the map. From the rock-covered glacier, turn right, walk up to a pass, turn right again and make for the summit. There is a trail in places, but mostly it's easy route-finding without wading or bushwhacking.

In the afternoon of 7/30/1992, the author did this climb in less than 5 hours round-trip. This would be the best access route for those wanting to climb the more difficult **Mt. Archibald**, where you'll need an ice ax crampons. Decoeli is an easy one-day climb; Archibald 2-3 days; or you can make a loop-hike around this massif, starting or ending at the MacIntosh Lodge, in about 3 days--depending on bushwhacking (?).

The author hasn't hiked to the peaks in the **Auriol Range**, but has passed through the region on several occasions. This is an area with some trails as shown on the map. The Auriol Trail should get you up near the tree & brush line, so there shouldn't be too much bushwhacking. In 1992, there was a rough trail up along Quill Creek; but it should be better by the time you get there. Either of these routes will get you up to some of the larger glaciers in this region.

Climbing **King's Throne** is a fun day-hike for the whole family. Near KM 220, turn west and park at Kathleen Lake Trailhead, then walk west along an old road shown as a trail on this map. After 2-3 kms, be looking for a rough trail on the left heading straight up the mountain. Once on this 2nd trail, it's easy to find the way up the ridge. At the top, you can walk south to even higher peaks. The author did this climb on 7/31/1992 in just over 4 hours, round-trip. If you stay on the old mining road, you can walk around this entire massif. It's about 85 kms, and may take 4-5 days for the average hiker; perhaps 3 days for someone in a hurry.

Maps *Dezadeash, 115A*, 1:250,000; or *Kathleen Lakes 115 A/11, Auriol 115 A/12, Mush Lake 115 A/6, Cottonwood Lakes 115 A/5, Kloo Lake 115 A/13 and Auriol Range 115 A/12*, all at 1:50,000 scale. Buy at Haines Junction Visitor Center, or Maps Canada, 615 Booth St., Ottawa,

Looking south from the Decoeli Peak area at the northern slopes of Archibald.

Map 352-1, Decoeli-Archibald, Kluane R., Yukon, Canada

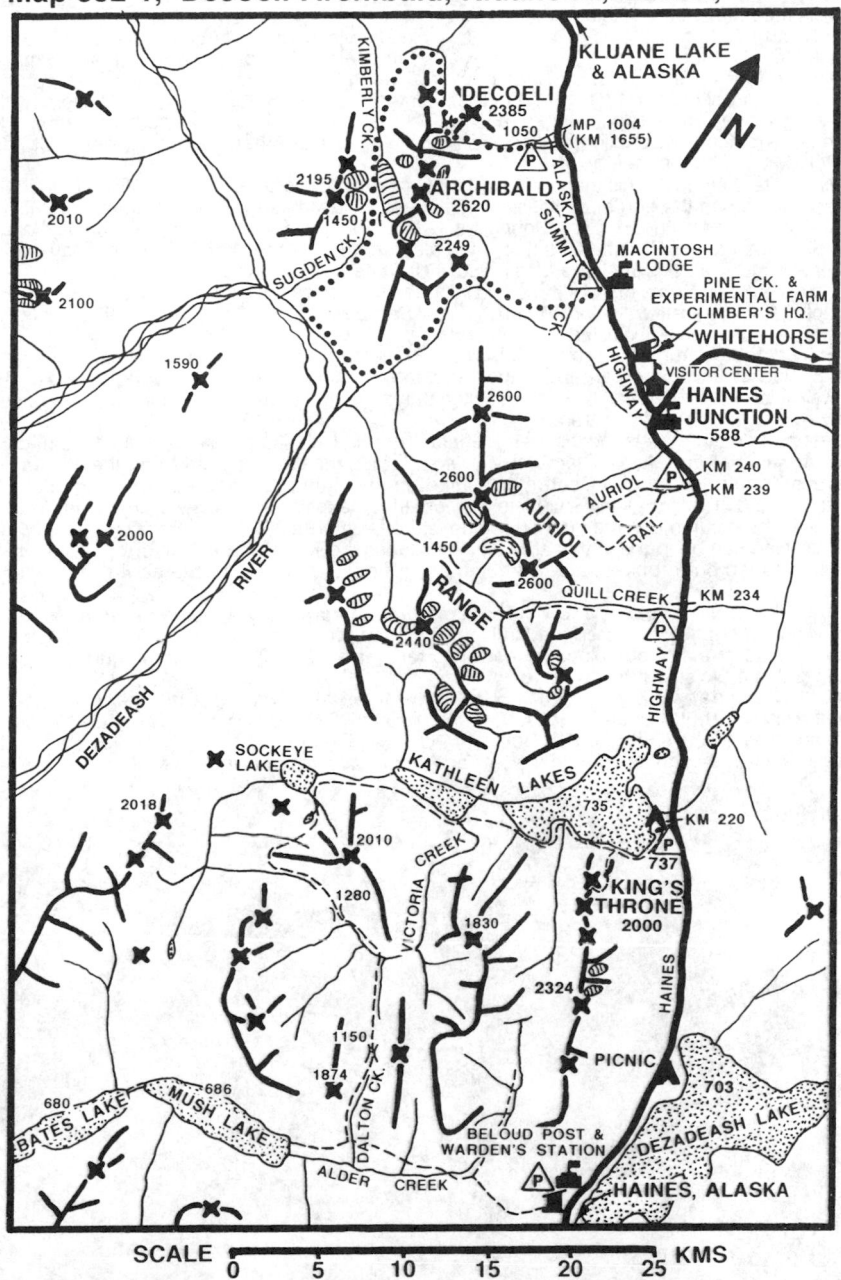

Ontario, Canada K1A OE8, see their website (www.nrcan.gc.ca:80/homepage/maps.shtml); and perhaps the books, **Kluane National Park Hiking Guide**, Darryl Bray; or **Kluane Park Hiking Guide,** Vivien Laugheed.

Fairweather, St. Elias Mountains, Alaska-BC, Canada-USA

This map shows mountains in southeast Alaska, the Yukon Territory and the northwestern part of British Columbia. This map obviously lacks details, shows a large area and should never be used for climbing. But it will give the reader an overall view of the area and some hints on how to get into the mountains. After deciding which mountains you want to attempt, more detailed maps will have to be found. For that, contact the USGS, Alaska Pacific University, 4230 University Drive, Anchorage, Alaska, 99508, Tele. 907-786-7011; or the Kluane National Park Headquarters, Haines Junction, Yukon, Tele. 867-634-7207; or their warden's office at 867-634-7279; or Maps Canada, see below.

There are 2 areas on this map which will be of interest to climbers. First, Mt. Fairweather, 4671 meters, located on the border of British Columbia and Alaska, is the highest summit on this map. Fairweather is part of the St. Elias Mountains, which is only one of many ranges running along the coasts of Alaska and British Columbia. It is also on the boundary of the Glacier Bay National Monument, all of which is in Alaska, and includes all areas around Glacier Bay.

Here are some places to call for undated information. Haines Visitor Bureau, Tele. 907-766-2234. Or contact Paul Swanstrom, at the *Mountain Flying Service* in Haines, Tele. 907-766-2665, or 3007; or see their website (www.flyglacierbay.com).

Fairweather is normally climbed this way. Planes are taken from either Haines or Yakutat, both in Alaska, to the area around Cape Fairweather on the coast of the Gulf of Alaska. Then the walk inland, approaching the summit ultimately from the southwest. Serious climbers take 2 to 3 weeks of supplies to the area.

The other main area is the **Juneau Icefields**, north of Alaska's state capital. Juneau can be reached via air or the Alaska State Ferry System, which runs to all points along the Alaska coast between Kodiak Island and Seattle, Washington, including stops at several Canadian cities along the way. If you're taking a vehicle on that ferry, make reservations well in advance.

The highest summit in the Juneau region is the **Devils Paw**, 2617 meters. Some very good rock climbing can be found in this area which includes the **Mendenhall Towers**. There are also big glaciers, so both rock and ice climbing equipment is needed for the peaks in the Juneau Icefields.

The hike to the Chilkoot and White Passes, and Skagway are included on the next map. Plenty of food supplies can be found in Haines, Juneau, or Skagway. Keep in mind this area is one of the stormiest of any place on earth, so take about 2 or 3 times the amount of food you think you'll need to sit out bad weather.

Maps USGS maps *Skagway, Atlin, Mt. Fairweather and Juneau*; and *Skagway, Atlin and Juneau*, all 1:250,000 scale, but also available in 1:62,500 (or 1:63,360) scale for serious climbers, from Maps Canada, 615 Booth St., Ottawa, Ontario, Canada, K1A OE9, or see their website (www.nrcan.gc.ca:80/homepage/maps.shtml) for a list of sales outlets.

The northern slopes of Mt. Fairweather (Bradford Washburn foto).

Map 353-2, Fairweather, St. Elias Mtns., Alaska-Canada

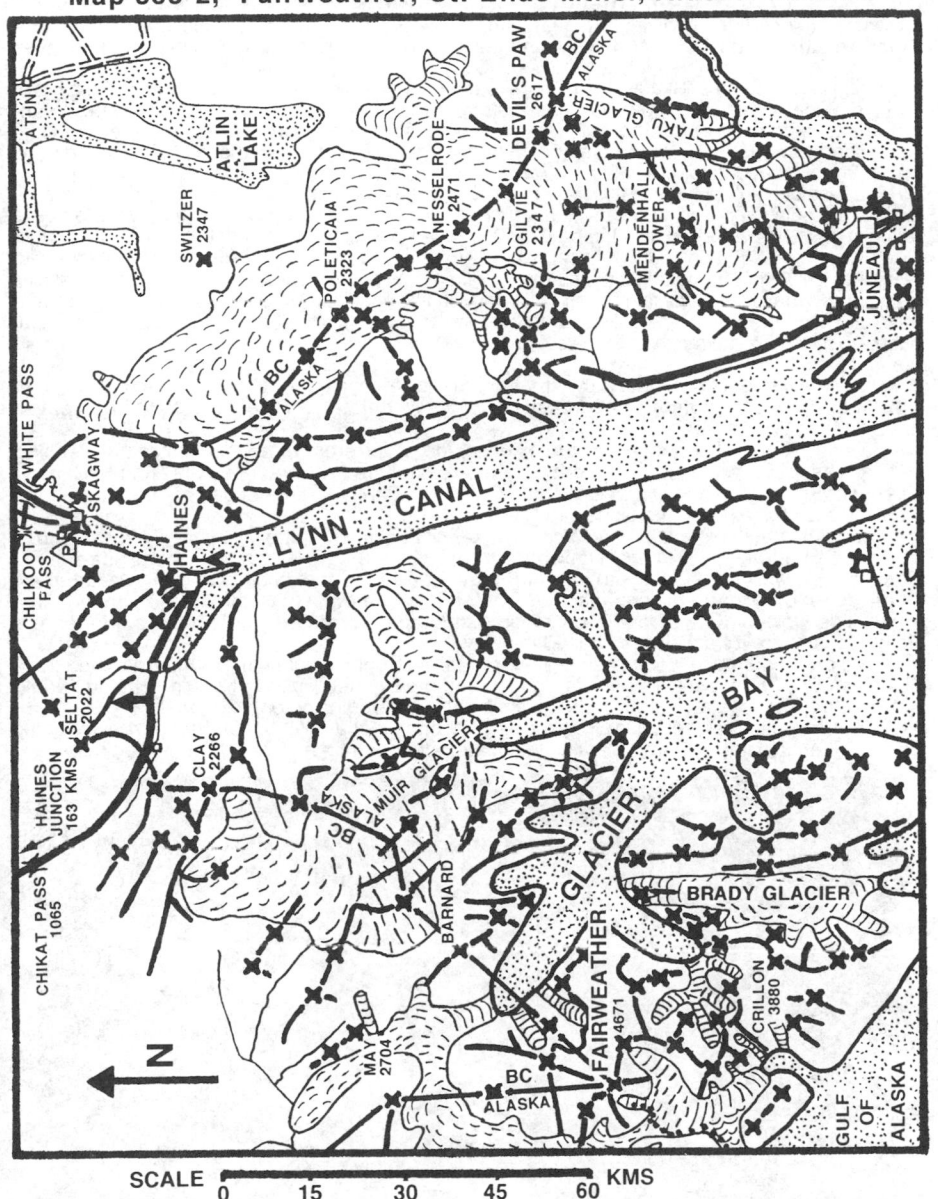

SCALE

0   15   30   45   60   KMS

Chilkoot Trail, Alaska-British Columbia (BC), USA-Canada

The **Chilkoot Trail** involves little if any mountaineering, but the historical significance of the **Klondike Gold Rush Trail of 1898** is worth taking a look at. This trail is 53 kms long and takes most people 3 days; others may linger for 4 or 5.

Most people begin in Skagway. It's not the exact beginning of the trail, but that's where you'll find the office of the *Klondike Gold Rush Historical Park*, which should be your first stop. Park rangers offer movies about the trail, Skagway, the White Pass Railroad, and the entire Gold Rush scene of 1898. They can also give you trail guides and other information, and sell you maps & books needed for the hike.

Because of the popularity of this pilgrimage, it's now under a quota system. Only 50 people are allowed to begin each day; 42 reserved, 8 walk-ins; and you must designate and reserve a campsite for each night on the trek. Expect to pay C$40 for a trip permit, plus C$11 for reservations. Within North America call 800-661-0486, or from outside NA or locally call 867-667-3910; or visit the website (www.nps.gov/klgo)--for updated information. Once in Skagway, stop at **The Trail Center** and pick up more information and pay for permits. Also, sign in at Canadian Customs, arrange transport to the trailhead, and from Bennett back to Skagway (or walk to Log Cabin). This is all very well organized, but make all transport arrangements before hiking.
before hiking.

Here's how to get to Skagway; by ferry from the towns and cities along the inland passage of Alaska and British Columbia; or by bus/train from Whitehorse, Yukon Territory; or by paved highway from Whitehorse.

Equipment and gear needed for the hike include: waterproof tent & clothes, warm sleeping bag, gloves, good boots and a camera. There are shelters (for winter use only) in the Canyon City area, Km 11, Km 17, and at Lindeman City, Km 42. Park rangers can be found at Sheep Camp, the Chilkoot Pass, and Lindeman City.

Everyone must take a tent and camp. The usual beginning of the hike is at Dyea; the end is at Bennett Lake & the Bennett Railway Station (Or you can take a train from Skagway to Bennett, and walk south to Dyea). From Skagway, either drive, hitch hike or hire a shuttle to Dyea (15 kms). Before hiking, check out the slide cemetery where those who perished in a snow slide were buried. From Dyea, walk 8 kms along a former road ending at Finnegan's Point. From there it's a well-used trail all the way.

On either side of Chilkoot Pass are remnants of structures built in 1898. From the site of Lindeman City, it's a fast walk to Lake Bennett and the Bennett Railway Station. The author did this hike in 2 1/2 days and about 17 hours total walk-time beginning on 8/20/1978.

From Bennett, hikers return to Skagway by train; or charter a boat to Carcross; or walk along the tracks to Log Cabin trailhead & parking lot located on the main highway. There are no roads to

The Golden Staircase in 1898 leading up to the Chilkoot Pass (National Park Service foto).

Map 354-1, Chilkoot Trail, Alaska-BC, USA-Canada

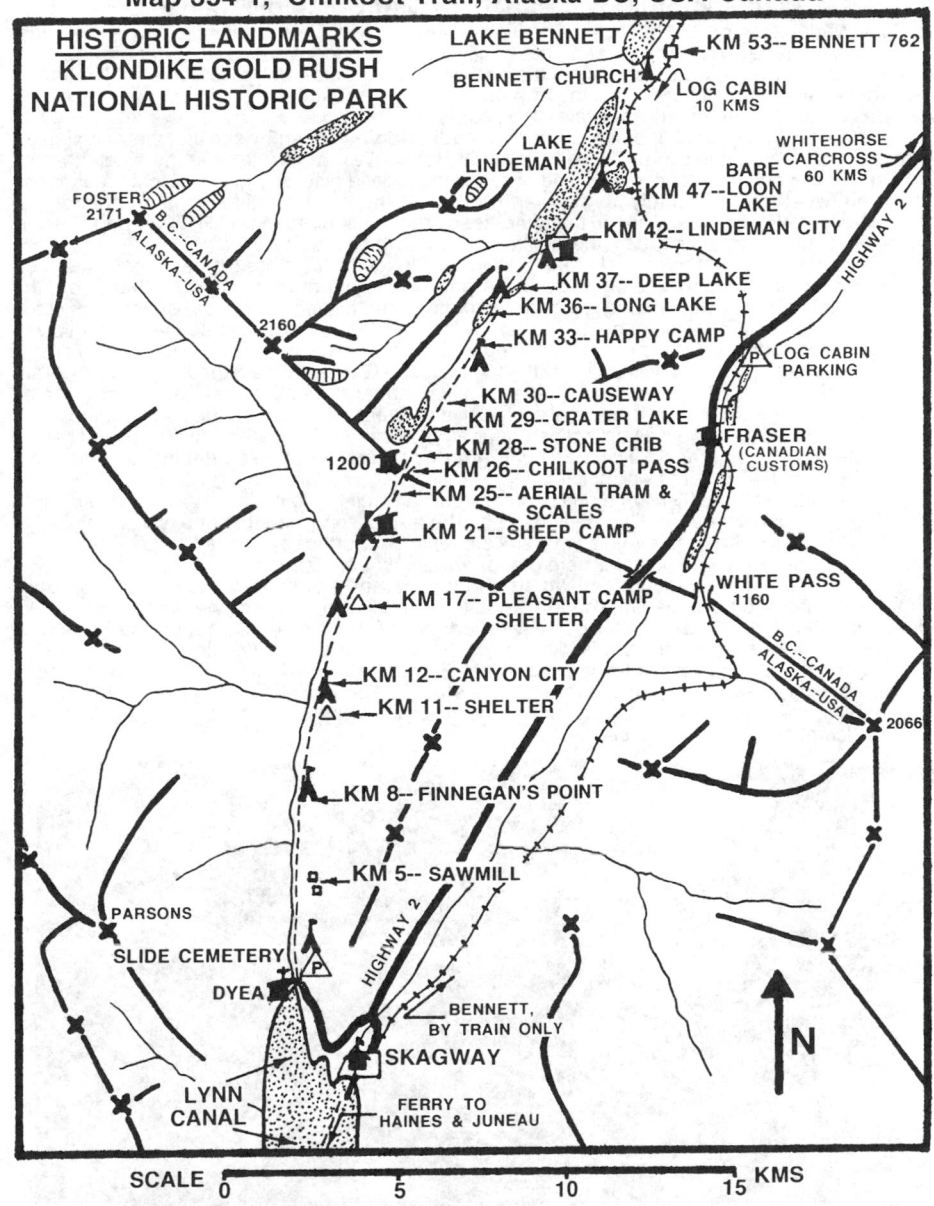

**HISTORIC LANDMARKS
KLONDIKE GOLD RUSH
NATIONAL HISTORIC PARK**

LAKE BENNETT

BENNETT CHURCH

KM 53-- BENNETT 762

LOG CABIN
10 KMS

WHITEHORSE
CARCROSS
60 KMS

LAKE
LINDEMAN

BARE
KM 47--LOON
LAKE

KM 42-- LINDEMAN CITY

FOSTER
2171

B.C.--CANADA
ALASKA--USA

2160

KM 37-- DEEP LAKE

KM 36-- LONG LAKE

KM 33-- HAPPY CAMP

LOG CABIN
PARKING

KM 30-- CAUSEWAY

KM 29--CRATER LAKE

KM 28-- STONE CRIB

FRASER
(CANADIAN
CUSTOMS)

1200

KM 26--CHILKOOT PASS

KM 25-- AERIAL TRAM &
SCALES

KM 21--SHEEP CAMP

WHITE PASS
1160

KM 17-- PLEASANT CAMP
SHELTER

B.C.--CANADA
ALASKA--USA

KM 12-- CANYON CITY

KM 11-- SHELTER

2066

KM 8-- FINNEGAN'S POINT

KM 5-- SAWMILL

PARSONS

SLIDE CEMETERY

DYEA

HIGHWAY 2

BENNETT,
BY TRAIN ONLY

SKAGWAY

N

LYNN
CANAL

FERRY TO
HAINES & JUNEAU

SCALE 0   5   10   15 KMS

Bennett! If coming from the Canadian side, you can drive, or take a bus to Fraser (or Skagway), or transfer to the daily train which now runs only from Skagway to Lake Bennett to pick up hikers. That train stops at Fraser to dropoff or pickup bus passengers. Hikers are requested to report to US and/or Canadian emigration & customs when arriving at either Skagway or Whitehorse after the hike.
Maps USGS map *Skagway,* 1:250,000; or several others at 1:62,500; but the best map is *The Chilkoot Trail,* 1:50,000?, which Parks Canada will send you when you make reservations; and any one of several **guide/history books** about the trail. Buy in Skagway.

Waddington, Coast Range, British Columbia, Canada

Mt. Waddington at 4017 meters, is the highest mountain in British Columbia and in the Coast Range of Canada. Waddington lies about due north of Vancouver Island, and near the west coast of BC. This mountain is very remote and difficult to get to. Because of the wild nature of the region, few attempts are made to climb the peak. For route descriptions, but no maps, see various editions of the American Alpine Club Journal.

In the past, the normal approach route to **Waddington** has been by sea and the Knight Inlet. Most people doing this climb will likely begin in Vancouver, or at one of many small harbors along the east coast of Vancouver Island. From one of these places, you could locate a boat and sail northwest and eventually up the Knight Inlet. At the head of this inlet is an abandoned lumber camp. From that old camp, the route heads northeast up the Franklin River and Glacier. It takes about 3 days to walk from the inlet to a base camp on Dais Glacier.

From Dais Glacier, the normal route is up the south face. Most groups have had extra food and supplies airdropped to a camp near the peak. It appears that with good luck from the weather, this climb could be done in less than 10 days, but this region is in the storm track much of the year, so plan on a lot longer stay than 10 days. The ultimate route up the peak involves steep snow couloirs, so go equipped accordingly. This is a real expedition and not for novices!

A **second route** up Waddington is via the Tiedemann Glacier. One expedition in 1975 (AAJ-1976) was flown into the area and left at a small lake near the end of the Tiedemann Glacier. From there they walked northwest up the glacier and eventually climbed the peak via the north ridge. They also had supplies airdropped near a place called *Rainy Knob* (which doesn't show up on the 1:250,000 maps). That particular group eventually traversed the massif and came down the Franklin Glacier to Knight Inlet.

As of 1980, apparently no one had been successful in climbing the mountain by walking into the region from Bluff Lake. The maps used by the author to create this one, shows a road to Bluff Lake, but it's likely more roads have since been made further down the Mosley River (?). If that's the case, the future may see more groups walking in from the north.

For someone interested in climbing around the **Homathko Icefield**, the normal approach route seems to be from the Chilko Lake and Nine Mile Creek (both to the east of Homathko Icefield and off this map). One group traversed the icefield and came out on the Heakamie Glacier. They finished the trip at Waddington Harbor, at the head of Bute Inlet.

The normal season for climbing in southern B.C. is July and August, which should be the same for this area. It's during that time the storm track usually heads north and effects southeastern Alaska and northern BC. For more detailed approach routes see any American Alpine Journal or Canadian Alpine Journal.

The upper west face of Mt. Waddington (Bradford Washburn foto).

Map 355-2, Waddington, Coast Range, BC, Canada

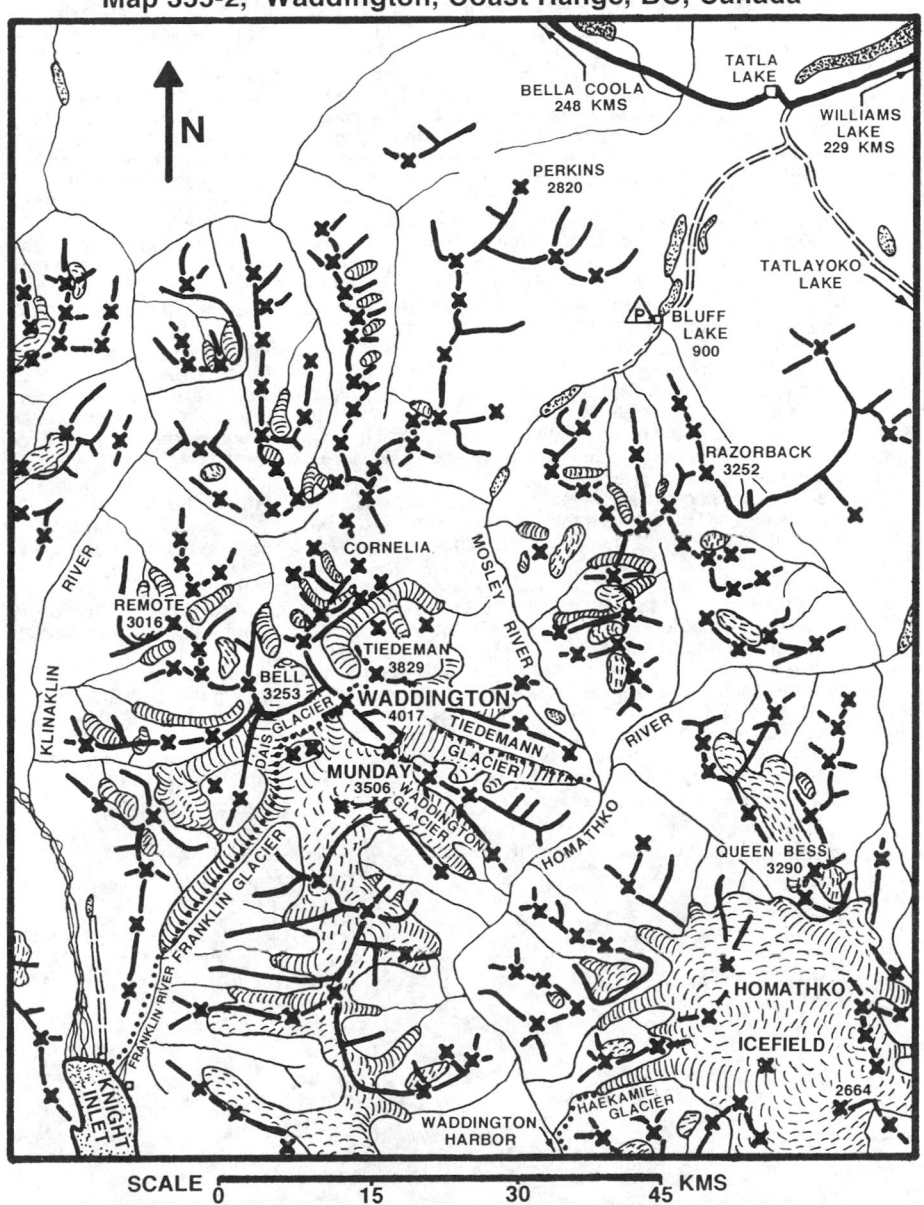

SCALE 0 — 15 — 30 — 45 KMS

Maps *Mount Waddington, 92-N,* 1:250,000; and *92-N-3 & 6,* 1:50,000, from Maps Canada, 615 Booth Street, Ottawa Ontario, Canada, K1A OE9; or their website (www.nrcan.gc. ca:80/homepage/maps.shtml); or in the USA contact OMNI Resources, 1004 South Mebane Street, Burlington, NC, 27216-2096, USA, Tele. 800-742-2677 (USA only), or 336-227-8300, or see their website at (www.omnimap.com).

Black Tusk, Garibaldi Provincial Park, Coast Range, BC, Canada

Featured here is the middle part of the Garibaldi Provincial Park, which is north of Vancouver and Squamish; and about 15 kms due north of Mt. Garibaldi. The main features here are The Black Tusk and Garibaldi Lake. This is one of the most popular hiking areas in British Columbia.

The Black Tusk is the remnant of a very old and eroded volcano--or more precisely, the remains of the throat of a volcano. Its geologic history is similar to Devil's Tower in Wyoming, USA. It started as an ordinary volcano or perhaps cinder cone; then slowly the softer outer part of the cone eroded away, leaving just the more weather-resistent throat or former vent standing. What you actually see today is a large vertical mass of black lava or basalt complete with columnar jointing. The last eruptions in this area were some time in the Holocene. Not far north of here is Mt. Meager, which last erupted in about 400 BC.

To get to the **Black Tusk**, drive north out of Vancouver on Highway 99. From Squamish, the largest town in the area, continue north on the same paved road for another 37 kms to the very small community of Garibaldi. From very near the dam on Daisy Lake, turn right or east and drive about 2 1/2 kms to the Rubble Creek Trailhead. At the trailhead is a large parking lot, toilets and an information board with a map of the area.

From the parking lot, a much-used trail heads southeast. Just before you reach Barrier Lake, the trail splits; one goes straight ahead to Garibaldi Lake where there's a backcountry campground and a summer-time park warden's station. The other trail heads northeast to the Taylor Creek camping site, Black Tusk Meadows, and finally to the top of The Black Tusk. Another hiking option would be to continue along the trail heading north to Cheakamus Lake; or to Panorama Ridge. You can also get to Black Tusk Meadows and The Tusk direct from Garibaldi Lake, as shown on the map.

The path to The Black Tusk leaves the main trail and zig zags north up the slope directly to the ridge just south of The Tusk. It then contours around the base of the peak to the west side, and finally straight up one of 2 couloirs to the top. This last part is very steep, but there are lots of good hand & foot holds and anyone can do it.

It's roughly 7 or 8 kms from the trailhead to Taylor Campground, then another 7 kms or so to the top of The Black Tusk. On 8/30/1992, the author hiked up to the park warden's headquarters on Garibaldi Lake, then on to the top of The Tusk in about 4 hours. He returned via Taylor Creek. Round-trip time was 7 1/4 hours for the 28 km hike.

Other hikes in the area would include going to **Panorama Ridge** for a good look at Mt. Garibaldi to the south. The approximate route is shown on the map. It might be a trail by the time you get there. East of Garibaldi Lake, and just off this map, are a number of high glaciated peaks that are for well-equipped mountain climbers only.

Do your shopping in Vancouver or Squamish. For more information about trails or roads, or maps, stop at the forestry department office about 5 kms north of Squamish, or in Squamish.

A postcard view of the Black Tusk from the southeast (Greg Griffith foto).

Map 356-1, Black Tusk, Coast Range, BC, Canada

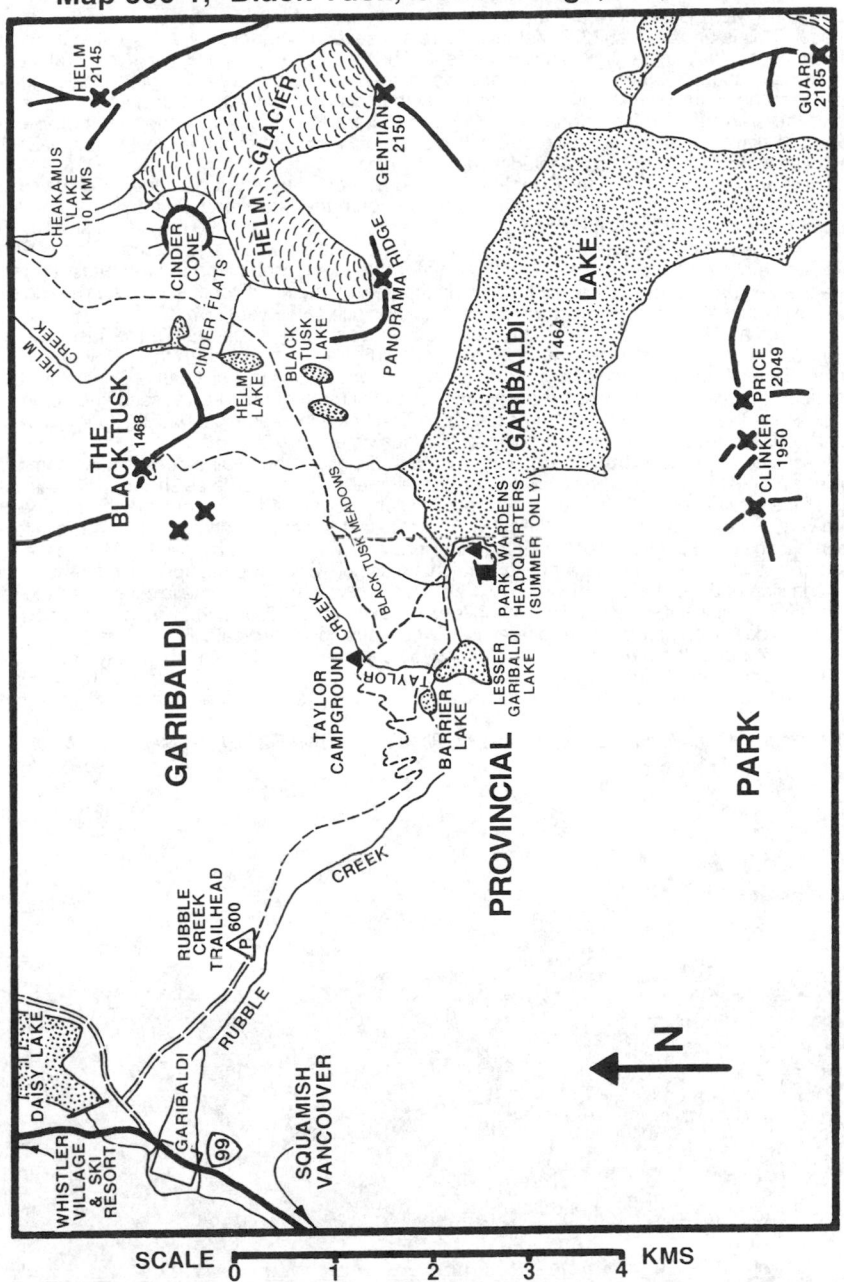

SCALE 0 1 2 3 4 KMS

Maps *Garibaldi Provincial Park map* (free handout); and *Cheakamus River, 92 G/14,* 1:50,000; from Maps Canada, or OMNI Resources (see the list of *Major Map & Guidebook Sales Outlets* in the back of this book), or buy in Squamish; or the book, **Climbing & Hiking in Southwestern British Columbia**, Fairley, Soules Publications.

Mt. Garibaldi, Coast Range, British Columbia, Canada

Featured here is the northern-most of the big volcanos along the west coast of the USA and Canada. This is Garibaldi at 2678 meters. There are several other old volcanos just to the north of this summit, but they aren't as high and prominent. The most recent eruption in this mapped area was Opal Cone in about 8055 BC. It exploded with ash, then had lava flows. Compared to the other big volcanos to the south, Garibaldi is one of the lowest, but also one of the most glaciated. This region is one of the stormiest in the world, so you'll have to be a little lucky with the weather to have a successful climb. Of all the normal routes in this chain of big volcanos, the easiest route on Garibaldi is perhaps more difficult and complicated than on any other.

There are 2 starting points for **Garibaldi**. First, drive north out of Vancouver on Highway 99 to a point about 5 kms north of Squamish, then turn east onto the Mamquam Road signposted for the *Diamond Head Area*. Follow this good gravel road to the trailhead at 1000 meters as shown. From there, walk or ride a mtn. bike up the blocked-off 4WD road for 11 kms to the Elfin Lakes Shelter. Most people climbing Garibaldi sleep in this shelter one night, then climb the mountain and return home the next day. Some stay a second night in the shelter, but most considered it a weekend climb. Near the shelter is a warden's cabin, which is occupied much of the year now.

From Elfin Lakes, walk north on the main trail signposted for Mamquam Lake (just east of this map). Just after you cross the stream below Garibaldi Glacier, head north to the lower end of the glacier. Once there, route-find northwest up through the crevasses to just south of Tent Peak, thence west up through a steep icefall on the west face to the summit. Lots of crevasses and some steep climbing near the top. An alternate route begins at Elfin Lakes and goes up past the Gargoyles to just east of Atwell Peak, then the same route up as previously mentioned.

A **second approach route** is for people with a 4WD, or someone who doesn't mind some road-walking. An old logging road begins just south of the smaller Brohm Lake as shown. It's a fairly good road all the way up to the Black Tusk Snowmobile Club Lodge at 1475 meters, but there's one steep place which stopped the author's VW Rabbit. There's a gate near the bottom end, so see the forestry department near the beginning of the Mamquam Road to see if that road is open (?). Above the lodge, the road is steeper and rougher. A mtn. bike might be useful. Once you get up high, ridge-walk east to the north side of Garibaldi, then head up to the summit as shown. This route is considered the safest and easiest. Bad weather stopped the author's climbs here on 9/2 & 9/3/1992 when he got close from both routes described above. He also failed in 1978 because of rainy weather .

Ice ax & crampons are mandatory. Soloing is possible, but risky. Climb in May or June when crevasses are covered; but there's less snow in August or September, the driest months. During the winter months everything is frozen and more stable, so in good weather, winter is a good time to climb.

Maps *Garibaldi Provincial Park* map (free); or *Cheakamus River 92 G/14, & Mamquam Mountain 92*

Mt. Garibaldi left, the Elfin Lakes and Warden's Hut & shelter to the right.

Map 357-1, Mt. Garibaldi, Coast Range, BC, Canada

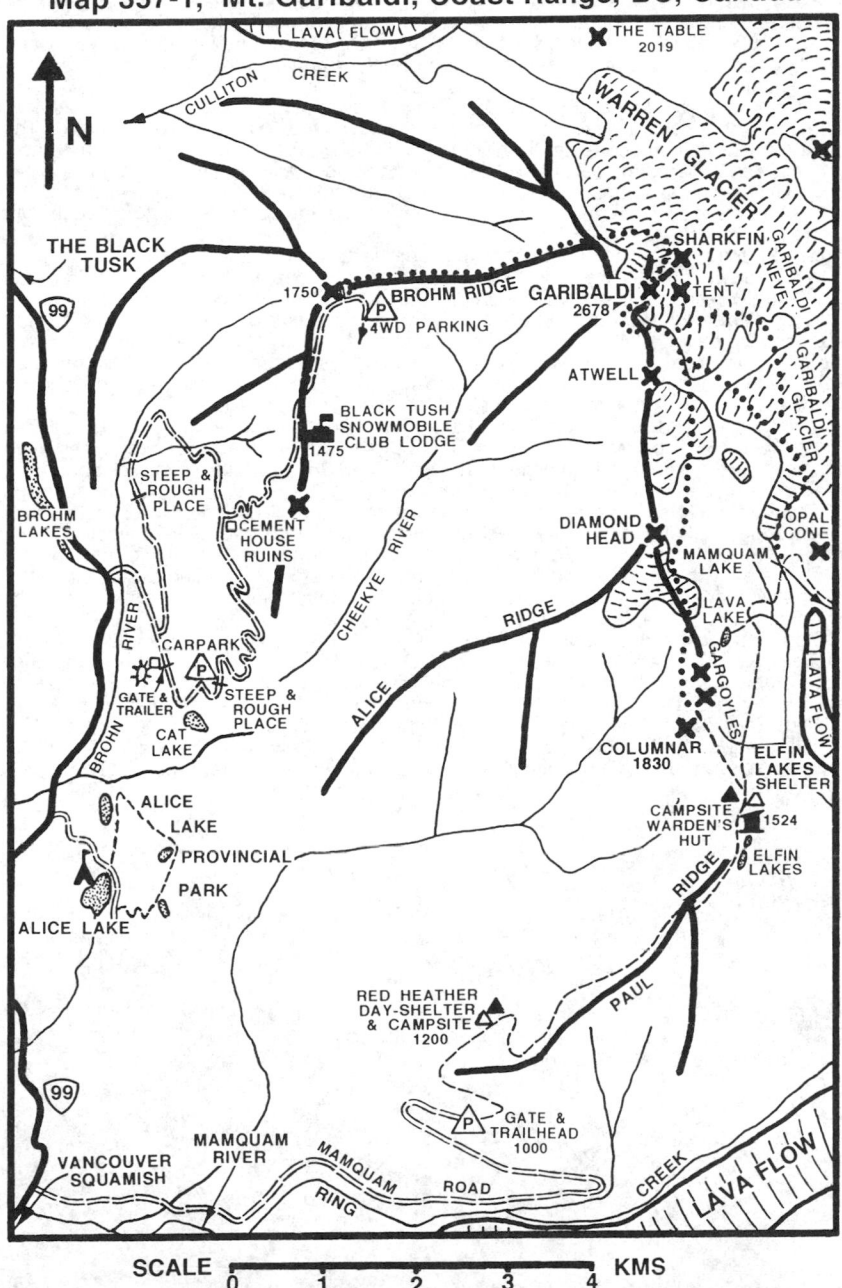

SCALE | 0 1 2 3 4 | KMS

G/15, 1:50,000; see Maps Canada website (www.nrcan.gc.ca:80/homepage/maps.shtml); or OMNI Resources, 1004 South Mebane Street, Burlington, NC 27216-2096, USA; or call 800-742-2677 (USA only), or 336-227-8300, or see their website (www.omnimap.com); or the book, **Climbing & Hiking in Southwestern British Columbia**, Soules Publications.

Golden Hinde, Strathcona P. Park, Vancouver Island, BC, Canada

Featured here is the highest mountain on Canada's Vancouver Island. This is The Golden Hinde at 2200 meters. It's located in about the middle of both the island and the Strathcona Provincial Park. The rocks in these parts are mostly granitic, or some other metamorphic or crystalline type.

To climb here, your first objective is get to Vancouver Island. There is ferry boat service from Seattle and Port Angeles in Washington state, to Victoria on the southern tip of the island. There is also ferry service from Anacortes in Washington state to Sidney, north of Victoria. From Vancouver, BC, to the island, there are boats from Horseshoe Bay and Tsawwasssen (actually in Washington state!), to Nanaimo. All ferries from Vancouver cost the same in 1992, which was about US$17.50 (C$25.50) for a car and one driver. Landing at Nanaimo is the quickest way to get to the island's mountains. This is the route the author took.

From Nanaimo, drive, hitch hike or take a bus northwest on the main highway running to Courtenay and Campbell River. Be sure you to do your shopping in one of these 3 small cities before actually going into the mountains. From Campbell River, drive west & southwest in the direction of Gold River, but when you reach the northern end Buttle Lake, turn left and drive south along the paved Western Mine Road. At the south end of Buttle Lake, the paved highway veers west and ends at the Western Mine (Westmin Resources). Lots of trucks on this road, which may help hitch hiking, if you don't have your own car. At the western end of this huge mining & mill complex is a public parking place for hikers.

From this trailhead, walk north up a zig zag trail to Arnica Lake on the **Phillips Ridge**. This trail has about 75 switchbacks and rises about 850 meters. From Arnica Lake, a less-used trail heads westward toward the high point of this ridge. On 9/1/1992, the author climbed the peak marked 1732 meters in about 6 1/2 hours, round-trip.

To climb **The Golden Hinde**, continue west along Phillips Ridge, then veer north staying on the main ridge. At Schjelderup Lake, veer northwest, bypass Burman Lake, then climb the south slopes of The Golden Hinde. From the top of Phillips Ridge, the actual climb of The Golden Hinde looks easy, but the ridge-walk getting there is time consuming. The best of climbers, and someone who is familiar with the route, could do it in 3 days, round-trip; but it's normally a 4 or maybe 5 day hike, depending on what time you get started.

To get additional Information about this climb, stop at the Strathcona Park Lodge (Box 2160G, Campbell River, BC, Canada V9W 5C9, or call 604-286-8206, or 3122), located on the shores of Upper Campbell Lake, about halfway between the town of Campbell River and the Western Mine. They take some of their guests on this climb and their guides know the route well. Or stop at Strathcona Park HQ., located between Upper Campbell Lake & Buttle Lake.

Take raingear, and an ice ax & crampons, but these likely won't be needed if you're there late in the season. Best time to climb is in July, August or early September. The road to the

From the top of the Phillips Ridge looking northwest at Golden Hinde.

Map 358-1, Golden Hinde, Vancouver Island, BC, Canada

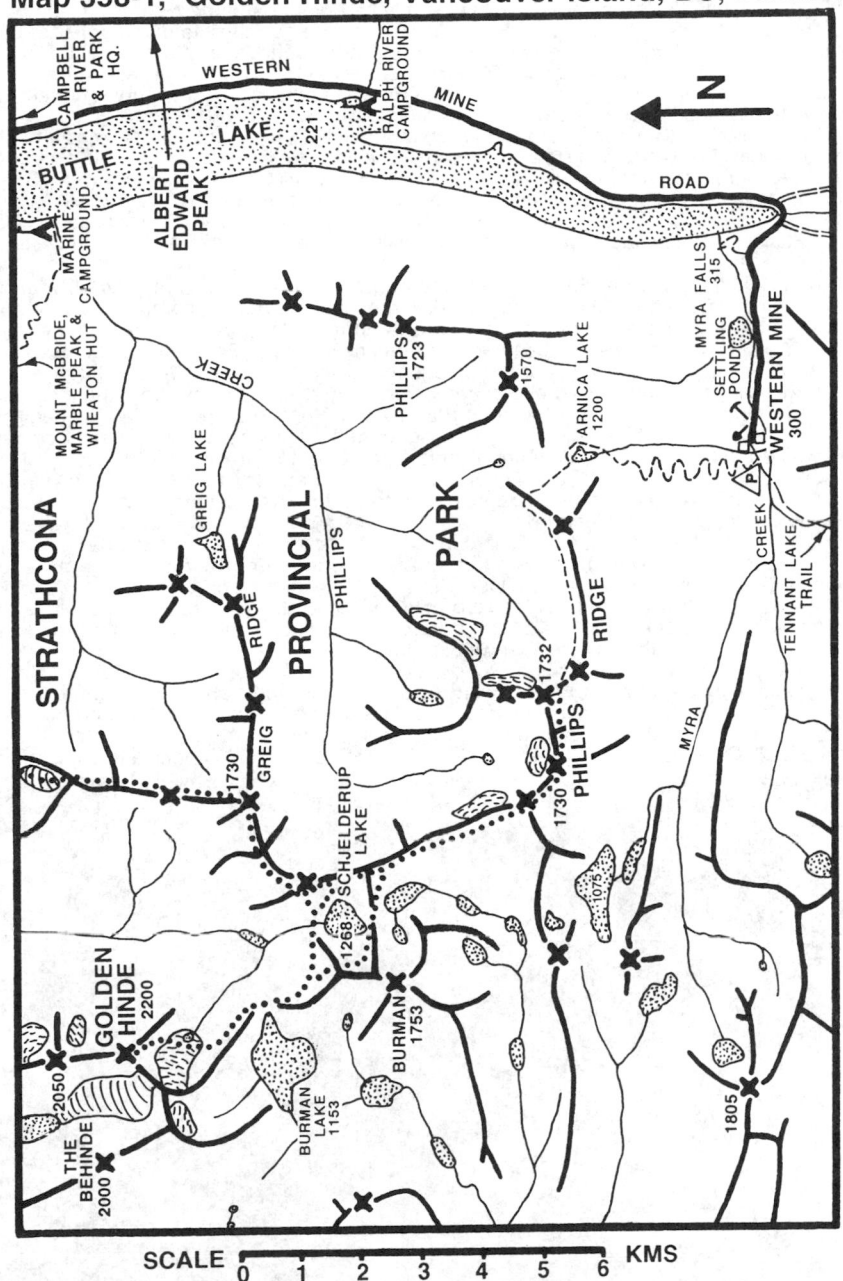

Western Mine will be open year-round, for winter climbing enthusiasts.
Maps *Buttle Lake, 92 F/12,* 1:50,000, from Maps Canada, Ottawa; or the books, **103 Hikes in Southwestern British Columbia**, The Mountaineers; or **Climbing & Hiking in Southwestern British Columbia**, Soules Publishing.

Mt. Albert Edward, Strathcona P.P., Vancouver Island, BC, Canada

Are you looking for a place to climb few people has ever heard of? If so, this might be one spot for you. It's the mountains on Vancouver Island just off the mainland coast of British Columbia. Featured here is a group of summits within the boundaries of Strathcona Provincial Park. The highest peak on this map is Mt. Albert Edward at 2094 meters. These mountains are the folded variety consisting of metamorphic or crystalline-type rock. If memory is correct, most of the rocks on Albert Edward are granitic (maybe quartzite?).

The first thing you'll have to do is get to Vancouver Island. There is ferry boat service from Seattle and Port Angeles in Washington state, to Victoria on the southern tip of the island. There's also ferry service from Anacortes in Washington state to Sidney, north of Victoria. From Vancouver, BC, to the island, there are boats from Horseshoe Bay (most used) and Tsawwasssen (actually in Washington state!), to Nanaimo. All ferries from Vancouver cost the same in 1992, which was about US$17.50 (C$25.50) for a car and one driver. Landing at Nanaimo is the quickest way to get to the island's mountains.

From Nanaimo, drive northwest along the coast highway to the small city of Courtenay. Right in the middle of town is a sporting goods store that sells good topo maps, but the author has forgotten the name of the place. Ask around for that store, and the way to the Mt. Washington Ski Resort. There's a paved road from the middle of Courtenay to the base of this mountain, then a good all-weather gravel road to the ski lodges above. When you arrive, locate the Nordic Lodge, which is for cross-country skiers. Across the street from the lodge is the trailhead for those hiking to the **Forbidden Plateau**, and Helen Mackenzie, Hair Trigger, Circlet and Moat Lakes. Take this trail, which is well-signposted, all the way to just before Circlet Lake, then veer left at that trail junction. After a short distance veer right and climb the steep slope to the west. Above the treeline, which is at about 1400 meters, the route is marked with stone cairns. This cairned-trail continues along a ridge to the top of **Mt. Albert Edward**. Round-trip distance from the lodge to Albert Edward is somewhere between 30-35 kms. Fast walkers can do this in one long day. The author did it round-trip in just over 7 hours on 8/31/1992.

A second way of getting to this mountain is to continue northwest from Courtenay to Campbell River, then turn west toward Gold River. At the northern end of Buttle Lake, turn south onto the Western Mine Road. Look for signs of the trailhead along this road west of Mt. Mitchell. This trail from Buttle Lake zig zags up to the top of Augerpoint Mountain, then along the ridge to Albert Edward. The author isn't familiar with this trail.

Buy all your supplies in Nanaimo, Courtenay or Campbell River's big shopping mall. July, August and early September generally have good weather, but always be prepared for rain. Access is good to the ski resort in winter for cross country skiing. Ice ax & crampons are needed in winter through early summer, but not in late summer.

Maps *Forbidden Plateau, 92 F/11,* and *Buttle Lake, 92 F/12,* 1:50,000 from Maps Canada; or the

The top of Albert Edward Peak as seen from the upper east ridge.

Map 359-1, Albert Edward, Vancouver Island, BC, Canada

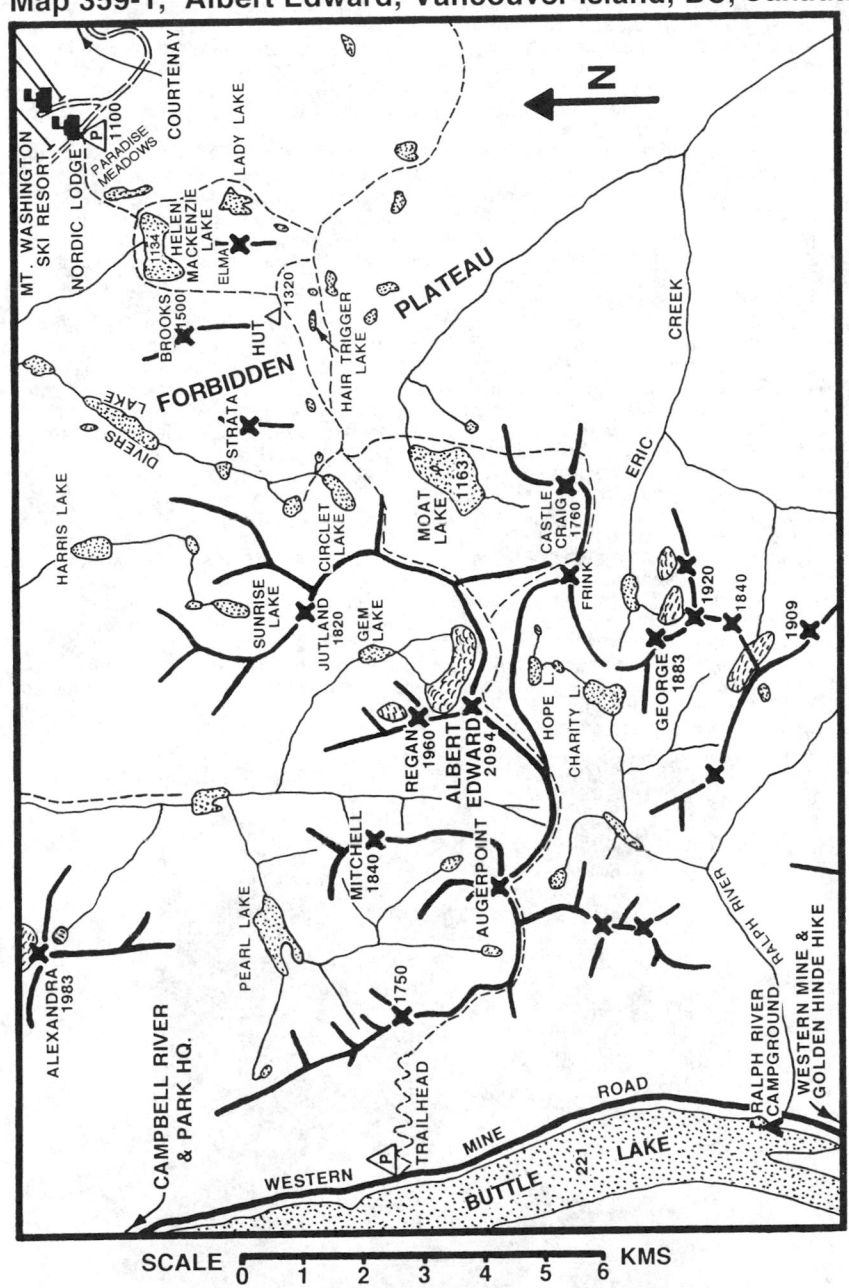

SCALE
0 1 2 3 4 5 6 KMS

books, **Hiking Trails III, Central and Northern Vancouver Island**; or **103 Hikes in Southwestern British Columbia**, The Mountaineers; or **Climbing & Hiking in Southwestern British Columbia**, Soules Publishing. Look for these maps & books in Courtenay, or elsewhere.

Sir James MacBrien, Logan Mtns., Northwest Territories, Canada

If you long for out of the way places that are hard to get to, here's one for you. Try the Logan Mountains of the Northwest Territories of Canada. They're located just east of the Yukon Territorial boundary and almost due north of Watson Lake, which is a small town but a major stop on the Alaska Highway. This massif is actually part of the greater MacKenzie Mountains, and on some maps they're labeled as the Rugged Range. The author hasn't been here, but it seems these peaks are made up mostly of granitic-type rock. Because of this, it's a popular place for rock climbing specialists.

There are 2 ways to get there. One way might be by road and a 4WD vehicle. All the area maps show a graveled road running north from Watson Lake to Ross River. This is the Robert Campbell Highway, or Highway 4. About 150 kms north of Watson Lake and at a place called Tuchitua, turn east or northeast onto the Nahanni Range Road, which runs for 201 kms to a place called Tungsten. This is an old abandoned mine. In 1992, the author was told you could drive about 100 kms along this road to a campground, but not much more because of a washed-out bridge. With a good 4WD, it appeared you might get to Tungsten (?). Check the situation out in Watson Lake. However, that old mine is a long way from the highest peaks.

The other way in, and the way that's most-used now, is to fly from Watson Lake and land on Glacier Lake, 10 kms south of **Mt. Sir James MacBrien**. Here's the name of a company which flies out that way; *Watson Lake Flying Service*, Box 7, Watson Lake, Yukon Territory, Y0A 1C0, Tele. 867-536-2231. This outfit flies Otters, Beavers, and Cessna 185's and 206's equipped with floats, wheels or skis. They can probably land on any of the larger lakes in this region; or any flat place with snow. They were charging about US$600 for a flight to Glacier Lake in the C-185, which is able to handle 2-3 people plus baggage; or about US$850 for one trip in their Beaver which carries 4 people plus baggage. You would of course have to pay the same price for the pickup at the end of your trip. If it's split about 4 ways, it isn't too bad. If you were there at the right time, you might catch a ride out in an otherwise empty plane going to pickup some other party. This could be about half the normal price and would be a good deal for everyone. By the time you arrive, the pilots may have discovered some other landing sites for wheeled aircraft. They can also brief you on approach routes from Glacier Lake and routes up the peaks.

Another outfit to contact might be *Tagish Air Service,* in Whitehorse, Yukon, Tele. 867-668-0503. Flights from Whitehorse however would be about double the distance as from Watson Lake. June through August is the best time to climb. This country is a lot drier than the West Coast Ranges, but there are some glaciers around, so go prepared for some ice & snow and a real wilderness experience. The altitude of some of these peaks is approximate. You can shop in Watson Lake as it's getting bigger every year, but it's also expensive! Try to buy all supplies in some larger city before arriving. You can hitch hike, drive or take a bus to Watson Lake.

This may be Sir James MacBrien Peak from Glacier Lake (Watson Lake Flying Service foto).

Map 360-3, Sir James MacBrien, Logan R., NWT, Canada

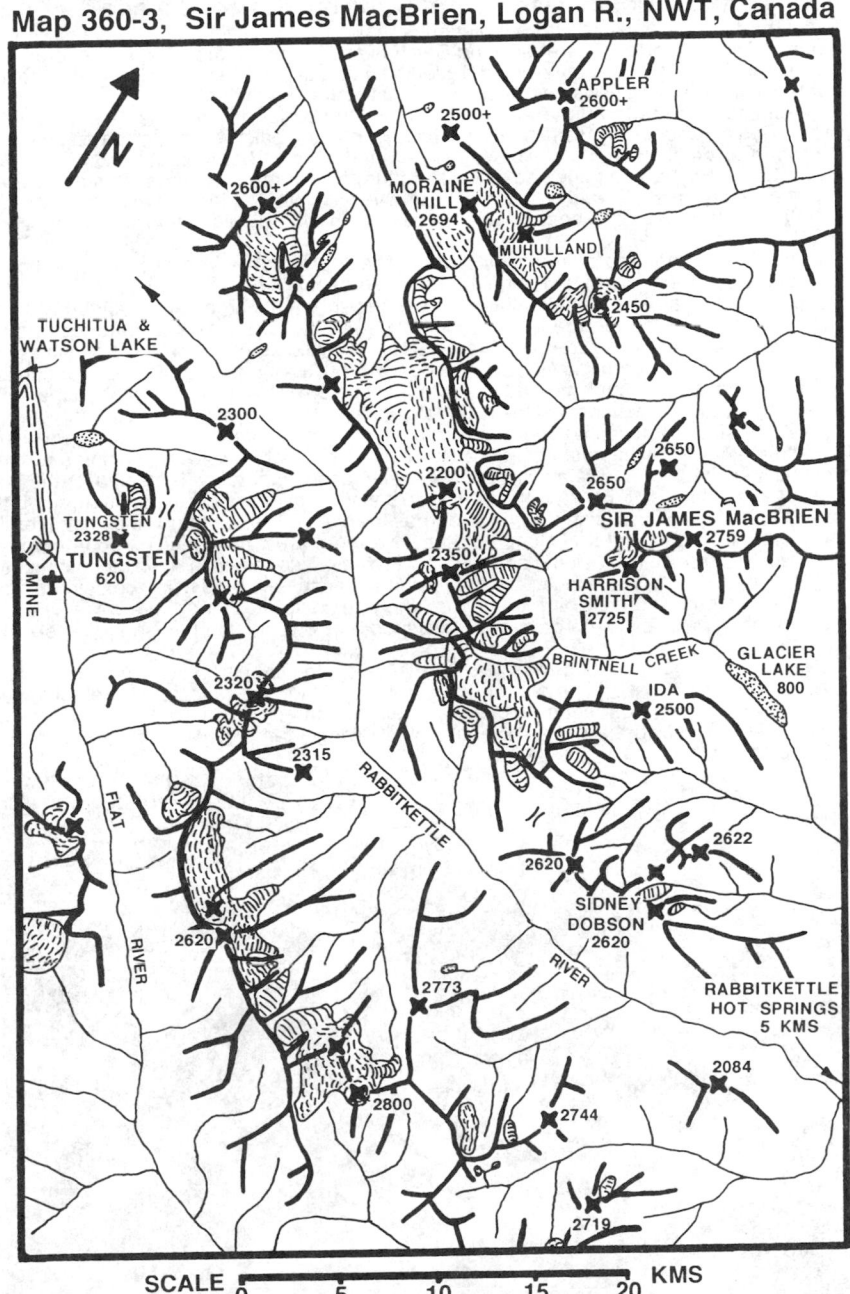

SCALE 0 5 10 15 20 KMS

Most people drive north on the Alaska or Alcan Highway.
Maps *Frances Lake, Flat River, Glacier Lake & Little Nahanni River,* 1:250,000; or many others at 1:50,000 scale. Buy from Maps Canada; see their website (www.nrcan.gc.ca:80/homepage/maps.shtml); or OMNI Resources website (www.omnimap.com).

Asgard, Baffin Island, Northwest Territories, Canada

One of the most unusual and far out places on earth for rock climbing is in the Northwest Territories of Canada and more precisely, on Baffin Island. Much of this island is covered with ice, but the coastal areas, for the most part, resemble parts of southwestern Greenland, having some grassy places, but with swampy muskeg dominating the river bottoms.

The best known part of Baffin Island is called the Cumberland Peninsula. It's here at the head of the South Pangnirtung Fjord, that you'll find a group of peaks which rank among the best in the world for rock climbing. The highest peak around is **Tete Blanche**, at 2156 meters; but the best known and the most spectacular is the flatopped summit of **Asgard** rising to 2011 meters. They're both just above the Arctic Circle in a very isolated region and rise vertically from a base of about 400 meters. These peaks have been shaped by glaciation with many sheer walls made of solid granite.

The only way to reach this area is by plane. There are flights from Montreal and other locations to the small settlement of Pangnirtung. The number of flights per week changes with the season. For the latest information on what airlines serve this area call Auyuittuq National Park at 867-473-8828; or see the Parks Canada website at (www.parkscanada.pch.gc.ca). These flights are expensive, so check with a travel agent on flights once you get the name of an airline. Your backcountry permit is also expensive, C$100 (US$67) as of 2000. Pangnirtung is a former Eskimo settlement, but is now a bit of a tourist place; with a hotel, campground, a small *supermarket*, and the headquarters of the national park.

From Pangnirtung, you can walk all the way, but most groups hire a boat or snowmobiles to get from the airfield to the head of the fjord. This eliminates a lot of walking and some wading. From the head of the fjord, where a national park shelter and campground is located, to the area of Summit Lake is about 40 kms. In the late 1980's an improved trail was constructed up the Weasel River Valley. There is now a bridge across the Weasel River near Windy Lake, and a cable crossing near the outlet of Summit Lake. National park wardens will update you on bridges, wading, etc. Just to visit the area around Summit Lake takes an absolute minimum of one week. But you can't do too much climbing with that much time, and using boats requires a limited time frame dictated by high tides, so take extra supplies and have a very flexible schedule. Also have a few extra days at your disposal. Take plenty of mosquito repellent in summer.

The normal climbing & boating season is from mid-July to October; May is drier, but colder. Tents are mandatory; take a good one. People tell the author the wind never stops blowing! Parks Canada has erected 7 emergency-only shelters named; Overlord, Windy Lake, Thor Peak, Summit Lake, Glacier Lake, Owl River and North Pangnirtung Fjord. Go prepared for wet, windy and cold weather anytime.

Mt. Asgard with its famous square flat top from the north (John Cleare foto).

Map 361-3, Asgard, Baffin Island, NWT, Canada

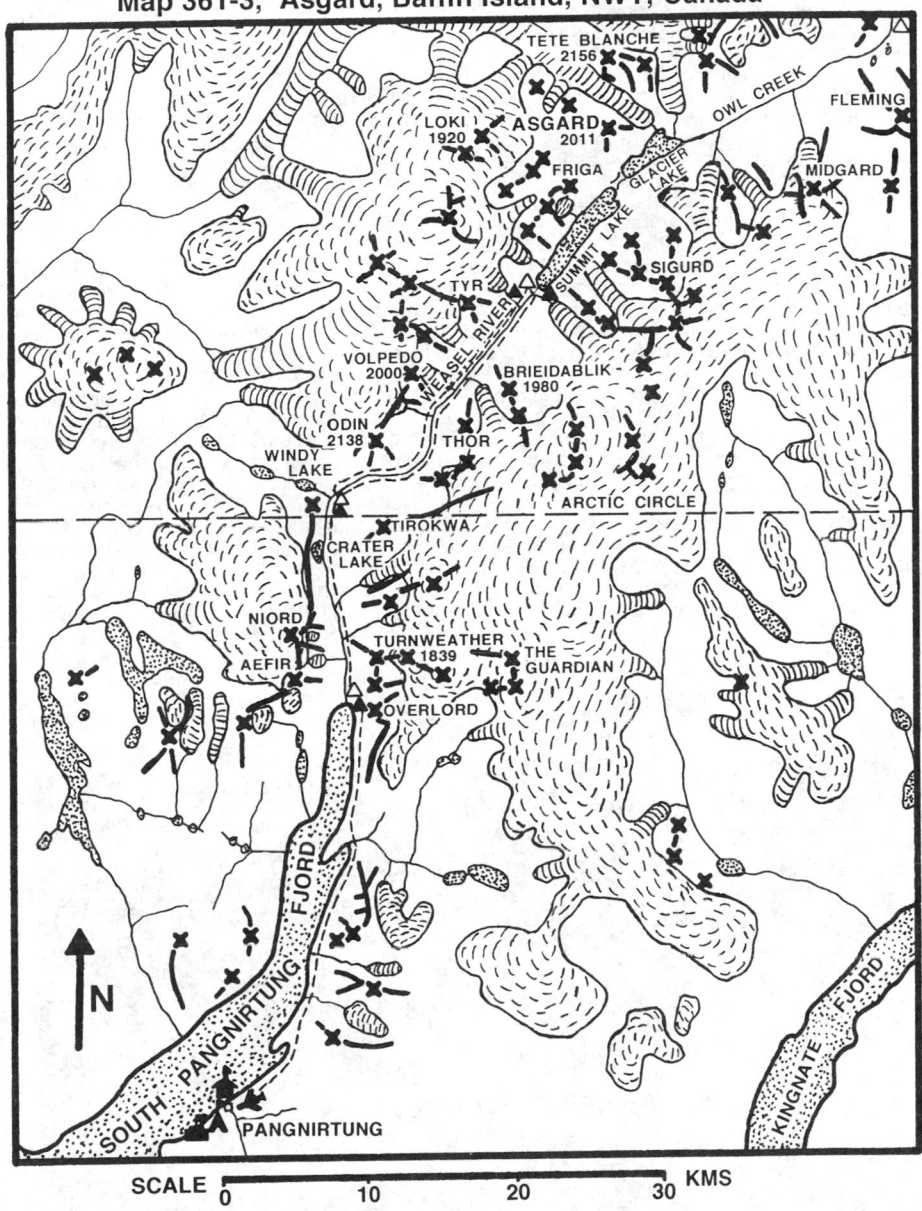

Maps *Pangnirtung, 261,* 1:250,000; and hopefully new maps at 1:50,000; see the Maps Canada website (www.nrcan.gc.ca:80/homepage/maps.shtml). Or call Tigit Geomatics at 867-873-8438, or in Canada call toll free 800-465-6277, for more map information. The national parks office in Pangnirtung will have simple maps with current campground & hut locations.

Muncho Lake Provincial Park Climbs, Rocky Mtns., BC, Canada

Featured on this map is a small section of the Rocky Mountains of northern British Columbia. This region is in the middle of a huge wilderness, but the Alaska Highway passes right through the middle giving easy access to a group of peaks similar to the Rockies further south in southern Alberta and even into the USA. Because of the scenery, this massif has been made into the Muncho Lake Provincial Park by the BC government.

The mountains here are not really high by international standards; the highest being an unnamed peak rising to 2342 meters. There aren't any glaciers in the group, just a few small snowfields that barely stay the summer. But the scenery and easy accessibility make for some interesting hiking at 59° north latitude. Above treeline, which is roughly 1400 meters elevation, it's just like climbing in southern Alberta or even as far south as Colorado. Since these peaks are part of the Rocky Mountains, many of the rocks are limestone that have been folded and uplifted.

As shown on the map, the best climbing areas are between mile posts 450 & 460. Most higher peaks are east of the highway. To get to the highest summit, stop at a convenient place near mile post 450 (roughly Km 725) where an old road construction camp used to be. Make your way to one of the stream channels, which in this area is normally a dry gully. Head east along one of these creek beds which is a lot easier than bushwhacking. Once into the canyons, you'll usually find water and can then look for an easy ridge route to any of the higher peaks.

The author didn't climb this particular peak, but did make it up to one of about the same altitude just east of the privately owned lodge, store, gas station-garage complex called **Muncho Lake**. This is just south of the lake itself. Just north of that settlement is a side road running east into a huge outwash plain coming out of a big canyon. It's dry to begin with, but further up there's good running water. The author finally got onto an open ridge, then climbed **Peak 2164** in 4 3/4 hours round-trip from the parking symbol. That was on 8/1/1992. If you were to stay right in the bottom of that canyon, you can easily climb the summit marked 2315 meters.

Because of the scenery, fishing and hiking possibilities, a number of private and provincial park campgrounds and picnic sites have been developed along the east side of Muncho Lake. It's not exactly a destination, but lots of people stop here a night or two on their long drive up or down the Alaska Highway. There are several lodges and small stores in the area, but you're well advised to buy all or most of your supplies elsewhere if possible.

The Alaska Highway was completely paved by 1992 on its 50th anniversary, and as a result, there are now public buses available which can drop you off anywhere. July, August and early September would be the best times to hike. During this time period you shouldn't need an ice ax or crampons; but in June, or earlier, you would. Most climbs here would be considered rather easy day-hikes.

Looking north from the peak marked 2164 meters. Typical limestone Rocky Mountains.

Map 362-1, Muncho Lake Climbs, Rockies, BC, Canada

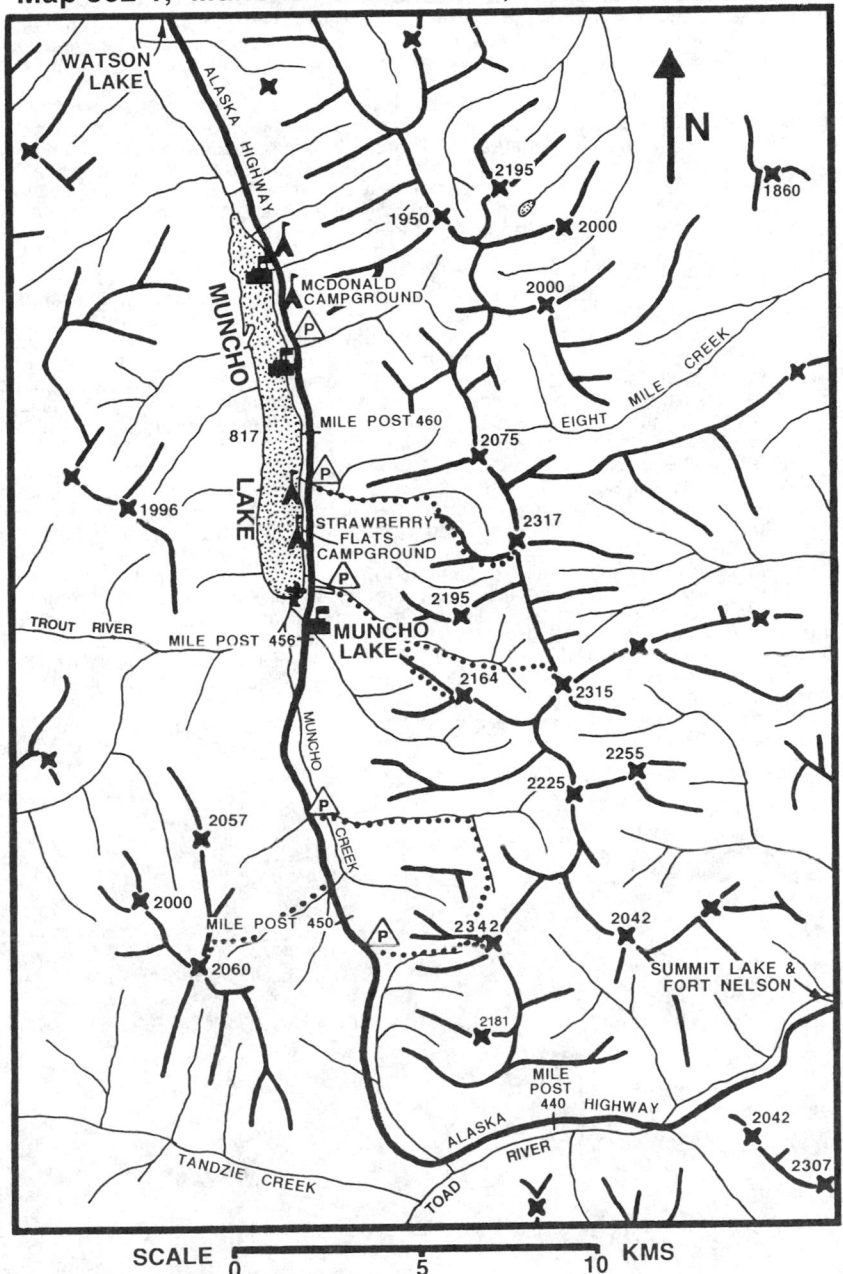

Maps *Toad River, 94N* and *Tuchodi Lakes, 94K,* 1:250,000, and several others at 1:50,000 scale from Maps Canada; or OMNI Resources, and their website (www.omnimap.com).

Stalin, Roosevelt & Churchill, Stone Mtn. PP, Rockies., BC, Canada

At about Km 553 (Mile 343) along the Alaska Highway, sits Summit Lake in the heart of Stone Mountain Provincial Park. Summit Lake has a highway maintenance shop, nearby campground, and a gas station-cabins-store-restaurant complex.

Here are some interesting hikes for those tired of the long drive along the Alaska Highway. Immediately on either side of Summit Lake, are easy climbs up to about 2200 meters. One trail heads north toward **St. Paul** at 2126 meters. This climb might take only half a day, or you can spend an entire day or more in this area. To the south, is a road running up to a microwave station. Halfway up is a parking place and a trail leading off toward Flower Spring Lakes. The area surrounding these lakes offers a number of easy climbs up to about 2300 meters. On the morning of 8/2/1992, the author headed north and climbed Peak 2014 round-trip in 1 3/4 hours. Later, he made the loop-hike of **St. George** and Flower Spring Lakes in 4 hours, all from Summit Lake.

To the south and southwest of Summit Lake, are a number of glaciated peaks with elevations of about 2750 to 2900 meters. They include **Yedhe, Roosevelt, Churchill,** and **Stalin** the highest at 2896 meters. But it's not easy getting to these mountains. A 1966 expedition used a float plane to make access easier. It's possible to fly to Tachodi and Wokkpash Lakes, or possibly to a landing strip built for the old Churchill copper mining operation northwest of Roosevelt Peak. Look into chartering a plane out of Ft. Nelson, the closest airport.

You could also use a 4WD road running south from the Alaska Highway and up Racing River and Delano Creek to the old Churchill Copper Mine, but this road was abandoned in 1992 and the bridges washed out. It starts where the highway crosses One Thirteen (113) Creek. If you were to go late in the season with low water levels, say August or September, then a 4WD **might (?)** get you across some of these rivers and up to the mine and nearby Roosevelt & Yedhe Peaks. A good mtn. bike might help, but heavy baggage crossing rivers would be a problem. Or you could just walk along this road, but crossing MacDonald Creek and the 2 fords halfway to the Churchill Mine are big problems.

Another good hike that's becoming popular, is to park at the Rocky Mtn. Lodge, then head south up MacDonald Creek and eventually end at Wokkpash Lake. You might then return to the highway via Wokkpash Creek and the Churchill Mine Road. That would be about 70 kms round-trip and take from 4 to 5 days (?). Or at Wokkpash Lake you could continue south for another day or two, *depending on bushwhacking,* for a try at Mt. Stalin. Depending on how difficult Stalin is, this would take between 9-11 days for a round-trip hike. Inquire about this hike, and most importantly *stream crossings,* at the Rocky Mtn. Lodge.

Some glaciers on these higher peaks are extensive, so go prepared. These peaks are mostly limestone, and much like climbing in the Rockies further south. Do all your shopping in

From the top of St. George Peak looking southwest toward Roosevelt Peak.

Map 363-1, Stalin, Roosevelt & Churchill, Rockies, BC, Canada

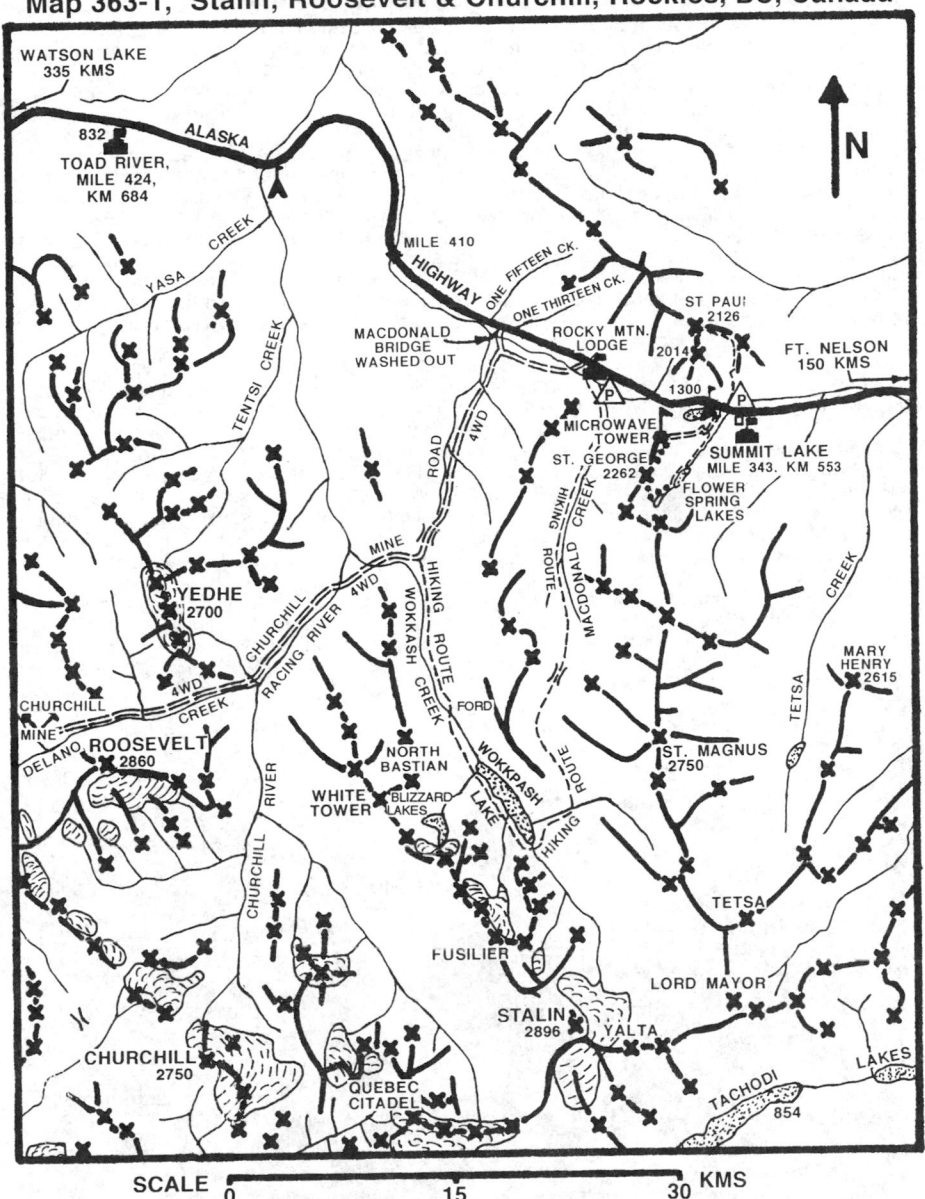

SCALE 0 — 15 — 30 KMS

Ft. Nelson or points south. Get maps of the area at Ft. Nelson, or Dawson Creek (beginning of the Alaska Highway). July, August or early September is the normal climbing season.

Maps *Tachodi Lakes, 94-K*, 1:250,000; or several maps at 1:50,000 scale, from Maps Canada, 615 Booth Street, Ottawa, K1A OE9, websites (www.nrcan.gc.ca:80/homepage/maps.shtml); or (www.geocan.nrcangc.ca/misc/contacte.html); or try OMNI Resources, and their website (www. omnimap. com); also, the book **Climber's Guide to the Rocky Mountains of Canada--North**, AAC.

Mt. Robson, Robson Provincial Park, Rocky Mountains, BC, Canada

Mt. Robson is the highest mountain in the Canadian Rockies at 3954 meters. Most of the peaks and glaciers seen on this map are part of the Mt. Robson Provincial Park, located just west of Jasper National Park and northeast of Tete Jaune Junction. Highway 16, which connects Jasper with the Fraser River Valley to the west, offers access to this park and mountain. Besides Highway 16, you can also get there by railway; however, there are no scheduled stops within the park itself. If you're coming to the area by train, it would be necessary to get off at either Jasper or Valemount, then take a bus, drive, or hitch hike to Robson Village. Needless to say, train or bus service is not good in these parts.

Mt. Robson is a magnificent peak, made up mostly of limestone rock, which has been folded and uplifted. Robson is capped with and surrounded by many glaciers.

Near Robson Visitor Center, is a gas station & store, which has limited amounts of food, but it's best to buy your supplies elsewhere. There are also 2 campgrounds nearby. Be sure to stop and register at the visitor center, where you can get additional maps and the latest information on trails, snow and weather conditions, the rules of the park for climbers, and the condition of the one hut on the mountain. Or call 250-566-4325, or see the website (www.elp.gov.bc.ca/bc parks).

To begin a hike to **Berg Lake**, or to climb this mountain, start at the Robson Visitor Center. From there, a short paved road runs north along the Robson River for 2.4 kms to a parking lot & trailhead. From this trailhead you can easily walk to the base of **Robson** and other sites in the park. This trail is heavily used up to Berg Lake at 1638 meters. Berg Lake is the most popular destination in the area; it's there you can fotograph the northeast slopes of the mountain.

High on the south ridge of Robson is located the Ralph Forster Hut, more commonly called the Robson Hut, at about 2440 meters. Its capacity is only 8 climbers, so make inquiries at the visitor center as to its condition and how many other climbers are using it. It's a difficult climb up to this shelter, especially with a large pack. On 8/5/1992, it took the author 3 1/2 hours to reach the hut from the trailhead with just a day-pack; 7 hours round-trip. On 2 previous trips to the area, he was stopped by continuous rain.

Climbing Robson along the **South Face** or **Wishbone Arete** is at least a 3 day climb, likely more. If conditions aren't just right, these can be dangerous routes because of unstable ice falling between the hut and the Wishbone Arete. The steep east or **Kain Face** is now considered the normal route. This is a 4-5 day trip from the visitor center. However, weather is an important factor and it can be bad for long periods of time. One is advised to take extra food if the weather looks less than perfect and be prepared for a longer stay. Other often-used routes are shown on the map. Normal climbing season is July through mid-September. Ice ax & crampons are required on all routes. *This is for experienced and well-equipped climbers only.*

Jasper town would be an important stop because it has a good shopping center and tourist

This is the upper south face of Mt. Robson and the Robson Hut.

Map 364-1, Mt. Robson, Rocky Mountains, BC, Canada

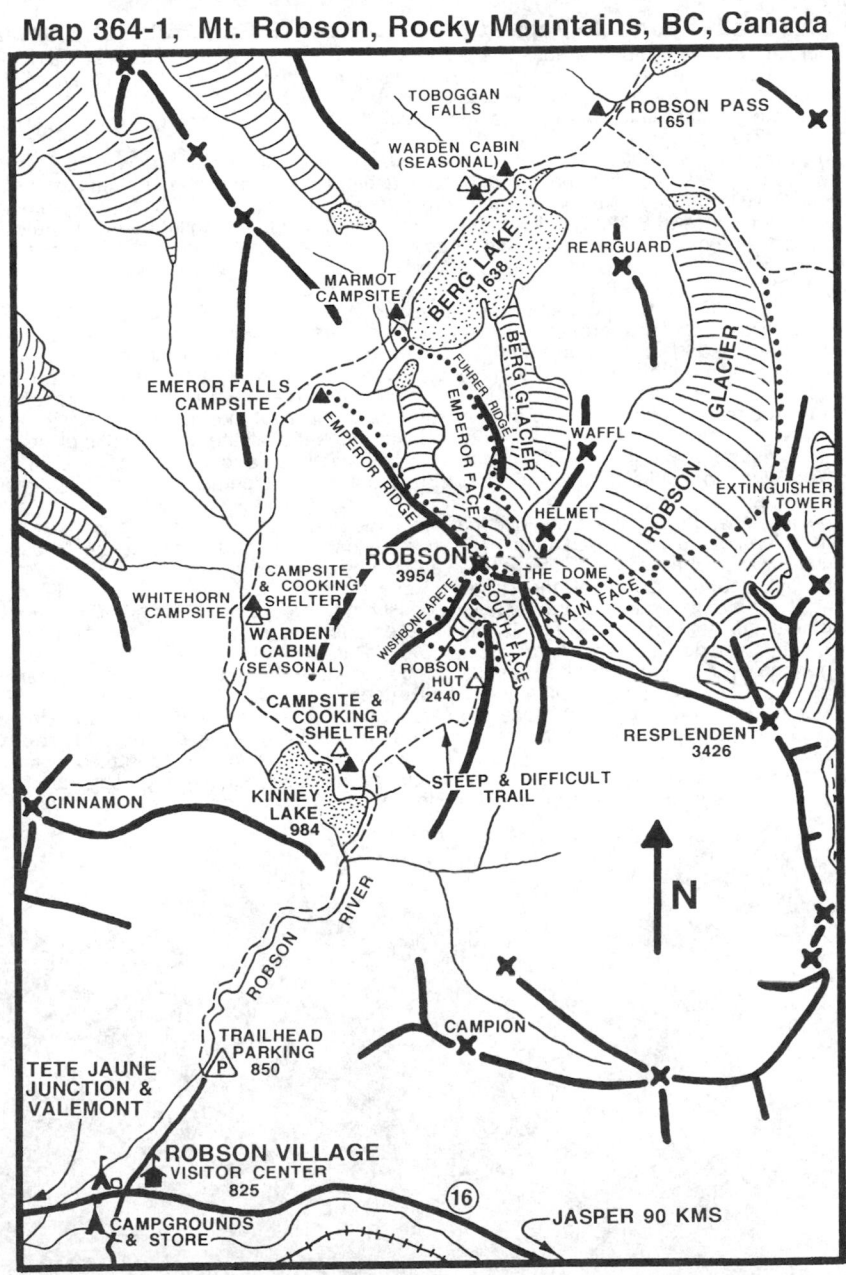

TOBOGGAN FALLS

▲ ROBSON PASS
1651

WARDEN CABIN
(SEASONAL)

REARGUARD

MARMOT
CAMPSITE

BERG LAKE
1638

BERG GLACIER

EMEROR FALLS
CAMPSITE

FUHRER RIDGE

EMPEROR FACE

WAFFL

ROBSON GLACIER

EMPEROR RIDGE

HELMET

EXTINGUISHER
TOWER

CAMPSITE
& COOKING
SHELTER

ROBSON
3954

THE DOME

ROBSON

WHITEHORN
CAMPSITE

WARDEN
CABIN
(SEASONAL)

WISHBONE ARETE

SOUTH FACE

KAIN FACE

ROBSON
HUT
2440

CAMPSITE &
COOKING
SHELTER

RESPLENDENT
3426

CINNAMON

KINNEY
LAKE
984

STEEP & DIFFICULT
TRAIL

N

ROBSON RIVER

CAMPION

TRAILHEAD
PARKING
850

TETE JAUNE
JUNCTION &
VALEMONT

ROBSON VILLAGE
VISITOR CENTER
825

CAMPGROUNDS
& STORE

(16)

JASPER 90 KMS

SCALE 0 1 2 3 4 5 6 KMS

information & weather offices.

Maps *Mt. Robson Park,* 1:125,000; or *Mount Robson, 83 E-3,* 1:50,000; buy at the visitor center, Robson Village, or at stores and the warden's offices in Jasper, Alberta; also the book, **Selected Alpine Climbs in the Canadian Rockies**, Rocky Mountain Books, Calgary.

Edith Cavell & Tonquin Valley Climbs, Jasper N. Park, Alberta, Canada

There are 2 main climbing areas featured here; Edith Cavell at 3368 meters, and a number of peaks mostly at the head of the Astoria River in the Tonquin Valley. These 2 areas are a couple of the most popular climbing destinations in Jasper National Park. Edith Cavell is made of sedimentary rocks--limestones and some shells, but the peaks forming The Ramparts are mostly quartzite.

To get there, drive southeast out of the town of Jasper about 8 kms on Highway 93, then turn west onto Highway 93A. From that junction, drive another 5 or 6 kms, and turn right again onto the Edith Cavell Highway. This paved road ends after about 15 kms at the bottom of the glacier below the north face of Edith Cavell. That place is a big tourist parking lot beneath one of the most impressive mountain walls around. About 2 kms before this road ends is another big parking lot next to a youth hostel; this is where you park and begin the hike to the Tonquin Valley, or the *route normal* on Edith Cavell.

To get to the Portal Creek Trailhead, observe the map closely. Follow the road toward the Marmot Ski Resort, but stop on Portal Creek at 1550 meters, to begin the hike to Maccarib Pass and Amethyst Lake. The trail from either of these trailheads will get you to the Tonquin Valley.

To climb **Edith Cavell**, park next to the youth hostel, then take the trail past the stables and up the Astoria River. After 4 or 5 kms, and just before you come to Verdant Creek, turn left onto an unmarked trail. Follow this south, then southeast and east into the cirque basin on the southwest side of the mountain. There's now a hiker-made trail all the way into this basin, then up to the west ridge and finally to the summit. This is a walk-up and the normal descent route for those doing more difficult climbs. On 8/6/1992, the author climbed Edith Cavell via this easy route in 7 1/4 hours round-trip.

The next most popular route, and one that's for experienced climbers, is the east ridge route. Park at the end of the paved road, then make your way on one of several trails to the base of the east ridge, thence to the summit. This is rated a III 5.3 by Dougherty.

To climb peaks surrounding the **Tonquin Valley**, make your way up from either of the trailheads to Amethyst Lakes, or the Wate-Gibson Hut at Outpost Lake. This hut sleeps 40, has a summertime attendant, and you must make reservations at the tourist information office in Jasper before you go. It belongs to the Alpine Club of Canada and you must pay a fee to use it.

There are some really good routes to various peaks in this area, most of which are for experienced and well-equipped climbers. See Dougherty's book below for details. There are however, a couple of easy climbs. One is up the east ridge of **Paragon Peak** at 3030 meters. It's rated the same as the *route normal* on Edith Cavell. Also, there's one easy route up **Outpost Peak** as shown on the map (approximate location). Most or all other routes require an experienced climber usually with some kind of equipment. July through early September is the normal climbing season. Do all your shopping in Jasper; for maps, guidebooks, food, camping

Looking east from along the summit ridge of Edith Cavell.

Map 365-1, Edith Cavell, Jasper NP, Alberta, Canada

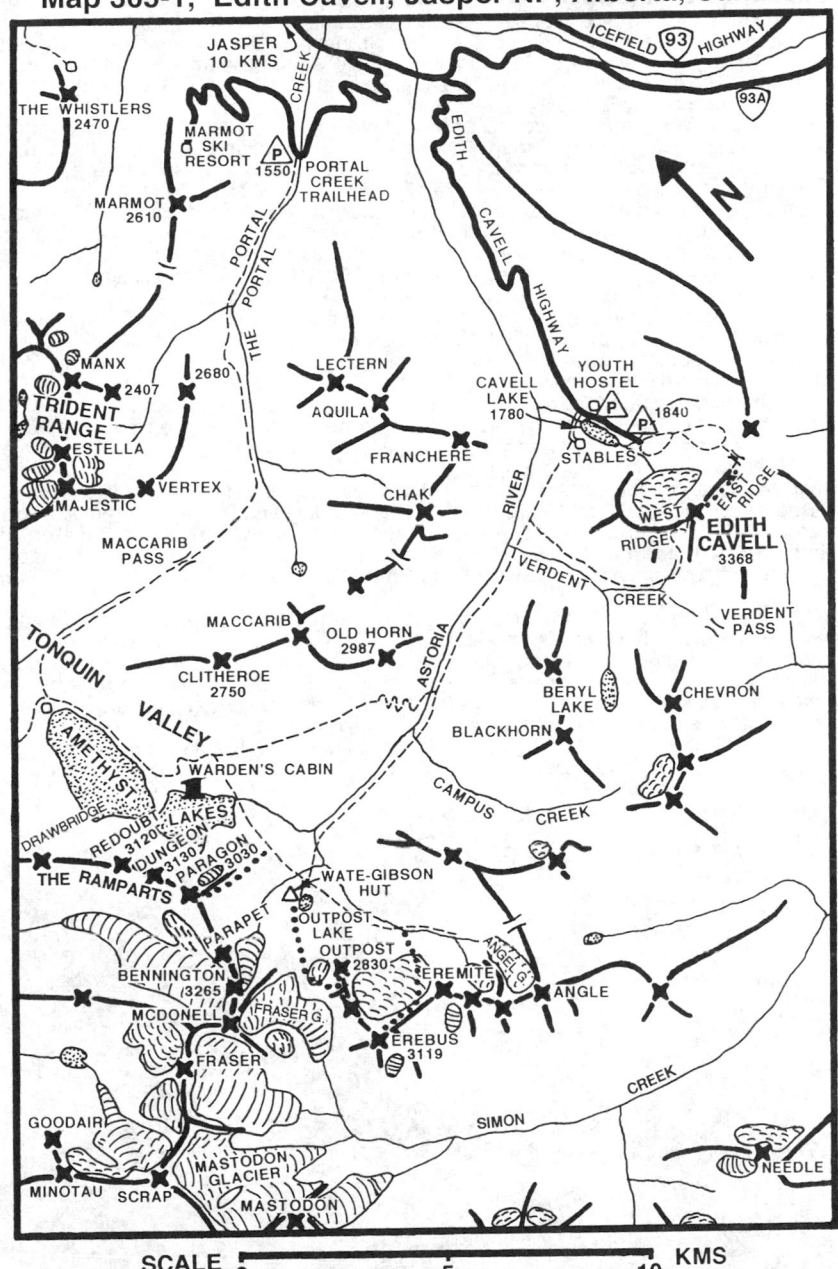

SCALE 0 — 5 — 10 KMS

permits, information, etc. Or call the visitor center 780-852-6177, or (www.parkscanada.gc.
ca/jasper).
Maps *Jasper National Park,* 1:200,000; or *Amethyst Lakes, 83 D/9,* 1:50,000, from Maps
Canada; or guidebooks, **Selected Alpine Climbs in the Canadian Rockies,** Dougherty, Rocky
Mountain Books (best), or **Climber's Guide to the Rocky Mountains of Canada--North,** ACC.

Columbia, Alberta, Snow D. & Athabasca, Jasper N. P., Alberta, Canada

Featured here are some of the best climbs in the Canadian Rockies, plus one of the most popular destinations around. That destination is the Columbia Icefield, sitting on the boundary of Jasper and Banff National Parks. The highest summit is Mt. Columbia at 3747 meters, the highest peak in Alberta. As with nearly all the mountains in the Canadian Rockies, these peaks are made of sedimentary rock, mostly limestone.

When arriving in this area, first go to the Icefield Visitor Center near the bottom of the Athabasca Glacier. They'll sell you maps, and will have information on weather, trails, routes, etc. Or see the website (www.parkscanada.gc.ca/jasper), or call the visitor center at 780-852-6688 (open May 1 to October 15) or 780-852-6177. Several climbs can be made right from the visitor center, or a parking lot 400 meters away. The closest peak is **Athabasca** at 3491 meters. From the visitor center, drive south, then turn southwest onto the snocoach road. See map. Just after you start up the snocoach road, and just before you reach the locked gate, park on the right. From there, walk up a trail, or the road another 300-400 meters, then strike out on a trail on the right side of the glacier coming down the north face of Athabasca. At the top of this moraine ridge, get onto the glacier and head up. The normal route is a walk-up, rated II, but *the author had to cross 8 or 9 crevasses; half he felt were risky.* Solo climbers beware! He hurried up in 2 1/2 hours; round-trip was 4 1/2 hours. This was on 8/12/1992. Be sure you buy and use Dougherty's book listed below, which shows the routes on all these peaks.

For **Andromeda**, located 2 kms west of Athabasca, drive up the snocoach road to the parking lot, then walk straight ahead or south over moraines to the glacier coming down from the summit. Cross it to the south, then angle up to the right to the west ridge. This is classed as a II, but looks more difficult in Dougherty's foto.

From the snocoach road, climbers head up the Athabasca Glacier, then continue west--often on skis, heading straight for the summit of **Columbia**. The last part is easy, but remove skiis on the rocky ridge. While in the area, you can easily climb **Snow Dome**, 3520 meters, and **Kitchener**, 3480. These are often done on skis in May or June. By using the same Athabasca Glacier approach, you can also climb **North** and **South Twin Peaks**, again on skis for the most part.

To reach **Mt. Alberta**, 3619 meters, drive along the Icefields Parkway to a point about 12 kms north of the Icefields Visitor Center marked 1600. Then ford the Sunwapta River, in the morning hours if possible. Use a long walking stick or pole and face upstream as you cross. *A risky operation!* On the other side, walk up the trail & route to the Alberta Hut (sleeps 6, has foam pads, and stove). Make reservations for the hut ahead of time at the ACC in Canmore, Alberta. **Wooley** and **Diadem** have easy routes; Alberta is difficult.

Climb the difficult **Mt. Bryce**, 3507, via the Saskatchewan Glacier, and the northeast ridge or north face. Or you can drive northwest from Golden, BC, then on good logging roads to the

Athabasca left, Andromeda right, as seen from near the Icefields Highway.

Map 366-1, Columbia, Jasper NP, Alberta, Canada

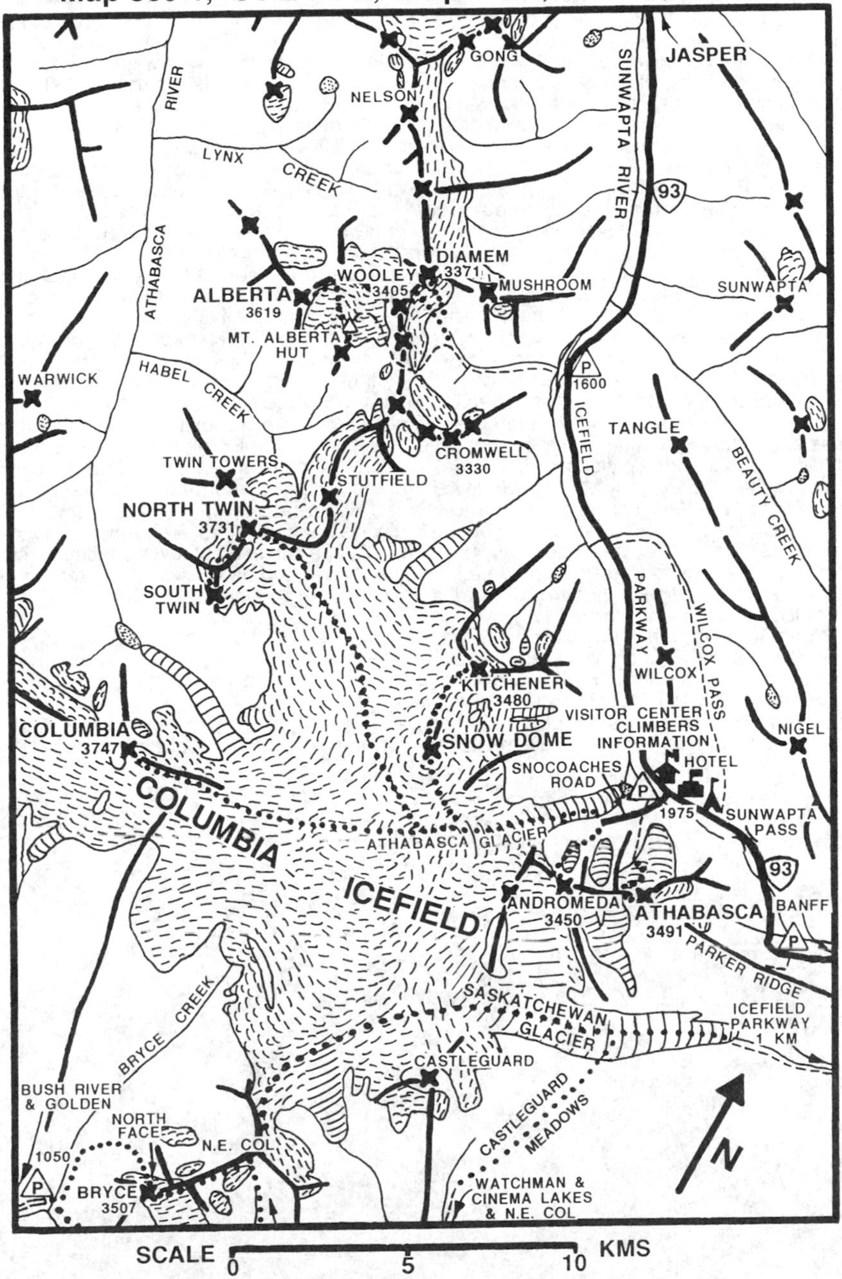

JASPER

GONG

NELSON

LYNX CREEK

SUNWAPTA RIVER

RIVER

93

ATHABASCA

ALBERTA
3619

WOOLEY
3405

DIAMEM
3371

MT. ALBERTA
HUT

MUSHROOM

SUNWAPTA

WARWICK

HABEL CREEK

P
1600

TANGLE

ICEFIELD

BEAUTY CREEK

TWIN TOWERS

STUTFIELD

CROMWELL
3330

NORTH TWIN
3731

SOUTH
TWIN

PARKWAY

WILCOX PASS

KITCHENER
3480

WILCOX

VISITOR CENTER
CLIMBERS
INFORMATION

NIGEL

COLUMBIA
3747

SNOW DOME

SNOCOACHES
ROAD

HOTEL

P

1975

SUNWAPTA
PASS

COLUMBIA

ATHABASCA GLACIER

93

ICEFIELD

ANDROMEDA
3450

ATHABASCA
3491

BANFF

P

PARKER RIDGE

BRYCE CREEK

SASKATCHEWAN
GLACIER

ICEFIELD
PARKWAY
1 KM

CASTLEGUARD

BUSH RIVER
& GOLDEN

NORTH
FACE

N.E. COL

CASTLEGUARD MEADOWS

1050

P

BRYCE
3507

WATCHMAN &
CINEMA LAKES
& N.E. COL

N

SCALE 0   5   10   KMS

base of the mountain.
Maps *Jasper National Park,* 1:200,000; or *Columbia Icefield 83 C/3, & Sunwapta Peak 83 C/6,* 1:50,000; also the books, **Selected Alpine Climbs in the Canadian Rockies**, Dougherty, Rocky Mountain Books; or **Climber's Guide to the Rocky Mountains of Canada--North**, ACC.

Mt. Forbes, Banff National Park, Rocky Mtns., Alberta, Canada

Mt. Forbes at 3628 meters, is the highest summit on this map, and the highest in Banff National Park. The area included here is the northern section of Banff with a small portion of Yoho National Park, north of Field. Most of the higher peaks shown lie west of the Icefields Highway or Parkway (Highway 93), but some over 3300 meters exist on the east side. The Freshfield and Lyell Glaciers are the largest in Banff National Park. As with all of the Canadian Rockies, these mountains are made of limestone and/or other sedimentary rocks.

Despite having a major highway nearby, parts of this area have few trails and bridges, and access can be difficult. The problem for part of this area is that 2 large streams must be crossed, the Bow or Mistaya, before the higher peaks west of the highway can be reached. For the most part these streams are braided, so with care and selection (and late in the season), they can be crossed. However, river crossings are always a problem to consider, therefore the summits west of Bow Pass and the Weed Campground are seldom climbed.

To climb **Mt. Forbes**, cross the Saskatchewan River on a foot bridge near the junction of Highways 11 & 93, then hike west up Howse Creek to Glacier Lake; a half day hike. To reach the west ridge of Forbes, which is the normal route, walk west from Glacier Lake on the south side of the stream (take wading shoes). Further up, veer right to get up past a headwall, then left and camp at the foot of Mons Glacier. Next day, climb up the Mons Glacier toward the west ridge, then ridge-walk east to the summit. This climb normally takes 3 long days from the highway and the Saskatchewan River. See Dougherty's book below for a better description.

The southwest ridge of Forbes is another possible, but more difficult route. To do that, walk across a footbridge over the lower Mistaya River, then up Howse Creek to the lower end of the Freshfield Glacier, then up along Forbes Creek. Finally, climb up the southwest ridge. Or climb up the Freshfield Glacier to **Mt. Freshfield**. The author has no information on that route, but there used to be a shelter called the Lawrence Grassi Hut, as shown on the map.

When climbing these higher peaks, you must always have an ice ax & crampons, along with adequate rain gear. Weather is generally better in July and August, but snow conditions should be better in August and September. The author has always had bad luck with weather in these parts; as a result, he has only climbed Sarbach in 3 1/3 hour round-trip on 8/6/1982. This is an easy half day climb along a trail.

Golden, Jasper, Banff and Lake Louise are the only places in the area to buy supplies. To get better maps, especially topos, stop at any warden's office, especially the one at Lake Louise. They can inform you of the park rules and help in finding the best routes into the area shown on this map. Or call them at 403-762-1550 or see the website (www.parkscanada.gc.ca/banff).

Maps *Banff National Park*, 1:190,080; and *Yoho Park*, 1:126,720; and for Forbes, *Mistaya Lake 82 N/15*, 1:50,000; and other larger scale maps from information centers in both parks; or from Maps

Substituting for Forbes is Sarbach as seen from the northeast.

Map 367-1, Mt. Forbes, Banff NP, Rocky Mtns., Alberta, Canada

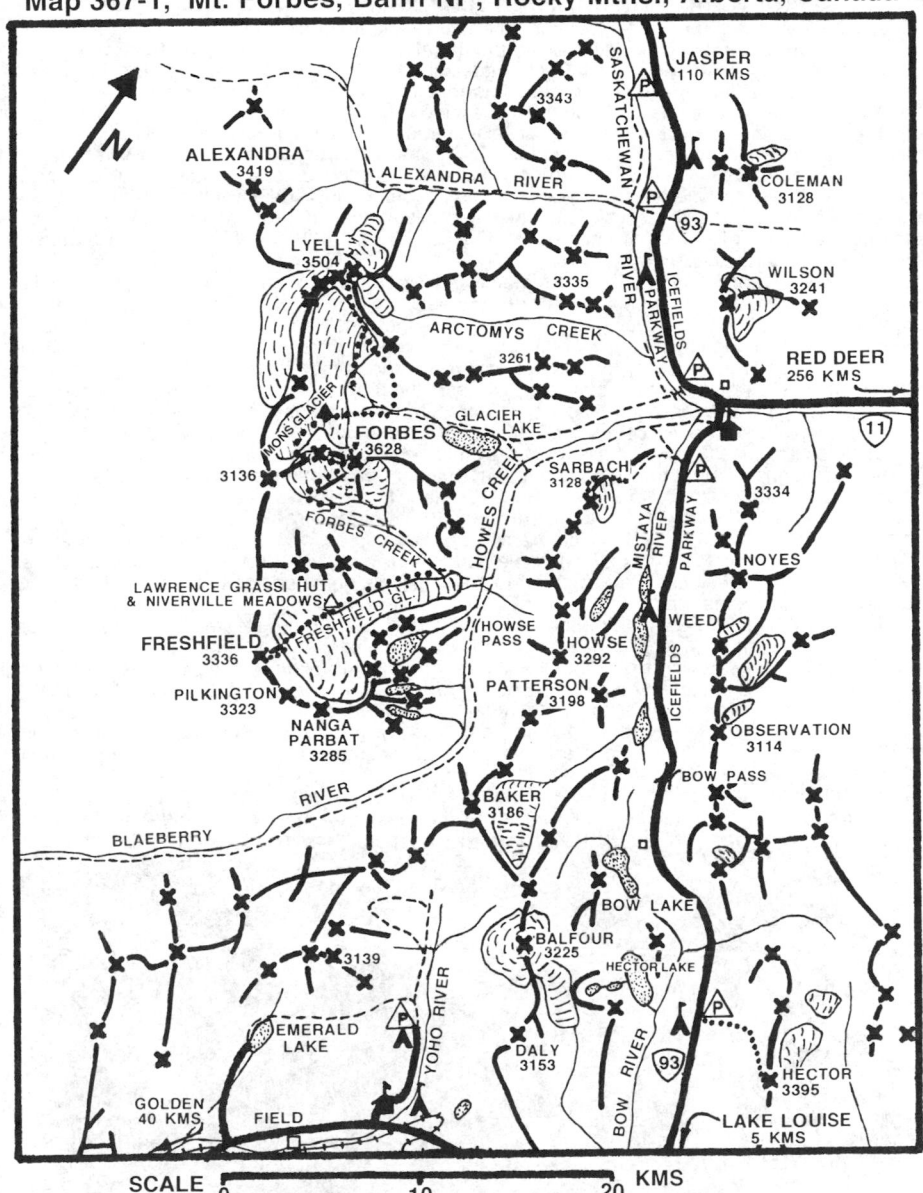

Canada; or OMNI Resources, 1004 South Mebane Street, Burlington, NC, 27216-2096, USA; or call 800-742-2677 (USA only), or 336-227-8300, or see their website (www.omnimap.com); and the books, **Selected Alpine Climbs in the Canadian Rockies**, Dougherty, Rocky Mountain Books, Calgary; and **Climber's Guide to the Rocky Mountains of Canada North,** AAC.

Hector & Richardson, Banff National Park, Alberta, Canada

Just east and northeast of the town of Lake Louise and the main highways running along the Bow River, are a number of moderately high summits. This is just one of many areas where easy to moderate climbs are found in Banff (and Jasper) National Park. These mountains like all others in the Canadian Rockies have been folded and uplifted and are mostly limestone rocks. Lots of fossils here, as seen in the names of Brachiopod & Fossil Mountains.

Your first destination would be the town of Lake Louise, situated just below & east of the lake of the same name, and on Canada's Highway 1. Lake Louise has several gas stations, a bus & train depot, book & map store, a small & expensive grocery store, and a good visitor information center. Buy all your food supplies elsewhere for much lower prices. Canmore or Calgary would be the best places. Be sure you stop at the visitor center to get the latest information on trails, weather, mountains huts, etc., before hiking. Their telefon number is 403-522-3833 or 403-762-1550 and/or the website (www.parkscanada.gc.ca/banff).

Perhaps the best known peak on this map is **Mt. Hector** at 3494 meters. Drive or hitch hike north from Lake Louise to a point just north and east of Hector Lake. On the east side of the highway is a small stream coming down from the east called Hector Creek. There's a trail-of-sorts running up along the south side of it. Use this to get up through the forest. Once above all the brush, make your own way up a minor northwest and north ridge; or up the gently sloping north glacier. This glacier route is an easy climb in summer, as well as a popular ski ascent in winter. If using the glacier route, take ice ax & crampons and beware of crevasses. The author climbed Hector in the 1970's, but can't remember which summer.

Because it's close to Lake Louise, the area just northwest of the town is very popular for day-hikes, and climbs. To get there, drive east out of town and above the freeway overpass, then continue east and north toward the Ski Lake Louise Resort. This is about 2-3 kms from the visitor center. Just before the ski lodge, turn east on the Fish Creek Road. After another km, park at the Fish Creek Trailhead, as car traffic is not allowed beyond that point. From there hike or mtn. bike 4 kms up the road to the Temple Lodge, which is part of the ski resort. From there, it's hiking only on a well-used trail. Some foot traffic on this path goes on to the Skoki Lodge, 13 kms from the end of the road.

Three or 4 kms from Temple Lodge, is the Halfway Hut on the right which anyone can use without permission or paying a fee. First come, first served. At that point take a trail north toward Hidden Lake, which sits just below 3 peaks. To climb **Richardson**, head left from just above the lake and make your way to the south ridge. You'll have to route-find up through the ledges, but it's a trail-of-sorts right up to the summit. The author did this climb on 8/13/1992 in 5 3/4 hours round-trip. From Hidden Lake, you can also climb **Pika** and **Ptarmigan Peaks**. From the top of any of these, you'll have a fine view of Lake Louise and the peaks of Temple and Victoria to the west.

Other high summits in the area, but unknown to the author, are Mts. Douglas, St. Bride, and further north, Cataract Peak at 3334 meters. See Kane's book below for some of these hikes.

This is Halfway Hut looking north at Richardson left, Ptarmigan right.

Map 368-1, Hector-Richardson, Banff NP, Alberta, Canada

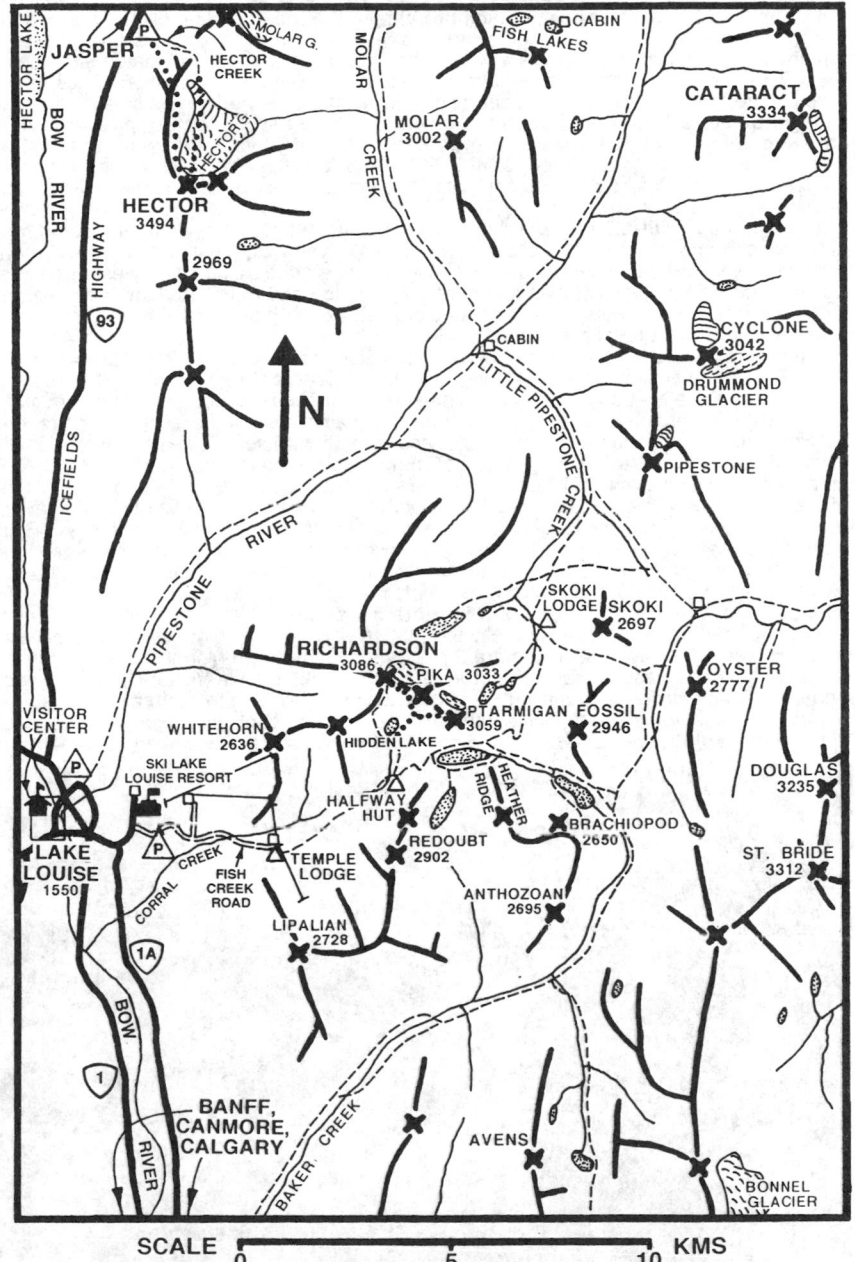

JASPER

HECTOR LAKE

BOW RIVER

P

MOLAR G.

HECTOR CREEK

HECTOR G.

HECTOR
3494

2969

HIGHWAY

93

ICEFIELDS

N

MOLAR CREEK

MOLAR
3002

CABIN

FISH LAKES

CABIN

LITTLE PIPESTONE CREEK

RIVER

PIPESTONE

CATARACT
3334

CYCLONE
3042

DRUMMOND GLACIER

PIPESTONE

SKOKI LODGE

SKOKI
2697

OYSTER
2777

RICHARDSON
3086

PIKA 3033

PTARMIGAN FOSSIL
3059   2946

VISITOR CENTER

P

WHITEHORN
2636

SKI LAKE LOUISE RESORT

HIDDEN LAKE

HALFWAY HUT

HEATHER RIDGE

DOUGLAS
3235

BRACHIOPOD
2650

LAKE LOUISE
1550

P

CORRAL CREEK

FISH CREEK ROAD

TEMPLE LODGE

REDOUBT
2902

ANTHOZOAN
2695

ST. BRIDE
3312

1A

LIPALIAN
2728

BOW

1

RIVER

BANFF, CANMORE, CALGARY

BAKER CREEK

AVENS

BONNEL GLACIER

SCALE   0   5   10   KMS

Best months for climbing are July through September.
Maps *Banff National Park,* 1:200,000; and/or *Lake Louise, 82 N/8, Hector Lake 82 N/9, and 82 0/5 & 82 0-12,* 1:50,000, from Maps Canada; and the books, **Scrambles in the Canadian Rockies**, Kane; and **Selected Alpine Climbs in the Canadian Rockies**, both from Rocky Mountain Books, Calgary.

Victoria, Temple & Ten Peaks, Banff NP, Rocky Mtns., Alberta, Canada

This map has 2 groups of peaks which are among the most popular climbing areas in the Canadian Rockies. One group surrounds Lake Louise and involves some of the most fotographed mountain scenes anywhere. The other is just to the south and features Mt. Temple, Valley of The Ten Peaks and Moraine Lake. To get there, your first destination will be the town of Lake Louise, which is situated on Canada's Highway 1. Lake Louise is a small town and an expensive place, so do your shopping elsewhere if you can. Located in town is a large information center and nearby book & map shop, both of which you'll want to visit before climbing. Contact the visitor center at 403-522-3833, or 403-762-1550, or see the website (www.parkscanada.gc.ca/banff). You can get to this place by car, bus, and train. Hitch hiking in these parts appears very slow.

There are many difficult routes in this region, but also some easy climbs up some tough-looking peaks. First, from the town of Lake Louise, make your way up to the valley holding Lake Louise itself and the majestic hotel or chateau. Locate the trail running west up the valley along the north side of the lake, then another trail going to Lake Agnes and the teahouse there. From Agnes, head up the valley southwest to a col between **Niblock** and **Whyte**. From the col, climb either peak, both of which are nearly walk-ups.

Or, from the chateau, head up the Valley of Six Glaciers toward **Mt. Victoria**, 3464 meters. At the head of the valley you'll pass through the *Death Trap* before you reach the Abbot Hut; apparently this route isn't as dangerous as it used to be (?). Because of this risky avalanche corridor, most climbers head for Lake O'Hara via Highway 1 and Cataract Brook, and reach the Abbot Hut from there. From O'Hara, to the hut and summit of Victoria is nearly a walk-up. It can be climbed in one long day from O'Hara, but many people make reservations at the ACC in Canmore and stay in the Abbot Hut one night. This hut has a guardian and sleeps 32, for a fee.

To climb **Mt. Temple** at 3543 meters, head south from Lake Louise to Moraine Lake and The Valley of Ten Peaks. From the lodge, locate the trail to Larch Valley and Sentinel Pass. Right at this pass, veer right or east and walk a well-used hiker's trail running up the southwest ridge to the top. The author's round-trip time from Moraine Lake on 8/7/1992 was just over 5 hours. It's a real easy walk-up, but other routes up the mountain are as tough as any around.

South & west of Moraine Lake is a mountain wall called **The Ten Peaks**. The first destination for serious climbers is normally the ACC *Neil Colgan Hut*, on the ridge between Mt. Little and Bowlen; it sleeps 24. There are 2 routes to this hut from Moraine Lake, but with big packs, neither is real easy, so talk to the rangers at the Lake Louise Visitor Center, or consult Dougherty's book below. From this hut, you'll be in a good position to climb all, or most, of the Ten Summits. Most routes are up the southern slopes of each peak, which can also be reached from the south and Prospectors Valley and the Banff-Windermere Highway. Lots of fairly easy

Looking west across Lake Louise at Mt. Victoria and the Plain of Six Glaciers.

Map 369-1, Victoria-Temple, Banff NP, Alberta, Canada

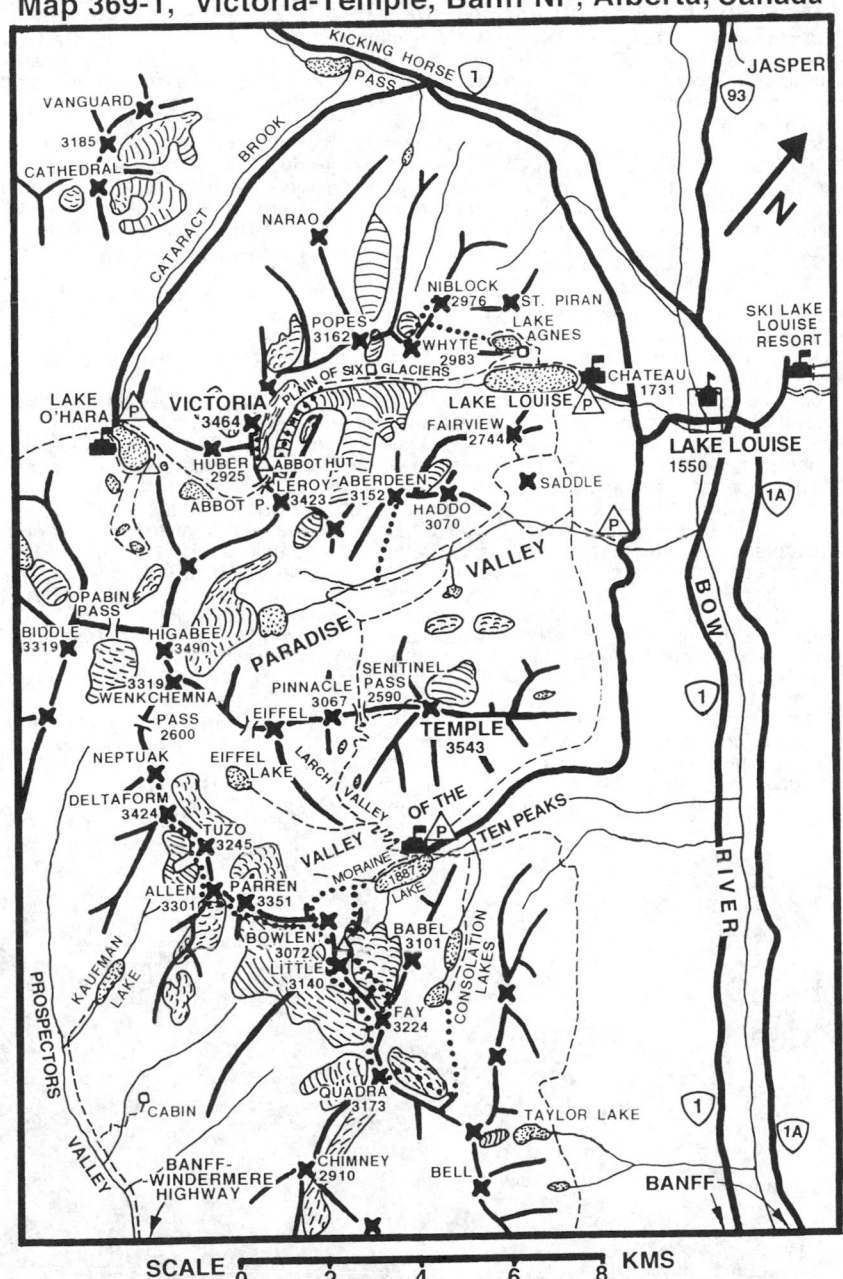

climbing routes from that direction, but always take ice ax & crampons and be prepared for bad weather even in July, August or early September.

Maps *Lake Louise 82 N/8*, 1:50,000; or the books, **Selected Climbs in the Canadian Rockies**, Dougherty (best); or **Scrambles in the Canadian Rockies**, Kane, both from Rocky Mountains Books; or **Climber's Guide to the Rocky Mountains of Canada--South**, ACC.

Assiniboine, Assiniboine Provincial Park, BC-Alberta, Canada

The prominent peak on this map is Mt. Assiniboine at 3618 meters. It's located on the boundary between British Columbia and Alberta, and was the main attraction in the creation of Assiniboine Provincial Park of BC. This is one of the premier alpine peaks in North America and is known for its Matterhorn-like appearance. The rocks in these parts are sedimentary, and mostly limestone.

There are several ways to get to **Assiniboine**; however, by far the best, shortest and most popular route is from the east via Canmore and the good road running past Spray Lakes Reservoir. In 1992, this road was a very good gravel all-weather highway, but it should be paved when you arrive. Or you can approach from the south and the Kananakis Lakes. When you reach the Mt. Engadine Lodge, turn northwest and drive 4 kms to the Shark Mtn. Trailhead.

From the trailhead, walk west on an old blocked-off road for a ways, then it turns into a good wide path for hikers, mtn. bikers, and horses. You are permitted to go all the way to Magog Lake via the Assiniboine Pass on a mtn. bike, which makes this a very popular trail, especially on weekends. At Magog Lake, stop at the park headquarters to register and get last minute information. You'll have to pay a small fee to camp; or double the price of a camping fee will get you into one of the Naiset Cabins. Helicopters fly most lodge customers in--which detracts from the otherwise wilderness setting.

From Magog Lake, walk past the camps on the west side of the lake, then up through some ledges and eventually to the Hind Hut. People have been killed on the approach to this hut, so see the route foto in Dougherty's book below. He's got it just right. There's a pretty good trail there now so it isn't the problem it once was. The Hind Hut is free to use on a first come, first served basis. It has foam pads and room for 12-18 people.

The *route normal* is the north (or maybe northwest) ridge which is in full view from the hut. It's the most-climbed way up the mountain and the descent route for climbers using other more difficult routes of ascent. In good weather and when the mountain is snow-free, this is an easy climb except for 2 rock bands. They're rated a II 5.5. Both the Red and Gray rock bands have rappel stations, so even if you climb it solo, take a rope to make it easier and safer to get down these 2 pitches. In good conditions you can down-climb, but with some risk.

Nearby is the *north face*, which has the same rating of difficulty, but with some snow climbing. All other routes are much more difficult. The author started on 8/8/1992 with 3 days of food, walked up to the Hind Hut in just over 8 hours, then had a big snowstorm that night, which ended everyones attempts on the summit. Next day he returned to his car in 8 hours.

Buy all supplies in Canmore or elsewhere. Take a rope, and ice ax & crampons, although you probably won't need them on the *route normal*. In good weather it's a 3 day climb from the trailhead, but take more food and supplies so you can wait out bad weather. Best time to climb is mid-July through September. For updated information call the Assiniboine Lodge at 403-

Looking south at the northern slopes of Assiniboine.

Map 370-1, Assiniboine, Rockies, BC-Alberta, Canada

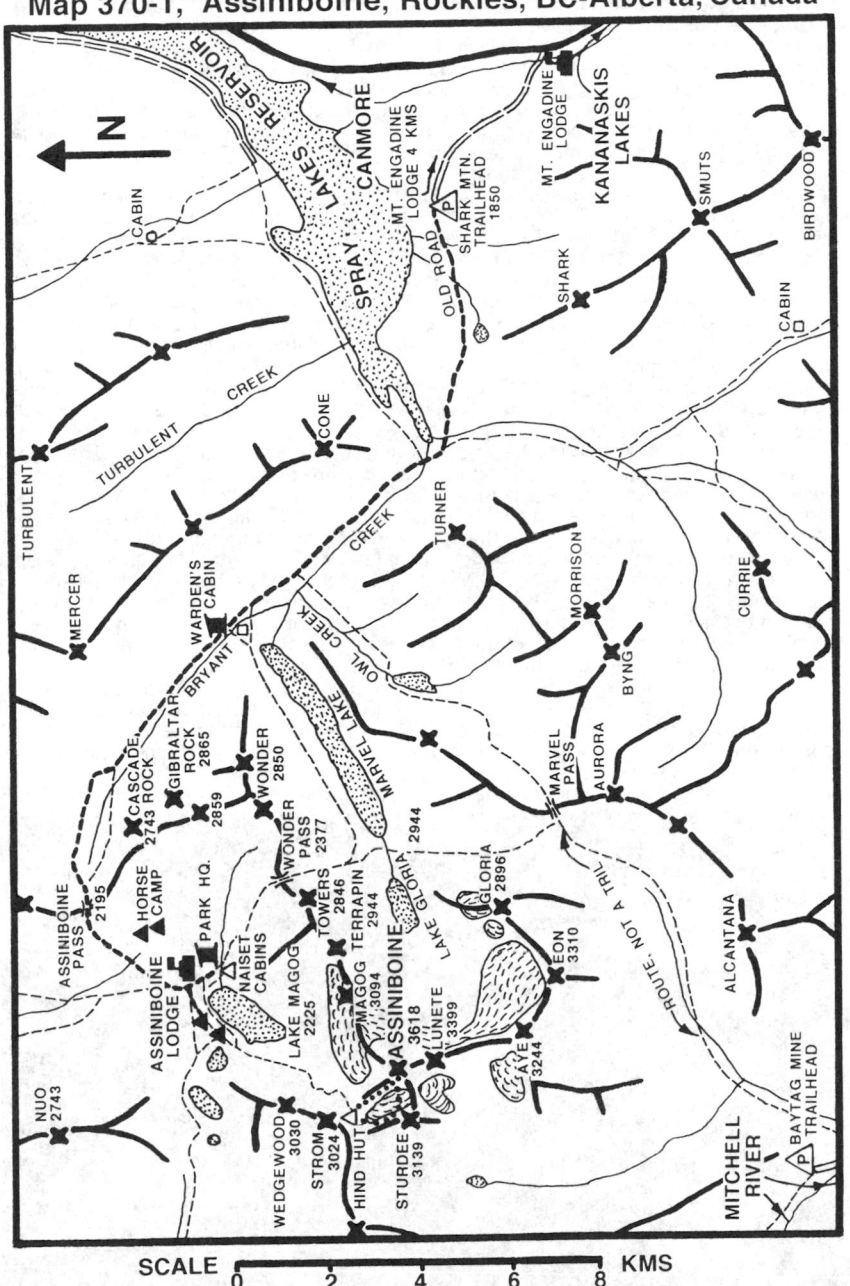

SCALE 0 2 4 6 8 **KMS**

678-2883. Or try BC Provincial Parks, Tele. 250-422-4200.
Maps *Banff National Park,* 1:200,000; and *Mount Assiniboine 82 J/13,* 1:50,000; and the books,
Selected Alpine Climbs in the Canadian Rockies, Dougherty, Rocky Mountains Books (best);
or **Climber's Guide to the Rocky Mountains of Canada--South,** ACC.

Sir Douglas & Joffre, Lougheed Provincial Park, Alberta, Canada

There are 2 high and well-known peaks on this map. Mt. Sir Douglas is in the north at 3406 meters; and in the lower left-hand corner of this map, Mt. Joffre, at 3449. Joffre is the highest summit between the Can-Am border and Mt. Assiniboine. As in all the Canadian Rockies, these peaks are made of sedimentary rocks, mostly limestone. Each peak has it's share of difficult routes, but only the easiest ones are discussed here. Almost all the area on this map is included in the Peter Lougheed Provincial Park, which was formerly Kananaskis Park. For current updated information call the visitor & climbing information center shown on the map at 403-591-6322, or visit Alberta Provincial Parks website at (www.gov.ab.ca/env/parks).

The normal way to the northwest face of **Sir Douglas**, is to park at the trailhead near Mud Lake on the Smith-Dorrien & Spray Lakes Highway. From there, take the trail heading southwest up Burstall Creek. Head for Burstall Pass, but just before that, turn south and route-find toward Burstall Pass South. From there continue south toward the 2 glaciers shown. You can walk up either glacier and do a northwest face and/or west ridge route. The northwest face is rated a III in Dougherty's book listed below. There are some crevasses on both glaciers, so solo climbers take note. Most do this climb in 2 or 2 1/2 days, but it might be possible to do it in one very long day. You could also get to this region via the west and the Albert River, but that's a long drive on old logging roads.

The author never did climb Sir Douglas, but on 8/10/1992, and in less than perfect weather, he did climb **Mt. Chester** via Chester Lake in 3 1/4 hours round-trip from his car which was parked at the Mud Lake Trailhead.

To climb **Joffre**, first drive to the visitor center near Lower Kananaskis Lake. There you can buy maps and get the latest information on trails & routes for all peaks in the park. Then continue south up the road to the trailhead on Upper Kananaskis Lake at 1700 meters. Take the very good and well-used trail west along the south shore of the lake for 5 or 6 kms, then not far beyond the springs welling up out in the lake, turn left or southwest and take a good, but unmarked trail to Hidden Lake. From Hidden Lake, this hiker-made trail heads up the slopes to the south, eventually arriving at Aster Lake at 2200 meters. From there, first head southwest, then veer south and head up along the creek as shown. As you near the first glacier, veer right, and walk up to the next level & glacier above. Once on the lower part of Mangin Glacier, your route will be in full view. You can either go straight up the glacier and north face; or veer left and climb up a steep chimney to the north ridge. Both are rated a III by Dougherty.

This glacier has some crevasses but they can be avoided so any danger is minimal. Most people do this climb in 2 or 2 1/2 days, but it can be done in one. The author started early on 8/11/1992, and climbed Joffre's north face, but broke one crampon near the top on solid ice! He make it OK, then descended via the north ridge & couloir. Round-trip time from his car was 11 1/2 hours.

Do all you shopping in Calgary or Canmore (which has 2 small supermarkets). Ice ax &

From a ways above Aster Lake looking at Joffre which is the snow peak to the upper right.

798

Map 371-1, Sir Douglas & Joffre, Alberta, Canada

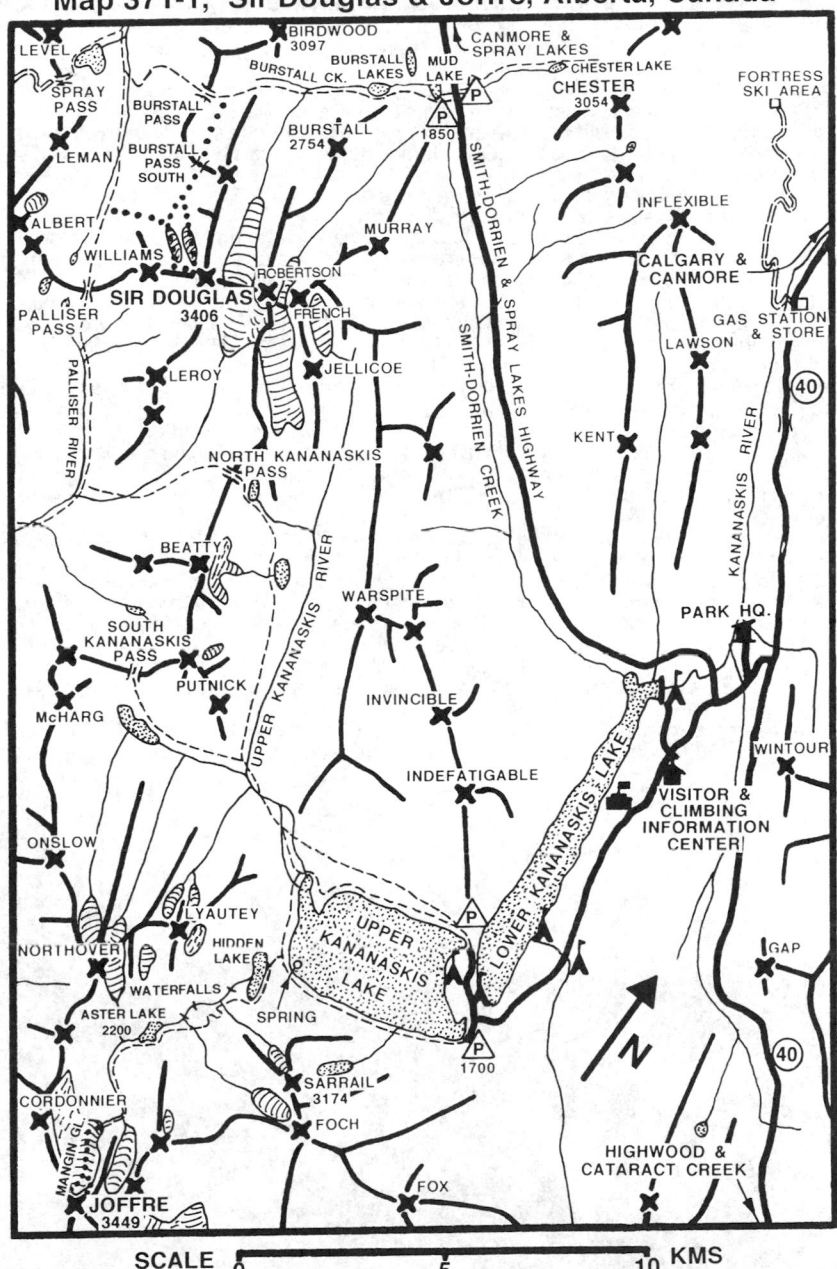

SCALE 0 ___ 5 ___ 10 KMS

crampons are required on both mountains. Normally, climb from July through September.
Maps *Banff National Park*, 1:200,000; and *Kananaskis Lakes, 82 J/11 & Kananaskis Lakes, 82 J/14* (for the approach to Sir Douglas), 1:50,000; and the books, **Selected Climbs in the Canadian Rockies**, Dougherty; and **Scrambles in the Canadian Rockies**, Kane; both from Rocky Mountain Books, Calgary.

Glacier National Park, Selkirk Mountains, British Columbia, Canada

Glacier National Park of British Colombia is located west of Banff and in the Selkirk Mountains. There are no dominating summits here, but a number of peaks over 3300 meters are found in an area south of National Highway 1 and Rogers Pass. The highest peaks there are Wheeler at 3354 meters, and Fluz at 3348. There's another group of high peaks north of Rogers Pass. The highest and best known summit there is Mt. Rogers at 3206 meters.

The author has passed through this park on several occasions but it was raining continuously each time. He made it to the Hermit Hut once--carrying an umbrella. It seems you'll have to have some luck and help from the weather gods to climb here. For current park information call the visitor center at Rogers Pass, Tele. 250-814-5232; or call the warden's office at 250-814-5202 for climbing or routes information.

Highway 1 cuts through the middle of this national park, giving good easy access, at least to areas near the paved road. Also, the main rail line for the Canadian Pacific Railroad runs over, now under, Rogers Pass, but there are no scheduled stops within the park.

Glacier Park seems to lie in the storm track much of the year, having precipitation on 15 to 20 days of each month, with lesser amounts received during the months of May through August. Because of the heavy snowfall, 12 percent of the park is covered with glaciers. Snow and ice climbing is most popular, but there are some rock routes as well.

Access is limited to a handful of trails, all of which are well-marked. Some of the trails marked on the map are fire-break roads and closed to private motor vehicles.

To reach the higher summits south of the main highway, you could use the trail running south up the length of **Beaver Creek** or River. However, the trail is on the opposite side of the river from the mountains and that river may or may not be fordable. Maps do show one trail running west up to Glacier Circle & Hut in the area just north of Fluz Peak. You cross the river on a cable car at that point.

Another possible way to reach peaks such as **Fluz, Wheeler** and **Purity**, would be to walk up the Flat Creek Trail to Flat Creek Pass, but there is no maintenance on that trail and they're giving it back to the bears. Another way of reaching the 3 peaks just mentioned is via Asulkan Creek, the Asulkan Hut, and Asulkan Pass, and perhaps as far as Donkin Pass, the Bishop Glacier, thence to any or most of those peaks. See or call the warden's office before setting out to do any climbs in that area. Also see the books below.

A couple of trails run up to some peaks north of Highway 1. One leaves the highway just north of Rogers Pass, and leads to the now-unusable and abandoned Hermit Hut, and nearby Campsite. From there, climb north to **Mt. Rogers**.

For more maps, guidebooks and information, contact the park headquarters in Revelstoke, Tele. 250-837-7500, located to the west; or the visitor center at Rogers Pass. Use Revelstoke

This is the Hermit Hut located a short distance north of Rogers Pass.

Map 372-1, Glacier National Park, Selkirk Mtns., BC, Canada

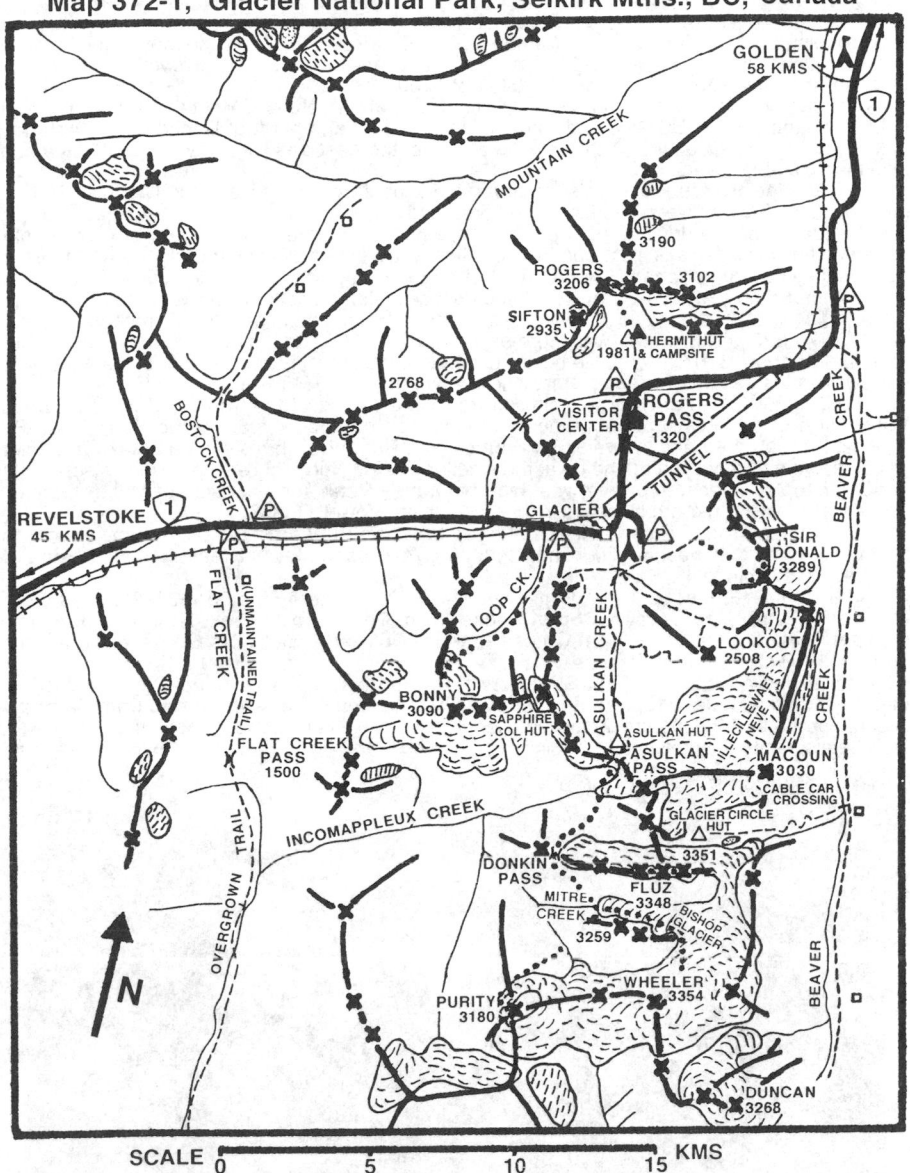

or Golden as your shopping centers. There's a Best Western lodge and dining facilities at Rogers Pass, as well as a gas station, but little else.

Maps Chrismar map *Rogers Pass: Glacier National Park,* 1:50,000 (from Mt. Rogers to Glacier Circle Hut); *Glacier Park-British Columbia,* 1:126,720; contact OMNI Resources website (www.omnimap. com), or Maps Canada website (www.nrcan.gc.ca:80/homepage/maps.shtml), or the wardens office, Rogers Pass; and the books **Climber's Guide to the Interior Ranges of British Columbia--North,** AAC; or **Climber's Guide--The Columbia Mountains of Canada,** AAC.

The Bugaboos, Purcell Range, British Columbia, Canada

The Bugaboo Group is a small cluster of sheer granite spires which rank among the best rock climbing areas of Canada, North America, and the world. Probably the most famous peak in the group is Bugaboo Spire at 3186 meters. This area now is a BC Provincial Park. For updated information about the place call 250-422-4200.

The area covered on this map is located in the northern Purcell Mountains, southeast of Glacier National Park (BC), west of Radium Hot Springs, and north of Duncan and Kootenay Lakes. Most roads & access into this area are from the east and Highway 95, which is along side the Columbia River.

To reach the **Bugaboos**, here's the normal approach route. Drive along Highway 95 to a point about halfway between Golden in the north, and Radium in the south. At Spillimacheen (or Brisco), turn west and drive up Bugaboo Creek, as shown on the map. This is (or was) an old logging road which ends at Bugaboo Forks, where you'll find the Gmoser Lodge. From there a good trail takes you up to the Conrad Kain Hut and Boulder Camp at 2200 meters. This takes about 4 hours with a full pack. Boulder Camp now has a large shelter to accommodate about 50 people. This is a popular place, so using this hut now requires reservations. To reserve a place, call 403-678-3200. The author was there on 8/8/1982 and hiked from Gmoser Lodge to the hut and back in about 3 1/4 hours. He did no climbing otherwise. From the shelter it's about a 2 hour walk to the base of **Bugaboo Spire** and **Snowpatch** at 3064 meters.

The Boulder Camp or Conrad Kain Hut route is also one of the traditional ways to reach **Vowell** and **Conrad Groups**, both located to the north and northwest of the Bugaboos. By walking through the pass between Snowpatch and Bugaboo Spire, you can make a glacier traverse to the northwest and end up at the smaller Shaft 7 Hut. This shelter, which sleeps only about 8 people, is located on the west face of Osprey Peak and east side of Malloy Glacier. From this hut you can climb all peaks in the Conrad and Vowell Groups.

You can also reach these 2 peaks and the hut from the northeast. Drive to Parson on Highway 95 and turn west, and continue south up Vowell and Malloy Creeks. From the end of the road, hike south to the Shaft 7 Hut.

Here are some other peaks or groups and the access routes: **Ethelbert**, 3159 meters, from Dunbar or Templeton Creeks; **Septet Peaks**, from Templeton Creek; **Howser Spire** and **Howser Peak**, 3094 meters, from Gmoser Lodge; **Quintet Peaks** from Gmoser Lodge; and **Taurus**, 2972 meters, from Frances Creek.

Further south, climb the **Four Squatters** from Healy, on Duncan Creek; **Eyebrow**, 3354 meters and **Stockdale**, 3125, from Horsethief Creek; climb **Peter** and **Jumbo** from Farnham Creek; **Farnham**, 3458 meters, from Horsethief Creek; and finally **Mcbeth** from Glacier Creek.

There's plenty of snow and rock climbing here, but bad weather too; that's why there are so

Bugaboo Glacier and the Bugaboo Group as seen from the Bugaboo Lodge.

Map 373-1, The Bugaboos, Purcell Range, BC, Canada

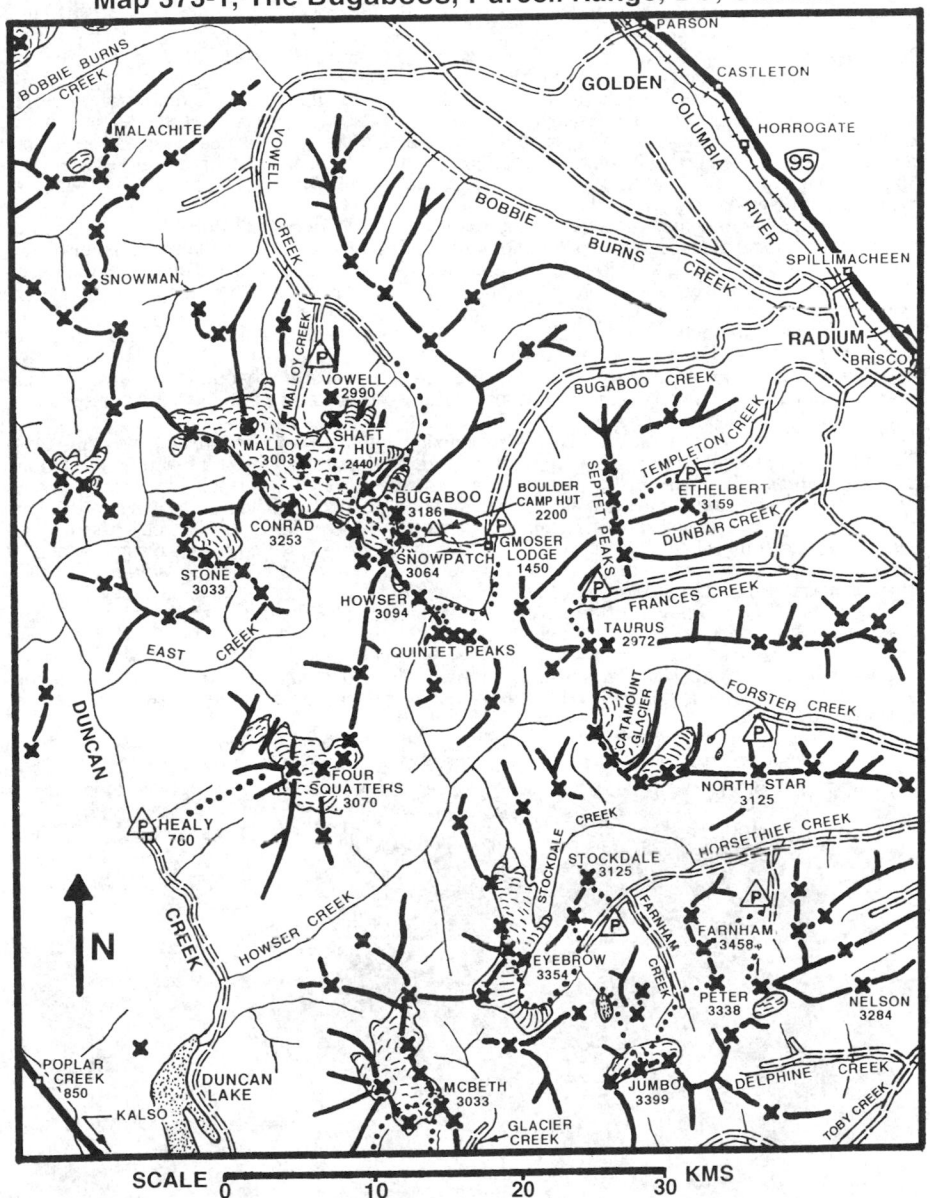

many glaciers around. Buy food in either Golden or Radium Hot Springs, or better still before you arrive in the area.

Maps *Lardeau, 82-K,* 1:250,00; or *82 K-10 & 82 K-15,* 1:50,000, all from Maps Canada, see their website at (www.nrcan.gc.ca:80/homepage/maps.shtml); and the book **Climber's Guide to the Interior Ranges of British Columbia--South,** AAC.

Mt. Olympus, Olympic Mtns. & NP, Washington, USA

Mt. Olympus at 2428 meters, is the highest summit in the Olympic Mountains of Washington state. These mountains are located in the middle of the Olympic Peninsula just across the Puget Sound west of Seattle. Much of the area is now part of the Olympic National Park. The Olympics are uplifted mountains with metamorphic-type rocks at the heart of the range.

To climb **Mt. Olympus** via the normal route, first drive to the west side of the range along Highway 101, then turn east on the paved highway running to the Hoh Ranger Station. Before you get to this point, be sure to buy all supplies for your trip, because there are no stores or large towns in the immediate area. For current climbing information call the Wilderness Office at Park HQ. in Port Angeles, Tele. 360-452-0300, or Hoh Visitor Center at 360-452-0330, or see their website (www.nps.gov/olym/).

While at the visitor center, get a backcountry camping permit for a small fee, and the latest maps and perhaps a local guidebook and other information. Then walk east through a high latitude rain forest. Some of the trees are up to about 95 meters tall and 4 or 5 meters in diameter at the base. These are among the biggest trees in the world! After 9 kms you'll come to a camping area and an emergency shelter called Happy Four. After that it's the Olympic Ranger Station cabin. It's occupied in summer only, with another crude shelter nearby. Further on you'll cross the Hoh River Bridge at 408 meters altitude. From there, the steep part of the trail begins. At Elk Lake there's another emergency shelter and camping area, then near the tree line is Glacier Meadows. There you'll find 2 more shelters, a couple of toilets and campsites. Just up the trail and still in the trees is a summertime ranger station which is a large tent.

From the ranger's tent, there's a 2 km trail running southeast up to the lateral moraine of the Blue Glacier. The real climb begins there. From the moraine, just follow the route-line on the Mount Olympus Climber's Map listed below. You first walk west across the lower glacier, then climb up and over rock & snow to the top of The Dome. From there head south toward the summit, but turn 90° east and pass through a notch in the northeast ridge before heading southwest. Finally, you'll pass over or beside the false summit before making a rock climb to the higher **West Peak**. In late summer and in good weather and with a trail in the snow, this can be very easy and relatively safe for climbing although at first glance it looks pretty fearsome to some. But in bad weather it's another story!

The author was in a hurry as usual and in the late afternoon of 8/13/1991 made the hike to Glacier Meadows in 6 3/4 hours. The next morning it took 2 1/2 hours to reach the summit; round-trip from Glacier Meadows, 4 1/3 hours. That afternoon he walked all the way back to Hoh Ranger Station & Visitor Center in 6 hours. His total walk-time for the trip was just over 17 hours, and the whole trip was completed within a 31 hour time period. Most people prefer 3 days for the climb: Day 1-in, Day 2-climbing, Day 3-out.

Take ice ax & crampons and a tent, because all the shelters are open on one side and the mosquitos will eat you alive. This region is one of the wettest places in North America so rain gear is

Looking southwest across the Blue Glacier. The Dome right, summit upper left.

Map 374-1, Olympus, Olympic Mtns. & NP, Wash., USA

essential. During July and August good weather spells are common, so this is the best time to go.
Maps *Olympic National Park,* 1:125,000; or *Mount Olympus Climber's Map,* 1:62,500 (best); and the book, **Climber's Guide to the Olympic Mountains**; or perhaps (?) **Olympic Mountains Trail Guide**, both from The Mountaineers; buy all these at the Hoh Ranger Station.

Mt. Baker, Cascade Mountains, Washington, USA

Mt. Baker at 3286 meters, is one of the highest of the volcanic peaks in the American Northwest and is heavily glaciated. It is located due east of Bellingham, west of Mt. Shuksan, and not far south of the Canadian border. The normal way to get there is to exit Interstate Highway 5 at Bellingham and drive east through Deming, Kendal and to either Glacier, or the Austin Pass ski area.

Mt. Baker is still considered an active volcano. Its last eruption was from the Sherman Crater (just south of the main summit) on 9/7/1880. That has been rated a small category VEI-2 explosion. Activity continued until 11/27/1880. Also, in about 1300 BC, there was a large VEI-4 explosion at the Schreibers Meadow Cone, located about 8 kms due south of the summit.

There are about 3 main routes to choose from. The first way is actually from the south and Concrete, then north on Forest Road (FS) 11 to near Baker Lake, then north and west on FR 12, then FR 13. The ascent is up the **Easton Glacier** (with lots of crevasses) on the south side of the peak. This route was being used a lot in the summer of 1991, when the road up Glacier Creek was partially washed out. However, this southern approach route is longer and more complicated using dirt or gravel roads.

Perhaps the second most-used route on the mountain is from the end of the paved road at Austin Pass. From there, a well-used trail runs southwest to Coleman Peak and **Camp Kiser**, then the summit climb is made along various routes on the northeast side of the mountain. This approach and climb usually takes 3 days.

Over the years the normal route up **Mt. Baker** has been to first stop at the Glacier Ranger Station (between mile posts 33 & 34, Tele. 360-599-2714) which is open from late May to early October, to pick up any maps and information on roads, trails or routes, or the new *parking fee*. Good news, no permits are needed for climbing. From there, drive up Glacier Creek to the trailhead, climb over Heliotrope Ridge, then southeast up Coleman Glacier and finally the upper part of Deming Glacier.

In 1991, a bridge on the paved road up along Glacier Creek had been washed out the previous winter and climbers were required to road-walk 8 kms from the bridge marked on the map to the actual trailhead. From there, a good trail zig zags up to the southeast to where the Kulshan Cabin used to be located. It's gone now. Some people occasionally camp on some moraine meadows just below the snow on Heliotrope Ridge, then continue southeast and east up the south side of Coleman Glacier. This is a very easy walk-up route, but higher on the glacier are lots of crevasses to negotiate. This may be the most dangerous *route normal* of any of the northwest volcanos, at least from a solo climber's aspect. The last part of the route up Deming Glacier is steeper, but easy, and no crevasses.

On 8/14/1991, the author walked up the Glacier Creek road climbing the *route normal* and made the summit in 5 1/2 hours. Round-trip from his car was just under 10 hours. This was a warm sunny day in August with ideal snow conditions. Most people using that route in 1991, were camping one or 2 nights and doing the climb in 2 or 3 days. By parking at the actual trailhead, this should be an easy

From the upper Coleman Glacier looking east at Baker's summit.

Map 375-1, Baker, Cascade Mtns., Washington, USA

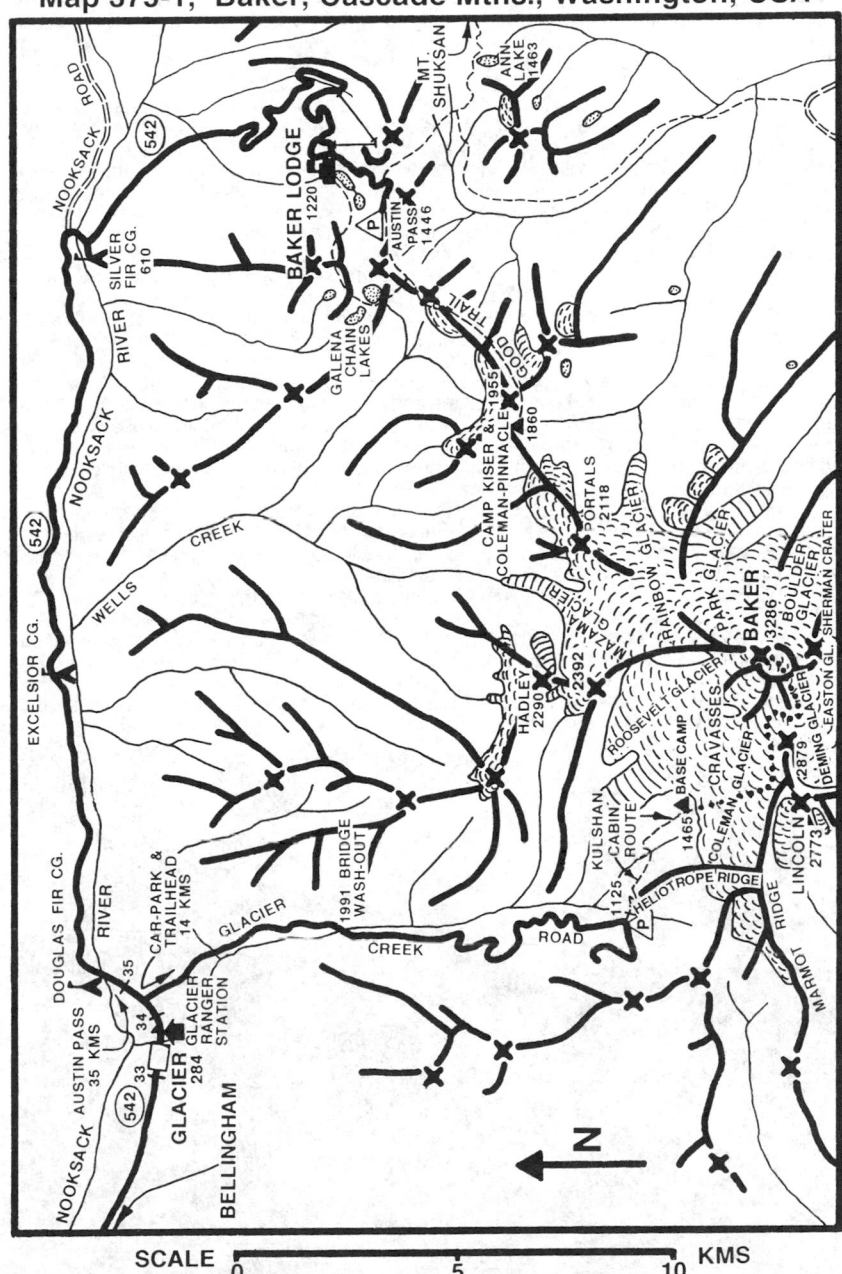

one-day climb in late July, August or early September, which is the best time to climb.
Maps USGS maps *Mt. Baker* & *Mt. Shuksan,* 1:62,500; or *Mt. Baker, Mt. Shuksan, Lake Shannon* and *Hamilton,* all at 1:69,500 scale from Green Trails, Bothell, Washington; or the *Mt. Baker--Snoqualmie National Forest* map, 1:168,959, buy all these at the Glacier Ranger Station; and the book, **Challenge of the North Cascades**, The Mountaineers.

Shuksan, Challenger, Fury & Terror, Cascades, Washington, USA

For those interested in some good, challenging snow, ice and rock climbing, this part of the northern Cascade Mountains of Washington state might be the place for you. The most famous peak on this map is Mt. Shuksan at 2783 meters. Other well-known summits are Challenger at 2511meters; Fury, 2585; and Mt. Terror at 2485 meters. All of these peaks are in the North Cascades National Park and in a wilderness setting. It will take at least a day, usually more, just to reach a base camp. This part of the Northern Cascades has been folded and uplifted and is made mostly of metamorphic-type rocks. Mt. Baker and other volcanos are just to the west.

To get to these mountains by the normal approach, drive north from Seattle on Interstate Highway 5, and exit at the small city of Bellingham. From there, drive east through Deming, Kendal, Glacier and toward the Baker Lodge and the Austin Pass ski area. See the previous map on Mt. Baker for part of the access route to these mountains. While driving to this area, it's recommended you first stop at the Glacier Ranger Station in the small town of Glacier, for road, trail and weather information, and the latest on any new camping restrictions, Tele. 360-599-2714. You can also buy more maps. This information (and map) is meant to be an introduction only.

To climb **Mt. Shuksan**, stop right at Austin Pass and look for the trailhead parking and the beginning of Trail 600. Walk southeast along this very good trail to Ann Lake at 1463 meters. Continue east from the lake to the Fisher Chimney, then veer northeast and climb along the northwest slope. Finally you'll arrive at the Upper Curtis Glacier west of the main summit, then head due south a little more than one km, round the corner to the east, and onto Hourglass Glacier, then north to the summit. The Green Trails, *Mt. Shuksan Map 14*, shows these landmarks. Take that map to the Glacier Ranger Station (or buy it there) and they can mark the route. This is a popular climb, so there should be a trail in the snow during the climbing season. The author was in this area twice and weather prevented him from climbing both times.

To reach **Mt. Challenger**, drive along the Nooksack River. Near the Silver Fir Campground, turn east onto the Nooksack Road. Drive to Camp Hannegan and Trailhead, then walk the good trail over Hannegan Pass to Whatcom Pass. From there head south up the ridge along the approximate routes shown on the map. See the book below for more details.

To climb **Fury** and **Terror**, you can get there via the Whatcom Pass, but you'll have to traverse around a lot of ridges and glaciers, and it seems a very difficult way. Or take a boat north on Ross Lake and walk west up trails along Big Beaver Creek from Big Beaver Campground to reach Mt. Terror and Fury; or walk west up Little Beaver Creek from Little Beaver Campground to reach the east side of Mt. Challenger. The North Cascades map shows these trails.

Keep in mind, none of these peaks are for beginners. Some routes are easier than others, but they're all on the difficult side. Take ice ax & crampons, ropes and a good tent. This is a wet area so

Mt. Shuksan as seen from Lake Ann (calender foto ?).

Map 376-1, Shuksan, Fury, Terror, Cascades, Washington, USA

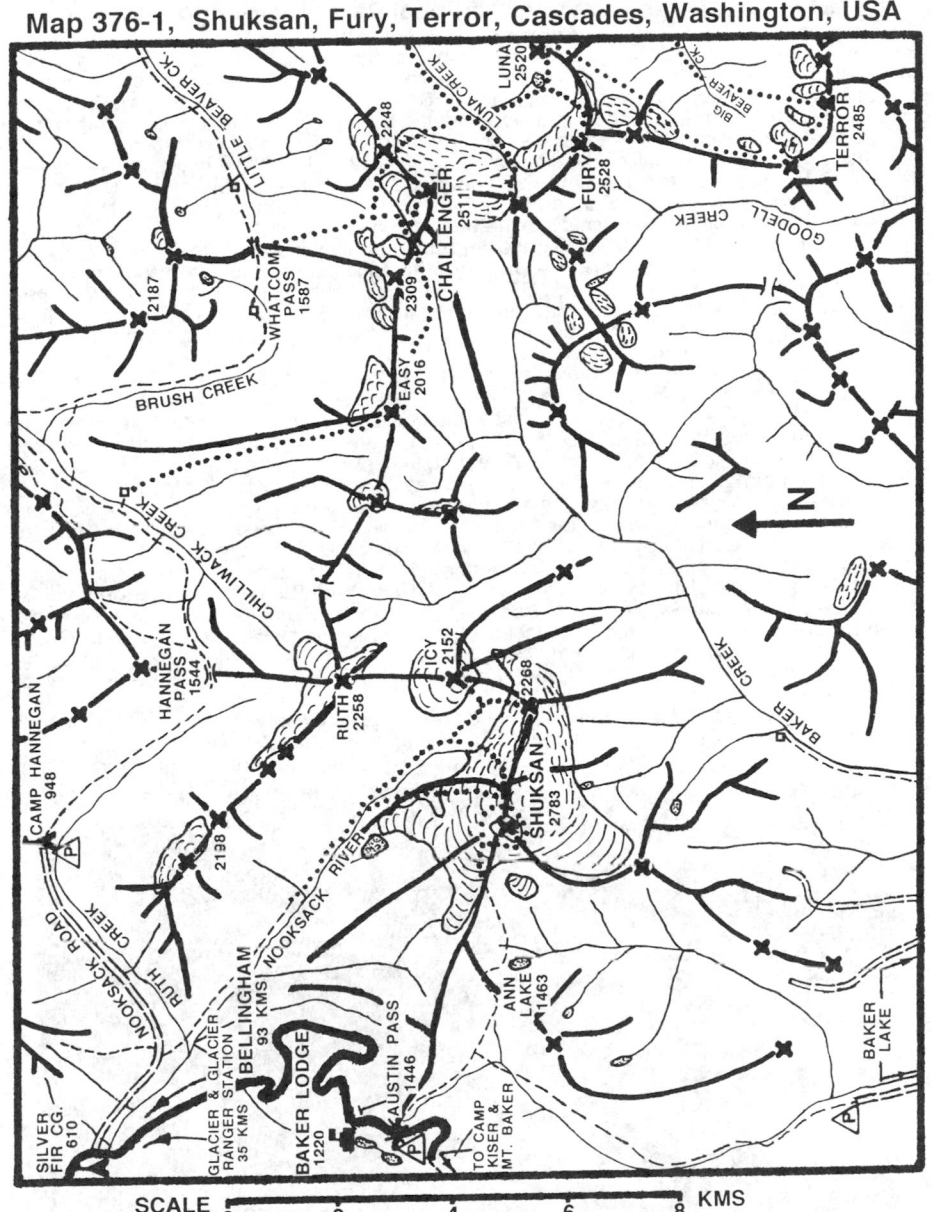

SCALE

0   2   4   6   8 KMS

go prepared for bad weather. The best time to climb in good weather is during July through the first part of September.   Best to buy all your supplies in the Bellingham region.

Maps Green Trails maps *Mt. Shuksan, 14,* and *Mt. Challenger, 15,* 1:69,500; and *North Cascades National Park,* 1:100,000; and the book, **Challenge of the North Cascades**, The Mountaineers.

Eldorado, North Cascades National Park, Washington, USA

Shown here is a group of peaks in the central part of the North Cascades National Park, located in north central Washington state. This national park begins on the US-Canadian border just east of Mt. Baker, and runs south to the northern end of Lake Chelan. Almost due west of this area are the cities of Mt. Vernon, Burlington, Sedro Woolley, Concrete and Marblemount. Highway 20, the North Cascades Highway, makes a big loop from Marblemount north of this mapped area and nearly to Ross Lake, then continues east to Winthrop and Okanogan.

This is the most heavily glaciated section of the national park, and the peaks are very steep and rugged, much like Mts. Shuksan, Challenger and Terror, located further north. The best known summit in the group is Eldorado at 2703 meters. Most of the rocks in this area are metamorphic, totally unlike the volcanos to the west.

The simplest way to get there is to drive north from Seattle on Interstate Highway 5, exit at Burlington and head east toward Sedro Woolley, where the park headquarters is located. For current information call them at 360-856-5700, or see their website (www.nps.gov/noca/). From there, drive east through Rockport and Concrete to Marblemount, where a NPS-USFS ranger station/visitor center is located. You can also reach the area from the east side of the Cascades along the North Cascades Highway .

Perhaps the most-used access route to these peaks is from Marblemount. From there, turn east onto a gravel road running towards the Mineral Park Campground. Using this road allows access to the west & southwest side of most of the peaks. A second way is to drive north from Marblemount to the Newhalem CG. & Information Center, and hike south from there up Newhalem Creek. The third main access route, and the best from the north, is from the Colonial Creek Campground. From there, the Thunder Creek Trail heads south to the center of this group of peaks and to the east side of the major summits on the map. You can also reach the middle part of this mapped area via the Panther Creek and Fisher Creek Trails on the east, as well as along a dirt road running north from the north end of Lake Chelan.

This map shows routes up some of the more prominent peaks, almost all of which are difficult climbs. Some of the easier routes are as follows. Climb **Buckner** and **Boston** from the Black Warrior Mine, and **Sahale** from Cascade Pass along the Sahale Arm or southwest ridge. Climb **Eldorado's** southwest face (not real easy!) and **Triad** from the Hidden Lake Trail. Get to that trail from the Cascades Pass Road, then FS Road 1540. See the national park map for the beginning of that trail. On 8/17/1991, that author climbed Triad in 7 hours round-trip from the Hidden Lake Trailhead.

Climb **Tricouni** and **Primus** from the bridge on the Fisher Creek Trail and via the northern ridge and/or glacier. Climb **Pyramid, Colonial, Pinnacle** and **Snowfield** from the trail running south from Diablo just below the Diablo Dam, to Pyramid Lake (just northeast of Pyramid Peak

The western slopes of Eldorado as seen from the Marble Creek Cirque.

Map 377-1, Eldorado, North Cascades NP, Washington, USA

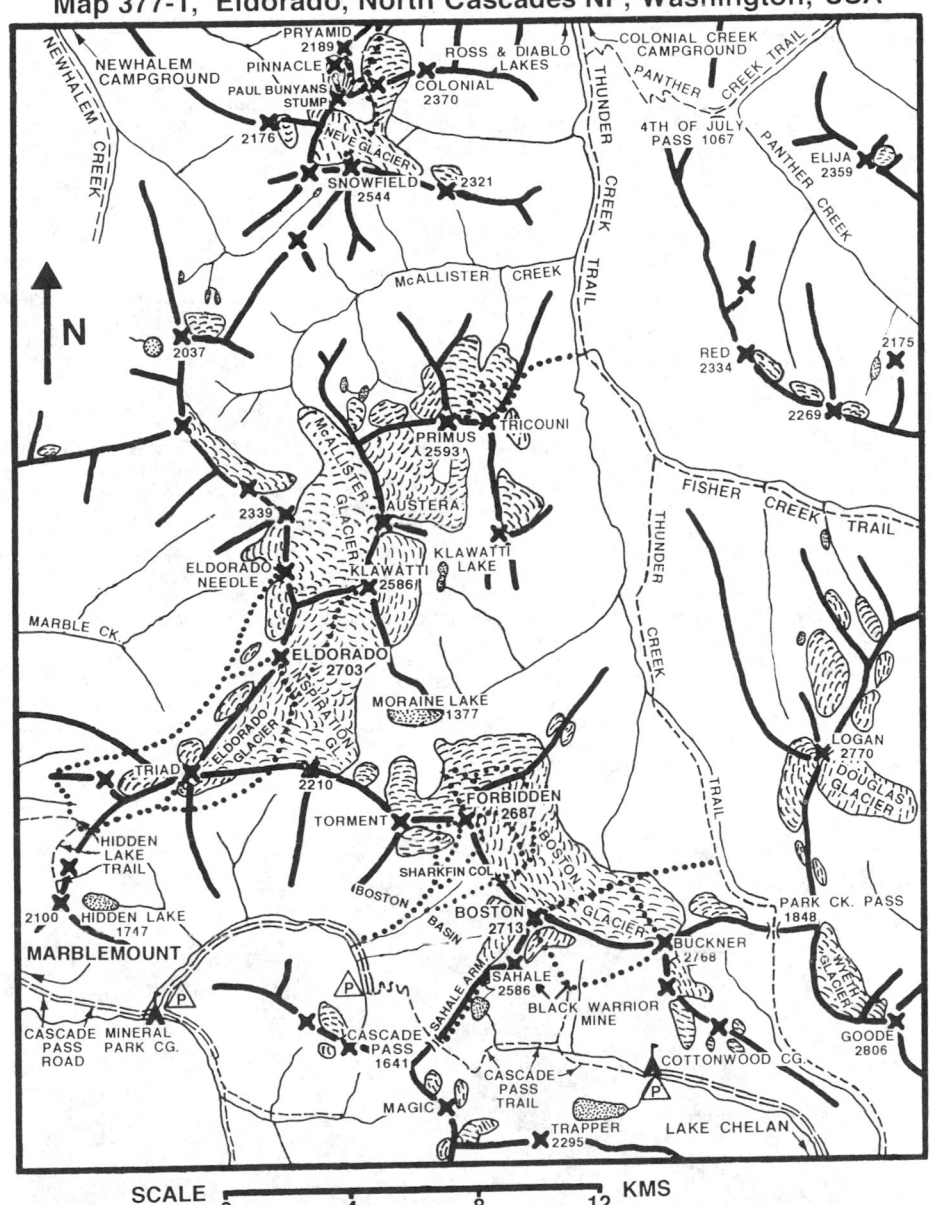

and off this map). From there climb south onto a ridge, then to Colonial Creek and onto Colonial Glacier. Take and use an ice ax & crampons on all routes. A rope would be helpful on many of the glacier routes, as some of the glaciers are fairly big and many have real crevasses.

Maps *North Cascades National Park*, 1:100,000, from any of the park visitor centers; and the books **Cascade Alpine Guide, Stevens Pass to Rainy Pass**; and **100 Hikes in Washington's North Cascades National Park Region**, both from The Mountaineers.

Glacier Peak, Cascade Mountains, Washington, USA

Glacier Peak, at 3222 meters, is one of the better and popular climbs in the state of Washington. It involves some wilderness hiking and camping and a variety of routes, some very easy--others more difficult. Since it's one of the highest mountains in the American Northwest, there are a number of glaciers on the peak, most of which are on the north and east slopes.

Glacier Peak appears to be a rather old volcano, but it's had a number of eruptions during human history. The book, **Volcanos of the World**, gives approximate dates on 7 eruptions: 3550 BC, 3150 BC, 850 BC, 200 AD, 900, 1300 and 1700. All eruptions were from the summit area, and the one in 200 AD was estimated to be a category VEI-4 explosion.

Glacier Peak is located east of Everett and in the Mt. Baker-Snoqualmie National Forest and Glacier Peak Wilderness Area. Access is easy with all the westerly approaches beginning from the town of Darrington. Darrington can be reached by leaving Interstate Highway 5 at the Arlington Exit, and driving east. In Darrington, stop at the Forest Service visitor center for current information or Tele. 360-436-1155. From Darrington, the shortest way to Glacier Peak is to drive southeast along the Sauk River, until the White Chuck River enters. Then drive east along the White Chuck River to the Owl Creek Campground. The trail begins just beyond the campground, and takes you to the western slopes of the mountain. From Owl Creek CG., it's less than a 2 hour walk (8.2 kms) to the Kennedy Hot Springs. From there you can take any one of a number of routes up.

The easiest way to the summit is along the **Gerdine or South Ridge.** To get there, continue walking south from the hot springs to the area below or west of the White Chuck Glacier. From the Pacific Crest Trail, there are 2 routes up to the glacier and the Gerdine Ridge. The White Chuck Glacier is not dangerous, but take an ice ax anyway. From the top of the glacier, turn north and ridge-walk up the very easy South Ridge to the summit. On 8/12/1982, the author hiked from Owl Creek Campground in the rain, but didn't get much further than the Kennedy Hot Springs and a small shelter there..

If you're interested in a slightly more difficult route, walk up along the Sitkum Creek drainage and ascend the ridge just north of the Sitkum Glacier. Or walk part way up Sitkum Creek, then contour south to the head of Chetwot Creek, and up a southwest face route of your choice. You could also leave the Pacific Crest Trail and climb up the Kennedy Glacier on the northwest side of the peak, but this is a more complicated route.

Another way to the mountain is to drive north from Darrington, then turn east into the Suiattle River drainage, and drive to the Sulphur Creek Campground. From there walk up the Suiattle River to the east slopes and climb from there. One easy route is up Streamline Ridge. However, it'll take at least one long day to reach a base camp on the east slope, then a day for the climb, and maybe a third day to return. If you use the White Chuck River trail, it's normally an easy 1 1/2 or 2 day climb, up and back.

Glacier Peak as seen from the Kennedy Ridge Trail (Ira Spring foto).

Map 378-1, Glacier Peak, Cascades, Washington, USA

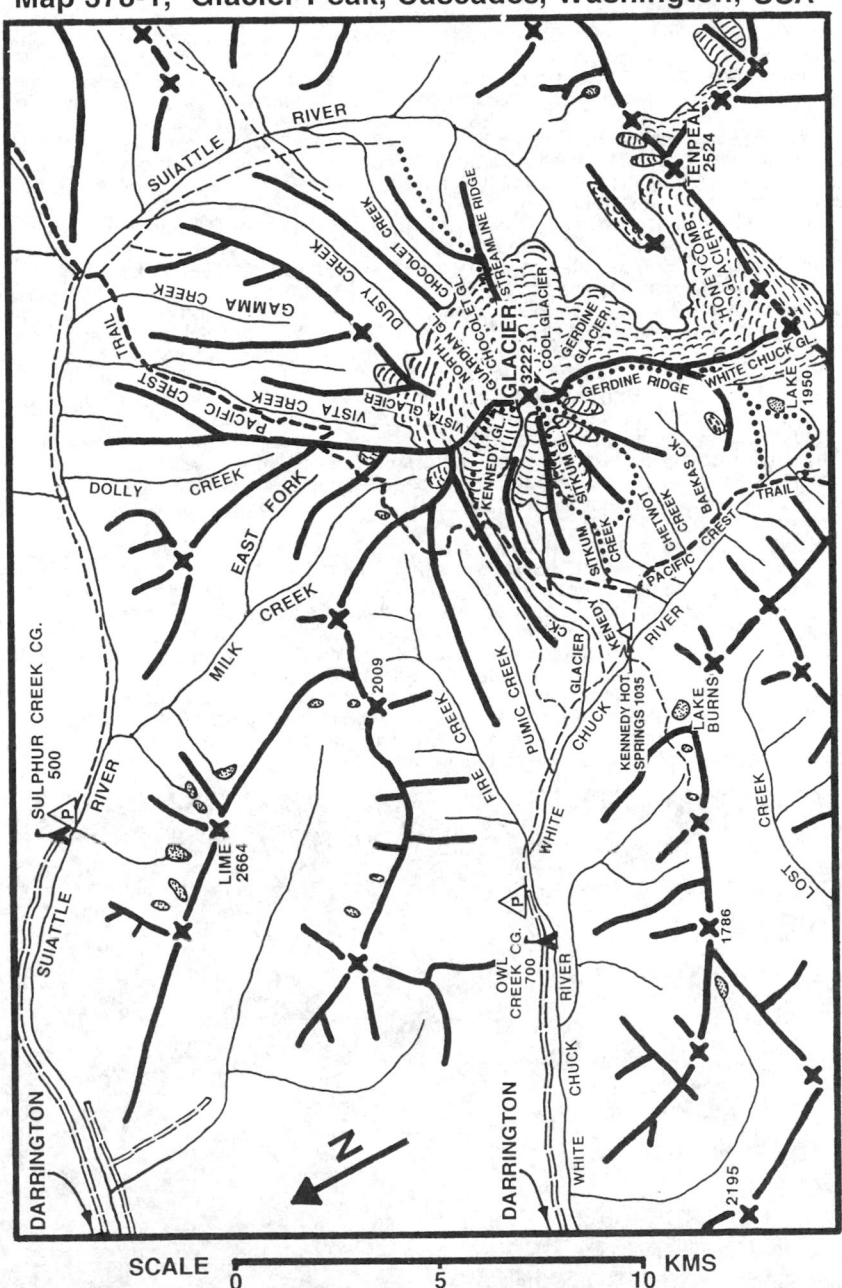

Map *The Glacier Peak Wilderness,* 1:100,000, from the Forest Service office, Darrington; and the books, **Cascade Alpine Guide, Stevens Pass to Rainy Pass**, Becky; and **100 Hikes in Washington's North Cascades National Park Region**, Spring/Manning; or **100 Classic Hikes in Washington, etc,** Spring/Manning; all from The Mountaineers.

Mt. Rainier, Cascade Mountains, Washington, USA

This map shows Mt. Rainier at 4393 meters, the highest peak in Washington state, in the northwest USA, and in the entire Cascade Range. Mt. Rainier is located southeast of Seattle and Tacoma, and is now the cornerstone for a national park. When taking all things into account, Rainier has some of the best snow & ice climbs in the USA; with the exception of some Alaskan mountains. Rainier's glaciers are often the training ground for expeditions heading for the Himalayas and Mt. Everest.

Rainier is a stratovolcano. About 5000 years ago, there was an eruption from the Sunset Amphitheater which sent a lahar all the way to the coast near Seattle. Geologists have studied about 7 eruptions during the 1800's, but they are all questionable. The last eruption (?) from the central crater was on 11/21/1894.

Getting to Rainier is quite easy. The most popular destination is Paradise on the south side of the mountain. To get there, leave Interstate Highway 5 about anywhere and drive east to the park and Paradise. You can also get there from the east; see a state highway map for route selection. The other main starting point is called Sunrise on the northeast side of the mountain.

Before climbing, here are some regulations. You now need a **climbing permit** to go above 3000 meters or Camp Muir--cost US$15 per person. Get this at Longmire, Paradise or Sunrise. To camp anywhere on the mountain or stay in the public shelter at Camp Muir, you need a free **permit**, and for weekends, maybe reservations (US$20). But 40% of all sites are for walk-ins (no reservations and free, no charge). Solo climbers need permission from climbing rangers at Longmire. Call park HQ., located at Ashford, at 360-569-2211; or for reservations call 360-569-4453 (summer only); or see their website (www.nps.gov/mora) for updated information.

The most-used route up **Rainier** starts at **Paradise**. From the visitor center, walk up a good trail, then onto snowfields to Camp Muir. Most people camp there, or sleep in the hut. Day 2 is for the summit climb, and return to your car. In favorable conditions, strong climbers do this in one day easy.

The author arrived late in the afternoon of 8/7/1978, walked 2 hours and camped at Anvil Rock. Next morning it took 2 1/2 hours to reach the summit in perfect conditions, another hour back to camp (he had good knees then!). Ate lunch and in one hour was at Paradise. Total walk-time was about 6 1/2 hours. In good weather, there are lots of people on the mountain and a trail in the snow, which makes a very easy climb.

From **Sunrise**, take a trail/route to Camp Schurman on the northeast side of the mountain, then to the summit, a more difficult route. In good conditions, this is a 2 day climb. Both of these access points offer easy climbs, along with many more difficult routes as well.

Pay attention to the weather forecasts issued by the ranger stations/visitor centers. These places have books and national park maps and the latest information on routes, weather, snow conditions, and the number of people on the mountain.

The upper part of the Ingraham Glacier and the rocky east ridge.

Map 379-1, Mt. Rainier, Cascade Mtns., Washington, USA

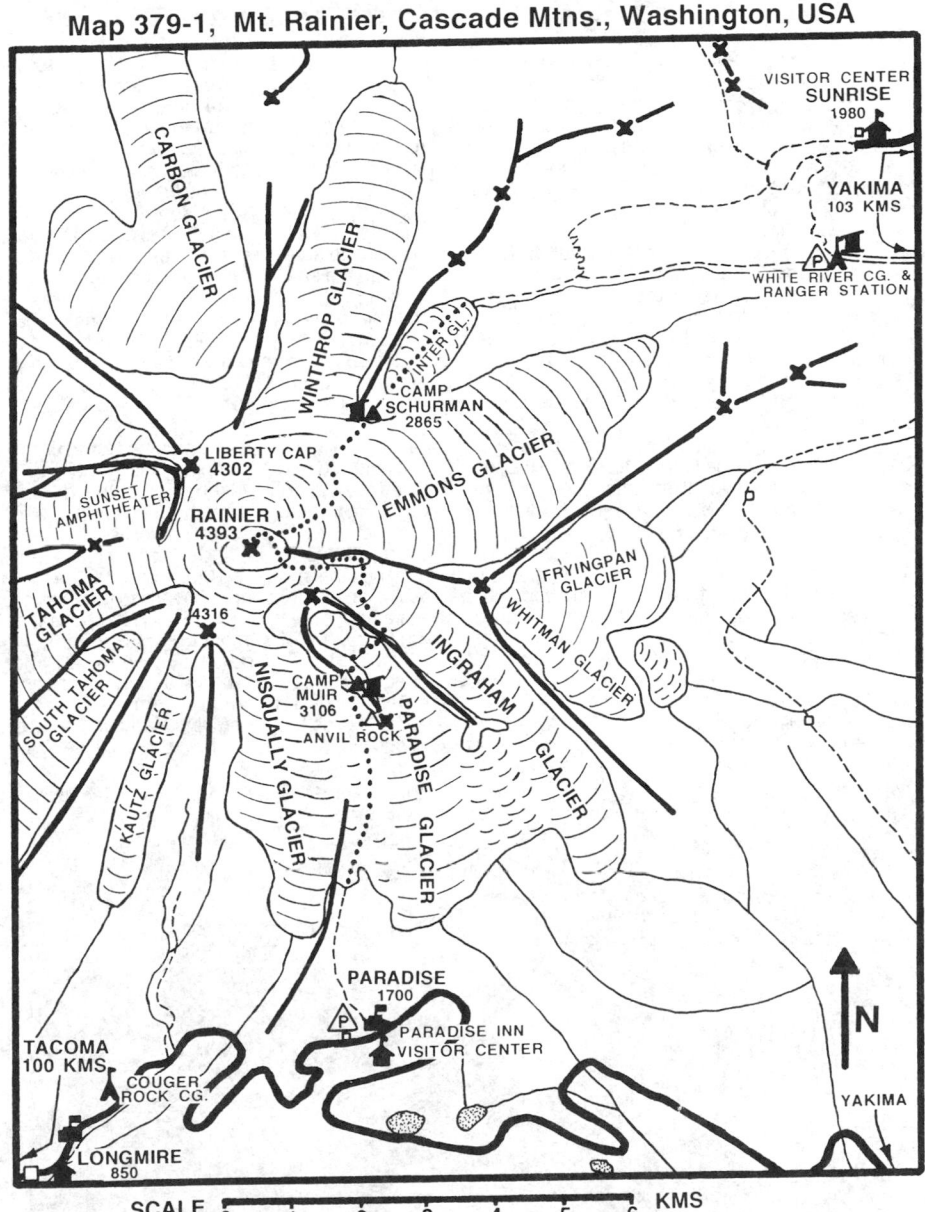

Do your shopping before entering the area, such as in Yakima, Seattle, Tacoma or Portland. Warm clothing and ice ax & crampons are a must, along with other expedition type clothing, especially if the weather looks less than perfect.

Maps *Mt. Rainier National Park,* 1:50,000; or *Stanley Friedman's climbing maps,* from the park visitor centers; and the books, **Climbing Mt. Rainier,** Beckey; or **Mt. Rainier, a Climbing Guide,** Gauthier; or **Cascade Alpine Guide, Columbia River to Stevens Pass,** Beckey; all from The Mountaineers.

Mt. Adams, Cascade Mountains, Washington, USA

This is Mt. Adams, the second highest mountain in the American Northwest and the state of Washington at 3758 meters. It is a moderately eroded volcanic cone with a number of extensive glaciers. The territory surrounding the mountain is part of the Mt. Adams Wilderness Area, and is one of the more inaccessible volcanic mountains in the northwest. The immediate area is almost unpopulated, but places outside the wilderness area have been, and continue to be, logged by the lumber industry. The eastern half of the mountain is part of the Yakima Indian Reservation.

There seems to be no studies or research which would date the last eruption from the summit crater; perhaps before the Holocene, or prior to the last 10,000 years, but in about 7535 BC, there was an explosive eruption on the south flank from the White Chuck Fissure. Volcanologists got that date using tephrochronology. But this mountain may not be completely dead. In the 1930's, a mine was operated at the top for the recovery of sulfur. Horses were used to haul miners food and supplies up to the summit camp and to haul sulfur down. Today, and late in the season when the summer snow is gone, you can see the remains of a cabin & the mine near the top.

The normal route to the top of **Adams** is on the south flank. To reach the trailhead, first make your way to the small town of Trout Lake which is immediately south of the mountain. At the west end of town is a Forest Service Ranger Station where you can pick up a climbing permit, either inside when it's open; or on the front porch after hours. In 2000, the permit cost US$15 per/person to climb on Fridays through Sunday; or US$10 per/person from Monday through Thursday. For updates, Tele. 509-395-3400.

From the ranger station, turn north at the sign indicating the road to Randle and the South Climb Trail. It's about 22 kms to the trailhead. The first 10 kms of the road is paved, the last 5 kms is very rough, at least it was in 1991, and it seems to be that way in 2000. The last portion of this drive is Forest Road 8040. Most cars make it all the way to Cold Springs where you can bivouac for the night. If it's too crowded there, then camp at Morris Creek CG., another rather primitive campsite.

From the trailhead is a very wide path going up through the trees, but soon you'll arrive at timberline. The trail is still obvious at that point, until it reaches the snowline. Most climbers get right on the snowfields, but late in the season, you may be able to stay on solid ground nearly to the summit. It's an easy route with no crevasses, but take an ice ax & crampons anyway. On 8/10/1991, the author made it to the summit in just over 3 hours, with a round-trip time of just over 5 hours. For most people, it's an all-day climb. You'll find lots of people on these slopes on good weather weekends.

Other standard routes are from Killen Creek Campground almost due north of the mountain; and from the area near Bird Lake, which is on Yakima Indian Reservation land. Trout Lake has a couple of small stores plus a gas station, but it's best to buy all your supplies before arriving. July and August are the driest months of the year in Washington and the best time to climb. Always stop at the Trout Lake Ranger Station for updated information and to buy maps.

Looking at the south slopes and south ridge of Mt. Adams.

Map 380-1, Mt. Adams, Cascade Mtns., Washington, USA

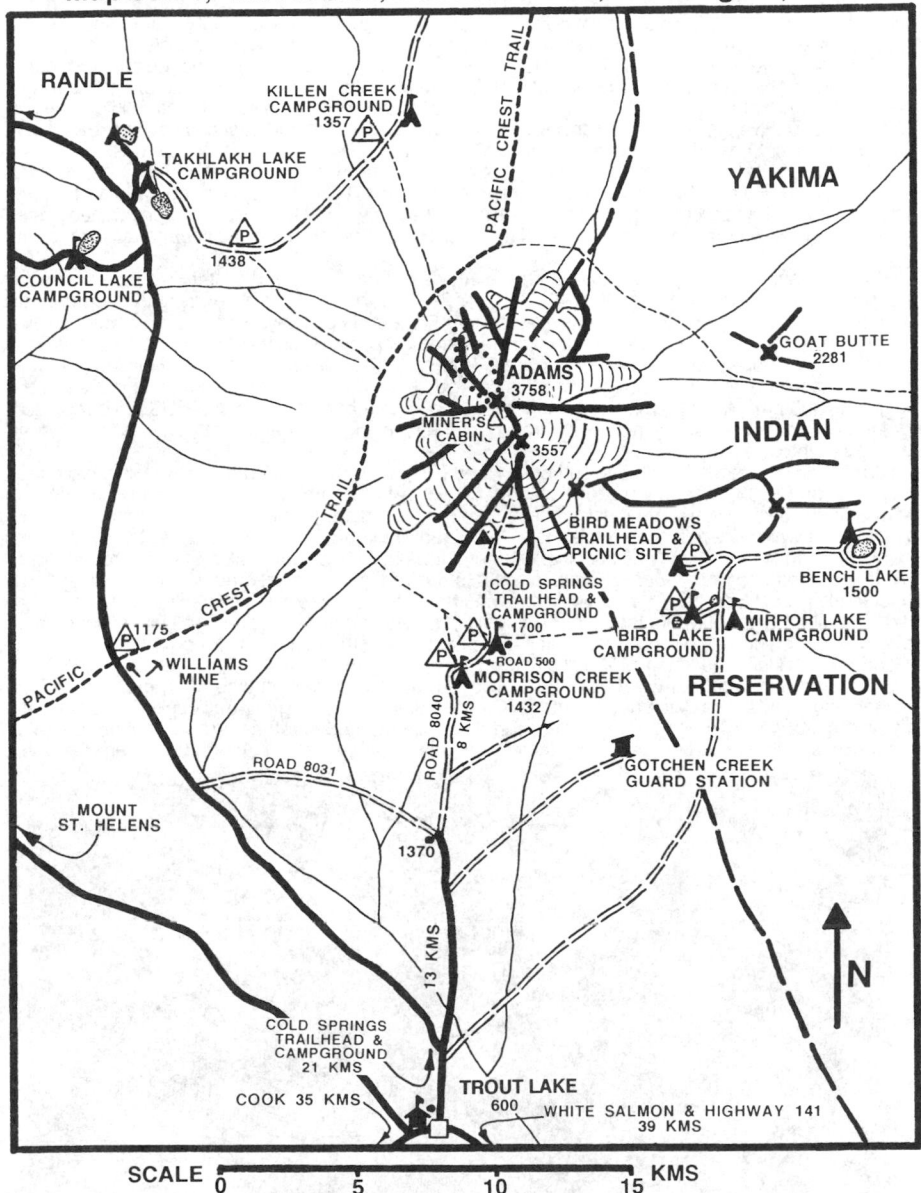

RANDLE

KILLEN CREEK
CAMPGROUND
1357 P

PACIFIC CREST TRAIL

YAKIMA

TAKHLAKH LAKE
CAMPGROUND

P
1438

COUNCIL LAKE
CAMPGROUND

GOAT BUTTE
2281

ADAMS
3758

INDIAN

MINER'S
CABIN
3557

TRAIL

CREST

BIRD MEADOWS
TRAILHEAD &
PICNIC SITE P

BENCH LAKE
1500

P1175

PACIFIC

WILLIAMS
MINE

COLD SPRINGS
TRAILHEAD &
CAMPGROUND
1700

ROAD 500

P

MORRISON CREEK
CAMPGROUND
1432

P

P

BIRD LAKE
CAMPGROUND

MIRROR LAKE
CAMPGROUND

RESERVATION

ROAD 8031

ROAD 8040

8 KMS

GOTCHEN CREEK
GUARD STATION

MOUNT
ST. HELENS

1370

N

13 KMS

COLD SPRINGS
TRAILHEAD &
CAMPGROUND
21 KMS

COOK 35 KMS

TROUT LAKE
600

WHITE SALMON & HIGHWAY 141
39 KMS

SCALE 0   5   10   15 KMS

Maps *Mt. Adams Wilderness,* 1:31,680, buy at the Trout Lake Ranger Station, or any Gifford Pinchot National Forest office or visitor center. The main office is at 500 West 12th Street, Vancouver, Washington; also the book, **Cascade Alpine Guide, Columbia River to Stevens Pass,** Beckey, The Mountaineers.

Mount St. Helens, Cascade Mountains, Washington, USA

On the morning of May 18, 1980, Mt. St. Helens erupted with a VEI-5 explosion, the first time in over 100 years and killed nearly 70 people. Before 1980, the altitude was 2950 meters; the present elevation is about 2549 meters. For volcano updates, see the website (www.volcano.si.edu/gvp/).

For several years the mountain was closed to visitors, but in 1987 it was opened for sightseeing and climbing. The area is now called the Mount St. Helens National Volcanic Monument and is run by the Gifford Pinchot National Forest. The easiest way to get there is to exit Interstate Highway 5 at Woodland and drive east on State Highway 503. Another way is from the east and southeast via White Salmon and Trout Lake (the jumping off point to Mt. Adams).

You can climb St. Helens, but there's one small problem. It operates under the *Quota System*. This means the Forest Service will limit the daily hikers to 100 climbing above the 1460 meter level between May 15 and October 31. Their excuse is *to save the mountain*--as if it hasn't already been blown to kingdom come--from too many climbers, rather than creating facilities to accommodate bigger crowds.

Here's what you're supposed to do. This is information as of 7/2000. After February 1, call the monument HQ. in Chelatchie at 360-247-3960 (or 3900) and request a date to climb the mountain. During the busier summer season they reserve up to 50 permits per day. If you can't or won't do this, and very few of us can, then go to the mountain the afternoon before you want to climb and do this: stop at Jack's Restaurant & Store, located right where Forest Road 90 leaves State Highway 503 near mile post 31 in the general area of Cougar, which is between Lake Merwin and Yale Lake. Sign the register beginning at 5 pm. At 6:00 pm, they give the first 50 people a permit, which costs US$15 per/person, for the next day--come hell or high water, rain or shine. Check their website at (www.ss.fed.us/gpnf) for updated information.

From Jack's, proceed northeast on Forest Road (FR) 90 to near the dam on Swift Reservoir, then turn north on FR 83. After 5 kms, turn left onto FR 81. After another 3 kms, turn right onto FR 830. After another 5 kms, you'll arrive at Climber's Bivouac (the trailhead) where you can camp--but take all your own water--there's none there. The Ptarmigan Trail starts out from near the toilets and runs up Monitor Ridge. It's 3 kms to timberline, another 7 kms to the crater rim; about 20 kms round-trip.

If you don't like their *Quota System*, protest to the radicals who created the policy by writing a letter to the Forest Service. They count letters, and base public policy on that. Or you could protest by climbing without a permit--like the author did. On 8/11/1991, he visited the main trailhead, then drove to Windy Ridge and walked south on the trail to the east side of the mountain. He climbed the east face in about 2 1/2 hours; round-trip was took 5 hours.

Or, to protest, start early from Climber's Bivouac, but come down a different route, to avoid the ranger who climbs it daily to check permits. Or you could walk along the trail circling the mountain and climb any one of many routes. Some can do this in half a day, others will want a full day. The mountain is stable now, but the crater rim isn't, so stay back a ways. July and August are the driest

Mt. St. Helens with the lava dome in the blown-out crater, as seen from the northeast.

Map 381-1, St. Helens, Cascade Mtns., Washington, USA

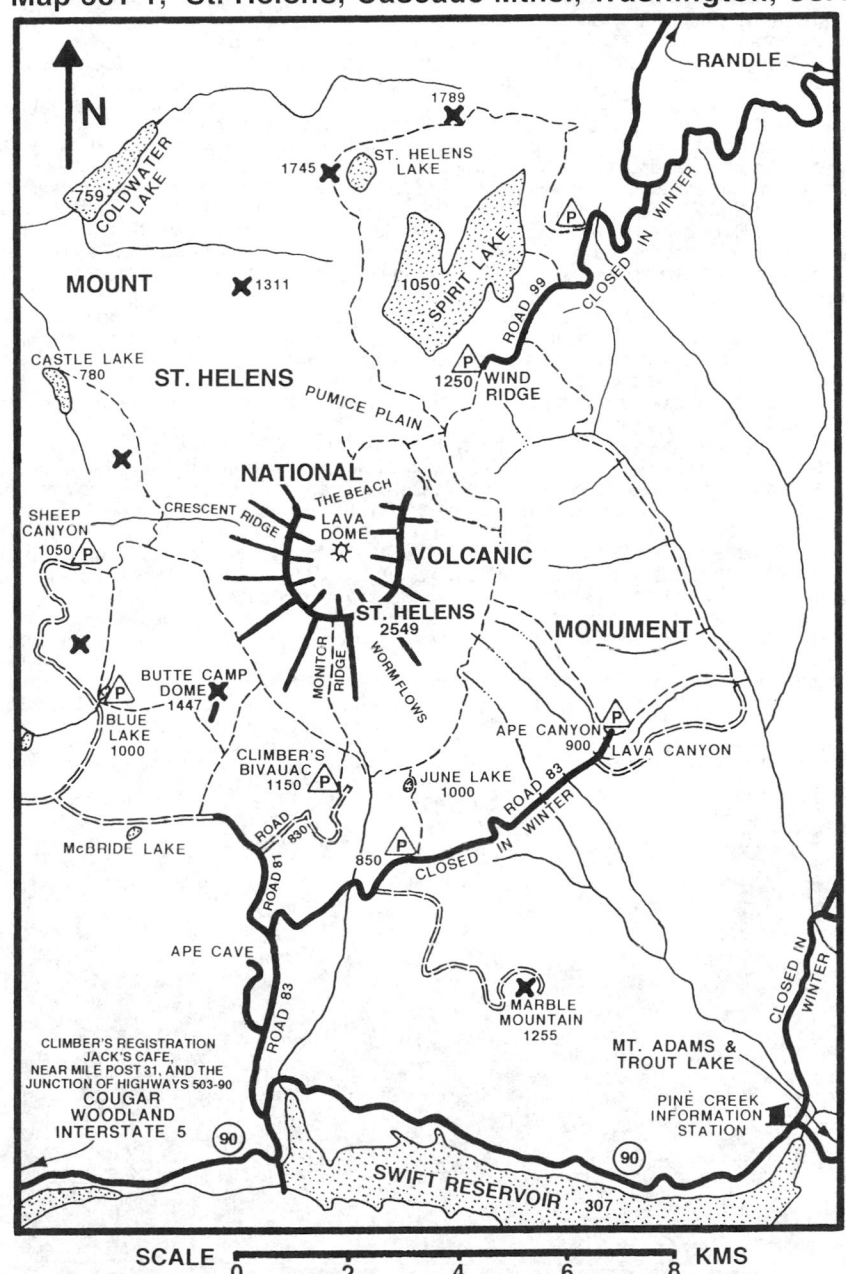

SCALE 0 2 4 6 8 KMS

months in the northwest.

Maps *Mount St. Helens National Volcanic Monument,* 1:100,000; and the books, **Mount St. Helens, a Pocket Guide,** Williams; or **A Complete Guide to Mount St. Helens National Volcanic Monument: For Hiking, Skiing, Climbing & Nature Viewing,** Vielbig, both from The Mountaineers.

Matterhorn Peak, Wallowa Mountains, Oregon, USA

In the northeast corner of Oregon is the Wallowa Range. These mountains are not as high or as rugged as say the best parts of the Swiss Alps, nor is the area large. But it is wild. The higher central part of these mountains is officially designated the Eagle Cap Wilderness Area. The highest point is known as the Matterhorn Peak, reaching 3050 meters. Several other summits in the group are near the 3000 meter level. A large part of the Wallowa Mountains is made of granitic rock, with some outcroppings of limestone around the perimeter.

Here's how to get there. Most people will reach this area via Interstate 80N, which roughly runs north-south on the west side of the range. From this major highway, you can reach all parts of the wilderness area. If coming from the south, you might stop at Baker and get a better map at the Forest HQ. or call 541-963-7186 or see their website (www.fs.fed.us/r6/w-w) for current information. From the exit just north of Baker, drive east on Highway 86 until you reach Halfway, then head north to Cornucopia, as shown at the bottom of this map. Or leave the freeway 2 exits north of Baker and exit east onto Highway 203; head northeast to Medical Springs, then continue toward the Boulder Park Resort on Eagle Creek.

But the best roads and the most popular route if going to **Matterhorn Peak**, is to leave I-80N at La Grande, and drive north on Highway 82 through Elgin and Wallowa, to Enterprise, where you'll find a small visitor center and can buy maps and get up-to-date information, or call 541-426-5546. From there, drive south through Joseph to either Hurricane Creek and the Falls Creek CG.; or to Wallowa Lake and the trailhead just beyond. This is where you park if you only want to climb Matterhorn Peak.

From the trailhead above Wallowa Lake, walk south along the Wallowa River on a good trail. After about 4 kms, turn west at the junction and walk on the trail going to Ice Lake. From the lake, continue west straight toward Matterhorn Peak. There's a trail there now, and an easy climb. The author climbed Matterhorn Peak on 8/17/1982. He was on top in about 3 hours; 5 1/4 hours round-trip.

From the same trailhead south of Wallowa Lake, peaks such as **Sacajawea, Eagle Cap** and **Aneroid** can all be climbed as well. Here's a warning; best not to camp in Lakes Basin. It's getting popular now and one day they may impose some kind of restrictions on the place.

Two other access routes can be used from the north; one is from Lostine & Lostine Creek; the other is up Hurricane Creek. To get into those canyons, see the map below and always carry an Oregon State Highway map.

On the south slopes are 3 other entry points. From Medical Springs follow the signs up Eagle Creek to the Boulder Park trailhead and hike from there to Eagle Cap Peak at 2950 meters. Or from Cornucopia, drive north 3 or 4 kms and park. However, there aren't any really high peaks in these parts; nor will you find any high summits above the Kettle Creek CG.

Do your shopping in Baker or La Grand. The road from La Grand to Wallowa Lake is paved

Matterhorn Peak, in the clouds, as seen from Ice Lake.

Map 382-1, Matterhorn, Wallowa Mountains, Oregon, USA

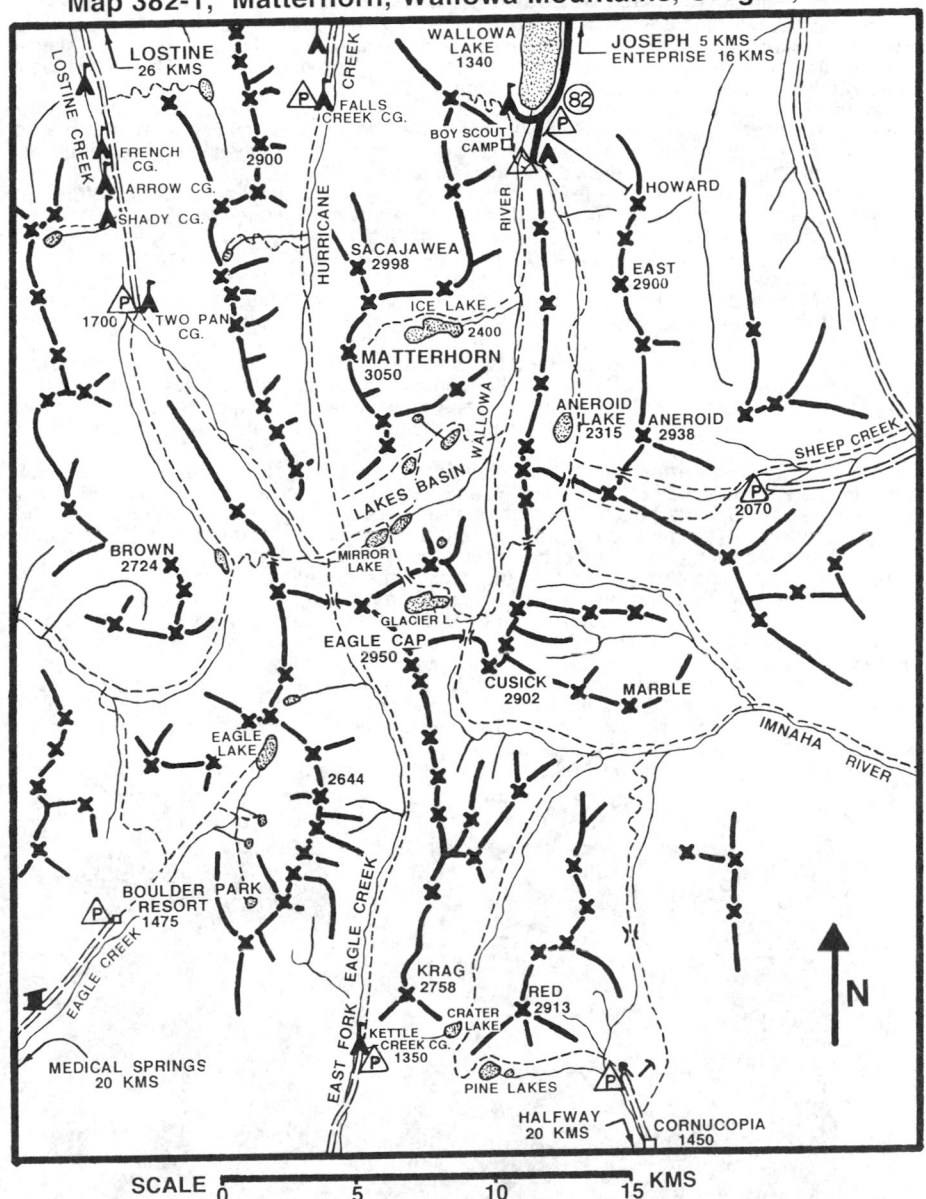

all the way. There are no glaciers in the Wallowas and no need for any ice ax & crampons, except in winter or early summer. Most peaks have both very easy and more difficult routes. The Eagle Cap Wilderness Area is less crowded than other places in Oregon.
Maps Forest Service map *Eagle Cap Wilderness*, 1:62,500, from the Wallowa Ranger Station, or Wallowa-Whitman N.F. Headquarters at Baker, Oregon; or the books, **Hiking the High Wallowas & Hell's Canyon**; or **50 Hikes in Hell Canyon & Oregon's Wallowas**, The Mountaineers.

Mount Hood, Cascade Mountains, Oregon, USA

This map shows Mount Hood at 3425 meters, the highest peak in the state of Oregon, and one of the highest in the American Northwest. Hood is located in northwest Oregon and almost due east of Portland. It's also due south of Hood River, and southwest of The Dalles, both located on the Columbia River and Interstate Highway 80N.

Mount Hood is a volcano with an almost perfect conal shape. The summit crater has not erupted in historic times, but the south flank peak called Crater Rock has had what are believed to be 7 eruptions since 1800. But there are questions regarding all of these eruptions. The last was on 8/28/1907. It may have been a phreatic explosion.

You can get to the mountain from 3 different ways. First, most people come from the Portland area via Highway 26. The second route is to first make your way along I-80N which follows the Columbia River, then turn south at Hood River onto Highway 35. The third way to reach Mount Hood is from the south and the central Oregon area along Highway 26. All 3 of these roads converge on the south side of the mountain at a place called Government Camp.

Hood is one of the most climbed mountains in the USA. The reasons are; it's close to the large Portland metropolitan area, the area has good access roads which are kept open year-round, and the south face route is rather easy and safe to climb.

The normal or tourist route up **Mt. Hood** is via Government Camp and the Timberline Lodge. At this lodge are rooms, restaurants, small gift shops and an office of the Mt. Hood National Forest which gives out information and sells maps of the area (for updates call the Hood River forest office at 541-352-6006). The rangers prefer hikers to sign in before they climb, but that's not required.

The south face or Mazama Route begins at the Timberline Lodge, and follows or parallels along the east or right side of the ski lift. You can't get lost. Above the top of the lift, which operates year-round, a trail heads straight for the summit via the right side of Crater Rock. This is the so-called volcanically active part of the mountain. From there, continue up a steep snowfield, then an icy couloir. The author hiked 2 hours in the late afternoon of 8/6/1978, and camped. Next morning it was to the top, and back to the lodge in 2 1/2 hours; or 4 1/2 hours total 2-day walk-time. Needless to say, this is a fast & easy climb.

Another route high on the mountain and from the south, heads further to the right or east, and up a kind of ridge called Castle Crags. This route is a bit more difficult. Ice ax & crampons are required for both routes. All routes from the south are day-climbs.

The climb can also be made from the Hood Meadows ski resort not far east of the Timberline Lodge; and from the Cloud Cap area, located on the northeast side of the mountain. Climbing from Cloud Cap and any northern route involves more glaciers & ice climbing than those on the south side of the mountain.

Above the ends of the roads there's little or no running water, so fill up water bottles before

The southern slopes of Mt. Hood as seen from just above the Timberline Lodge.

Map 383-1, Mt. Hood, Cascade Mountains, Oregon, USA

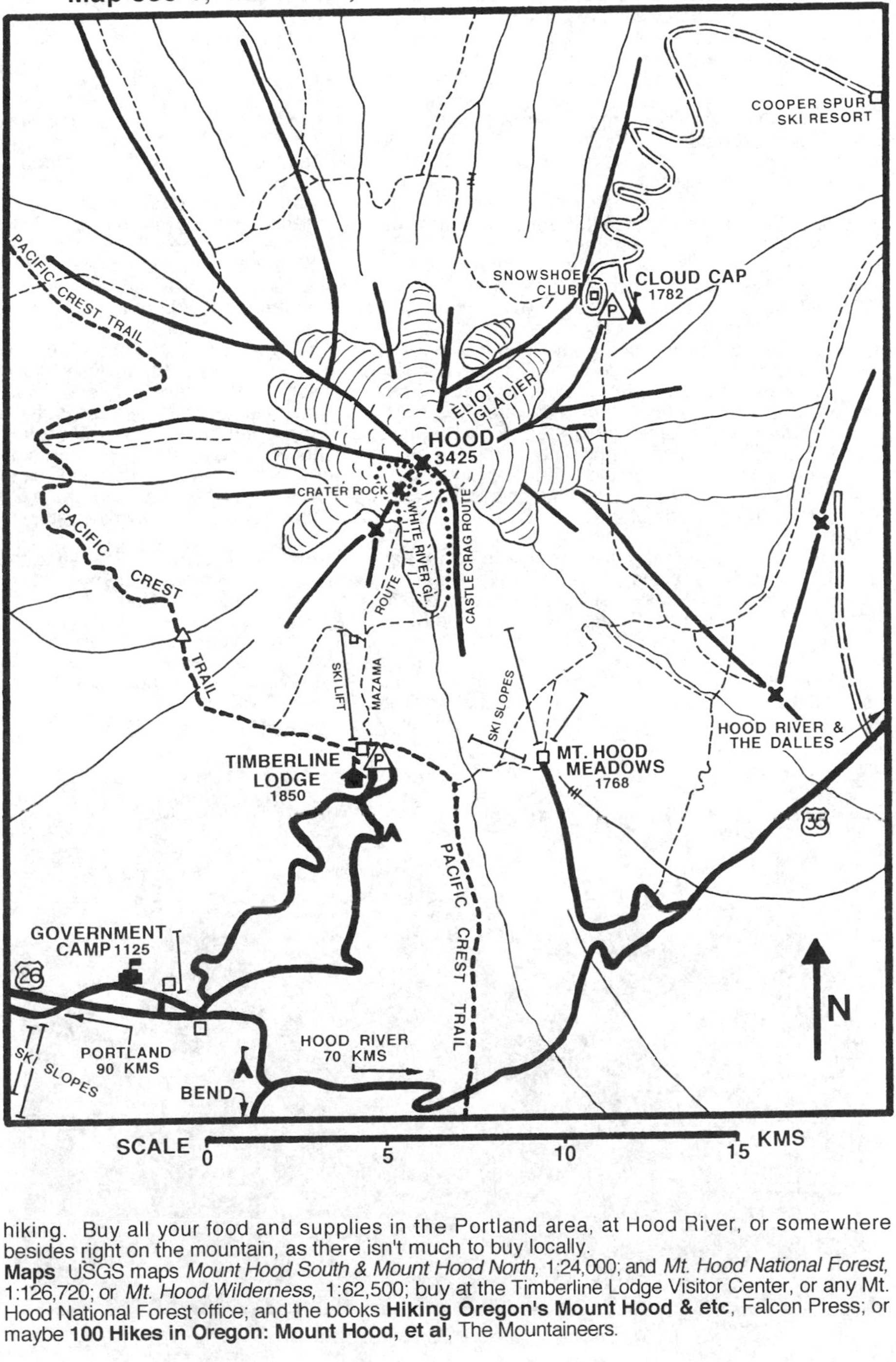

COOPER SPUR
SKI RESORT

PACIFIC CREST TRAIL

SNOWSHOE
CLUB

CLOUD CAP
1782

ELIOT GLACIER

HOOD
3425

CRATER ROCK

WHITE RIVER GL.

PACIFIC CREST

CASTLE CRAG ROUTE

ROUTE

MAZAMA

SKI LIFT

TRAIL

SKI SLOPES

HOOD RIVER &
THE DALLES

TIMBERLINE
LODGE
1850

MT. HOOD
MEADOWS
1768

35

PACIFIC CREST TRAIL

GOVERNMENT
CAMP 1125

26

N

SKI SLOPES

PORTLAND
90 KMS

HOOD RIVER
70 KMS

BEND

SCALE 0   5   10   15 KMS

hiking. Buy all your food and supplies in the Portland area, at Hood River, or somewhere besides right on the mountain, as there isn't much to buy locally.
Maps USGS maps *Mount Hood South & Mount Hood North*, 1:24,000; and *Mt. Hood National Forest*, 1:126,720; or *Mt. Hood Wilderness*, 1:62,500; buy at the Timberline Lodge Visitor Center, or any Mt. Hood National Forest office; and the books **Hiking Oregon's Mount Hood & etc**, Falcon Press; or maybe **100 Hikes in Oregon: Mount Hood, et al**, The Mountaineers.

Mount Jefferson, Cascade Mountains, Oregon, USA

Mt. Jefferson is the second highest mountain in Oregon and is one of many volcanos in the northwest USA. Jefferson at 3200 meters altitude is one of the older and more eroded stratovolcanos in the area. The north and east sides of the mountain are glaciated, but these glaciers are not nearly as large nor as crevassed as those found on other peaks such as Mt. Rainier.

The last eruption from the summit of Jefferson has not been determined, but it was sometime in the late Pleistocene. A wild guess would be from 10,000 to 20,000 years ago. However, Forked Butte issued lava in about 4500 BC; while South Cinder Peak had an eruptive period in about 950 AD.

Good access roads make this climb fairly easy, but **Jefferson** is at the center of the Mount Jefferson Wilderness Area, so there are no tourist lodges or ski resorts anywhere near. From Salem, take Highway 22 east, then southeast, past Detroit and Idanha to the Whitewater Road (you can also get to this point from the south and the town of Sisters). From the highway turn east on first the Whitewater Road, then Forest Road 2243 until you reach the trailhead marked 1225 meters. From there, walk east to Jefferson Meadows on the north side of the mountain. From Scout Lake, there's a trail up the north ridge to the summit. The author climbed Jefferson on 8/13/1982 via this northern route in just under 6 1/2 hours round-trip from his car. Or, by using this northern approach, there are other more difficult non-standard routes to choose from.

The second most popular approach route is from the west and the Pamelia Creek Road, located about 3 kms south of the Whitewater Road. This logging road takes you to near Pamelia Lake, where many people camp, then climb the mountain on the southwest side. There are many other access roads, from the north and the south, most of which were used by loggers on the lower slopes and outside the wilderness area, but they are much longer and more difficult to locate. On the east side of the mountain is Warm Springs Indian Reservation, thus for the most part, eliminating that side of the peak as an access route. You can enter from that side, but you have to get a special permit from the tribe.

At times in late summer, it's possible to find an all-rock route up Jefferson, eliminating the need for ice ax & crampons, but you're well advised to take this equipment along anyway. Also, be aware of the new **Northwest Forest Parking Pass** which is required for parking at trailheads in Washington & Oregon. Pickup a year or single trip pass at any Forest Service office.

For those coming from the north or west, do all your shopping in Salem or its suburbs. The towns of Idanha and Detroit are very small roadside villages and offer little in the way of mountain climbing supplies. If you're coming from the south shop in Sisters, and/or contact the Forest Service office there for updated information (Tele. 541-549-7700).

The 3 summer months of June, July and August have the best weather for climbing. There's a fair

Mt. Jefferson from the trail northwest of the peak.

Map 384-1, Mt. Jefferson, Cascade Mountains, Oregon, USA

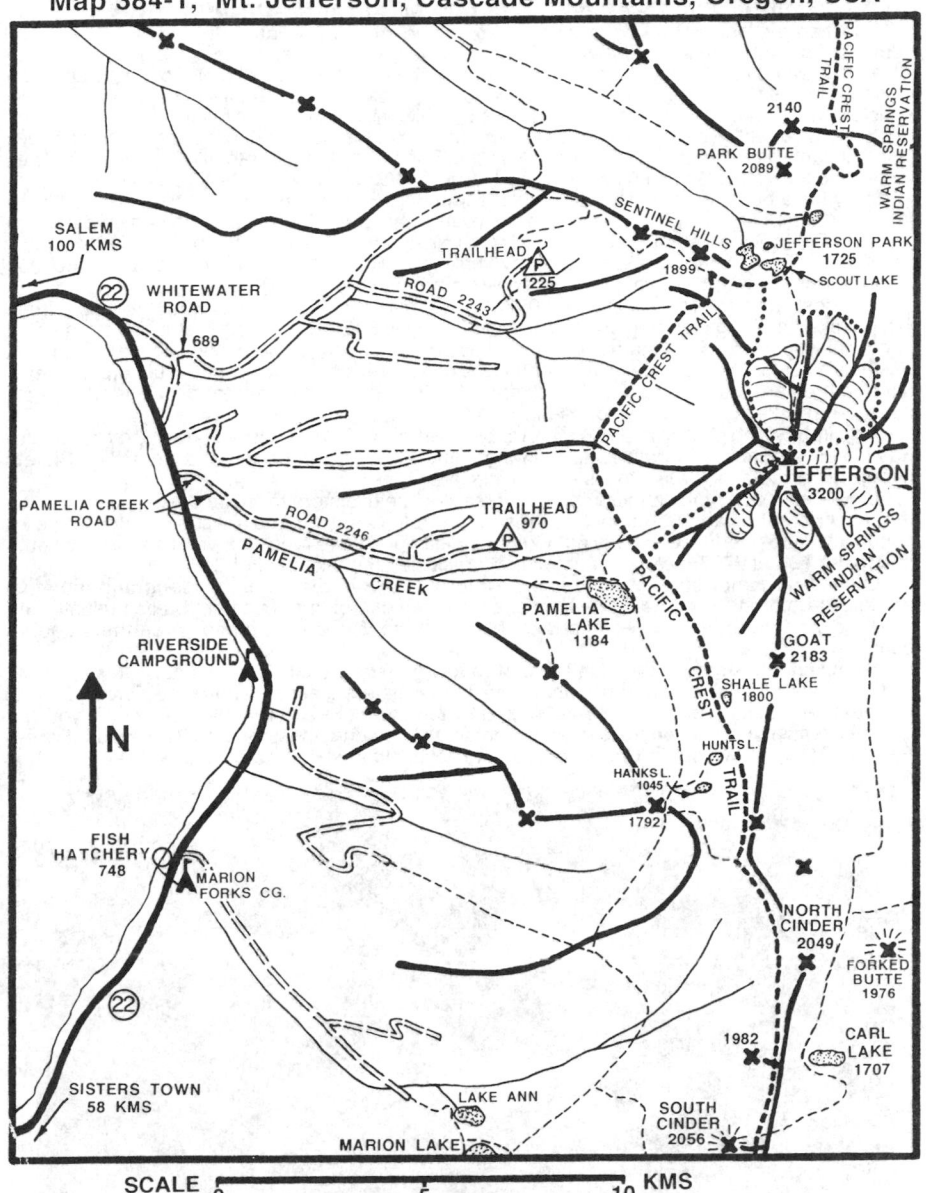

SCALE

0   5   10   KMS

amount of traffic on Highway 22, so hitch hiking is possible, if you're on foot. There's a fish hatchery at Marion Forks and the guard station is gone.

Maps *Mt. Jefferson Wilderness*, 1:62,500, from Mt. Hood, Deschutes, and Willamette National Forests, and any of their ranger stations; USGS maps *Mount Jefferson*, 1:24,000; and *Madras 44121-E1* & perhaps *North Santiam River 44122-E1*, 1:100,000; and maybe the book, **100 Hikes in the Central Oregon Cascades,** Navillus Publishing.

Three Sisters Peaks, Cascade Mountains, Oregon, USA

The Three Sisters Peaks are a group of volcanic cones located due west of Bend and southwest of Sisters town, in the central Cascade Range of Oregon. Access is quite good with State Highway 242 running along the west and north side of the area, while to the south is the Cascade Lakes Drive, beginning at Bend and running west, then south, from the area. All of the middle part of this map is part of the Three Sisters Wilderness Area.

Everything on the map is volcanic with a number of sites being rather young. North Sister's last eruption was in the late Pleistocene, but Sims Butte last blewup in about 7350 BC. No dates mentioned for Middle Sister (in the book, **Volcanos of the World**), but it still has a conical shape and may have been active in the early Holocene or late Pleistocene. Collier Cone issued large lava flows in about 350 AD, and is one of the youngest craters in the area. No certain dates are given on South Sister, but it may have had an explosion from the central crater in 7/1853. Also, just south of South Sister is a large lava flow making up Rock Mesa which dates from about 350 BC. Nearby is Devil's Hill with lots of lava being ejected in about 50 BC.

The best ways to **North Sister** at 3077 meters, and **Middle Sister** at 3065, are from Lava Camp Lake and Frog Camp, both located near Highway 242. See map. Just follow trails south or southeast to the base of the peaks, then climb a route of your choice. A west face route might be the easiest for Middle Sister. The north ridge of North Sister is the normal route up that peak. Other routes are shown. The author climbed North Sister in bad weather on 8/14/1982 from Lava Camp Lake in 7 3/4 hours round-trip.

To climb **South Sister** at 3158 meters, begin at one of the trailheads near Devils Lake or Fall Creek. From these trailheads, paths or routes lead north on either side of The Sisters Group, but a south face route looks easiest for South Sister.

On the east side, you can approach the area from near Sisters town, by driving southwest on the good Forest Road 1524 about 21 kms to the Pole Creek Spring Trailhead. You'll need a good map to do this. Also, by driving northeast past Todd Lake, you'll arrive at a trailhead south of **Broken Top** at 2797 meters, a rugged looking cluster of peaks east of South Sister.

Of the four major summits in this area, North Sister is the oldest volcano and the most eroded, therefore the one having the most difficult routes. In late summer you can usually find an all-rock route up any of these peaks, but an ice ax & crampons should be the standard equipment.

Shopping areas can be found in Bend, with a large business district; and at Sisters town, 34 kms northwest of Bend and northeast of the Three Sisters Peaks. There are Forest Service offices in both Bend (Tele. 541-383-4000) and Sisters town (Tele. 541-549-7700) where you can get the latest information on trails, roads, weather, snow conditions, the new **Northwest Forest Parking Pass,** and where the latest maps of the national forest can be bought.

This is the north face of South Sister as seen from the summit of Middle Sister.

Map 385-1, Three Sister Peaks, Cascades, Oregon, USA

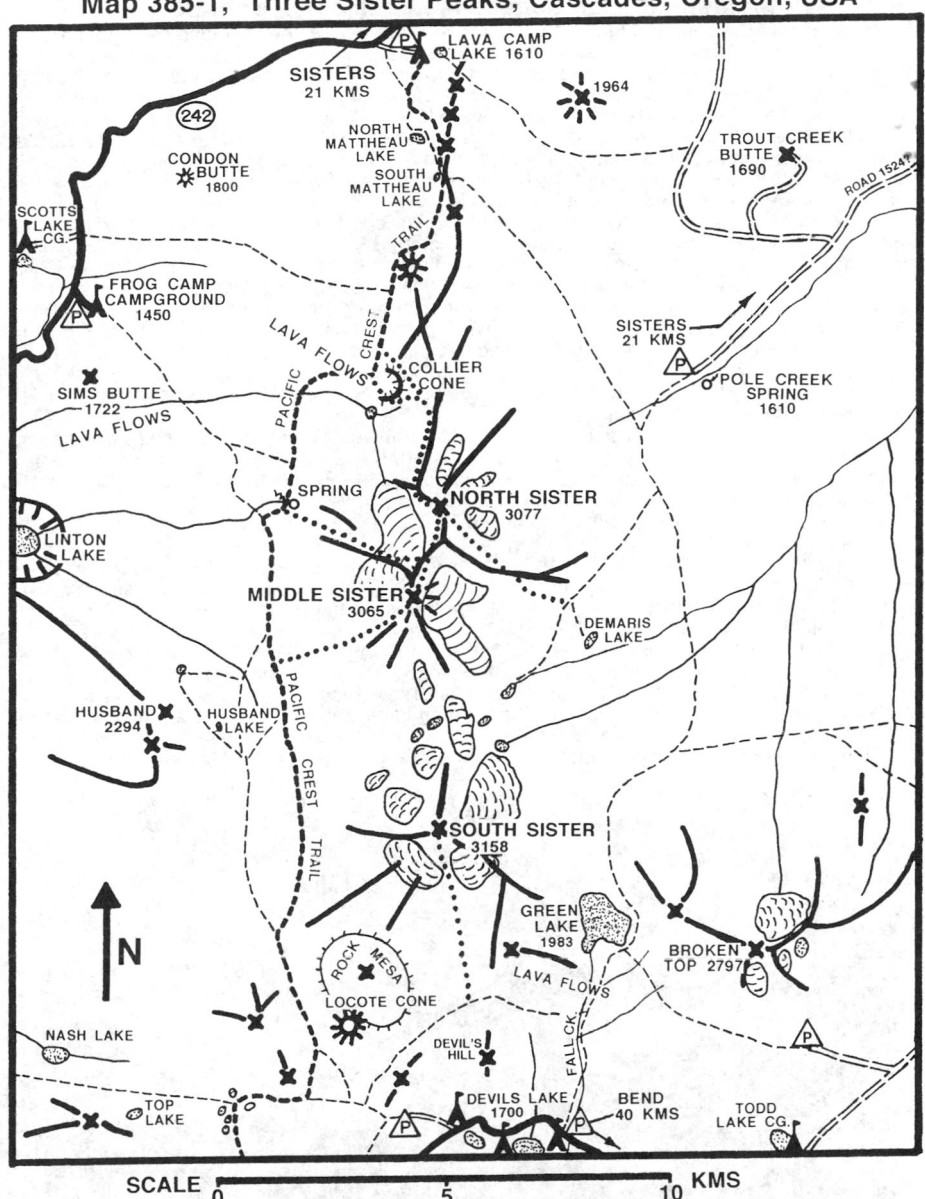

The best weather conditions usually exist in the summer months, but September and October often have good weather as well. Normally, the 9 months excluding summer, are subject to continuous cyclonic storm activity.

Maps *Three Sisters Wilderness*, about 1:95,000, from the Deschutes and Willamette National Forests, and any nearby ranger station, especially those at Sisters and Bend; or USGS maps *North Sister, South Sister*, and for the east side approaches *Broken Top* and *Trout Creek Butte*, 1:24,000; and the book **100 Hikes in the Central Oregon Cascades**, Navillus Publishing; or **Hiking Oregon's Three Sisters Country**, Falcon Press.

Diamond Peak, Cascade Mountains, Oregon, USA

Located near the center of the Cascade Range in Oregon, is the Diamond Peak Wilderness Area. Within this small primitive roadless section is Diamond Peak at 2665 meters. This elevation doesn't seem very high to some, but this whole massif rises well above the treeline. This wilderness area is so small, that a strong hiker with day-pack could walk across it in one day. The area is full of small lakes, but few have fish.

All the rocks in this area are volcanic in origin, but they're all pretty old. Diamond Peak's last eruption was probably in the middle Pleistocene sometime (perhaps a half million years old?), but Crater Butte and Redtop are much younger, probably late Pleistocene.

Diamond Peak is located just southwest of Highway 58 which runs between Eugene in the northwest, and Crescent Junction southeast of this area. Due south about 65 kms is Crater Lake National Park. The easiest way to get to Diamond Peak is to drive south from Baker on Highway 97 until you reach Odell Lake. Or head southeast from Eugene on Highway 58; or drive north from Crater Lake on Highway 97, then 58 until you reach Odell Lake.

The normal and simplest way to begin hiking to **Diamond Peak** is via Highway 58 and Odell Lake. Other access back roads offer shorter walking distances, but it's much easier to drive to Odell Lake on good paved roads. The Pacific Crest Trail crosses Highway 58 near Willamette Summit, but you can get on this same trail going to Diamond Peak by parking near the lake and walking over the railway tracks near the tunnel as shown. See map. By starting there, it shortens the hike by about 2 kms.

From the lake, follow the Pacific Crest Trail southwest then south, to a point just east of Diamond Peak, then route-find west up to the north ridge, then south to the main summit. Another easy route would be to walk further south along the Pacific Crest Trail and climb north along the south ridge. There are small snow fields in a couple of north facing cirque basins, but in some years they dwindle to nothing. The Pacific Crest Trail in this area is well-kept, but has little foot traffic.

You could also walk the trail to Yoran Lake, as shown on the map, then bushwhack (which is easy) in a westerly direction until you come to the Pacific Crest Trail, then on to the summit. The author hiked this trail/route to the peak, then returned via the Pacific Crest Trail in just over 5 hours round-trip. This was done on 8/16/1982.

A route which involves less walking, but some travel on graveled and dusty roads, would be to drive to Oakridge (not on this map) on Highway 58 about 40 kms northwest of Willamette Summit, and take Forest Road 21 south from Hills Creek Reservoir. This paved highway turns to gravel near Summit Lake. From near the Summit Lake Campground find and use the same Pacific Crest Trail and walk north to the top. This hike might take only a half-day for some.

There are a few cabins around both Crescent and Odell Lakes, but few places to buy

The Diamond Peak Massif seen from Yoran Lake.

Map 386-1, Diamond Peak, Cascade Mountains, Oregon, USA

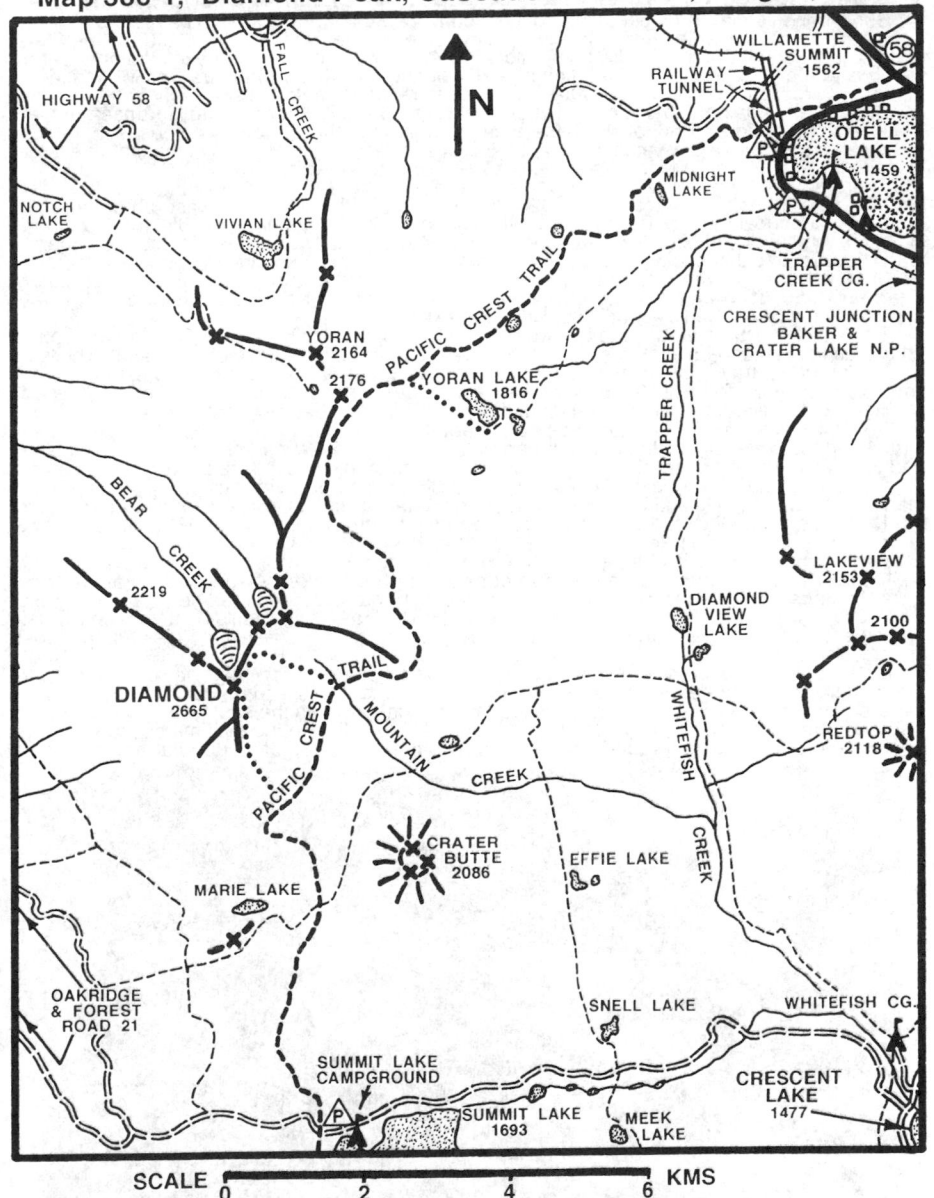

HIGHWAY 58

WILLAMETTE SUMMIT 1562

RAILWAY TUNNEL

58

ODELL LAKE
1459

NOTCH LAKE

VIVIAN LAKE

MIDNIGHT LAKE

TRAPPER CREEK CG.

FALL CREEK

PACIFIC CREST TRAIL

CRESCENT JUNCTION
BAKER &
CRATER LAKE N.P.

N

YORAN 2164

2176

YORAN LAKE 1816

TRAPPER CREEK

BEAR CREEK

2219

DIAMOND VIEW LAKE

LAKEVIEW 2153

2100

DIAMOND 2665

MOUNTAIN TRAIL

CREEK

WHITEFISH

REDTOP 2118

PACIFIC CREST

CRATER BUTTE 2086

EFFIE LAKE

CREEK

MARIE LAKE

SNELL LAKE

WHITEFISH CG.

OAKRIDGE & FOREST ROAD 21

SUMMIT LAKE CAMPGROUND

P

SUMMIT LAKE 1693

MEEK LAKE

CRESCENT LAKE 1477

SCALE 0   2   4   6 KMS

supplies. Buy everything you need before entering the region, either at Eugene, Bend, or Oakridge. Because this isn't a really high peak, an all-rock route can be found after about mid-July, so ice ax & crampons are normally not needed.

Map Willamette and Deschutes National Forest map *Diamond Peak Wilderness,* 1:62,500; or Willamette and Deschutes National Forest maps; or USGS maps *Diamond Peak, Willamette Pass, Emigrant Butte, Cowhorn Mountain,* 1:24,000; and perhaps the book, **100 Hikes in the Central Oregon Cascades**, Navillus Publishing.

Mt. Thielsen & Crater Lake, Cascade Mountains, Oregon, USA

Shown on this map is an old and eroded volcano called Mt.Thielsen at 2799 meters. This is one of the lesser known high summits in the Cascade Range. Also shown is Mt. Bailey, 2549 meters, just across Diamond Lake from Thielsen. Also included is Crater Lake (National Park), which is actually the remains of a much higher volcano known posthumously as Mt. Mazama. This area is located in south central Oregon not far north of Klamath Falls.

Crater Lake has had an explosive history. In about 5065 BC, a north flank eruption at Llao Rock was classified a VEI-6, of which there have been 34 in the world. By comparison, Mt. St. Helens had a VEI-5. A few years later, in 4895 BC, a *colossal* explosion took the top off a large volcano that we now call Mt. Mazama. The Volcanic Explosivity Index was a VEI-7.

There have only been 4 historical volcanic explosions in human history that are classified VEI-7: Crater Lake (Mt. Mazama) in 4895 BC; Kikai in the Ryukyu Islands south of Japan in 4350 BC; Changbai Shan or Baitoushan on the China-North Korea border in 1050; and Tambora in Sumbawa, Indonesia, in 1815. Tambora released about 100 cubic/kms of tephra, compared to 2800 cubic/kms that came out of the Toba Caldera in northern Sumatra 74,000 years ago.

More volcanic activity in roughly 4750 BC, created Wizard Island inside Crater Lake. Later, in about 2050 BC, more activity took place west, northwest of Wizard Island. This was apparently the last volcanic activity in the immediate area.

To climb **Mt. Thielsen**, drive to the area just north of Crater Lake and to the large recreation area around Diamond Lake. From the southeastern corner of this lake, look for the Mt. Thielsen Trail. You can park on the lakeshore highway, or on Highway 138 (and save walking about 1 km). From the lake to the intersection of the Pacific Crest Trail is about 5 kms and is well-used, as climbing Thielsen is a popular summertime hike. From the Pacific Crest Trail, continue east up the Mt. Thielsen Trail which zig zags up the southwest slopes of the peak. Go more or less straight up the scree slopes to the upper part of the peak. The last part steepens to a scramble, and the last 15 meters is near vertical; but almost anyone can climb it because of the nature and composition of the rock which is the former throat of the volcano. This last part is much easier than it first appears. Up and back takes about half a day for most people. Length of the hike is 6.5 kms, one way. The author climbed Thielsen in the morning of 8/15/1982 in just under 3 hours round-trip from the lake.

Another nearby hike is to the top is **Mt. Bailey**, located west of Diamond Lake. To find this trail, walk or drive along the paved road connecting the Broken Arrow and Thielsen View Campgrounds. At the southwest corner of the lake is a Forest Service road heading southwest. Just beyond that turnoff is the beginning of the Mt. Bailey Trail. This should be another easy half day hike for most people. From the top of Bailey you'll have a good view of Thielsen, the most spectacular peak around.

Crater Lake National Park has little to offer climbers because of the highway circling around the caldera rim. The best hike however is to walk up a trail to the top of **Scott Peak** at 2721 meters. This trail begins just east of the Cloudcap parking area on the east side of the lake. On 8/9/1991, the author hurried to the top for pictures of the lake in a round-trip time of 1 1/4 hours.

There are many campgrounds in the area, but the entire region is popular and crowded.

A NPS aerial foto of Crater Lake looking east. On the far side to the right is Scott Peak; the younger volcano in the lake is Wizard Island. Thielsen & Diamond Lake are to the left out of sight

Map 387-1, Thielsen & Crater Lake, Cascades, Oregon, USA

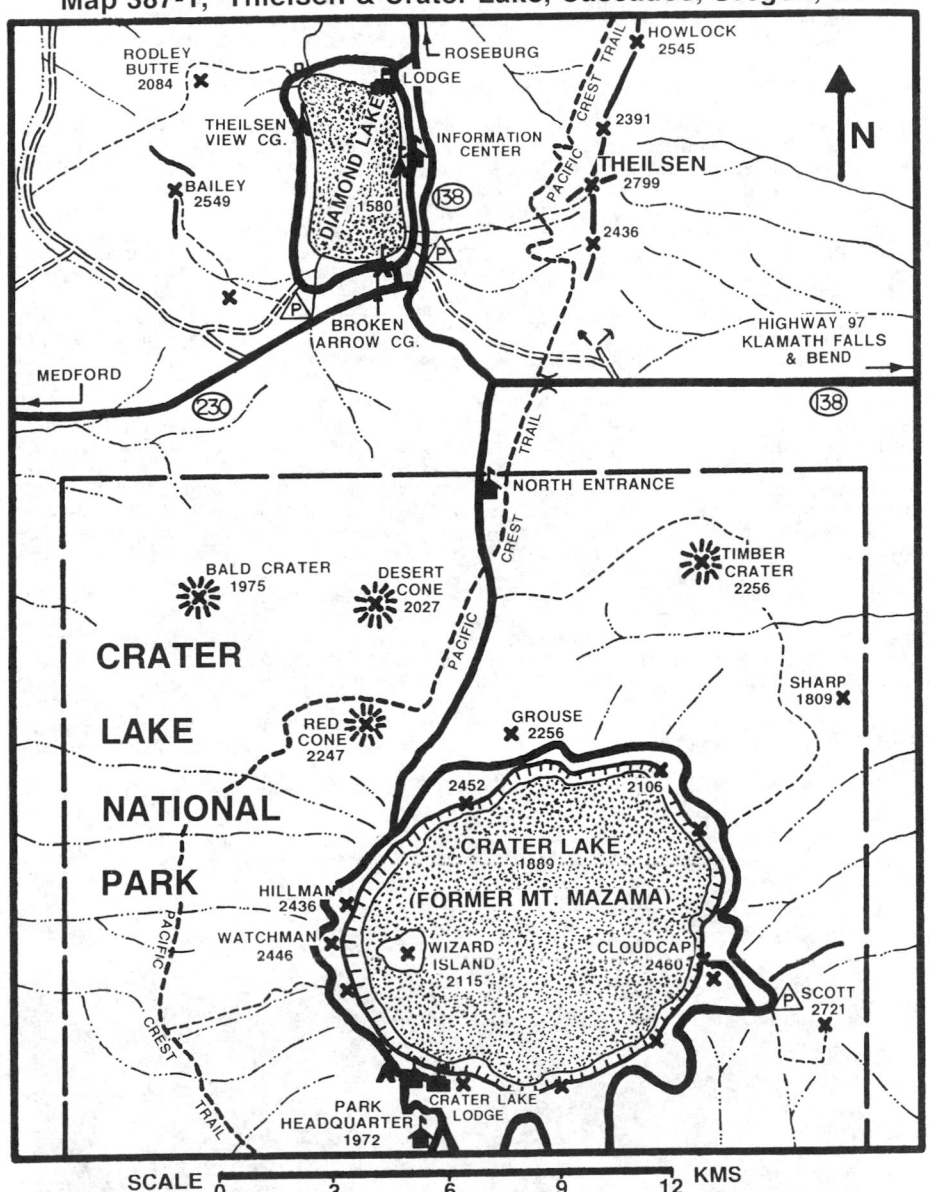

Given its national park status, everything is severely regulated, so plan to spend the night elsewhere. Buy all your food and supplies elsewhere too, perhaps in Klamath Falls, or Bend which is north of this area. For current information about Crater Lake National Park, call 541-594-2211, or the website (www.nps.gov/crla/).
Maps *Rogue River, Winema, or Umpqua National Forests* maps, 1:126,720; USGS maps *Crater Lake West, Crater Lake East, Pumice Desert East & Pumice Desert West*, 1:24,000; or pickup free maps of Crater Lake & buy guidebooks at the national park visitor center near the Crater Lake Lodge.

Mt. McLoughlin, Cascade Mountains, Oregon, USA

In southern Oregon not far north of the California state line, stands another of the lofty volcanic peaks in the Cascade Range. This is Mt. McLoughlin rising to 2894 meters. It's located about halfway between Medford on the west and Klamath Lake and the city of Klamath Falls on the east. It's also just north of Fish Lake & Campground, and Highway 140, which is your main access route.

McLoughlin is one of the oldest of the major volcanos in the American Northwest. Apparently no one has tried to estimate the age of McLoughlin, but a good guess is its last eruption was 25,000 to 30,000 years ago. It has an eroded crater which is breached on the north; perhaps blown out during its last eruption. McLoughlin has no glaciers, and even the north-slope snow fields sometimes melt completely during some summers. There is a trail to the summit where you'll find a cement building, probably the remains of an old fire lookout station.

To climb **McLoughlin**, drive northwest out of Klamath Falls on Highway 140; or north, then east from Medford, again on Highway 140. At a point about 2 kms east of the Fish Lake Turnoff, and between mileposts 32 & 33, you'll find Forest Road (FR) 3650 heading northeast. Drive northeast about 5 kms to where there's a large parking lot on the west side of the road. Another way to the trailhead, and along a better road as of 2000, is to leave Highway 140 at the north end of Lake of the Woods. From there drive northwest along FR 3661 to a junction, then turn south to the trailhead on FR 3650.

Just a few meters beyond the beginning of the trail you'll cross a stream (actually a canal) and the only water you'll find along the way, except perhaps during late spring or early summer. After a ways, the Mt. McLoughlin Trail joins the Pacific Crest Trail for a short distance, then veers left and heads up the eastern slopes.

Once above treeline, the one trail turns into several that zig zags upslope to the summit. This is a popular climb for residents of southern Oregon and the author found 30-35 hikers there on Sunday afternoon, 8/15/1982. His round-trip time was about 3 1/4 hours. Good trail and nice hike. No special equipment needed if doing the climb in summer or fall. The north face has a large cirque basin and could offer more challenging climbs.

In the southeast corner of this map is the **Mountain Lakes Wilderness**. It's very small as wilderness areas in America go, only 10 kms square, but it does offer some interesting hikes. These peaks are rounded summits and not considered real mountaineering goals. No peaks rise above treeline, with perhaps the exception of Aspen Butte at 2502 meters, which has a north facing cirque. These mountains offer trail hiking with small lakes, the larger of which have been stocked with fish. Easiest way to these mountains is by way of the Aspen Point Campground or the Varney Creek road and trail. With a better map than this, you can also get there from the southwest along the Clover Creek Trail. There's apparently no public access from the east side.

This region is noticeably drier than points north. Summers and the dry season tend to be a

Mt. McLaughlin as seen from the northeast. The east ridge is to the left.

Map 388-1, Mt. McLoughlin, Cascade Mountains, Oregon, USA

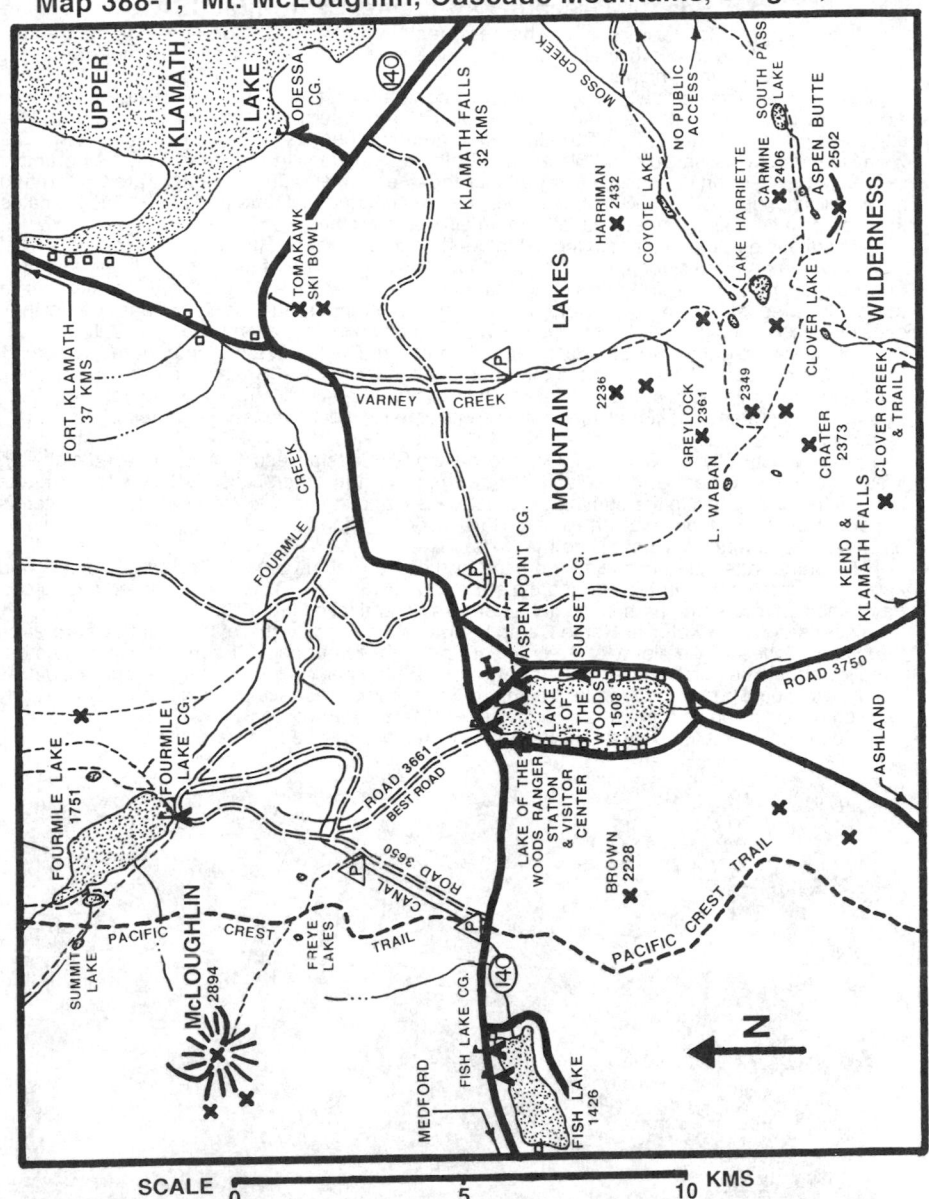

SCALE 0 _____ 5 _____ 10 KMS

lot longer here than around the US-Canadian border. June through September is the normal hiking season, although ski touring is becoming popular. Do all your shopping in Klamath Falls, Medford or Ashland. While in either of these small cities, you might look for a local hiking guide to the area. For updated information call the Rogue River National Forest Office in Medford at 541-858-2200; or in Ashland call 541-482-3333; or in Klamath Falls call Winema National Forest office at 541-885-3400.

Maps *Rogue River or Winema National Forest* maps, 1:126,720; or USGS maps *Mt. Mcloughlin, Lake of the Woods North, Lake of the Woods South,* and *Aspen Lake,* 1:24,000.

Mt. Shasta, Cascade Mountains, California, USA

Mt. Shasta at 4317 meters, is the highest peak in northern California and is the second highest in the American Northwest & the Cascade Mountains. Of all the volcanos in the Cascades, only Rainier is higher.

Shasta is an symmetrically-shaped volcanic cone, and not very old. According to the book, **Volcanos of the World**, the last eruption on Shasta's summit crater was in 1786. That explosion ranked a VEI-3. There are other young eruptive centers on the mountain as well. The west side craters of Shastina and Black Butte both had eruptions in about 7415 BC. An eruptive center somewhere on the north flank, perhaps the one marked 2680 or North Gate Crater, had its last eruption in 7350 BC. Shastina also issued lava during that time period. All this indicates the mountain still has the possibility of coming alive at any time.

Shasta has glaciers, but not to the extent as the more northerly Rainier. These glaciers exist mostly on the northern slopes, while the south face is largely free of snow & ice in late summer. For the most part, the region north of Shasta is part of the Marine West Coast Climate; that to the south, Mediterranean. Summers are hot and dry in this area, but it's far enough north to escape the real long periods of drought which are common in central and southern California.

Here's how to get to **Mt. Shasta**. Head for northern California along Interstate Highway 5. About 15 kms south of Weed, exit to the east on Highway 89 and Shasta (rather Shasta City). Before leaving town, stop at the Shasta-Trinity National Forest Office & Visitor Center (Tele 530-926-4511) to get any additional information regarding road conditions or buy maps. Also stock up on water in Shasta.

From Shasta City, drive about 23 kms to the old Ski Shasta Resort site on a paved highway. Most people park there and hike straight up the mountain, then cross left over the ridge to Avalanche Gulch, then to the summit. A second way, and the normal trailhead during winter, is to park at Bunny Flat, and walk the trail to Horse Camp Lodge (camp for $5), then to the summit of Shasta, or its western sister, **Shastina**, 3759 meters.

The author attempted this climb from the end of the road on 9/11/1978, but failed. He had knee-deep fresh snow up high from a big storm the day before. This is considered a long one day climb by the average person, so get an early start and take a good lunch.

There's plenty of water at Horse Camp Lodge, but otherwise there's little surface water on the higher slopes. Take plenty of water in your car and in your pack. Food, gasoline and other supplies should be purchased in Shasta City, which is the last such place on the route. Ice ax & crampons should be taken regardless of the route or time of year, although in late summer--early fall, some routes can be climbed almost entirely on bare ground or rock.

The normal climbing season for Shasta is June through September, with the remaining 8

Looking north at the south face and south ridge of Mt. Shasta.

Map 389-1, Mt. Shasta, Cascade Mountains, California, USA

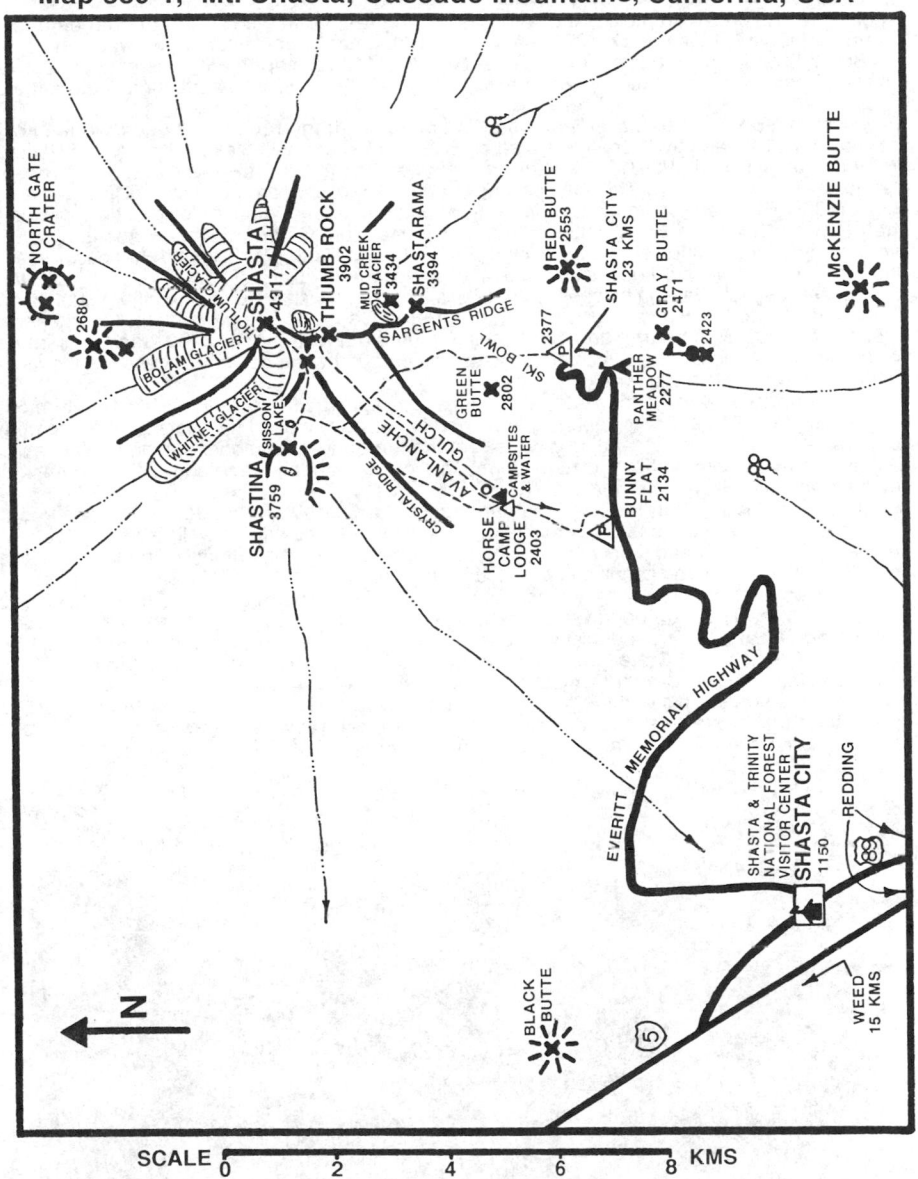

months subject to frontal passages. However, climbing is done throughout the year, because someone plows the road up to Bunny Flat Trailhead throughout the winter. The old Ski Shasta resort at the end of the highway has been removed.

Maps USGS map *Shasta*, 1:62,500; or the *Shasta National Forest* map from Shasta City Forest Service Office; or the Selters & Zanger map *Mount Shasta* 1:24,000, and the book, **The Mt. Shasta Book**, both from Wilderness Press.

Lassen Peak, Lassen Volcanic National Park, California, USA

Lassen Peak at 3188 meters elevation, is the highest point within the boundaries of the Lassen Volcanic National Park. This park is located in northern California, between Redding and Susanville. From Redding, drive east on Highway 44 to the north entrance and Manzanita Lake; or from Susanville take either Highway 44 or 36 west and follow the signs with a state highway map.

Since Lassen's last eruptive period starting 5/30/1914, the region has been made into a national park. That eruptive period climaxed on 5/22/1915 with a VEI-3 explosion. Activity lasted about 3 years, or until 6/29/1917. There are also other peaks in the park with some recent eruptions. There was activity at Chaos Crags in about 1650; plus an eruption at Cinder Cone in about 1635. There are some big lava flows northeast of Lassen running down to the highway; and between Snag and Butte Lakes. That flow came from Cinder Cone. In addition, other symetrically-shaped cones or craters include; Raker, Crater Butte, Fairfield and Prospect Peaks. And there are more in the area, most of which are Holocene in age.

In some respects Lassen belongs to the Sierra Nevada, which includes the high peaks south of this area. In other ways it seems to belong to the Cascade Range, which extends north through Oregon, Washington and into British Columbia. With much of the Cascades being volcanic in origin, most people categorize Lassen as part of that range. In this case, it's the most southerly in that great chain of volcanos.

Access to the park is good, except in winter when Highway 89 running north-south through the area is closed. Generally speaking, this road is normally closed from late October to mid-June, but ski touring is popular during winter around the park. The ranger station at Manzanita Lake is open year-round. For updated information, call park headquarters at 530-595-4444, or see their website (www.nps.gov/lavo/).

About halfway through the park is a parking lot & trailhead at the base of **Lassen Peak**. From that point it's a very easy walk to the top via a well-maintained and well-used trail. Lots of people are on the trail and it only takes one or 2 hours to reach the summit. The author made this hike on 9/12/1978 and it took only one hour going up.

If you don't like crowds, you might try some of the nearby peaks such as **Eagle, Diller and Loomis**. The park has a good system of trails throughout, and all are well-marked. A good starting place to reach the central parts of the park is at the Summit Lake Campground & Trailhead. **Fairfield** and **Crater Butte** can be reached from there. Or drive south from Highway 44 to Butte Lake, to see **Cinder Cone** and the big fresh lava flow nearby.

Near the south entrance of the park is the Lassen Chalet which is open year-round, but the information booth there is closed in winter. This is the best winter access point (the road between Lassen Chalet & Manzanita Lake is not plowed). If you expect to spend time in this

This is Lassen Peak fotographed from the highway and lake 3 kms south of the summit.

Map 390-1, Lassen Peak, Lassen Volcanic NP, California, USA

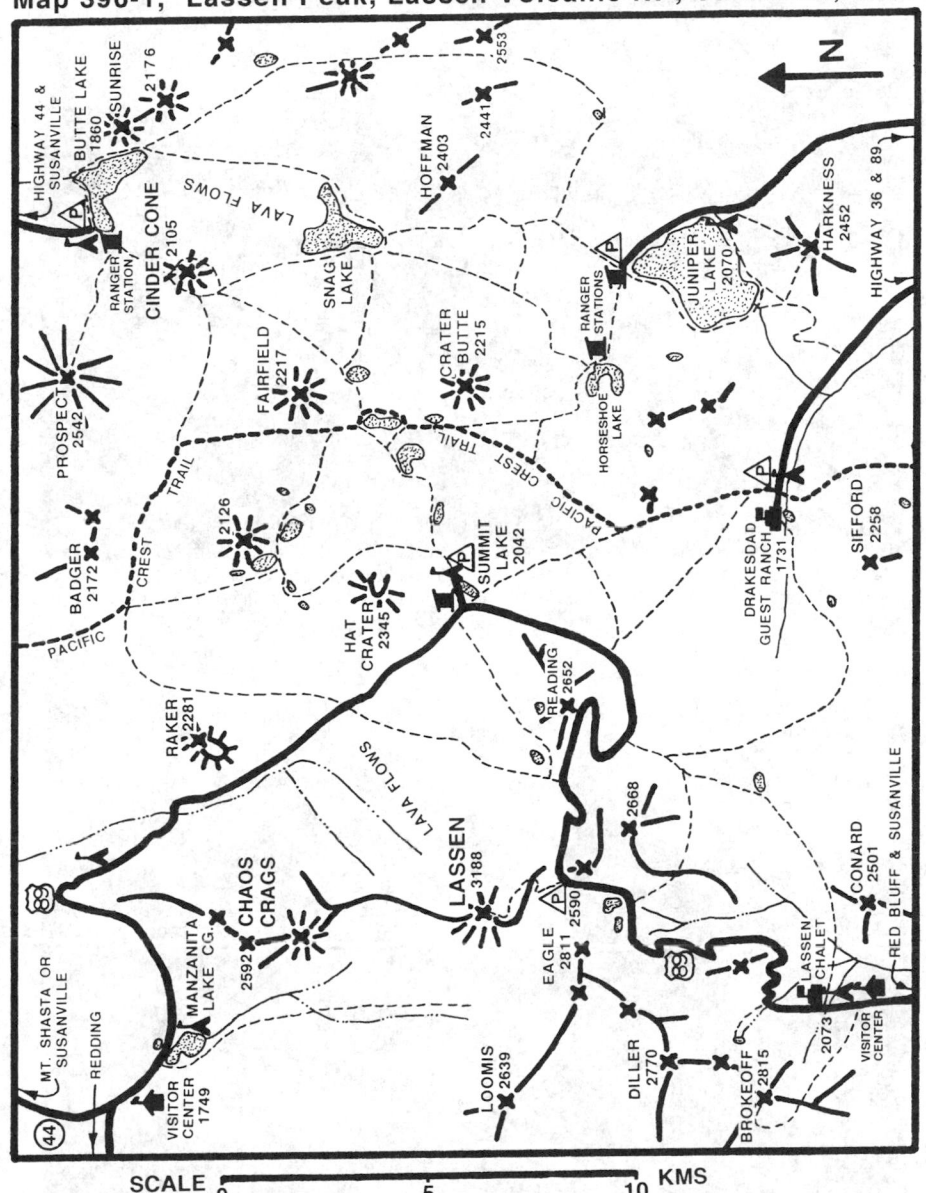

area, plan to buy food & supplies before arriving, preferably in Susanville, Redding, or Red Bluff. There are no towns in the immediate area, only roadside motels, dude ranches and gas stations. There's no public transportation in this immediate area.

Maps USGS map *Lassen Volcanic National Park,* 1:62,500; or *Hiking Map & Guide, Lassen Volcanic National Park,* 1:48,000, from Earthwalk Press; or *Hiking Trails of Lassen,* Perkins; buy these at Manzanita Visitor Center.

The author and the plane at the landing site on the Hulahula River north of Mt. Michelson in the Brooks Range, Alaska. Above the plane in the distance is the pass marked 762 meters (Map 337, page 731).

This foto was taken at or near the summit of Thompson Peak and looking west. Thompson is the highest point in the Trinity Alps of Northern California (see next page).

A late summer fotograph of Mt. Shasta from the south. The lower peak
on the left is Shastina (Map 389, page 835).

The highest peak in the middle background is Bear Creek Spire as seen
from the summit of Mt. Morgan (Map 396, page 851).

Thompson Peak, Trinity Alps, California, USA

Here's a group of peaks few people outside northern California know about. It's the Trinity Alps, located roughly halfway between Redding and the coastal city of Eureka. This small group of alpine peaks is part of the much larger Salmon Mountains, which some might classify as part of the Coastal Range. The highest parts of the range have been made into the Trinity Alps Wilderness Area. The elevations here aren't the highest, but scenically, they are at or near the top of anyones list.

The highest summit is Thompson Peak at 2743 meters. Two other prominent peaks are Mt. Hilton at 2732, and Sawtooth Mtn. at 2708 meters. The Salmon Mountains are made up of various metamorphic rocks such as slates and gneisses, but the higher summits are mostly a light colored granite. Largely because of the rock, and partly because of the altitude and higher precipitation, these higher peaks rise well above treeline. There are 2 small glaciers on the north side of Thompson Peak.

There are several access routes to the Trinity Alps. One way to the north face of Thompson would be from the northwest and a place called Cecilville, then Grizzly Lake. Another route would be on the northeast along Coffee Creek and the Big Flat Campground. On the west you could approach the peaks from a wide-place-in-the-road called Helena, then drive north, and hike from the Hobo Gulch Trailhead.

However, the best way into the middle of the highest summits and **Thompson Peak** is to first go to the small logging town of Weaverville. This place is roughly halfway between Redding on the east, and Eureka and Arcata on the west. The road connecting Redding and Eureka is Highway 299. Weaverville has now become a little tourist town, partly because of the Trinity Alps, but also its proximity to Clair Engle Lake, located just to the northeast. In Weaverville, you can buy books and maps of the area, plus do all your shopping. At the west end of town is a visitor center & ranger station of the Trinity National Forest, Tele. 530-244-2978. Be sure to stop there for more maps, information, and your free backcountry camping permit--if you plan to backpack and stay overnight in the wilderness area.

From Weaverville, drive west about 13 kms on Highway 299 in the direction of Eureka. At Junction City, which is right at mile post 43.50, turn north onto a paved road and drive about 19 or 20 kms to the Canyon Creek Trailhead. You can bivouac at the trailhead, or camp 1 1/2 kms back down the road at the Ripstein Campground; a primitive backpackers campsite.

While the author climbed Thompson Peak (on 9/5/1992) in a round-trip time of just under 9 hours from the trailhead, many people prefer to backpack 12 kms or so to the Canyon Creek Lakes, camp there, then make several hikes or climbs using the lakes as a base camp. The distance from the trailhead to the top of Thompson is about 16 kms one-way, or 32 kms round-trip; a long one-day trek for most people. Above the lakes there's no trail, so you'll just route-find, which slows things down some.

Ideal time to climb here would be in July, August and early September, but there's usually good

From the Canyon Creek Lakes looking northwest at Thompson Peak (far background).

Map 391-1, Thompson Peak, Trinity Alps, Calif., USA

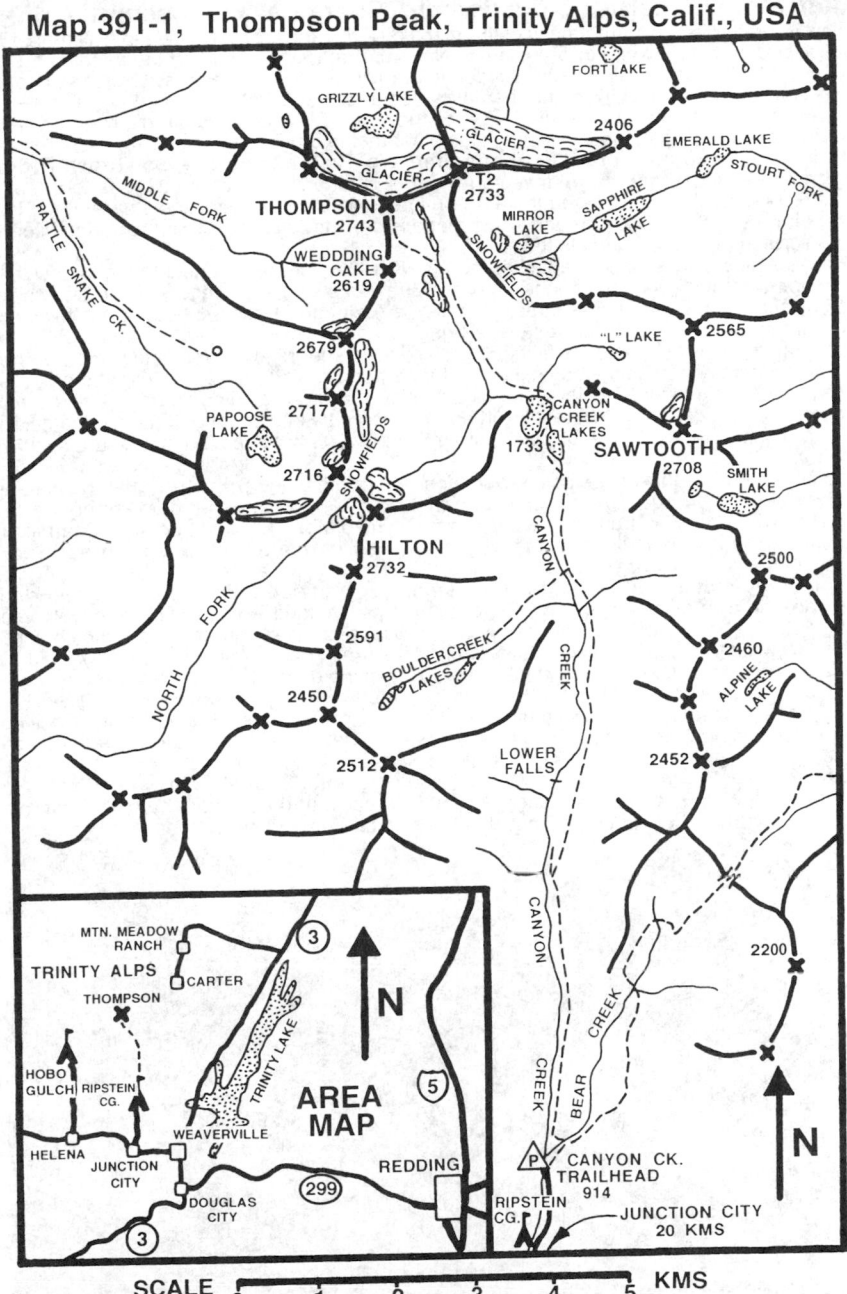

weather in these parts from June to October. There are both easy and difficult routes on these peaks.
Maps *Trinity Alps Wilderness (Shasta-Trinity, Klamath, Six Rivers National Forests)*, 1:63,360 (best); or *Hiking Map & Guide--Trinity Alps Wilderness Area*, 1:62,500, from Earthwalk Press; and the guidebook, **The Trinity Alps**, Linkhart, Wilderness Press.

Matterhorn, Excelsior & Dunderberg, Sierra Nevada, California, USA

This is the first and most-northerly of the maps covering the Sierra Nevada in California. The western third of this map is part of Yosemite National Park, while much of the middle part is in the Hoover Wilderness Area. This is included in the Toiyabe National Forest which has a ranger station & visitor center just to the northeast at a small town called Bridgeport (Tele. 760-932-7070, & open year-round). As with most of the rest of California's Sierra Nevada, these mountains are made up of mostly granite, plus other metamorphic-type rocks.

Featured in the northern half of this map are **Twin Lakes**, the **Sawtooth Ridge & Matterhorn Peak**. To get there, drive south out of Bridgeport for about 21 kms to the Mono Village Resort as shown. Located there on private land is a small store, restaurant, cabins, a fishing tackle store and campground. This place is crowded in summer, but you don't see too many people in the high country to the south.

Here's a nice hike & climb the author did on 9/6/1992. He parked next to the lake with the fishermen's cars, then walk south looking for the one trail over a footbridge. On the other side is a sign pointing the way up Horse Creek. There's a pretty good trail to about the halfway point along that creek, then it begins to fade. Higher up, the trail is marked in places with stone cairns. When you reach the pass marked 3260 meters, veer right or west and climb northwest up a climber's trail direct to the summit of the Matterhorn at 3738 meters. Most of the peaks in this region are pretty steep, as the name *Sawtooth Ridge* implies. The author did this climb in just over 6 hours, round-trip. Take a lunch and plan on an all-day outing. There's another long hike to a group of moderately high peaks directly west of Twin Lakes, but not all are shown on this map.

Southeast of Twin Lakes are some even higher peaks, namely **Dunderberg** at 3772 meters, and **Excelsior**, 3794, the highest summit on this map. To reach either of these peaks, drive along Highway 395, which runs between Carson City and Mono Lake. At Conway Summit, turn west and drive about 10 kms to the Virginia Lakes. Located there is a Forest Service Campground and the Virginia Lakes Resort. The author was there in 9/1978 and can't remember too much, but expect to find a small store of some kind, probably catering to fisherman, and a cafe and cabins (?). There is some private land, so expect some development. To climb Dunderberg, start in the area somewhere west of the campground and climb straight up the slope toward the summit. The author reached the top in only 1 1/4 hours on 9/13/1978. But it's a fairly steep scramble, so it might be easier to climb the east ridge route, as shown.

To climb Excelsior, you'll have to walk west on the trail from the campground, then hike up and over one pass, then route-find south or southwest to the summit. The author hasn't climbed this one, but by following the route symbols, you should get there. These peaks are moderately rugged.

By using a better map than this, you can also get into this country via Green Creek, from Highway 395. You'll have limited shopping in Bridgeport and Lee Vining, so it's best to buy supplies elsewhere. July through October is the normal climbing season; no need for ice ax or

Looking southwest at Whori Peak from the summit of Matterhorn Peak.

Map 392-1, Excelsior-Dunderberg, S. Nevada, Calif., USA

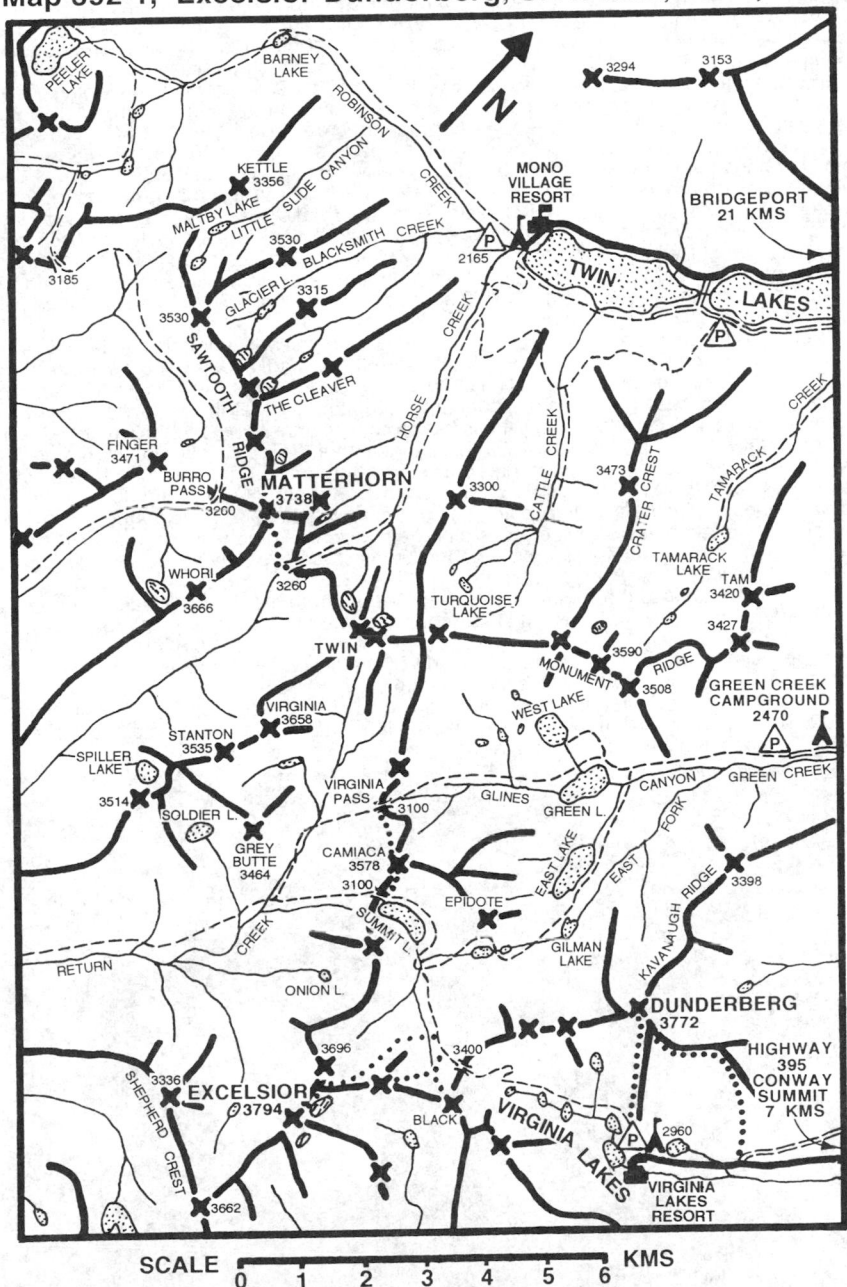

crampons then. Winter climbing is possible with reasonably easy access.
Maps Topo map *Hoover Wilderness,* 1:63,360; or *Toiyabe National Forest--Bridgeport Ranger District,* 1:126,720; or USGS map *Yosemite National Park and Vicinity,* 1:125,000; and perhaps the book, **A Climber's Guide to the High Sierra**, Sierra Club.

Dana & Conness, Sierra Nevada, California, USA

This is the second of 8 maps covering the higher and more interesting peaks in California's Sierra Nevada. Featured here is Mt. Dana, 3979 meters, and Mt. Conness at 3837. Both of these peaks are the highest in the immediate area, and both sit on the eastern boundary of Yosemite National Park. All points west of these 2 peaks and Tioga Pass, are in the park.

Down the canyon a few kms to the east of this map is the small town of Lee Vining. There's a Toiyabe National Forest visitor center just north of town on the south shore of Mono Lake where you can buy maps and guidebooks to the entire area (Tele. 760-647-3044). This should be your first stop in the area. The rocks in these parts are almost all granite, but the author seems to remember there was some quartzite as well, at least east of Saddlebag Lake.

Here's how to reach **Mt. Dana**. From Lee Vining, or the northern part of Yosemite Park, drive to Tioga Pass along Highway 120. Park somewhere at or near the pass, then look for the trail signposted for Dana Lake. After walking about 2 kms, veer right or south, and ascend the northwest ridge of Dana. This should be an easy walk because all the way up it's all above timberline with no bushwhacking and it's not too steep. Or continue on up to Dana Lake, then look for another way up from there. The north face of Dana has a small ice field, which could prove to be an interesting route.

To climb **Conness**, make your way to the junction just downhill or north of the Tioga Pass Resort, as shown on the map. There's a small store there, and it seems like it sold gasoline in 1992 (?) Turn north on the gravel road heading toward Saddlebag Lake & Campground. About one km before you reach the dam at Saddlebag, stop and park at the entrance to the walk-in Sawmill Campground. Walk to and past this backcountry campsite, and to the Carnegie Institute Experimental Station, which is a small cabin. Beyond that, the trail slowly fades, but just head west, then as you near the mountain, veer right and climb up over some steeper places. Eventually, you'll come to the steep east face of Conness. Head straight up, sometimes following cairns marking the easiest route. Follow the route symbols on the map.

From on top of the east shoulder, walk along a hiker's trail running west or northwest to the summit. Parts of this climb are steep, but normally easy & safe for anyone, as a route is marked out much of the way. Many people are climbing it these days.

The author made it to the summit in just over 2 hours from the dam on Saddlebag Lake and along the east ridge, but that route is longer than the one just described. He returned via the *route normal* with a total round-trip climb-time of 4 1/3 hours. Most people will want 6 or 7 hours round-trip. The north face of Conness has one of the largest glaciers in the Sierra Nevada, which could make some difficult routes for the technically inclined.

During the summer and early fall months, there will be no need for an ice ax or crampons here. The campgrounds you see are all fee-use sites and often full, especially on weekends. Buy all your food and supplies in larger towns before arriving in this area.

Looking southwest at the north face of Conness and the Conness Glacier.

Map 393-1, Dana & Conness, Sierra Nevada, Calif., USA

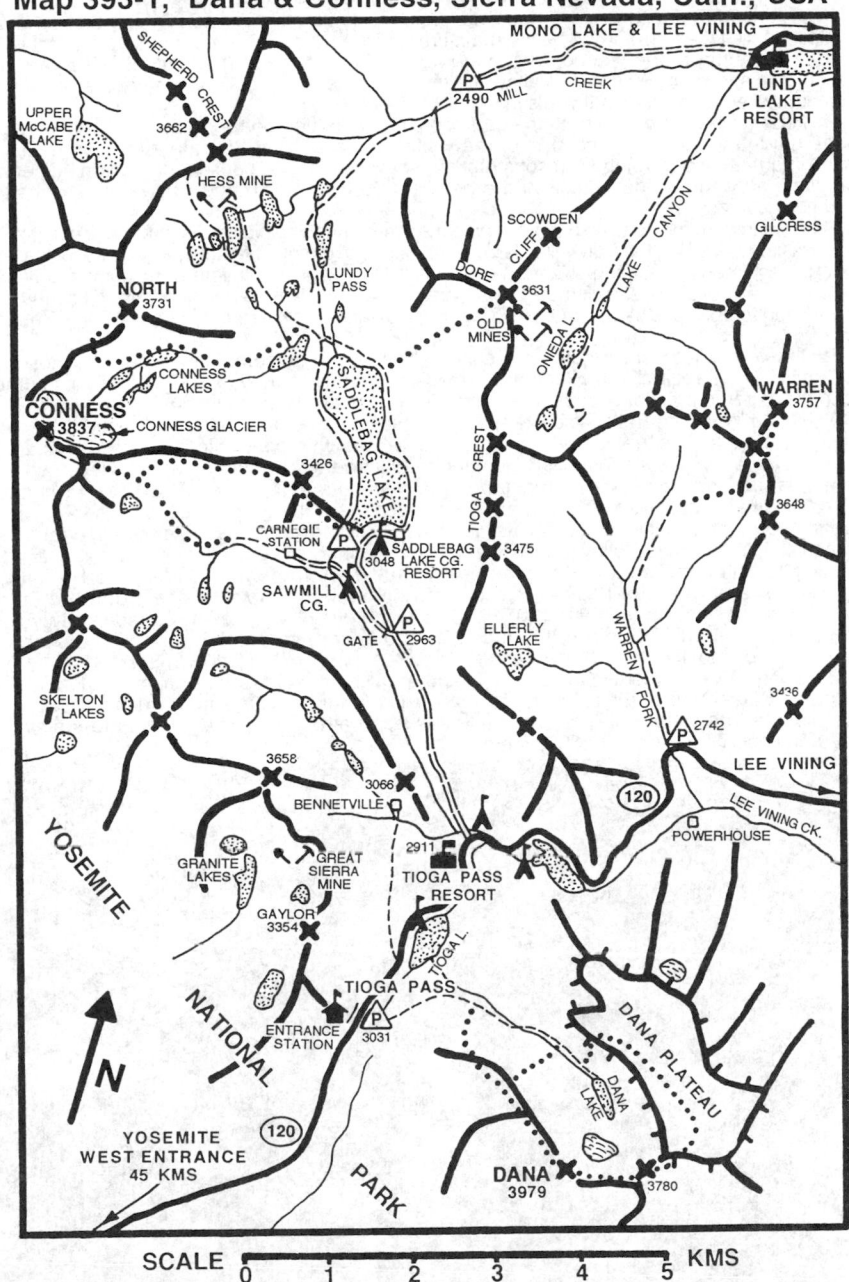

MONO LAKE & LEE VINING

SHEPHERD CREST

UPPER McCABE LAKE
3662

HESS MINE

P 2490 MILL CREEK

LUNDY LAKE RESORT

SCOWDEN CLIFF

GILCRESS

NORTH 3731

LUNDY PASS

DORE

3631

LAKE CANYON

CONNESS LAKES

OLD MINES

ONIEDA L.

WARREN 3757

CONNESS 3837

CONNESS GLACIER

SADDLEBAG LAKE

TIOGA CREST

3648

3426

CARNEGIE STATION P

3048 SADDLEBAG LAKE CG. RESORT

3475

SAWMILL CG.

GATE P 2963

ELLERLY LAKE

WARREN FORK

3436

P 2742

SKELTON LAKES

LEE VINING

3658

3066

BENNETVILLE

120

LEE VINING CK.

POWERHOUSE

YOSEMITE

GRANITE LAKES

GREAT SIERRA MINE

2911

TIOGA PASS RESORT

GAYLOR 3354

TIOGA L.

TIOGA PASS

ENTRANCE STATION

P 3031

DANA PLATEAU

NATIONAL

DANA LAKE

N

YOSEMITE WEST ENTRANCE 45 KMS

120

PARK

DANA 3979

3780

SCALE   0   1   2   3   4   5   KMS

Maps Topo map *Hoover Wilderness,* 1:63,360; or *Toiyabe National Forest--Bridgeport Ranger Dirtrict,* 1:126,720; or USGS map *Yosemite National Park and Vicinity,* 1:125,000; and the book, **A Climber's Guide to the High Sierra,** Sierra Club.

Yosemite National Park, California, USA

This is the third of a series of 8 maps, covering most of the high regions of the Sierra Nevada of California. All these maps follow the main crest of the range from north to south, but this one includes a section to the west of the divide on the San Joaquin Valley side. This very non-detailed map shows the Yosemite Valley and the Yosemite National Park, one of the best-known and most-visited of the national parks in the USA.

This is merely a introduction to the park, so plan on getting better maps, perhaps a recently printed guidebook, and contact one of the visitor centers for up-to-date information. To get current information regarding road construction, snow conditions, backcountry camping permits, rock climbing information, etc., call the park at 209-372-0200, and/or see their website at (www.nps.gov/yose/).

This region is known for its big trees, alpine meadows, hanging waterfalls, and most of all, for the sheer granite cliffs facing the Yosemite Valley. This is one of the most famous, if not the most famous, rock climbing areas in the world. Names such as Half Dome and El Capitan stand out in the climbing journals as some of the best rock routes anywhere. However, this map and generalized information is not intended for rock climbers; it merely shows a generalized view of the southern 2/3's of Yosemite Park.

For those who like peace, quiet, and solitude, it's best to go someplace else. For those who do want to hike or rock climb, expect big crowds and many regulations. All of this of course is due to the extreme popularity of the area and the large nearby population in California.

Within the Yosemite Valley itself, that's in the middle part of this map, there used to be many campgrounds, picnic sites, horse stables, and a village with post office, chapel, clinic, lodge, hotels, restaurants, gas stations, and the park headquarters & visitor center. However, some of these campgrounds were washed out in some big floods during the 1990's, and will not be replaced. Other concessionaires may also be phased out in the valley itself (?). The author was there in 1992, and it will likely be his last visit! They are now using shuttle buses to take most visitors into the Yosemite Valley thus eliminating cars in that area--at least in summer time.

If you're still interested in doing any backpacking in the park, Wilderness Permits are required for any overnight travel into the park's backcountry. The telefone number for **Wilderness Information** is 209-372-0745. During the busy backpacking season, July, August and perhaps early September, you may need to make reservations to the more popular campsites. To actually make **Wilderness Permit Reservations**, call 209-372-0740.

More people visit Yosemite in June, July and August, much fewer in December, January and February. September or October can be the best time for backpacking or rock climbing. The bottom of the Yosemite Valley is rather mild, as it's at a relatively low 1200 meters elevation. Most of the backcountry is over 3000 meters.

From the Yosemite Valley looking east at Half Dome.

Map 394-1, Yosemite National Park, California, USA

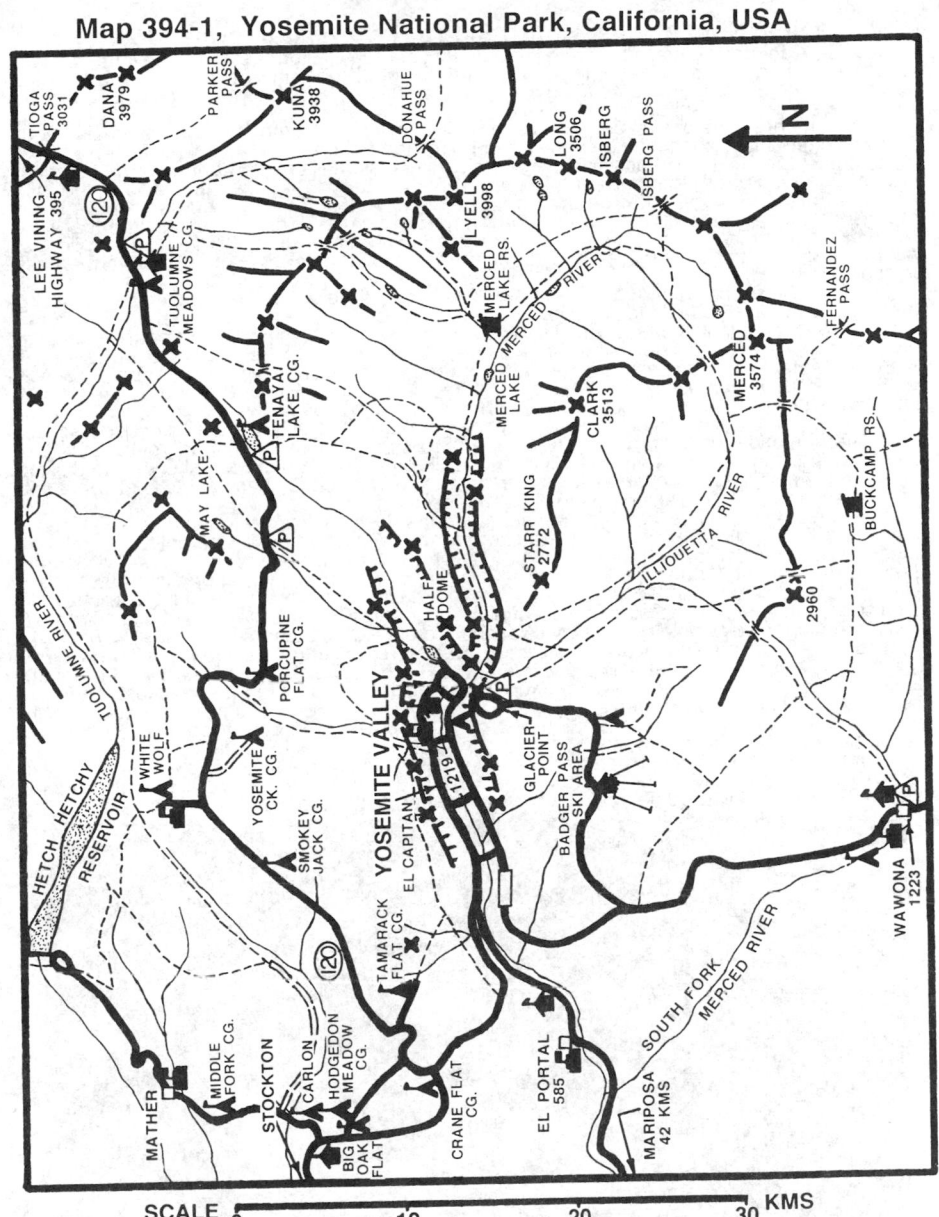

SCALE 0   10   20   30 KMS

Maps USGS map *Yosemite National Park and Vicinity,* 1:125,000; or the plastic Trails Illustrated map *Yosemite National Park,* 1:100,000; and the book, **Yosemite Trails,** Western Trails Publications; or **A Climber's Guide to the High Sierra,** Sierra Club; buy these at any park ranger station or visitor center.

Kuna, Koip, Lyell & Ritter, Sierra Nevada, California, USA

This is the fourth of 8 maps covering the highest peaks in California's Sierra Nevada. Shown here are a number of mountains in the area just west of the June Lake Loop Road, which connects June, Silver and Grant Lakes with Highway 395. The western quarter of this map is part of Yosemite National Park.

To reach one of the best access points, drive Highway 395 south of Mono Lake using your California state map. First look for June Lake Loop Road, then make your way to Silver Lake, where one of the main trailheads is located. This immediate area is just northwest of Maria Lakes. To reach another important trailhead, drive to Mammoth Lakes, but stop at the Inyo National Forest Visitor Center on the east side of town, to get better maps and the latest information on trails, roads and perhaps permits for backcountry camping. Call them at 760-924-5500. From Mammoth Lakes town center, start in the direction of the Devil's Postpile, but make your way to the Agnew Meadows Campground instead, which is another important access point and trailhead.

To climb **Ritter**, begin at Agnew Meadows Trailhead. Take the trail running northwest along the North Fork of the San Joaquin River to Shadow Lake, as shown on this map. From there, first head west on a trail, then route-find up to the ridge between Banner and Ritter, then south to the summit. The Sierra Club rates this a class 3 climb, which is generally not quite for the beginner. Actually, the easiest route up Ritter is on the west slopes, which they rate a class 2, but that is from a very inaccessible region. All the peaks in the Ritter area are on the difficult side, some being granitic-type rock, while others are volcanic in origin.

To climb to **Mt. Lyell**, which is the highest peak in Yosemite National Park (although it sits on the western boundary), first drive to Silver Lake. From Silver Lake, the normal route is the trail past Gem & Waugh Lakes, then to Donohue Pass. From there drop down to the west and climb up the north-facing glacier to the saddle between Lyell and Maclure, then east to Lyell's summit. This is classed as a 2-3. Take an ice ax & crampons.

You can also climb Lyell from Maria Lakes and the east ridge or arete, but this is classed a 3, and is a slow climb. On 9/7/1992, the author started from Silver Lake, and got to a point very near Lyell's summit from Maria Lakes, but had to turn back because of the short days of September. The total round-trip time was 11 1/4 hours. Climbing Lyell in one long day is very difficult, but you can do it in 2 easily, or for some in 3 days. If you camp overnight, you'll have to get a backcountry permit, either from Yosemite N.P., or at the Silver Lake Trailhead or Mammoth Ranger Station Visitor Center, or call Inyo National Forest HQ. in Bishop at 760-873-2400.

You can also climb **Kuna**, **Koip** and **Parker** from Silver Lake, but it's a long walk from there. The best way would be to get onto the Parker Lake Road, which leaves the northern part of the June Lake Loop. From the trailhead marked 2438 meters, walk first to Parker Lake, then follow the stream bed up to a trail, then south to the pass at 3750 meters. From there you can climb one or more peaks, or perhaps all 3, in one day. In 9/1978, the author got the to pass and nearly climbed Parker in a snowstorm.

Normally, ice ax & crampons aren't needed in these parts in late summer or early fall. Try to buy all your supplies before getting to the east slope of the Sierra's; or you'll pay high prices, even at Bishop. Climb anytime from July through mid or late October.

Lyell's northeast slopes and glacier as seen from the southeast ridge above Maria Lakes.

Map 395-1, Kuna, Koip, Lyell, Ritter, S. Nevada, Calif., USA

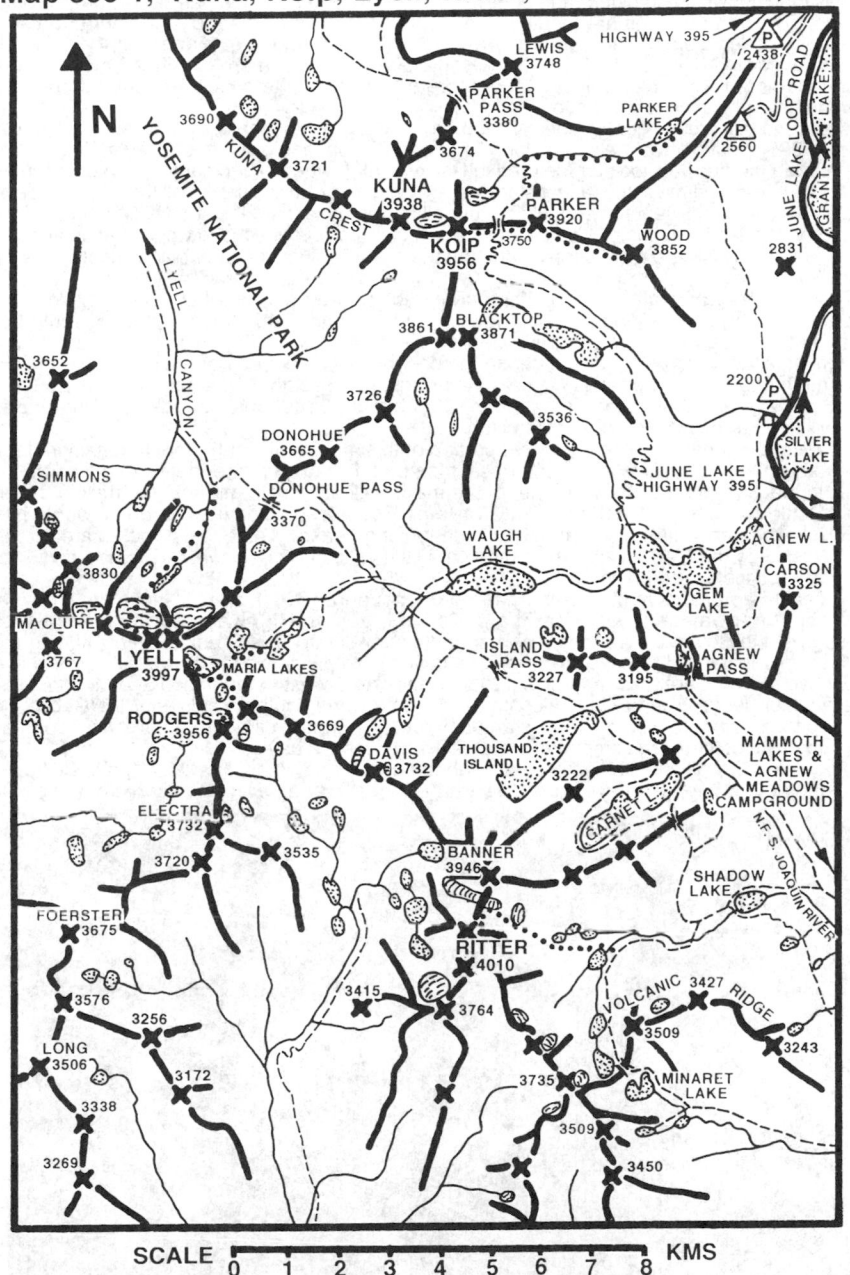

Maps Forest Service map, *Ansel Adams Wilderness,* 1:63,360; *Inyo National Forest,* 1:126,720; and the book, **A Climber's Guide to the High Sierra,** Sierra Club.

Morgan, Abbot & Gabb, Sierra Nevada, California, USA

This map shows some higher and better known peaks in the middle part of California's Sierra Nevada. These mountains are located due west of the town of Bishop, and south of a small community called Tom's Place on Highway 395. Mt. Morgan is the highest at 4191 meters, followed by Mills, Abbot, Dade, Bear Creek and Gabb, all of which are over 4000 meters. Most of the rock here is granite, but just east of Morgan, where all the mines are located, there are other metamorphic-type rocks present.

Access to this area is good, especially the areas along Rock Creek. To get there, drive along Highway 395 about halfway between Mono Lake and Bishop, and exit the freeway at Tom's Place. After leaving the freeway, look for the road to Rock Creek (If you want to camp in the backcountry, you'll have to get a permit at the ranger station in Mammoth Lakes or Bishop; call the numbers below. In July, August to mid-September you'd better call for reservations! If just day-climbing or hiking, then you won't need a permit). Drive south up along the Rock Creek road to where it ends at a large parking lot. This is where most people park, but there are a couple of other places nearby you can begin hiking from.

To climb **Morgan**, walk east from the parking lot on the trail to Eastern Brook Lakes, then head south along a minor ridge coming down from the southeast. Or, walk straight south from the end of the road on the main trail, then after about one km, turn east and route-find up through the scattered trees until you get on the previously mentioned ridge. It's steep getting up to the north ridge, but not difficult. Once on the ridge, head south, and southeast to the summit. On 9/8/1992, the author reached the top in 1 3/4 hours; 4 1/3 hours round-trip. The average hiker will need all day for this round-trip climb.

To climb other peaks in the northwest portion of this map, walk south from the main trailhead in the direction of Ruby Lake and Mono Pass, then up **Mt. Starr**, or other peaks to the north.

Or for peaks in the southwest corner of the map, walk straight south from the trailhead along upper Rock Creek toward **Mills, Abbot, Dade or Bear Creek Spire**. The guide book listed below tells the various routes up these difficult-looking peaks. The easiest routes are rated at about class 3 by the Sierra Club, which may be a little difficult for beginners. On Mills and Abbot you may need ice ax & crampons.

To reach mountains in the southern or southeast portion of this map, make your way to a point about halfway between Bishop and Tom's Place on Highway 395. Locate the road heading west to Rovana, then continue west and southwest up Pine Creek to an old mining area and former tungsten mill, as shown. There's a paved road all the way to a new public parking lot & trailhead. From there, one trail (an old road) heads northwest to the mines and Morgan Pass; while another heads west to Pine Lake, Italy Pass, and to the southern slopes of **Mt. Gabb**. The climb up the southeast face of Gabb is an easy route. A strong climber can probably do this in one long day; but for most, camp near Lake Italy and do it in 2 days.

If you can, buy all supplies before reaching the east slope of the Sierras; or go to Bishop for food, and books & maps at the Forest Service information center in the middle of town. Call

From the northwest ridge of Morgan looking south at Bear Ck. Spire (L), Dade, Abbot & Mills.

Map 396-1, Morgan, Abbot & Gabb, S. Nevada, Calif., USA

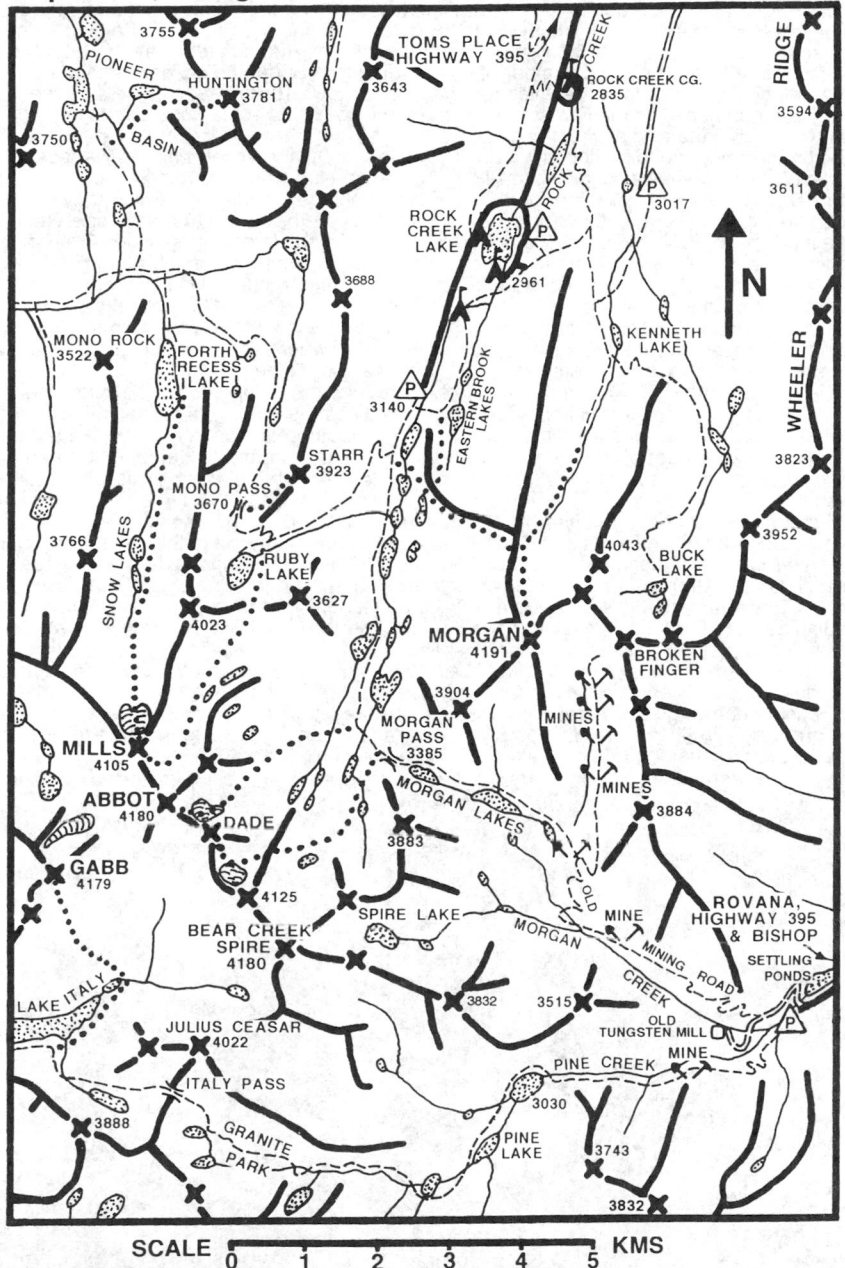

760-873-2400, or the ranger station across the street at 760-873-2503. Climb from mid or late June through October.

Maps *John Muir Wilderness & National Park Backcountry,* a set of 3 good Forest Service topo maps covering the crest of the Sierra from about Mammoth Lakes to Mt. Whitney, 1:63,360; or *Inyo National Forest,* 1:126,720; and the book **A Climber's Guide to the High Sierra**, Sierra Club.

Humphreys & Muriel, Sierra Nevada, California, USA

This map features a group of high mountains just southwest of Bishop in the middle part of California's Sierra Nevada. This is the 6th of 8 maps covering the Sierras. The highest peaks here are Mt. Humphreys at 4263 meters, the highest in the immediate area; and Mt. Muriel at 4173 meters. There are also a number of peaks with small cirque-type glaciers lined up on an east-west ridge going by the collective name *Glacier Divide*. There seems to be an absence of names for these peaks on the Forest Service map, but you'll find some good climbs there, some of which will require an ice ax & crampons.

Before climbing, go to Bishop, the largest town in the Owens Valley which is just east of the Sierra crest. Bishop has a couple of small supermarkets, plus a large Forest Service information center. Buy guidebooks and maps there, and if you're planning to do any backcountry camping, pick up your permit. From July 1st to September 15, you may want to make reservations to insure a campsite. Call 760-873-2503 or 760-873-5500, for the latest information They can also give you a permit and/or information on camping inside Kings Canyon National Park, which covers the southwest quarter of this map. If you're day-hiking, no permit is needed.

From the center of Bishop, drive west on paved State Road 168 running toward Lake Sabrina. You can do some climbing from Sabrina, but for now turn west from just below (or north of) that reservoir and follow the signs to North Lake, where you'll find a campground and a large separate parking lot and horse wrangler's camp at the trailhead.

To climb **Humphreys**, walk from the trailhead, through the campground and follow the signs to Piute Lake & Pass and into Humphreys Basin. Before you get to the pass, you might consider climbing **Emerson**. Do that from the southwest or west slopes. Each route ranks a class 3. From about 2 kms west of Piute Pass, route-find north to the base of Humphreys, then climb either the south ridge or southwest face, both of which are rated class 4. This is not quite for beginners.

Muriel has some easy routes from the east or west sides. From the Alpine Col, which is along the ridge between Muriel and Goethe, you can climb southwest to the summit of **Goethe**, which rates class 3. Reach **Lamarck** from North Lake Trailhead, but take the trail to Grass and Lamarck Lakes, then walk southwest to Lamarck Col and climb the southeast ridge to the summit. This route rates a class 2, a walk-up. **Mts. Mendel** and **Darwin** (not quite on the map) are climbed from Evolution Valley and the Pacific Crest National Scenic Trail. The southwest face of Mendel, and the western slopes of Darwin are both rated class 3.

Climb here from late June through October. Some routes may require an ice ax & crampons, especially early in the season. Here's a example of time and distance for those who don't want to bother getting a backcountry camping permit. After the author slept in his car at the North Lake Trailhead, he climbed Emerson via the southwest face, then made his way to Muriel via the east side and Lost Lakes. This day-climb on 9/9/1992, took just over 8 hours,

From the summit of Emerson looking northwest at Mt Humphreys.

Map 397-1, Humphreys & Muriel, S. Nevada, Calif., USA

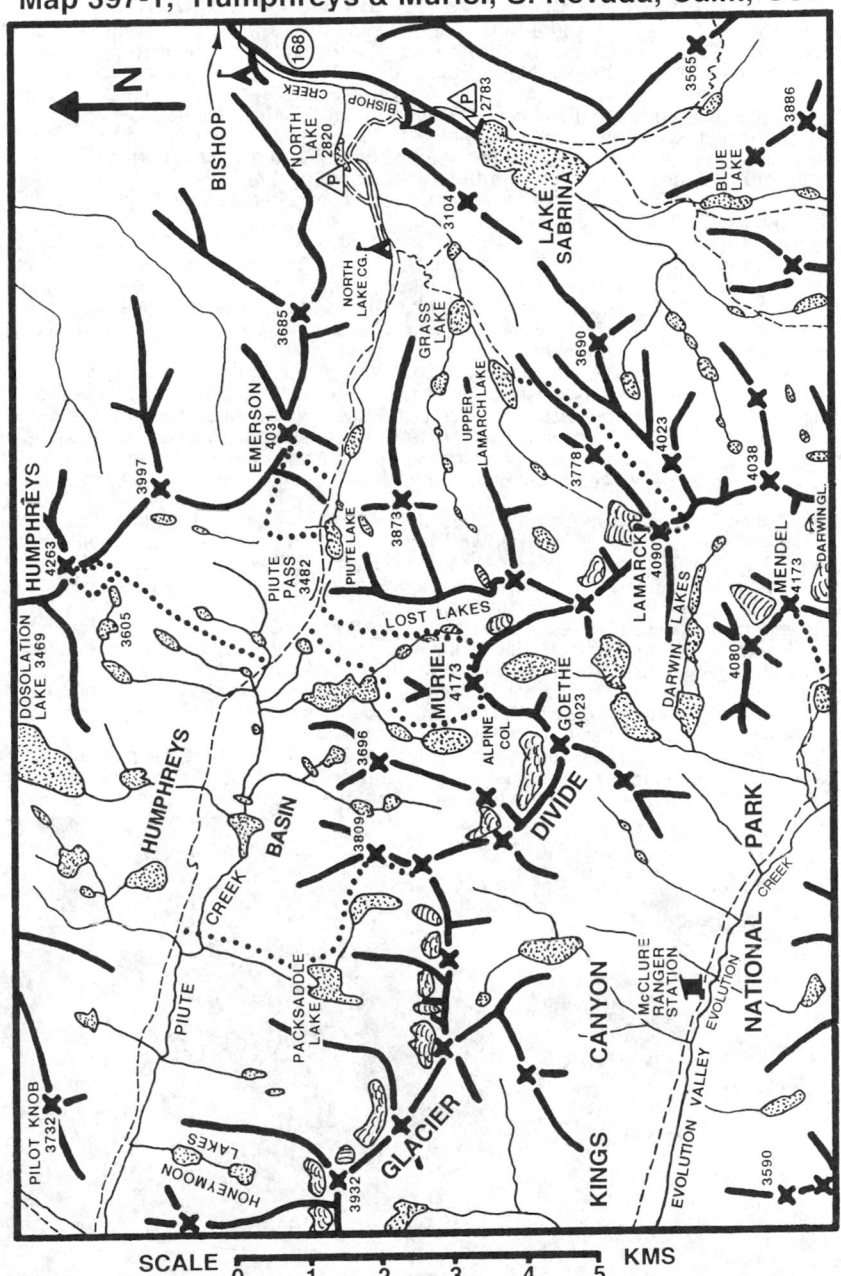

SCALE 0 1 2 3 4 5 KMS

round-trip.

Maps *John Muir Wilderness & National Park Backcountry,* a set of 3 good Forest Service topo maps covering the crest of the Sierra from about Mammoth to Mt. Whitney, 1:63,360; and/or *Inyo National Forest,* 1:126,720; and the book, **A Climber's Guide to the High Sierra**, Sierra Club.

Palisade Ridge, Sierra Nevada, California, USA

Featured on this map are some of the highest mountains in the Sierra Nevada and the continental USA. The most famous peaks here are The Palisades, a wall of steep pinnacles all over 4000 meters. The highest is North Palisade at 4341 meters, not much lower than Mt. Whitney, which is just a few kms to the south. This area is due west of Big Pine and southwest of Bishop, both of which are in the Owens Valley east of the Sierra. All the rocks here, at least those along the main crest, are granite and part of the one huge batholith.

If you intend to camp in the backcountry, stop in Bishop and pick up a permit from the Inyo National Forest office (where you can buy guidebooks and maps too). From July 1st to September 15, you may want to make reservations to insure a campsite. Call 760-873-2503 or 760-873-5500, for the latest information.

There are 2 main access roads into the east slope. First, there's a good paved road (State Road 168) running west, then southwest out of Bishop to South Lake. By parking there at 2950 meters, you can climb all the peaks in the northern part of this mapped area. From the trailhead, take the well-used trail south toward Treasure Lakes to climb Mts. **Gilbert** and **Johnson**. The southern slope of Gilbert is a class 1 hike, which is like walking on a trail. Its east ridge is a class 2. The west ridge of Johnson is also a class 2; again very easy.

By taking the other trail to Bishop Pass at 3649 meters, you'll be able to reach the southwest slopes of the Palisade Ridge. The easiest climb here, at least among the 4000 meter peaks, is **Mt. Agassiz**. Climbed from Bishop Pass, it's rated a class 2 hike. The author slept in his car at the South Lake Trailhead, then with an early start on 9/10/1992, went to Bishop Pass and climbed the peak northeast of Columbine just to have a good look at the west side of the Palisade Ridge. Later he climbed the unnamed peak marked 3856 and returned. Round-trip walk-time was just under 8 1/2 hours.

From Bishop Pass to the southwest slopes of the Palisade Ridge, you'll either have to route-find over one ridge; or take the trail down Dusy Creek to King River, then another trail up Palisade Creek. From there, the easiest route up **North Palisade** is a class 3 climb up the southwest side. A southwest couloir up **Thunderbolt** is a class 4. Be sure to consult the book listed below for a good description of many routes up all of the major peaks here.

The other main access road is the one running west from Big Pine. Follow the paved county road all the way to Big Pine Creek Campground as shown on the map. From there one trail runs up the North Fork. By using this you can climb the East Arete of **Winchell**, a class 3 climb. There are class 4 routes up Thunderbolt from Palisade Glacier, the largest in the Sierra Nevada. There's also a class 4 climb up **North Palisade** from the same icefield. Nothing easy here! Beginners should stand back and take fotos.

If you take the trail up the South Fork of Big Pine Creek, you'll be able to make a class 3 climb up **Gayley**, or climb the southeast face of **Temple Crag**, also a class 3. You can also reach the normal route up **Middle Palisade**, which is a class 3 climb up the east face. Take ice

From the peak north of Columbine looking north at Agassiz left, Winchell right.

Map 398-1, Palisade Ridge, Sierra Nevada, Calif., USA

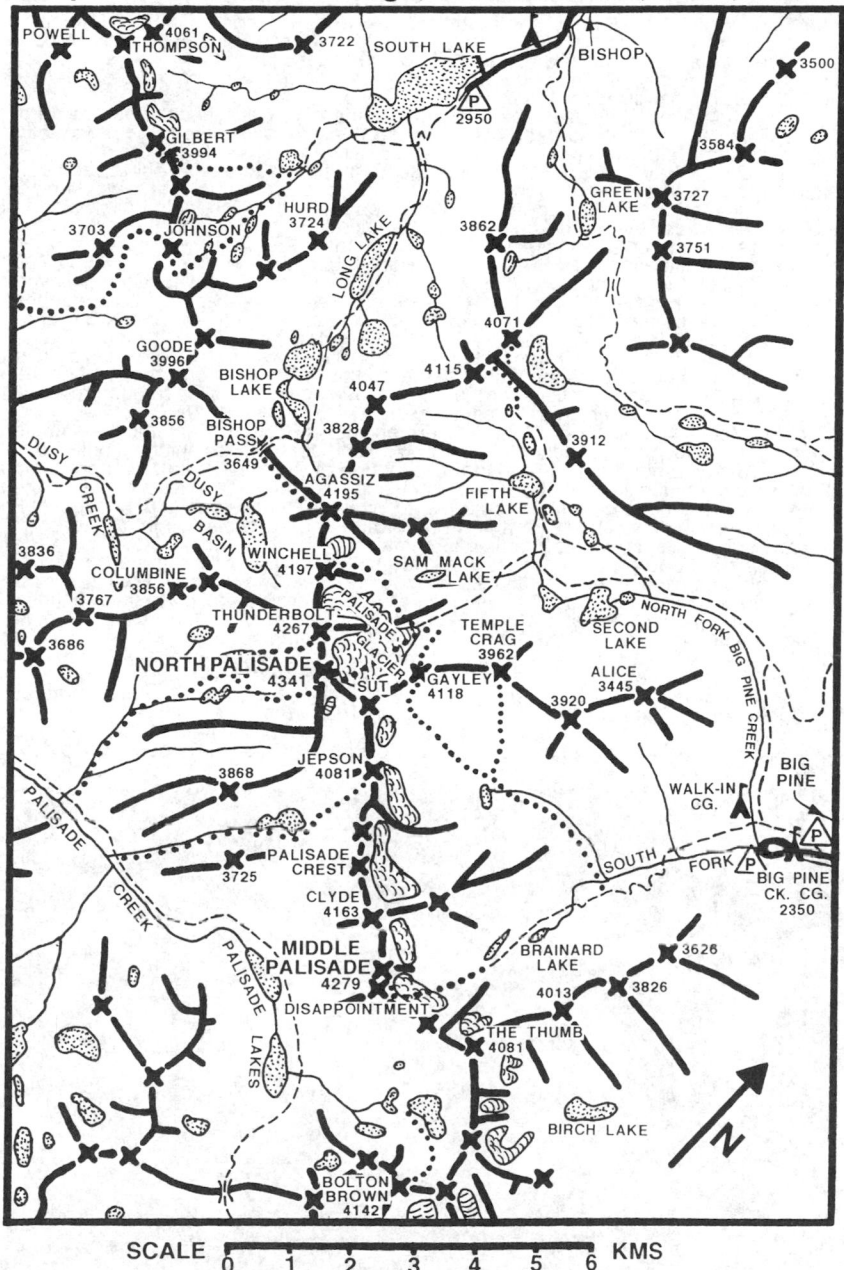

POWELL 4061
THOMPSON ✕3722 SOUTH LAKE BISHOP
✕3500

P
2950

GILBERT
3994
3584
GREEN
LAKE ✕3727
HURD
3724 3862 3751
3703 JOHNSON
LONG LAKE

4071
GOODE
3996
BISHOP
LAKE 4047 4115
✕3856 BISHOP 3828 3912
PASS
DUSY 3649 AGASSIZ
CREEK 4195 FIFTH
DUSY LAKE
3836 BASIN WINCHELL SAM MACK NORTH FORK
COLUMBINE 4197 LAKE SECOND
3767 ✕3856 THUNDERBOLT PALISADE LAKE BIG PINE CREEK
3686 4267 TEMPLE
CRAG ALICE
NORTH PALISADE GLACIER 3962 3445
4341 SUT GAYLEY 3920
4118
BIG
JEPSON PINE
3868 4081 WALK-IN
CG. P
PALISADE PALISADE BIG PINE
CREST SOUTH FORK P CK. CG.
3725 2350
CLYDE
4163
MIDDLE BRAINARD ✕3626
PALISADE LAKE
4279 4013 3826
PALISADE DISAPPOINTMENT
THE THUMB
LAKES 4081
BIRCH LAKE
N
BOLTON
BROWN
4142

SCALE 0 1 2 3 4 5 6 KMS

ax & crampons for glacier routes, and locally, buy all your supplies in Bishop.
Maps *John Muir Wilderness & National Park Backcountry,* a set of 3 good Forest Service topo
maps covering the crest of the Sierra from about Mammoth to Mt. Whitney, 1:63,360; and/or
Inyo National Forest, 1:126,720; and the book, **A Climber's Guide to the High Sierra**, Sierra
Club.

Mt. Whitney, Sierra Nevada, California, USA

This map shows Mt. Whitney, the highest peak in the continental USA. The altitude is variously listed at 4418, 4419 or 4555 meters, depending on the source. Whitney is located in the southern part of the Sierra Nevada just west of the small town of Lone Pine & Highway 395. This is as popular as any hike in the USA. Whitney is made of a light colored granite, making it a favorite for alpine rock climbing as well.

You'll be sad to hear they have setup a **quota system** for regulating the number of people on **Mt. Whitney** and this wilderness area. If you disagree with this radical way of crowd management, then write to Inyo National Forest, 873 N. Main, Bishop, California, USA, 93514. Or call 760-873-2503 or 760-876-6200. They do count letters and base public land policy on comments. This writer suggests a wider trail, a parking lot down on the flats, a weekend shuttle bus up to Whitney Portal Trailhead, and unlimited day-hikers on the main trail--which will not quite be the wilderness everyone would like, but would allow **you** to climb the mountain on the day you choose--not when some bureaucrat wants you to!

To get this permit, call the Mt. Whitney Ranger Station in Lone Pine, Tele. 760-876-6200, Fax 760-873-2484, for current information. Also see their website (www.r5.fs.fed.us/inyo), then double click *Wilderness Permit--(year)*, and *Wilderness Permit Application*. You're supposed to fill out a form with the date you want to climb and fax it to them in February for the upcoming season. They allow 150 day-hikers & 50 overnighters per/day. Making reservations costs US$15 per/person. This quota system lasts from May 15 to November 1. The most sought-after time is late July and August. As the author gathered this information on 6/15/2000, there were only 20 people who had reservations for that day. If quotas are not filled through reservations, walk-ins can pickup permits on a first come, first served basis--free.

Before climbing, stop at the Mt. Whitney Ranger Station & Visitor Center in the south end of Lone Pine. There you can buy better maps & books, and get the latest information. From Lone Pine drive west on a good paved road in the direction of Whitney Portal, the normal starting point. Along the way are several BLM campgrounds, plus a number of places to pull off the road to park & camp for the night. Just as you arrive at Whitney Portal, you'll find a couple of Forest Service campgrounds which are on a first come, first served basis. Right at the end of the paved road is a small store & cafe at about 2550 meters altitude.

From the trailhead parking, locate the trail which begins by making a big loop to the northeast. From bottom to top the distance is about 17 kms (34 kms round-trip), so get started early and take a good lunch and 2-3 liters of water. There are several places along the way up to Trail Camp where you can get water, but it's best to carry your own. If camping overnight, you must stay at either Outpost or Trail Camp sites. At Trail Camp you'll get your first good look at Whitney. From there to the summit are lots of switchbacks. On top is a small rock shelter.

On 9/16/1978, the author climbed Whitney in 8 hours round-trip. On his second climb, 9/11/1992, he carried a 6 kg pack with water, extra clothes & boots, lunch and cameras, and walked to the top in 3 hours, 21 minutes (7 1/3 hours round-trip). He was disappointed to later find the record time for the climb up was 2:21, set in the 1970's by a marathoner. But 3:21 isn't too bad for a 49 year old just out hiking! Most people need 10-15 hours round-trip to day-climb Whitney.

From Trail Camp at 3650 meters, looking northwest at the east face of Whitney.

Map 399-1, Mt. Whitney, Sierra Nevada, California, USA

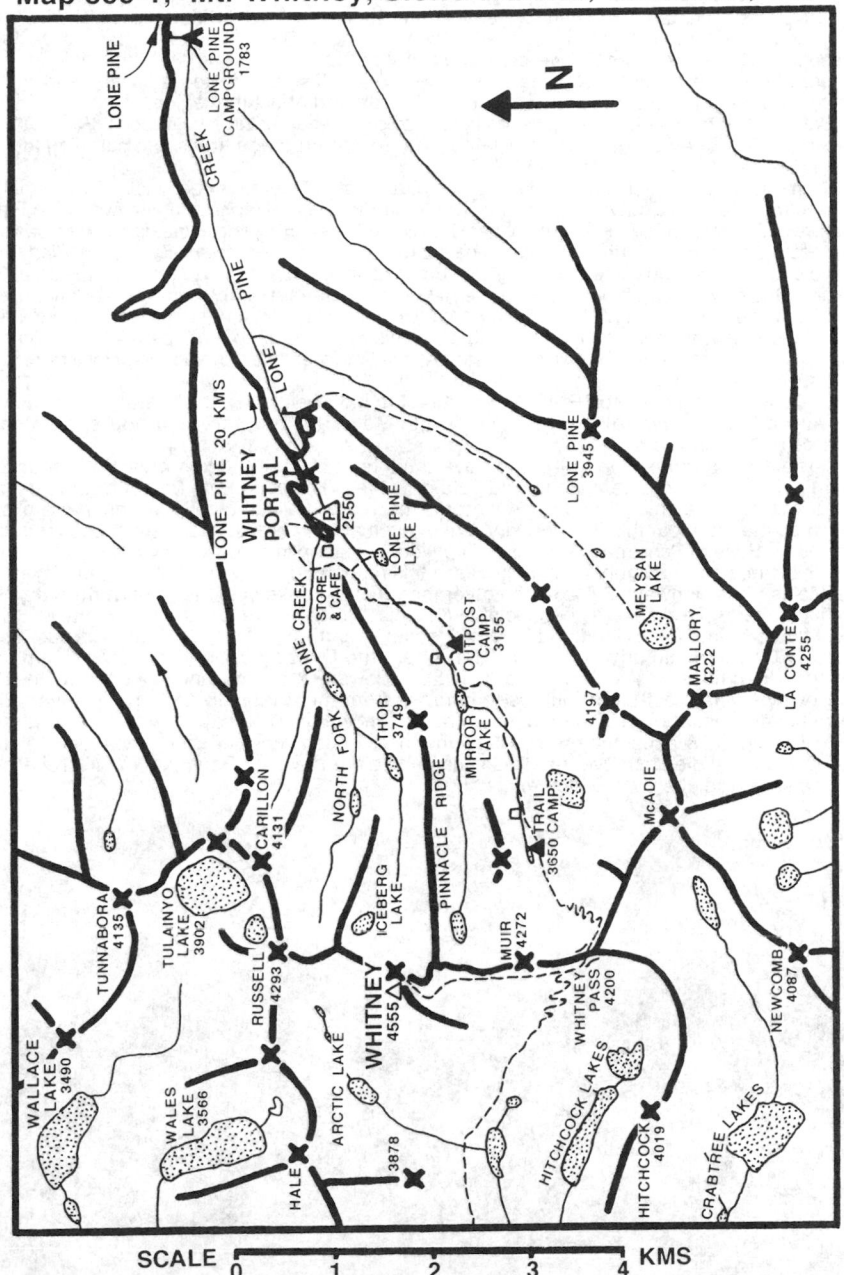

SCALE |0 1 2 3 4| KMS

Maps *John Muir Wilderness & National Park Backcountry,* a set of 3 good Forest Service topo maps covering the crest of the Sierra from about Mammoth to Mt. Whitney, 1:63,360; and/or *Inyo National Forest,* 1:126,720; and/or the books, **Climber's Guide to the High Sierra**, Sierra Club; and/or **Climbing Mt. Whitney**, La Siesta Press.

White Mtn. & Boundary Peak, White Mtns., California-Nevada, USA

White Mountain at 4342 meters is the highest summit in the White Mountains. This very high & dry mountain range is located just east of Bishop and the Sierra Nevada in central California. These mountains are near the western boundary of the Great Basin and the Basin & Range system which covers most of Nevada and western Utah. It's been folded & uplifted and consists of many different rock types. Many old mines are scattered about the region.

Before going to any of these peaks, it's best to stop in Bishop at the Inyo National Forest Office & Visitor Center. They can give you the latest information on roads, trails and camping facilities. Telefon them at 760-873-2400 or 760-873-2503.

White Mountain itself is rather easy to get to, at least in summer or early fall. The normal way to these mountains is to drive south out of Bishop on Highway 395 to the small town of Big Pine, a distance of 24 kms. In Big Pine, turn northeast on State Road 168 going in the direction of Oasis, but after about 20 kms, turn north onto another paved road going to the *Ancient Bristlecone Pine Forest.* Above or beyond the Schulman Grove, it's an unmaintained dirt track up to the locked gate at 3600 meters. See map. You'll have to park there--if you can get there at all, then road-walk north in the direction of the the University of California Barcroft Research Laboratory, which was still in operation as of 2000. Beyond that, continue walking on an old rough track to the top of White Mountain, a distance of about 11 kms from the locked gate. At one time there was another research station there, but that's now abandoned.

The author did this trip on 9/17/1978, but had to park about 4 kms short of the locked gate. He walked fast and made it to the top of White Mountain and back in 6 hours, a round-trip distance of 30 kms.

If you go this route, don't forget to have a full tank of fuel and lots of water, especially if you're planning to camp near the locked gate or in the Bristlecone Pine Forest just to the south. In that forest are picnic sites, but no water! There are several small springs in the area as shown on the map, but this is a very dry region even at high elevations. The access road from Westguard Pass to Schulman Grove is now paved, but steep in places.

While there are a number of other peaks in this range and many short roads heading into the mountains from Highways 6 & 264, the other most-popular hike is to the top of **Boundary Peak** at 4006 meters. This is the highest point in Nevada. To get there, drive along Highway 6. You could go up Morris Creek from 2 different directions, and route-find up what ever route seems easiest. Or you could drive up toward the Albert and Queen Mines, hike a trail (?) up to Mt. Kennedy, then ridge-walk southwest to Boundary. Beware of private land along this route (?).

However, the most-used route is to come in from the east side and Trail Canyon Road, which heads west about 100 meters south of the junction of Highways 264 & 773. 2WD's can make it to a pond & aspen trees. You'll run into a little bushwhacking along the creek bed up to Trail Canyon Saddle, then over one false summit, before reaching Boundary Peak. Take lots of water on this hike, the pond & stream may be dry!

From Highway 6 looking east at Boundary Peak left, Montgomery right (Richard White foto).

Map 400-1, White Mountain & Boundary Peak, White Mountains, California-Nevada, USA

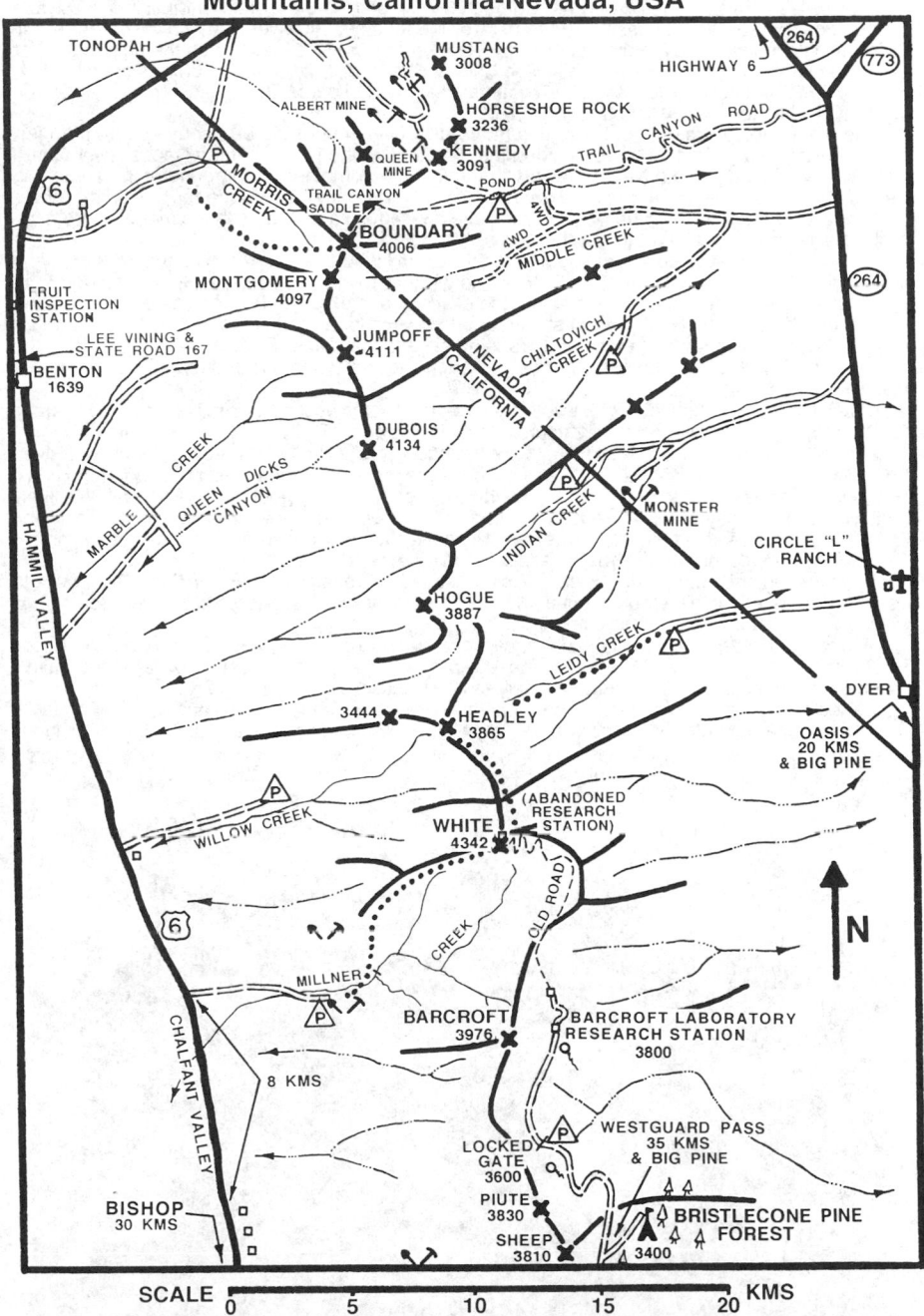

Maps *Inyo National Forest* map, or USGS maps *White Mtn. Peak* and *Barcroft,* 1:62,500 (if still available); or *Benton Range,* 1:100,000; or *Boundary Peak* and *White Mountain Peak,* 1:24,000; and the book, **Hiking the Great Basin,** Sierra Club.

Toiyabe (Arc) Dome, Toiyabe Range, Nevada, USA

Toiyabe Dome, sometimes called Arc Dome at 3590 meters is the highest summit in the Toiyabe Range of central Nevada. These mountains are about halfway between Austin in the north and Tonopah to the south. They're also just south of Bunker Hill which is featured on the next map. For updated information of any kind, call the Austin Ranger Station at 702-964-2671; or the Tonapah office at 775-482-6286. These folded & uplifted mountains are typical of the Great Basin ranges which run north-south and are composed mostly of quartzites.

There are several access routes to this mountain. One way would be to drive south from just west of Austin on a good country road along the west side of the range. At the Reese River Guard Station, turn southeast and drive up Stewart Creek to the Columbine Campground at the end of the road. From there, hike southeast to **Toiyabe Dome**. You could also drive further south on the westside county road and walk up Reese Creek or Cow Canyon and approach the mountain from the west. Use the map listed below to see these possible routes.

However the **most-used way** in getting to the summit would be a route from the northeast and along either South Twin or North Twin Rivers. To get there, drive along State Highway 376, which runs roughly between Austin and Tonopah on the east side of the range. Between mile posts 59 & 60, or between mile posts 62 & 63, turn westward and follow the loop-road numbered 080, as shown on the map. This puts you at one of the trailheads on either stream mentioned above. Water from the creeks is now diverted into pipes at the mouth of each canyon. There are also campsites at or near each stream-crossing.

The author has climbed this peak twice; once he hiked southwest up South Twin River. He made it to the summit and back in about 7 1/2 hours. That trip was on 9/17/1978.

His second trip was on 8/5/1991. That time he made a loop-hike by walking up North Twin River, then south up to a pass east of a north peak. From there he ridge-walked west up to that north peak, then south to another pass, and finally up to the main summit on a good trail. This trail was likely originally built by surveyors who first used this peak as a heliograph or triangulation station back in the 1880's. Stone shelters and tent platforms can still be seen at the summit. Many of these ruins are no doubt much more recent than the 1880's, as each survey party added to the site.

From the top, the author ridge-walked southeast and eventually down South Twin River back to his car. That round-trip hike took about 8 1/2 hours. It's best for most people to walk up South Twin making it a shorter and less-complicated trip.

You could also camp in one of the upper canyons, as there's running water everywhere, and climb it in 2 days. There are cattle and sheep in these canyons in the summer months so be careful when it comes to drinking water. Take it from a spring source if possible.

As you go up either canyon, you'll see remnants of old mines, stone cabins and other old artifacts. There is an especially interesting mill site up South Twin. You can get gas and some groceries in the

Toiyabe or Arc Dome seen from the north and the ridge south of North Twin River.

Map 401-1, Toiyabe (Arc) Dome, Toiyabe Range, Nevada, USA

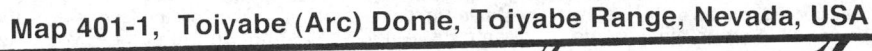

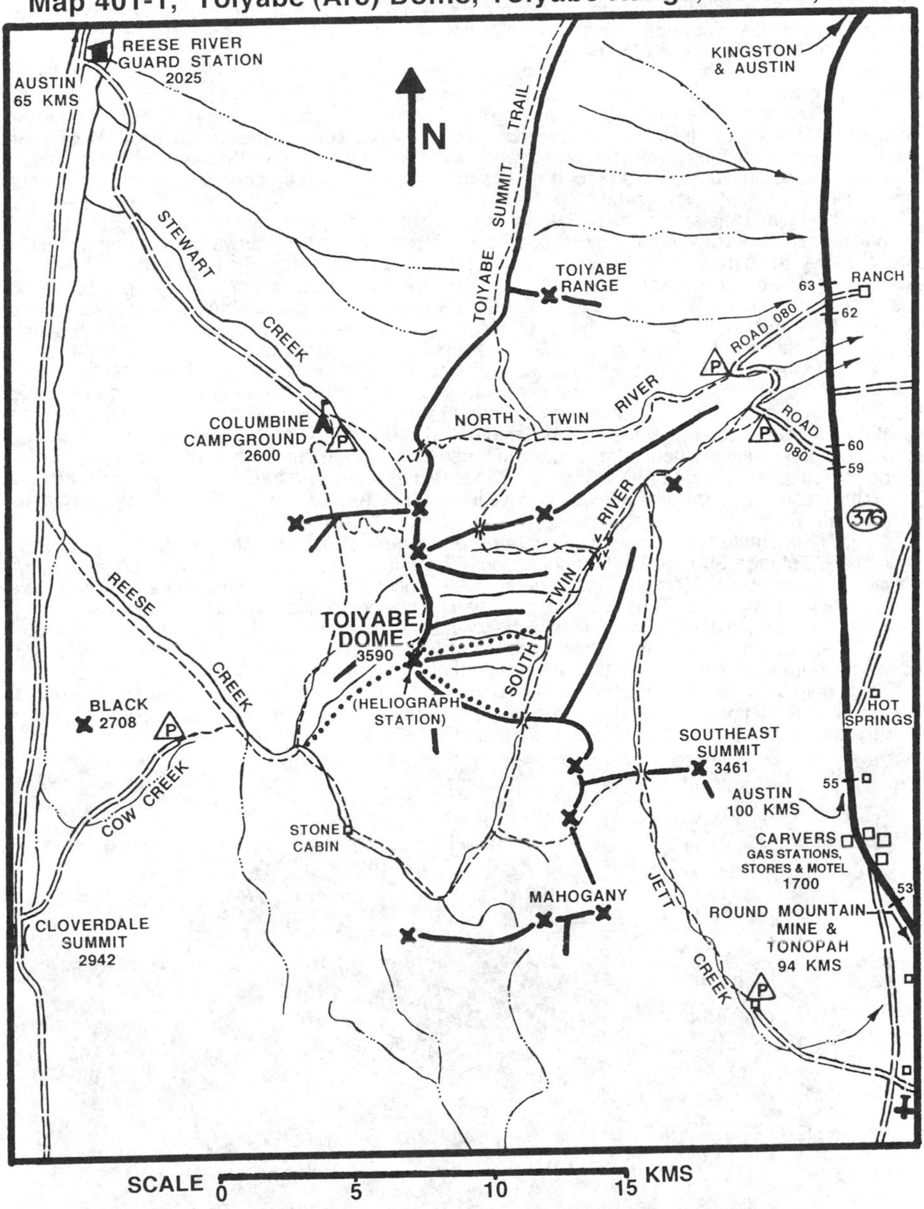

AUSTIN
65 KMS

REESE RIVER
GUARD STATION
2025

KINGSTON
& AUSTIN

N

STEWART

CREEK

TOIYABE SUMMIT TRAIL

TOIYABE
RANGE

63 — RANCH

— 62

ROAD 080

P

COLUMBINE
CAMPGROUND
2600

P

NORTH   TWIN   RIVER

P

ROAD
080

— 60

— 59

376

REESE

CREEK

TOIYABE
DOME
3590

SOUTH

TWIN   RIVER

(HELIOGRAPH
STATION)

HOT
SPRINGS

BLACK
2708

P

COW CREEK

SOUTHEAST
SUMMIT
3461

55 —

AUSTIN
100 KMS

STONE
CABIN

CARVERS
GAS STATIONS,
STORES & MOTEL
1700

53

CLOVERDALE
SUMMIT
2942

MAHOGANY

JETT

CREEK

ROUND MOUNTAIN
MINE &
TONOPAH
94 KMS

P

SCALE 0   5   10   15 **KMS**

area at Austin and Carver (a couple of gas stations & small stores, and motel), but there's no gas or store at the mine site called Round Mountain, just a few kms southeast of Carver and east of the main highway. You can climb in these parts from sometime in June through October.

Maps *Toiyabe National Forest, Northern Section,* 1:126,720, from the Tonopah or Austin Forest Service Ranger Stations; or USGS maps *South Toiyabe Peak, Arc Dome, Carvers & Carvers NW,* 1:24,000; or the book, **Hiking the Great Basin**, Sierra Club.

Bunker Hill, Toiyabe Range, Nevada, USA

Bunker Hill at 3498 meters, is the highest peak in the northern half of the Toiyabe Range of central Nevada. This mountain is made up of limestone and shales, but on the summit you'll find metamorphic slates. For updated information of any kind call the Austin Ranger Station at 702-964-2671; or the Tonapah office at 775-482-6286.

Here's how to get there. The normal access road to Bunker Hill is via Nevada State Highway 376. This paved road runs north-south on the east side of the range roughly between Austin on the north and Tonapah on the south. Drive along this highway to between mile posts 2 & 3 just east of the mining town of Kingston, then turn west and continue past a number of homes at the mouth of Kingston Canyon. Just inside the canyon, the way becomes a good gravel road which heads up past Grove's Lake, the Kingston Guard Station (open and used in summer only) and eventually over a pass and down to the Big Creek Campground.

The best place to start a climb of **Bunker Hill** is to drive to a point just north of the guard station, then turn east into a canyon named Mahogany Gulch, and drive a 4WD or walk about one km to the end of a very steep road. From there, climb up a prominent ridge in a southeast direction. When you meet the main west ridge, veer left or east and ridge-walk to the south summit. From there it's a short distance north to the main peak. On the highest summit are a couple of small solar powered radio towers. They must have been installed with the aid of a helicopter, because there's no real trail up this mountain. This peak is rather wild and pristine except for this summit clutter.

Another way up would be to drive further north from the guard station and to the mouth of Sawmill Canyon northwest of the summit. From there walk southeast up an old road a ways, then use sheep trails to gain access to the mountain from the north ridge. Forest Service maps show a trail running east over a pass and down to the northern end of Kingston, but the author saw little or no sign of it. Walking cross-country without a trail is easy in these parts as you'll find either an open forest of pine or quaking aspen, or sage brush. On 8/4/1991, the author made a loop-hike climbing Bunker Hill using the 2 canyons and routes described above in 4 1/3 hours. However, you'll want most of a day for this climb.

If you're interested in a longer hike either north or south of Bunker Hill, you could use the well-maintained **Toiyabe Summit Trail**. If going south, begin at the upper end of Grove's Lake; or at the trailhead located about 400 meters further north. If heading north, park at the end of the road northeast of Big Creek Campground. The author has not been on any part of this north-south summit trail.

There are a number of small streams in the west-side canyons of Bunker Hill, but there are lots of sheep around in summer, so take water from springs if you can. The best policy is to have some in your car before arriving in the area. Climb here from about June 1 through October.

The main mountain road running from Kingston to the guard station and on past Big Creek CG. and north to Austin on the west side of the range is a good road for cars in dry conditions. The only place in the immediate area to buy food is at Austin. In 1991 & 2000, there was a gas station near mile

Looking north from the Toiyabe Summit Trail at the southern slopes of Bunker Hill.

Map 402-1, Bunker Hill, Toiyabe Range, Nevada, USA

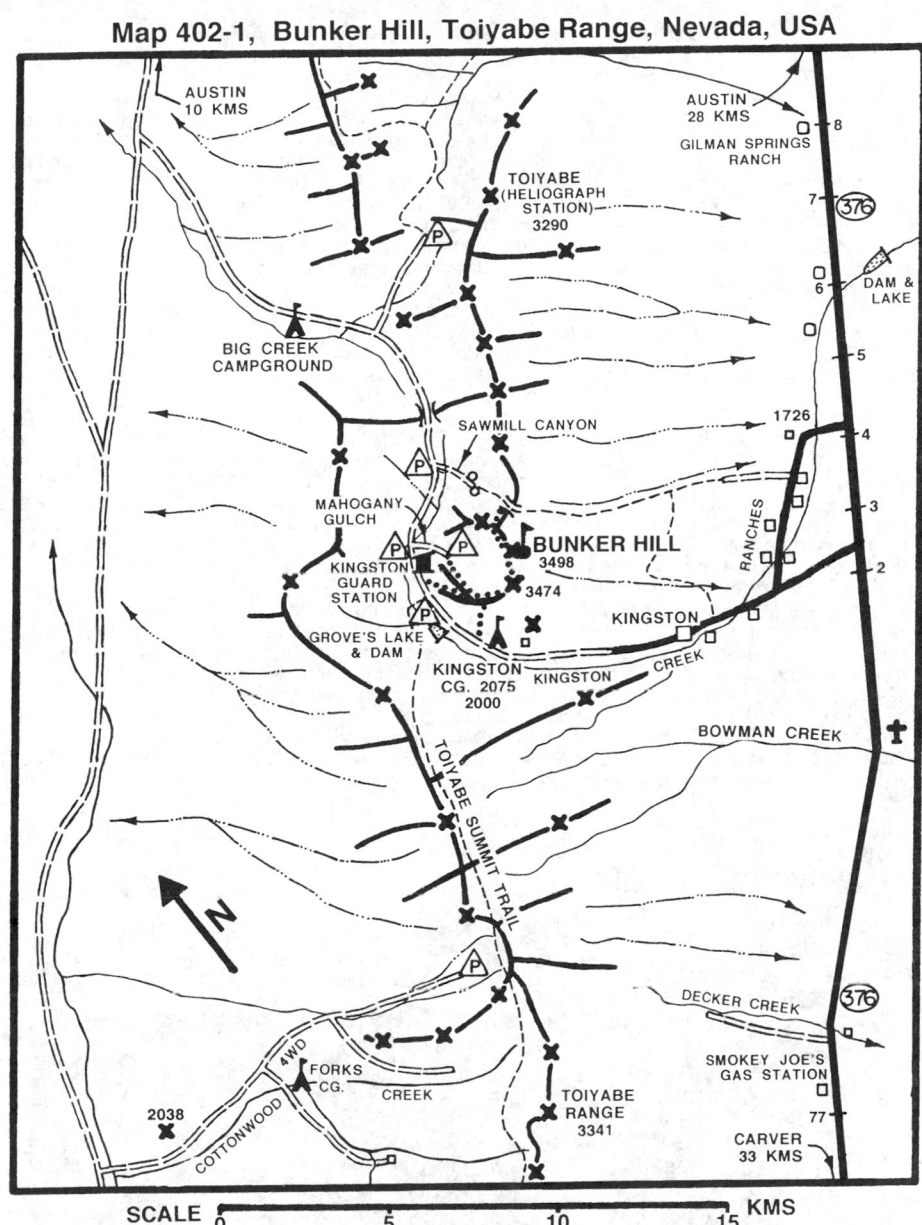

SCALE 0 — 5 — 10 — 15 KMS

post 77. By now there may be someplace to buy food or gas near Kingston (?).
Maps *Toiyabe National Forest, Northern Section,* 1:126,720, buy at the Tonapah or Austin Ranger Stations; or USGS maps *Austin* and *Millett Ranch,* 1:62.500 (if available); or *Bunker Hill, North Toiyabe Peak, Kingston & Brewer Canyon,* 1:24.000; or the book, **Hiking the Great Basin**, Sierra Club.

Mt. Jefferson, Toquima Range, Nevada, USA

The south peak of Mt. Jefferson at 3640 meters is the highest mountain in all the central Nevada ranges. It's located in the Toquima Range, which is due north of Tonopah and Highways 6 & 396, and south of Austin and Highway 50. East of Jefferson is the Monitor Valley and Range; to the west the Toiyabe Range, which is covered on the 2 previous maps. All of the ranges in the Tonopah district are included in the Toiyabe National Forest maps North & South.

The Toquima Range is forested, and during the early years of settlement of Nevada, was an important lumber-cutting region. This area has long been a mining center as well. The rocks at the summit appear to be mostly quartzite, but a variety of other rock formations exist within the range. Old mining settlements such as Belmont and Jefferson are now largely ghost towns.

There are several ways of approaching the **summit plateau and Jefferson**, but perhaps the best all-around route is via Pine Creek & Campground located on the east side of the range. This area can be reached via County Road 82, from Tonopah on the south, or from Highway 50 and the Austin/Eureka area on the north. See a Nevada state highway map. When you reach a point due east of the mountain, look for a sign pointing out the way to Pine Creek Campground.

By using the trail beginning at the campground, a loop can be made climbing 3 of the highest summits on the same long day-hike. To do all 3 in one day would be too much for some people however, but a 2 day or day-and-a-half hike could be enjoyable, as there is water in all canyons for camping.

To reach the **North Peak**, walk up the South Fork of Pine Creek, then enter the 3rd canyon on the right about 5 or 6 kms above the campground. The cattle trails fade in the upper canyon, so route-find up to the summit plateau and veer north. Or head south and over the top of **Middle Peak**, then the **South Peak**, as shown on the map. Trails fade in places, but cows usually keep them open. Not many hikers in these parts; which is the best reason for going to these mountains. The author got to the South Peak around mid-day on 9/18/1978, but was caught in a snowstorm and had to to retreat the same way instead of making a loop-climb. It likely took about 5 hours (?) for the round-trip hike.

There are other route possibilities as well. A trail going up the South Fork of Morres Creek, will take you to the North Peak. From the south, the Meadow Canyon Road can be taken in order to reach the South Peak (which may be the best route for climbing all the higher summits). From the southwest, you can drive about 10 kms east from Round Mountain town & mine, to the historic site of Jefferson. From there, you can easily *bushwhack* in a northeasterly direction to the South Peak; or use the trails shown on the map.

Best places to get supplies are in Tonopah, Eureka or Austin (there are Forest Service ranger stations in these towns as well), with the very closest place being Carvers (see Toiyabe Dome map) due west of Mt. Jefferson. For updated information of any kind, call the Austin

Looking south at the South Peak of Mt. Jefferson.

Map 403-1, Mt. Jefferson, Toquima Range, Nevada, USA

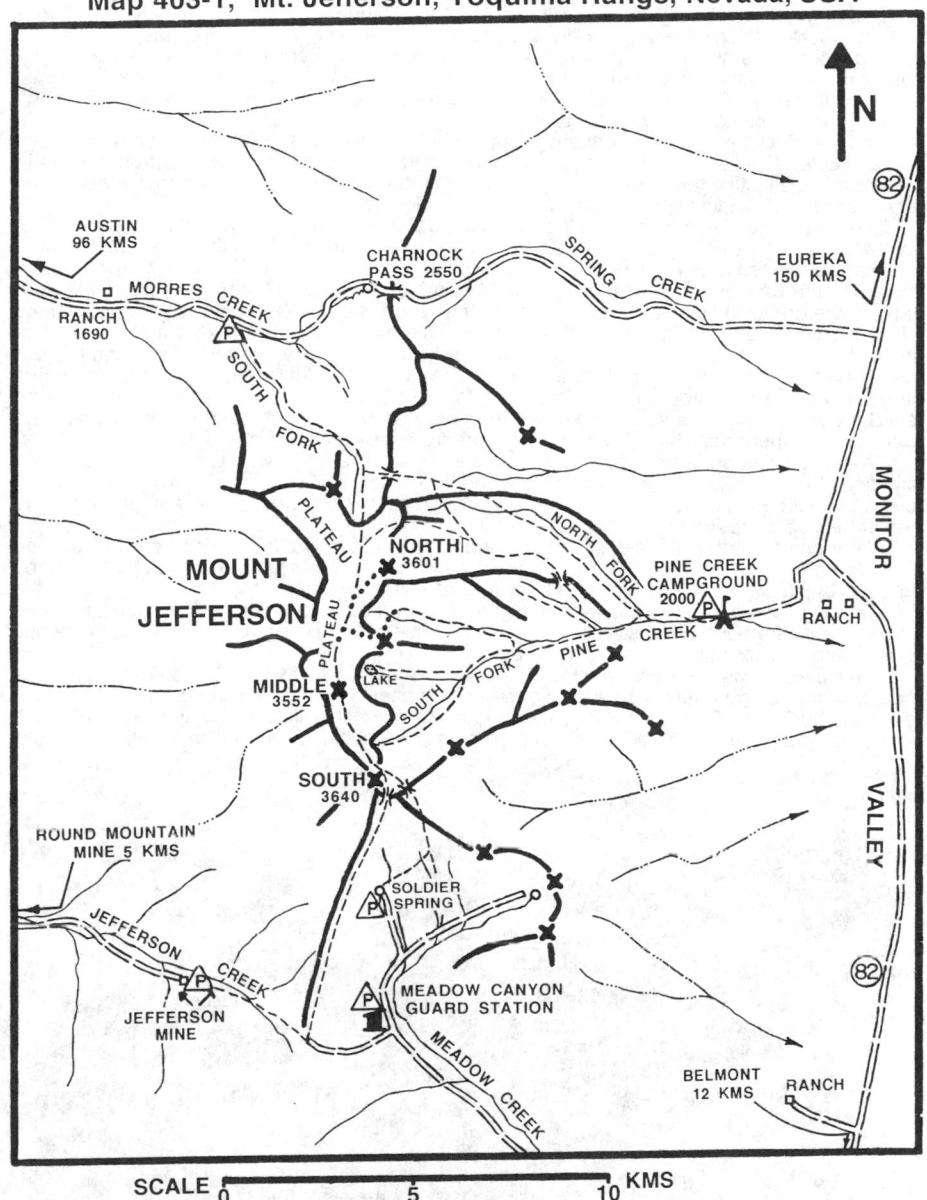

SCALE 0 ——— 5 ——— 10 KMS

Ranger Station at 702-964-2671; or the Tonapah office at 775-482-6286. Have a full tank of fuel, lots of water, and be prepared for long dusty rides on good, but graveled roads. Water is not plentiful, but can be found in all the main canyons around Mt. Jefferson.
Maps *Toiyabe National Forest, Southern Section,* 1:126,720, from the Tonopah or Austin Ranger Stations; and USGS maps *Mt. Jefferson, Pine Creek Ranch,* and perhaps *Jefferson & Corcoran Canyon,* 1:24,000; and the book, **Hiking the Great Basin**, Sierra Club.

Troy and Whitepine Peaks, Grant Range, Nevada, USA

This map shows the highest summits in the Grant Range of south central Nevada. These mountains are located southwest of Ely and Currant, due west of Pioche, and east of Tonapah. The highest point is Whitepine Peak at 3444 meters, while Troy Peak is listed at 3435. They are not high even by Nevada standards, but because of the extreme isolation, the chances are good you won't find other climbers or backpackers in the area to spoil an interesting climb. This is one place where you can get away from it all.

On top of Troy Peak are the remains of an old heliograph or triangulation station dating back to the 1880's. A heliograph was a mirrored instrument used for sending signals from mountain to mountain reflecting the suns rays. For anyone interested in ghost towns, there's also the remains of the old mining town of Troy on the west side of the range.

One way to get there (and you'll need a Nevada state highway map to do this) is to drive southwest out of Ely on Highway 6 to Currant, then leave 6 and head south and southwest on a graded county road until you reach the junction marked 1485 meters. Or, from Warm Springs located to the west on Highway 6, drive east & south on Highway 375 about 25 kms, then turn east on the graveled county road heading for the Grant Range. Once at the junction marked 1485, turn southeast and drive about 6 kms to the Troy ghost town. If you have a 4WD, you can drive into either canyon a ways; or park at Troy and walk from there. From either canyon, make your way up either **Troy** or **Whitepine**. There are no trails in the area, but these mountains aren't very rugged, and route-finding is easy. On 9/19/1982, the author climbed Troy Peak and found the summit area made of limestone with a grove of bristlecone pine trees on top, plus the remains of the heliograph site. His round-trip time from Troy ghost town was 4 3/4 hours.

The Grant Range is very isolated, yet there's a paved highway within 50 kms in any direction. Because of its desert environment and lack of any real streams, there's an absence of towns or ranches in the area. However, even with all these minuses, there is one primitive Forest Service campsite on Cherry Creek.

Water can be a problem in the Grant Range. There are only a few springs around, and *no permanent live or running water* to speak of. In spring and early summer there is limited amounts of water available, however. **Carry lots of water in your car!**

There's not much traffic around these mountains, especially once you leave Highway 6, but what travelers there are would surely stop for someone in trouble. This is one place you'll have to have you own car and it should be in good running condition.

You are well advised to stock up on food and supplies in either Las Vegas, Ely, or Tonapah. What may appear to be small towns on state highway maps, may only be a crossroads or road junction, ranch, or ghost town! Best time to climb in the Grant Range is late spring, early summer, or fall. With a bit of snow around, water will be less of a problem. For updated information, call the Humboldt

A grove of bristlecone pines growing near the summit of Troy Peak.

Map 404-1, Troy & Whitepine Peaks, Grant Range, Nevada, USA

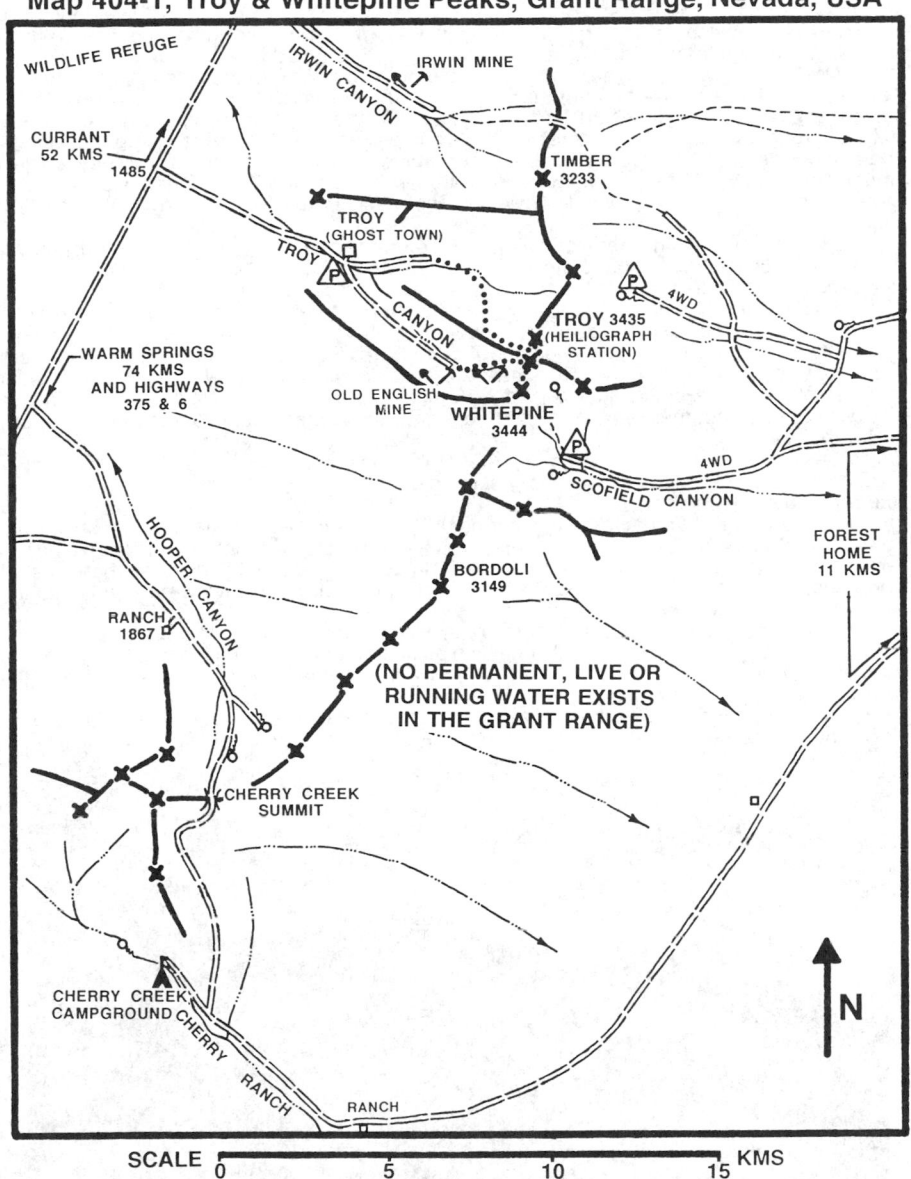

WILDLIFE REFUGE

IRWIN CANYON

IRWIN MINE

CURRANT
52 KMS
1485

TIMBER
3233

TROY
(GHOST TOWN)

TROY

TROY 3435
(HEILIOGRAPH
STATION)

4WD

WARM SPRINGS
74 KMS
AND HIGHWAYS
375 & 6

CANYON

OLD ENGLISH
MINE

WHITEPINE
3444

SCOFIELD CANYON

4WD

FOREST
HOME
11 KMS

HOOPER CANYON

BORDOLI
3149

(NO PERMANENT, LIVE OR
RUNNING WATER EXISTS
IN THE GRANT RANGE)

RANCH
1867

CHERRY CREEK
SUMMIT

CHERRY CREEK
CAMPGROUND

CHERRY RANCH

RANCH

N

SCALE 0   5   10   15 KMS

Ranger Station in Ely at 775-289-3031, as this range is part of the Humboldt National Forest. The
Toiyabe Ranger Station in Tonapah may offer some help, Tele. 775-482-6286.
Maps Any *Nevada state highway map*; and *Humboldt National Forest--White Pine Ranger District*
map, 1:126,720, from the Ely Ranger Station; USGS maps *Troy Canyon* and *Horse Spring Hills*,
1:24,000; and the book, **Hiking the Great Basin**, Sierra Club.

Currant Peak, White Pine Mountains, Nevada, USA

Currant Peak at 3510 meters elevation, is the highest summit in the White Pine Mountains. This range is located in east central Nevada, southwest of Ely and the Ruth Copper Mine, north of the small junction town of Currant, and west and northwest of US Highway 6.

The White Pine Mountains are similar to all the other mountain ranges in the Great Basin of Nevada and western Utah. They run north-south, and are covered with a pine (often bristlecone), spruce or fir forest at higher elevations. On the lower slopes you'll find sagebrush, sometimes other brush and open forests of aspen in places, then the coniferous forests above. The author doesn't recall seeing any bristlecone pines in these mountains, but they're likely around somewhere. For those unaware, researchers have found bristlecones pines on other Great Basin mountains to be the oldest living organisms on earth. See Wheeler Peak, Map 407, page 873.

The central portion of the White Pines is composed of solid and largely unfractured limestone, which dips about 45° to the east. The upper east portion of Currant Peak has some steep and smooth slabs of limestone slickrock, which makes climbing interesting.

The White Pine Mountains and **Currant Peak** are relatively easy to get to. There are 3 approach roads to the eastern side of the range, all of which take off from Highway 6. The best & easiest way is the road beginning near the Currant Creek Campground and running northward alongside Currant Creek. It may have some bad sections, but it's the most-direct way to Currant Peak. Park your car near the pass marked 2490 meters and route-find west from there. There's no trail to the top, but there's no need for one, as a good route is easy to find with little if any bushwhacking.

The author was here in the afternoon of 9/20/1978 and climbed up the east face in just under 2 1/2 hours. His diary states it was tricky coming down on steep slickrock, and the round-trip time was about 4 1/4 hours.

A second way to approach the highest peaks is to leave Highway 6 just east of Currant Summit, and drive up White River, along which are located 2 primitive campgrounds or campsites. At the junction marked 2140 meters, drive southwest and park somewhere east of **Duckwater** (3408 meters) or Currant Peaks. There appear to be relatively easy routes up the east face of Duckwater Peak too.

Nevada is a dry state, but these mountains are high and large enough to produce their own weather and sufficient water to feed 3 streams big enough for fish. Camping in the White Pines is quiet and free, with few visitors. If you're sick & tired of the crowds and restrictions in the Sierra Nevada, this is one place for you.

The nearest town to this area is Ely located about 62 kms northeast of Currant Summit. That's the best place, almost the only place, to buy supplies nearby as it's the biggest town in

From the White River Road at 2140 meters looking southwest. Currant Peak is to the right.

Map 405-1, Currant Peak, White Pine Mtns., Nevada, USA

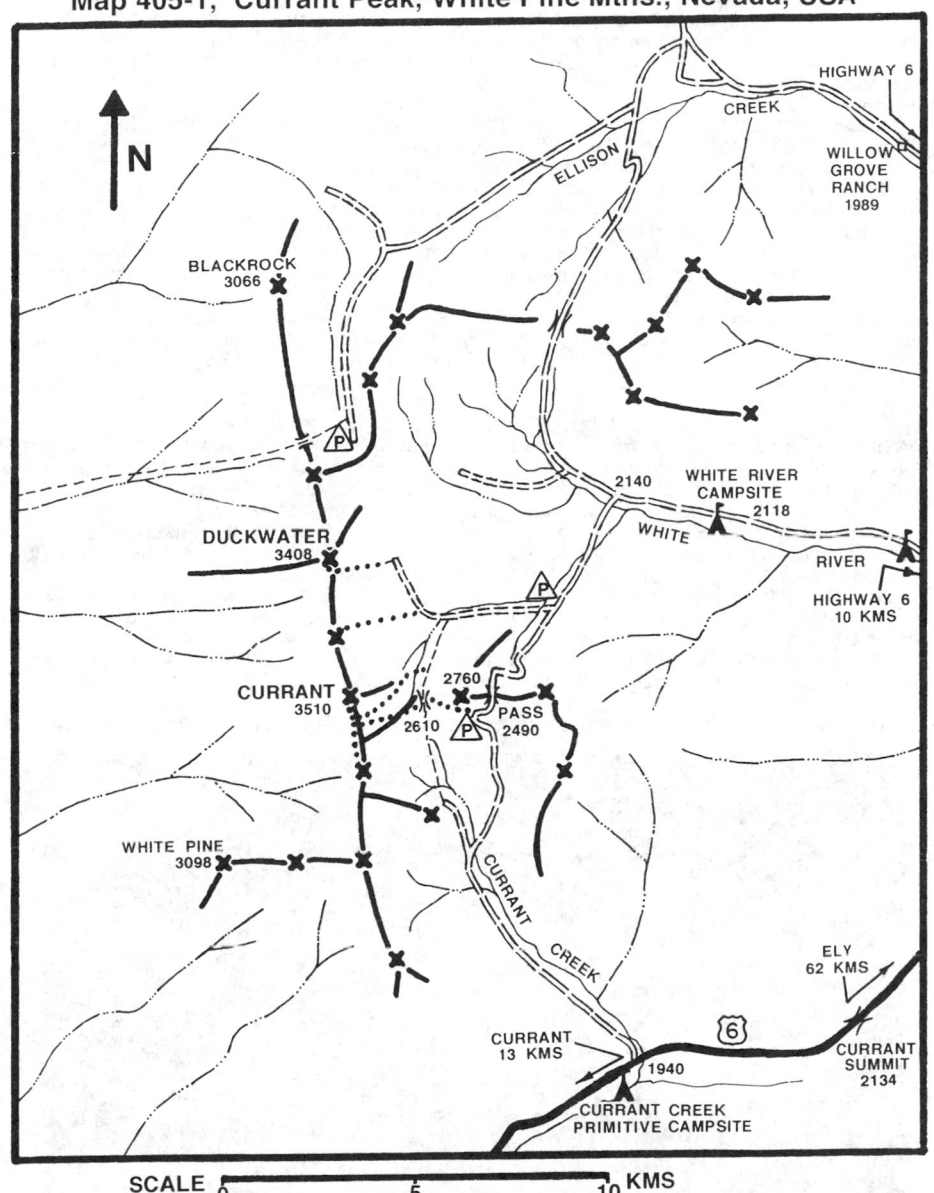

SCALE | 0 .... 5 .... 10 KMS

eastern Nevada. If you're coming from the west, stop and shop in Tonapah. For Forest Service maps and the latest information on roads and campsites, see the Humboldt National Forest Office in Ely, Tele. 775-289-3031.
Maps *Humboldt National Forest--White Pine Ranger District,* 1:126,720; and/or USGS maps *Currant Mountain, White Pine Peak, Currant Summit & Horse Track Spring,* 1:24,000; and the book, **Hiking the Great Basin**, Sierra Club.

North & South Schell Peaks, Schell Range, Nevada, USA

Shown here is the Schell Range located in extreme east central Nevada not far from the Utah state line. This part of the range is located northeast of Ely, east of McGill, and northwest of both Mt. Moriah and Wheeler Peak--both of which are shown on the next 2 maps. The highest peak in the range is North Schell at 3623 meters. Next is South Schell at 3587, and Taft, 3577 meters.

Like all the mountains of the Great Basin, the Schell Range runs north-south, is long & narrow, and is covered with a coniferous forest at the higher elevations. There are various kinds of rocks in these mountains, but in the area of North Schell Peak, it's mostly limestone.

The summits of the Schell Range are not very rugged, instead are mostly rounded over. From Cleve Creek Peak on the south, to about Bird Creek in the north, there are no real passes or low points on this one long summit ridge. There are a few trails in these mountains, but for the most part only cattle and local residents use them. From any of the access roads shown on the map, it's an easy day hike to the summit of one or more peaks. However, many of these short side roads are for 4WD vehicles only.

To climb **North Schell**, drive north out of Ely, and past McGill while on Highway 93. About 8 kms north of McGill, turn east on State Road 486, the road giving access to the west side of the range. About 4 kms beyond (south) the Duck Creek Dam & ranch, turn southeast at the sign stating *Timber Creek,* and drive to the end of the road. There are 2 campgrounds and a small stream at the head of this canyon. One of the facilities is a Girl Scout Camp. From the end of the road, walk up the trail to the north into what might be called the North Fork of Timber Creek, and at one of many locations, route-find up to the east while aiming for the summit. You can also stay on the trail as it winds its way up to the pass marked 3325 meters, then ridge-walk southeast to the summit. The author climbed North Schell on 9/21/1978 from the end of the road. No time was recorded, but it likely took about half a day round-trip.

To climb **South Schell** or **Taft Peaks**, continue south up Duck Creek on State Road 486, and turn southeast up along Berry Creek. Park at or near the end of the road, then walk along a trail going up to the pass between the 2 summits, then climb both on the same short hike.

Few if any difficult routes can be found in the Schell Range, but some north or east faces are steeper. The only equipment needed is a good pair of boots. Running water can be found in all major canyons.

Ely is the largest town in the area, making it the best place to shop. It's also the place to get more maps and/or information as there's a ranger station of the Humboldt National Forest located there, Tele. 775-289-3031.

Heavy snows fall in these mountains in winter, but very little rain in summer. Best time to climb

From the summit of North Schell looking south, with Wheeler Peak in the far left background.

Map 406-1, North & South Schell, Schell Range, Nevada, USA

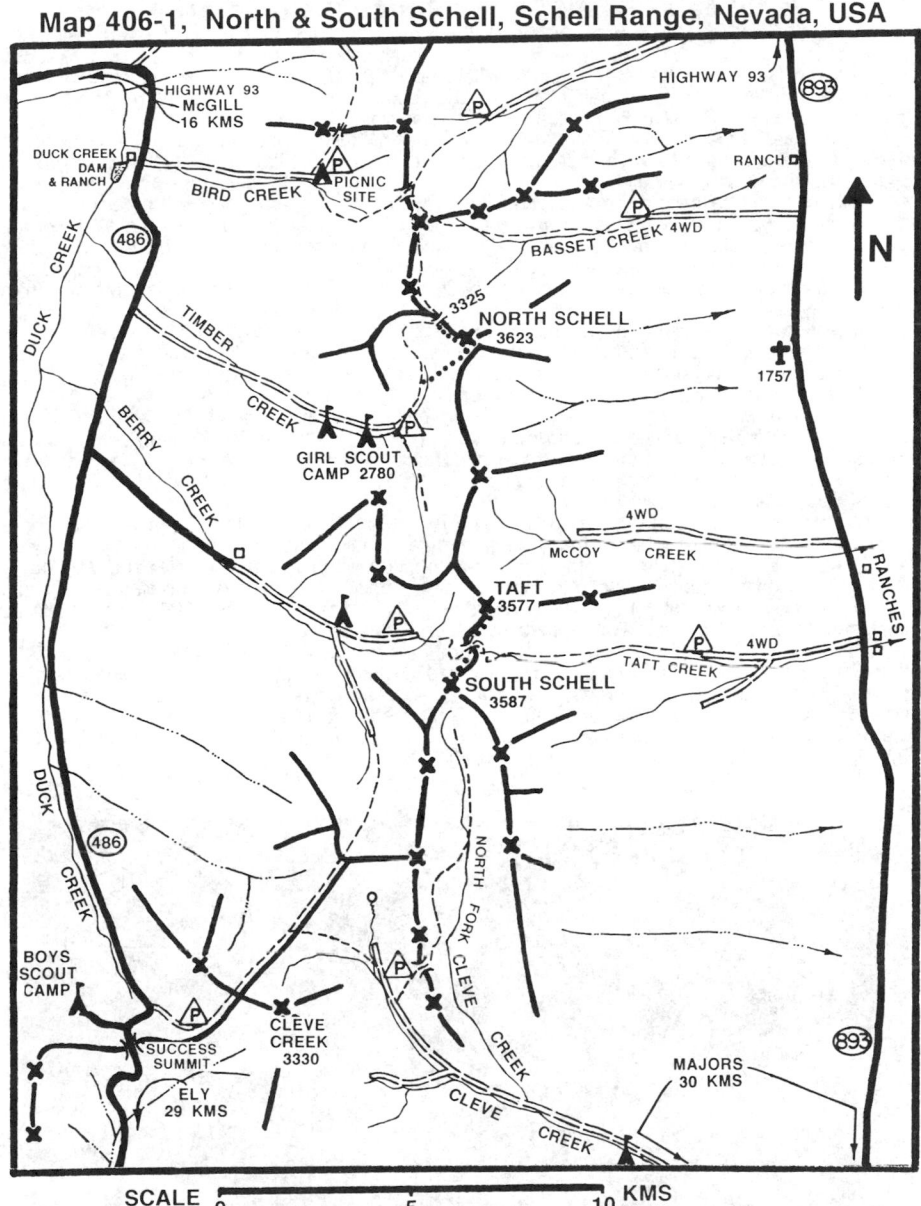

SCALE ⊢————————————————⊣ KMS
      0   5   10

is from June through October.
Maps *Humboldt National Forest--Ely Ranger District,* 1:126,720, from the Ely Ranger Station; USGS maps *Duck Creek Valley, Clove Creek Baldy, North Schell Peak & South Schell Peak,* 1:24,000; and the book, **Hiking the Great Basin**, Sierra Club.

Wheeler Peak, Snake Range, Nevada, USA

Featured on this map is Wheeler Peak at 3982 meters. It's located in the southern half of the Snake Range of eastern Nevada not far west of the Utah-Nevada state line. This is the highest and most impressive peak in the Great Basin. In October 1986, much of this range was made into the Great Basin National Park. The main features in the park are the Lehman Caves (formerly a national monument), Wheeler Peak, and bristlecone pine trees as old as 4900 years.

The Snake Range is similar to other mountain ranges in the Great Basin of Utah and Nevada in that it's been uplifted and folded and consists of mostly quartzite and limestone, with some marble in the Lehman Caves area.

Within the Snake Range are a number of cirque basins with steep north faces. Wheeler Peak has a very impressive cirque (with small permanent icefield) and northeast face. On top of Wheeler are the remains of an old heliograph or triangulation station, first used by the US Coast and Geodetic Survey in the 1880's as a signal point when they surveyed east to west along the 39th parallel. Still remaining are a number of stone shelters and platforms dating from that time period, but also from more recent surveys.

Access to the mountain is easy, with Highway 50 & 6 nearby. Normally, the best and easiest way there is from the east side of the range. Food, gasoline and other supplies can be purchased in Baker, Nevada, 8 kms east of Lehman Caves, but it's a very small town. Best to stock up on food in Delta, Utah to the east; or in Ely, Nevada located to the west.

The normal way to climb **Wheeler** is to first drive west from Baker almost to Lehman Caves & Park Headquarters, but turn right and follow the signs up to the Wheeler Peak Campground. From the trailhead just west of the campground, walk the trail running west up to the big North or Northwest Ridge, then south up the big hogsback to the summit. It's 8.5 kms one way, and can be done in as little as half a day. Most people take all day.

The author first climbed Wheeler on 9/22/1978, but in 1988, he wrote and published the book mentioned below. That book tells of many different routes up this outstanding peak.

This map also shows various other, and more difficult routes to both Wheeler and **Jeff Davis Peak**. There's also a good well-used trail into the cirque basin to the bristlecone pine forest. Within this forest, one tree was cut down in 1964 for further study. It was found to be 4900 years old! It was the oldest living thing on earth. They named it WPN-114.

The road to the campground is open by around the first week or two in June, and is snowed in again by about November 1. This road is not plowed in winter. Summer climbing is during this time period. Because the road to Lehman Caves is open year-round, you'll have easy access to the east side for winter climbing. Use the Lehman Creek Trail or the east ridge in winter. The visitor center is also open year-round at Lehman Caves. Stop there for last minute updates or maps. Or Tele. 775-234-7331, or see their website (www.nps.gov/grba/).

Looking south from Bald Mountain at Wheeler Peak in winter.

Map 407-1, Wheeler Peak, Snake Range, Nevada, USA

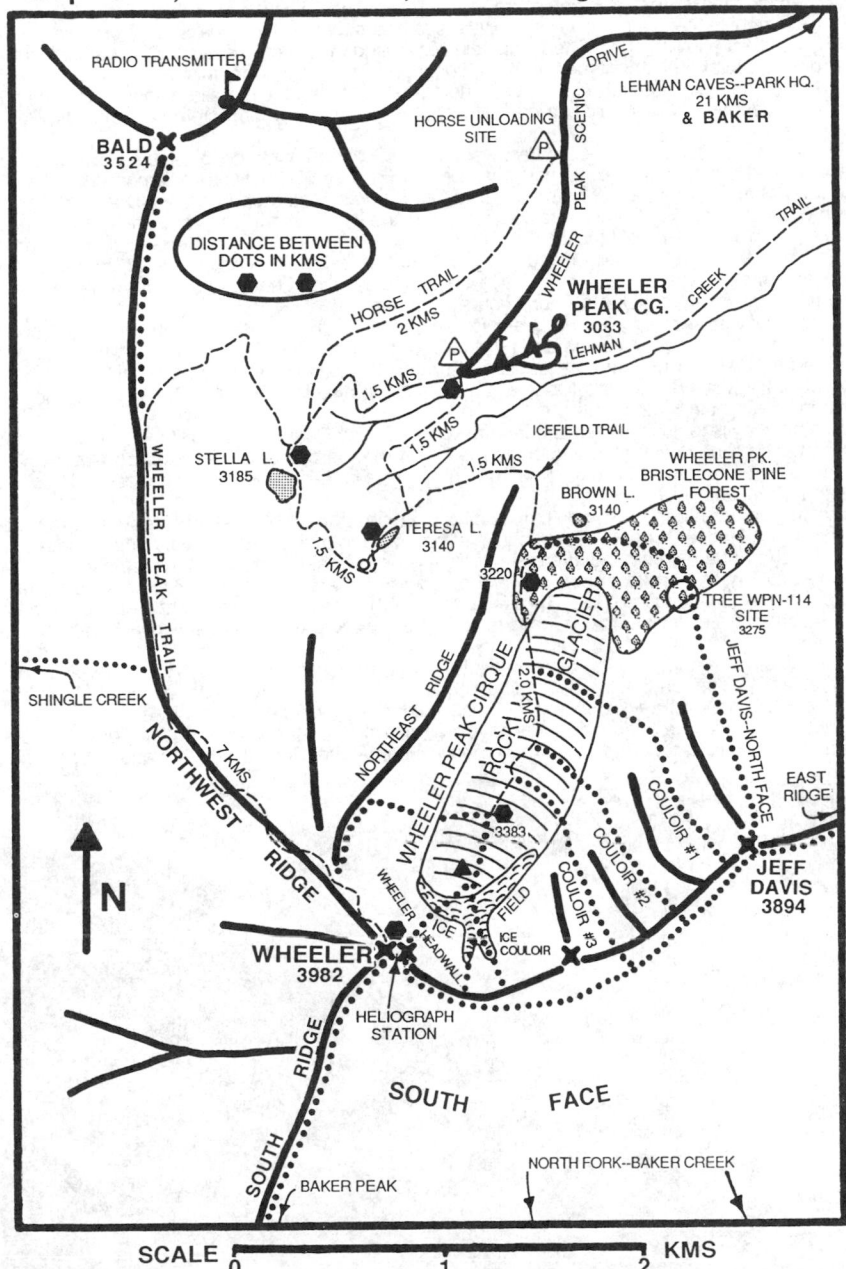

Maps USGS or BLM maps *Ely* and *Garrison*, 1:100,000; or *Wheeler Peak, Windy Peak & Lehman Caves*, 1:24,000; one of the geology maps *MF-1343 A, B, or C*, 1:62,500; or *Humboldt National Forest*, 1:126,720; and **Hiking and Climbing in the Great Basin National Park**, Kelsey.

Mt. Moriah, Snake Range, Nevada, USA

Mt. Moriah at 3674 meters is part of the Snake Range, same as Wheeler Peak to the south, but in reality it's a mountain and a range in itself. What separates these 2 high peaks is US Highway 50-6.

Mt. Moriah is a folded and uplifted mountain composed mostly of limestone and quartzite, but with outcroppings of various other types of rock. Because of the limestone, this mountain probably has more bristlecone pines than anywhere else. There are 6 basic routes or trails leading to the summit of Moriah, but serious hikers should see the author's other book below for more details on both Wheeler Peak and Moriah.

For those with 4WD vehicles, the best way to climb **Moriah** might be to use the **Four Mile Road** located on the northwest side of the mountain. Leave Highway 50-6 between mile posts 80 & 81, drive north for 11 kms, turn east just before a fence, and drive up a steep rough 4WD road toward the Moriah Cabin and the Big Canyon Trailhead. That place is just off this map one km and west of The Table, a high plateau north of Moriah. From there, walk a little east, then south 5 kms to the summit.

Also from the west, you can drive up **Negro Creek** to the end of a drivable road, then hike an old abandoned track up to the west face. This is a long all day hike. The author did this route for the first time on 9/27/1978. It probably took 7 or 8 hours round-trip (?).

To reach the east-side routes which are shown on this map, drive Highway 50-6 to a point one km east of the Utah-Nevada state line and turn north onto the Callao Road (extreme right side of this map). After 12 kms you come to a junction. Turn northwest onto a good road until you reach the trailhead on **Hendrys Creek**. It's a long all day round-trip hike from there; or take a pack and camp higher up, making it in 1 1/2 days.

Another way is to drive 6 kms further north on the Callao Road to the old Robinson Ranch. Turn west from there and drive to the end of the road near the Garnet Mine on **Hampton Creek**. From there a good trail heads to the summit via The Table. This is likely the easiest, shortest and best route to the top of Moriah.

Still further north on the Callao Road is a large spring and an old red ranch house. From there drive west into **Horse Canyon**. There's a trail from the end of this rough road, but it's seldom used today. This is not a recommended route. Or from just north of the red ranch house, turn northwest and drive into **Smith Creek Canyon**. From the upper trailhead, you can follow another seldom-used trail up Smith and Deep Creeks to The Table, then to the summit. Part of that trail seems to have deteriorated and is difficult to find. Once the author just walked up Deep Canyon with no trail, which was easy.

He has also climbed Moriah twice in winter; once using the Four Mile Route, once going up Hendrys Creek. The roads approaching those 2 areas are the best for winter access. All the roads listed above are good for any car in dry conditions except the upper part of Four Mile Road.

Each of the above mentioned routes have water available (carry water on the Four Mile route), along with good campsites. Stock up on supplies in either Delta, Utah, or Ely, Nevada. Nearby Baker

Looking at the summit of Mt. Moriah from the southwest.

Map 408-1, Mt. Moriah, Snake Range, Nevada, USA

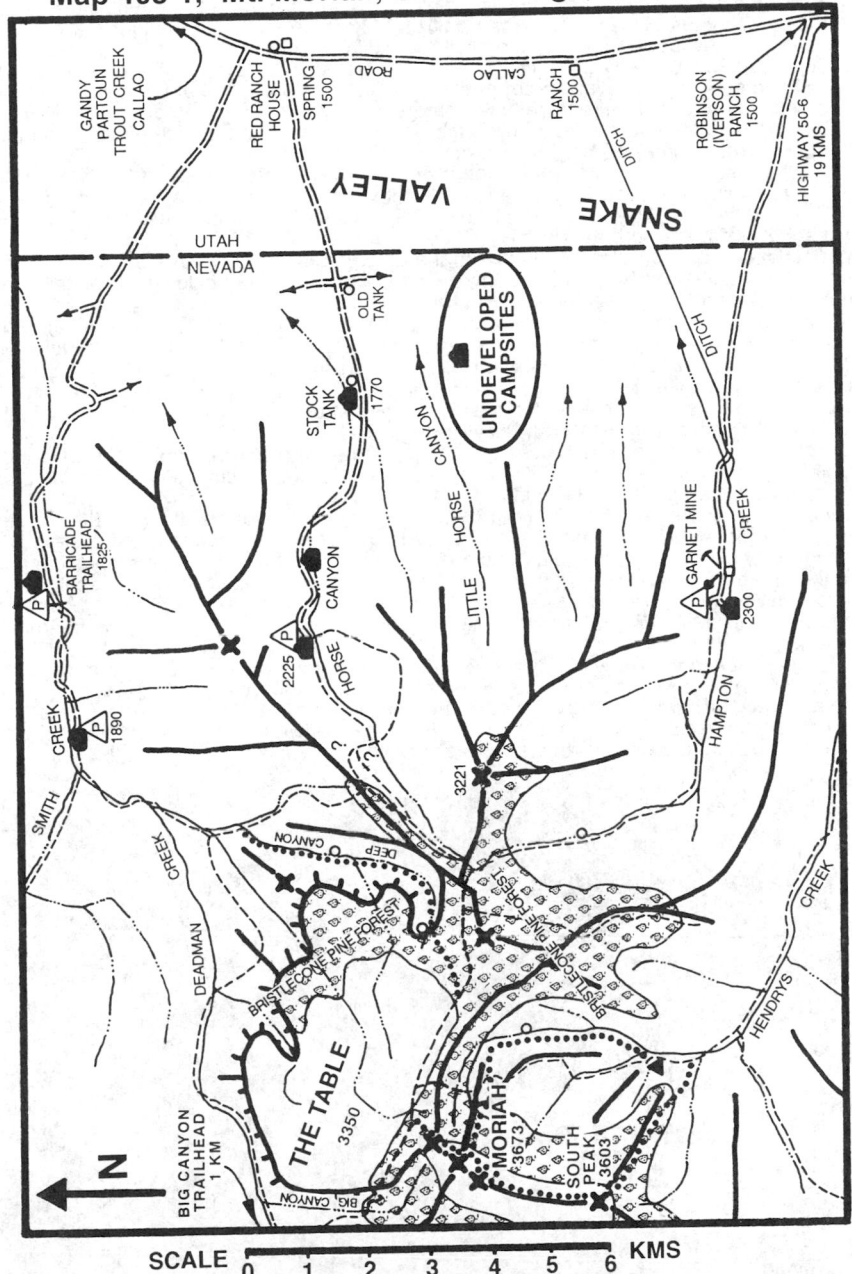

SCALE
0 1 2 3 4 5 6 KMS

and Garrison are pretty small ranching communities and don't have much in the way of shopping facilities. Normal hiking season is from June through October.

Maps USGS maps *Ely*, 1:100,000; or *Sixmile Canyon, Mount Moriah, Little Horse Canyon, The Cove & Old Mans Canyon*, 1:24,000; and/or *Humboldt National Forest*, 1:126,720; and the book, **Climbing and Hiking in the Great Basin National Park**, Kelsey.

Ruby Dome & Thomas Peak, Ruby Mountains, Nevada, USA

Ruby Dome at 3471 meters altitude, is the highest summit in the Ruby Mountains located in northeastern Nevada. Nearby Thomas Peak at 3450 meters is second highest. The Ruby Mountains are fairly rugged, some of the most rugged in all of Nevada. The rock appears to be mostly quartzite, but with some granite. There are "U" shaped valleys and many cirque basins, often holding small lakes, evidence of past glaciation. It's evident that because of its more northerly position, this area receives much more precipitation than the central and eastern Nevada ranges to the south. The treeline is also much lower, about 3200 meters, indicating most of the moisture received falls in the form of snow.

Public access can be a problem, but there's one easy way into the area; that's via Lamoille Creek Road, which takes you to the heart of the Ruby Mountains Scenic Area. Best way to get there is to start in Elko at the Humboldt National Forest Office where you can get any last minute information updates and better maps. Or call them at 775-738-5171. From there, drive southeast out of town on State Road 227 in the direction of Lamoille. About one km west of Lamoille, turn south onto the Lamoille Canyon Road. From a number of locations on this paved highway, you can reach most of the summits worth climbing.

Most people drive to the very end of the road at 2850 meters. From there, hike northwest on one trail toward Island Lake. From the lake, climb west up to a ridge, then north to **Thomas Peak**; or south to **Peak 3407** meters, or **Snowlake Peak**. Or hike south on another trail to Liberty Pass & Lake and other summits beyond. On 9/26/1978, the author climbed Thomas on a quick hike, but didn't record his hike-time--probably 2-3 hours round-trip (?). Later that afternoon, he hiked up the Right Fork Canyon but didn't have the time to reach Ruby Dome.

As of 2000, the best all-public access route to **Ruby Dome** was to park at Camp Lamoille (Boy Scout camp), walk upcanyon on a trail, bushwhack a short distance up to the west, then continue ridge-climbing west to the summit.

Much of the western side of the range is Te-Moak Indian lands. At times in the past they have allowed non-Indians access to forest lands to the east--but this wasn't the case in 2000. However, they may change the policy and charge a fee in the future. If or when this happens, start at the Elko Ranger Station for information, then drive east on State Road 227, south on 228 for about 20 kms, then turn east toward Lee. From Lee, head north, then east along Echo Creek as shown on this map. From somewhere along Echo Creek route-find up Ruby Dome from the southwest.

The few trails in the Ruby Mountains Scenic Area are supposed to be well-marked, and because of the nearness of Interstate 80 which runs through Elko, this is one of the most-popular mountain areas in Nevada (but not nearly as popular as Wheeler Peak & Mt. Charleston). An eastern approach to this range could be easy in some cases, but the foothills are covered with ranches under private ownership, with no public access.

From Island Lake looking north at the south face of Mt. Thomas.

Map 409-1, Ruby Dome & Thomas Peak, Ruby Mtns., Nevada, USA

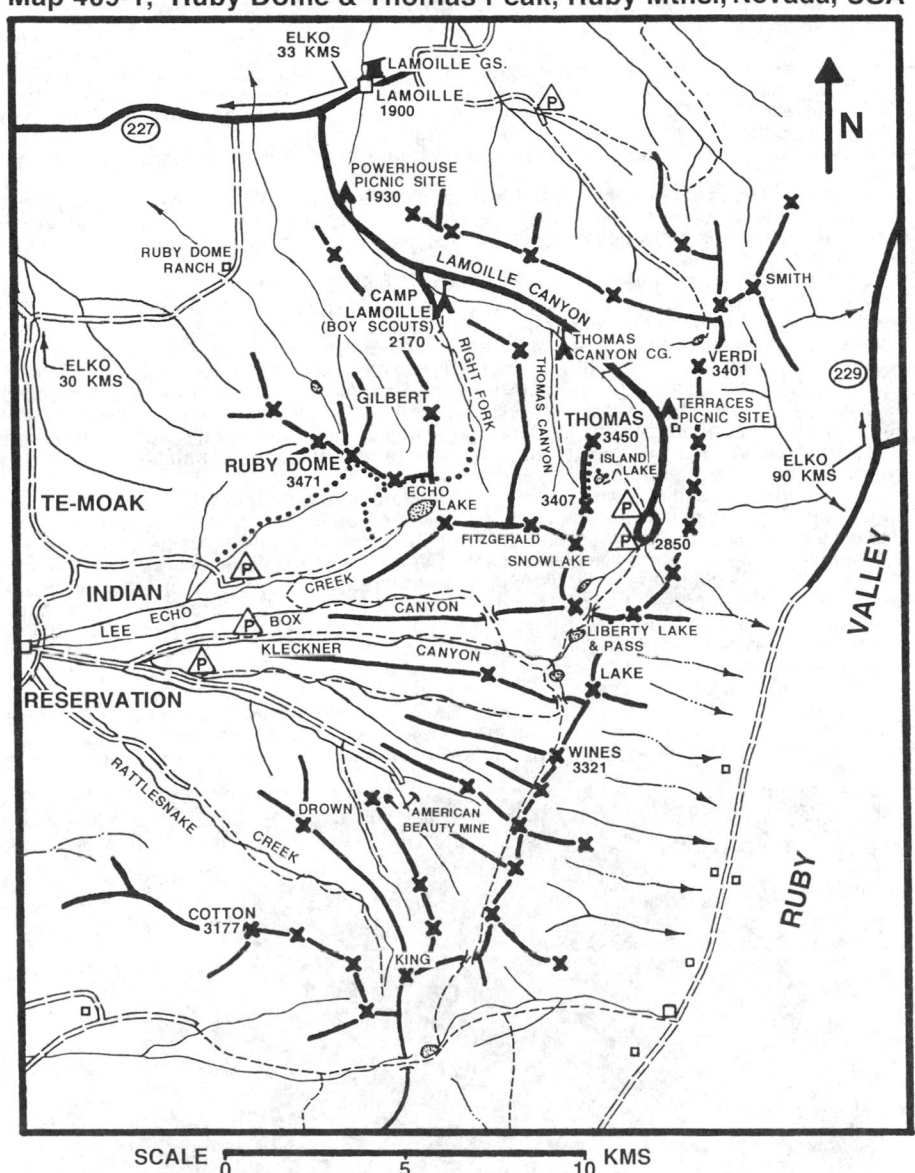

The best place to buy food, gas and supplies is Elko, but Lamoille has a small store & gas station. Roads in the area are generally well-used, but mostly graveled. The road up Lamoille Creek is paved with heavy traffic (by Nevada standards) in summer. Other mountains in the area include the East Humboldt Range northeast of the Ruby Mountains; however, they too have public access problems. About the only way to get there is via Wells and the Angle Lake Road. From the campground at Angle Lake, you can climb several peaks.

Maps *Humboldt National Forest--Ruby Mountains Ranger District,* 1:126,720, from the Elko Ranger Station; USGS maps *Lamoille, Verdi Peak, Lee, Ruby Dome & Ruby Valley School,* 1:24,000; and the book, **Hiking the Great Basin**, Sierra Club.

Matterhorn, Jarbridge Mountains, Nevada, USA

Few people know of this small wilderness area in the northeast corner of the state of Nevada; even the author was unfamiliar with it until Mark Cox of Ogden, Utah, wrote him a letter. This is the Jarbridge Wilderness, which covers the higher parts of the Jarbridge Mountains. The highest summit is Matterhorn Peak at 3304 meters. These mountains are located just south of the Idaho state line and due north of Elko and Wells, Nevada. At the northwest boundary of the wilderness, is the very small community of Jarbridge, a former gold mining center, but which is now nearly abandoned. Jarbridge town has a small store for buying simple supplies, but sells no gasoline.

There are 3 ways to reach this area. First, from the south drive along Interstate 80 to a point roughly halfway between Wells and Elko, exit at Deeth, and turn north onto a graveled county road. After more than 100 kms (?), you'll arrive at the tiny settlement of Jarbridge. Long drive on an all-dirt road!

Or if starting in Elko, drive north on paved State Road 225 (number 51 on old maps) for 88 kms, then turn right or northeast onto a gravel road for another 75 kms to Jarbridge. The problem with both of these routes is, you must go over 2 high passes on less than perfect dirt roads which are open for only 3 or 4 months each year. But in summer any car can make it.

Probably the best way in would be to start in Twin Falls, Idaho, and drive west, then south on US Highway 93 in the direction of Wells, Nevada. At Rogerson, Idaho, turn west, then south and pass through Three Creek, where the last gasoline station is located. The pavement ends at Three Creek. From there south to Jarbridge town is a good graveled road. Rogerson to Jarbridge is about 134 kms--another long lonely drive. For updated information call the Elko Ranger Station at 775-738-5171.

Once in the area and ready to climb, drive south out of Jarbridge town up to the end of the road at the Pine Creek Campground, where there's a parking lot and trail register (or if the *shovel brigade* is successful in reopening the road, then you might drive up to the *old trailhead* at 2117 meters?). If you want to climb **Matterhorn Peak** quickly, then walk up the old washed-out road for about 2 kms to the *old trailhead*, then southeast up the prominent ridge between Snowslide and Dry Gulches. You may have a little bushwhacking. This takes you straight to the summit with the least amount of walking. The author did this hike, then returned by way of Dry Gulch, as shown on the map. He found water about halfway down Dry Gulch. He did this on 9/17/1982 in just over 3 hours round-trip. The average hiker can do this in half a day. For slower walkers it's a full day-climb.

You could also walk further up the Jarbrige River to the Norman Mine and nearby Jarbridge Pond, then turn left and walk north along the summit ridge over **Cougar Peak** to Matterhorn. Another good climb would be to walk up to the Success Mine on an old road or trail (?), then

This is another Matterhorn Peak. Looking south at the northeast cirque basin.

Map 410-1, Matterhorn, Jarbridge Mountains, Nevada, USA

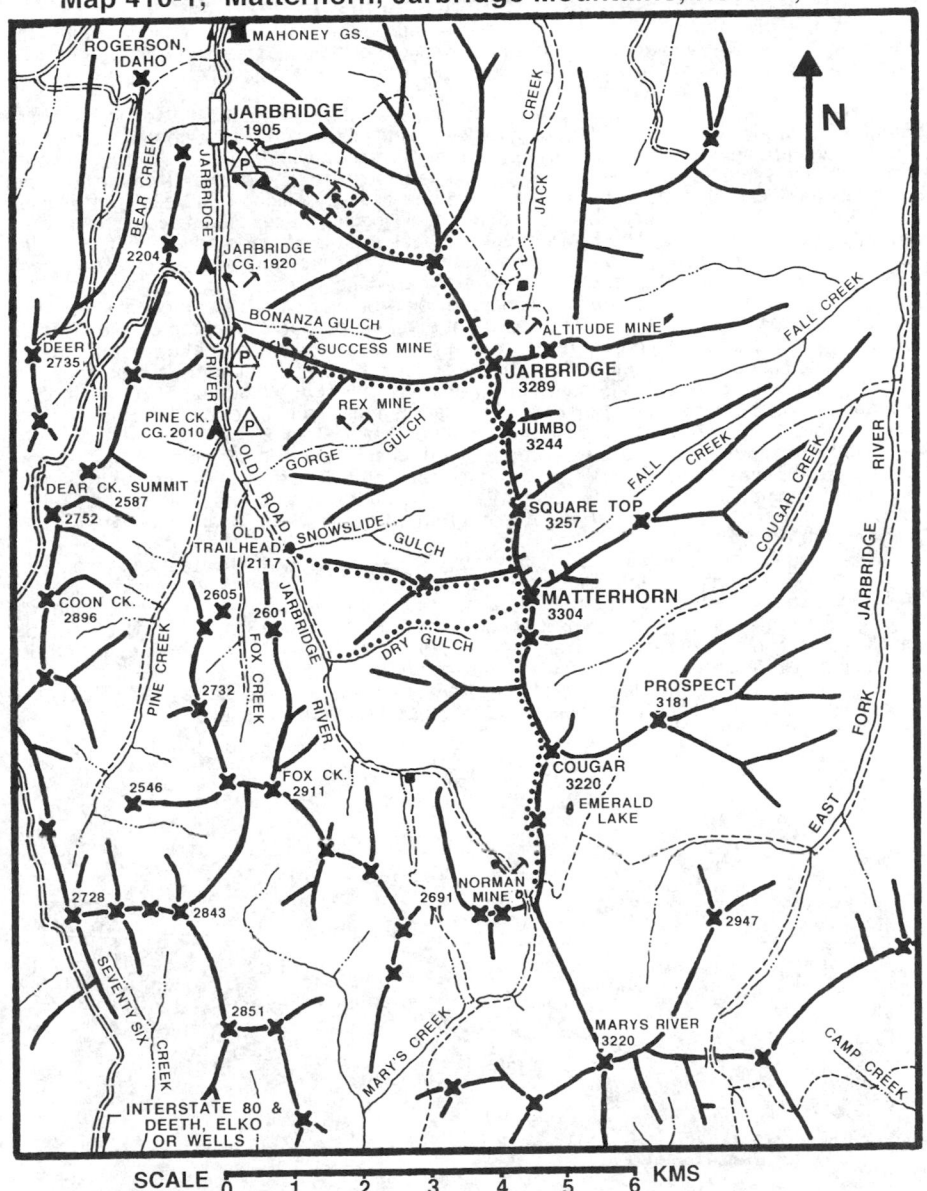

SCALE 0 1 2 3 4 5 6 KMS

ridge-walk east to **Jarbridge Peak** at 3289 meters. From there continue south along the ridge to Matterhorn. These ridges are not very rugged, so ridge-walking is easy.

Camp anywhere in the canyon bottoms as you'll find lots of water, and best of all, few if any other people. Climb from early June to October, using the Idaho access route; but perhaps a little shorter season if you come in from the south. Best to buy supplies at Elko or Twin Falls.
Maps *Humbolt National Forest*, 1:126,720; or USGS maps *Jarbridge North, Jarbridge South & Gods Pocket Peak*, 1:24,000; buy these at the Humboldt National Forest Ranger Station in Elko or maybe Jarbridge town store (?).

Thompson, Sawtooth Mountains, Idaho, USA

Shown on this map is the Sawtooth Range, located in central Idaho, just southwest of the resort town of Stanley, and about 100 kms northwest of Ketchum and the Sun Valley region. To get there drive north from the Twin Falls area on Highway 75 until you reach Stanley. Many of the peaks in this section are composed mostly of granitic-type rock.

These are some of the most spectacular mountains in the USA, at least when viewed from Stanley. They also offer some of the best rock climbing possibilities in the country. However, there is one problem; the place is very popular and over-run with tourists. Much of the area covered by this map is part of the Sawtooth Wilderness Area, and/or the Sawtooth National Recreational Area. As a result, places along the main highway, linking Sun Valley with Stanley and ultimately Challis, are very crowded with road-side lodging places, gas stations, campsites, and other tourist facilities. The Sawtooth Wilderness Area is affected adversely too; it's the road-less area covered by the southwest half of this map. It's recommended you visit this place in September if you can, rather than mid-summer, to avoid the crowds.

The only settlement of any size in the entire region is Stanley. It has a number of stores, gas stations and restaurants. About 5 kms south of the main part of town is the Stanley Ranger Station. There's also a visitor center located further south at Redfish Lake. These are the logical places to get more detailed maps of the mountains, as well as information on camping, climbing, etc. For up-to-date information call the Sawtooth N.R.A. at 800-260-5970. That office is located 84 kms southeast on Highway 75 not far north of Ketchum; or call the Redfish Lake Visitor Center at 208-774-3536; or the Stanley Ranger Station, Tele. 208-774-3000.

The highest summit in the Sawtooths is Thompson Peak at 3285 meters. In the same cluster are Williams, 3242; Baron, 3142, and Heyburn at 3119 meters. To find the trail to the summit of Thompson, park near the Stanley Ranger Station, or near the trailhead on Redfish Lake. Talk to those people first and they'll update you on where exactly to park and the beginning of the trail.

Observing this map carefully, walk from either of these trailheads to the west and onto a long straight hill, which is actually an old lateral glacier moraine. At the western end of the moraine, the trail faded some on the author's trip on 8/20/1982, then it was simply walking west along the south side of the peak and making the finally ascent up the southwest face to the top. Someone told the author, as of 2000, there's now a distinguishable trail all the way to the top. The author made this climb from the visitor center on Redfish Lake in just under 7 hours round-trip.

Other trails to the high country begin at the trailheads on Iron Creek, at Stanley Lake, Pettit Lake and near Wapiti. For further information, contact the rangers at the visitor center.

Looking southwest from Stanley at the northeastern slopes of the Sawtooth Mountains.

Map 411-1, Thompson, Sawtooth Mountains, Idaho, USA

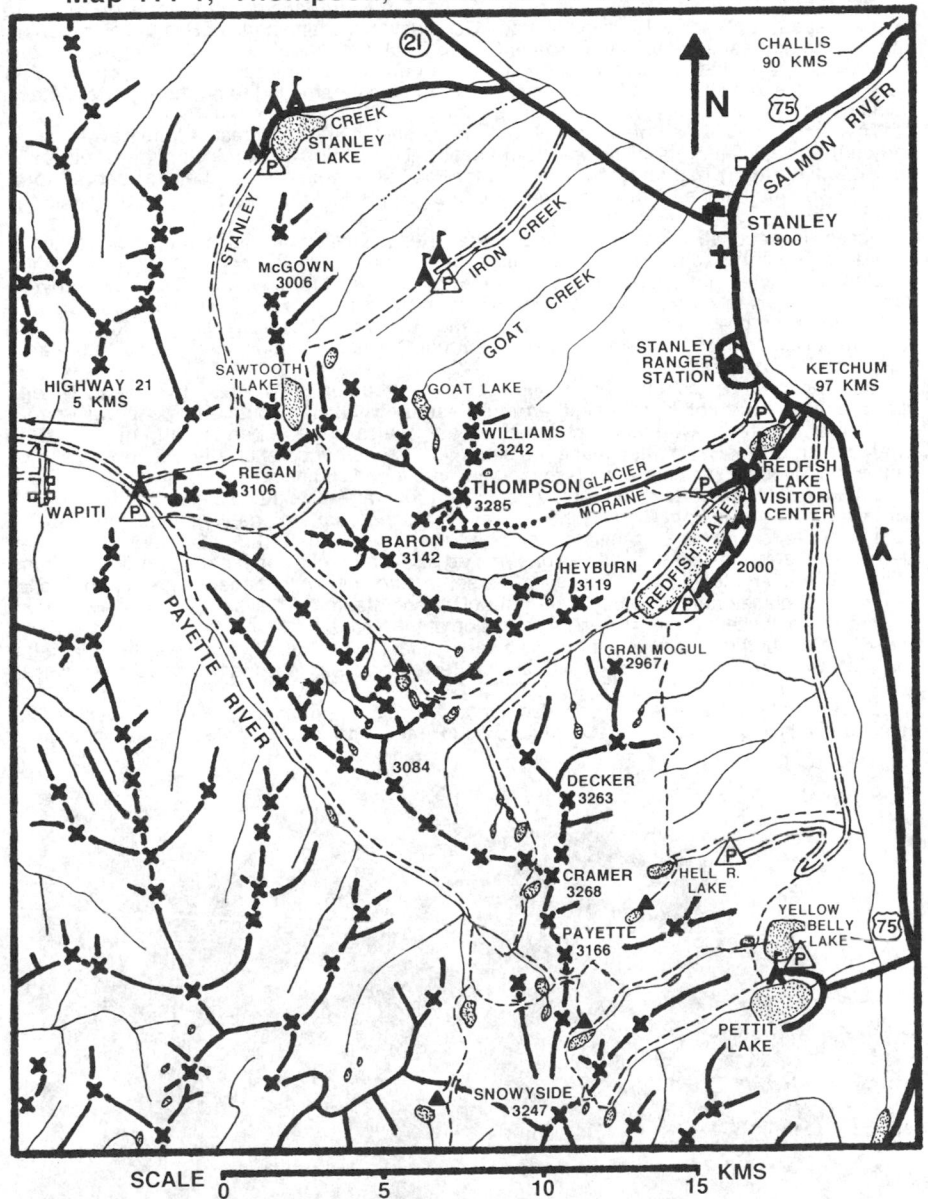

Maps *Boise, Challis and/or Sawtooth National Forest* maps, 1:126,720; or USGS maps *Stanley, Lake Stanley, Warbonnet Peak & Mt. Cramer*, 1:24,000, buy at the Stanley Ranger Station; and the book, **Trails of the Sawtooth & White Cloud Mountains**, Signpost Books.

Castle Peak, White Cloud Peaks, Idaho, USA

The White Cloud Peaks are part of the Sawtooth National Recreational Area, and are located just east of Stanley, Redfish Lake and US Highway 75, and north of Sun Valley in central Idaho. The highest summit in the area is Castle Peak at 3602 meters. Much of this area is composed of granitic-type rock; as a result, some peaks are fairly rugged and fotogenic, and there are many old abandoned mines, most of which are located in the northern parts. These would be on the north side of the granite intrusion.

This range is not a part of an official wilderness area, but it is protected from development and off-road vehicles by its inclusion into the national recreation area. Much of this area is still very wild with many high altitude lakes, which makes fishing the number one recreational activity. The mountains themselves aren't quite as rugged as their neighbors to the west, the Sawtooths.

Access is reasonably easy but you must drive several kms on dirt roads from any direction in order to get near the higher peaks. One thing to remember; there are thousands of people in the area each summer mostly visiting the Sawtooths to the west, so if you want to avoid crowds, approach these peaks from the east side and the road running up the East Fork of the Salmon River. However, probably the easiest way to reach the highest peaks is via the Fourth (4th) of July Creek Road, which begins about 5 kms south of Obsidian. It ends after 15 kms in the area below Fourth of July Lake.

The author chose this route for his climb of **Castle Peak** on 8/19/1982. He drove to the end of the road on Fourth of July Creek, then hiked east a ways, then south on a good trail up to a pass. From there he walked cross-country east over a ridge, down into the upper part of Chamberlain Creek Basin, then made the climb up the south face of Castle. His trek is shown on the map as route symbols, and his round-trip climb took 6 3/4 hours.

On the East Fork of Salmon River, a good road runs as far as the Livingston Mine and Mill, but this is a long way from Castle Peak. To climb Castle from the east, continue south up the East Fork Road and park at the trailheads on the lower ends of Little Boulder, Wickiup or Germania Creeks. There should be signs posted at each creek & trailhead. The distance and difficulty of each route appears to be about the same, and using either one will get you to Castle.

The best places nearby to buy food & supplies are Stanley, Challis or Ketchum. For more information and better maps of this entire area, stop at the Yankee or Stanley Ranger Stations, Tele. 208-774-3000, or the visitor center at Redfish Lake, Tele. 208-774-3536. If you're coming from the south and the Sun Valley side, stop at the National Recreation Area Headquarters, about 15 kms north of Ketchum on Highway 75, Tele. 800-260-5970.

This entire region is especially crowded during the summer months of July and August, so the best time for hiking or climbing in the White Cloud Peaks is after the first weekend in September,

The south face of Castle Peak, the highest summit in the White Cloud Peaks.

Map 412-1, Castle Peak, White Cloud Peaks, Idaho, USA

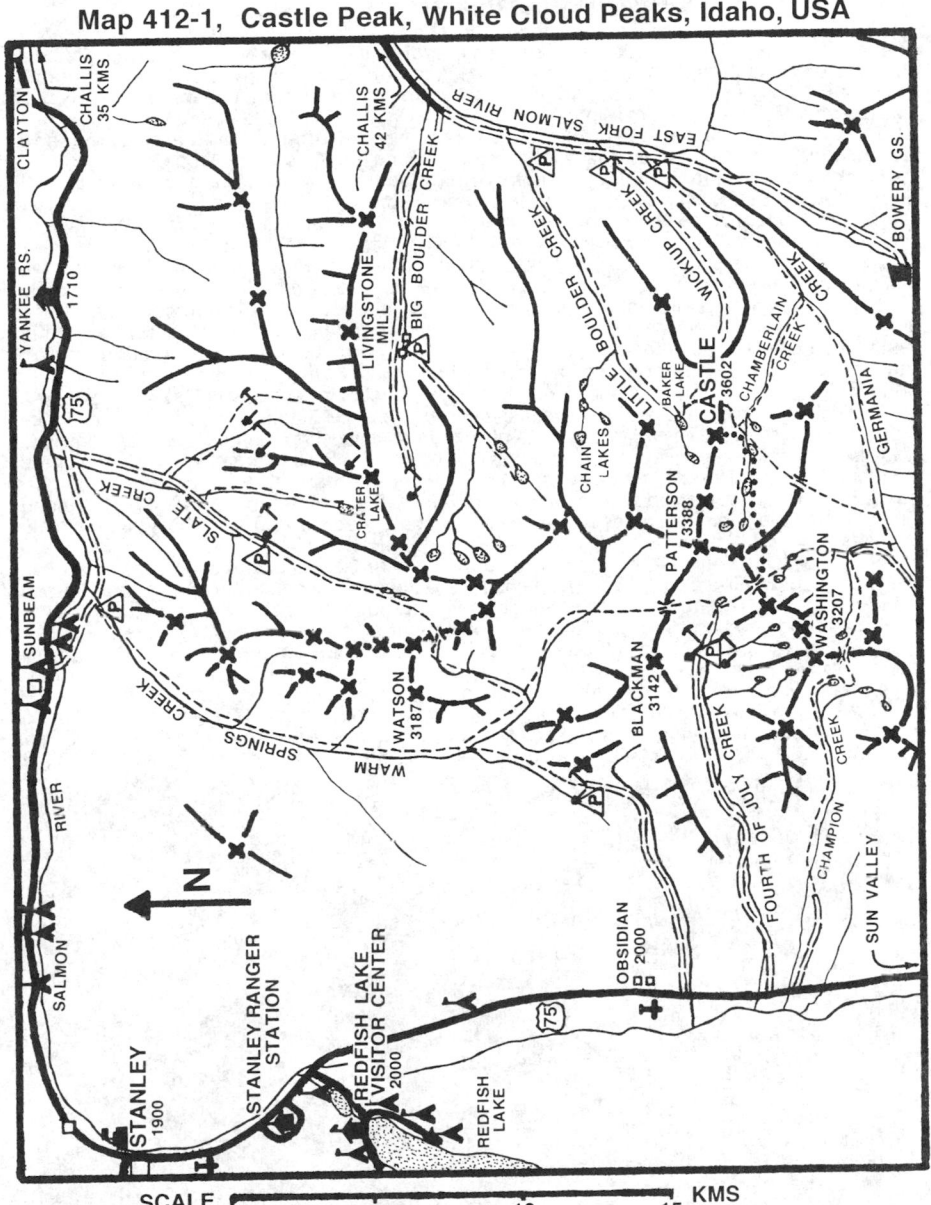

which is the 3-day Labor Day weekend (an American holiday the first Monday of September), through the first part of October.

Maps *White Cloud Peak Area,* and/or *Challis National Forest,* 1:126,720, from any local ranger station, especially the Stanley Ranger Station; also the books, **Trails of the Sawtooth & White Cloud Mountains**, Signpost Books; or **Exploring Idaho's Mountains**, The Mountaineers.

Hyndman & Ryan Peaks, Pioneer Mountains, Idaho, USA

Hyndman at 3682 meters, is one of the highest peaks in Idaho, and the highest in the region east of Sun Valley. These peaks are in an area known as the Pioneer Mountains. Standhope at 3567 meters is another high summit east of Hyndman. Also included here are parts of the southern Boulder Range located in the northwest corner of this map with peaks such as Ryan at 3628 meters, plus Kent and Glassford.

These mountains have all been folded, squeezed & uplifted, and are composed of metamorphic-type rock such as quartzite, along with some granite and limestone.

Much of this region is wild and roadless, but none of it is part of any wilderness area. Unfortunately, the *tourist trap* of Sun Valley near Ketchum, makes many parts of this area congested throughout the year. However, there are some places with access for 4WD vehicles only, making the area attractive despite all the of tourists just down the road.

To climb **Ryan** or other nearby summits, drive north out of Ketchum to the Sawtooth NRA HQ. then continue north up the North Fork of Wood River, past Camp Manapu to the end of the road. For those who prefer solitude this is, or it was, a great place even through it's close to Sun Valley. From the end of the road, walk the trail heading up to West Pass, then route-find east to the summit. The author climbed Ryan on 8/5/1978 in about 6 1/2 hours round-trip. You can also climb **Kent Peak** from the same West Pass route. Or, you could get there from the North Fork of Big Lost River, as shown on the map. That should be an even less-used canyon.

To climb **Hyndman** and the high summits nearby, there are 3 approach routes you can take. Probably the least-used is via Mackay or Challis, then southwest up Big Lost River and finally up Wild Horse Creek to the campground at the end of the road. You'll need an Idaho state highway map for this trip. This route involves a longer drive on gravel roads, but it's more scenic and has less traffic. The author climbed Hyndman on 8/3/1978 via this northern route in 7 hours round-trip. Once on the peak, he first got up on the north ridge, then finished by climbing up the steep northeast face.

From the Sun Valley side, you can drive northeast to and along Corral Creek, then walk east over a pass, downhill a ways, then up the southwest slopes to Hyndman's summit. But this is a long hike! However, the easiest and most-used approach and route to Hyndman is via the Gimlet area, located on Highway 75 south of Ketchum. From Highway 75, locate, then drive northeast up the East Fork of Wood River to Hyndman Creek Trailhead for roughly 20 kms, much of which is now paved. From the parking area, there's a trail running northeast to the base of the peak, then you'll have to route-find up the southeast slopes.

Three towns in the area best for buying food supplies are Ketchum, Mackay and Challis. For more information and maps, stop at the ranger stations in these same small towns. Or call Ketchum R.S. at 208-622-5371; Mackay R.S., Tele. 208-588-2224; or the Sawtooth NRA HQ. at

Hyndman Peak as seen from the northeast ridge.

Map 413-1, Hyndman & Ryan, Pioneer Mtns., Idaho, USA

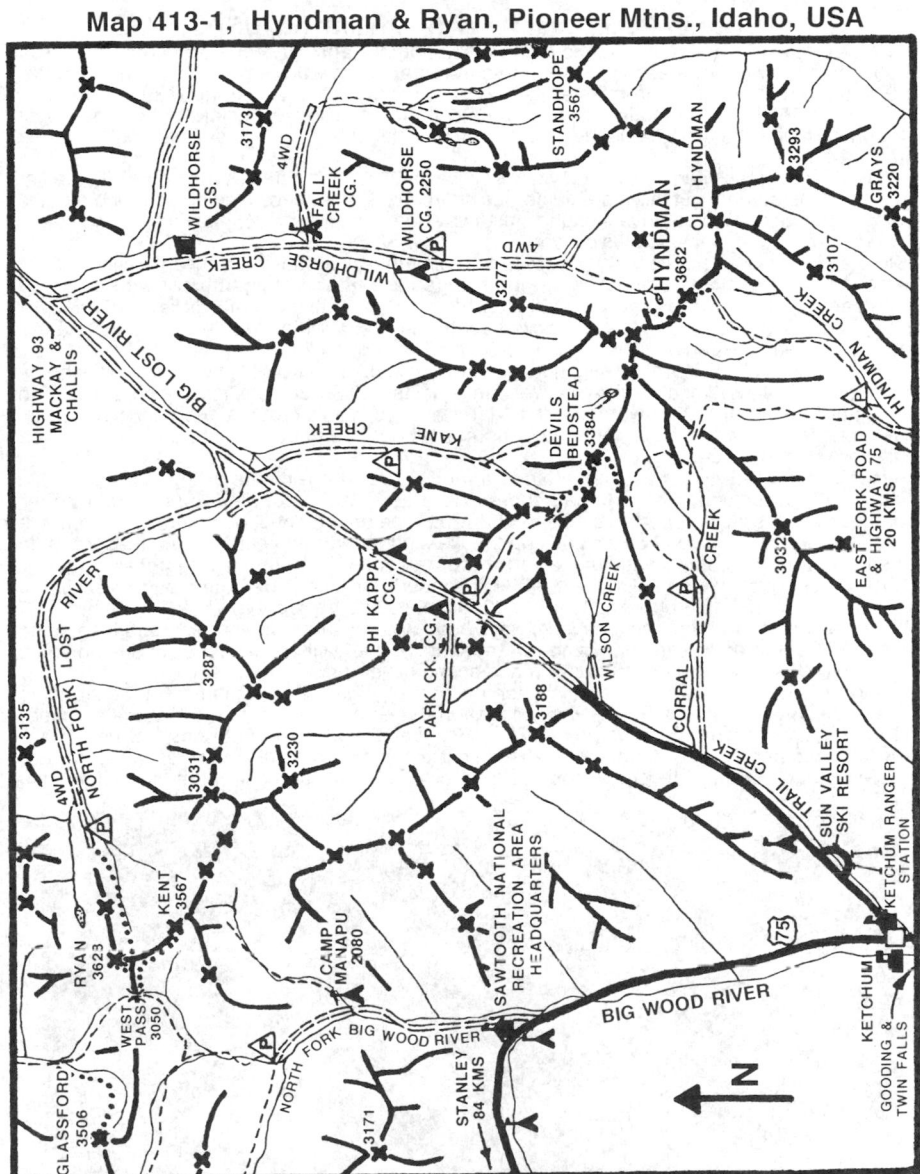

SCALE 0 5 10 15 KMS

800-260-5970.
Maps *Challis National Forest,* or the *Sawtooth National Forest,* both 1:126,720, from the Ketchum or Stanley Ranger Stations, or at Sawtooth NRA HQ.; or USGS maps *Ryan Peak, Amber Lakes, Phi Kappa Mountain, Standhope Peak & Hyndman Peak,* 1:24,000; and the book, **Exploring Idaho's Mountains**, The Mountaineers.

Borah Peak, Lost River Range, Idaho, USA

Borah Peak at 3858 meters is the highest summit in Idaho. It's located in the Lost River Mountains northwest of Mackay. Also in this mountain range are several other high peaks, making it the highest group in the state. Two of these are Leatherman at 3729 meters, and Breitenback, 3698. These mountains rise abruptly from the valley, especially on the southwest side, where fault lines mark the landscape. Rocks consist of various types, including limestone and quartzite.

Any of these peaks can be climbed via US Highway 93, which parallels the range. There are few if any trails around, but there are numerous short, 4WD-type roads leading up to the mouths of most drainages. As you drive along this highway, look for signs which indicate the names of the creeks flowing from the various canyons.

Because this is a relatively dry area with a minimum of vegetation, you can easily walk up the open ridges to most summits. But these routes are often hot in summer with no water. Some canyons have water and vegetation, which makes walking more difficult. The lower slopes and those exposed to the sun have sagebrush; the middle altitude slopes have a few pine trees, quaking aspen or junipers; and above treeline only rocks.

Here's how to climb **Borah**. Drive northwest out of Mackay on US Highway 93 and past the turnoff to Sun Valley. About halfway between mile posts 129 & 130, look for a good gravel road running northeast straight towards Borah. After a ways, you'll cross a ditch carrying Cedar Creek water to a nearby ranch. This water normally would be good to drink, but there may be cattle upstream, so take care.

Just before the base of the mountain is a fault scarp, the remains of the October, 1983 earthquake. Cars used to have to park there in a large clearing but the road has finally been improved over this little dropoff so cars can now (2000) be driven about one more km. From the end of the road a well-used trail zig zags up the west ridge to the summit. From the carpark to the summit and back is an easy day-hike for most people. The author attempted Borah on 6/3/1971, but got snowed off. On 8/21/1982 he climbed Borah in 3 1/2 hours round-trip. In the evening of 8/27/1992, he hurried up to about 3200 meters and back in 2 1/4 hours.

There's no water at the trailhead, so always have a good supply in your car, and take some on the trail. There are some springs and water south of the trailhead however. You can camp anywhere in this area, as it's all public land and a long drive from any large city.

Mackay is the only town in the vicinity, so make it your gas, food and information stopping place. The Challis National Forest Ranger Station there can provide you with the latest maps and information concerning trails and 4WD roads. Call them at 208-588-2224. Summer and early fall is the best time to climb. Winter ascents are common and fairly easy because this is a dry area with generally little snow, and you'll be on a ridge route most of the way. If snow is

An early June hike up Borah Peak turned out to be more like a winter climb. This foto was taken near the summit looking west.

Map 414-1, Borah Peak, Lost River Range, Idaho, USA

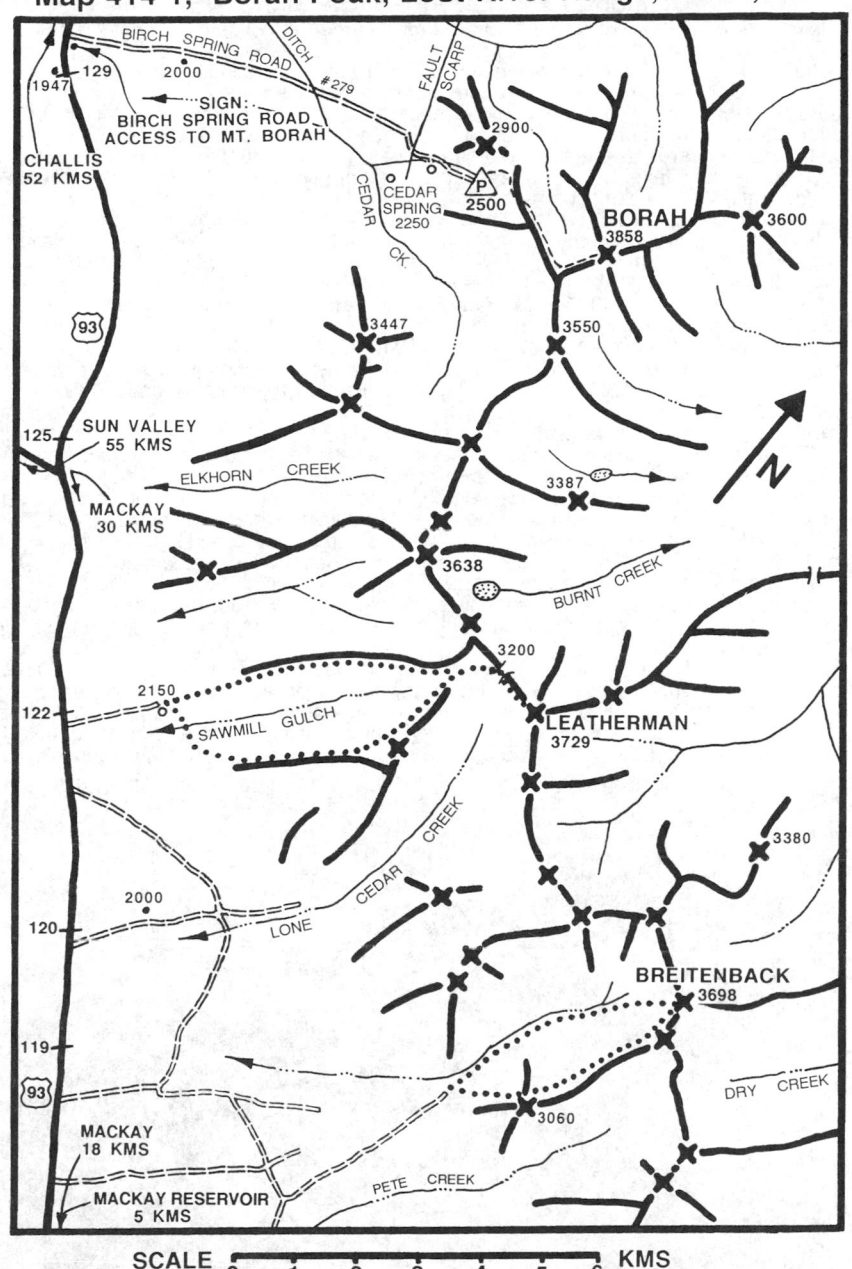

deep, you can at least walk the 4 kms from the highway to the trailhead without too much trouble.

Maps *Challis National Forest,* 1:126,720, from Mackay Ranger Station; or USGS maps *Borah Peak,* 1:100,000; *or Borah Peak, Leatherman & Elkhorn Creek,* 1:24,000; and the books, **Hiker's Guide to Idaho**, Falcon Press; or **Exploring Idaho's Mountains**, The Mountaineers.

Diamond Peak, Lemhi Range, Idaho, USA

This map features the highest part of the Lemhi Range, one of several ranges running in a northwest to southeast direction in south central Idaho. These mountains are long and narrow and rather dry. At the mouths of most major canyons water is available, but most everywhere else it's nonexistent. Like other nearby ranges, these peaks are made of various rock types, but are mostly metamorphic. Notice the mining symbols along Badger Creek and on Mt. Foss.

The highest summit in the Lemhi Range is Diamond Peak at 3719 meters. In the northern part of the mapped area, is the second highest peak, Mt. Bell, 3540 meters. Climbing in the Lemhi Range is likely to be lonely, as not many hikers or climbers make it to these mountains. But maybe that's the best part of going to places like this--no noisy neighbors.

Here's how to reach the **Diamond Peak** area. First make your way to eastern Idaho and have a state highway map in hand. From the north, drive south from Salmon toward Challis, but veer left or southeast on State Highway 22 signposted for Howe or Arco. Look for a sign pointing out Badger Creek Road 148. There are no real landmarks or towns in this area, so you'll have to have to the Challis National Forest map in hand and watch the mountains, canyons and signs carefully.

From the southeast, drive along Interstate Highway 15, but get off at Exit 143 and head west on Highway 33. Later you could turn northwest on Highway 28 bound for Salmon; or stay on 33 until you reach Howe. From there, turn northwest on Highway 22 and drive about 37 kms to the Badger Creek Road.

Once you locate the Badger Creek Road, drive about 8 kms up to the area near the Badger Mine. There's a little private land in that immediate area, so beware of this. The parking symbol is at the beginning of the private land. From that spot, which is likely where a bridge is washed out and won't be replaced, continue upcanyon on foot to the very end of the road, then route-find up to the summit along a ridge or follow the creek bed; whichever seems easiest. The author parked where Bunting Creek comes down and walked to the summit and back in 6 hours. That was on 8/22/1982, but in talking to rangers in 7/2000, it appears little has changed in that area.

You could also access this area from the east side and Highway 28. Drive to the Birch Creek Inn, or what ever business is presently located there, then head southwest up along Pass Creek to the Transfer Campsite. Like on Badger Creek, this climb, perhaps up the east ridge, should be a one day-hike.

To climb **Mt. Bell**, use the approach road reaching Black and Basinger Creeks, then route-find to the summit. This is from the west and Highway 22. Mt. Bell can also be ascended from the east and from Highway 28, but routes on that side appear to be more complicated.

There are no trails up either mountain, and few if any trails in the range, so plan to route-find all the way. For additional information about access roads or routes, stop at the ranger stations

The south face of Diamond Peak with the east ridge on the far right.

Map 415-1, Diamond Peak, Lemhi Range, Idaho, USA

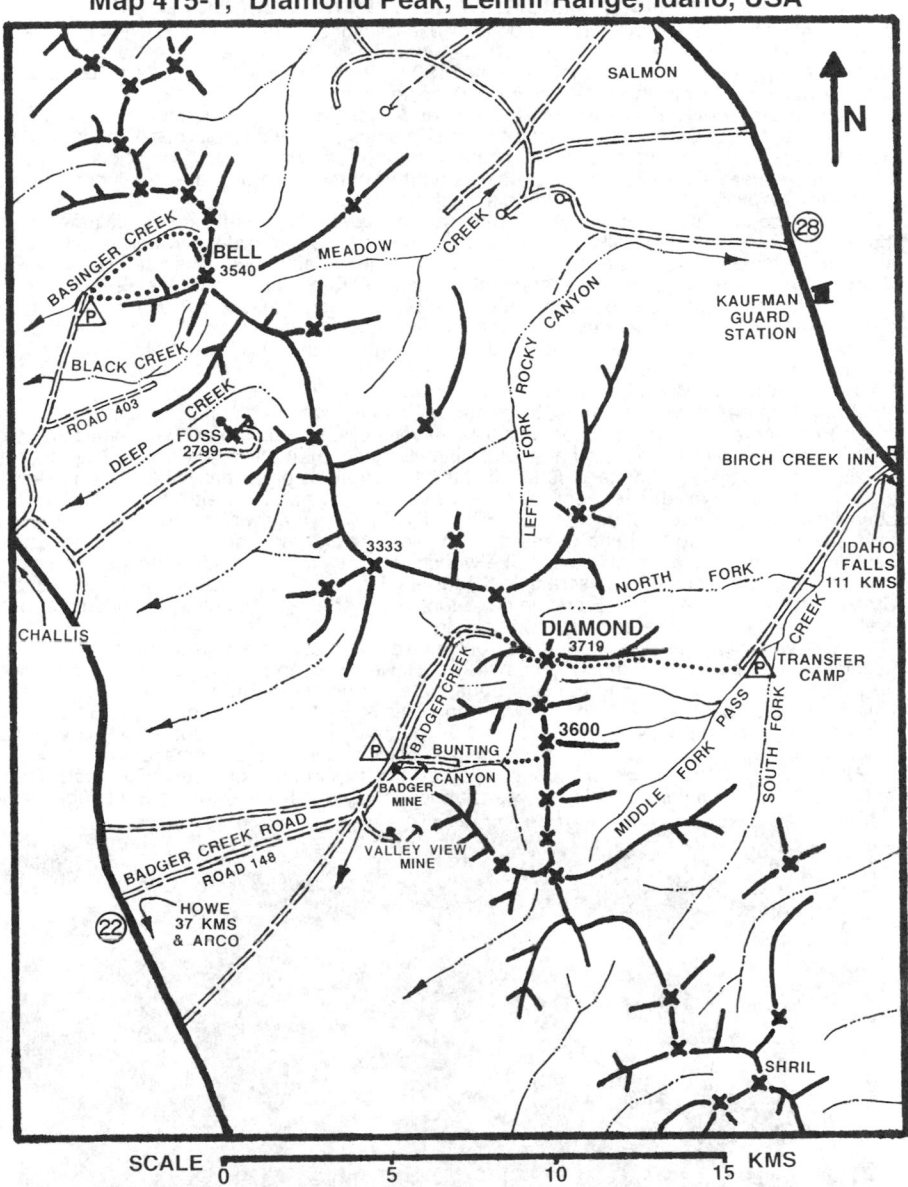

SCALE 0 5 10 15 KMS

in St. Anthony, Arco, Mackay (Tele. 208-588-2224), Challis or Salmon, or maybe the Kaufman Guard Station in summer. This is a very isolated area, so you must buy supplies in one of these towns, as there's nothing else in between. Pack a lot of water in your vehicle as well.
Maps *Challis or Salmon National Forests,* 1:126,720, from Mackay or Challis Ranger Stations; or USGS maps *Borah Peak,* 1:100,000; or *Badger Creek, Diamond Peak and Fallert Springs,* 1:24,000; and maybe the books, **Hiker's Guide to Idaho**, Falcon Press; or **Exploring Idaho's Mountains**, The Mountaineers.

Mt. Cleveland, Glacier National Park, Montana, USA

This map includes a small part of Waterton Lakes National Park of Alberta, Canada, plus the northern section of Glacier National Park in Montana, USA. The highest peak here, and in the entire international park, is Mt. Cleveland at 3190 meters. The rocks in these mountains are sedimentary in origin, mostly limestone, but with some shale.

There are several ways to get to **Mt. Cleveland**, most involving long backpacking trips. If you arrive at the mountain on the east side, you'll find some very difficult routes to the summit. However, the west side of the peak has some relatively easy walk-up routes. The best way to get to the western slopes is to walk or take a boat from the town of Waterton, located at the north end of Waterton Lake on the Alberta side of the border.

Start at the town of Waterton Lake, located just above the upper left side of this map. From there, one way would be to walk a trail running south along the west side of Waterton Lake. This appears to be roughly 12 kms and will take a little more than half a day. This trail will take you to **Goat Haunt**, which has a part-time ranger station and a US customs post. It's also the landing site for summer-time cruise boats. If you walk to Goat Haunt, it means a 3 day trip for most to climb Cleveland. So in the interest of time, many people take a boat which leaves Waterton at 9 & 10am, and 1, 4, & 7pm daily from about July 1 through August 31. Fewer boats run from mid-May to mid-September. From Goat Haunt, boats return to Waterton at 10:35 & 11:25am, and 2:25, 5:25 & 8:05pm. Round-trip boat fare was US$12 in 1992.

From Goat Haunt, walk south on the main trail about 3 kms and look for a faint trail on the left or east marked by a bright ribbon on a tree. If you miss it, but come to a very small trickle of water running under the trail in a half-meter diameter pipe, then backtrack north along the trail for 257 steps--roughly 257 meters. Once on this hiker's trail, it's pretty easy to follow up to a little steam coming down off the west face of Cleveland. Cross it, then soon you'll have to bushwhack through about 300 meters of thick alders laid down by winter snows. As you begin to bushwhack, look up & ahead to see a large pile of boulders. This will be your immediate destination. Once there, you'll be out of the woods and have an easy walk up to the head of the valley where you'll veer left and scramble & route-find up the steep slope to the ridge between Stoney Indian and Cleveland. From the ridge-top, walk north to the summit. An alternate route is shown, but it may involve some bushwhacking.

Those walking all the way from Waterton will want at least 3 days, round-trip; while those taking the boat usually do it in 2 or 3 easy days. However, strong hikers can do it in one long, very fast-walking day by taking the 9am boat out, climbing the mountain, then getting back in time for the 8:05 pm boat returning to Waterton. This is what the author did on 8/16/1992. He hurried to the top in about 4 1/4 hours, then 3 3/4 hours for the return; about 8 1/3 hours round-trip from Goat Haunt. However, few climbers can do this and it's not recommended.

No need for an ice ax or crampons if you do this trip in late summer. Buy food before arriving at Waterton if you can--it's an expensive tourist trap. July through mid-September is the

Straight ahead is Stoney Indian Peak, with the south face of Cleveland on the left.

Map 416-1, Mt. Cleveland, Glacier N. Park, Montana, USA

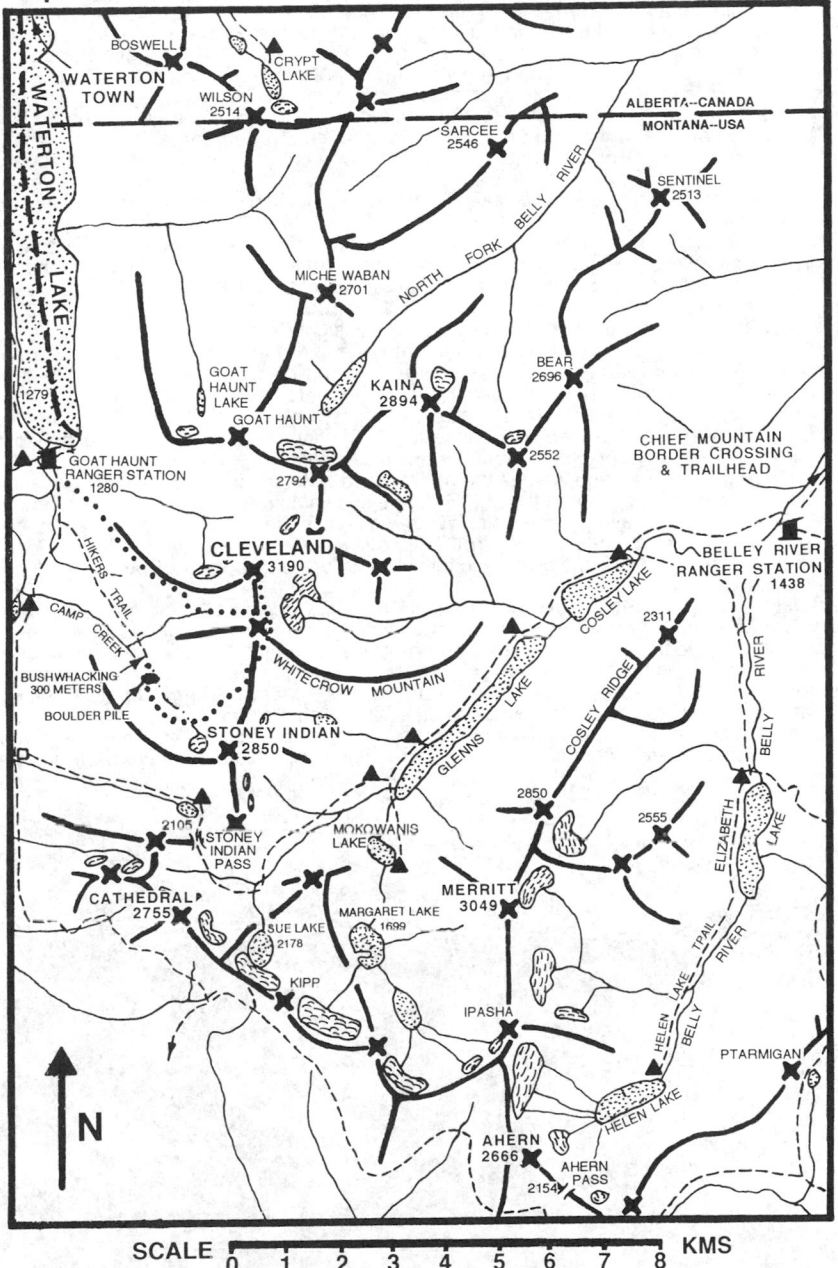

SCALE 0 1 2 3 4 5 6 7 8 KMS

best time to climb. For updated national park information (USA), contact the website (www.nps.gov/glac) or Tele. 406-888-7800.
Maps Trails Illustrated map *Glacier National Park/Waterton Lakes National Park,* 1:125,000; or the book, **A Climber's Guide to Glacier National Park**, Sierra Club.

Mt. Jackson, Glacier National Park, Montana, USA

There are a number of nice peaks on this map, but the best-known is Mt. Jackson at 3064 meters. Jackson is believed to be the third highest mountain in Glacier National Park, behind Cleveland and Stimson. This mapped area shows the middle of the park and the only road running across it. It's called the Going-to-the-Sun Highway. Use this for access to all these peaks. The rocks in this area are mostly limestone with some shales.

To climb **Jackson**, you have a choice of 2 trailheads to hike from. One would be to drive to Lake McDonald and park near the Lake McDonald Hotel. The author isn't familiar with that trailhead, but anyone working at the hotel can tell you where it is. This trailhead is at about 961 meters altitude. From the hotel, walk east up the trail toward Glacier Basin, then south past Sperry Chalets, then east to and past Lake Ellen Wilson, and finally to Gunsight Pass and down to Gunsight Lake.

The other trailhead, and the one that's considered the normal starting point for climbing most of the peaks in the middle of this map is at a place called the Jackson Glacier Viewpoint. This parking place is located about 3 kms west of the west end of Lake St. Mary. Park on either side of the road, then locate the trail leading downhill about 2 kms to another trail. Turn right and walk southwest up the well-used trail signposted for Gunsight Pass.

When you come to the east end of Gunsight Lake, and immediately after you cross the bridge, there is a less-used trail veering to the left and heading southeast around the bottom of the northeast ridge of Mt. Jackson. Take this trail, and after about one km, look for an easy route up through the brush and dwarf trees. You may find a trail, but if not, it's not far to scramble until you're out of the brush. See the map. Continue up this east ridge to the summit. This is perhaps the easiest of the 2 normal routes up Jackson.

The other normal route, and the one the author used, is to continue up the main trail running high above Gunsight Lake, then at the big "S" curve shown on the map, head up the mountain, but veer left just a little to avoid some cliffs. When you reach the main ridge, veer right and walk to the summit along the northeast ridge. You'll see a few stone cairns so finding the easiest way is no problem. On 8/14/1992, the author did this climb from the highway viewpoint in about 8 1/2 hours round-trip.

To climb **Logan** and **Blackfoot**, take the faint trail from Gunsight Lake southeast to Jackson & Blackfoot Glaciers, then aim for the low point between the 2 summits. Once on the ridge, you can climb either one fairly easily. **Gunsight Mountain** is normally climbed beginning at Lake McDonald and taking the trail toward the Sperry Chalets. From Glacier Basin, continue northeast up to the headwall, then make your way across the Sperry Glacier toward the northeast ridge & slopes. The approximate route is shown on the map.

Better take an ice ax & crampons for all climbs, but they may not be needed in late summer. Buy your supplies in larger communities long before you reach this area, because there are no

From the summit of Jackson looking southeast down on the Jackson Glacier.

Map 417-1, Mt. Jackson, Glacier NP, Montana, USA

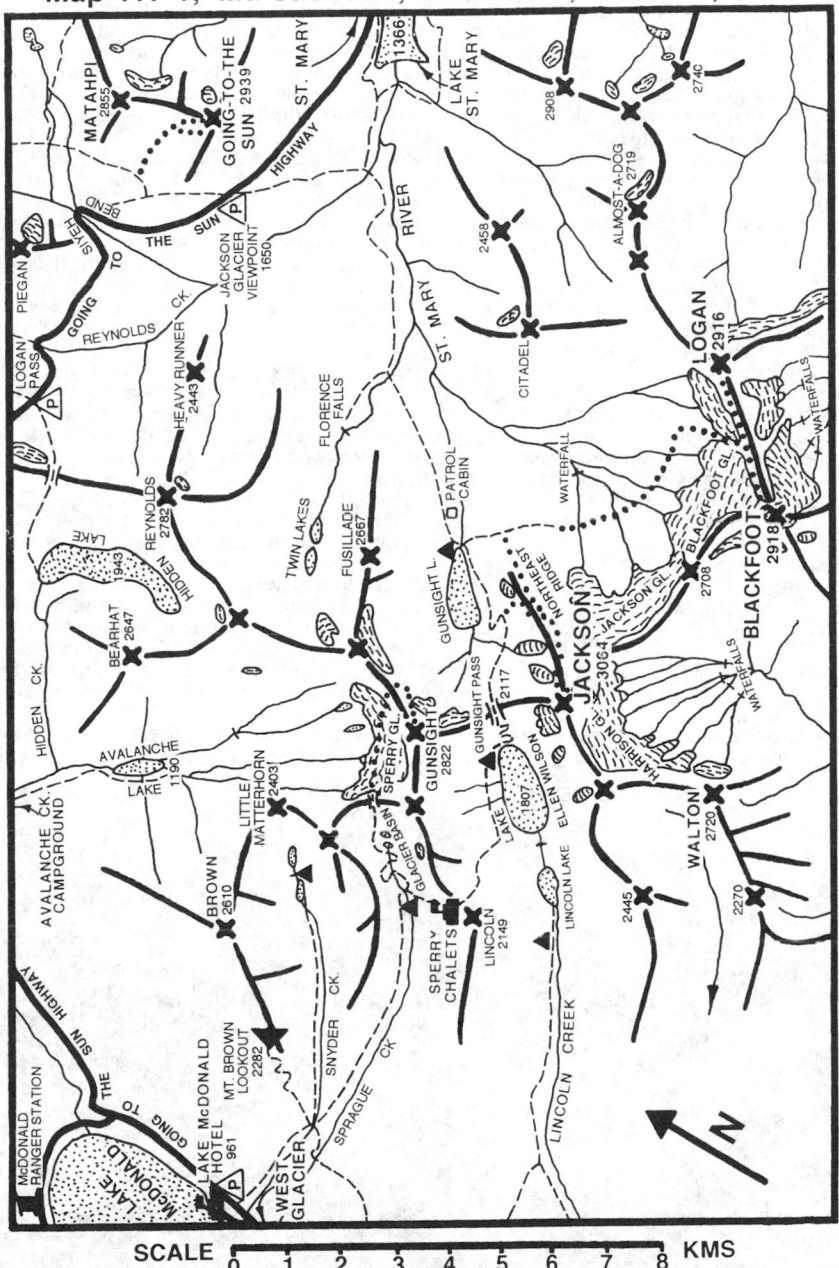

SCALE 0 1 2 3 4 5 6 7 8 KMS

large towns close to the national park. West Glacier and St. Mary have only small stores. For updated national park information, contact the website (www.nps.gov/glac) or Tele. 406-888-7800.

Maps Trails Illustrated map *Glacier National Park/Waterton Lakes National Park,* 1:125,000; and the book, **A Climber's Guide to Glacier National Park**, Sierra Club.

Stimson & Rising Wolf, Glacier National Park, Montana, USA

This map shows many of the higher peaks in the southeast corner of Glacier National Park in Montana. Featured here is the second highest point in the park, Mt. Stimson at 3091 meters, and Two Medicine Lake. Near this large lake is a ranger station & visitor center, and campground. Nearby is Rising Wolf Mountain at 2900 meters. The rocks in these parts are again mostly limestone, but with some red and yellow shales and/or sandstone.

The biggest problem with climbing **Mt. Stimson** is the long walk in. In the past, the normal way to get there was to wade across the Middle Fork of the Flathead River at a place called Nyack on the railway line, which is next to Highway 2. That place is due west of the peak & this map, and on the main highway running between West Glacier and East Glacier. However, wading across that river is only possible in late summer and fall. If the river is high, you'll have to walk along the east bank all the way from West Glacier. That river represents a real headache, so for this reason, a route beginning at Two Medicine Lake might sound more appealing to some. If you do try this way, first head north around the east end of Rising Wolf Mountain, then west to Old Man Lake, over Cut Bank Pass, and west toward the northwest side of Stimson. Once at the base of the peak, one of the easier routes is up the northwest face and ridge, approximately as shown on the map. This involves wading the swift Nyack Creek, then scrambling up some steep slopes.

The author hasn't gotten to this mountain yet, but he has seen it from Mt. Morgan to the southwest, and from Mt. Flinsch to the east. It appears the southeast ridge is a moderately easy climb, but you'll find some bushwhacking getting up to the saddle. One possible route is shown, but it may not be feasible. Regardless of the approach, Stimson is at least a 3 day hike & climb, maybe longer. This would be a climb for the adventurous-type person.

For those who want a good climb but with easy access, try **Rising Wolf**. Park at the campground trailhead at the east end of Two Medicine Lake. Walk across the bridge and head west along the north shore. Near the west end of the lake, and as you see the creek coming down off the mountain, turn right or north, and route-find straight up along side the creek bed. Higher up, veer right to avoid cliffs. Once on the east-west ridge, head west to the summit.

To make a loop, continue ridge-walking west to the trail running beneath Flinsch Peak, which looks a lot like the Matterhorn as seen from Rising Wolf. Climb **Flinsch** via the southeast face. From this peak and nearby Dawson Pass, you can return on the same trail you started on. On 8/15/1992, the author climbed both of these peaks, then hurried north along the trail and returned via Old Man Lake and Dry Fork. His round-trip loop-hike was about 28 kms and took 8 3/4 hours. It's recommended that most people return directly to Two Medicine Lake from Dawson Pass.

Buy all your supplies in bigger towns or cities elsewhere if you can. Shopping in the towns of East or West Glacier isn't too good, plus everything is expensive. Climb in July, August &

From near the top of Rising Wolf, looking west at Finsch, with Stimson far behind.

Map 418-1, Stimson & Rising Wolf, Glacier NP, Mont., USA

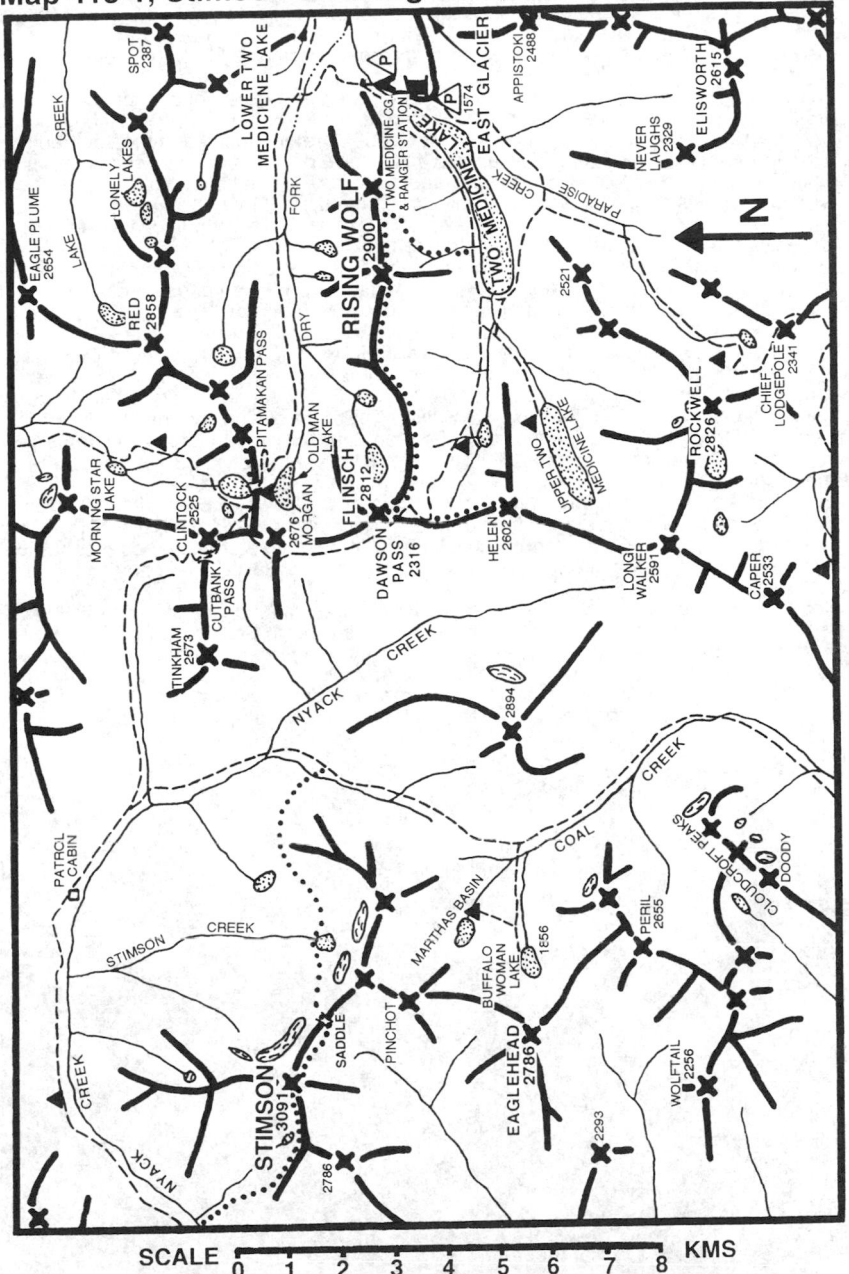

SCALE |0 1 2 3 4 5 6 7 8| KMS

September. Under normal conditions, ice ax & crampons are not needed during this time period. For updated national park information, contact the website (www.nps.gov/glac) or Tele. 406-888-7800.

Maps Trails Illustrated map *Glacier National Park/Waterton Lakes National Park,* 1:125,000; and the book, **A Climber's Guide to Glacier National Park**, Sierra Club.

Trapper Peak, Bitterroot Mountains, Montana,

The area included in this map is in the extreme southwestern corner of the state of Montana just south of Hamilton. The left hand side of the map is part of Idaho, but for this part of the Selway-Bitterroot Wilderness Area, one must approach from the Montana side and from US Highway 93 or State Road 473.

The Selway-Bitterroot Wilderness is a very large area and is part of a much larger primitive region of Central Idaho. It goes under various names in different places. The highest and best-known mountain in this region is Trapper Peak at 3094 meters, located in the southern part of the map and west of Conner and the Trapper Creek Job Corps Center. Only one other summit, El Capitan, is over the 3000 meter mark. All others are less in height, but not in ruggedness. All higher peaks on this map have some difficult climbing routes. Most also have easy routes, but not all. There are some lakes, but most are small. Fishing and hiking, and later in the season, hunting are the popular outdoor activities in this range.

Trapper Peak is in full view from the main highway in the region of Conner and to about as far north as Darby, both in the Bitterroot Valley. It has a very steep and impressive north face which can only be climbed by using ropes and other equipment. But there is a trail to the summit via the south face which is a gentle slope similar to a titled plateau.

To find this trail and climb **Trapper**, drive south from Darby and Conner on Highway 473, along the West Fork of the Bitterroot River. About 8 or 9 kms southwest of the Trapper Creek Job Corps Center and about 3 kms before the Boulder Creek Campground turnoff, turn right or west at the sign indicating the Trapper Peak Road. This is an old logging road but it was in good condition as of 2000. After driving this road about another 8 or 9 kms, there is a large signboard on the left and several places to park. This is the beginning of the 8 km trail to the top of Trapper Peak.

About halfway up to the summit is a small spring, the only water available on the mountain except in early summer. It's a good trail and easy to follow as this is a popular hike. It can be climbed in as little as half a day and is considered an easy hike or climb because the gain in altitude is only about 1100 meters. The author was there on 7/28/1982 and made the round-trip hike in exactly 3 hours.

Rock climbers or anyone who likes more difficult routes might be interested in **El Capitan**, a Matterhorn-like peak southwest of Lake Como. Approach it from Rock or Little Rock Creeks.

Hamilton is the biggest town in the valley and is the best place to do your shopping, but Darby has some stores. Hamilton and Darby also have Forest Service offices or ranger stations you can contact for additional information. Call Darby Ranger Station at 406-821-3913; or closer to Trapper Peak is the year-round fully-staffed West Fork Ranger Station, Tele. 406-821-3269.

From the Bitterroot Valley looking west at Trapper Peak left, North Trapper right.

Map 419-1, Trapper Peak, Bitterroot Mtns., Montana, USA

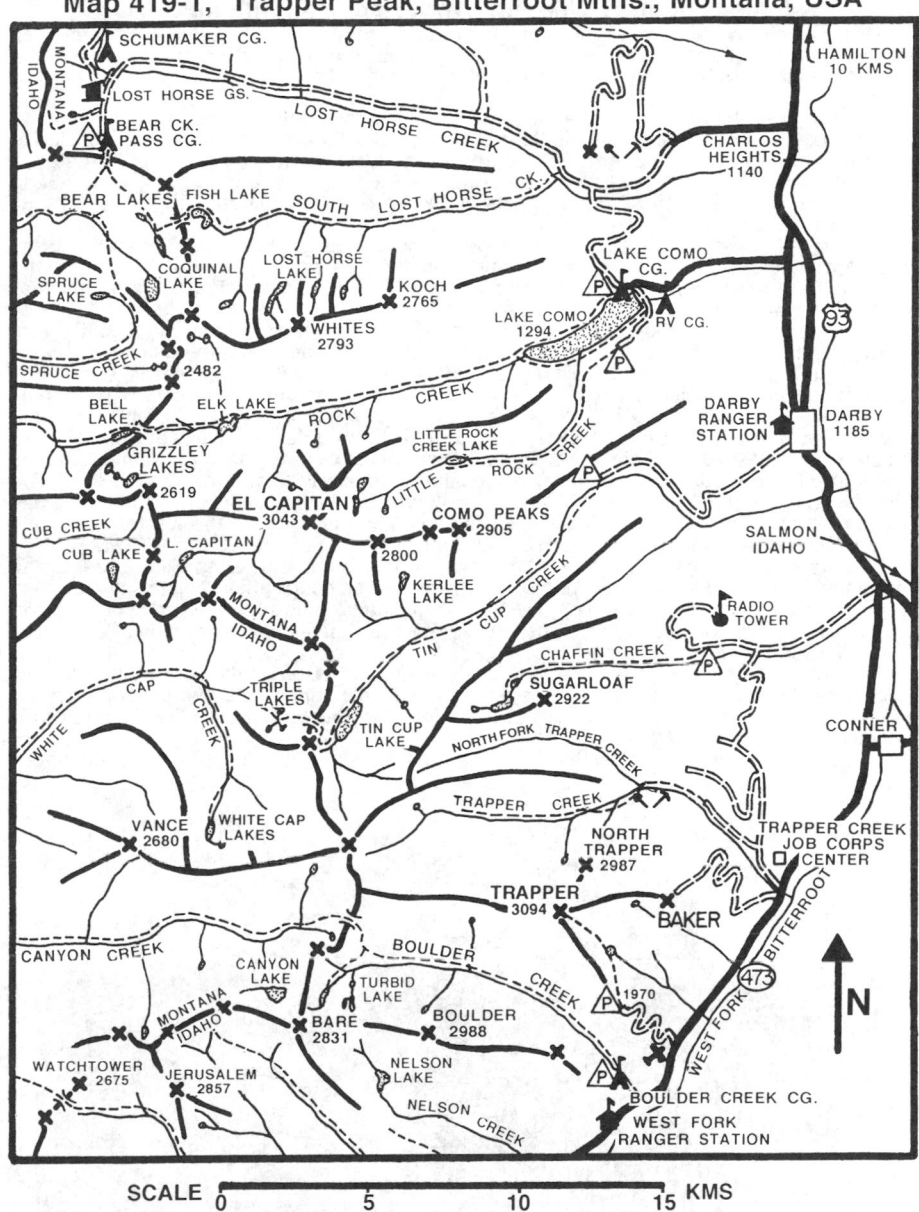

SCALE 0 5 10 15 KMS

Summer climbing and hiking is from mid-July through September.
Maps *Bitterroot National Forest*, 1:126,720; and USGS maps *Trapper Peak, Boulder Peak, Burnt Ridge*, 1:24,000; or *Nez Perce Pass*, 1:100,000; and perhaps the book, **Hiker's Guide to Montana**, Falcon Press.

Homer Youngs Peak, Bitterroot Range, Montana, USA

This map shows part of the Bitterroot Range running along the Montana-Idaho line, in an area not far north or northeast of Salmon, Idaho, and south of Wisdom, Montana. Most of the area on the map is in Montana, with just the extreme left-hand side of the map showing eastern Idaho.

You can enter this mountainous area from either Idaho or Montana, but most of the popular access routes seem to be from the Montana side, thus all attention here is given to that side of the state line. Both the Beaverhead (Montana) and Salmon (Idaho) National Forests are represented here. The closest ranger station is in Wisdom, Montana, Tele. 406-689-3243. There's a small Forest Service guard station, workshop & residence near Jackson, but it's not open to the public.

The highest summit in this part of the range is Homer Youngs Peak at 3237 meters. It sits inside Montana about 3 or 4 kms, and wholly within the Beaverhead National Forest. Homer Youngs is a prominent peak that stands alone for the most part, being much higher than surrounding summits.

It's an easy hike to the top of **Homer Youngs**, and here's how to get there and do it. From Highway 278 just south of the small ranching community of Jackson, drive almost due west about 20 kms to Lower Miner Lake via a good and well-used gravel road. At the lake is a large campground with all facilities. From the campground, you can drive any car or pickup about another 3 or 4 kms west to the trailhead where a locked gate is located. Immediately beyond the gate and before Kelly Creek, is a trail running north, then west, to the vicinity of Heart Lake at the base of the east ridge. From there, simply continue west up the ridge to the summit which is a walk-up. There should be water in several locations, but always start out with your own. The author was in this area on 7/26/1982, and climbed the peak via the east ridge, returning by way of Rock Island Lakes, all in about 4 1/4 hours. Like all other hikes in the western USA and Canada, he has updated this information by calling the nearest ranger station or NP office.

Another way up Homer Youngs would be to walk from the trailhead along Miner Creek all the way to the Rock Island Lakes at the head of the basin. Some people may want to camp and fish there. From the Rock Island Lakes it's an easy hike up the obvious southwest ridge or the south face. This would be the best way for most people, but the east ridge route may be a little faster. Either route can be done in one day by anyone.

The second highest summit in the area is believed to be **Squaw Peak** located not far from Twin Lakes & Campground. It too is a prominent peak standing alone and towering over its neighbors. It can be reached via Twin Lakes; or from the Big Swamp Creek side of the mountain. Another easy climb.

Since this area is in southwestern Montana (or east central Idaho), you can expect good

Home Young's Peak as seen from the town of Jackson.

Map 420-1, Homer Youngs, Bitterroot Range, Montana, USA

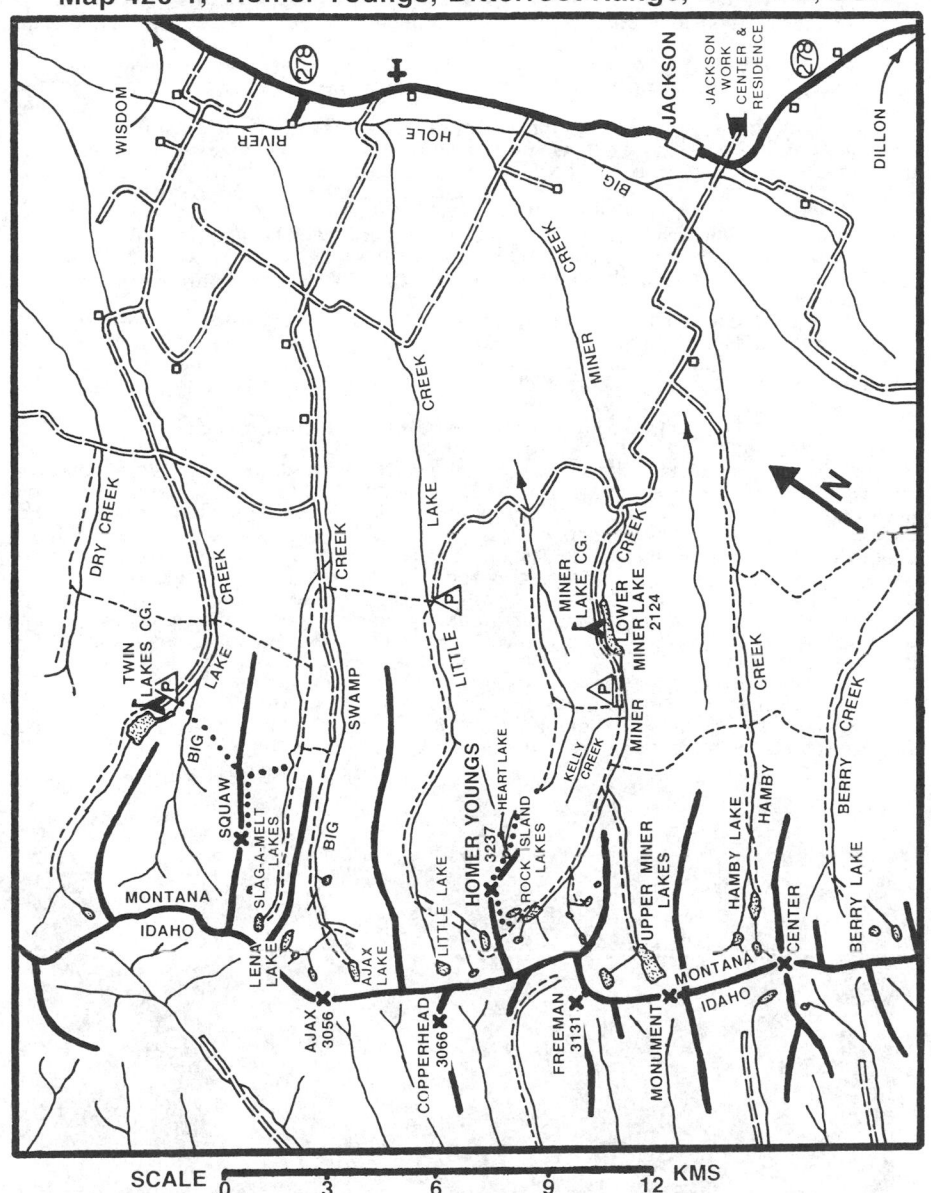

SCALE $\quad$ 0 $\quad$ 3 $\quad$ 6 $\quad$ 9 $\quad$ 12 $\quad$ KMS

weather during the summer months, in direct contrast to regions in the northern part of the state. The drier climate is reflected in the vegetation. Here you can walk through the forest very easily, with or without trail; again unlike the more northerly regions, which is always a bushwhack. Do your shopping in Dillon or Wisdom.

Maps *Beaverhead National Forest,* 1:126,720; or USGS maps *Salmon,* 1;100,000, or *Homer Youngs Peak,* 1:24,000; for a route from the Idaho side, see the book, **Hiker's Guide to Idaho**, Falcon Press.

Tweedy & Torrey Peaks, Pioneer Mountains, Montana, USA

All of Montana's higher mountain ranges are located in the southwestern part of the state. One of these is the Pioneer Mountains, just northwest of Dillon, southwest of Butte, and west of Interstate Highway 15. It's not a large range, but has 2 summits at or near 3400 meters. The highest peak is Tweedy at exactly 3400 meters. However, the best-known mountain seems to be Torrey Peak at 3398 meters.

Access into this mapped region is pretty good. There is one newly paved road running north-south along the west side of these high peaks; and the dirt and/or graveled roads seem to be well maintained. For those wanting to climb **Torrey Peak**, the Birch Creek Road is the best way to get there. To use this road, begin by driving along Interstate 15. Leave the freeway at Exit 74, which is about 18 kms north of Dillon (Exit 63), then head west to and along Birch Creek. Continue up the Birch Creek Road past the Dinner Station Campground. If you have a car, better leave it at the campground. Just beyond Dinner Station CG., which is at about 2130 meters altitude, is about 1 km of rough road, then a gate. This gate will likely to be locked, so if you make it that far, park and continue on foot.

On 7/27/1982, the author walked about one hour or about 4 to 5 kms beyond the gate, then bushwhacked north up to the ridge, and finally west up along the east ridge, an easy route to the summit. He returned via Pear and Boot Lakes and the trail from that basin back to his car. His round-trip time was about 4 1/4 hours. For strong climbers this is a half day hike; for others plan on an all-day trip.

To climb **Tweedy**, this would probably be the best access route. Drive along I-15 south of Anaconda and Butte, and leave the freeway at Exit 102 at Divide. From there head west on State Highway 43 for about 20 kms and stop at the small town of Wise River. While there, you could stop at the Wise River Ranger Station (Tele. 406-832-3178) for maps and information, then continue south up along Wise Creek in the direction of at least 4 Forest Service campgrounds as shown on this map. This is now a paved road. Stop at or just above Mono Creek Campground. From there, hike east on a trail that follows David Creek. Near the head of the David Creek Basin and Torrey Lake, route-find up the western slopes of Tweedy.

You could also get to the eastern slopes of Tweedy by leaving the Birch Creek Road above the Aspen Picnic Site, and driving over a pass or ridge and down to Willow Creek, then upcanyon as far as possible. From where you park, hike up toward Gorge Lakes and to the top of Tweedy. Walking the ridge between Tweedy and Torrey is a difficult passage and time consuming. Some of the peaks here are fairly rugged, others are easy walk-ups.

Several high peaks in the south such as Baldy and Alturas 1 & 2 can be ascended from Rattlesnake Creek and Kelly Reservoir; or from the area around Polaris along Grasshopper Creek. You can also access peaks in the north via the town of Melrose and Trapper Creek.

From the summit of Torrey Peak looking north at the south face of Twiddy.

Map 421-1, Tweedy & Torrey, Pioneer Mtns., Montana, USA

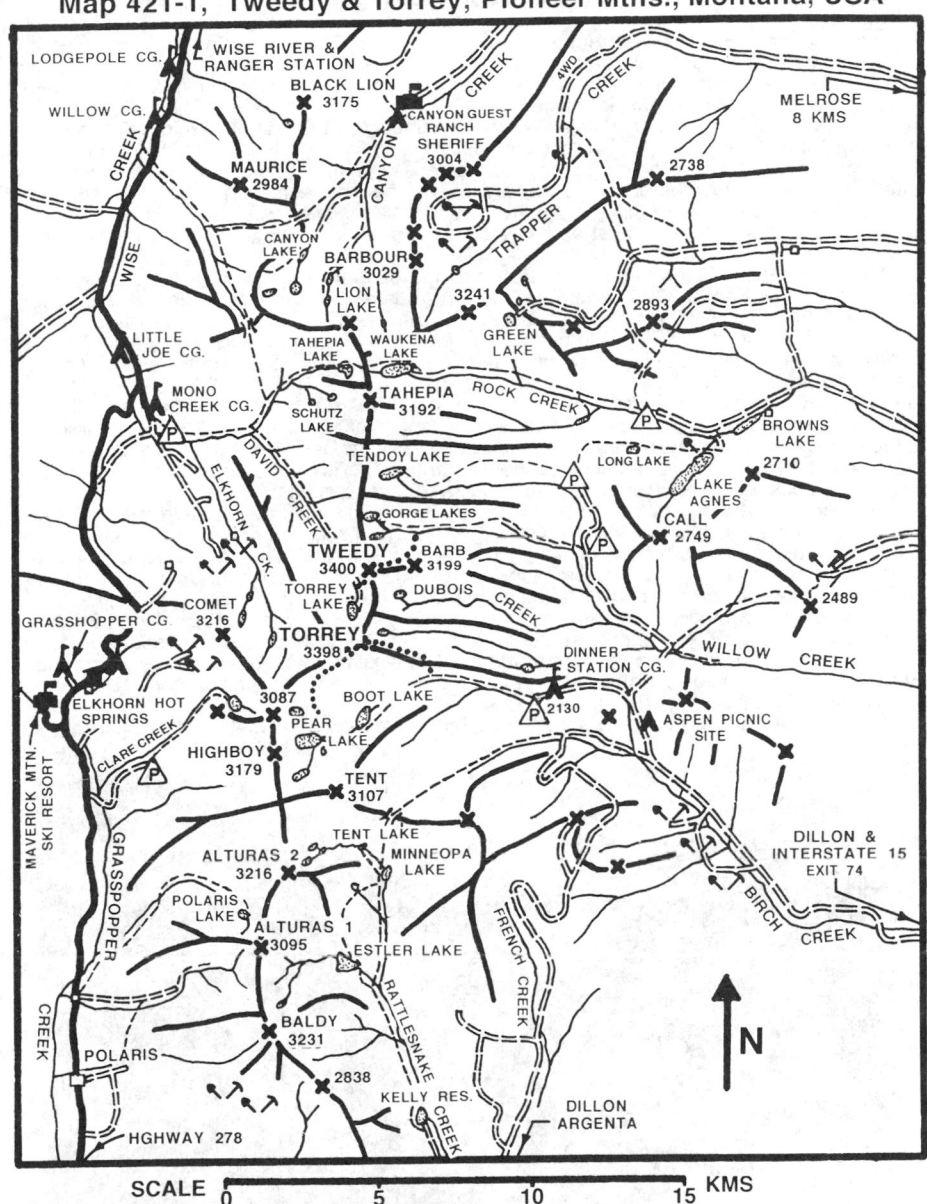

SCALE 0   5   10   15 KMS

Lots of old mines in that area, as well as around Elkhorn Hot Springs.
    The larger towns in the area include Butte to the northeast and Dillon to the southeast. The Beaverhead-Deerlodge National Forest headquarters is located in Dillon, Tele. 406-683-3900; as is the Dillon Ranger District office, same telefone number. This office(s) can sell you Forest Service maps and give you the latest information on road conditions, etc.

Maps *Beaverhead-Deerlodge National Forest,* 1:126,720; or USGS maps Dillon, 1:100,000; or *Mount Tahepia & Torrey Mountain,* 1:24,000.

Jefferson & Hollow Top, Tobacco Root Mountains, Montana, USA

Another of the small and compact ranges in southwestern Montana is the Tobacco Root Mountains, located southeast of Butte and directly west of Bozeman. Formerly there were 2 national forests involved in administering these public lands, but they have now been combined into one; the Beaverhead-Deerlodge National Forest. For updated information, or to buy maps, stop at the Madison Ranger District Office in Ennis, Montana, or call 406-682-4253.

The rocks found in these mountains are mostly crystalline or metamorphic of various kinds, including quartzite and granite. The area is crisscrossed with patches of private land which in the past have been old mining claims, or in some cases old mining camps or towns. Just a few kms south of this mapped area is Virginia City, one of the most famous old mining towns in the western USA. As a result of this mining, the area is well-endowed with old roads, miners trails and old mine sites. By now most of the original roads have reverted to trails, making it an interesting place for hiking.

The highest peak in the range is **Mt. Jefferson** at 3232 meters. However, the best known might be **Hollow Top** at 3205 meters, just south of Jefferson. Between these 2 peaks is a saddle which is easy to traverse, making it simple to climb both peaks on the same hike.

The easiest and standard way to get there seems to be from Harrison on Highway 287 just northeast of the high part of this mountain range. From Harrison, drive southwest on a paved road to the small town of Pony. From there, continue southwest up North Willow Creek Road for about 2 kms to where most cars must be parked. From the trailhead, walk along an old road, then trail, up to Hollow Top Lake. From the west side of this lake, simply walk through the forest to the base of either mountain, then make the climb straight to each summit; or perhaps head for the saddle between, then climb either or both from there. The author was here on 7/24/1982 and climbed both summits in terrible weather in 5 1/2 hours round-trip.

Another easy access route to either of these peaks would be to drive south from Cardwell on Interstate Highway 90 to Jefferson; then south for another 7 kms or so, and turn right up South Boulder Creek. Drive as far as possible, perhaps to within 2 kms of Louise Lake, and park. From there, route-find up the western slopes of either summit. However, this route involves driving a fair distance on dirt roads, and the upper part of the way may be pretty rough.

Besides the 2 approach routes above, you can also get in to these mountains from Sheridan on the southwest, as well as 2 or 3 different routes from McAllister on the southeast side of the range. The high peaks you could climb from the southwest or southeast would be **Thompson, Branham, Lonesome** or **Granite**. Before using any of these roads, call or stop at the Forest Service office in Ennis for road updates.

All the higher summits in the Tobacco Root Range are over 3000 meters, so there is a good

Hollow Top Peak left, Jefferson Peak right, as seen from Hollow Top Lake.

Map 422-1, Jefferson & H. Top, Tobacco Root Mtns, Montana, USA

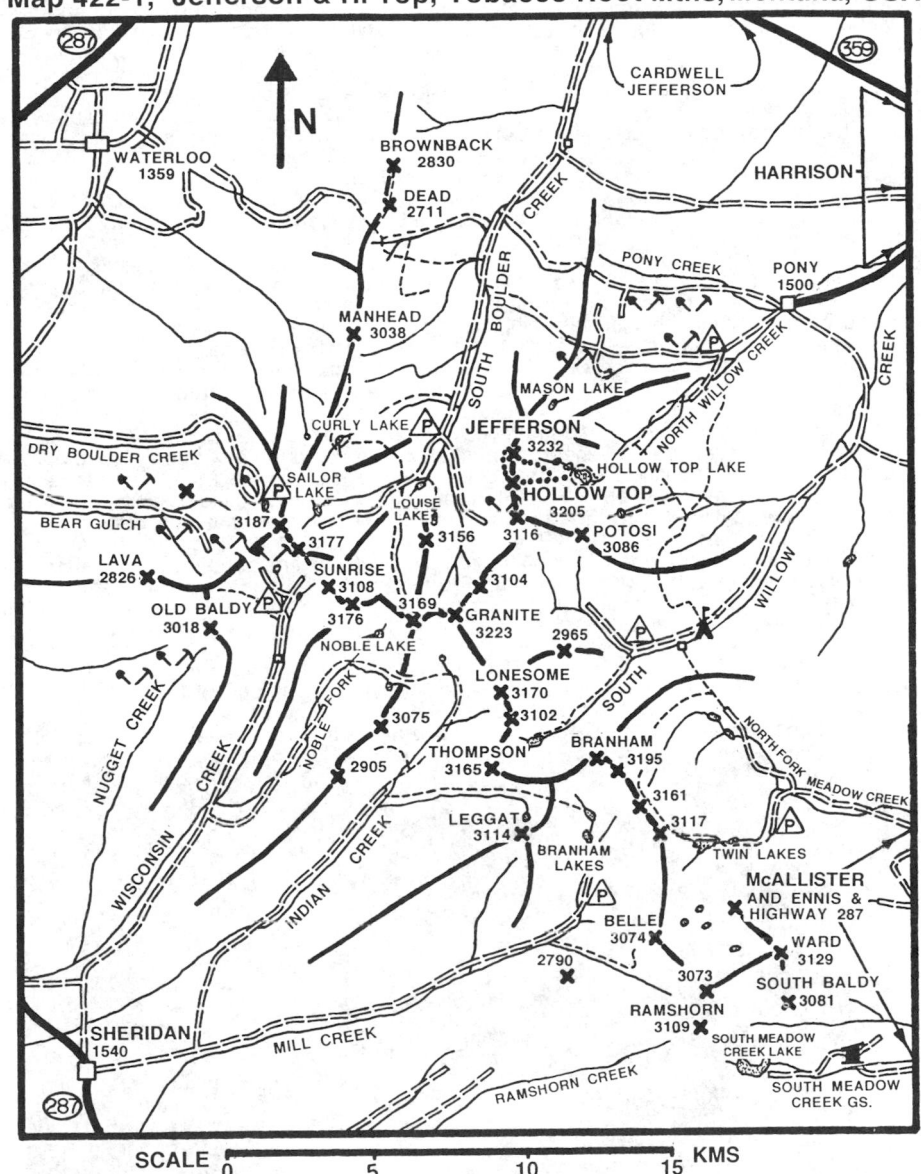

SCALE 0   5   10   15 KMS

selection of climbs to choose from. Do any shopping in Butte, Bozeman, Dillon or Ennis.
Maps *Beaverhead-Deerlodge National Forest,* 1:126,720; and USGS maps *Manhead Mountain, Pony, Noble Peak and Potosi Peak,* 1:24,000; and the book, **Hiker's Guide to Montana,** Falcon Press.

Mt. Hilgard, Madison Range, Montana, USA

Mt. Hilgard at 3450 meters is the highest summit in the Madison Range of southern Montana, which is just west and northwest of Yellowstone National Park. In this group of peaks, located just north of the Earthquake Lake National Memorial Site, are several summits over 3400 meters. These peaks are composed mostly of quartzite and other metamorphic rocks, with some difficult rock climbing routes on the eastern side of the higher summits.

Because of the 1959 earthquake, which caused a mountain to collapse creating Earthquake Lake, the southern portion of the range along the Madison River Gorge is heavily visited. Near the earthquake dam is a visitor center explaining what happened that fateful night.

To climb **Hilgard**, one access route is the Beaver Creek Road. It runs north from the Beaver Creek Campground on Highway 287, along Beaver Creek to the Beaver Creek Guard Station & Cabin (which you can rent) and trailhead. That road is good enough for most cars. From that trailhead, you can reach most peaks in the area.

From a trailhead about one km south of the guard station, walk southwest up a trail which follows the West Fork of Beaver Creek. Once into the upper basin, veer right or northwest and head for Avalanche Lake, as shown on this map. From the lake, route-find north and a little west hopefully to the summit--but that side of the mountain is pretty rugged looking! Some may want to backpack in and camp at the lake and attempt to climb it in 1 1/2 or 2 days.

Here's what the author did on 7/22/1982. He had a late start, and didn't bother to take an ice ax or crampons, then hiked up the West Fork of Beaver Creek, but instead of going to Avalanche Lake, he continued past Blue Danube Lake to the high peak just to the west. That was the wrong way to Hilgard! So he returned to his car in the round-trip time of 4 3/4 hours.

Another option and probably the *route normal,* is to drive to the end of the Beaver Creek Road and look for the Sentinel Creek Trail. Once at the head of Sentinel Creek, route-find south hopefully along a former trail toward Hilgard Basin, located northeast of the summit. From there route-find up Hilgard. This may take 3 days. The author hasn't seen that area, but it looks like easy climbing on some fotos.

Another option is on the west side of the range. Drive one km up Papoose Creek along a public easement to a trailhead with toilet. From there walk up an old road, then trail into Papoose Creek Basin. This route was closed to the public when the author was there in '82, but from the highway, that side of the mountain looked like an easy walk-up. From somewhere close to Hilgard simply route-find to the top.

To climb **Koch Peak** and others to the north, first get a better map than this, then drive up the Taylor Creek Road to a trail which heads southwest along South Fork of Taylor Creek. Look for this road and creek about 21 kms south of Big Sky on Highway 191.

Get more information or maps from the ranger stations at Bozeman (Tele. 406-522-2520);

Looking north from above Blue Danube Lake at the south face of Hilgard.

Map 423-1, Mt. Hilgard, Madison Range, Montana, USA

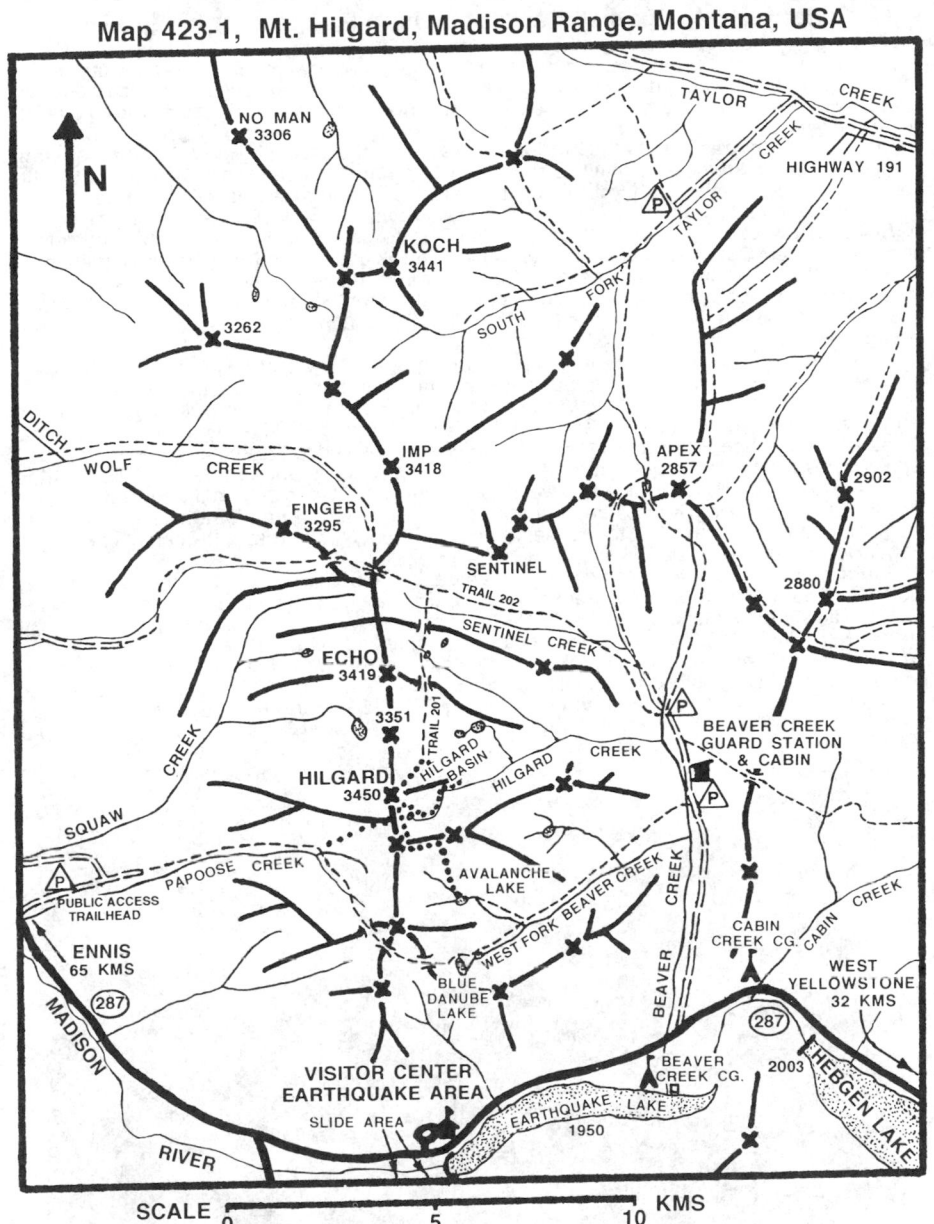

SCALE

0   5   10   KMS

West Yellowstone (Tele. 406-646-7369); or maybe Ennis (Tele. 406-682-4253). Do your shopping in these places. July through September is the normal climbing season.
Maps *Gallatin National Forest, Southern Half,* 1:126,720; or USGS maps *Hilgard Peak, Pika Point* and *Earthquake Lake,* 1:24,000; and the book, **Hiker's Guide to Montana,** Falcon Press.

Gallatin Peak, Spanish Peaks, Madison Range, Montana, USA

Gallatin Peak at 3358 meters is the highest summit in a group known as the Spanish Peaks Wilderness Area. These mountains are just north of the small town of Big Sky and southwest of Bozeman, Montana. This range is not large, but does have some interesting peaks and lakes in an official wilderness area. The mountains here consist of many different rock types, including granite, schist and gneiss.

Access is very easy, as both US Highway 191, and the Gallatin River, form the eastern boundary of the wilderness. From this highway, which runs between West Yellowstone on the south to Bozeman on the north, you can get to the high peaks from several different locations.

One main route to **Gallatin** is up Spanish Creek. From Highway 191 just north of the peaks, you'll first turn west on a graveled road, then after 7 or 8 kms it turns to pavement and continues up to the trailhead and the Spanish Peaks Cabin. This is used periodically by forest personnel working in the area; or you can reserve & rent it for up to several days. To do this, or gather other information about the area and to buy maps, contact the Bozeman Ranger District Office at 406-522-2520, or see their website at (www.fs.fed.us/r1/gallatin). Or contact the ranger's office in West Yellowstone at 406-646-7369.

From the cabin & trailhead, hike up the trail along South Fork to the upper basin, then walk northeast over a pass, drop down to Summit Lake, then climb up to the southwest ridge, thence northeast to the summit of Gallatin. Anyone who is halfway fit should be able to do this in one long day; or camp in one of the basins and do it in 2. You can also hike up Little Hell Roaring Creek to Indian Ridge, down to North Fork Creek, then route-find to the summit.

Probably the most popular route up Gallatin is the one running up the North Fork of the Gallatin River. To find this trail, head west from Highway 191 and stop in the town of Big Sky and at the Chamber of Commerce Tourist Information Office. They, or about anyone living there, can tell you where to find the trailhead, which is about 3 kms west of the center of Big Sky. Hopefully it will be signposted.

From the trailhead, walk up an old road, then trail to Bear Basin, then over the pass at 3010 meters and down into upper Hell Roaring Creek, and route-find to the summit as shown. This is what the author did starting on 8/1/1978. He didn't realize how easy it was, so he lugged his big pack to Bear Basin (2 2/3 hours), then went to the summit and back in probably 2 hours (?). The next morning he returned to his car, with a total 2-day walk-time of about 6 1/3 hours. This can be done in one day. Another way to Gallatin Peak would be via the Hell Roaring Creek Trail.

Another nice hike would be to drive to the Big Sky Ski Resort and park somewhere, then walk west along the Middle Fork Trail. As you near **Lone Peak** at 3413 meters, look for a route to the summit. This should be an easy one day climb.

The best place to shop is in Bozeman on the north, or West Yellowstone to the south. Big

Looking west at Lone Peak from the church in the town of Big Sky.

Map 424-1, Gallatin, Spanish Peaks, Madison R., Montana, USA

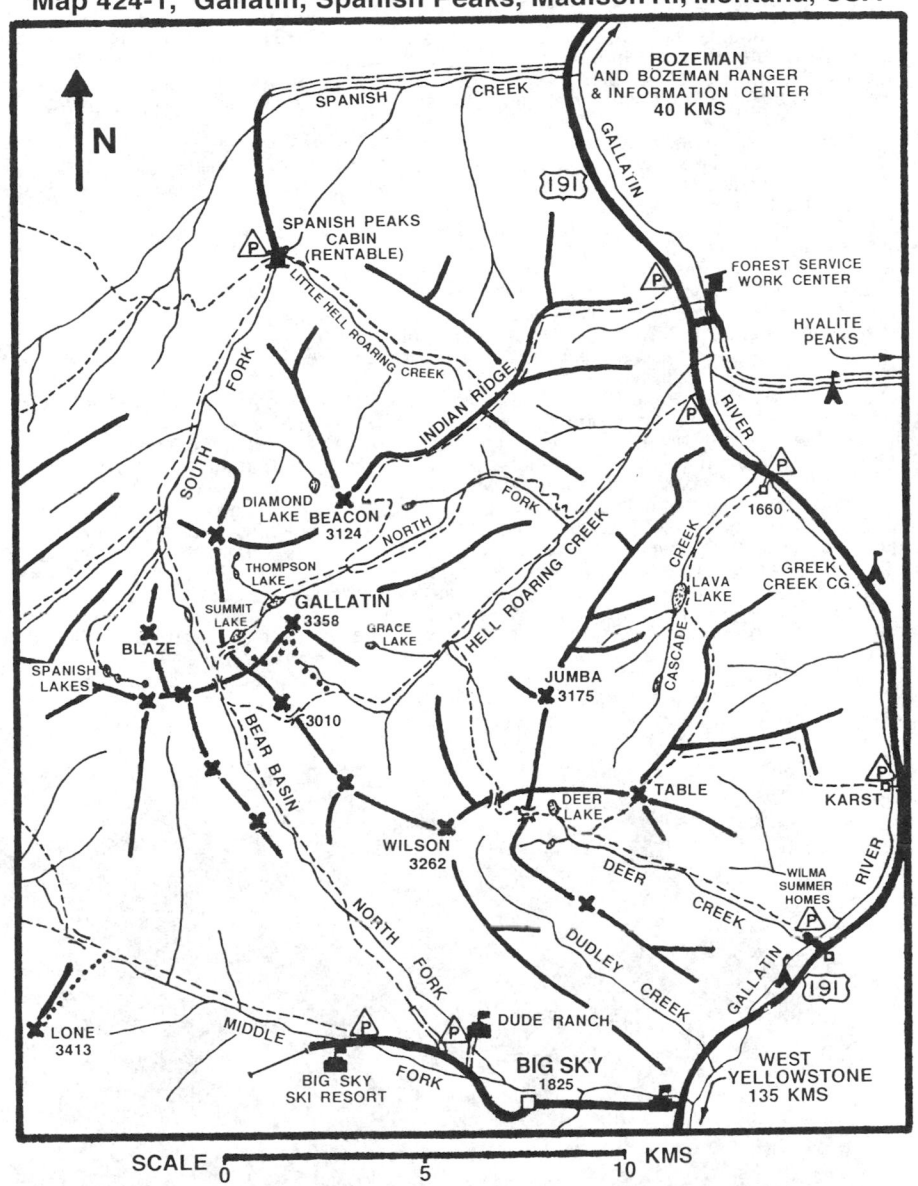

SCALE

0   5   10   KMS

Sky is a plush, retirement-type community and is a very expensive place.
Maps *Gallatin National Forest, Southern Half,* 1:126,720, from ranger stations in Bozeman or West Yellowstone; or USGS map *Gallatin Peak,* 1:24,000; and the book, **Hiker's Guide to Montana,** Falcon Press.

Mt. Douglas, Absaroka Mountains, Montana, USA

The Absaroka Mountains run from about the southeast corner of Yellowstone National Park, northward to about Livingston, Montana, and Interstate Highway 90. Covered on this map is part of the northern section, the part directly north of Yellowstone. Some of the higher peaks here include: Cowens, 3416 meters; Monument at 3352; and Douglas, 3444 meters, which is the highest in this part of the range. These mountains consist of various rocks types, from volcanic lava to granite.

Part of this region has a history of mining but that's been abandoned and the ghost towns of Independence and Lake City, both at the headwaters of Boulder River, still remain and could be an interesting destination. The area just north of Yellowstone Park (the bottom part of this map), is now part of the Absaroka Primitive Area, so that part is wild and roadless.

The main access road featured here is the one up Boulder River, which begins at Big Timber on Interstate Highway 90. Before leaving town, stop at the Gallatin National Forest Office for better maps and updates on road conditions, etc. Or call them at 406-932-5155. From Big Timber, drive southwest on State Road 298 through McLeod and along Boulder River. This road is paved to the national forest boundary (just north of the top of this map), then it's dirt and gravel from there to the Box Canyon Guard Station or Workshop. Along this road are 5 national forest campgrounds. From various points on this road, you can hike to many of the high peaks on this map.

To climb **Mt. Douglas**, park at or near the Hicks Park Campground, then take Trail 26 running southeast along Upsidedown Creek past Horseshoe Lake to the west side of the Lake Plateau. At some convenient point, leave the trail and route-find north to and beyond Rainbow Lake, and up to the ridge south of Douglas, then ridge-walk north to the top. You'll certainly need a better map than this, but the route is fairly simple.

Here's what the author did. He camped at the campground, then on 7/21/1982 with an early start, walked up past Horseshoe Lake, then east and north to the summit of Douglas in 5 hours; then straight down the west face, across the basin and up the peak southwest of Douglas (to get this foto), then back to his car. Total round-trip time was 8 3/4 hours. Long hike! Most people would prefer to camp in the basin south of Douglas, and do it in 2 days.

Another access route is via Highway 89, which runs between Livingston, Montana, and Yellowstone Park & Gardiner. This highway is the northern approach to Yellowstone. From that highway, drive east on Pine or Mill Creeks, and perhaps climb something in either area.

It's possible to get into this wilderness area from the east and south, but that's a along way to walk. This is a huge road-less area, one of the biggest in the continental USA, so if it's wilderness you want, this is it.

Looking east at the western slope of Mt. Douglas.

Map 425-1, Douglas, Absaroka Mountains, Montana, USA

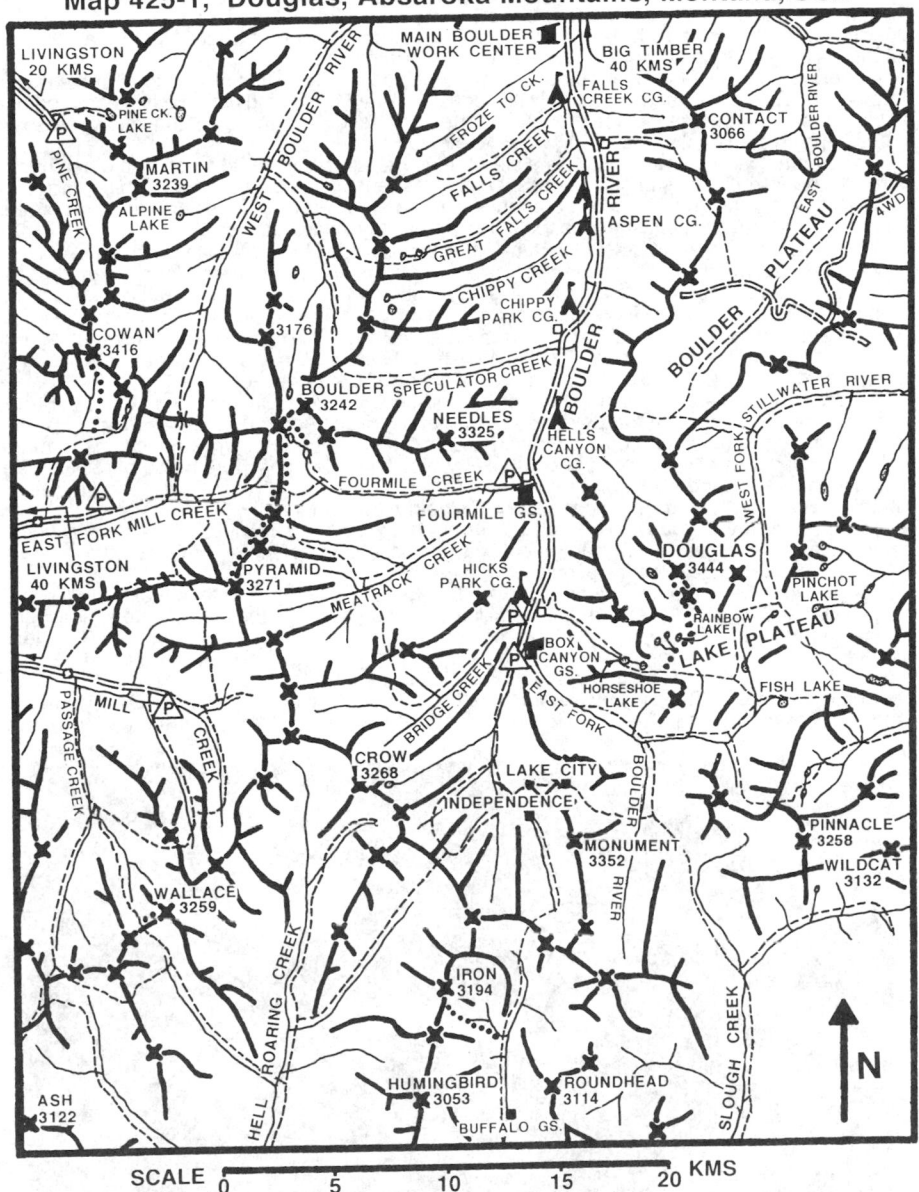

No special equipment is needed here, except for those intentionally seeking out a difficult climbing route. The 2 best places to shop for food are Livingston (Ranger Station Tele. 406-22-1892) and Big Timber. For Forest Service maps and other information, stop at the ranger stations in these 2 towns.
Maps *Gallatin National Forest, South Half,* 1:126,720; and USGS map *Mount Douglas,* 1:24,000; or *Gardiner,* 1:100,000; and perhaps the book, **Hiker's Guide to Montana,** Falcon Press.

Granite Peak, Beartooth Mountains, Montana, USA

Granite Peak at 3902 meters, is the highest summit in Montana. It's located in the Beartooth Mountains, northeast of Yellowstone National Park and west of Red Lodge, Montana. These mountains are made up mostly of granite, but also quartzite and other rocks.

Generally speaking, the Beartooths are not rugged as glaciated mountains go. For the most part, the area is merely a large plateau with occasional canyons or big cirque basins created by glacier erosion during the last ice age. Often the north faces are steep and have ice patches, but other places are gently sloping haystack-type mountains.

The summit part of Granite Peak is a steep and challenging climb, at least for the beginner. Normally, no special equipment is necessary for experienced climbers on the *normal route*, but beginners better take an ice ax & crampons and/or a short rope for crossing one short steep *snow ridge*. Everyone should take ice ax & crampons early in the summer.

There are 2 normal ways to **Granite Peak**. The first starts in Roscoe, which is northeast of Red Lodge, and southwest of Columbus on Interstate Highway 90. From there, drive about 23 kms southwest on a partly-paved road to East Rosebud Lake and Alpine. The trailhead is just north of Alpine. Or drive southwest from Columbus and the freeway, but after Absarokee, and before Roscoe, turn right and head up West Rosebud Creek past Emerald Lake to the hydroelectric station parking lot. There's a good trail connecting these 2 trailheads. If you start at the hydroelectric station, which is a little higher altitude than Alpine, the climb to Granite will be a little shorter and easier.

Normally, this is a 2 day climb, but fast & strong climbers can do it in one long day. From either trailhead you'll reach the Divide at 3100 meters, then veer southwest and climb up to a plateau which tilts down to the north. There's a trail across these gently sloping flats marked with cairns, or piles of stones. At several places you'll find wind shelters made of rock where you can pitch a tent and not be blown off the mountain. These usually form a half circle or circle. The highest and last campsite is near **Tempest Peak** at 3804 meters.

From there, a trail goes down to a pass or col between the summits, then up the obvious eastern ridge. It's a steep climb, and probably a little scary for beginners. Higher up, you'll cross a knife-edge snow ridge, then the summit.

Here's what the author did starting 7/26/1978. He camped at Alpine, then took his full pack. He stopped at Slough Lake and caught 2 small brook trout--this was the last time he ever fished. Then on up to the campsite marked 3550 meters. This must have taken 6 or 7 hours (?). Next morning, he made the climb and returned to camp in 3 2/3 hours. Then back to his car (3 or 4 hours?) and drove to Red Lodge before the Forest Service office closed.

Best places to go shopping locally would be Red Lodge, Columbus, or Cooke City, Montana. July, August and September are the best months to climb here, but sometimes June and

North face of Granite Peak. The normal route is up the left-hand skyline.

Map 426-1, Granite, Beartooth Mountains, Montana, USA

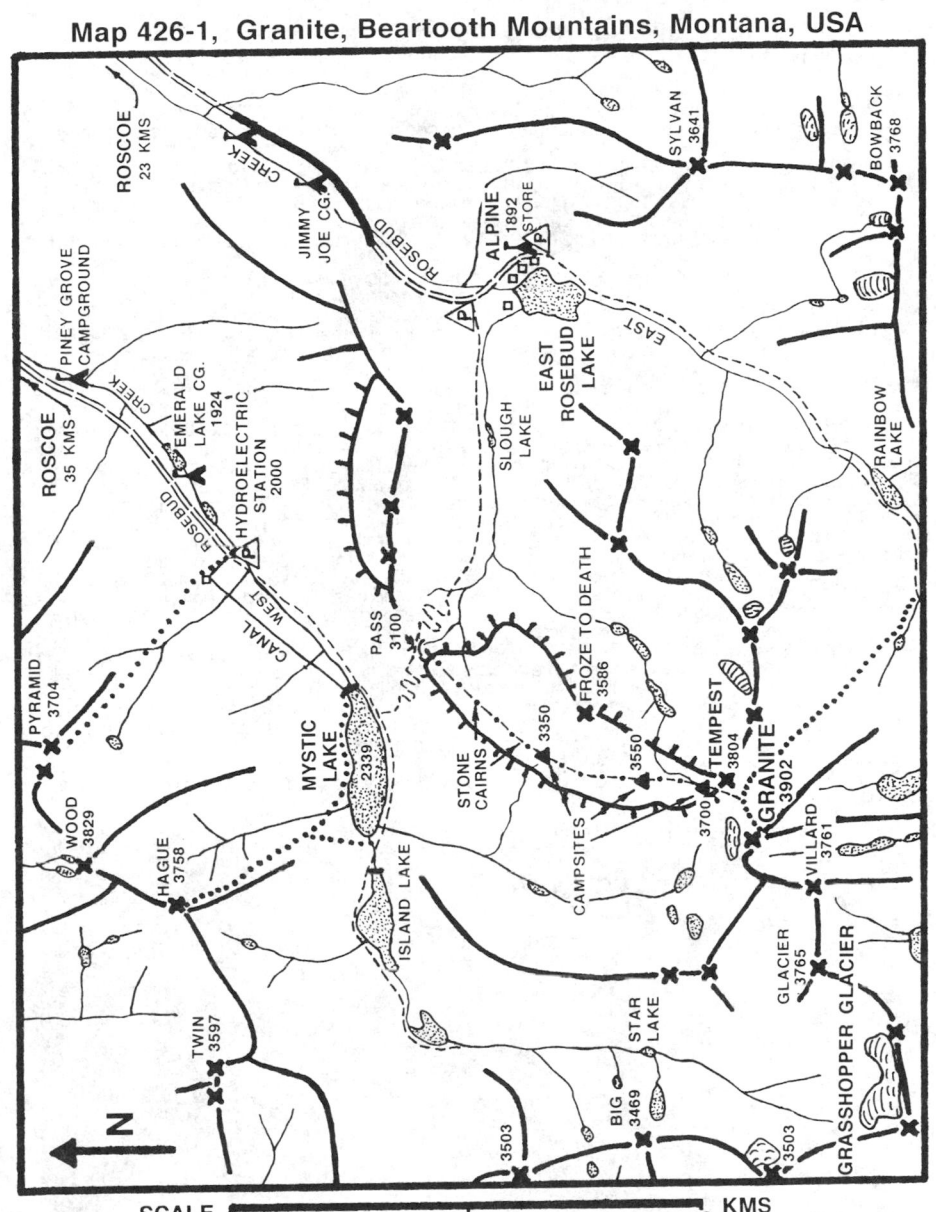

October have fine weather. For more information and Forest Service maps, see the Beartooth Ranger Station in Red Lodge, Montana, or call them at 406-446-2103.
Maps *Custer National Forest, Beartooth Division,* 1:126,720, from ranger stations at Red Lodge, Cooke City or Big Timber; and USGS maps *Granite Peak & Alpine,* 1;24,000; and the book, **Hiker's Guide to Montana**, Falcon Press.

Cloud Peak, Big Horn Mountains, Wyoming, USA

This map features Cloud Peak at 4017 meters, the highest summit in the Big Horn Mountains. This range is located in north central Wyoming, west of Sheridan and Buffalo, and east of Lovell, Greybull and Worland. Covering the higher portions of this range is the Cloud Peak Wilderness Area. The Big Horn Range is similar to other mountains in the west like the Wind Rivers and the Uintas. They were uplifted and dome-like, with granite exposed in the center, with quartzite and sandstone exposed around the outer edges.

There are several ways you can get to the heart of this range and **Cloud Peak**. If you're coming from the west, first make your way to Worland, and perhaps the Big Horn Ranger Station there, then head east on State Highway 16. Drive to and past the small town of Tensleep, then after about 30 more kms, you'll arrive at Meadowlark Lake. This is at a big curve where the highway turns east. On the west side of this lake, turn north and drive to West Tensleep Lake and park at the trailhead on the east side.

From the trailhead, walk north along a good trail past Misty Moon Lake, then as the trail turns left or west toward Lake Solitude, look for the path heading north and a little east. This hiker's trail takes you to the summit of Cloud Peak. In the past, this was the best and most-used route.

Here's what the author did beginning on 7/28/1978. He got maps and info at the Worland Ranger Station, then drove to West Tensleep Lake and packed food for 2 days. He hiked up to just beyond Misty Moon Lake and camped--rained all night. Next morning he found the trail and in 2 hours was on top. Then it was down to the car and drove all the way to the Crazy Mountains in central Montana to sleep for the night. He didn't record his time, but it was likely around 9-10 hours total walk-time, which means if you're in good shape, this is a one day climb; or 1 1/2 days of those who like to camp.

If you're coming from the east side, make your way to the town of Buffalo, due east of this mapped area. From there, drive west on State Highway 16. After about 25 kms, and just as the road makes the big turn to the south, you'll come to the turnoff to the North Fork Picnic Site and Hunter Creek Guard Station, both just to the west of the curve. Cars can be driven 2-3 kms from the highway to the Hunter Creek Trailhead. 4WD's can go another 7 kms to the North Fork Trailhead in Buffalo Park.

From Hunter Creek, walk or drive west past the 4WD trailhead and on to Florence Lake. From that area look for a new trail heading north to Golden Lakes, then it circles around the east side of Bomber Peak and down to Sapphire Lake, then west and up over a broad pass or divide and finally north to Cloud Peak. As of 2000, this is the best way from the east side, and apparently the most-used route up the mountain. Strong hikers might do this in one long day; otherwise, backpack in to Golden Lakes or Sapphire Lake, and finish the climb on Day 2.

Here's what the author did on 8/18/1992. He came up from Buffalo and turned off at Hunter Creek GS. It must have been muddy, so he parked somewhere near the guard station on Hunter Creek (?). He walked to the 4WD Trailhead in 2 1/4 hours!, then continued west over Florence Pass, but then made the mistake of walking north from there and landed on Bomber instead of Cloud Peak. There's a big gap between the 2 summits, and he didn't have the energy or time to backtrack and finish, so he returned arriving back at his car after 8pm. Round-trip time was just under 11 hours. Long hike!

Another east-side route suggested by Brad Solon, is to hike over Ant Hill Pass, west past Mead Lake, then joining the steep trail up to the gap between Cloud and Bomber Peaks. You may need 2, or maybe 3 days.

From Bomber Peak looking north at the south side of Cloud Peak.

Map 427-1, Cloud Peak, Big Horn Mountains, Wyoming, USA

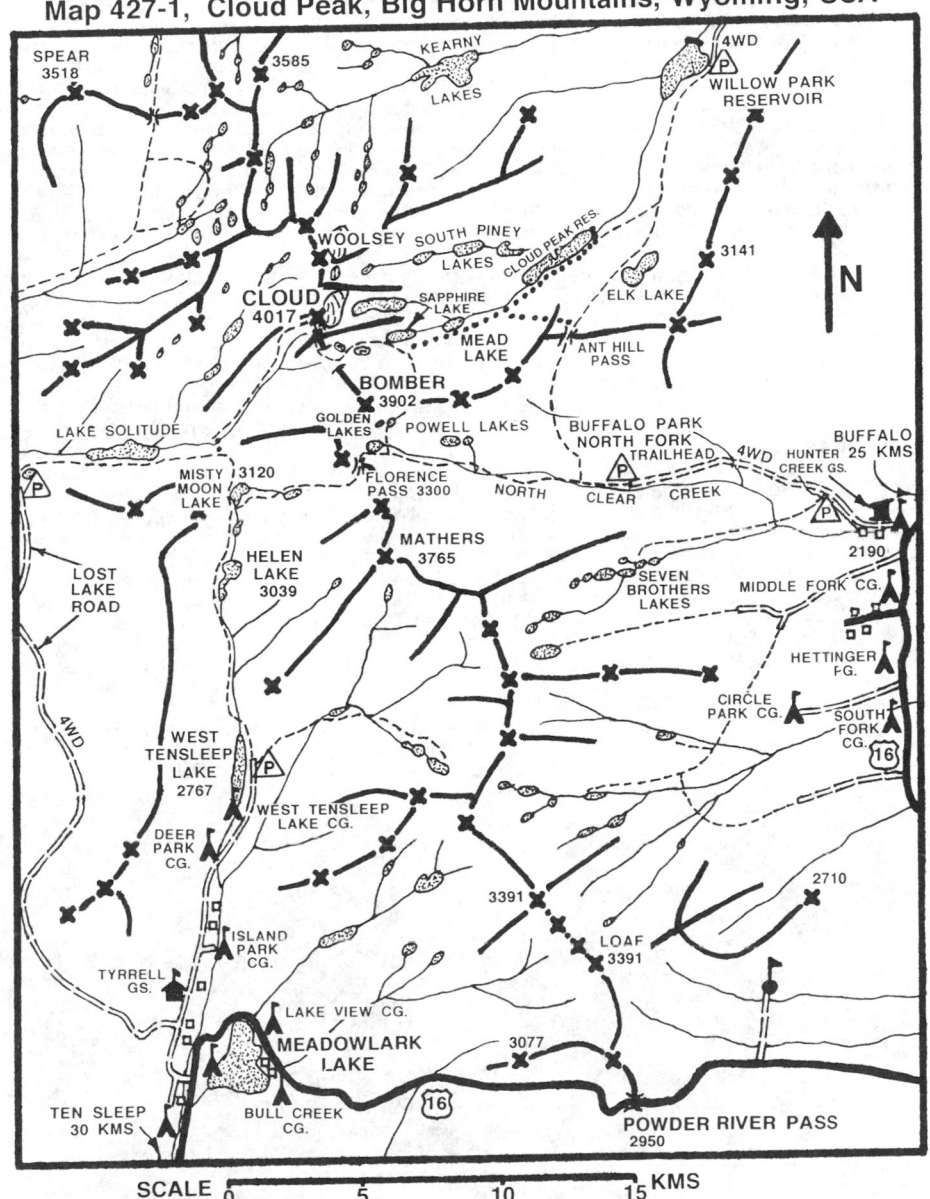

SCALE 0 5 10 15 KMS

The best places to shop are Sheridan or Buffalo on the east; or Thermopolis, Worland or Greybull on the west. District Ranger Stations, where you can buy maps and get undated information, are found at Buffalo, Tele. 307-684-7981, and Worland, Tele. 307-347-8291. Climb from mid or late July through mid or late September.
Maps *Bighorn National Forest,* 1:126,720; or USGS maps *Hunter Mesa, Lake Angeline, Meadowlark Lake, Lake Helen and Cloud Peak,* 1:24,000; or *Worland & Buffalo,* 1:100,000; and the books, **Cloud Peak Wilderness Trail Guide**, Tensleep Press; or **Hiking Wyoming's Cloud Peak Wilderness**, Falcon Press.

Trout & Dead Indian Peaks, Absaroka Mountains, Wyoming, USA

This map shows 2 of the highest peaks in Wyoming outside the Wind River Mountains. They are Trout Peak, 3734 meters, and Dead Indian Peak at 3723 meters. They are situated in the eastern part of the Absaroka Mountains, immediately northwest of the Buffalo Bill Reservoir, which is just a few kms west of the town of Cody along the Yellowstone Highway 14, 16 & 20. The rocks making up these 2 peaks, as well as most other parts of the Absaroka Range, are volcanic in origin.

The easiest, fastest and shortest way to these peaks is to approach from the south and the Yellowstone Highway. From Cody, drive west toward Yellowstone Park. Just after you pass the Yellowstone Valley Inn, and between mile posts 32 & 33, look for a good road heading north up to a bench. This road is number 6GV, and it may be signposted for Jim Creek Trailhead (?). Drive up this steep grade about 3 kms, then turn left or west, cross Jim Creek, and continue west onto a rougher dirt & gravel road. You leave private land and enter public domain as you pass through a gate.

For **Trout Peak**. From the trailhead, walk north on a well-used trail. It starts in sagebrush, then enters the forest at Jim Creek. From there on up, it's an open forest with grass between the trees. Soon you'll come to a junction at about 2600 meters; take the trail to the left running up Jim Creek. Follow it northwest to a big open meadow at the beginning of running water. From there you have 2 choices. First, you can go over a low divide to the northeast, then skirt around the east side of what this writer is calling *Flat Top Mtn*. With Trout Peak in full view, take the easiest way to the summit. You could also go up into a horseshoe-shaped canyon with a waterfall to the top of Flat Top, and walk northwest to Crag Summit at 3673 meters, then ridge-walk northeast to Trout Peak.

On 8/19/1992, the author started after 11am, and made it to the top of Crag Summit, but had to stop there; so he hasn't been along the ridge northeast to Trout Peak. It looked like an easy walk, but may have difficult places (?). Other route options are shown on the map, which may or may not work. With that late start, he made it to Crag Summit and back in about 8 3/4 hours. It's a very long all-day climb to Trout Peak and back; too long for most people.

If you want to climb **Dead Indian**, forget the trail up Big Creek, because all the land near the highway and up to the ranch shown on the map is private. There is no public access to Forest Service lands beyond. Therefore it's best to head for Trout Peak, walk over the pass between Trout and Crag, then get on Trail 761 and head west. Dead Indian is a steep climb, but you'll have a good look at it as you approach. An alternate route to either peak would be up along Trout Creek as shown. A fit climber could likely climb both these mountains in 3 days, with a camp in upper Trout or Dead Indian Creeks.

Cody is the only town nearby, so shop in supermarkets there, buy maps in the one bookstore, and visit the Shoshoni National Forest Ranger Station before climbing for maps and updated information on trails and public access problems. Or call 307-527-6241. Late June through October is the normal

From the south end of Flat Top Mountain looking north at the south side of Trout Peak.

Map 428-1, Trout, Absaroka Mtns., Wyoming, USA

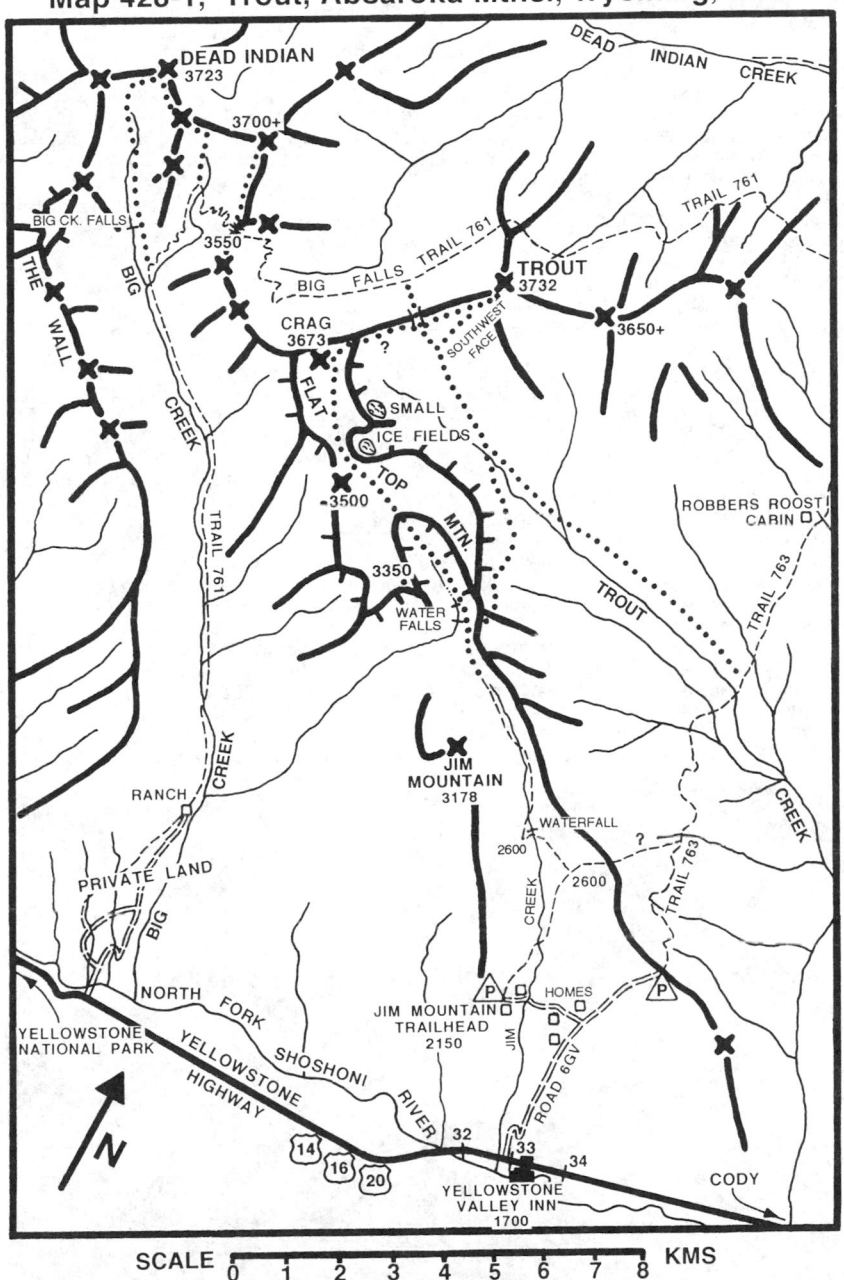

climbing season. No ice ax or crampons needed after about mid-summer.
Maps *Shoshoni National Forest, North Half,* 1:126,720; or USGS maps *Cody & Carter Mountain,* 1:100,000; or *Dead Indian & Jim Mountain,* and maybe *Wapiti,* 1:24,000; and maybe the book, **Hiking Wyoming,** Falcon Press.

Fortress Mountain, Absaroka Mountains, Wyoming, USA

Fortress Mountain at 3681 meters is the highest summit in an area along the southeastern boundary of Yellowstone National Park. It's located southwest of Cody, Wyoming, and south of US Highway 14, 16 & 20. This road is known locally as the Yellowstone Highway.

Most of the rocks in these mountains are volcanic in origin, especially those peaks and valleys to the west surrounding Yellowstone Lake. According to volcanologists who have researched the area, Yellowstone Lake is in the middle of an ancient giant caldera. Roughly 2 million years ago, there was a colossal eruption which displaced 2,500 cubic kms of ash & rock. There may have been bigger eruptions in earth's history, but the evidence is long gone. That explosion ranks up there with the Toba eruption 74,000 years ago on the island of Sumatra, Indonesia. That one blew out 2,800 cubic kms of ash & rock. Also, about 660,000 years ago, there was another eruption in Yellowstone nearly as big as the first. This is the reason there are so many hot springs and geysers in Yellowstone National Park.

The best way to get to these mountains is by way of US Highway 14, 16, & 20, which connects Fishing Bridge in Yellowstone Park with Cody, Wyoming. This highway is open for only about 7-8 months a year, but is heavily used when it's open, especially from mid-June to the first week of September. There are numerous campgrounds, motels, cabins, scout camps and resorts along this thoroughfare.

From this highway are several trails leading south along Eagle, Kitty, Fishhawk, and Blackwater Creeks. The best way to reach **Fortress** is via Blackwater Creek. About one km east of the Newton Creek CG, and just behind the Blackwater Lodge and fire memorial, is Forest Service Road 435 heading south for about 2 kms. That road is for 4WD's only and may be blocked off soon (after 2000), so park just behind the lodge and road-walk to the trail going to Blackwater Natural Bridge. From the end of the trail, route-find about one more km south to the summit of Fortress Mtn. On 7/19/1982, the author did this hike in 7 1/2 hours round-trip.

Another interesting hike is to the top of **Clayton Peak**. That trail begins at or near the end of FS Road 435, and is maintained to the summit. Somewhere near the top is another memorial to a group of fire fighters who were run over by a big blaze and perished back in the 1930's.

To reach the southern peaks, you can leave this main highway near Yellowstone Lake, and walk along the Yellowstone River to Mountain or Thorofare Creeks, but that would be a week-long trip if more than one peak were to be climbed.

Another access route (not shown on the map) is via the South Fork of the Shoshone River, southwest of Cody. Begin a hike at the South Fork Guard Station. See next map. This is due east of **Kingfisher Peak**, and is the shortest route to the southern part of this mapped region.

For those wanting more challenging climbs, head for **Chaos, Overlook** and **Ishawooa Peaks**, which have some small snowfields on their north and east slopes. Reach this area via Fishhawk Creek. You'd likely need about 3 days to do much climbing in that upper basin.

Looking at Fortress Peak from the northeast. The south face is more interesting.

Map 429-1, Fortress Mtn., Absaroka Mountains, Wyoming, USA

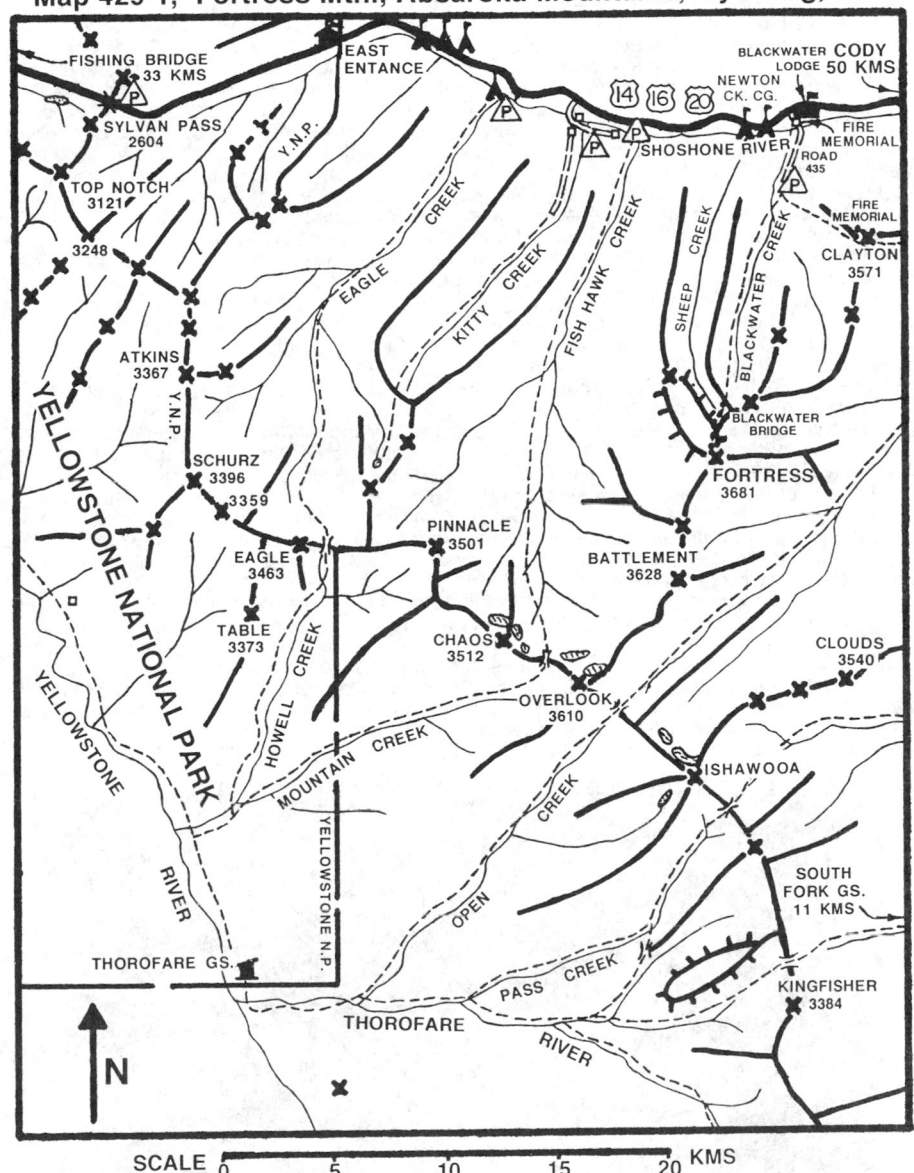

SCALE 0   5   10   15   20 KMS

If coming from the east, stop and shop in Cody, the biggest town around. While there, stop at the Shoshoni National Forest Office for more detailed maps and the latest information about trails outside the park. Call them at 307-527-6241. If coming from the west, Yellowstone Park has some grocery stores, but they're pretty expensive. For information on climbing within the park, enquire at the Fishing Bridge Ranger Station.

Maps *Shoshone National Forest, Northern Half,* 1:126,720 or *Yellowstone National Park,* 1:125,000, from any Yellowstone Park Ranger Station, or the Shoshoni National Forest Office in Cody; or USGS maps *Chimney Rock, Clayton Mountain, Sheep Mesa & and more,* 1:24,000.

Francs Peak, Absaroka Mountains, Wyoming, USA

Francs Peak at 4006 meters, is the only 4000 meter summit in the Absaroka Range of northwest Wyoming and southern Montana. Francs Peak is located in the South Absaroka Wilderness Area, southwest of Meeteetse, and southeast of Yellowstone National Park. This is a little known area, as most tourists and hikers head for the Tetons, the Wind Rivers or Yellowstone. Since there aren't many lakes in this area, you won't see many fishermen either.

Part of this region is one of the most remote areas in the western USA. One of the best approach routes is via Wyoming Highway 291, running southwest out of Cody. This paved road heads southwest for about 70 kms, ending near the South Fork Ranger Station. The last part of that road is reasonably good for all vehicles. To walk from the end of that road will mean some long hikes, perhaps into the southeastern corner of Yellowstone Park.

However, if your intention is to climb **Francs Peak**, here's the best way. From Cody, drive south on State Highway 20 to Meeteetse. From there, head west and southwest on State Road 290 in the direction of the Wood River GS. and Brown Mtn. Campground, as shown on this map. Above that, there's a 4WD road leading into the mountains near the abandoned mining settlement of Kirwin on the Wood River. There's been mining in that area in the past and this road beyond the 2 campgrounds and ranger station is for 4WD's only.

The best way to reach Francs Peak is to drive 2-3 kms past Brown Mtn. Campground, to or near the old Double D Ranch and park at the trailhead. This is a good road to that point. From there, walk southwest along the old road. After about 3 kms or so, you'll come to the first major canyon coming down from the northwest. This is called Meadow Creek. At that point, look for a trail or walk into the canyon and find the trail, then continue northwest as shown on the map. You'll reach one summit, then ridge-walk north to Francs Peak.

The author had some bad luck here on 7/18/1982. He parked at the trailhead, which used to be a locked gate, then road-walked to Kirwin. From there he climbed northwest to near Crosby, then started toward Francs along the ridge, but decided that was too long and the wrong way, so he gave up and returned, all in 6 1/2 hours. If you use the route up Meadow Creek, most hikers can climb Francs in one long day.

You can get to the area from the southwest too. From Dubois, are several 4WD-type roads into the southern section of this mapped area. From Dubois, take the road heading up Horse Creek, which ultimately leads onto the Wiggens Creek drainage, and eventually to the Double Cabin Guard Station and CG. This is the best entry point to the southwestern part of this area.

Use Cody, Meeteetse or Dubois for shopping, and be sure and have a full tank of fuel before leaving any of these towns. Check at one of the Forest Service ranger stations for more information about roads, trails, snow conditions and for much better maps than this. In Cody, Tele. 307-527-6921; in Meeteetse call 307-868-2536; or in Dubois call 307-455-2466.

Looking north at the south ridge of Francs Peak.

Map 430-1, Francs Peak, Absaroka Mountains, Wyoming, USA

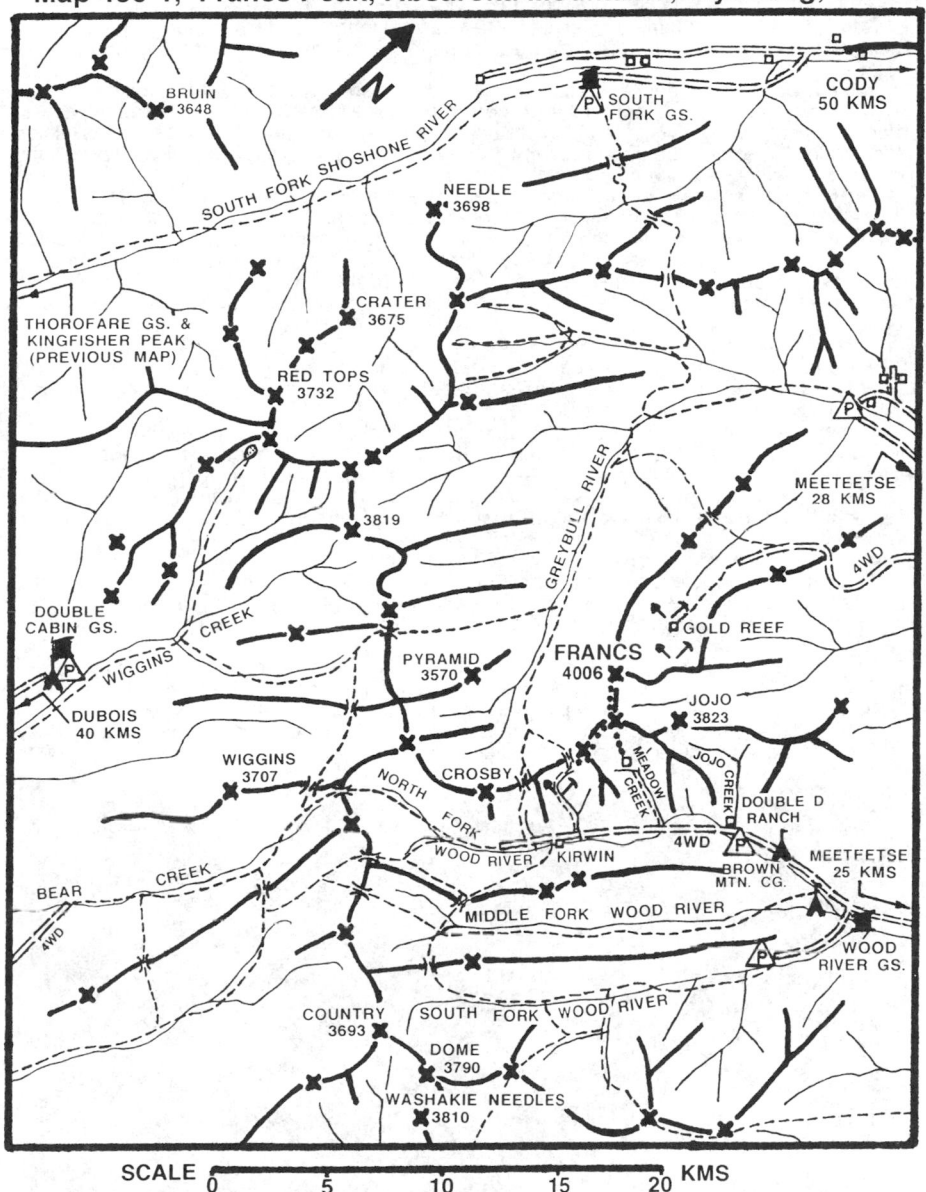

There are no glaciers or snowfields to speak of, so ice ax & crampons are not needed except in winter and spring. July, August and September are the best months for climbing.

Maps   *Shoshone National Forest, Northern Half*, 1:126,720; or USGS maps *Francs Peak*, 1:24,000; or *Carter Mountain & The Ramshorn*, 1:100,000.

Gannett Peak, Wind River Mountains, Wyoming, USA

Gannett Peak at 4208 meters, is the highest summit in the Wind River Mountains and in the state of Wyoming. The Wind Rivers are located in west central Wyoming and southeast of Yellowstone National Park.

In the area around Gannett Peak, the rock is almost entirely granite which makes for some very fine rock climbing. Not only is the rock good, but there's some snow & ice climbing as well. There are small glaciers, most of which are on the eastern sides of the highest summits. These glaciers hardly exceed the cirque variety, therefore almost no crevasses exist. There's little danger on these glaciers even for the solo climber.

The best access points are from the western side of the range, the most popular being from Pinedale to the Elkhart Park entrance. A good paved road runs between Pinedale and Elkhart Guard Station where you'll find the Trails End Campground and trailhead. The host couple at the guard station can sometimes have helpful information. Also, before leaving Pinedale, it's a good idea to stop at the Pinedale Ranger Station (Tele. 307-367-4326) of the Bridger-Teton National Forest, and buy the latest maps, and get up-to-date information on road, trail or snow conditions.

Here's the normal way to **Gannett Peak**. From the Elkhart Park Trailhead, walk east along the well-used trail going past Seneca Lake, north to Island Lakes and into the Titcomb Basin & Lakes. At that point you'll be at the western base of Fremont Peak, 4190 meters, the second highest peak in the range and the state.

A well-used trail continues north past the Titcomb Lakes, then just a steep route up to and over Dinwoody Pass & Glacier and finally up the east ridge of Gannett. This is a snow route early in the season and for most of the year. Ice ax & crampons are mandatory year-round.

The author was here for 4 days from 7/21 to 7/24/1978. He had lots of snow in the upper basins, but managed to climb Jackson's west face, and Gannett via Dinwoody Pass & Glacier and an east ridge. From his camp in upper Titcomb Basin, it took 7 1/2 hours to climb Gannett, round-trip. The 4 day trip took an estimated 27 1/4 hours total walk-time.

Another popular route is via Daniel, the Green River Lakes, Knapsack Pass, Dinwoody Pass, and then the same as the previously mentioned route. For the climber properly equipped, one could make a west face attempt, perhaps from Mammoth Glacier on the southwestern side of Gannett.

Another way to Gannett would be from the north and eastern side of the Wind Rivers. From Highway 26 about 6 kms southeast of Dubois, turn south to Torrey, then to Trail Lakes. From the end of that road, take the trail which passes Phillips Lake, later following Dinwoody Creek to Dinwoody Glacier, then the east ridge which is the same as on the routes mentioned previously.

The last places to get food are at Pinedale on the west, and either Dubois or Lander on the

From around Jackson Peak looking north at the east face of Gannett Peak
(in the far distance left), with Fremont Peak in the near foreground left.

Map 431-1, Gannett, Wind River Mountains, Wyoming, USA

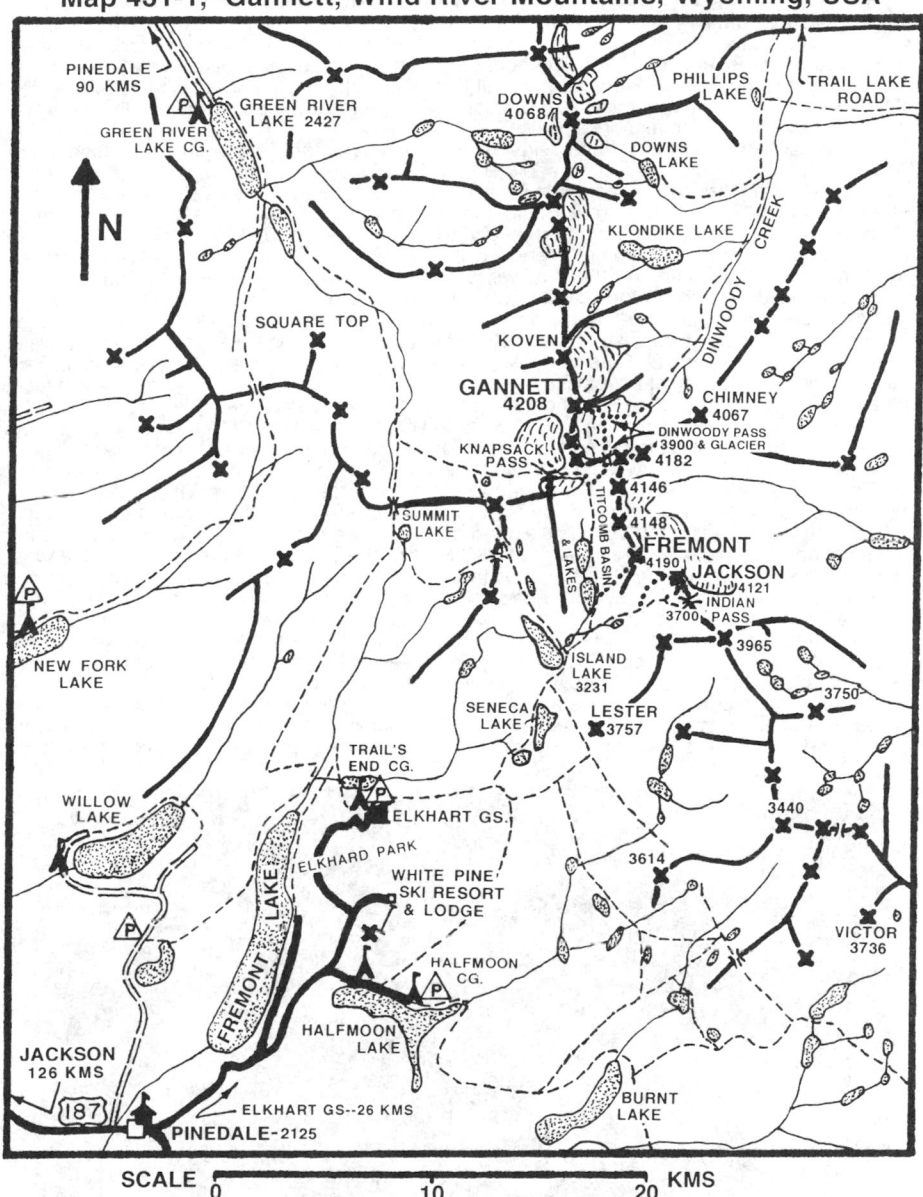

east. Late July, August and early September are the best times to climb in the Wind River Mountains.

Maps *Shoshone National Forest, South Half,* 1:126,720, from the Pinedale Ranger Station, or those at Lander or Dubois; USGS maps *Gannett Peak & Bridger Lakes, and maybe Fremont Peak North & Fremont Peak South,* 1:24,000; or *Gannett Peak,* 1:100,000; and the book, **Climbing and Hiking in the Wind River Mountains**, Joe Kelsey (no relation), Sierra Club.

Wind River Peak, Wind River Mountains, Wyoming, USA

The highest summit In the southern half of the Wind River Mountains is Wind River Peak at 4085 meters. Although this is the highest mountain around, it's not necessarily the most impressive or challenging to climb. The peaks surrounding Lonesome Lake, sometimes known as the *Cirque of the Towers,* is one of the best technical rock climbing areas in the USA. All the region in the center of this range is part of a large wilderness area which makes some very fine solitary backcountry hiking and/or climbing.

To reach **Wind River Peak**, the easiest way is via Lander, the Popo Agie River Road to the Bruce Picnic Site, then Worthen Meadow Reservoir. As of 2000, this was a good improved gravel road all the way to the reservoir & trailhead. From the reservoir, take the trail heading west in the direction of Stough Creek Basin, then up Tayo Popo Creek to Tayo Lake, a distance of about 20 kms. From just above that lake you'll have 2 routes to choose from going up the south or southeast ridge or slopes of Wind River Peak. The author hasn't climbed this one yet, but it's not a technical climb. Most people will want most of 3 days for this hike & climb.

If you're heading for the **Cirque of the Towers** (surrounding Lonesome Lake), then one route is via Fort Washakie, 23 kms north of Lander. One km south of Fort Washakie, turn west onto the Dickinson Park Road, and drive to Dickinson Park (don't go to Moccasin Lake, because you'll have to have a special Indian permit). Cars can easily make it there on a good road. From Dickinson Park Campground, begin on one of 2 trails heading south (if you plan to use these trails, inquire about them in Lander Ranger Station, as the author got lost there once) which can ultimately lead to the Cirque of the Towers. Or from the Dickinson Park Guard Station, head west to **Cathedral** and South Fork Lakes, then south and west to Lonesome Lake. The author was here for an early season climb of Cathedral Peak on 7/17/1982 and made it to the summit and back to the guard station in 6 1/3 hours.

On the west side of the Wind River Range are several roads (some 4WD) leading into the mountains from a settlement called Big Sandy. From Big Sandy the main road heads south, then northeast to the Big Sandy Campground on the Big Sandy River. It's a good road to the campground. This is the shortest route to the **Cirque of the Towers**. From the end of the road, take the trail running to Big Sandy Lake, then northward over a pass dropping down into Lonesome Lake as shown. If you're heading for **Hooker** or **Pyramid Peaks**, the Big Sandy Trailhead is the best place to start.

For Forest Service maps and up-to-date information, stop at the ranger station at Lander, Tele. 307-332-5460. The eastern part of the Wind Rivers is in their district. Or contact Pinedale Ranger Station, Tele. 307-367-4326, which covers the western part of the range..

Best places to buy supplies are at Pinedale, Big Piney or Lander. Late July, August and early September are the best months to climb. All the summits have easy routes, but also some difficult ones. Ice ax & crampons are generally not needed, except in early summer, or on a few

From near Cathedral Peak, looking west at Lizard Head Peak.

Map 432-1, Wind River, Wind River Mountains, Wyoming, USA

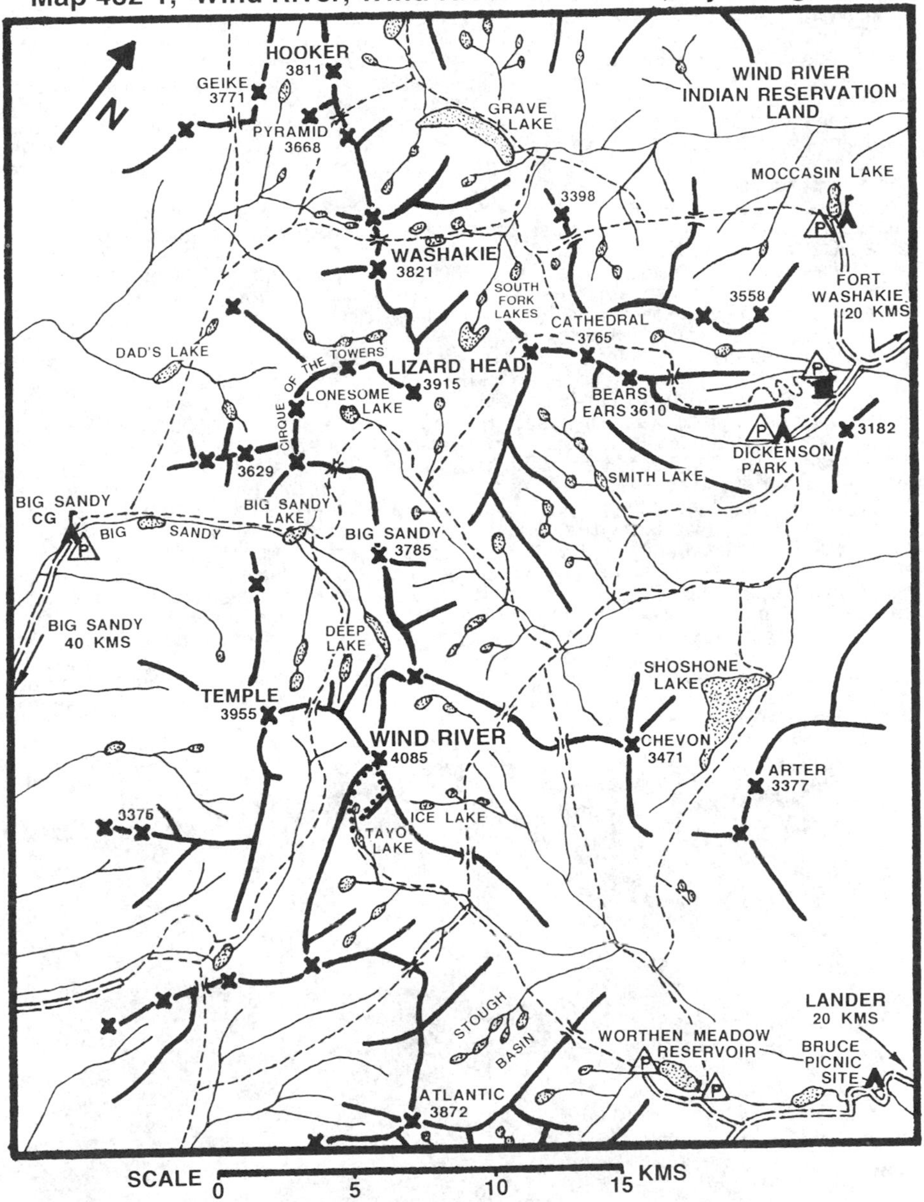

HOOKER
3811

GEIKE
3771

PYRAMID
3668

N

GRAVE
LAKE

WIND RIVER
INDIAN RESERVATION
LAND

MOCCASIN LAKE

3398

WASHAKIE
3821

SOUTH
FORK
LAKES

CATHEDRAL
3765

3558

FORT
WASHAKIE
20 KMS

DAD'S LAKE

TOWERS

LIZARD HEAD
3915

CIRQUE OF THE

LONESOME
LAKE

BEARS
EARS 3610

3182

DICKENSON
PARK

3629

SMITH LAKE

BIG SANDY
CG

BIG SANDY
LAKE

BIG
SANDY

BIG SANDY
3785

BIG SANDY
40 KMS

DEEP
LAKE

SHOSHONE
LAKE

TEMPLE
3955

WIND RIVER
4085

CHEVON
3471

ARTER
3377

3376

ICE LAKE

TAYO
LAKE

LANDER
20 KMS

STOUGH
BASIN

WORTHEN MEADOW
RESERVOIR

BRUCE
PICNIC
SITE

ATLANTIC
3872

SCALE 0 ⊢————— 5 ————— 10 ————— 15 ⊣ KMS

north facing routes.
Maps *Shoshone National Forest, Southern Half*, 1:126,720, from the Dubois or Lander Ranger
Stations; or *Bridger-Teton National Forest, Southern Half (?)*, from the Pinedale Ranger Station;
USGS maps *Lizard Head Peak, Dickinson Park, Temple Peak and Sweetwater Gap*, 1:24,000; or
Gannett Peak, 1:100,000; and the book, **Climbing and Hiking in the Wind River Mountains,** Joe
Kelsey (no relation), Sierra Club.

Grand Teton, Teton Range, Wyoming, USA

In the northwest corner of the state of Wyoming and just south of Yellowstone, is the Grand Teton National Park. The western border of the park runs along the crest of the Teton Range, which is small in square kms, but contains some of the most spectacular scenery and best climbing possibilities in the continental USA. This map covers a large area with many peaks and is meant to be more of an introduction rather than a detailed climbing guide.

These mountains run along a fault line which gives the east face of the range great local relief, and an unobstructed rise from about 2000 meters up to 4200. The highest peak is Grand Teton at 4197 meters. The higher part of this peak, and many others in the range, are composed of granite.

There are 2 ways to get to this area; via Yellowstone Park on the north, or from Jackson on the south. To do any climbing, your first stop should be the **Jenny Lake Ranger Station** which is the HQ. for climbers. Nearby is a campground where climbers from everywhere hang out and swap information & adventure stories. As of 2000, here's how to get currant information. The Ranger Station telefon number is 307-739-3343. They are open from sometime in June and close in early September. Weather and snow conditions dictate opening and closing dates. You can also visit their website at (www.nps.gov/grte/). For day-hikes or climbs, no permit is needed. But if you intend to camp on the mountain or in the backcountry, then you must stop at the Ranger Station the day or afternoon before and pickup a backcountry permit.

The normal route to the **Grand Teton** is via Jenny Lake, then a 2 km drive southwest to the trailhead at Lupine Meadows, up the trail to the south col, then north to the summit. This is the most-popular climb around, so there is a well-beaten path. It's about 12-13 kms to the top and the record time is 3:06:25 seconds, up and back (that was a guy named Bryce Thatcher). The average climber who attempts it in one day needs 6 to 12 hours, round-trip.

Mt. Owens, the second highest in the range at 3946 meters, is ascended by going up the same trail as going toward Grand Teton, but once the terrain starts to level out a bit, look for a climbers trail or route veering northwest. The normal way to **Mt. Moran** at 3870 meters, is to start at the Leigh Lake Trailhead. Walk north, then when you're due east of the east face, turn left or west and head up. There's no real easy climbs on Moran, but the easiest route is on the east face and up the Skillet Glacier. Each year is different, but you must have an ice ax & crampons for this one, as well as on Owens. Strong climbers can climb either peak on a long day-climb, while most prefer 2 days for each climb.

The author climbed Grand Teton in 1/1/2 days in 8/1968; Owens sometime in the early 1960's (?); and Moran in 8/1969 in 1 1/2 days, all while working during the summer season in Yellowstone National Park. But all information here has been updated as of 8/2000.

On some routes an ice ax & crampons are required, but for others, especially later in the

From left to right: Middle Teton, Grand Teton, Mt. Owens (behind with snow patches), and Teewinot on the far right.

Map 433-1, Grand Teton, Teton Range, Wyoming, USA

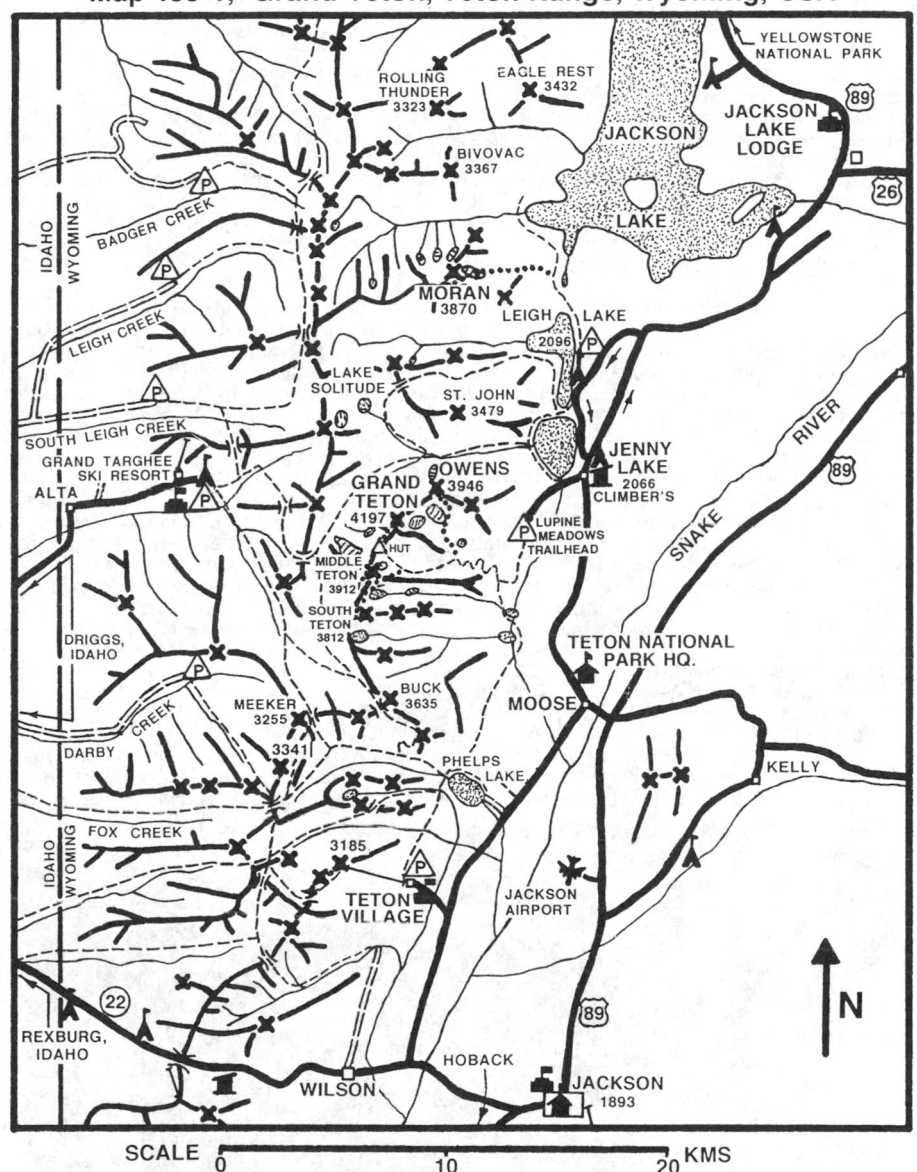

SCALE 0   10   20 KMS

season, only a good pair of boots are needed, especially for the Grand Teton.   Inquire at the Jenny Lake Ranger Station before doing any climbing. Jackson has become a real tourist trap, but it has large supermarkets and sporting goods stores. It's a good place to buy everything.
    There's a Forest Service ranger station in Jackson, Tele. 307-739-5450, and the national park headquarters is near Moose, in addition to the ranger station for climbers at Jenny Lake. Buy books and/or maps there. These are the best places to get the latest information.
Maps *Grand Teton National Park,* 1:62,500; and the book, **Climber's Guide to the Teton Range,** Ortenburger & Jackson, The Mountaineers.

Kings Peak, Uinta Mountains, Utah, USA

Included here are several of the highest summits in the Uinta Mountains of northeastern Utah, and the highest in the state. They are Kings Peak, 4123 meters; Kings Peak South, 4119; and Gilbert at 4097 meters. While you can reach these mountains from the south along the Yellowstone and Uinta Rivers, or from China Meadows, the normal route is from the north and the Henrys Fork drainage. Rocks in the higher parts of the Uintas are all quartzite.

Get there by driving into southwest Wyoming along Interstate Highway 80 and exit at Fort Bridger. From there, drive south to Mountain View and get updated information at the Wasatch-Cache National Forest office (Tele. 307-782-6555), then drive west & south on paved State Road 410. After about 14 or 15 kms, instead of turning west to Robertson, continue south on graveled County Road 246. Further along, turn left or southeast and follow the signs toward Henrys Fork. After you cross the Utah state line, it's about 6 kms of good graveled road to a major junction where the snowmobilers park in winter. From that junction, it's another 6 or 7 kms to the trailhead and campground. The Wasatch-Cache National Forest map below shows this entire route from the freeway.

Here's how to climb **Kings Peak**. From the Henrys Fork Trailhead walk up the well-used trail along Henrys Fork into Henrys Fork Basin. Many people using this trail are out to climb Kings Peak. Most camp somewhere in Henrys Fork Basin and finish the climb and return the next day.

From the upper basin, here's the normal route to Kings Peak. Follow the trail up through Gunsight Pass, then down on the other side, turn right or west, and continue up toward Anderson Pass. Right at Anderson, turn left or south and use a trail-of-sorts going up the ridge to the summit. Or from Henrys Fork Basin, it might be easier and faster to make a shortcut. Simply head for a low pass just west of what this writer is calling West Gunsight Peak. It's steep, but will save several kms on the round-trip. The author has climbed Kings Peak 7 or 8 times between the early 1960's and 2000, in summer and winter.

To climb **Gilbert**, use the main trail up to about Dollar Lake, then route-find east up to the high ridge and on to the summit. Easy climb. Climb **Gunsight** or **West Gunsight** right from Gunsight Pass. West Gunsight can also be climbed from around Anderson Pass.

To climb what this writer is calling **Henrys Fork Peak** and **West Henrys Fork Peak**, start either at Anderson Pass and climb west; or start along the trail on the west side of Anderson Pass, and climb up, as shown on the map. The north face of Henrys Fork Peak and that entire east-west ridge, is perhaps the steepest face in the Uintas, but it's made of rotten rock and not suitable for rock climbing.

To climb **Mt. Powell**, begin somewhere around Henrys Fork Lake and head west, then south, until you reach the summit. There are 3 little humps on top, all just over 4000 meters.

It's about 25 kms from the Henrys Fork Trailhead to Kings Peak if you stay on the trail all the way; or if you take the shortcut direct to Anderson Pass from the middle of Henrys Fork Basin, then it's closer to 19 kms. Many people do this climb in 3 days in summer, but those are the ones who enjoy camping. Many others do it in 2 days and on a regular weekend. Fit people can

From the middle of Henry's Fork Basin you can see Kings Peak to the upper left.

Map 434-1, Kings Peak, Uinta Mountains, Utah, USA

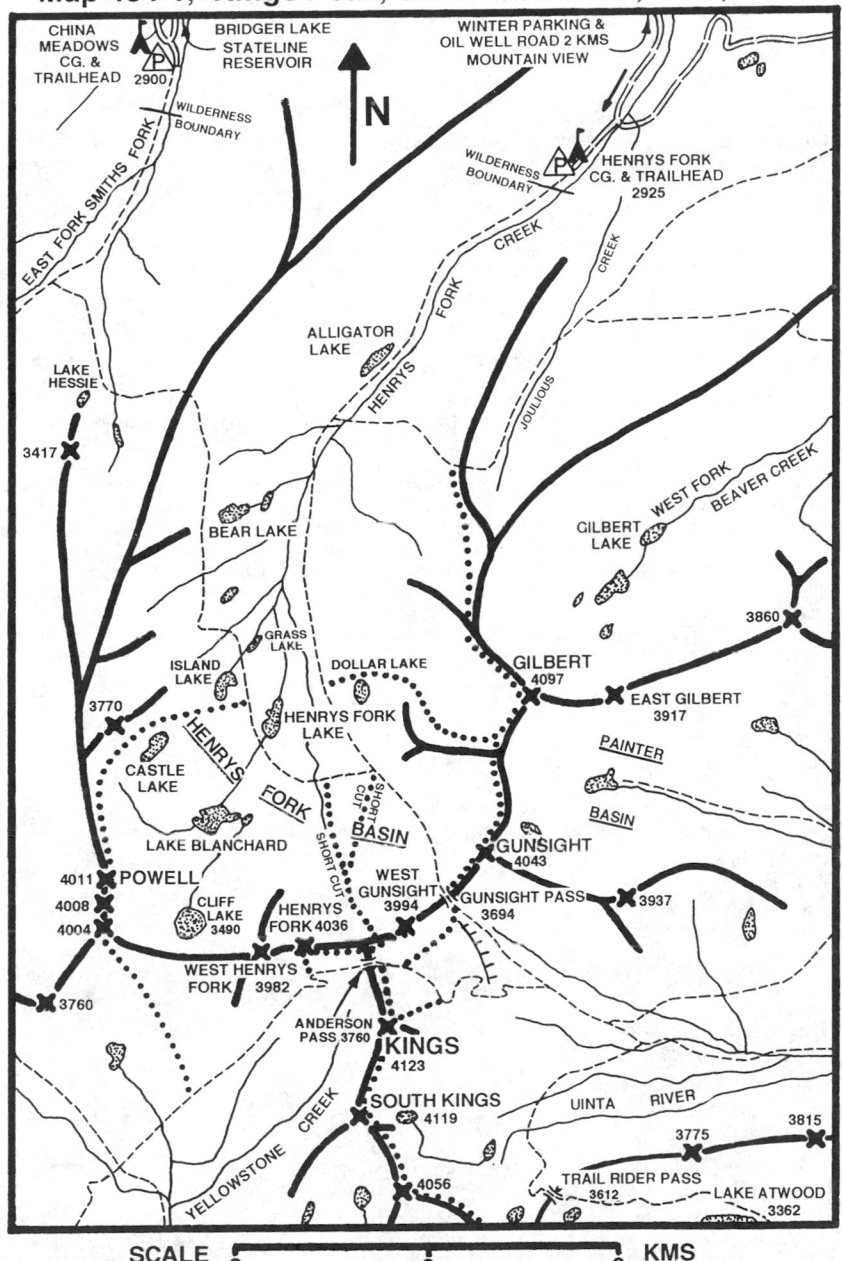

SCALE 0   3   6   **KMS**

do it in one long day from the trailhead in summer; or 2 days in late winter-early spring. In about 4 or 5 days in summer, you should be able to climb all the high peaks on this map. Climb from July through September.

Maps Trails Illustrated map *High Uintas Wilderness,* 1:75,000; and *Wasatch-Cache National Forest,* 1:126,720; and **Utah Mountaineering Guide**, Kelsey, Kelsey Publishing.

Mt. Timpanogos, Wasatch Mountains, Utah, USA

Utah's most-famous mountain is Mt. Timpanogos (Timp for short), at 3581 meters. Timp is located north of Provo and just northeast of Orem and Pleasant Grove. This huge massif has one single dominant ridge running northwest to southeast with nearly a dozen peaks along its crest. On the northeast side of that ridge are 7 high and separate cirque basins, one of which still holds a small perpetual snowfield called the Timp Glacier. For a closer look at the mountain and lots of historical aspects, see the author's book on Timp listed below.

The normal route to the top of **Timp** is from Aspen Grove on the east side of the mountain. Get there by driving up Provo Canyon on Highway 189. Right at the summer home complex of Wildwood, turn north into the North Fork drainage on State Road 92. Just a few kms beyond is Robert Redford's Sundance Ski Resort, then a place called Aspen Grove. In that area is a BYU summer camp, campground and the Timp Trailhead.

Between 1912 & 1970, this was the starting point for the Annual Timp Hike. In its last year or two, there were 7000 to 8000 people on the mountain on one single day, so it was decided to discontinue the hike to save the mountain.

From Aspen Grove, the trail heads west zig zagging up the slopes of a lower cirque basin and into the upper basins to Emerald Lake & Shelter at the bottom of the Timp Glacier. From that emergency-type where up to a dozen people could sleep on the floor, the summit trail runs west to a pass on the ridge crest, then zig zags southeast up to the summit. It's 13.3 kms from Aspen Grove. There's another small metal shelter on top, but it gives almost no protection from the elements. From the summit, most people return a slightly different way. They walk south along the ridge and return to the lake via the Timp Glacier. Early in the season the top of this icefield is rather steep, but most use the route anyway because they make a fast slide down, usually on the seat of their pants.

A second normal route up Timp is from the north and the Timpooneke Trailhead. Get there by driving up American Fork Canyon and along the Alpine Scenic Loop Road (State Road 92). Watch for signs pointing the way to the trailhead off to the right from the main loop road, as shown. This route is known as the Timpooneke Trail and is a little longer than the route from Aspen Grove. This trail connects with the Aspen Grove Trail in the high Timp Basin, then west and up to the summit.

Other routes you might use to reach the summit are up from Pleasant Grove along Grove and Battle Creek Canyons. You can also use the Dry Canyon Trail from northeast Orem to gain access to the southwest face. From Provo Canyon there's a south ridge route beginning near Bridal Veil Falls. These routes are all covered in detail in the Timp book below.

Normally the hiking season for Timp begins around mid-July and ends in mid-October. However, the road to Aspen Grove is open year-round so this allows easy access for winter climbs (the best snow conditions are in March). There is water all along the 2 main trails mentioned, except high on the ridge. Most people need 5 to 8 hours for this hike, but the record time during the old Annual Timp Hike was set in 1967 by this writer. He got to the top in 1 hour 30 minutes, and returned in 45 minutes (his first climb was in 1954). Since then a marathoner made it up in about 1:28, but the trail is a little

Emerald Lake Hut and Timp Glacier behind. Timp's summit is to the right out of sight.

Map 435-1, Timpanogos, Wasatch Mtns., Utah, USA

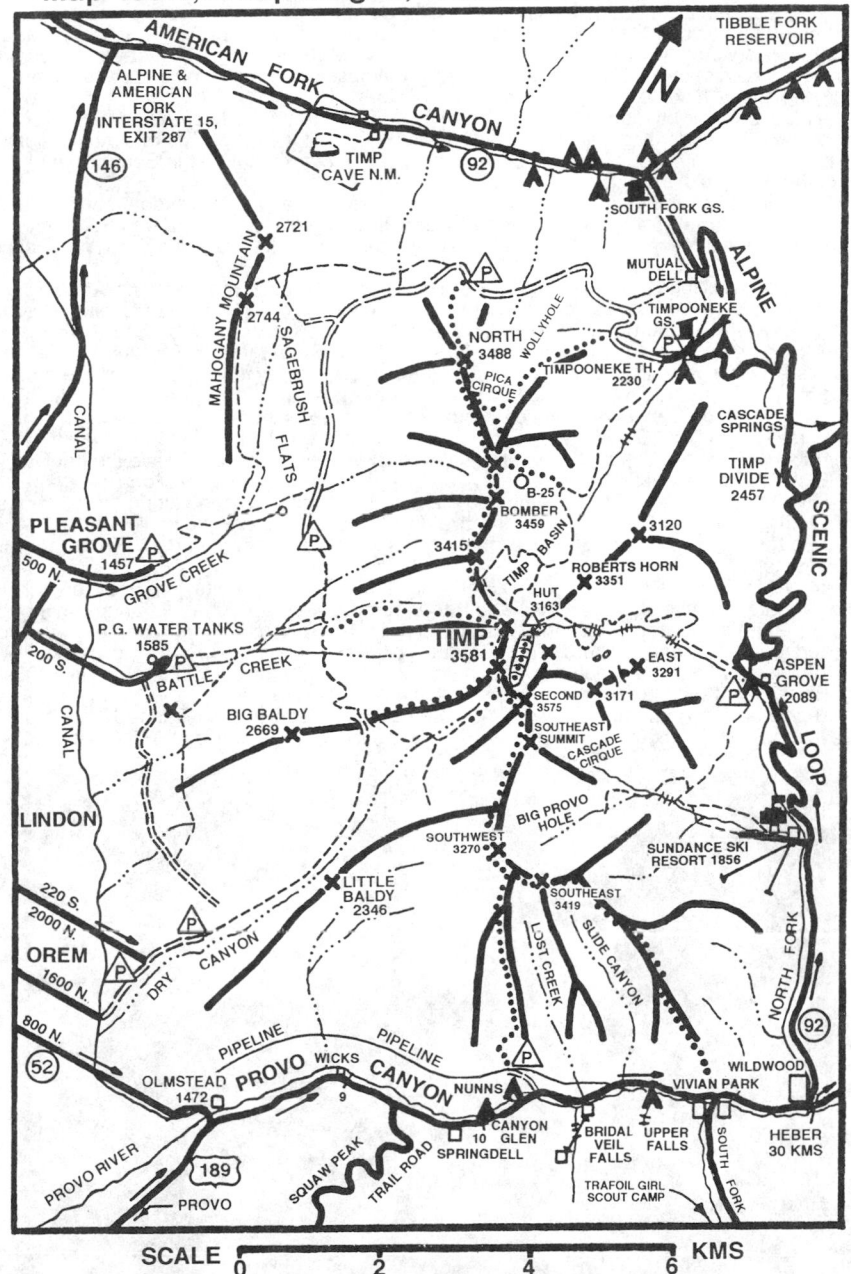

SCALE 0   2   4   6 KMS

longer and less-steep these days. For the very latest information call the Pleasant Grove Ranger
Station of the Uinta National Forest at 801(or 385)-785-3563.

Maps *Uinta National Forest,* 1:126,720; USGS maps *Timpanogos Cave, Aspen Grove, Orem* and
maybe *Bridal Veil Falls,* 1:24,000; or *Orem,* 1:62,500 (if available); or the books, **Climbing and
Exploring Utah's Mt. Timpanogos**, or **Utah Mountaineering Guide**, Kelsey Publishing.

Mt. Nebo, Wasatch Mountains, Utah, USA

The highest summit in Utah's Wasatch Mountains is Mt. Nebo at 3637 meters. It's located at the extreme southern end of the range, south of Provo and just east of the little town of Mona. What otherwise would be an unimpressive elevation, Nebo rises from 1498 meters at Mona, to the summit; a gain of over 2100 meters in one step. Almost all the rock making up this mountain is limestone, but with some quartzite in areas to the north.

Mt. Nebo was one of many mountains in the Great Basin that was used by the U.S. Army during the 1880's as a triangulation or survey station. One of their methods of sending signals was with a mirrored contraption called a *heliograph*. Very near the top of the South Summit are some of the remains of the surveyors camp.

Mt. Nebo is one very long high ridge with a number of peaks. The middle summit is the highest, but the main trail more or less stops at the South Peak, which is 3621 meters. However, in the last few years, there appears to be a developing hiker's trail running north along the ridge to the highest point.

Here's how to climb **Nebo**. There are 2 trails to choose from. One is the **Andrews Ridge** route on the eastern slopes. To get there, drive along Interstate Highway 15 to Nephi just south of Mona, exit on the east side of town and head east up Salt Creek on State Road 132. Between mile posts 39 & 40, and very near the KOA Campground, turn north. After 7 kms, the road splits; on the right is the Nebo Loop Road running north to Payson. But, take the one to the left another 3 kms and turn west at the trailhead. From there, the trail zig zags up the Andrews Ridge, turns north on the Nebo Bench or Basin Trail, then up to the main summit ridge. There, you'll intersect the Willow Creek Trail which heads north to the summit.

For most people, the **Willow Creek Trail** is the easiest route to get to. Leave the freeway (I-15) at Exit 236, drive west into Mona, then south, then east again out of Mona on Cemetery Lane. Cross over I-15 and at the electric sub-station turn south. Continue along the most-used dirt road into Willow Creek Canyon to the trailhead. Most cars can make it. Walk the trail leading up through the pine and spruce trees to the wide-open summit ridge. From there it's north to the top.

From Willow Creek to the summit is roughly 8 kms; the Andrews Ridge Trail is about 11 kms. On either route, the average hiker will need 5 to 8 hours round-trip. There may or may not be any water along either trail, so take all you want for the entire climb. In summer, each person may need 2 liters or more. There are good campsites on Willow and Andrews Creeks. The author has climbed Nebo by each of these routes about 4 times, plus a winter climb in 1996 up Cedar Ridge. That's the best route in winter.

For up-to-date trail information and conditions, call the Spanish Fork Ranger Station of the Uinta National Forest at 801 (or 385)-798-3571; or the small Nephi office at 435-623-2735. To

From the South Summit of Mt. Nebo looking north along the summit ridge.

Map 436-1, Mt. Nebo, Wasatch Mountains, Utah, USA

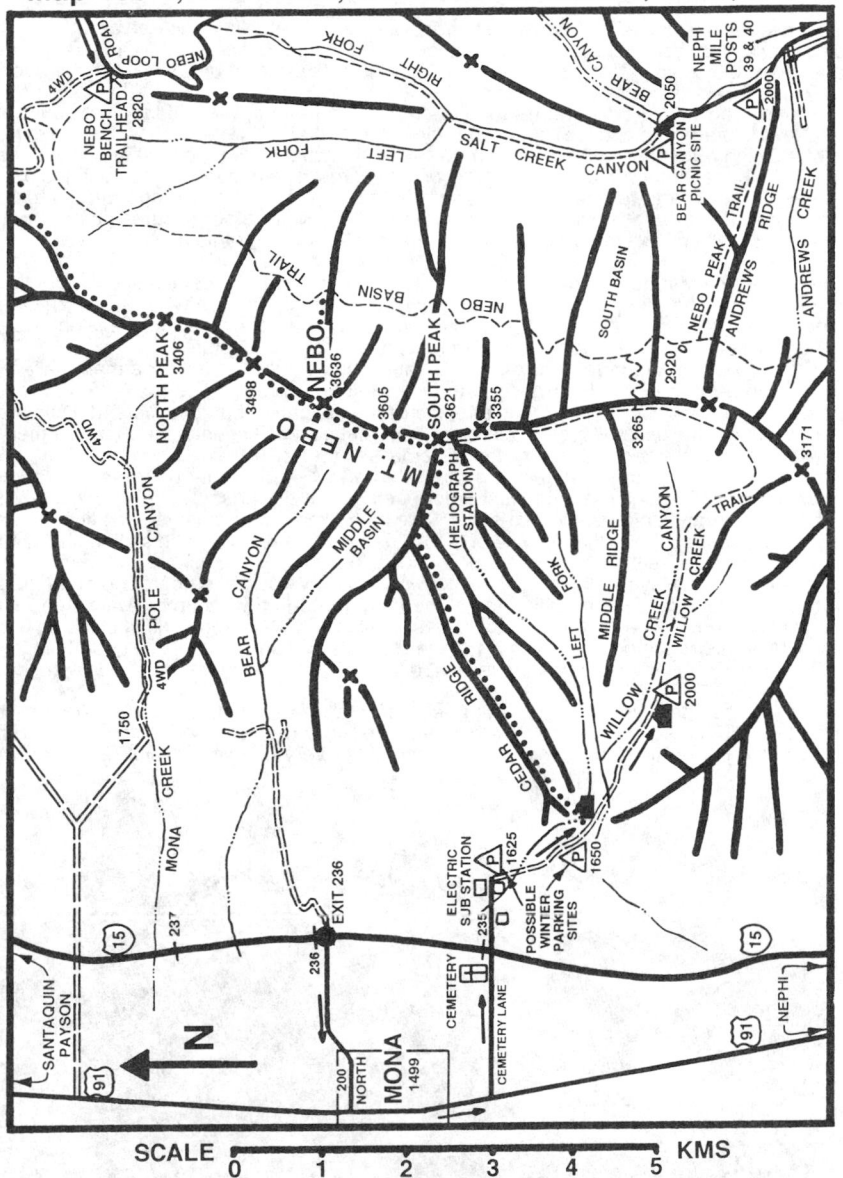

buy maps, best to stop at the Spanish Fork office, which is about 40 kms north of Mona.
Climbing season on Nebo is normally from mid-June through mid-October.
Maps Trails Illustrated map *Uinta National Forest,* 1:48,000; or *Uinta National Forest,*
1:126,720, from the Nephi, Spanish Fork or Provo Ranger Stations; and the author's other book,
Utah Mountaineering Guide, Kelsey Publishing.

Ibapah & Haystack Peaks, Deep Creek Mountains, Utah, USA

This map shows the highest mountains in Utah's West Desert and the Deep Creek Range. Included here are Ibapah Peak at 3684 meters, and Haystack Mtn., 3664. The Deep Creek Mountains are located just east of the Utah-Nevada state line and the Goshute Indian Reservation. They're also about halfway between Wendover in the north and the Garrison, Baker and the Great Basin National Park area to the south. Most rock in the Deep Creek Range, at least between Chimney Rock Pass and Red Mountain, is granite.

Probably the best way to get there is to drive Interstate Highway 80 to Wendover on the Utah-Nevada state line, and turn south on Highway 93A. Later, turn southeast and drive to Gold Hill and Callao on a graded & graveled road. The other route from the east and Salt Lake City would be to drive through Tooele to Dugway on paved roads, and continue south to the old Pony Express Route Road, then head west toward Fish Springs Wildlife Refuge and on to Callao. Also, from Eureka and Vernon--see Area Map. You could also get there by going to the Garrison, Baker and Great Basin National Park country south of this mapped area, then drive north.

Be sure to have a good running car with lots of water, food and especially fuel, and a state highway map. The last places to fuel-up will be Wendover (and maybe Ibapah?), Dugway, Vernon, and Stateline, just north of Garrison. Go well-prepared for this trip, it's a long way from nowhere! Once on gravel roads, lower tire pressure to prevent punctures.

The normal route to **Ibapah Peak** is via Granite Creek Canyon. Leave the main Callao-Trout Creek Road near the Douglas Ranch and drive west on a pretty good road into the mouth of Granite Canyon. This road gets rough after it crosses the creek, but most cars, driven carefully, can get to about the second stream crossing. After that it's 4WD country for about another km to where the road is blocked off at about the wilderness boundary.

Above the 4WD parking place, the old vehicle track gradually becomes a trail. Walk upcanyon near a small stream, but just before going over the pass at 3375 meters, route-find north toward Ibapah on a faint trail-of-sorts. This trail is more of a route, so just find the easiest way. On top of Ibapah are the remains of an old triangulation & heliograph station and campsite. From Ibapah, ridge-walk north to Haystack.

Another way to **Haystack Mtn.** is to drive west from the CCC Campground and into Indian Farm Creek Canyon. At or near the end of the road, route-find west up the east face. There's brush on the lower slope, but higher up it's easy walking. Don't even think of climbing from the west side of this range because it's part of the Goshute Indian Reservation and off limits to all non-Indians. The author has been here on 4 different trips, first in the mid-1960's, then winter climbing in 3/1997.

From the car-park, most people will need 4 to 5 hours to climb Ibapah, and 6 to 9 hours round-trip. To include Haystack on the same hike, may require 8 to 12 hours round-trip, or more! Some may want to backpack in and camp at the very head of Granite Creek, then finish

From the summit of Red Peak looking north at Ibapah Peak.

Map 437-1, Ibapah-Haystack, Deep Ck., Mtns., Utah, USA

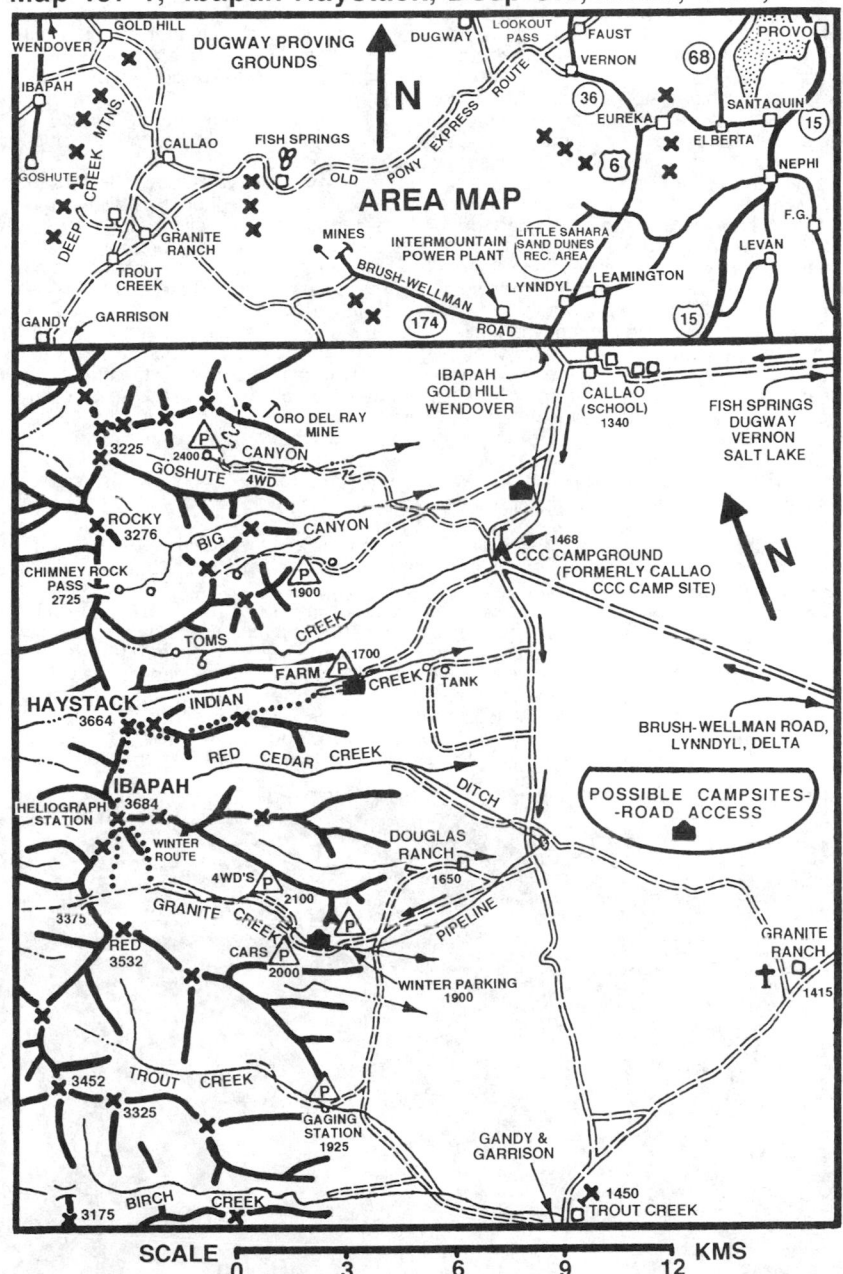

the trip the next day. There is water on Farm Creek and Granite Creek, but not high on the peaks. The water quality should be good, if there are no cattle around.

Maps USGS (or BLM) map *Fish Springs*, 1:100,000; or *Ibapah Peak, Indian Farm Creek, Goshute, and Goshute Canyon*, 1:24,000; and the author's other book, **Utah Mountaineering Guide**, Kelsey Publishing.

Delano, Belknap & Baldy, Tushar Mountains, Utah, USA

Featured here are the highest peaks in the Tushar Mountains of south central Utah. This range is located between Beaver on the west, and Junction & Marysvale to the east. From north to south here are the important summits: Baldy, 3683 meters; Belknap, 3699; Delano, the highest at 3709; and Holly, 3657 meters. This entire mountain range is composed of old volcanic rocks which date back about 23 million years.

Mt. Belknap is the one with an old triangulation or heliograph station located on top. Some of those structures may date from the early 1880's. Mt. Holly is the peak for which the original Mt. Holly ski resort was named. That resort is now called Elk Meadows.

To get to the **Tushar Mountains**, exit Interstate Highway 15 at Beaver. In the middle of town, turn east and drive 31 kms up to the ski resort. Once there, continue uphill from the main facilities to a day-lodge and upper parking lot. From there you can climb **Holly and Delano**. From the day-lodge, walk northeast uphill along some of the ski runs aiming for the first ridge. Once on the ridge you can see Mt. Holly straight ahead. It's an easy climb with little to slow you down. If you like, you can continue northwest along the summit ridge all the way to Delano.

Probably the normal way to reach **Delano**, and **Baldy & Belknap**, is to drive to a point about 3 kms below the ski resort and between mile posts 16 & 17, then turn north at the dirt road going to Big John Flat. In summer, when conditions are dry, this road is good for cars up to the highest pass marked 3400 meters near Belknap. As you drive along, be watchful of Delano to the east. At the upper end of Big John Flat, you should see an old road, now apparently a designated trail, heading off to the east. From there make your way up the slope toward **Delano**. This is an easy walk through alpine meadows. Or you might start on the trail as shown, walk southeast a ways, then strike out cross-country for the summit.

If you're heading for Belknap and Baldy, continue up the road in the direction of Marysvale. Park at the highest point along the road and at the pass if you can. This would be the starting point for climbing the 2 northern-most summits.

From that pass, you could walk along an old mining track in the direction of **Belknap**; or you could get on the prominent ridge, whichever way seems easiest. There's a trail you can use once you get to the base of the peak.

The best way to **Baldy**, is to ridge-walk southwest from Belknap. There's no trail, but it's easy walking and above timberline. From Baldy you can return the same way, or head down the steep southeast slope, cross the upper end of Blue Lake Creek, and climb up the other side back to the car-park. You may be able to use an old trail or mining track part way, as shown.

The author has been here several times; in 12/1993, he parked at the day-lodge and spent the next 3 days ridge walking over the tops of all 4 summits using snowshoes and/or crampons, returning via Big John Flat. Three-day walk-time was 16 2/3 hours. There is water on the lower slopes, but take your own on the peaks. Summer hiking is from mid-June through October; or

Looking northeast at Belknap from the summit of Bald Mountain.

Map 438-1, Delano & Belknap, Tusher Mtns., Utah, USA

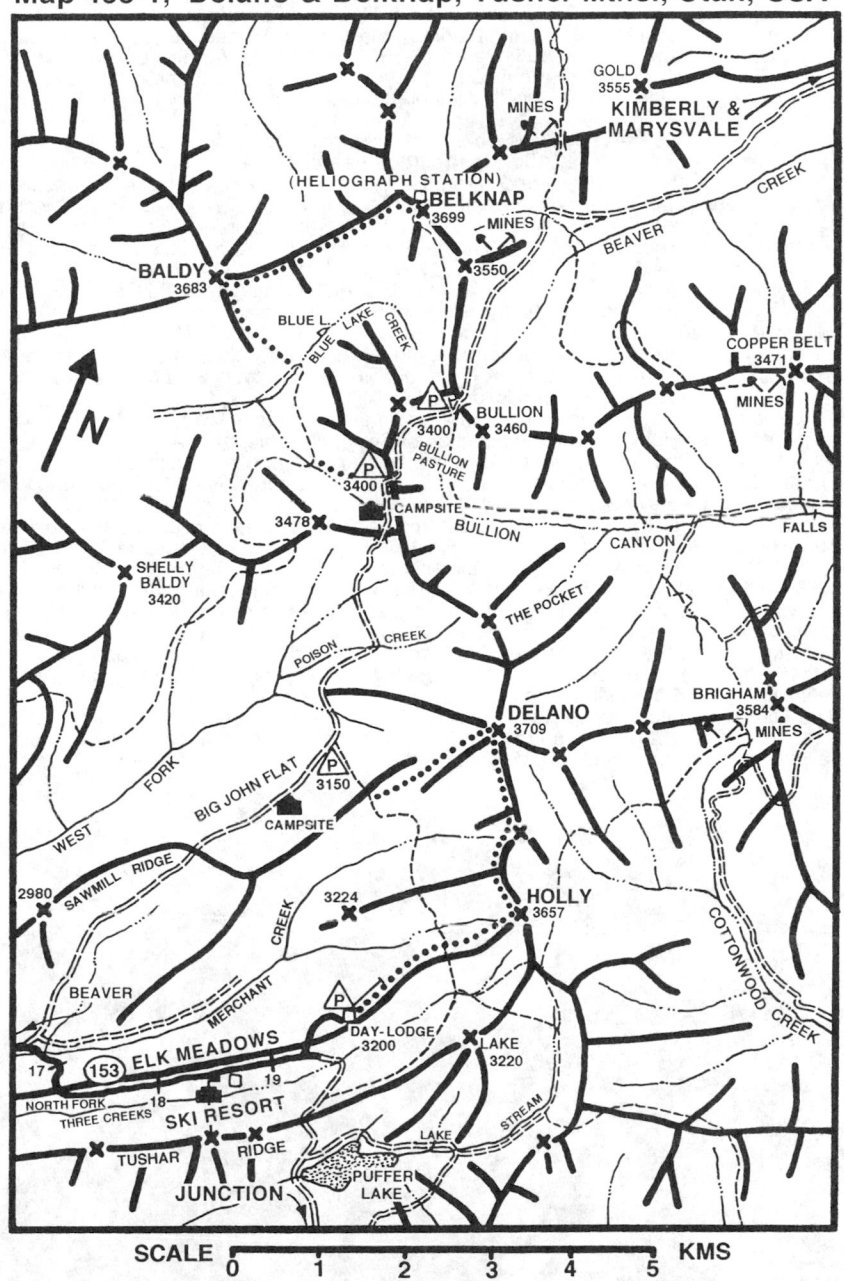

SCALE

0 1 2 3 4 5 KMS

winter-climb anytime with ski resort access.

Maps USGS maps *Beaver,* 1:100,000; or *Mount Belknap, Shelly Baldy Peak & Delano Peak,* 1:24,000; or *Fishlake National Forest; Fillmore, Richfield, Beaver and Loa Ranger Districts,* 1:126,720; and the book, **Utah Mountaineering Guide**, Kelsey Publishing.

Mt. Peale, La Sal Mountains, Utah, USA

This map shows the southern half of the La Sal Mountains of southeastern Utah. This is the range that dominates the skyline east of Moab. Three of the highest summits are: Mellenthin, 3855 meters; Tukuhnikivatz, 3805; Peale at 3877, the highest in the La Sals, and South Mountain, 3596 meters. There are also several other high peaks in the northern half of the range. Most of the higher summits in these mountain are made of fine-grained diorite porphyry belonging to a Tertiary intrusion.

The best access to these peaks is via the La Sal Mountains Loop Road. To get on it, drive south out of Moab on Highway 191. In the southeastern end of Moab Valley, look for the junction and turnoff to the left very near mile post 118. This is the paved La Sal Mountains Loop Road, which circles up and along the western slope of the La Sals. You can get to the northern end of this Loop by driving north out of Moab, east along the Colorado River and Highway 128, then south from between mile posts 15 &16 into Castle Valley. In the southern end of that valley, turn right onto the Loop Road.

Once on the Loop, and with a better map than this, make your way to the Geyser Pass Road. About one km beyond the cross-country skiers winter parking place, turn right or south and use an old driller's road to reach Gold Basin, a distance of about 2 kms. This is probably the best place to park to climb all the highest peaks in this part of the range. Under normal conditions, any car can be driven nearly to Geyser Pass. For those with low-clearance cars, a mtn. bike might help you avoid some rough roads, or road-walking

To get to the south end of the range, drive south out of Moab until you reach La Sal Junction then head east on Highway 46 in the direction of Slickrock, Colorado. About 8 kms east of the small settlement of La Sal, look for the sign pointing out the road leading to forest lands and La Sal Pass. The La Sal Creek Road gives access to South Mountain and the southern slopes of Mt. Peale, but it's likely to be too rough for the average car.

From the end of the road in Gold Basin, head south up a prominent ridge toward **Tukuhnikivatz**. You can then return the same way; or ridge-walk east to **Peale**. You could then head north and climb Mellenthin on the same climb, if you're up to it. It's about 5 or 6 kms from Gold Basin to Peale, and will take 2 to 3 hours up; 4 to 6 hours round-trip, maybe longer for some. You could also do a similar climb from about the halfway point on the Gold Basin Road. To climb only **Mellenthin**, begin from, or near, Geyser Pass. See these routes on the map.

From or near La Sal Pass, you can simply route-find north up the south slope of Peale, and perhaps come down the south ridge of Tukuhnikivatz to the pass. From the pass, you could ridge-walk south to **South Mountain**.

The La Sal Mountains Loop Road is now plowed of snow throughout the winter. Also, the Geyser Pass Road is plowed up to a parking place for cross-country skiers at about 2950 meters, as shown. For winter climbing this is the only route to take. The author has climbed

Looking west from the summit of Mt. Peale to Tukuhnikivatz on the far left.

Map 439-1, Mt. Peale, La Sal Mountains, Utah, USA

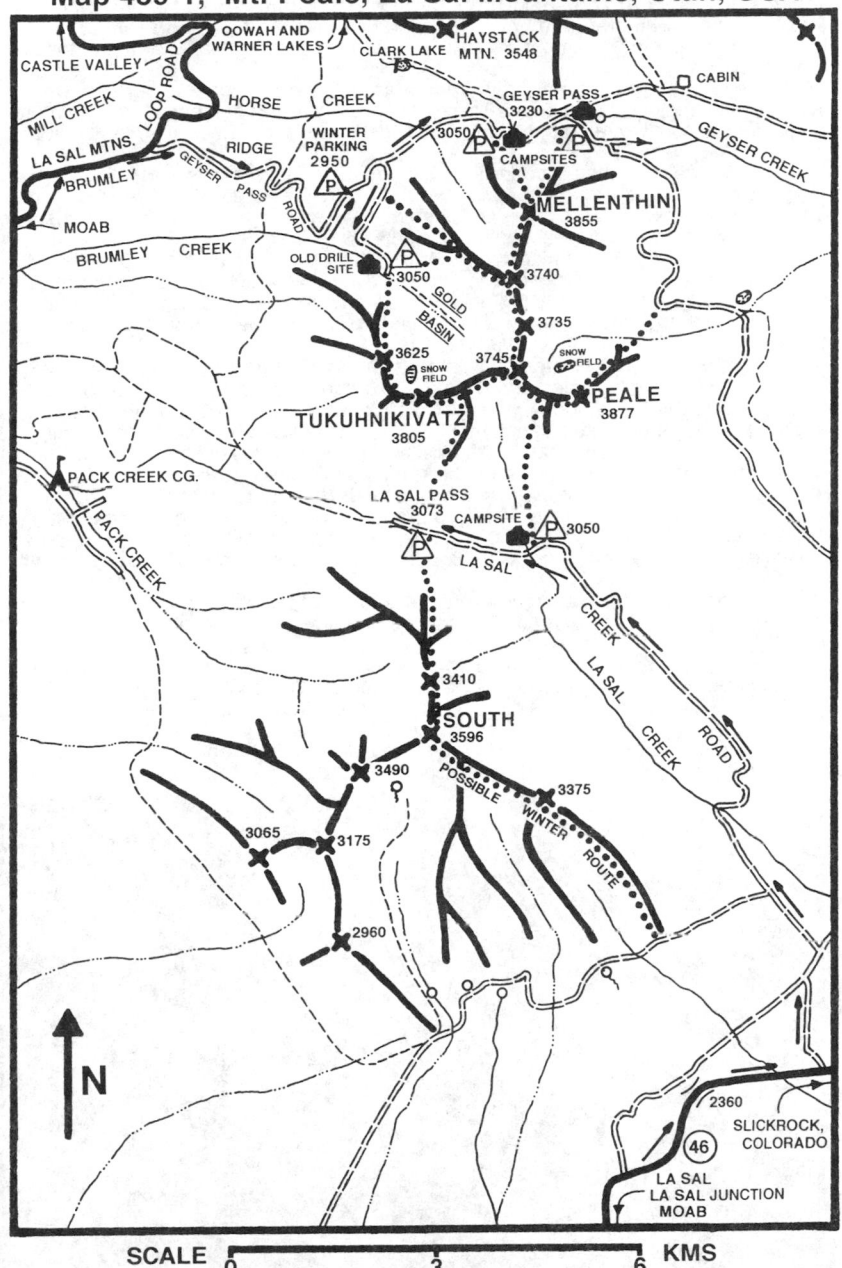

SCALE 0 3 6 KMS

here several times, in summer & winter. Water isn't always convenient so take plenty in your car and in your pack.

Maps USGS maps *Moab & La Sal,* 1:100,000; or *Warner Lake, Mt. Waas, Mt. Tukuhnikivatz & Mt. Peale,* 1:24,000; and books, **Utah Mountaineering Guide**, Kelsey Publishing; or **La Sal Mountains**, Canyon Country Publications, Moab.

Mt. Humphreys, San Francisco Mountains, Arizona, USA

The highest peak in Arizona is Mt. Humphreys at 3862 meters. Humphreys is located immediately north of Flagstaff and not too far southeast of the the South Rim of the Grand Canyon in northern Arizona. Humphreys and other nearby peaks together form the tops of the San Francisco Mountains.

Humphreys is the highest point on the rim of an old late Pleistocene volcano which still retains a little of its original conal shape. There are several other more recent or newer cones in the area, namely Sunset Crater to the east. That cinder cone last erupted in 1065 AD, according to dendrochronology data.

Access is very easy to these mountains, especially to Humphreys and Mt. Agassiz, the second highest peak in the group at 3766 meters. The easiest and normal way there starts in Flagstaff. While there buy any groceries first, then perhaps stop at the Coconino National Forest HQ. office at 2323 East, Greenlaw Lane, Flagstaff, 86004, Tele. 520-527-3600; or call the Peaks Ranger Station on the east end of Flagstaff near the Eldon Peak Trailhead at 520-526-0866.

From the west end of Flagstaff, look for US Highway 180 which heads in a northwesterly direction signposted for the Snow Bowl and Grand Canyon. About 12 kms out of Flag, you'll come to the turnoff to the Snow Bowl Ski Lodge and **Mt. Humphreys**. From the turnoff north to the ski resort is another 12 kms on a paved road.

The Snow Bowl Lodge & Ski Resort is located on the western slopes of **Agassiz** at 2927 meters altitude. The lodge is open year-round and serves meals and snack-type food. Just before you arrive at the lodge, look for a sign pointing the way to the trailhead parking. From there you have a choice of 3 ways up the mountain. First, you can ride the gondola or lift which runs year-round; or you can hike east up the trail which more or less follows the lift. From the top of the ski lift, continue east up a trail to the summit of Agassiz. From there, turn north and ridge-walk along a good trail all the way to the summit of Mt. Humphreys. As you climb, notice the trees as you approach timberline. These are bristlecone pines. In other parts of the west, these trees have been found to be 4900 years old (see Wheeler Peak, Map 407, page 873). The author climbed Humphreys on 9/30/1978, but didn't record the time. Probably 3 or 4 hours round-trip (?).

As this book goes to press, someone wrote the author stating there was a newer trail leaving from near the lodge and zig zagging up through the forest more or less direct to the summit of Humphreys. This is now the best way, but it's not shown on this map.

There's another possible route beginning near some water storage tanks (small livestock reservoirs) southeast of the high peaks, but there's some private land and a maze of 4WD roads in the area, so finding the trail may be difficult. From those water reservoirs, a trail leads up over Fremont Pass and eventually to the top of Humphreys.

If you're planning any long hikes or overnight backpacking, keep in mind there is no live water or streams on the mountain, only a few springs in the Inner Basin, which is inside the old

Looking east up toward Mt. Agassis from the lower ski runs near the Snow Bowl Lodge.

Map 440-1, Mt. Humphreys, San Francisco Mtns., Arizona, USA

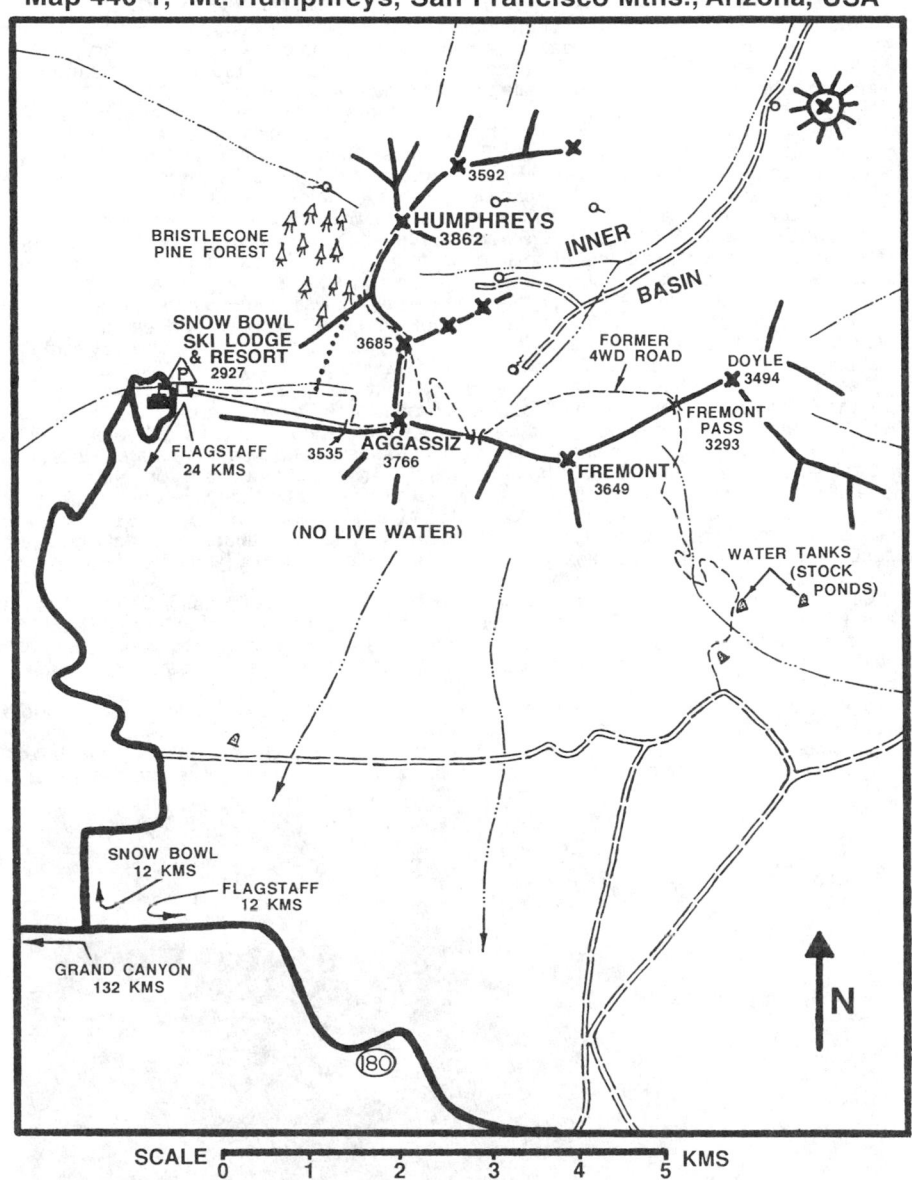

caldera. Humphreys is in a dry region, but heavy rains come at times in July, August and September; and sometimes heavy snows fall in winter. For warm weather hiking make the climb during the months of June through October. Winter climbing should be very enjoyable, because of the easy year-round access. March would be the best month for winter ascents.

Maps *Coconino National Forest,* 1:126,720, from the Peaks Ranger Station, east Flagstaff; or USGS maps *Humphreys Peak,* 1:24,000; or *Flagstaff,* 1:100,000; and perhaps the book, **100 Hikes In Arizona**, The Mountaineers.

Truchas Peak, Sangre de Cristo Mountains, New Mexico, USA

Truchas at 3995 meters, is the 2nd highest summit in New Mexico, and the highest in the Pecos Wilderness Area. Truchas Peak is near the southern end of the Sangre de Cristo Range, which extends south from central Colorado. These mountains are folded and uplifted and composed of many rock types, from granite to sandstone and quartzite.

These peaks are typical of all the central and southern Rockies; mostly dome-shaped summits, with old & small glacier cirques with rugged north faces which make easy climbs.

There are 3 ways to get into the Pecos Wilderness. One way is from Santa Fe; drive from the downtown area northeast on State Road 475 toward the Santa Fe Ski Basin. You really can't get to Truchas from there, but you can climb **Santa Fe Baldy** at 3848 meters.

The second way to the heart of the wilderness and to **Truchas** is to drive east from Santa Fe on Interstate Highway 25; or west on I-25 from Las Vegas (New Mexico). Leave the freeway on State Road 63 and drive north to and beyond the small town of Pecos. Right at the end of that paved road is Jacks Creek Campground which is about 30 kms due north of Pecos. You could also start at the Panchuela CG. From either of these places, walk north on a trail in the direction of Truchas. Once on the east side of the peak, route-find west up the east ridge to the summit. This hike is about 18 kms one-way, or 36 kms round-trip. A little long for a one day climb for most people, but it can be done. Most people would want to do this in 2 days.

The 3rd way to Truchas is the shortest and apparently the most-used route. This is the route from the northeast and the pueblo of Truchas. From Santa Fe head north toward Española, then turn northeast on State Road 76 going to Peñasco, but stop in Truchas just before the Rio de Truchas. To use the road along the Rio de Truchas, stop and locate the store *Los Sietes,* and ask someone for permission to drive across the Truchas Land Grant (private property). Hopefully there will be a sign pointing out the way (But don't bet on it!). Once you find the right road drive 10 or 11 kms southeast on a poor dirt road, which follows Truchas Creek. There are many good camping sites along this creek. This same 4WD road continues to the national forest boundary, where a good trail begins and follows Quemado Creek to a large cirque basin, then south to Truchas.

Or to avoid the hassle of private land, and with a Carson or Santa Fe National Forest map in hand, turn south off Highway 76 at State Road 4, and after 2 kms turn east on Forest Road 306 and drive 18 kms to the Borrego Mesa Campground. Park cars there, then walk or use a 4WD going up to the wilderness boundary, then follow Trail 153 to the base of the mountain and route-find to the top.

Most hikers can make this climb in one day, but many do it on a weekend. The author did this hike from along the Rio de Truchas on 10/2/1978; 3 hours up, 5 hours round-trip.

Truchas Village has stores, gas stations, garages and a Forest Service guard station, but it's only a work shop and seldom open or used. Good weather is common, with late summer and

From the top of Truches Peak looking north along the summit ridge.

Map 441-1, Truchas, Sangre de Cristo Mtns., New Mexico, USA

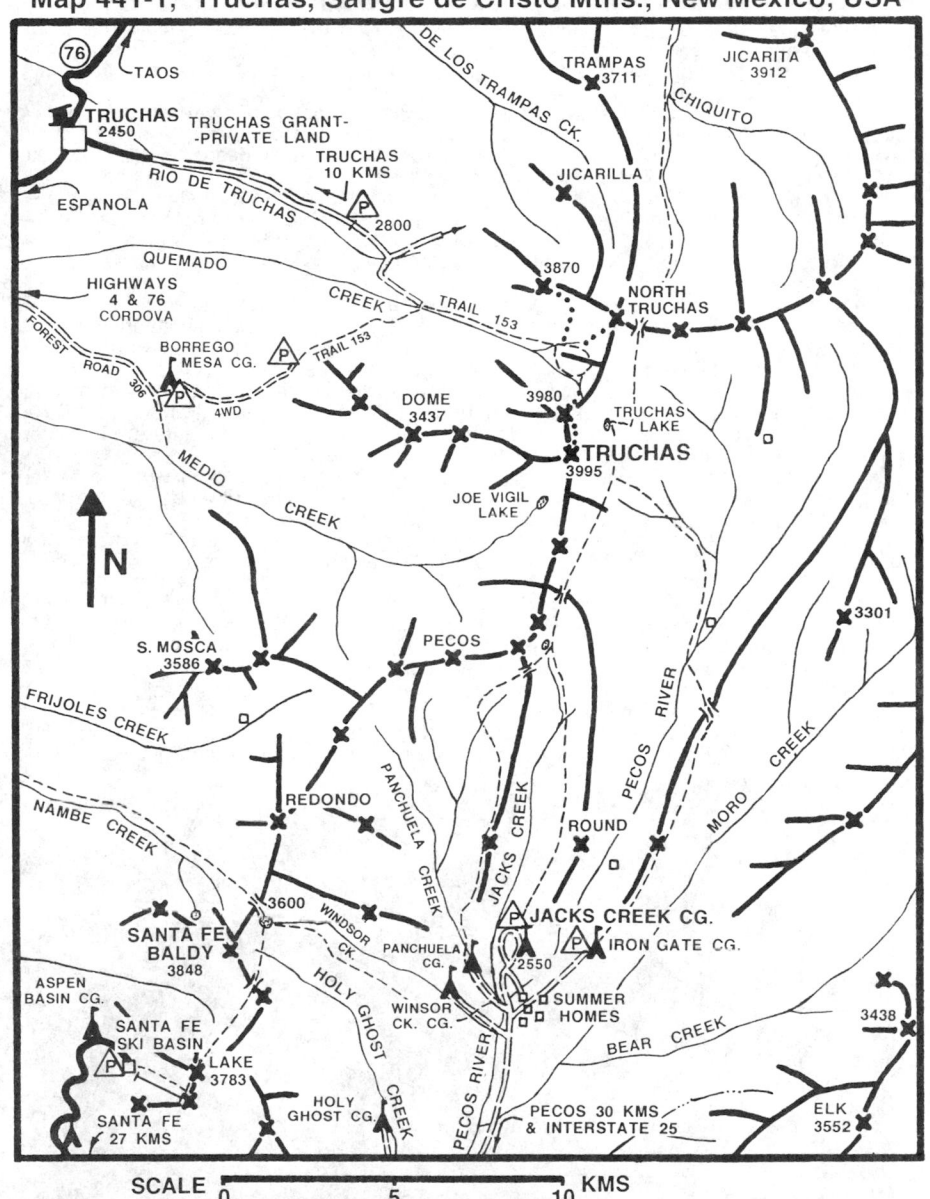

SCALE 0 ___ 5 ___ 10 KMS

December and January being the months of heaviest precipitation.

For more information and maps of this area stop at the Santa Fe National Forest Headquarters in Santa Fe, Tele. 505-438-7840; or head north to Española and the district office there, Tele. 505-753-7331. Or if using the southern approach stop at Pecos District Ranger Station, Tele. 505-757-6121.

Maps *Santa Fe National Forest*, 1:126,720; or USGS maps *Truchas, El Valle, Truchas Peak, Cowles,* 1:24,000; or *Santa Fe & Taos,* 1:100,000; and the book, **New Mexico's Wilderness Areas.**

Wheeler Peak, Sangre de Cristo Mountains, New Mexico, USA

Wheeler Peak at 4012 meters is the highest mountain in New Mexico. It's located near the southern end of the Sangre de Cristo Range and just south of the Taos Ski Bowl. Wheeler Peak and the ski resort are both northeast of Taos. The rocks in these parts seem to be mostly quartzite or other metamorphics.

By far the least-complicated way to **Wheeler Peak** is first make your way to northern New Mexico and to the small city of Taos. From there head north out of town on Highway 3 for about 7 kms, then veer right and head for Arroyo Seco. From Arroyo Seco, head northeast on State Road 150 for about 16 kms. There at the end of the paved road will be the Taos ski area.

From the ski resort parking lot, or the Twining Campground, one route first heads northeast towards the Bull-of-the-Woods Pasture and the pass at 3400 meters; then it doubles back to the south and runs along the prominent ridge all the way to Wheeler Peak. This is one of the longer routes, but you'll have some fine views all the way along the ridge. Take plenty of water, there's none up high.

The shortest route from the Taos ski resort is on a trail that used to cross private land, but apparently it's not the problem it used to be as of 2000 (?). From behind the restaurant and the general parking lot at the ski resort, there are signs pointing out the trail which runs south up along the west side of Lake Fork Creek. Halfway up, you'll cross the creek. The trail ends at Williams Lake. From this lake, at 3350 meters, you can climb (no trails) Wheeler or a number of peaks which range up to 4000 meters. Timberline here is rather high at about 3650-3700 meters (the highest trees the author has seen are in Peru at about 4580 meters). In winter, access would be good to the ski resort, so you can climb any time.

Once the author camped at the Twining Campground. Next morning, 10/3/1978, he walked up to Bull-of-the-Woods Pasture, then south to Wheeler and down via Williams Lake. He didn't record his hike-time but it must have been about 5 or 6 hours round-trip (?).

Another way to get to Wheeler is to drive north from Taos on Highway 3 to the town of Questa, where you'll find the District Ranger Station. There you can buy maps and get the latest information (Tele. 505-586-0520). From there head east to the town of Red River, then south up along the Red River to the end of the paved road. From the Middle Fork Trailhead, you'll find a trail going up Middle Fork then south and west to the summit via Horseshoe Lake, as shown. Or with a 4WD, you might use the road going up the East Fork of Red River.

Good weather is never far away, but in July, August and early September some heavy showers can be expected. In winter, December and January have more precipitation than other winter months.

For more information, call or visit the Carson National Forest Ranger Station in Taos, Tele. 505-758-6200, or in Questa. Forest Service maps are available at these 2 locations. Some food

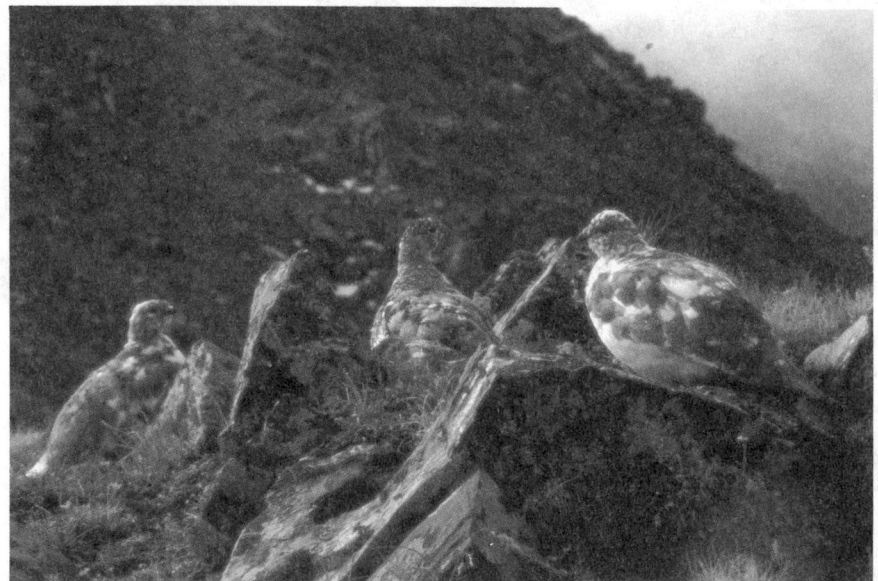

At the summit of Wheeler Peak the author was able to touch these ptarmigans.

Map 442-1, Wheeler, Sangre de Cristo Mtns., New Mexico, USA

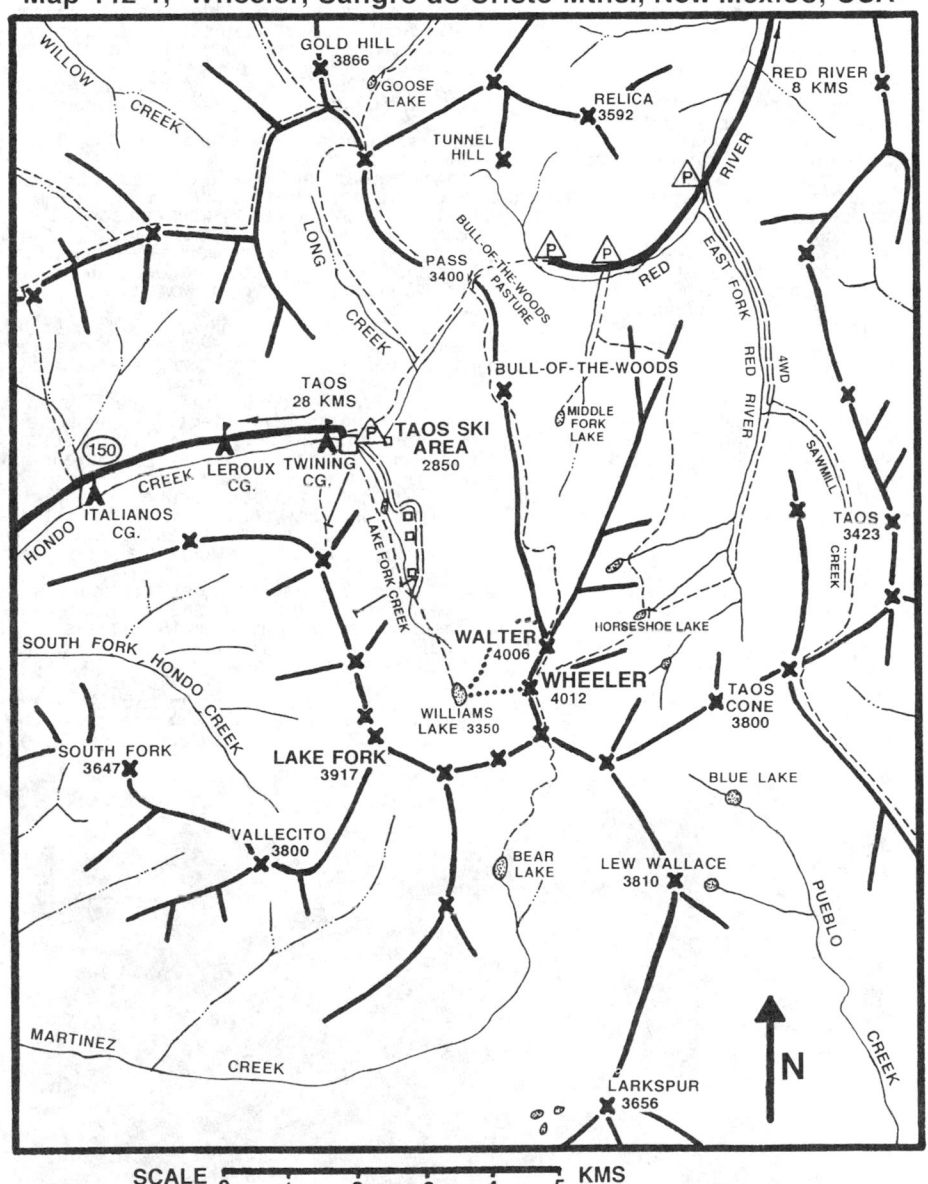

GOLD HILL 3866

GOOSE LAKE

RELICA 3592

RED RIVER 8 KMS

TUNNEL HILL

WILLOW CREEK

LONG CREEK

PASS 3400

BULL-OF-THE-WOODS PASTURE

RED RIVER

EAST FORK RED RIVER

4WD

SAWMILL

TAOS 28 KMS

TAOS SKI AREA 2850

BULL-OF-THE-WOODS

MIDDLE FORK LAKE

150

LEROUX CG.

TWINING CG.

CREEK

ITALIANOS CG.

HONDO

LAKE FORK CREEK

TAOS 3423

TAOS CREEK

SOUTH FORK

HONDO CREEK

WALTER 4006

WILLIAMS LAKE 3350

HORSESHOE LAKE

WHEELER 4012

TAOS CONE 3800

SOUTH FORK 3647

LAKE FORK 3917

BLUE LAKE

VALLECITO 3800

BEAR LAKE

LEW WALLACE 3810

PUEBLO CREEK

MARTINEZ

CREEK

LARKSPUR 3656

N

SCALE 0 1 2 3 4 5 KMS

and some supplies can be found at the ski village, or better still in Taos or Questa.
Maps *Carson National Forest,* 1:126,720; or the USGS maps *Wheeler Peak,* 1:24,000; or
Wheeler Peak, 1:100,000; or maybe the books, **75 Hikes In New Mexico,** The Mountaineers; or
New Mexico's Wilderness Areas.

Windom, Eolus & Sunlight Peaks, Needle Mountains, Colorado, USA

Included on this map are 3 of Colorado's 14'ers. This small group of high summits is in the Needle Mountains, which are part of the greater San Juan Range in southwest Colorado. They're located about 40 kms northeast of Durango, which is the largest city in the region; and at the western edge of the Weminuche Wilderness Area. The highest peak is Windom at 4295 meters, followed closely by Eolus, 4294, and Sunlight, 4286 meters. These elevations vary according to which survey you read. Remember, a 14,000 foot mountain, of which Colorado has 55 at last count, is equal to 4268 meters.

The Needles Range is composed of different rock types. The western parts have Eolus Granite, while other places have slate, conglomerate and quartzite.

These peaks are part of one of the more isolated groups of 14'ers in Colorado. If you're coming from the south, drive north from Durango on Highway 550 in the direction of Ouray and Montrose, but stop at the Purgatory Campground and look for the nearby trailhead parking. Or you can come from the north on the same Highway 550. Purgatory is the most popular starting point. Another popular place to start hiking is a little ways north of the Vallecito Reservoir. Get there by driving northeast from Durango. Another option in summer, would be to take the steam train between Durango and Silverton and get off at Needleton. This would shorten the hike, but is more complicated and not as convenient for car lovers.

From Purgatory Campground, head east and southeast to the railway bridge over the Animus River, then turn northeast to Needle Creek. Follow Needle Creek southeast & east and eventually into Chicago Basin. Make a camp in the upper end of the basin from where you can climb all 3 peaks.

To give an example of distance, it's normally a one day hike from the trailhead at Purgatory to the Chicago Basin, a distance of about 26 kms. It's normally another day to climb the 3 summits, and a third day to return to Purgatory. Looking at the map, the distance from the Vallecito Trailhead Campground to Chicago Basin seems about the same, but you'll have to go over Columbine Pass at about 3870 meters, which will take a little time and energy.

Once inside the Chicago Basin, **Sunlight** and **Windom** can best be climbed together by walking east from the 2 lakes in the upper basin to the slopes between the peaks, then to both summits. **Eolus** can also be climbed from the same 2 lakes, but head west skirting around the south side of a buttress and up the eastern slope; or head up to North Eolus, then ridge-walk south to the main summit. All routes discussed here are walk-ups.

The author did this trip on 9/30 & 10/1/1980. It took 5 2/3 hours to get to a campsite in Chicago Basin. Next morning, he climbed all 3 peaks in just over 5 hours; then packed up and walked back to Purgatory in just under 6 hours. His total 2-day walk-time was 16 2/3 hours.

July, August and September are the best months for climbing in these parts, but the author has made 2 trips to Colorado at the beginning of October and found the weather very stable and pleasant. But each year is different!

For all 3 routes, it's recommended you begin your journey in Durango. It's a good place to shop and you'll find 2 offices of the San Juan/Rio Grande National Forest located there. The forest headquarters is at 701 Camino Del Rio, Tele. 970-247-4874; or the District Ranger Station

From the summit of Eolus looking east at Sunlight left, Windom on the right.

Map 443-1, Windom, Eolus & Sunlight Peak, Needle Mountains, Colorado, USA

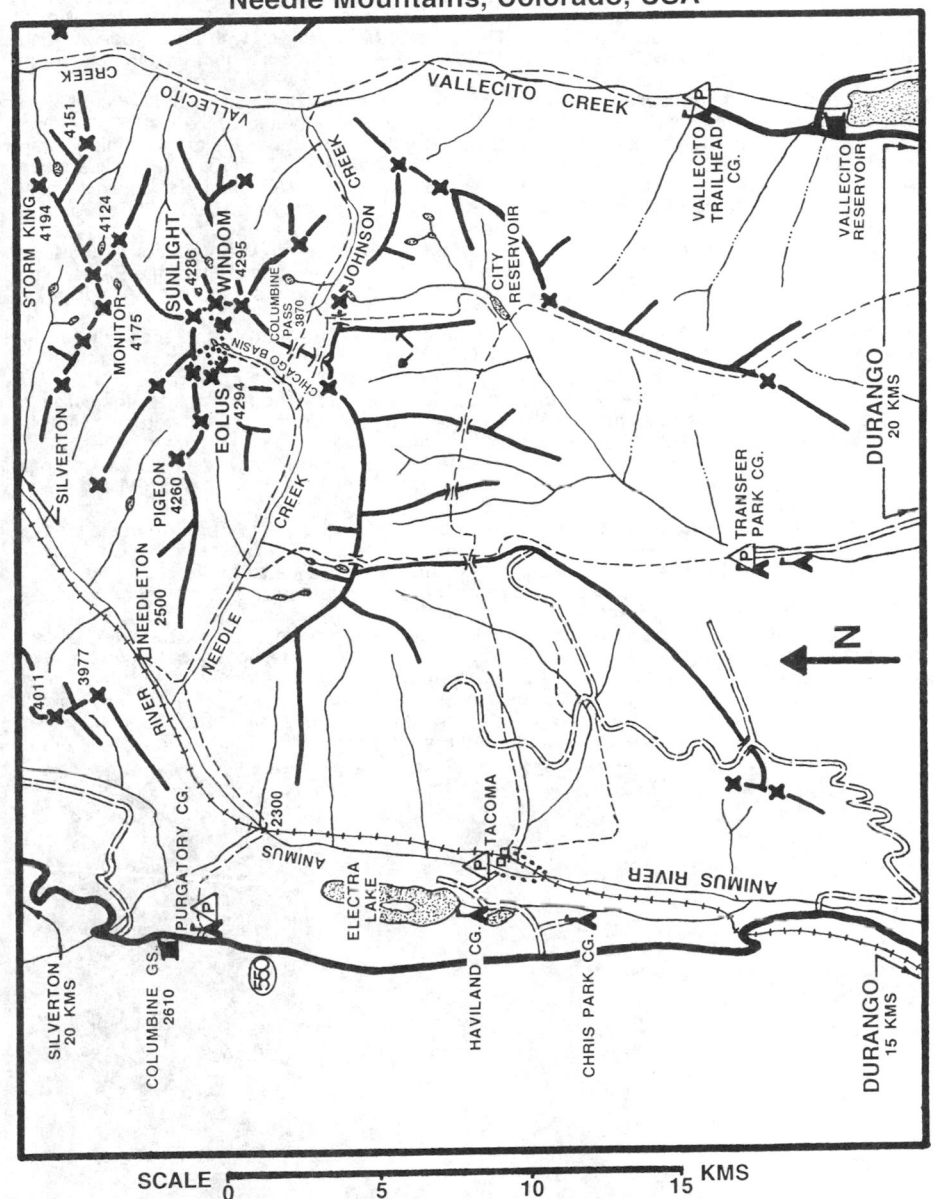

SCALE
0   5   10   15   KMS

at 110 West, 11th Street, Tele. 970-385-1283. The district office is probably the best place of the 2 to get the latest information about road, trail or snow conditions.

Maps *San Juan/Rio Grande National Forest,* 1:126,720; or USGS map *Columbine Pass,* 1:24,000; or the books, **A Climbing Guide to Colorado's Fourteeners,** Pruett Publishing; or **Colorado's Fourteeners: From Hikes to Climbs**, and *Colorado's Fourteeners, Map Package,* both from Fulcrum Publishing.

Wilson Peaks, El Diente & Sneffels, San Miguel Mtns., Colorado, USA

Included on this map are 4 of the 14'ers in Colorado. Three of them: Mt. Wilson, 4343 meters; Wilson Peak, 4273; and El Diente, 4317 meters, are located in the San Miguel Mountains not far southwest of Telluride. The other is Mt. Sneffels, with an altitude of 4313 meters. It's located in the extreme northwest section of the San Juan Mountains and just north of Telluride.

Sneffels can best be reached from the town of Ouray situated on Highway 550. From Ouray drive southwest up Canyon Creek to Camp Bird; that's where the better road ends. From Camp Bird, there's a rougher road heading in a northwesterly direction. It passes an old mining camp called Sneffels, then after another km you'll come to the Yankee Boy Basin Trailhead. Cars can be driven up to that point. From the trailhead, walk along an old mining road to Blue Lakes Pass, then route-find up the south face of Sneffels. The author did this route on 10/2/1980. From his car to the top and back took only 3 1/4 hours--a short easy hike.

Sneffels can be ascended from an east pass or col, as shown on the map; both routes are easy, but each involves some scrambling. Sneffels could also be climbed from the East Dallas Creek Trailhead on the north side of the mountain, but this requires a much longer drive on dusty roads.

To reach the other three 14'ers, drive about 10 kms southeast from Placerville in the direction of Telluride on Highway 145. At an old mill site called Vanadium, turn south at the sign (hopefully) pointing out the way to Silver Pick Basin along the Big Bear Creek Road. After driving 10 or 11 kms you'll come to the trailhead. There are old mining roads above the carpark, but they are no longer used by motor vehicles. This is by far the best route if you only want to climb **Wilson Peak**, but all 3 peaks can be climbed from this trailhead.

From the trailhead, walk another 2 or 3 kms to the old Silver Pick Mill site where you can camp if you like. From the Silver Pick Basin, climb up to a pass, then turn east to Wilson Peak, a distance of about 2 1/2 kms.

To climb **El Diente** and **Mt. Wilson**, walk down into Navajo Basin from the pass west of Wilson Peak, then immediately look for an easy route to the top of El Diente and/or Mt. Wilson. You can take one route straight to the top of Diente, then ridge-walk east to Wilson.

Navajo Basin can also be reached by starting in Doloras and driving northeast on Highway 145. When this highway turns east away from the West Doloras River, you veer left and follow this river up to Dunton and beyond to the Burro Bridge Campground. About 600 meters above the campground, park at the Navajo Lake Trailhead. From there, walk up the trail along the river toward Navajo Lake and Navajo Basin (if camping around Navajo Lake or in the Basin, you must use a stove--no open fires). Once there, you can climb all 3 peaks.

The main towns in the area are Silverton, Ouray, and Telluride. All 3 have plenty of places to buy supplies. For additional information and Forest Service maps of the area, stop at the

Looking west at an old miners shack near the base of Mt. Sneffels to the far right.

Map 444-1, Mt. Wilson, Wilson Peak, El Diente & Sneffels, San Miguel Mountains, Colorado, USA

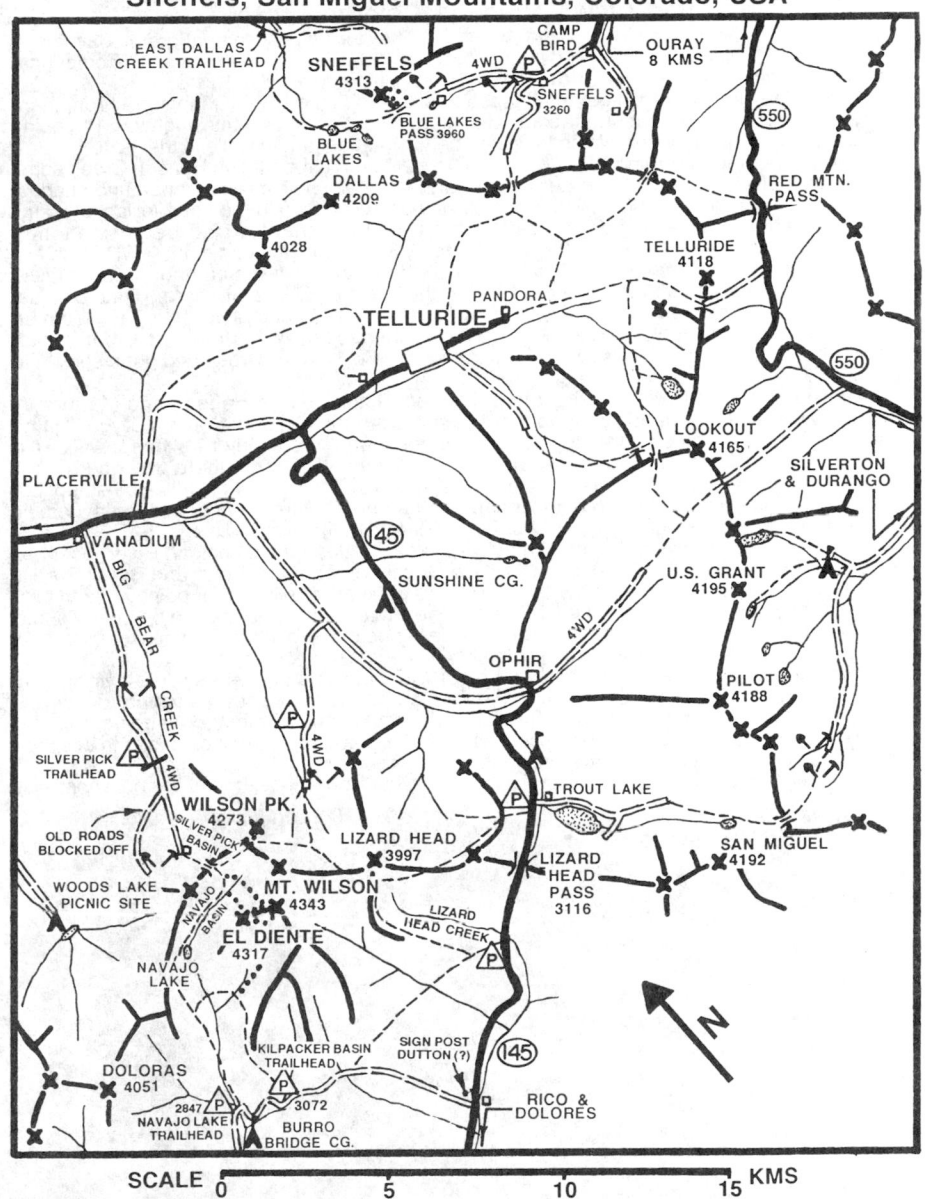

ranger stations at Montrose, Tele. 970-240-5300, located to the north; or Doloras, Tele. 970-882-7296 to the south.

Maps *Uncompahgre National Forest,* 1:126,720; or USGS maps *Mt. Wilson, Dolores Peak, or Mt. Sneffels,* 1:24,000; and the books, **Climbing Guide to Colorado's Fourteeners,** Pruett Publishing; or **Colorado's Fourteeners: From Hikes to Climbs**, and *Colorado's Fourteeners, Map Package*, both from Fulcrum Publishing.

Uncompahgre, Wetterhorn, Handies, Redcloud & Sunshine Peaks, San Juan Mountains, Colorado, USA

Included on this map are 5 of Colorado's 14'ers. They include: Uncompahgre, 4362 meters; Wetterhorn, 4273; Handies, 4283; Redcloud, 4279; and Sunshine, 4268 meters. Uncompahgre is the best known of the group and is the 6th highest in Colorado.

Probably the easiest way to get to all these peaks is to first drive to Gunnison. From there head west on Highway 50, but after about 13 kms, turn southwest on State Highway 149 going to Lake City. This small former mining town can be your headquarters while in the area.

To climb **Uncompahgre** and **Wetterhorn**, drive west from Lake City up Henson Creek about 8 kms to where Nellie Creek comes in from the north. At that junction is a campground at about 2850 meters. From there, a 4WD road winds its way up the canyon to the north for about 5 kms to a 4WD parking place at about 3490 meters. At that point a trail begins reaching Uncompahgre from the south side. The summit is only 3 kms from the end of the 4WD road.

This is what the author did on 10/3/1980. He left his camp at the campground on lower Nellie Creek and walked up the 4WD road and to the summit of Uncompahgre. That took just over 2 1/2 hours. From Uncompahgre, he headed west cross-country over 2 ridges (see map and follow the route symbols) and climbed up the south ridge of Wetterhorn. That part took 2 hours. From Wetterhorn, he walked down the trail & road to Henson Creek and got a short ride for about 3 kms back to his car. The entire trip took just under 7 hours.

Wetterhorn is usually climbed by itself. It's best reached from Henson and Matterhorn Creeks. With a HCV you can probably get to the main trailhead; with a 4WD you can go beyond the normal trailhead parking, as shown on the map. From either trailhead, walk up a trail, then veer west and climb up the south ridge. On the author's trip, there was no trail, but there's likely one there by now, especially near the summit. The summit pitch is a bit steep, but still easy. Strong climbers can do both Uncompahgre and Wetterhorn in one long day, as did the author, but a car or a mountain bike shuttle would shorten the climb a little.

To reach the other 14'ers, drive south out of Lake City along the Gunnison River, past Mill Creek Campground about 9 or 10 kms to where Grizzly Gulch, Lake Fork, and Silver Creeks meet. That's at 3170 meters and may take a HCV to get that far. From that point you can hike up Grizzly Gulch to the top of **Handies**, but this is the longer way. Best to drive up Lake Fork to a regular trailhead or 4WD parking place on the west side of the peak, then walk south to near the head of the basin, and finally up the south side of the peak.

There's a trail up Silver Creek and by now a trails-of-sorts shown as route symbols up **Redcloud** from the north & east which is the easiest; or up the west face which is steeper. **Sunshine** is normally climbed along with Redcloud, with the final summit route being from the north as shown. You can walk the ridge between these 2 peaks, but it may be easier to descend from one peak to the upper basin, then climb the other mountains.

Lake City has several small stores and gas stations, but for better selections do your shopping in

Near the trailhead at 3490 meters, looking west at Uncompahgre Peak.

Map 445-1, Uncompahgre, Wetterhorn, Handies, Redcloud & Sunshine, San Juan Mountains, Colorado, USA

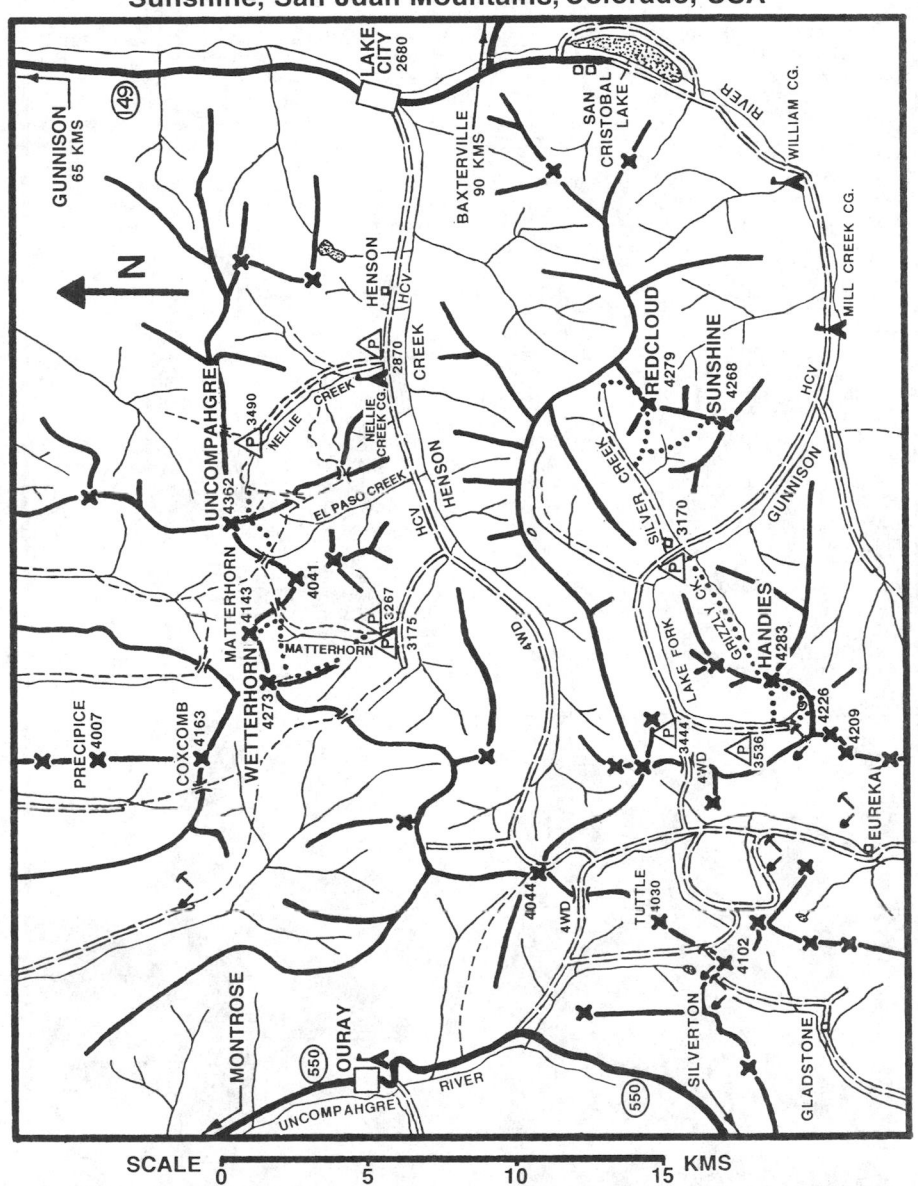

SCALE 0 5 10 15 KMS

Gunnison or some larger place before arriving in the area. There are ranger stations in both Gunnison, Tele. 970-641-0471, and Montrose, Tele. 970-240-5300 where Forest Service maps can be found.

Maps *Uncompahgre National Forest,* 1:126,720; or USGS maps *Uncompahgre Peak, Redcloud Peak, Wetterhorn Peak,* 1:24,000; and the books, **Climbing Guide to Colorado's Fourteeners**, Pruett Publishing; or **Colorado's Fourteeners: From Hikes to Climbs**, and *Colorado's Fourteeners, Map Package,* both from Fulcrum Publishing.

San Luis Peak, San Juan Mountains, Colorado, USA

The 50th ranking peak in the state of Colorado is San Luis, listed at 4272 meters. At present this is the only 14'er on this map. However, before some of the more recent surveys were taken, another nearby peak was listed as one of the 53 highest in the state. That's **Stewart Peak**, now set at 4263 meters. The author can't remember what kind of rocks were in the area, but it's likely they are some kind of metamorphics (?).

San Luis is one of the more isolated of the 14'ers. There are some rough roads surrounding the peak, but they are very much for 4WD vehicles. There are no sizable towns or cities in the immediate vicinity; however, there is the small mining community of Creede located just to the south.

One of the more normal routes to **San Luis** is via Gunnison, then Powderhorn, and south to the small community known as Cathedral. From there follow the 4WD road up Spring Creek to where the road ends--or where you must park your vehicle--then continue up the trail to a point west of the peak. Any place on the western front can be used for the ascent.

A second route of approach is from the northeast and the Upper Dome Reservoir, located between Gunnison and Saguache. You'll need a Rio Grande National Forest map to use this route. From the south end of the reservoir, look for Forest Road 794 heading southwest. Near the end of that road, and about 25 kms from the lake, you'll come to Stewart Creek (or possibly drive a little further on to Cochetopa Creek). From the trailhead shown, walk southwest and climb either Stewart, Baldy Alto, or San Luis Peak. Stewart Creek seems to be the more normal route from that side of the mountain. There appears to be no problem in crossing private land on this route, as is the case on some other high peaks in Colorado.

A third approach route, and one used by the author, is the one south of the peak and from the direction of Creede. This small town is on Highway 149 about halfway between Alamosa to the southeast, and Gunnison on the north. To climb **San Luis Peak** from Creede, drive up the Bachelor Road, first west and then north, out of town. Any vehicle can make this trip, at least to the old Equity Mine. Some people might want to park their cars at the mine, or the beaver ponds just to the south marked 3350 meters.

From the Equity Mine, walk or drive up the 4WD road along Willow Creek. This rough track gradually fades away into a trail at the pass shown. Then the trail heads in an easterly direction, crossing a 2nd pass before reaching the south ridge of San Luis. From that pass at 3850 meters, ridge-walk north to the summit. This is an easy one day walk from the mine.

Here's what the author did. He camped one night near the Equity Mine, then the next morning, 10/4/1980, he did the climb just described and returned to his car before noon, or just over 5 hours round-trip.

There's a guard station in Creede but it isn't manned very often, so for more information

San Luis Mountain is an uninspiring peak, but it's over 4268 meters.

Map 446-1, San Luis, San Juan Mountains, Colorado, USA

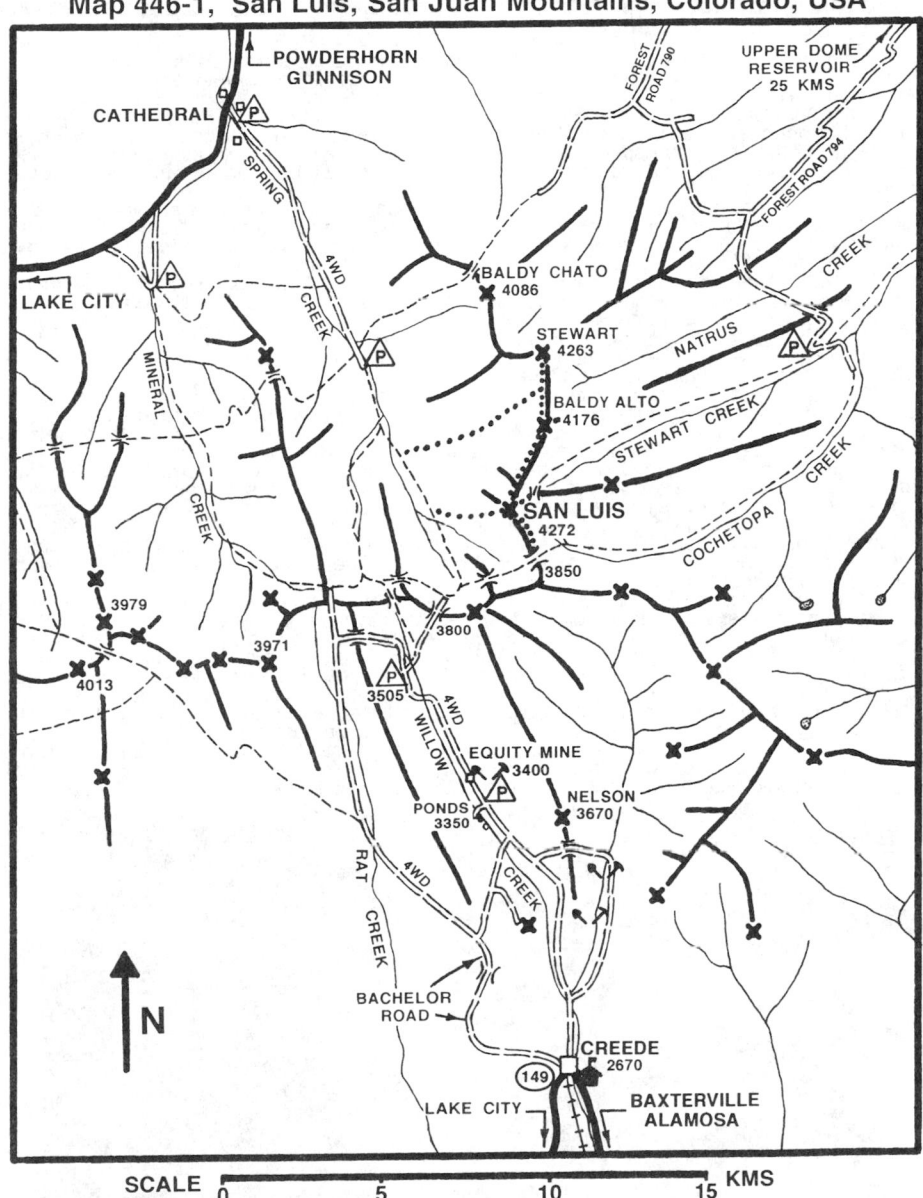

SCALE

0   5   10   15   KMS

contact the Gunnison National Forest Ranger Station in Gunnison at 970-641-0471; or possibly the Rio Grand National Forest office in Saguache at 719-655-2547. Both offices have information centers where you can get updates on routes & roads and buy maps.

Maps *Gunnison* or *Rio Grande National Forest,* 1:126,720; or USGS maps *San Luis Peak & Creede,* 1:24,000; and the books, **Climbing Guide to Colorado's Fourteeners,** Pruett Publishing; or **Colorado's Fourteeners: From Hikes to Climbs**, and *Colorado's Fourteeners, Map Package,* both from Fulcrum Publishing.

Capitol, Snowmass, North Maroon, Maroon, Pyramid, and Castle Peaks, Elk Mountains, Colorado, USA

In the area just south and southwest of Aspen--possibly Colorado's most-famous ski resort-- are found 6 of the state's 14'ers. These 6 summits form the highest portion of the Elk Mountains. The 14'ers are: Castle, the highest at 4349 meters; then Maroon, 4316; followed by Capitol, 4308; Snowmass, 4296; Pyramid, 4275; and North Maroon at 4272 meters. All are within the boundaries of the White River National Forest and the Maroon Bells-Snowmass Wilderness Area. None of Aspen's ski slopes are close to the high peaks, instead are confined to the lower slopes just above town. The rocks here consist of horizontal beds of mostly limestone and shale.

You can get to this general area from the east via Leadville; or the west via Glenwood Springs and Interstate 70--and Marble & Carbondale; and from the south, via Gunnison, Crested Butte and Gothic. Locally, these peaks are in 4 groups and all can be approached by way of 3 main roads from Aspen which is the recommended place to begin.

To climb **Castle Peak**, drive south from the western part of Aspen along Castle Creek to the end of the paved road, a distance of about 20 kms. Then walk, or drive a 4WD, up a rough track to just beyond the Montezuma Mine. From there, climb southwest into a basin, then southwest to a ridgetop, and south to the highest summit. (Some literature counts a north peak of Castle as one of the 14'ers. It's called Conundrum Peak at 4286). The author climbed Castle Peak on 10/9/1980, but didn't record the time it took.

The Maroons (or Maroon Bells as older literature seems to call them) and Pyramid can best be reached from the end of the surfaced road running southwest out of Aspen along Maroon Creek to the Maroon Lake CG. *In summer there are restrictions on driving this road,* so call ahead or go to the ranger station in Aspen to inquire. Call them at 970-925-3445.

To climb **North Maroon**, walk southwest up the trail to Crater Lake, turn right at the trail junction, then after half a km, veer left and route-find south, then west up the east ridge to the top. To climb **Maroon**, continue south past Crater Lake on a good trail to a point southeast of Maroon, then route-find west up the east face and finally ridge-climb north to the summit. To climb **Pyramid**, start again at Maroon Lake, walk up the trail 1 1/2 kms, then route-find southeast and south up into a cirque basin, then straight east up to the northeast ridge, and finally ridge-climb southwest to the summit.

To reach Capitol and Snowmass, drive northwest out of Aspen about 10 kms, turn southwest and drive past West Village to the end of the road at Snowmass Creek CG. To climb **Capitol**, walk southwest up Snowmass Creek, then up West Snowmass Creek, past Moon Lake and west and south into an upper basin and finally up to the ridge & summit. Using a better map than this, you can also reach Capitol from along Capitol Creek. For **Snowmass**, continue south up Snowmass Creek to Snowmass Lake all on a trail, then climb due west up to the summit. You can also reach Snowmass from Carbondale and Marble and the Crystal Trailhead, but those routes are longer and there's more backroad driving, perhaps with a 4WD (?).

Be aware that these peaks are more difficult than most of the other 14'ers in Colorado. Castle & Snowmass are the easiest, while Pyramid, North Maroon and the last part of Capitol are more difficult. But lots of people do them, so they can't be that technical. To help beginners

The Maroon Bells are some of the most rugged peaks in Colorado.

Map 447-1, Capitol, Snowmass, North Maroon, Maroon, Pyramid & Castle Peaks, Elk Mountains, Colorado, USA

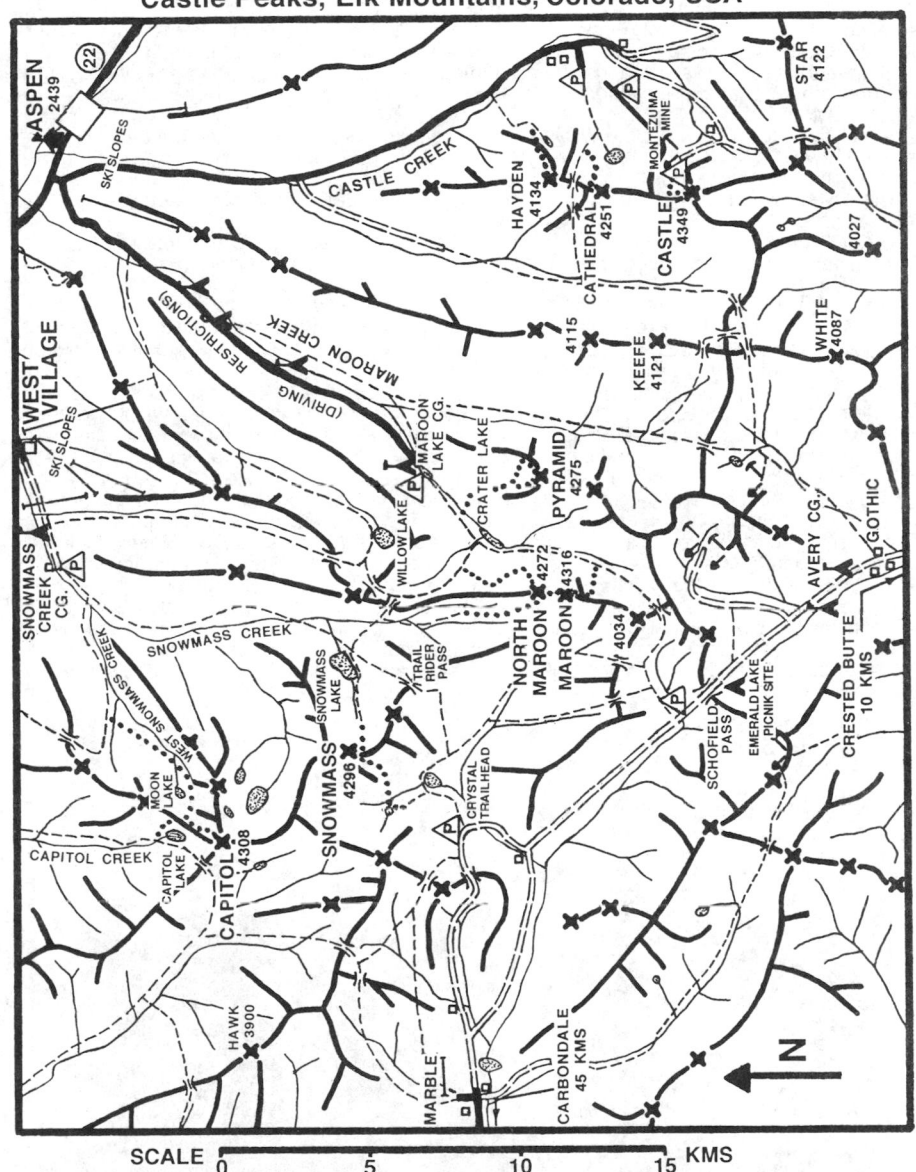

SCALE 0 5 10 15 KMS

in your group, you may want to take a short rope.

Gunnison, Aspen, and Crested Butte all have shopping centers and Forest Service Ranger Stations where the latest information can be found, but the White River National Forest office in Aspen is the closest and best place.

Maps *White River National Forest,* 1:126,720; or USGS maps *Hayden Peak, Maroon Bells; Capitol Peak and Snowmass Mountain,* 1:24,000; and the books, **Climbing Guide to Colorado's Fourteeners,** Pruett Publishing; or **Colorado's Fourteeners: From Hikes to Climbs**, and *Colorado's Fourteeners, Map Package,* both from Fulcrum Publishing.

Mount of the Holy Cross, Sawatch Mountains, Colorado, USA

This map shows one of Colorado's 14'ers; that is, peaks over 14,000 feet or 4268 meters. By some people's count there are 55 peaks in the state over the 4268 meter mark. This summit is called the Mount of the Holy Cross at 4269 meters, and is tentatively ranked at number 52 or 53 in the state, depending on whose list you're reading. Holy Cross is located at the extreme northern end of the Sawatch Range, almost immediately south of Interstate Highway 70 and the Minturn Ranger Station. It's also north of Leadville, and generally northeast of Aspen in the heart of Colorado.

Getting to Holy Cross is quite easy. If you're coming from the south and the Leadville side, take Highway 24 north over Tennessee Pass, to a dirt road about 3 kms north of Gilman. If you're coming from the north and Interstate 70, get off at Exit 171 and Highway 24, a place previously known as Dowde Junction; then drive south about 7 kms to the same dirt road just mentioned.

From Highway 24, drive southwest about 13 kms to the Halfmoon Campground situated at 3200 meters. That road is pretty bad and you'll need a car with a little clearance or you'll scrape bottom.

From the Halfmoon Campground you have a choice of 2 trails and 2 possible routes to the mountain. The normal way to the **top** of **Holy Cross** is to take the trail running west up to the Halfmoon Pass at 3536 meters, then down to Cross Creek at about 3320 meters, and finally up the north ridge to the summit; a very easy climb.

The bad part about this hike is the return trip from Cross Creek back up to the pass. Most people hate that part because they're usually tuckered out! At Cross Creek you'll find an old cabin with a dirt floor, which can be used as an emergency shelter. The author camped near the Halfmoon Campground, then on the morning of 10/9/1980, hurried to the top and back in exactly 4 hours. There are other more interesting routes to the summit as shown on the map.

Holy Cross first became famous because on its east face is a configuration in the shape of a cross. It's a specially shaped gully system and when filled with snow, gives the appearance of a cross. This can be viewed best from the east and from another peak named **Notch Mountain**. In the *notch* itself, is a small shelter (some call it a chapel), which is seen in many fotos. To reach this shelter, take the Notch Mountain Trail south from Halfmoon Campground.

Leadville is the closest town to the area of Holy Cross; therefore, the logical place to do the last minute shopping. Or if you're coming from I-70, then perhaps you should stop in Glennwood Springs on the west, or Denver to the east. Minturn has limited services, but includes the Holy Cross Ranger Station of the White River National Forest, Tele. 970-827-5715. Leadville also has a ranger station for the San Isabel National Forest, where Forest Service maps can be

An early morning foto of Holy Cross from Halfmoon Pass. The normal route is up the north ridge which is on the right.

Map 448-1, Holy Cross, Sawatch Mountains, Colorado, USA

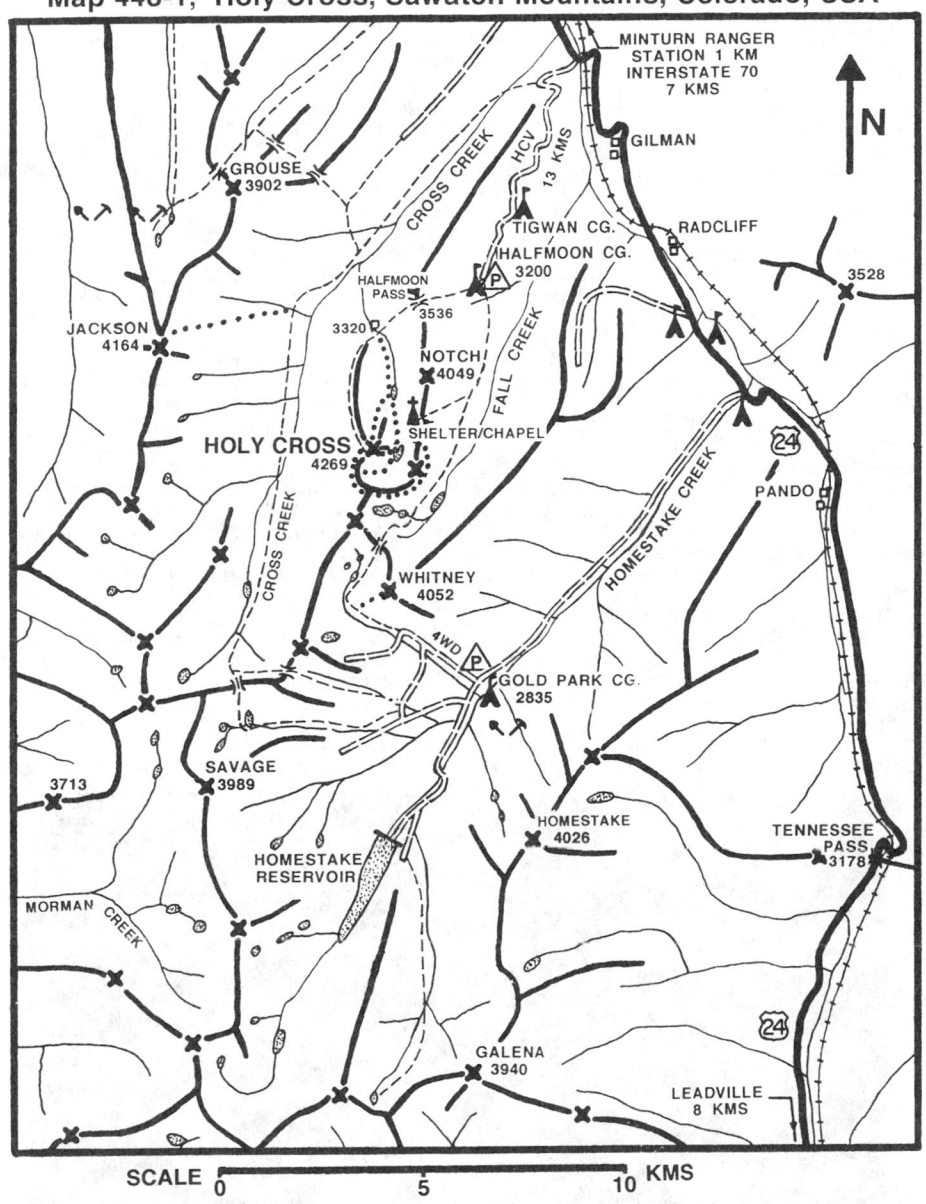

SCALE 0 5 10 KMS

bought. Or call them at 719-486-0749.
Maps *White River National Forest,* 1:126,720; or USGS map *Mount of the Holy Cross,* 1:24,000; and the books, **Climbing Guide to Colorado's Fourteeners,** Pruett Publishing; or **Colorado's Fourteeners: From Hikes to Climbs**, and *Colorado's Fourteeners, Map Package,* both from Fulcrum Publishing.

Massive, Elbert & La Plata, Sawatch Mountains, Colorado, USA

This map includes 3 of the highest summits in Colorado. They include Elbert at 4400 meters, Massive at 4397, and La Plata at 4372 meters. These are the 1st, 2nd and 5th highest peaks in the state. Because they're so near each other, they're often climbed together--but not on the same day. These summits are located in the northern part of the Sawatch Mountains, southwest of Leadville, east of Aspen, and northwest of Buena Vista.

As with the rest of the Sawatch, these peaks are rounded and dome-like, and make easy climbs or hikes. The rock is mostly quartzite, but different rocks are found in various places. North facing cirques and snow basins are almost non-existent here because of the light snowpack in winter. This is because the region is in the middle of a huge mountain mass and by the time clouds get that far, they've run out of moisture.

To climb **Massive**, most people drive west from an electric substation called Malta, then southwest along Halfmoon Creek to just beyond Halfmoon CG. Cars driven with care can make it to the trailhead marked 3063 meters. From there, walk north on the Colorado Trail a short distance, then either use the big southeast ridge route; or continue north for 4 more kms and turn left or west and use the east face trail. You could also walk northwest along a trail beside North Halfmoon Creek and climb Massive from the upper basin. All routes are easy hiking.

To climb **Elbert**, Colorado's highest, you could also begin at the trailhead marked 3063, then hike south on the Colorado Trail. After a couple of kms, veer right and walk up the northeast ridge along a trail. Further south is another trail going up the east face as shown on the map.

Another popular starting point for climbing Elbert, is to drive to Balltown on Highway 24, turn west on State Road 82, pass the Twin Lakes Reservoirs and look for a trailhead on the north side of the road maybe 300 meters east of the Elbert Lodge. This is the Black Cloud Trailhead. The trail heads upcanyon to the southeast ridge, then to the summit. The author climbed Elbert on 10/10/1978. He camped just off the highway along a 4WD road, then headed up the route just described. That was the last climb for the season and he left for home immediately afterwards; unfortunately he didn't keep good notes for that last climb.

You can also continue west to the Echo Canyon Trailhead at the mouth of Echo Canyon at 3048 meters. From there walk up a trail to the Golden Fleese Mine and route-find to the summit of Bull Hill, then ridge-walk to Elbert.

To climb **La Plata**, make your way along Highway 82 west of the Elbert Lodge to the trailhead marked 3079 meters. This starting point is at the beginning of an old 4WD road. After about 600 meters, veer left or east, round the north end of the ridge and walk up along La Plata Creek. About 2/3's the way up the canyon, veer left again and angle up the slope to the ridgetop, then south, southeast to the summit.

Leadville is the largest town in the area, so it's the best place to shop. You might find small stores at Balltown, Twin Lakes and the Elbert Lodge (?). There's a ranger station of the San

Near the head of Black Cloud Canyon is this old miners cabin.

Map 449-1, Massive, Elbert & La Plata, Sawatch Mountains, Colorado, USA

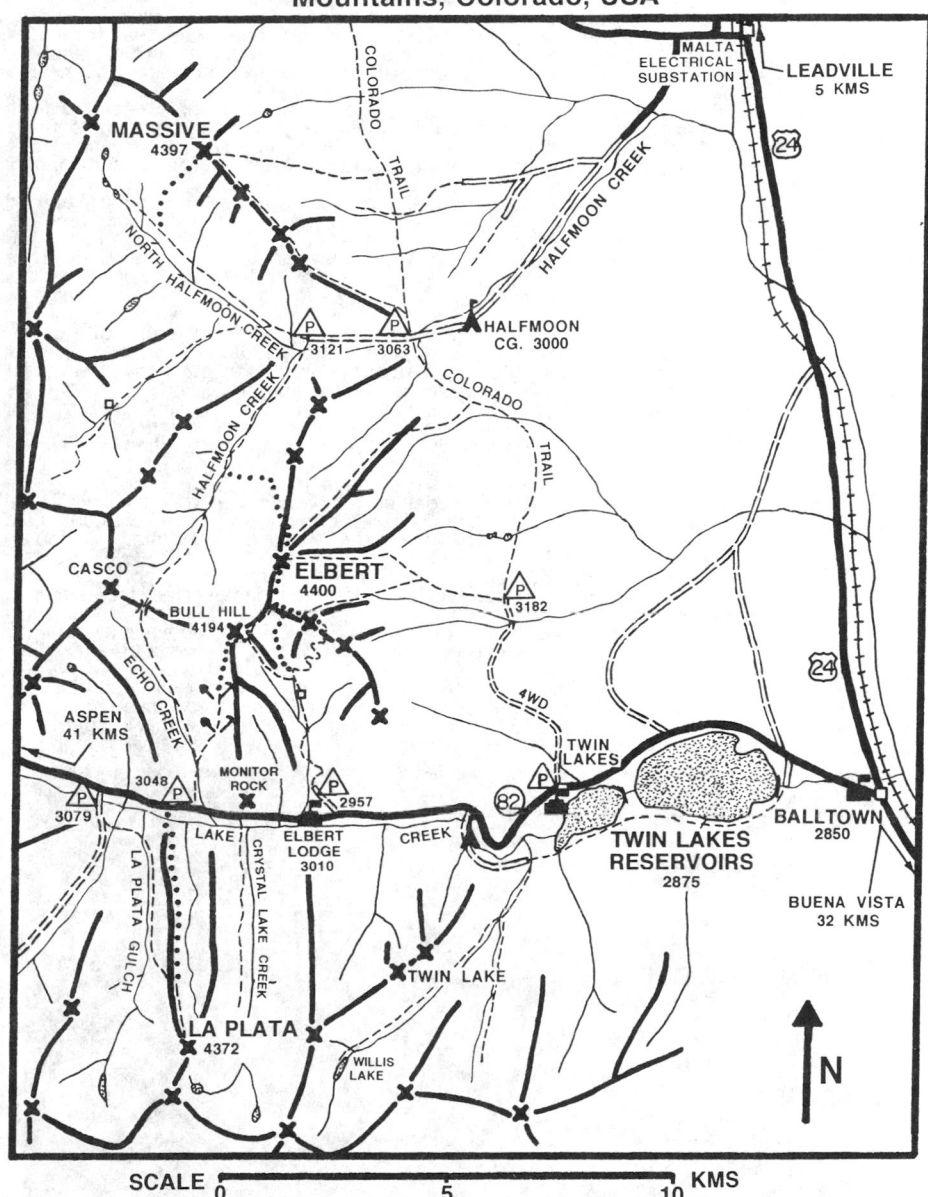

COLORADO TRAIL

MALTA ELECTRICAL SUBSTATION

LEADVILLE
5 KMS

MASSIVE
4397

NORTH HALFMOON CREEK

HALFMOON CREEK

HALFMOON CREEK

P 3121   P 3063

HALFMOON
CG. 3000

COLORADO TRAIL

CASCO

ELBERT
4400

P 3182

BULL HILL
4194

ECHO CREEK

4WD

ASPEN
41 KMS

MONITOR
ROCK

3048   P

TWIN
LAKES

P

3079
3079

LAKE

ELBERT
LODGE
3010

CRYSTAL LAKE CREEK

P 2957

CREEK

82

P

BALLTOWN
2850

TWIN LAKES
RESERVOIRS
2875

BUENA VISTA
32 KMS

LA PLATA GULCH

TWIN LAKE

LA PLATA
4372

WILLIS
LAKE

N

SCALE 0 — 5 — 10 **KMS**

Isabel National Forest in Leadville where you can get the latest information regarding trails or road conditions, or buy better maps than this. Call them at 719-486-0749.
Maps *San Isabel National Forest,* 1:126,720; or USGS map *Mount Elbert* and *Mount Massive,* 1:24,000; and the books, **Climbing Guide to Colorado's Fourteeners,** Pruett Publishing; or **Colorado's Fourteeners: From Hikes to Climbs**, and *Colorado's Fourteeners, Map Package,* both from Fulcrum Publishing.

Huron, Missouri, Belford, Oxford, Harvard, Columbia & Yale, Sawatch Mountains, Colorado, USA

Within Colorado's central Sawatch Mountains is a high area known as the Collegiate Range. The reason for the name is that many of the highest peaks have been named after eastern colleges and universities. Among these peaks is the third highest mountain in Colorado, Mt. Harvard, at 4396 meters. This area is south of Leadville, just northwest of Buena Vista, and west of Highway 24.

This map shows 7 of Colorado's 14'ers. These include: Huron, Missouri, Belford, Oxford, Harvard, Columbia, and Yale. All are reasonably easy to get to, and all are easy to climb. There's hardly a difficult route in the entire area. These rounded summits consist of various rock types, but are mostly quartzite. There are no glaciers and hardly any perpetual snowbanks, even in the north face cirques.

Huron, Missouri, Belford and Oxford are normally climbed from the improved gravel road running west from the Clear Creek Reservoir alongside Clear Creek. This road, good for cars, heads west to the old mining town of Winfield. **Huron** is often climbed from the Lake Fork Trail, but if you have a HCV and/or 4WD, you can drive nearly to Cloyses Lake and save about 6 kms of walking for the round-trip hike. Another way up is to park at Winfield and walk, or drive a 4WD, up Clear Creek about 3 kms, then angle up to the left and zig zag up the west face to a minor basin, then the summit.

To climb **Missouri, Belford** and **Oxford**, the normal starting point is at a site called Vicksburg at 2938 meters, located at the very bottom of Missouri Gulch. From the trailhead, walk south along a trail for about 2 kms, then veer left and route-find up the slope at an angle aiming for **Belford**. Once there, simply ridge-walk east to the summit of **Oxford**. Very easy hike. To reach **Missouri**, continue up Missouri Gulch to the head of the basin, then turn west and climb straight up the slope to the west, then ridge-walk southeast to the summit.

On 10/9/1978, the author walked up Missouri Gulch from his camp. He climbed Missouri via the northwest ridge, then more or less ridge-walked to Belford, and Oxford. On his return, he crossed Belford again and was back at his car in 6 1/3 hours round-trip.

Harvard and **Columbia** are usually climbed together. The recommended route is via North Cottonwood Creek. The best way to get there is to drive west from the north end of Buena Vista and follow the signs into North Cottonwood. From the end of the road at 3011 meters, head up the trail about 5 kms, then veer right and climb up to the ridge, then ridge-walk north to Columbia. From there you can drop down on the east side of the ridge running north and make your way up Harvard; or stay on the trail running north up Horn Fork and eventually route-find up the south ridge of Harvard.

Another possible route to Harvard is the trail running up Pine Creek. You could also park at a trailhead at or near a place called Riverside on Highway 24, and hike west up a trail then route-find to the top of both.

Yale is usually climbed from somewhere along Middle Cottonwood Creek west of Buena Vista. Most climbers park at the mouth of Denny Creek, walk up Denny Creek, then veer northeast and climb the south ridge to the summit. You can also get there from North Cottonwood and the trailhead marked 2865 meters. From there walk southwest along the

From the summit of Oxford looking west to the top of Belford.

Map 450-1, Huron, Missouri, Belford, Oxford, Harvard, Columbia & Yale, Sawatch Mtns, Colorado, USA

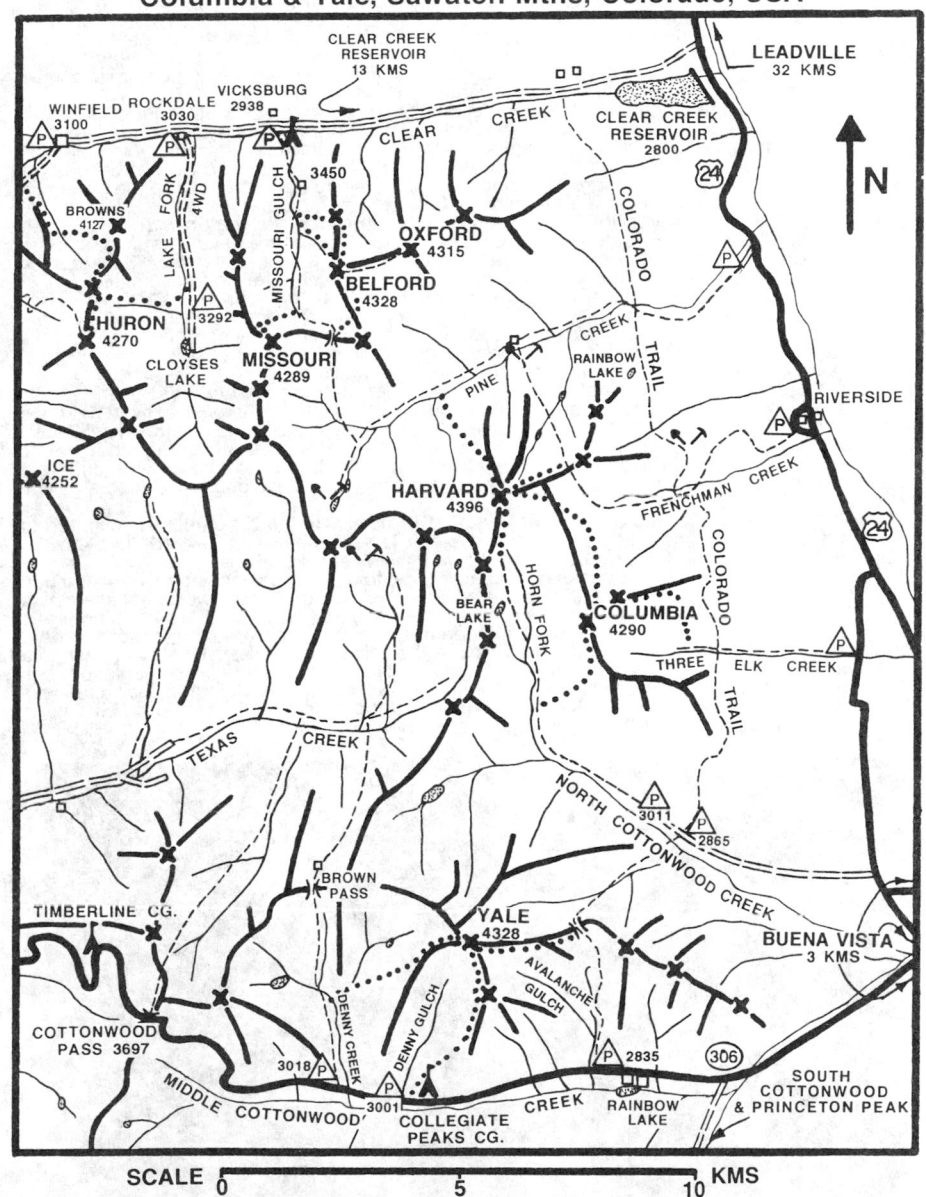

SCALE 0 ——— 5 ——— 10 KMS

Colorado Trail to a pass, then ridge-walk west to Yale.
   For updated information and Forest Service maps stop at the San Isabel Ranger Stations in Leadville, Tele. 719-486-0749; or Salida, which is southeast of this area on Highway 24, Tele. 719-539-3591. Last shopping place is Buena Vista.
Maps *San Isabel National Forest,* 1:126,720; or USGS map *Mount Harvard,* 1:24,000; and the books, **Climbing Guide to Colorado's Fourteeners,** Pruett Publishing; or **Colorado's Fourteeners: From Hikes to Climbs**, and *Colorado's Fourteeners, Map Package,* both from Fulcrum Publishing.

Princeton, Antero, Tabequache & Shavano, Sawatch Mtns., Colo., USA

This map shows the southern Sawatch Mountains and 4 of Colorado's 14'ers. They are, from north to south, Princeton, 4328 meters; Antero, 4350; Tabequache, 4316; and Shavano 4338 meters. One good thing about climbing in this part of the Sawatch is that the area has little private land surrounding the peaks, therefore access is no problem. Most of the land here is part of the San Isabel National Forest with little private land to worry about. If memory is correct, the rocks here seem to be quartzite and other metamorphics.

As with the majority of the mountains in this part of the world, most have rounded summits, with only a few north face cirques. The west winds are very dry when they reach the Sawatch, making the yearly snowfall too light to create any snowfields or glaciers. All climbs are walk-ups.

To climb Princeton, you could drive southwest from Buena Vista, up South Cottonwood Creek to Cottonwood Lake Campground, then walk south along Spruce Creek to the peak. Or, from Princeton's south side, it can be climbed via Grouse Creek, located between Princeton Hot Springs and Alpine. However, the normal route to the summit of **Princeton** is to drive to Mt. Princeton Hot Springs, which is due south of Buena Vista. From there head west past summer homes to the road going up the east face. Cars will have to be parked at about 2713 meters, but 4WD's can go further. From where you park, continue up the track & trail to the summit.

To climb **Antero Peak**, the normal route seems to be via Chalk Creek. Drive west from Princeton Hot Springs to the car-park at 2871 meters and walk from there; or drive a 4WD up to the end of the steep track along Baldwin Creek. From there take a trail southeast to the pass, then ridge-walk north to the summit. Another way for people with cars is to stop at the Cascade Campground at 2749 meters and route-find south to the summit.

To climb **Shavano** and **Tabequache**, the best approach is to drive west from Poncha Springs to Maysville, turn northwest and continue up North Fork of the Arkansas River 10 kms to the Shavano Campground (which doesn't appear on the latest USGS maps--but was still there as of 2000). From this campground, climb due north then northwest up a ridge just west of McCoy Creek. Or you can walk up McCoy Creek on its east side to avoid some cliffs and waterfalls. This route is being used a lot now, and is getting more developed by climbers as time passes.

Here's what the author did on the morning of 10/8/1978. He left his camp and climbed up the ridge just described and made a complete circle of Tabequache and Shavano, then down to an old mine and along McCoy Creek. Round-trip was just over 4 1/2 hours.

The normal route for these 2 peaks now seems to be to drive up to Jennings Creek and park at 3213 meters as shown (as of 7/2000, this trail was washed out somehow--so call the Salida RS for more information). Apparently this road is good for cars (?). From there head northeast up to the ridge, then circle around the summit ridge as the author did. Or for car drivers, another popular place to park is about 5 kms from Maysville, then climb northwest up the southeast ridge of Shavano. This route seems as good as any, but you'll be starting at a lower elevation, only 2798; which mean more meters to climb. Or, head west & north on the Colorado Trail, then west along a good trail called the **Blanks Cabin Route** to the summit of Shavano. This is the recommended route as of 7/2000 according to Forest Service rangers.

Old mining equipment from the 1800's still lie about the mine south of Shavano.

Map 451-1, Princeton, Antero, Tabequache & Shavano, Sawatch Mtns., Colorado, USA

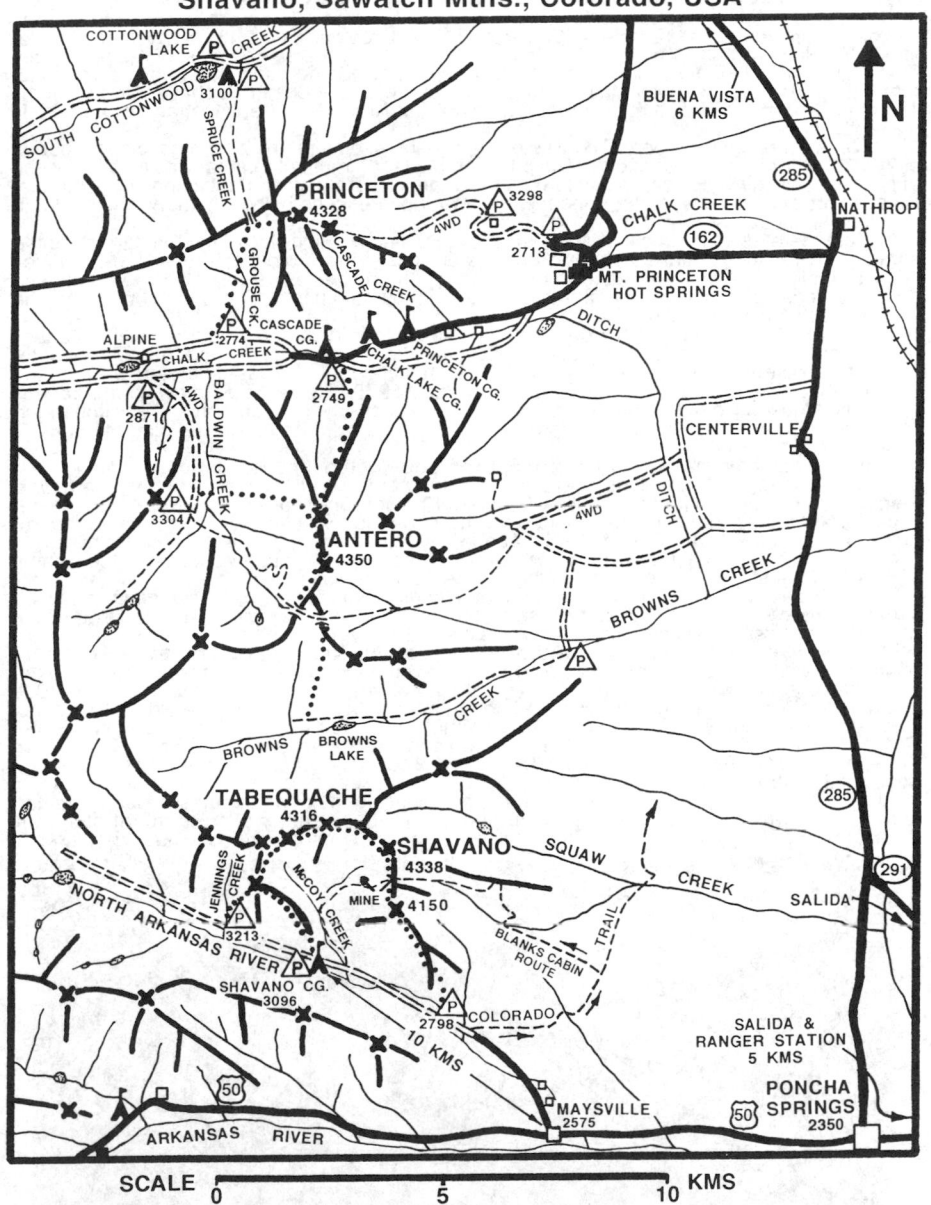

Plan to stock up on food supplies in Salida, 5 kms east of Poncha Springs, or Buena Vista. For updated information stop at the San Isabel National Forest Ranger Station in Salida, or call 719-539-3591.
Maps *San Isabel National Forest,* 1:126,720; or USGS map *Poncho Springs,* 1:24,000; and the books, **Climbing Guide to Colorado's Fourteeners,** Pruett Publishing; or **Colorado's Fourteeners: From Hikes to Climbs,** and *Colorado's Fourteeners, Map Package,* both from Fulcrum Publishing.

Challenger, Kit Carson, Crestone, Crestone Needle & Humboldt
Peaks, Sangre de Cristo Mountains, Colorado, USA

Featured on this map is the Crestone Group of 14'ers. They are, from northwest to southeast, Challenger, 4292 meters; Kit Carson, 4299; Crestone Peak, 4357; Crestone Needle, 4326 and Humboldt, 4291 meters. This group is located in the area northeast of Alamosa, east of Moffat and Crestone, southwest of Westcliff, and near the northern part of the north-south running Sangre de Cristo Mountains. These peaks are among the most challenging of all the 14'ers in Colorado. The rock is of various kinds, but Kit Carson Peak is made of very solid aggregate or conglomerate.

Access is reasonably good. The western approach seems the best for most climbs, but as of 7/2000, Gary Boyce of Crestone, who owns an old land grant in the area, was in the process of perhaps selling his 39 sections/square miles to the Forest Service. Best to inquire about that situation first; call the Saguache Ranger Station for updates (see below). Otherwise, inquire in Crestone about access from there.

To get there, drive north out of Alamosa about 60 kms on Highway 17 to Moffat; or drive the same highway south from Salida and Poncha Springs. From Moffat, turn east on a paved highway until you reach the small town of Crestone. From Crestone's post office, turn east and drive southeast for about 4 kms to South Crestone Creek, and park at what some are calling the Willow Creek Trailhead at 2707 meters.

To climb **Challenger** and **Kit Carson**, walk south then east on a good trail which passes over a ridge and down to Willow Creek. Follow the creek up to just beyond the Lower Willow Lake, then route-find southwest to the summit of Challenger, then 300-400 meters away to the top of Kit Carson. The author did this climb on 10/6/1978. He didn't quite reach the parking place shown because of the rough road, but it may be better when you arrive. He climbed the route shown, apparently over Challenger (?) to Kit Carson. The round-trip climb took 6 1/2 hours.

Another way from the west to **Crestone, Crestone Needle,** and **Humboldt,** is to drive west from Crestone town about 2 kms, turn south for another km and cross South Crestone Creek, then drive east and south across Willow Creek to Spanish Creek at 2518 meters. From there, walk 5 or 6 kms up Spanish Creek on a trail, then continue straight up the canyon to the low notch or pass as shown. From there you can ridge-climb southwest and south to the top of Crestone. This isn't technical, but not a walk-up. Or from the col, ridge-walk east to the summit of Humboldt. A strong climber might do these 2 peaks in one long day.

Another easier way up Crestone & Crestone Needle from the west is to use the Cottonwood Creek approach, then climb the south face of Crestone; or continue to the pass and ridge-walk northwest to Crestone Needle. Both routes are class 3 with route-finding.

Generally speaking, to climb **Humboldt, Crestone Needle** and **Crestone Peak,** an approach from the east is best; and as of 7/2000, maybe the only way to all these 14'ers! To get there, drive south from Westcliff on State Highway 69 for about 7 kms, then veer right (due south) onto Colfax Lane (County Road 119), to the intersection near where the old Becks School is located, then turn west on Road 120 to a trailhead. If you have a 4WD, continue up South Colony Creek to the end of the road, then walk up a trail to the upper South Colony Lake. From there, head north, then east to Humboldt; or circle around on either side of the Crestones and ridge-climb to those summits.

These peaks contain some difficult climbs, but by using the normal routes, most hikers can climb there without the use of extra equipment. A very healthy climber might climb the Crestones and Humboldt in one day from Colony Creek route, especially if you have a 4WD.

962   Looking at the northeast face of Kit Carson Peak from just above Willow Lake.

Map 452-1, Challenger, Kit Carson, Crestones, Humboldt Peaks, Sangre de Cristo Mtns., Colo., USA

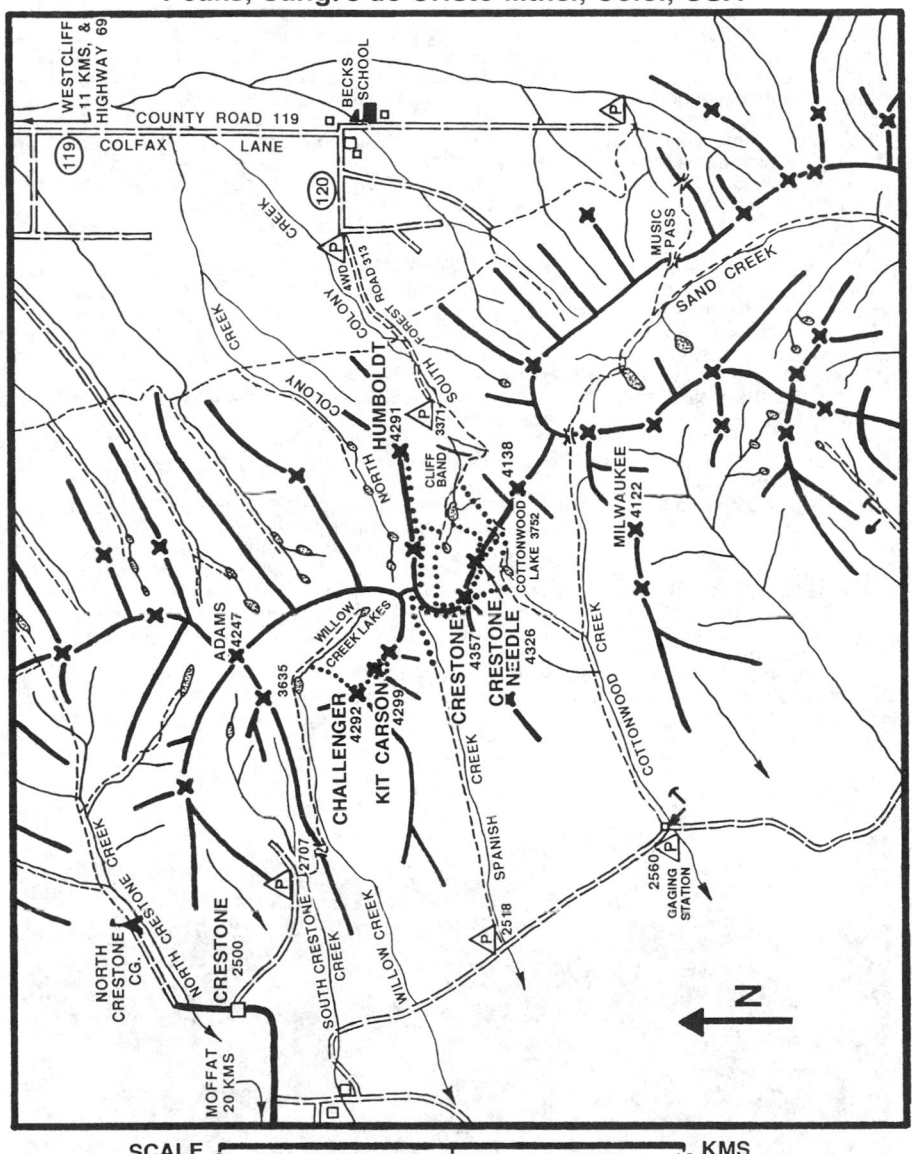

SCALE 0 ——————— 5 ——————— 10 KMS

Some supplies can be bought in Moffat, Crestone and Westcliff, but these are small towns and you're advised to shop in larger communities with supermarkets such as Alamosa. Call the San Isabel National Forest Ranger Station in Salida, Tele. 719-539-3591; or the Rio Grande National Forest offices in Saguache, Tele. 719-655-2547; or Canon City, Tele. 719-269-8500, for more current information concerning access roads.

Maps *Rio Grande* and/or *San Isabel National Forests,* 1:126,720; or USGS map *Crestone Peak,* 1:24,000; and the books, **Climbing Guide to Colorado's Fourteeners,** Pruett Publishing; or **Colorado's Fourteeners: From Hikes to Climbs**, and *Colorado's Fourteeners, Map Package,* both from Fulcrum Publishing.

Ellingwood, Blanca, Little Bear & Lindsey Peaks, Sangre de Cristo Mountains, Colorado, USA

This map features 4 of Colorado's 14'ers. From west to east they are; Ellingwood, 4281 meters; Blanca, 4373; Little Bear, 4279; and Lindsey at 4281 meters. Blanca is the 4th highest summit in Colorado; and the highest peak in the Sangre de Cristo Range, which runs south from central Colorado into northern New Mexico. This Blanca Group is just north of Fort Garland and northeast of Alamosa in the San Luis Valley. Access is quite easy to this mountain massif which is composed mostly of metamorphic-type rocks.

There are routes leading north from Blanca and Fort Garland towns, but these are entirely on private land (which dates back to the Spanish era), therefore won't be discussed here.

For those wanting to climb **Ellingwood, Blanca** and **Little Bear Peaks**, the best way is from the southwest. From Alamosa, drive about 42 kms east on Highway 160, then turn north on State Road 150 signposted for the Sand Dunes National Monument. You can also reach that point from the east and/or south. See a state highway map. Roughly 5.5 kms north of Highway 160, turn right or northeast and continue for about 3 more kms. Somewhere in that area cars will have to be parked, but 4WD's or HCV's can continue further along. Depending on Forest Service policy regarding 4WD's, and your vehicle, you may make it to as far as Como Lake (?).

From Como, walk east, northeast up a trail to a pass or col between **Ellingwood** and **Blanca**, then walk north or south to either summit. Normally, both of these peaks are climbed together on the same hike. This is a walk-up route all the way.

To climb **Little Bear Peak**, start 200 meters east of Como Lake and aim due south for a steep gully. Climb this, which can be filled with snow until late July, then head east up the west ridge. At one point there's a class 4 climb up a steep water-worn gully, then lots of class 3 scrambling to the summit. These 3 peaks are often climbed on the same weekend, and often times with a camp around Como Lake.

While it's possible to climb **Lindsey** from Blanca and the southwest, by far the best way there is to head for the small ranching community of Gardner, located on Highway 60 northeast of these peaks. From there, drive southwest to Red Wing and continue in the same direction up along Huerfano Creek to the area on this map. This is now public access. From the trailhead at 3249 meters, walk south on a good trail for about 1 1/2 kms, then veer left and route-find southeast. You'll eventually get on Lindsey's northwest ridge, then ridge-climb to the summit. At one point deviate east from the ridge, but this is also a walk-up. Lindsey is normally a one day climb and is usually climbed by itself.

The treeline in the Blanca Group is high, around 3600 meters. Since these peaks and the San Luis Valley are hemmed in by high mountains on all sides, most of the moisture has already been squeezed out of the clouds before they get here; therefore this region is very dry, with good weather the rule--bad weather the exception.

From the summit of Blanca looking east with Lindsey on the right, Iron Nipple left.

Map 453-1, Ellingwood, Blanca, Little Bear & Lindsey, Sangre de Cristo Mtns., Colorado, USA

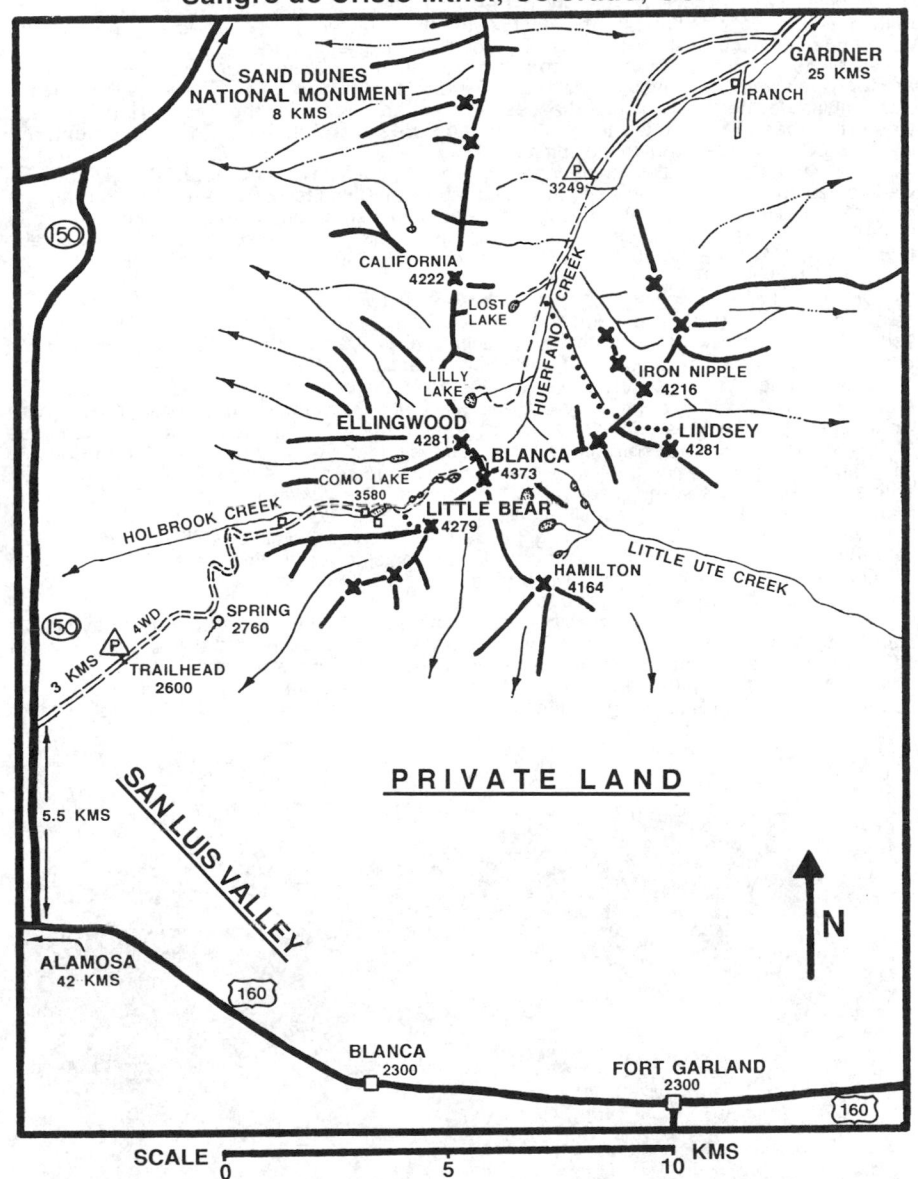

Food and supplies should be purchased in Fort Garland or Alamosa. Alamosa is a college town and the largest place in the San Luis Valley. The nearest Forest Service ranger station is located in La Hara, 20 kms south of Alamosa, Tele. 719-274-8971. Call or visit them to get the latest information on roads, trails and public access, or buy Forest Service maps.

Maps *Rio Grande National Forest*, 1:126,720; or USGS map *Blanca Peak*, 1:24,000; and the books, **Climbing Guide to Colorado's Fourteeners,** Pruett Publishing; or **Colorado's Fourteeners: From Hikes to Climbs,** and *Colorado's Fourteeners, Map Package,* both from Fulcrum Publishing.

Culebra, Sangre de Cristo Mountains, Colorado, USA

Culebra Peak at 4282 meters, is located east of San Luis and Chama in the southeastern corner of the San Luis Valley. This whole area is situated in south central Colorado not far north of the New Mexico state line. It's the most southerly of Colorado's 14'ers, and is in the southern part of the Sangre de Cristo Mountains. The rock here is mostly quartzite.

Of all the 14'ers in Colorado, Culebra is by far the most difficult to get to and climb. There are roads to within a relatively short distance of the summit, but it's all on private land. In the past, all land owners have refused access to climbers except for the **Taylor Ranch** on the western slopes. Taylor used to charge elk hunters several thousand dollars to hunt, and climbers US$40 for their shot at the summit.

However, as of 1999, the ranch changed hands and it's now the **Culebra Ranch**. Access was denied until 7/2000, when a group of Colorado Mtn. Club Members were allow to climb the mountain on a one day trip. Everybody is now holding their breath as to the future status, and the Club is negotiating for access for all of us. In the mean time, you might call the Colorado Mtn. Club at 303-279-3080, X-2; or in Colorado call 800-633-4417. You'll have to listen through a recording on both lines.

Or you might get a little information from the San Juan/Rio Grande National Forest office in La Jara, located to the west. Their number is 719-274-8971. This is not their land, but someone there usually knows something about the access situation. Make a telefon call or two before going out there, otherwise you'll run into a locked gate 2 kms from the Ranch HQ.

Once you get official permission--or whatever (?), then either drive to the large stone gate and cattle guard near the confluence of the El Valle and Carneros Creeks, where regular cars would best be parked nearby; or drive to and east from the Ranch Headquarters. In the late 1990's, driving the road east from the Ranch HQ. seemed the shortest route for people with cars. Ranch employees can put you on the best driving route. Car drivers will have to park at a trailhead at 2816 meters and road-walk to and beyond *The 4 Way Junction,* as shown on the map. It's about 7 kms from this trailhead to the end of the 4WD road at about 3566 meters. In that area is a small stream and spring right at tree line. You can camp there if you like.

From the end of the road, it's a simple walk up along a ridge to **Culebra's** summit, a distance of about 5 kms. With a 4WD, it's a climb of only about 700 meters--hardly enough to break a sweat! Car drivers will need most of one day for the climb.

Here's what the author did. He drove from Chama straight up the road to just beyond the stone gate, and camped for the night. The gates were all open because they were taking cattle off the mountain at the time. Next morning, 10/4/1978, he walked from Perdido Creek, past *The 4 Way* and on to the top in 3 hours; about 5 hours round-trip from his car. On the way out, he stopped at the Ranch HQ. and got all the latest information at that time. And got away without

This is *The 4-Way* road junction, with the summit of Culebra beyond just over the hill.

Map 454-1, Culebra, Sangre de Cristo Mtns., Colo., USA

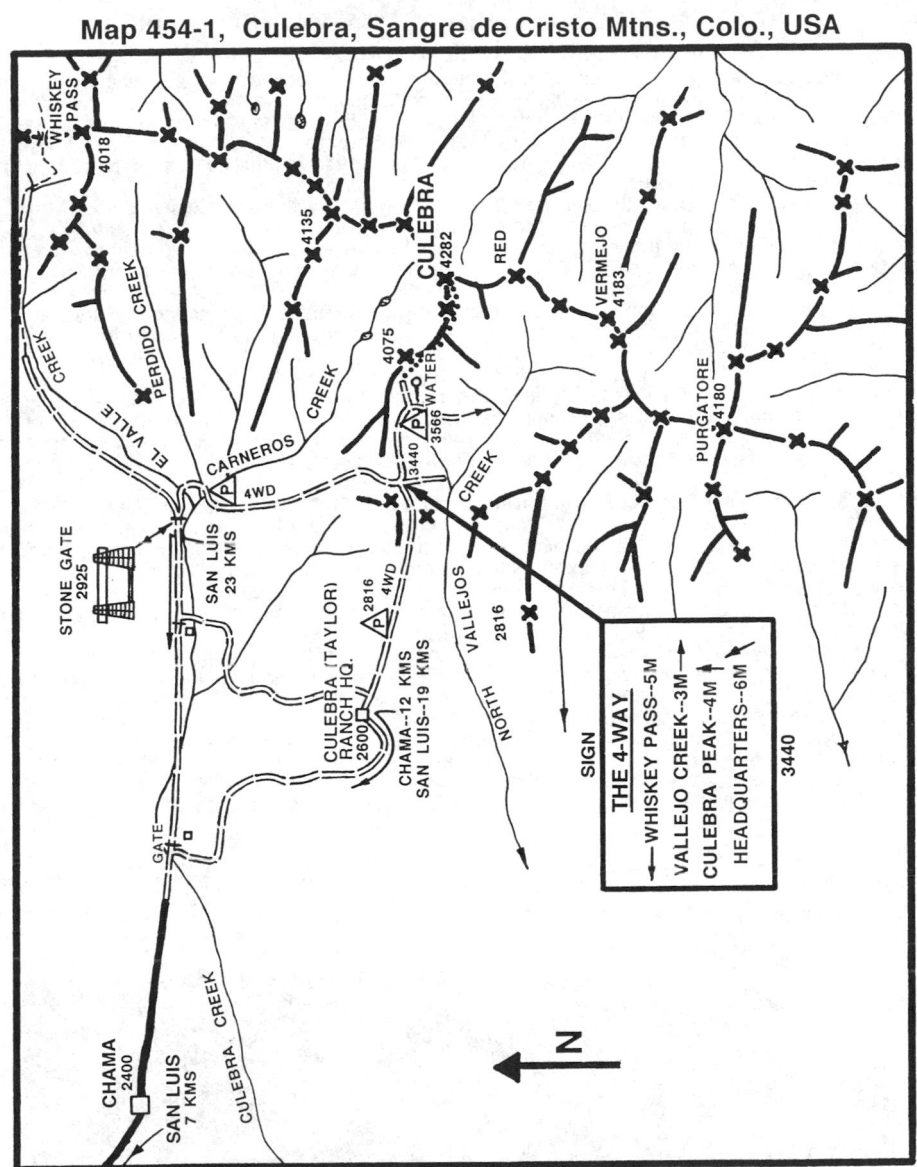

SCALE |___|___|___|___| KMS
0   2   4   6   8

paying a fee--which he was unaware of at the time!
   San Luis is the last place to buy groceries and gasoline, and the last place where garage services can be found, but Alamosa is a better place to shop.
Maps USGS maps *Taylor Ranch, El Valle & Culebra Peak,* 1:24,000; and/or *Alamosa,* 1:100,000; and the books, **Climbing Guide to Colorado's Fourteeners,** Pruett Publishing; or **Colorado's Fourteeners: From Hikes to Climbs**, and *Colorado's Fourteeners, Map Package,* both from Fulcrum Publishing.

Quandary, Lincoln, Cameron, Democrat, Bross and Sherman Peaks, Mosquito Range, Colorado, USA

Just east of Leadville and Climax, 2 of Colorado's high altitude lead & zinc mining towns, lies the Mosquito Range and 6 of the state's 14,000 foot/4268 meter summits. Here are the 14'ers, from north to south: Quandary, 4345 meters; Lincoln, 4355--the highest in this immediate area; Cameron, 4341; Democrat, 4311; Bross, 4320; and Sherman, 4279 meters. The Mosquito Range is rather narrow in this region, making access easy from either of 2 main highways on either side of these mountains.

As previously mentioned, this is a lead & zinc mining area, with many old mines, roads, mills, and other remnants of the mining era. Some mining continues today, and as a result, there are many used and unused roads in the region. In fact, there are more roads than trails--which are almost non-existent. Because of all the mining operations, it would be impossible to make the North Mosquito Range into a wilderness area.

All the 14'ers can be climbed from either side of the mountain range either from Highway 91 on the west, or Highway 9 on the east. The first thing you'll need to reach this area is a Colorado state highway map.

Quandary is usually climbed from the Blue Lake Basin south of the peak; or along the east ridge. Get there from Highway 9. Quandary is perhaps the easiest to get to of all 14'ers; as a result, there's now a trail-of-sorts along the east ridge. In the afternoon of 10/8/1980, after climbing Grays and Torreys Peaks in the morning, the author parked at the trailhead marked 3322 meters and climbed up the east ridge. He returned via Blue Lake in just over 2 1/2 hours, round-trip.

Best way to climb **Democrat, Cameron, Lincoln** and **Bross**, is to drive up the gravel road above Alma on Highway 9 to the Kite Lake Campground located just south of these 4 peaks. From this one trailhead, all 4 can be climbed. You could do it either direction, but one way would be to first climb Democrat, then ridge-walk to Cameron and Lincoln, then backtrack a ways, and head southeast for Bross, then route-find down the west face to Kite Lake. Any fit person can do all 4 of these in one day. However, someone coming direct from the lowlands may be in for trouble on the first day or 2, as this is high altitude country!

Sherman can be climbed from the east, southeast or west, but the least complicated way might be from Leadville up the road past Printer Boy Mine and into Iowa Gulch. With a 4WD, you can make it to the trailhead marked 3627 meters, which means it'll be a short climb southeast to a pass, then northeast to the summit. Most people in Colorado live east of the Rockies, so for them the fastest way to Sherman is to drive south 2 kms from Fairplay on Highway 285, then turn west onto County Road 18 going up Fourmile Creek. With a 4WD, continue past the 2 campgrounds to within one or 2 kms of the top.

There are San Isabel National Forest Ranger Stations in Leadville, Tele. 719-486-0749; and

Looking south from Quandary towards Lincoln, Democrat and Bross.

Map 455-1, Quandary, Lincoln, Cameron, Democrat, Bross & Sherman, Mosquito Range, Colorado, USA

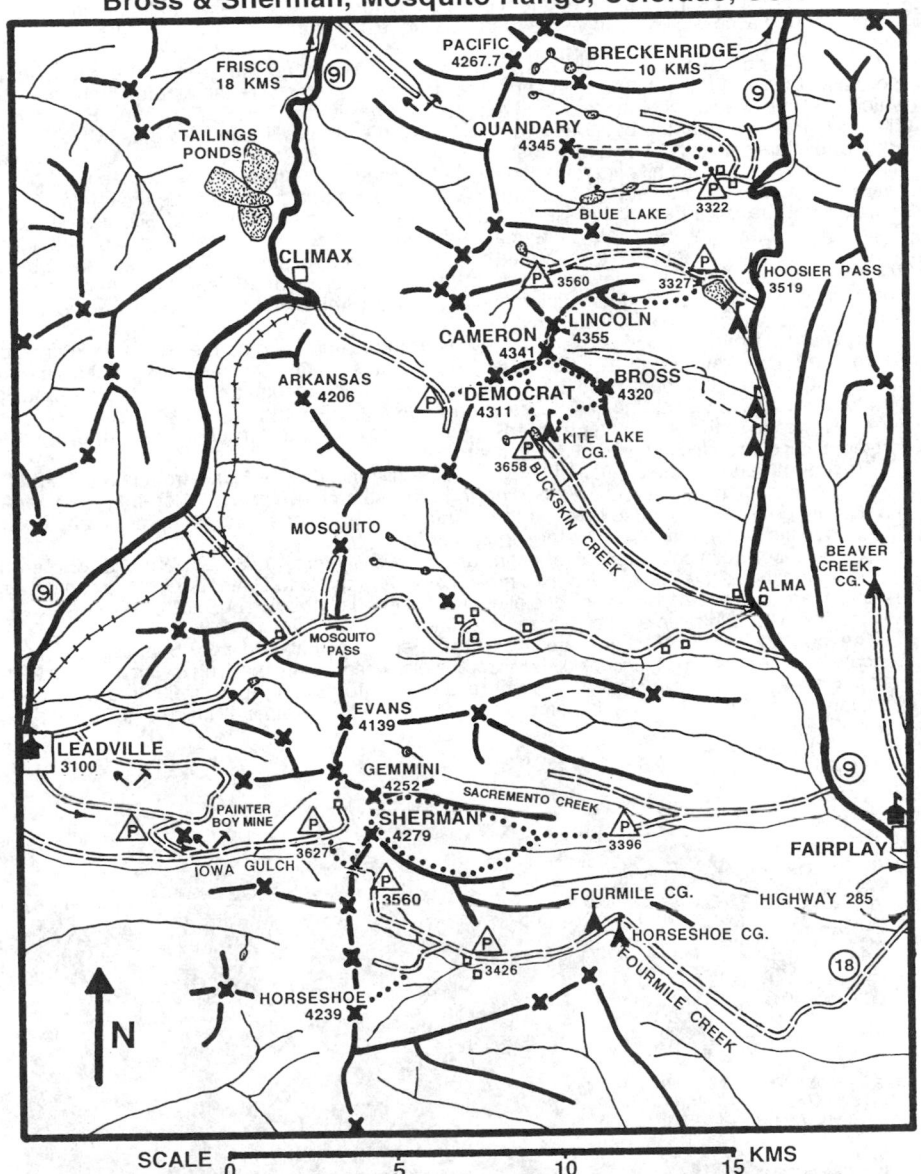

Fairplay, Tele. 719-836-2031, where Forest Service maps can be purchased and additional information gathered. There are 3 national forests sharing parts of the Mosquito Range, but the San Isabel National Forest map might be the best.

Maps *San Isabel, Pike, or Arapaho National Forest maps,* 1:126,720; or USGS maps *Climax, Mt. Sherman, Alma, and Breckenridge,* 1:24,000; and the books, **Climbing Guide to Colorado's Fourteeners,** Pruett Publishing; or **Colorado's Fourteeners: From Hikes to Climbs,** and *Colorado's Fourteeners, Map Package,* both from Fulcrum Publishing.

Torreys, Grays, Bierstadt & Evans Peaks, Front Range, Colorado, USA

In the region just east of Loveland Pass at the southern end of the Front Range are 4 of Colorado's 14'ers--peaks over 14,000 feet or 4268 meters. All 4 of these peaks are in a small area with good accessibility; in fact, one road, the highest in North America, winds its way to the summit of Mt. Evans.

The 14'ers on this map include Mt. Evans at 4349 meters, and just to the southwest, Bierstadt at 4287. Further to the west and closer to Loveland Pass are the others, the highest of which is Grays Peak, 4351 meters, and just one km north, Torreys Peak, 4350. Evans and Bierstadt are on or near the boundaries of the Arapaho and Pike National Forests, while Grays and Torreys are within the Arapaho Forest.

Access to these summits is easy, especially Mt. Evans, where a good surfaced road ends near the top at a research station. Fortunately, there are other routes to this mountain where climbers can be rewarded by climbing it. One popular route to Evans and Bierstadt is from Guanella Pass. To get there, leave Interstate Highway 70 at Exit 228 at Georgetown, and drive south to Guanella Pass, then hike east and southeast to both summits. Two other easy routes are from Summit Lake, as shown. Still another way is to begin at Echo Lake and walk up Chicago Creek. Most Coloradoans doing the 14'ers trip, climb Bierstadt and Evans at the same time from one of the suggested trailheads.

The normal way to reach Grays and Torreys is from the north and northeast. From Interstate 70, take the Bakersville Exit 221 (Bakersville has a gas station, bar and several homes-no more), and drive up the rough road into Stevens Gulch. Even though this is a very poor road fit mostly for 4WD's, cars with higher clearance and driven with care, can make it to or near the mine. Nowadays, the road ends at the Stevens Mine. An older track leads further up the canyon, but it's now blocked off and used as a trail only.

A good trail leads to the summit of Grays Peak, a distance of 4 or 5 kms from the trailhead & mine. You can then walk along the ridge north to the summit of Torreys. Normally, everyone climbs both peaks on the same hike. In the vicinity of the Stevens Mine, there are many good places to make camp with a good water supply nearby.

The author camped below the Stevens Mine and the next morning, 10/8/1980, climbed both peaks as suggested in exactly 3 hours. He then broke camp and drove to Quandary Peak, seen on the previous map, and climbed that 14'er in the afternoon. In this part of Colorado, most people, especially those with a 4WD, can climb several peaks in one day.

The towns in this immediate area are small, the largest being Idaho Springs. Some shopping can be done there, but it's recommended you buy supplies elsewhere before reaching the area. If you want Forest Service or topographic maps, or more currant information about trails, roads or snow conditions, stop at the Clear Creek District Ranger Station of the Arapaho National Forest in Idaho

Looking south from the top of Torres toward Grays Peak.

Map 456-1, Torreys, Grays, Bierstadt & Evans, Front Range, Colorado, USA

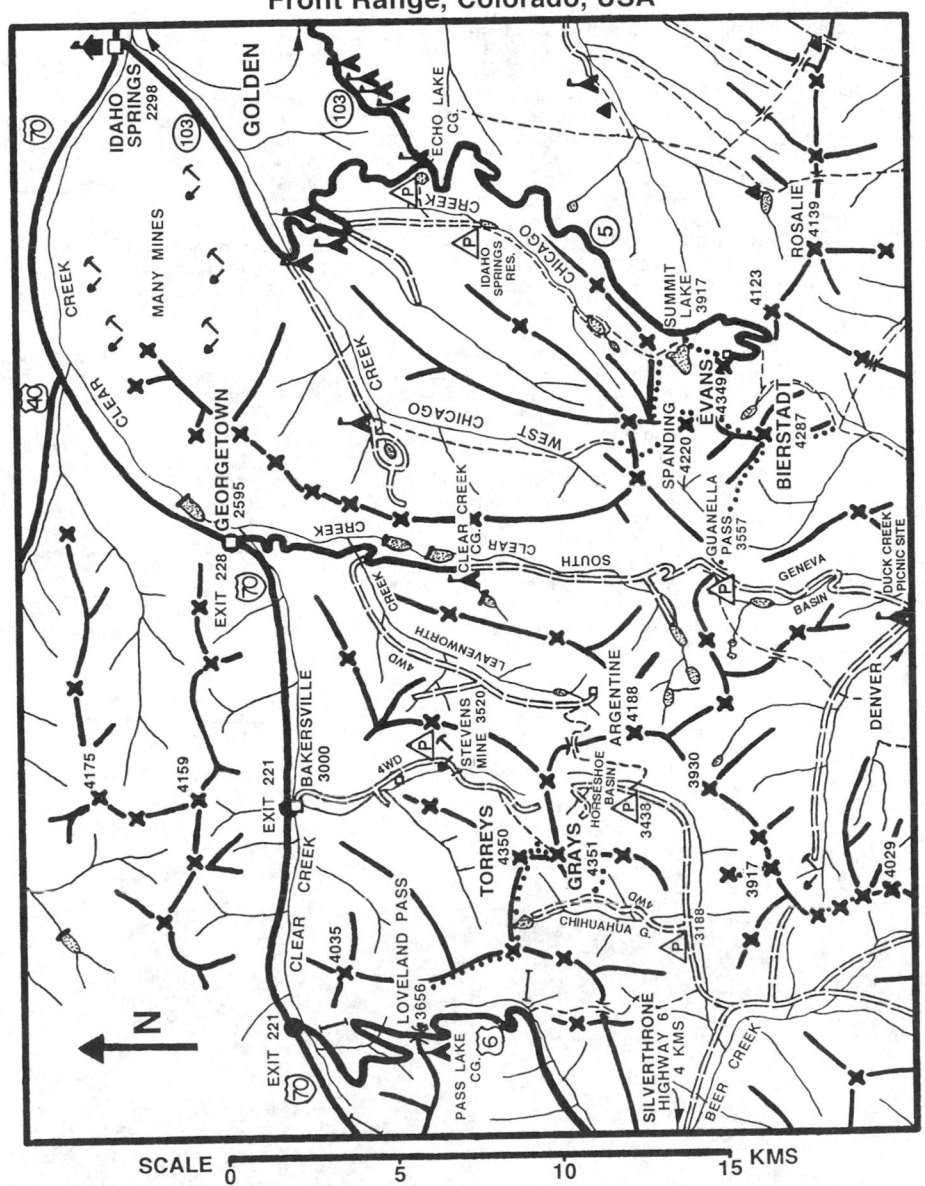

SCALE 0   5   10   15 KMS

Springs, Tele. 303-567-2901. It's open Tuesday through Saturday.
Maps *Arapaho National Forest*, 1:126,720; or USGS maps *Mount Evans & Grays Peak*, and perhaps *Montezuma & Georgetown*, 1:24,000; and the books, **Climbing Guide to Colorado's Fourteeners**, Pruett Publishing; or **Colorado's Fourteeners: From Hikes to Climbs**, and *Colorado's Fourteeners, Map Package*, both from Fulcrum Publishing.

Longs Peak, Rocky Mountain Nat. Park, Front Range, Colorado, USA

Included on this map is part of Rocky Mountain National Park, located in north central Colorado and in the northern part of the Front Range. This national park is west of Fort Collins and Greeley. Within the park is one of Colorado's 14'ers. It's Longs Peak at 4345 meters. If memory is correct, most of the rocks on Longs Peak are some kind of metamorphic, perhaps quartzite (?).

Access to this mountain is easy. If coming from the east, make your way to Loveland or Longmont and drive west on Highway 34 or 36. Or you can get there from Boulder to the south and along Highway 7. Get a state highway map. Nearer Longs Peak, get on Highway 7 in Estes Park and drive south; or drive north from someplace to the south. When you're due east of the peak, look for the paved side-road running west to the Longs Peak Ranger Station, which is the starting point for the easiest and shortest route up the mountain.

At that trailhead is a small campground and ranger station with a small climbers information center where you can buy books and maps, and get the latest information on snow and trail conditions. Good news; as of the summer of 2000, there was no fee for entering the park and using this route up Longs Peak. **But a warning:** if you're there on a weekend and have to park along the road, park completely off to the side beyond the white lines or the country will tow your car away!

From the **Longs Peak** Trailhead & Ranger Station the normal route to the summit heads due west up the shoulder of the mountain to a fork in the trail. One trail goes down to Chasm Lake below the summit and gives access to the famous east face. The other trail curves around a ridge, then enters a *boulder field* on the north slopes which is almost flat.

On the boulder field, you have a choice of 2 routes. The old route went up the north face, but it has one steep section which is difficult. Formerly there was a steel cable at that place, but it's been removed, making it a more difficult and dangerous climb rated at 5.4.

The normal route today is one leading from the boulder field to the rock hut and pass, located on the northwest ridge at about 4000 meters. From that small shelter, the route (marked with paint) heads south along the west face. Further along, the trail goes up to another pass and turns east along the south face, then north straight up to the flat summit. If there is fresh snow on the slope, this upper section can be difficult and dangerous, as there's some smooth rock to cross. This is a one day climb rated a class 3 from Longs Peak Campground. On 10/7/1980, the author parked at the trailhead and climbed via this normal route. He was on top in 2 2/3 hours; round-trip took 4 3/4 hours. You may need double this time.

Another access route would be from Estes Park and the trailhead located below Bear Lake. From there, one route or trail follows Boulder Brook; the other Glacier Gulch (or Gorge). But you'll have to pay a park entrance fee to use this route. One could also reach the peak via the eastern slopes of Mt. Meeker, 4241 meters; and/or Hunters Creek via Copeland Lake Trailhead,

Substituting for a Longs Peak foto is one looking southwest from the summit of Sneffels (Map 444, page 947).

Map 457-1, Longs Peak, Rocky Mtn. Nat. Park, Colorado, USA

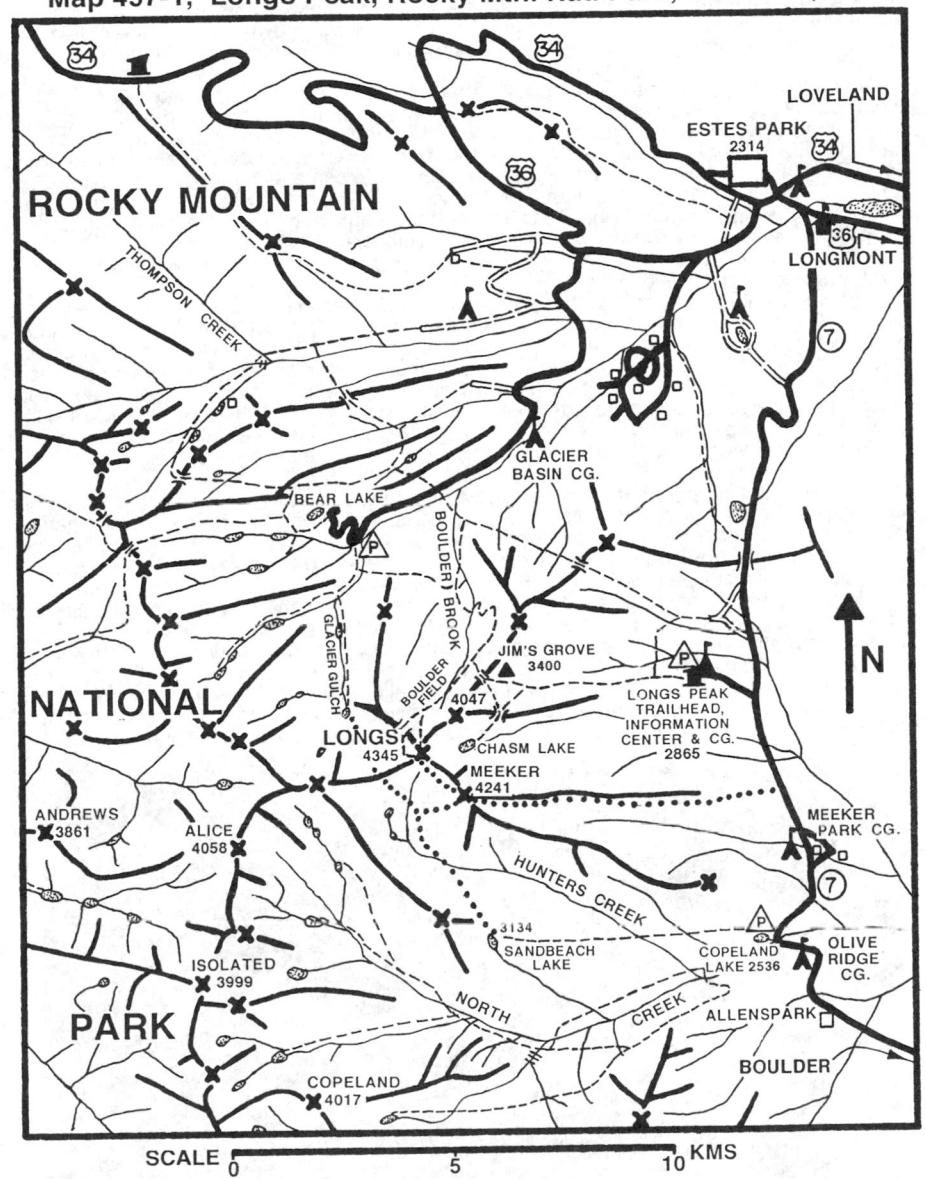

but there are few trails in either of those areas. No crowds either.
    The only place in this mapped area where you can buy food is in Estes Park. This is a growing community with at least 4 supermarkets. For currant information call 970-586-1242 for backcountry information; or Park HQ. at 970-586-1206; or see the park website at (www.nps.gov/romo/).
Maps *Roosevelt National Forest,* 1:126,720; or *Rocky Mountain National Park,* 1:62,500; and the books, **Climbing Guide to Colorado's Fourteeners,** Pruett Publishing; or **Colorado's Fourteeners: From Hikes to Climbs**, and *Colorado's Fourteeners, Map Package,* both from Fulcrum Publishing.

Pikes Peak, Front Range, Colorado, USA

Featured on this map is Pikes Peak, 4302 meters. It's one of Colorado's 14'ers and probably the most famous mountain in the state, and one of the better known peaks in the nation. If it weren't for these facts, the mountain probably wouldn't be in this book, because there's a highway and cog railway to the summit.

That highway is a toll road and the toll gate (Tele. 719-684-9138) is located one or 2 kms above Cascade, which is on Highway 24. See map. From the gate it's about 30 kms to the summit, with only the first 11 kms paved. It costs US$10 for one person in a car; but no more than $35 for a full car load. Higher up, there's a visitor center near Crystal Lake and the Crow Gulch Picnic Site. Above that is the Glen Cove Picnic Site and a lodge (open year-round). On top is the Summit House with restaurant and curio shop. The road is open year-round, except right after big winter storms. Also, each summer there's an automobile race. The Manitou and Pikes Peak Railway runs from mid-April to mid-November. In mid-summer they run 8 trains a day which costs US$24.50 per/person. For additional information call the Cog Railway office in Manitou Springs, Tele. 719-685-5401.

However, for those who can overcome their lazy streak there are several ways you can walk to the top via trails. The normal hiking route to **Pikes Peak** is called the **Barr Trail**. It begins just above the terminal of the cog railway at Manitou Springs at about 2000 meters elevation. By trail, it's about 21 kms to the summit. Be sure you take plenty of water as there's little along the way until you reach Barr Camp. Some people do the climb in 2 days, spending one night at Barr Camp at about 3000 meters. If you decide to camp there, you need reservations, so call 719-630-3934. Or, you can camp anywhere else on the mountain (but with few flat spots) for free with no reservations. At 3600 meters is a small emergency shelter. The second day is used to complete the climb and return to Manitou Springs.

However, *most people do the climb in one day*, and as of 2000, no reservations or permits were required. The vertical rise is 2300 meters, a pretty good workout for the average person. Most people do the 42 kms round-trip climb from Manitou in from 8 to 12 hours. On 10/6/1980, the author parked at the cog railway trailhead and did the round-trip hike in just under 6 hours. The record run at that time was 3 hours 16 minutes, round-trip.

There are other possible routes for a good hike. It could be done from the end of a dirt road not far from Cascade, then up to where that path meets the Barr Trail; or walk up Severy Creek to Barr Camp, then to the top. Still another possible route would be to walk (without trail) up Beaver Creek from the Gillette area.

However, the 2nd most popular way up is to begin at or near the Crags Campground located on the western side of the mountain. Use a state highway map or Pike National Forest map to get there. There's no actual trail to the top from the campground, but route-finding is not difficult.

This is an emergency shelter located about halfway between Barr Camp and the summit of Pikes Peak.

Map 458-1, Pikes Peak, Front Range, Colorado, USA

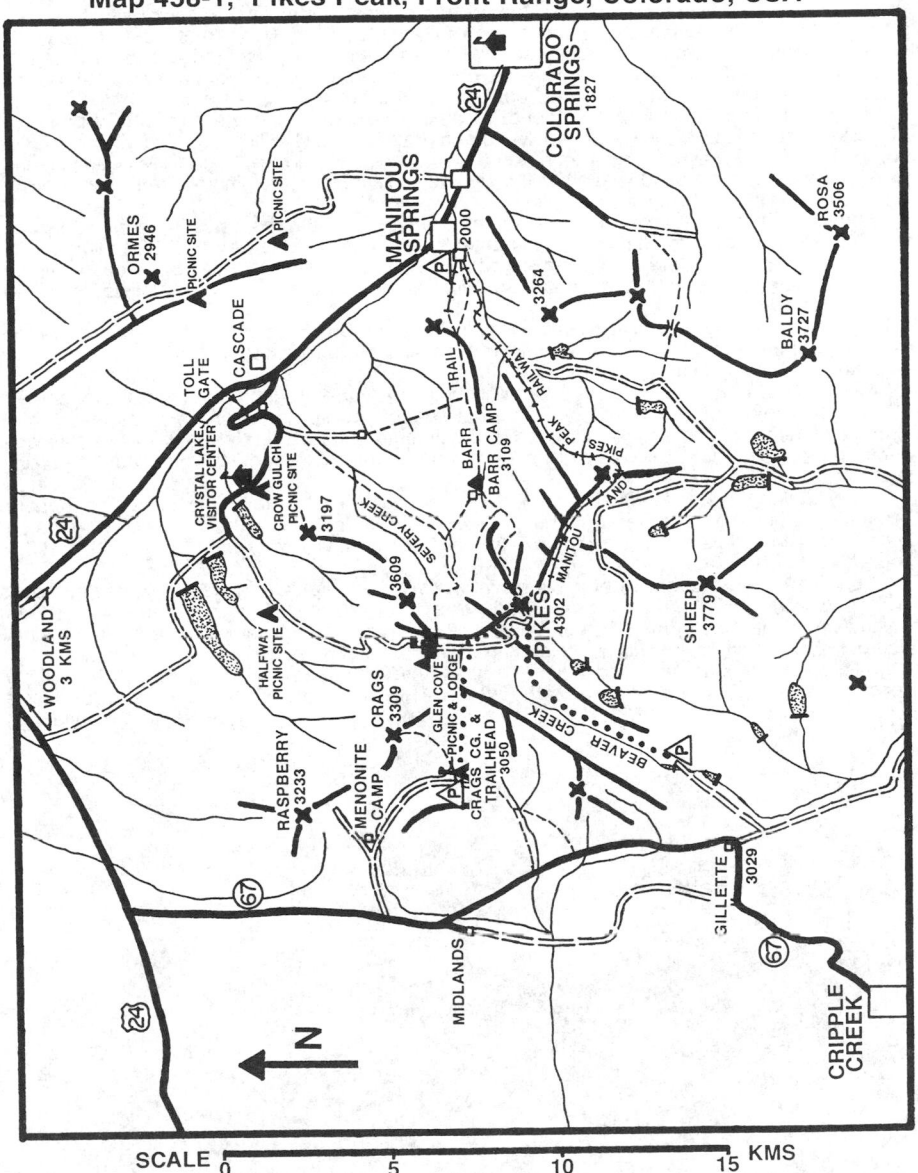

SCALE 0   5   10   15 KMS

Simply head east upslope. When you reach the road, you must get upon the ridge and follow a trail-of-sorts. Road-walking is illegal. Get additional information and maps at the Pike National Forest office in Colorado Springs, Tele. 719-636-1602.

Maps *Pike National Forest*, 1:126,720, or USGS map *Pikes Peak*, 1:24,000; and the books, **Climbing Guide to Colorado's Fourteeners,** Pruett Publishing; or **Colorado's Fourteeners: From Hikes to Climbs**, and *Colorado's Fourteeners, Map Package,* both from Fulcrum Publishing.

Harney Peak, Black Hills, South Dakota, USA

Featured here is Harney Peak, 2207 meters, the highest summit in the Black Hills of western South Dakota. Harney is located southwest of Rapid City and 7 or 8 kms west of the world famous landmark known as Mt. Rushmore National Monument. Rushmore is the solid granite mountain with the faces of 4 US presidents carved into the south side. Harney Peak is also made of granite with a number of spires, peaks and pinnacles dotting its slopes.

To get there from Rapid City, head south on US Highway 16 in the direction of **Mt. Rushmore**. After seeing the national monument, continue west on State Road 244. After about 8 or 10 kms, look to the south side of this paved highway for a sign pointing out the way to the Willow Creek Campground (horse camp). Drive about 400 meters to the carpark and campground. This trailhead is where you begin if climbing the peak from the north.

For access to Harney Peak from the south, which may be the most-used and most-popular route up, continue west on State Road 244 until you come to US Highway 16 & 385. Turn left or south and after 200 meters or so, turn left or south again onto State Road 87. Follow this for about 8 kms until you reach Sylvan Lake. You may want the Forest Service map listed below to do this drive.

At Sylvan Lake, you'll have to pay a small fee at the entrance gate, then proceed to the carpark just north of the lake. There's a small store and cabins located around the shore, which is a hangout for tourists and fisherman in summer.

Now the trails to **Harney Peak**. From Willow Creek Campground, take the trail signposted for Harney Peak. It's the one which first heads east, then south. From this trailhead to the summit it's about 8 kms and is well-used and well-signposted. The first part of this trail was once an old road. Most people can make it to the summit in 2-3 hours, or about half a day round-trip.

From Sylvan Lake, take either of the 2 trails signposted for Harney Peak. They meet about half a km northeast of Little Devils Tower. See map. From the lake to the top is about 5 kms on either trail. Strong hikers can make it up in an hour, but most will likely want 2 hours up, and 3-4 hours round-trip.

On 6/6/1992, the author slept in his car at the Willow Creek Campground (horse camp) & Trailhead, and with an early start made it to the top of Harney in less than 2 hours. He then walked south past Cathedral Spires to Sylvan Lake. From there he walked north along the west side of the mountain back to his car. Round-trip was about 23 kms and took 5 1/4 hours.

All trail junctions are well-signposted and trails are well-used and maintained. Most hiking here is from some time in May through October. It's not a steep mountain, so it could be climbed easily on skis in winter. Buy all your supplies in Rapid City. Any comfortable walking shoe will do here.

The summit of Harney Peak and a stone lookout tower which was probably once used as a forest fire observatory.

Map 459-1, Harney Peak, Black Hills, South Dakota, USA

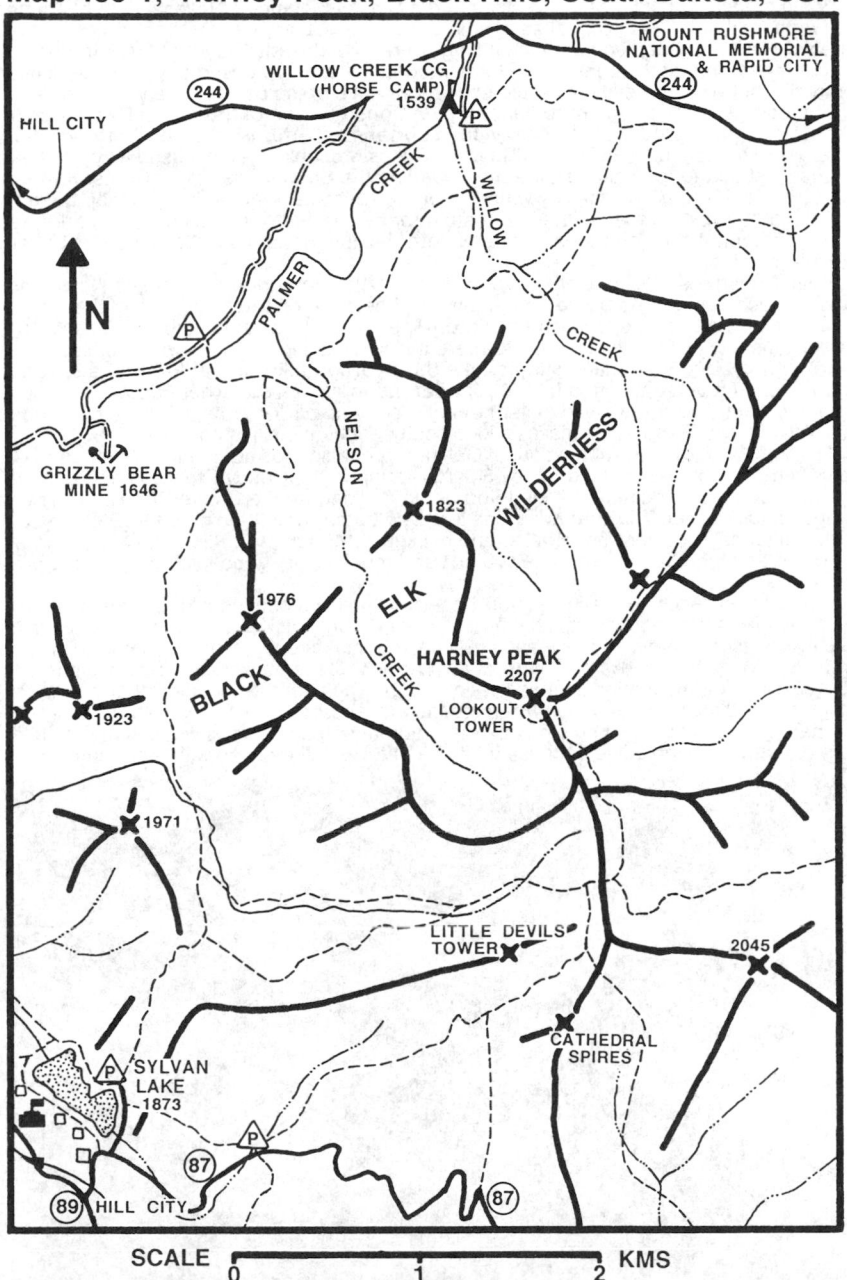

SCALE

0   1   2   KMS

Maps *Hiking Map of the Norbeck Wildlife Preserve,* about 1:20,000 (?), published by the Black Hills Group, Sierra Club; USGS maps *Hill City* and *Custer,* 1:24,000; or *Black Hills National Forest,* 1:126,720, from the Forest Service offices in Rapid City, Tele. 605-343-1567; Hill City, Tele. 605-574-2534; or the Black Hills National Forest HQ. at Custer,Tele. 605-673-2251.

Great Smoky Mountains National Park, Tennessee, USA

Featured here is the highest part of the Great Smoky Mountains National Park of Tennessee and North Carolina. The highest summit in the park is Clingmans Dome at 2025 meters; but there's a road to the top so not much hiking there. Next is Mt. Guyot at 2018 meters. Third highest is LeConte at 2010 meters. These mountains are composed of various sedimentary-type rocks, but you don't see many outcroppings as none of the peaks rise above treeline.

You can get to this region from many directions but one of the easiest would be to exit Interstate Highway 40 east of Knoxville, Tennessee, and drive south in the direction of Sevierville and the tourist town of Gatlinburg. This is probably the most-used way into the park, because just up the road and just inside the park is the Sugarlands Visitor Center & Park HQ., Tele 865-436-1200, or website (www.nps.gov/grsm/). It's recommended you stop there first to buy books & maps and get all the information for hiking and/or camping in the park. Keep in mind this information is only meant to be an introduction to the park. You'll need a better map than this for hiking.

From Sugarlands Visitor Center, you could head south and east using the Newfound Gap Road to reach **Clingmans Dome**; or the town of Cherokee on the south side of the mountains. You can also use this road to reach **LeConte**. The shortest way to the top is via the Alum Cave Trail which starts just south of the peak where the parking symbol is shown. From the trailhead to the top is about 8 kms, and should take the average hiker about 2-3 hours to reach the summit; about half a day round-trip. At or near the top is a lodge where about 50 people can sleep and another lean-to type shelter nearby. You can also get there from the Roaring Fork Motor Nature Trail Road which makes a loop southeast from Gatlinburg.

To climb **Mt. Guyot**, drive east out of Gatlinburg heading toward Pittman Center and Cosby. From there head south past the Cosby Guard Station to the Cosby Creek Campground at 762 meters. Locate the trailhead parking and begin walking up the Snake Den Ridge Trail, then continue south toward Tricomer Knob Shelter. The author was there on 5/29/1992, and did this hike to as far as Tricomer Knob Shelter and back in 6 1/2 hours. It was a rainy & misty day and he carried an umbrella part way. He couldn't see much or get good fotos but it was a pleasant hike anyway.

Here are some of the basic rules you'll need to know concerning hiking in the national park. If just day-hiking, you don't need a permit of any kind. But if you plan to camp or sleep in one of the shelters you will need a permit, and you'll have to make reservations for some of the popular campsites or shelters weeks or months in advance. Call the backcountry reservations office at 615-436-1231 for information and reservations. They can send you copies of all park rules and regulations and some simple maps which are quite adequate.

There is no public transportation into the mountain areas. This is wet country, so take rain gear; an umbrella works fine because you'll be in forest all the way with little wind. Hike from

In the fog, the Tricomer Knob Hut, located just southeast of Mt. Guyot.

Map 460-1, Great Smoky Mtns. NP, Tennessee, USA

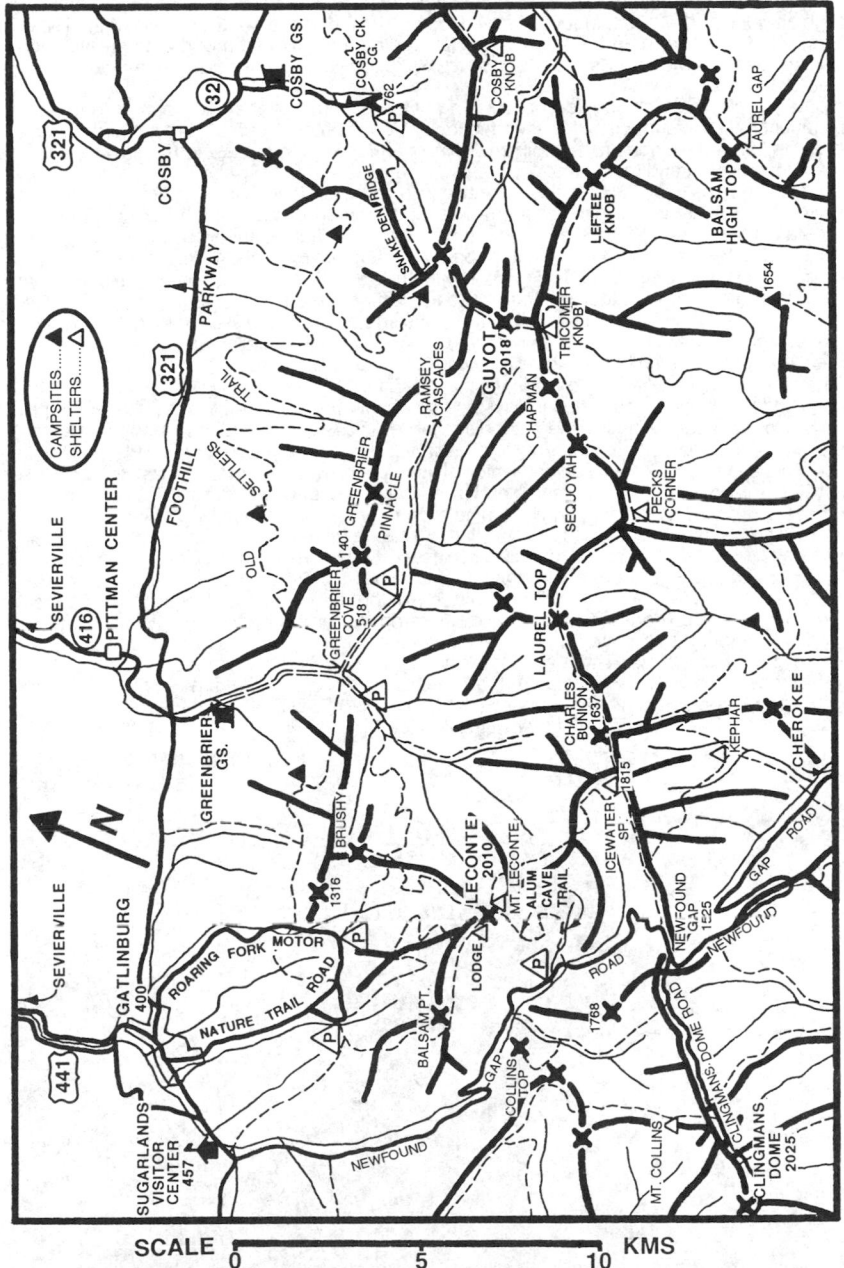

SCALE 0   5   10 KMS

April until mid-November.
Maps Earthwalk Press map *Hiking Map & Guide: Great Smoky Mountains National Park,*
1:62,500; and/or the handout *Great Smoky Mountains Trail Map and Guide,* National Park
Service, (no scale given). There are also guidebooks available at the Sugarlands Visitor Center
or in Gatlinburg stores.

Mt. Mitchell, Blue Ridge Mountains, North Carolina, USA

The highest mountain in the eastern half of the United States is Mt. Mitchell at 2037 meters. It's the highest point in the Black Mountains, which are located in the southern part of the Blue Ridge Mountains in the western end of the state of North Carolina. These mountains are all part of the greater Appalachian Mountain system. Because it's a popular place it's now been made into the Mt. Mitchell State Park.

Some people wouldn't considered climbing Mitchell because there's a paved road and some development near the summit. However, the lower slopes of the mountain are still very pristine, and are protected from development by the Pisgah National Forest. On top is a lookout tower, and nearby a picnic site, museum and restaurant.

Probably the best way to get to this mountain is to first go to the city of Ashville, located southwest of Mt. Mitchell. While in Ashville, gas-up and pick up a map of the Pisgah National Forest at the ranger station, Tele. 828-253-2352. From there, locate the Blue Ridge Parkway running northeast. You'll reach the turnoff to Mt. Mitchell after about an hours drive; about 48 kms from Ashville. But if you decide to climb it rather than driving up, continue in a northeast direction on the Parkway to the east side of the mountain. Look for the exit to the left (west) sign-posted for Busic. This is State Highway 80. From the cafe in Busic, follow the signs southwest to the Black Mountain Campground. Anyone in that area can show you the way if you get lost. Or you could start in Burnsville to the north. Head east out of town, then turn south on Highway 80 heading for Busic.

The normal hiking route to the top is via the **Mt. Mitchell Trail**. It begins at the Black Mountain Campground. This trail zig zags up the east face for about 10 kms, and will take the average person 3 or 5 hours to reach the summit. The author was there on 5/30/1992 and his round-trip hike took just over 5 hours. Along this trail and near Commissary Hill, are 2 small sleeping shelters. One has 10 wire bunkbeds, a fireplace, pit toilet, and water. These are open to visitors on a first come, first served basis. Get more information on camping and hiking on the mountain at the little Forest Service guard station in Busic on the road to the Black Mountain Campground (or in Ashville or Burnsville).

Here is some general information and rules to keep in mind if you plan to visit Mt. Mitchell. The road to the top is open year-round, but always closed at night. The Forest Service campgrounds on the lower slopes are open from about May 15 to October 15, depending on the weather. But if the roads are not snowed-in, you can get there and climb the mountain year-round. If you're there with lots of snow, the Blue Ridge Parkway may close temporarily, so get to Busic via Highway 80 from Burnsville. Camping is permitted only in designated campgrounds or campsites and operated on a first come, first served basis. There are some backcountry campsites, but mostly on the northern and eastern slopes. Fires and camping are not allowed along the trails. Get further information from the Pisgah National Forest, Burnsville Ranger Station, Tele. 828-682-6146, or at the Ashville R.S.; or call Mt. Mitchell State Park, 828-675-4611; or Parks & Recreation for North Carolina, 919-733-4181.

Another foggy day at the summit of Mt. Mitchell.

Map 461-1, Mitchell, Blue Ridge Mtns., N. Carolina, USA

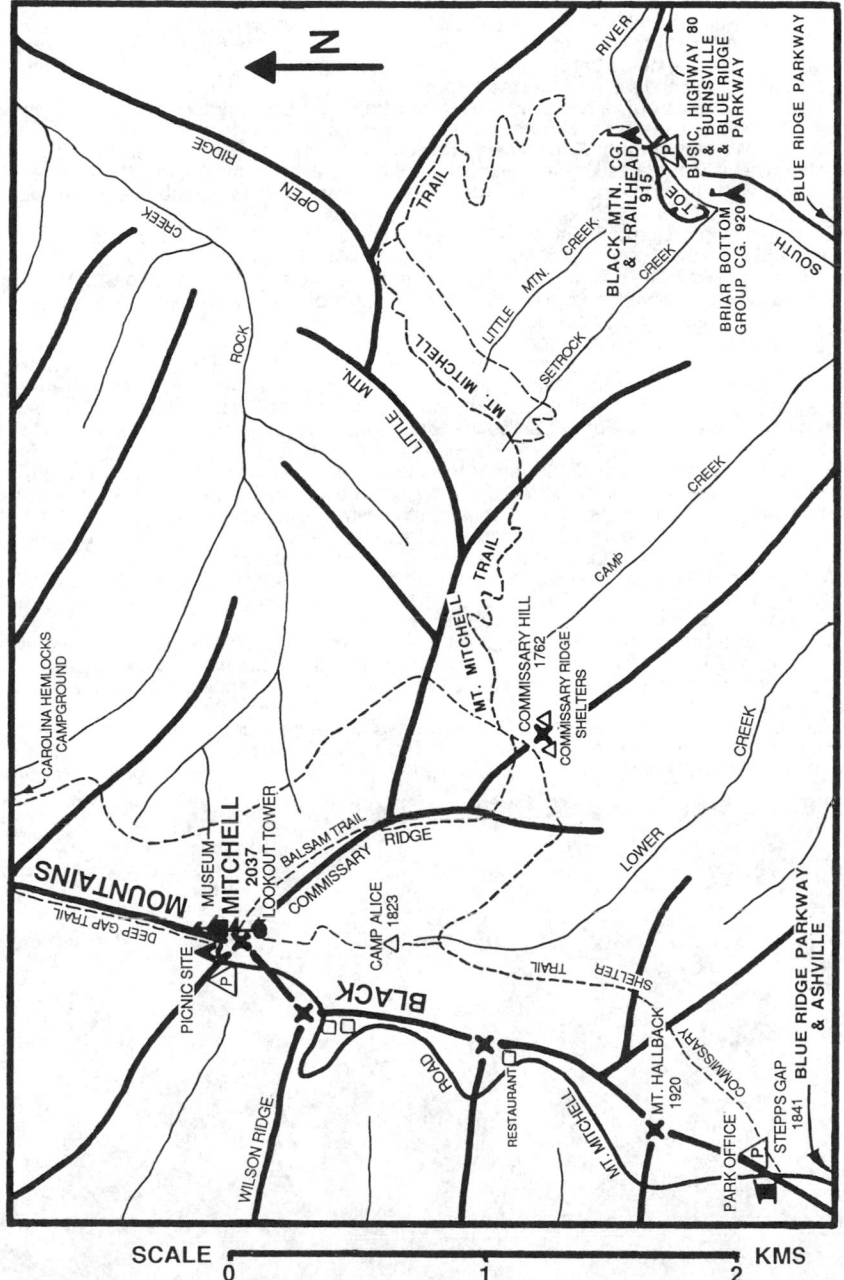

SCALE |————————————| KMS
0   1   2

Maps *South Toe River Trail Map,* 1:24,000; *Pisgah National Forest,* 1:100,000; or USGS maps *Mt. Mitchell, Celo,* and *Montreat,* 1:24,000.

Mt. Washington, White Mountains, New Hampshire, USA

The highest mountain in northeastern United States is Mt. Washington at 1917 meters. This summit is located in the middle part of the Presidential Range, which is just a small part of the much larger White Mountains of New Hampshire. These mountains are made of a very old granodiorite-type rock. This is one of the better hiking areas in the northeastern part of the United States even though there's a road and a cog railway to the summit.

To reach this region, get a New Hampshire state map, then drive north on Interstate Highway 93. Use Exit 35 and head east toward Fabyan and Mt. Washington. Just follow the signs.

The first **Mt. Washington Cog Railway** was completed in 1869. Since then it has seen many changes. The steam train starts at Marshfield and heads east to the summit. In summer you're forbidden to walk along the tracks, but in winter you can use the railway grade as a climbing or ski trail.

On the northeast side of the mountain is the beginning of the summit road. It was originally built between 1855 and 1861, and it's still known today as the **Carriage Road** (the numbers on the map indicate mile posts). The opening and closing dates of the Carriage Road and Cog Railway are determined by weather conditions, and of course the number of passengers, but generally they're both open from about mid-May until mid-October.

Of course no one is going to force you to ride or drive to the summit, so here's the healthy alternative; hiking. This map shows many trails, but on the mountain there are even more than indicated here. Be sure to buy a more detailed map when you arrive in the area. This map and description are meant to be an introduction only. Since much of this region is part of the White Mountain National Forest, a Forest Service map might come in handy (as well as the good AMC topo map listed below).

For those wishing to climb **Mt. Washington** the old fashion way, the best place to start is on the east side at Pinkham Notch and the AMC Camp & store. Locate the trail running west into Tuckerman Ravine. This is the easiest and shortest route up the east slope. Toward the upper end of this old glacier cirque basin are several huts or cabins. Inquire at the AMC Camp about using them and/or where you can camp. Above the shelters are several trails heading to the summit.

Another good hiking area is along the West Branch of the Peabody River, and in the peaks south of Randolph. This is on the north side of the range and you can enter on trails from Dolly Coop Campground, Glen House, or from near Randolph.

You can also start at the trailhead just below the cog railway station, and hike up either the Jewel or Ammonoosuc Trails. On 6/1/1992, the author went up the Ammonoosuc and returned via the Jewel. Round-trip time was just over 4 hours. Most hikers can make the summit and return in one day from most trailheads.

Take some extra clothing even on summer days as weather conditions can change quickly. There is no public transportation into this region. The AMC Camp store at Pinkham Notch seems to be one of the best place around to buy books and maps. Or contact the national forest office in

Mount Washington Hotel and Mt. Washington from Marshfield on the west side.

Map 462-1, Washington, White Mtns., N. Hampshire, USA

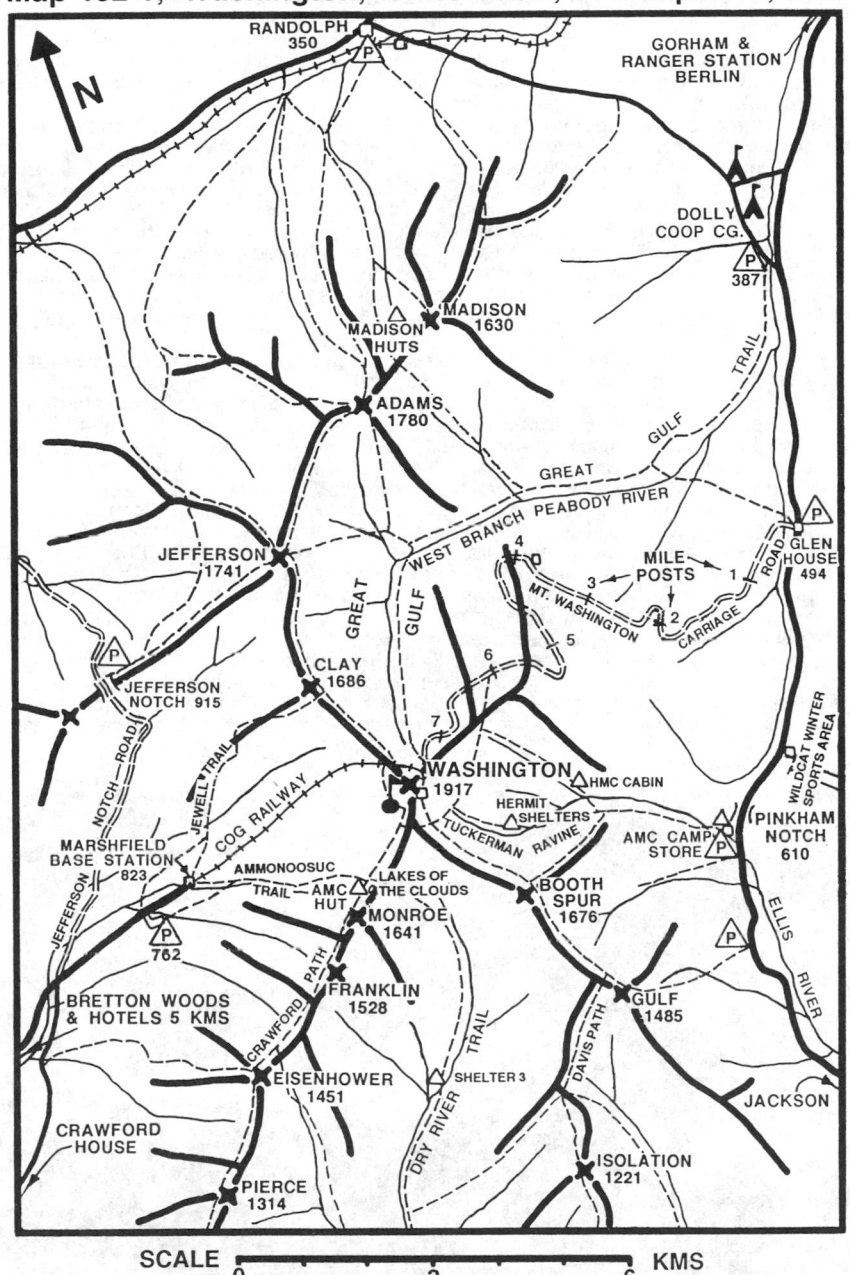

Gorham, New Hampshire, located just northeast of Mt. Washington, Tele. 603-466-2713.
Maps Appalachian Mountain Club (AMC) map, *Mount Washington and the heart of the Presidential Range,* 1:20,000; or DeLorme map *Trail Map & Guide to the White Mountain National Forest,* 1:100,000; or *White Mountain National Forest,* 1:126,720; and the book with map, **A.M.C. Guide to Mount Washington.**

Baxter Peak, Mount Katahdin, Maine, USA

Since the 2nd Edition of this book came out, 2 readers have written to the author suggesting one of the best hikes in the eastern USA was on Mount Katahdin located in north central Maine. The elevation of this mountain is only 1605 meters on Baxter Peak. But it's preserved in a wild natural area called Baxter State Park, and its northerly position puts these summits well above timberline. The higher peaks in this range are made of granite.

To reach the area of **Mt. Katahdin**, drive north on Interstate 95 toward Houlton on the Canadian border, but leave the freeway at Exit 56 at Medway. From there, head northwest on Highway 11 & 157 in the direction of Millinocket. From this sizable town, continue northwest toward Baxter State Park. Near the park entrance is a road junction. From there you have a choice of driving along the Roaring Brook Road toward Roaring Brook Campground, which is on the east side of Katahdin; or continuing northwest until you reach either the Abol or Katahdin Stream Campground. The Katahdin CG. is where the Appalachian National Scenic Trail crosses the road and heads for the top of the mountain.

The most-used route to **Baxter Peak** is the one beginning at the Katahdin Stream CG. From there a well-used trail runs northeast to the top. Trailhead to the summit is 8 kms. Most should be able to make the top in 3-4 hours, or about 5-7 hours round-trip. Part of this trail is over large granite boulders.

Another way up is along the Abol Trail. This path begins about 4 kms southeast of Katahdin Stream CG. as shown. It runs northeast into a valley and directly up to a shoulder of the mountain. The distance to the top on the Abol Trail is 6 kms, just a little shorter than on the Appalachian Trail.

The author did this hike on 6/2/1992. He slept in his *campwagon* (VW Rabbit) at the Katahdin Stream Campground and climbed up along the Appalachian Trail. That took a little over 2 hours. From the summit he came down the Abol Trail to the Abol Campground. Total trail time was 4 hours. He then road-walked back to his car; total hike-time for the trip was just over 4 3/4 hours.

Another entry point, not only for Katahdin, but to other wilderness areas to the north, is the Roaring Brook Campground. Locate and use one of 2 trails running west to the area of the Great Basin and South Basin. From that area are several trails heading for the summit. From the Roaring Brook CG. to the summit is about 9 or 10 kms, a little longer than on the 2 trails southwest of Katahdin. The advantage of using one of these eastern routes is you can make a circular hike of about 2 days, taking in Katahdin and some of the peaks and valleys to the north, then return to the same trailhead.

The last place to stock up on food is in the town of Millinocket, but it might be best to buy supplies before you get that far if possible. When heading for the high peaks, be sure to have some rain gear or warm clothing in your pack; or have a good weather forecast. The northerly position on this mountain can bring rapid changes in temperatures on top. Rainfall is evenly distributed throughout the year, but snow can fall anytime at the summit. All roads in the park are unpaved and likely to remain that way for some time.

Baxter Peak, the highest summit on Mt. Katahdin as seen from the south.

Map 463-1, Baxter Peak, Mt. Katahdin, Maine, USA

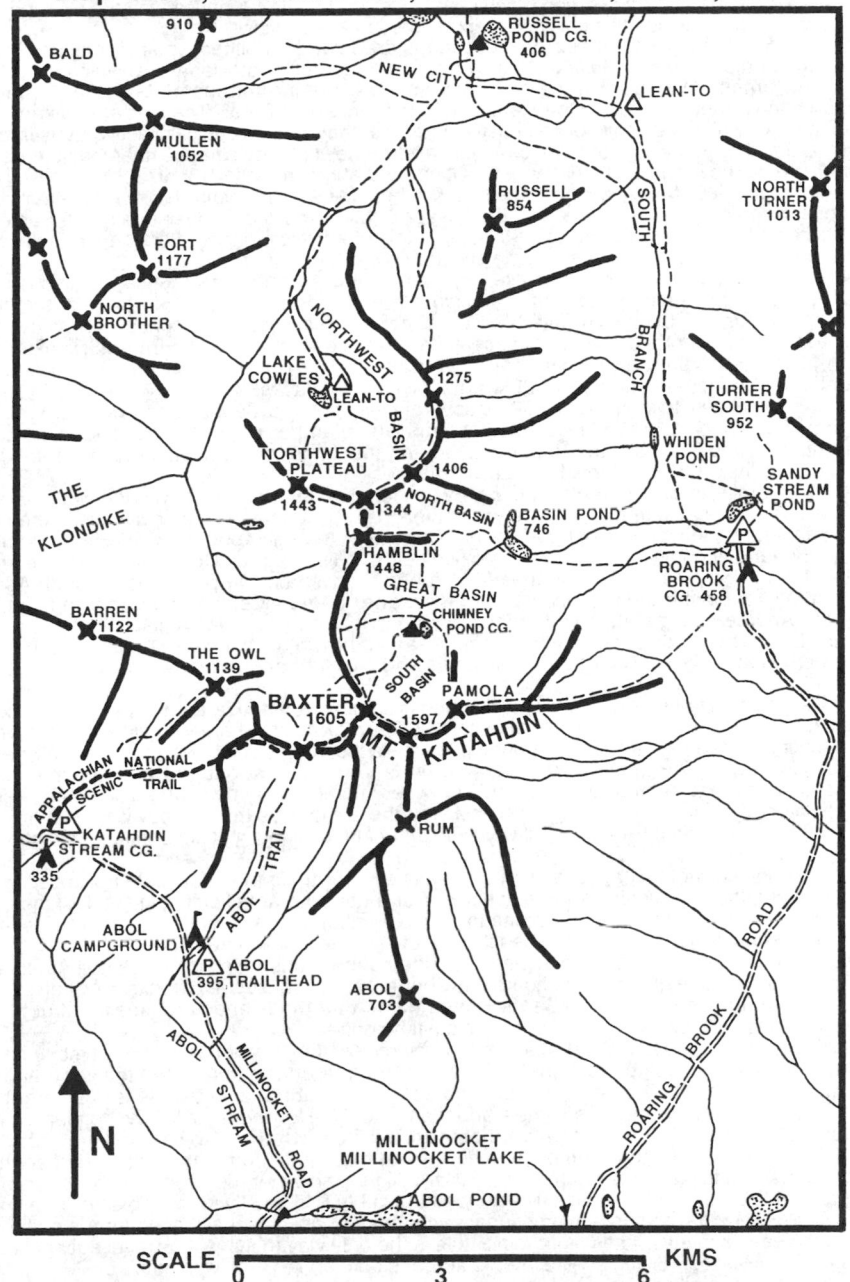

Maps USGS maps *Katahdin,* 1:62,500; or *Millinocket,* 1:100,000; or the book & map, **Katahdin: A Guide to Baxter State Park and Katahdin,** Stephen Clark, North Country Press, Unity, Maine.

Chapter 8--Mexico, Central America & the Caribbean

There are 52 maps in this section which covers Mexico, Central America, and the Caribbean. There are 28 different countries or islands represented in this section. About 1/5 of the higher summits on these maps are folded & uplifted type mountains. They are the mountain ranges in Mexico's Baja, on the islands of Cuba, Hispanola, which includes Haiti and Dominican Republic, the Northern Antilles, the mountains of Jamaica, Tobago, Trinidad and Curaçau, and the Cordillera Talamanca in Costa Rica. The rest are volcanic in origin, many of which are active or semi-active in one of the more volcanically active parts in the world. The author had the good fortune--almost misfortune--of being camped near the summit of La Soufriere on the island of St. Vincent when it erupted at 5:45am on 4/13/1979.

The 2 main areas of volcanic activity are from southern Mexico, southeast through Guatemala, to Irazu near San Jose in Costa Rica; and the Lesser Antilles or Windward Islands of the Eastern Caribbean. The island of Montserrat is the latest example of active volcanos. After 1995, most people there were evacuated to the UK or elsewhere and are just waiting to return.

Many people would classify this entire region as being part of Latin America, but this is not quite the case. The language spoken in Mexico, Central America, Cuba, Puerto Rico, and the Dominican Republic is Español (Spanish). But, Jamaica, Dominica, St. Vincent and Trinidad are populated by blacks (former slaves) and speak an African dialect along with English (Trinidad is about 40% East Indian, along with some Chinese). The French West Indies islands of Guadeloupe, Martinique and part of St. Martin, also have blacks, but they speak only French along with the whites. Der Nederlands has several islands in the Caribbean as well, and those people speak pigeon & some African dialect, plus Dutch and/or English. The Americans and British have or had islands in the Caribbean too and the language is English which is the best lingo to have when traveling through the Lesser Antilles.

As for weather, this entire region has a very similar climate throughout, with the wet and dry seasons about the same from one place to another. The best time to hike or climb is in the dry season and during the months of November or December through about April. During this time of year, the land becomes very brown in Mexico south to Nicaragua. Costa Rica and Panama have a shorter dry season. The Caribbean also has a dry season in December through April, but generally speaking these places are a bit greener than in Mexico and northern Central America. An interesting thing about the Caribbean is that on any of the small islands you will see both lush green vegetation on the east side---and a brown almost desert-like landscape on the western slope. This indicates the trade winds and moisture are perpetually coming from the east.

In this region the only place where you'll need crampons & ice ax are the tops of Popo, Ixty and Orizaba, all in Mexico. There seems to be very few rock climbing areas in the whole region.

As for crimes against travelers, the worst places are the large cities of Mexico and elsewhere including Managua & Panama City. These crimes involve someone grabbing your watch, camera, shoulder bag or small pack; either in crowded markets or at bus or train stations. Also, pick pocketers were active in Managua the last time the author was there. They work in a group of 2's or 3's on crowded buses. They always use bumping, pushing, jostling or other distractions and are very clever.

This is very similar to what goes on in Colombia and Peru; so for a complete list of security measures, see the Introduction for to this book. For those who are climbing in Mexico, there's little need for worry, except when traveling through big cities to the mountains. The Caribbean enjoys a reasonably good reputation when it comes to people stealing from tourists.

Mexico and Central America have relatively cheap public transportation. In Central America, travel is usually done in the daytime hours only, but in Mexico, buses and trucks travel all night long. The Caribbean is similar to Central America, in that the islands are small and getting anywhere takes only an hour or two during the daytime only.

Getting to the Caribbean Islands can be done by cruise ship, but you won't have time to hike or climb anything. Those people are real tourists and are on a different trip than you and I! There are few if any ferry boats in the islands so count boat travel out--unless you've got a yacht. The only sensible way to see the Caribbean is to fly. However, you'll have to plan a trip carefully, because there's not always flights going from where you are, to other nearby destinations. That's because sometimes there's not that much communication between the French, British, Dutch and American islands. Many flights, however, do have several stopovers along a flight line. One of the best airlines to contact is LIAT. They fly to more places than any other airline. They have various promotional packages or passes usually good for a month. If you want to see as many islands as possible, this is the only way to fly! Ask a travel agent about Caribbean Air Passes. Flying service on the author's last trip in 1998, was much better than in 1979, and not a whole lot more expensive.

Hitch hiking is good in Mexico (called dado), fair in Panama, and a little slow in the rest of Central America. It's slow in the French West Indies and most of the Lesser Antilles, good on Trinidad. But for most of us it's too hot to hitch hike in most places and generally speaking there's lots of competition in the transportation industry and fares are cheap, especially in Trinidad. In Mexico and Central America, food and hotels are cheap, but these same things are about 2 or 3 times as expensive in the Caribbean. The French West Indies are perhaps the most expensive islands for travelers.

This foto was taken from near La Joya looking at the south and western slopes of Ixty. (Map 468, page 997).

Looking east from the top of Acatenango at the west side of Volcan Agua. In the distance to the right is Pacaya Volcano, and below is the town of Alotenango (Map 476, page 1013).

Pico Diablo, Sierra San Pedro Martir, Baja, Mexico

This map shows Pico Diablo at 3095 meters. It's the highest point in the Sierra San Pedro Martir, which is now a national park. It's located in the northern part of the Mexico's Baja Peninsula. The core of these mountains is made of granite.

You can climb **Diablo** from the east or west slopes. To get to the drier eastern side, drive along Highway 3, which runs between Ensenada and San Felipe. Between Km posts 164 & 165, turn south onto a new road running along the east side of La Salada, a dry lake bed. When it's dry, you can use La Salada as a road, part of which is shown on the map. Near the southern end of the flats, look for a road heading west to Rancho Santa Clara. From there continue west on a good dirt road to the carpark at 675 meters. From the trailhead, walk northwest along the base of the mountain until you find the stream running out of Cañon del Diablo. Use a cable to pull yourself up over a waterfall; or backtrack a ways and go up around the waterfall to the north. Walk and wade up along this stream to Campo Noche campsite, then route-find east to the summit. This is a 3-day hike-climb; or maybe 4 days for some. Lots of wading, then a steep west face climb. The author was here on 5/22/1992, but wasn't prepared for a hike lasting several days and didn't get far into the cañon on his day-hike.

To get to the *ruta normal* on the west side of **Diablo**, drive south out of Ensenada on Highway 1. At the small village of San Telmo de Abajo, and just before you reach Km post 140, turn left or east onto the Camino (Road) de Observatorio. A sign there reads: *Observatorio, 106 kms, and Rancho Meling, 32 miles*. It'll take about 3 hours to drive to the entrance station of the parque nacional at about Km 84. This is an improved graded road all the way, but it's rocky in places. However, any car can make it.

From the park entrance, continue another 10 kms northeast on a smoother road made of granite sand through the ponderosa pines until you're on the eastern side of a big meadow called *Vallecitos*. Then look for a road heading southeast toward a small building where a well is located. Continue southeast until you reach a *steep rough place*. See map. Some cars will have to stop there; but the author, using a shovel, got his VW Rabbit over it and to the main carpark near the log cabin. It's 10 kms from Vallecitos to this log cabin. You can camp at either the *rough steep place*, or at or near the log cabin.

From the log cabin trailhead, walk up the stream valley to the northeast, then east. This is a trail-of-sorts, marked with stone cairns. Once you're north of the peak called **Cerro Botella Azul**, route-find north down to the bottom of the canyon. When you reach water, you'll have to wade down to Campo Noche (take wading shoes & long pants for stinging netal and other thorny bushes!), then climb east. This can be done in one very long day, but most people sleep at Campo Noche and finish the climb and return to their car on Day 2.

On 10/28/1992, the author got as far as the spring & running water, but didn't expect to wade and didn't want to ruin leather boots, so he gave up and returned to his car at the log cabin. The hike took 5 1/4 hours round-trip. If you have to park at the steep rough place, there is a partly marked (cairned) trail from there. Take a compass.

There are other routes up the mountain as shown, but Diablo is not an easy climb, and you'll have to do a lot of route-finding. Best time to climb is April, May and early June, to find running water on the plateau. However, always carry enough water in your car for your trip. There's

The western slopes of Pio Diablo as seen from just north of Botella Azul Peak.

988

Map 464-1, Pico Diablo, S. San Pedro Martir, Baja, Mexico

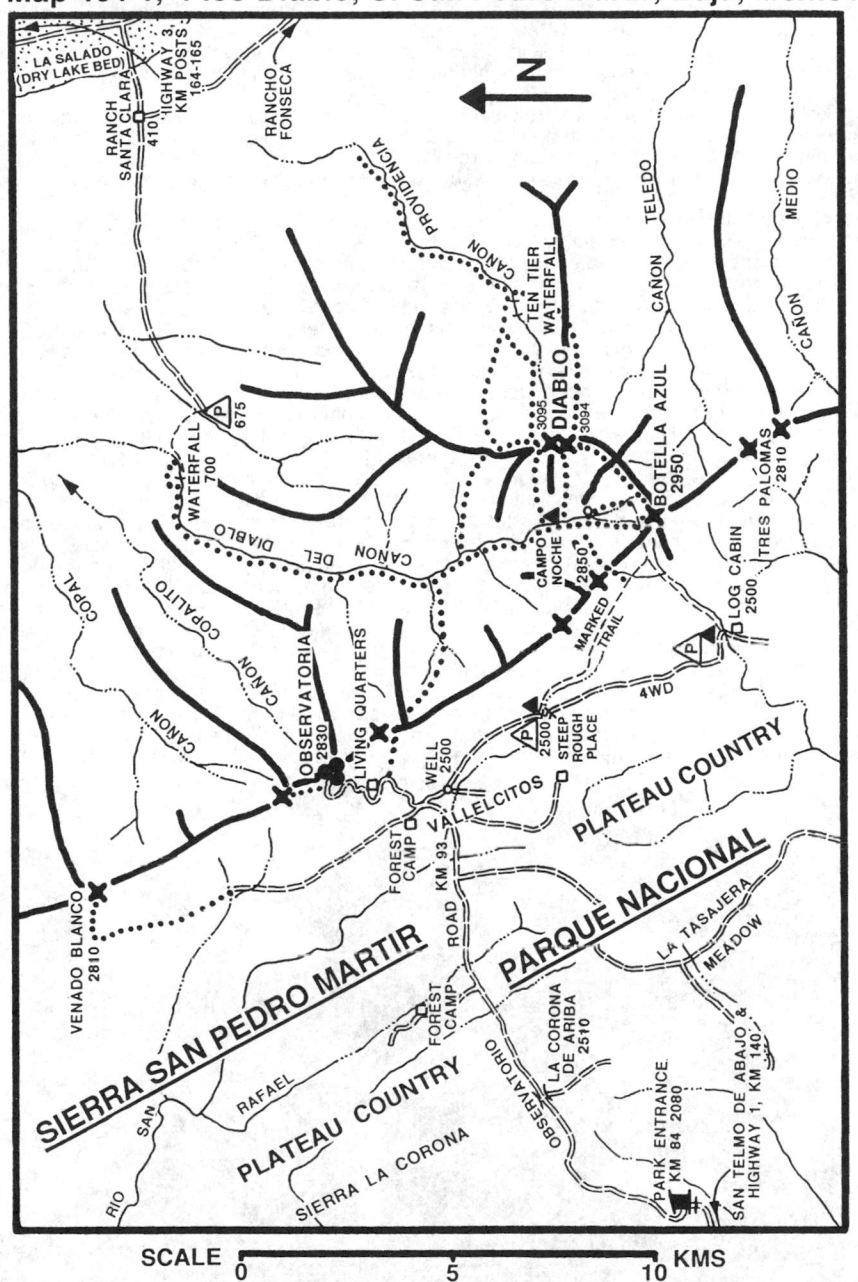

year-round water in Cañons Diablo, Providencia & Teledo. Winters are wet, summers dry.
Maps *Parque Nacional San Pedro Martir,* Centra Publications, Box 191029, San Diego, California, USA, 92159; and the book, **Camping and Climbing in Baja**, La Siesta Press.

Nevado & Volcan de Colima, Sierra Madre, Mexico

Featured on this map is one large mountain with 2 high summits. The highest is known as Nevado de Colima at 4240 meters (on some maps it's listed as high as 4320 & 4450 meters). The name nevado means snow mountain in Spanish. At times snow does fall on the high peak, thus the name. This nevado is a huge hulk of a mountain, and on top is an old volcanic crater with some erosion, but it still retains its conal shape.

The other peak is known as Volcan de Colima (known locally as Volcan Fuego) at 3820 meters. This is a new cone with no vegetation on its upper slopes. When the author visited the summit on 12/24/1982, it was emitting large amounts of smoke, but there was no trembling or explosions. The summit area was very warm with choking gases coming from vents inside the crater.

Volcan Colima is indeed an active volcano, and it's been erupting almost continuously since the Global Volcanism Program began in the early 1970's. On 2/10 & 5/10/1999, there were 2 big explosions which caused evacuations on the south side of the mountain. On 7/17/1999, there was another eruption which sent ash up to 11 kms. For the latest updates go to the websites (www.ucol.mx/volcan) or (www.volcano.si.edu/gvp/).

Here's what the author did. He started this trip at the terminal de buses in Guadalajara. He took a bus bound for Colima, a city southwest of the mountain. At Atenquique, he got out and got more information from locals, then walked up the road towards Paso Radon, but didn't get far that first evening. He camped just above the finca (farm) at 1540 meters. Along the way, there's no water anywhere, except at the finca (the author carried his water from Atenquique on the main highway). The next morning, 12/24/1982, he walked all the way to the top of Volcan de Colima and back to camp. That climb took nearly 12 hours; a very long and tiring hike! The third morning he returned to Atenquique and stopped a bus heading to Guadalajara.

The author's second day was far too long, so it's recommended if you're planning to walk all the way to either peak, get an early start and camp higher on the mountain. That would make the second day much shorter, but could also extend the trip into a third day. However, if you can speak a little Spanish and communicate, talk to people at the pulp & lumber mill at Atenquique, and they might help you get a lift part way up the mountain. Trucks passed the author's camp both mornings at about 5am. This would eliminate a lot of walking and carrying tons of water if you can get a lift. On this route, don't plan on finding water beyond the finca; water is a big problem on a walking trip. With your own 4WD, it can easily be climbed in one day.

There used to be a refugio at the Radon Pass, where 4 to 6 people could sleep on the floor. From there, a bushwhacking route can be found to the summit of **Nevado Colima**, but the normal route is up the northeast slopes along a steep road to the Miroondas just west of the summit cone. On weekends you can surely find a ride up either peak. Regardless, if you're using public transport, plan on 3 days of food and carry lots of water. Once on either mountain

Snow sometimes falls on the summit of Nevada Colima as we see here.

Map 465-1, Nevado & Volcan Colima, Sierra Madre, Mexico

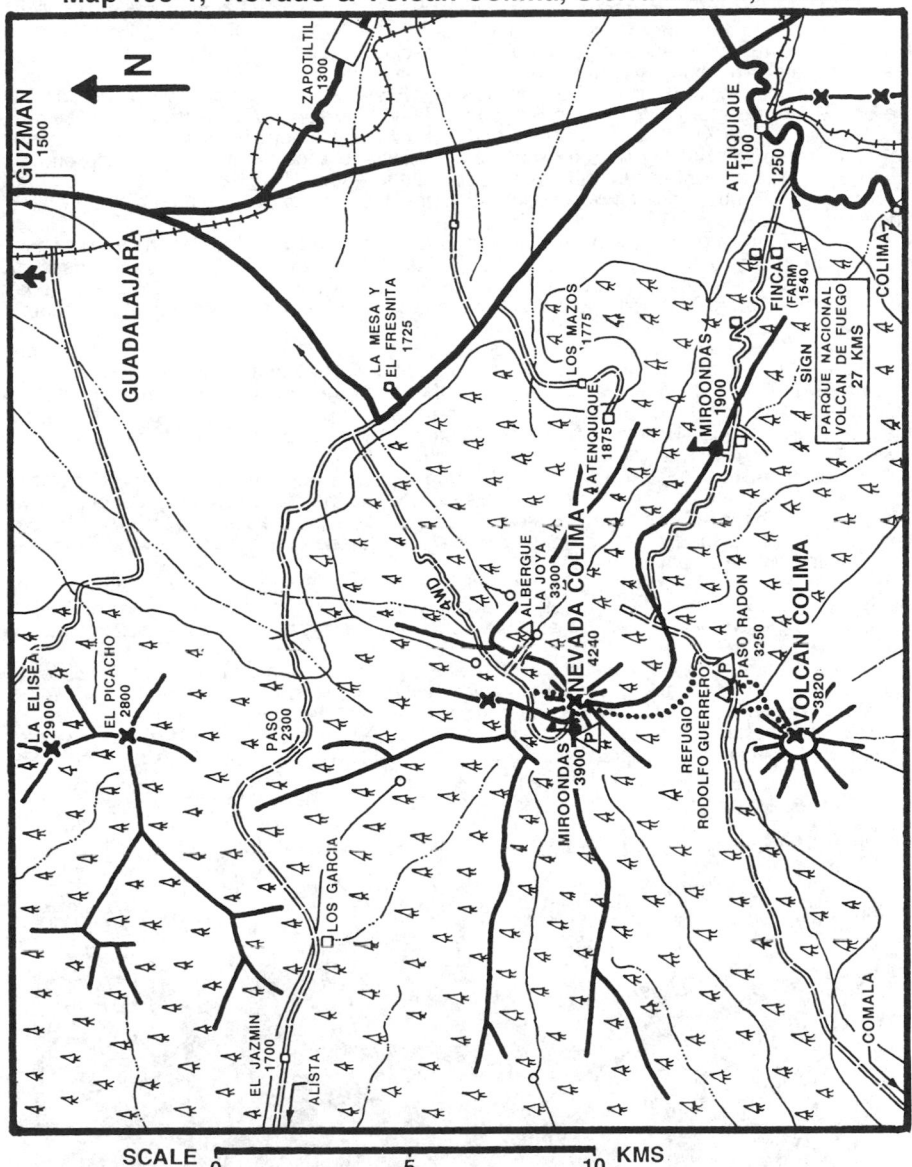

SCALE 0   5   10 KMS

the climbing is easy, but better take a tent. Greg Home of Jasper, Alberta, says you can hire a taxi from Guzman to La Mesa y El Fresnita, then ask for Agustin Ibarra (or someone else) for a ride up the mountain; or walk to the refugio (Albergue La Joya) at 3300 meters, then to the antennas or miroondas, and by trail to the summit. Normally it's 2 days round-trip for climbing Nevado de Colima along this road route. Dry season is from October to March.

Maps *Colima*, 1:250,000, (and maps at 1:50,000 scale) from the Direccion General De Geografia Del Territorio Nacional Mexico. Buy at DETENAL, Balderas 71, Mexico City; or check the website (www.omnimap.com), or in the USA call 800-742-2677, or 336-227-8300; and the book, **Mexico's Volcanoes**, The Mountaineers.

Volcan Parícutin, Sierra Madre, Mexico

Included in this book are many mountains, some of which are not high or difficult to climb, but are interesting for other reasons. On this map is just such a mountain. It's Volcan Parícutin at about 2744 meters, located in the state of Michoacan, in southwest Mexico. Large towns or cities in the area are Uruapan to the southeast and Zamora to the northeast.

A couple of things make this volcano interesting. First, it's a new or young mountain. This is the one which began erupting in a farmer's corn field on 2/20/1943. As the story goes, the man was in his field plowing. He looked behind and saw a crack develop and lava, steam and gases began to flow out. Over a period of weeks a hill grew into a mountain. The lava spread out covering valuable farmland and finally a small village named San Juan. At the end of the activity, a small cinder cone developed, which is now the highest point of the immediate area. The volcano has been quiet since 2/25/1952.

The second thing of interest is the San Juan Church. The lava surrounded the village finally engulfing it, and the only thing left of the pueblo of San Juan today is the church, which rises out of the lava near the edge of the flow. The lava covering the village is 3 to 5 meters deep. Today the mountain is quiet, but perhaps still steaming, and the church of San Juan has become a tourist attraction.

To get to this area, most people drive along Highway 15 which connects Zamora with Morelia. At the junction of Highways 15 & 37, and at a village called Carapan, turn south on Highway 37 in the direction of Uruapan. About halfway between Paracho and Uruapan, take the road west toward Los Reyes but stop at the village of Angahuan which is just south of the main road, as shown. You'll find lots of buses running along Highway 37, with less traffic going west toward Angahuan.

To get to **Parícutin** from Angahuan, there's an old road or trail heading south, then southwest to the north end of the lava flow. It's easy to find the church standing out of the lava. This scene is reminiscent of the Cagsawa Church & ruins on the southeast side of Volcan Mayon in The Philippines; or the church at the village of Saleaula near the Silisili Volcano on the island of Savaii, in Western Samoa.

Many routes can be taken to the top of the cinder cone of Parícutin, but there is a trail running south along the west side of the lava, which is the easiest way. Crossing the blocky lava flow is difficult, time consuming and it wears out shoes in a hurry. It's a long one day hike to see the church, climb the mountain, and return to Angahuan.

The author climbed Parícutin on 3/22/1972, his first climb in Latin America. He hitch hiked into the area in cars and in the back of a truck, and was invited into the home of Jose Cruz Gomez in Angahuan. The next morning he climbed the mountain and visited the church and left that afternoon.

Food and water can be found in Angahuan, as well as people who act as guides. However, any person in this village will be helpful in putting you on the right trail. Hitch hiking into the area is fairly

Lava has engulfed the village & church at San Juan. Parícutin is seen in the distance.

Map 466-1, Volcan Parícutin, Sierra Madre, Mexico

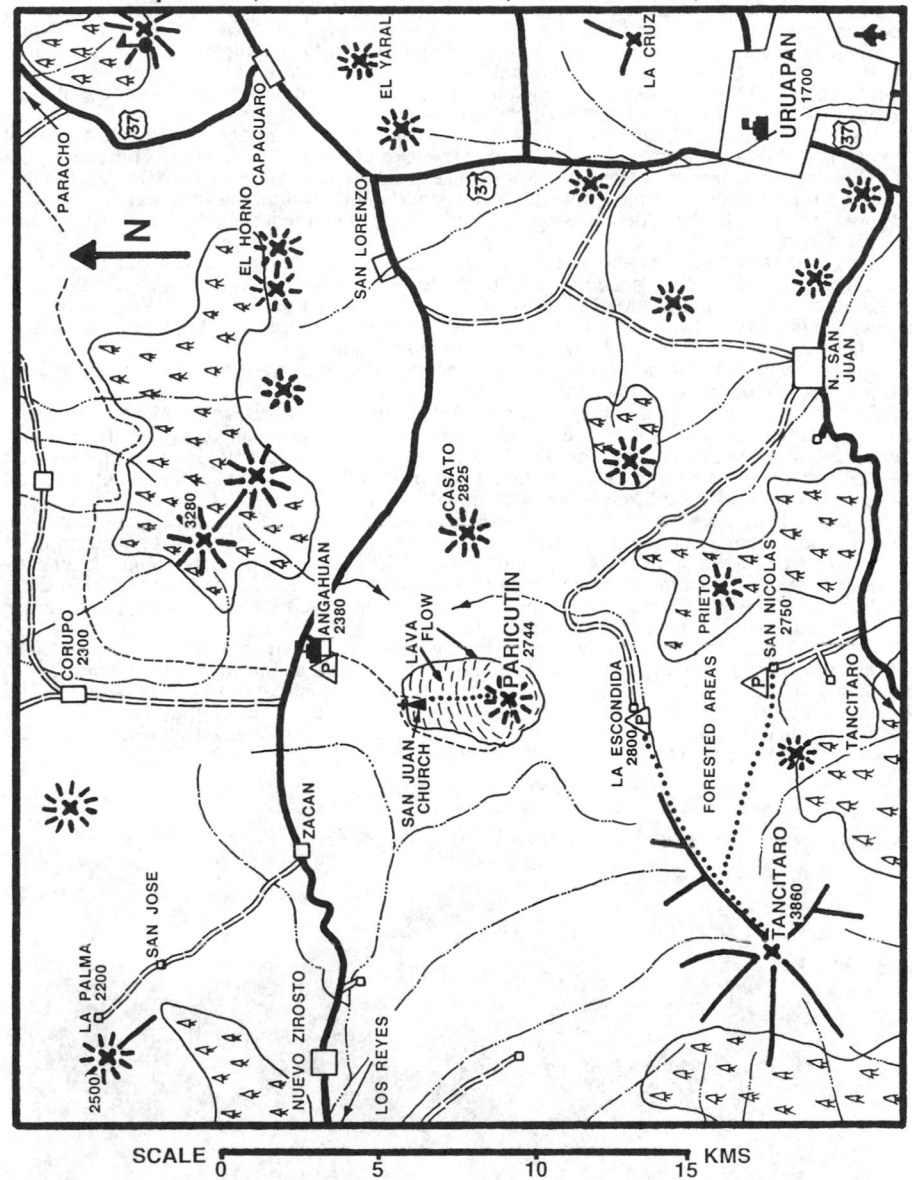

SCALE 0 5 10 15 **KMS**

easy, but traffic is light. There are a fair number of buses or minibuses going that way now. Also, there are several hotels or residencias in Angahuan as well.

Maps *Colima, E13-3,* 1:250,000 (and surely maps at 1:50,000 scale), from the Direccion General De Geografia Del Territorio Nacional Mexico. Buy at DETENAL, Balderas 71, Mexico City; or check the website (www.omnimap.com), or in the USA call 800-742-2677, or 336-227-8300;and the book, **Parícutin: The Volcano Born in a Mexican Cornfield**, Luhr & Simkin, Geoscience Press; and a travel guidebook to Mexico.

Nevado de Toluca, Cordillera Anahuac, Mexico

Nevado de Toluca is the high prominent peak southwest of the large city of Toluca, which is about 50 kms west of Mexico City. Nevado Toluca rises to an altitude of 4704 meters (4690 on some maps), making it the 4th highest mountain in Mexico. It too is an old and eroded volcano, but it still retains a conal shape, and has a large crater or caldera at the summit. The book, **Volcanos of the World**, doesn't even list this mountain, but an educated guess as to its age would be 20,000 to 25,000 years since it blew its top during the last eruption.

Inside the crater is a large lake and there are several radio-TV antennas on the north side of the mountain. There's also a 4WD-type road to the lake at about 4200 meters. Fortunately, the road beyond the albergue is steep and few vehicles make it to the crater lake. Despite the fact there's a road high on the mountain, it's still a good climb. Of all the mountains in Mexico featured in this book, Nevado Toluca seems to have more surface or running water. The reason for this is it's an older volcano.

This map shows the volcano and all or most of the possible hiking routes. It's possible to climb **Toluca** from the east, and the small pueblos of San Pedro Tlanisco, San Miguel Balderas or Zaragoza, but using these routes involves a 2 day climb for sure. The map the author used to create this one doesn't show any trail from the above mentioned villages, but there are trails all over this mountain, used mostly by wood cutters and shepherds.

But the recommended and normal route of access to **Toluca** is via the village of Raices and the refugios or albergues on the west side of the mountain.

The starting point is the city of Toluca. Get to the bus station and find a bus heading southwest to Raices and beyond to Sultepec. There will be a bus leaving every half hour all day long. Get off at Raices and walk or hitch hike 500 meters to the turnoff to the mountain. Just beyond that is the entrance gate for the parque nacional and the Posada Familiar where you can sleep. From that point it's 5 kms to the Albergue Ejidal at 3810 meters. On weekends you can likely get a ride up from Raices; if not, the walk is pleasant. The albergue is a regular hotel, with rooms, food, drinks and water. It's open year-round, and of course it's busiest on weekends. It has 64 bunk beds. You can also camp in the area. From the albergue to the summit is an easy half day hike. Just pick the route you want (If you continue along the road running toward the caldera, you'll find a government-run refugio which is said to be 6 kms from the crater and at 4050 meters altitude. The author didn't see this one).

On 12/26/1982, the author arrived in Toluca by bus, then got another bus going to Sultepec. He got off in Raices and bought most of his food, then walked all the way to the albergue. He continued up the mountain a ways and camped in the pines just below treeline. Next morning he climbed to the north summit called Pico Aguila in 1 1/2 hours. From that point it's hard to know which is the highest point and he didn't have a map. So he walked back to Raices and got a bus to Toluca and Mexico City that same afternoon.

Nevado Toluca seen from the albergue on the west side of the mountain.

Map 467-1, Nevado de Toluca, Cordillera Anahuac, Mexico

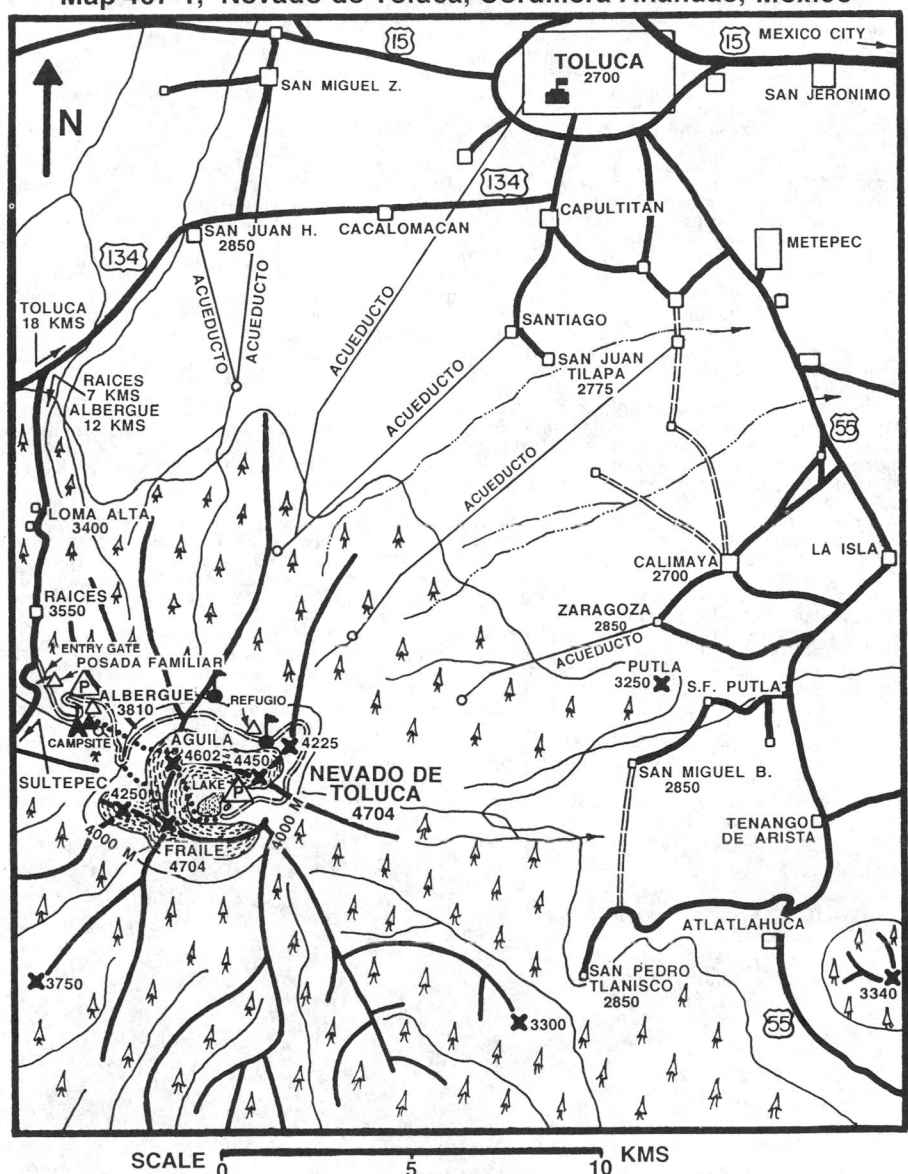

SCALE 0 — 5 — 10 KMS

Toluca is covered with a pine forest, which is open and easy to walk through. Snowline shown on this map is for the wet season, so winter climbing gear is not normally needed. But a walking stick or long ice ax might come in handy if there's new snow near the top. There are no perpetual snowfields on this mountain, but it can be windy, cold and snowy on top. Buy food in Toluca or Raices.

Maps *Ciudad De Mexico,* 1:250,000 (and surely maps at 1:50,000 scale) from the Direccion General De Geografia Del Territorio Nacional Mexico. Buy at DETENAL, Balderas 71, Mexico City; or check the website (www.omnimap.com), or in the USA call 800-742-2677, or 336-227-8300; and the book, **Mexico's Volcanoes,** The Mountaineers.

Popocatepetl & Iztaccihuatl (Popo & Ixty), Cordillera Anahuac, Mexico

The most famous mountain in Mexico is one of 2 high volcanos southeast of Mexico City. The highest is Popocatepetl (Popo) at 5452 meters, while its sister peak to the north is Iztaccihuatl (Ixty) at 5286 meters. Both peaks are crowned with snow and ice that form small glaciers at the higher elevations but there are few crevasses to be found. An ice ax & crampons are needed for a safe ascent on both summits. Both peaks are easy climbs but they both have the high altitude factor, which is a problem for people who live at or near sea level.

Ixty is the oldest and extinct. Its age is mid to late Pleistocene but it still has a somewhat conal shape. Popo is a very active volcano. It had historical eruptions through 1947, then was quiet until 12/21/1994. Since then it's had many small explosive-type eruptions, but then at about 7:30pm, 12/18/2000 it came alive with a fireworks show throwing lava perhaps 300 meters into the night sky; the biggest eruption in 1200 years. Thousands were evacuated.

To climb either mountain, you must first go to Amecameca, a small city at the western base of the peaks. Many buses go that way. In Mexico City, ask anyone which metro line will take you to the eastern bus terminal, from where you take a bus to Amecameca where you'll find a couple of hotels and a good mercado for buying food.

From Amecameca, there is no public transport to the mountain, but there are taxis and/or shuttle services you can hire. On weekends there's a fair amount of traffic so hitch hiking can be pretty good. The paved road up the mountain begins just south of Amecameca.

To climb **Popo**, make your way south from the Paso de Cortez (which has a visitor center, plus 25 beds) to the place called Tlamacas. At Tlamacas there's a small hotel and climber's hut where some food & drinks can be purchased.

From Tlamacas, you can climb to the top of Popo in one day, but because of the high altitude, some people sleep one night in one of the huts on the mountain, and make it to the top on the second day. If you're coming from sea level it's best to sleep at least one night (maybe more) at Tlamacas before climbing. Consult the latest travel guidebook or Secor's book below for up-to-date information on the condition of the huts and facilities at Tlamacas.

During the late 1990's, Popo was put on red alert and forbidden to climb; but it's your life and you can always get around the road block at Paso de Cortez if you so desire. But be warned, Popo's eruptions are always the explosive types which hurl lava block all over the summit area. Best to contact the tourist office in Mexico City first, or someone in Amecameca before going up. If its actively blowing up when you arrive, it could be you'll have to settle for Ixty only. For volcanic updates see the Global Volcanism Network at (www.volcano.si.edu/gvp/) or (www.cenapred.unam.mx) in Spanish.

To climb **Ixty**, turn left or north at the Paso de Cortez, and proceed to the end of the road and parking area called *La Joya*. Along the way and near the antennas is the *Altzomoni Lodge* where you can sleep. Higher on the mountain are 3 small huts close together where you may sleep. Ixty can also be climbed in one day, but again the high altitude makes it a 2-day trip for some. Your climbing speed depends mostly on your acclimatization. Ixty is the longer of the 2 climbs and involves a traverse of several high points along a high snowy ridge.

The author spent 4 days on these peaks beginning on 3/26/1972. He was joined by Del, Paul & Chip from Texas. On the first 2 days, he climbed Popo twice by 2 different routes taking 6 & 9 hours round-trip from Tlamacas. Beginning on the 2nd day, he had diarrhea and vomited every day (it wasn't an altitude problem, but bad food of some kind). On the afternoon of Day 3, he hiked to a hut on Ixty and finished the climb the next day; total walk-time for Ixty was about 9

From the summit of Ixty looking south at Popo.

Map 468-1, Popo & Ixty, Cordillera Anahuac, Mexico

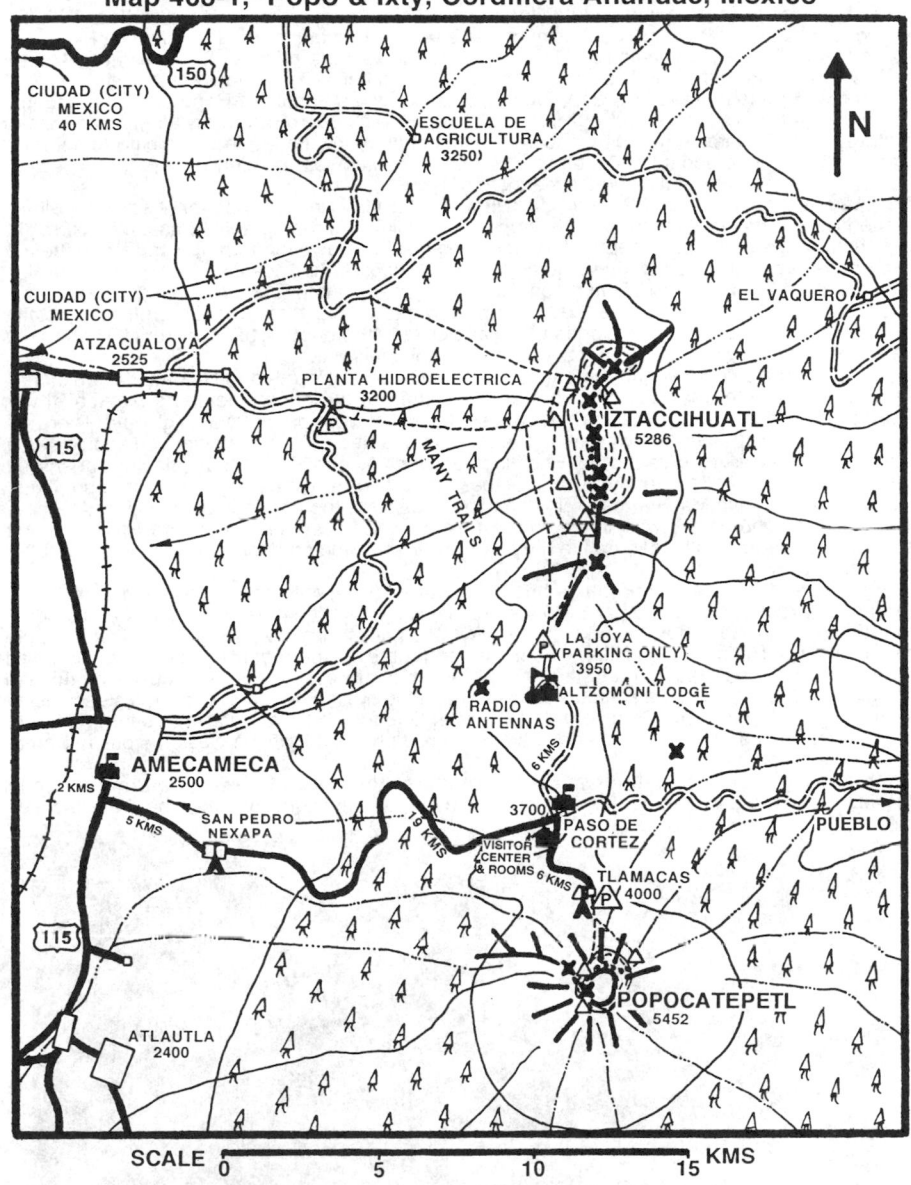

CIUDAD (CITY)
MEXICO
40 KMS

150

ESCUELA DE
AGRICULTURA
3250)

N

EL VAQUERO

CUIDAD (CITY)
MEXICO

ATZACUALOYA
2525

PLANTA HIDROELECTRICA
3200

IZTACCIHUATL
5286

115

MANY TRAILS

LA JOYA
(PARKING ONLY)
3950

ALTZOMONI LODGE

RADIO
ANTENNAS

AMECAMECA
2500

2 KMS

SAN PEDRO
NEXAPA

5 KMS

18 KMS

3700

6 KMS

PASO DE
CORTEZ

PUEBLO

VISITOR
CENTER
& ROOMS

6 KMS

TLAMACAS
4000

115

ATLAUTLA
2400

POPOCATEPETL
5452

SCALE 0   5   10   15 KMS

hours round-trip from La Joya.
      Water can be found at Tlamacas and at or near the huts on either mountain. All the huts are small, sleeping about 4-6 people each. Ask someone at the visitor center about their condition before climbing. Expect them to be full on weekends, especially in times of good weather. December through about April are the driest months. Many climbers are on the peaks during the North American Christmas Holidays.
Maps *Ciudad De Mexico, E14-2,* 1:250,000 (and others at 1:50,000 scale), from the Direccion General De Geografia Del Territorio Nacional Mexico. Buy at DETENAL, Balderas 71. Mexico City; or check the website (www.omnimap.com), or in the USA call 800-742-2677, or 336-227-8300; and the book, **Mexico's Volcanoes,** The Mountaineers.

La Malinche, Cordillera Anahuac, Mexico

For visitors to Mexico who would like an interesting hike, but one which lacks the higher altitudes of Orizaba, Popo or Ixty, this might be a good mountain to try. It's called La Malinche, rising to 4431 meters. This is about the same altitude as the highest peaks in the USA. La Malinche is an old and eroded volcano. It last erupted sometime in the late Pleistocene.

La Malinche is located between Orizaba and the twin summits of Popo and Ixty, and just northeast of one of Mexico's largest cities, Puebla. It's surrounded on all sides by major highways, so it's easy to get to. Once on the mountain, you'll find a beautiful pine forest from about 3000 on up to about 4000 meters. It's a fine mountain for camping, except for the lack of water high on the peak and along the standard routes.

There are several ways to reach the summit of **Malinche**. With several water pipelines (acueductos) coming down from springs on the east side, it's reasonable to assume you might walk up along one of these, then route-find to the summit. However, from the springs to the top it might be steep and there may be some bushwhacking. Other possible routes are from San Isidro on the southwest side of the mountain. The map the author used (scale 1:250,000) didn't show a trail, but it's likely one is there. Or from the town of Amozoc, south of the mountain, there's a road up the southern slopes to a place called Axaltenco at 3200 meters. There must be a trail to the summit from there, but this this not not confirmed.

Here's one *ruta normal* and the one used by the author. Proceed to Huamantla, which has several hotels. Get there by bus from several different directions including Mexico City or Puebla. Once there, walk or take a taxi to the west end of town on the main highway. There's a Pemex station at the junction where the road to Altamira begins. At that point you should see a sign, *Camino Rural-Altamira 8 kms*. From that junction you can likely find a colectivo, or shared taxi, and ride 3 kms to Matamoros. One of these colectives leaves every half hour or so; if not, just hire a taxi. From Matamoros, walk or maybe get a lift to the farming community of Altamira. Turn left at the church and walk to the end of the road which is at the school. From there it's first a 4WD track, then a well-used trail to the top. There are good campsites in meadows at 3800-4000 meters, but no water.

On 12/29/1982, the author took a bus from Ciudad (City) Mexico late in the morning, then went up this route and camped at 3420 meters. Next morning he hide his big pack and made it to the summit in 1 1/2 hours. After that he followed another well-used trail down to the old refugio (now in ruins). This is likely the most-used route on the mountain, but the author isn't sure about the road leading up to the ruins. You'll have to ask someone about using this *old refugio route*. From there he contoured east through the open pine forest back to his pack using an altimeter. Then down to Huamantla. Total walk-time for the 2 day hike was roughly 9 hours. This means you can climb it in one day from Huamantla. At 2:30 pm, he was on a bus to Perote and the next mountain.

In a recent travel guidebook to Mexico, it states there's a state-run *Centro Vacacional Malintzi* somewhere on the north slope which you get to from Highway 136. There are 3 buses

The summit of La Malinche rises far above the pines on the north slope.

Map 469-1, La Malinche, Cordillera Anahuac, Mexico

APIZACO

TLAXCALA

136

N

CHAPULTEPEC

TEACALCA
2900 2600

TLACHCO
2500
CUAUHTENCO

AZTATLA
2475

HUAMANTLA
2550

MATAMOROS
2660
ZARAGOZA
2525

TORRE
MICROODAS

ALTAMIRA
P 2975

AMOMOLOC

OLD REFUGIO
(RUINS)
3525

LOS PILARES
2700

ACUEDUCTO

S.J. IXTENCO
2500

CAMPSITE

3750

LA MALINCHE
4431

ACUEDUCTO

ACUEDUCTO

TRINIDAD
2500

F. JAVIER
2625

AXALTENCO
3200

ACUEDUCTO

SAN ISIDRO
2600
CANOO
2600

129

EL PINAL
3160

SAN JUAN TEPULCO

PUEBLA
LA RESURRECCION
2350

ACAJETE
2450

AMOZOC
CONCEPCION
CAPULAC
2440

AMOZOC

SCALE
0   5   10   KMS

per day going there from Apizaco and Tlaxcala. They have good tourist facilities and this is apparently the beginning of that *ruta normal* which runs past the *old refugio* mentioned above.

If using the Altamira route, do all your shopping in Huamantla, or surely not later than Matamoros. Also be sure and get water in Matamoros, as do the people in Altamira, with the use of donkeys--they probably use trucks by now! The dry season is October through March.

Maps *Ciudad De Mexico* and Veracruz, 1:250,000 (and other maps at 1:50,000 scale), from the Direccion General De Geografia del Territorio Nacional Mexico. Buy at DETENAL, Balderas 71, Mexico City; or check the website (www.omnimap.com), or in the USA call 800-742-2677, or 336-227-8300; and the latest edition of the book, **Mexico's Volcanoes,** The Mountaineers.

Cofre de Perote, Cordillera Anahuac, Mexico

Of all the mountains of Mexico covered in this book, this one is likely the least difficult or challenging. However, this old and very eroded volcano has some unique aspects which make it an enjoyable hike. This mountain is called Cerro Cofre de Perote at 4282 meters. It's located directly north of Mexico's highest mountain, Pico Orizaba, and due west of Veracruz and the much closer city of Jalapa. Perote is in the east-west belt of volcanic cones which dot the landscape in central Mexico.

The name *cofre* in Español means *coffin* in English, which is the way the summit rock appears. What you see on top is what remains of the throat or vent of this volcano. Its age is late Pleistocene and it's been perhaps 50,000 years since it's last throat-clogging eruption.

The mountain itself is a large and rounded mound with few canyons (except on the east side of the mountain where it drops to low elevations rapidly) and few interesting features. However, right on top is a huge rock, rising about 40 meters above the surrounding forest. This is the black coffin-like rock which gives the mountain it's name. What could be a good rock climb has been ruined by TV and radio antennas right on top. Despite the fact there's a road to the base of the summit rock this is still a good hike. There are many roads on the mountain, especially on the northern slopes, where you'll see many farms or fincas and ranchos. There are also many trails going in all directions, and in places, native forests which have been used in a small lumber industry. On the lower slopes just above Perote town is a pine forest, while further up it's more like a rain or cloud forest. Both forests are easy to walk through however.

This is the recommended route to **Perote**. Walk from the central plaza in downtown Perote toward the mountain, probably on Calle Allende (?). This dirt road passes a garbage dump, then turns left up the mountain, later turning into a trail. Take one of many trails going directly up the slope. There are springs somewhere high on the mountain you'll hear water gushing from a pipe at 2825 meters. See map. Otherwise the only places to find water on the mountain are at ranchos. Take perhaps 2 liters to begin the hike and a lunch.

You'll pass a fairly well-used road near Rancho Nuevo, then trails head straight up. You'll pass potato fields (harvest time is around Christmas), the highest of which is about 3550 meters. Higher up you can walk easily through the puno grass or along the 4WD road which leads to the summit.

Here's the author's experience. On 12/30/1982, he took an afternoon bus from Huamantla where he had just climbed Malinche. He checked into the Perote Hotel, had a quiet sleep, and the next day did the climb as described above. He was on the summit after 3 3/4 hours, while the round-trip was just under 7 hours. That afternoon he was on a bus to Vera Cruz and points south.

This is an all day hike, with the dry season being from October or November through March or April. But it can be climbed anytime. Perote town is on a busy highway and has at least 2

Looking southeast at Cofre de Perote from the main plaza in Perote.

Map 470-1, Cofre de Perote, Cordillera Anahuac, Mexico

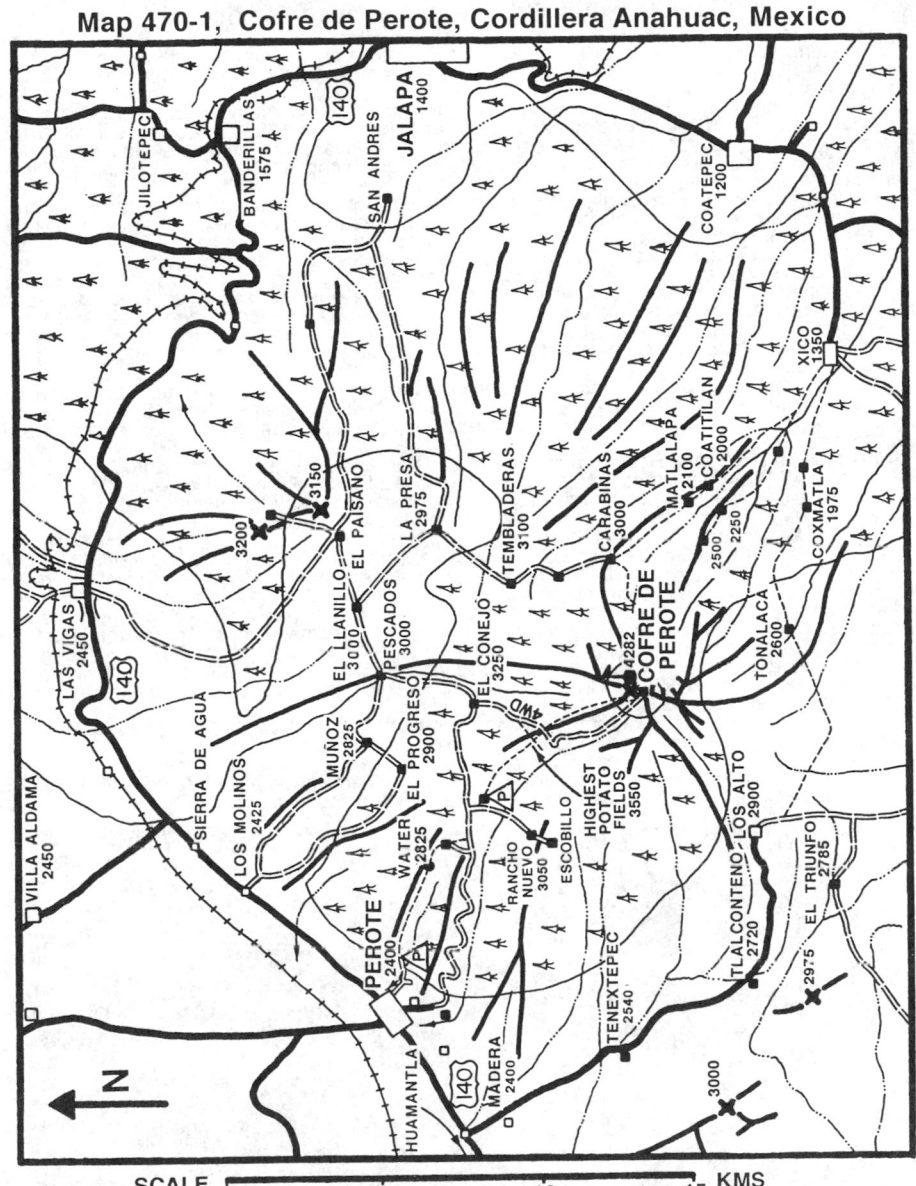

SCALE 0   5   10   15 KMS

small hotels, a supermarket, and many small stores. Nice town. Get to Perote by bus or even hitch hiking.

Maps *Veracruz,* 1:250,000 (and other maps at 1:50,000 scale) from the Direccion General De Geografia Del Territorio Nacional Mexico. Buy at DETENAL, Balderas 71, Mexico City; or check the website (www.omnimap.com), or in the USA call 800-742-2677, or 336-227-8300; and the book, **Mexico's Volcanoes,** The Mountaineers.

Pico Orizaba, Cordillera Anahuac, Mexico

The highest mountain in Mexico and the third highest in North America, is Pico Orizaba at 5760 meters. It's located just north of the city of Orizaba, east of Puebla and Mexico City, and west of Vera Cruz. It sits on the boundary of the states of Vera Cruz and Puebla and is not too far from the Gulf of Mexico.

Orizaba is an older but dormant volcano that still retains its symmetrical shape. According to the book, **Volcanos of the World**, Orizaba's last eruption was in 1687. That was a small VEI-2 explosion from the central crater at or near the summit. Researchers have detected 23 separate eruptions since 7450 BC, 7 of which occurred since Spanish colonization. But everything seems very quiet today.

Orizaba's summit is heavily glaciated, but these glaciers have few crevasses; certainly none to cause concern, even for a solo climber. Because it's the highest in Mexico, you'll find quite a few people climbing this peak.

Getting to **Orizaba** is relatively simple. The normal route is via the small town of Tlachichuca located northwest of the peak. You can get to Tlachichuca by bus, colectivo, or by hitch hiking from Highway 140, which runs from Acatzingo to Zacatepec and Jalapa. Get a Mexican highway map. Acatzingo is located on the main highway halfway between Puebla and Vera Cruz. If taking a bus, get off at Acatzingo and get another bus to Tlachichuca; or take a bus direct from Serdan; or get off at the Highway 140 junction 22 kms west of town and look for something else.

Tlachichuca is a small town, but there is at least one gasoline station, 2 hotels--the Panchita & Gerar, the La Casa Blanca Resturante, and several small shops where you can buy plenty of food for the climb. However, for better selections it's best to shop in larger towns before reaching this area.

At last report, a Señior Reyes was still there and operating the gas station, store & hotel. He also runs a 4WD shuttle service up to base camp called Piedra Grande. However, Reyes now has a competitor, so check out the prices before committing yourself to a hotel or transport to the mountain. Try the Gerar Hotel for lodging & transport to the mountain.

Beyond Tlachichuca, the dirt road is good to the pueblo of Hidalgo, then steep & rough in places and for 4WD's to Piedra Grande. If you're there on weekends it should be easy to get a lift all the way to the huts, but on other days, you'll either have to pay for the shuttle from Tlachichuca, or take a cheap taxi to Hidalgo and walk from there, which will help you acclimatize.

If you have your own vehicle, the climb could be made in one day from Tlachichuca, but because of the elevation, it's best to stay in Tlachichuca one night, then another night at Piedra Grande before attempting the summit (Piedra Grande has several huts, or you can camp nearby). Your speed of ascent will depend on the elevation where you live, and/or how well acclimatized you are when you arrive at the mountain. People who live at or near sea level are advised to spend a couple of nights at higher altitudes before climbing.

Also, beware that thefts are a chronic problem at the huts, so if possible have someone guard your stuff, or pack everything higher up the mountain and hide it out of sight.

The author hitch hiked from Popo & Ixty and landed at Tlachichuca about noon on 3/31/1972. He bought food & left baggage with Señior Reyes at the store, then walked a ways & got a lift to Piedra Grande. Slept in his tent, then made the summit in 3 1/3 hours; round-trip in 4 1/4 hours--he had good

The summit of Orizaba can be seen above the refugios on the north slope.

Map 471-1, Pico Orizaba, Cordillera Anahuac, Mexico

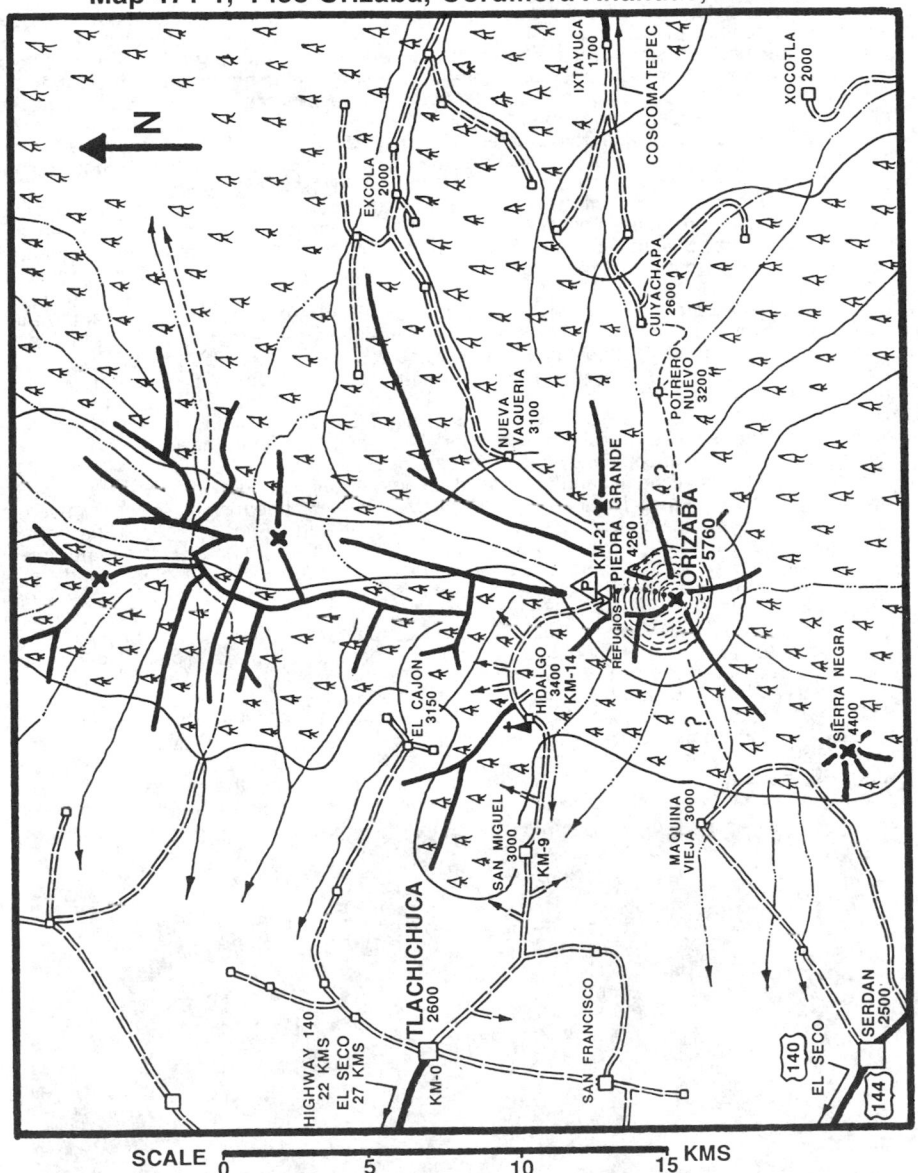

SCALE 0 — 5 — 10 — 15 KMS

knees in those days! He then walked and got a lift back to town and took a bus out of the area that afternoon.

Ice ax & crampons are required, as well as warm clothing, but it's not a difficult or dangerous climb. December through April are the dry months, with summertime (May through October) bringing heavy rains and snow to the mountain.

Maps *Veracruz, E14-3,* 1:250,000 (and other maps at 1:50,000 scale), from the Direccion General De Geografia Del Territorio Nacional Mexico. Buy at DETENAL, Balderas 71, Mexico City; or check the website (www.omnimap.com), or in the USA call 800-742-2677, or 336-227-8300; and the latest edition of the book, **Mexico's Volcanoes,** The Mountaineers.

Volcan Tacana, Mexico-Guatemala

Shown here is Volcan Tacana, 4110 meters, located on the Mexican--Guatemalan border near the Mexican city of Tapachula. Tacana is a forested composite stratovolcano that still retains a near perfect symmetrical shape. Between 1/1986 and 2/1988, there was local seismicity and several small phreatic eruptions from a vent on the northeast flank right on the international border at about 3800 meters. It's been quiet ever since and because it's covered with the pine forest it appears more dormant than active.

It's possible to climb Tacana from Guatemala, but it's a long bus ride to a remote part of the country. If you try it from Guatemala, make your way to Comitancillo, Ixchiguán, and Sibinal. From there, walk on a trail west to La Haciendita, then southwest to the summit.

However, it's easier to climb it from the Mexican side, which the author did on 1/7 & 1/8/1994. Begin in Tapachula. Locate the buses going to Cacaohatan. These begin every 20-25 minutes and take about half an hour for the run. Just north of the town center in Cacaohatan is a minibus station where all vehicles going north begin. About every half hour one will go to Unión Juárez.

From the main plaza in Juárez, walk north up the main street toward the mountain. At the edge of town continue along the cobblestone road through Cordova to Talquian. At the upper end of Talquian is the last store and the end of the cobblestone road at 1750 meters.

From Talquian, there's a very good trail running up to the Guatemalan border, which is marked by a large white cement monument. The border line has been clear-cut of trees and is called *La Linea*. This 10-meter-wide swath runs straight to the summit and you could scramble up along it, but there's a well-used trail almost parallel to the border that's easier.

From the white monument, head straight up La Linea until you find the first house where they grow flowers for the local market and perhaps for export. From there get on a regular trail which veers to the east and leaves La Linea. You'll pass a number of homes, all of which have tap water, which comes from springs higher up at about 2800 meters. After a while you'll veer back to La Linea, then continue straight up again until you come to a vertical cliff. From there veer right and walk through an open pine forest until you locate another trail coming up from the east side at about 3600 meters. Follow this to the summit. On top is a crater, which forms a moat, with the remains of a younger lava dome in the middle.

The last place to buy food is in Talquian, but Tapachula or Juárez have better selections. There's water at 1770, and from home taps as high as about 2600 meters. You can camp about anywhere, but this volcano can be climbed in one long day from Juárez. There's at least one hotel in Juárez where you can stay.

On 1/7/1994, the author took his full pack and walked 3 1/2 hours from Talquian and camped. Next morning, he broke camp, hid his pack, then reached the summit in 2 hours. Then down to Talquian. Total walk-time on Day 2 was 6 1/2 hours. Total 2-day walk-time was 10 hours. Had he stayed in a hotel in Juárez and climbed it in one day, the estimated time would be between 8 & 9 hours round-trip. The dry season is from November to April. Consider taking

The pine-clad upper slopes of Tacana with the clear-cut La Linea easily visible.

Map 472-1, Volcan Tacana, Mexico-Guatemala

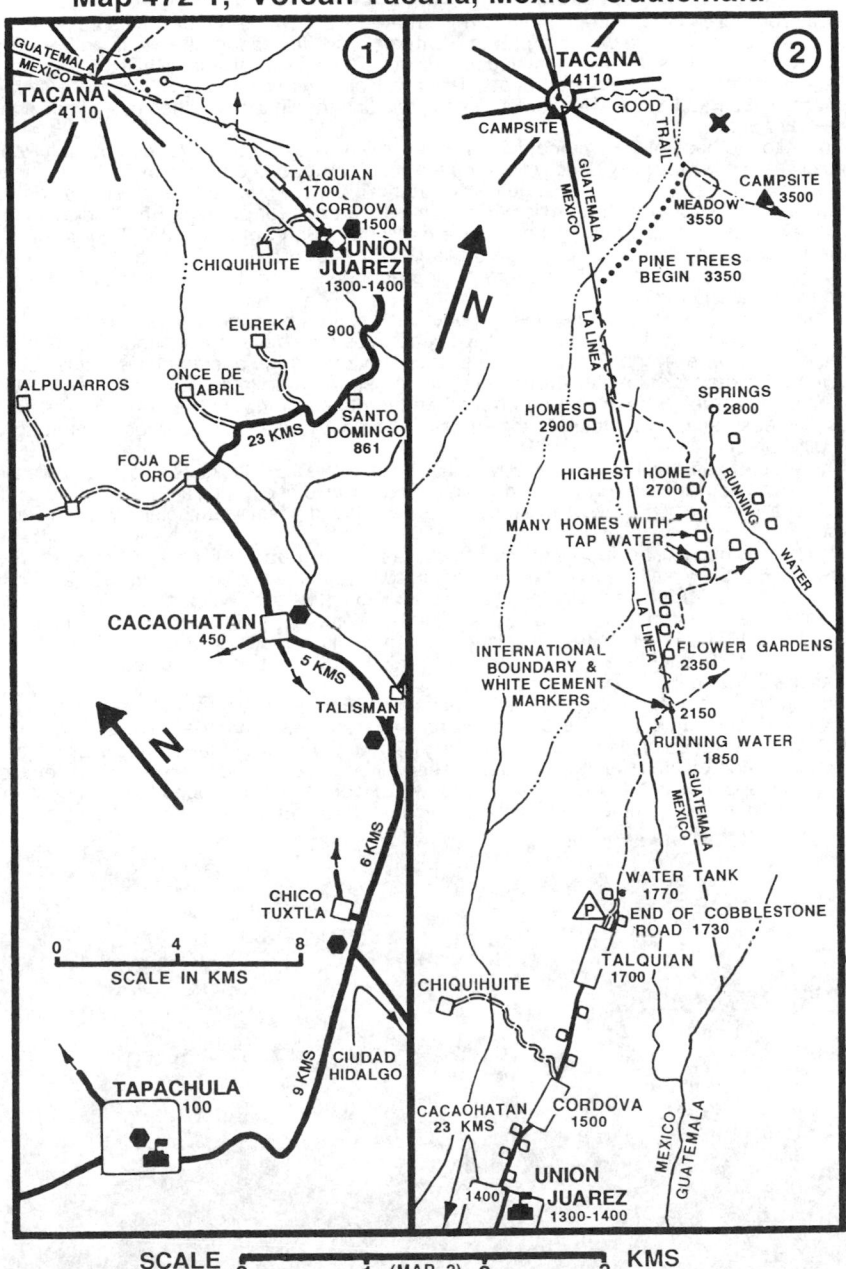

a light jacket for the summit.

Maps Mexican maps *Pavincul, D15B43,* 1:50,000, and perhaps *Huixtla, D15-2,* 1:250,000; or Guatemalan maps *Sibinal, 1761 II* and *Cuilco, ND 15-3, NE 15-11,* 1:250,000; and perhaps Guatemalan guidebook (in Spanish), **Guia de Los Volcanos de Guatemala,** Redondo; and any travel guidebook to Mexico.

Volcan Tajumulco, Guatemala

Featured here is the highest mountain in Guatemala. This is Volcan Tajumulco at 4220 meters. It's located in the western part of Guatemala not far east of the Mexican border and Volcan Tacana. This is an older, forested and extinct or dormant volcano with some erosion, but it still retains a mostly symmetrical shape. This is a Holocene volcano with 2 very questionable eruptions in 1821 and 1863. The author climbed this one in rain & fog so he couldn't see if there was a crater or not.

To get to the base of **Tajumulco**, first make your way to San Marcos (or nearby San Pedro). You can get to this small city directly from the Mexican border and the town of Talisman; or from the east and the city of Quezaltenango and Guatemala City. There are several buses going to San Marcos daily from either direction. Once in San Marcos (or perhaps San Pedro), look for one of several daily buses running north in the direction of San Sebastian and Tacana. Tell the driver or conductor you want to go to Tuichan, but be let off at the beginning of the trail to Tajumulco. There are several trails you could begin on, but try to be dropped off at a place called *Llano de la Guardia*.

From the road, head up to the west or southwest along a prominent hogsback ridge. There are a number of homes and farms in the first 2 kms. You may have to ask people along the way to make sure you're on the right path; but always stay on a ridge and continue a little south of due west. At about 3300 meters you'll enter the forest, then the trail is easier to follow. At the trail junction marked 3720 meters, turn right and continue going up the ridge; not down and across the east face. From there to the summit it's an easy walk along a good trail through an open pine forest.

The author did this climb during the rainy season on 9/18/1980. He took a bus from Quezaltenango to San Marcos and unknowingly checked into a *casa de puta* to begin with; then decided he'd rather sleep in peace, so he somehow got his money back and found a family run hotel called the *Pension Miranda*.

Next morning he shopped and had breakfast, then boarded a 10:30am bus for San Sebastian. His diary isn't clear, but he got off somewhere in the country, probably near Tuichan (?). It was raining hard for a while, then lightened up about the time he started hiking. He asked a farmer's wife if he could leave his big pack in her house and paid for that favor with several cans of food. He hurried to the summit in fog and rain in just under 2 1/2 hours. The round-trip was about 4 hours from the road. He got a lift back to San Marcos in a truck, arriving there at 6pm after a 2 hour ride.

The author isn't sure if there's a hotel or pension in San Sebastian or not. Ask someone, or check with a travel guidebook. From San Sebastian it's an easy one day climb. If you stay in San Marcos, get an early start and move quickly. There will be water taps somewhere near the beginning of the trail at Llano de la Guardia. This will be the only place on the trail to get water. Best to buy food in San Marcos or San Pedro, with Tuichan or San Sebastian next best. You could camp anywhere on the mountain, but you'd need to carry water from the road. The dry

This is the east ridge of Tajumulco in the clouds just below treeline.

Map 473-1, Volcan Tajumulco, Guatemala

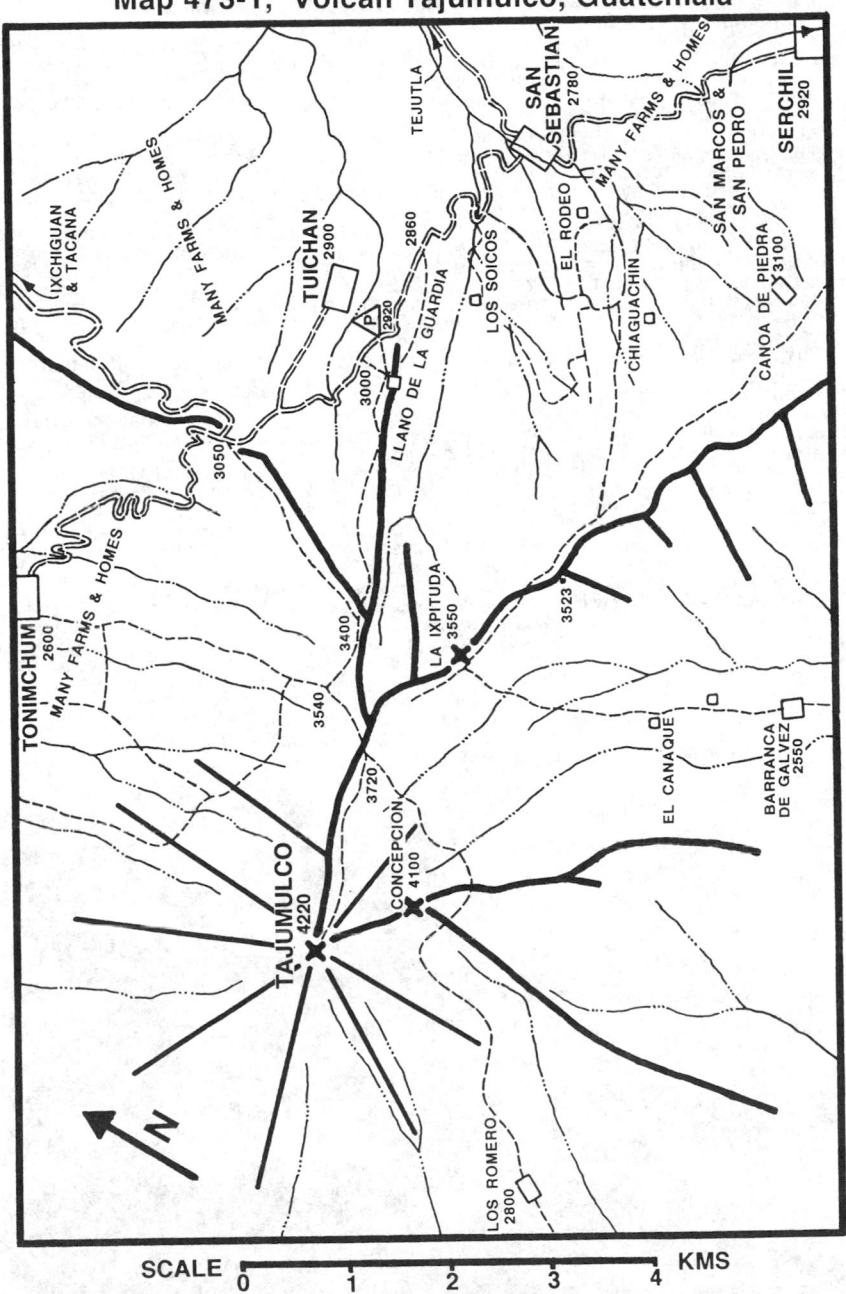

SCALE 0 1 2 3 4 KMS

season is from about November to April. It'll be chilly on top, so go prepared for cold.
Maps *Tajumulco, 1861 III*, 1:50,000; or *Cuilco*, 1:250,000, available from Servicio Cartografia Militar (or Nacional), Avenida Las Americas 5-76, Zona 13, Guatemala City; and perhaps the guidebook (in Spanish), **Guia de Los Volcanes de Guatemala**, Redondo; and the travel guidebook, **Central America**, Lonely Planet.

Volcans Santa Maria & Santiguito, Guatemala

One of the higher volcanos in Guatemala is Santa Maria, at 3772 meters. This one is located directly south of the city of Quezaltenango (called Shila in the local Indian language) in western Guatemala. The main peak of Santa Maria is a dormant volcano, but on its southwest flanks and at a much lower altitude, there's a new & very active volcano called Crater Santiaguito. It's altitude is about 2500 meters. It was active and erupting every little while in 1/1994 when the author was there.

While Santa Maria may be a Holocene volcano, Santiaguito is young, lively and deadly. On 10/24/1902 Santiaguito's predecessor blew up big time with a violent VEI-6 explosion creating a 1000 x 700 meter crater. And it's been more or less continuously active since 6/22/1922. In 1929, an explosion and pyroclastic flow killed as many as 5000 people. For volcano updates see websites (volcano1.pgd.hawaii.edu/goes/) or (www.volcano.si.edu/gvp/).

To climb **Santa Maria**, first make your way to Quezaltenango, which sits in a high, dry and cold valley at 2350 meters elevation. Lots of buses going that way every day and from all directions. Once there, ask about buses going in the direction of Llano de Pinal, which is a farming community in the south end of the valley. Every day but Sunday, there are many buses running from the middle of Quezaltenango to Llano de Pinal. You can also take a taxi or walk. It's about 7 kms from the center of the city to Cuatro Caminos or Esquinas (four roads or corners), where the hike usually begins.

Near Cuatro Caminos are several small shops and public water taps. From there, walk south on the one main road which runs into a prominent canyon. The road gradually turns into a trail. Further up near the head of the canyon, veer left or southwest. After another km, you'll reach a pass between Santa Maria and the peak marked 3060 meters. At that point, turn right or south, and walk through a meadow to the forest beyond and a well-used trail zig zagging straight up to the summit. The upper part of the climb is through an open pine forest.

On Sunday (no buses) 1/9/1994, the author walked part way to Llano de Pinal, then got a quick lift to Cuatro Caminos (Esquinas). He took his big pack up to just beyond the pass at 2950 meters, hid it in the forest, then hurried to the top. It took just over 2 hours to walk from Cuatro Caminos to the summit, and another hour down to the pass. A fast hiker can walk all the way from Quezaltenango to the summit and back in one long day. Or take a taxi or bus to as close to the mountain as possible, and make it a much shorter hike.

To reach **Santiaguito**, turn right or west from the main trail as shown on the map. Climb up to the pass at 2800 meters, then walk along a seldom-used road southwest for a km. Continue past one farm house, then along a trail that gradually becomes less-used. In the area before El Mirador (The Lookout), the trail fades a lot, and you may have to do some bushwhacking before reaching the rocky brush-less area near Santiaguito. The author walked that way after climbing Santa Maria, but had fog and lots of dust on the brush He could see nothing, so turned back. However, he did see it exploding earlier that same morning from the bus he took from Retalhuileu to Quezaltenango.

Best to buy all food in Quezaltenango, but you can get some food and water in Llano de Pinal. Water is piped from a spring somewhere on the mountain and is surely good to drink as is. The dry season is from November to April.

Looking south at Santa Maria from Llano de Pinal and Cuatro Esquinas.

Map 474-1, Volcans Santa Maria & Santiguito, Guatemala

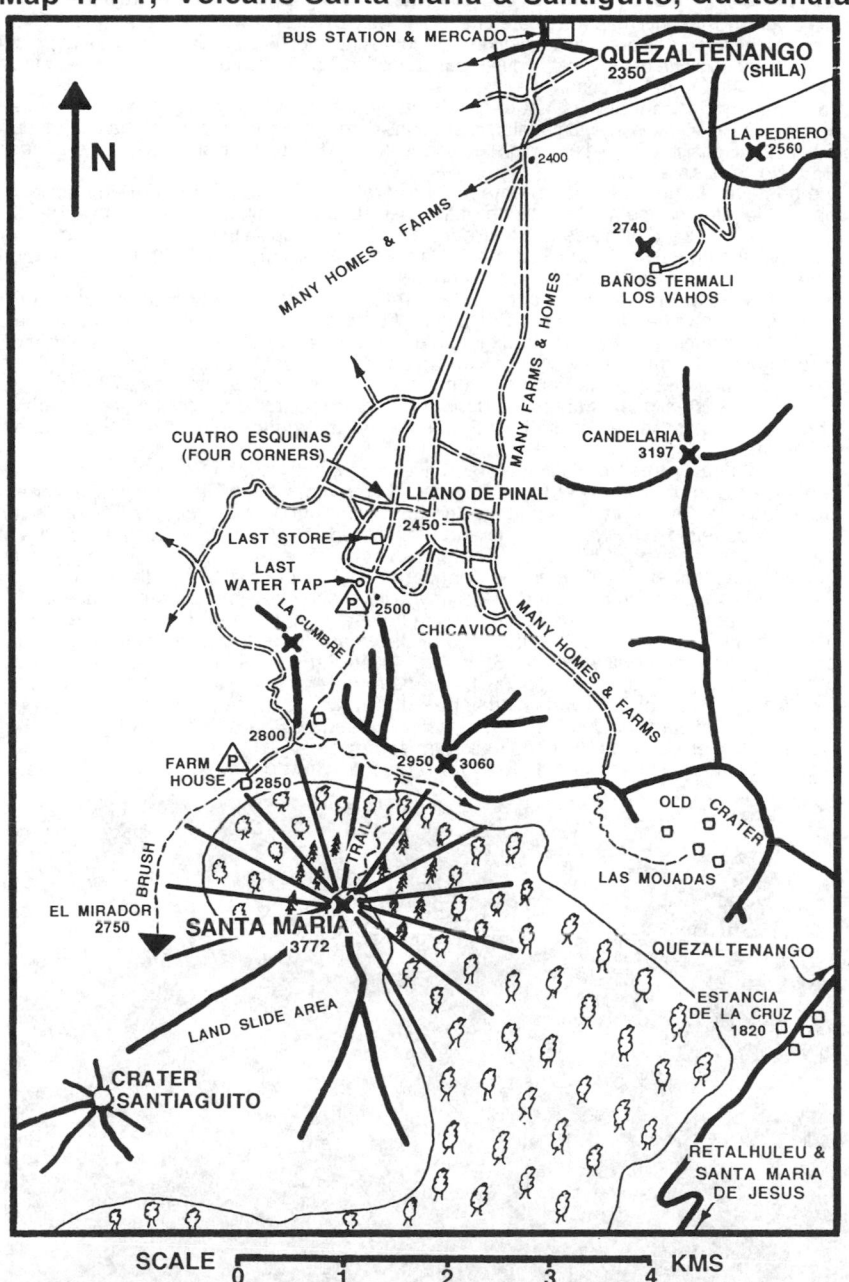

BUS STATION & MERCADO

QUEZALTENANGO
2350 (SHILA)

LA PEDRERO
2560

● 2400

2740

BAÑOS TERMALI
LOS VAHOS

N

MANY HOMES & FARMS

MANY FARMS & HOMES

CUATRO ESQUINAS
(FOUR CORNERS)

CANDELARIA
3197

LLANO DE PINAL

2450

LAST STORE

LAST
WATER TAP

P 2500

LA CUMBRE

CHICAVIOC

MANY HOMES & FARMS

2800

FARM P
HOUSE 2850

2950 3060

OLD CRATER

TRAIL

LAS MOJADAS

BRUSH

EL MIRADOR
2750

SANTA MARIA
3772

QUEZALTENANGO

LAND SLIDE AREA

ESTANCIA
DE LA CRUZ
1820

CRATER
SANTIAGUITO

RETALHULEU &
SANTA MARIA
DE JESUS

SCALE
0   1   2   3   4 KMS

Maps Guatemalan map *Colomba, 1860 II*, 1:50,000; or the guidebook (in Spanish), **Guia de Los Volcanes de Guatemala**, all of Guatemalas 37 volcanos are discussed; and the travel guidebook, **Central America**, Lonely Planet.

San Pedro, Toliman and Atitlan Volcanos, Guatemala

The 3 volcanos on this map are located next to Logo de Atitlan in western Guatemala. This lake sits in one of the largest calderas in the world. The combination of Guatemalan Indians, a big lake and volcanos makes this one of the most popular tourist destinations in the country. The scenery in these parts is the best in Central America.

San Pedro is dormant and its last eruption was in the early Holocene, or maybe earlier (?). Toliman is also Holocene in age, but Atitlan is still considered an active volcano. It has had eruptions throughout the Spanish Colonial era with 9 episodes in the 1800's. It's last certain activity began on 5/3/1853. No news since then.

The best way to get to these mountains is to first take a bus from about any direction to Panajachel, located on the northeast side of the lake--Lago de Atitlan. From Panajachel, about 6-7 passenger boats a day cruise to San Pedro and to Santiago Atitlan. There are also about 6 boats a day running between San Pedro and Santiago. There are also 3-4 buses daily running between Santiago and San Lucas Toliman, and beyond.

To climb **Volcan San Pedro** at about 3020 meters elevation, walk south out of San Pedro town on the dirt road heading toward Santiago. At the big bend shown on the map, is a sign indicating the beginning of the trail. Walk this path for 300-400 meters, then in the bottom of the prominent gully with smooth lava rocks, veer right uphill. Continue along the trail in the gully bottom for a ways, then veer left and stay on the most-used trail all the way to the top. You'll leave the cornfields (milpas) at about 2100 meters. The good trail ends on the east summit. On 1/11/1994, the author climbed up in about 2 hours; while the round-trip hike from San Pedro took about 3 1/2 hours.

To climb **Volcan Atitlan** at 3535 meters, make your way by bus to San Lucas Toliman, then walk southwest out of town toward the highway. At the highway, walk southwest another 300 meters to the intersection at 1670 meters and turn right onto a minor dirt road. Follow it as it veers right, then left, as shown. From the end of this road at 1700 meters, continue on the main trail right up to the pass called Chanan. There are several side trails along the way, so you may have to ask local farmers if you're on the right path. Just as the trail leaves the highest milpas, there's a shady campsite some groups use, but you'll have to carry lots of water if camping!

From the campsite, follow the less-used trail closely until it intersects with the other trail coming up from Santiago, which appears to be the main route to the summit. However, the author isn't familiar with that way from Santiago. From San Lucas Toliman to the summit took the author about 3 1/4 hours; and about 6 1/4 hours round-trip. That was on 1/12/1994. Take at least 2-3 liters of water on this warm all-day hike. Somewhere at the Chanan Pass is supposed to be a trail up **Toliman**, but it's apparently seldom used and hard to find and follow. By the time you arrive, there should be a good trail there somewhere (?).

Start early on all hikes to avoid afternoon clouds. The dry season is from November or

From the ferryboat docks at Panajachel looking southwest across Lago de Atitlan at Toliman left, and San Pedro to the right.

Map 475-1, San Pedro, Toliman & Atitlan, Guatemala

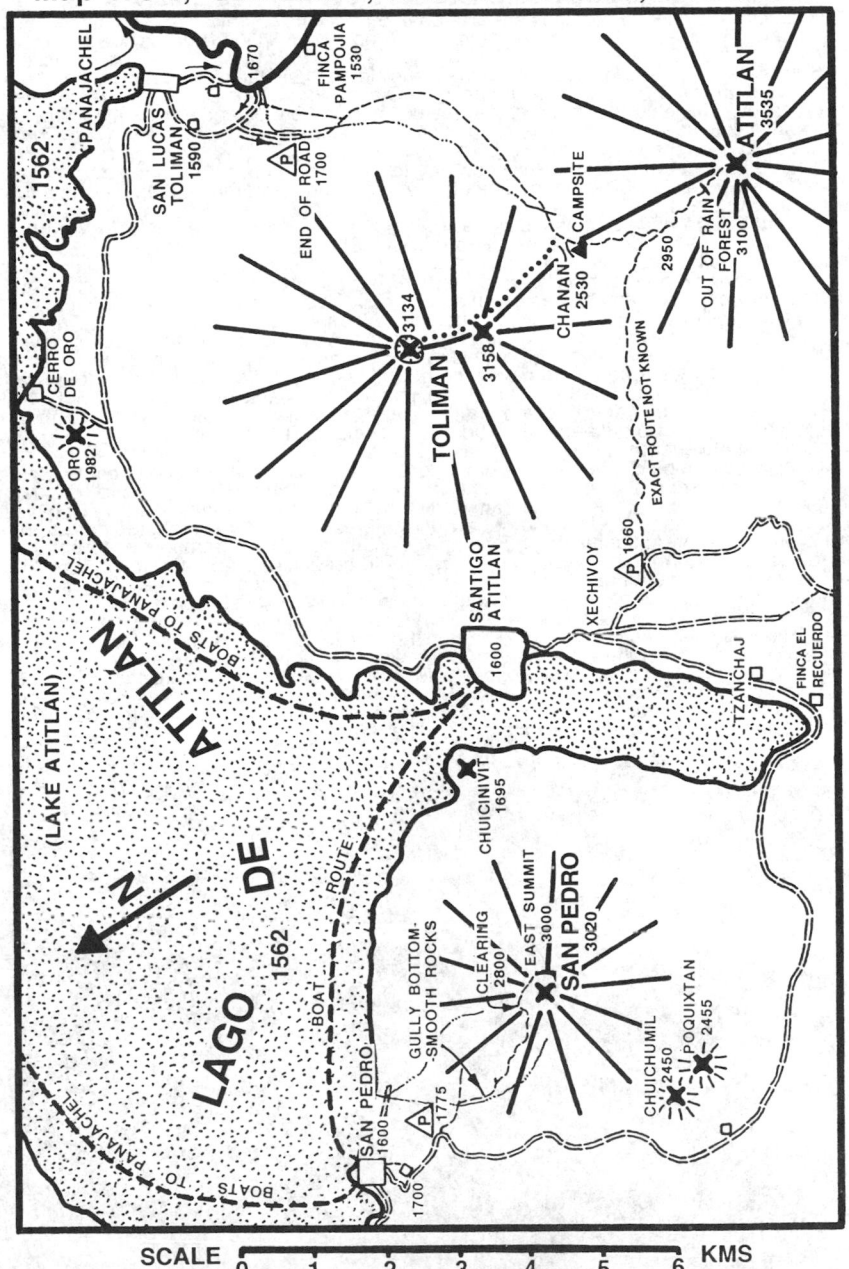

SCALE 0 1 2 3 4 5 6 KMS

December to April. There are many stores, hotels and tourists in San Pedro and Santiago, but fewer in San Lucas Toliman.
Maps Guatemalan maps *1960 III, 1959 IV, and 1959 I,* all at 1:50,000; or JOG map *Guatemala, ND 15-8,* 1:250,000; the hiking guide (in Spanish), **Guia de Los Volcanes de Guatemala**, Redondo; and the travel guidebook **Central America**, Lonely Planet.

Fuego and Acatenango Volcanos, Guatemala

Fuego and Acatenango volcanos are located about 15 kms southwest of Antigua, Guatemala. Acatenango is the oldest. Its northern summit, Pico Yepocapa at 3830 meters, is now extinct. It quit growing about 20,000 years ago, then Pico Mayor started. Pico Mayor's last activity lasted from 8/1926 until 5/19/1927. The last eruption on the mountain was from the crater between the 2 summits which erupted on 11/12/1972; thus the name 1972 Crater. Fuego is one of Central Americas most active volcanos. The latest reports indicate some boomers in 12/1999 and into 1/2000. Hopefully it'll be alive when you arrive. For updated information on volcanos check the websites (www.volcano1. pgd.hawaii.edu/goes/) or (www.volcano.si.edu/gvp/).

To climb these peaks, first make your way to Antigua. There are buses about every 15 minutes from Guatemala City. Antigua has lots of hotels and accommodations and is a favorite destination for tourists.

To climb **Fuego** and perhaps **Acatenango** on the same trip, take a bus from Antigua to Alotenango. Buses run about every half hour from 6:30am until 6 or 7pm (fewer buses run on Sundays). In 1994, there were no hotels in Alotenango (or Dueñas). From Alotenango's central plaza, walk downhill on the main road to the river bridge. About 100 meters past the bridge, head straight west along an old road set in a deep gully. You'll have to make 3 left turns before this very good well-used trail finally heads straight up the mountain.

Higher up, there may be a trail veering right toward **Acatenango**, but the author never saw it. But you can still climb Acatenango by this route by climbing to the pass at 3300 meters, then heading north. Very strong hikers can climb both peaks on the same day, but doing so from Antigua using buses would be very difficult. There are taxis available however, but at gringo prices! Take 3 liters of water to climb via this route; it's hot at the bottom! Camping means carrying tons of water up a steep trail! The author climbed Fuego on 1/16/1994 in 6 1/2 hours round-trip from Alotenango, but with Antigua as a base.

Acatenango can be climbed from Alotenango, but most use the good trail from La Soledad, which is 1000 meters higher and much cooler. First, take a bus from Antigua to (San Miguel) Dueñas. They run from about 6:30 or 7am, until 6 or 7pm. From Dueñas, start walking west on the road to La Soledad. You should get a ride quite easy, but it's sometimes hard to do this climb in one day from Antigua using buses and hitch hiking. Another option, and one to insure that you get back to Antigua on the same day, would be to hire a taxi--for maybe US$20-$30. There are also 2-3 daily buses running from Antigua to Yepocapa on the other side of the mountain, but normally using these only would require an overnight stay on the mountain.

At the junction in La Soledad, walk back up the road 300 meters to find the trail. In the first part, there will be 2 little left turns as you walk through the cornfields, then you reach the forest at about 2700-2750 meters. From there it's one trail all the way up. Along the way are 2 campsites, and a refugio near the top, which sleeps 6 people on the floor. If you were to sleep there one night, you could climb both peaks on a 2-day trip. The author climbed Acatenango in less than 4 hours round-trip from La Soledad; 7 1/2 hours from Antigua. He had great luck with buses & hitch hiking that day! This was on 2/12/1994 at the end of his Central American trip that year.

From the top of Volcan Agua looking west at the twin volcanic summits of Fuego left, and Acatenango to the right.

Map 476-1, Fuego & Acatenango Volcanos, Guatemala

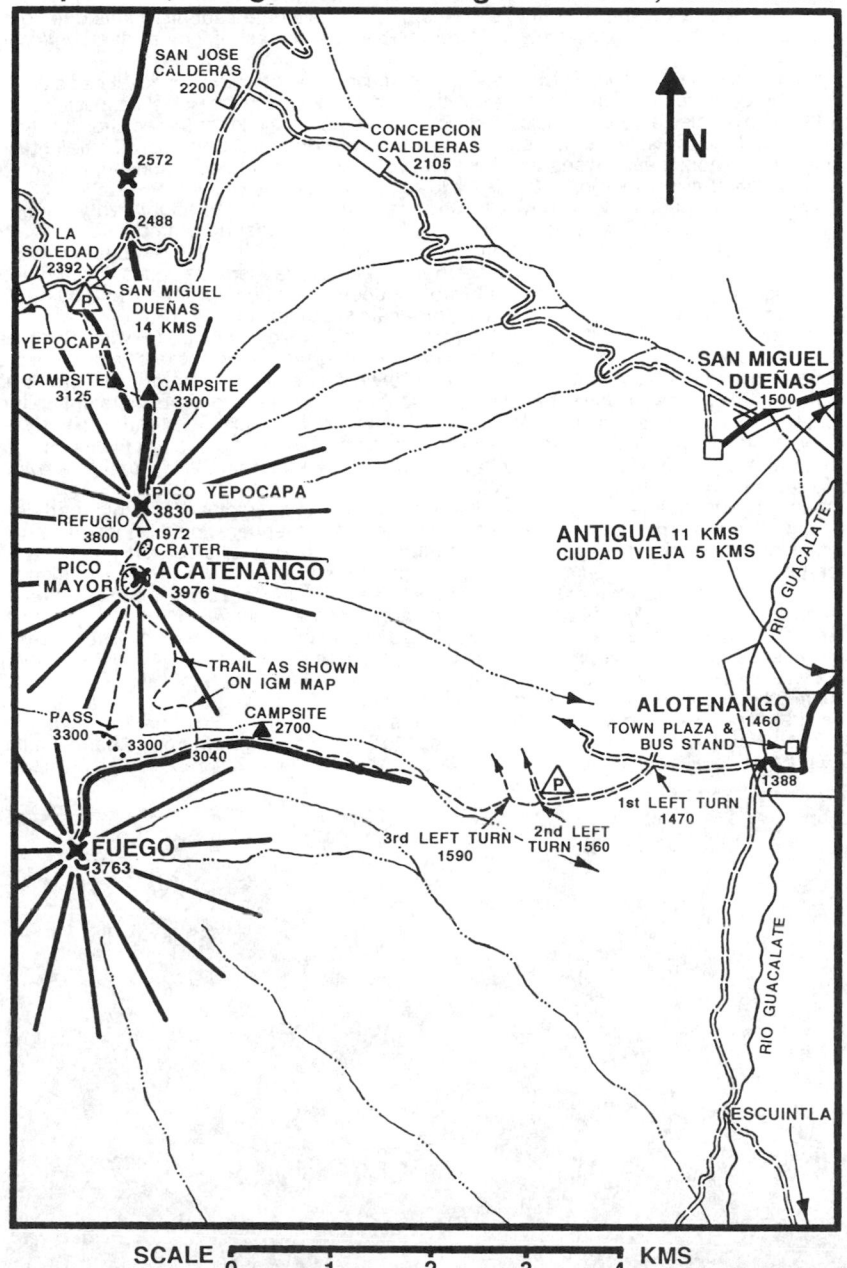

SAN JOSE CALDERAS 2200

CONCEPCION CALDLERAS 2105

N

2572

2488

LA SOLEDAD 2392

P

SAN MIGUEL DUEÑAS 14 KMS

YEPOCAPA

CAMPSITE 3125

CAMPSITE 3300

SAN MIGUEL DUEÑAS 1500

PICO YEPOCAPA 3830

REFUGIO 3800

1972

CRATER

PICO MAYOR

ACATENANGO 3976

ANTIGUA 11 KMS
CIUDAD VIEJA 5 KMS

RIO GUACALATE

TRAIL AS SHOWN ON IGM MAP

PASS 3300

3300

3040

CAMPSITE 2700

ALOTENANGO
TOWN PLAZA & BUS STAND 1460

P

1388

1st LEFT TURN 1470

3rd LEFT TURN 1590

2nd LEFT TURN 1560

FUEGO 3763

RIO GUACALATE

ESCUINTLA

SCALE | 0 1 2 3 4 | KMS

The dry season is from November to April. Buy all food in Antigua, but there are stores in La Soledad, San Jose Calderas and Alotenango.
Maps Guatemalan maps *2059 IV & 2059 III*, 1:50,000; or JOG map *Guatemala, ND 15-8*, 1:250,000; and the book (in Spanish) **Guia de Los Volcanes de Guatemala**, Redondo; and travel guidebook **Central America**, Lonely Planet.

Volcan Agua, Guatemala

Featured here is Volcan Agua at 3760 meters. Agua is located about 10 kms due south of Antigua, Guatemala's first capital city; and about 15 kms due east of 2 other nearby volcanos, Fuego and Acatenango.

Agua appears to be a young volcano and is very much symmetrically shaped. It has a crater on top that is breached to the north. Agua's last activity was sometime in the Holocene, but it has never had a historically-dated eruption. It's covered with a rainforest on the lower slopes, then higher up, a pine forest right to the summit. Located around the crater rim are a number of small huts and buildings which house employees who take care of several private communications antennas. There's also an old hiker's refugio just inside the lower part of the crater.

To climb **Agua**, first make you way to Antigua. There are buses about every 15 minutes arriving from Guatemala City. Antigua has lots of hotels and other accommodations for foreign tourists and is the number one destination city in Guatemala. It's also a quiet and basically crime-free place. Once there, look for buses heading for Santa Maria de Jesus, located about 9 kms due south of Antigua. These buses leave about every half hour from about 6:30am until 6 or 7pm from the Antigua bus station, or along the main street just to the east.

In Santa Maria, the bus will stop at or near the central plaza. From there, walk along one of the streets straight toward the mountain and cemetery. Once at the cemetery, turn right, then left, and follow a street, then a trail, along the northwest side of the cemetery wall. After about one km, the trail passes a small chapel on a good 2WD road, then continues straight up toward the peak. From the chapel, your choice is; walk up the trail, or along the road, which for some might be easier to follow than the trail. Higher up, the trail rejoins the road. At that point, stay on the road all the way to the top. If you have more money than time, you can hire a 4WD taxi and/or guide service in Antigua to take you there.

At about 3200 meters, the useable vehicle road ends at a big gully. This old road actually goes up to the crater rim, but because the mountain is so steep, erosion & floods have cut it in several places. So the upper part is only a trail and everybody walks. When you finally reach the crater, you'll be at a low point on the rim. From there, walk in either direction to the highest point. The crater is only 300-400 meters across. From various locations around the rim, you'll have good views of Antigua, as well as other volcanos such as Pacaya, Fuego and Acatenango.

This mountain is close to Guatemala City, therefore a popular hike, especially on weekends. There must have been 300 or more people on the mountain on Saturday, 1/15/1994, when the author was there. He walked up the road all the way, but returned to Santa Maria via the trail. It took him 5 hours round-trip. The average tourist needs 8-10 hours.

In 1994, there were no hotels in Santa Maria, so stay in Antigua. Get on the first bus out of Antigua so you can reach the summit before the clouds build up. Or you could camp on top, as many do--but you'll have to carry all your water up. Take no less than 2 liters of water and a

Loading buses in the early morning at Antigua with Volcan Agua behind to the south.

Map 477-1, Volcan Agua, Guatemala

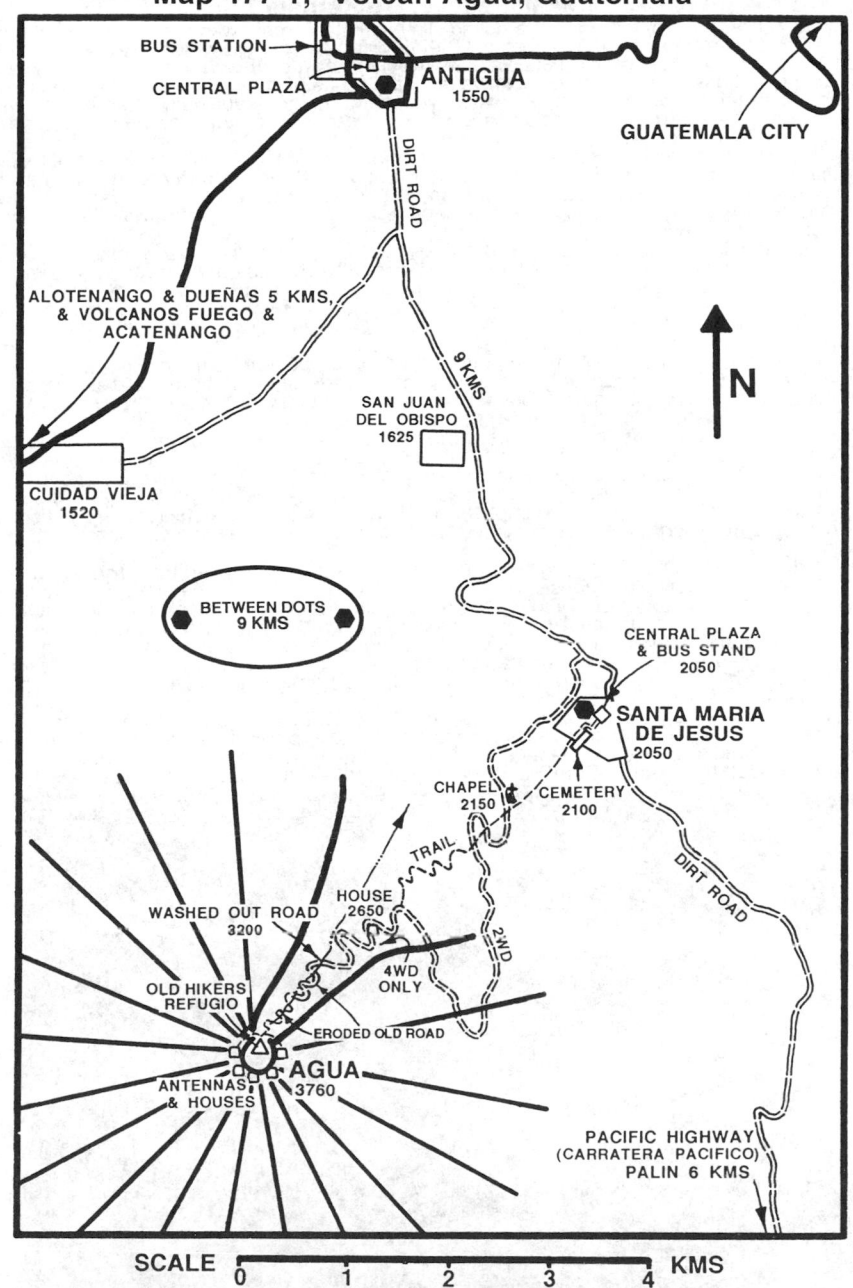

SCALE 0 1 2 3 4 KMS

lunch on a day-hike. The dry season is from November to April.
Maps Guatemalan maps *Amatitlan, 2059 II,* 1:50,000; or JOG map *Guatemala, ND 15-8,* 1:250,000, available from Servicio Cartografia Militar (or Nacional), Avenida Las Americas 5-76, Zona 13, Guatemala City; and perhaps the guidebook (in Spanish), **Guia de Los Volcanes de Guatemala**, Redondo; and the travel guidebook **Central America**, Lonely Planet.

Volcan Pacaya, Guatemala

During 1/1994, one of the most interesting climbs in Guatemala was the hike to the summit of Volcan Pacaya at about 2500 meters. At that time it was very active with Strombolian-type eruptions. There was a pool of liquid lava in the west crater and about every 4-5 minutes there was a release of gas, which blow red hot lava up in the air as high as 100 meters. As seen from the eastern summit about 100 meters away, it was quite a sight, especially after the sun went down. Some of the stronger explosions actually sent red lava bombs over the author's head, making it even more exciting.

Pacaya is a complex volcano sitting on the southern rim of the 14x16 km wide Pleistocene Amatitlan Caldera. Collapse of Pacaya Volcano about 1100 years ago produced a debris-avalanche deposit that extends 25 kms onto the Pacific coastal plain. If you want to know if Pacaya is still alive for your vacation see the websites (www.volcano1.pgd.hawaii.edu/goes/) or (www.volcano.si.edu/gvp/).

One word of caution: in 1991, there was group of tourists on this mountain who were robbed. Two people were killed. There may have been one other occasion where a large group of tourists were robbed at gun point by a group of armed men. So if this volcano is erupting, there will surely be lots of tourist visiting the place in the late afternoons, as well as the possibility of robbers. If this is the case, leave your passport, money and as many valuables as possible in a safe place, then have a fun and exciting trip.

If the mountain is erupting when you arrive, there should be tour companies in Antigua, and maybe Guatemala City, organizing little groups going there in vans or minibuses in the late afternoons and returning after dark. They will organize everything for the one day hike. In 1994, the cost was only about US$7 for the 6-7 hour trip from Antigua.

If you want to do it alone, and perhaps camp on the mountain, here's what you do. Take a bus from Guatemala City, or from anywhere on the Carratera Pacifico (Pacific Highway). Get off near Km post 37 and the road to San Vicente Pacaya. From that junction, there are about 3 or 4 buses per day running to Calderas. It's also easy to get lifts on trucks. Stop at the pueblo called San Francisco, which in 1994, had a couple of small stores and a little restaurant. You might be able to sleep on the floor of the restaurant (?); or there might be a pension you can stay by the time you arrive.

From the little church in San Francisco walk south on a good well-used trail. Higher up, turn left or east at the cement block house. Above that, just stay on the most-used trail as it winds up through the forest. At about 2300 meters, there's a meadow area with good grassy campsites. Above that, continue on the most-used trail which veers right and ascends the east ridge of Pacaya. There are many campsites around. If the mountain is having Strombolian eruptions, then go up in the afternoons to orient yourself; and stay until after dark for the best fireworks show around. Take a flashlight and extra batteries. If staying the night, camp down off the cone a ways so you don't get bombed in the night.

This is a climb of only about 600 meters from San Francisco, so it's fast and easy. The author carried his large pack to the east summit in 1 1/2 hours. This was on 1/12/1994. After dark he went back down to the pass at 2325 meters using a flashlight, and camped. Next morning, he walked down to San Francisco in 45 minutes, and later got a ride back to the

Fireworks at the summit of Pacaya, one of the world's most active volcanos.

Map 478-1, Volcan Pacaya, Guatemala

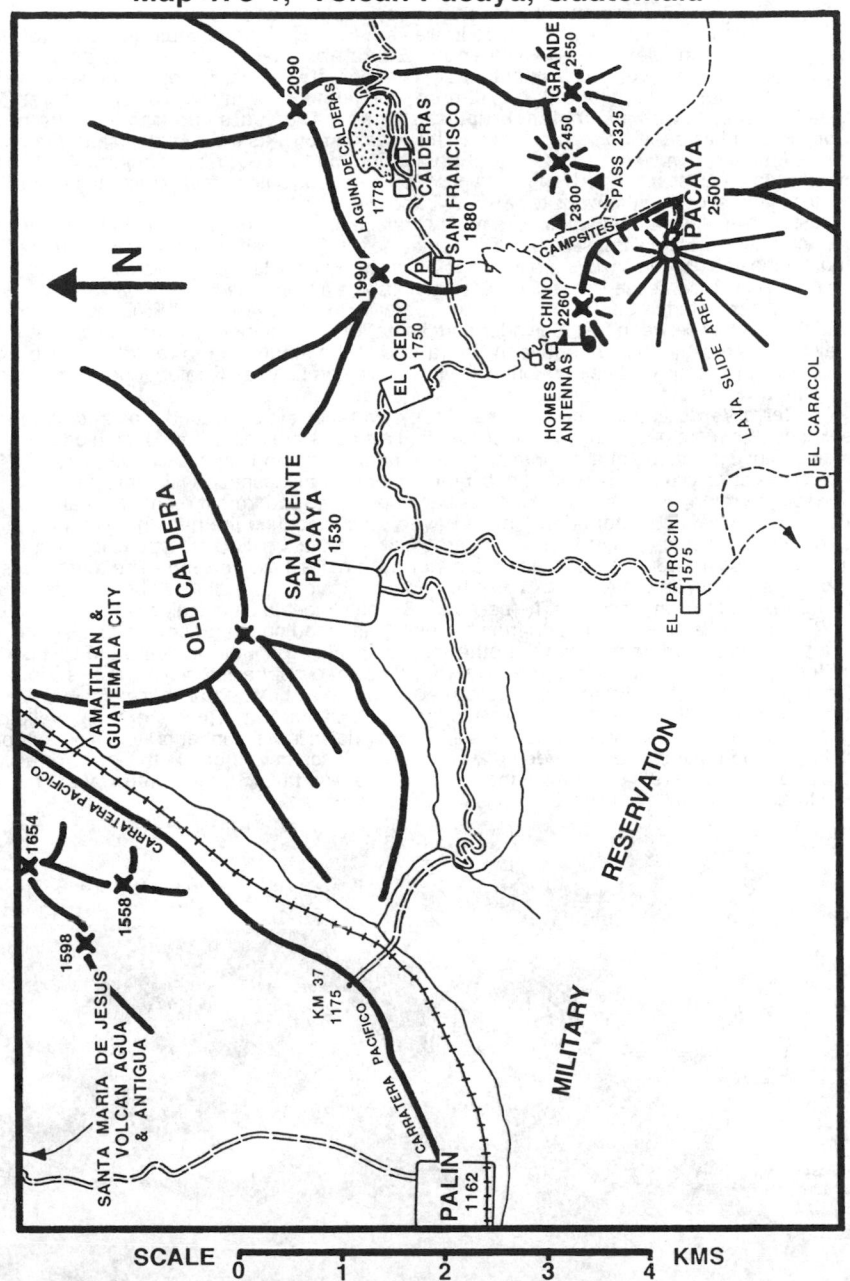

SCALE 0   1   2   3   4   KMS

highway. An interesting side note; there are no Indians in this valley, only white settlers. The
dry season is from November to April.
Maps Guatemalan map *Amatitlan, 2059 II,* 1:50,000; or JOG map *Guatemala, ND 15-8,*
1:250,000; and perhaps the guidebook (in Spanish), **Guia de Los Volcanes de Guatemala,**
Redondo; and the travel guidebook, **Central America**, Lonely Planet.

Santa Ana & Izalco Volcanos, El Salvador

On this map are 2 of the most famous volcanos in El Salvador; Santa Ana at 2365 meters, and Izalco, 1910 meters. They're located in western El Salvador due south of the city of Santa Ana. Both are considered active volcanos. Santa Ana's last eruption was on 1/12/1904. Activity lasted for 2 weeks and quit, but steam plumes were reported over fumaroles in 1978 & 1980. Izalco didn't exist until 2/23/1770, then it began to grow at the foot of the older Cerro Verde Volcano. It was in constant eruption for about 196 years and frequent strombolian eruptions could be seen from ships at sea. It became known as the *Lighthouse of the Pacific*. Izalco's last eruption was on 10/28/1966 from a vent on the southeast flank, but the summit crater has been quiet since 12/1/1957. A 12/1999 report indicated steam from the summit. For updated information see the website (www.volcano.si.edu/gvp/).

Just east of these 2 mountains is Lago de Coatepeque, the largest lake in the country, which occupies a huge caldera. Its last activity was sometime in the Holocene. The scenery in this region is almost comparable to the scenes around Lago Atitlan in Guatemala. If El Salvador can ever have a long period of political peace, this region will surely become a tourist mecca.

To get there, start in Santa Ana, or make your way to little town called El Congo, located on the main highway between San Salvador and Santa Ana. From there you can catch one of 4 or 5 daily buses making the run between Santa Ana to the mountain top resort of Cerro Verde. These buses run along the caldera rim with views down on Lago de Coatepeque. Get a seat on the right-hand side of the bus going up.

On **Cerro Verde** at 2030 meters, is a hotel, several picnic sites, and places to camp. On weekends with more people around, you may find a small store selling refrescos (soda pop) and snacks. Since it's on top of a mountain, water is hard to find and you may have to buy it. Take as much water as you can carry, and enough food for your trip, especially if camping.

To climb **Izalco**, walk about 150 meters back down the road from the national park entrance gate. Look for painted letters right on the paved road indicating the beginning of the trail. Or maybe a regular sign (?). At first you zig zag down through a Tarzan-type rainforest (lots of vines) to a pass at 1630 meters, then up a minor ridge of the bare volcano. The author was in a big hurry, so he made the round-trip hike to and from Izalco in about 1 1/2 hours. It's an easy hike up a perfectly shaped cone. The best view & place to get fotos of Izalco is from the hotel.

To climb **Santa Ana**, head north from the end of the road on one of several trails going over the top of Cerro Verde and down the other side. This is a popular hike and the trail is good. You'll first go down to a saddle, then walk along a road past a *futbol field* to the Finca Las Brumas at 1891 meters. From there you can either go up a shortcut trail that's highly eroded; or road-walk a ways, then use the main trail to the rim of Santa Ana. Once there, rim-walk to the highest point on the north side, or perhaps find a way down into the inner crater. The author did this hike round-trip from Cerro Verde in 2 1/4 hours. In fact, he climbed both these volcanos on the same day, 1/18/1994, and from the city of Santa Ana taking buses both ways. You may need to stay overhight and climb both volcanos in 1 1/2 days.

From the slopes of Santa Ana, looking south at Cerro Verde and Izalco (right).

Map 479-1, Santa Ana & Izalco Volcanos, El Salvador

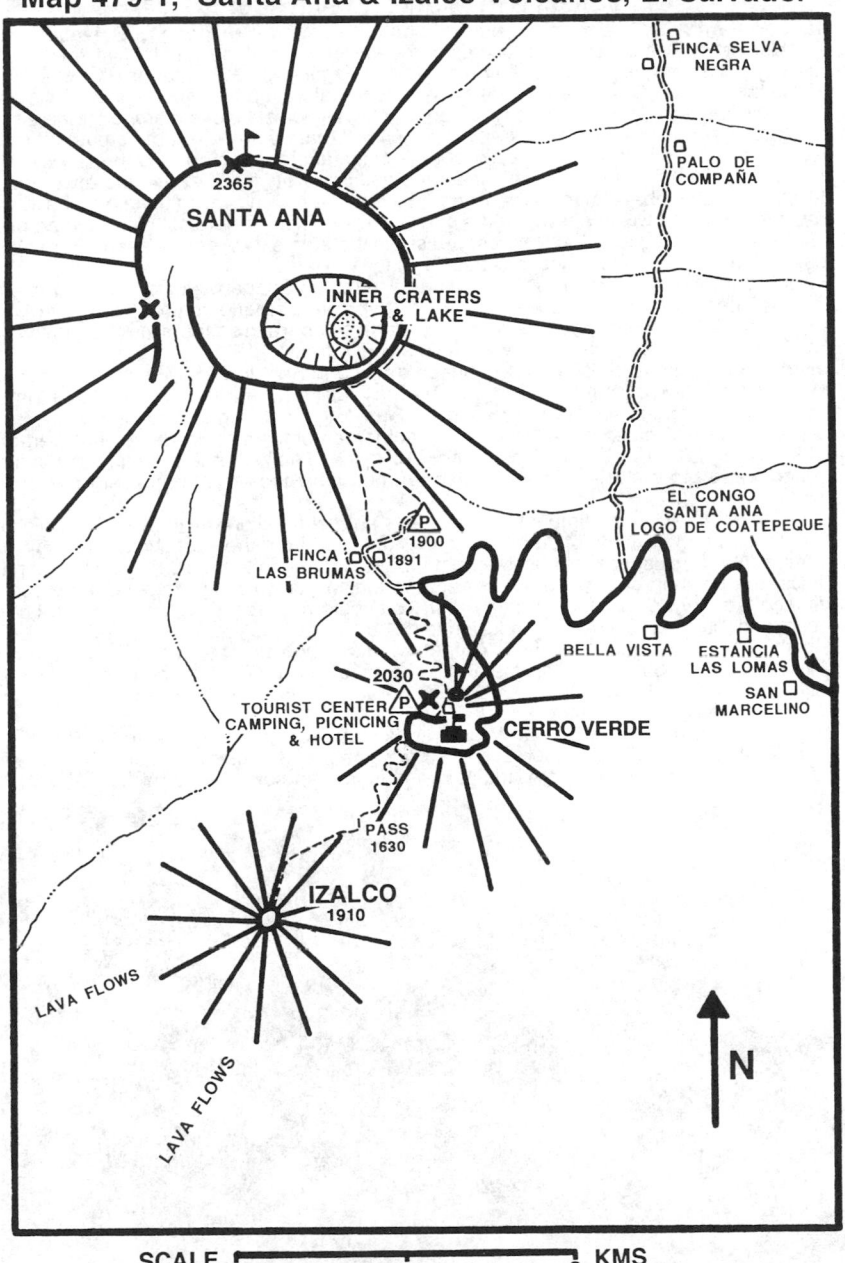

FINCA SELVA NEGRA

PALO DE COMPAÑA

2365

SANTA ANA

INNER CRATERS & LAKE

EL CONGO
SANTA ANA
LOGO DE COATEPEQUE

FINCA LAS BRUMAS

1891

P 1900

BELLA VISTA

FSTANCIA LAS LOMAS

SAN MARCELINO

2030

TOURIST CENTER
CAMPING, PICNICING & HOTEL

P

CERRO VERDE

PASS 1630

IZALCO
1910

LAVA FLOWS

LAVA FLOWS

N

SCALE 0   1   2 KMS

These mountains are part of a parque nacional, but you can camp anywhere; just bring lots of water and all your food. If staying in Santa Ana, catch the first bus out in the morning. The dry season is from November to April.

Maps El Salvador IGN maps *Santa Ana, 2257 I,* & *Sonsonate, 2257 I,* 1:50,000; plus any national highway map; and travel guidebook, **Central America**, Lonely Planet.

Volcan San Miguel, El Salvador

After Santa Ana and Izalco, perhaps the most interesting volcano in El Salvador is San Miguel. This perfectly shaped cone is located in the eastern part of the country just southwest of the small city of San Miguel. It's not a big mountain, rising to only 2130 meters; however, it sits on the coastal plain with its base near sea level, so it makes a pretty good climb. This same coastal plain is littered with old volcanos & cinder cones, some very old and eroded, others new.

San Miguel is an active volcano with lots of sulfur steam coming out of its summit crater. This volcano has been very active throughout the colonial era. One eruptive period was from 11/1985 through, and beyond, 2/1986. During the author's visit on 1/20/1994, there were rather recent-looking lava bombs & lava blocks sitting on the crater rim, indicating there may have been an unrecorded eruption within a few months of his arrival. There were also minor ash eruptions on 3/23/1995. According to the IGN maps, the summit crater is 344 meters deep. For volcano updates see the website (www.volcano.si.edu/gvp/).

To climb **San Miguel**, which is sometimes referred to as Chaparrastique, start in the small city of San Miguel. There are a number of inexpensive hotels around, many of which are found near the main bus station. Expect to find very warm temperatures there as the elevation is barely 115 meters. However, the mountain top is a cool retreat.

Inquire as to the location of where the buses running to San Jorge will be starting from. In 1/1994, they didn't leave from the main bus station, but from near the central plaza instead. There should be several buses per day running to San Jorge, but also several others going only as far as a baby clinic located at La Placita. The author remembers seeing buses numbered 90, 92, and 319 along the way. The bus the author used picked up lots of women and children and got very crowed before it stopped at La Placita; then it turned around and returned to San Miguel.

At La Placita, you'll find a number of small shops right at the highway intersection which sell coffee, refrescos and all kinds of snacks. Across the road from the shops is a building with a sign reading "Antel". Just east of that is an old road heading up the mountain. Walk along this farm (finca) road a short distance until it meets the main road which zig zags up the mountain through a coffee plantation. If you had a 4WD, you could probably drive up to the end of this very steep road, but you may need permission to do so (?).

From the end of the road at about 1475 meters, a trail begins. It winds its way up through brush, then at about 1650 meters, this main trail seems to vanish. From there, just head straight up a ridge using many little trails made by grazing horses. These gradually merge into one main hiker's trail which leads to the crater rim.

The author stayed in a hotel in San Miguel and got an early morning bus to La Placita. He made it to the top in about 1 2/3 hours; round-trip was about 3 hours. He found the mountain capped with clouds and very strong winds at the summit. He then headed back to San Miguel,

San Miguel as seen from about halfway between San Andras and La Placita.

Map 480-1, Volcan San Miguel, El Salvador

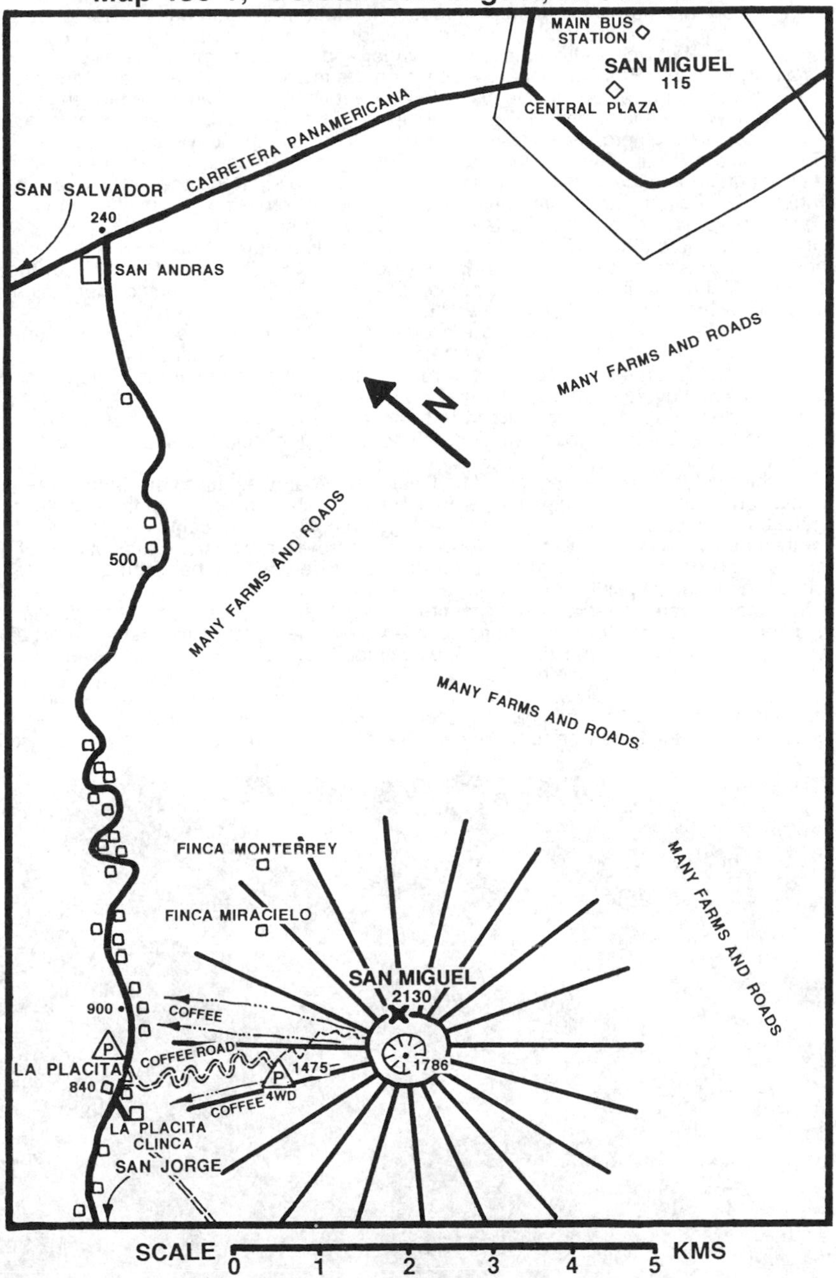

Map labels:
- MAIN BUS STATION ◇
- SAN MIGUEL 115
- CENTRAL PLAZA ◇
- CARRETERA PANAMERICANA
- SAN SALVADOR 240
- SAN ANDRAS
- MANY FARMS AND ROADS
- N
- 500
- MANY FARMS AND ROADS
- MANY FARMS AND ROADS
- MANY FARMS AND ROADS
- FINCA MONTERREY
- FINCA MIRACIELO
- SAN MIGUEL 2130
- 900 COFFEE
- COFFEE ROAD
- 1475
- 1786
- LA PLACITA 840
- COFFEE 4WD
- LA PLACITA CLINCA
- SAN JORGE

SCALE 0 1 2 3 4 5 KMS

had a shower, and got on a bus to the border, then another bus for a 3-hour ride to Choluteca, Honduras where he spent the night. Like the rest of Central America, the dry season here is from November to April, but you could climb it any time.

Maps IGN maps *Usulutan, 2556 III* & *San Miguel, 2556 II,* 1;50,000; and the travel guidebook, **Central America**, Lonely Planet for hotel and bus information.

Montaña de Celaque, Honduras

Featured on this map is the highest mountain in Honduras, Montaña de Celaque, at 2849 meters. This flat-topped mountain, perhaps more of a plateau or mesa, is located in western Honduras just east of where Guatemala, El Salvador and Honduras meet. It's also due south of the small city of Santa Rosa de Copán, which is on the main highway between Guatemala and the rest of Honduras. Celaque is one of the few mountains in the Central American part of this book that is not a volcano. However, it is made up of very old eroded Tertiary volcanic rocks.

Here's how to get there. If you're in Tegucigalpa, take one of many daily buses to the city of San Pedro Sula, then another one south to the town of Santa Rosa de Copán. From there, take a 3rd bus southeast to the town of Gracias (there might be a shorter route, so inquire). If you're coming from Guatemala, head for the Agua Caliente border crossing. From the Honduras side, take buses to Nueva Ocotepeque, Santa Rosa de Copán, then Gracias.

Gracias is a nice little town at about 800 meters elevation. It has 5 or 6 little hotels or hospedejas, and a small daily mercado for buying fruits & vegetables. Buy all your food and supplies in Gracias. While in town, stop at the COHDEFOR office for updated information about the mountain, which is now part of a *parque nacional*.

To climb **Celaque**, walk south from the middle of Gracias to Mejicapa, about one km. From the church there, walk (or hire a taxi) west across a bridge and small stream, then continue along the dirt road toward the pueblo Villa Verde and the centro de visitantes. This visitor center used to be a small hydroelectric plant, but it's now a national park hostel. It has 3 or 4 rooms with about a dozen beds, but you'll need to bring a sleeping bag. It also has a kitchen, with stove you can use, but bring your own food. The price, which includes an outdoor shower, was less than US$1 per night in 2/1994.

From the hostel, walk the signposted trail west and southwest up to the Campamento Don Tomas at 2060 meters. It has piped water for drinking or showering. From there to the second campsite the trail is less-used but you still can't get lost. This high camp is in the cloud forest with water nearby. This is a rather open forest of moss-covered pine trees without a lot of brush. From the high camp, plastic ribbons mark the route (slowly becoming a trail) to the undistinguished highest point 2-3 kms away.

The author arrived in Gracias late in the afternoon of 2/9/1994, bought some food, and started walking--too cheap to hire a taxi! He camped one km below the visitor center, then the next morning left his big pack at the hostel and took off for the summit. That took just over 6 hours round-trip from the hostel. He then returned, walking all the way to Gracias. The total 2-day walk-time from Gracias was about 9 2/3 hours. A really strong hiker could climb Celaque in one very long day from Gracias, with the aid of a taxi to Villa Verde, but it's recommended you arrive in the afternoon, sleep at the visitor center hostel, then finish the climb the next day. November through April is the dry season, and

The Campamento Don Tomas on the east side of Montaña de Celaque.

Map 481-1, Montaña de Celaque, Honduras

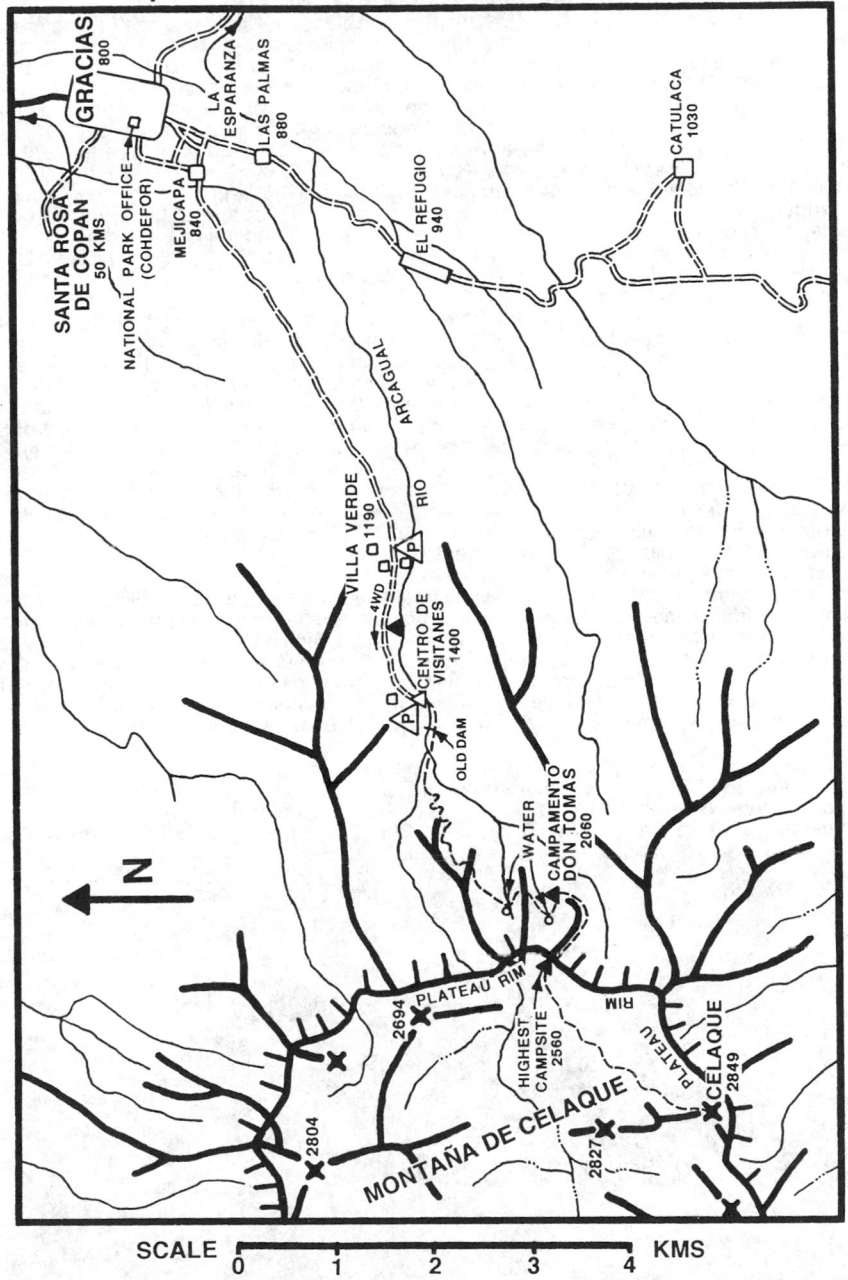

the water high on the mountain is good to drink as is.
Maps Honduras IGN map *Gracias, 2459 I*, 1:50,000; any national highway map; and the travel guidebook, **Central America**, Lonely Planet.

Volcan San Cristobal, Nicaragua

This map shows Volcan San Cristobal, the highest volcano in Nicaragua at 1745 meters. It's located in the extreme western part of the country just northeast of Chinandega. San Cristobal is an active volcano with lots of steam and sulfur rising from the summit crater. The mountain was quiet from 1685 until 5/3/1971, then phreatic eruptions with poisonous gases for several months killed all the trees on the upper slopes, the remains of which are still standing like ghosts in the clouds. It's been active ever since, with frequent eruptions and ashfall through 12/1999. But it was quiet in 2/1994 upon the author's visit. For volcano updates see the websites (www.ine.gob.ni/) or (www.volcano.si.edu/gvp/).

To get there, take one of many buses per day from Managua or Leon in the direction of Chinandega. Or if you're coming from Honduras, enter Nicaragua at the Guasule border crossing near Somotillo, then take a bus to Chinandega. Chinandega has a number of hotels, but most of these are next door to bars, which means noise, and traffic in and out all night long!

To climb **San Cristobal**, make your way to the middle of Chinandega and the mercado, then ask where the buses to Belen, La Mora and La Bolsa leave from. In 2/1994, it was from a little bus stand northwest of the mercado--not from the main bus terminal. At that time, one bus left for La Bolsa every hour on the hour. The first bus left at 7am; the last bus coming back left La Bolsa at 5 or 6pm. These old rattle-trap buses go through Belen, La Mora and to as far as La Bolsa, not far below the white water storage tank. It's a rough dirt road all the way. If you have lots of money, but less time, it's possible to hire a 4WD or taxi. Also, be aware that Hurricane David caused some colossal floods and a landslide & lahar on Volcan Casita just east of San Cristobal in 1998. This may have changed the driving route to San Cristobal (?). Will someone please send an update.

From La Bolsa, simply walk up the main road directly toward the volcano. There are a number of minor tracks branching off this one, but stay on the most-used road all the way to the vaqueria or dairy farm called Las Rojas at 720 meters. The peak should be in full view all the way. Above Miramar, this road is for 4WD's or tractors only.

Just before the gate at Las Rojas, turn right and walk up a minor road toward the mountain. The road soon turns into a trail. At first, you should see in a few places, an old water pipeline coming down from a dried-up spring. Further up you'll cross one gully, then at about 900 meters you'll come to a estacion sismica (seismic station). Continue up the trail made of loose scoria. At about 1100 meters you'll leave the living forest and enter a steep pasture with cows, skeletons of dead trees & many minor trails. Go straight up to the summit, but leave some kind of mark on a tree so you can find the trail back into the forest on your way down. It may cloud up later in the day! A compass will help, and always look back for landmarks as you're climbing up.

Here's what the author did on 2/7/1994. He took a bus to La Bolsa, then walked to the summit in just over 3 1/2 hours; round-trip from La Bolsa was less than 6 1/2 hours. The dry season is from November to April, but it can be climbed any time. Buy all your food in Chinandega, and take plenty of water--maybe 3 liters! Low altitude means hot weather. There

San Cristobal as seen from the southwest and from near Santa Teresa.

Map 482-1, Volcan San Cristobal, Nicaragua

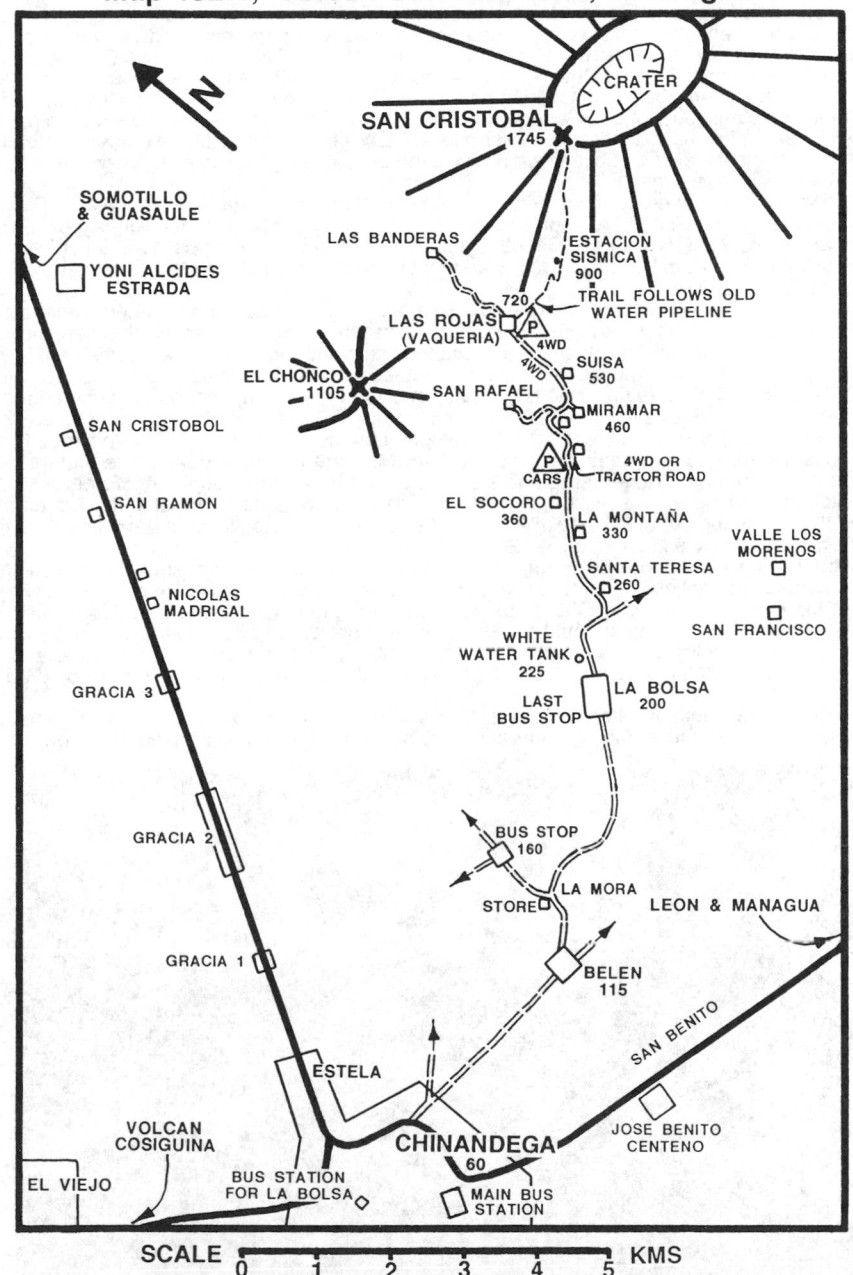

will be water at Las Rojas, but you may have to pay a little for it. Not featured in this book is Volcan Cosiguina, 807 meters, located northwest of this area. Adventurous hikers might try that one which last erupted in 1859.

Maps Nicaraguan IGN maps *Tonala, 2754 II & Chinandega, 2753 I*, 1:50,000; any national highway map; and the travel guidebook, **Central America**, Lonely Planet.

Volcan Telica, Nicaragua

Shown on this map are several volcanos, one of which is active. This is Volcan Telica at 1061 meters. Telica's activity is continually monitored by a solar powered *estacion sismica* (seismic station) located on the rim of an older nearby caldera. Telica was active throughout the late 1990's with small eruptions lasting through 2/2000. Also in the area are Volcan Santa Clara and Cerro de Aguero, both extinct. These mountains are located in western Nicaragua due north of the colonial city of Leon and the smaller town of Telica. They're also situated on the coastal plain which is not that far above sea level. Even though the altitude of these volcanos isn't great, the local relief is substantial. For volcano updates see the websites (www.ine.gob.ni/) or (www.volcano.si.edu/gvp/).

Getting to **Telica** is easy. If you decide to use one of the routes starting at or near La Piedra, first make your way to Leon. At Leon's main terminal, take a bus heading for San Isidro. These leave about every 20-30 minutes. Get off just before or not far after Km post 107. If you use the route starting at El Panal or Los Cocos, take any bus heading for Chinandega, and get off near Km post 103, as shown.

The author actually walked up a road, set in a deep dry gully beginning immediately east of La Piedra, but further up had to veer right or east to reach the ox cart road which begins across the highway from Santa Rita. He made it to the top using that route, but surely some people will get lost trying it. He returned via the route which passes through Colonia Maximo Jerez, which is the recommended route up. This is basically one road running up to 2 cornfield clearings in the forest, then onto a trail skirting the lower south side of Telica. From this trail, you can get upon one of 2 minor ridges to reach the old caldera just east of the main Telica Volcano. From there it's a walk through grass across the caldera floor to the main peak. The highest and newest volcano, has a rather large and steep-sided crater on top. Don't get too close to the edge of this 200 meter-deep crater; the rim could easily collapse! Lots of sulfur fumes and smoke were coming out of this one in 2/1994. The author's hike took just under 7 hours round-trip from the highway and La Piedra on 2/6/1994.

After having a good look down on the country side from the summit, and from the seismic station, this writer believes the least complicated route to **Telica** begins at Los Cocos. From there, the topo map shows a 4WD or ox cart road running north to sitio San Jorge, then on toward Agua Fria. The author could see this track just below the seismic station, and believes this is the route geologists used to construct that facility. It may be longer, but it appears to be less complicated. If finances aren't a problem, you could probably hire a pickup taxi or 4WD to do this route.

Be sure to take lots of water--at least 3 liters, as this country is at a relatively low altitude and hot year-round. November through April is the dry season, but it can be climbed anytime.

From the seismic station looking west at the active crater and summit of Telica.

Map 483-1, Volcan Telica, Nicaragua

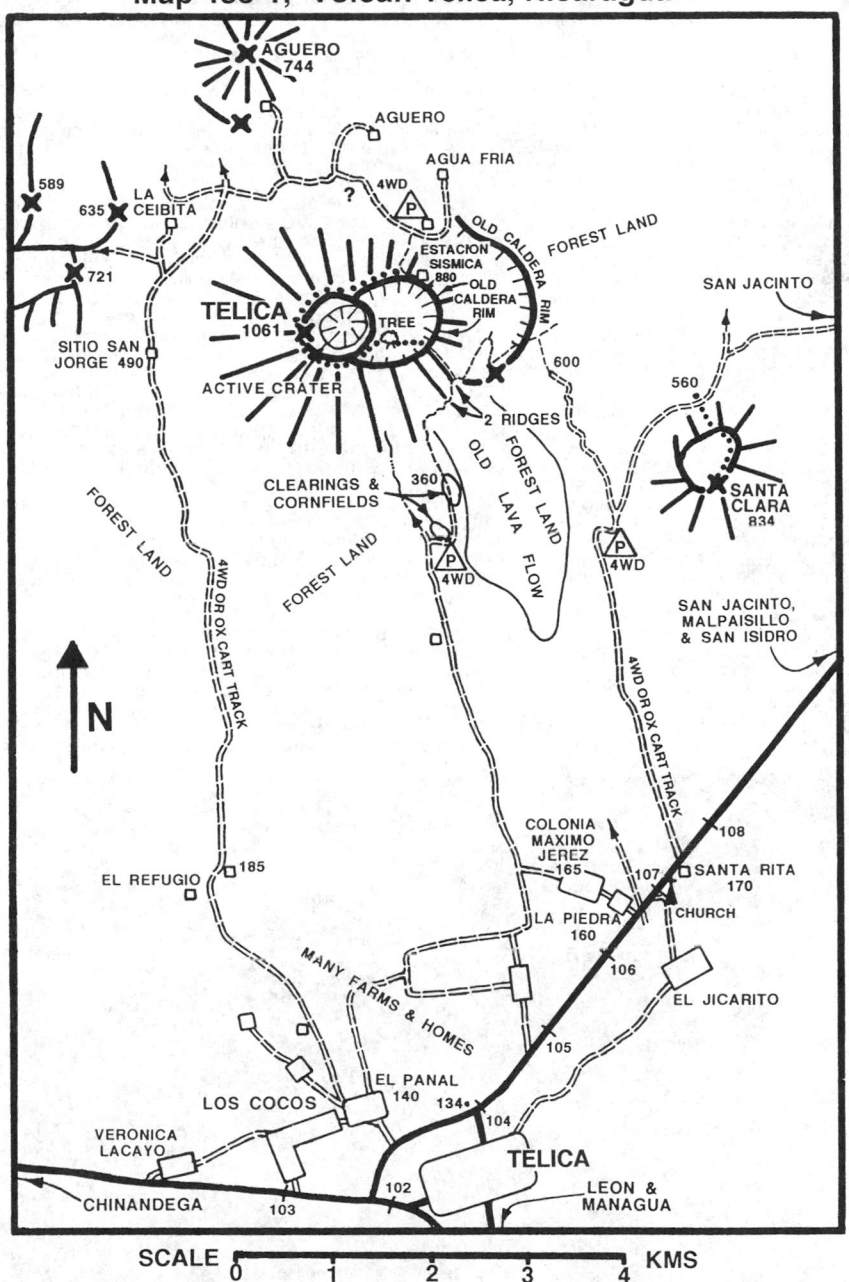

Maps Nicaraguan IGN map *Telica, 2853 IV,* 1:50,000; any national highway map; and the travel guidebook, **Central America**, Lonely Planet.

Negro, Hoyo & Momotombo Volcanos, Nicaragua

Featured here are several volcanos, 2 of which are very active. On the far left of the map is Volcan Negro at 726 meters; then Volcan El Hoyo, 1088; and Momotombo at 1297 meters. These are all located near the west end of Lago de Managua, north of La Paz Centro, and east of Leon.

Negro was born in 4/1850 and is Central Americas newest volcano. It's had frequent eruptions throughout the years. In 1968, 13 villages were evacuated. There were big-time explosions in 11 & 12/1995, with the last eruptions on 8/4 & 8/51999. Perhaps it's still ongoing (?). Momotombo started growing 4500 years ago and had its last big eruption in 1905 with lava flows. Since then it's had continuous fumarolic activity in it's tilted summit crater. For volcano updates see the websites (www.ine.gob.ni/) or (www.volcano.si.edu/gvp/).

A side feature to the volcanos is the geothermal electric power plant located at the foot of Momotombo next to the lake. It was started in the late 1970's and provides power to nearby areas; at least to La Paz Centro. In the travel guidebook below, it states you must have permission to climb Momotombo, but that's not true. You only need permission to visit the plant. Climb the west face starting just before the INE gate and hopefully there will be no problem.

To climb **Momotombo**, first make your way to La Paz Centro located between Managua and Leon. There were no hotels there in 2/1994! From the bus stand at the far east end of town, take one of about 7 buses per day heading for Puerto Momotombo. First bus leaves at 6:30am; last bus, 7pm. At Puerto Momotombo, walk (or maybe get a lift or hire a taxi) northeast on the road toward the power plant. Just before the INE gate, walk left along a 4WD or tractor road running to Laguna Monte Galan. About 100 meters before the pass at 200 meters, turn right on an ox cart trail used to haul wood. There were 2 tracks there in 1994, so take the first one up through the forest. When the track fades, walk up through the grass and scattered trees to where the forest ends at about 450 meters. From there to the summit it's steep with loose cinders or scoria. Near the top, veer left and skirt around to the north side to make the final ascent. Lots of hot steam and sulfur venting in 1994.

The author was invited into a home in La Paz Centro, then early on 2/5/1994, took a bus to Puerto Momotombo, left his big pack in a shop (for a small fee) and walked to the top of Momotombo and back in 7 3/4 hours. He took a bus from Puerto Momotombo to Leon for the night. For this hike, take at least 3 liters of liquids; it's hot. But the guards at the INE gate may give you a little water. Bathe in the stream 100 meters from the gate. There are several stores in Puerto Momotombo, but no hotels, so camp on the beach--or anywhere. While there, visit the ruins of Leon Veijo south of town. These date from the earthquake of 1610 AD.

Once the author went to Malpaisillo and walked south along the old railway grade to the foot of **Volcan Negro**, but failed to locate a way up through the thorny brush. Another route possibility is from Leon or La Paz Centro, then Miramar, or another place just off this map called Valle Los Urroz. From either of these places, there are ox cart or 4WD tracks up to near Negro and Las Pilas. Once near Las Pilas, it appears you can get up to **El Hoyo** rather easily. The author hasn't tried these routes, but the INETER maps are pretty actuate. Doing any of these latter climbs means camping overnight in the mountains, and carrying lots of water. The dry

From the Hacienda San Cayetano looking at the northwest slopes of Momotombo.

Map 484-1, Negro, Hoyo & Momotombo, Nicaragua

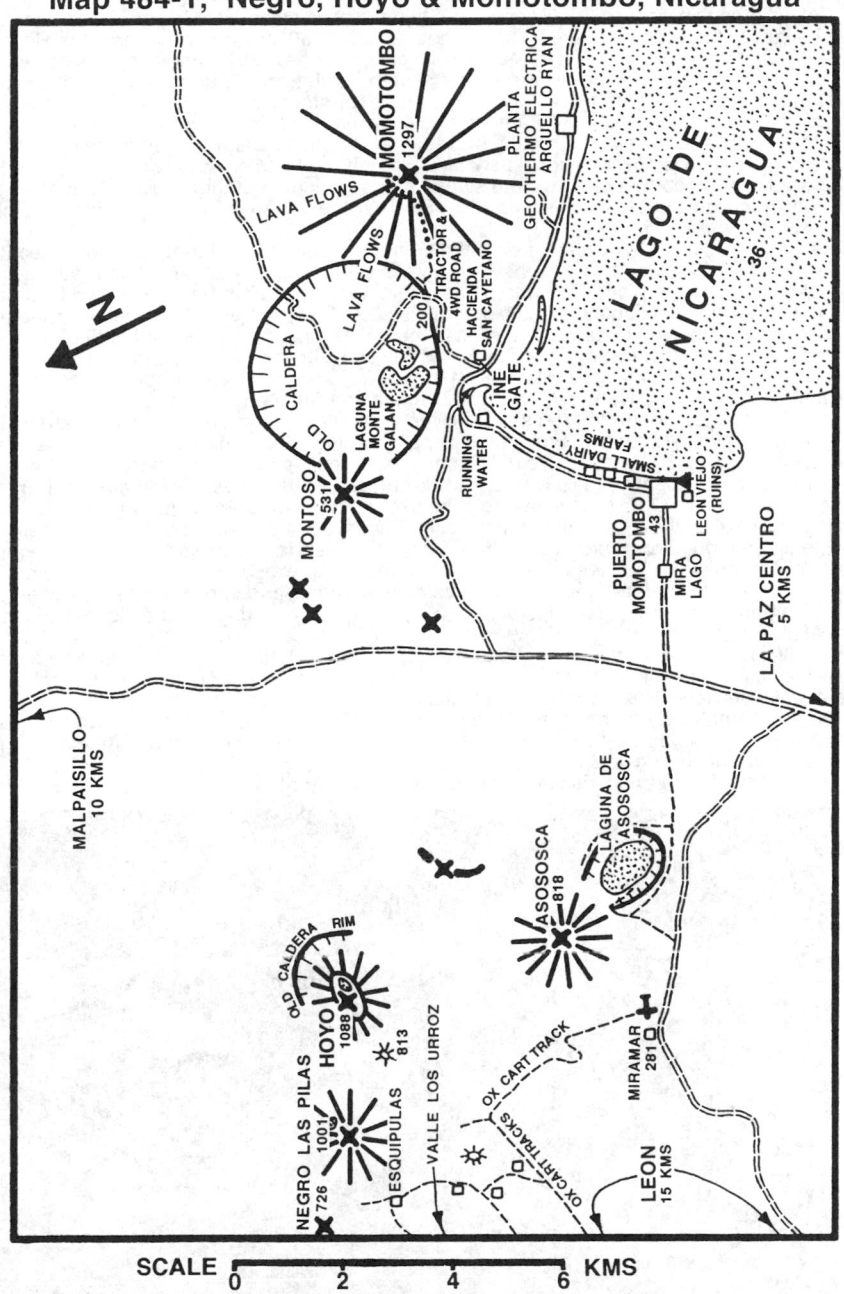

SCALE |0 2 4 6| KMS

season is from November to April, but it might be best to climb in the cooler wet season (?).
Maps Nicaraguan IGN map *La Paz Centro, 2853 II,* 1;50,000; and the travel
guidebook, **Central America**, Lonely Planet.

Masaya & Mombacho Volcanos, Nicaragua

Featured on this map are 2 of Nicaragua's better known volcanos; Masaya, 632 meters, and Mombacho at about 1345. These 2 mountains are located 30 kms apart, southeast of Managua. Santiago Crater is the active part of Masaya, which sits inside a 6x11-km-wide caldera. A major eruption in 1670 sent lava over the western caldera rim, and compressed a lake into the southeast corner. It's been in constant activity ever since, with degassing and minor ash explosions as late as 4/1999. The author was there on 1/23/1994 and found minor degassing from the red hot vent hole in the bottom of Santiago. Because this one is so close to Managua, it's visited often and is now a national park. Mombacho is a forested stratovolcano with 2 craters or blowouts on the northeast and south sides. It seems dead, but there are fumaroles and hot springs in the old craters. For volcano updates see the websites (www.ine.gob.ni/) or (www.volcano.si.edu/gvp/).

To reach **Masaya**, take a bus from the Huembes Terminal in Managua in the direction of Masaya. There's one leaving every 15-20 minutes. Get off the bus at the paved road leading to the volcano; the bus driver knows the place. This will be near Km post 23, which is about 17 kms from Managua, and about 7 kms before the city of Masaya. Pay a small entrance fee at the gate, then walk the short distance to the visitor center. From there to the end of the paved road it's about 4-5 kms. It's a fast one hour walk, but you can probably get a lift part way.

Once on Santiago's rim, you can walk on trails around each of the other summit craters. San Fernando is the oldest; Santiago the new & active one. It seems to be 200 meters deep, or more! There's also some foot trails around the central summit area, all of which are inside a much larger and older caldera. From the highway, walking around the summit craters and back, took the author only 3 1/3 hours. He did it in one day from Managua using buses.

To get to **Mombacho**, take a bus from Managua's Huembes Terminal heading in the direction of Rivas. Or if you're taking a bus from Rivas or Costa Rica in the direction of Managua, get off at the major intersection called Buenacate, near Km post 49. From there walk southeast up a good road past the coffee growing Hacienda Progresso, and all the way to a group of antennas on the western summit. The mountain was cloud covered on the author's visit, so he couldn't see a thing. If you have clear weather and can see where you're going, you'll likely find some trails, perhaps one running along the main ridge to the highest summit on the other side (?).

On 2/4/1994, the author took a bus from Managua to Buenacate and walked from the highway to the antennas and back in just over 3 hours. He then got on a bus back to Managua and another one to La Paz Centro for the night.

As an alternate, you might get off the bus at Cuatro Esquinas (4 corners) and walk to Los Ranchones, then south, east then north to El Crater. Have food and water before you reach this mountain; there's nothing at Buenacate.

As usual, the dry season is from November through April, but expect wetter conditions on

Looking down into the active Santiago Crater at the Masaya Volcano.

Map 485-1, Masaya & Mombacho Volcanos, Nicaragua

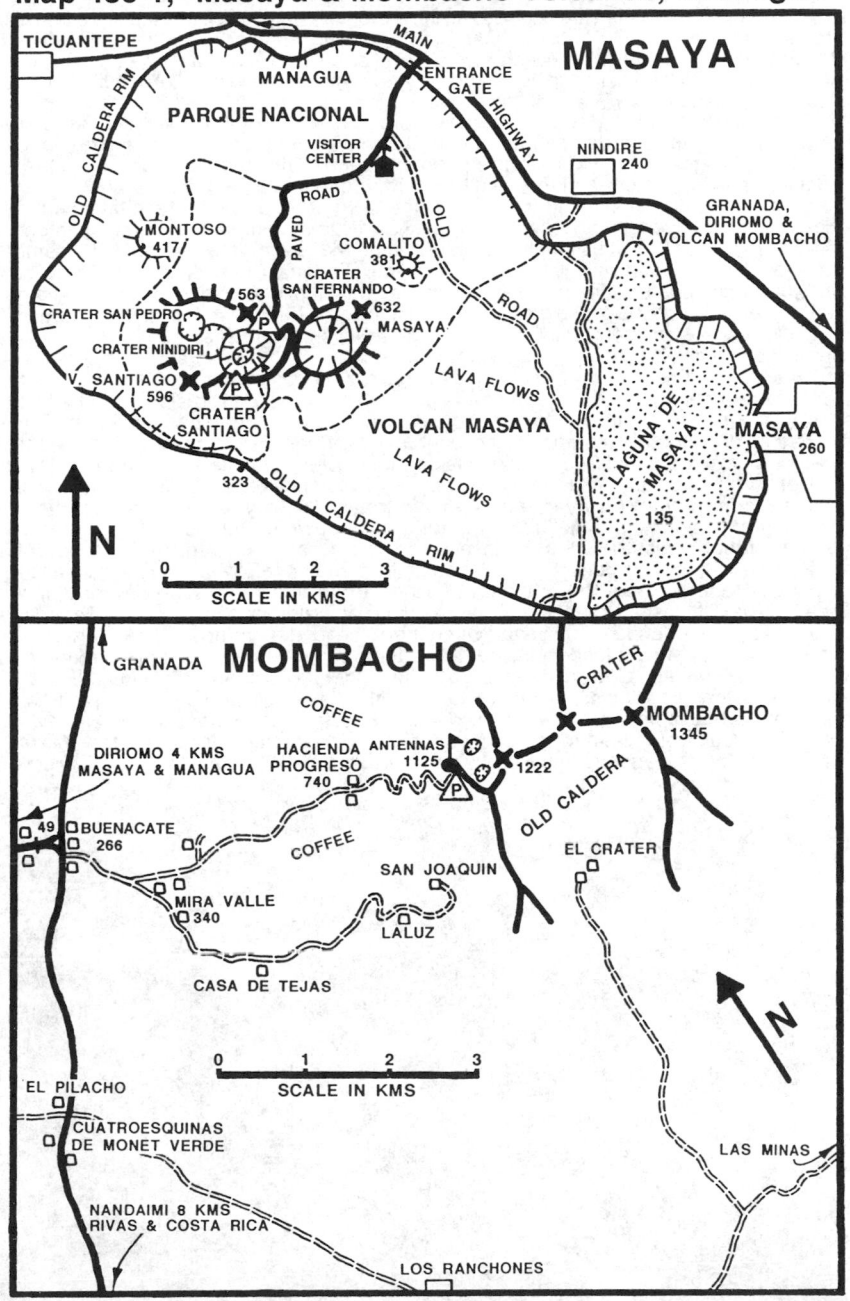

Mombacho, because of it's altitude & proximity to the western shore of Lago de Nicaragua.
Maps Nicaraguan IGN maps *Masaya, 2951 (for Masaya), plus Granada, 3051 IV, Isla Zapatera, 3051 III, and perhaps Nandaima, 2951 II, (for Mombacho)*, all at 1:50,000; and the travel guidebook, **Central America**, Lonely Planet.

Concepcion & Maderas Volcanos, Nicaragua

The 2 volcanos on this map are on an island in Nicaragua's Lago de Nicaragua; it's called Isla de Ometepe. Concepcion, 1610 meters, is an active volcano with some fairly new lava and little vegetation toward the summit. It's been active on & off since the 1970's with minor ash explosions. The last report from 2/2000 indicated ash eruptions for 3 days beginning on 12/27/1999. For volcano updates see the websites (www.ine.gob.ni/) or (www.volcano.si.edu/gvp/).

Maderas at 1394 meters, is older, heavily forested, with some erosion. It hasn't had a confirmed eruption in recorded history, but on 9/27/1996, a lahar came down the east flank wiping out the village of El Corozal killing 6 people. Police climbed to the beginning of the lahar and said they found a crater. A farmer said he heard rumbling sounds too.

To get to this island, first make your way to the town of Rivas west of the lake on the Pan American Highway. From there, take a bus or taxi 5 kms to the port of San Jorge; then one of 5 or 6 daily ferry boats to Moyogalpa, the largest town on the island. Moyogalpa has a number of small hotels and good food selections. A tourist place. To climb Concepcion, it might be best to stay in Moyogalpa, but to climb Maderas, and in one day, it might be best to stay in Altagracia. In 1994, there were about 8 or 9 buses per day running between these 2 towns. Altagracia has about 3 little hospedejas, many small shops, but few fruits or vegetables.

Here's how to climb **Concepcion**. The author stayed in Altagracia and on the morning of 2/3/1994, took a 5:30am bus toward Moyogalpa, but got off at La Union, a place with scattered houses. Someone showed him one of several trails heading up Concepcion. The trail he took was OK with a little route-finding, but at about 850 meters, ran into moss and brush 2 meters high. He then got into the gully shown and went up easily. About 125 meters from the top, the gully & trail ended in a sea of 2-meter-high plants with leaves as big as elephant ears. It was so steep, wet, windy and miserable, he failed to finish. To complete that route and return safely, you'll need to mark you're way carefully above that gully so you can find it on the return. Without that gully you'll have hell to pay getting back down in the clouds! Because of this problem, it might be best to go to San Jose, and use the trail or ox cart road shown. After 2 kms, simply walk up a prominent gully on the south face and hopefully right to the summit (?).

To climb **Maderas**, take the 5:30am bus from Altagracia (or maybe an early bus from Moyogalpa?) to Balgues. In 1994, there were no hotels in Balgues, only a couple of stores. Ask about the track to Hacienda Magdalena. Once there, head straight up on a regular trail. After 300 meters, pass through a fence and veer left; after another 300 meters, pass through a gate. After another 200 meters, cross another fence to the right to a cement box connected to a water pipeline. From there, a hiker's trail runs up to the crater rim and the lake inside. You'll wade in mud from about 950 meters up. It was cloudy, misty & wet on the author's trip on 2/2/1994, and he didn't see a trail along the rim; only one very steep slippery trail descending to the lake. He did this in 6 1/2 hours round-trip from Balgues, then caught the last bus to Altagracia. For some,

Concepcion Volcano as seen from the Santa Cruz-Balgues road.

Map 486-1, Concepcion & Maderas Volcanos, Nicaragua

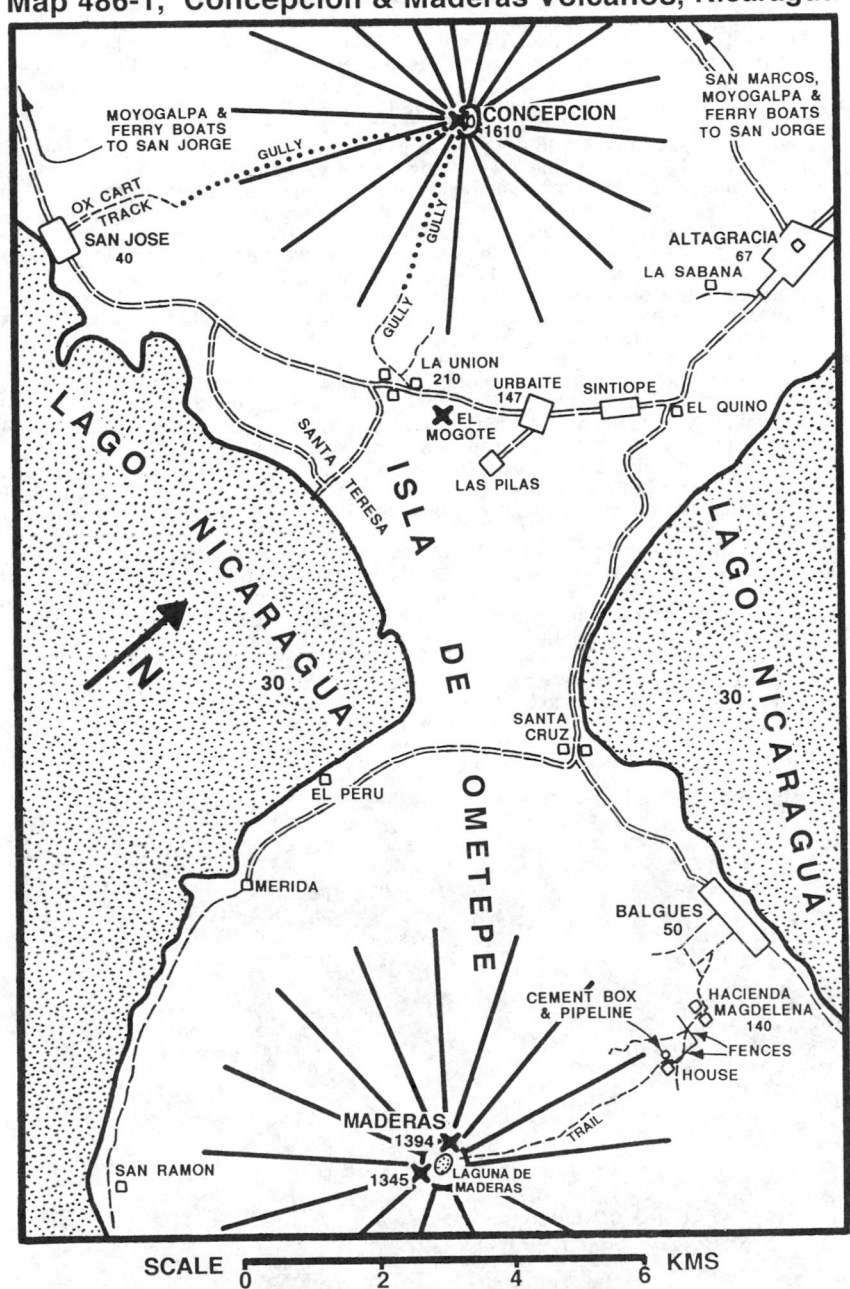

MOYOGALPA &
FERRY BOATS
TO SAN JORGE

SAN MARCOS,
MOYOGALPA &
FERRY BOATS
TO SAN JORGE

CONCEPCION
1610

OX CART
TRACK

GULLY

GULLY

GULLY

GULLY

SAN JOSE
40

ALTAGRACIA
67
LA SABANA

LA UNION
210

URBAITE
147

SINTIOPE

EL QUINO

✗ EL
MOGOTE

LAS PILAS

LAGO

NICARAGUA

30

SANTA TERESA

ISLA

DE

OMETEPE

SANTA
CRUZ

LAGO

NICARAGUA

30

EL PERU

MERIDA

BALGUES
50

CEMENT BOX
& PIPELINE

HACIENDA
MAGDELENA
140

FENCES

HOUSE

TRAIL

MADERAS
1394 ✗

SAN RAMON

1345 ✗

LAGUNA DE
MADERAS

N

SCALE   0   2   4   6   KMS

it might be best to camp near Balgues and not have to worry about catching a bus back to a hotel. Dry season is from November to April, but it's wet on top 365 days a year!
Maps Nicaraguan IGN maps *Moyogalpa, 3050 I & San Jose del Sur, 3050 II,* 1:50,000; and travel guidebook **Central America**, Lonely Planet.

Volcan Rincon de la Vieja, Costa Rica

Shown here are several volcanic craters, all of which make one the biggest mountains in Costa Rica. It's called Volcan Rincon de la Vieja. The highest point is actually Volcan Santa Maria at 1916 meters. However, the most interesting part of this massif is on the Von Seebach and Rincon de la Vieja craters at 1895 & 1740 meters. Rincon is one of 9 eruptive centers within a 15-km-wide caldera with the youngest cones to the southeast. Rincon's last magmatic eruption here was about 3500 years ago; since then all eruptions have been the explosive type. There were ash explosions in 1969 & 1991, and phreatic eruptions in 1998 & 1999. It's ongoing. Of special interest on the lower slopes are 4 areas with sulfurous ponds, thermal springs and boiling mud pots. These are found at Las Hornillas, Azufrales, Borinquen and Las Pilas. For volcano updates see the website (www.una.ac.cr/ovsi/) or (www.volcano.si.edu/gvp/).

To get to **Rincon**, get off the bus at a place called Cereceda on the Pan American Highway about 5 kms northwest of Liberia. From there you'll have to walk and hope for a lift part way; or hire a taxi. No public transport! It's 21 kms from the highway to the park entrance. This is a popular place especially on weekends so if you start walking, you'll surely get a lift part way.

After 10 kms there are 2 small stores in Curebande, your last place to buy food. Three kms above that is a gate where everyone pays a road tax of about US$2 for passing through the Hacienda Rincon de la Vieja. After another 3 kms is the hacienda itself, then it's 5 more kms to the entrance to the national park, visitor center, ranger's house and campground. Park fee and use of the campsite was about another US$2 in 1994. The campground has drinking water and a nice stream nearby for bathing. From the campground, there's a good trail running to a nearby thermal area called Las Pilas, with boiling mud pots and hot springs.

The trail to the volcanos begins next to the visitor center. It runs up through an interesting rainforest along a ridge between 2 small streams. There is water along the trail at about 1000 and 1450 meters elevation, but best take your own from the campground. You'll leave the forest at about 1450 meters.

The author started walking from the highway, but got 2 lifts which took him 3/4's of the way up. Next morning, 1/31/1994, he went up in clouds with rain and roaring winds above treeline. He couldn't see a thing, but did make it to the rims of the Von Seebach and Rincon craters. Be sure to take a compass for navigation in the clouds, plus a good wind & rain coat. An altimeter is useful as well. Trails are marked with painted stone cairns. If you can see and find the trail, you can make a loop-hike of the upper part of the mountain. The author did this one round-trip from the visitor center in 4 hours; most people need 5 or 6 hours. That same afternoon, he road-walked 18 kms before getting a lift to the highway.

About 3 kms below the park entrance is a mountain lodge or albergue for those who don't have camping equipment. They also serve meals. It's easy to get a ride back down to the highway from the visitor center, because this is one of the most popular hiking areas in Costa

One of the boiling mud pots at the base of Rincon de la Vieja Volcano.

Map 487-1, Volcan Rincon de la Vieja, Costa Rica

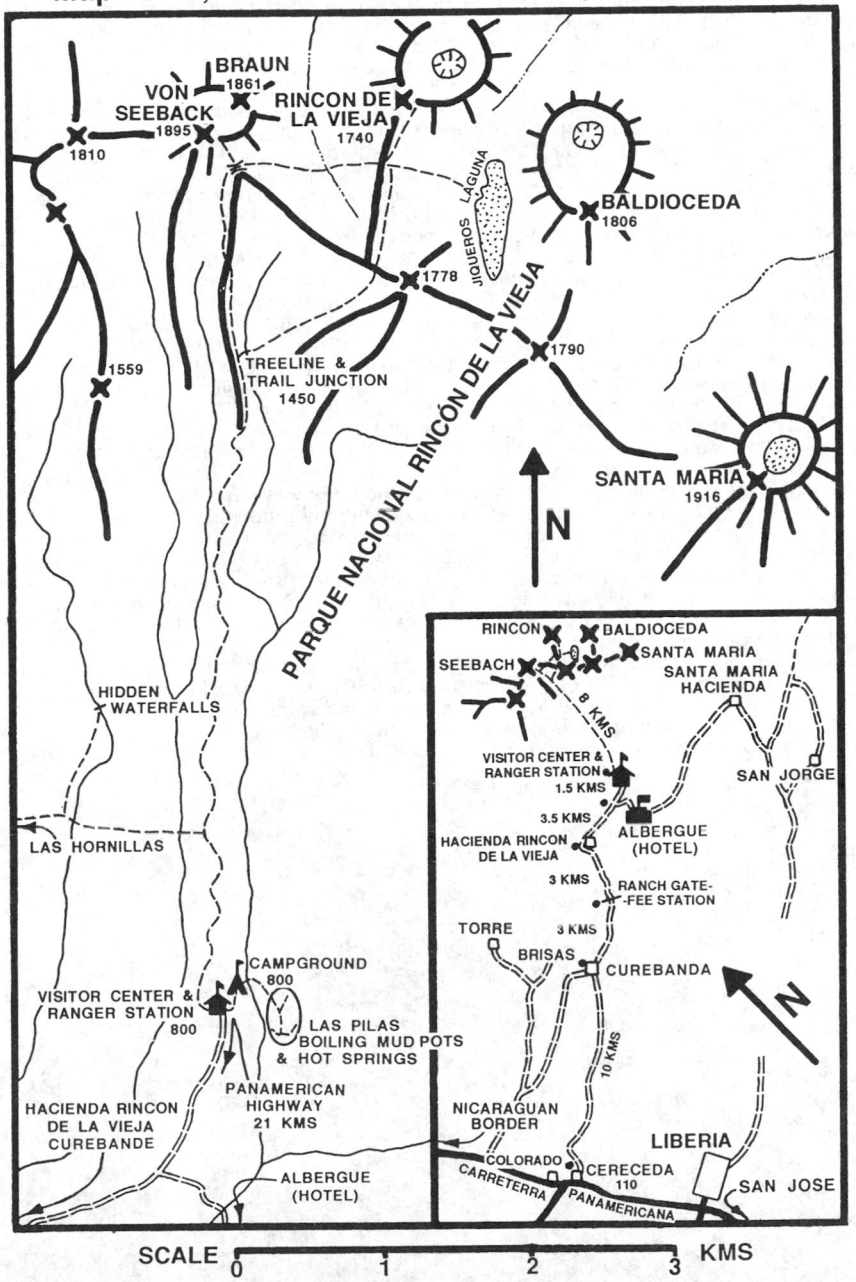

SCALE 0 1 2 3 KMS

Rica. The dry season is from December through April.
Maps IG de Costa Rica maps *Curebande, 3148 III,* 1:50,000; and *Liberia,* 1:250,000; and the books, **Costa Rica, Land of Volcanos**, Alvarado (very good); and the travel guidebook, **Central America**, Lonely Planet.

Volcan Arenal, Costa Rica

This map shows Volcan Arenal at about 1633 meters, located in the northwest part of Costa Rica and just east of the large lake, Laguna de Arenal. Arenal started growing only 2900 years ago. It grew quickly and diverted local drainages and formed Arenal Lake. Nearby Chato Volcano at 1140 meters, had its last eruption in the late Holocene, likely about the time Arenal took off.

Arenal's first historical eruption was a deadly Pelean-type explosion on 7/31/1968. That eruption buried 2 small villages killing 78 people. Lava blocks and bombs up to 4x6x10 meters were thrown out, some as far as 5 1/2 kms. Some impact craters were 4 meters deep & 25 meters in diameter. It's been in continuous eruption with mostly Strombolian-type canon-shot detonations ever since. On 8/26/2000, a sight-seeing plane crashed on the northeast side of the mountain and near the summit killing all 10 tourists onboard. For volcano updates see the websites (www.ine.gob.ni/) or (www.volcano.si.edu/gvp/).

Here's how to get there. It's best to begin in San Jose. First, visit the tourist office then buy a good topo map from one of several stores in the downtown area, then take a bus from the Coca Cola Bus Station to the city of Quesada. From there catch another bus to Fortuna.

Fortuna is a small town, and because of the active volcano, has become a real tourist hangout. There are lots of small hotels for less than US$5. Also, lots of little tour companies taking tourists around the mountain--when it's in a state of eruption. In 1994, there were also about 3 public buses daily running from Fortuna toward Tilaran, which you could take to reach the west side of the volcano. That's where the best views of eruptions are found. Or you can just hitch hike which is easy. Buy all your food and the volcano book listed below in Fortuna. Best to get your water there too if you plan to hike and/or camp on the mountain.

To climb **Arenal**, get out of the bus or car at the junction marked 530 meters and walk 4 or 5 kms to the base of the mountain. You might get a ride part way. The carpark at 700 meters is where most tourists, some in tour buses, were viewing the eruptions in 1/1994. At that time, canon-shot explosions about every half hour were blasting lava blocks in the air which rained down on the upper slopes. It would have been suicide to climb it then from the west side. However, if you were to loop around on the north or south side, then climb the higher east summit, it appeared it would have been reasonably safe. The best thing to do if it's having similar eruptions when you arrive, is to watch the mountain for a while from the carpark, then decide on a safe route to the top.

For the night of 1/29/1994, the author camped at the foot of Arenal, at the end of the trail as shown. After watching it for 2 hours, he climbed up to the river of blocky lava coming out of the active western crater. From a viewpoint at about 1200 meters, he saw several ear-shattering explosions up close. It threw lava block everywhere and he never made the summit. Later he wished he had gone around the north or east side and climbed the summit crater for a safer view

A cannon-shot type explosion seen close-up on the west side of the Arenal Volcano.

Map 488-1, Volcan Arenal, Costa Rica

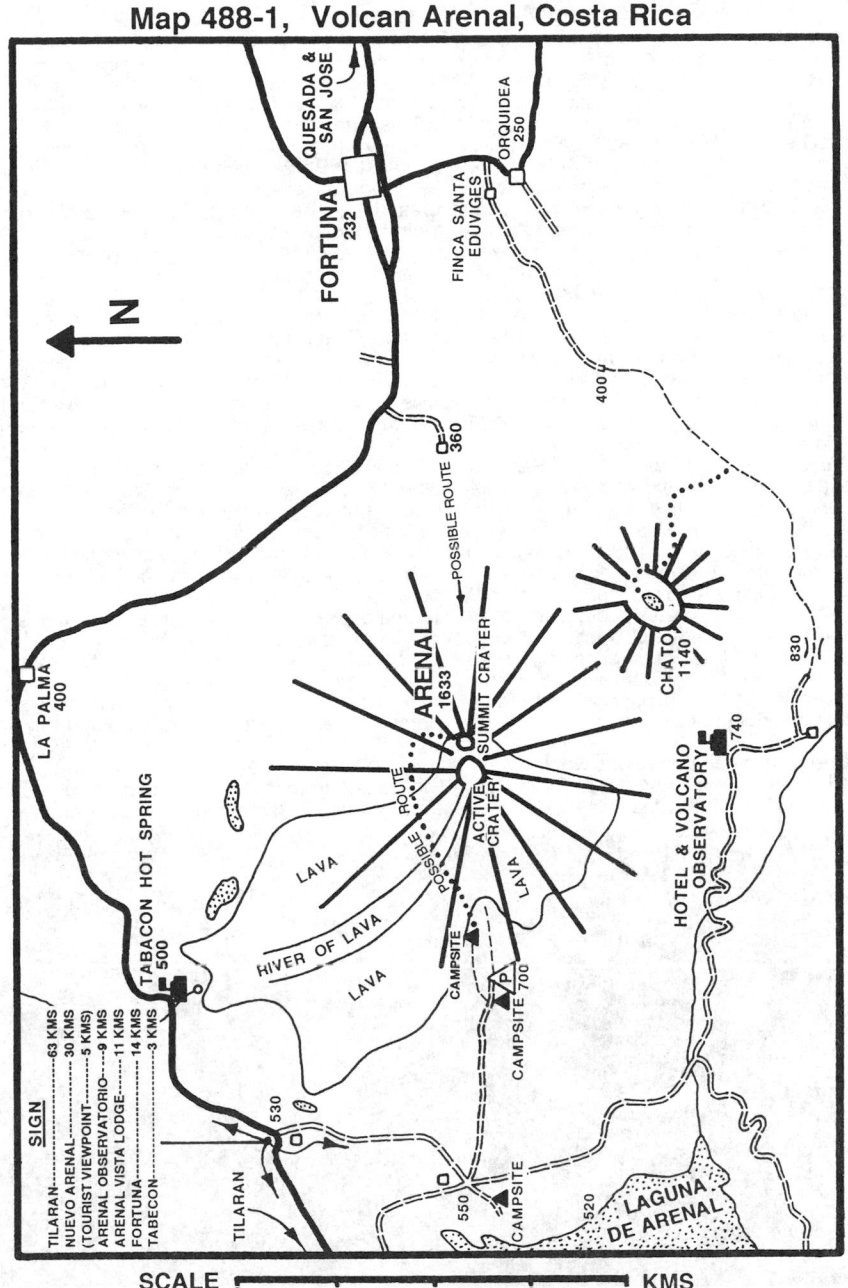

down on the blasting. Be sure to take some rugged hiking boots; the new lava rocks are very loose and the walking is difficult. It appears an east side route would have better footing. Ask about that in Fortuna. The dry season is from December through April.

Maps IG de Costa Rica map *Fortuna, 3247 II*, 1:50,000; and the interesting book, **Costa Rica: Land of Volcanoes**, Alvarado; and the travel guidebook, **Central America**, Lonely Planet.

Poas and Barva Volcanos, Costa Rica

Included on this map are 2 more of Costa Rica's volcanos; Poas, at 2704 meters, and Barva, 2906. Both are now national parks. Over the years Poas become famous because of steam and venting activity. It had a big eruption in 1953, a smaller one in 1969, then sporadic activity ever since, mostly minor phreatic eruptions and/or just big steam clouds. In the summit craters are 2 lakes; one clear, one colored and acidic. This latter one is in the active crater. Barva is an old & extinct volcano, but there are still several heavily forested craters with lakes inside. It's part of a national park, most of which is north and east of Barva's summit plateau. For volcano updates see the websites (www.ine.gob.ni/) or (www.volcano.si.edu/gvp/).

Because of the activity, interest in Poas increased over the years, and by 1968 a paved road was completed to the summit area and a viewpoint. Because of that, the author never did get there, thinking it wouldn't be interesting for hiking. However, there are a number of short trails leading to various parts of the volcano. If the mountain is really active when you arrive, it will certainly be worth the effort to make a visit.

To get to **Poas**, look for a bus in San Jose going in the direction of Puerto Viejo, but get off at the pass & junction marked 1936 and hitch hike or walk the 16 kms to the summit. Or make your way to Alajuela, then take one of about 2 buses daily to the pueblo of Poasita, then walk or hitch hike the last 10 kms. Or hire a car or go with a tour group. Inquire about tours at the very good tourist office in San Jose. At the end of the paved road on the mountain is a park ranger station, museum and a snack bar. Water is available, but you'd better take food for your trip. The park is closed at night and camping is not allowed.

To reach **Barva**, take a bus from San Jose to Heredia; they leave about every 10 minutes. From behind the big central market in Heredia, take another bus to Paso Llanos (Porrosati on IGN maps). In 1994, buses left at 6:30 & 11am, and 4pm. There are others going only as far as San Jose de la Montaña. From Paso Llanos, walk up the good road to Sacramento. There are several small restaurants along the way, but bring your own lunch. From Sacramento, continue walking up a very rough 4WD track to the park entrance. The latter part of this trail is now used by hikers and cows only. The ranger station is about 7 kms from Paso Llanos.

From the entrance, it's about 2 kms to the Laguna de Barva, and 3 kms to Laguna Copey, all through a rain and/or cloud forest. Maps show other trails, but they have apparently been blocked off and have been allowed to overgrow. About the only thing you really see here is a mountain rainforest and cow pastures on the lower slopes. There is day-hiking only in this park-- no camping. The dry season in Costa Rica is from December to April. From San Jose, be sure to get up early and take the first bus to either mountain, because it will surely cloud up by mid-day.

The author had marvelous weather on his hike to Barva on 1/28/1994. He took a bus from San Jose to Heredia, another to Paso Llanto and walked from there. He hid his large pack in trees near Paso Llanos then walked the paved road (4 kms) to Sacramento. He continued to the

A substitute for Poas/Barva is this picture of Turrialba with Irazu in the background (see next map).

Map 489-1, Poas and Barva Volcanos, Costa Rica

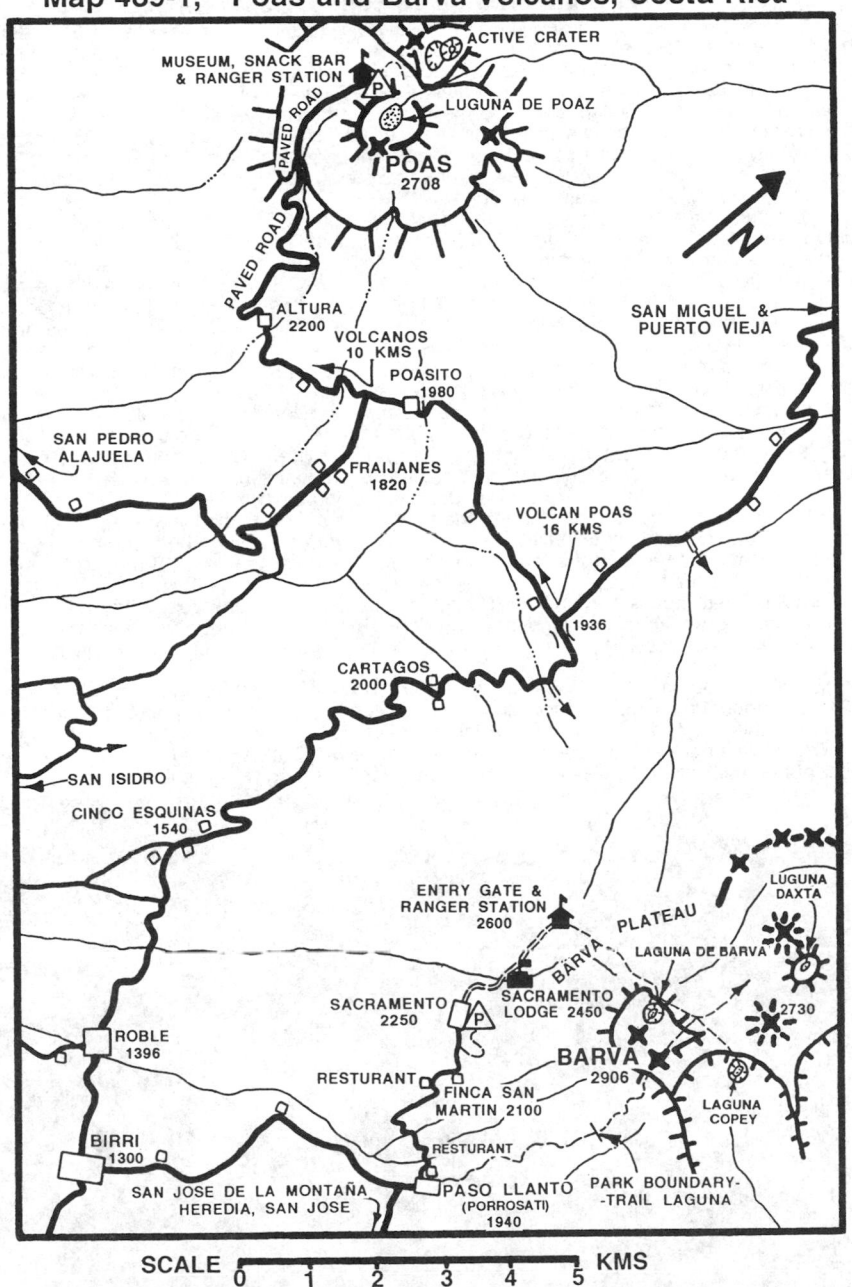

ACTIVE CRATER

MUSEUM, SNACK BAR
& RANGER STATION

LUGUNA DE POAZ

POAS
2708

PAVED ROAD

PAVED ROAD

ALTURA
2200

VOLCANOS
10 KMS

POASITO
1980

SAN MIGUEL &
PUERTO VIEJA

SAN PEDRO
ALAJUELA

FRAIJANES
1820

VOLCAN POAS
16 KMS

1936

CARTAGOS
2000

SAN ISIDRO

CINCO ESQUINAS
1540

ENTRY GATE &
RANGER STATION
2600

PLATEAU

LUGUNA
DAXTA

BARVA

LAGUNA DE BARVA

2730

SACRAMENTO
2250

SACRAMENTO
LODGE 2450

ROBLE
1396

BARVA
2906

RESTURANT

FINCA SAN
MARTIN 2100

LAGUNA
COPEY

BIRRI
1300

RESTURANT

SAN JOSE DE LA MONTAÑA
HEREDIA, SAN JOSE

PASO LLANTO
(PORROSATI)
1940

PARK BOUNDARY-
-TRAIL LAGUNA

SCALE 0 1 2 3 4 5 KMS

entry gate (3 kms) then to Laguna de Barva and returned, all in 4 1/3 hours. He got buses back to San Jose, and another afternoon bus to Quesado on the way to Arenal.

Maps IG de Costa Rican maps *Poas, 3346 I & Barva, 3346 II*, 1:50,000; and the books, **Costa Rica, Land of Volcanos**, Alvarado; and the travel guidebook, **Central America**, Lonely Planet.

Irazu and Turrialba Volcanos, Costa Rica

Featured here are the 2 highest volcanos in Costa Rica; Irazu at 3432 meters, and Turrialba, 3329. They're located near each other, and both are east of San Jose, northeast of Cartago, and northwest of the city of Turrialba. Irazu is the most famous because of its last great eruptions in 3, 7 & 11/1963. At that time San Jose and Cartago were buried in up to half a meter of ash. The story was told in the 7/1965 issue of National Geographic magazine. Irazu's last lava flows were 14,000 years ago; since then all eruptions have been ash explosions. Irazu's first historic eruption was in 1723, and it's had minor activity since. Turrialba is considered active by some, but it's last real eruption was in 1864-66. There is still some fumarolic activity in its 3 summit craters. For volcano updates see the websites (www.ine.gob.ni/) or (www.volcano.si.edu/gvp/).

The author hitch hiked up the paved road to **Irazu** on 4/24/1972, but it was raining and he couldn't see a thing. Having a paved road to the summit puts it in a negative list for most hikers, but there are some trails around the craters. There's no public transport there, so you'll have to take a bus from Cartago to Cot, and maybe as far as Tierra Blanca. From there, it'll be walking and/or hitch hiking. On weekends, there's lots of traffic. It's roughly 21 kms from Cot to the summit. Or you could hire a taxi in Cartago for about US$30 (1994 prices); or join a group in San Jose and go by bus. There are no facilities on the mountain except for a visitor center. You could likely camp out, but you'd have to hide your tent away from the rangers as this is another national park and camping is likely not allowed (?).

For hikers, **Turrialba** is the better of the 2 mountains, even though there's an old 4WD-type road up to the crater rim. To get there, take a bus from San Jose to the small city of Turrialba. From there take one of about 4 daily buses heading for Santa Cruz and Pastora. There are several stores in Santa Cruz, and one shop at the Pastora junction. You can also get to Pastora from Pacayas; in 1994, there were 2 buses per day making that run.

From Pastora, walk up a dirt road to the dairy farm called Finca Central, a distance of 14 kms. This road switch-backs up through pastures with lots of cows. About one km beyond the Finca Central is some kind of a lodge, but the author never saw it, so it may not be placed correctly on this map (?). From Finca Central, turn right and finish the climb passing Fincas Quemados & Mirahuajis enroute. 4WD's have a hard time getting past Quemados. On the crater rim are 2 antennas and a trail heading northeast along the ridge to the summit. For the energetic hiker, it's possible to walk from Finca Central to Irazu, but the IGN maps show some roads as private (?).

The author took buses from San Jose and arrived late in Pastora, then walked less than 1 1/2 hours before camping. Next morning, 1/27/1994, he hiked to Finca Central and hid his pack in bushes, then hurried to the summit. About noon he was in Pastora, walking all the way. That evening he was back in San Jose using buses all the way. Total walk-time for the 2 days was 8 1/3 hours, much of which was with a big pack. Last drinking water is at Mirahuajis. The dry

A tourist office foto of one of the craters on top of Irazu Volcano.

Map 490-1, Irazu & Turrialba Volcanos, Costa Rica

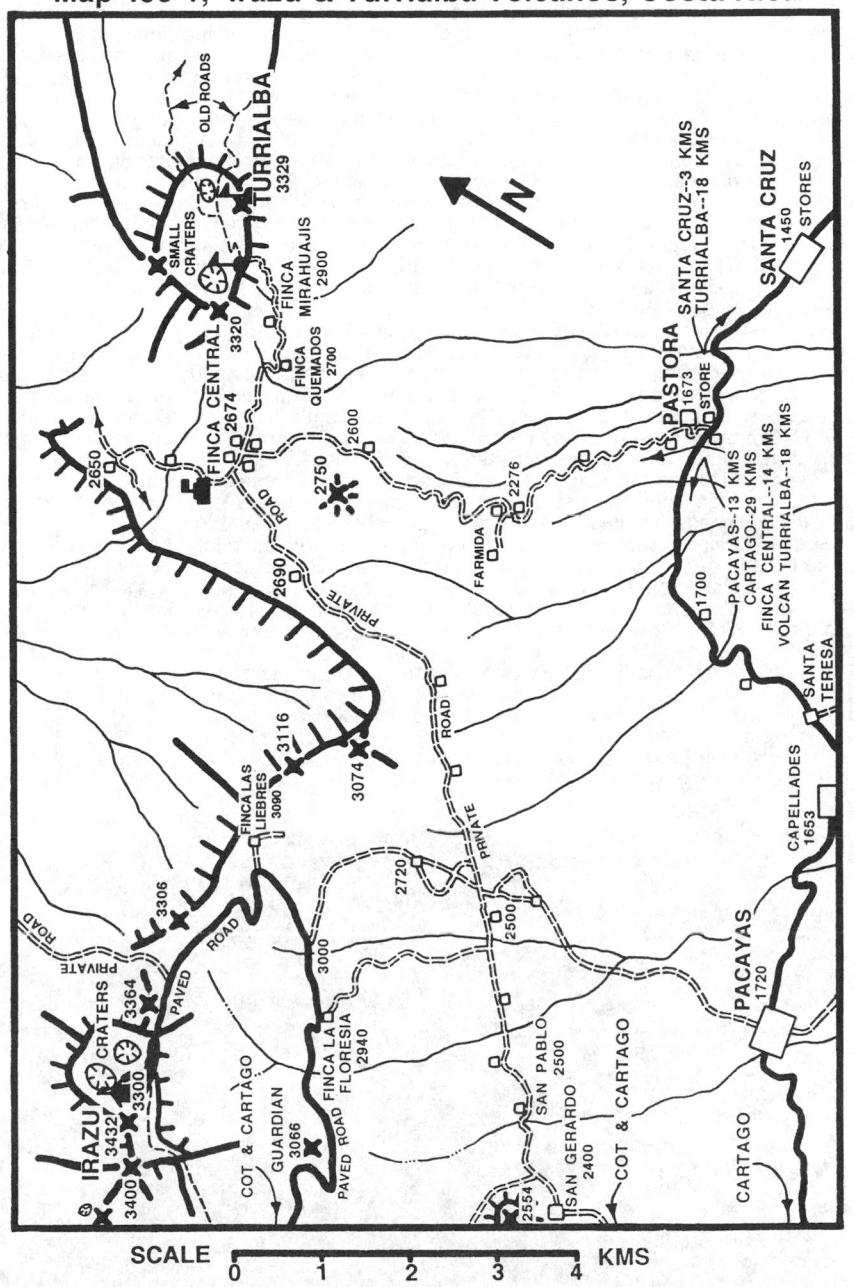

season is from December to April.
Maps IG de Costa Rican maps *Carrillo, 3446 III, and Cartago, 3445 IV,* 1:50,000; and the books, **Costa Rica, Land of Volcanos**, Alvarado; and travel guidebook, **Central America**, Lonely Planet.

Chirripo, Parque Nacional Chirripo, Cordillera Talamanca, Costa Rica

Costa Rica is famous for its active volcanos, but none of these are the highest mountain in the country. That distinction belongs to Cerro Chirripo rising through the clouds to 3819 meters. This summit is part of the Cordillera Talamanca running northwest to southeast in the southeastern part of Costa Rica. It's also just east of the Carretera Inter Americana (Pan Am Highway) and about halfway between San Jose and Palmar Norte. The rocks here are mostly metamorphic, as opposed to the lavas found in most other parts of the country.

The author was here on 9/7 & 9/8/1980, in the middle of the wet season! He stayed in a pension in San Isidro, then the next morning he shopped for food and started walking to San Gerardo. He got 4 shorts lifts, but walked about half of the 16 kms (other sources say 19 kms). He stored some baggage in the office of the *parque nacional*, then with a sketch map from the person there, headed up the trail. After 5 1/2 hours of walking in the rain, he stopped for the night in the first refugio at 3310 meters. Next morning he was at the summit of Chirripo in 1 1/2 hours; another hour down to the hut, and 4 more hours down to San Gerardo--12 hours total walk-time. Finally, on the way back to San Isidro, he got a lift with a power company line crew. Two long days from San Isidro.

Here's how you climb **Chirripo**. First, take a bus south from San Jose; or from anywhere south, take a bus north to the small city of San Isidro where you'll find 7 or 8 little hotels or pensions. In reviewing a recent guidebook, not a lot has changed since the author did this hike--except now there are at least 2 buses per day going from San Isidro to San Gerardo. One bus leaves at 5am, the other at 2pm. The trip takes 2 hours. At San Gerardo, there are now (1999) 3 or 4 small hotels. Before hiking, visit the national park office and get a map, updated information about waterholes, using the refugios and their condition, and pay an entrance fee.

From San Gerardo's church, walk up the road northeast crossing 2 streams. Not too far past the second bridge, is an entry gate then the trail runs south to the top of a ridge. Once on that ridge, the trail heads east and is easy to follow all the way to the summit.

Since the trail is on the ridge, water can be a problem with the heat & humidity. Start with at least 2 liters to get you to the spring & 1st refugio Llano Bonito, located at about 2525 meters. You'll pass a small stream at about 3125 meters, the next water supply on the route. The 2nd refugio at 3475 meters can accommodate 50-60 hikers and is where everyone must sleep, according to Richard White of Portland, Oregon, USA. With national park status, no camping is allowed in this area and everyone must sleep in the Refugio Centro Ambientalista El Paramo.

From the 2nd refugio, you'll have to go up and over 2 passes before you reach the summit of Chirripo. Normally, this is 2 day climb but a really fit climber might do it in one long day; but you'd have to sleep 2 nights, before and after the climb, in San Gerardo.

If you're starting this trip in San Jose, stop at the very good tourist office in the center of town and they can give you some updated information on the park, transport, refugios, etc. If you're there on a weekend, you should be able to get a lift to the mountain easy. Don't climb without

From near the summit of Chirripo looking north (Nature Conservancy foto).

Map 491-1, Chirripo, Cordillera Talamanca, Costa Rica

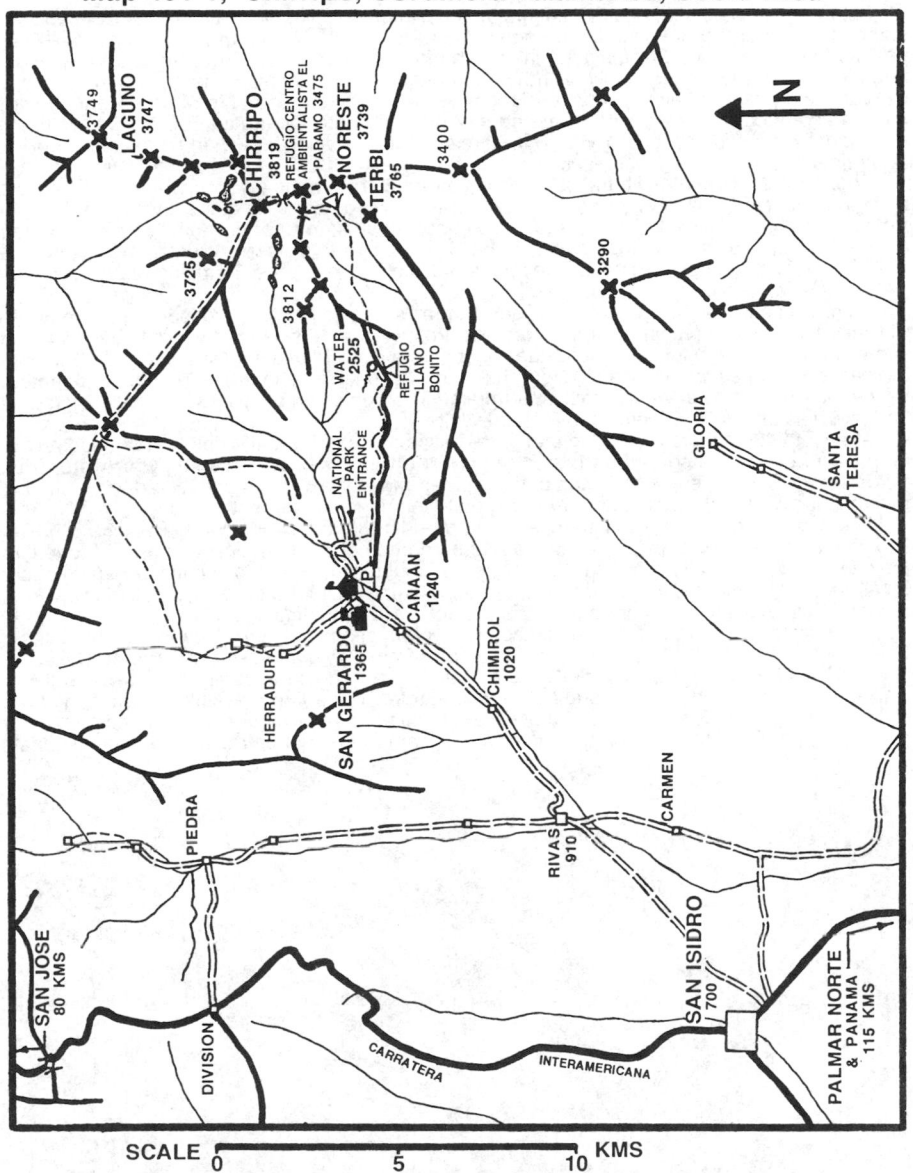

SCALE 0 ——— 5 ——— 10 KMS

first going to the national park office for updated information on refugios and to pay the park fee.
  Keep in mind these mountains are among the wettest places in Central America, so have rain gear with you even in the dry season. Food can be found in all the small villages en route to the mountain including San Isidro. Dry season is December through March.

Maps JOG or IG de Costa Rica map *San Jose, NC-17-9*, 1:250,000; or IG maps *Durika, 3544-III and San Isidro, 3444-II*, 1:50,000; and the books, **Costa Rica, Land of Volcanos**, Alvarado; and travel guidebook, **Central America**, Lonely Planet.

Volcan Baru (Chiriqui), Panama

In the extreme western end of Panama, just north of the cities of David and La Concepcion, stands the highest mountain in the country, Volcan Baru at 3474 meters. On some maps this peak is called *Volcan de Chiriqui*, after the name of the state in which it's located. Baru is an old and highly eroded volcano. Only slightly resembling a volcano today, the mountain has deep canyons and a mature rainforest on its slopes. According to the book, **Volcanos of the World**, there was an explosive eruption from one of 7 summit craters in about 600 AD, as well as a questionable eruption in about 1550. But there's nothing shaking today, and the author doesn't remember seeing anything that resembles a crater.

There are 2 ways to reach the summit of **Volcan Baru**, one is on a 4WD road, the other a trail. The most interesting way of course is the trail. This route begins at the town of El Hato del Volcan; locals just call it *Volcan*. It's located about 30 kms north of La Concepcion. You can easily hitch hike or take a small bus from La Concepcion to Volcan. Volcan, at a cool 1420 meters, has a couple of inexpensive pensions or hotels, and at least 3 small grocery stores as well as several restaurants.

From the center of Volcan, take the Cerro Punta Road to a junction about 3 kms to the north. At that point is a sign reading, *Parque Nacional Volcan Baru*, a side-road veers to the right and into a canyon on the mountain's west side. Just past a small house, turn left and walk down into the canyon and past an old shack. Near that 2nd old house is a spring, and about 300 meters beyond is where the trail heads up the mountain. The beginning of this trail is now easy to find and follow as of 1/2000, according to Richard White.

At about 2400 meters is a spring and place for camping. This is the only water found on the mountain beyond the spring at the end of the road (but it's best to take all your water from Volcan town). Most people don't camp, but instead make the climb in one long day. From this spring, head east--not up the other trail going up to the ridge on the west!

The author arrived in Volcan in the evening of 9/4/1980 and stayed in the Pension Omayra. Next morning he walked up the paved road, and veered right or northeast along a dirt road into the canyon. With directions from a local farmer, he found his way to the summit of Baru in about 5 1/4 hours. He returned in 4 hours for a round-trip time of 9 1/4 hours, walking all the way from Volcan. You could hire a taxi for part of this trip and save some time & walking.

The guidebook below updates the author's old information, and suggests the normal route up Baru is via Boquete. Take a bus or hitch hike north from David and ask about the 4WD road to Baru. The book says it's 8 kms (likely more ?) from Boquete to the summit and takes 6 hours walking one way. There are several hotels in Boquete. The author has little information about this road from Boquete to within 500 meters of the summit, but it's quite new and not on any of his maps. It's used to maintain the radio and TV antennas just below the summit. Tourists

Large cross at the summit of Volcan Baru, a typical site on Latin American summits.

Map 492-1, Volcan Baru (Chiriqui), Panama

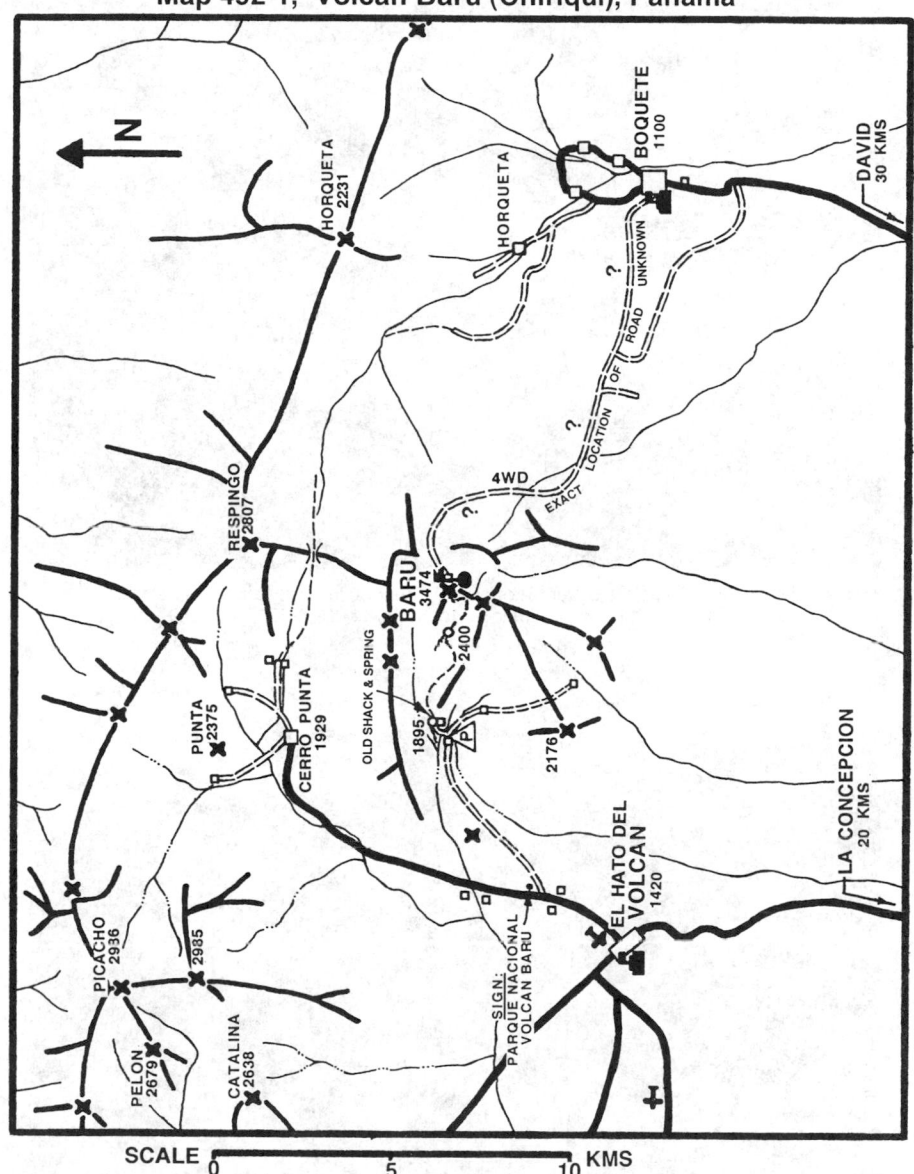

sometimes go that way in 4WD's.

The drier months are from December through April, but the mountain can be climbed any time. Just take good rain gear if you're climbing in the wet season.

Maps JOG or IGN map *Golfito (Costa Rica-Panama)*, *NC-17-13*, 1:250,000; or Panama's IGN maps *El Hato Del Volcan*, *3642-11*, or *Boquete*, *3743-III*, 1:50,000; and the travel guidebook, **Central America**, Lonely Planet.

This is the pool & cable at the small waterfall (700 meters) located at the lower end of Cañon del Diablo north of Pico Diablo in Baja, Mexico (Map 464, page 989).

From inside the crater (caldera) on the top of Soufriere Volcano on the island of St. Vincent, you can see the rope & vertical route extending 145 meters down from the crater rim (Map 510, page 1083).

One campsite the author saw during a rare moment when the clouds parted and mist stopped on top of Rorima Tepuy. These rocks are sandstone (Map 516, page 1097).

From near the point marked 4400 meters, looking east at Pico Humboldt left, and Pico Bonplano right, in the Sierra Nevada de Merida of Venezuela (Map 517, page 1099).

Pico Turquino, Sierra Maestra, Cuba

This map shows Pico Turquino, highest summit in Cuba at 1974 meters. It's in the Sierra Maestra which is on the far southeastern end of the island and due west of Santiago de Cuba. These mountains were formed by some kind of an intrusion and trusted upward, the result of which is the rocks on Turquino are mostly granite.

To get there, first go to Santiago de Cuba. Make your way to the central bus terminal, which in 1993 was just across the street from the train station in the western part of town. Buses leave Santiago several times a day going west along the coast to Chivirico, 75 kms away. In Chivirico, you'll have to get a second bus (or maybe a truck) going to Uvero and Ocujal, a distance of 45 kms. Buses going to Ocujal may also continue 7 kms west past the small pueblo called **La Cueva**, where the actual hike begins. (Back in Santiago, if you don't want to wait for a bus, then walk north, and west on the main road to the edge of town and hitch hike. Hitching is good, easy & safe in Cuba.)

There's a place to sleep in Ocujal called the Hotel Turquino. Also, just east of town about 3 kms is the Campismo Rio La Mula. There is one small store and a cafeteria in Ocujal, but in 1993, there was nothing to buy but *limonada*. Undoubtably that will change with more tourists arriving. Keep in mind, there were no good maps available to the public when the author was in Cuba in 1989 and 1993, so this map isn't quite drawn to scale. He used a tourist road map and his own sketch to create this one.

At La Cueva, get off the bus or truck at the big sign marking the beginning of the trail to **Pico Turquino**. Just above the sign is a rough road leading up past one house on the left. From that house, the trail is actually an old unused road which zig zags up a ridge. After about 3 kms you'll come to a flat place called La Esmajagua at about 600 meters. There you'll see a sign reading: *Alto de Cardero--2.7 kms*.

After another km the old road gives way to a real trail at about 950 meters. Then you'll come to **Alto de Cardero** at 1265 meters, a flat area with some old ruins of some kind just beyond, and to the right or east, a refugio apparently used by hikers. It was locked when the author arrived on 3/7/1993, but in summer it may be open (?). There's year-round water nearby which makes this the best place to camp on the mountain. Somewhere above that is another sign reading: *Al Pico Real Del Turquino--1.7 kms*. On top of the 1st summit is a sign stating: *Loma Redonda, 1872 meters*. (**BEWARE**: The author's notes were confusing when he got home, and the elevations given on some signs were much different than his altimeter readings; but this map will get you there!)

The author arrived at La Cueva after dark and camped not far above the first house. From there, and after hiding his big pack, he made it to the summit in 2 3/4 hours (less than 6 hours round-trip). The distance seemed like 10 kms or more, but according to the sign on the highway it's about 7 kms. Best to buy all your food for this trip in any tourist hotel store, but there's been big changes since 1993! In 1993, tourist stores with payment in US$ were the only places to buy hiking-type food.

Climb this peak year-round, but the dry season is from November through April. Only Americans need visas to Cuba, which used to cost $US26 at the Cuban Interests Section. Swiss

This foto shows the author's tent located at what is marked *Possible Campsite, 70 meters*, on the lower part of the trail up Turquino. The summit is to the far right out of sight.

Map 493-1, Pico Turquino, Sierra Maestra, Cuba

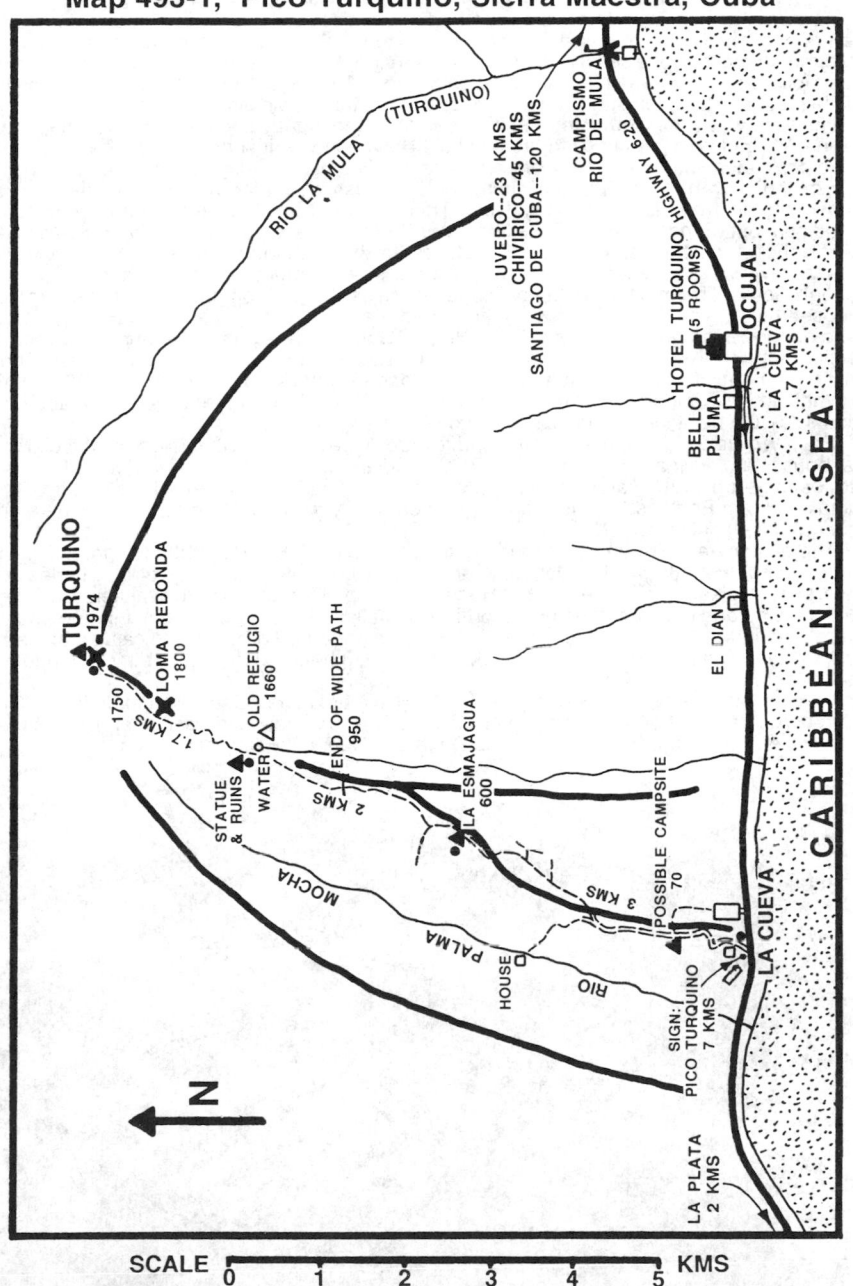

SCALE

0 1 2 3 4 5 KMS

Embassy, Washington, D.C. Buy the guidebook below because many things will change by the time you arrive--except for the route up the mountain.
Maps *Provincia Santiago de Cuba,* from any tourist hotel in Santiago; and the travel guidebook, **Cuba**, Lonely Planet.

Blue Mtn. Peak, Blue Mountains, Jamaica

Featured here is Blue Mtn. Peak, the highest point in Jamaica's Blue Mountains at 2256 meters. This high region is east of Kingston and immediately east of the town of Mavis Bank. Just prior to the author's second trip to Jamaica in 1993, this pristine region was made into the Blue Mountain & John Crow Mountain National Park. This should insure the more scenic places will be protected from farming & wood cutting, and the trails maintained.

Here's how to climb **Blue Mtn. Peak**. If you have the money and not so much time, you can hire a 4WD and be driven to as far as Whitfield Hall Lodge, or just beyond, on the south slopes of the peak; then you walk the rest of the way and will be back in Kingston late the same day.

For those with more time and using *public transport*, make your way to the center of Kingston to an area called Half Way Tree. This is where buses come and go in all directions, including most of the suburbs. Take bus 70 or 75 to the east side of the city to a place called Papine (bus numbers may change). Wait there for the bus going to Mavis Bank. If the bus is broken down or late, talk to drivers of private cars who might be going that way. You'll go through Gordon Town, Guava Gap or Ridge, to Mavis Bank. From there you have 2 routes to choose from. If you decide to stay on the paved road, you may get a ride to Hagley Gap, but there are no buses going that way. From Hagley Gap, where a good little store is located, turn uphill (north) and walk a very steep dirt road right up the ridge toward a place called Penlyne Castle. At Farm Hill turn right and walk the old road past the Wildflower Lodge (US$12 a night) to Whitfield Hall, a lodge near the end of the road. They have water and meals, and charge about US$10 a night for a room. If it's full, you can camp outside.

From Whitfield Hall, walk along the road toward Abbey Green, but turn uphill at the sign and first house, and walk a very good trail to Portland Gap, which now has a warden's office, picnic site, campground with water and even a shower. In 1993, they charged less than US$1 for camping. From Portland Gap, it's about 5 kms on a very good trail to the summit, where an old unused cement hut is located.

The author was here on his second trip to Jamaica on 3/1 & 3/2/1993. He got to Papine at noon, waited for a bus which never came, then finally got a lift all the way to Mt. Charles at 600 meters. He walked from there through Hagley Gap, up along the road to Whitfield Hall, then to Portland Gap and camped. The next morning he walked 5 kms to the summit in one hour. On the return trip from Portland Gap, he walked down a good horse trail; some call it a bridle path, from Penlyne Castle direct to Mavis Bank. That took 3 hours. He then got another ride in the back of a pickup going to Papine.

You can buy plenty of food at Papine, Mavis Bank, or Hagley Gap. Plan to do this in 2 days using public transport or hitch hiking, and walking. The dry season is December through March, but it can be climbed year-round. Be on top in the early morning to avoid clouds.

Looking northwest from the summit of Blue Mountain Peak.

Map 494-1, Blue Mtn. Peak, Blue Mtns., Jamaica

Maps *Kingston, Sheet L,* 1:50,000, from the Lands & Survey Office, 23 1/2 Charles Street, Box 493, Kingston; or from Sanford's, 12/14 Long Acre, London; and the travel guidebook, **Jamaica**, Lonely Planet.

La Sella, Massif du Sella, Haiti

The highest mountains in the Caribbean are concentrated on the island of Hispanola. This is the second largest island in the Antilles next to Cuba. On the eastern half of Hispanola is the Dominican Republic and highest mountain called Pico Duarte; on the west half is Haiti. Next to the summits around Pico Duarte, the highest peak on the island is in Haiti called La Sella at 2674 meters. La Sella is located southeast of Port au Prince, and not far from the border of the Dominican Republic.

Here's what the author did on 3/19/1979. While staying in Port au Prince, he got up early and found a mini bus called *tap tap* locally, going from Port au Prince to Petionville then Kenscoff. From there he walked south through Furcy and climbed one of the peaks south of the one marked 1696 meters. This is the wrong approach route for climbing La Sella, but it was a fun day-hike and it gave him an idea of what to expect in other parts. What he saw was a high cool area, with clouds in the afternoon, eucalyptus trees and vegetable gardens with corn & cabbage being grown on steep & terraced hillsides. An interesting cultural experience for trekkers.

The author never really got much information about climbing La Sella, but you can expect lots of farms & gardens on the lower slopes and very likely an open pine forest on the upper hill sides with some trails. The best way to get to La Sella is to take a bus or tap tap from Port au Prince to Ganthier then a tap tap or truck toward Fond Verrettes. However, in 1998, Fond Verrettes was wiped out by floods from Hurricane Georges. So you'll have to inquire in Port au Prince if there's anything left in that area (?). Apparently not much, plus they've had a couple of revolutions since the author's visit, so don't expect to see prosperity breaking out all over. Beyond Fond Verrettes, there's little traffic; likely only trucks going south toward the *Foret des Pins*. There's a road heading northwest from there toward La Sella, but you'd likely have to hire a 4WD to get up close. Or by carrying lots of water, you may be able to walk right from where Fond Verrettes used to be and into the mountains, but that would likely take a real tough hiker 2 or 3 days. Better find a better map than this!

There are many trails, villages and farms in the mountains, so trekking, perhaps from Kenscoff which is easy to get to, would be more enjoyable than trying to get to the more isolated La Sella. In the 1990's, some people were taking a tap tap to Kenscoff, then walking an old unused road over the top and down to Seguin and the hotel called Auberge de la Visite (US$50 a night, or camp nearby for free). This takes tourists about 5 or 6 hours. From there you may have to walk down to Marigot, and from there get a tap tap west to Jacmel and a bus back to Port au Prince. This is normally done in 2 days.

No matter where you go, a little knowledge of French comes in handy when trying to stay on the right path. From the end of one of the roads shown, you could walk cross-country up to and along the big east-west ridge to reach higher peaks or see villages. The northern slopes are steeper than the more gently sloping southern approaches. Also, public transportation in Haiti is

This foto was taken south of Kenscoff looking in the direction of La Vista Peak.

Map 495-1, La Sella, Massif du Sella, Haiti

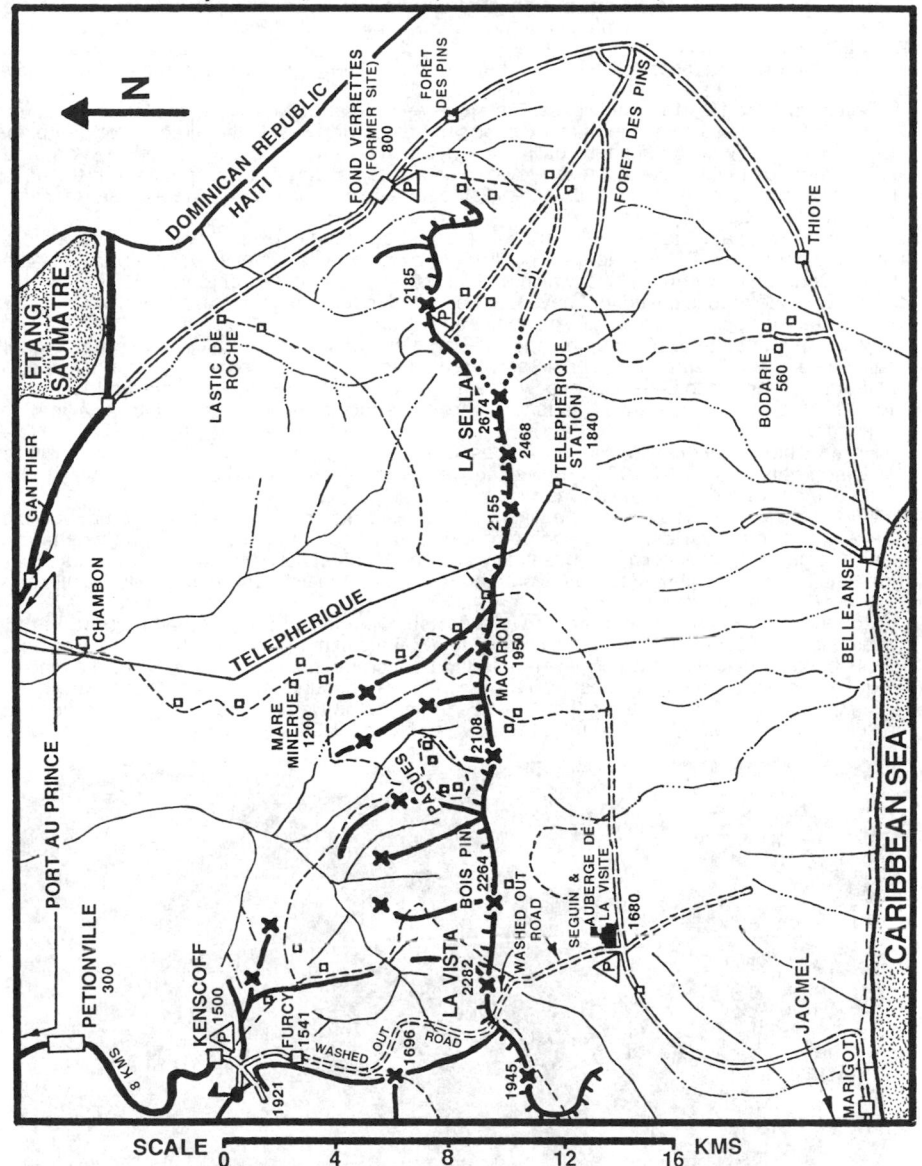

not as good as you might wish. And communication is a big problem, even for those speaking French.

Best time to climb is from December through April. Food should be bought in the larger towns, preferably at Port au Prince. For information concerning buses or where to buy maps, contact the Maison de Tourisme office in the capital, Tele. Inter+222-8659. The travel guidebook below has more telefon numbers.

Maps *Port-Au-Prince, 5771, Fond Parisien, 5871, Belle-Anse, 5770 & Grand Gosier, 5870,* 1:100,000, from Service de Geodesie et de Cartographis et les Forces Armees d'Haiti; and the travel guidebook, **Dominican Republic & Haiti**, Lonely Planet.

Pico Duarte, Cordillera Central, Dominican Republic

Pico Duarte at 3175 meters, is the highest mountain in the Dominican Republic. It's also the highest on the island of Hispanola and in the entire Caribbean. Second highest is La Pelona, 3087, then Rucilla at 3045 meters. Duarte is part of the Cordillera Central, which is a folded and uplifted range located near the center of the country. If memory is correct, most of the rocks making up this range are sedimentary in origin.

Getting to **Pico Duarte** is fairly easy. The journey normally starts in the capital city of Santo Domingo. From there, take one of many buses heading northwest in the direction of Santiago. About 3/4's of the way to Santiago you'll come to the small city of La Vega. Get off there, and take another bus to the mountain resort town of Jarabacoa situated at 529 meters. This town is a little cooler than the rest of the country, so it's been developed into a cool weekend retreat with many tourist facilities.

From Jarabacoa, there used to be no public transport in the direction of Manabao--but there is today. About every 2 hours there's a *publico or colectivo* (a car running along a route just like a bus). Or hire a taxi; or hitch hike, which on this rather lonely section of road is fairly easy. Up to Manabao, the road is paved, but beyond it becomes rougher and less-used, and you'll either have to hire a taxi, or walk the last 8 kms to the end of the road at La Cienega.

Between Manabao at 900 meters, and the beginning of the trail at La Cienega, are several small villages, all with small shops or stores where some food can be found. It's about another 3 kms from La Cienega to Casa Tablone, where the road used to end and where a work crew hut and gate used to be located. This is/was the entrance to the Parque Nacional Armanda Bermundez.

Here's what the author did. He took buses to as far as Jarabacoa, then had to hitch hike to Manabao. This was on 3/7/1979. He walked west from Manabao but got a lift part way to La Cienega; then walked the 3 kms to Casa Tablone.

Upon arrival at Casa Tablone, he was told that permission was needed to go beyond the gate and to climb **Duarte**. After begging that evening and the next morning, he was finally allowed to go up the mountain. He eventually climbed **Rucilla**, but went no further, as time was short, and he was not allowed to stay overnight. His round-trip time from Tablone to Rucilla and back was 6 hours.

However, during the 1980's, trails were constructed in the park and all restrictions for climbing lifted. According to the book below, 3000 hikers climb Duarte each year. It can be a hot climb, so carry plenty of water. There used to be a crude bush shelter and a small spring at about 2650 meters. But today most everyone continues on to the refugio & campsite known as *La Comparticion* and sleeps there, then finishes the climb on Day 2. The hike from La Cienega (vehicles are now parked at or near La Cienaga) to Duarte is 23 kms. This is normally a 2 day

The upper slopes of Duarte & Rucilla are covered with a pine forest.

Map 496-1, Duarte, Cordillera Central, Dominican Republic

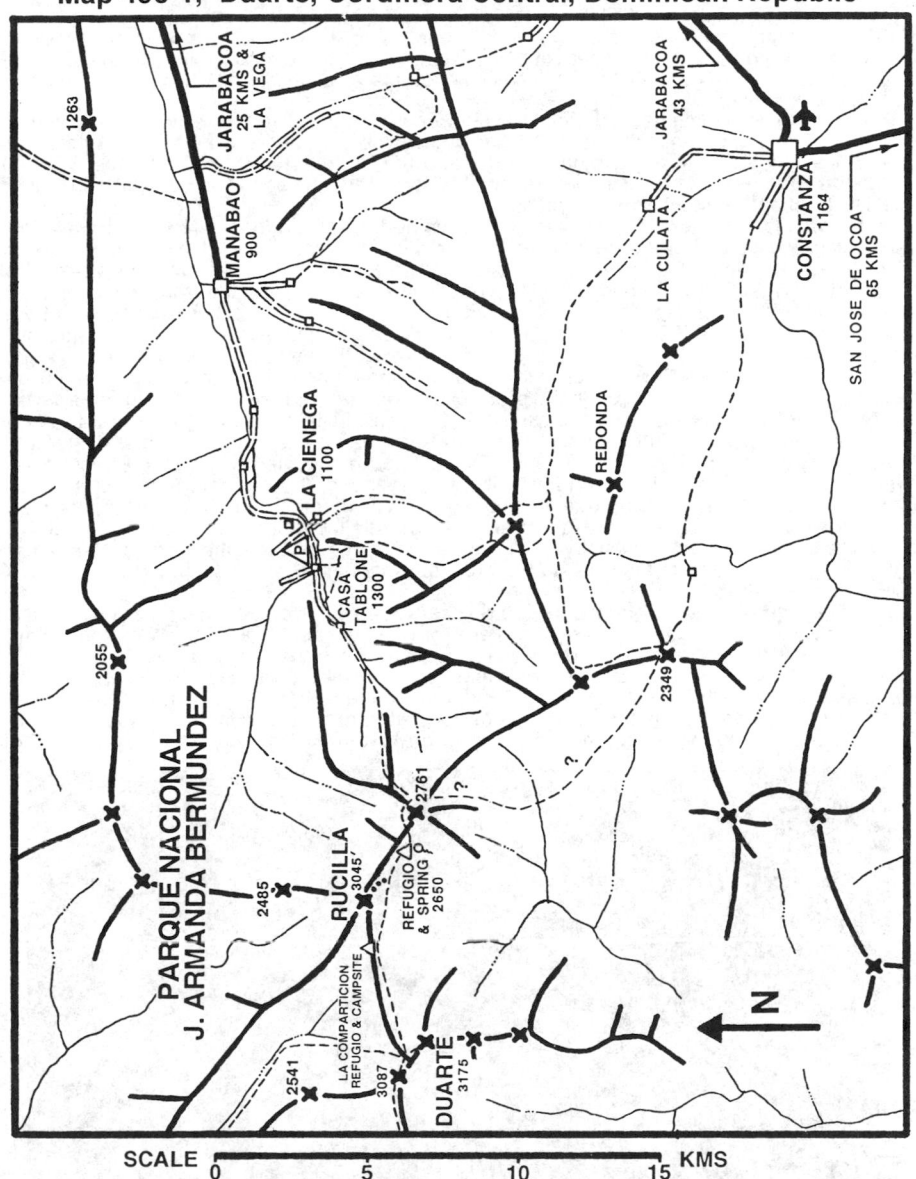

hike, but if you can manage an early start, a strong hiker might do it in one very long day (you have 13 hours or daylight only!). Buy food in Jarabacoa, or before. Dry season is from about December to April.

Maps JOG maps *Santiago, NE-19-1, San Juan, NE-1 9-5 and Santo Domingo, (?)* 1:250,000; or DMA & Instituto Cartografico Universitario map *Manabao, 6073-III,* 1:50,000; and the travel guidebook, **Dominican Republic & Haiti**, Lonely Planet.

El Toro & El Yunque, Sierra de Luquillo, Puerto Rico

El Toro at 1074 meters, is the highest summit in the Sierra de Luquillo, located in eastern Puerto Rico. To most this small, compact mountain range is known as El Yunque (pronounced *Junque*), same name as the second highest peak at 1065 meters. Tourists and natives alike come here to see and hike in the tropical rainforest, and it's one of the few places on the island where you can escape from the tropical heat.

Perhaps more should be said about the rainforest. It's different than any other the author has seen. There aren't so many large trees, as one sees in the forests of the Congo, Amazon or New Guinea; instead, there are palm trees (at least on the slopes of El Yunque) with an understory of ferns. Like most tropical rainforests, it has a high canopy, under which it is fairly open--at least open enough to walk through.

Most of the trails shown on this map are maintained by the Caribbean National Forest and used extensively, especially those between the summit of El Yunque and the visitor center. The author was here on 3/22/1979. He hitch hiked into the mountains from the north coast and Mameyes. It was a rainy day and carrying an umbrella all the way, and with a late start, he used the trails to climb from the visitor center to El Yunque and Britton. There is a road to both summits, but if memory is correct, it wasn't open to motor vehicles, so you have to walk (it's still closed as of 2000). Because of the weather and time factor he never did attempt El Toro.

One way to reach **El Toro**, which is in the most remote part of the island, is from Highway 191 which runs north-south through the area. Begin on the Trade Winds Trail not far from an aviary and the pass marked 753 meters and Km 13.5. This trail for the most part, follows a ridge in a westerly direction to the summit of El Toro, then descends, and ends at some kind of forestry ranger station called Cienega Alta. The last part of the way is called the El Toro Trail. You can also begin the hike at Km 20 on the south slopes of El Toro, 5 or 6 kms above Florida. Take at least 2 liters of water on this hike, maybe more. The altitude isn't that high so expect to sweat a lot. This is a one day hike from either trailhead with no need to camp. If you do decide to camp in the backcountry, you'll have to get a free permit at the visitor center. As of the summer of 2000, part of this trail to El Toro was closed by a landslide, but was to re-open soon.

As suggested above, **El Yunque** can be reached by a well-used trail which begins near the visitor center. On this path there is good water available but best to take some with you. Many people use this trail on week-ends, which is only about a 3 km walk to the top.

There is no scheduled bus service to this area, but hitch hiking was good for the author. The dry season is generally from December to April, but with the constant high humidity and tropical heat, the time of year for a hike matters little (except fotography is best in the dry season). The last place to buy food is in Mameyes, located on National Highway 3 to the north. Get

A small but pure stream of water runs down the slopes of El Junque.

Map 497-1, El Toro & El Yunque, Sierra de Luquillo, Puerto Rico

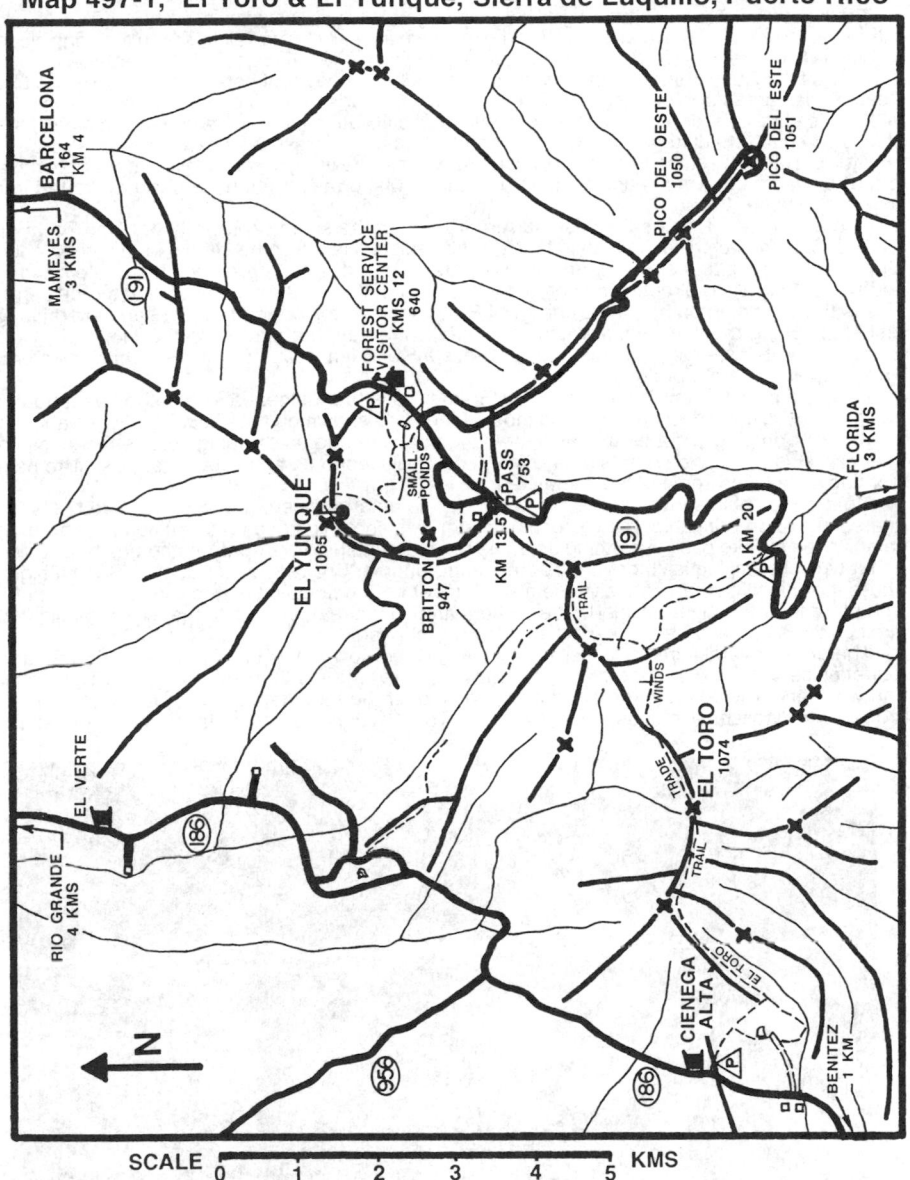

SCALE 0 1 2 3 4 5 KMS

information on trails at the Forest Service visitor center, or call 787-888-1810 or 1880.
Maps Forest Service map *Caribbean National Forest, Luquillo Experimental Forest,* 1:30,000, from the visitor center; or USGS map *Puerto Rico,* 1:120,000; and the travel guidebook, **Puerto Rico**, Lonely Planet.

Sage Mountain, Tortola Island, British Virgin Islands, Caribbean

The highest point in the British Virgin Islands is Sage Mountain located on the island of Tortola. It's only about 521 meters above sea level, but it does have a small tropical rainforest on the north slope and is one of the few places on the island where you can do a little hiking and get some exercise.

Most of the Sage Mtn. ridge has now been made into a national park, but it's surrounded by steep garden areas or cow pastures. A fence keeps wild or semi-wild goats out. As early as the 1700's, nearly all of Tortola was under some kind of cultivation including some of this small park of only 37 square hectares. Since national park status, the forest has been allowed to go back to nature. The north slope has some of what appears to be virgin forest, while other areas have faded remnants of terraces and former cultivation. Mahogany trees have been replanted in a couple of places.

The author flew into the Beef Island Airport east of the small capital city of Road Town on 1/22/1998, then hitch hiked into town to the tourist office. He did some shopping, bought a good topo map of the island at the nearby Survey Department, then started walking. He headed northwest along Main Street to the cemetery due west of the large roundabout, and turned uphill. This is the beginning of the paved Joe's Hill Road heading for **Sage Mtn.** He had several long rest stops along the way which was in the heat of the day, but made it to the Mountain View Restaurant with his large pack in 2 hours. That's a 5 or 6 km walk. Or you could hitch hike part way, which is generally pretty good.

Next to the restaurant & parking lot at 480 meters is the trailhead. The author went up the trail part way, hid his pack, and walked most of the trails shown on the *Close-up Map* in about 1 1/2 hours. Camping is not permitted in the park, but he ended up camping outside the fence on the north slope. On the south side are many other places to camp in cow pastures. The next morning he re-hiked some of the same area.

Next to the cabin shown on the *Close-up Map*, is a barrel where rainwater is stored. It's not guaranteed to be drinkable, but you can use it for washing if you end up camping in the area. If camping, be sure to pack everything up in the morning and hide your pack in the brush or forest. If that type of camping isn't for you, try the campground at Brewer Bay for about US$10 a night. That's the only thing that remotely resembles budget accommodation on the island. This is not a kind place for the budget traveler! The author camped in the bush next to the airport on his 2nd night on the island and caught a flight out the next morning.

There are several fairly large supermarkets in Road Town, plus the Survey Department and tourist office. There are some minibuses running along the south coast from Road Town east and west, and toward the airport, but none going over the mountain to the north slope. There are relatively inexpensive guest houses in Road Town, but they aren't cheap! The dry season is

On the south side of the summit of Sage Mountain is this observation platform.

Map 498-1, Sage Mtn., Tortola Island, British V. Islands

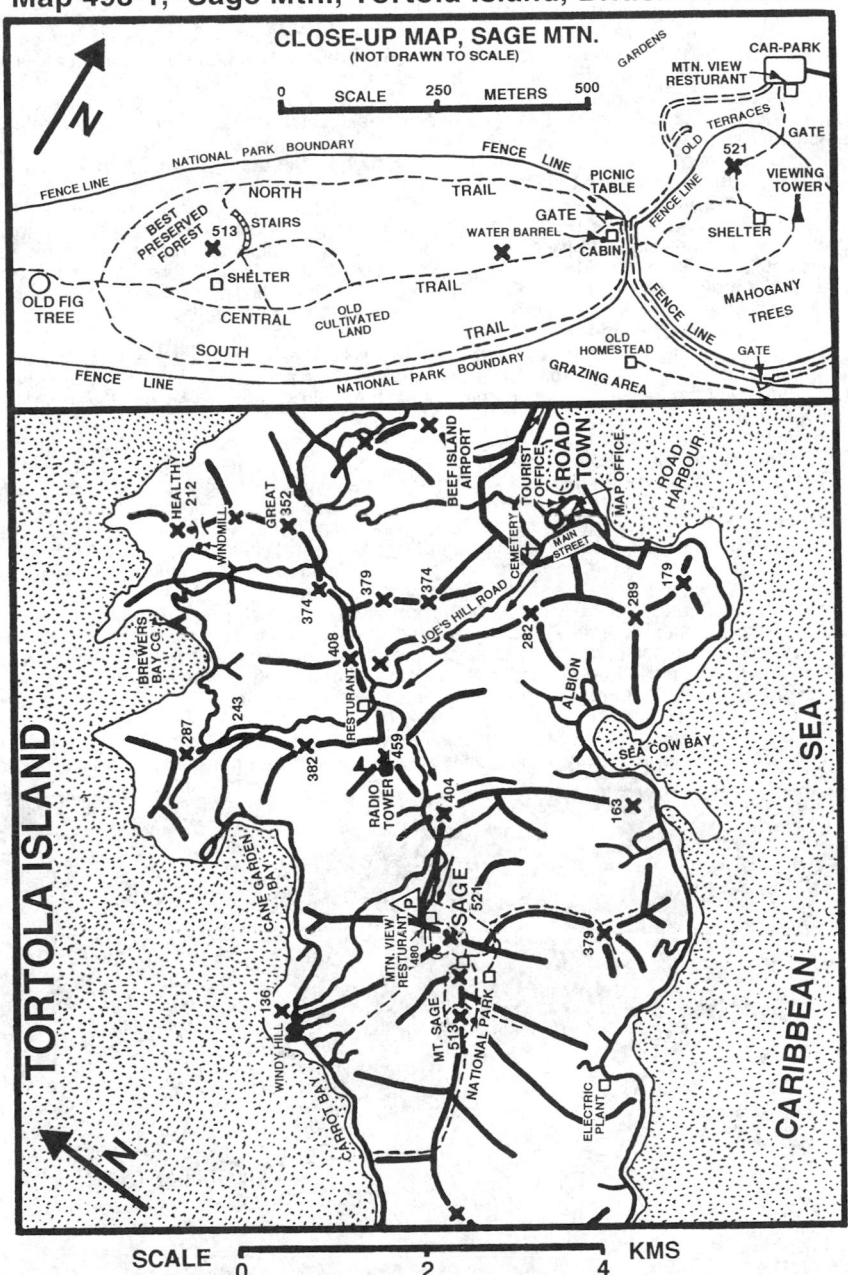

CLOSE-UP MAP, SAGE MTN.
(NOT DRAWN TO SCALE)

from November through March or April, but you can hike any time.
Maps *British Virgin Islands-Torola,* 1:25,000, or any simple tourist map from the airport, tourist office or travel agent; and maybe the book, **A Walking Guide to the Caribbean**, Adkins; and a travel guidebook to the Eastern Caribbean from Lonely Planet or Moon Publications.

Pic Paradis, St. Martin/Sint Maarten Island, Caribbean

Shown here is most of the island of Saint Martin/Sint Maarten, which is in the northern Lesser Antilles. The northern half of the island is a French Department--Saint Martin; while the southern half is part of Der Nederlands and the Dutch Antilles--Sint Maarten. This small island is split between 2 colonial nations, and has the oddity of having 3 languages and 3 currencies. Since most tourists come from North American, the US$ is accepted everywhere and is used the most, especially on the Dutch part. The natives speak Dutch or French, or both, and everyone seems to speak a little English.

Both sides have an airport, but all international flights land at the Juliana Airport on the Sint Maarten side about 3 kms west of Cove Bay. This island is wall to wall tourist development as far as your eyes can see. The hotels are large and expensive, the cheapest of which was between US$45-50 a night in 1998. They don't allow anyone to camp for free on beaches, but you can head for the hills and bivwak for nothing! There are minibuses running from the airport to Philipsburg, capital of Sint Maarten; and from either place to Marigot (pron. Mary-go), capital of Saint Martin side. Others run north to Grand Case. There are no border formalities of any kind and everything seems to run smoothly. The Dutch side has some very large supermarkets, which means lower prices than on the French side.

The highest mountain is Pic Paradis at 424 meters. This island may have originated as a volcano, but the hills are all one form of sedimentary rock or another--some kind of limestone no doubt. Even with the dense population, the higher mountains are relatively pristine, though they aren't very high.

The author arrived early on 1/29/1998 and took a minibus into Philipsburg, went to the tourist office, bought some maps at the Cadastral Survey at 132 Beck Street, made a couple of telefone calls home, bought food in a supermarket, then took a minibus to Marigot for US$1.50. There he took a 20 minute ferry ride to Anguilla, but didn't like the place--no mountains! He returned to Marigot in the afternoon, and took another bus north getting out at Rambaud (pron. Rambo). In the hot afternoon sun, he walked from Rambaud up the steep cement road to **Pic Paradis**. The last km or so is a rough dirt track, but cars can reach the summit. He found a rain barrel full of water next to a building, so he washed up and camped near the top. Next morning he walked down the mountain and eventually got to the airport and flew to Saba--see next map.

It was after he returned from Paradis, that he got more information on trails. On most of the highest ridges, and in some valleys, are constructed & well-maintained trails as shown. Most of the best hikes are on the French side; they being the most active alpinists. If you're serious about hiking, stop at the tourist office in Marigot and pickup a free booklet showing the various trails. Because the island is small, you could likely leave your hotel on the Dutch side early, take a minibus to Rambaud, and start hiking. Stay on the Sentier (Trail) Cretes as it winds its way south and ends above Cove Bay. This trail is marked with paint on trees or rocks. You should

Substituting for Paradis is this foto of Mt. Scenery taken from the town of Windwardside on the island of Saba (see next map).

Map 499-1, Paradis, St. Martin/Sint Maarten, Caribbean

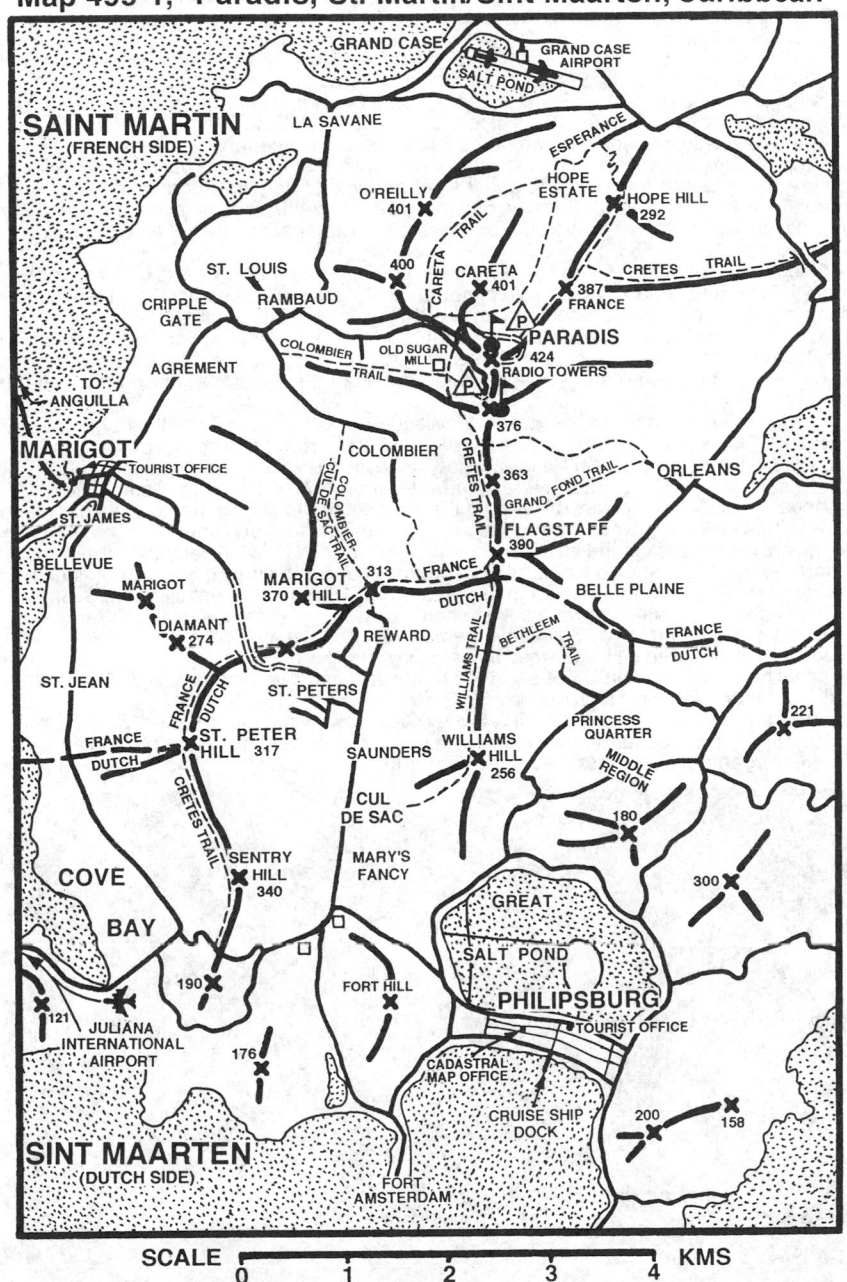

finish by the late afternoon. Start with 3-4 liters of water; it's low elevation and hot! The dry season is from December through April.

Maps *St. Martin,* 1:10,000 (?); or any of the free tourist maps, especially those from Marigot; and a travel guidebook to the Eastern Caribbean from Lonely Planet or Moon Publications.

Mt. Scenery Volcano, Saba Island, Caribbean

This map shows the island of Saba located in the northern Leeward Islands. It's part of the Dutch Antilles, which includes Sint Maarten and St. Eustatius (Statia). See Area Map. Saba is very small--only about 2 1/2 x 3 kms! The population is only 1200, plus about 300 students & facility at the Saba University School of Medicine. There is no crime, largely because half the population is of Dutch, Irish or Scottish extraction. This might be the second most-pleasant island in the Caribbean for hiking (Dominica is best), partly because everyone speaks English.

Saba is basically one volcano, with the highest peak Mt. Scenery at 870 meters. Here is a quote from a study conducted by the Dutch Government; it states, *Age dating and stratigraphic study reveal the last activity on Saba was the deposition of a thin ash surge layer on the area of The Bottom village. This ash layer overlies Amerindian archeological levels and immediately underlies the first European levels..... and has been radiocarbon dated at around 1600 AD.* Another source states <1636.

Besides Mt. Scenery, Mary's Point Mtn., Troy Hill, Bottom Hill, Peak Hill, Old Booby Hill, Thais Hill, St. John Flat, and the Peter Simmon's Hill & Maskerhorne complexes are old andesite volcanic domes. The next youngest volcanos are The Level & Booby Hill.

To get to Saba you must first fly to Sint Maarten, then via Winair, fly to Saba and/or Statia. The author did this three-legged trip in 1/1998 for US$99. If going to either island on the cheap, buy as much of your food & supplies as possible in one of the supermarkets in Philipsburg (see previous map).

You'll fly to Saba in a 20 passenger De Haviland Twin Otter which is built for short takeoffs & landings (STOL), because Saba's runway is very short. From the airport you can walk up the paved road to the capital town of Windwardside, or get in one of the waiting taxis for US$10.

Here's what the author did. He arrived late on 1/25/1998 but instead of looking for a guesthouse at US$40-50 a night, he walked the trails south of the airport and eventually found a hidden campsite (he got water from a tap at the Cove Bay school complex). The next day he broke camp, hid his pack in the bush, then walked up the road to Windwardside. While there, he got maps from the tourist office, checked out nearby shops and small supermarket, then right at the edge of town, got on the trail going to the top of **Mt. Scenery**. That climb up Scenery took just over half an hour, but most will want one hour going up.

He then walked down to The Bottom Village via Crispen. Later, he continued down to the wharf at Fort Bay, back north to the end of the road at Well's Bay, and down The Ladder to the coast. After that, the visited the library at Saba University, then road-walked all the way back to Windwardside, the airport & campsite. A pleasant 10 hour day.

You can also walk the Mary's Point & Sandy Cruz trails, which aren't used much. Or hike to Old Booby Hill or the sulfur mine on the north coast. Hopefully, wild goats will help keep the trails cleared and visible. Ask any local where these trails begin. The dry season is from

Just west of Windwardside town is the very beginning of the trail up Mt. Scenery.

Map 500-1, Mt. Scenery Volcano, Saba Island, Caribbean

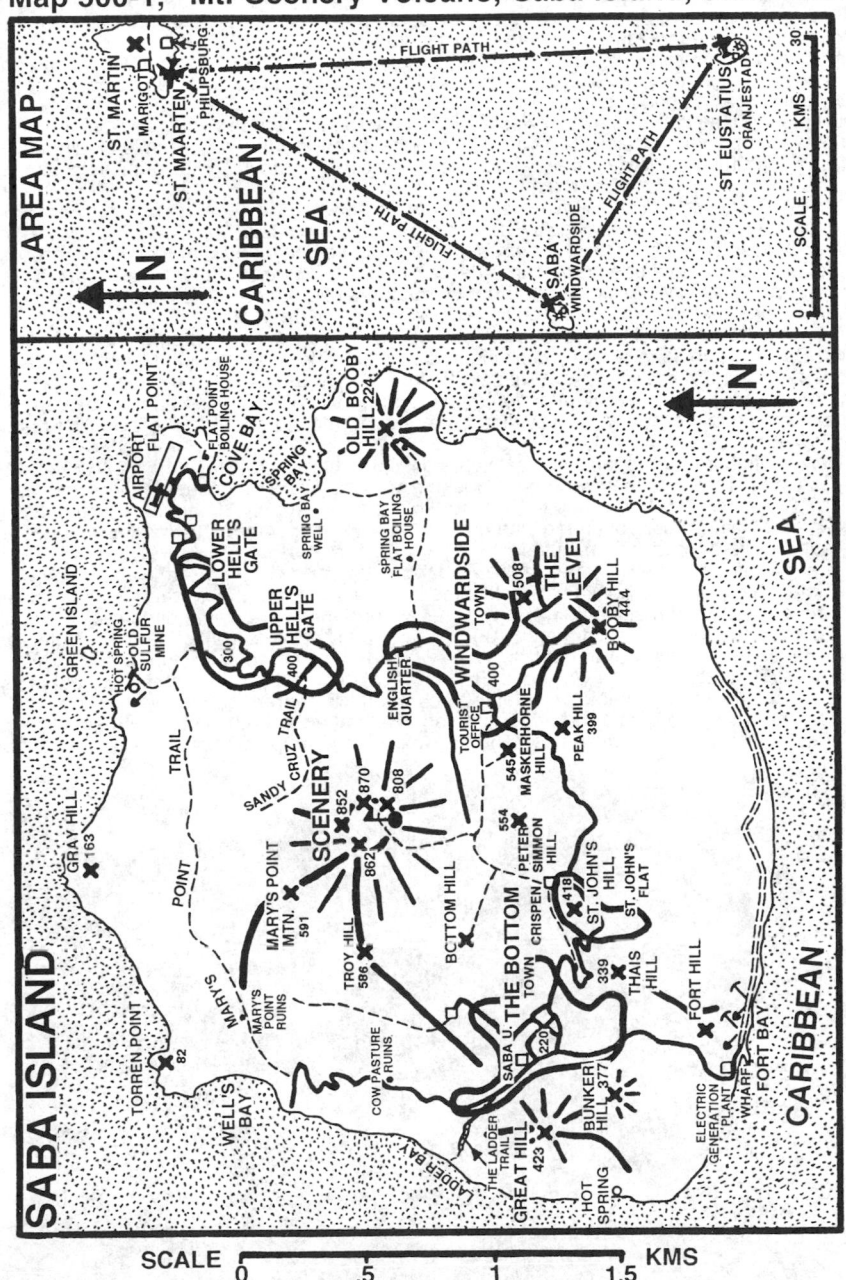

SCALE
0   .5   1   1.5   KMS

November or December to March or April.
Maps *Saba*, 1:10,000, from Der Nederlands Antilles Cadastral Survey Department, 132 Beck Street, Philipsburg, Sint Maarten; and maybe the book, **A Walking Guide to the Caribbean**; and a travel guidebook to the Eastern Caribbean from Lonely Planet or Moon Publications.

Mazinga Peak, The Quill Volcano, St. Eustatius, Caribbean

This is the island of St. Eustatius (Statia for short, pronounced Stay-sha), which is part of the Dutch Antilles. See the 2 previous maps. It's located in the northern part of the Leeward Islands in the Eastern Caribbean. Statia is very small, measuring only 3x8 kms, but was an important shipping center in the 1700's and has many old forts and historic sites. The population of about 1900 is almost all African in origin.

All the rounded hills in the northwest of Statia are old and eroded volcanos, but the highest and newest mountain is called The Quill. The highest peak on the crater rim is Mazinga at 600 meters. The Dutch Government once did a geologic study of the island to see if volcanic active was still possible. Here is a short quote from that report:

On St. Eustatius, the last activity was pyroclastic flows and surges but of a different type to those presenting a hazard on Saba. The last of Statia's pyroclastic flows are like those erupted from St. Vincent in 1979. These are produced by column collapse from open crater eruptions. As the last events have been radiocarbon dated at 1550+-35 years Before Present (1950), the hazard is probably still significant. In other words the last eruption was in about 400 A.D., and it's still possible that more eruptions could occur sometime in the future.

To get to Statia, you'll first have to fly to Sint Maarten to the north, then on a 20-passenger Winair De Havilland Twin Otter fly to Statia and/or Saba. There are about 6 flights per day, but that depends on the season. Many visitors fly from Sint Maarten in the morning, have a good visit, then fly back in the evening. If you're in the area, plan to stay a couple of days on Statia and another couple on Saba. If traveling on a budget, the big supermarkets on Sint Maarten have lower prices.

Here's what the author did. After 2 nights on Saba, he flew to Statia on 1/27/1998, left his pack in the tourist office, then walked up Rosemary Laan. Once he found the new trail near the *Tree at 140 meters,* he hurried up to **The Quill's** crater rim in only 30 minutes. From there he headed for **Mazinga**, but got on the wrong trail. He walked down from the crater rim on the old trail to the Welfare Road in 18 minutes.

That evening, he carried water to the Zeelandia area and camped--rather than pay US$50 for a hotel. Next morning he hid his pack in the bush, and went to the volcano again. This time he reached the top of Mazinga along a rough trail, one that's not well-maintained, but visible. From the pass at the crater rim marked 390 meters to Mazinga, it took about 45 minutes each way. He also got to the bottom of the crater with some nice campsites, in about 15 minutes each way. That afternoon, he walked to Fort de Windt, then back to his campsite, got his pack, walked to the new trail with lots of water, and camped 500 meters above the last house. Next morning, he walked to the airport in 35 minutes. He bathed at both campsites using water he carried in a jug from the tourist office. The dry season is from November or December to about

The Quill Volcano as seen from inside the historic Fort Oranje in Oranjestad.

Map 501-1, Mazinga, The Quill Volcano, St. Eustatius

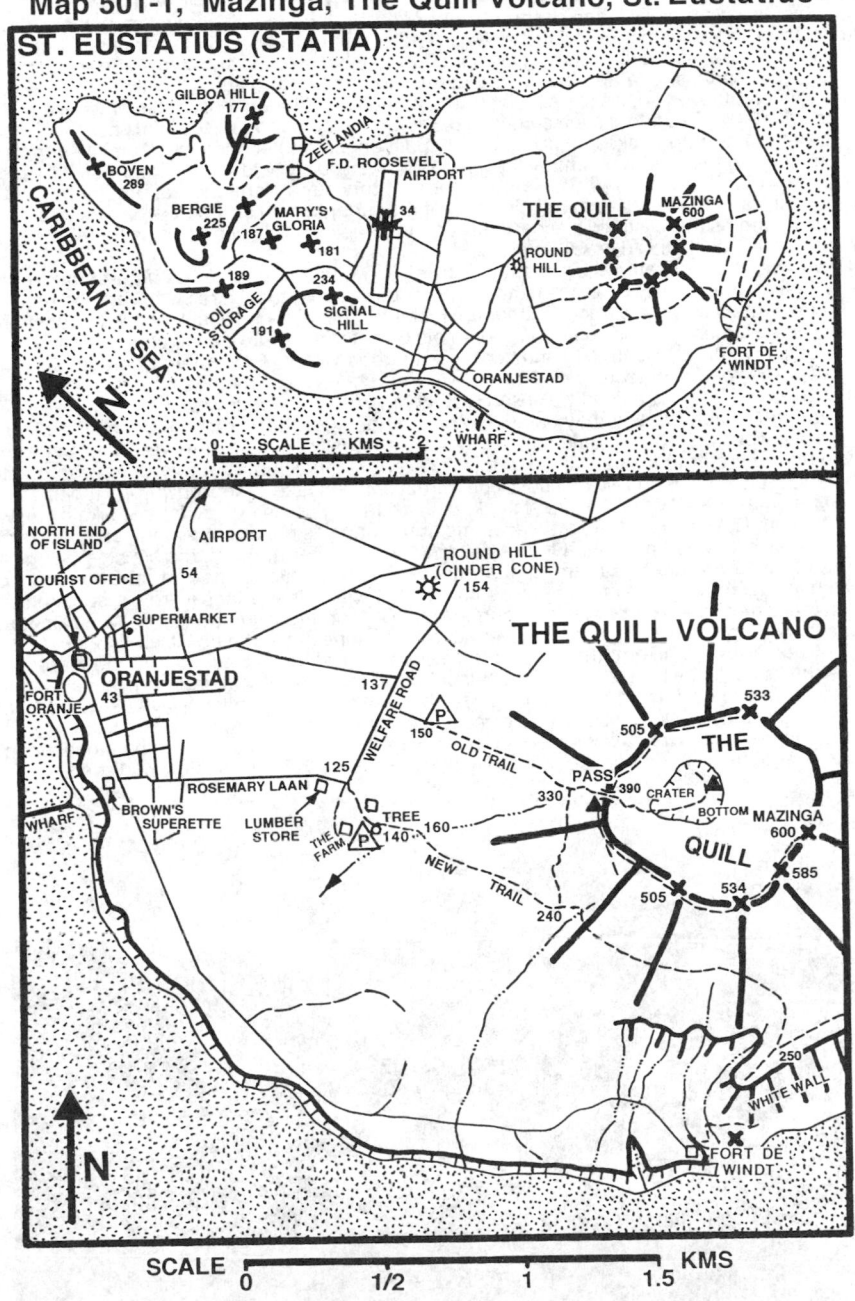

April.
Maps *Sint Eustatius*, 1:10,000, from Der Nederlands Antilles Cadastral Survey Department, 132 Beck Street, Philipsburg, Sint Maarten; and a travel guidebook to the Eastern Caribbean from Lonely Planet or Moon Publications.

Liamuiga Volcano, St. Kitts (Christopher) Island, Caribbean

One of the nicer hikes in the eastern Caribbean is to the top of Liamuiga on the island of St. Kitts, otherwise known as Saint Christopher. The summit is only 1156 meters high, but it rises abruptly from near sea level. Liamuiga is a moderately old volcano showing some erosion, but it still retains a conal shape and has a very steep-sided summit crater. It's also covered with a dense rainforest; even so, it's still considered to be active. It had questionable eruptions in 1692 and on 2/8/1843. This information comes from the book, **Volcanos of the World**.

To get to **Liamuiga**, take a mini bus (15-20 passenger van) or hitch hike from the capital city of Basseterre to the northwest end of the island. Make your way to the Belmont Estate, which is half a km west of the town of St. Paul's. Once at this sugarcane plantation, it's best to ask someone if it's OK to proceed in the direction of the mountain. You'll be walking across private land, but it seems there is public access through their fields. This seems to be the normal route to the mountain so it should be OK to proceed.

If you don't have water, there's a tap in front in the last house on the right at the Belmont Estate before you actually enter the cane fields. Proceed southeast directly toward the mountain on the most-used cane field track. Higher up, look for 6 palm trees. Just to the left or east of the palms will be a gully, and down in it will be an old 3-meter-wide sugarcane cooking pot, which is now a cattle watering trough, and another tap with good water. From there it's about one km to the end of the road and about 4 kms from Belmont Estate HQ. From the trailhead which is just inside the forest, there is a good well-used trail running up to the crater rim.

From the crater rim, you may be able to bushwhack in either direction to reach the highest peak, but it won't be easy. In time a better trail will gradually develop however. You can also go down into the crater to a small lake, but this is a very steep climb where you'll have to use tree limbs and roots on a normally wet and slippery trail. Guides take clients down with ropes.

If you go all the way to the highest peak, plan on taking an entire day for this hike if you walk from Belmont Estate. You can however, camp in the cane fields, or up near the end of the road. On 1/20/1993, the author walked to the trailhead in just over an hour, hid his big pack nearby and made it to the crater rim in 45 minutes. He started along the rim, but doesn't enjoy bushwhacking so he missed the highest summit. The water in the taps is from a spring located somewhere near the end of the road and should be good to drink as-is. Take a raincoat or umbrella, a good lunch, and plenty of water, as there's none along the trail itself.

For adventurous hikers, there's an old overgrown trail from Sadlers and the Harris Land Settlement direct to the highest peak. The author looked for that one, but gave up right from the start because if was a real bushwhack! Some guides have taken clients up that way, and in time it may become a good trail. Ask about that route at the tourist office in Basseterre.

The dry season is from November or December through April, but expect the mountain to be cloud-covered year-round with the probability of wet slippery trails all the time.

This is the crater on top of Liamuiga Volcano with the highest point on the far side.

Map 502-1, Liamuiga Volcano, St. Kitts Island, Caribbean

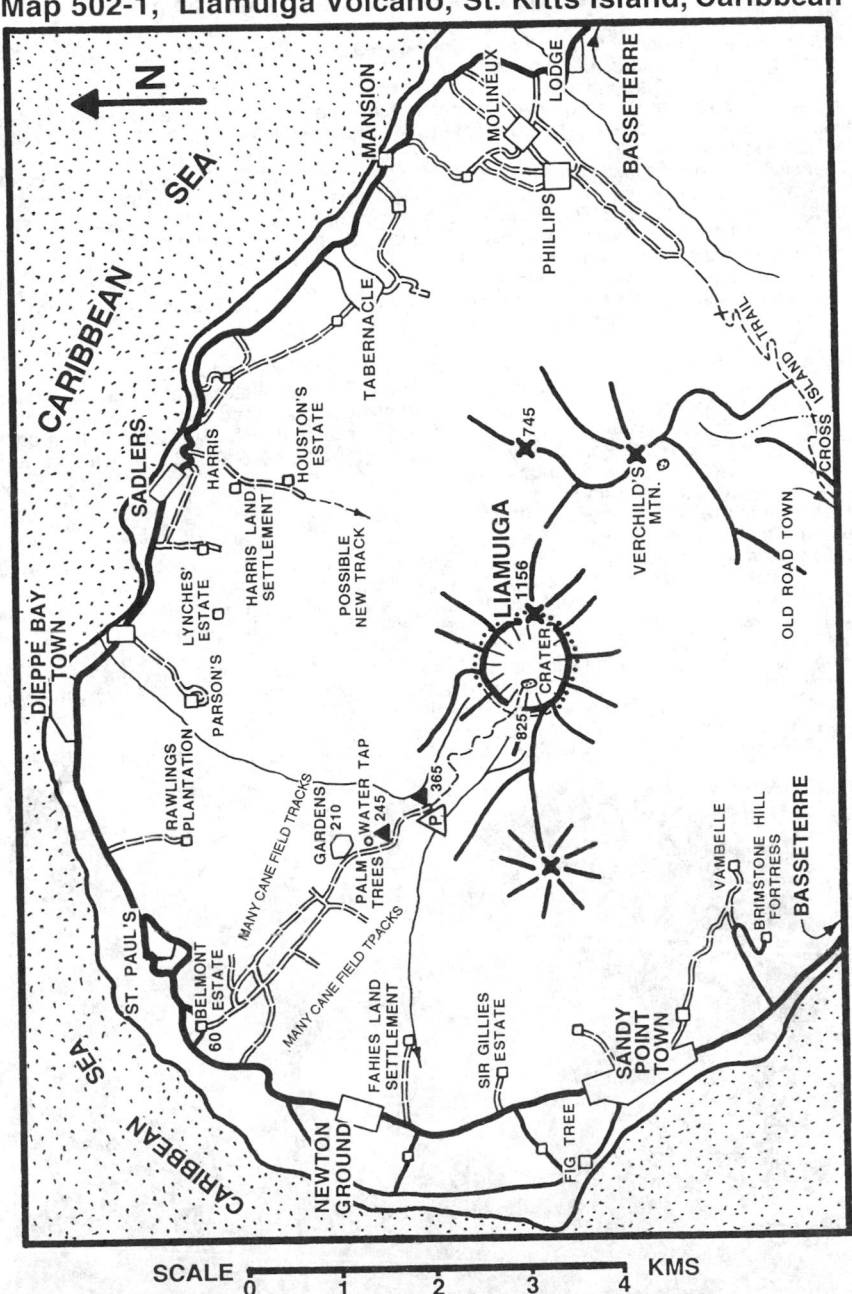

SCALE

					KMS
0	1	2	3	4	

Maps British Overseas Survey map *St. Kitts & Nevis,* 1:50,000, from any tourist bookshop in Basseterre; or from Stanfords, 12/14 Long Acre, London, UK, Tele Inter+171-836-1321; and perhaps the guidebook, **A Walking Guide to the Caribbean**, Adkins; and a travel guidebook to the Eastern Caribbean from Lonely Planet or Moon Publications.

Nevis Peak, Nevis Island, Eastern Caribbean

This map shows Nevis Peak at 985 meters, the only mountain on the island of Nevis. Nevis is an old and fairly eroded volcano. It's last eruption was sometime in the early Holocene, which is within the last 10,000 years.

Nevis is now part of an independent country composed of St. Kitts & Nevis. To get there you'll have to fly into the Basseterre Airport on St. Kitts, then take one of several daily ferries to Nevis. The ferries land at the jetty right next to the middle of Charlestown, the administrative capital of this island.

There are 2 good trails going up **Nevis**. First is the *Hamilton Mill Trail*. From the main street in Charlestown, locate Government Road, then walk due east as it meanders up towards the mountain. After about 2 kms, you'll pass the Hamilton Mill on the south side of the road. Continue east as shown on the map. Not far above the mill, will be a very narrow cement road. After a ways, and right where the pavement ends and the road veers southeast, the trail itself begins. It's a wide trail at first, then narrows when it turns east and heads straight uphill. Higher up you'll be on a knife-edge ridge and in a moss or cloud forest You'll eventually reach one summit, then go down a ways, then up to the main peak which rises above treeline. There's a hiker's register on top.

The other way is known as the *Zetlands Trail*. Take a minibus from Charlestown bound for the east side of the island. Tell the driver to drop you off at the Zetlands Road in Chicken Stone. Once there, walk north on a cement road past the old Zetlands Hotel. Not far beyond that is a "T" junction and the Upper Round Road. Turn left or west a few meters, then again head north uphill on another steep cement road. Just before you reach the white house with twin gables, and on the right at about 365 meters, will be the beginning of the Zetlands Trail. If you get lost ask anyone where the trail is. Everyone speaks English. The author found this trail, but walked up only a short distance and returned.

Here's what the author did on 1/19/1993. He took the first morning ferry from Basseterre to Charlestown. To save one night's lodging, the very cheapest of which was US$15 in 1993, the author walked up Government Road with a full pack to about where the campsite is located at 600 meters on the west side of the peak. He hid his pack there, then went to the summit in a total walk-time of 3 3/4 hours from Charlestown. He later slept at that campsite. Next morning he walked down and checked into a hotel, then explored the way to the Zetlands Trailhead and was a tourist for a while.

Here's a suggested hike. Walk right from your hotel in Charlestown up along the Hamilton Mill Trail to the top, then down the Zetlands Trail to the main highway. Flag down any minibus to get back to town. Lots of little buses run along the main highway. Take 2 or 3 liters of water and a good lunch, plus a raincoat or umbrella. The dry season is from December through April.

Maps British Overseas Survey map *St. Kitts & Nevis,* 1:50,000, from any tourist bookshop in

Near the top of Nevis Peak you'll walk through this cloud forest on a good trail.

Map 503-1, Nevis Peak, Nevis Island, Eastern Caribbean

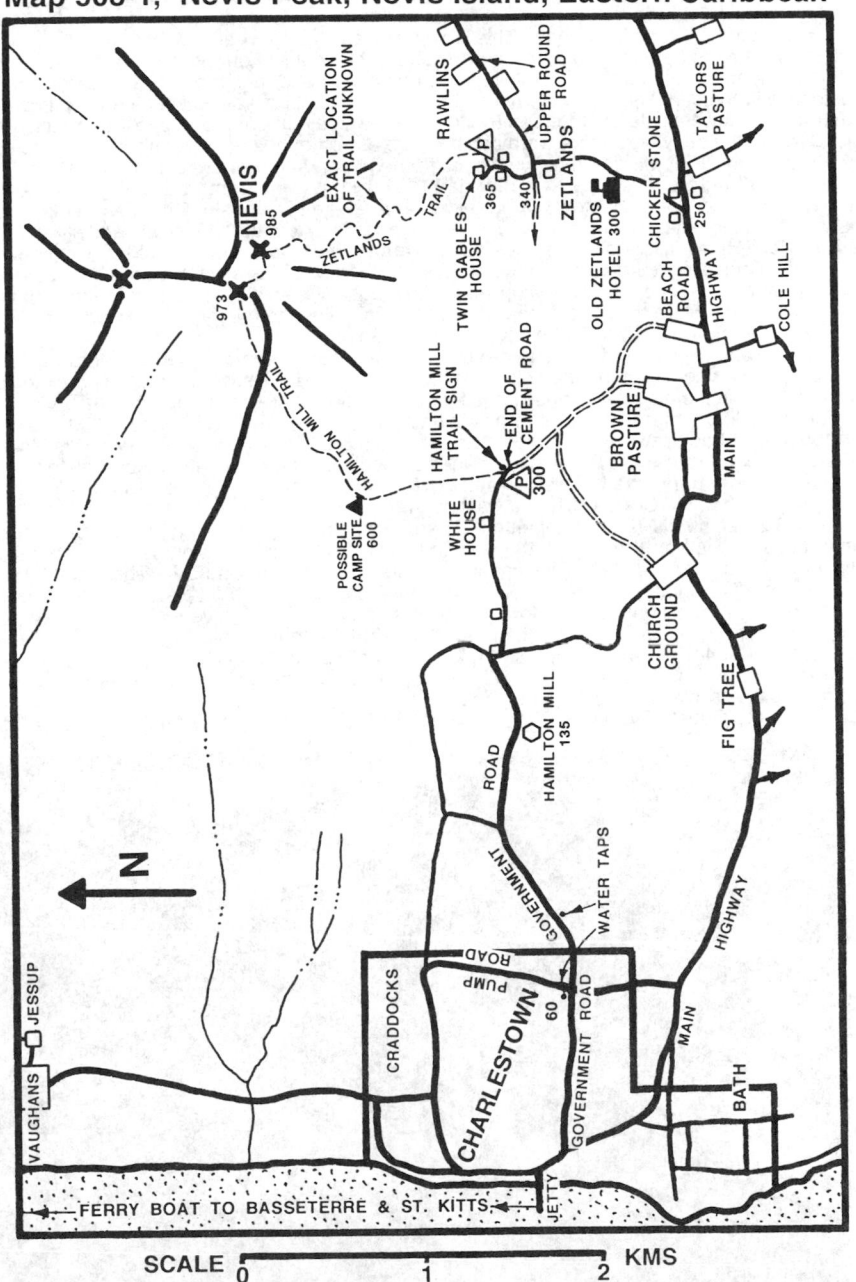

SCALE 0   1   2   KMS

Basseterre or Charlestown; or from Stanfords, 12/14 Long Acre, London, UK, Tele Inter+171-836-1321; and perhaps the guidebook, **A Walking Guide to the Caribbean**, Adkins; and a travel guidebook to the Eastern Caribbean from Lonely Planet or Moon Publications.

Soufriere Hills Volcano, Montserrat, Eastern Caribbean

The hike intended to be featured here was to the highest summit on the small island of Montserrat in the Eastern Caribbean. This is or was Chances Peak at 923 meters.

Here's what the author did beginning on 1/21/1993. He flew from St. Kitts to the Blackburne Airport on Montserrat and rode in a minibus to Plymouth, the former capital. He stayed in a little guesthouse in Victoria, just south of Plymouth. Next morning, he walked southeast past Fairfield and up the southwest side of **Chances Peak**. There was a cement road up to 425 meters, then a good trail to the top where there were cable & wireless antennas. It took only 1 1/2 hours up; 3 hours round-trip. That afternoon he went back to the airport and flew on to St. Lucia Island.

Since that time everything has changed. Everything, including a lot of history, on the southern half of the island is now buried under several meters of ash! Chances Peak in 1993 was an old and forested volcano. Just east of Chances was a crater. This was and still is called the **Soufriere Hills** with what used to be called **Castle Peak** (lava dome) inside. This is where violent eruptions have taken place beginning on 7/18/1995. That's when Castle Peak blew up and is no more. A series of explosive eruptions lasting well into 2000, has covered the southern half of the island. More than half of the population was evacuated either to the north end of the island, or temporarily resettled to the UK or other islands.

In 2000, plans were underway to develop about 7 new settlements in the northern parts. However, everything, including the activity of the volcano and resettlement plans is ongoing and who knows when the mountain will become totally quiet so that life will return to normal?

For this edition, the author has thrown away the map he created after his 1993 trip to the Caribbean and has drawn a new one. It shows Chances Peak & the Soufriere Hills Volcano and the former capital city of Plymouth. In addition, it shows the route the author took to the top, and where everything was before the activity & evacuations took place. But keep in mind, everything south of the Centre Hills is a wasteland of ash and dust.

As of 8/2000, here's what's happening. There is a daily ferry boat running from St. Johns on Antigua (just to the northeast), to Little Bay on the northwest side of Montserrat. There's also helicopter service from St. Johns, which lands somewhere in Gerald's Park. They may fly close to the volcano for a close-up look, if there's not too much ash in the air! As of 2000, there is very little in the way of accommodations for tourists and no one is allowed very close to the volcano. Before making any plans for visiting this island, telefon the tourist office located somewhere in Woodlands at 664-491-2230 for updated information regarding tourism. Or call the Montserrat Volcano Observatory at 664-491-5647; or keep track of the action on the websites (www.mvomrat.com/) or (www.volcano.si.edu/gvp/).

Maps The old British Overseas Surveys map *Tourist Map of Montserrat*, 1:25,000 is totally

The author along the well-constructed and well-maintained trail running up the west side of Chances Peak on his 1993 trip. This trail is now buried and long gone.

Map 504-1, Soufriere Hills Vol., Montserrat, Caribbean

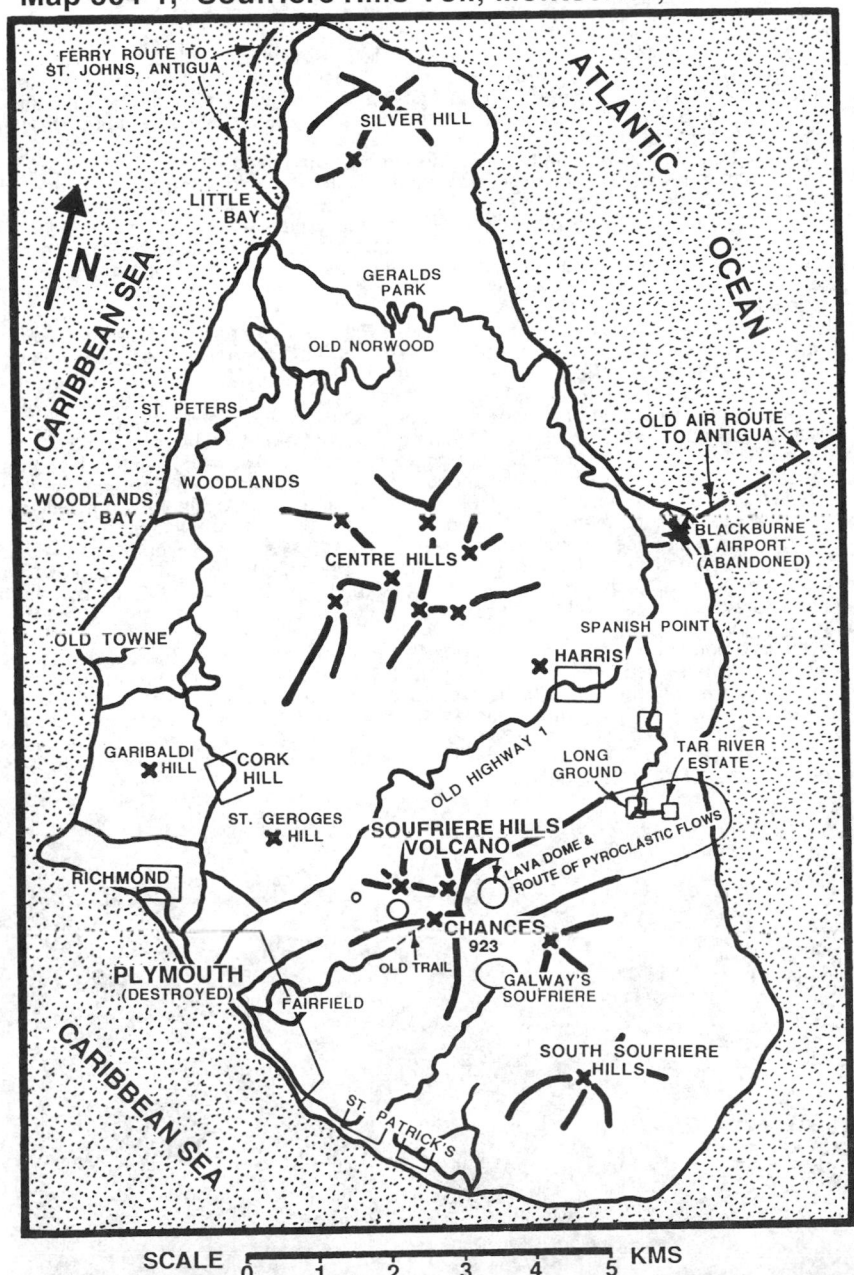

SCALE |0 1 2 3 4 5| KMS

outdated--so look for a new one in the coming years. Buy from the Ordnance Survey, Romsey Road, Southampton, England, UK, S09 4HD; or Stanfords, 12/14 Long Acre, London, Tele. Inter+171-836-1321; and a travel guidebook to the Eastern Caribbean from Lonely Planet or Moon Publications.

La Soufriere Volcano, Guadeloupe, French Caribbean

La Soufriere at 1467 meters is the highest summit on the French Caribbean Island of Guadeloupe which is a department or state of France. As with all the mountains & islands in the Lesser Antilles, which is the Eastern Caribbean, it too is a volcano. La Soufriere is located on the western or Basse-Terre half of the island, and has been active over the years with about 10 major eruptions during colonial times. The last period of activity was between 7/8/1976 through 3/1/1977. In those 8 months, there were 4 minor phreatic explosions which caused Pointe-a-Pitre, the capital city to be evacuated.

Here's what the author did. He flew into the airport near Pointe-a-Pitre and slept there the night. Next morning, 4/3/1979, he walked to and through the capital then hitch hiked south to the city of Basse-Terre on the southwest coast. From there he walked 5 kms up to St. Claude and camped in a nearby banana plantation. Next morning, he walked 5 kms up to the end of the paved road & parking lot at a place called Savane a Mulet at 1125 meters, hid his big pack, and in the wind, clouds & rain, and covered with plastic, hiked up to and around the crater rim and to as far as Carmichael Peak and back. After that, he hitch hiked back to the airport that same afternoon.

There's public transport available from Pointe-a-Pitre to as far as Montebello & Vernou on the north side of these mountains, and to Basse-Terre & St. Claude on the southwest side, so there's no need to hitch hike! Besides, it's too hot for that.

From the end of the paved road at Savane a Mulet, it's only about an hour's hike to the top of **La Soufriere**. This is also one of the popular places to begin a longer hike along the backbone of Basse-Terre. You can hike north from Savane a Mulet or from Matouba; and come out of the mountains at either Vernou or Montebello. By taking either the Merwart or Victor Huges trails, you can climb several of the highest volcanos in the Lesser Antilles. Most people can do this north-south traverse in one very long day, but many do it in 2. Check with the tourist office or a local guidebook to see if there are hotels or youth hostels in the towns on this map. These have no doubt changed a lot since the author's trip, so check with the latest travel guidebook.

There are 2 refuges in this area; one near Grande Decouverte, the other Ajoupa Maynac, near Morne Incapable. Both can be used, but you'd better get the latest information on their condition and availability at the Maison Forestiere in Matouba before hiking. It's best to hike from south to north.

Most trails around La Soufriere are very good and well-used; however, the Victor Huges and Merwart trails are less-used and in rougher condition. But that was the situation in 1979; they're likely better by now. For the longer hikes, wear boots unaffected by mud & water, especially if you're there in a wet spell. If camping, an extra set of dry clothing in a plastic sack would be good. On the higher summits, expect to find clouds and wet & cool conditions. The cities of Pointe-a-Pitre or Basse-Terre are the best places to buy food (most of which comes from France), but it's not cheap on this island!

Along the ridge-top trail which runs from La Soufriere to Vernou.

Map 505-1, La Soufriere Volcano, Guadeloupe, French Caribbean

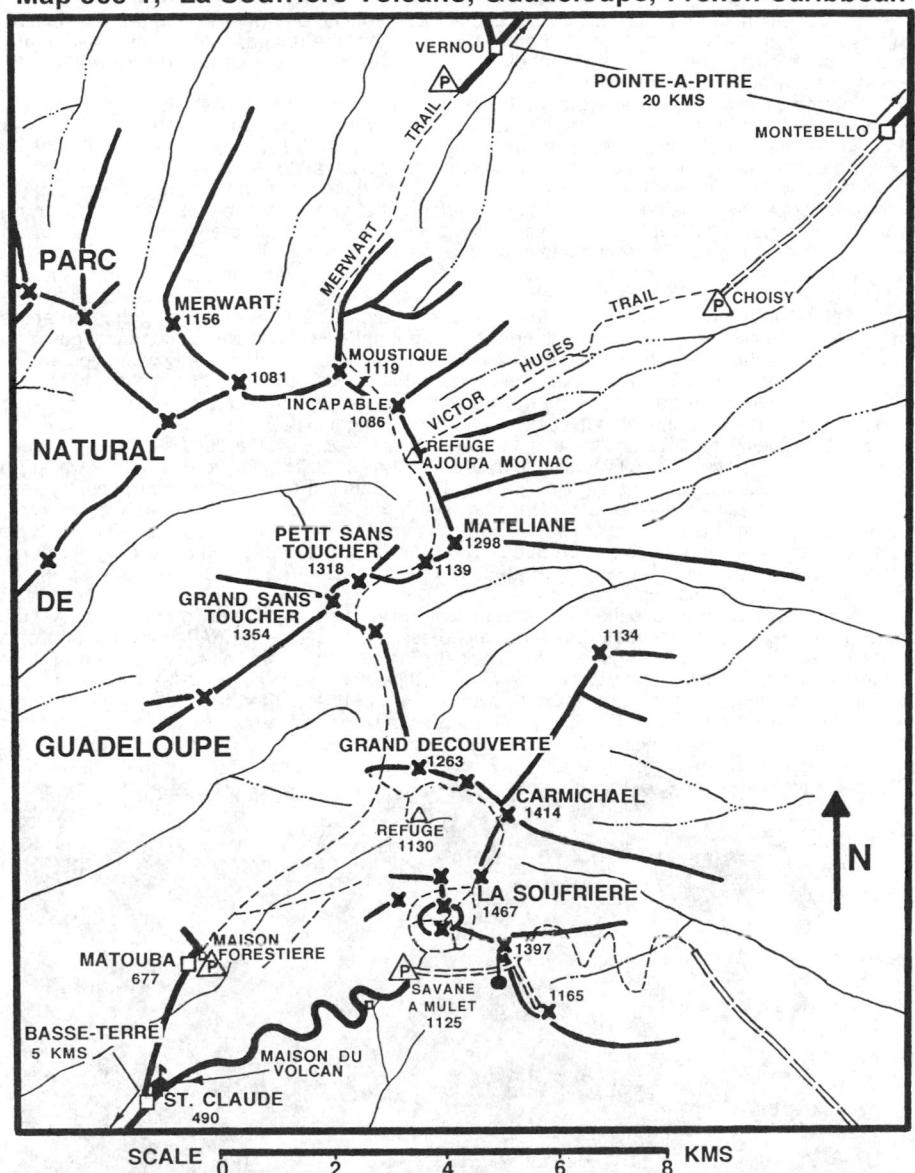

For updated information, stop at the Maison du Volcan in St. Claude, or the Maison Forestiere in Matouba, or the tourist office in Pointe-a-Pitre. As in all the Caribbean, the dry season is from about December to April. If you want dry trails go during that time.

Maps See the free booklet with maps, *Walks and Hikes (Promenades & Randomees)*, from the Parc Natural de Guadeloupe & Tourist Office of Guadeloupe, Pointe-a-Pitre; or *Guadeloupe, 510*, 1:100,000, from Institut Geographique National (IGN), 136 bis, rue de Grenelle, Paris, France, website (www.ign.fr); and the travel guidebook, **Eastern Caribbean**, Lonely Planet; or **Caribbean Handbook**, from Moon Publications.

Morne Diabloting, Dominica Island, Eastern Caribbean

The highest mountain on Dominica, and in the Eastern Caribbean, is Morne (Mt.) Diabloting at 1447 meters. Diabloting is located on the north end of the island just east of Dublanc and southeast of Portsmouth. It's also immediately east of the Syndicate Estate and in what is now the Morne Diabloting National Park.

Diabloting is an older stratovolcano believed to have last erupted at the very end of the Pleistocene, but there is still fumarolic activity somewhere around the mountain. It's been eroded to the point of having little resemblance to a volcano today. Like many mountains on Dominica, much of this area is covered with a pristine tropical rainforest.

The author was on **Diabloting** on 4/8/1979, but didn't quite reach the summit. In those days, very few people were hiking and the trail just faded to nothing; or maybe he was on the wrong trail (?). However, by 2/1998 the trail was much better. At that time there were lots of so-called eco-tourists roaming the island and one of their favorite activities is hiking.

During his second trip and on the morning of 2/17/1998, the author got in a minibus at the bus stand located one block east of the market in Roseau, which was bound for Portsmouth. He got off at the village of Dublanc, but should have stayed on for another km and gotten off at the turnoff to the Syndicate Estate. He started walking, but got a lift on a construction truck going up to Syndicate as they were upgrading the road. It will likely be paved all the way when you arrive.

From the major junction where a national park cabin in located, he walked the one km to the trailhead. He hid his large pack in the trees and proceeded uphill. None of this trail has been constructed with pick or shovel, but it's good and you can't get lost.

In the beginning, the trail runs through a marvelous rainforest, then the slope steepens, the trees get smaller, and you have to pull yourself up by roots and limbs. Still higher, you'll surely be wading in mud. In other places, you'll literally be climbing above ground through some short, squatty trees Tarzan-style, because no one up to that time had used a chainsaw to clear the trail. But it sure was a fun climb! This, and the climb up Morne Trois Pitons (see next map), are probably the 2 best *Jungle Jim-type climbs* the author has ever been on. The summit is windy, chilly and likely misty or raining. Cover your camera well! The author made it up in 1 3/4 hours; 3 2/3 hours round-trip from the trailhead. You may need double his times.

On the return, he walked to the small stream near the trailhead, had a bath, and walked down the road. He got a ride down the mountain, but camped near the main highway. A fair number of people from Portsmouth and Dublanc drive up to Syndicate Estate in the mornings to work on crops, then return in the late afternoon, so it's easy to get a lift. With an early start, this could be done in one long day from Roseau using public transport, but you'll surely get back after dark. Or you could camp some where near the trailhead. Or hire someone in Roseau to drive & escort you up.

Remember, all airlines fly into Melville Hall Airport, which is about 1 1/2 hours by minibus or taxi to Roseau (find minibuses in Marigot). The dry season is from December to April, but the

A huge tree at the edge of the rainforest next to the Syndicate Estate.

Map 506-1, Diabloting, Dominica, Eastern Caribbean

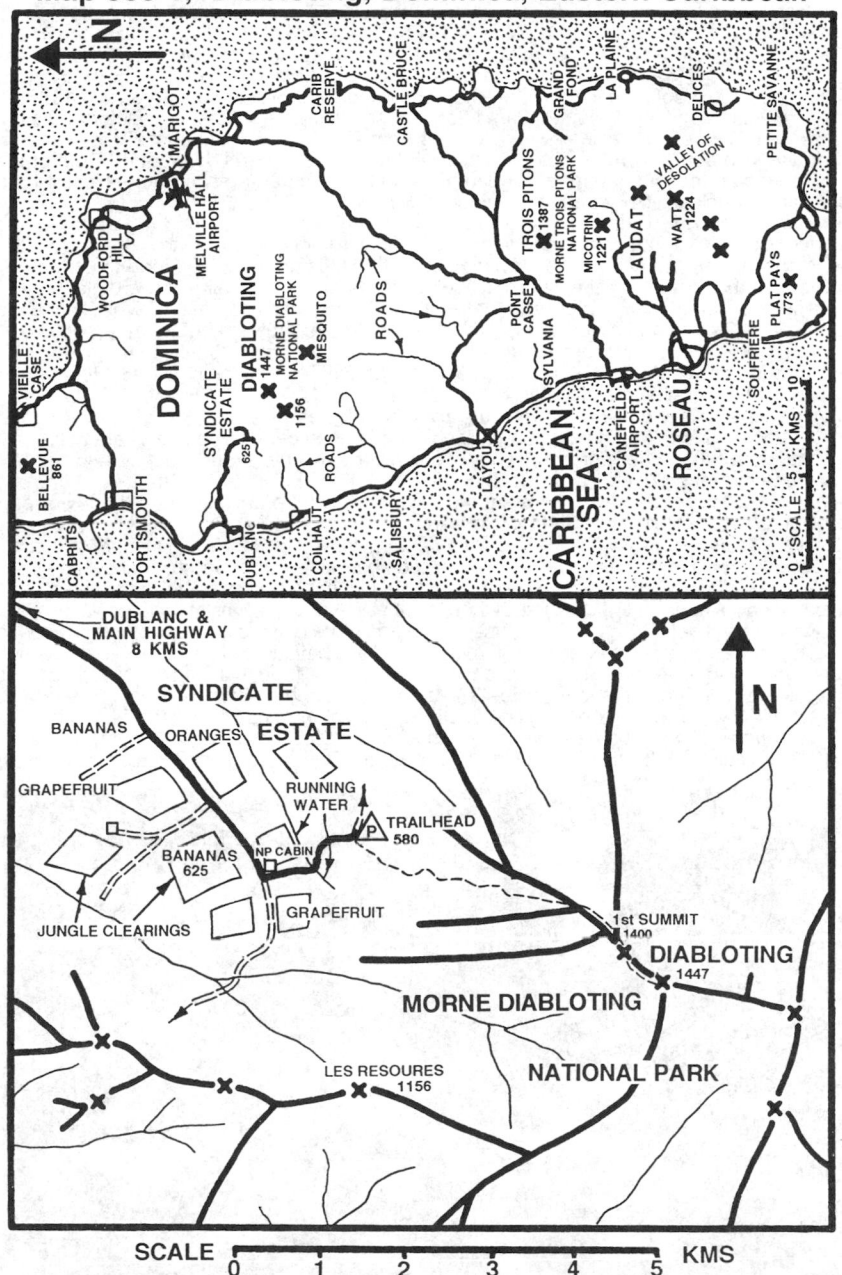

top of Diabloting will be wet all the time.
Maps Lands & Surveys maps *Dominica, Sheets 1 & 2,* 1:25,000, buy from their office along the road to Loudat in Roseau; and a travel guidebook to the Eastern Caribbean from Lonely Planet or Moon Publications.

Trois Pitons, Micotrin & Valley of Desolation, Dominica, Caribbean

Shown here is the second highest mountain on the Caribbean island of Dominica. It's Trois Pitons at 1387 meters. Nearby is Micotrin at 1221 meters. Also, in the southeastern part of this map is the Valley of Desolation with its Boiling Lake and steam pits which resembles parts of Kamchatka, Iceland, Waireki in New Zealand, or Yellowstone Park in the USA.

The Valley of Desolation is considered an active volcanic area because on 1/4/1880 there was a phreatic (steam) explosion and mud flows. Ash fell over a 4-km-wide sector at the coast 10 kms away. There were also seismic swarms from 2 to 5/1976. Also, both Trois Pitons and Micotrin are lava domes. In the case of Trois Pitons, maybe several domes (?). Both of these stratovolcanos are considered extinct. Southeast of this mapped area is Patates which had an eruption and pyroclastic flow in about the year 1500.

To climb **Micotrin**, walk through Roseau to the beginning of the road to Laudat, and ask about minibuses. One bus makes the 10 km run about 10 times a day, with more frequent trips in the mornings and late afternoons. It's about 10 steep kms on the paved road to Laudat. This hike begins at the turnoff and the Lake Trail Lodge at 580 meters. Walk eastward along a rough road in the direction of Freshwater Lake. After about 3 kms, you'll come to a big gully and metal bridge, then 300 meters of steep cement road. At the top of that, is another steep gully on the left, which is also at the national park boundary. Head straight up this gully to the summit. The author did this climb on 4/6/1979, but the pipeline and hydroelectric plant were built later, in the early 1990's. He revisited the place on 2/16/1998.

To reach the **Valley of Desolation**, walk from the middle of Laudat, down the paved road to the hydroelectric plant, then south along a rough road past a cement pond and along a pipeline to the intake facility & hot springs. This is the trailhead. Continue up a very good, well-maintained and much-used trail to Boiling Lake. It took the author 1 2/3 hours getting there; less than 3 1/2 hours round-trip from Laudat. He did this hike and revisited the lower part of Micotrin on 2/16/1998 on a day-trip from Roseau.

To climb **Trois Pitons**, take a minibus from near the market in Roseau bound for Marigot or the Carib Reserve on the east coast. Get out at the round-about called Pont Casse, or about one km east as shown. Look for a sign pointing to the start of the trail. In the beginning, this is an old plantation road, but when it steepens, the bush trail at that point has never been constructed. However, it's well-used and you can't get lost, as it's being used more and more by so-called *eco-tourists*. Higher up you'll come to a steep section of about 100 meters, and you have to pull yourself up by roots or tree limbs. People who never exercise may find this challenging. Above that, and in some places, you'll literally be crawling through squatty trees *Tarzan-style above the ground*--until someone takes a chainsaw to it! This is both challenging and exciting. The author rates this and the Diabloting hike as the 2 best *Jungle-Jim* climbs he's ever been on. Take a plastic bag to keep cameras dry. On 2/18/1998, the author took a minibus from his campsite near Dublanc & Diabloting to Roseau; then got

This is the beginning of the trail to the Valley of Desolation.

Map 507-1, Trois Pitons, Micotrin & Valley of Desolation, Dominica

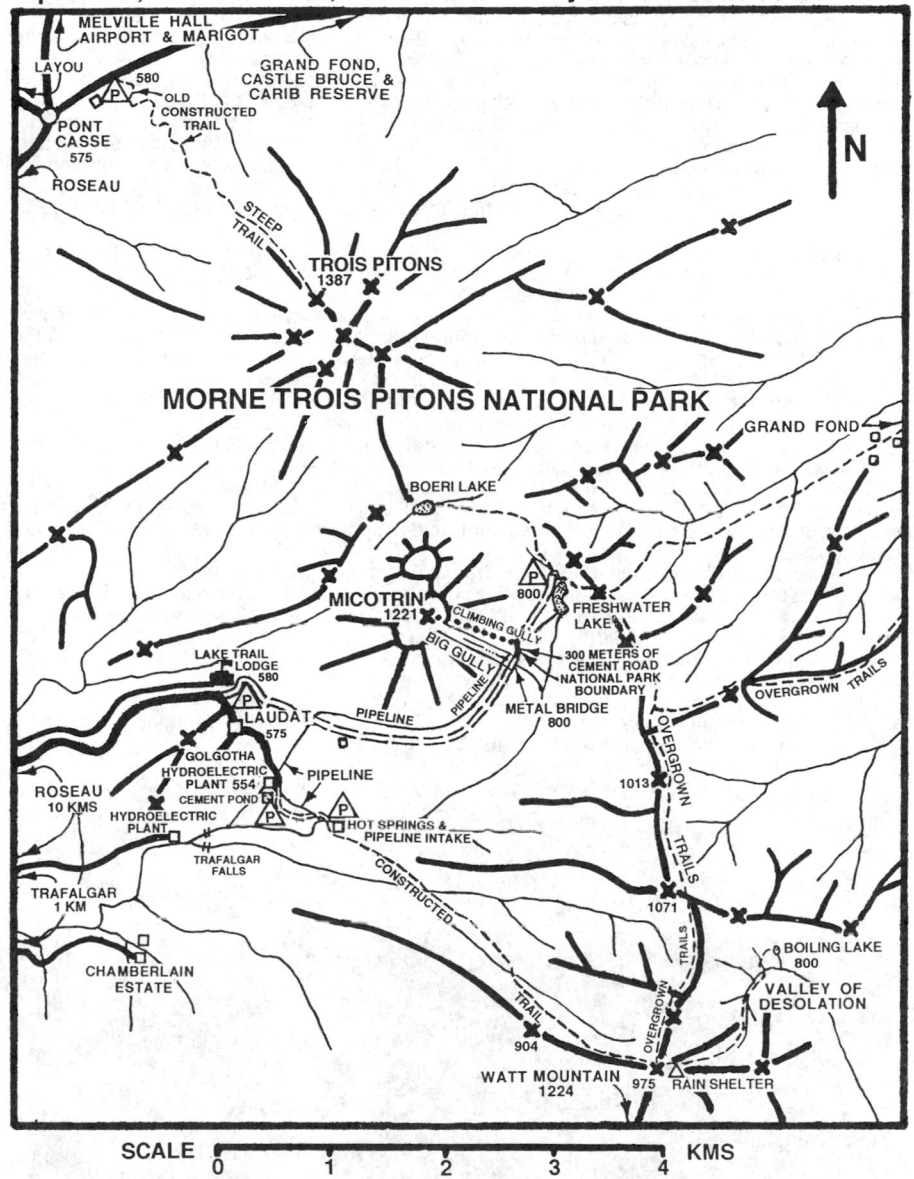

SCALE 0 1 2 3 4 KMS

information about the trail to Trois Pitons. Finally, he took a minibus to Pont Casse. He found the trail, hid his big pack, then made the summit in 1 1/2 hours; 3 1/3 hours round-trip. After that, he hitch hiked to the Melville Hall Airport and camped nearby for the night and flew out the next morning.

A guide is not needed on any of these hikes, and a fit hiker could do them all from a guesthouse in Roseau on separate day-trips. The dry season is from December through April.

Maps *Dominica, Sheets 2 & 3*, 1:25,000, from Lands & Surveys, Roseau; or Stanfords in London; and a travel guidebook to the Eastern Caribbean from Lonely Planet or Moon Publications.

Mt. Pelée Volcano, Martinique, French Caribbean

Mt. Pelée at 1397 meters, is the highest summit on the island of Martinique in the French West Indies which is in the Eastern Caribbean. Historically, Pelée is one of the most active volcanos in the Lesser Antilles. It's had 20 major eruptions in the last 5000 years. This modern volcano sits on the northeast rim of a caldera formed by slope failure of a former Pelée volcano. On 5/2/1902 it came alive for the first time since 1851. Then at 7:52am on the morning of 5/8/1902, it exploded and sent a superheated cloud down its southwest slope to annihilate the city of St. Pierre and killing more than 30,000 people. Only a condemned murderer in a protected subterranean jail cell survived the holocaust. That eruption, which registered a VEI-4, was the type-example of **Pelean Eruptions** and marked the beginning of modern volcanological studies of the behavior of pyroclastic flows, called *nuée ardente* in French. Later, beginning 9/16/1929, there was a 3 year period of activity, but it's been quiet since.

The author flew into Martinique on the night of 4/9/1979, slept at the airport, then took a publico (shared taxi, which carry several passengers and operate along a route, the same as buses) into Fort-du-France and bought maps, food, etc. Very expensive! Then hitch hiked north to St. Pierre and camped just out of town. Next morning, he got a lift to Le Morne Rouge and walked to the end of the road at 880 meters and the old Aileron Refuge. He hid his pack in the bush and climbed the mountain in fog all the way--never saw a thing! But the trails were good. He then hitch hiked back to Fort-du-France and the airport that afternoon.

Getting to **Pelée** is fairly easy. You can take a publico from Fort-du-France to St. Pierre where many ruins, including the famous jail cell, and a museum can be seen. Other publicos go on to Le Morne Rouge. Publicos can also be taken direct from Fort-du-France along Highway N-3 to Le Morne Rouge. Or you can join a group and be bused around.

From Le Morne Rouge, it's about 6 kms to the parking lot at the base of the peak. If you're traveling cheap, you may have to walk from Le Morne Rouge, as public transport is minimal from there on, but that distance is short. The author found hitch hiking poor on Martinique, but that's another possible way.

Pelée can be climbed in half a day from the parking lot at the end of the paved road. It's a cool hike and the area may be in clouds so start hiking early. Take a light jacket too, it'll be cold on top. On the summit, there are 2 small huts: one is some kind of volcano observatory which is always locked and can't be used by hikers; the other is a hiker's shelter and dilapidated to a point of giving no protection at all. There's a restaurant about one km down from the parking lot, but hikers should buy food in Le Morne Rouge or better still, Fort-du-France.

There are other trails to the summit leading from both Le Precheur on the west coast; and from Macouba on the north, but the author is unfamiliar with those trails. An educated guess is they are less-used and perhaps overgrown. Ask about them in the tourist office in Fort-du-

Below the deadly slopes of Volcan Pelée is the town of St. Pierre.

Map 508-1, Mt. Pelée Volcano, Martinique, French Caribbean

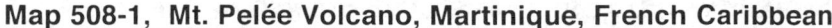

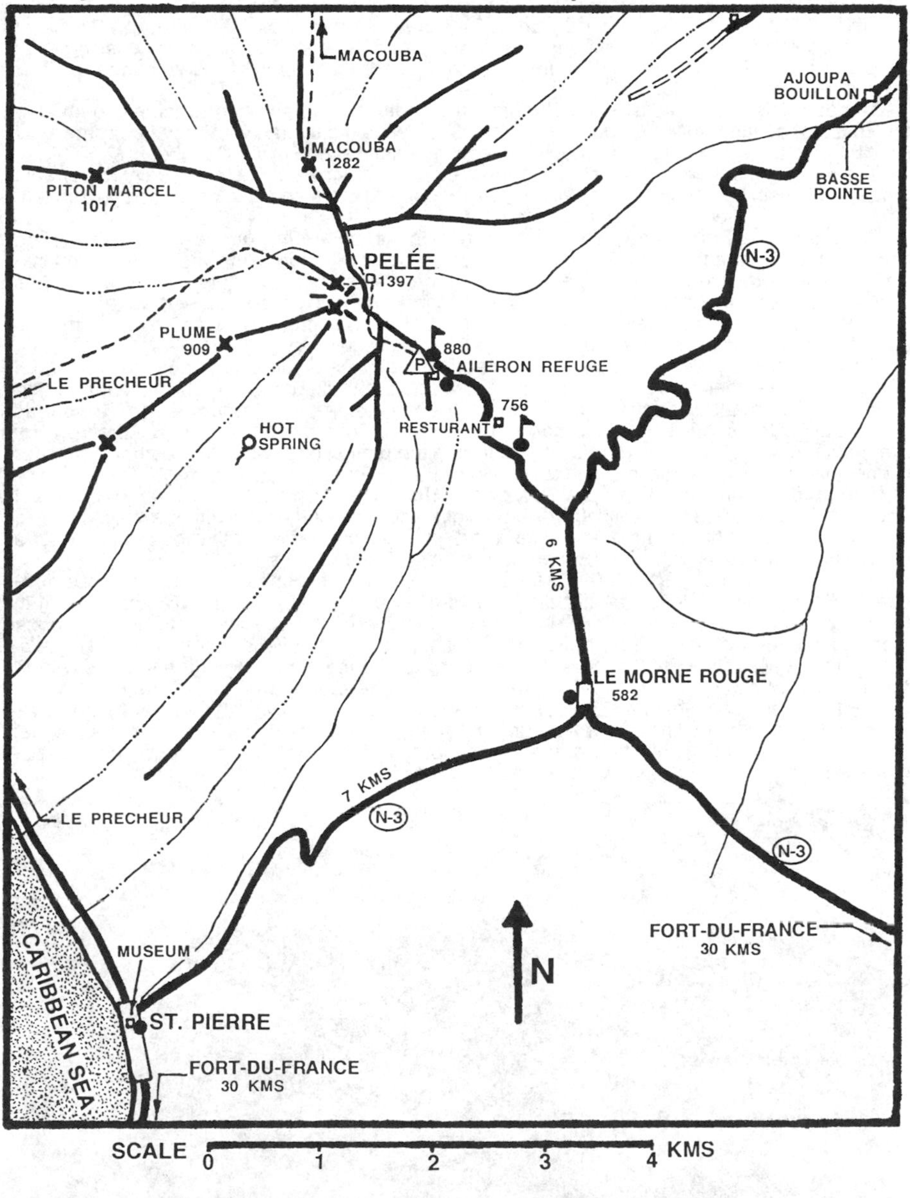

MACOUBA

AJOUPA
BOUILLON

MACOUBA
1282

BASSE
POINTE

PITON MARCEL
1017

(N-3)

PELÉE
1397

PLUME
909

880

LE PRECHEUR

P AILERON REFUGE

HOT
SPRING

RESTURANT 756

6 KMS

LE MORNE ROUGE
582

7 KMS

LE PRECHEUR

(N-3)

(N-3)

FORT-DU-FRANCE
30 KMS

MUSEUM

N

CARIBBEAN SEA

ST. PIERRE

FORT-DU-FRANCE
30 KMS

SCALE 0   1   2   3   4 KMS

France.
    Updated information can be found in the tourist office in Fort-du-France. Some bookshops there sell good topographic maps of Pelée and the island. The dry season is from December to April. For updated volcanic information see the Smithsonian website (www.volcano.si.edu/gvp/).
Maps *Fort de France-St. Pierre,* 1:50,000, or road map *511,* 1:100,000 (?), both from Institut Geographique National (IGN), 136 bis, rue de Grenelle, Paris, France, website (www.ign.fr); and the books, **Volcano Mondo,** Dieckmann, Pinnacle Books (history of the 1902 eruption); and a travel guidebook to the Eastern Caribbean from Lonely Planet or Moon Publications.

Petit and Gros Pitons, St. Lucia, Eastern Caribbean

Two of the most interesting and challenging climbs or hikes in the Caribbean are shown on this map. These peaks are Petit Piton at 743 meters, and Gros Piton, about 790 meters. They're located on the southwest coast of the island of St. Lucia. The author is guessing a little here, but these 2 very steep mountains appear to be the remains of old volcanos, perhaps volcanic throats, or lava domes (?).

To get to this area, take a minibus or hitch hike from the capital city of Castries south along the coast to the large town of Soufriere. From Soufriere's main jetty, you'll have a great view of Petit Piton to the south. This is probably the best mountain scene in the Caribbean!

The author was there in 1/1993. It's supposed to be dry then but he had heavy rains, which made it impossible to even try Petit Piton, the steeper and more challenging of the two. Instead, and with one dry afternoon, he climbed Gros Piton.

To climb **Gros Piton**, walk, hitch hike, or take a minibus from Soufriere south to a village called Etangs. From there, walk along an unpaved road down and southwest toward the Union Valle Estate and Union Valle village. At the village, ask anyone about the trail to Gros Piton. The right trail is one that heads southwest, and for the most part, contours at about the same elevation around the mountain to the west side. If you get confused or want to save time, ask one of the village boys to show you the way--but it's really quite easy to find.

Once on the trail, you'll soon come to a meadow area where some cows and pigs are tied up and left to graze, then further along you'll pass 2 or more trails branching off to the left running downhill. See map. When you finally get to the west side of the mountain, the trail heads straight up to the summit. It'll take about half a day to do this climb walking all the way from Etangs on the main highway. Or you can camp in the pig pasture, which the author did. There is one good public water tap in Union Valle, as well as at Etangs.

The author took a minibus from Castries to Soufriere, and another to Etangs in the late afternoon of 1/23/1993. He walked to Union Valle and had a boy show him the way. Near the pig pasture, he hid his big pack and racing the setting sun, hurried to the top in just under an hour; 1/3/4 hours round-trip. He camped near the pig pasture for the night.

In the afternoon of 12/17/2000, the author got a call from Richard White who was on St. Lucia. Here's how he described his climb up **Petit Piton**. Walk south out of Soufriere on the road going to the Jalousie Hilton Hotel. After roughly 2 1/2 kms, you'll come to a small parking place on the left or east side of the road, and a sign reading, *Pitons Warm Mineral Waterfall*. From there, backup about 20 meters (to the north) to find the beginning of the trail. *It's not the trail directly across the road from the parking place*. The trail heads toward the north side of Petit Piton, then veers right and contours west below a cliff or headwall. Once on the northwest side of the peak, the trail heads straight up. It's steep, but there are some ropes in the steepest places. An easy halfday climb. Soufriere has plenty of food shops and some of the cheapest hotels on the island, which are about US$15 to $20 a night.

Looking south at Petit Piton as seen from the wharf at the town of Soufriere.

Map 509-1, Petit & Gros Pitons, St. Lucia, Caribbean

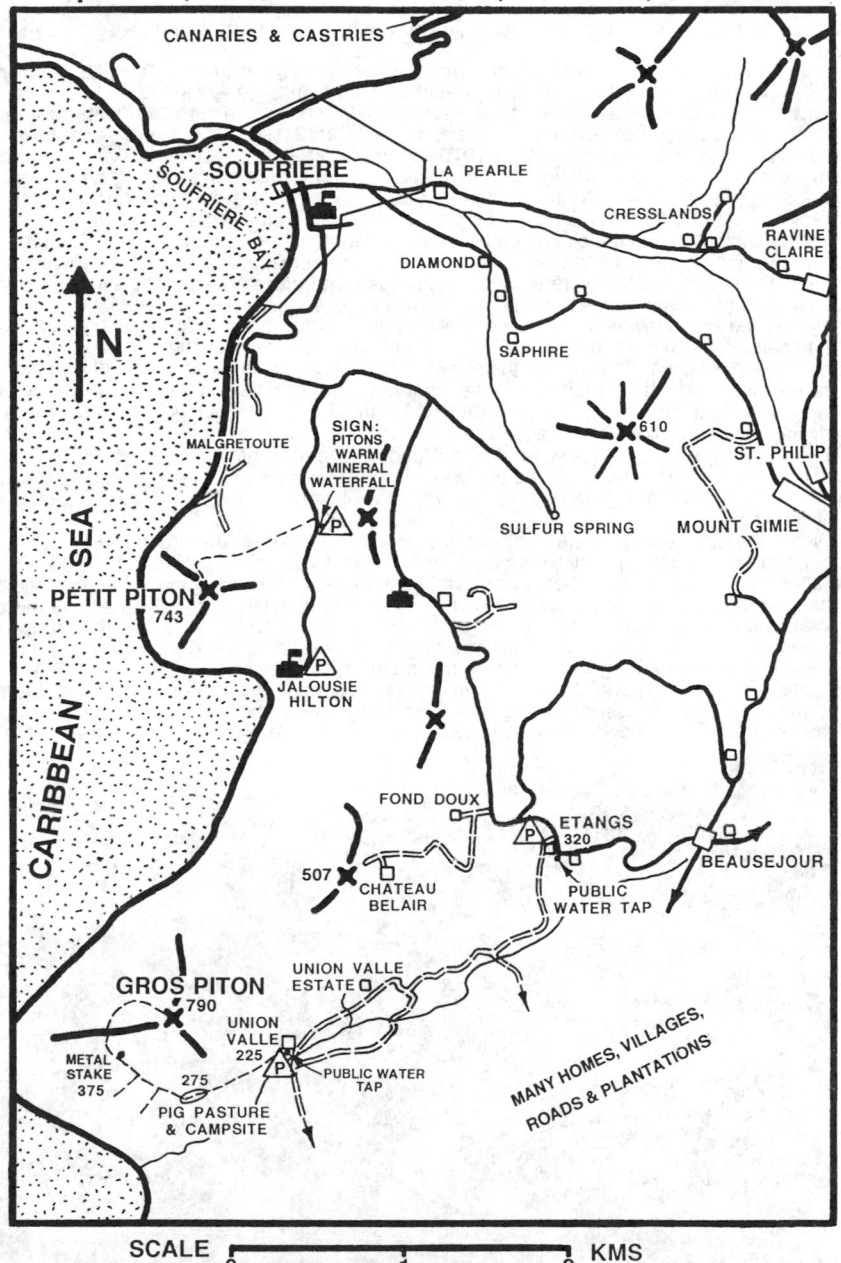

CANARIES & CASTRIES

SOUFRIERE

LA PEARLE

SOUFRIERE BAY

CRESSLANDS

RAVINE CLAIRE

DIAMOND

N

SAPHIRE

SIGN:
PITONS
WARM
MINERAL
WATERFALL

MALGRETOUTE

610

ST. PHILIP

SULFUR SPRING

MOUNT GIMIE

SEA

P

PETIT PITON
743

P

JALOUSIE
HILTON

CARIBBEAN

FOND DOUX

ETANGS
320

P

BEAUSEJOUR

507

CHATEAU
BELAIR

PUBLIC
WATER TAP

UNION VALLE
ESTATE

GROS PITON
790

UNION
VALLE
225

P

PUBLIC WATER
TAP

MANY HOMES, VILLAGES,
ROADS & PLANTATIONS

METAL
STAKE
375

275

PIG PASTURE
& CAMPSITE

SCALE
0   1   2   KMS

Maps Ordnance Survey map *St. Lucia Tourist Map,* 1:50,000; from the tourist office, or the
Survey and Mapping Department, Castries, St. Lucia; or Ordnance Survey, Romsey Road,
Southampton, UK, SO9 4DH; or Stanfords, 12-14 Long Acre, London, Tele. Inter+171-836-1321;
and a travel guidebook to the Eastern Caribbean from Lonely Planet or Moon Publications.

Soufriere Volcano, St. Vincent Island, Eastern Caribbean

The highest mountain on the island of St. Vincent is the Soufriere Volcano. The highest peak is 1219 meters located on an old caldera rim immediately north of the present-day summit crater.

Soufriere has had a history of violent explosions. The eruption of 1812 created the Northeast Crater and another blast from the main crater on 5/6/1902 killed 1600 people This was just hours before the beginning of the disastrous 1902 eruptions of Pelée on Martinique.

Here's the author's experience. On the night of 4/12/1979, the author was camped at Jacob's Well. The next morning, 4/13/1979, he was up at dawn, about 5:30am. At 5:45, he heard sounds like thunder and it began to get darker; then mud began falling on his tent. He broke camp, walked down the trail a ways, hid his pack in the bush, and hurried to the top between the 1st and 2nd eruptions. On the crater rim was 5 cms of new ash & mud. Ash had fallen back down through the clouds that capped the summit and turned to mud. See foto. The second eruption came as he was walking down. Other explosions with mushroom-type clouds that resembled atom bombs were viewed from Kingstown before he left the island. For volcano updates see the website (www.volcano.si.edu/gvp/).

In 1998, the author returned. He took a minibus from Kingston, the islands capital city, and stopped at Chapmans Barrio in the north end of Georgetown. Later he got on another minibus going to New Sandy Bay and got out at Rabacca and the paved road running up to the main trailhead. The trail going up the southeast side of the mountain is the most-used and is considered the normal route up the volcano. A word of advice, be patient in Kingstown and you'll find a bus going all the way to New Sandy Bay, instead of taking 2 like the author did.

The author got a lift part way to the trailhead on a banana truck, then at 9:20am started walking up the trail. He made it to the crater rim in 1 1/2 hours with a large pack, but 20 minutes of which was spent at the potholes visiting with other hikers. This is an easy climb on a well-maintained trail.

During the day he viewed the northeast crater, then went down the roped route to the crater floor. Anyone can climb up & down that rope which has a vertical drop of about 145 meters. He also attempted to reach the highest peak, but by then lacked the time & water to camp overnight on the mountain, so he headed down the very good Southwest Trail and reached the mouth of the Wallibou River at 5:30pm. He had a quick skinny dip, filled his water bottles, and walked back up the trail a ways to camp. Next morning he walked to Chateaubelair, getting a lift part way, and got on one of many early morning minibuses to Kingstown.

If you're fit and don't spend a lot of time on the mountain, you can do this climb, at least to the crater rim and back in one long day from Kingstown using public transport. Lots of minibuses go to Georgetown, New Sandy Bay and Chateaubelair. You can do it even faster if

The author was covered with muddy ash on the crater rim at about 7:30am
in between the 1st and 2nd eruptions of Soufriere on May 13, 1979.

Map 510-1, Soufriere Volcano, St. Vincent, Eastern Caribbean

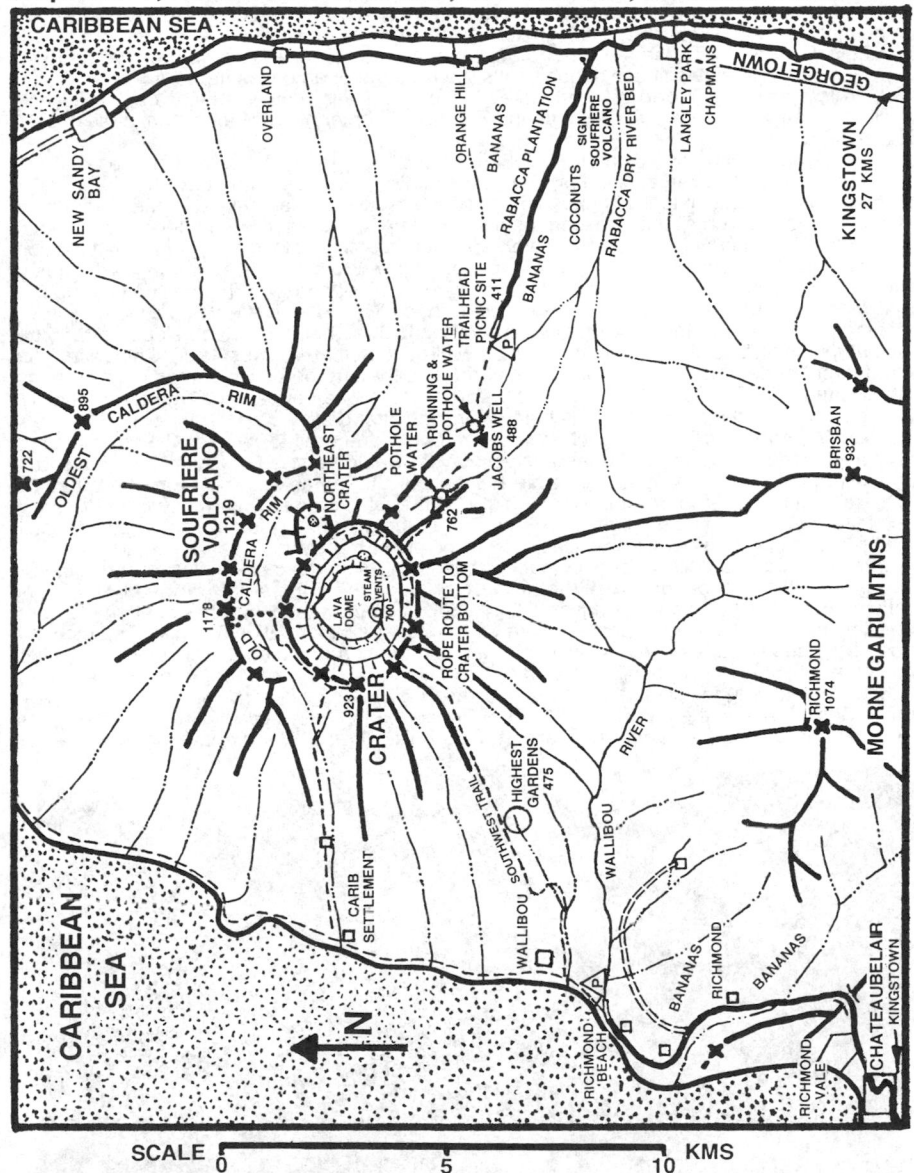

SCALE 0   5   10   KMS

you rent a vehicle like many tourists do.

If camping on the mountain, buy all your food and supplies in Kingstown. There are lots of small supermarkets in the city center near the marketplace & minibus station. Once on the mountain, load up with water from Jacob's Well (a very small stream) or the Wallibou River (the potholes at 762 meters aren't as reliable). The dry season is from December through April.

Maps Lands & Surveys map *St. Vincent North*, 1:25,000, Kingstown, St. Vincent; and a travel guidebook to the Eastern Caribbean from Lonely Planet or Moon Publications.

Mt. St. Catherine & Qua Qua, Grenada, Eastern Caribbean

The 2 hikes featured here are on the island of Grenada. One is to the top of Mt. St. Catherine, the highest summit on the island at 840 meters. The other is to the top of Mt. Qua Qua at 715 meters. These mountains are volcanic but show little sign of recent activity. However, St. Catherine's shape suggests it's the remains of an old caldera. According to the book, **Volcanos of the World**, St. Catherine's last erupted was sometime in the early Holocene, or within the last 10,000 years. Also, Grand Etang, the center piece of a national park, has the look of a crater lake.

Here's what the author did on 1/27/1993. He left St. George's (the capital of Grenada) and took a minibus to Grenville on the east coast. He hunted for a guide who gave him information about St. Catherine, then took another minibus northwest to the village of Mt. Horne. From there he located the Mt. Horne Road, which runs northwest up to a pass at 500 meters at the base of the peak. The author did this from the water tap at the beginning of the Mt. Horne Road in about one hour with full pack. From that pass, a trail goes down to a nice little stream inside the old caldera, west along the creek a ways, then finally to a trail-of-sorts which begins on the right or north side just below a couple of impassable waterfalls. This route first runs up a steep gully for 50 meters, then leaves the gully on the left and heads straight up the steep slope north to the main ridge running east-west. On this ridge, a well-used trail heads west to St. Catherine. The author first headed east to checkout the antennas at the end of the road, then got to within a short distance of St. Catherine's summit before turning back because of the late hour. He managed to get to the Mt. Horne Road before camping after dark.

This *Mt. Horne Road route* might be the better route if you want to camp on the mountain and have a little adventure, but by far the easiest way up would be to go to Paraclete by bus from Grenville, then road-walk up to the Cable & Wireless Station as shown. From there use the good trail running west to St. Catherine. This is a great place to see a very mossy cloud forest. This latter route would be 6-7 kms from Paraclete to the summit. A fast walker should be able do this hike in one long day from St. George's, using public transport.

Mt. Qua Qua is located in the middle of the island and near the main highway connecting St. George's with the east coast. All the area on this second map is part of the Grand Etang National Park. Just tell your bus driver to let you off at Grand Etang, which is right on the pass. Near the main road is a visitor center where you can get trail information and hiking maps of the area. From the visitor center you can easily locate the trail running up a ridge to the summit of Qua Qua, which is only about 2 kms away. The author did this hike round-trip in one hour on 1/28/1993. One suggested hike would be to climb Qua Qua, then walk down another well-used trail to Concord Falls, then west to the town of Concord and finally back to St. George's by bus. This can easily be done in one day from St. George's. *Grand Etang gets an unbelievable 4*

This picture was taken along the Mt. Horne Road below Mt. St. Catherine.

Map 511-1, St. Catherine & Qua Qua, Grenada, Caribbean

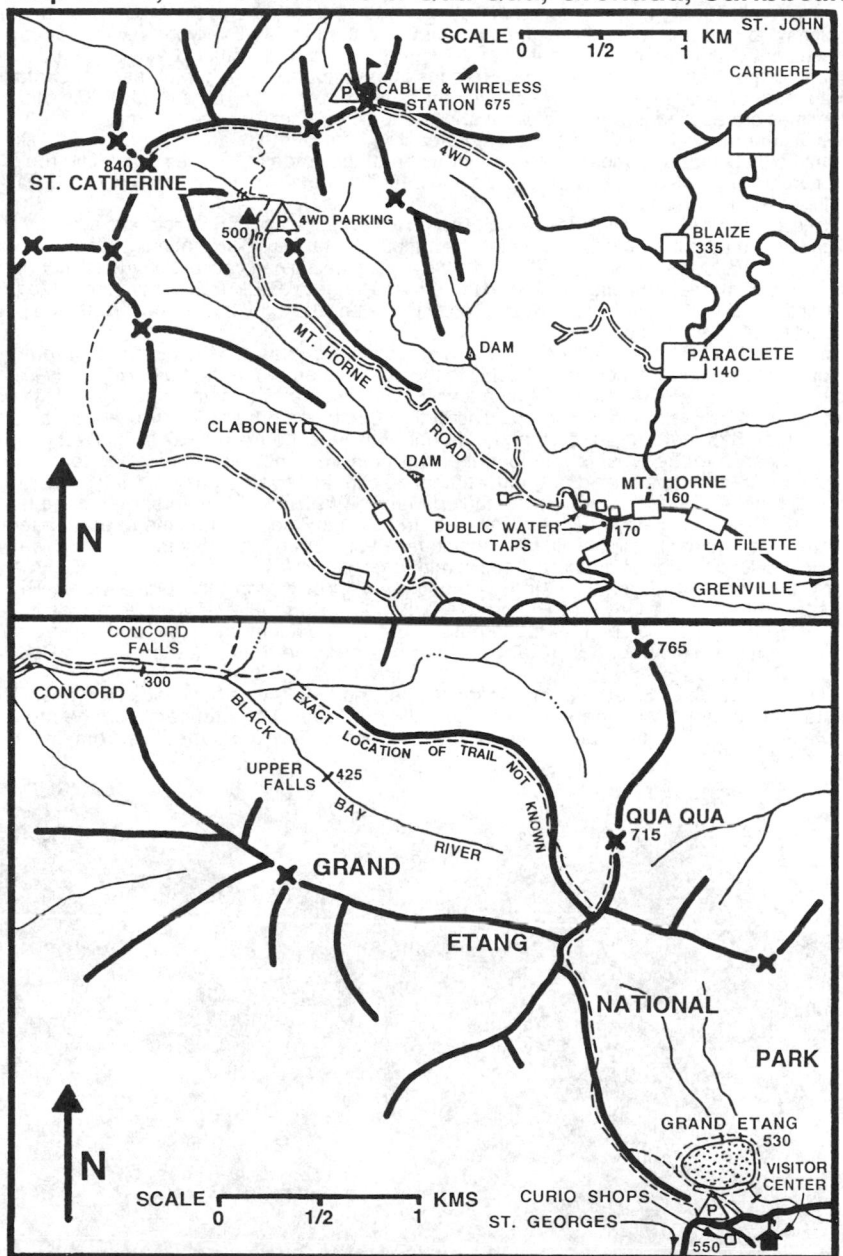

meters of rain a year, so take a raincoat or umbrella and expect slippery wet trails.

Maps *Grenada, Island of Spice,* 1:50,000, from the Grenada Tourist Board, or Lands and Surveys in St. George's; or from Ordnance Survey, Romsey Road, Southampton, UK, SO9 4DH; and a travel guidebook to the Eastern Caribbean from Lonely Planet or Moon Publications.

Man-of-War Hill & Pigeon Peak, Tobago, Eastern Caribbean

If you're vacationing on the island of Tobago, and you get tired of the beach, you might try climbing what appears to be the highest mountain on the island. Everyone told the author the highest point was Pigeon Peak, but after the climb and when he finally bought a good map, it appears Man-of-War Hill is the highest. Perhaps this is another name for the same mountain, or perhaps Pigeon is the name for the summit that's visible from Charlotteville (?). On this map, both names are applied to 2 parts of what appears to be one big rounded summit.

This mountain is located on the extreme eastern end of the island of Tobago and like the mountains of Trinidad, appear to be an extension of the Andes of Venezuela. The rocks are metamorphic or crystaline of various kinds and definitely not volcanic as the rest of the Eastern Caribbean islands are.

To get to **Man-of-War Hill/Pigeon Peak**, first go to the capital city of Scarborough, either by plane or daily ferry boat from Trinidad. From there take a bus or maxi-taxi (like a minibus) or shared route taxi going to Charlotteville. Have the driver drop you off at the trailhead about 200 meters north of the pass marked 210 meters altitude. A sign there reads, *Pigeon Peak Trail*. From there the faded remains of an old road heads southwest. Today this is only used by occasional hikers and people going out to cut grass for their cows.

After less than 2 kms, you'll come to a deep gully which has cut the old track. From there backup 10 meters, and head straight uphill to the south on an emerging trail. Hopefully it'll be a lot better when you arrive. After less than a km of walking in a nice mostly-open rainforest, you'll arrive on the almost-flat mountain top. The author continued on a fading trail which led to the point marked 525 meters. At the time he thought this was the main peak or highest point. In reality, the area to the west is a little higher but there may not be a trail going that way (?). However, with a compass and in good weather, it should be fairly easy to *jungle walk* to the southwest and arrive at the high point marked Man-of-War Hill, 550 meters, on the maps. But be warned; this is a big almost-flat summit area and you can't see through the trees to determine if you're on the highest point. This hike should take you about half a day from the highway and will give you a good look at a natural tropical rainforest.

If you're not up to bushwhacking, you could walk north along the Observatory Road to Flagstaff Hill for good views of Pigeon Peak and Charlotteville. The author was here on 1/29/1993. He got out of the bus at the pass, hid his big pack in the bush, and walked an old road to Flagstaff Hill. Round-trip was less than an hour. He then hiked up Pigeon Peak and back in 1 3/4 hours.

There are hotels in Speyside and Charlotteville; and both towns have nice beaches. There are stores in either town where you can buy all your food. You can camp on the mountain anywhere, but you'll have to carry water to a campsite. The dry season is from December through April.

The author's camp along the Observatory Road with Pigeon Peak beyond.

Map 512-1, Man-of-War/Pigeon Peak, Tobago, Caribbean

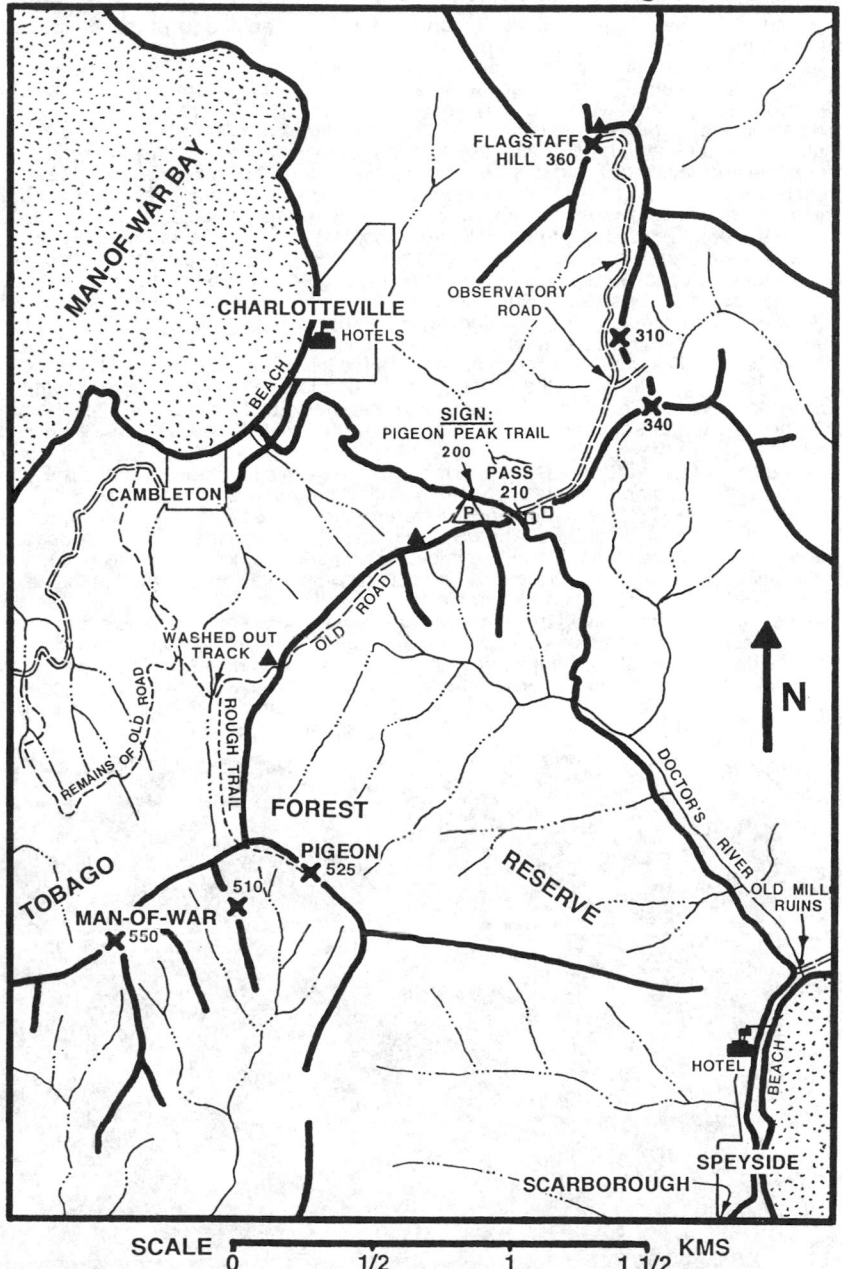

MAN-OF-WAR BAY

FLAGSTAFF
HILL 360

OBSERVATORY
ROAD

CHARLOTTEVILLE
HOTELS

BEACH

✗ 310

SIGN:
PIGEON PEAK TRAIL
200

✗ 340

CAMBLETON

PASS
210

P

WASHED OUT
TRACK

OLD ROAD

REMAINS OF OLD ROAD

ROUGH TRAIL

N

FOREST

DOCTOR'S RIVER

PIGEON
✗ 525

OLD MILL
RUINS

TOBAGO

510
✗

RESERVE

MAN-OF-WAR
✗ 550

HOTEL

BEACH

SPEYSIDE

SCARBOROUGH

SCALE   0   1/2   1   1 1/2   KMS

Maps   Lands & Surveys maps *Tobago, Sheet 3,* 1:25,000; or *Sheets 3B & 3E,* 1:10,000, from Lands & Surveys, 18 Abercromby Street, Port of Spain, Trinidad; or Stanfords, 12/14 Long Acre, London, UK, Tele. Inter+171-836-1321; and a travel guidebook to the Eastern Caribbean from Lonely Planet or Moon Publications.

Cerro Aripo, Bleu (Blue) Mountains, Trinidad, Eastern Caribbean

The highest mountain on Trinidad is El Cerro del Aripo at 941 meters. It's located in the central part of the Bleu (Blue) Mountains, northeast of Arima, southeast of Blanchisseuse and immediately south of Brasso Seco.

The Bleu Mountains of Trinidad run east-west and appear to be an eastward extension of the Andes of South American. The few observable rocks along Aripo's summit ridge appear to be some kind of sedimentary layers, probably limestone (?).

The author was in these mountains on 4/20/1979, but took the wrong ridge and didn't reach the summit. He returned on 2/5 & 2/6/1998. Here's his experience. He stayed with a friend in Port of Spain, the capital of Trinidad & Tobago. He took a maxi-taxi (minibus) from the outskirts of the city into the area where the main bus station is, which is immediately south of the city center and next to the old unused train station. At that bus station, you can either take a shared taxi, maxi-taxi, or a full-sized bus to Arima located about 30 kms due east of Port of Spain.

In 1979, there were mini buses running from Arima to Blanchisseuse on the north coast; but in 1998, your only option was to hitch hike, or take a regular private taxi from a point about 3 blocks northeast of the bus station & market in Arima. The author paid a little over US$3 for a private taxi going 10 kms up the main highway to the beginning of the *Lalaja Road* as shown. He then walked up the paved, but crumbling Lalaja Road, to a pass marked 550 meters, then on to what will be called the *trailhead at 440 meters*. This is the beginning of the old La Paria Road. At that point you'll find a home to the right (south of the road), and a small stream & waterfall to the left. This should be good water for drinking (?) or bathing and the last you'll find before the peak. The walk to the trailhead took the author 1 1/2 hours with a large pack, a distance of about 7 kms.

The first part of La Paria Road is regularly used then as this much-used road turns left, you continue straight ahead on an old wagon road that dates back to the 1800's. In 1998, the author hid his pack near the first pass marked 550 meters, then headed north and down to Brasso Seco. That took about 1 1/4 hours (3 1/3 hours from the Aripo Road). Brasso Seco has a couple of stores, a church & school, but no public transport--only taxis or hitch hiking from there. The walk back to his pack took 45 minutes. A nice rainforest hike. He returned to the waterfall, had a bath, and camped near Pass 550 meters.

The next morning, he walked the ridge trail east toward **Aripo**, but the trail gradually faded and was difficult to follow and slow walking in the second half of the hike. It's marked in places with plastic ribbons, but it's still not used a lot. As time goes on however, it should become a real trail. Due to prior commitments, he had to give up again less than a km from the summit and get back to town. It took 1 1/4 hours to walk from the waterfall back to the main road, then a lift down to Arima (US$1.63), and a bus to Port of Spain (about US$.50).

The little waterfall beside the road at Lalaja. This is where you turn left to reach Aripo.

Map 513-1, Cerro Aripo, Bleu (Blue), Mtns., Trinidad

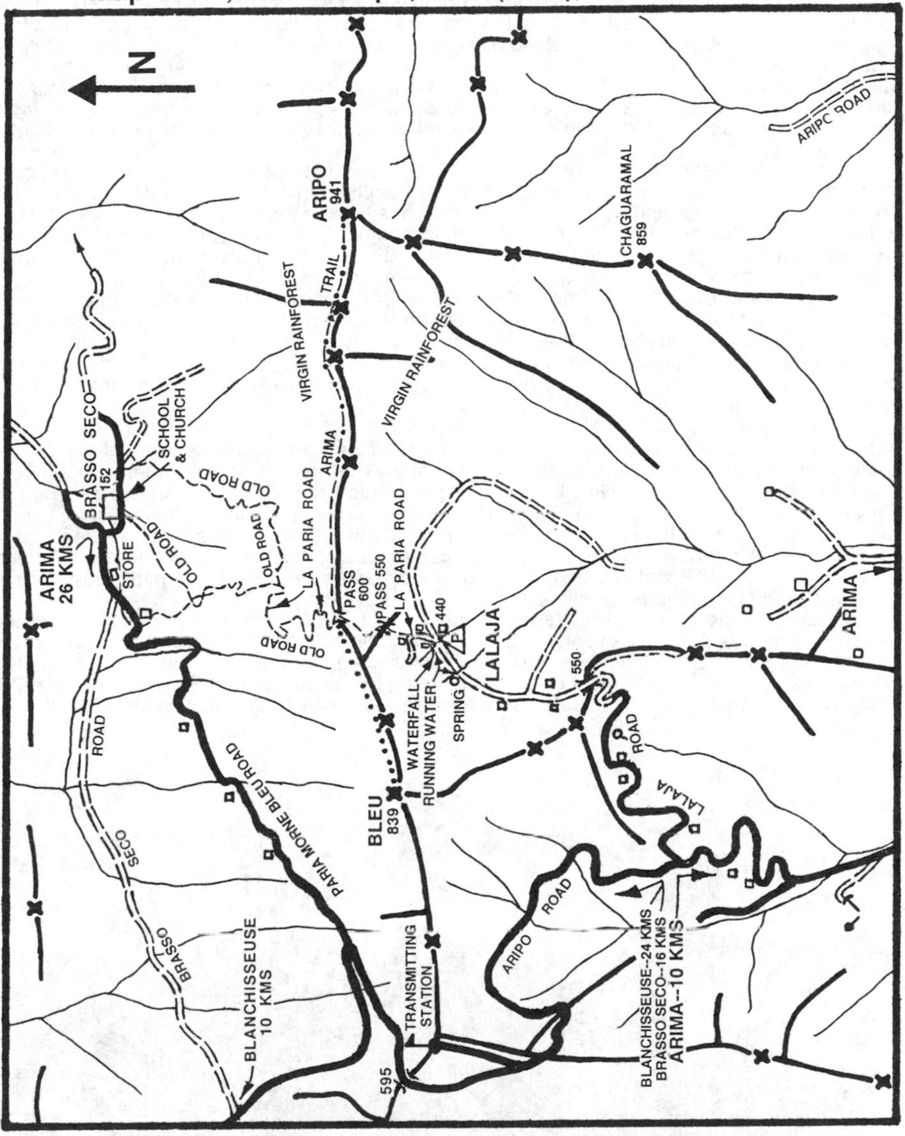

N

ARIPO 941

ARIPC ROAD

CHAGUARAMAL 859

VIRGIN RAINFOREST

TRAIL

VIRGIN RAINFOREST

BRASSO SECO 152

SCHOOL & CHURCH

OLD ROAD

OLD ROAD

OLD ROAD

OLD ROAD

ARIMA 26 KMS

STORE

ARIMA

LA PARIA ROAD

LA PARIA ROAD

PASS 600

PASS 550

440

LALAJA

550

ARIMA

WATERFALL RUNNING WATER

SPRING

LALAJA ROAD

ROAD

SECO

PARIA MORNE BLEU ROAD

BRASSO SECO

BLANCHISSEUSE 10 KMS

BLEU 839

TRANSMITTING STATION

595

ARIPO ROAD

BLANCHISSEUSE—24 KMS
BRASSO SECO—16 KMS
ARIMA—10 KMS

| SCALE | 0 | 1 | 2 | 3 | 4 | KMS |

You can buy all your food for this trip in Arima, as there's a good market next to the bus station. If you had you're own vehicle, and with an early start, you could do this climb in one long day from Port of Spain. The dry season is from December to April.
Maps *Sheets 14 & 15,* 1:25,000, from Lands & Surveys, Port of Spain; and a travel guidebook to the Eastern Caribbean from Lonely Planet or Moon Publications.

Mt. Christoffel, Curaçao, Dutch Caribbean

Included on this map is one of the smallest or lowest altitude mountains in this book, but the hike is one of the more interesting the author has made. This mountain is known as Christoffel and rises to 370 meters. It's on the island of Curaçao, which is part of the Dutch Antilles or West Indes. It's located about 100 kms north of the Venezuelan coast, and about halfway between Maracaibo and Caracas. Curaçao is only about 65 kms long and averages about 10 kms in width. The island is composed of limestone and is generally very flat. However, the upper-most part of Christoffel appears to be made of some kind of quartzite (?). This is the only mountain or hill on the island.

Get to Christoffel by hitch hiking or by bus. Since public transport is good on Curaçao, taking the bus is easiest. To start with, take a bus from the airport into Willemstad, the capital. To find the right bus heading north, go to the Ortobanda Bus Terminal which is across the harbor or inlet from the famous waterfront and swinging bridge. There are (or were in 1979) buses leaving each hour for the small town of Westpunt at the very northwestern tip of the island. Another way and sometimes even faster is to hitch hike.

Mt. Christoffel is part of the Christoffel National Park, a small but very interesting piece of land. The headquarters for the park is at Landhuis Savonet, about 40 kms northwest of Willemstad on the main highway. Before heading that way contact the tourist information office in Willemstad for the latest information about opening and closing times. In 1979 the park was open from 8am until 3pm, but it was necessary to enter before 12 noon. The entire park is enclosed in a 2-meter-high chainlink fence.

The thing that makes this peak, and all the park interesting, is the vegetation. On the trail from park headquarters to the peak, you'll pass through a forest composed entirely of cactus, some of which are 5 or 6 meters high. There are many roads in the area so when walking from Landhuis Savonet, always follow the white arrows along the main track known as *Voetpad Christoffel*, or Christoffel Foot Trail. There's no water in the park, so always have a good supply with you. As you near the summit of Christoffel the vegetation changes from cactus to other types of trees, some of which are draped in moss because of the morning (or afternoon?) cloud deck. The peak itself is rather steep and rugged, but there's a path to the summit. Any kind of boot or shoe will do on this easy half-day hike.

Here's what the author did. He flew from Trinidad to Curaçao on 4/22/1979. He left baggage in a locker at the airport, took a bus to town and bought food, took fotos of the fotogenic waterfront, then bused back to the airport and camped nearby. Next morning he left his big pack in a locker again, went to town, then got a bus to Landhuis Savonet. It was after 12 noon, so they wouldn't let him in, but he managed to find a hole in the chainlink fence and went

The wide trail passing through the forest of cactus along the way to Mt. Christoffel.

Map 514-1, Mt. Christoffel, Curaçao, Dutch Caribbean

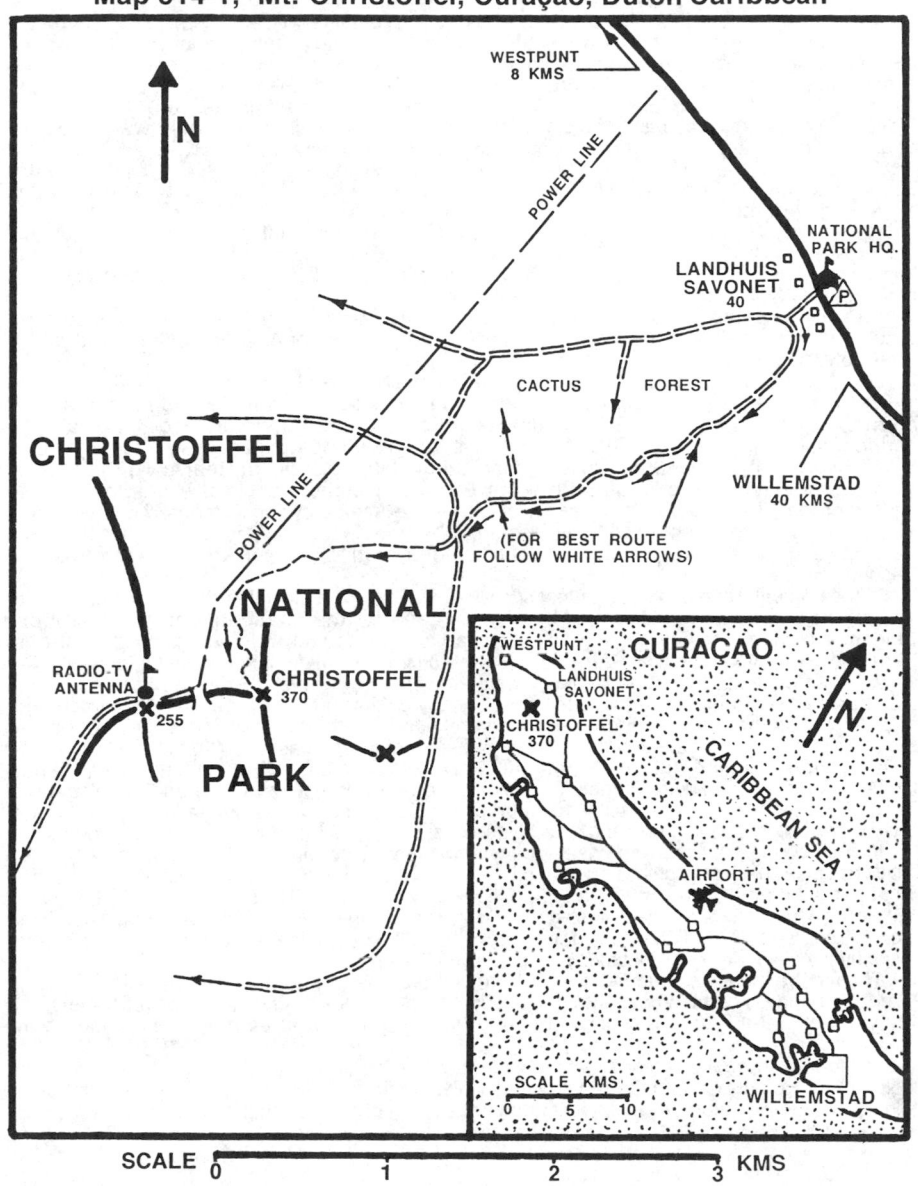

in anyway. He climbed the peak and returned via the correct way. He then hitched back to Willemstad, took night fotos of the waterfront, then bused to the airport, got baggage and camped again. He flew out the next morning.

Maps *Christoffel National Park*, (scale unknown), buy at the national park headquarters in Landhuis Savonet, or in Willemstad.

Chapter 9--South America

This chapter on South America includes 70 maps, beginning with the mountains just north of Caracas in Venezuela and ending with Antarctica. One nice thing about traveling on this continent is there is basically one language; Spanish. In Brazil they speak Portuguese, but it's almost the same as Spanish, and there aren't any real mountains there anyway.

If you look at a map of South America which shows the highest peaks, you'd be looking at mostly volcanos. A great many of the high mountains on the continent are either volcanic cones, or are built of volcanic lavas laid down long ago and eroded to form peaks.

The areas of most-recent volcanic activity are in southern Colombia and north central Ecuador, southwest Peru, western Bolivia, and along the frontier of Chile and Argentina down to about Puerto Montt.

Folded, fault-block or uplifted mountains are those in Venezuela, northern Colombia, and most of Peru from the Cordillera Blanca to Lake Titicaca. In Bolivia, the Cordillera Real east of La Paz is uplifted & folded, as are those in the extreme south of Chile-Argentina. Many of these mountain ranges have granitic-type rocks at the core.

Weather-wise, most of South America is in the tropics, but when you're in the high mountains and half-frozen, it seems otherwise. Only the southern third of the continent is south of the Tropic of Capricorn.

The Andes Mountains can be broken down into three generalized climatic regions. Two are in the tropical regions, which include all the mountains from Colombia south to the area of northern Argentina. From about the border of Peru-Ecuador north and including all of the northern part of the continent, the dry season is from November or December, through about April. South of that border, down to and including all the Cordillera Real in Bolivia, the dry season begins in May and ends about the last part of September. South of where Bolivia, Chile and Argentina meet is under the influence of the middle latitude cyclonic storms. However, most of the activity is from central Chile and south. The driest place in South America is from the Peru-Ecuador border south along the coast to central Chile. This in known as the Atacama Desert.

In the tropical Andes, the permanent snowline, or where the glaciers end, is at about 4600 to 4800 meters elevation. This is generally the case for the mountains of Venezuela and Colombia, south to the Cordillera Real in Bolivia. In the volcanic and dry regions of southwest Peru and south along the Chile-Argentine border to central Chile, is the highest snowline in the world. In some areas, permanent snow is near the 6000 meter level. However, throughout all of these areas mentioned, snow does fall (though very seldom!) down to below 4000 meters, but doesn't stay on the ground for long. From central Chile south, the snowline ranges from about 5000 meters down to where several glaciers in Tierra del Fuego cascade into the sea.

Difficulties in climbing range from the *best in the world* in Peru's Cordilleras Blanca, Huayhuash, Vilcanote and Vilcabamba; to some of the easiest anywhere on the volcanos of Peru, Bolivia, Chile & Argentina. The mountains of Ecuador and Colombia are generally very easy for experienced climbers, and some of the best rock climbing in the world is in Patagonia.

In each country of South America, the Instituto Geografico Militar (IGM), or in some the IGN (Nacional) publishes maps of their own region. These maps can be found in each capital city. For the most part all maps are available to the public, with some exceptions being those along some international frontiers. Best place to start looking for maps is the website (www.omnimap.com), or in the USA call toll free 800-742-2677, or Inter+336-227-8300. Look in the back of this book for other major map makers and/or distributors of maps around the world.

The most expensive countries in South America are/were; Argentina, Brazil and Chile, with Venezuela and Colombia about equal. The poorest countries and the cheapest for travelers, are Bolivia, Peru and Ecuador. This list changes with the current economic situation on the continent.

In regards to travel to places where there's crime against travelers, especially Peru and Colombia, which are among the worst places in the world, first read **Chapter 1--Introduction** to this book for information on what to do when traveling in crime-ridden places and how to protect yourself.

From the Laguna Rio Blanco looking southwest toward the summit
area of Mercedario (Map 570, page 1207).

In the Cordillera Real southeast of Illampu & Ancohuma is Cherroco left,
and Chachacomani right (Map 557, page 1179).

Pico Naiguata, PN El Avila, Cordillera de la Costa, Venezuela

Here's a nice hiking area for those who might find themselves with a little free time in Caracas, Venezuela. It's in the mountains immediately north of the city, and between Caracas and the coast. This is the Cordillera de la Costa, the highest part of which is included in the Parque Nacional El Avila. Locals simply refer to this area as **Avila**. It's especially popular for hiking and jogging because it's so close to the capital city of Caracas. These mountains are made of granite, same as the higher Andes to the west, and to as far east as Tobago.

Included on this map is the crest of the range and the northern part of Caracas. Avenida Boyaca, an autopista, forms the boundary between the city and the mountains. For we travelers, the first thing to do is go to any metro or subway station in the downtown area. Get on the metro and go to the *Parque del Este Station*. Once out of the station, walk 200 meters east to find the office of all national parks in Venezuela. Pick up the map listed below and/or any other information that's available. Then with a good city map, walk from one of the various metro stations due north to the base of the mountain. If you hire a taxi, you can save a 2 km walk from the metro.

You'll have a choice of many trails and entry points to choose from, but here's what the author did on 2/3/1993. He left his hotel early and walked a short distance to the subway and rode it to the Altamira Station. He then walked north and crossed the very busy Avenida Boyaca to find himself at the beginning of the trail to **Picos Occidental and Oriental** just below Sabas Nieve. Best to cross under the autopista at the north end of Avenida 2. Once on the trail, it was an easy but steep walk up to the ridge crest (Fila Maestra) between Picos Occidental and Oriental. He then turned east and ascended Oriental, which took just over 2 hours from the trailhead.

From Pico Oriental, he ridge-walked east and ended up at the summit of **Pico Naiguata** at 2765 meters, the highest point in **Avila** and the entire range. He ate lunch there, then backtracked a ways, and headed down the mountain on the trail to the Galindo entrance point. That trail was a little overgrown in places, but you can't get lost. He then walked the streets to the Petare Metro Station. His walk-time from trailhead to trailhead was just over 8 hours, while the total time walking from metro station to metro station was 9 3/4 hours.

The trails in these mountains are all well-used especially on weekends. With map in hand it's hard to get lost. Along the main ridge, the Fila Maestra, there are small campsites in many locations, but with garbage scattered everywhere. There is no water on the ridge, but canyon streams seem to flow year-round, as shown. There should be drinking water at all the little park entrance gates; fill your bottle(s) there. Hiking up the Quebrada Tocome should give you a good look at the tropical rainforest with bigger trees, whereas the ridges are usually just covered with brush. Hike up wearing T shirt & shorts, but it's much cooler on the high ridges, so take a jacket. The best part of hiking El Avila is the view of the city far below, especially at night. The dry

One of the peaks along the crest of the Cordillera de la Costa in the Avila National Park.

Map 515-1, Naiguata, Avila, Cord. de la Costa, Venezuela

season is from December through April.

Maps *Parque Nacional El Avila,* (no scale given), from the Parque del Este Office, Caracas; any *good city and metro map*; and the travel guidebook **Venezuela**, Lonely Planet; and/or **South American Handbook**, Footprint Handbooks.

Roraima Tepuy, Sierra Pacaraima, Venezuela

The mountain featured here is called Roraima Tepuy at about 2810 meters. It's located where the borders of Guyana, Brazil and Venezuela meet, but the only way to the top is from the Venezuelan side. The name *tepuy* is a local Indian name meaning *mesa*. Extending northwest from Roraima is a row of tepuys which are flat-topped sandstone mesas. This scene remotely resembles Monument Valley in Utah & Arizona, USA, but is green, not red.

To get there, take a day or night bus from Caracas to Cuidad Bolivar (9-10 hours), then another day or night bus going past Cuidad Guyana toward Santa Elena near the Brazilian border. It's a paved highway all the way into Brazil, but get off the bus at San Francisco de Yuruani, a ride of about 12 hours from Ciudad Bolivar. Or if you're in a hurry you can fly to Santa Elena, then take a bus north. From San Francisco, you can find a ride in a taxi (usually 4WD) going to the only town on the way to **Roraima** called Paraitepuy. To that village, it's generally good road. To rent an entire vehicle cost about US$50 in 1993, but paying for one seat colectivo-style was only US$12. Or you can walk from just south of San Francisco (Km 251) to Paraitepuy along the road. It's 22 kms to Paraitepuy, and another 22 (44 kms total) to the base of Roraima. As you ride or walk, you can see Roraima in front of you for most of the way across the Gran Sabana, which is a dry grassland or savannah hemmed in by a ring of tepuys. This whole valley is in the middle of the rainforest.

An old vehicle track runs from Paraitepuy to the base of **Roraima**, but it's washed out in places so now everybody walks or hires mules. Paraitepuy has 2 small stores selling cookies, crackers, sardines, rice, & sugar. From the school, walk the old track around the hill to the southeast and down across a valley to a little stream (Scott Patterson of Salt Lake City, Utah, USA, says as of the late 1990's, villagers at Paraitepuy had set up a gate & checkpoint just after the village and now requires everyone to hire a guide (If you're persistent you can likely walk around this problem). The *guardia nacional* may have a hand in this as well. Just beyond the creek, use a short-cut trail on the left to save 3-4 kms of road-walking. Further along, use another shortcut going to the campsite & good water at 1350 meters. There are other established campsites at Rio Tex and Rio Kukenan.

From the Rio Kukenan Campsite, follow the very good trail up the slope to meet the old 4WD track again. At 1450 meters, the vehicle track ends at a campsite. Further up is Campamento La Base with good water. From there the trail climbs to the left and runs up along a natural ramp or dugway to the top of the tepuy. All the way to Roraima it's usually sunny and almost a desert in places, but on top it's always misty, wet and cloudy. Take a good waterproof tent if you intend to camp on top. Also, have a **compass** and don't wonder too far on top or you'll get lost for sure in the boulders, mist and clouds. This is likely one reason why locals insist on *tourists* taking a guide (?).

From the Rio Tex Campsite at 1175 meters, there's also some kind of trail heading north & northeast to the top of Kukenan Tepuy. There's a steep gully to the top on the left or west of the waterfall. See map.

Starting 2/7/1993, the author walked all the way to Rio Kukenan the first day, then climbed Roraima and returned to the campsite at Rio El Guia at 1350 meters on Day 2. On Day 3, he walked back to San Francisco. Total walk-time for the 88 kms was about 24 hours in 2 1/2 days. Most people hire out local guides (there are several) who have 4WD's; then ride to Paraitepuy and do it in 3 easy days from there. The dry season is from January through March. Best to

East of Paraitepuy looking at Roraima straight ahead, with Kukenan Tepuy on the left.

Map 516-1, Roraima Tepuy, Sierra Pacaraima, Venezuela

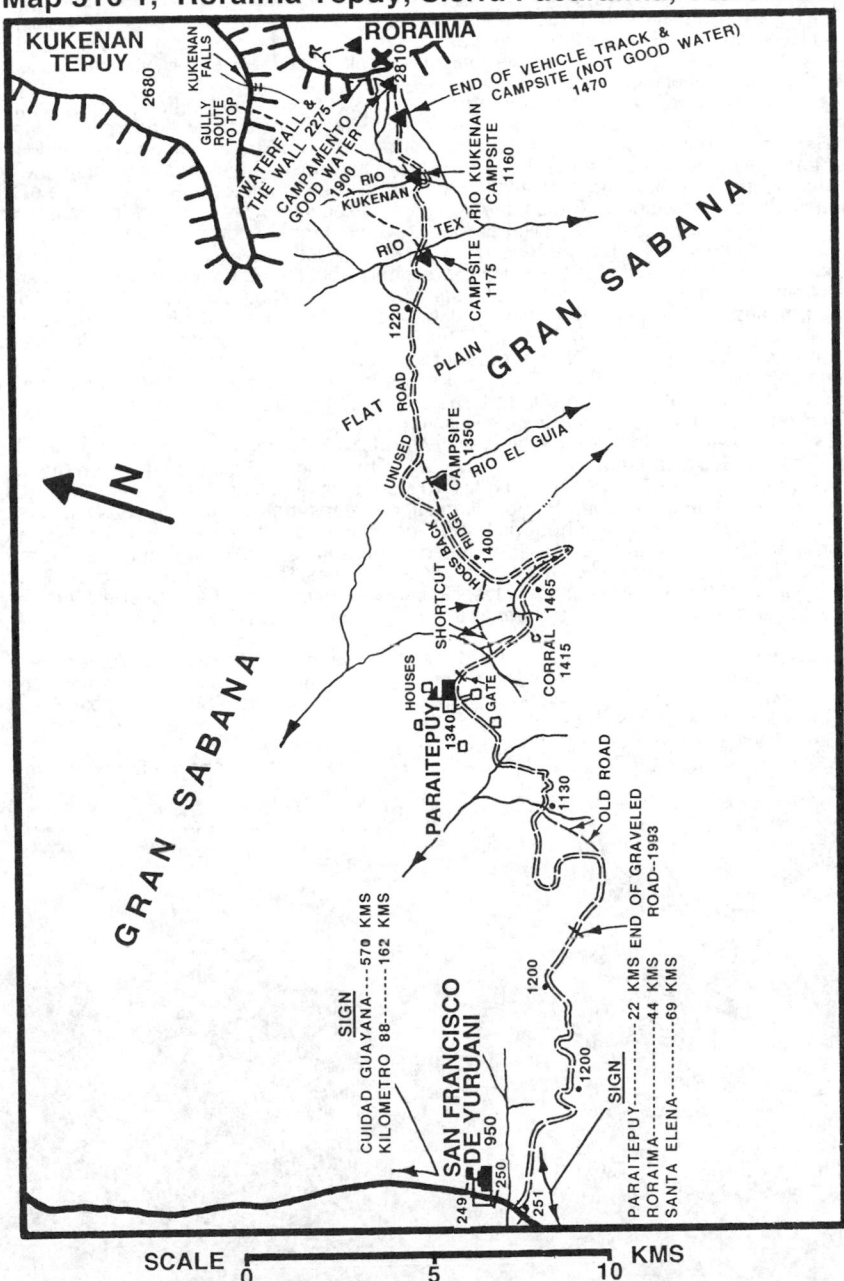

buy your food in Ciudad Bolivar, but San Francisco has several small shops with basic foods, plus several small rat & cockroach-infested hotels. Or camp at the *futbol field* just south of town; or carry water and camp outside of town.

Maps No good large scale maps available in 1993; look for the TPC map *L-27B,* 1:500,000; and the travel guidebooks, **Venezuela**, Lonely Planet; or **Venezuela** and/or **South American Handbook**, from Footprint Handbooks.

Pico Bolivar, Sierra Nevada de Merida, Venezuela

The highest mountain in Venezuela is Pico Bolivar at 5007 meters. It's located just southeast of the highland resort city of Merida in western Venezuela. Bolivar is the only summit in Venezuela over 5000 meters. All the higher peaks in this compact massif called the Sierra Nevada de Merida are made of granite or other metamorphics.

Here's what the author did beginning on 5/27/1972. He and 2 other climbers, one an American named Jerry Keaton, got on the teleferico which runs from Merida to the summit of **Pico Espejo** at 4765 meters. It was somehow a free ride (?). The afternoon was spent in the upper terminal because of never ending snow showers. That night, everyone slept on the floor of the upper station. Next morning all 3 headed up a steep couloir on the south face of **Pico Bolivar** in the clouds & snow. Carlos, the Venezuelan knew the way. Ice ax & crampons were used because of new snow. One climber was slow and it took 2 hours up, 4 1/2 hours round-trip. In normal conditions in the dry season it will likely take less time.

After that climb everyone rode down in the teleferico, but the author got off at the 3rd station called Loma Redonda at 4045 meters and camped nearby. Next day, he climbed **El Toro & Pico Leon**, and another peak in between. All were snow-free. He had intended to go down to the pueblo Los Nevados, but sore feet ended that. On Day 4 he walked down the trail to Merida.

The teleferico broke a cable in the upper section in 11/1991, and since then has been running only up to Loma Redonda Station. However, there's a good trail all the way up from Merida to the 3rd station and on up to Espejo from there. Taking the lift doesn't help the acclimatization process, so smart climbers walk up.

The author returned in 1993. He arrived in Merida at 7:30am on a night bus from Caracas on 2/12/1993. Extra baggage was left in a hotel on the promise he'd stay there on his return. He then bought food for 3 days and made his way to the national park office called INPARQUE, which is located near the airport. He got information & maps there, then at the bus station got a minibus to Tabay. From there he took a 4WD colectivo up to the entry post for the parque nacional and paid a small fee. He then hiked to Laguna La Coromoto in 2 1/2 hours and camped. Next morning he walked to Laguna Verde, then east to Pico Espejo and down to Loma Redonda in 8 1/4 hours. He ended up sleeping in a little lunch room that was open. On Day 3, he walked down a good trail to the lower terminal in 5 hours. Total 3 day walk-time was 15 3/4 hours.

The author's 1993 trip was primarily to the Caribbean, so he had only tropical clothes, running shoes and no ice ax. He made no attempt to climb Humboldt or Bonplano, both of which look easy. The 2 refugios along his hike are in poor condition, but the Espejo Station is open to *andinistas*, apparently free (?). Keep it clean! Also, the route from Espejo to the summit of Bolivar is now marked with painted rocks and very easy to follow.

Do all your shopping in Merida which has lots of hotels. The dry season is from December

From the summit of Torre looking east at Pico Bolivar.

Map 517-1, Pico Bolivar, S. Nevada de Merida, Venezuela

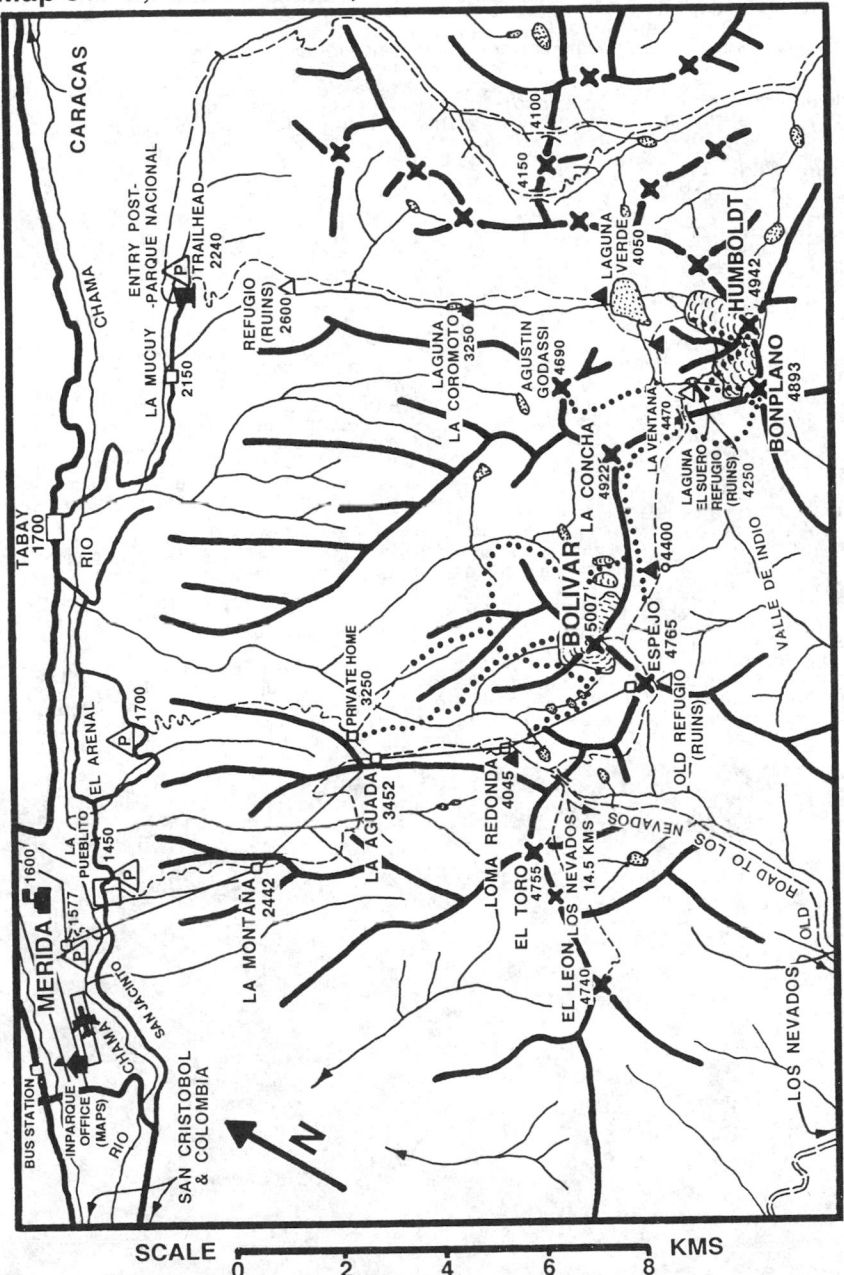

SCALE

0   2   4   6   8   KMS

through March or April. There are many buses going to Merida from San Cristobal or Caracas.
Maps *Parque Nacional "Sierra Nevada",* 1:50,000, buy in Merida national park office; and travel guidebooks, **Venezuela**, Lonely Planet; or **South American Handbook** or **Venezuela**, both from Footprint Handbooks.

Colon & Bolivar, Sierra Nevada de Santa Marta, Colombia

The highest mountain in Colombia is Pico Colon, 5778 meters, followed closely by Bolivar at 5776. These peaks are in the Sierra Nevada de Santa Marta, which rise directly from the Caribbean coast. The central part of these mountains are made of granite.

The normal staging point before climbing is the small city of Valledupar, which is just southeast of the range. One route involves taking a 4WD colectivo or shared taxi from near Valledupar's main market, 55 kms to Pueblo Bello (many shops and 3 hotels), which is on the south side of the mountains. From there you can hire another 4WD for the journey to Nabusimake (formerly San Sabastian); or you can walk this last 25 kms in 6-7 hours. At Nabusimake, you must get a permit to go further from the director of the village, which cost US$10 in 1993. From there take one of several trails to Duriameina, Mamancanaca, then over a 3rd pass to Lago Naboba. The author tried this route between 5/6 & 5/9/1972, but didn't have a map and had no idea where he was! Plus, he couldn't see the route in the clouds & rain! He also spent one night in Nabusimake just prior to the his 2nd trip discussed below.

For years the *normal* way to **Colon** was to take a small bus from near the main market in Valledupar to the town of Atanquez (many shops and one hotel) 44 kms to the northwest. From there look for a 4WD going to Chemesquemena (one good store); or walk the 7 kms. From there cross the bridge west of town and continue northwest on an old road as shown. Later, turn left uphill onto a very good trail which runs horizontally across the southeast face of Cerro Gueirua. There's some running water along this face. Later you'll drop down to a small store at 1380 meters. From there, continue up the Rio Donechui. The village of Donechui has a store, school and small infirmary. Above that is Sogrome with a store & school. All the stores in this valley have things like oatmeal, sugar, cookies, sardinas and matches, but they're not open all the time as the owners are often working in fields, or tending livestock higher in the valley.

Above Sogrome is a meadow and campsite called Secaracunge at 2000 meters. Above that you'll cross the river twice on good bridges. Above the treeline in the upper valley are many shepherd huts and cattle, sheep & goats. You'll go over one pass at about 4250 meters, then on to Lago Naboba. From there route-find north to the col between Picos Bolivar & Colon. Colon is supposed to be an easier climb; **Bolivar** more difficult.

Buy all supplies in Valledupar, but basic foods can be bought along the way. Before going, get permission from the Indians (Indios) at their headquarters called Casa Indigena in the north part of Valledupar. The tourist office in the Casa de Acultura can help--maybe (?) Count on at least 2 long days, maybe 3 to a base camp, and at least a week round-trip from Atanquez. In 1993, the author got to the pass at 4250 meters and returned to Atanquez. That hike took 3 days beginning 2/20/1993 and 25 hours total walk-time. He was on a tropical Caribbean trip and wasn't ready for cold weather camping or climbing.

Dry season is from late December through March. Better take an ice ax & crampons, but they may not be needed. If you can't get permission on one route, try the other. Lots of politics involved with these Indios, and apparently drug trafficers too (?). Check with your national alpine club or Colombian Embassy to see if permission is being given before leaving home. Last report from 1997 stated the Donechui route was closed, but the way through Nabusimake was

An Indian hut along the Rio Donechui Trail just above Bete, looking at Peak 5297.

Map 518-1, Colon-Bolivar, S. N. de Santa Marta, Colombia

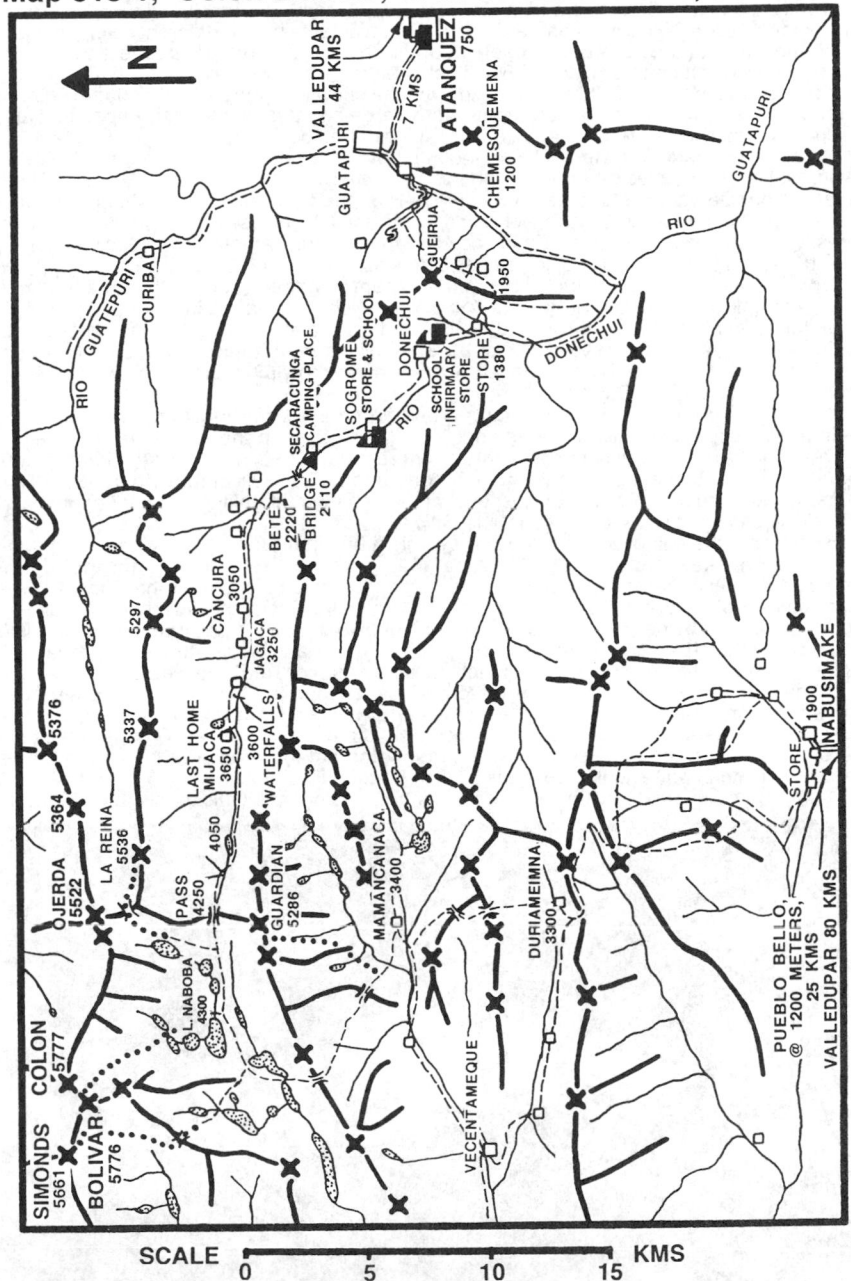

SCALE

0   5   10   15   KMS

open and apparently the only way to the high picos.

Maps   IGN maps *19, 20, 26 & 27*, 1:100,000, from the Instituto Geografico Augustin Codazzi, located in the tallest building in Valledupar; and travel guidebook, **Colombia**, from Lonely Planet and/or Footprint Handbooks; or **South American Handbook**, also from Footprint Handbooks.

Ritacuba Blanco, Sierra Nevada del Cocuy, Colombia

Located in eastern Colombia and in the Cordillera Oriental, is a small and compact mountain range known as the Sierra Nevada del Cocuy. These mountains are different from many others in Colombia in that they are not volcanic in origin; but consist of various metamorphics and granite. The highest peak is Ritacuba Blanco at 5493 meters.

The higher summits are all snow capped, with the snow line generally at about 4700 or 4800 meters. Glaciers are not large, but some fairly large crevasses do exist, especially around Ritacuba Blanco and to the south around Concavo and Pan de Azucar.

Most people reach this area via Bogota by night bus, generally a 14 hour ride. There are now (2000) about 6 buses per/day making this run, most via Le Cocuy, then Guican. The best place to organize your trip and begin walking is from the town of Guican, which is where bus service ends--or begins. In Guican, you'll find 3 or 4 small hotels, several restaurants and many stores, where all food needed for climbing can be found. You can also hire 4WD's to get closer to the peaks. El Cocuy has a couple of small hotels as well.

With Guican as a base, you can approach either the northern or southern sections of the range. From Guican walk uphill on Calle 6 to a trail which eventually joins the road just above a small country school. About 200 meters beyond that, another trail begins on the left and continues northeast to the area of **Ritacuba Blanco** and the Laguna Grande de Las Verdes. Scott Patterson of Salt Lake City, Utah, USA, says there's now a refugio on the way to Ritacuba Blanco. Ask about this in Guican.

You may also continue to following the road and make your way to the now-abandoned Hacienda La Esperanza at the road's end. See Map. Or take the short-cut trail direct from Guican. This is the best way to reach the southern portion of Cocuy. For trekkers, a popular week-long trip is to walk southeast from Guican and cross over the divide south of Pan de Azucar, head north past many lakes just east of the snowy crest until you reach Laguna Grande de Las Verdes, then walk southwest back to Guican.

Here's what the author did. He took an overnight bus from Bogota to Guican which took 15 hours. He checked into the Hotel Tourista and spent the day preparing for the trip. Next morning, 8/25/1980, he left Guican early and walked to a base camp near the little lake west of **Ritacuba Negro's** glacier. That took 5 1/4 hours. He set up camp, then climbed Ritacuba Norte and a second nearby peak in the clouds and rain showers; all in 4 1/4 hours. Next morning he climbed to within 100 vertical meters of Ritacuba Blanco and had to turn back because of a blizzard. There are some crevasses on that glacier so go prepared! He was back at camp after 3 1/2 hours, then packed up and walked to and just beyond the Hacienda La Esperanza and camped; 5 hours. On Day 3, he hiked in the rain up to Laguna Grande and back in 2 hours, then because of the weather, headed back to Guican (4 hours). Total 3 day walk-time was about 24 hours. This was in the middle of the wet season and not the best time to climb the highest peaks. That afternoon he took a 5pm bus back to Bogota.

A small party of strong climbers (or solo climber) could leave Guican, climb in the northern

From what is marked Ritacuba Norte looking south toward Ritacuba Negro.

Map 519-1, Ritacuba Blanco, Sierra Nev. del Cocuy, Colombia

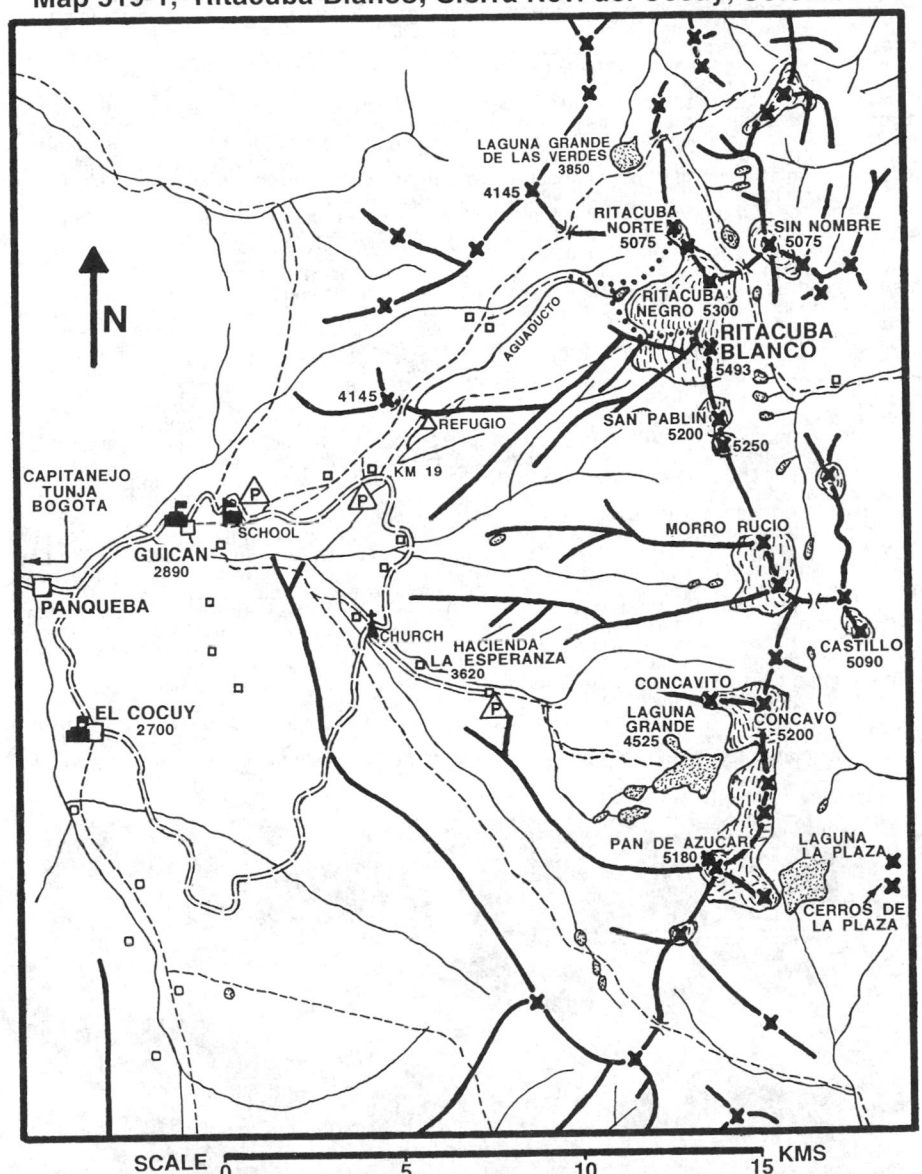

SCALE 0 ___ 5 ___ 10 ___ 15 KMS

sections, then walk and climb south along the western edge of the glaciers to the last high peak in the south, **Pan de Azucar**, then return to Guican, all in about one week's time. From what the author could see--which wasn't much--these peaks aren't as rugged or difficult to climb as say the Cordillera Blanco in Peru. The dry months are December through March. Take ice ax & crampons for safe climbing.

Maps Instituto Geografico Agustin Codazzi maps *planchas (sheets) 137 & 153,* 1:100,000, Bogota; and travel guidebooks, **Colombia** from Lonely Planet and/or Footprint Handbooks; or the **South American Handbook**.

Ruiz, Santa Isabel & Tolima, Cordillera Central, Colombia

Near the middle of Colombia and in the Cordillera Central, is a group of volcanic peaks, some of which are high enough to be capped with small glaciers. The highest is Nevado El Ruiz at about 5335 meters, followed closely by Tolima at 5215, and Santa Isabel at about 5100 meters. These mountains are south and east of Manizales and north of Ibague.

The last major eruption of Ruiz began on 9/11/1985 with moderate phreatic explosions. Then on 11/13/1985, a larger explosive eruption melted part of the summit ice cap and produced pyroclastic flows and surges . This resulted in a major mud flow down the east slope wiping out the city of Armero and killed 23,000 people. Only 3 other historic eruptions have killed more; Tambora in 1815 (92,000), Krakatau in 1883 (36,000), and Pelee in 1902 (28,000). Intermittent minor ash emissions with occasional phreato-magmatic eruptions continued until 7/1991. For updated volcano information see the website (www.volcano.si.edu/gvp/).

Tolima has had 5 eruptions during colonial times, the last being in 3/1943. Santa Isabel is also considered an active volcano having had lava flows in about 2800 BC.

Here's what the author did beginning on Sunday, 8/17/1980. He left Manizales at 9am on a tourist bus going to what was El Refugio on the west side of **Ruiz**, a distance of 51 kms. He left his pack at the refugio and hurried up Ruiz on a sunny day in one hour; coming down took 23 minutes. He then started walking south along the road going to Laguna Otun and met American Peace Corps worker Glenn Galloway who had just attempted Tolima. He camped west of El Cisne. On Day 2 he walked to a campsite between 2 lava flows with rain much of the way. Day 3 he climbed over 2 passes in rain & snow and camped west of Tolima. Day 4 he climbed up a northwest ridge of Tolima but when he came to crevasses very near the summit, he turned back because of no visibility and snow. That afternoon in heavy rain, he descended to the road at El Silencio and camped nearby. On Day 5 he walked for 1 1/4 hours to Juntas and got a ride on a milk truck to Ibague. Total walk-time was roughly 29 hours, much of it in rain or snow and low visibility. For better results, try it in the dry season, December through March!

The route of the long trek the author took is easy to find with the exception of the area between Laguna de Otun, across the 2 lava flows and over 2 passes marked 4410 & 4205 meters. A good map and compass are standard equipment.

Scott Patterson of Salt Lake City, Utah, updates the author's information from 1998. You'll now have to hitch hike or hire a 4WD in Manizales to reach Refugio Arenales and/or the new refugio at 4800 (about US$10 per/person with 4 other passengers). However, this new refugio is more of a coffee shop with apparently no rooms. Parque Nacional entry fee is US$10. The road is blocked off south of Ruiz, but you can still walk it. Climb **Santa Isabel** in 2-3 days walking from the new refugio. For **Tolima**, take a mini bus from Ibague to Juntas (at least one hotel & shops), then hitch hike on a milk truck or hire a taxi from there to El Silencio. Then walk to El Ranch Hot Springs (where there's a small refugio and a little food available), then hike up a trail to the campsites of Las Cuevas or Las Latas, where you should find water. There are no glaciers, but some high snow going to summit. Easy climb, but take ice ax & crampons.

Generally speaking, the snowline here is down to about 4700 or 4800 meters. Besides Ruiz & Tolima, Nevado Santa Isabel has a large enough glacier to require an ice ax & crampons.

Ruiz is in the process of rebuilding a new glacier but it still should be an easy climb via the

This was the former refugio on the west side of Ruiz in 1980. It's now gone, as is the icefield beyond. Today there's a new refugio nearby; see the next page.

Map 520-1, Ruiz, Santa Isabel & Tolima, Cord. Central, Colombia

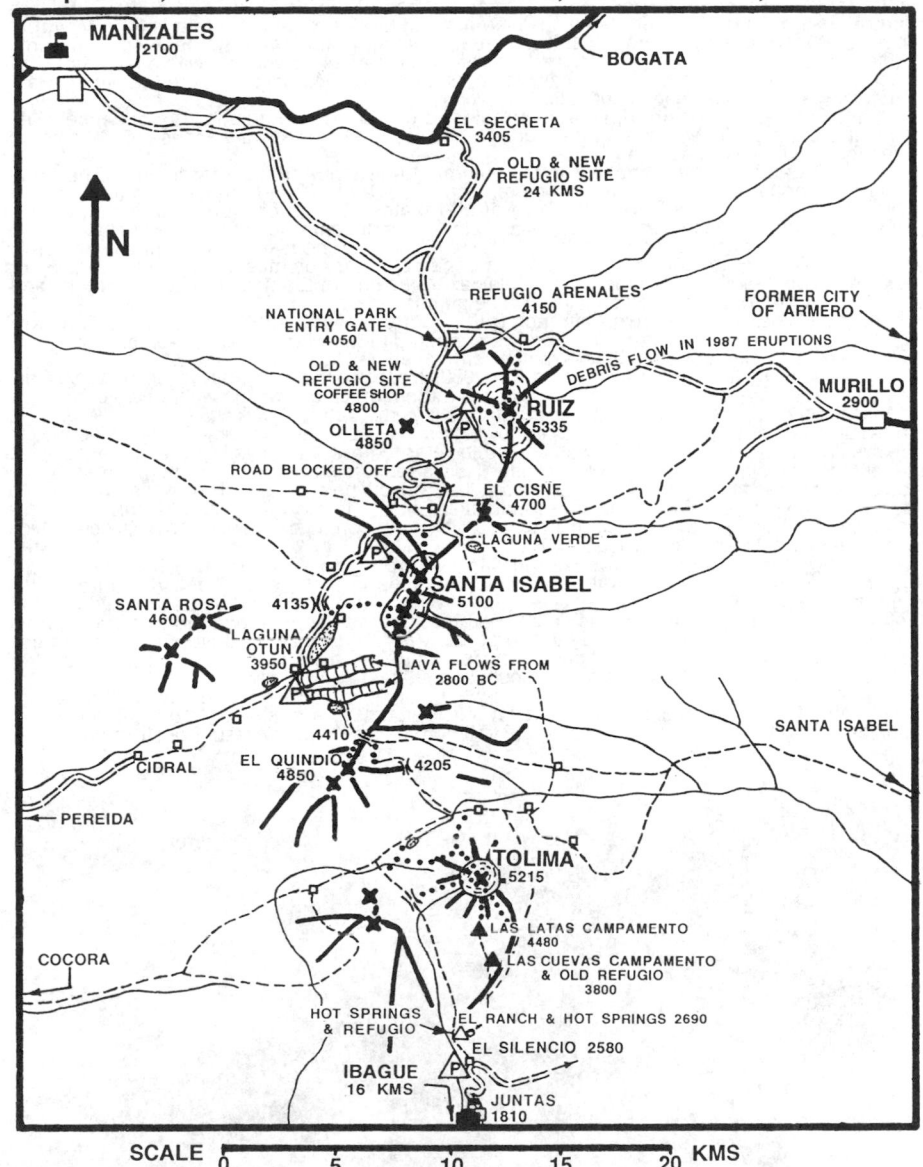

SCALE 0 ___ 5 ___ 10 ___ 15 ___ 20 KMS

west face. **El Cisne** is a walkup along the north ridge, which seldom has snow. Santa Isabel can be climbed from the north or westerly routes as well as from Laguna de Otun. **El Quindio** is generally climbed from the pass marked 4410 meters on the map.

In times of better weather, it's possible for a strong and determined climber, to do a trip similar to that of the author's, but climbing all the 5 major summits along the way in about one week or little more. The route from north to south is recommended. Or perhaps do Tolima on a separate trip. Buy supplies in Manizales, Ibague or Juntas.

Maps IGN maps *planchas (sheets) 206, 225, 244*, 1:100,000, buy from the Instituto Geografico Agustin Codazzi, Bogota, Manizales or Ibague; and travel guidebooks, **Colombia**, from Lonely Planet and/or Footprint Handbooks; or **South American Handbook**.

1105

Pico Mayor, Nevado Huila, Cordillera Central, Colombia

Located in the southwestern part of Colombia and at the southern end of the Cordillera Central, is the Sierra Nevado de Huila. The highest peak on the mountain is Pico Mayor at about 5750 meters--other maps list it as 5365. This mountain is at the center of a triangle formed by the cities of Popayan, Cali and Neiva. Huila is an older volcano with a fair amount of erosion and an ice cap, but even with all the apparent erosion it's still considered active. It's last eruption was an explosion in about 1555.

Huila is one of the more difficult mountains to get to in Colombia, partly because of its remoteness and partly because all the maps of the area are blanked-out because of cloud cover when the aerial fotos were taken.

Also, the author did not make it to the summit, largely due to misinformation. The route described and shown on the map is a composite of the author's personal information, that of Colombian climber Luis Fernando Toro of Manizales and other locals, and the Institute Geografico maps. The location of the trail and elevations of campsites are approximate.

Getting to the base of **Huila** is relatively easy. Buses can be taken from Popayan or Neiva, to the town of La Plata south of the mountain. Then another bus must be taken to the town of Belalcazar, sometimes known as Paez. Belalcazar has one or 2 small pensions or hotels, and many stores where all food and supplies can be purchased.

Beyond Belalcazar, there's not much traffic, but usually 2 small buses run to Toez and sometimes to Irlanda each day. You'll likely be required to walk from Toez, at approximately Km 20. The actual trail is supposed to begin near Km 44, at the Hacienda Verdun.

Here's what the author did beginning on 8/11/1980. He took a bus from Popayan to Belalcazar, but couldn't find the pensions or hotels. Ended up in a room of a local church where he stored some baggage. He bought food for 4 days and early the next morning started walking. No traffic all day! He ended up walking to a point somewhere just beyond Km 44. Long day, and no one was in the area to talk to where he camped There was a sizable river to cross (this was the rainy season), so discouraged, he started back the next morning. He walked to a point 3 kms south of Toez and got a ride out. The weather had been fairly good along the road, but he never saw the mountain and had no idea where he was, except for scattered km markers along the way. Toez and Irlanda both had a couple of small stores, but no hotels in 1980. In 6/19994, an earthquake caused an avalanche which partially destroyed Irlanda killing about 100 people.

At Km 42 there's some kind of building belonging to INDERENA, the government organization protecting national parks in which Huila is included. From Verdun a trail is supposed to go up through the rainforest in the direction of the first campsite known as the Polish Camp. This campamento is on the Paramo, or grasslands above the treeline, so from there you can usually find the way to the peaks with little difficulty-assuming you can see anything. Try sunrise! The normal base camp is Camp Piedras, on the northwest side of the ice cap, or another even higher place further south at 4600 meters.

From Toez, where your walk will undoubtedly begin, it could take 5 or 6 days for the round-trip climb. If you're with a group, hire a 4WD in Belalcazar and save lots of walking. Also, consider hiring some local to get you on the trail up through the rainforest. For Huila and for all

Substituting for Huila is this foto of the new refugio on the west side of Ruiz; see previous page (Sam Palsmeier foto).

Map 521-1, Mayor, Nevado Huila, Cordillera Central, Colombia

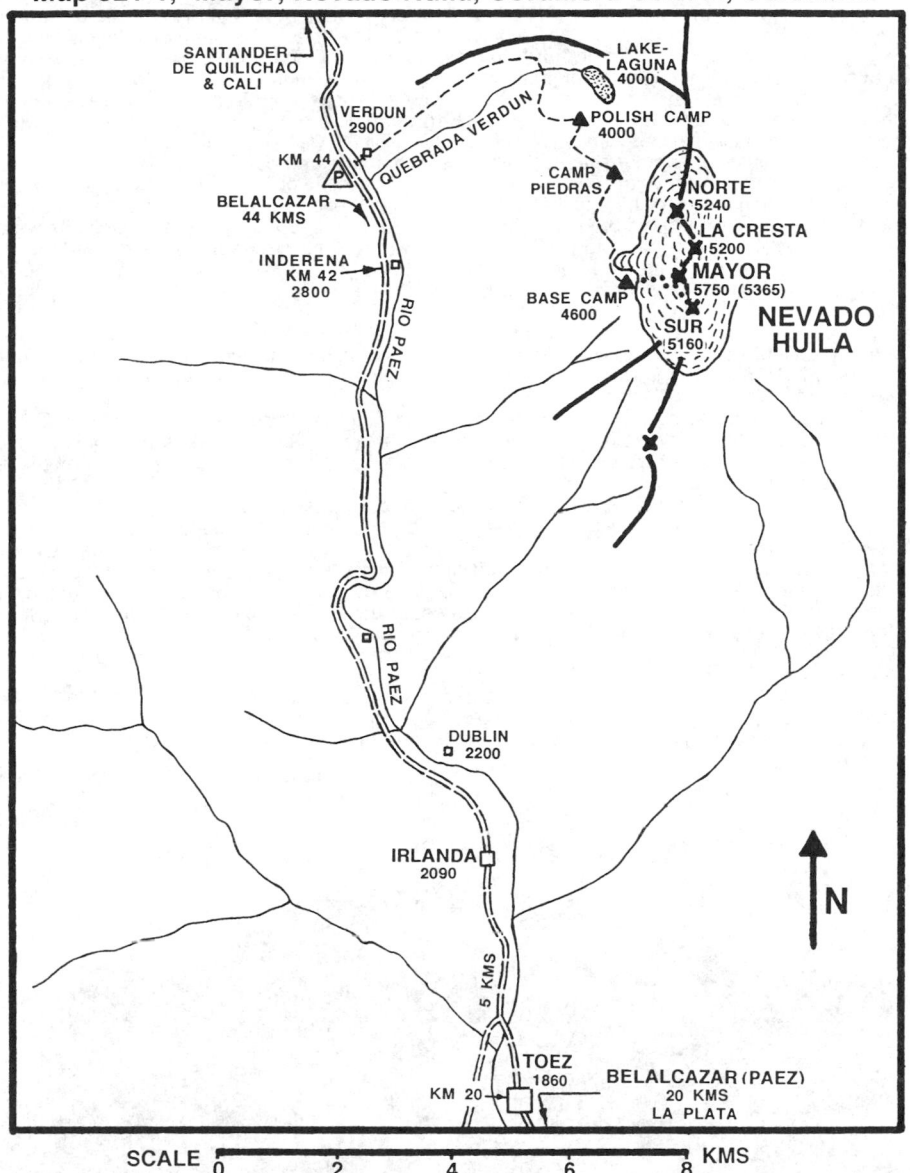

SCALE 0 2 4 6 8 KMS

the mountains of Colombia the best months for climbing are December through March. However, rain gear should always be part of your equipment, as well as ice ax & crampons. Everyone the author talked to about this mountain seemed to think it was difficult to climb, but none had actually climbed it. Anyone who has, and who wants to share information with the world, please contact the author.

Maps Maps are poor--half blanks and covered with clouds, but see *plancha (sheet) 321-IV-B & D,* 1:25,000, buy from the Instituto Geografico Agustin Codazzi in Bogota, Cali and perhaps Popayan (?); and the travel guidebook, **Colombia**, from Lonely Planet and/or Footprint Handbooks.

Volcan Purace, Cordillera Central, Colombia

In the southwest part of Colombia and in the extreme southern end of the Cordillera Central, are located a number of volcanos, some of which are still active. This band of volcanic activity extends from Sangay in Ecuador, north to Nevado Ruiz in Central Colombia. In this section between Pasto and Popayan, the highest and best known mountain is Volcan Purace, reaching a height of 4756 meters. To the southeast is Pan de Azucar at 4670 meters. Purace has no permanent snow or ice, but for some reason Pan de Azucar does. Purace is located directly east of the tourist city of Popayan, and on clear days is highly visible from the city center.

Purace consists of an andesitic stratovolcano with a 500-meter-wide summit crater that was constructed over a shield volcano. Purace is the most-northerly of 7 cones and craters, with Los Coconucos sitting between the 2 higher volcanos on either end. Purace has had 24 eruptions in the 1800's & 1900's, with the biggest being in 1849, 1869 & 1885. The last 2 explosions were 3/19 & 3/25/1977. Both explosions sent ash downwind 7 kms. Because of its activity and its nearness to some population centers, Purace has become a popular parque nacional. About half of the national park is shown on this map. For updated volcano information see the website (www.volcano.si.edu/gvp/).

Getting to Pilimbala and the beginning of the trail to **Purace** is easy. From Popayan take one of many daily buses traveling east to the city of La Plata on the east side of the mountain. Ask the driver to stop at the intersection known as Cruz Mina at Km 23. From there you'll have to walk the 2 1/2 kms up to Pilimbala.

Pilimbala is not a village, but a small tourist resort, with hot springs feeding 7 sulfur baños or baths at 28°C. There are cabins, a hotel or hospedaja, picnic sites, a restaurant and a building housing national park personnel. For additional information about the hike, ask someone at the *officina parque nacional*.

The trail up the mountain begins behind the tourist office and used to be a little obscure for the first 400 or 500 meters as it winds its way up through some cow pastures and past one small farmhouse. As of 1980, hikers were required to climb over 4 or 5 fences before the 2-meter-wide trail was reached; no doubt the trail has been improved since. Just after the building marked 3760 meters, you'll come to a new road running up to a seismic station & several telecommunications antennas guarded by the military (as of 2001, Colombia is essentially a war zone). The **South American Handbook** reports that new road is mined at night, but the mines are removed during the day time (?). Inquire about this situation in Pilimbala before climbing. From the *estacion sismica* it's a good trail to the top of Purace.

Here's what the author did. He stayed one night in Popayan. Next morning, 8/15/1980, he bought maps and food, and at 2pm, took a bus going to La Plata, but got off at Cruz Mina. He walked to Pilimbala, filled water bottles, then walked for 30 minutes and camped in the rain.

From along the trail can be seen Volcan Purace straight ahead (Scott Patterson foto).

Map 522-1, Volcan Purace, Cordillera Central, Colombia

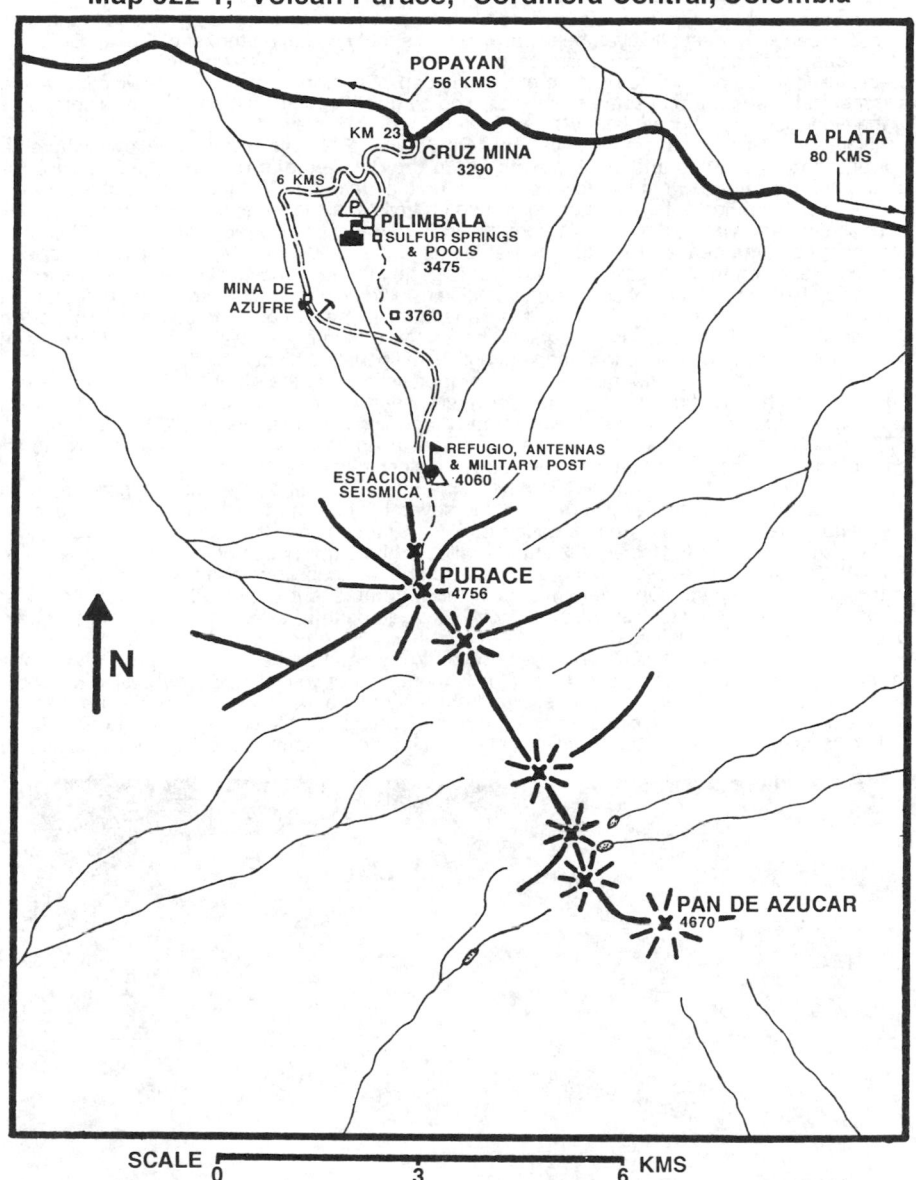

POPAYAN
56 KMS

LA PLATA
80 KMS

KM 23
CRUZ MINA
3290

6 KMS

P
PILIMBALA
SULFUR SPRINGS
& POOLS
3475

MINA DE
AZUFRE

3760

REFUGIO, ANTENNAS
& MILITARY POST
4060

ESTACION
SEISMICA

PURACE
4756

N

PAN DE AZUCAR
4670

SCALE
0   3   6   KMS

Next morning, he hid his big pack in tall grass and got to the top in 1 1/2 hours. It was a very cold day with wind & rain. He ran down to warm up and hitch hiked back to Popayan and took a night bus north.

With an early start, a fit hiker could climb this mountain in one day from Popayan. Or perhaps spend the night in Pilimbala. Buy all your food in Popayan.

Maps Simple map *Parque Nacional Purace*, (no scale given), from the Tourist Office, Popayan or at Pilimbala (maybe); and travel guidebook, **Colombia**, from Lonely Planet or Footprint Handbooks.

Cayambe Volcano, Cordillera Real, Ecuador

The third highest summit in Ecuador is Cayambe at 5840 meters. Cayambe is located 18 kms (25 road kms) east of Cayambe town, which is about 86 kms northeast of Quito. Because of its easterly position and nearness to the Amazon Basin, Cayambe receives heavy precipitation which has created a large glacier ice cap. Cayambe is a compound volcano with a symmetrical shape but with some erosion caused by glaciation. Its last eruption was sometime in the early Holocene, but no date has been determined for that event.

Here's what the author did on **Cayambe**. On 6/12/1972 he was in Cayambe town where he bought food for 4 days and started walking up the cobblestone road at 11am toward the mountain. He passed what is shown on maps as the Hacienda Monjas, but which everyone seems to call the Piemonte Alto; then continued up trails passing Indian huts & farms with small ditches diverting water to fields. At 2pm it rained and Indians invited him in for a while and offered green lima beans. He later camped somewhere near 3900 meters (his altimeter was stolen a week before in Colombia). Next morning, he left early and climbed 2 1/2 hours to the snowline, then through lots of crevasses to within 100 vertical meters of the summit, but turned back; it being too risky for a solo climber to continue. He made it down to camp in a round-trip time of 10 hours. Then it rained all night, 12 hours. Next morning, he walked about 2 hours and to within 3-4 kms of Cayambe town and got a lift. He spent that night in Quito.

There have been big changes since the author's climb. In the early 1980's, a refugio was built along with a road up to it. The author hasn't been there since, so only the approximate location of the road & refugio are shown on this map. The refugio at about 4660 meters, sleeps 37 in bunk beds. It has a kitchen, eating place, fireplace, electric lights and a radio for emergencies. It has a caretaker and cost US$10 a night in the late 1990's.

Make Cayambe town your pre-climb headquarters. It's right on the main highway running between Quito and Colombia. There you'll find several hotels and you can buy all your food for the climb. There's no public transportation from Cayambe town to the mountain, but you might get a lift in a pickup up to Hacienda Piemonte Alto; hire a taxi to that point. For the most part, it's a 4WD road from there on up, but vehicles can be found in Cayambe town which can take you right to the refugio. On weekends, you might be able to get a lift all the way. As a last resort, a tough climber can walk all the way from Cayambe town to the refugio in one long day; or 3 or 4 hours from the hacienda.

Cayambe is a one day climb from the refugio. You'll need an ice ax & crampons and a rope for each group. This is definitely not for solo climbers, unless you follow a new trail in the snow made by other climbers. The route shown is heavily crevassed, but finding a route through should be fairly easy. Unacclimatized climbers may want to stay a second night in the refugio before climbing. In nearby Quito, June & July are the 2 driest months, but Cayambe is similar to

The heavily crevassed upper west face of Cayambe.

Map 523-1, Cayambe Volcano, Cordillera Real, Ecuador

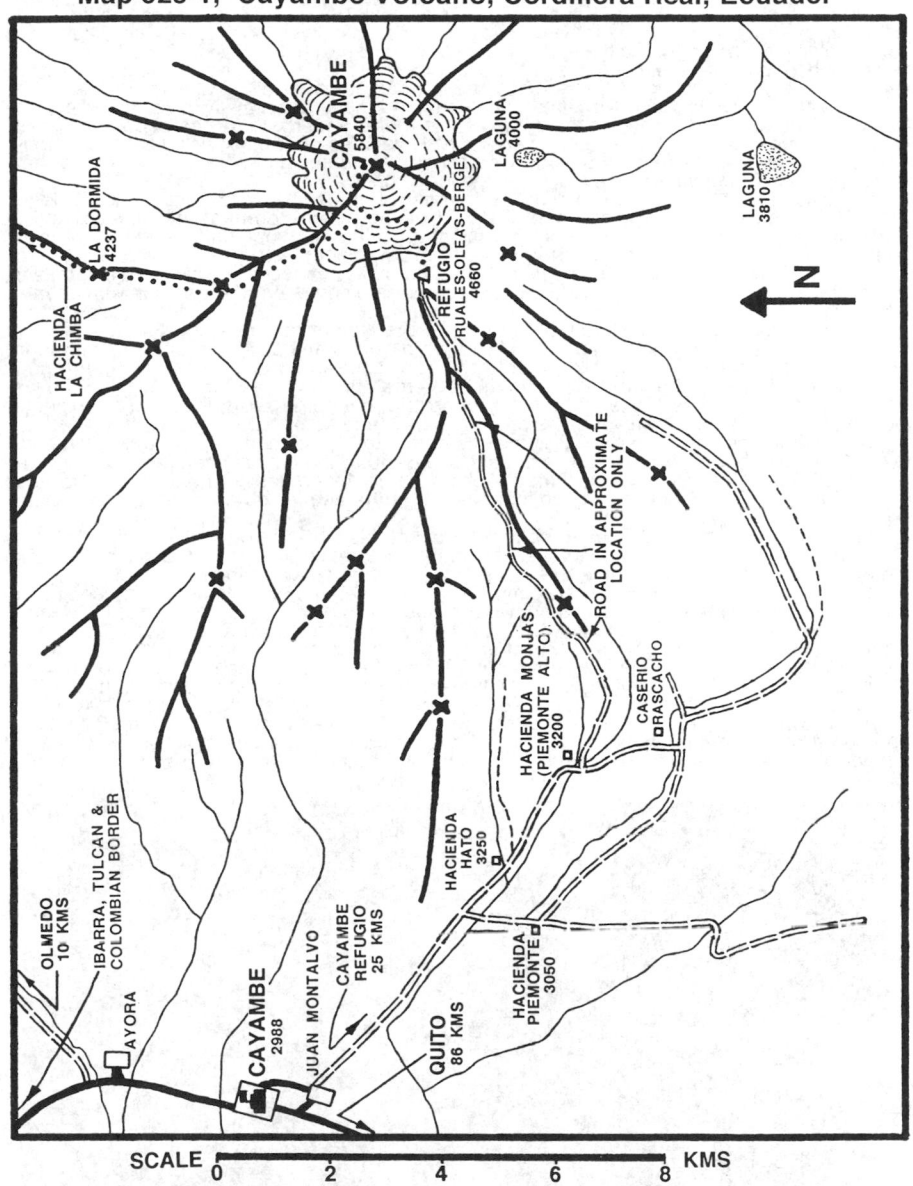

SCALE | 0   2   4   6   8 | KMS

other peaks in the Cordillera Real, in that June, July and August seem to be the wettest months
(?). However, go prepared for rain and/or snow whenever you go. Ecuador is a wet country!
Maps IGM maps *3994-11-SW & SE, 4094-111-SW, 4093-IV-NW, & 3993-1-NE & NW,*
1:25,000; or *Cayambe, 3994-11 & Nevado Cayambe, 4-94-111,* 1:50,000; and the books,
Climbing and Hiking in Ecuador, Bradt Enterprises; **South American Handbook**, or the better
Ecuador Handbook, both from Footprint Handbooks.

Antisana Volcano, Cordillera Real, Ecuador

The 4th highest mountain in Ecuador is Antisana at 5753 meters. Antisana is extensively glaciated and is said to have the largest icefield in the country. Antisana is a stratovolcano with a symmetrical shape but with a fair amount of erosion. Even with the erosion, it's still considered active. It had a questionable eruption in 1728, but then in 1801 & 1802 it had subglacier activity in the summit crater. During that time, it had one or more eruptions along with some lava.

There are 2 ways to reach **Antisana**. The usual, normal and best way is via Pintag and the Hacienda Antisana. But keep in mind this way is the normal route for the people living and working in Quito. But those using public transport, the northern or Papallacta is an option. One reader wrote saying he got lost so the northern route is for adventurers only! See author's experience below.

If you have a 4WD vehicle, you must get permission to use the road beyond the Hacienda Pinantura, located about 8 kms past Pintag. For the permit, contact the Associacion de Andinismo de Pinchincha or any other *club andino* in Quito. If you're on foot, public transport goes only as far as Pintag. Buses arrive there from Quito about every hour. Also, if you're on foot and plan to walk all the way to the mountain, a permit is not needed. This is old information, so check with the tourist office in Quito and they can locate someone who can help with updated information.

The road from Pintag is rough all the way to the Hacienda Antisana (34 kms) and the experiment station (3 1/2 kms more) at 4180 meters, but small pickup trucks make it alright. From the experiment station walk an old track northeast and make a base camp in one of several locations near the snowline at about 4600 meters. If you end up walking all the way from Pintag, the climb will take 4 or 5 days round-trip, but some short rides can be expected along the way. With your own vehicle, 2 or 3 days round-trip from Quito.

To reach the summit requires passing some large crevasses regardless of which route you take. One guidebook says to head southeast and climb to the col between the 2 peaks. The author tried this route solo, but was turned back on 5 different probes. Perhaps a safer route, at least for a solo climber, would be to go to the left or north, and make the final approach up the north face (?).

Another possible way for those using public transport is to get on one of several daily buses going from Quito to Papallacta (hydroelectric station) but get off at Luguna Papallacta and take the trail around the west end of the lake. The author camped there in the rain on 8/5/1980 after a 1 1/2 hour walk from Papallacta. Next morning he crossed the old lava on a little-used trail to a small lake, then with compass in hand headed due south in the fog & rain up mostly through tall ichu grass. It rained for most of the 7 1/4 hours it took to reach a camp at 4670 meters. Above 4300 meters walking was easy in short grass on near-level ground. On the west side of the peak there was a definite break in clouds & rain--much drier than north or south of the mountain. On Day 3, he went right up the west face with mostly fine weather, but with dark clouds north and south, and reached 5250 meters. There are lots of big crevasses on this mountain and not a good place for a solo climber! After 4 hours climbing round-trip, he packed up and walked 4 more hours before getting a lift in the back of a hacienda pickup. Later he got out about 6 kms before Pintag to camp for the night. Counting one more hour on Day 4, his total

There are lots of crevasses on the upper western face of Antisana.

Map 524-1, Antisana Volcano, Cordillera Real, Ecuador

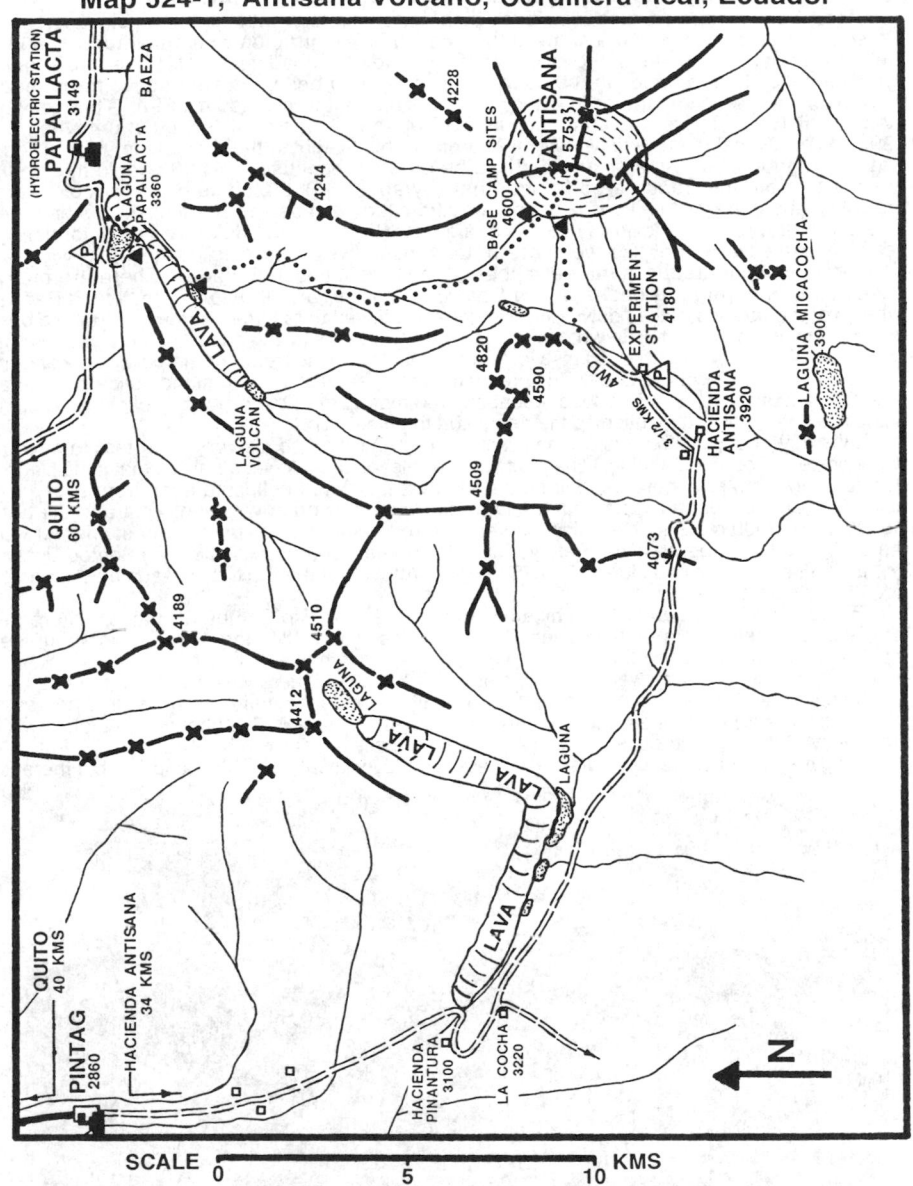

walk-time was about 17 3/4 hours for the trip. Ice ax, crampons and a rope are required for a safe ascent.

Both Pintag and Papallacta have a hotel or pension, and several small stores. Wettest months in the Cordillera Real seem to be June to August, so go in December through March.

Maps IGM maps *Pintag, Papallacta, La Cocha, Antisana, Lago Micacocha,* 1:25,000; or *Pintag,* 1:100,000; and books, **Climbing and Hiking In Ecuador,** Bradt Enterprises; and **Ecuador Handbook,** Footprint Handbooks.

Tungurahua Volcano, Cordillera Real, Ecuador

Of the 8 mountains in Ecuador included in this book, the one with the lowest elevation and the smallest amount of ice and snow at the summit is Tungurahua with an altitude of 5087 meters. Tungurahua is one of the most active volcanos in Ecuador. It's also one of the most symmetrically shaped cones in the country. Tungurahua has been very active throughout colonial times. Recently, the eruption in 1916 was one of the biggest at VEI-4. That activity lasted until 1925. There was some action in 1944, then it was relatively quiet until the late 1990's. The *Global Volcanism Network* first brought this to light in their reports in 9/99. There was an eruption on 10/5/1999, and perhaps before that, because ~25,000 people had been evacuated from the Baños area for months. By about 6/2000, some of the people were protesting about the military keeping them away from their homes and livestock; however there is real danger of pyroclastic flows heading straight for Baños. For updated volcano information see the website (www.geofisico.cybw.net/) in Spanish, or (www.volcano.si.edu/gvp/).

Getting to **Tungurahua** is the easiest of all the mountains in Ecuador. There are many buses each day running between Rio Bamba & Baños, and between Ambato & Baños. Whenever the volcano settles down and everyone is allowed to resume normal lives, take a bus to Baños, to find many hotels in what might be the taffy candy-making capital of the world! From the center of town, walk one or 2 kms west on the main highway to where the police checkpoint is located (in 1980 it was closed, but is presently used periodically). From the police control, a road veers southeast toward Pondoa, but about 100 meters from the highway look for a tall sign pointing out the trail and mentioning the refugio on the mountain.

Generally, the trail zig zags up the prominent north ridge, so it's very important to have a water bottle full when beginning. The relatively low elevation makes it a hot & exhausting climb. At about 2475 meters, there used to be a house whose owner collected a fee from everyone using the refugio. But a report from the late 1990's states you now pay the guard at the hut. Above about 2600 meters, the trail is marked with red paint on trees or fence posts right up to the shelter. Just at treeline is the Refugio Nicolas Martinez, or maybe it's now the Santos Ocaña (?), at 3835 meters. It can sleep 10 to 15 people. Above the hut the trail zigzags up the same ridge to the summit crater.

On 7/29/1980, the author hitch hiked with one ride from Rio Bamba to Baños. There he looked up the Residencia Anita and left some baggage, got a little more information about the mountain, bought more food, and started up. It took 4 1/4 hours to reach the refugio. Some poor altitude-sick Germans were just going down. At that time there was a stove in the hut, but maybe not today (?). Next morning was cloudy, but he made the summit anyway in 2 hours; 2 2/3 hours round-trip from the refugio. Then it was down to Baños in 2 1/3 hours. The total walk-time for the 2 days was about 9 1/2 hours. This is normally a 2 day climb.

Using the normal route, climbers can generally get by without ice ax & crampons, but there is

The summit of Tungurahua rises above the Refugio Nicolas Martinez at 3835 meters.

Map 525-1, Tungurahua Volcano, Cordillera Real, Ecuador

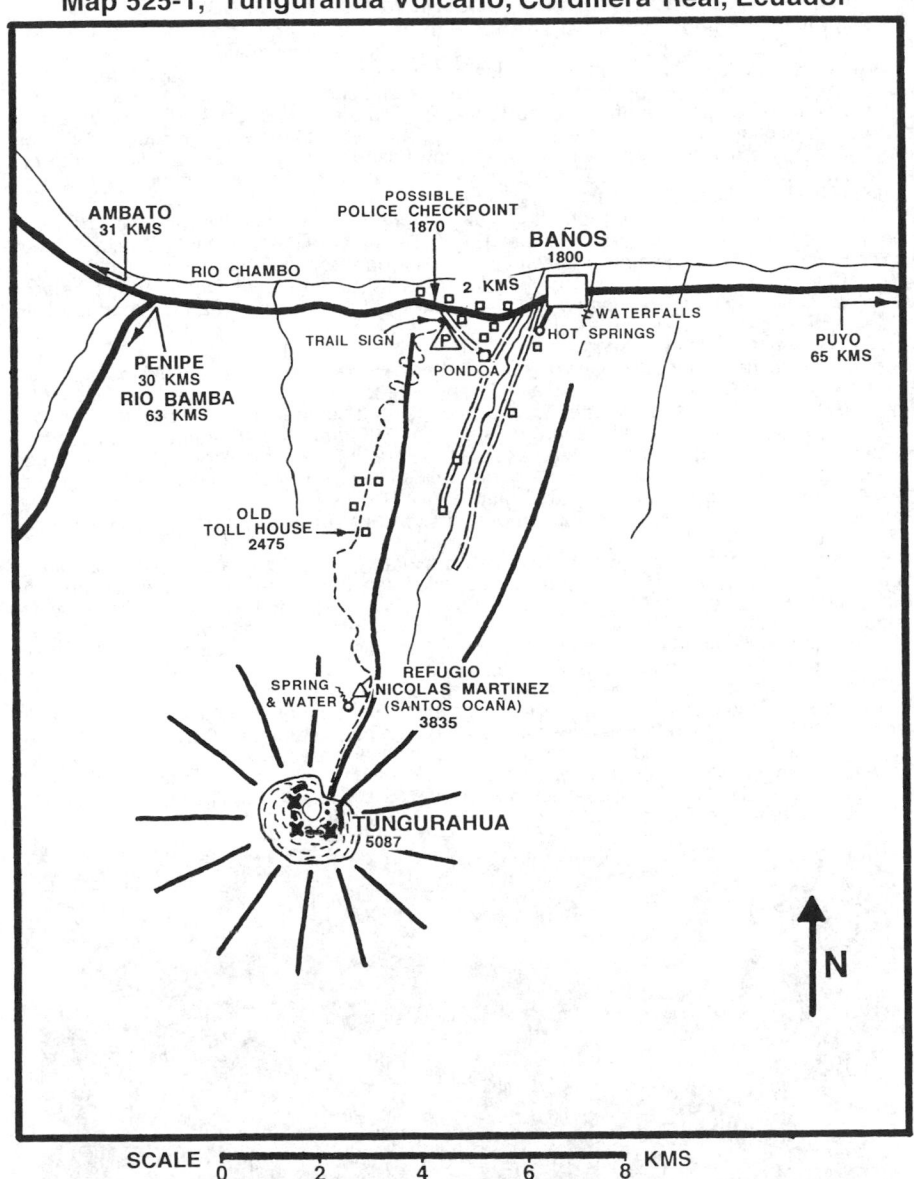

AMBATO
31 KMS

POSSIBLE
POLICE CHECKPOINT
1870

BAÑOS
1800

RIO CHAMBO

2 KMS

TRAIL SIGN

WATERFALLS

HOT SPRINGS

PUYO
65 KMS

PENIPE
30 KMS
RIO BAMBA
63 KMS

PONDOA

OLD
TOLL HOUSE
2475

SPRING
& WATER

REFUGIO
NICOLAS MARTINEZ
(SANTOS OCAÑA)
3835

TUNGURAHUA
5087

N

SCALE   0   2   4   6   8   KMS

a slope at the very summit where this equipment could come in handy for some people. June, July and August seem to have the most rain, with all other months about equal in the amount of precipitation. December through March might be the driest (?), but each year is different.

In the valley, the holiday resort town of Baños is a fine place to spend some time. Baños has many inexpensive hotels and thermal hot springs. Hopefully the volcano will spare the town and it will still be there when you arrive.

Maps IGM map *Volcan Tungurahua, 3989-IV,* 1:25,000; and the books, **Climbing and Hiking in Ecuador,** Bradt Enterprises; and the **South American Handbook** and/or **Ecuador Handbook,** both from Footprint Handbooks.

El Altar Volcano, Cordillera Real, Ecuador

If you were to choose the most spectacular, impressive and challenging mountain in Ecuador, it would have to be El Altar. The highest of many peaks around this old caldera rim is Obispo at 5465 meters (various other altitudes are sometimes given). Altar is the remains of an old volcano which blew its top some time in late Pleistocene (?). The book **Volcanos of the World** doesn't even list this one. Perhaps no one has attempted to date El Altar's last big blowout (?). Today, all that remains is the circular crater rim with the western section removed, and a lake by the name of Laguna Amarillo (Yellow Lake) inside. All areas above about 4700 meters are glaciated. The steepness of the walls makes this the most difficult climbing in Ecuador. Apparently Obispo wasn't climbed until 1963.

There are 2 main approach routes to **Altar**. The one the author used, and the one which seems to be the *ruta normal* is from Penipe. Get to Penipe by bus or hitching from either Baños or Rio Bamba. From Penipe, walk or with luck, get a ride (or inquire in Penipe about hiring a 4WD) 10 kms up to the pueblo of Candelaria. About 1 1/2 kms past Candelaria is Releche where you'll now find a green *parque nacional* building. El Altar is now part of a national park and you'll have to pay an entry fee there. From Releche, turn northeast for 1/2 a km to the hacienda. From there the trail begins.

Here's what the author did beginning on 7/25/1980. He left baggage in a hotel in Rio Bamba and got a morning bus to Penipe. He walked from there to Candelaria in 2 1/4 hours. He took a few fotos, bought a coke in the one shop, and continued southeast past Releche, then up a steep slope below the waterfalls and eventually to 3700 meters and camped--5 hours from Penipe. Next day he continued to the pass at 4150 meters, but was plagued by a sore knee. He hiked around that area without a pack, then decided climbing was a little on the risky side so he returned and camped at 3380 meters just above Releche. On Day 3, he walked back to Penipe for the Sunday *mercado* and got a bus/truck back to Rio Bamba. Three day walk-time was roughly 15-16 hours.

The trail the author walked was a well-used but muddy path. The only place it was hard to locate is where it runs through pastures about one km past the Hacienda Releche. Remember, it goes high on the west-facing hillside just below the small waterfall, but above the cultivated fields. Beyond that point it's easy to follow and there's water at various places. This route is used by those wanting to climb peaks on the northern slopes, but can also be used to reach Obispo. Follow the route symbols on the map.

Another route used by climbers attempting Obispo, is the one via Quimag, Chanag and the Hacienda Sali. You may have to hire a 4WD for this. The author is unfamiliar with the middle sections; that's the reason for the question marks on the map. Keep in mind there are no good maps of the area east of Candelaria, so locations of trails and roads are approximate. For sure, there is a road to as far as the Hacienda Sali, and some kind of a trail to the *vaqueria*, which consists of several huts used by shepherds pasturing & milking cows. Make inquiries locally as you get near the areas in question.

A morning foto showing Altar and its giant crater to the east.

Map 526-1, El Altar Volcano, Cordillera Real, Ecuador

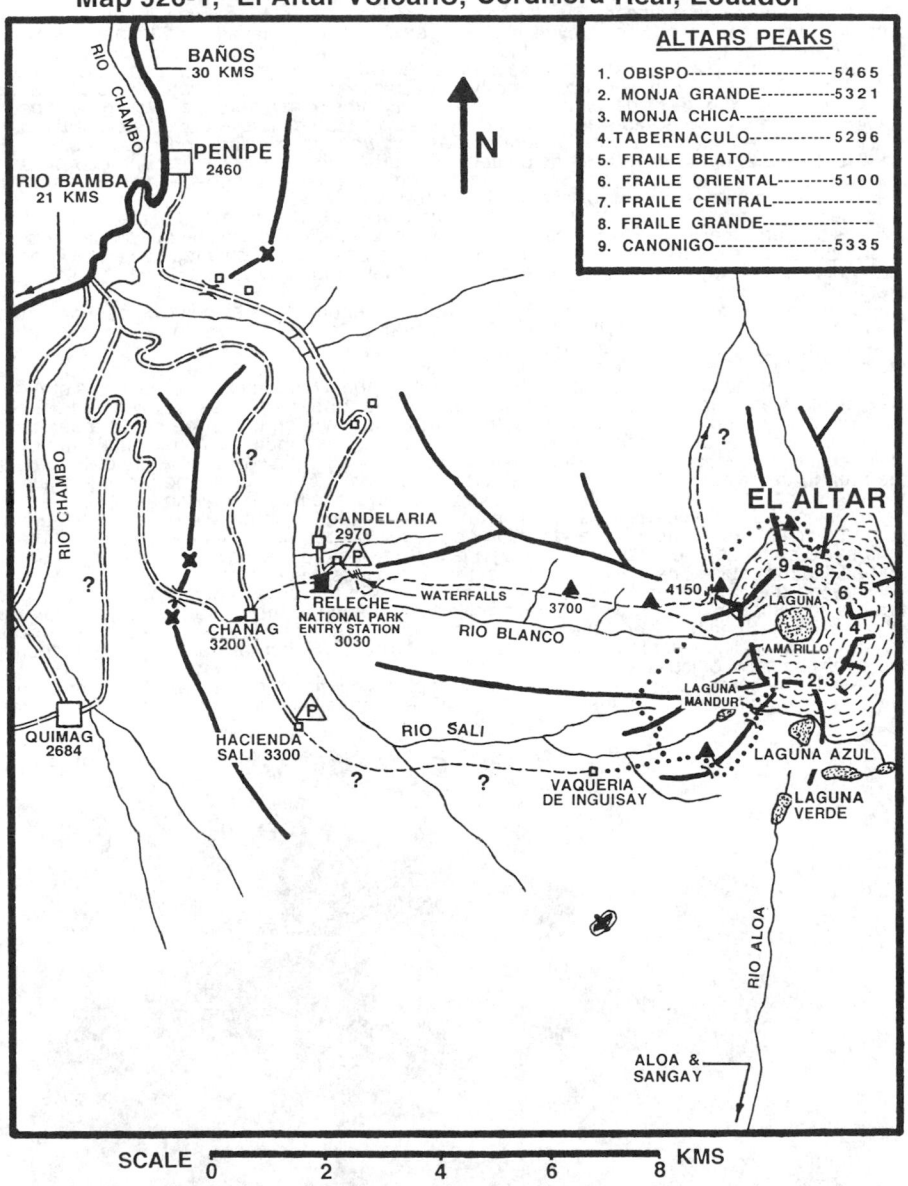

ALTARS PEAKS

1. OBISPO----------------------5465
2. MONJA GRANDE------------5321
3. MONJA CHICA----------------------
4. TABERNACULO-------------5296
5. FRAILE BEATO--------------------
6. FRAILE ORIENTAL---------5100
7. FRAILE CENTRAL----------------
8. FRAILE GRANDE----------------
9. CANONIGO------------------5335

SCALE 0   2   4   6   8 KMS

Altar and all the summits in the Cordillera Real, seem to have an endless rainy season, but June-August seem to be the wettest. Penipe and Quimag each have several small stores, and there's even one in Candelaria, where the author found adequate, but poor selections of food.
Maps Look for IGM map Ñ4D (?), 1;100,00 (if it's completed) on the website (www. omnimap.com), or in the USA call 800-742-2677, or Inter+336-227-8300; or see the magazine *Andinismo, Volumen 1, Noviembre 1979*; the IGM map *Chimborazo, Ñ4C*, 1:100,000, covers areas west of Candelaria; and the books, **Climbing and Hiking in Ecuador,** Bradt Enterprises; and **South American Handbook** and/or **Ecuador Handbook**, both from Footprint Handbooks.

Sangay Volcano, Cordillera Real, Ecuador

Of all the high mountains in Ecuador, the very active Sangay Volcano is the most isolated and most difficult to get to. The elevation of Sangay is generally placed at 5230 meters. From the *Volcanic Activity Reports* of the Smithsonian Institution (www.volcano.si.edu/gvp/) it states: ....*This steep-sided, glacier-covered volcano grew within horseshoe-shaped calderas of 2 previous [calderas], which were destroyed by collapse to the east. Sangay towers above the tropical jungle on the east side; on the other sides flat plains of ash from the volcano have been sculptured by heavy rains into steep-walled canyons up to 600 meters deep. The earliest report of an historical eruption was in 1628. More or less continuous eruptions took place from 1728 until 1916, and again from 1934 to the present.* Reports of its activity are few and far between because of its isolation. For current volcanic conditions see the websites (www.geofisico. cybw.net/) in Spanish, or (www.volcano.si.edu/gvp/).

One of the major obstacles to climbing **Sangay** is the lack of good maps of the region. The 2 maps that are available, Rio Sangay and Lago Tinguichaca, are preliminary drafts showing rivers and lakes, but no elevations or vegetation. To see about new maps see the website (www.omnimap.com). Another factor is the area is pretty much surrounded by natural forests and is all but uninhabited.

There are 2 access routes, both beginning at the hacienda and pueblo known as Aloa. Aloa is located 38 kms southeast of Rio Bamba, 20 kms from Licto, and 15 kms from Pungala. There are several buses each day leaving Rio Bamba ending at Pungala. From there to Aloa, you must walk, hitch hike, get a ride on a hacienda vehicle or milk truck; or hire a taxi.

On the morning of 7/23/1980, the author hitch hiked from Rio Bamba to within 4 kms of Aloa. He got information from 2 people, then crossed the Rio Aloa 2 kms west of town and walked east on a very rough 4WD road to a pasture area above which is a stream and a series of waterfalls. He walked along the trail which zig zags south up to the pass marked 4065 meters-- all in the rain. He made camp near the pass. On Day 2 he spent a couple of hours walking over the pass in the rain, then was in his tent the rest of the day. On Day 3, hope ran out--again in the rain, so he packed up and walked back to town and got one ride to Rio Bamba.

In times of good visibility, this should be an interesting trip. From the pass at 4065 meters, continue down this trail to a hacienda cabin or shelter located about halfway to the mountain. This same cabin can be reached by taking a trail from Aloa to the Hacienda Eten, then south and east to the cabin. The trail used by the author is the most-used route.

Beyond the cabin there's apparently no trail (?), but the area is high and mostly above treeline so not too much bushwhacking is involved (?). Once the Rio Xamayacu is reached, one of several routes can be taken. The normal route seems to head up the river to a good campsite called *La Playa*. The safer route is up the southwest slopes. Better take an ice ax & crampons; there may be snow or ice near the summit.

Before attempting this mini-expedition, it's strongly recommended you make Rio Bamba your information headquarters. First see the tourist office, then talk to the people at the office of the

Aerial foto of the upper part of the very active Sangay Volcano (National Geographic foto).

Map 527-1, Sangay Volcano, Cordillera Real, Ecuador

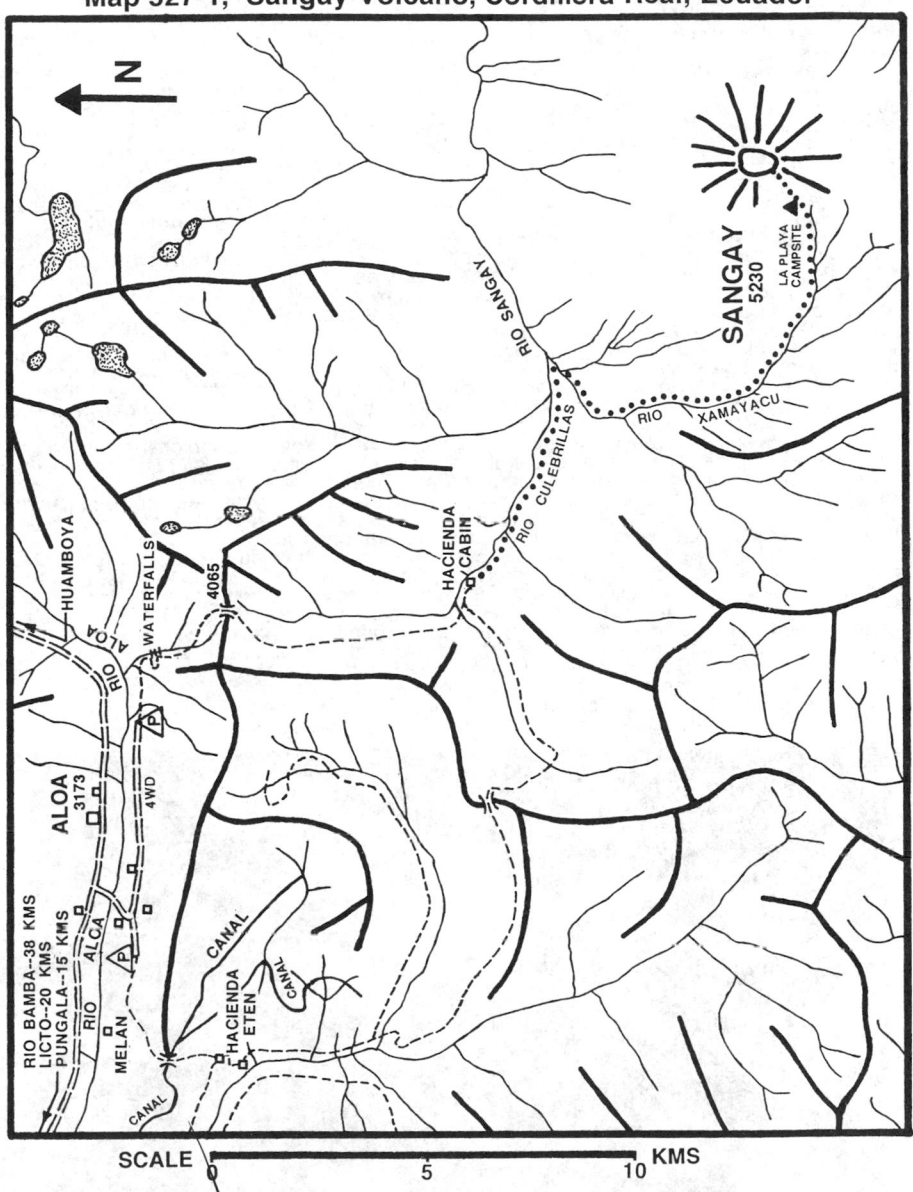

Parque Nacional Sangay. That's located in the western part of Rio Bamba north of the roundabout at the end of Avendia Isabel de Godin, Tele. 963-779, mornings only. They'll give you names of guides or outfitters who can take you there--if success is important. Remember, June through August are the wettest months, but there's no real dry season any time. Take rain gear and compass and food for 7 or 8 days. There are several small shops in Aloa, but Rio Bamba is the best place to buy supplies.
Maps IGM maps *Guamote*, 1:50,000, and 2 preliminary maps, *Rio Sangay & Lago Tinguichaca,* 1:50,000; and the books, **Climbing and Hiking in Ecuador,** Bradt Enterprises; and **South American Handbook**, and/or **Ecuador Handbook**, both from Footprint Handbooks.

Cotopaxi Volcano, Cordillera Real, Ecuador

After Chimborazo, the highest mountain in Ecuador is Cotopaxi, with an altitude of 5897 meters. Like all summits in these parts over about 5000 meters, Cotopaxi is snow capped and has some sizable glaciers & crevasses.

Cotopaxi is considered an active volcano. This cone is capped by 2 craters, one inside the other. Lahars along with explosive eruptions have frequently devastated adjacent valleys. The most violent historical eruptions took place in 1744, 1768 and 1877. Pyroclastic flows descended all sides of the volcano in 1877 and lahars traveled more than 100 kms into the Pacific Ocean and western Amazon basin. The last significant eruption took place in 1904, but between 9 & 11/1975, vapor plumes were reported rising from the summit crater. For a quick check of current volcanic conditions check the website (www.geofisico.cybw.net/) in Spanish.

Cotopaxi is located about 80 kms south of Quito in central Ecuador and about another 20 kms east of the Pan American Highway. This makes access to the mountain fairly simple. Buses can be taken from anywhere on the Pan Am Highway to the junction west of Cotopaxi, as shown on the map. From there a good dirt road heads northeast in the direction of Laguna de Limpiopungu and the Cotopaxi Turnoff. There's usually enough traffic on this section of road on weekends to get a fast lift with a thumb. However, on weekdays there's very little traffic, so it might be best to stop in Machachi, Lasso or Latachunga and hire a taxi. It'll be cheap for a small group and as of 9/2000, you'll pay in US$.

From the highway to the Cotopaxi Turnoff is about 28 kms, then other 7 kms to the parking lot at 4600 meters. Nearby is an old refugio which is useless as a shelter. About one more km uphill is the new refugio known simply as Refugio del Cotopaxi, or Refugio Jose Ribas. It's well-equipped with beds, stove, cooking facilities, and a watchman--but no food, bring your own. Payment is required for the use of this hut.

Most people spend a night in the refugio before making the summit climb on the second day. With your own vehicle, it can be climbed in 2 short days or one very long day from Quito. Ice ax & crampons are required, and for beginners, a rope. There are crevasses on the *ruta normal*, but they can be skirted easily. Just stay on the trail in the snow. If you're planning to use the refugio, it might be best to do the climb during the week, as on weekends it can be crowded. Cotopaxi is perhaps the most-climbed big mountain in Ecuador.

Or you can do it like the author did. On 6/17/1972, he hitch hiked out of Quito to the main junction 10 kms south of the turnoff to the NASA Station. Started walking, but got a lift from fishermen to the Laguna de Limpiopungu. He ended up walking 3 hours from the lakes to the refugio. He stayed there the night and with a 5:30am start, made it to the summit in 3 1/4 hours. He then ran down (good knees then!) to the refugio in 30 minutes, packed up and walked to the Cotopaxi Turnoff, and soon had one lift to the highway and another one to Ambato for the start of his Chimborazo climb. It used to be great hitch hiking in Ecuador and it probably still is, but there is lots of cheap transport on the highways now too.

If you're coming out of Quito, buy your food there. However, any small store on the highway has the kinds of food that are needed for this short climb. The Andes of Ecuador are moist and

The normal route to the summit of Cotopaxi goes below this large outcropping. A June, 1972 foto. Some climbers say the glacier is getting smaller.

Map 528-1, Cotopaxi Volcano, Cordillera Real, Ecuador

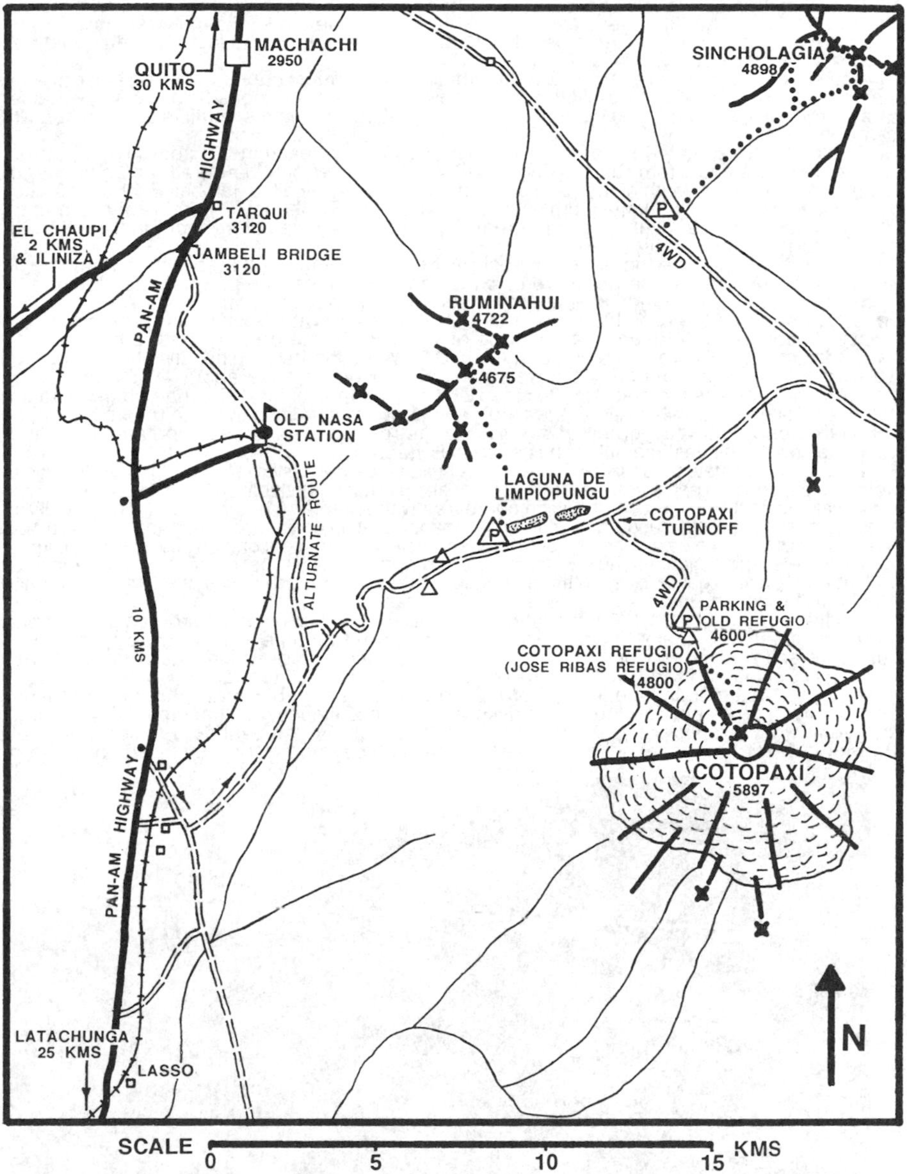

MACHACHI
2950

QUITO
30 KMS

SINCHOLAGIA
4898

HIGHWAY

TARQUI
3120

EL CHAUPI
2 KMS
& ILINIZA

JAMBELI BRIDGE
3120

P

4WD

RUMINAHUI
4722

4675

PAN-AM

OLD NASA
STATION

ALTURNATE ROUTE

LAGUNA DE
LIMPIOPUNGU

P

COTOPAXI
TURNOFF

4WD

PARKING &
OLD REFUGIO
4600

COTOPAXI REFUGIO
(JOSE RIBAS REFUGIO)
4800

10 KMS

COTOPAXI
5897

PAN-AM HIGHWAY

LATACHUNGA
25 KMS

LASSO

N

SCALE

0   5   10   15   KMS

rainy for the entire year, but for Cotopaxi which is centrally located in the highlands, June & July are the driest months--or at least they are in Quito. For maps & information, contact the tourist office and/or Instituto Geografico Militar in Quito.
   Maps IGM maps *Sincholagua, 3992-III, & Cotopaxi, 3991-IV,* 1:50,000; and the books, **Climbing and Hiking in Ecuador,** Bradt Enterprises; and **South American Handbook** and/or **Ecuador Handbook**, both from Footprint Handbooks.

Iliniza Sur & Norte, Cordillera Occidental, Ecuador

Less than one hour's drive south of Quito stands the twin summits of Iliniza. The highest of the 2 is Iliniza Sur at 5305 meters. Iliniza Norte is 5116 meters. This mountain is a very old volcano, with more erosion than most of Ecuador's high summits. Its last eruption could have been 50,000 to 100,000 years ago (?).

The snowline on Iliniza is around 4900 meters. Iliniza Sur is capped with a glacier and has many small, but steep ice falls. Iliniza North has no glaciers, but does have some permanent snow. Normally, the north peak is a rock scramble, while the south summit is a difficult snow & ice climb.

Getting to **Iliniza** is the second easiest big mountain to reach in Ecuador (Tungurahua is easiest). The distance from Quito is only about 40 airline kms, and there's a road up to near the refugio. About 6 kms south of the town of Machachi, is a place called Jambeli Bridge; from there drive, hitch hike or walk 7 kms southwest to the village of El Chaupi. There's not much at this village except a plaza, church, government building and 2 small stores, but that's where the author bought all food for his climb.

From El Chaupi, take the dirt road west past the church about 3 kms, where another road turns south and enters a large grove of pine trees. Amongst the pines is the Hacienda El Refugio. From this hacienda & pine grove, continue up the road southwest. As you walk or drive, you can see the road higher on the mountain as it switchbacks up a prominent ridge. Most vehicles can be driven to an altitude of about 4300 meters, or about 8 kms from the hacienda; then it's 2 more kms along a 4WD road to where the trail begins. It's about a one hour walk from the end of the road to the Refugio Nuevos Horizontes at about 4775 meters. This cinder block shelter is large enough to sleep 25 or 30 people, but in 1972, had no beds, tables, chairs or stove. It was also free at the time! Ask about its condition in Quito before going. (As you walk along the 4WD portion of the road to the refugio, small trees can be seen at about 4300 meters; the highest the author has seen in Ecuador).

Don't underestimate these peaks. The rhyme build-up on the eastern slopes of Iliniza Sur was the worst the author has seen since the Ruwensori, making climbing both difficult and dangerous. There is no walk-up route on Iliniza Sur, which compares with some of Altars peaks in difficulty. Climb southwest from the refugio angling up to the right, then route-find up the northwest slopes. Iliniza Norte is an easy climb up the east ridge. If you've got a vehicle, this can be a one day climb from Quito, but most people spend a night on the mountain. For travelers like us, it's best to take a bus to Machachi and look for a taxi to get as close to the mountain as possible. Or use buses, then walk and/or hitch hike from the Jambeli Bridge.

On the morning of 7/31/1980, the author hitch hiked from Baños and Tungurahua to Ambato, then to Jambeli and finally El Chaupi in 3 fast rides. At that time, drivers were on strike and buses weren't running, so the only way around was hitch hiking--which was very good! At El Chaupi, he bought food and stored some baggage in one store, then walked 4 hours non-stop to the refugio. Next morning, he made 2 probes toward the summit of Iliniza Sur, and was higher than the north peak, but considered the risks too high, mainly because the mountain was totally fogged in with zero visibility. Never did see Iliniza Sur! So he packed up the walked to El Chaupi in 2 1/4 hours; repacked, walked to the highway and got a fast lift to Quito before

The Refugio Nuevos Horizontes on the north side of Iliniza Sur.

Map 529-1, Iliniza Sur & Norte, Cordillera Occidental, Ecuador

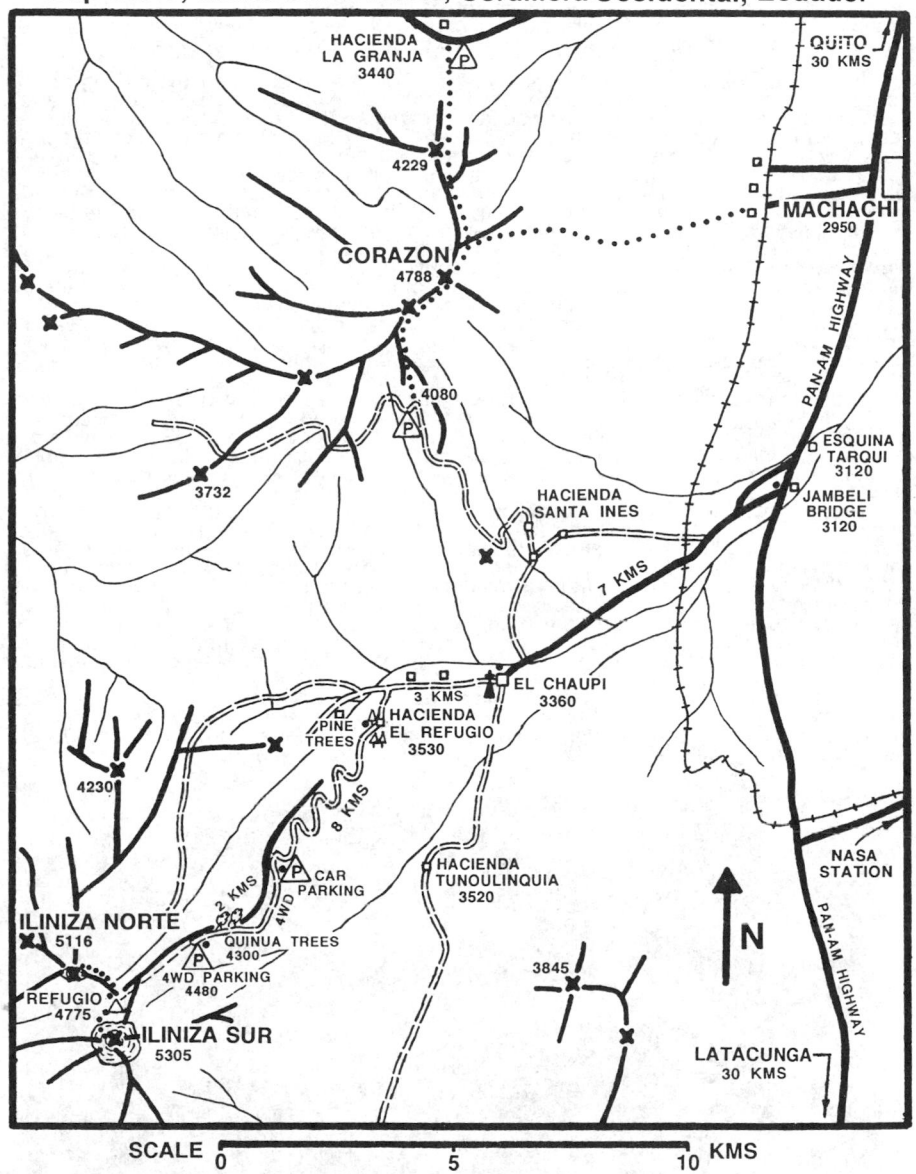

embassies closed that afternoon.
 The weather on Iliniza is similar to Quitos, with the 2 driest months being June and July. The vegetation in these parts leads one to believe this is perhaps the driest place in Ecuador.
Maps IGM maps *Machachi,* 1:100,000; or *Machachi,* 1:50,000; and the books, **Climbing and Hiking in Ecuador,** Bradt Enterprises; and **South American Handbook**, and/or **Ecuador Handbook**, both from Footprint Handbooks

Chimborazo, Cordillera Occidental, Ecuador

The highest mountain in Ecuador and one of the most famous summits in South America, is Chimborazo at 6310 meters. Chimborazo is a volcano which has not shown activity in recorded history. Because of its elevation and location (in wet and humid Ecuador), it has a large ice cap with many glaciers & crevasses.

There are now 2 normal ways to **Chimborazo**. First, there's the time-honored Pogyos and Refugio Fabian route, located on the northwest side of the mountain. There are now a few buses and trucks running between Ambato and Guaranda which can be taken to, or near, the pass called Pogyos with the antennas. However, Pogyos covers the area between the pass and a few huts at 4000 meters. From either trailhead shown, a trail leads to the old Refugio Fabian at 4700 meters. This hut is in ruins and no longer usable so a tent & camping is required. The climb from the hut involves going straight up, then veering right at the red cliffs, thence to the summit. This takes one long day. Climbing this route normally takes 2 or 3 days, depending on your physical fitness, acclimatization and your time of arrival in the area.

As of 1980, to celebrate the 100 years since the mountain was first climbed by Edward Whymper, a new hut was constructed on the southwest slopes at about 5000 meters. This refugio bearing Whympers name, is on the route of the first ascent. By using this route the elevation gained between hut and summit is less than on the northwest route, and according to Greg Horne, it's a lot less dangerous than climbing Cotopoxi. There's a refugio at the parking lot at the end of the road below Whymper's Refugio. It sleeps 8 or 10, has water, electricity, toilets. The Refugio Whymper has beds for 40, 5 separate rooms, stoves, kitchen facilities, all for US$10 a night.

Getting to these huts may be a bit more difficult, as the traffic using the road between Pogyos and Pulingui is less than on the Ambato-Guaranda road. As a last resort you can walk to the Refugio Whymper from either Pogyos or Pulingui, but for only a few US$ you can hire a taxi in Rio Bamba for the ride to the parking lot below Whymper's Refugio. Rio Bamba might be the best place to make headquarters before making this climb. Get updates from the tourist office first.

The author was invited into the home of Hector Vasquez in Ambato for one night, then the next morning, 6/19/1972, he walked out of town and hitch hiked to the Pogyos area and got off at the trailhead marked 4000 meters. He walked straight for the mountain and later found a cairned-trail up to the old refugio. That took 2 3/4 hours. He slept in the hut which was half open & breezy, then at 5am the next morning, he left for the summit taking 4 1/2 hours. He skirted around several minor harmless-looking crevasses but felt no danger. It has rained hard a day before and as a result he had knee-deep powder snow on the big broad rounded summit. There are several bumps on top, but no visible crater. He was back at the hut in one hour, and was at the road at 1pm. He immediately got the first of 3 lifts on the way to Quito arriving at 6:30pm.

Northeast of Chimborazo is a very old and eroded volcanic peak known as Carihuayrazo at 5106 meters. The map shows the normal approach route to this peak, which begins near Pogyos; or from the east and Mocha. To do Cerro Mocha, head for the town of Mocha by bus or hitching, then either walk or hire a taxi or pickup to get closer to the peaks.

This is the old Refugio Fabian as it was in 1972. It's unusable today!

Map 530-1, Chimborazo, Cordillera Occidental, Ecuador

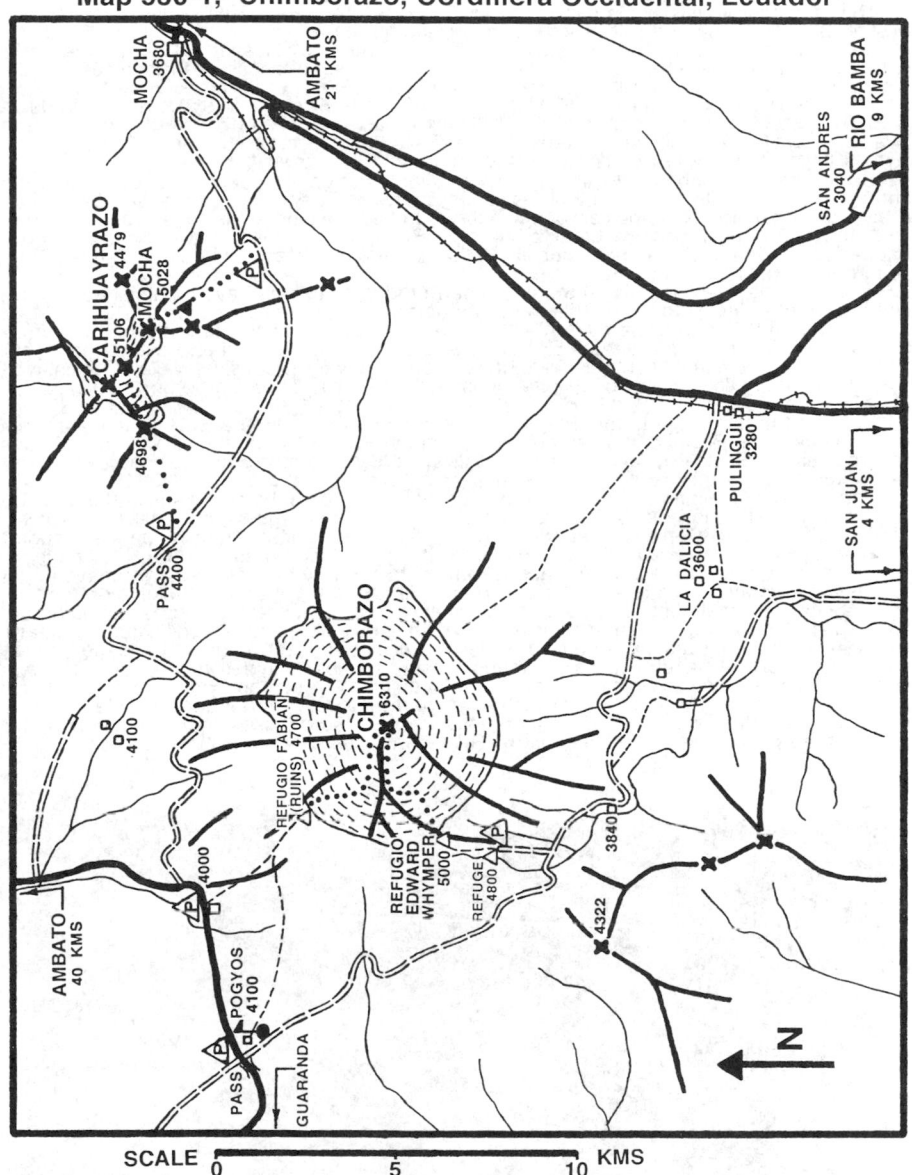

June and July are generally considered to be the best months for climbing either of these summits, but bad weather can come at any time. The cities of Rio Bamba and Ambato are the best places to buy food and supplies.

Maps IGM maps *Chimborazo*, 1:100,000; or *Chimborazo, 3889-IV & Quero (for Carihuayrazo), 3889-I*, 1:50,000; and the books, **Climbing and Hiking In Ecuador**, Bradt Enterprises; and **South American Handbook**, and/or **Ecuador Handbook**, both from Footprint Handbooks.

Volcan Wolf, Galapagos Islands, Ecuador

The Galapagos Islands, or the Archipelago de Colon as it's known in Ecuador, lies 1000 kms due west of the South American mainland and Guayaquil, and right on the equator.

These islands are all volcanic in origin, with the older islands & volcanos in the east; the newer volcanos migrating toward the west and northwest. Most of these volcanos take their names from the islands themselves. On small islands there's only one volcano and nothing more. Here's a rundown on some of the more recent eruptions: Pinta last erupted in 1928; Marchena on 9/25/1991; Sierra Negra in 1979 (?); Darwin in 1913; and Wolf on 8/28/1982 which lasted about a week. It had explosions and lava flows from the central crater and radial fissures. Also, Fernandina erupted for 5 days beginning on 4/19/1991. There is very likely one live volcano in the islands at any one time.

Getting to the Galapagos Islands isn't too difficult, but getting around from one island to another is. Apparently there are 2 ships sailing between Guayaquil and the islands. These ships, carrying passengers and cargo, make the rounds to the different islands to deliver goods and pick up products (such as cattle or hides). Presumably they stop at the 5 main ports: Baquerizo, on San Cristobal; Seymour, on Baltra; Villamil, on Isabela; Flores, on Santa Maria; and Puerto Ayora, on Santa Cruz.

In just the past few years with the increase in tourism, airlines have established several flights a week from Quito via Guayaquil to the island of Baltra and/or San Cristobal. Most tourists end up at Puerto Ayora on Santa Cruz after the flight, which is a bus/ferry/bus ride from the airport. It's at the port (near the Darwin Research Station) called Puerto Ayora, that boats taking tourists out to the different islands dock. Some are very expensive, while other fishing-type boats are cheaper. Some boats offer beds on board, while others have you camp on shore at night. Lots of options.

Once in the islands you can live relatively inexpensively, with a wide range of tourist accommodations. Plenty of food can be bought in the Puerto Ayora market, with lots of fruits and vegetables. Santa Cruz and San Cristobal islands have lots of locally grown food. Imported items from the mainland are more expensive.

The higher mountains are mostly on the largest island of Isabela. This island makes up about half of the total land area of the group and has 5 volcanos. The highest peaks are **Volcan Wolf**, 1707 meters & **Cerro Azul** at 1689 meters. The third highest summit is on the island of Fernandina and simply called Volcan Fernandina. Its highest point is **La Cumbre**, 1494 meters.

Since these islands are one big national park with an entry fee of US$80, you have to get permission to camp (designated places only) and climb in many areas (for wildlife protection). The way tourists get around is by boat and normally in groups. Boats go to designated areas, and captains make all arrangements for you. Expect to pay more for a special chartered boat if you want to climb volcanos, as opposed to viewing wildlife. **Alcedo** appears to be the highest peak you can climb without permission. It has geysers and lots of turtles in the crater. There is now an airport at Puerto Villamil, formerly a penal colony, so you can fly or take a boat there, where you'll find 6 or 8 hotels. Maps show a road up to St. Tomas and to a place called Alemania, and a trail on to the crater rim of Sierra Negra. There's also a trail from Bellavista up to the craters of Chacras (or Media Luna) on Santa Cruz. Surely arrangements can be made to

This is part of the crater on Volcan Wolf. You may have to get special permission to climb this one.

Map 531-3, Volcan Wolf, Galapagos Islands, Ecuador

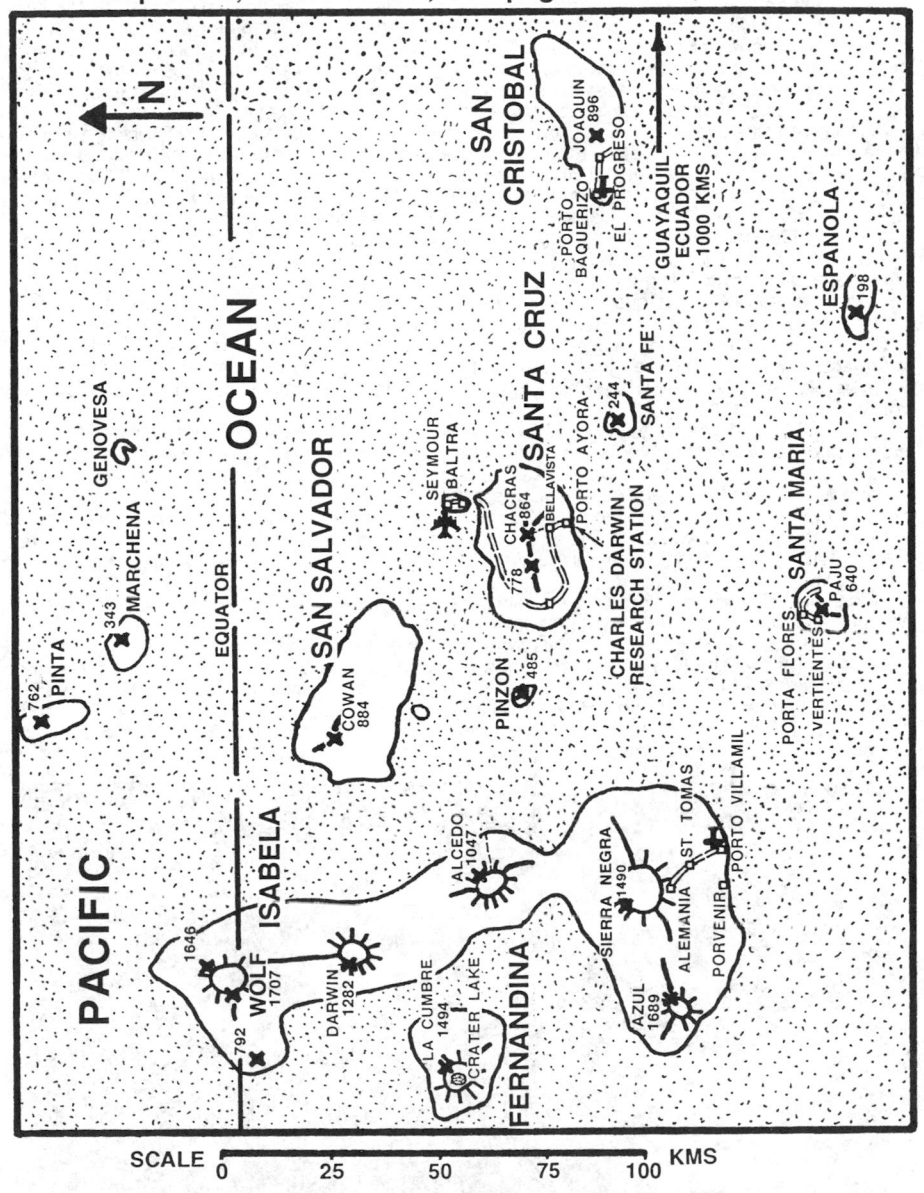

get to Wolf or Fernandina--for a price! Someone in Puerto Ayora can give you information on where you can and cannot go. This is merely an introduction, so buy one of the several guidebooks available.

Maps Buy good maps and guidebooks at the national park headquarters--Puerto Ayora, including the books, **Galapagos Guide,** White, Epler & Gilbert, Charles Darwin Foundation for the Galapagos Islands; or **The Galapagos Islands,** The Mountaineers; and the **Ecuador Handbook**, Footprint Handbooks.

Champara, Cordilleras Blanca & Rosco, Peru

Included on this map is the Cordillera Rosco and the extreme northern end of the Cordillera Blanca. *Rosco* is the name more commonly known is climbing circles for this compact range, but the IGM maps in Peru call it *Pacra*. Regardless of the name, this small group of peaks is the most northerly of Peru's snow-capped summits. Many people would classify Rosco as part of the Cordillera Blanca, but there is a wide gap between it and the Champara Group. Both groups are made up of essentially the same type of rock, mostly granite.

Getting to this region is quite easy, at least to the Champara Group. There are several buses each day running between Huaraz, the center of government & tourism along the Cordillera Blanca, and the coastal city of Chimbote. Get off the bus at Yuramarca, then wait for still another bus or truck heading in the direction of Corongo--or just start walking and hope for a lift. From Corongo take the trail to Aco and Cusca, then up the quebrada (canyon), to the area of the Laguna Rutu. This is where most base camps are set up. If you're looking for help getting up to Rutu, Corongo is the place to look for mules. There is likely at least one store in Corongo (?).

Since the 5/30/1970 earthquake, the route to the **Champara Peaks** has been altered a bit. At one time the trail along the aquaducto above Santa Rosa was used to reach Laguna Qollurcocha northwest of Champara, but the quake broke the aguaducto leaving that trail high, dry and hot. The author has no information on whether it's been fixed--or is used today (?). Ask someone in Yuramarca which route is the best to reach Laguna Qollurcocha. Actually, the route from Santa Rosa isn't bad, but it's a long, hot climb to the first water.

As of 1980, the best way to the lake was to walk or catch a ride to a place called Ranhuas. From there a trail winds up the mountain to some shepherd huts called Tayabamba, then heads over the pass to the south and down into Qollurcocha Lake basin. Apparently, this is the route used to drive grazing animals to the high pastures.

Another possibility is from the Hacienda Mirasanta up to Tayabamba then over the pass; or follow another aquaducto east and upstream from Mirasanta. However, the author was told there's a 450-meter-long tunnel you must walk through, in knee deep water before reaching the high basin!

Once at Qollurcocha, climb south to reach a col on the west ridge, then cut across the steep north face to the summit. All peaks here look difficult.

On 7/18/1980, the author took a bus from Huaraz heading north for Chimbote, but got off at Yuramarca (at 1300 meters & hot!). Bought some food in a shop, left a little baggage there, then walked to the Santa Rosa Hacienda and up the trail along the dry aguaducto, but returned and talked to locals who said to go to Mirasanta instead. He camped at Mirasanta, then on Day 2 climbed up past Tayabamba, but returned because Champara doesn't look good for a solo climber. Returned to Yuramarca in 2 1/2 hours, and got on a bus to Chimbote (3 1/2 hours).

One of many snow peaks east of Huaraz, largest city near the Cordillera Blanca.

Map 532-1, Champara, Cordilleras Blanca & Rosco, Peru

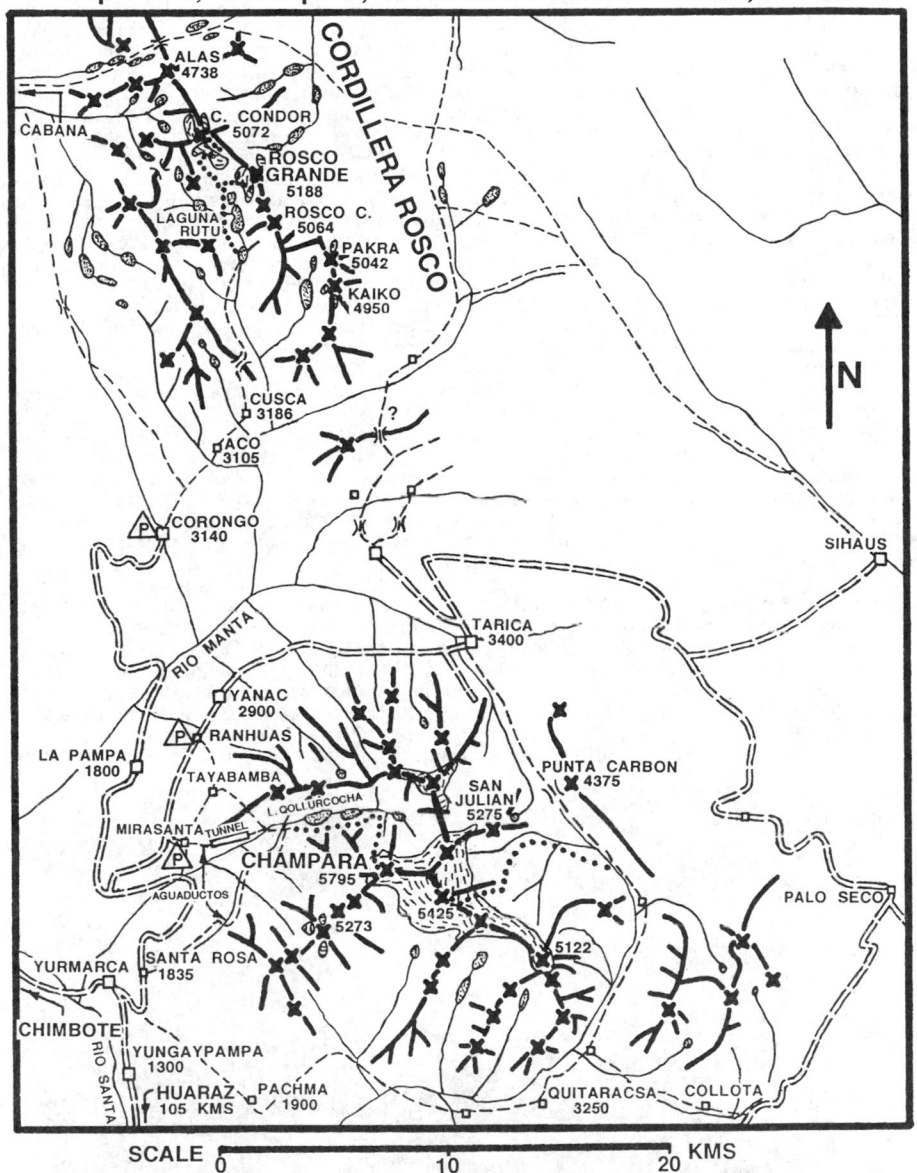

SCALE | 0 | 10 | 20 | KMS

From Yuramarca, better plan on at least 4 or 5 days or a week to reach either Champara or Rosco, do a climb, and return. The dry months here are May into September and the best places to buy food are in Huaraz and Chimbote. Also, be prepared for some difficult climbing with ice ax & crampons and ropes.

Maps IGM maps *Pallasca and Corongo,* 1:100,000, from the Instituto Geografico Militar, 1190 Av. Aramburu, San Isidro (barrio), Lima; and the book, **Yuraq Janka (Cordilleras Blanca and Rosko),** American Alpine Club; **Peruvian Andes**, Beaud, Cordee Books; or **Climbing in the Cordillera Blanca**, Sharman; and travel guidebook **Peru**, from Lonely Planet and/or Footprint Handbooks.

Huandoy & Alpamayo, Cordillera Blanca, Peru

This is the second in the series of maps covering the Cordillera Blanca. Well known areas and mountains included here are Cañon de Pato, Alpamayo, Huandoy, the Lagunas Llanganuco & Peron, and the new village of Yungay. The highest mountain in this section in Huandoy at 6395 meters. If it weren't for the presence of Huascaran just south of the Llanganuco Lakes, Huandoy would undoubtedly be much better known. This range is made of granitic-type rocks.

There are only 2 ways into this area; one is from Chimbote, north and west of this area and on the coast. There are several buses each day making the run up to Huaraz. But normally, climbers & trekkers make their way to Huaraz from Lima, then take buses north to this region.

Most climbers & trekkers visiting the region make Huaraz their headquarters. Huaraz is at a relatively high elevation of 3050 meters, and is a good place for acclimatizing. It's also a good place to buy maps & books and to visit with other climbers. Huaraz has many hotels and a good selection of food. For information, stop at the tourist office near Plaza de Armas; or the Casa de Guias at Plaza Ginabra in the center of town. That's the best place to get information about guides, transportation or any other information pertaining to climbing or trekking. Or see the office of the National Park in the eastern part of the city on Avenida Raymondi.

The author has been up and down this valley to and from Huaraz several times, but the only hiking he did here was some simple walking around the upper Laguna Llanganuco on 7/1/1972. He was with some other climbers in a Jeep so there wasn't much exercise that day. Yungay National Cemetery was also visited on that day. That's where on 5/30/1970, an avalanche, triggered by an earthquake, came off Huascaran and wiped out the entire town killing up to 20,000 people.

The normal route to **Huandoy** begins at the new village of Yungay (see the next map). Get there by taking a bus north from Huaraz. There are trucks leaving Yungay daily for the Llanganuco Lakes, and sometimes to the pass just beyond, marked 4737 meters on this map. There are also tourist buses going to Llanganuco in season (June to August). You can also walk and hitch hike, or hire a taxi in Yungay. Not far from the upper lake, turn left or northwest, and walk up the slope as shown. The difficult part is in reaching the col, after that it's straightforward. Plan on a 4 or 5 day climb from Yungay.

Probably the best known mountain on this map is **Alpamayo**. This is a pyramid-shaped peak, with steep fluted faces and knife-edged ridges; a good prize for any climber. Getting to Alpamayo is a longer hike than to most other peaks in the Cordillera Blanca. One route would be; bus to Caraz, walking to Baños, then up the Quebrada Alpamayo. One could also begin at the Hacienda Colcas, or at Los Cedros, at the beginning of the spectacular Cañon de Pato, a canyon perhaps unrivaled in the world. Once in the upper basin, the western face, then the south ridge is the normal route. Climbing Alpamayo could take close to one week and is a very technical climb.

Many trekkers walk from Yungay to the Lagunas Llanganuco, then circle the Huandoy

This foto was taken just north of Catac showing the Cordillera Blanca southeast of Huaraz.

Map 533-1, Huandoy & Alpamayo, Cordillera Blanca, Peru

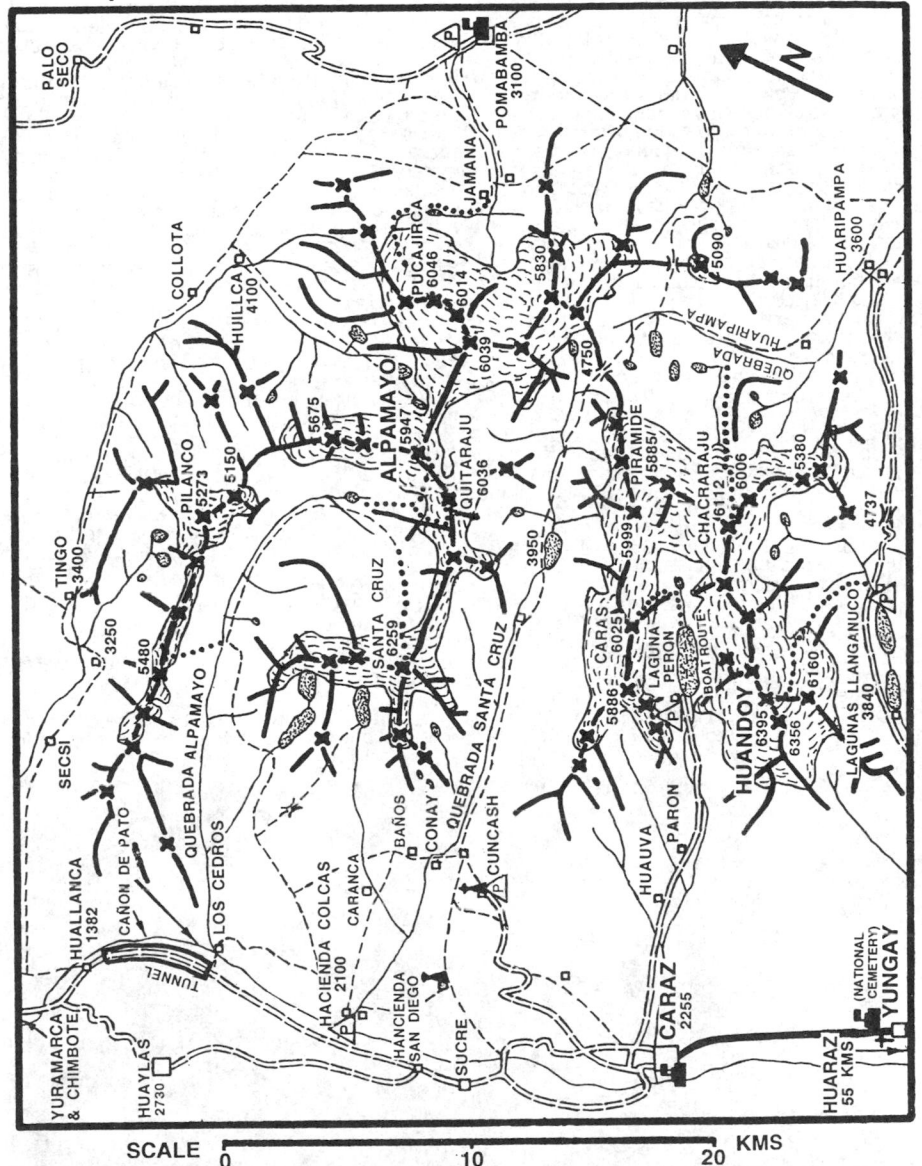

SCALE 0   10   20   KMS

Massif, and come down the Quebrada Santa Cruz to Caraz. Beware of thieves on this route.
May through early September is the climbing season. Mountains on this map are for experienced and well-equipped climbers only.
Maps IGM maps *Corongo and Carhuas,* 1:100,000, from the Instituto Geografico Militar, 1190 Av. Aramburu, San Isidro (barrio), Lima; check South American Explorers Club website (www.samexplo.org); and the books, **Yuraq Janka (Cordillera Blanca),** American Alpine Club; **Peruvian Andes**, Beaud, Cordee Books; or **Climbing in the Cordillera Blanca**, Sharman; and travel guidebook, **Peru**, Lonely Planet and/or Footprint Handbooks.

Huascaran, Cordillera Blanca, Peru

This is the 3rd map in the series of 5 covering the Cordillera Blanca. This covers the middle part of the range, including the highest summit in all of Peru, Huascaran at 6768 meters. It has twin summits with the south peak being the highest. The north peak is 6654 meters. Huascaran is composed of metamorphics and granite rock.

Despite its elevation, Huascaran is one of the easier mountains to climb in the entire cordillera. However, it does have many crevasses & an icefall which make it an interesting but hazardous climb. This is not a good place for solo climbers!

The normal route to **Huascaran** is from the west face and the villages of Mancos and Musho. There are many buses on the main road running up and down the Rio Santa Valley, especially between Huaraz and the national cemetery at Yungay; so it's easy to reach Mancos. Hitch hiking can also be good. In Mancos, you can hire a taxi to reach the actual trailhead at Musho, but most groups have transport arranged all the way from Huaraz. Or you can walk to Musho along a steep road. From Musho it's a well-beaten path up to base camp at or near the edge of the glacier at about 4600 meters. Anyone at Musho can put you on the right trail.

Because of the altitude, it's necessary to make at least one camp on snow, but most groups prefer making 2 camps on the ice before the summit climb. For reasonably fit & acclimatized climbers, it's about 5 days to the top and back to Musho, but many prefer a 6th day. Last minute supplies can be found in Mancos or Musho, but it's best to stock up before leaving Huaraz. With so many groups on the mountain there's a well-beaten path in the snow to the top. Even so, there have been climbers killed in the area of the icefall called *Garganta* between the 2 peaks, so take a rope and of course ice ax & crampons. It's basically an easy climb, but with risks from crevasses.

Here's what the author did starting 7/7/1972. He hitch hiked from Huaraz to Mancos, bought lunch, then walked to Musho in 2 1/4 hours with a 39 kg pack. Camped next to an Argentine group, then headed for the highest of the *base camps* next to the glacier at 4600 meters in 6 1/2 hours. There he joined an Adventist group led by David Taylor. Another climber joined the group, he was Hans Peter Dutton from Switzerland and *Four Against Everest* fame and their illegal 1962 attempt. To Camp 2 at 5250 meters took 3 hours, then one day was spent taking some food & supplies up to Camp 3 at about 5900 meters. Day 4 to Camp 3 was made in 4 1/2 hours with some snow showers. On Day 5 to the summit in about 5 hours and back to camp in 2. Then down to Musho in 6 1/4 hours on Days 5 & 6. Roughly 30 hours total walk-time. During this entire trip the author had diarrhea every night and averaged about 2-3 hours sleep! It wasn't altitude--but just going native and eating bad food in Huaraz!

Other high peaks include **Hualcan**, 6125 meters. This is considered an easy climb, but there is the threat of crevasses. It's usually climbed from the Hacienda Copa Chica, located north of Marcara. You'll likely have to walk from the main highway, or look for a vehicle in Marcara. **Cerro Copa** at the southeastern end of the same snow massif, has an altitude of 6188 meters. It too can be climbed from the village of Marcara and the Hacienda Copa Grande.

The city of Huaraz is a short distance south of this mapped area. That's the place to buy your supplies and get information from other climbers at the **Casa de Guias** on Plaza Ginabra in the city center, or the Huascaran National Park or tourist office. Huaraz has lots of cheap and/or

Musho is the beginning of the trail to Huascaran. The trail runs left, then to the glacier.

Map 534-1, Huascaran, Cordillera Blanca, Peru

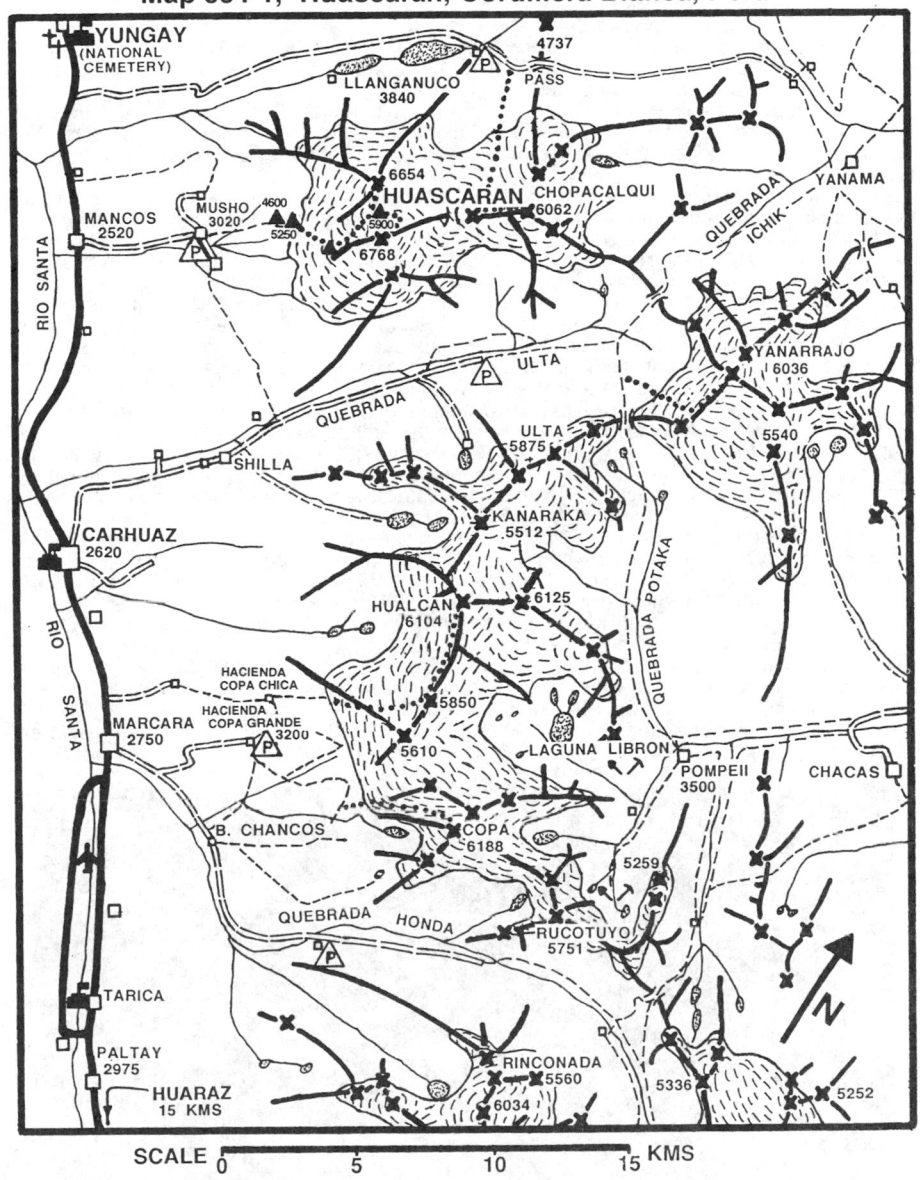

YUNGAY
(NATIONAL
CEMETERY)

LLANGANUCO
3840

4737
PASS

6654

HUASCARAN CHOPACALQUI
6062

MANCOS
2520

MUSHO
3020 4600

5250

6768

QUEBRADA
ICHIK

YANAMA

RIO SANTA

ULTA

QUEBRADA

YANARRAJO
6036

SHILLA

ULTA
5875

5540

CARHUAZ
2620

KANARAKA
5512

RIO SANTA

HUALCAN
6104

6125

QUEBRADA POTAKA

HACIENDA
COPA CHICA

5850

MARCARA
2750

HACIENDA
COPA GRANDE 3200

5610

LAGUNA LIBRON

POMPEII
3500

CHACAS

B. CHANCOS

COPA
6188

5259

QUEBRADA HONDA

RUCOTUYO
5751

TARICA

N

PALTAY
2975

RINCONADA
5560

5336

5252

HUARAZ
15 KMS

6034

SCALE 0   5   10   15 KMS

expensive hotels, a good mercado and many food stores. This is where climbers & trekkers
gather before, after and in between climbs. Visit these mountains from May through the
beginning of September for the best climbing weather.
Maps *Carhuaz and Huari,* 1:100,000, from the IGM, 1190 Av. Aramburu, San Isidro (barrio),
Lima; check South American Explorers Club website (www.samexplo.org); and the books,
Yuraq Janka (Cordillera Blanca), American Alpine Club; **Peruvian Andes**, Beaud, Cordee
Books; or **Climbing in the Cordillera Blanca**, Sharman; travel guidebook, **Peru**, from Lonely
Planet and/or, Footprint Handbooks.

Huantsan & Chinchey, Cordillera Blanca, Peru

This is the 4th in the series of 5 maps covering the Cordillera Blanca. This one shows Huaraz, the largest city in the Rio Santa Valley and the gathering place for trekkers & climbers. Around Huaraz, the valley is more open than it is to the north. Also, this map shows the mountains from Quebrada Hondo in the north, to Aco and Ollerros in the south. The rocks here are mostly granite or other metamorphics.

Most climbers & trekkers make their way from Lima to the Cordillera Blanca and Huaraz by bus, many of which make the 7 or 8 hour run at night. These buses use the Pativilca route. You can also reach Huaraz from the north, and from Casma or Chimbote, both located on the coastal highway.

For some climbs, you can walk directly from downtown Huaraz, however there's a maze of roads, trails, farms, fields and scattered huts you must pass before reaching the canyons or quebradas. On the map are drawn the more important roads and trails, along with probably the easiest or at least the earliest routes climbed up some of the more prominent peaks in this area. The summits here are only slightly lower than peaks to the north near Peru's highest mountain Huascaran, but are still just as rugged and present some routes as difficult as any in this range.

Some of the more prominent peaks include **Huantsan**, 6395 meters, the highest in the region. It's accessible from Janco and the Quebrada Scallap. Also, **Cashan**, 5723 meters, and **Uruasa**, 5735; both south of Huantsan and climbed via Quebradas Cashan and Rurek. Going north, **Cayesh**, 5721 meters, one of the most difficult and jagged pyramids in the range is reached via the Quebrada Quilcayhuanka (Qelcahuanca). **Ranrapalica**, 6162 meters, one of the most dominant peaks overlooking Huaraz can be climbed via Quebrada Ishinca or Laguna Perolocha at 4840 meters. And **Chinchey (Rurichichay)**, 6309 meters. The best way there might be from Tingo and the Mina San Jose on the east side of the range. All these summits are for experienced and well-equipped climbers only (also, beware of many conflicting names in this part of the range as a result the various maps used by the author).

The author arrived in Huaraz on 6/29/1972 from the north. He camped for 3 nights near the Hotel Baños Termales Monterrey with the hot spring & swimming pool, then spent 3 nights at a construction camp at the lake called Laguna Llaca at 4300 meters. This is right under Ranrapallca. He never did get very high, about 5500 meters a couple of times. He was constantly plagued by diarrhea which lasted into his Huascaran trip right after that. ADVICE: always carry some good diarrhea medicine!

All the author's food came from Huaraz, which has good enough selections for any climb. If it's additional information you want, contact the tourist or Huascaran National Park offices, or find other climbers at the **Casa de Guias** at Plaza Ginabra in the center of the city.

Most climbing is done during June, July and August, when it's very dry. It's also possible to have long spells of good weather in May and September. The rest of the year is wet and cloudy.

This is Ranrapallca as seen from the southwest.

Map 535-1, Huantsan & Chinchey, Cordillera Blanca, Peru

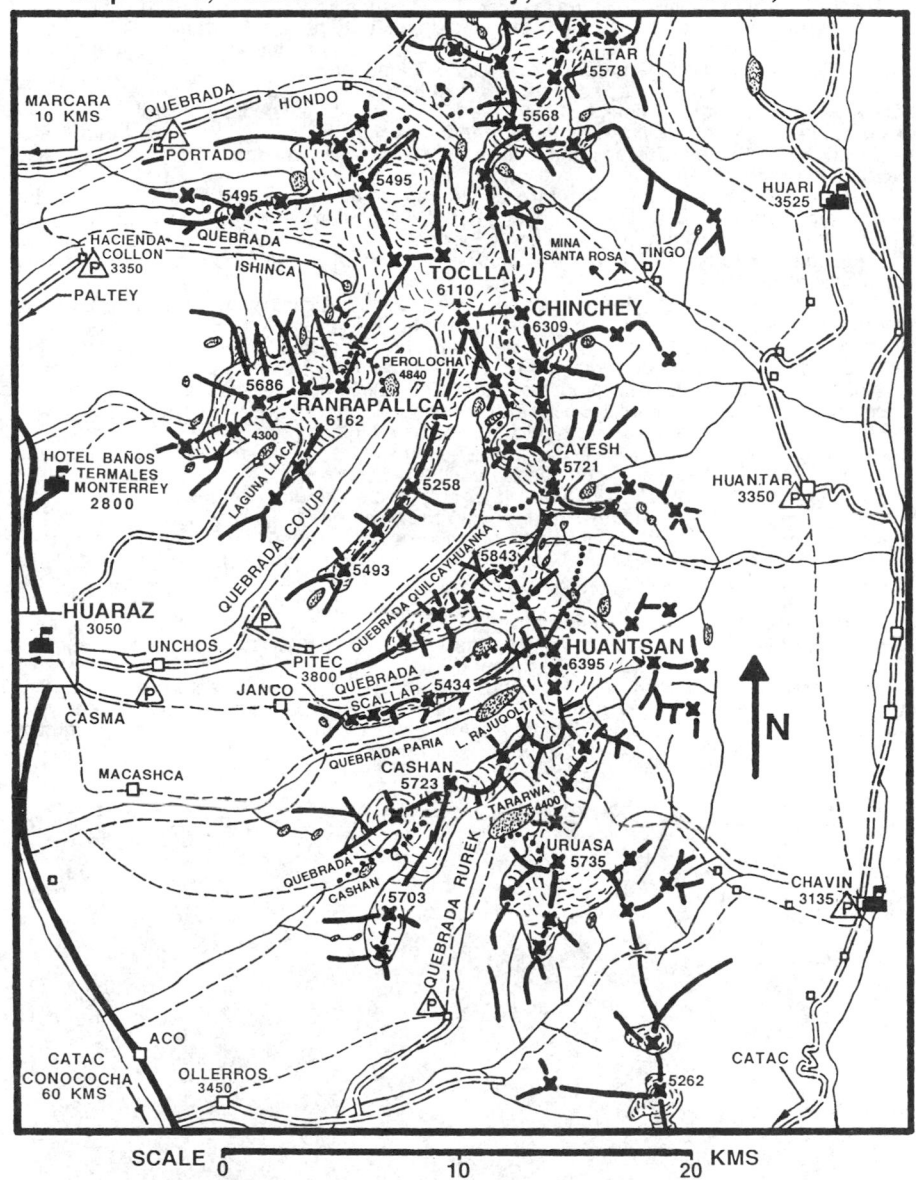

SCALE 0   10   20 KMS

Remember, with the sun to the north, the north facing slopes have the more consolidated snow; while the south faces have more powdery, light snow. Peru is one of the worst countries in the world when it comes to thief, so it might pay to leave a good portion of your money in a hotel safe, especially if you're trekking alone or in a small group.

Maps *Huari and Recuay*, 1:100,000, from the IGM, Lima; check South American Explorers Club website (www.samexplo.org); and the books, **Yuraq Janka (Cordillera Blanca)**, American Alpine Club; **Peruvian Andes**, Beaud, Cordee Books; or **Climbing in the Cordillera Blanca**, Sharman; and travel guidebook, **Peru**, Lonely Planet and/or Footprint Handbooks.

Pongos Group, Cordillera Blanca, Peru

This is the last of 5 maps covering the Cordillera Blanca of north central Peru. This map is the most southerly of the 5, and includes the most southerly peak in the range, Rajo Cutac at 5355 meters. The highest peak on the map is the highest in a cluster known as the Pongos Group. It's shown on the IGM maps as Murrorajo, 5688 meters.

One problem the author has had in creating this and all the maps of the Cordillera Blanca is, there are different names of peaks on the various maps. He has used the Instituto Geografico Militar maps, as well as the maps and information in John Ricker's book, **Yuraq Janka**. Also used were the author's own maps and diaries. Some names may be different and elevations vary, but these maps themselves are reasonably accurate.

The peaks in this region are not nearly as high as the mountains to the north in the central portion of the range, nor are they as rugged and difficult to climb. For this reason they are well-suited for climbers who enjoy mountaineering but don't want to put their lives on the line. This is also a good place to begin climbing in the Cordillera Blanca in order to acclimatize for higher peaks such as Huascaran.

This part of the range may also be attractive to people interested in botany. The rare plant known as *Puya Raimondi,* is found here and in few other places in the range, or in Peru. The author personally visited 2 groups of these plants. One is at the head of the Quebrada Qeshqe, the other is in the Quebrada Ingenio. This latter group is near a visitor center, which may or may not be open, or even exist, when you arrive. Both groups are at 4200 to 4300 meters altitude, and are on the north facing slopes. These plants grow to about 8 to 10 meters in height.

This part of the range is easy to get to. The paved highway on the left of this map is the busy road connecting Huaraz with Lima, so there is lots of traffic. Take a local bus south from Huaraz to Catac, about 38 kms, where there are a couple of hotels.

You can walk southeast right from Catac, or continue south on the highway. For climbers, the best access route might be the road leaving the main Lima-Huaraz Highway at Km 159. This road was used in the 1980's by trucks bringing ore from several mines, the most important of which was the Mina Santon. It's not difficult to get a ride on an ore truck, either up or down--if the operation is still running (?). By using this road you can reach the heart of the area covered by this map.

Or you can walk, as did the author direct from Catac to the **Pongos Group** and northern Puya Raimondi area. He left Huaraz on the morning of 7/16/1980 on a bus to Catac. That took just over an hour. He then walked southeast to the 3 lakes just west of the Pongos in 4 1/2 hours. There are trails everywhere. Weather and a still-sore knee prevented him from doing any serious climbing. Next day in the rain, he walked over the pass marked 4600 meters and down to some kind of visitor center or traffic control point. He then got a lift back to the highway and walked the 7 kms to Catac where he got a bus back to Huaraz.

These are the rare Puyo Raimondi located just west of the Pongo Group of peaks.

Map 536-1, Pongos Group, Cordillera Blanca, Peru

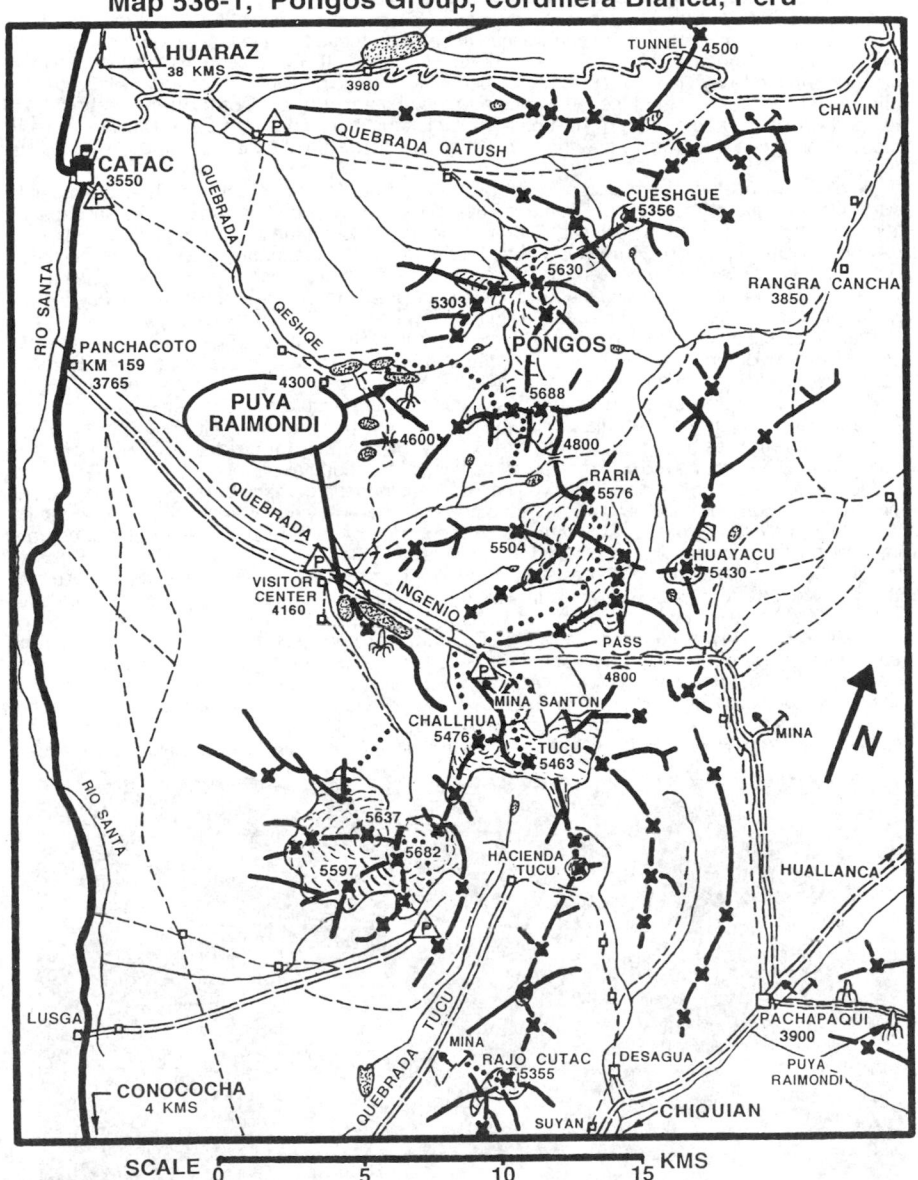

HUARAZ 38 KMS
TUNNEL 4500
CHAVIN
3980
QUEBRADA QATUSH
CATAC 3550
CUESHGUE 5356
QUEBRADA
5630
QESHQE
5303
RANGRA CANCHA 3850
PANCHACOTO KM 159 3765
PONGOS
4300
PUYA RAIMONDI
5688
4600
4800
QUEBRADA
RARIA 5576
5504
HUAYACU 5430
VISITOR CENTER 4160
INGENIO
PASS 4800
MINA SANTON
CHALLHUA 5476
TUCU 5463
MINA
RIO SANTA
5637
5682
5597
HACIENDA TUCU
HUALLANCA
N
LUSGA
PACHAPAQUI 3900
MINA
RAJO CUTAC 5355
DESAGUA
PUYA RAIMONDI
CONOCOCHA 4 KMS
QUEBRADA TUCU
SUYAN
CHIQUIAN

SCALE 0   5   10   15 KMS

Food can be bought at Catac, the only town shown on the map, which is in the least populated section of the Rio Santa Valley. But it's best to make your headquarters in Huaraz, then catch one of many buses each day to this region. Many climbs are relatively easy here, but ice ax & crampons will still be needed.

Maps *Recuay,* 1:100,000, from the IGM, Lima; check South American Explorers Club website (www.samexplo.org); and the books, **Yuraq Janka (Cordilleras Blanca),** American Alpine Club; **Peruvian Andes,** Beaud, Cordee Books; or **Climbing in the Cordillera Blanca**, Sharman; and travel guidebook, **Peru,** Lonely Planet and/or Footprint Handbooks.

Cerro Burro, Cordillera Huallanca, Peru

Everyone knows of the Cordilleras Blanca and Huayhuash in central Peru, but few know of a small and compact mountain range sandwiched in between these 2 higher, larger and more famous ranges. This obscure massif is called the Cordillera Huallanca. If you've been to Chiquian, the main entry points to the Huayhuash, you may remember the road heading northeast out of town. This is the only practical way of reaching the Huallanca and the highest summit, Cerro Burro, at about 5450 meters. Burro is the name of the highest peak on IGM maps, but some call it *Cerro Huallanca*. More precisely, this range is located just northeast of Chiquian, and east of the Pongos Group (see previous map).

Here's how to get to **Cerro Burro**. First take a bus from Huaraz or Lima to the pleasant little town of Chiquian just to the south of this map. There are buses running from Chiquian to Pachapaqui, but it may not run every day. However, if you were to hang around the central plaza in Chiquian, it's likely at least one vehicle of some kind will be found going to Pachapaqui each day. Most likely it would be a mining truck taking passengers and cargo. You could also reach the east side of the range by way of Cerro de Pasco, then Huanuco, La Union, and finally to the town of Huallanca, but this is a very long trip and it seems most traffic to the Huallanca is from the Chiquian side anyway.

Pachapaqui is a small mining community with a refinery just east of town. It has several small stores, but they don't have much to sell. Chiquian is much larger and a better place to make headquarters while in this area, but Huaraz is by far the best place in the region to stock up on food.

From Pachapaqui, there's a good but dusty road heading east to some mines near the base of Cerro Burro (or you can walk along a trail on the other side of the small river). It's likely you could get a ride to these mines in a company truck if you were to make inquires at the mine office in Pachapaqui. Otherwise it's a 6 or 7 km walk to the base of the mountain.

From near Cara (some Indian huts), there's you can walk southeast and reach other high peaks, namely **Chaup Janca** (perhaps called Nevado Soltario on some maps?), and other snow capped summits. The author has drawn some route symbols on the map for climbing Burro, but has not actually climbed it; he has however climbed on Chaup Janca instead.

On 6/20/1982, the author rode in a rattle-trap bus from Chiquian to Pachapaqui. After he got off the bus, he walked east for half an hour and camped. Next morning, he continued upcanyon and finally hid his pack at 4300 meters and continued toward Chaup Janca, but got on the wrong route and had to look for a better one. Never did reach the summit as these are quite challenging peaks. After that disappointment, he returned to Pachapaqui but ended up walking the 15 kms to Aquia. There were trucks going up, but none down. While Aquia has one little hotel it must have looked pretty bad, because he continued for another km and camped instead. Next morning he walked about 15 more kms to Chiquian and got a bus to Lima around mid-day.

The rocks in the Huallanca are of various kinds from limestone to slates and shales; and maybe a

Substituting for Cerro Burro is this foto of El Misti from the east (Map 553, page 1171).

Map 537-1, Cerro Burro, Cordillera Huallanca, Peru

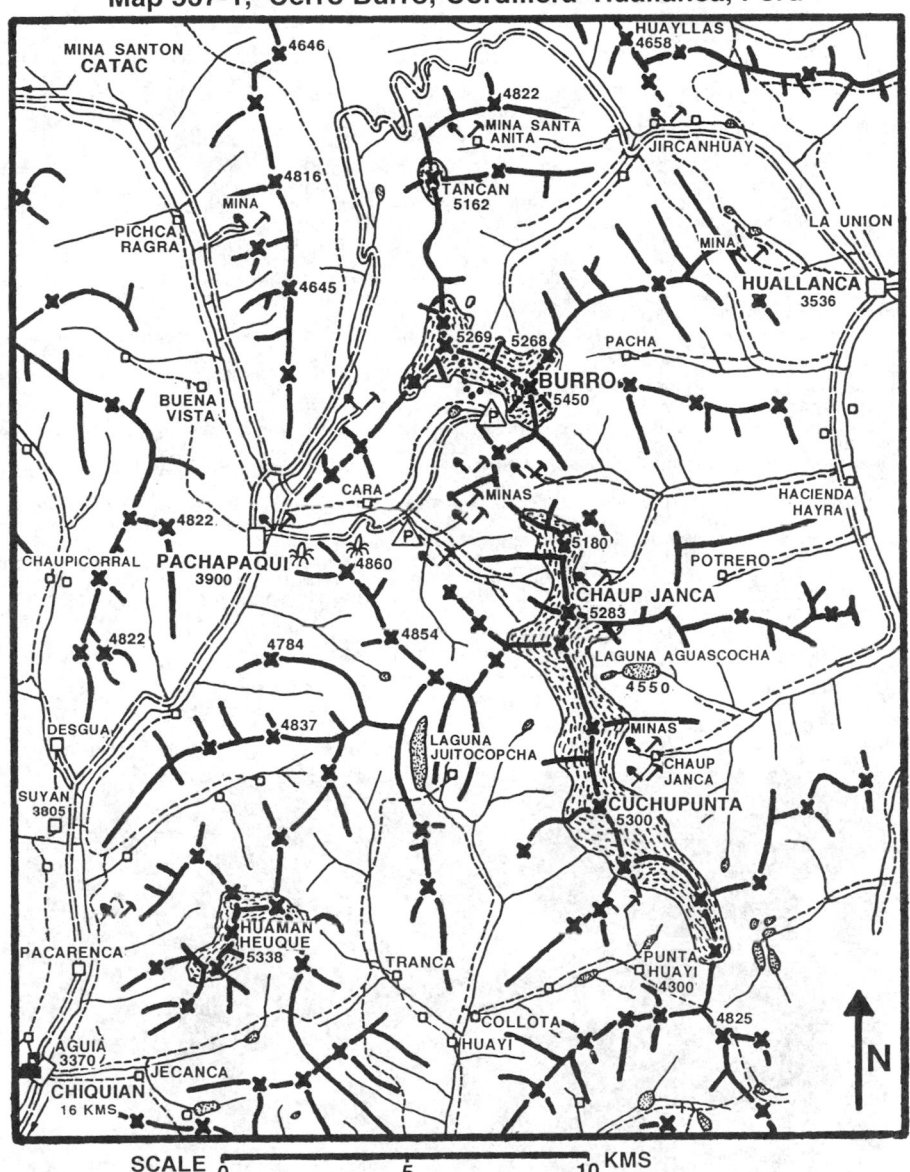

little granite (?). All of these higher peaks are for experienced climbers, but they're not as difficult as the more rugged peaks in the Cordillera Blanca. You'll need at least an ice ax & crampons for all peaks over 5000 meters; and maybe a rope. Note the rare Puya Raimondi just east of Pachapaqui on north facing slopes. May to September is the dry season.

Maps *Recuay, La Union, and Chiquian,* 1:100,000, from the IGM, 1190 Av. Arumburu, San Isidro (barrio), Lima; and perhaps the books **Peruvian Andes**, Beaud, Cordee Books; and travel guidebook, **Peru,** Lonely Planet and/or Footprint Handbooks.

Yerupaja, Cordillera Huayhuash, Peru

One of the most spectacular peaks in South America, and in the world for that matter, is Yerupaja, 6617 meters. This peak dominates the skyline of the Cordillera Huayhuash, a compact but towering mountain range located just southeast of the Cordillera Blanca in west central Peru.

The physical makeup of the range is similar to that of the Cordillera Blanca, consisting of rock such as granite at the center of the range. There's no such thing as a *walk-up* route in the whole Yerupaja Massif, as these peaks are some of the most challenging in the world. There are 7 peaks over 6000 meters.

In recent years the Cordillera Huayhuash has become rather popular among trekkers and climbers. There are many small companies or individuals, who take groups of hikers into these mountains, usually making a circular route around the range. For both climbers & trekkers, the traditional starting point for entering the Huayhuash has been **Chiquian**.

Chiquian is located 32 kms east of Conococha (120 kms from Huaraz), which is on the main highway linking Lima and Huaraz. Chiquian is still a quiet little town with many small shops, at least 2 inexpensive hotels, and a good daily market with lots of little food stalls & coffee shops. There are daily buses (mostly at night) going to or from Lima, plus 3 daily buses, plus non-scheduled trucks linking Chiquian to Huaraz.

It's also possible to begin a trek at the town of **Cajatambo**, southwest of the range and at the bottom of this map. There are 2 daily buses to/from Lima, plus 3 small hotels. Another way in or out of the area is via Oyon (Oyun), which is southeast of this massif. See that town on the next map of San Rosa and the Cordillera Raura.

The author made it to Chiquian on 2 occasions. The first time was on 7/12 & 7/13/1980. This was about 2 weeks after tearing cartilage in one knee so it was mostly a rest stop. But he did walk out of town to the south and had a good look at the mountain and talked to returning trekkers. Next trip was on 6/22/1982 as he was returning from Cerro Burro and Pachapaqui--see previous map.

From Chiquian, start walking the trail southeast out of town. There are many trails, so continually inquire about the correct route along the way. The normal base camp for climbers in the Huayhuash, especially for those climbing **Yerupaja**, is the area around Lugunas Jahuacocha & Solteracocha at the bottom of the northwestern slopes. For most, this is a 2 day hike from Chiquian. Many trekkers go that way too and since most of them today are basically tourists, require a minimum of 5 days round-trip. It'll take several more days to climb Yerupaja.

For many trekkers, the normal thing to do is to walk completely around the range, taking 10 to 12 days for the circuit. Tough climbers can do it in nearly half that time! Although many groups bring food from their home country, the author found adequate food supplies in Chiquian. However, for better selections, shop in Lima or Huaraz.

The dry season for the Huayhuash is the same as for all of Peru, from about late May through early September. For further information and/or maps stop in Lima at the national tourist office or Instituto Geografico Militar; or in Huaraz at the Casa de Guias (best) or tourist office. If you're looking for a helping hand in transport, advice, maybe even a guide service,

Yerupaja as seen from near Lago Solterococha. Yerupaja Chico left (E. Bordogni foto).

Map 538-1, Yerupaja, Cordillera Huayhuash, Peru

SCALE

			KMS
0	5	10	15

Huaraz is the best place to do that. While there, you'll also be acclimatizing at over 3000 meters.

Maps *Chiquian & Yanahuanca*, 1:100,000, from the IGM, Lima; check South American Explorers Club website (www.samexplo.org); and the books, **Trails of the Cordilleras Blanca & Huayhuash of Peru** (if still available) Bartle; and perhaps the books **Peruvian Andes**, Beaud, Cordee Books; and travel guidebooks, **Peru**, Lonely Planet and/or Footprint Handbooks, or the **South American Handbook**.

Cerro Santa Rosa, Cordillera Raura, Peru

Just southeast of the Cordillera Huayhuash and Yerupaja, is another group of peaks known as the Cordillera Raura. Some people would classify them as part of the Huayhuash, but officially they're listed as a separate mountain range. The highest peak in this group is Santa Rosa, 5706 meters. Like the neighboring ranges to the northwest, this peak and the entire group, is glaciated and steep and challenging for climbers.

One advantage of trekking or climbing in the Raura, is that you'll likely not see or meet other climbers or trekking groups. It's still unknown to the average traveler in Peru or to the armchair climber at home. Despite the fact it's unknown, it has some very good climbing possibilities. Perhaps one reason it's been overlooked is that right in the middle of the highest peaks is a big mining operation called the Mina Raura.

Getting to the village of Oyon, which is probably the easiest and least complicated route of approach to the peaks, is not so difficult, but may be time consuming. There are at least 2 buses running between Lima and Oyon daily, but finding these small bus companies in Lima can be difficult. It may be easier to take any bus and go 149 kms north of Lima along the coast to a city named Huacho. From there it would be much easier to find a bus or truck to Sayan, Churin and finally Oyon. You could also take a bus or truck to the town of Cajatambo west of Raura, but this involves a much longer hike to the peaks.

There's at least one hotel in Oyon and several small stores where most basic food items can be found. However, in this case it's better to purchase food and supplies in Lima or another larger city before arriving in this region. From Oyon, trucks or 4WD's can be found going to the many mines or haciendas in the valley to the north and closer to the mountains. Look for something going to the Mina Raura which is a group of mines scattered around the 3 lakes shown on the map. It's about 32 kms from Oyon to Mina Raura.

The easiest route up **Santa Rosa** is from the Mina Raura. From near the end of the road, climb south into the glacier basin and to the summit via the north face. This should be a long one day climb from a camp at the bottom of the glacier.

Here's what the author did. This was the next to last climb he made, or rather attempted, before flying home from Lima after a 6 month tour of South America in the first half of 1982. He left Lima on 6/18/1982 in the 11am bus (another bus leaves at 7am). The route was north along the coast to Huacho & Huaura, then northeast past Sayan & Churin and another 32 kms to Oyon, arriving there at 7:30pm. To avoid a crowd, he walked 2 kms north out of town and camped in the moonlight. Next morning, he got a ride on top of a Coca Cola truck (cold!) going to the Mina Raura. He left his big pack at the main entry gate, and if notes are correct, climbed an easy 5000 meter peak just to the east and got some good fotos of the area, including this one of the northern slopes of Santa Rosa. All high summits in these parts are a little too much for a safe solo climb so he returned to the mine, and got a lift back down to the coast arriving long after dark.

Looking at the north side of Santa Rosa from the Mina Raura at 4800 meters.

Map 539-1, Cerro Santa Rosa, Cordillera Raura, Peru

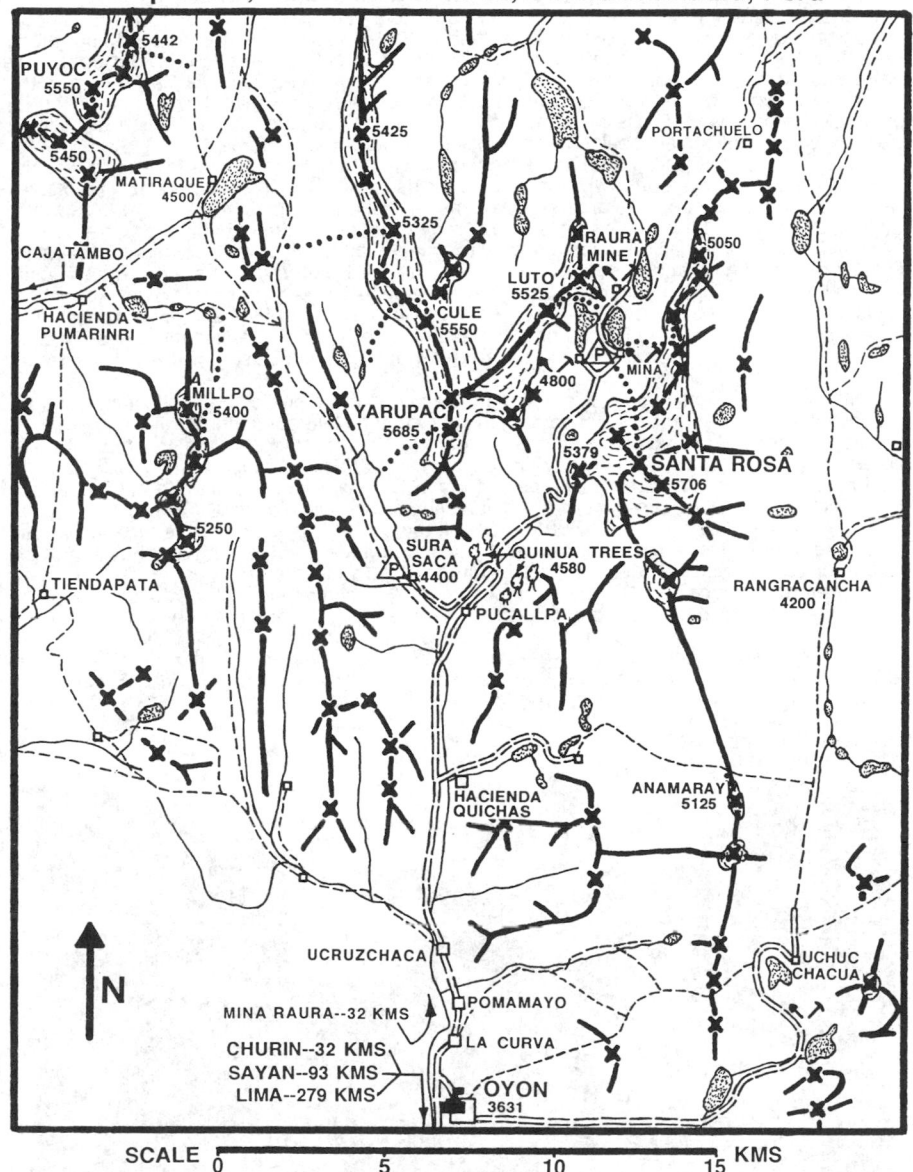

SCALE 0   5   10   15 KMS

Other routes on other peaks shown are approximations, made by using the IGM maps. **Yarupac**, 5685 meters, can be climbed from Sura Saca and the western slopes. **Cule**, at 5550 meters, from the same approach route and a final climb up the north face. **Luto** 5525, can be climbed from the Mina Raura and a northeast ridge. Climbing season is normally from late May through early September.

Maps *Yanahuanca and Oyon,* 1:100,000, from the IGM, Lima; and perhaps the books **Peruvian Andes**, Beaud, Cordee Books; and travel guidebooks, **Peru**, Lonely Planet; or **Peru** or **South American Handbooks**, Footprint Handbooks; also check the South American Explorers Club website (www.samexplo.org) for other publications.

Cerro Raujunte, Cordillera La Viuda, Peru

In central Peru not far northeast of Lima, is a mountainous region with scattered snow-capped peaks known as the Cordillera La Viuda. Even though they're close to Lima, these summits seem unknown in mountaineering circles. The likely reason is these peaks are scattered and there isn't one massif or group that is outstanding such as Yerupaja and the Cordillera Huayhuash. Because they're not so popular, that may make it more interesting for some trekkers because it's possible some Indians in the most-remote villages have never seen a foreign traveler. The highest peak on this map is Raujunte about 5650 meters.

This region is populated in the lower sections, with many livestock trails leading into the higher valleys. It's also an area with small mines, plus many lakes, the result of past glaciation. The author passed through this area several times on this long trips in 1972-73, 1980 & 1982, both by tren (train) and bus, but never took the time to stop and do any climbing.

From Lima there's a major paved highway running northeast through Matucana, Casapalca, Morococha, La Oroya, and on to Cerro de Pasco and/or Huancayo. There are many buses traveling this line so finding transport is easy. From various towns on this main highway such as Chicla, Casapalca or Morococha, entry can be made to all or most of the summits. There's also the rail line and trens running from Lima to Huancayo and beyond. Consult the tourist office in Lima about which may be the best. The author would choose buses, then look for trucks running off from the main highway.

For traveling the secondary roads one idea would be to take one of many buses heading for La Oroya or beyond, get off at Casapalca and look for a truck heading north to mining areas or haciendas. The road to Ondores is the main access to Marcapomacocha, the only real village in this region away from the main highway. If you can't find a truck carrying passengers, you might look for a taxi to get a little closer to the peaks. Or just start walking and hope for a lift. Many of the higher mountains here are within walking distance of the main highway.

Here's how you can reach **Raujunte**. Get off the bus at Casapalca, or better still, Curvas just up the road 3 kms. From Curvas, start walking up the graveled road and hope for a lift. After 11 or 12 kms, you'll be at the foot of Raujunte. One suggested route is up the west ridge which is supposed to be easy. The routes shown to other summits are guesses only, made by using the 1:100,000 maps from the IGM in Lima. They may or may not be the best climbing routes.

Being so close to Lima, that's the best place to buy food and obtain information about the mountains, buses, etc. Also, the best maps available can be purchased in Lima. First contact the tourist office downtown or at the airport for the up-to-date addresses of the IGM, the South American Explorers Club (www.samexplo.org), various club andinos and addresses of bus stations and/or companies.

This *tren* station is Galeria, the highest railway in the world.

Map 540-2, Cerro Raujunte, Cordillera La Viuda, Peru

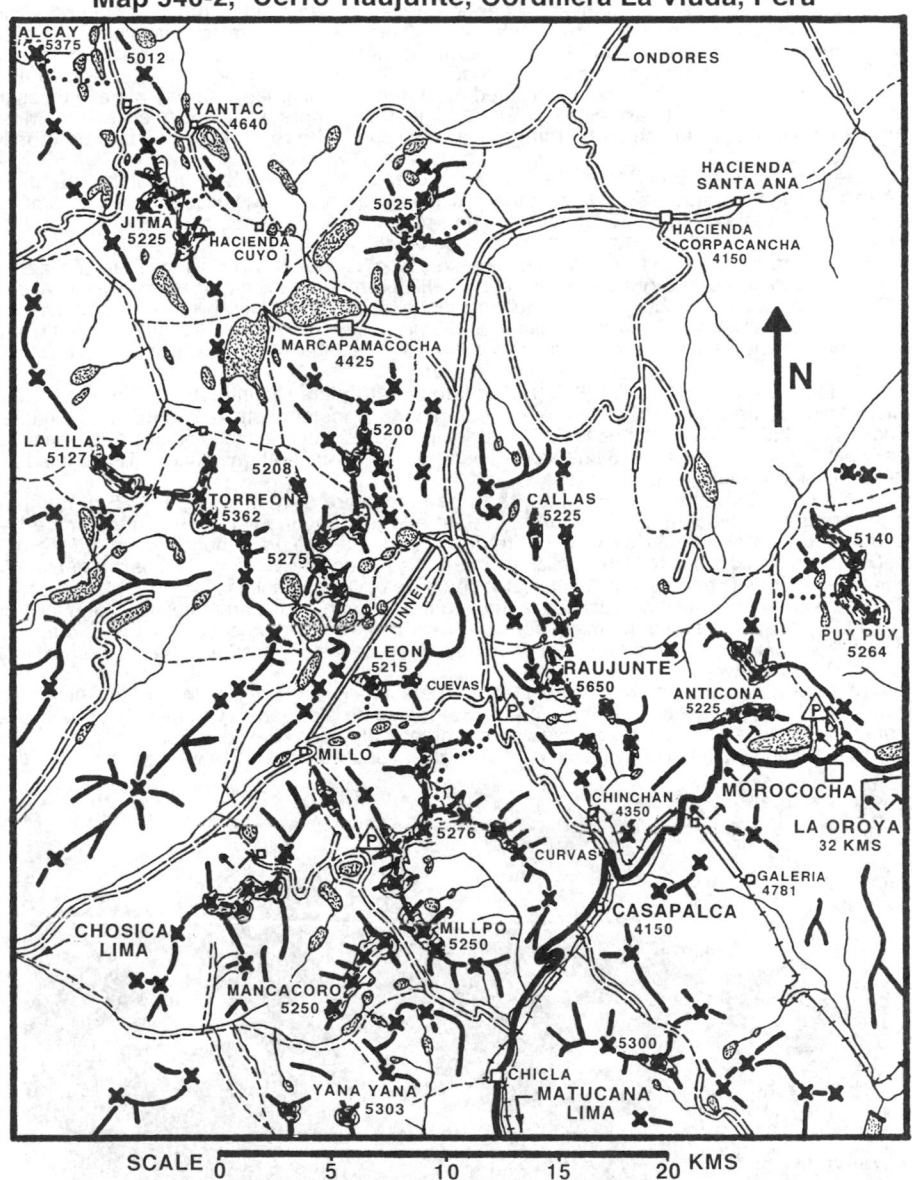

SCALE 0   5   10   15   20 KMS

May through the first part of September is the best time to climb. These are fairly rugged mountains, but not as difficult as in other ranges in Peru, such as in the Cordillera Huayhuash or Blanca. You'll need ice ax & crampons for all the higher summits over about 5000 meters.

Maps *Matucana and maybe Ondores,* 1:100,000, from the IGM, 1190 Av. Aramburu, San Isidro (barrio). Lima; and perhaps the books **Peruvian Andes (?)**, Beaud, Cordee Books; and travel guidebooks, **Peru**, Lonely Planet; or **Peru** or the **South American Handbook**, Footprint Handbooks.

Cerro Tunshu, Cordillera Central, Peru

Due east of Lima is a group of snow capped peaks known as the Cordillera Central. The highest summit on this map is Cerro Tunshu at 5730 meters. This peak stands alone, just east of the main ridge where most of the high summits are located. Within this section of the Cordillera Central are many peaks with altitudes of 5400/5500 meters, and several others in the 5600 meter range. They have been glaciated much more in the past, resulting in many lakes in the high valleys. These peaks are fairly rugged and are for more experienced climbers. Most higher peaks require an ice ax & crampons and a rope. The rocks here seem to be mostly metamorphic.

The mountains around Cuzco, the Cordillera Blanca and Huayhuash get all the attention, while this range is almost unknown. For those seeking new routes and possibly even unclimbed peaks, this might be the place for you. It's one place you'll likely not meet other climbers or trekkers. In other words, it's not a part of the *gringo trail!*

Here's what the author did. In Huancayo he bought food & supplies for 4 days, left extra baggage at the Hotel Baldeon, then early on the morning of 6/9/1982, boarded a tren heading towards Lima. After 2 1/2 hours, he got off at a country station called Pachacayo and walked 3 kms to the town of Canchayllo. After a snack, he walked 20 kms to the Hacienda Cochas arriving at 4:20pm. Not much traffic on that road. He borrowed a hammer, repaired boots, then walked another 40 minutes and camped at 4150 meters.

On the morning of Day 2 at -8°C, he walked toward Mina Bicunita, but left the road and walked directly west toward **Tunshu**. Made camp at 4870 meters right at the bottom of the east ridge. Day 3 at -7°C, climbed up to 5575 meters in 2 hours, put crampons on, but felt it was too risky getting around the 1st of 3 buttresses near the summit, so he turned back. This should be fairly easy for a small group with a rope.

He returned via the Bicunita Mine, then headed more or less straight for Suitucancha through some swampy areas in 3 hours, then to and just beyond Huay Huay and camped at 3935 meters. Morning of Day 4 in -8°C temperatures, he walked without breakfast for 1 1/2 hours, jumped into a bus to Huari, which is on the main highway & railway line between Lima & Huancayo. Got into another bus for the 2 1/2 hour ride back to Huancayo.

There are 4WD or mining truck roads leading to the heart of this area, but you'll find little or no public transport beyond the main highway linking Lima and Huancayo, except for one or 2 buses a day to Huay Huay. From Lima, there are many buses and trucks on the paved highway running to Huancayo.

To visit the western part of this group, stop at the small village of San Mateo and walk, and hope for a lift southeast to some mining areas along some old roads. You can also ride a bus from Lima to Huarochiri, in the southwest corner of the map, then hike north from there.

Your starting point will likely be Lima, so buy most supplies there. The villages shown on the

Tunshu and its east ridge as seen from the valley east of the peak.

Map 541-1, Cerro Tunshu, Cordillera Central, Peru

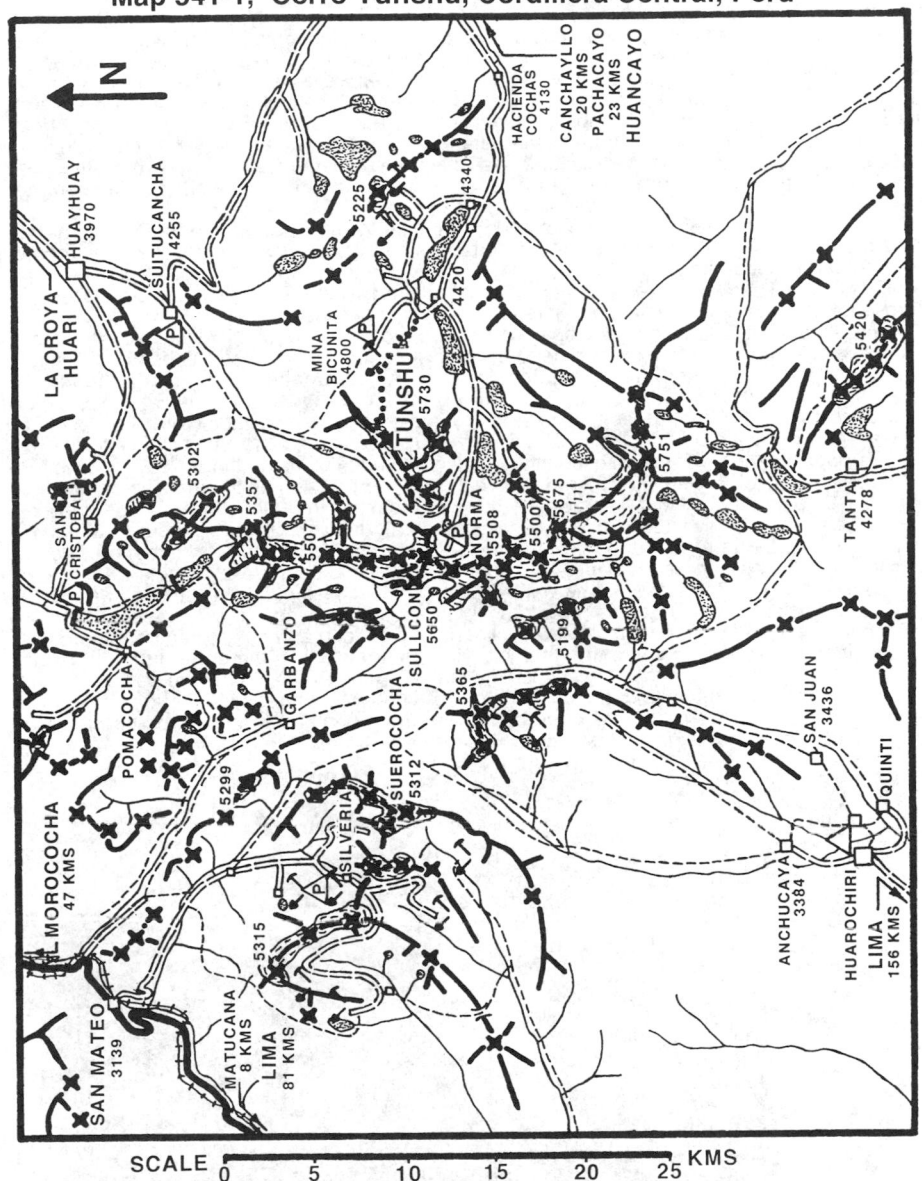

SCALE 0 5 10 15 20 25 KMS

map will stock basic foods only. Huancayo is a small city with very good food selections, plus a good tourist office which will help you locate buses or trucks heading for the mountains. Huancayo at nearly 3300 meters is a good place to acclimatize and/or rehabilitate between climbs. The dry season is generally from late May through early September. The skies were clear on the author's trip, which makes some cold nights!

Maps *Matucana, Oroya, Huarochiri & Yauyos,* 1:100,000, from the IGM, Lima; and perhaps the books **Peruvian Andes (?)**, Beaud, Cordee Books; and travel guidebooks, **Peru**, Lonely Planet; or **Peru** or **South American Handbook**, Footprint Handbooks.

Nevado Ticlla, Cordillera Central, Peru

This is the second of 2 maps covering the Cordillera Central located in central Peru. This section is directly east of Lima and west of Huancayo. Even though this mountain range is fairly close to high population centers, it's still very isolated, with no paved highways shown on the map. The highest peak in this southern section of the Cordillera Central is Nevado Ticlla, rising to 5897 meters. This summit is located in about the center of the high peaks on this map. There are some mines in this area with mostly metamorphic-type rocks.

One route of approach to **Ticlla** is via Asia (on the main coastal highway south of Lima), Coayllo, Omas and finally to the village of Ayaviri at the end of the road. From Ayaviri, there are trails on both sides of the river heading east, then northeast, to a large lake named Huascacocha. There may be a route up Ticlla from there (?).

Another approach is from the south and the coastal town of Cañete. From Cañete, a road heads northeast to the town of Yauyos, located about halfway between the coast and Huancayo. From near Yauyos, the same road continues to the village of Tinco Miraflores, east of Ticlla. This approach seems to have more trails, shepherds and livestock than the western slopes, the presence of which are advantageous in reaching the high peaks.

Whichever route is taken, take any bus running along the coastal highway south of Lima, and stop at Asia or Cañete. From either of these places, trucks or buses can be found going to the upper valleys. (Later information tells of daily buses running from Lima to the town of Yauyos). One disadvantage with starting on the coast is the low altitude and lack of acclimatization. For that reason it's best to first make your way to Huancayo at nearly 3300 meters elevation for a breath of thin air. It's 6-7 hours by bus from Lima on a paved highway.

Perhaps the best way to these mountains is the one used by the author from Huancayo. He stayed in the Hotel Baldeon and stored extra baggage there. Then on the morning of 6/4/1982, took the 6:40am three-or-four-times-weekly bus which passes through Tomas, Tinco Yaricocha, Tinco Miraflores and eventually to Yauyos. He got off at Tinco Miraflores at about 12:30pm and walked 9 kms to the terraced & half-abandoned village of Miraflores. From there it was due west toward the place called Banadera. At 5pm, he stopped to camp at 4240 meters.

The morning of Day 2 at -7°C, he walked for an hour, hid his pack, and climbed Peak 5422 for a good look at the area & fotos. At 2:30pm (7 hours after leaving camp) he reached the pass (Paso Ticlla) at 4945 meters just east of Ticlla, but it's a steep and risky climb from there for a solo climber, so he abandoned the attempt. He headed down to the north, turned east and eventually stopped at 5pm to camp at 4360 meters. Morning Day 3 at -9°C, he walked for 1 1/3 hours to Miraflores and on to near Tomas before getting a short ride. Later he got another ride to near Huancayo, but had to camp for the night in the moonlight. On the morning of the 4th day, he got one short ride in a truck back to Huancayo.

The south ridge of Ticlla to the left, seem like an easy but crevassed climb.

Map 542-1, Nevado Ticlla, Cordillera Central, Peru

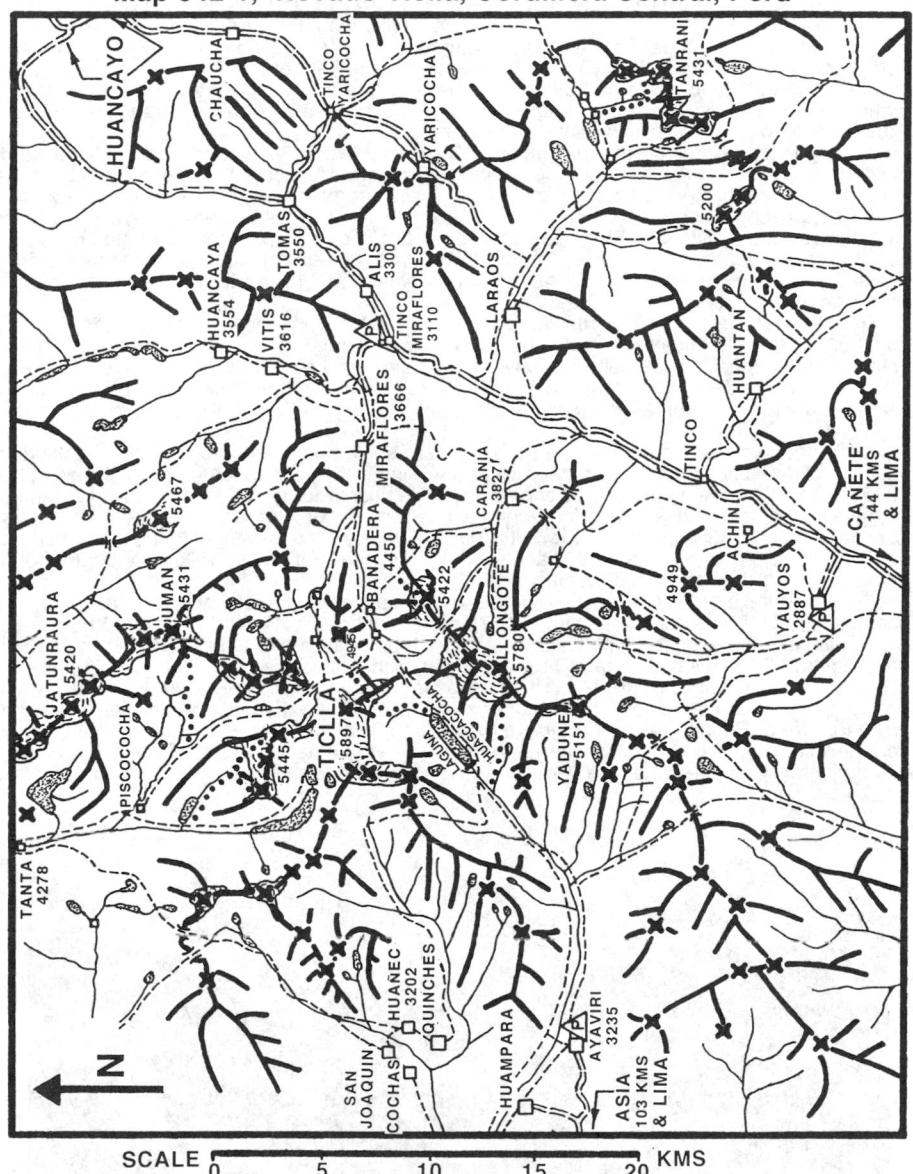

SCALE
0   5   10   15   20   KMS

Villages on this map are small, but each usually has several small shops for all the basic foods, but best to buy supplies in Huancayo. Peaks over about 5400 meters are for experienced & well-equipped climbers; peaks under 5400 are generally safe for solo climbing. Climb from late May to early September. Also, the canyon below Tomas is interesting.

Maps *Huarochiro and Yauyos,* 1:100,000, from the IGM, 1190 Av. Aramburu, San Isidro (barrio), Lima; and perhaps the books **Peruvian Andes (?)**, Beaud, Cordee Books; and travel guidebooks, **Peru**, Lonely Planet; or **Peru** or **South American Handbook**, Footprint Handbooks.

Cerro Jallacata, Cordillera Huaytapallana, Peru

If you're interested in out-of-the-way places where few mountaineers dare venture you might try the Cordillera Huaytapallana. This small compact mountain range or massif is located just northeast of the city of Huancayo and the Mantaro Valley in central Peru. There are many tourists visiting Huancayo, especially on Sundays to see the weekly mercado, but very few mountaineers or andinistas going to these peaks, although getting there is easy and there's some very good and challenging climbs to be found.

The highest peak in the Huaytapallana is Jallacata rising to 5557 meters. It's located toward the southern end of a big high ridge. To get there, first go to Huancayo. Get there from Lima by daily tren over the highest railway in the world; or by one of many daily buses. You can also get there from Cuzco, Ayachcho and Huancavelica to the southeast. Once there, inquire at the local tourist information office about the exact location of the departure area for buses and/or trucks going in the direction of Pariahuanca. In 1982 it was located on Calle Cajamarca where it intersects the railway line just south of the railway station. But departure places change from time to time.

Here's what the author did on **Jallacata** which was right after his attempts on Ticlla & Tunshu. On the morning of 6/14/1982, he got on a truck bound for Pariahuanca located on the east side of the mountains. It left at 11am. At 1:45pm, it reached the pass marked 4575 meters which is at or near Km 29. He got off and started walking in the direction of Laguna Lazo Huntay, but stopped soon after and climbed a peak at about 5075 meters for a look around in the clouds.

After that he walked to the lake where there were some abandoned construction work crew huts and camped nearby at 4600 meters. Next morning in -7°C temperatures, he climbed up to 5300 meters before being blocked by crevasses. With poor visibility and storm clouds gathering, he gave up; but it looks fairly easy for 2 people on a rope. It took less than 2 hours to get there from camp, and about 45 minutes down. He packed up quickly and walked to the main road for lunch, then walked halfway back to Huancayo before getting a lift. Meanwhile, 7 or 8 buses and trucks passed him going toward Pariahuanca.

There are several vehicles a day going to Pariahuanca, but usually only one takes a lot of passengers. Get off at the pass marked 4575 meters at Km 29. From there it's a 2 hour walk with a big pack to the base of the southwest face of the peak. Make base camp at the Laguna Lazo Huntay. From the lake ascend the west ridge which is likely the easiest and safest route.

This mountain range has big glaciers & crevasses which extend down to about 4800 meters on the drier western face. For all the higher summits you'll need an ice ax & crampons and a rope & partner. Before leaving Huancayo have all supplies on hand. Huancayo is a city with good selections of food in a large market place. Everything needed for a climbing expedition can be found there, and it's a good place to visit and acclimatize before going to the mountains.

The highest peaks of the Cordillera Huaytapallana as seen from the west side.

Map 543-1, Cerro Jallacate, Cordillera Huaytapallana, Peru

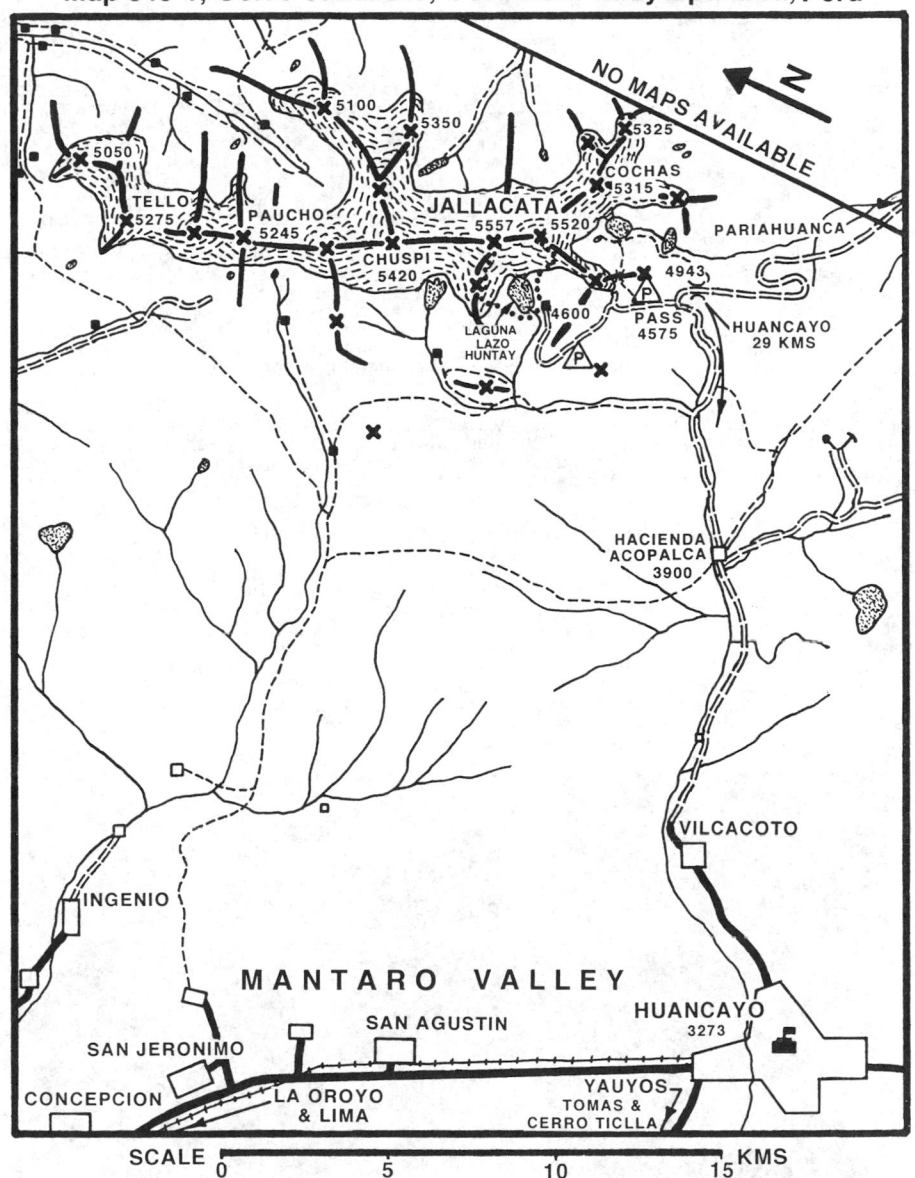

There are many hotels to choose from as it's a tourist city. Remember, the Huaytapallana is a wetter area than the ranges west of Huancayo. Best to go prepared with raingear even in the May-to-September dry season.

Maps *Jauja and Huancayo,* 1:100,000, from the IGM, Lima; and perhaps the books **Peruvian Andes**, Beaud, Cordee Books; and travel guidebooks, **Peru**, Lonely Planet; or **Peru** or **South American Handbook**, Footprint Handbooks; also check the South American Explorers Club website (www.samexplo.org) for other publications.

Salcantay & Humantay, Cordillera Vilcabamba, Peru

This map shows part of the mountain range called the Cordillera Vilcabamba. It lies northwest of Cuzco in west central Peru. The highest summit here and in the entire Vilcabamba is Salcantay (Salkantay) at 6271 meters.

There are 3 ways to get to **Salcantay**. The access route most commonly used is the one beginning at Km 88 on the railway line running between Cuzco and Machu Picchu. This is also the normal starting point for the thousands of tourists who walk the *Inca Trail* between Km 88 & Machu Picchu. From Km 88, which is only a stopping point on the line, the trail heads south, past Huayllabamba (where most turn right for Machu Picchu) and Pampacahuana, then over a pass and down to Soray and finally to another possible starting point, Mollepata.

To reach Mollepata, take a bus or truck from Cuzco or Abancay, to the road junction below Mollepata, then either walk or catch another ride up to the village, then continue upvalley to the north. If the author were to do this trip again, he'd take a bus or truck to Mollepata to avoid the thieves on the local tren to Machu Picchu!

You could also get to Salcantay by taking the same tren from Cuzco on down the line past Machu Picchu to the town of Santa Teresa. From there walk (or hire a vehicle) south along the road to Punta Carretera, then hike to Colcapampa and turn east to Salcantay.

Once you get to the mountain, the normal route up Salcantay is the northeast ridge. This is reached via the East Pass at 4720 meters as shown on the map. An experienced & tough climber might do the ridge solo, but it's not an easy climb and conditions would have to be perfect. All other routes up this peak require experienced climbers with snow & ice climbing equipment.

The walk from Km 88 to a base camp at the foot of the northeast ridge will take 2 days for most. The summit climb is normally one day, then another day back to Km 88. That's perhaps 4 days for fit and already acclimatized climbers with good luck & fair weather. However, the author recommends taking 5 or 6 days or more of food, and much more if other routes or summits are to be attempted. **Humantay**, at 5917 meters, is the second highest peak on the map, and it too is a difficult climb. The easiest route is from another pass marked 4620 meters and up the northeast ridge or buttress.

On the morning of 7/2/1980, the author got up early and got on the 6:30am local tren out of Cuzco. Got off at Km 88 about 9:30am along with about 100 other *gringos* heading for the Inca Trail. All had to go across the river on a cable car, then walking began at 9:45. At Huayllabamba, the *88'ers* turned right to Machu Picchu, but the author continued south and alone up past Ocollo and made camp at 4100 meters after 6 1/2 hours walking. On Day 2 it was snowing, so with an 11am start, he walked up a good trail over the East Pass to a base camp on the other side at 4650 meters and camped. About 2 hours walking (?), and it snowed all afternoon! The morning of Day 3, at -3°C, was a little better, but with new snow on the rocks of the lower northeast ridge it wasn't fit to climb, so he headed down and up to the Southeast Pass at 4895 meters, then down across a moraine and up to the other pass at 4620, and on down to a camp at 4200 meters; 7 1/3 hours walking. It snowed on & off all that day too! Read about his next 3 days on the next map featuring Pumasillo.

Humantay, second highest peak in the Salcantay Group, as seen from the northeast.

Map 544-1, Salcantay & Humantay, Cordillera Vilcabamba, Peru

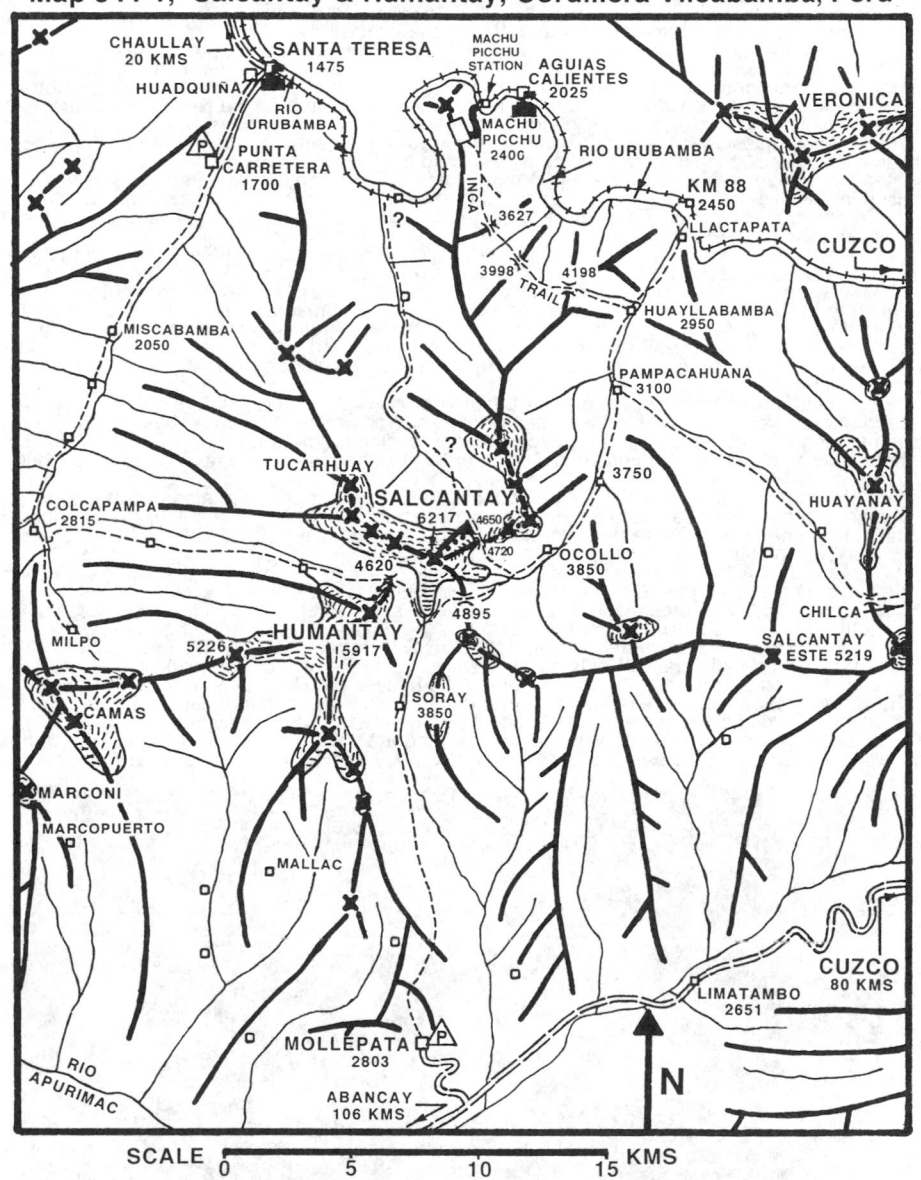

SCALE 0 ── 5 ── 10 ── 15 KMS

If it's the **Inca Trail** you want, plan on from 2 to 4 days to make the hike. Buy all your food in Cuzco. Bigger towns are Santa Teresa, Aguas Calientes and Mollepata. In the valley above (south) Santa Teresa, families are now offering some meals to trekkers. As usual in Peru, the dry season is from May to the beginning of September.

Maps *Carta de la Region Norte del Cusco,* 1:200,000, from the IGM, 1190 Av. Aramburu, San Isidro (barrio), Lima, or *Landstat Foto 2190-14131 (I-10),* from the IGM Lima, or Eros Data Center, Sioux Falls, South Dakota, USA; and perhaps the books **Peruvian Andes**, Beaud, Cordee Books; **Backpacking and Trekking in Peru and Bolivia**, Brandt Enterprises; and travel guidebooks, **Peru**, Lonely Planet and/or Footprint Handbooks.

1153

Pumasillo & Lasunayoc, Cordillera Vilcabamba, Peru

This map includes the central portion of the Cordillera Vilcabamba. The highest summit is Lasunayoc at about 6100 meters, but more famous is Pumasillo at 6070.

Everyone should know that good maps of this mountain range are still lacking. The map used by the author is called *Carta de La Region Norte del Cuzco*, put out by the IGM in Lima. Most climbers consider it to have many inaccuracies. However, the author used it when he visited the area between Km 88 & Santa Teresa and a brief climb on the Nevado Quishua, and found these parts to be reasonably good. That map does not include trails, and was compiled in 1959. Where question marks are shown on this map, it means the location of the trail or road is uncertain. The 5000 meter contour line was used to mark the snowline on this map.

As you travel in this region, keep in mind that all major canyons or quebradas have trails used to take livestock to the high pastures. The lower valleys are all tropical and the first day on the trail will be very warm. Farmers living in the lower valleys near the railway line, grow tropical fruits for their livelihood.

To reach Pumasillo & Lasunayoc there are 2 possible approach routes, both originating at Santa Teresa. Take the tren from Cuzco *past Machu Picchu* to Santa Teresa, then walk up the major canyon southwest above Huadquiña. There must be a trail in that canyon, but that is not confirmed. That would put you on the northeast slopes of **Pumasillo**. The other way would be to find/hire a truck (or walk) going to Punta Carretera then hike to Colcapampa, Paso Yanama, Yanama and to a place called Paccha. From there head north to the west ridge, but avoid a buttress on the left, then continue up the ridge. This is difficult and may take 2 or 3 days from base camp.

It might be possible to find a route to **Lasunayoc** by walking northeast from Totura; but one source states you cross over to the west side of Paso Yanama then follow a valley north to a col just south of the summit. But then ascend the east slopes and a ridge to the top. This map won't help much, so talk to a guide in Cuzco, or locals, and plan on a day or two to scout out a route.

If the southern or Yanama route is used, plan on about 3 days to Yanama or Paccha, and if a serious attempt is to be made on any of the major summits, a total of about 10 days supply of food should be taken. These peaks are all glaciated and challenging and require snow and ice climbing equipment. Ice climbing experience helps too!

Here's the 2nd half of the author's experience with Salcantay and Pumasillo. Read the first part on the previous page. On the morning of 7/5/1982, Day 4, it was -7°C at 4200 meters. He walked down to Colcapampa where he found a small store and got information, then headed up to Totura where he found another store & school, and was invited in for lunch by a pack train cowboy. Camped at 3675 meters above Totura. Day 5 started at -4.5°C, then he bushwhacked south up toward Quishua, but only got to 5000 meters. Returned, and walked down to near Colcapampa and camped at 2850 meters near the bridge. On Day 6, it took 7 hours to walk all the way to Santa Teresa where he had a very tender knee which had torn cartilage from June 26 at Urcos. Walking fast downhill to catch the 3pm tren back to Cuzco really hurt!

Have all your food and supplies before boarding the train in Cuzco, but Santa Teresa has many small shops with basic foods. Also, you can buy some food and meals at Colcapampa

From the slopes of Quishua, looking toward Lasunayoc left, Pumasillo, right.

Map 545-1, Pumasillo & Lasunayoc, Cordillera Vilcabamba, Peru

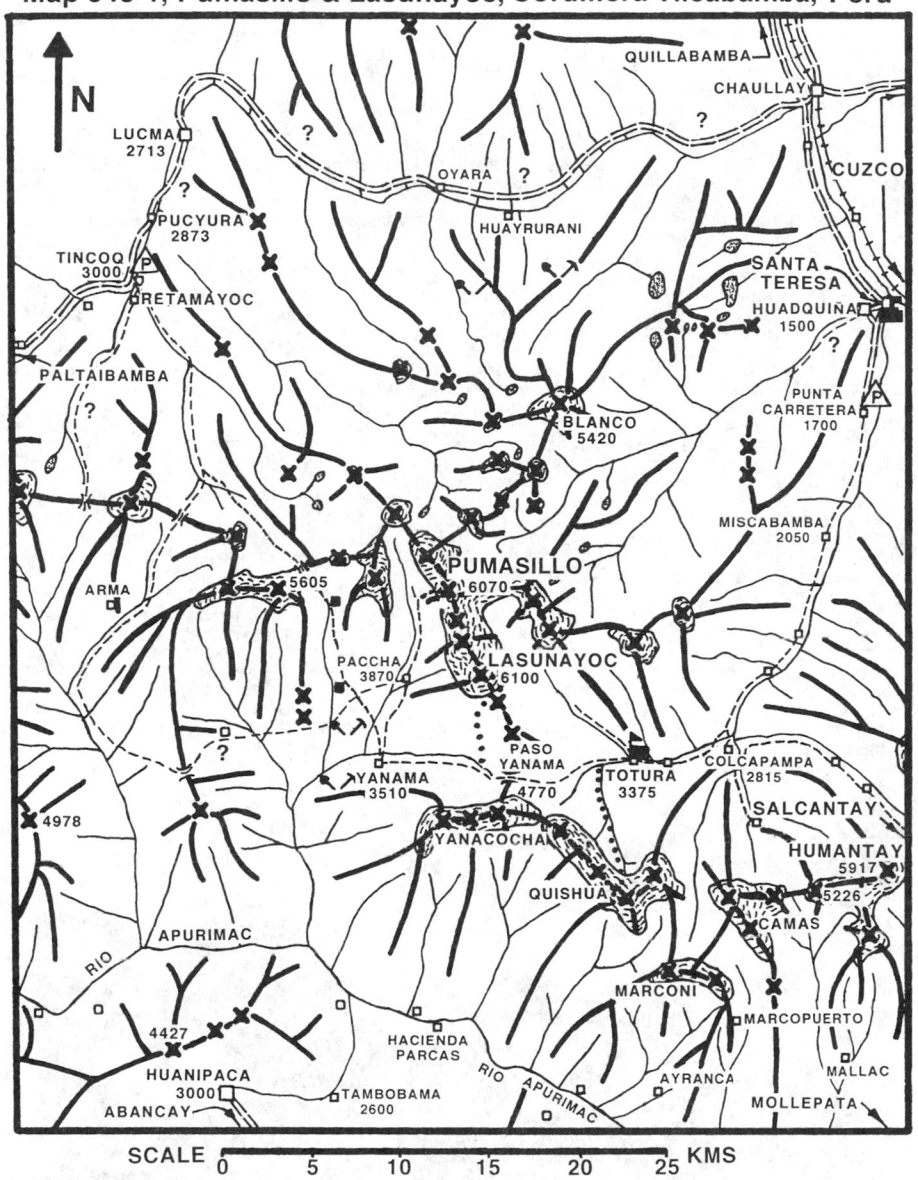

SCALE 0 5 10 15 20 25 KMS

and Totura, and possibly at Lucma and Retamayoc (these are rumors from other trekkers). Chaullay is also a larger town. And each small village seems to have a store. Late May through the beginning of September is the dry season.

Maps *Carta de la Region Norte del Cuzco*, 1:200,000, from the IGM, Lima; or *Landstat Foto 2190-14131(I-10)*, from the IGM, Lima, or EROS Data Center, Sioux Falls, South Dakota, USA; and the books **Peruvian Andes (?)**, Beaud, Cordee Books; **Backpacking and Trekking in Peru and Bolivia**, Brandt Enterprises; and travel guidebooks, **Peru**, Lonely Planet and/or Footprint Handbooks.

Huaycay Huilque, Cordillera Urubamba, Peru

This map shows the Cordillera Urubamba, located northwest of Cuzco and southeast of Manchu Picchu in southeastern Peru. Some climbers may not recognize some of the names on this map. The author has used his own maps and experience talking to locals, maps from **Le Ande**, by Mario Fantin, the Tambo Treks map, *Ollantaytambo-Amparaes*, and *Landstat Foto 219-14131 (I-10)* in creating this map.

The highest peak here is Huaycay Huilque, sometimes spelled Waqaywillka, and sometimes known as Veronica. In the small pueblo of Pisca Cocha, the name Veronica was applied to the peak north of that village, and not the highest summit they call Huaycay Huilque. There's also a lot of confusion on the names of peaks just north of Urubamba. Locals call it Media Luna (Half Moon), and sometimes Chicon. Other maps, especially in *Le Ande*, have totally different names, although elevations given here are from that book.

Keep in mind, these mountains are on the boundary between the Amazon Basin and the Peruvian Altiplano; therefore, during the rainy season, heavy amounts of rain & snow can be expected; thus heavy glaciated and very rugged peaks. These climbs are for experienced & well equipped *andinistas* only. The dry season is from late May into September.

One report indicated the most normal route to the top of **Huaycay Huilque** is from the east and Abra Malaga, but the south ridge looked good; or at least possible. The summit of **Veronica** has been climbed from Pisca Cocha and the south face and then by walking west along the ridge, as shown. Another important group of summits is around **Media Luna**. This is one big ridge with many peaks. Climbers have made ascents from both Urubamba and Yucay, with possibly another route of access from the Hacienda Huaran and Cancha.

There are several other groups along the Urubamba River, but none so high as the 2 mentioned. However, there is one more group of some importance located to the north of the main range. This is **Terijuay**. Climbers have penetrated into this area from Abra Malaga (possibly the best route) and from along the road running from Amparaes to Colca. Little is known of these peaks but they'll make a good expedition.

Reach the Rio Vilcanota Valley by bus from Cuzco or take one of several daily trens to Ollantay(bambo) or Chilca. Best to buy food in Cuzco, but Ollantay, Urubamba and Yucay are bigger towns with many shops and some hotels. Contact Tambo Treks (formerly Robert Randall) at El Albergue; or Andean Treks in Cuzco (formerly Tom Henderson), or any of many new trekking outfits for more detailed & updated information.

With Cuzco his headquarters, the author left extra baggage at a hotel and left town at 8am by bus on 5/27/1982. He rode for 2 1/4 hours and got off at Chilca. At that time the road was paved to Ollantay, but it could be paved all the way to Chilca by now (?). With his full pack, he walked to the end of the road at Pisca Cocha and up the canyon above. He wasn't climbing on this short trip, only gathering information and taking fotos. Later he walked up the other 2 canyons leading toward Huaycay Huilque. There are trails into each canyon. He camped in the 3rd quebrada at 2875 meters. Next morning he talked to different people about names of places and walked to Tanqaq, got on the 10am train for the 10 minute ride to Ollantay. Talked to Robert Randall at El Albergue, then rode to Urubamba in the back of a small pickup for bus fare. Walked up the Quebrada Chicon to the base of Media Luna, then back along the highway to Yucay and got a bus to the Hacienda Huaran. Walked into

This is Huaycay Huilque to the right as seen from just north of Ollantaytambo.

Map 546-1, Huaycay Huilque, Cordillera Urubamba, Peru

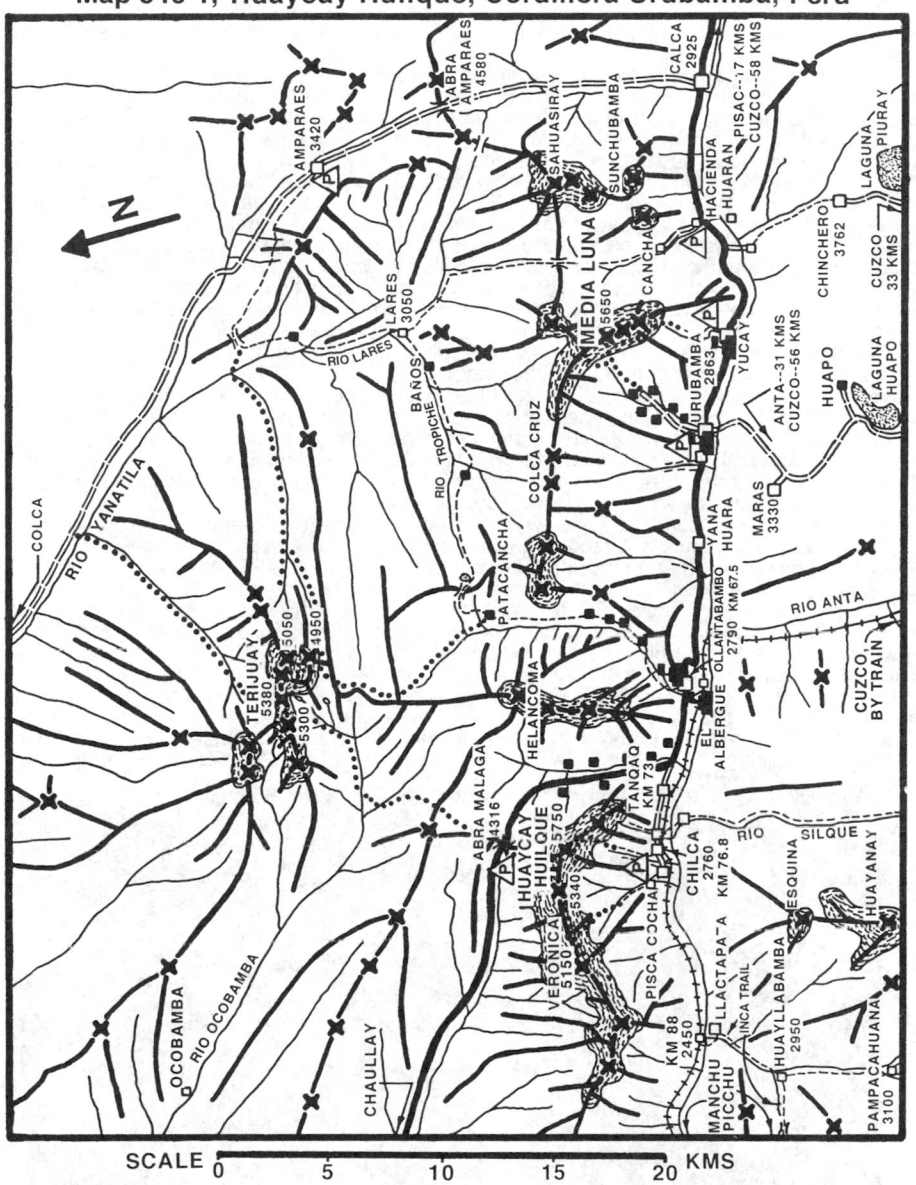

SCALE 0 5 10 15 20 KMS

the canyon near Cancha for a campsite. Next morning walking down and got in a pickup and a quick visit to the ruins of Pisac and on to Cuzco. Perfect weather for 2 1/2 days.

Maps *Landstat Foto 2190-14131 (l-10)*, from the IGM, Lima, or EROS Data Center, Sioux Falls, South Dakota, USA; TPC map *N-25C*, 1:500,000; and perhaps the books, **Peruvian Andes (?)**, Beaud, Cordee Books; **Backpacking and Trekking in Peru and Bolivia**, Brandt Enterprises; and travel guidebooks, **Peru**, Lonely Planet and/or Footprint Handbooks.

Nevado Ausangate, Cordillera Vilcanota, Peru

In the region southeast of Cuzco and east of Urcos in the Cordillera Vilcanota, are some of the most rugged and spectacular peaks in Peru. The highest and most visible is Ausangate at 6372 meters.

There are several ways of approaching the Cordillera Vilcanota, but by far the easiest is via Cuzco (or Juliaca to the south) to Urcos, then east along the road passing through Ocongate and ending at the Amazon city of (Puerto) Maldonado. From along this road, one of many trails can be taken to any part of the Vilcanota. The valley above Ocongate, the largest town on this map, is sparsely populated with small settlements and trails everywhere. There are shepherd huts in every valley up to about 4300 meters, with about 3 snarling barking dogs to each hut!

In recent years trekkers have discovered this area along with climbers. A popular trekking route is via Ocongate, Chillca, and Pitumarca, passing beneath Ausangate.

To reach **Ausangate** and the normal climbing route up the south face, you should first take a bus from Cuzco south; or from Juliaca north; and stop at Urcos (with several small hotels). Wait at the police checkpoint in Urcos for truck convoys going to Maldonado. With luck you'll likely now find a bus. Get off at either Yanama or the Hacienda Tinqui, about 5 and 9 kms along the road above Ocongate. The author stopped at Ocongate and walked from there, but it may be shorter if you use the trail from Tinqui and Upis (but if using that route you'd have to wade one stream). It's about the same distance either way.

The south face of Ausangate is one continuous icefall, with literally hundreds of crevasses to negotiate. If you're following the tracks of someone else in hard snow, it may take only one day to reach the summit from a high base camp, but you should plan on at least one night on the face. It has apparently been climbed solo (?), but that's not recommended. Ausangate and the high peaks in that area are for experienced and well-equipped climbers only. For less-experienced climbers, try something below about 5500 meters.

On the morning of 6/23/1980, the author left baggage at a hotel in Urcos on the main highway between Juliaca & Cuzco, and waited 4 hours at the police checkpoint for a ride. Finally got on a truck going to Maldonado but got off at Ocongate. Walked out of town & camped. Next morning in -7°C temperatures, he walked to Yanama, the Hacienda Labramarca and on to the last village of Jalacocha. Higher up he passed 2 big lakes called Pacacocha and Grande. Just above Grande was a Japanese expedition base camp. He finally made camp at 4800 meters after 8 long hours of hiking. The morning of Day 2 was warmer, only -4 1/2°C. He climbed over the pass marked 4900 meters, down the other side and up to a pass to the east. Finally climbed up to 5510 meters to have a good look, but one peek at this mountain made him decide trekking was just fine! No easy routes on Ausangate! Back to camp and heading down. Camped at 4450 meters. On Day 3, he walked all the way back to Ocongate by 12:20pm, about 4 1/2 hours walking. At 3:30 got on another truck bound for Urcos. Arrived there at 8pm and

From near the Hacienda Labramarca, Ausangate can be seen to the southeast.

Map 547-1, Nevado Ausangate, Cordillera Vilcanota, Peru

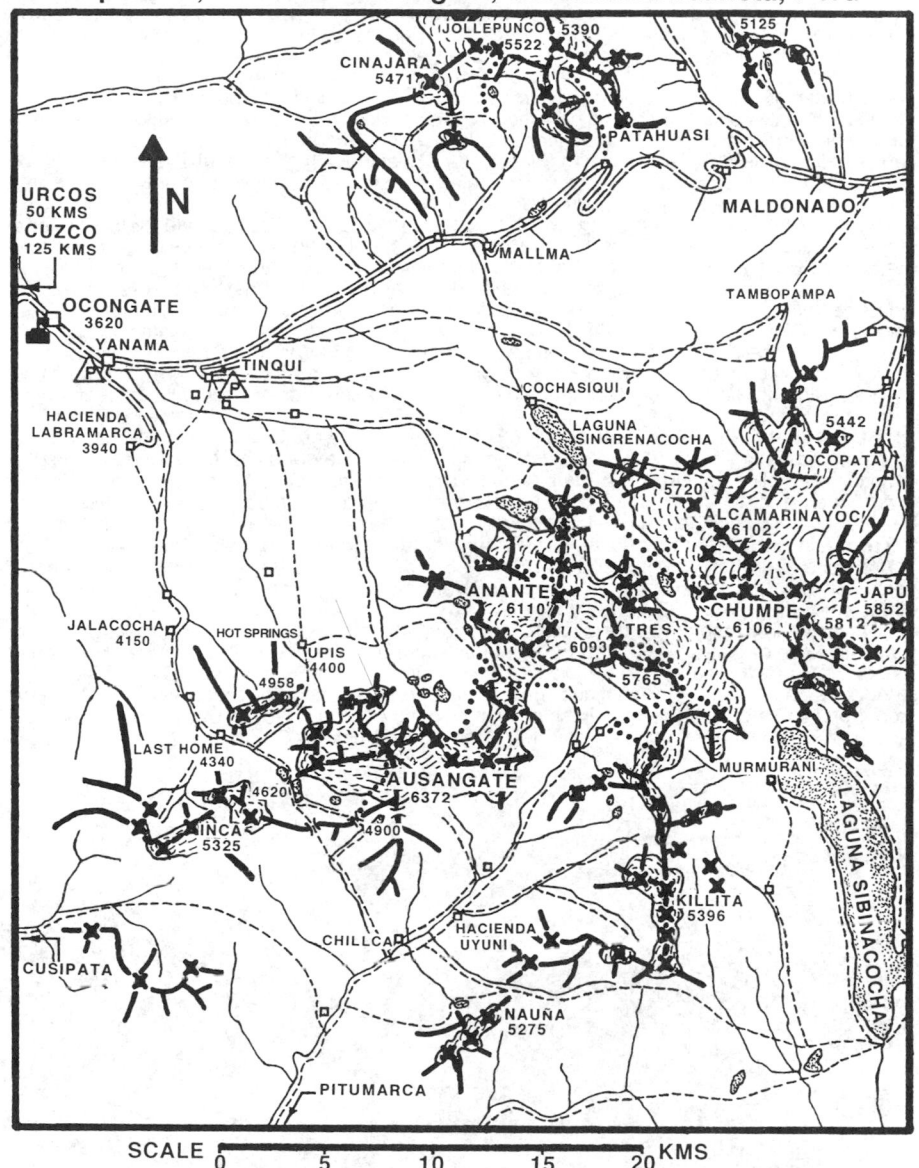

couldn't find a decent room, so he walked to the edge of town to camp. In the process, he stumbled and tore cartilage in his right knee, an event he'll never forget.

Supplies can be purchased in the cities of Cuzco or Juliaca, but can also be bought in Urcos, or Ocongate with 2 alojamientos (small hotels which often include bed bugs) and many shops. Yanama also has several shops. Climbing season is from May to early September.

Maps *Ocongate,* 1:100,000, from the IGM, 1198 Av. Aramburu, Surquillo, Lima; TPC map *N-25C,* 1:500,000; and perhaps the books, **Peruvian Andes**, Beaud, Cordee Books; **Backpacking and Trekking in Peru and Bolivia**, Brandt Enterprises; and travel guidebooks, **Peru**, Lonely Planet and/or Footprint Handbooks.

Yana Cuchilla & Cunurana, Cordillera La Raya, Peru

This map includes the higher portions of the Cordillera La Raya. This area is about halfway between Cuzco and the Juliaca & Lake Titicaca area, and mostly just east of the main highway and railway line linking these 2 important cities. The La Raya is not one massive mountain range, but a cluster of individual peaks, most of which are within easy reach of the main highway and railway line. The highest peak is Yana Cuchilla at 5472 meters. Next is Chinchina at 5463, and Cunurana at 5420 meters. This latter peak may be the best known of any in the cordillera and is an important landmark for travelers making the trip from Juliaca to Cuzco. One reason it's well-known is it's the snow capped peak behind the large town of Santa Rosa. All of these higher summits are glaciated, but mostly on the southern slopes. There are no really large snowfields anywhere partly because it's a good distance from the Amazon moisture source.

Because there are no really high and difficult peaks here, it's a good place for the beginner or intermediate climber and to acclimatize. There are of course difficult routes on all peaks, but not to the extent you'll find on most of the well-known ranges in Peru. There are many buses and trucks on this route all running between Juliaca to Cuzco. Last report the author has indicates this main highway is now paved all the way from Juliaca to Cuzco, but that hasn't been confirmed. You can also pass through the area by tren. Tren service begins at Cuzco in the north, and Juliaca on the south, with connecting lines coming in from Puno and Arequipa.

You should buy and have all or most of your food before entering this mapped area. But if you stop at Santa Rosa everything needed can be purchased there. There's at least one hotel or residencial in Santa Rosa.

Here's what the author did on 5/23/1982. He got up early from his hotel in Juliaca and was on a 6am bus going north, with a breakfast stop at Pucara. He got off at Santa Rosa and left his big pack at a police station and started hiking toward **Cunurana** at 10:25am. He walked directly toward the mountain then circled around to the north side with a lot less snow and climbed what he thought was the highest summit, but it was the 2nd peak. Since there was a big gap between the two, and since there was only a few meters difference in altitude, he returned. It took 3 3/4 hours up; 2 hours to get back to Santa Rosa. He must have taken an ice ax but can't recall using crampons on this easy climb. Much later, he got on a night-bus to Cuzco which took 6 hours.

Shown on this map are some possible routes on the 3 highest summits. For **Cunurana**, hike from the town of Santa Rosa into the basin southeast of the peak and circle around to the backside for the ascent by an all rock route; or you can pass between Cerro Negro and Cunurana, and make a more difficult snow & ice climb up the south face. For **Yana Cuchilla**, stop 4 or 5 kms north of La Raya Pass and walk up a trail running to the pass north of the main peak and make the final ascent from the north ridge. To climb **Chinchina**, get off the bus at

Cunurana's south slopes as seen from near the town of Santa Rosa.

Map 548-1, Yana Cuchilla & Cunurana, Cordillera La Raya, Peru

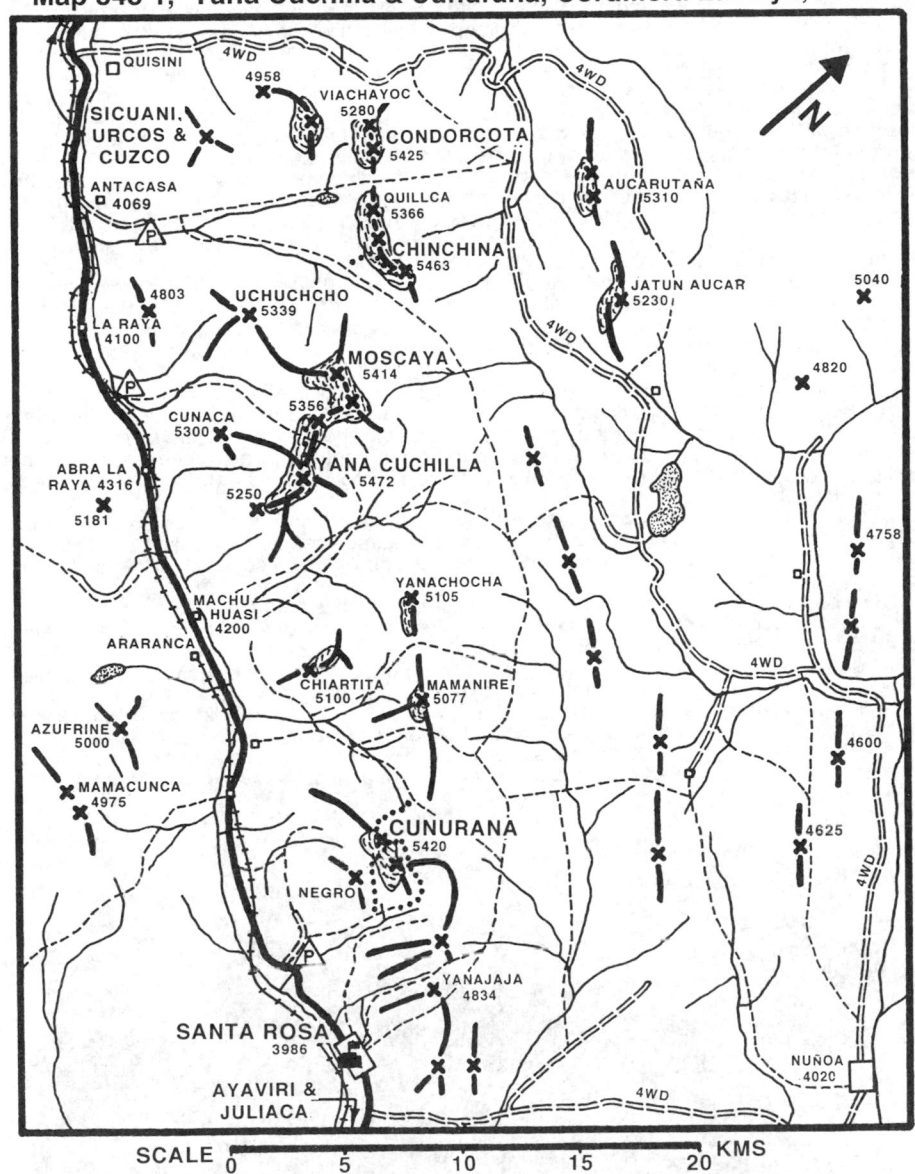

Antacasa and walk a road, then trail, northeast about 10 kms to the south face; or skirt around to the north side. Keep in mind north face routes are generally rock climbs; south faces have small glaciers and ice ax & crampons are required. The dry season is from May through September with hardly a cloud in the sky.

Maps *Ayuvin, Nutioa and Sicuani,* 1:100,000, from the IGM, 1190 Av. Aramburu, Isidro (barrio), Lima; TPC map *N-25C,* 1:500,000; and perhaps the books **Peruvian Andes**, Beaud, Cordee Books; and travel guidebooks, **Peru**, Lonely Planet and/or Footprint Handbooks; also check the South American Explorers Club website (www.samexplo.org) for other publications.

Nevados Allin Ccapac & Quenamari, Cordillera Carabaya, Peru

The area covered by this map is an isolated part of the Andes essentially unknown to the outside world. There have been very few groups into these peaks, and because of the lack of maps, long distances, and poor public transportation & roads, it's a cinch you won't find other climbers around. The highest peak seems to be called Allin Ccapac at 5825 meters.

On 5/20/1982, the author was in Juliaca looking for transport to Macusani, but only found a truck going to Rosario. He left Juliaca at 8am, arrived in Rosario at 3:30pm (about 103 kms?), then he walked about 10 kms and camped at 4155 meters. Next morning it was -8°C. He walked another 11 kms to the cruz, or turnoff going to the Mina Quenamari (or Carabaya?), then got a ride in a Suzuki pickup to the mine. He left his pack there and climbed **Nevado Quenamari (or Carabaya?)** at 5294 meters, an easy hike. He drew a map and took fotos of the group of nevados to the north, then walked back down the road about 11 kms and got a truck ride to Rosario, then another ride to Asillo by 7pm. Remember, trucks in Peru masquerade as buses and you always pay. You also ride on top with the Indians.

He walked out of Rosario and camped in the dark at 3900 meters. Next morning, -10°C. Under clear skies, the altiplano does get cold at night! It then took lots of waiting, 3 truck rides, and about 11 hours to travel the 70 kms to Juliaca arriving after dark. At that time there were no buses going to Macusani, and not that many trucks either. Most of those seem to be going to mines. And things don't seem to have changed a lot since 1982!

The name **Allin Ccapac** comes from the TPC map N-25C, but in earlier editions of this book the name **Schio** was used. Schio comes from Mario Fantin's book, **Le Ande** and is likely the wrong name. Elevations of other peaks are estimates made by the author, and could be way off the mark. None-the-less, the summits he could see around Allin Ccapac are very rugged and present a challenge for any climber. These are folded and uplifted mountains, so count on the rock being largely metamorphic.

To create this map the author used the Macusani IGM map, his own map drawn from Quenamari, the TPC map N-25C, and one Landstat foto (see below). The Allin Ccapac Group lies just north of 14° north, and the mapped region, so there's not much detail on that part of the map. Information on roads in this section come from a national highway map.

The best way to reach the valley around Macusani, which is the more important town in the region, is to proceed to the large market city of Juliaca, just north of Lake Titicaca. That seems to be the place where all transport trucks begin. Inquire at the north end of town as to the exact location where Macusani-bound trucks park. There are several trucks going that way each week. The truck route passes through Ayaviri on the main highway and another possible boarding place, then veers right or north to Asillo, San Anton, the Hacienda Rosario, and finally to Macusani, perhaps a 12 hour day, or longer. But don't be surprised if it takes 2 days.

Macusani should be your base, unless you're climbing something to the east on this map. In that case take the road leading to the town of Coasa (it also passes Ajoyani). Macusani is a

From Quenamari looking northeast at Allin Ccapac left, and Macusani left out of sight.

Map 549-1, Allin Ccapac & Quenamari, Cordillera Carabaya, Peru

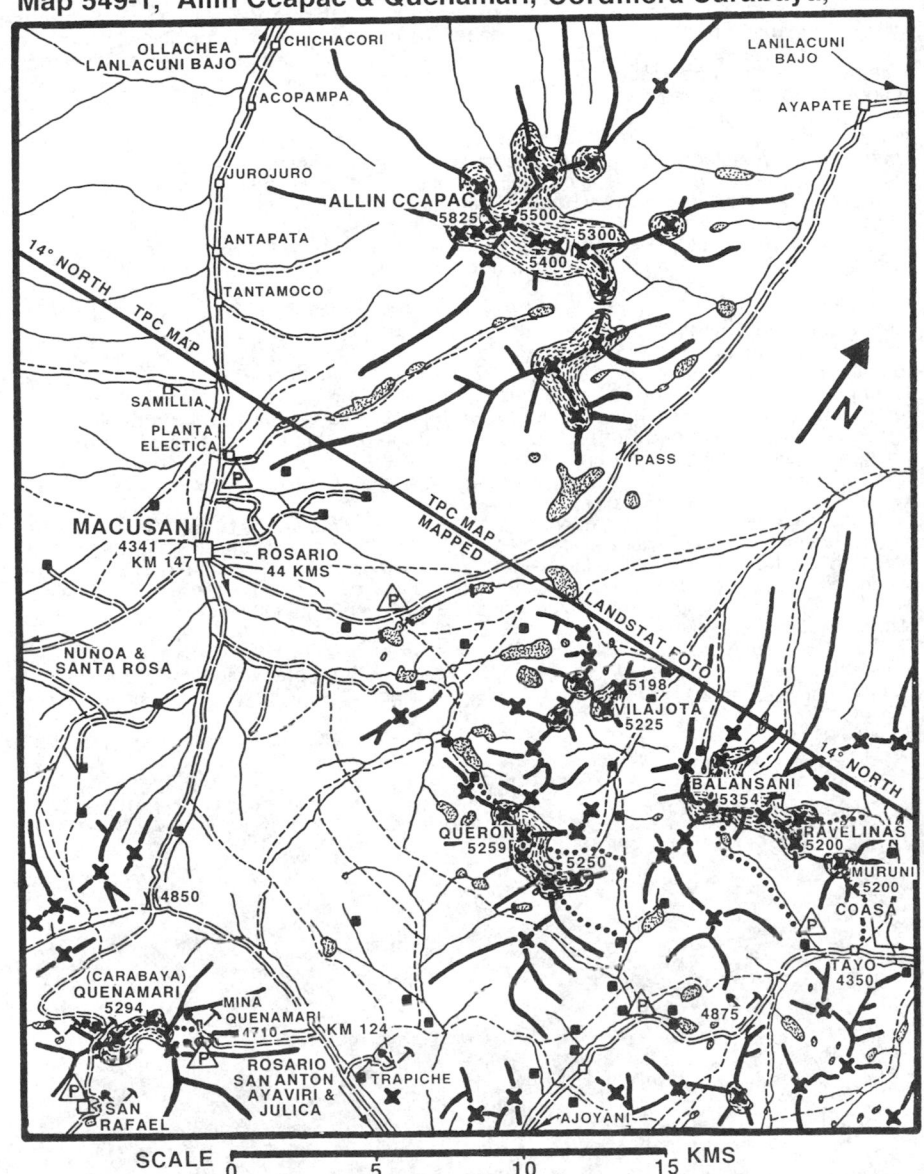

good sized village at the bottom of a large, dry valley, where plenty of food and supplies can be found. It's not certain, but it's likely there's some kind of hotel or alojamiento to sleep in. Best to stock up on supplies in Juliaca, and be prepared for a long, cold, dusty, truck ride (on top). From Macusani, plan on 4 or 5 days to climb Allin Ccapac, maybe longer (?). The dry season in Peru lasts from about May through September. The Allin Ccapac Group sits on the east side of the altiplano and should be a lot wetter than places to the west.

Maps *Macusani*, 1:100,000, and *Landstat foto 2170-14030 (K-11),* both from the IGM, Lima; TPC map *N-25C*, 1:500,000; and perhaps the book **Peruvian Andes (?)**, Beaud, Cordee Books; and travel guidebooks, **Peru**, Lonely Planet and/or Footprint Handbooks.

Nevado Aricoma, Cordilleras Carabaya, Peru

The peaks on this map are surely unknown to climbers or anyone living outside these valleys. The author isn't even sure of the name of the mountain range, although it appears to be part of the Cordillera Carabaya. But it also could be the Cordillera Aricoma (?). This is not a large range nor are the summits really high, at least by Peruvian standards. The highest peak is Aricoma at about 5350 meters. The one good map of the area does not show exact elevations, with only one exception. So all the higher summits are estimates and all appear to be about the same height. Ipante is about 5225 meters, as are 2 summits of Nevado Pinquiyumi Orjo. Jalahuana, 5325 meters is another higher peak southeast of Aricoma.

These summits are a fair distance due north of Lake Titicaca, and directly west of the larger town of Sandia. On your highway map of Peru, find the towns of Crucero, Patambuco, and Limbani. These peaks are in the center of a triangle formed by these towns.

The author has not been to this mapped area, but has seen the snow summits from the northwest not far from Macusani and the northern Carabaya; and from the south and Cerro Ananea in the Cordillera Apolobamba. Count on these peaks being fairly easy climbs, as snow mountains in Peru go. Remember, nearly all the higher nevados (snow peaks) in Peru are for experienced climbers with at least ice ax & crampons.

The best place to look for trucks going into these mountains is in Juliaca (there are probably no buses). Juliaca is the main market town or city in the mountains of southern Peru. Trucks begin there going to such places as Macusani, Ananea, Sandia, and Cojata, so it's likely they begin in this same city for trips to Crucero, Limbani and Patambuco. The probable route is through Ayaviri, Asillo and San Anton, but some could reach the area by way of the road reaching Sandia and Ananea. Which ever route is ultimately taken, find a truck going to Limbani or Para (Phara), and get off in the region of Lago Aricoma. It's also possible to catch trucks in Ayaviri. The ride may take one day, but possibly 2.

If any easy route is found up **Aricoma**, it'll be a one day climb from the road and pass at 4800 meters, but it may take a day or 2 to locate an easy route. To climb **Ipante**, start at the same pass. To climb **Jalahuana**, head for the place called Totora Cocha and walk/climb northeast. These suggested routes may or may not go! Maps show quite a bit of snow and/or glaciers, but the altitude would indicate small glaciers near the summits and above 4800 to 5000 meters only. The bigger glaciers will be on the southern slopes.

This is a grazing area for livestock; llamas, alpacas, cattle and sheep. There are hundreds of trails and small homes or shepherd huts in the valleys. There are some mines, but not in the immediate area. Buy all food in Juliaca or Ayaviri, but limited supplies can be found in the small towns enroute.

This part of the Carabaya is on the eastern side of the altiplano, not far from the Amazon Basin.

Substituting for Aricoma is a foto of Ananea from the south (see next map).

Map 550-3, Nevado Aricoma, Cordillera Carabaya, Peru

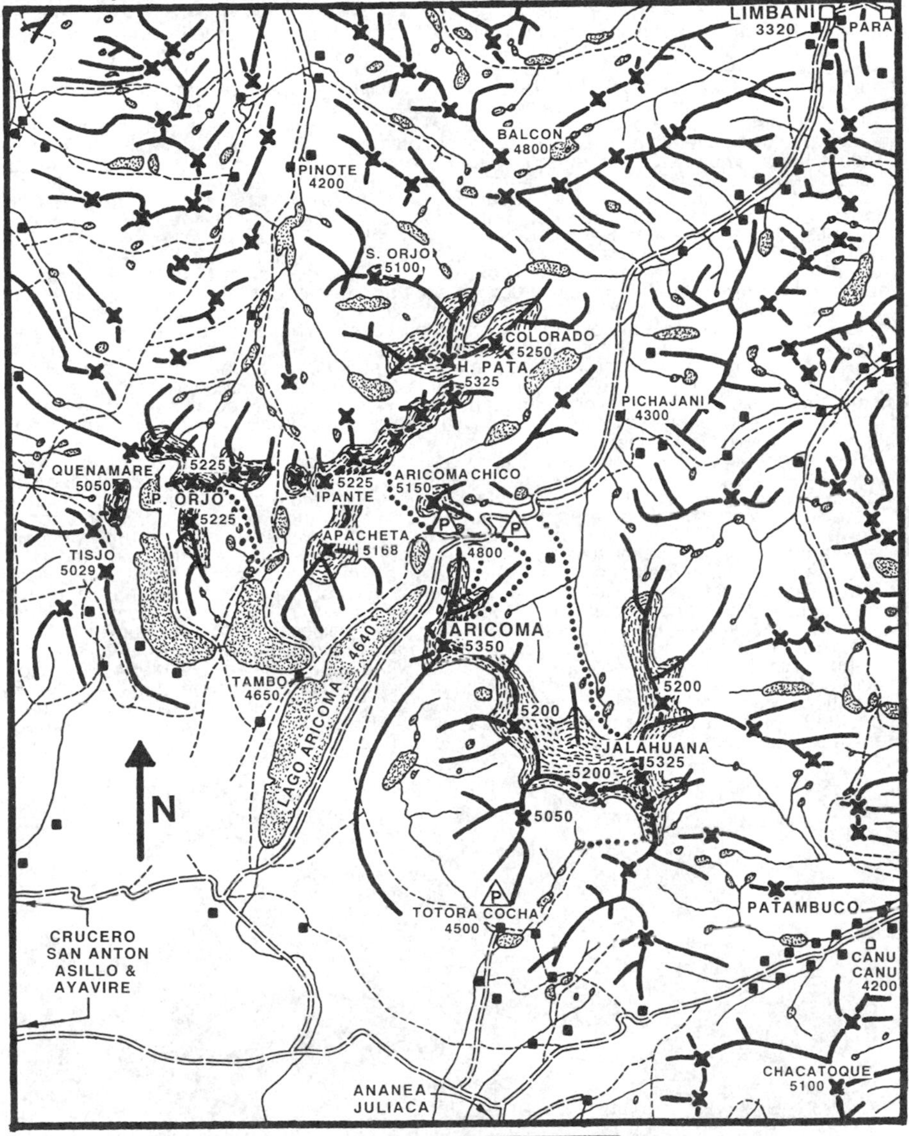

LIMBANI
3320 PARA

BALCON
4800

PINOTE
4200

S. ORJO
5100

COLORADO
5250

H. PATA
5325

PICHAJANI
4300

QUENAMARE
5050

5225

P. ORJO
5225

5225
IPANTE

ARICOMACHICO
5150

P

P
4800

APACHETA
5168

TISJO
5029

ARICOMA
5350

LAGO ARICOMA 4640

TAMBO
4650

5200

5200

JALAHUANA
5325

5200

5050

N

P

TOTORA COCHA
4500

PATAMBUCO

CRUCERO
SAN ANTON
ASILLO &
AYAVIRE

CANU
CANU
4200

CHACATOQUE
5100

ANANEA
JULIACA

SCALE 0 ____ 5 ____ 10 KMS

Therefore, it gets a little more precipitation in the rainy months than areas to the west. The dry season is from sometime in May until early September.

Maps *Limbani*, 1:100,000, from the IGM, 1190 Av. Aramburu, San Isidro (barrio), Lima; TPC map N-25C, 1:500,000; and perhaps the book **Peruvian Andes (?)**, Beaud, from Cordee Books might help; and travel guidebooks, **Peru**, Lonely Planet and/or Footprint Handbooks; also check the South American Explorers Club website (www.samexplo.org) for other publications.

Ananea & Chaupi Orco, Cordillera Apolobamba, Peru

The mountains on this map are known as the Cordillera Apolobamba. Shown here is the northern part of that range which is just inside southeastern Peru. Most of the Apolobamba is in northwest Bolivia. This region is mapped by the IGM of Peru, at least their side of the frontier, but those maps are classified, and the public is not allowed to purchase them (see website www.omnimap.com for updated information). Therefore, this map has been created from a map in the Club Alpino Italiano book, **Le Ande**, by Fantin, with the use of a Landstat Foto, the TPC map below, and the author's own map and notes from his experience there.

Here's what the author did beginning on 5/13/1982. Left extra baggage in a hotel in Juliaca, got on a truck which left at noon bound for Sandia but got off after dark at Pampilla Cruz, 7pm--gringo & Indians huddled together on top like frozen rats! Got water at the trucker's stop and camped nearby. Snow in the night. Morning Day 2, -9 1/2°C. At 7am he began walking to Ananea with many shops & food for gold miners with Alaska-type dredges--no hotels. Walked past Mina Poto and more dredge gold mining operations, and past Laguna Parinani to the highest little lake southeast of Nevado Ananea. Camped at 4790 meters with snow.

Morning Day 3, -4°C. Attempted an east face route up Ananea but didn't make 5300 meters in knee-deep snow and big crevasses. Broke camp, walked over pass 4945 to Paso Sina, and south on the road to the house at 4630, then east and camped at 4865 meters below Peak 5630. More snow showers. Morning Day 4, -4 1/2°C. Attempted Peak 5630 meters, but only got to 5545 meters before almost going into big crevasse. That was enough! From camp, 3 hours climbing round-trip. Then back to house at 4630, and on the road towards Cojata. No traffic. Walked to within 18 kms of Cojata and camped at 4465 meters after 13 hours of climbing & walking. Morning Day 5, -7°C under clear skies. Started walking, but quickly got on a truck to Cojata, one hour; then on to Juliaca with many stops & mechanical problems arriving after dark at 6:30pm. Five long days from Juliaca--2 days riding on top of trucks in bitter cold, and roughly 33 hours of climbing & walking.

Remember, all trucks leaving for this area begin at the large market town of Juliaca. Ask in Juliaca where the parking place is for trucks leaving for Sandia or Cojata. Buy all your food and supplies in Juliaca, as everything is available there, although there are a number of small stores in both Ananea and Cojata where basic supplies can be found. There is likely not a hotel in either of these small towns, but if you know Español, a place for sleeping can surely be found. The Ananea region has lots of gold mines while Cojata is a cattle, llama & alpaca raising valley. There are many llama & alpaca trails throughout this entire mapped area, with an occasional Indian hut here and there, mostly in the lower valleys. But not many people around. The region is elevated very high and has night time temps of between -5 to -10 C in the dry season (from May to mid-September). Sometimes the lower valleys are colder than near the glaciers.

The routes shown on the map to various peaks are those taken by several different Italian groups in the past and those of the author. Snowline here is down to about 4800 meters; glaciers 5000 and above; but snow falls down to about 4000 meters, then melts quickly. Full expedition and snow climbing equipment is needed as these peaks are heavily glaciated. These are folded mountains and are similar in appearance and in difficulty of climbing as the Cordillera Real of Bolivia. Climbing season from mid-May to mid-September.

The northern slopes of Chaupi Orco as seen from the east end of Pico Ananea.

Map 551-1, Ananea & Chaupi Orco, Cordillera Apolobamba, Peru

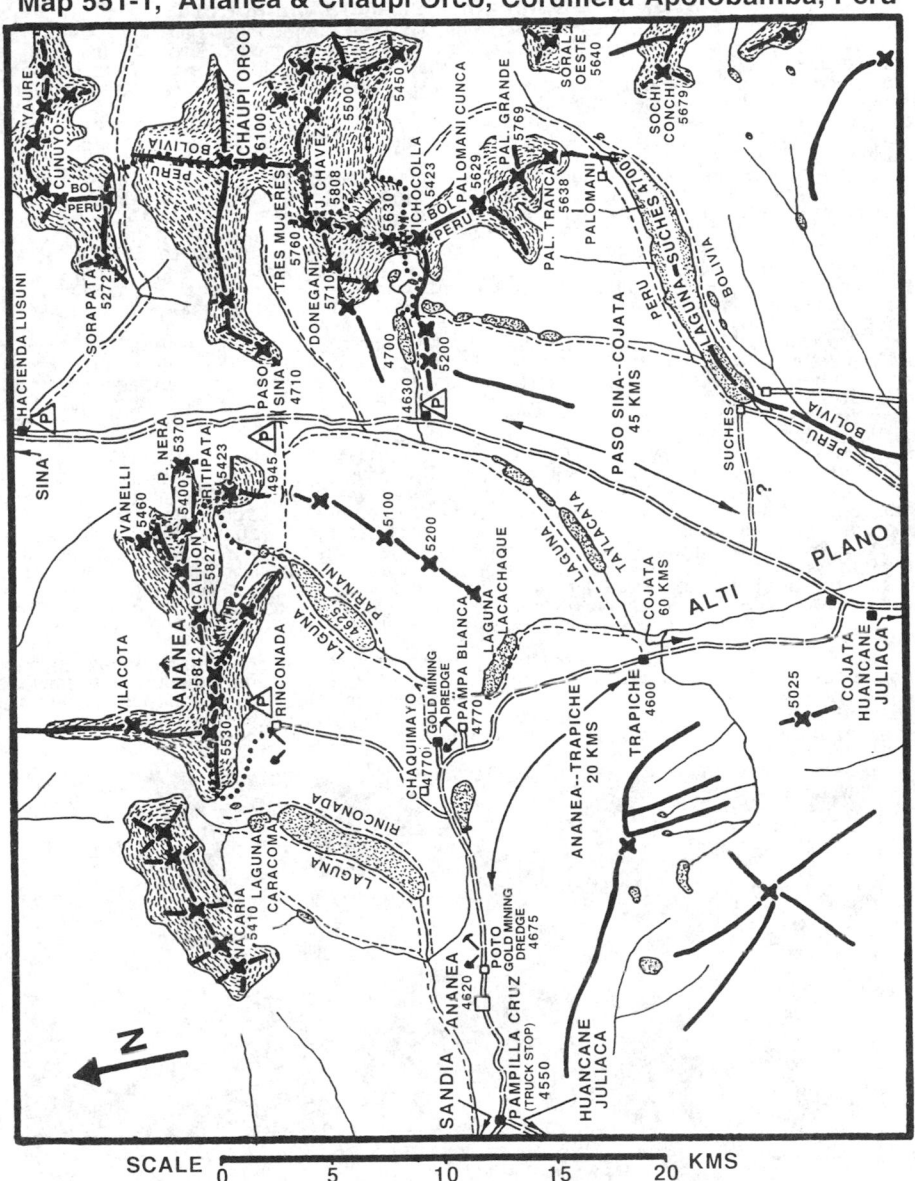

SCALE 0 ————— 5 ————— 10 ————— 15 ————— 20 KMS

Maps IGM maps if ever available (also see South America Explorers Club websites (www.samexplo.org) or email to Lima (montegue@amauta.rcp.net.pe); maps from book, **Le Ande**; map *Departamento de Puno, 1:670,000*, IGM; or *Landstat Foto 2223-13554*, from IGM Lima, or Eros Data Center, Sioux Falls, South Dakota, USA; TPC map N-25C, 1:500,000; and perhaps the book **Peruvian Andes**, Beaud, from Cordee Books might help; and travel guidebooks, **Peru**, Lonely Planet and/or Footprint Handbooks.

Coropuna & Solimani, Cordillera Chila, Peru

Some of Peru's highest, yet some of the most easy-to-climb mountains are in the southwest part of the country in the region of Arequipa, Peru's second largest city. This is an area dotted with volcanos, some new like El Misti (see next map); some very old and eroded like Solimani. Coropuna is an older ice capped volcano with twin summits which last erupted in the early Holocene. It still has a conal shape.

Because of their location in the central part of the Atacama Desert, these mountains have very little snowfall. However, all the peaks above about 5200 or 5300 meters are capped with permanent snow.

There is one route of approach to all the summits on this map. Most people begin the journey in Arequipa, where buses can be found at the main bus terminal. In the late 1990's, there were 2 daily buses leaving in the early afternoon for Cotahuasi taking 12-13 hours. They arrive at Cotahuasi in the early morning darkness and apparently return that afternoon (?). The route they take is west to a junction on the main highway called Mejas (or El Alto?), then northwest to Aplao in the lower Colca (Mejas) River valley at only 650 meters. From there north to the higher village of Chuquibamba, 2900 meters, where you'll find at least one hotel and last decent place to shop for food or fuel. From Chuquibamba, there will be several trucks and one day-time bus going to the town of Cotahuasi.

Coropuna is the highest mountain in the region, and one of the highest in Peru at about 6400 meters. Ask the driver of the vehicle to let you out near a lake named Pallacocha. It can't be seen from the road, but that area is the closest the road comes to the mountain. From just above the lake head for the south summit, the one on the right. There are many good campsites near the snowline at about 5200 meters, or near the last running water at 4900. From the lake to the top and return takes one long day for most climbers.

Here's the author's experience. On the morning of 6/16/1980, he left Arequipa but spent the entire day getting as far as Aplao, only 164 kms! Stayed in a hotel; next morning while waiting for a bus, was given a ride in a government pickup which went past Chuquibamba (56 kms) and later dropped him off at a little stream just up the road and below Laguna Pallacocha at 4700 meters. He climbed for an hour or 2 and camped at 5220 meters above all the shepherds & thieves. Next morning with -12°C, he made the summit in 3 hours; 4 1/2 hours round-trip from his tent (prior to climbing he had spent time in Bolivia acclimatizing) Then for some stupid reason decided not to go on to Solimani! So he went down to the lake & road and walked 7 or 8 kms and got a ride down to Chuquibamba where he stayed in the hotel. On Day 4, it again took all day until about 9pm to get back to Arequipa. Transport is a lot better in 2000 than it was in 1980!

For **Solimani** at 6093 meters, take the same approach route as to Coropuna, but continue on the bus or truck to a place called Visca Grande at 4670 meters. From there walk southwest cross-country to shepherd huts called Sora. From there, climb up the north face to the summit. Depending on when you arrive at Visca Grande, better plan on 2 days, maybe a 3rd day, from the road for this climb. No information on difficulty, but apparently not technical (?).

The western slopes of Coropuna as seen from Laguna Pallococha.

Map 552-1, Coropuna & Solimani, Cordillera Chila, Peru

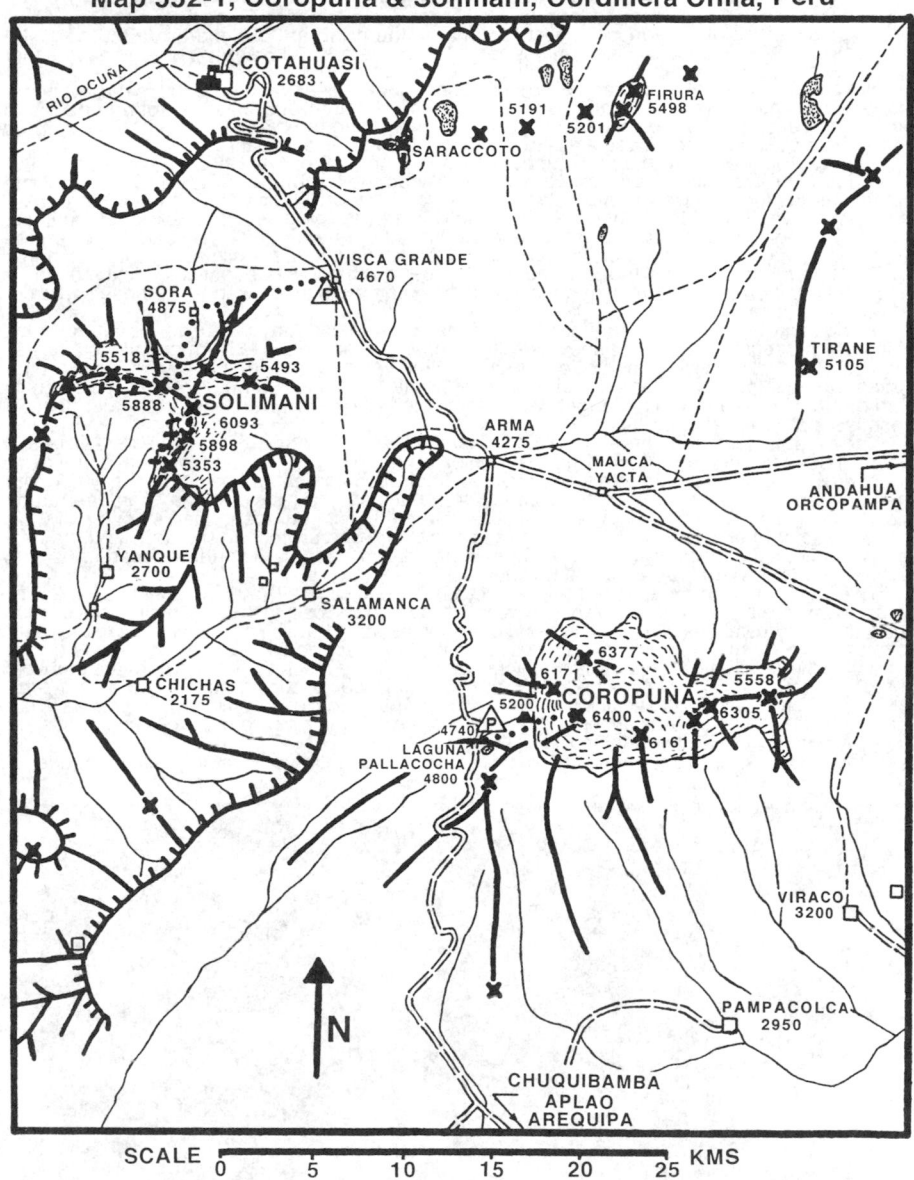

SCALE 0 5 10 15 20 25 KMS

Coropuna is high, has big glaciers, but some very easy routes with little or no danger from crevasses. There are some icefalls and crevasses on the peak, but they can easily be avoided. Solimani is a jagged peak with some very difficult routes. The snowline shown is for the wet season. The climbing season is from May through September, but it's a dry area so climb anytime. For updated information contact the tourist office or the club andino in Arequipa.

Maps *Cotahuasi and Chuquibamba,* 1:100,000, from the IGM, Lima; for access use the TPC maps *P-26A & N-25C,* 1:500,000; and perhaps the book **Peruvian Andes**, Beaud, from Cordee Books; and travel guidebooks, **Peru**, Lonely Planet and/or Footprint Handbooks.

Chachani, El Misti & Pichu Pichu, Cordillera Volcanica, Peru

Shown here is Peru's second largest city, Arequipa, along with 3 nearby volcanos. From Arequipa's central plaza you can see Chachani to the north at 6057 meters; El Misti to the northeast at 5822; and Pichu Pichu on the east at 5510 meters. All 3 are reported to have some kind of Incan ruins at or near their summits.

Nevado Chachani is an old and eroded volcano, but the peak marked 5180 is the youngest summit having had its last eruption sometime in the Holocene. El Misti is young and has a perfect conal shape. It had 5 questionable eruptions during the 1800's and is still considered active. Pichu Pichu is the oldest of all and no longer resembles a volcano.

Here's what the author did on **Chachani**. On the morning of 5/4/1982, he got on one of 4 daily buses in Arequipa bound for Chivay. That bus took about 2 hours to reach what the author's notes indicate was *Pampa Canaguas* at 4175 meters (maps show the same area as *Kutypampa*) and Km 47. He got off the bus and walked west on a vehicle track for 20 minutes, then hid is big pack in tall puno grass, and continued up the sandy 4WD road. High on the mountain he met a Swiss climber, then continued to the summit. Easy climb. About 5 1/2 hours up; 2 2/3 hours down; round-trip 8 1/4 hours. He set up camp in the moonlight. Next morning it was -10°C; but on the altiplano when the sun comes up, it feels much warmer in these super dry & calm conditions.

To do this trip, contact the tourist office at Plaza de Armas or any bus driver about transport along this *old route to Chivay*. It seems (?) that most traffic now goes to Yura and along a newer road paralleling the railway line up to Cañahuas, then veers left toward Chivay. If there are no buses traveling past Kutypampa, you may have to hire a taxi; or somehow make your way to Cabreria at Km 20 and walk a longer & warmer route from there. Carry all your water; there's none around except at snowline.

The most famous peak here is **El Misti**. Here's what the author did on 7/20/1972. He and Doug Rose, who was living & working in Arequipa at the time, packed food for 2 days and at 12 noon, drove east to Chihuata and to the tiny pueblo of Cachamarca and paid one family to watch the car. From there it took 4 hours to walk to a round stone corral where they camped (today there's some kind of shelter (?) at a place called Monte Blanco, but the author is unsure of what it is or exactly where?). They slept inside the corral for wind protection (no tent) and the next morning climbed along a trail to the summit in about 6 1/2 hours. Then they headed back to Cachamarca and were in Arequipa at 6:15pm.

There's no water beyond the last village, so you'll have to carry all you'll need for this 2 day trip. To get there, take a city bus to Baños de Jesus and a police checkpoint, then catch another bus or truck going up to Chihuata, and start walking along one of many llama trails. You can also make the climb from the *embolsa* or reservoir called *Aguada Blanca* (its exact position on this map may not be correct). Check with the tourist office for information on how to reach the lake. There are probably buses going that way (?) or take a taxi. Also, the S.A. Handbook suggests there is now a trail up the southwest slopes of El Misti beginning in the suburb of Apurimac. This would be a shorter walk, but with more elevation gain. Ask about it at the tourist office. Or for climbing questions contact Carlos Zarate (or his son Tito) at the Club Andino de Peru.

For **Pichu Pichu**, take any bus or truck going in the direction of Puno or Juliaca, but get off

The eastern side of the Chachani Group as seen from Km 47 and Kutypampa.

Map 553-1, Chachani, El Misti, Pichu Pichu, Cord., Volcanica, Peru

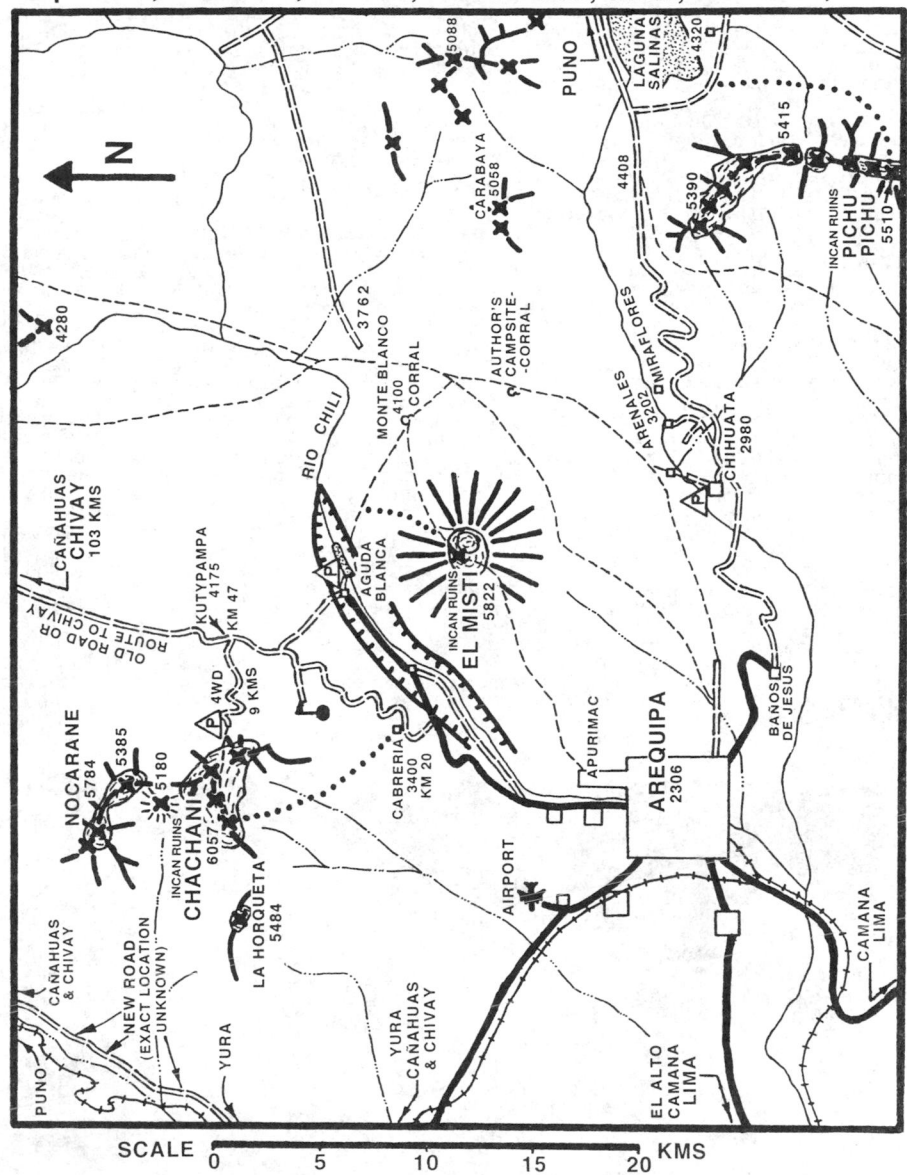

SCALE 0   5   10   15   20 KMS

just before reaching Laguna Salinas at about 4300 meters. From there walk south along the foot of the high ridge, then veer west toward the highest peak. No water there either except for a little snow up high. Better take enough for 2 days. However, maps show huts on the south side of the lake. If someone is living there, they should have some *agua dulce* (sweet water).

Make Arequipa your headquarters when climbing in this region. It has many hotels, a good tourist office, lots of tour operators and a club andino for route & water information.

Maps *Characato & Arequipa*, 1:100,000, from the IGM, Lima; TPC area map *P-26A*, 1:500,000; and the books **Peruvian Andes**, Beaud, Cordee Books; and travel guidebooks, **Peru**, Lonely Planet; or **Peru** or **South American Handbooks**, Footprint Handbooks.

Ampato & Sabancaya, Cordilleras Ampato & Chila, Peru

In southwest Peru not far north of Arequipa, stand a number of snowcapped peaks, the highest of which is Ampato at 6360 meters. Other peaks included in the Cordillera Ampato are Sabancaya, Hualca Hualca, Ananto and Huarancante. This range is south of the Colca River. To the north of the Colca is the Cordillera Chila with a number of peaks in the 5500 meter range. Surihuiri, 5556 meters, is the highest in this group.

All the peaks of the Cordillera Ampato are volcanos, with Ampato still retaining the conal shape, and Sabancaya the active one. Sabancaya has a fairly recent lava flow heading southeast from the summit. It also had a good eruption on 5/29/1990 sending ash 7 kms high. It was active through the 1990's and at last report had some ash explosions in 9/1998. For updates see website (www.volcano.si.edu/gvp/), and the 11/1999 issue of National Geographic for a story of finding a frozen mummy on top of Ampato. The Cordillera Chila is made of very old volcanics, but none is considered a volcano today.

Starting at 4:30am on 7/26/1972 the author and Carlos Zarate and son Tito got on a bus in Arequipa bound for Chivay. Got off at 4825 meters and walked direct toward **Ampato** for 7 hours and camped at 4800 meters. Day 2, walked 11 1/2 hours and camped at 5100 meters near Ampato. The author had to return and help friends to camp. Day 3, walked 2 1/2 hours to base of Ampato, had to melt snow for water. Day 4, the author climbed Ampato in 4 1/2 hours up through solid & safe icefall, but had to wait 3 1/2 hours for Zarates and a group foto. The author ran down in 45 minutes, but Zarates took 12 3/4 hours round-trip. Tito had a little snow blindness--no goggles! Day 5, all walked to the road, then down into a big quebrada or canyon to Huanca in 9 1/2 hours. While waiting for a midnight bus back to Arequipa, all were invited to a party with drunk Indians & chicha (corn beer). Also the prettiest Indian women the author has ever seen! Arrived in Arequipa at 3:30am on Day 6!

If your plans are to climb **Sabancaya** & Ampato, consider taking a bus from Arequipa to Huanca and climbing north out of the canyon from there. Or take a bus from Arequipa to Chivay and/or Cabana Conde and climb south from along that road toward **Hualca Hualca**. Little or no traffic going by way of Lluta. Better still, make a traverse from north to south, or vise versa. Perhaps a group can hire a vehicle in Arequipa or Chivay to save walking. It's very dry on this altiplano; water in only a few places. Always carry lots of water and inquire about its location.

Here's another climb the author made starting on 5/5/1982. On the morning after climbing Chachani (see previous map), he walked back to Kutypampa and got on a pickup as a paying passenger and rode to Chivay. After a quick look around he walked west across a bridge to Coporaque, then north to a camp at 4750 meters near the base of **Nevado Mismi**. About 5 hours walking. Next morning, -9°C. He left the tent and climbed Mismi in exactly 2 hours. Back at the tent in on hour, then down to Chivay and stayed in the Hotel Modero for the night.

Mismi is an easy climb and accessible from Coporaque. **Surihuiri** and **Sepregina** can both be ascended from Mina Madrigal. Take a bus or truck from Chivay to the mina. Just above this mine are quinua trees at 4575 meters, some of the highest the author has seen, and about a dozen Puya Raymondi plants across the canyon. See the next map for the rest of the author's adventure in that area.

All of the larger villages on this map now (2001) have a store or small restaurant. Achoma &

Looking at the east face of Ampato from a camp at the edge of the lava flow.

Map 554-1, Ampato & Sabancaya, Cordillera Ampato & Chila, Peru

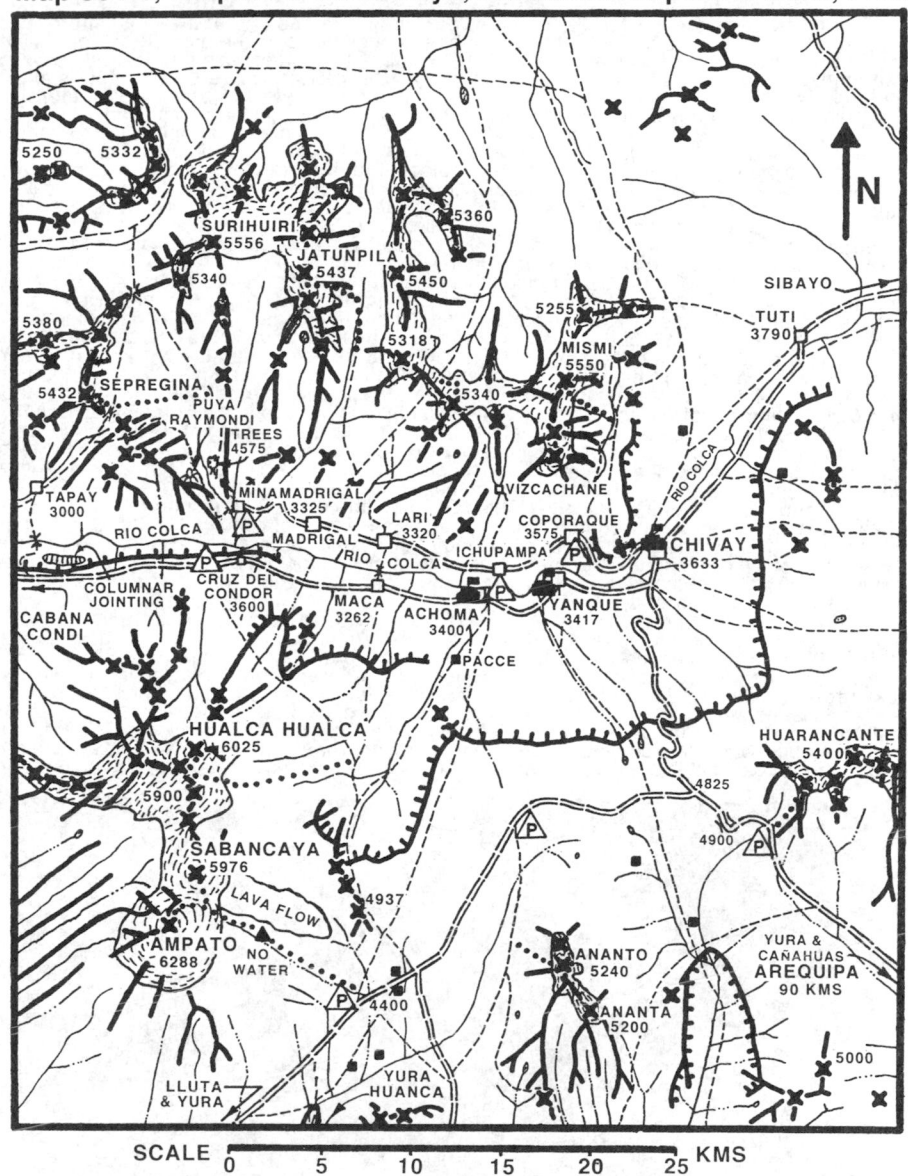

Yanque have one hotel each; Cabana Conde, 4 hotels. Chivay is the largest and best known town in the valley, with 7 or 8 hotels and several buses and many trucks running to Arequipa each day. It's very easy walking cross-country as the entire area is crisscrossed with livestock trails. All the higher peaks will require an ice ax & crampons. The snowline shown on this map is for the wet season--it's much higher (over 5000 meters) in the dry months of May through September.

Maps IGM map *Chivay*, 1:100,000; for access try TPC maps *P-26A & N-25C*, 1:500,000; and the books **Peruvian Andes**, Beaud, Cordee Books; and travel guidebooks, **Peru**, Lonely Planet; or **Peru** or **South American Handbooks**, Footprint Handbooks.

Nevado Chila & Rio Colca Canyon, Cordillera Chila, Peru

This map shows the western half of the Cordillera Chila and one of the most impressive canyons in Peru. This is the Rio Colca, which has its beginnings on the high divide separating the Amazon basin and the Atacama Desert. The Rio Colca runs between the Cordilleras Chila and Ampato, and passes the larger town of Chivay. This canyon is deep; 2200 meters at the bridge between Tapay and Cabana Conde (CC), and from there climbs to 5432 meters on Sepregina; or to 6025 meters on Hualca Hualca; each of which are just few kms apart.

The canyon has a number of small and isolated villages containing populations of Indian and/or mixed-Indian blood (?), with attractive & fine-featured women. Also, above Tapay and on the opposite wall, is the best example of a geologic feature known as *columnar jointing* the author has seen. And between about December and June, you can buy and eat a fruit called *tuna*, from cultivated cacti. Also just off this map (see previous map) and above the Mina Madrigal, is a group of 11 or 12 unusual plants called Puya Raymondi, and some of the highest quinua trees the author has seen at about 4575 meters. These mountains are made of old volcanics, but there are younger cones near Andahua.

Here's the rest of what the author did in this area. See the 2 previous maps. On 5/7/1982, and after climbing Chachani & Mismi, he waited half a day for a bus or truck from Chivay to CC. Finally he got a ride in a small truck, and later had 2 more rides, then walked about 1/4 the way to CC. He inquired about bridges across the river, then headed down to the one at 2200 meters in 1 1/2 hours. Camped on the other side at 2600 meters below Malata. Next morning at a warm 9°C, he packed up, hid his big pack and walked almost to Llatica and returned, then headed up past the half-empty pueblos of Malate & Tapay, where people called the author *viracocha* (?) instead of *gringo!* Camped at 4650 meters below Sepregina. Morning of Day 3, -6°C, a slow walk to the pass at 4960 meters, left pack, climbed **Sepregina** in one hour--easy climb, then on down to the Mina Madrigal and a slow 3 hour ride to Chivay in a loaded mining truck. Ate supper on the street and walked west out of town to camp. Next morning along with a dozen locals, hitched a free ride on a canal company truck to Arequipa.

For climbers, the highest summit is **Chila**, 5665 meters, with **Casiri** close behind at 5631. These peaks can both be scaled from Andahua and Chachas. Both should be easy climbing as big mountains go in Peru. The higher peaks may have small glaciers or icefields. Take an ice ax & crampons if climbing the big ones. Snowline shown is for wet season. There are many trails in this region, both in the canyon and in the mountains which are used by Indians with herds of llamas, alpacas, sheep & cattle.

There are 2 ways of reaching this area. The easiest is from Chivay (see 2 previous maps), and the longer one via Andahua. Get to Chivay from Arequipa on one of several daily buses. Ride to Andahua in a 4-times-weekly bus from Arequipa, or perhaps on mining or cargo trucks. Some trucks go on to Chachas. There are one or more buses a day from Chivay to CC, and another from Chivay to Mina Madrigal, plus trucks. A long hike from Mina Madrigal or CC to Andahua is recommended, perhaps doing one or more climbs along the way. About 5 days walking from CC to Andahua. Known bridges are shown, but inquire about river crossings at the end of the bus routes and along the way. Some rain or snow can be expected from October to about April or May, but this is a very dry area. All higher valleys have water. Best to buy food in

The bridge over the Rio Colca between Malata and Cabana Conde.

Map 555-1, Nevado Chila & Rio Colca C., Cordillera Chila, Peru

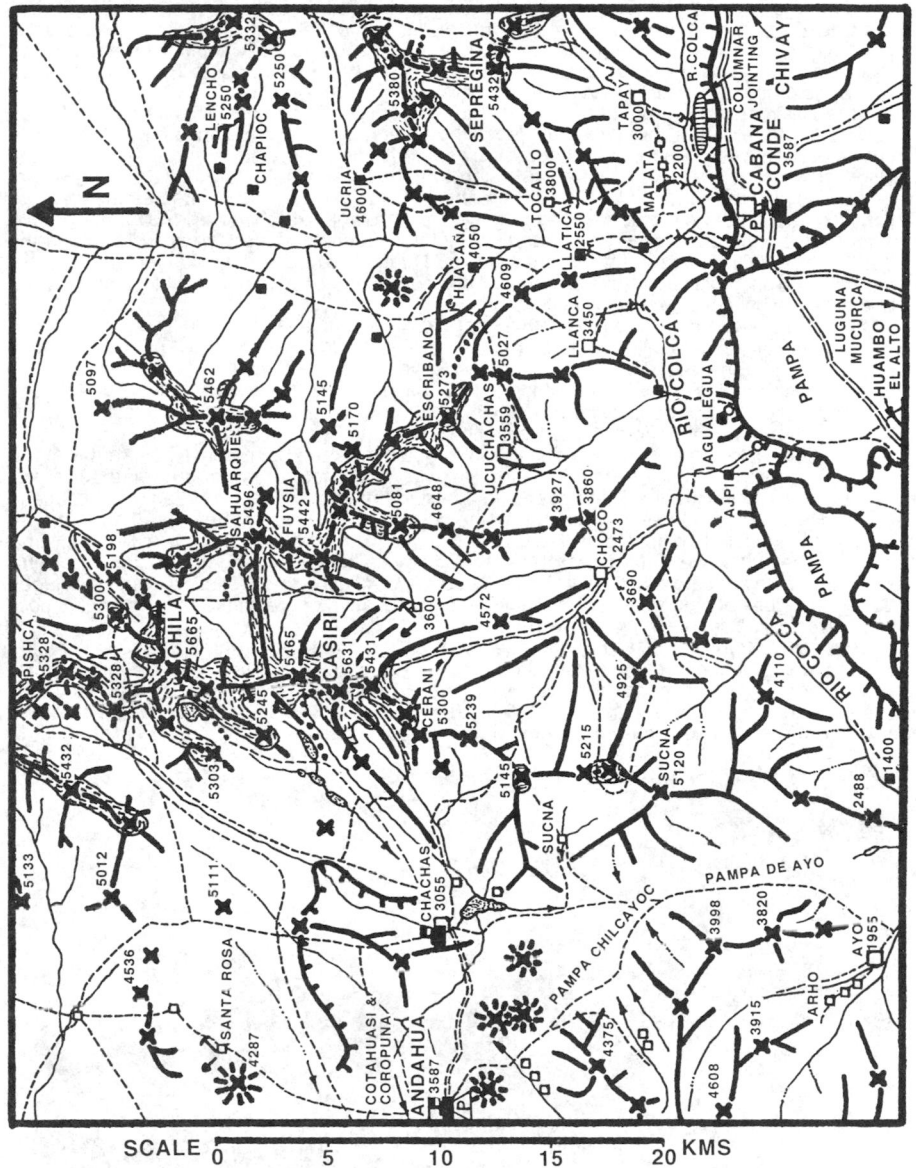

SCALE 0 5 10 15 20 KMS

Arequipa, but all larger villages along the roads have stores. Chivay has 7 or 8 hotels; CC has 4, and Andahua & Chachas have one each. The author can't remember seeing other gringos in the 1970's, but there are some tourists around now--after 2001.
Maps IGM maps *Huambo, Orcopampa, Chivay, & Cailloma,* 1:100,000; for access TPC maps *P-26A & N-25C,* 1:500,000; and the books **Peruvian Andes**, Beaud, Cordee Books; and travel guidebooks, **Peru**, Lonely Planet; or **Peru** or **South American Handbooks**, Footprint Handbooks.

Southern Cordillera Apolobamba, Bolivia

The mountains on this map show the southern end of the Cordillera Apolobamba. These mountains are located in western Bolivia, immediately north of Lake Titicaca, and just across the frontier from Peru. The Apolobamba stradles the frontier of Peru & Bolivia and is on boundary of the altiplano or high plain where Titicaca is situated, and the Amazon Basin. The northeast side of the range drops steeply to the Amazon rainforest.

There are virtually no topo maps available to the public of this region. Peru has good ones of their side of the border, but you can't see or buy them, and they wouldn't help much for the Bolivian part anyway. And Bolivia has apparently not completely surveyed their side of the frontier, or is just withholding information! Therefore, this map was created by using provincial and national highway maps of both countries, the TPC map below, the Landstat (satellite) foto which lies just north of the one covering Laguna Titicaca, and sketches drawn by other people and the author. So don't expect his map to be totally accurate. Most stream valleys and the larger lakes are in their proper places, but roads and high altitude peaks and ridges are probably out of place. Nonetheless, this sketch should help more than going completely blind into an area that is basically unknown to mountaineers.

The author climbed on 2 mountains in the northern Apolobamba, and viewed these peaks on the last 2 days of that trip from the road leading to the town of Cojata. See Map 551, Ananea & Chaupi Orco, page 1167. These are nevados or snow peaks, and the highest summit in each major group is estimated to be about 5500 meters in altitude. The appearance and makeup of these mountains, and the difficulty of climbing, appears similar to the high summits in the Cordillera Real located south of this area. The dry season is from May to September.

Access can be a problem. Since it's in Bolivia, you'd think the approach is best from Bolivia, but it might be easier from Peru (?). On the Bolivian side, look for transport going northwest from La Paz through Huarina & Achacachi, and along the eastern shore of Laguna Titicaca to Puerto Acosta, which is located just south of the border of Peru. From there head north on the road going to the lonely outposts of Ulla Ulla or Suches. But there are likely very few trucks on the road. The author viewed & fotographed this valley as he walked south from the Paso Sina area nearly to Cojata before getting a lift. He never saw anything that looked like trucks, villages or any kind of habitation on the Bolivian side. In fact, because of the altitude and relatively poor feed for livestock, it seemed all but deserted.

Or you could try from the Peru side. Begin in Juliaca and look for the 2 or 3 times-weekly truck and/or bus heading for Huancane and Cojata. From there, perhaps hire a vehicle (?), or start walking toward Suches to hopefully cross the largest stream in the area on a bridge. The rivers aren't that big, but this valley is high & cold, so you don't want to wade! If there's a frontier post somewhere, best to check with them so you're not suspected of being a smuggler. It is an

From Cojata looking east at the south half of the Apolobamba in Bolivia.

Map 556-2, Southern Cordillera Apolobamba, Bolivia

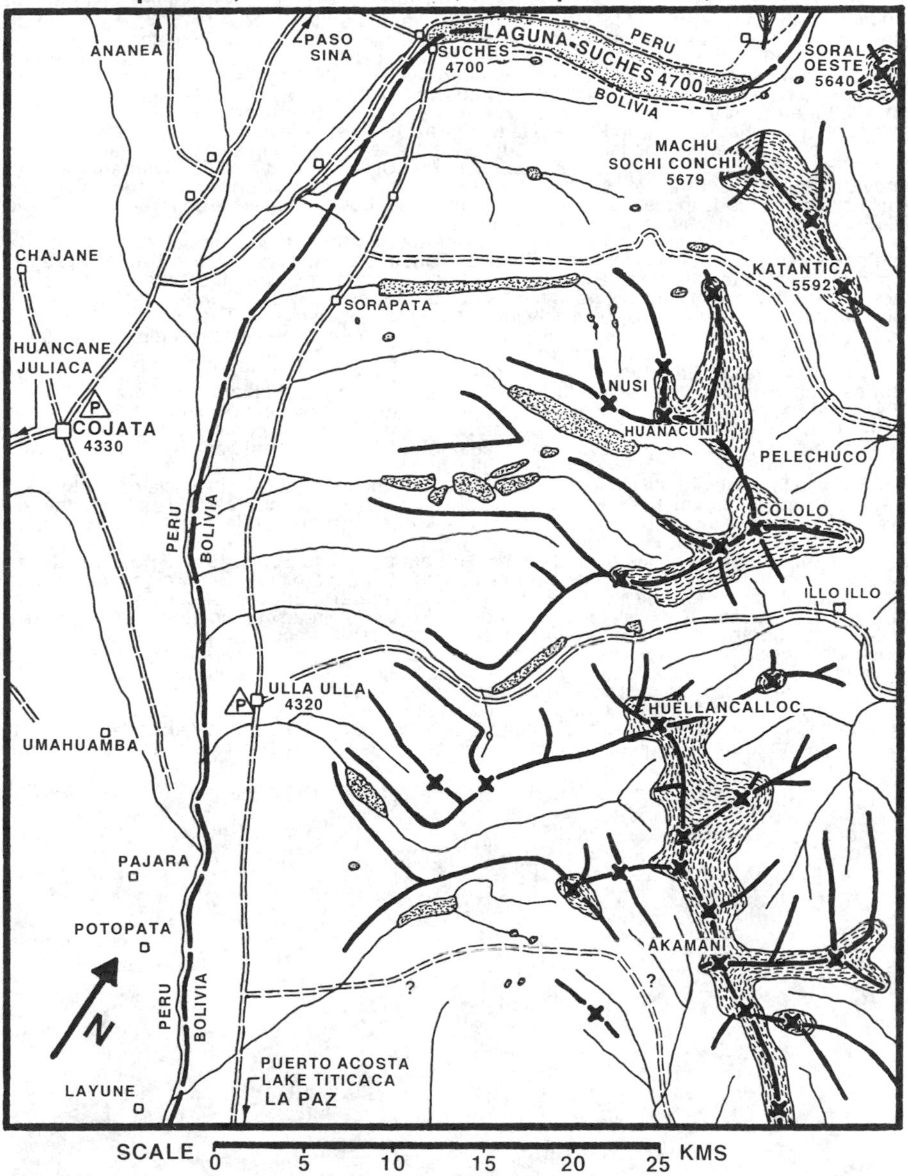

SCALE 0 5 10 15 20 25 KMS

international border! With a **visa to Bolivia**, there should be no trouble--even if you should meet a border patrol--which is unlikely.

Maps *Landstat foto 2223-13554,* from the IGM, Lima, or from Eros Data Center, Sioux Falls, South Dakota, USA; a little help is TPC map *N-25C,* 1:500,000; *national highway maps of Bolivia and Peru*; check with the IGM, Estado Mayor Gen. Av. Saavedra Final, Miraflores in La Paz for new maps made public; and the books **Trekking in Bolivia**, and **Bolivia--A Climbing Guide**, both from The Mountaineers; and travel guidebooks, **Bolivia**, Lonely Planet and/or Footprint Handbooks.

Illampu, Ancohuma & Chearoco, Cordillera Real, Bolivia

This is the first of 4 maps covering the Cordillera Real of western Bolivia. The highest summit is Ancohuma at 6427 meters, followed by Illampu at 6362. Many other summits nearby are over 6000 meters such as Chearoco, 6127, and Chachacomani at 6094 meters.

On 8/29/1972, the author hitch hiked north out of La Paz to Achacachi, then had a short ride of 7 or 8 kms and started walking. He walked through Millipaya and a village called *Taipi Pararani* and slept in the school while it snowed all night. Next day he climbed east and camped at 4700 meters in the snow. Never saw a thing, so with 30 cms of snow on the ground, he walked back to the highway and got a bus to La Paz. He's still not certain where he was!

Next trip was better; it began on 6/7/1980. He made contact with a couple of Yanks working in La Paz named John Greenough& Doc Odle, one of whom had a 4WD. With an early start they drove north, perhaps to Huarina, then zig zagged east and stopped at Chiar Jokho--with lots of real bad roads to that point. Then the author set out on foot alone and walked up the Rio Kellhuani to the lake and camped at 4800 meters.

Morning of Day 2 was -7°C--about the same each morning. He then climbed up to 5100 meters, which would be a safer campsite away from shepherd boys & thieves, then zig zagged up to the summit of **Chearoco** and back; 6 1/4 hours round-trip. Near the top and in the shade he sank in up to 25-30 cms, but good hard snow otherwise. Day 3, he climbed the west summit of **Chachacomani**, which may be a little lower than the east peak (?). That day took 6 1/2 hours round-trip from camp. Both peaks have crevasses, but he can't remember feeling endangered. Steepness was up to 45° and simple routes.

Day 4; he walked back to the tiny village of Chiar Jokho, and north on the 4WD road and into the canyon just below Paso Casala. He camped at the highest lake called *Laguna Verde* at 4800 meters; an 8 1/2 hour day. Day 5, he walked to the pass and back in 1 1/2 hours, then went down to Laguna San Francisco but had cloudy skies, so he continued west past Ancullo (Estancia Jankho Huyo) and finally to the road north of Achacachi, after another 7 hours walking. Then a 2 hour bus ride to La Paz. A long 5 day trip.

For you to climb around Chearoco, take a bus to Huarina and hire a vehicle or start walking east--it's a maze of roads! Ask locals for the directions to Kellhuani. Then do as the author did.

For **Calzada**, take a bus to Achacachi, then walk east past Hacienda Tacamarca and up the river to Paso Casala, and climb from that area.

For **Ancohuma**, take one of 10 daily buses from La Paz to Sorata (8 or 9 hotels and many shops), then walk south, east and southeast as shown--according to Ben Folsom of Salt Lake City, Utah, USA. Head for the small lake at 5038 meters, and beyond. Looks like some glaciers & crevasses, and risky for solo climbers! Folsom's already-acclimatized group did it in 4 days. For **Illampu**, get a truck from Sorata to the pueblo Ancohuma, then head south and southwest as shown. Looks like some steeper sections on both rock and snow. As an LDS missionary, Ben Folsom apparently climbed **Huacana**, 6200 meters alone from Laguna San Francisco. Apparently an easy route--at least in good weather!

Some climbers have gone to the Mina Candelaria and Cocoyo (one food store there), and hiked up to Leche Khoto, made base camp & climbed from there. Some trekking outfitters are taking clients around the Illampu Massif in 5 to 7 days. Bolivia isn't what it used to be with

From somewhere above Tacamarca, the summit of Ancohuma can be seen.

Map 557-1, Illampu, Ancohuma, Chearoco, Cordillera Real, Bolivia

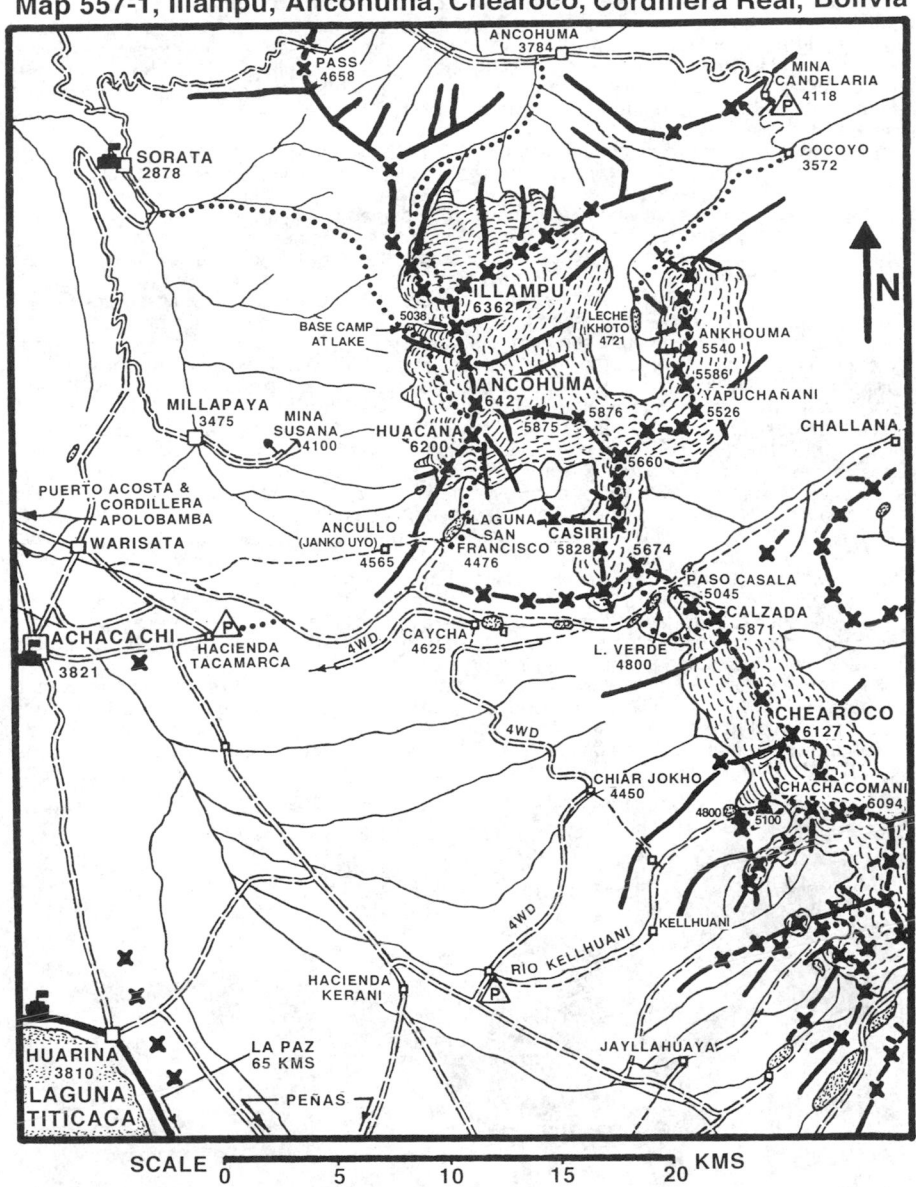

robberies reported. Best to go with a larger group and always leave a guard at base camp.

The tourist office in La Paz can help in locating buses or trucks, and can direct you to the local *club andino* or trekking outfitters; and the present location of bookstores or the IGM for maps. All maps listed below are now available at IGM, La Paz. Climb in Bolivia from May through early September.

Maps German Alpine Club map *Cordillera Real Nord (Illampu)*, 1:50,000; and/or IGM maps 5846-I, 5846-II, 5946-IV, 5946-III, 5845-I, 5945-I, all at 1:50,000; or *SE 19-3 & SD 19-15*, 1:250,000; and the book **Trekking in Bolivia**, and **Bolivia--A Climbing Guide**, both from The Mountaineers; and travel guidebook, **Bolivia**, Lonely Planet or Footprint Handbooks.

Nevado Condoriri, Cordillera Real, Bolivia

This is the second of 4 maps covering Bolivia's Cordillera Real. This map shows the area between just north of Huayna Potosi and 16° south. The highest summit here is Condoriri at 5648 meters. However, there are many other peaks over 5500 meters, so Condoriri is only slightly above the rest. For residents of La Paz, both locals and foreign diplomats & businessmen, this is one of the more popular climbs in the area, because of its easy access. Most of them have their own 4WD's.

Here's the author's experience starting on 4/25/1982. After storing baggage in a hotel in La Paz, he went to the Plaza San Francisco and met Stan Shepherd who worked for USAID. They drove up to the Chacaltaya Ski Resort at 5180 meters, the highest ski resort in the world (see next map). Stan and his Bolivian friends apparently stayed to ski, but the author walked up to the top (5290 meters on his altimeter) of the lifts and down the other side right to Milluni at 4550 meters. From there he walked for almost 8 hours until he was nearly to Laguna Chiar Kkota and camped at 4650 meters.

Next morning at -4°C, he climbed west, then northwest, then up along the southwest ridge to 5475 meters, but turned back because of snow showers, poor visibility, soft snow and the diarrhea bug. He was back at camp in about 4 hours round-trip. He was upset at not getting to the top, since Shepherd had climbed it solo the year before, so he moved his camp up to 4850 meters to be safer from thieves. Next morning, Day 3, he went again, but had snow off & on the whole trip and only got to 5535 meters on the knife-edge ridge and had to return. Back at the tent in 4 hours round-trip; packed up and road-walked southwest, got a bus ride nearly to the highway and camped. Next day he got to La Paz fast.

Getting to **Condoriri** is easy if you have a vehicle. Drive from La Paz towards Chacaltaya ski resort, then to Milluni and left to Tuni & Laguna Chiar Kkota. This lake can also be reached via the paved main highway leading northwest out of La Paz, then 20 kms northeast on the good dirt road to a turnoff leading to Chiar Kkota. If you're using public transport, inquire at the tourist office as to the location of where buses or trucks load up every day taking cargo and passengers to Tuni, and the twice daily buses to Milluni. Or take any bus north from La Paz to the turnoff to Tuni and walk the 20 plus kms to the lake. This should take one long day.

From Tuni, the road follows a small canal. At roads-end, walk up the valley to just beyond Chiar Kkota, then turn left and climb steep slopes, eventually reaching & climbing a prominent south ridge. Condoriri can also be climbed from the Mina Palcoco, but that's a more difficult climb, and there is almost no traffic going in that direction.

To climb other peaks further north such as **Yankho Huyo**, 5512 meters, you should use the road from Peñas to the Mina Navidad, about 32 kms. That's one very long day on foot. There's no public transport to this mine or the Mina Santa Rosa, which is now abandoned.

Condoriri is normally climbed on a weekend (2 days), but a strong climber could do it in one day with a 4WD from La Paz. For other peaks, and by taking trucks and walking, plan on 3 to 5

One of the best climbs in Bolivia is Condoriri and its southwest ridge.

Map 558-1, Nevado Condoriri, Cordillera Real, Bolivia

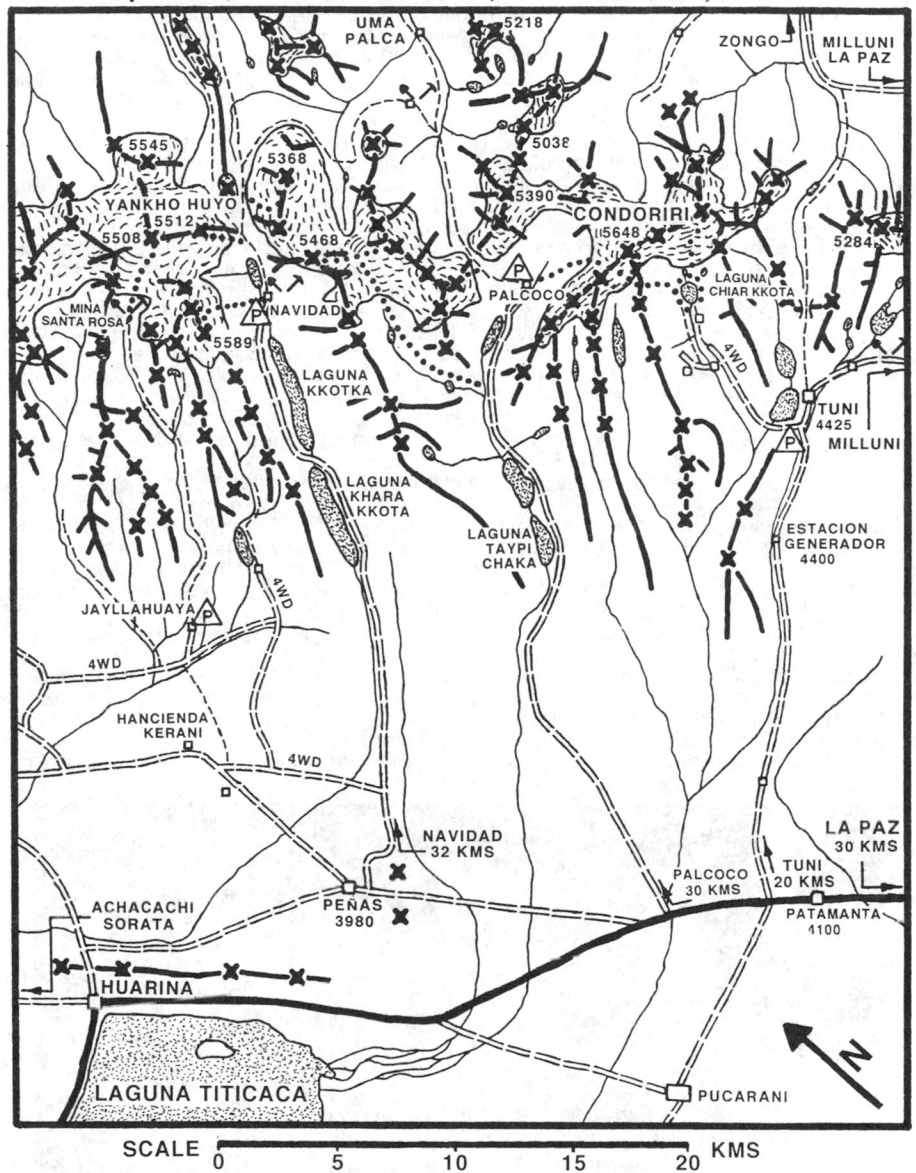

SCALE 0   5   10   15   20 KMS

days if only one peak is to be climbed. Peñas and Huarina are the only places on the map where food supplies can be purchased. In the months of May through early September, the snow is good and hard, but not in April, as the author found out! The rock is metamorphic & granite on most peaks.

Maps *Lago Khara Khota, Peñas, Zongo & Milluni,* 1:50,000, from the IGM, Estado Mayor Gen. Av. Saavedra Final, Miraflores; TPC map *P-26A,* 1:500,000; and the books **Trekking in Bolivia**, and **Bolivia--A Climbing Guide**, both from The Mountaineers; and travel guidebook, **Bolivia**, from Lonely Planet or Footprint Handbooks.

Huayna Potosi, Cordillera Real, Bolivia

Included on this map is La Paz, the highest capital city in the world, and the central portions of the Cordillera Real. This is the third in the series of 4 maps covering this mountain range. The highest peak in the area is Huayna Potosi at 6088 meters. Of interest to skiers, the Chacaltaya ski resort has a day-use refugio at 5180 meters, with the ski lift rising to about 5300 meters, highest in the world. Huayna Potosi is perhaps the most climbed mountain in Bolivia. The reason is obvious, it's very near and easy to reach from La Paz.

Here's what the author did on 8/8/1972. Transport wasn't as good in those days, so people in La Paz suggested he contact the Bolivian Power Company which was partially owned by a Canadian company. They have a hydroelectric plant just below Laguna Zongo. So he did, and a Canadian guy showed him some good maps of **Huayna Potosi** and gave permission for him to get a ride in a company truck for about 30 kms to Laguna Zongo.

Once there, he walked along a canal which gathers water from streams on the east side of the mountain and channels it to the lake. Being in the middle of a bad case of the flu, it took 3 hours to reach a campsite at 4800 meters just above the canal and at the beginning of the route up. Next morning, he headed up and almost due west weaving around exposed crevasses with good hard snow. He reached the summit in 3 1/3 hours. The last part was along one of the sharpest knife-edged ridges he has ever climbed. On the way down he gathered some fixed rope left by a Japanese expedition. From camp, the climb took exactly 5 hours round-trip. There are quite a few crevasses, but at that time of year you can see them and the author felt safe alone. He walked back along the canal to the lake in 1 1/3 hours. Total walk-time from Laguna Zongo was 13 hours. Later, another power company truck came and he had a quick ride back to central La Paz arriving at 6pm.

In La Paz, ask someone at the tourist office about public transport to Milluni and the nearby mines, and perhaps to Zongo (?). There are likely no buses to Zongo, so take one of 2 or 3 daily buses to Milluni, then walk 5 or 6 kms to Zongo. Or hire transport through the Hotel Continental. With your own vehicle, it's less than 2 hours from downtown La Paz to the lake. According to Ben Folsom, there is now (as of 1999) a refugio at Laguna Zongo, but most everyone camps along the canal as shown; or a little above and away from thieves, then does the climb and returns to La Paz on Day 2. Never leave an unguarded camp--lots of thieves in this area. Near the summit the route steepens, but in the months of May through early September, the snow is very hard, making the climb both easy and interesting.

To make climbs in other areas, go to the tourist office in La Paz and find out where trucks load up taking passengers and cargo to the area of the Mina San Francisco and the very popular **Inca Trail** to **Khasiri**. For climbs further southeast, there's heavy traffic over the pass known as Cumbre. From somewhere along that road you can reach **Rosario** or **Charquini**.

The route symbol shows some of the normal routes up other mountains. Half the peaks on

Halfway up the east face of Huayna Potosi. The route is easier than it first appears.

Map 559-1, Huayna Potosi, Cordillera Real, Bolivia

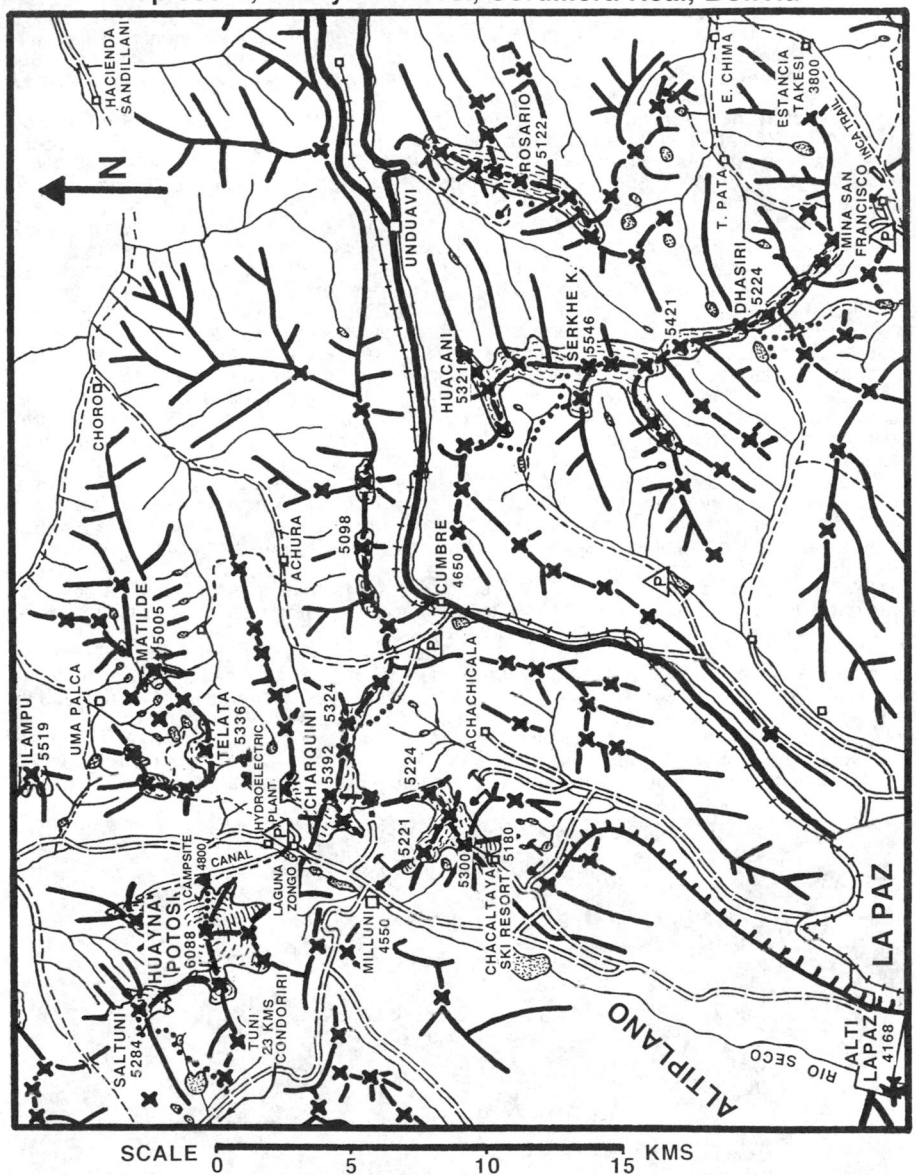

SCALE 0   5   10   15 KMS

this map can be climbed from the Milluni area. Buy all food and supplies before leaving La Paz, as there are almost no other places where food can be found. The snowline is about 4800 meters, making ice ax & crampons required equipment on most peaks.

Maps *Milluni, La Paz (Norte), Chojlla & Palca,* 1:50,000; and/or *La Paz,* 1:250,000, from the IGM, Estado Mayor Gen. Av. Saavedra Final, Miraflores, La Paz; TPC map *P-26A,* 1:500,000; and the books **Trekking in Bolivia**, and **Bolivia--A Climbing Guide**, both from The Mountaineers; and travel guidebook, **Bolivia**, from Lonely Planet or Footprint Handbooks; also check the South American Explorers Club website (www.samexplo.org) for other publications.

Illimani & Mururata, Cordillera Real, Bolivia

This is the last and most-southerly of the 4 maps covering the Cordillera Real. The highest mountain here is Illimani at 6402 meters. It's Illimani that dominates the southeastern skyline of La Paz. The second most important summit is Mururata, with its highest peak set at 5868 meters (the large area shown as snow east of Mururata is not glaciation, only the normal snow line during the rainy season. IGM maps are misleading).

Here's what the author did on **Illimani** beginning 8/21/1972. He took a city bus from downtown La Paz about 10 kms southeast to the suburb of Calacoto. He waited at the police checkpost there and finally got a ride on top of a truck going to the Mina Bolsa Negra. It was packed with people! At 3:15pm he was let off just before Paso Pacuani, then started walking south on the road along the west side of Illimani. He walked 3 1/4 hours and camped after dark. Day 2, he road-walked another 1 1/2 hours, then started climbing, but wasn't in the right place. He finally did get on the west ridge and went up to about 5500 meters and camped at 1pm; 5 1/4 hours walking. Melt snow. There's a climber's trail and many campsites on that ridge, but no running water. Day 3, he headed straight up the west ridge to the top of the south summit. The climb took 3 3/4 hours; 1 1/4 hours going back to camp. Easy climb, as he easily skirted around only 3 crevasses. This is a lot safer for a solo climber than Huayna Potosi!

He broke camp and headed straight down the ridge to the road, taking one hour, and about 14 1/2 hours total walk-time at that point. He camped next to the road near a pond at the base of the west ridge. There used to be an old building next to the road where the ridge trail begins. Late information states many climbers camp one night near a bridge called *Puente Roto*, apparently at the base of the west ridge (?). Next morning he broke camp and waited beside the road for 3 hours for a truck to pass, then got a ride back to La Paz arriving at 2:30pm.

Evidentially, the road from Paso Pacuani to Cahone is not used much because of a washed-out bridge (?). So according to the latest information from the **South American Handbook** (1998), some climbers are now taking an irregular truck from La Paz, past Palca to the *Estancia Una* (or Ena?), hiring mules, then apparently walking northeast to Pinaya and to the base of the west ridge.

However, the easiest way as of 2000 seems to be to take one of 2 daily buses from somewhere in La Paz (ask directions at the tourist office) to Cahone, then road-walk northeast and north about 12-13 kms to the base of the west ridge.

Mururata. On 6/3/1980, the author took one bus to Calacoto and at the police checkpoint found a truck going to the Mina San Francisco, so he & 10 Israeli Jews got on--they going to the Inca Trail. Got to the mine at 12:30pm. The author backtracked, then walked to Junani and up past 2 mines to a campsite just below snowline at 5040 meters; about 4 hours walking (?). Next morning it took less than 2 hours to reach the summit with rock-hard snow and no crevasses. Just over 3 hours round-trip from camp. Then another 2 1/2 hours down to the main road (less than 10 hours total walk-time), and soon a free ride in a pickup down to La Paz. With your own

The northeast side of Illimani as seen from the summit of Muturata.

Map 560-1, Illimani & Mururata, Cordillera Real, Bolivia

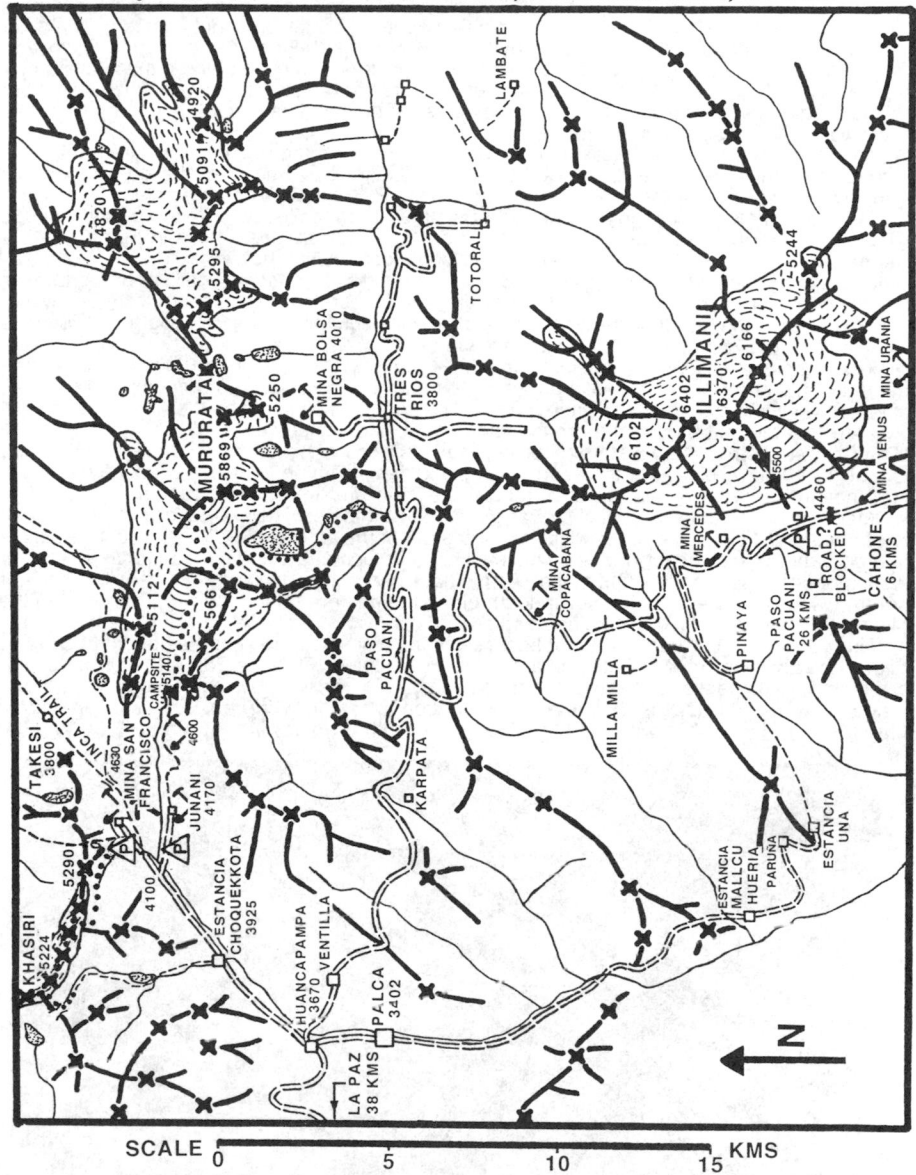

4WD, a strong & acclimatized climber could do Mururata in one long day from La Paz. This is the easiest-to-climb big mountain in Bolivia.

Of the villages on the map, only Palca, Huancapampa and Bolsa Negra have stores. Best to buy everything in La Paz. Dry season is from May to early September. Trekkers should check out the Inca Trail, between the San Francisco Mine and Takesi and beyond.

Maps IGM maps Chojlla, Palca, Chulumani, Cohoni, and Lambate, 1:50,000, and La Paz, 1:250,000 (best for access), from IGM, Estado Mayor Gen. Av. Saavedra Final, Miraflores, La Paz; and the books **Trekking in Bolivia**, and **Bolivia--A Climbing Guide**, both from The Mountaineers; and travel guidebook, **Bolivia**, from Lonely Planet or Footprint Handbooks.

Gigante Grande, Jacha Pacuni, Cordillera Quimsa (Tres) Cruz, Bolivia

This map covers the highest part of the Cordillera Quimsa Cruz, a small & compact mountain range due north of Oruro and southeast of La Paz. Lots of confusion about names of peaks on mountaineering maps and those put out by the IGM of Bolivia. First of all the name *Quimsa* in Quechua (language of highland Indians) means three or tres. On most Bolivian maps this range is called *Tres Cruzes*, but it appears most mountaineers know it as the Quimsa Cruz. Names of several peaks don't correlate either. But regardless of names, this range has a number of fine peaks which can challenge any climber.

To reach the Quimsa Cruz take any bus out of La Paz bound for Oruro; or in Oruro take any bus north toward La Paz; and proceed to the small village of Panduro located on the main highway (one source say the actual turnoff is at Konani & Km 149). At Panduro look for either a bus, or more likely a truck, going to Caxata (55 kms), then to Rodeo (30? more kms), and to Viloco (another 50 kms). Bus transport ends there, but you can take a truck to Araca where a German man owns the Hacienda Teneria and a lodge for travelers.

Sometime in the late 1990's, there was a bus leaving El Alto (somewhere near the La Paz Airport) from Calle Jorge Carrasco between Calle 4 & 5, bound for Viloco about 4 times a week. Ask someone at the tourist office in La Paz, and check it out the day before departure. That bus used to depart at 7am and took 10 hours to reach Viloco.

The highest summit is **Gigante Grande** at 5748 meters, the highest point on **Nevado Jacha Pacuni**. This and other high peaks are glaciated and require ice ax & crampons and perhaps other snow climbing equipment. There is a trail leading to an old mine on the western slopes of Gigante, but the route up from there is near vertical. An easier way would be to begin at the Mina Chojña Kkota at 4800 meters (directly below the electric transformer). Route-find north up to a big nearly level glacier to the base of the peak, then climb up the steeper east face. From that same glacier you can also climb **Don Luis**, the 2nd highest peak in the range.

Many peaks here are especially attractive to rock climbers. There are literally hundreds of unclimbed granite peaks, most of which are in the northern part of the range. One source states one good place to climb granite is 6 kms east (?) of Viloco at a place called **Mocaya**; but that name doesn't appear on the IGM maps. A trek that's becoming popular for the very few who get out that way is the trail running north-south along the eastern base of the range between the Mina Caracoles and Viloco. That should take 2-3 days.

Buy all food in Oruro or La Paz for best selections, but some food can be bought at Caxata, Viloco, the Estancia Rancho Pata and at the Mina Caracoles. From La Paz, into the range, and climbing say two peaks, and return to La Paz will take a week to 10 days. Expect to find bad roads, slow trucks or buses and no accommodation except for your tent. Dry season is from May to September. The western slopes are drier with the snowline at about 5000 to 5200

Gigante Grande, the highest peak in the Quimsa (Tres) Cruz (S. Calegari foto).

Map 561-1, Gigante Grande, Cordillera Quimsa (Tres) Cruz, Bolivia

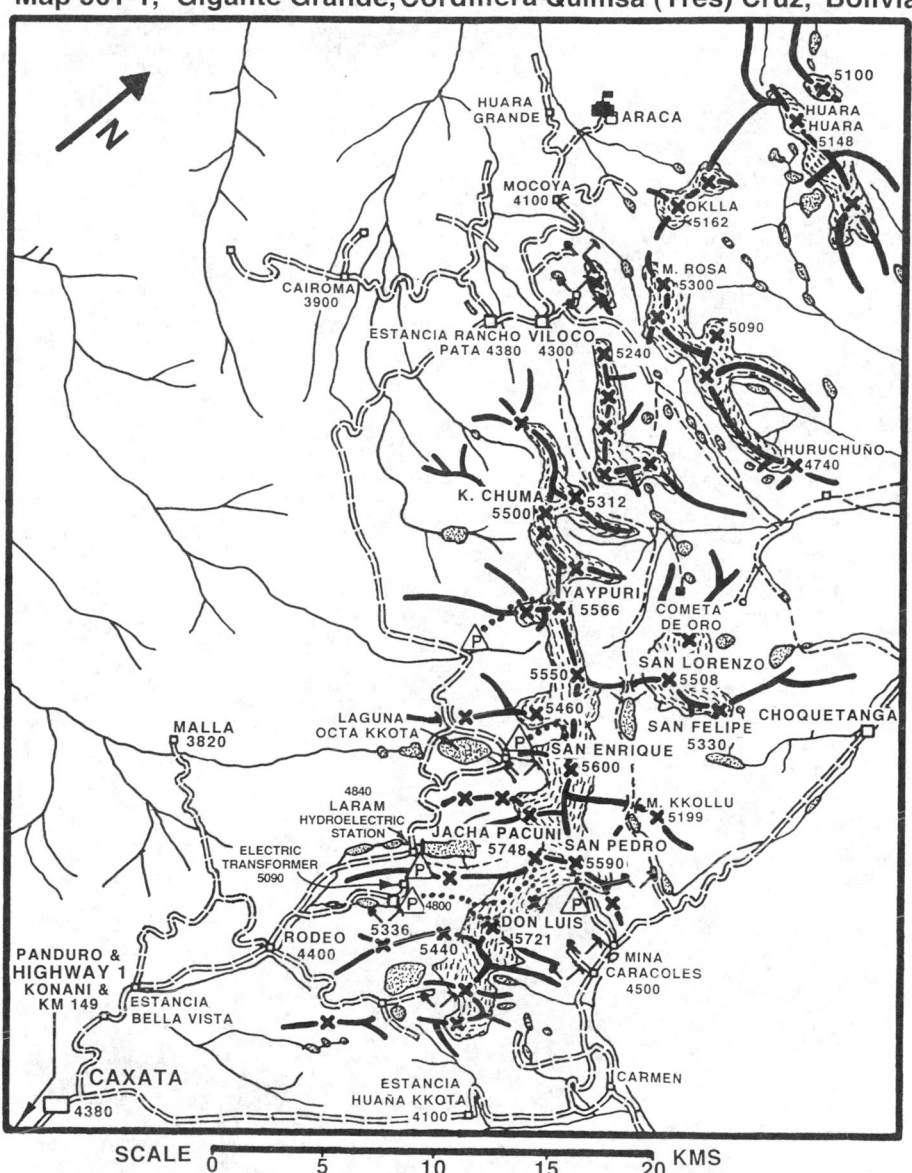

SCALE 0   5   10   15   20 KMS

meters, whereas the eastern face is wetter with a snowline at about 4800 or 5000 meters.
Maps *Mina Caracoles, Araca, Estancia Choquetanga, Chico Yaco, Cairoma*, 1:50,000, or maps
SE-19-4 and SE-19-8, 1:250,000, from the IGM, Estado Mayor Gen. Av. Saavedra Final,
Miraflores, La Paz; TPC map P-26B, 1:500,000; and the books **Trekking in Bolivia**, and
Bolivia--A Climbing Guide, both from The Mountaineers; and travel guidebook, **Bolivia**, from
Lonely Planet or Footprint Handbooks; also check the South American Explorers Club website
(www.samexplo.org) for other publications.

Nevado Sajama, Cordillera Occidental, Bolivia

This map features the highest mountain in Bolivia, Nevado Sajama at 6520 meters. Also, not far west of Sajama and right on the border with Chile, are 2 more symmetrically shaped snow capped volcanos over 6000 meters. They are Pomerape, 6240, and Parinacota at 6330 meters. These 2 volcanos are on boundary between the Parque Nacional Lauco in Chile, and Parque Nacional Sajama in Bolivia.

Southwest of Sajama about 45 kms are 3 more high peaks, 2 of which are over 6000 meters. Guallatiri is 6060, and Acotango at 6050 meters. A 6th major summit on this map is Tacora, 5988 meters. Tacora had questionable eruptions in 1930 & 1937. This is the volcano which forms part of the skyline for both Tacna, Peru and Arica, Chile. All the above mentioned volcanos last erupted in the Holocene or late Pleistocene.

Here's how the author climbed **Sajama**. He met power company employee Pete Williams in La Paz, drove to Oruro, stayed one night, then on 8/13/1972, drove west in a 4WD to as far as Turco. Pete & wife returned, but the author stayed and bought some food, then at 8pm a truck came going to Chachacomani. Arrived at 2:30am half frozen. Slept on a dirt floor of a military frontier post the rest of the night; then walked north for 1 1/3 hours and got on the same truck as the night before and rode to Lagunas. From there he walked 4 1/2 hours to a camp at the base of Sajama at 5000 meters (?).

Day 3, he climbed Sajama in 5 1/2 hours on the southern route. Ran down in 1 1/4 hours-- good knees then!, and another 2 1/2 hours to Lagunas. Slept on another dirt floor in the school teacher's room, that of Nestor Lima Torrey. Next morning a truck came at 11am and went to Sajama, loaded cargo, and got as far as Curahuara de Carangas. Slept in an extra room of an army school barracks. Day 5, left Carangas at 9am, standing with the sheep, and in sheep dip, all the way to La Paz arriving at 6pm. While crossing the Rio Desaguadero on a ferry, all passengers had to help pull the boat across with a rope by hand. That was then, but now you'll find a paved road & bridge and can drive from La Paz to Sajama in 4-5 hours, or less.

Sajama was an easy climb, but the author had to chop 8-10 steps up a short icy wall, otherwise a walkup with no crevasses. Take an ice ax & crampons on all 6000'ers. Climb **Parinacota & Pomerape** direct from Sajama village; and **Guallatiri & Acotango** from Chachacomani. Carry water from the lower stream valleys which are crawling with llamas & alpacas; or camp high near snowline for water. Bring all your food & supplies from La Paz (or Arica). Dress warm and have a warm sleeping bag.

By the 1990's, the road was paved all the way from La Paz to Arica. It goes south from La Paz to Patacamaya, 104 kms; west to Puente Japones on the Rio Desaguadero, then to C. de Carangas, Tameripi and Sajama with a dirty alojamiento (hotel), school, restaurant & store. Lagunas, now a truck stop, has the Bolivian Customs & military garrison, a hotel & restaurant, school, petrol & shops. No water or electricity in either pueblo. Take candles. Cold nights.

Before the border called Paso Tambo Quemado is the Bolivian immigration & police, then after another 7 kms, the Chilean border post. Further along is some kind of refugio on Chungara Lake (with lots of wildlife), plus 2 more refugios along the way to Putre with several hotels and park headquarters, then on to Arica. Several buses per week now run from La Paz to Arica (11 hours), but you can go as far as Sajama & Lagunas on the same buses. Also trucks going to

Sajama as seen from the south near Lagunas. Both llamas & alpacas graze here.

Map 562-1, Nevado Sajama, Cordillera Occidental, Bolivia

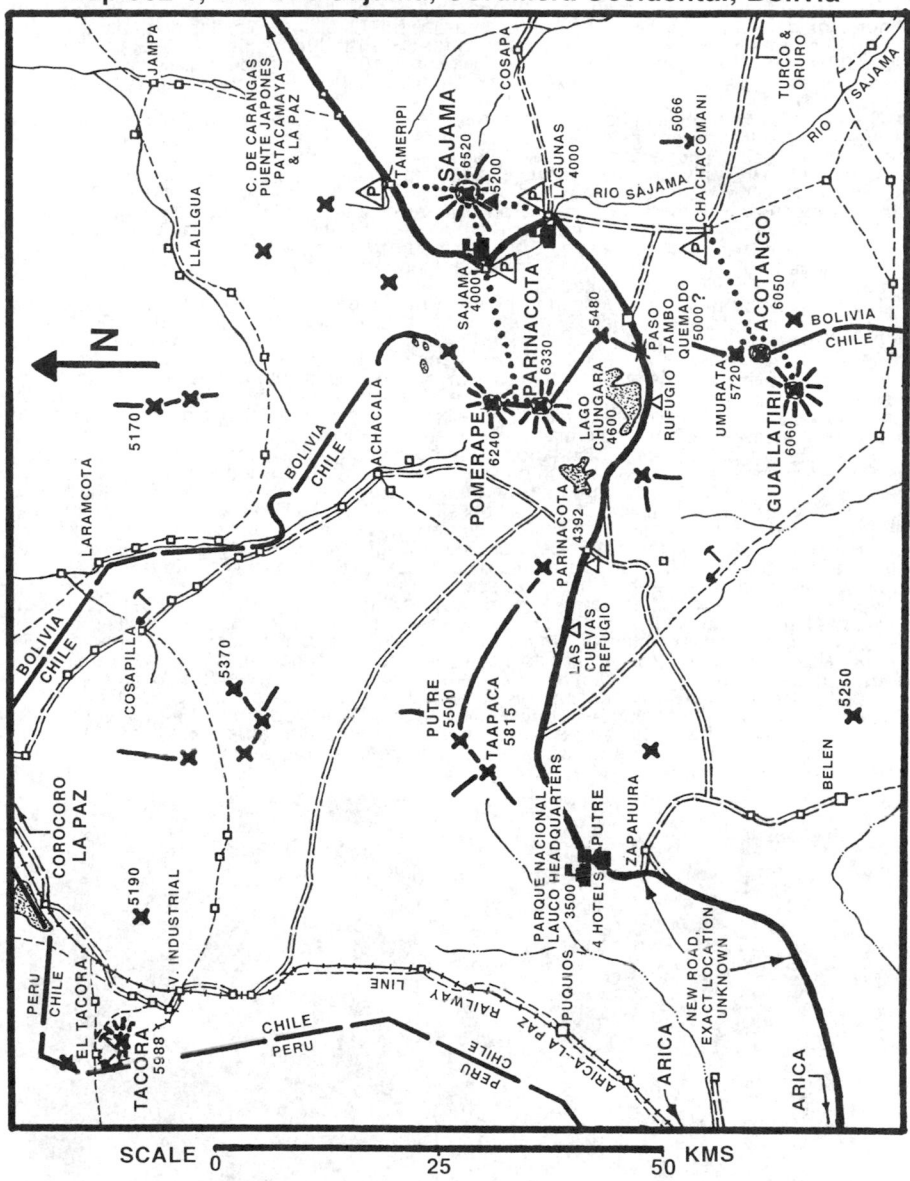

SCALE 0 ——— 25 ——— 50 KMS

Sajama area.
Maps *Arica,* 1:500,000, from the IGM, Santiago; or check with IGM, La,Paz, maybe maps at 1:50,000 are ready, and buy *Gorque (Bolivia) SE 19-11,* 1:250,000; perhaps TPC map *P-26A,* 1:500,000; and the book **Bolivia--A Climbing Guide**, The Mountaineers; and travel guidebooks, **Bolivia** and/or **Chile**, both from Lonely Planet or Footprint Handbooks; or **South American Handbook**.

Aucanquilcha, San Pedro & Ollagüe, Cord. Occidental, Chile-Bolivia

The area covered by this map is north and east of Calama & Chuquicamata, 2 important copper mining towns in northern Chile's Atacama Desert. Of all the volcanos on the map, 3 are over 6000 meters. However, there are dozens more near that mark, and all peaks shown are over 5000 meters. Ollagüe may have had an eruption in 1903; San Pedro had its last confirmed activity beginning 5/25/1901 lasting to 8/1901. Otherwise all volcanos here last erupted before the Holocene (last 10,000 years).

The actual ascent of any peak here is hardly a problem. There are no glaciers and only a few snow fields at the summits of the highest peaks. The problems you'll have however, are limited transportation, poor accessibility, and lack of water.

As for water, the only flowing stream is the Rio Loa, which is the source of water for Calama and the mines. There are hot springs and geysers at Tatio, but that water is undrinkable. The further east you go, the more precipitation and grass you'll find, but this entire region is desert. The lakes shown are all salty. What this all means is you'll have to carry water from a railway station or Calama, and plan to camp very high on the peaks and melt snow. Permanent snow is usually above 5500 meters, but when stormy weather comes it snows down to as low as 4000 meters. Plan on carrying lots of water!

The only reliable means of transport is the tren (train) running from Antofagasta and Calama, to the border town of Ollagüe, then a Bolivian tren to Uyuni and La Paz. In 1980 and in the late 1990's, there was a once-a-week scheduled passenger tren running each way on the line. However, there are periodic unscheduled runs and freight trains which can be boarded with permission. Stops are made at the stations shown on the map, all of which have water in tanker cars. Ollagüe has a so-called hotel by the name of Residencia Derby, a bar and 2 very small stores, but no running water or electricity. This information is from 1980, but the author is certain it's about the same as of 2000, according to the latest guidebooks.

Here's the author's experience on **Aucanquilcha & Ollagüe.** He returned from Licancabor and San Pedro de Atacama about noon on Wednesday, 5/7/1980, and found there was a tren heading for Ollagüe and the border at 1pm, then a return tren on Saturday. So he left extra baggage in a hotel, bought as much food as possible, and got on the tren. The tren stopped in San Pedro, and the author had a quick visit with the station master and made tentative plans to climb the nearby peaks on the way back, then on to Ollagüe at 7pm. He got off along with other passengers getting on the Bolivian tren heading for La Paz. He checked into the Residencia Derby, a cold, miserable, bed-bug infested place.

Next morning he got a lift in a mining truck to Amincha & mine HQ. Tried to get permission to visit the highest mine in the world at 5800 meters, but no permission; so he walked back to Ollagüe, got pack & water bottles full and walked directly toward the mountain, camped at 4385 meters. Next morning, cloudy, windy, snowy and very cold. Headed up but wasn't prepared for super cold even with a down jacket, so he turned back at 5100 meters, the coldest he's ever been (the old tramway is now unusable)! Returned to Buenaventura and got a ride to the sulfur mines near the summit of Ollagüe. Round-trip ride was 2 3/4 hours and 15 kms one-way by road. Walked out of town and camped. Next morning it was calm, clear & cold, -15°C! A cold front must have gone through, but when the sun came up it was pleasant. At 2pm, the tren came and took 6 hours to reach Calama.

Volcan Ollagüe as seen from the railway depot of Buenaventura.

Map 563-1, Aucanquilcha, San Pedro & Ollagüe, Chile-Bolivia

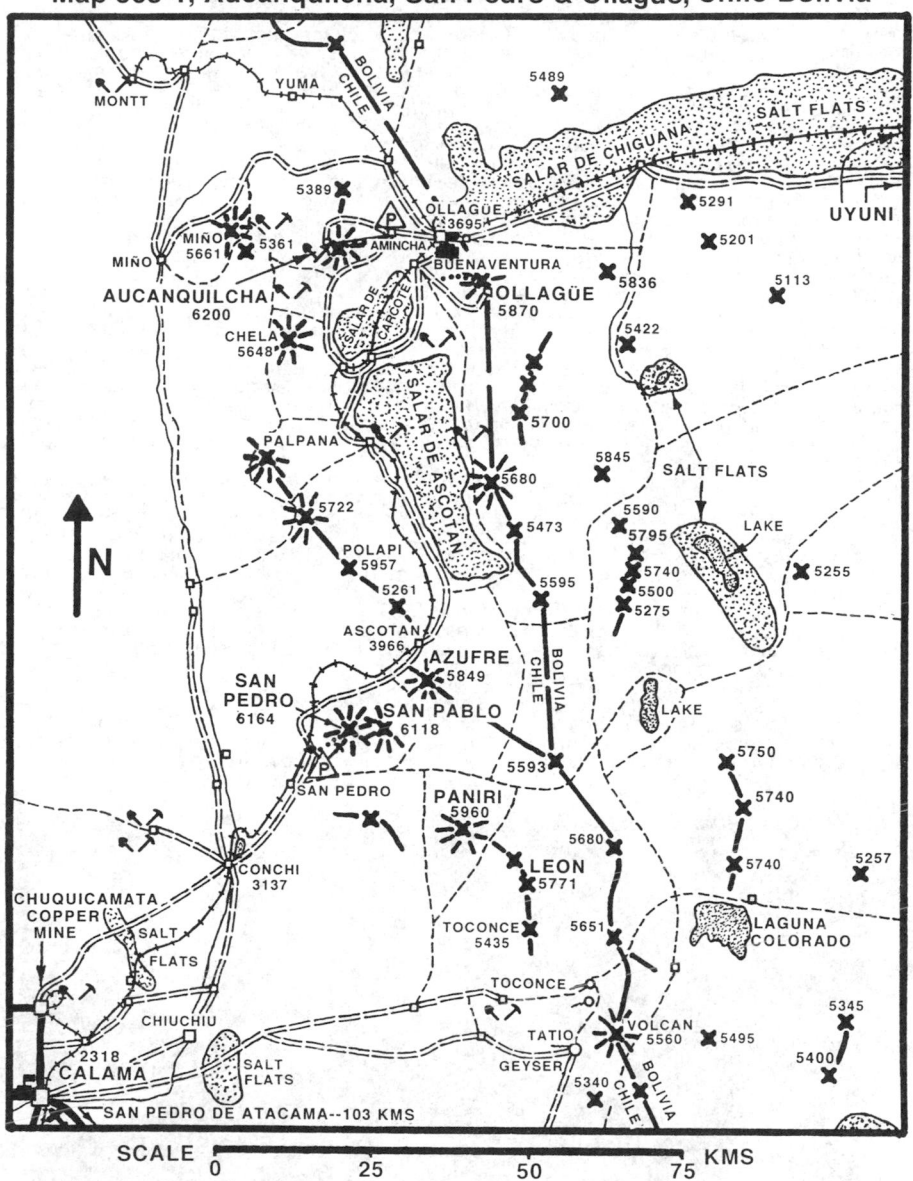

SCALE
0   25   50   75   KMS

To climb either of these peaks, walk right from Ollagüe or Buenaventura. To climb **San Pedro**, 6154 meters, or **San Pablo**, 6118 meters, stop at San Pedro station and walk from there, or from the mine just up the road. Be prepared to wait a day or 2 to get in or out of Ollagüe or San Pedro (perhaps by truck too). Buy all food and supplies in Calama for all climbs. To climb other mountains away from the railway you'll have to walk or hire a vehicle. Get tren, road & traffic reports at Calama's tourist office. This is a desert, but some rain or snow can fall from November through March.

Maps *Zapaleri & Calama*, 1:500,000, from the IGM, Santiago; or TPC map *P-26D*, 1:500,000; and travel guidebooks, **Bolivia** and/or **Chile**, from Lonely Planet or Footprint Handbooks.

Licancabur, Pili & Volcan Lascar, Cordillera Andes, Chile

This map shows the mountainous region where Chile, Bolivia and Argentina meet. This is the Atacama Desert; high, dry and cool & cold. The problems climbers have here are lack of water and poor accessibility; not mountaineering difficulties. Every summit on this map is a volcano at one age or another, and every peak marked is over 5000 meters. Many of these volcanos are Holocene in age, or older, except one. Lascar at 5592 (or 5154?) meters is the most active in the northern 2/3's of Chile. It has had at least 18 eruptions during the 1900's. Sometime after 1/30/1993 one explosion registered a VEI-4. It threw lava bombs 3 1/2 kms from the crater. Last reports from 7/1996, indicate huffing & puffing vapors & steam only.

Here's what the author did on **Licancabur**, 5921 meters, starting on 5/3/1980. From Calama he hitch hiked to the small town of San Pedro de Atacama and stayed in the Residencia Florida, with water, but no electricity. Next morning bought some food, gathered information, and started walking up the road toward the Purico Sulfur Mine carrying water for 24 hours. There were big quebradas to his left so he stayed on the road until south of the mountain, then headed north. He walked about 30 kms in 8 hours & camped at 3750 meters. Morning of Day 2, -7°C. Walked for 4 hours to where there was lots of snow at 4370 meters and camped. He was short on fuel, so he used the sun to melt snow the rest of the day. Morning Day 3, -6 1/2°C. He climbed to the summit in 2 3/4 hours, took fotos of the Incan ruins and all the wood they carried up, and returned. About 4 1/2 hours round-trip from camp. Walked another 3 hours to the road and immediately got a ride to San Pedro saving 5-6 hours walking.

As of 2000, access & transport is a lot easier. Make your way to the mining town of Calama, then take one of several daily buses to San Pedro, the largest settlement in the area. There are many tourists going that way these days, as well as mining trucks. You can walk to Licancabur as the author did; or hire a vehicle in Calama or San Pedro which can take you up a 4WD road to the western base of Licancabur. If you're acclimatized, it's a long day-climb from the end of the track, and 2 days from San Pedro.

As of 2000, there is daily bus service from San Pedro (with Chilean Customs post) to Toconao; and twice-a-week bus service from Antofagasta & Calama, to Salta in Argentina, apparently via San Pedro, Toconao, Comar, Socaira, and the *Paso de la Laguna Sico* at 4079 meters. This has apparently replaced the Guaitiquina Pass as the way into Argentina (?). There's another route to Argentina called the *Paso de Jama*. It's used by some trucks and runs southeast from San Pedro to Jama, but the **South American Handbook** isn't clear on the exact route after that.

So there's more traffic in the area now than in 1980, so you should be able to hire a vehicle in Calama or San Pedro (?) to get out to the **Lascar** area. With a group to split costs, this is the best way. With a vehicle, you can carry all the water you'll want; and if returning by foot, you can cache water along the road.

Or you can walk. Take a bus to Toconao, and walk to Soncor and Talabre, both with spring water, then hike cross-country to **Lascar** and other peaks nearby, including **Pili** at 6050 meters, the highest in the area. You should find some snow for water up high. December through February has more rain or snow (down to below 4000 meters), making water less of a problem.

Food should be purchased in Calama, with plenty of shops, hotels and a tourist office.

Licancabur as seen from the south. It has Incan ruins at the summit.

Map 564-1, Licancabur, Pili & Lascar, Cordillera Andes, Chile

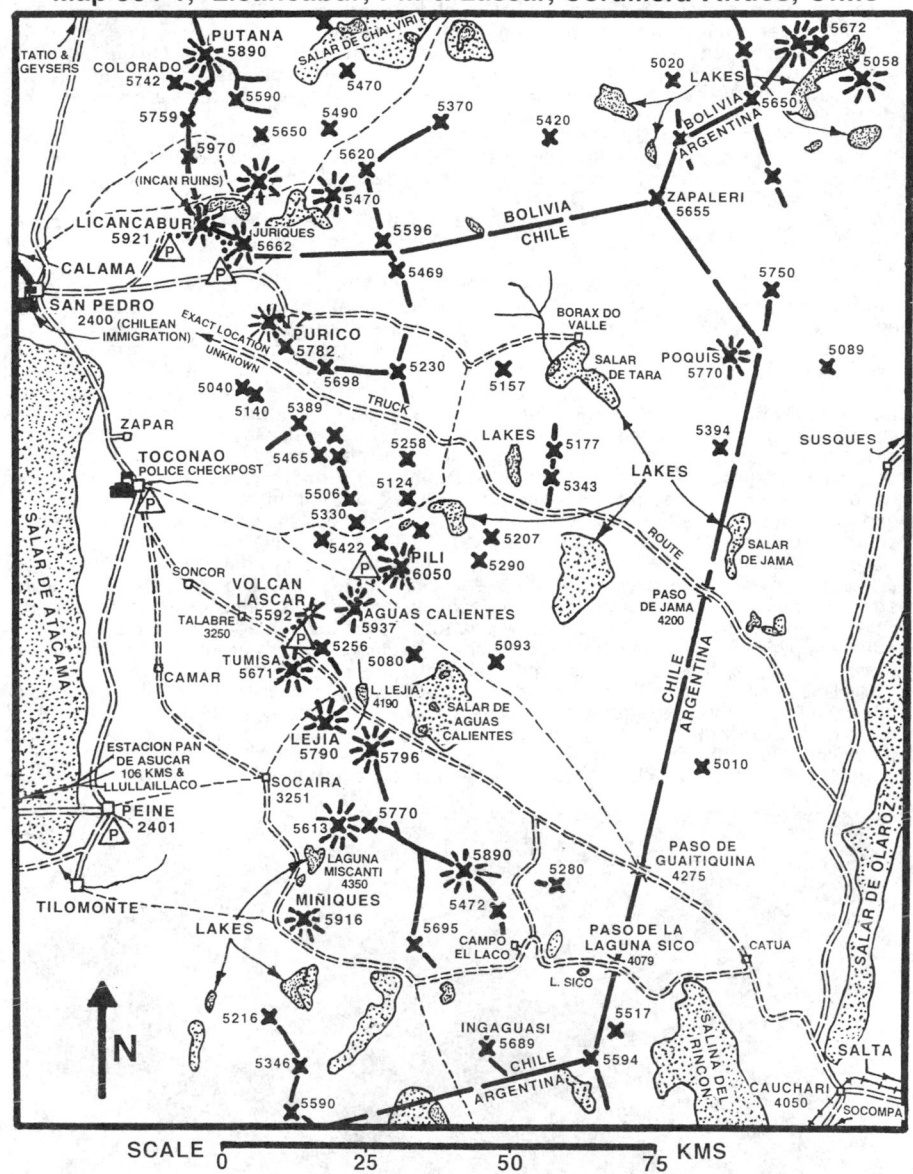

Because of the world famous museum of Belgian Father Le Paige of San Pedro, that town now has 15 or more small hotels and many shops. Toconao has 3 residenciales, and a store or two. **Maps** *Calama, Antofagasta, Zapaleri & Socaire,* 1:500,000, from IGM, 384 O'Higgins, Santiago; or TPC maps *P-26D & P-26C,* 1:500,000; and travel guidebooks **Chile**, from Lonely Planet; or **Chile** or **South American Handbook**, both from Footprint Handbooks. As of 12/2000, it appears that both Chile and Argentina now have newer & better maps at 1:250,000 scale available. A quick way to check this out is to see the website (www.omnimap.com). Or some of the other companies or websites listed in the back of this book under *Major Map and Guidebook Sales Outlets.*

Libertador, Chañi & Queva, Cordillera Andes, Argentina

Included on this map are 4 ranges all of which have peaks at or above 6000 meters. The highest is Libertador at 6720 (or 6380 on some maps) meters. This summit is part of the Nevado de Cachi. Other summits in this range are: Palermo, 6350 meters; Quemado, 6120; and Cienaga, 6030 meters. Other major summits in the area include Chañi, 6200 meters; Queva, 6130; and Nevado Acay, at about 6000 meters. All of these mountains are west of Jujuy and/or Salta, in the extreme northwest part of Argentina.

These mountains are relatively close together, with similar climates. Only Queva, which is further west than the others, is noticeably drier. For this region the months of November through March (the Southern Hemisphere summer) is the rainy season. Therefore the preferred climbing season is from about April through October.

Maps used by the author show some glaciers on the higher summits, but these are small. All or most peaks may be climbed without ice ax or crampons; however, better take them on all the higher peaks just in case.

Here's the author's experience with **Chañi**. On 1/8/1982, he left Jujuy by bus late in the afternoon heading north. Got off at Leon and walked west 45 minutes and camped at 1700 meters. Day 2, walked 8 1/2 hours in cloudy, misty weather--never saw a mountain! At one point he crossed the stream to the north side, then up and over a ridge and down again, then up to within one km of the ovejeria and camped at 3250 meters. Morning, Day 3, 4°C, walked to the ovejeria (sheep shepherd huts), then headed northeast over a ridge and down to the next valley and camped at 4760 meters after 7 hours walking. Cloudy all day long! There's supposed to be a refugio somewhere, but never saw it (?). Morning Day 4, -3 1/2° C, clear for a while and bad battery in camera! Climbed up a northeast ridge, easy at first, then with pinnacles; got to within 40 vertical meters of the summit, but turned back because to finish would have been very time consuming; 3 hours up, 5 hours round-trip from camp. Supposed to be Incan ruins on top. Headed back down for 3 1/2 hours in clouds and camped at 3570 meters. Morning Day 5, only 3°C, then walked to the road in 8 hours and a bus back to Jujuy.

A couple of days later he was in Salta heading for Cachi & **Libertador**, but it had rained very hard for 2 days with flooding, so he left the area looking for the sun! According to travel guides, there's one bus a day running from Salta to Cachi, another bus from Molinos to Cachi--a tourist town with 6 hotels & shops. From town, walk northwest in the quebrada and up the south side with snow up high. Three or 4 days (?), depending on fitness & acclimatization. Or hitch hike to Pueblo Viejo, and spend 4-5 days climbing **Quemado**, **Cienaga** or **Palermo**.

To climb **Acay**, take the almost-daily bus from Salta to San Antonio de los Cobres, but get off at, or just beyond Encrucijada, and climb south from there. The upper west face might be easier. Hitch hike out. To get to **Queva**, which also has Incan ruins at the summit, take the bus, or a once-weekly *tren* from Salta to San Antonio (4 hotels & some shops), then go to the police checkpost & Argentine immigration, and wait for a truck going to Olacapato (or ask around town); or possibly get on a once or

A picture of a shepherd home at the ovejeria just south of Chañi.

Map 565-1, Libertador, Chañi & Queva, Cordillera Andes, Argentina

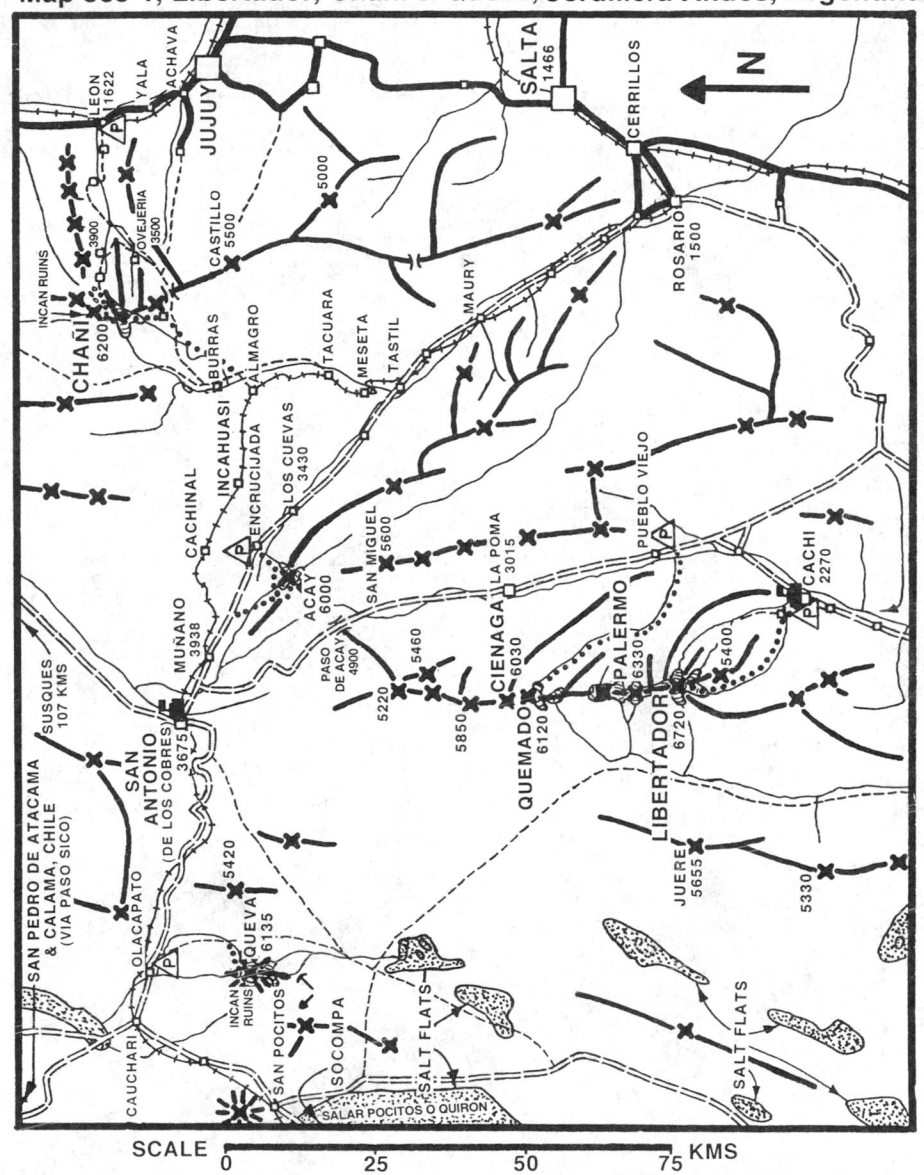

SCALE 0 25 50 75 KMS

twice weekly *freight tren* going to Antofagasta, Chile. You may have to wait a day or 2, but you'll be acclimatizing at 3675 meters. Climb south from Olacapato, but carry lots of water, and ask of its whereabouts! A 3 or 4 day climb. Buy supplies for all climbs in Jujuy or Salta

Maps *Socaire & Nevado San Francisco*, 1:500,000, from the IGM, 384 O'Higgins, Santiago, Chile; or check website (www.omnimap.com) for newly released maps; or TPC map *Q-27A*, 1:500,000; and the *Carta Vial de Zona--Catamarca, Jujuy, Salta and Tucuman*, from Automovil Club Argentino, Buenas Aires; and travel guidebook **Argentina**, from Lonely Planet or Footprint Handbooks.

Llullaillaco, Cordillera Andes, Chile-Argentina

Featured on this map is Llullaillaco at 6723 meters, the 4th or 5th highest peak in South America. Llullaillaco is claimed by some people to be the highest volcano in the world. However, Ojos del Salado, on the next map south, is slightly higher. Llullaillaco had 3 eruptions in the 1800's, the last being in 5/1877, but the author found no sign of activity on this climb.

Llullaillaco is in that part of the Atacama Desert that is widest; therefore, it is very dry. This lack of water coupled with the near absence of roads or railways, makes access very difficult. All mountains on the map are over 5000 meters, and all are volcanic.

The **Llullaillaco** adventure for the author started in Antofagasta, Chile. He boarded the once-weekly *tren* running to Argentina in the late afternoon and rode all night. Because of the crowded conditions that night, he had a bad case of the flu when the tren arrived at Socompa in the early afternoon, 5/15/1980. He went through Argentine immigration, left extra baggage at the aduana (customs) and camped nearby. Bad flu, not much sleep, but next morning better, with 1°C & light snow. Filled water bottles and walked south. Crossed over 2 passes, past the nearby salty Laguna Tecar and to a 3rd pass, camped at 4250 meters, 6 1/2 hours walked, light snow all day. Morning Day 2, -9 1/2°C, walked south over the 4th pass or low divide, saw one ostrich-like bird running like hell, then turned west and walked into and up a V-shaped canyon to the plateau above. After 1st day, melting snow for water. Camped behind boulders for wind protection at the base of Llullaillaco at 4700 meters. Snow showers all day, walked 8 hours. Morning Day 3, -10°C, made the summit in 6 1/4 hours, saw Incan ruins at 6250, 6500 & 6700 meters. One minute on top, cold! Down to camp in 2 1/2 hours, afternoon snow, camped in same place. Morning Day 4, -11°C, walked back along same route, saw a fox near Tecar Lake. After 8 hours walking, camped at 4200 meters with snow showers. Morning Day 5, -4 1/2°C, walked about 3 hours to Socompa. Victor, of Argentine customs, invited author to sleep on the floor of the aduana with stove, toilet & water. Paradise! Next day, visited 1000 mummified cattle that died in a blizzard years before. Last day, trens came from both sides, exchanged passengers, and returned. The author continued into Argentina, 19 hours to Salta.

As of 2000, there are no more passenger trens crossing the border at Socompa, but there is about one freight tren per week, and passengers are allowed on, at least on the Argentine side. There seems to be no truck traffic at Socompa. If coming from Salta, immigration may be in San Antonio de los Cobres (?). Inquire in Salta or Antofagasta.

If you make it to Socompa, you might climb **Nevado Socompa** just north of the tren station in one long day or 1 1/2 days--if you're acclimatized! In the upper part of this map are 4 mountains with Incan ruins or some proof that Indians were there first. They are Socompa, Pular, Salin & Aracar. You'd have to have your own 4WD to reach them.

In the 1990's one way to Llullaillaco was to hire a 4WD in Calama, drive past San Pedro, Toconao (see previous page) and south to the railway and Estacion Pan de Azucar & the north end of the Salar Punta Negra, then to the Quebrada de las Zorritas where running water is found. From there an easy day hike to a base camp as high as possible, then summit and back to Zorritas on Day 2 or 3! Start inquiries at tourist office in Calama.

However, according to Bob Villarreal, Livermore, California, the best way now is to start in Antofagasta, take a truck or hire a 4WD and go to Mina La Escondida which is 10 kms west of Estacion Imilac (see map), then head east, and south across Salar Punta Negra and to Quebrada Zorritas. This seems the simplest, but you'll need to set a date to be picked up. You've also got to acclimatize somewhere, or someone could die! Maybe spend 2 days at Escondida (?), and hire someone there to take you on.

A third way, one done by Villarreal, is hire a 4WD, drive along main highway 174 kms south

Arriving at the base of Llullaillaco from the northeast.

Map 566-1, Llullaillaco, Cordillera Andes, Chile-Argentina

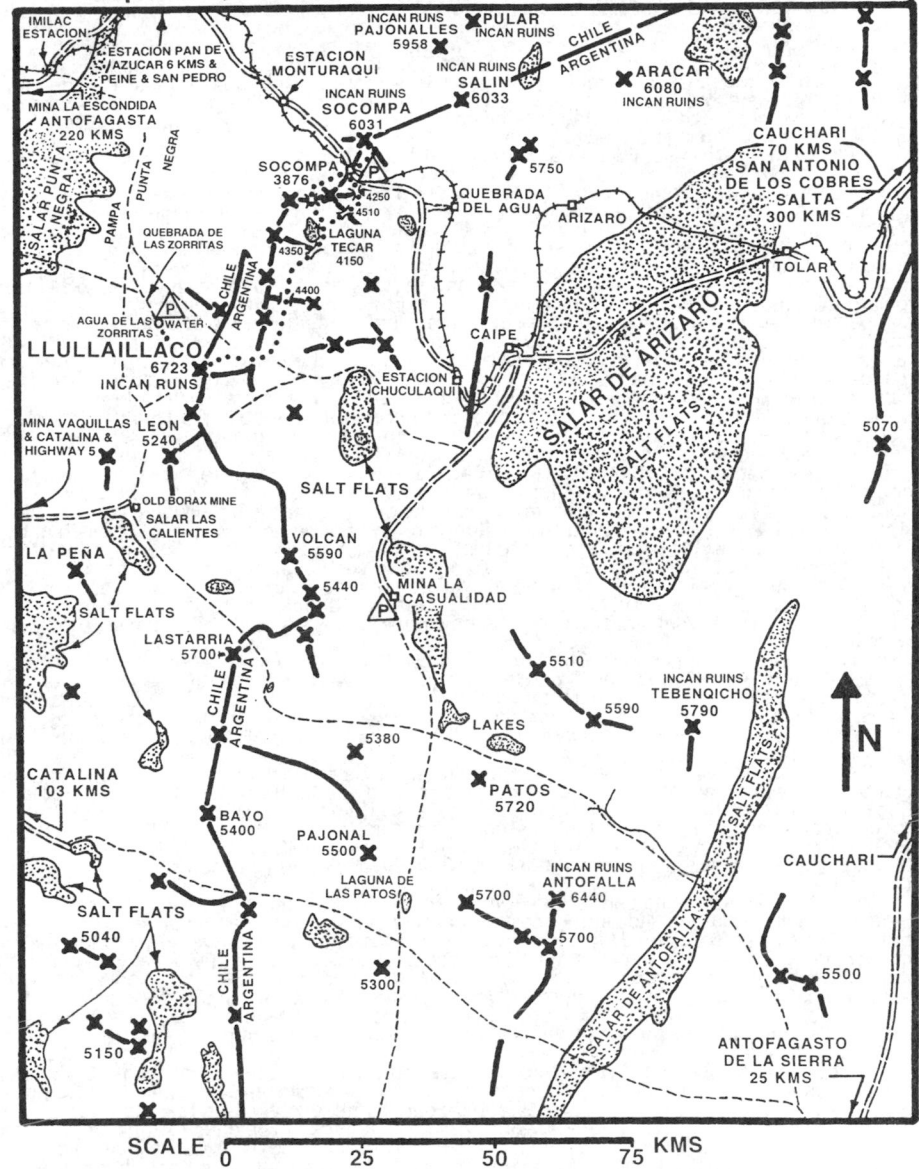

SCALE
0   25   50   75   KMS

of Antofagasta to Oficina Chile, turn east to Catalina, then Mina Vaquillas and to old Borax Mine at Solar las Calientes, and finally north to Llullaillaco. A costly expedition! Nearby is an unreported, but active (?) volcano named Lastarria.

Buy all food in Salta, Calama or Antofagasta. Take extra supplies, especially water and fuel! New fallen snow would ease water problem, otherwise the snowline is very high. What little snow does fall usually comes in winter, May through October. December may be the best month to climb

Maps *Antofagasta, Nevado San Francisco & Socaire*, 1:500,000, from the IGM, Santiago; or TPC map *Q-27A*, 1:500,000; and *Carta Vial de Zona-Catamarca, Jujuy, Salta and Tucuman*, from the Automovil Club Argentino; check websites (www.omnimap.com) or (www.samexplo.org); and travel guidebooks **Argentina** or **Chile**, from Lonely Planet or Footprint Handbooks.

Ojos del Salado, Pissis & Incahuasi, Cordillera Andes, Chile-Argentina

The highest mountain in Chile or on its border is Ojos del Salado at 6880 meters. This older volcanic peak is due east of both Copiapo and Chañaral, Chile. For many years it was considered to be the 2nd highest summit in the western hemisphere, but late reports state Pissis at 6882 meters may be the 2nd highest. However, Ojos is the highest volcano in the world.

This region has more 6000 meter peaks than anywhere outside the Himalayas. The area surrounding the Paso de San Francisco is very dry and near the southern limits of the Atacama Desert. There are Incan ruins on top of Copiapo (6080 meters); and maybe Ojos del Salado (?), but the author was too cold & tired to look around.

It was here on **Ojos del Salado** and **Incahuasi** the author had one of his best adventures. He arrived in Copiapo on 1/12/1973 and soon learned of a group of government workers driving over the Paso de San Francisco to Argentina for 11 days then returning the same way. It was late in the day when he got permission to go halfway with them, so he rushed around town, buying food, fuel & water jugs, then waiting at someone's house all night. They finally started at 5am. It was afternoon when the convoy of 3 pickups dropped him off near Km marker 270. His last words were, *My life in is your hands, please come back!*

He made a stone marker and left some baggage beside the road, then walked one hour toward Incahuasi and camped at 4600 meters. Next morning, Day 2, walked 5 1/2 hours and camped at what he thought was 5100 meters. In his tent it was hot in the afternoon, no sleep-- much warmer than on Llullaillaco a few years later. Day 3, to the summit of **Incahuasi** in 6 hours--tired! From sea level to 6610 meters in 56 hours! In the first few days, he coughed up mucus with blood, had headaches & was weak, partly because of elevation, and partly because he wasn't sleeping good at night with a leaky air mattress (foam pads are much better!).

Day 4, he walked 6 or 7 hours west to near El Muerto and camped at perhaps 5400 meters. Day 5, he walked south for about 6 hours and camped at 5500 meters with running water nearby. Fixed leaky air mattress and rice doesn't cook in 45 minutes at that altitude! Day 6, he left early and made the summit of **Ojos del Salado** in 8 hours--really tired; back to camp in 4 hours, for a 12 hour day. Another night there, then on Day 7 spent roughly 6 hours walking north to the salty Laguna Verde and camped near the bridge over the fresh water stream called *Agua Dulce* at 4300 meters. Built a pile of stones on the bridge so no one could pass him by! That night he had his first good sleep on the trip! You always sleep well after coming down from high altitudes. Day 8, he walked up to Km 270 and retrieved his extra bags; 4 1/4 hours round-trip. Day 9, just pooping around waiting, & walked west and visited a road workers cave, 3 hours. At 10pm on Day 10, 3 cars came by but all were full; at 3am on Day 11, a Jeep came by, but it was also full. At 2pm that afternoon, the government workers came back and in 5 hours all were in Copiapo.

Things have changed on the **Chilean** side since 1973. Here's the latest as of 2000 with some help from Bob Villarreal and Greg Horne. Ojos del Salado seems to be the only mountain in Chile that requires permission to climb. To get that, go to tourist office (SERNATUR) in Copiapo. They will direct you to another office where you'll get the permit in about one day. Be sure to get this piece of paper because the police checkpost at the base of the mountain will want to see it.

Also in Copiapo, contact someone at the Hotel La Casona. They have a 4WD and take climbers to remote mountains, but any vehicle can take you to the police checkpoint north of Ojos at *Barrancas Blancas* at 4300 (4500?) meters. If you're not acclimatized, the author recommends you camp there 2 nights or more; or at Laguna Verde, a 4 hour walk to the east. From the checkpoint, a 4WD track heads south 20 kms to the *Refugio Universidad de Atacama* at roughly 5050 meters. It sleeps 4 in bunks & 15 on the floor, plus running water 300 meters to the west.

Seven kms above the first hut is the *Refugio Tejos* at 5735 meters. It sleeps 6 in bunks, 20 more on the floor, plus small dining & cooking area. With a 4WD you can be driven to the Tejos hut, and even a little above. However, it would cost a lot less to be driven only to the police checkpoint (to be pickup up later, or hitch hike back), sleep 2 nights, and in 2 easy days reach the highest hut, then on Day 5 or 6 to the summit, and other day back to the checkpoint. Plan on about a week to reach the top. Remember, you've got to acclimatize somewhere! Hiring a 2WD in Copiapo might cost US$50 to $75 a day to be dropped off and another day to be picked up. As of 2000, the road was paved for the first 75 kms toward Ojos, and plans are to pave it into Argentina--maybe!

Also, as of late 2000, the *Albergue Ojos del Salado* which was built in the late 1990's by the mining company *Placer Dome Latin America* of Copiapo, was still there, but closed. If the price of what ever they're mining goes up, they could open the mine again, and that albergue would be open. It's located at Piedra Pomez, somewhere west of the police checkpoint at Barrancas Blancas. For updated information, contact Maria Ester Rodillo at the Hotel La Casona, Inter+56-52-217277 (Tele. & Fax), or email (lacasona@entelchile.net). There are also other people in Copiapo who can drive you to the mountains.

Another option would be to rent a vehicle in Copiapo, and spend 2 nights in a refugio near Laguna Santa Rosa, then continue toward Barrancas Blancas and to **Tres Cruces**, **Ojos** or **Incahuasi**.

If coming from the **Argentina** side, take a daily bus to Tinogasta, then Fiambala. Contact Jonson Reynoso at the FM radio station. He can connect you with someone to take you to Cazadero Grande where you can hire *mulas*, then head up the Rio del Cazadero for 1 1/2 or 2 days to where the flowing water begins at Agua Calientes at 4280 meters. Mules can continue to Agua del Vicuña at 4950 meters in one more day. From there, hike another day or 2 to a base camp near and the summit of **Ojos del Salado**. About 5 to 7 days from Fiambala to the top; this

Map 567-1, Ojos del Salado, Pissis & Incahuasi, Chile-Argentina

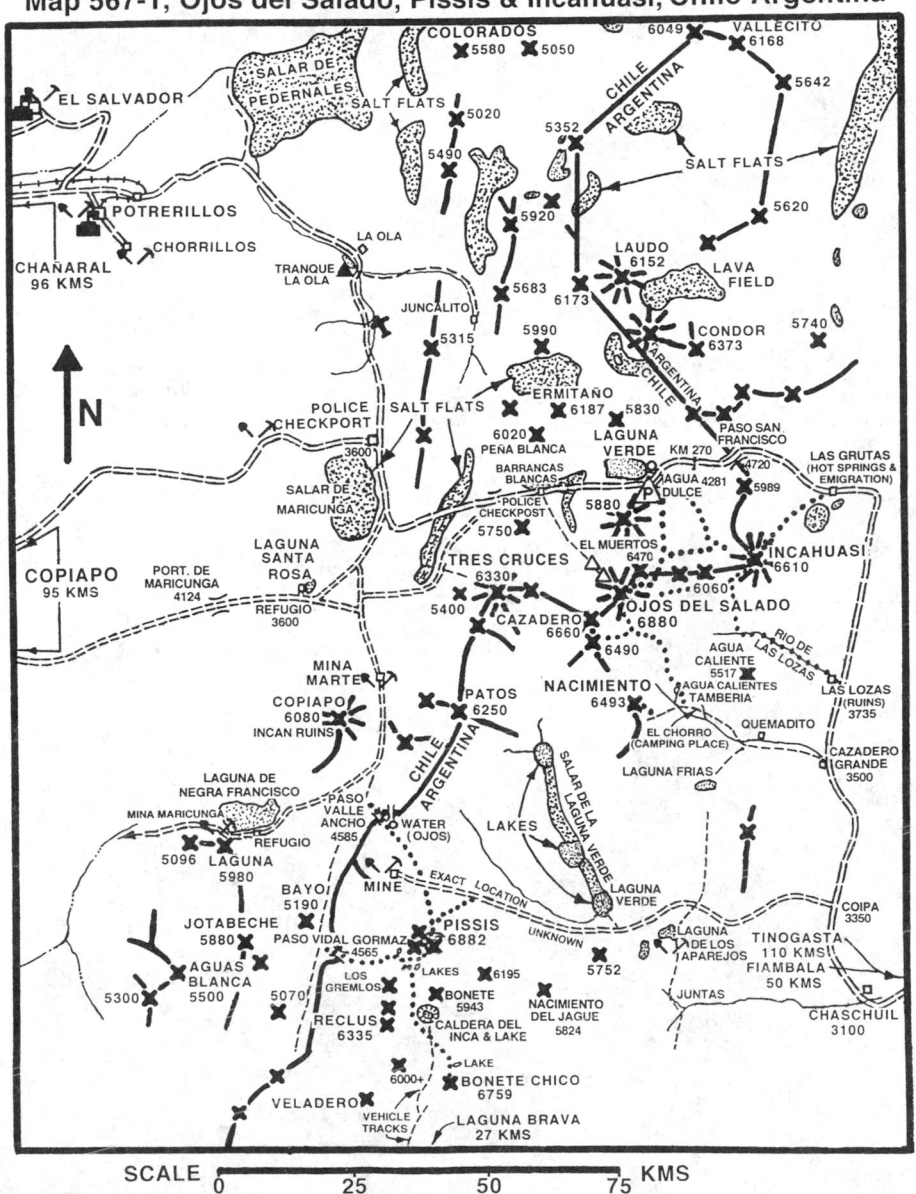

SCALE 0   25   50   75 KMS

according to Greg Horne of Jasper, Alberta. You can also climb many other peaks in this area like **Cazadero** at 6637 meters or **Nacimiento**, 6493, so load up on supplies. You could also hike up, or return, via the Rio de Las Lozas which has a canyon full of water & trout. From Lozas at 3735 meters, you might get a lift back with fishermen. If you make it to that area, you'd be able to climb Incahuasi too. If climbing **Incahuasi** you could be driven to Las Grutas and the Argentine Emigration post with hot springs, and hike from there. The Argentine side has more water than the Chilean side.

Another climb is to **Pissis**, 6882 meters, or **Bonete Chico** at 6759 meters. Bob Villarreal & Greg orne have been there several times with the now-deseased former-owner of the Hotel La Casona in Copiapo. They stayed in the refugios at Laguna Santa Rosa or Laguna Negro del Francisco to acclimatize, then headed east and south over Paso Valle Ancho (water on the east side) and southeast to the foot of Pissis, *at $US350 a day* (this price is for rugged travel beyond the roads)! Wild 4WD country! Pissis has a large flattish glacier between 4 of its half dozen summits. Bonete Chico is a 1 1/2 or 2-day walk south of Pissis (Greg Horne) passing the 5-km-wide **Caldera del Inca**. Between these 2 peaks are several places with water. At last report from the late 1990's, the Mina Marta was closed, but guards were still there so you might get a lift that far or hire a vehicle, then walk over the border (If the Mina Maricunga is open when you arrive, you might get a lift there). If so, they would have some water, and maybe transport. Ask about that situation in Copiapo.

Another option for Pissis, is to head for Fiambala and be driven to a road junction called Coipa at 3350 meters, then west and northwest toward a new (1997) gold mine somewhere northwest of Pissis (closed in 1999). This map shows the approximate location of the mine & road. Someone in Fiambala will have the latest information. This would be the best approach to Pissis, especially if the mine is still operating when you arrive.

To climb **Bonete Chico**, you could get there via Laguna Brava, but you might have to hire a vehicle in Chilecito--very expensive! For us, it's best to hire a vehicle in Fiambala and be driven close to Pissis, then walk south, perhaps climbing Pissis on the way and looking into the Caldera del Inca. Take extra food & bottles of water to be deposited along the road for the long walk back to the main highway. The map indicates walking routes by Greg Horne.

Shown in the northwest section of this map are 2 mining towns whose population depends on the price of metals or minerals they mine. These are El Salvador and Potrerillos. Reaching these 2 mining camps is a lot easier than the Paso San Francisco. There is apparently a club andino in Potrerillos and they may help with information and/or transport to some high peaks in that area.

Buy all supplies in either Tinogasta, Fiambala or Copiapo & Chañaral. The winter months of May through October may be the best time to climb here. It would be colder, but there would also be more snow for water. November & December (spring time) still have snow drifts for water, and it's warmer. Greg Horne likes February or March. Little or no need for ice ax & crampons.

Maps Chilean maps *Copiapo, Chañaral, Ojos Del Salado, and Nevado San Francisco*, 1:500,000; or even better are Argentina maps *Fiambala (2769 IV & III), Tinogasta (2969 II) & Paso de San Francisco (2769 II)*, 1:250,000, all from the IGM, Chile and/or Argentina; or website (www.omnimap.com) or in USA call 800-742-2677 or Inter+336-227-8300; or TPC map Q-27A, 1:500,000; and/or *Carta Vial de Zona-Catamarca, Jujuy, Salta, and Tucuman*, from the Automovil Club Argentino, Buenas Aires; and travel guidebooks **Argentina** or **Chile**, from Lonely Planet and/or Footprint Handbooks.

Looking east at the western slopes of Incahuasi.

This is a 1973 foto of a salt-encrusted mummified horse on the south side of Laguna Verde.

Camp with Mulas Muertas (or El Muertos?) in the background.

Cerro Belgrano, Nevado del Famatina, Argentina

West of La Rioja, and southwest of Catamarca in northwest Argentina, stands one of the highest of the *interior ranges* in Argentina. This is the Nevado del Famatina. The highest summit is Cerro General Belgrano, listed on various maps from 6250 to 6450 meters in elevation. The author's altimeter indicated something closer to 6100 meters, but it's effected by weather & pressure. Whatever the altitude, these are high mountains and are located just northwest of the small city of Chilecito at 1074 meters.

Climbing these peaks is very easy for several reasons. First, there's a road from the village of Famatina to Corrales and on to the Mina Mejicana. This mine has been closed for many years, but still standing is the old *cablecarril* running from the mine to the railway at Chilecito. It was built in 1902 and is 39 kms long. Another reason for the ease of climbing is the dry climate. There are some small glaciers at and near the summit, but there's little or no need for even an ice ax, at least in their summer, which is from about December through March. This is a slightly wetter period than the rest of the year but it's the normally climbing season.

There are many daily buses running to Chilecito from various locations, namely Patquia and La Rioja. From Chilecito you'll find one tourist hotel and a hospedeja run by Antonio Chabis (?). From this apple & grape growing valley you must walk, hitch hike or hire a vehicle going up the road to Corrales, about 22 kms. There's a little traffic on this part of the route. Corrales used to be a work-crew camp for those improving the road to the mines in the mountains. Inquire at Famatina or Corrales about vehicles going up to the Mina Mejicana.

Here's what the author did. He arrived in Chilecito from Salta, Tucuman & La Rioja by bus. Chilecito is a tourist & old mining town. He got information at the tourist office, then got on the 12 noon bus to Famatina. He checked into the hospedeja, and found everything in town closed until 5pm--it's hotter than hell there in January! Later bought food for the trip.

Next morning, 1/17/1982, he walked up the road for 8 hours and camped somewhere below Km 10. There's not much traffic on that road, but there's water about every 5 kms or so. Day 2, he walked to La Cueva Perez by 11am, and 5 more kms up to the abandoned Mina Mejicana at 4375 meters, then continued up to a campsite at 4510. That site had poor tasting water! Morning of Day 3 was -3°C. Climbed up to the summit in 3 1/4 hours; 5 1/4 hours round-trip from camp. Packed up and started walking; at 3pm had a ride back to Famatina. Next morning he was driven to Chilecito in Antonio's old Fiat, and later got a bus to Patquia, then a night bus to San Juan.

With luck from rides, or with your own vehicle, this could be an easy 2 day climb. However, a slower ascent is recommended because of the altitude. Water in the Rio Amarillo (yellow) is undrinkable. If you're walking this road at the lower levels, it's going to be warm, so carry lots of

Picture taken from La Cueva Perez looking at the first ridge above Mina Mejicana.

Map 568-1, Cerro Belgrano, Nevado del Famatina, Argentina

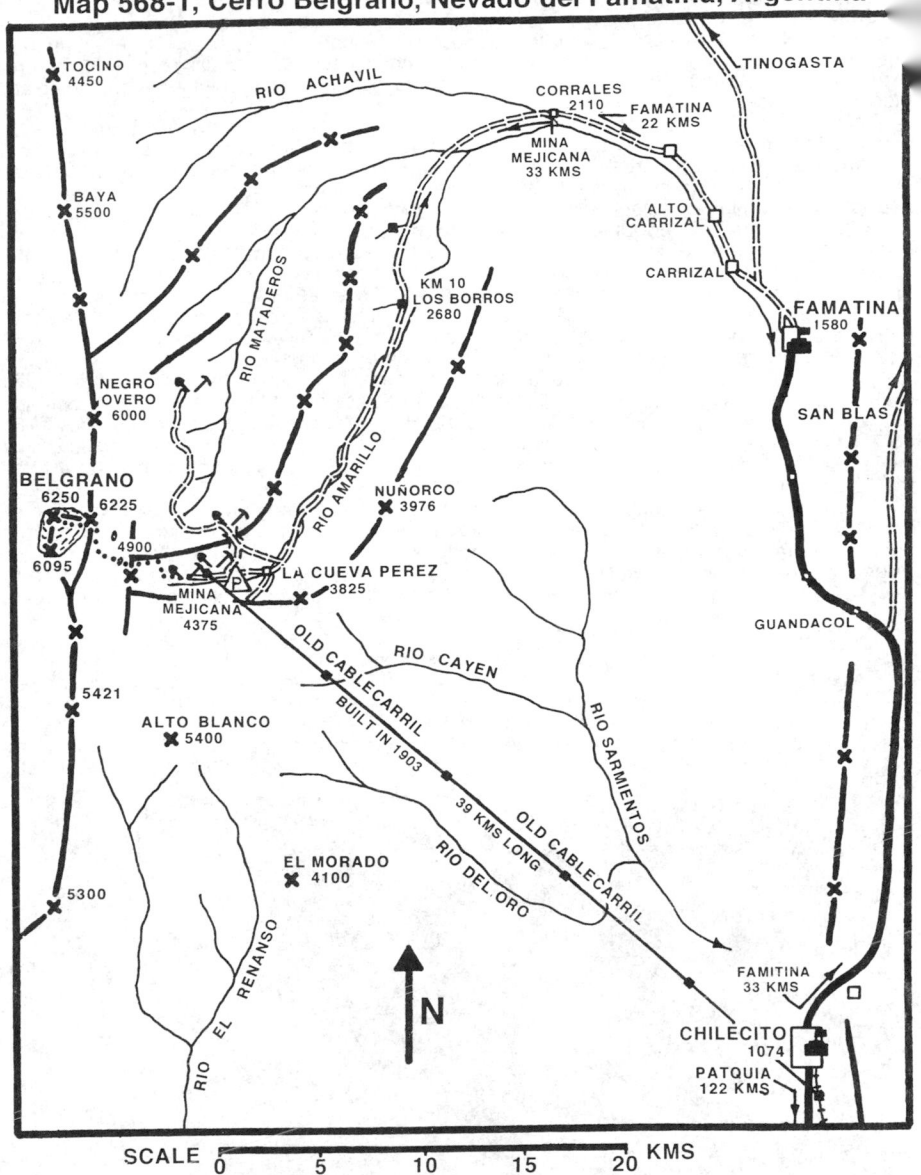

TOCINO
4450

RIO ACHAVIL

TINOGASTA

CORRALES
2110

FAMATINA
22 KMS

MINA
MEJICANA
33 KMS

BAYA
5500

ALTO
CARRIZAL

CARRIZAL

FAMATINA
1580

RIO MATADEROS

KM 10
LOS BORROS
2680

NEGRO
OVERO
6000

SAN BLAS

BELGRANO
6250   6225

RIO AMARILLO

NUÑORCO
3976

4900

6095

LA CUEVA PEREZ
3825

MINA
MEJICANA
4375

GUANDACOL

OLD CABLECARRIL

RIO CAYEN

5421

BUILT IN 1903

ALTO BLANCO
5400

RIO SARMIENTOS

39 KMS LONG

OLD CABLECARRIL

5300

EL MORADO
4100

RIO DEL ORO

RIO EL RENANSO

FAMITINA
33 KMS

N

CHILECITO
1074

PATQUIA
122 KMS

SCALE 0   5   10   15   20   KMS

water at all times. Chilecito has a tourist office, many small hotels or residenciales and many shops. Famatina is the last place to buy food.
Maps Unknown map at 1:250,000 available, maybe at 1:100,000 or 1:50,000 scale too (?), check website (www.omnimap.com); *Carta Vial de Zona--Catamarca, Jujuy, Salta, and Tucuman*, from the Automovil Club Argentino, Buenas Aires; and travel guidebook **Argentina**, from Lonely Planet and/or Footprint Handbooks, or the **South American Handbook**.

El Toro, Tortolas & Olivares, Cordillera Andes, Chile-Argentina

Shown on this map is the region north of Santiago and due east of La Serena, Chile; and ᴐrthwest of San Juan in La Rioja state of Argentina. Included are 3 peaks over 6000 meters. ᴖhe highest is El Toro at 6380 meters. Next is Las Tortolas at 6332, and Olivares, 6252 meters. ᴖncan ruins are found at the summits of Toro, Tortolas and Doña Ana. All these mountains are made of old volcanics, but are not volcanos.

This is a transitional area between the Atacama Desert to the north and the Mediterranean climatic zone to the south. The area is dry, but not to the same degree that you see from Copiapo north and in the area of Ojos del Salado. These mountains receive enough winter snow to make streams and block roads at higher elevations. There's also more water for heavier concentrations of people, as you can see in the valley between La Serena and Vicuña.

Accessibility to the central Andes gets better and easier the further south you go, in both Chile and Argentina. South of this mapped area, there's more water and more farming and grazing; therefore, better access roads to the heart of the mountains. The main access road for this area is the one running from La Serena, Vicuña and over the Paso de La Agua Negra, and down to Las Flores, Rodeo, San Jose de Jachal and from there south to San Juan, the capital of La Rioja state. There is no bus service over the pass, only a few trucks and private cars. It's closed by snow in winter and open only from about January through March.

To climb **Olivares**, stop in La Serena and get on one of 10 buses a day going west to Vicuña (with several hotels & tourist office). At the tourist office ask about hiring a vehicle, or perhaps getting a ride in a mining truck going to up to the El Indio Mine at Aguas del Volcan. However, from that junction it's probably 80 kms to the pass! You could probably hitch hike in summer, but it might be best to hire a taxi or other vehicle in Vicuña to get to the base of the peak at or near the big south bend in the road.

Or in Argentina, take a bus to San Juan, then Jachal. You may have to get a colective or hitch hike to Rodeo. Look for a vehicle, or maybe even hitch hike to the eastern base of the peak and climb from there. The eastern slope looks easier on topo maps. It's 114 kms from Rodeo to the Paso de la Agua Negra, but you'd stop and start climbing before the pass. From the road plan on about 3 or 4 days for the climb, depending on your acclimatization, then the return trip.

For **Tortolas**, proceed to Vicuña by bus, then look for vehicles going to Baños del Toro, or the mine at Aguas del Volcan. From either place, plan on 2-3 days climbing round-trip.

To reach **Toro**, the Chilean side might be best. From Vallenar, take a bus going southeast to Alto del Carmen, or maybe further (?). Then look for someone to drive you up to Conay and beyond. With a 4WD, you can likely get all the way up the Rio Valeriano to the Laguna Valeriano (?) and climb from there. Check the transport situation out before leaving Vallenar. You may have to hire a 4WD there, at a pretty good price. Climb Toro in 2-3 days; either directly

One of many Incan ruins near the summit of Llullaillaco (Map 566, page 1197).

Map 569-3, El Toro, Tortolas & Olivares, Chile-Argentina

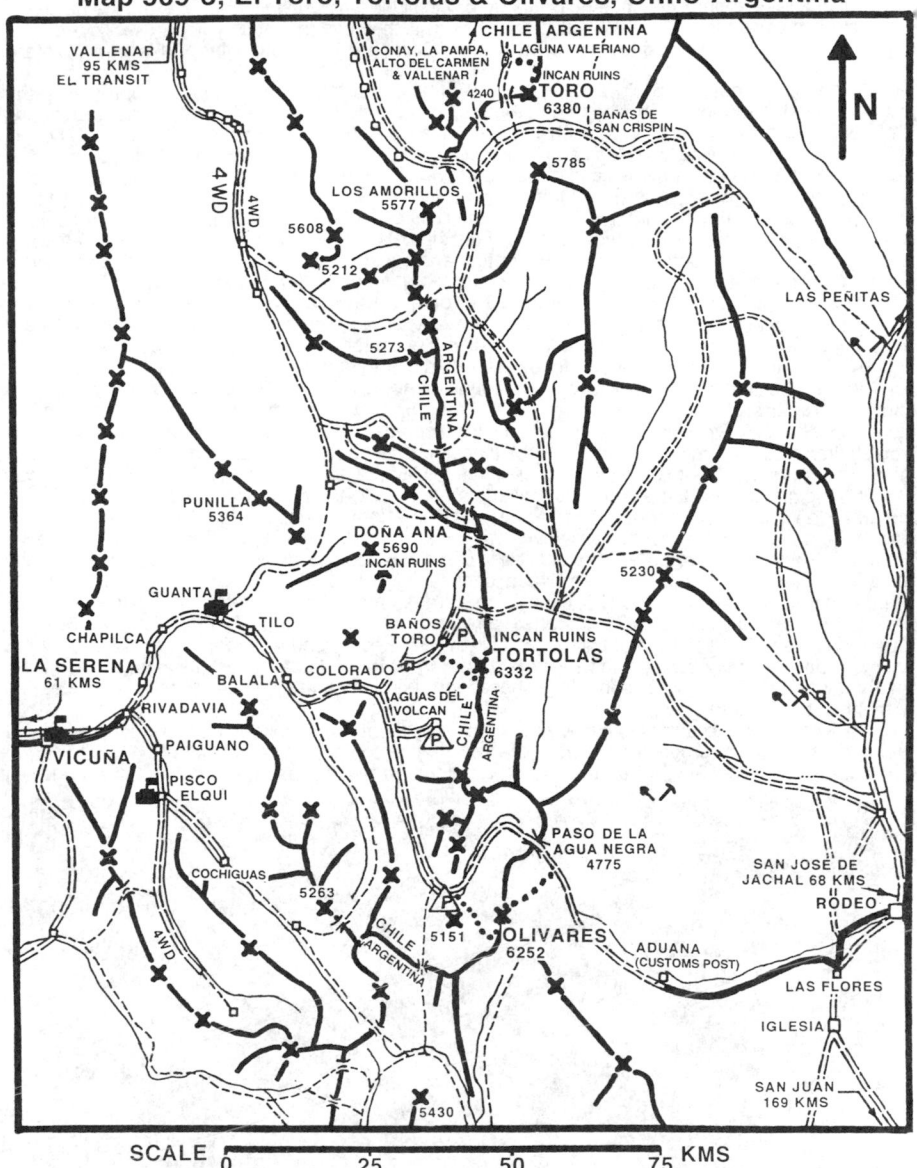

from the lake, or via the pass to the south at 4240 meters.

Best to buy all food and supplies in San Juan or Jachal, or La Serena, Vicuña or Vallenar. Take ice ax & crampons, though they may not be needed. Climb here from late December through March.

Maps Chilean IGM maps *SH-19-10,* 1:250,000, or *La Serena,* 1:500,000, from the IGM, Santiago; or TPC map *Q-26C,* 1:500,000; or *San Juan Province,* by the Automovil Club Argentino, Buenos Aires; a good *Chilean highway map*; and travel guidebooks **Argentina** or **Chile**, from Lonely Planet and/or Footprint Handbooks, or the **South American Handbook**.

Mercedario, Cordillera Andes, Argentina-Chile

Mercedario at about 6770 meters, is the 3rd or 4th highest mountain in the Western Hemisphere, depending on whose top 10 list you're looking at. This is the huge mountain you can see to the north from the upper slopes of Aconcagua. It sits on the Chilean-Argentine border and is a very old and eroded volcano.

Mercedario is not a difficult climb, in fact it may be easier than Aconcagua. The problems are; just getting to the mountain and the ford of the Rio de Los Patos. Here's what the author did starting 1/21/1982. He stayed in a hotel for one night in San Juan, the capital of San Juan Province, and bought about 8 days of food. Next morning he took one of 2 daily buses 176 kms west past Calingasta and on to Barreal. This is a farming town and military camp, with one residencia (as of 2000 about 4 hotels), several food stores and a municipal campground. He made inquiries at the army post to see if they had a patrol going to the mountains, but they weren't sure. He then camped one night in the Barreal Campground and stored extra baggage there. Late the next morning, with no rides in sight, he started walking through the desert (the river is never too far away, but carry water anyway, it's hot there is summer). After 3 hours, a mining truck stopped and gave him a lift all the way to a mining camp called La Molles. That truck had no trouble fording the river at La Juntas which is near Casa Amarillo, but cars couldn't have made it, as it was nearly a meter deep. Later in the season, maybe in March, it surely can be waded; but otherwise, if you're on foot you may have to go upstream to a bridge at Las Hornillas. Or better still, for most it would be better to just hire a vehicle in Barreal.

From La Molles, the author walked for a couple of hours or about 5 kms, and made Camp I, as shown on the map. Next morning, Day 2 at a warm 15°C, he walked past the landslide which has created the Laguna Rio Blanco, then to an old mining company house (refugio on map) the army uses as a shelter while they're out on patrol. Twice that day he climbed up the canyon wall to have a better look at the route since he had no map. Later he made Camp 2 at 3500 meters. Morning of Day 3 was -3 1/2°C; he climbed to Camp 3 at 5200 meters, but passed 2 other campsites at about 3800 & 4400 meters. He walked a short distance to find running water from a small glacier. Next morning, Day 4, with the temperature at -11°C, he walked upslope to the south, then west to the summit in 4 1/3 hours. Good weather and easy climbing. He returned to camp in 6 hours round-trip and headed down. At the refugio, he met an army patrol, then continued to the lake where his Camp 4 was set up. That night he slept 10 hours! Next morning, Day 5, the soldiers came early and all walked down together to a truck parked just below the lake, then on to Barreal arriving at 12 o'clock noon. The trip lasted a little more than 4 days from Barreal, but the author got lucky rides! He camped in Barreal a 2nd night, then got another ride in an army truck south to Uspallata, then west to Punta de Vacas (just east of Puente del Inca), which is due north of Tupungato. These were just a couple of similar good experiences the author has had with the Argentine army.

Take an ice ax & crampons, but you may not need them. Also, take at least a week's supply of food, maybe more. Remember, you've got to acclimatize somewhere! The author prefers to carry a big pack and walk slowly, rather than hiring a vehicle, traveling fast, then have to sit around and

The eastern side of Mercedario as seen from just above the refugio at 3160 meters.

Map 570-1, Mercedario, Cord. Andes, Argentina-Chile

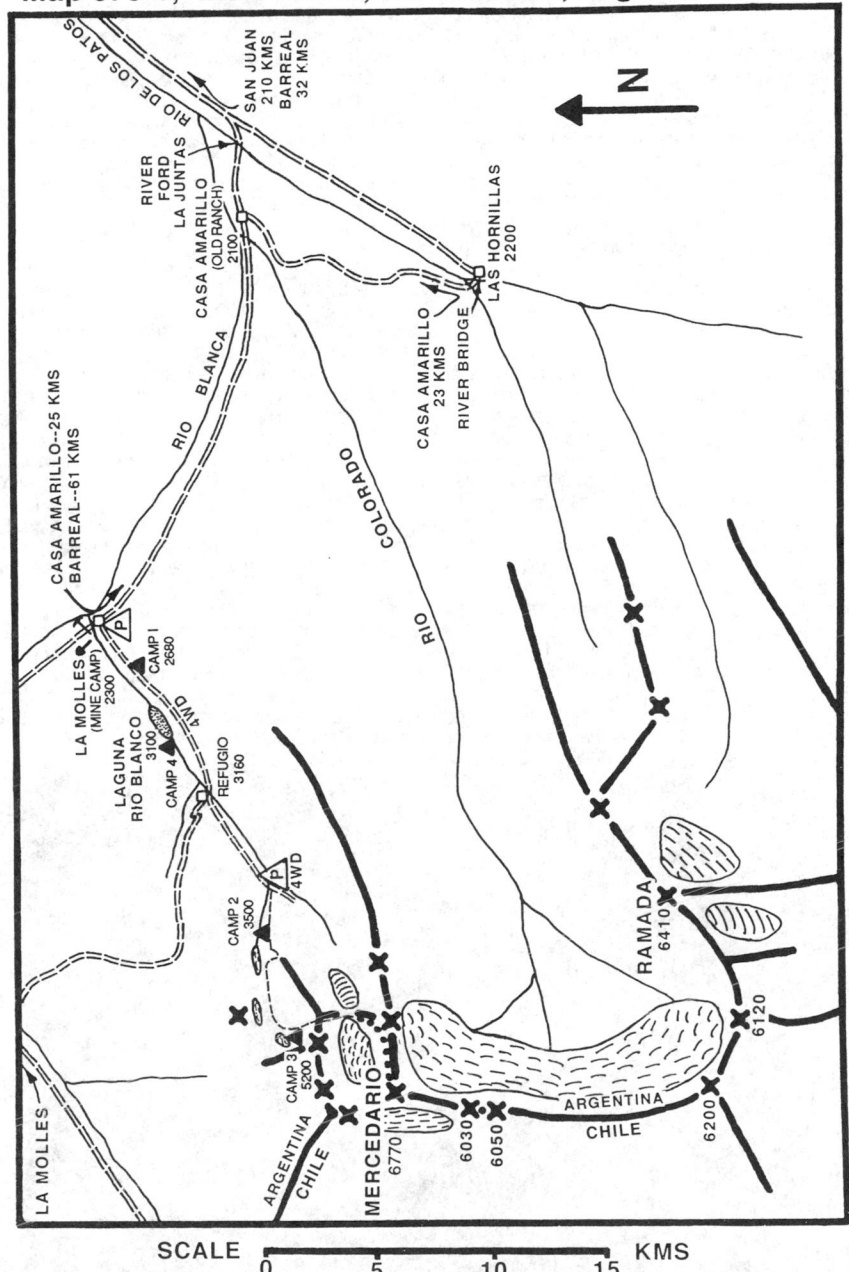

SCALE 0 5 10 15 KMS

acclimatize someplace. Climb between late December and March.
Maps *San Felipe*, 1:500,000, from the Chilean IGM, Santiago, or see website (www.omnimap.com) for new maps at 1:100,000 scale; maybe TPC map *Q-26C*, 1:500,000; a road map of *San Juan Province*, Argentina; and travel guidebooks **Argentina**, from Lonely Planet and/or Footprint Handbooks, or the **South American Handbook**.

Aconcagua, Cordillera Andes, Argentina

The highest mountain in the Western Hemisphere is Aconcagua at 6959 meters. This mountain is ᴄated just east of the international boundary with Chile. Gateway to the mountain is the small tourist ᾽ military settlement of Puenta del Inca at 2735 meters. It's 189 kms west of Mendoza.

Most people get to Puenta del Inca by taking a bus, colectivo (shared taxi) or hitch hiking, either from Chile or Mendoza along the international highway running south of the mountain. If you're coming direct from overseas, fly to Buenas Aires, then Mendoza; or Santiago, then take a bus over the pass & border. There are trekking companies in Europe and North America which can help organize a trip. In that case just open your wallet, submit an EKG (electro kardiogram--heart test), and go straight to Puenta del Inca and up the mountain. Your outfitter will take care of the rest. If traveling independently, head for Mendoza and locate the office of the *Parque Provincial Aconcagua* and get a **permit**. In 1998, it cost US$120 in January, $80 in December & February, and $20 in March. This takes about one hour, then head for higher altitudes quick.

Here's the author's story on **Aconcagua**. In about 1 1/2 days, he hitch hiked south from Copiapo (where he spent 11 days alone around Ojos del Salado at high altitudes) to Puenta del Inca. Bought all his food there in an ejercito (army) PX shop & another store. Stored extra baggage, then on 1/26/1973, Day 1, walked to Confuencia in 4 hours, camped. Next morning, Day 2, waded the river and in 4 1/4 hours was at the old army refugio (ruins) and another hour to old Plaza de Mulas. Slept with 3 Germans. Day 3, climbed up to Refugio Antarctica in 3 3/4 hours, rested & ate lunch, then 2 more hours to Refugio Berlin, alone that night. Day 4, climbed to Refugio Independencia in 1 2/3 hours, then to the summit and back down quickly to Berlin--5 hours round-trip. Then on down to the army refugio and slept there. Day 5, to Confluencia in 3 hours, and by 2:30pm was in Puenta del Inca.

If you're flying in on your vacation of a lifetime to climb Aconcagua, take 2 full weeks off work and take 10 or 12 days of food to the mountain. This will allow you time to acclimatize and sit out any bad weather and still make the summit. Also, don't be in a big hurry getting up to Plaza de Mulas; lack of acclimatization kills on this mountain! Ten people died in 1998! Most people take mules and do it all very easy. The author recommends you carry one big pack and go slow--at the same time acclimatizing. The problem many people have is, the climb is too easy with the mules, refugios and trail to the summit, so they're tempted to go up too fast. Any healthy person can climb Aconcagua--just acclimatize for 5 or 6 days above Puenta del Inca, dress warmly and expect cold winds on top.

Everyone has to take and use a tent, as there are hundreds of climbers on the mountain from late December through February. As of 1998, there is a permit checkpoint & ranger station at Laguna Harcones, at Confluencia you'll find a bridge (no more waist-deep wading!) plus a coffee shop-hamburger stand, and a big new Refugio Hotel 2 kms west across the glacier from Plaza de Mulas. No more refugio at Plaza de Mulas--only summer-time ranger's tents. All refugios on the mountain are in ruins or poor condition, or will be used by park rangers. Above Plaza de Mulas, there are now

This is the trail above the Refugio Independencia and near the summit of Aconcagua.

Map 571-1, Aconcagua, Cordillera Andes, Argentina

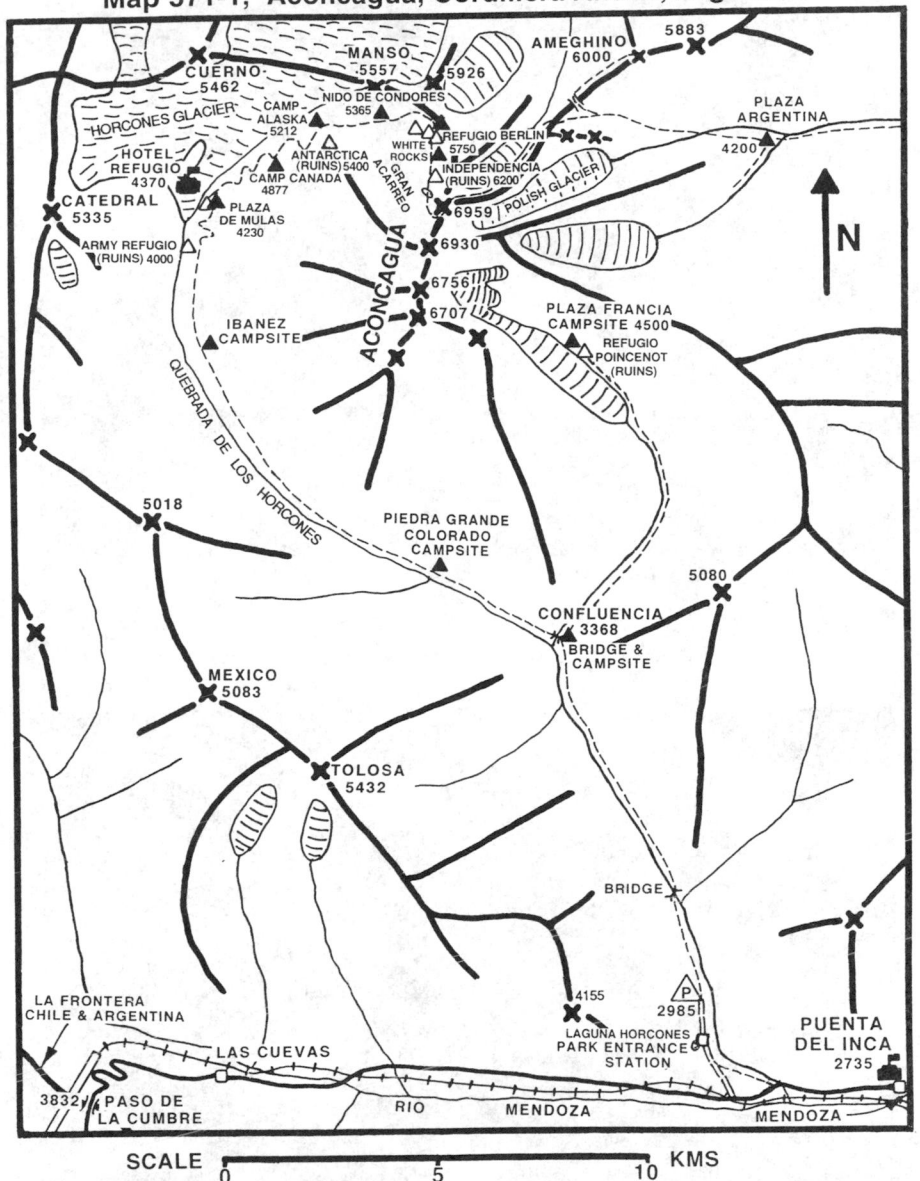

campsites called Camp Canada, 4877 meters; Camp Alaska, 5212; and Nido de Condores, 5365 meters. Don't buy expensive plastic boots for this climb; any Soral-type insulated snowmobile boots will do on the *ruta normal*. Take ice ax & crampons but they may not be needed.

Maps *Aconcagua*, 1:50,000, American Alpine Club; or IGM maps *3369-7-4, 3369-13-2, 3369-14-1 & 3369-8-3*, all at 1:50,000; the guidebook **Aconcagua**, The Mountaineers; and travel guidebook **Argentina**, from Lonely Planet and/or Footprint Handbooks, or **South American Handbook**.

This is a 1/1973 foto of the 2 old refugios at Plaza de Mulas.

A 1/1973 foto of the Refugio Antarctica at 5400 meters. It's in worse condition now and is totally unusable.

This is Pissis as seen from the northwest. There's a rather large glacier in between about 4 major summits (Bob Villarreal foto, Map 567, page 1199).

Looking south at the Refugio Tejos at 5735 meters on the north side of Ojos del Salado (James Garrett foto, Map 567, page 1199).

Tupungato & San Jose, Cordillera Andes, Chile-Argentina

his map shows the region east of Santiago and south of Aconcagua and includes the ;national highway running between Santiago & San Felipe, Chile; and Mendoza, Argentina. he bottom of the map is Baños Morales and Volcan San Jose. The highest peak on this map is **Tupungato** at 6550 meters. This old volcano lies very near e center of the map and can be approached from 3 different directions. The distance and the ength of time needed for this climb is about the same from either approach. Not shown on this map is Tupungatito, a lower 6000 (or 5682?) meter subsidiary peak of Tupungato just to the south. It's an active volcano and its last phreatic explosion was on 1/20/1986.

Chilean climbers normally drive or take a bus to a place called Cuayacan, then drive, hitch hike or walk northeast to the end of the road at Alfalfal. From there they walk or hire mules for the 3 or 4 day trip to the northern slopes of the mountain, then up the north ridge. The climb is normally done in a week to 10 days, depending on climber's fitness. Mules are usually hired to help get across streams.

For Argentine climbers the *ruta normal* is from the small village & military camp of Tupungato. It takes about one week for the trip. Contact the army post at Tupungato for information and/or possible use of mules.

A day after climbing Mercedario, and on 1/28/1982, the author got a ride in an army truck to Punta de Vacas. He stored extra baggage at a worker's compound, and got a ride up the canyon 23 kms, then walked another 5 kms, but couldn't ford the river, so he turned back. That northern route might be OK in cooler weather, but not in the heat of summer with melting glaciers. Or hire some mules to make stream crossings.

He went to Mendoza for a night, bought food, and headed for another disappointment. He was told to go to Manzano Historico and hike west. He did, and it took 2 days; 6 & 5 1/2 hours walking to reach the Refugio Real de la Cruz, but that's not the right way--he couldn't even cross the stream to climb Marmolejo, so he walked about 9 hours back to Manzano. The normal route is via the village of Tupungato, and hopefully no really big streams to cross going that way.

A popular climb for Chileans is **Volcan San Jose** at 5821 meters. It's also active with it's last eruption in 1960. In 5/1991, a new fumarole field was observed on its south flank. On 4/11/1982, the author took one of several daily buses from Santiago to El Volcan taking 2 3/4 hours (on weekends there are buses to Baños Morales), then walked & hitch hiked upcanyon to where the trail begins near a mining area called Lo Valdez (13 kms above El Volcan). From there the trail crosses a stream going north, then gradually turns east. He walked 5 hours and camped at 2675 meters. Next morning (8°C) he walked past the rather good *Refugio San Jose* at 3130 meters. It had 8 beds & table. He continued east above the refugio to a campsite at 4400 meters near a lateral moraine, water nearby. Morning Day 3, -11°C, he made the summit in 3 hours, 1 2/3 hours back to camp; then another 5 or 6 hours back to within one km of Lo Valdez and camped at 1900 meters. Next morning he walked to & beyond El Volcan before getting a ride back to Santiago. Normally ice ax or crampons are not needed.

Another peak of interest is **Marmolejo**, 6110 meters. Make this climb from the Embolsa del Yeso & Termas del Plomo. **Pabellon & Piuquenes**, 6152 & 6017 meters, are normally climbed from Tupungato or Manzano Historico; or Termas del Plomo. **Juncal**, 6110 meters, is usually

From just north of the Refugio Real de la Cruz looking at Tupungato (with snow).

Map 572-1, Tupungato & San Jose, Andes, Chile-Argentina

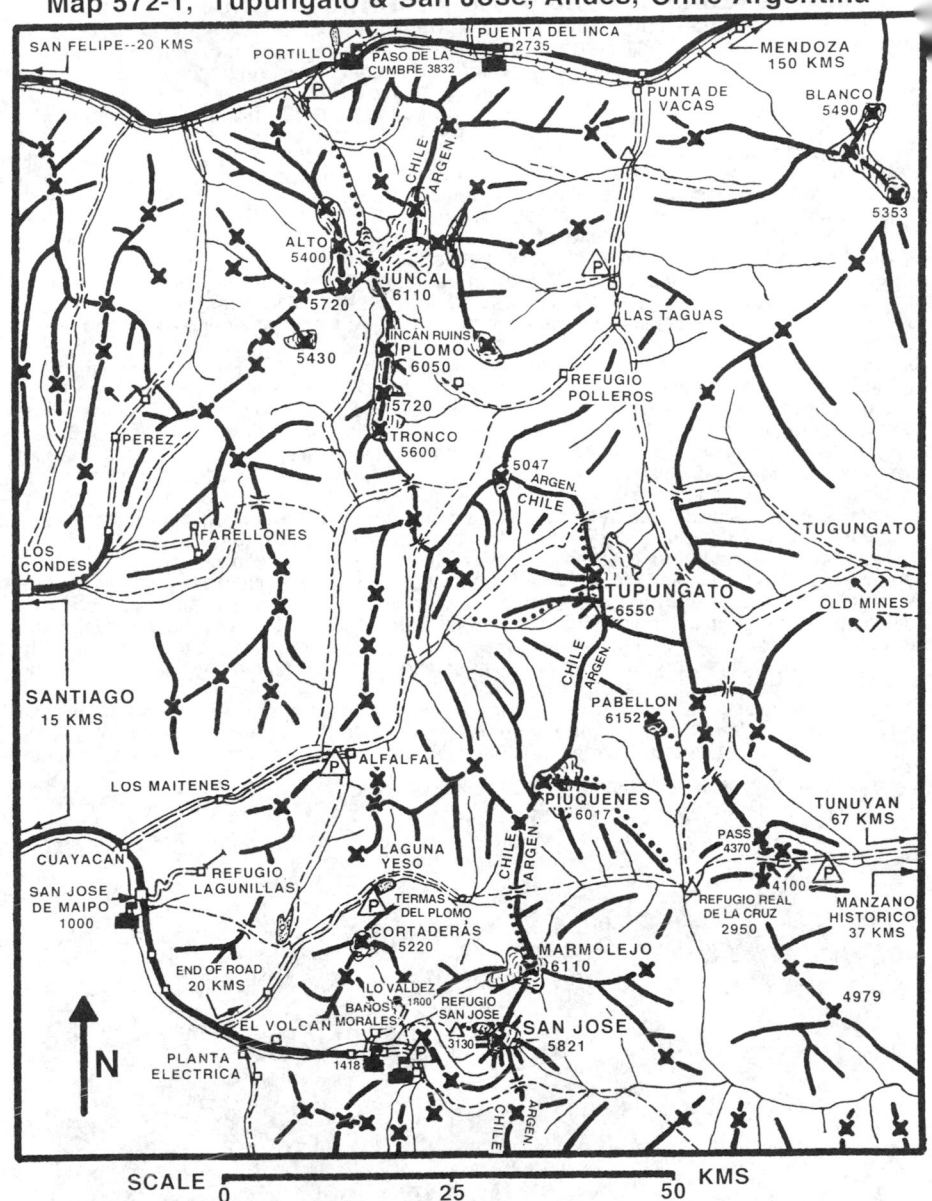

climbed from the north and from near the Portillo Ski Resort. **Plomo**, 6050 meters has Inca ruins near the summit. Climb between Christmas and end of March. Take ice ax & crampons on higher peaks. Always inquire about big river crossings which is a problem in this region.
Maps *Santiago, Volcan Tupungato & San Felipe*, 1:500,000; or maps *3300-7000* for Juncal, *3330-6945* for Marmolejo, & *3345-6945* for San Jose, all 1:50,000; or *3300-6900* for Tupungato, Puquenes & Pabellon, 1:250,000, all from the IGM, Santiago; or the book, **Guia de Excursionismo para la Cordillera de Santiago,** in bookstores in Santiago; and travel guidebooks **Argentina** or **Chile,** from Lonely Planet and/or Footprint Handbooks.

Castillo & Volcan Maipo, Cordillera Andes, Chile-Argentina

Covered on this map is the region southeast of Chile's capital, Santiago. The northern boundary is near Volcan San Jose which is discussed on the previous map, while the southern part is due east of the city of Curico and includes the semi-active Tinguiririca volcano and the nearby crash site of a plane in 1972 which inspired the book & movie, **Alive**.

The highest mountain on this map is Castillo at 5485 meters, while its eastern summit is 5375. The next highest peak and surely the most famous in this part of the Andes is Volcan Maipo at 5290 meters. As with most of the mountains along the Chile-Argentina frontier, these are volcanic in origin. Most have lost all signs of volcanism, but Maipo still retains a conal shape. It had eruptions in 1905 & 1912. Tinguiririca also had a questionable eruption in 1917. The most southerly 5000 meter peak in South America is Sosneado at 5189 meters.

This area is in that part of Chile which has a changing weather system. It's within the Mediterranean climate zona, but receives heavy precipitation in the 6 months or so of winter. As a result, ice fields, even though small, are appearing on mountains with less elevation than others to the north. Note that all the glaciers and perpetual snow is on the western or Chilean side of the frontier. Moisture comes from the west, leaving Argentina in a rainshadow and drier.

Approaching the area may be better from the Chilean side, but few of the high peaks along the border are easily accessible. Fortunately, **Castillo** and the border area shown on the northern part of the map is easier to reach. There are many daily buses leaving Santiago going to as far as El Volcan or higher. From there, drive, hitch hike or walk to the end of the road, then hike southeast for one or 2 days to a base camp on Castillo's north slope. Or veer southwest and follow trails south for perhaps 3 or 4 days to the base of **Maipo** (see Tupungato map for more information on San Jose, 5821 meters). However, the streams in the Tupungato area to the north get rather large making them difficult to cross on foot, and many people hire mules to help get across. A similar situation may exist here, so contact the tourist office in Santiago and get the names of *club andinos* for updated information on stream crossings & hopefully bridges.

However, to reach **Maipo**, it appears the best way is via the Argentina side and from an area southwest of San Carlos and west of San Rafael. Ask about roads and trails going to Laguna Diamante at the tourist office in Mendoza or San Rafael. The approach seems a little complicated on Argentine highway maps, but at least there's some kind of road to the lake and no big rivers to cross. You can surely hire a vehicle to get you all or part way, then walk & climb. The east side is drier country, so water on the approach could be a problem if walking. From the lake, it might take a couple of days to climb Maipo.

For the ice fields around **Arrieros**, walk from Coya in the north; or from the end of the road running southeast from San Fernando, then head north. On the Argentine side, there's some kind of tourist place at Termas Sosneado and a mine above that, which could offer easy access

Volcan Maipo, one many volcanos along the Chilean border (E. Echevarria foto).

Map 573-1, Castillo & Volcan Maipo, Andes, Chile-Argentina

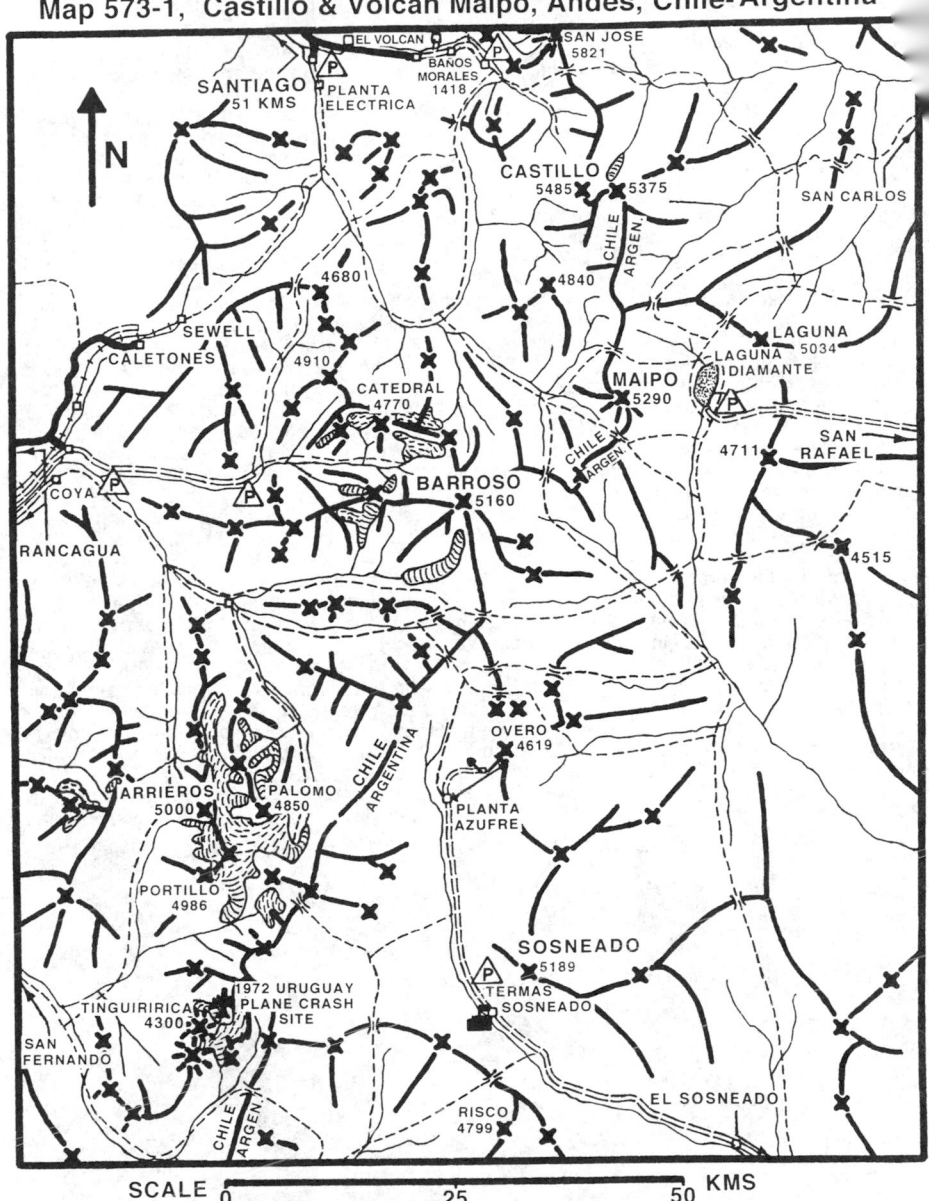

N

EL VOLCAN

SAN JOSE
5821

SANTIAGO
51 KMS

BAÑOS
MORALES
1418

PLANTA
ELECTRICA

CASTILLO
5485   5375

SAN CARLOS

CHILE ARGEN

4680

4840

SEWELL
CALETONES

4910

LAGUNA
5034
LAGUNA
DIAMANTE

CATEDRAL
4770

MAIPO
5290

CHILE ARGEN

SAN
RAFAEL

4711

COYA

BARROSO
5160

RANCAGUA

4515

CHILE ARGENTINA

OVERO
4619

ARRIEROS
5000

PALOMO
4850

PLANTA
AZUFRE

PORTILLO
4986

SOSNEADO
5189

TINGUIRIRICA
4300

1972 URUGUAY
PLANE CRASH
SITE

TERMAS
SOSNEADO

SAN
FERNANDO

CHILE ARGEN

RISCO
4799

EL SOSNEADO

SCALE 0   25   50 KMS

to some parts of this region, including **Sosneado**.

Buy supplies in Santiago, Rancagua, Mendoza or San Rafael. Take an ice ax & crampons to all the higher peaks. Best time to climb is January through March.

Maps *Santiago & Volcan Tupungato*, 1:500,000 (1:250,000 scale maps now available), from the IGM, Santiago; a *Provincial map of Mendoza*; a *Chilean highway map*; and travel guidebooks **Argentina** and/or **Chile**, from Lonely Planet and/or Footprint Handbooks.

Antuco, Velluda, Callaqui & Copahue, Chile-Argentina

Shown on this map are 3 volcanos and another major summit, plus the Rio Bio Bio. It's this ver that arbitrarily separates the dry from the wet climates in Chile. The highest summit here is . very old volcano called Sierra Velluda with one peak at 3385 meters. However, the most amous mountain is Volcan Antuco, 2985 meters. Lava flows from Antuco dammed Laguna Laja's outlet in 1853 and raised lake levels by 20 meters. It has had fumarolic activity ever since its last major eruption in 1869. Further south is an active volcano known as Callaqui at 3164 meters. It had a pretty good blast in 1751 and periodic reports of other activity since. On 4/6/1982, the author heard thundering degassing events every half hour. Another featured peak is Copahue at 2969 meters. This map doesn't show it, but it sits inside a 600,000-year-old, 8-km-wide caldera, which is within the bigger & older Pliocene 15x20-km-wide Del Agrio Caldera. It had it's last eruptive period beginning on 7/1/2000 and continued through 10/19/2000. From that time active seemed ongoing. For volcanic updates see the websites (www.dgf.uchile.cl/salsa/ovdas/ovdas.html) or (www.volcano.si.edu/gvp/).

For **Callaqui**, the author took one of several daily buses leaving the rural bus terminal in Los Angeles destined for Ralco, then got a short ride of 2 kms to Pague, then walked up the road toward the ranch at 960 meters and camped at 1280 meters. Next morning, 4/6/1982, he bushwhacked up the slope with lots of old logging roads and got to the arucana forest, but recent forest fires had put the shade on the ground and bamboo grass was growing everywhere. Difficult climbing! Discouraged and on a tight schedule, he returned from 2400 meters and camped near Ralco. Next morning he hitch hiked and took buses to Los Angeles & Antuco.

From Ralco to the hacienda on the northwest slopes of Callaqui is about 15 kms. Some cattle and wood hauling trucks go part way up this road, but they are few and far between. The house is one km past the bridge. From the house take an old logging road south to the burned-over area on the western slopes. The final ascent should be up the southwest ridge, as the northern slopes have some steep faces. This may be a 2-3 day climb from Ralco, where you'll find at least 2 small stores and a bar.

Copahue. On various days some buses run from Ralco to Queuco, then you would likely have to walk/hitch hike from there to Trapa Trapa and southeast to Baños Copahue and climb from there. But the simplest way is from the Argentine side where some traffic goes all the way to Baños Copahue. Start in Neuquen, capital of Neuquen state, then head west to Las Lajas, north to Loncopue, then to the mineral baths at the base of Copahue.

Reach **Antuco** by taking one of many daily buses from the rural bus terminal in Los Angeles to Chacay. The author did that on 4/7/1982. From Chacay to the ski resort of Antuco is 14 kms. He walked & hitch hiked that part. He camped up the mountain a ways above the ski resort and the next morning made the summit in 2 1/3 hour; 3 2/3 hours round-trip from camp. He walked most of the way back to Chacay, then a bit later got one ride to Santiago.

In summer, there's no snow on the *ruta normal* up Antuco, just follow the ski lift to about 2000 meters, then climb straight up. From the ski resort you can also reach the eastern face of

From the summit of Antuco looking southwest at the eastern side of Velluda.

Map 574-1, Antuco, Velluda, Callaqui, Copahue, Chile-Argentir

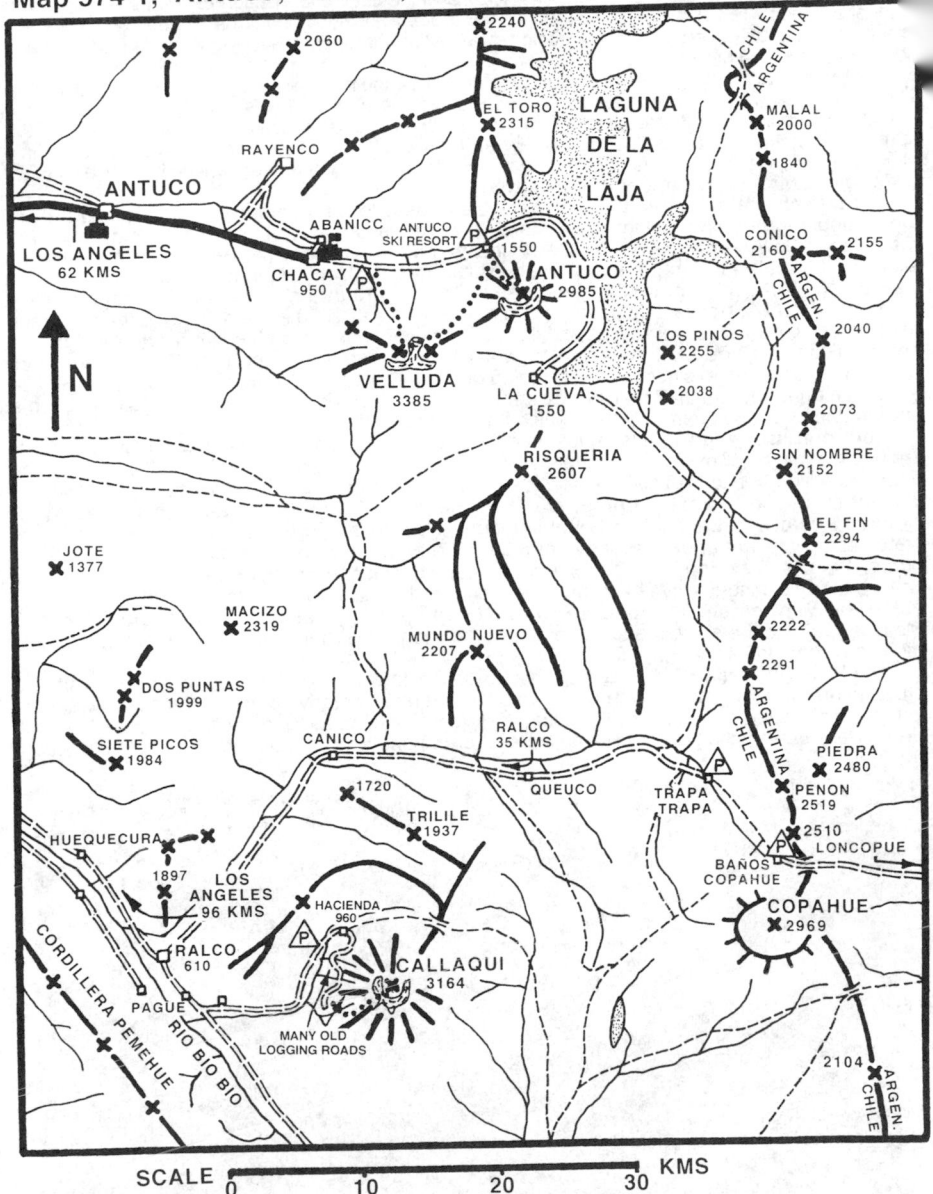

SCALE 0   10   20   30   **KMS**

Velluda, by far the best climb in this mapped area. This peak will require experienced climbers with proper equipment, including ice ax & crampons and maybe a rope. But it's mostly rock climbing on old volcanics. The north face can also be reached from the road near Chacay. There are places to buy food at Antuco, Chacay, Abanico and Rayenco. This valley is both a summer & winter ski resort area, but much drier than areas to the south, with less snow on the peaks. You can count on good summer weather here from December through April.

Maps *Laguna de la Laja*, 1:500,000 (1:250,000 also available), from the IGM, Santiago; *Chilean highway map*; and travel guidebook **Chile**, from Lonely Planet and/or Footprint Handbooks.

Llaima & Lonquimay, Cordillera Andes, Chile

Shown on this map are 3 of the many volcanos which dot the landscape of southern Chile. The ghest and best-known is Volcan Llaima at 3180 meters. Next is Lonquimay at 2890 and Tolhuaca Tolguaca) at 2708 meters. Llaima is located due east of Cherquenco & Temuco, while Tolhuaca and Lonquimay are east of Curacautin and Victoria.

Llaima had a very large VEI-5 explosion in 6880 BC and has been very active since the 1700's. The author was greeted to loud degassing explosions at the summit in 1982. It's last explosion was in 11/1998. Lonquimay began its latest activity 12/25/1988 from a flank fissure 3 1/2 kms northeast of the summit. It ejected lava, and ash up to 7 kms. Activity stopped about 1/24/1990. Tolhuaca is a Holocene volcano with no historic eruptions. For volcanic updates see (www.dgf.uchile.cl/salsa/ovdas/ovdas.html) or (www.volcano.si.edu/gvp/).

For **Llaima**, the author took one of many daily buses leaving Temuco for Cherquenco. That took 2 hours for the 58 km ride. From there he walked east toward Llaima, but got a lift the last 7 or 8 kms. No buses on this road. It's 21 kms from Cherquenco to the Refugio Llaima, where a ski resort is located with reportedly the largest log hostel in South America; also buildings of the Parque Nacional. He got water and walked up the mountain a ways and camped. Next morning, 4/1/1982, he went up past the end of the ski lifts at 1900 meters, then up the west face after crossing an ash covered glacier. It's steep as volcanos go, with some falling rock, but he got on a rock rib and took off his crampons. From camp to the top took 3 1/4 hours, then enjoyed several gas explosions before going down in 2 hours; 5 1/4 hours round-trip. Take ice ax & crampons though they may not be needed. He walked down the road a ways, bathed in a stream, then got one ride to Temuco which has a good tourist office.

For **Lonquimay** and Tolhuaca, take the tren from Victoria, getting off at either Curacautin or the tiny logging town of Malalcahuello. Or take a bus from Victoria or Temuco. The author rode a bus from Temuco to Malalcahuello in 3 3/4 hours, got more information from Cordoba Salazar & camped nearby. Next morning, 4/3/1998, he walked from Malalcahuello 13 kms to the Refugio Puelche at the base of Lonquimay in 2 1/3 hours. This is an old ski hut with spring water nearby. That afternoon, he climbed up the eastern ridge, then to the summit in 2 3/4 hours; 4 hours round-trip from the refugio. He bathed, washed clothes & camped; next morning walked to Malalcahuello in 2 1/4 hours and hitch hiked west, then north toward Antuco. If you're there early in the season take an ice ax & crampons. A strong hiker could walk from Malalcahuello to the summit and return in one very long day, but that's not recommended. For most it's a one day affair from the refugio.

To climb **Tolhuaca**, stop at Buena Vista, about 6 kms east of Curacautin, and walk up the old logging road toward the base of the volcano. At one of many points on the southwest face leave the road and climb toward the southwest ridge, passing Laguna Caracole at 1427 meters. From there walk up the ridge. Take an ice ax & crampons even though they may not be needed.

Longquimay Volcano seen from the southeast and near the old Refugio Puelchi.

Map 575-1, Llaima & Longquimay, Cordillera Andes, Chile

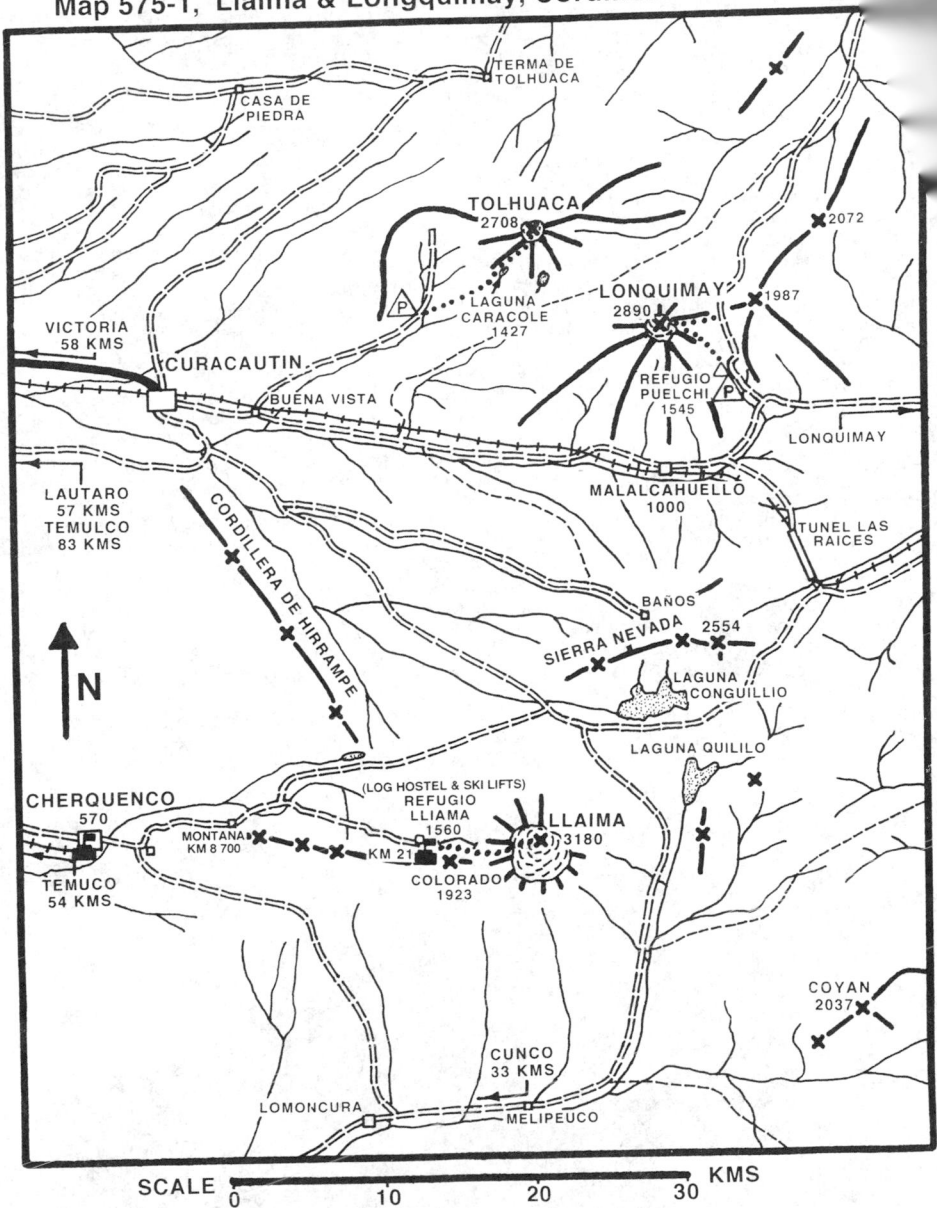

SCALE
0   10   20   30   KMS

Of interest to botanists are the arucana pine trees. They are all over this area above about 1400 meters. Climbing season is from late December to March or April. Lots of blackberries too in the valleys in March and April.

Maps *Laguna de la Laja,* 1:500,000 (1:250,000 maps also available now), from the IGM, Santiago; a *Chilean highway map;* and travel guidebook, **Chile**, from Lonely Planet and/or Footprint Handbooks.

Lanin & Villarrica, Cordillera Andes, Chile-Argentina

e 2 major peaks on this map are in the Lakes District of southern Chile. First is Lanin at 3845
s. This is a Holocene volcano that hasn't had an eruption in recent human history. It sits on the
-Argentine frontier about 55 kms northwest of the Argentine resort town of Junin (de Los Andes).
other major summit is Volcan Villarrica, located 12 kms south of the Chilean summer & winter
resort of Pucón. This volcano has been almost continuously active since the Europeans landed.
roughout 1998, there were explosions extending into late 1999 according to the latest *Global
olcanism Program* reports. The author was treated to thundering degassing explosions at the top of
illarrica in 1982. An eruption sometime prior to '82 destroyed the ski resort on the north slopes of the
peak. Because of its activity, it's sometimes closed to climbing. For volcanic updates see the
websites (www.dgf.uchile.cl/salsa/ovdas/ovdas.html) or (www.volcano.si.edu/gvp/.).

To climb **Lanin**, take one of the 3 or 4 weekly buses running between Temuco, Chile, and
Junin, Argentina, and get off at the Argentine border checkpoint of Tromen. In summer you can
combine walking & hitch hiking from Junin and with luck get to Tromen just as fast. That's what
the author did on 3/6/1982. Tromen is where the *ruta normal* begins. There's a refugio on the
northeast ridge at about 2525 meters, but you're supposed to get permission to use it at the
ejercito (army) post in Junin. If you don't have permission when you arrive at Tromen, tell them
you'll use your tent. The army is supposed to give you a key, but the refugio seems to be
unlocked! The author failed to understand this in 1982, so he walked back down the road 2-3
kms, and walked up along a stream on the east face and camped. Next morning he made the
summit in just over 4 hours; 6 1/2 hours round-trip from camp. On that lower east face route,
there is some tall bamboo grass to wade through but it's fairly easy walking. The *east face* and
ruta normal are walk-ups. Take an ice ax & crampons just in case. This is a 2 day climb from
Tromen; maybe 3 or 4 days from Junin or Temuco. Get updates on this climb at the tourist
offices listed below.

To climb **Villarrica**, take one of many daily buses from Temuco to Villarrica, then Pucón.
Just before reaching Pucón, turn right and walk or hitch hike up the gravel road to the remains of
a old ski resort. On weekends in summer there is lots of traffic on this road. There's water at
the old ski resort, but it's now closed and out of business; but there are still several picnic or
camping sites just below the refugio. The author was there on 3/30/1982 and from his camp
above the ruined resort, made the summit in 2 1/2 hours; 3 1/2 hours round-trip from camp. This
is a walk-up. Then another 2 1/2 hours walking 12 kms down to Pucón. Recent guidebooks
state you must climb in a group with a guide; or show proof of membership in an alpine club in
your country before you're allowed to climb!

There's a trail running up the mountain beside the old ski lift to near the glacier, then you
must have an ice ax & crampons to finish the climb. There are no crevasses on the north face.
With good timing--a 2 day climb from Temuco. Lots of hotels in Pucón.

Lanin from the east. The *ruta normal* and refugio are on the right-hand skyline.

Map 576-1, Lanin & Villarrica, Cordillera Andes, Chile-Argen

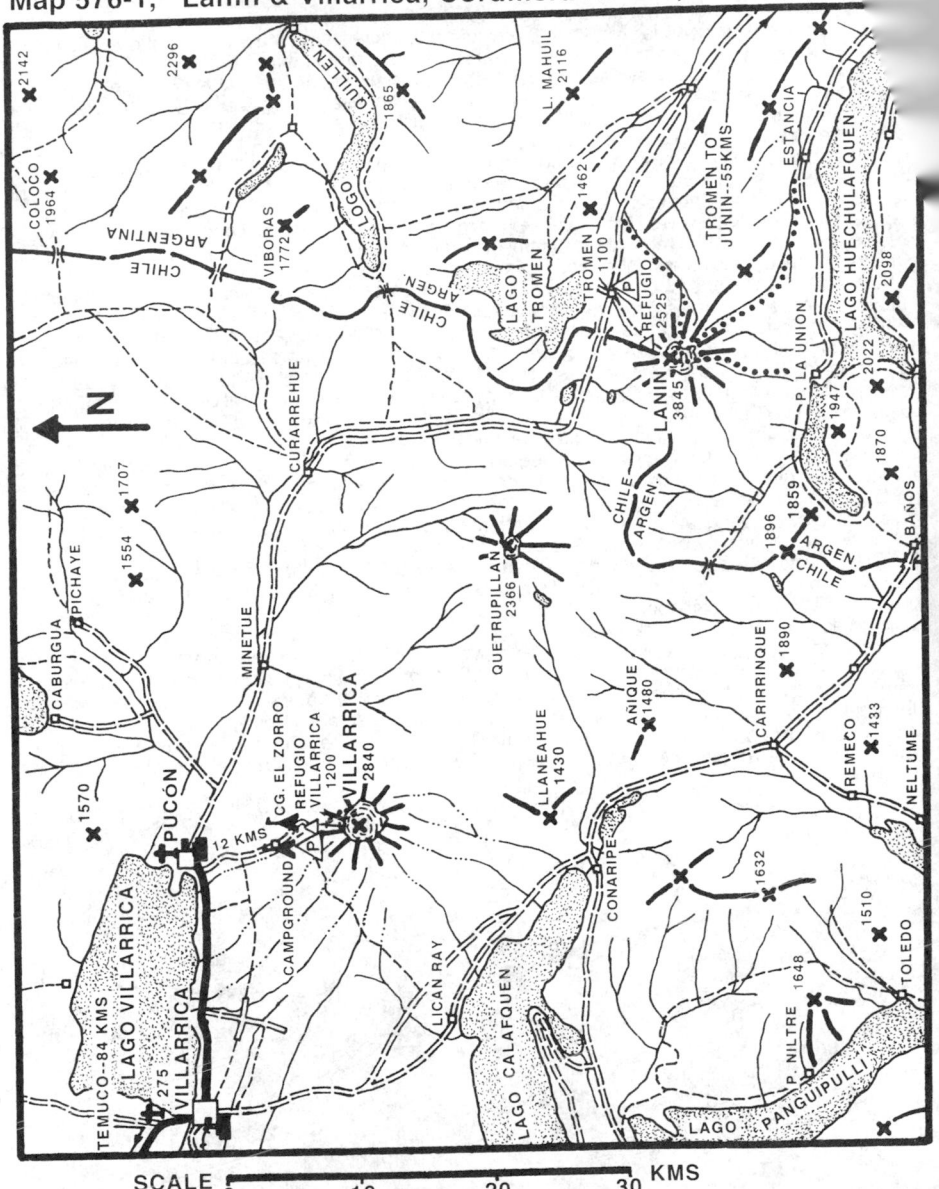

SCALE | 0 | 10 | 20 | 30 | KMS

If you're in Argentina, buy all your food in Junin, the last place to do so. If you're in Chile, buy all food for either climb in Temuco, Villarrica or Pucón. Lots of free blackberries around Pucón in March & April. Junin, Villarrica, Pucón and Temuco each have tourist offices for updated information. There are lots more hotels and spas (baños) on the Chilean side than are shown on this map. Arucana pines are found here, especially around Lanin.

Maps *Volcan Villarrica*, 1:500,000, and *other maps at larger scale*, from the IGM, Santiago; a *Chilean highway map;* and travel guidebook, **Chile**, from Lonely Planet and/or Footprint Handbooks.

Pico Catedral, Cordillera Bariloche, Argentina

...ne mountains featured here are a group of peaks just west of the world famous year-round resort ...f Bariloche. Bariloche is located in the extreme southwestern corner of Argentina's Rio Negro ...ince, and not far from the border of Chile. The author is calling this range the Cordillera ...loche, for a lack of a better name. Locally they may call it something else (?). The author has ...en to Bariloche several times, has hiked up an insignificant peak called **Cerro Otto** just west of the ...y, went to Pampa Linda and Tronador, and crossed into Chile via Lago Frias, but has not actually ...een to the mountains in the center of this map.

These mountains are very popular both in winter and summer. The ski resorts which have made ...Bariloche famous are located here, and in summer there is lots of rock climbing, backpacking and mountaineering. The highest and most famous summit in the area is **Pico Catedral** at 2409 meters. To most this doesn't seem very high compared to the rest of the Andes, but keep in mind this area gets lots of snow in winter, thus most of the central massif is well above timberline. In these mountains are a number of cirque basins and lakes and half a dozen refugios built by andinistas over the years.

On this map are a number of suggested trails and routes. These are well-outlined in the book by Arko listed below (in Spanish). All of his routes are shown as trail symbols, but some are not actually trails. Some are simply routes over the tops of peaks or high ridges. Along some of the more westerly of the trails (routes) shown between Laguna Frias and Pampa Linda, there may be some bushwhacking through tall bamboo grass at lower elevations. You can get to any of these trailheads by hitch hiking, hiring a taxi in Bariloche, or getting on one of the many local buses. The number of buses changes with the season or time of year. The author once took a late afternoon bus to Mascardi, then hitch hiked to Pampa Linda, all in just over one hour.

There are 3 main trailheads to this region. One is on the main road north of Refugio Lopez; another is at Villa Catedral on the eastern side; and the last is at Pampa Linda, which is the normal starting point for those climbing Tronador. See next map. There are other trailheads but you may have problems locating less-used trails. For those of us using public transport or hitch hiking to get around, it's best to start at one of the first 2 trailheads mentioned above.

Greg Horne of Jasper, Alberta, has written to the author stating that he once started on the main road north of Refugio Lopez, then walked south to the Refugio San Martin. From there, he hiked east to Villa Catedral. That trip took 5 days. He did some exploring and climbing along the way, as this could be done in as little as 2 or 3 days.

Bariloche is probably the best place in Argentina to look for guidebooks and maps. There are a number of stores specializing in outdoor books and/or sports, plus several supermarkets, in addition to many hotels & hostels, campgrounds and a good tourist office. It's a real tourist place something like Chamonix or Zermatt, with lots of young people around during summer and winter.

Maps Buy maps from bookstores in Bariloche; also sold locally is the book, **Excursiones, Andinismo y Refugios de Montaña en Bariloche,** by Toncek Arko, Guias Regionales Argentinas,

Refugio Emilio Frey with Cerro Catedral to the left (Toncek Arko foto).

Map 577-1, Pico Catedral, Cord. Bariloche, Argentina

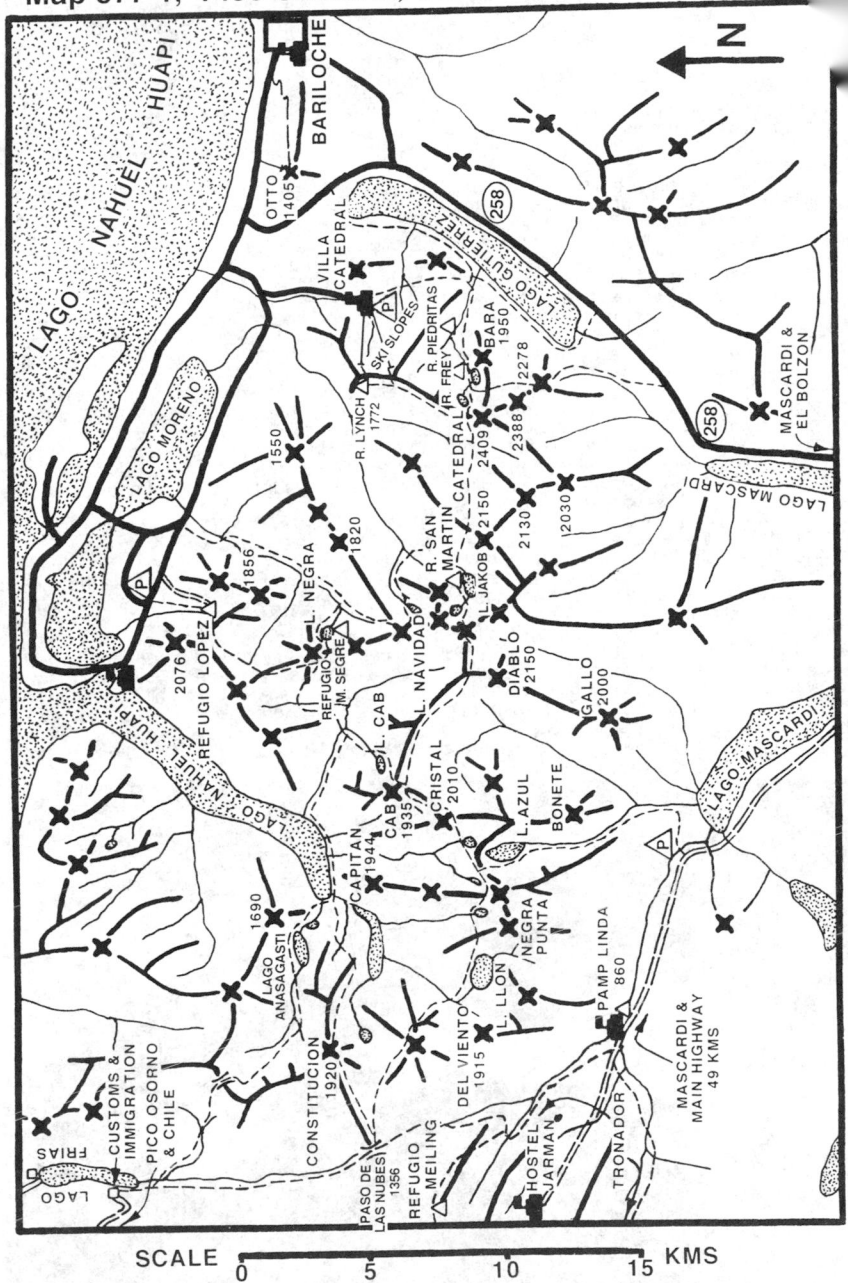

Neumeyer 60, San Carlos de Bariloche; any *Argentine highway map;* and travel guidebook,
Argentina, from Lonely Planet and/or Footprint Handbooks.

Tronador & Osorno, Cordillera Andes, Chile-Argentina

this map are 2 of the better known mountains in the southern part of South America. One is ̣dor at 3554 meters; the other is Osorno, 2661. These are both volcanos; Osorno being the ̣ger and more conal-shaped and having had its last eruptions in the 1800's. Tronador is older, ̣er and heavily glaciated.

This area is along the boundary of Chile and Argentina. On the Chilean side are the important ̣s of Puerto Montt & Puerto Varas just to the southwest of Osorno, and the city of Osorno northwest ̣his mapped area. In Argentina, Bariloche is east of Tronador. Bariloche is the most important city ̣the area. It's a summer & winter ski resort complex and likely the best-known & best-equipped in ̣outh America. If climbing Tronador, Bariloche is the place to gather more information, maps, books, ̣ood and supplies.

Here's what the author did beginning on 3/10/1982. He hiked up Cerro Otto in the morning then, bought food, visited the tourist office, left the campground in Bariloche & got on a 6pm bus heading south. Got off at Mascardi & got a quick ride to Pampa Linda. Next morning, headed up the trail to Refugio Meiling in 4 1/2 hours. Slept there. Day 2, climbed the 2nd highest peak on Tronador, Pico Argentina in 4 1/2 hours round-trip (many crevasses, especially going up to the highest summit); then headed down and camped on the south side of Paso de las Nubas. Day 3, walked over pass and down to Lago Frias, but had some tall bamboo grass on the way. At the lake, checked out of Argentina, walked a ways, got picked up by an empty tourist bus & rode past the caribineros and got off just before Peulla and camped. Next morning, checked through Chilean emigration, but had to spend a 2nd night there before taking a 4pm ferry boat across the lake on 3/15/1982. At Petrohue he hitched to Ensenada and camped. Bad weather ended dreams of climbing Osorno.

To get to **Tronador**, take a bus southwest out of Bariloche to Mascardi, then hitch hike northwest to Pampa Linda. See previous map. Pampa Linda is where 2 trails begin going up the mountain. One trail runs west and up the south ridge to the Refugio Tronador at 2270 meters. The other paths heads north in the direction of Lago Frias. After 3 kms along an old blocked-off road, take the left-hand trail, which leads to the Refugio Otto Meiling. From Meiling, the route goes up the eastern slopes which is the *ruta normal*. Both routes are 2-3 day climbs. Beware, Tronador gets lots of snow, bad weather and has big glaciers & crevasses.

To get from Tronador to Osorno, continue north on the trail down to Lago Frias, then take a bus with other tourists to Peulla. From there take the daily boat across Lago Todos Los Santos to Petrohue, then another bus or colectivo, or hitch hike to Ensenada.

Volcan Osorno can best be reached from a point 2 kms north of Ensenada. Take the secondary road at that point running 12 kms northeast to 2 refugios, at 900 & 1200 meters (you can also get there via Puerto Klocker and the north slope and La Picada). The highest is the Refugio Teski & resort. It's a one day climb with ice ax & crampons. Reports from recent guidebooks state you must have a guide to make this climb; but if you have the will, you can always route-find around the bureaucrats. The reason for the concern is the lousy weather. Take a compass, altimeter & have a good weather forecast! Get to Ensenada in summer by daily bus from Puerto Varas, or hitch hike. Hitch hike, walk or hire a taxi to get to the refugio. It's best to buy supplies for the climb in Puerto Varas or Puerto Montt, but there are several small stores in Ensenada.

Maps Valdivia, Puerto Montt, Volcan Villarrica, Lago Vidal Gormaz, 1:500,000, *plus new maps at*

The Refugio Otto Meiling with Tronador in the background to the west.

Map 578-1, Tronador & Osorno, Andes, Chile-Argent.

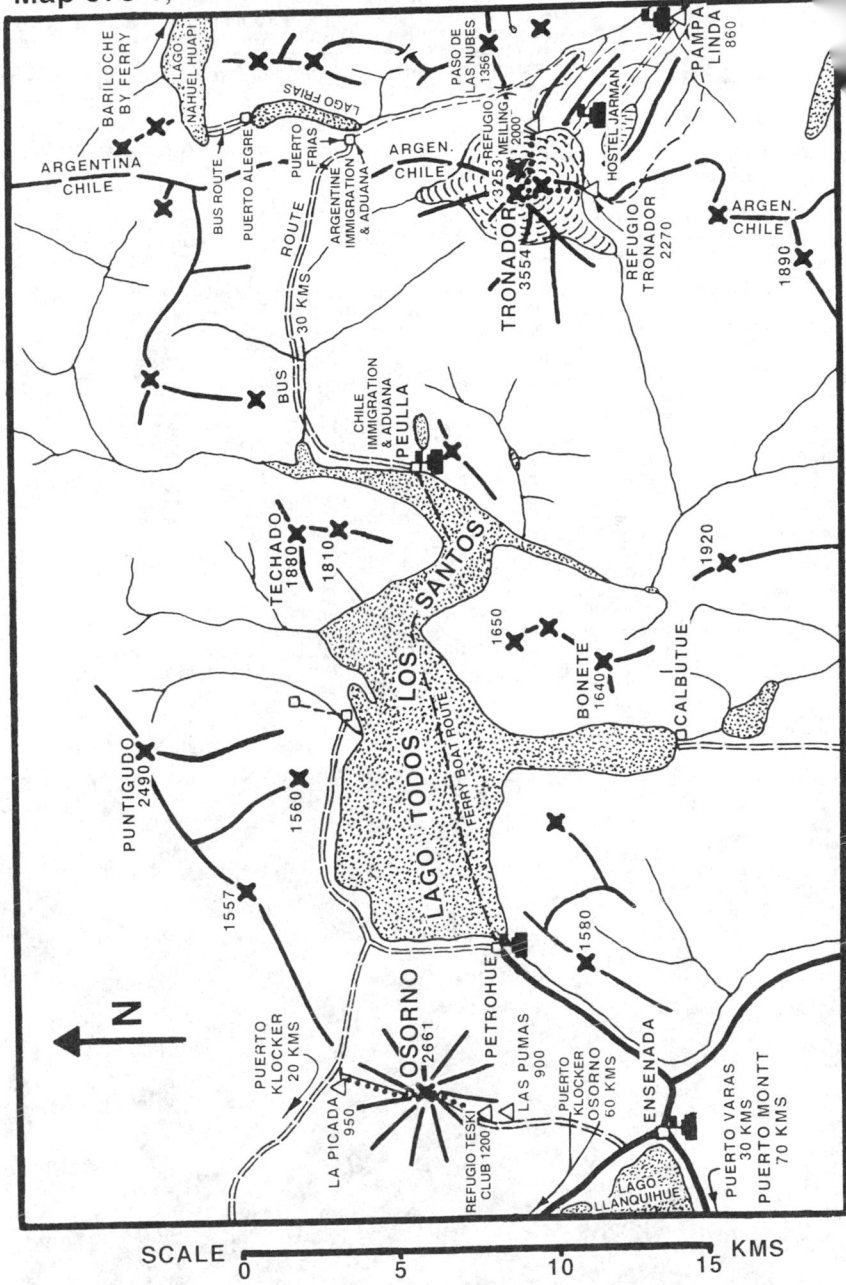

SCALE 0 — 5 — 10 — 15 KMS

larger scale, from the IGM, Santiago; or the book **Excursiones, Andinismo y Refugios de Montaña en Bariloche,** Toncek Arko, buy in Bariloche; an *Chilean highway map*; and travel guidebooks, **Chile** & **Argentina,** from Lonely Planet and/or Footprint Handbooks.

Monte Fitzroy & Cerro Torre, Campo de Hielo, Chile-Argentina

s map shows part of southern Argentina's Patagonia which is in the province of Santa Many of the high peaks here are on the Chile-Argentina frontier, but all access is from the tine side. On the Chilean side is a massive ice cap known as the Campo de Hielo Sur. ce & snow accumulates on the wetter Chilean side, but part of the ice flows east into ntina and into 2 lakes--Viedma and Argentino. While in the area you must visit the Glaciar eno west of Calafate, or go on a boat tour to the icebergs in the Brazo Norte of Lago gentino

By far the most famous peak in this area is a granite pinnacle named Monte Fitzroy at 3441 eters. Next is the highest peak in another nearby group called Cerro Torre at 3122 meters. ach of these groups have several peaks which cannot be shown in detail on this map

The entire eastern half of this map, at least up to the Chilean border, is included in the Parque Nacional Los Glaciares. The region is very remote, but slowly, roads and facilities are improving. There are improved gravel roads into and through the area, but still traffic is light. There are many ranches or estancias with sheep & cattle grazing freely and that's about all. However in recent years, due to the national park status, the area now has a booming tourist industry.

One of the main access roads runs west from Santa Cruz to Lago Viedma, then south to the only real town in the area, **Calafate**. From Calafate, the main highway runs southeast to the small city of Rio Gallegos. This is now a paved highway, and there are several buses each day running between Calafate and Rio Gallegos and other places. You may also find several buses each week going to Rio Turbio on the Chilean border near Torres del Paine. Or you can fly into Calafate from at least 9 different cities in the southern part of Argentina. Check the price of air fares; sometimes they're cheaper than buses! Hitch hiking into the area is very slow! Once at Calafate, you can hitch hike (slow) or join a bus tour going to different places.

This is what the author did beginning on 2/12/1982. He hitch hiked to Calafate and because getting around was so difficult he ended up taking one minibus tour to the Glaciar Moreno, a boat tour to see icebergs in the Brazo Norte and got on the once-a-week bus to what was then called Fitzroy. It had one small store & hotel with 6 rooms and a small ranger station. The bus returned the same day. He was in the area for one week, then took 2 days to hitch hike out of Calafate and on his way to the Falkland Islands.

In summer there is still light traffic going in the direction of Fitzroy and the small nearby tourist community now known as **El Chalten**. In the late 1990's, there were daily buses running from Calafate to Chalten, plus tour buses.

From Chalten, one trail goes north & west to the base camp of **Fitzroy**, located just east of the peak. There are 3 small huts, maybe more. Fitzroy is normally climbed via the east face. Another road & trail heads for the north side of Fitzroy. For **Torre** and that group, walk west from Chalten to Lago Torre, where base camp is normally set up beside one refugio. The normal route up Torre is on the northeast face. Some glacier travel is required on both before the granite peaks can be climbed. Both these peaks are for expert rock climbers. Get more information and maps in Calafate and Chalten.

Buy all food before reaching this area if you can, or pay high prices at Calafate, or sky-high

Cerro Fitzroy and nearby peaks as seen from the Rio Blanco Valley (foto?).

Map 579-2, Fitzroy & Torre, Campo de Hielo, Chile-Argent

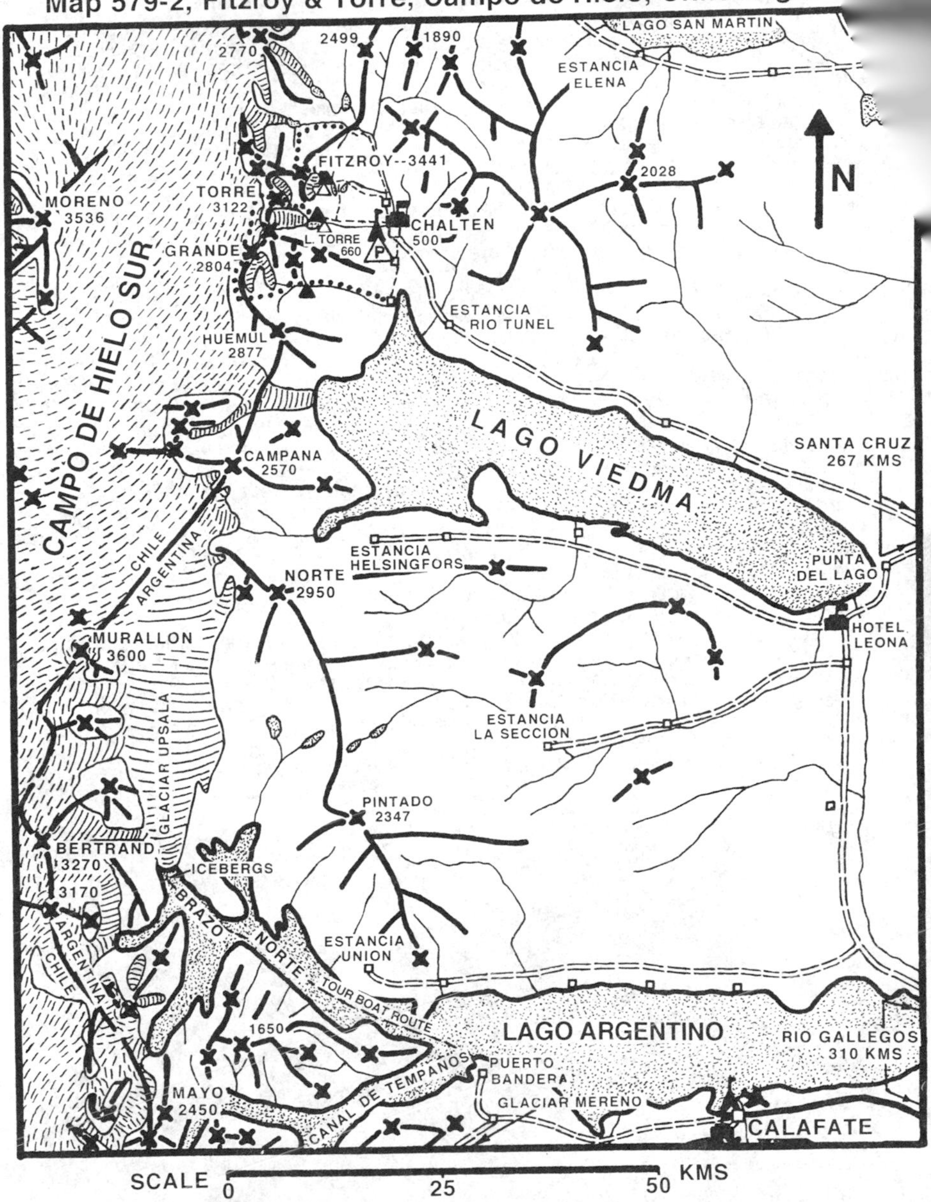

LAGO SAN MARTIN

2499   1890

2770

ESTANCIA
ELENA

FITZROY--3441

2028

N

MORENO
3536

TORRE
3122

CHALTEN
500

GRANDE
2804

L. TORRE
660

P

ESTANCIA
RIO TUNEL

HUEMUL
2877

CAMPO DE HIELO SUR

LAGO VIEDMA

CAMPANA
2570

SANTA CRUZ
267 KMS

CHILE

ARGENTINA

ESTANCIA
HELSINGFORS

NORTE
2950

PUNTA
DEL LAGO

MURALLON
3600

HOTEL
LEONA

GLACIAR UPSALA

ESTANCIA
LA SECCION

PINTADO
2347

BERTRAND
3270

3170

ICEBERGS

BRAZO NORTE

ARGENTINA

CHILE

ESTANCIA
UNION

TOUR BOAT ROUTE

1650

LAGO ARGENTINO

RIO GALLEGOS
310 KMS

MAYO
2450

CANAL DE TEMPANOS

PUERTO
BANDERA

GLACIAR MERENO

CALAFATE

SCALE 0   25   50 KMS

prices at Chalten. Within this mapped area, Calafate is the only real place to buy food or
anything else. By 2000, there were 25 or 30 hotels in Calafate, and nearly a dozen in Chalten.
Each place also has campgrounds. Go prepared for bad weather, especially around the peaks.
East of the mountains it's dry & windy in the rainshadow.
Maps   *Ecomapa: Parque Nacional Los Glaciares*, 1:250,000; and *Monte Firzroy & Cerro Torre--
Trekking-Mountaineering*, 1:50,000, both from Zagier & Urutty, contact the website (www.omnimap.
com), or hopefully buy these maps in Calafate; an *Argentine highway map*; and travel guidebook
Argentina, from Lonely Planet and/or Footprint Handbooks.

Torres del Paine, Cordillera de Paine, Chile

ar the southern tip of South America in the region known as Patagonia, is a small
ict massif called the Torres del Paine, or Towers of Paine. These granite peaks & spires
nt some of the best challenges for rock climbers in the world. These peaks are now part
rational park.

The highest summit is Paine Grande at 3050 meters, which is largely covered with snow &
. There are also several peaks rising immediately northwest of Lago Nordenskjold and are
own as the Cuernos del Paine, the highest of which is about 2100 meters. Behind or north of
ese, are the actual **Torres del Paine**, with **Paine Sur**, 2500 meters, **Central**, 2460, and
orres Norte, 2250 meters. These 3 are the most spectacular.

There are 2 problems with climbing or hiking in this region. First is getting there, but things
are improving. The starting point is Puerto Natales (PN), 254 kms north of Punta Arenas and
140 kms south of Paine by gravel road. There are now several daily buses running from Punta
Arenas to PN, plus flights from Puerto Montt. PN is the only city (15,000 people) in the region
and for the most part, the only place to buy food and supplies. The area between PN and Paine
is wind-swept and occupied only by a few scattered ranchos or estancias with sheep & cattle. In
other words, this country is still rather isolated.

During summer, there are now 2 daily morning buses running from PN to park headquarters,
plus an occasional truck. In PN your first stop should be the tourist office. They will either sell
you the good trekking map listed below, or will direct you to a bookstore that does. Other
trekking and regional maps and guidebooks are also available. During the summer season,
tourism is really big business, so there are all kinds of guide services and package tours. As of
2000, PN has 25 or 30 hotels or residenciales.

Before leaving PN, have all the food & supplies you'll need for the trip, as there's little to buy
in the park. At park headquarters is a small hostel, campers store and a campground. As time
goes on, and as this area gets even more attention from climbers, trekkers & tourists, things can
only improve as far as transportation and facilities go. If entering Chile from Argentina, there are
now several daily buses running between the coal mining area of Rio Turbio to PN. You can
also enter/exit between Cerro Castillo & Cancha Cerrera, with buses going to Calafate or Rio
Gallegos; or at the Casas Viejas crossing east of PN.

The second problem is the weather. It's seemingly always bad, at least for those attempting
the peaks. Storms come in one after another. Wind & waterproof gear is important; especially a
tent & coat. Away from the peaks to the east, the weather is often clear, but always windy.

Climbing in the **Paines** is for the most part on granite, but some snow is usually
encountered. The map shows some of the access routes to the peaks. One recent guidebook
states a climbing fee of **US$800** is now charged--as of the late 1990's! Park entry fee for
foreigners is US$12. For those who want a good hike & fotography, there's a reasonably easy

Torres del Paine from the east (John Cleare foto).

Map 580-3, Torres del Paine, Cordillera de Paine, Chile

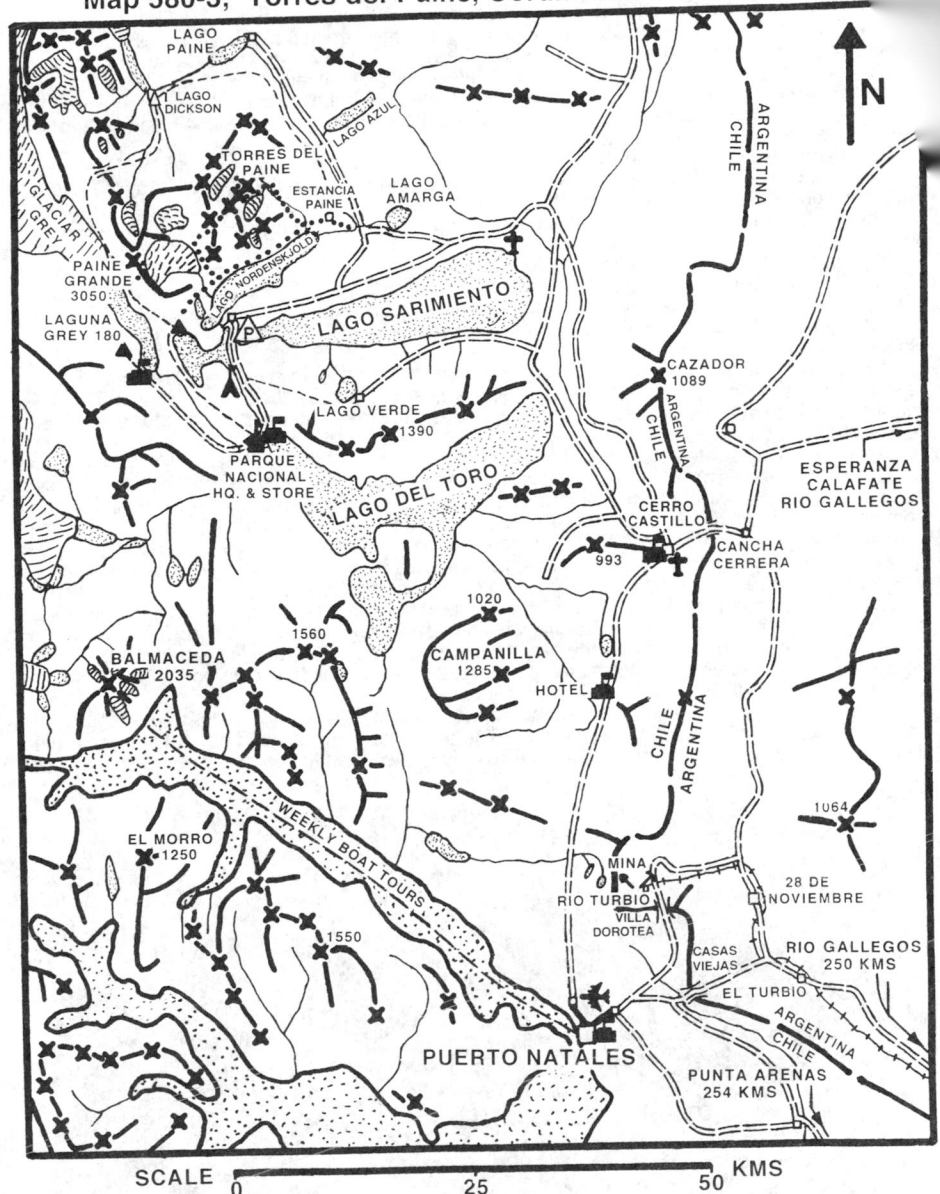

trek around the entire cordillera, which can take from 5 to 7 days from any of several starting points. There are refugios along the way, but *you must take a low profile tent* in case you're caught by bad weather between huts. A better map than this will show the refugios. The best time for visiting this region is from about Christmas through March.

Maps Trekking map *Sociedad Turistica Kaoniken*, buy in PN or Punta Arenas; *Cerro Fitzroy & Puerto Natales*, 1:500,000 (1:250,000 available) from the IGM, Santiago; or *Parque N. Torres del Paine, Club Aleman de Excursionismo*, by Günther Jüllich; see website (www.omnimap.com) for new maps; travel guidebooks **Argentina** and/or **Chile**, from Lonely Planet and/or Footprint Handbooks.

Cerro Darwin, Cordillera Darwin, Chile-Argentina

...is map covers the most southern land masses in South America and Tierra del Fuego. ...ded here is the Cordillera Darwin, a heavily glaciated peninsula of Tierra del Fuego, which ...ost resembles an ice cap; and the most southerly city in the world, Ushuaia (just to the south ...oss the channel is the small Chilean military garrison town of Puerto Williams). Most of the area ...own is Chilean territory, but the eastern part is Argentina. The highest peak in the range is Cerro ...arwin at 2488 meters. Others include Shipton, 2469; Italia, 2350; Buckland, 2043; and perhaps the ...ost climbed peak, Sarmiento at 2234 meters.

There are 2 ways to get to this area. One is overland by bus, hitch hiking or driving. Make your way to Punta Arenas (PA) just north of this mapped area; or to Ushuaia on the south side of Tierra del Fuego and on the Beagle Canal or Channel. There are daily buses now from Rio Grande to PA and/or to Ushuaia. The other way is to fly to either one of these summer-time tourist towns. Consult a travel guidebook.

Perhaps the biggest problem to climbing in this area is transport and/or accessibility. There are no roads into the Cordillera Darwin itself, and only a few trails, all in the extreme eastern end not far from Ushuaia. So the only real means of access is by boat, and from one of 3 starting points; Ushuaia in Argentina, and Porvenir and PA, both located to the north in Chile and both on the Estrecho de Magallanes.

If your group wants to climb in the northern sections of the range, then either PA or Porvenir would be the likely starting point. PA is the larger of the two, which makes it the best choice. In PA, make your first inquiries at the tourist office in the center of town. They can direct you to tour agents or to people who have boats for hire.

Likewise, if you're interested in peaks on the southern part of the cordillera, go to Ushuaia and make inquires at the tourist office. Ushuaia is a very popular tourist spot these days, with many hotels & posadas (rooms in private home), and tour outfitters that can be hired to take groups to about any isolated place. If you're interested in a good climb close to civilization, then hitch hike north out of Ushuaia for 7 or 8 kms on the road to Rio Grande and stop at the foot of **Monte Olivia** (see foto). On the west side is a steep gully heading straight up where an ice ax & crampons are required near the summit. This can be done in one day hitch hiking round-trip from Ushuaia.

During the month of 12/1972, the author hitch hiked south through Patagonia and across Tierra Fuego to Ushuaia. The further south he got, the better the hitching was. In Ushuaia, and on 12/19/1972, he got a ride while still in town right to the foot of Monte Olivia. He headed straight up the steep couloir to the summit. It was steep at the top, but he made it, then came down very carefully. On the highway, he had a ride in 5 minutes back to town.

The next problem with climbing here is the weather. It's often stormy in the western sections, but the further east you go, the better the weather. The author had several good days of fine weather in Ushuaia in late December, when he climbed Olivia. However, from March to December the weather

Looking northeast from Ushuaia, Pico Olivia left, Cinco Hermanos in the center.

Map 581-1, Darwin, Cordillera Darwin, Chile-Argentina

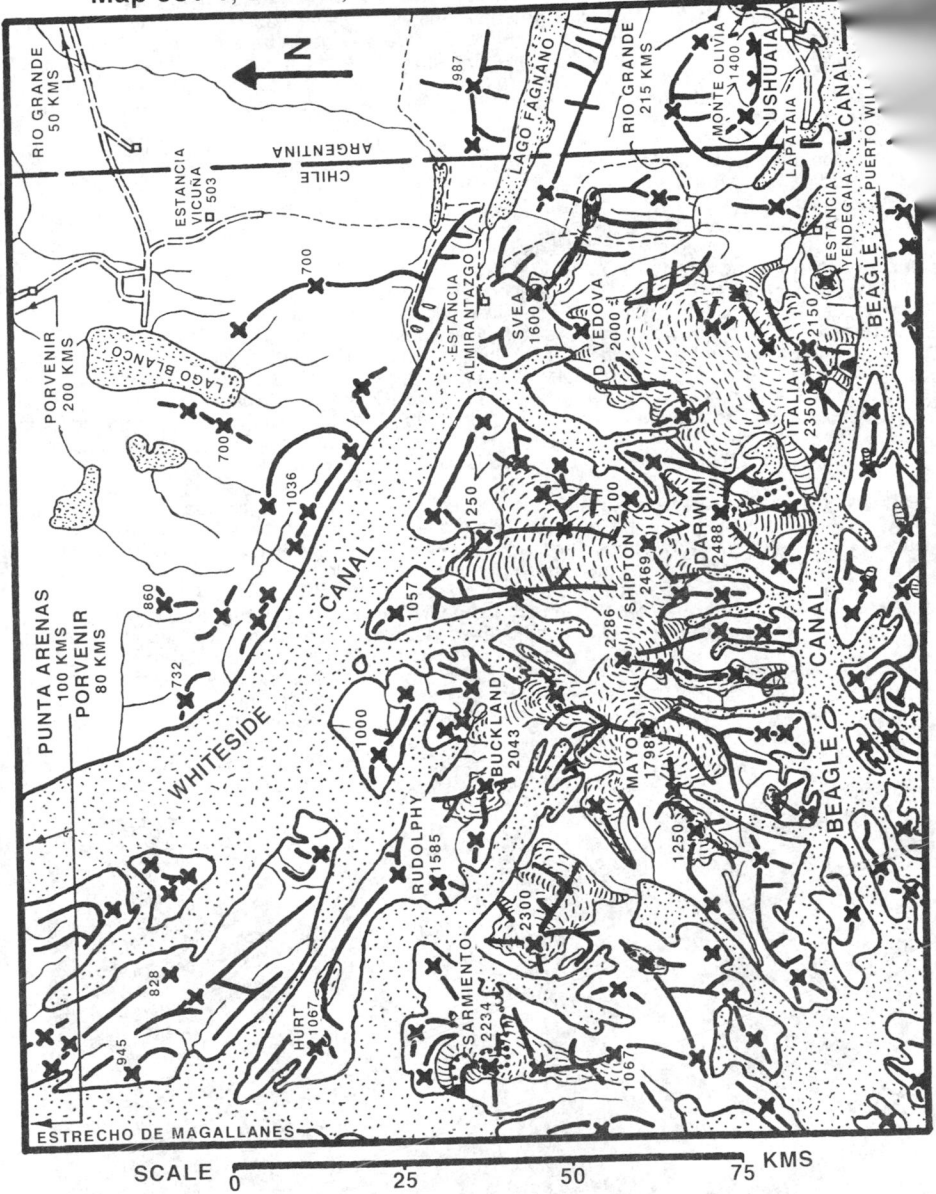

SCALE 0 — 25 — 50 — 75 KMS

is notoriously stormy. Summers aren't so bad, but often windy. The only places in the area where climbers can buy food & supplies are PA, Porvenir, Rio Grande and Ushuaia (very expensive!). The map shows several routes taken by previous climbing parties to various peaks in the region. Needless to say, go prepared for wet stormy weather and lots of glacier travel & snow climbing.
Maps *Punta Arenas,* 1:500,000 (1:250,000 maps now available) from IGM, Santiago; *Chilean & Argentine highway maps*; and travel guidebooks, **Chile** & **Argentina**, from Lonely Planet and/or Footprint Handbooks; or the **South American Handbook**.

Usborne, Falkland (Malvinas) Islands, South Atlantic, UK

alkland Islands are located in the South Atlantic, 600 kms east of Tierra del Fuego, and
ns almost due south of Buenas Aires. There seems to be some dispute over the
hip of the islands; Argentina lays claim to them and call them *Islas Malvinas* on Argentine
However, the people in the Falklands claim to be part of the British Commonwealth, and
. Britain officially claims them as part of the British Antarctic Territories, along with South
gia, South Sandwich, South Shetlands, and South Orkney islands.

The people in the Falklands are of British descent and speak English. About half of the total
d area is owned by the Falkland Islands Company. That outfit own dozens of small sheep
ations dotting the landscape. The only exports from the Falklands are wool and some hides.
ll supplies and most food are imported. The company headquarters is in London. Stanley gets
0 cms of rain a year and little if any snow. Summer temps average 10°C; winter 3°C.

Getting around the islands is not easy. Float planes have now replaced boats for taking
most passengers and mail to the outlying areas. Boats are still used to transport wool & sheep,
and maybe a few tourists, but nothing is scheduled. You can now rent a car or Land Rover in
Stanley, or hire a vehicle with driver. Hitch hiking used to be good in 1982.

Stanley is the only real town in the islands, and about 1800 of the islands 2200 residents live
there (this doesn't count British military personnel based at or near Mt. Pleasant Airport). The
rest of the people live in the *camp* as the countryside is called, and at sheep stations. Darwin is
second in size to Stanley on an all-weather road. By the late 1990's, Stanley had 3 or 4 hotels,
several pubs and/or restaurants, and a couple of stores. There are now a fair number of tourists
visiting the islands, with more than one tour agency taking groups out in boats or Land Rovers to
view penguins and other wildlife. You can now telefon home via satellite.

The highest peak in the islands is **Mt. Usborne**, 705 meters. Inquire around Stanley as to
people heading in the direction of Darwin or Goose Green, as there are no buses. Or rent some
kind of vehicle, or walk and hope for a ride. Before turning south toward Darwin, head north to
Darwin Hut, then the peak which is a walkup. It's a windy and boggy place these Falklands, so
go prepared with a good sturdy waterproof tent and rain/wind clothing.

The author left extra baggage at a campground in Comodoro Rivadavia, Argentina, and from
there flew to Stanley on 2/23/1982. He camped near Stanley, then changed money, walked to
Fitzroy, then got a ride to Goose Green and stayed in a bunkhouse for free with the local drunks
for 2 days & nights with rodeo-type games & sheep shearing contests (late February each year).
Then walked north to Darwin Hut (2 bunks, table & stove) which used to be on a pair of skids,
and climbed Usborne on 2/27. Later that day walked to about where the new airport is now, &
camped. Next day, walked & got ride to Bluff Cove to visit penguins, then a ride to Stanley,
camped for 2 nights before flying back to CR on 3/3/1982. Argentina invaded on 4/2/1982.

Big changes have occurred since the Falklands/Malvinas War of 1982. Now you can fly from
the UK. The RAF operates 2 Tri-Star flights a week from Brize Norton, Oxfordshire, via

The Darwin Hut and sheep corral located at the base of Mt. Usborne.

Map 582-1, Usborne, Falklands (Malvinas), South Atlantic, U

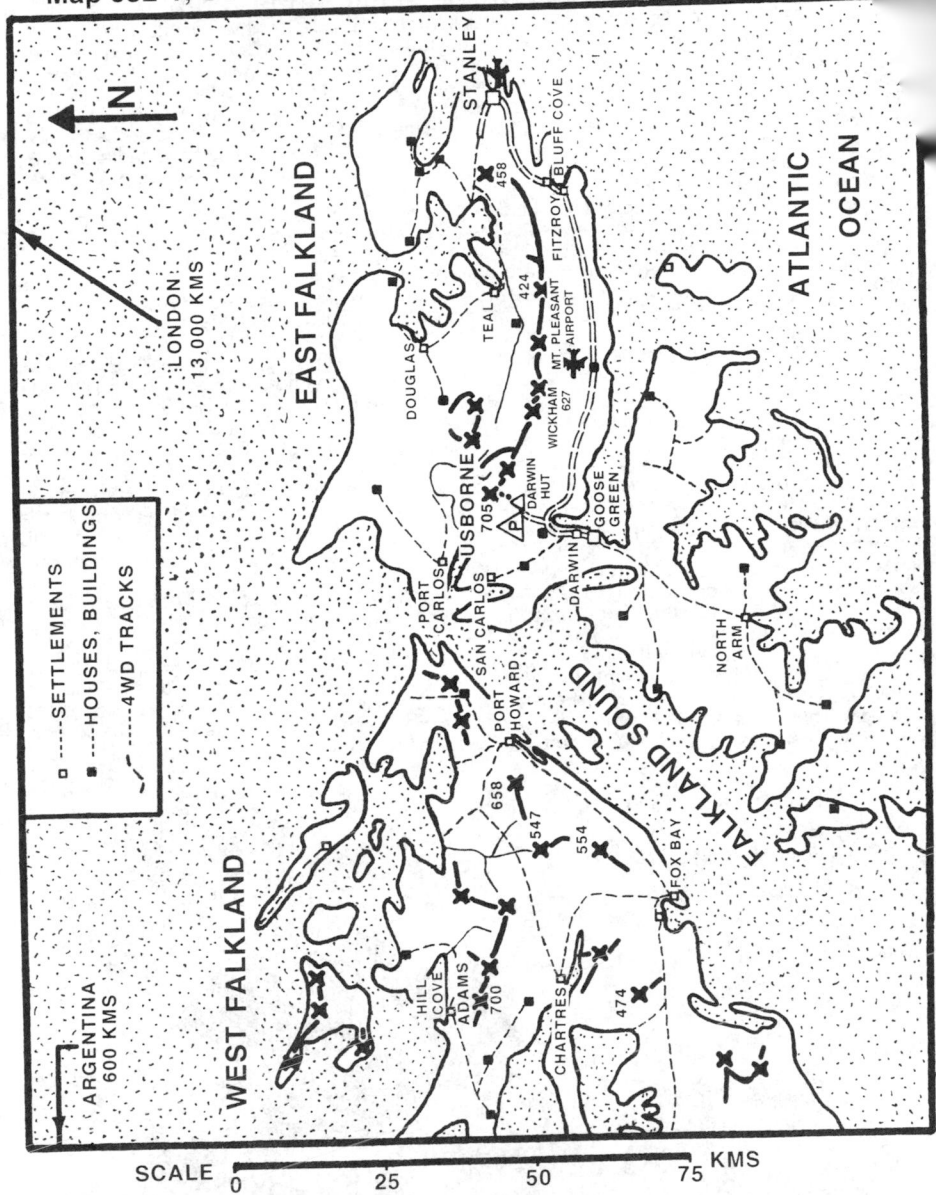

Ascension Island to the new Mt. Pleasant Airport 56 kms west of Stanley. Also one flight per week via Areovias DAP from Santiago, Chile, via Punta Arenas to Mt. Pleasant. This connects with a BA flight from London. Make inquires at Falkland Islands Government Office, London, Falkland House, 14 Broadway, Westminster, Tele. Inter+171-222-2542. Or call Falkland Islands Tourist Board, Stanley, Tele. Inter+010500-22215 or 22281.
Maps *East & West Falklands (2 maps)*, 1:250,000, plus *larger scale maps* from the British Directorate of Overseas Surveys, Secretariat, Stanley, or at Stanfords 12-14 Long Acre, Covent Garden, London, Tele. Inter+171-836-1321; or **South American Handbook**, Footprint Handbooks.

Erebus Volcano, Ross Island, Antarctica

eatured here is one of those far away mountains few people will ever have the chance to visit. It's
=rebus at 3794 meters, located on Ross Island in the Antarctic. This mountain and the entire
nd is volcanic. Erebus is the world's most-southerly active volcano. A summit plateau at about
)0 meters marks the rim of the youngest caldera, within which a newer cone has been built. On top
this new cone is a 500-meter-wide crater and lava lake. The first report of activity was in 184. In
ore recent times, it was continuously active from 1972 through 12/1995, which is the last report from
ne *Global Volcanism Network* (www.volcano.si.edu/gvp/). For all these years, it has had a lava lake
with periodic strombolian eruptions. Other volcanos in Antarctica active since 1900 are Mt.
Deception and on Penguin Island.

Located on the southern tip of the island are 2 permanent research stations; the American
McMurdo Station and Scott Base operated by New Zealand. In summer (January-February) ships
resupply both bases, while the nearby Ross Ice Shelf allows planes to land almost any time. Also on
the island are several old wooden shelters built by early-day explorers. These sites include
Shackleton's and 2 of Scott's cabins. These were used in the first years after 1900 and were the
staging sites for the race to the South Pole. These huts are the same as when they were left and still in
excellent condition.

The biggest problem confronting climbers in the Antarctic is simply getting there. In the case of
Erebus & Ross Island, this may be the easiest of all locations to find transport to because of it's
seaside location and because there are many ships heading that way. However, these are cruise
ships specializing in wildlife viewing, not mountaineering outfitting. Here are some contacts. Try
website **(www.expeditiontrips.com)** or in the USA call Expedition Trips at 877-412--8527. They are
a *middle man*, lining up clients with ship owners who go to the Antarctic.

Or contact an outfit called *Mountain Madness* in Seattle, Washington, USA at 206-937-8339, or see
their website **(www.mountainmadness.com)**. This company specializes in taking clients to the
highest summits on each continent, including Mt. Vinson. In 2000, they charged US$89,000 to climb
all Seven Summits: Kilimanjaro, Aconcagua, Denali, Elbrus, Carstenz Pyramid, Everest & Vinson.
Or contact *Adventure Associates* from Sydney, NSW, Australia, Tele. Inter+61 2-9389-7466, or Fax
Inter+61 2-9369-1853, or see their website **(www.adventureassociates.com)**. They specialize in
South America & the Antarctica. For more outfitters see ads in sports magazines like *CLIMBING*, or
the *Sierra Club* magazine.

Shown on this map are the routes of 2 fairly recent expeditions to the top of Erebus. This
information comes from the Italiano mountaineering atlas, **Atlante di Alpinismo Italiano nel Mondo**
by the Club Alpino Italiano. It appears the easier of the 2 routes shown would be up the west face of the
mountain. That side seems to have the fewest glaciers, but the entire mountain is snow & ice covered
year-round. However, if you hope to climb Mt. Terror as well, then a route similar to C. Mauri's in

Erebus Volcano from the American McMurdo Station (National Geographic foto).

Map 583-3, Erebus Volcano, Ross Island, Antarctica

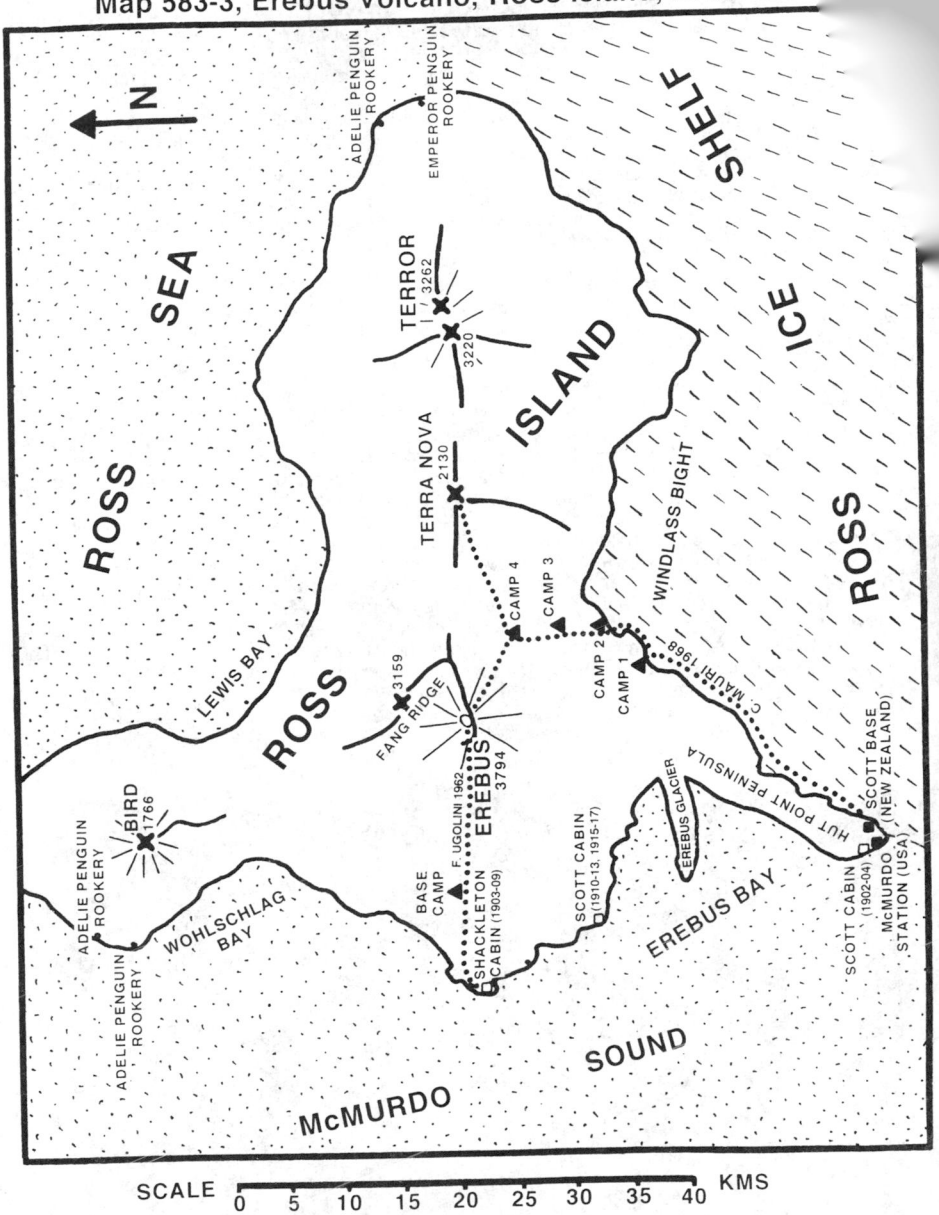

1968 might be the best. Climbing any of these mountains is not difficult, but there will be crevasses in many areas. This would be the only danger other than bad weather and isolation. Obviously you must go well-prepared in this part of the world, but your outfitter will take care of the details.
Maps American USGS map *Ross Island, Sheet 57-60/6*, 1:250,000; the book above; and *McMurdo Sound Area, Antarctica*, American Alpine Club; the annual **South American Handbook** should have an up-to-date list of contacts.

on Massif, Sentinel Range, Ellsworth Mtns., Antarctica

've been dreaming about climbing the highest mountains in Antarctica, you can now
...aming. The chances of getting there are better every day. One way would be to go with
...ific expedition doing some kind of research in the mountains, or if you're filthy rich hire
...ne to fly you and equipment there.

...: try this. Make contact with an outfitter specializing to going to far away places. To start
...ebsite (www.expeditiontrips.com) or in the USA call *Expedition Trips* Tele. 877-412-8527.
y're a *middle man*, lining up clients with outfitter who go to the Antarctic.

Or contact *Mountain Madness* in Seattle, Washington at 206-937-8339, or see their website
...ww.mountainmadness.com). This company specializes in taking clients to the highest
...ummits on each continent, including Mt. Vinson. In 2000, they were charging US$89,000 to
...limb all Seven Summits: Kilimanjaro, Aconcagua, Denali, Elbrus, Carstenz Pyramid, Everest &
Vinson.

Or contact *Adventure Associates* in Sydney, NSW, Australia, Tele. Inter+61-2-9389-7466, or
Fax Inter+61-2-9369-1853, or see their website (www.adventureassociates.com). They
specialize in South America & Antarctica. For more outfitters see ads in sports magazines like
CLIMBING, or the *Sierra Club*.

The area featured here is the **Ellsworth Mountains**, but one small part of that massive
range is called the **Sentinel Range**. Approximately the southern half of the Sentinels is included
here; plus the highest peak in the range, and in all of Antarctica, **Mt. Vinson** at 5140 meters.
Next in height is **Tyree**, 4965 meters; then **Shinn**, 4801; and fourth is **Gardner** at 4688 meters.

The information about these mountains comes from *National Geographic Magazine*, June,
1967, and the *American Alpine Club Journal, 1967*. It was a 10 member American group
sponsored by the National Geographic Society, the National Science Foundation, and the
American Alpine Club, with the help of the US Navy, which went to this remote corner of the
world and made 6 climbs in about one month in 1966-67. If the author is not mistaken, this was
the second expedition to visit the Sentinel Range, but there's probably one group going there
each year now. (In 1957 an American survey team established elevations of the important
peaks, but make no ascents. This range was only discovered in 1957.)

The American Expedition climbed the 4 highest peaks previously mentioned, then later climbed
Ostenso, 4170 meters, and Long Gables, 4151 meters (just off the map). The routes they used are
shown with the exception of Long Gables. The group was flown in to a point about 30 kms from where
the mountains emerge from the ice. They used snowmobiles and Nansen sleds to haul supplies to the
base of each peak. They then set up camps, 3 intermediate camps on Vinson, and reached the
summits rather easily. Only Tyree was difficult, and only 2 climbers reached its summit. Long

Base camp somewhere in the Vinson Massif (Hall & Ball, Adventure Consultants foto).

Map 584-3, Vinson, Sentinel Range, Ellsworth Mtns., Anta

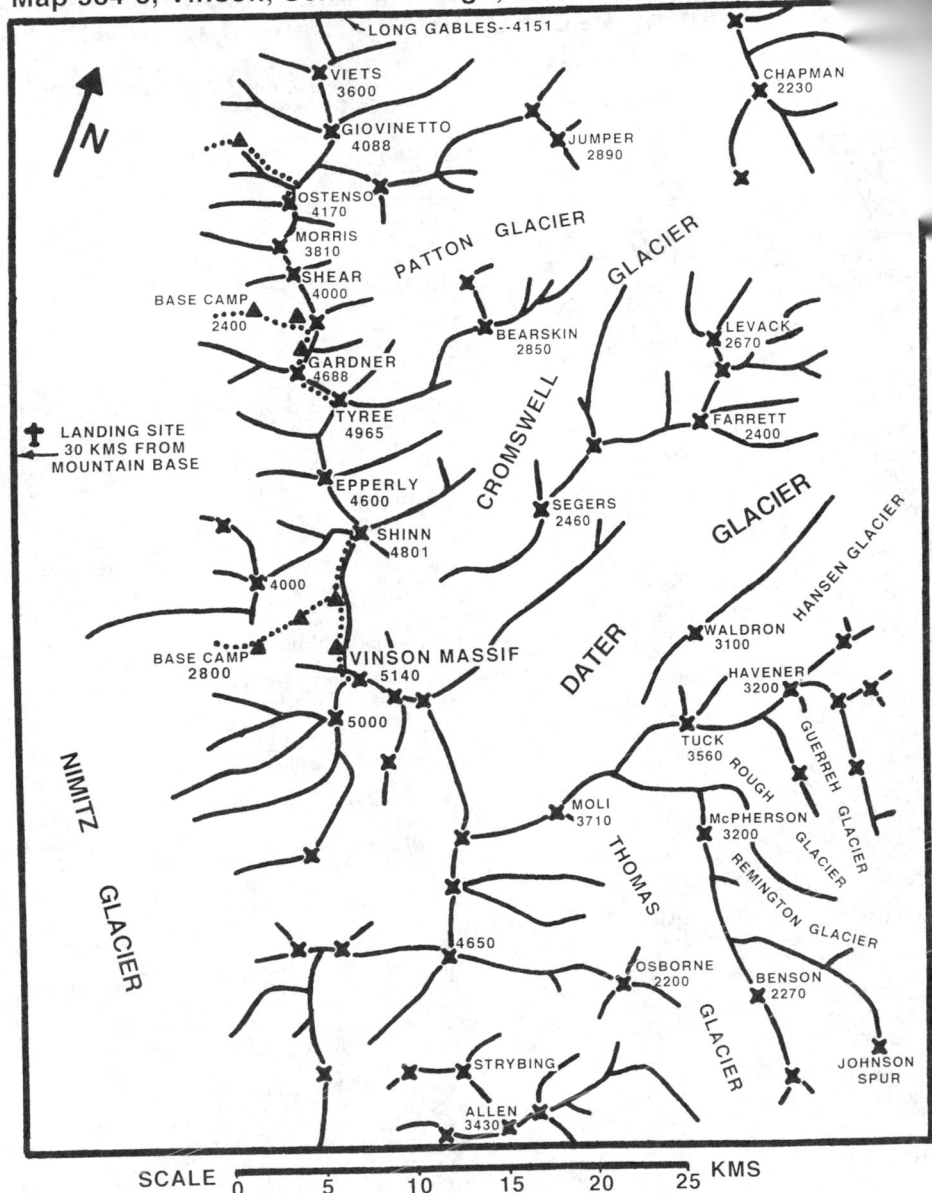

SCALE 0   5   10   15   20   25 KMS

Gables was next most difficult. They had good weather for the most part, but howling blizzards pinned them down on occasions. Temperatures averaged around -30°C. The obvious time to visit Antarctica is January & February. Your outfitter will take care of the details.

Maps USGS map *Vinson Massif,* 1:250,000, see list of mapping agency address in the back of this book; and the publications mentioned above.

...l Addresses for the International Mountaineering ...nd Climbing Federation Associations (UIAA)

...ational Headquarters Address
Monbljoustraße 61, Postfach, CH-3000, BERN 23, Switzerland, Tele. Inter+41-31-370-1828, Fax
+41-31-370-1838, Website (www.mountaineering.org), E-mail (uiaa@compuserve.com).

Country	Member Initials	E-mail Address
Andorra	FAM	fam@andorra.ad
Australia	ASCF	ascf@climbing.com.au
Austria	OEAV	office@alpenverein.at
Austria	VAVOe	vavoe@aon.at
Bulgaria	BAC	bac@netbg.com
Canada	ACC	alpclub@telusplanet.net
Canada	FQME	fqme@fqme.qc.ca
Chile	FACH	fedandinismo@transtar.cl
China	CMA	cma@sport.gov.cn
Croatia	HPS	hps@zg.tel.hr
Ceska	CMF	horolez@cstv.cz
Denmark	DB	dbpresid@post11.tele.dk
Denmark	DSF	mette.mc@mail.tele.dk
Finland	FCA	rockoski@netti.fi
Makedonia	MMSF	shara@mt.net.mk
France	FFME	info@ffme.fr
France	CAF	CLUB.ALPIN@wanadoo.fr
Georgia	MCAG	stc@ip.osgf.ge OR beno_k@hotmail.com
Germany	DAV	info@alpenverein.de OR jdav.@alpenverein.de
Great Britain (UK)	BMC	office@thebmc.co.uk OR gensec@thebmc.co.uk
Greece	EOOA	press@climbing.org.gr
Hong Kong	HKMU	hkmu@hkstar.com
Hong Kong	SCAHK	scahk@hongkong.com
Hungary	MHK	nsanyi@hoya.kee.hu
Iceland	ISALP	ps@tm.is
India	IMF	indmount@del2.vsni.net.in
Indonesia	FPTI	fpti@cyber.or.id
Ireland	IAA	mci@eicom.net
Iran	I.R.IMF	irmountfed@neda.net
Israel	ILAC	relkatz@yahoo.com
Italy	CAI	
Italy	AVS	office@alpenverein.it
Italy	FASI	fasi@iol.it
Kazakhstan	KMC	office@asiatour.org
Korea	CAC	cac@unitel.co.kr
Korea	KAF	KOCKAF@chollian.dacom.co.kr
Latvia	LAA	valde@climbing.lv
Lithuania	LMA	ksc@tdd.lt
Malaysia	MAM	pmm@tm.net.my
Mexico	FMEM	marilu.martinez@rez.com
Nepal	NMA	office@nepalmountaineeringassociation.com
Netherlands	NKBV	info@nkbv.nl OR sportklimmen@nkbv.nl
New Zealand	NZAC	nzal@voyager.co.nz OR climber@voyager.co.nz
Norway	NTK	Egil.Fredriksen@ntk.no OR ntk@sn.no
Norway	NK	klatring@klatring.no
Pakistan	ACP	alpineclub@meganet.com.pk
Peru	FEPADI	fepadi@superred.com.pe
Poland	PZA	biuro@pza.org.pl OR wsalp@poczta.pdi.net
Portugal	FPC	info@fpcampismo.pt
Romania	FRAE	badralexe@pcnet.ro
Russia	UMCR	lvd@risk.ru
Singapore	SMF	davelim@cyberway.com.sg
Slovakia	JAMES	shsjames@ba.telecom.sk
Slovenia	PZS	info@pzs.si
South Africa	MCSA	mcsacc@iafrica.com
Spain	CEC	cec.centre@mx3.redestb.es
Spain	FEDME	fedmebcn@sct.ictnet.es
Sweden	SKF	skf.kansllet@swipnet.se
Switzerland	SAC	info@sac-cas.ch
Taiwan	CTMA	roc523@hello.com.tw
Taipei (Taiwan)	CTMA	hsing3@ms1.seeder.net

Ukraine	UMF	slavin@ugp.viaduk.net
United States	AAC	getinfo@americanalpineclub.org
United States	ALAC	logic@mosquitonet.com
Venezuela	FEVME	cicela@cantv.net

OBSERVER MEMBERS

Switzerland (?)	UIAGM	ivbv-uiagm@bluewin.ch
Chile (?)	UPAME	juval@entelchile.net

From near the village of Lagunas, looking west at Parinacota on the left, and Pomerape on the right. Notice the morning ice on the stream in the foreground, along with grazing llamas & alpacas (Map 562, page 1189).

Carlos Zarate took this picture on 7/26/1972. It shows Ampato in the far background, along with the author and an Indian couple behind a small herd of pack-carrying llamas (Map 554, page 1173).

List of Government Map Making Agencies

ıs a very incomplete list of national or governmental map making agencies around the
. much of the world good maps that can be used for climbing or trekking are either non-
., highly restricted or are in an alfabet/script we in the west cannot read. For this reason,
uidebook authors and/or publishers seldom go to the bother of listing the addresses/Tele.
ers of these map making organizations. For up-to-date information on where to buy maps,
in the country you're going to, and/or at home, **see the latest travel guidebook** to that
.ntry. A list of major publishers is found below. Readers are asked to add or update address
.d/or Tele. numbers listed below.

1. Europe

Austria Freytag und Berndt (private company), Kohlmarkt 9, A-1010, Wien.
Danmark Geodætisk Institut, Copenhagen.
France Institut Geographique National (IGN), 136 bis, rue de Grenelle, Paris, France;
website (www.ign.fr).
Germany Mairs Geographischer Verlag (private company), Stuttgart.
Ireland Ordance Survey of Ireland, Phoenix Park, Dublin.
Italy Institut Geografico Militare (IGM), Via Cesare Battisti, Firenze; or Kompass-
Fleischmann (private company) S.a.r.L., Via Max Valier Strasse 4, 139100 Bozen.
Norway Norges Geografiske Oppmaling (NGO), 3500, Honefoss.
Portugal Instituto Geografico e Cadastral, Lisboa.
Spain Instituto Geografico Nacional, General Ibanez de Ibero, 3, Apartado 3007, Madrid-3.
Sweden Generalstabens Litografiska Anstalt, Kart Centrum, Vasagatan 16, 1120
Stockholm.
Switzerland Eidg. Landestopographie, 3084 Wabern, Bern.
UK Ordnance Survey International, Romsey Road, Southampton, UK, SO19 4GU, England;
Website (www.ordsvy.gov.uk); email (enquiries@ordsvy.gov.uk); Local UK Helpline: 8456 05 05
05; Worldwide Tele. Inter+44-23 8079 2912; Fax Inter+44-23 8079 2615.

2. Africa

Algeria (French IGN) Institut Geographique National (IGN), 136 bis, rue de Grenelle, Paris,
France; website (www.ign.fr).
Cabo Verde Direcção-Geral do Turismo, Caixa Postal No. 211, Praia, Cabo Verde; or
Instituto Geografico e Cadastral, Lisboa, Portugal.
Cameroun Geographique National, Avenue Vogt, BP 157, Yaundi.
Kenya Director of Surveys, Nairobi.
Madagascar FTM (Institut National de Geodesie et Cartographie), Lalana Dama--NTSOHA,
JJB, BP 323, Tananarivo, 101.
Malawi Map Sales, Department of Surveys, PO Box 349, Blantyre.
Mauritius Chief Surveyor, Ministry of Housing, Lands and the Environment, Edith Cavell
Street, Port Louis.
Morocco (French IGN) Institut Geographique National (IGN), 136 bis, rue de Grenelle,
Paris, France; website (www.ign.fr).
Namibia Surveyor General, Justitia Building, Independence Avenue, Private Bag 13182,
Windhoek.
Seychelles Islands Director of Surveys & Lands, PO Box 199, Independence House,
Victoria.
South Africa Government Printer, Private Bag X85, Pretoria.
Sudan Lands and Survey Office, Khartoum.
Tanzania Surveys and Mapping, Ministry of Lands, Housing and Urban Development, Dar
es Salaam.
Uganda Lands and Surveys, Entebbe.
Zimbabwe Department of Surveyor General, Electra House, Sanora Machel Avenue,
Harare.

3. Asia

China Buy from Xinhua Bookstores throughout China.
Iran Gita Shenasi (private company), at 15 Ostad Shahrivar Street, Razi Street, Vali-yé Asr
Cross-roads, Enghelab Avenue; PO Box 14155/3441, Tehran, Tele. 21-679-335, or Fax 21-675-
782.
India Lands and Surveys of India, New Delhi.

Myanmar Myanmar Travels & Tours (MTT), Yangon.
Pakistan Lands and Surveys of Pakistan (?), Islamabad.
Thailand Thai Army Map Department (Krom Phaen Thii Thahaan), or another m
Survey Department, near Interiour Ministry, Ko Ratanakosin, Bangkok.
Tibet Mapping Bureau of the Tibet Autonomous Region, Lhasa.
Turkey Harita Genel Müdürlügu (General Mapping Directorate), part of Ministry of
Ankora
   Russia Geodesi & Kartografiya Rossiyskoy Federatsi, near Kurski Metro Stantsiya, M
Buy at private shops.
Singapore Periplus Travel Maps (private company), Singapore.
Sri Lankla Survey Department Map Sales Centre, Fort Colombo, Sri Lanka.
USSR, Former Republics of, Institut Geodezi & Kartografia in each capital city.
Yemen General Tourist Corporation or Survey Authority, both in San'a.

4. The Pacific
   Australia Central Mapping Authority, Panarama Avenue, Bathhurst, 2795, New South
Wales.
   Fiji Lands & Surveys, Suva.
   Indonesia Bedan Koordinasi Survey dan Pemetaan Nasional **(BAKOSURTANAL)**, Jalan
Raya, Jakarta-Bogor, Km 46; Tele. 807-2062, Fax 021-879-3075. This place is located about 10
kms north of Bogor, and 46 kms south of Jakarta on the Raya Highway.
   New Calcdonia See French IGN.
   New Zealand Topo-Hydro, Land Information, PO Box 5501, Wellington; or (private
company) Craig Potton, 98 Vickerman Street, Nelson, NZ; Tele. Inter+64-3-548-9009, Fax
Inter+64-3-548-9456, website (www.craigpotton.co.nz) or email (info@cpp.co.nz).
   Philippines NAMRIA (formerly the Bureau of Coast & Geodetic Survey), Barranca Street,
San Nicolas, or in Fort Bonifacio, Makati, Manila.
   Papua New Guinea National Mapping Bureau, Box 5665, Melanesian Way, Port Moresby;
Tele. 276465.
   Samoa, Western Lands and Survey, Apia.
   Soloman Islands Lands & Surveys sales office (it used to be behind, or just south of the
main post office) in Honiara, Guadalcanal Island.
   Tahiti & French Polynesia See French IGN.
   Vanuatu Department of Land Surveys, Port Vila, Efate Island.

5. North America
   Canada Maps Canada, Center for Topographic Information Geomatics Canada 615 Booth
Street, Room 703, Ottawa, Ontario K1A 0E9, Canada; websites (www.nrcan.gc.ca:80/
homepage/maps.shtml); or (www.geocan.nrcangc.ca/misc/contacte.html); Tele. 613-995-4921;
Fax 613-947-7948.
   United States USGS, Map Sales, USGS, PO Box 25286, Denver, Colorado, 80225; website
(www.usgs.gov); in USA call 888-ASK-USGS (275-8747); or Tele. 303-202-4200 (Denver); Fax
303-202-4693.

6. Mexico, Central America & the Caribbean
   British Virgin Islands Survey Department, Road Town, Tortola Island.
   Costa Rica Instituto Geográfico de Costa Rica, San Jose.
   Dominica Lands & Surveys, Loudat Road, Roseau.
   Dominica Republic Instituto Cartografico Universitario, Santo Domingo.
   El Salvador IGN Ingeniero Pablo Arnoldo Guzman, Minsterio de Obras Publicas, San
Salvador (?), in collaboration with the Servicio Geodesico Interamericano (IAGS).
   Grenada Lands & Surveys, St. George's; or Ordnance Survey, Romsey Road,
Southampton, UK.
   Guatemala Servicio Cartografia Militar (or Nacional), Avenida Las Americas 5-76, Zona 13,
Guatemala City.
   Guadeloupe & Martinique Institut Geographique National (IGN), 136 bis, rue de Grenelle,
Paris, France; website (www.ign.fr).
   Haiti Service de Geodesie et de Cartographis et les Forces Armees d'Haiti, Port au Prince.
   Honduras Instituto Geográfico Nacional, SECOPT, Tegucigalpa, D.C.
   Jamaica Lands & Survey, 23 1/2 Charles Street, Box 493, Kingston.
   Mexico Direccion General De Geografia del Territorio Nacional Mexico, buy at DETENAL,
Balderas 71, Mexico City.
   Nicaragua IGN, Managua.
   St. Kitts & Nevis British Overseas Survey, Romsey Road, Southampton, UK, SO19 4GU,
England. See UK, Europe for Tele. numbers.

Survey & Mapping Department, Castries.
Maarten, Saba & St. Eustatius Der Nederlands Antilles Cadastral Survey , 132 Beck Street, Phillipsburg, Sint Maarten.
ent Lands & Surveys, Kingstown.
ad & Tobago Lands & Surveys, 18 Abercromby Street, Port of Spain.

th America

Argentina Instituto Geografico Militar, Cabildo 301, near the Ministro Carranza Metro on, Casilla 1426, Buenos Aires.
Boliva IGM, Estado Mayor Gen. Avenida Saavedra Final, Miraflores, La Paz.
Chile IGM, Calle Dieciocho 369, San Antonio 65, or Avenida O'Higgins 240, Santiago.
Colombia Instituto Geografico Agustin Codazzi, Avenida Ciudad de Quito y (and) C 45, Bogata; Tele. 368-3666.
Ecuador IGM, on a hill east of El Ejido Parque, uphill on Paz y Miño & behind military hospital. Or try the Centro de Difusion Geografica, Casa de Sucre, Venezuela 573. Or mail order maps from Latin American Travel Consultants, PO Box 17-17-908, Quito, Ecuador; or website (www.amerispan.com/latc); email (LATA@pi.pro.ec).
Peru Instituto Geografico Nacional, Avenida Arumburu 1198, Surquillo, Lima 34; Tele. 475-9960; Fax 473-3075; or private company, South American Explorers Club, Avenida Republica de Portugal 146, Breña, Lima; email (montague@amauta.rcp. net.pe); Telefax 511-425-0142; or the New York office, website (www.samexplo.org); email (explorer@samexplo.org); Tele. 607-277-0488; Fax 607-277-6122.
Venezuela Cartografia Nacional, Edifiscio Camejo, 1st Floor, Avenida Este 6 (south side), Caracas.

Major Map & Guidebook Sales Outlet

Australia
Macstyle Media, 20-22 Station Street, Sandringham, Victoria, Australia, 3191. Tele. Inter+61-39-521-6585, Fax Inter+61-39-521-0664, or toll free 800-818-764, website (www.macstyle.com .au), or email macstyle@netspace.net.au).

Canada
International Travel Maps, 530 West Broadway, Vancouver, BC, V5Z 1E9, Canada; website (www.itmb.com); email (order@itmb.com), Tele. 604-879-3621, Fax 604-879-4521. Specializing in maps of Canada, and publishing & selling travel maps to the world.

Germany
GeoCenter Scientific Cartography, Schockenriedstrasse 44, D-70565 Stuttgart, Germany; Tele. Inter+49-711-781-94670, Fax Inter+49-711-781-94671, website (www.geokatalog.de), email (kl@geokatalog.de).
Customers in the North America East View Cartographic, 3020 Harbor Lane N., Minneapolis, MN 55447, USA. Tele. 612-550-0961, Fax 612-559-2931, email (maps@eastview. com).

UK
Cordee, 3a De Montfort Street, Leicester, England, UK, LE1 7HD; website (www.cordee.co.uk), Tele. from UK 0116-254-3579, or Inter+44 116-254-3579, Fax from UK 0116-247-1176, or Inter+44-116-247-1176. Europe's largest book & map distributor/wholesaler.

Stanfords Maps-Charts-Books, 12-14 Long Acre, Covent Garden, London WC2E 9LP, UK; website (www.stanfords.co.uk), email (sales@stanfords.co.uk), Tele. Inter+171-836-1321, Fax Inter+171-836-0189. Claims to be the world's biggest map shop, plus guidebooks.

USA
Adventurous Traveler Bookstore, 245 South Champlain Street, PO Box 64769, Burlington. Vermont, USA, 05406-4769; website (www.adventuroustraveler.com); Tele. in the USA 800-282-3963; or 802-860-6776.

Alpenbooks, 3616 South Road, Building C, Suite 1, Mukilteo, Washington, 98275, Tele. 425-

290-8587, or 800-290-9898, (www.trailstuff.com), email (cserve@alpenbooks.c

Amazon.com, (www.amazon.com). They sell lots of guidebooks.

Map Link, 30 S. La Patera Lane, Unit #5, Santa Barbara, California, USA, 93117, Tele. c
Fax 805-692-6787, website (www.catalog.maplink.com), email (custserv@maplink.com,

National Geographic Maps (they now own Trails Illustrated maps), P.O. B
Evergreen, Colorado, USA, 80437, Tele. in the USA 800-962-1643 or 303-670-3457, .
(www.trailsillustrated.com), (www.geographic.com) or (www.topo.com), email (xyztof
com).

National Imagery and Mapping Agency, NOAA, Riverdale, Maryland, USA. In the USA
800-638-8972; or Tele. Inter+301-436-8301; Fax 301-436-6829. Call and they'll send you a fr
catalog. This is the agency that made the Defence Mapping Agency (DMA) maps 1:250,000 r
many parts of the world after World War II. They now make and sell the new version of some or
the old DMA maps now called Joint Operations Graphic (JOG) (in North America and/or some
individual countries) and the Tactical Pilotage Charts (TPC) maps 1:500,000 listed in this book.

Origin Books, 415 North, Neil Armstrong Road, International Center, Salt Lake City, Utah, USA,
84116, Tele. 801-972-8060, or 888-467-4446, email (rsandack@originbooks.com).

OMNIMAP Website (www.omnimap.com); in the USA call 800-742-2677; or 336-227-8300.
This place has maps and guidebooks from all over the world. Maybe the best single source for
topo maps, plus guidebooks.

South American Explorers Club, 126 Indian Creek Road, Ithaca, New York, 14850, USA;
website (www.samexplo.org); email (explorer@samexplo.org); Tele. 607-277-0488; Fax 607-
277-6122.
        Peru Avenida Republica de Portugal 146, Breña, Lima; email (montague@amauta.rcp.
net.pe); Telefax 511-425-0142. The SAEC sales many guidebooks & maps for South America,
plus some for Central America.

Treasure Chest Books, 1802 West Grant Road, Suite 101, Tucson Arizona, 85745, Tele. 520-623-
9558, or 800-969-9558, email (info@rionuevo.com). They sell guidebooks on the western USA.

Major Guidebook Publishers

Bradt Publications Hiking guides to Africa and Latin America and the world.
U K 19 High Street, Chalfont St. Peter, Bucks SL9 9QE, England; website (www.bradt-
travelguides.com); email (enquiries@bradt-travelguides.com); Tele. 01753-893444; Fax 01753-
892333.
USA Distributor The Globe Pequot Press, P.O. Box, 480, 246 Goose Lane, Guilford,
Connecticut, 06437, Tele. 203-458-4500, or to order books call 800-243-0495.

Cicerone Press 2 Police Square, Milnthorpe, Cumbria, LA7 7PY, UK; Website (www.cicerone.
co.uk); email (info@cicerone.co.uk); Tele. Inter+44-1539-562-069; Fax Inter+44-1539-563-417.
Hiking guides to UK, Europe and some of Asia & North Africa.
Diadem Books International hiking and climbing books.
        U K Hodder and Stoughton, Mill Road, Dunton Green, Sevenoaks, Kent TN13 2YA,
England.
        USA Menasha Ridge Press, 3169 Cahaba Heights Road, Birmingham, Alabama, USA,
35243.
        Distributed by Cordee Books, 3a De Montfort Street, Leicester, England, UK, LE1 7HD; website
(www.cordee.co.uk); Tele. from UK 116-254-3579; or Inter+44-116-254-3579; Fax from UK 116-247-
1176; or Inter+44-116-247-1176. Europe's largest book & map distributor/wholesaler.

Falcon Press Helena, Montana, website (www.falcon.com); email (cs@falcon.com), Tele. 406-
442-6597; Falcon Press has recently been aquired by Globe Pequot Press, P.O. Box, 480, 246
Goose Lane, Guilford, Connecticut, 06437, Tele. 203-458-4500; or to order books call 800-243-
0495 in the USA. Hiking guides to the western USA.

Rest stop along the trail between Pico Ruivo and the pass at Encumeada on the island of Madeira (Map 20, page 59).

From near the summit of Sajama looking west. The 2 snow capped peaks are Parinacota on the left, Pomerape to the right. The pueblo of Sajama is somewhere near the center of the foto (Map 562, page 1189).

If you climb Sabalon Kuh of northwest Iran you may see nomadic people like these (perhaps Kurds?) around the base of the mountain (Map 213, page 467).

A 1980 foto of Socompa Volcano and the Socompa railway station in the distance. In the foreground are the mummified remains of nearly 1000 cattle. They were being shipped by *tren* from Argentina to Chile when they were delayed by a blizzard and froze to death (Map 566, page 1197).

oks website (www.footprintbooks.com); email (enquiries@footprintbooks.
ɔbooks to Latin America, but other countries too.
side Court, Lower Bristol Road, Bath BA2 3DZ, England; Tele. Inter+44 1225-
ɛr+441225-469-461.
ublished by NTC Passport Books, 4255 West Touhy Avenue, Lincolnwood
nois, 60646-1975; email (ntcpub2@aol.com); Tele. 847-679-5500, Fax 847-679-

uides Hiking and travel guidebooks to the world.
ed by **Cordee,** and **Geocenter International**; website (www.insightguides.com); email
@gbs.tbs-ltd.co.uk); Tele. Inter+44 1256-817-987; Fax Inter+44 -1256-817-988.

ıy Planet website (www.lonelyplanet.com). Travel guidebooks to most countries.
Australia PO Box 617, Hawthorn, Victoria 3122; email (talk2us@lonelyplanet.com.au),
ɛe. 3-9819-1877, Fax 3-9819-6459.
UK 10A Spring Place, London NW5 3BH; email (go@lonelyplanet.co.uk), Tele. 171-428-
4800, Fax 171-428-4828.
USA 150 Linden Street, Oakland, California, USA 94607; email (info@lonelyplanet.com),
Tele. 510-893-8555, or in the USA Tele. 800-275-8555, Fax 510-893-8563.
France 1 Rue de Dahomey, 75011, Paris; email (bip@lonely planet.fr), Tele. 1-55-25-33-
00, Fax 1-55-25-33-01.

Moon Travel Handbooks--Publishers Group West Travel Guidebooks to most countries.
USA Corporate Office, 1700 Fourth Street, Berkeley, California, 94710; website
(www.moon.com), email (travel@moon.com), Tele. in the USA 800-788-3123, or 212-614-7888.
Canada 250A Carlton Street, Toronto, Ontario, M5A 2L1; Tele. 416-934-9900.

The Mountaineers 1001 SW Klickitat Way, Suite 201, Seattle, Washington, USA 98134;
website (www.mountaineersbooks.org), Tele. 206-223-6303, or toll free in USA 800-553-4453,
Fax 800-568-7604. Climbing and hiking guidebooks to the world.

Rocky Mountain Books, Spruce Center #4 Southwest, Calgary, Alberta, T3C 3B3, Canada;
Tele. 403-249-9490, Fax 403-249-2968, website (www.rmbooks.com), email (orders@rmbooks
.com). Hiking and climbing guides to Canada.

West Col Goring Reading Berks, RG8 9AA, UK; Tele. Inter+44-14-9168-1284. Trekking and
climbing guidebooks to just about everywhere.

Looking south toward Ojos del Salado to the left far away, from the bridge (with pile of stones)
over the small stream of drinkable water called Agua Dulce (Sweet Water). Laguna Verde is
just to the right out of view (Map 567, page 1199).

Other Guidebooks by the Author
Books listed in the order they were first published.
(Prices as of April, 2001. Prices may change without notice)
Climber's and Hiker's Guide to the World's Mountains (4th Edition), Kelsey, 1248 pages, 584 maps, 650 fotos.
Utah Mountaineering Guide (3rd Edition), Kelsey, 208 pages, 143 fotos, 54 hikes, ISBN 0-944510-14-0. US$10.95 (Mail orders US$13.00).
Canyon Hiking Guide to the Colorado Plateau (4th Edition), Kelsey, 320 pages, 118 hiking maps, 185 fotos, ISBN 0-9605824-16-7. US $14.95 (Mail orders US$17.00).
Hiking and Exploring Utah's San Rafael Swell, 3rd Edition, Kelsey, 224 pages, 32 mapped hikes, plus History & Geology, 198 fotos, ISBN 0-944510-17-5. US$12.95 (Mail orders US$15.00).
Hiking and Exploring Utah's Henry Mountains and Robbers Roost, *Including The Life and Legend of Butch Cassidy,* (Revised Edition), Kelsey, 224 pages, 38 hikes or climbs, 158 fotos, ISBN 0-944510-4-3. US$9.95 (Mail orders US$12.00).
Hiking and Exploring the Paria River (3rd Edition), Kelsey, 224 pages, 30 different hikes from Bryce Canyon to Lee's Ferry, 155 fotos, ISBN 0-944510-15-9. US$11.95 (Mail Orders US$14.00).
Hiking and Climbing in the Great Basin National Park --*A Guide to Nevada's Wheeler Peak, Mt. Moriah, and the Snake Range*, Kelsey, 192 pages, 47 hikes or climbs, 125 fotos, ISBN 0-9605824-8-7. US$9.95 (Mail Orders US$12.00).
Boater's Guide to Lake Powell (4th Edition), with hiking emphasized, Kelsey, 288 pages, 256 fotos, ISBN 0-944510-10-8. US$13.95 (Mail Orders US$16.00).
Climbing and Exploring Utah's Mt. Timpanogos, Kelsey, 208 pages, 170 fotos, ISBN 0-944510-00-0. US$9.95 (Mail Orders US$12.00).
River Guide to Canyonlands National Park & Vicinity, Kelsey, 256 pages, 151 fotos, ISBN 0-944510-07-8. US$11.95 (Mail Orders US$14.00).
Hiking, Biking and Exploring Canyonlands National Park & Vicinity, Kelsey, 320 pages, 227 fotos, ISBN 944510-08-6. US$14.95 (Mail Orders US$17.00).
Life on the Black Rock Desert, *A History of Clear Lake, Utah,* Venetta B. Kelsey, 192 pages, 123 fotos, ISBN 0-944510-03-5. US$9.95 (Mail Orders US$12.00).
The Story of Black Rock, Utah, Kelsey, 160 pages, 142 fotos, ISBN 0-944510-12-4. US$9.95 (Mail Orders US$12.00).
Hiking, Climbing & Exploring Western Utah's Jack Watson's Ibex Country, Kelsey, 272 pages, 224 fotos, ISBN 0-944510-13-2. US$9.95 (Mail Orders US$12.00).

This is Mt. Blackburn as seen from Willow Lake on the Richardson Highway between Glennallen and Valdes (Map 349, page 755, George Herben foto).

Distributors for Kelsey Publishing

Primary Distributors All (or most) of Michael R. Kelsey's books are sold by these companies. If you'd like to order a book, please call one of the following:

Alpenbooks, 3616 South Road, Building C, Suite 1, Mukilteo, Washington, 98275, Tele. 425-290-8587, or 800-290-9898, (www.trailstuff.com), email (cserve@alpenbooks.com).

Canyon Country Distribution, Box 400034, Thompson Springs, Utah, 84540, Tele. 435-285-2210, Fax 435-285-2252, email (archhunter@moci.net).

Origin Books, 415 North, Neil Armstrong Road, International Center, Salt Lake City, Utah, 84116, Tele. 801-972-8060, or 888-467-4446, email (rsandack@originbooks.com).

Treasure Chest Books, 1802 West Grant Road, Suite 101, Tucson Arizona, 85745, Tele. 520-623-9558, or 800-969-9558, email (info@rionuevo.com).

Some of Kelsey's books are sold by the following distributors.

Anderson News, 1709 North, East Street, Flagstaff, Arizona, 86004, Tele. 602-774-6171.

Books West, 5757 Arapahoe Avenue, D-2, Boulder, Colorado, 80303, Tele. 303-449-5995, Fax 303-449-5951.

Canyonlands Publications, 4860 N. Ken Morey Drive, Bellemont, Arizona, 86004, Tele. 520-779-3888 or 800-283-1983.

Crown West Books (Library Service), 575 E. 1000 S., Orem, Utah, 84058, Tele. 801-224-1455.

High Peak Books, Box 703, Wilson, Wyoming, 83014, Tele. 307-739-0147.

Wide World of Maps, 2626 West, Indian School Road, Phoenix, Arizona, 85012, Tele. 602-266-1043, or 800-279-7652, Fax 602-279-2350, (www.maps4u.com).

Nevada Publications, 4135 Badger Circle, Reno, Nevada, 89509, Tele. 702-747-0800.

Peregrine Outfitters, 105 South Brownell Road, Suite A, Williston, Vermont, 05495, Tele. 802-860-2977, or 800-222-3088. Or **Adventurous Traveler** at (www.adventuroustraveler.com)

Recreational Equipment, Inc. (R.E.I.), P.O. Box C-88126, Seattle, Washington, 98188, Mail Orders Tele. 800-426-4840, website (www.rei.com), or check at any of their local stores.

For the UK and Europe, and the rest of the world contact:

CORDEE, 3a De Montfort Street, Leicester, England, UK, LE1 7HD, Tele. Inter+44-116-254-3579, Fax Inter+44-116-247-1176, website (www.cordee.co.uk).

For Australia and New Zealand:

Macstyle Media, 20-22 Station Street, Sandringham, Victoria, Australia, 3191. Tele. Inter+61-39-521-6585, Fax Inter+61-39-521-0664, or toll free 800-818-764, website (www.macstyle.com.au), or email macstyle@netspace.net.au).

From above Tuni and looking north at Laguna Chiar Kkota with Condoriri above and to the left (Map 558, page 1181, Willy Kenning foto).